ENCYCLOPAEDIA JUDAICA

ENCYCLOPAEDIA JUDAICA

SECOND EDITION

VOLUME 5
Coh–Doz

Fred Skolnik, *Editor in Chief*
Michael Berenbaum, *Executive Editor*

MACMILLAN REFERENCE USA
An imprint of Thomson Gale, a part of The Thomson Corporation

IN ASSOCIATION WITH
KETER PUBLISHING HOUSE LTD., JERUSALEM

THOMSON
GALE

Detroit • New York • San Francisco • New Haven, Conn. • Waterville, Maine • London

THOMSON
GALE

ENCYCLOPAEDIA JUDAICA, Second Edition

Fred Skolnik, *Editor in Chief*
Michael Berenbaum, *Executive Editor*
Shlomo S. (Yosh) Gafni, *Editorial Project Manager*
Rachel Gilon, *Editorial Project Planning and Control*

Thomson Gale
Gordon Macomber, *President*
Frank Menchaca, *Senior Vice President and Publisher*
Jay Flynn, *Publisher*
Hélène Potter, *Publishing Director*

Keter Publishing House
Yiphtach Dekel, *Chief Executive Officer*
Peter Tomkins, *Executive Project Director*

Complete staff listings appear in Volume 1

For more information, contact
Macmillan Reference USA
An imprint of Thomson Gale
27500 Drake Rd.
Farmington Hills, MI 48331-3535
Or you can visit our internet site at
http://www.gale.com

LIBRARY OF CONGRESS CATALOGING-IN-PUBLICATION DATA

Encyclopaedia Judaica / Fred Skolnik, editor-in-chief ; Michael Berenbaum, executive editor. -- 2nd ed.
v. cm.
Includes bibliographical references and index.
Contents: v.1. Aa-Alp.
ISBN 0-02-865928-7 (set hardcover : alk. paper) -- ISBN 0-02-865929-5 (vol. 1 hardcover : alk. paper) -- ISBN 0-02-865930-9 (vol. 2 hardcover : alk. paper) -- ISBN 0-02-865931-7 (vol. 3 hardcover : alk. paper) -- ISBN 0-02-865932-5 (vol. 4 hardcover : alk. paper) -- ISBN 0-02-865933-3 (vol. 5 hardcover : alk. paper) -- ISBN 0-02-865934-1 (vol. 6 hardcover : alk. paper) -- ISBN 0-02-865935-X (vol. 7 hardcover : alk. paper) -- ISBN 0-02-865936-8 (vol. 8 hardcover : alk. paper) -- ISBN 0-02-865937-6 (vol. 9 hardcover : alk. paper) -- ISBN 0-02-865938-4 (vol. 10 hardcover : alk. paper) -- ISBN 0-02-865939-2 (vol. 11 hardcover : alk. paper) -- ISBN 0-02-865940-6 (vol. 12 hardcover : alk. paper) -- ISBN 0-02-865941-4 (vol. 13 hardcover : alk. paper) -- ISBN 0-02-865942-2 (vol. 14 hardcover : alk. paper) -- ISBN 0-02-865943-0 (vol. 15: alk. paper) -- ISBN 0-02-865944-9 (vol. 16: alk. paper) -- ISBN 0-02-865945-7 (vol. 17: alk. paper) -- ISBN 0-02-865946-5 (vol. 18: alk. paper) -- ISBN 0-02-865947-3 (vol. 19: alk. paper) -- ISBN 0-02-865948-1 (vol. 20: alk. paper) -- ISBN 0-02-865949-X (vol. 21: alk. paper) -- ISBN 0-02-865950-3 (vol. 22: alk. paper)
1. Jews -- Encyclopedias. I. Skolnik, Fred. II. Berenbaum, Michael, 1945-
DS102.8.E496 2007
909'.04924 -- dc22
2006020426

ISBN-13:

978-0-02-865928-2 (set)
978-0-02-865929-9 (vol. 1)
978-0-02-865930-5 (vol. 2)
978-0-02-865931-2 (vol. 3)
978-0-02-865932-9 (vol. 4)
978-0-02-865933-6 (vol. 5)
978-0-02-865934-3 (vol. 6)
978-0-02-865935-0 (vol. 7)
978-0-02-865936-7 (vol. 8)
978-0-02-865937-4 (vol. 9)
978-0-02-865938-1 (vol. 10)
978-0-02-865939-8 (vol. 11)
978-0-02-865940-4 (vol. 12)
978-0-02-865941-1 (vol. 13)
978-0-02-865942-8 (vol. 14)
978-0-02-865943-5 (vol. 15)
978-0-02-865944-2 (vol. 16)
978-0-02-865945-9 (vol. 17)
978-0-02-865946-6 (vol. 18)
978-0-02-865947-3 (vol. 19)
978-0-02-865948-0 (vol. 20)
978-0-02-865949-7 (vol. 21)
978-0-02-865950-3 (vol. 22)

This title is also available as an e-book
ISBN-10: 0-02-866097-8
ISBN-13: 978-0-02-866097-4
Contact your Thomson Gale representative for ordering information.
Printed in the United States of America

10 9 8 7 6 5 4 3 2

TABLE OF CONTENTS

Initial "C" at the opening of II Chronicles in the Bible of Saint Martial of Limoges, *France, 12th century, depicting Solomon enthroned, Paris, Biblithèque Nationale, Ms. Lat. 8, Vol. II, fol. 102.*

COH–CZ

COHEN, Italian family of majolica makers, active in Pesaro and Ancona from 1614 to 1673. The following names are known: ISAAC (Pesaro, 1613–14), JACOB (Ancona, 1654), and ISAAC (II; Ancona, 1673–77). Together with the *Azulai family, the Cohen family produced most of the majolica *seder* dishes that were made in Renaissance Italy. In the case of dishes made by Jacob Cohen, the manufacturer's mark is a crown to denote priesthood, instead of the usual Star of David.

BIBLIOGRAPHY: C. Roth, in: *Eretz Israel*, 7 (1964), 106–11.

[David Maisel]

COHEN, prominent U.S. family in the 18th–19th centuries, mostly in Baltimore. JACOB I. (1744–1823) was the first of the family to go from Oberdorf, Germany, to the U.S. (1773). He served in the Revolutionary Army, and in 1780 settled in Richmond. A successful banker and merchant, he was much honored by the citizens of his city. Like other leading Jews of that period, Jacob I. Cohen was active in Masonic affairs. He was also active in Jewish affairs and was a founder of the first Richmond synagogue, Beth Shalom. The last 17 years of his life were spent in Philadelphia. He was the pillar of the city's Mikveh Israel Congregation and served as its president during 1810–11. In his will he provided that upon his death his black slaves were to be freed and each one given $25.00. The progenitor of the Baltimore branch of the family was Jacob's brother, ISRAEL I. (1751–1803), who arrived in the U.S. from Germany around 1784. He too settled in Richmond, where he became a leading citizen and was very active in Jewish affairs. In 1808 his widow Judith (Salomon) moved with her seven children to Baltimore, where Israel's descendants became prominent as financiers, scientists, physicians, and public servants.

JACOB I. (1789–1869) eldest of Israel's sons, started out in the lottery business in Baltimore and branched out into banking, establishing J.I. Cohen, Jr. and Bros. The bank had a considerable reputation, with a branch in Philadelphia. It was also a fiscal agent of the Rothschilds. In addition to banking, Jacob I. Cohen's other enterprises included a directorship of the Baltimore and Ohio Railroad and the presidency of the Baltimore-Philadelphia Railroad. Although U.S.-born, Cohen was active in the affairs of the German Society of Maryland. He held a *minyan* for services in his palatial home. He is best remembered for his participation with Solomon *Etting in the protracted struggle for Jewish equality in Maryland. In a memorial presented by him to the legislature he stressed that Jews were not asking for privileges, but rights, and that "to disqualify any class of citizen is for the people to disqualify themselves." After the passing of the so-called "Jew Bill," Cohen was elected a councilman of the city (1826), later serving as president of the city council during 1845–51. He never joined any Baltimore synagogue, but did participate in the organization of a short-lived Sephardi congregation (1856–58). MENDES I. (1796–1879), brother of Jacob I., was born in Richmond and spent a few years in the banking business. He then traveled abroad during 1829–35, visiting practically every country in Europe and the Near East, including Palestine. He was a prolific writer and his letters and diaries are a rich source of information about Jewish life in the countries he visited. Cohen was the first American to explore the Nile, and presented his important collection of Egyptian relics to Johns Hopkins University. Cohen also served in the Maryland State Assembly during 1847–48. BENJAMIN I. (c. 1798–1845) and DAVID I. (1800–1847), brothers of Jacob and Mendes, were noted bankers who helped establish the Baltimore Stock Exchange in 1837. As Orthodox Jews, they neither attended meetings on the board of the Stock Exchange nor transacted business on the Sabbath. Benjamin was an officer of the German Society. He served in the Maryland militia and was active in passing the Maryland "Jew Bill." JOSHUA I. (1801–1870), another brother, was born in Richmond, and became a physician and one of the early American otologists. A recognized authority in this field, he was elected president of the Medical and Chirurgical Faculty of the University of Maryland, where he was also professor of mineralogy and geology. Cohen's valuable Judaica collection, cataloged by Cyrus Adler (1887), is housed in Dropsie College. Like his elder brother Jacob, Joshua was actively engaged in securing Jewish rights in Maryland. Even after passage of the "Jew Bill", discriminatory laws remained on the books. The doctor attended the state constitutional conventions of 1851, 1864, and 1867 and struggled with limited success for equal rights. Cohen was active in Jewish communal affairs, and like his brothers was Orthodox but never joined any local synagogue. His voluminous correspondence in Isaac Leeser's *Occident* in Philadelphia contributes much on the history of the Baltimore Jewish community.

MENDES (1831–1915) son of David. Mendes was born in Baltimore. An accomplished engineer, he was president of a number of railroad companies, and served as president of the American Society of Civil Engineers. Cohen was interested in many communal affairs, especially the Maryland Historical Society, of which he was secretary (1875–1904) and president (1904–14). He purchased rare collections of documents for the society and bequeathed it $5,000. A founder of the American Jewish Historical Society, Cohen was a member of its executive council. He contributed to Jewish causes in Baltimore.

BIBLIOGRAPHY: Rosenbloom, Biog Dict, s.v.; Baroway, in: *Maryland Historical Magazine*, 18 (1923), 355–75; 19 (1924), 54–77; H.T. Ezekiel and G. Lichtenstein, *History of the Jews of Richmond* (1917), 352; H. Simonhoff, *Jewish Notables in America 1776–1865* (1956), 394; S.R. Kagan, *Jewish Contributions to Medicine in America* (1934), 26–27; DAB; Adler, in: AJHSP, 25 (1917), 145–7.

[Isaac M. Fein]

COHEN, family distinguished in Anglo-Jewish life for almost two centuries. LEVI BARENT COHEN (1747–1808) went to England from Amersfoort (Holland) in the third quarter of the 18th century. He was presiding warden of the Great Synagogue, London, and the first president of the Jews' Hospital. One daughter, Hannah, married Nathan Meyer *Rothschild and another, Judith, Sir Moses *Montefiore; a granddaughter married Sir David *Salomons and a great-granddaughter Samuel Montagu, the first Lord *Swaythling. His male descendants included AARON *COHEN, who was appointed a queen's counsel, and LIONEL LOUIS COHEN (1832–87). The latter succeeded his father, LOUIS COHEN (1799–1882), as head of the family firm of foreign bankers and brokers, and subsequently became a manager of the Stock Exchange. He was an authority on Indian railways and Turkish finance. A political Conservative, he was elected to parliament in 1885 and during his short but brilliant political career served on royal commissions on the trade depression, on gold and silver, and on endowed schools. In communal affairs, he became honorary secretary of the Jewish Board of Guardians (now Jewish Welfare Board) on its foundation and its president in 1878. He was followed in this office by his brother SIR BENJAMIN LOUIS COHEN (1844–1909), his son SIR LEONARD LIONEL COHEN (1858–1938), his niece HANNAH FLORETTA COHEN (1875–1946), and his grandson Lord Lionel Leonard *Cohen. He played a leading part in the founding of the United Synagogue in 1870. In 1881 he initiated the movement to help oppressed Russian Jewry, which led to the first relief fund being established in England on their behalf. His descendants include Sir Andrew Benjamin *Cohen (1909–1968), colonial governor and civil servant, and RUTH *COHEN (1906–1991), principal of Newnham College, Cambridge. The WALEY-COHEN family are descendants of his brother NATHANIEL (see Cohen, Sir Robert *Waley).

BIBLIOGRAPHY: JHSET, 16 (1952), 11–25 (address by Lord Justice Cohen); V.D. Lipman, *Century of Social Service, 1889–1959* (1959); C. Roth, *History of the Great Synagogue* (1950), index; P.H. Emden, *Jews of Britain* (1943). **ADD. BIBLIOGRAPHY:** C. Bermant, *The Cousinhood* (1961), 175–98, index; Michael Jolles, *Directory of Distinguished Jews, 1830–1930* (2002), index; ODNB online for Sir Andrew Cohen, Sir Benjamin Cohen, Louis Cohen, and Ruth Cohen.

[Vivian David Lipman]

COHEN, family of Liverpool (England) merchants and public servants. LOUIS SAMUEL COHEN (1846–1922) was born in Sydney (Australia), and went to England in 1859. In 1864 he joined a relative, David Lewis, who owned a clothing store, becoming head of the business on the death of David Lewis in 1885 and developing it into Lewis', Ltd., one of the largest department chain stores in the north of England. A generous supporter of local charities, he was prominent in local synagogue life and Jewish institutions. He became a member of the Liverpool city council in 1895 and served as lord mayor in 1899–1900. His eldest son, HAROLD LEOPOLD (1873–1936), succeeded his father as chairman of Lewis'. Among his benefactions was a gift

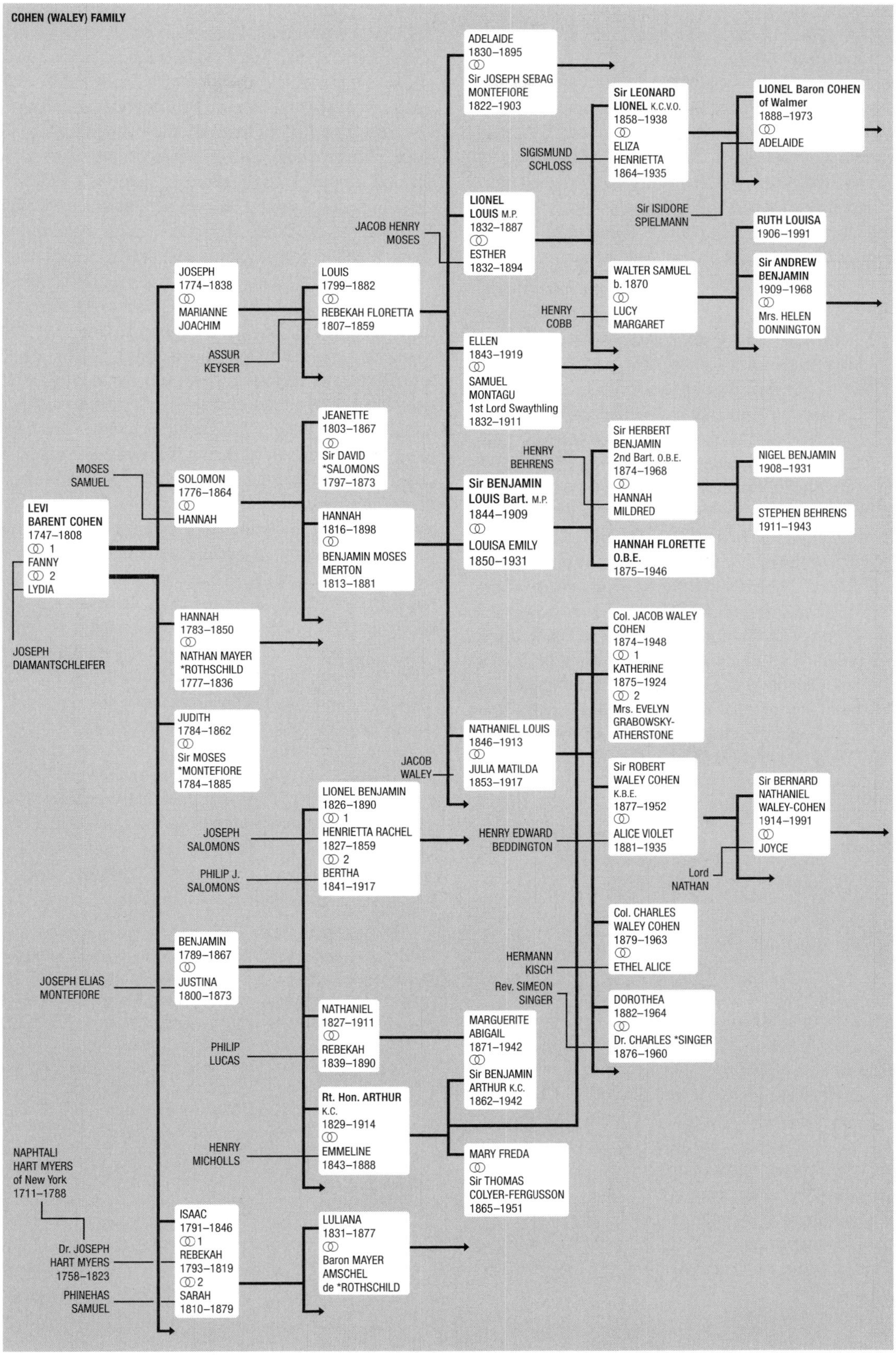
COHEN (WALEY) FAMILY
LEVI BARENT COHEN 1747–1808 ⚭ 1 FANNY ⚭ 2 LYDIA
JOSEPH DIAMANTSCHLEIFER
MOSES SAMUEL
JOSEPH 1774–1838 ⚭ MARIANNE JOACHIM
ASSUR KEYSER
LOUIS 1799–1882 ⚭ REBEKAH FLORETTA 1807–1859
JACOB HENRY MOSES
ADELAIDE 1830–1895 ⚭ Sir JOSEPH SEBAG MONTEFIORE 1822–1903
LIONEL LOUIS M.P. 1832–1887 ⚭ ESTHER 1832–1894
SIGISMUND SCHLOSS
Sir LEONARD LIONEL K.C.V.O. 1858–1938 ⚭ ELIZA HENRIETTA 1864–1935
Sir ISIDORE SPIELMANN
LIONEL Baron COHEN of Walmer 1888–1973 ⚭ ADELAIDE
HENRY COBB
WALTER SAMUEL b. 1870 ⚭ LUCY MARGARET
RUTH LOUISA 1906–1991
Sir ANDREW BENJAMIN 1909–1968 ⚭ Mrs. HELEN DONNINGTON
ELLEN 1843–1919 ⚭ SAMUEL MONTAGU 1st Lord Swaythling 1832–1911
SOLOMON 1776–1864 ⚭ HANNAH
JEANETTE 1803–1867 ⚭ Sir DAVID *SALOMONS 1797–1873
HANNAH 1816–1898 ⚭ BENJAMIN MOSES MERTON 1813–1881
HENRY BEHRENS
Sir BENJAMIN LOUIS Bart. M.P. 1844–1909 ⚭ LOUISA EMILY 1850–1931
Sir HERBERT BENJAMIN 2nd Bart. O.B.E. 1874–1968 ⚭ HANNAH MILDRED
NIGEL BENJAMIN 1908–1931
STEPHEN BEHRENS 1911–1943
HANNAH FLORETTE O.B.E. 1875–1946
HANNAH 1783–1850 ⚭ NATHAN MAYER *ROTHSCHILD 1777–1836
JUDITH 1784–1862 ⚭ Sir MOSES *MONTEFIORE 1784–1885
JACOB WALEY
NATHANIEL LOUIS 1846–1913 ⚭ JULIA MATILDA 1853–1917
Col. JACOB WALEY COHEN 1874–1948 ⚭ 1 KATHERINE 1875–1924 ⚭ 2 Mrs. EVELYN GRABOWSKY-ATHERSTONE
Sir ROBERT WALEY COHEN K.B.E. 1877–1952 ⚭ ALICE VIOLET 1881–1935
Sir BERNARD NATHANIEL WALEY-COHEN 1914–1991 ⚭ JOYCE
Lord NATHAN
JOSEPH SALOMONS
PHILIP J. SALOMONS
LIONEL BENJAMIN 1826–1890 ⚭ 1 HENRIETTA RACHEL 1827–1859 ⚭ 2 BERTHA 1841–1917
HENRY EDWARD BEDDINGTON
Col. CHARLES WALEY COHEN 1879–1963 ⚭ ETHEL ALICE
HERMANN KISCH
Rev. SIMEON SINGER
DOROTHEA 1882–1964 ⚭ Dr. CHARLES *SINGER 1876–1960
JOSEPH ELIAS MONTEFIORE
BENJAMIN 1789–1867 ⚭ JUSTINA 1800–1873
PHILIP LUCAS
NATHANIEL 1827–1911 ⚭ REBEKAH 1839–1890
MARGUERITE ABIGAIL 1871–1942 ⚭ Sir BENJAMIN ARTHUR K.C. 1862–1942
HENRY MICHOLLS
Rt. Hon. ARTHUR K.C. 1829–1914 ⚭ EMMELINE 1843–1888
MARY FREDA ⚭ Sir THOMAS COLYER-FERGUSSON 1865–1951
NAPHTALI HART MYERS of New York 1711–1788
Dr. JOSEPH HART MYERS 1758–1823
PHINEHAS SAMUEL
ISAAC 1791–1846 ⚭ 1 REBEKAH 1793–1819 ⚭ 2 SARAH 1810–1879
LULIANA 1831–1877 ⚭ Baron MAYER AMSCHEL de *ROTHSCHILD

of £100,000 for the building of Liverpool University Library. Another son, REX D. COHEN (1876–1928), remained in the family business and left over £1.6 million upon his death. Louis Samuel's eighth child, SIR JACK BRUNEL COHEN (1886–1956), lost both legs in World War I. From 1918 to 1931 he was a member of parliament representing Liverpool and for many years was national treasurer of the British Legion. SIR REX ARTHUR LOUIS COHEN (d. 1988), grandson of Louis Samuel (1906–1988), was chairman of Lewis' from 1958 to 1965, when the business passed from family control. For several years he was president of the Liverpool Jewish Welfare Board.

[Sefton D. Temkin]

COHEN, ABRAHAM (1887–1957), Anglo-Jewish clergyman, scholar, and communal leader. Cohen, who was born in Reading and grew up in the East End of London, was educated at London and Cambridge Universities. He became a minister in Manchester in 1909 and in 1913 minister to the Birmingham Hebrew Congregation, where he remained for 36 years. Cohen was active in the World Jewish Congress and in the Zionist movement. He was the first minister to preside over the *Board of Deputies of British Jews (from 1949 to 1955), which he greatly strengthened by a combination of firmness and diplomacy. Cohen edited the Soncino Books of the Bible, himself translating the Psalms, and participated in the Soncino translation of the Talmud and Midrash. His writings include *Everyman's Talmud* (1949^2), *An Anglo-Jewish Scrap-Book* (1968^2), and *Teachings of Maimonides* (1927). Cohen assisted Chief Rabbi Joseph *Hertz with his *Pentateuch Commentary*, the first English commentary written by Jews. His *Everyman's Talmud* was republished as a paperback in 1995.

BIBLIOGRAPHY: *The Times* (London, May 30, 1957); JC (May 30, 1957); Roth, Mag Bibl, 172; Lehmann, Nova Bibl, 12, 20.

[Vivian David Lipman]

COHEN, ALBERT (1895–1981), French novelist whose four outstanding novels, written over a period of four decades, form one of the most outspoken series in modern Jewish literature. Cohen, who was born in Corfu, was educated in France, then studied law in Geneva, where he became active in various international organizations and pursued a sporadic literary career. His first published work was a volume of poems, *Paroles juives* (1921), whose tone, by turns violent, opulent, tender, and lyrical, foreshadowed that of his later writing. In 1925, with the encouragement of Chaim *Weizmann, Cohen founded a short-lived periodical, *La Revue juive*. He later became the Zionist Organization's delegate to the League of Nations. During the Nazi occupation Cohen fled to London, where he became the Jewish Agency's special representative to the Allied governments in exile. After the defeat of the Nazis, he worked at the UN headquarters of the International Refugee Organization.

The most important themes in Cohen's writings are the problem of personal integrity in a world of untruth, the eternal message of Israel to humankind, and the place of the Jew in the modern world. These themes recur in various forms in the four novels: *Solal* (1930: Eng. tr. *Solal of the Solals*, 1933); *Mangeclous* (1938; *Nailcruncher*, 1940); *Belle du Seigneur* (1968), which won the Grand Prix de l'Académie française, and *Les Valeureux* (1969). In *Solal*, the eponymous hero escapes from his native Greek island of Cephalonia and narrow Jewish environment into the glittering gentile world, where he is eventually destroyed by his own success and by a fatal passion for a non-Jewess. After a terrible struggle, Solal returns to his own oppressed people, "the poetic people of genius," and finds redemption. *Mangeclous*, a Rabelaisian extravaganza, has as its setting a semi-mythical Jewish Orient peopled by grotesque but innocent and lovable inhabitants. Under the burlesque absurdity, a profound Jewish wisdom is often brought to the fore. In *Belle du Seigneur*, which returns to the *Solal* story, the hero has achieved his ultimate ambition as an undersecretary at the League of Nations, but is haunted by the impending Nazi destruction of the Jews. Aware of his own helplessness and of the nations' indifference, Solal seeks escape in an impossible romantic adventure, but the lovers fall victim to a self-destructive passion from which only death can release them. *Les Valeureux*, a burlesque sequel to the epic begun in *Mangeclous*, tells about the five jolly cousins from Cephalonia, nicknamed the "Valorous Ones." This last novel contrasts the Jewish love of life and truth to the falsity and hypocrisy of the outside world. Other works by Cohen are the one-act play *Ezéchiel* (1956), produced at the Comédie Française in 1933, and the autobiographical *Le livre de ma mère* (1954), dedicated to the author's mother, who died in occupied France, and to the simple grandeur of maternal love.

Cohen, like his hero, can best be described as extreme – extreme in his love for his people, extreme in his satire (particularly concerning international organizations), extreme in his condemnation of sexual passion. Cohen's work is original, varied, and rich, containing humor, tragedy, drama, lyricism, satire, tenderness, violence, and anger.

BIBLIOGRAPHY: A. Lunel, in: *Revue juive de Genève*, 1 (1932–33), 120–2, 165–70; A. Berchtold, in: *La Suisse romande au cap du XXè siècle* (1963); D. Goitein, *Jewish Themes in French Works Between the Two World Wars* (Columbia University Thesis, 1967); A. Pesses, in: *Les nouveaux cahiers* (1969). **ADD. BIBLIOGRAPHY:** D.R. Goiten-Galperin, *Visage de mon peuple:essai sur Albert Cohen* (1982); H. Nyssen, *Lectures d'Albert Cohen* (1986); J. Blot, *Albert Cohen ou Solal dans le siècle* (1995); C. Auroy, *Albert Cohen, une quête solaire* (1996); V. Duprey, *Albert Cohen: Au nom du père et de la mère* (1999); J.I. Abecassis, *Albert Cohen: Dissonant Voices* (2004).

[Denise R. Goitein]

COHEN, ALEXANDER H. (1920–2000), U.S. producer. Cohen began investing in the theater at the age of 21, and became known on Broadway as the "millionaire boy angel." He scored his first success with *Angel Street* in 1941. Subsequently, he staged more than 30 productions in New York and London. His Nine O'Clock Theater for intimate review opened in 1959 with *At the Drop of a Hat*, and presented such diverse performers as John Gielgud, Yves Montand, and the Karmon Israel Dancers. In 1962 he imported *Beyond the Fringe* from England, directing it himself. His production of *Hamlet*, starring Richard Burton and directed by Gielgud, won widespread critical acclaim.

His many Broadway productions included *Of V We Sing* (1942), *King Lear* (1951), *An Evening with Mike Nichols and Elaine May* (1960–61), *The School for Scandal* (1963), *Baker Street* (1965), *The Homecoming* (1967), *Black Comedy/White Lies* (1967), *6 Rms Riv Vu* (1972–73), *Good Evening* (1973–74), *Words & Music* (1974), *Comedians* (1976–77), *I Remember Mama* (1979), *A Day In Hollywood / A Night in the Ukraine* (1980–81), and *Waiting in the Wings* (1999–2000).

In 1967 Cohen won a Tony for Best Play for *The Homecoming*. That year, he conceived and originated the national Tony Awards telecast, an annual special TV presentation in which the American Theater Wing presents awards to the best plays and musicals of the season. After a long stint of producing the show (1967–86), Cohen was pressured to step down as presenter of the awards when he publicly made a disparaging remark about a particular theater critic and implied that he spoke not only for himself but for the American Theater Wing as well.

A compilation of 17 musical numbers from several editions of the Tony Awards shows Cohen produced is captured on *Broadway's Lost Treasures* (2003), a 110-minute DVD. In 1973 Cohen was honored with the Theater World Special Award for "his contribution to cultivating theater audiences by extending Broadway, not only nationally but internationally, with his exemplary television productions."

[Ruth Beloff (2nd ed.)]

COHEN, ALFRED MORTON (1859–1949), U.S. lawyer, politician, and Jewish civic leader. Cohen was born in Cincinnati, Ohio. He graduated from the University of Cincinnati Law School (1880), in the same class as his lifelong friend, William Howard Taft. At the age of 25, Cohen served the first of several terms on Cincinnati's city council and in 1896 he was elected to the state senate, where he served two terms. Cohen was a staunch advocate of equal rights for blacks and was active in the Urban League. In 1876, when he was only 17, Cohen organized a local chapter of the Young Men's Hebrew Association, and in 1890 he helped to create a national Y.M.H.A. organization, whose presidency he held for several years. A member of B'nai B'rith for over 60 years, he was president of his Cincinnati lodge (1906) and served as international president of the order from 1925 to 1938. In 1933 he helped found the Joint Consultative Council, a body composed of B'nai B'rith, the American Jewish Committee, and the American Jewish Congress, whose purpose was to achieve Jewish unity in the struggle against Nazism. That same year he represented B'nai B'rith at the World Conference of Jews held in London on the subject of German Jewry. In 1936 B'nai B'rith funded the creation of a colony in Palestine named Moledet B'nai B'rith, in tribute to Cohen.

BIBLIOGRAPHY: E.E. Grusd, *B'nai B'rith* (Eng., 1966), index.

[Robert Shostek]

COHEN, SIR ANDREW (1909–1968), British colonial administrator, brother of Ruth Louisa *Cohen. Cohen began his career in the Inland Revenue Department of the British government and a year later was transferred to the Colonial Office. During World War II he organized the food supply to Malta. In 1947 Cohen became undersecretary of state at the Colonial Office. In this post he did much to prepare the African colonies for independence at a time when it was not generally believed that independence for Africa was imminent. From 1952 to 1957 he was governor of Uganda and introduced widespread political and economic reforms, although he encountered much trouble when he deported the Kabaka of Buganda in 1953. He was the British representative on the United Nations Trusteeship Council from 1957 to 1961, and in 1961 was appointed secretary of the newly created Ministry of Overseas Development. This ministry was set up to deal with the problem of relations with newly independent states in the post-colonial period. Cohen wrote *British Policy in Changing Africa* (1959).

BIBLIOGRAPHY: *New York Times* (June 19, 1968), 47; *The Times* (London, June 19, 1968). **ADD. BIBLIOGRAPHY:** ODNB online.

COHEN, ARMOND E. (1909–), U.S. Conservative rabbi. Cohen was born in Canton, Ohio, and ordained at the Jewish Theological Seminary in 1934. He spent his entire career as rabbi of the Cleveland Jewish Center (renamed Park Synagogue in 1951), which, under his stewardship, grew to some 2,000 families. A proponent of interdenominational cooperation, Cohen was active in both civic and Jewish communal affairs. He was also a staunch Zionist, serving as president of the Ohio chapter of the Zionist Organization of America and later honorary president of the entire organization. He was an advocate of pastoral psychology and lectured in the Department of Religio-Psychiatry of the Jewish Theological Seminary (1969–74), as well as at the American Foundation of Religion and Health (1965–75), which he also served as a member of its Board of Directors. As chairman of the Rabbinical Assembly's Committee on Marriage and the Family (1958–60), he lobbied successfully for marriage counseling to be provided under the auspices of the Rabbinical Assembly and the Seminary. He was also a member of the Seminary's Board of Overseers and of the Executive Council of the Rabbinical Assembly (1950–58). In 1945, he published *All God's Children: A Jew Speaks*, a collection of open letters on Jewish-Christian relations and Jewish tradition that had previously appeared anonymously in his synagogue's bulletin.

BIBLIOGRAPHY: P.S. Nadell, *Conservative Judaism in America: A Biographical Dictionary and Sourcebook* (1988).

[Bezalel Gordon (2nd ed.)]

COHEN, ARTHUR (1829–1914), English lawyer. Born in London, a grandson of Levi Barent Cohen, Cohen was admitted to Magdalene College, Cambridge, after his uncle Moses *Montefiore had persuaded the prince consort to sponsor his candidacy. He became president of the Cambridge Union and was Fifth Wrangler in 1853 but was able to take his degree only in 1858, after the passage of the Cambridge University Reform Act. In that year he became the first practicing Jew to graduate from Cambridge. Admitted to the bar in 1857, he built up a substantial practice and in 1872 he was named junior counsel in the critical Alabama arbitration between Great Britain and the United States. In 1874, Cohen was made a queen's counsel and sat in Parliament as a Liberal from 1880 to 1887. In his later years he received many honors, becoming a member of the Privy Council (a rare distinction for one who held no governmental position) and being elected chairman of the Bar Council. From 1893 until 1914 he was standing counsel to the India Office.

Cohen was active in Jewish affairs and from 1880 to 1895 was president of the Board of Deputies of British Jews in succession to Moses *Montefiore.

BIBLIOGRAPHY: L. Cohen, *Arthur Cohen* (1919); P. Emden, *Jews of Britain* (1943), 178–84; I. Finestein, in: J.M. Shaftesley (ed.,), *Remember the Days: essays … C. Roth* (1966). **ADD. BIBLIOGRAPHY:** ODNB online; C. Bermant, *The Cousinhood* (1971), index; I. Finestein, *Jewish Life in Victorian England* (1993).

[Moshe Rosetti]

COHEN, ARTHUR (1864–1940), German economist and statistician. Cohen was born in Munich. After studying law and economics he joined the Bavarian public finance administration. In 1906 he turned to teaching and research at the Technical University in Munich, working at the same time at the Munich Chamber of Commerce. With the advent of the Nazis in 1933 he was dismissed from his posts, but continued to live and work privately in Munich until his death. Cohen's professional interests ranged from economic history, monetary theory, and finance to agricultural and labor economics as well as to Jewish topics. He published several monographs on the history of the Jews in Munich.

[Joachim O. Ronall]

COHEN, ARTHUR A. (1928–1987), U.S. novelist, publisher, art historian, and theologian. Born in New York, Cohen received his B.A. (1946) and M.A. (1949) from the University of Chicago and then continued with studies in medieval Jewish philosophy at the Jewish Theological Seminary. He founded, with Cecil Hemley, Noonday Press in 1951; in 1956 he began Meridian Books. From 1960 to 1974, when he founded Ex Libris Publishing Company, he worked as an editor. He wrote essays, works of non-fiction on Jewish subjects, and novels.

His *The Natural and the Supernatural Jew* (1962) sets the most insistent theme of his theological writings. Since Enlightenment, he avers, Jewish thought and imagination have with ever-increasing measure focused on the "natural" Jew enmeshed in immediate social and political concerns. Cohen fears that this understandable attention to the interests of the natural Jew, abetted by secular attitudes and biases of the modern period, has led to the neglect of the "supernatural" Jew, the Jew of the covenant conscious of his transcendent responsibilities. Accordingly, the urgent task of contemporary Jewish religious thought is to develop a strategy to reintegrate the natural and the supernatural Jew, otherwise the prospect looms that although the supernatural Jew may survive, Judaism will perish. Because of the experience of the modern, secular world, however, the supernatural vocation of the Jew could no longer be naively affirmed. To be spiritually and intellectually engaging, Cohen holds, the presuppositions of classical Jewish belief must be first "theologically reconstructed." Cohen's conception of this endeavor is inspired largely by the German Jewish thinker Franz *Rosenzweig whose uncompromising affirmation of theistic belief – grounded in the experiential categories of creation, revelation, and redemption – was supplemented by an equally unyielding adherence to rigorous philosophical reflection and honesty. For Cohen, the task of theological reconstruction is rendered all the more urgent by the Holocaust, which in disclosing "the *tremendum* of evil," has so radically challenged the presuppositions of Jewish belief that to avoid this task is to relegate Judaism to blind faith and atavistic sentiment. Clearly, as Cohen argues in *The Tremendum. A Theological Interpretation of the Holocaust* (1981), the retreat to an unthinking, platitudinous posture endangers the recovery of Judaism as a supernatural vocation. These themes are echoed in Cohen's novels, among them *The Carpenter Years* (1967), *In the Days of Simon Stern* (1973), *A Hero in His Time* (1976), *Acts of Theft* (1980), and *An Admirable Woman* (1983). He coedited, with Paul Mendes-Flohr, *Contemporary Jewish Religious Thought* (1987).

[Paul Mendes-Flohr (2nd ed.)]

COHEN, BARRY (1935–), Australian politician. Born in Griffith, New South Wales, Barry Cohen was an Australian Labor Party member of the House of Representatives for the seat of Robertson in New South Wales from 1969 to 1990. During much of this time he was the only Jewish member of the Australian parliament. He held ministerial office in Bob Hawke's Labor government from 1983 to 1987 as minister for home affairs and the environment and then as minister for the arts, heritage, and the environment.

[William D. Rubinstein (2nd ed.)]

COHEN, BENJAMIN (1726–1800), Dutch financier and tobacco merchant. Taking over his father's tobacco company, he made it into one of the most prosperous and influential firms in Holland. Cohen conducted large-scale financial operations first in Amersfoort and from 1786 in Amsterdam. He owned tobacco plantations in Holland and exported to the Baltic area; in 1788 his firm contracted to import 40,000 carats of diamonds annually from Brazil. It was then probably the only Jewish firm in Amsterdam to issue loans, and in 1793 and 1796 made two loans to the Prussian government of five and three million guilders. Via his sister Cohen was related to the *Goldsmids in London, who opened their bank for new issues in this period. He acted as financial adviser to Prince William V of Orange, who was his guest in Amersfoort in 1787 during the Patriotic Revolt. A patron of Jewish letters, he sponsored the publication of Hebrew mathematical and philosophical works, such as works by Naftali Herz Ulman. As a *parnas* of the Ashkenazi community in Amsterdam, he was one of the leading Jews and at the same time a deeply committed member of the Orangist faction in Dutch politics.

BIBLIOGRAPHY: J. Zwarts, *Het verblijf van Prins Willem v in Amersfoort ten huize van den Joodschen tabaksplanter Benjamin Cohen* (1921). **ADD. BIBLIOGRAPHY:** J. Michman, *The History of Dutch Jewry during the Emancipation Period: Gothic Turrets on a Corinthian Building* (1995), 15–16; J. Meijer, *Zij lieten hun sporen na, joodse bijdragen aan tot Nederlandse beschaving* (1964), 98–103.

[Frederik Jacob Hirsch / Bart Wallet (2nd ed.)]

COHEN, BENJAMIN VICTOR (1894–1983), U.S. lawyer and presidential adviser. Cohen was born in Muncie, Indiana. He was admitted to the Illinois Bar in 1916. Cohen served as secretary to Judge Julian W. *Mack in New York until 1917, then as attorney to the U.S. Shipping Board. During 1919–21 he was counsel to the U.S. Zionists negotiating the Palestine Mandate terms at the London and Paris Peace Conferences. Returning to New York, he practiced law, specializing in corporate reorganization and legal counseling to lawyers. As Harvard protégés of Felix *Frankfurter, Cohen and Thomas G. Corcoran became members of an inner circle of advisers to President Franklin D. *Roosevelt from 1933. They provided ideas, facts, and statistics for many New Deal programs and drafted such important legislation as the Securities Act (1933), the Securities Exchange Act (1934), the Public Utility Holding Company Act (1935), and the Fair Labor Standards ("Wages and Hours") Act (1938). Cohen, who skillfully drafted the legislation, and Corcoran, who managed it through Congress, were both bitterly attacked and highly praised for the roles they played. Cohen's offices in government included associate general counsel to the Public Works Administration (1933–34) in charge of railroad loans; general counsel to the National Power Policy Commission (1934–41); and special assistant to the U.S. attorney general in public utility holding company litigation. In 1941 he was appointed adviser to the U.S. ambassador to Great Britain. Cohen was director of the Office of Economic Stabilization (1942–43); general counsel, Office of War Mobilization (1943–45); counselor, U.S. Department of State (1945–47); legal adviser, International Monetary Conference, Bretton Woods, N.Y. (1944); and member of the U.S. delegation to the Dumbarton Oaks Conference, Washington, D.C. (1944), and to the peace conferences held after World War II in Berlin, London, Moscow, and Paris. He is reputed to have helped write the United Nations Charter, and served the U.S. delegation to the UN at several General Assemblies. In 1961 Cohen delivered the Oliver Wendell Holmes Lectures at Harvard Law School, published as *United Nations: Constitutional Developments, Growth, and Possibilities* (1961). A friend of President Lyndon Johnson, Cohen studied the problem of oil reserves during his administration.

[Julius J. Marcke]

COHEN, BERNARD (1933–), British painter; brother of the painter Harold *Cohen. Bernard was born in London. While visiting the U.S., he was profoundly impressed by Abstract Expressionism. He was included in the Venice Biennale of 1966 and a retrospective at the Tate Gallery, London, in 1973 established him as a leading contemporary British artist. Bernard Cohen is essentially a romantic painter and his quasi-mystical manner has more in common with postwar American painting (especially the work of Jewish artists such as *Rothko and Newman) than his English contemporaries. His later work sought a new purity and spirituality. The Tate Gallery in London held 48 of his works in 2004.

[Charles Samuel Spencer]

COHEN, BOAZ (1899–1968), U.S. rabbinic scholar. Cohen was born in Bridgeport, Connecticut, and in 1924 was ordained by the Jewish Theological Seminary, where he began teaching the following year and remained for the rest of his career. He was awarded a Ph.D. from Columbia University. He was secretary of the Committee on Jewish Law of the Rabbinical Assembly of America, 1933–45, and chairman, 1945–48. He wrote thousands of opinions responding to every facet of Jewish life in America as he considered the request of rabbis and the needs of their congregants, including adoption and conversion. His judgment was restrained. Halakhah could not solve every problem and its processes must be respected and its authority protected. He led a committee to study the issue of the **agunah*, but out of respect for the unity of the Jewish people would not permit unilateral action by the Conservative Rabbinate. He was a leading expert on Jewish divorce law, and at a time when denominational lines were less rigid than they are in the early 21st century, the divorce documents that he supervised were recognized and respected by Rabbi Joseph *Soloveitchik and the Rabbinical Council of America despite the fact that Cohen was on the faculty of the Jewish Theological Seminary.

A man of gentle disposition and immense erudition, his knowledge was far-ranging, including Greek and Roman, Canon, Islamic, and American law and Assyrian and Babylonian literature. Cohen was one of the first American-born and American-educated scholars to make significant contributions to the scientific study of rabbinic literature. His *Kunteres ha-Teshuvot* (1930), an annotated bibliography of the rabbinic responsa of the Middle Ages, was one of the first attempts to classify and describe the responsa literature and has remained a standard reference work. He published bibliographies of his father-in-law Israel Friedlaender (1936), Louis Ginzberg (1945), and Alexander Marx (1950[2]). In addition, he prepared the voluminous index to Ginzberg's *The Legends of the Jews* (1938). Cohen's main scholarly activity was in the field of comparative law, his principal works being *Law and Tradition in Judaism* (1959) and *Jewish and Roman Law* (2 vols., 1960). His work reveals a mastery of the relevant literature and ancient languages.

ADD. BIBLIOGRAPHY: P.S. Nadell, *Conservative Judaism in America* (1988) pp. 53–55; S. Greenberg, *Foundations of a Faith* (1967) 90–112; *Proceedings of the Rabbinical Assembly* (1969),173–75.

[Michael Berenbaum (2nd ed.)]

COHEN, CHAPMAN (1868–1954) English philosopher. Born in Leicester, Cohen became involved in the free thought movement in England as a result of the work of Charles Bradlaugh and G.W. Foote. He began writing on religious topics in the 1890s. He attacked religious beliefs and the activities of religious organizations. In 1915 he became the editor of the *Freethinker* and president of the National Secular Society. Cohen was an advocate of materialism, and lectured against and debated religious thinkers. He opposed the English laws against blasphemy. Cohen wrote many books and pamphlets including *Determinism or Free Will?* (1912), *Religion and Sex: Studies in the Pathology of Religious Development* (1919), *Theism or Atheism* (1921), *A Grammar of Freethought* (1921), *The Other Side of Death* (1922), *Materialism Re-Stated* (1927), and *Essays in Freethinking* (1923–39). In 1940 he published a work about himself, *Almost an Autobiography: The Confessions of a Freethinker*.

ADD. Bibliography: ODNB *online*.

[Richard H. Popkin]

COHEN, DAVID (1883–1967), Dutch historian and prominent Jewish and Zionist leader. Cohen, who was born at Deventer, east Holland, was professor of ancient history at the universities of Leiden and Amsterdam from 1924 to 1953 (except for the years of Nazi occupation). His involvement in Jewish affairs started in 1903; while a student he established an organization to assist Jewish refugees from Eastern Europe who passed Deventer by train, and afterwards he became involved in a variety of local, national, and international organizations for Jewish refugees and migrants. In the 1920s, while living in The Hague, he headed the committee for the poor of the local Jewish community. A Zionist from his youth, he was for many years one of the leaders of Dutch Zionism, establishing branches and youth organizations, writing in its publications, and representing it abroad. In 1933, immediately after the ascendance of the Nazis to power in Germany, Cohen co-founded and led – with Abraham *Asscher – the Comité voor Bijzondere Joodse Belangen (Committee for Special Jewish Affairs) to combat Nazi antisemitism and policies and to help refugees from Germany; for this purpose a special Subcommittee for Jewish Refugees, headed by Cohen, was established, and became one of the most powerful organizations in Dutch Jewry of the 1930s. In this position he was instrumental in having Alfred Wiener with his documentation on Nazism and antisemitism move from Germany to Amsterdam (1933). From 1933 to 1939 he was chairman of the Jewish Central Information Office, under the auspices of which Wiener constantly enlarged his collection; in 1939 Wiener once again moved, now to London, where the collection finally settled and became known as the *Wiener Library. The Refugee Committee continued its activities also after the German invasion in May 1940. In December 1940 Cohen joined the Jewish Coordination Committee, an initiative to organize Dutch Jewry vis-à-vis the Germans. From February 12, 1941, to September 1943 Cohen acted as cochairman (with Abraham Asscher) and dominating personality of the *Joodsche Raad voor Amsterdam*, the Amsterdam Jewish Council, appointed by the German occupation authorities (see *Amsterdam), which gradually expanded its authority over all Jews in the Netherlands. In this position he conducted the controversial policies of the Council, which were characterized by servility towards the German authorities. He was finally arrested on the eve of Rosh ha-Shanah (September 1943) and sent as a "prominent Jew" to Theresienstadt, where he stayed from 1943 to 1945. In 1947 he was arrested on charges of collaboration with the Germans, but was soon released. However, a Jewish "honorary" court excluded him from participation in all Jewish functions. In 1955 Cohen published reminiscences, *Zwervend en Dolend*, dealing with his work for Jewish refugees in the 1930s; a second, planned volume, intended to explain his policies in the 1940s, was never published. However, a part of it was published in 2000 in a biography of Cohen. His and his colleague Abraham Asscher's behavior and policies have been a major theme of Dutch and general historiography as well as of popular discussion of the fate of the Dutch Jews, of whom about 75% perished during the Holocaust, and of the Jewish Councils in general.

BIBLIOGRAPHY: A.J. Herzberg, *Kroniek der Jodenvervolging* (1951); J. Presser, *Ashes in the Wind: The Destruction of Dutch Jewry* (1968). **ADD. BIBLIOGRAPHY:** L. de Jong, *Het Koninkrijk der Nederlanden in de Tweede Wereldoorlog*, vols. 1, 4, 5, 6, 7, 14 (1969–89); J. Michman, in: *Studia Rosenthaliana*, 4 (1970), 219–27; idem, in: *Yad Vashem Studies*, 10 (1974), 9–68; D. Michman, "The Jewish Refugees from Germany in The Netherlands, 1933–1940," ch. 3 (Ph.D. thesis, 1978) (Heb.); H. Knoop, *De Joodsche Raad. Het Drama van Abraham Asscher en David Cohen* (1983); N.K.C.A. in 't Veld, *De Joods Ereraad* (1989); J. Meijer, *Prof. Dr. David Cohen: Joodse jeugdjaren in Deventer, 1882–1901* (1992); I. Scheltes, *Cohen: professor in oorlogstijd* (1995); W. Lindwer (with J. Houwink ten Cate), *Het fatale dilemma. De Joodsche Raad voor Amsterdam, 1941–1943* (1995); B. Moore, *Victims and Survivors: The Nazi Persecution of the Jews in the Netherlands, 1940–1945* (1997); D. Michman, in: *Studia Rosenthaliana* 32 (1998), 173–89; J. Michman, H. Beem, and D. Michman, *Pinkas. Geschiedenis van de joodse gemeenschap in Nederland* (1999); N. van der Zee, *Um Schlimmeres zu verhindern. Die Ermordung der niederländischen Juden: Kollaboration und Widerstand* (1999); P. Schrijvers, *Rome, Athene, Jeruzalem. Leven en werk van Prof. Dr. David Cohen* (2000); J.C.H. Blom, R.G. Fuks-Mansfeld, and I. Schöffer (eds.), *The History of the Jews in the Netherlands* (1992).

[Shaul Esh / Dan Michman (2nd ed.)]

COHEN, DAVID (known as "*Ha-Nazir*," the Nazirite; 1887–1972), rabbi, talmudist, philosopher, and kabbalist. Cohen was born in Maisiogala, near Vilna, the scion of a distinguished rabbinic family. In his youth he studied in the yeshivot of the Ḥafeẓ Ḥayyim (*Israel Meir ha-Kohen) in Radun, Volozhin, and Slobodka. Even then his restless and inquiring mind led him to extend his studies beyond the traditional subjects taught in the yeshivot. Thus he turned to the *Ḥorev* of Samson Raphael *Hirsch and the early writings of Rabbi A.I. *Kook. He also studied Russian to prepare himself for entrance to the university. During the Russian Revolution of 1905 he was twice arrested but was not detained. His spiritual unrest and the desire to widen his intellectual horizon led him to enroll in the Academy for Jewish Studies established by Baron David Guenzburg, where one of his close fellow students was Zalman Rubashov (Shazar), later president of Israel. From there he proceeded to Germany to study at the University of Freiburg. At the outbreak of World War I he was interned as an enemy alien, but was released and made his way to Switzerland, studying philosophy, classical literature, and Roman law at Basel University. He was for a time chairman of the Jewish Students' Society there and delivered lectures on Jewish philosophy. It was then that he took upon himself a life-long Nazirite vow, which involves complete abstention from cutting one's hair and partaking of any products of the vine. But his asceticism went much further. It included an extreme vegetarianism, which encompassed not only food but any garment made of leather, and a self-imposed silence every Rosh Ḥodesh eve (Yom Kippur Katan) and from Rosh Ḥodesh Elul to the morrow of Yom Kippur. In addition, he refused to speak anything but Hebrew. However, he was not a recluse, and did not hesitate to express his views on important topical problems.

The turning point in his life came with his meeting with Rabbi Kook, who was then in St. Galen in Switzerland (1915). "My life then stood in the balance," he noted. "I listened to him and was turned into a new man … I had found a master." He decided to abandon his secular studies and devote himself entirely to Jewish thought. In 1922 he received an invitation from Rabbi Kook, who had returned to Ereẓ Israel, to become a tutor in the yeshivah which he had established, and helped to draw up the curriculum which was also to include history, philosophy, ethics, Hebrew grammar, and Bible. He was appointed lecturer in Talmud, ethics, and philosophy. The two used to meet daily and Rabbi Kook entrusted him with the editing of his philosophical works, to which, along with disseminating Kook's ideas, he dedicated his life, hardly publishing any of his own works, although he left over 30 works in manuscript. The principal exception was the *Kol Nevu'ah*, of which the first volume appeared shortly before his death. It is the fruit of his life's work and is in two parts, "The Foundations of Jewish Religious Philosophy" and "The Foundations of Inner Wisdom." The work is based on the premise that there is an original Jewish philosophy and a spiritual Jewish system of logic which is not intuitive-speculative but spiritual-acoustic: "Sound and light are the two angels of thought which accompany man everywhere" but "hearing is greater than seeing." The prophetic power is the beginning of Jewish wisdom, and he was convinced that the renewal of Jewish life in Israel would produce a new generation to which would even be vouchsafed the return of the spirit of prophecy.

A passionate adherent of the doctrine of Rabbi Kook that the Return to Zion and its various stages, of which the establishment of the State of Israel was the latest, was itself only a stage in the fulfillment of the Divine Promise which would bring about the Complete Redemption and the Messianic Age, he did not hesitate to reprove those rabbis who did not accept this belief. He saw in Moses Ḥayyim *Luzzatto the harbinger of this redemption, pointing out that the three significant movements, Ḥasidism, Musar, and Haskalah, had each made certain of Luzzatto's works their classics, and he claimed that both Rabbi Kook and he himself followed his doctrines.

Cohen's only son, Rabbi Shear-Yashuv Cohen, was Ashkenazi chief rabbi of Haifa, and his only daughter the wife of Israeli Chief Rabbi Shlomo Goren.

In 1977 there was published a three-volume *Festschrift* in his honor entitled *Nezir Eḥav*.

BIBLIOGRAPHY: Tidhar, 1 (1955), 2082–84; *Ha-Ẓofeh* (Sept. 6, 1972); H. Lifshitz, in: *Sinai* 438/9 (1972); A. Ẓoref, *Havveiha-Rav Kook* (1947), 122–5.

[Chaim Lifschitz]

COHEN, ELI (1924–1965), Israel intelligence officer, executed by the Syrian government. He was born in Alexandria, Egypt, and educated at a Jewish primary school and a French high school. In 1949 Cohen and all other Jewish students were expelled from Farouk University. His activities in local Zionist organizations, in which he had been involved from childhood, led to several investigations on the part of the Egyptian authorities. During the Sinai Campaign (October 1956) he was arrested and detained until January 1957, and upon his release was expelled from Egypt. He settled in Israel in February 1957, thereafter serving with the Israel intelligence service. In January 1965 he was arrested in Damascus as an Israel secret agent. His public trial before a military tribunal attracted worldwide publicity. The prosecution contended that he had established close ties with various departments and high-placed officials in the Syrian government. Cohen was convicted on a charge of espionage and sentenced to death. Requests that he be represented at his trial by a foreign or even local lawyer were refused. Despite strenuous efforts to persuade the Syrian government to commute the death sentence, including the intervention of Pope Paul VI and the heads of the French, Belgian, and Canadian governments, Cohen was publicly hanged in the Damascus city square. Streets, squares, and parks in

Israel were named in his honor, but repeated requests to Syria to release the body for burial in Israel have been refused.

BIBLIOGRAPHY: Y. Ben-Porat and U. Dan, *The Spy from Israel* (1969); E. Ben Hanan, *Eli Cohen, Our Man in Damascus* (1967); Bar-Zohar, in: *Midstream*, 14, no. 9 (1968), 35–53.

COHEN, ELISHEVA (1911–), Israel art designer. Born in Frankfurt-on-Main, Cohen immigrated to Israel in 1933. She was curator of the Israel Museum and specialized in arranging three-dimensional art exhibitions in which she was considered a pioneer in Israel. In 1977 she was awarded the Israel Prize for art and sculpture.

COHEN, ELIZABETH D.A. MAGNUS (1820–1921), pioneering woman physician in the southern United States. Cohen was born and educated in New York City. Married to Dr. Aaron Cohen and mother of five children, Magnus decided to study medicine at the age of 33, following the death of her young son. She enrolled in the recently created Women's Medical College of Pennsylvania in Philadelphia, from which she graduated in 1857. She then joined her husband in New Orleans, becoming the first woman to practice medicine in Louisiana. She helped combat yellow fever epidemics in 1857 and 1858, but thereafter treated mostly women and children in her private medical practice. For two decades she was listed in the New Orleans City Directory as a midwife and then as a "doctress," but in 1876 she finally achieved recognition as Mrs. Elizabeth Cohen, physician. She retired in 1887, following the deaths of her husband and children, and lived for the rest of her very long life in the Touro Infirmary, later known as the Julius Weis Home for the Aged, where she continued to serve as a volunteer. Elizabeth Cohen was an ardent supporter of women's rights and women's suffrage; only after her death at the age of 101 did the first woman receive a medical degree in New Orleans, from Tulane University.

BIBLIOGRAPHY: P.E. Hyman and D.D. Moore (eds.), *Jewish Women in America*, 1 (1997), 243–44; *New Orleans Times-Picayune* (Feb. 22, 1920); J. Duffy (ed.), *The Rudolph Matas History of Medicine in Louisiana*, 2 (1962); *Encyclopedia Louisiana* (1998).

[Harriet Pass Friedenreich (2nd ed.)]

COHEN, ELLIOT ETTELSON (1899–1959), U.S. journalist. Born in Des Moines, Iowa, Cohen was managing editor of *The Menorah Journal* from 1925 to 1931 and headed a group of writers who gave the journal its vitality and integrity. In 1945, he became editor of the newly founded magazine **Commentary*, which was designed to be larger in scope than the previous organ of the American Jewish Committee, *The Jewish Contemporary Record.* Established as a liberal anti-Communist journal, *Commentary* had Cohen as its editor and driving force from its inception until his death. As his successor Norman *Podhoretz stated, "Everyone knows that Elliot Cohen created *Commentary* and edited it for fourteen years, but I doubt that anyone except the people who in one capacity or another were close to the actual workings of the magazine ever appreciated the extent to which *Commentary* was Elliot Cohen." Cohen wrote *Commentary on the American Scene: Portraits of Jewish Life in America* (1953).

BIBLIOGRAPHY: L. Trilling, "On the Death of a Friend," in: *Commentary*, 29 (Feb. 1960); *Jewish Belief: A Symposium Compiled by the Editors of Commentary Magazine* (1966).

[Ruth Beloff (2nd ed.)]

COHEN, EMIL WILHELM (1842–1905), Danish mineralogist and geologist. Born in Aakjaer, Denmark, and a convert to Lutheranism, Cohen began his career as an assistant at the Heidelberg University and in 1878 was appointed professor of petrography at the University of Strasbourg. In 1885 he became professor of mineralogy at the University of Greifswald. In 1886 he explored the gold and diamond fields of the Transvaal, South Africa, and made several geographical explorations in various countries of South America. In the Franco-Prussian War he served as a noncombatant with the Germans, although he was a Danish subject. A nickel compound, Cohenite, is named for him. Among his works are *Sammlung von Mikrophotographien* (1881, 1899^3), on the microscopic structure and chemical composition of rocks and stones, and *Meteoritenkunde* (1894–1903), a study of the structure of meteorites.

COHEN, ERNST JULIUS (1869–1944), Dutch physical chemist. His father, Jacques Cohen, also a chemist, went to Holland from Germany and founded the Netherlands Coal Tar Distillery. Ernst Julius was born in Amsterdam, and became the leading disciple of van't Hoff. From 1902 he was professor of inorganic and general chemistry at Utrecht. He explained the previously mysterious phenomenon of "tin disease" and pursued research on the polymorphism and physical metamorphosis of numerous solid substances, notably iodides. Cohen established the historical committee of the Dutch Chemical Society and its historical library, and the Dutch Society for the History of Medicine, Natural Sciences, and Mathematics. He was the first president of the Dutch Chemical Society, chairman of the Dutch Committee on Coinage, and president of the International Union of Pure and Applied Chemistry. Among his many books are *Piezochemie kondensierter Systeme* (1919), in collaboration with W. Schut, *Physico-Chemical Metamorphosis and Some Problems in Piezochemistry* (1926), and textbooks for medical students and on physical chemistry and inorganic chemistry.

In 1941 his property was seized by the Germans. Two years later he was arrested and sent to a concentration camp, but released after an appeal by the Dutch Chemical Society. Early in 1944, he was advised to flee the country, but he refused. He was arrested, and transported to the gas chambers of Auschwitz.

BIBLIOGRAPHY: Donnan, in: *Journal of the Chemical Society* (1947), 1700.

[Samuel Aaron Miller]

COHEN, FANNIA (1885–1962), U.S. labor movement activist. Cohen was born in Kletsk, Russia, and immigrated to the United States with her brother in 1904. After working briefly with new immigrants on Ellis Island as the representative of the American Jewish Women's Committee, Cohen began studies for entrance to a college of pharmacy before deciding to take a job at a garment factory and work in the labor movement. In 1909, Cohen was elected to the executive board of her local union; she served as its chair from 1913 to 1914. In 1914, while president of the Kimono, Wrappers and Housedress Workers Union in New York City, Cohen was among early graduates of the Training School for Women Organizers, a year-long curriculum of academic and field work. In August 1915, she led workers in the first successful strike of Chicago's dress and white goods; later that year she was the first woman elected as vice president of the International Ladies' Garment Workers Union. She went on to become one of the foremost leaders of the ILGWU Education Department, where she was a staunch proponent of Unity Centers, places for women workers to learn and socialize. In 1921, Cohen helped establish Brookwood Labor College, the first residential college for workers in the United States; in 1923, she began working with Pioneer Youth of America, which sponsored summer camps for worker's children. Cohen spent the rest of her career creating additional educational programs, opportunities, and events for workers despite declining funding and opposition from others in the labor movement. In the course of debates about organizing women workers, Cohen became isolated from radical feminists and ultimately lost much of her power base in the union. In 1925, Cohen was not re-elected to the ILGWU General Executive Board and over the next few years, to the outrage of many, the new director, Mark Starr, restricted Cohen's work almost completely. Cohen continued as a relatively powerless executive secretary until she was forced into retirement in August 1962; she died four months later of a stroke.

BIBLIOGRAPHY: H.B. Long and C. Lawry, "Fannia Mary Cohn: An Educational Leader In Labor and Workers' Education, Her Life and Times." Research sponsored by University of Oklahoma: www-distance.syr.edu/long.html. **WEBSITE:** Jewish Virtual Library: www.jewishvirtuallibrary.org/jsource/biography/fcohn.html

[Marla Brettschneider (2nd ed.)]

COHEN, FRANCIS LYON (1862–1934), British rabbi and writer on Jewish liturgical music. Born in Aldershot, England, and trained at Jews' College, London, Cohen became a recognized expert on Jewish liturgy. He was preacher at South Hackney, London (1883–85), in Dublin (1885–86), and at the Borough New Synagogue, London (1886–1904), and chaplain in the British army. Ordained a rabbi in 1905, he became chief minister of the Sydney Great Synagogue in the same year and was senior Jewish chaplain to the Australian army (1914–34). In Australia, Cohen became one of the leading anti-Zionists of the Jewish community, opposing "political Zionism" as anti-British. Using the pseudonym "Asaph Klesmer" as well as his own name, Cohen wrote articles for the commemorative volume of the Anglo-Jewish Historical Exhibition (1887) and the Jewish Historical Society of England (1894), and was music editor of *The Jewish Encyclopedia* (1901–06). He edited collections of Jewish music, including *A Handbook of Synagogue Music for Congregational Singing* (with B.L. Mosely, 1889) and *The Voice of Prayer and Praise* (with D.M. Davis, 1899, 1914[2]). His arrangements of old melodies were published in *Lyra Anglo-Judaica* (pt. 1, 1891). Cohen married the daughter of a cantor, Marcus *Hast, and one of his nieces was the pianist Harriet *Cohen.

BIBLIOGRAPHY: JC (April 8, 1904), 18; (May 4, 1934), 10; Sendrey, Music, index. **ADD. BIBLIOGRAPHY:** R. Apple, "Francis Lyon Cohen: The Passionate Patriot," in: *Australian Jewish Historical Society Transactions*, 12, Pt. 4 (1995), 663–747, being a comprehensive biography; *Dictionary of Australian Biography*; H.L. Rubinstein, Australia I, index.

[Dora Leah Sowden]

COHEN, GERSON D. (1924–1991), Jewish historian and leader of Conservative Judaism. Educated at Camp Massad, where he cultivated a life-long commitment to Hebraism and Zionism, at the *Jewish Theological Seminary of America (JTS), and at Columbia University, Cohen specialized in the study of Jewish history and historiography. After the death of Alexander *Marx, Cohen served as librarian at JTS, also teaching Jewish history and Talmud there. He left in 1967 to succeed his academic mentor, the historian Salo W. *Baron, as director of the Center for Israel and Jewish Studies at Columbia University. After the Vietnam-era student riots at Columbia, Cohen returned to JTS as the Jacob Schiff Professor of Jewish History and inaugurated the school's Ph.D. program in Jewish history.

Cohen's scholarly work transplanted and updated the *Wissenschaft des Judentums model of research in the light of 20th-century Conservative Judaism. In his publications, he combined meticulous textual study, epitomized by his critical edition of Abraham ibn Daud's *Sefer Ha-Qaballah*, with an inter-textual focus. Cohen's scholarly essays, no less than his programmatic ones, encompassed the many permutations of rabbinic culture, both classical and medieval. He highlighted the leadership roles of Jewish intellectuals in their societies, especially in medieval Spain, but also in ancient and modern Jewish centers. Cohen's scholarly and administrative insights coincided in his thesis that Jewish continuity has always depended on the creative tension of maintaining the centrality of Jewish religion to Jewish history, on the one hand, and openness to influences from the broader cultural context, on the other. Among his books are *Studies in the Variety of Rabbinic Cultures* (1994) *and Jewish History and Destiny* (1997).

In 1971, Cohen and Bernard *Mandelbaum jointly succeeded Louis *Finkelstein as leaders of JTS. The division of the presidency and the chancellorship roles did not last for long. Within a year, Mandelbaum having resigned, Cohen became the chancellor of JTS, leading and transforming the institution until his retirement in 1986.

Cohen's leadership of JTS featured five emphases, in part continuations of the work of Finkelstein, but in large measure representing new departures: (1) The continued development of JTS as a center for Judaic Studies, and in particular, the physical reconstruction of its world-class library devastated by a fire in the mid-1960s. (2) The continued cultivation of JTS as a force for inter-religious dialogue. While maintaining his predecessor's initiative, the Institute for Religious and Social Studies, Cohen focused on inter-faith academic collaboration, fostering arrangements for student cross-registration and scholarly interchange with the Union Theological Seminary, a leading liberal Protestant divinity school in New York. (3) The administrative restructuring of JTS and the development of an independent graduate school of Jewish Studies. In 1974, Cohen replaced the existing JTS graduate program, the Institute for Advanced Studies in the Humanities, with a non-sectarian graduate school encompassing all non-theological graduate training. Under Cohen's aegis, the JTS graduate school became the largest institution of its kind in the Diaspora, training many of the scholars filling the expanding number of Judaic Studies chairs in North American Universities in the late twentieth century. (4) The active engagement of JTS as a resource for the development of Conservative (later, Masorti) Judaism in Israel. Cohen championed the twin concepts that JTS could offer a unique contribution to Jewish life in Israel and that, to serve the movement worldwide, Conservative rabbis needed extensive first-hand experience in Israel. Cohen raised the profile of JTS in Israel, expanding the school's Jerusalem campus, Neve Schechter, creating Midreshet Yerushalayim, a Conservative *yeshivah* program there, regularizing Israel residency requirements for JTS rabbinical students and, in 1984, opening an autonomous Israeli Conservative rabbinical school, the *Beit Hamidrash Lelimudei Hayahadut.* (5) Most consequentially for American Judaism, the active reorientation of JTS to a stance of closer involvement in the development of the Conservative movement. The leading issue that precipitated this change of course was the debate over the ordination of women as Conservative rabbis. Although initially opposed to that change, in 1977, Cohen consented to a *Rabbinical Assembly resolution that JTS conduct a movement-wide study of the issue, and in the course of that process, he became an ardent proponent of women's ordination. While characterizing the proposed reform as fully within the parameters of Conservative Judaism, Cohen also argued that JTS risked forfeiting its position as "fountainhead" of the denomination if it failed to ordain women, seeing that the Rabbinical Assembly was moving closer to admitting women candidates ordained privately or at other rabbinical seminaries. Although unsuccessful in his first attempt to persuade the JTS faculty to approve the proposed reform, in 1979, four years later, when movement pressure for women's ordination had mounted and the composition of the JTS faculty had changed, Cohen succeeded in changing school policy in this regard.

BIBLIOGRAPHY: J. Wertheimer (ed.), *Tradition Renewed*, 2 vols. (1998).

[Michael Panetz (2nd ed.)]

COHEN, GEULAH (1929–), Israeli politician, member of the Eighth to Twelfth Knessets. Cohen was born in Tel Aviv. Her father immigrated to Eretz Israel from Yemen and her mother was born in Eretz Israel to a family that had arrived there in the 19th century from North Africa. As a youth, she became a member of *Betar and joined the *Irgun Tzeva'i Le'ummi in 1942. In 1943 she joined the *Loḥamei Ḥerut Israel (Leḥi), becoming its radio broadcaster. Because of her involvement in Leḥi she was obliged to leave her studies at the Levinsky teachers' seminary, was detained by the British, and was sentenced to 19 years in prison. She escaped from the prison hospital in Bethlehem, and continued to broadcast.

Cohen received an M.A. from the Hebrew University of Jerusalem in philosophy and Bible studies. In 1948–60 she was a member of the editorial board of *Sulam*, a political monthly published by Israel *Eldad. Later she wrote a social-political column in *Ma'ariv*, and was a member of its editorial board in 1961–73. After the Six-Day War Cohen was involved in the campaign for Soviet Jewry, and in 1972 joined the *Ḥerut movement. Under the auspices of the movement Cohen founded the Midrashah Le'ummit educational institution in the spirit of Leḥi. She was elected to the Eighth Knesset in 1973 on the *Likud list. In the course of the Ninth Knesset, following the political upset of 1977, Cohen became chairperson of the Knesset Immigration and Absorption Committee. Following publication of Prime Minister Menaḥem *Begin's peace proposals, she established an internal opposition within the Likud, but finally left the Ḥerut movement in 1979, and together with MK Moshe *Shamir established the Teḥiyyah-Banai parliamentary group.

In October 1979 she established the Teḥiyyah Party, which was based on cooperation among three main groups: defectors from the Ḥerut movement, the Movement for Greater Israel, and *Gush Emunim. The new party objected to Israel's withdrawal from any territories in Ereẓ Israel.

In December 1980 Cohen proposed Basic Law: Jerusalem the Capital of Israel, and a year later the law extending Israeli law and administration to the Golan Heights. She failed to get a law passed that would extend Israeli law and administration to Judea, Samaria, and the Gaza Strip. In 1986, following the *Vanunu affair, Cohen called for the purge of left-wingers from the secret services. In the course of the Twelfth Knesset she was active in efforts to obtain the release of Jonathan *Pollard, found guilty in the United States of spying for Israel.

In the government established by Yitzḥak *Shamir in June 1990, Cohen was appointed minister of science and technology, and was active in connection with the absorption of immigrants from Ethiopia. In November 1991, following the Madrid Conference, she left the government together with her party. Following the failure of Teḥiyyah to pass the qualifying threshold in the elections to the Thirteenth Knesset in 1992, she returned to the Likud but failed in her efforts to get elected to its list for the Fourteenth Knesset. She wrote the autobiographical *Sipurha shel Loḥemet* ("Story of a Warrior," 1962), *Ha-Tapuz she-Ba'ar ve-Hetzit Levavot* ("The Orange That Burned and Lit Up Hearts," 1979), and *Mifgash Histori* ("An Historic Meeting," 1986). In 2003 she received the Israel Prize for her special contribution to Israeli society. Her only son, Tzaḥi Hanegbi, was a member of the Knesset for the Likud from the Twelfth Knesset and a member of several governments.

[Susan Hattis Rolef (2nd ed.)]

COHEN, GUSTAVE (1879–1958), Belgian historian of medieval French literature and theater. Cohen studied at Brussels, Liège, and Lyons, and received his doctorate from the Sorbonne. He taught at Leipzig (1906–09), was professor of French language and literature at Amsterdam (1912–19), and in 1932 was appointed professor of the history of medieval French literature at the Sorbonne. After the fall of France in 1940, Cohen fled to the United States. In 1941 he was appointed visiting professor at Yale, and in the following year he became dean of the Faculty of Letters of the Ecole Libre des Hautes Etudes which he had founded in New York. After the liberation of France in 1944, Cohen resumed his chair at the Sorbonne. Among the many honors bestowed on him was that of laureate of the Académie Française (1921) and laureate of the Académie des Inscriptions et Belles Lettres. Cohen's most important works are the *Histoire de la mise en scène dans le théâtre religieux du moyen-âge* (1906) and *La comédie latine en France au XIIe siècle* (1931). He founded and led a group called the "Théophiliens," which presented medieval plays. Cohen was decorated for military service in World War I. He was a convert to Catholicism.

BIBLIOGRAPHY: *Publications of the Modern Language Association*, 75 (1960), Supplement p. 132; *Mélanges … Gustave Cohen* (1950), 13.

[Howard L. Adelson]

COHEN, HAROLD (1928–), British painter. Harold Cohen was born in London and studied and later taught at the Slade School of Art. He represented Britain at the 1966 Venice Biennale with his brother Bernard *Cohen (1933–), with whom he shared a distinctive style, as both were influenced by traditional European expressionism and later American abstract expressionism. He designed the Ark curtains for the synagogue of Jews' College, London. In later years he lived in America and was involved, with considerable international publicity, in using computers to simulate human drawing. Bernard Cohen was also born in London and educated at the Slade School. From 1988 he was Slade Professor of Fine Art at London University and also director of the Slade School. A highly regarded abstract expressionist, he frequently exhibited in Britain and America.

BIBLIOGRAPHY: Friedmann, in: *Arts Magazine* (Feb. 1965), 34–40; Russell, in: *Art News* (Summer 1965), 48–49; Thompson, in: *Studio International* (June 1966), 233–45. **ADD. BIBLIOGRAPHY:** P. McCorduck, *Aaron's Code: Meta-Art, Artificial Intelligence, and the Work of Harold Cohen* (1991).

[Charles Samuel Spencer / William D. Rubinstein (2nd ed.)]

COHEN, HARRIET (1901–1967), British pianist. She made her debut at Queen's Hall, London, in 1914. By the age of 20 she had established her reputation as a virtuoso whose keyboard style combined elegance with spontaneity. Her interpretations of Bach were distinguished by clarity, precision, and vitality. Edward Elgar, Ralph Vaughan Williams, Arnold Bax, and William Walton all wrote compositions for her. In 1934 she took part in a London concert to aid refugee scientists at which *Einstein accompanied her on the violin. Shortly before World War II, when she visited Palestine to play with the Palestine Symphony Orchestra, she presented a collection of music manuscript autographs to the Jewish National and University Library. In Britain, she was active in supporting Jewish, and especially Israel, causes. In 1954 she was granted the freedom of the City of London. An injury to her right wrist in 1948 almost ended her concert career. It was two years before she appeared in public again, playing a concerto for the left hand written for her by Sir Arnold Bax. Failing eyesight compelled her to retire in 1960. Her writings include *Music's Handmaid* (1936) and memoirs, *A Bundle of Time* (1968).

BIBLIOGRAPHY: *New York Times* (Nov. 14, 1967); JC (Nov. 17, 1967).

COHEN, HARRY (1885–1969), U.S. surgeon, inventor, and author. Cohen was born in Austria and taken to the U.S. as a baby. In the course of a 60-year medical career in New York, Cohen was a medical inspector for the New York Department of Health (1912–13), and a surgeon at several institutions. He invented the clamp tourniquet (1934), the ligature guide (1936), and a surgical forceps for intravesical use (1930). Cohen, who was extremely active in Jewish affairs, was coeditor of *Jews in the World of Science* (1956), and chief editor of *American Jews: Their Lives and Achievements* (1958). His other publications include: *Simon Bolivar and the Conquest and Liberation of South America* (1955); *The Religion of Benjamin Franklin* (1957); and numerous medical monographs.

BIBLIOGRAPHY: *New York Times* (Jan. 31, 1969); S.R. Kagan, *Jewish Medicine* (1952), 462–3.

COHEN, HENRY (1863–1952), U.S. Reform rabbi and humanitarian. Cohen was born in London. He studied for the rabbinate at Jews' College, interrupting his studies during 1881–83 to work in South Africa as an interpreter of native dialects. He occupied pulpits in Kingston, Jamaica (1884–85), and Woodville, Mississippi (1885–88), then was rabbi of the Reform Congregation B'nai Israel of Galveston, Texas. An important shipping and commercial center with an affluent Jewish community, Galveston was the site of a hurricane in 1900 that took the lives of over 3,500 people. Cohen achieved national prominence for his heroic relief efforts after the disaster. In 1907 Cohen was drawn into the "*Galveston plan," which undertook to divert a part of the stream of East European Jewish immigration from the overcrowded slums of the Eastern sea board to the interior of the country, where there was a shortage of labor. Galveston was selected as port of entry, and over 10,000 Jews were served by the Jewish Immigrants' Information Bureau under Rabbi Cohen during 1907–14. Throughout his Galveston ministry, Cohen carried on a vigorous campaign against inhumane conditions in the Texas penal system and against public indifference to released prisoners. He was a pioneer in the rehabilitation of former convicts. Cohen was appointed a member of the Texas Prison Board by the governor (1927) and later chairman of the advisory committee of the Southwestern Probation and Parole Conference (1936). He was deeply involved in many other humanitarian activities.

BIBLIOGRAPHY: A. Cohen et al., *Man Who Stayed in Texas* (1941); A. Dreyfus (ed.), *Henry Cohen, Messenger of the Lord* (1963).

[A. Stanley Dreyfus]

COHEN, HENRY, BARON (1900–1977), British physician. Cohen, who was born in Birkenhead, became one of Britain's leading medical administrators and was involved in the establishment of the country's National Health Service. He was professor of medicine at Liverpool University from 1934 to 1965, and his contributions to the practice of medicine, particularly in the field of diagnosis, gained him an international reputation. His innumerable appointments to medical and allied bodies included the presidency of the British Medical Association, the General Medical Council, the Royal Society of Health, and the Royal Society of Medicine. He was made a baron in 1956. In 1973 Lord Cohen resigned as president of the General Medical Council, a position which he had held since 1961, on account of ill health. He was made a Companion of Honor in the 1974 New Year's Honors List for services to medicine. In 1970 he was appointed chancellor of Hull University. Lord Cohen was active in the affairs of the Liverpool Jewish community; he was on the council of the Anglo-Jewish Association and a governor of the Hebrew University of Jerusalem. His published lectures include *New Pathways in Medicine* (1935), *Nature, Method, and Purpose of Diagnosis* (1943), *Evolution of Modern Medicine* (1958), and *Sherrington: Physiologist, Philosopher, and Poet* (1958). He also contributed many papers on biological, neurological, and other medical subjects.

COHEN, HERMANN (1842–1918), German Jewish philosopher. Born in Cowsig, the son of a cantor, Cohen studied at the Jewish Theological Seminary at Breslau, but gave up his initial plans to become a rabbi. He turned to philosophy, studying first at the University of Breslau and then at the University of Berlin. He received his doctorate at the University of Halle in 1865. In 1873 he was invited by F.A. Lange, the well-known author of *The History of Materialism*, to become a *privatdozent* (lecturer) in philosophy at the University of Marburg. Appointed full professor after only three years, Cohen taught in Marburg until 1912. He spent the last years of his life in Berlin, where he taught at the Hochschule fuer die Wissenschaft des Judentums.

Interpretation of Kant and the Marburg System

Cohen's early works were devoted to a critical evaluation of idealism as embodied in the thought of Plato and, particularly, of Kant. "Die platonische Ideenlehre" (1886; see: *Schriften zur Philosophie und Zeitgeschichte*, 1928) was followed by *Kants Theorie der Erfahrung* (1871), *Kants Begruendung der Ethik* (1877), *Von Kants Einfluss auf die deutsche Kultur* (1883), and *Kants Begruendung der Aesthetik* (1889). These critical works brought Cohen to a new interpretation of Kant's philosophy, which came to be known as the Marburg School of neo-Kantianism. This approach found its expression in his three systematic works: *Logik der reinen Erkenntnis* (1902), *Die Ethik des reinen Willens* (1904), and *Die Aesthetik des reinen Gefuehls* (1912). These works reflect Cohen's attempt to renew Kantian philosophy and place it again at the center of the philosophic discourse, despite the prevailing Hegelian philosophy.

The starting point of Cohen's philosophic system, like that of Kant's, is the existence of scientific knowledge expressed mathematically. Like Kant, Cohen believed that the task of the philosopher is to unfold the logical conditions underlying this type of knowledge. However, Cohen criticized Kant for according sensation a special role in the establishment of scientific knowledge. While Kant had maintained that the sense content of our knowledge is a "datum," which, once given, is organized and synthesized by thought, Cohen puts forth the extreme idealistic thesis that thought produces everything out of itself. According to his "principle of origin" (*Ursprungsprinzip*) objects are constructs of thought. Thus he opposed Kant's notion of the "thing-in-itself" (*Ding an sich*), according to which there lies behind the object that we know an object which can never be known as it really is. For Kant, the action of reason is confined to the creation of associations between sensations, which are given. For Cohen, sensation merely describes the problem posed to thought.

Describing the method of science, Cohen holds that the scientist posits certain basic principles which help him to determine the facts, but as his research progresses he is required to revise these underlying principles and to conceive new hypotheses, which, in turn, lead to the discovery of new facts. In accordance with this view, our knowledge of reality at any given time is determined by the particular stage of this process, and since this process has no end, a person can never have a final knowledge of reality.

Considering ethics, Cohen held that human freedom is the basis of ethics, and constructed a parallel system to that of natural science, ruled by causality. Human dignity is central to Cohen's ethical thought. A proponent of humanistic socialism, he regarded a nation's treatment of its working classes as an index of its level of morality. While he called Marx "God's historical messenger," he rejected historical materialism as well as the atheistic trends prevalent in the workers' movement. He viewed religion, represented by the Biblical prophetic call for justice, as a revolutionary step towards systematic ethics. Cohen accordingly perceived Judaism, based on this prophetic vocation, which manifested itself in radical notions like that of the Sabbath, as a cornerstone of moral culture.

Defense of Judaism

A short time after his appointment as professor at Marburg, Cohen was obliged to declare publicly his attitude to "the Jewish question." When the historian Treitschke attacked the German Jews in his *Ein Wort ueber unser Judentum* (1879), defining Judaism as the "national religion of an alien race," Cohen countered with his *Ein Bekenntnis zur Judenfrage* (1880), in which he professed the total integration of German Jewry into the German society "without any double loyalty," yet demanding at the same time that the Jews take their religion seriously. In 1888, Cohen was called upon to testify in a lawsuit against an antisemitic teacher who had clamed that according to the Talmud, Jews are permitted to rob and deceive gentiles. Cohen published his testimony in a pamphlet called "Die Naechstenliebe im Talmud" (Love of the Neighbor in the Talmud, 1888), in which he set out to harmonize two apparently contradictory notions that are the basic of Judaism: the idea of the election of Israel, and the idea of the messianic unity of mankind. The connecting link is provided by the concept of God as the protector of the alien. The vocation of Israel begins with the fact of its chosenness, but since God is conceived from the outset as one who loves the stranger, Israel's chosenness is directed primarily at the unity of mankind.

Throughout his Marburg period Cohen viewed religion as merely a popular, nonconceptual form of ethics and believed that its aim is to be realized within ethics. Nevertheless, the idea of God played a much more central role in his ethics than in Kant's theory. Ethics provides mankind with an eternal ideal, whereas nature knows no eternity. It is here that Cohen introduces his postulate of God. This formulation of the postulate of God reflects Cohen's strong emphasis on ethics as the will to realize the ethical demand and make it part of reality, rather than the Kantian emphasis on the ethical as "practical reason."

Change in Attitude toward Religion

Cohen's move from Marburg to Berlin at the age of seventy was more than a change of place; it reflected an attempt to deepen his preoccupation with Jewish philosophy and life, and to focus on religious philosophy in general and Jewish thought in particular. This shift was manifested, among other things, in his journey to meet Polish Jewry in 1914 in order to assist in the foundation of an independent institute of higher learning for Jews who found it difficult to be admitted to universities, and his contact with the life of the Jewish masses in Vilna and Warsaw. From 1912 till his death he was primarily a Jewish philosopher and educator.

Although he had already dealt with religion in his previous books, it was only now that Cohen started to realize his old idea of dealing systematically with the role and content of religion. In 1915 he published *Der Bergriff der Religion im System der Philosophie* ("The Concept of Religion within the System of Philosophy," second edition, Zurich, 1996). In contrast with his earlier understanding of religion, Cohen now sought to determine the role and conceptual content of religion, and to define its place within the rational universe of philosophy. Religion is no longer a nonconceptual popular ethics, but rather a teaching that borders metaphysics, ethics, aesthetics and psychology. Furthermore, religion can be scientifically understood only through an analysis of these boundaries, although no solely rational approach has the capacity of exhausting its quality and content. Nevertheless, Cohen makes clear that religion can maintain this unique independent content only through its strong attachment to ethics.

At the heart of religion and of its relationship to ethics is the concept of the individual, which ethics as a philosophical system must ignore, and at the same time desperately needs. Ethics is based on the notion of duty that the individual has, his or her moral decisions and responsibility. At the same time, ethics, as it was being thus understood in the Kantian and neo-Kantian tradition, must "overcome" the individual. A deed is moral only when it is the right deed for every human being in the given situation. Neither the doer of the moral deed nor the person towards whom it is being aimed can be really seen as individuals, only as particular manifestations or examples of universal humanity. Only monotheistic religion, focusing on the correlation between the one God and the individual, can allow us to focus on the concept of the individual, and thus provide ethics with grounding and stability.

It is apparent that Cohen was not fully satisfied with his 1915 formulation of religion and reason. A very short time after releasing this book he started to work on his last book, *Religion der Vernunft aus den Quellen des Judentums*, which was published posthumously in 1919 (2nd edition, 1928; English: *Religion of Reason Out of the Sources of Judaism*, New York, 1972; also in Hebrew and other languages). Three main new focuses were emphasized in this title. First, when in the former book Cohen spoke about "religion" in general, meaning monotheism, now he clearly wishes to focus on Judaism and its sources as the *Urquelle*, ground-sources, of religion of reason. Second, the universe in which he places that religion is no longer "philosophy" but "reason" (*Vernunft*), a concept that should include not merely philosophy but also the unique teachings of religion in general, and Judaism in particular. The last emphasis is that religion can be analyzed and investigated only through a hermeneutical effort to understand its literary sources. These sources of Judaism – initially, the Hebrew Bible, but also rabbinic literature as well as medieval Jewish philosophy – bear a unique body of knowledge and reason. Analyzing religion's boundaries with ethics and aesthetics, and to a lesser extent with history and psychology, can be useful, but religion can be genuinely comprehended only from within, from its sources. These three elements, especially the last one, deeply manifest Cohen's life-long attachment to Maimonides, an attachment that was balanced only by his parallel attachment to Kant.

Cohen's new approach to the essence of religion can be fully traced in his notion of religious love. In his early works, Cohen viewed love as a mere affection, used by religion in a way that is legitimate, but proves that religion is of no scientific, rational nature. His *Religion of Reasons* reflects a fundamental change in his approach. The book's first chapter deals with the monotheistic concept of God, and emphasizes that in the religion of reason, the qualitative uniqueness of God (*die Einzigkeit Gottes*) as the only true Being is more essential than the quantitative oneness of God (*Die Einheit Gottes*). In chapter 2, Cohen, (clearly, if implicitly, reflecting the influence of Friedrich Schleiermacher) asks how one can depict the monotheistic person. Cognition cannot suffice, for cognition always has many objects; it is only love that can determine the monotheistic focus of human life. Here, love is no longer an affection but rather a course of life and an act of reason.

Love as an approach that represents the religion of reason, is directed foremost to our fellow humans. Ethics deals only with the person that I find besides me, the *Nebenmensch*. It defines my duties to that individual without relating to her or his individuality. Religion teaches me to relate to that person as the one who is with me, my *Mitmensch*, as an individual, whose uniqueness, her or his being here-and-now, are the source of my love and responsibility to him or her. Through the *Mitmensch* one also learns to perceive oneself as an individual. The other's individuality is manifested in his or her suffering, whereas the self's individuality is manifested in his or her sinfulness. In both cases, individuality is marked by incompleteness.

Nevertheless, sin cannot and should not rule life, nor should it define the "I." Cohen, following the teachings of the prophets Ezekiel and to a lesser extent Jeremiah, places repentance and atonement at the heart of religion. Every individual can free himself or herself from sin, can recreate himself anew. Repentance is thus the ground for the correlation between God and the human, and for human freedom and responsibility. Repentance (as a human act) and forgiveness (the divine reply to this act, that expresses God's goodness) depict the essential core of religion, and the ground of ethics provided by Jewish monotheism.

The concept of correlation is a key concept in Cohen's philosophy. It appeared already in his early books, referring to a logical reciprocal relationship between concepts that are developed from each other according to the "principle of origin." In *Der Begriff der Religion* the concept was used for the first time to describe the mutual relationships between God and the human, clearly referring to both as theoretical concepts rather than personalities. In *Religion der Vernunft*, correlation plays a major role, and refers to the dynamic relationships, to the *Mitmensch* and also to the divine-human reciprocal relationship. Cohen's readers developed different understandings of the meaning of these relationships. Some scholars follow Franz Rosenzweig's reading that correlation refers here to the biblical notion of covenant, arguing that in *Religion der Vernunft*, Cohen's God is no longer mere idea but rather personality. Others stick to Cohen's usage of the concept in his early philosophy, depicting *Religion der Vernunft* as a direct continuum of Cohen's early philosophy rather than a breakthrough from his idealism.

Cohen emphasizes that Judaism is not the sole manifestation of the religion of reason, though his approach to Christianity, the only other religion being referred to in the book, is quite polemical. As a unique form of monotheism, carrying the quality of an *Urquelle*, the existence of Judaism, and hence of the Jewish people, is of universal significance. Cohen clearly views the Jews as a people rather than merely a community of faith, yet draws from this view no Zionist conclusion. To the contrary, he sharply opposed Zionism, viewing it as a betrayal of Judaism's messianic universalistic horizons, and advocated the continued existence of the Jewish people as a national minority ("nationality") within the various nation-states ("nations"). This anti-Zionist approach was expressed in his article "Religion und Zionismus" (1916; *Juedische Schriften*, 2 (1924), 319–27).

The religious significance of Jewish existence was one of the bases for Cohen's devotion to Jewish religious law. Using Kantian terminology and criteria, he argues sharply against Kant's notion of autonomy and the philosopher's negation of Jewish law. Cohen interprets "*mitzvah*" to mean both "law" and "duty." The law originates in God, the sense of duty in man. The law is at the same time duty; duty at the same time law. God issued commandments to man, and man of his own free will takes upon himself the "yoke of the commandments." With the "yoke of the commandments," one simultaneously accepts the "yoke of the kingdom of God." Thus, the law leads to the messianic ideal.

ADD. BIBLIOGRAPHY: *Hermann Cohen: Juedische* Schriften (3 vols., Berlin, 1924), intro. F. Rosenzweig; abridged Eng. tr. E. Jospe, *Reason and Hope: Selections from the Jewish Writings of Hermann Cohen* (1971, 1993)); *Hermann Cohen: Werke*, critical edition (1996–); A. Poma, *The Critical Philosophy of Hermann Cohen*, tr. J. Denton (1997); S. Moses et al. (eds.), *Hermann Cohen's Philosophy of Religion* (1997); H. Holzhez et al. (eds.), *Religion der Vernunft aus den Quellen des Judentums – Tradition und Ursprungsdenken in Hermann Cohens Spätwerk* (2000); H. Wiedebach, *Die Bedeutung der Mationalitaet fuer Hermann Cohen* (1997); J. Melber, *Hermann Cohen's Philosophy of Judaism* (1968): M. Zank, *The Idea of Atonement in the Philosophy of Hermann Cohen* (2000).

[Samuel Hugo Bergman / Yehoyada Amir (2nd ed.)]

COHEN, HIRSH (1860–1950), Canadian rabbi. Cohen was born in Budwicz, Russian Poland, and was educated at the Volozhin Yeshivah. He obtained his *semikhah* from R. Jacob David *Willowski (Ridbaz). He immigrated to Montreal, Canada, in 1889 or 1890. After a short period in Chicago, during which he qualified as a *shoḥet*, he returned to Montreal as a *shoḥet*, teacher, and preacher. He became superintendent of

Montreal's Talmud Torah in 1901 and began functioning as a rabbi. Supported by his older brother, Lazarus Cohen, a prominent communal leader, and by Hirsch *Wolofsky, publisher of Montreal's Yiddish daily, *Keneder Adler*, Cohen began a protracted struggle to become preeminent in Montreal's immigrant Orthodox rabbinate in the area of the supervision of *kashrut*, facing such rivals as Rabbis Simon Glazer and Yudel *Rosenberg. His efforts culminated in 1922 with the founding of the Jewish Community Council of Montreal (*Va'ad ha-Ir*). He became head of the Council's rabbinical body (*Va'ad ha-Rabbanim*), and thus widely recognized as Montreal's chief rabbi. He struggled to maintain the integrity of the Council and its monopoly over *kashrut* supervision in Montreal in the face of numerous challenges. He was active in Jewish communal issues, in particular those related to Jewish education and Zionism. He was well known as a public speaker in Yiddish and often published his speeches in the *Keneder Adler*. He retained the title of chief rabbi to his death, though he was not active in his last years due to illness.

BIBLIOGRAPHY: *Keneder Adler* (Nov. 19, 1950); I. Robinson, *Canadian Ethnic Studies* 22 (1990), 41–53.

[Ira Robinson (2nd ed.)]

COHEN, H. RODGIN (1944–), U.S. lawyer. Born in Charleston, W. Va., Cohen graduated from Harvard University in 1965 and Harvard Law School three years later. He also earned a law degree from the University of Charleston in 1998. After two years in the Army, Cohen joined the old-line law firm Sullivan & Cromwell in 1970 and was assigned to the firm's banking practice. For more than 30 years, Cohen was a sought-after counselor to chief executives of the industry's largest institutions, including the Bank of New York, First Union, and Societé Générale, advising on 10 of the 15 largest bank mergers in the 1990s. As part of a team in late 1980, Cohen represented several banks in the exchange of billions of dollars worth of frozen Iranian assets for American hostages held in Iran. He was involved in the consolidation wave, including the mergers of Chemical and Chase Manhattan, Wells Fargo and Norwest, and First Union and Corestates. He became chairman of Sullivan & Cromwell in 1999. The firm had more than 525 lawyers and its clients included Disney, Goldman Sachs, and Microsoft, making it one of the most profitable law firms in the United States.

[Stewart Kampel (2nd ed.)]

COHEN, I. BERNARD (1914–2003), U.S. historian of science. Cohen was born in Far Rockaway, New York. He was an expert on Benjamin Franklin and Sir Isaac Newton. Most of his professional life was spent at Harvard University, where in 1937 he received his B.Sc. in mathematics, subsequently becoming the first American to receive a Ph.D. in the history of science (1947). He transformed Harvard's undergraduate and postgraduate program on the history of science into a department and in 1977 became Victor S. Thomas Professor of the History of Science. After retiring in 1984, Cohen continued to teach at Harvard, Brandeis University, and Boston College. The fruits of his polymath skills included *Science and the Founding Fathers* (1995), which deals with the contribution of scientific thought to the authors of the American Constitution, and the first English translation of Newton's *Principia Mathematica* (with Koyre and Whitman) since 1729 (1999). He served as president of the most influential national and international organizations concerned with the history of science and was accorded the discipline's most prestigious honors.

[Michael Denman (2nd ed.)]

COHEN, ISAAC KADMI (1892–1944), French Zionist writer and lawyer. Born in Lodz, Poland, and educated at the Herzliah gymnasium, Tel Aviv, Kadmi Cohen later settled in Paris, where he became a lawyer. A man of the French left, he was a Zionist of the extreme right, surpassing the Revisionists in his *Etat d'Israël* (1930), which called for a Jewish empire stretching from the Nile to Iraq. While interned at Compiègne in 1941–42, he organized the Massadah Zionist club to counteract the prevalent assimilationism of other imprisoned French-Jewish intellectuals. Believing a Nazi victory to be inevitable, he concluded that the Germans might agree to a mass evacuation of European Jews to Ereẓ Israel and reputedly sent a memorandum to Hitler recommending this "solution." He was finally deported to the Gleiwitz concentration camp and is thought to have died in Auschwitz.

Kadmi Cohen's son by his marriage to a French Catholic was the writer JEAN-FRANÇOIS STEINER (1938–). Distressed by the terrible death of a father whom he had never known and haunted by the conflicts of his own identity, Steiner spent a year in Israel at the age of 17 in search of an answer to his dilemma. This eventually took the form of a book, *Treblinka* (1966; Eng. ed., 1967), a dry and unemotional mixture of fact and fiction based on the documents he had studied at *Yad Vashem and interviews with concentration camp survivors. Although it contained gripping descriptions of Jewish resistance to the Nazi genocide program, *Treblinka's* rejection of the Diaspora – an unconscious echo of Kadmi Cohen's views – and its underlying assumptions met with wide protest. Steiner advanced his own theory of Jewish "complicity" in the "final solution," based on his idea of the sanctity of life in Jewish tradition. The book aroused controversy and survivors whose names had been used published *La vérité sur Treblinka* (1967), in which documented facts were printed in opposition to Steiner's theory. In 1967 Steiner married the granddaughter of Field Marshal Walter von Brauchitsch, the commander in chief of Hitler's army.

BIBLIOGRAPHY: M. Novitch, *La vérité sur Treblinka* (1967); Winegarten, in: *Commentary*, 45 no. 1 (1968), 27–35.

COHEN, ISRAEL (1879–1961), writer and Zionist. Born in Manchester, the son of a tailor, and educated at Jewish schools, Manchester Grammar School, and London University, Cohen was active in the Zionist movement from the mid-1890s. In

1910 he became the English-language secretary of the Zionist Central Office in Cologne, which later moved to Berlin. During World War I (until 1916) he was interned in a prison camp in Germany. In 1918 Cohen rejoined the secretariat of the World Zionist Organization, and was professionally active in the Zionist movement for the rest of his career. Touring Poland and Hungary to investigate the condition of Jews after the war, he reported on the current pogroms and discrimination. On behalf of the Zionist Organization he visited the Jewish communities of Egypt, Australia, China, Manchuria, Japan, Java, India, and of other countries. From 1922 he was secretary of the Zionist Organization in London and edited the reports of the Zionist Executive to several Zionist Congresses. One of the early Zionist journalists and writers in Great Britain, Cohen published articles in Jewish, Zionist, and other English-language journals. His books include *Jewish Life in Modern Times* (1914), *The Zionist Movement* (1945), *Contemporary Jewry* (1950), *A Short History of Zionism* (1951), *Travels in Jewry* (1953), and *Theodor Herzl: Founder of Political Zionism* (1959). He also published pamphlets on Jewish affairs, Zionism, and antisemitism. In 1956 he published an autobiography, *A Jewish Pilgrimage*.

ADD. BIBLIOGRAPHY: ODNB online.

[Josef Fraenkel]

COHEN, ISRAEL (1905–1986), Hebrew literary critic and editor. Cohen spent his childhood in Galicia and Czechoslovakia and later studied in Buczacz and Lemberg. Active in Zionist youth movements, he immigrated to Palestine in 1925, and was a leading member of Ha-Po'el ha-Ẓa'ir and later Mapai. In 1934 he was appointed to the editorial board of the weekly **Ha-Po'el ha-Ẓa'ir* and was its editor from 1948 until it ceased publication in 1970. Active in the writers' association, he edited many of its publications, including the monthly *Moznayim*. Cohen wrote extensively on literature. His books include: *Ha'arakhot u-Vavu'ot* (1938) and *Gesharim* (1955), essays on the labor movement. In 1962 four volumes of his selected works appeared: *Sha'ar ha-Soferim, Sha'ar ha-Havḥanot, Sha'ar ha-Te'amim*, and *Ishim min ha-Mikra*. He also published several compilations of epigrams, including studies of parallel Hebrew, German, and English sayings (1954, 1960). Cohen's articles are excellent examples of eclectic analysis. His essays, written in an outstanding Hebrew style, generally describe and define the literary scene and the works or their authors. On his 75th birthday, Nurit Govrin edited *Sefer ha-Yovel* (1980). Cohen's correspondence with *Agnon and with David *Ben-Gurion, *Ḥilufei Mikhtavim*, appeared in 1985.

BIBLIOGRAPHY: *Israel Cohen, Bibliografyah 1924–65* (1965), 1,430 items by and on him; **ADD. BIBLIOGRAPHY:** H. Hoffman (ed.), *Israel Cohen: Bibliografyah 1979–1987* (1987).

[Getzel Kressel]

COHEN, JACK JOSEPH (1919–), Reconstructionist rabbi and educator. Cohen was born in Brooklyn, New York, earned his B.A. from Brooklyn College in 1940, and received his M.H.L. and ordination from the Conservative movement's *Jewish Theological Seminary in 1943. He studied at the Hebrew University of Jerusalem even before the creation of the State of Israel and received his Ph.D. in education from Columbia University's Teachers College in 1958. He was awarded honorary D.D. degrees from both the Jewish Theological Seminary (1968) and the Reconstructionist Rabbinical College, which simultaneously bestowed on him its Keter Torah Award (2000).

After serving as educational director of the Park Synagogue in Cleveland, Ohio (1943–45), Cohen was named director of the Jewish Reconstructionist Foundation, where, for the next 10 years he oversaw the activities and institutions of the growing movement. In the cause of promoting Reconstructionist Judaism, he published educational material (such as *Zionism Explained, The Theology of the Jewish Prayer Book,* and a study guide for Milton *Steinberg's *A Partisan Guide to the Jewish Problem*); created *havurot*; lectured widely throughout the United States; and was associate editor of the *Reconstructionist* magazine. But his efforts to convince the Reconstructionist laity to support the opening of an office in Israel, to establish a camping program, to develop a training program for teachers, and a variety of other activities were ultimately frustrated. During his tenure, the Federation of Reconstructionist Congregations was formed. In 1953, he became educational director of the Society for the Advancement of Judaism, the Reconstructionist congregation founded in New York City 30 years earlier by Mordecai *Kaplan. In 1954, Cohen was also named rabbi of the SAJ, where he is credited with a number of educational innovations, including setting up experimental schools and establishing a year-long program of study for bat- and bat mitzvah students and their parents.

Although clearly identified with Reconstructionism, Cohen remained associated with the Conservative movement. He was a lecturer at the Jewish Theological Seminary (1955–61) and chairman of the United Synagogue Commission on Jewish Education (1960–61). In 1961, Cohen moved to Israel and assumed the directorship of the B'nai B'rith Hillel Foundation at the Hebrew University, serving until 1984. He maneuvered skillfully to permit expressions of religious pluralism while resisting Reform and Conservative attempts to import denominational divisions into Israel. He also worked to improve Arab-Jewish relations on campus and widened the scope of Hillel. In 1970, Cohen joined the faculty of Jerusalem's David Yellin College of Education (1970–83), on whose board he also served. He also taught students of the Reconstructionist Rabbinical College who were studying in Israel (1970–2002).

In 1962, Cohen was instrumental in founding the egalitarian Congregation Mevakshei Derekh, widely considered the first Reconstructionist synagogue in Israel. He served as the first chairman of Mevakshei Derekh for several decades and, although he never took the official title of rabbi, has always been acknowledged as its de facto spiritual leader. In

1984, the congregation was able to move into its own permanent building.

Cohen wrote numerous articles for Anglo-Jewish and Hebrew journals, as well as many chapters in scholarly compilations. He also wrote eight books, including several on philosophy and education. These include *The Creative Audience* (with Rebecca Imber, 1954), *The Case for Religious Naturalism* (1958), *Jewish Education in a Democratic Society* (1964), *The Reunion of Isaac and Ishmael* (1989), *Morim Lizman Navokh* (Hebrew, 1993; English version: *Guides for an Age of Confusion: Studies in the Thinking of Avraham Y. Kook and Mordecai M. Kaplan*, 1999), *Major Philosophers of Jewish Prayer in the 20th Century* (2000), *Judaism as an Evolving Civilization* (with Yosef Begun, in Russian, 2001). Cohen also served on the editorial board of the *Reconstructionist.*

In Israel, Cohen became a member of the Ministry of Education's Committee on Culture and Leisure Time and chairman of the Israel Interfaith Association, which brings together Jews, Christians and Muslims for dialogue.

BIBLIOGRAPHY: P.S. Nadell, *Conservative Judaism in America: A Biographical Dictionary and Sourcebook* (1988).

[Bezalel Gordon (2nd ed.)]

COHEN, JACOB RAPHAEL (1738?–1811), U.S. *ḥazzan.* Cohen was born in North Africa. He served as *ḥazzan* in England before being sent to Montreal's Congregation Shearith Israel in 1778. Bound again for England, Cohen was detained in New York, and became minister of Congregation Shearith Israel there (1782–85). Later he replaced *ḥazzan* *Seixas in Philadelphia's Congregation Mikveh Israel, remaining in that office until his death. Cohen was frequently called upon to fulfill all ritual functions. He kept a meticulous record of marriages, circumcisions, deaths, and memorial prayers, an important source of data for Jewish history in Montreal, New York, and Philadelphia. He was assisted by his son, Abraham Hyam Cohen (d. 1841), who succeeded him.

BIBLIOGRAPHY: "Record Book of Jacob Raphael Cohen" (in AJHQ, 59 (1969), 23ff.); Rosenbloom, Biogr Dict (1960), 24; H.S. Morais, *Jews of Philadelphia* (1894), 18, 20, 43.

[Malcolm H. Stern]

COHEN, JACOB XENAB (1889–1955), U.S. Reform rabbi. Cohen was born in New York City and began studying for the rabbinate only after starting a career as a civil engineer. He received his rabbinic ordination and M.H.L. degree at the Jewish Institute for Religion in 1929 and was appointed associate rabbi and executive secretary of the Free Synagogue in New York that same year. He also served as executive secretary of its philanthropic institute, the Free Synagogue Social Service Inc., and bursar of the Jewish Institute for Religion. In 1939, he became president of the New York Board of Jewish Ministers (renamed the New York Board of Rabbis in 1946) and was credited with revitalizing the organization and its various missions. He was the first to recognize the importance of public relations for the Jewish community, of cooperation with other religious and philanthropic bodies, and of the special impact of radio for educating the general public about Judaism. During his chairmanship, the Board was recognized to be on a par with the Catholic Diocese and the Protestant City Mission Society for the designation of chaplains, and Cohen was appointed the first Jewish member of the Mayor's Committee on Chaplaincy. In 1948, as chairman of the New York Board of Rabbis' Chaplaincy Committee, Cohen inaugurated, with the Psychiatric Department of Mount Sinai Hospital, a Chaplaincy Institute for the scientific training of chaplains serving in city, state, and federal institutions. An activist, Cohen was a member of the Governing Council of the American Jewish Congress, and chairman of its National Commission on Economic Problems; his widely circulated reports – *Jews, Jobs and Discrimination, Helping to End Economic Discrimination,* and *Towards Fair Play for Jewish Workers,* among many others – called attention to the issue of antisemitism in the workplace. At the same time, he spoke out about discrimination against other minorities as well. He also investigated the problem of restrictive quotas against Jewish applicants to U.S. medical and dental schools for the AJ Congress Special Committee on Discrimination in Medical Schools. He traveled widely throughout the world, interviewing government leaders in North America, Latin America, and Europe, warning about the rise of Nazism and documenting antisemitic outbreaks for the World Jewish Congress. Cohen also chronicled *Jewish Life in South America,* publishing a book under this title in 1941. He is the subject of a biography, *Engineer of the Soul,* written by his wife, Sadie Alta Cohen (1961).

[Bezalel Gordon (2nd ed.)]

COHEN, SIR JOHN EDWARD (**Jack**; 1898–1979), British businessman and philanthropist. Born Jacob Edward Kohen in the City of London, Cohen worked in his father's ladies' tailoring shop in the East End, before joining the Royal Flying Corps in World War I. After the war he used his army bonus of $150 to open a food stall in a London market. By World War II he had built up a company of over 100 grocery stores in London and in Great Britain. After the war he built a chain of more than 500 supermarkets, groceries, and discount houses. He incorporated these into Tesco Stores (Holdings) Limited and associated companies and was chairman of its board. By the 1960s Tesco was one of the best known of High Street retail chains, and Sir Jack Cohen was virtually a household name as a prominent entrepreneur. In 1967 Cohen opened the first Tesco Superstore, vastly larger than previous branches. He was an active worker for the Joint Palestine Appeal. He established the Shirene Home apartments for elderly people at Herzliyyah, Israel. Cohen was knighted in 1969 and retired in 1970.

BIBLIOGRAPHY: S. Aris *Jews in Business* (1970), index. **ADD. BIBLIOGRAPHY:** M. Corina, *Pile It High, Sell It Cheap: The Authorised Biography of Sir Jack Cohen* (1971); D. Powell, *Counter Revolution: The Tesco Story* (1991); DBB, I, 724–29; ODNB online.

COHEN, JOHN MICHAEL (1903–1988), English critic and translator. A businessman turned writer, Cohen published many Penguin Classics that bear the stamp of mature reflection and wide reading. His works include translations of Cervantes' *Don Quixote* (1950), Rabelais' *Gargantua and Pantagruel* (1955), and *Montaigne's Essays* (1958); *History of Western Literature* (1956); *The Penguin Dictionary of Quotations* (1960); *Latin American Writing Today* (1967); and a series of comic verse anthologies.

COHEN, JOHN SANFORD (1870–1935), publisher, U.S. senator. Cohen of was the scion of an old American family. His father, Phillip Lawrence Cohen (1845–1882), who had surrendered with Lee at Appomattox, was descended from Portuguese Jews who had settled in Savannah, Georgia, in the early 18th century. His mother, Ellen Gobert (Wright) Cohen, was the daughter of Major General Ambrose Ransom Wright, "a distinguished commander in the Confederate army and a lieutenant-governor of Georgia," and Mary Hubbell Savage, "a descendant of Thomas Savage (1594–1627), who came from England and settled in Virginia in 1607."

Cohen received a private education at various prep schools in Virginia and Maryland. After a year at the United States Naval Academy in Annapolis, Maryland, he returned to Augusta, where he served a two-year apprenticeship on the *Augusta Chronicle*, one of the South's oldest and most respected newspapers and long owned by Cohen's maternal grandparents. At 18, he went to Mexico as secretary to Captain William G. Raoul, the builder of the Mexican National Railroad. In 1889, he moved to New York, becoming a reporter on Joseph *Pulitzer's *New York World*. The following year, Cohen returned to Georgia, where he went to work for the *Atlanta Journal*, a connection he would maintain for the rest of his life.

During President Grover Cleveland's second administration (1893–97), Cohen became Washington correspondent for the *Journal* and private secretary to Interior Secretary Hoke Smith. On the outbreak of the Spanish-American War in 1898, he sailed to Cuba with the American fleet as a correspondent for the *Journal*. When the call went out for volunteers, he returned to Georgia and was commissioned as a first lieutenant in the Third Georgia United States Volunteer Infantry. Promoted to major, he went with the army of occupation to Cuba. After the war, Cohen became the *Atlanta Journal*'s managing editor; eventually he was named the paper's president. Under his guidance, the *Journal* became the first newspaper in the South (and the second in the nation) to establish a radio station – WSB, the "Voice of the South," which went on the air from the roof of the Journal Building in March 1922. A visionary, Cohen directed his paper to use wire-service photos as early as 1930.

"The Major," as he was known, was elected Democratic national committeeman for Georgia in 1924. He was reelected to that post in 1928 and 1932. In April 1932, Georgia's senior Senator, William J. Harris, unexpectedly died. Cohen was appointed to replace him until a special election could be held. Cohen, who had been named vice chair of the Democratic National Committee, decided not to run for the remaining four years of his Senate term. He decided that it would be better to put all his political energies into campaigning for Franklin D. Roosevelt. A patron of art, music, and education, Cohen was instrumental in reestablishing the Lee School of Journalism at Washington and Lee University in Virginia.

BIBLIOGRAPHY: K.F. Stone, *The Congressional Minyan: The Jews of Capitol Hill* (2000) 61–62; J. Mellichamp, *Senators From Georgia* (1976).

[Kurt Stone (2nd ed.)]

COHEN, JOSEPH (1817–1899), French publicist and lawyer. Born in Marseilles, he practiced law in Aix-en-Provence, and was delegated by the French government to study the condition of Algerian Jewry. In 1845 he was appointed head of the Algerian *consistory. He returned to Paris in 1848, thereafter devoting his time to journalism. He edited (1860–62) the first Jewish weekly in France, *La Vérité israélite*, contributed to the monthly *Archives israélites*, and was editor of *Le Pays* (1853), *La France* (1860–68), and *La Presse* (1871). His works include *Les Déicides* (1861), a critical investigation into the life of Jesus and the Gospels, and *Les Pharisiens* (2 vols., 1877). Cohen represented the Algerian Jews at the Central Consistory from 1868.

BIBLIOGRAPHY: Rosenstock, in: JSOS, 18 (1956), 41–42, 48–49, 51–52.

COHEN, JOSEPH ISAAC (1896–1981), Sephardi congregational rabbi and communal leader in Havana and Atlanta and active Zionist. Born in Istanbul, Cohen was educated at an Alliance Israélite Universelle school, the prestigious Galata Saray gymnasium, and studied law at the university. In the Turkish army, he rose to the rank of captain in intelligence and served from 1915 to 1918 in the Dardanelles, Syria, and Ereẓ Israel. He was taken prisoner by the British in Beersheba. After the war, he remained in Ereẓ Israel, working for the Jewish Agency and the Jewish National Fund; he then immigrated to Cuba in 1920. He set up a Jewish day school, Colegio Herzel, and served as its headmaster, and as an active Zionist, he was cofounder of the Zionist Organization and the Jewish National Fund in Cuba. He served as an active spokesman for the Jewish community in its dealings with the Cuban authorities. In 1930, after being ordained privately by local rabbis in Cuba, he became head of the Sephardi congregation *Shevet Ahim Union Hebrea* in Havana.

Cohen subsequently served the Atlanta Sephardi Congregation Or Veshalom of Rhodian and Turkish Jews from 1934 until his death in 1981. In 1935, he reorganized the Talmud Torah, added a Sunday religious school for pre-kindergarten until 10th grade, and hired accredited teachers for both.

He encouraged his Sephardi congregants to become active and integrate into the general Jewish community and

Federation philanthropic activities. He placed emphasis on giving to charity locally for orphans, Jewish welfare needs, and causes in Israel and elsewhere abroad, i.e., through the Jewish National Fund, and the return of *Marranos to Judaism in Oporto, Portugal.

For his efforts, he received the Bringer of Light award from the Jewish National Fund of America, and in 1969 he was elected president of the newly formed Atlanta Rabbinical Association.

Upon retirement in 1969, he was elected rabbi emeritus of his congregation and continued serving the congregation and community until his death. He was succeeded by Rabbi S. Robert Ishay, a native of Morocco, who had served previously in Manchester and Rhodesia.

BIBLIOGRAPHY: S. Beton (ed.), *Sephardim & a History of Congregation Or VeShalom* (1981), 108–110; J. Papo, *Sephardim in Twentieth Century America, In Search of Unity* (1987), 281–83.

[Yitzchak Kerem (2nd ed.)]

COHEN, JUDAH (c. 1700), community leader of Algiers and diplomat serving the ruler of Tunisia, Murād Bey. In 1699 Cohen was authorized by the bey and his council to negotiate a peace treaty and trade agreement with the Dutch government. This assignment involved regular contacts with Tripoli, Tunisia, Algeria, and the Netherlands. A number of Jews helped him to carry out the negotiations, but they were conducted in a careless manner and lasted six years, 1702–08, instead of the sixteen months originally stipulated. Cohen made use of his high position to benefit the Jews.

BIBLIOGRAPHY: Hirschberg, Afrikah, 2 (1965), 124–6.

COHEN, JULIUS BEREND (1859–1935), British organic chemist. Born in Manchester. Cohen taught there until 1891, when he joined the Yorkshire College, Leeds, faculty. When this became University of Leeds (1904), he was appointed its first professor of organic chemistry. He is known for three textbooks: *Chemistry* (1902); *Organic Chemistry for Advanced Students* (1907); and *Class Book of Organic Chemistry* (1917). He was a Fellow of the Royal Society.

COHEN, LEONARD (1934–), Montreal-born poet, novelist, and songwriter whose work was uniquely influential through the late 1960s and early 1970s. Cohen's background differentiated him from the Jewish writers of Montreal, who had grown up before him on the hardscrabble streets of the downtown. His family were pillars of the community, ensconced in a grand Westmount home near the hilly Murray Hill Park, which he turns into an iconic landscape in his fiction.

Although Cohen's poetic career was nurtured by the rich literary life of Jewish Montreal, and the burgeoning modernist movement centered around a few older poets and teachers, his broader impact as a writer came with his ability to enter the international scene through his songwriting. There are thus two Cohens – one a contributor to an established line of poetic inheritance, intimately linked to his birthplace; the other a pop troubadour whose songs speak to audiences in Poland, Finland, and New York as directly as they do to Canadians.

In the early 1960s this division was not so easily felt, as poems that appeared in his early books were reworked into successful songs. His first album, *Songs of Leonard Cohen*, appeared in the same year that his *Selected Poems* was published. The particular style and tone of his poetry were well suited to the blend of folk, country, and blues that informed such records as *Songs from a Room* (1969). In the early 1970s Cohen began to express a diffidence with his poetic gifts and distanced himself from his audience in the darkly ironic poems collected in *The Energy of Slaves* (1972). This persona of the divided poet returns in his collection *Death of a Lady's Man* (1978). In it, the left-hand page presents a poem, which is then critiqued on the facing page. Around the same time, Cohen released *Death of a Ladies' Man*. This project distanced Cohen from the constituency of listeners who had fallen for songs like "Suzanne" and "Bird on the Wire." Cohen's movement through poetry, novels, and on to popular songwriting suggested a restless and multitalented artist who is both drawn to and repelled by fame.

Much of Cohen's work is informed by his Jewishness, although often in shadowy and ambiguous ways. *Let Us Compare Mythologies* (1956), *The Spice-Box of Earth* (1961), and *Flowers for Hitler* (1964) revealed a voice informed by subtle humor, Judaic imagery, and pop cultural savvy. His first novel, *The Favourite Game*, is a lyrical portrait of a charmed Westmount adolescence, not unlike Cohen's own. Among his best albums is *New Skin for the Old Ceremony*, which reworks Jewish liturgical imagery (especially that of Yom Kippur) in powerfully strange and simple folk-blues anthems. Even *Beautiful Losers* (1966), Cohen's final novel, is underwritten by the predicament of what his narrator provocatively calls the "New Jew," inheritor of a tradition transformed into some grotesque yet compelling version of its once more coherent self. But the novel reaches beyond Cohen's established themes and lyrical tones for a more all-encompassing portrait of Canadian identity in a nascent multicultural era. The combination of cultural influence in the novel is representative of Montreal's mixed heritage, as French, English, Mohawk, and Jewish settlements on the banks of the St. Lawrence are explored. The book in which Cohen places the greatest emphasis on Jewish language and imagery is his last published collection of new poetry, *Book of Mercy* (1984). In short psalm-like sections, the poet returns to the familiar subject matter of private and poetic pain, yet he does so in language that repeatedly echoes traditional Jewish prayer: "Blessed are you who has given each man a shield of loneliness so that he cannot forget you."

Leonard Cohen's oeuvre stands at the end of a line of inheritance beginning with the earliest Yiddish writers who settled in Montreal, followed by A.M. Klein and Irving Layton, both of whom influenced Cohen in his youthful work. Readers have had to accept a relative silence from Cohen since the mid-1980s, when song and his growing position as a cultural icon took precedence over literary output.

[Norman Ravvin (2nd ed.)]

COHEN, LEVI-ABRAHAM (1844–1888), Moroccan journalist. Cohen was born in Mogador and lived in Tangiers. Here he founded *Le Réveil du Maroc* and also acted as correspondent not only for Jewish papers but also for the Agence Havas and the London *Times*, for which he wrote articles on the unfortunate situation of the Jewish and Muslim masses. Supported by such personalities as Sir Moses *Montefiore, Cohen acquired a considerable influence in the political and diplomatic circles of Morocco.

BIBLIOGRAPHY: JC (Nov. 16, 1888); Miège, Maroc, 3 (1962), 280, 319, 338; 4 (1963), 49, 325, 352.

[David Corcos]

COHEN, LIONEL LEONARD, BARON (1888–1973), English judge and jurist. Born in London, he was admitted to the bar in 1913, made a king's counsel in 1929, a judge of the Chancery Division of the High Court in 1943, and Lord Justice of Appeal and a privy councillor in 1946. In 1951 he was named a peer as Baron of Walmer and sat in the House of Lords as a "Lord of Appeal in Ordinary" until 1960. He was chairman of the Company Law Amendment Committee (1943–45) and acquired renown as the author of the Companies Act of 1948, which became a model for company legislation in many countries. Notable among his public offices were his chairmanship of the Royal Commission on Awards to Inventors (1946–56) and of the Council on Prices, Productivity, and Incomes (1957–59) which was known as the Cohen Committee. Cohen followed his family tradition of general and Jewish public service. He was an active president of the Jewish Board of Guardians and also president of the Jewish Historical Society of England and of the Union of Liberal and Progressive Synagogues. He was vice president of the Board of Deputies.

BIBLIOGRAPHY: P. Emden, *Jews of Britain* (1943), 177. **ADD. BIBLIOGRAPHY:** ODNB online.

[Israel Finestein]

COHEN, LYON (1868–1937), Canadian businessman, Jewish community leader. Cohen was the most eminent Montreal Jew of his time. He was born in Poland and immigrated to Montreal with his family in 1871. A successful businessman, Cohen began as a coal merchant and dredging contractor. He added a brass foundry and a major Montreal men's clothing manufacturing company to his business holdings. He eventually became head of the Montreal Men's Clothing Manufacturers' Association and led this organization during the bitter labor strikes of 1916 and 1917, finally agreeing to union demands for better working conditions.

Cohen was also associated with virtually all the major causes in the Jewish community's development. In 1897, Cohen, with Samuel Jacobs, founded Canada's first Jewish newspaper, *The Jewish Times*. The paper provided the Jewish community with a window on the rest of the Jewish world, a forum for debate, and a tool for educating new immigrants. He joined the drive to obtain equal rights for Jews in Quebec elementary schools, headed the Baron de Hirsch Institute, and spearheaded efforts to create the Federation of Jewish Charities. He presided over the Canadian Jewish Congress and committees to aid World War I sufferers in Eastern Europe. Cohen was active in the *Jewish Colonization Association, the Jewish Immigrant Aid Society, the Montreal Y.M.H.A., and other welfare efforts; he served for many years as president of Sha'ar Hashamayim synagogue.

[Gerald Tulchinsky (2nd ed.)]

COHEN, MARCEL (Samuel Raphael; 1884–1974), French linguist and philologist. Born in Paris, he studied at the Paris School of Oriental Languages from where he went on a study mission to Algeria. The results of this mission were summarized in his book, *Le parler arabe des Juifs d'Alger* (1912). In 1910 he was sent by the French Ministry of Education to Abyssinia where he collected material for his scientific research on linguistics and ethnography. Upon his return to Paris, the following year, he was appointed lecturer in Amharic at the School of Oriental Languages. After serving for four years as a soldier in World War I, Cohen became director of Ethiopian studies at the school. In 1924 he published his *Le système verbal sémitique et l'expression du temps* and in 1936 *Traité de langue amharique*. In these works he substantiated the proofs for *Benfey's thesis that all Semitic idioms and all branches of the Semitic-Hamitic language are of the same parentage. During World War II, he participated in the underground anti-Nazi resistance movement. After resuming his academic activities in 1945, Cohen published another important work in the field of Semitic linguistics, *Essai comparatif sur le vocabulaire et la phonétique du chamito-sémitique* (1947), and founded the research center for comparative Semitics, Egyptian, etc., called GLECS (*Group linguistique d'études du chamito-sémitique*). During this latter phase of his academic career he concentrated his research on the evolution of the French language and its social and cultural functions. In 1955 Cohen's friends published a jubilee volume to mark his completion of 50 years of academic activity. This book, *Cinquante années de recherches linguistiques* (1955), contained a list of all his books, essays, and articles.

COHEN, MARY MATILDA (1854–1911), journalist, belletrist, educationist, communal worker, and proto-feminist. Cohen was born into an intellectually distinguished upper middle-class Philadelphia family. Never marrying and financially independent, Cohen devoted her energies to a variety of religious, cultural, and communal causes in Philadelphia. She was a capable and enthusiastic organizer, serving as superintendent of the large Hebrew Sunday School started by Rebecca Gratz, acting as the first corresponding secretary of the Jewish Publication Society, sitting on synagogue committees and philanthropic society boards, and joining numerous literary and cultural organizations. Cohen was at ease among the American Orthodox elite that associated with Mikveh Israel and was accepted within Philadelphia's progressive intelligentsia. She was a prolific writer, contributing to both the Jewish and general press under her own name as well as the pseudonym "Coralie." Cohen's literary output ranged from biography, social commentary, and essays on Jewish themes to short stories and poetry. The concerns that Cohen expressed in her writing reflected those of her intellectual and social milieu. She sought to advance the acceptance of acculturated Jews within American society by authoring articles that satirized prevailing prejudicial norms and criticized creeping racial antisemitism. She also sought to counter gender inequality within the Jewish community and wider society. Cohen was an advocate of universal education and argued for open access for women to professional training. She also pushed for improved religious education for Jewish girls, a greater role for women in the Jewish public sphere, and the ordination of female rabbis.

BIBLIOGRAPHY: D. Ashton, in: *American Jewish History*, 83, 2 (1995), 153–76; H. Morais, *The Jews of Philadelphia* (1894), 316–17; *American Jewish Yearbook*, 7 (1905), 48–49.

[Adam Mendelsohn (2nd ed.)]

COHEN, MATT (1942–1999), Canadian writer. Cohen was born in Ottawa and then moved with his parents to Kingston, Ontario. Later, he moved to Toronto and took advantage of a rich cultural moment, when the few square blocks around Spadina and College were becoming one of Canada's most exciting cultural and artistic centers. Despite frequent travels abroad, Toronto remained his most intimate personal landscape.

Cohen's most sustained attention to Jewish themes appeared in a trio of novels published in mid-career. Their themes were disparate: *The Spanish Doctor* (1984) explored the experience of Spanish *Marranos, while *Nadine* (1986) and *Emotional Arithmetic* (1990) focused on postwar Jewish identity, including the Holocaust. In the posthumously published *Typing: A Life in 26 Keys* (2000), Cohen expressed frustration with the Canadian reception of these books, suggesting that it was his foray into books with overtly Jewish themes that guaranteed them a chilly reception at home. The response of the Canadian literary establishment was abrupt and largely dismissive.

Cohen's was not a career in any way circumscribed by Jewish upbringing, Jewish values, or Jewish literary influences. He swam in the waters of the late-1960s counterculture without completely committing himself to its idealism; he took part in the explosion of small press publishing in Toronto; and he guided the Canadian Writers' Union. He is best known for a set of works dubbed his Salem novels, set in the countryside around Kingston, Ontario. He received acclaim for his final two novels, *Last Seen* (1996) and *Elizabeth and After* (1999). Other literary achievements include numerous excellent short stories, poetry, translations from French to English, and popular children's books, which he wrote under the pseudonym Teddy Jam. *Typing* takes the reader by surprise, with its recollection of the impact on Cohen of his immigrant grandparents and with its portrait of the particular struggle of one Jewish writer to find footing for himself in Canadian literature.

[Norman Ravvin (2nd ed.)]

COHEN, MAXWELL (1910–1998), Canadian legal scholar and teacher, public servant, international jurist. Cohen grew up in a secular middle-class family in Winnipeg's North End, and received his B.A. (1930) and LL.B. (1934) from the University of Manitoba, and LL.M. (1936) from Northwestern University with a thesis on Habeas Corpus. In 1937–38 he was research fellow at Harvard Law School studying anti-trust law. This led to a position as counsel for the Combines Investigation Commission (1938–40) and with the Department of Munitions and Supply (1940–41). Following a year freelancing for the *Christian Science Monitor* and several Canadian journals, he joined the Canadian army, reaching the rank of major, and in 1945–46 was head of Economics and Political Science at the Khaki University for Canadian soldiers in England. Drawn to education, he joined McGill University Law School in 1946 where he became an innovative legal educator. As dean of the Law School (1964–69), he introduced the National Programme combining training in common and civil law, subsequently McGill Law School's most distinctive characteristic. An acknowledged expert in international, constitutional and labor law, in 1951 he was named special assistant to the director general of the UN Technical Assistance Program and in 1959–60 a member of the Canadian delegation to the UN. He was frequently called upon to chair public inquiries.

Wartime revelations of Nazi atrocities and the birth of Israel awakened a sense of Jewish identity, and Cohen became very active in Montreal and national Jewish life, particularly through the Canadian Zionist Federation and Canadian Jewish Congress. As an English-speaking federalist in Quebec, he joined the Liberal Party and served as adviser on foreign and constitutional policies and relations with Israel in the 1950s. In 1965 he hoped to run for election in the heavily Jewish Montreal federal riding of Mount Royal but withdrew his candidacy in favor of Pierre Elliott Trudeau. He went on to head a Special Committee on Hate Propaganda in 1965–66 and the Royal Commission on Labour Legislation in Newfoundland in 1969–72 and was special counsel on constitutional law for the Government of New Brunswick (1967–70), president of the Quebec Advisory Council on the Administration of Justice (1972–74), and chair of the Federal Advisory Committee on the Law of the Sea (1971–74). From 1974 to 1979 he chaired the Canadian section of the International Joint Commission examining Canada-U.S. boundary waters. Leaving McGill as emeritus professor in 1978, he became professor of law and scholar in residence at the University of Ottawa (1980–89) and adjunct professor at Carleton University. From 1981 to 1985 he represented Canada as ad hoc judge at the International Court of Justice, the Hague. A prolific writer throughout his career, the range and significance of his interests are apparent from the chapters he wrote in a 1993 Festschrift: international law, human rights, dispute settlement, public law, legal history, and the theory and practice of legal education. He received honors from the Canadian Bar Association, the Canadian Council of International Law, the Council of Christians and Jews, the Manitoba Bar Association, and Columbia University, and was awarded eight honorary doctorates and the Order of Canada (1976).

BIBLIOGRAPHY: W. Kaplan and D. McRae (eds.), *Law, Policy, and International Justice: Essays in Honour of Maxwell Cohen* (1993).

[James Walker (2nd ed.)]

COHEN, MORRIS (1911–), U.S. metallurgist. Born in Chelsea, Mass., Cohen received his doctorate from the Massachusetts Institute of Technology in 1936. He then joined the staff at MIT as an assistant professor, becoming an associate professor in 1941. He became professor of physical metallurgy in 1946 and professor of materials science and engineering in 1962. In 1975 he was nominated as Institute Professor at MIT and in 1982 Institute Professor Emeritus. During World War II he was associate director of the Manhattan Project investigating atomic fission. Among his many awards he received the National Medal of Science and Presidential Award in 1977. He wrote *Heat Treatment of High Speed Steel* (1946) and *Titanium in Steel* (1949). Cohen's major works were published from 1962 to 1983 in the fields of phase transformations, metallography, heat treatment of metals, diffusion in the solid state, thermodynamics of metal systems, mechanical behavior, tool steels, age-hardening of metals, and dimensional stability. In 1994 he published *Societal Issues in Materials Science and Technology*, followed in 1995 by *Societal Implications of Microalloying Steels*.

[Gali Rotstein (2nd ed.)]

COHEN, MORRIS ABRAHAM (1887–1970), military adviser. Cohen was born in London and sent by his father to Canada at the age of 16. There he made a living as a ranchhand, peddler, gambler, and real estate speculator, ultimately drifting to Edmonton, Alberta, where he became a ward boss in the Chinese quarter of the city. He lobbied successfully in 1913 in the provincial legislature for the repeal of the head tax clause in the Chinese Immigration Act, an action that earned him the gratitude of the local Chinese population.

In 1908 Cohen had become friendly with Sun Yat-sen, the Chinese nationalist leader then in exile. Cohen joined Sun Yat-sen in China as an aide in 1922, and later was also adviser to his successor, Chiang Kai-shek. Cohen helped organize the Kuomintang Army, which awarded him the rank of general, and from 1926 to 1928 functioned in all but name as the Nationalist war minister. He took part in military campaigns against both Communist rebels and the Japanese, and carried out several secret missions to Europe to purchase arms and organize support for the Nationalist forces. He was probably known as Two-Gun Cohen. In 1941 he was taken prisoner by the Japanese after their capture of Hong Kong and two years later he was repatriated to Canada. After 1949 Cohen visited China several times in an attempt to reconcile the split Chinese factions. He subsequently settled in Manchester, England.

BIBLIOGRAPHY: C. Drage, *The Life and Times of General Two-Gun Cohen* (1954).

COHEN, MORRIS RAPHAEL (1880–1947), U.S. naturalist philosopher. Born in Minsk, Belorussia, Cohen went to New York at the age of 12. He studied at City College, and later with the Scottish philosopher Thomas Davidson. At Harvard University, where Cohen earned his doctorate, he studied under William James and Josiah Royce. Cohen, known as an outstanding teacher, was appointed professor of philosophy at City College in New York in 1912 and continued teaching there until 1938. From 1938 to 1941 he was professor of philosophy at the University of Chicago. He was president of the American Philosophical Association in 1928. In the later years of Cohen's life, as a result of the rise of Nazism, he began to champion Jewish interests. In 1933 he founded the Conference on Jewish Relations, an organization that assumed responsibility for scientific research on Jewish problems. He relates the details of this organization's activity in his autobiography, *A Dreamer's Journey* (1949), which also is valuable for its commentary on the Jews of Cohen's generation. An early interest in the plight of the working class – his parents had actively participated in the Jewish workers' movement in New York – eventually led Cohen to the study of legal philosophy. Reacting to the conservatism of American judges, who at that time tended to support anti-labor legislation, Cohen attacked the 18th-century concepts of natural law upon which this conservatism rested. He analyzed legislation strictly according to empirical criteria and his results were clearly socialistic; the sum of his work in this field is found in *Law and the Social Order* (1933). Cohen's naturalistic viewpoint and involvement with scientific methods as exemplified in his work in legal philosophy had been worked out earlier in his first, and perhaps most important, work, *Reason and Nature: An Essay on the Meaning of Scientific Method* (1931). *An Introduction to Logic and Scientific Method* (1934), written together with the American philosopher Ernest *Nagel, became a standard textbook in American universities and in the armed forces. *A Preface to Logic* (1945) is about the foundations of logic and its relation to the sciences. Cohen's interests also include ethics and the philosophy of history. In his work *The Meaning of Human History* (1947) he develops the theory that human history is expressed by a cyclical process of fruition and degeneration, not by a lineal progression. The optimistic note in this otherwise discouraging view is that

Truth, despite its continuous repression and opposition, succeeds in reasserting itself from time to time. Similar views are expressed in his collection of essays *The Faith of a Liberal* (1946). In 1939 Cohen founded the organ for Jewish social research, *Jewish Social Studies*. He was also one of the editors of the *Journal of the History of Ideas*. *Reflections of a Wandering Jew*, a collection of short essays on Judaism, was published posthumously in 1950.

[Samuel Hugo Bergman]

His son, FELIX (1907–1953), was a legal philosopher. Born in New York, he was a solicitor in the U.S. Department of the Interior, 1933–48. He wrote *Ethical Systems and Legal Ideals* (1933), *Handbook of Federal Indian Law* (1941), and *Readings in Jurisprudence and Legal Philosophy*, which he edited with M.R. Cohen (1951). After his death, a collection of Cohen's articles was published as *The Legal Conscience* (1960), edited by L.K. Cohen and with a foreword by Felix *Frankfurter. The divisions of this work show the range of Cohen's interests: Logic, Law and Ethics, the Indian's Quest for Justice, and the Philosophy of American Democracy. Like his father, Cohen was a legal realist, who insisted that law cannot escape dealing with ethics.

[Richard H. Popkin]

Bibliography: *A Tribute to Professor Morris Raphael Cohen: Teacher and Philosopher* (1928); Feuer, in: *Philosophy and Phenomenological Research*, 11 (1949–50), 471–85; S.W. Baron et al. (eds.), *Freedom and Reason: Studies in Philosophy and Jewish Culture in Memory of Morris Raphael Cohen* (1951); M.A. Kuhn, *Journal of the History of Ideas* (1957), supplement; H. Cairns, in: *Vanderbilt Law Review*, 14 (1960–61), 239–62; L. Rosenfield (Cohen), *A Portrait of a Philosopher: Morris R. Cohen in Life and Letters* (1962).

COHEN, MORTIMER JOSEPH (1894–1972), U.S. rabbi and author. Cohen, who was born in New York City and educated in public schools in Charleston, South Carolina, and New York, earned his B.S. at the City College of New York (1915) and was ordained at the Jewish Theological Seminary in 1919. He served as rabbi of Congregation Beth Shalom in Philadelphia. While serving as rabbi, he attended Dropsie College and earned his Ph.D. (1935). His thesis on *Jacob Emden: A Man of Controversy* was published in 1937 and described in its historical, psychological, and sociological contexts the feud between *Emden and Jonathan *Eibeschuetz.

Jews who had left older Orthodox and Conservative congregations formed Beth Shalom with 25 families, which under Cohen soon established itself as a Conservative congregation, putting up its first building in 1922. Established in the heart of Philadelphia's Jewish neighborhood in the aftermath of World War I, it boldly moved out of the city after World War II when Cohen persuaded his congregation to follow the Jewish population into the nearby suburbs. At first, it only built an educational and synagogue center in Elkins Park and services were conducted in the city and in the suburbs. As Jews moved to the suburbs in the 1950s, the suburban branch brought with it a new membership that sought to find full religious services locally. Cohen then hit upon an innovative idea and the congregation commissioned Frank Lloyd Wright, a preeminent American non-Jewish architect, to design its new sanctuary. Working closely with Cohen, whom he credited as co-designer, Wright designed an exterior that represented Mount Sinai and an impressive interior. The American Institute of Architecture recognized the distinguished quality of the design, adding greater visibility to the synagogue and prestige to the newly arrived Jews who commissioned such a brilliant building. A model of the synagogue is shown at *Beth Hatefutsoth, the Museum of the Diaspora, in Tel Aviv.

As a writer, Cohen was editor of *Pathways Through the Bible* (1946), a popular condensation of the Bible for the general reader, which went through numerous editions and was translated into Spanish and Portuguese. He was one of the founders, and editor for six years, of the Jewish Welfare Board's *In Jewish Bookland* and *The Jewish Book Annual*. He was president of the Jewish Book Council and of the Philadelphia Board of Rabbis. A man of many talents, he also composed four oratorios with the congregation's musical director Gedaliah Rabinowitz and wrote a number of plays. He also wrote on the design of the synagogue in *Beth Shalom Synagogue: A Description and Interpretation* (1959). His wife, Helen Kalikman Cohen, co-authored with P.T. Davis the story of his collaborative work with Wright in *Together They Built a Mountain* (1974).

Add. Bibliography: *The Beth Shalom Story, 1919–1969* (1969); P.S. Nadell, *Conservative Judaism in America: A Biographical Dictionary and Sourcebook* (1988).

[Jack Reimer / Michael Berenbaum (2nd ed.)]

COHEN, NAOMI WIENER (1927–), scholar of American Jewish history. Cohen was born in New York City and educated at Hunter College and the Jewish Theological Seminary of America, receiving her Ph.D. in history from Columbia University in 1955. She taught for 30 years at Hunter College and the Graduate Center of the City of New York and also served as adjunct distinguished service professor at the Jewish Theological Seminary. In 1948, she married Gerson D. *Cohen, a historian who later became chancellor of the Jewish Theological Seminary of America. Following her retirement in 1996, Cohen moved to Israel.

Cohen focused her research on various aspects of American Jewish history. One special area of interest was the German Jewish community in the United States; scholarly works in this area includes *A Dual Heritage: The Public Career of Oscar S. Straus* (1969), *Not Free to Desist: The American Jewish Committee, 1906–1966* (1972), *Encounter with Emancipation: The German Jews in the United States*, 1830–1914 (1984), and *Jacob H. Schiff: A Study in American Jewish Leadership* (1999). Cohen addressed the distinctiveness of American Zionism in three books, including *American Jews and the Zionist Idea* (1975) and *The Americanization of Zionism, 1897–1948* (2003).

Cohen also made an important contribution with her work on the complex interaction between American Jews and

Christians and on the separation of church and state in the United States. Articles on the legal arguments made by American Jews in defense of equal rights and religious freedom, as well as on their positions on religion in the public schools, appeared in the 1970s and 1980s, followed in *Essential Papers on Jewish Christian Relations in the United States: Imagery and Reality* (1990), an edited volume on Jewish-Christian relations in the United States. *Jews in Christian America: The Pursuit of Religious Equality* (1992), which details American Jews' efforts simultaneously to secure equality in American life and to protect their distinctive identity as non-Christians in a Christian country, is considered a landmark work on the separation of church and state.

Cohen received numerous awards for her work, including the American Jewish Committee's Akiba Award for Scholarship and Teaching; the Jewish Cultural Achievement Award in History; the National Federation for Jewish Culture Award in Historical Studies; and two National Jewish Book Awards for Jewish history.

BIBLIOGRAPHY: T. Kaplan, "Cohen, Naomi W.," in: P.E. Hyman and D. Dash Moore (eds.), *Jewish Women in America: An Historical Encyclopedia*, 1 (1997), 246–47.

[Jennifer Sartori (2nd ed.)]

COHEN, NATALIE (1912–), leading tennis player in the Southern United States and certified official of men's and women's tennis matches. Born in Atlanta, Georgia, the daughter of Dewald A. and Meta Leinkauf Cohen, she began playing competitive tennis at age eight and continued tournament play until age 81, earning the sobriquet, "Atlanta's First Lady of Tennis." At the University of California, Berkeley, where she earned a B.A. in political science, Cohen was president of the Women's Athletic Association in 1934. Cohen won numerous titles in Atlanta, Georgia, and Southern Tennis Association championships. In 1954, at age 42, she won the Georgia state singles title and the Atlanta city and state doubles titles. She competed in doubles in the 1955 National Clay Court Tennis Championship in Atlanta, reaching the quarterfinal round.

Cohen officiated for over 50 years as a United States Tennis Association stadium umpire and referee. Overcoming entrenched gender boundaries, Cohen became the first woman to serve as a chair umpire for a men's National Collegiate Athletic Association championship, and she was the first Southern woman to serve as a chair umpire at the Forest Hills Tennis Championships, the annual U.S. tennis championship. During her career she was chair of umpires for the Southern and Georgia Tennis Associations. Cohen received the Marlborough Award from *World Tennis* (founded by Gladys *Heldman) in 1962 and was selected Umpire of the Year by both the Southern and Georgia Tennis Associations. She was inducted in the Southern Tennis Hall of Fame and the Georgia Sports Hall of Fame for her distinguished career in tennis.

BIBLIOGRAPHY: G. Asher, "How She Played the Game," in: *Georgia Trend*, 19 (Jan. 2004), 114; J. Cook (ed.), "Cohen, Natalie," in *Who's Who in Tennis* (1983), 145; B.H. Weiner, "Cohen, Natalie," in: P.E. Hyman and D. Dash Moore (eds.), *Jewish Women in America: An Historical Encyclopedia*, 1 (1997), 247–48.

[Linda J. Borish (2nd ed.)]

COHEN, NATHAN (1923–1971), Canadian critic and journalist. Cohen was born in Sydney, Nova Scotia, and graduated in English from Mt. Allison University. Attracted to the left, Cohen entered journalism as a reporter for the labor press in Cape Breton. Moving to Toronto, he wrote for a number of newspapers and journals including the English-language pages of the leftist *Vokhnblat* and *Canadian Jewish Weekly*. By the late 1940s, Cohen's interests shifted from political journalism to arts review, particularly theater criticism. Increasingly respected for his uncompromising pursuit of artistic excellence, he became Canada's foremost arts and theater critic, eventually gaining an international reputation for the quality of his comments. Regarded by many as irascible and iconoclastic, his theater reviews and criticism were seldom shy about what lay behind the theater's facade.

No elitist when it came to the arts, Cohen's voice became familiar across Canada as a broadcast critic for CBC and for ten years as radio and television moderator of *Fighting Words*, a freewheeling program of social and political debate. With a well-earned reputation as broadcaster and print journalist who helped chart the course of Canadian theater, in 1959 Cohen became drama critic and entertainment editor for the Toronto *Star*, the largest circulation newspaper in Canada, an association he maintained until his death. Cohen was also a fluent Yiddishist who was known in Jewish circles for his translations of Yiddish poetry and prose.

BIBLIOGRAPHY: W.E. Edmonstone, *Nathan Cohen: The Making of a Critic* (1977).

[Harold Troper (2nd ed.)]

COHEN, NATHAN EDWARD (1909–2001), U.S. social work educator. Born in Derry, New Hampshire, Cohen took his doctorate at Harvard. He worked as executive director of the Roxbury Y.M.H.A., Boston, with the Jewish Community Welfare Fund in Springfield, Massachusetts, and as the director of various divisions of the National Jewish Welfare Board.

He became a professor at Columbia University's New York School of Social Work in 1954 and served as associate dean from 1955 to 1958. He co-founded the National Council on Social Work Education, helping to shape curricula across the country. He was then appointed dean of the School of Applied Social Sciences at Western Reserve University, Cleveland, of which he became vice president in 1963. In 1958, as a professor at Western (now part of Case Western Reserve), Cohen led a group of students to Selma, Alabama, to march with Martin Luther King, Jr.

In 1964 he was appointed professor of social welfare at the University of California at Los Angeles. Cohen formed a team of researchers to investigate the social causes underlying the Watts riot of 1965, writing "The Los Angeles Riot Study." He served as dean of UCLA's School of Social Welfare from 1964 to 1979. Cohen stressed that professional social work must contribute to changes in society by leadership and action and that social services are an enduring function of the social economy. Cohen was chairman of the National Conference of Social Welfare and was the co-founder and president of the National Association of Social Workers. At Berkeley, he and his wife, Sylvia, founded the Association for Lifelong Learning. Practicing what he preached, Cohen continued to lead current events discussions until 2000 at age 90.

His writings include *Social Work in the American Tradition* (1958); *The Citizen Volunteer*, which he edited (1960); *Social Work and Social Problems* (1964); and *The Los Angeles Riots: A Socio-Psychological Study* (1970) as well as many articles in professional journals and collections such as *Social Work* and *The Social Welfare Forum*. At UCLA a foundation for the Nathan E. Cohen Doctoral Student Award in Social Welfare has been established.

[Jacob Neusner / Ruth Beloff (2nd ed.)]

COHEN, PAUL JOSEPH (1934–), U.S. mathematician. Born in New Jersey, Cohen was a student at Brooklyn College from 1950 to 1953 and he received his M.Sc. in 1954 and his Ph.D in 1958 from the University of Chicago. From 1959 to 1961 he was a fellow at the Institute for Advanced Study at Princeton and in 1961 he was appointed to the faculty at Stanford University. In 1964 became a professor of mathematics at Stanford University. At the same time Cohen received the Bocher Memorial Prize from the American Mathematical Society, and in 1966 Cohen was awarded the Fields Medal for his fundamental work on the foundations of set theory. Cohen used a technique called "forcing" to prove the independence in set theory of the axiom of choice and of the generalized continuum hypothesis. Cohen's main interests were set theory, harmonic analysis, and partial differential equations. He wrote *Set Theory and the Continuum Hypothesis* (1966).

[Bracha Rager (2nd ed.)]

COHEN, SIR PHILIP (1945–), British biochemist. Cohen was born in Edgware, Middlesex, and earned his B.Sc. (1966) and Ph.D., under the supervision of Michael Rosemeyer (1969), in biochemistry from University College, London. After a postdoctoral fellowship with Edmond Fischer at the University of Washington, Seattle (1969–1971), he joined the staff of the University of Dundee, where he progressed to full professor (1981) and Royal Society Research Professor (from 1984). He also became director of the Medical Research Council Protein Phosphorylation Unit and the University's School of Life Sciences. Cohen's research centered on kinases, large families of enzymes which attach phosphate to proteins, and protein phosphatases, enzymes which have the opposite effect. He made pioneering contributions to elucidating these systems, which provide signals regulating normal cell behavior and which are perturbed in many diseases, including cancer and rheumatoid arthritis. In particular, his group identified the enzymes which control the conversion of blood glucose to tissue glycogen and have major implications for understanding diabetes. These discoveries are being applied to the design of novel drugs for treating diseases such as diabetes and cancer. His publications are currently the world's second most cited in biology and biochemistry. His many honors include election to the Royal Society of London (1984), knighthood (1998), and the Bristol-Myers Squibb Award (2002). In 2005 he became president of the British Biochemical Society. His leadership had a major influence in transforming a depressed area of Scotland into a center of scientific and biotechnological excellence. He also delivered many major lectures to Israeli academic institutions.

[Michael Denman (2nd ed.)

COHEN, PHILIP MELVIN (1808–1879), pharmacist and civic leader in Charleston, South Carolina. Cohen, born in Charleston, was the son of Philip Cohen, lieutenant in the War of 1812. During the Second Seminole War Cohen served as surgeon to a detachment of troops in Charleston Harbor (1836). In 1838 he became city apothecary. He was a member of the city board of health (1843–49), and its chairman (1850–54). Cohen was a director of the Bank of the State of South Carolina (1849–55). He was one of the citizens who served as honorary guard at the funeral of John C. Calhoun in 1850.

BIBLIOGRAPHY: A. Elzas, *Jews of South Carolina* (1905), 189.

[Thomas J. Tobias]

COHEN, PHILIP PACY (1908–1993), U.S. biochemist. Cohen was born in Derry, New Hampshire. He studied science at Tufts University, Boston, and received his Ph.D. in physiological chemistry in 1937 and M.D. in 1938 from the University of Wisconsin. His main interests were transamination reactions, nitrogen metabolism, and urea synthesis, including developmental aspects of these processes, on which he became a world authority. After graduating, he worked with Hans Krebs in Sheffield, England, and at Yale University before returning to the University of Wisconsin in 1941. He became a full professor in 1947 and Harold Bradley Professor of Physiological Chemistry in 1968. His administrative skills were also highly regarded. He was elected to the National Academy of Sciences and was a member of many key scientific committees in the U.S. and abroad responsible for research and education. He had strong research and organizational links with Mexico and many South American and Asian countries.

[Michael Denman (2nd ed.)]

COHEN, ROBERT (1889–1939), French historian of ancient Greece. He served in the French Army in World War I, was seriously wounded, and was decorated for bravery. Cohen taught at the Lycée Henri IV in Paris. He collaborated with his former teacher, Gustave Glotz, and Pierre Roussel on the four volumes of the *Histoire générale* dealing with Greece (*Histoire grecque*, 1926–38). Other works include *La Grèce et l'hellénisation du monde antique* (1934) and *Athènes, une démocratie de sa naissance à sa mort* (1936). Cohen's work is distinguished by an appreciation of the importance of ancillary disciplines and exhaustive bibliographies to historical studies.

BIBLIOGRAPHY: *Dictionnaire de Biographie Française*, 9 (1961), s.v.; *Revue des études grecques*, 52 (1939), 25.

[Irwin L. Merker]

COHEN, SIR ROBERT WALEY (1877–1952), British industrialist and Jewish communal leader. He was the son of Nathaniel Cohen, who pioneered labor exchanges and university appointment boards in Britain, and of Julia, daughter of Jacob Waley. In 1901 he joined the staff of Shell Company under the future Viscount *Bearsted and represented the company in the negotiations which led to its amalgamation with the Royal Dutch Petroleum Company. For many years he was, in effect, second in command of "The Group." During World War I Waley Cohen played a vital part in ensuring the supply of fuel oil to the Allies and was knighted for his services in 1920.

He rose to high office in the Anglo-Jewish community and was in turn treasurer, vice president, and president of the *United Synagogue. His concept of the overriding role of the lay leadership brought him into constant conflict with the chief rabbi, J.H. *Hertz, who believed that the traditional authority of the rabbinate must be paramount. The conflict was exacerbated by the incompatibility of two dominant personalities. Waley Cohen was largely responsible for establishing in 1919 the Jewish War Memorial (later Jewish Memorial Council) for improving religious and educational conditions in the Anglo-Jewish community. In 1942 he was one of the founders of the Council of Christians and Jews. In spite of some collaboration with Chaim *Weizmann in the 1920s, he remained basically opposed to political Zionism, though he contributed to the economic development of Palestine as chairman of the Economic Board for Palestine and of the Palestine Corporation. It was he who selected the site for the Haifa oil refinery. His son SIR BERNARD WALEY-COHEN (1914–1991) was lord mayor of London 1960–61, when he was named a baronet. He was a vice president of the United Synagogue.

BIBLIOGRAPHY: R. Henriques, *Sir Robert Waley Cohen* (1966). **ADD. BIBLIOGRAPHY:** ODNB online.

[Vivian David Lipman]

COHEN, ROSE GOLLUP (1880–1925?), U.S. author and memoirist, was born in Belarus, the eldest child of Abraham (Avrom) Gollup, a tailor, and his wife, Annie (maiden name unknown). Rose immigrated with an aunt to New York City in 1892, joining her father, who had arrived in 1890. The rest of the family followed a year later. Cohen's 1918 autobiography, *Out of the Shadow* (rep. 1995), offers a rich account of her childhood in Russia, immigration to the United States, and life in New York City's Lower East Side, including a detailed view of sweatshop garment work. She recounts union organizing in her shop, her attendance at a mass union meeting, and joining a union, probably the United Hebrew Trades. She also describes a brief stint as a domestic servant, her rejection of an arranged marriage, and increasing health problems. During one illness, Lillian *Wald, the noted settlement worker, visited Cohen's home and sent her to uptown Presbyterian Hospital where she met wealthy non-Jews who sponsored summer outings for immigrant children. Cohen worked successive summers at a Connecticut retreat, and, like other immigrants found herself torn between Old World traditions and broader American culture. Wald also referred Rose Gollup to a cooperative shirtwaist shop under the direction of Leonora O'Reilly, later a board member of the National Women's Trade Union League. When O'Reilly began teaching at the Manhattan Trade School for Girls in 1902, she recruited Rose Gollup as her assistant.

Little is known about Cohen's later life. She married Joseph Cohen and stopped working upon the birth of her daughter, Evelyn. She continued her education after marriage, attending classes at Breadwinners' College at the Educational Alliance, the Rand School, and University Extension at Columbia University. In addition to her enthusiastically received autobiography, which also appeared in French and Russian translations, Cohen wrote eight short pieces published in New York and Philadelphia magazines between 1918 and 1922. A short story, "Natalka's Portion," was reprinted six times, appearing in the prestigious *Best Short Stories of 1922*. In 1923 and 1924 Cohen attended the MacDowell Colony in Peterborough, New Hampshire, where she met the American impressionist painter Lilla Cabot Perry and the poet Edwin Arlington Robinson. An untimely death, perhaps a suicide, cut short her promising literary career. Her autobiography survives as her legacy, a moving account of a cultural journey shared with many other Jewish immigrant women at the turn of the 19th century.

BIBLIOGRAPHY: T. Dublin, Introduction to *Out of the Shadow* (1995); L. O'Reilly, "Rahel and 'Out of the Shadow,'" in: *Life and Labor* (May 1919), 103–5; A. Yezierska, "Wild Winter Love," in: *Century Magazine* 113 (Feb. 1927): 485–91.

[Thomas Dublin (2nd ed.)]

COHEN, RUTH LOUISA (1906–1991), British economist, specializing in the field of agricultural economics. The granddaughter of Louis Lionel *Cohen, she was educated at Newnham College, Cambridge, and was a teaching fellow at Stanford and Cornell universities in the U.S. from 1930 to 1932. Upon her return to England, she became a research officer of the Agricultural Economics Research Institute at Oxford (1933–39). She returned to Newnham College in 1939 and served as its principal from 1954 until 1972. She was chairman of the Committee on Provincial Agricultural Economics in 1957. In addition to numerous articles, her writings include *History of Milk Prices* (1936) and *Economics of Agriculture* (1939).

ADD. BIBLIOGRAPHY: ODNB online.

[Joachim O. Ronall]

COHEN, SAMUEL HERBERT (1918–1969), Australian labor politician. Born in Bankstown, New South Wales, of Russian Jewish parents, Cohen practiced law in Melbourne, becoming a queen's counsel in 1961. He was a member of the Victoria Central Executive and of the Australian Labor Party's foreign affairs and defense committee. Cohen was elected to the Senate in 1961 (the first Jew elected to the Australian Senate) and became deputy leader of the labor opposition party there in 1967. He was Labor spokesman on education, and was responsible for the party's state aid program in the 1969 elections. From his youth he was involved in Jewish community affairs, particularly in combating antisemitism, and was a patron of Montefiore homes and welfare projects. A leftist and an early opponent of the Vietnam War, in 1962 Cohen became involved in a fierce controversy within the Melbourne Jewish community when he failed to support an opposition measure condemning Soviet antisemitism, arguing that Soviet Jews enjoyed equal rights. Cohen's stance sparked considerable outrage in sections of the Jewish community. Despite this incident, Cohen was much respected and his early death at only 51 was widely regretted.

BIBLIOGRAPHY: *Australian Jewish News* (Oct. 10, 1969), 3. **ADD. BIBLIOGRAPHY:** P. Mendes, "The Senator Sam Cohen Affair: Soviet Anti-Semitism, the ALP, and the 1961 Federal Election," in: *Labor History*, 57 (2000), 179–97; idem., "Samuel Herbert Cohen," in: *Biographical Dictionary of the Australian Senate*, vol. 3 (2006); W.D. Rubinstein, Australia II, index.

COHEN, SASHA (Alexandra Pauline; 1984–), U.S. Olympic figure skater. Cohen was born in Westwood, California, and named after Alexandra Rajefrejk, the favorite ballerina of her mother, a native of the Ukraine. Cohen began skating at age seven after first starting with gymnastics at age five and progressing to level five of the sport's 10 levels. She decided to take skating seriously at age 10, working first with coach Yvonne Nicks and then with Yvonne's husband, John Nicks. Cohen placed second at the U.S. Junior Championships in 1999, and shocked the skating world by placing first in the short program at the U.S. Senior Championships in 2000, and second overall to World Champion Michelle Kwan. A back injury limited Cohen to only two competitions in the 2000–1 season, but she bounced back to place second at the U.S. Championships in 2002, again behind Kwan. This landed her a spot on the U.S. Olympic team for the games in Salt Lake City, where Cohen sat next to President George W. Bush at the opening ceremonies and made national news when she asked him to talk on her cell phone to her mother. Cohen then finished fourth behind Sarah Hughes, Russian Irina Slutskaya, and Kwan, in a controversial competition that some felt should have included Cohen among the medal winners. Cohen then competed in her first World Championships, where she placed fourth. She won her first major international title at the 2003 Grand Prix Final, and placed fourth overall at the 2003 World Championships. A supreme stylist, she won silver medals at the 2004 Grand Prix Final and, despite coaching changes made directly beforehand, at the 2004 and 2005 World Championships. She placed second after Kwan at the U.S. Championships in January 2005, her otherwise flawless performance marred when she fell on a triple lutz jump and put her hand down on a triple loop. Cohen won a silver medal at the 2006 Winter Olympics. Her autobiography, *Sasha Cohen: Fire on Ice,* was published in 2005.

[Elli Wohlgelernter (2nd ed.)]

COHEN, SAUL BERNARD (1925–), U.S. geographer and educator. Cohen, the son of a Hebrew teacher, was born in Malden, Mass., and studied at Harvard University, where he obtained his doctorate in 1955. He taught at Boston University from 1952 to 1964, and in 1965 became the director and a professor of the Graduate School of Geography at Clark University in Worcester, Mass. In 1967 he became the dean. He served as president of Queens College of the City University of New York (1978–85), and then for ten years as professor of geography at Hunter College, also of CUNY. Among his many appointments was that of coordinator and co-chairman of the United States–Israel Geographic Research symposium held in Jerusalem in 1969. A member of the American Geographical Society, Cohen specialized in the economic and political geography of the Middle East. He was a visiting professor at the U.S. Naval War College and the Hebrew University of Jerusalem, and served as consultant on geography to the National Science Foundation. His fieldwork took him to Israel, Puerto Rico, Sweden, and Venezuela.

Cohen served on numerous government committees devoted to educational improvement. From his arrival in New York in 1978, he was involved in various city and state policy committees. He was elected to the New York State Board of Regents in 1993 and chaired the Elementary, Middle, and Secondary Committee when it established new academic standards for the schools (1995–98). He chaired the Regents Committee on Higher Education and led the effort to reform teacher education.

Cohen received awards from the Association of American Geographers (1965 and 1979). In 1990 and 1992 his work was recognized as Best Content Article by *The Journal of Geography*. In 1994 the National Geographical Society named him Distinguished Geography Educator, and in 1998 he received the Rowman and Littlefield's Author Laureate Award.

In 2004 Cohen received an honorary doctorate from the University of Haifa. Acknowledged for having laid the foundations for the field of political geography, he was praised for "his wide-ranging and in-depth scientific contribution to the study of political geography; his educational and public activity to advance the teaching of geography; his societal involvement and dedication to the Jewish community in the United States; and his support of academe in Israel."

He was editor of *The Oxford World Atlas* (1973), served as geographic consultant for the fifth edition of *The Columbia Encyclopedia* (1993), and was editor of *The Columbia Gazetteer of the World* (1998). Among his publications are *Geography and Politics in a World Divided* (1963, 1964, 1973); *American Geography – Problems and Prospects* (1968); *Jerusalem – Bridging the Four Walls* (1977); *Jerusalem Undivided* (1980); *The Geopolitics of Israel's Border Question* (1986); and *Geopolitics of the World System* (2002).

[Ruth Beloff (2nd ed.)]

COHEN, SELMA JEANNE (1920–), U.S. dance historian. Cohen taught at New York City's High School of Performing Arts and later at the Connecticut College School of Dance. She wrote on dance for the *New York Times* and the *Saturday Review* and edited *The Modern Dance – Seven Statements of Belief* (1966). She was co-founder with A.J. Pischl of *Dance Perspectives* magazine (1959) as a series of monographs; she continued as sole editor from 1965 until 1976 and was the editor of the Dance Department of the *Encyclopaedia Judaica*. She was the founding editor of the International *Encyclopedia of Dance* published in 1998, which crowned her initiatives on behalf of dance scholarship.

[Amnon Shiloah (2nd ed.)]

COHEN, SEYMOUR J. (1922–2001), U.S. Conservative rabbi. Cohen was born in New York City, ordained at the Jewish Theological Seminary in 1946, and earned a Ph.D. in economics from the University of Pittsburgh in 1953. He studied at the Hebrew University of Jerusalem in pre-Israel Palestine and worked with Holocaust survivors in Italy and France (1946–47). Cohen served as rabbi of the Patchogue Jewish Community Center in Patchogue, New York (1947–51) and B'nai Israel, Pittsburgh, Pennsylvania (1951–61), before taking the pulpit at the formerly Reconstructionist Anshe Emet Synagogue in Chicago in 1961, a post he held for 29 years before being appointed rabbi emeritus. Cohen joined with other neighborhood clergy and resisted the temptation to flee the city and was instrumental in the congregation's remaining in Chicago and thus in stabilizing the renewal of the neighborhood. Although considered a scholar-rabbi and compelling orator, Cohen was also a gifted pastor who devoted much time and considerable energy to serving the needs of his congregants and others.

Cohen rose to the highest positions of leadership in several major American Jewish organizations. While serving as chairman of the American Jewish Conference on Soviet Jewry, he led the first Eternal Light Vigil for Soviet Jews in Washington D.C. (1965). As president of the Synagogue Council of America (1965–67), he worked to further Jewish-Christian relations and was founding co-chairman of the Interreligious Committee Against Poverty. As president of the Rabbinical Assembly (1980–82), he introduced a number of services benefiting working rabbis.

Also known as a scholar, Cohen edited and translated the Hebrew classics *Orchot Tzadikkim: The Ways of the Righteous* (1969, 1982[2]); *Sefer Hayashar: The Book of the Righteous* (1973), and *Iggeret Ha-Kodesh: The Holy Letter* (1976). He published two collections of sermons, *A Time to Speak* (1968) and *Form, Fire and Ashes* (1978), and wrote the book *Affirming Life* (1986). He was also the co-author (with Byron L. Sherwin) of *How to Be a Jew: Ethical Teachings of Judaism* (1982). In 1991, Abraham J. Karp, Louis Jacobs, and Chaim Zalman Dimitrovsky edited a *Festschrift* in his honor: *Threescore and Ten: Essays in Honor of Rabbi Seymour J. Cohen on the Occasion of His Seventieth Birthday*.

BIBLIOGRAPHY: P.S. Nadell, *Conservative Judaism in America: A Biographical Dictionary and Sourcebook* (1988).

[Bezalel Gordon (2nd ed.)]

COHEN, SEYMOUR STANLEY (1917–), U.S. biochemist. Cohen was born in Brooklyn, New York, and received a B.Sc. degree at CCNY in 1936 and a Ph.D. at Columbia University College of Physicians and Surgeons in 1941. He was a National Research Council Fellow in plant virology with Wendell Stanley at the Rockefeller Institute and then explored the properties of the typhus vaccine for the Army during World War II. In 1945 and 1946 he began his biochemical studies of bacteriophage multiplication in the Department of Pediatrics of the University of Pennsylvania. Following research with André Lwoff at the Pasteur Institute in Paris in 1947 and 1948, and research and teaching at the University of Pennsylvania, he was appointed American Cancer Society (ACS) Research Professor of Biochemistry in 1957, and chairman of the Department of Therapeutic Research in 1963. After initiating studies on nucleoside analogues and on polyamines, he continued work on these subjects from 1971 to 1976 as ACS Professor of Microbiology at the University of Colorado Medical School, and from 1976 to 1985 as Distinguished Professor of Pharmacology at the State University of New York at Stony Brook. In 1985 he retired to Woods Hole, Massachusetts. His studies on plant and bacterial viruses led to discoveries on the structure, composition, and metabolism of viral nucleic acids. He was the codiscoverer of a new phage pyrimidine and its biosynthesis, thereby describing a new set of viral functions, which were presented in his 1968 book *Virus-Induced Enzymes*. This phenomenon has become significant in viral reproduction generally and a key to the treatment of human viral diseases such as AIDS, herpes infections, and influenza. Cohen's studies with polyamines resulted in two books, *An Introduction to the Polyamines*, presented at the Collège de France in 1970, and *A Guide to the Polyamines* (1998). Cohen was elected to the American National Academy of Sciences in 1967. In later years he took a working interest in the history of early American science.

[Sharon Zrachya (2nd ed.)]

COHEN, SHALOM BEN JACOB (1772–1845), Hebrew writer, poet, and editor. Born in Mezhirech, Poland, he studied German and read the new Hebrew literature, particularly *Ha-Me'assef. His first book, *Mishlei Agur* (1799), was a collection of Hebrew fables in rhyme, with German translation, aimed at teaching Jewish children simple and clear Hebrew. Cohen went to Berlin in 1789 and taught in the Ḥinnukh Ne'arim school and in private homes. After the publication of several works he renewed the publication of *Ha-Me'assef* and served as its editor (1809–11). In 1813 Cohen left Germany, spent a short period in Amsterdam, and moved to London where he tried unsuccessfully to establish a Jewish school. In London, in 1815, he printed his catechism, *Shorshei Emunah* (with an English translation by Joshua van Oven), in which he stressed the divinity of the Written and Oral Law and its immutability. From London, Cohen moved to Hamburg (1816 or 1817), where he spent three controversy-laden years. In a posthumously published poem he attacked the hypocrisy of the "reformists" for their lack of religious belief and national feelings and considered the establishment of the Reform temple in Hamburg an act of blasphemy. However, he refrained from public intervention on this controversy. In 1820 Cohen was invited by Anton Schmid to serve as head proofreader in the Hebrew section of his printing press in Vienna where he remained for 16 years. In 1821 Cohen established the annual *Bikkurei ha-Ittim, three issues of which appeared under his editorship. In 1834 he published his poetic work, *Nir David*, a description of the life of King David, one of the first romantic works in Hebrew literature. In 1836 Cohen returned to Hamburg, where he lived until his death. His last extensive work was *Kore ha-Dorot*, a history of the Jewish people (1838). His other works include: *Matta'ei Kedem al Admat Ẓafon* (1807), poetry; *Amal ve-Tirẓah* (1812), an allegorical and utopian drama, a sequel to M.Ḥ. Luzzatto's *La-Yesharim Tehillah*; and *Ketav Yosher* (1820), a literary miscellany.

BIBLIOGRAPHY: Klausner, Sifrut, 1 (1960), 275–90; R. Mahler, *Divrei Yemei Yisrael*, 1, pt. 2 (1954), 275–9; Zinberg, Sifrut, 5 (1959), 267–71; 6 (1960), 25f; J.L. Landau, *Short Lectures on Modern Hebrew Literature* (1939), 121–34; Waxman, Literature, 3 (1960), 153–8.

[Gedalyah Elkoshi]

COHEN, SHAYE J.D. (1949–), leading historian of Jews and Judaism in the world of late antiquity. Cohen received his B.A. from Yeshiva College (1970), rabbinic ordination from the Jewish Theological Seminary (1974), and his Ph.D. from Columbia University (1975). He taught at the Jewish Theological Seminary (1974–91), where he also served as dean of the Graduate School, and at Brown University (1991–2001), where he served as Ungerleider Professor of Judaic Studies and director of the program in Judaic studies. From 2001 he served as Littauer Professor of Hebrew Literature and Philosophy at Harvard University.

Cohen is the author or editor of nine books, including *From the Maccabees to the Mishnah* (1987), which is widely used as a textbook in colleges and adult education courses, and *The Beginnings of Jewishness* (1999), and dozens of articles.

The focus of Cohen's research is the boundary between Jews and gentiles and between Judaism and its surrounding cultures. What makes a Jew a Jew, and what makes a non-Jew a non-Jew? Can a non-Jew become a Jew, and, if so, how, and can a Jew become a non-Jew, and, if so, how? How does the Jewish boundary between Jew and non-Jew compare with the Jewish boundary between male Jew and female Jew? Building on sources in Hebrew, Aramaic, Greek, and Latin, Cohen argues for the fluidity of identity markers in the ancient world. He also insists that the Jewish reaction to Hellenism in antiquity and to Christianity from ancient to modern times consisted of both resistance and accommodation, and both stances had a far-reaching influence on the history of Judaism.

[Jay Harris (2nd ed.)]

COHEN, SHLOMO (1947–), Israeli attorney. Born in Tel Aviv, Cohen received LL.B. (1971) and LL.M. (1973) degrees from Tel Aviv University Law School and LL.N and J.S.D. degrees from New York University School of Law (1976 and 1978). He is the founder of Dr. Shlomo Cohen & Co., a law firm specializing in intellectual property and served as adjunct professor (intellectual property) at New York University School of Law (1976–95), the Hebrew University School of Law (1980–92), and the Tel Aviv University School of Law (from 1988). He has written extensively in the field of intellectual property and chaired the Justice Ministry Committee to revise the Registered Design Act. He also served on the Justice Ministry Committee to revise the Patents and Copyright Acts and founded the Israeli Chapter of the International Licensing Executives Society (LES) and served as its president from 1994. He was a member of the Israeli Civil Rights Association, serving on its board for two terms, and was a founding member of Betselem, the human rights watch organization. Cohen was a member of the Israeli Bar Association from 1971. As its president (from 1999), he initiated a pro bono program and an annual evaluation survey by lawyers of judges and other programs. He was also a member of the Israeli Forum (an organization dealing with Israeli-Diaspora relations), serving on its board in 1988 to 1992.

[Leon Fine (2nd ed.)]

COHEN, SIMON (Sam; 1890–1977). South-West African businessman who was known as the "uncrowned king of South-West Africa" by reason of his extensive commercial and financial interests. Born in Russia and educated in London, he went to South Africa as a child with his father. In 1906 he went to Swakopmund, in South-West Africa (then a German colony), to run his father's store. After the South African occupation of the territory he settled, in 1916, in the capital, Windhoek, where he built up a large business organization, comprising commercial, industrial, agricultural, mining, transport, and fishing concerns, which spread to South

Africa, Rhodesia, and other neighboring countries. His energy and enterprise played a pioneering role in furthering the economic development of South-West Africa, a mandated territory under South African control. Cohen was an honorary life president of the Windhoek Hebrew Congregation.

[Louis Hotz]

COHEN, STANLEY (1922–), U.S. biochemist and Nobel Prize laureate. Cohen was born in Brooklyn, New York. After studying at Brooklyn College (B.A., 1943) and Oberlin College (M.A., 1945), he received his Ph.D. in biochemistry from the University of Michigan in 1948. From then until 1952 he worked at the University of Colorado. Cohen then proceeded to Washington University in St. Louis in 1952 where he was a fellow of the American Cancer Society. There he worked with Dr. Rita *Levi-Montalcini and they isolated the protein which is recognized as the nerve growth factor (NGF). In 1959 Cohen moved to Vanderbilt University as an assistant professor of biochemistry, where he discovered epidermal growth factor (EGF), which oversees cell development in the skin. In 1986 he shared the Nobel Prize with Levi-Montalcini for physiology and medicine for having "opened new fields of widespread importance to basic science with these discoveries."

Cohen remained at Washington University until 1967 when he became a professor of biochemistry at Vanderbilt University. He was an American Cancer Society research professor in 1976 and in 1986 a distinguished professor. He was a member of the National Academy of Science. He and Dr. Levi-Montalcini were also the co-recipients of the 1986 Lasker Award.

ADD. BIBLIOGRAPHY: Le Prix Nobel.

COHEN, STANLEY N. (1935–), U.S. geneticist. Cohen was born in Perth Amboy, New Jersey. He graduated from Rutgers University with a degree in biology and as an M.D. from the Pennsylvania School of Medicine (1960). After research training at the National Institutes of Health, Bethesda, he joined the faculty of Stanford University (1968), where his appointments included chairman of the Department of Genetics and then professor of genetics and medicine and director of the S.N. Cohen Laboratory. His early research dealt with the ability of plasmids to alter the properties of the bacteria they colonize, a subject of fundamental importance to the development of antibiotic resistance. His pioneering research interests involved isolating, cloning, and propagating mammalian genes in other species, including bacteria (also known as recombinant technology). This work laid the foundation for biotechnological techniques enabling the production of large quantities of pure proteins for diagnostic and medicinal purposes. His many honors include the Lasker Award (1980), the Wolf Prize (1981), the Albany Medical Center Prize (2004), election to the U.S. National Academy of Sciences and National Medals in both Science and Technology.

[Michael Denman (2nd ed.)]

COHEN, WILBUR JOSEPH (1913–1987), U.S. social welfare authority. Born in Milwaukee, the son of Jewish immigrants, Cohen left his home in the early 1930s to attend the University of Wisconsin. He served with the U.S. Committee on Economic Security in 1934-35 and participated in the drafting of the Social Security Act. From 1936 to 1956 he was employed in the Social Security Administration and helped secure the adoption of measures that would provide for shared financing by the federal government and the states in programs for the aged, dependent children, the totally disabled, and the blind. Cohen was responsible for the passage by Congress in 1946 of legislation enabling the federal government to offer financial aid in hospital construction. He aided Jewish organizations in their support of social security and welfare legislation. In 1952–53 he advised the Israeli government when the state undertook the establishment of its own social security program.

For five years (1956–61) he was professor of public welfare at the University of Michigan, during which time he served as consultant to the U.S. Senate Committee on Labor and Public Welfare and to the White House Conference on Aging. He returned to government service in 1961 when President John F. Kennedy appointed him assistant secretary of the Department of Health, Education, and Welfare. During the Johnson administration he was named undersecretary of Health, Education, and Welfare and saw the enactment of Medicare and Medicaid programs, which he had recommended three decades earlier. In 1968, he assumed the post of secretary of the department (1968–69). He initiated extensive changes in the department and reorganized its public health division. As a part of the reorganization, the National Institute of Health, the National Institute of Mental Health, and the National Library of Medicine were brought into a new agency called the Health Services and Mental Health Administration. In 1969, when President Johnson left office, Cohen assumed the position of dean of the University of Michigan's School of Education.

As one of the key players in the creation and expansion of the American welfare state, Cohen was dubbed by President Kennedy as "Mr. Social Security"; President Johnson praised him as the "planner, architect, builder, and repairman on every major piece of social legislation" [since 1935]; and the *New York Times* described him as "one of the country's foremost technicians in public welfare."

Cohen wrote extensively on the field of welfare. Papers he presented before the National Conference of Social Welfare appear in *The Social Welfare Forum* (1954, 1957, 1961). Among his books and articles are *Readings in Social Security* (with W. Haber, 1949); *Retirement Policies in Social Security* (1957); *Social Security: Programs, Problems and Policies* (with W. Haber, 1960); and "The Problem of Financing Social Services" in J.E. Russell's (ed.), *National Policies for Education, Health and Social Services* (1961). He was one of four contributors to *Income and Welfare in the United States* (1962). He wrote *Toward Freedom from Want* (with S.A. Levitan and R.J. Lampman, 1968), *Social Security: Universal or Selective?* (with

M. Friedman, 1972), *Demographic Dynamics in America* (with C.F. Westoff, 1977), and *The American Economy in Transition* (1980). He also edited *The New Deal Fifty Years After: A Historical Assessment* (1984).

BIBLIOGRAPHY: M.O. Shearon, *Wilbur J. Cohen, the Pursuit of Power* (1967^2), incl. bibl.; *Business Week* (March 30, 1968), 35f. **ADD. BIBLIOGRAPHY:** E.D. Berkowitz, *Mr. Social Security: The Life of Wilbur J. Cohen* (2000).

[Joseph Neipris / Ruth Beloff (2nd ed.)]

COHEN, WILLIAM S. (1940–), U.S. congressman, senator, secretary of defense, author. One of three children of a Russian-Jewish immigrant father and an Irish-Protestant mother, Cohen was born in Bangor, Maine, in 1940. As a youngster he came to an understanding with his father, Reuben Cohen, who ran a small local bakery: he would play basketball at the local YMCA one Saturday morning a month, and attend Sabbath services at the local synagogue the other three.

Cohen remembers that during these early years in Bangor, he had "the worst of two worlds." As a Jew, the local bigots reviled him; as the child of mixed marriage, he was not fully accepted by the close-knit Bangor Jewish community. Cohen was told, shortly before his 13th birthday, that he could not become *bar mitzvah* without first submitting to a *hatafat dam berit* (symbolic circumcision) and his mother's completing conversion. Neither event took place; Cohen never became *bar mitzvah*. The trauma of his religiously bifurcated childhood led the adult Bill Cohen to affiliate with the Unitarian Universalist Church.

In 1958, Cohen entered Bowdoin College, where he excelled both in his major, Latin, and on the basketball court, where he was named to both the All-State and the New England Hall of Fame teams. Following his graduation in 1962, he entered Boston University Law School to study for his LL.B., which he received *cum laude* in 1965. While a student at BU, he was a member of the law review and served on its editorial board. His first year out of law school, he was employed as assistant editor-in-chief of the *Journal of the American Trial Lawyers Association*.

In 1971, he was elected mayor of Bangor.

In 1972, Cohen decided to run for the United States House of Representatives. Cohen came to national attention during his first term when, as a member of the House Judiciary Committee, he "resisted political pressure by voting to recommend the impeachment of President Richard Nixon for complicity in the Watergate cover-up." Crossing party lines, Cohen cast what turned out to be the deciding vote on a Democratic motion that informed President Nixon of his failure to comply with the committee's subpoena for White House documents and tapes. Cohen's mostly Republican constituency saw his impeachment vote as a matter of conscience; he was reelected in 1976 and again 1978, this time with 77 percent of the popular vote.

In 1978, Cohen was elected to the first of three terms in the United States Senate. During his 18 years in the upper chamber, Cohen became an acknowledged expert on military affairs. From his seat on the Armed Services Committee, Cohen led the fight for a stronger, more efficiently financed American military. In 1980, Cohen ran into trouble with the American Jewish political establishments when he cast a "reluctant vote" in favor President Reagan's proposed sale of five Airborne Warning and Control System (AWACS) surveillance planes to Saudi Arabia. Heretofore a committed Zionist, his last-minute vote in favor of AWACS was seen as a betrayal of the Jewish community which, in this instance, chose to see him as being "one of the family." During his years in the Senate, Cohen became well known for both his political moderation and independence of thought. As chair of the Senate Committee on Aging, Cohen played a pivotal role in the health care reform debates of the 1990s. As a committed environmentalist, he became the only Republican endorsed by the League of Conservation Voters.

In December 1996, President Bill Clinton, seeking to fulfill his wish for a bipartisan cabinet, nominated Cohen to become the nation's 20th secretary of defense. Easily confirmed by his former colleagues in the Senate, Cohen served as defense secretary throughout the remainder of the Clinton years (1997–2000).

Throughout his more than 30 years in public life, Cohen published nearly a dozen books. Among these are two volumes of poems (*Of Sons and Seasons* and *A Baker's Nickel*), three novels (*The Double Man, Murder in the Senate*, and *One-Eyed Kings*) and several works concerning government policy.

BIBLIOGRAPHY: K.F. Stone, *The Congressional Minyan: The Jews of Capitol Hill* (2000), 63–64.

[Kurt Stone (2nd ed.)]

COHEN, WILLIAM WOLFE (1874–1940), U.S. stockbroker, congressman. Cohen was born in New York City in 1874. His father, like his mother a German Jew, was a prosperous shoe manufacturer. Following a public school education, William entered his father's business; on his 21st birthday, his father made him a partner. In 1903, a year after his marriage, William left his father's shoe manufacturing concern and went into business for himself, forming the stock brokerage firm of William W. Cohen & Co., in which he was active for the rest of his life. Cohen prospered as a stockbroker, even purchasing a seat on the New York Stock Exchange. Greatly respected by his fellow brokers, Cohen became a director of the New York Cotton Exchange and the Chicago Board of Trade and a member of the Commodity and New York Curb exchanges. Always interested in diversification, Cohen eventually bought up a copper-mining company in the American west. In the early 1920s, he decided to sell his seat on the New York Stock Exchange, netting a nearly $100,000 profit. By age 50, he was set for life.

Always active in Democratic political circles, Cohen served as chairman of the Tammany Hall Finance Committee for more than a decade. In 1926, he ran for the 17th Congressional District seat being vacated by Congressman Ogden L. Mills. Cohen served a single term (1927–29), subsequently declining to run for reelection and returning to New York.

Aside from his many business ventures, Cohen was a lifelong supporter of the New York City Fire Department, who honored him by making him an honorary deputy fire chief. Active in Jewish communal organizations, Cohen served as president of the Jewish Council of Greater New York and the New York branch of the American Jewish Congress. He was also a member of the Reform Temple Emanuel and president of the American Committee for the Settlement of Jews in Birobidzhan, a remote Soviet region near Siberia.

BIBLIOGRAPHY: K.F. Stone *The Congressional Minyan: The Jews of Capitol Hill* (2000), 65.

[Kurt Stone (2nd ed.)]

COHEN, YARDENA (1910–), dancer, choreographer, teacher. Cohen was one of the pioneers of Israeli dance and in the vanguard of modern dance in pre-State Israel. She was born in Haifa, a sixth-generation Israeli. In 1929, she went to Vienna and studied at the Academy for the Arts and, after two years, left for Dresden and studied with Gert Palucca. In 1933, she returned to Haifa and began teaching.

The solo compositions Cohen produced were dramatic portraits of biblical women: *Eve in the Garden of Eden*, *Lot's Wife*, *Hannah in Shiloh*, *The Sorcerer's*, *Jephtah's Daughter*, and *Hagar* are but a few. Contrary to Central European Expressionism in dance (*Ausdruckstanz*) practiced by other dance pioneers who had recently arrived from Europe, Cohen's dance was rooted in the soil of the Land of Israel. Accompanying her on the drums were Oriental Jewish musicians. In 1937, Cohen was awarded first prize in a national dance competition in Tel Aviv.

Cohen was a forerunner in organizing the holiday pageants that took place in agricultural settlements (*kibbutzim*) where the members wanted to relive and celebrate the ancient holidays as in former times, albeit with a modern approach. The pageants took place outside and people of all ages participated. There was a medley of dancing, singing, and instrumental performances as well as readings from special texts. The "*Bikkurim*" Festival (First Fruits) (1943) and Vineyard Festival (1944) at kibbutz Ein ha-Shofet were famous, as was the pageant dedicated to the biblical story of Jael and Sisera that took place at kibbutz Sha'ar-ha-Amakim (1945), located at the spot where the narrative took place, and the "*Mayim Mayim*" (Water, Water) Festival (1947) at kibbutz Ginnegar, celebrating the installation of running water at the settlement. Some of the dances created for these pageants became folk dances.

Cohen was also a leader in the new field of dance therapy, which she called "convalescent dance." She wrote two books: *With Drum and Dance* (1963) and *The Drum and the Sea*. (1976). She continued to teach in Haifa well into her nineties.

BIBLIOGRAPHY: R. Eshel, *Dancing with the Dream – The Development of Artistic Dance in Israel 1920–1964* (1991), 24–26, 74, 89–90.

[Ruth Eshel (2nd ed.)]

COHEN, YIGAL RAHAMIM (1940–), Israeli plant pathologist. Cohen was born in Jerusalem and received his Ph.D. in agriculture from the Hebrew University of Jerusalem, Rehovot (1969). He joined Bar-Ilan University as a lecturer in plant pathology (1969) and was a full professor from 1980. His research discoveries concern the epidemiology of plant diseases, genetic resistance to disease and their prevention by immunization, genetic selection, and pesticides and other agents. His work has important practical implications, including collaboration with seed-producing companies, and has led to the development of tomato and potato strains genetically resistant to the potentially devastating infection by the fungus *Phytophthora infestans* and muskmelon lines resistant to other fungi. He was also the first to show that certain amino acids and polyunsaturated fatty acids induce resistance against late blight. His contributions were recognized internationally and in 2004 he was among the world's 250 most cited researchers. His honors include the Israel Prize for agriculture (1999). At Bar-Ilan University he served as dean of the Faculty of Natural Sciences (1977–80), member of the Senate, and member of the Board of Trustees. He was also president of the Israel Phytopathological Society.

[Michael Denman (2nd ed.)]

COHEN GAN, PINCHAS (1942–), Israeli artist. Cohen Gan was born in Meknes, Morocco, and immigrated to Israel in 1949. In 1970 he graduated from the Bezalel Art School. He studied at the Central School of Art at London in 1971 and then joined Bezalel as a teacher. In 1973 he received his M.A. degree in sociology and history of art from the Hebrew University of Jerusalem and in 1977 an M.A. in art from Columbia University. From 1990 he was an associate professor in Bezalel. In 1968 he was severely injured by a terrorist car bomb.

Cohen Gan is considered an avant-garde artist and was a major voice in bringing back the figure and subject matter to a modern art under the influence of Pop Art and minimalism. His art reflects deep political and social concerns. It directly confronts man's condition while challenging and commenting on his fellow artists. His work is influenced by his childhood memories as an immigrant. He exhibited in many museums and art galleries the world over, among them the Israel Museum, Tel Aviv Museum, galleries in New York, and the Los Angeles Museum. He represented Israel at the Documenta in Kassel, Germany, the Sao Paulo Biennale, and the Biennale of Venice. In 1991 he published *And These Are the Names* with 100 drawings representing 100 lost Jewish communities destroyed by the Nazis in Europe and North Africa. He also participated in a traveling exhibition to Israel's provincial settlements aimed at attracting their population to art. He won an America-Israel Cultural Foundation grant in 1978, the Isaac Stern Creativity Prize, Sandberg Prize of the Israel Museum (1979), Minister of Education Prize (1991), Eugene Kolb Prize for Israeli Graphics (1991), and Acquisition Prize of Tel Aviv Museum (1991).

[Shaked Gilboa (2nd ed.)]

COHEN GELLERSTEIN, BENJAMIN (1896–1964), Chilean diplomat. Born in Concepción, he graduated as a lawyer specializing in international law from the University of Georgetown in Washington. In 1923 he served as secretary of the Chilean delegation to the fifth Panamerican Conference. Later he served for five years as head of the Diplomatic Department of the Ministry of Foreign Affairs. In 1939 he was named ambassador to Bolivia. After his retirement he was appointed subsecretary in charge of information at the United Nations.

[Moshe Nes El (2nd ed.)]

COHEN MELAMED, NISSAN (1906–1983), authority on music and liturgical melody of Oriental Jews. Born in Shiraz, Persia, he came to Ereẓ Israel with his parents at the age of two, and as a child, became an expert in the cantillation of Oriental Jews. He studied music at the Jerusalem Conservatory of Music and did research on cantillation under Prof. Solomon *Rosowsky. In 1927 he was appointed by Chief Rabbi *Ouziel as cantor of the Sephardi Great Synagogue "Ohel Moed" in Tel Aviv and director of the Pirḥei Kehunah College for Sephardi *ḥazzanut*. From 1956 to 1962 he served as *ḥazzan* and school principal in Mexico City and as head of the Koresh Jewish School in Teheran. On his return to Israel he joined the faculty of Jewish Music of Bar-Ilan University. In 1980 the Israel Academy of Music in Tel Aviv released a recording of cantorial liturgies, cantillation of the Torah, *haftarot*, and the five *megillot*, sung by Nissan Cohen Melamed as arranged by Yehezkel Braun.

[Akiva Zimmerman (2nd ed.)]

COHEN-TANNOUDJI, CLAUDE (1933–), French physicist. Cohen-Tannoudji completed his Ph.D. in 1962 at the Ecole Normale Supérieure in Paris. He was then professor at the University of Paris in 1964–73, and from 1973 professor of Atomic and Molecular Physics at the Collège de France in Paris. He is a member of the French Académie des Sciences and a foreign associate of numerous other academies of science.

He has written about 200 theoretical and experimental papers dealing with various problems of atomic physics and quantum optics: optical pumping and light shifts, dressed atom approach for understanding the behavior of atoms in intense RF or optical fields, quantum interference effects, resonance fluorescence, photon correlations, physical interpretation of radiative corrections, radiative forces, laser cooling and trapping, Bose-Einstein condensation.

He is the recipient of many awards, including the Harvey Prize in science and technology, the Quantum Electronics Prize of the European Physical Society, and the Gold Medal of the Centre National de la Recherche Scientifique. He published the two-volume *Quantum Mechanics* (1977), written with Bernard Diu and Franck Laloë; *Photons and Atoms* (1989), an introduction to quantum electrodynamics, with Jacques Dupont-Roc and Gilbert Grynberg; and *Atom-Photon Interactions* (1992), also with Jacques Dupont-Roc and Gilbert Grynberg. He in addition published a collection of selected papers under the title *Atoms in Electromagnetic Fields* (1994) and *Lévy Statistics and Laser Cooling – How Rare Events Bring Atoms to Rest* (2001), written with Alain Aspect, François Bardou, and Jean-Philippe Bouchaud.

[Bracha Rager (2nd ed.)]

COHN, Swiss family. ARTHUR COHN (1862–1926) served as the rabbi of Basle from 1885 until his death. He was a graduate of the Orthodox Rabbinical Seminary of Berlin and the leader of Orthodox Jewry in Switzerland. In 1907 helped to found the Central Association for Observant Jewry in Switzerland. His call to Orthodox Jewry during the Tenth Zionist Congress in 1911 to establish an independent organization to deal with religious issues contributed to the founding of *Agudat Israel in 1912. Some of his essays and sermons were published posthumously in *Von Israels Lehre und Leben* (1927). His son MARCUS (Mordecai) COHN (1890–1953), jurist and Zionist leader, in the sphere of Jewish law wrote *Die Stellvertretung im juedischen Recht* (1920) on agency and *Juedisches Waisenrecht* (1921) on orphans. He was also active in communal affairs and the Swiss Zionist movement. He represented the Mizrachi party at several Zionist Congresses and from 1931 to 1936 was president of the Swiss Zionist Federation, establishing the Palestine office in Switzerland in 1933. In 1935 he became a member of the court of the Zionist Congress. He was a member of the executive of the Federation of Jewish Communities in Switzerland from 1938 until 1950, when he settled in Israel. During the last three years of his life, Cohn served as assistant attorney-general to the Israeli government.

His son ARTHUR (1928–) is a Hollywood film producer whose six Oscars is a record. His films sometimes have Jewish themes, as in *The Garden of the Finzi-Continis* (1970), based on a story by Giorgio Bassani. Cohn maintains his ties to the Swiss Jewish community, contributing to the Jewish Swiss weekly *Tachles* of Zurich.

BIBLIOGRAPHY: A. Weil, *Gedenkrede fuer Rabbiner Dr. Arthur Cohn* (1927). **ADD. BIBLIOGRAPHY:** Th. Nordemann, *Zur Geschichte der Juden in Basel* (1955).

[Uri Kaufmann (2nd ed.)]

COHN, ALBERT (1814–1877), French scholar and philanthropist. Cohn, who studied philosophy and Oriental languages at Vienna University, was fluent in Arabic, Hebrew, German, and Italian. In 1836 he settled in Paris, where he became closely associated with James de *Rothschild, and was put in charge of his philanthropic works. In this capacity he traveled frequently to Morocco, Algeria, and Turkey, where he was instrumental in improving the condition of the Jewish communities, and to Palestine, where he promoted the establishment of Jewish hospitals and schools in Jaffa and Jerusalem. From 1860 to 1876, Cohn taught at the rabbinical seminary in Paris. He was also a member of the central committee of the *Alliance Israélite Universelle. Cohn wrote various scholarly and religious works, including his partly autobiographical "Lettres Juives" (in *L'Univers Israélite*, 20, 1864/65).

BIBLIOGRAPHY: I. Loeb, *Biographie d' Albert Cohn* (1878).

COHN, BERTHOLD (1870–1930), German astronomer, mathematician, and historian. Cohn, who was born in Ravicz (now Poland), studied in Basle, Breslau, and Strasbourg. He was appointed astronomer at Strasbourg Observatory. Some of his astronomical publications addressed Gaussian mathematical methods; the theory of logarithms; tables on the beginning of twilight; the first visibility of the moon; determinations of the orbits of three comets; and the comparison of various star catalogues (1912). His first historical paper dealt with the structure of the Jewish calendar (in the *Zeitschrift der Deutschen Morgenlaendischen Gesellschaft*, 59 (1905), 622–4). In "Die Anfangsepoche des juedischen Kalenders," Cohn suggested that the total solar eclipse of June 6, 346 C.E. (4106), fixed the time of the original new moon (of the creation period) as the point for back-dating the Jewish calendar (*Sitzungsberichte der Koeniglich-Preussischen Akademie der Wissenschaften*, no. 10 (1914), 350–54).

[Arthur Beer]

COHN, CILLA CYPORA (née **Rabinowitz**; 1910–2005), Danish Holocaust author. Cilla Cohn was born into an Orthodox family in Austria and immigrated with her family to Denmark during World War I. She studied history and literature at the University of Copenhagen. In the *Aktion of* October 1943, Cohn was arrested together with her family, and sent to Theresienstadt, where she remained until she was liberated through the intercession of Sweden's Count Bernadotte in 1945. Her experiences of this period form the basis for her novel, *En Jodiskfamilies saga* ("The Saga of a Jewish Family," 1960), which gained considerable general popularity and is used as textbook in high schools throughout Scandinavia. In the novel Cohn discusses the general historical basis for antisemitism, at the same time taking the reader on a veritable tour of Jewish history, folklore, and customs. Her novel *Sven-Adam's Kibbutz* (1973) also uses the Holocaust as the focal point, this time for a discussion of past history, and the birth and growing pains of the State of Israel. In addition to her participation in the public debate and espousal of Jewish causes through radio appearances and many articles in various Danish publications, Cohn was consistently active in the Danish Jewish community. She was one of the founders of WIZO in Denmark and secretary of its first board, and served as a member of the Governing Board of the Federation of Zionist Organizations in Denmark. From 1975 she served as Chairman of the Association of Danish Former Inmates of Theresienstadt.

[Robert Rovinsky]

COHN, EDWIN JOSEPH (1892–1953), U.S. biochemist. Born in New York, Cohn became professor of biological chemistry at Harvard and head of the department in 1938. Cohn's fields of research were the chemistry of the liver, plasma, and other tissue proteins. He discovered a method of fractioning blood plasma, and the varied subjects of his papers included aminoacids, peptides, the separation of gamma globulin, liver extract, thrombin, fibrinogen, and isohemagglutinin. Cohn wrote *Proteins, Amino Acids, and Peptides as Ions and Dipolar Ions* (1943) and *Research in the Medical Sciences – the March of Medicine* (1946). Cohn received awards and decorations from many governments and the Medal of Merit from the U.S. government in 1948.

[Samuel Aaron Miller]

COHN, ELKAN (1820–1889), U.S. Reform rabbi. Cohn was born in Kosten, province of Posen, then in the Kingdom of Prussia. He was an orphan whose grandparents sent him to Braunschweig to be tutored in Talmud by the traditional Rabbi Isaac Eger. But there Cohn also fell under the influence of historian Levi *Herzfeld, one of the earliest Jewish practitioners of the critical method and later a prime mover in the German Reform movement. Cohn spent the decade of the 1840s in Berlin, where he earned a doctorate in classics at the university, and, studying under Leopold *Zunz among others, his rabbinical degree. He chafed under the authoritarian rule of the Hohenzollern king and supported the revolution of 1848.

In 1850 Cohn was appointed rabbi of Brandenburg. Four years later he immigrated to America and succeeded Isaac Mayer *Wise as rabbi of Congregation Anshe Emeth in Albany, New York. Cohn took part in the Cleveland Rabbinical Conference of 1855 and was elected vice president. In 1860, accepting the challenges of a frontier pulpit, he became the rabbi of Congregation Emanu-El of San Francisco, where he remained almost three decades until his death. Like his friend Thomas Starr King, the famed Unitarian minister who arrived in San Francisco the same year, Cohn preached ethical universalism, presided over the building of a magnificent house of worship, and helped "save California for the Union" during the Civil War. After Lincoln's assassination, Cohn was one of 38 distinguished citizens of the West who served as pallbearers in a large procession of mourners in San Francisco. The tribute that he delivered in his synagogue to the fallen president was a passionate oration by a man otherwise not known as a gifted speaker or powerful writer.

Congregation Emanu-El, comprised largely of Bavarians, followed the German Orthodox ritual, but Cohn, in the face of opposition from within and without the synagogue, initiated Reform practices. His introduction of a new prayer book led to the secession of 55 families in 1864 who formed their own congregation, Ohabai Shalome, which for many decades continued to adhere to the Minhag Ashkenaz that Cohn had compromised. In the summer of 1877, shortly after Isaac Mayer Wise's eventful visit to San Francisco, Emanu-El joined the fledgling Union of American Hebrew Congregations, the first synagogue in the American West to do so. Toward the end of Cohn's tenure, he inaugurated radical reforms such as banning skullcaps, moving Friday evening services to Sunday morning, and replacing the *shofar* on High Holidays with a cornet or trombone. Although Sunday morning services lasted only a year, the Classical Reform orientation of the synagogue was firmly established and would become even more pronounced during the rabbinate of Cohn's protégé, Jacob *Voorsanger (1889–1908).

Cohn's greatest achievement was the erection in 1866 of the imposing Sutter Street Temple, modeled after the Gothic cathedrals of medieval England. With its two tapered towers, each topped with a bronze-plated dome, it was a prominent feature of the San Francisco skyline until its destruction in the earthquake and fire of 1906. The grand temple reflected the strength and style Elkan Cohn had brought to Reform Judaism in Northern California.

BIBLIOGRAPHY: F. Rosenbaum, *Visions of Reform: Congregation Emanu-El and the Jews of San Francisco, 1849–1999* (2000); J. Voorsanger, *Chronicles of Emanu-El* (1900).

[Fred S. Rosenbaum (2nd ed.)]

COHN, EMIL MOSES (pen name **Emil Bernhard**; 1881–1948), German rabbi, writer, and active Zionist. Cohn, who was born in Berlin, was the son of the pro-Herzl Zionist Bernhard Cohn. He received both a Jewish and Zionist education at home. As a student, he organized a Zionist student group together with J.L. *Magnes, A. *Biram, and others. In 1906 he was appointed *prediger* (preacher and teacher of religion) by the Jewish community in Berlin, but was forced to resign in 1907 because of his Zionist views. The resignation caused a scandal and gave rise to much polemical literature (cf. his own statement in *Mein Kampf ums Recht*). After serving as rabbi in Kiel (1908–12), in Essen (1912–14) and in Bonn (1914–26), he returned to Berlin, where he served as rabbi in Grunewald. After several arrests by the Nazis, he emigrated to the Netherlands, then in 1939 to the U.S., where he lived until his death. Cohn published plays (mostly under the pseudonym Emil Bernhard), some of which were performed in Germany and abroad. One of them, *Brief des Uriah* (1909, printed in 1919), was performed by the *Habimah theater. He also wrote poetry, ideological essays on Judaism and Zionism, a book entitled *David Wolfsohn, Herzls Nachfolger* (1939; Eng. tr. 1944), and a translation of Judah Halevi's *Diwan* into German (1920). In the field of Zionism he was one of the editors of *Zionistisches ABC Buch* (1908) and published his Zionist and Jewish credo called *Judentum, ein Aufruf der Zeit* (1923, 1934²). He also published *Juedischer Kinderkalender* (1928, then *Juedischer Jugendkalender* 1929–31 and 1934).

BIBLIOGRAPHY: Tramer, in: BLBI, 8 (1965), 326–45 (including bibliography). **ADD. BIBLIOGRAPHY:** M. Zimmermann, in: YLBI 27 (1982), 129–53; R. Heuer (ed.), *Lexikon deutsch-juedischer Autoren*, 5 (1997), 208–25.

[Getzel Kressel / Marcus Pyka (2nd ed.)]

COHN, FERDINAND JULIUS (1828–1898), German botanist and pioneer bacteriologist. Cohn was born in Breslau, the eldest son of Isaac Cohn, who held the post of Austro-Hungarian consul. He joined the faculty of the University of Breslau in 1851 as a lecturer in botany and in 1872 was appointed professor, the first Jew in Prussia to be granted that rank. Cohn long advocated the establishment of botanical gardens for the rigorous study of functional botany and in 1888 founded the Institute of Plant Physiology. He is generally credited with pioneering the investigation of heat production in plants and encouraging a generation of students to pursue careers in other phases of plant physiology. Cohn's most significant work, however, involved his seminal contribution to the nascent science of bacteriology. He was the first to classify bacteria as plants rather than protozoa, and in 1872 initiated a systematic classification of bacteria based upon their morphological as well as their physiological characteristics. He devised methodological tools which not only afforded a means for assessing biochemical characteristics of bacteria but which also led to the isolation of pure cultures. As the author of the first monograph on bacteria, *Untersuchungen ueber die Entwicklungsgeschichte der mikroskopischen Algen und Pilze* (1854), he directed the attention of both medical men and biologists to the research and clinical opportunities associated with microbiology at the Botanic Institute in Breslau. He founded and for a long time edited the *Beitraege zur Biologie der Pflanzen*. Cohn was awarded the Linnaeus Gold Medal. On his 70th birthday he was made an honorary citizen of Breslau and after his death a monument was erected to his memory.

BIBLIOGRAPHY: P. Cohn, *Ferdinand Cohn: Blaetter der Erinnerung* (1901).

[George H. Fried]

COHN, FRITZ (1866–1922), German astronomer. Cohn was born in Koenigsberg, and was appointed professor at the university there in 1905. In 1909 he became director of the leading center for astronomical calculations and professor at the University of Berlin. Cohn, who did outstanding work in the field of celestial mechanics, dealt with the determination of the orbits of planets, asteroids, comets, double stars, and satellites, in his researches. He also investigated the values of the astronomical constants, the theory of errors, transit observations, fundamental star catalogs, and the orbital identification of minor planets. Cohn wrote *Neue Methoden der Bahnbestimmung* (1918), on celestial mechanics, and edited ten volumes of the *Astronomischer Jahresbericht* (1910–20), the basic bibliographical work in astronomy.

[Arthur Beer]

COHN, GEORG (**Arye**; 1887–1956), Danish international law expert and diplomat. Born in Frankfurt-on-Main into an old Danish-Jewish family, Cohn came to Copenhagen as a child. After law studies at the University of Copenhagen, he joined the Danish Foreign Ministry in 1913, remaining there for 43 years. In 1918 Cohn was appointed head of the ministry's new department of international law; from 1921 he held the position of advisor in international law and in 1946 received the title of minister.

During World War I Cohn was instrumental in maintaining Denmark's neutrality and in arranging help for wounded prisoners of war. For these efforts he received a knighthood of the Dannebrog Order and the Danish Red Cross Award. At the League of Nations in Geneva, where he was a delegate in 1920, 1925, and 1929, Cohn was concerned with problems of neutrality for the smaller states. From that point forward, he was preoccupied with the prevention of war and the need to define a new concept of active neutrality. This is reflected in his *Neutralité et Société des Nations* (1924) and *Kriegsverhuetung und Schuldfrage* (Frankfurt, 1931) and further developed in the seminal *Neo-Neutralitet* (1937; revised as *Neo-Neutrality*, 1939). The last two works earned him doctoral degrees at the Universities of Frankfurt and Copenhagen, respectively.

From 1929 Cohn was a member of the Permanent Court of Arbitration at The Hague. He negotiated the resolution of the age-old dispute over the Oresund Straits separating Denmark and Sweden (1931). In 1932–33 he successfully presented Denmark's case at the Permanent Court of International Justice at The Hague, in the sovereignty dispute with Norway over Eastern Greenland. A part of N.E. Greenland bears his name. In 1936 Cohn was elected a member of the International Diplomatic Academy in Paris. He lectured at the Academy of International Law at The Hague in 1939.

In October 1943 Cohn fled with his family to Sweden, joining the Danish Embassy in Stockholm. Returning to Denmark in 1945, he was a delegate to the United Nations General Assembly at Lake Success (1946). In 1948 he headed the international committee which dealt with states' rights over the continental shelf. As head of Denmark's delegation to the International Red Cross conference in Geneva (1949), he strongly supported the recognition of Israel's *Magen David Adom.

An observant Jew and a founder of the *Machzikei Hadat* synagogue in Copenhagen (1910), he later received rabbinical ordination. With his brother Naphtali, a lawyer at the High Court of Denmark, he purchased the original S.R. Hirsch synagogue in Frankfurt (1924) to keep it in Jewish hands. He was among those consulted by David *Ben-Gurion on issues of religion and state. He visited Israel in 1950.

He was the recipient of numerous international awards. He edited and published with his brother the monthly law journal *Juridisk Tidsskrift* (1915–30). His legal and philosophical writings include *Platons Gorgias* (1911), *Etik og Soziologi* (1913), *Kan Krig forhindres?* ("Can War Be Prevented?" 1945), *Existentialisme og Retsvidenskab* ("Existentialism and the Science of Law," 1952).

BIBLIOGRAPHY: P. Fischer and N. Svenningsen, *Den Danske Udenrigstjeneste, Vol. II, 1919–1970* (1970); E.C.Roi, *Ḥatzrot Kopenhagen* (2003).

[Emilie Roi (2nd ed.)]

COHN, GUSTAV (1840–1919), German economist. Cohn, who was born in Marienwerder, taught at the Riga Polytechnic from 1869 to 1872 and, after a few years in England, went to Switzerland in 1875 to become professor at the Zurich Institute of Technology. In 1885 he was called to the University of Goettingen, Germany, where he remained for the rest of his life. Cohn was not only a theoretician. Besides writing textbooks and studies of classical economic doctrines, he made important contributions to transportation and public finance. His investigations of the British railroad system in which he strongly advocated railroad amalgamation and public ownership became the basis of subsequent treatises on railroad theory. Together with Adolf Wagner (1835–1917), he was a leading representative of German Kathedersozialismus ("armchair socialism") during the second half of the 19th century. His publications include *Untersuchungen ueber die englische Eisenbahnpolitik* (1874–75), *Finanzlage der Schweiz* (1877), *System der Nationaloekonomie* (3 vols., 1885–98), and *Volkswirtschaftliche Aufsaetze und Nationalekonomische Studien* (1886).

BIBLIOGRAPHY: Wininger, Biog, 1 (1925).

[Joachim O. Ronall]

COHN, HAIM (**Hermann**; 1911–2002), Israel jurist. Cohn was born in Luebeck, Germany, and settled in Palestine in 1930. He studied at Merkaz ha-Rav yeshivah in Jerusalem, then gained a law degree in Germany in 1933. Cohn practiced law in Palestine, joining the Legal Council of the Jewish authorities in Palestine in 1947. From 1948 to 1950 Cohn was state attorney and in 1950–52 and 1953–60 he served as attorney general, contributing to the founding of the Israel legal and judicial system during the formative years of statehood. In 1952–53 he was minister of justice and in 1960 he was appointed a justice of the Israel Supreme Court. On March 5, 1980, Cohn was appointed deputy president of the Israel Supreme Court; he retired in 1981. He then became president of the Association for Civil Rights in Israel and of the International Center for Peace in the Middle East. From 1975 he was member of the International Commission of Jurists in Geneva and president of the International Association of Jewish Lawyers. His decisions were characterized by a liberal approach to problems connected with *halakhah*. During 1957–59 and 1965–67 Cohn served on the UN Commission on Human Rights. He also served as a law professor at the Hebrew and

Tel Aviv universities. He published *Foreign Laws of Marriage and Divorce* (1937); *Glaube und Glaubensfreiheit* (1967); *Mishpato shel Yeshu ha-Noẓeri* (1968; *The Trial and Death of Jesus*, 1972), dealing with the trial of Jesus in the light of contemporary Roman and Jewish law; and *Human Rights in Jewish Law* (1984). In 1980 he was awarded the Israel Prize for law. During his last years he devoted himself to issues of human rights. The Haim Cohn Institute for Legal Protection of Human Rights gives free legal assistance to people in need. Cohn was editor of the department of Criminal Law and Procedure in the *Encyclopaedia Judaica* (first edition).

[Benjamin Jaffe]

COHN, HARRY (1891–1956), movie pioneer; president and executive producer of Columbia Pictures Corporation. Born in New York, he entered show business as a piano player in nickelodeons, moved to music publishing, and then became an exhibitor of road show films. Later he was an associate producer at Universal Films. In 1919 he and his brother Jack, together with Joe Brandt, organized the CBC Film Sales Corporation, producing and distributing the *Hallroom Boys* comedies. This company was reorganized as Columbia Pictures in 1924. He acquired the Brandt holdings in 1932 and became president of the company the same year. Among the directors who worked for him were Frank Capra, Rouben Mamoulian, and Fred Zinnemann.

[Jo Ranson]

COHN, JONAS (1869–1947), German philosopher and educator. Cohn was a distinguished teacher of aesthetics, who based his conclusions on actual aesthetic experience. Born in Goerlitz, he studied philosophy under Wundt, Fischer, Paulsen, Barth, and Kuelpe at the Universities of Leipzig, Heidelberg, and Berlin. In 1901 he was appointed professor of philosophy at Freiburg im Breisgau. In March 1939 Cohn fled to England, returning to Germany after World War II. A noted neo-Kantian, Cohn developed a perceptive-critical idealism which went beyond Kant's synthesis of rationalism and empiricism and was centered between the Marburg (see Hermann *Cohen) and the South German neo-Kantian schools of thought. Cohn's most valuable contribution was in the study of aesthetics. Among his important works are his *Wertwissenschaft* (1932) and *Wirklichkeit als Aufgabe* (1955).

BIBLIOGRAPHY: J. Cohn, in: R. Schmidt (ed.), *Philosophie der Gegenwart in Selbstdarstellungen*, 2 (1923), 61–81; Earl of Listowel, *A Critical History of Modern Aesthetics* (1933), passim; J. Cohn, *Wirklichkeit als Aufgabe* (1955), appendix by J. von Kempski. **ADD. BIBLIOGRAPHY:** J. Cohn, *Jonas Cohn* (*Die Philosophie der Gegenwart in Selbstdarstellung*, vol. 11 (1923)); I. Idalovichi, "Die Unendlichkeit als philosophisches und religiöses Problem im Denken des Neukantianismus unter besonderer Beruecksichtigung von Jonas Cohn," in: *Theologische Zeitschrift* 46:3 (1990), 245–65; M. Heitmann, *Jonas Cohn – Das Problem der unedndlichen Aufgabe in Wissenschaft und Religion* (1999).

[Shnayer Z. Leiman]

COHN, LASSAR (later **Lassar-Cohn**; 1858–1922), German chemist, born in Hamburg. Cohn became professor of chemistry at University of Koenigsberg and was the head of the Jewish community there. His *Die Chemie im taeglichen Leben* (1896; *Chemistry in Daily Life*, 1896) ran to seven editions and was translated into several languages, including Hebrew. His other works included *Arbeitsmethoden fuer organisch-chemische Laboratorien* (1891), and *Moderne Chemie* (1891).

COHN, LEOPOLD (1856–1915), classical and Hellenistic scholar. Cohn was born in Zempelburg, West Prussia, and taught at Breslau University, from 1892 as professor. From 1902 he was also librarian of the university's library, and for some time he lectured at the Breslau Theological Seminary as well. Apart from studies in Greek literature, grammar, and lexicography, Cohn wrote on Judeo-Hellenistic philosophy. Together with P. Wendland he prepared an authoritative edition of *Philo's writings *Philonis Alexandrini Opera quae Supersunt* (7 vols., 1896–1915), of which he was responsible for volumes 1 (1896), 4 (1902), 5 (1906), and 6 (1915), and for the introduction. Cohn was associated with a German translation of Philo (*Die Werke Philos von Alexandria*), editing the first three volumes (1909–19) and translating most of the fourth.

BIBLIOGRAPHY: J. Guttmann, *Trauerrede fuer Leopold Cohn*. (1915). **ADD. BIBLIOGRAPHY:** D.T. Runia, "Underneath Cohn and Colson – The Text of Philo's 'De Virtutibus,'" in: *Society of Biblical Literature* (Atlanta), 30 (1991), 116–34.

[Joseph Elijah Heller]

COHN, LINDA (1959–), U.S. sportscaster; anchorwoman for ESPN's signature SportsCenter news and information program. Raised on Long Island, Cohn played goalie for the boy's ice hockey team as a senior at Newfield (N.Y.) high school and on the women's ice hockey team at SUNY-Oswego college, from where she graduated in 1981. She began her career in Patchogue, N.Y., as a news anchor and sports reporter for WALK-AM/FM. She worked at radio stations WGBB-AM, WCBS-FM, and WCBS News Radio 88; as sports/news anchor and reporter for WLIG-TV on Long Island, N.Y.; and as anchor, news director, and chief correspondent for Long Island News Tonight. Cohn became the first full-time female sports anchor on a national radio network (ABC) in 1987. She was a sports anchor for WABC TalkRadio, hosted a call-in show and provided sports updates at WFAN radio in New York, was sports reporter for both SportsChannel America and News 12 on Long Island, and then moved to Seattle, where she was weekend sports anchor/reporter at KIRO-TV. Cohn joined ESPN as an anchor/reporter on SportCenter in July 1992 and has hosted ESPN's Baseball Tonight, National Hockey Night, ESPN2's NHL 2Night and RPM 2Night, and SportsCenter's NBA All-Star Game coverage. She has provided weekly "Extra Point" commentaries on ESPN Radio since 1998.

[Elli Wohlgelernter (2nd ed.)]

COHN, MESHULLAM ZALMAN BEN SOLOMON (1739–1811), rabbi and halakhic authority. Cohn was born in Rawicz (Posen region) and was orphaned at the age of four. He studied in the yeshivot of Posen and Zuelz, and in Altona, under Jonathan *Eybeschuetz who ordained him. He served as rabbi in Rawicz, Krotoszyn, Kempen, Zuelz, and finally in 1789 in Fuerth, where he remained until the end of his life. Cohn was one of the signatories of the indictment against the *Frankists in Offenbach in 1800. Questions were addressed to him from Germany, Poland, Hungary, and Bohemia, and his responsa reflect his acumen and great erudition, particularly in the area of matrimonial law and in cases dealing with *agunot*. He vigorously opposed all attempts to tamper with traditional customs. His published works are *Bigdei Kehunnah* (Fuerth, 1807), responsa; *Mishan ha-Mayim (ibid.*, 1811), an aggadic commentary on the Pentateuch; and *Naḥalat Avot* ("The Inheritance of Parents," *ibid.*, 1818), moral exhortations to his children and pupils. He wrote this last work at the age of 70 and explained its title as implying that when children walk in the way of the Lord, they bring a boon upon their parents, who, in consequence, inherit the world to come.

BIBLIOGRAPHY: A. Walden, *Shem ha-Gedolim he-Ḥadash*, 2 (1864), 6a, no. 48; Neubuerger, in: MGWJ, 22 (1873), 192; Back, *ibid.*, 26 (1877), 239; Loewenstein, in: *Blaetter fuer juedische Geschichte und Literatur*, 3 (1902), 44–46; idem, in: JJLG, 6 (1908), 203–7, 219, 225, 229–30; J. Rabin, *Die Juden in Zuelz* (1926), 32.

[Josef Horovitz]

COHN, MILDRED (1913–), U.S. physical and biochemist. Cohn was born in New York City and earned a B.A. from Hunter College and Ph.D. in physical chemistry from Columbia University. Her life-long interests were metabolism and enzyme mechanisms, and she was a pioneer in applying stable isotopic techniques and electron spin and nuclear magnetic resonance to in vivo metabolic studies. Her work greatly influenced other areas of research, including the development of anti-cancer agents. She worked at George Washington University (1937–38), Cornell University Medical School (1938–46), Washington University Medical School at St. Louis (1946–58), and the University of Pennsylvania in Philadelphia (1960–82), where she became professor of biophysics and physical biochemistry in 1961 and then Benjamin Rush Professor Emerita of Physiological Chemistry. Her many honors include election to the National Academy of Sciences (1971) and the National Medal of Science (1982). She succeeded in her field despite discrimination against women early in her career and worked all her life to upgrade the status of women in science.

BIBLIOGRAPHY: *Chemical and Engineering News* (Feb. 4, 1963), 92.

[Michael Denman (2nd ed.)]

COHN, MORRIS MANDEL (1898–1975), U.S. public health engineer. Cohn was born in Schenectady, New York, where he was successively sanitary chemist, sanitary engineer, director of environmental sanitation, and city manager. He lectured on public health at Albany Medical College, Union University, University of California, Georgia Institute of Technology, and was professor at City College, New York. He acted as consultant to the U.S. Atomic Energy Commission, New York State Legislature and U.S. Public Health Service, and was editorial director of *Wastes Engineering* and *Water Works Engineering*. Cohn was a consultant to several Israel institutions.

COHN, NORMAN (1915–), British historian. Educated at Oxford, Norman Cohn was a lecturer and later professor at Sussex University. He is best known for his work *Warrant for Genocide: The Myth of the Jewish World Conspiracy and the Protocols of the Elders of Zion* (1981), which presents a comprehensive history and account of the notorious antisemitic forgery. Cohn has also written on aspects of European history, in works like *Pursuit of the Millennium: Revolutionary Messianism in Medieval and Reformation Europe* (1957) and *Europe's Inner Demons* (1975).

[William D. Rubinstein (2nd ed.)]

COHN, OSCAR (1869–1936), German socialist politician. A lawyer in Berlin, he was a socialist member of the Reichstag from 1912 to 1918 and from 1921 to 1924. After the Russian Revolution of October 1917, he became legal adviser to the Soviet embassy in Berlin. He acted as counsel for the defense in the trials following the naval mutiny of 1917 and the general strike of January 1918. Cohn was often legal consultant in Jewish affairs and was active in various Jewish charity organizations. In the German Reichstag he combated the postwar campaign against the *Ostjuden*. In 1920 he went to Poland as a member of the commission set up by the International Socialist Conference to investigate the situation of the Polish Jews, and contributed to the report on their findings: *La situation des Juifs en Pologne. Rapport de la Commission d'Etude désignée par la Conférence Socialiste Internationale de Lucerne* (by Oscar Cohn, Pierre Renaudel, G.F. Schaper, and Thomas Shaw, 1920). In 1925 he was elected as representative of the *Po'alei Zion Party to the assembly of deputies of the Jewish communities of Berlin. He died in Geneva, and his remains were interred, according to his will, in kibbutz Deganyah.

BIBLIOGRAPHY: E. Hamburger, *Juden im oeffentlichen Leben Deutschlands* (1968), 503–8. **ADD. BIBLIOGRAPHY:** M. Brenner, in: *Terumah*, 3 (1987), 101–27; L. Heid, *Oscar Cohn* (Ger., 2002).

COHN, TOBIAS BEN MOSES (1652–1729), physician and Hebrew author. Tobias' father was a rabbi in Metz who died when Tobias was 9 years old. He was then sent to his relatives in Cracow, where he got a traditional Jewish education. Later he went to Frankfurt on the Oder to study medicine. He even got a scholarship from the elector of Brandenburg. He studied at the University of Padua and then went to Turkey where he served as a court physician until the age of 62, when he went to Jerusalem in order to concentrate on the study of Torah.

His main work *Ma'aseh Tuviyyah* (Venice, 1707) is an encyclopedia dealing with theology, astronomy, cosmography, geography, botany, with medicine taking up about half of the entire work. He describes the system of Copernicus but rejects it on religious grounds. On the other hand, he enthusiastically supports the Harvey system of blood circulation. At the request of friends from Poland, he deals at length with the disease then common in Poland, *plica polonica*. He stresses the chemical aspect of stomach diseases, in contrast to the then still prevalent system of Galen.

Although Tobias Cohn adhered to the old system of medicine, he was fully conscious of new trends, especially in surgery and in chemistry. He applied exact measurements in his scientific work, especially in thermometry. One of Cohn's innovations was the comparison of the human body to a house. The head was the roof, the eyes the windows, and the mouth, the doorway; the chest was the upper storey, the intestines were the middle storey, the lungs were water tanks and the legs, foundations. His remedies were laxatives, emetics, cupping glasses, and bleeding, but he demolished many superstitions and criticized the anti-Jewish professors of Frankfurt on the Oder as well as Jews who were devoted to Kabbalah and blindly believed in miracles. His theories relating to infant care and pediatrics were advanced for his age.

Ma'aseh Tuviyyah was printed in 5 different editions and is the only Hebrew work on medicine which was profusely illustrated. The work is also rich in historical references, e.g., on Shabbetai Ẓevi, and has considerable significance in the history of science.

BIBLIOGRAPHY: D.A. Friedman, *Tuviyyah ha-Rofe* (1940); A. Levinson, *Tuviyyah ha-Rofe ve-Sifro Ma'aseh Tuviyyah* (1924); E. Carmoly, *Histoire des médecins juifs* (1844), 248ff.

[David Margalith]

COHN-BENDIT, DANIEL (1945–), student leader and politician in Germany and France. Born to German-Jewish emigrants in Montauban (France), Cohn-Bendit grew up in Paris. As a young lawyer in Weimar Germany, his father, Erich, had made a name for himself defending left-wing activists and fled to France already in 1933. He returned to Germany in the early 1950s and began working as a restitution lawyer in Frankfurt, with his wife, Herta, and younger son, Daniel, following him there in 1958. After the early death of his parents and his graduation from high school (the well-known Odenwaldschule boarding school), he went on to university studies in Paris, where he became one of the leaders of the student protest movement of 1967/68 at the University of Nanterre. He founded the group "22nd March" and received the nickname "Danny le rouge" (Danny the Red). He distanced himself from Western capitalism as well as from Soviet-style communism. When he left France for a brief visit to Germany in May 1968, he was refused permission to return. On May 22, 4,000 French students marched through the streets of Paris under the slogan "We are all German Jews." He continued to study sociology in Frankfurt and remained active in the radical left student movement as founder (in 1976) and editor of the "*Sponti*" ("anarchist") journal *Pflasterstrand*. Only in December 1978 was he allowed to return to France. From the mid-1980s, he was active in the politics of the Green Party in Frankfurt, where, together with Joschka Fischer he dominated the so-called "realistic" faction against the "fundamentalists" and ran for the office of mayor in 1987. In 1989, he was appointed official for multicultural affairs of the City of Frankfurt and remained in this position for eight years. From 1994 he was a member of the European Parliament, elected both in Germany and France.

Cohn-Bendit does not identify himself as a Jew religiously but emphasizes that he identifies himself as a Jew as long as antisemitism exists. He keeps a distance from Israel, but in contrast to many of his contemporaries from the 1968 student protest he did not develop an explicit anti-Zionism. During the 1985 protests of the Jewish community against the staging of the allegedly antisemitic play by Rainer Werner Fassbinder, *Die Stadt, der Muell und der Tod*, he maintained a mediatory position between those for and against performance. In 1993 he filmed a documentary about the Frankfurt Jewish community.

BIBLIOGRAPHY: L. Lemire, *Cohn-Bendit* (Fr., 1998); S. Stamer, *Cohn-Bendit* (Ger., 2001).

[Michael Brenner (2nd ed.)]

COHNHEIM, JULIUS (1839–1884), German pathologist and pioneer in experimental histology. Cohnheim, who was born in Pomerania, held professorships in pathology at the universities of Kiel, Breslau, and Leipzig. Cohnheim discovered how to freeze fresh pathological objects for examination and how to trace nerve endings in muscles by using silver salt impregnation. His studies on inflammation and suppuration revolutionized pathology. He demonstrated that the main feature of inflammation is the passage of leukocytes through the capillary walls and that in this way pus is formed out of the blood. His work on the pathology of the circulatory system and on the etiology of embolism resulted in innovations in the treatment of circulatory diseases. He inoculated tuberculous material into the eye of a rabbit and thus demonstrated that tuberculosis is a contagious disease. A monument in Cohnheim's memory was erected in Leipzig.

BIBLIOGRAPHY: S.R. Kagan, *Jewish Medicine* (1952), 223–4.

[Suessmann Muntner]

COHN-REISS, EPHRAIM (1863–1943), Ereẓ Israel educator. In 1888 he was appointed principal of the Laemel School in his native Jerusalem. From 1904 to 1917, as the representative of the *Hilfsverein der deutschen Juden, he contributed greatly to the foundation and expansion of the network of modern Jewish education in Ereẓ Israel by planning and establishing the Hilfsverein's schools and kindergartens. He became a controversial figure during the language conflict (1913–14) when he supported the Hilfsverein's insistence on German as the language of instruction for technical subjects. Gradually his opposition to Zionism as a whole became so violent that during World War I he sent letters to the Hilfsverein in Berlin, through the German diplomatic service, denouncing the Zionists. In 1917 he went to Berlin, and did not return to Jerusalem, as the "German" Hilfsverein schools had been closed by the British Army authorities. He moved to France in 1938 and died there. In 1933 he published his memoirs, entitled *Mi-Zikhronot Ish Yerushalayim.*

BIBLIOGRAPHY: Y.Y. Rivlin, in: E. Cohn-Reiss, *Mi-Zikhronot Ish Yerushalayim* (1967²), 11–25 (first pagination).

[Moshe Rinott]

COHN-SHERBOK, DAN (1945–), British professor of Judaism, author, and rabbi. Born and educated in the United States and at Cambridge University, Dan Cohn-Sherbok has held academic posts at the University of Kent and, since 1997, at the University of Wales-Lampeter in Wales, where he is professor of Judaism. An ordained Reform rabbi, Cohn-Sherbok is a truly prolific author, with more than 50 books to his credit on all aspects of Judaism and Jewish history. Among the more notable are *The Blackwell Dictionary of Judaica* (1992), *The Crucified Jew: Twenty Centuries of Christian Anti-Semitism* (1992), and *Judaism: History, Belief, and Practice* (2003). He is also the author of an amusing autobiography, *Not a Job for a Nice Jewish Boy* (1993).

[William D. Rubinstein (2nd ed.)]

COHN-WIENER, ERNST (1882–1941), German art historian. Cohn-Wiener was born in Tilsit. After studying the history of art, archaeology, and philosophy, Cohn-Wiener worked as an art historian at the *Juedische Volkshochschule* and the Humboldt Academy in Berlin. Initially a specialist in German gothic sculpture, his principal fields of interest became Islamic and Jewish art as well as study of the Near and Far East, which he visited during a research expeditions in Russia, Asia Minor, Turkestan, and China (1924–5). His chief works are *Die Juedische Kunst* (1929) and *Turan* (1930). In 1933 he emigrated to Great Britain and in 1934 to India, where he was appointed as manager of the museums and art school in Baroda. There he modernized institutions like the Gallery of Baroda and established new departments for Islamic art and Indian miniatures at the University of Bombay. His wife, Lenni, an archaeologist, assisted him. In 1939 he settled in the United States and taught at the American Institute for Iranian Art and Archaeology until his death in New York 1941. Cohn-Wiener's works on Jewish and Islamic art were seminal, but remained isolated for a long time.

ADD. BIBLIOGRAPHY: E.G. Lowenthal, "Ernst Cohn-Wiener. Forscher, Historiker und Lehrer bildender Kunst," in: *Allgemeine juedische Wochenzeitung* (Jan. 9, 1953); U. Wendland (ed.), *Biographisches Handwörterbuch deutschsprachiger Kunsthistoriker im Exil. Leben und Werk der unter dem Nationalsozialismus verfolgten und vertriebenen Wissenschaftler*, vol.1, A-K. (1999), 101–104.

[Sonja Beyer 2nd ed.]

COHON, GEORGE A. (1937–), U.S. entrepreneur and philanthropist. Cohon was born in Chicago, Illinois, and graduated from Northwestern University Law School. After serving in the American military, he was practicing law when he met Ray Kroc, the founder of McDonald's. Kroc offered Cohon the McDonald's franchise for Eastern Canada. In 1967 Cohon moved his young family to Toronto and began opening restaurants in Canada. In 1971 Cohon sold his rights back to McDonald's in return for company stock, becoming the second largest shareholder in McDonald's after Kroc himself. While Cohon stayed at the helm of McDonald's Canada, in 1976 he began negotiating the opening of McDonald's restaurants in the Soviet Union. His efforts culminated with the first Moscow McDonald's in 1990. In addition to introducing fast food marketing, mechanization, and management techniques to the Soviet Union, McDonald's demand for quality ingredients led to the introduction of innovative agricultural and food-processing methods to the Soviet Union. McDonald's, for example, spent over five times more building a huge food-processing plant than it did on the restaurant itself. During his prolonged period of negotiations with Soviet officials, Cohon came to know Soviet power brokers at the highest level. He quietly used these connections to advocate on behalf of Soviet Jews. Cohon was honored with the Order of Friendship from Russian President Boris Yeltsin. His philanthropic endeavors, including his work as patron for the chain of Ronald McDonald Houses which provide accommodations for families whose children are receiving medical treatment, have earned Cohon the Order of Ontario, Honorary Doctorate (Haifa), the Canadian Council of Christians and Jews Human Relations Award, Israel's Prime Minister's Medal, and an appointment as Officer of the Order of Canada.

BIBLIOGRAPHY: G. Cohon (with D. MacFarlane), *To Russia with Fries* (1997).

[Paula Draper (2nd ed.)]

COHON, SAMUEL SOLOMON (1888–1959), U.S. Reform rabbi and theologian. Cohon was born in Minsk, Belorussia. He received a traditional yeshivah education before his family immigrated to the United States in 1904. He received his B.A. from the University of Cincinnati (1911) and was ordained at Hebrew Union College in Cincinnati in 1912. Subsequently, he served as rabbi in Springfield, Ohio (1912–13), and in Chicago at Zion Temple (1913–18) and then at Temple Mizpah (1918–23), which he organized. In 1923 he returned to Hebrew Union College as professor of theology. He was active in the affairs of the *Central Conference of American Rabbis. Cohon took a more favorable attitude toward traditional Jewish observances, the Hebrew language, and the idea of Jewish peoplehood than did the earlier generation of American Reform rabbis; his viewpoint is reflected in the statement of position called the "Columbus Platform," of which he was the principal draftsman and which was adopted by the Central Conference in 1937 and essentially overthrew the earlier Pittsburgh Platform of Reform Judaism. As a theologian, he built on the Reform writings of Abraham *Geiger and Kaufmann *Kohler, but parted company with them when they departed from the historical development of Judaism. Cohon participated in editing the *Union Haggadah* (1923) and the *Rabbi's Manual* (1928). He wrote *What We Jews Believe* (1931) and a number of papers in the yearbooks of the Central Conference and in the Hebrew Union College Annual. He was a significant participant in the revision of the *Union Prayer Book* and served on the Committee that revised the *Union Home Prayer Book*. He was editor of the department of theology for the *Universal Jewish Encyclopedia* (1939). In 1956 Cohon retired from HUC in Cincinnati and became a fellow at the Hebrew Union College-Jewish–Institute of Religion, Los Angeles Campus, and later chairman of its graduate department. His library collection, now housed at Hebrew Union College, is one of the finest collections of Jewish theology and philosophy on the West Coast. His *Jewish Theology: A Historical and Systematic Interpretation of Judaism and Its Foundations* was published posthumously in 1971.

BIBLIOGRAPHY: M.A. Meyer, in: *Judaism*, 15 (1966), 319–28. **ADD. BIBLIOGRAPHY:** K.M. Olitzsky, L.J. Sussman, and M.H. Stern, *Reform Judaism in Amer/ica: A Biographical Dictionary and Sourcebook* (1993), 32–33; S.E. Karff, *Hebrew Union College-Jewish Institute of Religion at One Hundred Years* (1976), 403–07; I. Landman (ed.), *The Universal Jewish Encyclopedia* (1942), 262.

[Sefton D. Temkin]

COIMBRA, city in central Portugal; a major center of Jewish population until the forced conversions of 1497. The Jews of Coimbra suffered frequent attacks, the most serious occurring in 1395 under the leadership of a church prior and several priests. Coimbra was the center of considerable Marrano Judaizing in the 1530s and 1540s, and a century later Antonio *Homem, professor of canon law at the University of Coimbra, led a conventicle of distinguished Marrano Judaizers. Many Marranos in addition to Homem attended the University of Coimbra, among them the distinguished dramatist and martyr, Antonio José da *Silva (d. 1739), while others such as Antonio Fernando Mendes (d. 1734), later a convert to Judaism in England, were on its faculty. Many of the New Christians arrested as Judaizers in Ferrara in 1581 were refugees from the Coimbra region. Three of them, including Joseph Saralvo, who boasted of returning 800 Marranos to Judaism, were put to death in Rome two years later. Coimbra was also the seat of an inquisitional tribunal, one of the four operating in Portuguese territory, besides Lisbon, Évora, and Goa. The tribunal in Coimbra, which tried many distinguished Conversos, disposed of more than 11,000 cases between 1541 and 1820. The trials sometimes lasted for months or even years, during which the accused were held in prison. The accused came in great numbers from Bragança, Braga, Porto, Viseu, Aveiro, Guarda, and Coimbra. Considering the claim that the accusations were mostly motivated by the wish to confiscate the property of the accused, it is noteworthy that the most frequent professions and crafts were, in descending order, shoemakers, merchants, priests, farmers, tanners, and weavers. From the sermons preached at the auto-da-fé we learn that mothers and grandmothers were held responsible for maintaining Jewish practices and beliefs among the Conversos. Thus, during the first century of its existence, more women than men were tried by the Inquisition of Coimbra. The hardest hit were those who lived in distant and mountainous areas. As late as June 17, 1718, over 60 secret Jews appeared at an auto-da-fé there, some for a fifth or sixth time. Two were burned at the stake and the rest penanced, among them Dr. Francisco de Mesquita of Bragança and Jacob de *Castro Sarmento.

BIBLIOGRAPHY: M. Kayserling, *Geschichte der Juden in Portugal* (1867), index; J. Mendes dos Remedios, *Os Judeus em Portugal*, 1 (1895), 362, 430ff.; E.N. Adler, *Auto de Fé and Jew* (1908), 145ff.; N. Slouschz, *Ha-Anusim be-Portugal* (1932), 11, 85ff.; Roth, Marranos, index. **ADD. BIBLIOGRAPHY:** A. de Oliveira, in: *Biblos*, 57 (1981), 597–627; J. do N. Raposo, in: *REJ*, 141 (1982), 201–17; I.S. Révah, in: *Bulletin des Etudes Portugaises*, n.s., 27 (1966), 47–88; E.C. de A. Mea, in: *Inquisição*, vol. 1 (Lisbon, 1989–90), 201–19.

[Martin A. Cohen / Yom Tov Assis (2nd ed.)]

COINS AND CURRENCY.

Jewish and Non-Jewish Coins in Ancient Palestine

THE PRE-MONETARY PERIOD. Means of payment are mentioned in the Bible on various occasions; the relevant passages in their chronological order reflect the development of these means from stage to stage. When compared with the material extant from contemporary cultures of the region, these passages show that the underlying concepts were region-wide in the Near East. The earliest form of trade was barter. Certain commodities became generally accepted means of payment such as cattle and hides. This is reflected in Genesis 21:28–30: "Abraham set seven ewe lambs of the flock by themselves" (in connection with the settlement with Abimelech in Beersheba) and Genesis 13:2, "Abraham was very rich in cattle, in silver and in gold." This last quotation, however, reflects the fact that Abraham lived in the period of transition from the use of cattle to the use of weighed quantities of metal, which is the next stage in the development of the means of payment – a fact which is well illustrated when he weighs four hundred shekels of silver as payment for the cave of Machpelah in Hebron (Gen. 23:15–16). Onkelos renders 100 kesitah, paid by Jacob for a field in Shechem (Gen. 33:19), by 100 lambs (*hufrin*). Cattle as a means of payment is reflected in many usages, such as the Latin *pecunia* (derived from *pecus*, sheep), the Greek *polyboutes* ("rich in oxen," a rich man), and the cattle-shaped weights depicted on Egyptian tomb wall-paintings found in excavations. The shekel was a unit of weight of 8.4 grams in the time of Abraham, based on the Babylonian *šiqlu*, which was divided into 24 gerah (Babyl. *giru*); 60

Babylonian shekels were one minah and 60 minah one kikkar (Babyl. *biltu*).

The shape of the metal ingots varied. Egyptian tomb wall-paintings depict them as shaped like bracelets or oxhides. In Genesis 24:22 Eleazar "took a golden ring of half a shekel [*beka*] weight, and two bracelets for her hands of ten shekels weight of gold." When Joshua conquered Jericho, Achan took booty against orders, among other things 200 shekels of silver and a "golden wedge" of 50 shekels weight (Josh. 7:21). Such a "golden wedge" was discovered during the excavations of Gezer. In the pre-monarchy period the word *kesef* ("silver") was frequently used instead of shekel (Judg. 9:4; and II Sam. 18:11; et al.). During the period of the kingdoms of Israel and especially of Judah, payments are mentioned in the Bible in the shekel weight, the unit used to weigh the metal bars which were in those days the main means of payment. Jeremiah bought a plot of land and weighed his payment (silver) on scales (Jer. 32:9). Subdivisions of the shekel were the beka or half-shekel (Gen. 24:22; Ex. 38:26) and the gerah, then a 20th of the shekel (Ex. 30:13). The shekel, in turn, was a 50th part of the maneh, and the maneh was a 60th part of the kikkar, which thus was equal to 3,000 shekels. The maneh and the kikkar, however, were only units of account and remained so during the Second Temple period when the shekel became a coin denomination. Gold, silver, and bronze ingots were discovered during excavations conducted in Ereẓ Israel and so were scales and weights of the shekel unit and its multiples and fractions.

INTRODUCTION OF COINS IN ANCIENT PALESTINE. The earliest known coins originate in Lydia in northwest Anatolia in the late seventh century B.C.E. (i.e., before the destruction of the First Temple). No coins of that period have yet been discovered in Ereẓ Israel. The earliest coins found on Palestinian soil are from the second half of the sixth century and the first half of the fifth century B.C.E. They are Greek coins from Athens, Thasos, and Macedon, brought apparently to the country by Greek merchants. In the late fifth and first half of the fourth centuries Palestine was under Persian rule and Phoenician coins, especially those from Sidon and Tyre, circulated in the northern part of the country and the coastal strip down to south of Jaffa. At the same time there was an abundance of small coins of the obol and hemi-obol denomination, struck in the Gaza area in a great variety of types, which are also artistically interesting. During that period the Athenian coinage, bearing the head of Pallas Athene and the owl, her holy bird, were the hard currency of the eastern Mediterranean. The owl type coin was so widely imitated on a local level that the local money had the same value as the Athenian coins.

THE COINS OF JUDEA IN THE LATE FIFTH AND FIRST PART OF THE FOURTH CENTURY B.C.E. Alongside the above-mentioned issues, imitations of the Athenian coinage were also issued in Judea. These silver coins are rather rare, but at least six coin types are known with the inscription *Yehud* (Aramaic: Judea). Some follow the "head/owl" type, while others show a falcon, a fleur-de-lis, a Janus head, a god seated on a winged chariot, and a bird of an unidentified kind. It cannot be determined whether the Jewish high priest or the local Persian governor was the issuing authority. On one coin, however, the Hebrew name Hezekiah (Yeḥezkiyyah) can be deciphered and could be related to the high priest mentioned by Josephus (Apion, 1:187–9). The largest denomination of this type which has been discovered is the drachm, but the bulk is composed of oboloi and hemi-oboloi.

THE HELLENISTIC PERIOD. During the third century B.C.E. Palestine was ruled by the Ptolemies and their currency not only circulated there but was struck in local mints at such coastal towns as Acre (then already called Ptolemais), Jaffa, Ashkelon, and Gaza. This changed after the battle of Panias in 198 B.C.E., when the Ptolemies were replaced by the victorious Seleucids. The latter used the local mints of Acre, Ashkelon, and Gaza for the production of their own currency, besides the many mints they had in other parts of their kingdom. Their coins circulated in Palestine at least until the first coins were issued by the Hasmonean rulers. The Ptolemies issued gold, silver, and bronze coins, some of the latter of heavy weight in place of the small silver. Their silver standard was lighter than that of the Seleucids, which still leaned on the Attic standard.

The Jewish Coinage

THE HASMONEAN COINAGE (135–37 B.C.E.). The consecutive history of ancient Jewish coinage begins after the establishment of the independent Hasmonean dynasty in the 2nd century B.C.E. The bulk of Hasmonean coins were of the small bronze denomination, namely the perutah or dilepton. In accordance with the Second Commandment no likeness of living beings, men or animals, are found on them. Most of the emblems, for example the cornucopia – single or double – the wreath surrounding the legend, the anchor, the flower, the star, and the helmet, were copied from emblems found on the late issues of the Seleucid coinage. All Hasmonean coins bear Hebrew legends, but those of Alexander *Yannai and Mattathias *Antigonus also have legends in Greek. The Hebrew legend, written in the old Hebrew script, almost always appears in the formula, "X the high priest and the **ḥever* of the Jews" (*ḥever* probably means the assembly of the elders of the state). The Hasmonean rulers are thus styled on most coins as high priests. The only exception is Alexander Yannai who eventually also styled himself king on some of his Hebrew legends. On the Greek legends the Hasmonean rulers styled themselves throughout as "king." With one exception all Hasmonean coins are undated, which presents scholars with difficulties in arranging them chronologically, especially as different rulers went by the same names. In spite of earlier opinions, *Simeon, the first independent Hasmonean ruler (142–135), never issued any coins. According to I Maccabees 15:2–9, Antiochus VII granted Simeon the right to issue coinage, but it has been proved that this grant was withdrawn before Simeon could make use of it. The series of *Shenat Arba* (the "Year Four") formerly assigned to him were actually issued during the Jewish War (66–70 C.E.). It has been suggested that Simeon's son John *Hyrcanus I (135–104 B.C.E.) did not start issuing coins immediately on succeeding his father, but only considerably later, probably in 110 B.C.E. This suggestion is based on the fact that cities in Phoenicia and in Palestine received the right to coin their own money from the declining Seleucid kingdom: Tyre in 126 B.C.E., Sidon in 110 B.C.E., and Ashkelon in 104 B.C.E. John Hyrcanus' coins are the main pattern for the whole series of Hasmonean coins. The obverse depicts a wreath surrounding the legend, "Johanan [Yehoḥanan] the high priest and the *ḥever* of the Jews," while the reverse depicts a double cornucopia with a pomegranate. All his coins are of the perutah denomination. The coins of his successor, *Aristobulus I (104–103 B.C.E.), are in brass with the same denomination and type, but the name was replaced by Judah (Yehudah). At the beginning of his reign Alexander Yannai (103–76 B.C.E.) issued coins of the same type as his predecessors, changing the name to Jonathan (Yehonatan). Later, he issued another series of coins (in Hebrew and Greek) on which he styled himself king. Their emblems are star, anchor, both sometimes surrounded by a circle, and flower. A lepton or half-perutah with a palm branch, and a flower also belong to this "king" series. One type of this series, the star/anchor surrounded by a circle, is very frequent. This is the only coin type in the whole series of Jewish coins which bears an Aramaic legend written in square Hebrew letters and which has been dated. The Hebrew as well as the Greek date 25, which is the 25th year of reign of Alexander Yannai (78 B.C.E.), were recently discerned. As in the Greek legends and this Aramaic one as well, his name is given as "Alexandros." Alexander Yannai also apparently issued lead coins which belong to his "king" series. It is believed that in his final issues he reverted to the early Hasmonean coin type, styling himself again as high priest but altering his Hebrew name from Yehonatan to Yonatan probably in order to avoid the formula of the tetragrammaton. The bulk of the coins of John Hyrcanus II (67, 63–40 B.C.E.) are in the same shape as those of John Hyrcanus I. There are, however, varieties which are peculiar to his issues. Greek letters, single or as monograms, eventually appear on his coins. An A is to be found on the obverse and sometimes on the reverse; other letters are Δ, Λ or Π. These letters probably refer to the magistrates who were responsible for the mint. A change in the traditional legend, namely "Johanan [Yehoḥanan] the high priest head of the *ḥever* of the Jews," may indicate the privileges bestowed upon Hyrcanus II by Julius Caesar who confirmed him as high priest (Jos. Wars 1:194). Besides the regular coin type, Hyrcanus II also issued lepta or half perutot of the same type as did his father Alexander Yannai, bearing the palm-branch/flower. One larger trilepton shows a helmet and a double cornucopia. On all his coins he styled himself high priest.

During the short reign of the last Hasmonean ruler, Antigonus Mattathias (40–37 B.C.E.), a fundamental change occurred in the coin issue of the Hasmoneans. His Hebrew name Mattityahu (Mattathias) is only given on his perutah denomination. The pomegranate between the double cornucopia is replaced by an ear of barley. He issued two larger denominations which can be compared with the Seleucid chalcous and dichalcous. Antigonus was the only Jewish ruler who depicted the holy vessels of the Temple of Jerusalem on his coins, i.e., the table of shewbread and the seven-branched candelabrum. In his Hebrew legends he styles himself high priest and in his Greek legends "king." His Hebrew name is known to us only from his coins.

THE COINAGE OF THE HERODIAN DYNASTY (37 B.C.E.–C. 95 C.E.). The coins of Herod the Great (37–4 B.C.E.), all of bronze as those of his successors, can be divided into two groups: those which are dated and those which are not. The dated coins all bear the same date, the year three. As Herod no doubt reckoned his reign from his appointment as king of Judea by the Romans in 40 B.C.E. and not from his actual accession three years later, the "year three" is equal to 37 B.C.E. All legends on his coins are in Greek and no Hebrew legends appear on the coins of the Herodian dynasty. The legends render his name and title, Βασιλέως Ἡρώδου. The emblems on his coins are the tripod, thymiaterion, caduceus, pomegranate, shield, helmet, aphlaston, palm branch, anchor, double and single cornucopia, eagle, and galley. It may be concluded from this selection of symbols that Herod the Great did not wish to offend the religious feelings of his subjects. The denominations of his coins were the chalcous and hemi-chalcous (rare), the trilepton, and frequently the dilepton or perutah.

The coins of Herod Archelaus (4 B.C.–6 C.E.) are undated and bear mainly maritime emblems, such as the galley, prow, and anchor. Other types are the double cornucopia, the helmet, bunch of grapes, and wreath surrounding the legend. His main denomination was the perutah, but he also issued a trilepton. Herod Antipas (tetrarch of Galilee 4 B.C.E.–C. 39 C.E.) began to issue coins only after he founded and settled his new capital Tiberias. All his coins are dated. The earliest date is from the 24th year of his reign (19/20 C.E.). On his coins he is called Herod, but they can easily be distinguished as they bear his title "tetrarch." The emblems on his coins are all of flora such as the reed, the palm branch, a bunch of dates, and a palm tree. Though the emblems are the same on all denominations, three denominations can be distinguished. The obverses show a wreath that surrounds the legend "Tiberias"; only the series of the last year refers to Gaius Caligula. As the territory of the tetrarch Herod Philip I (4 B.C.E.–34 C.E.) was predominantly non-Jewish, he allowed himself to strike coins with a representation of the ruling Roman emperor and the pagan temple erected by his father in his capital Panias. His coins are dated from the year 5 to the year 37 of his reign, though not all dates occur. Three denominations can be observed, though their units cannot be distinguished.

The most common coin struck by King Herod Agrippa I (37–44 C.E.), grandson of Herod the Great, was a perutah of the year 6 of his reign (42/3 C.E.), depicting an umbrella-shaped royal canopy and three ears of barley. This coin was obviously struck for Judea. For the other districts of his kingdom he issued coins that would have offended Jewish religious feelings as they carried his own portrait or that of the Roman emperor and even gods or human beings in the Greco-Roman style of the period. On one very rare coin two clasped hands are shown; the legend seems to refer to an alliance between the Jewish people and the Roman senate. All Agrippa's coins are dated, and in his non-Jewish series two different groups of two denominations each can be discerned belonging to the reigns of Caligula and Claudius respectively. Herod of Chalcis (41–48 C.E.), brother of Agrippa I, regularly put his portrait on his coins, calling himself "friend of the emperor." Some of his extremely rare coins bear the date "year 3," others are undated; a system of three denominations can be observed in this coinage too.

From the time of the son of Herod of Chalcis, Aristobulus of Chalcis (57–92 C.E.), only a few rare specimens have been preserved. They bear his portrait and sometimes also that of his wife *Salome. His coins can be identified by their legends which mention him and his wife Salome as king and queen.

Because of his long reign, the series of coins assigned to Herod Agrippa II (c. 50–93 C.E.) is the largest and most varied among the coin series of the Herodians. Two types bear his likeness, and others issued in the year 5 of Agrippa with the name of Nero have a legend surrounded by a wreath. There are two coins which have a double date (the years 6 and 11) and which belong to the two different eras used on his coins. These double dated coins bear "inoffensive" symbols such as double cornucopias and a hand grasping various fruits. All his coins, like those of his father Agrippa I, are of bronze and dated, making it easy to arrange them in chronological order. There are however some difficulties. The first is the parallel issue of coins in the name of Vespasian and in the name of his sons Titus and Domitian. It has been accepted that all his Greek coins belong to an era starting in the year 56 C.E. The Latin series issued in the name of Domitian belongs to an era starting in 61 C.E. The bulk of his coins were struck during the reign of the Flavian emperors, with Tyche, the goddess of destiny, and the goddess of victory as emblems. A unique specimen, with the victory inscription on a shield hanging on a palm-tree, refers to the Roman victory in the Jewish War (66–70 C.E.). Agrippa thus put himself into the Roman camp against his own people. His coinage, as described above, shows the most far-reaching deviation from Jewish tradition among the ancient coinage issued by Jewish rulers.

THE COINAGE OF THE JEWISH WAR (66–70 C.E.). By the time the Jewish War broke out, the Tyrian mint had ceased to issue silver shekels but shekels were needed by every Jewish adult male for the payment of the annual Temple tax of a half-shekel (Ex. 30:11ff.; II Kings 12:5ff.). This reason and the resolve of the Jewish authorities to demonstrate their sovereignty over their own country led to the decision to strike the well-known "thick" shekels and half- and quarter-shekels dated from the first to the fifth year of the era of the war. These are the first silver coins Jews struck in antiquity. They are of an extraordinarily good quality, artistically as well as technically. The emblems are as simple as they are beautiful: a chalice with pearl rim and three pomegranates. The legends which are, of course, only in Hebrew and written in the old Hebrew script, read, *Yerushalayim ha-Kedoshah* ("Jerusalem the Holy") and *Shekel Yisrael* ("Shekel of Israel") with the abbreviated dates: ש'א', ש'ב', ש'ג', ש'ד', ש'ה' (*shin alef, shin bet* for *sh*[*enat*], *a*[*lef*], "year one," *sh*[*enat*] *b*[*et*], "year two," etc.). Small bronze coins of the perutah denomination were struck during the second and third year of the war, and three larger denominations were issued during the fourth year, two of which indicate the denomination as *revi'a* ("quarter") and *ḥaẓi* ("half"). The emblems of the bronze coins are the vine leaf, the amphora, the *lulav*, the *etrog*, the palm tree, the fruit baskets, and the chalice.

THE COINAGE OF THE BAR KOKHBA WAR (132–135 C.E.). During this war the last Jewish coin series in antiquity was issued. Bar Kokhba became the head of the Jewish community, and the bulk of the coins issued bear the name Simeon and eventually his title "prince of Israel." However, other coins exist from that period which bear the name of one "Eleazar the Priest" or simply that of "Jerusalem" as the minting authority. The coins were issued over a period of a little more than three years (i.e., during the entire war). The coins of the first two years are dated, but the formula of the era changed from "Year one of the redemption of Israel" to "Year two of the freedom of Israel." During the third year and until the end of the war, the coins issued were undated and bear the war slogan "For the freedom of Jerusalem." These coin types, too, are as numerous as they are beautiful, and artistically rank first in the series of Jewish coins. During this war as well coins were issued in silver and in bronze. What makes this series exceptional from all other coin series in antiquity is the extraordinary fact that the whole issue was overstruck on coins then current in Palestine, such as on the Roman provincial tetradrachms (mainly from Antiochia) and on the Roman denarii or provincial drachms, as well as on local bronze city coins mainly from Ashkelon and Gaza. Bar Kokhba possibly obtained the gentile coins needed for overstriking by means of a public loan for the national war effort.

There are two silver denominations, the tetradrachm or sela and the denarius or zuz. The Temple front and a *lulav* and *etrog* appear on the tetradrachms, while a rather large number of emblems occur on the denarii, such as a wreath surrounding the legend, a bunch of grapes, a juglet, a lyre, a *kithara*, a pair of trumpets, and a palm branch. These emblems are used in many die combinations, thereby creating a large number of coin types. The bronze coinage can be divided into four denominations, a system taken over from the city coinage then current in Palestine and which was reused for the Bar Kokhba issues. On the large denomination, which was issued during the first and second year only, a wreath surrounding the legend and an amphora are depicted. On medium bronze 'א, which is the commonest denomination, a palm tree and a vine leaf are shown. On medium bronze a wreath surrounding a palm branch and a lyre or a *kithara* appears. The small bronze denomination shows a palm tree and a bunch of grapes. In general, the Bar Kokhba coinage is based on the tradition of the coinage of the Jewish War, 66–70. The amphora, vine leaf, and palm tree occur on the coins of that period, and the similarity of the legends is all the more striking, with the name of Zion replaced by the name Israel during the Bar Kokhba War.

Non-Jewish Coins During the Roman Rule

THE ROMAN PROCURATORS (6–37 AND 44–66 C.E.). After the banishment of Herod Archelaus in 6 C.E., his territory (Judea and Samaria) came under direct Roman rule administered by a procurator of equestrian rank. Some of these procurators issued coins of the perutah denomination as follows: coin types with a palm tree and an ear of barley; coin types with a wreath surrounding legend, a double cornucopia, olive spray, three lilies, a vine leaf or leaves, *kantharos*, amphora, and a palm branch; coin types with three ears of barley, *simpulum*, *lituus*, and a wreath surrounding the date of issue; and coin types with a wreath surrounding legend, two crossed spears, a palm tree, and a palm branch. It is believed that these coins were issued at *Caesarea Maritima, the administrative center of the Romans in Palestine. All coins bear the regal years of the respective Roman emperors and can therefore be arranged in chronological order without difficulty.

JUDEA CAPTA COINS AND LATER ISSUES OF THE ROMAN ADMINISTRATION. After the destruction of the Second Temple in 70 C.E., Palestine became a separate administrative unit called *provincia Judaea*. The Flavian emperors appointed a *legatus pro praetore* as head of the local administration and he was also the commander of the military forces stationed in the province. During the reigns of Vespasian (69–79 C.E.) and Titus (79–81 C.E.) the coins issued refer in their types and legends to the Roman victory; the legends are the Greek equivalent to the well-known legend *Judaea Capta*. Under Domitian (81–96 C.E.) four series of coins were issued, which do not refer to the victory over the Jews, but to Domitian's victories in Germany and Britain. All but the last two coin types of Domitian are undated and their chronological order was conjectural until recently.

THE PALESTINIAN CITY COINS. The following cities in Palestine proper struck coins in antiquity: *Aelia Capitolina (Roman Jerusalem), Anthedon, Antipatris, Ashkelon, Caesarea Maritima, Diospolis, Eleutheropolis, Gaza, Joppa (Jaffa), Neapolis (Shechem), Nicopolis-Emmaus, Nysa-Scythopolis, Raphia, Sepphoris-Diocaesarea, and Tiberias. Other cities beyond the border of ancient Palestine struck coins as well, such as Dora and Ptolemais (then part of Phoenicia), and the following cities in Transjordan: Abila, Dium, Gadara, Gerasa, Hippos, Kanatha, Kapitolias, Panias, Pella, Petra, Philadelphia, and Rabbath-Moab. Older cities which struck coins were Ashkelon, whose era began in 104/3 B.C.E., and Gaza, whose era began in 61/60 B.C.E. The era beginning between 64 and 60 B.C.E., which was adopted by many of the above cities, refers to Gabinius' invasion of the Hasmonean kingdom under Pompey, when many cities became independent, especially the so-called *Decapolis in the northeast. The coin types are numerous. City coins issued under Roman rule customarily had the head of the emperor on the obverse while the reverse bore images referring to the city, such as temples built there, the gods worshiped by their inhabitants, and military garrisons stationed in them. The legends frequently indicated the status of the city within the Roman empire, such as *colonia*, autonomous, etc. The archaeological finds suggest that the circulation of these coins was not restricted to the city by which they were issued, but was countrywide. In some cases (Ashkelon, Gaza, Neapolis, Sepphoris, and Tiberias) the money systems consisted of three or more denominations. Their equivalency with the Roman coin system cannot be ascertained. All these coins are of bronze. The only city in Palestine that issued an autonomous silver coinage was Ashkelon (between 51 and 30 B.C.E.) – coins bearing portraits of Ptolemy XIV, Ptolemy XV, and Cleopatra VII. The city coinage came to an end in about 260 C.E. when it became known that the value of the metal was greater than their nominal value. It was then replaced by debased Roman imperial coins.

[Arie Kindler]

Coins in Talmudic Literature

The currency system most commonly found in tannaitic literature is a syncretic one, based on the Greek drachm-obol – 6 obols = 1 drachm – but otherwise following the Roman monetary system both in terminology and metrological structure. Its standard was linked to that of the Tyrian tetradrachm (sela). In tabular form it appears as follows (above the talmudic terms are the Roman ones from which they derive.

Bronze				Silver		
	Quadrans	Semis	As	Dupondius	Denarius	
Perutah	Kardionts or Kuntrun(k)	Musmis	Issar	Pundion	Ma'ah	Dinar
192	96	48	24	12	6	1
32	16	8	4	2	1	
16	8	4	2	1		
8	4	2	1			
4	2	1				
2	1					

There were also two (silver) tarapiks (quinarii) to the dinar, 24 or 25 dinars to the gold dinar (aureus), and 100 dinars to a maneh (theoretical unit of Babylonian origin).

The Talmud (Kid. 12a) also records what is apparently an earlier system, of uncertain origin.

Bronze			Silver		
Perutah	Shamin	Niz or Hanez	Darosa or Hadris	Ma'ah	Dinar
144	72	36	18	6	1
24	12	6	3	1	
8	4	2	1		
4	2	1			
2	1				

However, by the second century C.E. these systems were already of the nature of archaic literary heritages (from Hasmonean times, most probably), so that, for example, no ma'ot were actually in circulation. Coins in daily use were denarii and sela'im from imperial mints (Antioch, etc.), while "small change" copper coinage was minted locally in a number of cities (see above). These city coinages had their own metrological systems, still insufficiently understood, and a number of strange talmudic monetary terms, quoted much later than the coins were actually used, may be related in some way to these local systems; e.g., the trisit (tressis) of Tiberias and Sepphoris (Tosef., Ma'as. Sh. 4:13, 94), termissis (Roman as, denarius?), asper, riv'a (Roman sestertius, ¼ denarius?), tib'a (didrachm), and ragia (tridrachm, or cistophoric tetradrachm). The only silver coins minted in Palestine during this period were "revolt coins" of the Jewish War (66–70) and the Bar Kokhba War (132–135). In the Talmud those of the first war are called "Jerusalem coins," after their legend "Jerusalem the Holy," and those of the second "Kosiba coins" (Tosef., Ma'as Sh. 1:6).

The third century was one of inflation throughout the Roman Empire, so much so that by the 270s the denarius, instead of being 1/25 aureus was 1/1000 (See TJ, Ket. 11:2, 34b). The effects of this inflation were to force the closure of all local (copper-producing) mints, and by the time of Diocletian (284–309) to usher in a completely new monetary system, based on a gold standard, unlike the earlier silver-based one. A number of new terms appear in talmudic literature from the late third century onward, corresponding to units of the new system; e.g., lumma (nummus, Av. Zar. 35b), leken (leukon, meaning white, whitish silver-washed follis?; TJ, Ma'as. Sh. 4:1, 54d, etc.), follsa, follarin (follis), argaron (argurion, siliqua?; TJ, Pe'ah 8:7, 21a). Throughout the fourth century, which was one of continued economic instability, these units were subject to constant depreciation and revaluation. Even gold solidi, which had superseded the aurei, were at times viewed with mistrust because of their adulteration and pure bullion was preferred to gold coin (cf. Cod. Theod. 12:6, 13).

In Babylonia during the Sassanid period (from the early third century onward), the standard silver unit was the Sassanid drachm, called in the Talmud zuz (from Akkadian *zuzu* – "to cut," but according to Jastrow "glittering"), while smaller copper coins of varying sizes were called peshitte.

HALAKHAH. According to talmudic law, "coin" cannot effect a transfer of property; only "produce" (*pere*) can. All "coin" can do is cause an obligation to complete a contract. Hence there is much discussion on what [coins] constitute "coin" and what "produce," or in modern terminology the relative "fiduciariness" of the elements of a trimetallic monetary system (BM 44a–b, etc.). There is also some discussion as to when coins cease to be legal tender (BM 4:5; BK 97a–b, etc.).

In Post-Talmudic Literature

There are two main contexts in which monetary terms appear in post-talmudic literature, halakhic and lexicographic-metrological (partly related to halakhic), and there are also incidental references.

HALAKHIC. There were constant attempts to translate monetary *shi'urim* ("halakhic measures"), such as the five sela'im of "the redemption of the *firstborn," the perutah of the *marriage act, and the 200 zuz of the *ketubbah* in terms of contemporary coinage. Already in the Talmud (Bek. 50a) there is a geonic gloss which gives the Islamic equivalent of the five sela'im as "20 mitkalei [gold dinars], which are 28½ dirham [silver coins] and ½ danka." Though this reckoning is repeated in various early sources, subsequent commentators give a number of different calculations in terms of their own respective time and country (e.g., Persia, *Halakhot Gedolot*; Egypt, Maimonides; Aragon, Naḥmanides; etc.).

LEXICOGRAPHIC-METROLOGICAL. In several lexicographic works biblical and talmudic monetary terms are explained, for example, Jonah ibn Janaḥ's *Sefer ha-Shorashim*, Nathan b. Jehiel's *Arukh*, David Kimḥi's *Mikhlol*, etc. There are also a number of halakhic-metrological studies in which biblical and talmudic coins are discussed in current terms, as in the work of Joseph b. Judah ibn Aknin (12th–13th century) and Estori ha-Parḥi (*Kaftor va-Feraḥ* (c. 1322), ch. 16), which confusingly cites Arabic, Provençal, and French coins, right up to H.J. Sheftel's *Erekh Millim* (1906), a very rich dictionary of halakhic metrology.

INCIDENTAL REFERENCES. There are innumerable incidental references to coins in the responsa literature, for example to Islamic coins in *Teshuvot ha-Ge'onim* (ed. by A. Harkavy (1887), nos. 386, 424, 489, et al.); Spanish, in Solomon b. Abraham *Adret (responsa 2:113); Portuguese, in *David b. Solomon ibn Abi Zimra (responsa 2:651), etc. In some cases local monetary terms are translated literally into Hebrew, thus florins (*peraḥim*); gulden (*zehuvim*); albi or whitten (*levanim*); doblas (*kefulot*). Coins of pure silver are variously called *tabor, naki, ẓaruf, mezukkak*, or *zakuk*. Often a local term is equated with a talmudic one, at times with confusing results. Thus, for example, a pashut or pashit may stand for esterlin, sol, denier, dinaro, pfennig, etc.

[Daniel Sperber]

Currency of Palestine

EREẒ ISRAEL UNDER OTTOMAN RULE. Both Turkish and European coins circulated in Ereẓ Israel during Ottoman rule. Tokens issued by various communities, such as the Jews and the German Templers, and by some business firms, were also in circulation. The reasons for this variety of currency were lack of trust in Turkish coinage, shortage of coins, disparities in the value of Turkish coins of high denomination in different parts of the country, and the capitulations which granted special rights to some European powers and resulted in French gold napoleons and Egyptian coins being brought into circulation alongside Turkish coins. Egypt, though nominally under Turkish rule, enjoyed coinage rights from the middle of the 19th century, and its currency also circulated in Ereẓ Israel.

[Yitzhak Julius Taub]

PALESTINE UNDER THE BRITISH MANDATE 1917–48. On the British occupation of Palestine, the Egyptian pound was made legal tender in the territory. It was replaced in 1927 by the Palestine pound (œ-P), administered by the Palestine Currency Board in London. The Palestine pound was divided into 1,000 mils, and all subsidiary coins issued for Palestine were denominated in mils. A one-pound gold coin, equal to the British sovereign, was authorized but never issued. The first coins of Palestine were placed in circulation on Nov. 1, 1927. Their denominations were 1 and 2 mils in bronze, 5, 10, and 20 mils in cupro-nickel, and 50 and 100 mils in silver. The designs, prepared by the Mandatory government, were intended to be as politically innocuous as possible, the only feature besides the inscriptions being an olive branch or wreath of olive leaves. The inscriptions were trilingual, giving the name of the country, Palestine, and the value, in English, Hebrew, and Arabic. As a concession to the Jewish community, the initials, א״י ("Ereẓ Israel") appeared in brackets following the name Palestine. Perhaps in order to stress the colonial nature of the coinage, the 5, 10, and 20 mils coins were holed in the center.

The design of the Palestine coins remained unchanged, with the exception of the date, throughout the period of the Mandate. The only changes introduced from 1942 to 1944 were the minting of the 5, 10, and 20 mils in bronze due to wartime shortage of nickel, and a slight change in the composition of the 1 and 2 mils (from 1942 to 1945) in order to save tin, which was scarce. Coins were not minted annually, but according to local requirements as reported by the Mandatory government to the Currency Board. They were all minted at the Royal Mint, London. The last coins to be minted were those of 1947, but the entire issue bearing this date was melted down before leaving the Mint, except for two sets, one in the British Museum and the other in the Ashmolean Museum in Oxford. The entire series of coins actually in circulation numbers 59. Some of these exist in proof state as well. The Palestine Currency Board also issued bank notes (see Table).

[Dov Genachowski]

Denomination	Obverse design	Reverse design	Main color
500 Mils	Rachel's Tomb	David's Tower	lilac
1 Pound	Dome of the Rock	David's Tower	green
5 Pounds	Tower of Ramleh	David's Tower	red
10 Pounds	Tower of Ramleh	David's Tower	blue
50 Pounds	Tower of Ramleh	David's Tower	purple
100 Pounds	Tower of Ramleh	David's Tower	green

In the Concentration Camps and Ghettos

In the concentration camps, which had been established in Germany as soon as the Nazis came to power in 1933, the possession of currency, German or foreign, by the inmates was strictly prohibited. Amounts which they were allowed to receive every month from their relatives had to be exchanged for *Lagergeld* ("camp money"), a kind of scrip issued in denominations of 10 and 50 pfennig and 1 and 2 RM. Such camp money was in use in Oranienburg, Dachau, and Buchenwald. A substantial part, however, of the prisoners' monthly transfers was confiscated by the camp administration under the heading of "deduction for damage to camp inventory," and was channeled into the special accounts maintained by the SS.

GHETTO CURRENCY (PAPER). In several of the ghettos established by the Nazis, the Jewish administration was ordered by the SS to set up special banking and postal departments. The purpose was to deprive the Jews of all the money in their possession by forcing them to convert it into bank notes of a nonexistent currency. In the Lodz (Litzmannstadt) ghetto, established on April 30, 1940, all contact with the outside "Aryan" world was prohibited on pain of death. As early as June 1940, special 50 Pfennig notes were issued by the *Judenrat*, on orders of the ghetto commandant, in order to enable the ghetto inmates to purchase postcards bearing a postage stamp. The notes were overprinted in black with smaller denominations – 5, 10, and 20 Pfennig – which could be cut out for separate use. In July of the same year six more notes were issued, in denominations of 1, 2, 5, 10, 20, and 50 marks. This series, like the first, was printed by the German authorities outside the ghetto. The notes, called *Quittungen* ("receipts"), showed the respective denominations on one side, and the serial number, the Star of David, and the signature of the *Aeltester der Juden in Litzmannstadt* on the other; the denomination was repeated and, in addition, there was a *menorah* and a statement threatening severe punishment for any forgery of these notes. In April 1942, 10-Pfennig scrips totaling 2,000 marks were in circulation in the Lodz ghetto in order to meet the demands on its postal department. Additional series of 10 Pfennig notes were issued in the course of the year.

GHETTO COINS. The first coins specially minted for use in the ghetto, made out of an aluminum-magnesium alloy and issued in the denomination of 10 Pfennig, were put into circulation on Dec. 8, 1942. They were withdrawn after a few days because they lacked the inscription *Quittung ueber* ... ("receipt for ...") and were replaced by a newly minted coin bearing the missing inscription. In 1943 more coins were minted in denominations of 5, 10, and 20 marks. On one side the coins showed the respective denomination, and on the reverse the Star of David, the word "ghetto," and the year of issue.

THERESIENSTADT "BANK NOTES". In the Theresienstadt ghetto the *Aeltestenrat* was ordered by the SS commandant to establish a ghetto bank at the end of 1942. In the spring of 1943 on the eve of a visit by a Red Cross commission, a hasty effort was made to prepare the ghetto for the visitors: shops were opened, in which items confiscated from new arrivals were put on sale; a "cafe" and "concert hall" for the "entertainment" of the starving prisoners were established; the only thing missing in the show was money. Thereupon the "technical department" of the ghetto was ordered to design bank notes on the spot, which were printed in a rush by the Prague National Bank in denominations of 1, 2, 5, 10, 20, 50, and 100 Kronen. The "money" was deposited in the ghetto "bank." Desider *Friedmann, a prominent Austrian Zionist, was appointed bank manager and was forced to report to the commission on the ghetto currency, the bank reserves, and the progress of the "savings accounts." This tragi-comedy reached its climax when the prisoners had to form a long queue in order to deposit their "money." Soon after the commission's visit, the bank and the ghetto currency became the subject of a Nazi propaganda film. Once again "banking transactions" were performed and filmed. Part of the film was discovered after the war; it shows emaciated old people waiting outside the bank in the old Theresienstadt town hall, with ghetto currency and savings books in their hands. Soon after, the "actors" in the film were sent to the Auschwitz death camp. Several series of Theresienstadt ghetto banknotes have been preserved. They vary in color and show Moses with the Ten Commandments, a Star of David, and the inscription *Quittung ueber... Kronen* on one side, and *Quittung*, a Star of David, the date of issue (Jan. 1, 1943), the signature of the *Aeltester der Juden*, Jacob *Edelstein, and the serial number on the reverse.

FORGING FOREIGN CURRENCY AT SACHSENHAUSEN. A different story altogether was the "production" (i.e., forging) of foreign bank notes by Jewish prisoners in the Sachsenhausen concentration camp for use by the Nazis. This was known as "Aktion Bernhard," after the officer in charge, *Sturmbannfuehrer* Bernhard Krueger, and began in 1942. Experts in graphic art and printing among Jewish prisoners were sent to Sachsenhausen. They were kept in a separate block, surrounded by barbed wire and isolated from the rest of the camp. A total of 130 prisoners was engaged in the work; the monthly output of sterling notes alone was as high as £400,000 but gold rubles, dollars, and foreign stamps were also forged. Shortly before the end of the war, a similar project was organized at the Mauthausen concentration camp.

[B. Mordechai Ansbacher]

The State of Israel

On the establishment of the State of Israel, the Palestine pound and its subsidiary coins continued to be legal tender until Sept. 15, 1948, when the Palestine pound was replaced by the new Israel pound (I£, in Hebrew *lirah* (לִירָה) abbreviated ל״י). The Palestine coins continued in circulation until 1949, disappearing, however, even before their demonetization when the I£ was devalued against the pound sterling.

LEGAL AND ADMINISTRATIVE ARRANGEMENTS IN ISRAEL. While the issue of banknotes was carried out for the State from 1948 until 1954 by the Issue Department of Bank Leumi le-Israel (before 1950 the Anglo-Palestine Bank Ltd.), the issue of coins during the same period, that is until the establishment of the Bank of Israel, was the responsibility of the government, exercised by the accountant-general in the Ministry of Finance. This responsibility was transferred to the Bank of Israel under the Bank of Israel Law, 5714 – 1954. A treasury note for I£4.1 million was issued to the bank on its opening day, Dec. 1, 1954, to cover the liability arising from coins in circulation on that date. This note was redeemed in 1965.

The Bank of Israel continued, between 1954 and 1959, to issue mainly the same coins issued previously by the Treasury. The first series of Bank of Israel trade coins was issued in 1960, while the first Bank of Israel commemorative coin was issued in 1958. The issue of coins is handled in the Bank of Israel by the Currency Issue Unit, charged with planning and producing the currency, while its placement in circulation comes under the Issue Department of the Bank. Coin designs are chosen by tender among qualified artists, or in some cases by open tender, by the Advisory Committee appointed for this purpose, which submits its recommendations to the governor of the bank. In order for the coins to become legal tender, the approval of the minister of finance and publication of the particulars of the coin in *Reshumot*, the official gazette, are required.

THE 25 MILS OF 5708–9. Following independence in 1948 the shortage of coins in Israel became acute. Firms, municipalities, and bus companies started illegally issuing coin-tokens, out of sheer necessity. As a result, in August of that year the Treasury decided to mint the first Israel coins. The first coin minted, denominated 25 mils (the term perutah replaced mil only later), was made of aluminum, carrying the design of a bunch of grapes taken from a coin of the Bar Kokhba War. It was at first minted by a private factory in Jerusalem, and later by one in Tel Aviv. It was not a successful coin and was placed in circulation only because of the pressure of demand. It established, however, the principle of design governing Israel trade coins – all designs are taken from ancient Jewish coins, those of the Jewish War (66–70) and of the Bar Kokhba War (132–135), and all are dated according to the Jewish year. The 25 mils coins are the only ones that were actually demonetized in Israel following the establishment of the perutah as the subdivision of the Israel pound.

THE PERUTAH SERIES. The perutah series, commencing in 1949 and ending in 1960, comprised eight denominations: 1, 5, 10, 25, 50, 100, 250, and 500 perutot. Various changes occurred during the period as regards the 10 perutot coin (minted in bronze and aluminum, four types in all), and the 100 perutot (two sizes) – there are several varieties, as distinct from types, in each coin of the series. The 250 perutot was minted in cupro-nickel for general use and in silver for sale to numismatists. The 500 perutot was minted in silver only, for numismatists' use, and was never in actual circulation. In all, the series includes 25 types for the eight denominations and numerous varieties. Until 1954 all perutah coins were minted for the Israel government by two private mints in Britain: the ICI Mint and The Mint, Birmingham. In 1954 the Israel Mint was established in Tel Aviv, as a division of the government printer, and gradually took over the minting of Israel's coins.

THE AGORAH SERIES. The law amending the Currency Order of 5719 – 1959 abolished the division of the I£ into 1,000 perutot and introduced instead its division into 100 agorot. Following this enactment, the Bank of Israel began in 1960 to issue the new series, denominated in agorot. Four denominations were introduced in 1960: 1 agorah made of aluminum, and 5, 10, and 25 agorot of cupro-nickel-aluminum. In 1963 the series was completed by the addition of half-pound and one pound coins in cupro-nickel. The one pound coin introduced that year proved unpopular owing to its similarity to the half-pound coin and its design was changed in 1967, this being the only change in the series. Complete sets of all six denominations were issued for each year since 1963 with the exception of 1964. By the end of 1968 the series comprised 47 coins. For some of these there are several varieties. Coins of the agora series were minted by the Israel Mint, the Royal Dutch Mint at Utrecht, and the Swiss National Mint, at Berne. The Israel Mint was moved from Tel Aviv to Jerusalem in 1966, and all 1967 trade coins were minted in Jerusalem, this being the first year in which no foreign mint took part in the minting of these coins.

COMMEMORATIVE COINS. The first commemorative coin of Israel was issued by the Bank of Israel in 1958 to mark Israel's tenth anniversary. It proved to be a success, and established the series of Israel's commemoratives as one of the most popular in the world. The basic series of commemoratives is the Independence Day coin, of which the 1958 coin was the first. These were issued until 1967 in the denomination of I£5 and from 1968 in the denomination of I£10, in silver. Two other series of commemorative coins were started but discontinued after a period: half-pound "half-shekel" series issued for Purim, of which two coins were issued in cupro-nickel, and one pound Ḥanukkah series, six coins also in cupro-nickel. Special (*hors-de-série*) commemorative coins were issued on several occasions: a 20-pound gold coin to mark the centenary of the birth of Theodor Herzl; 50- and 100-pound coins in gold to mark the tenth anniversary of the death of Chaim Weizmann; a 50-pound coin in gold to mark the tenth anniversary of the Bank of Israel; a 10-pound coin in silver and a 100-pound coin in gold to commemorate the victory in the Six-Day War; and a 100-pound coin in gold to mark Israel's 20th anniversary and the reunification of Jerusalem. Most of the commemorative coins were issued in both proof and uncirculated conditions. In all they were minted by four mints – the Utrecht and Berne mints already referred to, the Italian State Mint at Rome, and a private mint in Jerusalem. Under an amendment to the Bank of Israel Law, passed in 1968, the government granted the distribution rights of Israel's commemorative coins to the Government of Israel Coin and Medals Corporation. Its profits, deriving from the surcharge on the face value of coins and from the sale of state medals, are devoted to the maintenance and reconstruction of historical sites in Israel.

BANK NOTES. Until the Bank of Israel was established in 1954 there were two series of bank notes issued by the Bank Leumi. The first series bore the former name of this financial institute, Anglo-Palestine Bank Ltd., and was printed in denominations of 500 mils, 1, 5, 10, and 50 P£. A second series was printed in denominations of 500 perutah, 1, 5, 10, and 50 I£ under the new name of the bank, Bank Leumi Le-Israel. The Bank of Israel has issued two series of bank notes – the first in denominations of 500 perutah, 1, 5, 10, and 50 I£ and the second in denominations of one-half, 1, 5, 10, 50, and 100 I£. In 1969 the government of Israel voted to change the name of the standard currency from that of the Israel (pound) lira to the shekel.

[Dov Genachowski]

BIBLIOGRAPHY: IN ANCIENT PALESTINE: L.A. Mayer, *A Bibliography of Jewish Numismatics* (1966); G.H. Hill, *Catalogue of the Greek Coins of Palestine* (1914); T. Reinach, *Jewish Coins* (1903); F.W. Madden, *Coins of the Jews* (1881; repr. with introd. by M. Avi-Yonah 1967); A. Reifenberg, *Ancient Jewish Coins* (19472); L. Kadman, *Coins of the Jewish War of 66–73* C.E. (1960), includes bibliography, 153–79; Y. Meshorer, *Jewish Coins of the Second Temple Period* (1967), includes bibliography, 110–2; L. Kadman and A. Kindler, *Ha-Matbe'a be-Ereẓ-Yisrael u-ve-Ammim mi-Ymei Kedem ve-ad Yameinu* (1963). IN TALMUDIC TIMES: B. Zuckermann, *Ueber talmudische Muenzen und Gewichte* (1862); Krauss, Tal Arch, 2 (1911), 404–16, 712–20; S. Ejges, *Das Geld im Talmud* (1930); Sperber, in: JQR, 56 (1965/66), 273–301; idem, in: *Numismatic Chronicle*, 8 (1968), 83–109; Carson, in: A. Kindler (ed.), *International Numismatic Convention, Jerusalem 1963* (1967), 231–61. IN POST-TALMUDIC TIMES: Zunz, Gesch, 535–43; Y.Z. Cahana, in: *Sinai*, 25 (1949), 129–48. UNDER BRITISH MANDATE: Palestine Currency Board, *Annual Report* (1926–48). STATE OF ISRAEL: Bank of Israel, *Annual Report* (1954–to date); *Israel Numismatic Bulletin*, nos. 1–5 (1962–63); Israel Coins and Medals Co., *Israel's Coins* (1965); Israel Numismatic Society, *13 Years of the Israel Numismatic Society: 1945–1959* (1959); *Israel Numismatic Journal* (1963–); *Alon ha-Ḥevrah ha-Numismatit le-Yisrael* (1966–); S. Haffner, *History of Modern Israel's Money, 1917 to 1967* (1967); F. Bertram, *Israel 20 Year Catalog of Coins and Currency* (1968); L. Kadman, *Israel's Money* (1963^{2}); F. Pridmore, *Coins of the British Commonwealth of Nations*, pt. II: *Asian Territories* (1962); Deputy Master and Controller of the Royal Mint, *Annual Report* (1926–48).

°**COLBERT, JEAN BAPTISTE** (1619–1683), comptroller-general of finances under Louis XIV of France. Contrary to the prevailing attitude of his day, Colbert was in favor of the presence of the Jews. He believed them advantageous to the economy because of their trade, their manufactured products, and their capital investments. Therefore, he protected the *New Christians of *Bordeaux and Marseilles in the face of pressure from Catholic circles. He was also anxious that the Jews should remain in the French colonies – though at the same time restricting the public manifestations of their religious life – for the sake of their investments and the impetus they gave to agriculture.

BIBLIOGRAPHY: J.B. Colbert, *Lettres...*, 6 (1869), 159, 188, 193, etc.; C.W. Cole, *Colbert...*, 1 (Eng., 1939), 351, 362; 2 (1939), 42.

[Bernhard Blumenkranz]

COLCHESTER, country town of Essex, England. In the Middle Ages the town harbored a Jewish community, which ranked ninth in importance among the English Jewries in the *Northampton Donum of 1194. On the organization of the *Exchequer of the Jews, Colchester became the seat of an **archa* for the registration of Jewish transactions. The Ashmolean Museum holds a mid-13th century bowl engraved in Hebrew probably owned by Joseph of Colchester. In 1277 a number of local Jews and Christians were involved together in a breach of the Forest Laws. On the expulsion of the Jews from England in 1290, nine houses owned by the Jews on Stockwell Street, as well as the synagogue, escheated to the crown. A short-lived Jewish community was established at the close of the 18th century. A congregation was established in 1957, and 27 Jews were living there in 1967. In 2004 the Jewish population numbered approximately 100.

BIBLIOGRAPHY: Roth, England, index; Roth, in: AJA, 3 (1957), 22–25; J. Jacobs, *Jews of Angevin England* (1893), passim; J. Jacobs, *Jewish Ideals* (1896), 225ff.,; Neubauer, in: REJ, 5 (1882), 246ff. **ADD. BIBLIOGRAPHY:** JYB 2004; D. Stephenson, in: *Essex Arcaeol. & Hist. Jnl.* 16 (1983–84), 48–52; *VCH Essex*, 9 (1994), 27–28; M.M. Archibald and B.J. Crook, *English Medieval Coin Hoards* I, BM Occasional Paper 87 (2001), 67–142; H.G. Richardson, *English Jewry Under the Angevin Kings* (1960), index.

[Cecil Roth / Joe Hillaby (2nd ed.)]

COLE, KENNETH (1954–), U.S. footwear and clothing designer, entrepreneur, civic activist. Cole, president and chief executive officer of Kenneth Cole Productions, not only founded an international footwear and clothing business, but through his company's advertising, managed to raise social awareness of such issues as AIDS, homelessness, gun safety, and women's rights. Many of his ads carry the message: "To be aware is more important than what you wear." Born Kenneth Cohen, he was raised on Long Island and began working part time while still a teenager. He was a stock boy at a local shoe store and sold peanuts at two of New York City's most notable sports arenas, Shea Stadium and Madison Square Garden. After earning a B.A. from Emory University, Atlanta, Cole joined El Greco, his family's footwear business. Under the leadership of his father, Charles, the Brooklyn-based company produced the highly successful Candies shoes for women in the 1970s. In 1983, Cole left El Greco and launched Kenneth Cole Productions. It grew into a publicly owned corporation with more than 50 retail stores in the U.S.; distribution in Europe, Asia, and Latin America; licensees covering more than two dozen product categories for men and women; and more than a billion dollars in retail sales. Cole ran his first "awareness" ad in 1986. It depicted nine top models posing with children. The copy read: "For the future of our children … support the American Foundation for AIDS Research [Amfar]. We do." In keeping with the non-commercial aspect of the ad, the models were barefoot. Cole, a director of Amfar since 1987, is also its vice chairman and director of creative services. His company also supports HELP USA, a major provider of housing, jobs, and services for the homeless. He is married to Maria Cuomo, the daughter of former New York governor Mario Cuomo. Cole, who has received numerous awards for his innovative advertising, was named humanitarian of the year by Divine Design (1996), the Council of Fashion Designers of America (1997), and the National Father's Day Committee (2002). He wrote about his company and its ad campaigns in *Footnotes* (2003).

[Mort Sheinman (2nd ed.)]

COLEMAN, CY (1929–2004), U.S. composer, pianist. Born in the Bronx, N.Y., Coleman (Seymour Kaufman) was a child prodigy, giving a recital at Steinway Hall at the age of six and Carnegie Hall by nine. At 17 he was playing Manhattan supper clubs. While a student at the New York College of Music in 1948, Coleman turned away from classical music and formed a trio. He began to attract attention with songs recorded by Frank Sinatra, including "Try to Change Me Now," and "Witchcraft" and "The Best Is Yet to Come," the latter two written with Carolyn Leigh. The songs established Coleman's reputation as a master of the swiveling sexy come-on, a critic for *The New York Times* wrote. The partnership produced several hits and two Broadway musicals, *Wildcat*, which starred Lucille Ball, in 1960, and *Little Me*, a vehicle for Sid *Caesar in 1962.

In 1964 Coleman met Dorothy *Fields, a successful songwriter earlier in her career who was revitalized by working with the much younger Coleman. Their first project became the Broadway smash musical *Sweet Charity* in 1966 with songs like "Big Spender." They worked on two other shows, an aborted project about Eleanor Roosevelt and *Seesaw*, which reached Broadway in 1973. Fields died the following year. Coleman continued to write for the stage and produced the scores for the following shows: *I Love My Wife*, with lyrics by Michael Stewart, in 1977; *On the Twentieth Century*, with lyrics by Betty *Comden and Adolph *Green, 1978; *Barnum*, with Michael Stewart, 1980; *City of Angels*, with lyrics by David Zippel, 1989; *Will Rogers Follies*, Comden and Green, 1991 (which won a Grammy award); and *The Life*, with lyrics by Ira Gasman, 1997.

Other hits that became standards in the American songbook include "Hey, Look Me Over," "Real Live Girl," "Here's to Us," "Why Try to Change Me Now?", and "The Riviera."

[Stewart Kampel (2nd ed.)]

COLEMAN, EDWARD DAVIDSON (1891–1939), writer and bibliographer. A native of Suwalki, Poland, Coleman emigrated to the United States at a young age and studied at Harvard University. In 1931 he became the librarian of the American Jewish Historical Society and later its secretary and assistant to the president. He helped organize the Herzl Zion Club, the first Hebrew Zionist youth organization in the United States. Coleman's main scholarly interest was the Jew in English literature and American Jewish bibliography. Among his main works are *The Bible in English Drama* (1931), and *Plays of Jewish Interest on the American Stage, 1752–1821* (1934). He prepared the second volume to A.S.W. Rosenbach's *American Jewish Bibliography*, which, like most of his literary estate, has remained unpublished. Coleman's private library is now part of the Jewish National and University Library in Jerusalem.

BIBLIOGRAPHY: Rivkind, in: AJHSP, 37 (1947), 458–60.

°**COLENSO, JOHN WILLIAM** (1814–1883), English Bible scholar, Anglican bishop of Natal (South Africa). In 1853 Colenso was appointed bishop of Natal, where he learned Zulu, for which he compiled a grammar and dictionary; he also translated parts of the Bible and the New Testament into Zulu. Prompted by questions put to him by Zulus, his mind turned to difficulties and inconsistencies in the Pentateuch. He wrote *The Pentateuch and Book of Joshua Critically Examined* (7 parts, 1862–79), in which he denied the Mosaic authorship of the Pentateuch; Deuteronomy, he asserted, was written by Jeremiah. Such views caused much scandal and controversy; he was repudiated by his church but continued to minister to his followers. For a long time he was a solitary English representative of Higher biblical criticism. The popular *Speaker's Commentary* on the Bible was issued mainly to combat Colenso's views. In the English-Jewish community his views also caused a stir, and Chief Rabbi Hermann *Adler and A. *Benish joined his critics.

BIBLIOGRAPHY: G.W. Cox, *The Life of John William Colenso* (1888), 2 vols.; EB, 6 (1947), 1; *Encyclopedia Americana*, 7 (1955), 224.

COLLATIO LEGUM MOSAICARUM ET ROMANARUM (or **Lex Dei**), one of the rare examples of a systematic comparison of two different legislations, the Jewish and the Roman. It was probably compiled in Rome, between the years 294 and 313 C.E. At one time the author was thought to have been a Christian; however, Volterra's view that the author was a Jew who wanted to prove the priority and superiority of the teachings of Moses (*Scitote, iurisconsulti, quia Moyses prius hoc statuit*, Coll. 7:1) appears to be preferable and is accepted by Levy. The *Collatio* contains 16 chapters dealing particularly with penal law; the first extract in every chapter is the biblical one, normally preceded by the phrase *Moyses dicit* ("Moses says") or *Moyses Dei sacerdos haec dicit* ("Moses, the priest of God, says the following"), followed by the paragraphs from the Roman jurists and the imperial constitutions. The biblical extracts (taken exclusively from Exodus, Leviticus, Numbers, and Deuteronomy) are carefully translated into Latin, probably by the same author, who used the text of the Septuagint and Latin translations before Jerome, frequently comparing the Hebrew text and also bearing in mind at times the traditional Jewish interpretation. The author often alters the text in order to make it more comprehensible juridically, or to make it agree with Roman precepts. Cassuto assumed that the translation of the biblical texts contained in the *Collatio* might be a reflection of "the tradition of the Italian Jews" who needed a Latin translation of the Bible for use in their synagogues and schools (*Annuario di Studi Ebraici*, 1 (1934), 105). The work, preserved in three manuscripts, was discovered in the 16th century and first published by P. Pithou (Basel, 1574). Among the principal editions should be mentioned those by Bluhme (Bonnae, 1833), by Mommsen (Berlin, 1890), by Girard (4th ed., Paris, 1913), by Hyamson (Oxford, 1913), and by Baviera (2nd ed., Florence, 1940).

BIBLIOGRAPHY: E. Volterra, in: *Memorie della Reale Academia Nationale dei Lincei*, series 6, vol. 3, fasc. 1 (1930), contains earlier literature; E. Levy, in: *Zeitschrift der Savigny Stiftung fuer Rechtsgeschichte (romanistische Abteilung)*, 50 (1930), 698ff.; G. Scherillo, in: *Archivio Giuridoco F. Serafini*, 104 (1930), 255ff.; idem, in: *Novissimo Digesto Italiano*, 3 (1959), 446–8; N. Smits, *Mosaicarum et Romanarum Legum Collatio* (Dutch, 1934); Schulz, in: *Studia et Documenta Historiae et Iuris*, 2 (1936), 20–43 (Ger.); idem, in: *Symbolae Van Oven* (1946), 313–32 (Ger.) A.M. Rabello, in: *Scritti sull' Ebraismo in Memoria di G. Bedarida* (1966), 177–86; idem, in: RMI, 33 (1967), 339–49, with the most recent literature.

[Alfredo Mordechai Rabello]

COLLEGIO RABBINICO ITALIANO, Italian rabbinical college, the first modern institution of its kind, inaugurated in 1829 at Padua under the name Istituto Convitto Rabbinico through the efforts of I.S. Reggio and under the direction of L. Della Torre and S.D. Luzzatto. Among its alumni were L. Cantoni, S. Gentilomo, A. Lattes, E. Lolli, F. Luzzatto, A. Mainster, and M. Mortara. After Luzzatto and Della Torre's deaths, the institute underwent a series of crises and closed in 1871. It was reopened in Rome under its above name in 1887 and was directed by M.M. Ehrenreich. In 1899, after a period of suspended activity, it was moved to Florence under the direction of S.H. Margulies, with H.P. Chajes and I. Elbogen among its teachers; under them the college flourished. Among its alumni were E.S. Artom, U. Cassuto, D. Disegni, A. Pacifici, and D. Prato, who all exerted a marked influence on Italian Judaism. After the death of Margulies in 1922 the college, whether in Florence or in Rome, was never the same again. Back in Rome in 1934 and directed by the rabbi of the Rome community, R.A. Sacerdote, the collegio had U. Cassuto, I. Kahn, and D. Lattes among its teachers. After being closed during the later stages of the Fascist regime, the college was reopened in 1955. It published the *Rivista Israelitica* from 1904 until 1915, and the *Annuario di Studi Ebraici*, at intervals 1935–1969.

BIBLIOGRAPHY: A. Toaff, in: *Scritti in onore di D. Lattes* (1938), 184–95; G. Castelbolognesi, in: RMI, 5 (1930/31), 314–22; S. Alatri, *Per la inaugurazione del Collegio Rabbinico Italiano* (1887); R. Prato, *Brevi cenni sul collegio Rabbinico Italiano* (1900); N. Pavoncello, *Il Collegio Rabbinico Italiano* (1961).

[Alfredo Mordechai Rabello]

COLLINS, LOTTIE (1865–1910), British actress and music hall singer. Collins' family name was originally Kalisch. Her father, William Alfred Collins, was a wood turner and music hall entertainer. Lottie Collins gained fame in London in 1891 with the song, "Ta-ra-ra-boom-de-ay," originally a boating song from the lower Mississippi. She accompanied it with a swift, high-kicking dance and made it her main act for years. Her daughter, JOSE COLLINS (Cooney; 1887–1958), also became famous in musical comedy, especially in *The Maid of the Mountains* (1917) which ran for three years. She used the title for her memoirs (1932). They were relatives of the architect HYMAN HENRY COLLINS (c. 1832–1905), one of the few Jewish architects in Victorian Britain. Hyman Collins built several London theaters, including the Strand Music Hall, and worked extensively on housing projects for the poor. He was also a major synagogue architect, building at least five synagogues in London and several others in provincial cities. The well-known Hollywood stars JOAN COLLINS (1933–) and her sister JACKIE COLLINS (1939–), also a best-selling author, are members of this family.

ADD. BIBLIOGRAPHY: ODNB.

COLM, GERHARD (1897–1968), U.S. economist. Colm, who was born in Hanover, served in World War I as an officer in the German Army and was decorated. In 1922 he began his professional career as a government statistician and became deputy director of the Institute for World Economy in Kiel. In 1933, with the advent of Hitler, he emigrated to the United States, and was professor of economics at the New School for Social Research in New York, 1933–39, and an adviser to the Department of Commerce, Bureau of the Budget, and the Council of Economic Advisers. In 1952 he joined the National Planning Association, and was frequently called upon as consultant to the government. His publications include: *Economic Theory of Public Finance* (1927); *Economic Consequences of Recent American Tax Policy* (with Fritz Lehmann, 1938); *Essays in Public Finance and Fiscal Policy* (1955) contains a list of his writings; *The Economy of the American People* (1958); and *Integration of National Planning and Budgeting* (1968).

[Joachim O. Ronall]

COLMAR, capital of Haut-Rhin department, E. France, in Germany until 1681. Jews probably settled in Colmar toward the middle of the 13th century; they are mentioned as living there in a document from 1278. In 1279, the synagogue was destroyed by fire but it is not known whether through foul play or an accident. The Colmar community became the refuge of the Jews from *Rouffach in 1293, and from Mutzig and other localities in 1330 and 1337–38 during the *Armleder persecutions. The first community owned a synagogue, a *mikveh*, a "dance hall," and a cemetery. The Jewish quarter was situated between the western rampart, the present Rue Chauffour, and the Rue Berthe Molly (formerly the Rue des Juifs). In 1348, at the time of the *Black Death persecutions, all the Jews of Colmar were condemned to death and at the beginning of 1349 were burnt at the stake, at the place which is still called "Judenloch." From 1385, Jews were again admitted into Colmar, and town officials allowed them to establish a cemetery. The community was said to include at least 29 adults (or possibly heads of families) in 1392. Their number decreased from the second half of the 15th century, however, until in 1468 there were said to be only two families. In 1510, the emperor authorized the town to expel its remaining Jews, though the expulsion was not carried out until 1512. Nevertheless, Jews from Colmar who had settled in the surrounding localities continued their commercial relations with the burghers of the town. From 1530 they were forbidden to lend to the burghers except against movable pledges. In 1534 they lost the right to trade within Colmar, and in 1541 were forbidden to enter its bounds even when markets and fairs were held. It was as a result of this decision that *Joseph (Joselmann) b. Gershon of Rosheim brought an action against the town which went on for several years, the result of which is unknown. The Jews of Alsace maintained commercial relations with the burghers of Colmar throughout the 16th century, however, as evident from the numerous court cases recorded in that period (*Archives Communales de Colmar*, esp. pp. 33 and 39ff.). In 1547, about sixty Marranos from the Low Countries were arrested in Colmar. They were only liberated after having taken the oath that their destination was a Christian country, and not Turkey.

The attitude of the burghers toward the Jews remained unchanged, even after Colmar was formally annexed to France in 1681. From the 18th century, a few Jews were authorized to live in eating houses and inns in the town in order to prepare ritual food for Jews visiting Colmar to trade. As late as 1754, the Jew Mirtzel Lévi of the neighboring city of Wittelsheim was martyrized after an iniquitous trial. After the outbreak of the French Revolution in 1789, Jews were again allowed to settle in Colmar. In 1808 it became the seat of a *Consistory, with 25 dependent communities. In 1823 Colmar also became the seat of the chief rabbinate of Alsace (Haut-Rhin). The Jewish population numbered approximately 1,200 in 1929.

[Bernhard Blumenkranz / David Weinberg (2nd ed.)]

Holocaust and Postwar Periods

The Jews in Colmar shared the fate of the other Jews in Alsace and Moselle in World War II. They were expelled from their homes, and their synagogue, which was built in 1843, was completely ransacked. After the war the survivors rebuilt the

Jewish community, restored the synagogue, and set up new institutions, including a community center. In 1969 there were over 1,000 Jews in Colmar.

[Georges Levitte]

BIBLIOGRAPHY: Lévy, in: Communauté israélite de Colmar, *La Maison de la Communauté* (1961); Mossmann, in: *Revue de l'Est* (1866), 105ff., 238ff.; Loeb, in: *Annuaire de la Société des Etudes Juives*, 1 (1881), 123ff.; Krakauer, in: REJ, 19 (1889), 282ff.; Ginsburger, *ibid.*, 83 (1927), 52–58; Z. Szajkowski, *Franco-Judaica* (1962), index; Germ Jud, 2 (1968), 415–20.

COLOGNA (De), ABRAHAM VITA (1754–1832), Italian rabbi. Cologna, then serving in *Mantua, was a delegate to the *Assembly of Jewish Notables convened by Napoleon in 1806. In 1807 he was appointed vice president *(ḥakham)* of the French *Sanhedrin and in the following year one of the three *Grand Rabbins* of the central *Consistory, of which he was president from 1812 to 1826. In 1827 Cologna became rabbi of Trieste. He published a collection of sermons and apologetic writings, besides many occasional poems.

BIBLIOGRAPHY: Roth, Italy, 441, 443; Graetz, Gesch, 11 (1900), 258, 260ff., 270, 281.

[Attilio Milano]

COLOGNE (Ger. **Köln**), city in Germany. Founded in 50 C.E. as the Roman Colonia Agrippinensis, seat of the provincial and military administration, it is likely to have attracted a Jewish population at an early date. A Jewish cemetery, assumed to have existed from Roman times, is attested there from the 11th century. It was in use to the end of the 17th century and came to light in the 1930s. Two edicts of Constantine (Cod. Theod. 16:8, 3–4) of 321 and 331 respectively imposed the onerous *Curia* duties on the Jews of Cologne and exempted the officials of their community from the obligations incumbent on the lower class of citizens. No further information on Jews in Cologne is available until the 11th century.

In 1012 (or 1040) a synagogue was erected which, though destroyed, was three times rebuilt on the same site, until, after the expulsion of 1424, it was turned into a chapel, though it served various purposes in the course of time. Allied bombing during World War II laid bare the foundations of the ancient building where unique examples of a *genizah* cellar under the *bimah* and a cistern (in the forecourt?) have been discovered. During the 12th century rabbinical opinion was divided over the religious propriety of its stained glass windows depicting lions and serpents. A chronicler of the first half of the 12th century describes the Cologne community at the end of the 11th century as "a distinguished city… from where life, livelihood, and settled law issued for all our brethren scattered far and wide" (Solomon b. Samson in *Sefer Gezerot Ashkenaz ve-Ẓarefat*, ed. by A.M. Habermann (1945), 43). The central importance of the Cologne fair and the community there for Jewry throughout the Rhine valley is further attested by the description of the *synods held in the city: "all the communities came to Cologne to the fairs three times a year and deliberated at its synagogue" (*ibid.*, 47). The First Crusade of 1096 brought death and destruction to Cologne Jewry. Though the archbishop tried to protect the Jews of the diocese, many were massacred; the Jewish quarter and synagogue were sacked and burned down. The number of those killed indicates a community of approximately 1,000. The martyrs included Moses Kohen Ẓedek, rabbi and cantor, originating from France and respected for his scholarship and piety, as well as other scholars. One of the martyrs had come from Italy, another was a proselyte. A few saved their lives by accepting baptism, but were subsequently permitted by imperial decree to return to Judaism. However, a group of converts remained, who, themselves or their descendants, attained positions of importance in the Church and civil administration.

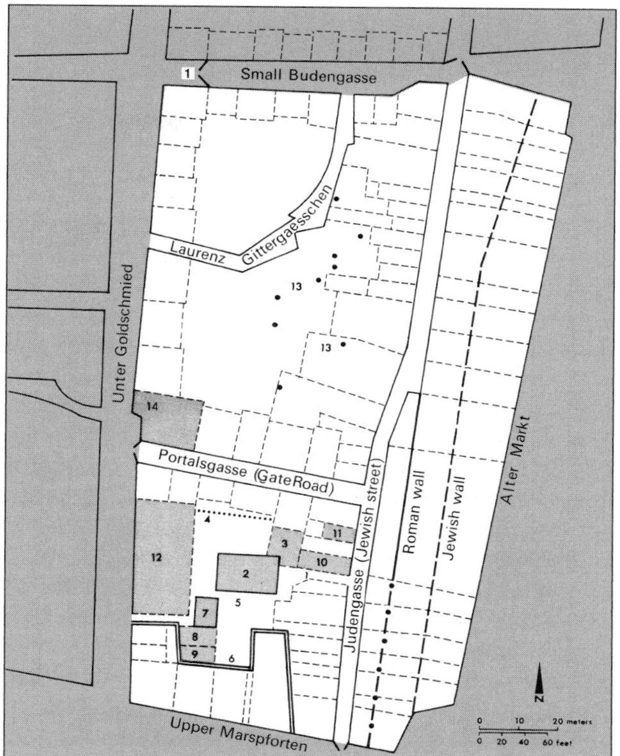

1. Gateway 2. Synagogue 3. Women's synagogue 4. Court of the Synagogue (Curia Judaeorum) 5. Court next to the synagogue 6. Wall to separate Jewish from non-Jewish buildings 7. Mikveh 8. Baths 9. Bakery 10. Hospital 11. The quarters of the synagogue beadle 12. Dance and wedding hall 13. Holes where coins from 1372 were found 14. Coin makers' quarters.

Medieval Jewish quarter in Cologne. Zvi Asaria, Die Juden in Koeln, *1959.*

The community was afterward reconstructed. When a new city wall was built in 1106, the Jews were assigned their own gate (*Porta Judaeorum*) for the defense of the city. In the Cologne land register (*Schreinsbuch*), from 1135, the extent to which Jews owned property there is revealed: from 30 houses at the beginning of the period, to 48 in 1170, 50 in 1235, 60 in 1300, 70 in 1325, and 73 in 1349. Many also lived in leased or rented houses. The land register also yields information on the provenance of the Jews of Cologne, mentioning over 20 places in the Rhineland and beyond (such as Frankfurt, Wuerzburg,

Arnhem in Holland, and even England). The Second Crusade of 1146–7 left Cologne Jewry more or less unharmed, due mainly to Archbishop Arnold, who put the fortress of Wolkenburg at their disposal as a refuge. The imperial Jewish tax as well as the jurisdiction over Jews for serious criminal offenses were in the hands of the archbishops. From 1252 onward they issued periodical letters of protection or privileges to the Jewish community, by which the Jews were assured of protection of life and limb, freedom of commerce and worship, freedom from forcible conversion, and the right to untaxed burial for any Jew in the Jewish cemetery. The rabbinical courts had exclusive jurisdiction over cases involving Jews. For these "privileges" they had to pay heavily in the form of taxes or lump sums. The 1266 privilege, granted by Archbishop Engelbert II, was engraved on stone and can still be seen in the wall of the cathedral. During the 14th century power in the city passed from the archbishop to the patrician city fathers who had defeated him in the battle of Worringen (1288); subsequently the latter were asked to endorse the archepiscopal privileges granted to the Jews, and in 1321 the city itself issued them a letter of protection valid for ten years. It is an indication of the growing insecurity of Jewish life in Cologne that this sort of charter had to be frequently reissued. The cost of the letter of protection to the Jewish community was the considerable sum of 1,600 marks in 1321, rising to 1,800 in 1331. From 1341 acquisition of property by Jews required the consent of the city council, which also intervened in internal disputes.

Disaster overtook Cologne Jewry during the Black *Death. The plague had reached the city in the summer of 1349; the mob stormed the Jewish quarter on St. Bartholomew's Night (Aug. 23–24), letters of protection notwithstanding. Part of the community had assembled in the synagogue; they themselves set fire to it and perished in its flames. The rest were murdered. Among the martyrs were the last three "Jews' bishops" of Cologne (see below) and a number of distinguished rabbis. The archbishop, the municipality, and the count of Juelich now laid claim to the derelict Jewish property. When the "protectors" had at last settled their quarrel, the property was sold and the proceeds used for church and city buildings.

In 1372 Jews were readmitted to Cologne, once more under a privilege from the archbishop renewed in 1384 and every ten years until 1414. The city council also granted a privilege similar to earlier ones, stipulating that no claims could be raised arising out of property owned prior to 1349. Interest rates were limited to 36 1/2% per annum. A new spirit of discrimination was shown in the special dress regulations introduced for Jews and the prohibition on employing Christian nurses, contained in documents of 1384. The golden penny (*goldene Pfennig*) poll tax, imposed on German Jewry in 1342, is recorded as being collected in Cologne in 1391. The post-1372 community was small, never comprising more than 31 taxpaying households and 200 persons. All the more burdensome was the enormous tax which this small group had to pay, though it must have included some fairly rich people. However, the days of the community were numbered. The city refused, after prolonged pleadings before the archbishop, emperor, and pope, to renew the residential privilege which expired in October 1424. This brought the history of medieval Jewry in Cologne to a close.

Communal Structure

Cologne Jewry, like other ethnic and economic groups, formed a corporation with its own council (of 12?) and leader, referred to as the *Judenbischoff* (**Episcopus Judaeorum*; seven holders of this office are known by name between 1135 and 1417), apart from its religious and judicial organization with rabbis, *dayyanim*, readers, *shoḥatim*, beadles, etc. The office of "bishop" and rabbi were not identical, though occasionally united. The Jewish quarter, its synagogue (with a separate building for women), and the cemetery have been mentioned above. Other communal property included a *mikveh* (in addition to a public bath), a dance and wedding hall (*Spielhaus*), a bakehouse, a "hospital" for wayfarers, and accommodation for officials. The synagogue court (*curia Judaeorum*) served for public assemblies, wedding ceremonies, and perhaps for the rabbinical court. A wall separated the Jewish quarter to the south from the adjoining area, while a gate led into it from the east. The *mikveh* was discovered and partly restored during the 1956–57 excavations. The Jews of Cologne were mainly merchants, and later moneylenders. The Cologne fairs, to which traders from near and far brought both raw materials and finished goods, were one of Europe's most important mercantile events. Jewish visitors came from as far as the Ukraine. Transactions at this fair form the subject of an opinion by *Gershom b. Judah (10th–11th century; *Ma'aseh ha-Ge'onim*, ed. by A. Epstein (1909), 70; Rashi's *Pardes*, ed. by H.L. Ehrenreich (1924), 73). Powerful financiers who established themselves in the banking business in the 13th and 14th centuries were largely a law unto themselves, as shown by their repeated conflicts with the community, but their wealth and ostentation often proved their undoing. Many pursued more modest trades and occupations. Some physicians are mentioned toward the end of the 14th century. Among a long line of notable Cologne rabbis (*rabbanei Kolonya*) were *Eliezer b. Joel ha-Levi of Bonn ("Ravyah"), and *Asher b. Jehiel ("ha-Rosh") who was active in Cologne before his emigration to Spain in 1303. *Alexander Suslin ha-Kohen of Frankfurt (martyred in Erfurt, 1349) lived for some time in Cologne. To the kabbalistic school belonged *Abraham b. Alexander of Cologne. The Cologne community early established its own liturgical rite, partly based on Palestinian custom. Maimonides' *Mishneh Torah* was copied in four volumes of vellum in 1295–6 by Nathan b. Simeon of Cologne. This manuscript, now at Budapest, is one of the finest examples of Ashkenazi calligraphy and miniature painting of the period.

From 1424 to the end of the 18th century Jews were rigorously excluded from residence in Cologne. Even those few admitted for business were not permitted to stay overnight, not excepting Jewish physicians who were frequently called in by the local population from nearby towns such as *Bonn and *Deutz. In the 16th century Cologne became the center of the *Pfefferkorn-*Reuchlin controversy. The University of Cologne (founded 1388) had a chair of Hebrew from 1484.

Printing

The Pfefferkorn-Reuchlin controversy led to the publication of many books and pamphlets, some containing Hebrew letters printed from woodcuts, such as Pfefferkorn's *Judenveindt* and *Osternbuch* (1509). In 1518 a polyglot psalter (in four languages) was edited by Johann Potkin, and printed by Jacob Soter and again in 1539 by Johann *Boeschenstein. In 1553 Soter printed the books of Obadiah and Jonah with a rhymed Latin translation by the apostate Johann Isaac ha-Levi and in 1555 Jacob *Anatoli's *Ru'aḥ Ḥen* with a Latin translation also by ha-Levi. In 1563, in partnership with P. Horst, he printed the book of Malachi, with translations. The Cologne imprint of a Bible of 1603 by J. Lucius (of Helmstedt) is doubtful, and it may have to be assigned to Hamburg. A Passover *Haggadah* with German translation and music by the Cologne cantor Judah, father of the composer Jacques *Offenbach, was published in 1838 by Clouth and Company.

Modern Period

The annexation of the Rhineland by revolutionary France in 1794 brought Jewish residents again to Cologne from 1798. A new congregation, formed by 17 households, was established in 1801. Solomon *Oppenheim represented it on the *Assembly of Jewish Notables convoked by Napoleon in 1806, and its rabbi, S.B. Rapaport, on the French *Sanhedrin of 1807. Under the decree of 1808, the Cologne congregation was administered first by the *Krefeld and (from 1817) by the Bonn *Consistory.

Residential permits were required even after the Rhineland had been incorporated into Prussia in 1815; 33 were granted in 1817, and 134 in 1845, when the community numbered approximately 1,000. Among the lay leaders of this period was David Hess, father of Moses *Hess. It was not until 1861, however, the year of the opening of a new synagogue magnificently endowed by the banker Abraham von Oppenheim, that the Cologne congregation achieved the status of a public corporation under the Prussian community law of 1847. Civic equality was finally obtained in 1856. Cologne Jewry numbered 4,523 in 1880, 9,745 in 1900, and approximately 20,000 (2 1/2% of the total population) in 1933. It had four synagogues and several *battei midrash*, two elementary schools and a secondary school, apart from religious schools, a hospital, an orphanage, a children's home, a home for apprentices, and many ancillary societies and institutions. Among rabbis who officiated in Cologne before World War II were the scholars Isidor *Scheftelowitz and Adolf *Kober. From 1867 an independent Orthodox congregation (*Adass Jeshurun) was active; a Jewish teacher's training college was closely associated with it. When David *Wolffsohn, a resident of Cologne, succeeded Theodor Herzl as president of the Zionist Organization in 1904, its offices were transferred to Cologne where they remained until 1911. Max *Bodenheimer was another leading Zionist in Cologne.

[Alexander Carlebach]

After the Nazis came to power in 1933, Jews (and other political opponents) were tortured and even murdered. The turning-point in the life of Cologne Jewry was April 1, 1933, the "Boycott Sabbath." The boycott affected not only shops and businesses but doctors, lawyers, and other professionals as well. Lawyers were driven through the street on garbage trucks. The subsequent dismissal of Jews from the civil service on April 7 affected physicians, teachers, and professors as well. It was a two-way boycott, many Christian shops refusing to serve Jews and it continued in some quarters as the city ceased purchasing from Jewish merchants. On May 10, 1933, "Jewish" books were burned on the University plaza. The Jewish community reacted to all this by carefully worded protests and declarations of loyalty to Germany, but also by assisting emigration, by increased welfare efforts, and by organizing professional retraining courses and trade schools. Discrimination, including the closure of playgrounds and athletic facilities, intensified. By 1935 Jews were barred from public baths. Jews responded by emigrating, leaving Cologne if possible, but there was also movement in the other direction as Jews from the small towns and villages of the Rhineland sought refuge in Cologne. The community organized its own cultural life through the local "Kulturbund," the second largest in Germany after Berlin's. As elsewhere, religious life revived, and Jewish schools could hardly accommodate the number of pupils seeking admission. By the end of 1936 2,535 people required communal assistance. In March 1938 the two Cologne congregations were deprived of their status of public law corporations. The November 9–11, 1938, pogroms known as *Kristallnacht led to the destruction by fire or vandalism of all synagogues. Jewish shops and offices were plundered and great numbers of Jews thrown into prison or concentration camps. More than 400 Jews were arrested and sent to Dachau. Emigration intensified. Over 100 children were sent to Great Britain on the *Kindertransport*. In total, more than 40% of the Jewish population emigrated before September 1939. In May 1939 the Jewish population was 8,406 with another 2,360 *Mischlinge*, persons of mixed Jewish ancestry. When war came in September 1939, the remainder of Cologne Jewry became subject to an all-night curfew, their special food rations were far below that of the general population, they were officially forbidden to use public transport and, when allied bombing began, to use public air raid shelters. Jews had to move out of houses owned by non-Jews; later they were restricted to certain parts of the town, and finally to Jewish-owned houses or institutions, and living conditions grew steadily more desperate. Toward the end of 1941 Jews were interned at a camp in the suburb of Muengersdorf with exemptions for those working in the armament industry and hospitalized patients. Jewish hospital patients were moved into the camp on May 31, 1942, with seriously ill patients temporarily housed in the Adass Jeshurun school building.

The first deportation was that of Polish Jews in October 1938. On October 21, 1941, some Cologne Jews were deported to Lodz. Later deportations were to Theresienstadt, Lodz, Riga, Lublin, and Auschwitz. Many died or were murdered before the end of the journey. Of special note was the deportation to Minsk on July 20, 1942, of Jewish children and some of their teachers. The last to be deported in 1943 were Jewish communal workers. After that deportation the only Jews remaining were those in mixed marriages and their children, many of whom were deported in the fall of 1944. Approximately 40–50 Jews survived in hiding.

[Alexander Carlebach / Michael Berenbaum (2nd ed.)]

A new community came into being after 1945, consisting of the few survivors, displaced persons, and a trickle of returnees (600 in 1946), and in 1967 numbered 1,321. The Roonstrasse synagogue was rebuilt in 1959. Rabbis active in Cologne in the postwar period were Zvi Asaria and E. Schereschewski. The *Monumenta Judaica* exhibition, reflecting 2,000 years of Jewish history and culture in the Rhineland, was shown in 1963–64. Besides a youth center the community maintained a Jewish home for the aged. The Jewish community numbered 1,358 in 1989 and 4,650 in 2003.

[Alexander Carlebach]

BIBLIOGRAPHY: Z. Asaria (ed.), *Die Juden in Köln* (1959); A. Kober, *Cologne* (1940); S. Braun (ed.), *Jahrbuch der Synagogengemeinde Köln* (1934); A. Pinthus, in: ZGJD, 2 (1930), 109–10, 127; K. Schilling (ed.), *Monumenta Judaica-Handbuch* (1963), index, s.v. *Köln*; A. Carlebach, *Adass Yeshurun of Cologne* (1964); K. Bauer, *Judenrecht in Köln bis zum Jahre 1424* (1964); Germ Jud, 1 (1963), 69–85; 2 (1968), 420–42; PK; B. Friedberg, *Toledot ha-Defus ha-Ivri be-Augsburg…* (1935), 33; A. Marx, *Studies in Jewish History and Booklore* (1944), 321–3; Roth, Dark Ages, index. **ADD. BIBLIOGRAPHY:** A. Kober, *Grundbuch des Kölner Judenviertels* (1926); *Köln und das rheinische Judentum* (1985); S. Doepp, *Juedische Jugendbewegung in Koeln* (1997); K. Serup-Bilfeldt (ed.), *Zwischen Dorn und Davidstern* (2001); M. Schmandt, *Judei, cives et incole* (2002); B. Bopf, *"Arisierung" in Koeln* (2004).

COLOMBIA, South American republic; population 43,800,000 (2003); Jewish population estimated at approximately 3,400.

History

Jewish settlement in the country dates back to the arrival of the *Crypto-Jews during the Colonial Period. The first to reach the area came with the Spanish conquerors during the 16th century. From the beginning of the 17th century, in the wake of the establishment of the Inquisition in Cartagena, the dangers increased for those who practiced Judaism in secret. The Inquisition authorities also specialized in persecuting Jews captured in their ships off Spanish-held coasts, mainly in the Caribbean Sea. Merchandise was confiscated, and if the captives were *New Christians reconverted to Judaism, they were tried, and in many cases executed. It is said, however, that a secret synagogue functioned in Cartagena at the beginning of the 17th century in the house of Blas de Paz Pinto.

The church was traditionally very powerful in Colombia, even after the country achieved independence, and its status was one of the main issues of political struggle. Until 1853 Roman Catholicism was the only religion permitted. Between 1861 and 1886 the influence of the liberals brought about freedom of religion and the restriction of the church's power, but from then until 1936 Roman Catholicism was the national religion protected by the state. The constitution of 1886, reformed in 1936 and 1945, guarantees freedom of religion as long as its practice is "not contrary to Christian morals or to the laws."

It was only at the end of the 18th and the beginning of the 19th century, however, that the first Jews openly began to settle in Colombia. (See the map "Jews in Colombia.") They came from the Antilles islands of Jamaica and Curaçao and by the middle of the century had settled in Barranquilla, Santa Marta, Ríohacha, and Cartagena, as well as in other port cities. In 1844 a cemetery was established in Santa Maria. In 1853 the Jews of Barranquilla were granted a plot of ground by the government to be set aside as a cemetery; in 1874 the Jews, together with the Protestants and the Catholics, set up a new communal cemetery divided into sections. On March 6, 1874, the Caribbean Jews in Barranquilla organized themselves as the "Colombian Jewish Community." Barranquilla developed into the main Colombian port, and the important Jewish houses of the Senior, Solas, Alvarez Correa, Rorg Mendes, Cortizos, and Curiel families were founded. The originator of transport on the Magdalena River, the main artery between Bogotá and the

Map of Colombia showing 19th-century and contemporary Jewish settlement.

sea, was David Lopez Penha. The major banks were managed by Moises de Sola, and the "Company of Water Resources" was headed by Augustin Senior, in whose home the Jewish prayer services were conducted. In 1919 Colombian air transport was established by Ernesto Cortissoz.

Smaller Jewish communities existed on the Caribbean coast, Riohacha and Santa Marta. Among their members were the generals Efrain and Abraham Juliao.

In the cultural field, in the 19th century the Barranquilla Jew Abraham Zacarias Lopez Penha became one of the main Colombian poets. Raised in the valley of the Cauca was one of the most famous Latin American writers, Jorge Ricardo Isaacs (1837–1895), author of the classic novel *Maria,* who was of Jewish origin, stemming from a family that came from Jamaica. The descendants of those settlers from the Caribbean have almost completely assimilated into the local population.

The contemporary Jewish community was established at the beginning of the 20th century. Sephardi Jews from Greece and Turkey and Jews from Syria came during the post-World War I period and constituted the first group of practicing Jews in the country. They engaged in commerce in manufactured articles and founded two silk factories in Barranquilla. At about the same time, Jewish immigrants began to arrive from Eastern Europe, mainly from Poland, as well as from Palestine. At first they engaged in peddling and then gradually entered manufacturing and business, considering Colombia only a temporary haven. The rise of Nazism in Germany changed the transient character of the community and also brought the last major wave of Jewish immigrants, who came from Germany and Central Europe. Of the 3,595 Jews who arrived between 1933 and 1942, 2,347 were German. According to official population statistics, in 1935 there were 2,045 Jews in Colombia. Of those, 1,100 were in Bogotá, 400 in Cali, 150 in Medellín and Barranquilla, and the rest in other places. (See the map "Jews in Colombia.") Two years later the number was estimated at over 3,000, and by 1943 the Jewish population reached 6,625. In 1934 active anti-immigration propaganda was instigated by the Chambers of Commerce. The press voiced its unanimous opposition to aliens, and in October 1938 the government passed new laws directed especially against Jews. In 1939 immigration ceased completely, and between 1945 and 1950 only 350 Jews entered the country.

Most of the immigrants entered the fields of minor industry and crafts and have played an important role in the economic and industrial development of the country. Attempts at agricultural settlement failed for the most part; of the 200 settlers in 1938 and 1939, only 46 were left by the end of 1942. The chief causes for this failure were the difficult and unknown climatic and agricultural conditions and especially the low standard of living of the farmers in Colombia. On the other hand, Jews played a prominent role in business.

Contemporary Period

Until World War II Colombian Jewry was rather loosely organized. The responsibility for this lay to a great extent with the authorities, who in 1940 still refused to approve the establishment of a central organization of the Jews of Bogotá and Cali, claiming that such a body would prevent the community's assimilation. The Holocaust, however, spurred communal organization, and today the Jewish community is united under the umbrella organization Confederación de Asociaciones Judías de Colombia, which is based in Bogotá. The Jewish community of Bogotá (946 Jewish families in 2005) includes three main groups: the Ashkenazim, the Sephardim, and the Germans. Each has its own communal institutions: the Centro Israelita de Bogotá (founded 1928), the Comunidad Hebrea Sefaradí (reorganized 1943), and the Asociación Israelita Montefiore. In addition, other cultural and Zionist organizations such as *B'nai B'rith, *WIZO, *General Zionists and *Maccabi serve the community. The Colombo Hebrew School in Bogotá educated about 280 students from kindergarten through high school, and religious life centers around the four synagogues in the city: two Ashkenazi, one Sephardi, and one German.

The Jewish communities in the other principal cities were also well organized. A total of 344 Jewish families lived in Cali in 2005. All the organizations within the city, as well as those in the small towns in the region, have united to form the Unión Federal Hebrea, which offers religious and social services. The community has two synagogues, one Ashkenazi and one Sephardi, and a school, the Colegio Jorge Isaacs, with 120 students (2005). It also sponsors a summer camp for children, the only one of its kind in the country. In Barranquilla, which is the third largest Jewish community in the country, 203 Jewish families were counted in 2005, of whom approximately half were East Europeans, one-third Sephardim, and the rest Germans. Economically, the Jews are in a favorable position, but they are not involved in general public life. Their organizations include the Club Unión, a social organization which encompassed the community as a whole; religious institutions maintained individually by each sector; general organizations such as B'nai B'rith, etc.; and an umbrella organization that includes all the organizations. The day school has a student enrollment of 300; the number of mixed marriages is small.

The cultural life of the Jewish community in Colombia is not exceptionally active. A good part of the social life centers on institutions of entertainment and leisure. At the same time, great affinity was evinced for the Zionist Movement, whose Colombia branch was founded in 1927, and for the State of Israel. Between 1962 and 1964, 146 Colombian Jews migrated to Israel, and there were 62 youths from Colombia among the volunteers who went to Israel after the *Six-Day War (1967). Jewish participation in political life in Colombia is minimal. There are no Jewish members of parliament or Jewish statesmen. The relations between the Jews and the Roman Catholic Church are cordial and were strengthened during Pope Paul VI's visit to the country in 1969, when a delegation of leaders of the Jewish community was received by him. Throughout the years, a variety of Jewish publications have appeared in the country. By 1970 only two remained, both in Bogotá: *Menora*, established in 1950, had a Zionist-Revisionist orientation, stressed political problems, and presented community news; *Ideal*, Zionist and nonpartisan, published cultural and general news, both local and international.

Colombia did not vote for the partition of Palestine in 1947, nor did it recognize the State of Israel immediately upon its establishment. Later, however, it maintained an embassy in Jerusalem and Israel has established an embassy in Bogotá. Cordial relations exist between the two countries. A large number of Colombians participated in technical courses offered in Israel and even established an organization called Shalom.

The very unstable security situation initiated a wave of Jewish emigration from Colombia. The number of Colombian Jews in Israel has reached almost 2,000, with others settling in the United States and Spain or in other Latin American countries. In Bogotá Jewish activity has dwindled and the Jewish day school has fewer and fewer Jewish children. The number of members in the Jewish communities in Cali, Medellín, and Barranquilla are in steady decline.

BIBLIOGRAPHY: C.S. Rosenthal, in: JSOS, 18 (1956), 262–74; Jewish Central Information Office, Amsterdam, *Position of Jews in Columbia* (1937); J. Beller, *Jews in Latin America* (1969), 58–67; J. Shatzky, *Yidishe Yishuvim in Latayn Amerike* (1959), 195–205; A. Monk and J. Isaacson (eds.), *Comunidades Judéas de Latinoamérica* (1968), 57–63; Asociación Filantrópica Israelita, Buenos Aires, *Zehn Jahre Aufbauarbeit in Suedamerika* (Ger. and Sp. 1943), 250–75. **ADD. BIBLIOGRAPHY:** I. Croitoru Rotbaum, *De Sefarad al Neosefardismo* (1967); D.M. Bermudez and J. Watnik Baron, *Nuestra Gentes* (1994); D. Mesa Bernal, "Los Judios en la epoca colonial," in: *Boletin de Historia y Antiguedades*, 73 (1986): 381–99; A. Beker (ed.), *Ha-Kehillot ha-Yehudiyyot ba-Olam* (1997); M. Arbell, *The Jewish Nation of the Caribbean* (2002).

[Moshe Nes El / Mordechai Arbell (2nd ed.)]

COLOMBO, SAMUEL (1868–1923), Italian rabbi and scholar. Born in Pitigliano, Colombo completed his rabbinical studies at Leghorn under Israel Costa and Elia Benamozegh and graduated from the University of Pisa. From 1900 he served as rabbi and head of the rabbinical seminary in Leghorn. In 1912 he was accused before an Italian court of having applied Jewish law by refusing to conduct the wedding of a *mamzer* (see RMI, 29 (1963), 207ff.), but he won his case. Colombo was president of the Italian Rabbinical Federation and a keen Zionist. Among his published writings are *Babel und Bibel* (1904) against Delitzsch, *Il pensiero religioso di G. Mazzini* (1905), *La coscienza di un popolo* (1923), *Una questione di Divorzio secondo il Diritto Ebraico* (1895), and *Sepoltura o Cremazione*? (1908); *Vivere per un' Idea* (1958), *L'Idea dell'Ebraismo* (1958), *Verso Sion* (1920).

BIBLIOGRAPHY: A.S. Toaff, *S. Colombo* (1948); A. Pacifici, *Interludio* (1959); G. Laras, *S. Colombo* (1968); Y. Colombo, in: RMI, 35 (1969), 21ff.

[Alfredo Mordechai Rabello]

COLOMBO, YOSEPH (1897–1975), Italian educator. Colombo was born in Leghorn, the son of Samuel *Colombo; he studied philosophy and pedagogy at the University of Pisa and taught history and philosophy in high schools. He was one of the founders of the Hebrew High School of Milan and its head from 1938 to 1945, when governmental schools were closed to Jews. He taught Hebrew language and literature at the University of Milan and began editing *Rassegna Mensile di Israel* in 1965. Colombo contributed to Italian encyclopedias as well as to Italian-Jewish periodicals and Festschriften. Among his published works are *Problema della Scuola Ebraica in Italia* (1925); *Concezioni ebraiche e teorie moderne* (1926); an Italian translation of and commentary to Avot (last reprinted, 1996), the prefaces to E. *Benamozegh's selected writings, *Scritti Scelti* (1955), and his work on the immortality of the soul in the Pentateuch (1969).

[Alfredo Mordechai Rabello]

COLON, JOSEPH BEN SOLOMON (c. 1420–1480), Italian halakhist, surnamed Trabotto, also known as **Maharik**. Colon was raised in Savoyard, capital of Chambéry, where his family had migrated after the expulsion of the Jews from France (1394). Colon's primary teacher was his father, an eminent talmudist in his own right, though he mentions having studied under other scholars in Chambéry. In his early thirties he migrated to the Piedmont, where he maintained himself through a combination of teaching children and older students and occasional loan-banking. In the late 1450s he headed a yeshivah in Savigliano. Subsequently, we find him in Mestre (before 1467), Bologna, and Mantua (apparently from 1467). According to a report in Ibn Yaḥya's *Shalshelet ha-Kabbalah*, in Mantua he and *Judah b. Jehiel Messer Leon became involved in a dispute, as a result of which they were both banished by the authorities. Colon afterward moved to Pavia, where he continued to teach and write responsa until his death. From an early age, scholars from Germany, Turkey, and Italy sought his decisions on Jewish law. After his death his responsa were collected and have since been frequently reprinted and published (Venice, 1519 etc.). His decisions had massive influence upon all subsequent legal development. His influence is particularly notable in the Ashkenazi orbit, as reflected in Moses Isserles' glosses on the Shulḥan Arukh. Colon was the central pillar of later Italian *halakhah*, and there is scarcely an Italian rabbi of the 16th, 17th, and 18th century who does not quote him.

Colon's responsa are distinguished by his encyclopedic knowledge and methodical analysis of sources. He attempted to identify the basic principles underlying his sources and to elucidate the conceptual framework within which he rendered his rulings. His legal method also resembled the mode of analysis known as *pilpul*. Established custom played a unique place in his thinking and he defined its authority. In this context, he served as the defender of a uniquely French school of Ashkenazi law and lore. The *Mishneh Torah* of *Maimonides enjoyed a preeminent place in his writings. His extensive comments thereupon, scattered throughout his responsa and lecture notes, helped to set the agenda for later scholars. Colon's responsa are marked by tremendous deference to authorities of the past. Hesitating to decide between them, he resorted to methods of legal determination which removed or minimized this necessity (e.g., *Halakhah ke-Batra'i*). Possessed a strong sense of justice, he spoke out courageously against decisions that were widely accepted at that time, but that he deemed unjust. He also displayed great independence *vis-`a-vis* his contemporaries. Firmly, though respectfully, he reproved Israel *Bruna for overstepping the bounds of his authority. When a blood libel was made against some Jews of Regensburg, and the neighboring communities refused to be taxed for their ransom (although agreeing to make voluntary payments), Colon decided that it was their duty, to pay the tax. Colon's zeal for halakhic truth and integrity led him into a dispute with Moses b. Elijah *Capsali of Turkey. Having been wrongly informed that the latter had made grievous errors in decisions concerning marital law, Colon wrote to the leaders of the Constantinople community, threatening to place Capsali under a ban if he did not cancel his decisions and do public penance. This unprecedented attack on the rights of the community aroused a furor in Constantinople. Capsali answered the attack vehemently. Soon many of the leading rabbis of the day were embroiled in the dispute, which ended when Colon learned that he had been the victim of intrigue. With this discovery, Colon's remorse was as swift and thorough as had been his rebuke, and he did all within his power to make amends to the victim of his unjust attack, to the degree of sending his son Perez to travel to Constantinople and beg forgiveness of Capsali. In addition to his previously published responsa, new material under the title *She'elot u-Teshuvot u-Fiskei ha-Maharik ha-Ḥadashim* has been edited by E.D. Pines (1984²). Colon was the author of a commentary on the *Sefer Mitzvot Gadol* of *Moses b. Jacob of Coucy, part of which was published in Munkacs (1899). A fuller edition was also published by E.D. Pines under the title, *Hiddushe u-Ferushe Mahatrik* (1984). His *Seder ha-Get* appeared in Judah Minz's *She'elot u-Teshuvot* (Venice, 1553). Other material has been published in various journals, while a significant amount remains in manuscript.

BIBLIOGRAPHY: Marmorstein, in: *Devir*, 2 (1923), 213–243; H. Rabinowicz, "The Life and Times of Rabbi Joseph Colon" (doctoral diss., Univ. of London, 1947; idem, in: JJS, 6 (1955), 166–70; idem, in: JQR, 47 (1956/7), 336–44; idem, in: *Historia Judaica*, 22 (1960), 61–70; Tamar, in: *Zion*, 18 (1952/53), 127–35; Colorini, in: *Annuario di studi Ebraici*, 1 (1934), 169–82. **ADD. BIBLIOGRAPHY:** Freimann, in: *Leket Yosher*, 2 (1904), XXXIII, no. 61; S.A. Horodetzky, in: *Le-Korot ha-Rabbanut* (1914), 45–55; I.H. Weiss, *Dor Dor ve-Dorshav*, 5 (1924), 269–73; U. Cassutto, *Encyclopædia Judaica*, 5 (1930), 629–31; Rosenthal, in: *Tarbiz*, 34 (1965), 74–76; Ben-Hayyim, in: *Moriah*, 2 (1970), 67–69; Y. Yudelev, in: *Sinai*, 67 (1970), 321–23; A. Fuchs, "Historical Material in the Responsa of Rabbi Israel Bruna" (doctoral diss., Yeshivah University, 1974); idem, in: *Zion*, 37 (1972), 183–96; M. Güdemann, *Geschichte des Erziehungswesens*, trans. A. Friedberg, 3 (1972), 186–90; Green, in: *Sinai*, 79 (1976),147–63; Sh. Simonsohn, *The History of the Jews in the Duchy of Mantua* (1977), 704–5; idem, *The Jews in the Duchy of Milan*, 2 (1982), 749 n. 1826; Booksbaum, in: *Shut u-Piskei Maharik ha-Ḥadashim*, E.D. Pines (ed.) (1984), xix–xlviii; R. Segre, *The Jews In Piedmont*, 2 (1986), 284 n. 617; J. Woolf, "The Life and Responsa of Rabbi Joseph Colon ben Solomon Trabotto" (doctoral diss., Harvard University, 1991); idem, in: *Sidra*, 10 (1995), 57–60; idem, in: *Tarbiz*, 66 (1996), 1–15; idem, in: *Italia*, 13 (1997); idem, in: AJS Review, 25 (2000–2001) and idem, in: *Be'erot Yitzhak* (2005).

[Abraham Hirsch Rabinowitz / Jeffrey R. Woolf (2nd ed.)]

COLONNE, JULES EDOUARD (**Judah**; 1838–1910), French violinist and conductor. Born in Bordeaux, he learned to play several instruments there. In 1855 he went to Paris and in 1857 entered the Paris Conservatory, where he won first prize for harmony and for violin. He became the leading violinist of the Paris Opéra and in the Lamoureux Quartet. In 1873 he founded the Organisation du Concert National, which became the Concerts du Châtelet, and finally the Concerts Colonne, which under his conductorship played an important role in fostering the performances of works by contemporary French and foreign composers; it was on performances of the works of Berlioz that his success was based. He was also the conductor of the official ten concerts at the Trocadero during the Paris Exposition Universelle of 1878, and appeared as visiting conductor in Europe and New York. In 1892 he joined the Paris Opera as artistic adviser and conductor.

BIBLIOGRAPHY: NG2, s. v.

[Amnon Shiloah (2nd ed.)]

COLOPHON, inscription at the end of a manuscript, of a book or part of a book written by the copyist, in which he records details of his work. Colophons were not added to every manuscript, and many of them have been lost because usually the last (and first) pages of the book were damaged. The colophon contains a number of details for the study of the text, for history in general, for the history of culture, and for paleography. It is generally written in the first person and tends to include the following details: the name of the copyist, the title of the work, the date of the completion of the copying, the place where it was copied, the name of the person for whom the work was copied or whether the scribe copied it for himself, and good wishes for the owner and for the copyist. Not all these details are included in every colophon, and their order is not always the same. Some colophons are very extensive. Others are brief, containing only the date of completion.

Names and Formulas of Blessings

The names mentioned in colophons usually include that of the father and at times also the family name. In Yemenite and Karaite manuscripts, several generations and even very lengthy genealogies are listed. The names are accompanied by colorful expressions of blessings for the living and the dead, which almost always take the form of *abbreviations. Some of these formulae are common to various cultural regions of the Middle Ages, while others are characteristic only of the land of origin. For example, the formula of blessing for the living, יי״א (= יִרְאֶה זֶרַע יַאֲרִיךְ יָמִים אָמֵן), "May he see his seed prolong his days" – based upon Isa. 53: 10 – and ישר״ו (= יִחְיֶה שָׁנִים רַבּוֹת וְטוֹבוֹת, "May he live many and pleasant years," or יַעֲמֹד וְיִחְיֶה שָׁנִים רַבּוֹת, "May he exist and live many years"), is characteristic of Italy, probably only from the middle of the 14th century. The formula of blessing for the dead, רי״ת (= רוּחַ ה׳ תְּנִיחֶנּוּ, "May the Spirit of the Lord cause him to rest" – Isa. 63:14), is characteristic of Oriental countries. The copyist often bestows flowery honorific titles on his customer. In later Yemenite manuscripts, it became customary for the copyist to precede his name by expressions of humility.

Places of Origin and Dates

The copyists were accustomed to note, in addition to the place of the copying, their own or the owner's places of origin, thus providing interesting historical information. Details of this category are especially found in manuscripts written in Italy. For example, an Oxford manuscript (Bodleian Library, Ms. Opp. Add. 302, fol. 37), was copied in Ancona in 1402, by a copyist from Perpignan for someone from Rome then living in קסא. The date was given according to the eras customary among Jews. In Italy, from the 15th century onward, a mixed date consisting of the Jewish year and the Roman month came to be employed. In Hebrew manuscripts written by apostates, the Christian year is also to be found. In many manuscripts, especially from the 15th century onward, the year is given in the *gematria* form of a word or words from a biblical verse. In many colophons, the day of the week and of the month is also given, thus making it possible – with the help of chronological tables – to verify the dates. In some manuscripts, the dates in the colophons were forged by changing the letters or by erasing and re-writing the date with the aim of antedating the manuscript. In others, whole colophons, which do not belong to the copyist, have been added, but these can be identified by the difference of handwriting. It appears that only in about one-third of the medieval manuscripts which have colophons is the place of copying mentioned. This is most often omitted in manuscripts written in Germany. It is sometimes difficult to identify the name of the place, because of the Hebrew spelling of the special Hebrew appellation of localities during the Middle Ages.

Felicitations

The final part of the colophon, the concluding felicitations, is often the longest. In manuscripts written for a specified person, it contains good wishes and blessings addressed to the future owner, and in many cases there are some for the copyist particularly when the manuscript is written for himself. Most express the wish that the owner or the copyist, his children, and his descendants would be allowed to study the book. Appropriate biblical verses were also added, the most popular being Joshua 1:8, as in one of the oldest European manuscripts (Prophets, Codex Reuchlin 3 of the Badische Landsbibliothek, Karlsruhe): "This Book of the Prophets, the Targum and the Text, was completed by Zerah b. Judah, the most humble of scribes, in the year 4866 of the Creation [1105/6] and in the year 1038 of the Destruction of the Temple, may it be speedily rebuilt in our days; may we be granted to study them [the Prophets] and to teach [them] without affliction or misfortune. May the verse be fulfilled in him: 'This book of the law shall not depart out of thy mouth, but thou shalt meditate therein day and night, that thou mayest observe to do according to all that is written therein; for then thou shalt make thy ways prosperous, and then thou shalt have good success.'"

Concluding Formulas

Next to the colophon, the copyists usually wrote further concluding formulas containing praises to the Creator or a blessing for the copyist. Various formulas are known, some written out in full and others in abbreviated form, either before or after the colophon. Some formulas of this category are, for example: בד״ח לב״א (= ברוך דיהב חילה לעבדיה בר אמתיה, "Blessed be the All Mercifull Who hath given strength to His servant the son of His maidservant"), בנל״כ ואע״י (= בָּרוּךְ נוֹתֵן לַיָּעֵף כֹּחַ וּלְאֵין אוֹנִים עָצְמָה יַרְבֶּה, "Blessed be He Who giveth strength to the faint and to him that hath no might increaseth power" (Isa. 40:29)); בילא״ו (= בָּרוּךְ ה׳ לְעוֹלָם אָמֵן וְאָמֵן, "Blessed be the Lord forever, Amen"); יֶשַׁע יִקְרַב ("May salvation come soon"); ברוך רחמנא דלצלן מריש ועד כאן ("Blessed be the All Merciful Who helped us from the beginning till now"); תַּם וְנִשְׁלַם שֶׁבַח [תְּהִלָּה] לְבוֹרֵא עוֹלָם ("[It is] finished and completed, praise [or "glory"] unto the Creator of the world"); ת״ל (= תּוֹדָה לָאֵל, "Thanks unto the Lord"); חֲזַק הַכּוֹתֵב וְאַמֵּיץ הַקּוֹרֵא ("Strengthen the writer and give courage to the reader"); כְּבוֹדְךָ ה׳ ("Thy glory, O Lord!"); and many others. One of the most famous formulas is חֲזַק וְנִתְחַזֵּק, הַסּוֹפֵר יֻזַּק לֹא הַיּוֹם וְלֹא לְעוֹלָם עַד אֲשֶׁר יַעֲלֶה חֲמוֹר בַּסֻּלָּם אֲשֶׁר יַעֲקֹב אָבִינוּ חָלַם ("Be strong and let us be strengthened, may the writer not come to any harm, neither today, nor ever after, until the ass ascends the ladder, of which Jacob our father dreamt"), which is found first in Ashkenazi manuscripts but which may have its origin in anti-Muslim polemics (cf. A. Altmann, in *Studies in Mysticism and Religion presented to G. Scholem* (1967), 1–33). Copyists usually inserted their names in this formula as well.

The Oldest Colophon

The most ancient colophon known is at the end of a manuscript of prophetical books of the Bible, found in the Karaite Synagogue of Cairo. It was written by Moses b. Asher in Tiberias in the year 827 after the destruction of the Temple (895/6 C.E.). This lengthy colophon contains all the details and rhetorics which are likely to appear in a colophon. In Ashkenazi manuscripts, the tendency is to write the colophon in very large letters. According to *Sefer Ḥasidim* (ed. Wistinetzki-Freimann, (1924), no. 700), it is forbidden to write the colophon in the actual manuscript of the biblical text. Colophons were also written in the form of poems, especially during the late Middle Ages, with the name of the copyist or the owner in acrostics. At times one can find in the colophon other valuable details, such as the time taken by the copyist (*Maḥzor Worms*, Jerusalem National Library, Ms. Heb. 4° 781) in the colophon of the year 1272 (it was copied in 44 weeks); the salary of the copyist; his adventures and biography; echoes of historical events and valuable information for the criticism of the text, the condition and quality of the original from which the copy was made, working conditions. Occasionally the copyist apologizes for mistakes made. The information as to whether the manuscript was copied by a professional copyist or not is naturally of importance for the criticism of the text. Besides the colophons of copyists, those of masoretes and punctuators in biblical and liturgic manuscripts are also found. In case the copyist also wrote the masorah and punctuated the manuscript, he usually pointed this out explicitly, as in a Jerusalem manuscript (Heb. 8° 2238): "I, Isaac ben Abraham ha-Levi, have written, punctuated, and added the masorah, with the aid of the Almighty, in the year 1418 of the Seleucid era [1106/7 C.E.]." The colophons of masoretes are sometimes hidden in letter decorations of the masorah. On rare occasions, the proofreader wrote the colophon. Those who completed the missing parts of manuscripts sometimes added their own colophons.

[Malachi Beit-Arie]

In Printed Books

When books were first printed, the colophon was used by the printer to convey information about himself and his assistants and about the date of the beginning and/or finishing of printing, as was the practice of manuscript copyists. It often contained apologies for mistakes or self-praise for their absence and sometimes, paeans in honor of the new and wonderful art of printing. One also finds in colophons the name of the ruler under whose protection the production took place, thanks to financial backers of the venture, the number of copies printed, and so on. The Jewish printer also used the colophon to give thanks to God for permitting him to accomplish his holy task and to pray that he might be enabled to continue his work and witness the restoration of the Temple. Warnings to respect the printers' copyright for a stated number of years, with references to the sanctions of rabbinic law, such as excommunication, were also inserted in the colophon. These appeared later in the approbations (see **Haskamot*). The formulas were much the same as those used in manuscripts. For the date the Jewish era was normally used, the year being given in general by complicated chronograms, which lead to much confusion in determining the exact dates.

The colophon in printed books is a source not only of bibliography but of the history of printing and Jewish genealogy in general, e.g., the colophon of Judah Halevi's *Kuzari* (Fano, 1506), which provides important data on the Yaḥya family. Colophons varied in size: in Rashi's commentary on the Pentateuch published by Soncino (Rimini, c. 1525) the colophon occupies a whole page. The length and shape was influenced by the space available, the idea being that, as in the Scroll of the Law (Sof. 1:12), no blank space must be left at the end. In works appearing in several volumes one occasionally finds a different colophon at the end of each volume, e.g., Meshullam Cusi's *Turim* (Pieve di Sacco, 1475 and after). Colophons were sometimes rhymed verse with an acrostic giving the name of the printer or even the proofreader.

The type used for the colophon was sometimes larger than that in the text, e.g., the Augsburg *Turim* (1540) or Ẓahalon's *Yesha Elohim* (Venice, 1595). Sometimes the colophon was printed in the shape of funnel, diamond, goblet, pyramid, or, very often, an inverted cone, the lines tapering off to a short line or a word. At a later stage the more elaborate title pages and approbations made the use of colophons superfluous.

BIBLIOGRAPHY: MANUSCRIPTS: M. Steinschneider, *Vorlesungen ueber die Kunde hebraeischer Handschriften* (1897), 44–56 (Heb. tr., *Harẓa'ot al Kitvei Yad Ivriyyim*, ed. by A.M. Habermann (1965), 61–75, 120–1); A. Freimann, in: zhb, 11 (1907), 86–96; 14 (1910), 105–12; idem, in: *Alexander Marx Jubilee Volume* (1950), 231–342; L. Zunz, in: ZHB, 18 (1915), 58–64, 101–19; C. Bernheimer, *Paleografia Ebraica* (1924), 149–63, 253–68. BOOKS: A. Berliner, *Ueber den Einfluss des ersten hebraeischen Buchdrucks* (1896); D.W. Amram, *Makers of Hebrew Books in Italy* (1909); A. Freimann (ed.), *Thesaurus typographiae hebraicae saeculi XV*, 8 pts. in 1 (1924–31); M. Steinschneider and D. Cassel, *Juedische Typographie* (1938).

COLORADO, U.S. state. Colorado was still an untamed wilderness when the discovery of gold near Pike's Peak in 1858 brought the area to the nation's attention. By the spring of 1859, fortune seekers began to arrive in droves. During the "big excitement," as the year of the gold discovery was called, at least 12 Jews of German descent migrated to Colorado to join the hunt for freedom, new opportunities, and wealth. Few Jews were miners, but most established small businesses in new towns and mining camps throughout Colorado. The first Rosh Hashanah service was held in Denver in 1859, and as men married and children were born, the fledgling Jewish community began to stabilize. Colorado Jews soon established a burial society, and in 1872 B'nai B'rith was founded in *Denver followed by the incorporation of Congregation Emanuel in 1874. Smaller Jewish communities were established in towns around the state such as Leadville, Cripple Creek, Central City, Colorado Springs, Trinidad, Ft. Collins, and Boulder, and synagogues were formed in each of these towns.

Jews became a vital component in the economic, social, and political development of Colorado. Fred Salomon opened the first general mercantile company in Colorado in 1859, David May located the first store of what was to become the May Company chain in Irwin, Colorado, in the 1870s, and in 1910 Jesse Shwayder and his brothers opened a small luggage factory that became one of the largest producers of luggage in America – the Samsonite Corporation. Wolfe Londoner, Denver's Jewish mayor, took office in 1889 and Simon *Guggenheim, part of the illustrious family whose fortune was rooted in mining activity in Leadville, Colorado, served as Colorado's only Jewish senator from 1906 to 1912.

By the turn of the century, Colorado had also become a mecca for health-seekers, primarily victims of tuberculo-

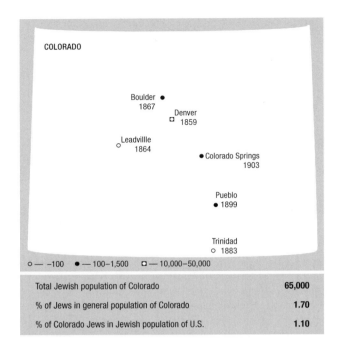

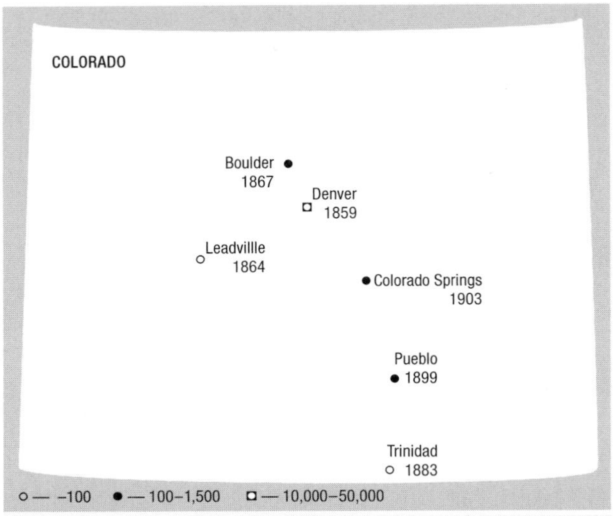

Total Jewish population of Colorado	**65,000**
% of Jews in general population of Colorado	**1.70**
% of Colorado Jews in Jewish population of U.S.	**1.10**

Jewish communities in Colorado and dates of establishment. Population figures for 2001.

sis, and was nicknamed the World's Sanitorium. The Jewish community was the first to step forward with aid for consumptives. Frances Wisebart *Jacobs, known as "Colorado's Mother of Charities," spearheaded a movement that resulted in the founding of National Jewish Hospital for Consumptives, largely by German Reform Jews, which opened in 1899. A large percentage of the health-seekers were East European Jews, who flocked to Colorado after 1900 and significantly augmented the state's Jewish population and established Denver's west side Orthodox Jewish community. In 1904, a second Jewish sanitorium, the Jewish Consumptives' Relief Society, was founded by East European Jews who wished to provide a more traditional Jewish setting for its patients. Both hospitals gave their services free of charge, served patients from throughout the United States, and were formally nonsectarian, although the vast majority of patients at both sanatoria were Jewish.

From the first, most of Colorado's Jews resided in its capital, the "Queen City" of Denver, although active Jewish congregations still exist in Boulder, Colorado Springs, Pueblo, Ft. Collins, Greeley, and Grand Junction, and newer small congregations have been established in the resort towns of Aspen, Vail, Steamboat Springs, Breckenridge, and Durango. While metro Denver hosts nearly 25 congregations, Boulder now claims five synagogues as well as a growing Jewish day school. Chabad is active in most Colorado communities. A small group of Jews was active in Aspen from its beginnings as a mining town. Hyman Avenue, one of the central thoroughfares in Aspen, is named in honor of Jewish pioneer David Hyman, an early investor. Because of their beautiful mountain locations, both Aspen and the much newer ski town of Vail have been popular sites for many national Jewish conferences and meetings.

A wide array of Jewish religious, cultural, and educational institutions abound. Denver hosts several day schools. Hillel Academy, the oldest of the day schools, was organized in 1953 as an Orthodox elementary school; Herzl Day School is described as a community Jewish day school; the Denver Academy of Torah is a Modern Orthodox elementary school. On the high school level, Yeshiva Toras Chaim is an Orthodox yeshivah high school for young men with a talmudic college-level religious studies program as well, and Beth Jacob High School serves young Jewish women. The Rocky Mountain Hebrew Academy (RMHA) is a co-ed private Jewish day school for secondary school students. In the late 1990s, Herzl and RMHA combined forces to open the new Denver Campus for Jewish Education. The Central Agency for Jewish Education serves as a coordinating agency for a number of Jewish educational programs in the area, and the Center for Judaic Studies at the University of Denver provides a variety of courses in Jewish studies for college students as well as housing the Rocky Mountain Jewish Historical Society and Beck Archives, and the Holocaust Awareness Institute. The Hillel Council of Colorado sponsors Hillel branches for Jewish students at the University of Colorado at Boulder, CU – Denver, Colorado State University, and the University of Denver.

Today, Colorado also hosts many charitable and social service organizations, some with a long history such as the Allied Jewish Federation of Colorado, B'nai B'rith, Hadassah, the National Council of Jewish Women, the American Jewish Committee, The Anti-Defamation League, the Jewish Family Service, and Shalom Park, an award-winning continuum retirement complex and nursing home. The last formal population survey conducted in 1998 estimated the Jewish population of the state as approximately 63,000, and in 2004, informal estimates placed the Denver-Boulder population alone at between 65,000 and 70,000.

[Jeanne E. Abrams (2nd ed.)]

COLORNI, VITTORE (1912–), Italian jurist. Born in Mantua, he lectured on the history of Italian law at the University of Ferrara, where he was appointed professor in 1956. Colorni was much esteemed as a pioneer in the study of the legal situation of the Jews in Italy from the Roman period to medieval times. In his major work, *Legge ebraica e leggi locali* (1945), Colorni examined the special status of the Jews and how far Jewish private law was recognized in Italy, tracing the history of rabbinical courts in the medieval Italian states. Colorni also wrote many articles on Mantuan Jewish history, on the names and history of ancient Jewish families, and on subjects of general interest, including "Teologi cristiani dell' Ottocento, precursori del Sionismo" (RMI, 21 (1955), 170–85) and the books, *Gli ebrei nel sistema del diritto comune fino alla* *prima emancipazione* (1956) and *L'uso del greco nella liturgia del giudaismo ellenistico* (1964).

ADD. BIBLIOGRAPHY: M. Perani (ed.), *Man Tov le Man Tovah. Una Manna buona per Mantova. Studi in onore di Vittore Colorni per il suo 92 compleanno* (2004), incl. bibl. of. Calorni's writings.

[Alfredo Mordechai Rabello / Alfredo Rabello (2nd ed.)]

COLUMBUS, capital of Ohio, U.S. The Jewish population of Columbus and the rest of Franklin County was estimated at 22,000 out of a total of 1,080,000 (roughly 2% of the total population) in 2001. Chosen for its central location, Columbus was founded in 1812 to serve as the state capital and was incorporated as a city in 1834. By 1840, the first Jewish families, the Nusbaums and the Gundersheimers, settled in the city. They had emigrated from the village of Mittelsinn in the northwest corner of Bavaria (Lower Franconia), and they earned their living in Columbus as peddlers and merchants. They were soon joined by a few other families from Mittelsinn and elsewhere in Germany. In 1851 the first congregation, B'nai Jeshurun, was organized. Orthodox services were held in a variety of locations and were led by educated laymen such as Simon Lazarus, who volunteered to serve as the new congregation's first religious leader. The following year, the city's first Jewish cemetery was established. By 1868, religious tensions led to a split in the small community, and 19 families organized a Reform congregation, B'nai Israel (now Temple Israel). Those supporting Reform included all of the surviving founders of B'nai Jeshurun, men who were now prosperous and well-established Columbus merchants. Within two years, B'nai Israel hired the city's first full-time ordained rabbi and dedicated the city's first synagogue building. Soon thereafter, B'nai Jeshurun folded and its members joined B'nai Israel. The growth of the congregation to over 100 families required a larger synagogue, which was completed in 1904 among the grand homes of the city's Olde Towne East neighborhood.

The arrival of Jews from Eastern Europe beginning in the 1880s brought greater diversity to religious life. In 1889, Agudas Achim was incorporated as an Orthodox congregation, formalizing a *minyan* that had been meeting for several years. Other Orthodox congregations developed to represent a particular ethnic group or style of worship. Those familiar with the Polish-Sephardi ritual (instead of the Ashkenazi ritual in place at Agudas Achim) organized Beth Jacob congregation in 1897. Hungarian immigrants formed Tifereth Israel in 1901. In 1913, another group desiring to use the Polish-Sephardi ritual created Ahavas Sholom. These congregations initially lacked the wealth and resources of Temple Israel. Their services took place in locations in the impoverished neighborhood where most East European Jews lived, immediately south and east of downtown. Agudas Achim dedicated its first synagogue building in 1896, moving to a larger structure in 1907. In 1908, the congregation hired its first ordained rabbi. Beth Jacob laid the cornerstone for its first synagogue in 1909. Tifereth Israel established its first permanent house of worship in 1915, while a converted stable next door to Agudas Achim served as home to Ahavas Sholom. Tifereth Israel joined the Conservative movement in 1922 and built a synagogue in 1927 in Olde Towne East. The structure, with additions and renovations in subsequent years, remains Tifereth Israel's home. It is the oldest synagogue building in continuous use in Columbus.

After World War II, most Jews moved farther east into the prosperous suburban enclave of Bexley and the surrounding Columbus neighborhoods of Berwick and Eastmoor. This area is still home to the greatest concentration of Jewish institutions: the Leo Yassenoff Jewish Center, Wexner Heritage Village (a care and housing facility for the elderly), Jewish Family Services, the Columbus Community Kollel, as well as synagogues Agudas Achim, Ahavas Sholom, and Beth Jacob. The Orthodox congregation Torat Emet was established in Bexley in 2001. Agudas Achim joined the Conservative movement in 2004. Although the East Side remained the heart of the Columbus Jewish community, in the early 21st century a majority of Jewish households lived in the suburban and fast-growing northern section of Franklin County. Temple Israel moved to the Far East Side of Columbus in 1959, and two more recent Reform congregations are located in northern Franklin County suburbs. Beth Tikvah, founded in 1961, is in Worthington. Temple Beth Shalom, founded in 1977, is in New Albany. Most of the Jews living in the northern suburbs, however, were unaffiliated and did not actively participate in Jewish communal organizations.

In the early 21st century, Columbus natives represented only a minority of the Jewish community. Most Jews had moved to the area, with steady population growth accelerating in the decades after World War II. Between 1975 and 2001, the Jewish population of Franklin County grew by an estimated 60 percent and included the resettlement of more than 1,400 Jews from the former Soviet Union. This rapid influx made the dynamics of the Columbus Jewish community more akin to those of quickly growing Southern and Western U.S. cities than to other Ohio communities. In fact, at the beginning of the 21st century, the Columbus Jewish community was on the verge of overtaking Cincinnati as the second-largest in the state after Cleveland. New Jewish institutions were emerging. A second Jewish newspaper, *The New Standard*, began publication in 2003, in competition with *The Ohio Jewish Chronicle*, which started in 1922. The Columbus Jewish Day School, an egalitarian elementary school modeled on the Heschel School in New York, opened in 1998 as an alternative to Columbus Torah Academy, an Orthodox K-12 day school in operation since 1958.

In the early years of the community, many Jews in Columbus earned their living in retail activities. Simon Lazarus' descendants developed his clothing store into a major department-store chain in the Midwest which continued to bear the Lazarus name until 2005, when the stores were merged into Macy's. In the early 21st century, retail and real-estate development continued as important businesses for Columbus Jews, though many members of the community were involved in professions such as law and medicine. As a center of government, insurance, and education, Columbus provided employment opportunities for the highly educated Jewish community. In particular, Ohio State University has attracted many Jewish faculty and students (it was estimated that more than 3,500 Jewish students were attending Ohio State in 2005), and the university has a well-respected Jewish studies program, employing distinguished Jewish scholars such as Marvin Fox. The campus area is host to student centers from both the Hillel and Chabad organizations.

The Jewish community has enjoyed friendly relations with its non-Jewish neighbors. Antisemitism was restricted primarily to social organizations and was far more prevalent at the beginning of the 20th century than at the beginning of the 21st. Jews have taken prominent roles in local government in both the Republican and Democratic parties, most notably U.S. Congressman Robert N. Shamansky (Democrat, 1981–83), Columbus City Council members Melville D. Frank (Republican, 1930–37) and Maurice D. Portman (Democrat, 1966–96), Franklin County Treasurer Philip Goldslager (Democrat, 1967–73), and state representative and senator David Goodman (Republican, from 1998). For decades, Jews have regularly served as judges in elected and administrative courts in Franklin County. The community has gained international prominence through the Jewish philanthropy of Samuel M. *Melton (1900–1993), Leslie H. Wexner (1937–), and members of the Schottenstein family. Notable achievers who grew up in Columbus include cancer researcher Dr. Judah Folkman (1933–), author and columnist Bob Greene (1947–), and cabaret performer Michael Feinstein (1956–).

BIBLIOGRAPHY: M.L. Raphael, *Jews and Judaism in a Midwestern Community: Columbus, Ohio, 1840–1975* (1979).

[Michael Meckler (2nd ed.)]

COLUMBUS, CHRISTOPHER (1451–1500), discoverer of America, thought by some to have been of Marrano extraction. He was himself mysterious when speaking of his origin, apparently having something in his background which he wished to conceal. However, he boasted cryptically about his connection with King David and had a penchant for Jewish and Marrano society. Spanish scholars have attempted to explain the fact that this great hero of Spanish history was almost certainly born in Genoa, Italy, by the assumption that his parents were Jewish or ex-Jewish refugees from Spain. In fact, the name Colon (or Colombo) was not uncommon among Italian Jews of the late medieval period. A document recently discovered suggests that Columbus was of Majorcan origin, and almost certainly belonged to a Marrano family: but the authenticity of the document still remains to be proved. On the other hand, Columbus' mysterious signature, which he adjured his son always to use, is susceptible to a Hebraic interpretation, which is no more improbable than the many other solutions that have been proposed. It is remarkable moreover that Columbus began his account of his voyage with a reference to the expulsion of the Jews from Spain; that in one document he refers to the Second Temple in Jerusalem by the Hebraic term "Second House"; that he dates its destruction as being in the year 68, in accordance with the Jewish tradition; and that he seems to have deliberately postponed the day of his sailing until August 3, while all was ready for the purpose on the previous day, which was the unpropitious fast day of the Ninth of Av commemorating the destruction of the Temple. The mystery regarding Columbus' origins is largely the outcome of his own mendacity: and as a result it is equally impossible to exclude or to confirm the hypothesis that he was descended from a Jewish or ex-Jewish family.

The fact that he ultimately received the patronage of the Spanish sovereigns for his expedition was in large measure due to the enthusiasm and help of a group of New Christians around the Aragonese court, notably Luis de *Santangel and Gabriel *Sanchez as well as to some extent Isaac *Abrabanel. It was in fact to Santangel and Sanchez that Columbus wrote the famous account of his success on his return, which was immediately published and circulated throughout Europe in two recensions – one addressed to the former, the other to the latter. On his journeys, the explorer used the nautical instruments perfected by Jews such as Joseph *Vecinho, and the nautical tables drawn up by Abraham *Zacuto. It was formerly stated that several of the crew on his first voyage were of Jewish birth, but this was true in fact of only one of them – the interpreter Luis de *Torres, who had been baptized immediately before the expedition set sail.

[Cecil Roth]

The motivations behind Columbus' travels were varied. Alongside Franciscan-Joachimite traditions of the coming Third Age, Columbus had been interested for many years in biblical prophecies. He had collected them long before his first journey and later on as well, after his discoveries had verified his expectations. These prophecies are collected in his *Libro de las profecías*, where he uses well-known Catholic medieval authors. The chiliastic plans included not only the liberation of Jerusalem but the establishment of the Temple. The gold brought from the New World was supposed to serve for the coming crusade.

Unlike his entirely negative attitude to the Muslims, Columbus saw the Jews and Jewish tradition in a more positive light, as part of the religious quest of humanity.

The discoveries of Columbus were echoed in Jewish sources; a collection of correspondence from 16th century Italy (Firenze, Biblioteca Medicea Laurentiana, Ms. Plut. 88.12 p. 13v) refers to the return of the second expedition (1496). A Hebrew translation of a book describing the discoveries in the New World was made in Voltaggio (near Genoa) in 1557, refering specifically to "the new world found by Columbus."

[Roni Weinstein (2nd ed.)]

BIBLIOGRAPHY: M. Kayserling, *Christopher Columbus and the Participation of the Jews in the Spanish and Portuguese Discoveries* (1907); S. de Madariaga, *Christopher Columbus* (Eng., 1940); C. Roth, *Personalities and Events in Jewish History* (1953), 192–211; Cantera, in: *Atlántida*, no. 9 (May–June, 1964), 303–10; R. Llanas de Niubó, *El Enigma de Cristóbal Colón* (1964). **ADD. BIBLIOGRAPHY:** H.I. Avalos, "Columbus as Biblical Exegete: A Study of the 'Libro de las profecías,'" in: *Studies in Jewish Civilization*, 5 (1996), 59–80; G. Pistarino, "Christians and Jews, Pagans and Muslims in the Thought of Christopher Columbus," in: *Mediterranean Historical Review*, 10:1–2 (1995), 259–271; L.I. Sweet, "Christopher Columbus and the Millennial Vision of the New World," in: *Catholic Historical Review*, 72:3 (1986), 369–82.

COMA (Koma), HERZ, *dayyan* and leader of the Vienna community at the time of the 1670 expulsion. He was one of the signatories of the letter sent by the community to Manuel Texeira asking him to petition Queen Christina of Sweden to intervene. In another effort he and Leo *Winkler offered the emperor *Leopold I 100,000 florins if he would allow 1,000 Jews to stay in Vienna. After the death of Hirschel *Meyer (c. 1673–75), Coma became the leader of the Viennese Jews who had settled in *Mikulov (Nikolsburg). Acting through the archduchess of Innsbruck, he again endeavored to obtain the return of the Jews to Austria.

BIBLIOGRAPHY: D. Kaufmann, *Die letzte Vertreibung der Juden aus Wien* (1889), 132–4, 168–70.

COMAY, MICHAEL SAUL (1908–1987), Israeli diplomat. Born in Cape Town, Comay studied and practiced law in South Africa. He served in the South African Army from 1940 to 1945, reaching the rank of major. From 1946 to 1948 Comay represented the South African Zionist Federation in the political department of the *Jewish Agency, Jerusalem. From 1948 he held several positions in the Ministry for Foreign Affairs and from 1953 to 1957 was Israeli ambassador to Canada. In 1960 Comay was appointed Israel's permanent representative to the UN. He was named political adviser to the minister for foreign affairs in 1967 and was appointed Israeli ambassador to Britain in 1970. Comay's term of office as Israeli ambassador to Great Britain ended in 1973, when he reached the age of retirement.

[Benjamin Jaffe]

COMDEN, BETTY (Elizabeth Cohen; 1919–), U.S. theatrical writer. Born in Brooklyn, New York, Comden studied drama at New York University and graduated with a B.Sc. While a student, she acted with the Washington Square Players. She was a member of "The Revuers," a satirical nightclub act that included, among others, Adolph *Green (1914–2002). Comden went on to write the Broadway scores for *Wonderful Town* (1953), *Peter Pan* (1954), and *Do Re Mi* (1960). She was also the co-librettist for *On the Town* (1944), *Billion Dollar Baby* (1945), *Two on the Aisle* (1951), *Bells Are Ringing* (1956), *Say, Darling* (1958), *Subways Are for Sleeping* (1961), *Fade Out – Fade In* (1964), and *Hallelujah, Baby* (1967).

Joining ASCAP in 1945, she teamed up with Adolph Green as her chief lyrics, libretto, and screenplay collaborator; her main musical collaborators were Leonard *Bernstein, Jule *Styne, Morton Gould, and Andre *Previn. The team of Comden and Green became the longest-running creative partnership in theater history. They wrote the book for the Broadway play *Applause* (1970) as well as the book and lyrics for *On the Twentieth Century* (1978) and *A Doll's Life* (1982). In 1991, they wrote the lyrics for the Broadway musical *The Will Rogers Follies*. As performers, they appeared in *On the Town*, and later did an evening at the Golden Theater, entitled *A Party with Betty Comden and Adolph Green*, composed of material from their own shows and movies, and from their act, "The Revuers."

Their many film musicals include *Singin' in the Rain*; *The Band Wagon*; *On the Town*; *Bells Are Ringing*; *It's Always Fair Weather*; *Good News*; and *The Barkleys of Broadway*. Much to the credit of Comden and Green, *Singin' in the Rain* has been named one of the ten best American films ever made and, by a vote of international film critics, was chosen as number three of the ten best films of all time.

Comden's string of longstanding popular songs includes "New York, New York," "Lonely Town," "The Party's Over," "Just in Time," "Ohio," "A Little Bit in Love," "The French Lesson," "Long before I Knew You," "Never-Neverland," "Make Someone Happy," and "I'm Just Taking My Time."

Comden and Green were members of the Council of the Dramatists' Guild, were inducted into the Theater Hall of Fame and the Songwriters Hall of Fame, and received the Mayor of New York's Certificate of Excellence.

In 1953, they won the Writers Guild of America's Screen Award for *Singin' in the Rain* for Best Written American Musical and, in 1961, the same award for *Bells Are Ringing*. In 1991, they were the recipients of the Kennedy Center Honors Lifetime Achievement Award. In 2001, they received the Writers Guild of America's Laurel Award for Screen Writing Achievement. And in 2002, the Dramatists' Guild presented the duo with its third Lifetime Achievement Award in Theatrical Writing (the previous recipients included Arthur Miller and Edward Albee).

Comden received the Theatre World Award (1945), the Woman of the Year Award from the Alumni Association of New York University, and the Kaufmann Center's Creative Arts Award (2003).

As for Comden's own work, *Wonderful Town* won a Tony Award for Best Musical (1953). *A Party* received an Obie Award when it was first performed (1958). *Hallelujah, Baby* won two Tonys – Best Musical, and Best Composer and Lyricist (1968). *Applause* won the Tony in 1970 for Best Musical. In 1978, *On the Twentieth Century* won Tonys for Best Original Score and Best Book of a Musical. And in 1991, *The Will Rogers Follies* won a Tony for Best Original Score, and the cast recording won the Grammy Award for Best Musical Show album. In 1995, Comden published her autobiography, entitled *Off Stage*.

BIBLIOGRAPHY: A.M. Robinson, *Betty Comden and Adolph Green: A Bio-Biography* (1993).

[Ruth Beloff (2nd ed.)]

COMISSIONA, SERGIU (1928–), Israeli and American conductor of Romanian birth. Comissiona studied violin and conducting at the Bucharest Conservatory, making his conducting debut at the age of 17. After an early career as a violinist, he was appointed music director of the Romanian State Opera in Bucharest (1955–59). He immigrated to Israel in 1959, where he was music director of the Haifa SO (1959–66) and founder-conductor of the Ramat Gan Chamber Orchestra (1960–67). In 1963 he appeared in North America as conductor of the Israel Chamber Orchestra. A familiar figure in more than 25 countries, Comissiona led virtually all of the world's major symphony orchestras in performances acclaimed for their interpretative fire and musical and orchestral discipline. As music director, he transformed the Baltimore SO into a truly professional ensemble (1969–84) and brought the Vancouver SO back to musical health (1991–2000). He frequently conducted opera, chiefly at Covent Garden and the New York City Opera. In the early 2000s he held several important musical posts, among them as principal guest conductor of the Jerusalem SO and the Georges Enescu Bucharest Philharmonic. As conductor laureate of the Asian Youth Orchestra, he led the ensemble on its tour in the Far East (2004). Comissiona has a clear preference for Romantic and Impressionist repertory. Among his recordings are works by Saint-Saëns, Ravel, Britten, Blomdahl, and Wirén. He received honors and awards from the Romanian and French governments as well as from Johns Hopkins University and the Peabody Conservatory. Comissiona and his wife became American citizens on July 4, 1976.

BIBLIOGRAPHY: Grove online; Baker's Biographical Dictionary (1997); "Comissiona's 'Vitamins of Happiness,'" in: *Opera News*, 52 (July 1987) 26–27.

[Naama Ramot (2nd ed.)]

COMITÉ DES DELEGATIONS JUIVES (**Committee of Jewish Delegations**), body established at the end of World War I, at the initiative of the Zionist Organization, to alert the Paris peace conference to the grave situation of the Jews in various European countries and to obtain international guarantees for safeguarding their rights (see *Versailles, Treaty of). Apart from the French and British delegations – who refused to join the Committee on account of its "nationalist" demands – the Committee included all the Jewish delegations sent to Paris to bring the Jewish demands before the peace conference. Among them were the representatives of the Jewish National Assemblies, Councils, and Committees formed in most East and Southeast European Jewish communities after the war – the Jewish minorities whose fate was at stake. Other delegations represented the American and Canadian Jewish Congresses, the Constituent Assembly of Ereẓ Israel Jews, the World Zionist Organization, the American Jewish Committee, and B'nai B'rith, among others. Since most of these delegations had been elected on a democratic basis, the Committee could describe itself as representing 12 million Jews.

The memorandum of the Committee, dated May 10, 1919, but officially submitted on June 10, 1919, called upon the peace conference to include in the treaties with the new states, and those whose territory was to be considerably enlarged, specific provisions guaranteeing individual rights to the members of the minorities living in these countries, and collective national rights to each minority as a group (see *minority rights). The memorandum called, among other things, for the right of all inhabitants to protection of life, liberty, and property and of freedom of religion; the right of all citizens to enjoy equal civil, religious, national, and political rights; the right of the national minorities to use their own language in their public activities and to be recognized as distinct and autonomous organizations having the right to establish, manage, and control schools and religious, educational, charitable, and social institutions; to receive a proportionate part of the state and municipal budgets for these institutions; to tax their members; and have proportional representation in state, municipal, and elective bodies. These provisions were to be embodied in the fundamental laws of the country and recognized as obligations of international concern, subject to the supervision of the *League of Nations; furthermore, every state which was a party to the treaties, and every minority affected by their violation, was to have the right of appeal to the League or to any Tribunal that might be established by the League. The memorandum was drafted in general terms, referring to all minorities in the newly created or enlarged states, and was not restricted to Jewish minorities only. It had a profound effect upon the minority treaties as they were eventually adopted. Not all of the Committee demands were accepted; thus, the term "national minority" was replaced by the more cautious phrase "ethnic, linguistic, and religious minority"; nor were the minorities recognized as autonomous bodies, as the Committee had proposed, though they did grant them certain rights relating to language and culture, which – by their very nature – were group and not individual rights.

In another memorandum, the Committee demanded of the peace conference to hold the countries concerned responsible for the pogroms that might have taken place within their boundaries since the outbreak of the war, or might take place subsequently, and to pay compensation to the victims. A third memorandum supported the historic rights of the Jewish people to Ereẓ Israel and called for the creation of political, administrative, and economic conditions that would ensure the establishment of the Jewish National Home.

The Committee was not disbanded after the Peace Conference, and it remained in existence up to 1936, when the *World Jewish Congress succeeded it. Throughout this period the Committee was active in safeguarding the rights granted to Jews in the minority treaties, in combating antisemitism, and in promoting the participation of Jews as Jews in the work of international nongovernmental organizations. In the early postwar years the Committee concentrated on the struggle against the wave of anti-Jewish pogroms in Eastern Europe, especially the Ukraine. It also intervened to protect the right to nationality or to reasonable conditions for its acquisition by naturalization in several East and Central European countries, against the expulsion of Jewish war refugees, and against the *numerus clausus at the universities in such countries as Poland and Romania. The Committee was instrumental in the establishment of the World Jewish Aid Conference (1920), which was concerned with the economic rehabilitation of Jews in different countries. The Committee was also very active in assisting the defense of Shalom Schwarzbard, who in 1927 shot and killed *Petlyura to avenge the murder of Ukrainian Jews.

In 1933 the Committee took energetic steps following the rise of Hitler when the first Nazi anti-Jewish discriminatory legislation was introduced. Since Germany was not among the states on which the peace conference had imposed the system of international protection of minorities, there was no legal basis for bringing up before the League of Nations the question of the position of the Jews in the whole of Germany. The Committee therefore had to rely on the limited framework of the German-Polish Convention of 1922, under which Germany undertook, for a transitional period of 15 years, to guarantee the rights of all the minorities in Upper Silesia in line with the provisions of the minority treaties. On May 17, 1933, two petitions were submitted to the League of Nations: one signed by the Committee and other Jewish institutions and organizations, and the second by Franz Bernheim, a store clerk in Upper Silesia who had been dismissed under the new anti-Jewish legislation (see *Bernheim Petition). Despite all the efforts made by the Nazi representatives to prevent discussion of the affair, and even have it removed from the agenda, the Committee succeeded in having the petition publicly debated at the League. All the speakers denounced the persecution of the Jews in Germany and energetically condemned curtailment of Jewish rights.

This was the first time after Hitler's accession to power that his regime was censured from the platform of the League of Nations. Nazi Germany was forced to honor the rights of the Jews in Upper Silesia until 1937, the expiration date of the German-Polish agreement. In October 1933, as a result of the Committee's efforts, the League of Nations Assembly held a searching debate on the oppression of the Jews in Nazi Germany and decided on the appointment of a High Commissioner for Refugees (Jewish and others) from Germany; the Committee took an active part in the work of the Commissioner through its membership on the Advisory Council set up to assist him. Owing to the efforts of the Committee and other Jewish organizations, the Jews of the Saar Territory were allowed to leave the territory and take their belongings with them within one year from its return to Germany resulting from the plebiscite held in 1935.

The Committee was headed, successively, by Julian *Mack, Louis *Marshall, and Nahum *Sokolow. Its secretary-general was Leo *Motzkin, from 1924 also acting president; upon the latter's death, in 1933, Nahum *Goldmann was elected president and, in 1935, Stephen S. *Wise. During its period of existence, the Committee published a wide range of books, pamphlets, and bulletins on the Jewish problem in various languages.

BIBLIOGRAPHY: *Proceedings of Adjourned Session of American Jewish Congress Including Report of Commission to Peace Conference and of Provisional Organization for Formation of American Jewish Congress* (1920); D.H. Miller, *My Diary at the Peace Conference, with Documents* (1928); N. Feinberg, *La Question des Minorités à la Conférence de la Paix de 1919–1920 et l'Action Juive en Faveur de la Protection Internationale des Minorités* (1929); O.I. Janowsky, *Jews and Minority Rights, 1898–1919* (1933), 253–383; *Unity in Dispersion. A History of the World Jewish Congress* (1948), 9–41; Y. Tennenbaum, *Bein Milḥamah ve-Shalom* (1960); N. Feinberg, *Ha-Ma'arakhah ha-Yehudit Neged Hitler* (1957); idem, in: ILR, 3 (1968).

[Nathan Feinberg]

COMMAGENE, small kingdom on the upper Euphrates, between Cilicia and Armenia (modern southeastern Turkey). In 17 C.E. Commagene became a Roman province. However, the monarchy was restored by Claudius (41) and Antiochus IV Epiphanes reigned there until 72, when the land was reannexed to Syria by Vespasian. Several marital ties existed between the rulers of Commagene and the Herods of Judea. Tigranes, great-grandson of Herod the Great, married his son Alexander to Jotape, daughter of King Antiochus of Commagene. Drusilla, daughter of Agrippa I, was to marry Epiphanes, the son of Antiochus, but this agreement was canceled when Epiphanes refused to convert to Judaism. Antiochus of Commagene was among the kings entertained by Agrippa I at Tiberias, a gathering that aroused the suspicions of Marsus, Roman governor of Syria. During the Jewish rebellion of 66–70 C.E., contingents from Commagene were among those which fought for Rome.

BIBLIOGRAPHY: Jos., Wars, 2:500; 3:68; 5:461; 7:219–25; Jos., Ant., 18:53, 140; 19:276, 338, 355; 20:139; Klausner, Bayit Sheni, 4 (1950[2]), 292.

[Isaiah Gafni]

COMMANDMENTS, THE 613 (Heb. תַּרְיַ״ג מִצְווֹת, *taryag mitzvot*). The total number of biblical commandments (precepts and prohibitions) is given in rabbinic tradition as 613. R. Simlai, a Palestinian teacher, states: "613 commandments were revealed to Moses at Sinai, 365 being prohibitions equal in number to the solar days, and 248 being mandates corresponding in number to the limbs of the human body" (Mak. 23b). (See the table "613 Commandments.") The number 613 usually known by the Hebrew mnemonic, תַּרְיַ״ג (Ta-RYa-G – ת = 400, ר = 200, י = 10, ג = 3), is found as early as tannaitic times in the sayings of Simeon b. Eleazar (Mekh. Yitro, Ba-Ḥodesh, 5, only in ed. by I.H. Weiss (1865), 74 [75a]), Simeon b. Azzai (Sif. Deut 76 where the 365 prohibitions are mentioned), and Eleazar b. Yose the Galilean (Mid. Hag. to Gen. 15:1) and is apparently based upon an ancient tradition (see Tanh. B.,

A list of the commandments as enumerated by Maimonides. The subheadings do not appear in *Sefer ha-Mitzvot* but are added here as a guide to the general reader. It should be noted that the biblical sources are given according to the rabbinic interpretation, which is sometimes not the obvious meaning of the verse cited.

MANDATORY COMMANDMENTS		
	God	
1. Ex. 20:2 3. Deut. 6:5 4. Deut. 6:13 6. Deut. 10:20 7. Deut. 10:20 9. Lev. 22:32	The Jew is required to [1]believe that God exists and to [2]acknowledge His unity; to [3]love, [4]fear, and [5]serve Him. He is also commanded to [6]cleave to Him (by associating with and imitating the wise) and to [7]swear only by His name. One must [8]imitate God and [9]sanctify His name.	2. Deut. 6:4 5. Ex. 23:25; Deut. 11:13 (Deut. 6:13 and also 13:5) 8. Deut. 28:9
	Torah	
10. Deut. 6:7 11. Deut. 6:7 12. Deut. 6:8 13. Deut. 6:8 16. Deut. 31:12 17. Deut. 17:18 18. Deut. 31:19	The Jew must [10]recite the Shema each morning and evening and [11]study the Torah and teach it to others. He should bind tefillin on his [12]head and [13]his arm. He should make [14]ẓiẓit for his garments and [15]fix a mezuzah on the door. The people are to be [16] assembled every seventh year to hear the Torah read and [17]the king must write a special copy of the Torah for himself. [18]Every Jew should have a Torah scroll. One should [19]praise God after eating.	14. Num. 15:38 15. Deut. 6:9 19. Deut. 8:10.
	Temple and the Priests	
20. Ex. 25:8 22. Num. 18:4 24. Ex. 30:19 25. Ex. 27:21 26. Num. 6:23 30. Lev. 6:3 31. Num. 5:2 33. Ex. 28:2 34. Num. 7:9 35. Ex. 30:31	The Jews should [20]build a Temple and [21]respect it. It must be [22]guarded at all times and the [23]Levites should perform their special duties in it. Before entering the Temple or participating in its service, the priests [24]must wash their hands and feet; they must also [25]light the candelabrum daily. The priests are required to [26]bless Israel and to [27]set the shewbread and frankincense before the Ark. Twice daily they must [28]burn the incense on the golden altar. Fire shall be kept burning on the altar [29]continually and the ashes should be [30]removed daily. Ritually unclean persons must be [31]kept out of the Temple. Israel [32]should honor its priests, who must be [33]dressed in special priestly raiment. The priests should [34]carry the Ark on their shoulders, and the holy anointing oil [35]must be prepared according to its special formula. The priestly families should officiate in [36]rotation. In honor of certain dead close relatives, the priests should [37]make themselves ritually unclean. The high priest may marry [38]only a virgin.	21. Lev. 19:30 23. Num. 18:23 27. Ex. 25:30 28. Ex. 30:7 29. Lev. 6:6 32. Lev. 21:8 36. Deut. 18:6–8 37. Lev. 21:2–3 38. Lev. 21:13
	Sacrifices	
39. Num. 28:3 43. Lev. 23:36 44. Lev. 23:10 46. Lev. 23:17 47. Num. 29:1–2 49. Lev. 16 50. Num. 29:13 51. Num. 29:36	The [39]tamid sacrifice must be offered twice daily and the [40]high priest must also offer a meal-offering twice daily. An additional sacrifice (musaf) should be offered [41]every Sabbath, [42]on the first of every month, and [43]on each of the seven days of Passover. On the second day of Passover [44]a meal offering of the first barley must also be brought. On Shavuot a [45]musaf must be offered and [46]two loaves of bread as a wave offering. The additional sacrifice must also be made on [47]Rosh Ha-Shanah and [48]on the Day of Atonement when the [49]Avodah must also be performed. On every day of the festival of [50]Sukkot a musaf must be brought as well as on the [51]eighth day thereof. Every male Jew should make a [52]pilgrimage to the Temple three times	40. Lev. 6:13 41. Num. 28:9 42. Num. 28:11 45. Num. 28:26–27 48. Num. 29:7–8 52. Ex. 23:14

53. Ex. 34:23	a year and [53]appear there during the three pilgrim Festivals. One should	
Deut. 16:16	[54]rejoice on the Festivals.	54. Deut. 16:14
55. Ex. 12:6	On the 14th of Nisan one should [55]slaughter the paschal lamb and [56]eat	
56. Ex. 12:8	of its roasted flesh on the night of the 15th. Those who were ritually	
57. Num. 9:11	impure in Nisan should slaughter the paschal lamb on [57]the 14th of	
	Iyyar and eat it with [58]mazzah and bitter herbs.	
59. Num. 10:10;	Trumpets should be [59]sounded when the festive sacrifices are brought	58. Num. 9:11;
Num. 10:9.	and also in times of tribulation.	Ex. 12:8
60. Lev. 22:27	Cattle to be sacrificed must be [60]at least eight days old and [61]without	61. Lev. 22:21
62. Lev. 2:13	blemish. All offerings must be [62]salted. It is a mitzvah to perform the	
64. Lev. 6:18	ritual of [63]the burnt offering, [64]the sin offering, [65]the guilt offering, [66]the	63. Lev. 1:2
66. Lev. 3:1	peace offering, and [67]the meal offering.	65. Lev. 7:1
68. Lev. 4:13	Should the Sanhedrin err in a decision, its members [68]must bring a sin	67. Lev. 2:1; 6:7
	offering which offering must also be brought [69]by a person who has	
69. Lev. 4:27	unwittingly transgressed a karet prohibition (i.e., one which, if done	
	deliberately, would incur karet). When in doubt as to whether one has	
70. Lev. 5:17–18	transgressed such a prohibition, a [70]"suspensive" guilt offering must	
	be brought.	
71. Lev. 5:15, 21–25;	For [71]stealing or swearing falsely and for other sins of a like nature, a	
19:20–21	guilt offering must be brought. In special circumstances the sin offering	
	[72]can be according to one's means.	72. Lev. 5:1–11
73. Num. 5:6–7	One must [73]confess one's sins before God and repent for them.	
74. Lev. 15:13–15	A [74]man or [75]a woman who has a seminal issue must bring a sacrifice;	75. Lev. 15:28–29
76. Lev. 12:6	a woman must also bring a sacrifice [76]after childbirth. A leper must	
	[77]bring a sacrifice after he has been cleansed.	77. Lev. 14:10
78. Lev. 27:32	One must [78]tithe the one's cattle. The [79]firstborn of clean (i.e., permitted)	79. Ex. 13:2
	cattle are holy and must be sacrificed. The firstborn of man must be	
80. Ex. 22:28;	[80]redeemed. The firstborn of the ass must be [81]redeemed; if not, [82]its	81. Ex. 34:20
Num. 18:15	neck has to be broken.	82. Ex. 13:13
83. Deut. 12:5–5	Animals set aside as offerings [83]must be brought to Jerusalem without	
84. Deut. 12:14	delay and [84]may be sacrificed only in the Temple. Offerings from	
85. Deut. 12:26	outside the land of Israel [85]may also be brought to the Temple.	
86. Deut. 12:15	Sanctified animals [86]which have become blemished must be redeemed.	
87. Lev. 27:33	A beast exchanged for an offering [87]is also holy.	
89. Ex. 29:33	The priests should eat [88]the remainder of the meal offering and [89]the	88. Lev. 6:9
	flesh of sin and guilt offerings; but consecrated flesh which has	
91. Lev. 7:17	become [90]ritually unclean or [91]which was not eaten within its appointed	90. Lev. 7:19
	time must be burned.	
	Vows	
92. Num. 6:5	A Nazirite must [92]let his hair grow during the period of his separation.	
93. Num. 6:18	When that period is over, he must [93]shave his head and bring his	
	sacrifice.	
94. Deut. 23:24	A man must [94]honor his vows and his oaths which a judge can [95]annul	95. Num. 30:3.
	only in accordance with the law.	
	Ritual Purity	
96. Lev. 11:8, and 24	Anyone who touches [96]a carcass or [97]one of the eight species of reptiles	97. Lev. 11:29–31
98. Lev. 11:34	becomes ritually unclean; food becomes unclean by [98]coming into	
	contact with a ritually unclean object. Menstruous women [99]and those	99. Lev. 15:19
100. Lev. 12:2	[100]bedridden after childbirth are ritually impure. A [101]leper, [102]a leprous	102. Lev. 13:51
101. Lev. 13:3	garment, and [103]a leprous house are all ritually unclean. A man having	103. Lev. 14:44

105. Lev. 15:16	[104]a running issue is unclean, as is [105]semen. A woman suffering from	104. Lev. 15:2
106. Lev. 15:19	[106]running issue is also impure. A [107]human corpse is ritually unclean.	
107. Num. 19:14	The purification water (mei niddah) purifies [108]the unclean, but it makes	108. Num. 19:13, 21
109. Lev. 15:16	the clean ritually impure. It is a mitzvah to become ritually clean [109]by	
110. Lev. 14:2	ritual immersion. To become cleansed of leprosy, one [110]must follow	
	the specified procedure and also [111]shave off all of one's hair. Until	111. Lev. 14:9
	cleansed, the leper [112]must be bareheaded with clothing in disarray	112. Lev. 13:45
	so as to be easily distinguishable.	
113. Num. 19:2–9	The ashes of [113]the red heifer are to be used in the process of ritual	
	purification.	
	Donations to the Temple	
114. Lev. 27:2–8	If a person [114]undertakes to give his own value to the Temple, he must	
116. Lev. 27:14	do so. Should a man declare [115]an unclean beast, [116]a house, or [117]a	115. Lev. 27:11–12
	field as a donation to the Temple, he must give their value in money	117. Lev. 27:16, 22–23
	as fixed by the priest. If one unwittingly derives benefit from Temple	
118. Lev. 5:16	property, [118]full restitution plus a fifth must be made.	
119. Lev. 19:24	The fruit of [119]the fourth year's growth of trees is holy and may be eaten	
	only in Jerusalem. When you reap your fields, you must leave [120]the	120. Lev. 19:9
121. Lev. 19:9	corners, [121]the gleanings, [122]the forgotten sheaves, [123]the misformed	122. Deut. 24:19
124. Lev. 19:10	bunches of grapes, and [124]the gleanings of the grapes for the poor.	123. Lev. 19:10
125. Ex. 23:19	The first fruits must be [125]separated and brought to the Temple and	
	you must also [126]separate the great heave offering (terumah) and	126. Deut. 18:4
127. Lev. 27:30;	give it to the priests. You must give [127]one tithe of your produce to	
Num. 18:24	the Levites and separate [128]a second tithe which is to be eaten only	128. Deut. 14:22
	in Jerusalem. The Levites [129]must give a tenth of their tithe to the	129. Num. 18:26
	priests.	
	In the third and sixth years of the seven-year cycle, you should	
130. Deut. 14:28	[130]separate a tithe for the poor instead of the second tithe. A declaration	
131. Deut. 26:13	[131]must be recited when separating the various tithes and [132]when	132. Deut. 26:5
	bringing the first fruits to the Temple.	
133. Num. 15:20	The first portion of the [133]dough must be given to the priest.	
	The Sabbatical Year	
134. Ex. 23:11	In the seventh year (shemittah) everything that grows is [134]ownerless	
135. Ex. 34:21	and available to all; the fields [135]must lie fallow and you may not till	
136. Lev. 25:10	the ground. You must [136]sanctify the Jubilee year (50th) and on the	
	Day of Atonement in that year [137]you must sound the shofar and set	137. Lev. 25:9
	all Hebrew slaves free. In the Jubilee year all land is to be [138]returned	138. Lev. 25:24
139. Lev. 25:29–30	to its ancestral owners and, generally, in a walled city [139]the seller has	
	the right to buy back a house within a year of its sale.	
	Starting from entry into the land of Israel, the years of the Jubilee must	
140. Lev. 25:8.	be [140]counted and announced yearly and septennially.	
141. Deut. 15:3	In the seventh year [141]all debts are annulled but [142]one may exact a	142. Deut. 15:3
	debt owed by a foreigner.	
	Concerning Animals for Consumption	
	When you slaughter an animal, you must [143]give the priest his share	143. Deut. 18:3
	as you must also give him [144]the first of the fleece. When a man	144. Deut. 18:4
145. Lev. 27:21, 28	makes a ḥerem (a special vow), you must [145]distinguish between that	
	which belongs to the Temple (i.e., when God's name was mentioned	
	in the vow) and between that which goes to the priests. To be fit for	
146. Deut. 12:21	consumption, beast and fowl must be [146]slaughtered according to the	

	law, and if they are not of a domesticated species, [147]their blood must	147. Lev. 17:13.
	be covered with earth after slaughter.	
148. Deut. 22:7	Set the parent bird [148]free when taking the nest. Examine [149]beast,	149. Lev. 11:2
150. Deut. 14:11	[150]fowl, [151]locusts, and [152]fish to determine whether they are permitted	151. Lev. 11:21
	for consumption.	152. Lev. 11:9
	Festivals	
153. Ex. 12:2	The Sanhedrin should [153]sanctify the first day of every month and	
Deut. 16:1	reckon the years and the seasons. You must [154]rest on the Sabbath day	154. Ex. 23:12
	and [155]declare it holy at its onset and termination. On the 14th of Nisan	155. Ex. 20:8
156. Ex. 12:15	[156]remove all leaven from your ownership and on the night of the 15th	
157. Ex. 13:8	[157]relate the story of the exodus from Egypt; on that night [158]you must	158. Ex. 12:18
159. Ex. 12:16	also eat maẓẓah. On the [159]first and [160]seventh days of Passover you	160. Ex. 12:16
	must rest. Starting from the day of the first sheaf (16th of Nisan), you	
161. Lev. 23:35	shall [161]count 49 days. You must rest on [162]Shavuot and on [163]Rosh Ha-	163. Lev. 23:24
162. Lev. 23	Shanah; on the Day of Atonement you must [164]fast and [165]rest. You must	165. Lev. 16:29, 31
164. Lev. 16:29	also rest on [166]the first and [167]the eighth day of Sukkot during which	167. Lev. 23:36
166. Lev. 23:35	festival you shall [168]dwell in booths and [169]take the four species. On	168. Lev. 23:42
169. Lev. 23:40	Rosh Ha-Shanah [170]you are to hear the sound of the shofar.	170. Num. 29:1
	Community	
171. Ex. 30:12–13	Every male should [171]give half a shekel to the Temple annually. You	
172. Deut. 18:15	must [172]obey a prophet and [173]appoint a king. You must also [174]obey	173. Deut. 17:15
175. Ex. 23:2	the Sanhedrin; in the case of division, [175]yield to the majority. Judges	174. Deut. 17:11
176. Deut. 16:18	and officials shall be [176]appointed in every town and they shall judge	
	the people [177]impartially.	177. Lev. 19:15
	Whoever is aware of evidence [178]must come to court to testify.	178. Lev. 5:1
	Witnesses shall be [179]examined thoroughly and, if found to be false,	179. Deut. 13:15
180. Deut. 19:19	[180]shall have done to them what they intended to do to the accused.	
	When a person is found murdered and the murderer is unknown, the	
181. Deut. 21:4	ritual of [181]decapitating the heifer must be performed.	
	Six cities of refuge should be [182]established. The Levites, who have	182. Deut. 19:3
183. Num. 35:2	no ancestral share in the land, shall [183]be given cities to live in. You	
	must [184]build a fence around your roof and remove potential hazards	184. Deut. 22:8
	from your home.	
	Idolatry	
	Idolatry and its appurtenances [185]must be destroyed, and a city which	185. Deut. 12:2; 7:5
186. Deut. 13:17	has become perverted must be [186]treated according to the law. You are	
187. Deut. 20:17	commanded to [187]destroy the seven Canaanite nations, and [188]to blot out	188. Deut. 25:19
	the memory of Amalek, and [189]to remember what they did to Israel.	189. Deut. 25:17
	War	
	The regulations for wars other than those commanded in the Torah	
190. Deut. 20:11–12	[190]are to be observed and a priest should be [191]appointed for special	
191. Deut. 20:2	duties in times of war. The military camp must be [192]kept in a sanitary	192. Deut. 23:14–15
193. Deut. 23:14	condition. To this end, every soldier must be [193]equipped with the	
	necessary implements.	
	Social	
194. Lev. 5:23	Stolen property must be [194]restored to its owner. Give [195]charity to the	195. Deut. 15:8;
196. Deut. 15:14	poor. When a Hebrew slave goes free, the owner must [196]give him gifts.	Lev. 25:35–36
197. Ex. 22:24	Lend to [197]the poor without interest; to the foreigner you may [198]lend at	198. Deut. 23:21

	interest. Restore [199]a pledge to its owner if he needs it. Pay the worker	199. Deut. 24:13;
200. Deut. 24:15	his wages [200]on time; [201]permit him to eat of the produce with which	Ex. 22:25
201. Deut. 23:25–26	he is working. You must [202]help unload an animal when necessary, and	202. Ex. 23:5
203. Deut. 22:4	also [203]help load man or beast. Lost property [204]must be restored to its	204. Deut. 22:1;
205. Lev. 19:17	owner. You are required [205]to reprove the sinner but you must [206]love	Ex. 23:4
206. Lev. 19:18	your fellow as yourself. You are commanded [207]to love the proselyte.	207. Deut. 10:19
208. Lev. 19:36	Your weights and measures [208]must be accurate.	
	Family	
209. Lev. 19:32	Respect the [209]wise; [210]honor and [211]fear your parents.	210. Ex. 20:12
212. Gen. 1:28	You should [212]perpetuate the human race by marrying [213]according	211. Lev. 19:3
213. Deut. 24:1	to the law. A bridegroom is to [214]rejoice with his bride for one year.	
214. Deut. 24:5	Male children must [215]be circumcised. Should a man die childless, his	
215. Gen. 17:10;	brother must either [216]marry his widow or [217]release her (halizah). He	216. Deut. 25:5
Lev. 12:3	who violates a virgin must [218]marry her and may never divorce her.	
217. Deut. 25:9	If a man unjustly accuses his wife of premarital promiscuity, [219]he	
218. Deut. 22:29	shall be flogged, and may never divorce her. The seducer [220]must be	
219. Deut. 22:18–19	punished according to the law. The female captive must be [221]treated	221. Deut. 21:11
220. Ex. 22:15–23	in accordance with her special regulations. Divorce can be executed	
222. Deut. 24:1	[222]only by means of a written document. A woman suspected of	
	adultery [223]has to submit to the required test.	223. Num. 5:15–2.7
	Judicial	
224. Deut. 25:2	When required by the law, [224]you must administer the punishment	
	of flogging and you must [225]exile the unwitting homicide. Capital	225. Num. 35:25
226. Ex. 21:20	punishment shall be by [226]the sword, [227]strangulation, [228]fire, or	228. Lev. 20:14
227. Ex. 21:16	[229]stoning, as specified. In some cases the body of the executed [230]shall	229. Deut. 22:24
230. Deut. 21:22	be hanged, but it [231]must be brought to burial the same day.	231. Deut. 21:23
	Slaves	
232. Ex. 21:2	Hebrew slaves [232]must be treated according to the special laws	
	for them. The master should [233]marry his Hebrew maidservant or	233. Ex. 21:8
234. Ex. 21:8	[234]redeem her. The alien slave [235]must be treated according to the	
235. Lev. 25:46	regulations applying to him.	
	Torts	
	The applicable law must be administered in the case of injury caused	
236. Ex. 21:18	by [236]a person, [237]an animal, or [238]a pit. Thieves [239]must be punished.	238. Ex. 21:33–34
237. Ex. 21:28	You must render judgment in cases of [240]trespass by cattle, [241]arson,	239. Ex. 21:37–22:3
240. Ex. 22:4	[242]embezzlement by an unpaid guardian and in claims against [243]a paid	241. Ex. 22:5
242. Ex. 22:6–8	guardian, a hirer, or [244]a borrower. Judgment must also be rendered	244. Ex. 22:13
243. Ex. 22:9–12	in disputes arising out of [245]sales, [248]inheritance, and [246]other matters	248. Num. 27:8
245. Lev. 25:14	generally. You are required to [247]rescue the persecuted even if it means	247. Deut. 25:12
246. Ex. 22:8	killing his oppressor.	
PROHIBITIONS		
	Idolatry and Related Practices	
1. Ex. 20:3	It is [1]forbidden to believe in the existence of any but the One God.	
2. Ex. 20:4	You may not make images [2]for yourself or [3]for others to worship or for	3. Lev. 19:4
4. Ex. 20:20	[4]any other purpose. You must not worship anything but God either	

5. Ex. 20:5	in [5]the manner prescribed for His worship or [6]in its own manner of	6. Ex. 20:5
	worship.	
7. Lev. 18:21	Do not [7]sacrifice children to Molech.	
8. Lev. 19:31	You may not [8]practice necromancy or [9]resort to "familiar spirits";	9. Lev. 19:31
10. Lev. 19:4	neither should you take idolatry or its mythology [10]seriously.	
11. Deut. 16:22	It is forbidden to construct a [11]pillar or [12]dais even for the worship of	12. Lev. 20:1
13. Deut. 16:21	God or to [13]plant trees in the Temple.	
14. Ex. 23:13	You may not [14]swear by idols or instigate an idolator to do so, nor may	
15. Ex. 23:13	you encourage or persuade any [15]non-Jew or [16]Jew to worship idols.	16. Deut. 13:12
17. Deut. 13:9	You must not [17]listen to or love anyone who disseminates idolatry nor	
18. Deut. 13:9	[18]should you withhold yourself from hating him. Do not [19]pity such a	19. Deut. 13:9
	person. If somebody tries to convert you to idolatry, [20]do not defend	20. Deut. 13:9
21. Deut. 13:9	him or [21]conceal the fact.	
22. Deut. 7:25	It is forbidden to [22]derive any benefit from the ornaments of idols. You	
	may not [23]rebuild that which has been destroyed as a punishment for	23. Deut. 13:17
24. Deut. 13:18	idolatry nor may you [24]have any benefit from its wealth. Do not [25]use	25. Deut. 7:26
	anything connected with idols or idolatry.	
26. Deut. 18:20	It is forbidden [26]to prophesy in the name of idols or prophesy [27]falsely	
27. Deut. 18:20	in the name of God. Do not [28]listen to the one who prophesies for idols	28. Deut. 13:3, 4;
29. Deut. 18:22	and do not [29]fear the false prophet or hinder his execution.	Deut. 13:4
30. Lev. 20:23	You must not [30]imitate the ways of idolators or practice their customs;	
33. Deut. 18:10–11	[31]divination, [32]soothsaying, [33]enchanting, [34]sorcery, [35]charming,	31. Lev. 19:26; Deut. 18:10
34. Deut. 18:10–11	[36]consulting ghosts or [37]familiar spirits, and [38]necromancy are	32. Deut. 18:10
35. Deut. 18:10–11	forbidden. Women must not [39]wear male clothing nor men [40]that of	36. Deut. 18:10–11
37. Deut. 18:10–11	women. Do not [41]tattoo yourself in the manner of the idolators.	38. Deut. 18:10–11
40. Deut. 22:5	You may not wear [42]garments made of both wool and linen nor may	39. Deut. 22:5
42. Deut. 22:11	you shave (with a razor) the sides of [43]your head or [44]your beard. Do	41. Lev. 19:28
45. Deut. 16:1;	not [45]lacerate yourself over your dead.	43. Lev. 19:27
Deut. 14:1; 45.		44. Lev. 19:27
also Lev. 19:28		
	Prohibitions Resulting from Historical Events	
46. Deut. 17:16	It is forbidden to return to Egypt to [46]dwell there permanently or to	
47. Num. 15:39	[47]indulge in impure thoughts or sights. You may not [48]make a pact	48. Ex. 23:32; Deut. 7:2
49. Deut. 20:16	with the seven Canaanite nations or [49]save the life of any member of	
50. Deut. 7:2	them. Do not [50]show mercy to idolators, [51]permit them to dwell in the	51. Ex. 23:33
52. Deut. 7:3	land of Israel, or [52]intermarry with them. A Jewess may not [53]marry	53. Deut. 23:4
	an Ammonite or Moabite even if he converts to Judaism but should	
	not refuse (for reasons of genealogy alone) [54]a descendant of Esau or	54. Deut. 23:8
55. Deut. 23:8	[55]an Egyptian who are proselytes. It is prohibited to [56]make peace with	56. Deut. 23:7
	the Ammonite or Moabite nations.	
57. Deut. 20:19	The [57]destruction of fruit trees even in times of war is forbidden as is	
58. Deut. 7:21	wanton waste at any time. Do not [58]fear the enemy and do not [59]forget	59. Deut. 25:19
	the evil done by Amalek.	
	Blasphemy	
60. Lev. 24:16;	You must not [60]blaspheme the Holy Name, [61]break an oath made by	61. Lev. 19:12
rather Ex. 22:27	It, [62]take It in vain or [63]profane It. Do not [64]try the Lord God. You may	63. Lev. 22:32
62. Ex. 20:7	not [65]erase God's name from the holy texts or destroy institutions	
64. Deut. 6:16	devoted to His worship. Do not [66]allow the body of of one hanged to	66. Deut. 21:23
65. Deut. 12:4	remain so overnight.	

	Temple	
67. Num. 18:5	Be not [67]lax in guarding the Temple.	
68. Lev. 16:2	The high priest must not enter the Temple [68]indiscriminately; a priest	
69. Lev. 21:23	with a physical blemish may not [69]enter there at all or [70]serve in the	70. Lev. 21:17
	sanctuary, and even if the blemish is of a temporary nature, he may	
71. Lev. 21:18	not [71]participate in the service there until it has passed.	
	The Levites and the priests must not [72]interchange in their functions.	72. Num. 18:3
	Intoxicated persons may not [73]enter the sanctuary or teach the Law. It	73. Lev. 10:9–11
74. Num. 18:4	is forbidden for [74]non-priests, [75]unclean priests, or [76]priests who have	75. Lev. 22:2
	performed the necessary ablution but are still within the time limit of	76. Lev. 21:6
	their uncleanness to serve in the Temple. No unclean person may enter	
77. Num. 5:3	[77]the Temple or [78]the Temple Mount.	78. Deut. 23:11
	The altar must not be made of [79]hewn stones nor may the ascent to	79. Ex. 20:25
80. Ex. 20:26	it be by [80]steps. The fire on it may not be [81]extinguished nor may any	81. Lev. 6:6
	other but the specified incense be [82]burned on the golden altar. You	82. Ex. 30:9
83. Ex. 30:32	may not [83]manufacture oil with the same ingredients and in the same	
84. Ex. 30:32	proportions as the anointing oil which itself [84]may not be misused.	
85. Ex. 30:37	Neither may you [85]compound incense with the same ingredients	
	and in the same proportions as that burned on the altar. You must	
86. Ex. 25:15	not [86]remove the staves from the Ark, [87]remove the breastplate from	87. Ex. 28:28
88. Ex. 28:32	the ephod, or [88]make any incision in the upper garment of the high	
	priest.	
	Sacrifices	
89. Deut. 12:13	It is forbidden to [89]offer sacrifices or [90]slaughter consecrated animals	90. Lev. 17:3–4
91. Lev. 22:20	outside the Temple. You may not [91]sanctify, [92]slaughter, [93]sprinkle	92. Lev. 22:22
94. Lev. 22:22	the blood of, or [94]burn the inner parts of a blemished animal even if	93. Lev. 22:24
95. Deut. 17:1	the blemish is [95]of a temporary nature and even if it is [96]offered by	96. Lev. 22:25
97. Lev. 22:21	Gentiles. It is forbidden to [97]inflict a blemish on an animal consecrated	
	for sacrifice.	
98. Lev. 2:11	Leaven or honey may not [98]be offered on the altar, neither may	
99. Lev. 2:13	[99]anything unsalted. An animal received as the hire of a harlot or as	
100. Deut. 23:19	the price of a dog [100]may not be offered.	
101. Lev. 22:28	Do not [101]kill an animal and its young on the same day.	
102. Lev. 5:11	It is forbidden to use [102]olive oil or [103]frankincense in the sin offering or	103. Lev. 5:11
104. Num. 5:15	[104,105]in the jealousy offering (sotah). You may not [106]substitute sacrifices	105. Num. 5:15
107. Lev. 27:26	even [107]from one category to the other. You may not [108]redeem the	106. Lev. 27:10
108. Num. 18:17	firstborn of permitted animals.	
109. Lev. 27:33	It is forbidden to [109]sell the tithe of the herd or [110]sell or [111]redeem a	110. Lev. 27:28
111. Lev. 27:28	field consecrated by the herem vow.	
112. Lev. 5:8	When you slaughter a bird for a sin offering, you may not [112]split its	
	head.	
113. Deut. 15:19	It is forbidden to [113]work with or [114]to shear a consecrated animal. You	114. Deut. 15:19
115. Ex. 34:25	must not slaughter the paschal lamb [115]while there is still leaven about;	
116. Ex. 23:10	nor may you leave overnight [116]those parts that are to be offered up	
117. Ex. 12:10	or [117]to be eaten.	
118. Deut. 16:4	You may not leave any part of the festive offering [118]until the third	
120. Lev. 22:30	day or any part of [119]the second paschal lamb or [120]the thanksgiving	119. Num. 9:13
	offering until the morning.	
121. Ex. 12:46	It is forbidden to break a bone of [121]the first or [122]the second paschal	122. Num. 9:12
	lamb or [123]to carry their flesh out of the house where it is being eaten.	123. Ex. 12:46
124. Lev. 6:10	You must not [124]allow the remains of the meal offering to become	

125. Ex. 12:9	leaven. It is also forbidden to eat the paschal lamb [125]raw or sodden	
126. Ex. 12:45	or to allow [126]an alien resident, [127]an uncircumcised person, or an	127. Ex. 12:48
	[128]apostate to eat of it.	128. Ex. 12:43
	A ritually unclean person [129]must not eat of holy things nor may	129. Lev. 12:4
130. Lev. 7:19	[130]holy things which have become unclean be eaten. Sacrificial meat	
131. Lev. 19:6–8	[131]which is left after the time-limit or [132]which was slaughtered with	132. Lev. 7:18
	wrong intentions must not be eaten. The heave offering must not be	
133. Lev. 22:10	eaten by [133]a non-priest, [134]a priest's sojourner or hired worker, [135]an	134. Lev. 22:10
136. Lev. 22:4	uncircumcised person, or [136]an unclean priest. The daughter of a priest	135. Lev. 22:10
137. Lev. 22:12	who is married to a non-priest may not [137]eat of holy things.	
	The meal offering of the priest [138]must not be eaten, neither may	138. Lev. 6:16
139. Lev. 6:23	[139]the flesh of the sin offerings sacrificed within the sanctuary or	
140. Deut. 14:3	[140]consecrated animals which have become blemished.	
141. Deut. 12:17	You may not eat the second tithe of [141]corn, [142]wine, or [143]oil or	142. Deut. 12:17
143. Deut. 12:17	[144]unblemished firstlings outside Jerusalem. The priests may not eat	144. Deut. 12:17
	the [145]sin-offerings or the trespass-offerings outside the Temple courts	145. Deut. 12:17
146. Deut. 12:17	or [146]the flesh of the burnt-offering at all. The lighter sacrifices [147]may	
147. Deut. 12:17	not be eaten before the blood has been sprinkled. A non-priest may	
	not [148]eat of the holiest sacrifices and a priest [149]may not eat the first	148. Deut. 12:17
	fruits outside the Temple courts.	149. Ex. 29:33
150. Deut. 26:14	One may not eat [150]the second tithe while in a state of impurity or [151]in	151. Deut. 26:14
152. Deut. 26:14	mourning; its redemption money [152]may not be used for anything other	
	than food and drink.	
153. Lev. 22:15	You must not [153]eat untithed produce or [154]change the order of	154. Ex. 22:28
	separating the various tithes.	
155. Deut. 23:22	Do not [155]delay payment of offerings – either freewill or obligatory –	
	and do not [156]come to the Temple on the pilgrim festivals without an	156. Ex. 23:15
	offering.	
157. Num. 30:3	Do not [157]break your word.	
	Priests	
158. Lev. 21:7	A priest may not marry [158]a harlot, [159]a woman who has been profaned	159. Lev. 21:7
160. Lev. 21:7	from the priesthood, or [160]a divorcee; the high priest must not [161]marry	161. Lev. 21:14
162. Lev. 21:15	a widow or [162]take one as a concubine. Priests may not enter the	
163. Lev. 10:6	sanctuary with [163]overgrown hair of the head or [164]with torn clothing;	164. Lev. 10:6
	they must not [165]leave the courtyard during the Temple service. An	165. Lev. 10:7
166. Lev. 21:1	ordinary priest may not render himself [166]ritually impure except for	
	those relatives specified, and the high priest should not become impure	
167. Lev. 21:11	[167]for anybody in [168]any way.	168. Lev. 21:11
	The tribe of Levi shall have no part in [169]the division of the land of Israel	169. Deut. 18:1
170. Deut. 18:1	or [170]in the spoils of war.	
171. Deut. 14:1	It is forbidden [171]to make oneself bald as a sign of mourning for one's	
	dead.	
	Dietary Laws	
172. Deut. 14:7	A Jew may not eat [172]unclean cattle, [173]unclean fish, [174]unclean fowl,	173. Lev. 11:11
174. Lev. 11:13	[175]creeping things that fly, [176]creatures that creep on the ground,	175. Deut. 14:19
176. Lev. 11:41	[177]reptiles, [178]worms found in fruit or produce, or [179]any detestable	177. Lev. 11:44
178. Lev. 11:42	creature.	179. Lev. 11:43
	An animal that has died naturally [180]is forbidden for consumption,	180. Deut. 14:21
181. Ex. 23:19	as is [181]a torn or mauled animal. One must not eat [182]any limb taken	182. Deut. 12.23
183. Gen. 32:33	from a living animal. Also prohibited is [183]the sinew of the thigh (gid	
184. Lev. 7:26	ha-nasheh), as are [184]blood and [185]certain types of fat (helev). It is	185. Lev. 7:23

186. Ex. 23:19	forbidden [186]to cook meat together with milk or [187]eat of such a mixture.	187. Ex. 34:26
188. Ex. 21:28	It is also forbidden to eat [188]of an ox condemned to stoning (even if it	
	has been properly slaughtered).	
189. Lev. 23:14	One may not eat [189]bread made of new corn or the new corn itself,	
190. Lev. 23:14	either [190]roasted or [191]green, before the omer offering has been brought	191. Lev. 23:14
192. Lev. 19:23	on the 16th of Nisan. You may not eat [192]orlah or [193]the growth of mixed	193. Deut. 22:9
194. Deut. 32:38	planting in the vineyard (see Mixed Species). Any use of [194]wine	
195. Lev. 19:26;	libations to idols is prohibited, as are [195]gluttony and drunkenness.	
Deut. 21:20	One may not eat anything on [196]the Day of Atonement. During Passover	196. Lev. 23:29
197. Ex. 13:3	it is forbidden to eat [197]leaven (hamez) or [198]anything containing an	198. Ex. 13:20
199. Deut. 16:3	admixture of such. This is also forbidden [199]after the middle of the 14th	
	of Nisan (the day before Passover). During Passover no leaven may be	
200. Ex. 13:7	[200]seen or [201]found in your possession.	201. Ex. 12:19
	Nazirites	
202. Num. 6:3	A Nazirite may not drink [202]wine or any beverage made from grapes;	
203. Num. 6:3	he may not eat [203]fresh grapes, [204]dried grapes, [205]grape seeds, or	204. Num. 6:3
206. Num. 6:4	[206]grape peel. He may not render himself [207]ritually impure for his	205. Num. 6:4
208. Lev. 21:11	dead nor may he [208]enter a tent in which there is a corpse. He must	207. Num. 6:7
209. Num. 6:5	not [209]shave his hair.	
	Agriculture	
210. Lev. 23:22	It is forbidden [210]to reap the whole of a field without leaving the corners	
211. Lev. 19:9	for the poor; it is also forbidden to [211]gather up the ears of corn that	
	fall during reaping or to harvest [212]the misformed clusters of grapes,	212. Lev. 19:10
213. Lev. 19:10	or [213]the grapes that fall or to [214]return to take a forgotten sheaf.	214. Deut. 24:19
215. Lev. 19:19	You must not [215]sow different species of seed together or [216]corn in	216. Deut. 22:9
217. Lev. 19:19	a vineyard; it is also forbidden to [217]crossbreed different species of	
	animals or [218]work with two different species yoked together. You must	218. Deut. 22:10
219. Deut. 25:4	not [219]muzzle an animal working in a field to prevent it from eating.	
220. Lev. 25:4	It is forbidden to [220]till the earth, [221]to prune trees, [222]to reap (in the	221. Lev. 25:4
222. Lev. 25:5	usual manner) produce or [223]fruit which has grown without cultivation	223. Lev. 25:5
	in the seventh year (shemittah). One may also not [224]till the earth or	224. Lev. 25:11
	prune trees in the Jubilee year, when it is also forbidden to harvest	
225. Lev. 25:11	(in the usual manner) [225]produce or [226]fruit that has grown without	226. Lev. 25:11
	cultivation.	
227. Lev. 25:23	One may not [227]sell one's landed inheritance in the land of Israel	
228. Lev. 25:33	permanently or [228]change the lands of the Levites or [229]leave the	229. Deut. 12:19
	Levites without support.	
	Loans, Business, and the Treatment of Slaves	
230. Deut. 15:2	It is forbidden to [230]demand repayment of a loan after the seventh	
231. Deut. 15:9	year; you may not, however, [231]refuse to lend to the poor because	
232. Deut. 15:7	that year is approaching. Do not [232]deny charity to the poor or [233]send	233. Deut. 15:13
	a Hebrew slave away empty-handed when he finishes his period of	
	service. Do not [234]dun your debtor when you know that he cannot pay.	234. Ex. 22:24
235. Lev. 25:37	It is forbidden to [235]lend to or[236]borrow from another Jew at interest or	236. Deut. 23:20
237. Ex. 22:24	[237]participate in an agreement involving interest either as a guarantor,	
	witness, or writer of the contract.	
238. Lev. 19:13	Do not [238]delay payment of wages.	
239. Deut. 24:10	You may not [239]take a pledge from a debtor by violence, [240]keep a poor	240. Deut. 24:12
241. Deut. 24:17	man's pledge when he needs it, [241]take any pledge from a widow or	
242. Deut. 24:6	[242]from any debtor if he earns his living with it.	

243. Ex. 20:13	Kidnapping [243]a Jew is forbidden.	
244. Lev. 19:11	Do not [244]steal or [245]rob by violence. Do not [246]remove a landmarker	245. Lev. 19:13
246. Deut. 19:14	or [247]defraud.	247. Lev. 19:13
248. Lev. 19:11	It is forbidden [248]to deny receipt of a loan or a deposit or [249]to swear	249. Lev. 19:11
	falsely regarding another man's property.	
250. Lev. 25:14	You must not [250]deceive anybody in business. You may not [251]mislead	251. Lev. 25:17
	a man even verbally. It is forbidden to harm the stranger among you	
252. Ex. 22:20	[252]verbally or [253]do him injury in trade.	253. Ex. 22:20
254. Deut. 23:16	You may not [254]return or [255]otherwise take advantage of a slave who has	255. Deut. 23:17
	fled to the land of Israel from his master, even if his master is a Jew.	
256. Ex. 22:21	Do not [256]afflict the widow or the orphan. You may not [257]misuse or	257. Lev. 25:39
258. Lev. 25:42	[258]sell a Hebrew slave; do not [259]treat him cruelly or [260]allow a heathen	259. Lev. 25:43
260. Lev. 25:53	to mistreat him. You must not [261]sell your Hebrew maidservant or, if you	261. Ex. 21:8
262. Ex. 21:10	marry her, [262]withhold food, clothing, and conjugal rights from her. You	
263. Deut. 21:14	must not [263]sell a female captive or [264]treat her as a slave.	264. Deut. 21:14
265. Ex. 20:17	Do not [265]covet another man's possesions even if you are willing to	
266. Deut. 5:18	pay for them. Even [266]the desire alone is forbidden.	
267. Deut. 23:26	A worker must not [267]cut down standing corn during his work or [268]take	268. Deut. 23:25
	more fruit than he can eat.	
269. Deut. 22:3	One must not [269]turn away from a lost article which is to be returned	
270. Ex. 23:5	to its owner nor may you [270]refuse to help a man or an animal which	
	is collapsing under its burden.	
271. Lev. 19:35	It is forbidden to [271]defraud with weights and measures or even [272] to	272. Deut. 25:13
	possess inaccurate weights.	
	Justice	
273. Lev. 19:15	A judge must not [273]perpetrate injustice, [274]accept bribes, or be [275]partial	274. Ex. 23:8
275. Lev. 19:15	or [276]afraid. He may [277]not favor the poor or [278]discriminate against the	276. Deut. 1:17
278. Ex. 23:6	wicked; he should not [279]pity the condemned or [280]pervert the judgment	277. Lev. 19:15, rather Ex. 23:3
279. Deut. 19:13	of strangers or orphans.	280. Deut. 24:17
281. Ex. 23:1	It is forbidden to [281]hear one litigant without the other being present.	
282. Ex. 23:2	A capital case cannot be decided by [282]a majority of one.	
283. Ex. 23:2	A judge should not [283]accept a colleague's opinion unless he is	
284. Deut. 1:17	convinced of its correctness; it is forbidden to [284]appoint as a judge	
	someone who is ignorant of the law.	
285. Ex. 20:16	Do not [285]give false testimony or accept [286]testimony from a wicked	286. Ex. 23:1
	person or from [287]relatives of a person involved in the case. It is	287. Deut. 24:16
288. Deut. 19:15	forbidden to pronounce judgment [288]on the basis of the testimony of	
	one witness.	
289. Ex. 20:13	Do not [289]murder.	
	You must not convict on [290]circumstantial evidence alone.	290. Ex. 23:7
291. Num. 35:30	A witness [291]must not sit as a judge in capital cases.	
292. Num. 35:12	You must not [292]execute anybody without due proper trial and	
	conviction.	
293. Deut. 25:12	Do not [293] pity or spare the pursuer.	
	Punishment is not to be inflicted for [294]an act committed under	294. Deut. 22:26
	duress.	
295. Num. 35:31	Do not accept ransom [295]for a murderer or [296]a manslayer.	296. Num. 35:32
297. Lev. 19:16	Do not [297]hesitate to save another person from danger and do not	
298. Deut. 22:8	[298]leave a stumbling block in the way or [299]mislead another person by	299. Lev. 19:14
	giving wrong advice.	
300. Deut. 25:2–3	It is forbidden [300]to administer more than the assigned number of	
	lashes to the guilty.	
301. Lev. 19:16	Do not [301]tell tales or [302]bear hatred in your heart. It is forbidden to	302. Lev. 19:17

303. Lev. 19:17	[303]shame a Jew, [304]to bear a grudge, or [305]to take revenge. Do not	304. Lev. 19:18
305. Lev. 19:18	[306]take the dam when you take the young birds.	306. Deut. 22:6
307. Lev. 13:33	It is forbidden to [307]shave a leprous scalp or [308]remove other signs of	308. Deut. 24:8
	that affliction. It is forbidden [309]to cultivate a valley in which a slain	309. Deut. 21:4
	body was found and in which subsequently the ritual of breaking the	
	heifer's neck (eglah arufah) was performed.	
310. Ex. 22:17	Do not [310]suffer a witch to live.	
311. Deut. 24:5	Do not [311]force a bridegroom to perform military service during the first	
312. Deut. 17:11	year of his marriage. It is forbidden to [312]rebel against the transmitters	
313. Deut. 13:1	of the tradition or to [313]add or [314]detract from the precepts of the law.	314. Deut. 13:1
315. Ex. 22:27	Do not curse [315]a judge, [316]a ruler, or [317]any Jew.	316. Ex. 22:27
318. Ex. 21:17	Do not [318]curse or [319]strike a parent.	317. Lev. 19:14
319. Ex. 21:15	It is forbidden to [320]work on the Sabbath or [321]walk further than the	321. Ex. 16:29
320. Ex. 20:10	permitted limits (eruv). You may not [322]inflict punishment on the	322. Ex. 35:3
	Sabbath.	
323. Ex. 12:16	It is forbidden to work on [323]the first or [324]the seventh day of Passover,	324. Ex. 12:16
325. Lev. 23:21	on [325]Shavuot, on [326]Rosh Ha-Shanah, on the [327]first and [328]eighth	326. Lev. 23:25
327. Lev. 23:35	(*Shemini Azeret) days of Sukkot, and [329]on the Day of Atonement.	329. Lev. 23:28
328. Lev. 23:36		
	Incest and Other Forbidden Relationships	
	It is forbidden to enter into an incestuous relationship with one's	
330. Lev. 18:7	[330]mother, [331]step-mother, [332]sister, [333]half-sister, [334]son's daughter,	333. Lev. 18:11
331. Lev. 18:8	[335]daughter's daughter, [336]daughter, [337]any woman and her daughter,	334. Lev. 18:10
332. Lev. 18:9	[338]any woman and her son's daughter, [339]any woman and her daughter's	335. Lev. 18:10
336. Lev. 18:10	daughter, [340]father's sister, [341]mother's sister, [342]paternal uncle's wife,	337. Lev. 18:17
338. Lev. 18:17	[343]daughter-in-law, [344]brother's wife, and [345]wife's sister.	339. Lev. 18:17
341. Lev. 18:13	It is also forbidden to [346]have sexual relations with a menstruous	340. Lev. 18:12
343. Lev. 18:15	woman (see Niddah).	342. Lev. 18:14
344. Lev. 18:16	Do not [347]commit adultery.	345. Lev. 18:18
347. Lev. 18:20	It is forbidden for [348]a man or [349]a woman to have sexual intercourse	346. Lev. 18:19
	with an animal.	348. Lev. 18:23
350. Lev. 18:22	Homosexuality [350]is forbidden, particularly with [351]one's father or	349. Lev. 18:23
351. Lev. 18:7	[352]uncle.	352. Lev. 18:14
353. Lev. 18:6	It is forbidden to have [353]intimate physical contact (even without	
	actual intercourse) with any of the women with whom intercourse	
	is forbidden.	
354. Deut. 23:3	A mamzer may not [354]marry a Jewess.	
355. Deut. 23:18	Harlotry [355]is forbidden.	
	A divorcee may not be [356]remarried to her first husband if, in the	356. Deut. 24:4
	meanwhile, she had married another.	
	A childless widow may not [357]marry anybody other than her late	357. Deut. 25:5
	husband's brother (see Levirate Marriage).	
358. Deut. 22:29	A man may not [358]divorce a wife whom he married after having raped	
	her or [359]after having slandered her.	359. Deut. 22:19
360. Deut. 23:2	A eunuch may not [360]marry a Jewess.	
361. Lev. 22:24	Castration [361]is forbidden.	
	The Monarchy	
362. Deut. 17:15	You may not [362]elect as king anybody who is not of the seed of Israel.	
363. Deut. 17:16	The king must not accumulate an excessive number of [363]horses,	
364. Deut. 17:17	[364]wives, or [365]wealth.	365. Deut. 17:17
		[Raphael Posner]

Deut. 17; Ex. R. 33:7; Num. R. 13:15–16; 18:21; Yev. 47b) which crystallized in the school of R. *Akiva (see A.H. Rabinowitz, *Taryag*, 38–39). Doubt as to the validity of this tradition in the eyes of the sages of the Talmud has been expressed by *Naḥmanides, Abraham *Ibn Ezra, Simeon b. Zemaḥ *Duran, Schechter, and others, but the majority of scholars, including Naḥmanides and Duran, conclude that the tradition does in fact reflect the opinion of the rabbis of the Talmud. Works enumerating the commandments are numerous (see Jellinek, *Kunteres Taryag*, 1878), but the majority of the lists conform to one of four methods of enumeration: (1) The earliest lists, those of the anonymous *azharot, are divided simply into two lists of positive and prohibitive precepts, with little attention being paid to the internal classification, e.g., *Attah Hinḥalta, Azharat Reshit, Emet Yehegeh Ḥikki*. (2) The threefold division into positive commandments, prohibitions, and *parashiyyot*, first found in the list prefacing the *Halakhot Gedolot of R. Simeon Kayyara and subsequently in almost every enumeration of geonic times. (The basis for this division is to be found in Mid. Ps. 119:1 and indirectly in PR 22:111.) The section called *parashiyyot* lists precepts involving the public body but not the individual, e.g., setting aside cities for the levites, erecting the sanctuary. (3) Classification of the precepts under the tenfold headings of the *Decalogue. This method of classifying the precepts is at least as old as *Philo (Decal.), is mentioned in the Midrash several times (e.g., Num. R. 13:15/16), and is followed by *Saadiah Gaon, Isaac *Abrabanel, Ma'amar Haskel, and many others. (4) Independent logical classification of the two lists of positive and prohibitive precepts. This is the method of Maimonides and his school. There are in addition many literary curiosities in this field. Elijah Ettinger attempted to show that the 613 precepts are contained in the four verses of Moses' prayer (Deut. 3:23–6). *Shirah le-Ḥayyim* (Warsaw, 1817) attempts to insert the 613 precepts into the 613 letters of the song of *Ha'azinu* (Deut. 32:1–43). David Vital's *Keter Torah* construes a 613-line poem, each line defining one *mitzvah* and commencing with the letters of the Decalogue as they appear in the text. A *Taryag* enumeration amounts in principle to a codification of the major elements of biblical law – the 613 headings under which all the details of Torah legislation may be classified. Extracting and identifying these headings from the complex body of biblical law is the central problem of the vast literature which has grown up around *Taryag* enumerations. In this literature the term *mitzvah* is used in the limited sense of a mandate or prohibition which fulfills the conditions necessary for inclusion among the member *mitzvot* of *Taryag*. Since early tradition gives no precise criteria, the problem is immense and no logical system hitherto proposed is free from criticism. Although preceded by the logical systems of Saadiah Gaon and Ḥefeẓ b. Yaẓli'aḥ, and subsequently criticized by Naḥmanides, the principal method of enumerating the *mitzvot* is that defined by *Maimonides in his *Sefer ha-Mitzvot*. Maimonides introduces the work with a lengthy treatise in which he lays down 14 guiding principles governing the inclusion or exclusion of a *mitzvah* in a *Taryag* enumeration. This treatise formed the basis for subsequent literature on the subject, and the divergence of different *Taryag* lists, both preceding and succeeding Maimonides, is due to differences of opinion over these principles. *Taryag* lists are by no means confined to halakhic treatment. They range over the fields of ethics (Aaron of Barcelona, and Isaiah Hurwitz, among others) homiletics (Aḥai Gaon), philosophy (*Moreh Nevukhim*), and mysticism (David b. Solomon ibn Abi Zimra). An entire (though incomplete) section of the Zohar, the "*Ra'aya Meheimna*" ("Faithful Shepherd"), is devoted to enumerating *Taryag* and offers a mystical interpretation of the precepts. Taryag lists also entered the liturgy, during geonic times, in the form of *azharot*, which form an integral part of the festival prayer book.

BIBLIOGRAPHY: Bloch, in: REJ, 1 (1880), 197–211; 5 (1882), 27–40; J.M. (Michael) Guttmann, *Beḥinat ha-Mitzvot* (1928); Halper, in: JQR, 4 (1913/14), 519–76; 5 (1914/15), 29–90; H. Heller (ed.), *Sefer ha-Mitzvot le-R. Moshe b. Maimon* (1914); Maimonides, *The Book of Divine Commandments*, tr. by C.B. Chavel (1940).

[Abraham Hirsch Rabinowitz]

COMMANDMENTS, REASONS FOR (Heb. טַעֲמֵי הַמִּצְווֹת, *Ta'amei ha-Mitzvot*). The search for "reasons" for the commandments of the Torah springs from a tendency to transcend mere obedience to them by investing them with some intrinsic meaning. The Pentateuch itself offers reasons for some commandments (e.g., Ex. 22:26; 23:9; Deut. 11:19; 17:16–17; 23:4–5) and emphasizes the "wisdom" of the Law (Deut. 4:6–8). It also differentiates between *mishpatim* ("ordinances") and *ḥukkim* ("statutes") without, however, offering any clear principle of division. Classical rabbinic literature contains a more formal discussion of the problem. The *mishpatim* are said to represent laws that would have been valid even without having been "written" in the Torah, such as the prohibitions against robbery, idolatry, incest, and murder, while the *ḥukkim*, such as the prohibition of swine's flesh and the wearing of garments made of both wool and flax are "decrees" of God. It is to the latter class that "the evil inclination" and the gentiles object (Sifra, Lev. 18:4, par. 140). From the second century onward Christian attacks on "the Law" provoked many Jewish replies stressing the importance of the *mitzvot*: the commandments were given for the sole purpose of purifying man (Gen. R. 41:1 – for parallels see Theodor Albeck, ed. (1965), 424–5); they strengthen man's holiness (Mekh. 89a); they enable Israel to acquire merit (Mak. 3:16). R. Simeon b. Yoḥai is known to have favored the exposition of the reasons of Scripture (*doresh ta'amei di-kera*), but he did not go beyond offering exegetical observations (Kid. 68b, et al.). The *ta'amei ha-Torah* ("reasons of the commandments") are not revealed and should not be revealed (Pes. 119a; cf. Sanh. 21b); the "yoke of the commandments" is to be cherished without probing its reasons. No detailed rationalization of the commandments is to be found in the rabbinic sources.

[Alexander Altmann]

Although the rabbis do not present a systematic exposition of the "reasons for the commandments," and notwithstanding their presumed aversion to such "reasons," they frequently suggest the religious significance or ethical justification for the commands and their details. Thus, the "four species" held on the Sukkot festival are understood as symbolizing God or, alternatively, as different components of the Jewish people which, when held together, form an organic unity (Lev. R. 30, 9; 30, 12). Such explanations need not be symbolic: a married couple is commanded to keep apart during the woman's menstrual period so that "she returns to him as fresh as a bride on her wedding day" (Nid. 31b). This explanation – and many others – is introduced with the phrase, "Why did the Torah command?," a phrase betraying no discomfort with the enterprise of finding reasons for the commands. Frequently, it is the details of commandments that are subject to didactic moralizing: the ear of the Hebrew slave – and no other organ – is bored so as to signify the extension of his servitude (Ex. 21:6) because his ear "heard at Sinai 'the children of Israel are My servants,' yet he went and threw off the yoke of Heaven and took a human master for himself" (Tosef. BK 7, 5), a comment with an an obvious political moral as well.

[Gerald Y. Blidstein (2nd ed.)]

Hellenistic Literature

The need for a rational explanation of the Mosaic law was expressed for the first time in the Hellenistic period; it was motivated by a desire to present the Jewish religion to the pagan world as a legal system designed to produce a people of the highest virtue. The *Letter of Aristeas* describes the dietary laws and other commandments, e.g., those concerning sacrifices, wearing of *ẓiẓit*, the *mezuzah*, and *tefillin*, as divinely ordained means for awakening holy thoughts and forming character (cf. 142–4, 147, 150ff., 169). In IV Maccabees (5:23–24) divine law is identified with reason and held to be the chief aid to a virtuous life (cf. 1:15–17, 30ff.; 5:7, 25–26).

PHILO. Philo offered the first systematic exposition of the reasons for the commandments in several of his works. He presented the law of Moses as the ideal law envisaged by the philosophers, that is, the law that leads men to live according to virtue (H.A. Wolfson, *Philo*, 2 (1947), 200ff.). The laws of Moses are divided into positive and negative laws and into those relating to man and those relating to God, and they are all subsumed under the *Decalogue. Aside from these classifications, the laws of Moses also fall into the following four categories: (1) beliefs; (2) virtuous emotions; (3) actions symbolizing beliefs; and (4) actions symbolizing virtues. However, under the influence of Judaism this fourfold classification of philosophic virtues is expanded to include such religious virtues as faith, piety, prayer, and repentance. Unlike the natural law, the Mosaic law is revealed by God; nevertheless, it is in accord with human nature. Every law in it has a rational purpose (*ibid.*, 305–6). In the explanation of some laws, particularly those involving the sacrifices and festivals, Philo used the allegorical method. Elsewhere he tried to present the Mosaic legislation as a form of government that combines the best features of the three types of rule described as good by Plato and Aristotle, namely, monarchy, aristocracy, and democracy (382ff.).

Medieval Philosophy

SAADIAH GAON. *Saadiah Gaon was the first Jewish thinker to divide the commandments into those obligatory because they are required by reason (Ar. *ʿaqliyyāt*, Heb. *sikhliyyot*) and those given through revelation (Ar. *samʿiyyāt*, Heb. *shimiyyot*). In making this distinction he followed the parallel teachings of the Mu'tazilite *Kalām but also added a Platonic account. According to the Mu'tazilite exposition, the rational laws are divided into three kinds: gratitude, reverence, and social conduct; and from these three categories he derived many special laws. In his Platonic exposition he showed the rational character of certain laws by pointing out the damaging effects of the acts prohibited: theft and robbery, for example, undermine the economic basis of society, and untruthfulness destroys the harmony of the soul. Discussing the revelational laws, Saadiah holds that while they are primarily an expression of God's will, they have some rational aspects or "usefulness," although he repeatedly reminds himself that God's wisdom is superior to man's. For example, the holy seasons enable man to pursue spiritual matters and human fellowship; the priesthood guides and helps people in time of stress; and dietary laws combat animal worship (*Book of Beliefs and Opinions*, 3:5, 1–3).

KARAITES. While the Rabbanites eventually went on to formulate other "reasons of the commandments," the Mu'tazilite approach, exemplified by Saadiah, remained in force among the *Karaites throughout the medieval period. Joseph al-*Baṣīr and *Jeshua b. Judah emphasized the validity of the moral law prior to revelation. *Aaron b. Elijah differentiated between *mitzvot sikhliyyot* ("rational laws") and *mitzvot toriyyot* ("Toraitic laws"; *Eẓ Ḥayyīm*, ed. F. Delitzsch (1841) chap. 102). Elijah *Bashyazi (b. c. 1420) spoke of the rational ordinances as those precepts "established and planted in man's heart" and known prior to revelation (see L. Nemoy, *Karaite Anthology* (1952), 241ff.).

BAHYA IBN PAQUDA. Baḥya combined Saadiah's division of the commandments with another classification also derived from Mu'tazalite sources, that of "duties of the members [of the body]" (Ar. *farāʾiḍ al-jawāriḥ*, Heb. *ḥovot ha-evarim*) and "duties of the hearts" (Ar. *farāʾiḍ al-qulūb*, Heb. *ḥovot ha-levavot*). The "duties of the members" are of two kinds: duties obligatory by virtue of reason and duties neither enjoined nor rejected by reason, e.g., the prohibition of eating milk and meat together. The "duties of the hearts," on the other hand, are of an intellectual and attitudinal kind, such as belief in God, trust in Him, and fear and love of Him (*Ḥovot ha-Levavot*, Introduction). Baḥya emphasized "duties of the hearts" (3:3) and asserted that it is only on account of the weakness of the intellect that the revelational commandments are necessary. Unlike Saadiah, however, he does not try to explain the revelational laws in terms of usefulness for specific ends; they are simply expressions of piety and, thereby, effective aids to the attainment of the perfect life of attachment to God.

JOSEPH IBN ẒADDIK. Joseph ibn *Ẓaddik stressed gratitude as the most fundamental duty to God, who out of love created the world and gave it His commandments. Accepting the distinction between rational and revelational commandments, Ibn Ẓaddik held that even the latter have a "subtle meaning" (*sod dak, inyan dak*). The observance of the Sabbath, for example, teaches the createdness of the world and points to the bliss of the world-to-come (*Sefer ha-Olam ha-Katan*, S. Horovitz, ed. (1903), 59–64).

JUDAH HALEVI. Judah Halevi's classifications of the commandments were under three headings: (1) rational laws (*sikhliyyot*), also termed psychic laws (*nafshiyyot*), such as those having to do with belief in God, justice, and gratitude (*Kuzari*, 2:48; 3:11); (2) governmental laws (*minhagiyyot*), which are concerned with the functioning and well-being of society (*ibid.*); and (3) revelational laws (*shimiyyot*), or divine laws (*elohiyyot*) whose main function is to elevate the Jew to communion with God and whose highest manifestation is prophecy. God alone is capable of determining the revelational laws, which in themselves are neither demanded nor rejected by reason (1:98; 2:23; 3:53). For Halevi the revelational laws are supreme and the rational and governmental laws are only a "preamble" (2:48).

ABRAHAM IBN EZRA. Abraham *Ibn Ezra dealt with the subject of the commandments in his commentaries on the Torah and in his small treatise *Yesod Mora*. He distinguished between laws which are implanted in the human heart prior to revelation (*pikkudim*) and laws which prescribe symbolic acts reminding us of such matters as creation, e.g., observance of the Sabbath, and the exodus from Egypt, e.g., the observance of Passover (*Yesod Mora*, ch. 5; Commentary to Gen. 26:5; Short Commentary to Ex. 15:26). In addition he speaks of "obscure commandments" (*mitzvot ne'elamot*), which have no clear-cut reason. Certain of these commandments he tried to explain as prohibitions of acts contrary to nature, e.g., seething a kid in its mother's milk, and others, as serving utilitarian purposes, e.g., the separation of the leper as a sanitary measure (Lev. 13:45–46) and the dietary laws in order to prevent injurious influences to body and soul (Comm. to Lev. 19:23; 11:43). Astrological motifs are employed in the interpretation of the sanctuary and its parts, the garments of the high priest, and the sacrifices.

ABRAHAM IBN DAUD. Abraham *Ibn Daud, who initiated the Aristotelian trend in medieval Jewish philosophy, abandoned the Kalām terms "rational" and "revelational" and replaced them with "generally known" (Ar. *mashhūrāt*, a translation of the Greek *endoxa*; Heb. *mefursamot*) and "traditional" (Ar. *maqbūlāt*, Heb. *mekubbalot*). This change of terminology reflects the Aristotelian view that good and evil are not a matter of demonstrative knowledge but of opinion (*Topics*, 1:1; cf. Maimonides, *Millot ha-Higgayon*, ch. 8; Guide 1:2). Ibn Daud assumed that the "generally known" laws, i.e., the laws of social conduct, are identical in all religions and, therefore, that the formation of states composed of different religious communities is possible, no matter how opposed their religions may be (*Sefer ha-Emunah ha-Ramah*, ed. S. Weil (1852), 5:2, 75).

MAIMONIDES. Maimonides, like Ibn Daud, discarded as illegitimate the distinction between "rational" and "revelational" laws. In his view, all laws set forth in the Torah have a "cause" (Ar. *ʿilla*, Heb. *illah*), that is, a "useful purpose" (Ar. *ghāya mufīda*, Heb. *takhlit mo'ilah*), and follow from God's wisdom, not from an arbitrary act of His will. In some cases, such as the prohibitions against killing and stealing, their utility is clear, while in others, such as the prohibitions against sowing with diverse seeds, it is not. Maimonides identified the former commandments with the laws known as *mishpatim* ("ordinances") and the latter, with those known as *ḥukkim* ("statutes"). Although general laws, e.g., the institution of sacrifices, have a reason, particular laws, e.g., the number of animals for a particular sacrifice, do not (Guide, 3:26, 31). There are two overall purposes of the Torah: the welfare of the soul, in which man finds his ultimate perfection in this world and the next, and the welfare of the body, which is a means to the welfare of the soul. For the welfare of the soul the law promotes correct opinions, and for the welfare of the body it sets down norms for the guidance of society and the individual. To promote opinions, the law fosters two kinds of beliefs: absolutely true beliefs, such as the existence and unity of God, and beliefs necessary for the well-being of the state, such as God's anger in punishing evildoers (Guide, 3:27–28, 31–32).

Introducing a new method of interpretation of Jewish law, Maimonides regarded many *ḥukkim* of the Torah as directed toward the abolition of the idolatrous practices of the ancient pagans, as described in a tenth-century book by Ibn Waḥshiyya, known as the *Nabatean Agriculture*. He even maintained that it is the first intention of the law to put an end to idolatry (Guide, 3:29). Another method that Maimonides used to explain certain laws is described by the term "gracious ruse" (Ar. *talaṭṭuf*; Heb. *ormah*), which is borrowed from the Greek philosopher *Alexander of Aphrodisias (c. 200; see S. Pines' introduction to his translation of the Guide, lxxiiff.). Thus, for example, God graciously tolerated the customary mode of worship through animal sacrifice, but transferred it from idols to His own name and through this "ruse" effaced idolatry (3:32). However, in marked contrast to the utilitarian treatments of the commandments in Maimonides' *Guide of the Perplexed* is the deeply religious approach of his *Mishneh Torah*. The *ḥukkim*, including the sacrifices, appear in the latter work as important vehicles of the spiritual life (cf. Yad, Me'ilah, end; Temurah, end; Mikva'ot, end).

*Levi b. Gershom also set forth explanations of the commandments in terms of their utility; his commentary on the Torah largely follows Maimonides' *Guide* in this respect.

HASDAI CRESCAS AND JOSEPH ALBO. The approach of Ḥasdai *Crescas is of an entirely different nature. Crescas rejected the notion, implicit in the views of his predecessors, e.g., Maimonides, that the Torah had to adapt itself to the low level of religion prevalent at the time of its revelation, an assumption which tended to render part of the commandments obsolete. He was also the first to introduce theological instead of moral or metaphysical concepts for the interpretation of the commandments. In this context it is important to recall that Crescas was concerned with refuting Christian theological notions and the charge of the apostate *Abner of Burgos that Judaism had succumbed to philosophy. In his polemic with Christianity Crescas accepted the notion of original sin (*Or Adonai*, 2:2, 6), but argued that all *mitzvot* are means of redemption from the "poison" injected into Eve by the serpent. Unlike the Aristotelians who saw intellectual perfection as the final goal of the Torah, Crescas maintained that its ultimate purpose is to instill the love of God in man (*ibid.*, 2:6, 2).

Crescas' pupil Joseph *Albo continued his master's polemics against Christian attacks on the Mosaic law, arguing that it is more perfect than any other law and that the Gospels are really no law at all. Distinguishing three kinds of laws, Albo held that natural law (*ha-dat ha-tivit*) contains those rules that are indispensable for the merest association of men; that conventional law (*ha-dat ha-nimusit*) promotes virtues according to human opinion, or the "generally known" (*ha-mefursam*); and that divine law (*ha-dat ha-Elohit*) guides man to true happiness, which is the bliss of the soul and eternal life (*Sefer ha-Ikkarim* 1:7, and passim; see I. Husik, in HUCA, 2 (1925), 381ff.; R. Lerner, in *Ancients and Moderns*, ed. J. Cropsey, 1964).

A similar treatment is found in the work of Albo's predecessor, Simon b. Zemaḥ *Duran, *Keshet u-Magen* (12b). On the other hand, Shem Tov *Ibn Shem Tov in his work *Kevod Elohim* (1556) completely discarded the philosophical approach. He considered it wrong even to investigate reasons for the commandments, since the divine in principle cannot be explained by natural reasons (21b ff.). Only in a secondary sense can the commandments be called "rational"; primarily they are "decrees" based on the will of God, who must be presumed to have a purpose, but whose purpose we cannot know. This attitude became increasingly popular in the last phase of medieval Jewish philosophy and persisted until the dawn of the modern age.

Modern Jewish Thought

Modern Jewish thought, marked by a deep crisis of traditional beliefs and halakhic authority, has dealt with the subject of reasons for divine commandments on various levels.

MOSES MENDELSSOHN. Moses *Mendelssohn distinguished three layers within the body of Jewish teachings: (1) religion par excellence, consisting of eternal truths that all enlightened men hold in common; (2) historical truths concerning the origin of the Jewish nation, which faith accepts on authority; and (3) laws, precepts, commandments, and rules of life revealed by God through words and Scripture as well as oral tradition (*Jerusalem* (1783), 113–5). Revealed legislation prescribes only actions, not faith nor the acceptance of eternal truths. The actions prescribed by the revealed law are the "ceremonies," and the specific element of Judaism, therefore, is the ceremonial laws.

In opposition to *Spinoza, who considered the Mosaic legislation a state law designed only to promote the temporal happiness of the Jewish nation, Mendelssohn contended that Mosaic law transcends state law, because of its twofold goal: actions leading to temporal happiness and meditation on eternal and historical truths leading to eternal happiness (*ibid.*, 116). Every ceremony has a specific meaning and a precise relation to the speculative aspect of religion and morality (*ibid.*, 95). Since the Mosaic law is more than a state law, those of its parts which apply to the individual remain valid even after the destruction of the Jewish state and should be steadfastly observed (*ibid.*, 127–9). Moreover, it retains its important function as a bond between Jews everywhere, which is essential as long as polytheism, anthropomorphism, and religious usurpation continue to rule the earth (letter to Herz Homberg, in *Gesammelte Schriften*, 5 (1844), 669). Mendelssohn's polemics against Spinoza were taken up again in the late 19th–early 20th century by Hermann *Cohen (cf. his *Juedische Schriften*, ed. B. Strauss, 3 (1924), 290–372).

NINETEENTH-CENTURY PHILOSOPHERS. Isaac Noah *Mannheimer and Michael *Sachs wrote against the alarming neglect of observance of the ceremonial law in the period of Emancipation. They reemphasized the significance of ceremonial law in terms borrowed partly from Mendelssohn and partly from Kant's vindication of the *cultus* as a means of furthering morality. Of great moment was Leopold *Zunz's forthright stand on behalf of the rite of circumcision, which occasioned his study of the ceremonial law as a whole (*Gutachten ueber die Beschneidung*, in Zunz, Schr, 2 (1876), 190–203). Abraham *Geiger recognized only the validity of those ceremonies which proved capable of promoting religious and moral feelings (*Nachgelassene Schriften*, ed. L. Geiger, 1 (1875), 254ff., 324–5, 486–8). Under the influence of the German philologist Friedrich Cruezer and *Hegel, theologians began to view the rituals prescribed in the Torah, especially the sacrificial cult, as merely symbolic expressions of ideas (see for example, D. Einhorn, *Das Prinzip des Mosaismus*, 1854). Defending an orthodox position, Samson Raphael *Hirsch evolved a system of symbolism based chiefly on ethical values in order to give fresh meaning to the totality of *halakhah* (*Nineteen Letters*, sections *Edoth* and *Horeb*; see *Horeb*, trans. by I. Grunfeld, 1 (1962), 108).

TWENTIETH-CENTURY PHILOSOPHERS. In the 20th century Leo *Baeck spoke of two fundamental religious experiences, that of mystery (*Geheimnis*) and that of commandment (*Gebot*), which in Judaism are intertwined in a perfect unity

(*Essays*, trans. by W. Kaufmann (1958), 171, 173). For Franz *Rosenzweig there is a difference between commandment and law. God is not a lawgiver – He commands, and each act of *mitzvah* accomplishes the task of "unifying" Him, an assertion that Rosenzweig formulated in terms of kabbalistic doctrine (*Der Stern der Erloesung*, 3rd ed. (1954), 2:114ff.; 3:187–94).

[Alexander Altmann]

In Kabbalah

In Kabbalah the reasons for the commandments are integrated in the general system in relation to two basic principles: a symbolic view according to which everything in this world and all human acts, especially religious acts, are a reflection of divine processes and particularly those of the divine emanation; and the notion of reciprocal influence between the upper and lower worlds, which are not separated from each other but affect each other in all matters. Thus it appears that the commandments both reflect a mystical reality and the relations between heavenly forces, and also themselves influence this heavenly reality. On the one hand, a person who fulfills a commandment integrates himself into the divine system and into the harmony of the divine processes and thus confirms the order of the true universe as it should be. On the other hand, the actual performance of a commandment radiates backwards, strengthening the supernal system. Therefore there is a natural connection between the symbolic and the magical significance of every act; i.e., a direct connection between all planes of existence and the action of each plane on the others. While the symbolic evaluation gave rise to no particular doubts or vacillations and was also in tune with other religious and philosophical views in Judaism, the magical perception of reciprocal influence was bound to create problems. A major difficulty was how to define that divine world upon which the fulfilling of commandments acts. Because the kabbalists saw that world as the world of divine emanation (*Aẓilut*) which is divine, unique, and united by the ten *Sefirot* and by the other manifestations of the divine creative power, the question arose as to how anyone could presume to speak of the influence of human action on the divine world itself. The kabbalists found themselves in a dilemma on this issue: they believed in the existence of such a magical-theosophical link between God and man – a link which is the soul of religious activity – yet they shrank from an explicit and unequivocal formulation of this relationship, justifying it by weak explanations designed to soften the magical interpretation and make it seem as if it were only allegorical.

At first only a few commandments were kabbalistically interpreted in terms of the activity of certain *sefirot*. Thus the Sefer ha-*Bahir interprets the commandments involving acts (*mitzvot ma'asiyyot*) such as *tefillin*, *ẓiẓit*, the *lulav* of Sukkot and *terumah* ("tithe-offering") as indications of the last *Sefirah* and its relations with the other *Sefirot*, especially of *Binah* and *Tiferet* (here called *Emet*) and the *Yesod*. The early kabbalists in Spain also interpreted according to these principles only those commandments that have no rational explanations (*ḥukkim*, or, according to theological terminology, *mitzvot shimiyyot*), e.g., sacrifices and worship in the Temple in general, and the major prayers. Moral and rational commandments were not yet included. *Ezra b. Solomon of Gerona, in his commentary on the Song of Songs, was the first to explain the reasons for these commandments in a kabbalistic framework. He was succeeded by his colleagues, Jacob b. Sheshet *Gerondi and *Naḥmanides. From the late 13th century on, the reasons for the commandments became more widely discussed in the Kabbalah. Even those commandments whose principles seem manifest to reason, such as love of God, fear of God, and *yiḥud* ("the unity of God"), were interpreted in terms of man's relation to the world of the divine *Sefirot*. The reasons behind the commandments on the Sabbath, festivals, sacrifices, prayers, and many others are discussed in the main part of the *Zohar, according to the general rule that spiritual awakening on earth causes a divine awakening. The author of the Zohar saw in many commandments the act which symbolizes the union of the *Sefirah* of *Malkhut* with the *Sefirah* of *Yesod* or *Tiferet*. The details of the commandments were explained as reflecting the processes of the supernal emanation, and a man who fulfills the commandment integrates within the process of *shefa* ("emanation"), strengthening the divine life which pulsates in every creature.

Fulfilling the commandments also strengthens divine harmony in the universe; the *yiḥud* is not merely a declaration of faith in the One God but also an increase in the oneness of the living God through man's acts in the world and man's intention (*kavvanah*) during the performance of such activity. The disunited world becomes reunited by the performance of commandments. *Moses ben Shem Tov de Leon's *Sefer ha-Rimmon* (written in 1287), which deals solely with the reasons for the commandments, included interpretations of over 100 positive and negative commandments. In the same era two anonymous kabbalists also composed comprehensive and detailed works (one of which was attributed to Isaac ibn Farḥi of Salonika 250 years later), on the reasons behind the commandments; these have survived in manuscript. Around 1300 the *Ra'aya Meheimna*, a later layer of the Zohar which was highly influential, offered a lengthy exposition according to which all 613 commandments may be interpreted mystically. Two classic works on this subject were written in the 14th century: Menahem *Recanati's *Ta'amei ha-Mitzvot* (Constantinople, 1544, complete ed. London, 1963), and Sefer ha-*Kanah (Cracow, 1894) by an anonymous Spanish kabbalist who interpreted most of the commandments in detail and argued radically that the only correct interpretation of the statutes of the Oral Law, and not only those of the Torah (Written Law), is through Kabbalah. In Safed in 1556 *David b. Solomon ibn Abi Zimra wrote *Meẓudat David* (Zolkiew, 1862) summarizing previous literature.

With the development of Lurianic Kabbalah the commandments were interpreted according to its special theses; i.e., the doctrine of *tikkun* ("restitution") and the divine *parẓufim* ("countenances"). Many comprehensive works were devoted to this subject, beginning with Ḥayyim *Vital's *Sha'ar ha-Mitzvot* (Jerusalem, 1872). Noteworthy are *Mekor Ḥayyim, Tur Bareket*, and *Tur Piteda* (Amsterdam, Leghorn, 1654–55) on the reasons for the laws in the Shulḥan Arukh by Ḥayyim ha-Kohen of Aleppo, Vital's disciple; *Ez Ḥayyim* by Judah ibn Ḥanin of Morocco (late 17th century; published in part, Leghorn, 1793); *Devar ha-Melekh* (Leghorn, 1805) by *Abraham b. Israel of Brody; and *Yalkut Yiẓḥak* (Warsaw, 1895–1900) by Isaac Zaler, an important anthology on the reasons for the commandments. Special works are devoted to the *mitzvah* of circumcision: e.g., *Yesod Yiẓḥak* (Zolkiew, 1810) by Jacob Isaac ha-Levi and *Zekher David* (Leghorn, 1837) by David Zacuto; and to the *mitzvah of sheḥitah, Pirkei ha-Nezar* (Lublin, 1880) by Eliezer Shoḥat of Zhitomir.

[Gershom Scholem]

Kabbalistic "reasons for the commandments" are integrated into the overall scholarly argument regarding the relationship of kabbalistic thought to its rabbinic forebear. As with other topics in the field, G. *Scholem finds the kabbalistic perspective at odds with the rabbinic view, which "cut ritual off from its mythic substratum … rejected all cosmic implications." But M. *Idel writes of rabbinic theurgy that "long before the emergence of Kabbalistic theosophy, Jews envisioned their ritual as a God-maintaining activity … as universe-maintaining as well."

[Gerald Y. Blidstein (2nd ed.)]

BIBLIOGRAPHY: J. Heinemann, *Ta'amei ha-Mitzvot be-Sifrut Yisrael*, 2 vols. (1949–56²); A. Marmorstein, *Studies in Jewish Theology* (1950), passim; W. Bacher, *Die exegetische Terminologie der juedischen Traditionsliteratur*, 1 (1899), 66–67, 113; 2 (1905), 69–73; C. Siegfried, *Philo von Alexandria* (1875), 20ff., 182ff., and passim; A. Altmann, in: *Rav Sa'adyah Ga'on* (1943), 658–73; idem, in: BJRL, 28, no. 2 (1944), 3–24; G. Golinski, *Das Wesen des Religionsgesetzes in der Philosophie des Bachja* (1935); D. Rosin, in: MGWJ, 43 (1899), 125ff.; idem, *Die Ethik des Maimonides* (1876), 92ff.; C. Neuberger, *Das Wesen des Gesetzes in der Philosophie des Maimonides* (1933); Miklishanski, in: *Ha-Rambam* (1957), 83–97; S. Poznański, *Perush al Yeḥezkel u-Terei Asar le-Rabbi Eli'ezer mi-Belganẓi* (1913), 68, and passim; G. Vajda, *Recherches sur la philosophie et la kabbale* (1962), 161ff.; J. Wohlgemuth, *Das juedische Religionsgesetz in juedischer Beleuchtung*, 2 vols. (1912–19); Guttman, Philosophies, index; A. Barth, *The Mitzvoth, Their Aim and Purpose* (1949). KABBALAH: I. Tishby, *Mishnat ha-Zohar*, 2 (1961), 429–578; A. Altmann, in: KS, 40 (1964/65), 256–76, 405–12; Fr.J. Molitor, *Philosophie der Geschichte*, 3 (1839); G. Vajda, *Le commentaire d'Ezra de Gérone sure le Cantique des Cantiques* (1969), 381–424. **ADD. BIBLIOGRAPHY:** I. Heinemann, *Ta'amei ha-Mizvot be-Sifrut Yisra'el*, 2 vols. (1954–57); E.E. Urbach, *Ḥazal: Pirkei Emunot ve-De'ot* (1969); I. Tishby, *The Wisdom of the Zohar*, vol. 3 (1989), 1155–1328; G. Scholem, *On the Kabbalah and Its Symbolism* (1961), 118–58; M. Idel, *Kabbalah: New Perspectives* (1988), 156–99.

COMMENTARY, magazine founded by the *American Jewish Committee (AJC) in 1945 as a monthly journal of "significant thought and opinion, Jewish affairs and contemporary issues." While its policies were consistent with the parent organization, especially in its early years, over time it won its editorial freedom, a situation rare in organizational life.

Eliot T. Cohen, an experienced journalist in the Jewish, communal, field was named its first editor. For a community rapidly undergoing assimilation in the postwar years, both the AJC and Cohen sought to establish ties between its intellectual class, often alienated from ancestral ties, and its emerging middle class. Cohen assembled an outstanding group of editors including Clement Greenberg, Robert Warshow, Nathan *Glazer, and Irving Kristol and invited the finest minds, both gentile and Jewish, to contribute to the publication. In a few years, *Commentary* moved to the forefront of journals of opinion not only as the major publication in Jewish life but as a critical force in the broader community as well.

Commentary was among the first publications on the liberal-left to recognize that the Soviet Union with its army sitting astride Western Europe following the war and U.S. withdrawal of troops from Europe posed a threat to the West. Under Cohen, the magazine took a leadership role in mobilizing public opinion to the threat during the early stages of the Cold War, a posture it held firmly to until the collapse of the Soviet Union.

Commentary's scope, however, was wider. It became involved deeply in the literary and cultural scene. Under Cohen and subsequent editors, it introduced to a wider public such writers as Saul *Bellow, Joseph *Heller, Bernard *Malamud, Philip *Roth, Cynthia *Ozick, and the Yiddish into English work of Isaac Bashevis *Singer.

In 1960, after a brief hiatus following Cohen's death, he was succeeded by Norman *Podhoretz, a young literary critic. Initially, Podhoretz moved the magazine to the left, publishing a number of the New Left writers of the period including Edgar Friedenberg and Christopher Lasch. His sojourn on the left, however, was brief. Before long, *Commentary* began to strike out at New Age Thought and activities, including student campus disruptions. The magazine continued and expanded its criticism of the Soviet Union. By the late 1960s and early 1970s, *Commentary* came to be known increasingly as the voice of neo-conservatism, a characterization leveled at it by its critics, but which the magazine took as a badge of honor. During and following the Six-Day and Yom Kippur wars, Podhoretz came increasingly also to focus on Israel's safety and security.

Commentary's influence reached its height during the Ford and Reagan administrations. Podhoretz's book, *The Present Danger*, became the bible of efforts to move beyond detente with the Soviet Union supported by previous Democratic and Republican administrations to efforts to bring down the Soviet Union through a rapid defense build-up and challenging Soviet imperial designs in every part of the world. Following articles that appeared in *Commentary*, a number of neo-cons, including Jeane Kirkpatrick, who wrote on authoritarian and totalitarian government, arguing incorrectly as it turned out that totalitarian governments cannot make the transition to democracy, and Daniel Patrick Moynihan, entered the Ford and Reagan administrations. Both Kirkpatrick and Moynihan served as ambassadors at the United Nations.

With Podhoretz's retirement in 1995, his long-time associate Neal Kozodoy took over the reins of the publication. His main task has been to lead the magazine into the post-Cold War era following the collapse of the Soviet Union. He has continued to emphasize, however, many of the magazine's older themes, such as criticism of left-wing influences on the campus, in the media, and in American politics. In the period following 9/11, *Commentary* became one of the most forceful defenders of the Bush Doctrine calling for the use by the nation, with or without international support, of the preemptive strike in the battle against international terrorism, a move that was implemented by the administration in Iraq.

A new generation of younger, neo-conservative intellectuals and writers emerged, including Charles Krauthammer, William Kristol, and Robert Kagan and government officials Paul *Wolfowitz and Eliot *Abrams, whom historian John Ehrman has characterized as "*Commentary*'s Children," who continued to promote many of the ideas brought forward by *Commentary*.

BIBLIOGRAPHY: M. Friedman, *"Commentary" in American Life* (2005).

[Murray Friedman (2nd ed.)]

COMMUNISM, the international revolutionary Marxist movement that evolved under *Lenin's leadership from the Bolshevik faction (created in 1903 in the Russian Social Democratic Party) to become the ruling party of Russia after the October Revolution in 1917 and created the Communist International (Comintern) in 1919. The Communist movement and ideology played an important part in Jewish life, particularly in the 1920s, 1930s, and during and after World War II. Violent polemics raged between Jewish Communists and Zionists in all countries until the disenchantment with the anti-Jewish policies of *Stalin in his last years and, after his death, with the antisemitic quality of the treatment of Jews and Jewish life in the U.S.S.R., as well as the increasingly violent anti-Israel stand of Moscow in the Arab-Israel conflict.

Individual Jews played an important role in the early stages of Bolshevism and the Soviet regime. These Jews were mostly confirmed assimilationists who adopted their party's concept of the total disappearance of Jewish identity under advanced capitalism and socialism. They thus opposed the existence of separate Jewish workers' movements, particularly the *Bund and Socialist Zionism. The great attraction of communism among Russian, and later also Western, Jewry emerged only with the establishment of the Soviet regime in Russia. The mere fact that during the civil war in Russia following the October 1917 Revolution the counterrevolutionary forces were violently antisemitic, shedding Jewish blood in pogroms on an unprecedented scale, drove the bulk of Russian Jewish youth into the ranks of the Bolshevik regime. During Lenin's rule, the NEP ("new economic policy"), and the years preceding Stalin's personal dictatorship and the great purges of the 1930s, a dichotomy of Jewish life evolved in the Soviet Union and was greatly attractive to both assimilationist and secular Yiddish-oriented Jews outside Russia. On the one hand, Russian Jews enjoyed the opportunities of immense geographical and social mobility, leaving behind the townlets of the *Pale of Settlement and occupying many responsible positions in all branches of the party and state machinery at the central and local seats of power. On the other, a secular educational and cultural network in Yiddish and an economic and administrative framework of Jewish life, including agricultural settlement and Jewish local and regional "Soviets," were officially established and fostered, culminating in the mid-1930s in the creation of the Jewish Autonomous Region in the Far East (*Birobidzhan). Many Jews the world over therefore regarded the Soviet concept of the solution to the "Jewish question" as an intrinsic positive approach with the main options open for various Jewish trends – assimilation or preservation of Jewish (secular) identity and even Jewish territorialism and embryonic Jewish statehood.

During this period the position of world Jewry markedly deteriorated because of the severe economic and political crises in Palestine and the growing trend of oppressive antisemitism in the rest of Eastern Europe, Nazi and fascist influence in Central and Western Europe, and the economic crisis in the United States. Communism and support of the Soviet Union thus seemed to many Jews to be the only alternative, and Communist trends became widespread in virtually all Jewish communities. In some countries Jews became the leading element in the legal and illegal Communist parties and in some cases were even instructed by the Communist International to change their Jewish-sounding names and pose as non-Jews, in order not to confirm right-wing propaganda that presented Communism as an alien, Jewish conspiracy (e.g., the Polish slogan against "*Żydo-Komuna*" and the Nazi reiteration against "Jewish Bolshevism," etc.). Initially, the Stalin-*Trotsky controversy did not affect the attraction of Communism to Jews, though a number of intellectual Jewish Communists tended more toward Trotsky's consistent internationalism than to Stalin's concept of building "Socialism in one country" and subjecting the interests of the international working class to the changing tactical interests of the Soviet Union. The facts about the gradual liquidation of the Yiddish cultural and educational network and the stifling of the Birobidzhan experiment in the late 1930s did not immediately reach the Jewish public outside the Soviet Union. In addition, only a minority of Jewish Communists condemned the Comintern-directed policy at the end of the 1930s that branded any form of non-Communist Socialism as "social fascism" and the main enemy of the revolution, while simultaneously seeking cooperation with German Nazism. Even the Molotov-Ribbentrop Pact of August 1939 was a shock to only a minority of Jewish Communists (except confirmed oppositionists, mainly of the Trotskyite "Fourth International"). When World War II broke out in 1939, most Jewish Communists defended the Soviet anti-Western-flavored neutrality. But from June 1941, when Nazi Germany attacked the Soviet Union and the Communists in occupied Europe excelled in anti-Nazi resistance, and particularly after the war, when the Soviet Union actively supported the establishment of a Jewish state in Palestine, Jewish Communists the world over achieved the highest degree of inner contentment and intellectual harmony in the whole history of the Communist movement.

The relatively abrupt disenchantment began in the late 1940s and the beginning of the 1950s, when Soviet policy toward the State of Israel gradually reversed from support to hostility and the anti-*Cosmopolitan campaign, the *Slanský Trials in Czechoslovakia, and the *Doctors' Plot in Moscow revealed the antisemitic character of the Soviet regime in Stalin's last years. The disclosures, in 1956–57, of the brutal liquidation of all Jewish institutions and the judicial murder of most Yiddish writers and artists in the "black years" (1948–53), the growing Soviet-Arab cooperation against Israel, and the anti-Jewish policy of the Khrushchev and post-Khrushchev period, which culminated in the violent "anti-Zionist" and anti-Israel campaign after the *Six-Day War and the Leningrad Trial of 1970, rendered Jewish disenchantment with Soviet-style Communism almost complete. The *New Left groups that emerged in the later 1960s and enjoyed heavy support from Jewish youth, particularly in the U.S., France, and Germany, were not Soviet-oriented.

[Binyamin Eliav]

Bolshevik Theory (1903–1917)

The Bolshevik attitude to basic questions concerning the Jews was formulated in as early as 1903, with the emergence of the Bolshevik faction during the Second Congress of the Russian Social Democratic Party in Brussels and London. The Bolshevik faction (which in 1912–13 became the Bolshevik Party) contained a number of Jews who were active mainly in the field of organization and propaganda (rather than in theory and ideology, as was the case with the Jewish Mensheviks). They included such people as Maxim *Litvinov (Wallach), M. Liadov (Mandelshtam), Grigori Shklovsky, A. Soltz, S. Gusev (Drabkin), Grigori *Zinoviev (Radomyslsky), Lev *Kamenev (Rosenfeld), Rozaliya *Zemliachka (Zalkind), Helena Rozmirovich, Yemeli *Yaroslavsky (Gubelman), Serafima Gopner, G. Sokolnikov, I. Piatnitsky, Jacob *Sverdlov, M. Vladimirov, P. Zalutsky, A. Lozovsky, Y. Yaklovlev (Epstein), Lazar *Kaganovich, D. Shvartsman, and Simon *Dimanstein. Their number grew rapidly between the Russian revolutions of February and October 1917, when various groups and individuals joined the Bolsheviks; prominent among the new adherents were *Trotsky, M. Uritsky, M. Volodarsky, J. Steklov, Adolf Joffe, David Riazanov (Goldendach), Yuri *Larin, and Karl *Radek (Sobelsohn). Most of the Jews active in Bolshevik ranks before 1917 were assimilationist intellectuals. Few Jewish workers in Russia belonged to the Bolsheviks, and propaganda material designed to recruit Jewish members was restricted to a single Yiddish pamphlet, a short report on the Third (Bolshevik) Congress of the Russian Social Democratic Party (April–May 1905), which contained a special introduction by Lenin addressed "To the Jewish Workers."

It was, indeed, Lenin, the ideological, political, and organizational leader of Bolshevism, who also determined the party's policy toward the Jews. In the period 1900–06, Lenin expressed himself on three Jewish topics: antisemitism, Jewish nationalism versus assimilation, and the relationship between the Bund and the Social Democratic Party. From its very beginnings, Russian Marxism under the leadership of Plekhanov had rejected both the anti-Jewish tendencies in Russian populism and the evasive attitude of the Second International toward the struggle against antisemitism (Brussels Congress, 1891). On the subject of antisemitism, Lenin's attitude was at all times consistent; not only did he take a definitive stand against it, but, unlike Plekhanov, he was free of any personal prejudice against Jews and would never indulge in any anti-Jewish remarks, in public or in private. This held true in spite of the many bitter arguments he had with Jewish opponents in the revolutionary movement. Although generally relying on Marx on questions of fundamental importance, Lenin did not resort to Marx's famous essay "On the Jewish Question" when dealing with Jewish affairs, because of its anti-Jewish implications. He rejected outright any suggestion that the Bolsheviks should ignore anti-Jewish policy and propaganda in czarist Russia, let alone make use of its popular appeal. Lenin regarded the czarist anti-Jewish hate campaign as a diversionary maneuver, an integral part of the demagogic campaign against "the aliens" conducted by henchmen of the czarist regime. He believed that the Jewish worker suffered no less than the Russian under capitalism and the czarist government (*Iskra*, No. 1, December 1900). Later (1905) he went even further, pointing out that Jewish workers suffered from a special form of discrimination by being deprived of even elementary civil rights. Antisemitism was designed to serve the social interests of the ruling classes, although there were also workers who had been incited. As antisemitism was clearly against the interests of the revolution, the fight against it was an integral part of the struggle against czarism and had to be conducted with "proletarian solidarity and a scientific ideology." Lenin regarded the pogroms of 1905–06 as part of the campaign against the revolution and called for the creation of a militia and for armed self-defense as the only means of combating the rioters. He also waged a special press campaign against the pogrom in Bialystok. Nevertheless, Lenin lacked a proper appreciation of the intensity of the Russian antisemitic tradition, the complexity of the factors underlying it, and the special role that it played in the political and social life of the country.

The Bolshevik attitude toward the collective identity of the Jews and their future was theoretically part of their general views on the national question. Lenin did not consider nationalism a constructive and stable social factor. His approach to it was conditional and pragmatic, subordinate to the interests of the class struggle. At the beginning of 1903 he voiced the opinion that the Social Democratic Party was not required to provide positive solutions to national problems, such as the granting of independence, federation, or autonomy, except in a few special cases, and that it should confine itself to combating discrimination and russification of the non-Russian nationalities. The vague formula contained in the platform of the Social Democratic Party on the "right of nations to self-determination" was regarded as a mere slogan, designed to facilitate the organizational and political consolidation of the workers in the common fight against czarism and capitalism, irrespective of their national origin. Furthermore, this "right to self-determination" applied to nationalities having a territorial basis and did not refer to the Jews.

Lenin knew little of the history, culture, and life of the Jews. His view on the Jewish problem was of a casual nature and was not derived from any study or analysis of his own; this was one of the reasons for the shifts in his attitude within a single year. In February 1903 (in the article "Does the Jewish Proletariat Need an Independent Political Party?") he spoke of a Jewish "national culture," a view predicated upon the recognition of the Jews as a national entity, and said that it could not be foretold whether or not the Jews of Russia would assimilate. But in as early as October of that year (in the article "The Position of the Bund in the Party") he voiced categorical opposition to the view that the Jews are a nation and expressed the conviction that their assimilation is a desirable and necessary development. He based himself on a truncated quotation from the writings of Karl Kautsky, the Marxist theoretician, accepting the view that the Jews lack the two characteristics of a nationality: a common territory and a common language (presuming that Yiddish was not a language). The decisive motive behind Lenin's view, however, was the overriding role of the party in his conception of the political struggle and his determination to base the party on absolute organizational centralism. The Bund's demand for a federative structure of the party, in which the Bund would be "the sole representative" of the Jewish proletariat, was regarded by Lenin as counter to his revolutionary strategy. Even so, he did not regard this difference with the Bund as closed to compromise. In 1905–06, when the emphasis in the internal struggle raging in the Russian Social Democratic Party passed from matters of organization to tactical questions and the Bund's stand on certain important points proved to be close to that of the Bolsheviks, Lenin did not hesitate to do everything possible to facilitate the return of the Jewish organization to the party fold (the Bund left the Social Democratic Party in 1903). That the Bund had put even greater stress upon its demand for Jewish cultural autonomy at its sixth convention proved to be no deterrent.

Several leading members of a short-lived non-Leninist group of Bolsheviks, which came into existence in 1908, developed their own approach to Jewish questions. Thus, A. Lunacharsky, in dealing with religion, found that the Bible, and particularly the Prophets, contained revolutionary elements and that there was a link between the Old Testament and the new "Religion of Labor," the latter being, in his opinion, an essential part of socialism. The existence of the Jewish people and the contribution it had made to humanity were of vital importance (*Religiya i Sotsiyalizm*, pt. 1, 1908). Maxim *Gorky, in his condemnation of antisemitism, did not confine himself to its economic, social, and legal aspects, and his struggle against it was not motivated by mere utilitarian political considerations. His positive remarks on Zionism, first made in 1902, were reprinted in 1906, at a time when he had already joined the ranks of the Bolsheviks. He acknowledged the contribution of Jewish ethics and regarded "the creative power of the Jewish people" as a force that would be of help in establishing "the Law of Socialism" among mankind. These individual stands on the Jews taken by Lunacharsky and Gorky had a direct bearing on the attitude they were to adopt on Jewish questions, especially on Jewish culture, at a later stage, when the Bolsheviks had already come to power in Russia.

After the 1905 revolution, when there were nationalist stirrings in Russia, Lenin came to appreciate the importance of the national question and its possible use in the struggle against the czarist regime. In addition to the slogan of "the right of nations to self-determination, including separation," he also recognized the need to make concrete and positive proposals on the solution of national questions, based mainly on the concept of territorial autonomy. Lenin was ready to advocate the creation of autonomous districts based on a homogeneous national (i.e., ethnic and linguistic) composition, even on a minute scale. Such districts, he assumed, would seek to establish contacts of various kinds with members of the same nationality in other parts of Russia, or even in other parts of the world ("Critical Notes on the National Question," 1913). The pogroms and the *Beilis blood libel led Lenin to conclude that "in recent years the persecution of Jews has reached unprecedented proportions" and that "no other nation in Russia suffers as much oppression and persecution as does the Jewish nationality."

In a bill on equal rights for nationalities that Lenin drafted for presentation to the Duma by the Bolshevik faction (1914), special emphasis was put on the lack of rights suffered by the Jews. He was not, however, consistent in the terms he employed with reference to the Jews; he frequently spoke of the Jewish "nationality" or "nation" (as for example in the above-mentioned bill) and nearly always in the context of the national question in Russia. In general, he held that "the process of national assimilation as furthered by capitalism is to be regarded as a great historical advance" and that "the proletariat also welcomes the assimilation of nations," except "when this is based on force or on special privileges." "Each nation consists of two nations," and there are "two national cultures" in each national culture, including that of the Jews. He acknowledged the presence of "universal progressive qualities" in Jewish culture, such as that of "internationalism" and "the capacity to absorb the stream of contemporary progressive ideas" (the latter quality manifesting itself in the high percentage of Jews found in democratic and proletarian movements). In view of his general attitude on the Jewish question, the "progressive qualities" that he perceived in Jewish culture were of the kind that implied the impending assimilation of that culture to "international culture." He did, however, admit that equality of national rights included the right to demand "the hiring of special teachers, at government expense, to teach the Jewish language, Jewish history, etc." The debate on Jewish nationalism, linked with the question of "national cultural autonomy" as demanded by the Bund, increasingly became a part of the internal party struggle. Lenin held fast to the idea that national cultural autonomy would result in weakening the workers' movement by dividing it according to the nationality of its members.

Similar views were also expressed by Stalin. In an essay published in 1913 under the title "The National Question and Social Democracy" (later known under the title "Marxism and the National Question"), which had Lenin's approval and was devoted in large part to the Jews, Stalin gave a dogmatic definition of the concept of nationhood: "A nation is a historically constituted, stable community of people, formed on the basis of a common language, territory, economic life, and psychological make-up, manifested in a common culture." If even a single one of these characteristics is missing, there is no "nation." On the basis of this definition, Stalin contended that the Jewish communities living in the various countries did not constitute one nation. Although every one of them might be described as possessing a common "national character," they were to be regarded as "tribes" or "ethnic entities." When the Pale of Settlement was abolished, the Jews of Russia would assimilate. There was no farming class among them and they existed only as a minority in various areas where the majority population belonged to a different nation. They are therefore to be classified as "national minorities," serving the nations among which they live as industrialists, merchants, and professionals, and were bound to assimilate into these nations. It followed that the Bund's program of "national autonomy" referred to a "nation whose future is denied and whose existence has still to be proven."

Stalin, of course, also opposed Zionism. Unlike Lenin, he did not even have any modest positive proposals to make on the solution of national and cultural problems concerning the Jews. In accordance with the Bolshevik approach, he did, however, agree that the Marxist stand on national questions was not absolute, but rather "dialectic," and depended on the specific circumstances of time and place. Another prominent Bolshevik, S. Shaumian, who generally opposed any positive suggestions about the national question, did in fact concede (in 1914) that under certain conditions it might be possible to accept "national cultural autonomy." Only one leading Bolshevik, Helena Rozmirovich, is known to have favored such a solution at this stage in the history of the Bolshevik Party.

Soviet Practice (1917–1939)

After the October Revolution, the Jewish problem in Russia ceased to be a theoretical issue in interparty strife, and the Bolshevik government and party had to assume responsibility for the specific problems affecting the existence and development of the Jewish community. During the Revolution Jews played a prominent part in the party organs. The Politburo elected on Oct. 23, 1917, had four Jews among its seven members. The Military Revolutionary Committee, appointed to prepare the coup, was headed by Trotsky and had two Jews among its five members. In the early years of the Soviet regime, Jews were in many leading positions in the government and party machinery, although, as a rule, their number did not exceed the percentage of Jews in the urban population. (The number of Jewish members of the All-Russian Communist Party was 5.2% in 1922, 4.33% in 1927, and 3.8% in 1930; the corresponding figures in the Ukraine and Belorussia in 1927 were 12.1% and 23%, respectively.) The legal emancipation of the Jews, which had already been proclaimed in the February Revolution, seemed in Soviet practice to be implemented to an extent unprecedented in any other country. Their unrestricted admission to the universities and to all categories of employment served both the interests of the Soviet regime and the needs and aspirations of the Jews. The centrifugal nationalist tendencies among the peoples of the western border republics, which endangered Soviet centralism, inspired the regime to utilize compact, Jewish masses in these areas as a counterweight, which would swing the balance in the centralist regime's favor. The cultural russification of the Jews played a significant role in this respect. In 1922, as much as two-thirds of the Jewish membership of the Communist Party in the Ukraine was Russian-speaking. The Soviet regime also derived a propaganda benefit from the legal and political equality of Soviet Jews, in contrast to the neighboring states, such as Poland and Romania, which followed an antisemitic policy in practice and sometimes also in law. In both these countries a large Jewish population was concentrated in the border regions (Western Belorussia, Western Ukraine, and Bessarabia) that the Soviet Union considered as being only temporarily detached from its territory.

Antisemitism was branded as being counterrevolutionary in nature, and persons participating in pogroms or instigating them were outlawed (by a special decree issued by the Council of Commissars in July 1918, signed and personally amended by Lenin to sharpen its tone). A statement against antisemitism made by Lenin in March 1919 was one of the rare occasions on which his voice was put on a phonograph record, to be used in a mass campaign against the counterrevolutionary incitement against the Jews. The regime made every effort to denounce the pogroms and punish the persons taking part in them, even when they were Red Army personnel. When the civil war came to an end, a law was passed against "incitement to hatred and hostility of a national or religious nature," which, in effect, also applied to antisemitism, including the use of the pejorative epithet *Zhid*.

The theoretical approach to the Jewish question adopted by prerevolutionary Bolshevism was found to be unsuited to the new situation. The denial of the collective right of the Jews to nationhood, the forecast of the desirable and unavoidable assimilation, and the negation of a Jewish "national culture" and the use of Yiddish as a national Jewish language no longer formed a part of Soviet dogma. Although not all of these formulas were officially abolished or reinterpreted, the entire propaganda network was based on a variety of views that were often the very opposite of Lenin's and Stalin's utterances in prerevolutionary days. The list of nationalities, i.e., ethnic groups, in the Soviet Union included the Jews among the "national minorities" that had no defined territory of their own and that the czarist regime had sought to destroy by any means, not excluding the instigation of pogroms. It followed that the assurance of their right to "free national development" by the "very nature" of the Soviet regime was not enough and that it behooved the party to help "the toiling masses of these ethnic groups" utilize in full "their inherent right to free development" (Tenth Congress of the All-Russian Communist Party, 1921, speech by Stalin, Resolutions). Shortly after the Revolution Jewish affairs were officially included in the jurisdiction of the Commissariat for Nationalities; in addition, Jewish councils ("soviets") were appointed on a local, subdistrict, and district level. This trend found its clearest expression during the early stages of the Birobidzhan experiment (1928–34), when the head of the Soviet state, Mikhail Kalinin, declared that "the Jewish people were facing a great task – that of preserving their nationhood." Thus the prerevolutionary forecast of assimilation as the solution to the Jewish problem, even under advanced capitalism, was now replaced by a national and territorial solution under the new conditions created by the "dictatorship of the proletariat." Disregarding Stalin's findings in 1913 that there were no links between the Jewish communities living in various countries, the Soviet leaders now clearly took into account the influence of the Jews on the Revolution, not only in Russia itself but in other countries as well. Lenin also stressed the significance of abolishing completely the anti-Jewish discrimination practiced by the former regime (see Dimanstein, *Lenin on the Jewish Problem in Russia*, 1924), and this may well have been one of the motives for the project of establishing the nucleus of a Jewish republic (Kalinin at the second national conference of OZET). Although the party did not abandon its theoretical opposition to granting "national cultural autonomy" to ethnic groups lacking a territorial basis, the Jews were in fact permitted to develop a "national culture" of their own (in Yiddish) under the slogan of "a culture that was socialist in content and national in form." Assimilationism ceased to be an obligatory ideal for the foreseeable future. Stalin declared that "Lenin had good reason for saying that national differences will remain for a long time, even after the victory of the dictatorship of the proletariat on an international scale" (Collected Works, vol. 13, p. 7). The belief that Yiddish secular culture in the Soviet Union had a bright future became widespread the world over and attracted to the Soviet Union such non-Communist Jewish authors as David *Bergelson, Leib *Kvitko, David *Hofstein, Moshe *Kulbak, Peretz *Markish, Der *Nister, Max *Erik, Meir *Wiener, and Nakhum *Shtif during the 1920s. Jewish culture in the Soviet Union in this period recorded significant achievements in literature, linguistics, literary history, and some branches of historiography and demography.

This development of Yiddish culture and Jewish autonomy was partly influenced by the considerable influx of former members of Jewish workers' parties (the Bund, the "Fareynikte," *Po'alei Zion, etc.) into the ranks of the Communist Party, especially in the years 1918–21. Many of them tried at first to form Jewish Communist units, as, e.g., the "Kombund" or the "Komfarband," but had soon to conform to the centralist territorial organization of the party and disband all Jewish formations inside the Communist Party. They also had to abjure demonstratively their previous "nationalistic" errors and adopt the official ideology. Nevertheless, these former members of Jewish parties placed their stamp upon the party activities directed toward the Jews, especially through the *Yevsektsiya (which was shunned by the old Jewish Bolsheviks, except Dimanstein). They attempted to continue the tradition of the prerevolutionary Jewish labor parties, basing their activities on various slogans and programs that conformed to the general party policy toward the Jews, such as "productivization," the development of Yiddish culture, Soviet-Jewish territorialism, etc.

At an earlier stage, the Kombund had even had hopes of establishing Jewish organs that would enjoy a large measure of autonomy, based upon the existence of densely settled Jewish masses with a common language and a common way of life. Such endeavors were abandoned as early as 1920, when the Yevsektsiya became a simple propaganda organ of the party with the task of attracting the unorganized Jewish proletariat to the new regime. In accordance with the official line, which demanded that the Russian majority combat its own "chauvinism" and the minority nationalities overcome the "bourgeois nationalism" in their own sphere, the Yevsektsiya found its raison d'être by struggling against the "Jewish class enemy," i.e., Jewish religion, Zionism, and the use of Hebrew, and against any link with traditional Jewish culture. The last vestiges of technically legal Jewish labor groups outside the ruling party, as, e.g., the Communist Jewish Labor Party-Po'alei Zion and the legal *He-Ḥalutz, were officially closed down in 1928. The former was candidly told by the GPU (secret police): "You are disbanded, for we no longer have any need for your party." Two years later, in 1930, the Yevsektsiya itself was dissolved. The end of the Yevsektsiya, however, did not mean an immediate cessation of Yiddish cultural activities. Only in the second half of the 1930s did official policy toward the Jews undergo what was at first a gradual change and later developed into a radical departure from previous policy evolving into forced assimilation.

In the early 1930s, popular antisemitism in the Soviet Union seemed to be on the decline. This trend was used to justify omission of the subject in literature or the press. It was claimed that the "victory of Socialism" made any resurgence of antisemitism impossible. Later, during the Stalinist purges in the late 1930s, most Jewish cultural institutions, including all Yiddish schools, were closed down, and in the course of the far-reaching changes in government and party personnel, a tendency of restricting the number of Jewish cadres made itself felt. The geographic and social changes that had taken place among the Jews, their absorption into the economy of the country, and their growing assimilation to the Russian language and culture provided additional reasons for the gradual abandonment of developing Jewish culture and Jewish institutions and for a return to the original concept of total Jewish assimilation. This time, however, the authorities would force it upon the Jews (though they seemed to disregard the fact that the obligatory registration of the Jewish "nationality" on internal documents, particularly after the reintroduction of the old "passport system" in 1932, made total assimilation even formally impossible). The conscious disregard of any manifestation of popular antisemitism inside the Soviet Union now assumed a different meaning.

Only in the short period of Stalin's anti-Nazi stance from 1934, in the "Popular Front" era, did official Soviet opposition to antisemitism again assume international significance. While Nazi propaganda identified Jews with "Bolsheviks," the Soviet government stressed its opposition to antisemitism "anywhere in the world," expressed "fraternal feelings to the Jewish people" in recognition of its contribution to international socialism, and mentioned Karl Marx's Jewish origin (an item dropped from the 1952 edition of the Soviet Encyclopedia) and the part played by the Jews in building up the Soviet Union (Molotov, 1936). At this time also, a statement made by Stalin in 1931 to a correspondent of the Jewish Telegraphic Agency that "antisemitism, as an extreme form of racial chauvinism, is the most dangerous vestige of cannibalism" was even made public in the Soviet Union itself. But in the period of Soviet-German rapprochement (1939–41), the Nazi persecution and murder of Jews in the occupied territories of Europe was hardly mentioned in the Soviet press. Even after the outbreak of war between Germany and the Soviet Union (June 22, 1941), the authorities made no efforts to combat manifestations of popular antisemitism on Soviet territory, which were a frequent occurrence both in the rear and among the partisan units.

An exceptional phenomenon during the war was the establishment of the Jewish *Anti-Fascist Committee in Moscow (created to solicit support for the Soviet war effort among Western Jewry), whose existence reinforced feelings of solidarity between Soviet and world Jewry. Another exception was the change in Soviet policy toward Jewish endeavors in Palestine; there were signs of it already in 1945 and it culminated in 1947, when it strongly supported the establishment of a Jewish state. Andrei Gromyko's statement at the UN Special Assembly (May 1947) even stressed the historic connection between the Jewish people and Palestine.

Stalin's own infection with antisemitism, however (as witnessed by his daughter, Svetlana Aliluyeva, in her books *Twenty Letters to a Friend* and *Only One Year*), tallied with his new policy of encouraging Russian nationalism, which had traditionally been anti-Jewish. This trend came into the open in the "black years" (1948–53) with the campaign against "Cosmopolitans," the murder of Solomon *Mikhoels and other Jewish intellectuals, and the destruction of the last Jewish cultural institutions. The pro-Jewish turn in Soviet policy on Palestine did not have any effect upon the internal anti-Jewish campaign. From the end of 1948 the latter was relentlessly pursued and spread to other Communist countries as well, notably to Czechoslovakia. It reached its climax in the Slánský Trials in Prague and the Doctors' Plot in Moscow.

After Stalin's death (1953) the enforced cultural assimilation of Soviet Jews, as well as their individual discrimination in the universities and certain professions, continued. Events such as the singling out of Jews for "economic trials" and the publication of antisemitic literature in the 1960s, as, e.g., *Judaism Without Embellishment* by Trofim Kichko (1963), reconfirmed the anti-Jewish line of Stalin's last years in a somewhat attenuated and disguised form. The necessity to disguise this line, especially under pressure of world opinion, including Communist and pro-Soviet circles (see below), elicited some minor concessions, such as the publication of a Yiddish journal (*Sovetish Heymland), a few Yiddish books, and a temporary lull in the propaganda against the Jewish religion (at the end of the 1950s).

A worsening of the situation resulted from the Soviet Union's complete reversal of its policy toward Israel that began in the 1950s with the supply of large consignments of modern arms to the Arab states and continued to be manifest in the sinister role played by the Soviet Union in the sequence of events leading to the Six-Day War and the arrival of Soviet military personnel in Egypt. Soviet antisemitism presented itself from then on as "anti-Zionism."

The World Communist Movement

The Comintern, established in Moscow in the year 1919 and officially dissolved in 1943, had to deal with Jewish problems throughout the period of its existence. In theory, the Comintern recognized neither a "world Jewish people" nor the existence of a world Jewish problem; it conceded that such a problem may exist in certain countries, in which case it remained the responsibility of the local section of the Comintern. Antisemitism was officially regarded by the Comintern as a counterrevolutionary phenomenon, emanating from the dissolution of the petite bourgeoisie and providing a breeding ground for fascism. Its principal danger was that it diverted the attention of the proletariat from the class struggle, and it would disappear as a matter of course as soon as socialism triumphed over fascism and capitalism. There was hardly any mention of antisemitism at the Comintern congresses, the plenary sessions of its Executive Committee, and in its press.

From the very beginning, however, the Comintern was forced to deal with the issue of its relations with the Jewish workers' movement, which was itself a kind of miniature international. The Po'alei Zion had its World Union, and the Bund, although lacking a world organization of its own, wielded great influence among Jewish workers' organizations in Europe and America. The Jewish workers' movement in prerevolutionary Russia had also exerted ideological influence upon Jewish workers in other countries, and even upon Jewish groups that did not belong to the working class. Moreover, the Jewish workers' movement had intricate ties with general workers' organizations and with the international workers' movement, and it had in its ranks many experienced revolutionaries. But the rigid principles of organizational structure made any organized Jewish participation in the Comintern impossible. Efforts made by Communist-oriented groups of the Bund (the Kombund) to join the Comintern as an organization ended in failure, as did similar attempts made by the Polish Bund. The left wing of Po'alei Zion, which, unlike the Bund, had not been involved in the prerevolutionary struggle between Mensheviks and Bolsheviks, made even more determined efforts to be accepted by the Comintern; but in 1920, after prolonged negotiations, the Comintern rejected a proposal to create a Jewish section within the Comintern that would consist of all Communist bodies active among the Jewish proletariat (the Yevsektsiya, Kombund, and the Communist Po'alei Zion). Another proposal, made after the second congress of the Comintern, which provided for the World Union of Po'alei Zion to be accepted as a member of the Comintern while its branches would be permitted to form Jewish sections of the respective Communist parties and would retain a degree of autonomy in matters affecting the specific needs of the Jewish masses, was also rejected. The Comintern was ready to concede the creation of Jewish sections of local Communist parties, but was not prepared to accept the continued existence of a Jewish world union. In 1921 the executive council of the Comintern announced the formation of a bureau of Jewish affairs to direct Comintern propaganda among Jewish workers all over the world; however, nothing further was ever heard about the realization of this plan.

Another major Jewish issue confronting the Comintern was that of its attitude toward Zionism and the Jewish settlement in Palestine. The second congress of the Comintern (1920) denounced Zionism, which "by its claim to a Jewish state in Palestine, where Jewish workers form only a small minority, actually delivers the Arab workers to Britain for exploitation." The executive committee (August 1921) further elaborated upon this denunciation of Zionism by branding the idea of concentrating the Jewish masses in Palestine as "utopist and reformist," an idea "that leads directly to counterrevolutionary results, aiming as it does at settlement in Palestine, which eventually will only serve to strengthen British imperialism there." Throughout its existence, the Comintern adhered to this stand, instructing its Palestine section, as well as all Jewish Communists in other countries, accordingly. In the mid-1920s, however, the Communist Trade Union International (the "Profintern") made an unsuccessful attempt to establish ties with the Left Po'alei Zion in Palestine.

Though the Comintern did not arrive at an official definition of Jewish group identity, its general approach was expressed in the early 1930s in a widely distributed book written by a Jew, Otto Heller, *Der Untergang des Judentums* (1931). Its thesis was that West European Jewry was doomed to disappear as a result of its emancipation, the decline of religion, mixed marriages, and assimilation, and the loss of the special social functions that it had previously fulfilled in European society. A similar process was taking place in the western hemisphere countries to which many Jews had emigrated. In Eastern Europe, on the other hand, the Jews had retained certain national characteristics, and their ultimate fate was still in the balance. In the Soviet Union, they were recognized as a nationality; whether they would utilize the opportunity offered them by the Socialist regime to preserve their national existence and even advance from the status of nationality to that of a nation, with its own territory, was completely dependent on their desire to do so. Even in the Soviet Union, however, at least partial assimilation was an irresistible trend.

During the 1930s, until June 1941, the Communist parties everywhere, including Palestine, adhered strictly to the Soviet line – from its anti-Nazi stand during the Popular Front period to its denunciation of the Western powers and their "imperialist" war against Nazi Germany during the Soviet-German rapprochement (1939–41). The mental strain involved in Soviet-Nazi friendship and cooperation, particularly for Jewish Communists, vanished with the German attack on the Soviet Union and the latter's anti-Nazi alliance with the Western democracies.

IN POLAND. Communism among the Jews in Poland was of particular importance. During the early 1930s in the area inhabited by ethnic Poles (i.e., excluding the areas populated by Ukrainians and Belorussians), Jews accounted for 22 to 26% of the membership of the Communist Party. In the Comintern, the Polish Communist Party occupied a special place, being the oldest member party and providing a large share of its functionaries. Its special role was also related to Poland's geographical situation between the Soviet Union and Germany – the latter at that time being the major strategic objective of the Comintern's activities.

The Polish Communist Party (KPP) was founded at the end of 1918 by the merger of the Social Democratic Party of Poland and Lithuania (SDKPiL) and the Polish Socialist Party (PPS)-Left. Each of the two components had its own tradition of dealing with Jewish affairs. There was a large number of Jews in the leadership of the SDKPiL (among them Rosa *Luxemburg), but the party advocated full assimilation for Jews and even failed to take a strong stand against antisemitism. This attitude did not change during the first few years of the Polish republic; in spite of pogroms, antisemitic campaigns, and a special resolution adopted by it, the party remained rather indifferent to antisemitism, so much so that Comintern leaders, such as Radek and Zinoviev, found it necessary to draw the KPP's attention to this state of affairs. At its second congress (1923), 30% of the delegates were Jews, but of these, two-thirds described themselves as "Poles of Jewish descent." In the period 1919–22, groups (such as Kombund) and individuals who had previously belonged to Jewish workers' parties joined the KPP and took up important posts in it; some of them left their imprint upon the party's activities among the Jews. They included former Po'alei Zion members, such as S. Amsterdam-Henrikowsky, Gershon Dua-Bogen, S. Zakhariash, and A. Lewartowsky; ex-members of the "Fareynikte," such as Jacob Gordin and P. Bokshorn (later also Gutman-Zelikowicz); and from the Bund, A. Minc and A. Plug. Eventually the struggle against antisemitism came to play an important role in the activities of the KPP. It did not follow the SDKPiL tradition, and called even for national rights for the Jewish minority, equal opportunities for cultural development, equal rights for Yiddish in the administration and the courts, and the establishment of secular Yiddish-language schools. The party's activities among the Jews were in the hands of special "sections," "bureaus," or "groups," the autonomy of which remained a controversial issue throughout their existence. The staff of these Jewish "sections" participated in the incessant internal struggle that marked the KPP; when the party line so demanded, these Jewish functionaries fought bitterly against the Bund, the Zionist movement, and He-Ḥalutz. A considerable number of Yiddish periodicals, ostensibly non-Communist, were in reality published by the illegal KPP, and for a while, during the 1930s, even a daily (*Der Fraynd*). A large group of Jewish writers and cultural personalities was affiliated with the KPP or linked with its periodicals. In the period 1935–37, the party made strenuous efforts to induce various political groups (among them its political rivals) to join in a common struggle against fascism and antisemitism.

[Moshe Mishkinsky]

IN THE UNITED STATES. In the United States, the Bolshevik Revolution led to factional disputes within the two main left-wing parties in existence in 1917, the Socialist Party and the Socialist Labor Party, which had significant Jewish memberships, and also within the Industrial Workers of the World (IWW). Some of the more moderate Jewish socialist and labor leaders, such as A. Lessin, A. *Cahan, J.B. *Salutzky, B.Z. *Hoffman-Zivion, and H. Rogoff, temporarily sided with the Bolsheviks after the October Revolution, in part because the alternative to Bolshevism was the violently antisemitic "white" counterrevolution, but soon adopted a firm anti-Communist stand. Other Jewish socialists threw their lot in permanently with the Communists. As a result of the first split in the Jewish Socialist Federation, a Jewish Federation of the Communist Party was founded under the leadership of A. Bittelman (October 1919). In 1921 the Jewish Socialist Federation seceded from the Socialist Party and a Jewish federation of the Communist-sponsored "Workers' Party" came into being (1922). In the same year a Yiddish Communist newspaper, **Freiheit*, made its appearance, edited by M. *Olgin and S. Epstein, two former members of the Bund. Certain socialist leaders who were steeped in Jewish culture, such as M. *Vinchevsky and K. *Marmor, also lent their support to Communism, largely because of their belief in the prospects of a national Yiddish culture developing in the Soviet Union. There was also considerable Communist influence in trade unions with large Jewish memberships. Many of the Yiddish schools founded by the *Workmen's Circle were transferred to Communist sponsorship, and in 1929 Jewish Communists founded the International Workers' Order. It is estimated that in the 1920s as much as 15% of the American Communist Party's membership was Jewish, and the percentage of Jews among the Party leadership was undoubtedly higher. Unemployed or economically marginal Jews, especially in such professions as teaching and social work, and in the fur industry and some sectors of the garment trade, were powerfully attracted by Communist ideals and the widely propagandized achievements of Soviet Russia. Jewish membership fell off slightly as a result of Communist support of the Palestinian Arabs against Jews in the riots of 1929. During the Depression, Communist influence was again on the rise and could claim many sympathizers and "fellow travelers" among the American Jewish academic youth and intelligentsia. A further rise came in the mid-1930s, when the Nazis came to power in Germany and the Soviet Union adopted the Popular Front policy. It was at this time that the Yiddisher Kultur Farband (YIKUF) was founded by Communists in the United States. In the late 1930s the Moscow trials and the acceptance by the American Communist Party of the Soviet-Nazi rapprochement (1939–41) resulted again in a sharp drop in Communist influence among American Jews, which was only partly reversed by the events of World War II. Postwar revelations of Stalinist atrocities and systematic Soviet antisemitism permanently put an end to Communism as a serious force in American Jewish life. Fears that the trial and execution of the Communists Julius and Ethel Rosenberg for espionage would tempt the anti-Communist right in the United States to adopt a platform of antisemitism proved unfounded. The list of Jews who played a prominent role in the leadership and factional infighting of the American Communist Party from its inception is a long one and includes such figures as Israel *Amter, Max *Bedacht, Benjamin *Gitlow, Jay *Lovestone, Jacob *Stachel, William Weinstone, and Alexander Trachtenberg. Many American Jewish authors and intellectuals, some of whom later publicly recanted, were active in editing Communist publications and spreading party propaganda in the 1920s, 1930s, and even later, among them Michael *Gold, Howard *Fast, and Bertram *Wolfe.

After World War II

Although the newly established Communist regimes of Eastern Europe after World War II followed the Soviet line on the Jewish question and the policy toward Israel, there existed some fundamental differences. Most of them permitted the Jews to establish countrywide frameworks for religious and cultural activities, primarily in Yiddish (see *Poland, *Romania, *Hungary, *Czechoslovakia, and *Bulgaria). But, as a rule, the recognition of the Jews as a national minority was not based upon their obligatory individual registration as members of the Jewish "nationality" on identity documents (as in the Soviet Union), and Jews were able to describe themselves either as Jews or as belonging to the respective majority people; in theory, at least, they had the option of national assimilation. Jewish cultural institutions, whose Soviet counterparts had been liquidated in Stalin's time, continued to function, as, e.g., Yiddish theaters (in Poland and Romania), the Jewish Historical Institute in Warsaw, and a similar institute in Budapest. At one period or other, most of these countries permitted large numbers of Jews to migrate to Israel, in spite of the different Soviet policy in this respect.

Communist parties outside the Soviet bloc, including their Jewish sections and Jewish press, reflected the policy of the Soviet Union toward the Jews. In the last years of Stalin's rule, when every trace of Jewish culture and Jewish institutions had been obliterated in the Soviet Union, they tried to obscure the truth of the situation and even defended the Soviet Union against attacks by Jewish leaders and organizations against the anti-Jewish policy of 1952–53. A radical change occurred after the 20th congress of the Soviet Communist Party in February 1956, when Stalin's crimes were for the first time revealed in the Soviet Union, although the anti-Jewish element in these crimes continued to be ignored and suppressed. The first shock came with the publication (in the New York Jewish *Forward*) of news of the judicial murder of 26 outstanding Soviet Jewish writers and poets on Aug. 12, 1952. A great stir was caused in the entire Jewish world by an editorial that appeared in the Warsaw Communist newspaper, *Folkshtime*, in April 1956 headlined "Our Sorrow and Our Comfort." The article contained a detailed report of the process by which Jewish culture in the Soviet Union, its bearers, and institutions, had been liquidated, a process that had commenced in the 1930s and had reached its tragic culmination in the last years of Stalin's life. The article expressed the hope that this process would be reversed and Jewish culture and cultural institutions would enter a period of revival.

A storm of indignation swept the Communist movement in the West, especially among Jewish Communists. In Canada, the veteran Communist leader J.B. Salsberg published a series of articles in the Communist press that contained a report on the meetings of a delegation of the Canadian Communist Party, headed by him, with Khrushchev in Moscow in 1957 at which the Soviet leader's antisemitic inclinations had been clearly indicated. Salsberg seceded from the Communist Party, and many Jews and non-Jews followed his example. In Britain, another veteran Jewish Communist, Hyman *Levy, published a pamphlet entitled *Jews and the National Question* (1958), in which he denounced Soviet policy toward the Jews after an extensive visit to the Soviet Union and talks with Soviet leaders. He was promptly expelled from the party. In the United States, Howard Fast left the Communist Party under similar circumstances, stressing the Jewish aspect of his decision in *The Naked God* (1957); so did several members of the editorial staff of the *Daily Worker* (which thereupon turned into a weekly). In Latin America, sizable groups of Jews left the party and embarked upon the publication of their own organs (called, e.g., *Mir Viln Lebn*, "We Want to Live") expressing their opposition to Soviet policy of forced assimilation of Jews and destruction of Jewish culture and institutions; eventually, most of them joined Zionist Socialist parties. In non-Jewish Communist publications, such as *L'Unità* in Italy, and theoretical Communist journals in Britain, Australia, and other countries, the Soviet Union also received severe criticism of its discriminatory policy toward the Jews. In 1963, when Kichko's antisemitic book was published in Kiev, almost the entire Communist press in the West joined in a sharp protest, and the central committee of the Soviet Communist Party found itself obliged to disassociate itself publicly from the book.

Far-reaching changes also took place after the Six-Day War (1967), when the Soviet Union launched a worldwide campaign against "international Zionism" marked by violently antisemitic overtones. The Communist Party in Israel (see below) split into a pro-Israel and pro-Arab faction (Maki and Rakaḥ, respectively); a similar split, which in most cases did not, however, extend to organizational separation but confined itself to differences of political attitude, also occurred in several Communist parties elsewhere. In New York, the *Morning Freiheit* adopted a stand akin to that of Maki (which considered that in the Six-Day War Israel defended its freedom and existence), while *The Daily World* followed the anti-Israel line. In France, *L'Humanité* took a sharp anti-Israel stand, and reasserted the old Communist call to the Jews to assimilate to their host nations (editorial published on March 26, 1970), while the *Naye Prese*, the Communist Yiddish daily in Paris, was much more moderate in its attitude toward Israel and continued to affirm the Jewish right to an independent national culture. The "Jewish crisis" in the international Communist camp was further exacerbated by the events that took place in Czechoslovakia in 1968, and even more by the stringent antisemitic policy in Poland from March 1968, which was accompanied by what amounted to the expulsion of veteran Jewish Communists from the country. Adherence to the Communist Party and the affirmation of a positive Judaism of any kind had become mutually exclusive. With the collapse of Communism in Eastern Europe in the early 1990s, Jewish affiliation virtually ended, as only diehards remained associated with the small political groupings that clung to the old ideology under altered names.

[Moshe Mishkinsky]

IN EREẒ ISRAEL. A Communist group first appeared in Palestine during 1919, within the extreme left Mifleget Po'alim Soẓialistim (MPS), "Socialist Workers' Party," but it soon disintegrated. Under the British Mandate the Communist Party was outlawed. In 1921 the Palestine Communist Party was organized illegally, by a combination of extreme left splinter groups, and affiliated with the Comintern in 1924. Its entire history was a series of internal splits and secessions, as well as conflicts with Zionism and the British authorities. Its course was always clouded by alternating Jewish-Arab cooperation and friction within the Party.

From 1924 onward, on Comintern orders, efforts were

made to "Arabize" the Party, the argument being that the country would always remain Arab, since Zionism was at best utopian, and at worst a servant to British imperialism. Jewish leaders were ousted, but attempts made to recruit Arabs proved largely unsuccessful; the richer Arabs were averse to Communism, while others, if at all politically minded, favored Arab nationalism. Although sympathy with the Russian October Revolution was widespread in the Palestine labor movement, during the 1920s only a splinter group of the *Gedud ha-Avodah broke with Zionism and eventually migrated to the Soviet Union. From 1936 to 1939 the Party openly supported the Arab revolt, including the anti-Jewish terrorism. Still, in 1939 the Party was quite isolated from the Arabs, while its support of the Ribbentrop-Molotov agreement jolted the remaining Jewish members. From 1939 it operated in separate Jewish and Arab groups.

Further splits occurred over the Soviet Union's support of a Jewish state in 1948, when some of the Arab members of the party were against the Soviet Union's vote for partition. After the establishment of the State of Israel, the Party reunited under the name of "Maki" (Miflagah Komunistit Yisre'elit- "Israel Communist Party"). It operated legally, but, as an anti-Zionist party in a Zionist state, its influence was negligible. Its following among Jews rose in the 1950s, when mass immigration caused economic hardship and when a leftist splinter group of *Mapam, led by Moshe *Sneh, joined Maki; but it dwindled again with the prosperity of the 1960s. Although the party always looked for support among Israel's Arabs, it intensified its appeals to the Arabs in this period. In each election to the Knesset, Maki received greater support, proportionally, from Arabs than from Jews, e.g., in 1961 about half of Maki's 42,111 votes came from Israel Arabs, who then constituted only a ninth of the population. Some of the Arabs voted Communist in response to Soviet support of Arab nationalism, while, for precisely the same reason, many Jews refrained from supporting the Party. Tensions on this point were the main cause of the rift in Maki, generally on Jewish-Arab lines, which occurred in the summer of 1965. The Arab-led faction formed the New Communist List (Reshimah Komunistit Ḥadashah, or Rakaḥ), with a more extreme anti-government attitude and complete obedience to Moscow.

At first the Soviet Union tended to endorse Maki and Rakaḥ, but after the 1967 Six-Day War it recognized Rakaḥ only. After the split Maki took a line increasingly independent of Moscow in all matters pertaining to Israel-Arab relations, reflecting the fundamental Jewish nationalism of its membership. This became more pronounced after the Six-Day War, when Maki openly criticized Moscow's anti-Israel attitude and largely endorsed Israel government acts and policy. At its conference in 1968 Maki adopted a program which included not only pro-Israel plans but also, for the first time, a recognition that every Jew, even in a Socialist country, should be allowed to choose among assimilation, Jewish cultural life, or migration to Israel. Some Communist parties abroad, mainly in the West, but also that of Romania, continued to maintain "fraternal" relations with Maki, in spite of Moscow's denunciations of Maki's "chauvinism."

Although membership statistics were not publicized, the party would appear to have had close to 5,000 members in the 1950s and about 3,000 in the early 1960s. In 1961, according to the report of Maki's congress, 74.3% were Jews and 25.7% Arabs; 83.8% had joined after 1948 and 27% after 1957, an indication of the rapid turnover among the rank and file. The leadership, which had changed often in pre-state days, remained fairly constant from 1948 until the 1965 rift. In the late 1960s the Jewish leaders of Maki were Shemuel Mikunis and Moshe *Sneh, while Meir Wilner and the Arabs Tawfiq Toubi and Emil Habibi headed Rakaḥ. All five were Knesset members at one time or another.

The party always stressed continuous, often strident, propaganda. Many joined the V (Victory) League after June 1941, and later, the various friendship societies with the Soviet Union, several of which were front organizations. The Party's written propaganda increased before elections, and it maintained a continuous flow of newspapers and periodicals in Hebrew (*Kol ha-Am* ("Voice of the People")), Arabic, French, Polish, Romanian, Hungarian, Bulgarian, and Yiddish. After the 1965 split, both Communist parties continued publishing in Hebrew and Arabic, with Maki publishing in other languages, to reach new Jewish immigrants. After winning just one seat in the 1969 Knesset elections, Maki was transformed into Moked under Meir *Pa'il in the early 1970s and effectively vanished from the political map. Rakaḥ changed its name to Ḥadash (Ḥazit Demokratit le-Shalom u-le-Shivyon, "Democratic Front for Peace and Equality") before the 1977 Knesset elections, joined now by Jewish leftists, and was able to maintain a Knesset faction of 3–5 members into the 21st century as a nationalist Arab party, despite the disintegration of the Communist Bloc.

[Jacob M. Landau]

BIBLIOGRAPHY: R.L. Braham et al. (eds.), *Jews in the Communist World 1945–1962* (1963), a bibliography; I. Shein (ed.), *Bibliografye fun Oysgabes…* (1963), 13–28; *Gesher*, 12 (Heb.; 1966), nos. 47–48; G. Aronson et al. (eds.), *Russian Jewry 1917–1967* (1969); S.M. Schwarz, *The Jews in the Soviet Union* (1951); B.Z. Goldberg, *The Jewish Problem in the Soviet Union* (1961); *Yidishe Komunisten vegen der Yidn Frage in Ratenferband*, 2 vols. (1958); A. Yarmolinsky, *The Jews and Other Minor Nationalities under the Soviets* (1928); A. Leon, *The Jewish Question: A Marxist Interpretation* (1950); A. Bittelman, *Program for Survival; the Communist Position on the Jewish Question* (1947); E. Collotti, *Die Kommunistische Partei Deutschlands 1918–1933* (1961), includes bibliography; L. Poliakov, *De l'antisionisme à l'antisémitisme* (1970); C. Sloves, in: *The New Leader* (Sep. 14, 1959); H. Levy, *Jews and the National Question* (1958); M.K. Dziewanowski, *The Communist Party of Poland* (1959), index, s.v. *Bund* and *Jewish Problem*; J. Kovacs, in: JSOS, 8 (1946), 146–70; E.R. Kutas, in: *Journal of Central European Affairs* (Jan. 1949), 377–89; M. Epstein, *The Jew and Communism: The Story of Early Communist Victories and Ultimate Defeats in the Jewish Community, U.S.A. 1919–1941* (1959); S. Zacharias, *PPR un Kamf un Boy* (1952); idem, *Di Komunistishe Bavegung Tsvishn der Yidisher Arbetendike Befelkerung in Poyln* (1954); idem, *Menshen fun KPP* (1964); R. Garaudy, *Toute la vérité* (1970); M. Jarblum, *Soixante ans de prob-*

léme juif dans la théorie et la pratique du bolchévisme (1964); M. Decter, in: *Foreign Affairs* (Jan. 1963). IN EREẒ ISRAEL: W.Z. Laqueur, *Communism and Nationalism in the Middle East* (1961^3), passim; N. List, in: *Keshet*, 5–9 (1963–67); G.Z. Yisre'eli (Laqueur), MPS–*MAKI* (Heb. 1953); H. Bazhuza, *Ẓe'adim Rishonim be-Netiv ha-Komunizm ha-Yisre'eli* (1956); M.M. Czudnowski and J.M. Landau, *The Israeli Communist Party and the Elections for the Fifth Knesset 1961* (1965); J.M. Landau, *The Arabs in Israel: A Political Study* (1969), passim.

COMMUNITY, the designation of Jewish social units, used for the Hebrew terms *edah, kehillah*, and *kahal*. Ideally the community denoted the "Holy Community" (*Kehillah Kedoshah*), the nucleus of Jewish local cohesion and leadership in towns and smaller settlements. Particularly after the loss of independence, as the Jews became predominantly town dwellers, the community became more developed and central to Jewish society and history. From the Middle Ages on the community was a "Jewish city," parallel to and within the Christian and Muslim ones.

This entry is arranged according to the following outline:

ANTIQUITY

While the central and centralistic institutions of *kingship, *patriarchs, *prophets, *Temple, *tribe, and academies predominated – each in its time and its own way – there is only occasional mention of local leadership among the Jews. However, in *Shechem it was apparently the *Ba'alei Shekhem* who ruled the town, determining its enemies and friends (Judg. 9, passim). King *Ahab had to turn to "the elders and nobles, which are of his town, who sit with Naboth" (I Kings 21:8) and they passed judgment on Naboth (*ibid.* 11–13). It would seem that this local leadership, which combined preeminence in the town with noble family descent, was a central element in the life of the exiles in *Babylon. For more on community structure in the Bible see *Congregation (Assembly). The Book of *Judith tells of local self-government in the town of Bethulia in the days of Persian influence. The town was led by three men (*ibid.* 26) who had judicial power and the right to lead the defense of the city.

Later, under the Ptolemaic and Seleucid rule and influence, Hellenistic institutions began to shape local social life. In the Second Temple period the *Sanhedrin had the function of municipal council of the holy city, Jerusalem, as well as its more central functions in national life. From its foundation *Tiberias was a city with a decisive Jewish majority, structured and organized on the model of the Greek *polis*, with a city council and popular assemblies which sometimes met in the synagogue. At the head of the executive branch stood the archon and supervision of economic life was in the hands of the *agoranomos*. In the Hellenistic-Roman Diaspora the element of *autonomy granted by the non-Jewish sovereigns became a basic constitutive element in the life of the Jewish community, remaining central to it throughout centuries of Jewish history. In *Alexandria, Egypt, there existed a large Jewish community, which did not however embrace all the Jews living within the city; the synagogue became a center of communal leadership and at the same time a focal point for the emergence of a separate synagogue-community, existing alongside similar synagogue-communities within the same city.

By Ptolemaic times the Jews in Alexandria were already organized as a *politeuma* (πολίτευμα), one of a number of such administrative (non-Jewish) units in the city. At the head of the Alexandria community at first were the elders. In the beginning of Roman rule, the leadership of the Alexandria community was in the hands of an ethnarch; later, in the days of Augustus, the main leadership passed to the council of elders (*gerousia*), which had scores of members. The Berenice (*Benghazi) community in Cyrenaica had nine archons at the head of its *politeuma*. The Rome community seems to have been divided up, and organized in and around the synagogues. In Rome, as in other communities of the empire, there were titles like *pater synagogae, archisynagogus*, even *mater* or *pateressa synagogae*, and to a great degree such titles had become formal, hereditary, and empty. An imperial order to the *Cologne community of 321 is addressed "to the priests [*hierei*], to the heads of the synagogues [*archisynagogi*], to the fathers of synagogues [*patres synagogarum*]," thus showing that even in a distant community a wide variety of titles, some of a priestly nature, existed side by side.

Synagogue inscriptions and tombstones attest the importance attached to synagogue-community leadership. Up to the fifth century the patriarchs supervised and instructed this network of communities in the Roman Empire through sages (*apostoloi*). The epistles of *Paul are in a sense evidence of the strength and cohesion of synagogue-community life and discipline. The nascent organization of the underground Christian Church was modeled to a considerable degree on this Jewish community life and organization. Fast-day ceremonies show clear signs of local organization and sense of identity. Sectarian organizational life, like that of the *Essenes or the *Qumran group, reveals the tendency to create a closed community structure and life on principles very similar to those of the holy synagogue-community.

Some methods of communal organization – based on autonomy, the synagogue as the local center, and the synagogue as a separate communal unit within the locality – and some of the titles (in particular the Hebrew ones like *Tuvei ha-Ir*) were carried over into medieval and modern times.

[Haim Hillel Ben-Sasson]

MIDDLE AGES

Organized local communities functioning in Babylonia were highly centralized under the control of the *geonim* and exilarchs from approximately the eighth to the eleventh centuries. However, there are many indications that local autonomy was stronger and more active than these centralist institutions. The breakup in centralized authority and the growth of new patterns formed under conditions created by the emerging cities and states, in Christian Europe in particular, brought the local community more and more into the foreground. External and internal factors provided the dynamic force leading to self-perpetuation; among the former were collective responsibility for taxes (royal or seignorial) and ecclesiastical privileges, and the corporate organization of society in general. The inner cohesive forces were equally potent, if not more so. First there were the ancient traditions of Jewish group life as expressed in a variety of institutions; most powerful of these was the *halakhah*, the firm rule of religious law. Of paramount importance was the sovereign right of each *kehillah* to adopt its own fundamental communal law as formulated in **takkanot*. The *kehillah* retained its links with the Jews in the Diaspora as a whole through its adherence to tradition and law and shared messianic hope. Probably economic concerns of Jewish artisans and merchants constituted powerful common interests, yet the predominant binding forces were religious and cultural.

Character and Structures

Up to the expulsion from Spain (1492) the pattern of only one community board, or *kahal*, prevailed. It was only in the period of resettlement after the expulsion from Spain and in the modern period that the pattern of a community centered on its own particular synagogue reemerged strongly in many areas and splintered the original community. From the beginning of the 12th century, Western European civic tendencies began to penetrate the life and thought of the adjacent Jewish communities, which attempted to close their doors to newcomers (see **ḥerem ha-yishuv*). Membership in a community was acquired by birth or granted by formal admission. In extreme cases failure to submit to communal discipline could lead to expulsion. These tendencies clashed with the feeling of Jewish solidarity and belief that charity should extend beyond the city walls. As in the gentile city, in the Jewish community too there was a patrician tendency to limit election rights and – through various election clauses – to make the ruling circle a closed and self-perpetuating one. Membership of this ruling class depended on riches, learning, and patrician descent, in most cases a combination of all three. This oligarchic system was much more pronounced in the communities of Christian Spain until the expulsion, than in those of northern France or Germany. From time to time pronounced popular dissatisfaction led to reforms in election and tax-assessment methods and community institutions and structures. Different types of voting procedure were employed at meetings and there were rarely secret and fair elections. Some officers, such as judges and charity wardens, were chosen by direct ballot, but the indirect ballot, whereby some half dozen unrelated electors (*borerim*) were drawn by lot, was most popular. They constituted the electoral college which proceeded to select the major officers.

In a very small community a single officer managed affairs. The larger communities had many more elders, who went by a large variety of titles in the vernacular or in Hebrew, such as chiefs (*rashim*), aldermen (**parnasim*), best men (*tovim*), trustees (*ne'emanim*), supervisors (**gabba'im*), and many others. Special officers acted as tax assessors (*shamma'im*), tax collectors (*gabba'ei ha-mas*), morality boards (**berurei averah*), diplomatic spokesmen (**shtadlanim*), supervisors of the synagogue, of communal schools, charities, weights and measures, and a host of others. The chief officers were sometimes "elder of the month" (*parnas ha-ḥodesh*) in rotation. In Germany, Moravia, and western Hungary this *parnas ha-ḥodesh* was subject to the control of an executive committee; in Poland and Lithuania he later had full authority to act on his own. The community board was called *kahal*. The *shtadlan*, who represented an individual community, a region, or an entire country, was found in the larger cities. He was responsible for interceding with the authorities in defense of Jewish rights and in the alleviation of abuses. He had to know the language of the country and feel at ease with king, bishop, and courtier. As the representative of a subject people in an age when ideas of freedom and equality were hardly understood, he did not fight for Jewish rights: he pleaded for them, or gained his point through bribery. He was either a wealthy Jew who acted for his people out of a sense of civic duty, or he was an official who was paid handsomely for his exacting labors.

The designation of *rabbi (*rav*) of the community appears fairly early in Western Europe. By the 12th century it was frequently used, although not then very clearly defined. Many rabbis subsisted on irregular incomes. For a long time learned laymen administered justice in some countries; judges had to be elected. After a long period of uncertainty, the authority of the rabbi gradually became established. Large communities had rabbis who specialized as judges in civil (**dayyan*) or ritual (*moreh hora'ah*) matters, heads of academies, or preachers (*maggid). Other paid communal officials were the cantor (*ḥazzan), sexton (*shammash), ritual slaughterer (*shoḥet), *scribe (sofer), or recording secretary, who entered minutes in the *pinkas (community register or minute-book). Some of these communal workers possessed executive authority alongside the elected elders. Thus a shammash might be empowered to take punitive action against a recalcitrant inhabitant without first consulting the elder of the month. In some communities he was even charged with watching for infractions of the ordinances.

Functions and Duties

The community offered religious, educational, judicial, financial, and social welfare services to its members. It thus made possible a self-determined life for segregated Jewry. The cemetery and the synagogue were the primary institutions in each community. A single dead Jew required hallowed ground and for that reason graveyards were often the first property to be acquired. Ten adult Jews could meet in any private dwelling for public worship, but they soon needed a permanent prayer house. No membership fees were paid; the synagogue largely depended on income from the sale of *mitzvot*, the main one being the honor of being called to the reading from the Torah. Every sizable community had several houses of prayer, whether communal, associational, or private, which served as pivots and centers of communal life (see *Synagogue and cf. **Bitul ha-Tamid*); these maintained and supervised the abattoir for ritual slaughter, a ritual bath (**mikveh*), the supply of kosher foods, and the sale of citrons (*etrogim*).

Though teaching children and adult study were the responsibility of the individual Jew, supervision over schools and the provision of education for the poor were assumed by the community or an association. Special imposts were levied for educational purposes. The number of students per teacher, the quality of instruction, and competition among teachers were regulated. Schoolhouses were built, mainly for poor children and for higher learning. Synagogues and schools were supplied with libraries of sacred books. The adult study groups and the general pervasive character of educational endeavors maintained the Jews as the People of the Book.

Local communities were accorded extensive jurisdiction and discretion. The principle of **ḥerem bet din*, the right of each community to final jurisdiction and its security against appeals to outside authorities, was established in northern France from the 12th century. However, appeals to outstanding rabbinic luminaries outside the community were not entirely ruled out. At first knowledgeable elders ruled in disputes; soon ritual, civil, and criminal law became the province of properly trained rabbinic judges, and court proceedings were speedy and efficient. Excommunication – religious, social, and economic ostracism – was widely applied. Capital punishment was inflicted on *informers in Spain and in Poland. In some countries execution was left to state authorities. Other penalties included expulsion, the pillory, flogging, imprisonment, and fines. The community was the fiscal agent of the ruler and the bearer of collective responsibility for the collection of taxes from the Jews. It had to treat with the ruler on the type and amount of taxes, distribute the burden among its members according to its own principles, and to collect the sum. Thus it imposed direct and indirect taxes, import and export duties, tolls, and taxes in lieu of military service or forced labor. The prevailing method of tax collection was assessment by elected officials. Tax exemptions were sometimes granted by the state to influential individuals and some scholars and community officials also enjoyed tax immunity. The fiscal system worked tolerably well in the Middle Ages when communal controls were effective, but broke down with emancipation of the individual in the modern period.

The Jewish community regulated the socioeconomic life of its members. The principle of **ḥazakah* had wide applications in such areas as rent control, the acquired right of an artisan or a merchant to retain his customer (**ma'arūfiyya*), or the right of settlement. Lavish dress and sumptuous festivities were strictly regulated, a rule more often observed only in the breach. Polygamy was combated by communal action until it was eradicated in Christian lands and sexual morality was stringently regulated: there were ordinances against mixed dancing, gambling, and improper family life. Communal and individual charity provided for the impecunious; food, money, clothing, and shelter were dispensed. Itinerant beggars were kept on the move from one community to another. The sick were comforted by visitation, care, and medicines. Some towns maintained a **hekdesh*, a hospital for the ailing poor which only too often, as usual at the time, was unsanitary. Orphans and widows were provided for. "Redemption of *captives," the ransoming of victims of imprisonment, captives of war or of pirates, was ranked first among charities. Special chests for relief in Ereẓ Israel (**ḥalukkah*) were maintained.

[Isaac Levitats]

Individual Centers

THE MUSLIM CALIPHATE IN THE EAST. By unanimous Jewish testimony the first caliphs were sympathetic toward the representatives of the supreme institutions of the Babylonian Jewish community. Following the stabilization of Arab rule in the mid-eighth century, which did not interfere with the internal affairs of non-Muslims, a state of peaceful coexistence developed between the Muslim authorities and the leaders of the autonomous institutions of the non-Muslims, so that the Jews were able to reconstitute a system of self-government. The head of the "secular" autonomous administration was the *exilarch, an office originating in Parthian times and continuing under the Sassanids. The exilarch was of Davidic stock, and the office was hereditary. After a period of instability, *Bustanai b. Ḥaninai was recognized as exilarch during the rule of Omar I (634–44) and transmitted the office to his sons. The hereditary and elected representatives of Babylonian Jewry were charged with the administration of all taxes levied on Jews, with the representation of Jewry before the Muslim rulers, with autonomous judicial functions, the enactment of communal regulations, and the supervision of the yeshivot, etc. The traveler *Benjamin of Tudela, who visited Baghdad in about 1162, gives an eyewitness account of the honor and splendor surrounding the exilarch Daniel b. Ḥisdai (1150–74) at the caliph's court. He was received in official audience by the caliph every Thursday, when all Muslims and Jews had to stand before him; he sat beside the caliph while all the Muslim dignitaries remained on their feet. Another Jewish traveler, *Pethahiah of Regensburg, reports that the heads of the Jewish community in Mosul punished offenders even if the other party to the case was a Muslim (there was a Jewish prison in the city). Pethahiah also notes that the Jews did not pay taxes directly to the caliph, but paid one gold dinar per annum to the exilarch. When the Mongol khan Hulagu conquered Baghdad (1258), he harmed neither the Jewish community nor the exilarch, Samuel b. David. Jewish leaders of the House of David continued to reside in Baghdad until the days of Tamerlane (1401). During the decline of the Abbasid caliphate, when control was passing to the Seljuks (c. 1030), minor governments sprang up in Mosul, Damascus, and Aleppo; settling in these cities, scions of the families of the Babylonian exilarch obtained important positions which were confirmed by the governments. So dear to the people was the memory of the Davidic kingdom that the descendants of David were received everywhere with great honor: they were given the title **nasi*, and their dynastic origin placed them automatically at the head of the community as its recognized representatives. This fragmentation of the exilarchate into different territorial units began in the 11th century. The *nesi'im* collected tithes, poll tax, and other imposts, appointed communal officials and judges, and sat in judgment themselves. In contrast to their silence about other religious communities generally, and the Jews in particular, Arab sources frequently mention the exilarch. Alongside the "secular" autonomous administration was the "spiritual" administration, the **geonim*, heads of the two famous academies of Sura and Pumbedita, who also were empowered to appoint *dayyanim* in their respective districts and to supervise the administration of justice. Each of the two Babylonian academies had a *bet din gadol* ("high court") attached to it, headed by a president (*av*) who acted as deputy to the *gaon* and sometimes succeeded him after his death. Litigants from other countries could, by mutual consent, bring their cases before the *geonim* for an opinion. Moreover, by means of the responsa, the *geonim* exerted great influence over the organization, procedure, and uniformity of jurisdiction of the law courts. Characteristic of the management of the Jewish community in the medieval Muslim East (Babylon and its dependencies) was the bipolarity in the division of functions and powers between essentially central secular and essentially central religious and academic authorities; this generally persisted until the beginning of the 11th century. Afterward it was not an infrequent occurrence that the secular head (exilarch) was called upon to lead the academy and the great *bet din* attached to it as well; but on occasion the *gaon* also assumed the functions of the exilarch.

THE MUSLIM COUNTRIES IN THE WEST (EGYPT AND THE MAGHREB). More is known about the forms of organization of Egyptian and North African communities, which were different from those in the East. For political reasons the Fatimid caliphs in Egypt did not want the Jewish communities in their domains, which extended as far as present-day Morocco, to be subject to Jewish authorities outside their realm. Like the Umayyad rulers of Spain and part of Morocco, they therefore encouraged the severance of local Jewry from dependence on the Babylonian center. The several extant versions of letters of appointment of *negidim* in Egypt show that the **nagid*'s functions were partly similar to those of the exilarch in Babylonia in later times: he represented all the Jews and was their religious guide and judge; he drew up deeds of marriage and divorce and saw to it that prayers were said while facing Jerusalem, in contrast to Samaritan custom; and he was responsible for the implementation of the special measures applying to the **dhimmis* (non-Muslims given protected status). Among the best-known *negidim* were the descendants of Maimonides – five generations in all – who were the government appointed secular leaders of Jewry in Egypt and its dependencies, and, at the same time, spiritual leaders consulted on all matters of religion and law. The Egyptian *negidim* were also in charge of the fairly large Karaite and Samaritan communities. Palestinian and Syrian Jewry was headed by a local *nagid*, subordinate to the *nagid* in Cairo, whose deputy he was and without whose permission he could not be appointed. Apart from the *nagid*, two other functionaries represented the community: the minister (*ḥazzan*) and the prayer leader (*sheli'aḥ ẓibbur*). The office of *nagid* existed in Egypt until the Turkish conquest in 1517. A special situation prevailed in Egypt under Ottoman rule, when the *nagid* was appointed and sent to Cairo by the government authorities in Constantinople. In the middle of the 16th century, after 30 years of Ottoman rule, the rabbi of the Egyptian community excommunicated the *nagid* for having slighted him; the *nagid* complained to the Muslim governor, which shows that he was not empowered to anathematize him, but the dispute ended with the expulsion of the *nagid* from Egypt. Sambari, the 17th-century Egyptian chronicler, concludes: "From that day onward, he [the Muslim ruler] made it a law in Israel that no Jew who came from Konstantina [Constantinople] should be called *nagid*, but that he should be called *chelebi*; and this has been the law for Israel to this day" (Sambari, in Neubauer, Chronicles, vol. 1, pp. 116–7). Later sources indicate that the titles *chelebi*, *bazirgyan*, and *muʿallim*, still in use in early 19th-century Constantinople, were given to a prominent Jew who performed the function of official intercessor by virtue of his position in the financial and economic administration of the Egyptian rulers. Jewish dragomans in seaport towns similarly had influence with the authorities and used it for the benefit of their coreligionists.

LATER DEVELOPMENTS IN NORTH AFRICA. From the 16th century onward, regulations, chronicles of Fez and responsa written by the rabbinical authorities of Morocco mention the *nagid*, Jewry's official representative and spokesman at the court of the ruler. The *nagid* was probably chosen by the ruler, by agreement with the Jews, from among the persons who had dealings with the court. The office was frequently hereditary. Beside the *nagid* in Fez (or sometimes in Marrakesh, the original capital of the Saʿdi's), there was a *nagid* in Meknès during the reign of Maulay Ismāʿīl, who rebuilt the city and made it his capital. Other *negidim* resided at Sefrou and Salè. Sefrou was chosen as the seat of the *nagid* because it was close to Fez, where activities were frequently suspended because of the many disturbances which occurred there. The *nagid* in Salè (Rabat) was probably Jewry's representative to the independent sheikhs and pirates in control there. Presumably there were *negidim* in other cities as well. In addition to the *nagid*, there were usually seven notables (*tuvei ha-ir*) concerned with the manifold needs of the community. Regulations required the consent of the rabbinical courts and the entire community. Although the influence of the refugees expelled from Spain is usually evident, there were certain changes resulting from political conditions and from the need to establish a system which was also acceptable to the veteran Jewish residents.

The autocratic status of the dey of Algeria affected the position of the **muqaddim*, the Jewish representative at his court. In Spain, before the expulsion, this title was borne by a member of the community's leadership, and it seems that in Algeria, too, there were at first several *muqaddimūn* who looked after the affairs of the community; they are mentioned in a *sharīʿa* document of the early 18th century in connection with the purchase of land for a cemetery. In 1735 a change was introduced in the leadership of the community, and from then onward increasing reference is made to the *muqaddim* as the community's sole representative before the dey. Henceforth, the position became a monopoly of two or three families: *Bouchara, *Busnach and *Bacri (who were related), and the famous *Duran family. Their activities at the dey's court were internationally noted, especially from the early 19th century onward. After the conquest of Algeria by the French in 1830, one of the military administration's principal measures with respect to the Jews was the curtailment of the powers of their communal courts. This was done systematically by several decrees, issued between 1830 and 1842, which gradually restricted their jurisdiction in matrimonial matters to the holding of merely symbolic ceremonies and the offering of advice and written opinions; most matters were transferred to the jurisdiction of the French civil courts. The French policy makers were assisted in their efforts by the influence, encouragement, and cooperation of the leaders of Jewish religious institutions in France and French-Jewish citizens who settled in Algeria. Throughout the French era, until they regained full independence in 1962, Algerian Muslims jealously guarded their position as an autonomous community, not subject to French law in matters of personal status. The fate of the *muqaddim*, described by Christian writers as "king of the Jews," was similar to that of the rabbinical courts. On Nov. 16, 1830, Jacob Bacri was appointed *muqqadim* and empowered to supervise all Jews in town, execute judgments, and collect taxes. In the following year he was given three advisers, and after him Aaron Mu'atti was appointed head of the Jews. However, after five years the title of the *muqaddim* was changed to deputy mayor for Jewish affairs; he became a French official, drawing a salary from the government.

The head of Tunisian Jewry, known as the *qa'id*, was in a very strong position, since as tax collector and toll gatherer – and, in the capital Tunis, treasurer as well – he played an important part in the bey's administration. H.J.D. Azulai, in his *Maʿagal Tov* (1921–34), gives some idea of the wealth, prestige, and autocratic ways of the *qāʾid* Joshua Tanūjī. Some of the other *qāʾids* he mentions belong to the class which ruled supreme in both religious and wordly affairs of the community. The dependence of the office of the *qāʾid* on the bey sometimes resulted in its becoming hereditary. Mutually independent sources attest that the powers of the *qāʾid* as head of the community were very broad and that all matters of religious leadership, in addition to the management of communal property, were decided by him. These powers were not appreciably curtailed until the second half of the 19th century. From personal observation D. Cazès (*Essai sur l'histoire des Israélites de Tunisie*, 1888) states that the *qāʾid* represented the government authorities vis-à-vis the Jews, and that he proposed to the authorities, or himself appointed, the *dayyanim*, the seven notables, the men in charge of certain departments, the notaries, and the scribes. His signature appears first on official documents, even before that of the chief rabbi. Nothing was done in the community without his consent because he had a veto on all decisions of the *dayyanim*, the seven notables, and the leaders of the community. Every document, whether public or private, had to bear his signature or the notification that it had been drawn up with consent. The *qāʾid* was also in charge of the administration of justice among the Jews, on whom he might impose fines, whipping, and imprisonment. The city authorities were obliged to lend him their assistance, and the chief of police had to carry out his judgments. A decree of 1876 concerning the organization of the Tunis Relief and Charity Fund (the official designation of the body in Tunisia which carried out the functions of the community in the spheres of religious services and social welfare) prescribed that it should be headed by the *qāʾid* and that the chief rabbis should be subordinate to him. After long negotiations between subjects of the bey and persons under consular protection – on the distribution of the income of the abattoir among the needy – it was agreed that the committee dealing with the distribution should be headed by the *qāʾid*. A decree of the bey confirmed the agreement, of which one copy was delivered to the *qāʾid* and another to the French consul. Decrees issued by the bey up to 1898 concerning various communal matters still reflect the status and powers of the *qāʾid* as they evolved during the course of many generations. Only after the death of R. Elie Borgel in 1898 did a fundamental change occur in the powers of the head of the community. A decree of 1899 concerning the organization of the Tunis Relief and Charity

Fund mentions (in article 4) a president elected annually by the members of the board.

It may be assumed that, as in all the other eastern countries, the community of Tripoli (North Africa) was headed by a *sheikh* (an elder or chief), whose functions resembled those of the *qāʾid* in Tunisia. Nevertheless, it is not known if the *sheikh* performed the same functions – financial agent and treasurer – at the court of the pasha in Tripoli as the *qāʾid* in Tunisia or the *muqaddim* in Algeria. The only source of information is that supplied by a late chronicler on the basis of ancient material. According to him, the names of the leaders of the Jews, "both the new ones and the old ones," were not mentioned with the names of the *dayyanim* in the prayer for the dead on the eve of the Day of Atonement because they were not scholars. "Only a rich man, who was not a scholar, was elected to be the intermediary between the Jews and the government, and on his order the *bet din* would inflict the punishment of whipping on evildoers. He would, moreover, send to prison those who refused to accept his judgment or failed to pay their share of the poll tax." In another instance he notes: "The *sheikh* collects the money of the poll tax from the Jews for transmission to the government treasury. He receives no remuneration for this labor except that he is exempt from poll tax. Nevertheless, people go to enormous expense in order to obtain that office because they are ambitious, for the *sheikh* imposes and releases from imprisonment; he also has a fixed place among the governors in the council chamber where he is consulted like the other notables, and in most cases his advice is taken." The creation of the post of *ḥakham bashi* in the second half of the 19th century no doubt impaired the powers of the *sheikh* and lowered the latter's prestige with the authorities. From then onward the *ḥakham bashi* was recognized as the intermediary between local Jewry and the provincial governor and his assistants.

The duties of the recognized leaders of the community in the Maghreb, especially those of the *qāʾid* and *muqaddim*, were not easy. There is reliable evidence that these leaders included men of high moral caliber, anxious to be of service to their brethren. As regards those accused of abusing their position, it should be remembered that all communal leaders in these countries – especially in Algeria – were agents of the local rulers, in whose name and for whose benefit they engaged in a variety of dealings, sometimes dubious. All were the first target of the anger of the ruler or of incited mobs who held them responsible for every injustice in connection with taxes and toll duties, farming of government monopolies (*iltizam*), and various transactions with foreign states at the expense of the populations; particularly shocking was the fate of the *muqaddimūn* of the Busnach-Bacri family in the early 19th century (see *Bacri; *Busnach). Moreover, their position in relation to their coreligionists was not an easy one. They were responsible for the collection of the poll tax, whether it was imposed on each individual separately or whether an aggregate amount was fixed for the community, leaving it to the latter's representatives to apportion it among its members. They also had to ensure the payment of every fine or special charge the ruler saw fit to collect from the Jews. To protect themselves against serious personal loss, they made the community promise in writing to bear those disbursements. It was, of course, an unpleasant duty to have to impose internal taxes to finance the requirements of the community, although the necessary means of enforcement were available. The commonest tax of this kind was the *gabella*, an excise duty on meat, wine, etc. In Tripolitania this name was given to an internal tax (at the rate of 2–3 per mil) on imported goods. This latter impost, known also as *khābā*, served to maintain children of destitute parents at religious schools.

The wide jurisdiction of the secular authority was an outstanding feature of the Maghreb. The secular functionary appointed the *dayyanim*, or if they were elected by the people confirmed their election (incidentally, the people's right to elect *dayyanim* was limited, since according to hallowed tradition religious offices were hereditary and were limited to a few families). The *nagid* in Morocco and the holders of similar positions in the other Maghreb countries were responsible for conducting the community's relationships with the outside world.

THE OTTOMAN EMPIRE. Very little is known about the religious and secular administration of the *Mustaʿrab Jewish population in the East. Ottoman rule was extended over the Near East and Europe in the 15th and the 16th centuries. According to Sambari, Sultan Muhammad the Conqueror (1451–81) assigned three seats on his imperial divan (council) to official religious functionaries: the mufti, the patriarch, and the rabbi. The aged rabbi Moses *Capsali was appointed head of the Jews for certain purposes. Sambari continues: "And Sultan Muhammad imposed taxes on the whole country in the manner of kings: *kharāj*, *ʿawarīd*, and *rab aqchesi*. And all the Jewish communities were assessed for tax by the said rabbi, and it was collected by him and delivered to the treasury. And the sultan loved all the Jews" (Neubauer, Chronicles, vol. 1, 138). The *rab aqchesi* tax ("the rabbi's asper"), i.e., the tax of one "white" (*lavan*, silver coin) for the right to have a rabbi, contains an indirect recognition of the autonomous nature of Jewish organization. Its imposition is confirmed by Turkish archival sources.

Conforte, a contemporary of Sambari, also states that Moses Capsali was appointed rabbi and chief of the *dayyanim* of Constantinople: "He was rabbi of the *Romaniots, who were resident in the city in the time of the Greeks, and exercised jurisdiction over all Jews of the city by the sultan's command. And the *ḥakhamim* of the city in his generation were all submissive to him because of fear of the authorities and they had no power to speak to him about any matter or any decision he gave that did not commend itself to them" (*Kore ha-Dorot*, ed. Cassel, 28b). The common assertion in historical works and encyclopedias, that Capsali was appointed *ḥakham bashi*, resulted from a combination of these two reports. The title *ḥakham bashi* is not mentioned in any form in the Hebrew or Turkish sources of that period, and it is nowhere stated that Capsali was given jurisdiction over all Jews in the Ottoman Empire and appointed chief of all *dayyanim* and *ḥakhamim*. Thus, Sambari and Conforte cannot be quoted as evidence for the early establishment of the office of a *ḥakham bashi* for the whole empire. The silence cannot be accidental, for the same situation is reflected in the sources dealing with Elijah *Mizraḥi, who succeeded Moses Capsali after his death. Sambari exaggerates when he speaks of the three seats reserved on the imperial divan for the representatives of the three religions. In point of fact, even the *shaikh al-Islam* ("grand mufti of the empire"), who was equal in rank to the grand vizier, was not a member of the divan. Nevertheless, it seems that the Orthodox patriarch was given the honorary rank of "pasha with the rank of vizier," and it may be assumed that Capsali was granted similar status; at any rate, Sambari, drawing on the analogy of the Christian representative, believed this. Sambari's statement that Capsali was the recognized head of the then small Jewish community and was responsible to the authorities for its affairs and especially for the payment of taxes appears to be a true reflection of events.

After the capture of Constantinople (1453), Muhammad the Conqueror granted recognition to the *millet (the religious communal organizations of non-Muslims in his state) and conferred broad powers on its religious leaders. This does not contradict the assumption that a Jewish communal organization was already in existence for some time in the areas occupied by the Turks in the 14th and early 15th century. Capsali's wide and exclusive powers as chief of the *dayyanim* met with opposition from the Ashkenazi and Italian rabbis in Constantinople, who requested the intervention of a noted rabbi in Italy in the matter of a judgment which they believed erroneous. (This took place considerably earlier than the expulsion from Spain.) According to the sources and his own testimony, Capsali's successor, Elijah Mizraḥi (d. 1526), had jurisdiction "over the whole city of Kostantina" for more than 40 years.

The settlement in Greater Constantinople of *ḥakhamim* expelled from Spain – who were unwilling to accept Mizraḥi's authority – led to tension between Romaniots and Sephardim, who also did not recognize the manner of authorizing rabbis which was practiced in Constantinople. Since the Spanish *ḥakhamim* refused to recognize the leading Romaniot rabbi's claim to be the chief *dayyan* of Constantinople, the position lapsed after Mizraḥi's death.

The Jewish settlements in the cities and towns of the Muslim Middle East were far from being united communities. In accordance with old traditions, every new wave of settlers continued its separate life in its own *kahal*. In North Africa the newcomers from Majorca and Catalonia (1391), Spain and Portugal (1492–97), and Leghorn (17th–18th centuries) had their own synagogues and charitable institutions (see *Gorni, Tuansa, *Maghrebi). In the East the situation was even more complicated. Besides the Mustaʿrabs, Maghrebis, Romaniots, Italians, and Ashkenazim, there were numerous separate congregations in the large cities of the Ottoman Empire, e.g., in Safed (1555–56) 12 congregations and in Istanbul (16th century) almost 40. In Salonika the situation was yet more complex: some congregations formed by groups who came from the same city or country were divided into sections and factions – majority and minority – which quarreled, seceded, built new congregations, and so on. Every congregation, small or large, had its own rabbi, synagogue, charity funds, and burial society; each had an independent status, was a "town" in and of itself and no rabbi or lay leader was permitted to interfere with the prerogatives of another. Although unity was achieved when a common danger faced the whole community, or funds had to be raised to redeem captives, maintain the Jews in Ereẓ Israel, etc., the rivalries between the congregations weakened the community. The situation lasted for centuries, continuing after the introduction of reforms in the organization of the millet in the 19th century, and surviving into the mid-20th century. After a prolonged delay caused by friction within the community, the draft of the "organizational regulations of the rabbinate" (*ḥakham-khāne nīẓām nāmesi*) was submitted (1864) to the Ottoman authorities in Constantinople. The confirmation took place in May 1865. The regulations fall into five sections: (1) the status of the *ḥakham bashi* as the head of Jewry in the empire; his qualifications and election (clauses 1–4); (2) his powers and his replacement in the event of resignation or removal from office (clauses 5–15); (3) The general committee (*majlis ʿumūmi*), its election, and powers. It consisted of 80 members, presided over by the permanent deputy of the *ḥakham bashi*. Sixty secular members were elected by the inhabitants of Constantinople according to city districts, and they, in turn, elected 20 rabbinical members. These 80 members elected the seven rabbis who formed the spiritual committee (*majlis rūḥānī*) and the nine members of the secular committee (*majlis jismānī*). The elections required the approval of the Sublime Porte. At the time of the election of the *ḥakham bashi* for the empire, the general committee was temporarily reinforced by 40 members summoned from eight districts, where each officiated as provincial *ḥakham bashi* (from Adrianople, Brusa, Izmir (Smyrna), Salonika, Baghdad, Cairo, Alexandria, and Jerusalem; clauses 16–19). It should be noted that clause 16 failed to prescribe the committee's term of office; only in 1910 was it fixed at ten years. (4) The powers of the spiritual committee: the seven rabbis were to concern themselves with religious and other matters referred to them by the *ḥakham bashi*; the committee was not to prevent the publication of books or the spread of science and art unless it was prejudicial to the government, the community, or religion; it must supervise the activities of the city-district rabbis (*mara de-atra*) who acted under its instructions; it was headed by a president, who was also the head of the rabbinical court; he had two deputies (clauses 20–38). (5) The powers of the secular committee as regards the management of communal affairs and the carrying into effect of government orders: it apportioned the communal impost and ensured the integrity of the property of orphans and endowments (clauses 39–48). The regulations remained in force for the duration of the Ottoman Empire; under the republic they lapsed, without being officially replaced.

[Haïm Z'ew Hirschberg]

WESTERN EUROPE. At the same time the communities of the north – France, Germany, England, and northern Italy, which had been under Christian rule and out of touch with Muslim-ruled Babylonia – became the focus of experiment in community living. Lacking the solid basis of long experience, they had to build from the foundation up. Great debates ensued among the handful of renowned scholars who valiantly strove to find precedents in talmudic law for solving communal problems. As they found little to go by in the Talmud, considerable activity ensued. Most influential were the *synods of scholars and leading laymen convoked mainly in Cologne on days when the fairs were held. The influential scholars were *Gershom b. Judah, *Meshullam b. Kalonymus, Joseph b. Samuel *Bonfils (*Tov-Elem*), and *Rashi and his followers. It was understood that the final decision on their *takkanot* would rest with the local community. Justice, too, was localized by the *ḥerem bet din*. Finally, the principle was accepted that the elders were empowered to enforce communal decisions. The legality of a majority forcing its will upon a minority elicited much debate. Jacob b. Meir *Tam disagreed with it (c. 1150). The right to vote was granted only to *meliores* (*mehugganim*, "respected persons").

More specifically, the scholars in France and Germany tended to vest considerable powers in the local community and to define the rights of the individual. In religious matters the authority of the community remained undisputed. To prevent breaches of Jewish law its authority extended beyond its borders to the neighboring communities. An individual had the right of appealing to a higher court in private cases, or of suing his own community. In general, however, the community remained independent of outside interference. Each community was conceived as the Jewish people in miniature, having sovereign rights, no longer dependent on Palestinian ordination or exilarchic-geonic appointment. *Meir b. Baruch of Rothenburg, the 13th-century talmudic scholar in Germany, further elaborated the principles of community government in an intricate array of judgments. A majority could enact regulations on religious or public matters, in pursuit of their primary aim of strengthening the authority of the community over the individual.

The autonomous Jewish community in Europe developed during the period of the growth of towns. However, when burghers succeeded in obtaining for themselves supremacy as members of a *cummunitas*, of a *coniuratio* of autonomous rule, they swore an annual oath of allegiance within the community. The Jews, however, did not follow this practice since each of them was assumed to be bound by the covenant at Sinai to follow God's law and community regulations.

While the Central European communities were rather small in the 13th to 15th centuries and needed only the guidance of one scholar or of a few leaders, in the following three centuries they expanded considerably, thereby requiring a more complex structure of public institutions. Social stratification within the community based on wealth and learning also became more differentiated.

SPAIN AND RESETTLEMENT COUNTRIES. Until the persecutions of 1391 the struggle between the higher and lower social echelons was pronounced; frequent changes of leadership resulted, but in spite of this one family might rule in one locality for a century or more. Strife developed over methods of allocating taxes, the elite preferring the officers of the *kahal* to act as assessors, and the masses opting for each taxpayer's declaring his income. Sporadically contending factions had to resort to the king or governmental authorities to resolve their conflict. In general, the Spanish *kahal* was engaged in the broad function of regulating the social, economic, intellectual, and religious life of local communities.

Until the expulsion from Spain there was only one *kahal* in a community, but a new phenomenon developed in the countries of resettlement. In Holland, France, and England the Spanish refugees formed a separate congregation of Sephardi Jews if there was already an Ashkenazi community in existence, and centered their communal affairs on it.

[Isaac Levitats]

EASTERN EUROPE. The communities of Poland-Lithuania followed a way of life and experienced problems which were a kind of amalgam of Ashkenazi and Sephardi patterns (see *Councils of the Lands). Medieval forms of Jewish community organization persisted far into modern times in those countries where emancipation was delayed. In Russia the autonomous institutions of the *kahal* remained vigorous despite a tyrannical absolutist government which sought to harness it in the service of its oppressive designs. In addition to the usual burdens of collecting taxes, the *kahal* was charged with providing recruits for military service. Internally the age-old traditions of self-government retained their vitality into the 20th century. Even after the *kahal* was officially abolished by the government, the associations carried on the time-honored services. While it lasted, the *kahal* followed the procedures inherited from earlier ages, with the system of indirect elections from among the taxpayers continuing the oligarchical rule of the medieval community. The control of religious behavior and of the economic and social life of the individual by the *kahal* was powerful: the judiciary was firmly in Jewish hands and resort to non-Jewish courts was rare indeed. Many of these traditions survived up to the Revolution of 1917.

MODERN VARIATIONS

Introduction

By the middle of the 18th century signs of decline and disintegration of the autonomous Jewish community became evident. The central agencies gradually dissolved. In Germany the Jewish communities were increasingly controlled by the state (see **Landesjudenschaften*). The *kahal* in Russia was officially abolished in 1844. Internally there was economic ruin, oligarchic mismanagement, class struggle, rationalist enlightenment, and judicial independence of the individual. The communities had amassed stupendous debts by deficit financing which kept transferring fiscal burdens to coming generations. Wealthy Jews gained exemption from taxes by special state privileges; the central and regional boards shifted assessments onto provincial communities without affording them due representation; tax burdens became unbearable. The small urban unit with its intimate knowledge of everyone's finances was gradually replaced by the anonymity of the larger city. The imposition of heavy responsibilities on lay leaders by governments and the inherent social structure fostered oligarchic oppression. Emergent social consciousness sharpened the class struggle of the poor and the guilds. Individualistic tendencies militated against the social control of the *kahal*. The Haskalah movement in Central and Eastern Europe became religiously iconoclastic and anti-traditional, launching its most venomous onslaught on "the forces of darkness" in control of the *kahal* and on its despotic rule. The increasing complexity of business relations after the Industrial Revolution did away with the simpler transactions of the pre-capitalist era when Jewish civil law was adequate for judges to make decisions based on talmudic law. The old ban against gentile courts was increasingly disregarded; the Jewish civil judiciary shrank. Finally, the force of religious values, which underpinned medieval social control, gave way to secularist and humanist attitudes.

These factors must be viewed in the light of the emergence of the united modern state in central and southern Europe on the one hand, and the economic and political decline of Poland (which ceased to exist as an independent state in 1795) and the Ottoman Empire on the other. The French Revolution dissolved the estates and the corporations; in their stead the state dealt directly with the individual citizen in matters of taxes and other civic responsibilities. Count *Clermont-Tonnerre, a liberal deputy and friend of the Jews, stated in 1789 in the French National Assembly: "To the Jews as a nation we owe nothing; to the Jews as human beings we give everything." All this implied the dissolution of all communal, corporate, self-governing institutions, to be replaced by an emancipated, equal citizenry. Individualism was further stimulated by early capitalism. Competition in new methods of production and distribution, private initiative, and the end of the guild system and of economic regimentation dissolved the social control of self-governing groups. The individual Jew was catapulted into gentile society, where his own institutions were of little avail. Enlightened absolutism in German-speaking areas further dissolved the corporative structures. In some countries, rabbis and religious functionaries became state officials. The ghetto community, as one of the autonomous corporate bodies, fell under the heavy blows of state control. The process of disintegration of the *kehillah* was long and tortuous; its demise was nevertheless inevitable under modern conditions.

Western Europe

In modern times, until World War II, Western Europe followed the consistorial (see *Consistory) pattern established by Napoleon in France and her conquered territories. In Paris there were Orthodox, Liberal, and Sephardi congregations. The East European Jews had their own Federation of Societies. In the Netherlands, the consistory of 1808 was replaced in 1814 by the former Ashkenazi and Sephardi organizations. In 1817 a Central Commission on Jewish Affairs was established, consisting of seven members, to work with local rabbis and elders, but it was abolished in 1848 by the new constitution which offered churches state subventions. In 1870 a new central commission was formed for ten districts, each with its independent rabbi and government subsidies. In 1917 their rights were narrowed. In Belgium the consistorial system existed from the days of Napoleon and was renewed in 1835 when membership in the community was made compulsory. In 1873 the state offered subsidies to Jewish communities. Membership was made voluntary in 1892. In 1933 a Council of Jewish Organizations was established to coordinate nationally both religious and secular institutions.

Under French occupation during the Napoleonic wars Italy introduced the consistorial system. When the old order was reestablished, it varied in the several states. In united Italy central regulation ensued. The law of 1857 applying to Piedmont and later extended to most of the country provided for community membership in the place of domicile, unless otherwise declared. The community's religious and educational activities were tax-supported. In 1911 the Jewish communities were united in the Consorzio fra le Comunità Israelitiche Italiane. Under Fascist rule, by a law of 1931, membership was made compulsory, and the central union was guided by a consultative committee of three rabbis.

The 24 Jewish communities of Switzerland organized in 1904 the Union of Swiss Jewish Communities to regulate their external and internal affairs. In Great Britain there were several national synagogue bodies. One body, largely based on synagogue representation, served as the official voice of British Jews in external matters – the *Board of Deputies of British Jews founded in 1760. The Ashkenazi congregations clustered around the *United Synagogue headed by the chief rabbi. Other congregations were affiliated with the Federation of Synagogues, the Union of Orthodox Hebrew Congregations, and Liberal, Reform, and Spanish-Portuguese congregations. There was also a Jewish Board of Guardians and welfare. In the British Commonwealth, Canada has a central representative agency, the *Canadian Jewish Congress. South Africa, too, has a Board of Deputies and a Board of Jewish Education. Australia has an Executive Council of Australian Jewry as well as State Boards of Deputies.

Central Europe

The Jewish communities of Central Europe, especially in Germany, were highly organized and enjoyed much power. Each settlement had only one community organization to which each Jewish inhabitant belonged and paid internal taxes. The government recognized this organization by law, and in some cases helped subsidize its activities. Unions or federations of local units were formed for entire territories. The legal status of the Jewish community in Prussia was defined by a law of 1750 which made affiliation and taxation compulsory and under state control. In 1876 resignation from the community was permitted without renunciation of the Jewish faith. The Weimar constitution of 1919 relaxed government control, thus offering full autonomy to the community. Election procedures were made democratic, giving the franchise to women and providing for proportional representation. In 1921 a territorial union of communities (Preussischer Landesverband juedischer Gemeinden) was granted public legal status. Its function was to further religious life, to help financially weak communities, and to act as liaison with the government. Bavaria, Saxony, and Wuerttemberg also formed such unions. In Baden, where they were governed by a supreme council, the Jews had the power to tax members for religious needs.

In Austria, which did not have a uniform law until 1890, the situation varied. In Galicia the rabbis contested the right of laymen to control community life. Bohemia boasted a central representation of Jews, the Landesjudenschaft, while in Moravia 52 autonomous communities had their separate municipal administration and police. In the German-speaking provinces of Austria proper, mainly Vienna, Jews were empowered in 1792 to collect *Buechelgeld* for religious purposes. The law of 1890, which regulated the life of all the communities in the empire and remained in force in the republic after World War I, provided for compulsory membership and taxation, and one *kahal* in each locality to control all Jewish public activities.

In Hungary the medieval form of organization of the community was left undisturbed by *Joseph II's decree of 1783 regulating Jewish life. Until 1871 there was a struggle between Liberal and Orthodox leaders for control of the community, finally resolved by government approval of a threefold division of independent community unions consisting of Liberal, Orthodox, and "status quo," that is, those who were not involved in the struggle. Czechoslovak Jewry formed a supreme Council of the Federations of Jewish Communities in Bohemia, Moravia, and Silesia, which were later governed by the Austrian law of 1890. In the eastern provinces Slovakia had both *Neolog and Orthodox communities, but Carpathian Ruthenia was entirely Orthodox. In 1920 a state-recognized Organization of Orthodox Jewish Communities was established.

Eastern Europe

In Eastern Europe the old forms of community government were the most tenacious. As in most of Europe they persisted despite adverse government legislation. After World War I the concept of *minority rights was briefly favored and a number of countries helped maintain Jewish schools. Secularization of Jewish life produced a variety of political parties, each seeking to gain a decisive voice in communal affairs. Despite oppressive government legislation in Russia, Jewish community life retained its vigor into the 20th century. When the *kahal* was abolished (1844), the government handed over Jewish affairs to the police and the municipalities; yet the Jewish communities were still saddled with the two most burdensome responsibilities – state tax collecting and army recruiting (see *Cantonists). In 1835, government-appointed rabbis, who did not have to be ordained, were introduced to take charge of registration and other official requirements. In 1917 democratic Jewish communities were established by the provisional government. When the Bolsheviks seized power they put an end to Jewish community organization and formed a "Jewish commissariat," only to dissolve it in 1923. The *Yevsektsiya, the Jewish section of the Communist Party, was formed in 1918 and lasted until 1930. It helped suppress all traditional Jewish institutions and sought to develop a Yiddish press and Yiddish-speaking schools. In the meantime a committee (the Yidgezkom), supported by the *American Jewish Joint Distribution Committee, coordinated the vast relief activities of a number of previously existing social welfare organizations. In the short-lived, quasi-independent Ukraine wide autonomy was projected in 1917 with a minister of Jewish affairs and a national council. Bolshevik occupation put an end to these efforts.

Congress Poland (see *Poland) abolished the *kahal* in 1822, replacing it by a synagogue board (*Dozer boznicy*) consisting of a rabbi, his assistant, and three elders, whose task was limited to religion and to social welfare. After World War I the German patterns of community government were established in large parts of the new Polish state. Taxes were levied, and religious and other needs were provided for. In the sphere of social welfare the Joint Distribution Committee played an important role. Jewry became divided into factions – Orthodox, Zionist, *Po'alei Zion, *Bund, and others – each vying for a share of community control.

In the Baltic countries, the Lithuanian republic established in 1918 a Ministry of Jewish Affairs and a National Council to take charge of religion, education, social welfare, and other autonomous Jewish affairs. In 1924 these national agencies were dissolved. Autonomy granted in Latvia in 1919 extended only to Hebrew and Yiddish schools, often subsidized from municipal taxes, with a Jewish department in the Ministry of Education. In Estonia the National Cultural Autonomy Act of 1925 was the most liberal. Jewish schools received subsidies from state and municipal treasuries.

The Balkan countries exhibited a variety of attitudes to Jewish group existence. Some extended wide autonomy, especially under the provisions for minority rights; others curtailed it. Under the *ḥakham bashi*, until the abolition of the caliphate and the separation of church and state, Turkish Jewry had considerable autonomy and standing in the imperial court. In 1923 Turkey refused to honor the minority rights promised in the Treaty of Lausanne and Jewish autonomy was restricted to purely religious matters. In Greece Jews were permitted to levy compulsory taxation and were granted government subsidies. The presence in some areas of local courts backed by the authorities and of central democratically elected bodies was another outstanding feature.

Romania had largely voluntary associations until 1928, when Jews were required to belong to the local community, except for the Sephardim in Moldavia and Walachia and the Orthodox in Transylvania. The government contributed toward Jewish institutions. The chief rabbi represented the Jews in the senate. In Yugoslavia conditions differed according to regions. Croatian and Slavonian communities dealt with religious and charitable affairs. In Zagreb an executive committee of 36 controlled the synagogues and other institutions. In Serbia, Macedonia, and Bosnia there were chief rabbis and religious-educational activities. In 1929 a law united the communities of Yugoslavia and offered subventions. Control was in the hands of a council. The chief rabbi of Belgrade was accorded the same rank as a bishop and had a seat in the senate. Wider autonomy was enjoyed by Bulgarian Jewry. Even before 1920, when national minority rights were granted to them, the Jews could impose taxes; their chief rabbi was paid his salary by the state. Thereafter each community was governed by a council; the larger communities had religious courts whose decisions were executed by the authorities. Centrally they were governed by a legislative congress and an executive, democratically elected Consistoire Central.

[Isaac Levitats]

Developments in North Africa from the 19th Century

In Tunisia, owing to the influence of Algeria to the west, changes were introduced in the powers and structure of Jewish religious courts even before the country became a French protectorate. The bey, Muhammad al-Ṣādiq, who organized civil courts for all his subjects, restricted the authority of the rabbinical courts to matters of personal status. In 1898 he ordered the composition and jurisdiction of the Jewish religious court in Tunis to be reorganized. The new composition of the court was as follows: the chief rabbi of Tunisia, honorary president; one rabbi, presiding judge; two *dayyanim*; two deputy *dayyanim*; and one clerk. The sessions of the court were held in public under the chairmanship of the presiding judge, with two *dayyanim* or deputy *dayyanim* as assessors. The jurisdiction of the court was extended over the whole country, and it was possible to bring any matter, from anywhere, directly before it or to appeal to it against a judgment given by a *dayyan* in a provincial town. On the other hand, the court was denied the right to deal with matters concerning the personal status of Algerian Jews, since these were French nationals, or concerning persons under the protection of a foreign state. The salaries of the rabbi, of all the *dayyanim* belonging to the court, and of the clerk were paid from the bey's treasury. The chief rabbi of Tunisia was at first given wide powers over communal organization and religious life. According to the decrees of the bey concerning the organization of the committees of the Caisses de Secours et de Bienfaisance Israélite – the official designation of the Jewish communities in Tunisia – in several provincial towns, the chief rabbi proposed the members of some of them and submitted their financial reports to the prime minister. Elsewhere this right was reserved to the *contrôleur civil*, i.e., the district governor. The chief rabbi granted *kabbalot* (certificates of competency) to ritual slaughterers and licenses of communal notaries. These powers extended over the entire country, except for the towns where they were vested expressly in the local rabbi. The chief rabbi presided over the rabbinical council attached to the chief rabbinate and the examining board for notaries. The rabbinical council set up under a beylical decree of 1922 consisted of six members appointed by the prime minister, on the recommendation of the chief rabbi, for a period of one year (the appointment was renewable). The council was to advise on all religious matters concerning Tunisian Jewry. Its meetings were attended by a government representative, who acted as an observer.

A law promulgated by the president of the Tunisian republic, Ḥabib Bourguiba, in July 1958 dissolved the community council of Tunis. On the same day the Department of Justice summoned eight Jewish notables in order to appoint them as a "Provisional Committee for the Management of the Jewish Religion." The main task of the committee was to prepare elections for the leadership of the religious society, which was to take the place of the Tunis community council. The law provided that "religious societies" of a district should be managed by an administrative council elected by all Jews of either sex of that district who were Tunisian nationals and were above 21 years of age. Every administrative council was to consist of five to 15 members, depending on the size of the society. Each district was to have not more than one religious society, and there might be one society for several districts. The provisional committee, replacing the Caisse de Secours et de Bienfaisance Israélite in the Sfax district, was appointed by the district governor in November, and the one for Gabès in December 1958.

A different development took place in the Jewish community of Algeria, which from 1830 was a part of France. A decisive role was played by the Jews of French nationality who began to stream into the country after the occupation. As mentioned, they did not content themselves with the restriction of the powers of the rabbinical courts and the abolition of the office of *muqaddim*, but wished to organize the community on the model of the consistory, the political and religious body of French Jewry established by Napoleon I and based on the principle of the priority of obligations toward the state. In 1845 the regulations for the organization of the Algerian consistory were published; their functions were defined as (1) to ensure the orderly conduct of communal affairs; (2) to supervise the school attendance of the children; (3) to encourage Jews to engage in useful crafts; and (4) to supervise endowments and charitable funds. After the regulations came into force, consistories were established in Algiers and Oran in 1847 and in Constantine in 1848. A decree issued in 1867 imposed the authority of the Consistoire Central, the supreme religious body of French Jewry, on the three Algerian consistories. From that time on, and especially after the promulgation of the Crémieux Decree conferring French citizenship on the Jews of the three northern departments of Algeria (Algiers, Oran, and Constantine) in 1870, the status and organization of the Jews inhabiting these areas resembled more and more those of the Jews in France. The *Crémieux Decree did not apply to the military region in the south; consequently, the Jewish communities in Mzab and several other oases retained their traditional structure and organization. This split had an influence on the religious life of Algerian Jewry, which developed along two different paths.

Morocco retained its sovereignty until 1912. The events of World War I slowed down France's military efforts to gain control of the interior and of the south of the country (where the occupation and the subjection of the free tribes were completed only in the mid-1930s). Nevertheless, the French administration drafted two decrees (*ḍahīr*) which were published in May 1918 – in the name of the Moroccan ruler and with the signature of the French high commissioner. One of them dealt with the organization of the Jewish communal courts and the other with the organization of the Jewish communities. At first seven rabbinical courts (*tribunaux*) of first instance, each consisting of three *dayyanim*, were set up in Casablanca, Fez, Mogador, Meknès, Marrakesh, Oujda, and Tangiers. In 1953 a court of this nature began to function also in Rabat. Simultaneously, a High Court of Appeal was established in Rabat with a bench of three: the chief rabbi as president and two judges. The dispersal of the Jewish population over a wide area necessitated the appointment of *rabbins-délégués* for provincial towns where no courts existed. Their powers were less than those of the full-scale courts. During the 1960s, when the Jewish population of Morocco dwindled to one-fifth of its previous size (about 50,000), many communities disappeared completely and numerous posts of *rabbins-délégués* ceased to exist, as did – in 1965 – the High Court of Appeal.

The second decree issued in May 1918 dealt with the organization and powers of Jewish community committees in Moroccan towns. These committees were to consist of the president of the rabbinical court, the *rabbin-délégué*, and notables who were chosen by the grand vizier from a list submitted by the communities and whose number varied according to the size of the Jewish population; in 1945 this choice of notables was replaced, in theory, by the election by secret ballot of candidates from among whom the authorities were to select the members of the committees. The term of office of the members was four years. The functions of the committees were to maintain religious services, to assist the needy, and to administer endowments. A decree promulgated in 1945 established a council of Jewish communities, which had to coordinate the activities of the communities. It consisted of the heads of the various communities and met once a year in Rabat under the chairmanship of a representative of the Directorate of Sherifian Affairs. These meetings dealt with matters of budget, housing, education, and hygiene. The question of permanent representation of the communities was also mooted. In the early 1950s a permanent bureau was set up under a secretary-general. The bureau was to guide the community committees in preparing budgets, operating services, and providing education in *talmud torah* institutions and evening classes. Most of the revenue of the communities came from charges on ritual slaughtering and the sale of *maẓẓot*, as well as from the management of public endowments, which were not many, since most endowments were family ones. The council sent six delegates to the Moroccan (natives) Committee of the Council of Government. It published a four-page monthly under the title *La Voix des Communautés*. Upon the reinstatement of Sultan Muhammad V in 1958 and the rise to power of the nationalist Istiqlāl party, the composition of the community committees was changed by appointing persons acceptable to the ruling group. With this change in policy they lost what little independence and initiative they had possessed and became tools of the government.

[Haïm Z'ew Hirschberg]

United States

U.S. Jewry, with its frequent waves of immigration from a large variety of countries, has launched many and ambitious forms of community organization. Until late in the 19th century these remained for the most part purely local in character. Wherever they settled in sufficient numbers the original Sephardi immigrants to the United States formed burial societies, benevolent and charitable associations, hospitals, synagogues and Hebrew schools, rabbinical courts, etc., all patterned originally on similar institutions in the Old World. The German immigration of the mid-19th century created a parallel series of institutions, as did the large Eastern European immigration of the years 1880–1920. In addition the immigrants from Eastern Europe originated the **Landsmannshaften*, organizations which consisted of members hailing from the same town or region and which offered sick and burial insurance, free loans, poor relief, a place to pray, and perhaps, above all, conviviality and a sense of belonging in the New World. Thus, at the end of the 19th century the American Jewish community was largely composed of a proliferation of local synagogues and organizations, frequently formed along lines of national origin and often duplicating each other's efforts with little or no coordination between them. On a local level the first attempts at centralization began to appear late in the 19th century and continued with increasing scope into the 20th. The first city-wide Jewish welfare federation in America was established in Boston in 1895; the first municipal bureau of Jewish education, in 1910. An attempt under J.L. *Magnes to establish a *kehillah* in New York lasted for about a decade before breaking up. Local YMHAS and YWHAS developed into Jewish community centers offering a wide range of educational, social, and recreational activities in many American cities. In 1970 such local Jewish federations, community councils, and welfare funds, whose function it was to coordinate Jewish communal life and regulate the disbursement of funds to it, existed in one form or another in 300 cities in 43 states in which were concentrated at least 95% of the Jewish population of the United States. The center of local community life for the average Jewishly active individual, however, continued to be the synagogue. Far from serving exclusively or perhaps even primarily as a place of worship, the synagogue, especially in suburban areas, provided such varied services as Jewish education for children and adults, men's clubs, sisterhoods, youth and sport groups, social service, and catering private social affairs. Organization on a nation-wide level in American Jewish life originated with the German immigration of the mid-19th century. In the course of the 20th century such a consolidation has created an overall hierarchical structure of organization embracing practically every area of American Jewish life. Among the most prominent of such national organizations are the Jewish Community Centers Association (the national coordinating body of community centers, 1917), United Jewish Communities of North America (created out of the Council of Jewish Federation and Welfare Funds (1932), the United Jewish Appeal (1939), both of which went out of existence), and the American Association for Jewish Education (1939). By the second half of the 20th century few local Jewish organizations were not affiliated directly with one or another such national group, a fact that undoubtedly owed much to the general American aptitude for centralized and efficient organization. At the political level the organization of American Jewry remained relatively unstructured, a reflection of the traditional reluctance, if not inability, of the American Jewish community to identify itself as a distinct political bloc. On the whole, those Jewish organizations that have assumed political functions did so originally to defend specifically Jewish rights and interests against discrimination and prejudice both in the United States and abroad. The first organization of this type was the *Board of Delegates of American Israelites (1859–78). It was followed by the American Jewish Committee (1906), which was controlled by a wealthy elite of German Jews. In reaction to it the more representative and militant American Jewish Congress was first established in 1918 and refounded in 1930. Other such national organizations to be formed were the Zionist Organization of America (1897) and many other Zionist bodies, the Anti-Defamation League of B'nai B'rith (1913), and the *Jewish Labor Committee (1934). Conflicting outlooks and ideologies have for the most part restricted these groups' common action, but the national and local agencies concerned with Jewish public affairs and public policy established the National Community Relations Advisory Council (later the National Jewish Community Relations Advisory Council, now the Jewish Council for Public Affairs (1944)). Another body, the Conference of Presidents of Major American Jewish Organizations, established in 1954, serves as a roof organization for 51 national Jewish bodies. The mandate of the Presidents' Conference is to act as a spokesman to the Administration, on behalf of the American Jewish Community, on matters related to Israel. The Conference has issued joint declarations and has lobbied nationally for Jewish interests both at home and abroad, especially in connection with Israel. Since the 1950s many national Jewish bodies have adopted positions on a broad range of issues, of concern to the larger polity, on the public-affairs agenda.

Latin America

The transplantation of Jews with East and Central European backgrounds to Latin America, primarily in the 20th century gave rise to a replica of the European *kehillah* that did not enjoy the same official status but was tacitly recognized by Jews and non-Jews alike as the organized Jewish community. These communities had a distinct public character but were not directly recognized in public law. In the last analysis, they had relied entirely on the voluntary attachment of their members. In sum, they functioned in an environment that provided neither the cultural nor the legal framework for a European-model *kehillah*. Characteristically, the Ashkenazi communities among them, as opposed to the Sephardi communities, emphasized the secular rather than the religious side of Jewish life. Founded in the main by men who considered themselves secularists (regardless of the level of their personal religious observance), they were developed in the mold of secular Diaspora nationalism, a powerful ideology at the time of their creation. However, since the 1960s there has been a new trend, and even the Ashkenazim tend more to emphasize the religious basis of their organization.

The Latin American communities have been relatively successful in their attempt to maintain European patterns primarily because the great social and cultural gap between the Jews and their neighbors in those countries with a large population of Indian origin aided in giving the Jews a self-image as a special and distinct, indeed superior, group, which in turn helped keep them apart in a corporate way as well as individually. This fact has important implications for the character of their community organization. In the first place, while the communities themselves were all founded in the modern era, they are located in essentially homogeneous societies whose social structures originated before the beginning of that period. Moreover, they were founded by people coming for the most part from still-modernizing societies of a different kind in Europe. As a result, assimilation into the host society was far more difficult than in other countries of migration, while, at the same time, the Jewish founders were able to build their institutions upon a far stronger sense of communal self-government than that which prevailed among more emancipated Jews. The community-wide "roof" organizations they have created have thus been able to attract and keep virtually every Jewish organization and affiliated Jew within their structures on a formally voluntary basis, while gaining informal governmental recognition as the "address" of the Jewish community.

The same phenomena also contributed to the dominant pattern of organizing the Jewish immigrants according to their countries of origin. Just as the Jewish immigrants did not assimilate into their host societies, so, too, they did not assimilate among one another, following a pattern not uncommon in pre-Emancipation Jewish history by which Jews who settled in new lands frequently attempted to preserve the special cultural nuances of the lands of their birth. In the course of time, these communities loosely confederated with one another to deal with common problems that emerged in their relations with their environment, i.e., essentially those of immigration, antisemitism, and Israel. At the same time, each country-of-origin community retained substantial, if not complete, autonomy in internal matters and control over its own institutions.

In three of the large Latin American countries (including Argentina and Brazil, the largest), the indigenous federal structures of the countries themselves influenced the Jews to create countrywide confederations based on territorial divisions (officially uniting state or provincial communities which are, in fact, local communities concentrated in the state or provincial capitals). In the other 21, the local federation of the city containing the overwhelming majority of the Jewish population became the countrywide unit, usually with the designation "council of communities." The community councils of the six Central American countries (total Jewish population 5,650) have organized the Federation of Central American Jewish Communities to pool resources and provide common services.

With the revival of open Jewish settlement on the Iberian Peninsula, Jewish communities similar to the "council of communities" took shape in both Spain and Portugal, for many of the same reasons. Similarly, the small Jewish community of Monaco found that same pattern most suitable.

None of the tacitly recognized communal structures has been in existence for more than two generations, and the communities themselves originated no more than three or possibly four generations ago. Most of the smaller ones were in the 1970s entering their second generation, since they were created by the refugees of the 1930s and 1940s. Indeed, all gained substantially as a result of Nazism and the Jews' need to leave Europe before, during, and after World War II. Consequently, many, if not most, were still in the process of developing an appropriate and accepted community constitution.

The great postwar adjustment that has faced the Latin American communities centers on the emergence of a native-born majority in their ranks. This new generation has far less attachment to the "old country" way of life with its ideologies and country-of-origin communities making the whole community structure less relevant to them. Moreover, they are already beginning to assimilate into their own countries of birth, or at least into the local radical movements, in familiar Jewish ways. For them, the *deportivo*, or community recreational center, often seems the most relevant form of Jewish association. On the other hand, the host countries, whose aim is the cultural assimilation of all minorities into a common mold, are not particularly receptive to the perpetuation of communities built on a Diaspora nationalist ideology. At the same time, they are committed, at least theoretically, to guaranteeing full freedom of religion for all legitimate groups, thereby pushing Jews toward at least a formal religious identification in order to maintain their communal identity while conforming to local mores. Both developments are encouraging a trend toward a kind of associational Jewishness in place of the organic pattern of the founding generation. It is not surprising, then, that the organizational structure that at first reflected and then came to reinforce the interests of the founding generation is becoming increasingly obsolete, creating a constitutional crisis of first magnitude in the ranks of organized Latin American Jewry. To the degree that a territorially based communal structure has emerged, with its accompanying substructure of association activities whose participants are drawn in for reasons of interest rather than simply descent, this constitutional crisis is being overcome.

The tacitly recognized community structures of Latin American Jewry have become important forms of Jewish communal organization in modern times, with around 400,000 Jews living within their framework at the outset of the 21st century. Their decline during the last 30 years was provoked by occasional waves of out migration due to economic and political crises, low fertility, and out marriages. They are all located in very unstable environments, which do not necessarily encourage pluralism, although there are signs of greater tolerance in this respect. Consequently, Latin American Jewries are also more closely tied to the State of Israel as a surrogate homeland (*madre patria* is the Spanish term they use) than any others. Their attempt to create a unified communal structure on a voluntary basis under such conditions bears close examination.

COMMUNITY ORGANIZATION SINCE WORLD WAR II

Introduction

Jewish communal organization has undergone many changes since the inception of the Israelite polity somewhere in the Sinai Desert, but none has been more decisive than those which have affected it in the past four centuries, and none more significant than those of the period since the end of World War II. The inauguration of the modern era in the 17th century initiated a process of decorporatization of Jewish communal life that gained momentum in the following two centuries. Jewish corporate autonomy, a feature of Diaspora existence in one form or another since the Babylonian exile, never even took hold in the New World, whose Jewish communities were all established in the modern era. Developments after World War I weakened that kind of autonomy in Europe, where it had been on the wane for two centuries. Only in the Muslim countries did the old forms persist, until the nationalist revolutions of the post–World War II period eliminated them.

The process of decorporatization – perhaps denationalization is a better term – brought with it efforts to redefine Jewish life in Protestant religious terms in Western Europe and North America and in socialist secular ones in Eastern Europe and, somewhat later, in Latin America. In Europe,

Table 1. Total Jewish Population and Its Distribution by Continent (in thousands)

Year / Continent	1840 Total	1840 %	1900 Total	1900 %	1939 Total	1939 %	2003 Total	2003 %
Europe (incl. Russia)	3,950	87.8	8,900	80.9	9,500	56.8	1,551	12.0
Asia	300	6.7	510	4.6	1,030	6.2	5,138	39.7
Africa	198	4.4	375	3.4	625	3.7	84	0.6
North and South America	50	1.1	1,200	10.9	5,540	33.1	6,071	46.9
Oceania	2	1	15	0.2	33	0.2	107	0.8
Total	4,500	100	11,000	100	16,728	100	12,950	100

the process was promoted both from within the Jewish community and without by Jews seeking wider economic and social opportunities as individuals and by newly nationalistic regimes seeking to establish the state as the primary force in the life of all residents within its boundaries. In the Americas, it came automatically as individual Jews found themselves with the same status and opportunities as other migrants to the New World.

Out of decorporatization came new forms of Jewish communal organization on the countrywide and local levels: (1) the consistory of post-revolutionary France (which spread to the other countries within the French sphere of influence in Europe), an attempt to create a Jewish "church" structure parallel to that of the French Protestant Church; (2) the 19th-century Central European *kehillah*, essentially a ritual and social agency chartered and regulated by the secular government as a means of registering all Jews and binding them to some "religious" grouping; (3) the united congregational pattern of England and her overseas colonies and dominions, whereby Jews voluntarily organized synagogues which then banded together to create a board to represent Jewish interests to the host country; (4) the radically individualistic organizational pattern of the United States, whereby individual Jews banded together locally (and sometimes nationally) to create whatever kind of Jewish association they wished without any kind of supralocal umbrella organization even for external representation; and, early in the 20th century, (5) separate communal associations based on the *Landsmannshaft* principle, which became the basis for voluntary affiliation of the Jewish immigrants to Latin America. The common denominator of all these different forms was their limited scope and increasingly voluntary character.

While these organizational changes were taking shape, a two-pronged demographic shift of great importance began. In the first place, the live birth and survival rate among Jews rose rapidly, causing the number of Jews in the world to soar. In the second, the Jews began to migrate at an accelerating rate to the lands on the Western world's great frontier: the Western Hemisphere and southern Africa and Australia in particular, but also, in smaller numbers, to east Asia, initiating a shift in the balance of Jewish settlement in the world. Finally, the modern era saw Jewish resettlement of the Land of Israel. The first to go to the land as founders of entirely new settlements began to arrive in the 17th century and continued regularly thereafter, pioneering new communities of a traditional character within the framework of the Ottoman Empire's millet system. They were followed, in due course, by the Zionist pioneers who created new forms of communal life, beginning in the late 19th century as part of the last stage of the modern transformation of the Jewish people.

World War II marked the culmination of all the trends and tendencies of the modern era and the end of the era itself for all of mankind. For the Jewish people, the Holocaust and the establishment of the State of Israel were the pair of decisive events that marked the crossing of the watershed into the "postmodern" world. In the process, the entire basis of the Jewish polity was radically changed; the locus of Jewish life shifted and virtually every organized Jewish community was reconstituted in some significant way.

The Jewish world that greeted the new State was no longer an expanding one which was gaining population even in the face of "normal" attrition through intermarriage and assimilation. Quite to the contrary, it was a decimated one (even worse – for decimated implies the loss of one in ten; the Jews lost one in three) whose very physical survival had been in grave jeopardy and whose rate of loss from defections came close to equaling its birthrate. Moreover, the traditional strongholds of Jewish communal life in Europe (which were

Table 2. World Jewish Communities by Population, 2003

Country	Jewish Population (thousands)	Percent of Total Jewish Population
1. United States	5,300,000	40.9
2. Israel	5,094,000	39.3
3. France	498,000	3.8
4. Canada	370,500	2.9
5. United Kingdom	300,000	2.3
6. Russia	252,000	1.9
7. Argentina	187,000	1.4
8. Germany	108,000	0.8
9. Australia	100,000	0.8
10. Brazil	97,000	0.7
11. Ukraine	95,000	0.7
12. South Africa	75,000	0.6
13. Hungary	50,000	0.4
14. Mexico	40,000	0.3
15. Belgium	40,000	0.2
Total	12,606,500	97.0

Table 3. Geographic Arrangement of Countries Showing Type of Community Organization in Early Postwar Period
Numbers refer to Jewish populations in 1968

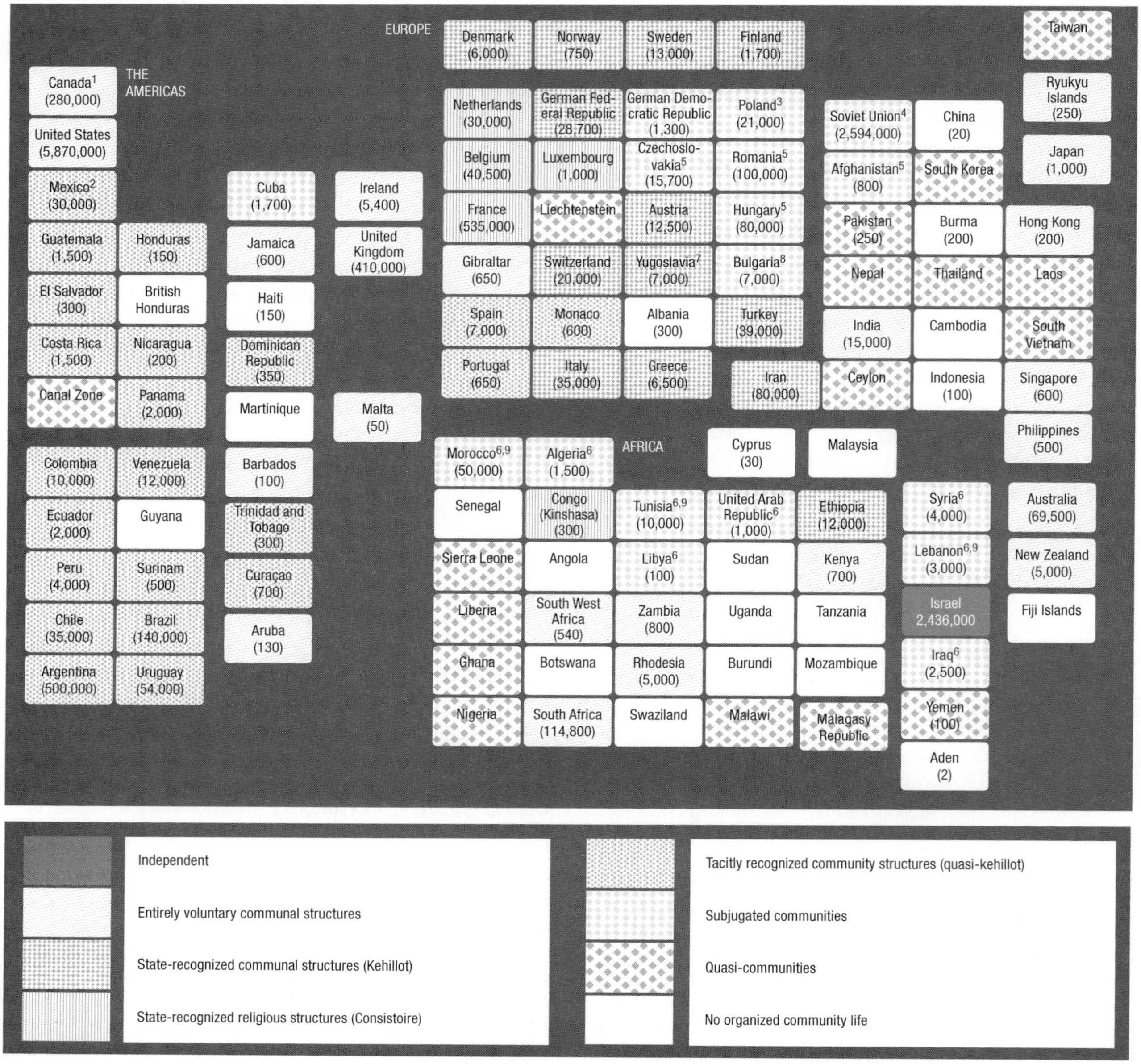
EUROPE
Denmark (6,000)
Norway (750)
Sweden (13,000)
Finland (1,700)
Taiwan
THE AMERICAS
Canada[1] (280,000)
United States (5,870,000)
Mexico[2] (30,000)
Guatemala (1,500)
Honduras (150)
El Salvador (300)
British Honduras
Costa Rica (1,500)
Nicaragua (200)
Canal Zone
Panama (2,000)
Colombia (10,000)
Venezuela (12,000)
Ecuador (2,000)
Guyana
Peru (4,000)
Surinam (500)
Chile (35,000)
Brazil (140,000)
Argentina (500,000)
Uruguay (54,000)
Cuba (1,700)
Jamaica (600)
Haiti (150)
Dominican Republic (350)
Martinique
Barbados (100)
Trinidad and Tobago (300)
Curaçao (700)
Aruba (130)
Ireland (5,400)
United Kingdom (410,000)
Malta (50)
Netherlands (30,000)
German Federal Republic (28,700)
German Democratic Republic (1,300)
Poland[3] (21,000)
Belgium (40,500)
Luxembourg (1,000)
Czechoslovakia[5] (15,700)
Romania[5] (100,000)
France (535,000)
Liechtenstein
Austria (12,500)
Hungary[5] (80,000)
Gibraltar (650)
Switzerland (20,000)
Yugoslavia[7] (7,000)
Bulgaria[8] (7,000)
Spain (7,000)
Monaco (600)
Albania (300)
Turkey (39,000)
Portugal (650)
Italy (35,000)
Greece (6,500)
Iran (80,000)
Soviet Union[4] (2,594,000)
China (20)
Ryukyu Islands (250)
Japan (1,000)
Afghanistan[5] (800)
South Korea
Pakistan (250)
Burma (200)
Hong Kong (200)
Nepal
Thailand
Laos
India (15,000)
Cambodia
South Vietnam
Ceylon
Indonesia (100)
Singapore (600)
Philippines (500)
AFRICA
Morocco[6,9] (50,000)
Algeria[6] (1,500)
Cyprus (30)
Malaysia
Senegal
Congo (Kinshasa) (300)
Tunisia[6,9] (10,000)
United Arab Republic[6] (1,000)
Ethiopia (12,000)
Syria[6] (4,000)
Australia (69,500)
Sierra Leone
Angola
Libya[6] (100)
Sudan
Kenya (700)
Lebanon[6,9] (3,000)
New Zealand (5,000)
Liberia
South West Africa (540)
Zambia (800)
Uganda
Tanzania
Israel 2,436,000
Fiji Islands
Ghana
Botswana
Rhodesia (5,000)
Burundi
Mozambique
Iraq[6] (2,500)
Nigeria
South Africa (114,800)
Swaziland
Malawi
Malagasy Republic
Yemen (100)
Aden (2)
Independent
Entirely voluntary communal structures
State-recognized communal structures (Kehillot)
State-recognized religious structures (Consistoire)
Tacitly recognized community structures (quasi-kehillot)
Subjugated communities
Quasi-communities
No organized community life

1. The Canadian Jewish Congress should be viewed as a Board of Deputies with a North American name.
2. Though Mexico is included among the neo-kehillah communities of Latin America, its lack of any overall structure uniting its region-of-origin communities in even the strictly formal sense really placed it somewhere between the common Latin American model and the pattern of the United States.
3. Poland was rapidly becoming a remnant community.
4. There was no organized Jewish life in the Soviet Union, except for services in a few synagogues.
5. The extent to which the Jewish communities of Czechoslovakia, Hungary, and Romania were actually subjugated varied from time to time but the basic fact of their total dependence upon the decisions of the Communist leadership placed them in this category. All were officially organized as modern keillot.
6. All those communities were formally traditional kehillot.
7. Though in part subject to the condition of the modern subjugated communities, Yugoslavian Jewry essentially perpetuated the kehillah pattern with formal government recognition.
8. Officially, Bulgarian Jewry was organized in a consistoire.
9. Lebanon, Morocco, and Tunisia did not officially restrict Jewish community life but in fact the communities were closely regulated.

Table 4. Early Postwar Changes in Continental Jewish Communities

Country	
Albania	Disappeared as an organized community after the Communist takeover.
Austria	Reconstructed and reconstituted with a substantially different population consisting, in the main, of World War II refugees concentrated in Vienna.
Belgium	Reconstructed and reconstituted as a consequence of a significant influx of Eastern European refugees. Brussels and Antwerp are the two major communities.
Bulgaria	Limited reconstruction after extensive emigration to the newly established State of Israel.
Czechoslovakia	Partially reconstructed and reconstituted under the Communist regime. Emigration increased after 1968.
Denmark	Reconstruction along pre-war lines with the return of the pre-war Jewish population.
Finland	Reconstituted and somewhat enlarged by the addition of a refugee population.
France	Reconstructed and reconstituted with a substantially new population from Eastern Europe immediately after World War II and subsequently further reconstituted in the wake of the North African influx of the early 1960s. Jewish population formerly concentrated in Paris and a few other major cities is now spread throughout the country to an extent unequaled since the Middle Ages.
Germany (Federal Republic)	Reconstructed and reconstituted with substantially different population including Eastern European refugees and "repatriates."
Gibraltar	No significant constitutional change or population shift.
Greece	Partially reconstructed and reconstituted around remnant population after World War II. Center of Jewish life moved from Salonika to Athens.
Hungary	Underwent partial reconstruction and limited reconstitution under the Communist regime. Flight of refugees in 1956 reduced the Jewish population somewhat but the community remains one of the largest and strongest in Eastern Europe.
Italy	Partially reconstructed after formal restoration of pre-war constitution. Jewish life divided between Rome and northern Italian communities.
Liechtenstein	Jewish community slowly disappeared through emigration.
Luxemburg	Reconstructed and reconstituted with little change in scope of communal activity.
Malta	No significant change; some population decline.
Monaco	Primarily a refugee community organized during and after World War II.
Netherlands	Partially reconstructed and reconstituted with remnant population as a far weaker community than before the war. Ashkenazi community is numerically dominant.
Norway	Reconstructed with addition of some refugees.
Poland	Extremely limited reconstruction under Communists with successive emigrations of surviving Jews culminating in the virtual expulsion of those born Jewish who had faithfully served the new regime.
Portugal	Reconstituted to include remnants of wartime refugees but essentially the same small well-integrated community.
Romania	Largest Jewish community in Eastern Europe outside the Soviet Union; underwent limited reconstitution under Communist regime after substantial emigration to Israel. Community organized on strictly religious lines.
Spain	Gained formal status as community by stages between 1931 and 1968 when it was officially recognized as a legal religious body. Wartime refugee settlers founded communal institutions in Madrid, Barcelona and Malaga.
Sweden	Reconstituted with addition of a substantial number of refugees and following the abolition of state-required community membership.
Switzerland	Reconstituted to include the few wartime refugees allowed to settle permanently.
Soviet Union	Virtually disappeared as an organized community, after World War II in the wake of the Stalin repression (1948–1952).
Yugoslavia	Reconstructed and reconstituted as a strictly ethnic community under Communist regime after substantial emigration to Israel.

also areas with a high Jewish reproduction rate) were those that had been wiped out. At the end of the 1940s, the centers of Jewish life had shifted to a decisive extent away from Europe to Israel and North America. Continental Europe as a whole ranked behind Latin America, North Africa, and Great Britain as a force in Jewish life. Its Jews were almost entirely dependent upon financial and technical assistance from the United States and Israel. Except for those in the Muslim countries (that were soon to virtually disappear), all of the major functioning Jewish communities had acquired sufficient proportions to become significant factors on the Jewish scene only within the previous two generations. Many of the shapers of those communities were still alive and in many cases still the active communal leaders. The Jewish world had been thrown back to a pioneering stage, willy-nilly.

The organization of Jewish communal life reflected these

shifts and their consequences wherever Jews were found. Thus in the late 1940s and 1950s reconstruction and reconstitution of existing communities and the founding of new ones was the order of the day throughout the Jewish world. The Jewish communities of Continental Europe all underwent periods of reconstruction or reconstitution in response to wartime losses, changes in the formal status of religious communities in their host countries, migration to Israel, and the introduction of new regimes. Table 4: Early Postwar Changes in Continental Jewish Communities summarizes these changes in the early postwar period. The most significant changes since that time occurred in Eastern Europe after the collapse of Communism. Despite large-scale emigration to Israel and the West, Jewish community life was revived in countries where it had formerly been repressed, and nowhere more impressively than in the former Soviet Union, where the Federation of Jewish Communities (founded in 1998) operates as an umbrella organization for its constituent communities, supporting an extensive network of synagogues, community centers, and day schools.

The Jewish communities in the Moslem countries were transformed in response to the convergence of two factors: the creation of Israel and the anticolonial revolutions in Asia and Africa. The greater portion of the Jewish population in those countries was transferred to Israel, and organized Jewish life virtually came to an end in all of them except Morocco. The changes in their situation are summarized in Table 5: Postwar Changes in Jewish Communities in Moslem Countries.

The English-speaking Jewries (and, to a somewhat lesser extent, those of Latin America) were faced with the more complex task of adapting their organizational structures to three new purposes: to assume responsibilities passed to them as a result of the destruction of European Jewry, to play a major role in assisting Israel, and to accommodate internal changes in communities still becoming acculturated. Their responses are summarized in Table 6: Postwar Changes in Major English-Speaking Jewish Communities and Table 7: Postwar Changes in Latin American and Caribbean Jewish Communities.

Many of the smaller Jewish communities in Asia and Africa were actually founded or received organized form in this period, while others, consisting in the main of transient merchants or refugees, were abandoned, as shown in Table 7: Postwar Developments in Asian and African Jewish Communities. Finally, all but a handful of the Jewish communities in the contemporary world have had to adjust to the new realities of voluntary choice, which, on one hand, gave Jews greater freedom than ever before to identify as Jews or not and, on the other, encouraged a wide variety of options for Jewish identification within each community.

Table 5. Postwar Changes in Jewish Communities in Moslem Countries

Country	
Aden	Entire community emigrated before Aden received its independence.
Afghanistan	Majority of the Jews emigrated leaving a small oppressed community behind.
Algeria	Virtually all the Jews fled the country in wake of the French evacuation, moving to France and Israel during the 1960s and essentially ending Jewish communal life.
Egypt	Successive oppressions and migrations to Israel after 1948 virtually ended the community's existence.
Iran	Community was reduced in size by emigration to Israel but continues to function as in the past with minor adjustment.
Iraq	Mass migration to Israel in the early 1950s reduced the community to a tiny oppressed minority which lived under severe government restrictions until the U.S. invasion of Iraq (2003).
Lebanon	With the help of a fairly sympathetic government, the community weathered the Arab-Israel conflicts but in 2005 was at the end of the process of self-liquidation through emigration, mostly to Latin America and Europe.
Libya	Migration to Israel accelerated after each Arab-Israel crisis and after the 1967 war the community finally ceased to exist as an entity. Very few Jews remain there.
Morocco	The community's slow decline through emigration to France and Israel after 1948 accelerated after Morocco received independence and picked up momentum after 1967 and 1979 wars.
Pakistan	Most of the small community emigrated, leaving a very small group to carry on minimal communal life in some cities.
Syria	Oppression after 1948 led to migration of a majority to Israel and Lebanon; government pressure increased against the remnant after the 1967 war. Practically all Jews emigrated, leaving no organized community life.
Tunisia	Despite official attempts to convince the Jews to stay, most migrated to Israel in successive waves after Tunisia's independence.
Turkey	Almost half of the 100,000 Jewish population left for Israel after 1948. The remainder were effectively reconstituted as a religious community with limited powers and under governmental supervision. Most of the Jews (nearly 20,000) live in Istanbul and a minority in Izmir (about 1,500) – the only two regularly organized communities.
Yemen	All but a tiny handful left for Israel immediately after the establishment of the state. The few remaining Jews mostly emigrated during the 1960s.

Community Structure in a Voluntaristic Environment

Whatever the form of community organization, the primary fact of Jewish communal life today is its voluntary character. While there are some differences from country to country in the degree of actual freedom to be Jewish or not, the virtual disappearance of the remaining legal and even social and cultural barriers to individual free choice in all but a handful of countries has made free association the dominant characteristic of Jewish life in the "postmodern" era. Consequently, the

Table 6. Postwar Changes in Major English-Speaking Jewish Communities

Country	
Australia	The postwar influx of refugees substantially enhanced Jewish life and necessitated changes in its communal structure, both locally and countrywide, to encompass the widened scope of Jewish activity and the more intensely "Jewish" Jews. These have continued into the 21st century, giving Australian Jewry comparatively favorable intermarriage statistics and continuing strong support for Zionism. Unlike the United States, a majority of Australia's Jews probably belonged to Orthodox synagogues.
Canada	Pressures of "Americanization," suburbanization and the general homogenization of Canadian society led to a weakening of traditional Canadian communal structure and the introduction of American-style "religious pluralism." But, characterized by a relatively strong sense of Diaspora identity, the Canadian Jewish community continued to grow, in large part through immigration. The community's center of gravity also continued to shift toward Toronto, now home to almost half of all Canadian Jews in the early 21st century. As in the United States, all of the denominations of Judaism are well represented in Canada, with the Orthodox stream very strong.
Ireland	Little significant constitutional change even though a native-born generation came to the fore. Some immigration from the former Soviet Union and elsewhere improved a declining situation.
New Zealand	Prior to about 1980, the continued emigration of the younger generation decreased the Jewish population and weakened the community structure. Subsequently, significant numbers arrived from the former Soviet Union and South Africa but emigration and assimilation continued.
Rhodesia (Zimbabwe)	The concentration of Jews from other countries of black Africa increased the size and importance of the Rhodesian community while the separation of Zambia and the Rhodesian secession increased its self-contained character. But with civil war and black independence the Jewish community began to shrink, leaving just a few Jews in the early 21st century.
South Africa	Changes in the regime and the rise of a native-born generation within the community shifted the emphasis of the communal institutions and the dominant mode of Jewish identification, weakening what had become the traditional structure. In the post-Apartheid era the tendency has been toward greater coordination and unity within the community.
United Kingdom	The rise to power of the last wave of immigrants and a native-born generation challenged the communal status quo from both left and right, weakening traditional institutions and strengthening new ones that reflected the community's greater diversity. The number of Jews in Britain has probably declined since its peak in the 1950s, with especially sharp declines in cities outside of London. On the other hand, in many respects Jewish consciousness has increased among Anglo-Jewry.
United States	The destruction of European Jewry transferred world Jewish leadership decisively to the American Jewish community. This plus the rise of a new generation and the disappearance of immigrant ideologies led to significant organizational changes to meet demands while also enabling American Jewry to become more rooted in the "religious pluralism" of the general society. Subsequently the traditional institutions, other than the synagogue became less significant as Jewishness tended more to find subjective expression.

first task of each Jewish community is to learn to deal with the particular local manifestation of this freedom. This task is a major factor in determining the direction of the reconstitution of Jewish life in this generation. The new voluntarism extends itself into the internal life of the Jewish community as well, generating pluralism even in previously free but relatively homogeneous or monolithic community structures. This pluralism is exacerbated by the breakdown of the traditional reasons for being Jewish and the rise of new incentives for Jewish association. At the same time, the possibilities for organizing a pluralistic Jewish community have also been enhanced by these new incentives and the "postmodern" breakdown of the rigid ideologies that divided Jews in the latter third of the modern era. Certainly the creation of the State of Israel has given the Jewish people a new and compelling focus that enhances the Jewish attachments of virtually all Jews. The state's crucial role as a generator of Jewish ties, regardless of other differences, was decisively demonstrated at the time of the *Six-Day War (1967).

Pluralism organized into more or less permanent structural arrangements leads to federalism, and federalism has been the traditional way in which the Jewish people has maintained its unity in the face of the pressures of diversity. This is one tradition that is not being abandoned today. The previous sections have suggested the wide variety of federal arrangements that presently exist in the organized Jewish communities of the world. In each case, the Jewish community adapts itself to the environment of the host country so that its own structure reflects local conditions while facilitating (as far as possible) the achievement of the main purposes of corporate Jewish life. In virtually every case, the structure that emerges from the adaptation is based on federal principles and uses federal forms. The pluralistic federalism of the voluntaristic community substantially eliminates the neat pattern of communal organization usually displayed as the model by those who concern themselves with rationalizing Jewish community life. Though smaller communities in different cultural settings are not likely to conform completely, more and more the seemingly anarchistic American pattern is revealed as the paradigm of their development, if not the vision of their future. Certainly the model of a hierarchic organizational structure does not offer an accurate picture of the distribution of powers and responsibilities in any Jewish community today. Even in the more formally structured communities of Central Europe and Latin America, the institution that appears to be at the top of the pyramid is really dependent upon and often manipulated by the institutions and organizations that would be placed farther down on the structure. The local community that "should" be on the bottom is, in fact, often the real center of power. For communities like the United States, even the modified model is useless. Nor is there a central governing agent in most communities that serves as the point at which authority, responsibility, and power converge. Even in the communities ostensibly dominated by a consistory, the erstwhile central body has been shunted aside to become just another specialized institution in an oligopoly of such institutions.

The structure of contemporary Jewish communities is best understood as a multidimensional matrix (or mosaic) that takes the form of a communications network; a set of interacting institutions which, while preserving their own structural integrity and roles, are informed by shared patterns of culture, activated by a shared system of organizations, and governed by shared leadership cadres. The character of the matrix and its communications network varies from community to community, with particularly sharp variations separating the six basic types. In some cases, the network is connected through a common center, which serves as the major (but rarely, if ever, the exclusive) channel for communication. In others, the network forms a matrix without any real center, with the lines of communication crisscrossing in all directions. In all cases, the boundaries of the community are revealed only when the pattern of the network is uncovered. The pattern itself is perceptible only when both of its components are revealed, namely its institutions and organizations with their respective roles and the way in which communications are passed between them.

The pattern itself is inevitably a dynamic one; that is to say, there is rarely a fixed division of authority and influence but, rather, one that varies from time to time and usually from issue to issue, with different elements in the matrix taking on different "loads" at different times and relative to different issues. Since the community is a voluntary one, persuasion rather than compulsion, influence rather than power are the only tools available for making and executing policies. This also works to strengthen its character as a communications network since the character, quality, and relevance of what is communicated and the way in which it is communicated frequently determine the extent of the authority and influence of the parties on the communication.

[Daniel J. Elazar]

Table 7. Postwar Changes in Latin American and Caribbean Jewish Communities

1. Communities entrenching, adjusting, and moving toward greater internal unity:	
Argentina	Guatemala
Brazil	Mexico
Chile	Panama
Costa Rica	Uruguay
El Salvador	Venezuela
2. Communities of emigration and decline:	
Bolivia	Haiti
Columbia	Honduras
Cuba	Nicaragua
Dominican Republic	Paraguay
Ecuador	Surinam
3. Communities undergoing "Americanization" through expansion of American business and leisure interests in the Caribbean:	
Barbados	Jamaica
Curacao	Trinidad and Tobago

Community and Polity

The discussion in the foregoing pages has been more or less restricted to the matrix of institutions and organizations that form a community on the countrywide plane. The Jewish polity as a whole, however, functions on several planes. The federal connections between local and countrywide communities and between Jewish communities around the world have also undergone important changes since World War II, and the feedback has begun to have a significant effect on the countrywide and local communities involved.

Before the modern era, although there were no formal organizations that functioned on a worldwide basis to unite the various Jewish communities, the common allegiance to halakhic Judaism and reliance upon traditional Jewish law gave the Jewish people the constitutional unity it needed. During the modern era, this unity was shattered, and nothing comparable developed to replace it. By the end of the 19th century, all that there was in the way of an organized worldwide Jewish polity was an informal alliance and organizations of Jewish "aristocrats" in the Western world who had taken it upon themselves to try and defend Jewish interests and protect the rights of individual Jews, so as to aid in their emancipation. These inadequate arrangements effectively perished in World War I, when the world which encouraged that mode of community action came to an end.

Meanwhile, tentative steps in the direction of a reorganization more appropriate to the 20th century were beginning to be made. The World Zionist Organization and its member organizations, the *American Jewish Joint Distribution Committee, the B'nai B'rith, and later the *World Jewish Congress

Table 8. Postwar Developments in Asian and African Jewish Communities

1. Communities founded or given new form:	
Hong Kong	Ryukyu Islands
India	Taiwan
Japan	Thailand
Philippines	
2. Communities abandoned or substantially reduced in size:	
Angola	Kenya
Burma	Malaysia
China	Singapore
Congo Republic	Uganda
Cyprus	Zambia
Indonesia	

began to offer more routinized and less elitist means of tying Jews together on a worldwide basis. All together, they began to create an infrastructure for a new Jewish confederation in the making.

After World War II, the structure of the Jewish confederation underwent further adaptation. This strengthening of the organizational aspects of the worldwide Jewish polity was partly a consequence of the changes taking place in its constituent communities. The other crucial factor is the State of Israel. The trend has been clear: the concentration in Israel of the major decision-making organs of the Jewish confederation and the organizations that serve it and the routing of their decision-making procedures through Jerusalem, even as the structures, centered in Israel, have at the beginning of the new century been experiencing considerable strain. This trend has become particularly noticeable since the Six-Day War, after which the Israel government began to take very explicit steps to reorganize and strengthen the institutions and organizations of world Jewry by tying them closer to the state. Israel's greater ability, as an independent state, to deal with political matters and its great stake in strengthening the worldwide Jewish confederation has led it to assume this role. Two major events – the Six-Day War in 1967 and the beginnings of the Soviet Jewry movement in 1963 – signaled that the American Jewish communal agenda would be more particularistic than it had been. Israel became the focal point of Jewish identification, the one Jewish phenomenon whose crucial importance is accepted by virtually all Jews and that has the ability to mobilize widespread public efforts in what is, after all, still a voluntary polity. Perhaps paradoxically, at the very moment that free individual choice in the matter of Jewish attachment has reached heights never previously attained, there has been a rediscovery of the Jewish polity, i.e., of the special political character of the Jewish community. In the first decade of the 21st century, however, new patterns in the American Jewish community – and especially in the consciousness of a younger cadre of Jews – had emerged. There was a diminution of the idea of a collective "community" as the meaning of Jewishness was increasingly defined in subjective individual constructs. American Jews found less meaning in formal Jewish organizations (except the local synagogue), political activity, philanthropic endeavors, and attachment to the state of Israel. The traditional institutions of community became less significant than they were to earlier generations of Jews in America. Because they feel that their identity as Jews is immutable, American Jews increasingly do not need the normative communal behaviors of the past in order to express their identity. This changing approach to "community" will have significant implications for the future of Jewish communal organizational structures, for communal fundraising, and for a range of communal involvements.

[Daniel J. Elazar / J. Chanes (2nd ed.)]

See also Communal *Amenities; *Autonomy; Judicial *Autonomy; Autonomous Jewish *Finances; Territorial *Federations of Communities; *Foundations (Community Federations); *Consistory; *Councils of the Lands; *AMIA; *DAIA; *Kultus Gemeinde; *Millet; *Landesjudenschaften; *Jewish Quarter; *Chief Rabbi; **Ḥakahm Bashi*; **Muqaddim*; **Takkanot*; **Shtadlan*; **Pinkas*; *Exilarch; **Ḥerem*; **Ḥerem ha-Yishuv*; **Ḥerem Bet Din*; *Minority Rights; *Synagogue. For communal organizations in the various countries, see entries for the respective countries.

BIBLIOGRAPHY: UP TO WORLD WAR II: Baron, Community; Baron, Social²; Baer, Spain; idem, in: *Zion*, 15 (1950), 1–41 (Eng. summary, i–v); M. Burstein (Avidor), *Self-Government of the Jews in Palestine since 1900* (1934); I. Levitats, *Jewish Community in Russia, 1772–1884* (1943); L. Finkelstein, *Jewish Self-Government in the Middle Ages* (1964²); M.S. Goodblatt, *Jewish Life in Turkey in the 16th Century* (1943); M. Franco, *Essai sur l'histoire des Israélites de l'Empire Ottoman* (1897); S. Rosanes, *Divrei Yemei Yisrael be-Togarmah*, 5 vols. (1930); W.J. Fischel, *Ha-Yehudim be-Hodu* (1960); J.M. Landau, *The Jews in Nineteenth Century Egypt* (1969); Hirschberg, Afrikah; idem, in: A.J. Arberry (ed.), *Religion in the Middle East*, 1 (1969), 119–225 (selected bibliography, vol. 2, 661–3); H.H. Ben-Sasson, *Perakim be-Toledot ha-Yehudim bi-Ymei ha-Beinayim* (1962); idem (ed.), *Toledot Am Yisrael*, 3 vols. (1969), index, s.v. *Kehillot*; I. Agus, *Urban Civilization in Pre-Crusade Europe*, 2 (1965), 421–553; M.J. Karpf, *Jewish Community Organization in the United States* (1938); B.M. Edidin, *Jewish Community Life in America* (1947). SINCE WORLD WAR II: *Bi-Tefuẓot ha-Golah* (Eng. ed., *In the Dispersion*; 1958); S. Federbush, *World Jewry Today* (1959); Institute of Jewish Affairs, New York, *Jewish* Communities *of the World* (1959); J. Katz, *Tradition and Crisis* (1961); O. Janowsky (ed.), *The American Jew: A Reappraisal* (1964); JYB; AJYB. **ADD. BIBLIOGRAPHY:** D. Elazar, *People and Polity: Organizational Dynamics of World Jewry* (1989); idem, *Community and Polity* (1995²); J. Chanes, *A Primer on the American Jewish Community* (1999²); idem (ed.), *A Portrait of the American Jewish Community* (1998).

COMMUNITY TOKENS, internal Jewish currency. The special conditions under which Jews lived in the Diaspora before Emancipation and in Ereẓ Israel especially up to World War I led to a kind of community similar to a miniature state. To preserve the character of the community, whose members did not enjoy the privileges of other citizens, Jews were obliged to create and provide for their own institutions, such as synagogues, rabbinic courts, schools, hospitals, homes for the aged, soup kitchens for the poor, etc. All these institutions were administered by the community and financed by its members through ordinary and extraordinary contributions. In order to cope with these tasks, the communal leaders at times resorted to issuing tokens of their own, with an internal value only and not generally acceptable outside the community. To not raise the suspicion of the authorities, they were often cast in a style that distinguished them from legal tender. Many communities issued tokens in metal or paper, and much information about them has been lost. Whenever a new kind of token is discovered, a fresh investigation has to be carried out.

Diaspora

Perhaps the oldest Jewish metal tokens are those issued by the community of Rome in the ghetto period. These were given to the *shoḥet* for the slaughter of a small chicken (1½ baiocchi) and a large one (3 baiocchi) and the proceeds went to the *talmud torah* fund. The Sephardi immigrants in *Constantinople had their own community centers and synagogues. They issued 5 para brass tokens on which the origin of the community is mentioned, such as Araico (Sarajevo), Shirigis (Saragossa), and Cordoba. The community of Beirut issued a brass charity token for the sick (*Bikkur Ḥolim*) in 1904. During World War I and in the first years after, many communities in Russia and Poland issued paper tokens. In the Austro-Hungarian Empire at least two metal tokens were issued: one in the Austrian community of *Mattersdorf with the initials I.G.M. (*Israelitische Gemeinde Mattersdorf*) and an equivalent abbreviation in Hebrew; and the other issued by the Hungarian community of *Satoraljaujhely in German and Hungarian (*Cultussteuer der israelitischen Gemeinde S.A. Ujhely*). In the 1830s the Jewish merchants of Belgrade obtained from Prince Milosh recognition of their custom of minting their own small change. Private issues were not uncommon; various Jewish enterprises issued their own tokens. Julius *Popper, owner of the gold mines in Tierra del Fuego, issued in El Paramo two gold coins of 1 and 5 grams respectively in his name: "Popper-Tierra del Fuego." The numismatic dealer Henry Seligmann, of Hannover, Germany, in 1921 issued porcelain tokens in the denominations of 25 and 50 Pfennig. Various Jewish enterprises in the United States, especially restaurants, circulated their own tokens.

Ereẓ Israel

Under Turkish rule in the 19th and 20th centuries, the communities in Ereẓ Israel issued a considerable number of tokens. A brass *Ẓedakah* token was issued in Jerusalem by the *Torat Ḥayyim* yeshivah, which also put out a small stamp-shaped paper token of ½ para and different kinds of paper currency in denominations of 1, 5, and 10 gold Napoleons. Other communities in Jerusalem, such as the various *kolelim*, also issued their own paper currency, as did Hebron yeshivah (in Jerusalem) during the British Mandate. There were other brass tokens, such as a square one bearing the legend שְׂכַר שְׁחִיטָה דַקָּה ("fee for the slaughter of a sheep or goat"), a rectangular one inscribed צְדָקָה תַּצִּיל מִמָּוֶת ("charity saves from death"), a round one with the legend קרש ("grush" = *piaster* = 40 para), and another round one with the abbreviation צל"ע (צְדָקָה לַעֲנִיִּים, "charity for the poor"). Turkish copper coins were also issued, countermarked with the same abbreviation. In the 1880s the colony of Zikhron Ya'akov and the agricultural school of Mikveh Israel issued brass tokens of 1, ½, and ¼ (presumably piaster), which, however, were declared illegal by the Turkish authorities. Another more primitive brass token was issued by the colony of Reḥovot, which also issued paper tokens inscribed in Hebrew and French in denominations of ½, 1, 3, 6, 13, and 26 piasters. The colony of Petaḥ Tikvah issued zinc tokens of 1 and 2 (undefined denominations), and in the early 1920s also issued paper tokens in denominations of ¼, 1, and 10 Egyptian piasters, then the legal currency in Palestine. In 1916 the city of Tel Aviv put into circulation paper tokens of 2⁄10, ¼, ½, and 1 beshlik and 1 franc as an emergency measure. However, this was prohibited by the Turks and had to be withdrawn. To overcome the lack of currency from 1914 to 1916, the Anglo-Palestine Co., the forerunner of the Anglo-Palestine Bank and today's Bank Leumi, issued checks in denominations of 5, 10, 20, 50 and 100 francs which were accepted by the *yishuv* as legal tender. In the early 1950s, during another shortage of small change, the Tel Aviv municipality issued paper tokens in denominations of 50 and 100 perutah respectively. The ½ mil of *kofer ha-yishuv* was a brass token that served as a self-imposed security tax during the British Mandate (from 1939) to meet the requirements of the Haganah. Paper tokens were issued by various bus companies in aid of the Magen David Adom. During the British Mandate there were private issues of small paper, mainly by restaurants.

BIBLIOGRAPHY: B. Kisch, in: HJ, 15 (1953), 167–82; Y. Shachar, in: *The Holy Land Philatelist*, 64–65 (1960), 1306–07; H. Feuchtwanger, in: *Israel Numismatic Bulletin*, 5 (1963), 2ff.; A. Kindler, in: *Museum Haaretz Bulletin*, 7 (1965), 66ff.; see also pls. x–xv.

[Alvin Kass]

COMO, city in Lombardy, northern Italy. In 1400 the Christian residents of Como requested the duke of Milan to segregate its few Jewish inhabitants. The Jews living in Como during the 15th century were mainly engaged in moneylending. They suffered considerably from the animosity aroused in the Christian populace by the preaching of the friars, but the duke did not yield to demands for their expulsion. However, in 1597 the Spanish government expelled the Jews from the duchy and the community in Como ceased to exist.

BIBLIOGRAPHY: Milano, Italia, index; Motta, in: *Periodico della Società storica comense*, 5 (1885), 7–44.

[Umberto (Moses David) Cassuto]

COMPASSION, norm governing the relationship between human beings and also regulating their behavior toward animals.

In the Bible

The biblical noun *raḥamim* and the verb *raḥam, riḥam*, frequently used to denote this behavior, are derived from the same root as is the noun *reḥem* ("womb"), hence some scholars have proposed that its original meaning was "brotherhood," "brotherly feeling" of those born from the same womb. Other terms, including *ḥesed* ("lovingkindness"), are also used, though in many instances this notion is not expressed explicitly and must be understood through the description of certain forms of conduct. For the writers of the Bible, the concept indicated an essential relation between God and Israel, rooted in the covenant: "He being full of compassion, forgives iniquity and does not destroy" (Ps. 78:38; see Ex. 33:19; Deut. 8:18; Isa. 9:16, etc.). It was made manifest by the preservation of Israel from destruction at the hands of its enemies and by divine intervention on its behalf: "In Your love You lead the people You redeemed" (Ex. 15:13; see Deut. 30:3; I Kings 8:23, etc.).

The human response to the disclosure of divine compassion is to be found in man's behavior toward his fellows: "Learn to do well; seek justice; relieve the oppressed; judge the fatherless; plead for the widow" (Isa. 1:17; see Micah 6:8; Jer. 21:12). "He that is gracious unto the poor, lends unto the Lord" (Prov. 19:17). "You shall not mistreat any widow or orphan" (Ex. 22:21). Nor is the stranger excluded from this obligation: "You shall not wrong a stranger or oppress him" (*ibid.* 22:20). Animals, too, are recognized as the objects of such solicitude: "When you see the ass of your enemy prostrate under its load and would refrain from raising it, you must nevertheless raise it with him" (Ex. 23:5; see Deut. 22:4). "You shall not muzzle an ox while it is threshing" (Deut. 25:4).

In Rabbinic Literature

Rabbinic Judaism enlarged and deepened the biblical concept, recognizing it as an indispensable characteristic of the Jew (Yev. 79a): "Whoever is merciful to his fellowmen is certainly of the children of Abraham" (Beẓah 32b). The Jews were popularly called *raḥamanim benei raḥamanim* – "compassionate scions of compassionate forbears." The rabbis conceived of the practice of compassion as an *imitatio dei*, for the ways of God in which man was commanded to walk (Deut. 8:6) were those set out in Exodus 34:6–7: "The Lord! The Lord! a God compassionate and gracious, slow to anger, rich in steadfast kindness, extending kindness to the thousandth generation, forgiving iniquity, transgression, and sin." These verses were understood to sum up and explain the divine attribute of compassion, and to set the norm for human conduct: "Just as God is called compassionate and gracious, so you must be compassionate and gracious, giving gifts freely" (Sif. Deut. 49). Maimonides declared that arrogant, cruel, misanthropic, and unloving persons were to be suspected of not being true Jews (Yad, Issurei Bi'ah, 19:17). The clear tendency of the Bible requiring compassion in dealing with animals was summarized in the talmudic phrase, "[relieving] the suffering of an animal is a biblical law" (*ẓa'ar ba'alei ḥayyim de-oraita*, BM 32b). According to a Midrash (Ex. R. 2:3) both Moses and David were chosen to lead Israel because of their kindness to animals. The ḥasidic teacher R. *Moses Leib of Sasov epitomized the concept in his statement, "to know the needs of men and to bear the burden of their sorrow – that is the true love of man."

BIBLIOGRAPHY: K. Kohler, *Jewish Theology* (1928), 126–33; S. Schechter, *Some Aspects of Rabbinic Theology* (1936), 201–2; S.H. Dresner, *Prayer, Humility and Compassion* (1957), 181–239.

[Lou H. Silberman]

COMPOUNDING OFFENSES. The injunction: "Ye shall take no ransom for the life of a murderer.... And ye shall accept no ransom for him that is fled to his *city of refuge" (Num. 35:31–32), was interpreted as an exception to the general rule that for all other offenses you may accept a "ransom" (*kofer*), except only for the offense of homicide (BK 83b; Rashbam to Num. 35:31). It seems that the capital offense of adultery was compounded in this way (Prov. 6:35). The rule that even the worst examples of personal injury (such as blinding or mutilating) were not to be punished by way of talion (as prescribed in the Bible, Ex. 21:24–25; Lev. 24:19–20), but were to be compensated for by the payment of damages, was based on the principle that as offenses short of homicide they were compoundable by money (BK 83b, 84a). The fact that the "ransom" was in these cases translated into "damages" (cf. Maim. Yad, Ḥovel u-Mazzik 1:3), caused some confusion and overlapping between civil and criminal law in this field. By the payment of damages the offender is relieved from criminal responsibility (see *Assault), the damages operating as "expiation money" (cf. Ex. 30:12, 15, and 16) in lieu of the otherwise expiating punishment. In the same way the owner of the ox that is a habitual gorer, who, though forewarned, fails to guard it so that it kills a man or a woman is liable to "be put to death," but may "redeem his life" by paying such ransom as "is laid upon him" (Ex. 21:29–30). The dispute between the *tannaim* as to whether the ransom is to be assessed according to the value of the killed man or of the owner of the ox (Mekh. Mishpatim 10; BK 40a), as well as the parallel dispute as to whether the ransom is in the nature of damages (*mamon*) or of expiation (BK 40a), reflect the underlying difference between purely civil and additionally criminal remedies. This distinction is not affected by the talmudic interpretation of the liability of the ox-owner to be put to death, as this relates only to the law of heaven (*bi-ydei shamayim*), the theory of expiation by payment of the ransom applying to *divine punishment as well (Sanh. 15b; Maim. Yad, Nizkei Mamon 10:4).

It is because the ransom underwent this transformation into damages that the injunction not to accept a ransom in cases of homicide was interpreted as addressed to the court (*ibid.*, Roẓe'aḥ 1:4). In fact, it was not only the court but more particularly such interested persons as *blood-avengers that were enjoined from compounding homicides – as was pointed out by later authorities (e.g., *Minḥat Ḥinnukh* 412). However it appears that such compounding had already been practiced by judges in biblical times and led to accusations of corruption (cf. Amos 5:12; and contrast I Sam. 12:3) – perhaps not so much because the judges corruptly enriched themselves (see *Bribery), but because of the inequality thereby created between rich offenders, who could afford to ransom themselves, and indigent offenders who could not (cf. Prov. 13:8; cf. Job 36:18). The elimination of this inequality in cases of homicide may have made it appear even more reprehensible in other cases, at least from the point of view of judicial ethics. In later periods courts allowed offenders to compound offenses for which previous courts had imposed severe punishments (such as flogging) by making payments to the injured person or to the poor (cf. e.g., Resp. Maharyu 146; *Eitan ha-Ezraḥi 7; Yam shel Shelomo* BK 8:49; Resp. Maharshal 28).

[Haim Hermann Cohn]

In the State of Israel

The Israel Supreme Court dealt with the matter of "ransom" or punishments in the case of Sheffer (CA 506/88, *Sheffer v. State of Israel*, 48(1) PD 87). The Court (Justice Elon) discussed the question of whether a terminally ill patient was entitled to request that he not be given any life-extending treatment. The Court cited in this context the biblical verse (Gen. 1:27): "In His image did God make man," which is the "analytical and philosophical basis of Jewish law's unique approach to the supreme value of the sanctity of human life" (*Sheffer*, 117). "The prayer of the Jew to the Almighty in the Days of Awe acknowledges not only that 'the soul is yours, and the body is your work,' but also that 'the soul is yours and the body is yours,' for man is created in the image of God, in the image of the world's Creator. This approach also serves as the rationale for a legal ruling. Thus, Numbers 35:31 – 'Do not accept ransom for a murderer' – is explained by Maimonides in his *Mishneh Torah* (*Roẓe'aḥ u-Shemirat ha-Nefesh* 23:4) as follows: 'The Court is warned not to accept ransom money from a murderer, even if he gives all the money in the world and even if the blood avenger is willing to acquit him [for it] – since the life of the person who was killed is not the property of the blood relative but rather that of the Almighty, as it is stated: 'Do not accept ransom for a murderer.' And there is nothing that the Torah deals with more seriously than with murder, as it is stated: 'Do not defile the land, etc., since the blood will defile the land' (Num. 35: 33)." These words have become the source of disputes among halakhic authorities with regard to the fundamental question of whether medical treatment can be forced on a patient against his wishes (*ibid.*, 118–19).

[Menachem Elon (2nd ed.)]

BIBLIOGRAPHY: J.M. Ginzberg, *Mishpatim le-Yisrael* (1956), 143f., 221–3; M. Greenberg, in: *Yeḥezkel Kaufmann Jubilee Volume* (1960), 5–28. **ADD. BIBLIOGRAPHY:** M. Elon, *Jewish Law, Cases and Materials* (1999), 600f.; A. Warhaftig, "*Lo Tikḥu Kofer la-Nefesh Meḥabel,*" in: *Teḥumin,* 6 (1985), 303–8.

COMPROMISE (Heb. פְּשָׁרָה, *pesharah*; apparently derived from the term *pesher*, "solution," Eccles. 8:1), deciding a civil law dispute (*dinei mamonot*) by the court or an arbitral body, through the exercise of their discretion and not according to the laws governing the dispute. In Jewish law, compromise is allied to *arbitration both with regard to the way it evolved and in some of its rules and trends (the two are treated contiguously in the Tur and Shulḥan Arukh ḤM 12 and 13).

Pesharah and Biẓẓu'a

In talmudic sources the term *biẓẓu'a* is synonymous with and equivalent to the term *pesharah*. (In Scripture *biẓẓu'a* was used to mean divide or cut (Amos 9:1), and to execute or carry out (Zech. 4:9)). Gulak makes the interesting conjecture – based partly on the fact that several talmudic sources indicate that *pesharah* and *biẓẓu'a* were two distinct matters – that there was a difference of principle between the two. *Pesharah* was carried

out by the court itself and in the opinion of all the scholars, was something permitted, and even desirable, for restoring peace between the litigants. On the other hand the court before which the matter was brought in the case of *biẓẓu'a* would refer investigation to other persons – knowledgeable and expert in the field of that particular matter – for its disposal by way of a compromise between the parties. Referral of a matter by the court in this way was customary in ancient law and when the Romans abrogated Jewish judicial autonomy after the Bar Kokhba War (132–135 C.E.), some scholars refrained from adjudicating according to strict law, preferring a compromise between the parties to be effected by others who were knowledgeable in the matter (TJ, Sanh. 1:1, 18b; Mekh. Yitro, 2; see also *Mishpat Ivri). Consequently there were scholars who came to regard *biẓẓu'a* as forbidden, since they looked with disfavor on the fact that the court evaded making its own decision in the matter. (Gulak stresses that a prohibition against compromising is always expressed in terms of *biẓẓu'a* and not *pesharah*, since the latter, effected by the *dayyan* himself, is a *mitzvah*.) In the course of time the difference between *pesharah* and *biẓẓu'a* came to be forgotten, as in both cases the object was to compromise between the parties and the rules laid down for the one came equally to govern the other. In this article the principles of compromise are treated in a like manner; i.e., the terms are regarded as applying to the same concept, as is the case in halakhic literature.

Desirability of Compromise

Three different opinions on the subject of compromise are found in the Talmud, all originating from the middle of the second century when the weakening of Jewish judicial autonomy encouraged a movement toward finding a replacement by way of arbitration and compromise. Joshua b. Korḥah based his opinion that "*biẓẓu'a* is a *mitzvah*" on the scriptural injunction: "Execute the judgment of truth and peace in your gates" (Zech. 8:16), commenting that justice which involved both peace and charity was to be found in *biẓẓu'a* (Sif. Deut. 17; Tosef., Sanh. 1:2–3; Sanh. 6b; TJ, Sanh. 1:1, 18b). A contrary opinion was expressed by R. Eliezer, the son of Yose the Galilean, who stated that "*biẓẓu'a* is forbidden and the *boẓe'a* ["arbitrator"] an offender… but let the law cut through the mountain, as it is written 'For the judgment is God's'" (Deut. 1:17; Tosef., Sanh. 1:2; Sanh. 6b). The third opinion, that of Simeon b. Menasya, was that compromise was neither a *mitzvah* nor prohibited, but simply permissible (Sanh. 6b). The *halakhah* was decided to the effect that it is a *mitzvah* to ascertain from the litigants beforehand whether they want their dispute resolved according to law or by compromise and that their decision must be abided by; moreover, "it is praiseworthy if a court always effects a compromise" (Maim. Yad, Sanhedrin 22:4; Tur and Sh. Ar., ḤM 12:2). It remains a *mitzvah* for the court to effect a compromise even after it has heard the pleas of the parties and knows in whose favor the suit is weighted, but once its decision has been given the court may no longer effect a compromise and "let the law cut through the mountain" (Tosef., Sanh. 1:2–3; Sanh. 6b; TJ, Sanh. 1:1, 18b; Yad, Sanhedrin 22:4; Tur and Sh. Ar., ḤM 12:2).

In the geonic period it was determined that even after judgment had been given a compromise could still be effected, at the hands of someone other than a judge and elsewhere than at the place where the court was situated (L. Ginzberg, *Ginzei Schechter,* 2 (1929), 126; Sh. Ar., ḤM 12:2). Similarly, it is permissible for the court to compromise between the parties, even after giving judgment if either of them is liable in law to take an oath, in order that the need for this be obviated by virtue of the compromise (Sh. Ar., ḤM 12:2). Since the equitable oath (*shevu'at hesset*) is imposed on one of the parties in practically all legal suits, great efforts were made to induce the parties to a compromise and thus avoid the gravity of the oath (see also Sh. Ar., ḤM 12:17). Compromise was permitted to the court even if this involved some waiver of the rights of orphans "so as to shelter them from disputes" (Sh. Ar., ḤM 12:3).

The scholars extended the discussion on the merits and demerits of compromise in monetary disputes between man and his fellow to the precepts governing man's relationship with God and man's conduct in general. Thus the statement of Eliezer b. Jacob – that a man who steals wheat and then, when making bread with it, says the blessing on separating the *ḥallah, is actually blaspheming God (quoted in connection with the meaning of the word *boẓe'a*; Sanh. 6b) – was explained by Simeon Kayyara (ninth century) as an example of a defective compromise: "since he compromised with the precepts of God, acting as if robbery were permitted but that he was in duty bound to separate the *ḥallah*; this is a *mitzvah* performed as the result of a transgression, something God hates" (*Halakhot Gedolot*, ed. Warsaw, 19a). Judah's compromise in rescuing Joseph from the pit and selling him to the Ishmaelites (Gen. 37:26–28) has been interpreted as unworthy conduct: "since he should have said 'Let us return him to our father'" (Rashi to Sanh. 6b), and as worthy conduct: since this compromise was imperative in the circumstances (*Ḥiddushei Halakhot ve-Aggadot*, Sanh. 6b).

Nature of Compromise

Compromise is comparable to a judicial decision and must therefore be made after weighty deliberation. Thus, "compromise too requires an application of the mind to the decision" (*hekhre'a ha-da'at*; TJ, Sanh. 1:1); "the *dayyan* must take as much care with compromise as with a legal decision" (*Lehem Rav* 87); "just as the law should not be perverted, so it is warned that a compromise should not lean more to the one than the other" (Sh. Ar., ḤM 12:2). Some scholars interpreted the injunction, "Justice, justice shalt thou follow" (Deut. 16:20) as meaning, "Justice, once for the law and once for compromise" (Sanh. 32b and Rashi ad loc.). Other scholars interpreted the verse, "In righteousness shalt thou judge thy neighbor" (Lev. 19:15) as referring to a judgment based on the law, and Deuteronomy 16:20 as relating entirely to compromise, since in compromise there is a two-fold need for justice as the arbitrator cannot have recourse to the governing law and therefore has to exercise great care and discretion "to see who of them is telling the truth and who deserves to be treated with greater severity" (*Yad Ramah* and *Beit ha-Beḥirah*, Sanh. 32b).

The Making of a Compromise and Its Validity

Compromise is generally effected by a court of three, but the parties may consent to two judges or even a single one. The court is not authorized to compromise between the parties unless they have previously consented to the court's taking this course rather than judging in accordance with the applicable law. In special cases, when the court is satisfied that there is no means of evaluating a matter on the strength of the evidence, it may give "a judgment in the nature of a compromise … and decide as it may deem fit according to its own estimate." This is so since the court is forbidden to let a dispute pass out of its hands without having given a decision on it, as "this will increase conflict and the imposition of peace in the world is the duty of the court" (Rosh, Resp. 107:6; Sh. Ar., ḤM 12:5). Unlike a judgment of the court or of arbitrators – which is given by majority decision – compromise must be unanimously arrived at by all the judges (Sh. Ar., ḤM 12:18). The parties may retract from the compromise – even if they had previously authorized the court to adopt this course – as long as a *kinyan* (see Modes of *Acquisition) has not been performed by them and provided that they did not undertake in writing to abide by the compromise. However, once execution of the compromise decision has been begun (Sanh. 6a; Sh. Ar. ḤM 12:7), the parties may no longer withdraw.

[Menachem Elon]

The Right and the Good

In Deuteronomy 6:17–18, we read: "You shall diligently keep the commandments of the Lord and his testimonies which he has commanded you. And you shall do that which is right and good in the sight of the Lord, that it may be well with you, and so you may go and possess the good land that the Lord swore to your fathers." Commenting on this verse in his Torah Commentary, Naḥmanides writes: "This is a matter of great consequence. Given that it is impossible for the Torah to explicitly enumerate all the ways in which people relate to their neighbors and fellow men and to cover all the numerous types of business and transactions and all the things necessary for the proper ordering of society and government, it first mentioned a great many such things … and then stated generally that in all matters one should do that which is right and good. This is the basis for compromise, for going beyond the letter of the law, regarding that which was set forth in connection with giving a preemptive right to owners of adjoining land."

Compromise and Justice

In the later halakhic literature (*aḥaronim*), and more recently in rulings by Israeli rabbinical courts, compromise is used extensively to supplement substantive law, where the court is unable to provide a just solution to the matter confronting it. R. Abraham Ḥayyim Schorr (Poland, 17th century), in discussing the term "to place a compromise" (*Torat Ḥayyim* on

Sanh. 32a), states that, where the circumstances relating to the litigants are identical, and it is impossible to decide whose right should prevail, the court is *obligated* to propose ("place") a compromise, and even *compel* its acceptance by the parties. This conclusion is based on the use of the terminology, "*to place* a compromise," as distinct from "*making* a compromise." The term "to place" indicates that, having proposed a compromise which was subsequently rejected by the parties, the judge is permitted to cast ("to place") a lot as a means of determining which party will receive the right in dispute, and which party will be indemnified for his loss.

The rabbinical courts have recently issued a number of rulings based on compromise. Even in cases where there was no basis under substantive law to obligate the litigant to pay money, although there was an obligation according to "the law of Heaven." An example of this is a case in which the damage was consequential. In *Gerama and Garme the rabbinical court does not make a financial award under the *law of damages*, but rather in accordance with the law of *compromise.* The institution of compromise has been put to similar use in cases involving an act committed in breach of a negative precept, but which did not give rise to a financial obligation, such as deception in the payment of a day-worker. Additional examples are cases in which there are no grounds for imposing a financial obligation under strict law, either because in monetary matters we do not follow the majority opinion, or because the litigant invokes the *kim lei* claim (i.e., the litigant's reliance on a certain rabbinical opinion in a matter disputed among halakhic authorities, as a means of preventing a monetary ruling against him). In such cases, where the law itself offers no remedy, the rabbinical court may have recourse to compromise as a means of doing justice (see, e.g., *PDR*, Kiryat Arba-Hebron, vol A, p. 205, and index there; V. Goldberg, "*Shivḥei Pesharah*," *Mishpetei Ereẓ*, 2002)

Method of Effecting a Compromise

The Rabbinical Court of Appeal, relying on the view of *Leḥem Rav,* overturned a ruling of the Regional Rabbinical Court, which had given a compromise ruling without having properly heard the claims of one of the litigants. The Court of Appeal stated that: "From the determination and ruling of *Leḥem Rav* we learn that failure to listen to a litigant's claims infringes the principle of doing justice, and that the rabbinical judge's duty to hear the parties' claims is a precondition for his ability to rule in accordance with the law, as may be inferred from the aforementioned words of the *Tur.* The rabbinical judge added that even a ruling by way of compromise is only valid if prior thereto the rabbinical judge heard the litigants' claims" (A. Sherman in File 734/59, *Judgments*, vol. 188; given in 1999).

In another ruling, the Jerusalem Rabbinical Court of Appeals nullified a compromise ruling of the Regional Court when it became clear to them that the compromise ruling had been issued as a substitute for adjudication, without either of the litigants having given their advance consent. As such, it should be regarded as *no more than a compromise proposal* (Yosef Kapach, 328/43, given 1984, published in *Mishpetei Ereẓ* collection, 2002.)

In Israeli Supreme Court Case Law

The conception and status of compromise in Jewish Law were the basis of a number of Supreme Court rulings in recent years.

In *Sobol v. Goldman* (CA 807/77, 33 (1) PD 789), an appeal was filed in the Supreme Court against a District Court judgment, the question adjudicated being the validity of a rabbinic court judgment given by way of compromise, when the Law directs it to rule "according to the religious law." The Supreme Court's judgment (per Justice Elon) included a detailed exposition of the status of compromise in Jewish Law. The court discussed the conflicting opinions on the status of compromise in adjudication during the talmudic period (see above: "Desirability of Compromise"), and the approach that was ultimately accepted in Jewish Law in the Codes and by earlier and later authorities (*rishonim* and *aḥaronim*) regarding the positive role of compromise ruling in the world of *halakhah* and its integration as a substantive element in Jewish Law. Justice Elon added that:

> In Jewish Law the institution of compromise, its nature and its procedure, comprised many purely legal aspects. Hence it was determined that compromise cannot be the product of an arbitrary decision, but requires serious deliberation: "Compromise, too, requires careful thought" (TJ Sanh. 1:1). An entire chapter in the *Tur* and *Shulḥan Arukh* is devoted to the laws of compromise (ḤM 12), consisting of 19 sections of detailed explanation of how a compromise is effected, under what circumstances it is binding, etc. These rules establish compromise as an institution of a clearly legal character .... The conclusion of a compromise by the rabbinical court is neither in conflict with, nor beyond the boundaries of, the religious legal system in which it operates, but is in fact an integral part of it ... distinguished by the clear legal principles and rules of procedure applicable to it (*ibid.*, 799, 802).

The Supreme Court was confronted with a similar question in the *Gabbai* case (HC 2222/99 *Gabbai v. Rabbinical Court of Appeals*, 54 (5) 401). In a petition submitted to the High Court of Justice, a woman contested the decision of the Rabbinical Appeals Court to affirm the regional rabbinical court's ruling on the division of property between herself and her husband in the wake of their divorce. She claimed that the ruling contradicted the "joint assets rule." The Rabbinical Court of Appeals held that the regional rabbinical court had decided between the disputants by way of an imposed compromise where there was no possibility of deciding the facts.

Justice Proccaccia elucidated the essence of compromise in Jewish Law, comparing it with compromise in the civil law. Relying on Justice Elon's ruling in the *Sobol* case (see above), she determined that compromise was an intrinsic part of the system of religious law. She further quoted statements made by E. Shochetman as to its importance, which derives from "the supreme importance conferred by Jewish Tradition to the value of making peace between man and his fellow" (p.

420 of judgment). Justice Proccaccia pointed out that, unlike civil law, Jewish law also validates a compromise concluded without the parties' agreement – even though such is generally based on the parties' consent – when there is no evidence that can tilt the law one way or another, or when the admissibility of evidence is impugned. Justice Proccaccia cites the ruling of Asheri (*Teshuvot* 107:6):

> When the judge is confronted by a matter which he is unable to resolve, it is forbidden for him to withdraw from adjudication leaving the parties to fight one another, as it states: "Execute the judgment of truth and peace (in your gates)," for justice brings peace to the world, and the judge was therefore permitted to adjudicate and to decide as he wishes, even without supporting reasons and evidence, all in order to bring peace to the world …

and the ruling of the *Shulḥan Arukh:*

> The judge must be permitted to give judgment by way of compromise in cases where the matter cannot be clarified, and he is not allowed to give a partial, incomplete judgment. (*ibid.*, 421–22).

Justice Yitzhak Englard, too, agreed that the rabbinical court is empowered to impose a compromise. He further added that a compromise should only be forced on the parties when there is a substantial doubt arising from evidence submitted by the parties, precluding judicial resolution of factual questions. (See also R. Ḥayyim David Halevi, "The Compromise Ruling Where There Is an Obligation to Take an Oath" (*Teḥumin*, 12 (5751 – 1991) 330: "There may be different levels of non-clarification. The *Rosh* apparently did not intend to rule that wherever the *Bet Din* is in doubt it should give a compromise ruling, for there would be no end to it, and there is always the possibility that one of the litigants is lying. His rule would therefore appear to be applicable only in those cases in which the evidential picture and the pleadings of the litigants create a real doubt among the *dayanim*. (*ibid.*, 429).)

The dispute between the judges only related to the issue of whether the circumstances were such as to compel the rabbinical court to rule in accordance with the joint property rules (see *Husband and Wife; *Dowry).

Another matter that came before the Supreme Court (CA 61/84 *Biazi v. Levi*, PD 42 (1) 446) concerned two parties to a dispute who concluded an agreement whereby the results of a polygraph test would be considered as conclusive evidence in the determination of facts in dispute between them. This agreement received the force of a judgment. After the results were received, the party whose factual account was confuted by the test results filed an appeal in which he contested the binding nature of their agreement.

The minority view (Justice Bach) allowed the appeal, whereas the majority view (Justices Goldberg and Elon) dismissed it. The judgment regarded the agreement between the parties as a compromise agreement, relying upon the sources of Jewish Law referred to above, and additional sources. It further emphasized (Justice Elon) that:

> Many reasons have been given for the preference of compromise over strict law. As stated, compromise engenders peace between the parties, a basic goal of doing justice. A particularly apposite expression of this idea appears in the following halakhic midrash (*Mekhilta de-Rabbi Ishmael, Masekhta de-Amalek*, §2). Commenting on the verse in Exodus 18:15, 'When they have a dispute, it comes before me, and I decide between one person and his friend,' it states: "'And I decide between one person' – this refers to a judicial proceeding where there is no compromise. 'And his friend' – this is a judicial proceeding which involves compromise; both parties depart from one another as friends." Moreover, compromise obviates the feeling of the losing party that justice was not done and the truth abandoned. "Compromise is agreed to and chosen by the parties, which is not the case when the decision is in accordance with substantive law. The person found liable in such a case [against whom judgment is given – ME] does not waive his complaints against his adversary, even though the latter won in court (R. Samuel Edels, *Ḥiddushei Maharsha*, 17th century Poland; on *Sanh.* 6b, *s.v. ohev shalom*).

Further on, the ruling extols another benefit of compromise, which in the view of Jewish Law makes it preferable to ruling by law. Compromise ensures rapid judgment and resolution of the dispute, thereby preventing postponement of judgment that may be the result of ruling according to strict law. In support of this consideration, the judgment cites the following statement by Maimonides, in his *Introduction to the Commentary on the Mishnah*:

> He [the judge] must attempt in all cases to have the parties compromise. If he can consistently avoid deciding a case, by always effecting a compromise between the two rivals – how good and how pleasant that is; but if he is unable to do so, he must apply strict law. Neither should he be hasty [impatient and hurrying – ME], but should give the rival litigants a long time and allow each of the rival litigants to plead his case all day long – even if they are garrulous and speak nonsense …"

Maimonides' guideline is that the judge must do his best to achieve a compromise, and only if he fails to affect a compromise between the parties should he rule by strict law. In that eventuality the examination of the facts and the hearing of the parties may be a protracted process, because the judge is duty-bound to allow the parties to exhaust all of their procedural options.

It is noteworthy that the same judgment also cites U.S. Supreme Court rulings praising compromise as an efficient and commendable means of resolving disputes, in the spirit of the aforementioned sources of Jewish Law (*Holman Mfg. Completion Works. v. Dapin 193 NW 986* (1923) pp. 988; *Sanders v. Roselawn Memorial Gardens, Inc. 159 SE 2d 784* (1968), pp. 795). Further on in the judgment, Justice Elon characterizes the positive approach to the compromise agreement concluded between the parties as "what has long been regarded as appropriate legal policy … and which today may well be one of the lifelines enabling the conduct of adjudication and rulings in accordance therewith, which is the ultimate purpose of the rule of law" (*ibid.*, 480–81)

Another example of the influence and application of Jewish Law in the Israeli legal system is provided by CA 287/88 *Manof v. Saleima*, 44 (3) PD 758. This judgment concerns an application filed by a party to disqualify the judge in the previous instance, in view of the following compromise proposal which the judge made to the litigants at the outset of proceedings: "In view of the above, the Court suggests that if the background explanation provided by plaintiff's attorney is correct (and its veracity may be reasonably presumed, in view of the letters), then the defendant ought to indemnify the plaintiff for all such expenses and damages as he may specifically demonstrate to the defendant's attorney, and they will compromise on a sum to be determined by the Court…" The judge rejected the application, claiming that she had not intended to establish that the background explanation provided by plaintiff's attorney was in fact correct. Rather, she had described the proceedings and pleadings that had been raised so far and which would continue to unfold in the course of the litigation. The Supreme Court ruled (per Justice Elon) that under these circumstances there were no grounds for impugning the judge's objectivity. He further added that the judge's proposal to bring the parties to a compromise was "correct, commendable, and blessed," and that "every court that effects a compromise is deserving of praise" (MT, *Sanhedrin*, 22:4), because "it brings about peace between a man and his fellow" (*Mekhilta, Tractate De-Amalek, Yitro*, §2), and it constitutes appropriate legal policy."

The *Hoffman* ruling (HC 699/89 *Anat Hoffman v. Jerusalem Municipal Council*, 48 (1) PD 678) exemplifies the use of the same principles of Jewish Law, affirming the judicial recourse to compromise – but in this case the dispute was not between individuals, but between an individual and the sovereign authorities. The ruling concerned a petition filed by the representatives of the non-Orthodox streams of Judaism against the Jerusalem Municipality. They objected to the decision not to approve their candidacy in the elections to the Religious Council. The Supreme Court judgment invalidated the municipality's decision, and in the beginning of its judgment the Court (Justice Elon) described its efforts at persuading the parties to compromise:

> After hearing the argumentations we made a compromise proposal to the parties. Our efforts were to no avail and the file was adjourned for a number of memorandum sittings, in an additional effort to induce the parties to compromise. We felt at the time, and still feel, that the dispute before us should be resolved consensually. And what makes this case so special? Because in their pleadings before us both parties presented extensive argumentation regarding the existence of divergent streams in matters related to world-views, each according to his own path and world-view. But that was not the question confronting us, and there was neither place nor need to discuss it or anything connected therewith in order to resolve the specific dispute before us, as we shall presently explain. It was regarding circumstances of this kind that our Sages stated (*Sanh.* 6b) "Settlement by compromise is a meritorious act, for it is written, (Zech. 8:16) 'Execute the judgment of truth and peace in your gates.'" http://www.come-and-hear.com/sanhedrin/sanhedrin_6.html – Folio 6b ref. 10 Despite our efforts, we were unsuccessful, and for this I am truly sorry (*ibid.*, p. 684 of judgment).

The Law in the State of Israel

In 1992 Israeli Law was amended (The Courts Law (Consolidated Version) 5744 – 1984), by the addition of provisions which established the position of the compromise as an integral part of the judicial procedure:

> **79A Compromise**
>
> (a) A court adjudicating a civil matter may, with the consent of the litigants, rule on the matter before it, wholly or in part, by way of compromise.
>
> (b) Nothing in the provisions of sub-section (a) shall derogate from the authority of the court to propose a compromise settlement to the litigants, or to give effect, upon the litigants' application, to a compromise settlement concluded between them.
>
> **79B Arbitration**
>
> (a) A court adjudicating a civil matter may, with the consent of the litigants, submit the matter before it, wholly or partially, to arbitration; and the court is also permitted, with their consent, to define the conditions of the arbitration. […]
>
> **79C Mediation**
>
> (a) In this section "mediation" – a procedure in which the mediator meets the litigants in order to bring them to an agreement for the resolution of the dispute, without him having any powers of resolution […]
>
> (b) The court is permitted, with the litigants' consent, to submit the action to mediation.
>
> […]
>
> (g) Where the litigants conclude a mediation settlement, the mediator will give notice thereof to the court, and the court is permitted to grant the force of a judgment to their settlement.

The impact of Jewish Law and the Supreme Court rulings cited above are clearly discernible in the provisions of the new law. The law permits the court to suggest compromise settlements to the parties; it enables them to reach an agreement whereby the judge will not adjudicate in accordance with the substantive law, but rather by way of compromise, and his decision is binding. The law also allows the court to refer the parties to alternative proceedings outside the court: mediation, in which an attempt is made to bring the parties to a consensual settlement; and arbitration, in which a ruling is given, but not necessarily in accordance with the substantive law (see *Arbitration). The explanatory notes accompanying the draft law (HH 5751, p. 319), emphasize the efficiency of the compromise mechanism: "It is proposed to confer upon compromise frameworks – mediation and arbitration – formal standing in the principal legislation, the intention being to enable the litigants to choose additional paths for the resolution of their dispute. This establishes possibilities for speeding up the resolution of the dispute, on the one hand, and easing the burden imposed by the litigation itself, on the other."

[Menachem Elon (2nd ed.)]

BIBLIOGRAPHY: Gulak, Yesodei, 4 (1922), 177f; Gulak, Ozar, 281–6; *idem*, in *Yavneh*, 3 (1941/42), 19–34; Herzog, Instit, 2 (1939), 33–35. **ADD. BIBLIOGRAPHY:** M. Elon, *Hamishpat ha-Ivri* (1988), 1:150–56; idem, *Jewish Law* (1994), 1:169–73; idem, Jewish Law: *Cases and Materials*, (1999), 361–67; E. Shochetman, *Seder ha-Din* (1988), 208–16; B. Lifshiz, "Pesharah," in: *Mishpetei Ereẓ* (2002); M. Elon and B. Lifshitz, *Mafte'aḥ ha She'elot ve-ha-Teshuvot shel Ḥakhmei Sefarad u-Ẓefon Afrikah*, vol. 2 (1986), 393–94; B. Lifshitz and E. Shochetman, *Mafte'aḥ ha She'elot ve-ha-Teshuvot shel Ḥakhmei Ashkenaz, Ẓarefat ve-Italyah* (1997), 290. For further bibliography see *Arbitration.

COMPUTER SCIENCE. The term Computer Science encompasses three different types of research areas: computability, efficiency, and methodology.

General Introduction

Computability deals with the question of what is "mechanically" computable. The most natural way to describe a "problem" is as a numerical function, i.e., as an operation that gets numbers as input and produces numbers as output. A crucial observation is that there is an inherent property in functions that makes them "computable in an organized fashion," e.g., by a series of rules. Most numerical functions do not have this property and the field of computability is concerned with the functions that do. In order to rigorously define "organized fashion" one needs to define formal models of computation. The conclusion of decades of different models that were developed in the beginning of the 20th century was the "Church-Turing Thesis." This thesis states that all reasonable models of computation are equivalent. Thus the property of being "computable" is considered to be inherent to the function and not dependent on an external computing machine.

Once it is established that a function is computable, it is important to find out whether it is efficient. Efficiency is also inherent in the function, rather than the machine computing it. A faster machine will only be able to compute a function faster by a constant multiple. However, a function that is not efficiently computable will cease to be realistically computable when presented with larger inputs, even on a fast machine. Consider, as an example, the sorting problem. Given a list of n numbers, we would like to sort them in ascending order. The naive way of doing it is to choose the smallest number and move it to the front. Then choose the next smaller and move it to the front, and continue until all numbers are sorted. This scheme takes in the order of n^2 operations. Thus, sorting 1,000 numbers will require roughly 1,000,000 operations. Suppose we have two machines, one of which is 10 times faster than the other. Suppose also that someone came up with a scheme that sorts n numbers in time n, rather than n^2. The slow machine would sort the 1,000 numbers using 1,000 operations using the faster scheme. The fast machine would use 1,000,000 operations using the first scheme, but being 10 times faster than the other machine, it would do it in the time the slow machine would be able to do 100,000 operations. Nevertheless, the slow machine wins by a factor of 100.

We conclude that the computation scheme, and not the machine, is the main contributor to the efficiency of computing a function. This computation scheme is called an "algorithm" in computer science, and the efficiency of the algorithm is called its "complexity."

The fields of Computational Complexity and Design and Analysis of Algorithms are the two main fields of computer science dealing with the efficiency of programs. Computational complexity can be likened to the study of the "forest" of functions, and the different traits causing different classes of complexity. Algorithm design and analysis is the study of methods that can lead to efficient algorithms for specific problems.

The final part of the science of computing is the methodology part. In view of the above discussion one can study computability and efficiency even in a world without computers and electricity. Nevertheless, the existence of computing machines creates many new problems. A machine that computes functions must deal with numerous peripheral devices and multiple functions being computed at the same time. The best ways of organizing these tasks are studied in the research area called operating systems. People who want to write down the code for very large and complex algorithms, need ways that would make it easy to write in the most error-free ways, easy to test, and easy to maintain and understand. These topics are researched in the areas of programming languages and software engineering. Dealing with huge data sets requires ways to index, search, and retrieve data efficiently. These methods are studied in the research areas of databases and information retrieval. The field of Natural Language Processing aims at the goal of having computers understand our speech. The desire to have systems that see and react, e.g., for self-driving cars, necessitates the area of computer vision and image processing. The proliferation of computers requires that they communicate, which leads to the areas of networks and communications. Robotics and Artificial Intelligence allows machines to be able to autonomously perform a range of tasks. All above research areas are concerned with methods that enable easier, better, and more efficient use of computing machines.

Computer Science in Jewish Sources

It is clear that one will not find too many hints of the methodology part of computer science in Jewish sources, since that branch of computer science evolved around the computer. Artificial life or robotics seems to be hinted at by the golem concept. The Talmud (Sanh. 65b) mentions that *Rava created a man and sent it to Rav *Zeira. There are additional midrashic and later references to the power of creating "artificial life" by use of the Holy Name. The relationship between these passages and Artificial Intelligence is only superficial. The point made in these passages seems to be the creative power of holiness, rather than the potential of the physical sciences.

A pervasive method in web technologies and digital libraries is the hypertext method. This method has been very successfully used in Jewish literature. The traditional page format in the Vilna Shas, for example, is a pure use of hypertext. The main text is centered in large letters, the main commentators are arranged around it in smaller letters, and links to appropriate passages in the Bible and in the main *posekim* are suitably incorporated. The printings of many other Jewish texts are in a similar format (e.g., Rambam, Shulḥan Arukh). These Jewish texts represent the most extensive use of windows and hypertext technology prior to the end of the 20th century. Some research papers in computer science were motivated by the hypertext in Jewish texts.

Computability and efficiency, especially the algorithmic part, do not require a machine, therefore it is not surprising that such topics are considered in the ancient world as well as in Jewish sources. Algorithms have a natural place in mathematics. For example, the sieve of Eratosthenes is a method for automatically finding prime numbers.

Such algorithms abound in the Judaic literature. Most of these algorithms deal with the methods of arriving at the *halakhah*. The *baraita* of Rabbi *Ishmael (Sifra 1:1) gives the 13 rules by which the Torah is interpreted. Even after the codification of the Mishnah, the problems of deciding *halakhah* were not solved, since the Mishnah leaves many issues in a state of dispute (*maḥeloket*). The Talmud, although far from settling the disputes in the Mishnah, does offer numerous rules to settling mishnaic disputes. Examples are "*yaḥid verabbim – halakhah ke-rabbim*" (in a dispute between one and many the *halakhah* follows the many), "*halakhah ke-veit Hillel*" (the *halakhah* is according to the House of Hillel), "*halakhah ke-Rav Akiva me-ḥaverav*" (the *halakhah* follows Rabbi Akiva's view when he is opposed by his colleagues). Nevertheless, in numerous places, the Talmud and its commentators have declared that *halakhah* is not to be deduced from the Mishnah (TJ, Hag. 1:8; Rashi, Sanh. 100:2, "Rava Amar Ipkha") The Rif goes further and says that *halakhah* cannot be deduced from the Talmud either (Er. 11:2). Rabbi Ovadiah *Yosef (*Yabi'a Omer*, introduction) states that it is not in our power to derive the law from the Talmud without consulting the **rishonim* and **aḥaronim*. These opinions discourage the *posek* from applying the rules as an algorithm.

A research project in Machon Lev gathered the given rules and meta-rules of deciding *halakhah* in the Mishnah and constructed a rule-based system to compare decisions deduced strictly by the algorithm with the *halakhot* as decided by the Shulḥan Arukh, or the Rambam when the Halakhah did not appear in the *Shulḥan Arukh*. The system was run and tested on Mishnayot in the tractates *Yoma*, *Ta'anit*, and *Ḥagigah*. The system achieved 90.3% success,

Jewish Contribution to Computer Science

The study of computability began in the early 20th century, before the advent of computers. Among the leading scientists who studied models of computation was the Jewish mathematician Emil Leon Post (1897–1954), who was born in Poland and educated in New York. He invented the model of computation named after him, the Post Machine, and proved results similar to those of Gödel, Church, and Turing. Post was the inventor of recursive function theory – the formal theory dealing with computability.

Most undecidability results (functions that are inherently not computable) are proved by a technique called diagonalization. In this technique values are placed in an infinite two-dimensional matrix and then a perturbation of its diagonal is proven not to be a row in this infinite matrix, leading to a contradiction. This method was first studied by Georg Ferdinand Ludwig Philipp Cantor (1845–1918), born to a Jewish Danish father, who converted to Protestantism, and a Danish Catholic mother. Cantor was the first to introduce Hebrew to modern mathematics. He used the letter א to denote infinite continuous sets, such as the total number of numerical functions, and אo to denote countable infinite sets, such as the number of computable functions. He also proved that אo is strictly less than א.

For a rigorous study of an algorithm's complexity, one needs a carefully defined model. The model on which most algorithmic analysis is calculated is the sequential von Neumann model. Johann von *Neumann (1903–1957) was born into a Jewish Hungarian family. He spent most of his adult life in the U.S. and was one of the original six mathematics professors at the Princeton Institute for Advanced Study. He was one of the leading mathematicians of the 20th century. His ideas on logic design were used in the development of the first computers and he pioneered game theory, fault tolerance in systems, and cellular automata.

Recently, newer models of computation have been sought. These models do not enhance the power of computation but it is hoped that they can achieve greater efficiency. For example, one of the most famous currently open problems in computer science and mathematics is the P=? NP problem. The question is whether non-determinism adds computation power. The computation in the von Neumann model is deterministic, i.e., there is a unique instruction that follows every program instruction. In non-deterministic computation the next instruction is "guessed" following certain rules. One of the scientists who introduced non-determinism is Michael Rabin (1931–) of the Hebrew University of Jerusalem. Intuitively, non-determinism should allow us to compute problems faster, using the power of the "guesses." However, it is still an open question whether there exist problems that can be computed efficiently non-deterministically yet cannot be computed efficiently deterministically. Specific efficient non-deterministic problems have a unique trait that if they can be computed efficiently deterministically, then all efficient non-deterministic problems can be efficiently computed deterministically. These problems are called NP-complete problems. The major theorem in the study of NP-completeness proves that deciding whether a logical formula can be satisfied is NP-complete. This theorem was proven independently by Steve Cook and Leonid Levin (1948–), a Jewish Russian computer scientist who emigrated to the U.S. in 1978. The theory of NP-completeness took off when Richard Karp (1935–), an

American computer scientist, published the first set of NP-complete problems.

New models of computation were suggested, which, possibly, compute efficiently problems that are inefficient in the von Neumann model. Some notable examples are Quantum Computation, pioneered in the 1980s by Paul Benioff, Richard *Feynman, and David Deutsch. The quantum model assumes that bits behave in a quantum fashion. An alternate model, basing computing on DNA, has been introduced by the American scientist Leonard Adelman (1945–).

One may mention another fundamental concept in complexity, that of Kolmogorov complexity. Kolmogorov complexity is the minimum size necessary to encode a function. It is named after Kolmogorov, who wrote a paper on it in 1965. Nevertheless, a year earlier, the Jewish mathematician Ray Solomonoff (1926–), published two papers on what is termed Solomonff induction and algorithmic probability, that independently tackle many of the same concepts.

Jewish contributions in the area of algorithms is also quite prominent. Some fundamental algorithmic methods were invented by Jewish scientists. Examples are linear programming and dynamic programming. Linear programming problems are optimization problems where one needs to optimize a linear function, i.e., a function that describes a line, subject to constraints that are also linear functions. This field of optimization is important since many problems in operations research, such as multi-commodity flow problems and scheduling problems, can be defined as linear programs. Linear programming was discovered by the Soviet mathematician and Nobel laureate in economics Leonid Vitaliyevich *Kantorovich (1912–1986). One of the most widely used algorithms for solving linear programs is the SIMPLEX method, developed by the American mathematicians George B. Dantzig (1914–2005).

Dynamic programming is a method of solving a large problem incrementally, by first solving it for small instances and subsequently constructing solutions for larger and larger instances based on previously computed solutions to the smaller cases. It is the core of many important algorithms in all areas of Computer Science. Dynamic Programming was invented by the American mathematician Richard Bellman (1920–1984).

Jewish contribution abounds in the methodology part of computer science as well. Artificial Intelligence is the science and engineering of making intelligent machines, especially intelligent computer programs, where the term "intelligent" is left as an intuitive notion. The field tries to make programs behave more as "intelligent" entities than programmed functions. among its most notable founders are the American scientist Marvin Minsky (1927–), Nobel laureate in economics Herbert *Simon (1916–2001), whose father was Jewish, and Boston scientist John McCarthy (1927–), who had a Jewish mother.

The field of cryptography deals with the ability to encrypt information. This is especially critical for information that gets transmitted publicly, as over the Internet, and is what makes electronic commerce possible. Public-key cryptography was co-invented by American computer scientist Martin Hellman (1945–). He was one of the co-authors of the Diffie-Hellman algorithm for secure key distribution over non-secure channels. The most widely used public-key algorithm today is the RSA algorithm, named after MIT scientist Ronald Rivest, Adi Shamir (1952–) of the Weizmann Institute, and Leonard Adleman (1945–).

The A.M. Turing Award is given annually by the Association for Computing Machinery to a person selected for lasting and major contributions made to the computing community. The Turing Award is often recognized as the "Nobel Prize of computing." It is sponsored by Intel Corporation and currently is accompanied by a prize of $100,000. Almost a third of the Turing Award winners to date are of Jewish descent. These are Alan Perlis (1966), Marvin Minsky (1969), John McCarthy (1971), Herbert Simon (1975), Michael Rabin (1976), Richard Karp (1985), William Kahan (1989), Edward Feigenbaum (1994), Manuel Blum (1995), Amir Pnueli (1996), Adi Shamir (2002), Leonard Adleman (2002), and Robert Kahn (2004).

It should be noted that three of the above 14 names are Israelis in Israeli universities. Indeed Israel is an international power in computer science. Israeli research is at the cutting edge of the scientific research. Five of the top 100 most cited computer scientists in the world are Israelis. Israeli universities are ranked at the top of international lists of leading computer science department.

Computer applications are not in the scope of this article, but we will mention in passing that many ubiquitous applications, such as the BASIC programming language, spreadsheets, the automated electronically switched telephone network, spread spectrum communications, the Internet, Google, and more, were co-invented by Jews.

Computer Science as an Aid to Judaism

The proliferation of electronic databases has not skipped the Jewish world. There are currently over a dozen different Jewish databases on the market, both as text and as scanned images. In addition there are numerous Internet sites on Jewish topics ranging from providing candle lighting times all over the globe to hospitality information in different communities. The first Jewish database was the Bar-Ilan Responsa Project.

The project was conceived in 1963 by Weizmann Institute scientist Aviezri Fraenkel and later migrated to Bar-Ilan University. Fraenkel was the project's director from 1963 to 1974, succeeded by Ya'akov Choueka, who headed the project from 1974 to 1986. The idea was to create an electronic library of the responsa with a search engine to enable easy access to information. The project required research and solutions in areas such as information retrieval, data compression, Hebrew computational linguistics, and Human-Computer Interaction. It led to many graduate theses and publications in computer science and for many years was at the cutting edge of technology. In its beginnings the database resided on an IBM mainframe. From 1979, it also became usable in a time-sharing mode from terminals on the Bar-Ilan campus, in Israel, and abroad. During Uri Schild's tenure as project director, it was decided to compress the database to a single compact disk. This made the system accessible to every home, scholar, rabbi, and *dayyan*. Because of the care the Project takes in seeking error-free text, it is unique in the fact that it is indeed a tool for *pesikat halakhah*, and used by many *posekim* today.

An emotionally charged and controversial current phenomenon is the Torah codes, or *Bible codes. This issue has involved Jews and Christians, scholars, scientists, and laymen, and has even produced best-selling books such as *The Bible Code* by Michael Drosnin.

Underlying the codes is the traditional Jewish idea that there are several layers to the Torah, and that the *remez* is a valid form of learning Torah. Rabbi *Jacob ben Asher's *Baal ha-Turim* commentary to the Torah is perhaps the most famous early concerted use of this form of learning. The modern code methods involve Equidistant Letters Sequences (ELS) and the idea is to find names, dates, and "prophecies" encoded as ELS's in the Torah. The first scientific claim to the statistical validity of the codes appeared in a 1988 paper by the mathematician Eliyahu Rips. It was followed by the 1994 paper by Doron Witztum, Eliyahu Rips, and Yoav Rosenberg and generated a very emotional response. Without taking a stand in the controversy, it is important to note that this entire line of research and school of thought is almost impossible without computers.

BIBLIOGRAPHY: S. Homer and A.L. Selman, *Computability and Complexity Theory* (2001); H.A. Simon, *The Sciences of the Artificial* (1996); Y. HaCohen-Kerner, "On the Sages' Rules for Deciding in Controversies Opposing Tannaitic Authorities Against Each Other," *Journal of Torah and Scholarship*, No. 14 (2004), 99–116; Y. Choueka and A. Aviad, "Hypertalmud – A hypertext system for the Babylonian Talmud," in: Proc. of the 25th Conference of Israeli Information Processing Association (Jerusalem, 1990), 281–290 (Hebrew). **WEBSITE:** http://citeseer.ist.psu.edu/allcited.html; http://www.acm.org/awards/taward.html.

[Amir Amihood (2nd ed.)]

COMTAT VENAISSIN, former papal territory in S.E. France, corresponding approximately to the present department of Vaucluse. Ceded in 1274 to the Holy See, to whom it belonged until the reunion with France in 1791, it became a distinct territory along with the town of *Avignon (though the later remained independent in local administration). Apart from Avignon, Jews do not seem to have settled in the Comtat earlier than the 12th century. The major Jewish communities, known as the "four holy communities," were those of Avignon, *Carpentras, *Cavaillon, and *L'Isle-sur-la-Sorgue. There were, however, smaller communities of a more ephemeral nature in Caromb, Entraigues-sur-la-Sorgue, Malaucène, Monteux, Mormoiron, Mornas, Pernes-les-Fontaines, and Vaison-la-Romaine. The Comtat became a haven of refuge for the Jews of the two provinces of Languedoc and Provence after various expulsions – in 1306, 1322, and 1394, and later around 1500. The Jews of the Comtat spoke a *Judeo-Provençal dialect, which they also employed in some semi-liturgic poetry, and had their own synagogue rite, now fallen into disuse (see *Liturgy). The reconstituted communities of the region, e.g., at Carpentras, were formed in the mid-20th century, mainly by Jews of North African origin.

BIBLIOGRAPHY: Gross, Gal Jud, 202; A. Mosse, *Histoire des Juifs d'Avignon et du Comtat Venaissin* (1934); L. Bardinet, in: *Revue Historique*, 12 (1880), 1–47; 14 (1880), 1–60; idem, in: REJ, 1 (1880), 262–92; 6 (1883), 1–40; 7 (1883), 139–46; E. Sabatier, in: *Famille de Jacob*, 17 (1876), 348ff.; 18 (1876), 367ff.; R. Boyer, in: *Evidences*, 8 (1956), 27ff.; C. Roth, in: *Journal of Jewish Bibliography*, 1 (1939), 99–105; Z. Szajkowski, *Franco-Judaica* (1962), index.

[Bernhard Blumenkranz]

COMTINO, MORDECAI BEN ELIEZER (1420–d. before 1487), Bible commentator, philosopher, philologist, astronomer, and mathematician. Born in Constantinople, Comtino studied religion and philosophy under Ḥanokh Saporta, a distinguished Catalonian scholar. Comtino was one of the leaders of the Hebrew cultural movement that flowered in Constantinople. He considered the dissemination of general knowledge his major task. Of those who thought that learning should be confined to the Talmud, he said: "The Talmud will be of no use to them and they will not comprehend it unless they study all sciences… including exact expression, which is logic and helps us to understand the meaning of the words of the Talmud." Like most enlightened Jewish scholars of his age, he was an admirer of Maimonides and Abraham ibn Ezra; he regarded the latter as an ideal man, and wrote commentaries to most of his works. However, he did not hesitate to criticize Ibn Ezra's opinions, and to those who regarded such criticism as an insult to the "greatest of the commentators," his reply was that even a man of Ibn Ezra's caliber is capable of error. Comtino followed in the footsteps of his teacher Saporta in seeking to spread religious and secular knowledge among both the Rabbanite and Karaite Jews; he did not regard the latter as outcasts or enemies. In this he influenced the attitude of R. Elijah *Mizraḥi, one of his most eminent students (see Mizraḥi's responsa, no. 57). The Karaite sages in Turkey, such as Elijah *Bashyazi and Caleb *Afendopolo, were also among his pupils. In the 1450s, when the plague broke out in Constantinople, Comtino fled to Adrianople and remained there for a while, teaching such disciples as the Ashkenazi rabbi Isaac Ẓarfati. He had a reputation as a sage and astrologer also among non-Jews, who sometimes consulted him.

Comtino wrote many books and treatises in Hebrew on mathematics and astronomy, the manuscripts of which are to be found in the Leningrad, Parma, Paris, London, and Cambridge libraries. They include *Sefer ha-Ḥeshbon ve-ha-Middot*, on arithmetic and geometry; *Perush Luḥot Paras* ("Interpretation of the Persian Tables"), essays on the construction of astronomical instruments; *Tikkun Keli ha-Ẓefiḥah*, on the construction of the sundial; a commentary on Euclid; *Sefer ha-Tekhunah* ("The Book of Astronomy"); *Ma'amar al Likkui ha-*

Levanah..., on "lunar and solar eclipse as seen in nature, based on philosophy and the natural sciences"; a commentary on Maimonides' work on logic, *Millot ha-Higgayon*; a commentary on Abraham ibn Ezra's *Yesod Mora*; a commentary on Ibn Ezra's *Sefer ha-Shem* ("Book on the Divine Names"); a commentary on Ibn Ezra's *Sefer ha-Eḥad* ("Book of the Unity"); a commentary on Aristotles' *Metaphysics; Iggeret Senapir ve-Kaskeset*, on clean and unclean fish; and *Keter Torah*, or *Kelil Yofi*, a commentary on the Pentateuch, in which Comtino reveals himself as a scholar of wide erudition, a liberal thinker, and an unbiased critic. R. Shabbetai b. Malkiel wrote a criticism of the last-mentioned work, to which Comtino wrote a reply (*Teshuvot al Hassagot R. Shabbetai Kohen*). Two of his *piyyutim* were published by Solomon b. Mazal Tov in *Shirim u-Zemirot ve-Tishbaḥot* (Constantinople, 1545–48, 127, 220), and were adopted in the Karaite prayer book.

BIBLIOGRAPHY: Gurland, in: *Talpioth*, 1 (1895), 1–34 (special pagination in *Toledot Anshei Shem* section); I. Zinberg, *Toledot Sifrut Yisrael*, 3 (1958), 16–24, 339f.; Rosanes, Togarmah, 1 (1930), 25–32; Obadiah, in: *Sinai*, 6 (1940), 76–80; Silberberg, in: JJLG, 3 (1905), 277–92; N. Ben-Menahem, in: *Hadorom*, 27 (1968), 211–20.

[Ephraim Kupfer]

CONAT, ABRAHAM BEN SOLOMON (15th century), Italian physician and one of the earliest printers of Hebrew books. Conat was probably of Ashkenazi origin. He lived in Mantua, where he may have been active as early as 1475. In 1476 he printed Jacob b. Asher's Tur *Oraḥ Ḥayyim* and began to print *Yoreh De'ah* as well; however, this was completed in Ferrara by *Abraham b. Ḥayyim of Pesaro, which suggests that Conat died about 1477. Other works printed by him (all apparently in Mantua, 1475–77) are *Sefer Eldad ha-Dani*; Jedaiah Bedersi's *Beḥinat Olam*; Mordecai Finzi's *Luḥot*, astronomical tables; Judah Messer Leon's *Nofet Ẓufim*; Levi b. Gershom's Pentateuch commentary; and *Sefer Josippon*, the pseudo-Josephus. Conat's work is particularly beautiful, and his type has been imitated in modern luxury editions. Abraham's wife, ESTELLINA CONAT, was equally active in the printing of these books and is the first woman who is named as an editor in a printing house. *Beḥinat Olam* was both arranged and printed by Estellina Conat. She is called the *kotevet* and in a colophon at the back of the book, she wrote: "I, Estellina Conat, the wife of my lord, my husband, the honored Master Abraham Conat ... wrote this pamphlet, *Beḥinat Olam*, with the help of the youth Jacob Levi of Provence, of Tarascon, may he live, Amen." In the early days of printing, no Hebrew word yet existed for the process and Abraham Conat explained that his books were "written with many pens, without the aid of a miracle."

BIBLIOGRAPHY: D. de Guenzburg, in: *Recueil des travaux rédigés en mémoire du jubilé scientifique de D. Chwolson* (1899), 57–66; D.W. Amram, *Makers of Hebrew Books in Italy* (1909), 30–34; A. Freimann (ed.), *Thesaurus Typographiae Hebraicae* (1924), A 4–10; A.M. Habermann, *Ha-Sefer ha-Ivri be-Hitpatteḥuto* (1968), 81–84, 86, 172; B. Friedberg, *Toledot ha-Defus ha-Ivri be-Italyah* (1934), 10–11, 17, 31. **ADD. BIBLIOGRAPHY:** A.M. Habermann, *Nashim Ivri'ot be-Tor Madpisot, Mesadrot, Motzi'ot le-Or ve-Tomekhot be-Meḥabrim* (1932–33), 7.

[Umberto (Moses David) Cassuto / Emily Taitz (2nd ed.)]

CONCIO, JOSEPH BEN GERSON (d. c. 1628), Italian poet, scholar, and printer. Originating from *Asti in Piedmont, Concio established a Hebrew printing press in nearby *Chieri, where he began printing mostly his own small books which were generally in verse, in 1626. These included: *Ateret Ẓevi*, together with *Ẓefirat Tifarah* (1626) broad-sheets; *Besamim Rosh* (1627), Purim songs; *Ot le-Tovah* (1627), talmudic maxims and some poems; *Arba'ah Rashim* (1628), rhymed Midrash explanations; and *Solet le-Minḥah* (1628), devotional prayers. In Asti itself Concio printed in Italian *Cinque enimmi* (1627) and *Conto di Jehudit* (1628), the apocryphal Judith story. His son Abraham, piously continued to publish his father's writings: *Divrei Ester* (1628), allegorical commentary on Esther; *Ma'gal Tov* (1628), talmudic maxims in verse; *Mareh Ḥayyim* (1629); *Mekom Binah* (1630), commentary on Job from 28:12 onward; and *Ḥelek le-Shivah* (1632), poem for Lag ba-Omer. The only book by another author known to have been printed by the Concio family at Chieri is Isaac Lattes' *Perush Ma'amar she-be-Midrash Rabbah* (1628/9).

BIBLIOGRAPHY: D.W. Amram, *Makers of Hebrew Books in Italy* (1909), 393.

CONCUBINE, marital companion of inferior status to a wife.

In the Bible

The term in Hebrew is *pilegesh*, the equivalent of Greek *pallakis* (παλλακίς) and Latin *pellex*. Among the Assyrians the concubine (*esirtu*) gained the rank of wife only after the veiling ceremony conducted by her spouse, if he so chose to elevate her (Assyrian Code A, 41). The legal formalities, if any, are not described in the Bible. A concubine did not always reside in her husband's home (Judg. 8:31), but such was not the general rule (Judg. 19–20). Her spouse was called the son-in-law (*ḥatan*) of her father, who was the father-in-law (*ḥoten*). Therefore, the concubinage relationship could partake of many aspects of regular marriage. Two famous concubines are mentioned in the Bible. Rizpah the daughter of Aiah the concubine of Saul (II Sam. 3:7) whose moving display of maternal love so moved David that he had her children buried in the family sepulcher (21:8–14) and the concubine of Gibeah whose rape and murder brought about the death of 25,000 members of the tribe of Benjamin and the ban against members of the other tribes intermarrying with them (Judg. 19–21).

Royal concubines were standard among the kings of Israel and Judah, just as in any ancient Near Eastern kingdom (Song 6:8–9). They were clearly distinguished from the wives (II Sam. 5:13; I Kings 11:13; II Chron. 11:21). To lie with a monarch's concubine was tantamount to usurpation of the throne (II Sam. 3:7; 16:21–22). For this reason Abner took Rizpah (II Sam. 3:7). The same concept stands behind Ahitophel's advice to Absalom, to "go into his father's concubines" (16:21), and Adonijah's request for Abishag the Shunamite was clearly associated with this custom (I Kings 2:21–24). The harem was usually in the charge of a eunuch (Esth. 2:14; cf. II Kings 9:32). The role of the concubine as the mother of venerable ethnic groups is not overlooked in the genealogies. Their descendants are usually classed as secondary or subsidiary tribes (Gen. 22:24; 36:12), especially the Abrahamic groups (Gen. 25:6; I Chron. 1:32). Within Israel, some of the clans were also the offspring of concubines (I Chron. 2:46; 7:14). In one instance, the term concubine is applied to a handmaiden (*shifḥah* and *a'mah*) who had borne children to her mistress' husband (Gen. 35:22). Such a relationship was usually established because the legal wife was barren (Gen. 16). Ancient marriage arrangements often stipulated that if the wife was barren, she must provide a handmaiden for her husband (cf. Code of Hammurapi, paragraphs 144–5 and the adoption contract from Nuzi in Pritchard, Texts, 220). Naming the handmaiden given to the bride by her father in such cases was evidently related to this practice (Pritchard, loc. cit.; Gen. 29:24, 29). If the wife later bore children of her own, they took precedence in the inheritance over those of the handmaiden (Gen. 21:12; cf. Code of Hammurapi, 170), although the latter did receive a share (usually on condition that their father had granted them legal recognition; Code of Hammurapi, 171). Israelite law provided safeguards for the rights of Hebrew girls sold as handmaidens who were to be wed to their purchaser or to his son (Ex. 21:7–11). If the handmaiden bore children for her mistress and then sought to place herself on an equal footing, she normally could not be sold, although she could be reduced to the status of a slave again (Code of Hammurapi, 146; cf. Gen. 21:12–14, where the slave-concubine and her child are both expelled, but only on the advice of a divine oracle.).

[Anson Rainey]

In the Talmudic Period and the Middle Ages

There is no evidence of actual concubinage in the Talmud, nor is there any evidence of it in practice during the Middle Ages. In the responsa of *Asher b. Jehiel (no. 32:1) there is a reference to a concubine, but it seems to be merely the case of a man cohabiting with a woman without going through a marriage ceremony with her, and not to a formal concubine. In the Middle Ages concubinage was formally forbidden by the rabbis as immoral, only one authority, Jacob *Emden (responsum no. 15) expressing the opinion that it should be permitted.

[Louis Isaac Rabinowitz]

In Jewish Law

A concubine may be defined by Jewish laws as a woman dedicating herself to a particular man, with whom she cohabits without *kiddushin (see *Marriage) or *ketubbah. "What is the difference between wives and concubines? R. Judah said in the name of Rav: Wives have *ketubbah* and *kiddushin*, concubines have neither" (Sanh. 21a; Maim. Yad, Melakhim 4:4; Leḥem Mishneh and Radbaz, ad loc.). Not all the scholars adopt this reading, however, and Rashi, for instance, comments: "wives with *kiddushin* and *ketubbah*, concubines with *kiddushin* but without *ketubbah*" (Comm. to Gen. 25:6; see also Comm. Hagra, EH 26, n. 7). This latter reading is apparently that of the Jerusalem Talmud too (TJ, Ket. 5:2, 29d and Hagra, *ibid.*; but see *Mareh ha-Panim* thereto). The majority of the *posekim accept the former reading as the correct one (Radbaz to Yad, Melakhim 4:4; *Kesef Mishneh* and *Leḥem Mishneh*, as against the *Maggid Mishneh*, to Yad, Ishut, 1;4; Radbaz, Resp., vol. 4, no. 225; vol. 7, no. 33; Naḥmanides, commentary to Gen. 19:8; 25:6; Ralbag to Judg. 19:1; Rashba, Resp., vol. 4, no. 314). Hence a concubine is to be distinguished both, on the one hand from a married woman, i.e., by *ḥuppah* ("marriage ceremony"), *kiddushin*, and *ketubbah*, and on the other from a woman who does not dedicate herself to one particular man exclusively, but who prostitutes herself; i.e., the harlot (*Hassagot Rabad* to Ishut 1:4 and see also Rema to EH 26:1).

The Prohibition against Concubinage

There are divided opinions in the codes on the question of whether the taking of a concubine is prohibited or permitted. Some of the *posekim* are of the opinion that neither pentateuchal nor rabbinical law forbids it, if the woman observes the rules concerning the *mikveh* so that the man should not cohabit with her during her period of menstruation (Rema in the name of Rabad, EH 26:1). Others are of the opinion that although it is not legally prohibited, one should refrain from taking a concubine, and they caution against her, "lest knowledge of the permissibility encourage licentiousness and sexual relations with her at a time when she is sexually unclean" (*Sefer Teshuvot ha-Rashba ha-Meyuḥasot le-ha-Ramban*, no. 284). The majority of the *posekim*, however, are of the opinion that it is forbidden to take a concubine, although they differ as to the substantive nature of the prohibition. Some are of the opinion that taking a concubine is a transgression of a prohibition of the pentateuchal law, based on the negative command: "There shall be no harlot of the daughters of Israel" (Deut. 23:18), to be punished with lashes (Rema to EH 26:1 in the name of Maimonides; Rosh, and Tur), while others expressed the opinion that the prohibition stems from a positive command of the pentateuchal law, the Torah saying, "when a man takes a wife" (Deut. 24:1) – i.e., he should take her by way of *kiddushin*. According to another view, the prohibition is rabbinical law only. (On the different views and their reasons, see *Oẓar ha-Posekim*, EH 26:3–8.) All the foregoing applies only to a woman who is unmarried; a married woman is by pentateuchal law at all times prohibited to have sexual relations with any man but her husband (*issur eshet ish*; see Prohibited *Marriages; *Bigamy; *Marriage).

Since more recent times it is unanimously accepted that the taking of a concubine is prohibited: "At the present time a woman is permitted to no man except through *kiddushin, ḥuppah, sheva berakhot*, and *ketubbah*" (Radbaz, Resp., vol. 4, no. 225; vol. 7, no. 33). This applies even more in the case of a married man, in the same way as he is prohibited from taking an additional wife (see *Bigamy), both for the protection of his wife and because his taking a concubine – since he is aware that he must not take an additional wife – can only be for the purpose of prostituting, and this is forbidden in the opinion of all the *posekim* (Rashba, Resp., vol. 4, no. 314; *Oẓar ha-Posekim*, EH 1, n. 4; 26, n. 5).

Personal Status and Pecuniary Rights of a Concubine

Inasmuch as a concubine does not acquire the personal status of a wife (*eshet ish*: Tur EH 26; Sh. Ar., EH 26:1), she has no *ketubbah*; therefore, in accordance with the rule providing that the "terms and conditions of the *ketubbah [tena'ei ketubbah]* follow the [prescribed] *ketubbah*" (Ket. 54b; Rashi *ibid.* s.v. *tena'ei ketubbah*) she does not acquire any of the wife's pecuniary rights – especially she is not entitled to maintenance – as all those rights stem from the *ketubbah*. Nor does living with a man as his concubine create a kinship as an impediment to marriage between herself and any of the man's relatives, or between the man and her relatives, as would be the case if she would be considered to be his wife (Rosh, Resp. no. 32:1; *Oẓar ha-Posekim*, EH 26, n. 3). For the same reason there is no need in principle for her to obtain a *get* (see *Divorce) in order to be permitted to marry any other man (*Oẓar ha-Posekim*, loc. cit.; *Sefer ha-Tashbez* 3:47). However in the opinion of some of the *posekim*, for the sake of appearances, in view of the parties having lived together, the matter should be approached stringently and the woman should not be permitted to marry another man without obtaining a prior "*get* out of stringency" (*get me ḥumrah*) from the man with whom she has lived; but whenever the latter's refusal to grant her the *get* is likely to entail the risk of her becoming an *agunah, she may certainly be permitted to marry without getting such *get* (*Oẓar ha-Posekim*, EH 26, n. 3). Moreover, since the prohibition against concubinage is intended solely against the concubine's connection with her spouse, this fact alone and as such does not impair the personal status of children born of the union, nor their rights of inheritance according to law (Rashba, Resp. vol. 4, no. 314).

Legal Position in the State of Israel

Since the question of concubinage touches on the issue of the requirements necessary for conferring on a woman the status of a wife, the question is a matter of "marriage" – within the meaning of the Rabbinical Courts Jurisdiction (Marriage and Divorce) Law, no. 64 of 5713/1953 – and therefore in the case of Jews who are citizens of the State of Israel, governed by Jewish law (sec. 1). However, legislation enacted for the first time after the creation of the state has given recognition to the concept of the "common law wife," i.e. a woman living together with a man to whom she is not married, but is so regarded (erroneously) by the public (*yedu'ah ba-ẓibbur keishto*) and in some laws the same applies, vice versa, to such a "husband" – granting her certain rights, mainly with regard to pension and tenant's protection. According to decisions of the courts, such a woman is entitled to the said rights even if she is lawfully married to another man (CA 284/61, in PD, 16 (1962), 102–12). As to the actual definition of the term "a woman known to the public as his wife" and the modes of proving the necessary facts, widely differing opinions have been expressed in decisions of the courts. It is generally accepted, however, that the said legislation does not entail any change in the personal status of the woman, whose position is to some extent similar to that of a concubine.

[Ben-Zion (Benno) Schereschewsky]

Decisions of the Israel Supreme Court

The distinctions in Jewish Law regarding the status of a woman who lives with a man to whom she is not married formed the basis of the Supreme Court's ruling in the case of *Agbara v. Agbara* (CA 4946/94, 49(2) PD 508). The case concerned a divorced couple, whose divorce agreement stipulated that "the husband's obligation to pay the entire sum of maintenance … will apply until each of the children has reached 21 years of age or until the wife remarries, if she remarries, whichever the later" (p. 510 of judgment). Following the husband's remarriage and subsequent separation from his second wife – without a *get*, due to the second wife's refusal to accept it – the original couple resumed living together as "common law spouses." Eighteen years later the husband left the home. The woman claimed that the original divorce agreement was still in force, as she had not yet married, and the man was therefore liable for maintenance payments. The husband claimed that his obligation under the agreement lapsed at the point that the wife had received a secure financial framework, and that the agreement was void by implication because their actions, upon returning to live together, attested to its annulment

The Supreme Court (Justice Zvi Tal) ruled that, in accordance with Jewish Law, the agreement was no longer valid because the condition regarding the woman's remarriage had been fulfilled, and the woman was considered as both betrothed and married to the man.

> Regarding an ordinary couple who are common law spouses, there are many opinions as to whether or not the woman requires a *get*, and it also depends on the circumstances of the case. There are those who at the very least require her to receive a *get le-ḥumra* (a writ of divorce to cover possible halakhic uncertainty as to her status), based on the presumption that "a man does not intend his sexual relations to be promiscuous" and the evidentiary presumption – *anan sahadi* – that there was marital intention. On the other hand, there are those who make the application of this presumption conditional upon whether the life style of the couple in question validates its application in their particular case. Furthermore, if they could have married officially, and refrained from doing so, this is deemed as a declaration on their part that they are not interested in marrying, and hence the presumption does not apply to them.
>
> But irrespective of what the situation is regarding an ordinary couple, it differs with respect to spouses who were married, divorced, and then resumed living together. Regarding such a couple the *Mishnah* states (Git. 9:10):
>
> "If a man has divorced his wife and then stays with her overnight in an inn, Bet Shammai say that she does not require

from him a second *get*, but Bet Hillel say that she does require a second *get* from him ...."

The halakhah was decided according to Bet Hillel, and codified accordingly (Maim., Yad, *Gerushin* 10.17; Sh. Ar., EH 149:1):

"Now, if this is the rule regarding one night in an inn, then *a fortiori*, it would apply to cohabitation for almost 20 years, during which time the couple were regarded as husband and wife; hence, she requires a *get* from him if she wishes to remarry. For if on the basis of one night together in an inn the woman is considered as "definitely betrothed" (the terminology of *Shulḥan Arukh*), and betrothal alone does not obligate the man to support her, then it is clear that cohabitation for close to 20 years would be deemed a marriage, creating an obligation of support. Indeed, the essence of *huppah* – which confers the status of marriage upon a betrothed woman – is their shared domicile in one house as man and wife. The fact that the couple did not remarry by way of a proper marriage ceremony with *ḥuppah and kiddushin* is not indicative of their intention not to marry, for the husband was still officially married to his second wife. It seems clear that, under the circumstances, the respondent should be considered a married woman who requires a *get* from the appellant, and as such he is obligated to support her by dint of his personal status – albeit not by force of the agreement. Regarding the divorce agreement, the condition stipulated for the termination of the agreement – "until she marries" – should be regarded as having been fulfilled, and therefore the obligation to pay support pursuant to the divorce agreement is vitiated. (*ibid.*, pp. 513–14)."

The question which the Supreme Court was required to decide in the framework of the appeal was limited to the issue of the validity of the agreement. Regarding this question, the Court's conclusion was that the agreement is invalid, inasmuch as the couple was considered as still married. Therefore, the woman can demand support from the man on the basis of her status as his married wife, but she can only do so in the framework of a separate proceeding.

It is noteworthy that Justice Tal emphasizes that the ruling does not constitute a decision on the validity of the marriage, an issue residing within the exclusive jurisdiction of the rabbinical court. The Supreme Court's decision relates solely to a secondary question, required for the clarification of the main question: the financial question of the validity of the agreement – for which the Supreme Court has jurisdiction.

[Menachem Elon (2nd ed.)]

BIBLIOGRAPHY: In the Bible: De Vaux, *Ancient Israel*, 521–22. Talmud and Middle Ages: Z. Falk, in *De'to*, 27 (1965), 35ff. In Jewish Law: L.M. Epstein, in *PAAJR* 6 (1934/35), 153–88; B.Z. Schereschewsky, *Dinei Mishpahah* (1967), 92, n.39. **ADD. BIBLIOGRAPHY:** M. Elon, *Ha-Mishpat ha-Ivri* (1988), 3:1415f.; idem, *Jewish Law* (1994), 4:1684f.; idem, *Ḥakikah Datit* (1968), 119–54; M. Elon and B. Lifshitz, *Mafte'aḥ ha-She'elot ve-ha-Teshuvot shel Ḥakhmei Sefarad u-Ẓefon Afrikah*, 2 (1986), 356; B. Lifshitz and E. Shochetman, *Mafte'aḥ ha-She'elot ve-ha-Teshuvot shel Ḥakhmei Ashkenaz, Ẓarefat ve-Italyah* (1997), 245. M. Shawa, "Mashma'ut 'Ben Zug,'" in: *Ha-Ḥakikah Le-Or Ḥok Yesod: Kevod ha-Adam ve-Ḥeruto, Minḥah Le-Yizḥak* (1999), 197; S. Lifshitz, "Yedu'im be-Ẓibbur," in: *Iyyunei Mishpat*, 25(3), 741–849. Corinaldi, *Status, Family & Succession, Between State and Religion*, (2004) 31–37.

°CONDER, CLAUDE REGNIER (1848–1910), British army officer in charge of the Survey of Western Palestine on behalf of the Palestine Exploration Fund. He worked first with C.F. Tyrwhitt-Drake from 1872–78. During this first survey Conder was attacked and seriously wounded at Safed in 1875. In 1881 he returned to Palestine for the Fund when he worked with H.H. Kitchener (later Lord Kitchener), and discovered Kadesh and also began a survey of Transjordan, discovering many megaliths. He was the coauthor (with H.H. Kitchener) of the *Memoirs* (vol. 1, pts. 1–3 of *Survey of Western Palestine*, 1881–83). Conder also wrote *Tent-Work in Palestine* (1878); *Heth and Moab* (1883); *Latin Kingdom of Jerusalem* (1897); and edited (with C. Wilson) *Palestine Pilgrim's Texts*. His later years included service in Egypt (1884–85), Bechuanaland (1895), and Ireland.

BIBLIOGRAPHY: Elath, in: *Eretz Israel*, 7 (1964), 158–70. **ADD. BIBLIOGRAPHY:** ODNB online; Y. Ben-Arieh, *The Holy Land in the Nineteenth Century* (1979).

[Michael Avi-Yonah]

CONDITIONS (Heb. תְּנָאִים, *tena'im*).

Definition

Conditions is an ambiguous word inasmuch as it refers not only to the external factors upon which the existence of an agreement is made to depend but also to the actual terms of the contract itself. Thus, one speaks of *tena'ei ha-ketubbah*, which really means the terms of the *ketubbah*. Similar ambiguities exist in English law (see G.C. Cheshire and C.H.S. Fifoot, *The Law of Contract* (19605), 118ff.). In Jewish law, there is a further contingency: *tenai* consists not only of the stipulations of the contracting parties but also refers to legislative provisions, as evident in the expression *tenai bet-din* (see *Takkanot). As to conditions proper, i.e., stipulations (qualifications or limitations) attaching to a principal agreement, the basic concept in Jewish law seems to be very much the same as that in other systems of law. For example, distinctions between conditions precedent and conditions subsequent, differentiations between affirmative and negative conditions, between authoritative, casual, and mutual conditions or between expressed and implied conditions, and much more are found in all legal systems, although in Jewish law they may not be so clear-cut terminologically.

A vital characteristic of conditions in Jewish law is the provision referred to as *tenai benei Gad u-venei Re'uven*, based on Numbers 32. This was the occasion when Moses allocated land to the tribes of Gad and Reuben (and to half the tribe of Manasseh) on the east side of the Jordan River on the condition that they crossed the Jordan and assisted the other tribes in the conquest of the Holy Land. The Mishnah notes (Kid. 3:4) that when Moses made this stipulation he used a *tenai kaful* ("double condition"), expressing himself, i.e., both in the affirmative and the negative: if they fulfill the condition, they shall be entitled to the allocation; if they do not, they shall not. Significance is here attached to the fact that the affirmative precedes the negative (*hen kodem le-lav*). Moreover, it is required that the conditions be stipulated prior to the actual transactions – which means, according to some authorities, that, as a matter of formality, conditions should be referred to before mentioning the main transaction (*tenai kodem le-ma'aseh*). A fourth requirement, usually listed in the context, is that the condition must be *davar she-efshar lekayyemo*, i.e., something objectively capable or possible of fulfillment (Maim. Yad, Ishut, 6:1–13; Sh. Ar., EH 38:1–4).

It is remarkable that the codes just referred to cite these rules in the context of matrimonial law, but it is the express opinion of Maimonides (*ibid.*, 6:14) that they apply equally to other provinces of the law, e.g., to *sale and *gift, and he persists in his ruling, despite the fact that later *Geonim* (to whom he explicitly refers) would have the formal requirements of *tenai kaful* and *hen kodem le-lav* apply to *kiddushin* (see *Marriage) and *gittin* (see *Divorce) only, and not to matters covered by laws of *mamon*. Maimonides aptly argues that the biblical "precedent," from which the present law is derived, concerned *mamon* ("acquisition of property"), and it would therefore be illogical to consider it as applicable only to matrimony rather than to matters of *mamon*. Nevertheless, in light of the glosses and commentaries to Maimonides (Maim. Yad, Ishut 6:14, and Zekhiah u-Mattanah 3:8), there is good authority for restricting the said requirements to *kiddushin* and *gittin*; and there is logic, too, in freeing everyday transactions from unreasonable formal requirements, since the predominant factor should be the will of the parties – and if they want a certain condition to be fulfilled, it should stand even if formalities like *tenai kaful* have not been observed (Rabad ad loc). Moreover, *custom, which is a powerful agent in *Dinei Mamonot*, may have regarded such a requirement in the field of commercial transactions as obsolete (Haggahot Maimoniyyot to Ishut 6:14). Yet, even if the *halakhah* were to be decided as suggested by Maimonides, there still exist various means of evading the problems arising out of the formalistic requirements of *tenai kaful* and *hen kodem le-lav*. Maimonides himself notes (Ishut 6:17) that if the word *me-akhshav* ("from now") was used in the stipulation, which would seem to turn a suspensive condition into a resolutive one, the requirement of *tenai kaful* may be ignored. Equally, the use of the words *al menat* ("provided that"), as distinct from the simple *im* ("if"), has the same effect as *me-akhshav* (Sh. Ar., EH 38:3). Furthermore, if the condition is contained in a written document, the date of the document could have the effect of *me-akhshav* (Git. 77a).

Already in the Middle Ages, when most of the transactions among Jews were in chattel, there seems to have been a tendency to consider the *tenai benei Gad u-venei Re'uven*, if applicable at all, as being restricted to the transfer of landed property (as was the case, in fact, in the original "deal" with the tribes of Gad and Reuben); pure obligations (*in personam*), not involving the transfer of property, would then certainly be exempt from those rules (see Gulak, Yesodei, 1 (1922), 80). It may be mentioned in this context that some "reservations" (*shi'ur*) do not fall under the term "condition." For example, if one sells his house, but reserves the right to a certain part of it, this is not construed as the vendor having said that he would sell the house "on condition that…"; therefore the requirement of *tenai kaful*, etc., does not apply (Sh. Ar., ḤM 212:3).

The requirement that the conditions should be capable of fulfillment, which is the most reasonable requirement and applies regardless of the form of the stipulation, needs some elaboration. The consequence of stipulating an impossible condition is that the principal transaction remains valid, despite the "nonfulfillment" of the condition (Maim. Yad, Ishut 6:7). By contrast, in Roman law the whole transaction would be voided by the defect of the condition (for a further discussion of this point, see Gulak, loc. cit., 81). It should be said at once that this is not the case of a person being prevented from fulfilling a condition by reason of *force majeure* (see *Ones), but with conditions stipulating something which according to all human experience is a priori impossible. The example usually given in the sources is "if you climb to the sky." Moreover, only physical and not moral or legal impossibility is visualized in this context. For example, if one promises to give his horse to another on the condition that the prospective recipient commits a sin, the condition would stand, and if he committed the sin, he would have the horse; if not, he would not (Maim. Yad, Ishut 6:8; EH 38:4). For a discussion of the problems of *jus dispositivum jus cogens*, and illegal contract, see *Contract.

Implied Conditions

A final category, widely discussed, is that of implied conditions. The classic case is that of a man who sold his possessions because he intended to immigrate to the Holy Land, but made no mention of his intentions during the negotiations. His plans having been foiled, he then wanted to renege on the transaction, arguing that he only sold his possessions on the condition that his plans would be realized. The ruling here is that such mental reservations have no effect ("words which are in the heart are not words," Kid. 49b–50a). This does not mean that only explicit conditions are valid; in fact, it is sufficient if in the circumstances, the dependency of the transaction on certain events was clearly apparent. For example, if a person, in contemplation of death, donated all his property, it is assumed that he did so on the premise that his death was imminent (especially if the donation was made during a particular illness). Accordingly, if he survived, the donation is ineffective (BB 9:6; see also *Wills). On the general question as to whether and to what extent the parties are bound by the transaction before the condition is fulfilled (Maim. Yad, Ishut 6:15–16; Sh. Ar., EH 38:6–7), it should be noted that, here again, conditions introduced by the simple *im* would lack forcefulness, which can be remedied by the addition of *me-akhshav* or by using the formula of *al menat*, a differentiation discussed above in connection with *tenai kaful* (see also *Asmakhta). Special problems of conditions attaching to specific transactions are further discussed in the respective articles on *Betrothal, *Sale, *Wills, etc.

[Arnost Zvi Ehrman]

The Law in the State of Israel

Sections 27–29 of the Contracts Law (General Part), 5773 – 1973, contain the various rules governing conditions in contracts: a suspensory condition (in which the contract only becomes valid upon the fulfillment of the condition), as opposed to a resolutory condition (the fulfillment of the condition terminates the validity of the contract); the possibility granted to a party to rely on the performance or the non-performance of such conditions; a contract whose fulfillment is conditional upon the agreement of a third party or the receipt of a license; and the date on which the contract is canceled when the condition is not fulfilled.

Decisions of the Israel Supreme Court

In a further hearing in the case of *Ben Shachar v. Yosef Machlev* (DN 22/73, 28(2) PD 89), the question adjudicated by the Court was whether, after a decision had been rendered by a court giving effect to an agreement between two parties regarding the payment schedule for a debt, it was possible to extend the dates that had been fixed for the payments, in the event that the debtor was unable to pay due to *duress. In the case at hand, the debtor was unable to pay because he had become completely paralyzed and the Court granted his son's request to extend the payment deadlines that had been fixed, and rejected the creditor's petition to evict him from his home. The Court held that it had inherent power to change the decision rendered pursuant to the agreement in order to do justice in such cases.

In addition to this holding, Justice Haim Cohn ruled that even without such power, the agreement between the parties must be read as containing an *implied condition* to the effect that "if the debtor does not discharge his obligations in the time prescribed therefore, due to illness or other circumstances beyond his control, the Court is vested with the authority to extend the time limit for his performance of those obligations (*ibid.*, p. 100). Justice Cohn invoked sources from Jewish Law in support of this ruling, stating that "the justice that we are obligated and try to do will be more secure and institutionalized when it is based on our legal tradition and the wisdom of our ancestors, of blessed memory" (*ibid.*, p. 98):

> We found a kind of *implied condition* of the sort that forms the basis of the Mishnaic rule exempting one who makes a vow from fulfilling his vow if, on the date set,… he was prevented from doing so due to circumstances beyond his control ("duress"). The Mishnah defines "vows affected by duress" as vows whose timely performance was thwarted because the one who made the vow "became ill, or his son became ill, or the river prevented him" (Ned. 3:3). Rabbi Obadiah of Bertinoro explains that "from the outset the one who made the vow had no intention to fulfill it if he were to be prevented from doing so; this proves that "words of the heart, even if unexpressed, are words." In other words, even if the one who took the vow did not make an express statement, but only thought it to himself, and generally speaking thoughts are not words, we must read into his explicit vow the condition that was not expressly stated therein, because it was in his mind, i.e., that should circumstances beyond his control prevent him from carrying it out, the vow will not obligate him. This is what the Talmud teaches: "though we [normally] rule words of the heart, even if unexpressed, are words, it is different when it is made under duress" (Ned. 28a).

Further on in his comments, Justice Cohn cites the rule stipulating that, in the case where a plaintiff presented the court with writs attesting to his rights (in other words, submitted them for execution), and prior to the completion of the process he had to return home, and therefore declared to the court and the litigant that in the event of his not returning within thirty days his rights would be annulled, and thereafter, due to circumstances beyond his control, he was unable to return, *his rights are not annulled* (Maim., Yad, *Hil. Sanhedrin* 6:10; *Tur,* and *Shulḥan Arukh,* ḤM 21.1; based on Ned. 27a). Regarding this case, as well, Justice Cohen suggests that the reason for this ruling is the same—namely, that the creditor's words are construed as containing an *implied condition* exempting him in the event of circumstances beyond his control (*ibid.*, pp. 98–99).

Another case in which the Supreme Court dealt with the application of an "implied condition" was that of *Behem v. the Rabbinical High Court of Appeals* (HC 609/92, 47(3) PD 288). In that case, the Court was requested to invalidate the decision of the Rabbinical High Court of Appeals regarding the apartment of a couple that had divorced due to the wife's infidelity. The rabbinical court ruled that the husband should become the sole owner of the apartment, because when the husband gave his wife half of the apartment he did so under the condition that she would be faithful to him. Even though such a condition had never been explicitly stated or written, the rabbinical court concluded that there had been an *implied condition,* based on the expectations of the parties (this, in addition to its decision that the husband was no longer bound by his compromise offer to give the wife 30% of the value of the apartment, as she had rejected that offer). The petitioner's argument was that this decision contravenes the principles of civil law applicable in the State of Israel under the Women's Equal Rights Law, 5711 – 1951, and concerning the possibility of retracting a gift pursuant to the Gift Law, 5728 – 1968; in addition, he argued that the decision violates the provisions of Basic Law: Human Dignity and Freedom.

The Court (Justice Elon) ruled that, as it had been established that the apartment was purchased with the respondent's money and the issue concerned the legal act of a gift between spouses, the only question confronting the Court was the question of "the interpretation of this legal act according to the expectations and intentions of the parties," and it does not bear upon the wife's equal rights or basic rights (ruling, *ibid.*, p. 294). The Court further held that, as the rabbinical court is vested with the jurisdiction to decide in the case, it must rule according to Jewish Law. In view of both of these rulings, the Court rejected the petition and held that the rabbinical court had ruled in accordance with the law and that, according to Jewish Law, this gift must be viewed as a conditional gift, "subject to the understanding that if she leaves him, he would not be regarded has having given it to her" (*ibid.*).

Justice Elon showed further that, even pursuant to the civil Gift Law, a gift may be given conditionally, and that the existence of such a condition may be deduced on the basis of the parties' intentions, as reflected by the circumstances. In a number of cases the Supreme Court held that, regarding a gift to a spouse, the circumstances may on occasion indicate that a gift was given conditionally. Hence, from the moment the judicial instance interprets the contract as a conditional contract, that condition becomes part of the gift contract; it is thus clear that the rabbinical court was required to interpret the contract as containing a condition, in accordance with Jewish Law.

The Supreme Court further pointed out that [in another case] the rabbinical court had ruled that a spousal gift is given on the condition "that they will not divorce," even where the situation was the opposite – that is, where the wife gave half of her apartment to the husband, and he had to return his share of the apartment to the wife.

It bears mention that the rabbinical court views itself as bound by civil law regarding the wife's equal rights, provided that the issue concerned monetary matters and not questions of *issur ve-heter* (i.e., ritual laws of prohibited and permitted actions). This was the position taken in *Nagar v. Nagar* (BDM 1/81, 38(1) PD 365), by Rabbi Yosef Kappaḥ, a judge in the Rabbinical High Court of Appeals and one of the important halakhic scholars of recent years. (The late Rabbi Kappaḥ was a member of the Supreme Court panel that ruled in the case, pursuant to a special procedure provided by the law when a ruling is required on whether the rabbinical or civil court has jurisdiction.) Rabbi Kappaḥ stated as follows:

> The legislator's directive [to equate a woman and a man regarding any legal act, pursuant to the Women's Equal Rights Law, 5711 – 1951 – ME] was apparently given under the assumption that monetary matters do not occasion an infringement of religious law inasmuch as a legislative directive [in the civil law] has the same halakhic status as [the establishment of] a "financial condition," which is not considered as making a condition against what is written in the Torah. As such, it must be presumed that the legislator did not intend to infringe any matter that did not fall within the ambit of a financial condition (*ibid.*, p. 412).

[Menachem Elon (2nd ed.)]

BIBLIOGRAPHY: Gulak, Yesodei, index; N. Wahrmann, *Die Entwicklung der Bedingungsformen im biblisch-talmudischen Recht* (1929); idem, in: *Zeitschrift fuer vergleichende Rechtswissenschaft*, 45 (1930), 219–39; idem, *Die Bedingung* תנאי *und* אסמכתא *im juedischen Recht* (1938); Herzog, Instit, 2 (1939), 217ff.; B. Cohen, in: *H.A. Wolfson Jubilee Volume* (1965), 203–32; also separately: *Conditions in Jewish and Roman Law.* **ADD. BIBLIOGRAPHY:** M. Elon, *Ha-Mishpat ha-Ivri* (1988), 1:352, 520f., 574f., 735, 754f.; 2:1285; 3:1480; idem, *Jewish Law* (1994), 11:424; 2:632f., 707f., 906, 930f.; 3:1533; 4:1760f.; idem, *Ma'amad ha-Ishah* (2005), 114–15; M. Elon and B. Lifshitz, *Mafte'aḥ ha-She'elot ve-ha-Teshuvot shel Ḥakhmei Sefarad u-Ẓefon Afrikah*, 2 (1986), 536–39; B. Lifshitz and E. Shochetman, *Mafte'aḥ ha-She'elot ve-ha-Teshuvot shel Ḥakhmei Ashkenaz, Ẓarefat ve-Italyah* (1997), 360–61.

[Arnost Zvi Ehrman]

CONE, U.S. commercial and philanthropic family. HERMAN CONE (1828–97), the father of 13 children, emigrated from Bavaria to the U.S. in 1845 and ultimately established a successful wholesale grocery business in Baltimore. His two eldest sons, MOSES HERMAN (1857–1908) and CAESAR (1859–1917), began their careers as salesmen. During their travels through the South the two brothers were struck by the unstandardized goods and disorganized marketing methods of Southern cotton mills. In 1891 they founded the Cone Export and Commission Company, with a main office in New York, which served both as a banker and distributor for the Southern textile industry. The company helped the industry both to standardize and variegate its products and to free itself of its costly dependence on Northern finishers and distributors. During the financial panic of 1893 it saved many mills from bankruptcy. Moses and Caesar Cone established a mill of their own in Asheville, North Carolina (1892), and soon after founded three more mills in Greensboro, North Carolina. Within a few years they had joined the world's leading producers of flannels and denims and controlled 3% of the entire cotton industry of the South. Both Cone brothers became active in community affairs in Greensboro. They helped found schools and a YMCA, and Moses left a large part of his estate for the construction of a hospital named after him. Caesar was vice president of the American Cotton Manufacturers Association and held important local and state philanthropic positions. After his death ownership of the Cone mills passed to his son HERMAN. CLARIBEL (1864–1929), sister of Caesar and Moses Cone, studied medicine at Johns Hopkins University and was later professor of pathology at Women's Medical College in Baltimore. Together with her sister ETTA, she built up a large collection of French impressionist and post-impressionist painting, which is now housed in the Cone Wing of the Baltimore Museum of Art.

BIBLIOGRAPHY: DAB; Cone Export and Commission Co., *Half Century Book* (1941); *New York Times* (March 3, 1917), 9–15 (obituary).

[Harry Golden]

CONEGLIANO (Heb. קוניאן, *Conian*, as pronounced in the local dialect), small town in Venetia, northern Italy. Jewish moneylenders settled there before 1398. Attempts made by the municipality to expel the Jews in 1511, 1518, 1560, and 1567 were opposed by the Venetian authorities. Moneylending was prohibited to Jews in Conegliano between 1538 and 1541, and finally in 1548. A talmudic academy flourished there in the first decades of the 17th century under the direction of R. Nathan Ottolengo. Following restrictions on Jewish residence, construction of a ghetto began in 1637; it was moved to a different site in 1675. The number of Jewish residents in 1752 reached 58 people, including moneylenders, traders, owners of a silk factory and stores. In 1866 Marco Grassini was elected mayor of the town. By 1866 the Jews numbered 30, and subsequently almost all of them moved elsewhere. The community of Conegliano died out completely from the 1930s and in 1931 passed under the jurisdiction of the Jewish Community of Venice. The beautiful synagogue, built in 1701 but incorporating earlier elements, was transferred to Jerusalem in 1948 and reconstructed in the Italian Synagogue in 1952.

BIBLIOGRAPHY: F. Luzzatto, *La communità ebraica di Conegliano Veneto ed i suoi monumenti* (1957). **ADD. BIBLIOGRAPHY:** Archivio della Comunità ebraica di Venezia, Busta 92, Conegliano Veneto.

[Attilio Milano]

CONEGLIANO, Italian family, many prominent members of which were physicians; the name comes from the small Italian town of *Conegliano. Some members of the family called themselves Conian, according to the pronunciation in the local dialect. ABRAHAM JOEL CONEGLIANO (17th–18th centuries), mathematician, lived in Ceneda and Verona. He wrote a reply to the polemical book by L.M. Benetelli, *Le saette di Gionata* ("The Arrows of Jonathan," Venice, 1703), to which the latter replied in *I dardi Rabbinici infranti* ("The Broken Rabbinical Arrows," Venice, 1705). ISRAEL CONEGLIANO (c. 1650–c. 1717), of Padua, was a physician and politician. In 1675 he settled in Constantinople where he was consulted by the sultan and the grand vizier. In 1682 he was appointed physician to the embassy of Venice, but when Venice joined the Holy League against the Ottoman Empire, Israel had to limit himself to his private medical practice. He succeeded, however, in keeping the senate of Venice informed of political happenings in Constantinople through his elder brother SOLOMON (see below). Between 1687 and 1690 he was again in Venice and then returned to Constantinople, where he made the arrangements under which the protection of Venetians who had remained in the Ottoman Empire was assumed by Holland, instead of France. Israel had to leave for Venice after the expulsion of all Venetians from the Ottoman Empire in 1694. He was able to continue supplying useful reports to Venice through a third brother JUDAH who had remained in Constantinople. In 1698 Israel attended the Congress of Karlowitz, at which peace was negotiated between the European powers and the Ottoman Empire; the following year, as physician and secretary to the Venetian envoy Carlo Ruzzini he took a direct part in the delimitation of the borders between Venice and the Ottoman Empire. He was honored by the Venetian senate and, with his brothers Solomon and Judah, was given Venetian citizenship and exempted from wearing the Jewish badge. SOLOMON (1642–1719), born in Padua, practiced as a physician in Venice. He acted as intermediary in the exchange of correspondence between his brother Israel and the senate of Venice. He organized preparatory courses for young students, mainly Jews, who attended the medical university of Padua. He wrote the preface to the book *Ma'aseh Tuviyyah* (1709), by Tobias b. Moses *Cohn who was his student. Another member of the family was EMANUEL CONEGLIANO (1749–1833) who assumed the name LORENZO DA PONTE. A man of letters, he lived in New York and was a well-known author of libretti for Mozart's operas. CARLO ANGELO CONEGLIANO (1868–1901) of Modena was an economist and professor of financial sciences at the University of Modena. He founded the Italian Zionist review *Lidea sionnista* (1901–10).

BIBLIOGRAPHY: D. Kaufmann, *Dr. Israel Conegliano* (1895); F. Luzzatto, *La communità ebraica di Conegliano Veneto ed i suoi monumenti* (1957), 27–31; C. Roth, *Venice* (1930), index; Roth, Italy, index; Milano, Italia, index. **ADD. BIBLIOGRAPHY:** A. Fabris, "Le famiglie ebraiche di Conegliano tra Sei e Settecento," in *Zakhor*, 6 (2003), 147–81.

[Attilio Milano / Federica Francesconi (2nd ed.)]

CONFERENCE OF PRESIDENTS OF MAJOR AMERICAN JEWISH ORGANIZATIONS (Presidents Conference). The Conference of Presidents of Major American Jewish Organizations was organized in 1955 out of a growing awareness that unified action by major American Jewish organizations was essential to help strengthen American support for the state of Israel, which equated with strengthening peace and stability in the Middle East. Of all American Jewish organizations, the Presidents Conference has the highest visibility in the American media, a stature not unchallenged by other Jewish organizations such as the ADL and which is also challenged in Washington, where AIPAC is viewed as the powerful and successful key to American support for Israel. It meets on a regular basis for the purpose of receiving briefings from Israeli and American government officials, the contents of which are useful for the leadership and constituents of member organizations; and offers a number of substantive programs. The Presidents Conference carries the message of the government of Israel and the American Jewish community to the administration in Washington on Israel-related issues and on international matters, and vice versa. It is *the* address for foreign leaders who want to address American Jewish leadership and is often employed as a forum for improving relationship with the American Jewish community, which is often perceived as essential to improving relationship with the American government by foreign leaders.

There were multiple factors at work in the genesis of the Presidents Conference. The Israeli government was eager to have a table at which it could present its concerns and discuss them with the American Jewish community; the U.S. State Department, under Secretary John Foster Dulles, was not happy with the idea of many Jewish organizations coming to it with messages from the Jewish community, and was therefore receptive to the idea of a single instrumentality with which it would relate, and which would represent the multiplicity of Jewish agencies. Additionally, Nahum *Goldmann, who was also president of the *World Jewish Congress (which had no real base in the United States other than the *American Jewish Congress, which did not really serve as a vehicle for the WJC), wanted more of a voice on the American scene. Goldmann wanted a body that could coordinate and regulate the contacts of Zionist leaders with the State Department and handle political discussions surrounding Israel with American leaders. Goldmann played a key role, together with Philip *Klutznick, at that time the president of B'nai B'rith, in the creation of the Presidents Conference.

Other factors that were instrumental in the creation of the Conference of Presidents included the facts that Israel-related issues were not, at the time, priorities on the agenda of the National Community Relations Advisory Council (NCRAC, later NJCRAC), and that there was no community-relations vehicle that embraced the Zionist organizations, which were not members of the NCRAC.

The essential question – who speaks for the Jews of America? – was not answered fully by the creation of the Conference of Presidents; but the Conference was perceived by the Administration as the authorized voice of the Jewish community on Israel.

As early as 1951 a small group of American Jewish leaders, at the urging of Israeli official Abba *Eban, in a communication to Nahum Goldmann, began meeting with key Israeli officials for briefings and consultations. In 1955 a number of major organizations called a national conference in Washington on American-Israel relations. Thereafter the leaders and staff members of these organizations began to confer on a regular basis. An organizational structure developed and the Conference of Presidents was formally established in 1959. The 15 founding member organizations included eight Zionist groups, plus a number of "defense," religious, and fundraising agencies. The mandate of the Presidents Conference, as originally defined, is to act as a spokesman (not a policy-making body) on behalf of the American Jewish community to the American Administration on Israel. (The mandate was expanded in the mid-1960s to include other international issues as well.)

Originally the Conference was more of a "Presidents' Club" than a "conference," reflecting the views of Philip Klutznick, the powerful lay head of B'nai B'rith (the largest Jewish membership organization at that time), who was against a formal centralized, binding organization; he wanted an informal structure, "a forum for presidents to debate … matters pertaining to Israel." Before too long, however, the body became a formal Conference, with by-laws and procedures. In 1966, the Conference became a body of constituent *organizations*, rather than of presidents of organizations. During the same year it also decided to establish and maintain ongoing contacts with world Jewish bodies to facilitate the exchange of information, opinions, and ideas.

As of 2005, the Conference membership consisted of 51 national Jewish organizations – Zionist, "defense," and community-relations, social-service, religious, and fundraising – whose members collectively represent the overwhelming majority of the Jewish community of the United States. The Conference of Presidents seeks to develop consensus for collective action on issues of national and international Jewish concern. It endeavors to enhance the work of its member organizations to strengthen U.S.-Israel understanding, to assist Israel and to assure the physical safety and rights of Jews and Jewish communities overseas.

For the most part the Presidents Conference is not responsible for the deliberative process of shaping strategy on public-policy issues facing Israel. This process is a function of the range of the community relations and "defense" agencies, religious bodies, and Zionist organizations. The Conference's primary role, that of a spokesperson, is to present to the Administration the public face of the American Jewish community and of Israel.

The Conference also serves as the representative body to which officials of the Executive and Legislative branches of the American government, Israeli leaders, and foreign heads of state turn in dealing with issues of mutual concern. Leaders of Jewish communities in other lands and a wide variety of prominent personalities also appear before the Conference.

Conventional wisdom has it that the Presidents Conference languished until the Six-Day War. In fact, the conference was launched at a time during which the Eastern Bloc began shipping heavy arms to Egypt, and arms sales became an issue for the first time. Activity of *fedayeen* across Israel's borders was also of increasing concern for the Jewish community and was on the Conference's agenda. The 1956 Sinai Campaign, and the need to respond to the threat of sanctions from the White House, was the first critical issue facing the Presidents Conference. The Conference, together with the NCRAC (NJCRAC), convened regional conferences around the country during those years. Over the years, the Presidents Conference has remained a significant vehicle for the Israeli government to communicate, through the American Jewish community speaking with one voice, with the Administration.

The Conference's activities and accomplishments have focused on building a broad-based educational program in support of the principle that a militarily strong, politically secure, and economically sound Israel is in the best interest of the United States and of world peace. During the period of the Six-Day War the Conference convened a mass rally in support of Israel opposite the White House. In the wake of the Yom Kippur War, the Conference worked vigorously in support of the United States resupplying Israel. With the new *Likud government in Israel in 1977 – overturning three decades of familiar *Mapai/Labor rule – the Conference President, Rabbi Alexander *Schindler, who was informed by a politically liberal philosophy, was nonetheless able to establish a cordial relationship – personally and professionally – with Prime Minister Menaḥem *Begin, and was an instrument in the process of gaining public acceptance in the Jewish community of the new government. Following Egyptian president Anwar Sadat's 1977 visit to Jerusalem, the Conference undertook numerous activities to keep up the peace momentum – including acceptance of the first invitation to an American Jewish organization to meet in Egypt with President Sadat and other top Egyptian leaders. Throughout the 1980s the Conference opposed the sale of sophisticated arms to Arab countries at war with Israel. It worked to guarantee the rights of Jews in the former Soviet Union to emigrate and practice their religious faith and cultural heritage, and it continues to monitor the resurgence of antisemitism in the former Soviet Union and parts of Europe. The Conference also had a role in the rescue of Ethiopian, Syrian, and Yemenite Jews and other endangered Jewish communities.

The Conference worked for the rescinding of the UN resolution equating Zionism with racism, which was reversed in 1991, as well as in countering the Arab economic boycott of Israel. The Conference was a leader in the successful effort to secure $10 billion in loan guarantees for Israel in 1992 over the opposition of President George H.W. Bush, who portrayed himself as overwhelmed by the activism of Jewish groups on the issue – a manifest display, suggested Bush, of the power of the Jewish "lobby." Since the 1993 signing of the Oslo Accords, the Conference has undertaken a significant program of activities in regard to the Middle East process. As there were deep internal divisions within the organized Jewish community regarding Oslo, which was indeed a revolution, the Presidents Conference was slow to act. Dovish critics faulted the Israeli Labor government for bypassing the Presidents Conference as it did not require its enthusiastic support. The American Jewish community overwhelming supported Oslo, with the noted exception of the Orthodox community.

Other priority issues before the Conference from the mid-1990s into the 21st century are terrorism in the United States and abroad, the proliferation of weapons of mass destruction, Islamic fundamentalism, support for foreign aid, promoting tourism to and trade with Israel, strengthening the bond between American Jews and Israel, and global antisemitism.

On the "Who-is-a-Jew?" question – a successive iteration of issues that has generated divisions in the American Jewish polity – the Presidents Conference over the years studiously avoided any involvement in the issue; indeed, the Conference avoided discussion of the issue within its deliberative process. This issue was particularly sensitive for Orthodox groups in the Conference, who viewed "Who is a Jew?" as an effort by the non-Orthodox/secular camp in Israel to chip away at the hegemony of the Chief Rabbinate in "personal-status" and other matters. The view of the Conference of Presidents leadership was that, as an organization that promoted Jewish unity, having on the agenda an issue that caused painful divisions would compromise that mission.

In the 21st century the salient issues for the Conference – international terrorism, global antisemitism, the Palestinian dilemma and the peace process in Israel, Jewish communities outside the United States and Israel – have been increasingly addressed via programmatic initiatives, which had not been the case in earlier years. In the late 1980s and early 1990s some "defense" agencies felt that the Conference was moving too aggressively in functional areas rather than limiting its activities to spokesmanship and coordination. Withal, the core function of the Conference has remained one of articulating a consensus position of its member organizations. When the organization is riven with strife it cannot achieve a consensus and results can be quite embarrassing. Such was the case with regard to the response to the assassination of Israel Prime Minister Yitzhak *Rabin by a religious Israeli opposed to the peace process, and with the Oslo accords. Condemnation of the assassination was fine but no consensus could be achieved on supporting the policies of the elected government of Israel. Similarly, in 2005 there was a great reluctance, because of internal political differences and the pull of right-wing and religious-nationalist organizations, to support the withdrawal from Gaza, and the support of the Presidents Conference was lukewarm at best.

Among the programs of the Presidents Conference in 2005 were the Daily Alert, a news summary on the Middle East; Israel Campus Beat, a weekly e-mail for the university community on Israel-related issues; Secure Community Alert Network (SCAN), an integrated rapid-response system for emergency communications; and Justice for Jews from Arab Countries, a refugee advocacy arm.

In 2005 the budget of the Presidents Conference was $2 million. The chairman of the Conference of Presidents is chosen on a rotational basis, with a two-year term of office the norm. In order to be eligible for the chairmanship, an individual must have been president of his or her organization within the past three years. In 2005 James S. Tisch was the chairman of the Conference of Presidents. Chairmen have been widely regarded as *the* spokespersons for American Jews during their tenure in office. Several were particularly effective; others relied upon staff to lead. Malcolm Hoenlein has served as executive vice chairman since 1986. Hoenlein, who had been executive of the New York Jewish Community Relations Council, is considered one of the more canny, aggressive, and creative American Jewish professional leaders. He was preceded by Yehuda Hellman, a career professional, who served from 1959 to 1986. The staff is small, and the membership base is organizational and not individual. There has therefore been considerable leeway for a single able professional leader, such as Hoenlein, to shape the organization

The following is a list of the member organizations of the Conference of Presidents of Major American Jewish Organizations in 2005:

America Israel Friendship League
American Friends of Likud
American Gathering/Federation of Jewish Holocaust Survivors
American Israel Public Affairs Committee
American Jewish Committee
American Jewish Congress
American ORT, Inc.
American Sephardi Federation
American Zionist Movement
Americans for Peace Now

Amit
Anti-Defamation League
Association of Reform Zionists of America/World Union North America
B'nai B'rith
Bnai Zion
Central Conference of American Rabbis
Committee for Accuracy in Middle East Reporting in America
Development Corporation for Israel
Emunah of America
Friends of Israel Defense Forces
Hadassah, Women's Zionist Organization of America
Hebrew Immigrant Aid Society
Jewish Community Centers Association
Jewish Council for Public Affairs
Jewish Institute for National Security Affairs
Jewish National Fund
Jewish Reconstructionist Federation
Jewish War Veterans of the U.S.A.
Jewish Women International
Joint Distribution Committee
Labor Zionist Alliance
Mercaz USA, Zionist Organization of the Conservative Movement
Na'amat USA
National Committee for Labor Israel
NCSJ: Advocates on Behalf of Jews in Russia, Ukraine, the Baltic States & Eurasia
National Council of Jewish Women
National Council of Young Israel
Rabbinical Assembly
Rabbinical Council of America
Religious Zionists of America
Union of American Hebrew Congregations
Union of Orthodox Jewish Congregations of America
United Jewish Communities
United Synagogue of Conservative Judaism
WIZO
Women of Reform Judaism
Women's American ORT
Women's League for Conservative Judaism
Workmen's Circle / Jewish Labor Committee
World Zionist Executive, U.S.A.
Zionist Organization of America

Significantly enough, the Simon Wiesenthal Center, a defense, research, and advocacy organization with membership and regional operations, does not appear on the list; and for many years the American Jewish Committee did not join the President's Conference, but retained observer status. The American Jewish Committee traditionally viewed itself as a non-Zionist organization whose priorities were centered on the domestic American agenda. In 1991, with international affairs holding primacy of place on AJC's agenda, the agency joined the Conference.

Several organizations, most recently Meretz U.S.A., have been rejected for membership. Reasons offered for rejection identify membership, budget, and regionalization criteria. But critics suspect a political agenda.

[Jerome Chanes (2nd ed.)]

CONFERENCE ON JEWISH MATERIAL CLAIMS AGAINST GERMANY, umbrella organization established in New York in 1951 by 23 national and international Jewish organizations representing Diaspora Jewish life in the West. Its aims were to obtain funds for the relief, rehabilitation, and resettlement of Jewish victims of Nazi persecution, and the rebuilding of Jewish communal life; and to obtain indemnification for injuries inflicted upon victims of Nazi persecution and restitution for properties confiscated by the Nazis.

The suggestion to call the Conference was made by the Government of Israel, which in 1951 said it was entitled to claim reparations from Germany, because it was responsible for the absorption and rehabilitation of the survivors of the Holocaust. The Conference was convened by Dr. Nahum *Goldmann, chairman of the Jewish Agency; he was elected its president. West German Chancellor Konrad *Adenauer issued an invitation to negotiate in a speech on the eve of Rosh ha-Shanah 1951, when he said "unspeakable crimes were perpetrated in the name of the German people, which impose upon them the obligation to make moral and material amends."

The idea of negotiations with West Germany was strongly opposed by various Jewish circles. There were riots in the Knesset before the Israeli government narrowly agreed in January 1952 to negotiate with West Germany. Opponents argued that the wrong caused to the Jewish people by Nazi Germany was of such a nature and magnitude that it was irreparable. They also maintained that to exchange this wrong for some "blood money" was morally and historically repugnant and likely to lead gradually to a "forgive and forget" policy. The partisans for negotiations did not dispute the basic assumption of the irreparability of the wrong but emphasized the differences between material claims and moral-historical claims, the latter to remain unaffected by the former.

The government of Israel and the Conference opened formal negotiations with the German Federal Republic in March 1952 at The Hague. On September 10, 1952, an agreement signed in Luxembourg between the West German government and the Conference was embodied in two protocols. The first protocol called for the enactment of German legislation to provide compensation and restitution to Holocaust survivors. Three German Federal Indemnification Laws (known as Bundesentschädigungsgesetze, BEG) were passed between 1953 and 1965. These laws, which established the legal framework for compensation for "victims of National Socialist persecution," mandated payments for victims in the West for personal and professional injuries. The Federal Restitution Law (Bundesrueckerstattungsgesetz, BRUEG-EG) enacted in

1957 was designed to compensate Nazi victims for loss of personal valuables, bank accounts, and other movable properties confiscated by Nazi authorities. In 1964, as a result of Conference pressure, the German parliament enacted amendments to the BRUEG which enlarged the volume of compensation payments and expanded the scope of eligibility. By 2000, under the terms of the first protocol, West Germany had paid more than DM 100 billion in compensation to individual victims of Nazi persecution. The German term for the measures is *Wiedergutmachung*, which is not used by the Jewish community because the term means "to make whole."

Under the second protocol, the German government agreed to provide the Conference with DM 450 million, over a decade, for the relief, rehabilitation, and resettlement of Jewish victims of Nazi persecution. This payment was in recognition of uncompensated Jewish losses. Of the early allocations, 76% was applied to relief, rehabilitation, and resettlement of Nazi victims, 20% to cultural and educational reconstruction, and approximately 4% to administration, including costs of the Israel Purchasing Mission in Germany (see *Restitution and Indemnification). These projects included educational institutions, community and youth centers, synagogues and other religious institutions, homes for the aged, children's homes and kindergartens, summer camps, and medical institutions. Of 750,000 Jewish victims of Nazi persecution living in European countries other than the Soviet Union, 225,000 became beneficiaries of aid for relief, rehabilitation, and resettlement, often through Conference financing of programs, primarily of the American Jewish Joint Distribution Committee. Conference allocations to the *United HIAS Service assisted the migration of 49,000 Jews from European countries.

The Conference helped finance the United Restitution Organization, which provided hundreds of thousands of Nazi victims with legal aid in connection with their restitution and indemnification claims. Conference allocations for cultural and educational programs totaled $19,450,000. Four major institutions for the commemoration and documentation of the Holocaust were the principal beneficiaries of the Conference: the *Yad Vashem Authority, Jerusalem; the combined projects of the *YIVO Institute, New York, and Yad Vashem; the *Centre de Documentation Juive Contemporaire and the Memorial to the Unknown Jewish Martyr, Paris; and the *Wiener Library, London.

The Conference was the first organization to establish a special program recognizing the Jewish community's moral obligation to assist *Hassidei Umot ha-Olam*, the *Righteous Among the Nations, who at considerable personal risk had saved Jews and who later were in need of financial assistance.

Conference allocations from the second protocol ended in 1964. In 1965 the Conference established the Memorial Foundation for Jewish Culture to serve as a living memorial to the Jews who perished in the Holocaust. The Foundation activities began with a capital of $10,432,000 allocated by the Conference.

The Conference continued to negotiate with Germany for compensation for individual victims after the three indemnification laws had been enacted. It believed there were serious deficiencies in West Germany's indemnification laws, which originally were limited to certain Nazi victims who were in the West by October 1953. Scores of thousands of victims were subsequently able to flee from Eastern Europe and the Soviet Union. In 1980 the Conference reached an agreement with West Germany for the creation of the Hardship Fund, which provided one-time payments to victims, primarily from Eastern Europe, who arrived in the West after the BEG deadline. More than 250,000 victims received payments from the Hardship Fund in its first two decades.

East Germany never compensated Nazi victims. It argued that it was an anti-fascist state, and it did not consider itself a successor to Hitler's Germany. When the United States established diplomatic relations with the German Democratic Republic, the Conference initiated efforts to obtain compensation and restitution from East Germany. An agreement was not reached until after German reunification, when Holocaust survivors in the West who had received minimal or no previous compensation became eligible for annuities from Germany. A separate fund for Jewish victims in Central and Eastern Europe was established in 1998.

In its first decade, the Conference reached agreements with individual German companies – IG Farben, Siemens, Krupp, AEG, Telefunken, and Rheinmetall – to provide compensation for Jews who had been slave laborers during the Nazi era. In 2000 the Conference represented Jewish victims in a multilateral agreement with the German government and industry in which DM 10 billion was provided as compensation for slave and forced labor. Since 1952 the Conference has concluded some 25 agreements with European governments and industry.

The unified German government also designated the Conference as a "Successor Organization," which gave it title to unclaimed and heirless individual Jewish properties and the properties of dissolved Jewish communities and organizations in the former East Germany. About 80% of the funds generated by the Successor Organization were used for projects that provided social welfare services to survivors; 20% was used to finance research, documentation, and education about the Holocaust. From 1995 through 2000, the Conference allocated more than $400 million from the proceeds of heirless Jewish properties in the former East Germany to projects that aid survivors. About 60% of these funds were used in Israel, while some 25% were for projects in the former Soviet Union.

The Conference leadership and membership remained stable over a half-century. Goldmann remained president until his death in 1982; he was succeeded by Rabbi Israel Miller, who served until shortly before his death in 2002. The executive functions were subsequently divided between the president and chairman, Rabbi Israel Singer and Julius Berman, respectively. The first director of the Conference was Saul Kagan, who served until his retirement in 1998. He was succeeded by Gideon Taylor.

Survivors organizations – the *American Gathering / Federation of Jewish Holocaust Survivors and the Centre of Organizations of Holocaust Survivors in Israel – joined the Conference in 1989. Jewish organizations from Central and Eastern Europe were not specifically admitted to the Conference, although in 2000 the board was expanded. It included one "pan-European representative" and bolstered Israel's membership with "four eminent Israeli personalities."

The Conference was sui generis in Jewish life. The founding principle – that direct compensation be paid to individual surviving victims of atrocities – was unprecedented in 1951. It was also unprecedented that a voluntary consortium of Jewish organizations would be recognized as a legitimate negotiating partner with a sovereign state, West Germany. The Conference's member organizations reflected broad religious and ideological points of view that often were antagonistic and yet collaborated to pursue assistance that ultimately benefited more than a half-million victims of the Nazis.

BIBLIOGRAPHY: Claims Conference, *Twenty Years Later: Activities of the Conference on Jewish Material Claims Against Germany, 1952–1972; Annual Reports* (1954–); M. Henry, "Fifty Years of Holocaust Compensation," in: *American Jewish Year Book* (2002).

[Marilyn Henry (2nd ed.)]

CONFERENCE ON JEWISH SOCIAL STUDIES, U.S. organization. The idea of the Conference originated in April 1933 with Morris Raphael *Cohen and S.W. *Baron. Its objective was to create an association of scholars to assemble reliable data about the "position of the Jew in the modern world," for the benefit of both Jewish and general scholarship, as well as the public at large. It was felt that such dependable research would help in the struggle against the rapidly spreading Nazi world propaganda with its fabricated evidence and other falsehoods. Beyond the immediate issue, however, loomed the widely felt need in the Jewish community itself to possess fuller and more precise information about the Jewish population, its economic stratification, and other socially and historically relevant aspects of Jewish life. After initial conversations the Conference (until 1955 called "The Conference on Jewish Relations") was launched at a meeting in 1936, presided over by Albert Einstein, addressed by M.R. Cohen, Harold Laski, and S.W. Baron, and concluded with an appeal for funds by Henry Morgenthau, Sr. From its inception, the Conference sponsored a number of research projects and publications, among them the quarterly *Jewish Social Studies*, published regularly from January 1939. An index to the first 25 volumes was published in 1967. There have also been several organizational offshoots of the Conference, including the Jewish Occupational Council, and particularly Jewish Cultural Reconstruction, Inc., which was in charge of salvaging and redistributing throughout the world much of the Jewish cultural property (manuscripts, books, artistic and ritual objects) looted by the Nazis from communities and individuals in the occupied countries.

[Salo W. Baron]

CONFERENCES. Intercommunal consultation started early in the history of Diaspora Jewry. The dispersion on the one hand and an intense feeling of solidarity on the other combined to make the holding of conferences of Jewish leaders and representatives an acutely felt need and hence a relatively frequent occurrence.

In the Middle Ages

It is often difficult to differentiate between intercommunal conferences and predominantly rabbinical synods. A responsum of *Gershom b. Judah (c. 965–1028) relates that "the communities which were gathered there [at a certain commerical center] … framed ordinances under oath" relating to certain matters (ed. by S. Eidelberg, no. 67, p. 155). The early 12th-century chronicler of the massacres of 1096 during the First Crusade describes how in the 11th century "all the communities used to come to Cologne thrice yearly for the fairs" and that "as the heads of the communities would start to speak" at their meeting at the Cologne synagogue, the head of the host community would lead and dominate the deliberations (*Sefer Gezerot Ashkenaz ve-Ẓarefat*, ed. by A.M. Habermann (1945), 47).

In Spain few conferences are recorded. Each cluster of Aragonese communities organized as a *collecta* for tax purposes transacted its business through regular consultation. On occasion, the king assembled delegates from Aragon, Catalonia, Valencia, and other provinces to reapportion a total tax. A large assembly met in Barcelona in 1354 under the impact of the *Black Death massacres to elect an executive committee for the purpose of conducting the common affairs of the Aragonese communities and to deliberate other matters. In 1432 Don Abraham *Benveniste convoked the trustees and scholars of Castile in the city of Valladolid, aiming to restore, through detailed *takkanot*, the social and cultural life of Castilian Jewry to the high level it had attained before the catastrophe of the persecutions of 1391.

A conference held in *Mainz around 1307 sought to raise funds to settle Jewish refugees from France in Germany. Just as in England a "Jewish parliament" was called by the king in 1241 in Worcester for no other reason than to extort money, so the German emperors convoked four meetings of delegates from many communities between 1431 and 1471 for the sole purpose of collecting tax. A number of Jewish gatherings were held during the 16th century (1513, 1530, 1562, 1582, and 1603) which attempted to deal with social, legal, and moral problems in Germany (see also *Synods).

In Italian-speaking areas the first known Jewish gathering was held in 1238 on the island of Crete. On the peninsula the earliest recorded conference seems to have taken place in Rimini in 1399 to apportion taxes among the communities. Jewish delegates from the Papal States, Tuscany, Padua, and Ferrara met in Bologna in 1416, electing at the conference a vigilance committee which met two years later at Forlì. In addition to deliberations on a serious defense problem, the meeting adopted a set of *takkanot* partly dealing with sumptuary laws. The group seems to have met again in Perugia in 1423 and once again in 1428. Rabbinical assemblies in Tivoli and Ravenna sought revocation of a hostile bull issued by Pope *Eugenius IV in 1442. In Sicily all the communities met in 1447 and resolved to remove the chief judge. Royal privileges were confirmed at the request of an assembly four years later. In 1459 further privileges were obtained; yet another conference in 1466 was granted permission to establish a central Jewish college. In 1469 and again in 1488 meetings were held by order of the viceroy to allocate taxes. A year later the viceroy again convened in Palermo a meeting of one or two delegates from each community to request funds for a substantial contribution to the king for the expedition against Granada. A similar convention in 1492 sent envoys to Spain to plead for revocation of the expulsion order. Failing that, they proceeded to help plan an orderly exodus. These Sicilian "parliaments" had their own elected permanent officers, with a treasurer empowered to pay the expenses of the delegates. The northern and central Italian communities also sought amicable agreements on tax quotas at loosely organized conferences. The *Councils of the Lands in Poland-Lithuania represent a successful combination of intercommunal conference and synod.

In Bohemia, the Jewish council leadership of Prague and its chief rabbi spread their hegemony over the entire province. Around 1659 the provincial communities established a separate council of ten elders who joined the Prague community in assessing taxes (see *Landesjudenschaften). Though the earliest extant records of a session of the council of *Moravia date from 1653, the council must have operated much earlier. Along with the chief rabbi, the council regulated Jewish communal life in the area. The *Landesjudenschaften* of Germany often held their own conferences, frequently to ensure efficient taxation and general obedience to state regulations (see also *Cleves). The *Consistory introduced in Napoleonic France can be viewed as a continuation of this type of conference.

Modern Times

In the era of individualization, assimilation, emancipation, and greater use of communication, conferences and congresses – regional, national, and international – became increasingly feasible and acceptable as units of organization and a means of working for Jewish causes and interests. The general tendency in Europe and America to act through conventions and gatherings facilitated this development. Thus in modern times a diversified and variegated Jewish society found the conference most suitable for expression of its involvement with or hesitations about Jewish identity, solidarity, and self-help. Relief work, Zionism, the Jewish socialist as well as the Orthodox movement, utilize the manifold forms of conference as vehicles for unification, activity, and continuity. The form of synod remained reserved for rabbinical gatherings, in particular those in search of an authority on which to base reform and change.

The numerous organizations participating in representative conferences include the *Board of Delegates of American Israelites (established 1859), the *Alliance Israélite Universelle in France (1860), the *American Jewish Committee (1906), the *American (1918) and *World (1936) Jewish Congress, the U.S. *Jewish Labor Committee (1933), and *COJO – Conference of Jewish Organizations. In England the *Board of Deputies of British Jews has a committee on foreign affairs. Especially active after World War I was the Conjoint Foreign Committee formed by this organization and the *Anglo-Jewish Association (1871). In its time the *Hilfsverein der Deutschen Juden (1901) was especially active in defense and relief. So was the Israelitische *Allianz of Vienna. As examples of the tremendous communal energy involved in bringing together divergent groups for international action, the evolution of the American Jewish Congress and the struggle for *minority rights are briefly outlined here.

Years before World War I, proposals for a democratic representative assembly of American Jewry were made. The first practical step was taken at an extraordinary conference of American Zionists held in New York on Aug. 30, 1914, which resolved to organize a convention to consider world Jewish problems that might result from the war. Negotiations were begun with the American Jewish Committee, which offered to cooperate. After a number of meetings by sympathetic groups, a Jewish Congress Organization Committee was formed in 1915. After many conferences and with the support of Zionist groups, the first meeting of the American Jewish Congress took place from December 15 to 18. The two major items on the agenda were Palestine and minority rights, then the focus of attention of every major Jewish group throughout the world.

Most active were the various parties in existence during and after World War I. Demands for national rights for minorities were made by groups in many countries. A Russian Jewish Congress held a preliminary conference in Petrograd (Leningrad) in July 1917. Elections were held the following winter, but the unsettled conditions caused the organization to be dissolved. In its place a Jewish National Council was formed in 1918. In the Ukraine a Jewish National Council was formed on Oct. 1, 1917. In Kiev a Ukrainian Jewish Provisional National Assembly met in November 1918. A national council of Jewish national parties of German Austria was formed in Vienna in 1918. Representatives of Hungarian communities met at Temesvar on Dec. 15, 1918. In the same month a preliminary conference of Polish Jewish communal and city councils, meeting in Warsaw, decided to convene a congress in March 1919. A council commenced operation in Lithuania early that year. In Poznan a council was formed on Nov. 11, 1918. The *Canadian Jewish Congress, like all the abovementioned, adopted a strongly national resolution at its convention in March 1919. In Paris the Jewish delegations sent from various countries to the Peace Conference were unified after many meetings on March 25, 1919.

Fund raising and relief organizations sought to alleviate the suffering caused by Russian pogroms, the two world wars, the Nazi Holocaust, and the rebuilding of a national homeland. A host of other welfare, religious, civic, and educational organizations came into being. Foremost among the fund-raising agencies was the *United Jewish Appeal (1939) which in the United States combined the American Jewish Joint Distribution Committee (1914), the United Israel Appeal, and the New York Association for New Americans.

Another field of unprecedented conference activity is the Zionist movement, with its many factions and groups. After the First Zionist Congress in Basle in 1897 and the biennial congresses which followed several annual meetings, the movement proliferated into a complex array of organizations. There were differences along ideological lines, i.e., secularism versus religion, socialism of many varieties versus capitalism; many non-Zionist or anti-Zionist leanings emerged. Most countries have continued supporting branches of international or Israel-based agencies.

BIBLIOGRAPHY: Finkelstein, Middle Ages; O. Janowsky, *Jews and Minority Rights* (1933); Baron, Community, index, s.v. *Councils*; Elbogen, Century; Halpern, Pinkas; idem, *Takkanot Medinat Mehrin* (1952); M. Epstein, *Jewish Labor in U.S.A.* (1950); S. Federbush, *World Jewry Today* (1959); H.H. Ben-Sasson (ed.), *Toledot Am Yisrael*, 3 vols. (1969), index, s.v. *Asefot*; JYB; AJYB.

[Isaac Levitats]

CONFESSION. Along with admissions of fact from which any criminal responsibility may be inferred, confessions are not admissible as evidence in criminal or quasi-criminal proceedings, for "no man may call himself a wrongdoer" (Sanh. 9b). This rule against self-incrimination developed from the rule that a wrongdoer is incompetent as a *witness, being presumed to be unjust and untruthful (cf. Ex. 23:1). Since some people might admit to misconduct in order to disqualify themselves from testifying, to cure this mischief the rule was laid down that no man can be heard to say of himself that he is so guilty as to be an incompetent witness (Sanh. 25a; BK 72b). The rule was originally derived from the principle that no man is competent to testify in his own favor (Ket. 27a) – his confession being intended to confer the benefit of not being required to testify.

The rule against self-incrimination dates only from talmudic times. Several instances of confessions are recorded in the Bible (e.g., Josh. 7:19–20; II Sam. 1:16; cf. I Sam. 14:43), but these are dismissed by talmudic scholars either as confessions after trial and conviction, made for the sole purpose of expiating the sin before God (Sanh. 43b), or as exceptions to the general rule (*hora'at Sha'ah*; cf. Maim. comm. to the Mishnah, Sanh. 6:2; Ralbag to II Sam. 1:14). As all instances recorded in the Bible related to proceedings before kings or rulers, it may be that they did not consider themselves bound to observe regular court procedures (cf. Maim. Yad, Melakhim 3:10). Confessions are inadmissible not only in capital cases, but also in cases involving only *flogging, *fines (Rashi to Yev. 25b), or quasi-punishments (*ibid.*; cf. Resp.Rosh 11:5). Opinions are divided on whether a *ḥerem and public admonitions could be administered on the strength of a confession only.

Varying reasons were given for the rule against self-incrimination: the earliest and commonest is that the biblical requirement of the evidence of at least two witnesses for the condemnation of any man (Deut. 17:6; 19:15) implicitly excludes any other mode of proof (Tosef., Sanh. 11:1, 5). Maimonides adds that melancholy and depressed persons must be prevented from confessing to crimes which they have not committed so as to be put to death (Yad, Sanhedrin 18:6). Another theory was based on the prophet's words that all souls are God's (Ezek. 18:4), hence no man may be allowed to forfeit his life (as distinguished from his property) by his own admission, his life not being his own to dispose of but God's (David b. Solomon ibn Abi Zimra); still another scholar held that if confessions were accorded any probative value at all, courts might be inclined to overrate them, as King David did (II Sam. 1:16), and be guilty of a dereliction of their own fact-finding task (Joseph ibn Migash). A 19th-century jurist (Mordechai Epstein) pointed out that the real difference between civil admissions and criminal confessions was that by an admission an obligation was created which had only to be enforced by the court, whereas in a criminal conviction it is the court which creates the accused's liability to punishment. While it is nowhere expressed, the reason for the exclusion of confessions may well have been the desire to prevent their being elicited by torture or other violent means: it is a fact that – unlike most contemporaneous law books – neither Bible nor Talmud provide for any interrogation of the accused as part of the criminal trial, so that there was no room for attempts to extort confessions.

[Haim Hermann Cohn]

In the State of Israel

The question of reliance upon self-incriminating confessions has often arisen in the courts. In Cr.A. 614, 5561/80 *Al Bahiri v. State of Israel* 37 (3) PD 169, Justice M. Elon reviewed Jewish law on this question, stating that "Jewish law originally maintained that a defendant's self-incriminating confession was absolutely inadmissible, pursuant to the rule that 'since a person is related to himself, no one may incriminate himself [lit. 'a person cannot make himself out to be a wrongdoer]' (Yev. 25b). The confession of a crime was absolutely inadmissible, whether the accused confessed outside or in court, and even if there was corroboration. One could not be convicted unless there was sufficient evidence and testimony to the commission of the crime. During the course of time, with the changing needs of the times and of society, various changes were made towards easing the methods of proof in criminal law. Certain witnesses were deemed qualified who had previously been legally disqualified; and circumstantial evidence was held sufficient if it was strong and substantial. Within the framework of these major changes, it also became possible to convict a defendant on the basis of his confession (Resp. Rashba IV, 311), but the qualification was established that a defendant's confession alone was not sufficient unless, in addition, there had to be 'some measure of corroboration' to support the veracity of the confession: In such a case, it is the practice to accept the defendant's confession even in a capital case where there is no clear proof, in order that what he says, '*together with some measure of corroboration*, may clarify what occurred' (Resp. Ribash, 234)." The reluctance to rely upon self-incriminating confessions was due to the concern expressed by Maimonides that such a defendant may be subject to "inner pressure" to blame himself for a crime that someone else has committed: "Perhaps he is among the melancholy and depressed who wish to die [and] who thrust swords into their bellies or throw themselves down from the rooftops. Perhaps such a person will come and confess to a crime that he did not commit, in order that he may be killed" (Maim. Yad, Sanhedrin 18:6). In this case, one of the issues decided was that a failure to testify in court cannot be considered the "something in addition" which, added to the extrajudicial confession, suffices for conviction, the reason being that the very "inner pressure" that renders a confession unreliable without corroboration, may well be the basis for the defendant's unwillingness to testify in court. Moreover, in keeping with Jewish legal principles as they developed over time, the court suggested that the law be amended and that the "something in addition" required only in regard to extrajudicial confessions be also required in regard to confessions made in court. Justice Elon added that the danger of convicting an innocent man on the basis of his confession is very worrisome, and in this regard the principle was stated, "it is better and more desirable that a thousand guilty persons go free than that a single innocent person be put to death" (Maim. *Sefer ha Mitzvot*, Neg. Commandment, 290). In an earlier case that reviews Jewish law's stringent evidentiary requirements and mentions the above principle of Maimonides (Cr.A. 641, 622, 543/79 *Nagar et al. v. State of Israel*, 35 (1) PD 35 113), the question arose as to whether a conviction for murder could be based upon circumstantial evidence alone or upon an extrajudicial confession, supplemented by "something in addition." Here Justice Elon outlined the Jewish legal sources as they developed over time relating to circumstantial evidence, the admissibility of testimony of relations and of self-incriminating confessions, and showed, based on the responsa of Rashba (IV, 311) and Ribash (251, 234), that self-incriminating confessions, though inadmissible alone, could be admissible if supplemented by "something in addition." In a case at first instance in the Beersheba District Court (Cr.F. 76/93 *State of Israel v. Suleiman El Abid*), Judge N. Hendel, in a minority opinion, examined the sources of Jewish law relating to circumstantial evidence and the inadmissibility of self-incriminating confessions, linking this question, following U.S. Judge Douglas' statement that the Fifth Amendment (against self-incrimination) "is part of our respect for the dignity of man," with Israel's Basic Law: Human Dignity and Freedom, which is intended "to anchor in a basic law the values of the State of Israel as a Jewish and democratic state." Upon this foundation, the court discussed the admissibility of confessions in keeping with Jewish values, extensively examining the sources of Jewish law (Maim. Yad, Sanhedrin 18:6; Resp. Ribash, 233; Resp. Rashba III, 399; Radbaz on Sanh. 18, and R. Simeon Shkop on Ket. 18b, 5) that provide different reasons for the inadmissibility of self-incriminating confessions. The Ribash, in view of Jewish law's reservations as to ascetic behavior and its opposition to self-inflicted harm, questions the motive of one who wishes to confess; stating that it need be closely examined in case it is due to a self-destructive urge (cf. Maim. Yad, Sanhedrin 18:6) or a misplaced wish to placate the conscience. The Radbaz states that such a confession is ineffective as "his soul does not belong to him but rather to the Holy One, blessed be He" (see Ez. 18:4); thus a confession in regard to what is not his is of no effect. R. Shkop's reason for the inadmissibility of confessions is the danger that too great a weight would be ascribed to them since they seem to constitute strong evidence, with the result that the court would be dazzled and not reach a balanced judgment. However, over time in certain Jewish communities, the pressure of circumstances necessitated that confessions be admitted within the framework measures of exigency (Resp. Rashba III, 399) with the qualification that "something in addition" must supplement them (Resp. Ribash, 233). Finding the case exclusively based upon the defendant's confession, Justice Elon suggested adopting Jewish law's careful approach and in the absence of clear corroborative evidence ruled that El-Abid be acquitted. The difficulty of the case is apparent in its development: initially El-Abid was convicted (by majority) for murder and rape; on appeal to the Supreme Court, only the rape conviction remained (by majority), while in a further hearing, only the murder conviction was upheld (by majority). In another case (Cr.A. 168, 115/82 *Moadi v. State of Israel*, 38 (1) PD 197), Justice Elon held (257–65) that the rationale behind the requirement that a confession must be "voluntary" is solely to ensure the reliability and truth of the confession and that a judgment rendered in disregard of this would be contrary to the judge's duty to render a judgment that is "true to its very truth" (*din emet le-amito*) (Shab. 10a; Er. 54b; Meg. 15b; Sanh. 7a, 1 11b).

[Menachem Elon (2nd ed.)]

BIBLIOGRAPHY: ET, 1 (1951), 88–90, 225–7, 266; 7 (1956), 372; 8 (1957), 432–5; H. Cohn, in: *Journal of Criminal Law, Criminology and Police Science*, 51 (1960–61), 175–8; H.E. Baker, *Legal System of Israel* (1968), 226. **ADD. BIBLIOGRAPHY:** M. Elon, *Ha Mishpat ha-Ivri* (1988), 1:568f; 2:1465; idem, *Jewish Law* (1994), 2: 698; 4;1740; idem, *Jewish Law (Cases and Materials)* (1999), 206–12; A. Kirshenbaum, *Harsha'ah Aẓmit ba-Mishpat ha-Ivri* (2005).

CONFESSION OF SINS (Heb. וִדּוּי, *viddui*).

Biblical Literature

In the Bible, the confession of sin committed either individually or collectively is an essential prerequisite for expiation and atonement. Such confession is often followed by divine pardon. Thus the Lord mitigates His rebuke of Cain when the latter admits his sin (Gen. 4:13). David, censured by the prophet Nathan, confesses his iniquity in connection with Uriah and Bath-Sheba and is forgiven by God. David's confession and God's mercy are the subject of Psalms 32, 41, 51, and 69 in which God's righteousness is extolled. Other instances of individuals confessing their sins are Judah publicly acknowledging his inadvertent transgression with Tamar (Gen. 38:26; Sot. 7b); Achan, who had stolen from the forbidden spoils of Jericho, at the exhortation of Joshua avowing his sin (Josh. 7:19–21); and Saul asking forgiveness for having contravened God's commandment and permitted the people to retain Amalekite booty (I Sam. 15:24–25). Examples of biblical confessions for the nation, made by the leaders of the people, are Moses after the worship of the golden calf (Ex. 32:31), the high priest's confession on the Day of *Atonement (Lev. 16:6, 11, 21), and Ezra's (9:6, 7, 15) and Nehemiah's (1:6, 7; 9:2, 33–35).

The various sin and guilt offerings prescribed by the sacrificial ritual had to be preceded by confession. The sacrifice was brought to the altar by the offender who confessed his transgressions while placing both hands upon the head of the sacrificial animal (Lev. 1:4; Maim. Yad, Ma'aseh ha-Korbanot 3:6, 14–15). No formula for the exact wording of these confessions is given in the Bible; the Mishnah, however, records the confession of the high priest on the Day of Atonement: "O God, I have committed iniquity, transgressed, and sinned before Thee, I and my house. O God, forgive the iniquities and transgressions and sins which I have committed and transgressed and sinned before Thee, I and my house, as it is written in the Law of Thy servant Moses, 'For on this day shall atonement be made for you, to cleanse you; from all your sins shall ye be clean before the Lord'" (Lev. 16:30; Yoma 3:8).

Rabbinic Literature and Synagogue Ritual

Maimonides, basing his views on biblical and rabbinic traditions, ruled that it is a positive injunction to confess one's sins before seeking atonement: "Whether it is a positive or negative commandment which the individual has disobeyed, either willingly or inadvertently, it is a positive precept for him to confess the sin when desirous of repenting…." (Maim. Yad, Teshuvah 1:1). Confession of sin became an integral part of the synagogue ritual. It is especially characteristic of the Day of Atonement where the supplication for forgiveness of sin forms the focal point of the service. Although, according to the Talmud, the simple statement "Truly, we have sinned" (Yoma 87b) is sufficient for confession, elaborate formulas have gradually evolved, the earliest dating back to the third century C.E. One such formula composed for the eve of the Day of Atonement reads, "I confess all the evil I have done before Thee; I stood in the way of evil; and as for all (the evil) I have done, I shall no more do the like; may it be Thy will, O Lord my God, that Thou shouldst pardon me for all my iniquities, and forgive me for all my transgressions, and grant me atonement for all my sins" (Lev. R. 3:3); while another states: "My God, before I was formed, I was of no worth, and now that I have been formed, it is as if I had not been formed. I am dust in my life, how much more in my death. Behold I am before Thee like a vessel full of shame and reproach. May it be Thy will that I sin no more, and what I have sinned wipe away in Thy mercy, but not through suffering" (Yoma 87b).

Ashamnu ("We have incurred guilt"), a confession of sin listing sins in alphabetical order known as *Viddui Katan* ("Small Confession"), and **Al Ḥet* ("For the sin which we have committed before Thee"), known as *Viddui Gadol* ("Great Confession"), are first mentioned in geonic liturgy. To the sins enumerated, additions have gradually been made to include all possible transgressions, since the repentant individual may have forgotten some of the sins which he is required to mention explicitly. Confessions, being formulated as communal prayers, are thus recited in the first person plural, "We have sinned, transgressed, and rebelled," and a worshiper may confess all the sins stated even when certain that he did not commit some of them (Isserles to Sh. Ar., OḤ 607:2). These confessional prayers are not only recited on the Day of Atonement, they also form part of the **Seliḥot* services during the weeks preceding the Day of Atonement. Under the influence of the Kabbalah, *Ashamnu* was introduced into the daily service; in the Sephardi-Oriental, the Italian, and the Yemenite rites it is recited on Mondays and Thursdays only, and in the ḥasidic rite daily. The former custom is observed in most Israeli synagogues. Conservative and Reform rites have retained the confession-of-sins prayers, particularly as part of the High Holidays services.

Individual Confessions

Confession of sins also extends beyond the synagogal sphere and can be said by individuals during silent prayer and on diverse occasions. Confession, whether collective or individual, is always made directly to God and never through an intermediary, but some 16th-century kabbalist ascetics confessed sins to each other. The most important occasion for individual confession is on the deathbed. The Talmud advises that a person who is seriously ill should be exhorted to confess his sins (Shab. 32a), and a criminal about to be executed is also urged to confess. If he is unable to compose his own confession, he is prompted to say, "May my death be an expiation for all my sins" (Sanh. 6:2), and when he is too weak to recite the confession, it should be read to him (Shab. 32a). While no special form of deathbed confession existed in ancient times, a formula has become customary (see *Death). The dying person, if he is still conscious and has the strength to do so, recites the Day of Atonement confession in the singular. A brief confession, formulated in the 13th century but which is of much earlier origin, is also recited (Hertz, Prayer, 1064). It is also customary for a bridegroom to recite the Day of Atonement confession at the afternoon service before his wedding, with the wedding day being considered a sort of judgment day for the bride and groom.

BIBLIOGRAPHY: Baer, Seder, 415–21; Elbogen, Gottesdienst, 149–51; Idelsohn, Liturgy, 111f., 228f.; E. Levy *Yesodot ha-Tefillah* (1952²), 12–17; E. Munk, *The World of Prayer*, 2 (1963), 239–50; ET, 11 (1965), 412–55.

CONFINO, MICHAEL (1926–), Israeli historian. Confino's research work encompasses social, economic, and intellectual history, with emphasis on comparative history, agrarian problems, collective psychology of social groups, the structure of societies under the Old Regime, the revolutionary movements, and the evolution of the Jewish community in Bulgaria. He was born in Sofia, Bulgaria, and immigrated to Israel in 1948. From 1951 until 1953 he was *aliyah* emissary in North Africa and in 1960 in the U.S.S.R. He studied at the University of Sofia, the Hebrew University of Jerusalem, and the Sorbonne. In 1959 he joined the Faculty of Humanities of the Hebrew University and was the founder and the first chairman of the Department of Russian Studies from 1964 until 1969. In 1970 he joined Tel Aviv University and founded the Russian and East European Research Center and was its first director between 1970 and 1977. From 1980 until 1995 he held the Samuel Rubin Chair of Russian and East European History and Civilization. He was visiting professor at many universities in the United States, France, and Italy. During his academic years, Confino was president of the Israel Association for Slavic Studies, a member of the executive committee of the International Association for Slavic and East European Studies, vice chairman of the executive board and member of the scientific committee of the Yitzhak Rabin Center for Israel studies, president of the Scientific Council, and member of the Israel Academy of Sciences and Humanities. He was also involved in the Documents of Soviet History series (1995–2004). Confino wrote numerous books and scholarly articles, including *Domaines et Seineurs en Russie à la Fin du XVIIIe Siècle* (1963), *Daughter of a Revolutionary: Natalie Herzen and the Bakunin-Nechaev Circle* (1974), *Il Catechismo del Rivoluzionario* (1986), *From Saint-Petersburg to Leningrad: Essays in Russian History* (in Hebrew, 1993), and *The Power of Words and the Frailty of Reason: Propaganda, Incitement and Freedom of Speech* (Heb., 2002). In 1993 he was awarded the Israel Prize in history and in 2003 he was awarded the EMET Prize for art, science, and culture.

[Shaked Gilboa (2nd ed.)]

CONFISCATION, EXPROPRIATION, FORFEITURE. Confiscation is mentioned once in the Bible as a quasi-criminal sanction against disobedience to lawful orders (Ezra 10:8). Relying on this precedent, the rule was enunciated that courts are empowered to expropriate (*hefker bet din*; Git. 36b, Yev. 89b); and the power of the courts to impose pecuniary penalties – apart from fines, the amounts of which are already prescribed (e.g., Ex. 21:32; Deut. 22: 19, 29) – is derived from this general power of expropriation (MK 16a). This power was regarded as necessary, as the authority given to Ezra and his courts to impose pecuniary punishments (Ezra 7:26 – rendered in the AV as punishment of "confiscation of goods") is presumed to have derived from Persian and not from Jewish law. Thus, even legally prescribed penalties were already increased by talmudic courts in severe cases, e.g., for recidivists (BK 96b); and in post-talmudic times ample use was made of this expropriatory power in the judicial campaign against lawlessness and violence (Maim. Yad, Sanhedrin 24:6; ḤM 2). A talmudic source seems to indicate that semi-confiscatory powers for punitive purposes could also be vested in non-judicial authorities, e.g., a Temple inspector who found a guard asleep on duty was authorized to burn his clothing (Mid. 1:2), an authority said to be derived from the expropriatory powers of the courts (*Piskei ha-Rosh, ibid.*). In later times it was held by some scholars that the townsfolk (*benei ha-ir*) or the seven notables (*shivah tuvei ha-ir*), exercising both legislative and quasi-judicial functions in the prevention of and fight against crime, were by virtue of this expropriatory power also customarily authorized to impose pecuniary sanctions (*Rema* ḤM 2).

Judicial expropriations were not, however, confined to criminal or quasi-criminal sanctions. They were also used for public utility purposes on the authority of Joshua and the elders of his time who redistributed the land among the tribes and families (Josh. 19:51). Such redistribution presupposed not only the power to divest an owner of some of his property, but also the power to vest that property in someone else – while punitive confiscations need not, according to some scholars, result in the confiscated property being vested in anybody else (*Shitah Mekubbeẓet* BK 100a). But while punitive confiscation presupposes some guilt or blameworthiness on the part of the owner (Tos. to Yev. 90a), public utility expropriations could also lawfully deprive innocent persons of their property (Resp. Akiva Eger 105). In the perspective of legal history, the most important use made of the expropriatory powers of the court was quasi-legislative. This use is best illustrated by some examples: thus, the legal rule that a lost chattel is to be returned to the claimant although he cannot formally prove his ownership, provided he satisfies the finder as to his bona fides by means of tokens (distinctive marks, *simanim*), was explained as an expropriation by the court of any rights in the chattel in favor of the claimant (BM 27b and Rashi *ibid.*). Also, a disposition by a son of his father's property before the latter's death, in payment of his father's debts or other responsibilities, was validated as an authorized disposition of money expropriated by the court for these purposes (BM 16a). Dispositions by infants of property in their hands were – if they were to their benefit – validated as authorized dispositions of expropriated property vested in the court, where the infants were legally incapable of disposing of their own property (Git. 59a and Tos. to Git. 40b s.v. וכתב). Hillel's famous law reform, the Prosbul, which made all debts recoverable notwithstanding their remission under biblical law (Deut. 15:2), was later sought to be explained and justified by the expropriatory powers of the court (Git. 36–37). In all these (and many similar) cases, the expropriatory powers of the court were invoked in theory only, by way of legal fiction, and mostly ex post facto: the rules were not established by their actual exercise by any given court but were explained and justified by the mere existence of those powers, which, had they actually been exercised in any particular case calling for the application of the rules, could have brought about the desired result (see also *takkanot).

These powers were also used to do justice in particular and individual cases: for instance, by purporting to expropriate an amount of money from a defendant and vesting it in a plaintiff, the court exercised a jurisdiction based on law, even where there was no law under which the plaintiff could have claimed that money (cf. Maim. Yad, Sanhedrin 24:6). Or, marriages lawfully contracted which could not (but should) otherwise be dissolved – as, e.g., the marriage of a girl abducted from under her canopy (see *Abduction) – were invalidated by retroactively expropriating from the bridegroom the money (the ring) with which he had married the bride (Yev. 110a, cf. Yev. 90b). Similarly, it was sought to validate the will of a wife, if she bequeathed her estate to a third party, by retroactively expropriating the husband's right to inherit from his wife (Resp. Asheri 55:10). A judgment already enforced, though founded on an error, was upheld because of the special circumstances of that case, on the strength of the expropriatory powers of the court (*Tummim* 25; *Milḥamot* Yev. 37b). The same consideration may have led the court to leave a widow in undisturbed possession of her husband's estate, which she had unlawfully but in good faith appropriated to herself (TJ, Ket. 9:3, 33a and Kid. 1:3, 159d).

Finally, there are expropriatory powers vested in the king (or other head of the state; cf. Ezek. 45:8 and 46:18). According to biblical law, these powers appear to have been unlimited (cf. Eccles. 2:4 and 8; I Sam. 8:14), whereas under talmudic law they were limited to the king's military and road-building requirements, although the king alone decided what these requirements were (Sanh. 2:4). The story that Ahab could not buy Naboth's vineyard without the owner's consent and had to have recourse to unlawful means to attain it (I Kings 21) is explained by some scholars to the effect that since he could not purchase the land, as was his desire, in view of the refusal of Naboth to sell, he exercised his legal right of confiscation (*Haggahot Maimoniyyot* to Melakhim 4:6). Nevertheless, the claim of the king to the vineyard after Naboth's death could not be based on the royal right to forfeiture of lands and goods of persons executed by royal decree, because Naboth was executed by judicial process and as such his lawful heirs inherited (Sanh. 48b). The claim of Ahab is therefore made to depend on the fact that as a nephew of Naboth, he was in fact such an heir (Tosef., Sanh. 4:6). The law was eventually codified to the effect that the king was not allowed to confiscate money or goods (and, *a fortiori*, lands) without paying compensation for them, and if he did confiscate without this, it was sheer plunder (Maim. Yad, Melakhim 3:8); for everything that he expropriated he had to pay fair compensation (*ibid.*, 4:3, 6).

In modern legal terminology, "confiscation" and "forfeiture" usually indicate expropriations without compensation (such as smuggled goods), while the term "expropriation" is normally reserved for acquisitions for public purposes against payment of compensation.

BIBLIOGRAPHY: S. Assaf, *Ha-Onshin Aḥarei Ḥatimat ha-Talmud* (1922), nos. 141, 150, 157, 163; S. Zeitlin, in: JQR, 39 (1948/49), 6f.; ET, 3 (1951), 173; 8 (1957), 343; 10 (1961), 95–110; J.M. Ginzberg, *Mishpatim le-Yisrael* (1956), 39f., 85–87; H. Cohn, in: *Essays in Jurisprudence in Honor of Roscoe Pound* (1962), 65–68, 77f.; idem, in: *Divrei ha-Congress ha-Olami ha-Revi'i le-Madda'ei ha-Yahadut*, 1 (1967), 185–8, English abstract 267.

[Haim Hermann Cohn]

CONFLICT OF LAWS (also called Private International Law) is a branch of the law dealing with the adjudication of a matter which involves some foreign element, for instance, the fact that one of the parties is a foreign citizen, or that the matter at issue arose, wholly or in part, in another country – as in the case of a contract signed in one country and breached in another – and the like. Where there is a conflict of laws, two main questions arise: does the forum in question have jurisdiction to deal with the matter; if it has jurisdiction, what law shall be chosen to apply to the matter? The choice of laws available to the forum include the following main possibilities: (1) The personal law (*lex personalis*) by which the plaintiff or defendant is governed; the personal law may be determined either by the law of the party's place of domicile (*lex domicilii*) or by his national law (*lex ligeantiae*); (2) the law of the place where obligation was established, for instance, the place where the contract was concluded (*lex actus; lex loci contractus*); (3) the law of the place where the legal act is to be carried out, for instance, the fulfillment of a contract (*lex loci solutionis*); (4) the law of the place of situation of the property forming the subject matter of the dispute (*lex situs*); (5) the law of the place of situation of the forum seized of the dispute (*lex fori*). (See A.V. Dicey and J.H.C. Morris, 1967/8.)

This entry is arranged according to the following outline:

In Jewish Law
Multiplicity of Legal Rules
CONCERNING THE LAWS OF MARRIAGE
CONCERNING THE LAWS OF DIVORCE
CONCERNING LABOR LAW
CONCERNING THE LAWS OF PARTNERSHIP, LAND TENANCY (*ARISUT*), ETC.
Conflict of a Factual-Legal Nature
CONCERNING BONDS OF INDEBTEDNESS
CONCERNING THE *KETUBBAH*
Jewish and Non-Jewish Parties to the Same Suit
Conflict of Laws: Principles Where the Foreign Law Is Applicable
DISTINGUISHING BETWEEN MATERIAL AND PROCEDURAL LAW
LEX DOMICILII AS OPPOSED TO *LEX SITUS*

In Jewish Law

The subject of the conflict of laws is not a defined branch of Jewish law. This is attributable to a substantive quality of Jewish law, namely that it is a personal law purporting to apply to each and every Jew, wherever he may be – even if outside the territorial bounds of Jewish sovereignty or autonomy. For this reason the mere fact that a contract is concluded in one country but is to be fulfilled in another is of no consequence in Jewish law. Moreover, Jewish law – for the substantially greater part of its history – has functioned as a legal system generally enjoying Jewish judicial autonomy but not Jewish political sovereignty (see **Mishpat Ivri*); the result has been that in suits before the Jewish courts both parties have usually been Jews, with little occasion for questions of conflict of laws to arise in relation to the personalities of the litigants (although there are isolated *halakhot* in this regard; see below).

Nevertheless, the fundamental problems that arise in the field of the conflict of laws occur also in Jewish law, in which they derive from two material phenomena of this legal system. One is the multiplicity of diverse customs in regard to the same subject, a fact expressed in the doctrine, "all is in accordance with the custom of the country" (*ha-kol lefi minhag ha-medinah*; see below). This multiplicity was already in evidence in talmudic times and became increasingly pronounced from the 10th century onward, when in the different centers of Jewish life hegemony was no longer exercised by a single center over the whole Diaspora, thus leading to the enactment of numerous local ordinances (see **Takkanot*, especially *Takkanot ha-Kahal*), to the spread of new *customs, and to much local decision (see Mishpat Ivri). The natural outcome of this phenomenon was the problem of choosing between the different laws, for instance, when the matter at issue arose partly in one place and partly in another, not between Jewish law and other law, but between diverse customs and *takkanot* within the Jewish legal system. The second phenomenon which brought about the problem of conflict of laws in Jewish law has been the contact between Jewish law and secular law; from this contact there evolved the doctrine of *dina de-malkhuta dina ("the law of the land is law"), and pursuant to it the creation of a number of rules pertaining to the field of the conflict of laws.

Multiplicity of Legal Rules

The existence of varying rules deriving from different customs and *takkanot* on a particular legal subject is to be found in various fields of the law. Wherever this reality exists and the various stages of a legal obligation have to be fulfilled in different places where varying rules are practiced in regard to such obligation, the question arises whether to apply to the obligation, the law that is customary at the place and time of its establishment, or that which is customary at the place and time of its fulfillment, or any other law.

CONCERNING THE LAWS OF MARRIAGE. Even in ancient times varying local customs had evolved and were practiced concerning the pecuniary relations between spouses. In regard to the amount of *dowry, R. Simeon b. Gamaliel adopted the rule of "all in accordance with the custom of the country" (Ket. 6:4), and the *halakhah*, with reference to both the *ketubbah* and the dowry, was determined as follows: "a marriage without condition is transacted in accordance with the custom of the country; also the wife who has agreed to contribute (i.e., a dowry to her husband) must do so in accordance with the custom of the country, and when she comes to recover her *ketubbah* she recovers what is contained therein in accordance with the custom of the country; in all these and similar matters the custom of the country is an important principle and must be followed, but such custom must be widespread throughout the country" (Yad, Ishut 23:12; Sh. Ar., EH 66:11). Thus there were different customs concerning a widow's right to lodging and *maintenance from the estate; the custom in Jerusalem and Galilee was to make the continuation of this right a matter of the widow's choice, and only if she preferred to claim her *ketubbah* would her right to maintenance and lodging become forfeited; in Judea the custom was to leave the choice with the deceased's heirs, and if they offered to pay the widow's *ketubbah*, she would forfeit the right to maintenance and lodging (Ket. 4:12); the people of Babylonia and environs followed the custom of the Judeans, and those of Nehardea and environs followed the custom of the Jerusalemites and Galileans (Ket. 54a).

This diversity of custom created problems relating to the conflict of laws. In the case of a woman of Maḥoza (in Babylonia) who was married to a man from the area of Nehardea, it was decided that she was governed by the law as customary in Nehardea, i.e., that the deceased's heirs could not deprive her of her rights by paying her *ketubbah* as mentioned (Ket. 54a). In a case in the 13th century, husband and wife were from separate towns and married in a third town; in each of the three places different customs prevailed concerning the financial obligations between spouses. Since the latter had not themselves defined these in the *ketubbah*, Solomon b. Abraham Adret decided that the custom to be followed in their case was that of the place of celebration of the marriage, if that was where they intended to live, otherwise the custom of the place where they intended to live; if they had not decided on the place of residence, the custom at the place where the husband was resident was to be followed, since in law the husband determines the place of residence (Tosef., Ket. 13:2; Ket. 110a–b) – "for he marries in accordance with the conditions at his own place of residence, whereto he takes her" (Resp. Rashba, vol. 1, no. 662 and cf. vol. 3, no. 433). The same conclusion was reached by other scholars on the basis of the talmudic rule concerning the woman of Maḥoza who married a man from Nehardea (Nov.Ritba, Ket. 54a; see also *Beit Yosef* EH 66, toward the concl.; Resp. Maharashdam, ḤM no. 327) and thus the *halakhah* was decided – "if a person married a woman from a certain place with the intention that she live with him at his place, the custom of his place is to be followed" (*Rema* to EH 66:12). In a 17th century decision it was determined that since the amount of the *ketubbah* was 500 gold coins in Lithuania and 400 gold coins in Poland, "the custom of the place of marriage is not followed but only that of the place of domicile" (*Ḥelkat Meḥokek* 66, n. 46 and *Beit Shemu'el* 66, n. 27); moreover, the customary law of their chosen *domicile was held to be applicable to the parties even if they had agreed that they would settle there two or three years after their marriage (*ibid.*, 66, n. 46), and opinions were divided on the question whether to follow the custom of the place of marriage or that of the place of intended domicile in the event that the husband died before their having settled in the latter place (*ibid.; Beit Shemu'el*, 66, n. 27).

Some scholars held the opinion that the customary law of the place of celebration of the marriage governs the financial obligations between spouses: "a matter must be dealt with only according to [the law of] the place where the *ketubbah* was written, the husband having only undertaken liability therefore in accordance with the law of such place" (Resp. Ribash, no. 105). It was similarly decided in regard to differing customs deriving from the different communal *takkanot* relating to heritage of the dowry on the wife's death: "in all places local custom is followed, and even if they did not stipulate at the time of marriage, they are considered to have done so, for everyone who marries does so in accordance with the custom; even if he went to a place where the custom of the communities is not practiced, the law of the place where he married her is followed" (*Rema* to EH 118:19, based on Resp. Ribash, no. 105). Clearly, if the parties expressly stipulated that the custom of the husband's place of residence be followed, their position would be governed accordingly (see *Ḥelkat Meḥokek* to EH 118:19 and *Beit Shemu'el*, 118 n. 26, in which manner the apparent contradiction between Isserles' statements, here and in EH 66:12, is reconciled).

A dispute waged between prominent 16th-century scholars centered around the claim of Hannah Gracia Mendes – one of the *anusim (Marranos) from Portugal who had reached Turkey, where they openly reembraced Judaism – for half of her husband's estate, in accordance with the custom in Portugal, the place of celebration of the marriage. The dispute concerned the validity of an undertaking made at the time of marriage which was not celebrated in accordance with Jewish law; otherwise, however, all agreed that she was entitled to succeed in her claim in accordance with the law in practice in Portugal even if this was not the law in Turkey where the hearing took place (*Avkat Rokhel*, nos. 80–81; Resp. Maharashdam, ḤM no. 327; Resp. Maharibal 2:23; see also Civil Appeal 100/49, in *Pesakim shel Beit ha-Mishpat ha-Elyon*, 6 (1951/52), 140ff.). In Israel the rabbinical court has accepted the opinion of the scholars who held that the law of the place of celebration of the marriage must be applied – even if on the basis of *halakhah* the marriage is invalid. In the case of a Jewish couple who had emigrated from Russia, having been married in Russia in a *civil marriage ceremony only, in 1942, and were seeking a divorce before the above court, it decided that their common property should be divided in accordance with the law in practice in Russia in 1942 regarding the division of property between separated spouses (PDR 5:124ff.; see M. Elon, *Ḥakikah Datit* (1968), 169–72).

Some of the scholars dealing with the Mendes matter (see above) determined, as a matter of principle, that all contracts and acquisitions of property (*kinyanim*; see *Contract and *Acquisition), made among the Marranos themselves, in accordance with the general law of their land, were to have legal validity, even after the Marranos' open return to Judaism. One of the reasons advanced for this far-reaching determination was the fact of the Marranos' interest, for the sake of proper order in business matters, in ensuring that all their commercial and economic transactions have full legal validity – "and this is as a fixed custom among them, overriding the *halakhah*" (Mabit, in *Avkat Rokhel*, no. 80; see also **Minhag*). Of particular interest is a reason advanced by Samuel de Modena, paralleling one of the general principles in the field of the conflict of laws: "for if it were otherwise, none of the *anusim* who came from there [from Portugal and Spain to Turkey] would be able to live; if the transactions they had with each other there in accordance with local custom but not according to the law of the Torah, were now reopened; this is plainly inconceivable; as regards everything that was done there, we must say: what is done is done, from now on a new reckoning" (Resp. Maharashdam, ḤM no. 327).

CONCERNING THE LAWS OF *DIVORCE. An illustration of the conflict of laws in the above field, arising in Spain in the 13th century in regard to a *takkanah* prohibiting the divorce of a wife against her will, is to be found in the responsa collection of Solomon b. Adret (vol. 4, no. 186). At that time this *takkanah* was not followed everywhere in Spain, and the question arose whether a wife could be divorced against her will in the event that the *takkanah* was in force at the place of celebration of their marriage but not at the place to which they later moved – where the divorce proceedings were taking place – Solomon b. Adret replied: "for anyone marrying at a place where a wife cannot be divorced except with her consent is so bound, and he marries her in the knowledge that he cannot divorce her except with her consent … and even if he takes her away from the place of their marriage … to another place, he may not divorce her except in accordance with the custom of the place of their marriage."

CONCERNING *LABOR LAW. In this field, too, there evolved different local customs, and the rule, "all in accordance with the custom of the country," (BM 7:1) was applied with particular reliance on the principle that "custom overrides the *halakhah*" (TJ, BM 7:1; see also *Minhag). This diversity naturally led to cases of conflicting laws. The Mishnah records that there were places where it was customary for laborers to go to work early in the morning and return late in the evening, while in other places they did not set out so early or return so late (BM 7:1). In the Jerusalem Talmud it is stated that it was not customary for the people of Tiberias to start early and finish late, but this was the case with the people of Beth-Maon; it was stipulated that residents of Tiberias hired as laborers in Beth-Maon must act in accordance with the custom in Beth-Maon and laborers from Beth-Maon hired in Tiberias must act in accordance with the custom in Tiberias – i.e., that the determining law is the law of the place of fulfillment of the obligation; nevertheless, if an employer from Tiberias should hire in Beth-Maon laborers to work in Tiberias, they must start early and finish late according to the custom in Beth-Maon because the fact that the employer does not hire laborers in Tiberias, but comes specially to Beth-Maon for this purpose, proves his intention to find laborers who will start early and finish late, and it is as if he expressly agreed to such effect (TJ, BM 7:1).

CONCERNING THE LAWS OF PARTNERSHIP, LAND TENANCY (ARISUT), ETC. Instances of differing and conflicting customs are mentioned also in fields of the civil law such as partnership (BB 1:1, 2), lease, and land tenancy in return for a share of the crop (*arisut*; BM 9:1), etc. (see *Lease and Hire). In these cases too it was laid down that the custom of the place where the obligation is established must be followed (Resp. Rashba, vol. 1, no. 662). Of interest is the conflict of laws principle laid down in a responsum of Simeon b. Ẓemaḥ Duran, 14th-century scholar of North Africa, in relation to a business partnership (*Tashbeẓ* 2:226). A dispute between one partner and the others concerning distribution of the partnership profits was brought before "a certain merchant who adjudicated between them," i.e., a lay judge adjudicating in accordance with the trade custom and not Jewish law. In an appeal before Duran against this decision, Duran held that the merchant's judgment did not conform with that required to be given in accordance with Jewish law; the contention of the partners who succeeded in the first instance, that the matter was originally brought before a merchant-judge in accordance with the local trade custom and that his decision was binding on the parties, was answered by Duran to this effect: the custom in question, although followed in the locality where the partners then found themselves, was not in existence at the place where the partnership was established, hence the local custom of the former place, i.e., the place of operation of the partnership, was not to be applied to their case, but the matter had to be dealt with in accordance with the custom at the place of establishment of the partnership.

Confict of a Factual-Legal Nature

A conflict of laws, in the wider sense of the term, may arise not only when there are in operation divergent legal methods at the various stages of an obligation, but also when there exists, at these various stages, a divergence of legal facts.

CONCERNING BONDS OF INDEBTEDNESS. When a bond specifies a particular currency which is in circulation in two countries, but its value is greater in one country than in the other, the rule is that the amount stated is payable in accordance with the value of the currency in the country where the bond was drawn up and not its value in the country where the bond is presented for payment: "When a person seeks to recover payment of a bond from his neighbor, then, if it is recorded as having been written in Babylonia – he recovers in Babylonian currency; if in Ereẓ Israel, he recovers in the currency of Ereẓ Israel; if there is no qualification in the bond, then, if he seeks to recover in Babylonia – he recovers in Babylonian currency, and if he seeks to recover in Ereẓ Israel – he recovers in the currency of Ereẓ Israel" (Tosef., Ket. 13 (12):3 and BB 11:3; according to the version in Ket. 110b; Yad, Malveh 17:9; Sh. Ar., ḤM 42:14). The *posekim* were divided based on the reasoning for the second part of the above rule; some of them expressed the opinion that the bond is recovered according to the currency value at the place where the bond is presented for payment, because it is presumed that the bond was drawn up at the place where it is presented for payment; but if the presumption is rebutted, by proof that the bond was drawn up elsewhere, it will be payable according to the currency value at the latter place (Yad and Sh. Ar., loc. cit.; *Sefer ha-Terumot* 54:1); other *posekim* explained the rule on the basis that in the circumstances in question, the parties intentionally omit any mention in the bond of the place where it is drawn up in order that the amount be payable according to the currency value at the place where the bond shall be presented for payment, and, according to this explanation, the currency value will always be as determined at the place of presentation of the bond for payment (Ran to Alfasi, end of Ketubbot; pupils of R. Jonah, in *Shitah Mekubbeẓet*, Ket. 110b; Nov. Ritba Ket. 110b; see also *Kesef Mishneh* Malveh 17:9; *Rema* ḤM 42:14 and *Siftei Kohen* thereto, n. 34).

CONCERNING THE KETUBBAH. A similar problem was discussed in relation to payment of the amount specified in the *ketubbah*, in a case where the parties had married in Ereẓ Israel and were being divorced in Cappadocia (a country in Asia Minor which was famous for its coin mint – see S. Lieberman, *Tosefta ki-Feshutta*, 6 (1967), 389), and the same currency was in circulation in both countries, although at different values (Ket. 13:11; see also Tosef., Ket. 110b and BB 11:3). The scholars who differed from R. Simeon b. Gamaliel were of the opinion that the *ketubbah* and a bond of indebtedness were subject to different rules (Ket. 13:11). In regard to the substance of the difference, the opinions stated in the Jerusalem Talmud differ from those in the Babylonian Talmud. According to the former, the value of the currency was higher in Ereẓ Israel than in Cappadocia, and in respect of the *ketubbah* – a right of the wife flowing from the Torah, according to these scholars – the scholars were always careful to see that it was received by the wife according to the higher value, i.e., according to the value in Ereẓ Israel, even if the marriage took place in Cappadocia (TJ, Ket. 13:11). In the Babylonian Talmud it is held that the currency value was lower in Ereẓ Israel than in Cappadocia, and as far as concerned the *ketubbah* – in the opinion of these scholars a right given the wife by rabbinic enactment and not law (see *Oral Law and Written Law (*Torah)) – it was more leniently regarded by the scholars than any other bond of indebtedness, and therefore it was held to be payable in accordance with the currency in Ereẓ Israel, i.e., according to the lower value, even if the marriage took place in Cappadocia (Ket. 110b). R. Simeon's opinion, according to both Talmuds, was that the *ketubbah* was subject to the same law as any other bond of indebtedness (according to the Babylonian Talmud because in his view the *ketubbah* was an obligation of biblical law; according to the Jerusalem Talmud because it was an obligation of rabbinical law), and it was always necessary to pay according to the currency value at the place of establishment of the obligation, i.e., the place where the marriage took place.

It may be noted that the same problem was discussed in principle in relation to other halakhic matters. Thus it was established that a person transporting – other than in Jerusalem – second tithe fruits from a cheaper to a more expensive area, or vice versa, had to redeem the fruits according to their value at the place of redemption and not as valued at the place from which they were brought (Ma'as. Sh. 4:1; see also Ned. 8:4 in TB and TJ; see also *Domicile). For the validity of documents drawn up in non-Jewish courts, see *Shetar.

Jewish and Non-Jewish Parties to the Same Suit

According to a *baraita* of the talmudic law, if in a suit between a Jew and a gentile, before a Jewish court, there exists the possibility of favoring the Jew either according to the general law or according to the Jewish law, then this should be done by the court (BK 113a; cf. Sif. Deut. 16; Yad, Melakhim 10:12). This *halakhah* is quoted in the Talmud in the context of heavy and arbitrary tax quotas imposed on the Jews (see *Taxation); it is also to be understood as a reciprocal measure, i.e., as a reaction to the unequal treatment afforded Jews in the gentile courts (in like manner to the *halakhah* in BK 4:3, see BK 38a – "because they did not take upon themselves the seven *Noachide laws"; see also Albeck and other commentators to the Mishnah and *Gemara*, loc. cit.). Thus in the 13th century it was laid down that "at any rate this [the foregoing] was not said in regard to those who follow a defined religious faith; if they come before us to be adjudged, their way shall not be barred in the slightest manner, but the law shall cleave the mountain, whether in his favor or against him" (i.e., whether in favor of the Jewish or gentile party – *Beit ha-Beḥirah* BK 38a; and this is also the interpretation given in other similar cases: *Beit ha-Beḥirah* BK 37b–38a and Av. Zar., 3a, 6b, 22a, 26a). This talmudic *halakhah* is still quoted in Maimonides' *Mishneh Torah* but in the later Codes, such as the *Arba'ah Turim* and the Shulḥan Arukh it is not mentioned at all. The very discussion of this *halakhah* ceased to be of any practical significance since the non-Jewish party was not subject to the jurisdiction of the Jewish courts and acted in accordance with the general law (in many places the central government would appoint a special judge to deal with suits between Jews and non-Jews; see, e.g., Baer, Spain, 1 (1961), 51, 83, 87, 115, 131, 310; 2 (1966), 66; *Beit Yisrael be-Polin*, ed. by I. Heilprin, 1 (1948), 58f.).

From various talmudic *halakhot* it may be deduced that in a legal transaction involving both a Jewish and a non-Jewish party, the latter acted in accordance with the foreign law – a fact that was calculated, in certain cases, to influence the manner in which the issue was decided. Thus the following problem is discussed in the Talmud: the debtor dies leaving *orphans; thereupon the surety pays the creditor before notifying the orphans of the fact of payment and then seeks to recoup this payment from the orphans (see *Suretyship). The surety's haste in paying the debt without prior approach to the orphans arouses suspicion of a conspiracy, i.e., the possibility that the debtor had paid the debt before he died in order to avoid a claim against the orphans, and that the surety and creditor conspired to recover the debt a second time, from the orphans, so as to share the money (BB 174b). In the course of the talmudic discussion the opinion is expressed that the above-mentioned suspicion only arises in the event that the creditor is a Jew, for the reason that in Jewish law the creditor must first have recourse to the debtor – hence the debtor's fear that the creditor might have recourse to the orphans and his decision to forestall this possibility by paying the debt; however, in the case of a non-Jewish creditor, there would be no reason to suspect that the debtor paid the debt during his lifetime, since according to Persian law, to which the creditor was subject, the latter might have direct recourse to the surety, and the debtor would know that the creditor was going to do so and not have recourse to the orphans (BB 174b; the contrary opinion expressed here also takes cognizance of the fact that in Persian law the creditor may claim directly from the surety). Hence it was decided, in Spain in the 14th century, that when the law applicable to the non-Jewish creditor is identical to Jewish law, the case of the latter will be no different from that of a Jewish creditor (*Maggid Mishneh* Malveh 26:6). Also recorded is the case of a non-Jew who hypothecated his courtyard to a Jew, which he then sold to a Jew (see BM 73b; Yad, Malveh 7:6; Sh. Ar., YD 172:5).

Conflict of Laws; Principles Where the Foreign Law Is Applicable

From application of the doctrine of *dina de-malkhuta dina*, rules are often derived (see above) which may serve as guiding principles in the field of the conflict of laws, of which the following two examples may be noted.

DISTINGUISHING BETWEEN MATERIAL AND PROCEDURAL LAW. Elijah b. Ḥayyim, head of the Constantinople rabbis at the end of the 16th century, determined that even in the case where Jewish law is subject, by virtue of the doctrine of *dina de-malkhuta dina*, to the foreign law, it is subject only to the material and not the procedural part of such law; hence the laws of evidence are always to be applied in accordance with Jewish law – i.e., the *lex fori*, which is the intrinsic law absorbing the foreign law. The case under discussion (Resp. Ranaḥ no. 58) concerned the question of *imprisonment for debt. Elijah b. Ḥayyim held that even on the assumption that the doctrine of *dina de malkhuta dina* was applicable (according to the accepted view, this could not have been the case since the question of personal freedom is a matter of the ritual law (*issur ve-hetter*) to which the doctrine is not applicable), only the material provision of the law of the land was to be applied, i.e., the provision that a defaulting debtor was to be imprisoned if he had the means to pay, but not otherwise; however, the mode of inquiry into, and proof of, the debtor's financial position had to accord with Jewish law. Hence Elijah b. Ḥayyim concluded that in a case where it was not satisfactorily proved, in accordance with the foreign law, that the debtor lacked the means of paying this debt, but according to the rules of evidence in Jewish law, there was adequate proof of the debtor's lack of means to make payment, then the debtor was to be treated as such and could not be imprisoned (see M. Elon, *Ḥerut ha-Perat* (1964), 164 n. 200).

LEX DOMICILII AS OPPOSED TO *LEX SITUS*. The validity of a *will executed by a Marrano Jew in Majorca was the subject of a dispute between two 14th-century halakhic scholars, Isaac b. Sheshet Perfet and Simeon b. Ẓemaḥ Duran (Resp. Ribash nos. 46–52; *Tashbeẓ* 1:58–61). The testator bequeathed his estate to his daughters on condition that the estate pass to his wife on their death. When the daughters died, the civil court decided that the estate was to pass to the testator's widow in accordance with the will, and called on all persons holding estate assets to restore such to the widow. The heirs of the daughters challenged the will on the ground that in Jewish law, in such circumstances, the estate belonged to the natural heirs of the deceased beneficiary ("Inheritance has no interruption" – BB 129b; Sh. Ar., ḤM 248:1) and called for restoration of the estate assets to themselves. Bar Sheshet held it to be correct that the heirs of the daughters would succeed to the estate if the will "had been executed amongst Jews at a place where they judged according to Jewish law"; however, he added, "the testator was living in Majorca presumably as a gentile and the wife claiming under the will, as well as those claiming to inherit by virtue of kinship are also presumed to be living there as gentiles, and even as Jews they have been required to be adjudged in accordance with the law of the gentiles; for this has always been their practice of their own will; how then shall one of the parties go to a far place to be adjudged in accordance with Jewish law? Let them come before their own judge in Majorca, namely the bailus (*gizbar*), and whoever shall succeed and be held by the bailus to be entitled to the testator's property shall be the heir." Thus Bar Sheshet regarded the *lex domicilii* as the law which was intended by the testator to apply to the will and all concerned therewith, so that none of the possible heirs, or beneficiaries under the will, were entitled to demand that the validity of the will be judged according to any other law.

Duran took a different approach, determining at the outset that Jewish law continued to apply to all the parties, even though they had been Marranos (for the opinions of Mabit and Maharashdam in the matter of Gracia Mendes see above). He added, however, that even if the doctrine of *dina de-malkhuta dina* was applicable to the case, the fact remained that "the rulers of the land are concerned only with the property in such land"; and in regard to property outside of Majorca (i.e., North Africa in this case) "on the contrary, we must say that the same law is not to be applied on account of this very doctrine in order that the government of the land in which the property in issue is situated shall not be particular – when there are in such land those who have a claim of right – about the fact that the latter lose their right because of the opposing law of another land." In his opinion therefore the *lex situs*, the law of the place of situation of the property, was the proper law applicable to assets in a foreign country, and not the law of the place of domicile of the testator and beneficiaries, and since at the place of situation of the property there were those who claimed it in accordance with Jewish law, this law, being the *lex situs*, as well as the *lex fori*, was to be applied (see also *Public Authority; as for the interpretation of privilege granted by the central government to the Jewish community, see Resp. Ribash no. 228).

Further to our comments above (under "Concerning the Laws of Marriage") there is a noteworthy decision of the Israel Supreme Court, the *Miller* case, given in accordance with Jewish Law on the subject of conflict of laws (*Miller v. Miller* – CA 100/49, 5(3) PD 1305).

The *Miller* case involved an appeal against a District Court decision requiring the estate of the deceased husband to pay a fixed monthly amount to the respondent throughout the period of her widowhood. The deceased was British and his wife had also acquired British citizenship on the basis of her marriage to him. The deceased was a Jew, who had closed his business in England and immigrated to the Land of Israel (pre-State), where he remained, without leaving, for 13 years. These and other facts led the District Court to the conclusion that the Land of Israel was his permanent place of residence and that, accordingly, given that his personal law was Jewish law, the applicable law was therefore the law applying to Jews in the Land of Israel, namely, Jewish Law, which requires the estate to pay maintenance to the wife even if the husband provided otherwise in his will. In this case, the deceased was wealthy, and the wife was hence awarded a sizable monthly payment.

Counsel for the estate argued, inter alia, that even under the assumption that the decedent's place of residence was the Land of Israel, in view of the fact that the deceased was a British subject, the domestic court must put itself in the place of the British court and determine what the latter would have ruled in such a case: i.e., would British law have transferred jurisdiction in this matter to the place of residence. Because English Law does not recognize a cause of action in this case, the English court would not have transferred the matter for the adjudication of an Israeli court.

Justice Y. Olshan rejected this argument, citing an English decision in the matter of *De Nicols v. Curlier*, in which the facts were similar to those of the case under discussion. In that case, two French citizens married in France and moved to England, where the husband died; the House of Lords held that the French law regarding joint ownership of property was applicable, despite the fact that the English law did not recognize such rights for the widow. Regarding this issue, Supreme Court Justice Prof. S. Assaf cited the above-mentioned case of Gracia Mendes, which is astonishingly similar to those of the *De Nicols* case, as follows:

> By the way, it should be noted that a case very similar to the *De Nicols* case ... is found in our Responsa literature from the middle sixteenth century, namely, the famous case involving Hannah Gracia Mendes and her younger brother-in-law. The case was brought before the halakhic scholars of the time in Turkey and in Israel, and the most important responsa are those of Rabbi Samuel of Medina (*Maharashdam*), the leading rabbi of Saloniki ... and that of Rabbi Moses Mitrani, the Rabbi of Safed (*Hamabit*).

Justice Assaf also presented in detail the contents of the above-mentioned responsa, ending with the above-mentioned responsum of the Rashba, to the effect that the wedding should be performed in accordance with the law of the place in which it is performed

ADD. BIBLIOGRAPHY: M. Elon, *Ha-Mishpat ha-Ivri* (1988), 1:10, 58ff., 70f., 189f., 556f., 600, 711, 760; 2:1088, 1238f.; 3:1485ff.; idem., *Jewish Law* (1994), 1:9f., 64f., 78f., 212f.; 2:677, 743, 878; 3:1311, 1482f, 1766f.; idem., *Ma'amad ha-Ishah* (2005), 290f.; M. Elon and B. Lifshitz, *Mafte'aḥ ha-She'elot ve-ha-Teshuvot shel Ḥakhmei Sefarad u-Ẓefon Afrikah*, 1 (1986), 48; B. Lifshitz and E. Shochetman, *Mafte'aḥ ha- She'elot ve-ha-Teshuvot shel Ḥakhmei Ashkenaz, Ẓarefat ve-Italyah* (1997), 33.

[Menachem Elon (2nd ed.)]

CONFLICT OF OPINION (Heb. מַחֲלֹקֶת, *maḥaloket*; Aram. *pelugta*; Palestinian Aram. *taflugta*).

General

Rarely did a view in the Talmud go unchallenged, since every talmudic scholar was entitled to his own opinion, even if it conflicted with that of his greatest contemporaries (BK 43b). Consequently the Talmud is replete with undecided controversies. However, this was not always so. For the Jerusalem Talmud (Ḥag. 2:2, 77d; cf. Sanh. 88b; et al.) states that: At first there was no *maḥaloket* in Israel, except over the issue of ordination (**semikhah*). Then Shammai and Hillel arose (see *Bet Hillel and Bet Shammai) and they differed on four issues (cf. Tos. to Ḥag. 16a). When, however, the disciples of Shammai and Hillel grew numerous, and did not wait upon their masters sufficiently, *maḥaloket* became rife in Israel. They divided into two schools, the one declaring (something) ritually impure, while the other declared (it) pure and it (i.e., unanimity of opinion) will not return to its place until the Son of David come (cf. Eduy. 8:7). Thus from the early first century C.E. on, undecided controversies became more common, often represented by opposing schools, e.g., Hillel and Shammai, Rav and Samuel, Abbaye and Rava, etc. Occasionally, a later controversy was attributed to "pre-*maḥaloket*" personalities, even to King Saul and David (Sanh. 19b; see Urbach in bibl. and p. 54 n. 49).

The rabbis appreciated the value of positive controversy, expressing it thus: Only a *maḥaloket* which is for the sake of heaven (*le-shem shamayim*), such as those of Hillel and Shammai, will in the end be of lasting worth; one which is not for the sake of heaven, such as that of *Korah and his company, will not in the end be of lasting worth (Avot 5:17).

Rules of Controversy

Though everyone was entitled to argue his own views, there are certain rules determining which kinds of dissenting opinions are permitted. Thus a *tanna* (a sage of the mishnaic period) cannot express a view that runs counter to a biblical passage. Similarly, an *amora* cannot contradict a Mishnah or accepted *baraita*, unless he cites another tannaitic source to support his contention. However, the early *amoraim* Rav and Johanan had the right to contest mishnaic opinions (Er. 50b).

Rules of Decision

Scattered throughout the Talmud are rules on how to decide practically between differing opinions. The following are general rules: In all cases the view of the majority overrules that of the minority (Ber. 9a; et al.). If one Mishnah recorded a controversy of two *tannaim*, and a later one in the same order recorded one of those opinions anonymously (*setam*), then the opinion of the latter Mishnah is to be followed (Yev. 42b). In matters of mourning the lenient ruling is to be preferred (MK 18a); likewise in rabbinic institutions (Beẓah 3b).

Particular rules (tannaitic and amoraic) are recorded on how to decide in the case of a tannaitic controversy. Thus, with certain exceptions, Hillel's rulings are accepted in preference to those of Shammai (Er. 13b). Eliezer b. Jacob's Mishnah is *kav ve-naki* ("small in compass, but trustworthy," Yev. 49b). As Eliezer b. Hyrcanus was a *shammuti* (either "under a ban," or "a Shammaite") his views were not usually followed (Shab. 130b). Decisions of Simeon b. Gamaliel, except for three cases (Git. 38a), and likewise those of R. Judah ha-Nasi (BB 124b; cf. Pes. 27a) are always followed. Akiva and Yose b. Ḥalafta are followed rather than their opponents (Er. 46b, 51a), and Meir is followed in his *gezerot* ("decrees," Ket. 57a), but not in matters involving reasoning, as his reasoning was too subtle (Er. 13b). In a *maḥaloket* between Judah b. Ilai and either Meir or Simeon, Judah is followed, but in all laws of the Sabbath Simeon is followed (Shab. 157a). Nathan's rulings are always binding (BK 53a).

The following rules apply with regard to amoraic controversies: In civil law Rav's views overrule those of Samuel; in religious law, the reverse is the case (Bek. 49b; et al.). Similarly with R. Naḥman and R. Sheshet (Ket. 13a; cf. BK 96b; Sanh. 5a; et al.). In all controversies between Rav and Johanan, except three, Johanan is followed (Beẓah 4a). Likewise Johanan's views overrule those of Resh Lakish, in all but three cases (Yev. 36a). Rabbah's opinion prevails over that of R. Joseph in all but three cases (Git. 74b), and Rava's opinion over that of Abbaye in all but six cases (BM 22b). Perhaps the most important rule to be formulated in post-talmudic times was that of *halakhah ke-vatra'ei*, that is: wherever two *amoraim* are in conflict, and nowhere is it stated which opinion is to be followed, that of the later *amora* takes precedence (see e.g., B.M.Lewin (ed.), *Iggeret R. Sherira Ga'on* (1921), 38). There are many more such rules, but they do not apply where the Talmud expressly states the *halakhah* (Er. 46b). A considerable literature discussing these rules has grown up since the geonic period, such as *Seder Tanna'im ve-Amora'im* (1839) and *Mavo la-Talmud* of Samuel Hophni, attributed to Samuel ha-Nagid (Constantinople, 1510).

BIBLIOGRAPHY: ET, 9 (1959), 241–339, 341–65; S. Assaf, *Tekufat ha-Ge'onim ve-Sefrutah*, ed. by M. Margalioth (1955), 223–45; E.E. Urbach, in: *Sefer Yovel… Gershom Scholem* (1958), 43–45, 54 n. 49; Z.H. Chajes, *Kol Kitvei* (1958), 363–94; B. De Vries, *Meḥkarim be-Sifrut ha-Talmud* (1968), 172ff.

[Daniel Sperber]

CONFORTE, DAVID (1617 or 1618–c. 1690), rabbi and literary historian. Conforte was born in Salonika into a well-known Sephardi family of rabbis and scholars. He studied rabbinics and Hebrew grammar with the leading rabbis of his time and Kabbalah with teachers in Jerusalem and Salonika. Conforte left Greece for Jerusalem in 1644, stopping for about a year in Cairo, where he studied in the *bet midrash* of Abraham Skandari, and for some time in Gaza with Moses b. Israel Najara. He stayed in Jerusalem for two years, returned to Salonika in 1648, and in 1652 once more to Jerusalem where he founded his own *bet midrash*. In 1671 Conforte was rabbi in Cairo, where Mordecai b. Judah ha-Levi was chief rabbi; the latter mentioned him several times in his responsa *Darkhei No'am* (1697–98). Conforte's major work was *Kore ha-Dorot*. The manuscript was published in Venice in 1746 by David Ashkenazi without mentioning the author's name, and it is uncertain whether the author or the publisher gave the work its title. A new edition with a biographical introduction, notes, and registers was published by David Cassel (1846, repr. 1945 and photo reprint 1969). *Kore ha-Dorot* is a chronicle of authors and works from post-talmudic times until the author's own. For the material up to 1492, he leaned heavily on his medieval predecessors' works: Abraham *Ibn Daud's *Sefer ha-Kabbalah*, Abraham *Zacuto's *Sefer Yuḥasin*, and Gedaliah *Ibn Yaḥya's *Shalshelet ha-Kabbalah*. He supplemented the information in these works with material taken partly from manuscripts that have since been lost. Conforte was the first to prepare an alphabetical list of scholars of the Tosafist period; it was supplemented in 1845 by L. Zunz in his *Zur Geschichte und Literatur* (pp. 30–60) with the help of Jehiel Heilprin's *Seder ha-Dorot* (1769). Though subsequent research findings supersede some of Conforte's information, his work remains important for the biography and times of Jewish authors and leaders. *Kore ha-Dorot* is especially important for its information about Sephardi scholars who lived in Mediterranean countries in the 16th and 17th centuries. The author knew many of them personally or received reliable information about them from descendants. He also diligently extracted names of scholars from the responsa of his time. Conforte's information on Ashkenazi scholars, however, is sketchy and sometimes wrong.

A volume of Conforte's responsa is lost, but a single responsum is preserved in the manuscript responsa collection of his contemporary Moses Judah *Abbas. Gabriel Conforte, mentioned in the same collection and in Aaron Alfandari's *Yad Aharon*, may have been his son.

BIBLIOGRAPHY: S.Z. Rubashow (Shazar), in: *Ha-Goren*, 10 (1928), 122–31; Frumkin-Rivlin, pt. 2 (1930), 48–50.

[Moshe Nahum Zobel]

CONGREGATION (Assembly). A variety of terms are employed in the Bible for "the people of Israel" in its social, military, and sacral capacity. The most common are: "Israel," "the people" (*ha-ʿam*), "the assembly" (*ha-qahal*), "the congregation" (*ha-ʿedah*), "the children of Israel" (*benei Yisrael*), and "the men of Israel" (*'ish Yisrael*). These terms denote not the total population but the institutionalized body of Israel, that is, a given group acting on its behalf. This may be deduced from the fact that the expressions mentioned sometimes alternate with "the elders of Israel" or "the elders of the people." For example, according to Exodus 12:3, Moses is commanded to address "the congregation of Israel" (*ʿadat Yisrael*) in connection with the Passover sacrifice, while in the following passage (12:21ff.) describing Moses' address, it is the "elders of Israel" (*zikenei Yisrael*) who are addressed (see Mekh., Pisḥa 3:11; cf. also Ex. 19:7 with 19:8; 17:5–6 with Num. 20:7; II Sam. 17:4 with 17:14). The terms discussed are used synonymously and often occur together without any possibility of distinguishing between them. In Judges 20–21, when all the tribes unite following the crime of the Gibeathites, the acting body of the Israelites is named: "the assembly," "the congregation," "the children of Israel," "the people," "the assembly of the people of God," "the men of Israel," and "the elders of the congregation." Similar expressions occur in the narrative concerning the division of the kingdom (I Kings 12): "the assembly of Israel," "all Israel," "children of Israel," "all the people," and "the congregation."

This ambiguous use of terms in connection with social institutions is characteristic of the entire area of Mesopotamia and Syria-Palestine, and is particularly conspicuous in documents from the second half of the second millennium B.C.E. The representative institutions of the cities of Syria-Palestine at the period of Israel's penetration into the area are designated by "town [*ālu*] of N," "the men [*amēlu*] of N," "the sons [*mārú*] of N," and "the assembly" or "council" (*mwʿd*). Furthermore, the interchange of "the elders" with "the congregation," which appears in the Bible, also occurs in these documents, where "the elders" (*šibūtu*) seem to be identified with "the town" (*ālu*), or the two may overlap (cf., e.g., el-Amarna Letter no. 100). As in the Bible, so also here the author may use different designations for the same representative body in the same document. A similar type of flexibility exists in the tribal-patriarchal vocabulary. The terms "clan" (*mishpaḥah*), "family" (*bet 'av*), and "tribe" (*shevet*) are interchangeable (Num. 17:17; Josh. 22:14; Judg. 13:2; 17:7; 18:19) and may even enter the semantic range of "people" and "nation" (Gen. 12:3; Jer. 33:24; Amos 3:1). However, in documents of the ancient Near East, as well as in the Bible, each of the various terms for the social institutions also has a more precise, literal meaning, but the exact interpretation of the term is always dependent on the context. For example, when the subject is a large crowd, the term *qahal* is more suitable than the others; when the author refers to a small group of representatives, as in Leviticus 4:13, he uses "the elders of the congregation," and in a clearly military context the term *'ish Yisrael* is employed. The same applies to the tribal-patriarchal vocabulary. Although the terms for family, clan, and tribe overlap, the literal sense of each was strictly preserved when it was necessary to distinguish between the various units in the tribal hierarchy (Josh. 7:14–18; I Sam. 10:19–21). The choice of terminology was also dictated (if the documentary hypothesis is accepted), by the different scribal traditions. In the three major strands of the Pentateuch, the source JE (Jahwist-Elohist) mostly employs "the elders of Israel," the Priestly Code *ʿedah*, and Deuteronomy *qahal*.

Qahal and ʿEdah: Etymology and Semantics

Although *ʿedah* and *qahal* seem to be synonymous, they actually have different nuances: *qahal* (perhaps related to *kol (qol*, "voice"); cf. the usage of *qr'*, *ṣʿq*, *shmʿ* for "summon") is used in a more general sense and refers to a multitude of nations (Gen. 28:3; 35:11; 48:4), to hordes (Num. 22:4; Jer. 50:9; cf. Ezek. passim) and to masses (e.g., I Kings 8:65; Ps. 22:26). *ʿEdah* (from *yʿd*, "set a time [or place] for a meeting") has a more specific sense and a sacred connotation. *Qahal* appears in all strata of biblical literature and applies to all periods of Israelite history. *ʿEdah* mainly occurs in a sacerdotal context and is restricted to the pre-monarchic period. Its last occurrence in the historical literature is in I Kings 12:20, in connection with the division of the kingdom. Together with *ʿedah*, the term *i'sh Yisrael* went out of use, as did the patriarchal terms "the heads of the tribes" (*rashei ha-maṭṭot*) and "the heads of the contingents of Israel" (*rashe 'alfei Yisrael*). This fact, together with the absence of *ʿedah* in the books of Chronicles and Ezra-Nehemiah, militates against the view (e.g., of Wellhausen and Rost) that this term was coined in the post-Exilic community. When referring to Israel, *qahal* encompasses the entire population: men, women, strangers, etc. (Jer. 44:15; cf. Deut. 31:12), while *ʿedah* denotes the indigenous, mostly arms-bearing population (cf. Judg. 20:2). The laws which apply to the *ʿedah* do not apply to strangers; when the legislator wants to impose the law on the resident and the stranger alike, he makes *qahal* subject to the law (Num. 15:15).

ʿEdah: Character and Functions

In its classical sense the *ʿedah* is the assembly of the arms-bearing male population (cf. the *guruš* in the Sumerian cities and *ṣābē nagbātī* in the Hittite kingdom), and hence its military character. It connotes (especially in the Book of Numbers) a military camp moving to its goal, the Promised Land, and consisting of 12 tribes, each tribe having its place of encampment, standard, and ensigns (Num. 2:2). The center of the camp is the "Tent of Meeting" (*'ohel moʿed*) containing the Holy Ark, which guides the people on its way. To set the divisions in motion, signals are given by priests blowing two silver trumpets (Num. 10:1–8). The conscription of the *ʿedah* is done by a census (Num. 1); the enrolled are men from the age of 20 years and upward, who are able to bear arms (cf. Judg. 20:2). A census is also carried out in connection with the casting of lots for the division of the land (Num. 26), and sometimes involves the collection of money for the building of the tabernacle (Ex. 30:11–16). The description of the congregation and the tabernacle is very schematic and utopian, with the result that the picture as a whole appears anachronistic. However, it should not be regarded as pure fiction. The organization of the tribes has prototypes in the tribal-patriarchal society of the nomadic West Semitic tribes, as reflected in the documents from *Mari, the area that seems to have been the cradle of the Patriarchs. Like the tribes of ancient Israel, those of Mari were organized on the basis of clans and households (cf. *bet'av* with *bīt abi* and *abu bīti*) and were ruled by elders (*šibūtu*) and chieftains (*sugagu*). Their military units were based on gentilic principles, and like the tribes of Israel, they lived in tents and encampments (*nawûm*). The census played an important role there and occurs in the context of conscription and division of the land as in ancient Israel. A portable sanctuary is used by the Bedouin in their nomadic way of life, and there is no justification for the denial of the existence of the tabernacle during the wanderings of the tribes in the desert. The reality of the tribal life of the Israelites is reflected in the story of the Danites' search for land for their settlement. Like "the children of Israel" in the desert, the Danites lived in a camp (cf. 600 armed men, Judg. 18:11, with the 600 *'elef* men in Ex. 12:37), and on their march acquired divinatory objects and a priest. Also like the "children of Israel," they sent men to spy out the land that they planned to conquer. In light of the last analogy, too sharp a line should not be drawn between the *ʿedah* of the period of the wanderings and that of the judges. Since classical stories concerning the *ʿedah* refer to the time of the wanderings in the desert, which involved preparations for the conquest, its military character prevails. However, the *ʿedah*, as the ruling body of the nation, also functioned in a judicial, political, and sacral capacity. In this respect it was not different from the so-called primitive democracies in ancient Mesopotamia and Homeric Greece. The *ʿedah* was convened in the following cases: (1) Breach of covenant with God, i.e., violations of the basic religious principles of the congregation, such as blasphemy (Lev. 24:14ff.; cf. I Kings 21:9ff.), desecration of the Sabbath (Num. 15:33ff.), violation of the taboo (*ḥerem*, Josh. 7), major cultic deviation (Josh. 22:9ff.), and grave immoral behavior (Judg. 19–21). (Cf. also Deut. 13:10–11; 17:5, in connection with pagan worship, and Ezek. 16:40; 23:46, in connection with fornication, although the last examples do not refer to the tribal assembly, but rather to the city assembly; see below.) In all these cases, the assembly acts in its judicial as well as its executive power; (2) Holy gatherings and religious ceremonies, such as Passover sacrifice (Ex. 12:47; Num. 9:2), covenantal gatherings (Lev. 19; cf. Deut. 4:10; Ex. 24:3–8, Deut. 31:12), and holy days and sacred occasions (e.g., Ex. 23:17; Lev. 23:4ff.); (3) Political affairs: concluding treaties with foreign nations (Josh. 9:15–21), appointing a leader or a king (Num. 27:2; I Sam. 8:4; 10:17; 11:14; 12:1; I Kings 1:39; 12:1, 20; cf. II Kings 11:17), and proclaiming war (Josh. 22:9ff.; Judg. 20:1ff.; cf. I Kings 20:7ff.

"the elders of the land"); (4) Tribal-patriarchal affairs: inheritance and division of the land (Num. 27:1–11; Josh. 18:1–10; cf. Micah 2:5); and (5) National crisis or natural calamity (Ex. 16:2–3; Num. 14:1–10; 17:6–7; 20:2; 25:6).

The parallel democratic institutions in ancient Mesopotamia (*puḫrum*), the old Hittite Kingdom (*pankuš*) and ancient Greece (βουλή) were convened for similar reasons, and like the *ʿedah* in Israel, the democratic institutions there decreased in importance as the kingdom became more stable. With respect to religious crimes, the *ʿedah* has more affinities with Hittite and Greek institutions. The assemblies in Greece and among the Hittites were summoned in cases of violation of major religious laws, stealing of sancta, etc. In Greece transgressors of the last type were put under the ban (κατάρατος, "accursed"), as were transgressors in ancient Israel (Deut. 27:11–26). The ban involved excommunication either through execution or exile, punishments which seem to correspond in some way to "cutting off from the congregation" (Ex. 12:19) or from the assembly (Num. 19:20) in the Bible. The classical *ʿedah* convened at "the entrance of the Tent of Meeting" (*petaḥ ʾohel moʿed*). The word *moʿed* ("meeting") refers to the meeting of God with Moses and the congregation (e.g., Ex. 25:22; 29:43–44; 30:36), but it also has the sense of assembly (Num. 16:2) and is so attested to in Phoenicia (Byblos; "The Journey of Wen Amon") and in Ugaritic literature (*pḫr mʿd*, in reference to the divine assembly). It is therefore possible that in one of the stages of its development, the *ohel moʿed* also carried the meaning of "the tent of the assembly." As already indicated, the power of the *ʿedah* decreased with the growth of the monarchy. However, a revival of the concept *ʿedah* occurs in the Dead Sea sectarian scroll of the "War of the Children of Light against the Children of Darkness." This sectarian community at the end of the Second Temple period saw itself as the true and ideal Israel living in the desert, and patterned itself after the congregation of the Exodus generation. Although the specific connotation of the *ʿedah* as the tribal assembly was gradually lost, the concept *ʿedah* continued to be employed in the sense of the local court or tribunal (cf. the Akkadian *puḫrum* in the cities of Babylonia; see, e.g., Code of Hammurapi, 5:202). Thus in Proverbs 5:14, *qahal* and *ʿedah* are the public places of judgment; the same meaning is ascribed to the expressions "to stand up in the congregation" (*qum ba-ʿedah*) in the documents from Elephantine and "I stand up in the assembly [*qamti ba-qahal*] and cry" in Job 30:28. It would seem that some of the features of the later city assembly were projected by the priestly author upon the ancient tribal assembly, and similarly, characteristics of the city influenced the description of the camp of the Israelite tribes. For example, according to the law of the cities of refuge in Numbers 35, the *ʿedah* established the right of the slayer to refuge (35:12, 24–25), whereas in the parallel law in Deuteronomy 19, it is the elders of the city who act in this case (19:12). Therefore, the *ʿedah* in the priestly account (according to the documentary hypothesis) is apparently none other than the judicial body of the city where the homicide occurred. By the same token, when the priestly legislator prescribes that those afflicted with severe skin disease shall live outside the camp (Lev. 13:45–46; cf. Num. 5:1–4), he apparently alludes to the Israelite city, which kept those afflicted outside its walls (II Kings 7:3ff.). The *ohel moʿed* in the priestly literature, according to Kaufmann, reflects the local sanctuary of the later Israelite city.

See also *Dead Sea Sect; *Manual of Discipline; *War Scroll.

BIBLIOGRAPHY: G. Busolt and H. Swoboda, *Griechische Staatskunde*, 2 (1926), passim; A.L. Oppenheim, in: *Orientalia*, 5 (1936), 244ff.; L. Rost, *Die Vorstufen von Kirche und Synagoge im Alten Testament…* (1938); R.S. Hardy, in: AJSLL, 58 (1941), 214ff.; Th. Jacobsen, in: JNES, 2 (1943), 159–72; G. Evans, in: JAOS, 78 (1958), 1–11, 114–5; A. Malamat, *ibid.*, 82 (1962), 143–50; de Vaux, Anc Isr, 91–93, 213–28; H. Tadmor, in: *Journal of World History*, 11 (1968), 3–17; H. Reviv, in: *Journal of the Economic and Social History of the Orient*, 12 (1969), 283ff.; Kaufmann Y., Toledot, 1 (1937), 126–37. **ADD. BIBLIOGRAPHY:** N. Gottwald, *The Tribes of Yahweh* (1985); R.E. Clements, *The World of Ancient Israel* (1989); C. Meyers, in: D. Jobling et al. (eds.), *The Bible and the Politics of Exegesis … Essays Gottwald* (1991), 39–51.

[Moshe Weinfeld]

CONGRESS FOR JEWISH CULTURE, organization devoted to the promotion of secular Jewish culture and the recognition of Yiddish as an indispensable means of Jewish creative expression. Founded in New York in September 1948 at a world conference convoked by American Yiddish cultural agencies and Jewish labor organizations, and participated in by delegates from similar organizations in other lands, the Congress for Jewish Culture set for itself the following basic objectives: to preserve the continuity of Jewish cultural creativity; to foster Jewish education through Yiddish and Yiddish-Hebrew schools; to assist in the publication of literary and scholarly works in Yiddish; and to protect the cultural freedom of the Jews wherever their right to maintain and develop their own culture is threatened. The work of the congress since inception has been in line with these objectives. The congress is a loose confederation of organizations bearing the same names in different parts of the world. Among the publications that appeared from its main center in New York are a number of volumes of Yiddish poetry and fiction by writers who perished during the Nazi Holocaust or were executed in the Soviet Union; a lexicon of Yiddish literature and press; a two-volume encyclopedia of Jewish education; and a series of books containing selected works of leading Yiddish writers. It has granted a number of awards for outstanding literary accomplishments. Through its department of education, the Congress seeks to coordinate the activities of the various types of Jewish secular schools. Closely allied with the Congress, although operating independently, are the Yiddish monthly **Zukunft* and CYCO (Central Yiddish Culture Organization). The affiliates of the Congress outside the United States, while cooperating in the activities of the main center, conduct programs of their own. Most prominent is the Congress of Jewish Culture in Argentina, which brought out a Yiddish translation of Dubnow's history of the Jewish people and the complete history of Jewish literature by I. Zinberg. The congress has its own house in Buenos Aires. Some of the activities of the Congress were financially supported in the past by the *Conference on Jewish Material Claims against Germany. When funds were no longer available from that source, the congress was forced to curtail activities.

[Charles Bezalel Sherman]

CONNECTICUT, one of the six New England states located in the N.E. section of the United States. The earliest reference to a Jew in Connecticut is found in connection with an entry on November 9, 1659, in the General Court in *Hartford, of one named "David the Jew" who was arrested for peddling. Shortly thereafter, in 1661, reference is made to Jews living in Hartford in the house of one John Marsh, and the extension of permission to continue to live in "ye Town for sea[v]en months."

Little or nothing is known of the first Jewish settlers and settlements in Connecticut prior to the latter part of the 18th century and the beginning of the 19th century. Jews were settled in *New Haven as early as 1759 where a family named Pinto – the brothers Jacob, Solomon, and Abraham – were living in that year. Ezra *Stiles, president of Yale College at the time, referred to these Pinto brothers as "men who renounced Judaism and all religion"; but he also refers to a new Jewish family (unnamed), who settled in New Haven in 1771 and describes them as the "first real Jews… that settled in New Haven." He says that there were about eight or ten members in this new family and reports a Sabbath service held "by themselves" as being probably "the first Jewish worship in New Haven." Despite the seeming apostasy of the Pinto brothers, they were active patriots of the community. Jacob Pinto was reported a member of an important New Haven committee of patriots in 1775. Solomon served in the U.S. Army until he retired in 1783. Solomon was one of the original members of the Society of the Cincinnati in Connecticut, which was a short-lived group of aristocratic veteran officers of the Revolutionary War. Another brother, Abraham, also served.

There is very meager information about organized Jewish communities in Connecticut prior to the 19th century. Part of that may be due to the fact that no Jewish congregations were permitted to incorporate prior to 1843, when the Statutes were amended by the addition of the following: "Jews who may desire to unite and form religious societies may have the same rights, powers, and privileges as are given to Christians of every denomination by the laws of the State" (Revised Statutes of Connecticut, 1849, Title III, Section 149). There is no doubt, however, that groups of Jews lived in the state who would assemble for worship even without statutory permission. The first Jewish congregations on record are the Beth Israel of Hartford and Mishkan Israel of New Haven. Beth Israel in Hartford was organized in 1843, but there is reason to believe that they held services as early as 1839. Mishkan Israel, in New Haven, assembled for worship as early as December 1840. By reason of population movement to the suburbs, The

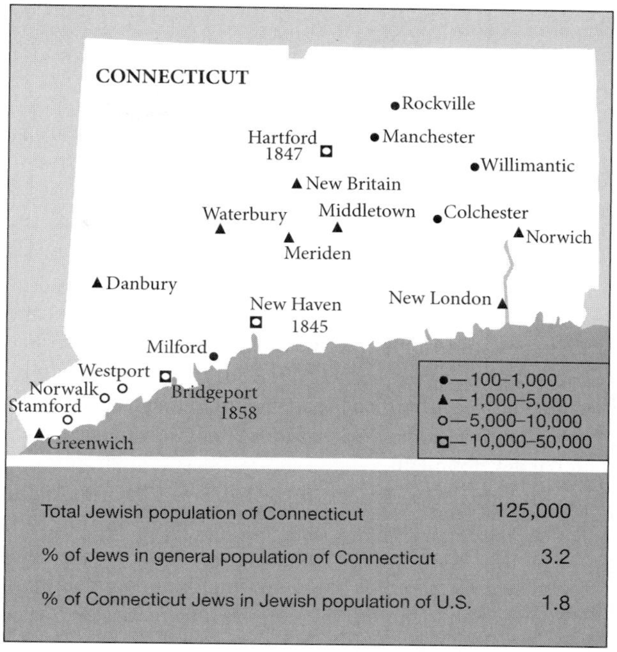

Jewish communities in Connecticut and dates of establishment. Population figures for 2001.

Congregation Beth Israel of Hartford (its corporate name) was located in the late 1960s in the town of West Hartford, and Mishkan Israel Congregation was located in the town of Hamden.

The Jewish population of Connecticut grew with the influx of Jews from overseas. Thus, it is estimated that in 1877 there were 1,492 Jews in Connecticut; in 1905, 8,500; in 1917, 66,862; in 1927, 91,538; and in 1937, 94,080. In 1969 it was estimated that the Jewish population of Connecticut was approximately 105,000. In the beginning of the 21st century, there were more than 125,000 Jews residing in the state. Out of 50 states in the U.S., Connecticut was ranked 10th highest for Jewish population.

The largest growth was in the Southern part of Connecticut, considered suburbs of New York City, mostly around the Westport and Greenwich areas. It is axiomatic that the closer to New York Connecticut residents live, the more they see themselves as part of the New York community though they affiliate locally with congregations, institutions, and organizations.

According to the Jewish Federation of the Western Communities of Connecticut, the most recent growth trend has been an increase of Jewish population in the western part of Connecticut, around Litchfield Co. The increase is better than 10%. The town of Waterbury, in western Connecticut, saw especially large growth in the Orthodox community after Yeshiva Gedolah opened its doors in 2000. In five years, membership grew to include 75 families and 175 students. Students come from all over the U.S. and the world. Yeshiva Gedolah anticipated membership growth of well over 30% in 2006. National grocery chains in the area responded by stocking kosher items for their new clientele.

The largest Jewish population in Connecticut was in Greater Hartford with 34,000 Jews. In the early 1900s, Hartford saw an influx of Jewish immigrants from Eastern Europe and at one point during the 20th century Hartford had at least 13 synagogues in the city. After World War II, Jews moved from Hartford to the suburbs and subsequently no synagogues remained in downtown Hartford. The second largest Jewish community is in Greater New Haven.

In the past, business was the major source of Jewish livelihood. Jews then moved into the professions as lawyers, doctors, and academics, and into real estate, mostly commercial. Two major real estate developers are both Holocaust survivors, David Chase and Simon Konover, with statewide and national developments.

Community Life

Connecticut had nine Jewish Federations and JFACT, Jewish Federation Association of Connecticut, a statewide government affairs office. The ADL and AJC both had statewide offices in Connecticut. The *Jewish Ledger* was a statewide Jewish newspaper. Around the state there were also 130 synagogues, six Jewish community centers (four big ones and two smaller ones in Sherman and Litchfield), three Jewish nursing homes, eight Jewish Family Service Offices, 13 Jewish day schools, and the Hebrew High School of New England. Connecticut saw a growth in Jewish day school enrollment throughout the state.

Jewish community centers were housed in splendid facilities, and the federations for the collection of philanthropic contributions were active. Mt. Sinai Hospital of Hartford was the only Jewish hospital in the state. B'nai B'rith was also active.

Connecticut Jews have played a distinguished role in the economic, social, political, and cultural life of the state. Herman P. *Koppelmann of Hartford (1933–38, 1941–43) and William M. Citron (1935–38) of Middletown served in the U.S. House of Representatives. Abraham A. *Ribicoff, who represented Connecticut in the House of Representatives (1945–52), was a member of the U.S. Senate (1962–1981), and governor of Connecticut (1955–61). Many Jews in the course of the years have served in the state legislature and on all levels of the judiciary. M. Joseph Blumenfeld of West Hartford was a Federal Court judge. Justices Samuel Melitz of Bridgeport and Abraham S. Bordon and Louis Shapiro of West Hartford served on the Supreme Court of Connecticut. Some men served as mayors of their communities, as U.S. referees in bankruptcy, and as Federal attorneys. In 2005, 14% of CT's State senators were Jewish (5 out of 36); they were Judith G. Freedman, Jonathan A. Harris, Edith G. Prague, Gayle S. Slossberg, and Andrea L. Stillman. Sam Gejdenson represented the greater New London area in Congress from 1981 to 2000. Born in 1948 in an American displaced persons camp in Eschwege, Germany, Gejdenson was the first child of Holocaust survivors elected to the U.S. House of Representatives. The most famous Connecticut political leader is Senator Joseph I. *Lieberman, who was first elected to the United States Senate in 1988, making him the first and only Orthodox Jew elected a senator. In 1994 he made Connecticut history by winning 67% of the vote, the largest ever in a Connecticut Senate race. In 2000, Lieberman was elected to a third term. He is perhaps best known as the Democratic candidate for vice president in 2000 and as the first Jew nominated for the position on a major party ticket. His career now spans more than three decades.

[Abraham J. Feldman / Robert Fishman (2nd ed.)]

°**CONON I**, one of the authors mentioned by Josephus (Apion 1:216) in the list of Greek writers who wrote in detail about the Jews. Some identify him with a writer of that name mentioned in Servius' commentary to Virgil (*Servius ad Aeneidem* 7:738), but this is doubtful. Still more doubtful is the identification of Conon with Conon II.

°**CONON II** (late first century B.C.E. and early first century C.E.), a mythographer, contemporary of King Archelaus of Cappadocia. Fragments of Conon's work have been preserved in the library of Photius. Among his tales is one linking the myth of Perseus' rescue of Andromeda with the town of Jaffa. This connection is in fact very old, and it can be traced to as early as the fourth century B.C.E. (in pseudo-Scylax).

CONRAD, VICTOR (1876–1962), Austrian meteorologist. Born in Vienna, Conrad studied under Josef Pernter, who offered him a post on the staff of the University of Vienna in the department of meteorology and magnetism. Conrad set up a section for the observation of electricity in the air. His results led the way to the discovery of cosmic rays several years later. In 1910, he was appointed head of the department of cosmic physics at the University of Czernowitz in Bukovina and worked there until the outbreak of World War I. With the cessation of hostilities in 1918, he returned to the University of Vienna and joined the Institute of Meteorology. Here he set up a seismographic station for the observation of earthquakes and other geophysical problems. From 1920 to 1938, he occupied himself to a large extent with bioclimatic questions. In 1926, Conrad was appointed editor of the geophysical quarterly *Gerlands Beitraege zur Geophysik*, which he edited until 1938. In the 39 volumes which appeared under his editorship, much important material on various problems in the field of geophysics was published. He also published two journals that dealt with physical-cosmic subjects and problems of applied geophysics. When the famous meteorologist Wladimir Koppen, who had settled in Austria after his retirement from the Meteorological Institute in Russia, began to publish his extensive *Handbuch der Klimatologie*, Conrad wrote the chapter on climatic elements and their dependence on terrestrial influences, which ran into a volume of over 500 pages. In 1938, when the Nazis annexed Austria, Conrad escaped to the United States in utter poverty. He lectured at the University of Pennsylvania from 1939 to 1940 and then went to Boston. There he was awarded a scholarship by Harvard University, where he remained until his death. During his years in the United States he published two works: *Fundamentals of Physical Climatology* (1942), and, together with Professor L.W. Pollak (of Dublin, Ireland), *Methods in Climatology* (1944, second edition 1950).

[Dov Ashbel]

CONRIED, HEINRICH (**Cohn**; 1848–1909), impresario. Born in Austria, he reached the United States in 1878 after a career in Germany, and directed various theaters. As manager of the Metropolitan Opera (1903–08), he achieved spectacular successes by engaging such celebrities as Caruso, Chaliapin, and Scotti, and producing operas new to the American public. He presented the first production of Wagner's *Parsifal* in the U.S. in 1903, overcoming the objections of the Wagner family, and in 1907 produced Richard Strauss's *Salome*, which aroused protests on moral grounds. He returned to Europe in 1908.

CONSERVATION.

Introduction

In consequence of the establishment in Israel of a Ministry for the Environment it is appropriate to take stock of the deep concern for the environment and its conservation which, from its earliest documents onwards, infuses Jewish tradition.

It is not our task here to analyze in detail the great ecological problems of our time or the ways in which they have recently manifested themselves in Israel, let alone to enumerate and describe the bodies, such as the Council for a Beautiful Israel, which are addressing them, or to list the contributions made by individual Jews, for instance scientists and economists, to the modern ecological movement. Rather, we seek to underpin Jewish involvement in conservation worldwide by drawing together the traditional source and highlighting their relevance to the contemporary scene.

We draw on a range of genres of traditional Jewish thought – the most distinctive is *halakhah*, or law, but history, myth, poetry, philosophy, and other forms of expression are also significant. And we must also be mindful that Judaism did not stop in the first century; it is a living religion constantly developing in response to changing social realities and intellectual perceptions. At the present time, it is passing through one of its most creative phases.

WHICH PROBLEMS ARE ADDRESSED? There is a worry prevalent today that people are destroying the environment on which living things depend for their existence. Many species are endangered as a result of human activity, the planetary climate may already have been destabilized, the protective ozone layer has been damaged, forests have been destroyed, species threatened or made extinct, and pollution in forms such as acid rain and other forms of water contamination is widespread.

Much of this destruction arises from the level of economic activity demanded by a rapidly increasing world population which is locally raising its living standards faster than ecologically sustainable levels of production.

In addition, there is a permanent worry that stockpiles of highly destructive weapons might actually be used and that the use of even a small part of the available arsenal would cause irreversible damage to the planetary environment, perhaps rendering impossible the survival of *homo sapiens sapiens* and many other species.

HOW IS RELIGION RELEVANT? It is not at first sight clear what these problems have to do with religious beliefs. After all, the only belief necessary to motivate a constructive response to them is a belief in the desirability of human survival, wedded to the perception that human survival depends on the whole interlinking system of nature. The belief is not peculiar to religions but part of the innate self-preservation mechanism of humankind; the perception of the interdependence of natural things arises not from religion but from careful scientific investigation.

Moreover, the discovery of which procedures would effectively solve the problems of conservation is a technical, not a religious one. If scientists are able to offer alternative procedures of the same or different efficiency the religious may feel that the ethical or spiritual values they espouse should determine the choice. But few choices depend on value judgments alone, and no judgment is helpful which is not based on the best available scientific information.

These considerations will be borne in mind as we examine the relevance of traditional Jewish sources to our theme.

Attitudes to Creation

GOODNESS OF THE PHYSICAL WORLD. "God saw that it was good" is the refrain of the first creation story of Genesis (chapter 1:1 to 2:4), which includes the physical creation of humankind, male and female. The created world is thus testimony to God's goodness and greatness (see Psalms 8, 104, 148).

The second "creation" story (Genesis 2:5 to 3:24) accounts for the psychological makeup of humankind. There is no devil, only a "wily serpent," and the excuse of being misled by the serpent does not exempt Adam and Eve from personal responsibility for what they have done. Bad gets into the world through the free exercise of choice by people, not in the process of creation, certainly not through fallen angels, devils, or any other external projection of human guilt; such creatures are notably absent from the catalogue of creation in Genesis 1.

Post-biblical Judaism did not adopt the concept of "the devil." In the Middle Ages, however, the dualism of body and spirit prevailed, and with it a tendency to denigrate "this world" and "material things." The Ereẓ Israel kabbalist Isaac Luria (1534–1572) taught that God initiated the process of creation by "withdrawing" himself from the infinite space He occupied; this theory stresses the "inferiority" and distance from

God of material creation, but compensates by drawing attention to the divine element concealed in all things. The modern Jewish theologian who wishes to emphasize the inherent goodness of God's creation has not only the resources of the Hebrew Scriptures on which to draw but a continuous tradition based on them.

Anthropocentrism. Certain theologians, such as Matthew Fox, are greatly exercised to replace traditional anthropocentric, fall/redemption, hence guilt-laden theologies with a "creation spirituality" of "original blessing." They invoke spirits, demons and earth goddesses, and do not rest satisfied until they have appropriated scripture itself to their purposes.

Perhaps they redress an imbalance in Catholic theology. But by what arbitrary whim do they confer authority on earth-centered Genesis 1–2:4 and deny it to people-centered Genesis 2:5–3:24? And by what further willfulness do they ignore the culmination of Genesis 1–2:4 itself in the creation of humankind in the image of God, at the apex of creation?

Do they not acknowledge that the Hebrew scriptures are a polemic against idolatry, and that the most significant feature of Genesis 1:2–4 is its denial, by omission, of the very existence of sprites, hobgoblins, demons, gods, demigods, earth-spirits, and all those motley beings that everyone else in the ancient world sought to manipulate to their advantages? There is only one power, and that is God, who is *above* nature (transcendent).

The Bible encompasses three realms: of God, of humankind, of nature. It does not confuse them. There is "original blessing" indeed – "God saw all that he had made, and it was very good" (Genesis 1:31) – but this includes people, maintains hierarchy, excludes "earth spirits," and remains subject to succeeding chapters of Genesis as well as the rest of scripture.

BIODIVERSITY. I recall sitting in the synagogue as a child and listening to the reading of Genesis. I was puzzled by the Hebrew word *le-minehu* ("according to its kind") which followed the names of most of the created items and was apparently superfluous. Obviously, if God created fruit with seeds, the seeds were "according to its kind"!

As time went on I became more puzzled. Scripture seemed obsessive about "kinds" (species). There were careful lists and definitions of which species of creature might or might not be eaten (Leviticus 11 and Deuteronomy 14). Wool and linen were not to be mixed in a garment (Leviticus 19:19; Deuteronomy 22:11), ox and ass were not to plow together (Deuteronomy 22:10), fields (Leviticus 19:19) and vineyards (Deuteronomy 22:9) were not to be sown with mixed seeds or animals cross-bred (Leviticus 19:19) and, following the rabbinic interpretation of a thrice repeated biblical phrase (Exodus 23:19, 34:26; Deuteronomy 14:21), meat and milk were not to be cooked or eaten together.

The story of Noah's Ark manifests anxiety that all species should be conserved, irrespective of their usefulness to humankind – Noah is instructed to take into his Ark viable (according to the thought of the time) populations of both "clean" and "unclean" animals.

The biblical preoccupation with species and with keeping them distinct can now be read as a way of declaring the "rightness" of God's pattern for creation and of calling on humankind not only not to interfere with it, but to cherish biodiversity by conserving species.

Scripture does not of course take account of the evolution of species, with its postulates of (a) the alteration of species over time and (b) the extinction (long before the evolution of humans) of most species which have so far appeared on earth.

Yet at the very least these Hebrew texts assign unique value to each species as it now is within the context of the present order of creation; this is sufficient to give a religious dimension, within Judaism, to the call to conserve species.

Perek Shirah. **Perek Shirah* (the "Chapter of Song," as found in large *Siddurim* (Prayer Books), particularly those of Jacob Emden and Seligmann Baer) affords a remarkable demonstration of the traditional Jewish attitude to nature and its species. The provenance of this "song" is unknown, though in its earliest form it may well have emanated from mystical circles such as those of the *heikhalot* mystics of the fourth or fifth centuries. Though occasionally attacked for heterodoxy, it is clearly rabbinic not only in its theology but even in the detail of its vocabulary and allusions.

More significant than its origin is its actual use in private devotion. It has been associated with the "Songs of Unity" composed by the German pietists of the 12th century who undoubtedly stimulated its popularity.

As the work is printed today it is divided into five or six sections, corresponding to the physical creation (this includes heaven and hell, Leviathan and other sea creatures), plants and trees, creeping things, birds, and land animals (in some versions the latter section is subdivided). Each section consists of from 10 to 25 biblical verses, each interpreted as the song or saying of some part of creation or of some individual creature. The cock, in the fourth section, is given seven voices and its function in the poem is to link the earthly song, in which all nature praises God, with the heavenly song.

We shall see in the section on hierarchy in creation that the Spanish Jewish philosopher Joseph *Albo draws on *Perek Shirah* to express the relationship between the human and the animal; yet *Perek Shirah* itself draws all creation, even the inanimate, even heaven and hell themselves, into the relationship, expressing a fullness which derives only from the rich diversity of things, and which readily translates into the modern concept of biodiversity.

STEWARDSHIP OR DOMINATION. There has been discussion among Christian theologians as to whether the opening chapters of Genesis call on humans to act as stewards, guardians of creation, or to dominate and exploit the created world. There is little debate on this point among Jewish theologians to whom it has always been obvious that when Genesis states that Adam was placed in the garden "to till it and to care for it" (2:15), it means just what it says. As Rabbi A.I. *Kook put it:

> No rational person can doubt that the Torah, when it commands people to "rule over the fishes of the sea and the birds of the sky and all living things that move on the earth" does not have in mind a cruel ruler who exploits his people and servants for his own will and desires – God forbid that such a detestable law of slavery [be attributed to God] who "is good to all and his tender care rests upon all his creatures" (Psalms 145:9) and "the world is built on tender mercy" (Psalm 89:3).

So perverse is it to understand "and rule over it" (Genesis 1:28) – let alone Psalm 8 – as meaning "exploit and destroy" (is that what people think of their rulers?) that many Christians take such interpretations as a deliberate attempt to besmirch Christianity and not a few Jews have read the discussions as an attempt to "blame the Jews" for yet another disaster in Christendom.

Hierarchy in Creation

"God created humans in His image ... male and female he created them" (Genesis 1:27). In some sense, humankind is superior to animals, animals to plants, plants to the inanimate. There is a hierarchy in created things.

The hierarchical model has two practical consequences. The first is that of responsibility of the higher for the lower, traditionally expressed as "rule," latterly as "stewardship." The second is that, in a competitive situation, the higher has priority over the lower. Humans have priority over dogs so that, for instance, it is wrong for a man to risk his life to save that of a dog though right, in many circumstances, for him to risk his life to save that of another human. Contemporary dilemmas arising from this are described in the section on animal versus human life.

The Jewish philosopher Joseph Albo (in *Sefer ha-Ikkarim*, book 3, ch. 1) places humans at the top of the earthly hierarchy and discerns in this the possibility for humans to receive God's Revelation. This is just a medieval way of saying what we have remarked. God's Revelation, *pace* Albo and Jewish tradition, is the Torah, from which we learn our responsibilities to each other and to the rest of creation.

According to Albo, just as clothes are an integral part of the animal, but external to people, who have to make clothes for themselves, so are specific ethical impulses integral to the behavior of particular animals, and we should learn from their behavior. "Who teaches us from the beasts of the earth, and imparts wisdom to us through the birds of the sky" (Job 35:11) – as the Talmud put it (TB Eruvim 100b): "R. Johanan said, If these things were not commanded in the Torah, we could learn modesty from the cat, the ant would preach against robbery, and the dove against incest." The superiority of humans lies in their unique combination of freedom to choose and the intelligence to judge, without which the divine Revelation would have no application. Being in this sense "higher" than other creatures, humans must be humble towards all. Albo, in citing these passages and commending the reading of *Perek Shirah*, articulates the attitude of humble stewardship towards Creation which characterizes rabbinic Judaism.

A Divergence Between East and West?. With regard to the hierarchical model there appears to be a radical difference of approach between Jews, Christians, and Muslims on the one hand and Hindus and Buddhists on the other.

The difference may be more apparent than real. Consider the following:

> I recall that in the year 5665 [1904/5] I visited Jaffa in the Holy Land, and went to pay my respects to its Chief Rabbi [Rav Kook]. He received me warmly... and after the afternoon prayer I accompanied him as he went out into the fields, as was his wont, to concentrate his thoughts. As we were walking I plucked some flower or plant; he trembled and quietly told me that he always took great care not to pluck, unless it were for some benefit, anything that could grow, for there was no plant below that did not have its guardian [Heb. *mazzal*] above. Everything that grew said something, every stone whispered some secret, all creation sang... (Aryeh Levine, *Laḥai Roi* (Heb., 1961), 15, 16).

Rav Kook, drawing on a range of classical Jewish sources from Psalm 148 to Lurianic mysticism, and without doubt accepting the hierarchical view of creation, nevertheless acknowledges the divine significance of all things – the immanence of God. Conversely, although Buddhists and Hindus teach respect for all life they do not conclude from this that, for instance, the life of two ants takes precedence over the life of one human being; in practice, they adopt some form of hierarchical principle.

CONCERN FOR ANIMALS. Kindness to animals is a motivating factor for general concern with the environment, rather than itself an element in conservation.

Kindness to animals features prominently in the Jewish tradition. The Ten Commandments include domestic animals in the Sabbath rest, and the "seven *Noachide laws" are even more explicit. Pious tales and folklore exemplify this attitude, as in the Talmudic anecdote of Rabbi Judah the Patriarch's contrition over having sent a calf to the slaughter (TB BM 85a and *Genesis Rabbah* 33).

Causing Pain or Distress to Animals. In rabbinic law this concern condenses into the concept of *ẓa'ar ba'alei ḥayyim* ("distress to living creatures"; see Cruelty to *Animals). An illuminating instance of halakhic concern for animal welfare is the rule attributed to the third-century Babylonian Rabbi that one should feed one's cattle before breaking bread oneself (TB Ber. 40a); even the Sabbath laws are relaxed somewhat to enable rescue of injured animals or milking of cows to ease their distress. Recently, concern has been expressed about intensive animal husbandry including battery chicken production.

Meat Eating. The Torah does not enjoin vegetarianism, though Adam and Eve were vegetarian (Gen. 1:29). Restrictions on meat eating perhaps indicate reservations. Albo (*Sefer ha-Ikkarim* 3:15) wrote that the first people were forbidden to eat meat because of the cruelty involved in killing animals.

Isaac *Abrabanel (1437–1508) endorsed this ("Commentary on Isaiah" (Heb., ch. 11 on the verse "The wolf shall lie down with the lamb."), and also taught (that when the Messiah comes we would return to the ideal, vegetarian state ("Commentary on Genesis" (Heb., ch. 2). The popular trend to vegetarianism has won many Jewish adherents though little official backing from religious leaders.

Hunting. On February 23, 1716, Duke Christian of Sachsen Weissenfels celebrated his 53rd birthday by a great hunting party. History would have passed by the Duke as well as the occasion had not J.S. Bach honored them with his "Hunting Cantata." The text by Salomo Franck, secretary of the upper consistory at Weimar, is a grand celebration of nature and its priest, Duke Christian, with no sense that hunting sounds a discordant note, and the cantata includes one of Bach's most expressive arias, *Schafe können sicher weiden* ("Sheep may safely graze").

Conditions of Jewish life in the past millennium or so have rarely afforded Jewish notables the opportunity to celebrate their birthdays by hunting parties. But it has happened from time to time and led rabbis to voice their censure.

N. Rakover sums up the halakhic objections to "sport" hunting under eight heads: (1) It is destructive/wasteful (see section on cutting down fruit trees). (2) It causes distress to animals (section on causing pain and distress to animals). (3) It actively produces non-*kasher* carcasses. (4) It leads to trading non-*kasher* commodities. (5) The hunter exposes himself to danger unnecessarily. (6) It wastes time. (7) The hunt is a "seat of the scornful" (Ps. 1:1). (8) "Thou shalt not conform to their institutions" (Lev. 18:3).

From this we see that although Jewish religious tradition despises hunting for sport, this is on ethical and ritual grounds rather than in the interest of conservation.[28]

The Land and the People – A Paradigm

Judaism, both in biblical times and subsequently, has emphasized the inter-relationship of the Jewish people and its land, and the idea that the prosperity of the land depends on the people's obedience to God's covenant. For instance:

> If you pay heed to the commandments which I give you this day, and love the Lord your God and serve him with all your heart and soul, then I will send rain for your land in season…. and you will gather your corn and new wine and oil, and I will provide pasture…. you shall eat your fill. Take good care not to be led astray in your hearts nor to turn aside and serve other gods…. or the Lord will become angry with you; he will shut up the skies and there will be no rain, your ground will not yield its harvest, and you will soon vanish from the rich land which the Lord is giving you (Deut. 11:13–17).

Two steps are necessary to apply this link between morality and prosperity to the contemporary situation: 1. The chosen land and people must be understood as the prototype of (a) all actual individual geographical nations (including, of course, Israel) in their relationships with land and of (b) humanity as a whole in its relationship with the planet as a whole. 2. There must be satisfactory clarification of the meaning of "obedience to God" as the human side of the covenant to ensure that "the land will be blessed." The Bible certainly has in mind justice and moral rectitude, but in spelling out "the commandments of God" it includes specific prescriptions which directly regulate care of the land and celebration of its produce.

To sum up – the Bible stresses the intimate relationship between people and land. The prosperity of land depends on (a) the social justice and moral integrity of the people on it and (b) a caring, even loving, attitude to land with effective regulation of its use. Conservation demands the extrapolation of these principles from ancient or idealized Israel to the contemporary global situation; this calls for education in social values together with scientific investigation of the effects of our activities on nature.

SABBATICAL YEAR AND JUBILEE.

> When you enter the land which I give you, the land shall keep sabbaths to the Lord. For six years you may sow your fields and for six years prune your vineyards but in the seventh year the land shall keep a sabbath of sacred rest, a sabbath to the Lord. You shall not sow your field nor prune your vineyard … (Lev. 25:2–4)

The analogy between the sabbath (literally, "rest day") of the land and that of people communicates the idea that land must "rest" to be refreshed and regain its productive vigor. In contemporary terms, land resources must be conserved through the avoidance of overuse.

The Bible pointedly links this to social justice. Just as land must not be exploited so slaves must go free after six years of bondage or in the Jubilee (50th) year, and the sabbatical year (in Hebrew *shemittah* – "release") cancels private debts, thus preventing exploitation of the individual.

The consequence of disobedience is destruction of the land, which God so cares for that he will heal it in the absence of its unfaithful inhabitants:

> If in spite of this you do not listen to me and still defy me … I will make your cities desolate and destroy your sanctuaries … your land shall be desolate and your cities heaps of rubble. Then, all the time that it lies desolate, while you are in exile in the land of your enemies, your land shall enjoy its sabbaths to the full (Lev. 26:27–35).

If in Israel today there is only a handful of agricultural collectives which observe the "sabbath of land" in its biblical and rabbinic sense, the biblical text had undoubtedly influenced the country's scientists and agronomists to question the intensive agriculture favored in the early years of the State and to give high priority to conservation of land resources.

CUTTING DOWN FRUIT TREES.

> When you are at war, and lay siege to a city…. do not destroy its trees by taking the axe to them, for they provide you with food (Deut. 20:19).

In its biblical context this is a counsel of prudence rather than a principle of conservation; the Israelites are enjoined to use only "non-productive," that is, non fruit-bearing trees, for their siege works.

In rabbinic teaching, however, the verse has become the *locus classicus* for conserving all that has been created, so that the very phrase *bal tashḥit* (lit. "not to destroy") is inculcated into small children to teach them not to destroy or waste even those things they do not need. In an account of the commandments specially written for his son, Rabbi Aaron Ha-Levi of Barcelona (c. 1300) sums up the purpose of this one as follows:

> This is meant to ingrain in us the love of that which is good and beneficial and to cleave to it; by this means good will imbue our souls and we will keep far from everything evil or destructive. This is the way of the devout and those of good deeds – they love peace, rejoice in that which benefits people and brings them to Torah; they never destroy even a grain of mustard, and are upset at any destruction they see. If only they can save anything from being spoilt they spare no effort to do so (*Sefer Ha-Ḥinnukh*, Mitzvah 529).

LIMITATION OF GRAZING RIGHTS. The Mishnah rules: "One may not raise small cattle [i.e., sheep, goats, etc.] in the Land of Israel, but one may do so in Syria or in the uninhabited parts of the Land of Israel (BK 7:7). The history of this law has been researched, and there is evidence of similar restrictions from as early as the third century B.C.E.

The Mishnah itself does not itself provide a rationale for the law. Later rabbis suggest: (a) that its primary purpose is to prevent the "robbery" of crops by roaming animals, and (b) that its objective is to encourage settlement in the Land. This latter reason is based on the premise that the raising of sheep and goats is inimical to the cultivation of crops and reflects the ancient rivalry between nomad and farmer; at the same time it poses the question considered by modern ecologists of whether animal husbandry is an efficient way of producing food. (The rabbis of the Talmud, however, did not envisage vegetarianism and did not ban the raising of large cattle in the Land. They assumed that meat would be eaten but tried to ensure that its production would not interfere with agriculture).

AGRICULTURAL FESTIVALS. The concept of "promised land" is an assertion that the consummation of social and national life depends on harmony with the land.

The biblical pilgrim-festivals all celebrate the Land and its crops, though they are also given historical and spiritual meanings. Through the joyful collective experience of these festivals the people learned to cherish the Land and their relationship, through God's commandments, with it; the sense of joy was heightened through fulfillment of the divine commandments to share the bounty of the land with "the Levite, the stranger, the orphan, and the widow" (a frequent expression, for instance, Deuteronomy 16:11).

Specific Environmental Laws

Several aspects of environmental pollution are dealt with in traditional *halakhah*. Although the classical sources were composed in situations very different from those of the present the law has been, and is, in a continuous state of development, and in any case the basic principles are clearly relevant to contemporary situations.

WASTE DISPOSAL. Arising from Deuteronomy 23:13,14 *halakhah* insists that refuse be removed "outside the camp," that is, collected in a location where it will not reduce the quality of life. The Talmud and Codes extend this concept to the general prohibition of dumping refuse or garbage where it may interfere with the environment or with crops.

It would be anachronistic to seek in the earlier sources the concept of waste disposal as threatening the total balance of nature or the climate. However, if the rabbis forbade the growing of kitchen gardens and orchards around Jerusalem on the grounds that the manuring would degrade the local environment (BK 82b), one need have no doubt that they would have been deeply concerned at the large-scale environmental degradation caused by traditional mining operations, the burning of fossil fuels, and the like.

Smell (see also the following section) is regarded in *halakhah* as a particular nuisance, hence there are rules regarding the siting not only of lavatories but also of odoriferous commercial operations such as tanneries (TB BB ch. 2; codified, with subsequent developments, in Shulḥan Arukh ḤM, ch. 145). Certainly, rabbinic law accords priority to environmental over purely commercial considerations.

ATMOSPHERIC POLLUTION AND SMOKE. Like smell, atmospheric pollution and smoke are placed by the rabbis within the category of indirect damage, since their effects are produced at a distance. They are nevertheless unequivocally forbidden.

The Mishnah (BB2) bans the siting of a threshing floor within 50 cubits of a residential area, since the flying particles set in motion by the threshing process would diminish the quality of the air.

Likewise, the second-century rabbi Nathan ruled that a furnace might not be sited within 50 cubits of a residential area because of the effect of its smoke on the atmosphere (BB 1:7); the 50-cubit limit was subsequently extended by the *geonim* to whatever the distance from which smoke might cause eye irritation or general annoyance (S. Assaf (ed.), *Geonic Responsa*, (5689/1929), p. 32).

The Hazards Prevention Law, passed by the Israeli Knesset on March 23, 1961, contains the following provisions:

> #3 No person shall create a strong or unreasonable smell, of whatever origin, if it disturbs or is likely to disturb a person nearby or passerby.
> #4a No person shall create strong or unreasonable pollution of the air, of whatever origin, if it disturbs or is likely to disturb a person nearby or passerby.

The subjectivity of "reasonable" in this context is apparent. Meir Sichel, in a study on the ecological problems that arise from the use of energy resources for power stations to manufacture electricity, and from various types of industrial and domestic consumption such as cooking, heating, and lighting, has drawn on the resources of traditional Jewish law in an attempt to define more precisely what should be regarded as "reasonable." Citing rabbinic responsa over an 800-year period he concludes that *halakhah* is even more insistent on individual rights than the civil law (of Israel), and that *halakhah* does not recognize "prior rights" of a defendant who claims that he had established a right to produce the annoyance or pollutant before the plaintiff appeared on the scene (M. Sichel, "Air Pollution – Smoke and Odour Damage," in: *Jewish Law Annual*, 5 (1985), 25–43).

In an exercise such as Sichel's there is no difficulty in applying traditional law to the contemporary context with regard to priority of rights, and also in clarifying the relationship between public and private rights. However, it is less clear that one can achieve a satisfactory definition of "reasonable," since ideas of what is acceptable vary not only from person to person but in accordance with changing scientific understanding of the nature of the damage caused by smells and smoke, including the "invisible" hazards of germs and radiation unknown to earlier generations.

WATER POLLUTION. Several laws were instituted by the rabbis to safeguard the freedom from pollution, as well as the fair distribution, of water. A typical early source says:

> If one is digging out caves for the public he may wash his hands, face, and feet; but if his feet are dirty with mud or excrement it is forbidden. [If he is digging] a well or a ditch [for drinking water], then [whether his feet are clean or dirty] he may not wash them (Tosef. BM 11:31 (ed. Zuckermandel).

Pregnant with possibilities for application to contemporary life is the principle that one may claim damages or obtain an appropriate injunction to remove the nuisance where the purity of one's water supply is endangered by a neighbor's drainage or similar works. It is significant that the *geonim* here also rejected the Talmudic distance limit in favor of a broad interpretation of the law to cover damage irrespective of distance (cited in Sh. Ar., ḤM 155:21).

Noise. Rabbinic law on noise pollution offers a fascinating instance of balance of priorities. The Mishnah lays down that in a residential area neighbors have the right to object to the opening of a shop or similar enterprise on the grounds that the noise would disturb their tranquility. It is permitted, however, to open a school for Torah notwithstanding the noise of children, for education has priority. Later authorities discuss the limit of noise which has to be tolerated in the interest of education (Rashi on TB BB 21a), and whether other forms of religious activity might have similar priority to the opening of a school (Sh. Ar., ḤM 156:3).

BEAUTY. Much could be said of the rabbinic appreciation of beauty in general. Here we concern ourselves only with legislation explicitly intended to enhance the environment, which is rooted in the biblical law of the Levitical cities:

> Tell the Israelites to set aside towns in their patrimony as homes for the Levites, and give them also the common land surrounding the towns. They shall live in the towns, and keep their beasts, their herds, and all their livestock on the common land. The land of the towns which you give the Levites shall extend from the center of the town outwards for a thousand cubits in each direction. Starting from the town the eastern boundary shall measure two thousand cubits, the southern two thousand, the western two thousand, and the northern two thousand, with the town in the center. They shall have this as the common land adjoining their towns. (Lev. 35:2–5)

As this passage is understood by the rabbis, there was to be a double surround to each town, first a "green belt" of a thousand cubits, then a two-thousand-cubit-wide belt for "fields and vineyards." While some maintained that the thousand-cubit band was for pasture, Rashi (on TB Sota 22b) explains that it was not for use, but "for the beauty of the town, to give it space" – a concept reflected in Maimonides' interpretation of the Talmudic rules on the distancing of trees from residences (see Maimonides, Yad., Shekhenim, ch. 10).

The rabbis debate whether this form of "town planning" ought to be extended to non-Levitical towns, at least in the land of Israel, designated by Jeremiah (3:19) and Ezekiel (20:6,15), the beautiful land."

The rabbinic appreciation of beauty in nature is highlighted in the blessing they set to be recited when one sees "the first blossoms in Spring":

> You are blessed, Lord our God and ruler of the universe, who have omitted nothing from your world, but created within it good creatures and good and beautiful trees in which people may take delight [in the name of Judah bar Ezekiel (third-century Palestinian) in TB Ber. 43b; a whole chapter of Sh. Ar., OḤ 226, is devoted to it.).

Sample Ethical Problems Relating to Conservation

ANIMAL VERSUS HUMAN LIFE. Judaism consistently values human life more than animal life. One should not risk one's life to save an animal; for instance, if one is driving a car and a dog runs into the road it would be wrong to swerve, endangering one's own or someone else's life, to save the dog.

But is it right to take a human life, e.g., that of a poacher, to save not an individual animal but an endangered species? I can find nothing in Jewish sources to support killing poachers in any circumstances other than those in which they directly threaten human life. If it be argued that the extinction of a species would threaten human life because it would upset the balance of nature, it is still unlikely that Jewish law would countenance homicide to avoid an indirect and uncertain threat of this nature.

Even if homicide were justified in such circumstances, how many human lives is a single species worth? How far down the evolutionary scale would such a principle be applied? After all, the argument about upsetting the balance of nature applies equally with microscopic species as with large cuddly looking vertebrates like the panda, and with plants as much as with animals.

Judaism, true to the hierarchical principle of creation (see above), consistently values human life more than that of other living things, but at the same time stresses the special responsibility of human beings to "work on and look after" the created order (Genesis 2:15 – see section-Stewardship or Domination).

PROCREATION VERSUS POPULATION CONTROL. The question of birth control (including abortion) in Judaism is complex, but there is universal agreement that at least some forms of birth control are permissible where a potential mother's life is in danger and that abortion is not only permissible but mandatory up to full term to save the mother's life. Significant is the value system which insists that, even though contraception may be morally questionable, it is preferable to abstinence where life danger would be involved through normal sexual relations within a marriage.

What happens where economic considerations rather than life danger come into play? Here we must distinguish between (a) personal economic difficulties and (b) circumstances of "famine in the world," where economic hardship is general.

On the whole, *halakhah* places the basic duty of procreation above personal economic hardship. But what about general economic hardship, which can arise (a) through local or temporary famine and (b) through the upward pressure of population on finite world resources?

The former situation was in the mind of the third-century Palestinian sage Resh Lakish when he ruled: "It is forbidden for a man to engage in sexual intercourse in years of famine" (TB. Ta'an. 11a). Although the ruling of Resh Lakish was adopted by the codes (Sh. Ar., OḤ 240:12 and 574:4), its application was restricted to those who already have children, and the decision between abstinence and contraception is less clear here than where there is a direct hazard to life.

Upward pressure of population on world resources is a concept unknown to the classical sources of the Jewish religion and not indeed clearly understood by anyone before Malthus. As Feldman remarks:

> It must be repeated here that the "population explosion" has nothing to do with the Responsa, and vice versa. The Rabbis were issuing their analyses and their replies to a specific couple with a specific query. These couples were never in a situation where they might aggravate a world problem; on the contrary, the Jewish community was very often in a position of seeking to replenish its depleted ranks after pogrom or exile.... (*Marital Relations, Birth Control and Abortion in Jewish Law* (1974), 304)

Feldman goes on to say "It would be just as reckless to overbreed as to refrain from procreation." As the duty of procreation is expressed in Genesis in the words "be fruitful and multiply and fill the earth" it is not unreasonable to suggest that "fill" be taken as "reach the maximum population sustainable at an acceptable standard of living but do not exceed it." In like manner the rabbis (TB Yev. 62a) utilize Isaiah's phrase "God made the earth ... no empty void, but made it for a place to dwell in" (45:18) to define the minimum requirement for procreation – a requirement, namely one son and one daughter, which does not increase population.

Of course, there is room for local variation amongst populations. Although as a general rule governments nowadays should discourage population growth there are instances of thinly populated areas or of small ethnic groups whose survival is threatened where some population growth might be acceptable even from the global perspective.

NUCLEAR, FOSSIL FUEL, SOLAR ENERGY. Can religious sources offer guidance on the choice between nuclear and fossil, and other energy sources?

They can have very little to say and – especially in view of the extravagant views expressed by some religious leaders – it is important to understand why their potential contribution to current debate is so small.

The choice among energy sources rests on the following parameters: (1) cost effectiveness; (2) environmental damage caused by production; (3) operational hazards; (4) clean disposal of waste products; (5) long-term environmental sustainability.

Cost effectiveness cannot be established without weighing the other factors. There is no point, however, at which religious consideration apply in establishing whether a particular combination of nuclear reactor plus safety plus storage of waste and so on will cost more or less than alternative "packages" for energy production.

It is equally clear that religious considerations have no part to play in assessing environmental damage caused by production, operational hazards, whether waste products can be cleanly disposed of, or what is the long-term environmental sustainability of a method of energy production. These are all technical matters, demanding painstaking research and hard evidence, and they have nothing to do with theology.

It is a matter of sadness and regret that extreme environmentalists are so prone to stirring up the emotions of the faithful for or against some project, such as nuclear energy, which really ought to be assessed on objective grounds. Much of the hurt arises from the way the extremists "demonize" those of whom they disapprove, and in the name of love generate hatred against people who seek to bring benefit to humanity.

GLOBAL WARMING. A very similar analysis could be made of the problems relating to global warming. The fact is that in mid-1990 no one knew the extent, if any, to which global temperatures have risen as a result of the rise in atmospheric carbon dioxide, and no one knew what would be the overall effects of the projected doubling of atmospheric carbon dioxide by the middle of the next century. Some consequences, indeed, may be beneficial, such as greater productivity of plants in an atmosphere with more carbon dioxide. Unfortunately, neither the techniques of mathematical modeling used to make the projections, nor the base of global observations at 500-kilometer intervals, can yield firm results. (See the summary provided by Robert M. White, "The Great Climate Debate," in: *Scientific American*, July 1990.)

So how can a government decide whether to spend hundreds of billions of dollars on reducing atmospheric carbon dioxide, and vast sums in aiding third world countries to avoid developing along "greenhouse" lines, when the draconian measures required greatly limit personal freedom and much of the expenditure might be better diverted to building hospitals, improving education and the like?

Essential steps, including better research, must be initiated, but it would be a lack of wisdom to rush into the most extreme measures demanded. It is clear that the decisions must be rooted in prudence, not in theology. Theology tends to absolutize and call for radical solutions where we have only relative and uncertain evidence, or conversely to commend us to faith in God when we ought to be taking initiatives ourselves.

DIRECTED EVOLUTION. After writing about the progress from physical evolution through biological evolution to cultural evolution, Edward Rubinstein states:

> Henceforth, life no longer evolves solely through chance mutation. Humankind has begun to modify evolution, to bring about nonrandom, deliberate changes in DNA that alter living assemblies and create assemblies that did not exist before.

The messengers of directed evolution are human beings. Their messages, expressed in the language and methods of molecular biology, genetics and medicine and in moral precepts, express their awareness of human imperfections and reflect the values and aspirations of their species. (E. Rubinstein, "Stages of Evolution and their Messengers," in: *Scientific American* (June 1989), p. 104.)

These words indicate the area where religions, Judaism included, are most in need of adjusting themselves to contemporary reality – the area in which modern knowledge sets us most apart from those who formed our religious traditions. Religion as we know it has come into being only since the Neolithic Revolution, and thus presupposes some technology, some mastery of nature. But it has also assumed that the broad situation of humanity is static, and this is now seen to be an illusion.

All at once there is the prospect, alarming to some yet challenging to others, that we can set the direction of future development for all creatures in our world. The Ethics Committees of our hospitals and medical schools are forced to take decisions; although the religious take part – and Judaism has a distinctive contribution to make to medical ethics – it has yet to be shown that traditional sources can be brought to bear other than in the vaguest way ("we uphold the sanctity of life") on the problems raised even by currently available genetic engineering.

Will religions, as so often in the past, obstruct the development of science? They need not. Jewish religious have ranged from Isaac Abrabanel, who opposed in principle the development of technology (see his commentary on Genesis 2), to *Abraham bar *Ḥiyya, who in the 12th century played a major role in the transmission of Greco-Arab science to the west. If Judaism (or any other religion) is to contribute towards conservation it will need to be in the spirit of Abraham bar Ḥiyya, through support for good science, rather than through idealization of the "simple life" in the spirit of Seneca and Abrabanel.

Conclusion – Religion and Conservation

Judaism, along with other religions, has resources which can be used to encourage people in the proper management of Planet Earth. We will now review the interaction of religion with conservation with special reference to the source cited.

1. We saw in the section on goodness of the physical world how Judaism interprets the created world, with its balanced biodiverse ecology, as a "testimony to God," with humankind at the pinnacle holding special responsibility for its maintenance and preservation. Certainly, this attitude is more conducive to an interest in conservation than would be emphasis on the centrality of the "next world," on the spirit versus the body, or on the "inferior" or "illusionary" nature of the material world.

2. One of the priorities of conservation at the present time is to control population so as not to exceed resources. Although Judaism stresses the duty of procreation we learned in the section on procreation versus population control that it offers the prospect of constructive approach to population planning, including some role for both contraception and abortion.

3. We have noted several specific areas in which Judaism has developed laws or policies significant for conservation. Prime among them (see the section: The Land and The People – a paradigm) were the laws regulating the relationship between people and land, for which the "chosen people" in the "promised land" is the model. Care of animals (section: Concern for Animals), waste disposal, atmospheric and water pollution, noise, and beauty of the environment were also treated in the classical sources. It would be neither possible nor fully adequate to take legislation straight from these sources; but it is certainly possible to work in continuity with them, bearing in mind the radically new awareness of the need for conserving the world and its resources as a whole.

4. Religions, Judaism included, discourage the pursuit of personal wealth. While in some instances this may be beneficial to the environment – if people want fewer cars and fewer books there will be fewer harmful emissions and fewer forests will be chopped down – there are also many ways in which poverty harms the environment – for instance, less research

and development means that such technology as remains (presumably for hospitals and other welfare matters) will be less efficient and the problems of environmental pollution less effectively addressed. Only rich societies can afford clean disposal of wastes.

5. Some religions remain strongly committed to evangelistic or conversionist aims which inhibit cooperation with people of other religions. Judaism is not currently in an actively missionary phase; some would say that it is unduly introspective, and needs to proclaim its values in a more universal context. All religions, however, must desist from ideological conflicts and espouse dialogue; conservation cannot be effective without global cooperation.

6. Mere information can motivate, as when someone who perceives a lion ready to pounce reacts swiftly. If ecological disaster were as clearly perceived as a crouching lion ideological motivation would be unnecessary. It is better that religions support conservation than oppose it, but the world would be safer if people would act on the basis of rational collective self-preservation rather than on the basis of confused and uncontrollable ideologies.

7. Several times, particularly in discussing energy sources and global warming, we had to stress the need to distinguish between technological and value judgments. Whether or not nuclear reactors should be built must depend on a careful, dispassionate assessment of their hazards; shrill condemnation of the "hubris of modern technology" merely hinders judgment, though it is right and proper that religious values be considered when an informed choice is made. Of course, the same need for objective assessment before value judgments are made applies to all other major conservation questions, such as how to reverse deforestation, control the greenhouse effect, restore the ozone layer.

8. Towards the end of the section on directed evolution we noted a characteristic religious ambivalence towards science. In the interest of conservation it is essential that the "pro-science" attitude of Abraham bar Ḥiyya, Maimonides, and others be encouraged. The extreme attitude of "simple life" proponents must be resisted. For a start, the present world population could not be supported if we were to revert to the simple life. Moreover, who would wish to do without sanitation, communications, electric light, books, travel, medical services and all those other benefits of "complex" civilization?

Finally, let us note that Judaism, like other religions, has a vital role to play in eradicating those evils and promoting those values in society without which no conservation policies can be effective. The single greatest social evil is official corruption, frequently rife in precisely those countries where conservation measures must be carried out. Next in line is drug addiction with its associated trade. But political animosities, such as those in the midst of which Israel finds itself, and which siphon off the world's resources into arms and destruction, surely head the list of human activities inimical to conservation. Religions must combat these evils and at the same time work intelligently for peace, not only between nations but among religions themselves.

For the Jewish contribution to the environmental sciences, see *Environmental Sciences. See also *Conservation.

BIBLIOGRAPHY: D. Ehrenfeld and P.J. Bentley, "Judaism and the Practice of Stewardship," in: *Judaism*, 24 (1985), 310–11; Israel Ministry of Justice, N. Rakover (compiler), *Protection of the Environment* (Heb., 1972); idem, *Protection of Animals* (Heb., 1976); S. Cooper, in: Harvey E. Goldberg (ed.), *Judaism: Viewed from Within and from Without* (1987), ch. 1; D. Novak, *The Image of the Non-Jew in Judaism* (1983), ch. 8; R. Schwarz, *Judaism and Vegetarianism* (1982); D.M. Feldman, *Marital Relations, Birth Control and Abortion in Jewish Law* (1974); I. Jakobovits, *Jewish Medical Ethics*, (1975^4); G. Allon, *History of the Jews in the Land of Israel in the Period of the Mishnah and the Talmud* (Hebrew), 1:173–78 and 359.

[Normon Solomon]

CONSERVATIVE JUDAISM (also known as **Masorti Judaism**), one of the three principal modern Jewish religious denominations, emerging, along with Reform and Orthodoxy, in the 19th-century era of emancipation.

After the denial of emancipation to Central European Jewry by the Congress of Vienna (1815), Jews found themselves frustrated in their desire to participate in the intellectual and political transformations of the day. *Reform Judaism arose as an attempt to reformulate Judaism, no longer as a comprehensive way of life and national identity, but as a western-style religion, so as to accommodate the desire of Jews to acculturate into their host societies while resisting total assimilation or conversion to Christianity. Radical and moderate wings of Reform emerged as its leaders debated the extent of changes from Jewish tradition. Zechariah *Frankel, chief rabbi of Dresden, Germany, a proponent of moderate Reform, broke with his more radical colleagues at the Rabbinical Conference of Frankfurt (1845), over the issue of retaining Hebrew as the language of prayer. Frankel called for "positive-historical Judaism." This formula connotes, first, a predisposition to accept much of the "positive," ceremonial substance of Jewish practice while allowing for moderate changes, and second, an attitude of respect for the historical nature of Judaism. The loyalties of generations of Jews to a particular practice, no less than a proof-text from an authoritative religious source, could sanctify that usage.

In 1854, Frankel concretized his conservative yet flexible approach to Judaism in a rabbinical school that he headed, the *Juedisch-Theologisches Seminar (Jewish Theological Seminary) of Breslau. Until destroyed by the Nazis in 1938, this rabbinical school trained the institutional leaders and served as a scholarly center for "Historical Judaism" in Central Europe.

In the United States

The principal development of Conservative Judaism took place in the United States. As in Germany, Conservative Judaism in the U.S. began with the creation of a school rather than of a congregational union. Developments within American

Reform Judaism strained the alliance of moderates and radicals. In a moment of high symbolism, the 1883 banquet celebrating the rabbinic ordination of *Hebrew Union College's first graduates featured a variety of nonkosher foods and became known as "the treifa banquet." In the ensuing, contentious atmosphere, the Radical Reform wing of the movement passed its 1885 Pittsburgh Platform, dismissing biblical and rabbinic rituals regulating diet and dress as anachronisms. In response, moderate rabbis and scholars, principally Sabato *Morais, Henry Pereira *Mendes, Alexander *Kohut, and Cyrus *Adler, called for the establishment of a new rabbinical seminary, more hospitable to traditional Judaism. By January 1887, the Jewish Theological Seminary Association opened in New York City, with the mandate to preserve "the knowledge and practice of historical Judaism."

Leaders of the new seminary did not seek to create a denomination; on the contrary, they hoped their school would become the unifying institution of all opponents of Reform. In addition to the moderate reformers of Sephardi or West European background, the Seminary's founders looked to secure the loyalty of the burgeoning East European Jewish population of New York. In this hope they were disappointed. Despite participating in the 1898 creation of the *Union of Orthodox Jewish Congregations, Seminary leaders were not able to create a congregational base comparable to what the Hebrew Union College enjoyed in its *Union of American Hebrew Congregations. Without significant congregational support, the Jewish Theological Seminary Association endured precarious finances during its first 15 years and was compelled to reorganize in 1902, but not before graduating 14 rabbis and three *ḥazzanim*, including Joseph H. *Hertz, who became chief rabbi of the British Empire, and Mordecai M. *Kaplan, preeminent theologian and founder of *Reconstructionist Judaism.

THE SCHECHTER YEARS. Although, prior to its 1902 reorganization, the Seminary had not successfully engaged traditionalist Russian Jewish immigrants, a group of prominent Reform lay leaders envisioned that the school could yet serve to Americanize that group, and thus simultaneously preserve the Jewishness of the new arrivals and reduce the social tension occasioned by their "un-American" ways. After the death of Morais in 1897, Adler mobilized Jacob *Schiff, a supporter of the school since 1888, and his colleagues, including Louis *Marshall, to set the school on a firmer financial basis and thus produce the leadership for the successful acculturation of the children of the new immigrants. Specifically, they raised the funds to engage Solomon *Schechter as the president of the faculty of the new organization, the *Jewish Theological Seminary of America (JTS). Educated in a traditional fashion as well as in modern, rabbinical seminaries, a first-rank rabbinic scholar with a gift for popularization, an orator equally at home in Jewish sources and in the classics of English rhetoric, Schechter personally exemplified the envisioned cultural type. Under his leadership, JTS was to fulfill its mission among American Jewry by producing religiously observant and intellectually open-minded rabbis.

For his part, Schechter held to the dream of Morais, to unify the non-Reform elements of the American Jewish community. In 1913, Schechter created the *United Synagogue of America, hoping that it would encompass congregations across the traditionalist and moderate ideological spectrum. But he was no more successful in this regard than Morais, because American Jewish Orthodoxy was gaining self-definition at that same time, promoting its own Rabbi Isaac Elchanan Theological Seminary (see *Yeshiva University).

Schechter did succeed, nonetheless, in making JTS the "fountainhead" of what would become a full-fledged denomination, Conservative Judaism. He engaged a faculty of leading scholars, including Louis *Ginzberg, Alexander *Marx, Israel *Friedlaender, and Israel *Davidson and oversaw the creation of the preeminent Judaica library in America. He transformed JTS into a graduate-level program. "Schechter's Seminary," as it was widely known, graduated an increasing number of Jewish communal leaders, at first rabbis, then also teachers, after the 1909 organization of its Teachers' Institute under the leadership of Mordecai Kaplan.

THE ADLER YEARS. After Schechter's death in 1915, his successor at JTS, Cyrus Adler, systematized the school's administrative procedures and presided over the construction of its new campus – including the Jewish Museum – which opened in 1930. Adler maintained the school's ideological posture and social program, to Americanize traditional Judaism. Adler also succeeded Schechter at the United Synagogue, and focused its efforts on obtaining congregational placements for JTS graduates. The JTS rabbinic alumni, first organized in 1901 and renamed the *Rabbinical Assembly in 1918, collaborated with him in this endeavor. Adler's tenure was one of building the infrastructure of Conservative Judaism, while discouraging partisan ideological pronouncements that might weaken its centrist coalition.

Nonetheless, the growing movement did have ideological "right" and "left" wings. Adler himself and Louis Ginzberg, representing the traditionalist point of view, controlled the direction and official pronouncements of the movement. Ginzberg founded and chaired the United Synagogue's Committee on the Interpretation of Jewish Law (191–27) which evolved into the Committee on Jewish Law of the Rabbinical Assembly (1927–) which was led until 1948 by traditionalists such as Louis *Epstein, Boaz *Cohen, and Michael *Higger.

Mordecai Kaplan was the leader of the movement's left wing. Kaplan's "Reconstructionist" definition of Judaism as an evolving religious civilization and his call to transform the modern synagogue into a comprehensive spiritual, intellectual, and cultural Jewish center resonated even among Conservative rabbis who took issue with his rejection of supernaturalism in formulating Jewish theology. During the 1930s, Kaplan's philosophical and liturgical publications spurred controversy among JTS faculty and in the broader movement, but the JTS administrative response, to assign Kaplan to teaching homiletics rather than Talmud, only increased his influence among generations of emerging professionals.

THE FINKELSTEIN YEARS. Conservative Judaism enjoyed its greatest period of growth during the two decades following World War II. Across the East, Midwest, and Sunbelt regions of the country, returning veterans and their growing families moved to the newly expanding suburbs, creating numerous houses of worship. Between 1945 and 1964, the United Synagogue grew from 190 to 778 member congregations. For the children of East European immigrants, the Conservative synagogue represented an acceptable balance of tradition and change.

As the movement expanded rapidly and faced the new conditions of Jewish life in suburbia, the tension between school and denomination also increased. Under the leadership of Louis *Finkelstein (1940–72), JTS aspired to influence American society at large, both Jewish and Gentile, without identifying the school's prime task as the support of its denomination; rather, it saw the Conservative movement as its own support network. Regarding himself as a "bridge-builder," Finkelstein created ecumenical institutes and expanded into radio and television programming, while further developing the school as an academic research center.

Rabbinical Assembly leaders such as Milton *Steinberg and Solomon *Goldman, critical of this focus, urged JTS to do more to build up the institutions of the movement. The Rabbinical Assembly took the lead in publishing a series of prayer books for use in Conservative congregations, more traditional than the Reconstructionist editions yet enriched with modern supplemental readings and, in selected passages, unorthodox in wording. The widespread adoption of Morris Silverman's *Sabbath and Festival Prayer Book* contributed to the nationwide scope of Conservative Judaism.

THE COMMITTEE ON JEWISH LAW AND STANDARDS. The Rabbinical Assembly's Committee on Jewish Law became the Committee on Jewish Law and Standards (CJLS) in 1948. This reorganization was a revolt against Boaz *Cohen and the traditionalists. As a result, the majority ruled in 1950 that it is permissible to ride to the synagogue on the Sabbath while a minority opinion forbade this practice. In the early 1950s, the CJLS was going to take unilateral action in order to solve the problem of *agunot* (chained women) whose husbands gave them a civil divorce but would not give them a *get* (religious divorce). Since Finkelstein did not want the CJLS to adopt a radical solution, he got Saul *Lieberman – the preeminent Talmudist at JTS – and the JTS faculty involved. Lieberman wrote the "Lieberman Ketubah" in 1954 which empowered a new Joint Bet Din of the Rabbinical Assembly and JTS – and by implication the secular courts – to force recalcitrant husbands to give their wives a *get*. The "Lieberman Ketubah" did not achieve the desired effect, but it did lead to greater cooperation between JTS and the Rabbinical Assembly.

SOCIAL AND EDUCATIONAL INSTITUTIONS. The movement provided religious and social programming for adult women and men at the synagogue level in Sisterhoods and Men's Clubs, organized nationally in the Women's League for Conservative Judaism (1918–) and the Federation of Jewish Men's Clubs (1929–).

During the post-war years of growth, Conservative Judaism developed educational and social institutions for youth. Kaplan and JTS created the Leadership Training Fellowship (LTF) in 1946 in order to prepare young men and women to study at JTS. One year later, Midwest Jewish leaders opened an educational summer camp, Ramah, and JTS became the camp's sponsor by 1948. The Ramah camp movement expanded, with numerous camps in North America, South America, Israel, and the Ukraine. It provided Hebrew and Jewish educational grounding for tens of thousands of youngsters, who became the nucleus of the lay and rabbinic leadership of the movement in the late 20th century. In 1951, the United Synagogue created United Synagogue Youth, which brought tens of thousands of young people closer to Judaism through its chapters, *kinnusim*, camps, Israel and European pilgrimages, and USY-on-Wheels.

In the formal educational setting, departing from a reliance on Sunday schools and afternoon Hebrew schools, Conservative educators such as Simon *Greenberg began to promote day schools. In 1951, Robert *Gordis opened a day school at his synagogue, Beth El of Rockaway Park, New York, and in 1965, a network of such schools formed the Solomon Schechter Day School Association. Day schools and supplemental schools currently coexist, with increasing numbers of Conservative families opting to give their children the more intensive schooling, especially in the primary grades.

UNIVERSITY OF JUDAISM. The national scope of Conservative Judaism after World War II contributed to the decentralization of denominational authority. In 1947, as America's West Coast was developing into a center of Jewish life, Mordecai Kaplan and Simon *Greenberg of JTS opened the *University of Judaism in Los Angeles, California. Under the leadership of David *Lieber, and later of Robert *Wexler, the school charted a course distinct from JTS, focused on Jewish liberal arts learning rather than professional training and on a very large adult education program. In 1996, the University of Judaism asserted its independence from JTS, by opening up its own Ziegler School of Rabbinic Studies.

THE SIXTIES. Conservative Judaism entered a more challenging era after 1965. The end of the postwar "baby boom" and the decay of urban and inner suburban neighborhoods hurt synagogue membership, and the number of United Synagogue member congregations dropped from its peak of 832 in 1971. Assimilation, including intermarriage, became more prevalent, and the social upheavals of the 1960s exacerbated the decline of the movement's appeal to young adults. Followers of Kaplan's Reconstructionist Judaism left the Conservative movement and opened their own rabbinical school in Philadelphia in 1968.

As a consequence of assimilation, the movement experienced a wide disparity between the high level of commitment to religious practice on the part of its rabbinic leadership and the lower degree observed by the majority of its laity. Moreover, the movement's minority of highly observant laity began to migrate to a revitalized American Jewish Orthodoxy. The resurgence of Orthodoxy, increasingly evident by 1970, both impressed and dismayed Conservative observers. Denominational leaders debated their response to the new conditions, traditionalists urging a reemphasis of commitment to *halakhah*, and liberals calling for outreach to the disaffected by means of bolder departures from tradition.

THE WOMEN'S ISSUE. The main subject of this debate in the 1970s-1980s was the role of women within the Conservative synagogue, an issue raised by the growth of feminism as an American social concern. In 1972, a small group of feminists named "Ezrat Nashim" came to the Rabbinical Assembly convention, demanding a greater role for women in the synagogue. In 1974, the CJLS voted in a near-tie to count women in the *minyan* (prayer quorum). From 1977 to 1983 the Rabbinical Assembly and the JTS faculty debated the ordination of women by JTS under its new Chancellor, Gerson *Cohen. After an initial defeat in 1979, women were admitted in 1983 after the death of Saul Lieberman and the defection of leading Talmud professors such as David *Weiss Halivni, Ch.Z. *Dimitrovsky, and Jose Faur. As a result, some Conservative rabbis set up the Union for Traditional Conservative Judaism in 1979 which later split from the movement as the *Union for Traditional Judaism (UTJ). It now has its own rabbinical association, law committee, and rabbinical school.

Amy *Eilberg was ordained by JTS as the first Conservative woman rabbi in 1985. Cohen's successor, Ismar *Schorsch, completed this process by admitting women to the Cantorial School in 1987. By 2004, 120 of the more than 1,500 members of the Rabbinical Assembly were women. A 2004 survey showed that women rabbis served in many rabbinic capacities, but had not yet achieved equality as congregational rabbis or in terms of compensation.

In recent years, the CJLS has debated the topic of women as witnesses. In any case, the attitude to women in Jewish law signaled a sea-change in the Conservative movement. It reflected the emergence of American-born, Conservative-movement educated faculty members as well as a greater degree of engagement between JTS and the denomination.

IDEOLOGY. The debate over gender roles within Conservative Judaism spurred both a self-definition and a reaffirmation of boundaries that the denomination had for so long avoided. In 1988, the various agencies of the movement jointly issued *Emet ve-Emunah: Statement of Principles of Conservative Judaism*. However, since it was written by a committee of 25 people from various aims and wings of the movement, many felt that it attempted to be all things to all people. Beginning in the 1970s, Conservative rabbis such as Seymour Siegel, Elliot Dorff, Joel *Roth, and David *Golinkin published a series of books and articles in which they explained and crystallized the Conservative approach or approaches to Jewish law. In 1995, Ismar Schorsch published "The Sacred Cluster" in which he enumerated seven core values of Conservative Judaism: God, Torah, *Talmud Torah*, *Halakhah*, the Land and State of Israel, *Klal Yisrael* (the collective Jewish People), and Hebrew. Interestingly enough, many of those same values were stressed by Louis Finkelstein in an address to the Rabbinical Assembly in 1927. Thus, despite many changes, the Conservative movement has maintained many of the same core values throughout its history.

COMMITTEES ON JEWISH LAW. Beginning in 1917, the Committee on the Interpretation of Jewish Law – which became the Committee on Jewish Law, which became the CJLS – became a meeting ground and a debating ground for the movement. The committee grew from five members to 15 members to 25 members and, as time went on, an attempt was made to appoint rabbis from the right, left, and center, and from the Rabbinical Assembly, JTS, and the United Synagogue. For many years, the CJLS issued majority and minority opinions. In more recent years, a *teshuvah* or responsum only became a valid opinion if it was supported by six members of the CJLS. Beginning in 1948, the CJLS and the RA developed the option of issuing Standards of Rabbinic Practice which are binding upon all members of the RA if approved by a two-thirds vote at the annual convention. To date, four standards have been adopted. A Conservative rabbi may not: participate in an intermarriage in any way; perform a wedding if the woman was divorced without a *get*; perform a conversion without circumcision and immersion; accept patrilineal descent.

PUBLICATION OF RESPONSA. From 1917 to 1975, *halakhic* authorities such as Louis Ginzberg, Boaz *Cohen, Michael Higger, and Isaac *Klein wrote hundreds of responsa both within the framework of the law committees and individually, but most of their responsa were never published. This changed drastically beginning in the 1970s as individual rabbis such as Isaac Klein, David Novak, and David Golinkin published their responsa along with the previously unknown responsa of Louis Ginzberg and six volumes of CJLS responsa.

THE VA'AD HALAKHAH. In 1985, the Rabbinical Assembly of Israel founded the *Va'ad Halakhah* chaired by Theodore *Friedman and later by David Golinkin. It dealt with halakhic questions from Israel and Europe in Hebrew, following procedures similar to the CJLS. It has published six volumes of responsa thus far, dealing with Israeli issues such as the Sabbatical year, entering the Temple Mount, and army service for women and *yeshivah* students, along with general halakhic issues such as conversion, medical ethics, and women in Judaism.

The Rabbinical Assembly's 1986 reaffirmation of the matrilineal principle of Jewish identity as a Standard of Rabbinic Practice, and the CJLS's retention of traditional strictures against homosexuality in 1992, served as counterweights to the liberalization represented by egalitarianism. In sum, they asserted in practice a Conservative denominational identity, over and against Reform and Reconstructionism, on the one hand, and Orthodoxy, on the other. The movement's attitude towards homosexuality has remained under debate to the present, but the growing equality of women in Judaism has become, in the main, an accepted part of the definition of Conservative Judaism.

LITURGY. Since the 1970s, the Conservative movement has published a series of new liturgical publications and a new *Humash*. Creative prayer booklets of the late 1960s–early 1970s were followed by Jules Harlow's *Mahzor* (1972) and *Siddur Sim Shalom* (1985). Leonard Cahan and Avram Reisner edited the new *Sim Shalom* in two volumes (1998–2002), followed by Reuven Hammer's *Or Hadash* commentary in 2003. The Masorti Movement in Israel published *Siddur Va'ani Tefilati* in 1998, while the Schechter Institute and the Rabbinical Assembly published *Megillot Hashoah* (*The* Shoah *Scroll*), a new liturgy for *Yom Hashoah* (2003). These publications reflect a growing sensitivity to spirituality, participatory prayer, gender awareness, and the level of knowledge of the average congregant.

Humash Etz Hayyim was published by the Conservative movement in 2001 in order to replace the outdated Hertz *Humash* of 1936. Edited by some of the leading rabbis and scholars of the Conservative movement, it aims to convey a synopsis of modern, critical scholarship along with the best of traditional *midrash*.

THE COHEN AND SCHORSCH YEARS. The Cohen years at JTS (1972–86) were marked by the transition from European-born to American-born faculty. This transition was epitomized by the struggle over the ordination of women described above. Cohen also built and dedicated the new library in 1983. The Schorsch era (1986–) has seen the expansion of JTS to over 700 students, thanks in large part to the founding of the William Davidson School of Education in 1996, which trains educators for day schools and afternoon schools. Schorsch expanded the endowment of JTS while rebuilding and expanding the campus. He steered a centrist course between the left and right wings of the movement. He was an avid supporter of expanding the roles of women in Judaism, while opposing the ordination of avowed homosexuals and gay commitment ceremonies.

EDUCATIONAL AND INSTITUTIONAL DEVELOPMENTS IN NORTH AMERICA 1970–2005. Beginning in the 1970s, Conservative Jews began to found *Havurot* (small fellowship groups) as a result of the counterculture and as a reaction to large, impersonal synagogue centers. This began with *Havurat Shalom* in Boston, but soon led to *Havurot* within existing Conservative synagogues. At the same time, large synagogues began to open alternative services for specific groups such as egalitarian services, family services, learners' *minyanim*, and singles' services.

Since many Conservative Jews did not know how to perform basic Jewish rituals, Ron Wolfson of the University of Judaism developed the Art of Jewish Living Series which teaches adults how to make Shabbat, run a seder, celebrate Hannukah, and mourn for relatives.

In 1963, Noah Golinkin developed the Hebrew Literacy Campaign which taught adults how to read the prayer book in 12 weeks. Adopted by the Federation of Jewish Men's Clubs in 1978, he wrote *Shalom Aleichem* (1978) followed by *Ein Keloheinu* (1981) in order to implement to Campaign. In 1986, Golinkin published *While Standing on One Foot*, which teaches adults how to read Hebrew in one-day Hebrew Reading Marathons. To date, over 200,000 Conservative and Reform Jews have learned how to read the prayerbook using these two methods.

All of these programs acknowledge that third- and fourth-generation American Jews did not receive a thorough Jewish education and must be taught basic Judaism using entirely new, user-friendly methods.

Since 1990, with the intermarriage rate among American Jews hovering at 50%, Conservative Judaism has witnessed an erosion at its periphery, resulting in lower numbers overall. In 2000, there were slightly over one million self-identified Conservative Jews, representing only 26% of American Jewry. The percentage of Conservative Jewish families affiliating with a synagogue also dropped to 33%. Mirroring similar developments in other sectors of American Judaism, the movement has simultaneously enjoyed an intensification at its core, with members of Conservative synagogues reflecting a more substantive Jewish education and demonstrating a more positive degree of identification with their denominational choice than in the previous generation. Whether assimilatory or revival trends will predominate is the critical question facing American Conservative Judaism in the 21st century.

While Conservative Judaism is most extensive in North America, in recent decades, it has expanded worldwide: in Israel, Latin America, and to a smaller degree in Europe and elsewhere.

The Masorti Movement in Israel

Unlike Reform and Orthodoxy, each of which has had non-Zionist and anti-Zionist wings, Conservative Judaism has been warm to the Zionist enterprise throughout the 20th century. The intensification of Zionist consciousness after the Six-Day War of 1967 spurred the growth of a wider presence of Conservative Judaism in Israel. While Solomon Schechter himself had been warm to Zionism, his successors, prior to Gerson Cohen, had not attempted to commit JTS to the renewal of Jewish life in Ereẓ Israel beyond the opening of an Academic Center in Jerusalem in 1963. A handful of Conservative rabbis had made *aliyah* and founded congregations in the early 1960s, but more Conservative rabbis and educators arrived after 1967. In 1979, they created a denominational umbrella organization, the *Masorti* ("Traditional") Movement, which has been led over the years by rabbis Moshe Tutnauer, Michael Graetz, Philip Spectre, and Ehud Bandel. This movement led the Conservative movement as a whole to become part of the World Zionist Organization as *Mercaz Olami* in 1987. Masorti has supported existing congregations and founded new ones, launched a youth movement, *Noam* (*No'ar Masorti*) and the Ramah Noam Summer Camp. By 2005, the movement had grown to approximately 50 *kehillot* (congregations) and *ḥavurot*.

Masorti Judaism continues to face political obstacles to recognition. Israeli government coalitions typically include Orthodox political parties, and under Israeli law, Orthodoxy enjoys a monopoly as the established form of Judaism. Masorti rabbis are generally not recognized by the state to perform Jewish marriages and divorces. The government has refused to register as Jews children converted by Masorti rabbis, and on four occasions, 1970 through 1997, the Knesset has entertained campaigns to change Israel's *Law of Return so as to discredit conversions conducted by Conservative and other non-Orthodox rabbis. In the wake of the last of these, the government empowered the Ne'eman Commission to explore methods of involving both Orthodox and non-Orthodox (Masorti and Reform) rabbis in conversions. Though the Israeli Chief Rabbinate rejected the commission's recommendations, the Knesset approved them and the Institute of Jewish Studies was established by the Israeli government and the Jewish Agency. It is run by Orthodox, Conservative, and Reform Jews, but the graduates are converted by an Orthodox Bet Din. Even so, the Masorti Movement continues to marry and convert people and to demand that these marriages and conversions be recognized by the State of Israel.

Masorti leaders seek to engage Israeli society beyond the movement's network of congregations. The Rabbinical Assembly of Israel's Va'ad Halakhah (Law Committee) deals with halakhic questions as described above. The movement operates special programs for *olim* (immigrants), especially those from Latin America. The Masorti Movement has also achieved symbolic recognition by being granted the use of the Robinson's Arch section of the Western Wall of the Temple Mount for worship services.

THE SCHECHTER INSTITUTE OF JEWISH STUDIES. The Seminary of Judaic Studies, later renamed the Schechter Institute of Jewish Studies, was founded in 1984 by JTS and the Masorti Movement for the purpose of training Masorti rabbis. Led over the years by Reuven Hammer, Lee Levine, Benjamin Siegel, Alice Shalvi, and David Golinkin, it slowly became the largest Conservative organization in Israel. It currently includes the Schechter Rabbinical Seminary for Israelis, which also hosts the one-year rabbinical school programs of JTS, the University of Judaism, and the Seminaro Rabbinico; the Schechter Institute of Jewish Studies, which is a graduate school for over 450 Israeli educators; the TALI Education Fund, which provides enriched Jewish Studies to over 22,000 Israeli children at over 120 TALI public schools and kindergartens; and Midreshet Yerushalayim, which provides Jewish education to thousands of new immigrants from the FSU and to Jews throughout the Ukraine and Hungary.

In Latin America

Conservative Judaism has established a major presence in Latin America. The pioneer rabbi in that region was Marshall *Meyer, a JTS graduate, who founded the *Seminario Rabbinico Latinoamericano* in 1962. Meyer later returned to New York, but the movement grew; 44 Conservative rabbis were serving in Latin America by 1999. In many Latin American countries, Conservative Judaism is the dominant stream. *Seminario* graduates have contributed to the development of the region's synagogue life, sponsoring the translation of the liturgy into Spanish and Portuguese, and fostering a modern spirit in worship, preaching, and life-cycle celebrations. *Seminario* alumni also serve in schools, summer camps, Hebrew sports clubs, and cultural centers, adding a religious component to institutions that had earlier been Jewish in a purely ethnic sense. Through the influence of the *Seminario*, Conservative Judaism has helped guide Latin American Jewry from an era of immigrant-created Jewish institutions to one in which native-born Jews express their distinctive religious identity.

In England

As in Latin America, a single rabbinic pioneer, Louis *Jacobs, was instrumental in founding Conservative Judaism in England. Denied appointment to a London synagogue by the English chief rabbi in 1963 on account of his unorthodox theological writings, Jacobs and his followers left the (Orthodox, English) *United Synagogue and opened the New London Synagogue. Members of that synagogue founded two kindred congregations closer to their northwest London homes, and in 1985, the three communities entered a formal partnership, the Assembly of Masorti Synagogues. Masorti in the United Kingdom describes its approach as "tolerant, non-fundamentalist, traditional." By 2000, the English Masorti membership had grown to 3,000 adults, led by young rabbis such as Jonathan Wittenberg and Chaim Weiner. Masorti U.K. comprised a youth movement, an organization for college students and young adults, and 11 congregations, one of which also sponsored a *ḥavurah*.

In France

Conservative/Masorti development in France began later than in the United Kingdom, despite the larger size of French Jewry. The first Masorti congregation, Adat Shalom in Paris, opened in 1988; a second congregation, in Nice, over a decade later. They are led by rabbis Rivon Krygier and Yeshaya Delsace. French Masorti Judaism faces the challenge of transplanting a movement into a new cultural milieu and engaging a largely Sephardi population.

Masorti Olami

Masorti Olami (The World Council of Synagogues) is the umbrella organization for all Conservative congregations outside of Israel and North America. In addition to England, France, and South America, there is a long-established community in Sweden. Other Conservative/Masorti congregations have recently opened in a number of other European countries, including Spain, Germany, Australia, and the Czech Republic. Rabbinic leadership in European Masorti institutions comes from the Schechter Rabbinical Seminary in Jerusalem. Worldwide, Conservative/Masorti Judaism is achieving a higher degree of coordination, as it confronts the weakening of Jewish identity due to assimilation and, at the start of the 21st century, a rise in worldwide *antisemitism.

BIBLIOGRAPHY: HISTORY: C. Adler, *I Have Considered the Days* (1943); N. Bentwich, *Solomon Schechter* (1938); N.B. Cardin and D.W. Silverman (eds.), *The Seminary at 100* (1987); M. Davis, *The Emergence of Conservative Judaism* (1963); E. Dorff, *Conservative Judaism* (1996²); D. Elazar and R.M. Gefen, *The Conservative Movement in Judaism* (2000); S. Ettenberg, *The Ramah Experience* (1989); R. Fierstien, *A Different Spirit* (1990); idem., *The Rabbinical Assembly: A Century of Commitment* (2000); idem. (ed.), *Solomon Schechter in America* (2002); N. Gillman, *Conservative Judaism: The New Century* (1993); S. and A. Goldstein, *Conservative Jewry in the United States* (1998); M. Greenbaum, *Louis Finkelstein and the Conservative Movement* (2001); P. Nadell, *Conservative Judaism in America* (1988); S. Rosenblum, *Conservative Judaism: A Contemporary History* (1983); J.Z. Sarna, *American Judaism* (2004); *Proceedings of the Rabbinical Assembly* (1927–); M. Sklare, *Conservative Judaism* (1972); M. Waxman (ed.), *Tradition and Change* (1958); J. Wertheimer, *A People Divided* (1993); idem, *Conservative Synagogues and Their Members* (1996); idem (ed.), *Tradition Renewed* (1997). WOMEN IN JEWISH LAW: D. Golinkin, (ed.), *Jewish Law Watch* (2000–3); idem (ed.), *To Learn and To Teach* (2004ff.); idem, *The Status of Women in Jewish Law: Responsa* (2001); S. Greenberg, (ed.), *The Ordination of Women as Rabbis: Studies and Responsa* (1988); S. Cohen and J. Schor, *Gender Variation in the Careers of Conservative Rabbis* (2004). JEWISH LAW: D. Golinkin, *An Index of Conservative Responsa and Halakhic Studies 1917–1990* (1992); idem (ed.), *The Responsa of Professor Louis Ginzberg* (1996); I. Klein, *A Guide to Jewish Religious Practice* (1979); idem, *Responsa and Halakhic Studies* (1975); D. Golinkin, D. Fine, K. Abelson et al. (eds.), *Proceedings of the Committee on Jewish Law and Standards, 1927–2000*, 6 vols. (1985–2005); D. Golinkin (ed.), *Responsa of the Va'ad Halakhah of the Rabbinical Assembly of Israel*, vols. 1–6 (1986–99); idem, *Responsa in a Moment* (2000); D. Novak, *Law and Theology in Judaism* (1974–76); S. Siegel and E. Gertel, (eds.), *Conservative Judaism and Jewish Law* (1977). ISRAEL AND LATIN AMERICA: H. Meirovich, *The Shaping of Masorti Judaism in Israel* (1999); T. Steinberg, "A Brief History of the Rabbinical Assembly in Israel," in: Robert Fierstien (ed.), *A Century of Commitment: One Hundred Years of the Rabbinical Assembly* (2000), 199–233; S. Szteinhendler, "The Rabbinical Assembly in Latin America," ibid., 234–43; E. Tabory, "The Israel Reform and Conservative Movements and the Market for Liberal Judaism," in: U. Rebhun and C. Waxman, (eds.), *Jews in Israel* (2004), 285–314. IDEOLOGY: *Emet Ve'emunah: Statement of Principles of Conservative Judaism* (1988); L. Finkelstein, *Proceedings of the Rabbinical Assembly*, vol. 1 (1927), 42–53; D. Golinkin, *Halakhah for Our Time: A Conservative Approach to Jewish Law* (1991) (in English, Hebrew, Spanish, French, Russian); R. Gordis, *Understanding Conservative Judaism* (1978); J. Roth, *The Halakhic Process: A Systemic Analysis* (1986); I. Schorsch, "The Sacred Cluster: The Core Values of Conservative Judaism," in: *Conservative Judaism*, 47:3 (Spring 1995), 3–12; idem, *Polarities in Balance* (2004).

[David Golinkin and Michael Panitz (2nd ed.)]

CONSERVATIVE PARTY, GERMAN (Deutsche Konservative Partei), party formed in 1848 for defending the economical and political interests of the Prussian Junkers. In 1866 the Free Conservative Party split off, which led to its reorganization in 1876. The newspaper *Kreuzzeitung* published the party's views for many years. The Conservatives, who stood for the old feudal ideal in Prussian society in opposition to the liberal, democratic, and social political theorists, affirmed their belief in the romantic vision of a state based on the virtues of monarchy, hierarchy, and, above all, military might. They also made "positive Christianity" basic to their platform. At first a loosely knit organization which had enormous influence at court, the Conservative Party did not adopt an antisemitic program until 1892. After Bismarck's retirement, however, the party constituted the opposition and the anti-parliamentarian groups within the Conservatives, particularly the *Kreuzzeitung* group with Adolf *Stoecker and Wilhelm von Hammerstein, joined hands to eliminate "Jewish influence." On the eve of the 1893 elections, the party called its first public conference at Berlin's Tivoli Hall (December 1892) and moved to demagogic antisemitism. The first paragraph of the new Tivoli party program stated: "We combat the obtrusive and debilitating Jewish influence on our popular life… We demand a Christian authority for the Christian people and Christian teachers for Christian pupils." Thus, at Tivoli, antisemitism moved up the social ladder and became respectable. It also proved to be a powerful attractor of votes, as the elections resulted in a joint victory for the Conservative and antisemitic parties, the antisemitic candidates winning 262,000 votes (2.9% of the total), and 16 seats in the German parliament. During World War I they worked against political and social reform, which led to their dissolution at the end of the war after the breakdown of the German state in November 1918.

BIBLIOGRAPHY: P.W. Massing, *Rehearsal for Destruction…* (1949), 64–66; P.G.J. Pulzer, *The Rise of Political Anti-Semitism in Germany and Austria* (1964), 118–26; K.S. Pinson, *Modern Germany…* (1954), 165–8. **ADD. BIBLIOGRAPHY:** J.N. Retallak, *Notables of the Right – The Conservative Party and Political Mobilization in Germany 1876–1918* (1988); J.N. Retallak, "Antisemitism, Conservative Propaganda and Regional Politics in late Nineteenth Century Germany," in: *German Studies*, 11 (1988), 3, 377–403; G. Eley, *Reshaping the German Right – Radical Nationalism and Political Change after Bismarck* (1980).

[Bjoern Siegel (2nd ed.)]

CONSIGLI(O), AVTALYON (Ottavio) BEN SOLOMON (c. 1540–1616), rabbi and financier of Rovigo, northern Italy. Consiglio studied under Samuel Judah Katzenellenbogen at Padua. To demonstrate his profound respect for his teacher, he commissioned an artist to paint his portrait and this was hung prominently in his *bet ha-midrash*. Like his teacher, Consiglio opposed *pilpul* in talmudic studies. Consiglio caused a heated controversy by disqualifying a *mikveh* in the house of his brother Jekuthiel, with whom he also had a financial dispute. The Italian rabbinate was divided on the matter. The rabbinate of Venice, headed by Hezekiah Finzi of Ferrara, strongly defended the halakhic fitness of the ritual bath in question. The matter became a *cause célèbre*, and several collections of responsa on the subject were published between 1606 and 1617, e.g., *Mashbit Nilḥamot* (Venice, 1606), *Mikveh Yisrael* (*ibid.*, 1607), and *Palgei Mayyim* (*ibid.*, 1608).

BIBLIOGRAPHY: Blau, in: *Jahresbericht der Landes-Rabbinerschule in Budapest*, 28 (1905), 119–20; 29 (1906), 129ff.; S. Bernstein (ed.), *Divan Leo de Modenas* (1932), 242 (epitaph); M. Szulwass, in: *Sinai*, 20 (1947), 198–205; I. Sonne, in: KS, 10 (1933), 360–4; A. Yaari, *Meḥkerei Sefer* (1958), 420–9; idem, in: *Sinai*, 34 (1954), 367–74.

CONSISTORY (Consistoire), official organization of the Jewish congregations in France established in 1808. The term was borrowed from Protestant usage by the Napoleonic administration to designate the committees of rabbis and laymen responsible for the administration of the Jewish congregations at the regional and national levels. By extension, the word applies to the whole organization subject to the authority of the "consistory."

Origins

The French Revolution abolished the existing internal structure of the Jewish communities. The adherence of a Jew to his communal organization then became voluntary, and created problems for the Jewish leadership, mainly concerning communal budget. In consequence, the reforms introduced by *Napoleon I were welcomed by some of the Jewish leaders in the hope that they would confer on Judaism a legal status similar to that given to the Catholic Church by the Concordat of 1801 and to the Protestants by the "organic articles" of 1802. The emperor himself was anxious to have an instrument at his disposal through which he could effectively supervise the Jewish community and at the same time integrate the Jews as individuals within French society. The statute establishing a Jewish religious organization was drafted at the *Assembly of Jewish Notables by the commissioners appointed by Napoleon in conjunction with the nine Jewish delegates. It was finally ratified by the Assembly on Dec. 9 and 10, 1806, although not without some opposition, and promulgated by imperial decree on March 17, 1808.

The decree provided that a central consistory was to be set up in Paris to head a group of regional consistories, which in their turn would control the local communities. A subsequent decree was issued on Dec. 13, 1808, establishing the location and jurisdiction of 13 regional consistories, to include also the Rhineland and northern Italy, then part of the French Empire. For every department with a Jewish population of at least 2,000 a consistory was established. Departments having less than this number might be combined with others. In the case of Paris the consistory controlled 16 departments. The central consistory comprised three *grands-rabbins* and two

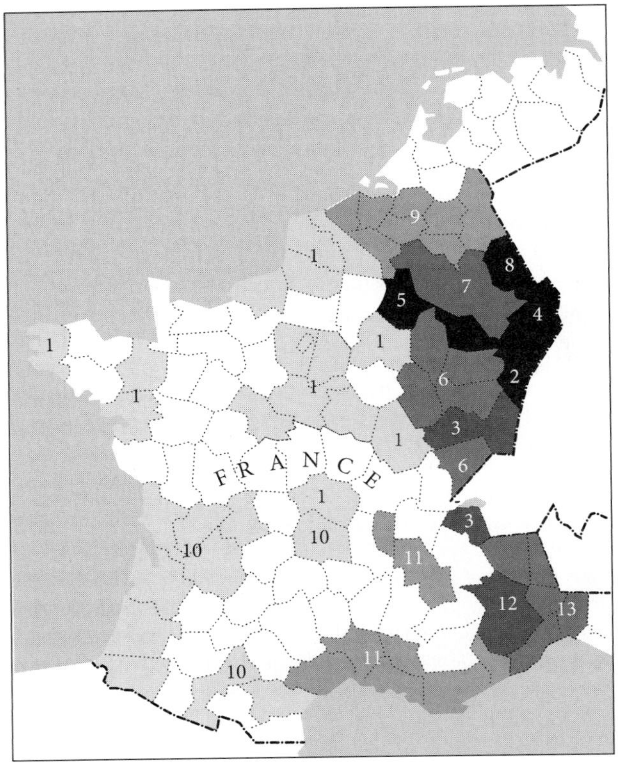

The Consistories of France according to the Napoleonic decree of 1808 (composition according to departments, darker shadings indicate greater density of Jewish population).

1. *PARIS: (Allier, Côte d'Or, Finistère, Ille-et-Vilaine, Loiret, Loiret-Cher, Loire-Inférieure, Marne, Nord, Pas-de-Calais, Seine, Seine Inférieure, Seine-et-Marne, Seine-et-Oise, Somme, Yonne).*
2. *STRASBOURG: (Bas-Rhin).*
3. *WINTZENHEIM: (Léman, Haut-Rhin, Haute-Saône).*
4. *MAINZ: (Mont-Tonnerre).*
5. *METZ: (Moselle Ardennes).*
6. *NANCY: (Doubs, Haute-Marne, Meurthe, Meuse, Vosges).*
7. *TREVES: (Forêts, Sambe-et-Meuse, Sarre).*
8. *COBLENZ: (Rhin-et-Moselle).*
9. *KREFELD: (Dyle, Escaut, Jemmapes, Lys, Meuse-Inférieure, Deux-Nèthes, Ourthe, Roër).*
10. *BORDEAUX: (Aude, Charente, Charente- Inférieure, Dordogne, Haute-Garonne, Gironde, Landes, Puy-de-Dôme, Basses-Pyrénées, Haute-Vienne).*
11. *MARSEILLES: (Alpes-Maritimes, Gard, Hérault, Isère, Rhôna, Bouches-du-Rhône, Var, Vaucluse).*
12. *TURIN: (Pô, Stura).*
13. *CASAL: (Génes, Doire, Marengo, Montenotte, Sésia).*

laymen, appointed by co-option, and the regional consistories one *grand rabbin* and three laymen. They were elected by 25 "notables" of the area who were designated by the members and confirmed in office by the local prefects. All nominations were subject to the approval of the government. Each head of a Jewish family was obliged to pay dues to the consistories. The budget was intended to cover the expenses of the Jewish religion in the narrow sense, i.e., the salaries of the rabbis and the maintenance of synagogues and their appurtenances. Welfare and educational activities were not included in the regular budget. The function of the consistories, according to the decree of 1808, was "to ensure that no assembly for prayers should be formed without express authorization, to encourage the Jews in the exercise of useful professions and refer to the authorities those who do not have an acknowledged means of livelihood, and to inform the authorities each year of the number of Jewish conscripts in the area." All those who wished to remain Jews had to register with the consistory. The duty of the rabbis was "to teach religions and the doctrines included in the decisions of the Great *Sanhedrin, to call for ... obedience to the laws, especially ... those related to the defense of the fatherland ... and in particular, every year, at the time of conscription, to induce the Jews to consider their military service as a sacred duty" in the performance of which they were exempted from any religious observances with which it could not be reconciled. The Jewish leaders generally accepted these regulations, which restored authority to the Jewish communities and also – an innovation in Western and Central Europe – gave them a centralized organization on the national scale. The consistories appointed a "commissioner" for each congregation whose absolute and often petty-minded authority replaced the traditional authority of the *parnasim* and who often clashed with the rabbis. Later, however, the system was dropped and thus the old communal organization continued to exist.

The decree of December 1808 established regional consistories in Paris, Strasbourg, Wintzenheim, Metz, Nancy, Bordeaux, Marseilles, Mainz, Treves, Coblenz, Krefeld, Turin, and Casal. In 1810 the annexation of central Italy brought the temporary addition of three new consistories, and in 1812 the annexation of Holland and a further portion of Germany added seven additional consistories. After the fall of Napoleon the communities of Belgium, Luxembourg, and Westphalia retained the consistorial system. New consistories were created in Saint-Esprit (Bayonne) in 1846 and in Lyons in 1857. The central consistory of Algiers and the regional consistories of Oran and Constantine were founded in 1845. They were linked to the metropolitan organization as three consistories of equal status in 1867. In 1872, after the annexation of Alsace-Lorraine to Germany and the consequent influx of Alsatian refugees, new consistories were founded in Lille and Vesoul.

Serious financial difficulties had endangered the existence of the consistories from the outset. As many of the members failed to pay their dues, in 1816 it was agreed that the state treasury would assume their collection in return for a percentage of the income. In 1831 King Louis-Philippe agreed to include the expenses of the Jewish religion, in particular the salaries of the rabbis and religious officials, in the national budget. An order of 1844 introduced important organizational changes. The central consistory was to be composed of a *grand rabbin* (the chief rabbi of France) and a representative of each of the regional consistories, while the regional consistories were to consist of a *grand rabbin* and five laymen. The right of veto in religious matters was granted to the rabbis. The system of election to the consistories was also drastically revised. Although the principle of "notability" of the electors was retained, the number of "notables" was augmented in accordance with the new principles of suffrage introduced in the French electoral system. The electoral college was first enlarged in 1844. In 1848, following considerable agitation, especially by the Orthodox members for the institution of general suffrage in consistorial elections, every male Jew aged over 25 was declared "notable" with the right to vote. During the Second Empire the central consistory again succeeded in limiting the popular vote, especially in the election of rabbis. In 1871 a government decree once more ordered democratic elections, only to be rescinded the following year as regards the election of rabbis. The provision of rabbinical training became one of the chief tasks of the central consistory. The rabbinical seminary of Metz, founded in 1829, was originally simply a modernized yeshivah. Later, however, the introduction of some reforms in synagogue ritual (1856), as well as the transfer of the rabbinical seminary to Paris, marked a more radical transformation.

In France the consistory remained the official French Jewish representative organization until the separation of church and state in 1905. Afterward, it was voluntarily retained, a new name, the Union des Associations Culturelles de France et d'Algérie, was given, to which the term "Consistory" is still applied. The three departments of Alsace-Lorraine, which retained their French institutions at the time of the German annexation in 1871 and did not renounce them either in 1918 or in 1944–45, still have a consistory despite the law of separation. Following the trend set by Napoleon and embodied in the motto of the Central Consistory "Religion and the Fatherland," a number of consistorial leaders endeavored to promote Jewish assimilation and preserve only the religious differences, which also became blurred with time. Others, notably in Alsace-Lorraine, used the consistorial organization as a force for maintaining cohesion and tradition within Jewish society.

Prior to World War I there was an influx of a large number of Jewish immigrants from Eastern Europe who formed their separate organizations. In 1935, 63 French and nine Algerian communities formally belonged to the Consistoire Central, the majority of Jews displaying little interest in communal affairs. After the German occupation of Paris in 1940 the central consistory was active in the free zone of France, continuously protesting against the anti-Jewish restrictions. However, its financial resources were soon depleted, since it could no longer rely upon the support of the wealthier Jews. Despite these odds, the central consistory aided various underground bodies of both native- and foreign-born Jews. By 1965 practically the entire Algerian Jewish community had settled in France, yet the central consistory still retained the former name which included both France and Algeria, their task restricted to the custody of remaining Jewish property. In June 1968, during the student uprising, some 60 Jewish youths seized the offices of the Paris consistory in protest against the alleged domination of French Jewry by "archaic and anti-democratic institutions" and calling for "a new community based on effective participation." The Consistoire Central continued to represent mainly Orthodox congregations in the 21st century, comprising less than 15% of France's Jews.

BIBLIOGRAPHY: P.C. Albert, *The Modernization of French Jewry: Consistory and Community in the Nineteenth Century*, (1977); A.E. Halphen, *Recueils des lois… concernant les Israélites* (1851); I. Uhry, *Recueil des lois… depuis 1850* (1887); R. Anchel, *Napoléon et les juifs* (1928); idem, *Notes sur les frais du culte juif en France de 1815 à 1831* (1928); M. Catane, in: *Gesher*, 9 nos. 3–4 (1963), 160–9; G. Wormser, *Français israélites* (1963), 17–46; L. Berman, *Histoire des Juifs de France* (1937); A. Manuel, in: REJ, 82 (1926), 521–32.

[Moshe Catane / Isaac Levitats]

CONSOLO, FEDERICO (1841–1906), violinist and composer. Born in Ancona, Italy, Consolo studied violin with Vieuxtemps and composition with Fétis and Liszt, but was forced to give up his career as a violin virtuoso in 1884 after a nerve injury. He then devoted himself to composition and musical research. His most important publication was his *Sefer Shirei Yisrael – Libro dei Canti d'Israele* (1892), an anthology of synagogue chants documenting the musical tradition of the Sephardi Jews of Italy. On the title page he called himself not only by his Italian name but also "Yehiel Nahmany Sefardi."

CONSTANCE (Ger. **Konstanz**), city in Germany. The first mention of Jews is in a royal tax list of 1241; the tax paid indicates that they had settled there some decades earlier. A responsum on divorce, written in Constance and published in R. *Meir b. Baruch of Rothenburg's responsa, has been erroneously ascribed to him. King Henry VII pawned the Jewish taxes to a nobleman in 1311, and Louis the Bavarian followed suit in 1330. King Wenceslaus (after 1393), Rupert (1401–02), and Sigismund (1413) transferred half the Jewish taxes to the city. In 1414 Sigismund assigned two Constance Jews to collect a levy for the Hussite War from Upper Swabian Jewry. Records of 1328, 1375, and 1425–29 show that Jews owned orchards, gardens, and vineyards in Constance. Moneylending by Jews to clerics, villagers, townspeople, and nobles is mentioned in 1293, 1300, 1346–48, and 1420–39; to the city in the 1370s; and a minor sum to the king in 1306. The city's usury law of 1383 referred to small scale moneylending by Jews. The records of the municipal court (1423–28) show that there were also Jewish traders, tailors, and metalworkers living in Constance. Twenty-seven Jews accused of *Host desecration were murdered in 1326. During the *Black Death (1349) 350 Jews were burned to death. Following a *blood libel in *Ravensburg, the Jews were imprisoned in 1429 and after a second one in the area in 1443; they were released each time after ransom was paid. From around 1375 until 1460 the Jews enjoyed burghers' rights. By 1424 there was a synagogue in the Ramungshof. The Jews lived in several streets. During the Council of Constance, in 1417, a delegation of German Jewry met Pope *Martin V who, in 1418, granted favorable privileges, confirmed by King Sigismund. A first expulsion order, in 1432, was not generally enforced, but it became final in 1533. Afterward Jews could only enter the town temporarily, though they continued to live in neighboring villages. In 1847 a group of Jews settled in Constance. After the *Baden emancipation law of 1862 a community was founded in 1863–66. The synagogue, consecrated in 1883, was burned down in November 1938. In 1910 the community numbered 574 persons (2.7% of the total) but declined to 537 in 1925 and 443 in 1933. In October 1940 the 110 Jews still remaining in Constance were deported to the internment camp in *Gurs (Southern France), and from there the majority were transported to *Auschwitz in 1942. Some 160 Jews liberated from displaced persons' camps lived in Constance between 1945 and 1948, most of whom subsequently emigrated. By 1968 fewer than 30 Jews lived in Constance; they were affiliated to the Jewish community of *Freiburg im Breisgau. An independent Jewish community was founded in Constance in 1988. It had 102 members in 1989, and as a result of the emigration of Jews from the former Soviet Union, their number increased to 502 in 2003.

BIBLIOGRAPHY: Germ Jud, 2 (1968), 445–50; L. Loewenstein, *Geschichte der Juden am Bodensee* (1879); H. Chone, in: ZGJD, 6 (1935), 3–16, 198–209; 7 (1937), 1–7; H. Maor, *Ueber den Wiederaufbau der juedischen Gemeinden in Deutschland seit 1945* (1961), 59; R. Overdick, *Die rechtliche und wirtschaftliche Stellung der Juden in Suedwestdeutschland im 15. und 16. Jahrhundert…* (1965); F. Handsnurscher and G. Taddey, *Juedische Gemeinden in Baden…* (1968). **ADD. BIBLIOGRAPHY:** H. Hoerburger, *Judenvertreibungen im Spaetmittelalter* (1981); E.R. Wiehn (ed.), *Novemberpogrom 1938* (1988); E. Bloch, *Geschichte der Juden in Konstanz…* (1989); W. Ruegert (ed.), *Juedisches Leben in Konstanz* (1999).

[Toni Oelsner]

CONSTANTA (in Greek and Roman antiquity **Tomis**, until 1878 *Kustendje*, Rom. **Constanța**), Black Sea port in S.E. Romania; within the Ottoman Empire until 1878. There was a small Jewish settlement in Tomis in the third century C.E. The Ashkenazi community of Constanta was founded in 1828. After a while a Sephardi community was established. The Jewish population increased with the development of the town. A Jewish cemetery was opened in 1854. In 1878, after northern Dobruja passed to Romania, Romanian nationality was automatically granted to the Jews in the region, including Constanta. As former Turkish subjects, they found themselves in a more favorable situation than the other Jews of Romania, the overwhelming majority of whom were deprived of rights. The Romanian authorities, however, attempted to expel individual Jews from Constanta. There were 957 Jews living in Constanta in 1899 (6.5% of the total population), most of whom were occupied in commerce and some in crafts, with two schools for boys, an Ashkenazi and a Sephardi one. In 1930 the Jewish population numbered 1,821 (3.1%) in the city and 1,981 in the province. In the fall of 1940, a German military representative was placed in the city and entry of Jews to the port was forbidden. After the outbreak of war against the U.S.S.R. (June 22, 1941) all the Jews were arrested and sent to the Cobadin camp. Men and women were also sent to forced labor. In November 1941 the Jews returned to Constanta, but to a special district. In 1942 there were 1,532 Jews in Constanta. In 1947, after the war, there were 2,400 Jews in the city, some of them refugees from *Bukovina. Until 1951 Constanta was a port of departure Jews emigrating to Israel, with the community consequently diminishing to 586 in 1956. There were 60 Jewish families in Constanta in 1969, with a synagogue and a rabbi. In 2004, 128 Jews lived there.

BIBLIOGRAPHY: M. Carp, *Cartea Neagra*, 1(1946), index; *Pe marginea prapastiei*, 1 (1942), 194, 231–33, 242; PK Romanyah, 1, 232–35. **ADD. BIBLIOGRAPHY:** D. Ofer, *Derekh ba-Yam* (1988), index; S. Sanie, in: SAHIR, 1 (1996), 1–27; FEDROM-Comunitati evreiesti din Romania (Internet, 2004).

[Theodor Lavi / Lucian-Zeev Herscovici (2nd ed.)]

CONSTANTINE (ancient **Cirta**), Algerian town. Constantine was named after Emperor Constantine in 313. Latin inscriptions give evidence of a Jewish colony there; its surroundings seem to have been inhabited by Judaized Berbers. The Arab conquest brought little change to Constantine. The Jews maintained their identity; their "elder" (*zaken*) led his followers to war like an Arab or Berber *sheikh*. According to the 15th-century rabbis of Algeria, Constantine was one of the most important Jewish communities in Muslim countries. Local scholars in the 15th century included Maimun Najjār, author of *Kunteres Minhagot*; Joseph b. Minir, called Ḥasid, whose tomb is venerated by Jews and Muslims to the present day and whose works, now lost, were quoted by Joseph *Caro; Joseph b. David; Isaac Kagig (also Kaçiç and Casès); and Samuel Atrani; in the 16th century, the poet Joseph Zimron and Moses Allouche; and in the 18th century, Masʿud Zerbib, author of *Zeraʿ Emet* (Leghorn, 1715). In the 18th century the community built its quarter. In 1818 the Turks from Algiers attacked Constantine; they pillaged, massacred, and carried off 17 young Jewish girls whom they brought to their commander. The girls were subsequently released. There were then 5,000 Jews in Constantine. After its capture by the French in 1837, many Jews left the city, and two years later the community numbered only 3,436. By 1934 the community grew to 12,000. In that same year on August 3–5, the Muslim population, provoked by the propaganda of the French antisemites, assaulted them. Twenty-five were killed and dozens wounded. When the Jewish resistance was organized, the massacres stopped; but French forces had not intervened, despite the appeals of Muslim leaders. The Vichy government severely persecuted this community in 1940 despite its large number of heroes in the two world wars.

[David Corcos]

Traditional Jewish education prevailed in Constantine for hundreds of years. In 1849 the Consistory of Constantine was instituted coordinating Jewish community life. The 1870 *Crémieux decree that granted French citizenship to Algerian Jews further accelerated the incorporation of Jews into the French school system, placing the *talmud torah* under strict supervision. The *Alliance Israélite Universelle, which strove to combine French modernity with Jewish tradition, started operating educational institutions in Constantine in 1902. The influence of French culture led to a gradual decline in the use of the local Judeo-Arabic dialect in favor of French. An intensive effort to preserve traditional Jewish culture and the Judeo-Arabic language was conducted by Rabbi Joseph Renassia (1879–1962), who wrote and translated over a hundred volumes in Judeo-Arabic.

[Ofra Tirosh-Becker (2nd ed.)]

During the Algerian FLN (Front de libération nationale) terrorist attacks in the late 1950s grenades were often thrown into the Jewish quarter. In 1962, when Algeria received its independence, there was a massive exodus of the Jewish community, which then numbered 15,000–20,000 – mostly to France and Israel. The local *talmud torah* with its 800 students closed down in July of that year. The synagogues were turned into the general headquarters of the FLN. By the end of the 1960s only a few Jewish families remained in Constantine.

[Robert Attal]

BIBLIOGRAPHY: A. Chouraqui, *Between East and West* (1968), index; E. Mercier, *Histoire de Constantine* (1903); M. Eisenbeth, *Judaïsme nord-africain … Constantine* (1931); R. Brunschwig, *Berbérie orientale sous les Hafṣides*, 1 (1940), 384ff., 406ff., 418–9, 421ff.; M. Ansky, *Juifs d'Algérie* (1960), 67–70; A. Hershman, *R. Isaac bar Sheshet Perfet and His Times* (1943); Hirschberg, Afrikah, index; *L'Arche*, no. 66 (1962), 11. **ADD. BIBLIOGRAPHY:** M. Abitbol, *From Crémieux to Pétain, Antisemitism in Colonial Algeria, 1870–1940* (1993), index (in Hebrew); S. Schwarzfuchs, *Les Juifs d'Algérie et la France, 1830–1855* (1981), 243–60, index; S. Ettinger (ed.), *Toledot ha-Yehudim be-Artzot ha-Islam*, Vol. 1 (1981), 121–96, 329–30, Vol. 2 (1986), 301–468, 479–82; Y. Charvit, *"Ha-Ḥinnukh ha-Yehudi be-Konstantin (Algeria) be-Idan shel Temurot (1837–1939),"* in: *Asufot* 14 (2002), 315–57; idem, *Elite Rabbinique d'Algérie et Modernisation* (1995).

°CONSTANTINE VII PORPHYROGENITUS, Byzantine emperor, 913–959. He was known for his learning, as evidenced by his great treatises on ceremonial, administrative, and army organization. According to some scholars, in response to a letter of protest addressed to Constantine's wife Helena by *Ḥisdai ibn Shaprut, he stopped the persecutions and forced conversions of Jews initiated in the empire by his co-emperor, *Romanus I Lecapenus. He also ceased attempts to force Christianity on the *Khazars. During his reign the condition of the Jews generally improved, earning him praises in the Hebrew apocalypse, "Vision of *Daniel."

BIBLIOGRAPHY: Baron, Social2, 3 (1957), 182–3; J. Starr, *Jews in the Byzantine Empire* (1939), 7–8, 153–6; Mann, Texts, 1 (1931), 10–16; 23–25.

[Andrew Sharf]

CONSTANTINER, JAIME (1918–2002), leader of the Jewish community of Mexico and generous promoter of Jewish education in Mexico and in Israel. Born in Butrimonys (Butrimanz), Lithuania, Constantiner studied in the *gymna-*

sium in Kovno (Kaunas). Owing to economic difficulties in 1928 his father immigrated to Mexico, where Constantiner and his mother joined him in 1934. Ten years after his settlement in Mexico City he graduated in surgery at the faculty of medicine of the Universidad Nacional Autónoma de México (UNAM). After completing his postgraduate studies in the United States, he was appointed professor at the UNAM and taught there until 1979.

During the 1940s Constantiner commenced his activities in the Jewish community as a physician in the field of welfare as well as in education, supporting the Hebrew Tarbut school. As the chairman of its *patronato,* he promoted special enrichment programs together with the Hebrew University of Jerusalem and the introduction of many new science and Hebrew courses in the Tarbut school.

He supported the activities of many Israeli and Mexican institutions: Tel Aviv University, the Tel Aviv Museum, the Philharmonic Orchestra of UNAM, San Carlos Museum, the Technion of Haifa as well as several special projects in the Hebrew University of Jerusalem and in the city of Jerusalem. He also supported special programs for Jewish studies in Mexico. He was awarded numerous prizes by Tel Aviv University, the Hebrew University of Jerusalem, and the city of Jerusalem.

[Efraim Zadoff (2nd ed.)]

CONSTANTINI, HUMBERTO (1924–1987), Argentinian author, poet, and playwright of Sephardi-Italian heritage. From his beginning in the 1950s, his works were deeply involved with the social and political situation of his country. His identification with leftist groups led him to choose exile when a military dictatorship seized power in 1976. In Mexico, where he lived in 1976–83, he wrote his most important novels: *De dioses, hombrecitos y policías* (1979; *Gods, the Little Guys and the Police*, 1984) and *La larga noche de Francisco Sanctis* (1984;*The Long Night of Francisco Sanctis*, 1985). Both deal with the practical and moral plight of people persecuted by state terrorism, in a combination of realistic themes with an expressionist, poetic, and even grotesque style. His collections of short stories (*Un señor alto, rubio, de bigotes*, 1963; *Una vieja historia de caminantes*, 1967; *Háblenme de Funes*, 1970) include some Jewish stories in Sephardi and ancient Jerusalem settings. Jewish history and identity also appear in his collection of poetry *Cuestiones con la vida* (1986). His unfinished novel *Rapsodia de Raquel Liberman* deals with the Jewish prostitution trade in Argentina in the 1920s. Costantini's plays and dramatic monologues were published in *¡Chau Pericles! Teatro completo* (1986). His works have been translated into English, French, Hebrew, German, and Russian.

BIBLIOGRAPHY: D.B. Lockhart, *Jewish Writers of Latin America. A Dictionary* (1997); A.E. Weinstein and M.E. Nasatsky (eds.), *Escritores judeo-argentinos: bibliografía 1900–1987* (1994); F. Reati, *Nombrar lo innombrable: Violencia política y novela argentina 1975–1985* (1992).

[Florinda Goldberg (2nd ed.)]

CONSTANTINOPLE (Byzantium; Heb. קושטנטיני, קושטנטינא, קושטאנדינא, קושטא), former capital of the *Byzantine and *Ottoman empires; now *Istanbul, Turkey. Under the Byzantine empire Jews were settled in various areas of Constantinople. In the fourth and fifth centuries they lived in the Chalkoprateia (copper market), where there was a synagogue as early as 318 (converted into a church in 422). From the 10th century to about 1060 they lived on the south shore of the Golden Horn. In the late 11th century they were transferred by the authorities to the suburb of Galata-Pera, the affluence of which was noted by *Benjamin of Tudela in the mid-12th century. In 1203 the Jewish quarter burned down.

There were Jewish workers in copper, finishers of woven material, dyers, silk weavers, and makers of silk garments. In the 11th and 12th centuries Jews were compelled to serve as executioners. Jewish physicians served various emperors despite church opposition to consulting them. Benjamin of Tudela also reports on the presence of Jewish tanners in the city and the complaints of wealthy Jews about the animosity among gentiles caused by the tanners.

Throughout the Byzantine period the Jews in Constantinople had close contacts with Christians. In the sixth and early seventh centuries Jews were active in the political factions of the *circus parties. In 641 Jews took part in a riot, during which the church of Hagia Sophia was broken into. Under *Leo III in 721–22, Jews were forced either to leave the city or to accept baptism. But this ruling apparently did not bring the community to an end. In about 874 *Shephatiah b. Amittai of Oria, Italy, according to a legendary report in the Aḥima'az Chronicle, went to Constantinople to plead with the emperor *Basil I to end the persecutions of Jews in Italy. Other prominent Jewish visitors to the city included a *Khazar in the 10th century, Benjamin of Tudela in the mid-12th century, and the poet Judah *Alḥarizi in the 13th century. Jews were among those banished from the city because they supported the princesses Zoe and Theodora against the emperor Michael V in 1042. Many were killed in a riot against Venetian and other Western merchants during the reign of Alexius II (1180–83). In 1204 the Latin Crusaders captured Constantinople and established the capital of the Latin Empire (1204–61) in Galata. The conflict of the great Christian powers awoke messianic expectations among the Jews of the city during the First Crusade.

In the Byzantine period the Jewish community was administered by a council of elders and by *archipherecites (heads of the academies). Benjamin of Tudela reports that five wealthy rabbis led the community. There were also religious officials, *didaskaloi* (teachers). The council of elders dealt with administrative, fiscal, and cultural-religious matters, and relations with Christians.

A Karaite community existed in Pera from the 11th century on and Constantinople became an important center of Karaite learning which attracted members of the sect from elsewhere. Celebrated leading Karaite scholars of Constantinople included *Tobias b. Moses ha-Avel (11th century) and Judah b. Elijah *Hadassi (mid-12th century).

From 1275 to 1453 the Venetian and Genoese Jews lived in Constantinople under the legal jurisdiction of their respective governments. From 1280 to 1325 the Venetian Jews lived together with the Byzantine Jews, but from 1325 to 1453 they lived in the Venetian quarter on the Golden Horn. The Genoese Jews lived in the Genoese quarter of Galata from 1275 to 1453. The Jewish quarter of Constantinople existed from about 1280 to 1453 in Vlanga, on the southern coast of the Golden Horn on the Sea of Marmara. During this period (from 1280) the Jews were involved in the tanning trade. The quarter was burned by the Turks in 1453. The fall of Constantinople appeared to Jews to herald the Redemption: the Targum for Lamentations 4:21 was held to prophesy the downfall of the "guilty city"; some predicted that redemption would occur in the same year, 1453.

For later history, see *Istanbul.

BIBLIOGRAPHY: J. Starr, *Jews in the Byzantine Empire* (1939); idem, *Romania* (1949); idem, in: JPOS, 15 (1935), 280–93; A. Galanté, *Les Juifs de Constantinople sous Byzance* (1940); Baron, Social², index; Baron, Community, index; Baer, Spain, index; A. Sharf, *Byzantine Jewry* (1970), index; D. Jacoby, in: *Byzantion*, 37 (1967), 167–227; M. Adler, *Itinerary of Benjamin of Tudela* (1907), 7, 10, 11–14.

[Andrew Sharf]

CONSTRUCTION. Jewish activity in this industry was restricted in the Diaspora and was narrowed down to the construction and repair of synagogues and houses for the community. Apparently Jews worked in the building crafts, such as carpentry, masonry, and bricklaying, throughout the Middle Ages and early modern times. The trade was organized on traditional lines, with established terms and conditions such as provisions for the meals of the masters. Where moneylending became the main Jewish occupation, the number of Jewish artisans in the building trade declined along with those in other crafts. In Christian countries Jews were excluded from guild membership, but were still occasionally found in building occupations. In countries where Jewish artisans were more common, as in Spain, Portugal, and Italy, this representation was correspondingly larger. It can thus not be generally assumed that all houses, or even synagogues, in the Jewish communities were built by Jewish contractors and workers. On the other hand the scanty mention of this profession in the sources is no conclusive evidence of its complete decline. Such mention is of great geographical variety. An account of building operations carried out in 1040 at the synagogue of the Ereẓ Israel community in Fostat (Old Cairo), Egypt, describes a Jewish master mason with his helpers, a carpenter and his "boy," and their working conditions. Jewish masons, layers of floor tiles, workers in clay, stucco workers, and their "boys," as well as their working terms, in Egypt are mentioned in Jewish sources. In Hebron, it is recorded that the whole community took part in pulling down a synagogue and erecting a new one. In the summer of 1045 seven masons in succession worked on a building. The 13th-century *Sefer Ḥasidim* castigates a Jewish householder, whose house was built by Jewish and Christian workmen, for not releasing his Jewish employees on Sabbath eve (Wistinetzky ed., no. 1499, p. 361). A contemporary Czech chronicle mentions a Jew, Podivi, who built the town of Podivin. In 1451 a Jew who won acclaim for building the royal palace in Palermo was made a master of the local Jewish carpenters' guild.

However, it was in Eastern Europe, from the 19th century on, that significant numbers of Jews first engaged in building. Visitors to backward Romania in the mid-19th century noted that the building trades, carpentry, masonry, plumbing, etc., were all exclusively represented by Jews, who built synagogues as well. Whereas no Jews engaged in the building profession in Poland before the 18th century, there were, in Congress Poland, excluding Warsaw, in 1856, 1,973 Jewish masons, 2,591 glaziers, 1,259 plumbers, and 1,289 locksmiths. In the eastern regions Jews were even more numerous in these trades, particularly for work on high buildings, steeples, and roofs, where Christian workmen were reluctant to go. Synagogues, which from the 18th century had often been embellished and decorated by wandering Jewish artisans, were now also built by them. With the rise of the *Court Jews, and the increasing numbers of Jewish army purveyors and bankers, numerous large-scale construction projects – palaces, fortresses, roads, and railroads – were organized and financed by Jews. In Poland in 1931, 23,745 Jews were engaged in the building and construction industry, about 10% of the total number, which approximated the proportion of Jews in the general population. Of these, 4,585 were glaziers (80% of the total in this occupation) and 8,034 house painters and decorators (30%); 17.7.% of independent employers in these trades were Jews, representing a much lower proportion than in others, such as clothing, textiles, and foodstuffs. Within the Russian *Pale of Settlement the proportion of Jews in the industry was even higher: 28.5% in Vitebsk government (province) in 1897, and 30.4% in Mogilev government (province), although these were employed mainly on repairs and building maintenance. This trend was manifested in countries to which these Jews immigrated. Thus, in Germany, the proportion was high, the majority being glaziers, painters, and decorators in small family firms. The Haberland family (Solomon Georg (1861–1933) and Kurt), a prominent exception, built parts of Berlin before World War I, and rebuilt cities in East Prussia after the war. Julius Berger founded the internationally known firm bearing his name which constructed tunnels and bridges.

The Jewish mass emigration from Eastern Europe coincided with the New York building boom around the beginning of the 20th century, and large numbers of Jews entered the trade. Harry *Fischel encouraged Jews to enter the building trades by enabling the keeping of the Sabbath and offering half-pay for those who did not work on that day. Many left the trade again, however, either because of a chance to better themselves or because of discrimination. The unions, in particular, in effect barred Jews from the better-paid types of construction work and forced them to become house painters, plumbers, or decorators, and to concentrate on repairs and remodeling. In 1890 there were nearly 900 Jewish house painters and carpenters on the Lower East Side, and associations of Jewish immigrants in these trades were to be found in many U.S. cities. As a result of the general upward mobility of the American Jewish population, however, few young Jews entered these occupations by mid-20th century. Similarly, in the East End of London, many Jews from Eastern Europe took up these trades around the beginning of the 20th century. Although many Jews in Britain were prominent in the development of housing schemes after World War II, they were mainly occupied in acquiring sites and developing new housing estates and modern blocks of offices. The actual construction was carried out by non-Jewish firms, but there was one large construction company, one of the foremost of its kind, "Bovis" founded by Sir Samuel *Joseph. Their managerial and financial abilities and experience also led Jews in the 20th century to enter the mass-construction industry in America through real estate brokerage, and Jews were especially prominent in the New York, Chicago, and Miami building booms of the 1920s. In New York City, the major part of the Bronx and the Borough Park and Bensonhurst neighborhoods of Brooklyn were built by Jewish contractors. Louis J. *Horowitz became president and general manager of the Thompson-Starrett Construction Company, builder of many skyscrapers in New York and other cities. Real-estate investors and developers who played a prominent role in reshaping the face of 20th-century America's cities and their environs include William *Zeckendorf, Benjamin *Swig, Percy and Harold *Uris, William *Levitt, and Samuel *Lefrak. The latter two in particular, the first in the suburbs and the latter in the central city, pioneered new approaches to mass-scale, low-cost housing that have permanently altered the American urban landscape. Builders of office space in major cities were involved in significant projects that also shaped the city skylines. And other major builders made their marks in other parts of the country, including Eli Brod on the West Coast, who built vast housing projects.

In the 19th and 20th centuries Jews developed real estate on an increasing scale. The large number of Jews who took up engineering and architecture had a place in the planning and supervision of construction projects (see *architecture, *engineering, etc.). In Ereẓ Israel building became an important Jewish enterprise. The building concern *Solel Boneh developed into a big construction and industrial combine. It and *Rassco built agricultural villages and housing estates designed for middle class settlement. Both these firms as well as a number of private ones have built roads, bridges, and public buildings in Asian and African countries.

BIBLIOGRAPHY: G. Cohen, *The Jews in the Making of America* (1924), 127ff.; S.D. Goitein, *Mediterranean Society*, 1 (1967), s.v. *carpenters, masons, stonecutters*; L. Rosenberg, *Canada's Jews* (1939), 202ff.; M.U. Schappes, *The Jews in the U.S.* (1958), 197; B. Brutzkus, in: *Zeitschrift fuer Demographie und statistik der Juden*, 4 (1908), 84; M. Rischin, *The Promised City* (1962), 27, 59f., 188f.; S. Kaznelson (ed.), *Juden im deutschen Kulturbereich* (1959), 84–86; R. Mahler, *Yehudei Polin bein Shetei Milḥamot Olam* (1969), 76f., 102f.; H. Kahn, *Die juedischen Handwerke in Deutschland* (1936).

[Henry Wasserman]

CONSUMER PROTECTION. Consumer protection is a new area of law; hence, the term does not appear in classical sources of Jewish law. The meaning of the concept is implied in the term itself: our generation is one of abundance, with great demands, numerous consumers, and extensive consumption. The consumers are not organized; each one consumes for himself and his household. On the other hand, there are large producers and distributors: manufacturers, monopolies, chain stores, merchants, suppliers, and agents of various kinds who are familiar with the markets and dictate its terms, including, inter alia, the consumer culture itself. Consequently, the consumer requires legal protection, as he does not always receive fair value for his money, both in terms of price and quality of goods.

This question is not confined to the sphere of commerce, but arises in the context of services as well. Contemporary society regards services as a commodity, and the service provided is not always commensurate with the price received for it.

But the term *consumer protection* is not only a matter of the relationship between consumer and supplier, or consumer and service provider, in terms of the contract between them and its execution. *Consumer protection* must be considered as part of the overall economic system. Does the economic system protect or even benefit the consumer? This question extends beyond the scope of our discussion, and we will only touch upon it briefly.

Although, as mentioned, the term *consumer protection* does not appear in our sources, Jewish law does deal with these problems. Some of the laws in the field relate to the overall economic system and the maintenance of fair trade, while others are designed to protect various weak parties, including the consumer. Most of the laws mentioned below also appear in the context of other entries, such as *Ona'ah (overreaching or misrepresentation), *Hafka'at She'arim (profiteering), and *Mistake; hence, we will treat those topics more briefly, referring the reader to the aforementioned entries for fuller discussion.

The Economic System

There are two major contemporary economic systems, albeit on a practical level each one includes elements of the other.

The first system, capitalism, advocates a free, competitive market, functioning according to the principles of supply and demand, without governmental involvement. The second, socialism-communism, espouses governmental involvement in the market economy, through the setting and supervising of prices, distribution and direction of the means of production, even to the extent of nationalization.

Each system has its advantages and drawbacks. The former system, practiced in the West, and most notably in the

United States, is attractive and alluring, but does not ensure wealth and happiness to all; there are many indigent people in need of welfare services. The latter system, in its extreme form, collapsed in the U.S.S.R. A number of reasons contributed to its collapse, among them the indomitable human spirit, man's yearning for freedom, including freedom of initiative, business, and property rights.

Jewish law takes the middle road. It accommodates initiative and competition, but in a limited fashion, thereby assuring the possibility of acquiring wealth, but without excessively impinging upon the poor and weak. This approach is manifested in a series of different laws. Given the casuistic nature of Jewish law, which deals with the particular and the concrete, inductive reasoning is necessary in order to infer general principles from the particular cases.

We will briefly mention a few pertinent laws in this field.

Interest-Bearing Loans

One who gives a loan fulfills a positive commandment (Ex. 22:24; and Rashi loc. cit.). Loans are also a vital element in economic development. One person has capital, while another has initiative and productive abilities, but requires capital by way of a loan in order to realize these potentials. Thus far, the loan serves the borrower's interest: if he is poor, it provides him with his immediate needs; if he has initiative, it provides him with the means for setting up a factory or business. However, the loan is also in the interest of the loaner. In addition to the kindness involved, he hopes to profit from the interest to be accrued. The risk involved is that the benefit attained by the borrower will instead become a source of damage, as the borrower who does not succeed in his business will need to pay back the principal and interest without any economic justification,. which the lender receives unconditionally, at no personal risk. The lender thus becomes enriched at the borrower's expense, while the latter becomes impoverished. Biblical law intervenes and forbids the taking of interest, thereby preventing the widening of the gap between the two. Biblical law thus protects the interest of the borrower, who is also a consumer. Other laws promote freedom and initiative, on the one hand, and concern for the poor and weak, on the other. These include the sabbatical and jubilee laws, and in particular the cancellation of debts in the sabbatical year, various forms of charity, limits on commercial competition and against unjustified withholding of wages, the right of the worker to terminate his service before the completion of work, and others.

Hafka'at She'arim (Profiteering)

A number of laws are intended expressly for the consumer's protection. They are intended to ensure fair prices within the framework of a free market, where there is an accepted, standard market price. Whoever deviates from the market price without the other's knowledge transgresses the prohibition on deceit, as explained below. Jewish Law also intervenes in the setting of prices. In a free market, there is a danger that manufacturers and merchants will employ artificial means to influence prices. Jewish Law therefore prohibits profiteering. The Talmud (Meg. 17b) states that the blessing in the *Shemoneh Esreh* prayer for the year's produce was instituted by the sages against "profiteers," on the basis of the verse, "Break the arm of the wicked," which Rashi explains there as referring to "those who overprice produce and inflate prices." In other words, they artificially hike up prices in order to profit at the expense of the poor. For example: merchants who hoard their wares in order to market them at exorbitant prices when there is a shortage. There are also merchants who market their wares through agents, thereby increasing the price paid by the consumer (BB 90b). The Talmud further states (ibid., 90a): "A merchant should not make a profit of more than one sixth." However, these laws only refer to those goods which are considered essential or "life supporting," and the authorities dispute whether this category includes all foodstuffs or only some of them (see *Maggid Mishneh* and *Kesef Mishneh* on Maimonides, Yad, *Hilkhot Mekhirah* 14:2; *Me'irat Einayim* on ḤM 231:36). Regarding all other goods, the market is free and "he can charge as much as he likes" (Maimonides, ibid.).

Another category of articles subjected to regulation includes items required for the fulfillment of positive commandments, such as shofar, lulav, tefillin, matzah, etc. With respect to this category the sages adopted supply-promoting measures that lead to price reductions: inter alia, by issuing lenient halakhic rulings (see Mish., Ker. 1:7 concerning the post-natal mother's sacrifice, and Suk. 34b regarding pruned myrtles on Sukkot). For details of the laws on this subject, see *Hafka'at She'arim (Profiteering).

The Services Market

In addition to protecting consumers of commodities Jewish Law also protects consumers of services from paying in excess of the value of the services rendered. Here, too, the tendency is to provide the consumer with the opportunity to receive essential services at reasonable prices. The policy of ensuring cheap prices for religious commodities also applied to religious services.

The Talmud (Ned. 37a) interprets the verse: "'God commanded me at that time to teach you … just as I [teach you] free, so shall you [teach others] for free." In other words, there is a positive obligation to teach Torah gratis. Similarly, the Mishnah states (Bek. 4:6) that payment is not to be accepted by persons fulfilling a positive commandment, such as a judge, witness, or one who prepares the waters of ritual purification (*mei ḥatat*) or sprinkles them on the ritually impure. The Talmud distinguishes, however, between wages paid for the actual performance of a commandment, and those paid for various preparatory labors involved in its performance. It is thus permitted to accept wages for transporting the ashes of the red heifer or for filling up the water used in that ritual. Similarly, the Mishnah states that one who, in order to perform a commandment, is compelled to take time off from work, may accept compensation for time lost. Thus, in the case of a judge adjudicating a legal dispute (even where there was no prior agreement to that effect), we estimate what proportion of a person's wages he would be prepared to forgo (in accordance with the wage level and the difficulty of his work) in order to fulfill a commandment rather than working (see Sh. Ar., ḤM 9:5). This method enables those who spread Torah, such as rabbis, judges, teachers, as well as doctors, to receive payment for their work. According to another view, it is permitted to take payment when paid by the community rather than by individuals (see Tos. citing R. Tam, Ket. 105a).

The level of the judge's wage is "enough for his livelihood" (Ket., ibid.). The Talmud does not consider the possibility that he might demand more than this. Maimonides adds: "Their livelihood: for them, their wives, their children, and the members of their households" (Maim., Yad, *Shekalim* 4:7).

Regarding the fulfillment of commandments by the consumer, such as one who requires the services of a scribe to write a Torah scroll, tefillin, or mezuzah for him, mention should be made of the appeal made by the *Tiferet Yisrael*, based on the Mishnah (Bek., ibid.) "… that it is not fitting to burden people [monetarily] too much in matters of Torah and mitzvot," i.e. special care is required not to financially burden people with respect to items they need to purchase for the performance of commandments.

Wage Rates in Private Sector

In general, wages in the free market are fixed according to supply and demand. Nevertheless, in two situations Jewish Law does intervene:

(a) Determination of fees by service providers. A professional association can determine a price for services provided by its members to the public. The danger is that the price may be excessively high, without economic justification. Jewish Law responded to this situation by requiring the approval of "an important person" to protect the consumers' interests (BB 9a; and Sh. Ar, ḤM 231:28).

(b) Where a private person charges more than the accepted price for his services. In certain cases, the consumer pays a higher price due to his ignorance of the accepted price (see the discussion of overreaching, below). On other occasions, he is aware of the accepted price but may be forced to pay an exorbitant price. This issue is discussed in Yevamot 106a:

> If he [an escapee] was fleeing from prison and reached a ferry and he said [to the ferryman]: "Take a dinar [which is an inflated price] and take me across," he [the ferryman] is entitled only to his [normal] wage.

The Talmud explains that the person who undertook to pay can say to the ferryman: "I was fooling with you [and did not intend to pay the inflated price]" (see Maim. Yad, *Hilkhot Gezelah ve-Avedah* 12:7; Sh. Ar., ḤM 264:7). However, the exemption is dependent on the fulfillment of two conditions: first, that the service provider inflated the price due to the customer's distress; second, that the service provider had other work at that time, which he lost because of the client.

Accordingly, the *Shulḥan Arukh* (ḤM 264:7) rules: "In addition, someone fleeing from prison … he [the service provider] receives only his [normal] wage, and if he [the service provider] was a hunter and he [the client] said to him: 'Stop hunting and help me across,' he must pay him whatever they agreed upon, and this applies to other similar cases." The Rema adds: "Some authorities contend that the ruling that he [the service provider] is only entitled to his [normal] wage applies exclusively to instances in which it is not customary to pay a high price, but where a high price is the norm – for instance, with swearing by demons (to find a lost article) or for medical treatment – he must pay him whatever they agreed upon."

Ona'ah (Overreaching)

This is another rule that protects the consumer, although the original intention was to protect both sides: the seller and the buyer. The Torah states (Lev. 25:14): "When you sell an item to your friend, or buy from your friend, do not defraud each other." The sages derived the law of overreaching from this verse. That is, if it transpires that the price of the transaction deviated from the accepted price by one-sixth of its value or more, the aggrieved party has the option of imposing a sanction upon the offender, irrespective of whether he acted intentionally or accidentally (see Sh. Ar., ḤM 227; and *Ona'ah).

Nowadays, due to the aforementioned market conditions, it is usually the consumer who is the overreached party, and the laws of *ona'ah* are intended to protect him from exaggerated prices.

Mistaken Transactions

We have thus far focused on issues of pricing, but at times the problem relates to the nature or identification of the transaction. In this context, Jewish Law protects the consumer in a variety of fields.

MISTAKEN IDENTITY: In some cases the contract may be legally executed, but at the time of performance a discrepancy emerges between what was agreed upon and the concrete situation. In this context, the Mishnah states (BB 5:6): "He sold him … olive wood and it turned out to be sycamore … both are entitled to cancel the deal." This is a case in which both parties make a mistake.

A MISTAKE IN THE OBJECT OF THE TRANSACTION: Sometimes the object of the transaction is transferred as required, but the consumer claims that there is a mistake related to the object of the transaction. We may distinguish between two different situations:

A. A Mistake relating to Quantity:

> Sometimes the seller permits himself a small deviation in terms of measure, weight, or quantity from a large number of customers, to "compensate himself" for his small profit margin. Therefore, the Torah warns (Lev. 19:35): "Do not defraud, in measurements, in weights, or in measuring; fair scales …" The in judgment sages' exegesis of this verse indicates the extremity of the measures taken in order to prevent the offense: first,

> extreme accuracy is required: the Talmud (BM 61b; BB 89b) interprets the verse as follows: "'In measurements' [of an] area of land – he must not sell to one during the summer and to another during the winter." This is because the rope used for measuring length is not the same length in the summer as in the winter. 'In weight' he should not dip the weights in salt. [Tosafot, in the name of Rabenu Tam, explained that this is because "salt lightens the weights").] 'In measure' [teaches] that one must not cause [the liquid] to foam. This means that it is forbidden for the seller to pour the wine from a height into the client's measuring vessel, because it foams … and appears full" (see Rashbam on BB, ibid.).

The passage clearly proves that the margin of accuracy required is 1/63 of a *log*, and the *Shulḥan Arukh* (ḤM 231:6) rules: "Even if [the measure] is very small, so that the foam is not worth one penny." Secondly, there are restrictions that extend beyond the strict scope of the prohibition: Not only is defrauding forbidden, but there is an a priori obligation to ensure the accuracy of the scales. Therefore: "Weights must not be made of tin, lead, or other types of metal, because they wear" (BB, ibid.). Moreover, based on the verse "you shall not have in your pocket …" the rabbis deduced that it is forbidden to possess an inaccurate measure in your house, so that it does not become an inadvertent stumbling block (Sh. Ar., ibid., 3). The court is responsible for taking precautions, by appointing inspectors charged with ensuring the accuracy of weights and measures (ibid., 2). Thirdly, in case of doubt, the seller must err in favor of the customer. This is derived from the verse (Deut. 25:15) "A full and righteous stone [weight] …" According to rabbinic exegesis: "Be righteous from yourself and give to him" (Sh. Ar., ibid., 14)

What remedy does the consumer have when he receives less than the agreed quantity of goods?

The Talmud (Kid. 42b) rules that the transacted object is returned. The authorities disagreed over the meaning of this ruling. Some hold that the transaction is annulled (Tos., BB 104a). Some distinguish between real estate and chattel: only with real estate must the defrauder supplement the amount or reduce the price as appropriate (Rashbam, BB, ibid.). Others distinguish between situations in which he can make up the lack, as with a shortfall in the weight or amount of a given product, and others which cannot be corrected, such as a house which is smaller than the agreed-upon size, in which case the transaction is annulled (see Naḥmanides on BB 103b; Sh. Ar., Ḥ.M. 232:1; *Me'irat Einayim* 4 and the novellae of the Gaon of Vilna, *ad loc.*). According to some authorities, if the transaction was made on the understanding that it is complete, but turns out to be deficient, the transaction is annulled. If, however, a sale of 100 eggs is agreed upon and it turns out that some are missing, the lack must be made up (Rabad's glosses on Maim., *Hilkhot Mekhirah* 15:2). According to another view, the transaction is always upheld, and the seller must make up the amount or, if this is not possible, reduce the price (Rashba, BB 103b).

B. A MISTAKE RELATING TO QUALITY.

The Mishna (BB 5:6) states: "If he sold him good wheat and it turned out to be bad, the purchaser may renege." Here, there is no remedy of supplementing the transaction, the only remedy is the annulment. Maimonides gives the following explanation (*Mekhirah* 15:2):

> We do not calculate the loss of value due to the fault … If the fault reduces its value by an *issar* [a negligible amount] he returns the vessel, and the seller cannot say to the buyer, "Take an *issar* in compensation for the loss of value" because the buyer can say to him, "I want a perfect item."

But not every change in the attributes or quality of goods annuls a transaction. Some changes are small, in which case the remedy lies in compensation or repair. Thus, for example, the *Shulḥan Arukh* rules in accordance with R. Asher regarding someone who sells a house in a different city, where it transpires that before the sale was complete Gentiles destroyed the windows and doors. In such a case, the transaction is not annulled. This is considered a "passing fault" that can be repaired. Therefore: "He [the seller] reduces the payment so that the buyer can restore the house to its previous state" (Sh. Ar., ḤM 232:5). There is also the case of a fault that is extraneous to the transaction and which can be remedied. For instance, if it transpires that a canal runs by the house, or another party has a right of passage through the house, the seller must remove this "obstacle," and the transaction is not annulled (Rema, ibid.).

What are the criteria for determining a mistaken transaction?

The more the customer details his original demands, the greater his opportunity to claim a mistaken transaction in the case of disagreement over the interpretation of the contract. A prior condition can serve to illuminate the parties' intentions (see Sh. Ar, ḤM 214:1). But regarding an actual fault, no prior stipulation is required: "It is assumed that any buyer wants a perfect article with no faults." In this context, a fault includes: "anything that the local residents agree is a fault, such as annuls a transaction of this kind" (Maim. Yad, *Hilkhot Mekhirah* 15:5; Sh. Ar., ḤM 2:6).

It follows that the local custom establishes the limits for a claim of mistaken transaction. The designated use of the item also influences the result of the consumer's claim. If a customer purchases a slave with a hidden blemish which does not prevent him from carrying out his work, such as a wart, he cannot claim this as a blemish, because the slave is intended for work and for no other purpose (Sh. Ar., ibid., 10). But if the item can serve several purposes, and the buyer failed to stipulate the purpose of his purchase, then even if the majority of consumers purchase it for the purpose he claims "we do not follow the majority in monetary matters." Hence, if someone purchases an ox, and it turns out to be a goring ox suitable for slaughter only and not for plowing, he cannot annul the transaction on the grounds of mistaken purchase (Sh. Ar., ibid., 23).

In some instances, the claim of mistaken purchase is contingent on the behavior of the purchaser: (a) If he knew in advance that the concrete reality did not conform with the terms of the agreement, the claim of nonconformity is not accepted, unless he made a condition to that effect (Rema, Ḥ.M. 220:10; Gra, ibid.); (b) If the purchaser used the item after seeing the fault he is considered "as if he has waived [his claim], and it is not annulled" (Sh. Ar., ibid., 3). Some hold that it is the purchaser's responsibility to check the item so that he can later claim that it is unsuitable (see *Maggid Mishneh* on Maim., *Hilkhot Mekhirah* 5:3). Others, however, limit this obligation to specific circumstances (see *Netivot ha-Mishpat* on Ḥ.M. 232:1; *Pitḥei Teshuvah* ad loc.).

The seller, for his part, can protect himself from the claim of mistaken transaction if he makes an appropriate condition in advance to the effect that the buyer waives his right to annul the transaction in that particular instance (see Sh. Ar., ḤM 232:7–9).

Commercial Advertising

The principal requirement of the seller relates to his presentation of the goods. He must be careful not to mislead the buyer. Not only is lying forbidden: concealing relevant information and misleading the buyer are similarly prohibited. Thus Maimonides rules (Yad, *Hilkhot Mekhirah* 18:1): "It is forbidden to defraud people in business or to mislead them. This applies equally to Gentiles and Jews. If he is aware of a fault in his merchandise, he must inform the buyer."

There are various kinds of actions that amount to misleading, but for our purposes we shall quote Maimonides (*De'ot* 2:6):

> It is forbidden to sell a Gentile the meat of a carcass instead of ritually slaughtered meat, or a shoe made from [the skin of] ritually slaughtered meat, or a shoe made from [the skin of] a carcass rather than one made from [the skin of] a slaughtered animal … rather [you should have] truth in speech, an honest spirit, and a heart which is pure of all deceit and wrongdoing.

Even if there is no difference between the price of slaughtered meat and the price of a carcass, the Gentile is grateful to him for selling him what he assumes to be slaughtered meat, which is considered of a higher quality.

At times the law depends on the behavior of the seller. Hence the ruling:

> It is forbidden to apply color [or apply makeup] to a person (i.e., a Canaanite slave), or an animal, or to vessels; for example, to dye the beard of a slave about to be sold to make him look young; or to give an animal bran water to drink, which causes it to swell and its hair to stand on end, so that it looks fat … (Sh. Ar., ḤM 228:9).

This does not mean that all advertising is forbidden. Improving the external appearance of merchandise without concealing faults is permitted. The Mishnah (Ar. 6:5) states: "… although they ruled that a slave sold with clothes is worth more, so that if you buy him a cloak worth 30 dinars, it increases his value by a maneh [i.e., 100 dinars]." Rashi explains that this is so "… because good clothing enhances them and adds to their value."

In his gloss on the Mishnah, *Tiferet Yisrael* adds that coloring the merchandise with intent to deceive is forbidden, but "… to wash and anoint him [the slave] to encourage the buyers to purchase him is permitted."

In certain instances, the seller's presentation of the product can be interpreted in different ways, and if the purchaser fails to verify the true significance, he has only himself to blame. The Talmud (Hul. 94b) gives the example of an announcement for the sale of meat to Gentiles. Here it is the responsibility of the gentiles to conclude that the meat is *terefah* (not ritually slaughtered in accordance with Jewish Law).

In principle, advertising directed at the emotions and imagination is permissible. The Mishnah therefore rules (BM 4:12):

> R. Judah said: a shopkeeper must not distribute parched corn or nuts to children, because he thereby accustoms them to come to him; the sages permit it. Nor may he reduce the price; but the sages say, he is to be remembered for good.

The ruling is in accordance with the sages' view. This demonstrates that free competition is more important than the possibility of deceiving people. However, it is still necessary to beware of overly seductive advertising, which obscures relevant information. The same Mishnah states: "One must not sift pounded beans: This is the view of Abba Saul. but the sages permit it." The sages ruling was accepted as the binding rule. In other words, the assumption is that the buyer will not be deceived into overrating the importance of the removal of the debris. However, the Mishnah continues:

> … but they agree that he may not remove the debris from the face of the dish only, because this amounts to creating a deceptive appearance. (This ruling was codified in the *Shulḥan Arukh*, ḤM 228:17.)

The *Tosafot YomTov* accurately point out that the phrase "creating a deceptive appearance" (literally "stealing the eye") implies that, even if the seller informs the buyer that he only sifted the top layer, he may nevertheless be deceived by the sight of clean merchandise, and receive the wrong impression.

An additional concern pertinent to the kind of commercial advertising common today is the use of immodest pictures and signs, etc. Similarly, one must beware of applying subliminal pressure to buy unnecessary merchandise, even to the extent of turning consumption itself into a value. This contravenes the words of Naḥmanides on the verse "You shall be holy …" (Lev. 19:2), where he states: "… that we should remove ourselves from luxuriousness."

The Legal Position in Israel

There are a number of laws relating to fair trade and the required agreement between a contract and its execution. We shall mention a few of these: the Standards Law, 5713 – 1953; the Sales Law, 5728 – 1968; the Contracts (General Part) Law,

5733 – 1973; the Standard Contracts Law, 5724 – 1964; the Contracts (Remedy for Breach of Contract) Law 5731 – 1971.

However, of special significance for our purposes is the Consumer Protection Law, 5741/1981. In the introduction to the explanatory note of the bill (Haẓaʾot Ḥok, 5780 p. 301), it was emphasized that "the proposal is deeply rooted in Jewish law, which provides extensive protection for the consumer within the framework of the laws of deception and fraud." In addition to some of the sources cited above, the words of the *amora* R. Levi are quoted: "The punishment for [false] measures is more rigorous than that for [marrying] forbidden relatives" (BB 88b).

The words of the Tosefta (BK 7:2) are also quoted: "There are seven types of thieves. Foremost among them – he who deceives people." The principles of Jewish Law pertaining to the topic are also quoted, as detailed above.

BIBLIOGRAPHY: Elon, *Ha-Mishpat ha-Ivri* (1988), I, 113, 642; II, 1078, 1106; idem, *Jewish Law* (1994), I, 127; II, 795; III, 1300, 1330; M. Elon and B. Lifshitz, *Mafteʾaḥ ha-Sheʾelot ve-ha-Teshuvot shel Ḥakhmei Sefarad u-Ẓefon Afrikah* 1 (1986), 213f.; B. Lifshitz and E. Shohetman, *Mafteʾaḥ ha-Sheʾelot ve-ha-Teshuvot shel Ḥakhmei Ashkenaz, Ẓarfat ve-Italiyah* (1997), 160f.; A. Levin, *Free Enterprise and Jewish Law* (1980); "Haganat ha-Ẓarkhan le-Or ha-Halakhah," in: *Tehumin* 1 (5740), 444; *Tehumin* 2 (5741), 470; *Tehumin* 3 (5742), 334; Keter, *Mehkarim be-Kalkalah al pi ha-Halakhah* (2004), pts. 1 & 2; N. Rakover, *Ha-Misḥar be-Mishpat ha-Ivri*, (1988), 17–49; M. Tamari, "Jewish Law and Economic Laws," in: *Niv ha-Midrashiyah* (1969), 127–32; S. Warhaftig, *Dinei Misḥar ba-Mishpat ha-Ivri* (1990), 51–115.

[Itamar Warhaftig (2nd ed.)]

CONTEMPT OF COURT. According to the Talmud, cursing a judge is a scriptural prohibition. The verse "You shall not revile God" (Ex. 22:27) is interpreted as referring to human judges (Mekh. *ibid.*; Sanh. 66a; Maim. Yad, Sanhedrin 26:1) as is a preceding verse "… the case of both parties shall come before God: he whom God declares guilty shall pay double to the other" (*ibid.*, 22:8). In both these verses the word *Elohim* is used and was taken to mean "judges." Cursing any person is an offense punishable with *flogging (see *Slander), cursing a judge, by virtue of the extra prohibition, is punished by a double flogging (Maim. (*ibid.*, 26:2). As in every offense punishable with flogging, so in contempt of court the offender must have been warned beforehand; however, insulting a judge or the court may be punished with anathema (see **Ḥerem*) or with admonitory lashes (*makkat mardut*), even though spontaneous and not punishable by law (Maim. *ibid.*, 26:5). The court may, however, at its discretion, condone such an unpremeditated insult and abstain from taking action on it, whereas a premeditated curse must be punished according to law and no apology can be accepted (Maim. *ibid.* 26:6).

It appears that in talmudic times the administrative, and not the judicial, officers of the court were the main target of contempt of court – demonstrated both in words and violence – and detailed rules were worked out to facilitate the perilous tasks of court messengers assigned to serve summonses and to execute judgments (BK 112b–113a; Maim. *ibid.*, 25:5–11; ḤM 11). The standard punishment for contempt of court messengers is anathema (*niddui*), after three prior warnings (*ibid.*); but admonitory lashes were also administered not only for insulting process-servers (Kid. 12b, 70b), but especially for failure to pay judgment debts (Ket. 86a–b). The source for the authority to proclaim anathema was taken to be Deborah's curse on those who did not come to the help of the Lord (Judg. 5:23). One scholar, invoking the wide authority given to Ezra by the Persian king for the punishment of offenders (Ezra 7:26), went so far as to authorize the infliction of imprisonment, shackling, and confiscation of goods (MK 16a), but in practice no such severe measures appear ever to have been adopted. No witnesses were required to prove such contempt: the complaint of the court official was accepted as conclusive – and expressly excluded from the applicability of the rules against slander (*ibid.*, and Maim., and ḤM *ibid.*).

In post-talmudic times, obedience to the courts had to be enforced by more rigorous means: both admonitory lashes (cf., e.g., Resp.Rosh 8:2 and 11:4) and imprisonment (cf., e.g., *Rema* and ḤM 97:15; Resp. Ribash 484) were widely used against persons who willfully persisted in disobeying the court. However, such extreme sanctions were resorted to only where previous public admonitions (cf., e.g., Resp. Maharam Minz 38, 39, 101), the exclusion from religious and civic honors, the disqualification from suing and testifying, and similar measures (including the anathema) had been of no avail (S. Assaf, *Battei Din…* (1924), 118 and passim). It has been maintained that all these sanctions were not punitive in nature but solely designed to execute the judgment of the court or make the adjudged debtor pay his debt (Elon) – a modern distinction which in most cases is rather academic. The talmudic formula, "he shall be beaten until his soul departs" (Ket. 86b et al.), has an unmistakably punitive undertone: compelling the debtor to pay coincides with punishing him for his contempt.

BIBLIOGRAPHY: M. Bloch, *Civilprozess-Ordnung nach mosaischrabbinischem Rechte* (1882), 24–27, nos. 35–42; S. Assaf, *Ha-Onshin Aḥarei Ḥatimat ha-Talmud* (1922), passim; Elon, in: *Sefer Yovel le-Finḥas Rosen* (1962), 171–201; idem, *Ḥerut ha-Perat be-Darkhei Geviyyat Ḥov ba-Mishpat ha-Ivri* (1964), 136, 256; ET, 3 (1951), 172; 8 (1957), 656–9, no. 6; 12 (1967), 119–28.

[Haim Hermann Cohn]

CONTRACT (Heb. חוֹזֶה, *ḥozeh*), in general law theory a legally binding agreement between two or more parties, in terms of which one party undertakes for the benefit of the other to perform or refrain from a certain act. As such, contract is the main source of the law of *obligations. The scriptural term closest to this meaning is the word *berit* ("covenant"), although it occurs mainly in the sense of a *covenant of love between man and his neighbor (I Sam. 18:3), or a perpetual covenant between the Almighty and man or the people of Israel (Gen. 9:9; 15:18; Ex. 31:16), as well as a covenant of peace between nations (Gen. 21:32; Judg. 2:2; II Sam. 5:4; Ezek. 30:5; Hos. 12:2). The word *ḥozeh* also occurs in Scripture, but not in any strict legal sense: e.g., "... with the nether-world are we at agreement" (Isa. 28:15). In the post-scriptural period no concrete legal significance was assigned to either of these terms, nor was there any embracing parallel term for contract in talmudic times (the word *kiẓa(h)* (Tosef. Ket. 4:7, et al.) is not a generic term for contract but represents a particular transaction only). In the rabbinical period (see *Mishpat Ivri), the term *hitkasherut* came into general use – a term rightly considered by Gulak to be a translation of the Latin *contractus* (from *contrahere*, "mutual binding together"), and one that aptly expresses the concept of contract. The term *ḥozeh* was used by I.S. Zuri (*Mishpat ha-Talmud*, 5 (1921), 1) as the equivalent of contract and this has come into general use in Hebrew legal parlance in the State of Israel.

The absence in Jewish law of a generic term for a concept paralleling that of contract in Roman law is apparently attributable to its preference for a concrete rather than abstract terminology (see *Codification of Law). The Jewish law principles of contract are to be gathered from the various laws of *sale, *lease, *gift, *loan, *suretyship, etc. and from the additional special laws accruing in the course of time.

Creation of Contractual Ties

In ancient Jewish law it was possible for contractual ties to be created in various symbolic ways, such as by "removing and handing over the shoe" (Ruth 4:7; see also TJ, Kid. 1:5, 60c) and by handshake (*teki'at kaf*, Prov. 6:1; 11:15; 17:18; 22:26; Job 17:3; see also Ezra 10: 19). The view of obligations as being of a concrete (*ḥefzi*) nature by giving the creditor a *lien over the debtor's assets (see Obligations, Law of) resulted in the fact that the modes of creating contractual obligations came to be the same as those for the creation of ownership rights in property (see Modes of *Acquisition). While Jewish law bases the conclusion of a contract on the *gemirut ha-da'at* (i.e., final intention or making up of the mind) of the parties to be bound, such intention may only be inferred from a formal and recognized *kinyan* ("mode of acquisition") executed by one of the parties. Hence, contrary to Roman law which allows for a contract to be concluded by the mere oral assent of the parties, Jewish law does not generally confer legal recognition on an obligation created merely orally (BM 94a; cf. Kid. 1:6; for exceptions to this rule, see below). Accordingly, the breach of a merely oral agreement involves "a breach of faith," carrying only moral sanction (BM 49a, opinion of R. Johanan, and Codes); and the obligation is not legally complete, even where the purchaser has paid the price but failed to observe the mode of acquisition proper to the transaction, and the sanction, if he should retract, is a "religious" one only: "He who punished the generation of the Flood and of the Dispersion will exact payment from one who does not stand by his word" (BM 4:2 and Codes). The reason for the existence of a religious or moral sanction in these circumstances is the underlying religio-moral duty of fulfilling a promise, i.e., an oral undertaking made without the execution of a formal *kinyan* (Ket. 86a; see also BM 9:7 and Pes. 91a).

Consideration

Jewish law attaches a great deal of importance to the existence of consideration in the creation of contractual ties, and in this respect shows an interesting similarity to English law (see Gulak, Yesodei, 2 (1922), 40ff.). This requirement finds expression mainly in the fact that the contract is only concluded upon the actual passing of the consideration, such as the borrower's receipt of the loan money, or the performance of an act representing the receipt of the subject matter of the transaction by the purchaser, donee, hirer, or borrower. Even with regard to the creation of a bailment, which gives the bailee no right in the property itself or its fruits, it was laid down that an act of *meshikhah* (lit. "pulling," see Modes of *Acquisition) of the subject matter established the obligation (BM 99a; see **shomerim*). Similarly, a contract of *partnership for profit-making purposes is concluded when each of the partners performs an act of receiving part of the subject matter of the partnership belonging to the other partners – whether in money or chattels (Ket. 10:4) – the rule being: "partners acquire one from the other a common interest in the partnership capital in the same manners that the purchaser acquires [from the seller]" (Maim. Yad, Sheluḥin, 4:1). In the same way, a contract for the hire of a laborer is concluded upon the laborer commencing his work, the work being the contractual consideration (Tosef. BM, 7:1; BM 76b). None of the obligations normally deriving from any of the above-mentioned transactions, such as payment of the price by the purchaser and the seller's responsibility for the subject matter, or payment of the bailment money by the bailor and the obligation of the bailee to take care of the bailment, etc., will be legally binding on any of the parties, except upon their execution of the act of *kinyan* offering some exchange of consideration.

A number of contractual obligations were originally capable of being established merely orally – these cases being explained on the basis of a "spiritual" consideration. Thus, in the case of a *dowry it was decided that the mutual promises of the parties achieved legal validity upon mere oral agreement ("matters concerning which *kinyan* is effected by a mere verbal arrangement," Ket. 102b); "owing to the pleasure in forming of a mutual family tie, they finally make up their minds to allow one another the full rights of *kinyan*." The distribution among the partners of partnership assets by lottery, even though effected orally only, was held to be legally binding for a similar reason (BB 106b). Similarly, the oral establishment of a suretyship obligation was justified because, "on account of the pleasure of being trusted [by the creditor, or court appointing him] he finally makes up his mind to undertake the obligation" (BB 173b, 176b).

The requirement of consideration for the creation of an obligation served to complicate the modes of formation of contractual ties, just as the need for real modes of acquisition complicated the manner of gaining a proprietary right. Beginning with the amoraic period, mention is made of "acquisition by the kerchief" (*kinyan sudar*) as a method both for the acquisition of a proprietary right and for the establishment of an obligation. This mode required that the promisee give the promisor some object belonging to him in return for which, as it were, the latter undertook the obligation; this procedure involved the handing over of a fictitious consideration – as the value of the object bore no relationship to the measure of the obligation and on completion of the formalities the object was returned to the promisee. Because it was convenient and easily executed, this procedure came to be widely followed from amoraic times onward as the mode of creation of different obligations (see BM 94a; BB 3a; etc.). In order to create mutual obligations between the parties, a *kinyan* would be effected by each in respect of his own undertaking.

Obligation by Admission (Hoda'ah) and by Deed

*Admission offered a further means for the creation of an obligation without consideration. Originally admission was an aspect of the procedural law: i.e., a man's admission that he was indebted to another or that a specified object of his belonged to another was enough to establish liability without any further proof, in terms of the rule that "the admission of a litigant is as the evidence of a hundred witnesses" (Kid. 65b). Accordingly, admission created no new obligation but merely confirmed an already existing one. Out of the procedural form of admission, Jewish law developed an admission of a substantive nature capable of creating a new obligation, so that the mere admission of liability for an obligation established its existence without further investigation, even if it was known not to have existed previously (Ket. 101b). In the opinion of most commentators, obligation stemming from admission may be created orally (before witnesses) without any need for a formal *kinyan* even if it is known by both parties and the witnesses that there was not any debt in existence (Maim. Yad, Mekhirah, 11:15; Sh. Ar., ḤM 40:1). The scholars found a basis for the existence of a unilateral obligation in a suretyship undertaking (see Ket. 101b; Yad and Sh. Ar., loc. cit.; and Siftei Kohen, ḤM 40:1, n.7). Admission, like a formal *kinyan*, served not only to establish an obligation but was also a method of alienation (*hakna'ah*) of property (BB 149a); in both events it was required that an oral formula be adopted, making clear the fact of an admission (*keẓot ha-ḥoshen*, ḤM 40:1). A written undertaking was also recognized by the majority of the commentators as a means of creating an obligation without consideration (Ket. 101b; BB 175b; Yad, Mekhirah 11:15; Sh. Ar., ḤM 40:1).

Obligations in Respect of Something Not Yet in Existence (Davar She-Lo Ba La-Olam)

The tenet of Jewish law that a person cannot transfer title of something not yet in existence or not in his possession (*She-eino bi-reshuto*; see Modes of *Acquisition), severely inhibited the development of trade. This problem was already referred to in tannaitic times in the statement: "one who declares, 'whatever I shall inherit from my father is sold to you, whatever my trap shall ensnare is sold to you,' has said nothing" (Tosef., Ned. 6:7); if however he says: "'whatever I shall inherit from my father to-day, whatever my trap shall ensnare to-day,' his statements are binding" (*ibid.*). Although in both cases the subject matter of the transaction is not yet in existence, the rule in the latter case resulted from a rabbinical enactment aimed at providing the promisor with money for the burial of his dying father, or for his own sustenance on that day (BM 16a–b). Similarly, it may be inferred from the plain meaning of the statement: "whoever sells products to his neighbor believing them to be in his possession, and it is then found that they are not, the other [party] does not have to lose his right" (Tosef. BM 4:1) that the seller is still legally obliged to deliver products to the purchaser, as undertaken (see also TJ, Ter. 6:3, 44b, statement of Abbahu). However, this *halakhah* was interpreted by the Babylonian *amoraim* as referring to the tradition of the moral sanction, "He who punished..." (BM 4:2) and not to a legal obligation (BM 63b; see also S. Lieberman, *Tosefot Rishonim*, 2 (1938), 111–2 on the wording of the Tosefta statement and attitude of the *rishonim* to it; cf. also BB 69b and Rashbam, ad loc.).

In the amoraic period an exception had already been stipulated to this general rule – something not yet in existence could be charged in a creditor's favor, even though no one could alienate it or transfer title to it; and the debtor could charge in favor of a creditor property which the former might acquire in the future (BB 157a; see *Lien). Out of this proposition there developed, in relation to something not yet in existence, a basic and substantive distinction between proprietary right and a right of obligation. Thus Solomon b. Abraham Adret (Rashba) made clear that a person who undertakes to give his neighbor all that he might earn in the following 30 days and charges all his property (whether existing or to be acquired in the future) to the latter is legally obliged to fulfill his undertaking, since this is not a case of transferring title of something not yet in existence, such as the fruit of the palm-tree, but a personal undertaking to give whatever the palm-tree shall produce during a specified period in the future; and "so far as obligations are concerned... the question of something that is not yet in existence is of no moment... because of the responsibility of the person himself" (Resp., vol. 3, no. 65; Rashba found a basis for the distinction in a man's undertaking to provide maintenance for a certain period which is valid even if he lacks the means for it at the time of the undertaking: Ket. 101b). The *halakhah* was also decided to the effect that the rule concerning something not yet in existence applied to a disposition couched in the language of sale or gift. If, however, it was couched in the language of obligation (e.g., "be witness that I oblige myself to *peloni* ["so-and-so"] for such-and-such"), the obligation in question would be effective and binding (Tur. and Sh. Ar., ḤM 60:6), because "the obligation rests on his person and he is in existence" (Sma, ḤM 60:6, n. 18).

Substantive Change in the Nature of Contractual Obligation in Jewish Law

The distinction described above was a convenient way in which the contractual obligation could be used to meet the requirements of a developing commercial life. Although it had its roots in talmudic *halakhah* (Rashba, loc. cit. and see also *Sefer ha-Terumot*, no. 64:2), the distinction was apparently accepted as an explicit legal principle only from the 13th century onward (Maimonides, for instance, does not mention it at all). Until its acceptance, the main emphasis in regard to an obligation was placed on the real nature of the right of lien over the debtor's property, but recognition of the validity of an undertaking, even one relating to something not yet in existence, strengthened the personal aspect of the obligation, for it was founded on the actual existence of the debtor's person.

This concept was developed further during the same period. A corollary of the "real-right" aspect of an obligation had been the legal conclusion that an undertaking could not be legally created unless the promisor owned property at that time, which would become charged in favor of the promisee. The statements of the *amoraim* concerning the extension of the lien to include assets which would be acquired subsequent to creation of the debt meant that the lien would take in such assets in addition to those owned by the promisor at the time the debt was created. Arising from this, the tosafists discussed the validity of the then current practice of a bridegroom's written undertaking in favor of his bride, "for a hundred pounds even though he does not have a penny," and they confirmed this practice for the reason that, "the subjection of his person established the debt forthwith" (R. Elijah, Tos. to Ket. 54b; Rosh, *ibid.*). The result was to shift the emphasis in a contractual obligation to the personal aspect of the undertaking – "even for something he is not liable for and even if he has no assets, since he binds and holds responsible his own person" (*Beit Yosef*, ḤM 60, no. 15). This doctrine was even more explicitly enunciated by Moses *Sofer in the 18th century (*Ḥatam Sofer*, nov. Ket. 54b). In this manner the contractual obligation underwent a substantial change, from being essentially real in nature to being essentially personal, with the property aspect subordinate to the personal.

The emphasis on the personal aspect brought in its train a series of additional halakhic rulings concerning contractual obligations. Thus, some of the *posekim* expressed the opinion that a person could validly give an undertaking in favor of someone not yet in existence – even though he was unable to transfer title in this manner – and hence it was decided, for example, that a stipulation in favor of a person yet unborn was binding "since the stipulator is at any rate in existence" (*Yad Malakhi, Kelalei ha-Dinim*, no. 127). Similarly, despite the rule that a person could not transfer title to an intangible thing, such as a right of usufruct or of occupation of a dwelling (Sh. Ar., ḤM 212:1 ff.), some *posekim* expressed the view that a person could validly give an undertaking of this nature (Resp. *Naḥal Yiẓḥak*, 60:3). The majority of the *posekim* were of the opinion that a person could validly give an undertaking in regard to an unspecified amount, such as maintenance, to extend even for a period of unspecified duration (Resp. Rashba, pt. 2, no. 89; *Hassagot Rabad* Mekhirah 11:16; Sh. Ar., ḤM 60:2; 207:21) and in the opinion of several *posekim* an undertaking could be given either to commit or to refrain from committing a certain act (Resp. Maharashdam, ḤM, no. 370; Resp. Maharsham, pt. 2, no. 18).

Developments in the Formation of Contractual Ties by Way of Custom

As has already been stated, it has been a general principle of Jewish law that mere oral assent is not sufficient to constitute the *gemirat ha-da'at* of the parties, which is a fundamental requirement for the validity of any transaction involving a proprietary right or contractual obligation and is complete only when expressed in one of the recognized modes of acquisition or accompanied by the existence of some "spiritual" consideration, except for certain exceptions laid down in talmudic law (as in the case where the parties are husband and wife or parent and child, BK 102b and Nov. Rashba, ad loc.; also in other special cases, Bekh. 18b and Tos.; see also *Ḥazon Ish*, BK no. 21:5).

By means of the legal source of custom (**minhag*), Jewish law came to recognize a way of creating orally a legally valid transaction. According to talmudic law, the existence of a trading custom whereby a transaction was concluded by affixing a mark (*sitomta*) on a barrel of wine was sufficient to render the sale legally complete, despite the absence of a *meshikhah* – the recognized mode of acquiring movable property (BM 74a). This rule was justified on the grounds that "custom abrogates the law in all matter of *mamon*" (i.e., monetary matters or the civil law; see *minhag) and therefore "acquisition is made in all manners customary among the merchants" (Rashba, nov. BM, 74a). In the course of the time it was decided, in line with the above principle, that a transaction concluded by way of a handshake or the payment of earnest money (*demei kadimah*, Piskei Rosh BM 74a) or the delivery of the key to the place of storage of the goods, enjoyed full legal validity if based on a local mercantile custom (Sh. Ar., ḤM 201). From the 13th century on the question was discussed whether a transaction concluded merely orally on the strength of local custom could be afforded full legal validity. *Asher b. Jehiel was of the opinion (Resp. 12:3) that an analogy could be made with the law of *sitomta* only so far as a custom provided for the performance of some act, like those mentioned above; but mere words alone could not suffice to conclude a transaction. In his opinion a custom of this nature could not override the basic attitude of Jewish law in requiring active formal expression of the *gemirat ha-da'at* of the parties, and custom could only vary the essential nature of the formal act. An opposing opinion was expressed by *Meir b. Baruch of Rothenburg (and R. Jehiel, quoted in *Mordekhai*, Shab., sec. 472–3) to the effect that the very existence of a custom to conclude a transaction orally justified the assumption that complete *gemirat ha-da'at* could also result from the use of words alone. This view was accepted in most of the Codes and confirmed, inter alia, in relation to an undertaking to perform a *mitzvah* (e.g., at a circumcision ceremony: Resp. Radbaz, pt. 1, no. 278) and to formation of a partnership, it having been decided that, despite the need for a formal *kinyan*, if there was a custom of establishing partnership by oral agreement, such agreement was sufficient, since "custom is a major factor in civil law" (*ibid.*, no. 380). This view was also accepted by the later *posekim* (see *Kesef ha-Kodashim* 210:1), and in terms of this full validity was afforded to public sales (*Mishpat u-Ẓedakah be-Ya'akov*, no. 33), to sales on the exchange (Resp. Maharsham, pt. 3 no. 18), and to similar transactions decreed by custom to be capable of being created in mere oral form.

Freedom of Stipulation

According to ancient *halakhah*, a condition stipulated by the parties that was contrary to the recognized provisions of the law was invalid: "any condition contrary to what is written in the Torah is void" (BM 7:11) – even in matters of civil law. For this reason a condition that the firstborn (see *Birthright) should not inherit a double portion or that a son should not inherit together with his brother was void (BB 126b and see *Succession; the explanation given for a distinction in regard to matters of succession does not accord with the plain meaning of the Mishnah). This was still the view of Simeon b. Gamaliel (Ket. 9:1) and R. Meir (Ket. 56a) around the middle of the second century. At this time R. Judah expressed the view that only in matters of ritual law (*dinei issura*; see *Mishpat Ivri) was it forbidden to contract out of the Pentateuchal law, such as a condition exempting a wife from the need to undergo a *levirate marriage on her husband's death. In matters of *mamon*, however, such as a wife's right to maintenance, a condition would be valid: "this is the rule: any condition contrary to what is written in the Torah is valid if relating to a matter of *mamon*; if relating to a matter other than *mamon*, it is void" (Tosef. Kid. 3:7–8, Ket. 56a). This view was also followed by the scholars who stated that the husband's right of succession could properly be varied by contract (Ket. 9:1) and that a bailee could stipulate for a different measure of liability than that provided for in the Torah (BM 7:10).

The *amoraim* developed the view that regarded matters of ritual law as being in the nature of *jus cogens* and therefore not subject to contrary stipulation; unlike matters of civil law, which were regarded as being in the nature of *jus dispositivum* (Ket. 83b–84a; BM 51a–b; TJ, Ket. 9:1, 32d; BB 8:5). The law was decided accordingly in the Codes (Yad, Ishut, 12:7–9; Shemittah, 9:10; Mekhirah, 13:3–4; Sh. Ar., EH 38:5, ḤM 67:9, 227:21). Hence the rule in Jewish law is that in matters falling within the purview of the civil law, the Torah itself prescribed no obligatory rules and therefore "a party may make a waiver [i.e., contract out] since the Torah does not require him to give an undertaking save of his own free will" (Nov. Ramban, BB 126b). A necessary requirement is that the condition be worded in the proper form; e.g., "on condition that *you* shall have no [complaint of] overreaching [*ona'ah*] against *me*" and not, "on condition that there shall not be any overreaching in the deal" (Mak. 3b, Rashi and Tos. *ibid.*, and Codes.)

Matters excluded, as a matter of principle, from being the subject of a stipulation include an agreement to submit to bodily injury or the curtailment of personal liberty. Hence an agreement to cut off another party's hand or put out his eye, even though they might be causing him pain, is void (BK 8:7 and TJ, BK 8:11, 6c; but cf. Tosef. BK 9:32). This applied even in the case of an ordinary beating – concerning which the opinion was expressed that as it did not amount to serious bodily harm no compensation was payable in respect of it (BK 93a; Resp. Ribash, no. 484 and see below Illegal Contracts). Similarly, a condition that the creditor shall have the right to imprison the debtor on his failure to repay the debt is invalid, since the imprisonment of an indigent debtor for non-payment is an infringement of his personal liberty (see *Imprisonment for Debt). In this connection, the scholars disputed the validity of an agreement between husband and wife not to cohabit with one another: the opinion in the Jerusalem Talmud was in favor of it being upheld as valid (BM 7:10, 11c), and this was followed by some of the *rishonim* (see *Oẓar ha-Ge'onim*, 8 (1938), 167 (first pagination) and commentary of Rabbenu Hananel, *ibid.*, 45); other *rishonim*, however (Rashi to Ket. 56a) and the *posekim* (Yad, Ishut, 6:9–10; Sh. Ar., EH 38:5; 69:6) held such a condition to be invalid since it was a *tenai she-ba-guf* (i.e., a condition involving bodily suffering).

The scholars further restricted the freedom of stipulation in matters where they saw the need for enforcement and preservation. Thus it was decided that a stipulation between husband and wife that she should forego her *ketubbah* is void (Ket. 57b and Sh. Ar., EH 69:6). Similarly, a stipulation of the parties that they shall submit to the jurisdiction of a gentile court even in monetary matters was held to be invalid, as it was regarded as tending to undermine Jewish judicial institutions (see Tur, *Beit Yosef*, and Sh. Ar., ḤM 26). The scholars also expressed different opinions on freedom of stipulation in certain fields of the law such as *suretyship and *succession (Yad, Nahalot 6:1; cf. the sources of Maimonides' statements, which are contradictory to the plain meaning of the talmudic statements, in Meiri to BB 126b). A stipulation contrary to good public order and morals is also void. On this ground Ḥayyim Jair *Bacharach decided that an agreement between local clothiers to refrain from suing each other on a complaint of unfair competition, trespass, etc., was void, since this could only lead to increased strife and disturbance of the public order (*Ḥavvat Ya'ir*, no. 163).

Illegal Contracts

Different systems reflect a varying approach to the question of illegal contracts, such as one involving the commission of a criminal offense or one made for an illegal purpose. Some European legal systems hold such contracts to be null and void *ab initio*, whereas English law does not void them initially but prescribes that the courts shall not enforce them or grant the parties any relief, all in terms of the two Roman Law maxims: *ex turpi causa non oritur actio* and *in pari delicto melior est pars possidentis*.

Jewish law reveals a materially different approach. Although fulfillment of a contract is not prescribed if this should involve the actual commission of an offense or transgression, the fact that it has been committed does not deprive the contract of its legal validity or preclude the court from granting relief in terms of it. Thus, in a transaction concerning lending at interest, prohibited by the Pentateuchal law to both lender and borrower (BM 61a and Codes; see *Usury), the lender cannot claim payment of the interest according to the agreement, since this involves the perpetration of the transgression itself, but the borrower may claim a refund of interest already paid by him, despite his transgression. Similarly, if the borrower has given the lender some object as a payment in lieu of interest money, the former may only claim the return of the amount of the interest but not the object itself, since "the transaction is binding and cannot be voided because it is in contravention of a prohibition" (BM 65a–b, Rashi and *Piskei ha-Rosh, ibid.*). In the opinion of R. Meir, the effect of a bond of indebtedness that includes interest is to fine the lender by precluding him not only from recovering the interest but also the principal (BM 72a); the *halakhah*, however, was decided according to the view of the other scholars, namely that the lender could recover the principal but not the interest (Yad, Malveh 4:6) except if in the bond an aggregate amount appears from which the separate amounts of principal and interest cannot be established (Sh. Ar., ḤM 52:1). The law was similarly decided with regard to any transaction prohibited in part; namely that the transaction is valid except that the illegal part must be severed from it (Sh. Ar., ḤM 208:1 and Rema thereto).

This basic approach was also followed in Maimonides' ruling that: "if a person sells or gives on the Sabbath, and certainly on festivals, even though he should be flogged, his act is effective" (Yad, Mekhira 30:7); so too with regard to an obligation contracted on the Sabbath: "if anyone performs a *kinyan* on the Sabbath, the *kinyan* is valid and the writing and handing over take place after the Sabbath" (Yad *ibid.*; Sh. Ar., ḤM 195:11; 235:28). This was held to be the case even with regard to a *kinyan* involving the desecration of the Sabbath according to Pentateuchal law (BK 70b).

This approach of Jewish law to the question of a contract involving a transgression illustrates its capacity to distinguish between the "legal" and the "religious" aspects of the *halakhah*, notwithstanding their common source and it is precisely because of the material link between law and morals that Jewish law deprives the transgressor of those additional "benefits" which result from the invalidation of the civil aspects of the contract. For the same reason the court will not grant relief to a party whenever enforcement of a transaction will, in the prevailing social circumstances, amount to an encouragement of criminal conduct. Thus the court will not order the refund of money paid for the procurement of false testimony, if the witness should fail to testify falsely (*Shevut Ya'akov*, vol. 1, no. 145; see also *Pitḥei Teshuvah*, ḤM 32:2, n. 1). A similar decision was given by the Great Rabbinical Court in a matter involving the contravention of the currency regulations in Ereẓ Israel (OPD, 63).

Stipulations in Favor of a Third Party

Unlike some legal systems, Jewish law shows no hesitation in recognizing the validity of a stipulation in favor of a person who is not party to the contract, provided that it confers a benefit and does not impose an obligation on him. In tannaitic times this rule was expressed in the doctrine that: "a benefit may be conferred on a person in his absence, but an obligation cannot be imposed on him in his absence" (Git. 1:6; BM 12a; etc.). The phrase "in his absence" (*she-lo be-fanav*) has been interpreted in the sense of *she-lo mi-da'ato* (i.e., without his knowledge or consent, Rashi to BM 12a). When the stipulation comes to the knowledge of the third party, he has the option either to accept it – in which case he may demand fulfillment by the promisor – or to reject it, since "a person cannot be compelled to accept a gift" (Yad, Zekhiah, 4:2 and *Maggid Mishneh*; Tur and Sh. Ar., ḤM 243:1–2; 190:4 in *Keẓot ha-Ḥoshen* 2). See also Law of *Agency.

Specific Performance

Each party to a contract must fulfill his obligations under the contract, from which he is exempt only in the event of *ones* ("inevitable accident or duress") and the court will generally oblige the parties to render specific performance of their contractual obligations. Hence, the sale of an object to someone other than the party to whom the vendor had previously undertaken, in a valid contract, to sell the same object at a determined price, will be set aside and the object given to the party with whom the undertaking was originally made (Av. Zar. 72a and Codes; *Torat Emet*, no. 133). If, however, the vendor has worded his undertaking thus: "If I sell, I shall sell to you at such and such a price," and later sells the same object to someone else at a higher price, the sale to the latter will be valid, since the vendor made his prior undertaking conditional on his desire to sell, and "he did not desire to sell, but sold only because of the increment given by the other, placing him in the position of one who sold under duress" (Yad, Mekhirah, 8:7; Resp. Maharik, no. 20).

In the opinion of some of the *posekim*, specific performance is not ordered unless the claimant is in possession of the object which the vendor undertook to sell to him (Rashba and author of the *Ittur*, quoted in *Maggid Mishneh* to Yad, Mekhirah 8:7). However, the majority opinion in the Codes is that specific performance is granted even if the claimant is not in possession of the subject matter of the contract (see Tur, ḤM 206 and *Baḥ* thereto, no. 1). The opinion was also expressed that both Rashba and the author of the *Ittur* were in favor of compelling specific performance, even if the subject matter of the undertaking was not in the claimant's possession, in the case of an undertaking worded in the terms: "I bind myself to sell the object to you" (Resp. *Torat Emet*, no. 133). Specific performance is not dependent on the prior payment of the purchase price and the contract must be executed even if the parties have entrusted other persons, or the court, with the determination of the purchase price (Av. Zar. 72a and Codes, *ibid.*).

Specific performance is not granted on contracts for personal service, such as a contract of employment, since compelling a person to work against his will involves an infringement of his personal liberty and a form of disguised slavery (BM 10a). This is even more so because of the general attitude of Jewish law that any engagement of a laborer, even of his own free will, is a form of restraint on personal liberty; thus the laborer has special rights for his protection (BM 10a; 77a; see also *Labor Law). Specific performance will be ordered, however, in the case of a contract of employment relating to a public service, if a breach of this would be harmful to the public. Thus, on the eve of a festival, if no other is available, a public bath-attendant, barber, or baker "may be restrained until he finds someone to replace him" (Tosef., BM 11:27; see also Resp. Maharam of Rothenburg, ed. Prague, no. 1016). Specific performance is accordingly recognized as a function of the law itself and not as a matter of equity, as in English law – from which Jewish law also differs in several other important respects on this subject.

Compensation and Penalty for Breach of Contract

Breach of contract renders the party in breach liable for the resulting damage, which, in talmudic times, generally included only compensation for the damage directly suffered by the other party and not for the loss of profit which, but for the breach, he would have earned. Since post-talmudic times, however, the tendency has been to extend liability in certain circumstances to cover also the loss of anticipated profits. Liability of this kind – i.e., consequential damages – is based on a category of damage known as *garmi* (see **Gerama*), or stems from an implied condition imputing an agreement between the parties to be liable to each other for the loss of profits in the event of either of them breaking the contract (see e.g., the statements of R. Jeroham, quoted in Tur, ḤM 176; *Beit Yosef, ibid.*, no. 21; ḤM 176:14). In order to bolster the effectiveness of contractual obligations, the practice was adopted from tannaitic times of specifying in the contract a fixed amount to be payable on breach of the contract by one of the parties (see e.g. Ned. 27b; BB 10:5). The question arose, however, whether such an undertaking was not to be regarded as defective on the grounds of **asmakhta* (an undertaking to forfeit an asset upon nonfulfillment of a condition). Since the founding basis of a contract in Jewish law is the *gemirat ha-da'at* of the parties to be bound, the scholars debated the validity of the additional undertaking to pay a fixed amount by way of a penalty, which they regarded as having been given solely on the strength of a "confident reliance" by the promisor on his ability to fulfill the principal contractual obligation, without his contemplating the possibility of having to fulfill the penalty obligation (BB 168a). The question was decided to the effect that in certain circumstances such an undertaking would be void for reasons of *asmakhta*, primarily if it appeared that the amount stipulated was exaggerated and beyond any reasonable estimate of the damage suffered by the other party and this would imply the lack of any serious intention by the promisor (BM 104b and Codes.)

The development of commercial life spurred on the search for a way of overcoming the invalidating effect of *asmakhta* on contractual stipulations. In talmudic times it had been decided that an undertaking effected by way of a formal *kinyan* before a court of standing excluded it from the operation of the law of *asmakhta* since in this manner the undertaking made with a complete *gemirat ha-da'at* would be clear (Ned. 27b and Codes). In the post-talmudic period the process of avoiding the invalidating effect of *asmakhta* on a penalty-undertaking was furthered by the enactment of a *takkanah* by the scholars of Spain. Thus the parties might undertake to pay each other, unconditionally, an amount specified in advance, each agreeing in advance to release the other from this undertaking in the event of the fulfillment of the principal obligation under the contract. Since, in terms of the *takkanah*, the undertaking to pay the amount fixed in advance is an unconditional one, it is valid and unaffected by the effect of *asmakhta* (Yad, Mekhirah 11:18; Tur and Sh. Ar., ḤM 207:16). Another way that was found to avoid the effect of *asmakhta* was by strengthening the penalty-undertaking with a vow, oath, or ban (Sh. Ar., ḤM 207:19). It was also decided that the law of *asmakhta* did not apply to certain obligations, such as an undertaking to pay a penalty for breach of a marriage promise (*betrothal) or for breach of contract by a teacher without his finding a replacement, these being valid undertakings.

In the State of Israel

In Israel the law of contract is based on various different sources – Ottoman and Mandatory law, as well as legislation after the foundation of the state. English Common Law and Equity represents an important source of the law of contract in Israel in all cases where the existing law provides no answer to the problems that arise (i.e., *lacunae*; cf. 46, Palestine Order in Council, 1922–1947). Various directions in the law of contract have been included in a number of laws of the Knesset, among them Contracts (Remedies for Breach of Contract), 1970; Hire and Loan Law, 1971; Contracts (General Part) Law, 1973; Contract for Services Law, 1974; and Insurance Contract Law, 1981.

[Menachem Elon]

A proposition has recently been put forth (see Bibliography, B. Lifshitz) that during the mishnaic and talmudic periods, and up to and including Maimonides, there was no recognition by Jewish Law of the binding nature of a promise. Contractual obligations, as currently understood, were not accorded legal effect. This indeed was the subject of a dispute between R. Yose and R. Judah, which the Talmud explains as being based on the question whether **asmakhta* is binding. (BM, 61a, BB 168a). The term *asmakhta* signifies reliance or support. The Hebrew equivalent of this Aramaic term is *devarim* (BM 47a–48a, BB 3a). Until the time of Maimonides (Mishneh Torah, Mekhirah, ch.11), the explanation for denying legal effect to promises was the subject of dispute: Was it due to the absence of a deliberate and final intention to be bound (*semikhut da'at*) or some other reason. Those who sought to make promises binding in particular instances adopted the first explanation, as did Maimonides, thus resulting in giving legal effect to a promise when there was a full intent to be bound.

In any case, according to the basic view of R. Judah as elucidated by the *geonim*, a transaction can be made binding only by giving it a contemporaneous effect, or assigning it a property character, or establishing a particular status for the obligor, such as borrower, bailee, debtor, employee, guarantor, etc, which would produce the result of a binding obligation. But there was no way to enforce a promise to perform an act in the future, simply as a promise, such as a promise to marry.

According to this approach, the creation of such a status is expressed in the formula, "He has concluded to bind his person" (*gamar – 'meshabed nafshei,* BB 173, etc.). In this way, the promise is comparable to an act of acquisition – *kinyan* – which attaches to the obligation and takes effect contemporaneously. "From the present time" thus becomes a key phrase in making a promise binding. It should be pointed out in this connection that establishing an obligation under Jewish Law is thus a unilateral act and not a bilateral undertaking, as in modern contract law.

Illegal Contracts

The Jewish Law on illegal contracts was elucidated and applied in the case of *Jacobs v. Kartoz*, 9 PD 401 (1955) in an opinion by Justice Silberg of the Israeli Supreme Court.

The plaintiff was a landlord who sued to evict a tenant on the ground that the lease of the apartment violated an important government regulation governing the amount of rent to be paid. Justice Silberg concluded that under the principles of Jewish Law, the claim of the landlord should be rejected.

This result is reached even though the tenant is essentially arguing that an illegal contract should be upheld. Jewish Law however distinguishes between the prohibition involved and the legal consequences of the transaction; the transaction is valid as long as it can be carried out in a permissible manner. For example, a sale effected in violation of a prohibition of the price to be paid is nevertheless valid, and the permitted price is to be paid.

As stated by Justice Silberg:

> Jewish Law deals very carefully with one who violates the law. Undoubtedly, the reason for this is the desire to avoid the unjust results which clearly follow from a rule that uniformly fails to recognize the legal validity of an illegal contract… The concept that the court should not "dirty its hands" by dealing with such claims has not been widely accepted in the philosophy of Judaism.

Howard v. Miarah., 35 (2) PD 505 (1980) involved a contract for the sale of land. At the request of the seller, the price stated was lower than the actual price, with the difference paid in cash. Upon discovering that part of the land had been expropriated by the municipality prior to the signing of the contract, the buyer requested a reduction in the price. When this was refused, the buyer stopped payments. The seller, claiming a material breach, rescinded the contract. The buyer thereupon sued for restitution of all sums paid.

The defendant seller argued that a transaction in which the true price is hidden is an illegal contract and the court should not hear a claim based on such a contract, both parties being *in pari delicto.* Justice Elon, however, found that under Jewish Law, the plaintiff buyer was entitled to restitution of the money paid.

The applicable principles of Jewish Law are that an illegal contract is generally valid as a matter of civil law; the parties should be held to their contractual obligations to the fullest extent permitted, and a wrongdoer should not be rewarded.

Comparing English Law to Jewish Law, Justice Elon stated:

> Under the English rule, the court does not dirty its hands by dealing with such a [n illegal] contract, and prefers to let the loss resulting from non-performance lie where it falls. This rule has caused great injustice … Under Jewish Law, an illegal contract is generally not invalid as a matter of civil law, and each party to the contract is entitled to pursue his remedies, so long as this does not result in the performance of the illegal act itself.

A decision by the Rabbinical Court of Appeals illustrates the view of Jewish Law that when it appears in a particular situation that giving effect to a transaction would serve to encourage the commission of an illegal act, the court should not lend its assistance to the enforcement of the contract.

In the case of A *v.* B (Warhaftig, *Ossef Piskei Din*, p.63, 1945) A sued B for a sum of money, alleging that A was entitled to the money as a result of the purchase of foreign currency, which B bought on A's behalf. At that time, trading in foreign currency was prohibited. The court held that since the claim was based on a transaction that violated a fundamental law of the state, the court should not entertain the action.

The Principle of Good Faith (Tom Lev)

Roth v. Yeshufeh (Construction) Ltd, 33 (1) PD (1979) was an action for damages for breach of contract. The claim was based on the failure of the defendant to transfer an apartment within the time period fixed in the contract. The apartment had been transferred to the plaintiff six months late.

The defense to the claim was based on a clause in the contract that provided that the purchaser's acceptance of possession shall serve as conclusive and final proof of the fulfillment of the seller's obligations under the contract. On the basis of this clause, the lower court rejected the claim.

On appeal to the Supreme Court, the decision was reversed and the case was remanded to the lower court.

The majority opinion was greatly influenced by the principles of Jewish Law. Israeli contract law provides that "a contractual obligation shall be performed and a right arising out of a contract shall be exercised in good faith" (*tom lev*). The opinion of Justice Elon examined the meaning of the term "good faith" (*tom lev*) in the light of the principles of Jewish Law.

In his opinion he explained:

> When we set out to interpret fundamental conceptual terms contained in the laws of the State of Israel, such as "good faith," which have a universal character, and which reflect legal and value judgments in every civilized legal system, we must examine the meaning of those terms primarily in the light of the principles of Jewish Law and the Jewish heritage. A universal principle such as this [good faith] manifests itself in the various legal systems of our own day, but its roots are embedded in the fundamental values which are humanity's heritage from ancient legal systems ... And if this is so with respect to the legal systems of other nations, it certainly applies to the laws of the State of Israel, whose fundamental principles are rooted primarily in its ancient heritage ...
>
> The very term "good faith" (*tom lev*) is an original Hebrew term... For this reason, when interpreting this term we are obliged to refer, first and foremost, to Jewish Law, which serves as the main source for understanding its content and meaning.

Among the Jewish Law sources cited were the following:

1. Mekhilta (Be-Shallah, Tractate De-Va-Yassah, sec. 1 Horowitz-Rabin ed., p.158): "If one is honest in his business dealings ... it is accounted to him as though he had fulfilled the entire Torah."

2. Shabbat 31a: "Rava said, When a man is brought in [before the Heavenly Court] for judgment, they ask him: 'Were you honest in your business dealings.'"

3. Deuteronomy 6:18: "Do what is right and good."

4. Nahmanides, Commentary on Leviticus, 19:2: One who obeys only the technical and formal sense of the law is a "scoundrel within the bounds of the Torah (*naval bi-reshut ha-Torah*)." The Torah states, "Do what is right and good" to establish an affirmative commandment to behave with uprightness and fairness.

The lower court was directed to determine whether the defendant acted in good faith, and if not, whether the conduct was sufficiently egregious to have legal consequences.

In the case of *Laserson v. Shikkun Ovedim Ltd.* 38 (2) PD 237 (1984) Justice Elon established that there are limits to the application of the principle of "good faith."

The issue in the case was whether the defendant was obligated to install a generator in the building it had constructed, which was necessary to operate the elevator in an emergency. The contract required the building of a chamber for a generator but it did not mention the generator itself. The question arose whether the obligation to perform the contract in good faith meant that the generator also had to be supplied.

In his opinion, Justice Elon pointed to the inherent problem in applying the principle of "good faith" – the tension between stability and flexibility in business transactions, and between predictability and uncertainty in the law. Thus in applying the command "Do what is right and good" great caution is required.

The conclusion reached was that for "proper and reasonable legal policy" the "good faith" principle should not be used to create new legal obligations which the parties did not contemplate and did not include in their contract. The principle should govern only the fulfillment of the obligations that were agreed upon.

In applying the command "do what is right and good" Jewish Law established some duties as legal obligations, and other duties as ethical precepts.

The rationale for refraining from categorizing all duties the performance of which may be considered to be "right and good" as legal obligations is given in the opinion as follows:

> The legal system cannot exist with the instability that would result from imposing unexpressed obligations never even contemplated by the parties ... One may discern in the Jewish legal system, in which morals and law combine in a unique pattern of decision making ... the utmost care that the principle of good faith should not extend the limits of legal enforceability further than is desirable and practical ...
>
> If it were otherwise, then a person would not – and could not – know what will be the end of the contract that he signed, and what new obligations are likely to be created in its framework, unbeknownst to him. The result would be that even a person of good faith would never know what obligations he undertook and how far they extended.

In this case, the lower court should determine whether in view of all of the circumstances, the contract could be interpreted as itself containing an implied agreement that the defendant should install the generator.

In regard to the basic principle of "good faith" in Jewish Law, the opinion quotes the characterization of "good faith" given by Professor R. Powell, who refers to the Hebrew terminology (Powell, *Good Faith in Contracts*, 9, *Current Legal Problems*, 16 (1956), 37–38):

> In the Hebrew language there is a simple phrase which satisfies that requirement. It is *derekh ereẓ*. It means "way of the land" but is also means "good manners."

INTERPRETATION OF DOCUMENTS. Various rules of Jewish Law govern the interpretation of contracts and other legal instruments. For example: The later part of a contract controls situations in which there is an inconsistency between an earlier and a later clause, which cannot be reconciled. It is presumed that the earlier statement was reconsidered and the later clause states the final intention.

Another rule is that if there is a doubt as to the meaning of a clause in a contract, the doubt will be resolved in favor the obligor. For an obligee to succeed, his claim must be free from doubt. However, this rule is applied only when the result will not destroy the essential validity of the instrument.

This rule was applied in the case of *Alperovitz v. Mizrahi*, 34 (4) PD 129 (1980), which involved an agreement for the purchase of an apartment. A memorandum of purchase fixed the price. It was accompanied by an initial payment and was to be followed by five additional payments. Possession was to be transferred at the time of the final payment.

The purchaser's contention that the memorandum implied that a detailed contract was to be executed was accepted by the court. The question that remained was when the further contract was to be made. Clearly this would not be at the end of all of the payments. But prior to which of the payments did the parties intend that the contract be executed?

The rule that doubtful questions are to be decided in favor of the obligor supported the conclusion that the contract was to be executed before any of the additional payments. Additionally, there was no logical basis for choosing the time of any one of the payments over the others.

The opinion by Justice Elon cited a responsum of R. Asher b. Jehiel (Resp. Asheri #68:14; beginning of the 14th century). A obligated himself to pay a sum of money to B "after Passover." The question was: which Passover does this refer to – the next succeeding Passover or the last Passover in the history of the world? There was no logical basis for choosing any Passover in between. In this instance, R. Asher b. Jehiel did not apply the rule that ambiguities should be resolved in favor of the obligor, because to do so would completely nullify the agreement.

The twelfth of the thirteen canons of (biblical) interpretation of R. Ishmael is that "an ambiguous word or passage is explained from its context or from a subsequent expression." This principle was the basis for the decision in *Katan v. Municipality of Holon*, 32 (1) PD 494, 1978.

The municipality sent out an invitation to a group of contractors to bid for a job. The invitation stated: "To validate the bid, the contractor shall provide a bank guarantee… for a period of sixteen months." An unsuccessful bidder claimed that the successful bidder did not provide the guarantee at the time it submitted its bid. The latter argued that the guarantee was not required to be submitted until the contract was awarded.

The court, in an opinion by Justice Elon, cited R. Ishmael's canon of interpretation, and held that in view of the context of the document and the surrounding circumstances, the successful bidder was correct. The duration of the work was set as sixteen months from the time of acceptance. The sixteen months of the bank guarantee was meant to cover the time during which the work was to be performed. The guarantee was thus to be submitted when the contract was awarded, not when the bid was submitted.

In addition, the submission of a guarantee is necessary to assure a degree of seriousness on the part of the bidder. In this case, the invitation to bid was not sent to the public as a whole, but to a limited number of contractors. It was therefore not necessary to assure the seriousness of their bids by requiring a guarantee at the time of the submission of the bids.

[Bernard Auerbach (2nd ed.)]

BIBLIOGRAPHY: M. Bloch, *Der Vertrag nach mosaisch talmudischem Rechte* (1893); Gulak, Yesodei, 2 (1922), 10–12, 31–82, 147–200; idem, *Toledot ha-Mishpat be-Yisrael*, 1 (1939), 15ff.; Herzog, Instit, 2 (1939), 19ff.; A. Shaky, in: *Sugyot Nivḥarot be-Mishpat* (1958), 470–508; B.-Z. Schereschewsky, *Kenas ve-Pizzuyim Ekev Hafarat Ḥozim Lefi Dinei Yisrael* (1950), 3–12; ET, 7 (1956), 138–49; 11 (1965), 245–59; B. Rabinovitz-Teomim, *Ḥukkat Mishpat* (1957), 2–4, 247–56, 269–73; M. Silberg, *Kakh Darko shel Talmud* (1961), 82–88; M. Elon, *Ḥerut ha-Perat be-Darkhei Geviyyat Ḥov ha-Mishpat ha-Ivri* (1964), 68ff.; idem, in: ILR, 4 (1969), 96–98; H.E. Baker, *Legal System of Israel* (1968), 101–9; Elon, Mafte'ah, 67–72; I.S. Zuri, *Mishpat ha-Talmud*, 5 (1921). **ADD. BIBLIOGRAPHY:** M. Elon, *Jewish Law* (1994), 96–99, 128–30, 183–89, 422–43, 1603–4, 1916–20, 1936; idem, *Jewish Law, Cases and Materials* (1999), 99–144; B. Lifshitz, *Promise and Acquisition in Jewish Law* (1998); idem, *Employee and Independent Contractor – Acquisition and Obligation in Contrast* (1993); idem, *Law and Action, Terminology of Obligation and Acquisition in Jewish Law* (2001); I. Warhaftig, *Undertaking in Jewish Law* (2001).

CONTRACTORS. Persons contracted for army supply and building, mainly road construction. While the initial possession of financial and commercial expertise and substantial resources was a necessary prerequisite for engaging in this occupation, it provided a successful means of enrichment and also opened the way to a certain measure of social acceptance and political influence from which as members of a hated group Jews were otherwise excluded. In Christian Spain Jews were prominent as military suppliers to kings. A noted example was Judah de la *Cavalleria, who supplied arms to the king of Aragon in 1276 for his wars against the Muslims in Valencia. The *Ravaya brothers supplied arms to King Pedro III of Aragon (1276–85) in his wars against the rebel nobility of Catalonia. The wealthy Muça de *Portella also supplied arms to Pedro III of Aragon. Isaac *Abrabanel was military supplier to Ferdinand and Isabella from 1489 to 1492, while Abraham *Senior was the chief supplier of military equipment to the Spanish troops who fought in Granada. Jews also played a prominent role in the production of military equipment, metal casting, and armaments manufacture. There is evidence of Jewish arms manufacture in Spain, and in 1495 large numbers of Jewish arms manufacturers entered Portugal after the king had promised them special rights, such as payment of only half the sum for entry imposed on Jewish immigrants from Spain. Portuguese chroniclers, among them Damião da Goes, recount that some members of the king's council opposed the expulsion of the Jews from Portugal on the ground that the Jews possessed many secret methods of armaments manufacture which should not be allowed to pass into the hands of the Turkish infidels. The Jewish chronicler Elijah *Capsali describes the exiles from Spain as having introduced firearms to the Ottoman Empire and army, this being one of the reasons why they were well received by the sultans. Among the experts on cannon and gunpowder manufacture in the 16th century were Jews who had immigrated to Ottoman territory after the Spanish expulsion.

Probably Jews served as military suppliers during this period in Central Europe also; there is no lack of evidence for their participation in the arms trade: a decision of the Bruenn (Brno) tribunal permitted the Jews of Uherske Hradiste to trade in arms. A number of Jewish military suppliers operated in Germany in the 16th century. Isaac Meyer was permitted to reside in Halberstadt in 1537 in order to supply the monastery with weapons. *Joseph (Joselmann) b. Gershon of Rosheim in 1548 was granted a writ of protection by the emperor which also specified his activities as a military supplier.

Portuguese Jews in Amsterdam in the 17th and 18th centuries were active as military suppliers to the armies of Holland, Morocco, and England. The internal wars in Morocco during the 17th century enabled many Dutch Jews, who acted as military suppliers to all sides involved in the conflict, to enter the arms trade. Amsterdam was the place of residence of Solomon Michael David, military supplier of Hanover in the second half of the 18th century.

The *Court Jews were regarded by their rulers as capable of supplying the whole range of military equipment: horses, food, uniforms, and weapons. Jewish commerce in Germany and Austria consequently prospered. Although the Court Jews themselves constituted only a minute proportion of the Jewish population, they required a widespread network of subcontractors, petty merchants, etc., who were also Jewish, in order to fulfill their functions as major contractor-suppliers, especially in wartime. Large-scale provisioning was achieved through contacts with Jewish dealers in agricultural products from Eastern Europe. Antisemites contended that in Germany at this time "all the military suppliers were Jews, and all the Jews were military suppliers." Samuel Julius was military supplier to Frederick Augustus, elector of Saxony. The *Model family were court suppliers and military contractors to the duchy of Ansbach during the 17th and 18th centuries. Joseph Suess *Oppenheimer acted as military supplier first to the landgrave Ernest Augustus of Hesse-Darmstadt, and then to Charles Alexander, duke of Wuerttemberg. The *Gomperz family of Cleves acted as military contractors and commercial agents to six Prussian rulers, notably Elias Gomperz, who founded his firm in Emmerich in the second half of the 17th century. His contemporary Israel Aaron, who had close commercial ties with Pomerania, Mecklenburg, Amsterdam, and Hamburg, also acted as military supplier to Prussia. The *Wertheimer, Mayer, and Herschel families, as well as others who were permitted to settle in Vienna during the rule of Emperor Leopold, also acted as military contractors.

The ability of the absolutist rulers to maintain organized and well-regulated armies under their control and command may be attributed to a considerable degree to both the acumen of the Jewish contractors and their connections with fellow Jews. The part played by Jews in supplying the armies of England in the 17th and 18th centuries was no less decisive. Abraham Israel (Antonio Fernandez) *Carvajal was the most important military contractor during the rule of Cromwell, and one of the five London merchants to sign a contract to supply the army with wheat in 1649. William of Orange was enabled to sail to England in 1688 by an interest-free loan of two million crowns made to him by Francisco Lopez Suasso of the Hague, while another Jew, Francisco de Cordova, was in charge of military supplies for the campaign in partnership with Isaac Pereira. Solomon de *Medina, military supplier to the Duke of Marlborough's troops, was granted a title in 1700 for his services to William III. In Ireland the firm of *Machado and Pereira provisioned the Duke of Schomberg's armies. During the War of the Spanish Succession, Robert Harley was accused of ruining the economy of England in order to enrich Jewish military suppliers. Joseph Cortissos, formerly a resident of Amsterdam, was in charge of military supplies during Peterborough's campaigns against the Spanish.

Jews can be found among French military suppliers as early as the 16th century. A number of Jewish families were permitted to settle in Metz in 1567 by Marshal de Vieilleville on the condition that they undertook to supply his troops, but their activities were limited to small-scale local operations. The part played by some of the wealthiest French Jews in military supplies reached considerable proportions during the reign of Louis XIV. Jacob Worms was chief military contractor to Louis XIV, and in the latter half of the 18th century Herz *Cerfberr rose to prominence in this field. When in 1776 it was decided to end the system of private contracting for military supplies, an exception was made in the case of Cerfberr, who remained the supplier for the army in Alsace-Lorraine. In 1785 he divided the management of his business enterprises, allocating his banking activities to his sons and sons-in-law, while concentrating his own efforts on military supplies. Moses Belin, military supplier in Metz, and Moses Eliezer Liefmann *Calmer of Hanover, military supplier from 1769, were among many other Jews prominent in this field in France. Most important was the wealthy Abraham *Gradis, who acted as military supplier to the French army in Canada and did much for French troops there, especially during the Seven Years' War. From 1748 to 1779 he organized, with the assistance of Raphael Mendes, Benjamin Gradis, and other Jewish shipowners, the embarkation of French warships from Europe to Canada.

Jews played a prominent part in supplying weapons and provisions to the English army in the colonies. Mathias Bush supplied the Pennsylvanian troops in the war against the French. The *Franks family, with branches in London and New York, acted as contractors to the English army in the American colonies. David Franks continued to serve the English crown even after 1775, supplying provisions and uniforms to English prisoners of war. Among other Jews, the Sheftall family of Georgia were suppliers to the American army as well.

In Russia in the 19th century contracting for construction of army buildings – fortifications and barracks – and for provisions was frequently combined with contracting for the construction of state-built roads and *railroads. The modern Jewish "white collar" worker first emerged in the network of offices as clerks or works supervisors of these contractors. Such a worker is Faby, the hero of J.L. *Gordon's poem *Koẓo shel Yod*, which in an indirect way chronicles the impact of railroad building on the various strata of Jewish society in the *Pale of Settlement in the second half of the 19th century. Several Jewish entrepreneurs rose in this way from the poverty of the Pale to opulence, such as Judah Opatow. After their initial success many of these contractors – better known under the Russian designation "Podryachiki" – combined contracting with banking, as for instance the houses of *Kronenberg and *Poliakoff.

BIBLIOGRAPHY: M. Grunwald, *Samuel Oppenheimer und sein Kreis* (1913); H.I. Bloom, *Economic Activities of the Jews of Amsterdam* (1937), index; B.G. Sack, *History of the Jews in Canada*, 1 (1945), 27 ff.; Kisch, Germany, 115, 414ff.; S. Stern, *Court Jew* (1950), 38–59; idem, *Der Preussische Staat und die Juden*, 2 vols. (1962); J.R. Marcus, *Early American Jewry*, 2 vols. (1951–53), index, s.v. *army purveyors*; idem, *American Jewry Documents* (1959), index, s.v. *army purveyors*; H. Schnee, *Die Hoffinanz und der moderne Staat*, 6 vols. (1953–67); Baron, Social, index; W. Sombart, *Jews and Modern Capitalism* (1962), 68–70; Roth, England, index, s.v. *army contractors*; A. Hertzberg, *French Enlightenment and the Jews* (1968), index, s.v. *army*.

[Joseph Kaplan]

CONVERSOS, designation used in Christian Spain and Portugal for Moorish or Jewish converts to Christianity. It was sometimes applied also to their descendants. Unlike the epithets *Marranos, *alboraycos, or *tornadizos*, the term Conversos has no derogatory implications.

COOK, SAMUEL (1907–1998), U.S. Reform rabbi. Cook was born in Philadelphia, ordained at Hebrew Union College in 1934, and received an honorary D.D. from HUC-JIR in 1959. He was director of the B'nai B'rith Hillel Foundation and a member of the faculty at the University of Alabama (1934–36) before assuming positions at congregations in Philadelphia and Altoona, Pennsylvania. After serving as U.S. Army chaplain in the Pacific (1943–46), Cook became director of the youth department at the Union of American Hebrew Congregations. In this capacity, he officially founded the National Federation of Temple Youth (NFTY), an organization he had conceived in 1941 in Pennsylvania, where he had formed and combined Reform youth groups of neighboring cities. His innovation had laid the cornerstone of the Middle Atlantic Federation of Temple Youth and marked the beginning of the regional structure system for NFTY (later renamed the *North American Federation of Temple Youth). Cook spearheaded the building of a summer camp system that grew to number 12 camps across the United States and Canada. He introduced experiential travel programs for teenagers to Israel, cementing a Reform commitment to Zionism for generations. Cook also instituted international exchange programs and social action projects. He chose a motto from the prophet Joel for the movement: "Your old shall dream dreams and your youth shall see visions" (3:1). In 1967, Cook was named executive director of the Union of American Hebrew Congregations Department of College Education, a position he held concurrently with the NFTY directorship until his retirement in 1973. In 1999, in recognition of his contributions the Reform movement established the Rabbi Samuel Cook Award for Outstanding Achievement in Youth Work, which is presented by the Central Conference of American Rabbis annually.

BIBLIOGRAPHY: K.M. Olitzky, L.J. Sussman, and M.H. Stern, *Reform Judaism in America: A Biographical Dictionary and Sourcebook* (1993).

[Bezalel Gordon (2nd ed.)]

°COOK, STANLEY ARTHUR (1873–1949), English Semitic scholar and historian of religion. Cook taught religion, Hebrew, and Aramaic at Gonville and Caius College, Cambridge, and was regius professor of Hebrew at Cambridge from 1932 to 1938. He served on the editorial staff of *The Cambridge Ancient History* and *The Encyclopaedia Britannica*, and was editor of the *Palestine Exploration Fund Quarterly* (1902–32).

Cook's main contribution was his archaeological, philological, and comparative religion studies. In a series of articles that appeared in 1903 he discussed the then oldest Hebrew biblical manuscript written in square Hebrew, the *Nash Papyrus. His *A Glossary of the Aramaic Inscriptions* (1898) was a study of Semitic epigraphy and Hebrew philology. The importance of historical methodology and archaeological research in the treatment of religious data was emphasized in his Schweich lectures of 1925, which were published as *The Religion of Ancient Palestine in the Light of Archaeology…* (1930). The fruit of his erudition was contained in copious notes to the third edition of W. Robertson *Smith's *Lectures on the Religion of the Semites* which Cook annotated in 1927. His views of the Bible and its religion as a whole were summed up in *The Old Testament: A Reinterpretation* (1936), a historical and anthropological assessment of the Israelite religion. He wrote important works on the study of religious methodology (1914), and he analyzed in the light of comparative religion the prophetic ideal of ethical monotheism (1932). He compared the laws of the Pentateuch with the Code of Hammurapi (1903), edited the Book of I Esdras in R.H. Charles' *The Apocrypha and Pseudepigrapha of the Old Testament* (1913), and wrote an introduction to the Bible (1945).

BIBLIOGRAPHY: H.F. Hahn, *The Old Testament in Modern Research* (1956), 77–78, 81; *Essays and Studies Presented to S.A. Cook…* (1950), includes bibliography. **ADD. BIBLIOGRAPHY:** ODNB online.

[Zev Garber]

COOKBOOKS, JEWISH. These compendia of instructions and recipes for the preparation of Jewish cuisine and/or guidelines for the Jewish cook constitute the single largest genre of literature created almost entirely by and for Jewish women.

Prior to 1900

By the first half of the 19th-century, a few Jewish manuscript cookbooks appear in Yiddish (Bohemia, Moravia, or neighboring areas); German ones appear in greater numbers throughout the century; and by the 1890s, there are Osmanli ones from Salonika. The first known published volume is J. Stolz's *Kochbuch der Israeliten, oder prakt. Unweisung, wie man nach dem juedischen Religionsgruenden alle Gattungen der feinsten Speisen kauscher bereitet* (Carlsruhe, 1815). During the 19th century, over a dozen Jewish cookbooks were published in German, more than in any other language. The most successful, *Kochbuch fuer Israelitische Frauen: Enthaltend die verschiedensten Koch- und Backarten, mit einer vollständigen Speisekarte so wie einer genauen Anweisung zur Einrichtung und Fuehrung einer religioes-juedischen Haushaltung* (Berlin, 1856) by Rebekka Wolf (née Heinemann), went through 14 editions. In print for almost 80 years, it was translated into Dutch (1881) and Polish (1904), and influenced the first known cookbook published in Yiddish, Ozer Bloshsteyn's *Kokhbuch far yudishe [sic] froyen* (Vilna, 1896; New York, 1898). These kosher cookbooks, which emphasized fine cuisine and gracious living, were part of a larger adaptation of mainstream bourgeois domestic values within an acculturating modern Orthodox community.

The first published English cookbook, *The Jewish Manual, or Practical Information in Jewish and Modern Cookery: With a Collection of Valuable Recipes & Hints Relating to the Toilette* (London, 1846), by "A Lady," aimed to refine the kosher table, but with an English and Western Sephardi emphasis. The anonymous author was recently identified as Judith Lady *Montefiore, who dedicated some of her philanthropic energies to educating Jewish girls for domestic service by establishing cookery classes at a Jewish orphanage and school. This book appeared in a single edition, although parts of it were reprinted, without attribution, in 1864 and 1867 in Australia. By the last decade of the 19th century, kosher gourmet cookbooks also appeared in Dutch, Hungarian, Russian, and Italian, and the German volumes were becoming larger and more elaborately bound. The grandest, Marie Elsasser's *Ausfuehrliches Kochbuch fuer die einfache und feine juedische Kueche unter Beruecksichtigung aller rituellen Vorschriften in 3759 Rezepten* (Frankfurt, 1901), was over 900 pages. The custom of giving cookbooks to brides accounts in part for the lavishness of such volumes.

American Cookbooks

The first known Jewish cookbook published in the United States is the *Jewish Cookery Book: On Principles of Economy, Adapted for Jewish Housekeepers, with the Addition of Many Useful Medicinal Recipes, and Other Valuable Information, Relative to Housekeeping and Domestic Management* (Philadelphia, 1876) by Mrs. Esther Levy. This volume brought a scrupulously kosher, yet elegant Anglo-Jewish cuisine to Philadelphia's well-to-do Jews.

Much more popular than *Jewish Cookery Book*, which appeared in only one edition, was the decidedly non-kosher, *"Aunt Babette's" Cook Book, Foreign and Domestic Receipts for the Household, A Valuable Collection of Receipts and Hints for the Housewife, Many of Which are not to be Found Elsewhere* (1889). *"Aunt Babette's" Cook Book* went through several editions in its first year, and stayed in print until the beginning of World War I. "Aunt Babette," the pseudonym for Mrs. Bertha F. Kramer, instructed her Reform Jewish readers in the niceties of the "Pink Tea" and in a non-halakhic approach to Jewish diet. "Aunt Babette" was by no means indifferent to *kashrut*. She declared, for example, that "NOTHING is *'Trefa'* that is healthy and clean," thus giving precedence to hygiene over ritual purity. At the same time not everything that is *treyf* made it into her cookbook. Shellfish, bacon, and rump roasts did, but lard did not. Ideology and hygienic purity aside, certain non-kosher foods were rejected on aesthetic grounds, a remnant of the internalization of religious taboo.

Many late 19th and early 20th century English cookbooks were intended to prepare Jewish girls, especially immigrants, for domestic service in kosher households. Marie Kauders' cookbook (Prague, 1891) and cooking school-trained cooks for Jewish restaurants and wedding catering. *The "Settlement" Cookbook* (Milwaukee, 1901), by Lizzie Black Kander, a German Jew, was written to prepare East European Jewish women for household employment and to raise money for the Settlement house where the classes were held. This remarkable volume has sold more than 2,000,000 copies and proceeds are still directed to charitable causes. Like *"Aunt Babette's" Cookbook* and the many German Jewish fundraiser cookbooks that appeared in the United States during this period, *The "Settlement" Cookbook* was a "*treyf* cookbook" and included recipes not only for Passover dishes, but also for oysters.

The first Yiddish cookbook published in the United States, apart from the 1898 New York edition of Bloshteyn's *Kokhbuch far yudishe [sic] froyen*, is Hinde Amkhanittski's *Lehr-bukh vi azoy tsu kokhen un baken* (1901), which was reprinted a few years later. The Yiddish cookbooks that followed, well into the 1930s, tried to Americanize Jewish eating habits, consistent with current nutritional ideas and an Anglo-American diet. Some promoted vegetarianism; Yiddish vegetarian cookbooks appeared in Europe as early as 1907 (Drohobitsh) and as late as 1938 (Vilna). Food companies used cookbooks, often bilingual in Yiddish and English, to market their products. Manischewitz's cookbooks, for example, showed how to use *maẓẓah* as an ingredient in everything from strawberry shortcake to tamales all year round.

By the end of World War I, with the mass immigration of Jews from Eastern Europe, the market for American Jewish cookbooks had changed. In response, Bloch Publishing replaced *"Aunt Babette's" Cook Book* with the strictly kosher *The International Jewish Cook Book: 1600 Recipes According to the Jewish Dietary Laws with the Rules for Kashering: The Favorite Recipes of America, Austria, Germany, Russia, France, Poland, Roumania, Etc., Etc.* by Florence Kreisler Greenbaum, an instructor in cooking and domestic science. Greenbaum made nutritional science palatable in Jewish terms. This cookbook and its successors, including Mildred Grosberg Bellin's many revised and enlarged editions, endured well into the 1980s.

Europe Between the Wars

While home economists were trying to reform the immigrant diet, Suzanne Roukhomovsky, a literary figure, waxed nostalgic for what she called "la cuisine maternelle" in *Gastronomie juive: cuisine et patisserie de Russie, d'Alsace, de Roumanie et d'Orient* (Paris, 1929). A year later a pirated translation of this book, with a few significant changes, appeared in Yiddish as

Di yidishe kukh in ale lender: poyln, rusland, rumenyen, daytshland, elsas, maroko, tunis, amerike, a.a.v. Dos beste un praktishe bukh far yidishe virtins (Warsaw, 1930). While Roukhomovsky's 36-page introduction offered a literary pastoral on traditional Jewish life, B. Shafran's "A word to our Jewish wives," in *Di yidishe kukh* advises Polonized Jewish women not to turn the health of their families over to servants but to pursue the culinary arts themselves.

During the interwar years, the *Juedischer Frauenbund (1904–38) offered home economics courses and published cookbooks, consistent with their emphasis on religious observance, Jewish national consciousness, and careers for women that were extensions of their traditional domestic roles. As M. Kaplan has noted, the Frauenbund's goal was to prepare unemployed East European Jewish women to work as domestics, supply middle-class families with qualified servants, create a pool of administrators and food specialists for public institutions, and make women better managers of their own homes. Their strictly kosher cookbooks included not only modern recipes, but also suggestions for children, invalids, and vegetarians, menus for institutional kitchens, recipes from "great-grandmother's kitchen," and "national dishes," as well as recipes from organizations in Palestine, many of them for eggplant. By 1935, after the Nazis enacted laws against kosher slaughtering, the Frauenbund published a cookbook to address difficulties in buying kosher meat which went through four editions in one year.

Palestine and Israel

Erna Meyer, a pioneer in kitchen ergonomics, brought her ideas from Germany to Mandate Palestine, where she published *Wie kocht man in Erez Israel?* (Tel Aviv, 1936) in German, Hebrew, and English, followed by a slim cookbook (Tel Aviv, 1940) dedicated to recipes and menus for cooking in a time of crisis. Meyer's cookbook was intended for the urban, urbane, and largely Central European cook in Mandate Palestine, who needed to learn to use a primus stove and local produce while maintaining high culinary standards and a Central European culinary repertoire. *Wie kocht man in Erez Israel?* was one in a series of *WIZO cookbooks that appeared in separate German and Hebrew editions as late as 1954.

Lillian Cornfeld wrote about Israeli cusine in *Complete Hebrew Cook Book* and *Ani Mevashelet.* Her *Israeli Cookery* (Westport, Connecticut, 1962) is organized by region, devotes several chapters to *sabra* foods and includes recipes from Israeli hotels and restaurants. In her preface, Cornfeld, who immigrated in the 1920s from Canada to Mandate Palestine, supervised domestic science for WIZO and worked as a food columnist and nutritional advisor, noted several challenges to the emergence of national cuisine in Israel. These include the diverse population, simplicity as a practical necessity (and ideological principle), and the absence of professional chefs. Her cookbook addressed the "urgent incentive to create an Israeli cuisine," by collecting recipes from national and international organizations that were actively trying to create a national meal pattern, as well as from kibbutzim. Molly Bar-David, a food columnist and culinary advisor for El Al, wrote *The Israeli Cookbook: What's Cooking in Israel's Melting Pot* (1964), based on recipes she collected on the airline's routes and in interviews with immigrants in Israel.

Since the 1980s, numerous Israeli cookbooks, many lavishly produced, have appeared. Individual volumes are dedicated to salads, soups, desserts, cakes, or breads, or to a particular fruit or vegetable. Each community's traditional cuisine (Yemenite, Kurdish, Moroccan) is celebrated, popular international cookbooks are translated, and special diets are the focus of their own cookbooks. In contrast with the austere *yishuv* outlook and Central European emphasis of earlier cookbooks, these new volumes are part of Israel's increasingly sophisticated and international culinary culture. Some of the cookbooks are also nostalgic, whether for foods associated with the *yishuv* and early years of the state or for the traditional cuisines of the country's many immigrant groups. Most recently, *The Arab-Israeli* Cookbook (London, 2004), a play and a cookbook based on the research of Robin Soans, Tim Roseman, and Rima Brihi in Israel, Gaza, and the West Bank, explores the everyday reality of conflict through the stories and recipes of those they met.

Fundraiser Cookbooks

This most prolific genre of Jewish cookbooks originates in Jewish women's voluntary associations, ranging from local efforts to support a hospital or Jewish school, to international organizations (*National Council of Jewish Women, *Hadassah, *ORT, WIZO) with local chapters. Spanning more than a century, such cookbooks have been published in locales ranging from New Zealand, Zimbabwe, India, and Panama to Turkey. While some are handwritten, others are professionally produced; some are illustrated with naïve drawings while others have full color plates. The earliest known example is *The Fair Cookbook* (Denver, 1888), published for a charity fair in support of the local synagogue, Temple Emanuel. Most often these cookbooks were created by women who were not professional cookbook writers. Some authors, like Suzie Fishbein, author of *Kosher by Design* (Brooklyn, 2003), a popular kosher gourmet cookbook published by ArtScroll, got their start working on a fundraiser volume.

The Home as Sanctuary

Starting in the 1920s, some cookbooks published by women's organizations, including *The Center Table* (Sisterhood Temple Mishkan, Boston, 1922) and *A Treasure for My Daughter: A Reference Book of Jewish Festivals with Menus and Recipes* (Ethel Epstein Ein Chapter of Hadassah, Montreal, 1950), presented cookbooks as a vehicle for transmitting Jewish religious observance from mother to daughter. *The Jewish Home Beautiful* (National Women's League of the United Synagogue of America, New York, 1941) provided recipes and a pageant script organized around aesthetically arranged holiday tables that was performed at synagogues and churches as well as in the Temple of Religion at the 1940 New York World's

Fair. According to the foreword to the third edition (1945), this book was used by Jewish service men and women during World War II.

New Trends

In the second half of the 20th century, Jewish cookbooks appeared in large numbers and variety, including comprehensive volumes by Florence Greenberg, Evelyn Rose, and Claudia Roden in the United Kingdom, and Joan Nathan and Gil Marks in the United States. Many recent volumes engage cuisine as heritage, including *Cookbook of the Jews of Greece* (1986) by N. Stavroulakis, *Bene-Israel Cook-book* (Bombay, 1986), *Recipes from the Jewish Kitchens of Curaçao* (Netherlands Antilles, 1982), Sephardi cookbooks in English, French, Hebrew, Spanish, and Turkish, and a cookbook devoted to the Marranos, *A Drizzle of Honey* (New York, 1999), by D.M. Gitlitz and L.K. Davidson.

Autobiographical cookbooks include Mimi Sheraton's *From My Mother's Kitchen: Recipes and Reminiscences* (1979) and Colette Rossant's *Memories of a Lost Egypt: A Memoir with Recipes* (1999). The most poignant examples of "memory cookbooks" are those created by women who, while starving to death in Nazi concentration camps, tried to appease their hunger by recalling recipes for delicious dishes they once cooked. They include *Ravensbrueck 1945: Fantasy Cooking behind Barbed Wire*, recipes collected by Edith Peer (Sydney, 1986), and *In Memory's Kitchen: A Legacy from the Women of Terezín* (Northvale, N.J., 1986), a translation of the recipe collection that Mina Paechter, who died in Terezín (Theresienstadt), entrusted to a friend with instructions that it reach her daughter, which it did, miraculously, around 1970. *Miriam's Kitchen* (1998), a memoir by Elizabeth Ehrlich, mixes recipes from the author's mother-in-law, a Holocaust survivor, with a story of personal reinvention.

Communities without a history of publishing cookbooks, particularly ḥasidim and *ḥaredim*, have now joined the fray. *The Spice and Spirit of Kosher-Jewish Cooking* (Brooklyn, 1977; revised edition, 1990) prepares the Lubavitcher *ba'alat teshuvah* to create a Jewish home, while *The Balebuste's Choice: Kosher Cookbook* (Brooklyn, 1999), published by Pupa ḥasidic women, raises money for *ẓedakah*. *Fun der mames kokh* (Jerusalem, 2003) by Sh. Zisl, in memory of her pious mother, appeared in Yiddish. *Out of Our Kitchen Closets: San Francisco Gay Jewish Cooking*, published by Congregation Sha'ar Zahav, communicates their "recipe for success" (San Francisco, 1987).

With the advent of new technologies, future Jewish "cookbooks" might take the form of online databases, such as the Yahoo group *jewish-food*, or Centropa's online recipe archive of the culinary culture of Central European Jews. Some contemporary blogs record an individual's daily culinary musings, including recipes, a practice reminiscent of writing recipes down in personal notebooks, the earliest form of Jewish cookbook.

BIBLIOGRAPHY: B. Kirshenblatt-Gimblett, "*Hebrew Cookery*: An Early Jewish Cookbook from the Antipodes," in: PPC *Petits Propos Culinaires*, 28 (1988), 11–21; idem, "Kitchen Judaism," in: J.W. Joselit and S. Braunstein (eds.), *Getting Comfortable in New York* (1991); idem, "The Kosher Gourmet in the Nineteenth-Century Kitchen," in: *Journal of Gastronomy*, 2:4 (1986–87), 51–89; idem, "'The Moral Sublime': The Temple Emanuel Fair and Its Cookbook, Denver 1888," in: A.L. Bower (ed.), *Recipes for Reading* (1997), 136–53; S. Sherman. "The Politics of Taste in *The Jewish Manual*," in: PPC *Petits Propos Culinaires*, 71 (2002).

[Barbara Kirshenblatt-Gimblett (2nd ed.)]

°**COOKE, GEORGE ALBERT** (1865–1939), English Bible scholar and Semitist. He taught at Oxford and was canon of Christ Church (1914–36). Cooke is remembered principally for *A Text-book of North Semitic Inscriptions* (1903), a pioneering effort to collate and interpret Hebrew, Moabite, Phoenician, Punic, Nabatean, Palmyrene, and Old Aramaic Semitic inscriptions. His commentaries for the "Cambridge Bible for Schools and Colleges" (Joshua, Judges, and Ruth, 1913) underscored the importance of philology in textual criticism. In his important commentary on the Book of Ezekiel (ICC, 1936, 1951), he argued that the book was written by one and the same hand with very little editorial expansion. Among his lesser-known works are an exposition on the Song of Deborah (1892), a study of the problem of revelation (1911), and a critical second edition of E.A. Edgehill's Book of Amos (1914).

[Zev Garber]

COOKING AND BAKING. In biblical times cooking or baking was generally done in the courtyard or kitchen, either in a hearth or an oven. In seasons of intensive labor in the field people encamped in the fields (Gen. 37:17), while in other seasons they returned to their homes. Accordingly, these conditions led to the development of cooking utensils for both the permanent kitchen and for the open field.

Cooking

As a rule, cooking utensils were made of earthenware (Lev. 6:21). Special attention was given to the preparation of these utensils, which had to be able to withstand heat. The clay was mixed with coarse solid matter, such as pebbles, shells, or sherds, in order to reduce the porosity of the utensil and to prevent its cracking under heat. Metal cookingware was rare in the biblical period. However, *sir* (סִיר) means specifically a copper pot (cf. Ezek. 24:11). Cooking vessels were of simple practical forms, usually without decoration. The bases of the vessels were rounded and wide to bring as much surface as possible into contact with the fire and to allow the heat to be distributed equally over the entire surface. As vessels were not placed on the ground or on a flat surface, the bases did not have to be flat. Instead, they were placed on stones, on a stand, or on any noncombustible object which held the utensils over the flame. Excavations in Palestine have revealed various methods of supporting cooking vessels. The simplest was a small pit in the ground with an opening at the side, which permitted feeding and fanning of the fire. A more sophisticated method was a low mound of rocks arranged in the shape of a horseshoe. The fire was fed through the opening and the utensil was placed on the rim. On the floors of rooms and kitchens at many sites small pits have been found which were coated with clay seared by the fire which continuously burned inside them. Each of these pits also contains an opening through which the flame could be reached. Beginning with the Early Bronze Age well-made portable stands of baked clay appear in the shape of a thick, high horseshoe with a flat base enabling it to stand on a flat surface. On the rim were at least three protrusions for supporting the cooking-pot. In later periods, beginning with the Middle Bronze Age, stands of cylindrical shape with openings for feeding and fanning the fire were widespread. These stands were designed to protect the fire from wind and to concentrate the heat under the base of the vessel. From the Early Bronze Age onward, handleless vessels with the width of the base greater than the height appear. These pots stood on stands while cooking, as well as during the meal, when the cooked food was scooped out with another vessel and served. In the Israelite period (Iron Age) various types of cooking vessels were common, some without handles, some with two handles, and some with more than two handles. In addition, smaller cooking vessels with only one handle were widely used. Apparently, vessels without handles were placed in the permanent pits or on fixed stands, where they could remain standing while the food was ladled into bowls for eating. Vessels with two or more handles were used in a slightly different manner: by means of a rope tied to the handles, they were hung from a tripod, with the fire beneath them. These vessels were perhaps used during the seasons of outdoor labor. The smaller one-handled vessels served for both cooking and pouring, the cooked food being poured into the eating vessels after its removal from the fire. Possibly, these vessels were used for thinner foodstuffs in contrast to the larger cooking vessels. While fruits and certain vegetables were eaten fresh, lentils and legumes, such as kidney beans, broad beans, and chick-peas, were made fit for eating by cooking them in water (as were eggs) and mixing them with other vegetables and seasonings, such as onions and garlic. This preparation was known by the general name *nezid* ("stew"; II Kings 4:38). Meat was a scarce commodity. Most frequently used was mutton, goat meat, or fowl, but sometimes veal or other types of meat were prepared. Meat prepared in various ways was served principally at special festive meals in which the entire family or tribe took part. One way to prepare meat was to boil it in water with seasonings. Softened by boiling, meat could easily be separated from the bones. Other methods of preparation were roasting on the open flame, baking in the oven, or frying in oil. It is not known whether meat was salted or smoked, but it is possible that these procedures were practiced.

Baking

While cooking hearths were open, baking ovens (Heb. *tannur*) were usually closed. The Hebrew word אפה, "to bake," and its derivatives specifically refer to the baking of bread (Gen. 19:3; Lev. 26:26; Isa. 44:15) and cakes (Ex. 12:39, I Kings 17:12–13), including the baking of the bread of display (Lev. 24:5) and baked offerings (2:4ff.). Baking, like cooking, was from the earliest periods an integral part of the everyday household chores. Only in later periods was baking somewhat industrialized and done by experts, or in national bakeries. The simplest method of baking involved placing the dough on glowing coals which baked it from below, while coals were spread also on top of the dough to bake it from above (Isa. 44:19). In a second method a bowl was placed upside down over the fire and when it was sufficiently heated, the prepared dough was placed on it for baking. Excavations of Middle Bronze Age settlements have revealed specially designed baking trays which are perforated in order to preserve the utensil for a long time and prevent the bread from sticking to it. The baking oven was a more sophisticated piece of equipment. Ovens made of clay or built of brick or stone have been found in various shapes – cylindrical, hive-shaped, semicircular and square.

Dough was stuck to the inner wall of the oven, while a fire heated the oven from the outside, thus baking the bottom of the bread; a fire inside the oven baked the top of the bread. A more perfected oven had two levels; the fire was kindled in the lower level, while the dough was placed on the floor of the upper level. Ovens operated in this manner served the needs of industrialized baking. As portrayed in ancient Egyptian paintings, an oven of this type was operated by two people; one fanned the flame and the other inserted and removed the bread. The oven had three openings: one for feeding the fire, the second for inserting and removing the bread, and the third for fanning the flame and letting out the smoke in the oven. The oven was heated with dried dung, with wood that had been gathered or chopped from trees and then dried, or with charcoal.

BIBLIOGRAPHY: Dalman, Arbeit, 4 (1935), 1ff.; pls. 17–19, 26, 27; C. Singer, et al. (eds.), *A History of Technology*, 1 (1954), 270–3; O. Tufnell et al., *Lachish*, 2 (1940), 39, pl. 54A; 338; G. Loud, *Megiddo*, 2 (1948), 60, fig. 132:3; R. Amiran, *Ha-Keramikah ha-Kedumah shel Ereẓ-Yisrael* (1963), 91, pl. 84.

[Ze'ev Yeivin]

COOPER, ALEXANDER (c. 1609–1660), English miniaturist; a convert to Judaism. Cooper was born in London, the brother of the better-known Samuel Cooper, the outstanding English miniaturist of his day. Alexander also worked in this medium. His sitters included members of the royal family and nobility. From 1647 he was at work in Sweden, where he was known as Abraham Alexander Cooper "the Jew." He apparently converted to Judaism shortly before this time, possibly in Amsterdam. There is no reason to believe that his brother Samuel had any connection with Judaism.

BIBLIOGRAPHY: G.C. Williamson, *History of Portrait Miniatures*, 1 (1904), ch. 7; F. Landsberger, in: HUCA, 16 (1941), 382–3; C. Roth, *ibid.* 17 (1942–43), 500–1. **ADD. BIBLIOGRAPHY:** ODNB online.

COOPER (Kuper), EMIL ALBERTOVICH (1877–1960), conductor. He studied violin with Hellmesberger in Vienna and composition with Taneyev in Moscow. After 1898 he conducted opera at Kiev, Moscow, and St. Petersburg, and between 1909 and 1914 conducted the Diaghilev troupe at its appearance in London and in the first Paris performance of Mussorgsky's *Khovanshchina* (1911). After the Russian Revolution he was director of the Petrograd Philharmonic Orchestra and the Mariinsky Opera Theater and taught at the Petrograd Conservatory. In 1924 he left Russia, and worked mainly in the United States, conducting at the Chicago Civic Opera (1929) and at the Metropolitan Opera in New York (1944–50).

COOPER, JACKIE (John Cooper Jr.; 1921–), U.S. actor. Cooper was born in Los Angeles. His father abandoned the family when he was two years old and his mother, Mabel, a stage pianist, then married Charles J. Bigelow, a studio production manager. With the help of his uncle, *Boys Town* director Norman Taurog, Cooper's entry into Hollywood was almost guaranteed. Between 1929 and 1931, he appeared in 15 Hal Roach *Our Gang* shorts and was cast in the title role of Tuarog's film *Skippy* (1931), which earned him an Academy Award best actor nomination (until 2004, the only actor below the age of 18 so honored). Cooper went on to star in *The Champ* (1931), *Treasure Island* (1934), *Tough Guy* (1935), *Streets of New York* (1939), and *Ziegfeld Girl* (1941). In 1943, he joined the Navy and rose to the rank of captain. After World War II, he moved to television as an actor, producer, and director. He directed episodes of *The Rockford Files*, *Kojak*, and *Quincy*, and received Emmys for an episode of *M*A*S*H* (1973) and the pilot of *The White Shadow* (1978). Before his retirement Cooper appeared as Perry White in the *Superman* series (1978–87) starring the late Christopher Reeve.

[Adam Wills (2nd ed.)]

COOPER, LEON N. (1930–), U.S. physicist and Nobel laureate. Cooper was born in New York City, where he got his B.A. (1951), M.A. (1953), and Ph.D. (1954) from Columbia University. After appointments at the Institute of Advanced Study (1954–55), the University of Illinois (1955–57), and Ohio State University (1957–58), he joined Brown University, where he became professor, and (from 1974) Thomas J. Watson Sr. Professor of Science and (from 1973) director of Brown University's Institute for Brain and Neural Systems. Cooper's earlier research was in theoretical physics. He was awarded the Nobel Prize in physics (1972) jointly with John Bardeen and Robert Schrieffer for providing a theoretical basis in quantum terms for the behavior of electrons whereby they "pair up" during superconductivity, the state in which electrical resistance reduces to zero at very low temperatures. Subsequently he led an interdisciplinary organization concerned with understanding learning and memory through theoretical models and experiment. While he remained interested in basic problems such as the limits of the laws of physics in understanding the universe, he also concentrated on the application of theoretical systems to drug development, electronics, and communications, including major involvement in industrial organizations with the same objectives. His many honors include the Comstock Prize of the U.S. National Academy of Sciences (1968).

[Michael Denman (2nd ed.)]

COOPERATIVES. The Jewish cooperative movement began toward the end of the 19th and beginning of the 20th century. Its development was part of the general spread of cooperatives throughout the world at that time, and was spurred additionally by the rising socialist and nationalist trends. The specific position of the Jewish artisan, often hemmed in by a hostile society and government, and having traditions as well as actual need of mutual help, led the Jewish cooperative movement from its beginning to lean heavily on artisan producer cooperatives and free-loan cooperatives (*gemilut ḥesed* associations). The main center of the Jewish cooperative movement before World War I was Russia, but it also began to develop in Galicia, Austria, and Bukovina, as well as countries outside Europe, especially Argentina (for Israel, see below Cooperative Movement in Israel).

Between the two World Wars the Jewish cooperative movement developed rapidly in Poland, Romania, and the Baltic countries, Soviet Russia (in the 1920s), other countries in Eastern and Western Europe, and Latin America. It became then an important instrument of Jewish defense against discrimination and efforts to oust Jews from their economic positions. Much financial help was extended to the movement by the *American Jewish Joint Distribution Committee. The Holocaust put an end to the Jewish cooperative movement in Europe, although in several countries, Poland, for example, efforts were made to revive it after the war. The movement continued to develop in South America, especially Argentina.

Russia

The growth of the Jewish cooperative movement in Russia was comparatively rapid, especially in the form of credit cooperatives, owing to the difficult credit terms that burdened the small Jewish trader and artisan (with compound interest as high as 30% or 40%). While in 1900 the number of Jewish credit cooperatives in Russia did not exceed 20, in 1914 there were 678, with a total membership of approximately 400,000, of which 36.0% were small merchants and shopkeepers; 32.6% craftsmen; 7.8% middlemen or agents; 7.4% farmers; 3.1% laborers; and 13.1% in miscellaneous occupations; the overwhelming majority of members came from the middle classes. With the members' families, about 1.5 million persons were served by Jewish cooperatives, approximately one-third of the total Jewish population in Russia. In addition to granting credit, the cooperative societies often engaged in ancillary activities, such as the provision of tools and instruments to artisans on long-term credit, the provision of storage facilities, as well as mutual insurance in case of death. Out of this latter service special insurance societies developed, which in 1912 numbered 95, with a membership of 52,000.

World War I and the subsequent civil war and pogroms in Russia resulted in the destruction of the Jewish cooperative movement there. However, when in 1922 the Soviet government introduced its New Economic Policy (NEP) a renewal took place. In 1929 the *Jewish Colonization Association (ICA) supported 208 cooperatives in the Soviet Union, with a total membership of 67,351. During this period the character of the Jewish cooperatives changed. Only wage earners were allowed to join. In 1929, 93.5% of the membership of the 400 Jewish cooperatives in existence were artisans, about half of the total number then in Russia. The societies' main activity was no longer the supply of credit, but of raw materials, a major problem at that time. Nevertheless, from 1930, Soviet legislation as well as the economic development during the following decade led to the gradual liquidation of the Jewish cooperative movement in the U.S.S.R.

Poland

Efforts made soon after World War I resulted in the establishment in independent Poland of 445 cooperative societies by 1925 and 774 by 1929, mainly saving and loan societies. Attempts to establish producer and consumer cooperatives mostly failed. This fast growth was interrupted during the 1930s partly as a result of the general economic crisis and partly because of anti-Jewish discrimination (see anti-Jewish *boycott).

Of 775 cooperative societies in Poland in 1938, 734 were loan and credit societies; 27 producer cooperatives; 9 agricultural cooperatives; 2 consumer cooperatives; and 3 miscellaneous. The total membership in 1937 was 143,608, serving some 600,000 persons (one-fifth of Polish Jewry).

Other European Countries

A comparatively strong Jewish cooperative movement existed in Romania between the two World Wars. In 1931 there were 88 Jewish cooperative societies having a membership of 67,000, with 30,000 living in Bessarabia, where even before World War I a ramified Jewish cooperative movement already existed. During the 1930s a sharp decline set in, mainly as a result of an economic crisis and antisemitic sentiments. By 1937 the total membership dropped to 52,000. In Czechoslovakia after World War I, a series of Jewish cooperative societies was established, which had a total membership of 7,136 in 1924, rising to 17,772 in 1937. In Bulgaria the first Jewish cooperative (Geulah) was established in 1921; by 1940 there were 23 Jewish cooperatives, of which 20 were credit cooperatives.

The Jewish cooperative movement in the Baltic countries, especially in Lithuania, was highly developed during the period between the two World Wars. In 1937 there were 85 Jewish cooperative banks, with a membership of 15,728. Low-interest loans were available especially to Jewish farmers and artisans. A central bank was established which serviced this cooperative network. Its credit policy aimed at enhancement of productivity. A special agricultural information center was established. In the late 1920s a Jewish cooperative movement began to develop also in Central and Western Europe. In 1928 there were in Germany a cooperative people's bank, Ivriah, which served especially emigrants from Poland and Russia, and a Jewish cooperative society for trade and commerce, founded largely by Berlin Jewish artisans. In the early 1930s efforts were made to establish Jewish cooperative societies in other German towns. At the same time, two cooperatives were established in Paris to assist Jewish migrants from Eastern Europe. Several Jewish cooperatives were also established in London, England.

Argentina

In Argentina the Jewish cooperative movement attained broad diversification.

AGRICULTURAL COOPERATIVES. These cooperatives developed in the Jewish agricultural settlements of Argentina from 1907, and dealt mainly with crop marketing (especially grain), as well as supply purchasing for farmers. Their activity in the sphere of credit was of secondary importance. These cooperatives declined in number as a result of the constant decrease of the Jewish agricultural population in Argentina.

COOPERATIVE BANKS. During the early 1960s there were some 40 Jewish cooperative banks in Argentina. Of special importance was the Jewish People's Bank in Buenos Aires, established in 1921. It developed rapidly, and by 1953 the number of shareholders reached 14,885. Another cooperative institution of this kind was the Mercantile Bank founded in 1917.

PEDDLER STORAGE COOPERATIVES. An original attempt was made to provide a convenient base and supply center for the Jewish peddler in Argentina. Storage depots were opened in various cities. The peddler could obtain his wares on credit with easy payment terms. Thus he could take samples to houses of far-flung customers, come with their orders to the depot, and supply the demand. He could also direct his clients straight to the cooperative stores in the city where they could make their wholesale purchases on the basis of the samples and recommendations of the peddler. There are also other Jewish cooperatives in Argentina, such as manufacturer societies (for manufacturers of wood products, fur products, knitted products, etc.) mainly for purchase of raw materials from a primary source. The total number of Jewish cooperatives exceeded 100 in the early 1960s. However, economic decline of the cooperatives set in after the bankruptcy of many of them at the beginning of 1970s.

United States

Jews have been particularly active in the general cooperative movements of the United States. During the first decade of the 20th century, the activity of the New York Cooperative League, whose members were mostly Jewish, stimulated consumer cooperatives throughout the United States. The League controlled a number of cooperative millinery stores and a hat factory. It developed a wide information activity, which had great influence among cooperative movements in the United

States which were largely Jewish, or had Jewish leadership, included the Growers Marketing Cooperative (serving Jewish farmers in the New York area), producer cooperatives, and housing cooperatives.

[Shaul Zarhi]

In Postwar Poland

One of the most important tasks that the Lublin Jewish Committee (see *Poland) took upon itself immediately after the defeat of the Nazis was to find productive employment for the Jewish survivors. As soon as the Central Committee of Polish Jews was established in Warsaw, economic subcommittees were appointed for each of the larger Jewish communities. They acted as a labor bureau; established a series of cooperatives, several trade schools, agricultural farms; and provided assistance to all those who decided to rebuild their workshops on an individual basis. According to the report of these subcommittees (August 1946), 27 cooperatives, with a membership of 753, were established during the first year of their activity. When the American Jewish Joint Distribution Committee (JDC) resumed its activities in Poland (July 1945), many of these cooperatives received assistance in the form of equipment, and *ORT provided facilities for retraining the Jewish survivors in the skills that were necessary under the new conditions. The coordinating body, known as Solidarity, provided raw materials and marketed the finished products. By the end of 1947 there were 200 cooperative societies with a membership of 6,000, according to the chairman of the Jewish Cooperative Association. The societies' membership grew to more than 9,000 in the following year and reached its peak of 15,500 members in 1949. During the period of Stalinization many of the Jewish economic achievements, which were made possible by the help of the JDC and ORT, were practically liquidated under the pretext of "unification" with the general Polish cooperative movement. With Wladislaw Gomulka's accession to power in 1956 and with the influx of some 40,000 Jews from the Soviet Union, the activities of the JDC and ORT were temporarily resumed and some of the Jewish cooperative societies, especially in Silesia and *Lodz, were revived. In their new form, the Jewish cooperatives maintained a certain liaison with their Polish counterparts. About 20% of their profits were earmarked for cultural and social work. In 1967–68, during the renewed anti-Jewish campaign in Poland, the Jewish cooperatives were once again "unified" with their Polish counterparts.

[David Sfard]

Cooperative Movement in Israel

BACKGROUND. The circumstances surrounding the birth of the cooperative movement in Ereẓ Israel were different from those in other countries, where the purpose of such movements was to combat the negative aspects of the capitalist system that resulted from the industrial revolution. Two factors in particular should be mentioned: Jewish settlement in Ereẓ Israel was a national movement. It was not modeled on colonization movements initiated by individuals (as in the United States, Australia, etc.), but was based upon a united effort of manpower concentrated into original forms of cooperation. Under the conditions prevailing in Ereẓ Israel, cooperation was the only way of facilitating mass settlement. Second, the ideological foundation of the cooperative movement in Ereẓ Israel differed from its European or American counterpart. It did not have its roots in socialism, anarchism, or any other political theory dedicated to ousting a repugnant and unjust order; rather, it was forced upon the Jewish settlers by extremely harsh conditions in the country that could not be overcome without the cooperative factor.

To these factors must be added the rapid development of the economy of Ereẓ Israel, in which cooperative enterprises and organizations played a particularly active and dynamic role (see *Israel, Economic Development), and enabled the cooperative movement to gain important advantages in various branches of the economy. Cooperative bodies were also able to record substantial achievements in the realm of technological progress and the modernization of production methods, as well as in vocational guidance and training of its members. These achievements were particularly important in the consolidation and progress of agricultural settlement. Furthermore, the cooperative movement received a special impetus from the inadequate growth rate of production and employment, which failed to keep up with the growing rate of immigration. A large number of immigrants, as well as some older settlers, could not be absorbed by the private sector and quite frequently solved their problem by joining cooperative establishments. It follows, therefore, that in addition to pursuing the aim held in common by cooperative movements around the world (i.e., improvement of the conditions of life for large numbers of people), the cooperative movement in Ereẓ Israel played an important role in the development of the economy, the advancement of agricultural settlement, and the absorption of immigrants, which has resulted in its present strength in the economic and social life of Israel.

BEGINNINGS OF THE COOPERATIVE MOVEMENT. The beginnings of cooperative organization were discernible in the economy of Ereẓ Israel as early as the second half of the 19th century. During that period, cooperative groups were instrumental in building new residential quarters, especially in Jerusalem, and the first signs of cooperative organization also appeared in the Jewish villages. However, it was not until the beginning of the 20th century that cooperation in its modern sense began to develop. At that time, the cooperative movement in the Jewish community displayed two distinctive branches: a "workers' sector," linked to the labor movement; and a "private sector," composed of agricultural smallholders and middle-class groups in the towns. The branch linked to the labor movement showed a substantial development in the period of the Second Aliyah (1904–14). Special organizational efforts were made in four fields: consumers' societies, contracting, agricultural settlement, and industrial cooperatives in the towns. The first efforts at cooperative consumption were the establishment of workers' kitchens, clubs, laundries, etc.; but these did not endure. The first consumers' cooperative, founded in Reḥovot in 1906, was also unable to survive. Other consumers' cooperatives were established in 1911 (in Jaffa) and 1915 (in Petaḥ Tikvah). During this period, small groups of workers, such as the stone-cutters' groups in Jerusalem, the Ḥaderah commune, etc., banded together to lead a completely cooperative life in the field of consumption. The single most important event in the history of cooperative consumption in Ereẓ Israel was the founding of the national consumers' cooperative, *Hamashbir, in 1916.

The first groups of organized contractors also appeared during this period, accepting projects and carrying them out on a cooperative basis. Numerous groups of this kind, usually of a temporary nature, established themselves in moshavot to undertake work in the orange groves and vineyards. In 1914 the contracting group "Aḥavah" ("brotherhood"), consisting of about 100 workers, was founded in Petaḥ Tikvah. Some workers' groups were also established in the towns, and others undertook projects on the farms that were then being established by the Zionist Organization. One of the latter groups, known as the "The Collective," undertook the cultivation of the training farm at Sejera in 1908 for the period of one year without a manager representing outside interests to direct it. The success of this enterprise received wide acclaim. A similar experiment was undertaken by the farm at *Kinneret in 1908, and the cooperative settlement *Deganyah, which became the first kibbutz in Ereẓ Israel, was founded there in 1909. On the eve of World War I, 14 kibbutz-type settlements existed, all based on complete collectivism.

Finally, this period also witnessed the beginnings of urban production cooperatives linked to the labor movement, such as the cooperative printing press Aḥdut (1910) and a cooperative shoe factory in Jaffa (1912). The development of "private" cooperatives actually preceded the cooperative labor movement. The first impetus toward the establishment and consolidation of private cooperatives arose from the needs and problems of the agricultural sector in the moshavot. The first such cooperative was apparently the Pardess cooperative society for the marketing of citrus, founded in Petaḥ Tikvah in 1900 by a small group of orange growers. Two years later, two more citrus-marketing societies were established in the moshavot. In 1906 the Association of Wine Growers of *Rishon le-Zion and *Zikhron Ya'akov was founded, taking over the vineyards originally established by Baron Edmond de *Rothschild. Other cooperative societies established in the moshavot before the war dealt with the marketing of milk and almonds, the development of irrigation, land amelioration, etc. From 1905 onward a network of cooperative credit societies began to develop in the moshavot and the towns, most of which had no connection with the labor movement. By 1914, 45 such societies were in existence, with a total membership of 1,833. Most of these societies were too weak to overcome the difficulties caused by the war and had to dissolve.

1918–1939. As a result of the intensive demographic and economic development in Palestine during the interwar period, the cooperative movement and its relative importance to the economy greatly expanded. This development was especially true of the labor-linked cooperative movement, whose growth was facilitated by the unification of the labor movement and establishment of the *Histadrut (General Federation of Labor). In the early years of the Mandatory regime, the cooperative movement concentrated mainly on two spheres of activity: agriculture and public works. The network of cooperative agricultural settlements grew in number and form: in addition to the constant increase of kibbutzim, moshevei ovedim ("workers' settlements") came into being, combining the principle of family holdings with marked cooperative tendencies such as mutual help and cooperative purchasing and marketing. The first moshav ovedim, *Nahalal, was founded in 1921. In 1926, a special cooperative organization, *Tnuva, was established to serve as the marketing instrument of the cooperative settlements. Public works, another important sphere of activity in the 1920s, were being carried out on a large scale. Some of the projects were contracted to groups of Jewish workers that functioned on a cooperative basis. In 1921, the Histadrut established an office for public works and building projects in order to centralize the work of these contracting groups. In 1924 this organization became the contracting firm *Solel Boneh, which operated in its initial phase as a cooperative organization.

From the middle of the 1920s, with the accelerated urbanization and industrialization, the cooperative movement began to branch out into new areas. Cooperation in production and services developed at a rapid pace, and a number of industrial enterprises, as well as transport and other service agencies, were formed. The number of workers in the cooperative enterprises dealing with production and services grew from 800 in 1926 to 2,796 in 1936 and 4,625 in 1946–47. The year 1925 also marked the first developments in a network of savings and loan institutions under the auspices of the Histadrut. Against the background of settlement in the towns and increased building activities, cooperative building societies that engaged in the founding of workers' residential quarters also appeared. A wide network of consumers' cooperatives was established, especially from 1930 onward. Simultaneously Hamashbir was reorganized into a cooperative company for centralized wholesale supply; in World War II, it also embarked upon large-scale industrial production. "Private" cooperatives also showed a considerable growth. In the moshavot, the cooperatives for the marketing of agricultural produce were strengthened and diversified, particularly as regards citrus and other kinds of fruit, and wine. The rapid growth of the Pardess cooperative was characteristic of this development: at its start, in 1903–4, it exported a total of 22,500 cases, whereas in 1938–39 its exports of citrus amounted to 3,300,000 cases. A new network of private credit institutions also arose in the 1920s in the towns and the moshavot; most of them were associated with the Merkaz supervisory union. The number of members of the credit institutions affiliated with Merkaz grew from 17,200 in 1930 to 58,706 in 1946.

1948–1970. Following the establishment of the State of Israel and the ensuing general growth of the population and the economy, the cooperative movement also grew remarkably. The existence of a relatively large cooperative sector became an outstanding characteristic of the economy and social fabric of the country, particularly in the field of agriculture. The population of the cooperative villages, which numbered 84,400 in 1948, rose to approximately 208,000 by the end of 1966. Cooperative villages continued to form the great majority of the rural population of the country (app. 80% in 1966); they retained their hegemony in agriculture, and their share in industrial production also rose (from 3% of the gross national industrial product in 1951 to 8% in 1965). Internal shifts, however, took place within the sector of cooperative settlement: the kibbutzim, which represented 64% of the total population of cooperative villages in 1948, represented 40% of the population at the end of 1966, while the percentage living in moshavim rose proportionately. The number of consumers' cooperatives also increased: in 1948 they served 140,000 persons, but by 1966 the figure had risen to 750,000, about a third of the total population. Similar growth was also recorded in other branches of cooperative enterprise.

Nevertheless, the general trend of the cooperative movement in this period was not toward further growth. Some branches of cooperation, especially industrial and credit cooperatives, ran into difficulties and were unable to compete with the private sector of the economy. The number of industrial cooperatives decreased from 287 in 1950 to 102 in 1966, and the number of their employees from 5,042 to 2,997; the number of credit cooperatives also declined, from 94 in 1955 to 17 in 1967 (as a result of the merger of Histadrut-affiliated cooperatives with Bank Hapoalim – the Workers' Bank – and the dissolution of most of the "private" credit cooperatives). This trend appeared to be the outcome of the growing process of concentration and the rise of large industrial and banking concerns. Housing cooperatives also began to lose their importance. Although the cooperative movement was still able to maintain its importance in the rural sector, it ran into great difficulties in urban areas. It also faced increasing social problems after the establishment of the state, particularly the employment of hired labor, which violated the movement's principles. This question also had economic implications stemming from the scarcity of manpower in the cooperative villages, which was caused by the slow growth of their population and the seasonal aspects of agriculture. Hired labor was also a pressing problem for the great transport cooperatives *Egged and Dan.

STRUCTURE OF THE COOPERATIVE MOVEMENT AND ITS PLACE IN THE ECONOMY. The scope of the cooperative movement and its activities in this period are reflected in the following data on the various cooperatives at the end of 1967:

After the establishment of the state, a new network of Arab cooperatives came into being. Whereas during the Mandatory period the Arab cooperatives concentrated on credit and marketing, they now engaged in irrigation and water supply (64 societies), general agriculture (10), production and services (20), and housing (16). It is estimated that approximately 30% of the population, i.e., some 800,000 people, were members of cooperatives.

From the functional aspect, cooperative societies in Israel can be divided into three kinds: (1) consumer cooperatives, which are not the source of their members' livelihood, but provide them with certain benefits – this group includes the consumers' societies, credit societies, housing cooperatives, etc.; (2) productive cooperatives, such as agricultural and industrial cooperatives; (3) "integral" cooperatives, which combine production and consumption. In Israel this group includes the kibbutzim, moshavim shittufiyyim, and the moshevei ovedim in their original form. The predominance of productive and "integral" cooperatives is characteristic of the cooperative movement in Israel, while the consumer cooperatives played a lesser role than in other advanced countries.

COOPERATIVE AGRICULTURAL VILLAGES. Cooperative agricultural villages exist in three forms – kibbutzim, moshavim, and moshavim shitufiyyim. In 1966 there were 228 kibbutzim in existence, comprising a population of 82,000. Most of the kibbutzim belonged to one of the following settlement movements: Iḥud ha-Kibbutzim ve-ha-Kevuẓot, Ha-Kibbutz ha-Arẓi, ha-Kibbutz ha-Me'uḥad, and Ha-Po'el ha-Mizrachi (see *Kibbutz movement). There were 365 moshavim including 22 moshavim shitufiyyim, with a total population of 126,000; most of them belonged to the *Moshav Movement or to the moshav union of Ha-Po'el ha-Mizrachi. The cooperative settlement movement established a diversified network of institutions and organizations designed to aid it in its economic and social activities that includes the central settlement organs, which engage in organization and policy making and have a distinct ideological trend; the regional councils in the areas settled by cooperative villages, which carry out municipal and economic activities within these areas; regional purchasing organizations, which serve to improve the flow of supplies and reduce their costs; financial institutions and various funds, which finance the operations of the cooperative villages; and trade organizations, which deal with specific problems of the various branches of agriculture. Apart from the agricultural settlements and their organizations, there were about 375 agricultural societies engaged in various aspects of agriculture – marketing, supplies, irrigation, mechanization, processing, etc. The central marketing organizations – Tnuva, Tenne, and Pardess Syndicate – played an important role in the economy of the country.

During the past three decades, the agricultural cooperatives have undergone profound changes. While in the 1960s and 1970s they enjoyed great prosperity, the inflationary 1980s brought on a severe crisis. Many of the kibbutzim failed to manage themselves efficiently and were faced with such nationwide processes as strong pressure for privatization, the decline in the power of the Histadrut, and the general economic crisis with its ruinous interest rates in a sector that lived by credit. The economic crisis was accompanied by social problems, such as an exodus of the young generation, who chose to live their adult lives elsewhere. The net result was a shift, starting in the 1990s, from collective living to a more privatized way of life, including paid salaries and the development of nonmember housing. This process was still unfolding in the first decade of the 21st century.

The moshavim also faced a severe economic crisis as a result of the general economic situation in the 1980s, accompanied by a cutback in subsidies for agriculture products and the opening of the market to the import of fruits and vegetables from abroad. Many moshav residents liquidated their farms and turned to tourism (letting out rooms) or rented their land to commercial enterprises, as well as seeking employment outside the moshav. Some of the moshavim shitufiyyim dissolved the collective structure and distributed common property among their members. Moshavim became attractive options for city dwellers seeking to live in the country without the onus of operating farms, and as a consequence moshav real estate prices soared.

In 2001 there were 268 kibbutzim in Israel with a population of 115,800, representing 1.7% of the general population; 409 moshavim with 163,300 inhabitants (3%); and 43 moshavim shitufiyyim with 13,100 inhabitants (0.2%). Of the central marketing organizations, only Tnuva survived, operating as a large-scale food corporation.

CONSUMER SOCIETIES. At the beginning of 1967 there were 219 consumer societies in operation, with a combined total turnover of IL 173,000,000. They were spread over 55 cities, development towns, and moshavot. During the 1960s they underwent a far-reaching reorganization: the total number of societies was reduced (due to the low turnover of some) and a comparatively large number of supermarkets and self-service stores were established. At the end of 1966 there were 40 supermarkets and approximately 130 self-service stores operated by consumer societies. Hamashbir Hamerkazi served as the central wholesale supplier both to the consumer societies and to the entire labor-controlled sector of the economy. It was also the largest commercial firm in the country, supplying the needs of a third of the population. In the 1990s, as the Histadrut sold off its assets, it passed into private hands.

THE PRODUCTIVE AND SERVICE COOPERATIVES. The productive and service cooperatives included a number of industrial concerns and service cooperatives that played a central role in the economy, particularly in the field of transport. Ha-Mashbir ha-Merkazi le-Ta'asiyyah was founded in 1963 in order to facilitate the development of consumer-goods industries linked to the labor sector of the economy; in 1966, the total sales of the factories owned wholly or in part by this company amounted to IL 103,000,000. They included the Shemen edible-oil factory, flour mills, metal, paper and food processing factories, etc. The service cooperatives and factories in this group belonged to a central body organized for this purpose, the Merkaz ha-Kooperaẓyah. Most of the industrial cooperatives were to be found in the food processing industry (35), metal and electrical industry (16), wood (15), and printing and paper (12). Over the years the majority of these factories were sold to private investors, and Ha-Mashbir ha-Merkazi le-Ta'asiyyah ceased to exist.

The cooperative transport companies play the leading role among the service cooperatives. *Egged runs the interurban bus lines in the country, operating 2,200 buses and employing 6,600 persons at the beginning of 1968. It also had a fleet of 200 tourist buses, 42 local offices, 8 subsidiary companies, and 20 modern garages. The second large transport cooperative is Dan, which serves the largest urban concentration in the country, with a population of 900,000 (including the cities of Tel Aviv, Ramat Gan, Petaḥ Tikvah, Bat Yam, Ḥolon, etc.). The company operated 795 buses on 80 urban lines with a combined length of 1,375 miles, transporting about a million passengers a day (at the end of 1967). In addition to the passenger transport companies, there were 24 cooperative freight forwarding companies operating all over the country and employing some 1,500 workers at the beginning of 1967. In 2004 Egged employed 6,309 workers, of whom 2,452 were Egged members. It owned 3,332 buses and operated on 1,308 bus routes. In all, it made 44,957 daily runs on these routes, serving about a million people over 810,000 km of roads. Dan employed about 2,400 workers in 2004, among whom 830 were members. The company served about 640,000 passengers a day. Most of the cooperative societies were linked to the labor movement. They could also be grouped as follows: institutional cooperatives, which included Hamashbir Hamerkazi, Tnuva, mutual aid credit cooperatives and others; and the cooperative economy, which included the cooperative agricultural settlements of various kinds (kibbutzim, moshavim, and moshavim shittufiyyim), as well as the productive and service cooperatives. Also included were the cooperative enterprises linked directly or indirectly to the cooperative settlements. Table: Cooperatives shows the extent of the activities of the two groups.

In its heyday the labor-affiliated cooperative sector occupied a relatively important place in the economy of Israel. In 1966 it employed 64% of the workers in the entire labor sector and about 15% of the total number of persons employed in the economy of the country. The percentage was higher in certain branches especially agriculture, where, as has been stated, labor-affiliated cooperatives were predominant. In transport, for example, the cooperatives employed 21% of the total; in commerce, banking, and finance, they employed 8–9% of the total; and in industry, 7% (especially industry based on the cooperative settlements).

[Leon Aryeh Szeskin / Shaked Gilboa (2nd ed.)]

BIBLIOGRAPHY: J. Lestschinsky, *Ha-Tefuẓah ha-Yehudit…* (1960); idem, *Ha-Pezurah ha-Yehudit* (1961); A. Stolinski, *Di Kooperative Bavegung* (1919), 203–19; M. Sakharov, *Fertsig Yor Tsu Dinst der Kooperatsie* (1940); Smilg, in: *Di Idishe Tsaytung Yovel Bukh* (1940), 291–308; *Der Idisher Kooperator*, 12 vols. (1922–33); H. Viteles, *A History of the Cooperative Movement in Israel*, 5 vols. (1966–1968); H. Drabkin, *Pattern of Cooperative Agriculture in Israel* (1962), incl. bibl.; H.F. Infield, *Cooperative Living in Palestine* (1946); Y. Avineri (ed.), *Lu'aḥ ha-Ko'operativi shel Medinat Yisrael* (1968); Histadrut, Makhon le-Meḥkar Kalkali ve-Ḥevrati, *Meshek ha-Ovedim 1960–1965* (1967); W. Preuss, *Ha-Tenu'ah ha-Shittufit ba-Olam* (1957), incl. bibl. **WEBSITES**: www.kibbutz.org.il; www.egged.co.il; www.dan.co.il.

COPÉ, JEAN-FRANÇOIS (1964–), French politician. Born in the Paris suburb of Boulogne-Billancourt, Copé studied civil government at the École Nationale d'Administration (ENA), France's most prominent school for civil servants. He wrote several reference books about local finances and was elected mayor of Meaux in 1995; from 1998 he held elective positions in the local government of the Ile-de-France region and he was a representative for the Seine-et-Marne subdivision in the national parliament from 1995 to 1997. This experience of local government led him to publish in 1999 a book describing the everyday life of a mayor and reflecting on the problems of civil service. Actively committed to the center-right RPR Party, in which he was given the position of deputy general secretary, he acted from 2002 to 2004 as the spokesperson for the French government before beginning a ministerial career: home secretary in 2004; deputy minister for state budget and budgetary reform from 2004 to 2005.

[Dror Franck Sullaper (2nd ed.)]

COPELAND, LILLIAN (1904–1964), track and field athlete, Olympic gold and silver medalist, member of the U.S. Track & Field Hall of Fame. One of the greatest field competitors in women's track and field history, Copeland was born in New York City to Polish immigrants. Copeland's father died when she was young, and after her mother married Abraham Copeland, the family moved to Los Angeles. Copeland excelled in all throwing events, especially in the shot put, winning the AAU championships in that event five times (1925–28, 1931) and setting the shot-put record in 1928 at 40' 4.25" (12.30 m.). Copeland also won the AAU discus throw title in 1926 with a 101' 1" (30.81 m.) world record, and again in 1927, and the javelin throw title in 1926 and 1931, breaking the world record in the javelin three times in 1926 and 1927. After setting a world discus record of 115' 8.5" at the U.S. Olympic trials in 1928, Copeland won the discus silver medal at the Olympic Games, the first Olympics to include women's track and field events (though not yet the shot put and javelin throw). Copeland also helped set a world record in the 440-yard relay at the 1928 time trials. Copeland then attended the University of Southern California Law School and semi-retired from competition, but she came back for the 1932 Olympics, where she won gold in the discus on her last throw of the day with a world record toss of 133' 2" (40.58 m.). She competed in the 1935 Maccabiah Games, winning the gold medal in discus, shot put, and javelin. Though planning to defend her discus gold medal at the 1936 Olympics in Berlin, Copeland joined the movement to boycott Hitler's Games.

[Elli Wohlgelernter (2nd ed.)]

COPENHAGEN (Dan. **København**), capital of *Denmark. The first Jewish congregation in Copenhagen was founded in 1684 when two Ashkenazi Jews, the court jeweler Israel David and his partner Meyer Goldschmidt, both of Hamburg, were permitted "to conduct morning and evening prayers in their homes on condition that these devotional exercises took place behind closed doors and without any sermon." In 1687 Abraham Salomon of Rausnitz in Moravia was appointed the first rabbi in Copenhagen. The first Jewish cemetery in Møllegade, established in 1693, is the oldest cemetery in northern Europe. Religious services – in some cases according to the Sephardi tradition – were held in private homes until 1766 when a synagogue with 320 seats was built in Laederstraede. This first synagogue was destroyed by the great fire of 1795, and services were thereafter held in 15 private homes. In 1827 the Liberal Party deemed it a matter of necessity to procure a rabbi with an academic education, and Abraham Alexander *Wolff, at the time *Landesrabbiner* in Upper Hessen, was appointed. A new synagogue in Krystalgade was built in 1833, on the initiative of Rabbi Wolff. A few strictly Orthodox members of the community were dissatisfied with some innovations introduced into the ritual in the new synagogue in Krystalgade, and a chapel was established in a private home in Laederstraede, where services in accordance with the traditional Polish rite were held from 1845 to 1955. After the consecration of the Krystalgade synagogue, the former Sephardi prayer rooms in Copenhagen were abandoned. There is no Reform synagogue in Copenhagen. The congregation *Mahzike Hadas*, established in 1910, and since 1914 affiliated with *Agudat Israel, maintains a synagogue in Ole Suhrsgade on a private basis.

The community is governed by a council of 20 delegates elected by approximately 1,800 dues payers; by a board of seven directors elected by the council; and by a board of seven trustees. The first old-age home, Meyers Minde, next to the synagogue, was erected in 1825 and rebuilt in 1925 and 1966. Three other old-age homes were erected in 1902, and a new old-age home and infirmary on the outskirts of Copenhagen were dedicated in 1961 in the presence of Queen Ingrid of Denmark. All Jewish welfare work in Copenhagen was carried out under the jurisdiction of the Jewish community until 1932, when Jews became subject to the same general social welfare legislation as all other Danish citizens. The Jewish community in Copenhagen, however, still has philanthropic institutions of long standing and applies the income from legacies to supplementary relief, medical aid, recreation, scholarships, dowries for needy brides, and assistance to Jewish transients. The all-day schools for boys and girls, founded respectively in 1805 and 1810, were united into one coeducational school, Carolineskolen, with 140 pupils after World War II. At the end of the 20th century its student body numbered close to 200 pupils. A Lubavitcher yeshivah founded in 1958 closed down, but 1997 saw the arrival of the first *Ḥabad representative in Copenhagen. In June 2004 the Danish Jewish Museum was inaugurated by the Queen of Denmark. The opening display showcased not only the exhibits but also Daniel Libeskind's architecture; it presented a far-ranging story of Jewish life in Denmark, emphasizing coexistence and identity over four centuries.

During World War I, the *World Zionist Organization established a central office in Copenhagen, and on Oct. 25, 1918, issued the Copenhagen program. This program contained the claims of the Jewish people which were to be presented to the Paris Peace Conference. A museum of ceremonial art objects was established in 1902. The Bibliotheca Judaica Simonseniana, part of the Royal Library in Copenhagen, is one of the great Jewish libraries of Europe. It comprises the library of Chief Rabbi David *Simonsen, the collection of the Danish maecenas Simon Aaron *Eybeschutz, and the library purchased from Lazarus *Goldschmidt. Rafael *Edelmann became its chief librarian in 1938.

For Copenhagen from the Holocaust onward, see *Denmark.

BIBLIOGRAPHY: J. Fischer, *Jødekirkegaarden i Møllegade* (1929?); R. Edelmann, in: *Exposition de 181 manuscrits, incunables et autres éditions rares de la Bibliotheca Judaica Simonseniana de Copenhague* (1952), 5–7; J. Margolinsky, *Minder fra Jødekirkegaarden i Møllegade* (1957); idem, *Chevra kaddischa 1858–1958* (1958); idem, in: AJYB, 63 (1962), 327–33.

[Julius Margolinsky]

COPISAROW, MAURICE (1889–1959), British chemist. Copisarow was born in Manchester. In World War I his research for the Ministry of Munitions was responsible for ending a succession of disastrous explosions in TNT factories. He also discovered methods of converting dangerous waste materials into dyestuffs and other useful products. Copisarow's continuous experimentation with TNT and phosgene, however, soon resulted in blindness, and he was forced to confine himself to theoretical work. This was both original and fruitful: he propounded a general theory of allotrophy and established new relationships between inorganic and living forms. In World War II Copisarow helped to meet Britain's food problems by his work in connection with grassland improvement, the reclamation of the brackenland, and fruit and vegetable preservation. After the war, he investigated enzyme and virus activity, and the biochemistry of influenza and of cancer.

[Samuel Aaron Miller]

COPLAND, AARON (1900–1990), U.S. composer. Copland was born in Brooklyn, studied with Rubin *Goldmark in New York, and with Nadia Boulanger in Paris. Returning to the U.S. in 1924, he became active as a composer, teacher, and conductor.

In his early years Copland attracted the attention of Serge *Koussevitzky, then conductor of the Boston Symphony Orchestra, who became an ardent champion of his music. His *Piano Concerto*, which he played with Koussevitzky in 1927, shocked the staid Boston audience by its aggressive jazz idiom. But Copland's talent soon won for him universal acceptance. At Koussevitzky's invitation, he joined the faculty of the Berkshire Music Center in Tanglewood, and for 25 years was the head of its composition department (1940–65). He traveled extensively in Europe, visited Russia in 1960, toured Latin America, and was guest conductor in Israel several times. Copland stopped composing abruptly and completely in 1970, but remained active as a conductor and lecturer until the mid–1980s. There were performances throughout the world to mark his seventieth, seventy-fifth, eightieth, and eighty-fifth birthdays, and New York City honored him with a "Wall-to-Wall" Copland Day tribute. He published several books: *What to Listen for in Music* (1939); *Our New Music* (1941); *Music and Imagination*, a collection of lectures delivered at Harvard University (1952); and *Copland on Music* (1960). In 1964 he received the Medal of Freedom from the U.S. government. Many of his works, such as the ballet *Billy the Kid* (1938), *Lincoln Portrait* for speaker and orchestra (1942), and the ballets *Rodeo* (1942) and *Appalachian Spring* (1944) were based on distinctly American themes. *El Salón México* (1937) for orchestra made use of authentic Mexican dance tunes, united in the form of a rhapsody; *Danzón Cubano* for two pianos (1942), a similar stylization of Cuban rhythms, was also arranged for orchestra.

Copland wrote much chamber music, notably: *Vitebsk* for piano, violin, and cello, based on a popular Jewish theme (1929), *Concerto* for clarinet, strings, harp, and piano (1950), *Piano Quartet* (1950) and *Nonet* for strings (1960). His piano works include *Variations* (1930); *Sonata* (1941); *Fantasy* (1957). In 1962, for the opening concert of Lincoln Center in New York, Copland wrote his first work explicitly composed in the 12-tone technique, entitled *Connotations*. He also wrote music for the play *Quiet City* and several film scores.

BIBLIOGRAPHY: A.V. Berger, *Aaron Copland* (Eng., 1953); J.F. Smith, *Aaron Copland, his Work and Contribution to American Music* (1955); Sternfeld, in: *Musical Quarterly*, 37 (1951), 161–75; G. Saleski, *Famous Musicians of Jewish Origin* (1949), 36–41; Grove, Dict; Baker, Biog Dict; Sendrey, Music, index; Riemann-Gurlitt; MGG.

[Nicolas Slonimsky]

°COPONIUS, first procurator of Judea, from 6 to 9 C.E. Of equestrian rank, he was sent to Judea by Augustus after the banishment of *Archelaus. He was accompanied by the Syrian governor, Quirinus, who was sent to take charge of Archelaus' property and to take a census in order to determine taxation. This census was customary in every land which became a Roman province, but the Jews, incited by *Zadok the Pharisee and *Judah the Galilean, regarded it as a sign of servitude and protested against it. Josephus mentions Judah as the founder of a new sect which has been identified variously with the *Zealots and the *Sicarii. As a result of the intervention of *Joezer b. Boethus, the high priest, the people were pacified and the census taken. During Coponius' period of office some Samaritans penetrated into the Temple and scattered human bones through its chambers, which led to an intensification of the vigil at the Temple (Eduy. 8:5; Tosef. Eduy. 3:3). No specific complaints were raised against Coponius as was the case with his successors, and he is believed to have maintained a satisfactory relationship with the Jews. One of the gateways to the Temple Mount, "the door of Coponius," was apparently named after him (Mid. 1:3).

BIBLIOGRAPHY: Jos., Ant., 18:1–10; 2:29; 31; Jos., Wars, 1:117–8.

[Lea Roth]

COPPERFIELD, DAVID (1956–). U.S. magician. As David Seth Kotkin, the son of Russian-Jewish immigrants (his father owned a small clothing store), Copperfield grew up in Metuchen, N.J. His grandfather taught him card tricks as a boy. Before his bar mitzvah he was performing magic at local community centers. He became the youngest person to be admitted to the Society of American Magicians. As a teenager, he said, he taught courses in magic at New York University. A week into his first year at Fordham University, he won the lead in the Chicago production of the musical *Magic Man*, and it launched his career. Under the name David Copperfield, suggested by a friend, he sang, danced, acted, and created all the magic in the show, which became a long-running production. His role led to his own television series, *The Magic of* ABC. CBS then signed him for a series of specials, *The Magic of David Copperfield*, and with each new special he introduced a new feat, always performing before a live audience. In one of his most famous tricks, in 1983, he seemingly made the Statue of Liberty vanish. He also walked through the Great Wall of China and escaped from the prison at Alcatraz, a trick no real prisoner ever managed to perform. Over 20 years his television specials were said to have reached more than three billion people. His face is on a postage stamp in four countries. His abilities as a businessman, as well as illusionist, paid off: he became one of the highest paid entertainers in the world. Copperfield, who was cited by the Library of Congress in 2000 as a living legend, started Project Magic, a program to help hospitalized people with physical and developmental disabilities.

[Stewart Kampel (2nd ed.)]

COPPER SCROLL, designation popularly given to the document at *Qumran officially listed as 3Q15. It was found in March 1952 in Cave 3, about two kilometers north of Qumran, in a much deteriorated condition. The use of the term "scroll" is perhaps incorrect, in so far as it was not intended to be frequently opened, read, and then rolled up like the rest of the Dead Sea scrolls. One suggestion is that it should be designated as a "rolled-up copper plaque."

Discovery and Unrolling

The document seems originally to have been a plaque of soft copper-base metal, about 8 × 0.9 ft. (2.46 m. × 28 cm.), made from three pieces riveted end to end. A hasty or clumsy attempt had been made to roll the plaque up, but the second row of rivets ceased to hold while this was being done, and the piece that remained was rolled up separately. The two scrolls were found embedded in the floor of Cave 3 in 1952. The writing, which had been punched out with about ten punching blows to a letter, was on the inside of the scrolls. From an examination of the lettering visible from the outside K.G. Kuhn concluded in 1953 that the document contained an inventory of the Qumran community's treasures and the places where they were hidden when its headquarters were abandoned. The metal was so utterly corroded and brittle that unrolling the scrolls or applying heat to reverse the process of decomposition was out of the question. The only means of exposing the inscribed surfaces was to cut the scrolls into strips, and even this was a precarious exercise in view of their condition. This was successfully achieved under the direction of H.W. Baker, then professor of mechanical engineering in the College of Science and Technology, Manchester, England. A spindle was put through the scrolls; they were coated with adhesive, warmed to 40°–50°C, and cut into 23 strips with a tiny high-speed circular saw. Each strip was photographed as it was cut, and dust and débris were removed from the remaining part stage by stage, by vacuum suction and a dental brush. When the strips were laid side by side with their inner surfaces exposed, the inscription could be read. It consisted of about 3,000 letters, and so carefully and skillfully had the operation been carried out that not more than five percent of the text was destroyed, while of the rest only about two percent was illegible. The language was colloquial mishnaic Hebrew; the writing was of the period 25–75 C.E., as suggested by various scholars, notably by Frank Moore Cross.

Contents and Significance

The first announcement of the contents of the document was made in 1956. It was said to contain an inventory of 64 hoards of treasure which had been deposited in various places, chiefly in the Buqeiʿa (Vale of *Achor) and its neighborhood and in the Jerusalem region. K.G. Kuhn's inferences from the limited amount of text visible in reverse in 1952 were vindicated. Three samples of the inventory were published in this first release: "In the cistern which is below the rampart, on the east side, in a place hollowed out of rock: 600 bars of silver" (item 11); "Close by, below the southern corner of the portico at Zadok's tomb, and underneath the pilaster in the exedras, a vessel of incense in pine wood and a vessel of incense in cassia wood" (item 53); "In the pit nearby toward the north, near the graves, in a hole opening to the north, there is a copy of this book, with explanations, measurements and all details" (item 64). A French translation of the whole text was published by J.T. Milik in 1959; a transcription of the text with English translation and notes was published by J.M. Allegro in 1960, while the official edition of text, translation, introduction, and notes by J.T. Milik, with photographic plates, appeared in 1962. One contribution of value made by this document concerns the topography of the areas where the treasures are said to have been deposited. For example, the name of the pool of Bethesda (mentioned in John 5:2) has been the subject of much debate because of the variant readings of the manuscripts; now it can be said definitely to be Bet-ʾeshda, "the place of outpouring," because this form (in the dual, Bet-ʾeshdatain) is mentioned under item 57 as the place where a cache of precious wood and resin was deposited. Some of the places mentioned are known either by geographical identification or by literary reference elsewhere (or both); others remain unknown. The references to sites around the Temple area are of particular interest. It is surprising to find one hiding place as far away as Mount Gerizim; there, "under the entrance to the upper pit," lot 61 was stored ("a chest with its contents and 60 talents of silver"). Josephus mentions the pretender in Pilate's time who promised to show the Samaritans the sacred vessels which Moses had hidden there (Ant., 18:85), but it may be that a hill in the vicinity of Jericho is meant (there is some patristic evidence for such a location).

A special problem is posed by the huge amounts of some of the caches; the gold and silver as listed would yield a grand total of about 200 tons or 200,000 kg. If the reference is to a collection of legends of buried treasure, there is nothing surprising in such a fantastic total; if the inventory is intended to be factual, it would have to be concluded that the amounts in some cases are in code for more realistic figures. Such use of a code is the less improbable because there are various cryptic signs and Greek letters in the document which appear to be intended to convey some meaning to those in the know. If the inventory is indeed intended to be factual, it may be asked if it lists the treasure seized from the Temple and elsewhere by the defenders of Jerusalem in the closing phases of the First Revolt to be used as sinews of war against Rome. The inclusion of incense, precious kinds of wood, tithe-jars, and so forth, along with the gold and silver suggests that some of the treasure may have come from the Temple. The use of such a durable material as copper for the inscription points to a factual inventory rather than to a collection of legends. But these and other questions raised by the inscription call for further examination. The fact that it was found in Qumran Cave 3 does not necessarily mean that it belonged to the Essenes or lists their property. Among other possibilities it may be considered that the Qumran headquarters were commandeered by Zealots or their Idumean allies as a useful strong point against the Romans, and that it was they who drew up the document and, at the approach of danger, rolled it up hastily and left it in a convenient hiding place. Its association with the Qumran scrolls on skin or papyrus need be no more than geographical.

BIBLIOGRAPHY: J.M. Allegro, *The Treasure of the Copper Scroll* (1960); Barthélemy-Milik, 3 (1962), 201–302, pls. xliii–lxxi; Kuhn, in: RB, 61 (1954), 193ff.; Baker, in: BJRL, 39 (1956–57), 45ff.; Ulendorff, in: VT, 11 (1961), 227ff. **ADD. BIBLIOGRAPHY:** S. Goranson, "Sectarianism, Geography and the Copper Scroll," in: JJS, 43 (1992), 282–87; J.K. Lefkovitz, *The Copper Scroll 3Q15: A Reevaluation. A New Reading, Tranlsation and Commentary* (1996); A. Wolters, *The Copper Scroll: Overview, Text and Translation* (1996).

[Frederick Fyvie Bruce / Shimon Gibson (2nd ed.)]

COPPER SERPENT, THE (AV, RV, "brazen serpent") (Heb. נְחַשׁ נְחֹשֶׁת; *neḥash neḥoshet*), a symbol set upon a standard by Moses at the Divine command (Num. 21:6–10). The instructions from the Lord followed a plague of "*seraph-serpents" sent against the people of Israel in the course of their wanderings through the desert. The purpose of the image was therapeutic; anyone bitten by a serpent could be healed by looking at it (cf. LXX, I Sam. 5:6 with MT, I Sam. 6:5). Since the peril was identified with the demonic power within the serpent, the copper image mounted on a staff constituted a counter-equivalent power which was an effective prophylaxis. Although the Pentateuch account regards the copper serpent as legitimate, King *Hezekiah broke it to pieces (II Kings 18:4) in the course of his reforms. It had come to be looked upon as idolatrous, on a par with the *bamot* ("High Places") and Asherah-groves, because the people had accepted it as a fetish, offering incense to it (the form *kitter* (*qiṭṭer*) instead of *hiktir* (*hiqṭir*) has a pejorative connotation). It is unclear from the end of II Kings 18:4 whether it was Hezekiah or the people who named the image Nehushtan. Some scholars regard the chapters in Numbers as an etiological account serving to justify the original adoption of this pre-Israelite cult-figure by the Jerusalemite priesthood, and as an attempt to emphasize the independent healing power of the Lord. The origin of the name Nehushtan is uncertain. Some regard it as having been formed from *neḥoshet* + the affirmative *-an*, and meaning "a copper object." Others note the play on words involving *naḥash* ("snake"), *neḥoshet* ("copper"), and perhaps also the verb *niḥesh* ("to practice divination"). It may be, however, that the *-an* suffix represents the Semitic dual ending.

Parallels from Other Cultures

Entwined serpents with wings indicating the equilibrium of the forces of life and death have been traced as far back as late third millennium Mesopotamia, in the design of the sacrificial cup of King Gudea of Lagash. Rituals designed to avert an evil power or concerning healing which involve serpents and images of them are known from Egypt and Mesopotamia. In addition, the serpent as a life-healing symbol was a common feature in the Canaanite fertility cult. It was associated with the mother-goddess Asherah on pendant reliefs and on incense altars. A small bronze serpent was found at pre-Israelite Gezer, and a bronze plaque with a woman flanked by two serpents was unearthed in Late Bronze Age Hazor. Finally, primitive religions frequently give examples of the conjunction of opposites, of serpents as symbols of sex and death or of death and rebirth. This concept was borrowed by the Greeks and served as the prototype of the caduceus, the staff with a handle of two intertwined serpents.

The Greek physician-god Asklepios, too, was associated with snakes.

[Michael Fishbane]

In the Aggadah

The Mishnah explains that the copper serpent was in itself ineffective as a healing agent. It merely signified that if the children of Israel would raise their eyes upward and subordinate their hearts to the will of the heavenly Father, they would be healed (RH 3:8). It also brought healing to those who had been bitten by other animals. In the case of the latter however, a casual glance sufficed for the cure, whereas in the former case they were healed only after a prolonged, insistent gaze (TJ, RH 59a). The appellation Nehushtan given to the serpent when it was destroyed by Hezekiah was regarded as a plural form, indicating that sacrifice to it involved the loss both of the present and future life (Yal., Num. 764, p. 524). The rabbis endorsed the action of Hezekiah in destroying this venerable relic, since it had become an object of idolatrous worship (Ber. 10b; Pes. 56a).

BIBLIOGRAPHY: G.B. Gray, *Numbers* (ICC, 1912), 274–8; J.A. Montgomery, *Kings* (ICC, 1951), 481; J. Gray, *I and II Kings* (1963), 608–9; Kaufmann Y., Toledot, 1 (1960), 670, 682–3; 2 (1960), 130, 265–6; Rowley, in: JBL, 58 (1939), 113–41; W.W. Baudissin, *Adonis und Esmun* (1911), 203ff.; R.A.S. Macalister, *The Excavation of Gezer*, 2 (1912), 399, fig. 488; Y. Yadin, et al., *Hazor*, 2 (1956), 117–8, pl. clxxxi, Barnett, in: *Eretz Israel*, 8 (1967), 3 (Eng. section); J.C. Henderson and M. Oakes, *The Wisdom of the Serpent* (1963); M. Eliade, *Patterns in Comparative Religion* (1958), esp. 164–71, 441–5, 457; Haran, in: VT, 10 (1960), 117–8. IN THE AGGADAH: Ginzberg, Legends, 3 (1947), 336, 480; 6 (1946), 115–6, 368–9. **ADD. BIBLIOGRAPHY:** B. Levine, *Numbers 21–36* (AB; 2000), 87–90.

COPPERSMITH, SAM (1955–), attorney and U.S. congressman. Coppersmith, was born in Johnstown, Pennsylvania, and educated in the local public schools, attending religious school from kindergarten through confirmation at the end of the tenth grade. He had his bar mitzvah at Johnstown's Conservative synagogue.

Coppersmith attended Harvard University, where he graduated *magna cum laude* in 1976. He earned a *Juris Doctor* at Yale in 1982 and then moved to Phoenix, Arizona, where he clerked in the Ninth Circuit Court of Appeals and eventually entered private practice. From the outset, Coppersmith became heavily involved in local civic and political affairs. In 1992, prodded by the local Democratic elite, Coppersmith declared for Arizona's First Congressional District seat against incumbent Republican Jay Rhodes. In Phoenix the first Congressional District seat had been occupied by a Rhodes – Jay and father John – for more than 40 years. Running as a "new-generation Democrat" (pro-choice and business-oriented), Coppersmith coasted to an easy victory in the Democratic primary and then scored an upset victory in the November general election.

Coppersmith took seats on the Public Works Committee and Science, Space and Technology Committee. During his one term in the House (1993–94), he kept a unique campaign promise: he turned down a congressional pay raise. He also gained attention with his leadership of an effort to eliminate the "Advanced Liquid Metal Reactor Program," an effort that brought praise from experts concerned about America's plutonium policy. Although largely unnoticed at the time, Coppersmith was also the first member of Congress to wire his office up to the Internet. In 1994 he gave up his House seat in order to run for the United States Senate; he lost that race and returned to Arizona for good.

After leaving Congress, Coppersmith practiced business and real estate law in Phoenix and wrote a weekly opinion column for the *Tribune* newspaper chain. In 1996, during his tenure as chair of the Arizona Democratic Party, Bill Clinton and Al Gore became the first Democrats to win Arizona since Harry S. Truman in 1948. In late 2004 he traveled several times to the Ukraine to serve on a panel of international observers monitoring the former Soviet republic's contentious presidential elections.

Coppersmith's wife, Beth Schermer, who practiced law with him, specialized in legal issues involving health care. One of Coppersmith's sisters, Dr. Susan N. Coppersmith, became a professor of physics at the University of Chicago. Their father, Louis Coppersmith, served 12 years (1969–81) in the Pennsylvania State Senate, where he chaired the Public Health and Welfare Committee and was known as the "Conscience of the Senate."

BIBLIOGRAPHY: K.F. Stone *The Congressional Minyan: The Jews of Capitol Hill* (2000), 66–68.

[Kurt Stone (2nd ed.)]

CORAL. The ancients regarded coral as wood, because of its tree-like appearance. Only at the beginning of the 18th century was it discovered to belong to the animal kingdom and to consist of the skeletons of marine polyps. Stone corals, found mainly in southern waters including the Red Sea and the Bay of Eilat, are the skeletons of the six-armed polyps (Hexacorallia), and are distinguished by their variety of shapes and their beautiful colors. To another group belong the eight-armed corals (Octocorallia), which include the Red Coral (*Corallium rubrum*). Found in the vicinity of Sicily and along North African shores, the red skeleton of the coral colony, which is extremely hard, is used for making ornaments. Red coral is probably to be identified with the biblical *peninim*, the color of which is red (Lam. 4:7). The identification of *peninim* as "pearl" is apparently wrong. The Talmud (RH 23a) tells of Arameans who brought up coral (Aramaic: *kesita*) from the bed of the sea. In Maimonides (Yad, Kelim 13:6) and in modern Hebrew the word *almog* is used to designate coral, but the identification is mistaken (see *Algum). Red coral was an important article in the commerce of Jews, especially those of Leghorn in the 17th–18th centuries.

BIBLIOGRAPHY: J. Margolin, *Zoologyah*, 1 (1962), 56f.; J. Feliks, *Animal World of the Bible* (1962), 141. **ADD. BIBLIOGRAPHY:** Feliks, Ha-Ẓome'aḥ, 204.

[Jehuda Feliks]

CORALNIK, ABRAHAM (1883–1937), Yiddish essayist and literary critic. Coralnik, who was born in the Ukrainian town of Uman, studied at the universities of Kiev, Florence, Berlin, Bonn, and Vienna. He mastered a dozen languages in the course of his travels. His main interest was philosophy. Coralnik's interest in Zionism led to his appointment as editor of the Viennese Zionist organ, *Die Welt*, in 1904. He also edited periodicals in Agram (now Zagreb, Croatian Republic) and Czernowitz, and served as correspondent for German and Russian newspapers in Rome, Berlin, and Copenhagen. In 1915 he joined the staff of the newly founded Yiddish daily *Der Tog*, for which he continued to work until his death, with a single interruption in 1917–20, when his enthusiasm for the Russian Revolution led him to edit Russian journals in Leningrad, Moscow, and Kiev. Although Coralnik was at first more at ease in Russian and German than in Yiddish, he gradually developed a lucid literary Yiddish. He claimed that civilization included far more irrational entities than rational ones and sought to explore the irrational core of artistic creation and national consciousness. In 1928 his essays were collected in five volumes, and three more volumes were published posthumously. In May 1933, he founded the American League for the Defense of Jewish Rights in response to the rise of Nazism, and with Samuel *Untermeyer organized the World Jewish Economic Conference in Amsterdam in an effort to coordinate an international anti-Nazi boycott, which met with little success.

BIBLIOGRAPHY: Rejzen, Leksikon, 3 (1929), 553–8; S. Bickel, *Shrayber fun Mayn Dor* (1958), 203–7; S.D. Singer, *Dikhter un Prozaiker* (1959), 284–90; M. Gottleib, "The Anti-Nazi Boycott in the American Jewish Community, 1933–1941" (Diss. Brandeis, 1967).

[Sol Liptzin / Sarah Ponichtera (2nd ed.)]

CORBEIL, capital of the department of Essonne, France. Jews lived there from at least the second half of the 12th century. They were expelled in 1180 with the other Jews in the kingdom of France, but are again mentioned in Corbeil from at least 1203. They owned a synagogue (*escholle*) whose building was preserved until the 14th–15th centuries. The *Rue des Juifs*, the ancient *Judearia*, still exists. The Jews were again expelled from Corbeil in 1306 with the other Jews in the kingdom, and returned in 1315. The community ceased to exist in 1321. Corbeil was an important center of Jewish learning in the Middle Ages. Its scholars included the tosafist Judah of Corbeil, *Jacob of Corbeil "the Saint," Samson of Corbeil, *Isaac b. Joseph, and *Perez b. Elijah. At the beginning of the German occupation of France in World War II (1941), 13 Jewish families were registered in Corbeil, but there was no Jewish community there after the war.

BIBLIOGRAPHY: J.A. Le Paire, *Histoire de Corbeil*, 1 (1901), 85, 88–89, 165, 169; E. Hamelin, *Les rues de Corbeil* (1908), 70–71; REJ, 9 (1884), 62f.; Gross, Gal Jud, 559ff.; Z. Szajkowski, *Analytical Franco-Jewish Gazetteer* (1966), 270.

[Bernhard Blumenkranz]

CORCOS, family originally from Corcos in the province of Valladolid, Castile. The scholar ABRAHAM CORCOS (c. 1275) lived in Castile; his son, SOLOMON CORCOS (d. after 1331), a disciple of Judah b. Asher, wrote a commentary on the astronomical work *Yesod Olam* of Isaac *Israeli in Avila. The wealthy financier JUDAH BEN ABRAHAM CORCOS (d. after 1493) of Zamora settled in Portugal in 1492. After 1492 members of the family were established in Italy and in Fez.

ABRAHAM, ḤAYYIM, YOSE AND JOSHUA CORCOS were among the leaders of the "Spanish Exiles" in Morocco. JOSHUA (d. after 1552) vigorously defended the "Castillanos" in the question of ritual slaughter traditions. A rabbinical authority, he was one of the promoters and signatories of the *takkanot* which determined the social and religious organization of the "Exiles of Castile" in Morocco. Renowned for his erudition and his piety, MOSES BEN ABRAHAM CORCOS (d. c. 1575) of Fez was appointed *dayyan* in Tunis, where his tomb is still the object of pilgrimage. One of the rabbinical authorities of Fez, JOSEPH CORCOS (d. c. 1710) had many disciples, several of whom achieved fame. JOSEPH BEN JOSHUA CORCOS (d. after 1800) lived in Gibraltar for some time and there he wrote his *Shi'ur Komah* (Leghorn, 1809; Jerusalem, 1934) which was regularly read in Morocco on Sabbath afternoons. He also wrote a homiletic work *Yosef Ḥen* (Leghorn, 1825). ABRAHAM BEN MOSES CORCOS (d. c. 1778), a talmudist, left several works of which only some decisions and a partially published work of responsa entitled *Ginnat Veradim* are extant. JOSEPH CORCOS known also as Maharik (Morenu ha-Rav R. Joseph Corcos; d. after 1575) was a Spanish-born talmudist. He traveled to Egypt, where he was head of a yeshivah, and finally settled in Ereẓ Israel, He wrote a commentary on the *Yad ha-Ḥazakah* of *Maimonides; several extracts have been published on Sefer Zera'im. His brother (?) ISAAC CORCOS (d. before 1540), first was rabbi in Egypt and later appointed *dayyan* in Jerusalem, where he was succeeded by his son Solomon. MAIMON BEN ISAAC CORCOS (d. 1799), one of the founders of the community of Mogador and an influential merchant, was one of the pillars of British politics in Morocco. SOLOMON BEN ABRAHAM CORCOS (d. 1854) was banker and adviser to the sultan. He was accredited as consular agent of Great Britain from 1822. His sons JACOB (d. 1878) and ABRAHAM (d. 1883), were entrusted with important missions by three successive sultans. In 1862 Abraham was appointed U.S. consul in Mogador. His influence at the palace of the sultan enabled him to considerably facilitate the mission of Sir Moses *Montefiore whom he received in Morocco. MEYER BEN ABRAHAM CORCOS (d. 1929) was appointed U.S. consul in 1884. He wrote *Ben Me'ir* (2 vols. 1912 and 1925) on the laws of the Sabbath and Passover. STELLA CORCOS (1857–1948) was born in New York and married MOSES CORCOS (d. 1903). She settled in Mogador, where she founded a free Jewish school which taught in English. She contested the growing influence of the Protestant missions over poverty-stricken Jews. She was the representative of the *Anglo-Jewish Association. ḤAYYIM BEN

JACOB (d. 1923), philanthropist and scholar, supported many yeshivot in Morocco. MONTEFIORE CORCOS (d. 1958), a pilot in World War I was a wing-commander in the Royal Air Force during World War II. JOSHUA BEN ḤAYYIM CORCOS (d. 1929), banker of the sultans and their advisers, played an important political role from 1885 to 1912. FERNAND CORCOS (1875–1956), advocate and active Zionist, defended the rights of the Jews of Morocco, Algeria, and Tunisia. He wrote *Le Sionisme au Travail* (2 vols., 1923 and 1925), as well as 15 volumes of international studies.

BIBLIOGRAPHY: REJ (1910), index to vols. 1–50, s.v. *Corcos, Carcause, Qorquossah*; Régné, *ibid.*, 63 (1912), 79–80; 65 (1913), 221f.; 68 (1914), 216; 69 (1919), 163, 189; J.M. Toledano, *Ner ha-Ma'arav* (1911), index; J. Ben-Naim, *Malkhei Rabbanan* (1931), passim; Baer, Urkunden, index, s.v. *Corcos, Caracosa, Carcosa*; Feldmann, in: *Sinai*, 58 (1966), 30–51; D. Grandchamp, *La France en Tunisie de la fin du XVI siècle…* (1920–30), viii, 221, ix, 33, 35; Hirschberg, Afrikah, 2 (1965), 308, 310, 369; Miège, Maroc, passim.

CORCOS, DAVID (1917–1975), historian of Moroccan Jewry. Scion of the prominent Spanish-Moroccan *Corcos family of merchants and diplomats, Corcos grew up as part of the elite of Mogador and Moroccan Jewry. Educated at the French High School and Higher Institute for Economy in Casablanca, he moved to Agadir as a young man and opened an import-export company and wholesale outlet that supplied southern Morocco and the Souss region with sugar, tea, and grain. He was a large-scale exporter to Europe of carob, almonds, wool, tea, sugar, and especially grain.

He immigrated to Israel in 1959 with a rare library of 1,500 books on North African and Moroccan Jewry as well as hundreds of manuscripts passed down from generation to generation that belonged to his great-grandfather. He lectured on Moroccan Jewish history on Kol Israel radio, published many scholarly articles on Moroccan Jewry in the *Jewish Quarterly Review, Zion*, and *Sefunot*, and in 1976 published *Studies in the History of the Jews in Morocco.* Corcos was the editor for the Maghreb of the first edition of the *Encyclopaedia Judaica*, writing over 250 entries on Moroccan, Algerian, and Tunisian Jewry. He also contributed to the *Enẓiklopediyah Ivrit*.

[Yitzchak Kerem (2nd ed.)]

CORCOS, HEZEKIAH MANOAH ḤAYYIM (Tranquillo Vita) THE YOUNGER (1660–1730), rabbi, physician, and preacher. Corcos was a member of the Rome branch of the *Corcos family which settled there after the expulsion of the Jews from Spain, becoming eminent for their rabbinical scholarship and financial acumen. His grandfather, of the same name (1590–1650), was among the foremost Italian rabbis of his day. In 1692 Corcos was elected to the Council of Sixty, the governing body of the Rome community, and was appointed rabbi and secretary of the community in 1702, after which he devoted even greater energy to communal affairs. In 1697 he appeared before the Congregation of the Holy Office to refute the anti-Jewish calumnies spread by the apostate Paolo Sebastiano Medici. Corcos' plea to Pope Innocent XII to authorize the reduction of the onerous rents paid in the ghetto was successful (1698). He also obtained some modification of the censorship of Hebrew books (1728), and secured the withdrawal of a *blood libel in Viterbo (1705).

Besides representing the interests of the Rome community, he attended to its daily needs within the confines of the ghetto, caring for the needy sick, superintending the local yeshivah, and encouraging secular instruction as well as delivering sermons. His firm and dignified demeanor was appreciated in the Vatican and generally in Rome. Corcos was perhaps the most illustrious personality of the Rome ghetto during its three centuries of segregation.

BIBLIOGRAPHY: A. Berliner, *Geschichte der Juden in Rom*, 2 (1893) 69ff.; Vogelstein-Rieger, index; A. Milano, *Ghetto di Roma* (1964), index s.v. *Corcos Tranquillo Vita il giovane.*

[Attilio Milano]

CORCOS, STELLA (1858–1948), educator. Stella Corcos was the daughter of an Algerian Jewish tobacco merchant, Avraham Duran, and Rivka Montefiore (1831–1929) of the famous London *Montefiore family. Stella married Moses Corcos, one of Mogador's wealthiest merchants, in England, and settled in Mogador in 1884.

In Mogador, with the assistance of the Agudat Aḥim philanthropic association of England headed by Claude Montefiore, she founded in 1885 an English-speaking school called "Kavod ve-Ometz" for lower class Jewish girls in order that they might escape the clutches of missionaries. The school attracted attention in the region and was visited by numerous diplomats and foreign dignitaries. The school outnumbered the local Alliance Israélite Universelle school in female students and thrived until 1915, when it closed. Through the influence of the school, English filtered into the Mogador Jewish community. Stella also introduced Jewish theater in the school and played a pioneering role in the introduction of Jewish theater in Morocco.

After her husband died in 1907, she was left alone with six children; among them her daughters Florence and Winnie, who were teachers in the school, and her sons Jacob and Mas'ud, the latter a London merchant. She used her influence with the Sultan of Morocco to better the living conditions of the Jews of the Mellah (Ghetto) of Mogador. On one occasion, she met with the Sultan in Marrakesh, riding to the meeting by horse. She maintained the school during periods of economic crisis, drought, epidemics, and even after the onset of French protectorate rule in 1912.

BIBLIOGRAPHY: S.S. Corcos, "English School for Girls in Mogador in Light of the Discovery Documents Unknown Until Now," in: *Brit*, 21, 31–43. (Heb.); D. Corcos, *Studies in the History of the Jews of Morocco* (1976), xii–xiii.

[Yitzchak Kerem (2nd ed.)]

CORCOS, VITTORIO (1859–1933). Italian portrait painter. Born in Livorno, Corcos studied with the Leghorn painter Giuseppe Baldini and from 1875 at the Art Academy in Florence. In 1877 he won a silver medal for his painting *Figura, copia dal vero*. The following year he won a scholarship for young painters. In 1880 his painting *Arabo in preghiera*, was bought by no less a personage than the King of Italy, Umberto I. In that same year Corcos left Italy for Paris, where he lived intermittently until 1886. He worked mostly for the art dealer Goupil. He presented paintings at the Salon, such as *A la brasserie* in 1881, *l'anniversaire* in 1882, and in 1885 a portrait. In 1886 he was back in Florence, where he took part in the First National Art Exhibition. He married, outside his faith, the widow Emma Rotigliano, née Ciabatti. His best-known portraits are those of the composer Pietro Mascagni (1891), the Italian poet Giosue' Carducci (1892), the German Kaiser Wilhelm II and his wife Augusta Victoria (1904), and Margherita of Savoy, Queen of Italy (1922). His last years were saddened by the death of his only son, Massimiliano, in 1916 at the front during World War I. Corcos is also remembered for his portrait paintings of beautiful women.

BIBLIOGRAPHY: I. Taddei (ed.), *Vittorio Corcos, Il fantasma e il fiore* (1997).

CÓRDOBA (**Cordova,** also **Corduba**), city in Andalusia, southern Spain. According to some sources, the Jews were entrusted with the city's defense immediately after the Muslim conquest in 711. The first references to Jewish settlement in Córdoba date from 840, in a polemical exchange between the Jewish proselyte *Bodo-Eleazar and Paul Alvarus. When Córdoba became capital of the Umayyad caliphate in Spain, it also became a center of a diversified and brilliant Jewish culture. This was due in great measure to *Ḥisdai ibn Shaprut, physician and diplomat in the service of the caliph ʿAbd al-Raḥmān III (912–961). Ibn Shaprut attracted the galaxy of philosophers, poets, and scholars, who made Córdoba a brilliant Jewish intellectual center. At this period, R. *Moses b. Ḥanokh, brought to Córdoba according to legend as a captive, was responsible for the revival of talmudic studies in Spain. A bitter dispute arose in the academy after his death when the succession of his son *Ḥanokh b. Moses was unsuccessfully disputed by his pupil Joseph *Ibn Abitur, upheld by the influential courtier Jacob *Ibn Jau.

During the 11th century, Córdoba declined as a result of the Berber conquest. After the revival of the community in the second quarter of the 11th century, Isaac b. Baruch *Albalia was the foremost rabbinical scholar in Córdoba. Scholars in the 12th century included Joseph b. Jacob *Ibn Sahl, a pupil of Isaac ibn Ghayyat, who was appointed *dayyan* of the community in 1113, remaining in office until his death in 1123. The noted poet and halakhic authority Joseph ibn *Ẓaddik served as *dayyan* from 1138 to 1149. At the beginning of the 12th century, messianic expectations were stimulated by the appearance of an Andalusian pseudo-messiah Ibn Arieh: excitement ran high until the communal leadership stopped the movement. Córdoba was the birthplace of Maimonides, born in 1135, who left the city as a result of the invasion of the *Almohades, when the Jews of Andalusia were compelled to adopt Islam and the community was destroyed.

The Jewish quarter during the Muslim period was situated near the *alcazar* ("fortress") southwest of the city; it continued in existence after the Christian reconquest and some parts may be seen today. A second quarter apparently existed in the northern part of the city, near the "Jewish gate" (*Bāb al-Yahud* – later the Talavera or León gate) which was standing until 1903. Shortly after the Christian reconquest in 1235–36 the ecclesiastical authorities in Córdoba were complaining that the new synagogue under construction was too high, and in 1250 Pope Innocent IV instructed the bishop of Córdoba to take steps against what he termed a "scandal" against Christianity. A synagogue still standing is that constructed by Isaac Moheb b. Ephraim in 1315 in the *mudejar* style. An adjacent room was probably used for teaching and the small assembly hall served for the *bet din*. The walls of the synagogue and women's gallery are embellished with quotations from the Psalms. The synagogue was declared a national monument in 1885. The Jews of Córdoba had helped to restore the economy of the city after the reconquest by Ferdinand III of Castile. Judah *Abrabanel served as a crown official there. Shortly afterward, however, anti-Jewish restrictions were introduced as elsewhere in Castile at this time. In 1254 Alfonso X ruled that Jews should pay tithes to the ecclesiastical authorities for real estate that had passed into their hands. The community in Córdoba at this period, although smaller than that of *Toledo, was evidently still important. Córdoba Jewry engaged in a wide range of crafts, specializing in the manufacture and marketing of textiles. An extraordinary measure passed by the communal board at the end of the 13th century provided that *dayyanim* were to be appointed for a period of one year only. In 1320–21 severe measures were taken by Judah *Ibn Waqar to tighten communal discipline and punish blasphemers (Resp. Rosh, 18:8). The annual tax paid by the community in 1294 amounted to about 38,000 maravedis, though the church claimed also a special annual payment of 30 denarii: this impost obviously had symbolic significance.

During the persecutions of 1391 anti-Jewish riots broke out in Córdoba in which most of the community was massacred. The annual tax of the reduced community in Córdoba in the 15th century was raised to about 1,200 maravedis in 1474 and amounted to 1,000 maravedis in 1482. A special levy of 18 gold castellanos was imposed on the communities of Córdoba and *Palma as their contribution to the war against Granada in 1485. From Córdoba, which was their headquarters during the war, Ferdinand and Isabella issued a series of anti-Jewish measures at the end of 1478. In 1483 the Jews were ordered to leave Andalusia, and except for a brief revival in 1485 the Jewish community in Córdoba ceased to exist. The Conversos living in Córdoba during the 15th century were fiercely persecuted; particularly violent attacks in 1473–74 made many flee to Sierra. The Conversos of Córdoba won a reputation for their attachment to Judaism, and a statement before a rabbinical court anywhere that a Converso had been educated or had studied in Córdoba was deemed sufficient evidence for him to be recognized as a Jew. The tribunal of the Inquisition established in Córdoba in 1482 comprised a large area in Andalusia within its jurisdiction, including Granada between 1492 and 1526. Many Conversos were martyred in the city in the 1480s. The inquisitor for Córdoba from 1499 until 1509, Diego Rodríguez Lucero, won a reputation for cruelty. The Inquisition in Córdoba remained active until the 18th century. Abraham Athias, father of the printer J. *Athias, was martyred there in 1665.

The 800th anniversary of the birth of Maimonides was officially commemorated in Córdoba in 1935, and in 1964 a Maimonides week was held. A statue was erected to his memory and a square in the former Jewish quarter was renamed Plaza Tiberias to perpetuate the connection of his birthplace with the city in Ereẓ Israel where he was buried.

BIBLIOGRAPHY: H.C. Lea, *History of the Inquisition in Spain* (1906), 190–209, 544; Baer, Urkunden, 1 (1929), 913; 2 (1936), index; M. Lowenthal, *A World Passed By* (1933), index; Baer, Spain, index; L. Torres, in: *Al-Andalus*, 19 (1954), 172ff.; Millás Vallicrosa, in: *Tarbiz*, 24 (1954), 48–59; F. Cantera, *Sinagogas Españolas* (1955), 3–32; Cantera-Millás, Inscripciones, 341; Suárez Fernández, Documentos, index; B. Postal and S.H. Abramson, *Landmarks of a People* (1962), 217–8; Ashtor, Korot, 1 (1960), 50–56, 194–7, 238–40; 2 (1966), 133; idem, in: *Zion*, 28 (1963), 50–51; Ibn Daud, Tradition, index.

[Haim Beinart]

CÓRDOBA

(1) Province in Argentina, area 64,894 sq. mi. (168,075 sq. km.); population 1,759,997 (1960). In 1943 Jews were living in 98 out of the 422 communities in the province. Their total number at that time was 7,675 persons. In 1964 there were organized communities affiliated with Va'ad ha-Kehillot (see *Argentina) only in seven cities and towns. The 1960 census indicated the overall Jewish population (above five years of age) in the province to be 8,639 persons, 7,409 of whom lived in the city of Córdoba. Each year large summer camps for the Jewish youth of Argentina are organized in Córdoba. There are also Jewish hotels in many villages. In Unquillo, the Liga Israelita Argentina Contra la Tubeculosis, originally in Buenos Aires, established in 1937 a large sanatorium which was transformed in 1956 into a summer resort for underprivileged children.

(2) Capital of the above province and third largest city in Argentina. Located in the center of the country, Córdoba had in 1960 a population of 589,153. The first Jewish families arrived in Córdoba at the beginning of the 20th century from the Jewish agricultural settlements in *Entre Ríos province. At the same time, the first Sephardi groups arrived from Lebanon, Syria, and Egypt. A census conducted by Jewish Colonization Association (ICA) in 1909 found about 600 Jews in Córdoba, the majority being Ashkenazim and the minority Sephardim. The same year two Ashkenazi *minyanim* and one Sephardi *minyan* were organized for the High Holy Days. A short time later the Ashkenazi community established two *kehillot* which united in 1915 to form the Centro Unión Israelita (Ashkenazi), under the presidency of Jaime Blank. The Sephardi community began to organize in 1917, when they founded the Sociedad Israelita Siria for Jews originating from Arab-speaking countries. In 1923 the Comunidad Israelita de Córdoba was established for Turkish and Greek Jews, and in the same year, with funds contributed by the Niño family, the first Sephardi synagogue was built. Each congregation has its own cemetery. In 1953 the Círculo Sefaradí was established as a social center for all Sephardi congregations of Córdoba. One of the main concerns of the community leaders has been the establishment of Jewish schools. The first Ashkenazi school, according to the annals of the Centro Unión Israelita, dates from 1917. The Sephardi community founded a school shortly after its communal organization began. A report dating from 1943 showed the city to have five supplementary Jewish schools (which gave instruction in Jewish subjects after regular school hours) whose total student enrollment was about 200. From 1944 the Centro Unión Israelita made efforts to improve school attendance by amalgamating the five schools and establishing a central day school. Their efforts finally succeeded in 1950 when the General San Martín school was officially recognized by the educational authorities of Córdoba. The establishment in 1957 of the Asociación Hebraica, which developed a club with sports facilities, has increased the social cohesiveness of the different communities. All Jewish community organizations belong to the local chapter of the *DAIA which, together with the Jewish National Fund, Keren Hayesod, and the youth movements, is housed in the large Centro Unión Israelita building. Originally employed in minor commerce (peddling, lottery tickets, cloth selling) the Jewish community has advanced to employment in the professions and heavy industry.

BIBLIOGRAPHY: J. Hodara, in: *Bi-Tefuẓot ha-Golah* 2, no. 3–4 (1960), 34–40; Centro Unión Israelita de Córdoba, 50 *Años 1915–1965* (1966).

[Joseph Hodara]

CÓRDOBA, ALONSO FERNANDEZ DE (late 15th century), Spanish silversmith, engraver, and typecutter, probably of a Marrano family. Córdoba worked from 1473 in Valencia but after leaving there was condemned to death *in absentia*, possibly on a charge of heresy. He then entered into a contract at Murcia with the Jewish silversmith Solomon Zalmati and the notary Dr. Gabriel Luis Arinyo for the production of the works of Bishop Jaime Perez. The partners were apparently also responsible for the publication of the Saragossan Catholic prayer book, *Manuale Caesaraugustanum* (Hijár, 1486). In this work, there is a beautiful border designed by Córdoba. This is also found in the Hebrew Pentateuch printed by Eliezer Alantansi in conjunction with Zalmati at about the same time. It has been suggested that Córdoba cut the incidental decorations and perhaps the Hebrew type used in the Hijár press.

BIBLIOGRAPHY: J. Bloch, *Early Hebrew Printing in Spain and Portugal* (1938), (=*N.Y. Public Library Bulletin*, May 1938); K. Haebler, *Typographie ibérique du 15e siècle* (1902), 11–12; A. Marx, *Studies in*

Jewish History and Booklore (1944), 293–4, 299–300; Roth, in: JJS, 4 (1953), 116–30.

[Cecil Roth]

CORDOVERO, GEDALIAH BEN MOSES (1562–1625), rabbi and kabbalist; son of Moses *Cordovero, he was born in Safed and after the death of his father, when Gedaliah was eight years of age, he studied under Solomon *Sagis. Before 1584 he was in Italy where he engaged in the book trade. While in Venice he published, with the assistance of Moses *Basola (see *Basilea family) and *Menahem Azariah of Fano, various kabbalistic works of the Safed scholars, including his father's *Perush Seder Avodat Yom ha-Kippurim* and *Or Ne'erav*. It seems that Gedaliah was also active in Italy as a preacher, expounding the imminent redemption; together with Israel *Sarug he was in Modena where they urged the adoption of the Safed customs of rising early to mourn for the destruction of the Temple and to pray for the redemption. Gedaliah went to Jerusalem after 1590 and was appointed chief rabbi of Jerusalem by the authorities, holding the title *Sheikh al-Yahūd* ("Chief of the Jews") until his death. In 1607 a quarrel broke out between him and the Jerusalem scholar, Menahem di *Lonzano, who had assisted him to obtain his high office. As a result of this quarrel, Lonzano was compelled to leave Ereẓ Israel. However after a short time he returned and peace was restored between them. Gedaliah was in Italy from 1609 to 1611 as an emissary of Jerusalem. In 1625 the disturbances during the tenure of office of Ibn Faruk, governor of Jerusalem, imposed a severe strain on Gedaliah in his capacity as chief rabbi and he died while the riots were at their height.

BIBLIOGRAPHY: Frumkin-Rivlin, 1 (1929), 136–8; 2 (1928), 15, 18f., 48; Benayahu, in: *Sinai*, 16 (1945), 82–90; Sonne, in: *Kobez al jad*, 5 (1950), 197–204; Yaari, Shelulḥei, index; Tishby, in: *Sefunot*, 7 (1963), 125f., 132f.

[Abraham David]

CORDOVERO, MOSES BEN JACOB (1522–1570), the outstanding kabbalist in Safed before Isaac *Luria. His birthplace is unknown, but his name testifies to the family's Spanish origins. He was a disciple of Joseph *Caro and of Solomon *Alkabeẓ, and a teacher of Isaac Luria. His first large systematic work is *Pardes Rimmonim*, which Cordovero completed by the age of 27. Ten years later he finished his second systematic book, the *Elimah Rabbati*, and also wrote a lengthy commentary on all the parts of the *Zohar which has been preserved in manuscript in Modena.

The doctrine of Cordovero is a summary and a development of the different trends in Kabbalah up to his time, and his whole work is a major attempt to synthesize and to construct a speculative kabbalistic system. This is done especially in his theology, which is based on the Zohar, and in particular on *Tikkunei Zohar* and *Ra'aya Meheimna*. Since Cordovero considered these texts to be by one and the same author, he felt constrained to harmonize their different and at times even opposing conceptions. Cordovero follows *Tikkunei Zohar* in his conception of God as a transcendent being: God is the First Cause, a Necessary Being, essentially different from any other being. In this concept of God, Cordovero is obviously drawing upon the sources of medieval philosophy (especially Maimonides). In accordance with the philosophers, Cordovero maintains that no positive attribute can apply to the transcendent God. In his opinion, the philosophers had attained an important achievement in purifying the concept of God of its anthropomorphisms. Yet, Cordovero stresses that the essential difference between Kabbalah and philosophy lies in the solution of the problem of the bridge between God and the world. This bridging is made possible by the structure of the *Sefirot* ("Emanations") which emanate from God.

In this way Cordovero tries to unify the concept of God as a transcendent Being with the personal concept. Thus, the central problem of his theology is the relation between *Ein-Sof (the transcendent God) and the question of the nature of the *Sefirot*: are they God's substance or only *kelim* ("instruments" or "vessels")? Cordovero's answer to this question is something of a compromise between the Zohar and *Tikkunei Zohar* – the *Sefirot* are substance and *kelim* at the same time. They are beings emanated outward from God, but His substance is immanent in them. Cordovero describes the *Sefirot* as instruments or tools with which God performs His various activities in the world, and as the vessels containing the Divine substance, which permeates them and gives them life, as the soul gives life to the body. By means of this attitude Cordovero wants to preserve, on the one hand, the concept of the simple and immutable God, and on the other hand to maintain God's providence in the world. Although this providence is sometimes described as a substantial immanence of God through all the worlds, Cordovero has reservations about it. In *Pardes Rimmonim*, a distinction exists between the transcendent God, who undergoes no process, and the light emanated from Him, spreading through the *Sefirot*. This emanated expansion is not of a necessary existence, but is activated by God's spontaneous will. This makes for the involvement of the will in every Divine act – the active God is the God united in His will.

It is quite understandable, therefore, why God's will has such a decisive place in Cordovero's system. Here again, the same question arises: what is the relation between God and His will? Cordovero's answer is dialectic in its character. By itself, the will is an emanation, but it originates from God in a succession of wills which approach God's substance asymptotically.

The process of emanation of the *Sefirot* is described by Cordovero as dialectical. In order to be revealed, God has to conceal Himself. This concealment is in itself the coming into being of the *Sefirot*. Only the *Sefirot* reveal God, and that is why "revealing is the cause of concealment and concealment is the cause of revealing." The process of emanation itself takes place through a constant dynamics of inner aspects inside the *Sefirot*. These aspects form a reflective process inside each *Sefirah*, which reflects itself in its different qualities; these aspects also have a function in the process of emanation, in being the inner grades which derive, each from the other, according to the principle of causation. Only this inner process, which is but a hypostasis of the reflective aspects, enables the emanation of the *Sefirot*, each from the other, as well. These inner processes are of special importance regarding the first *Sefirah* – the will. After the series of wills, which are the aspects of the "*Keter*" ("crown") in the "*Keter*," there appear in "*Ḥokhmah*" ("Wisdom") in the "*Keter*" aspects which express the potential thought of all the not yet actualized Being. Cordovero calls these thoughts: "The kings of Edom who died before the reign of a king in Israel." This idea appears in the Zohar, but Cordovero reverses its meaning. In the Zohar this is a mythological description of the forces of stern judgment (*din*) that were conceived in the Divine Thought, and because of their extreme severity, were abolished and died, whereas according to Cordovero these thoughts were abolished because they did not contain enough judgment (*din*). Cordovero conceives of judgment (*din*) as a necessary condition for the survival of any existence. What is too near to the abundance of God's infinite compassion cannot exist, and therefore the highest thoughts were abolished, so that the *Sefirot* could be formed only when emanation reached the *Sefirah* of *Binah* ("Intelligence"), which already contains judgment (*din*).

The whole world of emanation is built and consolidated by a double process, that of *or yashar* ("direct light") – the emanation downward, and *or ḥozer* ("reflected light") – the reflection of the same process upward. This reflected movement is also the origin of *din*.

The transition from the world of emanation to the lower world is continuous. Thus the problem of creation *ex nihilo* does not exist in relation to our world, but pertains only to the transition from the divine "Nothingness" (*Ayin*) to the first Being – the uppermost aspects of the first *Sefirah*. In spite of Cordovero's attempts to obliterate this transition, his stand is theistic: the first *Sefirah* is outside God's substance. This prohibits any pantheistic interpretation of Cordovero's system. The immanence of the Divine substance in the *Sefirot* and in all worlds is likewise clothed always in the first vessel, even though Cordovero hints several times at a mystical experience in which the immanence of God Himself in the world is revealed. In this esoteric meaning, Cordovero's system may, perhaps, be defined as pantheistic.

In addition to his two principal systematic books, *Pardes Rimmonim* (Cracow, 1592) and *Elimah Rabbati* (Lvov, 1881), the following parts of his commentary to the Zohar were published separately: the introduction to the commentary on the *Idras* in the Zohar, *Shi'ur Komah* (Warsaw, 1883); and an introduction to the Zohar "Song of Songs," *Derishot be-Inyanei Malakhim* (Jerusalem, 1945). Publication of the complete commentary has been begun in Jerusalem. Two volumes of the commentary had appeared by 1968.

Other published works are *Or Ne'erav* (Venice, 1587); *Sefer Gerushin* (Venice, c. 1602); *Tefillah le-Moshe* (Przemysl, 1892); *Zivḥei Shelamim* (Lublin, 1613), *Perush Seder Avodat Yom ha-Kippurim* (Venice, 1587); *Tomer Devorah* (Venice, 1589; tr. L. Jacobs, *Palmtree of Deborah*, 1960). In this work Cordovero laid the foundations for kabbalistic ethical literature, which proliferated in the 16th–18th centuries. In its short chapters he instructed every Jew in the right way to follow in order to come close and identify spiritually with each of the ten *Sefirot*. This short treatise influenced many later kabbalistic moralists in Safed and Eastern Europe. There are two existing abridgments of *Pardes Rimmonim: Pelaḥ ha-Rimmon* (Venice, 1600) by Menahem Azariah of *Fano, and *Asis Rimmonim* (Venice, 1601) by Samuel Gallico.

BIBLIOGRAPHY: S.A. Horodezky, *Torat ha-Kabbalah shel Rabbi Moshe… Cordovero* (1924); J. Ben-Shlomo, *Torat ha-Elohut shel Rabbi Moshe Cordovero* (1965).

[Joseph Ben-Shlomo]

CORFU, Greek island, the second largest of the Ionian group. The town of the same name is the largest on the island. *Benjamin of Tudela, in c. 1160, found only one Jew in Corfu. The number of Jews increased during the 13th and 14th centuries with the arrival of newcomers from the mainland. The Jews on the island were subject to violent attacks and persecution; they were forced to row on the galleys, to provide lodging for soldiers, were summoned to the law courts on Sabbaths and festivals, and as elsewhere in the Byzantine orbit had to act as public executioners. From time to time the authorities were forced to publish defense orders to protect them from the hostility of the general population. When Corfu surrendered to Venice (1386), the deputation of six persons sent to arrange the terms included the Jew David Semo. A decree of 1387 reaffirmed the previous rights of Jews under Byzantine rule, but in 1406 they were forbidden to acquire land and were ordered to wear a distinguishing *badge. Jewish women had to wear yellow veils. In 1408 they were forbidden to own land worth 2,000 ducats, later increased to over 4,000 ducats. The Venetian authorities frequently imposed heavy taxes on the Jewish community in order to finance the wars against the Turks. On the other hand, the Jews sometimes gave voluntary contributions and assisted in the fortification of the walls. The Jews lived at first in two streets between the Old Town and the fortress. When this area was included in the new fortifications, the two Jewish areas were eliminated and the Jews were scattered for a while throughout the city, but in 1622 they were confined to a ghetto. Despite these restrictions, the Venetian authorities were more liberal toward the Jews of Corfu than they were toward the Jews of Venice itself.

During the 16th century there were two congregations in Corfu, that of the *Romaniots who preserved the ancient Byzantine rite (known as *Minhag Korfu*), and that of the Italians. In the course of time the Italian community was enlarged by Jews from Apulia, Spanish exiles, Portuguese Marranos, and Ashkenazim, who ultimately adopted the Sephardi rite. The eminent Sephardi Spanish courtier and religious scholar Don Isaac *Abravanel stayed in Corfu for a short time in 1594, finished his commentary on Deuteronomy, was depressed at the state of the spiritual deterioration of Spanish Jewish exiles, and continued to Naples to reunite with his wife and other close family members. Relations between the two communities did not always run smoothly. The Romaniot community enjoyed special privileges and objected to the right of permanent residence being granted to the Italians. Between 1662 and 1664 all Jews in Corfu received equal status. Each of the communities had two "overseers" (*syndikoi*), two *kashrut* supervisors, and two *parnasim*. In 1563 the traveler Elijah of Pesaro reported that the Italians constituted the majority of the Jewish colony in Corfu. They imposed their language on all the Jews of the island, most of whom spoke the Apulian dialect interlaced with Greek words.

In 1522 there were about 200 Jewish householders; in 1558, about 400; and in 1663, 500. The Jews of Corfu engaged in dyeing, leather tanning, moneylending, trading, and the brokerage of goods between Venice and the Levant. The Jewish merchants of Corfu were granted privileges not granted to those of Venice itself. A New Testament in Judeo-Spanish was printed in Corfu in 1829, no doubt for missionary purposes. Hebrew printing by Jews began in 1853 and continued until 1896. Of 14 items published, 13 were by Joseph Nahamuli, who also supplied a Greek translation to some of the liturgical items. From 1861 to 1863, he published the Greek/Italian bilingual *Chronica Israelitika*. When in 1716 the Turks besieged Corfu, the Jews distinguished themselves in the defense of the island. The loyalty of the Jews of Corfu to the Venetian government lasted until Venetian rule ended in 1797. Under French rule of Corfu (1797–99 and 1806–15) Jews had equal rights with other citizens, and the community's rabbi enjoyed the same privileges as the religious heads of the other communities. Their condition deteriorated under British rule (1815–64); they were excluded from public office and disenfranchised, and Jewish lawyers were forbidden to plead in court. Judah *Bibas, known for his support of the ideal of the return to Zion and of the Haskalah movement, was rabbi of Corfu from 1831. He defended the regional *etrog* growers in Aya, Parga, and Rapeza in light of insinuations of non-kosher grafting by East European *etrog* importer Rabbi Eleazar Ziskind Mintz of Brody in the work *Pri Etz Hadar* (Lemberg, 1846). Rabbi Ephraim Zalman Margulies (1760–1828) of Galicia had previously defended the Corfu *etrogim*. From the late 1840s and in the 1850s, a small group of Corfiote Jewish cotton merchants settled in Manchester, attracted by its commercial and industrial growth, and were among the founders of the Cheetham Hill Road Sha'are Tefilla Spanish and Portuguese synagogue in 1873. The eminent Rabbi Israel Moses *Hazzan of Izmir succeeded Bibas and served from 1853 to 1857 before moving to Alexandria, Egypt. In 1855 the Jewish community comprised 4,000 persons and was visited by the philanthropist Sir Moses *Montefiore of England. In 1863, the Jewish community numbered 6,000, 9.23% of the local population. The local population maintained their old prejudice, and when equal rights were restored to the Jews upon the island's annexation to the kingdom of Greece in 1864, riots broke out, causing a large exodus of Jews to Greece and Italy. Despite, local Greek-Orthodox hostility toward the local Jews, the latter had significant political weight in the city of Corfu. Numerous Jews who worked as lawyers and notaries enjoyed a high public profile. Councilman and international olive oil merchant Eliias da Mordo was appointed as deputy mayor, and in 1870 he was elected mayor. In 1891, when the Jewish population of 5,000 still lived in their own quarter, a *blood libel caused a storm on the island and throughout Greece and brought in its train large-scale emigration. The ensuing riots lasted three weeks and some 22 Jews died. Foreign ships were sent to the island to quell the disturbances in light of the apathetic attitude of the Greek authorities. From then on the Jewish community waned; many Jews emigrated to Trieste and Alexandria, Egypt. The local Alliance Israélite Universelle representative, the philologist Lazaros Belleli, represented the Jewish community at the subsequent trial, which ended in a mockery in light of the acquittal of the perpetrators. Belleli did not find his place in academia in Greece and eventually migrated to London, where he became a professor of linguistics. The French novelist Albert *Cohen grew up in Corfu in the early 1890s and depicted the picturesque Jews of the island in many of his works. In 1897, the journalist and Jewish community leader Moïse *Caimis started the Zionist organization Mevasser Zion and from 1899 to 1901 edited the Zionist organ *Israelite Chronographos*. Under the influence of the Russian Hebrew teacher Bezalel Davidson, who passed through the island in 1906, the Zionist society Mekkitz Nirdamim was formed. In 1913, Haim S. Mizrahi formed the Zionist organization Tikvat Zion and in 1924 a new group, called Theodor Herzl, was formed and it eventually affiliated with the Zionist Revisionist movement. In World War I, the community suffered another blood libel with rioting mobs, but there were no casualties and the authorities assisted in the quelling of the disturbances. In 1923 about 3,000 Jews lived on the island, most of them small tradesmen who struggled to earn a livelihood. There were four synagogues in the town of Corfu all now following the Sephardi rite: the Greek synagogue, the Apulian, the Apulian-Spanish, and the Apulian *minyan*. In 1932, after Rabbi Judah Nehama failed to persuade members of the Italian Hevra to accept leadership positions in the Jewish community administration, since they refused to accept the authority of the Greek Hevra, the Supreme Court in Athens ruled that each Hevra would remain separate from the communal organization. On the eve of World War II the community numbered 2,000. During the occupation by the Italians (1941–43) there was relative quiet. The Germans occupied the island on September 27, 1943. On June 14, 1944, 1,800 Jews were deported to Auschwitz. By 1948, the number of Jews in Corfu was reduced to 170, in 1968 to 92. In the early 21st century fewer than 50 Jews remained, and only one of the four synagogues.

BIBLIOGRAPHY: C. Roth, *Venice* (1930), index; Romanos, in: REJ, 23 (1891), 63–74; Kaufmann, *ibid.*, 32 (1896), 226–34; 33 (1896), 64–76, 219–32; 34 (1897), 203–75; M. Horovitz, *Korfu* (1891); L.A. Schiavi, *Gli ebrei in Venezia e nelle sue colonie* (1893), 309–33; S.W. Baron, in: *Kovez Madda'i le-Zekher Moshe Schorr* 1944, 25–41; idem, in: *Joshua Starr Memorial Volume* (1953), 169–82. **ADD. BIBLIOGRAPHY:** B. Rivlin, "Corfu," in: *Pinkas Kehillot Yavan* (1999), 353–70; Y. Kerem, *History of the Jews in Greece 1821–1940,* Part I (1984), 415–94; P.L. Preschel, "The Jews of Corfu" (Diss., New York University, 1984).

[Simon Marcus / Yitzchak Kerem (2nd ed.)]

CORI, GERTY THERESA (née **Radnitz**; 1896–1957), Nobel laureate in medicine and physiology. Cori was born in Prague, where she graduated in medicine from the German University in 1920. That year she married her fellow student and lifelong scientific collaborator, Carl Cori, and converted to Catholicism from Judaism. The Coris joined the staff of the New York State Institute for the Study of Malignant Disease in Buffalo, New York (1922–31), before moving to Washington University, St. Louis, in 1931 where she was professor of biochemistry from 1947 until her death. The Coris became U.S. citizens in 1928. They were awarded the Nobel Prize in 1947 (shared with Bernardo Houssay) for their work on carbohydrate metabolism in which they discovered how glucose is stored as glycogen in the liver and muscles, and broken down to glucose as an energy source (a process termed the Cori cycle). They also described the effects of insulin and other hormones on glucose metabolism. The Coris' honors included election to the U.S. National Academy of Sciences.

[Michael Denman (2nd ed.)]

CORIANDER, plant called *gad* in the Bible and *kusbar* in the Mishnah and the Targum Pseudo-Jonathan. The *manna is described as being "like coriander seed, white" (Ex. 16:31), and "like coriander seed, and in color it was like bdellium" (Num. 11:7). Rashi stresses that the comparison is "in respect of the roundness" and not of the color of coriander, which is not white. It is the *Coriandrum sativum*, an annual plant of the Umbelliferae family; it has white flowers arranged in umbels and globular beige or brown fruit, and its leaves and fruit are used as a spice. It grows wild in the Judean mountains but not in Galilee, which explains the statement of the Talmud that the inhabitants used to mock the Galileans for setting such high store upon coriander (*kusbar*), saying: "*Kusbar, kusbarta*, who classed you among the spices?" (TJ, Dem. 1:1, 21d). Since its seed has a pungent taste, it was used for adulterating pepper (Tosef., BB 5:6). The eating of coriander was regarded as ensuring "fleshy children" (Ket. 61a).

BIBLIOGRAPHY: J. Feliks, *Olam ha-Ẓome'aḥ ha-Mikra'i* (1957), 180; idem, *Kilei Zera'im ve-Harkavah* (1967), 62f.; Loew, Flora, 3 (1924), 441f.

[Jehuda Feliks]

CORIAT, family of scholars originating in Marrakesh. The first known member was ISAAC (1) CORIAT (1580), *dayyan* of the community, kabbalist, and the author of works of which only fragments, published in the writings of his descendants, have survived. SOLOMON edited the *Azharot of Isaac b. Reuben *al-Bargeloni (Leghorn, 1650). The pious and learned ABRAHAM (1) settled in Tetuán, where his son JUDAH (1; d. 1788) was *dayyan*. Those of his works which survived the sack of the city in 1790 were published in a collection under the titles *Tofaḥ Saviv*, a selection of his father's religious decisions, and *Nofekh Sappir* (Pisa, 1812). His son ISAAC (2; d. Jerusalem, 1805) was the author of *Ma'aseh Rokem* (Pisa, 1806), containing (1) novellae on *Kiddushin* by Asher b. Jehiel (ha-Rosh), entitled *Simḥah La-Ẓaddik*; (2) his own commentary on *Kiddushin*, entitled *Paḥad Yiẓhak*; (3) his commentary on *Bava Meẓi'a*, entitled *Ma'aseh Nissim*. Judah's second son ABRAHAM (2; d. 1806) was *dayyan* at Tetuán, Mogador, Gibraltar, and Leghorn. His work *Zekhut Avot* (Pisa, 1812) contains information on the Jews of Morocco and Leghorn. Abraham's son JUDAH (2; d. 1787 in Tetuán) wrote *Ma'or ve-Shemesh* (Leghorn, 1838), a collection of extracts of various kabbalistic works, including some of the novellae written by his maternal grandfather, Judah (Abenatar) *Attar, rabbi of Fez. ABRAHAM (3), son of Judah (2), was *av bet din* in Mogador, where his poems and liturgical songs were destroyed during the bombardment of the city in 1844. He also wrote sermons and responsa, published under the title *Berit Avot* (1848). The son of Abraham (3), ISAAC (3; d. 1905), merchant, philanthropist, and scholar, wrote *Naḥalat Avot* (1899) on various religious questions and on the practices and customs of the Mogador community. NISSIM, son of Isaac (3), represented Holland at the court of the sultan at Marrakesh at the beginning of the 20th century. SAMUEL CORIAT (d. 1853) was farmer-general of revenues and government treasurer in Tetuán. He played an important role in the economic life of Morocco from 1818 as purveyor to the sultan. His nephew ISAAC (d. 1890) settled in Mogador in 1862 on the instructions of the government, and he became one of the five merchants of the sultan. Isaac distinguished himself during the Spanish-Moroccan war of 1859–60 by his devotion to public welfare.

BIBLIOGRAPHY: Benjacob, Oẓar, 33, no. 635d.; J.M. Toledano, *Ner ha-Ma'arav* (1911), 104, 107, 192, 200–1; J. Ben-Naim, *Malkhei Rabbanan* (1931), 9b, 45a, 75a; C. Didier, *Promenade au Maroc* (1844), 149–50; I. Benwalid, *Va-Yomer Yiẓḥak*, 2 (Leghorn, 1855), nos. 151, 153; Miège, Maroc, 2 (1961), 107, 140, 560; 3 (1962), 35; 4 (1963), 210.

[David Corcos]

CORINTH, Greek city. The earliest evidence of Jews in Corinth is contained in Agrippa I's letter to Caligula (Philo, *De Legatione ad Caium*, 281). The apostle Paul spent one and a half years in Corinth, preaching in the synagogue on Sabbaths (cf. the two Epistles to the Corinthians), and through his influence Crispus and his family were baptized. The Jews were embittered by Paul's activities; they brought him before Gallio, procurator of Achea, who, refusing to judge in a religious matter, said they would have to resolve their differences themselves (Acts 18:2ff.). Corinthian Jewry apparently belonged to the lower classes. Aquila and Priscilla, with whom Paul dwelt, were weavers, and he worked with them for his bread. These Jews went to Corinth from Rome when Claudius expelled the Jews from the city. There were no direct links between the Jews of Corinth and Ereẓ Israel, but

Corinthian products were known in the Holy Land. Josephus (Wars, 5:201) mentions the Corinthian copper that coated one of the Temple gates, the Gate of Nicanor (whose special copper is also noted in talmudic sources, Tosef., Yoma 2:4; Yoma 38a), and he similarly mentions the Corinthian candelabra in Agrippa II's house (Life, 68). Vespasian, after his victory in Galilee, sent 6,000 captive youths to Nero to dig at the Isthmus of Corinth (Wars, 3: 540). Conceivably, some of them might have escaped and found haven in the nearby settlements including Corinth.

[Lea Roth]

When the Visigoths invaded Corinth in 395 the Jews moved to the neighboring island of Aegina. Jews suffered persecution by the Byzantine emperors during the 9th and 10th centuries. Roger II, the Norman king of Sicily, brought Jewish dyers from Corinth to Sicily in 1147, thereby founding the Sicilian silk industry. The 12th-century traveler Benjamin of Tudela found 300 Jews there; they were silk-weavers. The Corinth community existed during the 13th and 14th centuries, but it seems to have disappeared in later years. In 1923 the Jewish community of Corinth again consisted of 400 persons, but ended during World War II.

[Simon Marcus]

BIBLIOGRAPHY: Schuerer, Gesch, 3 (1909), 55–56.

CORNEA, PAUL (Cohn; 1924–), Romanian literary historian and theoretician. After a short period in politics as a young Communist intellectual, Cornea devoted himself to an academic career and became one of the most important historians of Romanian literature and a specialist in comparative literature of international reputation. He wrote such important studies of Romanian romanticism as *Originile romantismului românesc* ("The Origin of Romanian Romanticism," 1972) and *Oamenii începutului de drum* ("The Men at the Beginning of the Road," 1974) as well as theoretical studies such as *Introducere în teoria lecturii* ("Introduction to the Theory of Reading," 1988).

BIBLIOGRAPHY: A. Mirodan, *Dicționar neconvențional al scriitorilor evrei de limbă română*, 1 (1986), 384–94; *Dicționar general al literaturii române*, 2 (2004), 386–98.

[Leon Volovici (2nd ed.)]

°**CORNILL, CARL HEINRICH** (1854–1920), German Protestant Bible critic. Cornill taught at Marburg (1877–86), Koenigsberg (1888–98), Breslau (1898–1910), and Halle (1910–20). In 1880 Cornill published his first important work *Jeremiah und seine Zeit*, which became the basis of his commentary on the book of Jeremiah published in 1905. He also wrote a commentary on Ezekiel (1886). His account of Israel's prophets (*Der israelitische Prophetismus*, 1894, 1920[13]; *The Prophets of Israel*, 1895) and history of Israel (*Geschichte des Volkes Israel*…, 1898; *History of the People of Israel*, 1898) were pioneering works in their day. Cornill is remembered principally for his *Einleitung in das Alte Testament* (1895, 1905[5]; *Introduction to the Canonical Books of the Old Testament*, 1907), the first important critical introduction to the Bible based on the literary and historical approach of the J. *Wellhausen and K.H. *Graf school of biblical criticism.

ADD. BIBLIOGRAPHY: R. Smend, in: DBI I, 227.

[Zev Garber]

CORO, colonial city of Venezuela whose streets still preserve the characteristics of the epoch. It is the capital of the Falcón State, with a population of 244,341 inhabitants (2004). The city was recognized by UNESCO as a Cultural Patrimony of Humanity in 1993. It is considered the cradle of the Venezuelan Jewish community.

Even though the government of Nueva Granada bestowed upon the members of the *Nación Hebrea* the right to settle in the country in 1819, granting them their religious freedom, it was not until the years 1823–24 that the first Jews from Curaçao started to strike roots in Coro. David Hoheb and Joseph Curiel were soon followed by the families Senior, Henríquez, Capriles, Dovale, Maduro, López Fonseca, DeLima, Correa, Castro, Da Costa, and others. All of them were of Sephardi origin and maintained intensive commercial ties with Curaçao and the West Indies.

The almost immediate economic success of this group aroused the envy and jealousy of the inhabitants of Coro, causing a wave of anti-Jewish outbursts in 1831 and a spree of riots, looting, and destruction of businesses and homes in 1855. Terrified, 168 Jews fled to Curaçao and made a claim against Venezuela demanding indemnity and the punishment of the guilty. Following an arrangement, they returned to Coro in 1859 and continued their activities in import-export and finances, achieving a high level of economic success and participation in the public and political life of the city, which helped bring about important changes in the region. Gradually the Jews became prominent in science, public health, journalism, finances, politics, and culture. Most of these Jews were Freemasons and Liberals. David *Curiel was among the founders of the first Masonic lodge in Coro.

By the end of the 19th century, however, the absence of a spiritual leader, intermarriage, the loss of liturgical elements and of the Hebrew language, and the assimilation of symbols of Catholic religiosity contributed to the erosion of group's identity. As a testimony to this prosperous community there remains in Coro a small room, restored in 1997, where Jewish worship was celebrated from the middle of the 19th century, and the cemetery that was founded in 1830 and is still in use. It was restored twice, in 1945 and 1970, and contains 175 graves. The first belongs to Haná Curiel, an eight-year-old girl who died in 1832, and the last to Sara Celinda López Fonseca, buried in April 2000. The cemetery, with its Angels' Corner, manifests unequivocally a process of cultural transference. Due to its exceptional characteristics, the municipal and regional authorities granted it the status of Cultural Patrimony in 2003, and in 2004 it was declared a Historic Monument of the Falcón State.

In homage to Elías David Curiel (1871–1924), one of the greatest *falconian* poets, the Elías David Curiel Biennial of Literature has been celebrated since 1998. Alberto Henríquez (1919–1990) collected in his residence valuable paintings and artistic objects which he bequeathed to the Miranda University and which are exhibited in the museum and gallery that bear his name. The Fundación del Patrimonio Cultural Hebreo Falconiano preserves the Sephardi cultural heritage and maintains the Salomón Levi Maduro Vaz Library. Of this first community established in Venezuela, the brothers Herman and Thelma Henríquez were the only two Jews living in Coro in 2004.

BIBLIOGRAPHY: I. Aizemberg, *La Comunidad Judía de Coro 1824–1900. Una Historia* (1983); J.R. Fortique, *Los Motines Anti-Judíos de Coro* (1973); J. Carciente, *Presencia Sefardí en la Historia de Venezuela* (1997); B. de Lima. *Coro: Fin de Diáspora* (2002).

[Jacob Carciente (2nd ed.)]

CORONEL, NAḤMAN NATHAN (1810–1890), talmudic scholar, author, and bibliographer. Coronel was born in Amsterdam where he studied at the Etz Haim yeshivah. At the age of 20 he immigrated to Ereẓ Israel and settled first in Jerusalem and later in Safed, where he suffered from the looting of 1834, the earthquake of 1837, and the Druze revolt. He thereupon returned to Jerusalem, where he became active in communal affairs. He was one of the few to support the establishment of the Laemel School, the first modern school in Jerusalem, as well as of the Battei Maḥaseh founded in 1859 to enable Jews from abroad to spend their last years in Jerusalem. He served also as an emissary of Jerusalem in Europe. Coronel became interested in acquiring manuscripts and gained world-wide renown as a bibliographer. While in Vienna in 1872, he exchanged manuscripts with the emperor Francis Joseph, from whom he received a decoration. He sold many manuscripts to various libraries and published others, among them: *Beit Natan*, comprising variant readings of *Berakhot* (Vienna, 1854); *Ḥamishah Kunteresim (ibid.*, 1864); *Seder Rav Amram Ga'on* (Warsaw, 1865; repr. 1956); *Teshuvot ha-Ge'onim* (Vienna, 1871); *Piskei Ḥallah* by Solomon b. Abraham *Adret (Jerusalem, 1876); and *Alfasi Zuta*, on *Berakhot*, by Menahem Azariah da *Fano (*ibid.*, 1885). His own works comprise *Zekher Natan*, a compilation of religious laws for travelers (Vienna, 1872) and *Ḥakor Davar* on the law of *ḥallah* outside *Ereẓ Israel* (Vienna, 1871).

BIBLIOGRAPHY: N. Sokolow, *Sefer Zikkaron…* (1889), 186ff.; *Ha-Asif* (1893), 139 (first pagination); Frumkin-Rivlin, 3 (1929), 271, no. 46; Back, in: *Talpioth*, 7 (1961), 484ff.; 8 (1962), 215ff., 626ff.

[Itzhak Alfassi]

CORONEL CHACON, SIR AUGUSTIN (c. 1600–1665), Marrano merchant. Born in Portugal, Coronel settled first in Bordeaux (1630–33), then in Rouen, and finally in London, where he acted as financial agent for the exiled Charles II. He was known on the Royal Exchange as the "little Jue," though it is doubtful whether he was circumcised or became a member of the later Jewish community. After the Restoration he acted as a Portuguese agent and is said to have first proposed the marriage of Charles II and Catherine of Braganza, for which he was knighted, having by now severed his Jewish connections. Subsequently he became bankrupt and was expelled from the Exchange. After a term of imprisonment he left England. His place of death is unknown. His widow was supported by the London Jewish community.

BIBLIOGRAPHY: JHSET, 1 (1893–94), 70–75; 5 (1902–05), 16–18; 14 (1935–39), 60–61; L.D. Barnett, *Bevis Marks Records*, 1 (1940), 7; A.M. Hyamson, *Sephardim of England* (1951), 21–22, 58.

[Cecil Roth]

CORREA, ISABEL (Rebecca) DE (c. 1650), Dutch Sephardi poetess. Born in Portugal, she lived in Flanders and later in Amsterdam. She was the second wife of Nicolas (Daniel Judah) de *Oliver y Fullana, the Majorcan author and cartographer, who reverted to Judaism. The poet *Barrios described her as being "as celebrated for her beauty as for her wit." Isabel Correa is remembered as the translator of Guarini's *Pastor Fido* (1694) into Spanish, an enterprise that apart from its literary value is a mirror of feminine writing.

BIBLIOGRAPHY: Kayserling, Bibl, 39; Brugmans-Frank, 455; Roth, Marranos, 335, 337; Scholberg, in: JQR, 53 (1962/63), 145f. F. López Estrada, in: *Hommage à Robert Jammes* I-III (1994), 739–53.

[Kenneth R. Scholberg / Harm den Boer (2nd ed.)]

CORSICA, Mediterranean island. Corsica is the only major Mediterranean island without a Jewish settlement either in ancient or in medieval times. "King" Theodore, the German adventurer who temporarily established his rule in Corsica in 1736, invited Jews and Protestants to settle under his protection, and among the accusations made against him was that he was addicted to magic and the Kabbalah and had induced Jews and Greeks to settle in his kingdom. When in 1757–68 General Paoli set up an independent Corsican regime, he attempted to encourage the settlement of Jews from Leghorn by promising them naturalization and autonomy. At the end of the 19th century a few families settled in Bastia and established a small community that maintained a stable population of up to 150 through the second half of the 20th century.

BIBLIOGRAPHY: C. Roth, *Essays and Portraits in Anglo-Jewish History* (1962), 152ff.

[Cecil Roth]

CORUNNA (Sp. **La Coruña, Coruniya**), Atlantic seaport in N.W. Spain. Fragments of tombstones found in Corunna show that Jews lived there in the 11th and 12th centuries. A street called Sinagoga is still to be found in Corunna. The Jewish community evidently began to expand in the 15th century along with other centers in northern Castile as Jews moved there from the south. The Jews of Corunna engaged in maritime trade with Castilian and Aragonese ports. In 1451 the community contributed 300 gold pieces toward ransoming a Jew of Murcia who had been taken captive. A tax of 1,800 maravedis was collected from the community in Corunna and others in the vicinity in 1474 by Jacob Aben Nuñez. One of the most beautiful illuminated Hebrew manuscripts in existence, the so-called Kennicott Bible in the Bodleian Library, Oxford, was completed in Corunna, for Isaac, son of Don Solomon de Braga, in 1486. The Corunna community apparently flourished until the expulsion of the Jews from Spain in 1492.

BIBLIOGRAPHY: H. Beinart, in: *Sefunot*, 5 (1962), 80, 90; C. Roth, *Gleanings* (1967), 316–9; I. Loeb, in: REJ, 6 (1883), 118–9; Cantera-Millás, Inscripciones, 31ff.; Suárez Fernández, Documentos, index.

[Haim Beinart]

CORVÉE, forced labor imposed by a conqueror on the conquered, or by a government on the citizens under its jurisdiction. Corvée labor is one of the most obvious features of the centralism in ancient Near Eastern states; it manifests itself in vast building projects requiring the labor of large forces of manpower over lengthy periods. The type of labor differed from place to place and from period to period. Various terms indicative of this function are also to be found in the context of landownership, occupations, conditions of tenancy, etc. Women as well as men could be drafted for forced labor, and even animals were requisitioned for some purposes. On the other hand, certain individuals, members of certain crafts, and various social strata and settlements might be exempted from the corvée, as a personal or collective privilege.

The diversity in the forms, terminology, and origins of the corvée is likewise reflected in the biblical text. Three separate terms are used, but they are sometimes juxtaposed, a sign that the original distinctions have become blurred (see Ex. 1:11–12): (1) *mas oved* (Gen. 49:10; Josh 16:10, etc.; "compulsory labor"), and sometimes *mas* alone (e.g., I Kings 4:6; 5:27). This expression is derived from Canaanite *massu*, "corvée worker," attested at *El-Amarna and *Alalakh. A Hebrew seal dating from the seventh century B.C.E. reads "belonging to Pelaiah who is in charge of the *mas*." (2) *sevel* (= Akk. *sablum*), a term found in the Mari documents (18th century B.C.E.). Its particularized meaning is a labor unit for emergency use. It appears three times in the Bible, I Kings 11:28; Psalms 81:7; and Nehemiah 4:11. Cognate nouns from the same stem are also found in scripture: *sivlot* ("burdens": Ex. 1:11; 2:11; 5:4–5; 6:6–7); *sabbal* ("burden-bearer": I Kings 5:29; II Chron. 2:1, 17; 34:13); *subbolo* ("his burden": Isa. 9:3; 10:27; 14:25). (3) *perekh*, sometimes said to be a term, Mesopotamian by origin, for forced labor; but its general meaning in the Bible seems to be "harshness" or "ruthlessness" (Ex. 1:11–12; Lev. 25:43, 46; Ezek. 34:4). The children of Israel became familiar with corvée labor (Ex. 1:11, et al.) in the course of their wanderings, inasmuch as the slavery in Egypt was a prolonged period of compulsory labor. During the Israelite conquest corvée labor was one of the indications of the nature of relations between the Canaanite population. According to the biblical account, sometimes the Israelites were tributaries of the Canaanites and sometimes the position was reversed (Gen. 49:15; Judg. 1:33, et al.). There are those who think that by compelling the Gibeonites to become "hewers of wood and drawers of water" (Josh. 9:21) Joshua was in fact imposing on them corvée labor. Corvée labor became a permanent institution only in the period of the monarchy. According to II Samuel 20:24, the minister who was "over the levy" was one of the highest officials in David's regime. It seems that he was a foreigner, attached to the royal staff for his expertise. The same official served Solomon and Rehoboam (I Kings 4:6; 12:18; II Chron. 10:18). Possibly, at first, only foreign elements in the country were obliged to submit to corvée labor (I Kings 9:20–22; II Chron. 8:7–9); only later was Solomon forced to demand compulsory labor from the population to carry out the vast building projects he had undertaken. Some scholars have supposed that *mas oved* was the term applied when foreign manpower was used and that *sevel* was indicative of an Israelite labor force. Yet such a distinction is not sufficiently evident, even if the corvée imposed by Solomon upon the tribes of the House of Joseph was called *sevel* (I Kings 11:28). Mendelsohn suggested that *mas* (or *sevel*) was the corvée exacted for short periods from freemen. According to his view, the term *mas oved* means "state slavery." The Bible states that Solomon sent thirty thousand men to hew cedars in Lebanon for the building of the Temple, in monthly shifts of ten thousand (I Kings 5:26–28). Similarly, he had at his disposal some seventy thousand "corvée workers" and eighty thousand "hewers in the mountains" (I Kings 5:29ff.). There is a hint of the continuation of the corvée tradition in the reign of Asa (I Kings 15:22). Asa built Geba Benjamin with stones taken by his subjects from Ramah: "Then King Asa made a proclamation unto all Judah; none was exempted…." (i.e., none could refuse the corvée). According to II Chronicles 34:13, King Josiah repaired the Temple with the labor of *sabbalim* ("corvée workers"). There was also corvée labor during the period of the return to Zion. The wall around Jerusalem was built by corvée laborers (Neh. 4:11).

BIBLIOGRAPHY: Artzi, in: BIES, 18 (1954), 66–70; Biram, in: *Tarbiz*, 23 (1951/52), 127–42; Maisler (Mazar), in: BJPES, 13 (1947), 105–14; Evans, in: *Revue d'Assyriologie*, 57 (1963), 65–78; Mendelsohn, in: BASOR, 167 (1962), 31ff.; J. Nougayrol, *Le palais royal d'Ugarit*, 3 (1955), index; Oppenheim, in: JQR, 36 (1945/46), 171 ff.; de Vaux, Anc Isr, 126–7, 138–40, 218–20; Held, in: JAOS, 88 (1968), 90–96. **ADD. BIBLIOGRAPHY:** M. Powell (ed.), *Labor in the Ancient Near East* (1987); CAD M/I I: 327; S. Ahituv, *Handbook of Ancient Hebrew Inscriptions* (1992), 126; S.D. Sperling, *The Original Torah* (1998), 54–56.

[Hanoch Reviv]

CORWIN, NORMAN LEWIS (1910–), U.S. radio and film writer, director, and producer. Corwin, who was born in Boston, first achieved prominence in the 1930s with dramatic scripts for CBS radio. His highly experimental programs in the series "Columbia Workshop" and "Columbia Presents

Corwin", many of them proclaiming the menace of Fascism, blazed a trail in radio script writing. His style gave his work a literary distinction new to radio, while his production technique had a vast influence on broadcasting both in the United States and in Great Britain. Some of his scripts were collected in *Thirteen by Corwin* (1942) and *More by Corwin* (1944). His most famous radio play was *On a Note of Triumph* (1945), written to celebrate the Allied victory in World War II. In 1949 he joined the United Nations as chief of special projects in radio and later went to Hollywood to write film scripts. He wrote and directed the Broadway productions of *The Rivalry* (1959), a documentary drama based on the Lincoln-Douglas debates over slavery and national unity, and *The World of Carl Sandburg* (1961), a dramatic mélange of the poems and sayings of the American poet.

[Jo Ranson]

COSAŞU, RADU (Oscar Rohrlich; 1930–), Romanian writer and journalist. Cosaşu drew attention with his novels *A înţelege sau nu* ("To Understand or Not," 1965), surveying Romanian society from the bourgeoisie to the Communists immediately after the Nazi defeat, and *Maimuţele personale* ("Private Monkeys," 1968), which deals with illusion and reality. From the early 1980s, he was recognized as one of the Romania's most important novelists. One of his most favorite themes is the decline of Communist and utopian illusions, especially among Jewish families, as in *Meseria de nuvelist* ("Novelist by Profession," 1980) and *Supravieţuirile* ("Surviving," 3 vols., 2002–5). The milieu of Romanian Jews who settled in Israel is described with a sympathetic irony in *Mătuşile din Tel Aviv* ("The Aunts from Tel Aviv," 1993).

BIBLIOGRAPHY: A. Mirodan, *Dicţionar neconvenţional al scriitorilor evrei de limbă română*, 1 (1986), 396–409; Dicţionarul *general al literaturii române*, 2 (2004), 393–95.

[Leon Volovici (2nd ed.)]

COSELL, HOWARD (Howard William Cohen; 1920–1995) U.S. sportscaster, commentator for ABC's "Monday Night Football" from 1970 to 1983; one of the most outspoken, colorful, and controversial national sports reporters and personalities in American broadcasting history. Cosell was born in Winston-Salem, North Carolina. His father had arrived in the United States from Lodz as a child and his mother was born in Worcester, Massachusetts, the daughter of a rabbi. After serving as an army major in World War II and a lawyer in New York City, Cosell joined ABC as a radio sports reporter in 1956 and first gained national attention in 1959 with his commentaries on world heavyweight fights, and then for his work on ABC's *Wide World of Sports*. But it was Cosell's relationship and interviews with the heavyweight champion Cassius Clay in the 1960s that thrust the sportscaster to the center of racial controversy in the United States. Cosell was the first person to use publicly the champion's black Muslim name Muhammad Ali, and in 1967 he vigorously defended him against charges of draft evasion. Cosell's meteoric rise as a sports journalist paralleled the equally meteoric career of Ali, as Cosell was the broadcast commentator for every one of Ali's fights in the 1960s and 1970s. But in the emotion-charged era of the Vietnam War and civil rights agitation, the relationship between the provocative black from Kentucky and the equally forthright Jewish lawyer from New York evoked a storm of protest and expressions of antisemitism, with many demanding that Cosell be fired. "I've been more vilified than [mass murderer] Charles Manson or Richard Nixon," he said.

In 1970, Cosell was hired to launch an innovative venture in television, the broadcasting of football in prime time, and the overwhelming success establishing "Monday Night Football" as an American tradition was attributed in large part to Cosell. Considered candid, opinionated, often insightful but also annoyingly verbose, his provocative style redefined sports play-by-play and "color" commentary. Cosell's shrill speaking style, incessant preaching, overbearing manner, and abrasive personality were irritants to many – "I tell it like it is" was his famous pronouncement – but they made him, according to one poll, both the most liked and most hated TV reporter in the country.

Cosell hosted his own show, *Saturday Night Live with Howard Cosell*, in the fall of 1975, but it was canceled after three months. He provided color commentary on ABC's "Monday Night Baseball" beginning in 1976 and hosted numerous other sports commentary shows on both television and radio, including *Speaking of Sports*, *Speaking of Everything*, and *Sportsbeat*. Cosell grew disenchanted with boxing and quit the sport after a brutal, one-sided fight between Larry Holmes and Randall Cobb in 1982, and he left "Monday Night Football" before the start of the 1984 season, claiming that the NFL had "become a stagnant bore." Cosell retired from ABC in 1985, and the following year he became a sports columnist for the *New York Daily News*.

Cosell was elected to the American Sportscasters Hall of Fame in 1993 and the National Sportscasters and Sportswriters Hall of Fame in 1993. In a July 2000 ranking of sportscasters of the 20th century by the American Sportscasters Association, Cosell finished second, followed by Mel *Allen.

The product of a non-religious family – his brother was bar mitzvahed though not Cosell, and his father would go to synagogue on holidays – Cosell never involved himself in the life of the Jewish community. That all changed after he covered the 1972 Olympics, with the kidnapping of Israeli athletes from Building 31 in the Olympic Village and their subsequent murder at the airport in Munich, West Germany. "I'll tell you when you know you're Jewish," he said in an interview, "you know you're Jewish when you're lying on the slope of a hill 30 feet from Building 31 and Dachau's [22] miles away.... When you undergo the experience that I underwent in Munich, you realize that no matter how you live, no matter what your feelings are about any formalized religion, in this world if you're born of Jewish parents you're Jewish. I married a gentile girl, my two daughters were not raised in the Jewish faith, but I'm Jewish." Cosell became a patron of the American Friends of the Hebrew University, which built the Howard Cosell Center for Physical Education in Jerusalem.

Cosell, who appeared as himself in Woody Allen's movies *Bananas*, *Sleeper*, and *Broadway Danny Rose*, is the author of *Cosell* (1973), *Like It Is* (1974), *I Never Played the Game* (1985), *What's Wrong with Sports* (1991), and *Cosell on Sports: An Unexpurgated Look at American Sports in the Age of Big Money, Easy Drugs, and Fast Sex* (1991). "In my field, not in conceit but in fact, I am historic," he said in 1981. "I changed the nature of my profession totally, completely. I brought it a whole new look. I brought it education, I brought it literacy, I brought it questing, I brought it journalism, and there's not going to be another like me – because of the corruption of my industry it won't be allowed. Circumstances were right for me and I was a freak. It's not going to happen again."

[Elli Wohlgelernter (2nd ed.)]

COSENZA, town in Calabria, southern Italy. Jews were apparently living in Cosenza in 1093 or even earlier. It is reported that in 1311 pledges belonging to the Jewish moneylenders there were stolen. Repeated attempts were made in the 15th century by the bishops of Cosenza to tax Jewish assets. An important source of revenue was the fair of Maddalena di Cosenza, which also attracted foreign Jews journeying to Calabria. The presence of Jews at the fair of Cosenza is mentioned in the ordinances of King Ferrante I in 1465. In 1473 the Jews of Rossano complained that the Jews of Cosenza had fixed the tax rate for the other communities of the Duchy of Crotone, and in 1487 the Jews of Cosenza loaned money to the royal treasury. In 1495 almost all the Jews in Cosenza, then part of the kingdom of Naples, were forced to accept baptism. In 1540–41 the few remaining were expelled with the rest of the Jews from the kingdom. During World War II, in 1940, 1,500 Jews whom the Fascist authorities had declared aliens were sent to a detention camp at Ferramonti near Cosenza.

BIBLIOGRAPHY: Roth, Italy, index; Milano, Italia, index. **ADD. BIBLIOGRAPHY:** C. Colafemmina, *Per la storia degli ebrei in Calabria* (1996); idem, "Presenza ebraica nel Marchesato di Crotone," in: *Studi Storici Meridionali*, 9 (1989), 287–308; idem, "Le iscrizioni ebraiche nel cimitero di Tarsia," in: F. Volpe (ed.), *Ferramonti: un lager nel Sud, Atti del convegno internazionale di studi* (1990), 101–16.

[Attilio Milano / Nadia Zeldes (2nd ed.)]

COSER, LEWIS A. (**Ludwig Cohen**; 1913–2003), U.S. sociologist. Born in Berlin, Coser left Germany in 1933 and went to France. In 1941 he immigrated to the United States, where during the war he worked for American government agencies. He taught at the University of Chicago (1948–50) and in 1951 was appointed professor at Brandeis University, where he founded the sociology department, and in 1968 at the State University of New York at Stony Brook, New York. Along with Irving *Howe and others, he founded the socialist magazine *Dissent* and was its co-editor for many years. Coser served as president of the Society for the Study of Social Problems (1967–68), the American Sociological Association (1975), and the Eastern Sociological Society (1983). He retired to Cambridge, Massachusetts, in 1987, where he was professor emeritus, first at Boston College and then at Boston University.

Coser was a leading proponent of conflict theory, as contrasted to equilibrium theory. Although he prided himself on separating his political and sociological thinking, he was critical of modern American sociology's abandonment of social criticism.

His best-known work is *The Functions of Social Conflict* (1956), which was listed in a 1997 *Contemporary Sociology* review as one of the best-selling sociology books of the century. Among Coser's other publications in political sociology and sociological theory are *The American Communist Party: A Critical History, 1919–1957*, with I. Howe and J. Jacobson (1957); *Sociological Theory*, with Bernard Rosenberg (1967[2]); *Sociology through Literature* (1963); a symposium on Simmel (1965); *Continuities in the Study of Social Conflict* (1967); *Men of Ideas: A Sociologist's View* (1970); *Masters of Sociological Thought* (1977); *The New Conservatives: A Critique from the Left* (with I. Howe, 1977); *The Pleasures of Sociology* (1980); *Books: The Culture and Commerce of Publishing* (1982); *Refugee Scholars in America: Their Impact and Their Experiences* (1984); and *A Handful of Thistles: Collected Papers in Moral Conviction* (1988).

[Pearl J. Lieff / Ruth Beloff (2nd ed.)]

COSER, ROSE LAUB (1916–1994), U.S. sociologist. Born in Berlin but educated in Antwerp, Rose Laub immigrated to New York with her parents in 1939. Three years later, she married Lewis A. *Coser (1913–2003), a fellow refugee from Nazi Europe, who, like Rose, was a committed socialist and also became an eminent sociologist. Both Cosers received their Ph.D. in sociology from Columbia University, Lewis in 1954 and Rose in 1957. Like many women in academia at that time, Rose Coser followed a much more difficult career path than her husband, working for many years as a research associate first at Columbia and then the University of Chicago and later in the psychiatry department of Harvard Medical School. She also held positions as an instructor and then assistant professor at Wellesley College (1951–59) and as associate professor at Northeastern University (1965–68). In 1968, Rose and Lewis Coser both became professors at the State University of New York at Stony Brook, where they remained until their retirement in 1987. Rose Coser published extensively and made many important contributions to the fields of medical sociology, sociology of the family, and gender roles. Her major works include *Life in the Ward* (1962), *The Family: Its Structure and Functions* (1964 and 1974), *Life Cycle and Achievement in America* (1972), *Training in Ambiguity: Learning Through Doing in a Mental Hospital* (1979), *Access to Power: Cross-National Studies of Women and Elites* (1981), *In Defense of Modernity: Complexity of Social Roles and Individual Autonomy* (1991), and *Women of Courage: Jewish and Italian Immigrant Women in New York* (1999, published posthumously). An ardent feminist and vocal supporter of affirmative action and social justice, Coser was a founder and frequent contributor to the journal *Dissent* and served on numerous editorial boards. She was also actively involved in professional associations, serving as president of the Society for the Study of Social Problems (1973–74) and the Eastern Sociological Society (1984), as well as vice president of the American Sociological Association (1985–86). Her papers are found at the John J. Burns Library at Boston College.

BIBLIOGRAPHY: P.E. Hyman and D. Dash Moore (eds.), *Jewish Women in America*, I, (1997) 290–92; M.J. Deegan (ed.), *Women in Sociology: A Bio-Bibliographical Sourcebook* (1991), 110–17; J.R. Blau and N. Goodman (eds.), *Social Roles and Social Institutions: Essays in Honor of Rose Laub Coser* (1991); C.F. Epstein, "In Memoriam: Rose Laub Coser 1916–1994," in: *Dissent*, 42 (Winter 1995), 107–10.

[Harriet Pass Freidenreich (2nd ed.)]

COSMETICS.

In Ancient Times

Cosmetics, for the care and adornment of the body, were widely used by both men and women in the ancient Near East. The use of cosmetics was widespread among the poor as well as the wealthy classes; in the same way that they used to wash the body, so they used to take care of it with substances that softened the skin and they would anoint (from the root *swkh*) the body with oils and ointments (eg., Ezek. 16:9), as is shown by the discovery of a great deal of pertinent archaeological material, dating from the third millennium B.C.E. Since the expensive cosmetic materials were used in small quantities, special containers were produced for them, and many bottles and small flasks made of porphyry, stone, bone, ivory, and glass have been found. Commonly discovered also are flat slate slabs with depressions in the center, which were used for grinding and mixing ingredients; small mortars, usually made of stone; and long thin metal, wood, bone, or ivory spatulas used for mixing or applying the cosmetics. Good examples of these implements, often lovely and in many diverse styles, were found in Gezer, Tel Beit Mirsim, Megiddo, and Hazor.

In the ancient Near East the use of cosmetics by men was mainly restricted to the rubbing of oil into the body and the spreading of the oil over the hair of the head and the beard (Ps. 133:2), but occasionally a facial cream or lotion was used to protect the skin against the heat of the sun. Women used preparations to beautify the hair, to color eyelids, face, and lips, to anoint exposed skin and the whole body (Esth. 2:12), and to care for the nails. Cosmetics were also used medically and were sometimes connected with cultic worship and witchcraft. They were made by expert craftsmen who imported the raw ingredients, especially from Arabia and India, and adapted them for local use. The very common creams for treating the skin, particularly important in the hot climate of the east, were compounded of oils and fragrances. Sometimes the oil in these creams was extracted from olives, almonds, gourds, sesame, or other trees and plants, but animal and fish fats, which were less expensive, were more widely used. There may even have been a certain amount of wine or alcohol added to these fats to thin them and make them evaporate. Other thick base materials for cosmetics were wood ash, beeswax, and mixed oils and fats. The fragrant ingredients were usually of vegetable origin: plant leaves, fruits, buds, stalks, roots, seeds, and flowers, especially cinnamon, jasmine, rose, mint, and balsam. The fragrant components were produced by squeezing the raw materials, by cooking and afterward compressing them, or by distillation. Several early Egyptian drawings show the ingredients being placed in strong cloth sacks which could be compressed by shrinking or twisting.

Women commonly put color around their eyes (Isa. 3:16; Jer. 4:30). In addition to beautification, this seems to have had some medicinal value, for covering the sensitive skin of the lids with color prevented dryness and consequent skin diseases. For the description of eye-painting the following terms are used: *kaḥal* (Akk. *guḫlu*), e.g., "painted your eyes and decked yourself with ornament" (Ezek. 23:40); *pukh* (II Kings 9:30, Jer. 4:30). Egyptian women colored the upper lid black, the lower one green, and painted the space between the upper lid and the eyebrow grey or blue. Mesopotamian women favored yellows and reds. These colors were usually mineral-based: black often being made from lead sulfate, greens and blues from colored stones (I Chron. 29:2) or from antimony stone (Heb. *pukh*), a precious blue stone which was ground and was used along with a mixture of oil base for the application of paint on the eyes, greens from copper oxide and reds from iron oxide. Such materials were generally powdered and mixed into a preservative oil base, possibly in combination with some fragrance. They were applied either with the fingers or with a stylized spatula. Red ocher or *henna may have been used on the face, and henna was also used for dyeing the hair, which was held in place with beeswax. Lips were colored with a cream made from oil combined with red ocher, and nails were painted with pigments mixed in ash or beeswax. Cosmetic colors were also produced from burned woods, ivories, and bitumen, mixed with strong fragrant compounds to eliminate their unpleasant odors.

[Ze'ev Yeivin]

A wealth of archaeological material has been found bearing testimony to the importance of beauty treatment in Roman and Byzantine Palestine. In every archaeological museum numerous tools and receptacles used to contain and apply make-up are to be found, such as metal and bone eyebrow pencils, containers for powders and creams in the form of small cylindrical pyxes, spoons and spatulae for applying make-up, small perfume bottles, mirrors (sometimes in pairs that fitted into one another, enabling one to see the back of one's head), tweezers, pins, brooches (fibulae), etc.

[Daniel Sperber (2nd ed.)

In the Talmud

The talmudic attitude toward the use of cosmetics is basically favorable, but it is combined with warnings against its utilization for immoral purposes. This applies to ointments, perfumes, paint, and powder. Olive oil was widely used as an ointment base. It was also used as a depilatory, when mixed with such substances as myrrh, flour, and chalk. The best-known ointment was the precious *balsam which was a highly praised product of the Jericho plain (Shab. 26a). Wanton women used to put it into their shoes together with myrrh, so that its scent would arouse passion in young men (Shab. 62b). This rare and costly commodity was subject to cheap imitations. There is a difference of opinion whether the biblical *ẓori* is to be identified with balsam (Ker. 6a) or whether it is a different substance (see Rashi and Naḥmanides to Ex. 30:34). However, its main use was medicinal rather than cosmetic. Besides these ointments, *rose oil, spikenard, foliatium, *laudanum, henna, most of which are already mentioned in the Bible, and others, were also utilized. Perfumes (*besamim*) were obtained in part by an admixture of dry aromatic substances to those already mentioned. The substances were both grown in Israel and imported from as far as Arabia and even India (See *Incense and Perfume). These perfumes were also utilized to sweeten the air in the home after meals (Ber. 6:6; Shab. 18a); or at weddings (Tosef. Shab. 7:16); and to perfume clothing (Ber. 53a). In the Talmud mention is made of such dyes as rouge (*sarak*), purple-violet (*pikas*, φύκες; cf. the term *pirkus*), white for the face, hair and finger- and toenails, and blue-black (*Kaḥal*) for the eyes. It was a wife's duty to beautify herself so as to appear pleasing to her husband (Tosef. Ned. 7:1, cf. MK 1:7 *ibid.*, 9b; Shab. 64b), and an enactment is attributed to Ezra that perfume peddlers should be allowed to circulate freely for this purpose (BK 82ab). The use of cosmetics during mourning (MK 20b; Ket. 4b) was forbidden. Prostitutes, of course, made a special art of painting themselves (Shab. 34a; TJ *ibid.* 8:3, 11b). For a scholar it was considered unbecoming to appear perfumed in public (Ber. 43b). An interpretation of Deut. 22:5 forbade men depilatories (Shab. 94b; Naz. 59a), which was understandable in a pagan world rife with pederasty. Against halitosis (which was a reason for divorce, Ket. 75a), women chewed peppercorns, ginger, cinnamon, and gum (Shab. 65a).

Talmudic literature contains a wealth of information on the manufacture and the marketing of cosmetic preparations. The *Avtinas family, who made the sacred incense for the Temple, took special care in its production and refused to share this art since it feared that unworthy persons would utilize its secrets for profane purposes (Yoma 38a). The Talmud also related that the women of Bet Avtinas never perfumed themselves lest people suspect that they were using sacred incense. The substances first had to be boiled in oil or seethed in water. After a time was allowed for absorption, they were poured into sealed containers, small tubes or boxes, with those for the more valuable substances made of alabaster (cf. Gen. R. 39:2). The perfume dealers had their shops in the market – Street of the Perfumers – where to this day there exists in the Old City of Jerusalem an ancient street still called by this name (*Shuk ha-Besamim*). Often such shops could be found in the "Market [street] of the Prostitutes," where the demand for perfumes was great (Ex. R. 43:7). The moral reputation of this trade was therefore not high, though it was considered indispensable and preferable to that of the tanner, who had to work with evil odors (Kid. 82a). The Mishnah decreed that a husband must give his wife ten dinars for her cosmetic needs. Rabban Gamaliel, however, said that the amount depended upon local customs (Ket. 66b). The Talmud states that Miriam, the daughter of Nakdimon b. Gorion, who lived at the time of the destruction of the Second Temple, used cosmetics to such an extravagant extent that the sages permitted her an allowance of 400 golden coins for her "perfume basket" (*Kuppah shel besamim*). The hair, both of men and women, was the subject of special care. In addition to its cosmetic aspect, there was also the hygienic consideration of keeping it free of vermin. It therefore was washed, anointed, combed, and sometimes dyed. It was cut (and thinned) regularly, and the higher the person was on the social scale the more frequently he went to the barber (Sanh. 22b). Hair was worn long, and arranged in various styles; even the special style of the high priest found ostentatious imitators (Ned. 51a). The stories of Joseph and Absalom gave the rabbis occasion to comment on the moral dangers of vanity in hairstyle (Gen. R. 84:7; Sot. 1:8). It was a religious custom to have one's hair cut before the Sabbath and festivals (cf. Shab. 1:2; MK 14a). A mourner (and someone put under the minor ban) was forbidden to cut his hair and beard for at least 30 days (MK 14aff.). Certain hairstyles, like the *belorit*, probably a kind of pigtail hanging down from the crown of the head while the rest of the hair was shorn short, and the one called *komei* (κόμη), a kind of tonsure, were forbidden to Jews "as *Amorite [pagan] custom" (Tos. Shab. 6:1), but a dispensation was made for the patriarchal family on account of its official contacts with the Roman authorities (TJ Shab. 6:1, 7d, Av. Zar. 2:2, 41a).

Beards received the same care as hair and were occasionally dyed (BM 60b; Naz. 39a). On the other hand, what was considered beautiful for men was deemed the opposite for women (TJ Ket. 7:9, 31c). Women, while not cutting their hair, would apply much care to it by arranging it skillfully in plaits and "building" it up, sometimes with the help of wigs (*pe'ah nokhrit*), using bands and nets, and adding *jewelry as well. So elaborate were these creations that it was forbidden to undo a woman's hairdo on the Sabbath because it involved transgressing the prohibitions of "building" and "demolishing" (Shab. 94b–95a). (For the requirement that married women cover their hair, see *Covering of Head.) Brides would wear their hair long on their wedding day (Ket. 2:10), as a sign of their virginity. Talmudic and midrashic sources contain much information about barbers and hairdressers, their lowly standing, and their implements and accessories. They also traded in perfumes and practiced manicure and pedicure, apart from carrying out certain medical functions such as bloodletting.

BIBLIOGRAPHY: R.J. Forbes, *Studies in Ancient Technology*, 3 (1955), 1ff. (incl. bibl.); C. Singer et al. (eds.), *A History of Technology*, 1 (1955), 285ff.; A. Lucas and J.R. Harris, *Ancient Egyptian Materials and Industries* (19624), 80ff.; C. Boreux, Mus'e National du Louvre, Departement des Antiquites Egyptiennes, *Guide-Catalogue Sommaire*, 1 (1932), 195–6, pl. xxiv; Pritchard, Pictures, pl. 93. IN THE

TALMUD: Krauss, Tal Arch, 233 ff.; J. Preuss, *Biblisch-talmudische Medizin* (1921[2]), 414 ff. **ADD. BIBLIOGRAPHY:** A.S. Herzberg, "*Yofyah ve-ha-Tipu'aḥ shel ha-Ishah bi-Zeman ha-Talmud*," in: *He-Atid*, 4 (1923), 1–53, and S. Krauss, ibid., 53–56; Antonio of Ambrosia, *Women and Beauty in Pompeii*, tr. G. Kelly (2001).

COSMOLOGY. Cosmological theories describe the physical structure of the universe. For cosmology in the Bible, see *Creation.

In the Talmud

According to R. Simeon b. Yoḥai, the earth and the heavens are like "a pot with a cover." This "cover" is the *raki'a*, the firmament. "The darkness of the firmament is that of a journey of 50 years. While the sun in the sky passes this journey of 50 years, a man can walk four miles." The distance between the firmament and the earth is the equivalent of a journey of 500 years (TJ, Ber. 1:1, 2c). The firmament is composed of water and the stars of fire, but they dwell harmoniously together (TJ, RH 2:5,58a). The heavens (*shamayim*) are an admixture of fire and water (*esh* and *mayim*) or made wholly of water (*Sham mayim*; Ḥag. 12a). Indeed, "the Holy One, blessed be He, took all the waters of the sea and with half He made the firmament and the other half the ocean. The firmament is like a pool, and above it is an arch" (Gen. R. 4:4 and 5). The earth is of the same thickness as the firmament (Gen. R. 4:5). Once every 1,656 years the firmament shakes on its foundations (Gen. R. 38:6).

There is however more than one firmament; according to R. Judah, there are two, according to Resh Lakish, seven (Ḥag. 12b). The sun and the moon are situated in the second firmament (Gen. R. 6:6). The above-quoted view of R. Simeon b. Yoḥai would imply that the world is wholly enclosed by the firmament. R. Joshua was also originally of the same opinion, that the world was "like a tent" enclosed on all sides, but later he came round to the view of R. Eliezer that it is like an *exedra*, closed on three sides only, but open on the north side, and it is from this opening that the north wind comes (BB 25b).

Originally the sun and the moon were both of the same size but God, realizing that "two kings cannot wear one crown," diminished the size of the moon. Thus what were originally "the two great luminaries" became "the greater luminary" and "the lesser luminary" of Genesis 1:16 (Ḥul. 60b). Eclipses of the sun are a sign of God's anger or displeasure (Suk. 29a). Beneath the earth is the abyss (*tehom*). There is a cavity which descends from the Holy of Holies to the abyss.

[Louis Isaac Rabinowitz]

In Medieval Jewish Philosophy

In medieval philosophy there were four types of cosmological theories: the Aristotelian-Ptolemaic, the neoplatonic, the Kalām theory, and the theory of the infinite universe.

ARISTOTELIAN-PTOLEMAIC. The medieval version of the Aristotelian-Ptolemaic cosmology asserts that the universe is a finite sphere whose center is the earth, around which nine other concentric spheres – the moon, the sun, the various planets, the stars, and the diurnal sphere – rotate. These spheres form a compact whole in which there are no gaps, or an inner vacuum, and around which there is nothing. The earth and the heavenly spheres differ in their composition. The latter are made up of a single element, ether, whose homogenous nature is free from change other than locomotion. The earth is composed of four elements, earth, water, air, and fire, whose continual transmutations make terrestrial substances subject to generation and corruption. Each of these moving spheres has a "soul," or internal moving force, which is set in motion by corresponding incorporeal substances, the Separate Intelligences. (According to some, "soul" and "intellect" are different aspects of the incorporeal substance.) According to *Maimonides, these incorporeal substances are identical with the angels (Maimonides, *Guide of the Perplexed*, 2:6). The ultimate source of motion is God, the Prime Mover, who "moves" the universe insofar as He is the most perfect substance, and therefore the object of love of all other substances (Aristotle, *Metaphysics*, 7:7; Maimonides, *Guide* 1:72; 2:1).

NEOPLATONIC. Medieval neoplatonic cosmology employs several Aristotelian notions but tries to overcome the terrestrial-celestial dichotomy inherent in the Aristotelian theory. Indeed, in some neoplatonic philosophies there is a decidedly pantheistic or monistic tendency (cf. the Christian philosopher Scotus Erigena). Solomon Ibn *Gabirol is the most neoplatonic of the medieval Jewish philosophers. In attempting to demonstrate the essential unity of the universe he applied the Aristotelian form-matter framework to every part of the universe except God and the Divine Will. The result of this extension is that every level of being that emanates from God (see *Emanation) exhibits a common universal matter and universal form. Each level of being, however, is further characterized by a specific material nature and a particular formal structure. In this way both homogeneity and diversity are accounted for. Typical of monistic cosmologies, Gabirol's system tends to be static: the emanation of the lower stages of being from God is described in non-temporal terms. The origin of the universe, as well as motion, is explained by Ibn Gabirol as the effect of God's will, which seems to serve as the mediating link between God and the universe.

KALĀM. The *Kalām cosmology employs the model of a universe consisting of atoms in a vacuum. These indivisible particles combine, separate, and recombine, forming the universe by these movements. The Kalām version of atomism differs from its Greek antecedents in that it rejects any notion of an infinite magnitude (Maimonides, *Guide*, 1:73). Atomism had virtually no impact upon the mainstream of Jewish philosophy, although a number of Karaite philosophers accepted its doctrines (see *Atomism). Abu al-Barākāt *Ḥibat Allah of Baghdad was a profound atomist but he had no influence upon Jewish thought, probably because of his conversion to Islam in his late years. Indeed, the most important Jewish representative of the Kalām, *Saadiah Gaon, was not an atomist.

INFINITE UNIVERSE – CRESCAS. One aspect of classical atomism, however, is found in the cosmology of Ḥasdai *Crescas. His philosophy constitutes a vigorous critique of Aristotle's physics and cosmology. Crescas reverts to the atomistic hypothesis of an infinite vacuum in which our universe, and perhaps others, are located. (The possibility of a plurality of universes is also found in rabbinic literature, but is rejected by Maimonides and other medieval Aristotelians; cf. Gen. R. 3; Maimonides, *Guide*, 2:30). Although Crescas does not explicitly introduce atoms into his physics, his theory of matter exhibits atomistic aspects. For example, unlike Aristotle, Crescas sees matter as requiring no external principle for its motion: bodies have a natural tendency to move. Consequently, Crescas eliminates the artificial system of intelligences as causes of motion. Finally, he rules out the distinction between the composition of the earth and the heavens in favor of the notion of a common matter characteristic of all bodies celestial and terrestrial. In several important respects Crescas' cosmology anticipates some ideas of Galileo and Newton.

[Seymour Feldman]

BIBLIOGRAPHY: Aristotle, *Physics* and *On the Heavens*; Munk, Mélanges; Maimonides, *Guide of the Perplexed*, ed. and tr. by S. Pines (1963); H.A. Wolfson, *Crescas' Critique of Aristotle* (1929); idem, in: PAAJR, 11 (1941), 105–63; A.C. Crombie, *Medieval and Early Modern Science*, 1 (1959), index; Hyman, in: Congrès International de Philosophie Médiévale, *La filosofia della natura nel Medioevo* (1966), 209–18. **ADD. BIBLIOGRAPHY:** J. Dillon, "Ibn Gabirol: The Sage among the Schoolmen," in: L.E. Goodman (ed.), *Neoplatonism and Jewish Thought* (1992), 77–110; P. Duhem, *Medieval Cosmology* (1985); I. Efros, *The Problem of Space in Jewish Medieval Philosophy* (1917); S. Feldman, "Platonic Themes in Gersonides' Cosmology," in: *Salo W. Baron Jubilee* Volume (1975), 383–405; G. Freudenthal, "Cosmogonie et physique chez Gersonide," in: REJ, 145 (1986), 295–314; L.E. Goodman, "Maimonidean Naturalism," in: *Neoplatonism in Jewish Thought* (1992): 157–94; A. Hyman, "From What Is One and Simple Only What Is One and Simple Can Come to Be," in: L.E. Goodman (ed.), *Neoplatonism in Jewish Thought* (1992), 111–36; T. Rudavsky, "Philosophical Cosmology in Judaism," in: *Early Science and Medicine* (1997), 149–84; N. Samuelson, "The Role of the Elements and Matter in Gersonides' Cosmogony," in: G. Dahan (ed.), *Gersonide en son temps* (1991), 199*233; H. Wolfson, *Crescas' Critique of Aristotle* (1929).

"**COSMOPOLITANS**," derogatory term applied in 1949 to Jewish intellectuals in the Soviet Union, at the peak of Russian chauvinism and its struggle against Western influence in Soviet culture and science. The change to a Soviet policy directed against the Jewish people and the State of Israel had in fact begun several months earlier (November 1948) with the arrest of Yiddish writers, the closing of the periodical *Einikeyt* and the *Emes* press, and the increasing attacks on Zionism. The campaign against the "cosmopolitans," however, marked the first public attack on Soviet Jews as Jews, and is thus considered as initiating what Soviet Jews call "the Black Years," which lasted until Stalin's death in March 1953.

The campaign against "cosmopolitans" who have no homeland was initiated in articles in the central organs of the Communist Party, in *Pravda* (January 28, 1949) and *Kultura i Zhizn* (January 30, 1949). Thereafter, over a period of two months, other Soviet newspapers and periodicals, led by *Literaturnaya Gazeta* (February 12, 16, 19, 20, and March 9, 1949) published severe attacks against "cosmopolitans" with Jewish names, in the fields of art and literature (Altman, Gurevitch, Levin, Danin, and others), out of all proportion to their real importance in their respective fields. The writers of anti-"cosmopolitans" articles then began to reveal the real names of Jews using pen names, such as Yakovlev (Holzmann), Melnikov (Melman), and Zhdanov (Lifshitz), in an attempt to show that Jews were concealing their identity behind Russian names. The "cosmopolitans" were accused of hatred of the Russian people ("Altman hates anything Russian, anything Soviet") and of insulting the Russian man; of representing the Russians and Ukrainians as turning their backs on the Jews when the Germans were leading them to their death (cf. Golovanivski in his poem "Abraham"); of supporting Zionism; of insulting the memory of great Russian writers by saying that they were influenced by such "cosmopolitans" or chauvinist-reactionary writers as Heine or Bialik (cf. Isbakh in his book "Years of Life"). The wave of attacks subsided in April–May 1949, probably as a result of violent reactions in the West. Anti-Jewish policy did not cease, however, and began to take even more extreme forms in succeeding years. The term "cosmopolitans" was also applied to Jewish intellectuals in other Communist countries at later nonconformist periods.

BIBLIOGRAPHY: *Bolshaya Sovetskaya Entsiklopediya*, 23 (1953), 111–4; *Filosofskaya Entsiklopediya*, 4 (1964), 74–76; S.M. Schwarz, *Jews in the Soviet Union* (1951), 208–10, 355–60; H.E. Salisbury, *Moscow Journal: The End of Stalin* (1961), 12, 15, 22–23, 29, 45.

[Benjamin Pinkus]

COSTA (**Mendes da Costa**), Anglo-Jewish Sephardi family, prominent in the 17th and 18th centuries. The founder was ALVARO (JACOB) DA COSTA (d. 1680), born a Marrano in Portugal, who escaped via Rouen to London. He was one of the prominent Anglo-Jewish personalities of the Restoration period, though he did not formally enter the community. He helped to finance Charles II during his exile. ANTHONY (MOSES; c. 1667–1747), his grandson, one of the wealthiest London merchants of his day, is (incorrectly) said to have been a director of the Bank of England. In 1727 he successfully brought an action against the Russia Company, which had refused him membership because of his religion. The company procured from Parliament a modification of its charter so as to reserve for itself the right of refusal. In 1729 he was one of the three Jewish subcommissioners appointed for the colonization of Georgia and in 1736 he was elected a member of the Royal Society. Catherine da *Costa (1679–1756), Anthony's wife, daughter of Dr. Fernando *Mendes and named after Catherine of Braganza, was a competent painter and JOHN (Abraham) was one of the three London merchants who in 1710 provided £300,000 for the provisioning of the English army in Flanders.

BIBLIOGRAPHY: J. Picciotto, *Sketches of Anglo-Jewish History* (1956²), 103–4; M. Gaster, *History of the Ancient Synagogue of the Spanish and Portuguese Jews* (1901), 97; Wolf, in: JHSET, 1 (1893–94), 71; 5 (1902–05), 20–22; A.M. Hyamson, *Sephardim of England* (1951), 99–100; Rubens, in: JHSET, 14 (1935–39), 95–97. **ADD. BIBLIOGRAPHY:** Katz, England, index; E. Samuel, *At the Ends of the Earth: Essays on the History of the Jews in England and Portugal* (2004), index; ODNB online for Anthony Moses da Costa and Catherine da Costa.

[Cecil Roth]

COSTA, CATHERINE DA (1679–1756), English miniature painter, daughter of Dr. Fernando Mendez, physician to Charles II. Catherine da Costa was the earliest known English Jewish artist and the first Jewish woman artist whose work has survived. A pupil of the famous drawing-master and mezzotint engraver Bernard Lens, she painted portrait miniatures of her family and of other members of the Jewish community. Among her works are portraits of her father in full 18th-century dress (1721) and of her ten-year-old son, Abraham da Costa (1714). She was married to Anthony Moses da Costa (1667/9–1747), a prosperous Sephardi merchant.

ADD. BIBLIOGRAPHY: ODNB online.

COSTA, EMANUEL MENDES DA (1717–1791), English scientist. Da Costa, who trained as a notary, became one of the eminent English scientists of his time. He was an omnivorous collector, wrote numerous papers on philosophical and scientific subjects, and belonged to several English and foreign learned societies, including the Royal Society and the Society of Antiquaries. His life was a continual struggle against adverse circumstances. In 1745–55 he was imprisoned for debt. In 1763 he was made clerk and librarian to the Royal Society, but was dismissed in 1767 for dishonesty. Subsequently, he was again imprisoned for debt in the King's Bench Prison, where much of the remainder of his life was passed. His remarkable collection of books, manuscripts, engravings, and specimens was seized and sold to pay his debts. Although his second wife was a Christian, he remained a member of the Jewish community. A large body of his correspondence with fellow savants is preserved in the British Museum (Add. Mss. 28534–44). His more important publications are *Elements of Conchology* (London, 1776), *Historia Naturalis Testaceorum Britanniae, or, the British Conchology* (1778), and an English edition of Cronstedt's *Essay Towards a System of Mineralogy* (London, 1770).

BIBLIOGRAPHY: J. Nichols, *Literary Anecdotes of the Eighteenth Century*, 2 (1812), 292; 3 (1812), 233, 757; 5 (1812), 712; 6 (1812), 80–81; 8 (1814), 200; 9 (1815), 607, 799, 812–3, 816; DNB, 6 (1923), 791; J.E. Smith, *Selection of the Correspondence of Linnaeus*, 2 (1821), 482–3; C. Roth, *Anglo-Jewish Letters* (1938), 122–3, 133; Margoliouth, Cat, 4 (1935), 15.

[Cecil Roth]

COSTA, ISAÄC DA (1798–1860), Dutch poet and writer. The precocious offspring of a distinguished Sephardi family in Amsterdam, Isaäc da Costa was brought up in the moderately Enlightened milieu that characterized the Portuguese Jewish elite of the early 19th century. In these circles much emphasis was put on the assimilation of Jews into Dutch society, and consequently Da Costa (at the early age of 13) became a member of Concordia Crescimus, a Jewish literary society. It testifies to his intellectual talents as well as to the incipient emancipation of Dutch Jewry in this period that, having obtained a higher education at the Amsterdam Atheneum, he went on to study law at the university of Leiden (1816–18). In the meantime, private tuition was provided by the Hebraist Moses *Lemans. It was Lemans who in 1813 first introduced Da Costa to the counterrevolutionary poet and philo-Judaist Willem Bilderdijk (1756–1831). In Leiden, where he attended Bilderdijk's idiosyncratic private lectures on history, Da Costa began to stress his identity as a Jew, albeit one of aristocratic ancestry. In the 1820s he expressly defended the (apparently common) belief that the Sephardim were superior by descent to the Ashkenazim. Moreover, since the Portuguese Jews had migrated to the Iberian Peninsula before the building of the Second Temple, they could not be reckoned as descendants of the Jews who had crucified Jesus. Perceiving the Enlightenment as a threat to his Jewishness, Da Costa's religious quest paradoxically resulted in his acceptance of a form of orthodox Calvinism in 1822. He shared Bilderdijk's strong interest in kabbalism and a chiliasm that focused on the second coming of Jesus Christ and the "national" conversion of the Jews. Thus, to him and to his wife, Hanna Belmonte (1800–1867), whom he had married in 1821, conversion to Christianity was both an alternative path to integration into Dutch society and a means of securing their identity as Jews. Da Costa soon became a prominent spokesman for the orthodox party within the *Hervormde Kerk* (Reformed Church). His *Bezwaren tegen de geest der eeuw* ("Grievances against the Spirit of the Times," 1823), in which he castigated contemporary Dutch society for what he regarded as its shallow liberalism, established his reputation as a disruptive controversialist. In the 1830s and 1840s, however, Da Costa concentrated on leading religious gatherings, editing periodicals, and giving private lectures on religious and historical topics. Although he had already achieved renown for his poetry, he began to be accepted as a Dutch poet of standing only after about 1840. His acclaim as a man of literature led to greater activity in public life. He developed an interest in the liberal constitution he had once rejected and labored for social and ecclesiastical reform. Da Costa always remained profoundly interested in the Jews. His *Israël en de Volken* (1848; translated as *Israel and the Gentiles*, 1850) is a history of the Jewish people from the biblical period to the middle of the 19th century, written from a Christian point of view. Many of Da Costa's poems have biblical themes. Of importance also are his studies of aristocratic Jewish families. Originally published in *Navorscher* (1857–59), they were reissued in English translation as *Noble Families among the Sephardic Jews* (1936).

BIBLIOGRAPHY: O.W. Dubois, *Een vriendschap in Réveilkring. De omgang tussen Isaäc da Costa en Willem de Clercq (1820–1844)*

(1997); G.J. Johannes, *Isaäc da Costa. Dwaasheid, ijdelheid, verdoemenis!* (1996); J. Meijer, *Isaac da Costa's weg naar het Christendom. Bijdrage tot de geschiedenis der Joodsche problematiek in Nederland* (1941); idem, *Martelgang of cirkelgang. Isaac Da Costa als Joods romanticus* (5715/1954); P.L. Schram, "Isaäc da Costa," in: *Biografisch lexicon voor de geschiedenis van het protestantisme*, 3 (1988), 85–88.

[Joris van Eijnatten (2nd ed.)]

COSTA, SIR MICHAEL (born **Michele Andrea Agniello Costa**; 1808–1884), conductor and composer. Born in Naples to a family of Spanish descent, Costa studied at the Collegio Reale, Naples, and produced his first two operas for the Conservatory theater: *Il delitto punito* (1826) and *Il sospetto funesto* (1827). In 1829, he was sent by Zingarelli to the Birmingham Festival to conduct one of that composer's works (by force of circumstance he had to sing the solo tenor part instead). Subsequently he became *répétiteur* at the King's Theatre in London, which later became Her Majesty's Theatre (1830), and he was its director and conductor from 1833 to 1846, during which time he was responsible for achieving a new state of excellence in the theater orchestra and ensemble. He was thereafter conductor of the Philharmonic Society (1846) and music director of the newly formed Royal Italian Opera, Covent Garden (1847–69), which attracted several of the outstanding singers of the age – Grisi, Mario, later Lablache – from Her Majesty's Theatre.

Costa was knighted in 1869 and became the leading festival conductor in Britain, making important annual appearances at the Festivals of Birmingham, Leeds, and Bradford, among others, at which he conducted the first performances of his oratorios *Eli* (1855) and *Naaman* (1864). In 1871, he again took on the leadership if Her Majesty's Theatre, where he remained until 1879. Costa's other works include the operas *Il Carcere d'Ildegonda* (1828; for the Teatro Nuovo, Naples), *Malvina* (1829; for the Teatro San Carlo, Naples), *Malek Adhel* (1839; for the Théatre des Italiens, Paris), and *Don Carlos* (1846; for Her Majesty's); together with symphonies and much vocal music. His reputation as an opera conductor in the middle years of the last century was virtually without equal.

[Max Loppert]

COSTA, URIEL DA (**Acosta**, alias **Adam Romes**; 1583/4–1640), philosopher and free thinker. He was born as Gabriel da Costa in Oporto, Portugal, into a New Christian or Converso family, his father being a devout Catholic. After studying Canon Law at Coimbra, he became a treasurer of the collegiate church, a lucrative and prestigious position. He took minor orders and received the tonsure. In his autobiography (see below), Da Costa claimed that examining the Bible brought him back to Judaism. Then, he said, he converted his family to the version of Judaism he had worked out from the Bible. In 1614 they fled to Amsterdam to avoid persecution by the Inquisition and to practice their religion freely. Shortly afterwards, Uriel and part of the family settled in Hamburg. Very soon after his arrival at Hamburg he addressed a polemical broadside to the leaders of the Sephardi congregation of Venice, in which he criticized rabbinic Judaism as incompatible with the Torah. The Venetian rabbi Leon *Modena rebutted Uriel's theses and advised the leader of the Hamburg congregations to excommunicate him. In spite of his excommunication at Hamburg in 1618, Da Costa did not leave the city before 1623. A year later Da Costa finished his *Examen dos Tradiçoens Phariseas Conferidas con a Ley Escrita* (1624), for which he was excommunicated, arrested, and fined, and the book was burned (at least three copies must have survived, however). Even before he finished his work on the subject, an answer had appeared by Samuel da Silva, *Tratado da Immortalidade da Alma* (1623). After his banishment, Da Costa lived for four years in Utrecht. When his mother died in 1628, Da Costa returned to Amsterdam, where he sought reconciliation with the Jewish community, though he had not altered his opinions. He felt the need to belong to the group and said that he would "become an ape among apes." Having rejoined the synagogue, he soon began doubting whether there was Divine sanction for the Mosaic Law, and whether religions were more than human inventions. He was led to deism or some kind of natural religion, denying any value to institutional religion. He gave up Jewish practices, and tried to prevent two Christians from converting to Judaism. This led to his second excommunication, after which he continued to live for seven years in Amsterdam. In 1640, he rejoined the Jewish community, submitted to a public recantation of his views, received 39 lashes, and prostrated himself so that the entire congregation could tread over him. He was so shocked by what was required of him that he wrote a few pages of his autobiography, *Exemplar Humanae Vitae* (published in Limborch's *Amica collatio...* 1687, repr. 1847), and then, according to the Hamburg Lutheran clergyman Johann Mueler, committed suicide.

Da Costa became a hero of the fight against religious intolerance, and a precursor of modern Bible criticism and naturalistic thought. He has been seen as a precursor and inspirer of *Spinoza. Practically all that is known about Da Costa comes from his autobiography (Eng. tr. in L. Schwarz, *Memories of my People* (1963), 84–94). On the basis of Portuguese Inquisition archives, it has recently been proposed that Da Costa's original version of Judaism was not that of the Bible, but rather an odd kind of Marrano Judaism, that some of his mother's family practiced, and that it was only in Amsterdam that he worked out his biblical religion and his deism. Da Costa became, for the Enlightenment and the Romantic Age, a symbol of the freethinker opposing religious orthodoxy. Though his doctrines are hardly known, he has had an important influence through the story of his life on anti-religious thinkers, and has been seen as a martyr to Orthodox Jewish intolerance and as a possible source of Spinoza's views.

[Richard H. Popkin / Harm den Boer (2nd ed.)]

In the Arts

Treatment of Uriel da Costa by writers, artists, and composers has generally tended to idealize him as a victim of obscurantism. The inspiring effect of a supposed link to the Spinoza case is obvious. The German dramatist Karl Ferdinand *Gutzkow, a "Young German" ally of Heine, wrote two works on the theme: the novella *Der Sadduzaeer von Amsterdam* (1834), and the five-act tragedy *Uriel Acosta* (1847). Gutzkow's heroic interpretation of the Sephardi philosopher, the first of significance in literature, inspired later works, including G. Schoenstein's brief parody in his *Humoristisch-jocoser Witz-und Lach-Almanach* (1851); a Hebrew version of the drama by S. Rubin (1856); and a Yiddish adaptation for the New York stage, with musical accompaniment, by Abraham *Goldfaden, produced in the late 19th century. Even as late as 1995 Gutzkow's depiction of Da Costa inspired the absurdist play by the Polish poet and playwright Lidia Amejko (1955–), *Męka Pańska w butelce* (The Lord's Passion in a Bottle; also produced in English and Italian). "Uriel da Costa" was one of H.M. Bien's *Oriental Legends and Other Poems* (1883), while *Uriel Acosta* (1900) was the title of a novel by the Yiddish writer John Paley. The most important 20th-century work on the subject was Israel *Zangwill's sketch in *Dreamers of the Ghetto* (1898), another idealized portrait. Later treatments of the theme were the U.S. writer Charles *Reznikoff's play *Uriel Acosta* (1921) and Yoḥanan *Twersky's biographical work of the same name in Hebrew (3 vols., 1934–45). Josef *Kastein devoted one of his literary-historical monographs to him (*Uriel da Costa, oder Die Tragoedie der Gesinnung*, 1932) and the American literary critic and poet Stanley Burnshaw (1906–) wrote an unpublished verse play entitled *Uriel da Costa* that he later made into Book I of *The Refusers* (1981).

In art there is a highly imaginative painting by Samuel *Hirszenberg depicting Uriel da Costa with the infant Benedict Spinoza. The Dutch Jewish artist Meijer Jacob Isaac de *Haan (1852–1895) is reported to have painted in 1888 the dramatic scene of his excommunication in antiquarian style.

All the musical works on the theme were inspired by Gutzkow's play, including *Uriel Acosta*, an opera by the Russian composer Valentina Serova and by general consent her most successful work, which had its première in Moscow in 1885. Subsequent compositions all took the form of stage music for Gutzkow's drama, especially for the Hebrew version by the *Habimah* company. Jacob *Weinberg's score (1921) has remained unpublished, but that by Karol *Rathaus for *Habimah's* Berlin production of 1930 has achieved a degree of permanence in the musical repertoire; later he reworked it into an independent piece in four movements.

[Bathja Bayer]

BIBLIOGRAPHY: C. Gebhardt (ed.), *Die Schriften des Uriel Da Costa* (1922), includes almost all known material by or about Da Costa; Révah, in: RHR, 161 (1962), 45–76 (new material); C. Michaëlis de Vasconcellos, *Uriel da Costa: notas relativas a sua vida e as suas obras* (1921), includes bibliography; A. de Magalhães Basto, *Alguins documentos inéditos sôbre Uriel da Costa* (1930). **ADD. BIBLIOGRAPHY:** S. Dorsey (transl.), *Uriel Acosta – A Tragedy by Karl Gutzkow*; see *Denow's Review*, vol. 6 (1869).

COSTA ATHIAS, SOLOMON DA (1690–1769), founder of the Hebrew collection in the British Museum. Da Costa Athias, who is also often referred to simply as Solomon da Costa, went from Amsterdam to London as a young man, amassed a considerable fortune as a broker, and became well known for his liberal views in Christian as well as Jewish society. Some Shabbatean works which he copied are still extant. He presented the newly opened British Museum in 1759 with its original Hebrew collection of 179 printed volumes and three manuscripts which had been collected and specially bound for Charles II.

BIBLIOGRAPHY: Hyamson, in: *Gaster Jubilee Volume* (1936), 260–6. **ADD. BIBLIOGRAPHY:** Katz, England, 371–72.

[Cecil Roth]

°**COSTA DE MATTOS, VICENTE DA** (16th century), antisemitic Portuguese writer. His book *Breve discurso contra a heretica perfidia do Iudaismo* ("A Brief Discourse Against the Treacherous Heresy of Judaism," Lisbon, 1622, 1634^2), in 27 chapters, was intended to justify the Inquisition's burning of Judaizing *Marranos. In 1625, a second part appeared, *Honras Christãas* ("Christian Virtues"). The work is a collection of libels and invective against Judaism; the Jews are described as "the pestilence of the world" and charged with homosexuality, ritual murder, etc.

BIBLIOGRAPHY: Kayserling, Bibl, 115; idem, *Geschichte der Juden in Portugal* (1867), 293; Mendes dos Remedios, *Os Judeus em Portugal*, 1 (1895), 398–402.

COSTA RICA, republic in Central America; general population 3,956,507 (2004), Jewish population 2,500.

History

Costa Rica was sparsely inhabited by Indians and in colonial times was considered unattractive to immigrants. Its inhabitants were mostly industrious farmers from Northern Spain who cultivated small landholdings, and their descendants are thus characteristically more European than any in any other Latin American country. There is no evidence of the presence of *Crypto-Jews in Costa Rica, and the myth of the Jewish ancestry of the Costa Ricans is not substantiated by historical evidence. In the 18th century Jews from Jamaica were involved in the illegal trade of cocoa with Cartago, but Jewish settlement in Costa Rica started only in the middle of the 19th century, with a few Portuguese Jewish families, such as Maduro, Robles, Piza, Sasso, and Chumaceiro. Originally from Curaçao and St. Thomas, these Sephardi Jews arrived in Costa Rica from Panama, which remained their religious center. Most of them settled in the capital San José, and a few in Cartago, Puntarenas, and Puerto Limón. Being affluent merchants they integrated into the local bourgeoisie, acquiring social and political prominence. A high rate of intermarriage resulted in assimilation, but a few still maintain the memory of their Jewish origin.

Following WWI and the imposition of restrictions on immigration to the U.S., a small number of Jews from Turkey arrived in Costa Rica. They were followed by Jews from Eastern Europe, particularly from Poland, who became the dominant Jewish group. Immigration until 1930 was relatively free, but Costa Rica was an unkown destination. From 1931 the government required a deposit from immigrants, but relatives of former immigrants were generally exempt. In all, 556 Jews entered Costa Rica between 1930 and 1936, the largest group coming from the Polish town of Zelechow. The Polish Jews engaged in petty trade, many of them as peddlers who provided cheap merchandise on credit to the lower classes, introducing to Costa Rica the idea of installment buying. Competition and rivalry with the local merchants, many of whom belonged to other groups of immigrants, such as the Spaniards, Lebanese, Italians, and Germans, provoked a wave of antisemitism. President Ricardo Jiménez was accused by his rivals of tolerating illegal immigration of *polacos* (Polish Jews). His successor, León Cortés (1936–40), restricted Jewish immigration, and his administration was considered to represent the high point of antisemitism in Costa Rica. Nevertheless, 159 Polish Jews were admitted during his term.

During the Holocaust period Costa Rica did not become a haven for refugees. In 1937, when the Refugee Economic Corporation acquired land around the area of Guanacaste for the purpose of settling Jewish refugees from Central Europe, a court ruling decreed that the purchase of land by a foreign company for settlement purposes was illegal. Jewish immigration to Costa Rica was interrupted between 1940 and 1945, and was partially resumed in the postwar period with the arrival of refugees from Poland, probably relatives of older residents, whose number was estimated at between 165 and 250. Jewish economic security was also imperiled in 1941 in the wake of the official nationalization of all foreign-held commercial establishments, but the legislation was not enforced. Again in 1944, an abortive attempt was made to prohibit peddling, which would have been a blow to the economic position of many Jews.

Following WWII the Jews became pawns of political struggles. During the presidency of Picado Michalsky (1944–48), the government party, led by Calderón Guardia, denounced Fascism and manifested solidarity with the Jewish cause. Its Communist image, however, was used against the Jewish community by antisemitic members of the opposition, particularly by Otilio Ulate, whose election to the presidency (February 8, 1948) was not accepted by the former administration. During the civil war of 1948 Jewish houses were sacked by revolutionary forces. Two emissaries of the Jewish community, Salomón Shifter and David Sikora, approached the leader of the armed revolt, José Figueres Ferrer, and obtained his promise to respect individual liberties.

Antisemitism in Costa Rica was directed explicitly against the Polish Jews. Oubursts of anti-Jewish feeling intensified with the appointment of Ulate as president, culminating in a wave of virulent antisemitism motivated by business competition (1951–52). The Junta Patriótica Costarricense agitated for a law restricting commercial activities to native Costa Ricans, attacking Jewish homes and institutions in San José. The situation began to improve with the presidency of José Figueres (1954–58), who publicly affirmed the principle of equal rights for all Costa Rican citizens.

Communal Organization

The early Sephardi immigrants worshipped in private homes on High Holidays, but permanent communal institutions were founded by the Jews from Poland. Around 1930 they purchased a plot for a Jewish cemetery and established a *Chevra Kadisha* and two years later they established a synagogue. The communal organization, Centro Israelita Sionista, was officially founded in 1934 serving both as a religious and a Zionist center. Costa Rican Jews were not very observant, and for several years they lacked rabbinical leadership. The strongest leader of the community was David Sikora (until his death in 1968), and religious functions were filled by Herman Reifer. With time, new institutions were formed as part of the Centro Israelita Sionista – *WIZO, *B'nai B'rith, Sociedad de Damas Israelitas de Beneficencia, several Zionist and youth groups, and a social and sports club. The community maintained ties with other Jewish communities in Central America through the Federación de Comunidades de América Central.

Jewish education in a complementary framework started in 1934 on the initiative of teachers, who saw to a Jewish religious and Hebrew education. During the 1950s the school system was modernized by Heszel Klepfish, who also introduced the study of Yiddish. In 1960 the Centro Israelita opened the Jaim Weizmann day school, starting with a kindergarten and first grade. Each year a new class was opened, and in 1970 it had a full program of primary and secondary grades with 300 students. Practically all the Jewish children in San José at primary level attend the Jewish school, and the number of students remained stable at around 300. Many young Jews completed their studies in Mexican or American universities, though of late most university students preferred to complete their studies in Costa Rica.

Religious life in Costa Rica centered around the Shaare Zion Congregation, the main Orthodox synagogue in San José. The Reform Congregation B'nei Israel was founded in 1984, building its own synagogue in 1989. In addition, there was a Chabad House in San José.

Relations with Israel

Costa Rica voted in favor of the partition of Palestine and was among the first nations to recognize the State of Israel in 1948. Diplomatic relations between the two countries were friendly, based on mutual values of freedom, tolerance, and democracy, Costa Rica being the only country (apart from El Salvador) that resisted international pressure and did not remove its embassy from Jerusalem.

BIBLIOGRAPHY: EJC, 3 (1948), 180–1. **ADD. BIBLIOGRAPHY:** M. Arbell, *The Jewish Nation of the Caribbean* (2002); J. Schifter Sikora, L. Gudmundson, and M. Solera Castro, *El Judío en Costa Rica* (1979); B. Baruch, *Judíos Costarricenses* (2000); L. Gudmundson, "Costa Rican Jewry," in: J.L. Elkin and G.W. Merkx (eds.), *Jewish*

Presence in Latin America (1987); D. Elazar, "The Jewish Community of Costa Rica," at: www.jcpa.org.

[Moshe Nes El / Margalit Bejarano (2nd ed.)]

°**COSTOBAR**, prominent Idumean of the first century B.C.E. (his ancestors served as priests of the Idumean god, Koz). At the time of Herod's capture of Jerusalem in 37 B.C.E., Costobar was given the task of blocking the city's exits to prevent the escape of all those opposing the new king. Convinced of his loyalty, Herod subsequently appointed him governor of Idumea and Gaza. Salome, Herod's sister, was given to Costobar in marriage, after her first husband's execution. Costobar seems to have plotted against the king. For twelve years he gave shelter to the sons of Baba, archenemies of Herod, and as governor of Idumea offered to support Queen Cleopatra of Egypt in her attempt to obtain control of territory. According to Josephus, he was pardoned by Herod after the plot was discovered, although he was eventually divorced by Salome, who revealed the full extent of her husband's treachery. As a result, Costobar, together with the sons of Baba, were seized and put to death (c. 25 B.C.E.).

BIBLIOGRAPHY: Jos., Ant., 15:253–66; A. Schalit, *Hordos ha-Melekh* (1964³), 82–84.

[Isaiah Gafni]

COTA DE MAGUAQUE, RODRIGO DE (fl. 1470), Spanish Converso poet. He was related to Diego Arias de Avila, the chief paymaster of Castile. Probably in the 1480s, Cota de Maguaque, incensed at not being invited to an Arias family wedding, wrote an *Epitalamio* ("Epithalamium") satirizing the groom. This contains many allusions to Jewish customs of the period. Cota de Maguaque was not content merely to convert. He felt or feigned hatred toward his former coreligionists, and sided with the "Old Christians" in their persecution of the Conversos. This animosity inspired the bitter satire directed against him by Antón de *Montoro. Cota de Maguaque was long credited, erroneously, with the authorship of many important 15th-century Spanish poems. There is no doubt, however, about his composition of the *Diálogo entre el amor y un viejo*, the deep humanity of which is in marked contrast to the superficiality and artificiality of the poetry of the period.

BIBLIOGRAPHY: A. Cortina, in: *Revista de la Biblioteca, Archivo y Museo*, 6 (1929), 151–65; Cotarelo y Mori, *Boletín de la Real Academia Española*, 13 (1926), 11–17; Baer, Spain, 2 (1966), 300–1, 311–2.

[Kenneth R. Scholberg]

COTLER, IRWIN (1940–) Canadian professor of Law, human rights activist, Jewish communal leader, and politician. Cotler was born in Montreal. He studied law at McGill University and did graduate work at Yale University. Returning to Canada, Cotler accepted an appointment at Osgood Law School in Toronto and, at the same time, became a special assistant to John Turner, federal minister of justice. In 1973 Colter moved to McGill Law School to teach international and human rights law.

Active in Canadian and Jewish affairs, he was counsel to the Deschenes Commission of Inquiry in the matter of bringing Nazi war criminals in Canada to justice, a member of the International Commission of Inquiry into the Fate and Whereabouts of Raoul Wallenberg, and the Canadian Human Rights Tribunal Active in Canadian Jewish life. In the early 1980s Cotler served as president of the Canadian Jewish Congress. A Zionist and advocate of Middle East rapprochement, Cotler helped found Canadian Professors for Peace in the Middle East and long worked to promote a dialogue between Israelis and Palestinians. As a passionate champion of human rights, Cotler served as legal council to many prisoners of conscience including Andrei Sakharov, Nelson Mandela, Jacob *Timmerman, and Natan *Sharansky. In 2003 Cotler helped win acquittal for Egyptian democracy advocate Saad Ibrahim, imprisoned by Egyptian authorities.

Asked to become a candidate for the federal Liberal Party, in 1999 Colter easily won election in the heavily Jewish Montreal riding of Mount Royal and was twice reelected. Passed over for cabinet office by former prime minister Jean Chretien, Coster was appointed in 2003 by newly installed prime minster Paul Martin as justice minister and attorney-general of Canada. Among his first and more controversial tasks, Cotler had to deal with the thorny issues of legalization of gay marriage, the decriminalization of marijuana, and the monitoring of the federal government's application of its anti-terrorism legislation.

Cotler's wife, Ariela, was no stranger to the political world, having worked in the office of Israeli Prime Minister Menaḥem *Begin.

[Harold Troper (2nd ed.)]

COTTBUS, city in Germany. Jews are first recorded in Cottbus in 1448. They were expelled in 1510 and not allowed to enter the city until 1712 and 1739, when Jewish wool merchants from Poland were permitted to stay temporarily for business purposes. From the middle of the 18th century a few individual Jews were allowed to settle permanently and to open businesses, but a community was not formed until 1858. It grew from around 40 in the first half of the 19th century to 128 in 1871 and 460 in 1895. The first rabbi was Marcus Dienstfertig (1872–95), followed by Solomon Posner (1895–1935). The synagogue was erected in 1902, and in 1933 the community had two charitable institutions, two cemeteries, and five cultural societies. In 1930 a training farm was established near Cottbus, under the auspices of the Reichsbund Juedischer Frontsoldaten. In 1933 there were around 450 Jews in Cottbus. From May 1933 the Jews were prohibited from taking part in the annual fair in Cottbus, and in June all Jewish employees were ousted from the trade unions and deprived of their jobs. The majority of the Jews emigrated from Cottbus after 1933, and by May 1939 only 142 were left. Most were deported in 1942. In 1943 Polish Jews were brought to a forced labor camp at Cottbus. The community was not reinstituted after the war.

BIBLIOGRAPHY: S. Posner, *Geschichte der Juden in Cottbus…* (1908); FJW, 64; Yad Vashem Archives, Arolson index. **ADD. BIBLIOGRAPHY:** J. Rueckert, in: I. Dieckmann (ed.), *Wegweiser durch das juedische Brandenburg* (1995), 5–82; S. Krestin (ed.), *Die juedischen Friedhoefe in Cottbus* (2004).

[Chasia Turtel]

COTTON, plant mentioned under the name *karpas* (derived from the Sanskrit *karpasa*) in the Book of Esther (1:6) in the description of the magnificent ornamentation of Ahasuerus' palace. In the Mishnah cotton is called *ẓemer gefen* ("vine wool") as its leaves resemble those of the vine (*gefen*). Mentioned several times in rabbinic literature, it was apparently an important crop. This is attested by the Greek scholar Pausanias, who in the second century C.E. wrote (5:5) that "the only Greek country that raises cotton is Elea. There it is delicate, like the cotton that grows in Judea, but less yellow." *Kutnah*, the modern Hebrew term for cotton, is derived, as is "cotton" itself, from the Arabic. In talmudic Hebrew and in Aramaic, however, its meaning is "flax" (cf. Shab. 110b). It is evident from the Mishnah (Kil. 7:2) that the cotton grown in Ereẓ Israel was a perennial, probably the species *Gossypium arboreum*. The annual or biannual species, *Gossypium herbaceum*, of Indian origin, began to be cultivated at a later date. Varieties of American cotton, though introduced to Israel only in the late 1950s, are grown extensively, and constitute one of Israel's major crops.

BIBLIOGRAPHY: Loew, Flora, 2 (1924), 235–43; J. Feliks, *Olam ha-Ẓome'aḥ ha-Mikra'i* (1968[2]), 285–7.

[Jehuda Feliks]

COTTON, JACK (1903–1964), British businessman. Born in Birmingham, Cotton became an estate agent in that city in the 1920s, and, after World War II, emerged as probably the best-known figure in the world of English property development. Realizing the enormous demand that peace would bring for homes and offices, he secured financing for major projects by giving a share in the development of properties to big companies which owned the land, especially banks and insurance firms. Cotton's City Centre Properties developed the Bull Ring area in central Birmingham and many areas of central London as well as the Pan Am Building adjacent to Grand Central Station in New York. A loyal Jew and Zionist, Cotton was vice president of the largest Birmingham Orthodox synagogue and donated three chairs to Israeli universities; he also funded the building of the Cotton Terraces at London Zoo.

BIBLIOGRAPHY: O. Marriott, *The Property Boom* (1967); ODNB online; DBB, I, 796–99.

[William D. Rubinstein (2nd ed.)]

°**COUDENHOVE-KALERGI, HEINRICH VON** (1859–1906), Austrian diplomat, philosopher, and author. He professed to having been an antisemite in his youth, but during a sojourn in Turkey and Japan became interested in Oriental religions and consequently in the Jewish legacy. Among 26 languages he knew Hebrew, which he acquired from the rabbi of Pobezovice (Ronsperg). Jewish scholars, among them Armand Aharon *Kaminka, were frequently guests at his castle. A practicing Roman Catholic, he used to leave mass demonstratively on Good Friday at the prayer for "perfidious Jews." In 1901 he published *Das Wesen des Anti-semitismus* (Eng. ed. 1935, *Anti-semitism throughout the Ages*), one of the most successful non-literary anti-antisemitic works of the 20th century. In this book he expressed the view that the Jews had always been a minority, first as monotheists in a polytheistic world, and later as non-Christians in a Christian world. He denied the validity of race and regarded the antisemitic movement in his day as a result of envy, semi-education, and intolerance. At present its root lay in the fanaticism instilled in the child when taught that the Jews had crucified Christ. Coudenhove welcomed Zionism but thought that Palestine was unsuitable for its aims. He suggested progressive assimilation for Western Jews and the founding of a Jewish state for East European Jews. An unsatisfactory solution of the Jewish question would endanger the future of Western civilization. His Judaic library and manuscripts were deposited in the synagogue of Pobezovice and destroyed with it by the Nazis in 1938. His son, RICHARD NICHOLAS (1894–1972), was the founder of the Pan-European movement after World War I. He re-edited his father's book with a preface of his own (1923), and in 1937 published *Judenhass*, in which he states that antisemitism in the 1920s had developed mainly as a weapon against Marxism and was an outcome of the pauperization of Central Europe. Zionism had turned the Jews from a despised caste into a hated nation. Basically the Jewish question was only one of the minority problems. It would find its solution when "nation" became a cultural definition rather than one of blood (see *Autonomism; S. *Dubnow). In 1937 he suggested Jewish colonization of Rhodesia, assuming that Great Britain might be interested in easing her position in Palestine in this way. His first wife, the Viennese actress Ida Roland (1884–1951), was of Jewish origin.

BIBLIOGRAPHY: R.N. Coudenhove-Kalergi, *An Idea Conquers the World* (1953), 1–59. **ADD. BIBLIOGRAPHY:** A.T. Levenson, in: YLBI, 46 (2001), 276–99; A. Ziegerhofer-Prettenthaler, *Die Pan-Europa-Bewegung* (2004).

[Meir Lamed]

COUNCIL OF FOUR LANDS, central institution of Jewish self-government in Poland functioning from approximately the middle of the 16th century until 1764, and representing the Jewish communities associated in their respective provinces ("Lands"), principally four in number. See *Council of the Lands.

COUNCIL OF JEWISH FEDERATIONS AND WELFARE FUNDS, association of U.S. Jewish community organizations. The Council was first organized in 1932 by Jewish Federations in 15 cities, absorbing the work of two predecessor organizations: the Bureau of Jewish Social Research and the National

Appeals Information Service. The Bureau of Jewish Social Research was founded in 1919 as a merger of the Bureau of Jewish Philanthropic Research, the Field Bureau of the National Conference of Jewish Social Service, and the Bureau of Information and Statistics of the American Jewish Committee. It conducted local studies of Jewish communities and special studies affecting Jewish Federations and the service areas of their affiliates. It also compiled statistics for various fields of local Jewish service. The National Appeals Information Service was organized in 1927 by 41 Jewish Federations.

The Bureau of Jewish Social Research acted as its agent in the preparation of reports on the programs and finances of national and overseas agencies. With the organization of the Council of Jewish Federations and Welfare Funds, the functions previously performed were extended to include community planning for local Jewish services and mutual aid to Jewish Federations and Welfare Funds in conducting local fund-raising campaigns.

The Council of Jewish Federations and Welfare Funds published annual reports on developments in specific fields (*Yearbook of Jewish Social Services*, 1930–67; and *Jewish Communal Services – Programs and Finances*, 1955–68), budget digests dealing with individual national and overseas agencies, and reports dealing with budgeting, campaigning, public welfare, public relations, and business management services. When the Council of Jewish Federations and Welfare Funds was organized in 1932, there were less than 70 Jewish Federations and Welfare Funds which were raising under $10 million a year. By 1995 Jewish Federations affiliated with the Council operated in 190 headquarter-cities, serving thousands of communities, and raised about $800 million in annual campaigns. About 95% of the Jewish population of the U.S. resided in federated communities. In addition, a special effort from 1967 for the Israel Emergency Fund, which was organized in the week preceding the Six-Day War, raised hundreds of millions of dollars through associated Jewish Federations. The idea of a second line to the annual campaign was used again in the Yom Kippur War and with the resettlement of Soviet Jews and Ethiopians and Argentinian Jews. Federations are the principal sources of financial support for the *United Jewish Appeal, *United Hias Service, *National Jewish Welfare Board, and community relations agencies (outside New York City). They also provide substantial financial support to about 50 other national and overseas agencies. In addition, each local Federation supports local welfare services (family, child care, aged care, refugee care), Jewish hospitals, centers, camps, youth services, Jewish education, and local community relations. Federations were allocating less than 30% of their funds for national and overseas agencies in 1932. By 1995 overseas agencies (mainly the UJA) were receiving 38.7%; national agencies were receiving 1%; and local agencies and Federation administration were receiving 55%. The remaining 5% is due to shrinkage. This was exclusive of about $20 million provided by nonsectarian United Funds and Community Chests for the support of local Jewish services. In response to pressures from local Federations that felt that there was not enough accountability to them regarding how funds were spent overseas, complaints of a redundancy of services and bureaucracies, and with the expectation of increased efficiency and actual dollar savings as well as increased fundraising capacity, the Council was merged with the United Jewish Appeal and United Israel Appeal in 1999 to form the United Jewish Communities. One proviso stemmed the tide of decreasing contribution to Israel and overseas needs by creating a floor beneath which the overseas contributions of the Federated Communities would not fall for a specific period of time.

BIBLIOGRAPHY: S.P. Goldberg, in: AJYB, 57–70 (1956–69); H.L. Lurie, *A Heritage Affirmed: The Jewish Federation Movement in America* (1961). **ADD. BIBLIOGRAPHY:** D. Elazar, *Community and Polity: The Organizational Dynamics of American Jewry* (1976, 1995²); G.B. Bubis and S.F. Windmueller, *From Predictability to Chaos?: How American Jewish Leaders Reinvented Their National Communal System* (2005).

[Samuel P. Goldberg / Michael Berenbaum (2nd ed.)]

COUNCIL OF JEWS FROM GERMANY, organization representing the German-speaking Jewish émigrés of the Nazi period from Central Europe. Originally known as the Council for the Protection of the Rights and Interests of Jews from Germany, the Council was established in 1945 by the American Federation of Jews from Central Europe, the Association of Jewish Refugees in Great Britain, Irgun Olej Merkas Europa (formerly Hitachduth Olej Germania w'Austria) in Tel Aviv, and also joined by some refugee organizations from Belgium and France, by Centra, and the Union of Jewish Communities in Latin America in Montevideo. The Council cooperated with leading Jewish organizations dealing with restitution and compensation from Germany and Austria, and was a founding member of the Conference on Jewish Material Claims Against Germany. It has established and supports social welfare agencies and looks after the various interests of German-speaking victims of the Nazi era living outside Germany and Austria, especially in the care of aging refugees, and maintains a link with the cultural past of German-speaking Jews through publications and conferences and the support of cultural institutions. The Council initiated the establishment of the United Restitution Organization (*URO) in March 1947 and in 1954 founded the *Leo Baeck Institute, Rabbi Leo Baeck serving as the first president of the Council. The goals of the Council are to act as the organizational framework for German-speaking Jews worldwide, and to commemorate and preserve the achievements of their heritage for future generations.

[Shalom Adler-Rudel / Saul Kagan (2nd ed.)]

COUNCILS OF THE LANDS, the central institutions of Jewish self-government in Poland and Lithuania from the middle of the 16th century until 1764. The bodies in question were the Council of the Four Lands (Heb. וַעַד אַרְבַּע אֲרָצוֹת) or council of the lands (Heb. וַעַד הָאֲרָצוֹת), the controlling body for the Jewish provinces ("Lands") of Poland, while the Council of the Land of Lithuania (Heb. וַעַד מְדִינַת לִיטָא or וַעַד הַמְּדִינָה) was the similar organization for the Lithuanian grand duchy, which was associated with the Polish crown. The two bodies were similar in structure and function. They were not constituted in either case as perpetual organizations, but were theoretically to the end ad hoc assemblies representing the permanent administrative entities, the local communities associated in their respective provinces or "Lands." The councils represent the highest form of Jewish autonomy within a regional or national framework attained by European Jewry, both in terms of territorial extent or of duration (see *Autonomy; *Poland).

Before the councils were established, the Polish government had made attempts to set up a centralized Jewish leadership. This official appointment was unpopular with the Jews. The beginnings of regional council leadership were seen in *Great Poland in about 1519. The Council of the Lands of the Polish Crown originated from the rabbinical court at the fairs held in *Lublin. It acquired the status of a central *bet din* because of its activity during the meetings of merchants and heads of the communities and because famous rabbis participated in its deliberations.

After 1533 documents refer to assemblies acting in the name of all the Jews of Lithuania. From the 1560s the tax administration of Lithuanian Jewry was centralized. In 1567 two delegates dealt with taxation matters "in the name of all Jewish communities in ... the duchy of Lithuania." Ordinances originating before 1569 issued from "the elected from all Lithuania" acting on behalf "of all the communities of Lithuania whose authority is vested in us." They enjoined the holding of assemblies every three years and the election of "nine heads of the Lands and three rabbis."

Even at the zenith of the activities of the councils, the autonomy of the individual community, which had its own dependent boroughs (*sevivot*), was undiminished. The older, firmly established communities were known in Poland as *kehillot rashiyyot* ("principal communities"), and in Lithuania as *kehillot rashei bet din* ("communities of heads of the courts"), the only constituents of this council. Later, growing communities contended for the status of "principal community." Among those which succeeded after strenuous effort were *Tykocin, in Poland, and *Vilna and *Slutsk in Lithuania.

The provincial council of the *galil* ("circuit") closely resembled the Polish regional Sejmik. The relationship of the provincial council to the Council of the Lands was paralleled by that of the Sejmik to the Sejm or national diet. The Council of the Lands of the Polish Crown comprised two distinct bodies: the assembly of the *rashei ha-medinot*, elders of the provinces, and the assembly of the *dayyanei ha-araẓot* ("the judges of the Lands" or "*bet din* of the Four Lands"), composed of the rabbis representing the principal communities and provinces. The *bet din* was competent to adjudge disputes among the constituents of the council, or between the council and its constituents. The two bodies frequently functioned in conjunction. These two sections of the council also cooperated frequently in Lithuania.

Constituents

The constituents of the council were, first, the principal communities, acting either as a recognized part of the delegation for "their province" or as an independent delegation, and, second, the provinces. The accepted designation of "Council of the Four Lands" generally denoted its principal constituents: the provinces of Great Poland (principal community: *Poznan) and Little (*Lesser) Poland (principal community: *Cracow); "the Lvov Land"; and the province of Volhynia. Reference is occasionally made to Three Lands, Five Lands, or even more. In 1717 the council comprised 18 entities, nine communities which acted in their own name and nine provinces. "The Council of the Land of Lithuania" had in 1623 three "communities of the heads of the courts": *Brest-Litovsk, *Grodno, and *Pinsk, each heading a wide area. However, even in Lithuania representatives of smaller communities were occasionally present at sessions of the council, with the right to petition on tax matters and other questions. In the regular sessions of the Council of the Lands between 20 and 30 delegates participated, in plenary sessions between 50 and 70. For the Lithuanian council a standing composition of 15 delegates was established in 1700 comprising the two heads and *av bet din* of each principal community (five at this date). The officials of the council included: (1) The "*parnas* of the House of Israel for the Four Lands," head of the council in both internal and external matters, who presided at the assemblies. He was elected from among the "heads of the Lands," not from the rabbinical delegates. (2) Second in the hierarchy was the "*ne'eman* ("trustee") of the House of Israel for the Four Lands," i.e., the treasurer and chief secretary. The position was salaried and open to rabbinical candidates. (3) The *shtadlan*, who received a high salary and was obliged to be on hand at court or at the place of the assembly of the royal Sejm to represent Jewish interests before the government. (4) There was also a *kotev* ("clerk") to the council, later joined by other clerks. (5) The function of the *shamma'im*, or assessors, was also important. The leadership of the Council of the Land of Lithuania was for a long time assumed by the *av bet din* of Brest-Litovsk. The other offices were generally similar to those of the Council of the Lands.

Both councils maintained an official minute book, a **pinkas*, which invested the record of resolutions and budgets with legal authority. Of the original *pinkas* of the Council of the Lands only a few remnants are extant (published by I. Halpern, 1945). The first detailed ordinance recorded there dates from 1580. The *pinkas* of the Council of the Land of Lithuania from 1623 until its end in 1764 is extant (ed. S. Dubnow, 1925).

The Congresses of the Councils

The Council of the Four Lands met twice yearly at the fairs of Lublin and Yarosłav. During the 18th century the meetings

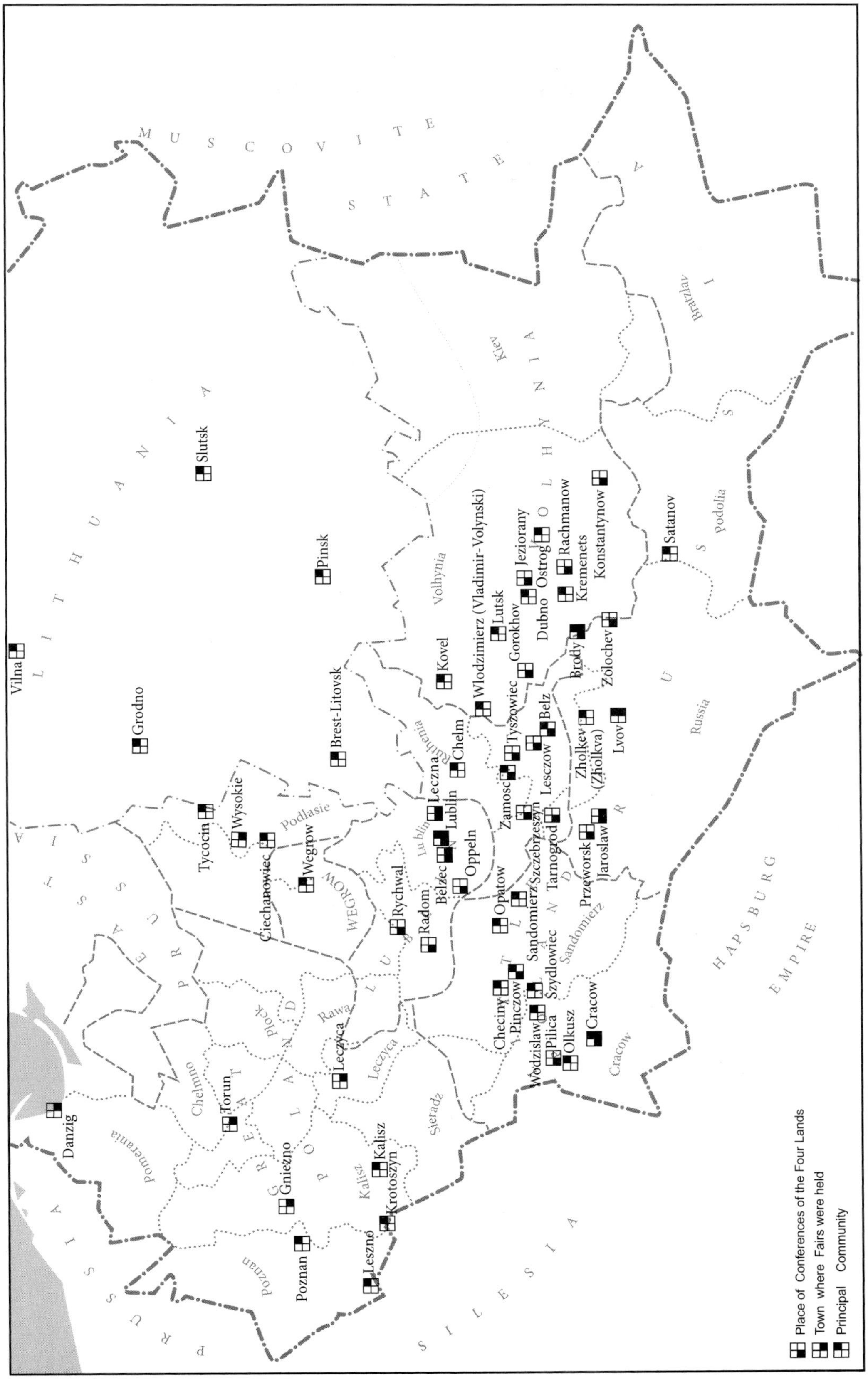

Main Jewish communities in Poland and Lithuania under the jurisdiction of the autonomous Jewish organization of the Council of Four Lands and the Council of Lithuania. After I. Halperin, Pinkas Va'ad Arba Araẓot *(1945).*

were less regular. The venue and time of meeting of the Lithuanian council were determined as circumstances required. Between 1623 and 1764 the Lithuanian council held 37 meetings in different places; of these 15 were held in its first 30 years of existence.

The principal communities in the Council of the Lands elected their delegates under varying systems and at different intervals. The proportion of electors among the householders in the community varied with its size and the number of its dependent boroughs. The residents of the boroughs, comprising about one-quarter, or even one-third of Polish Jewry, did not have the right of election. It has been estimated that in the latter period of the council's existence approximately 1,000 householders in only 35 communities participated in the elections, i.e., about 1% of the total 92,000 adult Jewish householders. In Lithuania the percentage of electors toward the end of the council's existence for all its five principal communities was 11.3% of the total of adult householders; for Vilna 7%; for Grodno 10%; and for Pinsk 20%. In relation to the total Jewish population of Lithuania the percentage of electors was only 0.7%.

Implementation of Decisions

In 1697 responsibility for implementation of the council's decisions rested with the "heads of the Lands, who, within their borders, will ensure that all ordinances shall be implemented." In 1666–67 the heads of the Cracow community ceased to attend meetings of the council. The council was forced to resort to persuasion and threats in order to bring them back. The Lithuanian council in 1628 decided that "all the ordinances from the beginning of the *pinkas* until its end are entrusted to the care of the heads of the Lands of each community." The means of enforcement and persuasion was excommunication (**ḥerem*), which was decreed at the fairs, and by announcements in the synagogues (in Yiddish, with an admixture of Hebrew words). R. Joel *Sirkes sharply condemned imposition of the *ḥerem* by the council and recommended a general prohibition on all such decrees to be replaced by a code of sanctions, including fines, expulsion, and handing over the accused to the non-Jewish authorities. He even suggested the establishment of a central supervisory administration under the council. The heads of the communities ignored his recommendations.

In 1596 the Council of the Lands constituted itself as the supreme court for hearing appeals and sentencing serious offenders. The Lithuanian council defined its jurisdiction and authority in 1626. Each congress would henceforward introduce ordinances on its own initiative without being bound by the proceedings of earlier congresses. Unanimous agreement to the introduction of new ordinances was demanded because of the federal nature of the council.

Relations between the Council of the Lands and the Council of the Land of Lithuania were occasionally strained. The Lithuanian council was dependent on the Council of the Lands for representation before the central government, while the Council of the Lands expected Lithuania to share in its "burdens," including gifts to magnates and the sovereign, which the heads of the Lithuanian communities often thought excessive. The two bodies also disagreed over the jurisdiction of the border communities and their boroughs, and over rights of commerce.

Competence

The competence of the council lay principally in relations with the Crown and central governmental institutions, in the representation of general Jewish interests, and in formulating legislation for the communities.

The government of Poland-Lithuania was aware of the existence of the councils as independent administrative bodies and accorded them tacit recognition. Formally, the councils were only bodies administering the collection of the Jewish tax from the generality of the Jewry of the kingdom. The councils conducted negotiations, often complicated, with the authorities on the amount of the taxation to be levied. A noteworthy achievement of the Polish council was that after 1717 the amount of taxes paid by the Jews was not increased despite depreciation of the currency. This was one of the main causes of the abolition of the council by the government.

The councils divided the total of taxes due into "sympla," units of payment of equal amount. It then directed a certain community or province to pay annually a certain number of "sympla." The council based assessment and collection on tax lists and estimates. In principle, taxes were allocated according to the means of the individual. The difficulties of raising the taxes forced the councils to try different methods. The social tension entailed by tax collection increased as the debts incurred by the councils and individual communities accumulated. Especially large amounts were expended on maintaining the Jewish representation before the government, defraying the cost of bribes, and physical protection necessitating swift and unobtrusive action. Such demands gradually swallowed the greater part of the budget at the councils' disposal. They were forced to raise loans at high interest rates to meet their obligations.

At the same time the communities themselves developed a new system of taxation, the **korobka*, or basket tax. This was first a commodity tax, mainly levied on *sheḥitah* and afterward extended to business transactions. In 1700 the Lithuanian council was forced to take over the basket tax. In the 18th century growing insolvency compelled the council to increase its demands while, on the other hand, the communities showed increasing independence. In 1721 it became known that a number of communities and provinces in Lithuania had united "to reject the assessment of the poll tax" which the previous council had imposed. The council issued a *ḥerem* against them. In fact, the dissidents had gone so far as to complain to the Lithuanian fiscal tribunal about the "oppressive practices" employed by the council in levying taxes. The principal communities tended to shift the burden from themselves onto the shoulders of the smaller communities and new settlements. The revolt of the latter against the council's "acts of oppression" and the aspersion on the fairness of its apportionment expressed the accumulated bitterness of opposition to the councils. The individual community became more determined to retain the revenues under its jurisdiction. The administration of tax collection may be seen as the criterion of the councils' ability to fulfill their functions.

The councils considered themselves empowered to direct the manifold social, ethical, and legal aspects of Jewish life, and to frame ordinances regulating the affairs of the communities and the conduct of its leaders. They regarded themselves as the guardians of Jewish autonomy. The councils seldom attempted to meddle in affairs between the community and its members; they tended to uphold the authority of the leaders of the communities and the federal character of the council organization. In Lithuania the principal communities sometimes intervened between the individual member and his community. A plaintiff first had to lodge a deposit. The councils arbitrated in disputes between communities or Lands. The majority of such cases were laid before the *dayyanim* of the "Land."

Structure of Leadership

The oligarchic character of the community leadership was reflected in the councils, especially in that of Lithuania. In 1628 the Lithuanian council instructed its three constituents to ensure that "no communal administrative board shall … divulge the deliberations and confidences of the board; and shall refrain from involving individual members of the community with matters concerning the board; and shall impose severe punishment in such cases." Heads of the communities were warned against attempting to rally their own factions in opposition to their colleagues.

The council supported the leaders of the community in countering attempts at rebellion or the organization of internal opposition against the community boards. In 1623 they reaffirmed the former *ḥerem* prohibiting such actions. Severe measures were to be taken against those suspected of these attempts. Any independent organization was prohibited: a plaintiff was instructed to appear before the community board "alone, or with one other, but not more."

The councils were vehement in their censures of the "common people," the "rabble in the streets and markets" who "make light of the acts of the town optimates." It was "the duty of the leaders of every community to deter these offenders with the severest sentences, reaching even to the gates of death." This was in reaction to the continual opposition which arose because the great majority of householders in the large towns, and all Jewish residents of the boroughs, were deprived of any influence or share in the leadership. The council repeatedly issued ordinances to enforce more severe sentences for "sedition" and "scorn." Concomitantly, the problem reflected the revolt of the ascendant against the old-established communities, and in the course of time it reflected the attitude of communities where lower social classes had attained leadership. In 1650 the ordinance against intrigues was extended to "communities, settlements, and boroughs" intriguing against the principal Lithuanian communities, members of the council. In 1687 "sedition" among the communities was also denounced. Opposition to the councils intensified and became more broadly based toward the end of their existence. Artisans apparently formed a major opposition group as in 1761 the council of Lithuania felt constrained to forbid expressly their participation in the main activities and institutions of the more important communities.

Economic Guidance

The councils undertook to provide guidance in the economic sphere, in particular on occupational problems originating in the 16th and 17th centuries from the leasing and management of farm estates and related branches. Consequently their legislative activity extended to both the socioeconomic aspects and the related socioreligious problems. In regard to the first, the council instituted the *ḥezkat orenda* (חֶזְקַת אוֹרֶנְדָא), its sanction of preemptive leaseholding (see **ḥazakah*); the Jewish lessee of a farm property or related enterprise from a Polish noble for a term of three years was henceforward upheld in possession against Jewish competitors for the lease, which might even devolve on his heirs. Similarly, it became possible to acquire preemption on houses rented from non-Jews and to establish a right after three years' undisturbed possession of market shops. As long as economic and social factors encouraged Jewish development, and the councils retained their influence, such regulations generally worked efficiently and prevented Jews from undercutting one another in dealings with the Polish nobility.

The councils also tried to ensure that Jewish religious precepts were strictly observed on rented properties – that Jews observed the Sabbath, refrained from employing Christian serfs on the Sabbath, from raising pigs, or gelding animals. The councils forbade isolated families to settle in the villages. In 1607, in an endeavor to reconcile economic realities with Jewish religious precepts, the council designated the rabbinical authorities to evolve a detailed code of ordinances regulating the permissibility of charging interest (see *Moneylending).

On one socioeconomic question the two councils adopted divergent approaches. The Council of the Lands prohibited Jewish contracting of customs duties, salt mining, and the like, since the Polish nobility themselves coveted such revenues and in pressing their own claims Jewish merchants could harm the whole community. This prohibition, however, was never obeyed to the letter, even within the limits of the Lands Council's jurisdiction, while the province of Great Poland evidently felt otherwise. The Lithuanian council several times expressed its opinion that the Jewish community would benefit if the customs revenues were in Jewish hands; the council promised its support to a group of Jewish contractors and accepted money from them. Nevertheless, the Lithuanian council agreed that it could be dangerous to contract for the mint and related operations.

Both councils applied strict safeguards to Jewish credit operations to inspire faith in Jewish business integrity. Special forms of credit instruments (*mamranot*) were authorized for the use of Jewish merchants. Numerous regulations dealt with the problems of absconding bankrupts, minors, or irresponsible persons who frivolously embarked on trade or contracted debts.

The Lithuanian council issued numerous **takkanot* against newcomers to protect the rights of community residence and membership (*ḥezkat *yishuv*), domicile in the towns (*ḥezkat ironut*), and business operations (see **ḥazakah*) within the communities. A similar trend is also discernible in ordinances introduced by the Council of the Lands. The foundations of Jewish solidarity became seriously undermined in the wake of the *Chmielnicki massacres (1648), when fugitives were deprived of rights in their places of asylum.

The councils maintained an effectual system of representation before the government and *self-defense to prevent the withholding of Jewish rights or to seek their renewal. They also tried to ensure that the murderer or assailant of a Jew should be brought to trial; similarly, they defrayed the cost for defense against anti-Jewish libels. On the other hand, the Lithuanian council warned, "Whosoever out of the violence of his heart shall go to provoke or assault a non-Jew … shall not be helped by a single penny, even if as a result he should be executed." The councils actively rebutted *blood libels and charges of desecration of the *host. Toward the end of their existence, they sent a representative to Rome to obtain papal declarations against the blood libel and undertook their publication.

Torah Study

Study had a prominent place in the councils' concerns. They attended to the supply of teachers and the fundamentals of Torah education. Similarly, by giving their approval to the publication of books, the rabbis participating in the council could exercise control over publications intended for the Jewish public. Great care was devoted to the *yeshivot. In 1652 the Lithuanian council ruled that "every congregation having a rabbi shall maintain a yeshivah for adults and youths according to their capacity, as formerly laid down: all existent agreements with the rabbi to diminish the numbers of the yeshivah shall be null and void." This instruction was endorsed in later assemblies. Scholars were exempted from paying tax. Yet the attitude toward scholars fluctuated, pointing to a certain tension; there were also changes in the definition of "scholar."

Social Problems

Social problems dealt with by the councils included assisting poor girls to marry and regulating matchmaking. Communities were directed to care for the fugitives driven from the west in the Thirty Years' War, and from the east of Poland-Lithuania after the Chmielnicki massacres. A nascent class-consciousness broke through sometimes in the ordinances relating to charitable matters: the poor bride was to be provided for – after doing service in a Jewish home. Jews were instructed to preserve modesty in dress and feasting so as to prevent dangerous excess of show. The councils arranged for the collection and dispatch of "money for Ereẓ Israel," and notables who went there were given assistance.

The authority of the councils was also recognized to some extent in Jewish communities outside Poland and Lithuania. The councils were consulted in the *Eybeschuetz-*Emden controversy, while the old established community of Frankfurt sought the advice of the Council of the Four Lands.

The councils' assemblies were brought to an end by a resolution of the Polish Sejm in 1764, which established a different system for collecting the Jewish poll tax. The resolution concluded: "Whereas the comprehensive Jewish poll tax, established by statute in 1717, is abrogated … henceforward there shall be no assemblies, apportionments or other kinds of injunctions, levies or compulsions relating to the Jews as customary hitherto … from Jan. 2, 1765 … we abolish them in perpetuity." The councils did not convene again. A committee authorized by the Sejm met in Warsaw for two years to wind up the commitments of the Council of the Four Lands. A similar committee was appointed for the Lithuanian council. The provincial councils continued to convene ad hoc, but no longer functioned regularly.

The Jews of Poland and Lithuania saw the councils as an expression and symbol of social majesty and political power. After the Chmielnicki massacres Nathan Nata *Hannover depicted them as "the pillar of justice in the Land of Poland, as in the days before the destruction of the Temple in Jerusalem"; "the *parnasim* of the Four Lands were like the Sanhedrin of the Chamber of Hewn Stone (see *Temple) and they had authority to dispense justice to all Israel in the kingdom of Poland, to safeguard the law, to frame ordinances, and to inflict punishment as they saw fit." Idealization though it was, this still reflected the Jewish attitude. When the councils were terminated in 1764, a burning shame was felt that their "captains, the heads of the Lands, have been dispossessed of their mite of greatness, and even this small honor has been taken from Israel." In later generations the councils served as a paradigmatic ideal, and were invested with exemplary qualities, especially by the advocates of Jewish *Autonomism, Simon *Dubnow and his followers, at the end of the 19th and in the 20th centuries. Exponents of this ideology represented the councils as the pilot institution for national organizations of central Jewish autonomy in the Diaspora.

BIBLIOGRAPHY: S. Dubnow, *Pinkas ha-Medinah* (1925); Halpern, Pinkas, index; idem, *Tosafot u-Millu'im le-Pinkas Medinat Lita* (1935); idem (ed.), *Beit Yisrael be-Polin*, 1 (1948), 59–65; idem, in: *Ha-Kinnus ha-Olami le-Maddaei ha-Yahadut*, 1 (1952), 439–45; idem, in: *Zion*, 21 (1956), 64–91; Mahler, in: YIVO, *Historishe Shriftn*, 2 (1937), 639–49; idem, *Toledot ha-Yehudim be-Polin* (1946), 188–215; Ben-Sasson, in: *Zion*, 21 (1956), 183–206; idem, *Hagut ve-Hanhagah* (1959); M. Schorr, *Organizacja Żydów w Polsce* (1899); *Istoriya Yevreyskogo Naroda*, 11 (1914), 157–210, 510–3; Schipper, in: MGWJ, 56 (1912), 458–77; L. Lewin, *Die Landessynode der gross-polnischen Judenschaft* (1926); J. Lewin, *Dzieje sejmiku Żydów wielkopolskich* (1935), 48–56; *Frunk and Brilling*, in: YIVOA, 11 (1956/57). **ADD. BIBLIOGRAPHY:** S. Ettinger,

Va'ad Arba Arẓot (1990²), 15–24; J. Goldberg, "Va'ad Arba ha-Arẓot be-Mishtar ha-Medini ve-ha-Ḥevrati shel Mamlekhet Polin-Lita," in: *Ha-Ḥevrah ha-Yehudit be-Mamlekhet Polin ve-Lita* (1999), 125–42; A. Leszczynski, *Sejm Zydow Korony1623–1764* (1994).

[Haim Hillel Ben-Sasson]

COURANT, RICHARD (1888–1972), German mathematician. Born in Silesia, Courant studied at the universities of Breslau, Zurich, and Goettingen. He remained at Goettingen as an instructor in mathematics until the outbreak of World War I, when he served in the German army. He taught at Muenster from 1919 to 1920 and then returned to Goettingen as professor of mathematics and director of the mathematics institute. Driven from his chair by the Nazi regime in 1933, Courant taught for a year at Cambridge, England. In 1936 he settled in the United States, becoming professor and head of the department of mathematics at New York University, where he remained until his retirement in 1958. In collaboration with David Hilbert, he developed methods of applying the theories of quantum mechanics to the problems of physics, which are credited with later paving the way for the practical use of electronic computers.

During World War II Courant organized a team of scientific scholars who worked on military projects. After the war he established an institute for mathematics and mechanics at New York University, which developed into one of the largest establishments of its kind in the Western world. In 1958 it was renamed the Courant Institute of Mathematical Sciences, and New York University established a Richard Courant Lectureship in his honor. On the occasion of its inauguration, Niels Bohr observed that "every physicist is in his debt for the vast insight he has given us into mathematical methods for comprehending nature and the physical world." On the occasion of his 60th birthday, a volume of *Studies and Essays* was tendered to him. Courant wrote many scholarly books and papers.

[Sefton D. Temkin]

COURLAND (Ger. **Kurland**), region of West and South Latvia, between the Baltic Sea and Western Dvina River. Throughout the centuries control of this region frequently changed hands and the attitude toward Jewish settlement there varied accordingly. During the 12th century, the local tribes were subdued by the Livonian Knights whose statutes prohibited the presence of Jews within their territories. Jewish tombstones of the 14th century confirm that there were exceptions in the case of individual Jews. The Order could not withstand its external enemies and was liquated in 1561. Under the suzerainty of Poland, Courland became a duchy. The act of surrender of the Order to Poland stipulated that "it is forbidden for the Jews of Livonia to engage in commerce or to lease the collection of taxes"; yet it was impossible to close to them the southern border between Courland and Poland-Lithuania where Jews had settled from the 13th century.

Duchy of Courland

Internal political partition resulted in a varied attitude toward Jewish settlement within the duchy. The region of Piltene, owned by the head of the Church of Courland, was regarded as the bishop's private property. The promise of gain induced him to authorize wealthy Jews to settle there. Because of its geographical position, Jewish merchants also arrived in the region by sea, from Prussia. In 1559 the bishop sold the region to the king of Denmark, who transferred it to his brother, Duke Magnus von Holstein. Piltene thus became a kind of enclave within the duchy of Courland – a situation which resulted in disputes, including military clashes with Poland. In 1585 the region was sold to Poland and two provinces were formed from the area: the province of Piltene with a Jewish population under the jurisdiction of Poland, and the other parts of Courland, where the prohibition of 1561 remained in force. The Jews in the province of Piltene were permitted to found organized communities and engaged in commerce and crafts. Following an alliance between the duke of Courland and the province, the status of the Jews deteriorated, and in 1717 an annual tax of two talers per person was imposed; it was doubled in 1719. Between 1727 and 1738, expulsion decrees were issued, but they were only partially applied. In 1750 the Polish Sejm decided to authorize Jewish residence in the province in exchange for a payment of 1,000 albertustalers. Its collection was entrusted to Jewish tax farmers. In 1783 the tax was fixed at 400 talers and the Sejm published an order on the "maintenance of the civic and economic rights of the Jews" since they paid the taxes levied on them. In 1795 when the province, together with Courland, became part of Russia, the Jews were authorized to register themselves in the merchant guilds and participate in the municipal elections, although without elective rights. In 1817 they were granted the same rights as the other Jews in Courland.

In the parts of Courland outside the province of Piltene, the number of Jews increased during the 17th century. They were regarded as "foreigners" and subjected to open hostility, especially on the part of the merchants and craftsmen, who considered them rivals. The attitude of the nobility was more tolerant: Jews acted as intermediaries in the sale of the agricultural produce of the estates of the landowners, and imported goods which were not locally manufactured; the sums collected from them to authorize their residence, or from fines, enriched the treasuries of the nobility. In times of emergency, even the duke did not refrain from leasing the collection of customs and interest to the Jews – an act which aroused the opposition of the Landtag, the legislative council of the duchy, on which sat delegates of the Church, the nobility, and the towns. In 1713 an expulsion order was issued and Jews who remained despite the order were compelled to pay one taler a day both for themselves and for those who did not pay. In 1719 Jewish residence was authorized in exchange for an annual payment of 400 talers. The payments were not made as agreed, and by 1727 the arrears amounted to 2,000 talers. The collection of these arrears was often a subject of discussion at meetings of the Landtags. Jewish assessors were appointed to collect the tax. In 1730 the residence of Jewish craftsmen and persons engaged in commerce was authorized. This did not prevent the publication of expulsion orders in subsequent years. The situation especially deteriorated in 1760, when the expulsion was brutally carried out. During the last years of the duchy's existence, the question of granting rights to the Jews was a subject of controversial polemics.

Within Czarist Russia (1795–1917)

In 1795, after the third partition of Poland, Courland passed to Russia. The number of Jewish males in Courland numbered 4,581 in 1797. When the Senate in St. Petersburg requested information on the number of Jews, their occupations, and the existing laws with respect to them from the governor of the province, the governor, influenced by the German inhabitants, sent a negative report. The "foreigners" had been living in the region illegally for several centuries; their economic situation was degenerate, and it was doubtful whether they could be transformed into useful citizens. The Senate was not convinced by his conclusions and issued instructions that regulations similar to those applicable in other parts of the country be prepared. In 1799 a law was ratified according to which the Jews of Courland became citizens with the right to reside in the province, to establish communities, and to engage in commerce and crafts. Courland was not included within the *Pale of Settlement in 1804, and the law of 1799 was therefore interpreted as applying only to those Jews who had lived in Courland at the time of its publication and to their descendants. By 1850 the number of Jews had increased to 22,734. Their material situation was unfavorable, and 2,530 persons immigrated to the agricultural colonies of southern Russia in 1840.

With the Russian economic recovery in the second half of the 19th century, the condition of the Jews in Courland improved. Their share in the import and export trade, and in commerce and industry, increased, and many Jews from neighboring areas settled there illegally; under the instructions issued in 1893, they were authorized to remain. The Jewish population of Courland numbered 51,072 (7.6% of the total population) in 1897, and approximately 68,000 on the eve of World War I. Several communities, notably those of Libava (*Liepaja), Mitava (*Jelgava), and Vindava (*Ventspils), were prosperous. Links with nearby Lithuania had some influence on Jewish life in Courland. A number of noted rabbis officiated in communities there; prominent rabbis of *Bauska included Mordecai *Eliasberg and Abraham Isaac *Kook.

In conformity with agreements with the other minorities, Courland sent a Jewish deputy to all the *Dumas which sat during the czarist period. The defeats suffered by the Russian Army during World War I aroused unfounded suspicions that the Jews were involved in treason. This resulted in the expulsion of the Jews from western Courland in May 1915. The number of those expelled to the provinces of the Russian interior reached 40,000. In 1918 Latvia, which included Courland, was proclaimed an independent republic. Some of the refugees and expellees returned, and in 1925 – when the highest Jewish population is recorded in Latvia – the number of Jews in Courland amounted to 22,548, still a decrease of 65% compared with the pre-war figure. For the history of the Jews in Courland from 1918, see *Latvia.

The prolonged duration of Jewish settlement in the same provincial locality, strict observance of Jewish tradition without profound comprehension of its relevance, and German Romantic cultural influences combined to create a specific type of "Courland Jew" who spoke a "Courland Yiddish" vernacular with more German elements.

BIBLIOGRAPHY: R. Wunderbar, *Geschichte der Juden in den Provinzen Liv-und Kurland* (1853); *Yahadut Latviyyah* (1953); E. Avotins et al. (eds.), *Daugavas Vanagi, Who Are They* (1963); M. Bobe, *Perakim be-Toledot Yahadut Latviyyah* (1965).

[Mendel Bobe]

COURNOS, JOHN (1881–1966), U.S. novelist. Born in Kiev, Cournos was raised in Philidelphia, where he experienced economic hardship. His earliest work of fiction was a trilogy based on his own life: *The Mask* (1919), *The Wall* (1921), and *Babel* (1922). His difficult years were described in his *Autobiography* (1922). Cournos converted to Christianity and in *Open Letter to Jews and Christians* (1938; Brittish edition, *Hear Oh Israel*, 1938) he appealed to other Jews to follow his example.

COURT JEWS (Court contractors and suppliers). Medieval princes used the commercial and financial services of individual Jews. However, as an institution, the Court Jew is a feature of the absolutist state, especially in Central Europe, from the end of the 16th century onward. Trying as far as possible to extend his power over the whole of his territory, the ruler set up a centralized administration as part of his court, which at the same time became the power center, presenting a lavish display of luxury. Economically, a Jew could be of great service to such a ruler. In Poland many landed estates were administered by Jews (see *Arenda) and a large part of the trade in agricultural products was in their hands (see *Agriculture). This, combined with the emergence of early Jewish capitalist commercial activity by Sephardim in the *Netherlands, with their connections with Levantine trade through Jews in the Ottoman Empire, made the Jew in Central Europe particularly suited to be an agent for provisioning armies with grain, timber, and cattle, as well as a supplier of diamonds and other goods for conspicuous consumption. As tax-collecting and enlargement of the scope of taxation often lagged considerably behind the growing expenditure of court, army, and bureaucracy, this type of regime developed an almost chronic financial deficit. Here the Jews with their organizational skill and their far-reaching connections could help, through the frequent supply of commercial credit or ready cash, as also through the supply of foodstuffs, cloth, and weapons for the army, the most important instrument of the prince's power. The institution of the Court Jew did not emerge suddenly but developed gradually during the 16th and 17th centuries. Early Court Jews like Michel *Jud and the mintmaster *Lippold were exceptions. Another phase is represented by Jews who were entrepreneurs of the mints during the "*Kipperzeit*" (a period of economic instability at the beginning of the Thirty Years' War, 1618–48, characterized by galloping inflation). The best known of this period, Jacob *Bassevi von Treuenberg of Prague (1570–1634), was the outstanding minting entrepreneur. Several Jews in the Hamburg region maintained close contacts with the courts of the neighborhood, such as Samuel Herscheider with the court of the archbishop of Bremen, Nathan Spanier with the count of Bueckeburg, and Alvaro Dinis with King Christian IV of Denmark. In the Thirty Years' War Jews were employed as army provisioners and spies by both the Swedish and imperial forces. It was only during the second half of the 17th century, with the further evolution of the mercantilist policy and baroque culture of the absolute state, that the Court Jew became a kind of requisite of the princes' court, a member of the group of officials through whom the state or territory was governed. Court Jews were then found in most of the principalities of the Holy Roman Empire, and in some of the adjoining states, such as Poland and Denmark. In some places they lived near the court, and in others the court made use of their services in one of the great commercial centers like Frankfurt or Hamburg. They were given a great variety of titles: *Hofjude, Hoffaktor, Hofprovediteur, Hoflieferant, Hofagent, Kabinettfactor, Proviantlieferant, Kommerzienrat, Kommerziendirektor*, and the higher appellations of *Oberhoffaktor, Obermilizfaktor*, or *Generalprovediteur*; many had titles from several princes. Their rights were similarly various; the chief privileges included a limited official standing, sometimes combined with a salary, direct access to the prince, exemption from the jurisdiction of the rabbinical courts (and submission to the jurisdiction of the royal court – *Hofgericht*), and freedom to travel and settle anywhere in the empire. Their highly varied activities included finance, commerce, and diplomacy, but they were responsible especially for providing the prince and his court with merchandise and money, supplying metal for the mint, provisioning the army, undertaking commercial and diplomatic missions, and investigating proposals for the promotion of trade and industry, e.g., tobacco.

Industrious and often restless, the Court Jews showed a strong drive toward success, both in business and social status, with the allied urge "to assimilate as completely as possible to his environment in speech, dress, and manners" (S. Stern, *Court Jew* (1950), 11). A decidedly dynastic attitude led them to prefer marriages with the families of other Court Jews and to attempt to secure their positions for their descendants, both contributing factors to the tendency of their families to form a particular group within Jewry. The personal relationship between the prince and the Court Jew was based not only on common interests but also on the isolation in which both lived: the prince in his omnipotence and inaccessibility and the Court Jew because of his descent and religion. Thanks to his privileged position, the Court Jew was often able to act as *shtadlan for the Jewish groups; frequently, he was the head of the community and could procure the right to establish new settlements and prepare the way for emancipation. On the other hand, his often adventurous and risky career, necessarily involved with the court intrigues, could end abruptly on the death of the prince, with the gravest consequences for the Court Jew's property, and even life.

Protestant and Catholic princes alike opened their courts to Jews. Among the earliest were Frederick William, elector of Brandenburg from 1540, and Christoph Bernhard von Galen, who was elected prince-bishop of Muenster in 1650. The latter, partly influenced by tolerant motives, was at the same time eager to include the Jews in his mercantilist-expansionist policy: in the 1650s he employed the services of the *Gomperz family on the lower Rhine; Nini Levi was made *Judenbefehlshaber* in 1651, and later Abraham Isaac became Court Jew. In the bishopric of Minden Behrend *Levi gained access to the court. From 1655 Israel Aaron was an army factor in Prussia; he was permitted to live in Berlin in 1663 and two years later became a salaried servant of the court. His widow Esther Schulhoff married Jost *Liebmann, who then succeeded to Israel Aaron's position and supplied the court with jewels. At the same time Simon Model, whose brother-in-law Bonaventura Sachs was influential at the court of Saxony, was Court Jew to the margrave of Ansbach, and Leffmann *Behrends served the court of Hanover; the latter's contribution was instrumental in the elevation of Hanover to an electorate, and he also made substantial loans to the Hapsburgs and other dynasties. Other Court Jews were his cousin Behrend *Lehmann at Halberstadt, who also gave financial assistane to Elector Frederick Augustus II of Saxony, and Aaron Beer at Frankfurt. Behrend Lehmann and his cousin both helped Frederick Augustus of Saxony to gain the throne of Poland, where he also employed Jewish factors. Samuel *Oppenheimer and Samson *Wertheimer made their careers at the imperial court in Vienna, where later they were followed by members of the *Arnstein, *Eskeles, and Pereira families. Emperor Charles VI favored employing Jews in his court; Prince Eugene of Savoy, commander of the Austrian army, depended heavily on Jewish army purveyors. During these decisive years, when Austria rose to the status of a great power through her wars with the Turks, Jewish loans probably accounted for one-third of the annual revenue. The Karlskirche in Vienna was financed by Jewish loans, as was Schoenbrunn Palace built by Maria Theresa. Five generations of the Gomperz family served at the Hohenzollern courts; later, members of the *Ephraim, Isaak, and Itzig families were mint masters. Also influential were Marx Assur, who received the title of *Hoffaktor* in Saxony and Sweden, and Behrend Lehmann's brother-in-law Jonas Meyer, who took up residence in Dresden, where Lehmann's son Lehmann Behrend also lived. The Saxon court probably used the services of the largest number of Jews; around 1707 it had connections with about 20 Jewish jewelers. At the court of Brunswick the David family, especially Alexander David, became firmly established.

As in the south, the greater number of Court Jews came from Frankfurt, so in the north, Hamburg (with Altona and Wandsbek) became a similar center. Various members of both the Sephardi and Ashkenazi communities were in the service of the Danish court, beginning with Alvaro Dinis (Samuel Jachia) at Glueckstadt; later, members of the de Lima and de Casseres families served as factors and financial or diplomatic agents. Gabriel Gomez (Samuel de Casseres) was made *Generalfaktor und Hofprovisor* by Christian IV, retaining his position on the succession of Frederick III and later being appointed *Finanzkommissarius* as well. Diego Teixeira de Sampaio (Abraham Senior) and his son Manuel (Isaac Ḥayyim) served Queen Christiana of Sweden as financial agents and resident ministers. In the service of the crown of Portugal abroad, notwithstanding their religious status, similar positions were held by Duarte Nuñes da Costa (Jacob *Curiel), his son Manuel, and his brother Jeronimo (the latter of Amsterdam), while Manuel Bocarro (Jacob *Rosales) was in the service of Spain, and Daniel and Joshua *Abensur in that of Poland. However, they were employed in diplomatic or consular, rather than financial, functions. From 1683 Jacob Mussafia, a mint master, was Court Jew of Duke Christian Albert of Schleswig-Holstein-Gottorp and later of Duke Frederick IV and his prime minister Wedderkop; he was followed by his son Joseph, who was involved in a famous law suit following the fall of Wedderkop. Other outstanding families of Court Jews in Hamburg were the Fuersts and the Goldschmidts: Samuel Fuerst served Bernhard and Johann Asolf, dukes of Schleswig-Holstein-Sonderburg; Jeremiah Fuerst became Court Jew of Duke Christian Louis of Mecklenburg in 1679 and of Sachsen-Lauenburg; Israel Fuerst served the court of Holstein-Gottorp. Bendix Goldschmidt and the Hindrichsen family were financial associates of the Fuersts; remaining in Hamburg, Goldschmidt became an agent of Goertz and later served the Danish court as a *Kammeragent*, while the Hinrichsen family took up residence in Mecklenburg-Schwerin. Ruben Hinrichsen became the salaried *Hofagent* of Duke Leopold II; Moses Josephs (Moses Wessely) of Glueckstadt was in the service of Peter I of Russia, and at the same time had dealings with the Danish court. All the petty German courts had their Court Jews: there was Moses Benjamin Wulff, Saul Samuel, and Moses Heyman at Weissenfels; Berend Wulff and Assur Marx at Sachsen-Merseburg and Sachsen-Zeitz; Samson von Baiersdorf at Bayreuth; the Van Geldern family at Duesseldorf; Simon Baruch at Kurkoeln; and the Heine family at Bueckeburg. Noah Samuel Isaac of Sulzbach, who helped finance the marriage of the Wittelsbach prince-elector Charles Albert to Princess Maria Amalia of Austria in 1722, was at the same time a banker of the elector of Cologne and of the Teutonic Order.

Joseph Suess *Oppenheimer, court factor of Duke Charles Alexander of Wuerttemberg, had dealings with many other rulers, including the elector of Cologne, the landgraf of Hesse, and the elector of the Palatinate, but it was in Wuerttemberg where his financial influence reached its peak. At the same time, he saw possibilities of political action which would transform the duchy into a modern absolutist state based on mercantilist principles. He failed, however, and was executed in 1738. By then the zenith of the Court Jew had already passed. Although Jews served the German courts as mint entrepreneurs well into the first half of the 19th century, in general, the French Revolution and the Napoleonic Wars, which gave rise to wide-ranging changes in patterns of finance, commerce, and international trade, put an end to the epoch of the Court Jews.

In all their varied activities, the Court Jews played a remarkable part in the development of international credit facilities especially in the Central European states and to some degree in northern Europe also, from the mid-17th to late-18th centuries. Generally, they were agents who arranged transfers of credit rather than possessors of vast capital in their own right; through their far-reaching commercial relationships and their organizing skill, they were able to provide funds more swiftly than most Christian bankers. Because of their specialization in the money business, they were able to furnish the silver for the mints more easily and could better act as army purveyors, once more because of their ability to organize and their network of family relationships. With their entrepreneurial spirit, they contributed in part to the process of industrialization within the frame of mercantilist policies. There is no doubt that they were instrumental in the growth of the modern absolute state, and at the end of the era there emerged a group of several important Jewish private bankers (see *Banking and *Bankers) who exemplify the transition to modern methods of economy and government, primarily the Rothschilds, the Goldschmidts, the Oppenheimers, and the Seligmanns. However, it should not be forgotten that the courts had their Christian bankers, entrepreneurs, and army agents, too, who also played a part in this development.

BIBLIOGRAPHY: S. Stern, *Court Jew* (1950); idem, *Der Preussische Staat und die Juden*, 4 vols. (1962); H. Schnee, *Hoffinanz und der moderne Staat*, 6 vols. (1953–67); J.R. Marcus, *Jews in the Medieval World* (1938, paperback 1965), 291, 415ff.; H. Kellenbenz, *Sephardim an der unteren Elbe* (1958); C. Roth, *Essays and Portraits in Anglo-Jewish History* (1962); idem, in: JSOS, 5 (1943), 355–66; R. Straus, *ibid.*, 3 (1941), 15–40; F. Redlich, in: *Explorations in Entrepreneurial History*, 3 (1951); Carsten, in: YLBI, 3 (1958), 140ff.

[Hermann Kellenbenz]

COUTINHO (also **Cotinio**, **Cothino**, **Cotinsio**, **Cutinho**, etc.), Portuguese *Marrano family, branches of which settled in Amsterdam, Hamburg, Brazil, and Jamaica in the 17th and 18th centuries. Notable among the Amsterdam branch were MOSES BEN ABRAHAM MENDES COUTINHO who in 1696 bought the printing house of David de *CastroTartas, which he owned until 1711. Among the works he printed was an edition of the Torah with the Targum Onkelos and Rashi's commentary, in 5,000 copies; SEBASTIAN COUTINHO (17th century) was one of the largest importers of sugar from Portugal and England in the 17th century; FRANCISCO DE SOUSA COUTINHO was representative of the king of Portugal in Holland and took part in an embassy sent by the king to the Scandinavian countries in 1641. The Amsterdam Jewish journal *Neiuwsblad voor Israëliten* was published by the firm S.M. Coutinho Jr. between 1884 and 1894.

GONSALVO LOPES COUTINHO (17th century) was among the first Portuguese Jewish settlers in *Glueckstadt near Hamburg, where he established a sugar refinery, an oil mill, and a soap factory. The brothers Abendana of Hamburg were sons of Manoel Pereira Coutinho of Lisbon, five of whose daughters were nuns in a convent in that city. The family HENRIQUEZ CUTINHO was among 12 Jewish families who settled in Curaçao 16 years after the Dutch conquest in 1634. LOURENÇA COUTINHO, the mother of the poet Antonio José da *Silva, was arrested by the Inquisition in Rio de Janeiro in 1713 as a Judaizer and taken to Lisbon. She was again arrested in 1737, and subsequently died in prison.

BIBLIOGRAPHY: J.L. D'Azevedo, *Historia dos Christãos Novos Portugueses* (1921), index; J.S. da Silva Rosa, *Geschiedenis der portugeesche Joden te Amsterdam 1593–1925* (1925), 31, 145; H.I. Bloom, *Economic Activities of the Jews of Amsterdam in the 17th and 18th Centuries* (1937), index; H. Kellenbenz, *Sephardim an der unteren Elbe* (1958), index.

COVENANT, a general obligation concerning two parties. It was confirmed either by an oath (Gen. 21:22ff.; 26:26ff.; Deut. 29:9ff.; Josh. 9:15–20; II Kings 11:4; Ezek. 16:8; 17:33ff.), by a solemn meal (Gen. 26:30; 31:54; Ex. 24:11; II Sam. 2:20), by sacrifices (Ex. 24:4ff.; Ps. 50:5), or by some other dramatic act such as dividing of an animal and the passing of the parties between the portions (Gen. 15:9ff.; Jer. 34:18ff.). The etymology of the Hebrew word *berit* is uncertain. Most probably it was used in the sense of binding (cf. Akkadian *birītu*, "fetter"), since the terms for covenant in Akkadian (*riksu*) and in Hittite (*išḫiul*) also signify binding. Hebrew has two additional terms for covenant, *ʿedut* (cf. the parallel terms *luḥot ha-ʿedut* and *luḥot ha-berit*) and *ʾalah*. These also have their counterparts in the cognate languages: *ʿdy[ʾ]* in old Aramaic (Sefire) and *adê* in Akkadian on the one hand, and *lʾt* in Phoenician, *māmītu* in Akkadian, and *lingai* in Hittite on the other. *ʾAlah* and the corresponding terms in Akkadian and Hittite connote an oath which actually underlies the covenantal deed. The terms *berit* and *ʾalah* often occur together (Gen. 26:28; Deut. 29:11, 13, 20; Ezek. 16:59; 17:18), rendering the idea of a binding oath, as does the Akkadian hendiadys *adê māmīt* or *adê u māmīte*. For concluding a covenant the Bible uses the expression "cut (*karat*) a covenant." The same idiom is used in Aramaic treaties in connection with *ʿdyʾ* (cf. *gzrʿdyʾ* in the Sefire treaties) and in a Phoenician document in connection with *lʾt* (cf. the incantation from Arslan Tash). It is quite possible that this idiom derives from the ceremony accompanying the covenant, viz., cutting an animal. The expressions *hekim* (*heqim*) *berit* and *natan berit* should not be considered synonyms of *karat berit*, used by different sources. The first term means "to fulfill a covenant (already made)"; the second signifies "the voluntary granting of special privileges."

Covenants are established between individuals (Gen. 21:22ff.; 31:44ff.; I Sam. 18:3; 23:18), between states or their representatives (II Sam. 3:13, 21; I Kings 5:26; 15:19; 20:34), between kings and their subjects (II Sam. 5:3; II Kings 11:4, 17), and also between husband and wife (Ezek. 16:8; Mal. 2:14; Prov. 2:17). The term is used figuratively in a covenant between men and animals (Job. 5:23; 40:28; cf. Hos. 2:20) and also a covenant with death (Isa. 28:15, 18). The covenant does not always constitute a mutual agreement; sometimes it represents a relationship in which a more powerful party makes a pact with an inferior one freely and out of good will. In this case the superior party takes the inferior under his protection, on condition that the latter remain loyal to him. The covenant of the Israelites with the *Gibeonites (Josh. 9) and the covenant requested by the people of Jabesh-Gilead (I Sam. 11:1–2) from the king of *Ammon belong to this category. That the covenant of the Israelites with the *Canaanite population was of a similar nature is shown in Deuteronomy 7:1–2: "When the Lord your God brings you to the land… and delivers them [the Canaanites] to you and you defeat them, you must doom them to destruction: do not cut a covenant with them [*loʾ tikhrot lahem berit*] and do not be gracious to them." J. Begrich (see bibl.) observed that this type of covenant is distinguished by the form "to cut a covenant to somebody," *karat berit le* –, in contrast with the other type of covenant which is phrased as "to cut a covenant with somebody," *karat berit ʿim*. Another type of covenant is that established through the mediation of a third party, especially when a covenant with the Deity is involved. Thus Moses (Ex. 24) and Joshua (Josh. 24) mediate the covenant between God and Israel. The priest *Jehoiada fulfills the same function (II Kings 11:17), when he serves as a mediator in a double covenant: that between God and king plus people on the one hand and between the king and the people on the other (apparently because the king was still a minor). Another example of this kind is mentioned in Hosea 2:20 where God is to establish a covenant between the people and the beasts of the earth, etc.

Sometimes the covenant is accompanied by an external sign or token to remind the parties of their obligations (cf. Gen. 21:30; 31:44–45; 52; Josh. 24:27, etc.). The "sign of the covenant," *ʾot berit*, is especially characteristic of the Priestly source of the Pentateuch. The *Sabbath, the *rainbow, and *circumcision are the "signs" of the three great covenants established by God at the three critical stages of the history of mankind: the *Creation (Gen. 1:1–2:3; cf. Ex. 31:16–17), the renewal of mankind after the *Flood (Gen. 9:1–17), and the beginning of the Hebrew nation. Circumcision came to be regarded in Jewish tradition as the most distinctive sign of the covenant, and is known as *berit milah* – "the covenant of circumcision."

The Covenant between God and Israel

The covenant par excellence in the Bible is that between God and Israel. Until recently this has been considered a relatively late idea (cf. J. Wellhausen). But S. Mowinckel (*Le Décalogue*, 1927), adopting the form-critical approach and *Sitz im Leben* method of investigation, concluded that it reflected an annual celebration involving a theophany and proclamation of the law. His arguments were based mainly on Psalms 50:5ff. and Psalms 81, where theophany is combined with covenant-making and decalogue formulas (cf. Ps. 50:7, 18–19; 81:10–11). He was followed by A. Alt (see bibl.) who argued that the so-called apodictic law had been recited at the Feast of Tabernacles at the beginning of the year of release (cf. Deut. 31:10–13) and that this periodical convocation was a solemn undertaking by the congregation which is reflected in the Sinai covenant. G. von Rad (see bibl.) inquiring into the significance of the peculiar structure of Deuteronomy – history (ch. 1–11), laws (12:1–26:15), mutual obligations (26:16–19), and blessings and curses (ch. 27–29) – suggested that this structure, and similarly that of the Sinai covenant – history (Ex. 19:4–6), law (20:1–23:19), promises and threats (3:20–23), conclusion of the covenant (24:1–11) – reflects the procedure of a covenant ceremony. This opened with a recital of history, proceeded with the proclamation of the law – accompanied by a sworn obligation –and ended with blessings and curses. Since according to Deuteronomy 27 (cf. Josh. 8:30–35) the blessings and curses had to be recited between Mounts Gerizim and Ebal, von Rad identified Shechem as the scene of the periodic covenant renewal in ancient Israel.

Although no real evidence for a covenant festival has been discovered so far, the observation made by von Rad that the literary structure of Deuteronomy and Exodus 19–24 reflects a covenantal procedure has been confirmed by subsequent investigations. It has become clear that the covenant form, as presented in these texts and especially in Deuteronomy, was in use for centuries in the ancient Near East. G. Mendenhall in 1954 found that the Hittite treaty has a structure identical with that of the biblical covenant. The basic common elements are: titular descriptions; historical introduction, which served as a motivation for the vassal's loyalty; stipulation of the treaty; a list of divine witnesses; blessings and curses; and recital of the treaty and deposit of its tablets. The Sinai covenant described in Exodus 19–24 has indeed a similar structure, although it is not completely identical. Thus, the divine address in chapter 19 opens with a historical introduction stressing the grace of God toward the people and its election (19:4–6), followed by the law (23:20–33), and finally the ratification of the covenant by means of a cultic ceremony and the recital of the covenant document (24:3–8).

Admittedly the analogy is not complete, since what is found in Exodus 19–24 is not a treaty, as in the Hittite documents, but rather a narrative about the conclusion of a covenant. Nevertheless, it is clear that the narrative is organized and arranged in line with the treaty pattern, which emerges in a much clearer fashion in Deuteronomy. This book, which is considered by its author as one organic literary creation (cf. the expression *Sefer ha-Torah ha-zeh*, "this Book of Teaching") and represents the covenant of the plains of Moab, follows the classical pattern of treaties in the Ancient Near East. Unlike the Sinai covenant in Exodus, which has no list of blessings and curses, Deuteronomy (like the treaties and especially those of the first millennium B.C.E.) has an elaborate series of blessings and curses and likewise provides for witnesses to the covenant, "heaven and earth" (4:26; 30:19), which are missing altogether in the first four books of the Pentateuch. Deuteronomy also makes explicit references to the deposit of the tablets of the covenant and the book of the Law in the divine Ark (10:1–5; 31:25–26). The Ark was considered in ancient Israel as the footstool of the Deity (the cherubim constituting the throne), and it was indeed at the feet of the gods that the treaty documents had to be kept according to Hittite legal tradition. As in the Hittite treaties, Deuteronomy commands the periodical recital of the Law before the public (31:9–13) and prescribes that the treaty be read before the king or by him (17:18–19).

The historical prologue in Deuteronomy (1–11) recalls to a great extent the historical prologue in Hittite state treaties. In this section the Hittite suzerain recounts the development of the relationship between him and the vassal, specifying, for example, the commitments and the promises of the overlord to the vassal's ancestors. This theme is echoed in Deuteronomy's recurring references to the promise made to the Patriarchs (4:37–38; 7:8; 9:5). The prologue also dwells on the insubordination of the vassal's ancestors and its consequences, a feature expressed in the historical introduction of Deuteronomy which deals fully with the rebelliousness of the generation of the desert. The Hittite historical prologue frequently refers to the land given to the vassal by the suzerain and its boundaries, a theme fully elaborated in Deuteronomy (3:8ff.). In a fashion similar to the Hittite sovereign, who urges the vassal to take possession of the given land, "See I gave you the Zippašla mountain land, occupy it" (Madduwataš, in: *Mitteilungen der vorderasiatisch-aegyptischen Gesellschaft* (= MVAG), 32 (1927), 17, 19, 46), God says in Deuteronomy: "I have placed the land at your disposal, go take possession of it" (1:8, 21). In this context the Hittite king warns the vassal not to trespass beyond the set boundaries. Thus for example, Muršiliš II says to Manapa-Dattaš: "Behold I have given you the Seḫa-river-land… but unto Mašḫuiluwaš I have given the land Mira… whereas unto Targašnalliš I have given the land Ḫapalla" (MVAG, 30 (1926), no. 3:3; MVAG, 34 (1930), no. 4:10–11). The historical prologue similarly states: "See, I place the land at your disposal" (1:21), "I have given the hill country of Seir as a possession to Esau" (2:5), "I have given Ar as a possession to the descendants of Lot" (2:9), "I have given [the land of the Ammonites] as a possession to the descendants of Lot" (2:19). The purpose of these reminders is to justify the command forbidding the trespass of the fixed borders of these nations.

Analogies have been drawn mostly from Hittite treaties as these have been preserved in fairly large numbers and in relatively good condition. However, the few treaties known from the first millennium B.C.E., i.e., the Aramaic treaty from Sefire, the treaty of Ashur-Nirâri V with Mati'el of Bīt-Agushi, and the treaty of Esarhaddon with his eastern vassals, do not differ in principle from those of the Hittites, and it seems in fact that there was a continuity in the treaty pattern for approximately 800 years. This might explain the fact that in a late book, according to the documentary hypothesis, like Deuteronomic elements are preserved which also occur in the Hittite treaties from the 14th–13th centuries B.C.E. In spite of this continuity, careful analysis reveals certain significant differences between the treaties of the second millennium and those of the first. This applies to the political treaties in the ancient Near East as well as to the theological covenants in Israel. While the Hittite treaties and similarly the Sinai covenant have a very short list of curses, those of the first millennium and the covenant in Deuteronomy have long lists. Furthermore, Deuteronomy has preserved in chapter 28 a series of curses which has an exact parallel in the Neo-Assyrian treaty Esarhaddon made with his eastern vassals regarding the coronation of his son Ashurbanipal (concluded in 672 B.C.E.). An investigation of these curses has shown that their origin is to be sought in Assyria, since their order can be explained by the hierarchy of the Assyrian pantheon while the order in Deuteronomy has no satisfactory explanation (see M. Weinfeld, *Biblica*, see bibl.). It has been supposed that a series of Assyrian treaty curses was incorporated into the section of curses in Deuteronomy, thereby making it clear that the pledge of loyalty to the Assyrian emperor had been henceforward replaced by the pledge to YHWH, a transfer which is to be understood against the background of *Josiah's liberation from Assyrian dominion. The shift of fealty, as it were, from one suzerain to another may also explain the striking similarity between the laws of sedition in Deuteronomy 13 and the warnings against sedition in the treaties of the first millennium B.C.E. and particularly in those of Esarhaddon with his vassals; compare also the Aramaic treaty of Sefire. Like the vassal treaties of Esarhaddon, Deuteronomy 13 warns against a prophet inciting rebellion and against any member of the family conspiring to break faith with the overlord. In the Aramaic treaty from Sefire there is a clause concerning a rebellious city which, like Deuteronomy 13, commands its destruction by the sword. In both sources the wording is almost identical: והן קריה הא נכה תכוה בחרב, "and if it is a city, you must strike it with a sword" in the Sefire treaty, and הכה תכה את ישבי העיר ההיא לפי חרב, "you must strike the inhabitants of this city with the sword" in Deuteronomy 13:16. Furthermore, the exhortations to keep faith with God in Deuteronomy are very close in form and style to the exhortations in the political treaties. As has been shown by W.L. Moran, the concept of "love of God" in Deuteronomy actually expresses loyalty, and it is in this sense that "love" occurs in the political documents of the Ancient Near East. The Book of Deuteronomy abounds in terms originating in the diplomatic vocabulary of the ancient Near East. Such expressions as: "to follow with the whole heart and with the whole soul," "to hearken to the voice of," "to be perfect with," "to go after," "to serve," "to fear (to revere)," "to put the words in one's heart," "not to turn right or left," etc. are found in diplomatic letters and state treaties of the second and first millennia B.C.E. and are especially prominent in the vassal treaties of Esarhaddon, which are contemporaneous with Deuteronomy. The scene of the concluding of the Josian covenant in II Kings 23:1–3 and the scene of the concluding of the covenant in Deuteronomy 29:9–14 are presented in a manner which is very close to the descriptions of the treaty ceremonies in Neo-Assyrian documents. The section stipulating the perpetual validity of the covenant occurs twice, both in the Esarhaddon treaty and in the Deuteronomy covenant, before the conditions and after them. The end of chapter 29 in Deuteronomy reads: "And the generations to come… and the foreigners… will ask 'Why did the Lord do thus to this land?…' and they will be told: 'Because they forsook the covenant of the Lord'" (21–24). The theme of self-condemnation (Deut. 29:21–24) is also encountered in the Neo-Assyrian texts in connection with a breach of a treaty. Thus the annals of Ashurbanipal state: "The people of Arabia asked one another saying: 'Why is it that such evil has befallen Arabia?' and they answered: 'Because we did not observe the valid covenant sworn to the god of Ashur'" (Rassam Cylinder, 9:68–72).

The difference between the Deuteronomy covenant, which reflects the treaty pattern of the first millennium B.C.E., and the earlier covenants reflecting the pattern of the second millennium will be appreciated if the covenant ceremonies in Genesis and Exodus are compared with that of Deuteronomy. The patriarchal covenants, secular and religious alike (Gen. 15:9ff.; 21:22ff.; 26:26ff.; 31:44ff.), and the Sinai covenant (Ex. 24:1–11) are validated by sacrifices and holy meals, similar to the covenants of the third and second millennia B.C.E. In the Deuteronomy covenant, on the other hand, as in the contemporary Assyrian and Aramaic treaty documents, it is the oath which validates the covenant and no mention is made of a sacrifice or meal (cf. especially Deut. 29:9ff.).

The Covenant with Abraham and David

Aside from the covenant between God and Israel described in Exodus and Deuteronomy, two covenants of a different type are found in the Bible. These are the covenant with *Abraham (Gen. 15, 17) and the covenant with *David (II Sam. 7; cf. Ps. 89), which are concerned respectively with the gift of the land and the gift of kingship and dynasty. In contradistinction to the Mosaic covenants, which are of an obligatory type, the Abrahamic-Davidic covenants belong to the promissory type. God swears to Abraham to give the land to his descendants and similarly promises to David to establish his dynasty without imposing any obligations on them. Although their loyalty to God is presupposed, it is not made a condition for God's keeping His promise. On the contrary, the Davidic promise as formulated in the vision of Nathan (II Sam. 7) contains a clause in which the unconditional nature of the gift is explicitly stated (II Sam. 7:13–15). By the same token, the covenant with the Patriarchs is considered as valid forever (*ʿad ʿolam*). Even when Israel sins and is to be severely punished, God intervenes to help because He "will not break his covenant" (Lev. 26:43).

In the same way as the obligatory covenant in Israel is modeled on the suzerain-vassal type of treaty so the promissory covenant is modeled on the royal grant. The royal grants in the Ancient Near East as well as the covenants with Abraham and David are gifts bestowed upon individuals who distinguished themselves in loyal service to their masters. Abraham is promised the land because he obeyed God and followed His mandate (Gen. 26:5; cf. 22:16–18), and similarly David is rewarded with dynastic posterity because he served God with truth, righteousness, and loyalty (I Kings 3:6; 9:4; 11:4, 6; 14:8; 15:3). The terminology employed in this context is very close to that used in the Assyrian grants. Thus the grant of Ashurbanipal to his servant reads: "Balta… whose heart is whole to his master, stood before me with truthfulness, walked in perfection in my palace…. and kept the charge of my kingship… I considered his good relations with me and established [therefore] his gi[f]t." Identical formulations are to be found in connection with the promises to Abraham and David. With regard to Abraham it is said that "he kept my charge" (Gen. 26:5), "walked before God" (24:40; 48:15), and is expected "to be perfect" (17:1). David's loyalty to God is couched in phrases which are even closer to the Assyrian grant terminology: "he walked before the Lord in truth, loyalty, and uprightness of heart" (I Kings 3:6), "followed the Lord with all his heart" (I Kings 14:8), etc. Land and "house" (i.e., dynasty), the subjects of the Abrahamic and Davidic covenants, are the most prominent gifts of the suzerain in the Hittite and Syro-Palestine examples; like the Hittite grants, the grant of land to Abraham and "house" to David are unconditional. Thus, the Hittite king says to his vassal: "After you, your son and grandson will possess it, nobody will take it away from them; if one of your descendants sins, the king will prosecute him… but nobody will take away either his house or his land in order to give it to a descendant of somebody else." The promises to Abraham and David, which were originally unconditional, were understood as conditional only at a later stage of Israelite history. The exile of northern Israel appeared to refute the claim to eternity of the Abrahamic covenant, and therefore it was stressed that the covenant is eternal only if the donee keeps faith with the donor. A similar interpretation is given to the Davidic covenant in the Books of Kings (I Kings 2:4; 8:25; 9:4–5).

Covenant Theology

Long before the parallel between the Israelite covenant and the Ancient Near Eastern treaty had been brought to light, W. Eichrodt recognized the importance of the covenant idea in the religion of Israel, seeing in the Sinai covenant a point of departure for understanding Israel's religion. Eichrodt explains that basic phenomena like the kingship of God, revelation, the liberation from myth, the personal attitude to God, etc. are to be explained against the background of the covenant. The discovery of the treaty pattern in the Ancient Near East strengthened this hypothesis, new developments in covenant research throwing light on the idea of the kingship of God. It now becomes clear that God as King of Israel is not an idea born during the period of the monarchy, as scholars used to think, but, on the contrary, is one of the most genuine and most ancient doctrines of Israel. In the period of the judges the tribes resisted kingship because of the prevailing belief that God was the real King of Israel and that the proclamation of an earthly king would constitute a betrayal. This is clearly expressed in Gideon's reply to the people's offer of kingship (Judg. 8:22–23), but is even more salient in Samuel's denunciation of the request for a king (I Sam. 8:6–7; 10:18ff.; 12:17). Earthly kingship in Israel was finally accepted, but this was the outcome of a compromise: David's kingship was conceived as granted to him by the Great Suzerain (II Sam. 7, see above). The king and the people alike were thus considered as vassals of God, the real Overlord (I Sam. 12:14, 24–25; II Kings 11:17).

It seems that this suzerain-vassal outlook has its roots in the political actuality of the period of the judges. As is well known, Syria-Palestine of the second half of the second millennium B.C.E. was dominated by two great political powers, the Egyptian and the Hittite empires, in turn. Either the king of Egypt or the king of the Hittites was overlord of the petty kingdoms in the area. The lands and the kingdoms of the latter were conceived as feudal grants bestowed on them by the great suzerain, in exchange for the obligation of loyalty to the master. Israel's concept of its relationship with God had a similar basis. The Israelites believed that they owed their land and royal dynasty to their suzerain, God. Furthermore, as the relationship between the suzerain and the vassal has to be based on a written document, i.e., a treaty, so the relationship between God and Israel had to be expressed in written form. It is not surprising, therefore, that the tablets of the covenant played so important a role in the religion of Israel. As already noted, the tablets had to be deposited in the sanctuary at the feet of the deity, a procedure known from the Hittite treaties. Moreover, it appears that, as in the judicial sphere, the written document expresses the validity of the given relationship. When the covenant is no longer in force the document must be destroyed. Thus the worship of the golden calf, which signifies the breaking of the covenant, is followed by the breaking of the tablets by Moses, the mediator of the covenant (Ex. 32). Indeed, the term for canceling a contract in Babylonian legal literature is "to break the tablet" (*tuppam ḫepū*). Following the judicial pattern, the renewal of the relationship must be effected by writing new tablets, which explains why new ones had to be written after the sin of the golden calf, and why the ritual decalogue was repeated in Exodus 34:17–26 (cf. Ex. 23:10–19). Renewal of a covenant with a vassal – after a break in the relationship – – by means of writing new tablets is an attested fact in Hittite political life.

The Covenant in Prophecy

This new examination of the covenant elucidates basic phenomena in Israel's prophetic literature. The admonitory speeches of the prophets are often formulated in the style of a lawsuit (Isa. 1:2ff.; Jer. 2:4ff; Hos. 4:1ff.; Micah 6:1ff.). God sues the people of Israel in the presence of witnesses such as heaven and earth, and mountains (Isa. 1:2; Micah 6:1–2), witnesses which also appear in the Ancient Near Eastern treaties and in the Deuteronomy covenant. International strife in the Ancient Near East provides parallels to prophetic denunciations; for example, before going out to battle with the Babylonian king Kaštiliaš, the Assyrian king accuses the latter of betrayal and violation of the treaty between them, and as proof he reads the treaty in a loud voice before the god Šamaš. In a similar way the prophetic lawsuit represents God's accusation of Israel before He proceeds to destroy the people for violating the covenant. This is clearly expressed in Amos 4:6–11, where a series of punishments, similar to those enumerated in Leviticus 26, is proclaimed, in the nature of a warning, before the final judgment or encounter (cf. Amos 4:12: "Be ready to meet your God, O Israel"). The warnings in Israelite prophecy are reminiscent of the curses in the Ancient Near Eastern treaties. Thus the calamities predicted in the prose sermons of Jeremiah are paralleled in contemporary treaty literature. The most prominent curses are (1) corpses devoured by the birds of heaven and the beasts of the earth; (2) cessation of joyful sounds; (3) exile; (4) desolation of the land and its becoming a habitation for animals; (5) dishonoring of the dead; (6) children being eaten by their parents; (7) the drinking of poisonous water and the eating of wormwood; and (8) cessation of the sound of the millstones and the light of the oven (or the candle). The treaty curses aim to portray the calamities that will befall the vassal as a consequence of his violation of the treaty. This is usually expressed through literary similes and also by a dramatic enactment of the punishment which will be visited on the transgressor. Both devices were in fact employed by the prophets. In the prophetic literature also the similes are drawn from various spheres of life, as for example Amos 2:3; 3:12; 5:19; 9:9. The dramatization of the punishment is also very close in form and content to the dramatic enactment in the treaties; compare, for example, the Sefire treaty, "As this calf is cleft so may Mati'el and his nobles be cleft," which is reminiscent of Jeremiah 20:2–4; 34:18 – "I will make the men who have transgressed my covenant… [like] the calf which they cut in two and passed between its parts."

The Origin of the Covenant

The idea of a covenant between a deity and a people is unknown from other religions and cultures. It seems that the covenantal idea was a special feature of the religion of Israel, the only one to demand exclusive loyalty and preclude the possibility of dual or multiple loyalties; so the stipulation in political treaties demanding exclusive fealty to one king corresponds strikingly with the religious belief in one single, exclusive deity.

The prophets, especially *Hosea, Jeremiah, and Ezekiel, expressed this idea of exclusive loyalty by speaking of the relationship between God and Israel as one of husband and wife, which in itself is also considered covenantal (cf. above and especially Ezek. 16:8). Although the idea of marital love between God and Israel is not mentioned explicitly in the Pentateuch, it seems to be present in a latent form. Following other gods is threatened by the statement: "For I the Lord your God am a jealous God" (Ex. 20:5; Deut. 5:9; cf. Ex. 34:14; Josh. 24:19). The root (קנא, *qn'*, "jealous") is in fact used in Numbers 5:14 in the technical sense of a husband who is jealous of his wife. Similarly the verb used in the Pentateuch for disloyalty is *zanah 'aḥarei*, "to whore after." Furthermore, the formula expressing the covenantal relationship between God and Israel, "you will be my people and I will be your God" (Lev. 26:12; Deut. 29:12, etc.), is a legal formula taken from the sphere of marriage, as attested in various legal documents from the Ancient Near East (cf. Hos. 2:4). The relationship of the vassal to his suzerain or of the wife to her husband leaves no place for double loyalty, and they are therefore perfect metaphors for loyalty in a monotheistic religion.

The concept of the kingship of God in Israel also seems to have contributed to the conception of Israel as the vassal of God. It is true that the idea of the kingship of God was prevalent throughout the Ancient Near East; nevertheless, there is an important difference between the Israelite notion of divine kingship and the corresponding belief of other nations. Israel adopted the idea long before establishing the human institution of kingship. Consequently, for hundreds of years the only kingship recognized and institutionalized in Israel was the kingship of God. During the period of the judges YHWH was actually the King of Israel (cf. Judg. 8:23; 1 Sam. 8:7; 10:19) and was not, as in other religions of the Ancient Near East, the image of the earthly king.

BIBLIOGRAPHY: TREATY TEXTS: J.A. Fitzmeyer, *The Aramaic Inscription of Sefire* (1967); E. Cavaignac, in: *Revue hittite et asiatique*, 10 (1933), 65ff.; J. Friedrich; in: *Mitteilungen der vorderasiatisch-aegyptischen Gesellschaft*, 31 pt. 1 (1926); 34 pt. 1 (1930); A. Goetze, *ibid.*, 32 pt. 1 (1927); E. Ebeling, in: *Mitteilungen der altorientalischen Gesellschaft*, 12 pt. 2 (1938); C.F. Jean, in: *Archives Royales de Mari*, 2 (1950), no. 37; L.W. King, *Babylonian Boundary Stones and Memorial Tablets inthe British Museum* (1912); J. Koehler and A. Ungnad, *Assyrische Rechtsurkunden…* (1913); M. Streck, *Assurbanipal und die letzten assyrischen Koenige bis zum Untergange Ninevehs*, 2 (1916); F. Thureau-Dangin, *Die sumerischen und akkadischen Koenigsinschriften* (1907); E.F. Weidner, *Politische Dokumente aus Kleinasien, die Staatsvertraege in akkadischer Sprache aus dem Archiv von Boghazköi* (1923); D.J. Wiseman, *The Vassal-Treaties of Esarhaddon* (1958 = *Iraq*, 20, pt. 1); idem, *The Alalakh Tablets* (1953); idem, in: *Journal of Cuneiform Studies*, 12 (1958), 124ff. STUDIES: Alt, Kl Schr, 1 (1953), 278ff.; K. Baltzer, *Das Bundesformular* (1960); J. Begrich, in: ZAW, 60 (1944), 1–11; E. Bickerman, in: *Archives d'histoire du droit oriental*, 5 (1950), 133ff.; W. Eichrodt, *Theology of the Old Testament*, 1 (1964); F.C. Fensham, in: ZAW, 74 (1962), 1–9; R. Frankena, in: OTS, 14 (1965), 122–54; I.J. Gelb, in: BOR, 19 (1962), 159–62; J. Harvey, in: *Biblica*, 43 (1962), 172ff. (Fr.); D.R. Hillers, *Treaty-Curses and the Old Testament Prophets* (1964); H.B. Huffmon, in: JBL, 78 (1959), 285ff.; V. Korošec, *Hethitische Staatsvertraege…* (1931); D.J. McCarthy, *Treaty and Covenant* (1963); G. Mendenhall, in: BA, 17 (1954), 50ff.; W.L. Moran, in: CBQ, 25 (1963), 77–87; S. Mowinckel, *Le Décalogue* (1927); J.M. Munn-Rankin, in: *Iraq*, 18 (1956), 68ff. (Eng.); G. von Rad, *The Problem of the Hexateuch and Other Essays* (1966); M. Weinfeld, in: *Biblica*, 46 (1965), 417–27 (Eng.); idem, in: JAOS, 89 (1969).

[Moshe Weinfeld]

COVETOUSNESS, condemned and prohibited in the tenth commandment of the Decalogue (Ex. 20:14; Deut. 5:18), and throughout the Bible and Jewish ethical literature, particularly in the Book of Proverbs (e.g., 3:31, 14:30, etc.). Since envy may be defined as a state of mind which wishes to change existing relations, there is an inherent relationship between the condemnation of covetousness and the maintenance of established social and economic conditions. Greed is regarded as the root of all social injustice (see Micah 2:1 ff.; Hab. 2:9, etc.). The talmudic rabbis and medieval thinkers as well as modern scholars argue, for example, that the tenth commandment summarizes all the previous ones (Pes. 107a ff.; Meg. 6; Naḥmanides' commentary on Ex. 20:14, etc.), because it is envy which leads to all the other sins. Avot 4:2 states that desire causes covetousness, which leads to robbery and tyranny (see also *ibid.*, 2:11, 28; Mekh. to Ex. 20:14; BM 107, etc.). In the 20th century, too, Hermann *Cohen repeated that greed causes envy which, in turn, causes hate, that leads to war (*Religion der Vernunft aus den Quellen des Judentums* (1929), 522). Since there is no limit to the objects of greed, envy is never sated, but is rather self-aggravating (Prov. 27:20; Eccles. 5:9; Eccles. R. 1:34; Ibn Ezra's commentary on Ex. 20:14, etc.), which explains the ethical warning that covetousness leads to the self-destruction of the one prey to it (Prov. 28:22; Sanh. 106; Sot. 9a). The cure for limitless greed lies in contentment and humbleness (Avot 4:1: "Who is rich? He who delights in his share"). Jewish tradition acknowledges, however, that the final abolition of envy will occur only with the advent of the messianic, i.e., the totally just society (see M.Ḥ. Luzzatto, *Mesillat Yesharim*, ch. 11, based on Isa. 11:13).

[Steven S. Schwarzschild]

COVILHÃ, city in central Portugal. A Jewish community existed there from the middle of the 12th century until 1496–97. A rabbi, called *ouvidor*, appointed by the **Arraby Mor* for the province of Beira Alta, resided in Covilhã. After 1497 Covilhã became an important Crypto-Jewish center. In 1543 a large *auto-da-fé was held in Covilhã with many judaizers sentenced to the stake. A number of the Crypto-Jewish families of Covilhã, such as the Mendes, De *Castro, Sousa, *Pinto, *Seixas, and *Mesquita families, emigrated from Portugal to other Western European countries, the Netherlands and England, where they returned to Judaism. The governor of Brazil in 1549 was Tomé de Sousa. The ambassador of Portugal in London in 1643 was Antonio de Sousa. Another important Crypto-Jewish family from Covilhã was that of Silvas. Some of the Silvas today live as Jews. During the civil wars in Portugal from 1806 to 1830, the Crypto-Jews of Covilhã were persecuted by the clergy, which suspected them, with good reason, of supporting the liberal side. It was stated that a Jewish community was established there at that time with its own rabbi. Due to the activities of A.C. de *Barros Basto and S. *Schwarz, many New Christians openly returned to Judaism under the republican government in the 1920s. The third community to be established in the country was in Covilhã (July 1929), where there were reported to be 6,000 Crypto-Jews. According to Slouschz, about a third of the city's population was of New Christian origin. Many of them still lived in what used to be the Jewish quarter before the forced conversions of 1497. A synagogue was established there named Sha'arei Kabbalah ("The Gates of Tradition"). With the establishment of the dictatorship in 1932 Jewish missionary activity among the descendants of crypto-Jews decreased in Covilhã as elsewhere in Portugal.

BIBLIOGRAPHY: M. Kayserling, *Geschichte der Juden in Portugal* (1867), index; E. da Costa, in: *Ha-Lapid* 16 (1929), 3–4; N. Slouschz, *Ha-Anusim be-Portugal* (1932), 68, 99 ff.; Portuguese Marrano Committee, *Marranos in Portugal* (1938), 8; Roth, Marranos, index. **ADD. BIBLIOGRAPHY:** J.L. Dias, *Notas biográficas de Simão Pinheiro Morão, escritor médico luso-brasileiro, natural de Covilhã* (1961).

COVO, family originating from Covo near Milan, which produced many rabbis who flourished mainly at Salonika. Among the most important are the following: (1) JUDAH (d. 1636), rabbi of Salonika. For the privilege of residing in Salonika the leaders of that community had undertaken to pay the Turkish authorities a special annual tax. Owing to the difficulty of finding the sum in cash, the authorities had agreed to accept in lieu clothes manufactured by Jewish craftsmen. Year by year a delegation of leaders of the community brought quantities of clothes to Constantinople where they were publicly sold and the proceeds made over to the authorities. In 1636 R. Judah headed the delegation. Because the clothes brought that year were regarded by government officials as inadequate in quantity and in value, R. Judah was summarily put to death and the other members of the delegation imprisoned and cruelly punished (Rosanes. Togarmah, 3 (1937/38), 396–8). (2) ELIJAH (d. 1689), rabbi and *rosh yeshivah* at Salonika. He was the author of *Aderet Eliyahu*, responsa and halakhic decisions. Together with those of Joshua Handali, they were published under the title *Shenei ha-Me'orot ha-Gedolim* (Constantinople, 1739). (3) JOSEPH BEN SHEMAIAH (d. 1727), chief rabbi of Salonika. He wrote a letter in support of the Shabbatean Nehemiah *Ḥayon, and was the author of *Givot Olam* (Salonika, 1784), responsa and homilies. (4) JOSEPH HEZEKIAH BEN ISAAC (d. 1762), rabbi at Salonika. Toward the end of his life he immigrated to Ereẓ Israel. He was the author of *Ben Porat Yosef* (Salonika, 1797) on the Shulḥan Arukh. On several occasions he traveled abroad on missions for Jerusalem. He was the father of (7), but is identified by some as father of (6). (5) RAPHAEL ḤAYYIM ABRAHAM (d. 1792), chief rabbi of Salonika from 1772. He wrote *Ḥayyei Abraham* (Salonika, n. d.), consisting of responsa on Jacob b. Asher's *Tur.* (6) ISAAC BEN HEZEKIAH JOSEPH called BEKHOR (d. 1807), *dayyan*. From Salonika he went to Jerusalem where he studied Talmud under Samuel Meyuḥas, the author of *Peri ha-Adamah*. He later became a member of Yom Tov Algazi's *bet din*. His signature appears on halakhic rulings, and on the *takkanot* of Jerusalem. (7) ISAAC BEN JOSEPH HEZEKIAH, called MORENU (1770–1854). In 1805 he went to Turkey as an emissary of Jerusalem. In his old age he returned to Ereẓ Israel and in 1848 was appointed *hakham bashi* in Jerusalem. In 1854, at the age of 83, he set out as an emissary of Jerusalem to Egypt and died in Alexandria. On an earlier mission he visited Germany. His writings have remained in manuscript. A brochure by him, entitled *Degel Maḥaneh* on the *Maḥaneh Efrayim* of Ephraim Navon, was published in the *Ateret Zahav* (vol. 2, Jerusalem, 1898) of Isaac Badhav. (8) RAPHAEL ASHER (1799–1875), chief rabbi and *rosh yeshivah* at Salonika. He was the author of responsa *Sha'ar Aḥer* (2 pts., 1877–79). (9) JACOB JOSEPH (d. 1899), rabbinic scholar and *dayyan* at Salonika. (10) JUDAH (d. 1907), chief rabbi of Salonika. He worked for the development of Jewish settlement in Ereẓ Israel and was the author of *Yehudah Ya'aleh*. (11) JACOB HANANIAH (1825–1907), chief rabbi of Salonika, where he established a yeshivah called Bet Yosef and a *talmud torah*. He was greatly respected by the Turkish authorities by whom he was decorated several times.

BIBLIOGRAPHY: Frumkin-Rivlin, 3 (1929), 39f., 126, 185, 274, 278f.; supplement, 90; M.D. Gaon, *Yehudei ha-Mizraḥ be-Ereẓ Yisrael*, 2 (1938), 615–7, 748; Ya'ari, Sheluḥei, index.

COWEN, SIR FREDERIC HYMEN (1852–1935), conductor and composer. Born in Jamaica, Cowen was taken to London as a child, and performed his own piano concerto there at the age of 13. He conducted the London Philharmonic Society, Halle Orchestra of Manchester, and many other orchestras. His works include four operas, four cantatas (including *The Veil*, 1910), six symphonies, orchestral and chamber works, songs, and marches. He published an autobiography, *My Art and My Friends* (1913); a humoristic glossary of musical terms, *Music as She is Wrote* (1915); and biographies of several composers. He was knighted in 1911.

COWEN, JOSEPH (1868–1932), a founder and leader of the Zionist movement in Great Britain. Born in Davenport, Cowen was initially indifferent to Jewish affairs. Persuaded to attend the First *Zionist Congress by his relative, Israel *Zangwill, he thereafter devoted himself to the Zionist movement, becoming *Herzl's chief associate in all matters concerning Great Britain and the Jewish community there. He was the moving spirit behind the foundation of the British Zionist Federation in 1899, and served several times as its president. Cowen accompanied Herzl during his audience with the Turkish sultan (1902), and Herzl made him a major character in his novel *Altneuland*, called Joe-Joseph Levy. He became director of the *Jewish Colonial Trust upon its foundation and held the post until his death. During World War I, Cowen was one of the few Zionist leaders to support Vladimir *Jabotinsky in his efforts to create a *Jewish Legion and was *Weizmann's right-hand man during the preparatory political work leading to the *Balfour Declaration. He was also a member of the *Zionist Commission to Palestine in 1918, treasurer of the Zionist Organization, a member of the Zionist Executive in 1921–22, and head of *Keren Hayesod in Great Britain. He should not be confused with his non-Jewish namesake Joseph Cowen (1829–1900), a prominent radical member of Parliament.

BIBLIOGRAPHY: T. Herzl, *Complete Diaries*, ed. by R. Patai, 5 (1960), index; N. Sokolow, *History of Zionism*, 2 (1919), index; Ch. Weizmann, *Trial and Error* (1949), index; JC (May 27, 1932); L. Jaffe (ed.), *Sefer ha-Congress* (1950^2), 153–5, 333–4. **ADD. BIBLIOGRAPHY:** S.A. Cohen, *English Zionists and British Jews: The Communal Policies of Anglo-Jewry, 1895–1920* (1982); D. Vital, *Zionism: The Formative Years* (1988).

[Getzel Kressel]

COWEN, PHILIP (1853–1943), U.S. publisher and author. Cowen was born in New York City, the son of German immigrants. He entered the printing business in 1878, and the following year, in cooperation with a group of distinguished New York Jews, founded the Anglo-Jewish weekly **The American Hebrew*. As its editor and publisher for 27 years, Cowen participated actively in the major issues and campaigns arising during the era of Jewish mass immigration. He was instrumental in publishing the works of such figures as Oscar S. *Straus, Max J. *Kohler, Henry Pereira *Mendes, Emma *Lazarus, Mary *Antin, and Alexander *Kohut. From 1905 to 1927 Cowen served as an official of the U.S. Immigration Service at Ellis Island and in 1906 went to Russia on a special mission to report on the causes of immigration from Eastern Europe, with emphasis on Jewish problems. His book *Memories of an American Jew* was published in 1932.

BIBLIOGRAPHY: *New York Times* (April 21, 1943).

[Morton Rosenstock]

COWEN, ZELMAN (1919–), Australian jurist and authority on constitutional law. Cowen, who was born in Melbourne, joined the Royal Australian Navy in 1941. After the war he was an adviser on constitutional problems to the British and U.S. military governments in Germany. From 1947 to 1950 he was a tutor at Oriel College, Oxford. In 1951 Cowen was appointed professor of public law at the University of Melbourne and was also dean of the faculty. In 1967 he became vice chancellor of the University of New England in New South Wales. Cowen's books on public law include *Australia and the United States: Some Legal Comparisons* (1954), *Federal Jurisdiction in Australia* (1959), and *The British Commonwealth of Nations in a Changing World: Law, Politics and Prospects* (1965). He also wrote a biography of Sir Isaac *Isaacs (1967) and numerous articles on constitutional problems. Cowen was president of the Adult Education Association of Australia. He was active in Jewish communal life. In 1970 he became the vice chancellor of the University of Brisbane. Cowen received a knighthood in 1976, and in November 1977 was appointed governor-general of Australia, the second Jew – Sir Isaac *Isaacs was the first – to occupy this position. Cowen took up this post at a critical time. In 1975 the previous governor-general, Sir John Kerr, had controversially dismissed the elected government of Gough Whitlam, although it continued to enjoy a majority in the Australian House of Representatives. The post of governor-general was thus under the spotlight. There is wide agreement that Cowen, who served as governor-general until 1982, did much to restore the post. Cowen subsequently lived in England for some years, where he was provost of Oriel College, Oxford from 1982 to 1990, and chairman of the British Press Council, before returning to Melbourne. He has received no fewer than 20 honorary degrees from universities around the world.

ADD. BIBLIOGRAPHY: W.D. Rubinstein, Australia II, 298–99.

[Isidor Solomon / William D. Rubinstein (2nd ed.)]

°COWLEY, SIR ARTHUR ERNEST (1861–1931), English Orientalist and bibliographer. Cowley's main interest from his school days was Hebrew and Jewish studies, but at Oxford he studied classics and his Semitic scholarship was largely self-taught. He became A. *Neubauer's assistant in the *Bodleian Library in 1896, succeeded him in 1899, and from 1919 was himself the Bodleian's librarian. Cowley's achievements in Jewish scholarship are paleographical, bibliographical, and interpretative. He published (at first with Neubauer) recovered Hebrew portions of Ecclesiasticus (1897, 1901), and (at first with A.H. Sayce) the Assouan (*Elephantine) Jewish-Aramaic papyri (1906, 1923). He completed vol. 2 of Neubauer's catalog of Bodleian Hebrew manuscripts and produced a concise catalog of its Hebrew printed books (1929, reduced from Steinschneider's catalog). Besides the papyri, Cowley edited – as his main work – *The Samaritan Liturgy* (2 vols., 1909). He taught rabbinics for the university, and a lectureship at Oxford in post-biblical Hebrew commemorates his name.

BIBLIOGRAPHY: T.W. Allen, in: *Proceedings of the British Academy*, 19 (1933), 351–9; G.R. Driver, in: DNB, 5 Supplement (1949), 194–5. **ADD. BIBLIOGRAPHY:** ODNB online.

[Raphael Loewe]

COZBI (Heb. כָּזְבִּי, Akkadian *Kuzābatum*, "voluptuous, well developed"), the daughter of Zur, who was one of the tribal leaders in Midian (Num. 25:15). When the Israelites committed harlotry with the Midianite women in the desert of Moab, *Phinehas son of Eleazar killed Cozbi together with her consort *Zimri son of Salu, a Simeonite chieftain. As a result of Phinehas' act, the plague which had afflicted the people was checked (*ibid.* 25:6–15).

COZEBA (Heb. כֹּזֵבָא). (1) Locality in Judah mentioned in I Chronicles 4:22. Some scholars identify it with Khirbat al-Dilba, 15 mi. (c. 24 km.) north of Hebron near ʿArrūb. Its name has been preserved in the neighboring Kirbat Kuwayziba. (2) Name of a dry river bed, now called Wadi al-Qilt. It is mentioned in the Dead Sea *Copper Scroll as one of the places where treasures were hidden. Many monasteries and hermitages were established there in Byzantine times, from the fifth century onward (Cyrillus Scythopolitanus, *Vita Sabae*, 44; John Moschus, PG, vol. 87, pt. 3, p. 2869). The Theotokós ("Mother of God") Chouzibiótissa, a Greek monastery, dedicated to St. George, still stands at the Deir (Dayr) al-Qilt.

BIBLIOGRAPHY: J.T. Milik, in: RB, 66 (1959), 321ff., pl. 34; Barthélemy-Milik, 3 (1962), 291, 14–15; Abel, Geog, 2 (1938), 300.

[Michael Avi-Yonah]

CRACOW (Pol. **Kraków**; Heb. קראקא, קרקא, קראקוב), city in S. Poland (within the historic region *Lesser Poland (Malopolska); in Western *Galicia under Austria). Cracow was the residence of the leading Polish princes during the 12th century, and later became the capital of Poland (until 1609). It was for many centuries the home of one of the most important European Jewish communities. It acquired the status of a city on the German model in 1257, and its situation on the Vistula river and the commercial route to Prague attracted an influx of immigrants from Germany, with whom the first Jews arrived. In 1335 King *Casimir the Great founded the rival city of Kazimierz near the southern extremity of Cracow (enclosed by a wall in 1422) and Jews settled there soon after its establishment. By the beginning of the 14th century (see below) they had an organized community, headed until the close of the century by an elected (or appointed) *Episcopus Judaeorum*; the first mentioned as such, in 1369, was a prominent financier, Samuel (Smoyl). A "Jewish Street" (*Platea Judaeorum*; now St. Anna street) in Cracow is mentioned in 1304. A synagogue, bath house, *mikveh*, and cemetery are first recorded in the 1350s; and a "Gate of the Jews" (*Valvae Judaeorum*) is mentioned in a deed of sale of 1366 as one of the gates of the city. From 1312, there is evidence that Jews acquired houses and building plots not only in their own quarter but also in neighboring parts of the city. The economic success and consolidation of the Jews in the city awakened among the townspeople an active hatred, already traditional among the burghers of German origin who were unused to Jewish commercial competition; the ownership of real estate by Jews was resented. The first protest against Jewish activities was submitted in 1369. In 1392 the municipal council requested that Jews should be allowed to sell their houses only to Christians.

15th Century

The struggle with the citizenry intensified during the 15th century (during 1408–70, 18 Jewish houses were sold to Christians), especially during the reign of Ladislas II Jagello (see also Zbigniew *Oleśnicki, Jan *Dlugosz). The assignment in 1400 of a building in a "Jewish street" to the university not only added to the overcrowding of the Jewish quarter, but for generations was a constant source of friction and danger to the Jews who were frequently attacked by students. A banker (*kampsor*), who was forced to provide loans to the students on interest not exceeding 25%, had to be appointed from among the Jews. In addition, the students extorted special payments from the Jews known as *kozubalec*. Mob outbreaks against the community and *blood libels also occurred (1407, 1423). In the 15th century Cracow Jews developed commercial ties with Breslau, Danzig, Lwow (Lvov, Lemberg), and Constantinople. The visit of the Franciscan preacher Johanes (Jan) *Capistrano to Cracow in 1454 led to severe anti-Jewish riots in which many Jews were killed and extensive damage was caused to property. In 1464 there were renewed disturbances. The heavy fines and financial sureties imposed by King Casimir IV Jagiello on the municipal council did not diminish the antagonism toward the Jews. In 1469 the community leaders had to sign an agreement to evacuate the street on which the university was located and to transfer their buildings to the university in exchange for a plot of land near the synagogue in Spiglarska Street (now St. Stefan Square). When a fire broke out in the city in 1477, the Jewish community was attacked. In 1485, its leaders – Moses *Fishel, Jacob b. Alexander, and Mordecai b. Jacob – were compelled to accept the dictates of the municipal council and signed "of their own free will and without coercion" an agreement to the effect that Jews would not compete in most branches of commerce and would only trade in pledges whose term of redemption had lapsed; this business was to be carried on only in their own houses, with the exception of Tuesdays, Thursdays, and market days, when they would be permitted to display the pledges publicly. Poor Jews and Jewesses were permitted to sell shawls, hats, and collars of their own manufacture. The Cracow Jews did not intend to abandon commerce, and a continuous struggle developed between the community and the burghers, in which both sides turned to the royal court for intervention. A fire which spread from a street inhabited by Jews to the Christian quarters in June 1494 led to riots against which the Jews took up arms in self-defense. The king ordered the arrest of the communal leaders, who were later set free largely through the intercession of the courtier and celebrated humanist Filippo Buonaccorsi (Callimaco Esperiente). The townspeople continued to insist on the expulsion of the Jews from the city. In 1495, the king expelled the Jews from the capital and they moved into adjacent Kazimierz.

Amalgamation with Kazimierz

The Cracow community amalgamated with that of Kazimierz, and, as customary after local expulsions, continued to visit Cracow from "their town" of Kazimierz and maintained a regular and often flourishing commerce there. For over four centuries, until the grant of emancipation in 1868, the Jews of Kazimierz continued the struggle, generally achieving some success, for rights to trade and work in Cracow. The Kazimierz community was already well established when it merged with that of Cracow. At the end of the 14th century construction was begun of a magnificent synagogue in Gothic style, completed about 1407, known as the Alte Schul. It is the oldest medieval synagogue still preserved in Poland. In the 1480s a Jewish bathhouse, a Jewish marketplace (*Circulus Judaeorum*), and a cemetery are mentioned in Kazimierz, all situated on the Breite Gass ("Broad Street"). From the 15th century on, the community was led by four elected "elders," who in 1454 were already empowered to judge lawsuits between Jews. On Feb. 27, 1494, the "elders" (*seniores*) Mark Simeon of Sącz, Joseph Kopelman, Moses Fishel, and Ulryk Samuel signed an agreement with the Christian butchers' guild (ratified by the *judex Judaeorum* Jan Goraj) which limited the number of Jewish butchers to four; they were forbidden to employ any assistants, either Jewish or Christian, or to sell meat to Christians, except wholesale.

Little is known about Jewish learning in Cracow-Kazimierz until the end of the 15th century (although the scholar Yom Tov Lipmann *Muelhausen had reputedly stayed there earlier in that century), when Jacob Pollak settled in Kazimierz and founded the first yeshivah from which talmudic learning spread throughout Poland. Several physicians lived there, including Moses of Przemysl, mentioned in 1465, who was also one of the community elders; Isachko, who practiced in Kazimierz after the expulsion from Cracow; Bocian, founder of the distinguished *Popper family; and Isaac of Spain (d. 1510) who served as court physician.

16th Century

At the beginning of the 16th century many Jews from Bohemia-Moravia settled in Kazimierz, but their desire to retain their separate cohesion and style of life was opposed by the Polish Jews, led by the *Fishel family. In the overcrowded conditions of the Jewish town tension between the two groups led to bitter conflict. After the resignation of Jacob Pollak from the Cracow-Kazimierz rabbinate the Polish congregation elected Asher Lemel, a friend of the Fishel family, while the Bohemian Jews elected another rabbi. In 1509 the king imposed financial sureties on both parties to compel them to maintain the peace. In 1519 he recognized the two congregations as autonomous communities, each electing its own rabbi, two elders, and a mediator to collaborate in the administration of the Jewish town. After the deaths of the two rival rabbis, this duality disappeared and the rabbinate was transferred to Moses Fishel of the Polish section. In addition to those from Bohemia-Moravia a large number of immigrants arrived in Kazimierz in the 16th century from Germany, Italy, Spain, and Portugal. These included wealthy men and physicians, some of whom acquired special personal privileges from the king of Poland exempting them from their financial obligations as members of the Jewish community. It was only in 1563, after numerous appeals from the communal leaders, that the king undertook to cease this practice.

Intensification of the overcrowding resulted in 1553 in official agreement to a small extension of the Jewish town and permission for the erection of a second synagogue. In 1564 a privilege was granted preventing non-Jews from acquiring residential or business premises in the Jewish town. By the 1570s, the Jewish population of Kazimierz numbered 2,060, and further extension of the Jewish quarter became urgent. In 1583 an agreement between the community and the municipality of Kazimierz on the expansion of the Jewish area was ratified by the king. The Jews undertook to erect the Bochnia Gate in the city walls and to liquidate the arrears in tax payments to the municipal treasury.

17th Century

In 1608 the king ratified an agreement with the municipality on the sale of an additional number of building sites and houses to Jews in return for an annual payment of 250 zlotys by the community to the municipality. The attempt of the community to retain control over the new acquisitions of real estate failed because of opposition from both Jews and Christians, and Jews were permitted to acquire real estate individually. By 1635, 67 houses, mainly occupied by wealthy persons (Isaac *Jekeles, Wolf *Popper, among others), had been erected in the section recently joined to the Jewish town. Throughout this period, the fierce struggle for Jewish commercial rights continued, in particular when Jewish traders had "invaded" the Christian sectors. In 1609 the community reached an agreement which in practice enabled the Jews to trade freely in Kazimierz and nearby Stradom, to rent shops and warehouses in the Christian city, and to engage in the fur and tailoring crafts for supply of their own requirements. They were prohibited from innkeeping and trade in fodder. Jewish economic activity within the limits of Cracow proper was dependent on bribery and the search for patrons among government and church circles or within the municipal council. While Christian property owners of Cracow were interested in Jewish trade in the town because they could lease warehouses and shops to Jews at exorbitant prices, the small tradesmen and craftsmen regarded the Jews as dangerous rivals. In 1576 the king had recognized the Jewish trade existing in the town through granting his protection to the practice. The struggle continued with varying success for both sides. The campaign against Jewish trade in Cracow was expressed in the polemic literature of the period in an anti-Jewish pamphlet by Sebastian *Miczyński. However, despite the influence of this tract and anti-Jewish outbreaks, Jewish trade in Cracow developed further in the 17th century, and was recognized de facto by royal decisions.

The 16th and first half of the 17th century was also a period of considerable cultural achievement in the Cracow-Kazimierz community. By 1644 the community had seven main synagogues, among them the Alte Schul and the Rema Synagogue (called after Moses *Isserles), erected in part by private persons and in one case with contributions from the goldsmiths' guild. From the second half of the 16th century a number of yeshivot were founded in Kazimierz whose fame made Cracow a most important center of Jewish learning. Among principals of the yeshivot during the second half of the 16th century were Moses Isserles, Mordecai b. Jacob of Cieplice, Joseph b. Gershon Katz, Nathan Nata Shapiro, Joshua b. Joseph Katz, Isaac b. David ha-Kohen Shapira, *Meir Gedaliah of Lublin, and Joel *Sirkes. About the middle of the 17th century Yom Tov Lippman *Heller was rabbi there. In 1666 the Shabbatean movement deeply stirred Cracow Jewry. The reformation movement among the Cracow burghers gave rise to charges of Judaizing, both true and unfounded, against its own radical wing. An earlier martyr of such accusations was Catherine *Weigel. The religious ferment and strife among the Christians made a strong impression on the Cracow Jews.

Communal Organization

By the end of the 16th century the patrician class had gained an oligarchic control of the communal administration mainly due to the exclusive system of elections. A statute for the community was formulated through various enactments, known after its main corpus as "the ordinances of (5) 355" (i.e. the year 1595; cf. M. *Balaban, "*Die Krakauer Judengemeinde-Ordnung von 1595 und ihre Nachtraege*," in JJLG, 10 (1913), 296–360; 11 (1916), 88–114). The community was headed by four *rashim* ("heads"), five *tovim* ("*boni vires*" or "notables"), and 14 *kahal* ("community council") members, a total of 23 leaders, i.e., the number constituting a "minor Sanhedrin." The duties of actual administration and supervision were assumed in rotation; every month one of the *rashim* publicly took an oath to fulfill his duties as *parnas ha-ḥodesh* ("leader for the month") conscientiously. Defined competencies and functions were assigned to other institutions of the community leadership. The community had numerous functionaries, some honorary and some paid, most of whom worked in committees and were allocated specific tasks, such as tax assessment, supervision of charity, and public market order. The persistent oligarchic trend inherent in the 1595 ordinances is shown in their regulation of judicial procedure which reveals a hierarchical system of three law courts, whose competence was graded according to the sums involved in the case, and payment was made to the two lower ones by both sides. These arrangements differ from strict halakhic conceptions of judicial practice.

Cracow-Kazimierz was one of the principal communities in the *Councils of the Lands; it headed the province (*galil*) of Lesser Poland. Taxes to the state were paid through and in conjunction with the Councils of the Lands (see also *Poland-*Lithuania). Provision for the regulation of internal taxation for providing defense against local persecution, for upkeep of officials, official functions, and charity is made in the 1595 ordinances and others (see B.D. Weinryb, "Texts and Studies in the Communal History of Polish Jewry," in PAAJR, 19 (1950), 77–98).

In the 1630s large numbers of Jews fled from Germany to Cracow during the Thirty Years' War. In addition, many others from Ukraine and Podolia sought refuge in Cracow in 1648–49 from the *Chmielnicki massacres.

The second half of the 17th century was a troubled period for the Cracow community. It suffered during the Swedish invasion, and in 1655, when Kazimierz was captured, many Jews fled. The Poles commanded by Stefan *Czarniecki looted Jewish shops and property, causing damage estimated at 700,000 zlotys. Much harm was also done to Jewish property during the two-year Swedish occupation. With the restoration of Polish rule, a monetary contribution was imposed on the Jewish community, who were accused of collaborating with the Swedes. The Jews of Cracow first had to pay large sums to the Polish army commanders, and, in the fall of 1657, 60,000 zlotys to the king; they were also charged 300 zlotys a week toward maintenance of the fortress garrison and the municipal guard, and were fined 10,000 zlotys following an accusation that they had handed over sacred objects from the cathedral to the Swedes. The Kazimierz Jews were excluded from Cracow under various pretexts.

During this period, attacks on Jewish houses by the students and the local population became increasingly frequent, while the royal authorities were powerless to take action against them. There were a number of blood libels. In 1663 Mattathias *Calahora was martyred at the stake. In 1664, the anti-Jewish outbreaks reached a new climax and intervention by the king and the fines imposed on the municipal council proved unavailing. In 1677 about 1,000 Jews in Kazimierz died of plague and the Jewish quarter was abandoned by most of its inhabitants. The stricken community could not pay its taxes; by 1679 the arrears of the poll-tax payments amounted to 50,000 zlotys and the king had to grant the Cracow community a moratorium on its taxes and other debts. The community began to reorganize in 1680 and reopened its yeshivah, but in 1682 anti-Jewish rioting by the populace and students again broke out accompanied by murder and looting, and army units had to be called in. The king punished the rioters severely and imposed heavy fines on the university, and the Jews were granted a further moratorium on their debts to the state treasury and individuals. The Cracow citizenry renewed its demands that Jews should be prohibited from practicing trade and crafts on the basis of the 1485 agreement (see above). Jews were prevented from entering Cracow on Sundays and Christian festivals. The most outstanding of the community's rabbis in the second half of the 17th century was Aaron Samuel *Koidanover.

18th Century

The history of the community in the 18th century was marked by fluctuations in the struggle of the Cracow citizenry to close the city, trade, and crafts to the Kazimierz Jews. In general, the Jews were able to withstand this pressure, with the support of the magnates and the king, since it was in their interest to have Jews acting as suppliers and financiers in Cracow itself. Anti-Jewish restrictions imposed by the city were mainly ineffectual and reflect the penetration of Jews into an increasing number of branches of trade and crafts, such as the trade in furs and hides, wax, soap, salt, tobacco, and haberdashery. Jews also traded in silver and gold, worked as goldsmiths, and engaged in large-scale import and export business, finance, and the lease and management of estates of the gentry (see *arenda). However the economic rise of the merchant and financier circles of the community was accompanied by increasing impoverishment among the majority of Kazimierz Jewry. These factors, combined with the growth of the artisan element, sharpened social tensions within the oligarchically led community. The expenses incurred in the struggle with the Cracow citizenry for providing defense against libels and for the constantly increasing requirements of charity forced the community to take loans and it thus became indebted to wealthy Christians and the Church. In 1719 the community owed a total of approximately 600,000 zlotys, of which about 350,000 was owed to churches and monasteries and the remainder to Polish noblemen and merchants. With the decline in status of the Kazimierz community its influence among the communities of the province also began to wane, and at the beginning of the 18th century these became largely independent of the mother community. In 1761 the Senate of Poland ratified a decree enforcing the prohibitions against Jewish commerce in Cracow. An attempt made by the municipality to confiscate the contents of the Jewish shops in the city was stopped by the authorities. During the troubled period between 1768 and 1772 the Jews in Kazimierz suffered at the hands of both the Polish and Russian armies. Many members of the community were arrested. One of its leaders, Gutman Rakowski, was tortured to death by the Poles. The Kazimierz community numbered 3,500 in 1775, and owned 212 houses; their property was valued at about 1,100,000 zlotys.

After the Polish Partitions

In 1772–76 Kazimierz passed to *Austria, while Cracow remained within Poland. The Austrian authorities demanded that Jews should be permitted to cross to Cracow, but the municipality tried to prevent them. In 1776 Kazimierz was returned to Poland, but the Senate prohibited Jewish commerce in Cracow and imposed a heavy sum on the Kazimierz community. Tension within the community continued under the new rule, and factions were formed among the oligarchy (see also *Jekeles family). Most of the Jews left Cracow and transferred their affairs to Kazimierz. The 92 Jews who remained were engaged in banking or moneylending, or owned inns. They occupied 38 houses. At the end of 1776 the king ratified an agreement between the community and the Kazimierz municipality extending Jewish commercial rights there. The Cracow municipal leaders then offered certain concessions to Jewish merchants in the city to prevent the complete transfer of Jewish business to Kazimierz. By the end of the 1770s, the 350 Jewish merchants and shopkeepers established in their new center at Kazimierz included 45 bankers and moneylenders, 52 textile merchants, 17 chandlers, 18 innkeepers, and several tailors, bakers, and furriers. In 1788 an explosives factory was established by a Jew in the vicinity of Cracow, and in 1790 a tannery. Many wealthy Jews left Cracow for Warsaw and other towns during this period.

During the 1780s the influence of *Ḥasidism began to penetrate to Cracow. This first circle of supporters of the movement in the city was established by Kalman *Epstein. In 1785 a *ḥerem* ("ban") was imposed on the Cracow Ḥasidim. Ḥasidism gained many adherents among the poorer classes of Jews in Kazimierz. Special houses of prayer were organized by the Ḥasidim, and the *Mitnaggedim* imposed a second *ḥerem* on them in 1797.

In 1795 Cracow and its environs were annexed by Austria, and in 1799 the Austrian authorities ordered the removal of all Jewish businesses from Cracow proper. Subsequently the communal leadership and nomenclature changed under the Germanizing influence and with the spread of *Enlightenment. The Austrian government attempted to introduce the specific taxes imposed on Jews within its territories, as well as the special systems of restriction and supervision of the number of Jewish families and marriages. The authority of the five *Vorstehers*, as the communal leaders were henceforth termed, was restricted to the synagogue, charities, and responsibility for the collection of taxes and the conscription of the quota of army recruits demanded from the Jewish quarter of Kazimierz. From 1800 both electoral and elective rights were determined by payment of the *candle tax, a new impost which constituted a heavy burden on the poorer sector in particular. This system required the payment of tax on at least seven candles a week in order to acquire the passive vote, and on eight candles to be eligible for election. Eligibility for the office of rabbi or *Vorsteher* required payment on ten candles a week.

This system did not change the social structure of the communal leadership. At the elections of 1807 there were only about 40 votes. In 1801 the income of the community from both direct and indirect taxes (e.g., on milk and butter) amounted to 55,000 zlotys and balanced its expenses. In 1806 it remained with a deficit of almost 30,000 zlotys, the income from direct taxation amounting to 8,000 zlotys. The community's deficit and debts rose with its increasing needs and the mounting rate of interest, and it was forced to increase the indirect taxes imposed on basic commodities.

In 1809 Cracow was incorporated into the grand duchy of Warsaw. Although certain of the regulations and restrictions imposed by the Austrian authorities were abrogated, others were introduced in their place. On Aug. 26, 1813, flood from the river caused extensive damage to the Jewish quarter of Kazimierz.

Cracow Republic

At the Congress of *Vienna the Cracow Republic (1815–1846) was established. The new state immediately issued regulations governing the position of the Jews there. They were permitted to reside in the Jewish part of Kazimierz and in some streets of the Christian sector. Only "cultured" Jews, entitled to civic rights, were permitted to acquire houses on the main street of the Christian sector. Outside Kazimierz only those Jews who qualified by a certain defined degree of education, who were assimilated in their dress, and who owned more than 5,000 zlotys were permitted to reside. (Only 196 out of a total of 13,000 Jewish residents qualified for this alleviation in 1848.) In addition, the community organization was abolished and replaced by a Committee for Jewish Affairs headed by a Christian chairman, a rabbi elected for three years and required to have a fluent knowledge of the Polish or German languages and to have gained a matriculation certificate, and two delegates elected by the highest category of taxpayers only. After some time, two deputy delegates were also included in the committee. The annual budget of the committee required the ratification of the republic's Senate. Collection of taxes from the Jewish inhabitants was placed under state administration. The books of the committee were kept in Polish. Among the 297 Jewish merchants and craftsmen in Kazimierz in 1811 there were 97 shopkeepers, 47 innkeepers and restaurateurs, about 20 market stallholders, 14 grain merchants, 12 textile and haberdashery merchants, 5 spice merchants, 5 hatters, 3 owners of timber depots, 3 goldsmiths, 3 barbers, 2 furriers, and one surgeon. 10,820 Jews were living in Cracow in 1833 (28% of the total population), 2,373 paid approximately 40,000 zlotys a year in taxes (income tax and business taxes), while of the 27,000 Christian inhabitants 2,296 paid approximately 25,000 zlotys a year in taxes. An elementary Jewish school was opened in 1830 and a number of commercial and vocational classes for boys and girls were added in 1837. In 1836/37, 146 boys and 239 girls were enrolled in this institution. Because of the lack of Jewish teachers, general subjects were taught by Christians. From 1832 the rabbi of Cracow, Dov Berush *Meisels, was the main influence in the community despite some opposition led by Saul Raphael Landau, who was elected rabbi by the Ḥasidim. In 1844 the Republic introduced a complicated system of its own for supervision of Jewish marriages, mainly to ensure that any additional Jewish families to the permitted number should be those with ample means; they were also to have a recognized non-Jewish education, and at least – in the case of poorer Jews – to discard their specific Jewish dress, and have reached the age of 30. In 1844 the first *Reform synagogue (Temple) was opened in Cracow. Some Jews were involved in the fighting in 1846 that preceded the liquidation of the Cracow Republic and its reversion to Austria.

Under Austria

The Austrians imposed a contribution of 55,000 guilders on the community and a tax on meat. The status of the Jews did not change basically, and their economic position became critical. The Jews of Vienna raised 6,000 guilders for distribution among 1,800 needy Jewish families in Kazimierz. During the 1848 revolution 12 Jews were elected to the municipal council of Greater Cracow, and the secretary of the community, Maurycy Krzepicki, was coopted to the municipal council. The Cracow Jews expressed their dissatisfaction with the communal system by demanding that the Jewish Committee should open its meetings to the public, and stormed the community building. They also demanded abolition of the kosher meat tax and the removal of its lessee, proposing instead taxation of poultry, which was mainly consumed by the wealthy, as well as reduction in the salaries of religious officials, abolition of all privileges of the oligarchy, and transfer of the hospital from the control of the *ḥevra kaddisha* to the Committee. In the 1848 elections to the parliament of Austria, Meisels was returned as deputy for Cracow. During the revolutionary ferment of 1848 the "Society for the Spiritual and Material Liberation of the Jews," an association with emancipatory and Polish-assimilationist aims, led by M. Krzepicki and A.J.

Warschauer, played a prominent role. The right of Jews to own real estate in the Christian sections of Cracow-Kazimierz was again restricted in 1853. When Meisels left Cracow for Warsaw, the struggle for the Cracow rabbinate ended in the election of the ultra-Orthodox Simeon Schreiber *Sofer, who later came into sharp conflict with the Reform-assimilationist group led by Joseph Ettinger and the rabbi of the Reform synagogue, Simon Dankovich. During the early 1860s the upper circles of Cracow Jewry inclined increasingly toward Polish assimilation. Many of them actively sympathized with the Polish rising of 1863–64.

The Period of National Awakening

After the grant of emancipation in 1867/68 to the Jews of Cracow, which carried with it the unrestricted right of settlement in Cracow itself, the community institutions were abolished and a Jewish Religious Council established in which the assimilationist *maskilim* and intelligentsia replaced the oligarchic leadership. In 1870, Simon Samuelsohn became chairman of the council. In 1869 there were 25 Jewish students (13% of the total) studying at the law faculty of the university, 14 (7%) at the faculty of medicine, and 10 at the technical college. During the early 1870s, about 200 Jewish pupils attended secondary schools and teachers' training colleges in Cracow. The first secular Hebrew public library in Cracow was founded in 1876. The first Hebrew school in the town, headed by the *av bet din* Ḥayyim Aryeh Horowitz, was established by the Shoḥarei Tov ve-Tushiyyah Society in 1874. A branch of the Alliance Israélite *Universelle was established at Cracow in 1867. In 1876 a talmud torah was founded and remained open until 1881. Later a school for the teaching of crafts was established by the Baron de Hirsch *Fund, as well as a vocational school financed by Arnold Rapoport, a member of the Austrian parliament.

Toward the close of the 19th century, the Jewish educational system of Cracow included *ḥadarim* and yeshivot (see also *Mahzike Hadas), as well as elementary and secondary schools with Polish and German as the languages of instruction. While Ḥasidic influence remained strong among the mass of Jews, with the influences of emancipation, *Haskalah, and assimilation many Jews became prominent in the Polish-German cultural and social life of Austrian Cracow, among them the professor of philology Leon Sternbach, the painter Maurycy Gottlieb, the jurist Joseph Rosenblatt, and the physicians Philip Eisenberg and Isidor Jurowich, who became director of the Jewish hospital in Cracow (see also *Aguddat Aḥim). Several Jews made fortunes in financial and industrial enterprises, notably Maurycy Datner, who became president of the Chamber of Commerce and Industry of the city. The Jewish population numbered 25,670 in 1900 (28% of the total), and 32,321 in 1910 (21%). (See Table: Jewish Population in Cracow 1900–2004.) A considerable number earned their livelihood in the grocery, haberdashery, leather, textiles, and clothing businesses. In addition to owning shops or stalls, many were occupied in hawking and the purchase of pig bristle and horsehair in the surrounding villages for industry. The wealthier Jewish merchants, a minority, owned wine and textile warehouses and were mainly engaged in the export of timber, feathers, and eggs. Among the artisans, most numerous were tailors, glaziers, and carpenters. There were 52 Jewish physicians in Cracow (out of the total of 248) and 47 Jewish lawyers (out of 110) in 1900.

Jewish Population in Cracow 1900–2004

Year	Jewish Population	Total Population	%
1900	25,670	91,310	28
1910	32,321	143,000	21
1921	45,229	164,000	27
1931	56,800	219,286	26
1938	60,000	237,532	25
1948	5,900	299,565	2
1955	4,000[1]		
1968	700[1]		
2004	150[1]	760,000	

1 Approximation.

*Antisemitism grew in Cracow at the close of the 19th century, amid the national rivalries in the city and demands that Jews should identify themselves with the Polish or German elements. At the same time the Jewish national revival began to penetrate to Cracow. The first *Ḥibbat Zion society, Rosh Pinnah, was established during the 1880s under the leadership of Simeon Sofer and Aaron Markus. During this period, the concepts of Hebrew revival were propagated; from 1892 the Sefat Emet Society and the Ḥevrah Ivrit le-Tarbut ("Hebrew Society for Culture"), headed by Israel Krasucki, the publisher of the periodical *Ha-Maggid he-Ḥadash* (published in Cracow), Jacob Samuel Fox, and later by the journalist Simeon Menahem Lazar, editor of *Ha-Miẓpeh*, was active there. From 1897 political Zionism won supporters, amoung whom Osias *Thon and Julius Schenweter were prominent, and an academic national society, Shaḥar, was founded. In 1906, the Jewish Nationalist Group was founded in Cracow. The organ of the Po'alei Zion, *Der Yidisher Arbeter*, was published in Yiddish in Cracow between 1905 and 1914. In 1900 the Group of Independents fighting for civic equality and the rights of the Jewish population was established, headed by Ignaz Landau and Adolf *Gross. The Committee of the Delegates of the Zionist Organizations of Western Galicia was established in Cracow under the leadership of Joseph Margolioth in 1905. During this period Cracow became an important center of Jewish cultural activity, with the historians Ḥayyim Nathan *Dembitzer and Feivel Hirsch *Wettstein, scholars such as Shlomo Rubin, the Hebrew author David Rotblum, and the popular Yiddish poet Mordecai *Gebirtig, who became celebrated in connection with the Holocaust.

After World War I

The rise of Polish nationalism and the movements connected with the upheavals of World War I, widespread unemployment, the return of armed soldiers and deserters, and famine throughout the city and vicinity, combined to intensify antisemitism. In 1918 the community was threatened with an outbreak of pogroms. The Endeks (*Endecja) elements attempted to direct the discontent of the Polish masses against the Jews. The Jewish youth in Cracow organized *self-defense, led by Jacob Billik and Y. Alster, and were joined by Jewish soldiers who had returned from the front. The entry of the troops of the antisemitic Polish General *Haller into Cracow set off a wave of riots which were warded off by the Jewish self-defense groups, who at the end of 1918 and the beginning of 1919 had a number of clashes with the rioters.

The Jewish population of Cracow numbered 45,229 in 1921, and according to the 1931 census, 56,800 (25.9% of the total), of whom 31% were occupied in industry and crafts (compared with 30% among non-Jews), 46% in commerce and insurance (non-Jews: 11%), 7% in communications (non-Jews: 8%), 2.5% in education and culture (non-Jews: 4%), approximately 1% in domestic employment (non-Jews: approximately 8%), and 13% in other professions (non-Jews: approximately 36%). Between the two world wars Cracow became an important center of Jewish political and social life in Poland. The Polish-language Zionist daily **Nowy Dziennik*, which had considerable public influence, was published there. Zionist movements were active. General Zionism, led by Osias Thon, who served for many years as rabbi of the liberal congregation, and by I. *Schwarzbart, had a strong following. The Bundist monthly *Walka* was published in Cracow between 1924 and 1927. In this period, as in former years, the mass of poorer Jews were concentrated in Kazimierz. Educational institutions included an elementary and a Hebrew secondary school in Cracow – during the school year 1937–38, 1,332 pupils were enrolled in these two institutions – a Hebrew *ḥeder*, the Taḥkemoni secondary school, a Jewish commercial school (opened in 1933), and the Orthodox women's teachers seminary for the Beit Yaakov girls schools in Poland. The president of the community between the two world wars was Raphael Landau. Antisemitism increased in Cracow from the early 1930s, especially among the Polish youth and the extremist (Fascist) Polish nationalist organizations, who made frequent attacks on Jewish shops and stalls, as well as on Jewish students at the university and technical high school.

[Arthur Cygielman]

Hebrew Printing in Cracow

Hebrew printing was first introduced in Cracow in 1534 by the brothers Samuel, Asher, and Eliakim Halicz, who had learned the craft with Gershom Kohen in Prague, whose style their productions betray. They printed the first edition of Isaac of Dueren's *Sha'arei Dura* – in Rashi type and with a beautifully decorated title page – in 1534, the year in which they received a license from King Sigismund I of Poland. A few other works followed, until in 1537 the three brothers converted to Christianity, which did not prevent them from continuing to print Hebrew books (a *mahzor* and the first two parts of the *Tur*), but their products were boycotted by the Jewish community. Eventually the king forced the Jewish communities of Cracow, Poznan, and Lvov to buy the Halicz's entire stock. Great success was attained by the Hebrew press set up in 1569 by Isaac b. Aaron of Prostitz (Prossnitz), who was trained in Italy and received a 50 years' license from Sigismund II Augustus. He acquired his equipment from the Venetian printers Cavalli and Grypho and also brought with him from Italy the scholarly proofreader Samuel Boehm. In the next 60 years Isaac and his successors (sons and nephews) produced some 200 books, of which 73 were in Yiddish. The Babylonian Talmud was printed twice (1602–08; 1616–20); a fine edition of the Jerusalem Talmud in 1609; Alfasi's *Halakhot* together with *Mordekhai* in 1598; and several editions of the Shulḥan Arukh with Isserles' annotations. Among kabbalistic literature was a Zohar (1603), and some of Moses Cordovero's writings. Other works included a Pentateuch and *haftarot* with the classical commentaries (1587), *Yalkut Shimoni* (1596), and *Ein Ya'akov* (1587, 1614, 1619). In his title-page decoration Isaac copied the Italian style. His printer's mark was first a hart, but from 1590 fishes. For the next four decades (1630–70), prominent Hebrew printers in Cracow were Menahem Nahum Meisels, his daughter Czerna, and his son-in-law Judah Meisels, a grandson of Moses Isserles. Menahem Nahum took over Isaac b. Aaron's equipment which he enlarged and improved, but he returned to the Prague style of printing, with Judah ha-Kohen of Prague as his manager. There was no Hebrew press active in Cracow in the 18th century. Between 1802 and 1822 Naphtali Herz Shapiro and his son Aaron Solomon issued such works as the *Midrash Tankhuma* (1803) and *Midrash Rabbah* (1805). Some "modernist" literature was also printed by Shapiro's son. Karl Budweiser printed various books between 1867 and 1874, before moving on to Lemberg (Lvov). Joseph Fisher, at first in partnership with B. Weindling, printed a good deal of Haskalah literature from 1878 until 1914, including a number of Hebrew periodicals such as *Ha-Tor*, *Ha-Zeman*, and *Ha-Maggid*. S.N. Deitscher and son were active as Hebrew printers from 1890 to 1940 and A. Lenkowitch from 1897.

Holocaust Period

There were 56,000 Jews living in Cracow on the eve of World War II. Persecution began soon after the German occupation (Sept. 6, 1939). On Sept. 17, 1939, Marek Bieberstein and Wilhelm Goldblatt became chairmen of the Jewish community and tried to restore community activities. The first *Aktion* took place on Dec. 5 and 6, 1939, when the Eighth District, inhabited mainly by Jews, was cordoned off, and searches and mass confiscations were carried out. The Germans burned down the Jewish Community Council building and several synagogues. That month the Germans appointed a *Judenrat, consisting of 24 members, including 11 of the former *kehillah* council and headed by Artur Rosenzweig. In April 1940, the German authorities issued an order for most of the Jews to evacuate the city within four months. Some 35,000 left, while about 15,000 Jews received special permission to remain. Another group was forced to leave in February 1941. About the same time, Cracow's two rabbis (Kornitzer and Rappaport) were murdered by the Nazis. On March 21, 1941, the ghetto was erected and close to 20,000 Jews, including 6,000 from neighboring communities, were crowded in. The physical extermination began in June 1942 when 5,000 victims were deported to the *Belzec death camp in three successive "selections." Several hundred were put to death in the ghetto itself. Among the deportees were Artur Rosenzweig and the 60-year-old poet Mordecai Gebirtig. The 70-year-old painter Abraham Neumann was shot in the street. In the next *Aktion* (Oct. 28, 1942) 7,000 Jews were shipped to Belzec, while the patients at the Jewish hospital, the old-age home inmates, and the 300 children at the orphanage were murdered on the spot. After new refugees arrived the ghetto population was now about 10,000, some of whom were in the work camp cordoned off from the rest of the ghetto by barbed wire. Final liquidation came in the middle of March 1943, when the inhabitants in the work camp were transferred to the nearby *Plaszow labor camp, and anyone found hiding was shot. The majority of the Jews in the other section were either killed on the spot or dispatched to *Auschwitz.

Resistance

The Cracow Jews began organizing resistance activities at the end of 1940. Their initially passive resistance soon turned into two organizations for armed resistance and sabotage: Bnei Akiva, consisting of Zionist youth and headed by Laban Leibowitz, Szymon (Shimon) Draenger and Adolf (Dolek) Liebeskind, which published a clandestine weekly in Polish; and a Ha-Shomer ha-Ẓa'ir group organized by leftist leaders H. Bauminger and Benjamin Halbrajch. The Bnei Akiva group established a base for military operations at a nearby village in the vicinity of the famous salt mines of Bochnia. Soon afterward both groups merged into the countrywide ŻOB ("Jewish Fighting Organization"). On Dec. 22, 1942, they attacked a group of German officers at Cracow's "Cyganeria Club," killing a dozen. This attack took on great significance. Several sabotage acts followed, including the derailment of trains. The Cracow ŻOB maintained contact with Jewish partisan groups in the Kielce district and with the *Warsaw Ghetto ŻOB leaders, one of whom, Yitzhaak Cukierman, was active in the Cracow ghetto for a period. When the Cracow ŻOB dissolved due to the final liquidation of Cracow Jewry, some of its members continued their activity at the Plaszow labor camp.

[Danuta Dombrowska / Stefan Krakowski]

Contemporary Period

By the end of World War II, only a few Jews who had been in hiding were saved. Only by the end of 1945 and in 1946 did Jews return to Cracow from Russia, where they had found refuge during the war years. The Jewish quarter of Kazimierz, however, was not reestablished by the Jews after the war because 3,000 among them sought residence elsewhere in the town, fearing the outbreak of a pogrom. The last Jew left Kazimierz in 1968. The new Jewish community used four of the ancient synagogues for their religious services. The oldest synagogue, "Hoyche Schul," was transformed into a Jewish museum. The old cemetery was renewed and reformed as a result of contributions from American and Canadian Jews. After the exodus of 1967–69, 700 Jews, mainly elderly ones, remained in the city. A few hundred were still present in the 1990s and just 150 or so in 2004.. A memorial book on Cracow Jewry, *Sefer Kraka Ir va-Em be-Yisrael*, was published in 1959.

[Arthur Cygielman]

BIBLIOGRAPHY: HISTORY: J.M. Zunz, *Ir ha-Ẓedek* (1874); H.D. Friedberg, *Luḥot Zikkaron* (1897, repr. 1969); Ḥ.N. Dembitzer, *Kelilat Yofi*, 2 vols. (1888–93, repr. 1960); F.H. Wettstein, *Kadmoniyyot mi-Pinkasot Yeshanim... be-Krakov* (1892); idem, *Le-Korot ha-Yehudim be-Polin u-ve-Yiḥud bei-Krakov* (1918, repr. 1968); F. Friedmann, *Die galizischen Juden im Kampfe um ihre Gleichberechtigung 1848–1868* (1929); B.; M. Balaban, *Historia Żydów Krakowie i na Kazimierzu*, 2 vols. (1931–36); I. Schipper (ed.), *Dzieje handlu żydowskiego na ziemiach polskich* (1937), index, s.v. *Krakow*; Halpern, Pinkas, index; R. Mahler, *Yidn in Amolikn Poylin in Likht fun Tsifern* (1958), 38, 62–64, 104, 126, 139, 150, 152, 156, 157, 175, 180, 187, 197; tables nos. 10, 18, 28, 42, 55, 57; H.H. Ben-Sasson, *Hagut ve-Hanhagah* (1959), index; S. Bronsztejn, *Ludność żydowska w Polsce w okresie międzywojennym* (1963), 31, 103, 114, 125, 141, 143, 146, 151, 167, 168, 170, 207–10, 232, 277, 280, 281. PRINTING: B. Friedberg, *Ha-Defus ha-Ivri bi-Krakov* (1900); idem, *Ha-Defus ha-Ivri be-Polanyah* (1950^2), 1–41; Balaban, in: *Soncino-Blaetter*, 3 (1929–30), 1–14, 31–34, 36–50; HB, 4 (1900), 135–6; Habermann, in: KS, 33 (1957/58); 509–20; Rivkind, in: *Bibliotekbukh* (Yid., 1934), 49–53. **ADD. BIBLIOGRAPHY:** "*Zeh Haya Bet ha-Sefer ha-Ivri be-Krakow*," in: A. Zbikowski, *Zydzi Krakowscy i ich gmina w latach 1869–1919* (1994); E.Reiner (ed.), *Kroke-Kazimierz-Cracow* (2001). HOLOCAUST PERIOD: J. Tenenbaum, *Underground* (1952), index; *Arim ve-Immahot be-Yisrael*, 2 (1948), 346–52; Nirensztajn, in: *Bleter far Geshikhte*, 5 no. 1–2 (1952), 226–63; G. Davidson, *Yomanah shel Yustinah* (1953); G. Reitlinger, *Final Solution* (1968^2), index; Y. Peled (Margolin), *Krakow ha-Yehudit 1939–1943* (1993); T. Pankiewicz, *Apteka w getcie krakowskim* (1947; *Bet Mirkaḥat be-Getto Krakow*, 1985); E. Duda, *The Jews of Cracow* (1998); PK.

CRAFTS.

In the Bible

Genesis 4:2, 17, 20–22 describes Cain and four of his descendants as the first to engage in crafts. Cain worked the land, Enoch engaged in building, Jubal, in music, Jabal (like Abel) was a shepherd, and Tubal-Cain worked with metals (i.e., copper and iron).

This division apparently reflects the social development of the ancient world from around the fifth or fourth millennium B.C.E. This period saw the beginning of the development of agriculture and the increase and diversification of the types of crafts connected with it. During this period, there was increased knowledge of each individual occupation, and many types of work were undertaken by experts who handed down their professional know-how from father to son as a family tradition or as a closed tribal tradition. For example, in the 12th century B.C.E., the Philistines held the monopoly in the processing of iron and the sharpening of iron implements (I Sam. 13:19–22).

The first known crafts were directly connected with the production and preparation of food. Other crafts that were also connected with agricultural production were the tanning of *leather and the manufacture of clothing. Examples of textiles preserved since the Bar Kokhba period were found in the *Judean Desert Caves. Evidence of weaving and dyeing are the loom weights and dye vats discovered in excavation. This group of crafts also included braiding, which consisted of the production of ropes and mats, and other similar industries. The development of agriculture and allied crafts also gave rise to the development of tools, such as the manufacture of plows, digging implements, vehicles of transportation, leather implements, and so on (see *Agriculture; *Carts and Chariots).

Another group of crafts are the various artistic crafts: the making of jewelry and of fine vessels of wood, stone, and ivory inlaying; the production of hammered metal objects; embroidery; and so on. There are biblical references to the work of the potter and many examples have been found in excavations (see *Pottery). This group of crafts developed with the building of palaces and temples:

> And I have filled him [Bezalel son of Uri] with the spirit of God, in wisdom, and in understanding, and in knowledge, and in all manner of workmanship. To devise skillful works, to work in gold, and in silver, and in brass. And in cutting of stones, to set them, and in carving of timber, to work in all manner of workmanship (Ex. 31:2ff.).

Artisans of various types were numbered among the slaves of the kings of Egypt, Mesopotamia, and other permanent settlements. The Bible does not mention craftsmen of this type, apart from *Bezalel, who worked on the construction of the Tabernacle, and the people of Tyre, who participated in the construction of the Temple in Jerusalem (I Kings 5:15–25). Gold and silver were used for vessels etc. to be used in the temples or palaces, for jewelry, figurines, sewing implements, pins and clasps, etc. These metals were processed by means of casting or hammering, and separate parts were joined together by means of welding and coating. Other products, especially jewelry and tiny vessels of precious metals, were formed from different shapes, such as squares, circles, and rectangles, which were welded together in various patterns, or joined together on a chain (II Chron. 3:16). Another artistic craft consisted of inlaying fine vessels and jewelry with precious and semiprecious stones as a decoration or for finishing other items. The biblical term *millu'at* apparently refers to this technique of inlaying (e.g., Ex. 28:17). Metal frames inlaid with precious stones have been found, dating to the second millennium B.C.E. Inlaid furniture and tablets dating to the third millennium B.C.E. have also been found, as well as another example of metal inlaid with stones from the second millennium B.C.E. and others. The Bible describes the stones of the breastplate (Ex. 28:15ff.) as being inlaid within their frames. Inlaying ivory ornaments into wooden furniture, walls, and other fine objects was also prevalent during the second millennium B.C.E. In general the Bible conveys the picture of the development by the Jewish people in Ereẓ Israel of manifold skills in the arts and crafts which they later carried with them throughout the Diaspora.

[Ze'ev Yeivin]

Post-Biblical and Talmudic Period

There is little information about crafts in the period between the return from the Babylonian captivity in 538 B.C.E. and the talmudic era. Carpenters and masons are explicitly mentioned in Ezra 3:7 as being among those who returned from the Babylonian exile, and they must have been active in the building of the Temple. Among those who took part in the building of the wall of Jerusalem under the guidance of Nehemiah are mentioned the *ẓorefim* ("refiners and workers in gold and silver"; Neh. 3:8 and 31), the perfumers (3:8), and the builders, who, in addition to the stonework, "set up the doors, the bolts, and the bars" of the various gates. Little is known of the life of the Jewish people in Judea during the period after Nehemiah until the establishment of Seleucid rule in 198 B.C.E. Discoveries at Tell al-Naṣba indicate that the manufacture of pottery was carried on by entire villages during this period. Aristeas described Jerusalem as "a city rich in crafts" (*Aristeas to Philocrates*, ed. M. Hadas, p. 147). Ben Sira (Ecclus. 38:27–32) describes in some detail the work of the various craftsmen of his time, wood carvers, signet engravers ("whose art is to make every variety of design; he is careful to make the likeness true"), metalsmiths, and potters, and concludes, "All these are deft with their hands, and each is wise in his handiwork; without them a city cannot be inhabited, and wherever they dwell they hunger not."

Arts and crafts were greatly fostered by the Hasmonean kings, as a result of the extensive building operations which they undertook. Simeon built the port of Jaffa to attract seaborne commerce, and the increased maritime trade also promoted the development of crafts. The description of the mausoleum which he erected for his parents and brothers in Modi'in (I Macc. 13:25) makes it certain that skilled craftsmen of every kind were employed in its erection and embellishment. The huge building projects undertaken by Herod, both in Jerusalem and Caesarea, but above all the rebuilding of the Temple, so vividly described by Josephus (Ant., 15:380ff.), called for skilled workers in many spheres – masons, carpenters, metalworkers, weavers and embroiderers, goldsmiths and silversmiths. Jews were employed for the building of the Temple as is specifically mentioned. Priests were trained as masons and carpenters for the edifice itself – as Josephus states, "Into none of these did King Herod enter, for he was forbidden, because he was not a priest. However, he took care of the cloisters and outer enclosures" (15:419–20). Excavations in Jerusalem have revealed the sarcophagus of "Simeon, the builder of the Sanctuary."

There were some families of craftsmen who were experts in skills required for the Temple service itself. The *Bet Garmu specialized in the preparation of the *shewbread and the house of Avtinas prepared the incense. These families actually monopolized their position. When they demanded higher wages, the Temple administration dismissed them and summoned shewbread and incense makers from Alexandria to take their place. The experiment failed because of the inefficiency of the new craftsmen, and the houses of Garmu and Avtinas were reinstalled. They only resumed work after receiving double their previous salary (Yoma 3:11, 38). That Jews engaged in the building of pagan edifices is specifically mentioned in the Mishnah with regard to the problems of conscience and *halakhah* for the Jewish workers. The sages ruled that "none may help them to build a basilica, scaffold, stadium, or judges' tribunal; but one may help them to build public baths or bathhouses, yet when they reach the cupola in which the idol is placed, it is forbidden to help them to build it" (Av. Zar. 1:7).

In ancient Jerusalem, before the city fell in 70 C.E., specified streets, markets, and districts were inhabited by artisans of the same trade. Bakers, cheese-makers, blacksmiths, goldsmiths, leatherworkers, dyers, weavers, fullers, potters, and other craftsmen were concentrated in their own quarters. The different trades seem to have had synagogues of their own. When passing through the city or a nearby village, the artisan was recognized by the distinctive badge he wore: the tailor had a needle stuck in the front of his dress; the worker in wool showed a woolen thread; the dyer carried different colored threads from which patrons could select the desired shade; the carpenter displayed a ruler; the leatherworker was recognized by the apron he wore; and the weaver carried a small distaff behind his ear and the scribe, a pen. Eleazar b. Azariah said of this practice of wearing badges: "There is something grand about artisanship; every artisan boasts of his trade, grandly carrying his badge in the street" (ARN^2 21, 45); and the rabbis stated that he who does not teach his son a craft, teaches him brigandage (Kid. 29a). The rabbis classified leather dressing among the coarser trades, but quilting or stitching in furrows was considered a clean and easy craft (Kid. 82a–b). The tanners of Palestine, like those of ancient Greece, practiced their trade outside the cities because of the unpleasant odor. Gold and silversmiths produced articles for the household as well as ornaments. An ornament produced for women was a "golden Jerusalem," which contained the picture or the engraving of Jerusalem (Shab. 59a). The institution of apprenticeship was frequently mentioned in rabbinic literature. The master was called *rav* and the apprentice, *talmid* or *shulyah*. The term of apprenticeship was agreed upon between the master and the parents of the boy. The son of an artisan generally followed the trade of his father, and orphans were instructed by members of the guild of their late fathers.

An impressive description is given by the rabbis of the massive basilica synagogue in Alexandria. The worshipers did not occupy their seats at random, but goldsmiths, silversmiths, blacksmiths, metalworkers, and weavers all sat together in groups so that when a poor man entered the place he recognized the members of his craft and on applying to that quarter obtained a livelihood for himself and for the members of his family (Suk. 51). The guild of Jewish weavers in Alexandria was registered according to Roman law as a corporation (J. Juster, *Les Juifs dans l'empire romain*, vol. 2, 306), and the Jewish coppersmiths of Alexandria were renowned. According to the Talmud the coppersmiths were employed to repair the bronze utensils in the Temple and were commissioned to make doors of Corinthian bronze for the Temple which "shone like gold" (Yoma 38a). The craftsmen of Jerusalem used to come out in groups to welcome the pilgrims bringing their first fruits to the Temple (Bik. 3:3). Both the Jerusalem and the Babylonian Talmuds have many references to craftsmen of every kind in Ereẓ Israel after the destruction of the Temple and an echo of their prosperity to which Ben Sira refers in the third century B.C.E. is heard in the proverb, "though a famine lasts seven years it does not pass through the gate of the artisan" (Sanh. 29a).

The textiles of Beth-Shean, referred to in the Talmud (TJ, Kid. 2:5) were famed for their quality and praised by Roman writers; Sepphoris had a synagogue of the weavers. Dyeing was a particular Jewish occupation; to the statement of a fourth century work, *Totius Orbis Descriptio*, that purple silk was manufactured in Sarafand, Caesarea, Shechem, and Lydda, the Talmud (Sot. 46b) adds a village, Luz, in Galilee, where the famous purple dye was made. As mentioned, whole villages engaged in pottery making, and Tiberias was a center for glass. Many beautiful mosaic pavements have been uncovered in Israel; that of the sixth-century synagogue in Bet Alfa is inscribed with the names of the craftsmen *Marianos and his son Ḥanina. In Babylon also, Jews worked in a multitude of crafts, including weaving, dyeing, tapestry making, leather work, metalwork, and wicker work (BB 22a; cf. Pauly-Wissowa s.v. *Babylonia*). Pumbedita was a center for the weaving of linen (Git. 27a; BM 18b). Josephus (Wars, 5:212) describes in detail a "truly wonderful" Babylonian-made curtain (*parokhet*) in front of the Holy of Holies in the Temple. The frequent references in the Babylonian Talmud to *rashei ommanot* ("heads of crafts") suggests that the craftsmen were organized in guilds, and in fact there are references to guilds of basketmakers and to weavers (Sot. 48a). Perfumers, carpenters, and art metalworkers were apprenticed (Krauss, Tal Arch, vol. 2, 255–6). Glassblowing seems to have been an occupation among Jews not only in Ereẓ Israel, but also in Egypt and Rome. Although a reference in the Talmud (Men. 28b) to Alexandrian goblets does not mention that they were of Jewish manufacture, names of Jewish glassblowers have been found in Oxyrhynchus and Thebes, and Roman glasswork of the third and fourth centuries decorated with typical Jewish symbols, the ark, the *menorah*, the Temple, and the *sukkah*, strongly suggest Jewish craftsmen in glass (*Classical Review*, 51 no. 4 (1937), 144–6).

From the Middle Ages to the End of the 18th Century

The Jewish occupational structure was gradually eroded with the destruction of the ancient Jewish social pattern and with the change in social attitudes through the relentless pressure from the Christian church, from the fourth century on. With the burgeoning of city life in the lands of Islam and the gradual exclusion from and relinquishment by Jews of agriculture under both Muslim and Christian rule, a process which had been accomplished more or less by the eighth century, crafts became almost the only economic sphere where Jews still worked with their hands. The respect paid to crafts in the period immediately preceding this profound change in Jewish life waned in the atmosphere of the medieval cities, where the merchant and trade had a more honored status.

Two entirely different patterns in the practice of crafts and their place in Jewish life and society are discernible throughout the Middle Ages. One characterizes the communities in countries around the Mediterranean, including in the south those in the continents of Asia and Africa, and in the north extending more or less to an imaginary demarcation line from the Pyrenees to the northern end of the Balkans. The other, in the Christian countries of Europe, was more or less north of the Pyrenees-Balkans line.

SOUTH OF THE PYRENEES-BALKANS. In the ancient places of Jewish settlement, crafts continued a major occupation of a large part of the Jewish population. The Karaite Benjamin b. Moses al-*Nahāwendī described in the ninth century those who "come to another's house, do his work and make what he needs for him for pay – like the tailor and the launderer, the worker in iron, in copper, tin, and lead, the dyer and the weaver as well as every other artisan" (in his *Massat Binyamin* [1834], 4b). There was thus a wide range of itinerant Jewish craftsmen in Persia and its vicinity. In the same century a hostile Muslim denigrated the Jews because among them are found "only dyers, tanners, bloodletters, butchers, and cobblers." This limitation in Jewish society must have been a figment of his imagination, but in any case he must have found many Jews in these occupations in Egypt and its surroundings in his time. The responsa of the *geonim* contain ample evidence of Jewish crafts and craftsmen throughout the Muslim Empire in the 10th and 11th centuries.

In the 11th and 12th centuries extensive Jewish activity in crafts is attested. S.D. Goitein has shown (*A Mediterranean Society*, 1 (1967), 362–7) how widespread and ramified were partnerships in crafts. He stated (p. 87) that these partnerships "range in date between 1016 and 1240.... Concerned are gold and silversmithing and other metal work..., dyeing (purple... indigo... silk),... the manufacture of glass vessels,... weaving,... silk work,... the making of wine,... and cheese, sugar factories,... and a pharmacy." The amounts of money and quantities of materials involved in these partnerships and in other craft enterprises (*ibid.*, 80–89) indicate a wide range in scale of the work. Sometimes the equipment of such a workshop is mentioned:

> An inventory of the workshop of a silk-weaver, dated 1157, contained 32 items... He possessed four looms, three combs connected with silk-weaving, three cylinders of wood on which the woven materials were rolled, two irons, one for the pressing of robes and another for the pressing of fabrics worn as turbans, wickerwork baskets full of warps, various quantities of bleached and other linen (which was woven together with silk), a small pot with weaver's reeds, copper threads covered with silver, and other items not preserved. The instruments taken away from a silk-weaver in Dahshū (the village famous for its pyramids) counted 26 items, of which nine were different from those just mentioned (*ibid.*, 86).

Most workshops were smaller, like the one whose "weaving tools" were sold for 12 dirhem only (J. Blau (ed.), *Teshuvot ha-Rambam* (1961), 85–86, no. 52).

*Benjamin of Tudela began to find Jewish craftsmen on his travels only on reaching Greece. At Thebes he found "about two thousand Jews. They are the good masters for preparing silk and purple clothes in the land of the Greeks, and among them are great sages in Mishnah and Talmud" (M.N. Adler (ed.), *Itinerary of Benjamin of Tudela* (1907), 12, Heb. section). He also found the Jews of Salonika, numbering about 500, among them scholars, "and they busy themselves in silk work" (*ibid.*, 13). At Constantinople he was told that Jews are hated mainly "on account of the tanners, who work in hides, because they throw out their dirty water into the streets at their doorsteps and they befoul the Jewish quarter. Therefore the Greeks hate the Jews, the good ones as well as the bad ones" (*ibid.*, 16). Benjamin's information not only expressed the usual superiority of merchants toward craftsmen in a medieval city, but also gave evidence of differing attitudes – an inimical one, toward "base" professions, like tannery, and a more friendly one, toward "better" professions like silk manufacture and dyeing, among Jews.

Throughout the later Middle Ages and up to modern times the same structure of Jewish society persisted in Islamic countries, in which a broad layer of various Jewish craftsmen was a distinct feature. Several crafts – like silk work and dyeing, in some countries also silver and gold work (e.g., in Yemen) – were considered a Jewish specialty.

Not only Sicily under Norman and Hohenstaufen rule relied on Jews for silk work and dyeing, but in Italy there were many Jewish craftsmen, in particular in the south. It would seem that Thomas Aquinas was referring to them in his letter *Ad ducissam Brabantiae* (March 7, 1274), advising Christian rulers that "they would do better to compel the Jews to work for their living as is done in parts of Italy" (*ut Judaeos laborare compellerent ad proprium victum lucrandum, sicut in partibus Italiae faciunt*). The same situation was found about 200 years later, by Obadiah of *Bertinoro. Writing in 1488, he describes the community of Palermo, which "contains about 850 Jewish families.... They are poverty-stricken artisans, such as coppersmiths and ironsmiths, porters and peasants... despised by the Christians because they are all tattered and dirty... They are compelled to go into the service of the king whenever any new labor project arises; they have to drag ships to the shore, to construct dykes, and so on. They are also employed in administering corporal punishment and in carrying out the sentence of death" (ed. A. Yaari, in *Iggerot Ereẓ Yisrael* (1943), 104). He found a similar situation at Messina, where he counted "about four hundred Jewish family heads… better off than those of Palermo, all of them craftsmen, though a few are merchants" (*ibid.*, 108). As in the 12th century, so in the 15th century, the Jewish onlooker from the north expresses shock at and a sense of superiority toward this artisan Jewish society.

CHRISTIAN SPAIN. In the kingdoms of Christian Spain, craftsmen made up a large and important sector in Jewish occupations and society. The family name Escapat, Scapat, derives originally from an Aramaic term for a shoemaker. In many communities artisans were the majority or formed at least half of the income earners. In Segovia, in the late 14th century, out of 55 Jewish earners, "23 were artisans – weavers, shoemakers, tailors, furriers, blacksmiths, saddlers, potters, and dyers" (Baer, Spain, 1 (1961), 198). "There was a street known as Shoemakers' Lane in the *judería* of Toledo in the 14th century" (*ibid.*, 197). "Conspicuous in Aragon are Jewish bookbinders, scientists who devise scientific instruments, and gold- and silversmiths" (*ibid.*, 426). Baer assumes that in the 14th century "at least half of the Jews of Barcelona… were artisans: weavers, dyers, tailors, shoemakers, engravers, blacksmiths, silversmiths (including some highly esteemed craftsmen who made Christian religious objects), bookbinders (who bound the registers of the royal chancery), workers in coral, and porters" (*ibid.*, 2 (1966), 37). The same holds more or less true for Saragossa (*ibid.*, 55–56). The anti-Jewish laws of 1412 stated that "Jewish artisans (blacksmiths, tailors, shoemakers, etc.) might not serve Christian customers" (*ibid.*, 168).

There is every reason to assume that the main outlines of Jewish society in the kingdoms of Christian Spain were a continuation of its structure in the kingdoms of Muslim Spain. The importance of artisans was evident in Jewish social and even cultural life there. The artisans were the mainstay of the opposition led by the mystic trend to the rule of the rationalist patrician stratum in Spanish communities. Artisan *guilds were behind many of the demands for democratization of community leadership and for equal distribution of taxes in communities like Saragossa and Barcelona in the 13th and 14th centuries. Shocked by the catastrophe of the persecutions of 1391, the moralist Solomon ibn Laḥmish *Alami demanded in 1415 of the Spanish Jew: "Teach yourself a craft, to earn your living by your work… for it is to the honor of men to live off their work and toil, not as the proud ones thought in their foolishness" (*Iggeret Musar*, ed. A.M. Habermann (1946), 29).

The artisans had always been the most faithful element in Spanish Jewry. During the mass conversions of 1391–1415, many devout artisans remained steadfast" (Baer, Spain, 2 (1966), 354). No wonder that King Alfonso v stated in 1417 that community leadership had passed to "the artisans and the little people" and Solomon *Bonafed complained about this time that in Spanish Jewry "the tailors render judgment, and the saddlers sit in courts (quoted by Baer, *ibid.*, 248).

The workshop of the Jewish artisan in Spain was not always a small one. Mention is made of workshops (*operatoria*) on a large scale for the manufacture of clothes in Saragossa and Huesca (Baer, Spain, 1 (1961), 425). About the beginning of the 14th century there came before *Asher b. Jehiel (the *Rosh*) the case of a dyer or saddler "who has an annual expense in the form of gifts to the judges and officials, to keep them from trumping up charges against him – the usual contribution that craftsmen are required to make out of their handiwork" (quoted by Baer, *ibid.*, 201). At the other end of artisan society there would be the case of that "worthless scamp among the artisans [who] will marry a woman here today and then become enamored of another and go and marry her elsewhere and return brazenly to his home town" (responsum quoted by Beer, *ibid.*, 424).

After the expulsion from Spain the exiled artisans merged into the artisan class of the communities in North Africa and the Ottoman Empire. It would seem that many other exiles took up crafts in their new straitened circumstances; some would even see it as a moral obligation, as formulated by men like Solomon ibn Laḥmish Alami (see above). The Safed community in its days of glory in the 16th century was based on a broad stratum of craftsmen practicing on a large and small scale. Stories about Isaac b. Solomon Ashkenazi *Luria (Ari) tell much about the social relationships and place of artisans in this holy community. One of the exiles who went to Jerusalem advised his correspondents: "Let anyone who wants to, come. For they can live out their lives earning through crafts. These are the worthwhile crafts here – gold- and silversmithery, tailoring, carpentry, shoemaking, weaving and smithery… I who know no craft except for my learning derive my needs from Torah study" (A. Yaari (ed.), *Iggerot Ereẓ Yisrael* (1943), 181).

NORTH OF THE PYRENEES-BALKANS (INCLUDING NORTHERN AND CENTRAL ITALY). Crafts played a very small role as a Jewish occupation, from the inception of Jewish settlement in this part of Europe. Around the beginning of the 11th century mention is made of a Jew in northern France who owned a furnace and made his living by working it with Christian hired men and letting it out for baking to other people (S. Eidelberg (ed.), *Teshuvot Rabbenu Gershom* (1956), 61–63, no. 8).

Neither the documents of privileges granted to Jews in these countries up to the 15th century nor their own writings reveal much concern with crafts or the presence of craftsmen. Certainly the Christian guilds prevented the growth of a Jewish artisan class in the cities of Western and Central Europe up to the 15th century. Since moneylending brought various articles in pawn into Jewish houses, to be able to return them undamaged or to sell them profitably the Jew had to learn to repair them and keep them in good condition. Hence a part-time, unspecialized kind of "pottering" artisanship always existed in those countries and times where Jews were engaged in moneylending. Jews attempted to maintain their own butchers for the sake of *kashrut*, although Christian butchers' guilds always tried, often with success, to thwart this aim. It is reasonable to assume that there were always at least part-time tailors among Jews everywhere, to avoid using the forbidden admixture of wool and flax (*sha'atnez*).

From these beginnings there developed from the 15th century a resumption of crafts among communities in Southern and Central Europe (Bohemia, Moravia, and Austria) and especially in Poland-Lithuania.

Rabbinical responsa tell of women – widows or spinsters – who worked in shawl-making and thread-making for gentile customers. Jewish craftsmen are mentioned in Poland in 1460. In 1485 the municipal council of Cracow permitted "poor Jewesses to sell every day shawls and scarves made by their own hands and craft." Jews increasingly penetrated crafts in the towns of Poland in the 16th century as the constant complaints of guilds and municipal councils abundantly show. The same development is reflected even more strongly in the various royal decisions and agreements between municipalities and Jews, or Christian guilds and their Jewish counterparts, all of which combine to give a picture of consistent, even if much hampered, penetration of Jews into various crafts.

In the grand duchy of Lithuania, the Jews of Grodno already had permission in 1389 in their charter of privileges "to exercise different crafts." In time, crafts became a well-developed sector of the Jewish economic structure. When needy, displaced refugee children from Germany arrived in Lithuania in the wake of the destruction of the Thirty Years' War, the Council of Lithuania (see *Councils of the Lands) gave the compassionate instruction: "It has been resolved and decided to accept 57 boys into our country to be under our protection, to divide them among the communities to feed them, to clothe and shoe them. Boys to whom God has granted wisdom that their study will be successful shall be induced to study Torah at school; boys whose abilities are not sufficient for the study of the Torah shall be induced to take service or to learn the work of some craft" (S. Dubnow (ed.), *Pinkas ha-Medinah* (1925), 73, no. 351). This indicates both that there was opportunity for learning a craft, and the disregard in which it was held by the leaders of Jewish society. Accordingly crafts are associated with intellectual incapability; it would be a sin, it seems, to send an able boy to be apprenticed to an artisan. The council also dealt with supervision of Jewish tailors to ensure that they should not transgress Jewish law in their work (*ibid.*, 178, no. 728). The increase in craftsmen is reflected in the hostile decision of the Council of Lithuania in 1761 forbidding craftsmen in all large communities from taking part in the assemblies of the community (*ibid.*, 268, no. 983). Indeed, in the bitter divisions in the Vilna community in the second half of the 18th century craftsmen played an important role in the opposition groups and activities.

Despite a general disparagement of crafts, *printing was considered an honorable profession. The Cracow community is found in 1595 trying to defend the printers of Cracow and Lublin against competition from Italian printers (M. Balaban, in JJLG, 11 (1916), 93, no. 79).

In the rapidly developing southeast of Poland a Jewish craftsman named Kalman, mentioned as a proficient tanner and furrier (*in arte pellificiaria bene versatus*) in *Przemysl, was important enough to be granted a special privilege by King Stephan Báthory in 1578 (M. Schorr, *Żydzi w Przemyślu* (1903), 88–89, no. 12). In the same town – which was certainly not exceptional in economic structure – the king defended in 1638 "the Jewish craftsmen who do their work for Jews only" against restrictions by the municipal authorities (*ibid.*, 143, no. 71). The Jews, however, penetrated the Christian market there. In 1645 the same king ratified an agreement between the municipal authorities and the Jews, paragraphs 5–14 of which show Jewish craftsmen as serious competitors to the Christian craftsmen in the branches of tanning, furriery, tailoring, barbering, goldsmithery, painting, cobbling, saddlery, baking, candle-making, hat-making, and sword-making; some of their products were intended by the Jewish craftsmen for the Jewish market only – or so their Christian competitors demanded. Some were entered on the Christian market with the reluctant agreement of the guilds (*ibid.*, 150–1, no. 74). By the end of the 17th century the citizens of Przemysl prepared a complaint which generalized that "every Jew is either a merchant or a craftsman." They state that the Jews had "totally ruined the goldsmiths', the tailors', the butchers', and the bakers' guilds." The method of competition used by the Jews is described. They employ mobility and initiative. "They [i.e., the Jews] have totally eradicated the barber-bloodletters' guild for there are several Jewish barbers who go with their physicians to the manor houses to the patients there letting blood, putting on suctions cups (*bańki*); the same they do in town. There were not a few Christian soap-makers; now there remains only one, and at that, very poor. But there are several Jews who make soap, carrying it down river and selling it in town too" (*ibid.*, 206–8, no. 129). In this town, as in others, Jewish guilds developed, and from the last quarter of the 17th century various ordinances and regulations are extant of the Przemysl Jewish tailors' guild – which called itself grandiloquently "the holy society of the dressers of the naked ones" (חברא קדישא דמלבישי ערומים) – showing relations between masters and apprentices, and between masters and hired workers, and demonstrating the strict supervision by the community and rabbi over the observance of *sha'atnez* laws by the tailors (*ibid.*, 259–74, nos. v–xxiii).

The situation in the west of Poland-Lithuania, i.e., Great Poland, is seen clearly in various ordinances of the Poznan community. In 1535 a council of community elders – usually very conservative and patrician in its attitude – admonished the Jews in their jurisdiction

> To remember for their good the clothes makers of Śwerzeniec community, a reminder of help and mercy, to look upon some among them with care and particular supervision – for we have seen that crafts are diminishing daily and many of our people have deserted craftsmanship, hence it is fitting to strengthen

the hands of the artisans, not to let them fall, for this is a great benefit and an important rule for the entire society (D. Avron (ed.), *Pinkas ha-Kesherim shel Kehillat Poznan* (1966), 55–66, no. 273).

The same council devised in 1747 a set of model ordinances for guilds in the community and for regulating their relations with other community institutions (*ibid.*, 398–403).

By the end of the 18th century the Poznan community had a well-developed artisan class. In 1797 there were in the town 923 Jewish and 676 Christian tailors; 22 Jewish goldsmiths and 19 Christian; 51 Jewish hatters, 24 Christian; 52 Jewish buttonmakers, 6 Christian; 238 Jewish ironsmiths, 6 Christian; 51 Jewish bakers, 607 Christian. In total there were 1,592 Jewish craftsmen, about one-third of the 4,921 craftsmen in Poznan in this year.

In Bohemia-Moravia also, as well as in southern Germany, Jews increasingly engaged in crafts. A community like that of Prague had long-standing and well-developed Jewish guilds by this period based on a ramified craft structure and professional life and organization.

Some circles of these craftsmen developed a specific ethos and pride in their own calling. As early as the 17th century there were tailors in Poland-Lithuania who asked to be buried with the boards of their tailoring tables, being certain of the honesty and righteousness of their life's work.

Modern Times

In the aspirations for emancipation of the Jews and spread of Enlightenment – and as a corollary of the program for "productivization" of the Jews – occupation in crafts became an issue of the ideological and political strivings for change and betterment in legal status and social standing. Christian W. von *Dohm regarded the encouragement to enter crafts as part of his proposals for "betterment of the Jews." Emperor *Joseph II included encouragement of crafts among Jews in his legislation for them.

Yet, the practical changes in crafts did not eventuate from this ideology or legal enactments, but from the actual economic and social situation among the masses of Jews in Poland-Lithuania and later on in the Pale of Settlement in czarist Russia. In the 18th century many Jewish craftsmen in the private towns of the Polish nobility began to bring their products to fairs and market days in the main royal towns. The general tendency, in which craftsmen were now working for the open market instead of producing to order, encouraged this development. The Jewish craftsman – being outside the guild structure – was unattached and ready to prepare stock and sell it in free competition. He thus became anathema to the Christian craftsmen and the guilds.

In the early 19th century Jews in the impoverished and overcrowded *shtetl* in the Pale of Settlement tended either to continue in the old crafts – mainly tailoring, textiles, and cobbling – or to enter new professions where not much training or outlay on equipment was needed, such as leather work, and carting. Many of those craftsmen peddled their work in villages around the townlets. Through the 19th century a specific Jewish crafts structure developed in Eastern Europe, as reflected in Table 1 for the end of the century.

This situation made for hardship and competition among Jewish crafts in the Pale of Settlement. It also gave rise to a specific way of life, and even folklore among the masses of Jewish workers. By the end of the 19th century, Eastern Europe had a strong element of class-conscious Jewish craftsmen who through their poverty and hardship formed an embryonic Jewish proletariat. Much of the force of the Jewish revolutionary movement and sentiment, the bitterness and impulsion to social activity, came from this stratum of Jewish society. The writings of *Shalom Aleichem and other writers of this generation immortalize the spirit of "*amkho, sher un eyzen*" ("our folk of the scissors and flatiron").

In the same period of the 19th and early 20th centuries, Jewish crafts in the old centers, for instance Prague and in Bavaria, disintegrated under the impact of flourishing capitalism and the crossing over of Jews in Central and Western Europe to the more profitable and "respectable" professions of the middle class. Emancipation in these countries brought about not productivization but practically the end of Jewish participation in crafts.

Jewish emigration in the second half of the 19th century, and in a large measure up to the 1930s, was predicated on and characterized by this craftsmen element.

Among the Jewish immigrants to the United States before World War I, over one-third were craftsmen, mostly tailors, whereas among non-Jews only 20% of the immigrants had a

Table 1. Crafts Structure in the Pale of Settlement, 1898

Crafts	Masters	Hired Workers	Apprentices	Total
Garment	108,527 (43.3%)	80,402 (32%)	61,923 (24.7%)	250,852
Food	43,665 (75.5%)	9,675 (16.7%)	4,547 (7.8%)	57,887
Woodwork	25,653 (51.7%)	14,119 (28.5%)	9,816 (19.8%)	49,588
Metalwork	25,499 (52.1%)	12,892 (26.4%)	10,530 (21.5%)	48,921
Construction	19,791 (62.7%)	7,094 (22.4%)	4,705 (14.9%)	31,590
Textiles	10,589 (57.4%)	4,582 (24.9%)	3,257 (17.7%)	18,428
Leather	6,123 (50.9%)	3,953 (32.8%)	1,964 (16.3%)	12,040
Paper and Print	5,998 (51.3%)	3,343 (28.6%)	2,354 (20.1%)	11,695
Chemicals	2,764 (76.4%)	594 (16.4%)	259 (7.2%)	3,617
Other Crafts	10,787 (65.9%)	3,874 (23.7%)	1,707 (10.4%)	16,368
Total	259,396 (51.8%)	140,528 (28%)	101,062 (20.2%)	500,986 (100%)

skilled profession. Of 106,236 Jewish immigrants to the United States in 1903–04 there were 16,426 tailors, 4,078 carpenters, 2,763 cobblers, 1,970 glaziers and painters, 1,400 butchers, 1,173 bakers, and 14,830 in miscellaneous crafts. (See Table 2: Jewish Craftsmen in New York, 1890). In Paris in 1910 Jewish immigrants from Eastern Europe included 16,060 craftsmen of whom 11,460 (71.4%) were in garment manufacture – 7,000 tailors, 2,000 hatters, 1,900 furriers, 1,200 cobblers – 2,700 (16.8%) iron workers, 1,000 (6.2%) wood-workers, 600 (3.7%) leather workers, and 300 (1.9%) in other crafts. The same structure held good for Eastern European Jewish immigrants in England as well as other countries.

Table 2. Jewish Craftsmen in New York, 1890

Tailors (General) 9,595	**Tailors (Women's Coats)** 2,084	**Tailors (Wholesale)** 1,043	**Cigarette Manufacturers** 976
Haberdashers 715	**Painters** 458	**Carpenters** 443	**Tinsmiths** 417
Butchers 413	**Gold + Silver Smiths** 287	**Bakers** 270	**Glaziers** 148
Typesetters 145	**Machinists** 143	**Shoemakers** 83	**Musicians** 67

Thus the sweatshop of New York, London, and other centers of Jewish immigration and the preponderance of Jews in tailoring and ready-made clothes businesses in countries of large immigration from Eastern Europe derived from the structure of the Jewish crafts world which had taken shape during the 19th and early 20th centuries in Eastern Europe.

This situation underwent many changes, mostly destructive, between the two world wars. In Soviet Russia the general trend against the practice of the independent craftsman and the industrialization of the country diminished the role of crafts among Jews. In the countries built on the ruins of the empires of czarist Russia and Austria-Hungary – like Poland, or Lithuania – the old enmity of the Christian craftsmen rapidly reasserted itself in modern guise. Jews were pushed out or barred from crafts either explicitly or more frequently by seemingly innocuous demands by the trade unions or authorities. Entry to the trade, for instance, was made conditional upon proper apprenticeship with proper masters (and Christian masters only were usually recognized as such); stringent demands for modern equipment and modern conditions of work were usually formulated in a way that hampered the Jewish craftsman in particular. The response of Jewish crafts to this challenge was pioneered by *cooperatives and loan banks; a stimulus was given to schooling and the establishment of educational systems; vocational training was provided by the *ORT organization.

In modern Ereẓ Israel the pioneering spirit of exaltation of work did not noticeably turn in the direction of crafts. Enthusiasm was mainly reserved for agricultural work and manual labor.

By the end of World War II, a large segment of Jewish craftsmen had disappeared as a result of the Holocaust. The specific technical requirements and social structure of the State of Israel and its growing prosperity, with the predominance of the middle-class, liberal and administrative professions governing the structure and ethos of Jewish economy and society in the countries of the West (Western Europe, the United States, Great Britain and the Commonwealth, South Africa, South America), have created a situation where in many places Jewish occupation in crafts is at a vanishing point, and in others they play an increasingly minor role. The large

Table 3. Professional Structure of Jewish and non-Jewish Population between the Two World Wars (approx.)

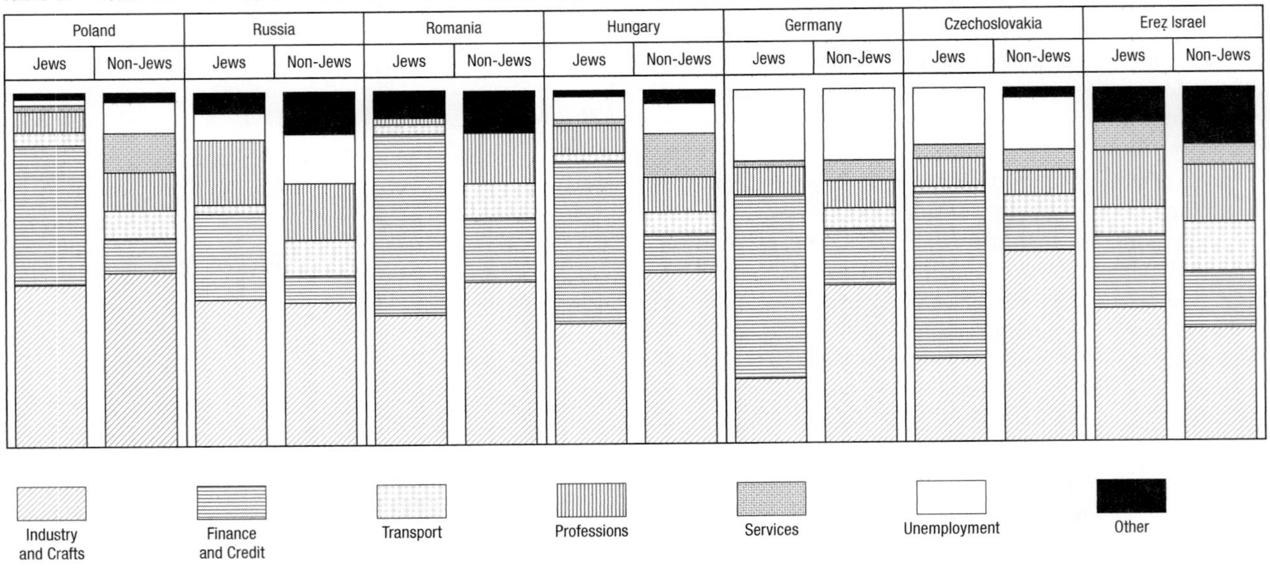

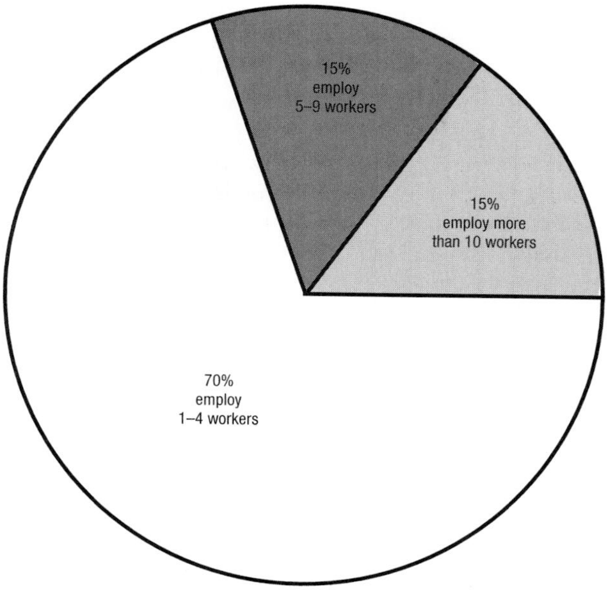

Figure 1. Share of small- and medium-scale enterprises in crafts and industry in Israel, 1968 (includes artisans' workshops – 24,500 workers)

concentrations of Jewish tailors and tailoring in New York, London, and elsewhere have almost disappeared in the lower echelons of the craft in particular.

A 1957 survey conducted by the U.S. Bureau of the Census found that 9% of employed male Jews were working in crafts. A similar breakdown in Canada put the percentage at 14%.

On the other hand, the large scale immigration of Jews from Near Eastern countries to Israel and the entry of survivors of the Holocaust to Israel and some western countries brought a certain temporary revival of Jewish crafts there as shown by Table 4. Craftsmen among Immigrants to Israel.

An indication of ORT activity in assisting young Jews to train for modern and sophisticated crafts in the postwar period is shown by Table 5. Crafts Specialization among Graduates of ORT. In keeping with this trend, from the late 1960s ORT schools began moving toward comprehensive education, academic as well as vocational, with an emphasis on technological occupations.

It now seems that despite efforts at modernization and the near disappearance of many of the old inimical forces, Jewish occupation in crafts and the role of craftsmen as an important factor in Jewish society are disappearing, as in other societies, through the influence of modern industrial techniques and organization.

CONCLUSIONS. Throughout the medieval and modern periods crafts played an uneven role and were differently evaluated in the various Jewish centers. The greatest continuity in position and constancy of attitudes toward crafts is found in the countries of the Middle East up to the end of the 19th century. Crafts and craftsmen weighed most importantly in the social and economic structure of the Jewries of Christian Spain (to the end of the 15th century) and those of Eastern Europe in the late Middle Ages and modern period. For a relatively brief interval they played a dynamic role in the new urban centers of Jewish immigration in the West.

Whereas in the Near East and Spain crafts were accorded – even if sometimes grudgingly – a positive evaluation and craftsmen had a certain recognized influence in Jewish

Table 4. Craftsmen among Immigrants to Israel (1950–1968)

	Clothing	Paper, Printing and Bookbinding	Wood	Leather	Food, Drink and Tobacco	Metal	Fine Mechanics	Machinery and Motor Vehicles	Electronics	Total Number of Craftsmen	Total Number of Immigrants
1950	7,139	422	1,632	2,394	1,587	1,009	1,408	1,071	702	17,364	169,405
1951	4,875	324	1,477	2,217	1,365	665	1,397	687	398	13,405	173,901
1952	791	66	327	407	145	155	141	225	113	2,370	23,375
1953	311	38	103	150	54	63	80	158	61	1,018	10,347
1954	664	63	261	404	88	117	124	203	92	2,016	17,471
1955	1,870	141	746	1,148	219	229	275	407	180	5,215	36,303
1956	2,594	209	931	1,236	308	427	358	565	350	6,978	54,925
1957	3,265	314	828	1,235	615	1,025	507	828	719	9,336	69,733
1958	805	66	242	275	223	191	189	286	179	2,456	25,919
1959	1,013	88	313	284	214	277	193	274	202	2,858	22,987
1960	973	90	315	215	187	283	182	326	222	2,793	23,487
1961	2,047	229	604	668	358	152	479	844	483	5,864	46,571
1962	2,366	244	643	1,171	375	154	443	747	380	6,523	59,473
1963	2,063	208	672	1,147	394	165	419	735	445	6,248	62,086
1964	2,731	243	738	822	515	235	385	1,053	664	7,386	52,193
1965	1,318	152	297	304	252	96	204	616	354	3,593	28,501
1966	435	47	132	178	97	41	81	270	155	1,436	13,451
1967	472	61	125	106	87	35	102	214	119	1,321	12,237
1968	573	85	162	137	76	35	126	291	190	1,675	18,087

society, in the centers of Ashkenazi Jewry, even in Eastern Europe, they had to wait until the late 19th century and for modern revolutionary tendencies to attain some positive evaluation and social standing. It would seem that both the slighting of crafts in modern Zionist thought, even if this is subconscious, and the ephemeral character of their prosperity in the West, are not solely to be ascribed to the advent of modern techniques and industrialization but also to the legacy of this long-standing negative Ashkenazi attitude.

Table 5. Crafts Specialization among Graduates of ORT (1950–1970)

Trade	Male	Female	Total	%
Metal and Mechanics	42,344	299	42,643	24.8
Electricity and Radio	28,404	347	28,751	16.7
Carpentry	5,973	8	5,981	3.5
Agriculture and Agro-mechanics, Telephones	1,629	290	1,919	1.1
Needle Trades	9,324	35,548	44,872	26.1
Leather Work	1,746	2,005	3,751	2.0
Textile	1,344	3,306	4,650	2.7
Industrial Arts, Drawing, Printing	6,671	2,285	8,956	5.2
Building, Plumbing	2,638	75	2,713	1.6
Chemistry Laboratory Assistants, Beauty Culture, Secretarial, Languages	11,785	15,996	27,781	16.2
Total	111,858	60,159	172,017	100.0

[Haim Hillel Ben-Sasson]

BIBLIOGRAPHY: M. Wischnitzer, *History of Jewish Crafts and Guilds* (1965); Krauss, Tal Arch; A. Ruppin, *Jews in the Modern World* (1934), 182–204; J. Lestschinsky, *Das wirtschaftliche Schicksal des deutschen Judentums* (1936; *Goralah ha-Kalkali shel Yahadut Germanyah*, 1963); E. Tcherikower (ed.), *Geshikhte fun der Yidisher Arbeter Bavegung in die Fareynigte Shtatn*, 2 vols. (1943–45); C. Singer et al. (eds.), *A History of Technology*, 1 (1954); Pritchard, Pictures, 305.

CRAIOVA, city in S. Romania. Sephardi Jews were living there from the first half of the 17th century. In 1790 they founded a *ḥevra kaddisha*, a Romanian landowner having granted them land for a cemetery. Ashkenazi Jews settled in Craiova in the mid-19th century, though their community was not officially founded until 1913. They owned two synagogues, the first built in 1842 and the other in 1880. Craiova was a center of Judeo-Spanish culture. In 1865 the Ashkenazi community established a boys' school which functioned until 1948. The Sephardi community maintained a separate school until 1887, when both schools were joined. There were 82 Jewish families in Craiova in 1831; 490 persons in 1860; 2, 891 in 1891; and 2,274 in 1930 (3.6% of the total population). In the Holocaust period, beginning in 1940, many Jews of Craiova were pauperized. Eighteen hundred Jews from northern Moldavia were forcibly transferred to Craiova.

After the war, the Jewish population was augmented by the influx of refugees from northern Bukovina, who chose not to return to their former homes under Soviet rule. A few years later the majority settled in Israel. In 1969, some 75 Jewish families lived in Craiova; they had a synagogue. In 2004, 89 Jews lived there. An Institute of Jewish Studies was established at the University of Craiova in 1998.

BIBLIOGRAPHY: J. Barasch, in: *Anuar pentru Israeliti*, 16 (1894), 45–181; M. Schwarzfeld, *Ochire asupra istoriei evreilor in Romania...* (1889), 16, 40, 47; idem, in: *Analele Societatii Istorice Iuliu Barasch*, 2 (1888), 33, 35, 39, 41, 46, 52, 74, 106; J.B. Brociner, *Chestiunea israelitilor romani*, 1 (1910), 103; PK Romanyah, 1, 236–40; M. Carp, *Cartea neagra*, 1 (1946), index. **ADD. BIBLIOGRAPHY:** A. Firescu, in: *International Symposium on Sephardi Jews in South-Eastern Europe* (1998), 39–45; A. Zimbler, ibid. (1998), 51–58; FEDROM-Comunitati evreiesti din Romania (Internet, 2004).

[Theodor Lavi / Lucian-Zeev Herscovici (2nd ed.)]

CRANE (Heb. עָגוּר, *agur*), the bird *Grus grus* (*Megalornis grus*), which passes over Israel twice a year, in autumn on its migration to Africa, and in spring on its return to Europe. At these times large flocks of cranes in arrowhead formation can be seen in the skies of Israel. Their name, based on Hebrew and Aramaic (*kurkeyah*), probably derives onomatopoetically from their cry. Hezekiah, king of Judah, says in his illness he cried out like a crane (Isa. 38:14), while Jeremiah (8:7) refers to the crane's precise knowledge of the times of its migrations. The gray crane is the tallest bird in Israel (55 in.; 140 cm.). It feeds on insects, worms, and water-plants, and resembles the stork, except that it is gray-colored and has a black neck.

BIBLIOGRAPHY: E. Semali, *Ẓipporim be-Yisrael* (1959^2), 110–2; Tristram, Nat Hist, 239–41; J. Feliks, *Animal World of the Bible* (1962), 85.

[Jehuda Feliks]

CRANGANORE, leading port and commercial center in ancient and medieval India, associated with the ancient port of Miziris, north of *Cochin. Medieval travelers (including *Benjamin of Tudela) refer to it as Shingli, Shinkali or Ginjalek. In the historical tradition of the Malabar Jews, Cranganore is regarded as their original home and chief dwelling place. Jewish immigrants reputedly established their first foothold on the Malabar coast, and from there branched out into neighboring places and villages. According to tradition, the leader of the Jewish settlement in Cranganore, Joseph Rabban, was accorded by the Hindu emperor a charter and privileges engraved on copper plates still in the hands of Cochin Jews. The suggested date of these inscriptions ranges from the 4th to the 11th centuries C.E. The Jews of Cranganore enjoyed cultural and religious autonomy under their leader, called *mudaliar*, appointed by the rajah. Their number may have given rise to the widely circulated notion that the Jews had an independent kingdom in Cranganore. Given the fact that Muziris was an important port, it is possible to suppose that the Jews of the town were engaged in trade. Another argument in support of this view is that when in 1341 the harbor of Cranganore became silted up and the town lost its significance as a port, the Jews moved to Cochin. The conquest of Cranganore by the Portuguese in 1523 led to the complete destruction of the Jewish community. As a result there was another wave of emigration to other places in Malabar, from which the city of Cochin benefited in particular. The memory of the Jewish settlement in Cranganore/Shingli has survived until today. Until recently there was a tradition of placing a handful of earth from Cranganore in the coffin of a deceased Cochin Jew. The Shingli form of pronunciation is a specific feature of the liturgy of the Cochin synagogue.

BIBLIOGRAPHY: D. Lopes (ed. and tr.), *Historia dos Portugueses no Malabar…* (1898); W.J. Fischel, *Ha-Yehudim be-Hodu* (1960). **ADD. BIBLIOGRAPHY:** J.B. Segal, *The Jews of Cochin* (1993)

[W.J.F. / Yulia Egorova (2nd ed.)]

CRANKO, JOHN (1927–1973), ballet choreographer and director. Cranko's father, Herbert, a lawyer in South Africa, was Jewish; his mother, Grace Hinds, was not. Cranko was born in Rustenburg, South Africa, and studied dancing in Johannesburg and Cape Town, where he joined the University of Cape Town Ballet (1942). His first creative work was a version of Stravinsky's *Soldier's Tale* (1942). Moving to London in 1946, he entered the Sadler's Wells Ballet school and company, directed by Ninette de Valois. Soon he was creating ballets, the first of which was *Tritsch-Tratsch* (1946). After his great success with *Pineapple Poll* (1951), he became resident choreographer of the Sadler's Wells Ballet (which later merged with the Royal Ballet). Subsequently, he did a series of works for the Royal Ballet Company, including *Bonne Bouche* (1952), *The Lady and the Fool* (1954), and his first full-length ballet *The Prince of the Pagodas* (1957).

Meanwhile, Cranko had also choreographed works for the New York City Ballet (*The Witch*, 1950), the Paris Opera Ballet (*La Belle Hélene*, 1955), the Ballet Rambert (*Variations on a Theme*, 1954), and La Scala, Milan. He also wrote a revue, *Cranks* (1955), which had a successful run in London. In 1960, he was invited to produce *The Prince of the Pagodas* in Stuttgart, following which he was appointed ballet director there, and created a company that ranked among the foremost in the world. The Stuttgart Ballet, which staged only Cranko's works, appeared at the Edinburgh Festival (1963) and made tours in America, Europe, and the Soviet Union.

Cranko first visited Israel with the Stuttgart Ballet in 1970. The programs included Romeo *and Juliet* and several shorter pieces. His second visit was in 1971 to create *Song of My People – Forest People – Sea* (set to Hebrew poems) for the Batsheva company, and lastly in 1972 to revise the ballet.

Cranko's choreography did not escape criticism. He was inclined to allow his inventiveness to crowd his work and to let his theatrical sense become too prominent. In his later works, however, and especially the short ones, he learned to prune his ideas. Although his *Romeo and Juliet* had enchanting moments, his most successful long ballets were *The Taming of the Shrew* (applauded for 20 minutes in Moscow) and *Onegin*. His greatest achievement was as the creator of the Stuttgart Ballet, which served to raise the standard of continental ballet. He died in an airplane crash when returning from the United States with the company.

ADD. BIBLIOGRAPHY: IED, vol. II, 265–68; IDB, vol. I, 312–15; J. Percival, *Theatre in My Blood: A Biography of John Cranko* (1983); ODNB online.

[Dora Leah Sowden]

°CRASSUS, MARCUS LICINIUS (d. 54 B.C.E.), prominent Roman toward the end of the republican period. Crassus served as consul together with Pompey in 70 B.C.E. He was consul again in 55, and was appointed proconsul of Syria for five years in order to wage war against the Parthians. The war began in 54 B.C.E., and continued until the following year, when Crassus was defeated and killed by the Parthians. Crassus was the first Roman to seize the funds of the Temple, to the amount of 2,000 talents of gold, despite the golden ingot offered him by Eleazar, the priest in charge of the curtains of the sanctuary.

BIBLIOGRAPHY: Schuerer, Hist, 104–5; M. Radin, *The Jews among the Greeks and Romans* (1915), 265–6, 397 n. 20; Regling, in: *Klio*, 7 (1907), 357–94; Jos., Ant., 14:105ff.; Jos., Wars, 1:179; Jos., Apion, 2:82.

[Menahem Stern]

CREATION AND COSMOGONY IN THE BIBLE. The Hebrew Bible commences with a majestic cosmological account of the genesis of the universe. According to Genesis 1:1–2:4a (the P account according to the documentary hypothesis), God created the world in six days and rested on the seventh day. The verb *brʾ* used in the very first sentence of the creation story does not imply, as most traditional commentators believed, *creatio ex nihilo*, a concept that first appears in II Maccabees 7:28, but denotes, as it does throughout the Bible, a divine activity that is effortlessly effected. The opening sentence in the story – many commentators think (but see Cassuto, *Genesis*, 1, pp. 19–20) – begins with a temporal clause, "When God began to create the heaven and the earth" (Gen. 1:1), continues with a circumstantial clause telling of the existence of the darkness and void (1:2), and then in two main clauses (1:3) relates the first act by which God, by divine fiat, created cosmic order out of primeval chaos: "God said, 'Let there be light,' and there was light." The six days of creation fall into a symmetrical pattern of three days each, in which the creation of light and of day and night on the first day, of the sky on the second, and of dry land, seas, and vegetation on the third are complemented by the creation of the luminaries on the fourth day, living creatures in the sea and sky on the fifth, and land animals and man on the sixth. The refrain "And God saw that it was good; and there was evening and there was morning" usually follows the completion of each day's activity. The final act of creation, man, is preceded by a solemn declaration of purpose announced in the heavenly council, "Let us make a man in our image, after our likeness" (1:26). Man is then blessed by God, "Be fertile and increase, fill the earth and master it," and entrusted with sovereignty over the "fish of the sea, the birds of the sky, and all the living things that creep on earth" (1:28). God, having found that all He had made was very good, ceased from further acts of creation and blessed and sanctified the seventh day (2:2). Another story of creation, Genesis 2:4b–24 (the J account according to the documentary hypothesis), describes a much more anthropocentric version of the origin of life on earth: with the ground watered at first only by a subterranean flow; the first man formed from the earth of the ground and animated by a breath blown into his nose, the first woman created from a rib of the man; and the two placed in the *Garden of Eden.

The main differences between the two accounts, whose sources reflect different epic traditions, are (1) the names of the deity: Genesis 1, *ʾElohim*; Genesis 2, YHWH; (2) in the first account the creation of plants (1:11ff., third day) precedes the creation of man (1:26, sixth day), but in the second before man there was no shrub in the field and the grains had not yet sprouted (2:5–7), trees being created only after the creation of man (2:8–9); (3) in Genesis 1:20–21, 24–25 animals were created before man, but in Genesis 2:19, after man; (4) the creation of man is repeated in the second account, but whereas in Genesis 1:27 male and female were created together, the woman was fashioned from a rib of the man in 2:21ff. The second account does not mention the creation of day and night, seas, luminaries, marine life, but commences immediately with the forming of man from the dust of the earth.

Conception of God

Though the style of the first account is much more hymnlike and sublime than the second, it does not reflect, as is usually assumed, a completely abstract, transcendental conception of God. First of all, though creation by divine fiat is found in connection with light (1:3), firmament (1:6), gathering together of the waters into one place and the appearance of dry land (1:9), vegetation (1:11), luminaries (1:14), marine life and fowl (1:20), animal life (1:24), there are also references to the actual making or creating of the firmament (1:7, *wa-yʿaas*), luminaries (1:16, *wa-yʿaas*), sea monsters, fish, and fowl (1:21, *wa-yivraʾ*), land animals (1:25, *wa-yʿaas*), and most important, the pinnacle of creation, man (1:26ff. *nʿaaseh, wa-yivraʾ*). Moreover, creation by divine fiat is not an abstraction first conceived by the author of the P account, but is found in earlier Egyptian (Pritchard, Texts, 5) and Babylonian cosmogonies. Second, that man was created in the image and likeness of the divine beings (Gen. 1:26) is interpreted by many modern exegetes in a physical sense, although the expressions must have lost their original corporeal sense in the biblical context (see Cassuto, *Genesis*, 1, p. 56). (For the image of the deity, cf. Ex. 24:10; 33:20–23; Isa. 6:1; Ezek. 1:26.) The terminology employed here has Near Eastern prototypes: In Egyptian literature, specifically in a cosmogonic context, man is described as being the image of his creator god (Wildberger; Pritchard, Texts, 417); in Mesopotamian literature the king is sometimes called the "image" (Akk. *ṣalmu*, Heb. *ẓelem*) or "likeness" (Akk. *muššulu*, Heb. *demut*) of his deity (for the views of Horst, Loewenstamm, and Wildberger, see bibliography). In Israel a "democratization" (Horst) took place in that not only the king but all of mankind is conceived as being created in the divine image. If this idea originally goes back to royal ideology, it would further explain man's unique task on earth. Just as the divine likeness of the king in Mesopotamia empowers him to be the sovereign of his people, so mankind is entrusted "to rule the fish of the sea, the birds of the sky, and all the living things that creep on earth" (Gen. 1:28). Finally, the plural verb *naʿaseh* ("let us make") and plural nouns *be-ẓalmenu* ("in our image") and *ki-demutenu* ("after our likeness"; Gen. 1:26) may refer to the divine council with which God consults before the important step of creating man; though other feasible explanations have been advanced (see commentaries). (For other references to the divine council, see Gen. 3:22; 11:7; I Kings 22:19ff.; Isa. 6:2 ff.; Job 1–2; Dan. 7:10; for the deity's taking counsel before creating man, see *Enuma Elish* 6:4, in Pritchard, Texts, 68.)

Mesopotamian Prototypes

The two versions of the creation story have often been compared to Mesopotamian prototypes. The translation given above in Genesis 1:1ff. and 2:4bff., "when … then," is analogous to the introductory style of Mesopotamian epics. Tracing a theme to the creation of the universe is a feature also found in as trivial a work as the "Incantation to a Toothache" (Pritchard, Texts, 100–1), and in as major a composition as the Sumerian King List (*ibid.*, 265–6), "history" commences with the dynasties before the Flood.

ENUMA ELISH. For specific cosmogonic details the most important piece of Mesopotamian literature is the Babylonian epic story of creation, *Enuma Elish* (*ibid.*, 60–72). Here, as in Genesis, the priority of water is taken for granted, i.e., the primeval chaos consisted of a watery abyss. The name for this watery abyss, part of which is personified by the goddess Tiamat, is the etymological equivalent of the Hebrew *tehom* (Gen. 1:2), a proper name that always appears in the Bible without the definite article. (It should be noted, however, that whereas "Tiamat" is the name of a primal generative force, *tehom* is merely a poetic term for a lifeless mass of water.) In both Genesis (1:6–7) and *Enuma Elish* (4:137–40) the creation of heaven and earth resulted from the separation of the waters by a firmament. The existence of day and night precedes the creation of the luminous bodies (Gen. 1:5, 8, 13, and 14ff.; *Enuma Elish* 1:38). The function of the luminaries is to yield light and regulate time (Gen. 1:14; *Enuma Elish* 5:12–13). Man is the final act of creation – in *Enuma Elish*, too, before his creation the gods are said to take counsel (*Enuma Elish* 6:4) – and following the creation of man there ensues divine rest. There is, furthermore, an identical sequence of events: creation of firmament, dry land, luminaries, man, and divine rest. Thus, it appears that at least the so-called P account echoes this earlier Mesopotamian story of creation.

Another reflection of very ancient traditions is found in Genesis 1:21. Since the entire story of creation refers only to general categories of plant and animal life, not to any individual species, the specific mention of "the great sea monsters" alongside, and even before, "all the living creatures of every kind that move about, which the waters brought forth in swarms" is striking. It is most likely part of the biblical polemic against the polytheistic version of a primeval struggle between the creator god and a marine monster which was the personification of chaos (see below). In Genesis this story has been submerged and only appears in the demythologized reference to the sea monsters as being themselves created by God, not as rival gods.

The second creation story, too, has Near Eastern prototypes: The creation of man from the dust of the earth (Gen. 2:7) is analogous to the creation of man from clay, a motif often found in Mesopotamian literature, e.g., the Gilgamesh Epic; the Hebrew name of the underground flow, *ʾed*, that watered the Garden of Eden, is related to either a cognate Akkadian word *edu* or to the Sumerian word ÍD, "river"; and the creation of woman from a rib may reflect a Sumerian motif (see Kramer).

Differences between Genesis and Enuma Elish

Nevertheless, the differences between the biblical and the Mesopotamian accounts are much more striking than their similarities; each of them embodies the world outlook of their respective civilizations. In Genesis there is a total rejection of all mythology. The overriding conception of a single, omnipotent, creator predominates. Cosmogony is not linked to theogony. The preexistence of God is assumed – it is not linked to the genesis of the universe. There is no suggestion of any primordial battle or internecine war which eventually led to the creation of the universe. The one God is above the whole of nature, which He Himself created by His own absolute will. The primeval water, earth, sky, and luminaries are not pictured as deities or as parts of disembodied deities, but are all parts of the manifold works of the Creator. Man, in turn, is not conceived of as an afterthought, as in *Enuma Elish*, but rather as the pinnacle of creation. Man is appointed ruler of the animal and vegetable kingdoms; he is not merely the menial of the gods (*Enuma Elish*). The story in Genesis, moreover, is nonpolitical: Unlike *Enuma Elish*, which is a monument to Marduk and to Babylon and its temple, Genesis makes no allusion to Israel, Jerusalem, or the Temple. Furthermore, the biblical story is non-cultic: unlike *Enuma Elish*, which was read on the fourth day of the Babylonian New Year festival, it plays no ritual role whatsoever in the religion of Israel.

EGYPTIAN ANALOGUES. In addition to Mesopotamian substrata, there are several Egyptian analogues to the biblical stories of creation, e.g., the existence of primeval water and its division; the breathing of life into the nostrils of man; man's being formed in the image of the creator god; the creation of plants, animals, fowl, and fish; and the light of day (see "Instruction for Meri-Ka-Re," Pritchard, Texts, 417; Junker, Hermann in bibl.).

OTHER BIBLICAL TRADITIONS. Outside Genesis there are a number of allusions to the vanquishing by YHWH of a great sea monster and his minions, with some traces of a belief that this was connected to the creation of the world. In the biblical version of this combat, known from Mesopotamia (Marduk-Tiamat) and Ugarit (Baal-Yamm), the forces of the watery chaos, called Yam, Nahar, Leviathan, Rahab, or Tannin, are either destroyed or put under restraint by God (cf. Isa. 27:1; 51:9–10; Jer. 5:22; Hab. 3:8; Ps. 74:13–14; 89:10–11; 104:6–9; Prov. 8:27–29; Job 7:12; 9:13; 26:10–13; 38:8–11). Recently it has been suggested (see Jacobsen) that this epic account, whose source was thought to be in Mesopotamia, may actually have originated in the West (though where in particular is not clear), and subsequently influenced both biblical and Mesopotamian literature. It is noteworthy, however, that the stories of Genesis meticulously avoid the use of such legendary material, even eschewing metaphorical figures of speech based on this mythological conflict.

Another poetic version of creation is reflected in Proverbs 8:1–31, where Wisdom relates that she attended God during the creation.

Weinfeld has drawn attention to the fact that four mythological motifs of Genesis 1 – the existence of primordial material (1:2); God's working and His rest; the council of God (1:26); and the creation of man in God's image (1:26–27) – are repudiated in the cosmogonic doxologies of Second Isaiah.

[Shalom M. Paul]

RABBINIC VIEW OF CREATION

"*Maʿaseh Bereshit*," "Act of Creation," was regarded in the Talmudic period, particularly the tannaitic, as belonging to esoteric lore, and the Mishnah (Ḥag. 2:1) states that it was "not to be expounded before two people." The Jerusalem Talmud, however (Ḥag. 2:1, 77c), explains that this was the view of R. Akiva, whereas R. Ishmael permitted it to be expounded. In point of fact, the interpretation of the first verse of Genesis, which is the basis of talmudic cosmogony, is the subject of a discussion between those two rabbis (Gen. R. 1:14), from which it is clear that R. Akiva was concerned with refuting gnostic views that God alone did not create the world, and the discussion of cosmogony during the tannaitic period seems to be concentrated on refuting gnostic and other heretical views which maintained either the eternity of matter or that God was not the sole creator. This emerges clearly from another passage: "A philosopher said to Rabban Gamaliel that God found good materials which He used in the creation of the world, '*Tohu, Bohu*, darkness, water, wind, and the deep' to which Gamaliel vigorously replied 'Woe to that man! The term creation is explicitly used of them'" (*ibid.* 1:9). This reply refutes both the existence of primordial matter and the view that God was not the sole creator.

There is a difference of opinion between Bet Shammai and Bet Hillel on two aspects of creation. The former maintained that the heavens were created first, and then the earth, while Bet Hillel maintained the opposite (*ibid.* 1:15). The former maintained that the intention ("thought") of creation was at night and the act by day, while Bet Hillel maintained that "both intention and act took place by day" (*ibid.* 12:14). On both of these statements, however, R. Simeon b. Yoḥai uses the identical words: "I am astonished! How could the fathers of the world differ" on this point. In the first case "both were created together like a pot and its cover," and in the other, "the intention was both by day and by night while the fulfillment was with the waning of the sun." It seems from this statement that by the time of Simeon b. Yoḥai, a disciple of R. Akiva, the need, so to speak, to disregard the prohibition against cosmogonical speculations was limited to the acceptance of one standard doctrine, the simultaneous and sole creation of heaven and earth, the "intention" being more important than the act, to which the Mishnah adds the avoidance of all metaphysical speculation: "What is above, what is below, what was before and what was after." The preeminence of the intention over the act is affirmed by the many passages, based on such verses as "By the word of the Lord were the heavens made" (Ps. 33:6), which emphasize that creation needed no action but merely the will of God ("not by labor, but merely by word," Gen. R. 3:2). The best-known expression of this belief is: "With ten words was the world created" (Avot 5:1). Especially vigorous was the rabbis' refutation of the gnostic idea that the world was created by angels. The angels were created by God (Gen. R. 1:3, 3:8) and it is specifically stated that "all agree that nothing was created on the first day, that no one should say that Michael stretched out [the firmament] in the south and Gabriel in the north, and the Holy One, blessed be He, made its measurements in the center" (the reading in Tanh. B., Gen. 1:12 is "that the sectarians should not say"). The angels were variously created on the second, or fifth days (Gen. R. 1:4). To this should be added the theory, which Philo attributes to the Stoics, that the present world was created after a number of previous experimental worlds were created, only to be destroyed (*ibid.* 3:7). R. Abbahu, for example, maintained that there were successive creations (Gen. R. 3:9; Eccles. R. 3:11, Mid. Ps. 34).

The world was created either in Nisan or Tishri (RH 11a). Special attention was paid to the problem of the creation of light, in view of the fact that the sun was not created until the fourth day. The anonymous sages opine that the luminaries were created on the first day, but they were not "suspended" until the fourth, while R. Jacob as well as R. Eleazar are of the opinion that the light created on the first day was a special light with which "one could see from one end of the world to the other," but it was hidden away and reserved for the righteous in the time to come because of the future corruption of the world in the days of the flood and the Tower of Babel (Ḥag. 12a). Only in the amoraic period does one find a distinct and strongly mythological element enter into rabbinic cosmology. Such statements as that of Judah in the name of Rav, "When the Holy One, blessed be He, desired to create the world, He said to the angel of the sea 'open thy mouth and swallow all the waters of the world,' to which he replied, 'Lord of the Universe, it is enough that I remain with my own.' Whereupon he struck him with his foot and killed him" (BB 74b), to which there are different variants in amoraic times (cf. PR 20:95), have no parallel in the tannaitic periods.

E.E. Urbach (see bibl.) sums up his comprehensive study of rabbinic cosmogony as follows:

"During the amoraic period the area of discussion was extended, and ideas which were previously regarded as esoteric penetrated into public discourses and into the teachings of the schools. There was a direct controversy against sectarian and other non-acceptable cosmogonies, but this polemic was not without influence and results. Ideas which prevailed in the hellenistic world found their place in the world of the rabbis. It seems that not a little of rabbinic exegesis on this subject are fragments of these cosmogonical and cosmological speculations. There are also notices of famous Babylonian *amoraim* of the fourth century who combined their cosmogonical speculations with theurgic and magic activity, but we do not know whether these esoteric doctrines attained a literary form."

He points out that it was only in the later kabbalistic literature such as the Sefer *Yeẓirah and the *baraita* of *Ma'aseh Bereshit* that a system was evolved (see *Kabbalah).

[Louis Isaac Rabinowitz]

Bible Commentators

Various attempts were made to explain the difficulties in the story of creation. Two general statements may be made: (1) the narrative was not generally taken literally as an act of creation in six days, and (2) the rabbis were fully aware of the difficulties which modern biblical criticism attempts to solve with the documentary theory, such as the different names of God and the double or treble parallel accounts, but they answered them on the basis of the unity of the account of Creation.

Although the fact of creation remains a prime article of faith, there is no uniform or binding belief as to how the world was created. Rashi interprets the first verse of the Bible as meaning that "when in the beginning the Lord created Heaven and Earth" and is not a chronology of creation. Similarly the differences in the names of God were fully recognized but it was explained that *Elohim* means God in His attribute of justice, the Tetragrammaton God in His attribute of mercy (Philo says the reverse), and the different nomenclatures and their combination teach that God first attempted to base the world on justice, but found that impossible; He then attempted to base it on mercy alone, but with similar results; and thereupon created it on the principle of justice tempered by mercy. Cassuto accepted the theory that the different names depict different attributes of God. Another explanation of the different accounts of Creation is the principle that at times the Bible states a generalization and later gives its details. Accordingly, the story of the creation of Adam in Genesis 1:27 relating that Adam and Eve were created together is a general description whose details are listed in 2:21ff., where it is related that the woman was formed from Adam's rib (Yal., Gen. 16).

Similarly, the brief description of the creation of animals in Genesis 1:24–26 is expanded in 2:19–20, and chapter 2 commences immediately with the creation of man from the dust of the earth in order to expand the narrative of the Garden of Eden. The contradiction between the statement in Genesis 1 that the plants were created on the third day and that of Genesis 2:5 that there were no shrubs in the field when Adam was created is answered in various ways. Rashi, in accordance with R. Assi (Yal., Gen. 8), explains that their creation took place on the third day but their growth began on the sixth. Naḥmanides makes the first apply to "plants of the earth," i.e., wild plants, while the second reference is to "plants of the field," i.e., cultivated plants which depended on man's activity. Malbim is the first of the modern traditional commentators to accept the view, later adopted by Cassuto and other scholars, that the biblical narrative is a conscious attempt to refute known mythological accounts of creation (see his commentary on Gen. 6:4).

CREATION IN PHILOSOPHY

Ever since the initial confrontation of the Jewish religion with Greek philosophy, Jewish philosophers have attempted to harmonize the biblical account of creation with philosophical theories that lend themselves to harmonization, and defend it against those theories that are incompatible with it.

Philo Judaeus

*Philo, for example, based his theory of creation on Plato's doctrine of creation in the *Timaeus*, but removed certain ambiguities, thus making Plato's theory compatible with the scriptural doctrine of creation (see H.A. Wolfson, *Philo*, 1 (1948), 180–380, passim.). Philo accepted Plato's conception of an eternal God who brought the world into existence, but he could not accept the Platonic theory that God created the world out of eternal preexistent matter. He solved the difficulty by stating that God created both the preexistent matter out of nothing, and the world out of the preexistent matter. The link between God and the created world is, according to Philo, the *logos. Beginning its existence as part of the essence of God, the logos was given by God an existence of its own. As this separate, incorporeal existence the logos contains within itself, and is the mind of, the intelligible world and the ideas which constitute the intelligible world. While both Plato and Philo described the creation of the world as an act which God "willed," they had differing notions of what is meant by the "will" of God. To Plato, God's "will" meant the necessary expression of God's nature, which led him to assume that God created the world by force of necessity, and that the world thus created could not have been any different. Philo, however, following the scriptural conception of God as an all-powerful free agent, interpreted God's "will" in creating the world to mean that the very act of creation was by God's free choice, as was the type of world created. This meant, according to Philo, that had God so willed, He could have either not created the world or created another kind of world.

Medieval Philosophy

In the subsequent development of Jewish philosophy the most pressing challenge came from the defenders of the Aristotelian-neoplatonic doctrine of the eternity of the universe, and most medieval Jewish philosophers had to come to grips with this claim. Since there were various philosophical frameworks within which medieval thinkers operated, it is possible to delineate several different philosophical accounts of biblical cosmogony in medieval Jewish philosophy: (1) Saadiah's version of the Kalām; (2) neoplatonic emanationism; (3) the "agnostic" approach of Maimonides; (4) the "Platonism" of Levi b. Gershom; and (5) the unique theory of Ḥasdai Crescas.

SAADIAH. The first systematic treatment of creation is to be found in *Saadiah Gaon. Employing the arguments of the *Kalām, Saadiah attempted to prove that the universe is created in time, that its Creator is other than it, and that it is created *ex nihilo*. In behalf of the first thesis Saadiah marshals four arguments in his *Book of Beliefs and Opinions*. According to the first argument, it is claimed that since Aristotle admits that the universe is finite in size, he cannot then say that it moves for infinite time, i.e., that it is eternal; for a finite body cannot have infinite power. The second proof is a variant of the argument from design: the combination and order of the parts of the universe imply the existence of a creator. The third argument purports to demonstrate creation on the grounds that the existence of accidental, i.e., contingent, properties in the universe implies that the universe itself is also contingent and hence not eternal. Finally, the thesis of eternity implies that past time is infinite. But if this were so, then since an infinite magnitude cannot be completed, past time would never reach the present, which is absurd. Saadiah's arguments for creation *ex nihilo* are designed to show that the assumption of an eternal primordial matter out of which the universe is allegedly created leads to various absurdities. For example, why should we expect that an eternal matter should be amenable to divine creative activity? (Saadiah, *Book of Beliefs and Opinions* 1:1–2).

NEOPLATONISM. The next major philosophical influence was *neoplatonism, of which Isaac *Israeli and Solomon Ibn *Gabirol were notable examples. Since neoplatonism exhibits a monistic tendency, it is not surprising that neoplatonists attempt to close the gap between God and the world. This tendency does not, however, easily accommodate itself to the biblical stress upon the hiatus between God and nature. Thus, in Jewish neoplatonism the problem of creation is especially vexing. Whereas the pagan neoplatonists, such as Plotinus, insist upon the eternal and necessary *emanation of the universe from God, Jewish neoplatonists were dogmatically constrained to find some place for creation *ex nihilo*. In Isaac Israeli there is a fundamental distinction between two primitive stages in the origin of the universe. In the first stage God's free creative power is manifested; whereas in subsequent phases nature and its forms necessarily emanate from the first products of God's power, primary matter and form.

In this manner Israeli adjusted the neoplatonic doctrine of emanation to the biblical conception of creation. Ibn Gabirol's version of neoplatonism exhibits this tension in a more exaggerated form. In his religious poem *Keter Malkhut* (*The Kingly Crown*, trans. by B. Lewis, 1961), he naturally stresses the doctrine of creation *ex nihilo*; in his philosophical work *Mekor Ḥayyim* ("The Fountain of Life"), he wavers between these two views, but tries to give primary emphasis to the voluntary origin of the universe. It would seem that modern scholars are more aware than Ibn Gabirol of this problem, but they have differed in their interpretations. In general, neoplatonic philosophies tend to be static and emphasize the timelessness of the emanation of the world from its ultimate source. Ibn Gabirol's venture into neoplatonic metaphysics is not free from this characteristic.

MAIMONIDES. Maimonides does not find the proofs of the Kalām convincing, chiefly because they rest upon certain physical and metaphysical assumptions that he rejects (Guide, 1:73–74). Moreover, he rejects the neoplatonic accounts of creation (Guide, 2:21). On the other hand, he argues that neither Aristotle nor his Muslim followers have succeeded in demonstrating the eternity of the universe. Hence, the issue cannot be decided on philosophical grounds alone. For Maimonides, however, it must be decided, since to adopt the eternity hypothesis is to give up belief in miracles; for the eternity hypothesis is tantamount to the claim that the universe and its laws necessarily emanate from God. The belief in miracles implies, however, that God can freely interrupt the course of nature. Thus the question of creation is especially perplexing: it must be decided, but philosophy cannot resolve it (Guide, 2:15, 21, 25). At this point Maimonides appeals to revelation as the ultimate arbitrator. In spite of this "agnostic" argument, Maimonides does present certain philosophical arguments in behalf of the creation thesis. These arguments are not decisive, he admits, but they do tip the balance in favor of the Bible. In general, these arguments attempt to show that Aristotle's theory of eternity cannot explain the existence of anomalous facts about the universe, in particular certain irregular features of the heavenly bodies. Consider, for example, the irregular motion of the planets or the difference in color exhibited by various stars. Given Aristotle's hypothesis that the universe is eternal, and that every natural phenomenon is explicable in terms of necessary law, it is difficult, as Aristotle himself admits, to account for these irregular facts; for why should one star give off bluish illumination and another reddish (Guide, 2:22, 24). However, if it is assumed that the universe has been freely created by God, all these irregular features of the heavens can be attributed to God's free will. Thus, although a decisive proof in behalf of the creation thesis is not available, the latter hypothesis can explain the phenomena more easily than the thesis of eternity, and hence can be accepted on philosophical grounds as well as for religious reasons. With respect to the question whether creation occurred *ex nihilo*, Maimonides claims that this issue is not crucial for religious faith. From the textual point of view the Bible states unequivocally that the universe is created; it is not so unambiguous on the details of creation. Nor does it matter on purely theological grounds, since even the Platonic theory of creation from primordial matter is compatible with divine freedom and the existence of miracles. Since the Platonic theory has not been proven, and the Jewish tradition has generally interpreted Genesis as implying creation *ex nihilo*, Maimonides follows tradition. However, it should be noted, he would be prepared to reinterpret Scripture if a proof of Plato's theory were forthcoming (Guide 2:25).

LEVI BEN GERSHOM. Maimonides' doubts about the provability of creation were dispelled by his two great successors, *Levi b. Gershom and Ḥasdai Crescas. Both of these philosophers attempt to prove creation, although they do so in different ways. According to Levi b. Gershom, Aristotelian physics implies creation, even if it is the case that Aristotle did not recognize it. For Aristotle's system is teleological: it ascribes ends and purposes to nature (Aristotle, *Physics*, 2). A teleological conception of nature, however, implies a creator who fashions the universe according to specified ends (Levi b. Gershom, *Milḥamot Adonai*, 6:1, 7). Moreover, Aristotle's laws of dynamics are falsified if the eternity hypothesis is accepted. For example, according to Aristotle, the velocity of a planet is a function of the number of rotations it makes around the earth in a given period of time; but if past time is infinite, the number of rotations for every planet in past time is the same – an infinite number of rotations. Consequently, the velocities of each planet would be identical; but this is false (*ibid.*, 6:1, 11). Unlike Maimonides, however, Levi b. Gershom maintains that God created the universe from an eternal formless matter (cf. Plato, *Timaeus*, 49ff.). Were creation *ex nihilo* adopted there would be no way to explain how God, who is incorporeal, could create a physical universe. Moreover, the theory of creation *ex nihilo* implies that prior to creation there was a vacuum, i.e., empty space. According to Levi b. Gershom, however, the notion of a vacuum has been proven to be absurd. He believes that the doctrine of an eternal formless matter is taught by the Torah and is, therefore, compatible with Jewish dogma (*ibid.*, 6:2, 1; Abraham Ibn Ezra also suggests the Platonic theory in his commentary on Genesis).

HASDAI CRESCAS. Crescas' doctrine of creation exhibits a different use of the term "creation" and displays an ambivalence on the issue of the eternity or temporal beginning of the universe. Whereas Maimonides and Levi b. Gershom construe "creation" as implying temporal beginning, Crescas understands this concept as meaning causal dependency. Accordingly, the universe is created insofar as it is causally dependent upon God, a thesis that Aristotle himself accepts. Creation so construed is a temporally neutral concept, such that the question of eternity is not decided by a proof that the universe is created. Indeed, for Crescas, "creation" means creation *ex nihilo* (cf. Thomas Aquinas, Summa Theologica, 1, question 44, a. 1–2; question 46, a. 1–2. There might have been some influence of Thomas' ideas upon Crescas). Insofar as the entire universe depends upon God, who is the only absolutely necessary being, everything is created *ex nihilo,* including matter, regardless of whether it is eternal or not. With respect to the question of eternity Crescas rejects all the arguments of Maimonides and Levi b. Gershom in favor of the temporal beginning of the universe. Indeed, he maintains that the teleological characteristics of the universe, which to the latter philosophers are evidence for temporal beginning, can be explained on the hypothesis of the eternity of the universe so long as we conceive of the universe as manifesting intelligence and perfection. This line of argument, then, would seem to suggest that Crescas believed in the eternity of the universe. Yet he claims that the traditional biblical view is that the universe had a temporal beginning. Perhaps the solution to this apparent inconsistency is to be found in his sympathy for the doctrine of eternal re-creation of many universes, a view that is found in rabbinic literature (see above). This doctrine preserves Crescas' predilection for the eternity thesis insofar as it postulates infinite time and is consistent with the traditional doctrine that our universe had a temporal beginning. Crescas actually relegates this problem to a secondary position: it is not, as it was for Maimonides, a doctrine whose denial undermines Judaism. What is crucial for Crescas is the belief that everything depends upon God, which for him means creation *ex nihilo* (Crescas, or Adonai 3:1, 4–5).

[Seymour Feldman]

IN MODERN THOUGHT

Baruch Spinoza's monistic system denies all medieval notions of creation, declaring God and Nature to be one substance (*Deus sive Natura*). The denial of creation serves as the basis of Spinoza's negations of most of traditional Jewish (and Christian) notions, like free will, providence, commandments, etc, and hence gives creation a significance that had a decisive impact on modern Jewish thought. In many of the 19th and 20th century Jewish philosophies, creation was treated as a theoretical concept, describing the nature of the world and its relationships to God, rather than a cosmogonist concept. According to Salomon Ludwig *Steinheim, the perception of nature as creation ex-nihilo is the substantial teaching of revelation, the decisive difference between true religion and idolatry, and the ground for human free will as well as that of God. In Hermann *Cohen's *Religion of Reason out of the Sources of Judaism* (*Religion der Vernunft aus den Quellen des Judentums*, 1919, ch. 3) creation is understood as the correlative logical relationship between God, the only *Sein* (Being), and the world, the eternal *Werden* (becoming). Using his *Ursprungsprinzip* (the concept of primary source) on the one hand, and the Maimonidean notion of negative Divine attributes on the other hand, Cohen refers to this concept as pointing not only to the unbridgeable gap between God and the world, but also as establishing the common context that combines them. In a similar way, revelation (see *ibid.*, ch. 4), namely the creation of reason, depicts the basic correlative relationships between the human (*Mensch*) and God. Franz *Rosenzweig depicted creation as the first of three relational theological events, alongside with revelation and redemption. Creation, like revelation and redemption, is at the heart of faith, namely the mutual context of Judaism and Christianity. Philosophy, as Rosenzweig maintained in the first part of *The Star of Redemption* (*Der Stern der Erloesung,* 1921), can perceive God, world, and *Mensch* only as isolated elements, and as theoretical concepts that have no common context. Nevertheless human experience, based on the very notion of revelation, depicts each of those three as relating to the two others, and as being revealed through the encounter with them. For the world, creation is the present status all the things, all the worldly phenomena, as "existence" and as creatures that are subject to Divine providence; for God creation is an absolute past. The only Divine attribute that Rosenzweig accepts is "Creator." Creation of *Mensch* in the image of God, the peak of the biblical narrative of Genesis, points to the strong connection between creation and revelation, between the consciousness of God's providence and that of His love (see *ibid.*, part II, 1–2). In Mordecai *Kaplan's reconstruction of Judaism, the value-concept of creation is "revaluated," and means that the "conception of creative urge" and self-revival reveal God within human life and endow life with Divine significance. The myth of creation intends to confront and deny pessimism and fatalism, without ignoring suffering and evil, and endorses human responsibility and progress (see *The Meaning of God in Modern Jewish Religion*, 1937, ch. 1).

[Yehoyada Amir (2nd ed.)]

IN THE ARTS

The biblical account of Creation formed the basis of episodes in various medieval mystery plays, including the 15th-century French *Mistère du Viel Testament* and the English Chester and York cycles. In England, too, there were the lesser-known Cornish mysteries, *Origo Mundi* and *Gwreans an bys* ("Creation of the World," ms. dated 1611, in the Bodleian Library, Oxford). Of the literary interpretations of the Creation story, the epic *Semaine* (1578) by the French Protestant *Du Bartas is one of the most celebrated and the most ambitious. In translation it had a great influence on later writers, particularly in England. Du Bartas' fellow Huguenot, the militant Agrippa d'Aubigné (1552–1630), also wrote his epic *La Création* on this theme, combining a kind of dictionary of Calvinist theology with a handbook of 17th-century scientific knowledge. Anders Arrebo (1587–1637), called the "father of Danish poetry," freely adapted the Du Bartas poem as *Hexaemeron* (1661).

In art, the Creation story is usually represented as a sequence, not so much following the biblical account as presenting pictorial combinations and condensations of the Six Days. Some early examples of this cyclic treatment are to be found in two manuscripts: the fifth-century Vienna Genesis and the seventh-century Ashburnham Pentateuch (Paris). Throughout the Middle Ages, the theme continued to inspire works of major historical and artistic significance, notably the bronze door of San Zeno at Verona, the mosaics of Monreale in Sicily, and the frescoes of Saint-Savin (12th century); the mosaics of San Marco in Venice, sculpture at Chartres, Laon and Salisbury, and stained glass windows in the Sainte-Chapelle in Paris (13th century); sculpture in the cathedral of Orvieto and the Florence Campanile (14th century); Ghiberti's doors in the Florence Baptistery (15th century); and Michelangelo's frescoes on the ceiling of the Sistine Chapel and the Vatican Loggia frescoes after designs by Raphael (16th century). An outstanding Jewish treatment of the Creation theme is the 14th-century Spanish *Sarajevo *Haggadah*, where the six days of creation are depicted with strength and boldness.

Musical compositions inspired by the Creation include various 18th-century settings of the "Morning Hymn" from *Paradise Lost* by John Milton, none of them of lasting importance. Milton was the inspiration behind Klopstock's *Morgengesang am Schoepfungsfeste*, which was set to music several times, mainly as a cantata. These included one by Carl Philipp Emanuel Bach (1784). An English libretto by an otherwise unknown Mr. Lidley (or Linley), written shortly before Handel's death in 1759, was intended to have been offered to him. The libretto was accepted by Haydn when he visited England in 1797, and his setting of the libretto as translated and revised by Gottfried van Swieten was privately performed in Vienna in April 1798. The worldwide popularity of Haydn's *Creation* began with its first public performance there in the following year. Some later works on the creation theme are a Norwegian one, J. Haarklou's *Skapelsen* (1891; first performed 1924); *The Creation* (1924) by Louis *Gruenberg; a ballet by Darius *Milhaud, *La création du monde* (1923), scored for 17 solo instruments in a jazz idiom and inspired not by the Bible, but by African creation myths; *In the Beginning – The Seven Days of Creation* (1947) by Aaron *Copland; and the oratorio *Genesis* (1958) by Franz *Reizenstein.

BIBLIOGRAPHY: IN THE BIBLE: F. Boehl, *Alttestamentliche Studien … Festschrift fuer R. Kittel* (1913), 42–60; H. Junker, *Die Goetterlehre von Memphis* (1940), 63; A. Heidel, *The Babylonian Genesis* (1951^{2}); S.A. Loewenstamm, in: *Tarbiz*, 27 (1957/58), 1–2; U. Cassuto, *Commentary on the Book of Genesis* (1961), 7ff.; S. Herrmann, in: *Theologische Literaturzeitung*, 86 (1961), 413–24; E.A. Speiser, *Genesis* (1964), 3ff.; H. Wildberger, in: *Theologische Zeitschrift*, 21 (1965), 245–59, 481–501; N.M. Sarna, *Understanding Genesis* (1967), 1–32; M. Weinfeld, in: *Tarbiz*, 37 (1967/68), 105–32. THE RABBINIC VIEW: A. Altmann, *Studies in Religious Philosophy and Mysticism* (1969), 128–39; E.E. Urbach, *Ḥazal* (1969), 161–9. For a general exposition of the traditional view see J.H. Hertz, *Pentateuch*, Genesis, Appendix A. CREATION IN PHILOSOPHY: Guttmann, Philosophies, index; Husik, Philosophy, index; N.M. Samuelson, *Judaism and the Doctrine of Creation* (1994); A. Altmann and S.M. Stern, *Isaac Israeli* (1958), 171–80; Z. Diesendruck, in: *Jewish Studies in Memory of G.A. Kohut* (1935), 145–58; S. Feldman, in: PAAJR, 35 (1967), 113–37; S. Wilensky, *ibid.*, 22 (1953), 131–50; idem, *Yiẓhak Arama u-Mishnato ha-Pilosofit* (1956), 97–120; H.A. Wolfson, in: *Saadia Anniversary Volume* (1943), 197–245; idem, in: *Essays… J.H. Hertz* (1942), 427–92; idem, in: JQR, 36 (1945/46), 371–91. IN THE ARTS: L. Réau, *Iconographie de l'art chrétien*, 2 pt. 1 (1956), 65–76, (1923), 1–34. **ADD. BIBLIOGRAPHY:** CREATION IN PHILOSOPHY: H. Davidson, *Proofs for Eternity, Creation and the Existence of God in Medieval Islamic and Jewish Philosophy* (1987); idem, "Maimonides' Secret Position on Creation," in: I. Twersky (ed.), *Studies in Medieval Jewish History and Literature* (1979), 16–40; W. Dunphy, "Maimonides' Not-So-Secret Position on Creation," in: E. Ormsby (ed.), *Maimonides and His Time* (1989), 151–72; S. Feldman, "Gersonides' Proofs for Creation of the World," in: PAAJR, 35 (1967), 113–37; idem, "The Theory of Eternal Creation in Hasdai Crescas and Some of His Predecessors," in: *Viator*, 11 (1980), 289–320; idem, *Philosophy in a Time of Crisis: Don Isaac Abravanel, Defender of the Faith* (2003), 40–66. A. Hyman, "Maimonides on Creation and Emanation," in: J. Wippel, *Studies in Medieval Philosophy* (1987), 45–61; A. Ivry, "Maimonides on Creation" (in Hebrew), in: *Jubilee Volume for Shlomo Pines*, Part II (1990), 115–37; idem, "Neoplatonic Currents in Maimonides' Thought," in: J. Kraemer, *Perspectives on Maimonides* (1991), 115–40; S. Klein-Braslavy, "The Creation of the World: Maimonides' Interpretation of Genesis I–V," in: S Pines and Y. Yovel (eds.), *Maimonides and Philosophy* (1986), 65–78; S. Klein-Braslavy, *Maimonides' Interpretation of the Story of Creation* (1987); T. Rudavsky, *Time Matters* (2000); N. Samuelson, *Judaism and the Doctrine of Creation* (1994); C. Touati, *La Pensée philosophique et theologique de Gersonide* (1973), 161–286; S. Wilensky, "Isaac Arama on the Creation and the Structure of the World," in: PAAJR, 22 (1953), 131–50; H. Wolfson, "The Platonic, Aristotelian and Stoic Theories of Creation in Hallevi and Maimonides," in: *Essays in Honor of the Very Rev. Dr. J.R. Hertz, Chief Rabbi of Great Britain* (1942), 427–42; idem, "The Meaning of *Ex Nihilo* in the Church Fathers, Arabic and Hebrew Philosophy, and St.Thomas," in: *Medieval Studies in Honor of J.D.M. Ford* (1948), 355–70; N.M. Samuelson, *Judaism and the Doctrine of Creation* (1994); J. Turner, "Franz Rosenzweig's Interpretation of the Creation Narrative," in: *Journal of Jewish Thought and Philosophy*, 4, 1 (1994), 23–37.

CRÉHANGE, ALEXANDRE (1791–1872), French author and communal leader. Créhange, who was strictly Orthodox in religious matters, was politically a republican and an advocate of universal suffrage. At the outbreak of the 1848 Revolution, Créhange and his Orthodox friends organized the Jewish Club Démocratique des Fidèles, with its own periodical, *La Vérité*. The club successfully demanded the reorganization of the Jewish *Consistories through democratic elections. Créhange was the oldest of the ten founders of the *Alliance Israélite Universelle and secretary of the Paris Consistory. He published several religious works, including an illustrated edition of the Psalms (1858). He edited two periodicals: *La paix, revue religieuse, morale et littéraire* (1846) and *Annuaire parisien du culte israélite* (1851–71). He also adapted the *Ẓe'enah u-Re'nah into French under the title *La Semaine israélite* (2 vols., 1846).

BIBLIOGRAPHY: Szajkowski, in: YIVOA, 2–3 (1947–48), 105ff.; A.E. Halphen, *Recueil des lois… concernant les israélites* (1851), 150; *Dictionnaire de biographie française*, 9 (1961), 1183.

CREIZENACH, MICHAEL (1789–1842), German mathematician, educator, and proponent of Reform. In his native Mainz, Creizenach received a traditional Jewish education as well as training in mathematics and philosophy. He founded a Jewish boys' school in Mainz and conducted it according to the principles of Reform Judaism. When the school closed, he continued his studies at Giessen University. Creizenach was appointed teacher and preacher at the Philanthropin high school in Frankfurt in 1825. During his tenure there he exercised a decisive influence toward the adoption of Reform. The Reform services he led attracted many worshipers, and an annual confirmation of boys was held at the school. The young rabbis, impressed when they went to preach there, spread the school's influence throughout Germany and beyond. Creizenach's publications cover a wide area of interest. He wrote a mathematical textbook for use in schools and participated in the editing of the periodical *Wissenschaftliche Zeitschrift fuer juedische Theologie* with Abraham Geiger (vol. 1 in 1835), *Israelitische Annalen* with J.M. Jost (1839–41), and the Hebrew periodical *Zion* (1840–42), also with J.M. Jost. He also published a periodical, *Geist der pharisaeischen Lehre*, of which only six issues appeared (1823–24). He edited Abraham ibn Ezra's *Yesod Mora* with a Latin and German translation (1840). Creizenach's most important work of Jewish interest was *Schulchan Aruch oder Enzyklopaedishe Darstellung des Mosaischen Gesetzes…* (4 vols., 1833–40). In this work he tried to prove that talmudic Judaism was a reform of biblical Judaism and, thus, that the Reform Judaism of his own time was a legitimate approach to Judaism.

BIBLIOGRAPHY: Loehren, in: *Philanthropin*, 1 (1904), 178; D. Philipson, *Reform Movement in Judaism* (1907), 109; M. Eliav, *Ha-Ḥinnukh ha-Yehudi be-Germanyah be-Ymei ha-Haskalah veha-Emanẓipaẓyah* (1960), 140, 245.

[Getzel Kressel]

CREMATION. Disposal of the dead body by burning is not a Jewish custom and inhumation is considered by traditional Jews to be obligatory and a religious commandment. The passage in Deuteronomy (21:23) "his body shall not remain all night upon the tree, but thou shalt surely bury him the same day" has been advanced as a scriptural proof, as well as other biblical sayings such as "for dust thou art, and unto dust shalt thou return" (Gen. 3:19). Cremation, however, was not unknown to the early Hebrews, and "burning" was one of the four death penalties imposed by the biblical code for a number of offenses (Lev. 20:14; 21:9). The ancient rabbis, however, found the execution of this death sentence so abhorrent that they refused to interpret the injunction literally (Sanh. 7:2 and TJ, Sanh. 7:2, 24b). In biblical times, cremation was clearly considered to be a humiliation inflicted on criminals (Josh. 7:15, 25; Isa. 30:33) and the practice as such was reprobated, even when it involved the burning of the remains of an Edomite king (Amos 2:1). I Samuel (31:11–12) seems to refer to the cremation of the remains of King Saul and his sons by the men of Jabesh-Gilead; but this is an isolated incident and the literal reading of the verse has been challenged by Driver who reads *sarap* ("anointed with spices") for *saraf* ("burnt"; ZAW, 66 (1954), 314–15; also Koehler-Baumgartner, supplement, 175). I Chronicles (10:12) merely records that "the bodies were buried." According to the Roman historian Tacitus, the Jews "bury rather than burn their dead" (Hist. 5:5). The Mishnah (Av. Zar. 1:3) considers the burning of a corpse to be an idolatrous practice, and the Talmud (Sanh. 46b) deduced that burial is a positive commandment prescribed in Deuteronomy (21:23). This is the ruling followed by Maimonides (*Sefer ha-Mitzvot*, 231, 536, positive command), and by the *Shulḥan Arukh* (YD 362). Tykoczinsky (*Gesher ha-Ḥayyim*, 2 (1947)) quotes the rabbinic idea that cremation is a denial of the belief in bodily resurrection and an affront to the dignity of the human body. On the other hand, some authorities permitted calcium to be spread over bodies already in the grave in order to stimulate decomposition (Responsa Rashba, pt. 1, no. 369; Isserles to Sh. Ar., YD 363:2). Others even suggested that interment was but a custom, supporting their statement with a passage from *Midrash va-Yosha* (Jellinek, *Beit ha-Midrash*, 1 (1938²), 37) in which Isaac begs his father at the sacrifice to be cremated completely. It was also suggested that as long as the body is brought into contact with the earth as soon as possible (in conformity with the injunction *Teikhef le-mitah kevurah*; "immediate burial after death"), it does not matter how the corpse is disposed of.

Modern European Orthodox authorities have insisted that burial is the proper method of disposal of a corpse, a view taken by the Italian chief rabbinate (see *Vessillo Israelitico*, 23 (1875), 12) and, in 1895, by the rabbi of Wuerttemberg (REJ, 32 (1896), 276). Chief Rabbi Marcus Nathan *Adler of Britain, though opposed to cremation, permitted the ashes of a person who had been cremated to be interred in a Jewish cemetery in 1887. The decision was sustained by his successor, Herman *Adler (1891), who quoted the authority of Rabbi Isaac Elhanan Spector. It was also the attitude of Chief Rabbi Zadoc *Kahn of France. American Reform rabbis, in accordance with a decision made at the Central Conference of American Rabbis in 1892, are permitted to officiate at cremation ceremonies. Reform rabbis of Europe also often officiate at cremations. A regulation of the United Synagogue of London Burial Society states that "if the ashes can be encoffined, then interment may take place at a cemetery of the United Synagogue, and the Burial Service shall be conducted there at the time of the interment." Ultra-Orthodox communities, however, do not permit the ashes of cremated persons to be buried in their cemeteries.

BIBLIOGRAPHY: JC (Oct. 2, 1891), 10; Schlesinger, in: CCARY, 2 (1891/92), 33–40; 3 (1892/93), 40–41; Felsenthal, *ibid.*, 3 (1892/93), 53–68; M. Higger, *Halakhot ve-Aggadot* (1933), 161–83 (complete survey of halakhic literature); M. Lerner, *Ḥayyei Olam* (1905); JE, 4 (1902), 342–4; H. Rabinowicz, *A Guide to Life* (1964), 25–30.

[Harry Rabinowicz]

CRÉMIEU, village E. of Lyons, France. Remains of the medieval gate leading to the Rue Juiverie could still be seen in the middle of the 19th century: the cemetery was near the Porte de Quirieu. The community apparently suffered during the *Black Death (1348–49): a Jew called Abraham "l'Espagnol" was imprisoned in Crémieu in 1349 and later brought to trial. A member of the community named Croissant contributed 500 francs of the total of 610 levied on the community in 1388.

From 1441, the Jews began to move away; in 1449, to induce them to return, the Dauphin Louis appreciably reduced taxes, but failed to attract them back. From the 16th century onward many Jews with the name Crémieu or Crémieux, Carmi, etc., resided in the area, especially in Carpentras, Avignon, and northern Italy.

BIBLIOGRAPHY: Gross, Gal Jud, 261–3; F. Calvet-Rogniat, *Crémieu ancien et moderne* (1848), 35; R. Delachenal, *Histoire de Crémieu* (1889), 81ff.; P. Saint-Olive, *La "Grande mortalité" en Bresse et en Bugey (1348–50)* (1913), 10; Z. Szajkowski, *Franco-Judaica* (1962), index; *Archives Juives*, 4 (1967–68), 38.

[Bernhard Blumenkranz]

CRÉMIEUX, BENJAMIN (1888–1944), French author and literary historian. Born in Narbonne, Crémieux was descended from an old Jewish family originating in the Midi. While serving in the French Army during World War I, he was wounded three times. After the war he became an authority on Italian literature and translated Luigi Pirandello into French. Crémieux was secretary-general of the French Institute in Florence and secretary of the French PEN Club. His best known works were *Le vingtième siècle* (1924), essays on contemporary writers, and *Inventaires; inquiétude et reconstruction* (1931), an essay on post-World War I writing. In his only novel, *Le premier de la classe* (1921), Crémieux tells the story of young Blum, the son of a Jewish tailor, who maintains his ancestral allegiances. After the French collapse in 1940, Crémieux joined the French underground and became a leader of the *Maquis*. He was captured and executed by a Nazi firing squad.

BIBLIOGRAPHY: A.A. Eustis, *Marcel Arland, Benjamin Crémieux, Ramon Fernandez; trois critiques de la "Nouvelle revue française"* (1961), 71–120, 209–12.

[Arnold Mandel]

CRÉMIEUX, ISAAC ADOLPHE (1796–1880), French lawyer and statesman. He was born in Nîmes of an old Comtat family which had adopted the revolutionary cause. He was among the first Jewish pupils to be admitted to the Lycée Impérial in Paris. He later studied at the University of Aix-en-Provence and was admitted to the bar at Nîmes in 1817. As a Jewish lawyer, Crémieux was required to take the humiliating *oath *more judaico* in court but he refused and won his case. He subsequently supported many liberal causes. In 1827 he won two cases brought against Jews who had refused to take the oath *more judaico*, and this finally led to its abolition. Crémieux thus acquired a reputation as a defender of Jewish rights. In 1828 he became a member of the College of Notables of the Marseilles Consistory. In 1830 he settled in Paris, where he became a member of the Central Consistory. He became vice president of the Central Consistory in 1834. In 1840, the *Damascus Affair and the consequent revival of antisemitism in Europe aroused intense emotion in all the Jewish communities of Europe. Crémieux accompanied Moses *Montefiore on a delegation to the East and secured the release of the Jews imprisoned in Damascus. Their success was the first step toward the new feeling of self-confidence in West European Jewry, based on the renewed sense of solidarity among Jews in different countries.

In 1842 Crémieux entered the Chamber of Deputies and became one of the main leaders of the opposition. On behalf of the Central Consistory he helped to draft the law of May 25, 1844, which was to regulate the life of French Jewry until 1848 and after 1905. Crémieux became president of the Central Consistory in 1843 but had to retire in 1845 when it became known that he had allowed his wife to have their children baptized. He took an important part in the 1848 revolution and until June 1848 was minister of justice in the provisional government. As such he was instrumental in promoting, among other things, the abolition of the death penalty for political offenses and of slavery in the colonies. Although he had supported the election of Louis Napoleon to the presidency of the republic, Crémieux opposed the latter's coup d'état. On Dec. 2, 1851, he was consequently arrested and remained for some time in prison. He returned to parliament in 1869 as one of the members for Paris. Again a leader of the opposition, he became minister of justice after the fall of the Second Empire. During his enforced retirement from public affairs, Crémieux concentrated on Jewish affairs. In 1864 he was elected president of the Alliance Israélite Universelle, and lent all the weight of his authority and political experience to many of the steps taken by the Alliance to help oppressed Jewish minorities. From 1866, Crémieux was active on behalf of Moroccan, Romanian, and Russian Jewry. In 1866 he traveled to St. Petersburg and intervened successfully in behalf of the Jews accused in the *Saratov blood libel.

After his return to the government Crémieux did not forget the problems encountered by Algerian Jewry. At that time French policy aimed at the complete assimilation of the Algerians, a process in which the Jews were also included. As minister of justice he signed the decree afterward known as the Décret Crémieux (1870) by which the Jews of Algeria received French citizenship en bloc. Defeated in the 1870 elections, he became deputy for Algiers in 1872 and sat on the left with the Union Républicaine. He was elected a life senator by the National Assembly in 1875. Despite old age, he continued to take an active part in the work of the Alliance as president. His interest in the Jewish communities of North Africa and the Orient was unfailing.

With his strong Jewish sense, Crémieux was the archetype of the extreme assimilated Jew who demonstrated that it was possible to combine a sense of Jewish pride with deep involvement in the affairs of his country.

BIBLIOGRAPHY: S. Posener, *Adolphe Crémieux*, 2 vols. (Eng., 1933–34), incl. bibl.; E. de Mirecourt, *Crémieux* (Fr., 1867); N. Leven, *Cinquante ans d'histoire: L'Alliance Israélite Universelle 1860–1910*, 2 vols. (1911–20); A. Chouraqui, *L'Alliance Israélite Universelle et la renaissance juive contemporaine* (1965). **ADD. BIBLIOGRAPHY:** D. Amson, *Adolphe Crémieux: l'oublié de la gloire* (1988); G. Weill, *Emancipation et progrès: l'Alliance israélite universelle et les droits de l'homme*

(2000); G. Renauld, *Adolphe Crémieux: homme d'Etat français, juif et franc-maçon: le combat pour la République* (2002).

[Simon R. Schwarzfuchs]

CREMIN, LAWRENCE ARTHUR (1925–1990), U.S. educator and authority on the progressive school system. A native of New York, Cremin received his Ph.D. from Columbia University in 1949 and began to teach at the university's Teachers' College. In 1957 he was appointed a full professor. In 1958 he became chairman of the department of philosophy and social sciences. In 1961 he became the Frederick A.P. Barnard Professor of Education as well as a member of Columbia's history department. He was president of the History of Education Society in 1959 and the National Society of College Teachers of Education, and then became vice president of the National Academy of Education. He directed the Teachers College's Institute of Philosophy and Politics of Education from 1965 until 1974, when he became the college's seventh president (1974–84). In that capacity, he established new centers, created new professorships, and raised funds while at the same time building on the college's existing strengths. He retired from the presidency in 1984 to return to teaching and research. In 1985, while remaining on the Columbia and Teachers College faculties, he became president of the Spencer Foundation, a Chicago-based educational research organization.

During his four decades at Teachers College, Cremin helped broaden the study of American educational history by promoting a more comprehensive approach: he examined the other agencies and institutions that educated children, integrated the study of education with other historical fields, and compared educational methods across international boundaries. He also played a leading role in many professional, governmental, and philanthropic organizations, including the U.S. Office of Education's Curriculum Improvement Panel, and the Carnegie Commission on the Education of Educators.

Cremin wrote *The Transformation of the School; Progressivism in American Education, 1876–1957* (1961), a history of the progressive education movement in the United States, for which he was awarded the Bancroft Prize in American History in 1962. His major work was a three-volume comparative history of education in the United States entitled *American Education*. The second volume, covering the period from 1783 to 1876, won the Pulitzer Prize for history in 1981. His other major works include *The American Common School: An Historic Conception* (1951), *A History of Education in American Culture* (with R.F. Butts, 1955), *Public Schools in Our Democracy* (with M.L. Borrowman, 1956), *The Republic and the School: Horace Mann on the Education of Free Men* (1957), *The Genius of American Education* (1965), *Isaac Leon Kandel (1881–1865): A Biographical Memoir* (1966), *Public Education* (1976), *Traditions of American Education* (1979), and *Popular Education and Its Discontents* (1990).

[Abraham J. Tannenbaum / Ruth Beloff (2nd ed.)]

CREMONA, city in Lombardy, N. Italy. Jews are first mentioned in Cremona in 1278 as loan bankers. The Jews were given protection by the Visconti dukes of Milan, who in 1387 granted the right of residence in Cremona. The Jews of Cremona did not confine themselves to banking but also engaged in commerce and farming, becoming the largest Jewish community in Lombardy. In about 1466 the commune requested that no more Jews be admitted into Cremona. Under the Sforza dukes, and after during the Venetian domination (1499–1509) and also during the French occupation, in 1509 and again later, the commune asked that the Jews should be excluded, but the requests were not met. In addition, the Jews suffered from the antisemitic preachings of the friars until Pope Paul III (1534–49) intervened to moderate their attacks. A few years previously (1525) the duchy of Milan (to which Cremona belonged) had passed to the iron rule of Spain. The *bull issued by Pope *Julius III in 1553 ordering that all copies of the Talmud should be burned was at first opposed by the governor of Milan. Cremona was then a center of Jewish scholarship. R. Joseph *Ottolenghi (d. 1570) gave special luster to the local talmudic academy and from 1556 printing of Hebrew works began. In 1557 the Inquisition urged the authorities of Cremona to enforce the bull of 1553. Although at first unsuccessful, the efforts of the Holy Office bore fruit in 1559. Following a dispute between the apostate Vittorio Eliano (in which he supported the equivocal Joshua de' Cantori) and Joseph Ottolenghi, the Inquisition seized 12,000 Talmudic codex and 10,000 Hebrew books and consigned them to the flames. In the same year, the archbishop of Milan, Carlo *Borromeo, enforced some of the anti-Jewish restrictions recently renewed by the Vatican, prohibiting Jews from lending money and compelling them to wear the Jewish *badge. In 1590, there were 456 Jews living in Cremona and most of them were moneylenders, traders of second-hand and dealers of new textiles. In 1591 Philip II, king of Spain, ordered all the Jews to leave the duchy of Milan. Several stays of the order were granted until 1597. In 1629 only the family Soave resided in Cremona as loan bankers and traders. Attempts to induce Jews to return to Cremona in 1619, 1626, and 1633 failed. Parts of the communal archives are preserved in the Montefiore Collection in London (Ms. 94).

Hebrew Printing

During the second half of 15th century were copied out some siddurim and commentaries. In 1550 Meir da Padova copied out some Torah scrolls for Joseph *Ottolenghi. The Christian Vincenzo Conti printed about 40 Hebrew books in Cremona between 1556 and 1567, the best known being the *Zohar* in 1559. The first production was Isaac b. Joseph of Corbeil's *Ammudei Golah* for which Conti had as his associates Samuel Boehm and Zanvil Pescarol. From 1558 until 1567 Conti continued to print Hebrew books whose contents had been sanctioned by the Inquisition. Until 1559 Conti used almost exclusively "Rashi" (cursive) type, as in his first edition of *Ẓiyyoni* by Menahem b. Meir, of which the Inquisition destroyed 1,000 copies. From then onward he used square type, as in the *Zohar* and the second edition of *Ẓiyyoni*. In Cremona Conti finished the Ashkenazi *Maḥzor* begun in *Sabioneta in 1557, while books printed there for Conti by Zifroni in 1567 (*Pirkei de-Rabbi Eliezer, Halikhot Olam, Ẓeidah la-Derekh*, and an Ashkenazi *siddur*) are continuations of Cremona work. Conti used a variety of title page decorations: in 1556, faun and nymph with the coat of arms of Cremona; 1557–67, the typical Cremona tailpiece inscribed SPQR; 1565–66, portals with turkey cocks; and, for folios, portals with *Akedah illustration. In 1576 another Christian printer, Cristoforo Draconi, printed (with the help of Solomon Bueno) Eliezer Ashkenazi's *Yosef Lekaḥ*.

BIBLIOGRAPHY: Roth, Italy, index; Milano, Italia, index; Milano, Bibliotheca, index; Joseph b. Joshua ha-Kohen, *Emek ha-Bakhah* (1852), 120, 130; G.B. De' Rossi, *Annali ebreo-tipografici di Cremona 1556–1586* (Parma, 1808); A. Pesaro, in: *Vessilo Israelitico*, 30 (1882/83), passim; 31 (1883), 4–7; Bergamaschi, in: *La scuola cattolica*, 34 (1906), 258–68, 617–37; J. Bianchi, *Sulletipografie ebraiche di Cremona nel secolo XVI* (Cremona, 1807); D.W. Amram, *Makers of Hebrew Books in Italy* (1909), 306ff.; I. Sonne, *Expurgation of Hebrew Books* (1943), 21ff.; H.D. Friedberg, *Toledot ha-Defus ha-Ivri be-Italyah* (1956^2), 80ff.; A.M. Habermann, *Ha-Sefer ha-Ivri be-Hitpatteḥuto* (1968), index; M. Benayahu, *Ha-Defus ha-Ivri be-Kremona* (1971). **ADD. BIBLIOGRAPHY:** S. Simonsohn, *The Jews in the Duchy of Milan*, 4 vols. (1982–86).

[Attilio Milano / Federica Francesconi (2nd ed.)]

CRESCAS (**Cresques**; Heb. קרשקש), personal or family name common among the Jews of southern France and Catalonia. It apparently comes from the Latin verb *crescere* ("to grow, increase"); compare the name Dieutecresse ("may God increase") common among the Jews of N. France and pre-Expulsion English Jewry, which is probably a French form of Joseph (["may God] increase," Gen. 30:24). Bearers of the family name include Ḥasdai *Crescas. It was also used as a personal name, e.g., by Crescas Solomon, a signatory of the communal regulations adopted for Aragonese Jewry in 1354; Magister Crescas Elijah, physician to Pedro IV of Aragon; and the astrologer *Cresques de Vivers and the Majorcan Jewish cartographer Cresques Abraham, mistakenly known as Abraham Cresques.

BIBLIOGRAPHY: Baer, Urkunden, 1 (1929), index; Baer, Spain, index; Gross, Gal Jud, index.; A.L. Isaacs, *Jews of Majorca* (1936), index.

CRESCAS, ASHER (Bonan) BEN ABRAHAM (first half of 15th century), author of religious and philosophical commentaries. Crescas lived in Provence. Before 1438 he wrote a commentary on Maimonides' *Guide of the Perplexed*, first printed with the Sabbioneta edition of 1553. In his commentary he quotes Shem Tov Ibn *Falaquera's *Moreh ha-Moreh*, a treatise by *Jedaiah ha-Penini (perhaps his *Midbar Kedemot* to the 25 propositions of Maimonides), Joseph *Caspi, *Levi b. Gershom, and *Alḥarizi's translation of the *Guide*. Crescas also wrote *Avvat Nefesh*, a supercommentary on Abraham *Ibn Ezra's commentary on the Pentateuch, extant in numerous manuscripts. Steinschneider identifies Crescas with Asher b. Abraham, the author of several liturgical writings still in manuscript in Cod. Paris 706.

BIBLIOGRAPHY: Steinschneider, Uebersetzungen, 425; Steinschneider, Arab Lit, 206; idem, *Berliner Festschrift* (1903), 351; A. Berliner, *Peletat Soferim* (Ger. and Heb., 1872), 43; Benjacob, Oẓar, 31, no. 614, 310, no. 802; Zunz, Lit Poesie, Supplement, 43.

[Moshe Nahum Zobel]

CRESCAS (or **Cresques**), **ḤASDAI BEN JUDAH** (c. 1340–winter 1410–11), Catalonian rabbi, philosopher, and statesman. Crescas was born into an old Barcelonan family of rabbis and merchants. He studied Talmud and philosophy there under Rabbi *Nissim b. Reuben Gerondi (c. 1310–1376) and together with Nissim's other outstanding disciple, Rabbi *Isaac b. Sheshet (1326–1408). In the 1360s, he served as one of the *ne'emanim* or "secretaries" of the Jewish community. By the 1370s, he was recognized as an authority on talmudic law, was requested by King Peter IV of Aragon to adjudicate certain cases concerning Jews, and received legal queries from Jews throughout the Kingdom of Aragon and abroad. He wrote poetry, and in 1370 participated in a competition between the Hebrew poets of Barcelona and those of Gerona. With the accession in 1387 of King John I and Queen Violante, he became a familiar of the royal household. In 1389 he moved to Saragossa, seat of the main royal court, and served there as rabbi. In 1390 he was empowered by the throne as judge of all the Jews of the Kingdom of Aragon. During the anti-Jewish riots of 1391, he worked together with the king and queen to protect the Jewish communities of the kingdom, but with only partial success: hundreds of Jewish communities in Valencia, Majorca, and Catalonia were destroyed, thousands of Jews killed, and more than 100,000 were converted to Christianity; but the Jewish communities in Aragon and Roussillon were saved. Despite Crescas' efforts to have his family protected, his only son was murdered in Barcelona. Crescas prepared a Hebrew chronicle of the massacres addressed to the Jews of Avignon, dated October 19, 1391 (trans. in Fritz Kobler, *Letters of the Jews through the Ages*, London 1952, pp. 272–75). The chronicle was presumably intended to provide information for Jewish intercessors meeting with the Avignonese pope. Its terse Hebrew bears theological allusions: the desolated centers of Jewish piety and learning become Jerusalem; and Crescas' son, "my only son, a bridegroom, a lamb without blemish," becomes Isaac. In the wake of 1391, Crescas, supported by the king and queen, devoted himself to the reconstruction of the devastated Jewish communities of the Kingdom of Aragon. He also secured passage for thousands of *Conversos* on ships sailing for places outside Christendom, like North Africa or the Land of Israel, where they could legally return to Judaism. He made efforts to reform the system of communal representation in Saragossa, and in 1396 framed regulations (no longer extant) for the community, which strengthened the powers of its administrators. Certain modifications were introduced to them in 1399 by Queen Violante, who extended the responsibility of the administrators and allowed the lower classes a greater share in the representation. Crescas helped to effect similar regulations in other communities. His influence was not confined to Aragon. Before 1391 he and Isaac b. Sheshet were approached for advice with regard to the succession of the chief rabbinate of France. Later his opinion was solicited by Joseph *Orabuena, chief rabbi of Navarre. In 1401 Crescas spent several weeks in Pamplona, perhaps to discuss with King Charles III the resettlement of Jews there. A document from Olite, the royal residence in Navarre, acknowledges the receipt of 40 florins from the king, and bears Crescas' signature in Hebrew and Spanish. After the martyrdom of his son, he received royal permission in 1393 to take a second wife, his first being no longer able to have children; and she bore him one son and three daughters. He died in Saragossa.

[*Encyclopaedia Judaica* (Germany) / Warren Zev Harvey (2nd ed.)]

Works

Crescas had limited time for writing, and what he did write was motivated by his commitment to salvage Judaism in Spain. As part of a campaign to combat the prodigious Christianizing literature aimed at Jews and Conversos he wrote his *Refutation of the Christian Principles* (1397–98) in Catalan (trans. D. Lasker, Albany, 1992). This work has survived only in Joseph ben Shem Tov's Hebrew translation entitled *Bittul Ikkarei ha-Noẓerim* (1451, 1860, 1904, 1990; trans. D. Lasker, Albany, 1992). He also composed at least one other Catalan work combating Christianity which is now lost, and he influenced Profiat *Duran to write his *Kelimmat ha-Goyim* ("Disgrace of the Gentiles"), another work criticizing Christianity. The *Refutation* is a non-rhetorical logical critique of ten principles of Christianity: original sin, redemption, the Trinity, the incarnation, the virgin birth, transubstantiation, baptism, the messiahship of Jesus, the New Testament, and demonology. Even his philosophic treatise *Or Adonai* ("Light of the Lord"), an anti-Aristotelian classic, written in Hebrew and completed in 1410 (Ferrara, 1555; Vienna, 1859–60; Johannesburg, 1861; Jerusalem, 1990), was conceived as a polemic. In this work Crescas attacked Aristotelianism because Aristotelian arguments had been used by Jewish intellectuals to justify their desertion of Judaism. Also extant is a philosophic and halakhic Sermon on the Passover (*Derashat ha-Pesah* or *Ma'amar Or le-Arba'ah 'Asar*, ed. A. Ravitzky, Jerusalem 1988), which contains a discussion of miracles, faith, and choice. Among Crescas' students were: Joseph Ḥabib, Joseph *Albo, *Zerahiah b. Isaac ha-Levi, Mattathias ha-Yiẓhari, Moses ibn *Abbas, and *Astruc ha-Levi. The last five scholars were delegates to the disputation of *Tortosa.

Or Adonai

Crescas had planned to write a comprehensive work *Ner Elohim* ("Lamp of God") which was to have been a reaction to the teachings of *Maimonides. He envisaged that the work would be composed of a philosophic-dogmatic part, *Or Adonai*, and a halakhic one, *Ner Mitzvah*; however, the latter section was never written. *Or Adonai* was directed against the *Guide of the Perplexed*, the main work of Jewish Aristotelianism. Crescas praised the immensity of Maimonides' learning, and acknowledged the desirability of his intent, but in justification of his critique he cited the rabbinic dictum, "... wherever the divine name is being profaned no respect is to be shown to one's master" (Er. 63a). *Ner Mitzvah* was to have superseded Maimonides' *Mishneh Torah* as a concise systematization of *halakhah*. The work was to have included Crescas' own novellae, and was to have incorporated logical and methodological features lacking in Maimonides' work, namely: alternate halakhic opinions, references to sources, and principles which would permit the application of commandments, general in their nature, to particular cases. Since this halakhic compendium was never written, Crescas is remembered as a philosopher, not a halakhist.

The disengagement of philosophy and belief from *halakhah*, symbolized by the projected two parts of his work, was crucial to Crescas. For example, Maimonides, combining the two, had interpreted the opening words of the Decalogue, "I am the Lord" (Ex. 20:2; Deut. 5:6), as constituting a positive commandment to believe in (or know) the existence of God. Crescas, by contrast, argued in the preface to his *Or Adonai* that it is absurd to speak of a divine commandment to believe in the existence of God, since such a belief cannot be a commandment itself, but must be a presupposition for any commandment. Before one can speak of a divine commandment one must already be convinced of the existence of a divine commander, God. Furthermore, in Crescas' psychology belief is involuntary; and one can only be reasonably commanded to do what one has the power to choose to do. Once again, therefore, belief in the existence of God is a presupposition of all the commandments, but it itself is not a commandment; it is pre-halakhic.

Or Adonai is divided into four books which analyze (1) the presuppositions or roots (*shorashim*) of Torah, (2) the fundaments (*pinnot*) of Torah, (3) other obligatory beliefs of Torah, and (4) some non-obligatory speculations. Following Maimonides, Crescas counts as roots God's existence, unity, and incorporeality. His analysis is tripartite: (1) a thorough presentation of the alleged Aristotelian roots of Torah, i.e., demonstrations of the 25 supposedly indubitable physical and metaphysical propositions that Maimonides had declared necessary premises of proofs of God's existence, unity, and incorporeality; and explanations of these proofs (cf. *Guide*, 2, Introduction); (2) a disproof of Aristotelianism, i.e., logical refutations of most of the propositions and all of the proofs; and (3) a new investigation of the roots. Crescas' critique of Aristotelianism was historically momentous; in arguing for the liberation of Torah, he was arguing also for the liberation of science. Crescas refutes the Aristotelian arguments against the existence of a vacuum and suggests that a medium is not a necessary condition of either motion or weight. It is not true that each element possesses an inner tendency toward its alleged natural place: rather, "all movable bodies have a certain amount of weight differing only quantitatively" and "those bodies which move upward do so only by reason of the pressure exerted upon them by bodies heavier in weight." Refutation of the impossibility of a vacuum enables Crescas to argue against the impossibility of infinite incorporeal and corporeal magnitudes and in the process to overthrow Aristotle's definition of place. In Aristotle's theory, according to which the universe is finite, "place" was defined as the adjacent surface of the containing body (*Physics* 4:4); this definition, observes Crescas, involves absurdities, e.g., the outermost celestial sphere has no essential place and the place of the part is sometimes not a part of the place of the whole. In Crescas' conception, space is infinitely extended; it is a vacuum, except where occupied by matter. Thus, space is the place of all matter, and the "place" of a thing is defined as "the interval between the limits of that which surrounds." To the Aristotelian argument that, according to such a definition, places themselves would have an infinite number of movable places, he replies that space is one and its dimensions immovable. Crescas notes that with the refutation of the impossibility of an infinite magnitude, the impossibility of a plurality of worlds is also refuted: there is now place for them. The objection that elements of the world would spill into another is quickly invalidated, even on Aristotelian terms, for each world could have its own proper places for its elements. Crescas does not explicitly posit the existence of an infinite number of worlds, but it is inferable; he does argue for an infinite number of coexisting magnitudes, and in two theological discussions he refers to *aggadah* about God's travels in (Crescas interprets "providence for") 18,000 worlds (Av. Zar. 3b). He rejects the Aristotelian view that the existence of an infinite number of causes and effects is impossible. In categorically affirming actual infinity, he contends that its denial by Aristotle was based on the fallacious assumption that the infinite is analogous to the finite. However, he argues, while finite magnitudes have boundaries and shape, the infinite by definition has no boundaries and is shapeless; while a finite number can actually be numbered, an infinite number possesses only the capacity of being numbered; while finite whole numbers can be subdivided exhaustively into even and odd, infinite numbers are not to be described by either evenness or oddness. On the other hand, regarding measurability, it is true that the predicates "greater than," "smaller than," and "equal to" are inapplicable to infinite numbers, but they are applicable to the numbers themselves. He rejects the Aristotelian view that the celestial spheres are rational, that is that they possess intelligence, and that their motion is voluntary; he argues that motion of terrestrial as well as celestial elements is natural rather than rational. Having dismissed Aristotle's theory of absolute lightness and weight, and having interpreted motion as a function of weight, he conjectures that the circular motion of the celestial spheres is due to their weightlessness. He rejects Aristotle's identification of form with actuality and matter with potentiality, and proposes that the substratum is "corporeal form." He rejects Aristotle's definition of time as an accident of motion; in his view, time exists only in the soul and is "the measure of the duration of motion or of rest between two instants." The critique of the Aristotelian propositions was also the critique of the premises of Maimonides' proofs of the existence, unity, and incorporeality of God; and the proofs fall with the propositions. Crescas does, however, recognize one short proof of the existence of God: regardless of whether causes and effects in the world are finite or infinite, there must be one cause of all of them as a whole. For were there nothing but effects, these effects in themselves would have only possible existence. Hence, in order to bring them into actual being, they need a cause, and this cause is God. He does not accept philosophic proofs for either of the other two roots: God's unity is known only from Torah, "Hear O Israel: the Lord our God, the Lord is one" (Deut. 6:4); His incorporeality is a corollary of His unity. Crescas concludes his dissertation on the roots by remarking that while philosophy cannot establish them, it does agree with them; the argument from design (see *God) suggested the existence of a Governor to Abraham, but only God's light dispelled Abraham's doubt (cf. Gen. R. 39:1).

Fundaments

Torah, in Crescas' conception, is "the product of a voluntary action from the Commander, Who is the initiator of the action to the commanded, who is the receiver of the action." Fundaments are concepts that follow necessarily (i.e., analytically) from his conception of Torah. They include the following:

1. God's knowledge of existents, for God could not have commanded the Torah without knowing what he commanded. Crescas argues that God as Creator knows a priori all existents across all time.

2. Providence, for God's voluntary giving of the Torah was itself providential. According to Crescas, God provides for individuals not, as Maimonides taught, in accordance with their intellectual excellence, but on the merit of their love.

3. God's power, for were He powerless, He could not have given the Torah. Crescas argues that He Who created all by virtue of His will is infinitely powerful, neither restricted by nor dependent on nature.

4. Communication between Commander and commanded, i.e., prophecy, for the Torah is the product of such communication. Prophecy, maintains Crescas, is the culmination not of philosophy, as Maimonides taught, but of love for God.

5. Man's power of choice, for the concept of commandment presupposes the commanded's ability to choose to obey. Yet Crescas accepts the philosophic position of determinism, maintaining that two hypothetical individuals with identical backgrounds would in the same situation choose identically. He accepts, also, the theological position of determinism, that God foreknows all, and he affirms R. Akiva's antinomy: "All is foreseen, but choice is given" (Avot 3:19). Man, he concludes, has a will, composed of appetite and imagination, though this will is determined by external causes, among them the commandments. Because of this will man is able to choose, and, furthermore, he is responsible for his choice, which, in turn,

becomes a cause, determining his reward or punishment. However, a man is not responsible for his beliefs, for belief, in Crescas' analysis, is independent of the will; thus, at Sinai the Israelites, coerced as if God had threatened to crush them with the mountain (cf. Av. Zar. 2b), were not rewarded for believing, but for the voluntary joy attendant on their belief.

6. The purposefulness of Torah, just as objects produced by men have a purpose, so, the Torah, produced by the Prime Intellect (God) must have purpose. It is the purpose of the Torah to effect in the one to whom it is addressed love for man, correct opinions, and physical felicity, which are all subsumed under one final goal – spiritual felicity, the infinite love for God. But even for God, the Commander, the Torah has a purpose, namely to bestow His infinite love upon His creatures.

Against both Platonism and Aristotelianism, Crescas argues that God's love for man is stronger than man's love for God, for God's infinite essence is the source of both loves. Man's love for God results in *devekut* ("conjunction" or "communion") with God; for among spiritual beings, as well as among physical objects, love and concord are the causes of perfection and unity. Love, the purpose of Torah, is the purpose also of man, and, further, of all that is. Maimonides had discredited the question of ultimate purpose, asserting that one could ask the purpose of every proposed purpose. Crescas replies that there is no infinite regress, because, ultimately, goodness is its own purpose, and it follows necessarily from God's essential and infinite goodness that He should boundlessly create good and joyfully will that His creatures attain the ultimate good, *devekut*.

Other Dogmas

Of the non-fundamental obligatory beliefs, Crescas distinguishes those independent of specific commandments, which include creation, survival of the soul, reward and punishment, resurrection, immutability of the Torah, the distinction between Moses and the other prophets, the efficacy of the Urim and the Thummim, and the Messiah, from those dependent on specific commandments, which include the efficacy of prayer and of the priestly benediction, God's readiness to accept the penitent, and the spiritual value of the High Holidays and the festivals. These beliefs differ only epistemologically from the fundaments: they are a posteriori, while the fundaments are a priori. One could logically conceive of the Torah without the nonfundamental beliefs but not without the fundamental ones. Yet, since the nonfundamental beliefs are affirmed by the Torah, their denial makes one a heretic. Crescas rejects Maimonides' contraposition of eternity and creation. For Crescas, whether or not the world is eternal is inconsequential; what is crucial is that the world is created *ex nihilo* by the absolute will of God, and that only the existence of God is necessary. Creation need not be in time: God is "creating each day, continuously, the work of the beginning" (liturgy). In his discussion of eternity, as in that of determinism, Crescas accepted a theory considered fatal to religion, and, instead of arguing against it, opted to establish its dogmatic inconsequence, and to show how it could be incorporated into an orthodox theology. In his discussion of the soul, Crescas rejects the Aristotelian theory that only the acquired intellect survives death. He argues that the soul is a simple and incorruptible substance, whose essence is not the intellect but something sublime and inscrutable. Crescas' teaching concerning the Messiah states that he will be greater than Moses and even the angels. Crescas recognizes only the Diaspora of 586 B.C.E.; the period of the Second Temple, being under foreign hegemony, did not constitute a redemption for him.

CONCEPT OF GOD. "The Place" (*ha-Makom*), a talmudic appellation for God, strikes Crescas as a remarkable metaphor: as the dimensions of space permeate the entire universe, so does the glory of God. Crescas, differing from Maimonides, speaks of positive attributes of God (e.g., eternity, knowledge, and power), maintaining that terms predicated of God are not employed absolutely equivocally, but amphibolously. Their generic meaning is the same when they are applied to God as when they are applied to created beings; yet, the attributes of created beings are finite, and thus incomparable with the infinite attributes of God. Attributes are infinite also in number; yet all are mental modifications of the attribute of goodness. Crescas considers both the Averroistic and the Avicennian identifications of God's existence with His essence as tautological. For Crescas existence, whether that of God or created beings, is simply extramental non-absence; it is essential to (i.e., a necessary condition of) essence, which, by definition, has extramental reality. Similarly, the attribute of unity, which is simply nonplurality, is essential not only to God, but to every existent substance. All divine attributes are essential in the way that existence, unity, animality, and rationality are essential to man. For Crescas, God is not the *intellectus-intelligens-intelligibile*, and, as is suggested in the astounding conclusion of *Or Adonai*, He even might not be unconditionally inscrutable. He is Goodness, and His happiness is in His infinite creation of good and in His infinite love for His creatures.

Influence in and Criticism of *Or Adonai*

Or Adonai was written within the tradition of the Jewish Aristotelianism it sought to refute; it is a continuation of the discussions in Maimonides' *Guide* and *Levi b. Gershom's *Milḥamot Adonai* ("Wars of the Lord"). Crescas makes significant reference to, among other Aristotelians, *Moses b. Joshua of Narbonne. Among Jewish non-Aristotelians, he refers sympathetically to *Judah Halevi and *Naḥmanides, recommends *Jonah b. Abraham Gerondi's treatise on repentance, and cites his teacher R. Nissim Gerondi, the spirit of whose philosophy pervades his religious thought. Of the medieval Islamic philosophers, whom it is assumed he knew only through Hebrew translations, Crescas is particularly concerned with *Averroes, the radical Aristotelian, whose physics and theology he attacks vigorously. He also discusses views of *al-Farābī, *Avicenna, al-*Ghazālī, *Avempace, and *al-Tabrīzī. Crescas' arguments show affinity to the revolutionary physics then being developed at Paris by students of Jean Buridan, especially Nicole Oresme. At times he seems influenced by Thomism, Scotism, and Ockhamist nominalism. However, since he did not write *Or Adonai* for a Latin audience and did not cite Latin schoolmen, the nature of his relationships to these movements is speculative. Aspects of Crescas' discussion of the will seem based on the work of *Abner of Burgos, a Jewish convert to Christianity.

Although *Or Adonai* was written for philosophers, not mystics, it is clear that Crescas was influenced by the Kabbalah, especially by the 13th-century Aragonese masters. He cites *Sefer Yeẓirah* and *Sefer ha-Bahir* and often interprets Scripture and Midrash kabbalistically. He emphasizes infinity (although he avoids the kabbalistic term *Ein-Sof*), love, and *devekut*; and he dismisses as preposterous the Maimonidean notion that the esoteric studies of *ma'aseh bereshit* and *ma'aseh merkavah* are physics and metaphysics. Aristotelians, such as *Shem Tov ben Joseph ibn Shem Tov, who rejected Crescas' arguments as "figments of the imagination" of a "perverse fool," were convinced that he could not understand Aristotle. Even Isaac *Abrabanel, who respected Crescas for his piety, considered his philosophic views often unintelligible or simpleminded. On the other hand, Joseph *Jabez praised "Rabbi Ḥasdai, who surpassed in intellect all the philosophers of his time, even the philosophers of Christendom and Islam, and how much more so the philosophers of Israel." Giovanni *Pico della Mirandola, quoting Crescas extensively, injected his critique of Aristotelian physics into the Latin literature, which later nurtured Galileo. The *Dialogues of Love* of Leone Ebreo (Judah *Abrabanel) might be seen as a poetic adaptation of Crescas' metaphysics. Giordano Bruno (1548–1600), the Christian Italian philosopher, seems to have borrowed arguments from him. *Spinoza's theories of extension, freedom and necessity, and love are marked by his close study of *Or Adonai*.

[Warren Zev Harvey (2nd ed.)]

BIBLIOGRAPHY: Baer, Spain, index; S. Pines, *Scholasticism after Thomas Aquinas and the Teachings of Hasdai Crescas and his Predecessors* (1967); Husik, Philosophy, 388ff.; Guttmann, Philosophies, 224ff.; H.A. Wolfson, *Crescas' Critique of Aristotle* (1929), incl. bibl.; idem, in: JQR, 7 (1916), 1–44, 175–221; S.B. Urbach, *Ammudei ha-Maḥashavah ha-Yisre'elit*, 3 (1961). **ADD. BIBLIOGRAPHY:** W.Z. Harvey, *Physics and Metaphysics in Hasdai Crescas* (1998); A. Ravitzky, *Derashat ha-Pesaḥ le-Rabbi Ḥasdai Crescas* (1988); D. Lasker, *Jewish Philosophical Polemics against Christianity in the Middle Ages* (1977); C. Sirat, *History of Jewish Philosophy* (1985), 357–70; D. Lasker, "Crescas," in: D. Frank and O. Leaman, *History of Jewish Philosophy*, ch. 17 (1997).

CRESQUES, ABRAHAM (d. 1387), Majorcan cartographer, son of Abraham Vidal and Astrugona. Contrary to what has been assumed in research, his name was Cresques Abraham and not Abraham Cresques. The latter is the name of his father. Hence his son Judah (son of) Cresques. In the Catalan-speaking lands and in Provence it was customary for Jews to bear two names, the second being the father's name. Cresques' grandfather Vidal Cresques was a leader of the community in Majorca. Cresques prepared maps and compasses for Pedro IV of Aragon and his son John, who conferred on him the title *magister mapamundorum et buxolarum*. His map of the world was sent by the infante as a gift to Charles VI of France in 1381. Both Cresques and his son Judah (see below) were granted royal protection in 1381 and exempted from wearing the Jewish badge. Pedro IV granted him revenues and the right to appoint the ritual slaughterers and inspectors in his community. The celebrated Catalan atlas, now in the Bibliothèque Nationale in Paris, is thought to be the work of Cresques. JUDAH CRESQUES (b. c. 1360) was also a cartographer. After his father's death he continued to make maps for John I and Martin of Aragon. He continued to reside in the *call* of Majorca, where he inherited a house from his father. During the anti-Jewish outbreaks in Spain in 1391, Judah became converted to Christianity, changing his name to Jaime Ribes. In 1394 he settled in Barcelona. From 1399 he is referred to in documents as *magister cartarum navegandi*. He is identical with the famous cartographer Mestre Jacome de Mallorca, employed in Portugal by Henry the Navigator during the 1420s.

BIBLIOGRAPHY: G. de Reparaz, *Maestre Jacome de Malhorca* (1930); idem, in: *Estudis Universitaris Catalans*, 13 (1928), 221; A. López de Meneses, in: *Estudios de Edad Media de la Corona de Aragón*,, 5 (1952), 724ff.; A. Pons, in: *Hispania*, 16 (1956), 251–5; Baer, Spain, 2 (1965), 52, 464; *Sefarad*, index to vols. 1–15 (1957), s.v. *Crescas*. **ADD. BIBLIOGRAPHY:** Cresques Abraham, *L'atlas catal de Cresques Abraham*, ed. L. Mercad I Nubiola (1975); J. Riera i Sans, "Cresques Abraham, jueu de Mallorca, mestre de mapa mundis I de Brúixoles," 14–22 (also in Spanish); Cresques Abraham, *Mapamundi, the Catalan Atlas of the year 1375*, ed. with commentary by G. Grosjean (1978); G. Llompart and J. Riera i Sans, in: *Bolletí de la Societat Arqueològica Luliana*, 40 (1984), 341–50

CRESQUES DE VIVERS (d. 1391), Spanish astrologer. Cresques, who apparently came from Vivers in southern France, was invited in 1384 by John, the heir apparent to the throne of Aragon, to serve him as astrologer. Cresques arrived in Aragon in 1386. When John became king in the following year he assigned Cresques an annual income of 500 Barcelona sólidos to be defrayed by the Jewish community of Perpignan. In 1389 he granted Cresques and his household royal protection, and also appointed him tax administrator (*procurador y gestor general*) of the Jewish communities in Aragon. Cresques was killed during the anti-Jewish outbreaks in 1391. After his death, his wife and sons became converted to Christianity, and in 1392 the king ordered the community of Perpignan to continue to pay them the income formerly received by Cresques.

BIBLIOGRAPHY: Baer, Urkunden, 1 (1929), 570; A. López de Meneses, in: *Sefarad*, 14 (1954), 99–115, 265–93.

CRESSON, WARDER (1798–1860), U.S. religious zealot, convert to Judaism, and visionary Zionist. Cresson, born into an old Philadelphia Quaker family, became successively a Shaker, a Mormon, a Millerite, and a Campbellite, while earning a living as a farmer outside Philadelphia. After associating with Isaac *Leeser for several years, Cresson determined in 1844 to visit the Holy Land. He received an honorary appointment as American consul at Jerusalem, but a protest by Samuel D. Ingham, a former secretary of treasury, who believed that Cresson had been "laboring under an aberration of the mind for many years," and that "his mania is of the religious species," resulted in the appointment being withdrawn. By then, however, Cresson had left for Palestine, and for a time believed that he was representing the American government. Four years of residence in Jerusalem persuaded him that he could find spiritual truth in Judaism; despite the discouragement of the chief rabbi of Jerusalem and of the *bet din*, he was circumcised and converted in 1848. Returning to Philadelphia to settle his affairs, Cresson was declared insane by a jury at the instigation of his wife and son, who felt that his conversion was an indication of mental imbalance. He appealed the decision and received a new trial, and in 1851 was found by the jury to be sane. They ruled that Judaism was a legitimate religion and that Cresson was not insane in converting. The Philadelphia Public Ledger commented that the case "settled forever … the principle that a man's religious opinions never can be made a test of his sanity." While in Philadelphia, he lived as an observant Jew and prayed at Mikveh Israel. Before returning to Palestine in 1852 as Michael Boaz, Israel ben-Abraham, he published a polemical volume entitled *Key of David, David the True Messiah* (1851). Back in Jerusalem, Cresson undertook propaganda campaigns against Christian missionary groups and on behalf of agricultural colonization of Jews in Palestine. He remained in contact with Leeser, who published many of his communications in his journal *The Occident*. Cresson lived in Jerusalem as a Sephardi and married a Sephardi wife, Rachel Moledano.

BIBLIOGRAPHY: Friedewald, in: *Jewish Comment* (Baltimore), 12 (Nov. 30, 1900), 1–2; Karp, in: American Jewish Historical Society, *Early History of Zionism in America* (1958), 1–20. **ADD. BIBLIOGRAPHY**: H. Obenzinger, *American Palestine: Melville, Twain and the Holy Land Mania* (1999).

[Bertram Wallace Korn / Michael Berenbaum (2nd ed.)]

CRETE (**Candia**), the fourth largest island, 160 mi. (248 km.) long, in the Mediterranean Sea and the largest Greek island, lying 60 mi. (96 km) from the Peloponnesus. Crete is apparently identical with the biblical *Caphtor, the original home of the *Philistines (Deut. 2:23; Jer. 47:4; Amos 9:7), who themselves, or certain groups of them, are referred to in the Bible as Cherethites (Ezek. 25:16; Zeph. 2:5; this is also the obvious meaning of I Sam. 30:14, cf. 30:16). David's bodyguard, which the Bible describes as Cherethites and Pelethites (II Sam. 8:18; 15:18; 20:7, 23 (Kere); I Kings 1:38, 44; I Chron. 18:17), was probably composed of Philistines ("Peleti" being a derivation of "Pelishti" analogous to "Kereti") and Cretans who had either recently emigrated from Crete or were already settled in the land of the Philistines but were still named after their place of origin. The Septuagint also translates Cheretim as Κρῆτας

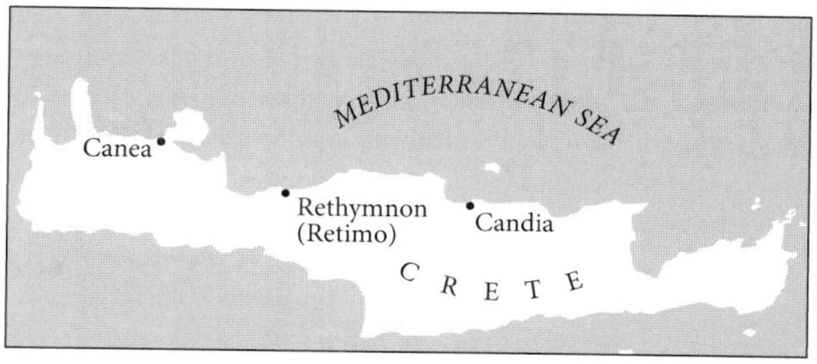

Major medieval Jewish communities in Crete.

(Ezek. 25:16; Zeph. 2:5); the verb כְּרִית in Zephaniah 2:6 is translated as Κρήτη; in Ezekiel 30:5 פוט is also given as Κρῆτες.

The earliest evidence of a Jewish community in Crete is to be found in a circular letter in support of the Jews, sent by the Roman Senate (142 B.C.E.) to various countries at the request of Simeon the Hasmonean. As this was also forwarded to the Cretan city of Gortyna (I Macc. 15:23), it can be assumed that there was a Jewish community in existence there. There is no doubt about the existence of Jewish settlements in Crete after its conquest by the Romans in 68–67 B.C.E. The false Alexander, who after Herod's death claimed to be his son, found ardent supporters and financial help among the Cretan Jews. *Philo of Alexandria mentions Crete among the countries with a large Jewish population (*Legatione ad Gaium*, 282). According to the New Testament (Acts 2:11) there were Cretan Jews living in Jerusalem. Josephus married, in Rome, a woman belonging to a prominent Cretan Jewish family (Jos., Life, 427). After the partition of the Roman Empire in 395, the island remained part of the Eastern Empire. Under the Byzantine emperor Theodosius II (408–50) the Jews of Crete, among others, were severely oppressed. Possibly in consequence of this in 440 they placed their faith in a pseudo-messiah, who claimed to be Moses sent from heaven to lead the Jews of Crete dry shod through the sea back to the Promised Land. Of those who did not drown after jumping from the cliff, most converted to Christianity. The Saracens, who invaded Crete in 823, founded a fortified city surrounded by a *khandak* ("ditch"), from which the city's present name Candia is derived. In 961 the Byzantines succeeded in reconquering Crete. The situation of the Jews under the Arabs and Byzantines is only vaguely known. In general the Muslim rulers gained the sympathy of the native population, while under the Eastern Empire their position, while not enviable, was probably no worse than elsewhere under Christian Byzantine rule. In the wake of the Fourth Crusade (1204) the island was sold to Venice and became known as Candia. In the period of Venetian rule (1204–1669), a fusion of various Jewish communities took place. The *Romaniots formed the upper class. Their Greek vernacular even penetrated the synagogue services. Jews settled on the island from both east and west throughout this period, and contacts with Jewish centers were maintained. In 1228 R. Baruch b. Isaac, on his way to Palestine, found a small Jewish community in Candia, which shocked him because of the laxity in observance of Jewish traditions.

A series of ordinances (*Takkanot Kandyah*; see bibliography) were then established against the abuses. In 1481 *Meshullam of Volterra found 600 Jewish families and four synagogues in Candia. The Jewish community of that city accorded a warm welcome to the exiles from Spain in 1492.

Nevertheless, even during the period of their prosperity, Cretan Jews did not number more than 1,160; they lived mainly in the harbor towns of Candia, Canea, and *Rethymnon (Retimo). The Jews formed a middle class between the Greek population and the feudal nobility, but they were nevertheless treated as *vilani* ("serfs") and depended on the favors of Venetian officials. From 1350 they were forced to reside in a specified quarter (*Ciudecca*), and not only to wear the Jewish *badge on their clothing but also to affix it to their houses. On Epiphany they had to donate a ducat a head to the church for the lighting of candles. There were also protests that the Jews had concentrated the major part of the commerce in their hands. When the Greek population rioted in 1364, the Jews of Castel Nuovo were massacred by the rebels. About a century later, in 1449–50, the Jews were accused of showing contempt for Christianity by crucifying the paschal lamb, an original departure from the *blood libel theme. Two years later, in 1452, an accusation was brought by a nun that the Jews had desecrated the *Host. Nine notables of the Jewish community of Candia were arrested, and tried in Venice, but were set free after two years' imprisonment.

In general the central government attempted to safeguard the Jews and these in turn proved their loyalty. A distasteful burden of the Jewish community was to supply an executioner. During the war with Turkey in 1538 a rumor that the Jews were hiding Turks in their quarter led to an attack by the Greek population. A massacre was averted by the intervention of Venetian troops and the day came to be celebrated as the "Purim of Candia." In 1568 the Greek patriarch in Constantinople dispatched a letter to the Christians of Candia taking them to task for their cruel treatment of Jews. However, when the fanatic Giacomo Foscarini ruled the island (1574–77), harsh anti-Jewish measures were undertaken to isolate the Jews of the island or compel them to convert. The Jewish community was heavily taxed and became the victim of extortions to finance the war against the Turks. Even so, the situation of the Jews was relatively secure. With some exceptions, they were Venetian subjects with the status of citizens. Only a limited number of them, however, were admitted to the wholesale commerce. Nevertheless they dominated the export trade of the island. They traded in sugar, wax, ironware, hides, female finery, indigo, and wine, while a certain group was engaged in moneylending and banking. These aroused considerable hostility, especially among the Greeks on the island. In 1416 Jews were restricted in the purchase of fields out of fear that all the land would come into their possession. In 1423 the Venetian senate forbade all Jews who were Venetian subjects to purchase land. Those who were already in possession of properties were required to transfer them to other owners within two years. Jews were also restricted in the renting of property. In 1433 they were forbidden to act as brokers. However, the majority of the Jewish population in Crete were artisans, such as tailors, shoemakers, bakers, silkweavers, and dyers. Some were lawyers, physicians, and book copyists. The *takkanot* of Candia (from the 13th century and the end of the 16th century) reveal that the Jews of the island had the right of self-government, especially in religious matters. At the head of the community stood the *condostablo* and after him the *ḥashbanim* ("accountants"). The *condostablo*, who was elected by the notables of the community and its wealthier members, represented the community externally, and was responsible for the efficient organization of communal affairs. He chose the *ḥashbanim*, who were responsible for financial affairs. The appointment of both the *condostablo* and the *ḥashbanim* required the approval of the government. In the city of Candia there were four synagogues: "The Great," "Kohanim," "Ashkenazim," and "The High."

The community produced many talmudic scholars and rabbis, especially of the Delmedigo and Capsali families. Among the famous scholars of Crete were the historian Elijah b. Elkanah Caspali, the philosophers Joseph Solomon *Delmedigo, *Elijah b. Eliezer, *Shemariah b. Elijah Ikriti, and Elijah Cretenses *Delmedigo, and the rabbi and poet Michael b. Shabbetai *Balbo. The Turkish period (1669–1898) marked a decline in the cultural life of the Jewish communities. In 1873 a blood libel was raised against the Jews and the French consul intervened effectively on their behalf. In 1875, local Jew Abba Delmedigo was elected to the Cretan Ottoman parliament. Abraham Evlagon served as chief rabbi from 1876 to 1934. When Crete became autonomous in 1897, it had a Jewish population of 1,150, with 200 families residing in Canea, 20 in Candia, and five in Rethymnon. In 1900 Canea had 726 Jews, speaking Greek. Crete became part of Greece after the Balkan wars of 1912–13.

Prior to World War II the community had dwindled to about 400. When the Nazis occupied Greece in 1941 many Jews fled to Crete. When Crete fell it came under direct Nazi administration. On May 20, 1944, the Jews of Canea were arrested and taken to Iraklion (Candia). On June 9, 1944, they were forced to board the *Danae* together with 400 Greek hostages and 800 Italian prisoners of war. The ship was then taken out to sea, identified by the British RAF (Royal Air Force) as a German boat without being aware of its human cargo, and bombed. After being abandoned by its German crew it sank with all on board. Only seven Jews survived the Holocaust.

BIBLIOGRAPHY: M. Steinschneider, in: *Mosé*, 2 (1879), 411–6; 3 (1880), 53–59, 281–5, 421–6; 4 (1881), 303–8; 5 (1882), 267–70, 401–6; 6 (1883), 15–18; Levi, in: REJ, 26 (1893), 198–208; Schiavi, in: *Nuova antologia di scienze, lettere ed arti*, 131 (1893), 309–33; Rosenberg, in: Festschrift… David Hoffman (1914), 267–80; S. Krauss, *Studien zur byzantinisch-juedischen Geschichte* (1914), passim; Finkelstein, Middle Ages, 82–85, 265–80; C. Roth, *Venice* (1930), 297–304, and passim; B.D. Mazur, *Studies on Jewry in Greece* (1935); E.S. Artom and U.M.D. Cassuto, *Takkanot Kandyah ve-Zikhronoteha* (1943); Schwarzfuchs, in: REJ, 111 (1961), 152–8; Marcus, in: *Oẓar Yehudei Sefarad*, 6 (1963), 135–9; 9 (1966), 84–101; idem, in: *Sinai*, 60 (1967), 63–76; idem, in:

Maḥanayim, 86 (1963), 138–43; J. Starr, in: PAAJR, 12 (1942), 59–114; M. Molho and J. Nehama, *Sho'at Yehudei Yavan 1941–44* (1965). **ADD. BIBLIOGRAPHY:** J. Humphrey, "The Sinking of the Danae off Crete in June 1944," in: *Bulletin of Judaeo-Greek Studies*, 9 (Winter 1991), 19–34; B. Rivlin, "Khanea," in *Pinkas Kehillot Yavan* (1999), 155–59.

[Simon Marcus]

CRIME.

INTRODUCTION

Jews in the Diaspora have generally been less involved in crime than the populations among which they lived. Their closely knit communities, cohesive family life, high educational standards, moderation in the consumption of alcohol, their solidarity, consciousness of mutual responsibility, and readiness for mutual help are regarded as the main causes for the generally low crime rates among Jews.

There are only a few countries where official crime statistics were recorded and published separately for Jews and non-Jews in certain periods. The limited data available – ranging from Czarist Russia prior to World War I to modern Canada – point to certain unmistakable trends. In the first place, crime rates were lowest where Jews were discriminated against and increased after Emancipation. Second, crimes committed by Jewish offenders were generally different in character in countries of discrimination and persecution from those committed by members of the dominant population groups. The more the Jews became emancipated and were enabled to participate in social, economic, and cultural life, the more the crimes committed by them became similar to those of the majority population.

In Czarist Russia, a country notorious for its discrimination against the Jewish minority, the conviction rate for Jews in 1907 was only about 67.5% of that for the dominant population group, while in Poland, another country where the overwhelming majority of the Jews lived in poverty and oppression, the ratio in 1937 was 63.9%. In Central Europe, Germany, Austria, and Hungary, the extent of criminality among Jews was somewhat higher. In Hungary, where the Jews were enjoying an ever-growing share in economic, social, and cultural life, the yearly average between 1909 and 1913 was 76.5%. Among German Jewry, from 1882 to 1910, when it had achieved formal emancipation and became the wealthiest and best educated Jewish community of the period, the crime rate rose from 76% to 91.7% of that for non-Jews. In Austria, in 1898, the ratio was 90%. Jacob *Lestschinsky notes that in 1918 the conviction rate for Austrian Jews was about 50% higher than for the poorer and less acculturated Jewish community of Galicia. Crime statistics for Nazi Germany in the mid-1930s seem to show that there is an inverse correlation between participation of Jews in crime and in the life of the country where they reside. However, after deducting the very high conviction rates of Jews for "racial pollution," passport exchange and industrial offenses – all results of discriminatory Nazi legislation – Jewish conviction rates for all other offenses combined were only about 30% those for non-Jews.

In the Netherlands, where Jews enjoyed genuine emancipation and equality for centuries, the crime rate for Jews, which was only 67.7% in 1902, was about equal to that of the general population in 1931–33.

With the exception of Canada, no separate criminal statistics are available for most of the democratic countries, where Jews are fully emancipated. The United States' census does not register crimes committed by Jews. The only relevant data available for the United States are some prison statistics; but there the participation of Jews in crime appears to be even lower than elsewhere, as the more dangerous criminals are sent to prison, while Jews generally commit offenses of less severity. In the ten-year period 1920–29, 6,846 Jews, on the average, were imprisoned annually in the United States – 1.74% of the total of 394,080 convicted offenders. As Jews constituted 3.5% of the population at the time, their share in the more serious offenses, which were punished with imprisonment, was therefore about 50% of the general ratio. Imprisonment figures for New York and Los Angeles confirm these findings. In the early years of the 20th century, Jews represented 17–18% of the population of New York City; the percentage of Jewish prisoners was 9.2% in 1902, 9.4% in 1903, and 14.7% in 1904. In 1947, Jews made up 4.7% of the prison population in New York State, about a quarter of their share in the population. In Los Angeles, while the Jewish share in the population rose from 5.8% in 1933 to 11.9% in 1947, their share in 15 out of 18 offense groups – including murder, burglary, robbery, assault, and sex crimes – ranged from 2.8% to 3.9%. The situation has been similar in Canada. The Jewish population in the province of Quebec, where the great majority of Canadian Jews live, is 2.5% of the total, while their share in the penitentiary population during the last three decades has been never more than 1%.

In Tunisia the share of the Jews in the prison population was 60% of their share in the total population in 1939, and only 21% in 1965. (According to André Chouraqui, the situation was similar in Algeria and Morocco.) The data about the United States and Tunisia show that two Jewish populations – one wealthy, emancipated, well acculturated, and living in an affluent society, and the other generally poor, culturally segregated, and living in a backward country in conditions of oppression and discrimination – are both equally underrepresented among the prison population of their countries and commit proportionally fewer serious crimes. Not less significant is the fact that when anti-Jewish persecution and discrimination increased in Tunisia following the establishment of the State of Israel, crime among Jews declined still further. This seems to support the assumption that criminality among Jews increases with the measure of their emancipation.

Soon after the establishment of the State of Israel, it came as a surprise that Jews committed serious offenses, including murder, rape, and burglary, in their own country. It seems that the full freedom had also resulted in crime to an extent and of a character not known before in modern Jewish history. This seems to suggest that normalization of life in general also results in a "normalization" of the extent of deviant behavior.

However, given the continuing rise of crime in Israel (see below), and particularly violent crime, in the post-Six Day War period, it may be suggested that the erosion of two particular psychological barriers has also been a decisive factor, namely, the Zionist ethos and, especially among Eastern Jews, the values of the traditional Jewish home.

IN THE DIASPORA

Offenses Against the Person

In all countries of the Diaspora, Jews committed proportionately far fewer offenses against the person than did non-Jews; their share in homicide was the smallest of all. This phenomenon was generally explained by the higher educational level of the Jews and their very moderate consumption of alcohol. In Europe before World War II, the share of Jews in cases of physical assault increased proceeding from east to west. In Russia, in 1907, Jewish convictions for aggressive crimes were about 25% of the corresponding rates for non-Jews, while in Poland in 1937 the proportion was about 55%. On the other hand, of the overall figure in Germany, taking the average for 1899–1902, Jewish participation in offenses against the person was 71.4% and in the Netherlands about 70% from 1931 to 1933. Arthur Ruppin showed that the figures for the city of Amsterdam alone were even higher, and he ascribes this to the existence of a sizeable Jewish working class employed in industries owned mainly by Jews. Thus it seems that where Jews had achieved the highest measure of emancipation and equality, Jewish laborers behaved more like other working-class people.

Statistics show that on the North American continent, in the United States and Canada, convictions for assault among Jews are very low. This was explained by the fact that a generation or two after immigration, Jews had moved up to the middle class, where such aggressive behavior is less common. The same, however, applies to Jews in North Africa, who were very rarely imprisoned for physical assault, despite the fact that the great majority were impoverished and uneducated. Oppression and discrimination obviously cause Jews to contain their aggressive urges. This seems to confirm views expressed by Gustav Aschaffenburg and others that the position of the Jews as a closely knit minority group served as a crime-preventing agency, since potential offenders were constantly aware of the danger that deviant behavior by an individual could pose for the group as a whole.

Offenses Against Morality

Jews were generally less involved in aggressive offenses against morality than non-Jews: least in Eastern Europe, somewhat more in Germany, and more again in the Netherlands. United States prison statistics and Canadian offender statistics also point to the very low rates for sex offenses among Jews. Prison statistics in Tunisia, however, show that in 1955, when Jews were only 1.7% of the general population, Jewish women represented 2% of the "*filles en cartes*," or prostitutes. This is an indication of the fact that where Jewish offenders belong to the poverty class, they tend to commit offenses characteristic of such populations. In some countries, however, convictions for nonaggressive offenses against morality, such as brothel-keeping, were proportionally more numerous among Jews than among non-Jews. In the previously Austrian part of Poland, the ratio was 228% during 1924–25 and in Germany during 1899–1902 it was 127%. In the latter years, conviction rates among German Jews for "diffusion of immoral writings" were 260% of those of non-Jews. All this seems to indicate that Jews in the Diaspora were more represented in commercial offenses against morality than non-Jews. Experts explain this by the fact that Jews lived mainly in urban centers and engaged in commerce.

Offenses Against Property

The participation of Jews in the common crimes against property in the Diaspora was generally still lower than their share in offenses against the person. It was lowest in Poland, where in 1937 conviction rates for Jews were only 20% of those for non-Jews (though it is possible that thefts committed by Jews within the closely knit Jewish communities were not always reported to the hated Polish police), while in Germany, from 1882 to 1916, the ratio ranged from 30% to 40%. In the Netherlands the rates were again the highest – 97.6% of those for non-Jews in the years 1931 to 1933. In the United States and Canada Jewish participation in common crimes against property was always very low. In Los Angeles, for example, it was only about one-third of the proportion of Jews in the general population during the period 1933–1947, while in Canada (1936–37) convictions of Jews were only about two-thirds, proportionally, of the general figure. In North Africa, the participation of Jews in property offenses was much lower than that of non-Jews. Contrary to the situation in Europe and America, however, theft and drunkenness were the offenses most often committed by Jews in North Africa. Chouraqui observes that they constituted almost all the offenses with which Tunisian, Moroccan, and Algerian Jews were charged in 1948.

Fraud

False pretenses, forgery, and fraud are offenses in which Jews in the Diaspora were often overrepresented. In Russia in 1907, conviction rates for "commercial swindlers" were 143%, while in Poland in 1937 rates for fraud were 137%, and for forgery 143% of those for non-Jews, while in Germany the ratio ranged during the years 1882 to 1916 from 183% to 217%. In the Netherlands, the average for 1901–09 was 160%, rising in the period 1931–33 to 249%. In Canada the adjusted conviction rates for fraud, comparing the urban populations only, are 160%. The higher conviction rates for "commercial" offenses are generally ascribed to the much higher proportion of Diaspora Jews than the non-Jewish population in commerce and in urban areas. In Germany, for example, there were proportionately about five times as many Jews as non-Jews, and in Poland about 20 times as many, in commerce. In Poland, between 1924 and 1937, fraud and forgery represented about 21% of all offenses committed by Jews. In Germany between 1882 and 1901 these offenses were about 13%, and in the Netherlands from 1931 to

1933 only about 5%, of all offenses committed by Jews. Thus, proceeding from east to west – from conditions of discrimination in Poland to those of emancipation in Germany and still further west to the Netherlands – the proportion of fraudulent behavior in all offenses decreased and crime among the Jews became more similar to that of the majority populations.

Offenses Against Public Order and State Security

In offenses against public order, the participation of Diaspora Jews is generally different from that of the non-Jews. In countries where Jews were discriminated against, their share is greater, while in countries of emancipation it is proportionally smaller. Thus, the conviction rates of Jews for these offenses seem to be a reflection of their treatment by governments and dominant populations. In Russia in 1907, when Jews were 4% of the population, they accounted for 17.1% of offenses against the security of the state and public order, including the circumvention of discriminatory anti-Jewish laws – over four times their due share. In Poland (1924 to 1937) such offenses represented 43.6% of all the violations committed by Jews. In Germany (1899 to 1902), on the other hand, they were only 25%, and in the Netherlands (1931 to 1933) only 6.2%, of all offenses committed by Jews. (The very low figure for the Netherlands is somewhat distorted because the available statistics include only the more serious offenses against the state, in which Jews were rarely represented.)

IN PALESTINE (BEFORE 1948)

From the First Aliyah (1882) to the establishment of the State of Israel in 1948, crime figures in the *yishuv* were extremely low for all types of offenses. As it was only during the last years of its existence that the mandatory government of Palestine published separate statistics for the different communities, figures for 1940, 1943, and 1945 give some indication of the incidence of criminality among Jews in Palestine. (See Table 1: Conviction Rates in Palestine shows the crime rates for Jews and non-Jews in Palestine.) The table shows that in 1940 conviction rates of Jews were only 51.4%; in 1943, 29.4%; and in 1945, 25.7% of those among non-Jews. The very low criminality rates obviously reflect the largely idealistic and pioneering character of the *yishuv*.

The general decrease in crime among Jews and the coincident increase among non-Jews should also be seen against the background of World War II. Most young Jews served in the army or the *Haganah, which reduced the number of potential offenders in the Jewish civilian population. Non-Jews generally did not join the forces, but many of them worked in military camps as laborers, often far from the social control of their families and communities.

Table 1. Conviction Rates Per Thousand of the Population for Jews and non-Jews in Palestine, 1940, 1943, 1945

Year	Jews	non-Jews	Ratio Jews: non-Jews
1940	7.1	13.8	1:1.9
1943	5.0	17.0	1:3.4
1945	5.5	21.3	1:3.9

IN THE STATE OF ISRAEL

The First Decades

The entire structure of crime among Jews changed rapidly with the evolution of the new society in the State of Israel. Practically no feature that had been regarded as characteristic of criminality among Jews in the Diaspora appeared in Israel's criminal statistics. The common offenses against the person – such as assault, physical injury, and homicide – and against property – such as theft and burglary – which in the Diaspora were less frequently committed by Jews, account for the overwhelming majority of convictions of Jews in Israel. It seems that crime became, as E. Durkheim expressed it, one of the normal expressions of life in society. This normalization is also reflected in the fact that fraud and forgery, which had constituted in Poland about 21%, in Germany about 13%, and

Table 2. Jewish Adult Offenders in Israel, 1951–1965

Offenses		1951	1952	Average 1956–65
All Offenses	Total	6,222	9,600	–
	Rate per 1,000	7.456	10.655	10.129
	Percentage	(100%)	(100%)	(100%)
Against Public Order	Total	568	1,084	–
	Rate per 1,000	0.685	1.203	2.870
	Percentage	(9.2%)	(11.2%)	(28.4%)
Against the Person	Total	1,434	2,124	–
	Rate per 1,000	1.717	2.356	2.894
	Percentage	(23.1%)	(22.2%)	(28.5%)
Against Morality	Total	138	142	–
	Rate per 1,000	0.165	0.158	0.267
	Percentage	(2.2%)	(1.5%)	(2.6%)
Against Property	Total	2,898	4,284	–
	Rate per 1,000	3.470	4.755	3.144
	Percentage	(46.5%)	(44.7%)	(31.6%)
Fraud and Forgery	Total	120	154	–
	Rate per 1,000	0.143	0.171	0.312
	Percentage	(1.9%)	(1.6)	(3.1%)
Economic Offenses	Total	814	1,464	–
	Rate per 1,000	0.974	1.625	0.226
	Percentage	(13.1%)	(15.2%)	(2.1%)
Administrative and Fiscal Offenses	Total	250	348	–
	Rate per 1,000	0.299	0.386	0.414
	Percentage	(4.0%)	(3.6%)	(3.9%)

in the Netherlands about 5% of all Jewish crime, made up only 3.1% in Israel (the average for the years 1956–65).

Another feature of crime in Israel is the fact that after an initial rise of about 30% – from 7.5 to 10.6 per thousand of the total population during the first years of mass immigration (1948 to 1952) – the crime rates for the Jewish population did not rise for over a decade. The average crime rate for Jewish adults from 1956 to 1965 was 10.1 per thousand. In spite of the upheavals and tensions accompanying Israel's birth, including the mass immigration of diverse ethnic groups, crime in Israel is relatively moderate in extent and characterized by the absence of brutal and ruthless offenses.

The changed physiognomy of crime in Israel, as shown in Table 2: Jewish Adult Offenders, is probably a consequence of the radical change in the occupational structure of the Jews.

A study of specific offenses committed by Jews and non-Jews in Israel will illustrate this further. (Figures given are conviction rates per thousand of the adult population concerned.)

Offenses Against the Person

The rates for all offenses against the person were on the average 2.9 among Jews and 8.8 among Arabs. The rates for homicide, rarely committed by Jews in the Diaspora, remained relatively moderate among Jews in Israel: 0.4 on the average for the years 1951 to 1965. Of the homicides, 34% were due to matrimonial and other emotional conflicts, 25% resulted from quarrels between neighbors and business partners, 14% were committed in the course of robbery and 8% during quarrels among criminals, 3% were connected with "family honor" in traditional Oriental families; 15% were committed for various other motives. Aggressive offenses involving bodily harm were 7.0% of all offenses against the person in 1964 and only 5.7% in 1965, which confirms the impression that crime among Jews in Israel is still less violent and brutal than in many other countries. Offenses against the Dangerous Drug Laws were rare: about 0.1 per thousand Jews and 0.2 for Arabs. There were 133 cases among Jews in 1964 and 135 in 1965. In most cases the offenders were immigrants from North Africa, Asia, and the Levant who acquired the drug habit in their countries of origin but did not pass them on to the next generation in Israel. Among the emerging class of habitual offenders in Israel, however, there were some who used drugs, trafficked in them, or induced others to become addicted in order to exploit them.

Offenses Against Morality

Offenses against morality were never characteristic of Jews in the Diaspora, and in Israel the conviction rates are also low – e.g., 0.29 for Jews and 0.45 for Arabs in 1964, a typical year. There were very few serious and brutal sex crimes, only 2.6% of all offenses against morality during the years 1956 to 1965. There were only eight convictions of rape or attempted rape in 1963, nine in 1964, and six in 1965. Most of the offenses against morality consisted of "indecent behavior," generally against minors. Cases of brothel-keeping and soliciting were also relatively few: 41 in 1963, 67 in 1964, and 59 in 1965.

Offenses Against Property

The common offenses against property are the most widespread. The rates were 3.13 among Jews on the average for the ten years 1956 to 1965 and 8.77 among Arabs, taking the average for five alternate years from 1956 to 1964. Theft from the person, which in some European countries was sometimes described as a "typically Jewish" offense, is rare in Israel and growing rarer: there were 44 convictions in 1951, and only 37 in 1965, when the Jewish population was almost twice as great. On the other hand, a class of habitual burglars is clearly emerging: there were 379 convictions in 1963, 468 in 1964, and 501 in 1965. Robbery, which entails direct contact with the victim, physical attack, and a threat to his life, is, however, comparatively rare: there were 7 cases in 1963, 9 in 1964, and only 3 in 1965. It seems that even the habitual criminal in Israel shies away from this aggressive form of offense against property.

Offenses Against Public Order and the Authority of the State

Offenses against public order and the authority of the state represent somewhat more than a quarter of all offenses committed by Jews and just over half among Arabs. This greater representation of Arabs is partly due to the political situation, Arabs being often convicted for illegal border crossings and other offenses connected with the emergency regulations. Violent disturbances of the peace in Israel make up more than half the total of offenses against public order – a very different situation from that in the Diaspora, where Jews are not generally involved in such behavior. Many of these violations have been aggressive acts committed against public servants, mainly due to the tensions arising out of mass immigration and absorption problems. All the other offenses in this main category are much less frequent in Israel than in the Diaspora. Evasion of military service is very rare. Corruption and abuse of office do not constitute a serious problem, but the public is deeply disturbed at the thought that they are committed at all, even if only occasionally. An average of 24.2 individuals per year were convicted for such offenses during the ten-year period from 1956 to 1965, and they have been on the decline in recent years: there were 33 cases in 1962, but only 19 in 1963, 18 in 1964, and 15 in 1965.

Share of Different Immigrant Groups

Statistics indicate considerable differences between the crime rates for those born in North Africa, Asia, and Europe, respectively. (See Table 3: Jewish Adult Offenders). The conviction rates for the various ethnic groups show that these dif-

Table 3. Jewish Adult Offenders in Israel, 1959 and 1965, by Place of Birth (per thousand of population group concerned)

Year	Israel	Asia	Africa	Europe and America
1959	10.185	13.580	22.607	4.812
1965	11.088	12.595	22.601	4.272

ferences have been fairly consistent during the first years of the State of Israel.

S.N. Eisenstadt, in his study, *The Absorption of Immigrants* (1954), has pointed to some of the factors which may explain the differences in deviant behavior between European and Oriental Jews in Israel. The European immigrants, particularly in the earlier years, were inspired by the ideal of Jewish labor – the desire to engage in basic productive occupations in agriculture, industry, and public works – which implies a readiness for occupational change and a striving to create a new society based on social justice. The Orientals, on the other hand, hoped "to be able to follow more fully and securely their own way of life" (pp. 93–94) after their immigration. Thus they were not consciously prepared for radical changes in their economic and occupational way of life.

This situation was aggravated by the fact that the Oriental Jewish communities were composed mostly of a small wealthy and educated class and great masses of the poor and uneducated. The latter, due to lack of education and training, were unable immediately to make good use of the opportunities offered by Israel's expanding society and economy. Some of them resented the pioneering, vitally necessary work they were offered in distant development areas in afforestation, agriculture, road construction and the like, leaving such areas and moving into slum areas in the urban centers. Thus problems and situations of frustration and tension were created, resulting, in many cases, in crime. But there were great differences in the crime rates among the Oriental Jews themselves, which seem to have been caused mainly by the conditions under which they were absorbed and integrated and the measure in which their expectations and aspirations were fulfilled in daily life.

ASIAN IMMIGRANTS. Crime rates for newcomers from Asian countries are much lower than those for the North African countries, but they are also very similar to each other, in spite of the fact that the immigrants come from extremely different social and cultural conditions. This is particularly noticeable in the case of those from Iraq and the Yemen, respectively. Among the immigrants from Iraq, there is a substantial class of well-educated, wealthy leaders, some of whom had taken an active part in the political, economic, and cultural life in the country of their origin and often even occupied official positions of importance. The Yemenite Jews, on the other hand, had lived, with few exceptions, in a culturally backward country in conditions similar to serfdom. They were regarded as the property of the Imam; they had no political or civil rights and no modern education. These extreme differences, however, seemed to have no influence whatsoever on the crime rates for the two communities in Israel: among the Yemenites 11.5 per thousand in 1956–57 and 10.9 in 1958–60, and among the Iraqis 11.5 and 11.3 respectively.

The common factor seems to be that during the long period of their Diaspora life both communities remained deeply immersed in the lifestream of the Jewish people. Both studied and observed the religious traditions, always felt part of the Jewish people, and after the establishment of the state returned to Israel practically in their entirety (121,512 Iraqis and 45,159 Yemenites) during the very short period between May 1948 and the end of 1951. The fact that they moved to Israel as intact and cohesive communities, with their religious and political leaders, rich and poor, young and old, gave them a sense of mutual responsibility, security and pride, which sustained them through the inevitable difficulties and strains of the initial period.

Though the Iraqis found no substantial community of common origin on their arrival, and there were no officials from Iraq to receive the masses who were transplanted within a couple of years, this highly developed community, with all its trusted leaders and rabbis, intellectuals, wealthy men, doctors, bankers, nurses, and social workers enabled the sick and the dependent to turn for advice, guidance, and support in their own language to their own countrymen, who had soon found positions in hospitals and clinics, labor exchanges, housing and settlement offices, social welfare bureaus, and other agencies concerned with the absorption of immigrants. These conditions substantially helped to lessen absorption problems among the Iraqi immigrants and thus kept crime in this group down to reasonable proportions.

Yemenite Jews had settled in Ereẓ Israel in substantial numbers (about 18,000) in the Ottoman and Mandatory periods, before the entire community of 45,000 was transferred to Israel immediately after its establishment. Although these early immigrants were unable to take up positions of influence in the newly emerging Jewish society, they had certain characteristics and skills which paved the way for smooth integration and speedy absorption after the state had been established. Most of the Yemenite Jews had been artisans and craftsmen, and some had worked on the land. As early as in the 1880s they had made a name for themselves as highly skilled, reliable, and competent workers. Their industry, cleanliness, modesty, and reliability soon made them a respected and welcome element in the pioneering laboring class. There was no need for occupational change; they were easily absorbed into the new social and economic system.

The Yemenites enjoy life in Israel as the fulfillment of their hopes and prayers and feel that they fully belong to its society. These favorable circumstances are obviously the main reason for the low crime rate among them. The similarity of the rates for the Iraqis, many of them wealthy and well educated, and the Yemenites, who came from conditions of backwardness and poverty, seems to indicate that traditional values and, in particular, the cohesiveness and solidarity of the community go a long way to explain the comparatively low crime rates among Jews everywhere. The same principle, from the opposite end, is illustrated by the North African immigrants.

NORTH AFRICAN IMMIGRANTS. Many Jews in the North African French protectorates had taken advantage of the promise of emancipation, equality, and full opportunities for participation in economic and social life offered to them by the French rulers. French became the language of every aspiring Jew and French culture was absorbed by the successful. They acquired the status of French citizens and ceased to cultivate their ethnic and religious autonomy. The younger generations of the better-educated Moroccan, Tunisian, and Algerian Jewish families thus became more and more estranged from Jewry and their own traditions. They took pride in being considered French, which they interpreted as being European. This led to severe disappointment, frustration, and tension when they came to Israel, where they were considered "Oriental" and were confronted with a society formed and led by European Jews with a background different from their own. Moreover, when the time had come for the exodus of the Jews from the North African countries – after they achieved independence and particularly with the establishment of the State of Israel – their political, intellectual, and economic leaders, with isolated exceptions, moved not to Israel but to France. The poor, the helpless, and the uneducated were left to their fate. Many of them had also lost contact with Jewish traditions, but they had been unable to acquire or share in French modern values. Hence many of them had become alienated from their own people and thus lost the moral and material support of group solidarity.

A mere thousand Jews went to Palestine from Morocco between 1919 and 1937; even in the early years of independence, 1948–51, when life in Morocco had become precarious for them, only about 45,000 immigrants came to Israel. The majority of Moroccan immigrants, about 88,000, left between 1955 and 1957, when Morocco had become independent and the Jews were threatened by mob violence. As the immigrants from North Africa consisted almost entirely of the less-educated and unskilled masses, they were unable, at first, to provide recruits for even the lower levels of Israel's political and social leadership. This fact was apparently the basic cause of the overrepresentation of North African Jews in crime in Israel. When 133,000 Moroccan Jews arrived in two waves, in 1948–51 and 1955–57, they found practically no members of their community to receive them and there were not enough educated people among them to be trained in a reasonable time to represent them in the administration and public services. This situation improved greatly with the evolvement of a local leadership in the development areas, particularly with the rapid acculturation of the young through army service and compulsory education, but the newly created slum population in the urban areas, as well as the disintegrating paternalistic structure and authority of the large families, still served as hotbeds of rebellious, antisocial attitudes, which often expressed themselves in crime (see below).

Juvenile Delinquency Before and Since the Establishment of the State

Although no reliable statistics are available on the subject, it is generally assumed that there was little juvenile delinquency among Diaspora Jews. In Mandatory Palestine as well, juvenile delinquency was probably very low, though no detailed statistics were published. During the years 1932–43, when the total Jewish population grew from about 175,000 to about 500,000, the number of juvenile offenders increased from 191 per year (average for 1932–37) to 322.5 per year (average for 1938–43). Among non-Jews the situation appears to have been similar during 1932–37, when differences in the demographic data and development are taken into consideration. During the period 1938–43, however, Arab juvenile delinquency increased by almost 100%, while the Arab population grew by less than 30%. As in the case of adult crime, this growth may be explained by the impact of the war and the opportunities for crime in and around military camps.

In the State of Israel, however, the incidence of juvenile delinquency among Jews started to increase. In 1951, the conviction rates for boys aged 9–16 and girls aged 9–18 were 4.5 per thousand of these age groups, while juvenile delinquency accounted for 12.1% of all crimes committed in Israel. Conviction rates for juveniles grew steadily to 9.8 per thousand in 1965, and juvenile delinquency now represented 23.8% of the crime total.

Of 4,453 young Jewish offenders in 1965, 430 were born in Europe or to European parents in Israel. The conviction rates were 7.4 per thousand for juvenile offenders born in Israel, 11.9 for the Asian-born, 23.0 for those born in North Africa and 3.6 for those born in Europe or America. One of the reasons for these developments has been the transition from one way of life to another. The Oriental family went through a severe crisis after immigration. The authority and functions of the family, and particularly those of the previously authoritative father, were substantially reduced or even shattered, while the young people did not yet feel the security that comes from integration into the new society. Many remained without a compelling system of values or effective social control and lived in a cultural and social vacuum. Most have cast off the yoke of religion and traditions without simultaneously achieving the educational and cultural standards of their peers of European origin. This created painful feelings of frustration and tension, which found expression in these comparatively high crime rates.

Juvenile delinquency among Jews in Israel consisted almost exclusively of offenses against property. Criminality figures for young Arab offenders were about twice those for Jews, and the forms of delinquency were also different. In 1961, for instance, only 46.7% of young Arab offenders committed offenses against property, as against 85.7% for Jewish juveniles. The other crimes were mainly offenses against the person, including acts of aggression resulting in physical injury. Trespassing on agricultural lands and illegal border crossing were also frequent. Arab juvenile delinquency is thus due partly to the traditional behavior patterns characteristic of rural societies in the Middle East and partly to tensions and conflicts arising out of the political situation in the region.

Crime Among Females

Authors always stressed the fact that crime among Jewish females in the Diaspora was very rare; some even claimed that the comparatively low general crime rates for Jews were due to the fact that crime was practically unknown among Jewish women. In Israel there has been only a slight increase in their share in crime, from 8.5% of crimes committed by Jews in 1951 to 13.8% in 1965. Crime rates for Jewish females were 1.3 per thousand in 1951 and 2.9 in 1965. Like the males, Jewish women were mainly convicted for offenses against public order and lawful authority, against the person and against property, the figures for these three types of offense being almost identical. Female juveniles committed mainly property offenses. Offenses against morality were rare: in 1961, a census year, 10 adult females and two juveniles were convicted of such offenses. The largest number of Jewish female offenders committed to prisons since the establishment of the state were sentenced for common theft, followed by disturbances of public order and common assault, including assaults on police officers. These facts also seem to reflect absorption problems in immigrant families, which express their dissatisfaction in aggressive behavior, mostly in governmental or other institutions dealing with public welfare and public health problems. Crime rates for non-Jewish females are somewhat lower than for Jewish ones due to the traditional patterns of the Arab village, where women are generally confined to the home. Offenses committed by non-Jewish females are mostly acts of assault and breach of the peace in public places, often in village feuds between clans. Offenses against morality are very rare among Arab women.

[Zvi Hermon]

After the Six-Day War

An extraordinary rise in crime in Israel was reported in 1966. During that year, the crime rate rose 13.5%, a jump not recorded by the Israel police at any other time during the decade. Two phenomena stand out in particular: growth in the number of robberies; breaking into box offices, booking offices, business firms, and private dwellings; various types of fraud; embezzlement; passing bad checks; and a rise in the crime rate among juveniles, whose share in the general crime rate reached 32.2% in that year.

The year 1966 was the climax of an economic recession, and the rise in offenses against property was possibly a consequence of the depressed condition of the economy. The rise in juvenile crime reflected the prevailing situation in the free world, though gangs of youngsters engaged in organized criminal acts, as found in other developed countries, had not been found in Israel, except small groups, organized ad hoc, for minor crime against property.

The year 1967 was one of war in Israel with the accompanying prewar and postwar periods. It is therefore possible to expect a large rise in crime, if one proceeds from the assumption that war naturally brings with it the collapse of restraints, a withdrawal from lawfulness and order, and a sense of permissiveness toward basic drives and impulses. The actual picture is therefore surprising, for in that year there was a 2.2% decline in crime. This is the only decline in the annual crime rate of the state since its establishment. It is possible that the reason for this decline is inherent in the mobilization – and thus removal from their regular activities – of the entire corpus of manpower, including the criminals; it is also probable that the general sense of danger, and the consciousness of national unity and civil cooperation, were also reasons for the drop.

Immediately afterward, in 1968, the situation returned to normal and there was another rise in the crime rate, this time of 10.6%. A study of the data proves that this percentage is approximately the average for the previous years, with slight fluctuations in both directions; but in comparison with the decline of the previous year, this was a sharp rise. It appears that the main factor behind the rise was the amnesty (albeit selective) declared after the war (July 1967), which set free a large number of criminals from prisons. More important than the widened scope of crime is that, beginning in 1968, the nature of the crimes committed became more serious. Violent crimes, involving the use of firearms and dangerous drugs, grew during that year. It appears that the rise in violent crimes (and not only those involving firearms) is more a reflection of the prevailing situation in most parts of the world, than a consequence of the war. The 1960s, which are sometimes described in other countries as the "Decade of Violence," left their mark on Israel as well. In reference to the use of arms, it is clear that many weapons, much more than in the past, were found in 1968–70 in the hands of citizens to protect their legitimate businesses (legally) and of hundreds of soldiers home on leave. Under such circumstances weapons found their way into the hands of unauthorized persons who used them to commit crimes. These conditions however, are a result of the prolonged emergency situation and only indirectly a result of the war itself.

The disturbing turn in events in the area of drugs after the Six-Day War is also merely an indirect result of the conflict. Many visitors who went to the country after the war – "volunteers" to work on kibbutzim and foreign students – brought with them drug habits and influenced some people of their age group. Another factor, which is also an indirect result of the war, is the fact that the usual routes for smuggling hashish were disrupted between the large supplier – Lebanon – and the large consumer – Egypt – by way of the Hashemite Kingdom of Jordan. As a result, many suppliers in the West Bank and East Jerusalem were left with large supplies of hashish and no marketing possibilities. This led to a drop in the prices of illegal drugs in Israel and the country therefore became a source at low prices for acquiring and smuggling hashish, which is more expensive than marijuana. The price in Israel fluctuated between $150–300 per kilogram whereas in the United States and Canada prices ran between $2,000–3,000 per kilogram.

Since the 1970s Israeli crime rates have been constantly rising, with the steepest rise in violent crime. Of the 243,719 crimes reported in Israel in 1985, 263 were cases of murder or attempted murder and 9,994 were cases of assault. By 1994 the figures had jumped to 4,629 and 18,368, respectively. In the same period sex crimes rose from 2,133 to 2,825. Drug offenses rose from 4,367 to 11,584.

The following decade showed a continuing rise in most crime categories, with murder, sex crimes, spouse and child abuse, and drug crimes increasing. Though not the highest in the Western world, Israeli crime rates were comparable to those in Germany and Austria. While in 1996, 454,622 files were opened, in 2004 the number grew to 517,238, among which 55% were offenses against property. The number of immigrants committing crimes rose from 11,287 in 1996 to 27,747 in 2004, reflecting problems of adjustment among Russian and Ethiopian immigrants. In 2004, the Arab share in Israeli crime was 36.8%, a further reflection of social and economic malaise. A relatively new phenomenon in Israel is what has been recognized as organized crime, involving such familiar agents as local crime families, a Russian Mafia, and foreign hit men and dealing in everything from money laundering to the white slave trade (the importation of women from the former Soviet Union). Of the 173 arrests for the latter offense in 2001–4, 80% were among Russian immigrants. There was also a steep rise in juvenile delinquency. Statistics for the 1990–2002 period show an increase in every category. While in 1990, 20,552 police files were opened for juveniles, by 2002 the number had jumped to 32,067. The nature of juvenile crime had also changed. While until 1965, 80% of juvenile crimes were against property, in 1999 the rate was only 45% as violent crime and drug abuse climbed commensurately. The growth of violence among teenagers, and even younger children – murder, rape, and assault, including violence in schools and disco clubs – has become a common occurrence in Israel, with a jump from 3,508 police files in 1990 to 14,696 in 2002.

[Yaacov Nash /Shaked Gilboa (2nd ed.)]

BIBLIOGRAPHY: B. Blau, *Die Kriminalitaet der deutschen Juden* (1906); R. Wassermann, *Beruf, Konfession und Verbrechen* (1907); A. Ruppin, *Die Soziologie der Juden*, 2 vols. (1930); idem, *The Jews in the Modern World* (1934); W.A. Bonger, *Race and Crime* (1943); A. Chouraqui, *Between East and West* (1968); L. Rosenberg, *Canada's Jews* (1939), 288–99; S.M. Robison, in: M. Sklare (ed.), *The Jews: Social Patterns of an American Group* (1958), 535–41; J. Lestschinsky, in: *YIVO Bleter*, 15 (1940), 202–16; N. Goldberg, *ibid.*, 24 (1944), 131–2; idem, in: *YIVO Annual*, 5 (1950), 266–91; J. Guttman, in: *Yivo Bleter*, 26 (1945), 210–7; I. Drapkin Senderey, *The Prevention of Crime and the Treatment of Offenders in Israel* (1965); S.N. Eisenstadt, *The Absorption of Immigrants* (1954); S. Shoham, in: *Journal of Criminal Law, Criminology and Police Science*, 53 (1962), 207–14; U.(C.) Schmelz and D. Salzman (Gavish), *Statistikah Pelilit be-Yisrael*, 2 vols. (1962–65); Israel Central Bureau of Statistics, *Statistikah shel ha-Mishpatim ha-Peliliyyim* (1952–); idem, *Avaryanut ha-Noʿar* (1960–). **ADD. BIBLIOGRAPHY:** S. Ben-Baruch, "Juvenile Delinquency," at www.police.gov.il; G. Eshed, "Organized Crime in Israel and in the World – Processes and Directions," at www2.colman.ac.il/law.

CRIMEA (Rus. **Krym** or **Krim**) (Heb. קְרִים), peninsula of South European Russia, on the Black Sea; from 1954 until 1991 an oblast of Ukrainian S.S.R. and from 1992 a republic of Ukraine.

Late Antiquity and Early Middle Ages

Jews first settled in the southeastern area and a Jewish Hellenistic community existed there by the end of the first century C.E. (based on inscriptions). *Jerome (d. 420; on Zech. 10:11, Obad. 20) heard from Jews that the Jewish settlers by the Bosporus were descended from families exiled by the Assyrians and Babylonians, and from deported warriors of *Bar Kokhba; the Bosporus was called by the Jews "Sepharad." In ancient and medieval times southeastern Crimea was linked to the Taman Peninsula, across the Kerch Strait. In the seventh to tenth centuries the *Khazar conquerors maintained their regional center there, from which they ruled much of the Crimea and confronted the Byzantine coastal base of Cherson, near the present Sevastopol. The Arab geographers Idrīsī and Abu al-fidāʾ call the Khazar city merely Khazariyya (Khazaria); it was located on the site of the town Sennaya (formerly Phanagoria), adjacent to the Jewish settlement mentioned by the Byzantine historian Theophanes, and is probably identical to the port Samkush (Samkerch) "of the Jews," referred to by the Arabic geographer Ibn al-Faqīh. Tombstones of Jews and Khazar proselytes have Jewish Hellenistic ornamentation. Similar Jewish tombstones have been found in Kerch and Partenit (Parthenita), near Yalta. The Byzantine chronicler Cedrinus relates that in 1016 a Byzantine Russian-assisted fleet subdued the region of Khazaria ruled by Georgios Tzoulos. The Russians were henceforth represented by a prince at Tmutorokan (Taman), while the Byzantines overlooked most of the Crimea from Cherson. The Khazars served as the prince's military auxiliaries in an inner Russian conflict in 1023, and in 1079 intervened with Byzantium in the competition for the princely office; this led to their massacre in 1083. From the 9th to 15th centuries the terms "Gazaria" (as the territory) and "Gazari" (as the population) were understood in Western Europe as the Taman peninsula and the adjacent changeable Crimean area. Gazaria is, according to Poliak, the "Kazariyya" mentioned by the 12th-century Jewish travelers *Benjamin of Tudela (in connection with the sea trade with Constantinople and Alexandria), and *Pethahiah of Regensburg (the Kuban delta). Isaac *Abrabanel commenting on Genesis 10:3 equates the "Qasari" in "Ashkenaz" with Gazaria, "below" (south of) the Azov Sea. In the 16th to 17th centuries "Gazaria" and "Crimea" were synonymous. This late usage led the Russian historian N.M. Karamzin (1816) to regard the Crimea as the ultimate domain of the Khazar kings, lost in 1016. After C.M.Y. Fraehn (1822) had dated the downfall of the Caspian Khazars to 969, the period 969–1016 was left for the duration of the mythical Crimean kingdom, considered from that point forward as Jewish. The early draft of H. *Graetz's "History of the Jews" (1860) included the history of the kingdom, written according to the manuscript discoveries claimed by the Karaite collector A. *Firkovich. After these claims had been attacked, the story was partly, but mechanically, deleted: in the late version

Major Jewish communities in Crimea, 1970.

the Crimean kingdom has a beginning but no end (Eng. ed., 3 (1949), 222ff.). Graetz's original coherent description continued to influence Jewish historians, notably S. *Dubnow (*History of the Jews in Russia and Poland*, 1 (1916), 28ff.). Firkovich also is the source of the idea that the Crimea was the cultural center which influenced the conversion of the Khazar royalty to Judaism, and that the Crimean Karaites were descended from ancient Israelite settlers and Khazar converts. The rival Karaite historian M. Sultanski (d. 1862) regarded the Crimean Karaites as purely medieval Jewish immigrants from various parts, while later Karaite authors held that they were basically Khazars-Turks. The Rabbanite *Krimchaks (i.e., "Crimeans") were also sometimes considered basically Khazars. All these views are founded on the late meaning of "Gazaria." Foreign Karaites (contrary to Rabbanites) in Khazar times never claimed that the Khazars had converted to Judaism and sometimes displayed intense hatred toward them (even expecting them to fight the Messiah in Ereẓ Israel): the sect was then seeking to uphold the Palestinian descent of the Jews and Judaism. In late antiquity and the early medieval period, Crimean Jewish tradition and records indicate that Jewish settlement existed in the following units.

THE CHERSONESE. The Chersonese (Cherson) Jews were living there at least in the 9th to 11th centuries. Excavations have shown that the locality never recuperated from a devastation in the late 10th century by the Russians (988?), and was ultimately destroyed at the end of the 14th (by Tamerlane's raiders, 1395–96?). The Hebrew letter attributed to the Khazar King Joseph (long version) lists among his tributaries in the 950s localities from Samkerch to "Gruzin" (Cherson?), including Kerch and "Bartenit." The Hebrew "Cambridge Document" claims that under him "Shurshun" was made tributary by a counteroffensive against Byzantium after the Byzantine-instigated Russian raid on Samkerch.

"GOTHIA". This is the medieval name for the rugged mountains north of Cherson, so-called after a Teutonic tribe which had remained there following the great migrations. The city of Partenit was the coastal mart of Gothia; a Jewish tombstone inscription there mentioned "Her(i)f(r)idil [a Teutonic name] ha-kohen [priest]." Around 787 the Khazars placed their garrison in Doros, the capital of Gothia; the *Life* of Bishop John tells of the unsuccessful revolt he instigated. Doros is assumed (despite temporary doubts of archaeologists in 1928–38) to be the "eagle's nest" later called Mangup (first in Joseph's Letter, as his tributary). In Ottoman-Tatar times (1475–1783) it increasingly became an all-Jewish (mostly Karaite) town.

CHUFUT-KALE. More to the north, a similar fortress town, known under the Tatars as Qirqyer (Qirqer), became referred to more frequently as *Chufut-Kale ("the Jews' Fortress," Heb. *Sela ha-Yehudim*). Excavations of 1946–61 showed that it existed on the site from the 10th or 11th century; a Christian cemetery (late 5th to early 9th centuries) attests to the corresponding beginnings of the enormous Jewish cemetery. Here, also, it was under Tatar rule that the town definitely became all Jewish (mostly Karaite); it later had a Hebrew printing press (1734).

Tatar Times

The conquest of Eastern Europe by the Tatars (Mongols) in 1236–40 made the Crimea the foremost link for the trans-Asian caravans with the Mediterranean and Western trade. The Crimean Tatar center was Solkhat or Qyrym (from which the name "the Crimea" derives); now Stary Krym, inland near the port of Kaffa (now Feodosiya), the city was made by the Genoese the center of their activities in Gazaria and on the Black Sea. The contact of the Crimean Jews with the outside world grew. The Jew "Khoza Kokos" was Muscovy's representative there in 1472–75. According to a Russian tradition, Jews from Crimea were among the instigators of the movement of *Judaizers in 15th-century Muscovy. There was a Jewish revival in Taman, by then ethnically Circassian and ruled by the Genoese Guizolfis (1419–82), who were considered Jews in modern Jewish historiography and Christians in Russian. In Muscovite documents the last ruler is called a "Jew" and "Hebrew" as well as "Italian" and "Circassian"; if so-called after the environment, this significantly emphasizes the Jewish resurgence. However the Tatar decline commenced early. The Karaites of Poland (western Ukraine) and Lithuania later considered that they had been deported from Solkhat by Lithuanian raiders under Witold (Vitort), 1392–1430. The Genoese extended their possessions from Kaffa, and their relatively mild attitude toward other communities (including the Jews) maintained prosperity in the area despite the shrinking geographical extent of trade. From around 1420 the Tatar realm of inner Crimea developed into a split kingdom. After the Ottomans conquered the Genoese possessions in 1475, they made the inland Tatars vassals, used them for raiding Muscovy and Poland-Lithuania, and protected them from reprisals by a vast belt of scorched earth (depopulated steppe). This led to a sharp economic decline and massive emigration. The remaining population was basically Tatar, which was then a Muslim Turkish-speaking blend under leadership of Mongol descent. The remaining Krimchaks and Karaites shared their tongue and many customs, though the two communities differed somewhat in these respects both from each other as well as from the Tatars. Their divergent existence is certain from Tatar times only. The Mongol influence, which made the Karaite anthropological type distinct, must be attributed to conversions, but of the early Tatar conquerors; a point unknown to former scholars who disputed the matter. Conversions to Judaism even took place at the home of Genghis Khan. Only this can explain the transfer of strategic strongholds to Jews (mainly Karaites), and the establishment by the Crimean Tatar kings of the unfortified valley suburb of the "Jews' Fortress" as the new capital Baghche-Saray (Bakhchisarai, 1454). It officially became a distinct town only in the 17th century.

Czarist Rule (1783–1917)

During the Russian conquest of the Crimea from the Turks the Jewish communities suffered severely. Many Jews left for Ottoman territory. In 1783, when the Crimea was annexed by Russia, there were 469 Jewish families (Rabbanite and Karaite) living in the peninsula. Tatar raids into the Ukraine and neighboring districts of Poland-Lithuania in the 16th centuries, in particular during the Tatar alliance with *Chmielnicki in 1648, brought into Tatar hands many Jewish captives, who were usually ransomed by Jews. After the Russian annexation of the Crimea it was included in the *Pale of Settlement (1791), although the major centers of development were later excluded, among them the military port of Sevastopol (1829–59, later admitting wealthier Jews), and the resort of Yalta (1893). Jewish settlers from Russia soon outnumbered the small local communities (Krimchaks, Karaites). There were 2,837 Jews living in the Crimea in 1847. The Karaites' successful struggle for exemption from the anti-Jewish czarist legislation (1863), and the abandonment of the common fortress towns (now ruins) because of the economic revival in the lowlands, definitely estranged the Karaite society from the rest of Jewry. From 1867 to 1900 Ḥayyim Hezekiah *Medini officiated as chief rabbi of Crimean Jewry and did much to raise the level of the spiritual and cultural life of the community. Among the few scholars of Crimean Jewry notable were Abraham *Kirimi, author of *Sefat Emet*, a commentary on the Torah, in the 14th century, and David *Lekhno, author of *Mishkan David*, in the 18th century. In the 19th century the archaeological discoveries of the Karaite scholar A. Firkovich, part of which were found to be forgeries, caused a sensation among scholars. There were 28,703 Jews living in the Crimea in 1897 (5.1% of the total population) and 5,400 Karaites. The Krimchak Jews numbered 3,300. The large communities were in *Simferopol (8,951 persons); *Kerch (4,774); Sevastopol (3,910); *Karasubazar (Belogorsk; 3,144, nearly all Krimchaks); *Feodosiya (3,109); and Yevpatoriya (Eupatoria).

[Abraham N. Poliak]

Soviet Rule

There were 39,921 Jews living in the Crimea in 1926 (6.1% of the total population), of whom 17,364 lived in Simferopol (19.6%); 5,204 in Sevastopol; 3,248 in Feodosiya (11.3%); 3,067 in Kerch; and 2,409 in Yevpatoriya (10.6%). In 1939 there were 47,387 Jews (8.1% of the total population), of whom 22,791 (15%) lived in Simferopol; 5,988 (5.5%) in Sevastopol; 5,573 (5.3%) in Kerch; 4,249 (9%) in Yevpatoria; 2,922 (6.5%) in Feodosia; 2,060 (6.3%) in Yalta; and 1,397 (7.1%) in Dzhankoi. In the early 1920s a movement for Jewish agricultural settlement in the Crimea began, pioneered by members of *He-Ḥaluẓ, who established the *hakhsharah* groups of Tel Ḥai (1922), Mishmar (1924), and Ma'yan (1925) in the Dzhankoi area. They were followed by numerous other Jewish groups. In 1924 the Soviet government initiated a large-scale settlement project to be implemented through *Komzet with aid from the *American Jewish Joint Distribution Committee. A number of Soviet Jewish leaders who were concerned with this project, such as M.(Y.) *Larin and A. Bragin, regarded it as the nucleus for establishing a Jewish Soviet Socialist Republic in the Crimea. However, by the beginning of the 1930s, when it became clear that the unoccupied land available in the Crimea was not adequate for large-scale settlement, the movement concentrated mainly on promoting settlement in *Birobidzhan. The state allocated 342,000 hectares of land for Jewish settlement in the Crimea, on which 5,150 families had settled by 1931, including a commune, named Voya Nova, established by a group of the *Gedud ha-Avodah, who had returned from Palestine. Many of the settlers left the colonies when collectivization was introduced in the early 1930s and with increasing industrialization in the Soviet Union. Some of the settlements were organized in two Jewish national districts: Freidorf (in 1930) and Larindorf (1935). By 1938 there were 86 Jewish kolkhozes in the Crimea cultivating an area of 158,850 hectares with 20,000 inhabitants (one-third of the total number of Jews in the Crimea). With the German occupation in 1941 the Jewish settlement and colonies in the Crimea were annihilated. The Nazis organized the systematic liquidation of the Ashkenazi Jews and Krimchaks, but did not include the Karaites, who were recognized by the Germans as Jews by faith but not by race. According to a provisional report from the beginning of 1942, 20,149 Jews from western Crimea alone had already been "liquidated." On April 16, 1942, the Crimea was declared *Judenrein*.

After the war Jewish settlement in the Crimea was renewed. Efforts were made to resettle Jews as farmers, but these were quickly abandomed. In 1959, the Jewish population numbered 26,374 (2.2% of the total population), according to the official census, of whom 11,200 lived in Simferopol (6%) and 3,100 in Sevastopol. In 1970 the Jewish population of the Crimea was concentrated in Simferopol, with an estimated Jewish population of 15,000; Sevastopol, where there was one small synagogue in the Jewish cemetery; Yevpatoria, with an estimated Jewish population of 8,000–10,000; and in smaller communities, e.g., Kerch, Yalta, and Feodosia. (See the map "Jews in the Crimea.") Crimea was involved in the affair of the Jewish *Anti-Fascist Committee, which led to the execution of its members. In the 1990s many Jews immigrated to Israel and the West.

[Yehuda Slutsky]

BIBLIOGRAPHY: A. Harkavy, *Altjuedische Denkmaeler aus der Krim* (1876); O. Lerner, *Yevrei v novorossiyskom kraye* (1901); A.N. Poliak, *Kazariyyah* (Heb., 1942); J. Golde, *Di Yidishe Erdarbeter in Krim* (1932); B. Nevelshtein, *Freydorfskiy Yevreyskiy Natsionalny Rayon* (1934); B. West (ed.), *Be-Ḥevlei Kelayah* (1963), 138–45.

CRIMEAN AFFAIR. Name used to refer to the closed antisemitic trial of the Jewish *Anti-Fascist Committee (JAC) held in Moscow from May to July 1952. One of the pretexts may have been a memorandum presented in the summer of 1944 by members of the Committee to the Soviet leadership containing a proposal to create a Jewish Soviet republic in the *Crimea (the Tatar population of which was exiled by Stalin by May 1944) on the territory of the former German republic of the Volga. Noting the successes of the Jewish national regions in the Crimea and in the Kerson region, the authors of the memorandum based their proposal on the lack of a geographical base of a significant part of the Jewish population of the Soviet Union and on the need to grant the Jews equality in governmental-legal terms with the other nationalities of the Soviet Union. They also expressed the hope that "the Jewish masses of all countries, in particular the United States would give substantial aid" to building up such a republic. Despite the rumors that some members of the Politburo of the Central Committee (Lazar *Kaganovich and Vyacheslav Molotov) were favorably disposed toward the idea of the "Crimean Plan," it was rejected in 1944.

The proposals of the memorandum contained nothing radically new. Projects for establishing a Jewish republic in the southern Ukraine or in the Crimea had been suggested earlier. For example, in 1923 the social leader A. Bragin had proposed that one be established on the Black Sea coast from Bessarabia to Abkhaz with its capital in Odessa, while Yuri *Larin supported, in opposition to the Birobidzhan plan, a Jewish autonomous area in the southern Crimean and Azov region centered in Kerch.

Another formal basis for initiating the case was false testimony, obtained by torture from the researchers I. Goldshtein and G. Grinberg, about the "anti-Soviet, nationalistic, and espionage activity" of the JAC secretary I. *Fefer, of the head of the Sovinformbyuro S. Lozovski, and of other members of the JAC.

After the murder by KGB agents of Solomon *Mikhoels, the chairman of the JAC, in January 1948, the arrest of JAC member David *Hofshtein in September 1948, the dissolution of the committee, and the closing of the newspaper *Eynikeit in November 1948, the liquidation of the "Emes" Publishing House in December 1948, and other centers of Jewish culture, almost all writers and artistic, social, and cultural figures with ties to Jewish life and institutions were arrested (as "bourgeois nationalists" and spies) in late 1948–early 1949. Among those arrested were D. *Bergelson, *Der Nister, B. Zuskin, L. *Kvitko, P. *Markish, I. Nisinov, I. Fefer, B. Shimeliovich (chief physician of the important Botkin Hospital in Moscow), L. *Stern, and I. Watenberg, Ch. Watenberg-Ostrovskaya, E. Teumin, and, subsequently, L. Talmi – employees of the JAC. In 1949 arrests were made of a number of Jews who were top officials in the Soviet Information Bureau (Sovinformbyuro), including Solomon Lozovski, M. *Borodin, and Yuzetovich. Since formally the Sovinformbyuro organizationally and Lozovski personally were responsible for the activity of the JAC, both groups were arrested and several years later, artificially linked in the Crimean case. Some of those arrested (Borodin, Der Nister, Nusinov, et al.) died under investigation, while another (S. Bregman, assistant minister of Goskontrol of the RSFSR) died before the trial began. At a secret trial the defendants were accused of espionage, anti-Soviet activity, and plotting the secession of the Crimea from the Soviet Union and establishing there a bourgeois Zionist republic which was supposed to become a base for American imperialism. All of the accused pleaded not guilty from the beginning with the exception of Fefer, who later retracted his testimony against others and his own admission of guilt. On July 18 the Military Board of the Supreme Court of the U.S.S.R. sentenced all the defendants to be shot (with the exception of Lina Stern, who was sentenced to five years internal exile). On August 12, 1952, the following were executed: Luzovski, Yuzefivich, Fefer, Shimeliovich, Kvito, Markish, Bergelson, Hofshtein, Zushkin, Talmi, the Watenburgs, and Teumin.

A number of additional trials involving other Jewish cultural figures and employees of the JAC were soon thereafter linked to the charges in the Crimean Affair. The Crimean Affair was the culminating act in the total liquidation of Jewish cultural and social life in the Soviet Union. It was followed by the accusations of "cosmopolitanism," which resulted in the dismissal of thousands of Jews in senior positions in almost all walks of Soviet life. It also served as a prelude to the antisemitic Doctor's Plot (1952–53). All those condemned in the Crimean Affair were "rehabilitated" in 1955. On December 29, 1988, a Politburo commission officially declared all of the accused to have been innocent and the whole affair to have been fabricated. After the dawnfall of the Soviet regime in the 1990s, all the details of the trial was published.

ADD. BIBLIOGRAPHY: G. Kostyrchenko, *V plenu u krasnovo pharaona* (1994).

[Mark Kipnis / *The Shorter Jewish Encylopaedia in Russian*]

CRIMINOLOGY. Traditional Jewish criminal law based the treatment of the offender on the idea of the freedom of will and on the principle that the severity of the punishment should fit the nature of the violation. Until modern times no consideration was given to the personality of the offender or any biological, psychological or socio-economic factors in crime causation and correction.

The Anthropological-Biological School

The first to stress the hereditary or biological aspect of crime causation was Cesare *Lombroso, a founder of the positivist school of criminology, who maintained that the true criminal was born as such and could be recognized in his physical features. Among later criminologists, Sheldon and Eleanor Touroff *Glueck, in their *Unraveling Juvenile Delinquency* (1950), made use of three basic somatic (body) types and showed their relationship to delinquency, but in a subsequent study, *Physique and Delinquency* (1956), they concluded that bodily structure was no longer to be considered the most important etiological factor in criminality. They emphasized, however, that the biological aspect of criminal causation was still "a promising focus of attention."

Psychiatric-Psychological School

The psychological and psychiatric approach to an understanding of crime causation was based on the teachings of Sigmund *Freud. Although Lombroso and Freud agreed on the biological origin of antisocial impulses, they differed fundamentally on the importance of environmental influences. Freud, in contrast to Lombroso, emphasized the prime importance of infancy and early childhood in the formation of character. Freud also stressed the possibility of altering the personality through psychoanalysis. Gregory Zilboorg (1890–1959) underlined the irrationality of antisocial behavior and asserted that mere punishment, which does not take this into account, served no useful purpose ("Psychoanalysis and Criminology," *Encyclopedia of Criminology* (1949), 398–405). Psychoanalytical interpretation became important for the development of progressive methods in correction. Morris *Ginsberg defended psychoanalysis against the claim that this method tended to free the criminal from his responsibility for his misdeed, pointing out that the object of psychoanalytical treatment was to help the patient face realities and become a responsible person. Herman *Mannheim, in his *Comparative Criminology* (2 vols., 1965), warned against the great dangers which the traditional penal methods held for society. In his view the character and measure of the punishments meted out by criminal courts everywhere tended to create in the offender feelings of unjust treatment and that this led to recidivism. An important concept of Freudian theory which helped to explain criminal behavior was the psychoanalytical theory of symbolism, according to which every object, action, or person could have an unconscious symbolic value. The application of symbolism to political murder is of particular interest. Wilhelm *Stekel, one of the earlier followers of Freud, maintained that a political attentat was a "displacement of a small personal conflict into the life of nations – perhaps Booth was beaten by a drunken father – so Lincoln died." Alfred *Adler, one of Freud's disciples, who later founded his own school of individual psychology, contributed to criminological thinking by the formation of the widely known and accepted concepts of the "inferiority complex" and the "masculine protest," which, under certain conditions, could become criminogenic factors.

The Sociological School

The sociological approach to criminology emphasized the fact that most behavior, including criminal behavior, was culturally patterned, and that crime had to be defined as a result of the relationships and interactions between a given society and its individual or corporate members. The best known and most influential proponent of the opinion that the class structure is the main determinant of social pathology, including criminality, was Karl *Marx. He saw in the class struggle the main cause of criminality and, therefore, predicted that in a future classless society there would be no crime. Hermann Mannheim, in his *Comparative Criminology*, 2 (1965), 499, stated that "by far the most important, comprehensive and influential of the class-oriented theories of crime and delinquency were those based upon the concepts of the criminal subculture and anomie."

The introduction of these two basic sociological concepts into criminological thinking was one of the great achievements of Emil *Durkheim. Robert K. Merton (1910–2003), who developed and classified the ideas of Durkheim on anomie, pointed out in his writings the criminogenic forces, i.e., the anomie situation in a society which preached the democratic idea of equal opportunities for everybody but by failing to give these opportunities to all was responsible for the creation of tension and crime. An outstanding contribution to the description and explanation of the phenomenon of a criminal subculture was made by Albert K. Cohen (1918–) who, in his *Delinquent Boys* (1955), described the overwhelming weight of class differences in crime causation. In a middle class society with its middle class ethics, standards, and values, the working class youth, brought up in a different value system, would, according to Cohen, be led inevitably into conflict and confusion and – part of it – into crime. The theories of anomie and criminal subcultures are, however, not generally accepted by contemporary criminologists. Herbert A. Bloch (1904–) repeatedly expressed the opinion that the tensions which always existed between the young and the old generations were still today far more important as an explanation of the phenomenon of juvenile and gang delinquency. Bloch and Gilbert Geis (1925–), in their *Man, Crime and Society* (1962), criticized the Durkheim-Merton theory of anomie and criminal subculture, and disagreed sharply with the view that there were hardly any lawful opportunities for upward mobility among lower class male adolescents.

The pertinent question which still occupies criminologists remains the problem of "differential response." Why do certain individuals living in a generally healthy environment become delinquent, while others, who are exposed to antisocial influences, do not? Daniel Glaser (1918–) formulated the theory of "differential identification." In his "Criminality Theories and Behavioral Images" (*American Journal of Sociology* (March 1956), 433–44) he expressed the opinion that an individual would act criminally when he identified himself with real or imaginary persons, in whose view his criminal behavior appeared to be acceptable. Thus the offender may identify with criminals presented in fiction, movies, television, or in the newspapers. Simon Dinitz (1926–), together with Walter C. Reckless (1899–1988), in *Critical Issues in the Study of Crime* (1968), approached this basic problem of differential response by asking the reverse question: "Why do some non-delinquent boys succeed in remaining within the law while living in high delinquency areas?" Their answer was that the insulation against a delinquent life consists in the self-image of the boy who experienced himself as being good. Jackson Toby (1925–), in his "Differential Impact of Family Disorganization" (*American Sociological Review* (Oct. 1957), 505–12), showed that the higher rate of broken homes among female delinquents was evidence that well-integrated families protected children against the antisocial influences exerted by neighborhood and peer gangs. The consideration of the problem of "differential response" led some sociologically orientated criminologists to the conclusion that it is impossible to explain crime exclusively in sociological terms. Sheldon and Eleanor Glueck, who spent decades in their search for the causes of delinquency, believed in multiple causation. In one of their later studies, *Family Environment and Delinquency* (1962), they provided many illustrations of the complex ways in which psychological, sociological, and biological factors might combine in one individual to produce delinquency.

Study of Criminology in the U.S.

After World War I, when crime began to become a major problem in the United States, and the study of criminology took its place in the universities, Frank Tannenbaum (1893–1969) and Nathaniel F. Cantor (1898–1957) wrote two of the first textbooks on criminology: *Crime and the Community* (1938) and *Crime and Society, an Introduction to Criminology* (1939). Later authors were Herbert A. Bloch and Gilbert Geis, *Man, Crime and Society* (1962); Richard R. Korn (together with W. McCorkle), *Criminology and Penology* (1959), gave a well balanced description of the different factors in crime causation, as did Ben Karpman (1886–1962) in *Case Studies in the Psychopathology of Crime* (1947^2). Other significant contributions to criminology were made by Leonard Savitz, who, in his "Delinquency and Migration" (in *The Sociology of Crime and Delinquency*, ed. by M.E. Wolfgang, et al., 1962, pp. 199–205), emphasized the criminogenic effect of black migration within the United States, and Stephen Schafter, in his *Restitution to Victims of Crime* (1960) and *The Victim and His Criminal* (1968), opened the way for the development of a new chapter – victimology – in the framework of modern criminology.

Other criminologists gave new insight into problems of penology and prison reform, among them, Joseph *Eaton in his *Stone Walls Not a Prison Make* (1962) and Sol Rubin in his *Crime and Juvenile Delinquency* (1970^3). The latter book criticized the very long prison sentences meted out in the United States and the way in which many of the prisons in that country were run. The role of the community in preventing crime was stressed by Solomon *Kobrin (1910–1996) in his research on the "Chicago Area Project, a 25-Year Assessment" (*Annals of the American Academy of Political and Social Science* (March 1959), 19–29).

The first significant work to determine systematically what psychodynamic theory could contribute to the development of more effective correctional methods was done by the New York State Department of Corrections in the late 1960s. It was carried out at the Diagnostic and Treatment Center of the Dannemora State Hospital at Clinton Prison, New York, under the direction of Ludwig Fink, a psychiatrist. He established a therapeutic community of 100 persistent offenders, subdivided into two units of 50, who received intensive psychotherapeutic treatment – in groups of ten – and in community meetings and psychodrama sessions.

British Contribution to Criminology

Much progress was made in Britain by Jewish criminologists. The great centers of criminological and penological study were all established by scholars who had emigrated from Europe. Hermann Mannheim established the first chair in criminology in the United Kingdom at the London School of Economics and was one of the founders of the Institute for the Scientific Study and Treatment of Delinquency in London. Mannheim and other outstanding psychoanalysts, including Anna *Freud, the daughter of Sigmund Freud, made notable contributions to the study of crime. Max *Gruenhut (1893–1964) was the first to be appointed to a chair in criminology at Oxford University.

Criminology in Ereẓ Israel

Criminological study in Mandatory Palestine and later in Israel grew out of the experience of those engaged in correctional research. Menachem Amir of the Hebrew University's Institute of Criminology published a bibliography in English and Hebrew containing an impressive list of Israel writers on criminology and the titles of their contributions during recent decades. Juvenile delinquency and its treatment under the mandate and in Israel is described in detail by E. Millo in *Child and Youth Welfare in Israel* (1960). The prison system in Israel's early years in the light of the Israel humanitarian ethos is analyzed fully by J.W. Eaton in the monograph *Prisons in Israel* (1964). He notes the existence of Massiyahu camp for more trusted inmates – a minimum custody facility. Between 1970 and 1988 nine volumes of *Israel Studies in Criminology* were published. A later publication was *Crime and Criminal Justice in Israel: Assessing the Knowledge Base Toward the Twenty-First Century* (1998), edited by Robert R. Friedmann.

The dominant approach to the understanding and treatment of the offender was psychological, psychiatric and especially psychoanalytical. Research was centered in the Hebrew University Institute of Criminology, the director of which was Israel *Drapkin, and at the Institute of Criminology and Criminal Law at Tel Aviv University, headed by Shlomo Shoham (1929–). Personality and psychopathic disorders in various origin-groups in Israel and crimes of violence in relation to the period of immigration is discussed by Louis Miller in *Social Psychiatry and Epidemiology of Mental Ill Health in Israel* (1967). In the first years of the State, strenuous efforts were made in the correctional field, including probation, after-care, and prison services, to set up and develop mental hygiene teams, consisting of psychiatrists, psychologists, and social caseworkers, who cooperated in the diagnostic and treatment process of offenders.

[Zvi Hermon]

CRIMSON WORM, biblical *tola'at shani* (Heb. תּוֹלַעַת שָׁנִי), which yields a dye, called in the Bible *shani, tola, karmil*, and in rabbinic literature *zehorit*, which was extracted from the body of the "crimson worm" (*carmine*), the *Kermes biblicus*. A brilliant, beautiful, and fast red dye, it was used for dyeing the curtains of the Tabernacle (Ex. 26:1) and the garments of the high priests (*ibid.*, 39:2); in the purification rites of a leper (Lev. 14:4–6) and of a house affected by leprosy (*ibid.*, 51–52); and it was added to the ashes of the red heifer (Num. 19:6). Crimson-dyed clothes were costly (Lam. 4:5). The Tyrians were experts in the art of crimson dyeing (II Chron. 2:6). Neither the Bible nor rabbinic literature describes the insect from which the crimson dye was extracted. The Tosefta (Men. 9:16) merely states that the best kind of crimson comes from "a mountain worm." Its color is "neither red nor yellow … it is crimson" (PdRK 98). According to Josephus, crimson symbolizes fire (Ant., 3:183; Wars, 5:213). The "crimson worm" is the "shield louse" which generally lives on a species of oak *Quercus coccifera*. In Israel, where this tree does not grow, the shield louse is found on the branches of the oak *Quercus ithaburensis*. There are two species of the insect, *Kermes nahalali* and *Kermes greeni*. In the early spring, when the females filled with red eggs and became pea-shaped, the red dye was squeezed out of them. The use of crimson dye was widespread in Ereẓ Israel until the cactus from Mexico was introduced at the end of the 17th century. The coccus, which lives on this plant, yields a red dye in larger quantities. Up to the end of the 19th century crimson dye was still used, but with the invention of synthetic dyes, it became obsolete.

BIBLIOGRAPHY: S. Bodenheimer, *Ha-Ḥai be-Arẓot ha-Mikra*, 2 (1956), 310–3; J. Feliks, in: *Sinai*, 38 (1955), 94–99.

[Jehuda Feliks]

°CRINAGORAS OF CARYSTUS (fl. 240 B.C.E.), elegaic poet, author of an epigram (*Palatine Anthology*, 7:645) which speaks of the philosopher Philostratus reposing under a monument on the banks of the Nile visible as far as Judea (the reading "Judea" is probable but not certain).

°CRISPIN, GILBERT (**Gislebertus**; c. 1046–1117), abbot of Westminster (England). A disciple of *Anselm of Canterbury, Crispin dedicated to him the record of a religious discussion which he had at Westminster with a Jew from Mainz with whom he had business connections. The discussion probably took place before 1096. The name of the Jew is not mentioned. Crispin commends his profound knowledge of both Jewish and Christian literature. The discussion recorded is greatly superior to others of this kind extant, in the courtesy and high intellectual standard it displays. In no other instance is so much space given to the Jewish arguments, which are often embarrassing to Crispin. The Jewish interlocutor refers to passages in the New Testament and reproaches Christians with abandoning observance of the Law. He also objects to the cult of the saints and pictorial representations of God. If the Christians refer to Isaiah and claim to find there the announcement of the coming of the Messiah, they must also agree that he has not arrived yet because the messianic era as described by the prophet (Isa. 2:4) has in no way been inaugurated. In his letter to Anselm, Crispin claims that, despite these objections, a Jew who was present at the discussion asked to be baptized. Crispin's record was rewritten during the 12th century, but in a rancorous tone and diluting the force of the Jewish arguments.

BIBLIOGRAPHY: J. Armitage, *Gilbert Crispin, Abbot of Westminster* (1911); B. Blumenkranz (ed.), *Gisleberti Crispini Disputatio Iudei et Christiani* (1956); ON THIS EDITION, SEE: Werblowsky, in: JJS, 11 (1960), 69–77; SEE ALSO: B. Blumenkranz, *Les auteurs chrétiens latins du Moyen Age* (1963), 279–87.

[Bernhard Blumenkranz]

CROCODILE (Heb. תַּנִּין or תַּנִּים), the largest surviving reptile, with a length of as much as 23 feet (7 m.) or more. The *tannim* or *tannin* of the Bible refers to the Nile crocodile (*Crocodylus niloticus*) and also to gigantic mythological animals said to have rebelled at the time of the creation against their Creator and hence to have been punished with extinction (Isa. 51:9; Ps. 74:13–14; Job 7:12); similar myths are found also in Ugaritic epics. The reference may be to prehistoric reptiles, remains of whose bones have been uncovered in various places in the Middle East region and which may have stirred the imagination of the ancients and formed the basis of these legends. Footprints of a prehistoric reptile have been discovered at Bet Zayit in the vicinity of Jerusalem. *Tannim* also refers to another gigantic, non-reptilian animal, the whale (cf. Lam. 4:3), usually called *leviathan, which word, however, also denotes a crocodile, as in Job 40:25–41:26, where the description, although poetical and mythical, applies to a crocodile. Thus, it is stated there that the leviathan has a tongue, a nose, enormous teeth, and shining eyes. Its head and neck are covered with protective scales impenetrable to spears. It is fearless and attacks every other animal. Mention is also made there of a bird that plays with it and of the covenant between them: this may refer to the crocodile plover (*Pluvianus aegyptius*) which pecks at the throat and teeth of the crocodile. This reptile was sacred to the Egyptians; hundreds of embalmed crocodiles have been found in cemeteries specially set aside for them. Plutarch relates that the Egyptians ascribed to them powers of prescience in that the female lays its eggs on the high water mark of the Nile. As it was a sacred animal, the Egyptians protected it, and it multiplied undisturbed in the country's waters. The sign performed by Aaron with his rod which became a *tannin* – a crocodile – (Ex. 7:9–10) may have been intended as a protest against its sanctity. Ezekiel calls Pharaoh king of Egypt "the great *tannim* that lieth in the midst of his rivers" (Ezek. 29:3; cf. Isa. 27:1), while Jeremiah (51:34) likens the king of Babylonia to a crocodile that preys on human beings. No longer found in the Nile, the crocodile is at present indigenous only in Central Africa. At the end of the 19th century crocodiles were still found in Ereẓ Israel, and a river in the Sharon is called Naḥal ha-Tanninim.

BIBLIOGRAPHY: Lewysohn, Zool, 220 no. 271; F.S. Bodenheimer, *Animal and Man in Bible Lands* (1960), 65; J. Feliks, *Animal World of the Bible* (1962), 94–95.

[Jehuda Feliks]

CROHMĂLNICEANU, OVID S. (**Moïse Cahn**; 1921–2000), Romanian literary critic. An authority on Marxist aesthetics, Crohmălniceanu was, during the 1950s and the 1960s, an authoritative literary critic and editor of important literary periodicals, preaching the ideology of socialist realism. Afterwards he successfully passed beyond this phase and gained prestige as an excellent analyst of modern and contemporary Romanian literature. He published a three-volume synthesis of Romanian literature between the two world wars (*Literatura română între cele două războaie mondiale*,1967–75), based on his courses as professor of Romanian literature at the Bucharest University. Another book, *Literatura română și expresionismul* (1971), is an original exploration of the expressionist traces in 20th-century Romanian literature. From 1992 he lived in Berlin. A book published after his death deals with the contribution of many Jewish writers and artists (e.g., Tristan *Tzara, Marcel *Janco, Benjamin *Fondane, Ilarie *Voronca, Sașa *Pană) to the Romanian avant garde movement (*Evreii în mișcarea de avangardă românească*, 2001).

BIBLIOGRAPHY: A. Mirodan, *Dicționar neconvențional al scriitorilor evrei de limbă română*,1 (1986), 425–33; *Dicționarul general al literaturii române*, 2 (2004), 489–92.

[Leon Volovici (2nd ed.)]

CROHN, BURRILL BERNARD (1884–1983), U.S. physician. Crohn was born in New York City and graduated as an M.D. from Columbia University College of Physicians and Surgeons (1906). He was gastro-enterologist and head of the department of gastro-enterology at New York's Mount Sinai Hospital. There he described the chronic inflammatory diseases of the ileum (terminal small intestine) termed regional ileitis (1932) or Crohn's disease and of the colon (1938) termed granulomatous colitis and also named after him. These remain major medical problems. Crohn was prominent in Jewish charitable causes.

[Michael Denman (2nd ed.)]

CROISSET, FRANCIS DE, pen name of Frantz Wiener (1877–1937), playwright. Born in Brussels, Croisset made his reputation in Paris, where he wrote many plays of the "boulevard" type, notably *Qui trop embrasse* (1899); *Chérubin* (1901), which was set to music by Jules Massenet; *Le paon* (1904); and *Le coeur dispose* (1912). He also wrote some plays in collaboration with R. de Flers; *Nos marionettes* (1928; *Our Puppet Show*, 1929); essays on the drama; a novel, *La Dame de Malacca* (1935; *Lady in Malacca*, 1936); and travel books such as *Le dragon blessé* (1936; *The Wounded Dragon*, 1937) on the Far East.

CROIX, LA, French Catholic daily newspaper, founded in 1883 by Father Bailly and sponsored by the Assumptionist Fathers. The newspaper was a success from its start and acquired considerable popular influence. Its daily circulation rose to 11,000 in 1889, 140,000 in 1890, and 180,000 in 1893 – more than double that of *Le Figaro*. By 1894 there also were 104 provincial supplements, and 2,000,000 copies of various *La Croix* publications were printed weekly. Always anti-democratic, *La Croix* also became violently antisemitic. In 1886 *La Croix* was the first newspaper to praise *La France Juive* and its author E. *Drumont. By 1890 it had become as vociferous as Drumont's *Libre Parole* in its daily attacks against Jew's, Protestants, and Masons, and after Alfred *Dreyfus' arrest in 1894 it became even more intemperate. Following the partially successful appeal of Dreyfus (1899) and the dissolution of the Assumptionist congregation (1900), *La Croix* withdrew from the political scene and returned to essentially religious tasks. *La Croix* continued to be published in Limoges during the German occupation in World War II although its provincial supplements disappeared. Now an evening newspaper published in Paris, *La Croix*, which remains the principal organ of the French Catholic press, avoids antisemitism.

BIBLIOGRAPHY: P. Sorlin, *"La Croix" et les Juifs (1880–1899)* (1967); F.R. Byrnes, *Anti-semitism in Modern France*, 1 (1950), 194–8; G. Hourdin, *La Presse Catholique* (1957).

CROLL, DAVID ARNOLD (1900–1991), Canadian lawyer and politician. Born in Mogilev, Belorussia, Croll was taken to Windsor, Ontario, at the age of three. He practiced law in Windsor from 1925 to 1930 when he was elected mayor of the city. In this office, he earned a reputation for helping the unemployed and homeless; he also successfully led the drive for the amalgamation of several municipalities into one city. In 1934 Croll entered the Ontario Legislature as Liberal member for Walkerville and was appointed to hold three cabinet portfolios in the Mitchell Hepburn government: minister of labor, public welfare, and municipal affairs. He resigned from the cabinet in April 1937 in protest against the Hepburn government's refusal to recognize the Oshawa automobile workers union, then on strike against General Motors. He was quoted as saying, "I'd rather walk with the strikers than ride with Mitch Hepburn." Immediately after the outbreak of World War II, Croll volunteered with the Essex Scots regiment of the Canadian Army and, while serving in Europe, rose to the rank of lieutenant colonel. Also while in the military, he wrote a handbook on despatch riding. In 1945 he was elected to the Canadian House of Commons for the Toronto riding of Spadina, then at the heart of Toronto's downtown, Yiddish-speaking Jewish community. In 1955 Croll became the first Jews ever appointed to the Senate of Canada. He served on the Canadian delegation to the United Nations at the time of the Suez crisis in 1956. A familiar figure in Canadian Jewish life, Croll was an enthusiastic supporter of the State of Israel, the Histradrut, and the Israel labor movement.

[Ben Kayfetz / Gerald Tulchinsky (2nd ed.)]

°**CROMWELL, OLIVER**, Lord Protector of *England, 1653–58. Cromwell was largely responsible for the readmission of the Jews to England. His puritan views, based largely upon the Old Testament, and his tolerant nature predisposed him to regard the Jews with favor; he was also quick to realize the material advantages of readmitting them. It was to Cromwell that *Manasseh Ben Israel presented his "Humble Addresses," petitions concerning the return of the Jews to England, and he was responsible for convening the Whitehall Conference in December 1655. When it became apparent that readmission would only be recommended under the most unfavorable conditions, Cromwell dissolved the conference after its fourth meeting. It was expected that he would issue a favorable reply to Manasseh Ben Israel on his own authority. However, in view of public opinion, Cromwell preferred to adopt an informal arrangement. The London Marrano community had to be satisfied with a favorable reply to a modest petition in which they merely requested authorization for the establishment of a cemetery and continuance of their freedom of worship. Cromwell's personal sympathies were manifested in the pension of £100 granted to Manasseh Ben Israel. His favorable attitude toward the Jews was so marked that, according to his enemies, Jews regarded him as their Messiah.

BIBLIOGRAPHY: L. Wolf, *Manasseh ben Israel's Mission to Oliver Cromwell* (1901); Roth, in: JHSET, 11 (1924–27), 112–42; Roth, England, 156ff.; idem, *Essays and Portraits in Anglo-Jewish History* (1962), 86–107. **ADD. BIBLIOGRAPHY:** Katz, England, 107–40, index; T.M. Endelman, *The Jews of Britain, 1656–2000* (2002), 15–27; E. Samuel, "Oliver Cromwell and the Readmission of the Jews to England in 1656," in: *At the Ends of the Earth: Essays on the History of the Jews in England and Portugal,* (2004), 179–89; C. Hill, *God's Englishman: Oliver Cromwell and the English Revolution* (1972); ODNB online.

[Cecil Roth]

CRONBACH, ABRAHAM (1882–1965), U.S. Reform rabbi, author, and teacher. Cronbach was born in Indianapolis, Indiana. He was ordained in 1906 at Hebrew Union College. He served at congregations in South Bend, Indiana (1906–15), and was assistant rabbi of the Free Synagogue, New York, under Rabbi Stephen S. *Wise (1915–17), and at Akron, Ohio (1917–19). He was also Jewish institutional chaplain of Chicago (1919–22). During these years Cronbach developed a passion for social justice, an unshakable belief in pacifism, and a "mutualistic" philosophy embodying ethical relativity and a concept of God as supreme ideal rather than source of power. As professor of Jewish Social Studies at Hebrew Union College from 1922 to 1950, Cronbach influenced a generation of rabbis in the struggle for social justice and peace.

Cronbach, an individualist, befriended the murderer Nathan *Leopold, was rabbi to the convicted American spies for the Soviet Union Julius and Ethel Rosenberg, and supported the anti-Zionist American Council for Judaism. As such he was under constant criticism by opponents. Although he was a Hebrew scholar, he was anti-Hebraist, opposing the use of Hebrew in American Jewish religious life.

Among his many writings are *Jewish Peace Book for Home and School* (1932), on the heritage of Judaism's pursuit of peace; *Judaism for Today* (1954), his philosophy in simple and popular terms; *Realities of Religion* (1957), his philosophy of radical empiricism; *Stories Made of Bible Stories* (1961), biblical stories rewritten to conform to his philosophy of pacifism and brotherhood; *Reform Movements in Judaism* (1963); and "Autobiography" (AJA, 2 (1959), 3–81).

BIBLIOGRAPHY: R.A. Seigel, *Biography of Abraham Cronbach* (unpublished M.A. thesis, Hebrew Union College, Cincinnati, 1965); A. Vorspan, *Giants of Justice* (1960), 201–99. **ADD. BIBLIOGRAPHY:** S.E. Karff, *Hebrew Union College-Jewish Institute of Religion at 100* (1976).

[Robert A. Seigel]

CRONENBERG, DAVID (1943–), Canadian filmmaker. Cronenberg was born in Toronto, Ontario. He showed an early interest in science, particularly the study of insects, and a skill for writing science fiction and fantasy short stories. He began experimental filmmaking while attending the University of Toronto, where he graduated at the top of his class with a degree in literature. He produced low-budget, psychologically intense horror films in the 1970s and mass entertainment horror/science fiction genre films in the 1980s. The release of *Dead Ringers* (1988) and *The Naked Lunch* (1991) increased Cronenberg's stature and gained him international recognition and awards. In 1999 he was chosen to chair the prestigious Cannes Film Festival jury. Cronenberg's themes explore society's collective unconscious and the boundaries of human physiology, sexuality, and psychology. Among film experts, he is considered a true auteur. His films defy easy classification; they shock, repel, provoke, and fascinate in equal measure. Throughout his career, Cronenberg wrote, directed, and produced many of his films. He also worked as an editor and cinematographer as well as acting in his own and other directors' films. He is among the very few directors who remained in Canada to make films yet achieved a solid international reputation. His films received numerous Canadian Genies as well as awards from the New York Film Critics Circle, the Cannes Film Festival, and the Toronto International Film Festival. In 1997 Cronenberg became an Officer of the Order of Arts and Letters in France. Additional films he directed are *Shivers* (1975), *Rabid* (1977), *The Brood* (1979), *Scanners* (1981), *Videodrome* (1983), *The Dead Zone* (1983), *The Fly* (1986), *M. Butterfly* (1993), *Crash* (1996), *eXistenZ* (1999), and *Spider* (2002).

BIBLIOGRAPHY: W. Beard, *The Artist As Monster: The Cinema of David Cronenberg* (2001); D. Cronenberg and C. Rodley (ed.), *Cronenberg on Cronenberg* (1997); S. Grunberg, *David Cronenberg* (2004); P. Handling et al., *The Shape of Rage: The Films of David Cronenberg* (1983).

[Paula Draper (2nd ed.)]

CROOL, JOSEPH (1760–1829), British scholar and writer; of Hungarian birth. Of wide if eccentric learning, he was rabbi at Manchester and Nottingham, where he published *The Importance and Necessity of a More General Knowledge of the Hebrew Language* (1805). He later taught Hebrew to members of Cambridge University. His *Restoration of Israel* (1812) resulted in controversy between him and the Anglican cleric Thomas Scott, who issued an elaborate answer (London, 1814). Crool was opposed to Jewish emancipation, fearing that it would lead to assimilation and on this subject wrote *The Last Generation* (Cambridge, 1829) and *The Fifth Empire, delivered in a discourse by Thirty-Six Men…* (London, 1829), and remained a loyal Orthodox Jew. His anti-emancipation writings were widely cited by Christian opponents of Jewish emancipation in Britain.

BIBLIOGRAPHY: H.P. Stokes, *Studies in Anglo-Jewish History* (1913), 231f.; JC (June 30, 1848); *Cambridge Independent Press* (June 11, 1848); Roth, Mag Bibl, index; C. Roth, *Rise of Provincial Jewry* (1950), 83, 87. **ADD. BIBLIOGRAPHY:** Katz, England, 377–79.

[Cecil Roth]

°CROWFOOT, JOHN WINTER (1873–1959), British Orientalist. Educated at Marlborough and Oxford, Crowfoot served as director of the British School of Archaeology in Jerusalem from 1927 to 1935 and as chairman of the Palestine Exploration Fund from 1945 to 1950. He excavated in the Tyropoeon Valley, Jerusalem, (1927–29), Jerash in Transjordan (1928–30), and Samaria-Sebaste (1931–33, 1935). Crowfoot was the author of *Churches at Jerash* (1931), *Churches at Bosra and Samaria-Sebaste* (1937), *Samaria-Sebaste* (3 vols., 1938–57), and *Early Churches in Palestine* (1941).

His wife, GRACE MARY CROWFOOT (1878–1958), was a specialist in the archaeology of pottery, glass, textiles, basketry, and mats. She contributed to the *Oxford History of Technology* (ed. by C. Singer, 5 vols., 1954–58) and also wrote about the linen wrappings of the Dead Sea Scrolls. She was the joint author (with Louise Baldensperger) of *From Cedar to Hyssop* (1935), a study of the folklore of Palestinian plants. Their daughter, Dorothy Crowfoot Hodgkin (1910–1994), was awarded the Nobel Prize in chemistry in 1964.

ADD. BIBLIOGRAPHY: ODNB online.

[Michael Avi-Yonah]

CROWN, HENRY (Henry Krinsky; 1896–1990), U.S. business executive. Crown was born and raised in Chicago, the son of Latvian immigrants. He left school at the age of 15 and went to work. After he was fired from his $4 a week job as a shipping clerk for dispatching a load of sand instead of gravel, he and his brothers, Sol and Irving, founded a materials supply firm. Through hard work and sound business practices, they steadily built up their company. Crown became the treasurer (1916), then the president (1921), and then chairman of the board (1941) of the multimillion-dollar Material Service Corporation in Chicago, which had become the largest materials firm in the world. During World War II Crown served as a colonel in the Corps of Engineers. The Crowns' corporation operated its own quarries, mines, lime and cement plants, and gravel and sand pits. Its fleet of tugboats traveled across Chicago's waterways, and the company's army of cement trucks churned through the streets on a daily basis. In 1959 the company merged into the General Dynamics Corporation, of which Crown served as director. He was also a director of several large firms, including Chicago Rock Island & Pacific Railroad, Hilton Hotels International, and was president and owner of the Empire State Building.

He diversified his business interests to include defense contracting, railroads, mining, farming, recreation, and trucking. With his disciplined risk-taking and financial acumen, he maximized on these investments to create Henry Crown and Company, one of the leading private investment groups in the U.S.

Crown served as director of the Chicago Jewish Welfare Fund and was a member of the Horatio Alger Association of Distinguished Americans.

The Crown family owned and managed operating companies and real estate investments. It also maintained significant investments in a broad range of publicly traded corporations, with extensive board of directors representation that includes General Dynamics, Hilton Hotels, Bank One, The Maytag Corporation, Alltel, and Sara Lee.

The Crown family established a worldwide reputation for philanthropy, donating funds to support academic and research programs. Some of the places and projects that bear Henry Crown's legacy include Henry Crown Field House on the University of Chicago campus; the Henry Crown Sports Pavilion /Norris Aquatic Center at Northwestern University; the Henry Crown Space Center Museum of Science and Industry in Chicago; the Aspen Institute's Henry Crown Fellowship Program, which seeks to develop the next generation of corporate and civic-minded leaders; the Henry Crown Symphony Hall and the Rebecca Crown Auditorium at the Jerusalem Theater; and the Henry Crown Institute of Business Research in Israel, under the auspices of Tel Aviv University's Faculty of Management, which aims to support research pertaining to business administration and management, with an emphasis on Israeli economy and society.

[Ruth Beloff (2nd ed.)]

CROWNS, DECORATIVE HEADDRESSES, AND WREATHS.

In the Bible

A crown is an ornate headdress which serves as a symbol of monarchy, high office, or some other position which marks its wearer as a distinguished person. Three different terms are used for such a headdress in the Bible: *nezer, ʿaṭarah* and *keter*. The first, *nezer* (from *nzr*), is also used to describe someone who is "God's chosen" by virtue of self-abnegation or complete devotion to worship (see *Nazirite). In biblical poetry the term is used to emphasize the dignity and independence of Israel. The loss of this *nezer* can symbolize the destruction of national and religious sovereignty, "Cut off your hair (Heb. *nizrekh*), and cast it away," (Jer. 7:29). The second term, *ʿaṭarah* (the root *ʿtr* means "to encircle"), is not used exclusively to indicate social position. Thus, in the phrase, "Beautiful crowns upon their heads" (Ezek. 23:42), it merely indicates an elaborate headdress. In other contexts, however, it is synonymous with the royal crown, e.g., "He took the crown of their king from his head" (II Sam. 12:30). The term also applies to the crown worn by a queen (Jer. 13:18), nobles (Esth. 8:15), and the bridegroom at his wedding (Song 3:11), and is often used in the Bible as a metaphor for anything conferring honor or authority, such as grandchildren (Prov. 17:6), or wisdom (Prov. 14:24). In Ezekiel 21:31 *ʿaṭarah* appears as part of the priestly headgear. *ʿAṭarot* were apparently made of precious materials – gold, silver, expensive cloths, and skins – as indicated in Zechariah 6:11, "Take from them silver and gold, and make crowns…." In biblical poetry, *ʿaṭarah* represents personal pride, "A good wife is a crown to her husband" (Prov. 12:4); and like the term *nezer* it also symbolizes national glory, "You shall also be a crown of beauty in the hand of the Lord…" (Isa. 62:3). The third term, *keter* (from *ktr*, "to encircle"), appears only in the Book of Esther where it clearly denotes royalty, "He set the royal crown on her head and made her queen…" (Esth. 2:17).

Excavations in Ereẓ Israel have yielded some decorative headdresses mainly of the *ʿaṭarah* type. Such a headdress of the Israelite period, made of gold, and probably originally attached to a strip of cloth meant to be bound around the head, was found in Tell Jemmeh (Yurza of the Egyptian sources?; W.M.G. Petrie, *Gerar* (1928), pl. 1:1). A gold band used as *ʿaṭarah* was also found in Gaza (Petrie et al., *Ancient Gaza*, 4 (1934), pl. 14). An ivory palette on which is carved a woman wearing a decorative headdress, possibly of Assyrian origin and dating from the Israelite period, was found in Megiddo (G. Loud, *The Megiddo Ivories* (1939), pl.4).

[Ze'ev Yeivin]

In Post-Biblical Literature

The technical distinction between crowns and wreaths – the former designating a symbol of royalty and of majesty, made of gold, and the latter signifying a circlet of leaves and twigs worn as a festive symbol – is often confused in talmudic literature, the two terms being used, sometimes indiscriminately, as synonymous. Thus the Talmud makes the Mishnah (Avot 4:5), "make not of them [the words of the Torah] a wreath [*ʿaṭarah*] to magnify thyself therewith," to refer to "him who makes [worldly] use of the crown [*keter*] of the Torah" (Ned. 62a).

By transference the crown was made the symbol of dignity in other cases, and R. Simeon states, "there are three crowns, the crown of Torah, the crown of priesthood, and the royal crown, but the crown of a good name excels them all" (Avot 4:13; cf. the elaborate treatment of this passage in ARN2 4, 3b).

The *aggadah* places a crown on the head of the Almighty, the "Supreme King of Kings." The archangel Sandalfon stands behind the divine chariot and wreathes a crown for his Maker, and pronouncing the divine name over it, places it on His head (Ḥag. 13b). The Midrash states that despite the fact that prayers take place at different times in different synagogues, when they are finished "the angel appointed over prayers takes all the prayers uttered in all the synagogues and makes of them a wreath which he places on the head of the Holy One, blessed be He" (Ex. R. 21:4). Although the word in that passage is *ʿaṭarah*, it is the basis of the *Kedushah* in the *Musaf* prayers of Sabbaths and festivals, according to the Sephardi ritual: "The hosts of angels above, together with Thy people Israel assembled below, make Thee a crown, O Lord our God." That wreath or crown the Holy One is destined to place on the head of the Messiah (*ibid.*, 8:1). The phrase *keter Torah* ("crown of the Torah") is also used for the ornament placed as an embellishment on top of the scroll of the law (see *Ceremonial Art, Torah Ornaments). The phrase *keter Torah* was particularly apposite because the numerical value of *keter* – כתר – is 620, which represents the 613 biblical commandments and the seven Noaḥide laws which constitute the primary message of the Torah. On this basis David Vital published his Keter Torah listing these commandments in Constantinople, 1536 (D. Sperber, *Minhagei Yisrael* 2, Jerusalem 1991, pp. 112–13).

The wreath belongs to a lower category of distinction than the crown, though like the crown, it has its place in otherworldly as in worldly matters. "In the world to come there is neither eating nor drinking but the righteous sit with wreaths on their heads" (Ber. 17a). Wreaths were worn on all joyous occasions. In the Apocrypha they are mentioned as being made of rosebuds (Wisd. 2:8) and of olives (Judith 15:13). In Temple times it was the universal custom for both brides and bridegrooms to don them, but according to the Mishnah the custom, with regard to bridegrooms, was abolished after the destruction of the Temple ("during the war of Vespasian") as a sumptuary measure or sign of mourning (Sot. 9:14). In the Talmud (Sot. 49b) Rav states that the prohibition applied only to a wreath made of "salt and brimstone," which Rashi explains as a crown made of a block of salt upon which figures were traced in brimstone. A wreath of roses or myrtle, however, was permitted. His colleague, R. Samuel, forbade the latter but permitted wreaths of reeds and rushes, while R. Levi forbade those. After the "war of Quietus" the prohibition was extended to brides, whose wreath was "a golden city" (Sot. 49a), probably a golden crown with a design of Jerusalem (cf. Shab. 59a). According to Shabbat 7d this was a three-layered gold crown (not wreath) (Abramson, *Leshonenu*, 29 (1965), pp. 75–76; cf. D. Sperber, *Leshonenu*, 40 (1976), p. 168), which R. Akiva was credited with having given to his wife. Nevertheless, at least in Babylonia the custom continued for brides to wear them. Mar, son of R. Ashi, explained to Ravina, who queried the correctness of his making a garland for his daughter, that the prohibition applied to bridegrooms (Git. 7a). The flowers used for making crowns and garlands were called in Greek στεφανþματα (Hesychius), and this term in medieval times was used for nuptials (אישטיפנומטא, responsum of Isaiah of

Trani, no. 39, Bari XIII cent.), indicating that the custom of garlanding the bride continued to be in use.

In the Mishnah (Ket. 2:1) it is stated that if a married woman could prove that on her wedding day she "went out with a *hinnumah*," it was accepted as evidence that she was a virgin. According to one opinion in the Talmud (Ket. 17b) the *hinnumah* is a myrtle wreath, and according to another a veil, but a suggestion has been made that it means "dyed with henna" (Bonfil).

Not only human beings were garlanded with wreaths. At the procession of the first fruits both horns of the sacrificial ox were garlanded with a wreath of olive leaves, and a garland consisting of either the seven species, according to R. Akiva or, according to R. Simeon b. Nanos, other species, was placed around the fruits themselves (Bik. 3:3 and 9). Wreaths of corn, which were used to adorn idols (cf. Acts 14:13), were forbidden for use by Jews (Av. Zar. 4:2).

[Louis Isaac Rabinowitz / S. David Sperling (2nd ed.)]

BIBLIOGRAPHY: IN THE BIBLE: M.G. Houston, *Ancient Egyptian, Mesopotamian and Persian Costume and Decoration* (1954²), figs. 1, 6, 13, 15, 17, 18, 27–32, 38–40, 45, 128a, 129, 138, 140, 148, pls. 2, 4, 7, 9; Pritchard, Pictures, 72, 296, 297; S.M. Paul, in: iej, 17 (1967), 259–63. IN POST-BIBLICAL LITERATURE: Krauss, Tal Arch, 1 (1910), 185f., 203 (no. 93); Bonfil, in: *Hagut Ivrit be-Eiropah*, ed. by M. Zohori and A. Tartakower (1969), 57–70. **ADD. BIBLIOGRAPHY:** H. Feuchtwanger, "The Coronation of the Virgin and the Bride," in: *Jewish Art*, 12/13 (1986–87), 213–24.

CRUCIFIXION, mode of execution by fastening the condemned to two crossed beams. Being the form of death to which *Jesus of Nazareth was sentenced by the Roman governor Pontius Pilate between 27 and 36 C.E., crucifixion subsequently acquired momentous historical, theological, and legal significance, providing subject matter for research and discussion until the present day. Its origins cannot be traced with precision; it is thought to have preceded hanging, of which there is early evidence (see *Capital Punishment). Hanging may have been introduced as a more humane and lenient mode of execution than crucifixion; at any rate hanging superseded crucifixion in most countries of Europe, after crucifixion had been abolished by the Roman emperor Constantine in the fourth century because of its Christian symbolism. In non-Christian, especially Far Eastern countries, it was practiced until early in the 19th century. Beheading was also practiced by the Romans (e.g., the beheading of John the Baptist), and it was apparently a more dignified procedure of execution because of the swiftness of the death experience as opposed to the prolonged suffering that crucified individuals endured. Stoning was the preferred method of execution practiced by Jews in the first century and earlier (Lev. 20:2, 27; 24:16; Num. 15:35; Deut. 21:21).

There are reports of crucifixions from Assyrian, Egyptian, Persian, Greek, Punic, and Roman sources. It has been said to have first been imported into ancient Israel by the Persians (cf. Ezra 6:11), but there is no report of a single instance of a crucifixion under the powers conferred on Ezra. If the hangings reported in the book of Esther (7:10, etc.) were crucifixions, they were carried out in Persia, where crucifixions seem to have been customary. Crucifixion was the standard Roman mode of execution for non-Roman criminals and enemies of the state, and hence was practiced on a large scale in Judea under the Roman occupation. The extent of such crucifixions is demonstrated by the legal rules which had to be elaborated to meet contingencies. As the exact time of death was not ascertainable, the fact that a man was seen hanging on a cross was not sufficient evidence of his death (Yev. 16:3). It might be otherwise when wild beasts or birds had already attacked him at vital parts of the body (Yev. 120b). The reason given for the rule that the crucified cannot be considered dead is that a rich matron may still come along and redeem him (TJ, Yev. 16:3,15c), an indication of the length of time often passing before death ensued, and of the amenability of Roman officers to bribes to save the lives of executed convicts. A man hanging on the cross may order a bill of divorce to be written for his wife. Even if his body has become weak, his mind is presumed to have remained sound (Tosef., Git. 7:1; Git. 70b). On such a bill of divorce being handed to the wife, she may remarry without evidence of death being required. As the blood from a dead body is impure, the question arose as to when the blood of the crucified becomes impure (Oho. 3:5). There is one benefit apparently derived from crucifixions; the nail of a cross is considered by some to have healing effects in cases of swellings or stings, and may therefore be carried around even on a Sabbath (Shab. 6:10; Shab. 67a; TJ, Shab. 6:9, 8c). Similarly, Romans used nails from crosses on which people had been crucified for healing epileptics (Pliny, *Natural History*, 28:36).

Josephus reports many incidents of crucifixion: Antiochus IV crucified Jews in Jerusalem who would not relinquish their faith (Ant., 12:256). Two thousand rebels were crucified by Quintilius Varus (Ant., 17:295). Tiberius Julius Alexander ordered two rebels, sons of *Judah the Galilean, to be crucified (Ant., 20:102). Seven years later (about 52 C.E.) there was another wholesale crucifixion of zealots at the hand of Quadratus (Wars, 2:241); Felix crucified not only zealots and rebels, but also citizens suspected of collaborating with them (Wars, 2:253). Florus had Jewish judges tortured and crucified before his eyes (Wars, 2:306–8). When Jerusalem was besieged, Titus ordered all Jewish prisoners of war to be crucified on the walls of the city and there were as many as 500 crucifixions a day (Wars, 5:449–51). Bassus erected a huge cross on the city wall for the execution of Eleazar, a young Jewish commander, whereupon the Jews surrendered to the Romans to spare Eleazar's life (Wars, 7:201–2). Josephus also reports crucifixions at the hands of the Jewish king Alexander Jannaeus, adding that this act of cruelty was an imitation of gentile usage. While he and his concubines were carousing, he ordered 800 Pharisees to be crucified and their wives and children killed before their eyes (Ant., 13:380–1), an atrocity said to be alluded to in the Qumran commentary on the Book of Nahum (4QpNah

2:13) with the postscript: "such a thing has never before been done in Israel, for the Scripture [Deut. 21:23] designates a man hung up alive as a reproach unto God." The hanging of people on trees (i.e., on wooden crosses) is also referred to in the Temple Scroll (11Q Temple 64.6–13). Some account of the laws and customs of crucifixion is contained in most books on the trial and death of Jesus. This crucifixion could only have taken place after the execution of John the Baptist in 28 C.E. and before the High Priest *Caiaphas had been removed from his position in 36 C.E. Hence, the latest possible date for the final Passover attended by Jesus in Jerusalem must have been in the spring of 36 C.E. The accepted view is that the death of Jesus took place late in the 20s or early in the 30s of the first century. It seems reasonable, therefore, that the crucifixion took place in the year 30 C.E. when Jesus was 36 years of age, and only two years after the beheading of John.

Archaeological evidence of crucifixion in Jerusalem emerged in 1968 during the excavation of a burial cave from the first century C.E. at Givat ha-Mivtar in Jerusalem. In one of the stone burial boxes (ossuaries) were the skeletal remains of a male named Jehohanan, whose right heel bone (*calcaneum*) had been pierced by an iron nail (length 11.5 cm). The anthropological study of these remains suggests that the arms of this individual were tied to the horizontal bars of the cross and that only his feet were nailed.

BIBLIOGRAPHY: H. Fulda, *Das Kreuz und die Kreuzigung* (1878); H. Hentig, *Die Strafe*, 1 (1954), 253ff.; E.G. Hirsch, *Crucifixion from the Jewish Point of View* (1921³); M.B. Saint Edme (E.T. Bourg), *Dictionnaire de la Pénalité*, 1 (Paris, 1824), 310ff.; E. Stauffer, *Jerusalem und Rom im Zeitalter Jesu Christi* (1957), 123ff.; S. Zeitlin, *Who Crucified Jesus?* (1964⁴); T. Mommsen, *Roemisches Strafrecht* (1899, repr. 1955), 918ff.; H. Cohn, *Mishpato u-Moto shel Yeshu ha-Noẓeri* (1968), 132–58; idem, *Reflections on the Trial and Death of Jesus* (1967), 39–49. **ADD. BIBLIOGRAPHY:** J. Hewitt, "The Use of Nails in the Crucifixion," in: HTR, 25 (1932), 2–45; V. Tzaferis, "Jewish Tombs at and near Giv'at ha-Mivtar," in: IEJ, 20 (1970), 18–32; M. Hengel, *Crucifixion in the Ancient World and the Folly of the Message of the Cross* (1977); J. Zias and E. Sekeles, "The Crucified Man from Giv'at ha-Mivtar: A Reappraisal," in: IEJ, 35 (1985), 22–27; W. Edwards et al., "On the Physical Death of Jesus Christ." in: *Journal of the American Medical Association*, 255 (1986), 1455–64; F. Zugibe, "Two Questions About Crucifixion," in: *Bible Review*, 5 (1989), 35–43; J. Zias and J.H. Charlesworth, "Crucifixion: Archaeology, Jesus and the Dead Sea Scrolls," in: J.H. Charlesworth (ed.), *Jesus and the Dead Sea Scrolls* (1992), 273–89.

[Haim Hermann Cohn / Shimon Gibson (2nd ed.)]

CRUMB, ROBERT (1943–), U.S. cartoonist. Born in Philadelphia, Crumb began his art career by drawing greeting cards in Cleveland. He soon began to work with Harvey *Kurtzman, creator of *Mad* magazine, on his post-*Mad* humor magazine, *Help!* When that magazine folded, Crumb moved in 1967 to San Francisco, where he drew comics for underground newspapers. In 1968, with his first wife, Dana, Crumb hawked copies of the first issue of *Zap Comix* from a baby carriage in the hippie Haight-Ashbury neighborhood. Crumb's comics mixed a nostalgia for comics' rich history with a psychedelic exuberance. Crumb became known as the godfather of underground comics when he created the characters Mr. Natural and Fritz the Cat and introduced the catchphrase "Keep on truckin'," which struck a note in the collective hip unconscious. Images of the characters and their odd mode of ambulating were made into merchandise, mostly without permission.

Crumb, who is credited with single-handedly creating the underground comic-book industry, acknowledged having taken LSD and other drugs in the 1960s and 1970s when he produced what he says is his best known work: the "Keep on truckin'" graphic, which continues to be seen on mud flaps; his cover for the album *Cheap Thrills* by Big Brother and the Holding Company (featuring Janis Joplin); and Fritz the Cat, who became the star of a full-length animated cartoon made by Ralph *Bakshi. Crumb hated the film.

In 1971, Crumb married Aline Kominsky (1949–). Kominsky-Crumb became known for her very personal comics, which look at life as a humiliating, dehumanizing experience. Her work generally focuses on the plight of a naïve heroine who believes in romance and in the infinite possibility of the world to be a perfect place. The Crumbs moved to Sauve, a small village in the south of France, in 1990. The film *Crumb*, a dark portrait of the cartoonist and his family, directed by Terry Zwigoff, won the top prize for documentaries at the 1995 Sundance Film Festival.

[Stewart Kampel (2nd ed.)]

CRUSADES, military expeditions of the European Christians in the 11th, 12th, and 13th centuries to conquer Ereẓ Israel from the Muslims or to repel their counterattacks. The explicit cause was the reports received from Jerusalem concerning the maltreatment of Christian pilgrims and the manner in which their access to the Holy Places was obstructed. In many of these reports, the malevolence of the Jews was also stressed, so that from the beginning the ground was prepared for including the Jews in the freshly stimulated animosity against the unbelievers: indeed, at the period of the analogous expeditions of French knights to assist the Spanish Christians against the Moors (c. 1065), the Jews of *Narbonne and elsewhere had been attacked notwithstanding the admonitions of Pope *Alexander II. It was originally intended that the crusaders should concern themselves solely with the success of their expedition overseas, without intervening in the affairs of the Christian countries of Europe. However, precisely because the crusaders ignored this stipulation, the Crusade was partially deflected from its initial course, with tragic consequences for the Jews of Europe.

The First Crusade

The Crusade was preached by Pope Urban II at Clermont-Ferrand (subsequently referred to as Har Afel, "the mount of gloom," by Jewish chroniclers of the Crusades) on Nov. 27, 1095, at the close of a council which had convened there. Those who obeyed the call affixed crosses to their outer garments, thus the name *croisés, crociati*, or crusaders. The Jews termed them *to'im* ("[misguided] wanderers"). At the outset, nothing in the proclamation of Urban II seemed to threaten the Jews, but it would appear that the Jews in France sensed danger, since they sent emissaries to the Rhine communities to warn them of the possible threat. The first group of crusaders gathered in France on their way to Germany. They may already have attacked some Jewish communities on their way, possibly in *Rouen, and more certainly in *Lorraine. It was already clear that the crusaders, or at least some of them, were gathering in the Rhine valley in order to follow the traditional route to the Orient along the Rhine and Danube rivers. The community of *Mainz was more troubled about the French communities and thought that those in the Rhineland had no reason for concern on their own account. However, their sense of security was soon to be brutally shaken shortly after the first muster of the crusaders and before the Jewish communities of Germany could take whatever precautions were open to them. The sight of the wealthy Rhenish communities acted as an incentive to the crusaders, who decided to punish "the murderers of Christ" wherever they passed, before their encounter with their official enemies, the Muslims. Soon it was rumored that Godfrey of Bouillon himself had vowed that he would not set out for the Crusade until he had avenged the crucifixion by spilling the blood of the Jews, declaring that he could not tolerate that even one man calling himself a Jew should continue to live.

The first bands of crusaders arrived outside *Cologne on April 12, 1096. For a month they left the Jews in peace, perhaps because the Jews of France had given Peter the Hermit a letter asking the Jewish communities he passed through on his journey to supply him and his followers with all the food they required, in exchange for Peter's undertaking to use his influence in their favor. However, the swelling throng of crusaders, which surpassed all expectations, and the religious frenzy preceding the departure of the army rapidly induced a change of mood which rendered the influence of Peter the Hermit ineffectual. Aware of the inherent danger in the situation, the leaders of the Mainz community hastily dispatched a delegation to Emperor Henry IV, who wrote immediately to the princes, bishops, and counts of the empire to forbid them to harm the Jews. Godfrey himself replied that he had never had any such intention. For their greater security, the communities of Cologne and Mainz each presented him with a gift of 500 pieces of silver, and he promised to leave them in peace, which he did.

Meanwhile, the Crusade had evolved into a ponderous machine made up of various elements: the greater nobility, the lesser nobles such as Count Emicho of Leiningen, and the people. It was the last element which proved particularly receptive to the anti-Jewish slogans spreading rapidly among its ranks and it was less amenable to discipline. Although the bishops and prominent nobles were generally opposed to such ideas, they had no wish to see Christians fight Christians over the Jews. Frequently their assistance to the attacked Jews was passive at the most. It was in the region where the crusaders assembled that violence broke out, in the weeks between Passover and Shavuot. The rioting continued until Tammuz (June–July). On the eighth of Iyyar (May 3, 1096), the crusaders surrounded the synagogue of *Speyer; unable to break into it, they attacked any Jews they could find outside the synagogue, killing eleven of them. One of the victims, a woman, preferring death to conversion, the only choice left open by the crusaders, inaugurated the tradition of freely accepted martyrdom. **Kiddush ha-Shem*, martyrdom for the glory of God, thus became the exemplary answer of Jews threatened in their life and faith by the crusaders. On the 23rd of Iyyar (May 18, 1096) *Worms suffered a similar fate. The crusaders first massacred the Jews who had remained in their houses, then, eight days later, those who had sought an illusory refuge in the bishop's castle. The victims numbered about 800; only a few accepted conversion and survived, the great majority choosing to be killed or suicide rather than apostasy. Hearing of the massacre, the Jews of Mainz asked for the bishop's protection, paying him 400 pieces of silver to this end. When the crusaders, led by Emicho, arrived outside the town on the third of Sivan (May 27, 1096), the burghers hastened to open the gates. The Jews took up arms under the leadership of Kalonymus b. Meshullam. Weakened through fasting, for they had hoped to avert the disaster through exemplary piety, the Jews had to retreat to the bishop's castle; however the latter could do nothing for them, as he himself had to flee before the combined assault of crusaders and burghers. After a brief struggle, a wholesale massacre ensued. More than 1,000 Jews met their deaths, either at the enemy's hands or their own. Those who managed to escape were overtaken; almost no one survived. A comparable disaster occurred in Cologne, where the community was attacked on the sixth of Sivan (May 30, 1096). The bishop dispersed the town's Jews in order to hide them in nearby localities: at Neuss, Wevelinghofen, Eller, Xanten, Mehr, Kerpen, Geldern, and Ellen. The crusaders located them and a bloodbath followed. At *Trier the bishop could not protect his Jews, as he himself had to go into hiding, and he consequently advised them to become Christians. The great majority refused, preferring suicide. At *Regensburg, all the Jews were dragged to the Danube where they were flung into the water and forced to accept baptism. At *Metz, *Prague, and throughout *Bohemia, one massacre followed another. These came to an end when Emicho's crusaders were decisively halted and crushed by the Hungarians, who, incensed by their excesses when they poured through the country, had risen against them. Seeing in this the hand of God, the Jews promptly set about reconstructing their ruined communities. There had been more than 5,000 victims.

The Jews who had been baptized under duress generally continued to practice Judaism in secret. As early as 1097, Emperor Henry IV allowed them openly to return to their former faith, an action which was strongly condemned by the antipope Clement III. Henry also ordered in May 1098 an inquiry into the manner of disposal of the property of massacred Jews in Mainz thus provoking the displeasure of the local bishop. In about 1100, Jews returned to Mainz, but their position was not yet quite secure, and the Jews of the upper town could scarcely communicate with those in the lower. In 1103, Henry IV and the imperial lords finally proclaimed a truce which, among other things, guaranteed the peace of the Jews.

THE CRUSADERS IN EREẒ ISRAEL. Meanwhile, the crusaders had reached *Jerusalem (June 7, 1099), and the siege had begun. The city was captured on July 15, with Godfrey entering it through the Jewish quarter, where inhabitants defended themselves alongside their Muslim neighbors, finally seeking refuge in the synagogues, which were set on fire by the attackers. A terrible massacre ensued; the survivors were sold as slaves, some being later redeemed by Jewish communities in Italy. The Jewish community of Jerusalem came to an end and was not reconstituted for many years, but the Jewish centers in Galilee went unscathed. However, the great community of *Ramleh dispersed, as did that of *Jaffa, so that overall the Jewish community in the Holy Land was greatly diminished.

The Second Crusade

On the loss of Edessa by the crusaders (1144) the West became troubled over the fate of the Latin Kingdom of Jerusalem, and a new Crusade to save it was preached by Pope Eugene III. The popes attempted to encourage the crusaders at the Jews' expense. Innocent III in 1198 ordered that no interest should be chargeable during the absence of crusaders on debts they incurred to the Jews and that anything already received should be returned. Since the return of a crusader was problematical, this restriction when it was observed implied at best the immobility of Jewish capital over prolonged periods, at worst the possibility of total confiscation (which was to become more widespread with the extension from the 13th century of the term "Crusade" to any campaign in any part of the world in which the popes might be politically interested). Naturally, this caused great difficulties to their Jewish creditors. In one way or another, as soon as the Second Crusade was announced, the clouds began to gather once more over the Jews of Europe. As early as the summer of 1146, a Cistercian monk, Radulph, while preaching the Crusade, violently attacked the Jewish communities of the Rhineland, exhorting the crusaders to avenge themselves on "those who had crucified Jesus" before setting out to fight the Muslims. The spiritual leader of the Crusade, *Bernard of Clairvaux, pointed out the theological error in his arguments, strictly forbidding any excess against the Jews, who were to be neither killed nor expelled. Although the anti-Jewish riots had begun before his intervention, he succeeded in preventing them from spreading so that, in the final count, they were far less extensive than those in the First Crusade. The persecution began in Elul (August–September). A few isolated Jews were put to death. At Cologne, the Jews bought the protection of the bishop and managed to find refuge in the fortress of Walkenburg. The bishop even went as far as having the leader of a mob blinded for killing a number of Jews. There were few victims at Worms and at Mainz, but more than 20 at *Wuerzburg. Scores of Jews sought refuge in the castles and the mountains. In Bohemia, about 150 lost their lives, and victims were equally numerous in *Halle and *Carinthia. As in the First Crusade, the community of France suffered less than the Rhineland communities. Jacob b. Meir *Tam was set upon a group of crusaders, who stabbed him in five places in memory of the wounds suffered by Jesus, but he succeeded in escaping with the help of a knight with whom he was acquainted. In England, the Jews were left in peace. Everywhere, Jews who had been converted by force were allowed to return to Judaism undisturbed. By the next summer, order had been restored, and the Jewish communities had everywhere recovered.

In the Holy Land, the Second Crusade had concluded with the conquest of *Ashkelon by the crusaders. *Benjamin of Tudela and *Pethahiah of Regensburg, who visited the crusading kingdom around 1160 and 1180 respectively, found well-established Jewish communities in *Ashkelon, *Ramleh, *Caesarea, *Tiberias, *Acre, among other localities, with scattered individuals living elsewhere: it seems that the Jewish settlement of Jerusalem was restricted to a handful of individuals, though a few years later Judah *Alḥarizi (1216) found a prosperous community there. The *Samaritans seem to have remained undisturbed in *Nablus as well as Ashkelon and Caesarea. It would therefore appear that the warriors of the Second Crusade left the Jewish communities relatively undisturbed.

Meanwhile the Latin Kingdom had begun to crumble under the blows of its enemies. When Jerusalem fell to Saladin in 1187, the Jews of Europe suffered the consequences of this defeat. It had already become habitual to harass the Jews whenever a Crusade was in the offing. In 1182, Emperor Frederick I took the Jews of the empire under his protection, receiving, as was customary, substantial payment for his pains. As soon as the news of the fall of Jerusalem reached Europe, he forbade all anti-Jewish sermons and renewed his promise of protection. At the beginning of 1188, a tragedy was narrowly averted in Mainz. Drawing a lesson from past experience, the Jews of Mainz, Speyer, *Strasbourg, Worms, Wuerzburg, and elsewhere left their towns to seek refuge in the nearby fortified castles. The few Jews who remained at Mainz owed their lives to the Diet which had convened there; and in the course of the proceedings the emperor and his son forbade on direst penalties any interference with the Jews, threatening death to anyone who killed a Jew. These warnings were echoed by the bishops, who threatened excommunication for those who persecuted Jews. All this had cost the Jews of the empire huge sums, and, more than ever before, they became dependent on the favors and the passing whims of their masters.

The Third Crusade and After

In *England, the Third Crusade had the most savage repercussions. England had taken little interest and no part in the first two Crusades, but her zeal was none the less intense when Richard the Lion-hearted decided to take part in person in the third. In January the first abuses struck the port of *Lynn, where the bulk of the Jewish community was massacred. The same occurred in *Norwich and *Stamford. At *Lincoln, the Jews were saved through the intervention of royal agents. The worst outrage took place in *York, where a number of local nobles, in heavy debt to the Jews, seized the opportunity to rid themselves of their burden. When attacked, the Jews took refuge in the Castle Keep, which the guard had opened for them; those who remained in the town were slaughtered. On their refusal to allow access to the keep, the Jews were besieged. On March 16, on the eve of Passover, the rabbi, *Yom Tov b. Isaac of Joigny, realizing that all hope was lost, asked his brethren to choose suicide rather than submit to baptism. First setting fire to their possessions, one after the other killed himself. More than 150 died in this way, and the few survivors were murdered by the mob, who also destroyed the register of debts to the Jews. In *Bury St. Edmunds 57 Jews were put to death. As the king was out of the country, where he neither could nor cared to intervene too vigorously, the perpetrators of the massacres also left England for the Crusade. There is little doubt that the Jews in England lost faith in the prospect of their continued survival in the West. The emigration in 1211 of 300 rabbis from Western Europe to the Holy Land may be connected with this general disillusionment. As the enthusiasm of the masses waned, the Jews in Western Europe were little troubled during the 13th-century Crusades. However, it appears that there was a massacre in central France around 1236 during the preparations for a Crusade; in fact, Pope *Gregory IX accused the crusaders of having slaughtered over 2,500 Jews.

Yet, at the very moment when the great wave of Crusades was ebbing, the Jewish community in France suffered most acutely from a popular Crusade, that of the *Pastoureaux (1320). Forty thousand of these "shepherds," aged on an average around 16 and without any clearly designated leader, marched through France from north to south. Although Pope *John XXII excommunicated all who set forth on this unauthorized march, this did not hinder the new crusaders from hurling themselves at the Jews in the manner of their predecessors. Their savagery was especially marked south of the River Loire, where they destroyed some 120 communities. Hoping to be protected there by the authorities, numbers of isolated Jews and small communities took refuge in the larger towns. Five hundred who had sought safety in the town of *Verdun sur-Garonne found death there. At *Toulouse there were 115 victims. In the *Comtat Venaissin, a direct papal dependency, there were many cases of forced conversion; the subsequent attempt to return to Judaism provoked the prompt intervention of the Inquisition. Meanwhile, the very abuses of the Pastoureaux aroused a violent reaction on the part of the Christian authorities: the governor of *Carcassonne even had some of the ringleaders executed. Those who had crossed the Pyrenees into Spain were routed by James II of Aragon and forced to disperse. Nevertheless, this uprising had struck a savage blow at the Jewish communities in the Midi and northern Spain.

The long era of the Crusades undoubtedly marked a turning point in the history of the Jews in medieval Western Europe. The Church herself was forced to reexamine and define her position of the problem posed by the large-scale persecution of the Jews. Clearly the situation of the Jews prior to the Crusades was not always free from danger: the animosity of the Christians toward the Jews was nothing new and the Crusades did not lead to any reappraisal of Christian doctrine. However, it was probably in the wake of the First Crusade that Pope *Calixtus II (1119–24) promulgated the bull *Sicut Judaeis*, which was renewed after the Second and Third Crusades and on at least five other occasions between 1199 and 1250. It stipulated that although no new privileges should be granted to the Jews, they should not be deprived of a single one of the rights secured to them. Christians should take special care not to endanger the lives of Jews, not to baptize them by force, and not to desecrate their cemeteries. Naturally papal protection was not extended to Jews who plotted against the Christian faith. It was sufficient for the Church to protect them from the excesses of the crusaders, especially since the latter, from the moment they took up the standard of the cross, were themselves placed under the jurisdiction of the Church. The Jews therefore requested the popes to intervene on their behalf: thus *Innocent III ordered the French bishops to take particular care that the crusaders did not harm the Jews. As mentioned, Gregory IX later (1236) accused the crusaders of conspiring to murder the Jews: such a crime committed in the name of sanctity could not be allowed to go unpunished. However, it would appear that these directives were in vain, although it is difficult to assess with any precision the measures relating to the Jews.

The Significance of the Crusades

In the memory of the Jews, the Crusades became the symbol of the opposition between Christianity and Judaism, and the tension aroused by the persecutions was far more severe than that which had existed since the origins of Christianity. The debate ceased to be a theological one, to the extent that this had ever been the case. The Christians saw the Jews as the implacable enemies of their faith and in this climate the *blood libel became widespread. From the 12th century comes the first expression of the idea of a Jewish plot against the Christian world: it was alleged that the Jews had to sacrifice one Christian each year, and held an annual council to decide the site of the sacrifice and the name of the victim. At *Blois in 1171, all members of the Jewish community were burned at the stake following such an accusation, and from the 13th century similar charges were raised in Germany.

The Jewish community found a source of inspiration in the memory of the martyrs. There being no hope of immediate vengeance, the massacre of the innocents was glorified and compared to the sacrifice of Isaac. The suicide of the martyrs was seen as a collective act for the sanctification of the Divine Name. Rather than a bitter memory of cruel affliction, it became an example of true piety and submission to the will of God. For the succeeding generations the martyrs were an object of admiration and even of envy, for they had been the generation whom God had put to the test and they had proved themselves worthy. A man of true faith could achieve no more than to be their equal. It therefore became important for the Jews to cherish the memory of their sacrifice, to retell it, and to be inspired by it. A number of *piyyutim* on the subject were incorporated in the liturgy, especially for the Ninth of *Av. It became customary in Western communities which had been closest to the massacres to recite the prayer of the martyrs, *Av ha-Raḥamim*, on the Sabbath before Shavuot and especially to remember their sacrifice in the fast of the Ninth of Av, which had fallen during the time of the massacres. The period of the counting of the **omer* acquired an especially sorrowful significance.

It was probably this era that gave rise to the custom, originating in Mainz, of reciting in public the deeds of the martyrs on the anniversary of their sacrifice, and recording their names and dates in a **Memorbuch*, which was kept in the synagogue. The most widely known martyrs and the most severely affected communities and regions figured in the *Memorbuecher* of all communities and not only locally. The martyrs became a symbol for the whole people, not just for their own communities; more than simply an object of pride, they became a common ideal in which the whole Jewish community, despite all its humiliations, could find inspiration. Their martyrdom was transformed into victory, for they had defied torture, finding in their faith the necessary strength for preferring death to apostasy. They had chosen death rather than conversion, even though the latter need probably have been only temporary. In their martyrdom lay the very justification of the sufferings of the Jewish people. Spiritual power proved the strongest force of all and the martyrs were seen as a demonstration of the absolute truth of Judaism.

Yet in fact the massacres attendant on the Crusades were far from being the worst persecutions which befell the Jews. The communities destroyed in the Rhine valley were quickly reestablished: Worms, Speyer, Mainz, Cologne, and Treves rapidly regained their former importance. The Jewish community in the kingdom of France proper, or at least in the north, hardly suffered throughout the course of the era. Italy and Spain were almost untouched. In England the royal authorities speedily put an end to local disorders. There is nothing to suggest that during this period the Jews in Western Europe lost their sense of security in the localities where they were living: no great exodus took place in 1096 or in 1146. The majority of those converted by force, at least until the Crusade of the Pastoureaux, were able easily to return to Judaism. It would seem that the actual number of Jews in Western Europe increased in this era and several communities became larger and more populous. For Jewish scholarship the 12th century was one of the most glorious in the West: it was the age of the Tosafists, renowned throughout France and Germany. Personal relationships between Jews and Christians apparently changed little; it was only at the beginning of the 13th century that they took a new turn. It would appear that the Crusades themselves did not play a decisive role in the evolution of the condition of the Jews in Europe. Placed in a larger context, they are only an element in the whole, though a far from negligible one.

At all events, the Crusades revealed the physical danger in which the Jewish communities stood and the impotence of their ecclesiastical protectors to defend them. On the outbreak of an actual attack, they pushed the Jews into the arms of the only powers capable of protecting them: duke, king, or emperor, and these secular protectors considered that they had a duty to protect the Jews only to the extent that they derived some benefit from them. The Crusades also encouraged the Jews to move to the fortified cities, where they would be less vulnerable in the event of an attack. The reactions on Jewish economic life were in their way disastrous. The former unique position of the Jews as intermediaries between East and West was undermined; henceforth, it was commonplace for western merchants to travel backward and forward between the two worlds, while at the same time the stimulation of religious fanaticism made the path of the Jewish merchant more dangerous. Hence it was the Crusades which marked the end of the heyday – at one time quasi-monopoly – of the international Jewish merchant. At the same time, they gave a stimulus *ipso facto* to the economic degradation of the Jew and his transformation, so far as Western Europe was concerned, into the recognized moneylender of the Christian world (see *moneylending). Partly this was due to the imperative necessity of finding a new outlet for their capital; partly to the increased demands on the part of the crusaders for ready cash to equip themselves and to carry with them on their travels. From now on therefore the Jewish moneylender became the typical Jewish figure of the Western European scene.

The Crusades and their attendant degradation were firmly imprinted on the historic consciousness of the Jews. This period became singled out in the popular mind as the start of and explanation for the misfortunes of the Jews, although in fact the excesses were only symptomatic of a process which had already been set in motion earlier. The Crusades marked in various ways a turning point in the history of the Western world, and this was reflected also in Jewish history. Indeed, it is from this point only that the history of the Jews in the Rhineland and Central Europe may be said to acquire continuity: whereas before the general picture has had to be constructed from scattered fragments and documents, henceforth the record is more or less sustained and complete. As in the case to some extent with general historiography, it is only at this period, with the remarkably graphic and moving records of the Rhineland massacres in 1096, that consistent Jewish *historiography, or at least chronography, begins to be preserved, even though there are fragmentary records written earlier. The history that now unfolded was predominantly a tragic one. Whereas in European Jewish history before this date episodes of violence and persecution are occasionally known, there now began a period of intermittently recurring massacre and persecution which colored European Jewish experience for centuries to come. The heightened religiosity of the age resulted in the sharpening of the system of anti-Jewish discrimination and of Jewish humiliation, culminating in the legislation of the Fourth *Lateran Council of 1215. The chronicles of *Solomon b. Samson, *Eliezer b. Nathan of Mainz, *Ephraim b. Jacob of Bonn, *Eleazar b. Judah of Worms, and many other whose names are not known, described the events of the Crusades, the scenes of the massacres, and the martyrs. They are also to be regarded as basic sources from which statistical accounts of the Crusades must start. Through capturing these events they magnified their significance, but thereby furnished an ideal of conduct which was constantly recalled to mind whenever severe persecutions befell the Jews.

BIBLIOGRAPHY: Graetz, Hist, index; Baron, Social^2, index; A.M. Habermann, *Sefer Gezerot Ashkenaz ve-Ẓarefat* (1946); Prawer, Ẓalbanim; Germ Jud, 1 (1963); S. Grayzel, *The Church and the Jews in the 13th Century* (1966^2), index; Roth, England; H. Liebeschuetz, in: JJS, 10 (1959), 97–111 incl. bibl. notes; S. Runciman, *History of the Crusades*, (3 vols., 1951–54); J. Katz, in: *Sefer… Y. Baer* (1961); idem, *Exclusiveness and Tolerance* (1969), 67–92; Baer in: *Sefer Assaf*, 110–26; S.D. Goitein, *Mikhtavim me-Ereẓ Yisrael mi-Tekufat ha-Ẓalbanim*; Neubauer-Stern, *Hebraeische Berichte ueber die Judenverfolgung waehrend der Kreuzzuege* (1892); Salfeld, Martyrol; N. Golb, in: PAAJR, 34 (1966), 1–63; M.N. Adler, *The Itinerary of Benjamin of Tudela*; Hacker, in: *Zion* (1966); M. Benvenisti, *Crusaders in the Holy Land* (1970). **ADD. BIBLIOGRAPHY:** J. Prawer, *The History of the Jews in the Latin Kingdom of Jerusalem* (1988).

[Simon R. Schwarzfuchs]

CRYPTO-JEWS, persons who while secretly remaining faithful to Judaism practiced another religion which they or their ancestors were forced to accept. Groups of Crypto-Jews came into existence after the forced conversions under the *Visigoths in Spain (7th century) and the *Almohads in North Africa and Spain (12th century). Other such groups were the *neofiti* in southern Italy from the end of the 13th to the 16th century, the *Conversos or *Marranos (Heb. *anusim*) in Spain after the persecutions of 1391 and the expulsion of 1492, as well as in Portugal after 1497. In Majorca these Jewish converts were known as the *Chuetas. A group coerced to adopt Islam were the *Jadīd al-Islām in *Meshed, Persia, in the 19th century. A different type of Crypto-Jew were the members of the *Doenmeh sect in Turkey and Salonika.

CRYSTAL, BILLY (1947–), U.S. actor. Born in New York, Crystal studied film and television direction under Martin Scorsese at New York University. He became known to television viewers as Jodie Dallas, the young homosexual in *Soap*, the satiric take-off on the soap opera genre (1977). In fact, Crystal made history by playing television's first openly gay character.

As a stand-up comedian on the comedy circuit, Crystal became famous for his Fernando Lamas and Sammy Davis Jr. impersonations. In 1984 he joined the cast of *Saturday Night Live*. Although he spent only one year with the show, he was one of the most popular members of the cast and was nominated for an Emmy for Best Individual Performance.

Crystal graduated to feature film work and built up a steady following with roles in *This Is Spinal Tap* (1984), *Running Scared* (1986), *The Princess Bride* (1987), *Throw Momma from the Train* (1987), and *Memories of Me* (1988), which Crystal co-scripted and co-produced with Alan *King. Crystal then catapulted to star status in the hugely popular *When Harry Met Sally* (1989), and he followed this with the equally successful *City Slickers* (1990). His next film was *Mr. Saturday Night* (1992), which he also directed. Subsequent films included *City Slickers II*, which he wrote (1994); *Forget Paris*, which he wrote and directed (1995); *Father's Day* (1997); *Deconstructing Harry* (1997); *My Giant* (1998); *Analyze This* (1999); *America's Sweethearts*, which he wrote (2001); and *Analyze That* (2002).

Crystal was the host of the annual Academy Award presentations in Hollywood from 1990 to 1993 as well as in 1997, 1998, 2000, and 2004. Widely acclaimed for his writing and performing talents, Crystal has won five Emmys and five American Comedy Awards, among many other honors and nominations. Crystal wrote *Absolutely Mahvelous* (with Dick Schaap, 1986), and the children's book *I Already Know I Love You* (2004).

[Ruth Beloff (2nd ed.)]

CSERGŐ, HUGO (1877–1944), Hungarian author and journalist. Csergő, who headed the Budapest social welfare department, was also a prominent Jewish community official. His works include *Versek* ("Poems," 1904) and the drama, *Az első hajnal* ("The First Dawn," 1923), but he is best remembered as editor of the anthology, *Száz év magyar zsidó kőltői* ("Hungarian Jewish Poets of the Last Century," 1943). He died following deportation.

CSERMELY, GYULA (1869–1939), Hungarian author. Csermely abandoned his law practice to write novels, plays, and short stories. Many of these have Jewish settings and deal with the conflict of the generations and the damaging effects of assimilation. They include *Ami két Miatyánk között van* ("Between Two 'Lord's Prayers,'" 1925), *Juda ben Tábbaj kulcsa* ("The Key of Judah ben Tabbai," 1927), and *Szent védekezés* ("Holy Defense," 1938).

CSUPO, GABOR (1952–), U.S. cartoon animator; founders/co-chair with Arlene Klasky, of Klasky Csupo. Csupo, born in Budapest, Hungary, learned animation at Pannonia Studio. He escaped Communist Hungary in 1975 and made his way to Stockholm, where he met Arlene Klasky. A graduate of California Institute of the Arts, Klasky worked as a designer for record labels such as A&M Records, served as a magazine and advertising art director, and then moved to special effects and graphics for film. The couple relocated to Los Angeles and formed Klasky Csupo, Inc. in 1982. In 1988, James L. Brooks awarded the company the job of animating *The Simpsons* for Fox's *The Tracey Ulman Show*. Klasky Csupo,

Inc. subsequently created such animated shows as *Rugrats* (1991), a cartoon told from a child's point of view, *Duckman* (1994), *The Wild Thornberrys* (1998), and *As Told by Ginger* (2000). *Rugrats* features Passover and Hanukkah episodes and its Jewish main character, Tommy Pickles, is based on Klasky's experiences with his sons Brandon and Jarrett. Feature films included *The Rugrats Movie* (1998), *Rugrats in Paris* (2000), *The Wild Thornberrys Movie* (2002), and the crossover film *Rugrats Go Wild!* (2003).

[Adam Wills (2nd ed.)]

CTESIPHON, in ancient times a city on the west bank of the Tigris, opposite the Hellenistic city of Seleucia, 25 mi. (40 km.) S.E. of modern Baghdad. Though greatly influenced by its Hellenistic origins Ctesiphon was basically a Persian city. A large Jewish community resided there and the town also served as a commercial center for the Jews of the surrounding area. When the Jews of Seleucia were persecuted about 41 B.C.E., they were able to take refuge in Ctesiphon (Jos., Ant., 18:374ff.) and when the city was taken by Carus in 283 C.E., it was found to have a large Jewish community (T. Noeldeke (tr. and ed.), *Geschichte der Perser und Araber… des Tabari* (1879), 49, n. 1). The Talmud (Yoma 10a) identifies Ctesiphon with the biblical Resen and the Targum Pseudo-Jonathan equates the city with Calneh (Gen. 10:10, 12). The *amoraim* *Ḥiyya b. Abba and Rabba b. Ḥiyya resided in Ctesiphon, both being termed "Ketosefa'ah" ("resident of Ctesiphon," Beẓah 38b; Yev. 104a; BB 93b). For commercial and legal purposes Ctesiphon was considered as a part of Bet-Ardeshir which controlled the other bank of the Tigris. This is illustrated by the fact that the inhabitants of Bet-Ardeshir were authorized to certify the signatures on bills of divorce from Ctesiphon, but not vice versa. For purpose of **eruv teḥumin* the two cities were considered one, and carrying between them was permitted (Eruv. 57b). The Arab conquest of Ctesiphon (637 C.E.) ended the city's growth, and the founding of Baghdad (762) brought about its total ruin.

BIBLIOGRAPHY: M. Streck, *Seleucia und Ktesiphon* (1917); O. Reuther, *Die Ausgrabungen… Ktesiphon-Expedition, Winter 1928–1929* (1930); J. Obermeyer, *Landschaft Babylonien* (1929), 351, index s.v. *Ktesiphon.*

[Abraham Schalit]

CUBA, archipelago of islands consisting of Cuba, Isla de Pinos, and 1,600 smaller islands; population (2004) 11,300,000; Jewish population (2004) approximately 1,200.

The Colonial Period

Columbus discovered Cuba during his first voyage (1492). His interpreter, Luis de *Torres, was the first converted Jew to set foot in America. He was sent to explore the island and discovered the tobacco leaves smoked by the indigenous people. After the occupation of Cuba by Spain (1508–11), converted Jewish women were forcibly sent there as wives for the settlers. In 1518 the immigration of *New Christians to the Indies was banned, but the local authorities disregarded the new laws, since many of the colonists abandoned the Caribbeans for the rich empires in *Mexico and *Peru. Cuba became a marginal colony in the Spanish empire, growing cattle, tobacco, and sugar, and living on contraband trade. *Havana, however, was chosen as the assembly point of the treasure caravans on their way back to Spain, becoming a cosmopolitan port with merchants from different countries and different faiths. The local officials were more interested in their personal profits than in the economic interests of the Spanish crown, and overlooked the entrance of heretics. It is believed that Jews were present among the buccaneers that raided the island as well as among the merchants who traded with it. Groups of Jews fleeing from Dutch Brazil following the Portuguese reconquest (1654) settled in Cuba, concealing their religious identity.

Cuban historians mention the presence of converted Jews among the early producers of sugar as well as among Spanish officials, but there is little evidence for the existence of *Crypto-Jews, since there was no tribunal of the *Inquisition in Cuba. During the 16th century Cuba belonged to the jurisdiction of New Spain (Mexico), but in 1610 was transferred to that of the newly erected Inquisition in Cartagena (*Colombia). At least 15 judaizers from Havana were sent to Cartagena for trial during the 17th and 18th centuries, the first being Francisco Gómez de León, whose death sentence in 1613 was commuted to life imprisonment. With time, however, the Crypto-Jews were totally assimilated into the Catholic population, leaving only sporadic memories of Jewish ancestry among the oligarchic families.

The admission of Jews to Cuba was officially prohibited until the fall of the Spanish empire (1898). Nevertheless, a few Jews from the Caribbeans, especially *Curaçao, settled in the island during the 19th century, concealing their Judaism. A few Jews were involved in Cuba's struggle for independence, such as Louis Schlesinger, a Hungarian Jew who participated in the military expedition of Narciso López (1851). According to Jewish sources (which are not accepted by Cuban historians), General Carlos Roloff, one of the heroes of the Ten Years War (1868–78), was a Polish Jew. José Martí, the greatest leader of the Cuban people, had a friendly attitude towards the Jews, which was manifested in his writings. His Revolutionary Cuban Party (1892) received contributions from the Jews in Key West (Florida). Joseph Steinberg was decorated as captain of the Cuban Army of Liberation and was among the first Jews who settled in Cuba after the Spanish-American War (1898).

The Republican Period (1902–1958)

THE LEGAL STATUS. The legal basis for Jewish existence was established under the U.S. Military Occupation (1898–1902), which granted freedom of religion and implemented the American immigration laws. The Cuban population was generally indifferent to religious questions and tended to identify the Church hierarchy with Spanish colonialism. The first constitution of the Republic (1902) introduced the principles of religious freedom and separation of church and state. Cuba maintained an open door immigration policy until the revolution of 1933, which adopted discriminatory legislation against aliens. The revolutionary government of Grau San Martín (1933) passed a law that at least 50% of the workers in each establishment must be Cuban natives and new jobs were to be given only to Cubans. The Law of Nationalization of Labor was included in the 1940 constitution and was the basis for Cuba's immigration policy during the Holocaust. Since only persons who could prove their financial independence were granted immigration visas, the admission of refugees was made possible only within the margins of the law, as tourists or passengers in transition. In April 1942 President Fulgencio Batista prohibited further immigration from Nazi-occupied countries, but granted the refugees who were already in Cuba the right of legal residence until the end of the war. By the end of World War II almost all the Jews who remained to live in Cuba had been naturalized, enjoying legal equality with the rest of the Cuban population.

FORMATION AND INSTITUTIONAL DEVELOPMENT. *American Jews.* The first Jewish immigrants arrived in Cuba from the United States during the military occupation (1899–1902) and following the foundation of the Cuban Republic (1902). At that time American firms were deeply involved in the development of the sugar industry and in exporting consumer products to Cuba. A small group, of about 100 Jewish families, formed part of the large colony of American businessmen that was established in Cuba. In 1906 they founded the first Jewish organization – the United Hebrew Congregation (UHC) – with the objective of acquiring land for a Jewish cemetery. Among the founders were Maurice Schechter (a nephew of Solomon *Schechter), John Zoller and Louis Djurick (who were born in Romania), and Manuel Hadida (from Algiers). The UHC organized services for the High Holidays, and in the 1920s established a Reform synagogue. In 1917 the women founded the charitable Ezra Society, whose leading philanthropist was Jeanette Schechter. The American Jewish community, estimated in 1925 at around 300 persons, was mostly affluent, and charity was directed to less privileged groups, especially among the Jewish immigrants from Eastern Europe. In 1927 the American Jewish women founded the Menorah Sisterhood as an auxiliary of the UHC, which was responsible for religious life and conducted a Sunday School.

Sephardi Jews. The *Sephardim, most of whom came from European Turkey, were the second Jewish group. Their immigration started prior to World War I and continued throughout the 1920s. Attracted by the Spanish language, which resembled their native *Ladino, they worked as itinerant peddlers selling their goods throughout the island, following the expansion of the sugar industry. In 1914 the Sephardi Jews established a community organization called Unión Hebrea Shevet Aḥim, with the objective of supplying all their religious and social needs. Among the founders were Moise Bensignor, Víctor Atún, and Samuel Amon. The Sephardim used the Jewish cemetery owned by the UHC, until they were able to purchase their own cemetery in 1942. Apart from that, there was little contact between these Jewish groups, who came from different backgrounds and belonged to different social strata. In 1918 Shevet Aḥim formed two auxiliaries: Bikkur Ḥolim, which cared for the sick and was responsible for burials, and the women's charity – La Buena Voluntad. Rabbi Guershon Maya, who immigrated from Silivri (Turkey), acted as the spiritual leader of the Sephardim (1923–52).

Sephardi immigration increased after World War I, as a result of the disintegration of the Ottoman Empire. The newcomers were assisted by Shevet Aḥim, as well as by informal Sephardi networks of social help, especially in the rural areas. During the 1920s several Sephardi communities were established in the provincial towns with local cemeteries and synagogues: Camagüey and Holguin (1921); Santiago de Cuba, Ciego de Avila, Camajuani, and Manzanillo (1924); Banes (1926); Matanzas (1928); Santa Clara, Colon, and Guantánamo (1929); and Artemisa (1930). In 1924 it was estimated that the Sephardim numbered 4,000 persons – 1,500 of them in Havana.

Ashkenazi Jews. The aftermath of World War I brought over to Cuba the third – and largest – Jewish group. Immigration from Eastern Europe began in 1920–21 as a result of restrictive U.S. immigration policy. Deluded by travel agents with the promise that subsequent voyage to the land of their dreams would be easy, immigrants viewed Cuba as a transit point on their way to the United States. Most of the immigrants who arrived between 1920 and 1923 had left Cuba by 1925. But as a result of the stiffening of U.S. immigration laws in 1924, thousands of immigrants found themselves compelled to stay in Cuba. It is estimated that between 1921 and 1930, 17,700 Jews from Eastern Europe entered Cuba, but only 50% remained on the island. The arrival of the destitute immigrants coincided with the collapse of sugar prices that shattered the Cuban economy. UHC and the Ezra Society did their utmost to supply food and shelter to their hungry and helpless Ashkenazi brethren, but in view of the growing influx of refugees, they called on Jewish welfare organizations in the United States to intervene on their behalf. From the end of 1921 *HIAS maintained its representative in Havana, and in 1922–23 the American Jewish Joint Distribution Committee (JDC) added its support. Their intention was to alleviate the difficult conditions in Havana, but also to prevent further immigration, since they did not consider Cuba as a desirable destination or transit station. The Quota Act of 1924, however, convinced the American Jewish welfare agencies that passage from Cuba to the United States was ultimately blocked, and they decided to develop a program that would facilitate Jewish settlement in Cuba and prevent illegal entry into the United States. In 1925 HIAS, in conjunction with the National Council of Jewish Women, established the Jewish Committee for Cuba. Later this body, whose center was in New York, was joined by the Emergency Refugee Committee. The Jewish Community for Cuba (JCC) assisted individual Jews to establish themselves in small business, particularly in workshops for shoes and garments. In addition, it was active in shaping local organizations, with the objective of creating a self-supporting community.

The JCC decided to turn the Centro Israelita – an organization that was founded by the immigrants in 1925 – into the central organ of the Jewish community. Led by David *Blis, Fiodor Valbe, Ben Dizik, and others, the Centro Israelita centralized a diversified range of actvities: aside from welfare assistance to immigrants, a clinic, a library, an evening language school, a student center, and a drama club. The Centro Israelita assisted in the establishment of other institutions, such as the religious Adath Israel organization (1925), the Unión Sionista (1924), and the Froyen Fareyn (1925). In the late 1920s, however, the JCC suspended its support, curtailing the activities of the Centro Israelita and causing the decentralization of the Ashkenazi sector. The Centro Israelita continued to represent the Jewish community vis-à-vis the authorities in matters of immigration, but it failed in its endeavor to become the Ashkenazi *Kehillah* – an objective that was achieved in the 1950s by the Patronato.

The religious services in the Ashkenazi sector were provided by Adath Israel, founded in 1925 by a group of Orthodox Jews who established a small synagogue in Old Havana. A rival synagogue – Knesset Israel – was established on the same street with Rabbi Zvi Kaplan as its spiritual leader (1929–39). Rabbi David Rafalín served in Adath Israel, until his immigration to Mexico (1932), where he became the spiritual leader of Nidjei Israel. Adath Israel, however, remained the central religious organization of the East European sector, with a Talmud Torah and a Chevra Kadisha.

The two major welfare institutions of the Ashkenazi sector were the Froyen Fareyn and the Anti-Tuberculosis and Mentally Ill Committee. Their functions reflect the difficult conditions of the immigrants, who suffered from diseases caused by poverty and difficulties of adaptation. The Women's Association established the Meidl Hey – a shelter for young women who arrived in Cuba alone and needed protection. Later it was converted into the Kinder Heym, where orphans or poor children of working mothers found asylum. In 1937, when poverty was less acute, the women founded the Ley Kasse – a loan fund that assisted small businessmen who needed credit.

ECONOMIC ADAPTATION AND CUBAN POLITICS. The Jewish upper class in Cuba was classified as American since most of its members were U.S. citizens who belonged to the UHC. Enjoying the tight economic relations between Cuba and the United States, they imported consumer goods, worked as high officials in American sugar companies and banks, or owned fashionable stores in the center of Havana. They resided in the fancy neighborhoods of Vedado and Miramar and adopted the way of life of the local American colony.

There were cases of rich Jews who did not belong to the Jewish community, married Catholic women, and assimilated into the Cuban bourgeoisie. One of them was Frank Steinhardt (1864–1938), who was born in Munich (Germany), immigrated to the United States, enlisted in the army, and was a sergeant during the war in Cuba. He became a successful businessman, served as U.S. consul general (1902–07), and became the owner of the Electric Railway Company in Havana.

A few of the early Sephardi immigrants were successful businessmen, like the fruit dealer Alejandro Rossich (Gabriel Cohen) from Macedonia. The majority, however, started as poor peddlers distributing consumer goods to the lower strata of the population, particularly in the provincial towns and around the sugar centers, where retail trade was scarce. Those who succeeded opened their own stores and supplied merchandise on credit to other peddlers. Though maintaining good relations with their Cuban neighbors, the Sephardim did not engage in Cuban politics. An exceptional case is that of Roberto Namer, born in Aleppo and resident of Holguin, who was appointed Cuban consul in Palestine in 1935.

Many of the Ashkenazi immigrants arrived from small shtetls in Poland, destitute, unskilled and with poor education, after having suffered the consequences of World War I. They crowded together in Old Havana in cheap hotels near the red light district of the port. According to the survey of Harry Viteles (1925), which served as the basis for the activities of the JCC, a few hundred Jews were engaged as day laborers in the construction of railroads, in the sugar centers, or on the docks. Most of them, however, were unable to cope with the physical hardships or to compete with the local cheap laborers.

Many of the early immigrants became peddlers, especially of cheap ware such as haberdashery and eskimo pie (ice-cream bars), or catered to tourists as street photographers and souvenir vendors. Among the Ashkenazim peddling was perceived as a temporary job, while waiting for an American visa, and most street vendors remained in Havana where competition was great. The retail trade in Cuba was dominated by the Spaniards, who saw the Jews as unfair rivals. Due to their influence the municipal authorities of Havana imposed heavy taxes on peddling permits and increased their control of illegal trade. In 1925 it was estimated that there were 500 East European peddlers in Havana and 300 in the interior. By 1933 there were only 150 in Havana. In addition to external pressure, the decision to remain in Cuba motivated peddlers to open a permanent business.

The economic crises that hit Cuba from 1920 on increased the demand for cheap local production that would compete with the expensive merchandise imported under the protection of the Reciprocity Treaty with the United States. Using their experience as shoemakers and tailors, East European immigrants started to produce shoes, underwear, and men's suits, especially for the lower classes. With the help of the JCC they acquired sewing machines and other working tools, opening workshops in the commercial center of Old Havana, where they employed other Jews. Morris Lewis, the director of the JCC, estimated in 1927 that there were between 1,500 and 2,000 Jewish workers in the sweatshops of Old Havana, working for low wages in the same difficult conditions that had existed in New York 25 years before.

The conflicting interests of the small entrepreneurs and their workers had an impact on political developments among the Ashkenazi Jews, especially in respect to the evolution of the Communists. The Jewish Communists established the Sección Hebrea in 1924, but with the foundation of the Cuban Communist Party (August 1925) gave up their separate organization. Three out of the ten founders of the party were Jews: Yoshke Grimberg, Avraham Simchovich (Fabio *Grobart), and Felix Gurvich. In 1926 they founded the Kultur Fareyn in order to attract Jewish workers to their banner. The rich cultural program, which included anti-religious parties on the eve of the Day of Atonement, became very popular in the Jewish neighborhood. The small, militant Communist group that led the Kultur Fareyn opened a cooperative restaurant that served as a secret meeting place for the party's activists. The Cuban CP was persecuted brutally by the government of Gerardo Machado (1924–33), especially from 1928, when the regime turned into a dictatorship. One of the first Communist victims was Noske Yalomb, a young Jewish worker from White Russia, whose body was found in Havana Bay. Four other Jews were murdered by the police between 1930 and 1933. Many others were expelled from Cuba as undesirable aliens, including the two Communist leaders Yoshke Grimberg and Chone Chazan. Grobart, who under the name of Simchovich was one of the founders of the party, returned secretly to Cuba after his expulsion, to become the liaison between the Komintern and the Cuban CP. In 1931 the Kultur Fareyn was closed by the authorities and its members were tried for revolutionary activity. In 1934 the organization was revived as the Yidishe Gezelshaft far Kunst un Kultur, but its cultural activities did not achieve their former popularity due to the decline of the Jewish working class after the 1933 revolution.

The 1933 revolution was based on a nationalist ideology directed against the domination of aliens in the domestic economy, combined with a struggle against the dictatorship and the corruption of the governing classes. The tremendous unemployment and the deplorable economic situation gave rise to an atmosphere of xenophobia. The slogan of President Grau San Martín was "Cuba for the Cubans." His decree that at least 50% of all workers should be native Cubans and that new jobs would be open only to Cubans became the symbol of the revolution. The political upheavals of 1933–34 were followed by the collapse of the revolutionary government and the intervention of the army, headed by Fulgencio Batista y Záldivar, who became the chief of staff and the strongman of Cuba (1934–40). Batista started to gain power through the repression of opposition. Among the victims of that period was Haim Grinstein, a member of the underground Joven Cuba group, who was sentenced to death by a court martial (1935). A few Jewish labor activists were imprisoned or went into exile. Moises Raigor (1914–36), son of the Yiddish printer Avraham Raigorodski, was a member of a cell of young Jewish Communists and became a leader in the Left Wing Students' Organization. After his release from imprisonment he joined the International Brigades and was killed in the Spanish Civil War.

In 1937 Batista started to build his image as a democratic leader by supporting the Spanish Republic and legalizing the CP. At the same time he adopted the banner of the Cuban revolutionary movement – the Law of Nationalization of Labor. This law restricted the rights of aliens to be wage earners, but encouraged them to engage in free enterprise that would create new jobs for Cubans. The discrimination against the Jews accelerated the process of deproletarization, since workers who were pushed out of the working class became self-employed or founded cooperatives with other associates. By 1944 there were only between 200 and 300 Jewish workers in Havana.

ANTISEMITISM AND THE REFUGEE PROBLEM. Until 1933 antisemitism was a marginal phenomenon in Cuba. The impact of the Catholic Church, and hence of religious antisemitism, was limited to the upper classes, who inherited Spanish colonial values. For the majority of the population, the *judíos* were diabolical mythical creatures who belonged to the realm of superstition, not to be associated with the immigrants from Eastern Europe whom they classified as *polacos* (Poles). Under Machado Jewish Communists were persecuted, but the Jewish community was not considered responsible for their acts. During the revolutionary period, apart from a few sporadic manifestations of anti-Jewish feeling, the Jews suffered the consequences of political agitation and anarchy together with the rest of the population.

The emergence of antisemitism was connected to the crisis of the Spanish minority after the 1933 revolution as well as with the rise of Nazi Germany. The Spaniards had enjoyed a privileged position in Cuba, and saw themselves displaced by the Jews from their traditional dominance in trade and light industry. Their classification as aliens by the revolutionary government gave rise to a wave of attacks against the Jews based on religious anti-Jewish arguments as well as on concepts of modern antisemitism. At the same time, Nazi Germany inundated Cuba with antisemitic propaganda, finding fertile ground among upper-class Spaniards who were influenced by right-wing elements in their homeland. During the Spanish Civil War the lower-class immigrants from Spain sided with the Republic together with the majority of the Cuban population, which identified the nationalist forces with their oppressors during the colonial era. The upper-class Spaniards, however, identified with Franco, establishing a Cuban branch of the Spanish Falange. Their leader was José Ignacio Rivero, editor of the influential newspaper *Diario de la Marina*, which became the most important organ in diffusing antisemitic propaganda from Nazi sources. The fierce anti-Jewish attacks had an impact on the problem of the Jewish refugees.

The refugees from Europe, who managed to slip in despite severe immigration laws and whose overall number in the years 1933–44 was estimated at about 10,000–12,000 (about 50% from Germany and Austria and the remainder from Poland and other countries), left Cuba, for the most part, after a few years. According to an estimate, in 1949, only 15% of them remained there. After World War II Jews did not reach Cuba in large numbers. The first refugees came from the United States in 1937 for a short stay, in order to obtain American immigration visas. They were aided by the JDC, which for this purpose founded the Joint Relief Committee in Havana. The number of refugees who came directly from Europe reached considerable proportions following the annexation of Austria (March 1938) and especially after *Kristallnacht* (November 1938). At that time the German quota for the U.S. consulate in Havana was cut drastically, and refugees were forced to remain in Cuba. Refugees had obtained entry permits using loopholes in Cuba's immigration laws, in semi-official arrangements based on graft. The sale of entry permits to the Jewish refugees was complicated by internal political conflicts between President Federico Laredo Bru and the military circle around Chief of Staff Batista, which reached its peak in the famous incident of the *Saint Louis*. The voyage of the Hapag Company's luxury liner *Saint Louis* was engineered by the German Ministry of Propaganda as proof that Jews were permitted to leave the Reich, but that democratic countries refused to admit them. A sustained anti-Jewish campaign was organized and financed by local and foreign Nazi elements in collusion with the German embassy. The Government of Laredo Bru invalidated the entry permits held by most refugees before the ship sailed from Hamburg, and it interpreted the arrival of the German ship as a violation of its laws. Disagreements between the president and Batista complicated the situation, but the direct victims of internal and international conflicts were the 936 Jewish refugees who, upon reaching Cuba on May 27, 1939, aboard the *Saint Louis*, were barred from entry and forced to return to Europe, in spite of the efforts of the JDC to reach an agreement. Four countries in Europe consented to admit the refugees to prevent their return to Germany – France, Belgium, Holland, and England. Unfortunately, only the fourth group was saved. Following the invasion of Western Europe many of the passengers who found refuge in France, Belgium, and Holland were deported to extermination camps, and the story of the *Saint Louis* became a symbol of the fate of the refugees.

The administration of Laredo Bru closed the gates of Cuba on the eve of World War II, but they were reopened when Batista was elected president (1940). Between 5,000 and 6,000 refugees were able to enter Cuba from October 1940 until April 1942. Many of them had fled from Western Europe after the German invasion. Like their predecessors, they were not allowed to work, and they depended on the assistance of the JDC or became self-employed in small industry or trade. The most important contribution of the refugees to the Cuban economy was the establishment of diamond workshops by immigrants from Antwerp (Belgium) that prospered during the war years and provided employment to Cuban workers as well as to the local Jews. In 1943 it was estimated that at least 1,200 workers and 100 proprietors worked in the diamond industry.

In December 1941 Cuba declared war against the Axis and in April 1942 President Batista prohibited further entry of passengers from Nazi-occupied countries, but at the same time granted the refugees permission to remain in Cuba until the end of the war. The passengers of two ships, *São Tomé* and *Guiné,* were refused landing, but the diplomatic representatives of England and other Allied countries pressed President Batista to avoid a repeat of the *Saint Louis* incident, and the 450 refugees remained detained in the immigrant camp of Tiscornia for eight months, before they were released.

The refugees from Germany and Austria founded the Asociación Democrática de Refugiados Hebreos (1941) and the Belgians established the Asociación de Refugiados Hebreos (1942). Since German spies entered Cuba disguised as Jewish refugees, these organizations fulfilled an essential function in identifying their members as authentic Jews who as victims of Nazism defended the Allied cause.

Political threats and antisemitic attacks were correlated with the attempts of the Jewish community to establish a central organization. At first, the Jewish community did not present a united front. Moderate factions, e.g., Americans and heads of the Centro Israelita, feared that large-scale Jewish action might be interpreted as disrupting public affairs and might thus evoke police repression. Nevertheless, a certain amount of community cooperation was obtained during the 1930s through the following institutions: The Federación Israelita de Cuba (1932); Comité Intersocial (1932–35), collaborating with the Comisión Jurídica (1933–34); among its functions was the liberation of Jews imprisoned during the political disturbances; Jewish Committee of Cuba (1935–36), in which Sephardim, Ashkenazim, and Americans collaborated. The Jewish Chamber of Commerce assumed the defense against antisemitism and represented the community on official occasions (between 1936–39). Only during the *Saint Louis* incident, when the antisemitic propaganda threatened their existence, did Cuban Jews finally reach accord. The Comité Central was organized in 1939, comprising all sectors of the community, and was recognized as its representative organ by the Cuban authorities. It joined forces with anti-Fascist bodies and supported the Allies in World War II. Antisemitism, however, started to decline shortly after the foundation of the Comité Central, since the German agents who instigated the anti-Jewish campaign left the island. After the outbreak of World War II propaganda of totalitarian countries was prohibited by law. The anti-Jewish activities practically disappeared by the time of the Japanese attack on Pearl Harbor. On December 9, 1942, when news on the extermination of the Jews in Europe reached Cuba, the Senate approved a resolution condemning the persecution of the "Hebrew race" by the German government.

After World War II there were rare manifestations of social discrimination against Jews, but on the whole antisemitism did not strike roots in the Cuban population.

EDUCATION AND CULTURE. The Jewish day schools in Havana were part of a large network of private schools that served different ethnic groups as well as the middle and upper classes. The only complementary Jewish school was the Sunday School of the UHC, which provided religious education for the American children who studied in prestigious private schools.

The first Jewish day school in Havana, Teodoro Herzl, was founded by the Sephardi community Shevet Aḥim in 1924. The leading force behind it was Ezra Behar, who expressed his educational principles in *Fundamentos de la moral hebrea* (1930). The school's orientation was a combination of religious tradition with a Zionist spirit.

The largest Jewish day school was founded by the Centro Israelita under the auspices of the JCC in 1927. At that time, the policy of the school was to help Jewish children in their process of integration. Parents discovered that acculturation could lead to assimilation, and they showed a growing concern about the content of the Jewish heritage transmitted in the school. Until 1939 the Yiddish school was part of the Centro Israelita, but a series of organizational and financial crises resulted in its reconstitution as the Autonomous School affiliated with the Centro Israelita (Oitonome Shul Beim Yiddishn Zenter). The director of the Autonomous School, Eliahu Eliovich, was considered a Bundist, but the school aimed to serve the entire Ashkenazi sector and to preserve its apolitical character by compromising among the conflicting political views. Emphasis was placed on the study of Yiddish and Jewish history, with a secular interpretation of the Jewish tradition. After World War II, and especially after the establishment of the State of Israel, the school became openly Zionist. In the 1950s the Centro Israelita ceased to exist, but the Autonomous School opened a high school (1954) and remained the central Jewish school.

A private Jewish school was founded in 1935 by Joseph Abrami, a Hebrew teacher who withdrew from the school of the Centro Israelita in protest against the domination of Yiddish. Abrami, a declared Zionist, opened the Yavneh Hebrew school, which operated until 1945. In 1940 left-wing elements, led by the Communist group, opened the Sholem Aleichem Shule – a Yiddish school for the working class. It was closed in 1949 together with other Communist organizations. The religious sector reopened a Jewish school following the fusion of Adath Israel and Knesset Israel in 1948. Rabbi Meir Rosenbaum, appointed spiritual leader of the new organization, Achdut Israel, founded the Orthodox school Taḥkemoni, which combined modern and religious education. Among the central figures in Jewish education was Ida Glazer de Castiel, a graduate of Havana University, founder of the Modern Jewish School (1944), who published several articles in the Jewish press with the objective of modernizing the Jewish school system. David Pérez, a teacher in the Sephardi school, left his imprint on Jewish education with the *preparatoria* – training courses for admission to high school that encouraged children, particularly in the Sephardi sector, to continue their studies.

The first Jewish university students founded the *Circulo de Estudiantes Hebreos* in 1928 with the aim of creating a bridge between the Jewish and Cuban cultures. The students published the first Jewish periodical in Spanish, *El Estudiante Hebreo* (1929–31), but all their activities were suspended when Machado closed the University of Havana. This periodical, however, is one of the few sources that records the ideological development of the Sephardi sector.

While the American and Sephardi communities conducted their social and cultural life inside their closed circles, the East European Jews left considerable written records on their cultural activities. In the 1920s immigrants showed a strong inclination toward the theater, literary evenings, and "literary trials." In 1927 the first Jewish book was published in Cuba – the poetry of N.D. Korman, *Oyf Indzler Erd*. A year later the poet Eliezer Aronowski (1904–85) published the book *Kubaner Lieder*. Aronowski became the most prolific Yiddish poet in Cuba, accompanying in his writings all the historical events in Cuban Jewish life. His last book, *Kuba*, was published in 1983, shortly after his emigration from the island. Aronowski and I.A. Pinis devoted poems not only to Jewish subjects, but also to the heroes of Cuban history. Avraham I. Dubelman wrote short novels describing the life of the immigrants. His first anthology, *Oyf Kubaner Erd*, appeared in 1935. Other prose writers were Pinchas Berniker, Avraham Weinstein, I.B. Mankelkern, and Osher Schuchinski. Among the few books written in Spanish was the poetry of Sonia Winer, *Compañeras*.

A considerable part of this literary work was published in the Jewish press. The *Havaner Lebn Almanaque* of 1943 lists the titles of 59 journals and periodicals that were published in Cuba – 11 in Spanish (four of the Sephardi community), four in German (by refugees), and 44 in Yiddish. Among the more important periodicals were *Oyfgang* (1927–30), organ of the Centro Israelita in its heyday; *Dos Idishe Vort* (1933–35), edited by David Utiansky with a pro-Communist orientation; and *Kubaner Yiddisher Vort* (1942–50), the organ of the Jewish Communists. The central newspaper of the Yiddish-speaking Cuban Jews was the *Havaner Leben-Vida Habanera* (1932–63), edited by Sender *Kaplan, whose content was pro-Zionist and dedicated to general and Jewish news. After World War II the number of publications in Spanish increased and they were directed also to the non-Jewish population. Abraham Marcus Matterín (the librarian of the Patronato between 1953 and 1983) edited a number of periodicals, including *Israelia, Hebraica,* and *Reflejos*. Marco Pitchon, president of B'nai B'rith (founded in 1943), was editor of its organ, *Fragmentos*.

THE ZIONIST MOVEMENT AND RELATIONS WITH ISRAEL. The founder of the Zionist Movement in Cuba was David *Blis who was nicknamed "The Grandfather of the Jewish Community." He settled in Cuba in 1913 and cooperated with Shevet Aḥim in its early Zionist activities, particularly after the *Balfour Declaration. Blis presented a memorandum on the Jewish question to prominent politicians, and thanks to his endeavors the Cuban Senate approved, on April 30, 1919, a resolution in favor of a Jewish National Home in Palestine.

In 1924 a group of East European immigrants founded the Unión Sionista de Cuba. Due to the small number of Zionists and to the constant outgoing migration, the founders decided to unite all Zionists in one organization, regardless of ideological divisions. In comparison with the lively cultural activities of the leftist circles, the beginnings of the Zionist organization were quite poor. Dr. Ariel Ben-Zion, the first emissary of *Keren Hayesod, who arrived in Cuba in 1926, had little confidence in the East European immigrants, and organized a new Zionist committee composed of a few wealthy Jews, mostly from the American sector. Ben Zion also ignored the Zionist leadership of Shevet Aḥim and founded a Cuban branch of a Zionist-Sephardi network that he formed in Latin America called Benei Kedem. This policy proved shortsighted, as both organizations vanished shortly after his departure, leaving those devoted to Zionist ideals without proper communication with the central Zionist offices in Jerusalem.

At first, the Unión Sionista was assisted by the JCC, but after a schism with the Centro Israelita it was reorganized with the cooperation of Shevet Aḥim. The president of the Unión Sionista, Avraham Kamioner (1928–34), came from Poland, but most of the board members were Sephardim. The secretary, José Cohen (Joseph Isaac *Cohen), was a rabbi from Istanbul who immigrated to Cuba from Jerusalem and served as a Hebrew teacher in the Teodoro Herzel school. Cohen conducted the correspondence of the Unión Sionista in Hebrew and published ideological articles in the local Jewish press. In 1934 he left Cuba to serve as rabbi of the Or Veshalom Congregation in Atlanta, Georgia. During its "Sephardi period" the Unión Sionista organized protests against the massacres of 1929 in Eretz Israel and against the immigration policy of the British government. It conducted small campaigns on behalf of the *Jewish National Fund and organized cultural events in Spanish. The East European Jews, however, rejected the religiously oriented Zionism of the Sephardim and the use of Spanish in their functions. New Zionist leaders from Lithuania and Poland founded the *He-Ḥalutz (1932) and *Ha-Shomer ha-Tzair (1933) youth movements with the object of reconstructing the ideological frameworks brought over from their communities of origin. The predominance of Yiddish removed the Sephardim from the common organization, and they founded their own Zionist frameworks, including the Maccabi youth movement (1934).

During the period of the Holocaust, Zionist activities in Cuba, as in other American lands, focused on campaigns on behalf of the Jews who found refuge in Eretz Israel. The tragic situation in their communities of origin, followed by destruction and extermination, increased the readiness of the Jews to contribute generously to the national campaigns, even if they did not adhere ideologically to the Zionist movement. Economic progress, particularly during the war years, increased their ability to give. The Communist group and the Zionists competed for the leadership of the Jewish community. Following the treaty between Hitler and Stalin, the Communists were expelled from the Centro Israelita and founded their own organization – Folks Tzenter. After the invasion of Russia by Nazi Germany, the Communists regained their influence, organizing campaigns on behalf of the Red Army and representing the Jewish community in Cuban anti-Nazi organizations. The Zionist movement, however, increased its influence and became the dominant factor in the Jewish community. The veteran activists, such as Chaim Shiniuk, Raphael Zilber, and Israel Luski, acted under the instructions of the Zionist emissaries sent by the World Zionist Organization. One of the most influential among them was Iosef Tchornitzky from Mexico, who organized the Keren Hayesod campaigns of 1942 and 1943. The local Zionists were also inspired by the refugees from Belgium who found temporary shelter in Cuba during the war. Many of the refugees from Belgium had been born in Poland, and they brought with them their former political and religious beliefs. The Orthodox established their own synagogue, Machazikei Torah, with Rabbi Samuel Alter as their spiritual leader. They organized a small school and a youth movement, Pirchei Agudath Isroel, which operated throughout the war. The Asociación de Refugiados Hebreos of the Belgian Jews opened a Zionist section and a youth movement, Banativ, but they were also accepted as leaders by the veteran Zionists, who admired their higher knowledge as well as their economic success in the diamond industry.

A turning point in the history of Cuban Zionism was the visit of Nathan Bistritski (see Nathan *Agmon), the emissary of the Jewish National Fund to Latin America, who reached Cuba in 1943. Bistritski focused his efforts on the ideological education of all the Jewish sectors, and at the same time established diplomatic contacts among Cuban intellectuals and politicians in order to create favorable public opinion for the foundation of a Jewish State in Palestine after the war. The Comité Cubano Pro Palestina Hebrea (CCPPH) was the first among similar organizations in other Latin American countries, and it was supported by prominent figures, including members of the cabinet, the Congress, and the Senate, from the liberal center to the Communist left. The secretary of the CCPPH was the director of the Office of War Propaganda, Ofelia Domínguez y Navarro, a Communist lawyer who remained a faithful defender of the Zionist cause under Castro's regime. One of the most ardent supporters of the CCPPH was Senator Eduardo Chibás, who passed a resolution that was approved unanimously by the Cuban Senate on October 29, 1945, that "it would view with satisfaction that Palestine, the historical homeland of the Hebrews, be constituted as soon as possible as a Hebrew independent and democratic state."

The solidarity of influential sectors, however, did not alter the decision of President Grau San Martín (1944–48) to oppose the United Nations Resolution on the Partition of Palestine of November 29, 1947, making Cuba the only Latin American state to oppose partition. Grau's decision rested on political considerations, including his bitter conflict with

Senator Chibás. When his successor, Carlos Prío Socarrás, ascended to the presidency, Cuba recognized the State of Israel and in 1951 Sender *Kaplan, editor of the periodical *Havaner Leben,* was named honorary consul, a role that he fulfilled until 1960. Raphael Zilber, one of the oldest Zionist leaders in Cuba, immigrated to Israel and became Cuba's commercial representative. Diplomatic relations between the two countries were established in 1954, with the ambassador in Mexico acting as Israel's representative. Only after the Castro revolution were the consulates converted into legations, and Israel was able to send a resident ambassador to Havana.

Towards the foundation of the State of Israel the Cuban Jewish community experienced an ideological transformation that resulted in the predominance of the Zionist movement. According to Sender Kaplan, the "Zionization" of the community was achieved through the women who founded WIZO in 1942. Organizing different committees of American, Sephardi, Ashkenazi, and refugee Jews, the women became a central factor in the education of the Jewish family. The decline of the Cuban CP during the Cold War had an impact on the Jewish Communists, and many of their longtime sympathizers changed their beliefs and embraced the Zionist cause. In 1947 two groups of Cuban Jews, almost all of them Sephardim, volunteered to fight in the War of Liberation, assisted by *Betar, which was founded in Cuba in 1940. The first group arrived onboard the *Altalena*, and two of its members – Daniel Levy and David Mitrani – were killed. Following the establishment of the State of Israel, the Sephardim founded the Consejo Pro Israel as the Zionist organ of Shevet Aḥim.

Throughout the 1950s participation in Zionist activities became the common denominator of all the Jewish sectors, which followed with zeal the development of the State of Israel. Zionist sources calculated in 1952 that the overall number of Jews in Cuba was 12,000, 7,200 of them Ashkenazim. About 75% were concentrated in Havana, and the rest were dispersed in Santiago de Cuba, Camagüey, Santa Clara, and other towns throughout the island. Only a limited number of Cuban Jews immigrated to Israel following its independence. Most of them were members of Ha-Shomer ha-Tzair who settled in the kibbutzim of Ga'ash (1949) and Devir (1954).

PROSPERITY UNDER BATISTA. The military dictatorship of Fulgencio Batista (1952–58) was a period of political upheaval and violent political repression, but for the small Jewish community it represented the peak of its achievements. Most Jews were integrated economically into the Cuban bourgeoisie and were able to raise their standard of living. The once poor immigrants residing in Old Havana moved into better residential areas, such as Santos Suarez and Vedado, or into the elegant Miramar. The Sephardim were concentrated in the provincial capitals and later moved to Havana, where economic prospects were better and where their children could find a Jewish spouse. Progress was less noticeable among the Sephardim, with a considerable number still engaged in peddling on the eve of the Castro revolution.

A growing number of the immigrants' children – Ashkenazim and Sephardim – studied at the University of Havana and turned to the liberal professions. A group of young intellectuals founded the Agrupación Cultural Hebreo-Cubana to increase understanding between Cubans and Jews. The 1940s and 1950s were a period of great political fermentation among university students, which turned into an open war against the regime of Batista. Jewish students, however, tended to avoid political participation, their integration into Cuban society being in its early stage. Only a small number of Jews took an active part in the Students' Revolutionary Directory or in Castro's 26 of July Movement. Most of them were active in Jewish organizations, such as the Ha-Shomer ha-Tzair and Ha-No'ar ha-Tziyyoni youth movements, or in the social clubs of the different communities.

Unaware of the coming revolution, the Jewish population felt confident of its future in Cuba, and its institutions moved from their rented premises into newly constructed buildings that reflected the prosperity of their members. The Orthodox sector, headed by Rabbi Meir Rosenbaum, tried to create a Kehillah – a united communal organization of the Ashkenazi sector that would rest on a religious base. After a series of conflicts a group of rich businessmen that included Herman Heisler, Leib Hiller, Isaac Gurwitz, and Julio Karity took the initiative and contributed the necessary funds for the construction of the Patronato – a beautiful modern building in Vedado, with the main Ashkenazi synagogue and spacious grounds for social and cultural functions. The Patronato – the House of the Jewish Community – was to become the representative organ of Cuban Jews and the center of all their activities.

The Orthodox Jews of Old Havana built a modern building for Adath Israel, with a large synagogue and a *mikveh*. The Unión Sionista had an old building not far from Old Havana and could not compete with the social services offered by the Patronato. The Sephardim followed the example of the Ashkenazi sector in building a luxurious synagogue in Vedado, but the new Sephardi Center was inaugurated when Castro was already in power. The American community, which celebrated its 50th anniversary in 1956, initiated a building project that never materialized. The American Jews were among the first to leave Cuba after the revolution, returning to the United States, which they considered their homeland.

The Revolutionary Period

THE IMPACT OF CASTRO'S REVOLUTION. The victory of the revolution on January 1, 1959, was welcomed by the Jewish community, which shared the euphoria of the Cuban population, believing that Fidel Castro would put an end to corruption and injustice. The new regime was not prejudiced against the Jews, and the political careers of those who were involved in the downfall of Batista were not hindered by their Jewish origin. The engineer Enrique Oltuski, who coordinated the revolutionary forces in the province of Las Villas, was appointed minister of communications (1959), becoming the first

Jewish member of the cabinet in the history of Cuban Jewry. In spite of ups and downs in his political career, Oltuski served in different governments, until recently as deputy minister of fisheries. Other Jews who were rewarded for their revolutionary actions were Máximo Berman, an activist of the 26 of July Movement, who became minister of commerce. Martin Klein and Victor Sarfati, who were both rebel revolutionaries, attained the rank of captain and colonel in the Armed Forces. The most prominent Jew was Fabio Grobart, the veteran Communist who remained a central figure in the Communist hierarchy. The revolutionary regime treated its Jewish subjects with equity and neither during the revolution nor after its success were any antisemitic attitudes adopted. But, by effecting profound changes in the social, political, and economic structure of the country, the revolution practically destroyed the economic stability of the majority of Cuban Jews.

Nationalization of private business by force, economic privations, and Fidel Castro's open identification with Marxist-Leninist ideology were among the causes of the large-scale emigration of upper- and middle-class Cubans as well as of the Jews.

Out of a Jewish population of about 12,000 before the revolution, in 1965 there remained about 2,500 Jews and in 1970 only about 1,500. In 1989 there were only 892 persons listed as recipients of products for Passover – 635 of them were Jews and 258 were their non-Jewish relatives; 82% of the Jews listed lived in Havana and the rest in provincial towns. The exodus of Cuban Jews, like that of their non-Jewish counterparts, was directed mainly towards *Miami, though many were relocated by HIAS in other cities in the United States or settled in other Latin American countries, like Puerto Rico, Venezuela, and Mexico. The Cuban government treated these emigrants as enemies of the revolution and their property was confiscated. The Jews who decided to make **aliyah* were treated with more respect, as fellow idealists. The Jewish Agency was able to charter from the Cuban Air Company three airplanes, bringing to Israel 420 *olim* (1961–62). The exodus started in 1960 with the wealthy merchants and industrialists, whose business activities were stopped by the INRA (National Institute of Agrarian Reform), but it included also the lay and religious leadership. A second wave of emigration, mostly of lower-middle-class Jews, was caused by the nationalization of small businesses in 1968.

The Jews who chose to remain in Cuba because they adhered to the revolutionary ideology preferred to stay aloof from the Jewish community, fearing that it would taint their reputations by identifying them as practitioners of religion. A relatively large number of these Jews turned to academic studies and integrated into the state economy in the liberal professions, a few attaining national fame for their remarkable achievements in science, music, literature, cinematography, and art. Among those who stayed were all the veteran Communists, whose merits were recognized by the new regime, but their attempts to represent the Jewish community were rejected by its members, who continued to identify with the Zionist movement. The new president of the community was Moisés Baldás (1961–81), born in Poland where he studied at a Tarbut school and was fluent in Hebrew. He had immigrated to Cuba in 1927 and become a successful businessman, but following the revolution he decided to dedicate himself to the declining community, presiding over the Patronato and the Unión Sionista and acting as the representative of the Jewish Agency. His functions included the protection of the Jewish community vis-à-vis the government as well as the provision of the spiritual and material necessities of those who remained affiliated with it. A large proportion of these Jews were elderly or handicapped, and they depended on the Jewish community for their sustenance. As individuals, these Jews lived in the margins of the revolutionary society, but the religious freedom of the Jewish community as an institution was protected and respected by Castro's government.

The Jewish institutions throughout Cuba were not dissolved by the government, and their existence depended on the activity of their members and not decrees from above. The five synagogues of Havana continued to function throughout the 1960s and 1970s. Temple Beth Israel of the American Jews was sold to the government around 1980 for lack of membership, and its property – including the Jewish cemetery – was transferred to Adath Israel. The three modern buildings of Adath Israel, the Patronato, and the Centro Sefaradi were permitted to rent out the unused parts of their spacious buildings to Cuban cultural organizations, so that rent received indirectly from the government covered the current expenses of the Jewish institutions. The synagogue of Shevet Aḥim in Old Havana was used until the late 1990s and was closed due to the deterioration of the building.

The Cuban government respected the Jewish dietary laws, and permitted Adath Israel not only to have their *shoḥet* use the government slaughterhouse, but also to operate the only private business – the kosher butcher shop where Jews were allowed to receive their meat rations. The Jewish community was permitted to receive packages of *matzot* and other products for Passover from abroad that were sent annually, from 1961, by the Canadian Jewish Congress. For the distribution of these products, which became the major form of identification with the Jewish community, Moisés Baldás organized the Comisión Coordinadora – a committee with representatives of the five synagogues that served as a central organization for Cuban Jewry.

The nationalization of education, in 1961, brought about the closure of all private schools, but Jews were granted special permission to impart Jewish education within the government system. The Autonomous School of the Centro Israelita was converted into a public school named after Albert Einstein, and in addition to the regular curriculum provided daily classes in Hebrew, Yiddish, and Jewish history. The government supplied transportation for Jewish children living in other parts of the city. This arrangement lasted until 1975, when it was suddenly stopped by government order. A small Sunday school was set up in the Patronato, where Baldás taught Hebrew and Jewish culture until his immigration to Israel in 1981.

The Unión Sionista continued to exist, and its members were able to carry on various cultural and educational activities within the limits of the revolutionary regime. Cuba was among the sponsors of the United Nations Assembly Resolution equating Zionism with racism (1975). It took, however, three years before the government realized that a Zionist organization was still functioning in Cuba. In 1978 the Unión Sionista was closed by government order and its building was confiscated and handed over to the PLO.

THE REVIVAL OF THE 1990S. The fall of the Soviet Union and the Communist Bloc in Eastern Europe caused a severe crisis in Cuba and shattered its economic base. Castro's government was forced to make ideological concessions to survive, including greater religious freedom and an influx of tourists and foreign investors. In 1990, when Castro declared the emergency policy of "the Special Period," the Jewish population had already been assimilated, and it shared with the rest of the Cuban people the economic difficulties as well as the crisis of values. The small community consisted of around 800 members and the intermarriage rate was over 90%. The Jewish presence was felt only in the Havana synagogues, where elderly people participated in the daily services of Adath Israel or the Sabbath prayers in the Patronato and Centro Sefaradi, to receive the modest meals offered after services.

From 1981 the community had been led by José Miller Ferdman, a dental surgeon born in Cuba who in the 1950s was secretary of the Agrupación Cultural Hebreo Cubana – an organization of Jewish intellectuals who tried to bridge between their Cuban and Jewish identities. Miller was one of the few Jews who remained faithful to Judaism while identifying with the revolutionary regime and achieving prominence in his professional field. Miller served as president of the Patronato from 1981 and is the representative of the Jewish community vis-à-vis the authorities. Adela Dworin, the main official of the Patronato, is one of the few Cuban Jews with a Yiddish background and Jewish education. She served as the librarian and secretary of the Patronato and was appointed vice president in view of increasing activities following the Jewish revival of the 1990s.

The revival of the community was engendered by the critical situation in Cuba but was made possible by spiritual and material assistance from abroad. From the mid-1980s Jewish tourists, particularly from Latin America, started to visit Cuba, and their donations became an important source of support to the declining community. A small Sunday school was reorganized in the Patronato in 1985, with Moisés Asis and Dr. Alberto Mechulam as volunteer teachers. They were assisted by the religious emissaries of *Ḥabad, who later focused their activities around Adath Israel, which became identified with the Orthodox movement. A small group of young Jews, born in mixed families and raised under the revolution, started to search for their roots in the Jewish community and to organize spontaneously, seeking spiritual guidance.

The growing need of the new generation to rediscover its Jewishness was met by the JDC, which started to assist the Jews of Cuba through its branch in Buenos Aires, providing religious and social leaders. The most influential among them was Rabbi Shmuel Szteinhendler, a graduate of the Seminario Rabinico of the Conservative movement in Buenos Aires, who served as rabbi in Guadalajara (Mexico). Throughout the revolutionary period the Jewish community of Cuba depended on the occasional visits of religious Jews to conduct services or perform religious ceremonies. During the 1980s the community had no *mohel*, and children grew up without circumcisions and bar mitzvahs. Rabbi Szteinhendler visited Cuba several times and in addition to his performance of Jewish rituals he trained local Jews to conduct their own services. He prepared persons who identified as Jews but were not halakhically Jewish to reaffirm their religion through conversion and religious marriage. About 150 males were circumcised before they were converted by a Bet Din of three rabbis that visited Cuba for this purpose, using the *mikveh* of Adath Israel. Szteinhendler also assisted in the revival of Judaism in the provincial towns, which had remained isolated from Jewish life since the revolution. Renovated communal institutions were established in Cienfuegos (1993), Guantánamo (1994), Santiago de Cuba (1995), Santa Clara (1995), Sancti Spiritus (1996), Manzanillo (1997), and Camagüey (1998).

The Jewish renaissance was accompanied by a trickle of *aliyah*, which increased considerably after 1994 following the quota imposed by U.S. President Clinton on immigration from Cuba. The main reasons for emigration were the difficult economic situation in Cuba, and many Jews did not hide their desire to use Israel as a stepping stone on their way to Miami. Lack of official relations between Cuba and Israel resulted in a secret arrangement between Cuba and the Jewish Agency, code-named Operation Cigar. In 1999 it became known that around 600 *olim* had reached Israel, but publicity did not hinder the *aliyah*, which continued on a small scale. The community today is a center of great activity, particularly of the younger generation, as well as a focus of interest and philanthropy for Jews in the Western Hemisphere.

[Margalit Bejarano (2nd ed.)]

Cuba-Israel Relations

Following Fidel Castro's revolution in 1959, and before Castro declared his intentions of introducing into Cuba a Socialist system based on the Soviet one, there was a period of fairly intense activity, which, inter alia, found expression in a series of trade agreements signed in 1959, 1960, and 1962. During Batista's administration Israel and Cuba were represented by their honorary consuls and by non-resident ambassadors. Diplomatic relations were strengthened under Castro, with the nomination of Dr. Jonathan Prato as the first resident ambassador in Havana (1961). Castro's sympathetic attitude towards Israel was partly due to his personal relations with Ricardo Subirana y Lobo (Richard *Wolf), a German Jew who had immigrated to Cuba prior to World War I and was appointed Cuba's ambassador to Israel (1961) in recognition of his generous support of the revolutionary struggle. Subirana y Lobo sent at his own expense agricultural and technical experts from kibbutzim to Cuba and used his personal contacts with Castro to protect the interests of Israel as well as those of Cuban Jews. Following the severance of diplomatic relations between the two countries (1973), he settled permanently in Israel and founded the Wolf Foundation.

The growing similarity of outlook on foreign policy between the Cuban government and the Soviet Union led to Cuban support of the Arab position. Cuba – alienated from its neighbors in the Western Hemisphere and suspended from participation in the Organization of American States – came to seek support, increasingly, among the countries of the so-called Third World, among which Egypt and Algeria played a prominent role. With the establishment in Havana of the Secretariat of the Tri-Continental Organization, which adopted the cause of the anti-Israel Palestine Liberation Movement (*PLO), Havana became increasingly active in spreading its doctrine. The press and radio of Cuba reflected this tendency, particularly after the Six-Day War (1967), in a one-sided editorial policy and selection of information. However, in spite of the heavy pressure brought to bear upon it, the Cuban government refused to break diplomatic relations with Israel and maintained its policy of recognizing Israel, and on various occasions manifested its support for Arab-Israel negotiations as a preferable means of resolving the Middle East conflict. At the United Nations, however, the Cuban government was consistent in supporting the Arab viewpoint against Israel from the mid-1960s and relations between the two countries continued to deteriorate.

In September 1973, during the Conference of Non-Aligned Nations in Algiers, Castro announced his decision to sever diplomatic relations with Israel. The attacks against Israel in the Cuban media became unrestrained, and Cuba endorsed a militant anti-Israeli and pro-Palestinian position in all the international arenas. In 1975 Castro's government co-sponsored United Nations Resolution 3379 declaring Zionism a form of racism. Propaganda against Israel and against Zionism has since been virulent, but the Cuban government was cautious not to slide into antisemitism or deny the legitimate existence of the State of Israel. The Cuban media made a clear distinction between anti-Zionism and antisemitism, and the Jewish community has never been attacked or discriminated against in spite of the hostile attitude towards Israel. Likewise, Cuba's permanent condemnation of Israel and its defense of the Palestinians were directed against the Israeli government and its policy, not against the people or the existence of the state. A Friendship League including members of the Israel Communist Party has been active since the 1960s.

The end of the Cold War did not alter Cuba's pro-Palestinian position, nor its anti-Israel pronouncements in all international forums. The official hostility towards Israel is nurtured by its close relations with the United States, manifested by its consistent voting in the United Nations in support of the American embargo. Quietly, however, there were signs of change in the economic and cultural spheres as well as a softening line in politics conditioned by prospects of peace in the Middle East. Private Israeli firms invested in Cuba's post-Soviet economy, and there were signs of rapprochement of non-political entities, such as academic and artistic institutions.

[Netanel Lorch / Margalit Bejarano (2nd ed.)]

BIBLIOGRAPHY: R.M. Levine, *Tropical Diaspora: The Jewish Experience in Cuba* (1993); B. Sapir, *Jewish Community of Cuba* (1948); H. Viteles, *Report on the Status of the Jewish Immigration in Cuba* (1925); L. Ran, in: *Algemeyne Entsiklopedye-Yidn*, 5 (1957), 421–36, includes bibliography; G. Minkowicz, *Tsifern un Fakten vegn Idishen Yishuv in Kuba* (1952). **ADD. BIBLIOGRAPHY:** M. Bejarano, "*Yahadut Kubah 1898–1939*," Ph.D. dissertation (1992); M. Asis, in: *Yahadut Zemanenu* 5 (1990, 325–39; M. Bejarano, *La comunidad hebrea de Cuba: la memoria y la historia* (1996); D.E. Kaplan, in: AJYB 101 (2001), 21–87; M.C. Capestani, *Presencia Hebrea en Cuba* (2004).

CUBAN, MARK (1958–), U.S. businessman, owner of the Dallas Mavericks basketball team. Cuban was born in Pittsburgh, Pennsylvania, his paternal grandparents having come to America from Dnepropetrovsk, Ukraine, and his maternal grandparents from near the Austrian/Russian/Polish border. Cuban began exhibiting acumen for business as a 12-year-old, when he sold garbage bags door-to-door. Attending business school at Indiana University, he put himself through school by giving disco dancing lessons and starting a chain letter that helped cover one semester's tuition. In 1983 Cuban co-founded MicroSolutions, a leading National Systems Integrator, later selling it to CompuServe, and then, in 1995, co-founded Broadcast.com, a leading provider of multimedia and streaming on the Internet, selling it to Yahoo! in July 1999.

Now a billionaire, Cuban purchased the Dallas Mavericks for $283 million on January 14, 2000, and immediately changed the face of the organization by becoming the first owner in team sports to encourage fan interaction through e-mail on his personal computer. His outspoken personality also got him into trouble with the National Basketball Association, which levied heavy fines for his criticism of officials and the league itself, totaling more than one million dollars. But Cuban's whatever-it-takes attitude and commitment to winning resulted in the team's finishing his first season, 2000–2001, with a 53–29 record and the team's first playoff appearance in 11 years. In 2001–2002, the team finished with a franchise-best record of 57–25 and an NBA-best road record of 27–14, advancing to the playoffs for the second consecutive year. In his third season the team went 60–22, and 52–30 in 2003–2004. "I spend every day thinking about the Mavericks," Cuban said. "That includes time dreaming about the Mavs while sleeping."

[Elli Wohlgelernter (2nd ed.)]

CUCUMBER. Three species of "cucumber" are mentioned in the Bible and in rabbinic literature: *kishu'im, pakku'ot,* and the *yerokat* (or *yerikat*) *ha-ḥamor.*

(1) *Kishu'im*: only the plural form occurs in the Bible, but the singular, *kishut*, occurs in rabbinic literature. The reference is to the chate cucumber (*Cucumis melo*, var. *chate*) which appears frequently in images from ancient Egypt. It was an important crop and a favorite food there, which explains the yearning of the Children of Israel for them during their sojourn in the wilderness (Num. 11:5). Botantically this "cucumber" belongs to the genus *Melon*, which is called *melafefon* in rabbinic literature (Mishnah, Kil. 1:2, regards the *melafefon* as belonging to the same species and modern Hebrew erroneously uses *melafefon* for the cucumber). In the mishnaic period the cucumber was an important crop, but its nutritious value was a matter of dispute. It was said that the large species "are as injurious to the body as a sword," while the small species "open the bowels" (Ber. 57b). A summer plant, it could be grown in the winter under special conditions. Thus it was stated of Judah ha-Nasi and the emperor Antoninus that their table never lacked cucumbers even in winter (*ibid.*). *Kishu'im* in modern Hebrew is applied to squash, which was introduced from America and was not known to the ancients.

(2) The *pakku'at sadeh* (bitter cucumber, colocynth, *Citrullus colocynthis*) is mentioned in the story of Elisha's disciple who, in time of famine, found a *gefen-sadeh* ("field vine") from which he gathered *pakku'ot*. He cooked porridge from it, which was poisonous, but Elisha provided an antidote by adding flour (II Kings 4:39–41). From the seeds of this plant the oil of the *pakku'ot* mentioned in the Mishnah (Shab. 2:2) is obtained. The bitter cucumber, a perennial plant of the family Cucurbitaceae, is widespread in the arid regions of Ereẓ Israel. It is of the same genus as the watermelon, being similar in leaf and fruit. Apparently edible, it in fact contains poisonous substances. The oil extracted from it has medicinal properties. In the coastal region south of Gaza, it is sometimes gathered for its seeds. The leaves of the bitter cucumber have an attractive shape and they appear as an artistic form in the ornamentation of ancient buildings. Some identify them with the *mikla'at peka'im* (AV, "carved knops") of the Temple of Solomon and the molten sea (I Kings 6:18; 7:24).

(3) *Yerokat ha-ḥamor* is mentioned in the Mishnah (Oho. 8:1) as a plant with crowded and hard leaves which serve as a screen against ritual defilement. The reference is to the *Ecbalium elaterium*. Its fruit resembles a small cucumber. When ripe, the slightest touch causes the fruit to burst open, squirting its juice a long distance. The mishnaic name is usually read as *yerokat ḥamor* ("the ass's vegetable"). In one manuscript, the reading is *yerikat ha-ḥamor* ("the ass's spittle") perhaps because the squirting of the juices resembled the spitting of an ass. The plant grows abundantly in Ereẓ Israel, mainly in refuse dumps.

BIBLIOGRAPHY: Loew, Flora, 1 (1928), 530ff.; H.N. and A.L. Moldenke, *Plants of the Bible* (1952), 78ff., 88ff.; J. Feliks, *Ha-Ẓome'aḥ ha-Mikra'i* (1957), 166, 202; idem, *Kilei Zera'im ve-Harkavah* (1967), 47–53. **ADD. BIBLIOGRAPHY:** Feliks, Ha-Ẓome'aḥ, 79, 101, 126, 144.

[Jehuda Feliks]

°**CUDWORTH, RALPH** (1617–1688), English Platonist. Cudworth was professor of Hebrew at Cambridge from 1645. His commentary on Daniel survives in manuscript form (British Museum, Ms. Add. 4986–87), and he is known to have been interested in the translation of the Mishnah into Latin by Isaac *Abendana (Cambridge Univ., Ms. Mm. 1. 4–9); his publications, however, were theological and philosophical. In a sermon preached before the House of Commons in 1647 Cudworth advocated toleration, and he was a member of the Whitehall Conference of 1655 concerning the readmission of Jews to England. He eulogized Cromwell and his son in Hebrew, as well as Charles II on his return by contributing a congratulatory volume called *Academiae Cantabrigiensis* Σῶστρα (1660). The auction catalog of his library (February 2, 1690/91) was printed, and contains a list of his Hebrew books among many others.

BIBLIOGRAPHY: J.A. Passmore, *Ralph Cudworth* (1950), includes bibliography. **ADD. BIBLIOGRAPHY:** ODNB online.

[Raphael Loewe]

CUENCA, city in Castile, Spain. Shortly after its reconquest in 1177, Cuenca was granted a *fuero* ("charter") which served as the model for other Castilian towns. This permitted Jews to settle freely and trade without restriction, but debarred them from certain offices and forbade sexual relations with Christian women, on pain of burning. Chapter XXIX in its entirety and seven scattered laws out of 983 laws of the *Fuero de Cuenca* deal with Jews. The *Fuero* establishes, in theory but not in practice, equality before the law for Christians, Jews, and Muslims. Toward the end of the 13th century the community of Cuenca numbered between 50 and 100 families, paying an average annual tax of 70,872 maravedis. The Jewish quarter was located near the cathedral. The Jews made loans to the city in 1318 and in 1326 at a high rate of interest. In 1355 there was an outbreak of anti-Jewish rioting in Cuenca led by the Christian and Muslim supporters of Queen Blanca. During the anti-Jewish riots of 1391, the leading citizens of Cuenca joined the populace in an attack on the Jewish quarter, which was completely destroyed. The community partly recovered during the 15th century. There was now also a considerable body of Conversos. A tribunal of the Inquisition began its activities in the district of Cuenca in 1489; the number of those sentenced reached into thousands. After the issue of the decree of expulsion of the Jews from Spain in March 1492, the Jews of Cuenca and Huete are said to have rioted, claiming that they had four years to leave Spain and threatening to take revenge on the Conversos. Some of the exiles from Cuenca in the Ottoman Empire adopted the name of the city as a family name. The Inquisition continued to operate in Cuenca throughout the 16th and 17th centuries. The last serious series of trials took place in the years 1718–25 when hundreds of Crypto-Jews or descendants of Conversos were cruelly persecuted and prosecuted by the local tribunal. This campaign was part of a general inquisitorial move under Philip v. The reason for this campaign in the region of Cuenca may have been the socioeconomic position of the Conversos. The confiscations contributed much to the finances of the Inquisition in Cuenca.

BIBLIOGRAPHY: Baer, Spain, index; H.C. Lea, *History of the Inquisition in Spain*, 1 (1906), index; R. de Ureña y Smenjaud, *Las ediciones del Fuero de Cuenca* (1917); Huidobro and Cantera, in: *Sefarad*, 14 (1954), 342; Suárez Fernández, Documentos, index; S. Cirac Estopañan *Registros de los Documentos del Santo Oficio de Cuenca y Sigüenza* (1965). **ADD. BIBLIOGRAPHY:** C. Carrete Parrondo, in: *Helmantica* 30 (1979), 51–61; M.F. García Casar, in: REJ 144 (1985), 27–37; R. de Lera García, in: *Sefarad* 47 (1987), 87–137; R. Carrasco, in: *Hispania* 166 (1987), 503–59; Y. Moreno Koch, in: *El Olivo* 27 (1988), 47–52.

[Haim Beinart / Yom Tov Assis (2nd ed.)]

CUENQUE (Cuenca?), ABRAHAM BEN LEVI (b. 1648), kabbalistic author and Shabbatean. He was born in Hebron, where he joined the Shabbatean movement, remaining among its followers even after *Shabbetai Ẓevi's conversion to Islam. In 1683 he went as special envoy to Europe, crossed Italy, France, Poland, and Germany and returned in 1693. At the request of a friend in Frankfurt, Cuenque wrote in 1689 his memoirs of Shabbetai Ẓevi, whom he had met in Hebron. The work constitutes "an almost idolatrous biography and a kind of Shabbatean gospel" (Graetz). Large sections of it are included in Jacob *Emden's *Torat ha-Kena'ot* (Amsterdam, 1752) under the title *Tofes Shelishi* (or *Nosaḥ Shelishi*). Cuenque also wrote a description of his travels (which has remained unpublished). He is also the author of the following works: (1) *Avak Soferim* (3 pts., Amsterdam, 1704), commentaries on the Bible and sermons; (2) *Minḥat Kena'ot* (Ms.), about envy, also containing a dialogue entitled *Vikku'aḥ al ha-Kinah u-Se'ifeha*; (3) *Avak Derakhim* (Ms.), a collection of sermons delivered on his travels. He died in Hebron.

BIBLIOGRAPHY: Graetz, Gesch, 10 (1896), 231, 312, 332, 431; D. Kahana, *Toledot ha-Mekubbalim*, 1 (1913), 119, 140; Scholem, Shabbetai Ẓevi (1967), index.

[Joseph Elijah Heller]

CUKIERMAN, ROGER (1936–), French banker, businessman, and community leader. Holding a doctorate in economy from Paris University, as well as a degree in law, Cukierman had a successful business and banking career in France and Israel, and headed the France-Israel Chamber of Commerce. Active in Jewish communal life and community leadership (vice president of the Alliance Israélite Universelle), he was eventually elected twice (in 2001 and 2004) to the presidency of the CRIF despite strong and sometimes controversial views on antisemitism and the future of the French Jewish community, which he does not fear to express frankly. His efforts helped promote awareness in political circles about the rise of a new antisemitism in France.

[Dror Franck Sullaper (2nd ed.)]

CUKOR, GEORGE (1899–1983), U.S. movie director. Born in New York City, Cukor began his theater career as an assistant stage manager and later directed several troupes (1921–29). His directorial work, included adaptations from novels and plays (including *Dinner at Eight*, 1933), and he directed many well-known actresses, including Katherine Hepburn, in *A Bill of Divorcement* (1932), *Little Women* (1933), *Philadelphia Story* (1940), and *Holiday* (1938); Greta Garbo, in *Camille* (1937); Ingrid Bergman, in *Gaslight* (1944); Judy Holliday, in *Born Yesterday* (1950) and *It Should Happen to You* (1954); Judy Garland, in *A Star Is Born* (1954); Marilyn Monroe, in *Let's Make Love* (1960); Audrey Hepburn, in *My Fair Lady* (1964); Anouk Aimée, in *Justine* (1969); Maggie Smith, in *Travels With My Aunt* (1973), Elizabeth Taylor and Ava Gardner, in *The Blue Bird* (1976); and Jacqueline Bisset and Candice Bergen, in *Rich and Famous* (1981).

[Jonathan Licht]

CULI, JACOB (c. 1685–1732), rabbi, editor, and initiator of an important series of *Ladino Bible commentaries known as *Me-Am Lo'ez. Born either in Jerusalem or Safed, Culi was descended on both sides from illustrious rabbinical families. His father was the son of a Cretan rabbi of Spanish origin and his mother the daughter of R. Moses ibn *Ḥabib. Culi left Safed for Constantinople in order to publish his grandfather's writings. He completed his studies under R. Judah *Rosanes (d. 1727), the chief rabbi of Constantinople, who appointed him *dayyan* as well as teacher of the community. After the death of Rosanes, Culi, who had by now published his grandfather's *Shammot ba-Areẓ* (Constantinople, 1727) and *Ezrat Nashim* (*ibid.*, 1731), the latter with two of his own responsa, was entrusted with the publication of the late chief rabbi's works. Adding introductions and notes he edited *Parashat Derakhim* (*ibid.*, 1728) and *Mishneh la-Melekh* (*ibid.*, 1731).

As the author of the *Me-Am Lo'ez* on Genesis and a portion of Exodus, Culi was one of the founding fathers of Judeo-Spanish (i.e., Ladino) literature. In this work, which he began in 1730 and in which he hoped to cover the entire Bible, Culi sought to provide the Ladino-speaking layman with translations of appropriate traditional texts. The result was an elaborate encyclopedic commentary on the Bible in the Ladino language. It dealt with all aspects of Jewish life, and cited a host of important rabbinic sources.

The success of Culi's *Me-Am Lo'ez* among the Jews of Turkey and the Balkans was unparalleled and the whole series was republished many times. Culi left, in addition to the printed commentaries on Genesis and Exodus (as far as the portion *Terumah; ibid.*, 1730–33), unpublished manuscripts of his work on other biblical books. The publication of the *Me-Am Lo'ez* continued after his death perhaps in part on the basis of his manuscript material. There were at least six editions of Genesis and eight of Exodus. New editions in Hebrew and Ladino were being prepared and published in the 1960s (see **Me-am Lo'ez*).

The subsequent increase of translations from Hebrew into Ladino testifies to the great success of Culi's works and to the demand which they created. His halakhic work, *Simanim li-Oraita*, was never published.

BIBLIOGRAPHY: M.D. Gaon, *Maskiyyot Levav* (1933); idem, in: *Mizraḥ u-Ma'arav*, 2 (1928), 191–201; idem, *Yehudei ha-Mizraḥ be-Ereẓ Yisrael*, 2 (1938), 305–08; A. Yerushalmi, *Yalkut Me-Am Lo'ez*, 1 (1967), introd.; Molho, in: *Oẓar Yehudei Sefarad*, 5 (1962), 80–94; Yaari, Sheluḥei, index; Rosanes, Togarmah, 5 (1938), 13–16; Azulai, 2 (1852), 96, no. 34.

CULLMAN (Kullman), family of U.S. business executives.

JOSEPH F. CULLMAN 3rd (1912–2004) was the longtime head of the giant tobacco company Philip Morris who, in the face of serious concern about smoking, built the company into one of the largest corporations in America and the maker of the best-selling product in the world. He was born into the business in New York, where his great-grandfather, FERDINAND KULLMAN, a cigar maker from Germany, settled in 1848. His son, the first JOSEPH CULLMAN, became a dealer in Ohio leaf. His son, eventually called JOE JUNIOR in the trade, led the General Cigar Company, which produced brands like White Owl, Van Dyck and Robert Burns; at one time he owned 1,800 acres of tobacco fields in Connecticut. Joe Junior had one daughter and four sons; the eldest came to be known as Joe Third.

After graduation from Yale, Joe Third spent a short time working as a clerk in a Schulte Cigar store in New York and then was sent to Havana to work at the H. Upmann cigar factory. During World War II, he spent three years as a gunnery officer aboard a cruiser that fought its way up the Coral Sea to Guadalcanal. When he returned to civilian life, he took over the management of a small company, Benson & Hedges, that his father had purchased in 1941. That company served the carriage trade with monogrammed gold-tipped and hand-rolled cigarettes. It also produced a luxury cigarette called Parliament, with a recessed mouthpiece and a cotton filter. The cigarette producer Philip Morris had no filters and other companies, perhaps with an eye on health concerns, were introducing filter-tipped cigarettes. In 1954 Philip Morris turned over stock valued at $22.4 million to Joe Junior for his interest in Benson & Hedges. In addition to the two brands, Parliament and Benson & Hedges, Philip Morris acquired Joe Third as a vice president. The next year he was named executive vice president and at the end of 1957 he became president and chief executive. He held both titles until 1967, when he was named chairman and chief executive, staying in that capacity until 1978.

From 1964 to 1969, cigarette sales for Philip Morris increased by 63 percent. One major reason was a shift in advertising. When Joe Third took over Philip Morris, the company and its flagship cigarette were represented by a short man in a hotel bellhop's uniform shouting "Call for Philip Morris," as if he were paging someone. As the company worked on a filter cigarette to challenge the industry leader, Winston, Cullman presided over the quest for the right mixture of tobacco, the appropriate filter, a new flip-top box, and the right image that would attract smokers to Marlboro, a new cigarette to be marketed under an old brand name that had once been aimed at women. The Chicago-based advertising agency Leo Burnett created a campaign involving rugged Western cowboys, inviting smokers to "come where the flavor is … come to Marlboro Country." In his memoir, Cullman said: "What was needed was a full-flavored filter brand that had a virile image." By 1983 Marlboro had become the best-selling product in the world.

Cullman had set the stage for the company's diversification in 1969, when Philip Morris acquired Miller Brewing, and then General Foods, Kraft and Nabisco Holdings, whose brands included Maxwell House coffee, Oreo cookies and Oscar Meyer sausages. Under his direction, Philip Morris rose from last in sales among the six major American producers to first in 1983, surpassing Reynolds Tobacco, the industry leader for 25 years. Philip Morris earned so much cash that it was driven to use its huge profits to acquire food giants like Kraft General Foods, Miller Beer, and Jacques Suchard and became the largest consumer products company in the world. It sold the most popular cigarette in the world (Marlboro) and the second most popular beer in America. But as the company grew, the basic product, cigarettes, was coming under increasing attack as perilous to health. As the evidence accumulated, Cullman led the company and the industry's effort to counteract those claims. He testified before Congressional committees, he deflected and delayed calls to curb cigarette smoking and advertising by scientists, public health specialists, legislators, lung-damaged plaintiffs, and personal injury lawyers. He led the unsuccessful effort against those seeking to put warnings on cigarette advertising and messages on cigarette packs. And he wrote countless letters to editors, arguing that smoking was a matter of personal choice. Cullman smoked for many years but eventually tapered off and quit.

Cullman involved Philip Morris, an $80 billion company in 2004, renamed the Altria Group, in countless philanthropies, especially in sports and the arts. He was a leader in creating the women's professional tennis tour, the Virginia Slims circuit, sponsored by one of his brands. The company gave millions each year to groups like the Dance Theater of Harlem, the Brooklyn Academy of Music, the Guggenheim and Metropolitan art museums and the Whitney Museum of American Art. An active conservationist, he was a former trustee of the New York State Nature and Historical Preserve Trust of the American Museum of Natural History and served on the national board of the Smithsonian Institution. He was also a member of the board of the World Wildlife Fund and director of the American Folk Art Museum.

One of his favorite philanthropic projects was the Gomez Mill House in Newburgh, N.Y. It is believed to be the oldest extant house in the United States built by a Jewish owner (1714). Cullman said he was a descendant of Louis Moses Gomez, who fled the Spanish Inquisition and built the house as a fortress where he traded with the Indians. A second floor was added during the period of the Revolutionary War. Gomez's descendants also include Supreme Court Justice Benjamin *Cardozo and Emma *Lazarus, the poet.

Cullman's second wife was JOAN PALEY CULLMAN, whose grandfathers were Nathan *Straus Sr. and Dr. Bernard *Sachs, a discoverer of Tay-Sachs disease, the hereditary neurological disorder. She became a Tony Award-winning producer of Broadway plays and vice chair of Linclon Center.

Joe Third's brother LEWIS B. CULLMAN (1919–) and his wife, DOROTHY (1923–), were philanthropists. In 1963, Lewis Cullman originated the idea of the leveraged buyout, acquiring the Orkin Exterminating Company, and continued to amass a fortune with this now-common business practice. He is the founder and former chairman of Cullman Ventures, which includes the jewel in his crown, the At-a-Glance Group, a manufacturer of 90 percent of the diaries and appointment books in the United States. He sold the company to Mead in 1999 so he could devote his energies to philanthropy in the arts, science and education. His philanthropies include many of the great institutions of New York City, including Lincoln Center for the Performing Arts, the Museum of Modern Art and Central Park. Dorothy is a television producer with an interest in aiding writers and artists, reading and human rights. They pledged more than $80 million, mostly to civic and cultural institutions in New York City, including the Metropolitan Museum of Art, the New York Public Library, the American Museum of Natural History and the New York Botanical Garden.

Another brother, EDGAR M. CULLMAN SR. (1918–) was chairman of the Culbro Corporation, manufacturers of premium cigars like Garcia y Vega and Macanudo brands. In 1961, Edgar bought a controlling stake in the General Cigar Company, which had been listed on the New York Stock Exchange since 1906. In 1976, General Cigar changed its name to Culbro, an echo of the family firm name. His son EDGAR JR. (1946–) became president and designated chairman of Culbro.

HOWARD S. CULLMAN (1891–1972), brother of Joseph F. Cullman, Jr., became president of the family firm. In 1927 he was appointed to the Port of New York Authority by Governor Alfred E. Smith. He became vice chairman in 1934 and chairman a few years later, serving until 1955. In 1929, Howard, a Yale graduate, and his brother formed Tobacco and Allied Stocks to invest and trade in securities in the tobacco industry. It was the first investment trust in the field. In 1931 he was appointed by Governor Franklin D. Roosevelt as chairman of a state committee to investigate problems connected with workmen's compensation. He served as a director of major corporations, and was a commissioner-general of the 1958 Brussels World's Fair. He also held prominent positions in Jewish communal affairs, serving with ORT and the Jewish Social Service Association. With his wife, MARGUERITE W. CULLMAN (1905–1999), he invested in such Broadway shows as *Life With Father*, *Oklahoma!*, *Carousel*, *Brigadoon*, *South Pacific*, *Annie Get Your Gun*, *Fiddler on the Roof*, *Teahouse of the August Moon*, *Death of a Salesman*, and *A Streetcar Named Desire*.

[Stewart Kampel (2nd ed.)]

CULT. The Israelite cult was a system of ritual acts by which the Israelites, individually and collectively, actualized their particular relationship to the God of Israel. In the pre-Exilic period (before 587–586 B.C.E.) this activity took the form of sacrificial offerings of various types. *Prayer as later known existed as a mode of religious expression, but it had not yet attained the status of an independently sufficient means for fulfilling religious obligations or for attaining ritual objectives. After the destruction of the First Temple the greater part of Jewry was dispersed. Since the Temple in Jerusalem was inaccessible to them on a regular basis, substitute ritual forms had to be acknowledged as sufficient, and prayer began to come into its own. It did not fully replace sacrifice until the destruction of the Second Temple in 70 C.E. After the return from exile and the rebuilding of the Temple, the Jewish communities inside and outside Israel continued to maintain their relationship to the Temple, and considered its cult indispensable to their religious and national life. Most information on the early Israelite cult comes from the Bible. Talmudic and other sources report on later practice in the Second Temple, which undoubtedly bore certain resemblances to the earlier cult. Archaeological excavations have unearthed many installations and vessels intended for cultic use, but it is generally difficult to identify them precisely with those described in the Bible. Uncertainty about the exact dates of the priestly codes of the Pentateuch complicates the problem of ascertaining the exact character of the Israelite cult, since it is from these codes that most information derives. Whatever may be suggested concerning the historicity of the "tabernacle" cult presented in these sources, there can be little doubt that it mirrors the cult of the First Temple in a significant way. The prophet Ezekiel lived at the end of the First Temple period; and in Ezekiel (40ff.) procedures are attested which closely resemble those in Exodus, Leviticus, and Numbers in much of their detail. The cult may be discussed with respect to diverse elements of Israelite culture. The concern here is to present the praxis of the cult, i.e., the principal types of sacrificial offerings and the manner of their disposition, which involved, in turn, certain vessels and tools.

Sacrifices of Animals and Fowl

The priestly codes prescribe sacrifices of large and small cattle, as well as pigeons and turtledoves (Lev. 1–7). Male animals predominate as sacrificial victims, no doubt because only a fraction of the males needed to be preserved for the reproduction of the herd. Why females are nevertheless prescribed for certain offerings is less obvious. The codes differentiate between pure and impure animals (Lev. 11; Deut. 14). An overall requirement is that sacrificial animals be free from physical defects (Lev. 22:20–25), although an animal with certain minor defects could be designated for "freewill offerings" (Lev. 22:23;

see *Blemish). In the case of the paschal sacrifice it is stipulated that the intended victims be observed for four days prior to the festival (Ex. 12:3, 6), a procedure which talmudic sages correctly understood to be for the purpose of discovering possible blemishes (Mekh. Bo, 5). The Bible says nothing of such procedures elsewhere, although they were undoubtedly necessary and widespread in the ancient Near East. Talmudic sources speak extensively of examination for defects, especially in the orders *Kodashim* and *Tohorot* of the Mishnah. The selection of sacrificial animals was also governed by consideration of age and, in certain instances, of the previous use of the animal. The requirement of physical perfection extended to the priesthood, and priests with certain physical defects could not officiate in the cult (Lev. 21:21–23; Deut. 15:21; 17:1). Once the animal was declared fit, it was designated a sacrificial animal and assigned as a certain type of offering for a particular time or occasion (cf. Lev. 16:9–10). This assignment normally involved "the laying [from the Heb. verb סמך, *samakh*] of hands" by the officiating priest on the head of the animal (Lev. 1:4; 3:2, 8, 13; et al.). Perhaps this act was accompanied by a declaration which has been lost. The method of slaughtering sacrificial animals was usually described by the verb *shaḥaṭ* (Ex. 12:6; Lev. 1:5), and in the case of fowl by *malak (malaq*; "to break the neck"; Lev. 1:15; 5:8). *Shaḥaṭ* involved the use of a knife or similar sharp instrument that would slit the gullet as well as the jugular vein, resulting in the rapid emission of most of the animal's blood. The Bible never describes the tool employed for this purpose, and the only clue is the term *ma'khelet* used in connection with Abraham's intended sacrifice of Isaac and elsewhere, but which is nowhere described (Gen. 22:6, 19; Judg. 19:29; Prov. 30:14; cf. the verb *nataḥ* ("to cut into sections") in Lev. 1:6; I Sam. 11:7; I Kings 18:23). This method of slaughtering was associated with the prohibition against eating *blood (Lev. 17:10–11). The blood of the sacrificial victim was caught in bowls (Heb. *mizrak; mizraq*) for further use in the performance of the sacrifice. In expiatory offerings some of the blood was dabbed or sprinkled on the horns of the incense altar, and in some cases on the *parokhet* ("curtain"), on the *kapporet* ("the lid [of the ark]") and elsewhere, as part of ritual procedure, usually designated by the verb *kipper* ("to perform an act of ritual expiation"; Lev. 4:6–7; 17–18; 16:14, 18–19; et al.), although the corresponding noun *kippurim* also occurs (Ex. 29:36; 30:10, 16; Lev. 23:27–28; 25:9; Num. 5:8; 29:11; see also **Kipper*). In all animal sacrifices most of the blood was poured or dashed against the side of the altar of burnt offerings so that it ran down to the ground (Lev. 1:5; 4:7). In the execution and disposition of sacrifices three principal parties were involved: the donors, the priests, and the deity. The various methods of disposition reflected the relative weight of these parties. There were two major categories of animal sacrifices: the *ʿolah* ("ascending offering") and the *zevaḥ* ("slain offering"). The *ʿolah* was burned to ashes in the altar fire, while most of the meat of the *zevaḥ* was cooked in vessels, and only certain portions, those assigned directly to the deity, were placed on the altar. According to Leviticus 1:9ff., the *ʿolah* was holocaust, i.e., an offering entirely consumed by the altar fire. This is also the sense of the term *kalil* (Lev. 6:15–16; Deut. 33:10; I Sam. 7:9; Ps. 51:21, and cf. Deut. 13:17; Judg. 20:40), although the exact relationship of these two terms is problematic. Some have suggested that *kalil* is an older term, which was later replaced by the term *ʿolah*. The two principal types of expiatory offering, *ḥaṭṭat* and *'asham*, although classified with the *ʿolah* in certain respects (Lev. 6:18), represented a distinct type of sacrifice since in some cases most of the meat of the *ḥaṭṭat* was assigned to the priests (Lev. 6:22; 7:6; Num. 18:9–10; Hos. 4:8). This was true of expiatory offerings brought by individuals, and according to rabbinic law also of the *ḥaṭṭat* of new moons and festivals (Num. 28:15; et al.), whereas certain communal offerings of these types were disposed of in different ways (Lev. 4–5; 16:27–28). The exact procedures are not entirely clear. If any blood of the sacrificial victim had been brought into the tent of assembly, all but the suet and the kidneys of the animal had to be burned separately outside of the altar area, since the animal had become a source of impurity (Lev. 4:12, 20; 6:23; 8:17, 32; 16:27). Problems remain in classifying the expiatory offerings of the Israelite cult, and it is likely that in the course of time the practices were altered. The dynamics underlying the *ʿolah* and all offerings of which any parts were burned on the altar was that the deity breathed in the smoke of the offering and in that way was considered to have consumed the sacrifice (Gen. 8:21; Lev. 26:31; Deut. 4:28; 33:10; I Sam. 26:19; Amos 5:21). This notion is conveyed in the term *i'sheh reʿaḥ niḥoʿaḥ* ("a fired offering of pleasing aroma"), which is often used to describe sacrifices (Ex. 29:18; Lev. 3:16; 8:21, 28; et al.). The odor of the burning meat was believed to be pleasing to the Lord (Lev. 1:9; et al.). In cultic terms, the parts of the animal most desired by the deity were the fatty portions (*ḥelev*) which covered the inwards of the animal (Lev. 3:3; et al.). Such fatty portions were forbidden for human consumption on somewhat the same basis as the prohibition of blood, since the fat belonged to the deity (Ex. 29:13; Lev. 3:16–17; 4:8, 31; 7:23–25; I Sam. 2:15–16; Ezek. 44:7, 15). From non-cultic sources it appears that the consideration of the fatty portions as choice was pervasive in the Israelite cult (Deut. 32:38; cf. Gen. 4:4; Isa. 1:11, 43:24). In addition to separate offerings containing incense, certain aromatic substances were probably cast into the altar fire, a widespread custom in antiquity. For the purpose of burning offered meat, a wood fire was maintained on the altar (Lev. 1:7, 12), and later sources mention a special appointment for supplying this material (Neh. 10:35; 13:31). The *zevaḥ* was conceived as a sacred meal of which the worshipers and the deity partook in common fellowship. In time, the officiating priesthood appropriated some of what originally had been eaten by the donors of the *zevaḥ*, i.e., the right shank and the breast (Lev. 7:31–34; cf. Num. 18:18). Perhaps a further stage in this development, affording even more to the priests, is to be seen in the Punic cult at Carthage, as known from inscriptions of the fourth–third centuries B.C.E. The fatty portions of the *zevaḥ* were consumed by the altar fire (Lev. 4:31; 6:5;

Deut. 32:38). The rest was boiled in pots. This is known from early biblical sources independent of the priestly codes (cf. Judg. 6:19), and from the prohibition against this manner of cooking the paschal *zevaḥ* in favor of broiling, a primitive practice (Ex. 12:9). This method was apparently abolished in Deuteronomy 16:7, where the regular technique of boiling (Heb. *bashal*) is prescribed. Other sources also speak of boiling the meat of the *zevaḥ* (Ex. 29:31; Ezek. 46:20, 24; II Chron. 35:13). That meat was regularly boiled is also presupposed by the prohibition against boiling a kid in the milk of its dam (Ex. 23:19; 34:26; Deut. 14:21). Those invited to partake of the *zevaḥ* were termed *keru'im* (*qeru'im*; "those called"; I Sam. 9:13, 22; cf. Zeph. 1:7). The flesh of certain offerings could be eaten only by those in a state of ritual purity (Lev. 7:19–20; 22:3) in a sacred place (Ex. 29:31; Lev. 6:19; 7:6; 10:13; 24:9; et al.). The Mishnah (Zev. 5–6:1) limits the latter requirement to sacrifices with the status of *kodshei kodashim* (*qodshei qodashim*). In certain cases there was also a time limit for eating sacrificial flesh, and what was not consumed by that time had to be destroyed (Lev. 7:18; 19:7). The burnt offering with its blood rites is an historical problem, since outside the sphere of Syria and Palestine it was rarely used until late antiquity. The Ugaritic texts show that it figured in the Ugaritic cult as early as the 14th century B.C.E. In Ugaritic ritual texts *šlmm* (Heb. *shelamim*), the most prominent type of *zevaḥ*, is paired with *šrp* (Heb. *saraf*), the burnt offering. Burnt offerings are also mentioned in Ugaritic epics. In Mesopotamia fire was used extensively in magical rites, which were often connected with the cult, but it was not employed for sacrifices until late Babylonian times.

Grain Offerings

Sacrificial offerings of grain prepared in various ways were widespread in the ancient Near East. In the biblical cult the most prominent form of grain offering was the *minḥah*, a general term. It was prepared from wheat or barley, normally ground into fine flour, and either baked in an oven, fried in pans, or deep fried (Lev. 2:4–7). Oil and frankincense were mixed with the dough or poured over the cakes. In contrast to other ancient Near Eastern cults, no honey was used (Lev. 2:11). As a rule the *minḥah* was made of unleavened dough *(maẓẓah)* rather than of leavened dough *(ḥameẓ)*, and the cakes were salted (Lev. 2:11, 13). The priest pinched off a fistful of the dough and placed it on the altar fire as an *ʾazkarah*. The meaning of this term is uncertain, but it probably conveys the notion that the deity was to be "reminded" by the ascending smoke of the burning cake. Two sizes of cakes, traditional in the ancient Near East, were prepared as *minḥah: ḥallot maẓẓot* ("loaves of unleavened dough") and *rekikei (reqiqei) maẓẓot* ("thin cakes of unleavened dough"; Lev. 2:4). The *minḥah* often accompanied animal offerings. However, other grain offerings were presented alone. These included the two loaves of the Pentecost (Lev. 23:17), the loaves of thanksgiving (Lev. 7:13), and the grain offering of first fruits (Num. 15:17–21). No part of these offerings was placed on the altar and for this reason they could be made of leavened dough. The rule was that no leaven could be placed on the altar (Ex. 23:18; 34:25; Deut. 16:3), but the converse was not consistently applied. This notion was somewhat related to the laws of Passover forbidding the eating of leaven (Ex. 12:15; 13:3, 7). The priestly codes specify that after the *ʾazkarah* was detached, the remaining cakes were to be eaten in a sacred place. In certain cases only the priest actually officiating at the rite could partake of the *minḥah* (Lev. 7:9–10). The *minḥah* offered on behalf of a priest was designated *kalil*, meaning that it was to be entirely burned on the altar (Lev. 6:15–16). As the Israelite cult became more standardized, procedures were probably instituted which afforded larger portions of the *minḥah* to the priests, a process also observed with respect to other types of offerings. The "bread of display" (*leḥem ha-panim*) represented another type of grain offering (Ex. 25:30; 35:13; 39:36; Lev. 24:5–9; Num. 4:7; I Sam. 21:7; I Kings 7:48; II Chron. 4:19). Twelve loaves were arranged in two rows on a table especially installed in the tent of assembly (*ʾohel moʿed*) outside the *parokhet* (Ex. 40:22–23). The loaves were removed each week to be eaten in a sacred place by the priests. A smoke offering of pure frankincense was offered in connection with these loaves in place of the *ʾazkarah* that usually accompanied the *minḥah*, since no part of these loaves was placed on the altar. The antiquity of the practice is attested by a story from the early career of David (I Sam. 21:7) involving the "bread of display" and by its inclusion in the Solomonic temple project (I Kings 7:48). The "bread of display" actually represents a distinct orientation to sacrifice paralleled by the offering of first fruits prescribed in Deuteronomy 26:10. Normally, the Israelite cult operated on the principle that the deity consumed sacrificial materials after they had been converted into smoke on the altar, by breathing in the smoke of the offering (see above). In the case of the "bread of display" and the first fruits the operative principle was the viewing of the offering by the deity, and his seeing it constituted either his acceptance or his actual consumption of it. The offering, therefore, was placed before him. The story of the theophany of Gideon (Judg. 6:19–21) seems to be a shift from the one principle to the other. Gideon first placed his offering before the angel, a divine manifestation, and was then told to make it a burnt offering instead. The method of sacrifice known as *tenufah*, usually rendered "wave offering," appears only in the priestly writings of the Pentateuch and though extended to mean "levy, tax" (Ex. 35:22; 38:24), its original sense derives from the act of "waving." *Tenufah* is associated with the common Near Eastern practice of showing the offering to the deity. Upon this method was imposed the more particularly Israelite practice of burning offerings on the altar instead of merely placing them there. *Tenufah* was utilized for animal as well as grain offerings, but in the case of animal sacrifices, and even of some grain offerings, the waving was only a preliminary to offering up the material on the altar fire, or to boiling part of the meat in pots (cf., eg., Ex. 29:24, 26; Lev. 7:30; 8:27, 29; 9:21; 10:15; Num. 6:20; et al.). Only in some fruit and grain offerings was showing the offering to the deity, in and of itself, a sufficient mode of sacrifice (Lev. 23:11–14, 15, 20). This corresponds with the presentation of the "bread of display." After the deity had had the opportunity to view the offering, it was removed from Him, and assigned to the priests.

Other Types of Sacrifices

LIBATIONS (*nesekh*). Libations normally accompanied other sacrifices (Lev. 23:37; Num. 28:14, 31; 29:6, 11). The priestly codes speak of wine as the material most frequently used in libations. Beer was widely used in the ancient Near East for cultic purposes, and while an interpretation of *shekhar* as beer in Numbers 28:7 is tempting, it means simply "intoxicant, liquor" and no doubt "wine" (Heb. יַיִן *yayin*) is to be restored near the beginning of the verse, as attested by some ancient versions (it was omitted due to הַהִין, *ha-hin*; *ibid*.; cf. Num. 28:14 and Ex. 29:40). According to the priestly codes, oil was used only for unction and purification, as an ingredient in grain offerings, and for kindling lights, but there are indications that it may have also been used for separate libations (Micah 6:7; Ezek. 16:18–19). The libation was poured from vessels termed *kasvah* (*qaswah*; Ex. 25:29; 37:16; Num. 4:7; I Chron. 28:17) and *menakkiyyah* (*menaqqiyyah*; Ex. 25:29). There is evidence for a water libation (II Sam. 23:16 = I Chron. 11:18), and talmudic sources speak of it as an ancient practice (Shek. 6:3; Suk. 4:1, 9; Zev. 6:2, Mid. 2:6).

INCENSE OFFERINGS (*ketoret, qeṭoret*). As distinct from the other uses of incense, there was a special offering on the "altar of incense," which stood in the tent of assembly. This offering was made by the high priest (Ex. 30:1–10). The altar was of gold and had four horns at the corners. Incense altars have been found in archaeological excavations, and the four-horned altar from Megiddo is of special interest. The high priest kindled incense as part of the *tamid* or daily sacrifice (Ex. 30:8). Its purpose was to delight the deity with a pleasant aroma. A special blend of incense, designated solely for this purpose, was employed (Ex. 30:34–38). The antiquity of these priestly regulations is not known, and in this respect a distinction should be made between the use of censers (*kaf*; Num. 7:14) and stationary incense altars.

[Baruch A. Levine]

FIRST FRUITS (*bikkurim*), see *First Fruits.

THE REGULAR PUBLIC OFFERINGS. The Torah prescribes a burnt offering of a yearling lamb twice daily – in the morning and evening of every day. Each lamb was to be accompanied by a *minḥah* of a tenth of an ephah of *solet* (semolina, the hard particles within wheat grain) and a *nesekh* of a quarter of a *hin* of wine (Ex. 29:38–42; Num. 28:3–8). This is called the *'olat tamid* ("regular or constant burnt offering"; Ex. 29:32; Num. 28:3, 10; et al.), and simply the *tamid* in Daniel 8:11–13; 12:11, and post-biblical literature. Additional offerings (*musafim* in rabbinic terminology) for Sabbaths, new moons, and annual festivals are listed in Numbers 28–29. There are further requirements in Leviticus 17 and 23. Numbers 10:10 prescribes that sacrifices be accompanied by trumpet blasts "on your seasons and new moons," but the Torah is otherwise silent about cultic music, in contrast to some of the hymns and thanksgiving songs in Psalms and especially to many of the superscriptions to Psalms (see *Psalms; *Chronicles).

[Harold Louis Ginsberg]

BIBLIOGRAPHY: G.B. Gray, *Sacrifice in the Old Testament* (1925), 1–82; F. Blome, *Die Opfermaterie in Babylonien und Israel* (1934); J.L. Kelso, *The Ceramic Vocabulary of the Old Testament* (1948); J. Licht, in: EM, 2 (1954), 902–4; M. Haran, *ibid*., 4 (1962), 39–45, 763–86; 5 (1968), 23–30, 883–6; idem, in: VT, 10 (1960), 113–29; R. de Vaux, *Studies in Old Testament Sacrifice* (1964); B.A. Levine, in: *Leshonenu*, 30 (1965), 3–11; idem, in: *Eretz Israel*, 9 (1969), 88–95; R. Rendtorff, *Studien zur Geschichte des Opfers im Alten Israel* (1967). **ADD. BIBLIOGRAPHY:** R. de Vaux, *Ancient Israel: Its Life and Institutions* (1961).

CULT PLACES, ISRAELITE, places at which sacrifices were offered to the God of Israel. Many such places are mentioned in the Bible, and modern archaeological excavations have added to the list. The definition of sacred space in the ancient Near East has seen much debate. The traditional view is that cult was characterized by permanence of location: sites noted for their sacredness, principally towns and their environs, continued to retain this attribute despite shifts in population and consequent changes in the dominant religion of the area. The Bible employs specific terms to refer to different types of cult places, although usage is not always consistent. Four general types can be identified by the terminology: *Bet* YHWH ("the house [*Temple] of YHWH"); *Mikdash* ("*sanctuary"); **Bamah* ("high place," raised cultic installation); and *Mizbe'aḥ* ("*altar"). In archaeological contexts structures defined as temples or shrines are more easily identifiable, with the addition of objects considered "cultic," such as figurines, statuary, standing stones (*maẓẓebot*), and altars.

Bet YHWH

Synonyms are *heikhal* YHWH (e.g., I Sam. 1:9; 3:3; II Kings 18:16; Jer. 7:4) and *bet ha-Elohim* (e.g., Judg. 18:31). Apart from several unspecified references, this term is applied exclusively to two places, *Shiloh and *Jerusalem (e.g., I Sam, 1:7; I Kings 3:1). The cult place established by David to house the *Ark after it was brought to Jerusalem was also designated as a *bet* YHWH (II Sam. 12:20). Since Shiloh and Jerusalem represent two successive stages in Israelite religion, it seems that use of this term and its synonyms implied the belief that the God of Israel had only one "residence" at any given time. This notion is expressed in Psalms 78:60ff.: "He [God] abandoned the tabernacle of Shiloh … He elected … Mount Zion which he prefers … and He made His sanctuary [*mikdash*] enduring as heaven, as the earth which He established forever."

Like the terms containing the element "house," the designation *mikdash* was also conceived of as designating a divine residence; and as in the passage first quoted, the Jerusalem Temple (and perhaps, on occasion, even Shiloh; see below) was also termed "sanctuary." All the Israelite sanctuaries so designated were founded long before the belief in a single divine residence became official doctrine in the late monarchy. Several of these sanctuaries coexisted with the Jerusalem Temple, serving specialized functions that were not in direct competition with the Temple's unique status. Scholars believe that Shiloh was either the principal sacred center in the period of the Judges, or, alternatively, following Noth, that it was one of a series of central shrines in pre-monarchic Israel, e.g., Shechem, Bethel, Gilgal, and Shiloh. The recent excavations at the site by Finkelstein suggest that Iron Age I Shiloh was not an ordinary village with a cult place but served as a religious *temenos*. The peak of Shiloh's prosperity was in the first half of the 11th century B.C.E. After Shiloh had been destroyed in the Iron Age I there is no evidence that it was subsequently used by Israelites for cultic purposes. Thus the belief in a single chosen residence for the God of Israel gained momentum in ancient Israel, ultimately producing a movement toward the elimination of all cult places other than the Jerusalem Temple. This could only take place after the fall of the Northern Kingdom where Beth-El, and perhaps other sites, enjoyed a particular status not accorded to any of the provincial sanctuaries in Judah. Beth-El was established as an avowed rival of Jerusalem after the death of Solomon, and, in general, political considerations produced a different cultic atmosphere in the Northern Kingdom.

While information on the Jerusalem Temple is available from biblical descriptions, little is known about the temple at Shiloh. Why Shiloh was chosen as an early Israelite cultic center is not clear. The selection of Jerusalem and most other important sites follows known patterns, but there is no evidence that the early Israelites were attracted to Shiloh by virtue of its prior religious, demographic, administrative, or strategic significance. Recent excavations, however, do indicate there were earlier cultic practices at the site during the Middle and Late Bronze Ages. Shiloh is located in the Ephraimite territory, several kilometers east of the ancient main road to Shechem (Judg. 21:19). It is reasonable to assume that it was selected as a cultic center for the Israelite tribes primarily because of its imposing position, and because it was fairly central in the early area of habitation. The ancient site is surrounded by lofty hills, and encircled on three sides by verdant valleys. The top of the site gives the impression of great height, but at the same time draws the eye to the hills rising above the cult place. Some have even compared the topography of Shiloh to that of Jerusalem.

Mikdash

The Jerusalem Temple was frequently termed *mikdash* and also *bet ha-mikdash*. The cultic installation at Beth-El was termed *mikdash melekh* ("a royal sanctuary") by *Amaziah, one of its chief priests during the reign of Jeroboam II in the eighth century B.C.E. (Amos 7:13). According to Joshua 24:26 a stele was erected "under the terebinth at the sanctuary [*mikdash*] of YHWH" after a convocation of the tribes at Shechem (24:1). If this is accurate, then there was a sanctuary in Shechem during the early Israelite period. However, the passage is problematic, and the Septuagint of Joshua 24:1 has Shiloh instead of Shechem. There is, consequently, no conclusive evidence for the existence of an Israelite sanctuary in Shechem at that time.

The site of Beth-El was partially excavated by W.F. Albright and further by J.L. Kelso. Massive remains were uncovered. Ancient Beth-El (now Beitin) is situated 3,965 ft. (880 meters) above sea level, about 10½ mi. (17 km.) north of Jerusalem on a site commanding major crossroads. The archaeological remains indicate the preeminence of Beth-El in pre-Israelite times and throughout almost the whole Israelite period. Among the finds was a cylinder seal with the images of a god and goddess and the name of the goddess Ashtoreth written in hieroglyphics showing that Beth-El was undoubtedly an important Canaanite cultic site later appropriated by the Israelites for their own use. Biblical sources contain ample evidence of the importance of Beth-El as a cult place in Israelite times. The tribes convened there during the period of the Judges (Judg. 20:18, 26; 21:2), and it was one of the principal cult places at which the prophet Samuel officiated (I Sam. 7:16). After the death of Solomon and the division of the kingdom, the heterodox Jeroboam established Beth-El, along with Dan, as a cultic center of the Northern Kingdom. His reasons for doing so related not only to its age-old importance as a cult place but to its location near the southern border of his kingdom, close to Jerusalem. Genesis 28 gives the origin of the sacred nature of Beth-El by associating it with the site of Jacob's dream (Gen. 35:13). Abraham also erected an altar near Beth-El (Gen. 12:18; 13:3–4). Perhaps no other cult place, with the exception of Jerusalem, achieved a comparable place in biblical tradition. The biblical account actually describes the sanctuary erected at Beth-El by Jeroboam as a *bet bamot* ("a temple of outdoor shrines"; I Kings 12:31–32), which suggests that Jeroboam enclosed a previously constructed *bamah* which had served as an open-air cult place. Perhaps the sanctuary of Beth-El mentioned in Amos 7:13 dates from this period.

In II Kings 23:15–16 it is recorded that Josiah destroyed the "altar" and the *bamah* at Beth-El. The passage speaks of the *bet bamot* as a frequent phenomenon in cities of the Northern Kingdom, but does not specify which ones. The *bamah* was the prime target of Josiah's reformist movement, and it is likely that the terminology of this passage is imprecise. There can be little doubt that a *mikdash*, and not just a *bamah*, stood at Beth-El at this period, and that it was destroyed by Josiah soon after 622 B.C.E. (The implications of Josiah's activities will be discussed below under the heading of *bamah*.)

No other specific cult place is designated *mikdash* in the Bible, except the desert *tabernacle, which represents a different sort of cultic phenomenon. Assuming that there must have been many sanctuaries in ancient Israel, scholars have employed various criteria in assigning the status of *mikdash* to other well-known cult places. Such criteria include the elaborate nature of the cultic ceremonies performed there and the undertaking of pilgrimages to the site. It is possible, of course, but far from certain, that at one time or another a *mikdash* used by Israelites stood at such places as Gilgal (exact location uncertain) and Mizpah, where the tribes convened in the early Israelite period, and at other places as well. It would appear that there was a sanctuary at *Nob, the city of priests, in the days of Saul (I Sam. 21:1–10).

Excavations undertaken by Y. Aharoni from 1962 to 1967 at *Arad, a Negev town in the vicinity of Beersheba, have uncovered the remains of a building that would qualify as a *mikdash* by virtue of its structure and contents, and in the light of what is known about the role of Arad during the period of the First Temple. The sanctuary building measured approximately 50 × 40 ft. (15 × 12 meters), and contained a niche with at least one *maẓẓevah* or cultic stele, a sacrificial altar, and other cultic appurtenances. It is likely that this building was in cultic use from the tenth to the late seventh or early sixth century B.C.E. The presence of levitical personnel at Arad is attested in the personal names which occur on the large numbers of ostraca found on the site. These brief communications and archival records reveal that Arad was in close communication with Jerusalem and leave no doubt that it was a legitimate cult place. Its location indicates that it was a border installation with combined cultic and administrative functions, two institutions which often go together.

The Arad excavations are of primary importance for an understanding of the ancient Israelite cult. The existence of a sanctuary near the southern border of Judah suggests that certain religious duties had to be fulfilled on departure from the land of the God of Israel. Perhaps the accounts of votive activity by the patriarch Jacob while on his flight to Syria (Gen. 28) and on his trek to Egypt (Gen. 46:1) reflect an early feature of Israelite religion, which rendered border sanctuaries necessary.

Since 1966 excavations have been conducted by A. Biran at *Dan, the site of Jeroboam's second cultic center, situated in upper Galilee. Although conclusive evidence of a sanctuary at Dan is still unavailable, there can be little doubt of its existence in ancient times. Judges 17–18 preserves a tradition about the establishment of the Israelite cult there. Indeed, a cultic temenos was unearthed by the spring at the northern flank of the site, and *maẓẓebot* were uncovered in a stone-paved piazza within the Iron Age gate.

Bamah

The term *bamah* is ambiguous. The Hebrew word (like Ugaritic *bmt*) means "back" or "shoulder." In many languages anatomical terms were transferred to architectural and topographic contexts, and in that process *bamah* ("back") acquired two related cultic connotations: (1) topographically – a high place, a cultic installation situated on a high elevation, such as a mountain top; and (2) architecturally – a raised platform, or the like.

The proverbial characterization of improper worship reflects these two aspects of the *bamah*: "Atop every high mountain [lofty hill] and under every verdant tree" (e.g., Deut. 12:2; I Kings 14:23; Jer. 3:6). The reference is undoubtedly to the **asherah* or cult pole, which was normally part of the *bamah* complex.

A well preserved pre-Israelite *bamah* dating from the early Bronze Age stands in the temple precincts at *Megiddo. It is a large circular platform of stones, with stairs leading up to it. It is likely that the altar stood on top of the *bamah* at Megiddo, since large quantities of bones and potsherds were found in the earth deposits immediately above. Elsewhere the altar may have stood in front of the *bamah*, which was kept for cultic stelae, statuaries, etc. There are biblical descriptions of cultic activity at the *bamah* that provide some details of its structure. Thus, Samuel ascended the *bamah* at *Ramah to bless the slain offering and subsequently to partake of it (I Sam. 9:13–14, 19). When the sacred meal was over, he and those "called" to the celebration descended from the *bamah* and reentered the city (9:25). The descent from the *bamah* is also recorded at Gibeah (I Sam. 10:5, 10, 13). The text even mentions a *lishkah* ("chamber") where the assembled company sat down to the meal. If all of this activity actually occurred at the *bamah*, then it was a very large and complex installation. In any event, the place of the sacrifice itself was probably an open-air installation not intended to serve as a residence for the deity, as in the case of the *mikdash*, but rather as a site that the deity would visit when invoked. The same was true of the altar. The *bamah* could, of course, be raised to the status of a residence for the deity, which is what the term *bet bamot* connotes. The Moabite *Mesha stele, in speaking of that king's cultic enterprises, uses both terms, *bamah* and *bet bamot* (Moabite *bmt* and *bt bmt*), perhaps interchangeably.

The account of Samuel at Ramah also states that the *bamah* was located outside the city. During the 1969 excavations at *Ashdod under M. Dothan a Middle Bronze installation of probable cultic function was unearthed outside the city wall, but it has not yet been fully interpreted. In 1966 the expedition under Kathleen Kenyon in the Ophel area of ancient Jerusalem discovered a cult installation with two stelae (stone monoliths) above which stood an altar. The installation was almost immediately outside the contemporary city wall. This site dates from the seventh century B.C.E., and was apparently a pagan site, one of those condemned by the writer of the Books of Kings (II Kings 23:4; cf. Jer. 31:39). The Bible also speaks of *bamotha-she'arim* ("the high places of the gates"; II Kings 23:8; cf. Ezek. 8:3).

Primarily on the basis of the *bamot* outside the city walls, Y. Kaufmann concluded that the Israelites did not convert pre-existing idolatrous cult places for their monotheistic needs, but withdrew to outside the city, or to other nearby sites, and there constructed new installations. Also citing the evidence pertaining to altars located outside the towns and in the open country, he thus minimized the extent of continuity between pre-Israelite and Israelite cultic activity. A verification of such a reconstruction of early Israelite religious practice would require greater knowledge of the history of particular sites.

Historically, the main problem with respect to the Israelite *bamah* is to determine when and to what extent it was considered a legitimate cult place by strict monotheistic standards. The "great *bamah*" at Gibeon (I Kings 3:4; cf. 9:2) was certainly legitimate when Solomon offered sacrifices and experienced a theophany there soon before construction of the Jerusalem Temple, notwithstanding the fact that the Ark had long before been brought to Jerusalem and was housed there (*ibid.*, 3:15). The redaction of the Books of Kings regards the *bamot* as illegitimate from the time of Solomon onward (I Kings 3:3; 15:14; 22:43–44; II Kings 12:4; 14:4; 15:4, 35), but these references are couched in the language of a later ideology. It is reasonable to assume that the Israelite *bamah* (as differentiated from the avowedly idolatrous one) came into official disrepute late in the monarchic era, at about the time of the Assyrian conquest of the Northern Kingdom, roughly the last quarter of the eighth century B.C.E. Ahaz came under Assyrian influence in cultic matters (II Kings 16–17), and his successor *Hezekiah actually took measures to eliminate the *bamah* as a legitimate Israelite cult place (*ibid.*, 18–19). There can be little doubt that Hezekiah's measures were aimed at bringing northern Israelites to Jerusalem, and at ridding the Israelite cult of foreign influences. Any success he might have achieved was temporary, because of the long period of Assyrian influence under King Manasseh, and it was not until *Josiah ascended the throne of Judah and Ashurbanipal, king of Assyria, died that the attempt to eliminate the *bamah*, which had become a focal point for cultic pollution, could be resumed in earnest. About the year 622 B.C.E. Josiah carried out a reformation which has correctly been considered a turning point in Israelite religion. He dismissed the priests who had officiated at the *bamot*, proceeded to destroy and render unfit for use the *bamot* in Jerusalem and its environs, and in the cities of Judah, and was especially concerned to destroy the cultic center at Beth-El, which had undoubtedly kept many worshipers from Jerusalem (II Kings 22–23).

It is interesting that Deuteronomy, which gives doctrinal expression to the illegitimacy of worship at local cult places, never uses the term *bamah* but rather *makom* ("place"; e.g., Deut. 12:3), a generic term for a cultic installation (cf. Ex. 20:21), known outside the Bible primarily in Phoenician inscriptions. There has been considerable speculation about the origin of the *bamah*-type cult place. W.F. Albright considers it to be primarily a funeral installation (cf. Isa. 53:9, and Abraham ibn Ezra's commentary), which later took on other functions. Indeed, Josiah destroyed a cemetery near the cult place of Beth-El, "there in the mountain" (II Kings 23:16–17). It is still impossible to be certain of this interpretation, however, and most of the evidence in support of it comes from Greek and other external contexts.

Mizbe'ah

The term *mizbe'aḥ* may be discussed either as a cultic appurtenance, considering its design and uses, or as the identifying feature of a cult place. It is the latter sense that will be examined here. Every cult place obviously included an altar. The problem is to ascertain whether the cult place designated as *mizbe'aḥ* was of restricted proportions and did not include a more elaborate installation such as a *bamah* or *mikdash*, or whether it did, in which case the designation *mizbe'aḥ* was imprecise. In ancient Israel a man might construct an altar at a site where he had experienced a divine revelation. Thus, Abraham set up an altar near Shechem "to the Lord who had appeared to him" (Gen. 12:7). Isaac built an altar at Beersheba after a theophany (26:25), and Jacob is commanded to go to Beth-El and to construct an altar, "to the God who appeared to you when you were fleeing from your brother Esau" (35:1). The dynamic relationship between theophany and altar-building underlies Jacob's earlier activities at Beth-El (Gen. 28), except that more was involved than simply an altar. The same dynamics applied to *Gideon at Ophrah (Judg. 6:12, 24) and to the parents of Samson at Zoreah (*ibid.*, 13:3, 19–20). Probably the most understandable circumstances for altar-building were the individual needs of worshipers for a place to offer sacrifice in proximity to their homes. Thus, Samuel constructed an altar in Ramah, where he lived (I Sam. 7:17), as did Abraham when he lived between Beth-El and Ai (Gen. 13:4), and when he pitched his tents near Hebron (Gen. 13:18), and Jacob when he purchased a plot of land in the area of Shechem (33:19–20).

Collectively, the Israelites constructed an altar when they were required to offer sacrifices at Mount Sinai, where no cultic installation stood (Ex. 24:4). Altars might be built in celebration of victory (Ex. 17:15; I Sam. 14:35), and abandoned altars could be restored as by Elijah somewhere on the Carmel range (I Kings 18). Most of this evidence indicates that altars were often built for particular purposes at cult places already noted for their importance. Of course many altars could be constructed at any one town, not necessarily in the same area. Yet it is significant that Samuel built his altar at Ramah where there was a large *bamah* installation, and the Bible clearly tells of Jacob building an altar at Beth-El, the very site where he had previously contributed to the establishment of a temple. Similarly, Isaac's altar at Beersheba was not the first "Israelite" cultic installation at that site, for Abraham had invoked God there (Gen. 21:33), and such an invocation (Heb. *kara be-shem* YHWH) is often associated with altar-building and evidently involved the offering of sacrifices. In some instances it can be assumed that the previous altar on a particular site might have fallen into disuse or been destroyed, but this cannot be said of all cases on record.

Building an altar could constitute the first step in establishing a site as an Israelite cult place. Thus, Gideon is commanded to destroy the altar of Baal and erect an altar to YHWH on the same site (Judg. 6:25–26). It seems clear that the Israelites did not use pagan altars, but they did tend to gravitate to localities considered sacred by the idolatrous peoples of the area. Scholars have tended to confuse these two aspects of the early history of Israelite religion, the sacredness of places and the fitness of cultic installations and appurtenances. Normally a locality was believed to be sacred in perpetuity, but the cultic installations of non-monotheistic peoples constituted an abomination. Deuteronomy (12:12) lays down the harshest legislation concerning the destruction of all of the *mekomot* ("places") where idolatry was practiced. Most of the information from biblical sources on the subject of altar-building suggests that it was a feature of the earlier periods of Israelite settlement in Canaan. This is certainly the impression that Genesis aims at and it is also implicit in Joshua, Judges, Samuel, and Kings.

BIBLIOGRAPHY: H. Kjaer, in: JPOS, 10 (1930), 87–174; Kaufmann Y., Toledot, passim; S. Zemirin, *Yoshiyyahu u-Tekufato* (1952), 33–65; J.L. Kelso, in: BASOR, 137 (1955), 5–10; 151 (1955), 3–8; M. Haran, in: EM, 4 (1962), 763–79; 5 (1968), 322–8 (incl. extensive bibl.); K. Kenyon, in: PEQ, 95 (1963), 7–8; 96 (1964), 7–13; S. Yeivin, in: EM, 2 (1965), 147–53; 5 (1968), 328–46 (incl. extensive bibl.); B.A. Levine, in: *Religions in Antiquity*, ed. by J. Neusner (1968), 78–79; W.F. Albright, *Yahweh and the Gods of Canaan* (1968), 193–207; Albright, Arch, 104, 163–4; idem, in: BASOR, 57 (1935), 18–26; Y. Aharoni, in: BA, 31 (1968), 2–32; idem, in: *Eretz Israel*, 9 (1969), 10–21; idem in: IEJ, 17 (1967), 64–65; W.F. Albright and J.L. Kelso, *Excavation of Bethel (1934–1960)* (=AASOR, 39, 1968); *New Directions in Biblical Archeology*, ed. by D.N. Freedman and J. Greenfield (1969), 25–39; M.-L. Buhl and S. Holm-Nielsen, *Danish Excavations at Tell Sailun, Palestine…* (1964). **ADD. BIBLIOGRAPHY:** W.G. Dever, "The Contribution of Archaeology to the Study of Canaanite and early Israel Religion," in: P.D. Miller, P.D. Hanson, and S.D. McBride (eds.), *Ancient Israelite Religion*. (1987), 209–47; J.S. Holladay, "Religion in Israel and Judah under the Monarchy: An Explicitly Archaeological Approach," in: P.D. Miller, P.D. Hanson, and S.D. McBride (eds.), *Ancient Israelite Religion*. (1987), 249–99; S.M. Olyan, *Asherah and the Cult of Yahweh in Israel* (1988); S. Ackerman, *"Under Every Green Tree": Popular Religion in Sixth-century Judah* (1992); I. Finkelstein (ed.), *Shiloh: The Archaeology of a Biblical Site* (1993); R. Albertz, *A History of Israelite Religion in the Old Testament Period*. vol. I: *From the Beginnings to the End of the Monarchy* (1994); A.G. Vaughn, *Theology, History and Archaeology in the Chronicler's Account* (1999); Z. Zevit, *The Religions of Ancient Israel: A Synthesis of Parallelactic Approaches* (2001); S. Gitin, "The Four-Horned Altar and Sacred Space: An Archaeological Perspective," in: B. Gittlen (ed.), *Sacred Time, Sacred Space: Archaeology and the Religion of Israel*. (2002), 95–123.

[Baruch A. Levine / Shimon Gibson (2nd ed.)]

°**CUMANUS VENTIDIUS**, Roman procurator of Judea from 48 to 52 C.E. He held office at a time of increasing unrest. The *Zealots, who were already active in the time of his predecessor *Tiberius Julius Alexander, extended their activities during his period of office. The tension which accompanied his appointment is to some extent attributable to his own corruption and readiness to accept bribes. This came to light in the quarrel between the Jews and Samaritans, when he failed to punish the latter for the murder of a pilgrim from Galilee to Jerusalem. In revenge the Jews, led by the Zealots *Eleazar son of Dinai and *Alexander, set fire to Samaritan villages and killed the inhabitants. According to the report in Josephus' *Antiquities*, Cumanus was in the pay of the Samaritans; in his *Jewish Wars* Josephus gives a different account. The disturbance was reported to Quadratus, the governor of Syria, by the Samaritans. After hearing both sides Quadratus executed a number of Jews and Samaritans and ordered Cumanus and the tribune Celer to report to the emperor in Rome. Cumanus was banished, after the emperor had been influenced by both his wife Agrippina and the young king *Agrippa II, and the tribune was sent to the Jews in Jerusalem for capital punishment. Two other riots were caused, one by the indecent behavior of a Roman soldier at the Passover festival and the other when a Roman soldier set fire to a Torah scroll in the course of a punitive mission to the villages near Beth-Horon, where Jews had robbed an imperial officer. Cumanus' period of office was marked by a deteriorating relationship between Jews and Romans.

BIBLIOGRAPHY: Jos., Ant., 20:103ff., 118ff.; Jos., Wars, 2:223ff., 232ff.; Tacitus, Annals, 12:54.

[Lea Roth]

°**CUMBERLAND, RICHARD** (1732–1811), English playwright and novelist who tried to reverse the image of the Jew created by Shakespeare in *The Merchant of Venice*. Educated at Cambridge, Cumberland began writing plays around 1759. His first stage Jew was Naphtali in *The Fashionable Lover* (1772). This was an unflattering portrait, but by the time he wrote *The Jew* (1794), his attitude had changed completely. In the person of Sheva, Cumberland brought a new kind of Jew to the English stage. Sheva, like Shylock, is a usurer, hustled and insulted by the gentlemen of the town as "the meerest muckworm in the city of London." But by the end of the play the audience is made to realize that not one of the unflattering epithets really applies to him, and he is acclaimed as "the widow's friend, the orphan's father, the poor man's protector, the universal philanthropist." In spite of touches of melodrama and sentimentality, *The Jew* did well on the stage and had an influence on the more serious drama of the period. It has been translated into Hebrew and Yiddish. Cumberland produced a collection of essays, *The Observer* (1785), in which he introduced the saintly original of Sheva, Abraham Abrahams. He also wrote an unsuccessful comic opera entitled *The Jew of Mogadore* (1808). Cumberland's philo-Semitism paved the way for other favorable depictions of Jews in English literary works.

BIBLIOGRAPHY: L. Zangwill, in: JHSET, 7 (1911–14), 147–76; L.I. Newman, *Richard Cumberland, Critic and Friend of the Jews* (1919); M.J. Landa, *Jew in Drama* (1926); H.R.S. Van der Veen, *Jewish Characters in Eighteenth Century English Fiction and Drama* (1935); E. Rosenberg, *From Shylock to Svengali* (1960), ch. 3. **ADD. BIBLIOGRAPHY:** Katz, England, 343–45; W. D Rubinstein and H.L. Rubinstein, *Philosemitism: Admiration and Support By Non-Jews in the English-Speaking World For Jews, 1840–1939* (1999), index; ODNB online.

[Harold Harel Fisch]

CUMIN (Heb. כַּמּוֹן, *kammon*; Isa. 28:25, 27), the spice *Cuminum cyminum*. In mishnaic times cumin grew extensively in Ereẓ Israel and was even exported (Dem. 1:1), the local variety being superior to that of Cyprus (TJ, Dem. 2:1, 22b). It was used as a spice for eating with bread, and it was popular though it was regarded as a luxury and was excluded from the commodities which it was forbidden to hoard in years of famine (BB 90b). Since cumin was effective in stemming the flow of blood, it was used to stem bleeding caused by circumcision (Shab. 19:2) and the menstrual flow (Shab. 110b). Today cumin is occasionally grown as a condiment in Ereẓ Israel. It scatters its seeds and thus grows wild in a number of places.

BIBLIOGRAPHY: Loew, Flora, 3 (1924), 435–9; J. Feliks, *Olam ha-Ẓome'aḥ ha-Mikra'i* (1968²), 182. **ADD. BIBLIOGRAPHY:** Feliks, Ha-Ẓome'aḥ, 85.

[Jehuda Feliks]

°**CUNAEUS (Van der Cun), PETRUS** (1586–1638), Dutch humanist legal scholar and poet. Cunaeus was appointed professor of Latin (1612), politics (1613), and law (1615) at Leiden University. From 1601 he had studied Hebrew under Ambrosius Regemorter at Leiden. Later he went to Franeker, where he learned Aramaic and read rabbinic texts with Johann *Drusius. His main work, *De Republica Hebraeorum libri tres* (Leiden 1617, with translations into English (1653), Dutch (1700), and French (1705)), was a comparative discussion of the political and theological institutions of the ancient Hebrews. Continuing similar studies by Carlo Sigonio and Cornelius Betram, Cunaeus forged political theory, historical research, and biblical studies into an integrated methodology. Taking *Josephus as his point of departure, he tried to show the superiority of the Israelite theocracy to the Greek and Roman polity. His exposition was one of the first to systematically rely on talmudic and medieval Jewish sources.

BIBLIOGRAPHY: A.J. van der Aa, *Biografisch Woordenboek der Nederlanden* III (1854), 914–20; P.C. Molhuysen et al., *Nieuw Nederlandsch Biografisch Woordenboek I* (1911), 658–60; *Nouvelle Biographie Universelle*, 10 (1858), 351–52; J.R. Ziskind, in: JQR, 68 (1978) 235–54.

[Irene E. Zwiep (2nd)]

CUNEO, city in northern Italy. The oldest Jewish community in the territory of the House of Savoy emerged in Savigliano, not far from Cuneo, at the beginning of the 15th century. It is estimated that by the middle of the 16th century, about 400 Jews lived under the dukes of Savoy. A turning point came in 1570, when Pope Pius V expelled the Jews from Avignon, where a flourishing community, called the "Pope's Jews," had long existed in proximity to the pontifical court. Emanuele Filiberto welcomed many refugees to the region of Cuneo, perhaps with the objective of filling the demographic gap that had developed in preceding decades following persecutions of the Protestants. A period of uninterrupted stability began in a large area between Cuneo and Monferrato; local administrations profited by the financial support of small but flourishing Jewish communities. Migrations from Provence continued for several decades. In 1630 the Jews of Cuneo were permitted to participate in artisan crafts and trade without the burden of taxes higher than those levied on non-Jews. The situation became much more critical in the 18th century as a result of the rigid attitude of Vittorio Amedeo II and his son Carlo Emanuele III. This was the period of the severe application of the Regie costituzioni (1723), forced conversions, and the imposition of the ghetto, an institution that arrived two centuries later than in the rest of the peninsula. The ghetto in present-day Mondovì, for example, dates from September 1724. Surviving documents reveal oppressive schemes in other cities under Savoyard authority, including attempts to organize anti-Jewish manifestations and conflicts during Carnival. By the end of the 18th century, the Jews had been progressively isolated, removed from any contact with the surrounding society. This condition continued in the following century right up to the Albertine Statuto (1848), the document that decreed the emancipation of religious minorities (Jews and Valdesians). The census of Napoleon I indicates that 215 Jews resided in Cuneo in 1806, a number that increased to 301 by 1816. These statistics indicate a community that in the 19th century witnessed the birth of several important representatives of Italian Jewish culture, including Lelio Della Torre. A significant transformation occurred at the beginning of the 20th century, following the industrialization of the Italian state created in 1861 and the consequent urbanization that attracted a considerable portion of the Jewish community to Turin. The census of Mussolini in 1938 established for Cuneo the figure of 182 Jews, but included Jews residing in Saluzzo, Mondovì, Fossano, Busca, Moretta, and Cherasco. The Jewish community lost its juridical autonomy after 1945 and is today part of the Jewish community of Turin.

Holocaust Period

Eight kilometers from Cuneo, at the point of confluence of the valley of the Gesso and the valley of the Stura, the two principal valleys of the Maritime Alps in Italy, the Germans established a concentration camp in the commune of Borgo San Dalmazzo a few days after their occupation of the area on September 12, 1943. They selected an old military barracks a few meters from the railroad station on the Nice-Cuneo line. In the 19th century the building had housed a spinning mill. Nothing remains today of the construction that hosted 349 "foreign" Jews, refugees from Central and Eastern Europe arrested by the Germans in the Province of Cuneo on or after September 18. They were from a group of about 1,000 Jewish refugees in enforced residence in St. Martin Vesubie, France, who had followed Italian soldiers retreating from formerly Italian-occupied France after the Italian armistice with the Allies was announced on September 8. They had struggled across the Alps through the passes of the Finestre, at 2,575 meters above sea level, and Ciriegia, at 2,551 meters, expecting to find the Allies in the Cuneo area rather than the Germans.

Also in the camp at Borgo San Dalmazzo in the autumn of 1943 were some Italian Jews arrested in Cuneo, but they were freed before a circular from Minister of the Interior Buffarini Guidi demanding their arrests went into effect. The "first camp" of Borgo San Dalmazzo functioned until November 21, 1943, when the 349 "foreigners" were taken from the barracks to the station where a freight train awaited them. Passing through Cuneo, Savona, and Nice, they were transferred to Drancy, outside Paris. The majority continued on to Auschwitz in convoy 64 on December 12, 1943. Only 10 are known to have survived. Most of the others from the original group survived, however, by hiding in the surrounding mountains or by moving south to Florence or Rome. They were aided by hundreds of local Italians in a rescue effort often coordinated by Don Raimondo Viale (1907–1987), who after the war was recognized as a Righteous Among the Nations.

The camp at Borgo San Dalmazzo was reopened a few days after the departure of the Jewish refugees, so that one speaks of a "second camp" between December 4, 1943, and February 15, 1944. The reopening was ordered by the police in Cuneo on December 9 in response to a decree on December 2. This time all Jews were eligible for arrest, without distinction. Most affected were the weak, the elderly, those living alone, all those who had not been able to hide. Jews from Cuneo who had escaped deportation from the "first camp" had gone into hiding, usually in the mountains. Those of Mondovì were warned in time. The fate of the Jews of Saluzzo, where Jews taking refuge from Turin were added to the few regular residents of the area, was different and more tragic. A total of 26 Jews from Saluzzo were deported, mostly women, registered in a list dated January 31, 1944. Phonogram number 01083 of the local police, dated February 15, 1944, ordered their transfer to Fossoli, from where they were ultimately deported to Auschwitz. Then on April 25, 1945, the day Cuneo was liberated, the Germans seized six "foreign" Jews from the local prison and shot them under the arches of the bridge leading into the city.

BIBLIOGRAPHY: R. Segre, *The Jews of Piedmont*, 3 vols. (1986–90); idem, "Gli ebrei piemontesi nell'età dell'assolutismo," in: *Italia Judaica. Gli ebrei dalla segregazione alla prima emancipazione* (1989), 67–80; M. Luzzati, "Banchi e insediamenti ebraici nell'Italia centro-settentrionale fra tardo Medioevo e inizi dell'età moderna," in: C. Vivanti (ed.), *Gli ebrei in Italia, Annali della Storia d'Italia*, vol. 11, 1, 208–10; P. Bianchi-Andrea Merlotti, *Cuneo in età moderna* (2003), 103–13, 301–14; A. Cavaglion, "Nella notte straniera. Gli ebrei di St Martin Vésubie e il campo di concentramento di Borgo S. Dalmazzo," in: *Cuneo: L'Arciere* (1981, 2004); A. Muncinelli, *Gli ebrei nella provincia di Cuneo* (1994); A. Cavaglion, "Borgo S. Dalmazzo," in: W. Laqueur, *Dizionario dell'Olocausto* (It. ed., 2004), 99–102.

[Alberto Cavaglion (2nd ed.)]

CUOMOTINI (Turk. **Gumuldjina**), city in northeastern Greece in the region of Thrace. Jewish settlement is known from the early 16th century when, according to a population census, the Jewish community numbered 100 people or 25 head of household. The first settlers came from Edirne and later Salonika, and a Jewish community, primarily Sephardi, existed until the Bulgarians deported the Jews of the city in World War II.

When *Nathan of Gaza, the key follower of the false messiah *Shabbetai Ẓevi, fled from Edirne and Ipsula, he found refuge in Cuomotini with Shabbateans. He was driven out of the city by opponents who placed a *ḥerem* against him.

A synagogue, immediately outside of the city walls, existed from the 18th century.

In 1786, the Jews were victims of an attack by a Turkish army rebel and his small force who revolted, attacked the walled city, locked themselves in, and forced the Jews who lived within the walls to collaborate with them and shoot at the army. They had to feed the captives and break the Sabbath. The Ḥakham Jacob saved the community by bribery and the Jewish women cared for the wounded insurgents. The Jews escaped prosecution from the authorities also by bribery, and the 22nd of Elul became a day of commemoration on which they did not work. An unfinished hymn was composed by Rabbi Daniel de Avila.

In the 1860s the Carasso, Abravanel, Nahmias, and Molho families of Salonika settled in Cuomotini. In the 1880s, the Jews lived within the walls and the gates were locked at night. According to legend, in 1888–89 the Jews did not live in the city but came daily as traders from Drama and elsewhere and were only permitted to live inside the walls after the sick wife of a Turkish official could not find a Jewish merchant who sold natural medicines, on condition that they would reside in the city permanently. Seventy houses in the Turkish Quarter were allocated to them and they were given permission to build a synagogue inside the walls.

In 1907 the Jewish community numbered 200 families. By the early 20th century, there were four philanthropic associations as well as a *ḥevra kaddisha* and a *bikkur ḥolim*. Since Jews were not admitted to Greek-Orthodox schools, a Jewish school was founded in 1889, but it closed down shortly afterward owing to financial difficulties. A boys school was established in 1899 and a separate girls school was also set up. A coeducational school was founded in 1910, which received assistance from the Alliance Israélite Universelle. In 1912 it had 246 students.

The community was under Bulgarian rule from 1912 until 1922. A branch of the Bulgarian Association for Hebrew Language and Culture was established in the city.

When Turkey ceded Thrace and Cuomotini became Greek, the Jews had to designate three buildings to house refugees. In 1928, the community numbered 1,159 people. New organizations included the cultural Cercle Israelite, the women's volunteer Rofeh Holim, and the Zionist Aḥdut and B'nai Israel. In 1934, Meir Dasa sat on the local municipal council.

In November 1940, after the commencement of the Albanian campaign, the government sequestered the Jewish school. In April 1941, the Bulgarians annexed Thrace. In early 1942, Jewish youth were seized for forced labor. The Bulgarians ran a harsh and violent occupation. While some 28 escaped, most of the Jews were arrested on March 4, 1943, and transported in 20 open train cars to the notorious Dupnitsa transit camp, and then dispatched from Lom by boat via the Danube. The Jews from Cuomotini and Kavala on the *Karageorge* were shot by the Bulgarians and the Germans; while three other boats, of which one held Cuomotini Jews, arrived in Vienna and from there the Thracian Jews were sent to Treblinka; where they were gassed upon arrival. The Bulgarians confiscated all of the Jewish properties and possessions.

Only 18 Jews returned to the city, left with nothing. Most did not stay, leaving for Athens, the United States, or Israel. The synagogue, which had been used as a stable during the war, was returned, but served as a storage facility until 1980. In the early 1990s the roof collapsed and the municipality tore down the structure in 1994.

BIBLIOGRAPHY: Y. Kerem, "The Jewish Community of Cuomotini. A Unique Case of Communal Organization and Philanthropic Consciousness," in: *Proceedings of the XIIth Congress of CIEPO, Archiv Orientalni, Supplementa VIII* (1998), 189–96; B. Rivlin, "Cuomotini," in: *Pinkas Kehillot Yavan* (1999), 339–47.

[Yitzchak Kerem (2nd ed.)]

CUPBEARER, a high ranking royal official primarily in charge of serving wine to the king. Since he was close to the person of the king, who feared intrigue and the possibility of poisoned food, the cupbearer was required to be a man of irreproachable loyalty capable of winning the king's complete confidence.

Genesis 40:1 mentions Pharaoh's cupbearer (Heb. *mashkeh, mashqeh*), who, in the next verse, is called the chief cupbearer (Heb. *sar ha-mashqim*). Indicative of the importance of the position is the fact that it was the cupbearer whom Joseph asked to intercede with Pharaoh in order to bring about his release from prison (Gen. 40:14). In I Kings 10:5 and II Chronicles 9:4, it is possible that the word *mashkav* (*mashqaw*) refers to Solomon's cupbearers who were among the king's many possessions which amazed the Queen of Sheba so much that "there was no more spirit in her." The word may, however, refer to Solomon's "drinking service," i.e., decanters and cups. Nehemiah's words, "For I was cupbearer to the king" (Neh. 1:11b), attests to a cupbearer at court as late as the Persian period.

An Aramaic inscription of the ninth century B.C.E. consisting of the word *lšqy'* ("belonging to the cupbearer"), has been found on a large stone jar at Ein Gev. It is assumed that *lšqy'* is the honorific title of a dignitary or royal official at the court of Ben-Hadad II or Hazael. The word was probably an imitation of such Assyrian titles as *šāqû*, or *rab-šāqê*, which denote an important official at the royal court. The title *rab-šāqê* appears in the Bible as *Rab-Shakeh, Sennacherib's chief cupbearer (II Kings 18:17ff.; Isa. 36:2ff.). That such a title could be honorary and also connected with practical duties is apparent from the context of II Kings 18:17–19 and Isaiah 36:2 where the Assyrian *rab-šāqê* challenges Hezekiah king of Israel. Assyrian palace reliefs indicate the importance of the cupbearer in relation to the king's other servants. Representations in pictorial art and literary sources show that cupbearers also existed at the courts of the various kings of Canaan.

BIBLIOGRAPHY: B. Mazar et al., in: IEJ, 14 (1964), 27–28.

CURAÇAO, an island near the northern coast of Venezuela, South America, under the Dutch Crown part of the Netherland Antilles. Sighted by the Conquistador Alonso de Ojeda in 1498, it was captured from the Spanish by the Dutch in 1634. The Dutch West India Company was interested in populating the island, and among others to attract Jews from Dutch Brazil and to stem the flow of experienced Jewish planters from Brazil to Barbados. The first organized group of Jews was headed by Joao de Yllan (1651), and a second group by David Nassi (1652). The Jews were given an area called the "Jewish Quarter," several miles from the fortress which today is Willemstadt, capital of the island. Their efforts to plant sugar cane and other tropical products were not successful on this arid island. In 1659, however, a grant was given to another group of Jews from Brazil to settle in Curaçao, led by Isaac da Costa. He received the right of free exercise of religion, the right to protection, and permission to build a synagogue. Contrary to the situation prevailing in other Dutch possessions, the Jews had to adjust to some restrictions. They were treated as foreigners and were not even allowed to be inside the fortress after nine o'clock in the evening. Upon his nomination as governor of Curaçao, Peter Stuyvesant tried his utmost to limit the Jews' rights. All this could not prevent the Jews from transforming Curaçao into the main commercial center of the entire area. The proximity of Venezuela and Colombia facilitated the promotion of so-called illicit trade with the Spanish colonies. Owing to the shortage of Spanish vessels, Jews of Curaçao dealt through the conversos in these countries for their import and export.

The community "Mikve Israel" was founded in 1659 and the Jewish cemetery consecrated that same year. The first synagogue was dedicated in 1674 and coincided with the arrival of the first Haham (rabbi), Joshiau Pardo of Salonika. The present-day synagogue was established in 1732.

Curaçao became the center of Jewish life in the Caribbean and was called "Mother of the Caribbean Jewish communities." The establishment of the yeshivah Etz Haim ve-Ohel Yahakov (1674) gave spiritual guidance of the Jewish communities in the area. Bodies of Jews who died in places with no Jewish cemetery (mainly those under Spanish colonial rule), such as Cuba, Puerto Rico, and Santo Domingo, were transported to Curaçao for burial. The *mohalim* (circumcisers) of Curaçao attended to persons who arrived from Europe or other parts of the Americas with the aim of reconverting to Judaism. Among those who came from Spain and Portugal were a Dominican friar, a Franciscan father, and a Catholic priest. This continued until 1821.

The Jewish population continued to grow. Jews came from Amsterdam and Bayonne, exiles arrived from Pomeroon (Guiana) and Martinique, and conversos from Spain and Portugal. By 1729, the Jewish population exceeded 2,000, about one-half the total white population of the island. The small island was overpopulated and this led to Jewish immigration to other areas. Curaçao, however, remained their center.

In 1693, a party of 70 Curaçao Jews joined the Jews from Barbados in Newport, Rhode Island. That same year a group of Leghorn Jews left Curaçao to found the enclave at Tucacas, on the Venezuelan coast. The enclave, with its community and synagogue, existed until 1720, when captured by Spanish forces.

Curaçao Jews settled on the Dutch islands of Sint Maarten (Saint Martin) and Aruba; in the towns of Coro, Barcelona, Barquisimiento, Valencia, Caroa, and Puerto de Caballo in Venezuela; Carabobo, Rio Hacha, and Santa Marta in Colombia; in St. Thomas and St. Croix of the Virgin Islands; in Cap Haitien in Haiti; and in the Dominican Republic, Costa Rica, Panama, Cuba, New York, New Orleans, and Mexico City. In each location they still remained attached to Curaçao which, in turn, attended to their spiritual needs.

The commmunal importance of Curaçao has diminished today, and with it its Jewish population. Reform Judaism came to Curaçao in 1863, causing a rift and dividing Curaçao into two communities. The Reform "Temple Emmanuel" was dedicated in 1867. The dispute led to many Jews distancing themselves from the community. The conflict continued for almost 100 years, harming Jewish life. To resolve the situation, in 1964, the two communities merged to form "The United Netherlands Portuguese Congregation Mikve Israel – Emmanuel," which adopted Reconstructionism and decided "to include Sephardi rites so long as these do not conflict with Reconstructionist principles." In 1969, the Ashkenazi community "Shaarei Tzedek" was founded and an Ashkenazi synagogue built.

As of 2000, some 300 Jews lived in Curaçao, with the Ashkenazim being the majority.

Israel is represented in the Netherlands Antilles by the ambassador in Caracas and an honorary consul in Willemstadt.

BIBLIOGRAPHY: M. Arbell, *The Jewish Nation of the Caribbean* (2002); I. Jesurun Cardozo, *Three Centuries of Jewish Life in Curaçao* (1954); A. Herbert Cone, "The Jews in Curaçao," in: PAJHS, 10 (1902): 147–52; J. Corcos, *A Synopsis of the History of the Jews of Curaçao from the Day of Their Settlement to the Present Time* (1897); I and E. Emmanuel, *History of the Jews of the Netherlands Antilles* (1970); R. Maduro, *Our Snoa, 5492–5742...Synagogue Mikve Israel* (1982); C.A. Arauz Monfante, *El Contrabando Holandes en el Caribe, Durante la Primera Mitad de Siglo XVIII* (1984).

[Mordechai Arbell (2nd ed.)]

CURIEL, Marrano family, active in Jewish life in Amsterdam and Hamburg under the name of Nuñez da Costa. The origin of the name is Curiel del Duero in Castile. Jews whose origin was from this village bore the name after they had left it. A certain David Curiel from Avila, who decided to leave Castile in 1492, probably settled in Coimbra, with which the Curiel family became identified. It seems that in Coimbra the family descended from Abigail Curiel, alias Guiomar da Costa, after the forced conversion of 1497. Abigail was kept as a mistress for several years by Jeronimo de Saldanha, a nobleman with some Jewish ancestry, who was the father of a son raised in Coimbra as a Jew or Crypto-Jew. Hence the claim of the Curiel family to Portuguese nobility. Part of the family moved to Lisbon, some escaped from Portugal and reverted to Judaism, others moved to the New World. Several members of the family were tried by the Inquisition in Coimbra. These trials reveal much about the Jewish practices maintained by the family. Several members of the family lived in Covilhã. The departure of the Curiel family from Portugal was the result of indiscreet correspondence between the Jewish branch of the family living in Italy and the Portuguese New Christian branch. JACOB CURIEL, alias Duarte Nuñez da Costa (1587–1665), born a Marrano in Lisbon, moved via Pisa and Florence to Amsterdam and later to Hamburg. Having made himself useful to members of the royal house of Portugal in Hamburg, he was made Portuguese diplomatic representative. His elder son, MOSES (Jerónimo Nuñez da Costa; died 1697), was Portuguese agent in Amsterdam, where he was prominent in the Sephardi community and represented his coreligionists in cases before the Dutch authorities. Jacob's younger son, SOLOMON (Manoel Nuñez da Costa), succeeded his father in Hamburg. The family held diplomatic positions in both cities until the late 18th century.

BIBLIOGRAPHY: Roth, Marranos, 303; ESN, 178; J. Caro Baroja, *Judíos en la España moderna y contemporanea*, 2 (1962), 243–4; I. Da Costa, *Noble Families among the Sephardic Jews* (1936), index; H. Kellenbenz, *Sephardim an der unteren Elbe* (1958), index; W.C. Pieterse, *Daniel Levi de Barrios als geschiedschrijver...* (1968), index. **ADD. BIBLIOGRAPHY:** E. Samuel, in: *Jewish Historical Studies*, 31 (1988–90), 111–36 (also in: E. Samuel, *At the End of the Earth*, (2004), 43–67).

[Kenneth R. Scholberg / Yom Tov Assis (2nd ed.)]

CURIEL, ISRAEL BEN MEIR DI (d. 1577), sage of Safed. Neither the place nor the date of his birth is known. Similarly, there is no precise idea as to the date of his arrival in Safed. Di Curiel studied under R. Joseph Fasi in Adrianople, and presumably he held a rabbinic office in one of the congregations there. He evidently spent some time in Istanbul as well. In Safed, Di Curiel studied under Jacob *Berab and was one of the latter's ordainees. Together with Joseph *Caro and Moses *Trani, Di Curiel sat in the Safed *bet din*. Among his disciples was R. Bezalel *Ashkenazi. He was one of the outstanding preachers of his time . A corpus of Di Curiel's homilies was published by S. Regev in addition to his *Or Ẓaddikim* (Salonica 1799), which was mistakenly attibuted to R. Joseph *Caro. The poet R. Israel *Najara was his grandson.

BIBLIOGRAPHY: M. Pachter, Kiryat Sefer, 55 (1980), 802–10; S. Regev, *Rabbi Israel di Curiel, Sermons and Homilies* (Heb.,1992), with biographical notes by M. Benayahu); A. David, *To Come To the Land: Immigration and Settlement in 16th Century Eretz-Israel* (1999), 151, 234.

[Abraham David]

CURRICK, MAX COHEN (1877–1947), U.S. Reform rabbi. Currick was born in Boston and ordained at Hebrew Union College in 1898. After serving as rabbi of United Hebrew Congregation of Fort Smith, Arkansas, he became rabbi of Congregation Anshe Hesed in Erie, Pennsylvania, a position he held from 1901 until his death in 1947. A journalist as well, Currick was editor of the *Erie Dispatch* (1910–12) and chairman of the board of editors of *Liberal Judaism*, the house organ of the *Union of American Hebrew Congregations. In 1927, he became chairman of the *Central Conference of American Rabbis Committee on International Peace and was active in assisting victims of Nazism. Currick rose to many leadership roles in the CCAR and co-sponsored a tough (although not adopted by the rabbinic organization) resolution vehemently condemning "immorality" in Hollywood films. He was elected vice president of the CCAR in 1935 and served as president of the organization during the time of Hitler's rise to international power (1937–39), calling for greater cooperation among American Jewry to meet rising antisemitism at home and abroad. Contrary to the views of some other American Jewish leaders, however, Currick was of the opinion that no new umbrella organization needed to be formed to confront this challenge; rather, he felt, the *Synagogue Council of America, with its bedrock foundation in the houses of worship of the three streams of Judaism, should be given a broader mandate to speak out and act on issues facing American Jewry. In addition to his CCAR roles, Currick served on the Boards of Governors of Hebrew Union College and of the B'nai B'rith Home for Children.

BIBLIOGRAPHY: K.M. Olitzky, L.J. Sussman, and M.H. Stern, *Reform Judaism in America: A Biographical Dictionary and Sourcebook* (1993).

[Bezalel Gordon (2nd ed.)]

CURRIE, EDWINA (1946–), British politician. Edwina Currie (née Cohen) was born and educated in Liverpool and then at Oxford and the London School of Economics. The daughter of Orthodox Jews, she served in Birmingham local politics and then as a Conservative member of Parliament from 1983 to 1997. Under Margaret Thatcher, she enjoyed a high profile career as under-secretary of state for health from 1986 to 1988, initiating many public and media campaigns on health matters. In December 1988 she was forced to resign from the government because of a safety scare when she unwisely declared that most of Britain's eggs were infected with salmonella. She then became a writer, producing such thrillers as *The Ambassador* (1999). Edwina Currie hit the national headlines in 2002 when she published her *Diaries, 1987–92*, which revealed that in the mid-1980s she had had a four-year affair with John Major (Britain's prime minister from 1990 to 1997) before he was a major political figure. Currie was defeated at the 1997 general election and has since become a well-known radio and television presenter. Major and Currie reportedly spent much of their time together discussing the Jews.

[William D. Rubinstein (2nd ed.)]

CURTIS, JAMIE LEE (1958–), U.S. actor. Daughter of Jewish actor Tony *Curtis (Bernie Schwartz) and Janet Leigh, Curtis spent her high school years at the Choate School in Connecticut. After graduation, she attended the University of the Pacific in California for one term before dropping out. Universal signed Curtis to a seven-year contract in 1977 that got her bit parts on television shows like *Operation Petticoat*, *Quincy*, and *Columbo*. She made her big-screen debut in John Carpenter's *Halloween* (1978), and became known as the "queen of scream" with such follow-up horror films as *The Fog* (1980), *Prom Night* (1980), *Terror Train* (1981), and *Halloween II* (1981). After portraying the lead in the TV film *Death of a Centerfold: The Dorothy Stratten Story*, Curtis followed with comedy roles in the films *Trading Places* (1983) and *A Fish Called Wanda* (1988). She married actor-director Christopher Guest in 1984, with whom she has a daughter, Annie, and a son, Thomas, both adopted. In 1989–92, she starred opposite Richard Lewis in the sitcom *Anything But Love*, winning a 1990 Golden Globe for best actress in a television comedy. A memorable performance in the film *True Lies* (1994) opposite Arnold Schwarznegger won her another Golden Globe (1995), the same year that she appeared in the screen version of Wendy *Wasserstein's *The Heidi Chronicles* (1995). She reprised her role as Laurie Strode in *Halloween H20* (1998). Curtis had a major hit with the Disney remake of *Freaky Friday* (2003) and continued her family-friendly roles with *Christmas with the Kranks* (2004). Curtis is also a successful children's book author, publishing *When I Was Little* (1995); *Tell Me Again about the Night I Was Born* (1996); *Today I Feel Silly* (1998); *Where Do Balloons Go?* (2000); *I'm Gonna Like Me* (2002); and *It's Hard to Be Five* (2004).

[Adam Wills (2nd ed.)]

CURTIS, TONY (**Bernard Schwartz**; 1925–), U.S. actor. Born in New York, the son of a Hungarian tailor, Curtis began his career on the stage in a settlement house in the Bronx. He then went from summer stock companies to off-Broadway shows, and finally to Hollywood. His first major dramatic role was in *Trapeze* (1956), followed by *Sweet Smell of Success* (1957). Adeptly handling both dramatic and comedy roles, Curtis starred in many films, including *Houdini* (1953), *The Defiant Ones* (1958), *The Vikings* (1958), *Some Like It Hot* (1959), *Operation Petticoat* (1959), *Spartacus* (1960), *The Rat Race* (1960), *Who Was That Lady?* (1960), *The Great Impostor* (1961), *The Outsider* (1962), *Taras Bulba* (1962), *Forty Pounds of Trouble* (1962), *Captain Newman, M.D.* (1963), *Goodbye, Charlie* (1964), *Sex and the Single Girl* (1964), *The Great Race* (1965), *Boeing, Boeing* (1966), *Don't Make Waves* (1967), *The Boston Strangler* (1968), *Lepke* (1975), *The Last Tycoon* (1976), *Casanova & Co.* (1977), *Little Miss Marker* (1980), *The Mirror Crack'd* (1980), *Insignificance* (1985), *Center of the Web* (1991), *The Mummy Lives* (1993), *Hardball* (1997), *Alien X Factor* (1997), *Stargames* (1998), and *Love Is a Survivor* (2004). Among his many television appearances, Curtis starred as Danny Wilde opposite Roger Moore in the adventure series *The Persuaders* (1971–72).

Adept at artwork as well, Curtis has been painting and drawing for more than 30 years. His works are on exhibit at art galleries and other venues around the world. Actress Jamie Lee *Curtis is the daughter of Curtis and his first wife,

Janet Leigh. In 1993 Curtis wrote *Tony Curtis: The Autobiography* (with B. Paris).

BIBLIOGRAPHY: A.A. Hunter, *Tony Curtis: The Man and His Movies* (1985).

[Ruth Beloff (2nd ed.)]

CURTIZ, MICHAEL (1888–1962), Hungarian director. Born Mihály Kertész in Budapest, Hungary, to carpenter Ignatz and opera singer Aranka. Curtiz grew up poor and made his acting debut in 1897 in an opera his mother had been cast in. He graduated from Markoszy University in 1906 and went to work for a traveling circus as a performer. He joined the Budapest Royal Academy of Theater and Art in 1910 and studied there for two years. After the academy, Curtiz became involved in the country's growing film industry and is said to have directed the country's first feature film, *Today and Tomorrow* (1912). In 1915, Curtiz married actress Lucy Doraine (nee Ilonka Kovács Perényi), who starred in many of his films from 1912 to 1919. Curtiz, who had served in the Austrian army during World War I, signed a contract with Sascha Studios in Vienna and relocated to Austria from Hungary in 1919 after the Communists nationalized the country's film industry. In 1923, he directed the acclaimed *Sodom and Gomorrah* and divorced his wife. In 1924 he directed the film *Die Sklavenkönigin*, released in the United States under the title *Moon of Israel*. The film inspired Jack Warner to extend an invitation to Curtiz to come and direct for the studio. His first films for Warner Bros. in 1926 were silent, but he gradually moved over to talkies between 1927 and 1929. Curtiz married screenwriter Bess Meredyth in 1929. In the late 1930s, he made several romantic adventures starring Errol Flynn, including *Captain Blood* (1935) and *The Adventures of Robin Hood* (1938). By 1937, Curtiz had become an American citizen, but was renowned for never having mastered the English language. Yet he directed some of the most iconic American films, such as the 1942 musical *Yankee Doodle Dandy* and what is considered the greatest American film, *Casablanca* (1942), the only film to earn him an Oscar for best director. He continued to work at a hectic pace, turning out 23 more films for Warner Bros., including the Oscar-winning *Mildred Pierce* (1945), *Life with Father* (1947), and *Jim Thorpe, All-American* (1951), but left in 1954, filming the popular *White Christmas* for Paramount that year. As the studios declined, so too did his career, but he continued to direct a wide variety of films, including Elvis Presley in *King Creole* (1958) and finishing the John Wayne film *The Comancheros* (1961) a few months before his death in Los Angeles.

[Adam Wills (2nd ed.)]

°**CUSA, NICHOLAS OF** (1401–1464), German theologian and philosopher. Nicholas was born in Cusa (Kues), Germany. He became a cardinal in 1448. At the ecclesiastical synod of Bamberg convened by him in his capacity of papal legate in 1451 Cusa had condoned the regulation obliging Jews to wear a distinctive *badge. His historical importance derives from his writings, in which he set forth an intensely spiritual interpretation of belief. For this task he developed philosophical concepts which enabled his work to serve as a link between the Middle Ages and early modern times. The conquest of Constantinople by the Turks in 1453 and the atrocities engendered by their fanaticism motivated him to write *De pace fidei* (1453; ed. by R. Klibansky and H. Bascour, 1956). His aim was to trace the common ground between different creeds and thus eliminate religious conflicts. In the work Nicholas portrays wise men of many nations representing a wide range of creeds and sects gathered in heaven to listen to esoteric teaching. According to it, the doctrinal essence of Christianity is defined as a cosmogonic process determining the relation of God and man, an interpretation that was intended as a basis of belief for all religions, even paganism. Nicholas knew very well that the Jews' explicit refusal to recognize the messianic character of Jesus, whose appearance on earth was the pivot of his metaphysical history, was an obstacle to the achievement of such harmony. But in the debate the Jewish speaker agrees that an understanding of the Trinity as the process of creation avoids ascribing the objectionable attribute of plurality to God (ch. 9). Further, Peter sets forth the argument that the real belief of the Jews transcends their own understanding: "They prefer death to any violation of the Law; but this attitude presupposes a belief in immortality, even though such blessing is not promised in the Torah for the mere fulfilling of the Law" (ch. 15). Nicholas' teaching was influenced by a tradition going back to the German Dominican theologian and mystic Meister *Eckhart (c. 1260–1327), whose writings introduced him to Maimonides. Nicholas' famous book *De docta ignorantia* (1440; tr. by G. Heron as *Of Learned Ignorance*, 1954) contains passages from Maimonides' *Dux neutrorum* (*Guide of the Perplexed)*, presented as the authority for the treatise's statements concerning the right approach to the understanding of the Divine Being (1:16; 26). They are identical with the corresponding quotations summarized in Eckhart's Exodus commentary. But in contrast to Eckhart, Nicholas names a Rabbi Solomon as the author of the texts. Possibly, at the time he did not wish to reveal his link with the daring 14th-century Dominican. About 1450 he made a search for a complete text of the *Dux neutrorum* and, having found it in a Dutch monastery, ordered a copy for the pope.

BIBLIOGRAPHY: E. Gilson, *History of Christian Philosophy in the Middle Ages* (1955), 534–40; H. Wackerzapp, *Der Einfluss Meister Eckharts auf die ersten philosophischen Schriften des Nikolaus von Kues, 1440–1450* (1962); P.E. Sigmund, *Nicholas of Cusa and Medieval Political Thought* (1963); Guttmann, in: MGWJ, 43 (1899), 251ff.; E. Roth, in: *Monumenta Judaica* (Handbuch, 1963). 75, 126 n. 111; Eckert, in: *Kirche und Synagoge*, 1 (1968), 273.

[Hans Liebeschutz]

CUSH (Kush). (1) Cush was the name of an ancient kingdom in N.E. Africa. The portion of the Nile Valley between the First and Sixth Cataracts was called Cush by the pharaonic Egyptians, though western nations preferred the Greek appellation Nubia. One of the earliest mentions of the name

Cush is found on an inscription of the early Middle Kingdom (c. 1970 B.C.E.). During the second millennium B.C.E. Cush was absorbed into the Egyptian empire, first as far as the Second Cataract under the Middle Kingdom rulers and then as far as the Sixth by the New Kingdom pharaohs. When the New Kingdom disintegrated (c. 1050 B.C.E.), Cush, which had been thoroughly Egyptianized, gained its independence under a line of native kings. It was probably the Cushite king Shabako (c. 707–696) who encouraged *Hezekiah of Judah to resist the Assyrians under Sennacherib and sent the relief army that the Assyrians crushed at the battle of Eletekh in 701 B.C.E., since Taharka (*Tirhakah), mentioned in II Kings 19:9 and Isaiah 37:9, had not yet come to the throne. In fact, the biblical account is believed by some scholars to be a conflation of two campaigns. After the Assyrian conquest of Egypt in 666 B.C.E., Taharka's successor Tanwentamani at first succeeded in freeing Upper Egypt as far as Memphis from the Assyrians in about 663–662 B.C.E., but he was driven out by the avenging armies of Ashurbanipal. The ancient capital of Thebes was so savagely plundered that 50 years later it served the prophet Nahum as an example for the forthcoming destruction of Nineveh (Nah. 3:8, 10). From this time on, Cush ceased to intervene in the affairs of Egypt.

(2) According to the Bible, Cush was the son of Ham (Gen. 2:13; 10:6–8; Ezek. 38:5; I Chron. 1:8–10) and the eponym of the N.E. African people. In several verses the name refers to other peoples; the distinction is not clear in every single case (Num. 12:1; II Chron. 14:8; 21:16). In the Septuagint the name appears in two forms: in those verses in which it designates the son of Ham it appears in the form Χους while in other cases it is Αιθιοπια, i.e., Ethiopia. Most modern translations follow the Septuagint. The whole of East Africa was called Cush by the Greeks, and in modern times "*Cushi*" is a Hebrew term for a black person.

BIBLIOGRAPHY: A.J. Arkell, *History of the Sudan* (1961²), 55–173; Lambdin, in: IDB, 2 (1962), 176–7 (incl. bibl.); Wilson, *ibid.*, 4 (1962), 652 (incl. bibl.).

[Alan Richard Schulman]

CUSHAN-RISHATHAIM (Heb. כּוּשַׁן רִשְׁעָתַיִם), the first oppressor of Israel in the period of the Judges (Judg. 3:8–10). Israel was subject to Cushan-Rishathaim, the king of Aram-Naharaim, for eight years, before being rescued by the first "judge," *Othniel son of Kenaz. The second element, Rishathaim ("double wickedness"), is presumably not the original name, but serves as a pejorative which rhymes with Naharaim. The combination Aram-Naharaim is not a genuine one for the period of the Judges, since at that time the Arameans were not yet an important ethnic element in Mesopotamia. In the view of some scholars, the story lacks historical basis and is the invention of an author who wished to produce a judge from Judah, and raise the total number of judges to twelve. Those who see a historical basis to the story have proposed various identifications for Cushan-Rishathaim: (1) Cushan is to be sought among one of the Kassite rulers in Babylonia (17th–12th centuries; cf. Gen. 10:8). Josephus identifies Cushan with an Assyrian king. Others identify him with one of the Mitannian or Hittite kings. (2) Cushan is an Egyptian ruler from *Cush in Africa (Nubia; cf. Gen. 10:6; Isa. 11:11, et al.). (3) The head of the tribe of Cush, which led a nomadic existence along the southern border of Palestine. Such Cushite nomads are mentioned in the Egyptian Execration Texts of the first quarter of the second millennium B.C.E. and in the Bible (Num. 12:1; Hab. 3:7; II Chron. 14:8; 21:16). (4) Aram (Heb. ארם) is a corruption of Edom (Heb. אדום) and Naharaim is a later addition. Thus, Cushan is an Edomite king who subjugated the tribe of Judah whose territory was adjacent to Edom. (5) Cushan is from central or northern Syria, and is to be identified with a North Syrian ruler or with *irsw*, a Hurrian (from the area of Syria-Palestine) who seized power in Egypt during the anarchic period at the end of the 19th dynasty (c. 1200 B.C.E.). In his campaign from the north to Egypt, he also subjugated the Israelites. Othniel's rescue of the Israelites is to be understood against the background of the expulsion of the foreign invaders from Egypt by the pharaoh Sethnakhte, the founder of the 20th dynasty.

BIBLIOGRAPHY: E. Taeubler, in: HUCA, 20 (1947), 137–42; A. Malamat, in: JNES, 13 (1954), 231–42; S. Yeivin, in: *Atiqot*, 3 (1961), 176–80.

[Bustanay Oded]

CUTH, CUTHAH (Heb. כּוּת, II Kings 17:30; כּוּתָה; II Kings 17:24), a Sumero-Akkadian and Babylonian holy and cult city; the present-day Tell Ibrāhīm, 31¼ mi. (50 km.) N.E. of Babylon, 12½ mi. (20 km.) W. of Jemdet Nasr (see *Mesopotamia). The Sumerian (or pre-Sumerian) name for Cuthah is Gudua, and the Akkadian (from which the biblical name was derived) is Kutû(m). In the Bible (II Kings 17:24, 30) Cuthah figures as one of the cities from which the king of Assyria brought colonists to the province of Samaria. The Talmud (BB 91a) and Josephus (Ant., 9:279) speak of it as a locality still known in their time. The former identifies it with the Ur of the Chaldeans, which was Abraham's original home according to Genesis (11:31; 15:7). Perhaps the modern name of the site of Cuthah, Tell Ibrāhīm, reflects this tradition. The city of Cuthah is known in cuneiform sources chiefly as the cult center of the god Nergal; his central shrine, É-MES-LAM, stood in Cuthah (cf. e.g., Laws of Hammurapi, Preamble, line 71), and the Cuthean colonists in the province of Samaria established this cult there (II Kings 17:30). Cuthah is mentioned in various hymns and cultic poems. One historical poem, formerly known as the "Legend of the King of Cuthah," is now called the "Legend of Naram-Sin" because its subject is King Naram-Sîn of *Akkad (see O.B. Gurney, *Anatolian Studies*, 5 (1955), p. 93ff.). Although Cuthah was also considered a holy city by the Assyrian kings, it was damaged and destroyed by Sargon II and Sennacherib, due to the active participation of its old and new inhabitants in the wars of independence and revolts. According to the first edition of Sennacherib's annals of his first campaign (lines 23ff.) he took the city because it served as a center of Babylonian resistance to Assyria, and Ashurbanipal had to chastise it for the same reason. (Rassam Cylinder, 3:130 (in: D.D. Luckenbill, *The Annals of Sennacherib* (1924), 61); meanwhile Cuthah served as a minor astronomical-astrological observations station.) Either one or both of these episodes may be connected with the transplanting of Cutheans to the territory of the former rump kingdom of Ephraim reported in the already cited biblical passages (II Kings 17:24, 30; cf. Ezra 4:1–2, 10). In rabbinic sources "Cuthean" (Heb. כּוּתִי) is the fixed term of "*Samaritan."

BIBLIOGRAPHY: Luckenbill, Records, index; A. Parrot, *Archéologie mésopotamienne* (1946), 93; D.O. Edzard, *Die zweite Zwischenzeit Babyloniens* (1957); A.L. Oppenheim, in: *Centaurus*, 14 (1969/70), 97–135.

[Pinhas Artzi]

CUTLER, BRUCE (1948–). U.S. criminal lawyer. Born in Brooklyn, N.Y., to a detective turned lawyer, Cutler graduated from Hamilton College and Brooklyn Law School, with honors, in 1974. He was supervising senior trial attorney with the Homicide Bureau of the Brooklyn District Attorney from 1974 to 1981, when he joined the private practice of Barry Slotnick, one of New York's premier criminal lawyers. In March 1985, he became the defense lawyer for John Gotti, who headed a notorious crime family by virtue of a murderous coup and flaunted his power during a flamboyant reign as a Mafia boss. Cutler provided a tenacious and highly publicized defense of Gotti against a government determined to bring Gotti to his knees. A ubiquitous presence at Gotti's side in and out of the courtroom, Cutler became almost as infamous as his client. And, as Gotti became a lightning rod for prosecutors seeking glory, reputation, or promotion, Cutler became a lightning rod for controversy. The government said Cutler may have gotten too close, and they set out to see that Cutler and Gotti paid the price. Cutler successfully defended Gotti in an assault case, a federal racketeering trial, and in a case in which he was accused of shooting a union official. But in a federal murder and racketeering trial in 1991 and 1992, with Cutler and an associate defending Gotti, the winning streak ran out. Prosecutors contended that both lawyers were house counsel for a crime family and thus became potential witnesses in the case against Gotti. They were removed at the government's behest. Cutler, the appeals court said, had "entangled himself to an extraordinary degree in the activities of the Gambino crime family." Gotti was later convicted and sentenced to life without parole. He died in 2002. A judge had warned Cutler not to talk to the media during the proceedings but Cutler did. In 1993 he was convicted of contempt for violating the court order. He was sentenced to 90 days of house arrest, ordered to perform 600 hours of community service, and fined $5,000. He was also suspended from practicing law for six months in 1995 and 1996. Eventually, Cutler returned to private practice. He wrote *Closing Argument* (2003) about his law career.

[Stewart Kampel (2nd ed.)]

CUTLER, HARRY (1875–1920), U.S. industrialist, public official, and communal leader. Born in Russia, Cutler went to the U.S. at the age of eight. He became a successful jewelry manufacturer in Providence, Rhode Island. From 1908 to 1911 he served with distinction as a state assemblyman in Rhode Island. Cutler was a colonel in the National Guard and an aide to General John J. Pershing during the Mexican border campaign in 1916. During World War I, he helped found the *National Jewish Welfare Board to serve the needs of Jewish servicemen and was chairman of its executive committee. Cutler was one of nine delegates sent by the American Jewish Congress to Paris in 1919 to represent Jewish interests at the Versailles Conference. His other communal activities were manifold, including membership in the executive committees of the American Jewish Committee, Zionist Organization of America, and American Jewish Joint Distribution Committee, as well as vice chairman of the American Jewish Congress and vice president of the Union of American Hebrew Congregations.

BIBLIOGRAPHY: *New York Times* (Aug. 20, 1920).

[Morton Rosenstock]

°CUZA, ALEXANDER C. (1857–1946), Romanian nationalist and antisemitic leader. Cuza taught political economy at Jassy University (1900). From 1890, he combined law teaching with a political career devoted to the propagation of racial antisemitism and xenophobia. In 1895, he founded the Alliance antisémitique universelle in Bucharest, with N. Iorga and J. de Biez. In 1910, together with Iorga, he formed the proto-fascist National Democratic Party (NDP), based on the "National Christian" idea. The main points of the party's program were the elimination of the Jews from professional life, the prohibition against Jews settling in the villages, and their removal from the army. Between the two world wars, Cuza was the principal promoter of "*numerus clausus" and of racialism in academic circles and students' organizations, particularly at Jassy University, which became a focal point of antisemitism in Romania. In 1923, Cuza created out of the NDP the National Christian Defense League, a fascist formation which later gave birth to *Codreanu's *Iron Guard formed in 1930. In 1925 he was among the organizers of a secret European antisemitic conference which convened in Budapest. On Hitler's rise to power in Germany, the German Nazi Party supported Cuza's party, which united with O. Goga's agrarian national party in 1935 and became the National Christian Party (Partidul național-Creștin). In December 1937 Cuza helped Goga to set up a government which paved the way for Ion *Antonescu's dictatorship. Among Cuza's works are *Naționalitatea în artaˇ* ("Nationality in Art," 1908); *Scaderea Proporației Creștine și înmulțirea Jidanilor* ("Decrease of the Christian Population and Increase of the Jews," 1910); *Jidanii în Raˇsboiu* ("The Jews in the War," 1919); *Numerus Clausus* (1923).

BIBLIOGRAPHY: *Politics and Political Parties in Rumania* (1936), 432–5; P. Pavel, *Why Rumania Failed* (1944), index.

C.V.-ZEITUNG (*Central-Verein-Zeitung*), weekly newspaper published in Berlin between 1922 and 1938 to replace the former monthly *Im Deutschen Reich* (founded 1895) as the official organ of the *Central-Verein deutscher Staatsbuerger juedischen Glaubens (CV). One of its subtitles was **Allgemeine Zeitung des Judentums* in reference to the venerable German-Jewish newspaper founded under this name by Ludwig *Philippson in 1837 and which ceased to appear in 1922. The *CV-Zeitung*'s chief editor between 1922 and 1933 was the director of the CV, Ludwig *Hollaender, followed up to the end by Alfred Hirschberg. The gradual deletion of the paper's subtitles reflects the hostile attitude of the Nazi regime to the "assimilationist" CV and its newspaper: as early as August 1933 the subheading *Organ des Centralvereins deutscher Staatsbuerger juedischen Glaubens* disappeared from the masthead. From April 1935 on the boldface line *Zeitung fuer Deutschtum und Judentum* had had to be omitted by government order, leaving *Allgemeine Zeitung des Judentums* as the sole subtitle. The *CV Zeitung* was the most widely read Jewish newspaper in Germany, reaching a circulation of 73,000 in 1926. It ceased publication, like almost all Jewish papers, after the pogroms of November 1938.

BIBLIOGRAPHY: A. Barkai, *"Wehr dich!" Der Centralverein deutscher Staatsbuerger juedischen Glaubens (CV)* (2002).

[Avraham Barkai (2nd ed.)]

CYNICS AND CYNICISM, Greek philosophy glorifying the unspoiled primitive life that left its imprint upon many ages and cultures. The Cynics used a fable-like witty anecdote, the *chria*, which immortalized the extreme actions and caustic *bon mots* of their favorite sages (often nonhistorical). They were followed in this by *Philo, *tannaim*, and *amoraim*, and some Church Fathers. Philo repeats many *chriae* and portrays the Jewish festivals and Moses' life in a cynicizing manner. It has recently been argued by Fischel that in the rabbinic stories of *Hillel and, to a lesser degree, *Eliezer b. Hyrcanus, *Joshua, *Meir, and *Akiva, are found cynic *chriae* or composites of chriic materials including their original social values, such as endurance, poverty, lowly toil, strenuous effort, and total non-worry (all non-biblical). Cynical invective, bawdiness, and offensive humor, however, are somewhat toned down in the talmudic stories or reinterpreted through *halakhah* and belief in a transcendental world. As in the Greco-Roman tradition these *exempla* were apparently used to increase the stature of a founder-sage.

Additional cynic-rhetorical favorites reworked in rabbinism include Heracles at the Crossroads (Eccl. R. on 1:14, etc.); the Laughing Democritus (Akiva) and the Weeping Heraclitus (Gamaliel, etc., Mak. 24a, etc.); the Forgetful Thales (Hillel, Pes. 66a, et al.); and anti-Alexander items (Tam. 31b, et al.). The cynical *thaumaston*, a *chria* on a visiting foreign sage (esp. the Scythian Anacharsis) who "marvels" (*thaumazei*) at the inner contradictions in the culture of his guests, may be the pattern for similar stories on Aesop, Jesus, and Hillel (TJ, Suk. 5:4, 55b; et al.).

The transition of cynic stances from the Greco-Roman scholar-bureaucracy to the Jewish-tannaitic one may have been facilitated by cynicism's superficial resemblance to biblical prophecy and by its critique of "paganism." Meir's reported disputations with the Cynic *Oenomaus of Gadara, although hardly genuine, may reflect some personal contacts, but then Oenomaus was a favorite target of Greco-Roman rhetoric. *Kinukos* (*kunikos*) as a destructive person occurs in the Jerusalem Talmud (Git. 7:1, 48c; et al.). Living under similar conditions the Cynics may have occasionally found rabbinic items congenial: Peregrinus Proteus' spectacular suicide at the Olympic Games of 167 C.E. resembles that of the Jewish high priest *Alcimus-Jakim according to the Midrash (Gen. R. 65:22).

BIBLIOGRAPHY: D.R. Dudley, *History of Cynicism* (1937); R. Höistad, *Cynic Hero and Cynic King* (1948); I. Heinemann, *Philon's griechische und juedische Bildung* (1932, repr., 1962); Fischel, in: *Religions in Antiquity, Essays… E.R. Goodenough* (1968), 372–411; idem, in: *American Oriental Society Middle West Branch Semi-Centennial Volume* (1969), 59–88.

[Henry Albert Fischel]

CYON, ELIE DE (Tsion, Ilya Faddeyevich; 1842–1912), Russian physiologist. Cyon, who was born in Samara (now Kuibyshev), graduated from the University of Kiev and later studied in Berlin and France. In 1870 he became the first Jewish professor in Russia when he was appointed to the chair of physiology at the University of St. Petersburg. In 1872 he was appointed professor at the Medico-Surgical Academy in St. Petersburg and reformed the teaching of physiology by introducing the method of illustrative experiments. His work on reflexes won him international renown. As a result of political intrigues, Cyon was obliged to resign from the Academy in 1875. He thereafter gave up his scientific career and left Russia for Paris. Cyon published original work on the physiology of the nervous system and the heart, the mechanism of blood pressure, the application of electrotherapy, and a monograph on the inner ear. His treatise on new methods and techniques in physiological experiments served as a guide in many European medical centers. His publications include: *Methodik der physiologischen Experimente und Vivisektionen…* (1876); *Gesammelte physiologische Arbeiten…* (1888); *Dieu et Science: Essais de psychologie des sciences…* (1910).

[Suessmann Muntner]

CYPRESS, the tree *Cupressus sempervirens* of which two varieties are known, the horizontal *Cupressus sempervirens horizontalis* and the vertical *Cupressus sempervirens pyramidalis*. The former grows wild in the high mountains of Gilead and the slopes of Lebanon. Scholars differ as to the biblical name for the cypress. In modern Hebrew it is identified with *berosh*, but the identification appears to be erroneous since the biblical *berosh* has been identified with the *juniper. It is almost certain that both the gopher and *te'ashur* of the Bible are the cypress. (1) Gopher: It was from this wood that Noah was commanded to build the ark (Gen. 6:14). Of all the suggestions put forward to identify this tree, the cypress seems the most likely, and its Greek name κοπάρισος appears to be related to the Semitic gopher. The wood is proofed against rot and is suitable for the building of seaworthy craft. Ships in ancient times were constructed mainly of cypress. (2) *Te'ashur* (AV "*box tree") is mentioned by Isaiah among the trees that will blossom on the way of the redeemed in the wilderness (Isa 41:19), and will be employed in the construction of the Temple (*ibid.* 60:13). Ezekiel, describing the ships of the Tyrians, states that they were made of *bat-ashurim* from the isles of the Kittites (Ezek. 27:6). Both Rashi (basing himself on the Targum) and Kimḥi read it as one word preceded by a preposition *bite'ashurim* ("with cypress wood brought from the island of Cyprus"). The cypress grows on that island, and some are of the opinion that the name of this island is actually derived from it. *Te'ashur* is apparently derived from "*yashar*" ("upright") because of the erect nature of the *C.s. pyramydalis*. The horizontal species resembles the cedar, and it would appear that the references in rabbinical literature to cedars growing in Israel are to the horizontal cypress. The cypress is not indigenous to Israel but is grown as an ornamental tree and as a windbreak in orchards. It is also planted in pine forests. The picturesque mixture of pine and cypress can be found in the forest at Sha'ar ha-Gai and at Ein Karem near Jerusalem.

BIBLIOGRAPHY: Loew, Flora, 3 (1924), 26–33; J. Feliks, *Olam ha-Ẓome'aḥ ha-Mikra'i* (1968²), 84–87.

[Jehuda Feliks]

CYPROS (first century C.E.), mother of *Herod. She was descended from a noble Nabatean family and married *Antipater, the Idumean, to whom she bore four sons, *Phasael, Herod, Joseph, *Pheroras, and a daughter, Salome. At the court of Herod, Cypros, supported by her daughter Salome, was in constant conflict with Herod's wife, *Mariamne the Hasmonean, and her mother Alexandra, who mocked at her descent. Cypros and Salome hence succeeded in inciting Herod against his wife. Before Herod left for Rhodes to meet *Augustus, he left the members of his family at Masada, but he sent Mariamne and her mother in the charge of two faithful servants to Alexandreion. The bitter domestic rivalry led directly to Herod's execution of Mariamne. A fortress near Jericho was named Cypros by Herod in honor of his mother (Josephus, Wars, 1:417; Ant., 16:143). The site is situated on the southern side of Wadi Qelt, opposite Nuseib 'Uweishira, 15 miles (22 km.) distant from Jerusalem. It was excavated by E. Netzer and E. Damati in 1974 revealing a sumptious palace with bathhouses (one with a large bathtub *in situ*) and reception rooms with painted walls.

BIBLIOGRAPHY: Jos., Wars, 1:181, 407, 438; 2:484; idem, Ant., 14:121; 15:81, 184, 213, 220, 239; A. Schalit, *Hordos ha-Melekh* (1960), 76–77, 79. **ADD. BIBLIOGRAPHY:** E. Netzer, *The Palaces of the Hasmoneans and Herod the Great* (1999).

[Lea Roth / Shimon Gibson (2nd ed.)]

CYPROS (first century C.E.), wife of Agrippa I, and daughter of Herod's brother Phasael and Salampsio. She bore her husband two sons, Drusus, who died in his childhood, and Agrippa, and three daughters, Berenice, Drusilla, and Mariamne. Cypros showed great loyalty to her husband whose reckless spending often caused him to get into debt. On one such occasion she prevented him from committing suicide. She then turned to his sister *Herodias, wife of Herod *Antipas, who secured a public appointment for Agrippa. He was however unable to hold it for long, and fell into debt again. Once more she came to her husband's rescue, persuading the alabarch *Alexander Lysimachus to grant a loan. Derenbourg considers that it was largely her influence which transformed Agrippa from a rather irresponsible and profligate young man into the king beloved of the rabbis.

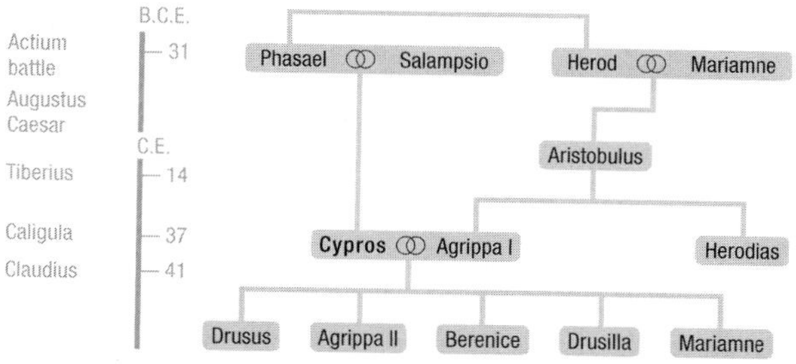

BIBLIOGRAPHY: Jos., Ant., 18:131ff., 148ff., 159ff.; Pes. 57–58; Sot. 7:8; Ket. 17a; Derenbourg, Hist, 209–10; Klausner, Bayit Sheni, 4 (1963), 288.

[Lea Roth]

CYPRUS, an island in the eastern Mediterranean, opposite the coast of northern Syria; c. 40 mi. south of Turkey and c. 65 mi. west of Syria.

Ancient Period

According to many scholars, the name Alashiya (Elishah, אֱלִישָׁה Gen. 10:4; I Chron. 1:7; Ezek. 27:7) refers to the island of Cyprus or a part of it. Alashiya is described in sources of the second millennium B.C.E. (Mari, Amarna, Ugarit, and Egyptian documents) as a place from which copper was exported – parenthetically it should be noted that Greek sources also bear witness to the fact that Cyprus was a source of copper for the Mediterranean countries (see *Metals). A stele of *Sargon II has been unearthed at Citium in Cyprus (*Kitti* in Phoenician, *Kittim in Isa. 23:1, and Ezek. 27:6). Sargon and Esarhaddon mention ten kings of the land of *Iadnāna* (or *ā'ā*) who paid them tribute. The names and residences of these kings indicate that the Cypriot population was not Semitic, and a relationship with indigenous peoples of Anatolia has been suggested. The Cypriot native language and the so-called Cypro-Minoan script or Cypro-Mycenean script from the Bronze Age remain undeciphered. The majority of the inscriptions in the so-called Cypriot syllabic script – which seems to have been

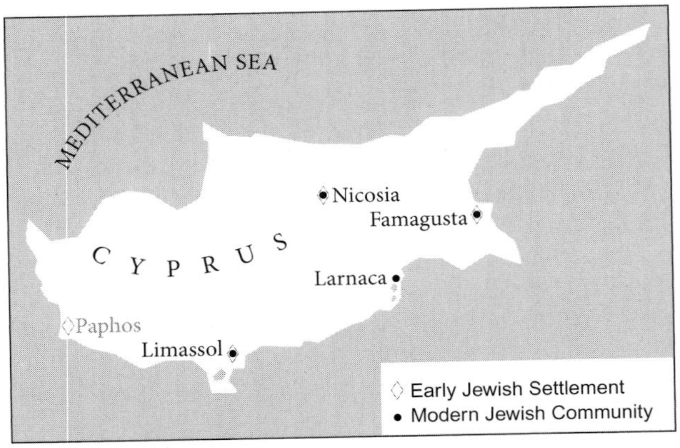

Major Jewish communities on Cyprus in medieval and modern times.

employed from about the sixth to the first centuries B.C.E. – is couched in Greek, and a few are in an undeciphered language.

[Bustanay Oded]

Like Ereẓ Israel, Cyprus came under Ptolemaic rule at the beginning of the third century B.C.E., at which period a Jewish settlement on the island apparently began to develop on a large scale. Actual evidence of such settlement, however, dates from the middle of the second century B.C.E., Cyprus being among the places to which the Romans sent letters in 142 B.C.E. requesting that the rights of the Jews there be safeguarded (I Macc. 15:23). In the days of John Hyrcanus the Jewish settlement in the island flourished (Jos., Ant., 13:284). Apart from the literary evidence that Jews lived in Cyprus in this period, Hasmonean coins have been discovered on the island. In 58 B.C.E. the island was annexed to the Roman province of Cilicia. During the Roman period there were contacts between Ereẓ Israel and Cyprus: Herod received from Augustus a portion of the revenue from the copper mines there and was entrusted with the management of some of them (*ibid.*, 15:128). It is possible that Jews were employed at the mines in an administrative capacity, or that they were sent to work there as a punishment for criminal offenses. After the death of Herod, his granddaughter Alexandra married an aristocratic Cyprus Jew, Timius of Cyprus (*ibid.*, 18:131). The existence of a large Jewish settlement in Cyprus is attested by a letter of *Agrippa I to the emperor Caligula in which he states that Jerusalem is the capital not of Judea alone, but of all Jews, including those in Cyprus (Philo, *Legatio ad Gaium*, 282). The Acts of the Apostles (4:36; 13:4–6; 15:39) also bear witness to a large Jewish population on the island. The apostles Paul, Barnabas of Cyprus, and John preached in the synagogues at Salamis and other places. The Jews were not favorably disposed to the spread of Christianity, and a certain Bar Joshua (Barjesus) attempted to obstruct the apostles' efforts to exert their influence on the Roman governor (Acts 13:6–8).

There is some evidence, though sparse, of Cyprus Jews in Ereẓ Israel: a Jew of Cyprus helped to persuade Drusilla, the daughter of Agrippa, to marry the procurator Felix (52–60 C.E.; Jos., Ant., 20:142); a certain Mnason of Cyprus lived at Caesarea (Acts 21:16); and there was apparently something of a community of Cyprus Jews in Jerusalem (*ibid.*, 11:19). Products of Cyprus were imported into Ereẓ Israel (TJ, Dem. 2:1, 22b, "cumin from Cyprus"; TJ, Yoma 4:5, 41d, "wine of Cyprus"; Jos., Ant., 20:51, "dried figs imported from Cyprus by Queen Helena of Adiabene during a famine"). Under Trajan, probably in 116/7 C.E., the Jews of Cyprus, led by *Artemion, together with those of Cyrene, Egypt, and Mesopotamia revolted (Dio Cassius 68:32; Jerome, *Chronica*, 196; et al.). The causes of the revolt in Cyprus are not entirely clear, but it was apparently due in part to the friction between Jews and non-Jews and not necessarily to their relations with the Roman administration. The Jews of Cyprus are reported to have killed 240,000 people and to have destroyed the city of Salamis. Jewish losses are not mentioned. After the revolt had been suppressed by Lusius and other generals sent by Trajan, Jews were strictly forbidden to set foot on the island, but this prohibition was not apparently in force for long. The belief held by some (on the basis of an inscription on a pillar) that Jews had already returned to the island in the second century is borne out by Jewish sources that mention R. *Akiva's visit to Ẓifirin (TJ, Av. Zar. 2:4; 41b; 113a; et al. – if Neubauer's identification of Ẓifirin as a place in Cyprus is to be preferred to that of Alon, who locates it in Cilicia). Another inscription, dating probably from the fourth century, refers to the renovation of a synagogue, apparently in the third century (Frey, Corpus, 2 (197), 735). In addition, a third century Jewish candelabrum with designs of a *lulav* and *etrog* have been found there. Jews, then, had resettled in the island by that time.

[Lea Roth]

Medieval Period

In the early seventh century there was a large community in Famagusta. The 12th-century traveler *Benjamin of Tudela mentions the existence of Rabbanite and Karaite Jews and a Jewish sect that apparently celebrated Sabbath on Sunday instead of Saturday. Under the Lusignan kings (1192–1489), Cyprus had the largest Jewish settlement in the islands off Greece. It included communities in Nicosia, Famagusta, Paphos, and Limassol. (See Map: Cyprus). Jews were discriminated against in law; however, attempts by the church to forbid Christians from visiting Jewish physicians were unsuccessful. Archbishop Giovanni del Conte (1319–1332) introduced the distinguishing yellow *badge for Jews. King Peter I (1359–1369) attracted Egyptian Jewish traders to Cyprus by promising equal treatment to Jews and non-Jews. The Genoese (1373–1463) plundered Jewish property in Famagusta and Nicosia. During the 16th century 2,000 Jews are said to have lived in Famagusta. One of the island's governors during Venetian rule (1489–1571) ordered the punishment of Jews who did not pay due respect to a religious procession. In 1495 a pupil of R. Obadiah of *Bertinoro mentioned the existence of many Jews who were artisans and traders in Cyprus. In 1552 R. Moses *Basola found 12 householders, originally from Sicily, in Famagusta. An attempt in 1568 to foment a rebellion on the island in favor of the Turks was attributed to the statesman Joseph *Nasi, who in 1563–64 set on foot an intrigue to offer the crown of Cyprus to the Duke of Savoy. Thanks to the efforts of Solomon *Ashkenazi a peace treaty was signed, in 1573, between Venice and Turkey which had conquered the island in 1561.

The sultans tried to settle Jews from Safed on the island in order to counterbalance the Christian element in the population, but subsequently the Jewish settlement on the island was insignificant.

Modern Period

In 1878, the English statesman Benjamin *Disraeli succeeded in having Cyprus placed under British administration. The few Jews who lived in Cyprus under British rule were mainly silversmiths and peddlers. Between 1883 and 1897 there were attempts to settle Jews from Romania elsewhere on the island. In 1900, the economist Davis *Trietsch made an attempt to settle Jews there after Herzl had failed in negotiations over Ereẓ Israel with the Turks. In 1902 and 1903 Herzl discussed with *Chamberlain a plan to settle Jews in Cyprus, but without success. Between 1933 and 1939 Cyprus was a sanctuary for 500 Jewish refugees from Germany. In 1941 the British began to evacuate the island, mainly women and children, for fear of a German invasion, and its Jews were also evacuated. After World War II, when the stream of "illegal" immigration to Palestine of the survivors in Europe assumed mass proportions, the British government forcibly transferred many thousands of them to deportation ships and sent them to detention camps in Cyprus. Their total number, from 1946 until 1948, was about 51,500. In the camps they were assisted by *sheliḥim* (emissaries) of the *Jewish Agency and the *Haganah to organize health and education services as well as some military training. With the establishment of the State of Israel they were released and quickly absorbed in the mainstream of mass immigration which began to arrive in the country (see *"Illegal" Immigration). In 1951 the Jewish population numbered only 165 persons who lived in Nicosia, Larnaca, Limassol, and Famagusta. They engaged in citrus growing, trade, industry, and farming; a few were mine owners. By 1970 there were only 25 Jews on the island and there was virtually no communal life. A cemetery was maintained at Margo and second one at Larnaca was no longer used.

The community began to revive in the early 21st century as the Jewish population grew to around 1,500 (300 families), mostly consisting of Israelis working in the burgeoning information and telecom industries there, as well as Jews from South Africa and the former Soviet Union. A community center was inaugurated in Larnaca in 2005 under the auspices of Chabad, with the island's only synagogue. Israeli-born Aryeh Ze'ev Raskin, who originally arrived as a Chabad emissary to stimulate the revival, became the community's rabbi. Sunday school classes were also inaugurated.

Relations with Israel

After the establishment of the State of Israel an Israel Consulate was opened in Nicosia. When Cyprus reached independence, in 1960, diplomatic relations were established on ambassadorial level, Israel being represented by a resident ambassador, Cyprus by a non-resident one. In its relations with Israel the government of Cyprus assumed a complex and sometimes contradictory attitude. While at the United Nations its representatives mostly sided with the Arab states against Israel, mainly under Egyptian pressure and under the influence of the Greek government (see *Greece), it simultaneously fostered mass-tourism from Israel to Cyprus, which reached around 60,000 Israelis a year by the beginning of the 21st century, and non-governmental ties (e.g., between labor movements, trade unions, agricultural organizations, etc.). Trade relations developed satisfactorily. There was also some technical cooperation between the two states. At the same time, from the 1980s on, Cyprus modified its pro-Arab stance and political relations with Israel began to warm.

[Simon Marcus]

BIBLIOGRAPHY: ANCIENT PERIOD: J.A. Knudtzon (ed.), *Die El-Amarna Tafeln…*, 2 vols. (1915), 279–98, 1076–86; C.F.A. Schaeffer, *Enkomi-Alasia*, 1 (1952); W. Helck, *Die Beziehungen Aegyptens zu Vorderasien* (1962), index, s.v. *Alasia, Cypern*; H.W. Catling, in: CAH2 (1966), fascicle 43, pp. 58ff.; C.F.A. Schaeffer et al., in: *Ugaritica*, 5 (1968), index s.v. *Alasia, Chypre*; D. Diringer, *The Alphabet*, 1 (1968), 120–3; Neubauer, Géogr, 369–70; Schuerer, Gesch, 1 (19014), 662ff.; 3 (19094), 56; G. Hill, *A History of Cyprus*, 1 (1940), 241–3, 247; A. Tcherikover, *Ha-Yehudim be-Miẓrayim…* (1963), 160ff.; A. Schalit, in: *Sinai*, 6 (1940), 367ff. 81; S. Shapira, *Ha-Aliyyah la-Regel bi-Ymei Bayit Sheni* (1965), 66–67; S. Appelbaum, *Yehudim vi-Yvanim be-Kirenyah ha-Kedumah* (1969), 231, 253–4; B. Lifshitz, *Donateurs et fondateurs dans les synagogues juives* (1967), 73–76; Reifenberg, in: JPOS, 12 (1932), 209–15. MEDIEVAL PERIOD: J. Starr, *Romania: Jewries of the Levant…* (1949), 101–10 (incl. bibl.); C. Roth, in: *Sefunot*, 8 (1964), 283–98; idem, *Duke of Naxos* (1967); J.M. Shaftesley, in: JHSET, 22 (1968/69), 88–107. MODERN PERIOD: O.K. Rabinowicz, *A Jewish Cyprus Project* (1967), 460ff.

CYRENE, ancient capital of Cyrenaica, on the northern coast of Africa. In 321 B.C.E. Cyrene came under Ptolemaic rule, remaining part of the Egyptian empire until 96 B.C.E. when it fell to the Romans. Josephus (Apion, 2:44) relates that Jews were sent by Ptolemy I Soter (304–282 B.C.E.) to "Cyrene and the other cities of Libya" to strengthen that king's hold upon the area. Strabo, in a passage quoted by Josephus (Ant., 14:115), describes the four classes of citizens in Cyrene in the year 85 B.C.E. "The first consisted of citizens, the second of farmers, the third of resident aliens (μέτοικοι), and the fourth of Jews." The Jews of Cyrene seem to have been at odds with the local Greek population as is shown by various Roman decrees supporting the rights of Cyrenean Jewry (I Macc. 15:23). Though under the Ptolemies Jewish civic equality (ἰσονομία) had been guaranteed, the Jews of Cyrene were persecuted by the local population and prevented from sending their donations to the Temple at Jerusalem. Only when Augustus and Marcus Agrippa intervened in 14 B.C.E. were these rights fully restored (Ant., 16:160ff.). The Jewish community in Cyrene maintained close ties with those in Palestine. A detailed history of the Hasmonean uprising was chronicled by *Jason of Cyrene (II Macc. 2:23), and in the first century C.E. numerous Jews of Cyrene resided in Jerusalem (Matt. 27:32; Mark 15:21; Luke 23:26; Acts 2:10; 6:9). This fact sheds light on the attempt made by some *sicarii under the leadership of a certain Jonathan to incite the Jews of Cyrene to rebellion after the fall of Jerusalem. This attempt would have been highly unrealistic had there been no intermediaries between Jerusalem and Cyrene. Though Jonathan made headway with the lower classes of the population, the leader of the Jewish community immediately reported his actions to the Roman governor, Catullus, who promptly put down the insurrection (Jos., Wars, 7:43ff.; Life, 424f.).

Far more serious was the Jewish uprising during the last years of Trajan (115–7), which spread across North Africa. The Jews of Cyrene, under their "king" called Lukuas or Andraeas, played a leading role in these bitter revolts, referred to by Greek authors as "the Jewish war" (ὁ ουδαικός πόλεμος). Various Greek and Latin inscriptions describe the destruction caused by the "Jewish tumult," which, although finally suppressed by the Roman legions, nevertheless left Cyrene in ruins (Eusebius, *Historia Ecclesiastica*, 2; Dio Cassius 68, 32).

BIBLIOGRAPHY: Hirschberg, Afrikah, 1 (1965), 8–11; Schuerer, Gesch, 4 (1911[4]), 41f. (index); *Corpus Papyrorum Judaicorum*, 1 (1957), 86–92; Allon, Toledot, 1 (1958[3]), 233–6, 239f.; Appelbaum, *Yehudim vi-Yvanim be-Kirenyah ha-Kedumah* (1969); idem, in: *Zion*, 19 (1953/54), 23–56; 22 (1956/57), 81–85; K. Friedman, in: *Miscellanea… H.P. Chajes* (It., 1930), 39–55; J. Gray, in: University of Manchester, *Cyrenaican Expedition 1912*; N. Slouschz, *Hébraeo-Phéniciens….* (1908), 223ff.

[Isaiah Gafni]

CYRUS (Heb. כֹּרֶשׁ; old Persian: **Kūruš**), king of Persia (reigned, 559–529 B.C.E.). At first, Cyrus II's dominion consisted of Anshan, southwest of the Iranian plateau, of which he was the legitimate king, being a descendant of the Achaemenian dynasty that had already reigned there for several generations. A number of differing accounts of his birth, youth, and ascent to the throne have come down from ancient writers (Herodotus and others), but they apparently belong mainly to the realm of legend. Extant inscriptions from his time, chiefly from Babylon, provide reliable sources of information about him (see Pritchard, Texts, 305–16). Cyrus' first important act was to conspire against Astyages, king of Media, toward which end he entered into an alliance with Nabonidus, king of Babylon. The army of Astyages betrayed him, and Cyrus seized control of the Median kingdom in 550 B.C.E. This conquest brought him into conflict with Lydia in Asia Minor, a kingdom that wished to profit from the fall of Media. In 546 Cyrus defeated Croesus and conquered his kingdom of Lydia. The conquest of Asia Minor was completed when Persia seized control of the many Greek cities on the coast. Apart from these wars with neighboring empires, he campaigned against various tribes, chiefly on the northern and eastern borders of his kingdom. In a battle with one of these tribes – the Massagetae – he was killed. His conquests had created the most extensive empire yet known.

Cyrus holds a special place in the history of Israel. He is mentioned in the prophecies of Deutero-Isaiah, in the Book of Ezra (and at the end of II Chronicles), and in the Book of Daniel (1:21; 6:29; 10:1). In these passages he appears both as one destined to save Israel and to fulfill for it a certain mission on behalf of the God of Israel (Deutero-Isaiah), and as one whose edict and command served as a foundation for the return to Zion and the erection of the destroyed temple (Ezra). Apparently the successes of Cyrus, particularly the preparations and steps that indicated that a struggle between him and Babylon was pending, were in part responsible for rousing Deutero-Isaiah to utter his prophecies on the imminent redemption of Israel and the impending destruction of Babylon. The hopes of the prophet are clearly expressed in chapter 45:1–13: God turns "to His anointed, to Cyrus," whom He helped in the past and will further help in the continuation of his activities ("I will go before you, and level the mountains; I will break in pieces the doors of bronze, and cut asunder the bars of iron"). Cyrus is to rebuild Jerusalem and restore the exilic community. While he does not yet know the God of Israel ("… I call you by your name, I surname you, though you do not know Me"), he may eventually do so, due to the great assistance he will receive from Him. Delivered before the event, this prophecy reveals the feelings and hopes of the prophet who awaits the conquest of Babylon and its punishment (cf. Isa. 46:1–2; 47). The prophecy in 44:28 apparently refers to Cyrus' edict and was certainly uttered after the event. Cyrus is mentioned in other places though not explicitly by name (e.g., 41:2, 25; 46:11). Nevertheless, the place occupied by Cyrus in Deutero-Isaiah should not be exaggerated. Although he occasioned many of the prophecies of Deutero-Isaiah, and his appearance was of great importance to the prophet, it is the people of Israel and its God that stand at the center of the prophecy. Cyrus is merely an instrument for the realization of the redemption of Israel through the will of its God. He is understandably a sympathetic figure, for he is a redeemer and not a "rod of anger," but it should not be assumed from his designation "anointed" and "shepherd" that he had an eschatological role or any function after the redemption of Israel (such as being their ruler in place of the House of David, etc.). It is doubtful if Cyrus was influenced in his congenial relationship with the Jews by the prophecies of Deutero-Isaiah concerning him, or by the part taken by the Jews of Babylon in the war between him and Nabonidus. An explanation of the relations between Cyrus and the Jews rests upon an understanding of his general policy, particularly in Babylon itself. This policy was based upon benevolence toward the conquered, support and sympathy for their gods, and a correction of the injustices done to them by the previous ruler Nabonidus, or in the case of the Jews of Babylon, by Nebuchadnezzar. In conformity with this policy, he restored the Babylonian gods to their temples, reconstructed temples that had been neglected in the time of his predecessor, and even returned exiles to their homes (see the Cylinder Inscription of Cyrus, Pritchard, Texts, 315–6). His policy toward the Jews was similar to that toward the Babylonians. These principles find expression in the Hebrew edict issued to the Jews of Babylonia (538 B.C.E.), which appears in Ezra 1:2–4 (see also II Chron. 36:23). There Cyrus attributes his decision to erect the temple to a command of God, just as he attributed his actions in Babylon to an order of Marduk. An additional document of his concerning the erection of the Temple is more administrative in nature and deals with the architectural and financial details of building (Ezra 6:3–5); this document is even written in Aramaic, the adminstrative language. As a result of the permission given by Cyrus, some of the Babylonian exiles returned to Judah, and with their return a new chapter in the history of Israel began – the period of the Second Temple.

[Uriel Rappaport]

In the Aggadah

Contradictory opinions are held about Cyrus, the Palestinian rabbis giving a rather favorable account of him while the Babylonians censure him. He was descended from Japheth who was thus rewarded for his commendable behavior toward Noah when drunk (PR 35). He was chosen by God together with Darius as the instrument of His vengeance against Babylon. Influenced by Daniel's prophecy to Belshazzar (Dan. 5:28) Darius and Cyrus slew him and vowed that they would permit the Jews to return to the Land of Israel with the Temple vessels (Song R. 3:4). His name is regarded as an anagram of the word *kasher* ("worthy"; RH 3b). He pledged to contribute to the Temple service and discovered the treasures that Nebuchadnezzar had hidden (Est. R. 2:1). He wept at the destruction of the Temple and as a reward the Medes received the domination of the world and he was thus vouchsafed to sit on the throne of Solomon (SER 20). Although he granted the Jews permission to rebuild the Temple he permitted the use of wood only, so that it would be easily destroyed should they rebel against him (RH 3b–4a). Moreover when he noticed that the Babylonian cities became desolate because of the emigration of the Jews he forbade them to leave the country (Song R. 5:5).

BIBLIOGRAPHY: E. Bickerman, in: JBL, 65 (1946), 249–75; H.T. Olmstead, *History of the Persian Empire* (1948), 34ff., 86–87; Klausner, Bayit Sheni, 1 (19512), 121–47; R.N. Frye, *The Heritage of Persia* (1962), index; Ginzberg, Legends, index.

°CZACKI, TADEUSZ (1765–1813), Polish historian, economist, and statesman. He is known for his book on the Jews and Karaites, *Rozprawa o Żydach i Karaitach* (Vilna, 1807), the first comprehensive historical survey of Polish Jewry. In general, Czacki's work maintains a fairly high standard of scholarship. For Polish history he makes use of archival material. He also occasionally utilized Hebrew sources in translation. For some generations his book served as the major textbook on the history of Polish Jewry. Between 1786 and 1792 Czacki held an important position in the Polish Treasury, then responsible for supervision of the affairs of the Jewish communities in the country. The last chapter of Czacki's work is based on personal experience; in addition to general data on the current Jewish position, he includes a detailed project for the amelioration of the status of the Jews, which had been drafted, as it subsequently transpired, by Czacki himself or with his active participation.

After the 1795 partition, this project was apparently brought to the notice of the imperial committee which drafted the statute of 1804 for Russian Jewry (see *Russia). In 1807 Czacki himself joined the committee, which recommended postponement of the article in the statute prescribing expulsion of the Jews from the villages. Czacki was appointed school inspector for the governments of Volhynia and Podolia in 1803, and in the course of his duties made contact with Jewish bodies. He also planned, inter alia, a Jewish teachers' seminary in conjunction with the high school which he established in *Kremenets. He was unable, however, to implement this project.

BIBLIOGRAPHY: D.B. Nathanson, *Sefer ha-Zikhronot* (1886), 151–2; J. Shatzky, *Kulturgeshikhte fun der Haskole in Lite* (1950), 157–8; I. Levitats, *Jewish Community in Russia 1772–1844* (1943), 30–31; Yu. Gessen, *Istoriya yevreyskogo naroda v Rossii*, 1 (1916), 182–3.

[Israel Halpern]

°CZARNIECKI, STEFAN (1599–1665), Polish army commander and leader of popular resistance to the Swedes in the wars with Charles X of Sweden (1655–60). In the fighting against the Protestant Swedes, Czarniecki's units, fired by Catholic fervor, attacked the Jews in many places through which they passed. They devastated synagogues and massacred important communities in Greater and Lesser Poland. A number of Jews perished as martyrs for their faith. These persecutions accelerated Jewish emigration from Poland westward. While a hero to the Poles, Jewish sources refer to Czarniecki as the *ẓorer* (enemy), *rasha* (cruel evildoer), or *talyan* (hangman) of Poland.

BIBLIOGRAPHY: Dubnow, Hist Russ, 1 (1916), index; L. Lewin, *Die Judenverfolgungen im zweiten schwedisch-polnischen Kriege* (1901). **ADD. BIBLIOGRAPHY:** M. Balaban, *Historja i literatura zydowska*, III (1925), 270–71.

°CZARTORYSKI, PRINCE ADAM JERZY (1770–1861), Polish statesman and patriot. After the third partition of Poland (1795), Czartoryski went to St. Petersburg and entered the Russian government service, becoming assistant to the minister for foreign affairs during the reign of *Alexander I, with whom he was on friendly terms. Appointed a member of the Jewish committees of 1802, 1806, and 1807, Czartoryski advocated a policy of Jewish assimilation which, while disguised by liberal utterances, was in its effects on the Jewish masses to all practical purposes anti-Jewish. When in 1813 a Jewish printer from Vilna requested permission to publish a Yiddish newspaper, Czartoryski – who was responsible for education in the region – refused on the ground that the Jews should use the language of the surrounding population to bring them close to their Christian neighbors, and eventually adopt Christianity. After Russia established the Kingdom of Poland in 1815, Czartoryski was appointed to deal with problems concerning the peasants and Jews there. He was then ready to support Jewish emancipation only after the Jews had undergone a long process of assimilation and achieved "better morals." In Paris, however, where he took refuge after the Polish insurrection of 1830–31, and became leader of the Polish émigrés, he was persuaded by the Polish writer and statesman Jan Czynski that the help of the middle classes and the Jews should be enlisted in the cause of Poland's liberation. Czartoryski then took a more positive stand on Jewish emancipation, and in a speech delivered on November 29, 1844, urged that the Jews should be given the same rights claimed by the other inhabitants of Poland. Czartoryski encouraged the Hebrew writer Mendel *Lefin (Satanover), a pioneer of Haskalah, who stayed on Czartoryski's estate and taught his children. At Czartoryski's suggestion he wrote a pamphlet in French calling for improvement of the situation of Polish Jewry.

BIBLIOGRAPHY: M. Wischnitzer, in: *Perezhitoye*, 1 (1908), 164–216; S. Mstislavskaya, in: *Yevreyskaya starina*, 2 (1910), 61–80, 235–52; A.G. Duker, in: *Joshua Bloch Memorial Volume* (1960), 165–79; R. Mahler, *Ha-Ḥasidut ve-ha-Haskalah* (1961), 216.

CZECH, LUDWIG (1870–1942), leader of the German Social-Democratic Party in Czechoslovakia. Born in Lemberg, Czech was the son of a minor railroad official from Moravia. While studying law in Vienna, he came under the influence of Victor *Adler and joined the Austrian Social Democratic Party. He practiced law in Bruenn and was an active figure in politics, editing the party organ *Volksfreund* from 1897 to 1901. Czech campaigned for universal suffrage and improvement in workers' conditions. In 1901 he obtained the support of Thomas G. *Masaryk, in organizing a textile workers' strike and demanded a reduction of the working day to ten hours. Following the independence of Czechoslovakia, Ludwig Czech became vice chairman (1919) and later chairman (1921) of the German Social Democratic Party in Czechoslovakia. He led the activist wing of the party which stood for collaboration with the republic. In 1929 he was made minister of social welfare. In this capacity he issued food vouchers known as "Czechkarten" to unemployed workers, no longer entitled to regular relief, during the depression of the early 1930s. Czech became minister of works in 1934. He continued in office until shortly after the German *Anschluss* with Austria in 1938 when he resigned from both his ministerial and party posts. He was deported, already ill, to *Theresienstadt in March 1942.

BIBLIOGRAPHY: J. Braunthal, *In Search of the Millennium* (1945), 292–6; J.W. Bruegel, *Ludwig Czech, Arbeiterfuehrer und Staatsmann* (1960), includes bibliography.

[Meir Lamed]

CZECH MEMORIAL SCROLLS, THE. The 1,564 sacred Scrolls which came to Westminster Synagogue on February 7, 1964, had been gathered together in Prague, from the desolated synagogues of Bohemia and Moravia, by the Nazi official in charge of the Czech "Protectorate." Much more synagogue booty, books, pictures, embroidered vestments, and ceremonial objects of silver and gold were similarly collected by the Nazis, and many of these articles are now in the State Jewish Museum in Prague. The Scrolls themselves lay piled in the disused Michle Synagogue for more than 20 years. It is believed that they were originally gathered for permanent exhibition as relics of a defunct culture.

At the end of the war the surviving remnant of the Prague Jewish community lacked the resources to maintain the museum, and it came under the control of the Czech state authorities. It was maintained conscientiously as a memorial to the vanished communities, but the *Sifrei Torah* (Scrolls of the Law) proved an embarrassment; they could not be effectively displayed as museum exhibits, and it was realized that they would eventually deteriorate if they remained rolled up and unused.

In 1963, a prominent British art dealer, who enjoyed the confidence of Artia, the Czech government agency responsible for cultural property, was able to arrange for the scrolls to be acquired by Ralph Yablon, a London businessman and philanthropist, on the understanding that they would be entrusted to a responsible noncommercial body; the honorary officers of Westminster Synagogue, an independent London congregation, accepted Yablon's invitation to undertake this responsibility. After a preliminary examination in Prague by Chimen Abramsky (later professor of Hebrew and Jewish Studies at the University of London), the scrolls were carefully packed and shipped to London.

On February 7, 1964, 1,564 *Sifrei Torah* – a consignment which must have been unprecedented in Jewish history – arrived at Westminster Synagogue. There they were housed in numbered cradles in specially constructed racks, while the work of inspection and classification was undertaken. Each scroll was expertly examined and a record made of the condition of the parchment, the state of the calligraphy, and (so far as these could be ascertained) the age and place of origin of the scroll. Many of the labels attached more than 20 years before had survived and provided valuable information; and in some cases despairing messages were concealed in the scrolls. On the basis of this painstaking study, the scrolls were classified into grades, ranging from those without serious defect and thus readily usable, to those beyond satisfactory repair and therefore suitable only for commemorative use. Between these were the middle grades, comprising many scrolls which could be made usable by repair, or had some parts which it was possible to restore. The task of inspection and classification was directed by Rabbi Harold Reinhart, the minister of Westminster Synagogue, who gave devoted attention to every aspect of the project until his death in 1969. A committee had been formed to take responsibility for the scrolls, and the formidable task of administering the work of repair and distribution was undertaken by Ruth Shaffer, daughter of the Yiddish novelist and dramatist Sholem Asch.

The completion of the preliminary study and classification was marked, in June 1965, by a solemn assembly at Westminster Synagogue; this was attended by representatives of all sections of the Jewish community and by ministers and scholars of other faiths. The memorial prayers were read by then Chief Rabbi Sir Israel Brodie and a message of good wishes was received from the president of the Prague Jewish community.

In the ensuing years visitors from many parts of the world have come to Westminster Synagogue to see the scrolls and often to witness the work of restoration in progress. Jews and non-Jews alike, including parties from schools and other institutions, have been deeply moved by the human tragedy implicit in what they have seen and by the scope and importance of the project.

The arrival of the scrolls in London had been widely reported, and requests for scrolls soon reached the committee from many parts of the world; the process of allocation and distribution, which started soon after classification had been completed, has continued without interruption up to the present time. In the allocation of scrolls, priority was given from the outset to congregations needing a *Sefer Torah* for use in services, but many scrolls that could not be made acceptable for this purpose have been distributed to synagogues, educational institutions, and other bodies wishing to have a memorial to the communities destroyed in the Holocaust. The scrolls are handed to recipients on "permanent loan," and congregations are invited to make a contribution to the cost of repair and distribution. Each scroll bears a brass identification tablet and is accompanied by a certificate recording its origin.

In many cases, allocations have been made to synagogues which include among their members some who have personal or family links with the communities from which the scrolls originated. Information about the origin of the scrolls and their new locations is now being systematically recorded with the aid of a computer system.

The work of restoration, with all its traditional techniques and discipline, has been progress for more than 20 years, achieving as much repair as possible – although few scrolls have been restored to full synagogue use. It was undertaken initially by the scribes who examined the scrolls, but since 1967 one highly skilled *sofer* (scribe) has devoted himself almost without interruption to the task. It is foreseen, however, that when all possible restoration is completed, a residue of scrolls and fragments of scrolls will remain, together with binders and other appurtenances. These will form the basis of a permanent exhibition at Westminster Synagogue, devoted to the history of the project and to the memory of the Czech communities. Since 1980, the constitution and activities of the Memorial Scrolls Committee have been governed by a Trust deed.

Czech memorial scrolls are now in use in many parts of the world. The United States, as might be expected, has been the main recipient; but many requests from Israel have been met, as have others from virtually every country in which Jewish communities flourish freely. In addition, scrolls appropriate as memorials are to be found at Yad Vashem, at Westminster Abbey, in the Royal Library at Windsor Castle, and in many other places where they serve, in Harold Reinhart's words, "to live, to commemorate, to inspire a saddened but not hopeless world, and to glorify the holy Name."

[Leo Bernard]

CZECHOSLOVAKIA, republic in Central Europe. Founded in 1918, it united within its political framework the Jewries of the "historic countries" (*Bohemia, *Moravia, and part of *Silesia), connected with the *Hapsburg Empire from 1526 and under its direct control from 1620, and of *Slovakia and Carpatho-Russia (see *Sub-Carpathian Ruthenia), both an integral part of *Hungary, from the tenth century. As of January 1, 1993, Czechoslovakia ceased to exist as a separate entity and its territory became two independent nations, the *Czech Republic and Slovakia. The Jewish communities of the various regions hence differed substantially in their demographic, economic, and cultural aspects, with influences of assimilation to the Czech and German cultures prevailing in the west, and the Hungarian in conjunction with the traditional Orthodox Jewish way of life in the east.

Demographic Structure

In the western part of Czechoslovakia Jewish life was mainly regulated by Austrian legislation (of 1890) and in the eastern areas by Hungarian (of 1870). The communal leadership was initially predominantly assimilationist-oriented to German, Hungarian, or Czech culture. Czechoslovakian Jewry was distributed as shown in Table: Czechoslovakian Jewry.

By 1930, over 80% of the Jews of Bohemia and Moravia-Silesia lived in towns with over 5,000 inhabitants (60% of these in towns with over 50,000 inhabitants, i.e., *Prague, *Brno (Bruenn)). Between 1918 and 1938 the number of Jews in the small towns decreased by 20% to 50%, while the Jewish population of Prague, Brno, *Ostrava, and several industrial centers in the Sudeten area increased. In 1930, the proportion of children up to the age of 14 was 13.04% among Bohemian Jews and 14.25% among Moravian-Silesian Jews, compared with 22.63% and 26.13% respectively among the general population. The occupational structure of the Jewish population was similar to that for the rest of West European Jewry.

Table 1. Distribution of Czechoslovakian Jewry

	1921 Absolute no.	% of Total pop.	1930 Absolute no.	% of Total pop.	% of Czech Jewry
Bohemia	79,777	1.19	76,301	1.07	21.4
Moravia	37,989	1.09	41,250 (Moravia and Silesia)	1.16	11.5
Silesia	7,317	1.09			
Slovakia	135,918	4.53	136,737	4.11	38.4
Carpatho-Russia	93,341	15.39	102,542	14.14	28.7
Total	354,342	2.6	356,830	2.42	100.0 %

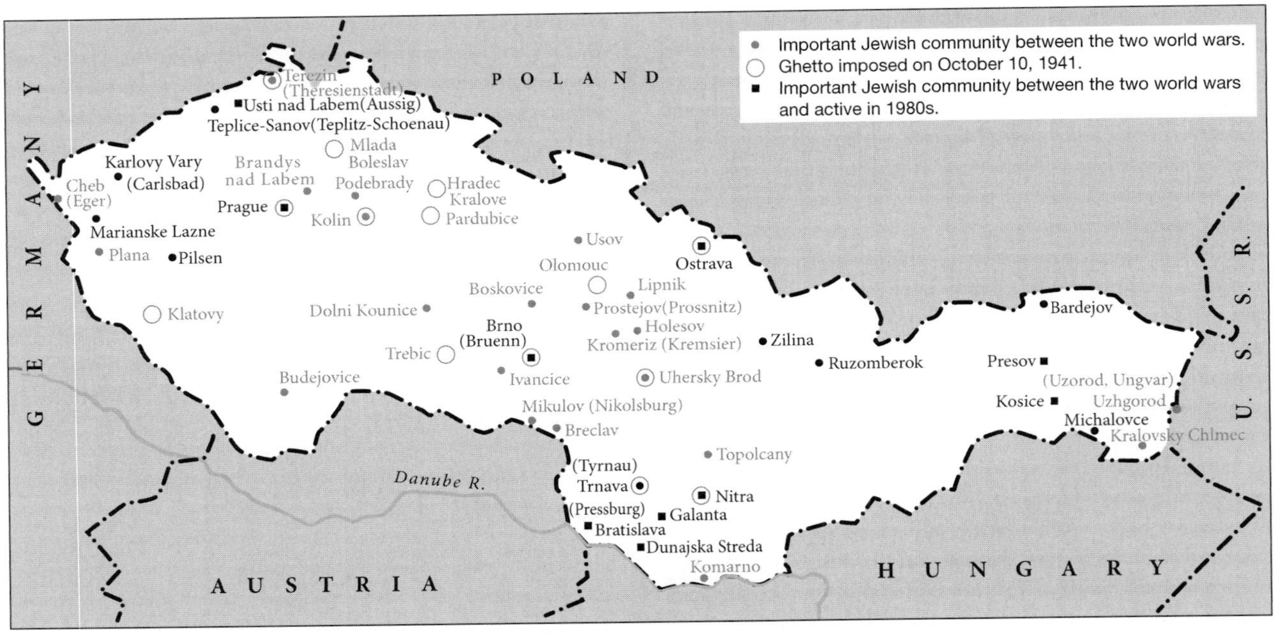

Major Jewish communities in Czechoslovakia from World War I to the 1980s (including involuntary settlement-ghettos as of October 1941).

During the century before World War I the number of Jews in Carpatho-Russia had increased almost fivefold because of the influx from Galicia, Romania, and Russia. In 1930, 65% were living in villages, constituting the highest proportion of rural dwellers among European Jewry. The communities in western Slovakia were closer to the way of life of the Moravian communities whose members had originally founded them. *Bratislava (Pressburg) had an individual character and was closely related to *Burgenland Jewry.

Communal Structure

The initiative to organize Czech Jewry within the new state came from Zionists. Ludwig *Singer had already suggested in November 1917 that the communities should be reorganized to provide a framework both for religious activities and toward achieving Jewish national and cultural *autonomy. On the initiative of Rudolph Kohn of the Prague *Po'alei Zion, the Jewish National Council (Národní rada Židovská) was established on Oct. 23, 1918, headed by Ludwig Singer, with the writer Max Brod and Karl Fischel as his deputies. On Oct. 28, at the proclamation of the republic, the council declared Jewish loyalty to the provisional government and put forward its principal claims: recognition of and the right to declare Jewish nationality, full civic and legal rights, democratization of the Jewish communities and expansion of their competences, establishment of a central supreme representation of the communities, cultural autonomy in Jewish education, promotion and use of Hebrew, and contact with the "center in Palestine." By November the federations of the communities of Moravia and Silesia had accepted the council's authority. On Jan. 4, 1919, a Prague conference of adherents to Jewish nationality adopted a program to convert the communities, as the "living cells of Jewish society," into the bearers of Jewish autonomy, but the program was not realized; nor could a unified communal organization be created. The conference decided to found the *Židovská Strana (Jewish party) as its instrument for electoral activities. Many communities reorganized themselves on democratic lines, granting franchise to women and to Jews from Eastern Europe who had settled there. Besides the demands urged on the authorities, as contained in the National Jewish Council's proclamation, the council also made demands on Jewish society itself, calling for a modern social policy to replace old-style philanthropy, establishment of Jewish secular schools, and provision of facilities for religious worship according to the wishes of the members of the community. The council dispatched a delegation to the peace conference in Versailles (Singer, Samuel Hugo *Bergmann, and Norbert Adler), which became part of the Jewish delegation there. Though Zionist influence predominated in the council, non-Zionists such as Alois Hilf and Salomon Hugo Lieben collaborated. The Czech assimilationist movement (see *Čechů-židů, *Svaz) and the extremist orthodox group contested the council's right to represent the whole of Czechoslovakian Jewry. The state under President Thomas Garrigue *Masaryk agreed to the council's basic claims, and the 1920 constitution expressly recognized Jewish nationality, corresponding to the conceptions of the *minority rights granted to all minorities in Czechoslovakia.

Political Affiliation

The 354,342 Jews by religion (Israelites) enumerated in 1921, and 356,830 in 1930, declared their nationality as shown in Table 2:

Adherents of the Jewish religion in 1930 represented 2.4% of the total population, and Jews by nationality 1.3%

of the total. While in general mother tongue served as the criterion for nationality, Jews could declare Jewish nationality irrespective of it: 156 persons who were not Jewish by religion declared their nationality to be Jewish in 1921, and 317 in 1930. After 1918 five regional federations of communities existed in Bohemia-Moravia; in 1926 they established the Nejvyšší rada židovských náboženských obcí (Supreme Council of the Jewish Religious Communities). It was first headed by the Czech-Jewish leader Augustin Stein and then by Joseph *Popper. The chief rabbi of Prague (then Ḥayyim Heinrich *Brody) was an ex officio member. In Slovakia and Carpatho-Russia, as in Hungary, three trends of community affiliation existed. The orthodox communities of Slovakia had an autonomous organization (confirmed in 1920) which from 1923 also included those of Carpatho-Russia. Its statute limited the franchise to dues payers. The *neologist and *status-quo-ante communities amalgamated into the Jeshurun federation in 1928. There was no supreme communal organization or chief rabbinate. From 1926 the salary of rabbis was augmented by the Kongrua, a government fund for the upkeep of religious life.

The Jewish party succeeded in achieving representation on a number of municipal councils. However, as it did not attain the minimum quota required for the parliamentary elections in any single electoral district, it succeeded in returning two representatives only in 1929, as a result of an agreement with the Polish minority (Ludwig Singer, succeeded after his death in 1931 by Angelo *Goldstein, and Julius Reisz) and in 1935, after an arrangement with the Czechoslovak Social Democrats (Goldstein and Ḥayyim *Kugel). The party was opposed by Czech, Slovak, German, and Hungarian assimilationists, as well as by the extreme Orthodox, who gave their votes to the strongest Czech party, the Agrarians. Jews, however, also attained leading positions in other political parties: Alfred Meissner and Lev Winter in the Czechoslovak Social Democrats, Ludwig *Czech and Siegfried Taub in the German, and Gabor Streiner in the Hungarian, Bruno Kafka in the Deutsche Arbeits-und Wirtschaftsgemeinschaft, and Rudolf Slánský and Viktor Stern in the Communist party. Jews were also active in political journalism. There were several Jewish weeklies, the Zionist *Židovské zprávy*, *Selbstwehr*, and *Medinah Ivrith* in Prague, Max *Hickl's *Juedische Volksstimme* in Brno, the *Juedische Volkszeitung* in Bratislava, and the *Juedische Stimme* in Mukačevo

Table 2. Declared Nationality of Jews in Czechoslovakia

Nationality	1921 (%)	1930 (%)
Jewish	53.62	57.20
Czechoslovak	21.84	24.52
German	14.26	12.28
Hungarian	8.45	4.71
Others	1.83	1.29
	100.00%	100.00%

Education

In Bohemia, Moravia, and Silesia Jewish children attended general schools on all levels: Prague and Ostrava both had a Jewish elementary school, while the only Jewish secondary school was in Brno. In most towns of Slovakia there were Jewish elementary schools where the language of instruction was Hungarian, most adopting the Slovak language subsequently. In Carpatho-Russia, Jewish education was substantially based on the traditional *ḥeder* and yeshivah. Government records of 1931 listed five yeshivot as institutions of higher education, in Bratislava, *Komarno, *Prešov, *Košice, and *Mukačevo; but there were others, as in *Galanta, *Dunajska Streda, and *Huncovce. A network of Hebrew schools developed; the first school was opened in Torun, and then, supported by the *Tarbut organization, expanded to nine elementary schools and two secondary, in Mukačevo (1925) and *Uzhgorod (1934). In 1934 the Supreme Council of the Jewish Religious Communities established a course for cantors and teachers of religion. A large number of Jewish children in Carpatho-Russia attended the Czech schools established for the children of civil servants and police officers. Many Jews attended universities and technical colleges, which also attracted numbers of students from countries where there was a *numerus clausus*. A number of Jews were appointed to professorships in Prague at the Czech and the German universities.

Economic Life

Jews played an important role in the economy and were among the pioneers of its development, notably in the textile, foodstuffs, and wood and paper industries. (It was estimated that 30%–40% of the total capital invested in Czechoslovakian industry in the 1930s was Jewish-owned.) The firm of *Petschek and Weimann was instrumental in the development of mining in north Bohemia, and Jewish enterprise was prominent in the steel industry and mining of the Ostrava area (see Wilhelm *Guttmann), insurance, and private banking. Jews were also instrumental in the Slovak wood industry. Later the concentration of capital in the national banks, agrarian reform, the development of agricultural and consumers' cooperatives, and the preference given to enterprises set up by veterans of the Czechoslovakian army tended to limit the extent and importance of Jewish economic activity, and the number of Jews in industry and commerce declined. The slump of 1929–30 affected many Jewish businessmen. After this crisis many Jews emigrated from Slovakia and Carpatho-Russia to the West; on the other hand, after 1918 Czechoslovakia received several thousand refugees from Eastern Europe, most of them in transit. They were supported through the Židovská ústředna sociální péče (Juedische Fuersorge-Zentrale), founded in 1921. After the Nazi advent to power in Germany in 1933, several thousand Jewish refugees, of whom 4,000 held Czechoslovakian citizenship, entered Czechoslovakia. A special committee was founded for their support. A particular problem was the provision of legal aid for the many Jewish stateless persons, who were permanently in danger of losing their permits of domicile and work. Prominent in social welfare work in the 1930s were Joseph Popper, and the *WIZO leaders Marie Schmolka, Hanna Steiner, and Gisi *Fleischmann.

Cultural Sphere

Jews contributed to all spheres of cultural activity, whether Czech, German, or Hungarian oriented. Many were outstanding authors in the Czech language (see *Czechoslovak literature). Gifted German-language authors were Adolf Donath, Friedrich Adler, and Hugo *Salus of the elder generation, and Franz *Kafka, Max *Brod, Franz *Werfel, Ludwig Winder, F.C. Weisskopf, and Egon Erwin *Kisch, among others (see *German Literature). Authors who wrote in German did not necessarily consider themselves German nationals, and some, like Max Brod, were active Zionists. Many Jews were intermediaries between the cultures, such as Otakar *Fischer in translating from German to Czech, and Kamil *Hoffmann, Max Brod, and Pavel Eisner in presenting Czech culture to the German-reading public. Jews prominent in music included the composer Jaromir *Weinberger and on the Czech stage the actors Hugo *Haas and Jiři Voskovec. Jewish journalists were on the staff of many newspapers, excepting those of the extreme right, and in all languages. Jews were active in all types of sports, within Jewish organizations as well as clubs of the other nationalities, notably the swimmers and water-ball teams of the Hagibor association in Prague and Bar Kochba in Bratislava. The refusal of the Jewish champions to represent Czechoslovakia at the Berlin Olympic Games in 1936 was a subject of heated public discussion. Jewish youth was organized in the numerous Zionist youth and student organizations, as well as in many organizations of the other nationalities.

Antisemitism

Antisemitism among all the nationalities of the republic was of old standing. At the time of the establishment of the republic in 1918 there were antisemitic riots in Prague and *Holešov (Moravia). In Slovakia, serious antisemitic violence continued until summer 1919. Among the Czech elements it was less noticeable, mainly because of the personal example of Thomas Masaryk and Eduard Beneš, and the democratic political philosophy as expounded by them, the author Karel Čapek, and other leaders of public opinion, including the head of the Czechoslovak Church Hromádka, and the writers Milena Jesenská, Emanuel Rada, and Pavla Moudrá. However, right-wing groups such as the Národni sjednoceni (National Union, founded by Jírí Stribrný in 1927), the Česká obec fašistická (Czech Fascist Community), headed by the former general of the Czech army Radola Gajda, and the Vlajka (Flag) group explicitly supported antisemitism in their platforms. Andrej Hlinka's Slovenská L'udová strana (Slovak People's Party) adopted an increasingly aggressive antisemitic policy. The Sudeten, where most of the Germans lived, was already a stronghold of racial antisemitism under the Hapsburg monarchy, and antisemitism grew even more violent, influenced by the rise of Nazism in Germany, the advent of Hitler to power, and the founding of Konrad Henlein's Sudetendeutsche Partei (1935). Antisemitism in Czechoslovakia was strongly associated with the general conflicts among the nationalities there: the Czechs would not forgive the adherence of many Jews to German language and culture and their support of the German liberal parties, and regarded them as a Germanizing factor. In Slovakia and Carpatho-Russia they were considered the bearers of Magyarization, and later, supporters of the Czech establishment. All groups alleged that the Jews were supporters of Communism, while the Communists claimed that they supported reaction. After Hitler's rise to power, his growing support for German extreme nationalist demands, and the enmity he manifested to the Czechoslovak establishment, the Jews drew increasingly closer to the state, which all Jewish groups supported in its stand against Nazism. Post-World War I Czechoslovakia, which was relatively progressive and stable, was a congenial milieu for Czechoslovakian Jewry. Hence, most of them failed to see the dangers threatening them even inside the country. However, the subdued popular antisemitism was soon to be rekindled. At the beginning of 1938 antisemitism gained in strength when in Romania the Goga government came to power and Jewish refugees tried to enter Czechoslovakia. Ferdinand Peroutka, the editor of a respected liberal weekly, published a series of articles in which he called for restriction of Jewish rights. A project for a rabbinical seminary, connected with the Prague Czech University, which was to begin functioning in 1938, was not realized. The problem of Jewish refugees became even more acute with the Nazi *Anschluss* with Austria, when many Jewish refugees, a large number holding Czechoslovakian passports, entered the country. Manifestations of antisemitism in Slovakia and the Sudeten area increased. At the time of the Munich conference (Sept. 29, 1938) the Jews from the Sudetenland (more than 20,000), which was handed over to Germany, fled to the remaining territory of the state. Parts of Slovakia and Carpatho-Russia, with a Jewish population of about 80,000, were ceded to Hungary by decree of Hitler and Mussolini as "arbiters" on Nov. 2, 1938. Antisemitism gained virulence in the truncated "Second Republic" mainly in Slovakia. The Second Republic did not last long. On March 14, 1939, Slovakia declared its independence and became a vassal of Nazi Germany; the next day the remaining parts of Bohemia and Moravia were occupied by the Germans and transformed into a German "Protectorate," while Hungary occupied Carpatho-Russia.

[Chaim Yahil]

Emigration and Exile (1938–45)

The emigration and escape of Jews from Czechoslovakia started immediately after the Munich conference (Sept. 29, 1938) and increased considerably after the German occupation (March 15, 1939). Half a million pounds sterling, part of a grant made by the British government to the Czechoslovak government, were earmarked for the financing of the emigration of 2,500 Jews to Palestine. In addition, about 12,000 Jews left with "illegal" transports for Palestine. Many others emigrated to the United States and South America or escaped to neighboring Poland, from where a number succeeded in reaching Great Britain, France, and other countries. He-Ḥalutz and Youth Aliyah transferred hundreds of children and youth to England, Denmark, and the Netherlands for agricultural training. The Anglican Church and missionary institutions succeeded in removing children. When after the outbreak of World War II the Czechoslovak National Council in London, later recognized as the government-in-exile and an ally, called upon army reservists in allied and neutral countries to enlist, many Jews responded. Even in Palestine, where many Jews from Czechoslovakia had already put themselves at the disposal of the Yishuv's war effort, about 2,000 Czech and Slovak Jews enlisted in Czechoslovak army units within the Allied Middle East Forces, where Jews constituted the great majority in these units. After the recognition of Czechoslovakia by the Soviet Union in 1941, a Czechoslovak division was established in the U.S.S.R. Up to 70% of the members of some of its units were Jews, many of them from Carpatho-Russia. The high percentage of Jews in these units created some tension and antisemitic reactions. The Czechoslovak government-in-exile in London, with Eduard Beneš as president and Jan *Masaryk as foreign minister, maintained good relations with Jewish organizations and supported the Zionist cause. In the State Council, Arnošt Frischer represented the Židovská *strana (Jewish party). Other Jews on the Council were Julius Friedmann, Julius Fuerth, and Gustav Kleinberg. Imrich Rosenberg represented Slovakian Jewry.

[Meir Lamed]

Holocaust Period

SLOVAKIA. According to the 1930 census, 135,918 Jews (4.5% of the total population) lived in Slovakia. The plight of Slovak Jewry actually began with the establishment of autonomous Slovakia (Oct. 6, 1938), when the one-party authoritarian system of the clerical Slovak People's Party of Hlinka (HSL's – Hlinkova Slovenská L'udová Strana) came to power. On March 14, 1939, Hitler made an independent state by causing the breakup of Czechoslovakia. A few days later Slovak leaders and the German Foreign Minister, von *Ribbentrop, signed the Treaty of Protection (Schutzvertrag), thus making Slovakia in effect a satellite of Germany. In the first months of Slovakia's "independence" anti-Jewish restrictions were sporadically introduced; however, fundamental changes in anti-Jewish policy occurred only after the Salzburg Conference (July 28, 1940), attended by Hitler, the Slovak leaders (Father Josef *Tiso, Vojtech Bela *Tuka, Saňo Mach) and the leader of the local German minority, the so-called Karpaten-Deutsche, Franz Karmasin. At this conference the Slovaks agreed to set up a national-socialist regime in their country.

At the end of August 1940, Dieter *Wisliceny, *Eichmann's emissary, arrived in Slovakia to act as "adviser for Jewish affairs," and with him came a score of advisers to assist the Slovak ministries. The Slovaks set up two institutes with the objective of "solving the Jewish problem": ÚHÚ – Ústredný Hospodárský Úrad (Central Office for Economy) whose task was to oust the Jews from economic and social life and "aryanize" Jewish property; the second was ÚŽ – Ústredňa Židov (Center of Jews). The ÚŽ, the Slovak equivalent of the Judenrat, was headed by the *starosta* ("Jewish Elder"), Heinrich Schwartz, chairman of the Orthodox-Jewish community. When Schwartz was arrested for non-cooperation, a more obedient *starosta*, Árpád Sebestyén, a former school director, was appointed by the authorities in April 1941. The Zionist leader Oskar Neumann replaced Sebestyén in fall 1943. The "aryanization" process was carried out by the ÚHÚ within one year: 10,025 Jewish enterprises and businesses were liquidated and 2,223 transferred to "Aryan" ownership. In order to solve the problem of employment of Jews, who were removed from economic life, the Slovak authorities ordered the erection of a number of labor centers and three large labor camps: Sered, Vyhne, and Nováky. In the fall of 1941, in an effort to clear the capital of Jews, a special ministerial order issued by Mach removed a greater part of the Bratislava Jews; some were sent to the labor camps and others to the towns of Trnava, Nitra, and to the region of Šariš-Zemplín in eastern Slovakia, where the majority of Slovak Jewry lived. Concurrently, during a visit to Hitler's headquarters, Tuka requested the assistance of the Reich in the removal of the Jews from Slovakia. News of the terrible fate of Jews in German hands filtered into Slovakia after fall 1941. At the beginning of February 1942, the German Foreign Ministry formally requested the Slovak government to furnish 20,000 "strong and able-bodied Jews." It was decided that the first transports would be composed of young men and women aged 16–35. However, on the suggestion of the Slovaks that in the "spirit of Christianity" families should not be separated, Eichmann gave his consent to deport families together. The Slovaks had to pay 500 Reichmarks "as charges for vocational training" for every deported Jew, receiving in return a guarantee that the Jews would not come back to Slovakia and that no further claims would be laid to their property. The organization of transports was performed by the Ministry of Interior, Department 14, headed by Gejza Kionka and afterward by Anton *Vašek, in collaboration with the Hlinka Guard and the Freiwillige Schutzstaffel (Voluntary Defense Squad of local Germans). The Jewish leadership, alarmed by rumors of the impending deportations, launched two appeals in the name of the Jewish communities (March 5, 1942) and in the name of the rabbis of Slovakia (March 6, 1942) warning the authorities that "the deportations mean physical extermination." On March 14, 1942, the Vatican sent a note of protest, and a few days later an oral warning was communicated on the direct instruction of Pope Pius XII by Slovakia's ambassador to Rome, Karol Sidor.

Between March 26 and October 20, 1942, about 60,000 Jews were deported as agreed with Berlin to *Auschwitz and to the *Lublin area, where they were killed. By the end of April the earliest evidence on the fate of deportees was received in Bratislava, when the first escapees from General Gouvernment of Poland arrived. Their eyewitness accounts were immediately forwarded to Jewish organizations in the free world. Thousands of Jews found refuge in neighboring Hungary (in 1944 some of them returned to Slovakia when the Hungarian Jewish community was in peril). Others sought protection through conversion to Christianity. From the end of July to the middle of September the transports were suspended for various technical reasons and perhaps also due to intercessions, mainly from religious circles.

During the interim, the underground "Working Group" (Pracovná Skupina; see also *Europa Plan) arose on the initiative of Rabbi Michael Dov *Weissmandel within the framework of úž with the objective of saving the remaining Jews of Slovakia. Led by Gisi Fleischmann, the Group was composed of Zionists, assimilated Jews, and rabbis. The Jewish underground succeeded in temporarily diverting the peril of deportation in the spring of 1943 as a result of negotiations with friendly Slovak ministers and bribes to Slovak leaders. Another achievement in 1943 was the rescue of fugitives from the ghettos of Poland, who were smuggled through Slovakia to Hungary with the help of the He-Ḥalutz underground. By that time about 25,000 Jews were left in Slovakia, some of them "submerged," so that only part of them were officially registered, mostly "economically vital" Jews who were granted "certificates of exemption." About 3–4,000 persons were engaged in productive work in the Slovak labor camps, and others lived on false "Aryan" papers or in hiding. On April 21, 1944, the first two escapees from Auschwitz reached Slovakia after a miraculous flight. Their account of the annihilation process was sent on to the head of the Orthodox Jewish community in Budapest, Rabbi Von Freudiger, to alert the world and forwarded through Switzerland to Jewish organizations in the free world with an appeal by Rabbi Weissmandel demanding the immediate bombing of the murder installations in Auschwitz. The Allies rejected the appeal.

In August 1944, an anti-Fascist uprising took place in Slovakia, and subsequently the German army invaded the country. Over 1,500 Jewish men and women enlisted in the Czechoslovak armed forces resisting the Germans. Among the enlisted Jews, a regular Jewish unit of about 250 fighters, under Jewish command and the name "Camp Novaky Unit," was active. Two hundred and sixty-nine Jewish fighters fell in the resistance.

Four parachutists from Ereẓ Israel reached Slovakia to extend help to the Jewish remnants and to organize resistance. However, the Jews had enlisted long before the arrival of the parachutists. Their cell included a woman, Ḥavivah *Reik ("Ada Robinson"). Three of the four, including Reik, were caught by the Germans, and subsequently executed. The *Einsatzgruppen* killed thousands of Jews during the Slovak revolt, and after its suppression (Oct. 28, 1944), about 13,500 of the remaining Jews of Slovakia were deported to concentration camps (including Auschwitz, *Sachsenhausen, and *Theresienstadt), under the pretext of reprisal for their participation in the revolt (October 1944–March 1945). On the eve of the liberation (April 30, 1945), there remained about 4,000–5,000 Jews in Slovakia hiding in the forests or with non-Jews or living clandestinely with "Aryan" papers. The losses of Slovak Jewry amount to over 100,000. In the part of Slovakia annexed by the Hungarian kingdom, there were about 45,000 Jews. Their fate was the same as the rest of Hungarian Jewry. In spring 1944, after the German occupation of Hungary, the Jews were deported to Auschwitz and most of them perished there. Some of those who eluded the deportations participated in the Slovak National Uprising. Only about 25,000 persons of the prewar community survived the Holocaust and the majority of them left Slovakia after the war, most of them for Israel.

[Livia Rothkirchen / Yeshayahu Jelinek (2nd ed.)]

PROTECTORATE OF BOHEMIA-MORAVIA. According to the 1930 census, Czechoslovakia had a Jewish population of 356,830 out of total of 14,000,000. Of these, 117,551 lived in Bohemia and Moravia and 102,542 in Carpatho-Russia. At the time of the Munich Agreement (September, 1938), the arrival of Jewish refugees from Germany and Austria increased the Jewish population in Bohemia and Moravia to approximately 122,000. In October 1938, when the German-speaking Bohemian-Moravian border areas were occupied by the Nazis, approximately 25,000 Jews fled their homes there to the unoccupied part of Czechoslovakia. On the basis of the Vienna arbitration decision of Nov. 2, 1938, the predominantly Hungarian parts of Slovakia and Carpatho-Russia were ceded to Hungary; these areas were inhabited by approximately 80,000 Jews. The remaining regions of Slovakia and Carpatho-Russia were granted autonomous status in the now federated Czecho-Slovakia. German pressure and a growing local anti-Jewish movement brought about increasing discrimination against Jews and persecution. In March 1939, when Slovakia seceded from the Republic, and the Protectorate of Bohemia and Moravia was established, the fate of the Jews in each of the two separate parts began to run its own course. In the Protectorate, the first synagogue, in Vsetin, was burned down on the day of the German occupation (March 15, 1939). At that time 118,310 persons in the Protectorate were designated as Jews according to the Nuremberg Laws; only 86,715, however, were members of the local Jewish communities. In the initial stage, the "Final Solution of the Jewish problem" proceeded, in part, on the basis of decrees issued by the Protectorate regime; in the course of time, Bohemia and Moravia came to be regarded more and more as part of the Reich, and the fate of the Jews in the two provinces was decided on directly by the *RSHA (Reich Security Main Office) in Berlin. The immediate consequences were the plunder of Jewish property, pogroms, and the burning of synagogues. Many Jews who were active in the general resistance movement were caught while a few Jews survived as "illegals." On July 27, 1939, Adolf Eichmann, the RSHA representative, established a branch of the Zentralstelle fuer juedische Auswanderung (Central Office for Jewish Emigration) in Prague. The Jews were forced to register for emigration, and divested of most of their property by a compulsory "Jewish emigration tax." Jewish books and periodicals were banned and the *Juedisches Nachrichtenblatt* was published in their place, controlled by the Zentralstelle. Jews were excluded from economic, cultural, and political life, and denied civil rights; an estimated 12,000,000,000 Kčs (about $343,000,000) in Jewish property were confiscated and, finally, an order issued on Sept. 1, 1941, forcing Jews to wear the yellow badge, resulted in their complete isolation. The Jewish communities reacted to the planned elimination of the Jews by stepping up their activities in Jewish and general education of the youth, giving foreign language instruction; retraining; and providing medical care, consulting agencies, and social welfare. These activities, which prevented the outbreak of panic and the community's dissolution, were later continued at the *Theresienstadt concentration camp. Efforts were made to promote legal and illegal Jewish emigration and, by the time emigration was totally banned (October 1941), 26,629 persons had succeeded in escaping from the country. In October 1939, the first group, comprising 1,291 Jewish men from Ostrava, was deported for the "settlement area of Nisko on the San." The Germans decided on the establishment of the Theresienstadt Ghetto on Oct. 10, 1941, in a secret meeting at the Prague Castle, chaired by Reich Protector Reinhard *Heydrich. The minutes of the meeting contain the following passage: "From this transit camp [Theresienstadt] the Jews, after a substantial reduction in their numbers, are to be deported to the East…." The Jewish communities were ordered to concentrate all the Jews living in their respective areas into a number of cities – Prague, Budweis (Budějovice), Kolín, Klatovy, Pardubice, Hradec Králové, Mladá Boleslav, Třebíč, Brno, Olomouc, Ostrava, and Uherský Brod. In October and November 1941, 6,000 Jews from Prague and Brno were deported directly to *Lodz and *Minsk. In the period Nov. 24, 1941–March 16, 1945, 73,614 Jews were dispatched to Theresienstadt in 121 transports. In this period also, 621 Jews were sent to Theresienstadt from towns in the Sudeten areas ceded to Germany. One of the leaders of Czechoslovak Jewry, Jacob *Edelstein, was appointed the "elder" of Theresienstadt. From Jan. 9, 1942, to Oct. 28, 1944, 60,399 Czech Jews were deported onward from Theresienstadt to the extermination camps in the East – Auschwitz, *Majdanek, Minsk, *Riga, *Sobibor, *Treblinka, and *Zamosc. Only 3,227 of the Jews deported from Theresienstadt survived the war. Following the assassination of Heydrich on Feb. 19, 1942, a "penal transport" of 1,000 Jews was deported from Prague to Poland, none of whom survived.

Jews joined the Czech resistance, both the pro-Western and the Communist wings. The sorely oppressed Czech population did not demonstrate exceptional courage in assisting the persecuted Jews. In the last period before liberation of the country, Jewish *Mischlinge* ("mixed" Jews considered Jewish under German law) were gathered to be shipped to extermination camps. Most of them survived.

In 1945, 10,090 Jews registered with the Jewish communities as returning deportees, out of a total of 80,614 who had been deported; 6,392 had died in Theresienstadt, 64,172 had been murdered in the extermination camps, and of the Jews who had not been deported, 5,201 had either been executed, committed suicide, or died a natural death. On the day of the restoration of national sovereignty in Prague, May 5, 1945, there were 2,803 Jews alive in Bohemia and Moravia, who had not been deported, most of them partners of mixed marriages.

[Erich Kulka]

Postwar Jewry

DEMOGRAPHY. Various estimates of the number of Jews living in Czechoslovakia in 1945 have been given, as postwar statistics do not classify the population according to religion. Many of the surviving Jews in Sub-Carpathian Ruthenia decided to leave in the brief period between its annexation to the Soviet Union (June 29, 1945) and the closing of its frontiers (September 30, 1945). They succeeded in fleeing to Bohemia, while only a few hundred moved to Slovakia. Most of the newcomers registered with the Jewish communities only later. In 1948, 19,123 Jews were registered with the communities in Bohemia and Moravia. The number of Jews in Slovakia in 1947 was estimated at about 24,500. This brings to 44,000 the number of Jews living in the whole of Czechoslovakia in early 1948, when the Communists came to power. However, this figure has to be augmented to include those who were in no way affiliated with organized Jewish communities, but in the past were classed as Jews by German authorities and registered after World War II as victims of racial persecution. In this category there were 5,292 persons living in Bohemia and Moravia in 1948. In Slovakia their number is not known; on the other hand, about 5,500 Slovak Jews, in an effort to save their lives, agreed to *pro forma* baptism during the war. It can therefore be estimated that out of the 356,830 Jews living in Czechoslovakia (including Sub-Carpathian Ruthenia) in 1939, less than a sixth remained in the country in 1948. The Communist coup of February 1948, and the establishment of the State of Israel in May of that year, led to a mass migration of Jews from Czechoslovakia. Between 1948 and 1950, 18,879 Jews went from Czechoslovakia to Israel, while more than 7,000 emigrated to other countries. When emigration was barred by the Communist authorities, in 1950, the number of Jews still remaining had dropped to some 18,000, while some 5,500 of them were still registered for migration to Israel. There were sporadic instances of Jewish emigration after 1954 but only from 1965 were 2,000–3,000 Jews allowed to leave Czechoslovakia. After the Soviet invasion in August 1968, 3,400 Jews left the country, according to a spokesman of the American Joint Distribution Committee in Vienna. It may therefore be assumed that at the end of 1968 there were less than 12,000 Jews left in Czechoslovakia. In June 1968, Rudolf Iltis of the Council of Jewish Communities in Bohemia and Moravia gave their average age as 60, while in the 15–20 age group there were only 1,000 Jews left. He also added that "with the exception of a few communities in Slovakia, the demographic situation of Czechoslovak Jewry does not necessitate religious instruction, because there are not enough children of school age."

ORGANIZATIONAL STRUCTURE. The renewed Council of Jewish Communities in Bohemia and Moravia held its first conference after World War II, under the chairmanship of Ernst Frischer, in September 1945. Delegates of 43 communities participated. In Slovakia a similar body, the Central Union of the Jewish Communities in Slovakia, was created at the end of 1945, presided over by Armin *Frieder. With the creation of the Union, the Orthodox and the Neolog-Status Quo organizations, separate before the war, were united. Both Frischer and Frieder were Zionists. In 1947 the two organizations set up a coordinating committee. At a Council conference in November 1963 representatives from only 16 communities took part and in 1968 the editor of the Council's publications listed only seven active communities in Bohemia and Moravia (Prague, Brno, Ostrava, Plzeň, Karlovy Vary, Ústí nad Labem, and Teplice-Sanov). Ten communities in Slovakia were listed as active (Bratislava, Košice, Prešov, Nitra, Michalovce, Žilina, Galanta, Trnava, Dunajská Streda, and Ružomberok). A small number of Jews were also living in some other places where, however, Jewish life had no organizational framework. The strongest communities in June 1968 were Prague, with 3,500 members (more than 4,000 in 1945), Bratislava, with 2,000 (8,000 in 1947), and Košice with 1,800 (4,000 in 1947). Religious life was practically limited to the High Holidays. On the Sabbath few places had a *minyan*. One of the main problems was the lack of rabbis. Religious education was nonexistent. The budget of the pauperized communities was covered entirely by State subsidies. The State Bakery in Zlaté Moravce supplied *mazzot* from 1965. There were four Jewish old-age homes, in Bratislava, Marianské Lázně, Brno, and Poděbrady; only in the first two was kosher food prepared. Of the 800 Jewish cemeteries only those were being kept in good order where a community was still in existence. A few, like the old cemetery of Prague, had become museums. The same applied to some old synagogues. In the years preceding the Communist coup of 1948, there were still signs of Jewish political life and of contacts with Jewish bodies abroad. In Slovakia, for instance, an Organization of Victims of Racial Persecution was created under the chairmanship of Vojtech Winterstein, a leading Zionist. The Central Union of Jewish Communities in Slovakia was affiliated to the World Jewish Congress from 1946, while the Council of Jewish Communities in Bohemia and Moravia joined the WJC only at the beginning of 1948. There were organized Zionist activities, and the American Joint Distribution Committee was permitted to undertake social work among the Jews of Czechoslovakia. All this was stopped when the Communists came to power in February 1948. After the Communist coup, Action Committees composed partially of Jewish Communists took over the leadership of the Jewish communities and eliminated noncommunists from their positions. At the beginning of 1949 the Zionists still succeeded in holding a conference at Piešťany; but by the end of 1949 the ties with the World Jewish Congress were broken, and at the beginning of 1950 the "Joint" was ordered to stop all activities and its workers were expelled. The Jewish Agency closed its Prague office voluntarily the same year, after all Jewish migration from Czechoslovakia had been stopped. The organ of the Council, *Věstnik židovských náboženských obcí*, and a quarterly in German, *Informationsbulletin*, became party mouthpieces, following the official line, including the hostile attitude to Israel. Some changes for the better could be discerned after 1964. In that year the *ḥevra kaddisha* of Prague was permitted to celebrate its 400th anniversary. The small Jewish Museum in Prague was enlarged during World War II by the Germans and later was taken over by the Ministry of Culture and officially reorganized. (In 1963 it was visited by 327,000 people.) In 1966 a more liberal-minded leadership, led by František Fuchs, succeeded the dogmatic Communist group in the Council of Jewish Communities, headed until then by František Ehrmann. The Prague community created a special Committee for Youth which, for the first time in a quarter of a century, organized lectures and seminars on Jewish themes, attended regularly by dozens of Jewish students. A delegation of the Council was received by the minister of culture and submitted a detailed plan for the celebrations of the millennium of Prague Jewry and the 700th anniversary of the Altneuschul, which were to have taken place in August 1968. Contacts with Jewish communities and organizations outside Czechoslovakia were renewed. In January 1967, the presidents of the Council and of the Central Union attended a World Jewish Conference in Paris and, on their invitation, Naḥum *Goldmann visited Czechoslovakia in the spring of that year. At the time, a series of stamps depicting Jewish subjects was issued. The stamps were taken out of circulation at the time of the *Six-Day War in June 1967, when Czechoslovakia, like other countries of the Soviet bloc, broke off diplomatic relations with Israel, but were reissued after the liberal community leadership of Alexander Dubček came into power in January 1968.

JEWS IN CZECHOSLOVAK PUBLIC LIFE. Thousands of Jews fought in the Czechoslovak armies formed both in the West and in the Soviet Union during World War II and many worked in various capacities in Beneš's government-in-exile. Many of those who returned after the war continued their work in the newly formed administration. The percentage of Jewish intellectuals among the Communists was also high, and after the Communist coup of February 1948, many of them were entrusted with responsible tasks in the government machinery. Thus, in 1948 there were three Jewish deputy ministers of foreign affairs, of defense, interior, foreign trade and finance. The Party's secretary general, Rudolf Slánský, was a Jew, and Jews played an important role in the party apparatus. This led to an increase of the antisemitism which was latent especially in Slovakia. Already in 1945, a delegation of the Council of Jewish Communities led by Ernst Frischer complained to President Beneš about anti-Jewish excesses in the Slovak towns of Prešov, Bardějov, and Topolčany. In 1945, in the village of Kolbasov in eastern Slovakia, a band of Ukrainian Bendera nationalists, together with local citizens, attacked Jews who had just returned from concentration camps, raped the women, and murdered all 14. The same year two Jews were killed in Žilina, and in 1946 and 1948 there were anti-Jewish riots in Bratislava. In Slovakia, from 1949, Benjamin Eichler generally headed the Central Association of Jewish Religious Congregations. After the emigration of his children in 1969, he was forced to resign and left the country in the wake of his children. The new leadership in Slovakia was composed of men already active in the Association. They did not act independently, until being replaced after the "Velvet Revolution" of 1989. Several congregations in Slovakia continued to carry on religious activities also after 1949, and even examined the possibility of setting up a yeshivah in Košice. Antisemitism knew no party barriers, and Communists were no more immune to it than others. As soon as the anti-Jewish line became official policy in the Soviet Union (see *Antisemitism: the Soviet Bloc), Communists in Czechoslovakia followed suit. The *Slánský Trial of 1952 had a clearly anti-Jewish character: 11 of 14 accused were Jews, and eight Jews among them were executed. In subsequent trials hundreds of Jews were sentenced to long-term imprisonment, hundreds were sent to hard labor without trial, and hundreds were dismissed from their posts. Jews became in fact, if not in law, second-class citizens. De-Stalinization was slower in Czechoslovakia than elsewhere. In April 1956, Prime Minister Široký admitted that "certain manifestations of antisemitism had been wrongly introduced in the Slánský trial," but in December 1957 the minister of justice still informed foreign correspondents that no revision of the trial was necessary; a special commission had checked the sentences and found them justified. Some Jewish prisoners were gradually released and some even rehabilitated, but in 1956 there were still about 300 Jews in jails, and their number increased in 1957, after the *Sinai Campaign, when many Jews, including 27 community leaders, were arrested as "Western spies" or on charges of "Zionist activities." It was only at the beginning of the 1960s that the way was reopened for Jewish participation in Czechoslovak public life. Not many Jews returned to the State administration or to politically important positions, though there were a few exceptions, such as František Kriegel (d. 1979), who became chairman of the National Front, and Ota Šik, the chief economic planner. The contribution of Jewish university professors, scientists, writers, musicians, theater and film artists, journalists, radio and television commentators to Czechoslovak cultural life again became considerable. A Jew, Eduard *Goldstuecker, vice rector of Prague University, was elected president of the Czech Writers Union, while the work of Jewish writers and journalists received a new impetus and became even more important after January 1968, when liberal reformers led by Dubček put an end to censorship and other fetters on spiritual freedom. This period was, however, short-lived. The Soviet invasion of August 1968 put an end to it, and a new wave of antisemitism, fed by Soviet, Polish, and East German propaganda, made further Jewish participation in public life impossible. Kriegel, the only member of the Czechoslovak delegation who refused to sign the Moscow "agreement" legalizing Soviet invasion, was, at Moscow's insistence, dropped from the Politburo and dismissed from all functions. Goldstuecker, who for a few days in August was also a member of the Politburo, and Ota Šik, deputy prime minister after the fall of Novotný, sought safety abroad. So did some 3,400 other Jews, many of them intellectuals. Antisemitism became an issue in the struggle between the liberal Communists and the pro-Moscow faction.

Czechoslovakia and Israel

Czechoslovakia was among the first countries in the world to recognize the State of Israel, though it was already ruled by Gottwald's Communist regime after the February 1948 coup. Moreover, during its *War of Independence, Israel enjoyed active and effective Czechoslovak assistance, including the supply of military equipment. The two countries exchanged diplomatic representatives. These initially promising relations rapidly deteriorated, however, when Moscow reversed her attitude to Israel. This process culminated in the expulsion of the Israel minister from Prague, Aryeh *Kubovy in December 1952. After the Slánský trial diplomatic missions of the two countries remained headed on both sides by a chargé d'affaires only, and all Israel efforts to bring about a political dialogue were frustrated by Prague. Limited trade relations continued until 1956, but after the Sinai Campaign even these were broken off, although Israel's trade with other Soviet bloc countries in the period between 1956 and 1967 showed a remarkable increase. In June 1967, Czechoslovakia, together with the rest of the Warsaw Pact countries (excluding Romania), broke off relations with Israel. The one-sided attitude adopted by Czechoslovakia in the Arab-Israel conflict, and Israel's rapid victory against an overwhelming Arab majority, caused second thoughts first among the Czech and Slovak intelligentsia and then among the whole people, and ultimately became a factor in the growing opposition to the Novotný regime. With Novotný's fall in January 1968 there was hope for an improvement in the relations between Prague and Jerusalem. Writers, students, even some political figures, openly advocated a resumption of diplomatic relations. The request found expression in the press, on television, in public debates with members of the government, and finally in a collection of signatures organized by students in the streets of Prague. New hopes also arose among the remnants of Czechoslovak Jewry. On April 7, 1968, the Council of Jewish Communities in Bohemia and Moravia adopted a resolution, unprecedented in Communist countries, expressing not only their approval of the new liberalization but also their protest against the "vehement anti-Israel campaign" of the previous Novotný regime, which was based on "unobjective, one-sided reporting, often explicable only as intentionally anti-Jewish." The resolution stated: "We cannot agree and never will agree, to the liquidation of the State of Israel and to the murder of its inhabitants. In that country, the cradle of our religion, victims of persecution found a haven. Our brothers and sisters live there, those who together with us spent years in concentration camps, who together with us arose to take up the fight against Nazism." In conclusion the resolution requested that the government condemn the antisemitic pronouncements in the political trials of the 1950s and rehabilitate Jews wronged during that period by judicial or administrative decisions; place victims of racial persecution on the same level as those of political persecution in all welfare legislation; not impede contact between the Jews of Czechoslovakia and Jewish bodies abroad; not to obstruct the religious education of Jewish youth with administrative difficulties. A similar declaration, issued on the same day by the Central Union of Jewish Communities in Slovakia, contained an additional request: "It is a minimal human postulate, that everyone asking to be reunited with his family should be allowed to do so, wherever his family may be living." A few months later, with the Soviet invasion of August 21, 1968, these hopes were shattered.

[Avigdor Dagan]

Toward Renewal

The International Council of Jews from Czechoslovakia in 1978 published its first report on Post-War Jewry in Czechoslovakia. It revealed a steady decline in the number of Jews, estimated to be 15,000, half the number registered in the census of 1950. The number of localities in which Jews resided had also fallen from 193 in 1968 to 174.

The largest number of registered congregants was in Prague, which, however, showed only 644 at the end of 1977, compared with 934 in 1968. Other centers showed similar decline: Brno 237 (from 295), Ostrava 122 (from 154) and Bratislava 88 (from 314).

There were no rabbis and only 8 communities still maintained a nominal existence in Bohemia and Moravia: Prague, Brno, Usti nad Labem, Olomouc, Ostrava, Levice, Pizen, Pribram; while in Slovakia there existed the six communities of Bratislava, Kosice, Presov, Galanta, Nove Zamky, Nitra.

The Council of Jewish communities of Bohemia and Moravia continued to function. Its chairman, engineer Frantisek Fuchs, who was appointed in 1966, was compelled to resign in August 1974, following attacks on him in the Czech press on the grounds that he had refused to sign a condemnation of the State of Israel during the Six-Day War. However, it seems that the real reason for the forced resignation was the fact that his son had left Czechoslovakia for the West. In March 1975 he was succeeded by Dr. Bedrich Bass, who died in 1979.

The Council of Jewish Communities in Bohemia and Moravia and the Central Union of Jewish Communities in Slovakia continued to publish the quarterly *Vestnik Zidovskych nabozenskych obci*, as well as the German language quarterly *Informationsbulletin*. The famous Pinkas Synagogue was closed because the rise in the level of sewage water surrounding it covered the monumental slabs bearing the names of 78,000 Czech Jews who perished in the Holocaust. The synagogue itself was in danger of total collapse.

Antisemitic propaganda, in the guise of anti-Zionism, still continued and came prominently to the fore in the struggle of the regime against the "Charter 77 Movement," whose manifesto – it was alleged – was drawn up "under order of the general staffs of anti-Communism and Zionism." But the antisemitism of the Czech Press was not restricted to the struggle against the protest movement; it was evident in purely ideological discussions, and its political hostility towards Israel continued. Commercial ties, however, which were severed in 1953, were re-established, and in 1976 Israeli exports to Czechoslovakia amounted to $4.767 million, while imports from Czechoslovakia were only $541,000. The respective figures for 1977 were $3.8 million and $600,000. In 1981 there was virtually no trade between the two countries.

The situation of Czechoslovakia's 6,000–10,000 Jews changed dramatically following the "Velvet Revolution" of November 1989, which ousted the country's hard-line Communist leaders. Restoration of religious freedom was one of the top priorities of the new, freely elected government headed by former dissident playwright Vaclav Havel.

Under communism, the regime tightly controlled religious observance and maintained a shrill anti-Zionist policy. Participation in Jewish religious, cultural, or educational activities was either discouraged or banned, and community leaders were appointed by the regime.

In some respects, the rigidity began to be eased somewhat in the 1980s. A major event was the traveling "Precious Legacy" exhibit put together by the State Jewish Museum in Prague, which introduced Czech Jewish culture to foreign audiences. In the late 1980s, some younger members of the Prague Jewish community formulated a letter openly criticizing the community leadership. Just one week before the "Velvet Revolution," World Jewish Congress President Edgar Bronfman paid his first official visit to Prague.

Havel's new government in February 1990 reestablished diplomatic relations with Israel, which had been broken after the Six-Day War in 1967, and in April 1990, Havel became the first leader from former Communist Eastern Europe to visit Israel – he took a planeload of Czechoslovak Jews with him. The trip coincided with the opening of "Where Cultures Meet," a major exhibit on the Jews of Czechoslovakia at Beth Hatefutsoth, the Museum of the Jewish Diaspora, in Tel Aviv. The exhibit was later presented in Prague and elsewhere in Czechoslovakia.

Jewish spiritual and cultural life began to blossom in the three major communities: Prague in the Czech Republic and Bratislava and Kosice in Slovakia, each of which has about 1,000 registered members. Community administrations were reorganized to rid them of their Communist-appointed leaders. In December 1989 the well-respected Desider Galsky became president of the Jews in the Czech Republic, and was highly active in restoring numerous contacts between Czech Jews and international Jewish organizations before his death in a car accident 11 months later.

New Jewish organizations, societies, clubs, publications, and study groups ranging from the B'nai B'rith lodge to a Franz Kafka Society sprang up in the three main communities, and legislation was passed that will enable Jewish communities to regain property that had been confiscated by the communists. Numerous new books on Jewish topics were published, ranging from local Jewish guidebooks to fiction by local Jewish writers to examinations of the Holocaust in Czechoslovakia. In 1991 a museum dedicated to Franz Kafka, whose works had been suppressed under the communists, was opened in Prague focusing on Kafka's Jewish identity. In the same year, a memorial museum dedicated to the Jewish Ghetto concentration camp was inaugurated at Terezin (Theresienstadt) north of Prague, and in the summer of 1992 work began to restore the Holocaust memorial in Prague's 500-year-old Pinkas synagogue – a list of every one of the more than 77,000 Bohemian and Moravian Jews who were killed by the Nazis, hand-painted on the walls of the sanctuary. Memorials commemorating Jewish Holocaust victims were erected for the first time in many provincial towns, too.

Prague became a symbol city for the rebirth of freedom. As such, it was chosen as the site of a key meeting between Roman Catholic leaders and the International Council for Interreligious Consultations (IJCIC) in September 1990, in which the Catholic leaders condemned antisemitism as a sin. The meeting issued a landmark joint statement that called for concrete measures to foster interreligious dialogue and spelled out recommendations for combating the upsurge of antisemitism in Central and Eastern Europe. In the spring of 1992, Prague hosted a major symposium on antisemitism in Eastern Europe.

One casualty of these changes was Prague-based Rabbi Daniel Mayer, the only rabbi in Czechoslovakia, who was forced to resign his post in June 1990 after he admitted he had served as a government informant for a decade under the communist regime.

In September 1992, Karol Sidon, a former dissident playwright who had been forced to leave Prague because of his views, became the new rabbi in Prague, and Australian Lazar Kleinman took up the post of rabbi in Kosice, in eastern Slovakia. Both new rabbis expressed the hope they could revive Jewish life and religious practice in the two communities. Kleinmann was later forced to resign his post because of activities which, inter alia, played into the hands of Slovak nationalists. The Jews faced many problems. Most community members were elderly. Young people, many of them just discovering or rediscovering their Jewish roots, knew little about Judaism. In the Czech Republic especially, where Jews traditionally were highly assimilated and intermarriage was common, many of the younger people who considered themselves Jews were not Jews according to *halakhah*.

Soon after the "Velvet Revolution" a number of antisemitic incidents were recorded in Slovakia, including the desecration of cemeteries, attacks in the Slovak nationalist press, and antisemitic slurs against Fedor Gal, the leader of the Slovak People Against Violence political movement, who was born in the Terezin ghetto concentration camp.

In addition, at one point there was a movement in Slovakia to rehabilitate Father Josef Tiso, the leader of the wartime clerico-fascist Independent Slovakia, which was allied with the Nazis. Nationalistic and antisemitic organizations celebrated a revival. This revival was accompanied by a wave of anti-Jewish publications, including the "Protocols of the Elders of Zion." However, the community increased its public and religious activities and renewed ties with Jewish organizations abroad.

[Ruth E. Gruber]

For subsequent events, see *Czech Republic and Slovakia.

Slovak Historiography

Slovakian Jewry was until 1918 an integral part of Magyar Jewry. Therefore, historians never paid particular attention to "Oberland Jewry" (i.e., the Jewry of Upper Hungary, as it was known), although it must have been clear that an ethnic-religious minority living within an alien population would develop special traits akin to the majority. Neither the Magyar masters nor Jews living within the Magyar nation would be willing to admit that the Jews of Upper Hungary were special and had a different life-path from the dominant Jews of Hungary.

Already during the 19th century there were Jewish figures and publicists in Upper Hungary who recognized the particularism of the Slovak nation and protested against its oppression. In several cases, this recognition was instrumental in attempts to close Jewish-Slovak ranks. This was not easy, however, given the Magyar insistence on the Magyarization of Upper Hungarian Jewry. Neither was the hostility of leading Slovak nationalists helpful.

Only the creation of the Czechoslovak Republic, and the introduction of the Slovak language into Jewish schools, spurred the development of an independent Slovakian Jewry. It was then that the Jews become cognizant of their independent tradition and existence.

The Bratislava Zionist Samuel Bettelheim was among the first to recognize the existence of an independent Jewish history in Upper Hungary, today Slovakia. He founded a historical journal, *Judaica*, and encouraged original historical research. Bratislava's archivist and librarian Ovidius Faust, not a Jew, joined hands with Bettelheim to promote Slovak-Jewish historiography. Faust compiled the first work telling the story of Bratislava's Jewry. The work of Jewish historiography was terminated with creation of the Slovak state in 1939. The publisher Hugo Gold also cherished the idea of recording the Jewish past in Slovakia. The manuscript he is said to have prepared has disappeared.

The trauma of the Holocaust created a desire to commemorate the tragic events. Immediately after the end of the war Friedrich Steiner started to gather historical evidence, which he eventually transferred to Yad Vashem in Jerusalem.

The daily press published the first descriptions of the horror. However, the Communist authorities, who singled out the Jews for hostile treatment, prevented any extensive and systematic analysis of the Holocaust. Therefore, it was Jews born in Czechoslovakia and living in Israel who were moved to look into the past of their community. Livia Rothkirchen, a native of Carpatho-Russia, published the pioneering *Destruction of Slovak Jewry, a Documentary History* in 1961. Graduates of the Hebrew University of Jerusalem, Yeshayahu A. Jelinek, Gila Fatran, Akiba Nir, and Yehoshua Robert Buechler, all survivors of the Holocaust, also described those bitter days. Thus Israel witnessed the foundation of modern Slovak-Jewish historiography. After the fall of Communism in Czechoslovakia, local historians followed in the footsteps of the Israelis. Ivan Kanenec wrote a dissertation on the Holocaust of Slovakian Jewry, but was not permitted to publish it. It only saw print in 1991 (*Po stopách tragedie*, "In the Footsteps of Tragedy"). Eduard Nižnianský commenced a systematic study of the first years of Jewish persecution in Slovakia. Katarina Hradská and Peter Salmer also devoted attention to the recent post. In Slovak academia the Holocaust is a subject of instruction and study. After escaping to Switzerland a graduate of Bratislava's university, Ladislav Lipscher, published *Die Juden im Slowakischen Staat 1939–1945* (1980). It is worth mentioning that most of this historical writing is devoted to Slovakian Jewry deals with the years 1938–45. Little has been published on its earlier history.

The most significant work on Czechoslovak (and naturally Slovak) Jewry is the American *Jews of Czechoslovakia* in three volumes (see Bibliography). It was prepared by the leading historians of Czech and Slovak Jewries living outside their native country. The most recent work on Slovakian Jewry is Yad Vashem's *Pinkas Kehillot Slovakia* (in the Encyclopedia of Jewish Communities series), edited by Yehoshua Robert Buechler and Gila Fatran (2004). Similar work has been published in Slovakia by Eugen Bárkány and Ludovit Dojč, *Židovské náboženské obce na Slovensku* ("The Jewish Religious Communities in Slovakia"). An older book of similar content is Lanyi Menyhert and Propperné Békefi Hermin's *Szlovenszkoi Zsidó Hitközsegek Törtente* ("The Story of the Slovak Jewish Communities). Dozens of books devoted to individual communities have been published in Israel, Slovakia, and overseas

The director of the Jewish Museum of Prague, Pavol Meštan, publishes the yearly *Acta Judaica Slovaca*, devoted to Jewish history in Slovakia. Meštan has published several books on the life of the Jewish community in Slovakia since the Velvet Revolution. Works on Slovak Jewry have thus become a frequent occurrence in Israel, the Slovak and Czech republics, Germany, the United States, England, Canada, Hungary, and Austria.

[Yeshayahu Jelinek (2nd ed.)

BIBLIOGRAPHY: *The Jews of Czechoslovakia: Historical Studies and Surveys*, 3 vols. (1968–1984); F. Steiner (ed.), *Tragedy of Slovak Jews* (1949); O. Muneles, *Bibliographical Survey of Jewish Prague* (1952); H. Gold (ed.), *Zeitschrift fuer die Geschichte der Juden in der Tschechoslowakei* 5 vols. (1930–38); V. Paleček, *Die israelitische Religionsgesellschaft* (1932); F. Friedmann, *Einige Zahlen ueber die tschechoslowakischen Juden* (1933); R. Iltis (ed.), *Die Aussaeen unter Traenen mit Jubel werden sie ernten* (1959); idem, in: *Le Monde Juif*, 24 no. 2 (1968), 37–42; A. Charim, *Die toten Gemeinden* (c. 1966), 13–42; J. Stanek, *Zrada a pád* (1958); O. Kraus and E. Kulka, *Noc a mlha* (1966); Ḥ. Yaḥil (Hoffmann), *Devarim al ha-Ẓiyyonut ha-Tshekhoslovakit* (1967); idem, in: *Juedische Wohlfahrtspflege und Sozialpolitik*, 6 (1936), 123–35; F. Weltsch (ed.), *Prag vi-Yrushalayim* (1954); L. Rothkirchen, *Ḥurban Yahadut Slovakyah* (1961), includes extensive English summary and bibliography; idem, in: *Yad Vashem Studies*, 6 (1967), 27–53; O.J. Neumann, *Be-Ẓel ha-Mavet* (1958); M.D. Weissmandel, *Min ha-Meẓar* (1960); J. Lettrich, *History of Modern Slovakia* (1956), ch. 2 and passim; G. Jacoby, *Racial State: The German Nationalities Policy in the Protectorate of Bohemia-Moravia* (1944), 201–64; International Military Tribunal, *Trial of the Major War Criminals*, 23 (1949), index; Institute of Jewish Affairs, New York, *European Jewry Ten Years after the War* (1956), 82–108; idem, *Position of the Jewish Communities in Eastern Europe…* (1957), 25–28; idem, *The Use of Anti-Semitism against Czechoslovakia* (1968); P. Meyer et al., *Jews in the Soviet Satellites* (1953), 49–204 (incl. bibl.); R.L. Braham, *Jews in the Communist World: A Bibliography 1945–1960* (1961), 20–22; Y. Gordon, in: *Algemayne Entsiklopedie – Yidn*, 4 (1950), 527–52; Moskowitz, in: JSOS, 4 (1942), 17–44; K. Stillschweig, in: HJ, 1 (1938–49), 39–49; 6 (1944), 52–59; G. Kisch, *ibid.*, 8 (1936), 19–32; B. Blau, *ibid.*, 10 (1948), 147–54; Bodensieck, in: *Vierteljahrshefte fuer Zeitgegeschichte*, 9 no. 3 (1961), 249–61; W. Benda, in: *Zeitschrift fuer die Geschichte der Juden*, 3 (1966), 85–102; O.D. Kulka, in: *Moreshet*, 2 no. 3 (1964), 51–78; *Gesher*, 15 no. 2–3 (1969); B. Blau, in: *Yidishe Ekonomik*, 3 (1939), 27–54, 175–93; *Selbstwehr*, 11–31 (1918–38); JGGJČ, 9 vols. (1929–38); Juedische Kultusgemeinde Prag, *Wochen-*, *Monats-*, and *Vierteljahresberichte*, 10 vols. (1939–42); *Judenerlasse im Protektorat Boehmen und Maehren* (1939–44); *Juedisches Nachrichtenblatt* (Prague, 1939–44); *Věstnik židovských náboženských obcí v československu* (1945–68); Rada židovských náboženských obcí v zemi české a moravskoslezské, *Informationsbulletin* (1961–68); *Gesher*, 59–60 (1969). For additional works, see "Slovak Historiography" above.

CZECHOSLOVAK LITERATURE. By force of historic circumstances, Jews in the Czech lands – Bohemia and Moravia – before World War I tended on the whole to identify themselves with the culture of the ruling Austrians, while Jews in Slovakia mostly absorbed Hungarian culture. Most of the internationally famous Jewish writers of Prague – Franz *Kafka, Franz *Werfel, Max *Brod, Egon Erwin *Kisch – to cite just a few examples – wrote in German. Jewish writers nevertheless also played an important part in Czech literature. It is true that a gap of 400 years separates the colorful 15th-century convert Pavel *Žídek from Siegfried *Kapper, the first modern Jewish author of significance to write in the Czech language. It must be remembered, however, that for three centuries the Czechs and Slovaks had been deprived of their national independence and that not until the 19th century was there a real revival of Czech nationalism and a consequent renaissance of Czech literature.

Long before the Czechs regained political independence Jewish writers were active in Czech cultural life, and in the period between the two World Wars the Jewish contribution to Czech literature was out of all proportion to the small minority of Jews in the country's population as a whole. It was during this period also that Jews first began writing in the Slovak language. The Jewish writers who succeeded in escaping from Nazi-occupied Czechoslovakia contributed to Czech literature while they were in exile, and those who returned after the end of World War II went on to play an important part in the cultural life of the country.

There is a marked difference in the treatment of Jewish themes in Czech and Slovak literature before and after World War II. Before the war, gentile writers were almost invariably biased and antisemitic, and anyone who created an authentic Jewish character nearly always proved to be of Jewish stock himself. One result of the Holocaust was the large number of openly pro-Jewish literary works produced by non-Jewish Czech and Slovak writers. In many cases this went hand-in-hand with expressions of sympathy for the State of Israel.

Biblical Influences

The proportion of writers attracted in one way or another by the Jew's fate, his behavior, and his place in the life of the nation was much greater in Czech literature than in the literature of most other countries. Surprisingly few biblical themes, however, were used by Czech authors, and these occur mainly in the works of Jewish writers. With the exception of Karel Čapek's play *Adam stvořitel* (1927; "*Adam the Creator,*" 1929), Stanislav Lom's drama about Moses, *Vůdce* (1916; "*The Leader,*" 1917), and some poems by Svatopluk Čech, J.S. Machar, and G.R. Opočenský, hardly a single work inspired by the Old Testament can be found in the writings of Czech non-Jews. Practically all the significant imaginative literature based on the Bible has come from the pens of two leading writers of mixed origin – Jaroslav *Vrchlický and Julius *Zeyer. J. Vrchlický, the most prolific Czech poet, wrote more than 100 poems on Jewish themes, at least half of them biblical, including the dramatic epic *Bar Kochba* (1897). Zeyer published a biblical drama, *Sulamit* (1883), a short story about Joseph in Egypt entitled *Asenat* (1895), and poems about Moses and about Solomon and the Queen of Sheba.

The Figure of the Jews and Jewish Themes

Several factors lend a distinctive character to the treatment of Jewish themes by Czech authors. One is that modern Czech literature developed at a time when the Czechs themselves did not have a state of their own. Hence, the many allusions to the homeless Jew longing for a country of his own, whose tragedy symbolized the Czech longing for statehood. An instance of this is the romantic, Byronesque poem *Cikáni* ("Gypsies," 1835) by the greatest of the early 19th-century Czech poets, Karel Hynek Mácha (1810–1836).

Another phenomenon is the extraordinary number of writers who concerned themselves with the question of whether or not a Jew could also be a loyal Czech. The first to discuss this problem publicly was Václav Bolemír Nebeský (1818–1882), who made Czech-Jewish assimilation the theme of several of his short stories. His view, expressed in a number of essays, was that Jews who had long been settled in the Czech lands should be regarded as Czechs of the Jewish faith and that they could be just as good patriots as Czechs of any other religion. Nebeský's thesis was repudiated by the great poet, journalist, and patriot Karel Havlíček-Borovský (1821–1856), who held that the Jews belonged not merely to a different religion but that their Semitic bond was much stronger than the one that bound them to the land of their birth. Nevertheless, Havlíček-Borovský was a supporter of Jewish emancipation and repeatedly explained to his readers that the Jews were not to be blamed for their shortcomings. This did not prevent him from writing a number of epigrams in which he accused them of crimes for which, on his own showing, they could scarcely be held responsible. Josef Jiří Kolár (1812–1896) posed the question of assimilation in dramatic form in his popular historical play, *Pražský žid* ("The Jew of Prague"), which remained in the repertoire of Czech theaters for more than 50 years after its première in 1871. The central character in this play about the historic battle on the White Mountain in 1620 is a dignified Jew who is at the same time a Czech patriot.

Literary Antisemitism

On the other hand, the contribution made to this discussion by Jan Neruda (1834–1891), possibly the best Czech poet of the 19th century, could hardly be called constructive. Although he was greatly influenced by some of the German-Jewish poets, especially Heinrich *Heine, and although he was originally inclined to be sympathetic toward the Jews, Neruda became an active antisemite. In 1869 he published a pamphlet entitled *Pro strach židovský* ("The Jewish Danger"), in which he excused his prejudice on the grounds that the Jews generally sided with the Germans and were intent on world domination. Far from emancipating the Jews, he said, what the Czechs needed was to emancipate themselves from Jewish control. Similar ideas are to be found in a number of Neruda's articles and epigrams, and this author of some of the most beautiful love poetry in all Czech literature even went so far as to express his regret when in 1881 the antisemitic riots in Berlin came to an end.

The case of another great 19th-century poet, Svatopluk Čech (1846–1908), is more complicated. When he dealt with historical figures – as in the collection of verse, *Sny palestýnské* ("Palestine Dreams," 1872), in his first long poem, *Adamité* ("The Adamites," 1873), and in several of the poems in *Modlitby k Neznámému* ("Prayers to the Unknown," 1896) – he was full of respect and sympathy. As soon as he turned to the contemporary scene, however, Čech's Jew invariably became a repulsive usurer, exploiter, or villain, whose only object was to enrich himself at the expense of his Slav hosts. Examples of such figures can be found in his novels *Jabloň* ("The Appletree," 1878), *Kandidát nesmrtelnosti* ("Candidate for Immortality," 1879), and *Člověk se zlatníkem v tobolce* ("The Man with a Gold Coin in his Purse," 1883). A few other Czech writers, notably A.E. Mužík, Bohdan Kaminský, and F.X. Svoboda, showed a more kindly attitude toward their Jewish characters, but none of them was of major literary importance.

It is another peculiarity of Czech literature that its expression of antisemitism was at least in part motivated by nationalist considerations. The fact that Jews in the Czech lands were traditionally closer to German than to Czech culture laid them open to the charge that they supported Austrian oppression of the Czechs. This is probably the first instance in literature of antisemitism being based on nationalism, whether from honest conviction or merely as an excuse for prejudice. Sometimes the two types of antisemitism – the social and the nationalist – appear together. For example, Viktor Dyk (1877–1931) wrote a poem about two Jews, the wealthy Kohn and the poor Bloch. As long as Kohn is rich, he speaks German; but when he loses all his money he begins to speak Czech, as the poor Bloch always did.

For the leading Czech social poet, Petr Bezruč (pseudonym of Vladimír Vašek, 1867–1958), the Jew was also the national as well as the social enemy. In his famous *Slezské písně* ("Silesian Songs," 1909), hatred of the Germans is repeatedly coupled with hatred of the Jews, whom he charged with committing every crime in the calendar in their dealings with the poor. Bezruč was probably the most bitter and most programmatic antisemite among the leading Czech poets, but he was certainly not the only one. The great symbolist Antonín Sova (1864–1928) wrote at least two openly antisemitic poems and the mystic poet Otakar Březina (1868–1929), who is generally regarded as the greatest of all Czech poets, made no secret in his published correspondence of his hatred of the Jews.

As far as the drama is concerned, the Jewish characters in the plays of Ladislav Stroupežnický (1850–1892), Jaroslav Hilbert (1871–1936), and F.F. Šamberk (1839–1904) are all either unpleasant or ridiculous. The rustic novel might be said to have an antisemitic tradition, originated by a Catholic priest, František Pravda (1817–1904), whose short stories are full of Jewish swindlers and opportunists battening on the Czech people. His example was followed by far more significant authors such as Alois Mrštík (1861–1925), who drew a whole series of unsympathetic Jewish portraits in his classic novel, *Rok na vsi* ("Year in a Village," 1904). Alois' brother, Vilém Mrštík (1863–1912), gave vent to anti-Jewish feelings of an even cruder sort in his short stories. It would almost seem that no Czech novel about village life could be complete without its Jewish villain, and he is to be found in such classics as *Naši* ("Our People") by Josef Holeček (1853–1929) and *Jan Cimbura* by Jindřich Š. Baar (1869–1925). Even Thomas Masaryk's close friend Ivan Herben (1857–1936) introduced a Jewish villain as a matter of course in his *Do třetího a čtvrtého pokolení* ("To the Third and Fourth Generation"). One of the most virulent antisemites in the annals of Czech literature was Rudolf Medek (1890–1940), a former general who wrote popular novels about World War I. The anti-Jewish tirades in his *Ohnivý drak* ("The Fiery Dragon," 1921) were unmatched by any other Czech author.

Hardly any figure recurs in Czech prose as often as that of the wicked Jew. The villain in the novel *Sup* ("Vulture," 1920) by Emil Vachek (1889–1964) is the old familiar stereotype; but Vachek at least appeared to realize that the Jew's faults might be attributable to his Diaspora environment. Even such important progressive social novelists as Antal Stašek (1843–1931) and Anna Maria Tilschová (1873–1957) were not above depicting negative Jewish characters in their novels.

Although he was attracted by the Jew, the Czech writer in general had too little knowledge of Jewish life and character to draw him as anything but a caricature. The few Czech writers with a wider outlook, such as Jaroslav Hašek (1883–1923) and the brothers Karel Čapek (1890–1938) and Josef Čapek (1887–1945), created Jewish characters without attempting to discuss problems affecting the Jews.

Objective Treatment

There were Czech authors, nevertheless, who created sympathetic Jewish characters. Among them must be included Alois Jirásek (1851–1928), Karel Klostermann (1848–1923), Karel Matěj Čapek-Chod (1860–1927), Gabriela Preissová (1862–1946), Josef Svatopluk Machar (1864–1942), Marie Majerová (1882–1958), Eduard Bass (1888–1946), and Benjamin Klička (1897–1943). On the whole, however, if the works of Jewish or partly Jewish authors are excluded, objective treatment was quite exceptional in Czech literature before 1945.

In Slovak literature, too, as in the realistic village novels of Martin Kukučín (1860–1928) and Jozef Gregor Tajovský (1874–1940), the Jew was most often depicted as the innkeeper and usurer who exploits the poor Slovak peasant and serves the Hungarian overlord. This generally hostile treatment of the Jews in Slovak literature virtually ceased in the democratic period between the two World Wars, but even then no Slovak author of distinction portrayed a sympathetic Jewish character. The omission was only remedied during World War II, when a leading Slovak writer, Janko Jesenský (1874–1945), in his short story *Strach* ("Fear"), and the then young author Margita Figuli (1909–1995) in her four-volume novel *Babylon*, expressed their horror at anti-Jewish persecution and their pity for the victims. Both works, of course, had to wait for publication until the war was over.

[Avigdor Dagan]

After World War II, in the years 1956–69, some Czech non-Jewish writers published stories and novels with Jewish themes and characters and wrote about Jews in a very positive way. Jan Otčenášek (1924–1979) in his short story "Romeo, Julie a tma" ("Romeo, Juliet and the Darkness," 1958) depicted a tragic love story between a Czech boy and a Jewish girl (made into a movie by the Jewish director Jiří *Weiss). Hana Bělohradská (1929–) later made her debut with the short story "Bez krásy bez límce" ("Without Beauty Without Collar," 1962) about a Jewish physician waiting for a summons to a concentration camp, which was made into a movie *…a pátý jezdec je strach* (" …and the Fifth Rider is Fear") by Zdeněk Brynych. Ladislav Fuks (1923–1994) published his novels and stories with Jewish topics between 1963 and 1969: *Pan Theodor Mundstock* ("Mr. Theodor Mundstock," 1963), *Mí černovlasí bratři* ("My Black-haired Brothers," 1964), *Variace pro temnou strunu* ("Variations for a Dark String," 1966), *Spalovač mrtvol* ("The Burner of Corpses," 1967), and *Cesta do zaslíbené země a jiné povídky* ("The Way to the Promised Land and Other Stories," 1969). Josef Škvorecký (1924-), who in 1958 published his best novel, *Zbabělci* ("The Cowards"), which shocked the governing Communist Party establishment, published his works with Jewish themes also in those years: a short story "Legenda Emöke" ("The Legend Named Emöke," 1963), a series of stories called *Sedmiramenný svícen* ("The Menorah," 1964), and *Babylónský příběh a jiné povídky* ("A Tale of Babylon and Other Stories," 1967). Last but not least the Slovak author Ladislav Mňačko (1919–1994), well known for his antifascist and anti-Stalinist novels and stories and who openly criticized official anti-Israeli Czechoslovak government policy in 1967, published the book *Die Aggressoren* ("Agressors," 1968) and left Czechoslovakia for Israel and later for Austria. He also started to publish stories, some of them with Jewish topics, in the 1960s, such as "Jizvy zůstaly" ("Scars Left," 1966).

The Jewish Contribution to Czech and Slovak Literature

A long list of Czech Jewish writers appears already in the second half of the 19th century including Siegfried *Kapper and publicists and authors connected with the Czech-Jewish assimilation movement. Linked to its ideas is Vojtěch *Rakous, a writer who described the life of Jews in the country in a masterly fashion. The following generation included František *Gellner, an anarchist poet, one of the first victims of World War I, Otokar *Fischer, Pavel *Eisner, and many others whose critical, literary, and public activities developed freely during the two decades of Masaryk's First Republic (1918–38). Some of them, Fischer, Eisner, Otto Pick, and Rudolf Fuchs, became famous as translators and mediators between the Czech and German cultures. Jewish writers, journalists, and editors also played an important role in the press of the First Republic, promulgating Masaryk's and Beneš' so-called "Castle" policy in the public at large. Jan and Jaroslav *Stránský, Gustav *Winter, Alfred *Fuchs, Josef Kodíček, František *Langer, Richard *Weiner, Karel *Poláček and others held decisive positions in many publishing houses (for example Orbis) and newspapers such as *Národní osvobození, České slovo, Prager Tagblatt, Prager Presse, Tribuna, Lidové noviny*, and *Přítomnost*, or regularly contributed to them. The only prominent Jewish journalist and editor who opposed the "Castle" policy was Lev Borský (in 1944 he perished in a concentration camp). There was an informal "Castle" institution called *Pátečníci* ("Friday visitors") which met regularly in the years 1924–37 in the presence of Tomáš G. *Masaryk and Edvard *Beneš. A quarter of them were Jews such as Julius *Firt, Otokar Fischer, Alfred Fuchs, Camil Hoffmann, Josef Kodíček, František Langer, Arne Laurin, and Karel Poláček. Poláček, in his stories and novels, portrayed the life of people in a district town before and during World War I. Fischer and Weiner laid foundations for Czech Jewish poets who were to follow, such as František *Gottlieb and Avigdor *Dagan, who were then succeeded by Ivo Fleischmann (1921–1997), Hanuš *Bonn, and Jiří *Orten.

[Milos Pojar (2nd ed.)]

The Jewish contribution to Slovak literature was less important than to Czech literature. The only Jewish author of any significance was Gejza Vámoš (1901–1956), a gifted writer of psychological short stories, the best of which were collected in *Editino očko a iné novely* ("Edith's Eye and Other Stories," 1925). His novel *Odlomená haluz* ("The Severed Branch," 1934), about Slovak-Jewish symbiosis, was at once a protest against antisemitism and an equally vehement criticism of the bigotry, exclusiveness, and materialism of the Jewish community in which he was raised. The few remaining Jewish writers in Slovakia before 1939 were of lesser importance, but both their number and their significance increased considerably after World War II. At least some of them deserve mention. Emil *Knieža, Juraj *Spitzer, and Ladislav *Grosman won distinction with their books on Jewish suffering during the Nazi occupation, Hela Volanská (1912–1996) and Leopold Lahola (1918–1998) were held in a labor camp in Nováky during World War II; Volanská was persecuted after 1968, Lahola went to Israel and died when he returned to Czechoslovakia in the late 1960s. Scriptwriter and writer of non-fiction literature Ján Ladislav Kalina (1913–1981) died in exile in Munich, Germany.

Another notable Jewish contribution to Czech and Slovak letters has been in the field of literary criticism. Those prominent in this sphere include Josef Kodíček (1892–1954), formerly the director of one of Prague's leading theaters, Pavel *Fraenkl (1904–1985), who settled in Norway, and Eduard *Goldstuecker. Jews, furthermore, played an important part in popularizing the works of Czech authors abroad and in translating the great foreign classics into Czech, thus enriching the literary life of Czechoslovakia. Max *Brod, Pavel Eisner, Paul Selver (a Londoner who translated Čapek and Hašek into English), Gustav *Winter, Otto Pick, Willy *Haas, Rudolf Fuchs, Emil and Erik Saudek, Bedřich Adler, Edmund Gruen, Arnošt Mandler, Jan Urzidil, and, not least, Otokar *Fischer, who was both a poet of the first rank and an important drama critic – the list is a long one, and yet these are only a few of the many gifted Jews who helped to spread a knowledge of Czechoslovak culture throughout the civilized world.

[Avigdor Dagan / Milos Pojar (2nd ed.)]

World War II brought immense losses to the ranks of Czech Jewish writers, authors, and journalists. Some perished in the Holocaust: Alfred Fuchs, Karel Poláček, Hanuš Bonn, Camil Hoffmann (from a German Jewish family); Jiří Orten was killed in 1941; many went into exile: František Langer, Pavel *Tigrid, Josef Kodíček, Julius Firt, Arne Laurin, the prominent novelist Egon *Hostovský, Viktor Fischl (later Avigdor Dagan), František Gottlieb, Eduard *Goldstuecker and Jiří Langer, who died in 1943 in Palestine. Some who returned to Czechoslovakia after World War II, went into exile again after the Communists came into power in 1948 (Tigrid, Firt, Hostovský, Fischl). Nevertheless, many Czech Jewish authors made important contributions to Czech literature after World War II, for example Norbert *Frýd, Josef *Bor, Arnošt *Lustig, František *Kafka, František R. *Kraus, Ruth *Bondy, Ivan *Klíma, who all survived the Holocaust. Some managed to escape Nazi persecution: Jiří *Weil, Ota *Pavel, Pavel Eisner, Zeno *Dostál.

The Thaw

The 20th Congress of the Soviet Communist Party and political events in Poland and Hungary in 1956 opened the gates for a more liberal period in Czechoslovakia in the field of culture, which lasted until the Soviet occupation in 1968. The Second Congress of the Union of Czechoslovak writers and its critical course, articles which appeared in *Literární noviny*, and works of young Czech and Slovak writers published in 1955–59 in the literary monthly *Květen* made it possible to start publishing "Jewish themes" again. In particular, another literary monthly, *Plamen* (1959–69), gave space to Czech and Slovak writers, publicists, translators, journalists, etc., both Jewish and non-Jewish, to publish their own stories, critical pieces, and translations pertaining to Czech-Jewish literature, the Holocaust, Jewish humor and extracts from the works of Jewish writers (Julian *Tuwim, Lion *Feuchtwanger, Isaac *Babel, Ilja *Erenburg, Franz *Kafka), philosophers, sociologists, psychoanalysts, etc. (Ernst *Fischer, Erich *Fromm, Lucien *Goldmann, Sigmund *Freud, and others). Similarly, a new bimonthly, *Světová literatura* (from 1956) started publishing works of world literature, especially those of American and Western writers, including Jews. In 1958, Pavel Eisner's translation of Kafka's *Proces* ("The Trial") appeared on the book market, followed by translations of Lion Feuchtwanger, Alberto *Moravia, Isaac Babel, Herman *Broch, and many others. In the growing liberal atmosphere of the late 1950s and 1960s (with many setbacks for new trends) Jewish writers also profited. In the beginning, they either published (from 1945) in *Věstník židovské náboženské obce v Praze* ("Gazette of the Jewish Religious Community in Prague"; from 1968 *Věstník židovských náboženských obcí v Československu*, "Gazette of Jewish Religious Communities in Czechoslovakia"), from 1991 in *Roš chodeš* or from 1954 in *Židovská ročenka* ("Jewish Yearbook") or in *Judaica Bohemiae*. Slowly, they started to publish their books, too. Ludvík *Aškenazy, F.R. *Kraus, Norbert Frýd, J.R. Pick and Jiří Weil, who could publish even in the 1940s and 1950s, were joined in the 1960s by Arnošt Lustig, Ivan *Klíma, Josef *Bor, František Kafka, František Langer, Ota Pavel, František Gottlieb, Ladislav *Grosman, Gabriel *Laub, and Efraim K. *Sidon. In these years works of deceased authors also appeared – František Gellner, Ivan *Olbracht (a staunch supporter of the Communist regime), Jiří Orten (already in 1958), Karel Poláček, and Richard Weiner. In 1963 and 1965 two international literary conferences were held in Liblice near Prague, co-organized by Eduard *Goldstuecker and others, on Franz Kafka and on Prague German literature, attended, for instance, by Anna *Seghers, Ernst *Fischer, Roger Garaudy, etc., followed by an edition of *Franz Kafka aus Prager Sicht* (1966) and *Weltfreunde. Konferenz ueber die Prager deutsche Literatur* (1967). Kafka and his work ceased to be taboo in Czechoslovakia (until 1968). In 1964 Max Brod visited Prague after 25 years. In 1963–1964 an open dialogue between Marxists and Christians came into being at the Faculty of Philosophy in Prague. It ran until 1968 and brought to Prague, among others Erich Fromm, Theodor *Adorno, Roger Garaudy. Allen *Ginsberg, J.P. Sartre, and Simone de Beauvoir. J.A. Jevtuschenko, Edward Albee, and John Steinbeck visited Prague, too. Eichmann's trial in Israel in 1961–62 and trials of German war criminals from Auschwitz in 1965 in Frankfurt were described in detail by Ladislav Mňačko and Erich *Kulka who took part in these trials, which attracted wide attention in the Czech public, including Jewish themes in general. The official Czechoslovak policy toward Israel in 1967 and after the Six-Day War brought on open criticism of Ladislav Mňačko and of some Czech writers at the Fourth Congress of the Czechoslovak writers. Three of them (Ludvík Vaculík, Milan Kundera, and Ivan Klíma) lost their membership in the Communist Party. "The Prague Spring" in 1968 lasted a mere eight months. A special board of the Czechoslovak Writers' Union discussed persecution cases of 168 authors discriminated against after 1948. Josefa Slánská (1967), Eugen Löbl, (1968), Artur London (1969), and Heda Margoliová-Kovályová (1973, from exile) published their testimonies about the *Slánský trial. Eduard Goldstuecker was elected president of the Czechoslovak Writers' Union. Censorship was abolished, books of exiled authors (for instance Egon Hostovský) were allowed to be published. Czech and Slovak writers took an active part in the process of the so-called "democratization" of the whole society. The mass media became free and the weekly edition of *Literární listy* (issued by the Czechoslovak Writers' Union) reached 300,000 copies. "The Prague Spring" was crushed by Soviet tanks in August and a process of liquidation of all the freedoms which had been achieved started and culture was not an exception. This period of "normalization" lasted 20 years with all its disastrous consequences also for Jews. An official state and party antisemitism (under the guise of anti-Zionism) emerged. The Czechoslovak Writers' Union was decimated, split into the Czech and Slovak unions, and a majority of important writers stayed outside. The ban on publication hit those who did not approve of the occupation of the country. Dozens of writers, publicists, journalists, editors, etc., went into exile, among them Ludvík Aškenazy, Ladislav Grosman, Eduard Goldstuecker, Gabriel Laub, Arnošt Lustig, Erich Kulka, and later Karol E. Sidon. Czech literature split into three sections: an official one, an underground (*samizdat*), and an exile literature published either in Czech exile publishing houses and smuggled back into Czechoslovakia or in translations in foreign languages. Some Czech Jewish authors stayed in the country and published abroad or in *samizdat* (Ivan Klíma, or Milan *Uhde); some of them (Arnošt *Goldflam, Zeno *Dostál, or Ota Pavel) were allowed to publish at home as long as they did not emphasize their Jewishness or write about Jewish themes. From the old Jewish authors rather occasionally Orten, Poláček, Gellner or Bor appeared.

The return of freedom to Czechoslovakia after 1989 physically brought back some Czech Jewish authors from exile (Goldstücker, Lustig, Sidon). In the 1990s Czech Jewish writers started to be published again. This trend continued into the 2000s.

[Milos Pojar (2nd ed.)]

BIBLIOGRAPHY: O. Donath, *Židé a židovství v české literatuře 19. století* (1923); idem, *Židé a židovství v české literatuře 19. a 20. století* (1930); P. Váša and A. Gregor, *Katechismus dějin české literatury* (1925); L. Páleníček, *Rukovět dějin československé literatury od roku 1918* (1961); Dagan and Hostovský, in: *Jews in Czechoslovakia*, 1 (1967); Lagus, in: *Judaica Bohemiae*, 3 (1967), 61; 4 (1968), 91; P. Eisner, in: *Jewish Studies in honour of Gustav Sicher* (1955), 50–61; Dagan and Lustig in *Gesher*, 59–60 (1969), 227–41. **ADD. BIBLIOGRAPHY:** *Československé spisovatelé v literatuře 20. století* (2000); *IV. Sjezd Svazu československých spisovatelů (Protokol) Praha 27.–29. června 1967* (1968); J. Čulík, *Knihy za ohradou. Česká literatura v exilových nakladatelstvích 1971–1989* (n.d.); P. Kubíková and P. Kotyk, *Čeští spisovatelé* (1999); J. Lehár et al., *Česká literatura od počátků k dnešku* (1998); V. Menclová et al., *Slovník českých spisovatelů* (2000); V. Mikula et al., *Slovník slovenských spisovatelů* (1999); A. Mikulášek et al., *Literatura s hvězdou Davidovou*, 1 (1998), II (2002); *Slovník českých spisovatelů* (Toronto, 1982); V. Sůva, *Jewish Literature in Bohemia* (2001); *Slovník zakázaných autorů* (1991).

CZECH REPUBLIC AND SLOVAKIA. (For earlier history of these regions, see *Czechoslovakia.) Czechoslovakia split peacefully into the Czech Republic and Slovakia on January 1, 1993. Israel established formal diplomatic relations with both new countries.

Czech Republic

Jewish life in the Czech Republic continued the process of revival that began after the fall of Communism in 1989. As the only rabbi in the country, Prague Rabbi and Czech Chief Rabbi Karol Sidon, who took up his post in late 1992, was a major catalyst in this. About 3,000 Jews in the Czech Republic, including 1,300 in Prague, identified with the community in the early 21st century.

There were numerous classes, conferences, cultural and social events. An old age home was opened in Prague in late 1993, and a Jewish kindergarten opened in 1994. The ritual orientation of the community was strictly Orthodox. This alienated some people, particularly younger people, products of mixed marriages, who felt a Jewish identity but were not Jewish according to *halakhah*. A number of them gravitated to an alternative Ḥavurah group, Bet Simcha, that functioned outside the mainstream of the official Jewish community and made a point of appealing to people who were not halakhically Jewish but wanted to take part in Jewish activities. In 1994 another "liberal" Jewish group, Bet Praha, was formed, mainly appealing to the hundreds of American, English, and Canadian Jews in the city. At the High Holidays in 1994, Reform services, conducted by a visiting rabbi, were held in Prague's High Synagogue.

A new segment of Czech Jewry were Jews from Carpatho-Russia, who in the years 1946–48 opted to settle in Bohemia and Moravia rather then remain citizens of the Soviet Ukraine. They chose to settle in the big cities, like Prague and Brno, and in the region formerly called "Sudeten," where the old German community was expelled to the German Federal and Democratic Republics. Remnants of Carpatho-Russia Jewry could also be found in Karlovy Vary (Karlsbad), Liberec, Usti nad Labem, and Teplice-Sanov. The Carpatho-Russian Jews comprised the pious element of Czech Jewry.

The former pious Moravian Jews were all but annihilated. Traditional Orthodox communities of the Silesia-Teschen region and the Orthodox of southern Moravia almost disappeared. The ancient synagogue and cemetery of Mikulov is a tourist attraction but does not represent Jewish communal life.

A large part of Prague's Orthodox Jews were also immigrants, newcomers from Slovakia and Carpatho-Russia. Therefore the recurring tension between Orthodox Jews and self-identified Jews sometimes also reflected the differences between the remnants of old-time Czech Jewry and the immigrants. Thus issues of faith, the generation gap, and intellectual differences upset the communal life of the Prague congregation. The center of Bohemian-Moravian communal life was nevertheless concentrated in Prague, which offered regular educational-intellectual and social activities and preserves a modicum of religious life.

The memory of Czech Jewry is preserved in the Pinkas synagogue, on whose walls the names of all Bohemain-Moravian Jews have been inscribed. The Jewish Museum of Prague, and naturally the Altneuschul and the adjacent ancient cemetery, preserve the memory of Czech Jewry. Memorials were erected in numerous towns and municipalities also care for surviving synagogues and cemeteries, but by and large it can be said that, except for Prague and Brno, intensive Jewish life, for all practical purposes, has ceased to exist in the Czech Republic.

The Czech Republic had very good relations with the State of Israel. Economic ties are close. Restitution of Jewish property remained an issue. A number of properties that had been owned by the Jewish community in 1938 were returned to the community. The most notable was the Prague Jewish Museum, including its priceless collection of Judaica and half-dozen synagogue and other buildings in which the collections were displayed, all of which was returned to the community in October 1994.

There was continuing concern at incidents involving right-wing and skinhead groups who primarily attacked gypsies but also shouted antisemitic slogans.

[Ruth E. Gruber / Yeshayahu Jelinek (2nd ed.)]

Slovak Republic (Slovakia)

While the exact number of Jews living in Slovakia is hard to establish, the estimate is that some 5,000 lived in the country in the early 21st century. Most of them lived in the capital, Bratislava, with the second largest Jewish community in Kosice in Eastern Slovakia.

In addition to these two congregations, nine more were active, serving all the Jews living in the towns of the vicinity. These nine were Galanta, Nove Zamky, Dunajska Streda, Komarno, Nitra, Zilina, Banska Bystrica, Presov, and Michalovce. The tendency was toward decline as the Jewish population abandoned the countryside or died out.

The British-born Lubavitcher rabbi, Baruch Myers, arrived in Bratislava in May 1993 as the city's first rabbi since the departure of Rabbi Elias Katz in 1968. He launched education and youth programs and for the first time, a huge Hanukkah menorah was in public in Bratislava in a ceremony attended by President Michal Kovac and the Israeli ambassador.

After the "Velvet Revolution" (1989), Jewish communal, religious, social, and political life received a big boost. Among the principal actors in this revolution in Bratislava were several Jews, in particular Fedor Gal, who was the leading figure in the organization called "Public Against Violence" (Verejnost Proti Nasiliu, VPN). He and other Jews were later squeezed out of political life.

The representative institution of Slovakian Jewry was the Central Association of Jewish Religious Communities in the Slovak Republic, with its seat in Bratislava. It represented local Jewry in all matters affecting its life, including activities for restoration and restitution of Jewish communal and private property, representing Jews in Slovak elected and communal bodies, organizing religious and social activity, and maintaining relations with Jewish organizations abroad, including the Israel Association of Jews from Czechoslovakia. Among its important political tasks was the struggle against frequently occurring antisemitism. Antisemitism made itself felt in the desecration of surviving Jewish cemeteries and synagogues, attempts at rehabilitation the Slovak state, the first satellite of the Third Reich, and its president Father Dr. Jozef. Also, and attacks on Jews in the media. Rabbi Myers was attacked in Bratislava on September 5, 1993, by skinheads. A survey in April 1993 showed that a large percentage of the population had negative feeling about the Jews, and this state of affairs has not changed. It also provides fertile ground for anti-Israeli Arab propaganda. Anti-Jewish publications, including "The Protocols of the Elders of Zion," are regularly published. In 1990 the Slovak Parliament made a public apology to the Jews and in October 1993 a landmark law aimed at partial restitution of property claims by churches and religious communities, including the Jews. The Jewish community listed over 300 properties, including over three dozen synagogues, buildings, and schools. In 2003 another law provided for the partial return of "Aryanized" or confiscated Jewish property.

In 2002, Slovakian authorities reached an agreement with the Association of Jewish Religious Communities on partial indemnification of Slovakian Jews who lost their property during the Holocaust. Slovakia has good relations with Israel, and Israeli figures like the president and the speaker of Parliament have visited Slovakia, as have the Slovak president and the prime minister visited Israel.

Among the important Jewish institutions in Slovakia mention should be made of the Jewish Museum, which is part of the Slovak National Museum, as well as the Holocaust Documentation Center and a variety of cultural enterprises, including the frequent publication of books of Jewish content by Jewish authors and the Ezra foundation for social and humanitarian activities. Within Comenius University an Institute for Jewish Studies is active.

Slovakia proclaimed September 9, the date of publication in 1941 of the so-called "Jewish Codex," based on the Nuremberg laws, as the National Day of Holocaust commemoration. A memorial was erected on the mass grave in Kremnicka, a memorial exhibit was constructed in Auschwitz, and in Sobibor. In Poland, where most of Slovakian Jews perished, a plaque was put up. The state supported all these undertakings financially and morally.

The Association cares for Jewish cemeteries and synagogues, including the construction of a mausoleum over the graves of famous Bratislava rabbis in the ancient cemetery, such as Moses Schreiber-Sofer (Ḥatam Sofer).

[Yeshayahu Jelinek (2nd ed.)]

CZENSTOCHOWSKI, WALTER (1924–1997), Zionist activist and leader in Venezuela. Born in Vienna in a Zionist and Yiddishist home, Czenstochowski immigrated to Palestine (Eretz Israel) with his mother in 1935 and studied in the agricultural school of Ben Shemen. He joined the *Palmach*, and when the IDF was established, he continued his military service in its air force. In 1953 he moved to Venezuela, where his father had found refuge. From that time on he participated in local Jewish public life and in political activity on behalf of the World Zionist Organization. At various times he presided over the Zionist Federation of Venezuela and the northern section of the Latin American Zionist Confederation. Czenstochowski was active in many Jewish Venezuelan organizations. He was president of the Confederación de Asociaciones Israelitas de Venezuela – CAIV (the central political organization of the Jewish community) and was a member of the Executive Committee of the World Zionist Organization as the representative of Latin America.

[Efraim Zadoff (2nd ed.)]

CZERNIAK, MOSHE (1910–1984), Israel chess master. Czerniak was born in Warsaw and in 1934 settled in Palestine. Three times champion of Israel, he was active in promoting the game in the country. He represented Israel in international tournaments and in the chess Olympics. He contributed articles in Spanish, Polish, Russian and Hebrew to many periodicals, including his chess column in *Haaretz*, and the Argentinian chess reviews *Estrategia* and *Revista Metropolitana* which he edited between 1942 and 1949. He was also editor of *64 Squares* (1956–59). His books include *El final* (1941);

Botwinnik's Best Games (1946[2]); *Sefer ha-Shaḥmat* (1963); and *Toledot ha-Shaḥmat* (1963).

[Gerald Abrahams]

CZERNIAKOW, ADAM (1880–1942), president of the *Warsaw Jewish Community Council from shortly after the outbreak of World War II and first head of the Warsaw *Judenrat. Czerniakow was born in 1880 in Warsaw to an assimilated Jewish family. He was trained as an engineer at Warsaw's Polytechnic Institute and studied industrial engineering in Dresden. His Polish was native, his German fluent, and his Yiddish more halting, which later hampered his communication with less assimilated, more traditional Yiddish-speaking ghetto inhabitants and their confidence in him. Czerniakow acquired considerable experience as a communal leader and was known especially as the organizer of the Jewish artisans, who constituted some 40% of all Polish Jewry. In 1927–34 he was an elected a member of the Warsaw Municipal Council, and ran unsuccessfully for the Polish Sejm. Before the outbreak of World War II he was a member of the Executive Council of the Warsaw Jewish community and served as its vice chairman. Several members of the Council, including its chairman, Maurycy Mayzel, fled Warsaw when the Germans invaded. Czerniakow had several such opportunities and rejected them all. It was a matter of responsibility, of basic integrity, for Czerniakow that leaders not abandon their people and save themselves.

On Sept. 23, 1939, the mayor of besieged Warsaw appointed Czerniakow to head the Jewish Community Council; his appointment was confirmed by the German authorities on October 3, 1939, when the 24-member Jewish Council (*Judenrat*) was constituted on *Heydrich's orders. Throughout this period Czerniakow kept a secret diary, notebooks containing 1,009 pages, which is an indispensable day-by-day account of his work and depicts conditions in the Warsaw Ghetto and throughout Poland.Under Czerniakow, the *Judenrat* evolved into a multi-layered municipality with a series of departments, including a Jewish police force to which he appointed Joseph Szerynski, who had converted to Christianity, as commander. It was a bad choice, made worse by the lack of trust between the ghetto inhabitants and the commander. He struggled in vain to serve two masters: the Germans, who viewed the Council as an instrument of their policies; and the Jews, whose ever-increasing needs they unsuccessfully tried to meet. Thus, his situation was compromised from the very beginning. Czerniakow was acutely aware of the precariousness of the *Judenrat*'s position. Twenty-four cyanide pills were in the drawer of his desk, one for each member of the Council. He reported to different German and Polish agencies who were in charge of ghetto operations, beginning with the leaders of Einsatzgruppe IV during the opening days of the war and then the city administration until the fall of 1940, followed by the German district administration's resettlement division as the ghetto was formed in the fall and winter of 1940–41. Much of Czerniakow's diary – especially on the buildup to the deportation – was written during the period in which he reported to the Komissar for the Jewish District Hans Heinz Auerswald. In the final days of the ghetto the SS Resettlement staff, under the leadership of Hermann Hofle, predominated. He could never be sure exactly who was his "boss": the ghetto commissar, the SS, the police, the governor of the district, the Transferstelle, or the Polish municipality.

His daily dilemma was overwhelming: how to run a municipal government that could provide adequate food and shelter, heat, medicine, religious services, education, and work to a starving population; how to care for the young and sustain the elderly; how to make life bearable in the ghettoes. The resources at this disposal were meager; his authority derived from the Germans. Funds were scarce and production, though increasing through the initiative of ghetto residents, was always inadequate to sustain the ghetto. To accomplish his task, he worked virtually all day, every day. He was preoccupied with the immediate. Seldom did he look at the larger picture or even think of the fate of his son Jas who lived in Lvov and from whom he had not heard from since the German invasion. Unlike other ghetto leaders such as Mordecai Chaim *Rumkowski of Lodz, whom he criticized, Czerniakow was not full of himself. He did not perceive himself as a grand strategist, but he tried his best. He did not deceive himself regarding his abilities or his achievements. His diary depicts his few successes and his many failures. Czerniakow, who remained at his post for nearly three years, was beset by constant budgetary difficulties and often faced contradictory demands from various offices within the Nazi bureaucracy and constant complaints from desperate individuals and competing groups within the ghetto.

As chairman of the *Judenrat*, he was charged by the Nazi authorities with effecting the community's fatal transition into a ghetto. He vigorously fought against the idea of ghettoization and the proposed boundaries of the ghetto, and so accumulated a vast documented correspondence with the Nazis. His direct exchanges with the Nazi authorities were usually held at a junior level, with lieutenants and sergeants. The chairman comported himself with dignity and honor. Nor was his position within the Jewish community a simple one. It was Czerniakow's difficult task to conciliate conflicting interests of various groups in the captive heterogeneous ghetto population. He personally did not escape Nazi brutality. He bore his situation with a certain stoicism. He often included criticism of German policy against the Jews in his memorandums and reports but they like his diary were self-censored. There were clear limits to what he could say or what he could write in private should his notebooks be discovered. He stubbornly fought for the inclusion of certain formerly Jewish streets within the ghetto limits in order to relieve the dangerous overcrowding, and also maintained open and clandestine contacts with leaders of the Polish population. He was in the words of Raul Hilberg and Satnislaw Staron, who edited the English-language version of his diary, "overwhelmingly ordinary, a non-villain, non-hero, non-exploiter, no saint and not a leader."

He encouraged secret educational and cultural activities, including technical and medical training, helped obtain food, raw materials, and tools for the artisans within the ghetto, and cared for the labor commandos outside and for their families left within, even though this required ingenious schemes of smuggling and outwitting, usually only temporarily, the Nazi authorities.

Almost until the end, Czerniakow refused to believe that the Germans were bent not on exploitation of the Jews but on their murder. He was preoccupied with the endless problems beleaguering the more than 400,000 Jews who lived in a position of increasing squalor and hunger, disease and malnutrition. He rejected the rumors and hints about the impending deportations and liquidation of the ghetto and used his influence to encourage the besieged community to be calm and continue to work and endure until the emergency would pass.

When he was asked by the Germans to sign children's deportation orders, he frantically ran to various Nazi offices in the hope that these orders might not have been issued by competent authorities and could be countermanded, but despite reassurances to the contrary from Auerswald, he realized the futility of the situation, and committed suicide by swallowing the poison which he always carried in his pocket. His final entry in the diary was: "I am powerless, my heart trembles in sorrow and compassion. I can no longer bear all this."

Even in death Czerniakow was a controversial figure. Those close to him saw his suicide as an act of personal courage that expressed his integrity and sense of public responsibility. Ghetto diarist Chaim Kaplan said: "Some people earn eternity in a single hour." Those active in the ghetto's militant underground were less charitable. Emanuel *Ringelblum, the chronicler of the Warsaw ghetto, wrote: "Suicide of Czerniakow – too late, a sign of weakness – should have called for resistance – a weak man." No doubt, he saw that his strategy of negotiations and of hoping to alleviate the plight of the Jews and to prolong their survival beyond a German defeat would not work. In the end, he chose to share the fate of his community, to die by his own hand rather than be killed by the Germans. The order for deportation appeared without his signature. On the day of his death, he completed the ninth of his notebooks. The diary has been published in Hebrew and Polish as well as English (*The Warsaw Ghetto Diary of Adam Czerniakow* [1979] and *Yomano shel Adam Czerniakow* [1968]). One notebook is missing covering the dates of December 14, 1940–April 22, 1941. The diary was probably intended to serve as source material for a book to be published after the end of the German occupation.

BIBLIOGRAPHY: A. Tartakower, in: *Yad Vashem Studies*, 6 (1967), 55–67; A. Hartglass, in: *Yad Vashem Bulletin* no. 15 (1964), 4–7; Y. Gutman, in: *Yalkut Moreshet*, no. 10 (1969), 122–43, see also 144–55. **ADD. BIBLIOGRAPHY:** R. Hilberg, S. Staron, and J. Kermisz, *The Warsaw Diary of Adam Czernaikow: Prelude to Doom* (1979); Y. Gutman, "Adam Czerniakow: The Man and His Diary," in: Y. Gutman and L. Rothkirchen (eds.), *The Catastrophe of European Jewry* (1976).

[Michael Berenbaum (2nd ed.)]

CZERNOWITZ YIDDISH LANGUAGE CONFERENCE, first international, interparty conference to deal with the role of Yiddish in Jewish life. It was held from August 30 to September 4, 1908. The idea of such a conference was first broached by Nathan *Birnbaum, and the original call was sent out by an organizing committee in New York consisting of Birnbaum, dramatists Jacob *Gordin and David *Pinski, the publisher A.M. Evalenko, and the philosopher Chaim *Zhitlowsky. The 70 delegates who went to Czernowitz (Chernovtsy), the principal Yiddish-speaking center of Bukovina, included representatives of all shades of Jewish opinion, from Zionist Hebraists to militant Bundists, and such diverse personalities as I.L. *Peretz, Abraham *Reisen, Sholem *Asch, H.D. *Nomberg, Noah *Prylucki, Matthias *Mieses, Mordecai *Spector, Gershom *Bader, and Esther (Lifshitz). The two leading Yiddish authors, S.Y. *Abramovitsh (Mendele Mokher Seforim) and *Shalom Aleichem, prevented by illness from attending the conference, endorsed its aims. The agenda included problems of orthography, grammar, literature, theater, press, translation of the Bible into Yiddish, and, above all, recognition of Yiddish as a national language of the Jewish people. Controversy raged between delegates who espoused Hebrew as the only Jewish national language and who looked upon Yiddish as a *galut* ("Diaspora") language to be discarded, and delegates who regarded Yiddish as the living Jewish language and Hebrew as the language solely of the past and of prayer. After long debates, a compromise resolution was adopted proclaiming Yiddish as a national language and asking for its political, cultural, and social equality with other languages. By using the expression "a national language" rather than "the national language," the conference wished to leave participants free to take any stand on Hebrew that accorded with their personal convictions. The conference aroused much discussion in the Jewish press. *Aḥad Ha-Am called it a Purim spectacle. Hillel *Zeitlin, Reuben *Brainin, and Morris *Rosenfeld ridiculed it, while S. *Niger and *Ba'al-Makhshoves defended it as an historic achievement. After the conference, Peretz, Asch, Reisen, and Nomberg undertook a tour of Jewish communities of Galicia and Bukovina to intensify interest in Yiddish language, literature, and culture. The conference heightened the prestige of Yiddish. It stimulated literary creativity, research, and publication in Yiddish, and laid the ideological basis for the later founding of *YIVO.

BIBLIOGRAPHY: YIVO, *Die Ershte Yidishe Shprakhkonferents* (1931); S. Liptzin, *Flowering of Yiddish Literature* (1963), 175–7.

[Sol Liptzin]

CZESTOCHOWA (Pol. **Częstochowa**), city in Poland, approximately 125 miles (205 km.) S.W. of Warsaw; the shrine of the Jasna Góra Madonna in Czestochowa was celebrated as a center of Catholic pilgrimage. Seventy-five Jewish residents are recorded in Czestochowa in 1765 and 495 in 1808, when an organized community was established. Although Jewish residence was prohibited in certain districts, the Jewish population in Czestochowa grew from 1,141 in 1827 (18.5% of the total) to 2,976 in 1858 (34.5%), and in 1862, with the abolition of the Jewish quarter, to 3,360 (37.3%). By 1900 it numbered 11,764 out of a total population of 39,863 (29.5%), in 1921, 22,663 and in 1939, 28,486. From the early 19th century, Jews played an important role in the development of industry and commerce in Czestochowa, and a number of Jewish social, educational and charitable institutions were established.

[William Glicksman]

Holocaust Period

The German army entered the city on Sept. 3, 1939. The next day, later called "Bloody Monday," a pogrom was organized in which a few hundred Jews were murdered. On September 16, a *Judenrat was established, chaired by Leon Kopinski. On December 25, a second pogrom took place and the Great Synagogue was set on fire. In August 1940 about 1,000 young men between the ages of 18–25 were sent to the forced labor camp in Cieszanow (Lublin Province), where almost none survived. Thousands more were sent to forced labor locally and the Judenrat managed to arrange licenses for 2,000 Jewish artisans as well as providing a wide range of community services, including the inoculation of 17,000 Jews against typhus under the auspices of the *TOZ organization. When a greater number of Jews from other parts of western Poland came to Czestochowa in 1940–41, the city's Jewish population grew by several thousands. On April 9, 1941, a ghetto was established. When it was sealed off (Aug. 23) the population suffered severe overcrowding, hunger, and epidemics. On Sept. 23, 1942 (the day after the Day of Atonement), the first of six large-scale *Aktionen* began. By October 5, about 39,000 people had been deported to *Treblinka and exterminated, while about 2,000 were executed on the spot. The ghetto, by now largely diminished and within new borders (now called the "small ghetto") had about 6,500 people, of whom about 1,000 were "illegal."

Resistance

Various Jewish underground organizations arose during the first months of German occupation, first engaging in sabotage and mutual aid activities. In December 1942, a unified Jewish Fighting Organization (ZOB) was set up. It had about 300 fighters and established contact with the *Warsaw Ghetto Fighting Organization. On Jan. 4, 1943, a group of fighters under Mendel Fiszlewicz offered the first armed resistance. Twenty-five fighters fell, while 300 nonfighting men were deported to Radomsko. The next day the Nazis shot 250 children and old people who had been living in the ghetto "illegally." On March 20, 1943, 127 of the city's Jewish intelligentsia were executed. The Jewish Fighting Organization tried to organize guerilla units in the nearby forests. Two large groups were dispatched to the forests of Zloty Potok and Koniecpol, but before they could begin partisan activities, they were murdered by Polish terrorists of the National Armed Forces (Narodowe Siły Zbrojne). A few smaller groups succeeded in contacting the Polish left-wing People's Guard and they conducted guerilla activities in its ranks. On June 26, 1943, the Germans began liquidating the "small ghetto." The Jewish Fighting Organization offered armed resistance, but they could not cope with the situation. About 1,000 people were deported and the ghetto was closed down. The remaining 4,000 Jews were transferred to two slave labor camps organized at the city's HASAG factories. On July 20, 1943, about 500 prisoners from these camps were executed at the Jewish cemetery. In 1944 the HASAG slave labor camps were enlarged, when a few thousand Jewish prisoners from *Płaszów concentration camp, Lodz Ghetto, and the slave labor camp of Skarzysko-Kamienna were moved there. Before leaving the city on Jan. 17, 1945, the Germans managed to deport almost 6,000 prisoners from the HASAG camps to the concentration camps of *Buchenwald, Gross-Rosen and *Ravensbrueck in Germany. The 5,200 prisoners who succeeded in hiding were saved by the Soviet army. The Jewish survivors tried to rebuild their community. In June 1946, 2,167 Jews lived in Czestochowa. Some kibbutzim to prepare Jewish youth for settlement in Palestine were active until 1948, a Jewish school existed until March 1946, and a Jewish Religious Society was active. After 1948 only the official communist Jewish Social-Cultural Society continued to function until the antisemitic campaign in 1968. Jews left Czestochowa and settled mainly in Israel in 1949 and 1957. After 1968 almost all those who remained left Poland. Organizations of Czestochowa Jews are active in Israel, the United States, Canada, Argentina, and France.

[Stefan Krakowski]

BIBLIOGRAPHY: J. Tenenbaum, *Underground* (1952), 184–208; W. Glicksman, in: *Yad Vashem Studies*, 6 (1967), 331–57; B. Orenstein, *Khurbn Tshenstokhov* (1948); *Tschenstokhover Yidn*, 2 vols. (1944–58); S. Waga, *Khurbn Tshenstokhov* (1949); L. Brener, *Vidershtand un Umkum in Tshenstokhover Ghetto* (1950); *Sefer Tshestokhov*, 2 vols. (1967–68). **ADD. BIBLIOGRAPHY:** R. Mahler (ed.), *Czenstochower Yiden* (1947); S. Krakowski, *The War of the Doomed. Jewish Armed Resistance in Poland, 1942–1944* (1984), 218–23; PK.

CZOBEL, BÉLA (1883–1976), Hungarian painter. Czobel, who was born in Budapest, went to Paris in 1903 and associated with the "fauve" painters. When his works were exhibited in Hungary, he was acclaimed as a leader of "the Eight," a group of artists who were introducing fauvism into that country. During World War I he lived in Holland and after the war moved to Berlin. He then returned to Paris, which became his base. Domestic subjects such as flowers, gardens, interiors and still lifes were among his favorites. His characteristic mood is still and meditative. Czobel's early works were influenced by Van Gogh and Cézanne and executed in flat patterns with strong outlines. His mature works are characterized by warmth and richness of color and *sfumato* effects which blur the outlines and permit the separate parts of a painting to merge.

BIBLIOGRAPHY: Roditi, in: *Arts Magazine*, 39 (Oct. 1964), 57ff.

Initial letter "D" for "Dixit," the first word of Psalm 53, from the Angoulème Psalter, *France, 13th century. The illustration shows King David and a fool who, in accordance with medieval iconography, is represented holding a club and eating cheese, Besançon, Bibliothèque Municipale, Ms. 140, fol. 62 v.*

Da–Doz

DABBŪRIYYA (Ar. دبُّرِيَّة), Muslim-Arab village in central Israel, west of Mount Tabor. A serpentine road leads from the village to the top of Tabor. First mentioned under its present name by a 13th century Arab geographer, the village has been identified with the biblical Daberath, while legend associates the village's name with the prophetess *Deborah. Remnants of a fortress and church with a mosaic floor, as well as rock-hewn tombs and cisterns, have been found there. In 1961 Dabbūriyya received municipal status. In 1968 it had 2,590 inhabitants, mainly engaged in farming, increasing to 7,690 in 2002. The village's area is 2.8 sq. mi. (7.3 sq. km.).

[Efraim Orni / Shaked Gilboa (2nd ed.)]

DABROWA GORNICZA (Pol. **Dabrowa Górnicza**), industrial town in Katowice province, S. Poland. Jews settled in Dabrowa Gornicza in the middle of the 19th century. They mainly engaged in small trade and metal crafts. There were 4,304 Jews living in Dabrowa Gornicza according to the 1921 census (11% of the total population).

[Arthur Cygielman]

Holocaust Period

The German army entered the town on Sept. 3, 1939. In the fall of 1940 several hundred young Jewish men were deported to slave labor camps in Germany. Several hundred more were deported in the course of 1941. At the end of that year a ghetto was established. On May 5, 1942, the first deportation took place in which 630 Jews were taken to Auschwitz and exterminated. In the second deportation, conducted on August 12, 1942, another few hundred Jews were sent to their death in Auschwitz. On June 26, 1943, the ghetto in Dabrowa Gornicza was liquidated and all its inmates were transferred to the ghetto in Srodula (a suburb of Sosnowiec), the only ghetto still existing in Upper Silesia. It too was liquidated and all its inhabitants, including the Jews from Dabrowa Gornicza, deported to Auschwitz and killed. After the war the Jewish community in Dabrowa Gornicza was not reestablished.

[Stefan Krakowski]

BIBLIOGRAPHY: *Yad Vashem Archives*, O-16/154, M-1/E/1064, 03/1246, 03/2728; B. Wasiutyński, *Ludnosć żydowska w Polsce…* (1930), 29. **ADD. BIBLIOGRAPHY:** N. Gelbart (ed.), *Sefer Kehillat Yehudei Dabrowa Gornicza ve-Ḥurbana* (1971); Y. Rapaport (ed.), *Pinkas Zaglembie* (1972), 81–87.

DACHAU, town near Munich, Bavaria, where the nearby concentration camp was established on March 10, 1933. It was the first of the *SS-organized concentration camps and became the model and training ground for all other camps when they were taken over by the SS in April 1933. The Dachau camp was established within 40 days of Hitler's ascent to power; it operated

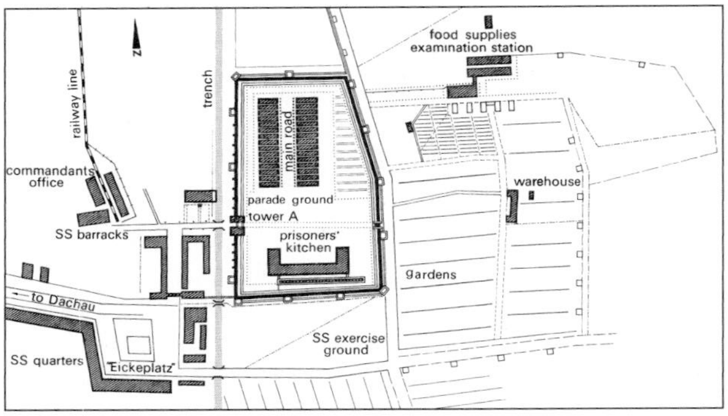

Plan of Dachau concentration camp. From A.J. Grand, Turm A ohne Neuigkeit, *Vienna, 1946.*

until the day before he died, less than ten days before the end of the war, when it was captured by the Americans on April 29, 1945. During World War II, approximately 150 branches of the main camp established in southern Germany and Austria were also called "Dachau." The main camp consisted of 32 huts in two rows, surrounded by an electrified fence, in which there was a gate surmounted by the slogan *Arbeit macht frei* ("Labor Liberates"). The camp's first commandant was Theodor Eicke, who planned and organized the brutal Dachau regime. He later went on to become inspector general for all camps. It was at Dachau that permission was first given to the guards to shoot a prisoner approaching the barbed-wire fence, and this practice was encouraged by granting leave to guards who hit their target. Dachau produced commandants for other camps, including Rudolph *Hoess.

From the first, Dachau was used to incarcerate "enemies of the regime," trade unionists, and political opponents. The Nazis used Dachau as an execution site for the SA Storm Troopers caught in the 1934 purge. Later gypsies, German – and after 1938 Austrian – male homosexuals, and Jehovah's Witnesses were imprisoned there. As the Germans invaded countries, Dachau continued to serve a political function as political opponents were imprisoned there. The Jews who first came to Dachau were incarcerated for their opposition to the regime, not because they were Jewish. In fact, Jews were a distinct minority of the prisoners at Dachau though their percentage in the general population varied with the general conditions of Jews under the Third Reich. After the *Anschluss* (annexation) in March 1938, thousands of Austrian Jews were sent to Dachau. Eleven thousand were sent there from Germany and Austria in the wake of **Kristallnacht* but nearly all of them were released if they could leave the country. No Jews were released, however, after the outbreak of World War II. Late in the war, the Jewish population again increased when Dachau received Jews on the death marches. The exact number of those who passed through Dachau is unknown. In the main camp 160,000 prisoners were registered on the files and about 90,000 in the camp's branches; but, during the last several days of the camp's existence, many transports of prisoners arrived which were not registered in the file. Some inmates remained in Dachau or one of its branches; others were sent further in "death transports"; most were murdered or died from starvation. Of the more than 200,000 prisoners at Dachau, at least 32,000 died of starvation and disease, many after the typhus epidemic that broke out during the extreme overcrowding in the winter of 1945.

It was at Dachau that German doctors and scientists first experimented on prisoners. Sigmund Rasher conducted experiments on decompression, high altitude, and freezing, ostensibly to find a way to help German fliers. Of the 200 inmates whom Rasher experimented upon, 4 in 10 died. Dr. Claus Schilling conducted malaria experimentation. Many died as a result of these pseudo-scientific experiments, and those who survived were often maimed for life. Dachau claimed many victims of want and starvation. From time to time there was also a "selection" in which the weak and crippled were sent to the gas chambers in other camps. Gas chambers were built in Dachau in 1942 but were never used. The exact number of people killed in Dachau is not known.

Dachau was used as a transit center. Mentally retarded and physically infirm Germans – whose Aryan status was never questioned – were incarcerated there and sent from there to Hartheim castle, where they were gassed as part of the "euthanasia operation." Jews were deported from Dachau to the death camps in German-occupied Poland, where they were subsequently gassed after "the Final Solution" became operational in 1942. In the waning hours of the camp, seven thousand Jews were forcibly evacuated from the camp in a planned death march. They were overtaken by American troops.

Prisoners were used for labor; at first the arrangement was local, but it was later consolidated by SS industries. The SS was paid for the laborers by German industries, particularly the armament industry. The prisoners were not paid.

As American troops approached Dachau on April 29, 1945, they found 30 coal cars filled with bodies, all in an advanced state of decomposition. The doors had been locked, and they were left to die. When Dachau was occupied by the American army, one of the uses made of the camp was for the concentration of German prisoners of war and war criminals, who were to be tried in the town of Dachau. The Americans tried 40 of the concentration camp officials; 36 were sentenced to death. Of the other war criminals, 260 were sentenced to death, and 498 to imprisonment. The camp was later a transit camp for refugees and foreign citizens freed from concentration camps. Part of the camp is preserved as a memorial.

BIBLIOGRAPHY: E. Kupfer-Koberwitz, *Die Maechtigen und die Hilflosen*, 2 vols. (1957–60); *Law Report of Trials of War Criminals*, selected and prepared by the UN War Crimes Commission, 11 (1949), case no. 60, 5–17.

[Nachman Blumental / Michael Berenbaum (2nd ed.)]

DA COSTA, ISAAC (1721–1783), merchant and shipping agent of colonial Charleston, South Carolina. Da Costa was born in London, scion of an eminent Anglo-Jewish family of Spanish-Portuguese origin. He received religious training from Isaac *Nieto, haham of the Sephardi congregation of London. Da Costa immigrated to Charleston in the late 1740s. He helped found Congregation Beth Elohim in 1749, serving as *ḥazzan* for some years. In 1764 he deeded a plot of land to the congregation for use as a communal cemetery, which exists today as Coming Street Cemetery, the oldest Jewish burial ground in the South. Da Costa is the earliest recorded Jewish Mason in South Carolina. He was in partnership with Thomas Farr, Jr., for about five years from 1758, handling exports of rice, indigo, lumber, and pitch, and imports and coastal shipments of European and Indian goods, rum, spermaceti, and slaves. An ardent partisan of the patriot cause, Da Costa was banished and his property seized by the British when Charleston fell in 1780. He took refuge with his family in Philadelphia, where, in 1782, he helped establish Congregation Mikveh Israel. Returning after the Revolution, he died in Charleston.

BIBLIOGRAPHY: B.A. Elzas, *The Jews of South Carolina* (1905), index; C. Reznikoff and U.Z. Engelman, *The Jews of Charleston* (1950), passim; J.R. Marcus, *Early American Jewry* (1953), index; J.R. Rosenbloom, *A Biographical Dictionary of Early American Jews* (1960), 28–29.

[Thomas J. Tobias]

DA COSTA, JOSEPH MENDES (1863–1939), father of modern Dutch sculpture. He was born in Amsterdam, where his father kept a stonecutting workshop, a circumstance which affected his choice of career. At the start of his career he produced a series of earthenware figures of great charm, including many on Jewish subjects, which reflected the long period he had spent in Amsterdam's Jewish quarter. He also made figures of animals, such as his *Melancholy Apes*, for which he became well known. He received an honorary degree of doctor of biology from Groningen University for this work. After 1905 Da Costa was frequently commissioned to provide sculptures for public buildings. For these he developed a highly stylized idiom. From 1907 to 1911 he sculpted portraits of famous personages, including Van Gogh, Jan Steen, and Spinoza. After 1917 he completed many important works, such as the monument to the Boer general De Wet, the bronze group "*De Liefde*" ("Love"), and the monument to President Steyn of the Orange River Republic called "*De Raadsman*" ("The Counselor"). He also sculpted a number of biblical subjects, among them *The Sacrifice of Abraham*, *Job and His Friends*, *Jeremiah*, and *David*. Da Costa's strong, robust style generally achieves expressiveness rather than outward beauty of form.

BIBLIOGRAPHY: Roth, Art, 869–70; *Art Journal*, 23 (1963), 108.

DAFNAH (Heb. דַּפְנָה), kibbutz in the Ḥuleh Valley, N. Israel, affiliated with Ha-Kibbutz ha-Me'uḥad, founded in 1939 as a "*tower and stockade" village and as the first of a complex of settlements called the "Ussishkin fortresses" (named after M. *Ussishkin). The first settlers were pioneers from Lithuania and Poland, later joined by immigrants from various countries. In 1968 the kibbutz had 540 inhabitants. In the mid-1990s Dafnah's population was approximately 639, dropping to 553 in 2002. Its economy was based on intensive farming (field crops, avocado and apple orchards, citrus groves, fishery, and dairy cattle) and plastic goods and confection factories. The kibbutz had guest rooms and a park with recreational activities. Near the kibbutz is the Ḥurshat Tal park. The kibbutz is called after the Greek name of a villa suburb of Panaeas (Caesarea Philippi, *Bāniyās) lying 3 3/4 mi. (6 km.) further east; its name means "laurel tree."

WEBSITE: www.dafna.org.il.

[Efraim Orni / Shaked Gilboa (2nd ed.)]

DAGAN, AVIGDOR (formerly **Viktor Fischl**; 1912–2006), Israeli diplomat and Czech writer. Born in Hradec Králové, Bohemia, he edited the Zionist weekly *Židovské zprávy* ("Jewish News"), and became secretary of the Jewish Party (*Židovská strana*) in the Czechoslovak parliament. His verse collections, notably *Jaro* ("Spring," 1933), *Kniha nocí* ("The Book of Nights," 1936), and *Hebrejské melodie* ("Hebrew Melodies," 1936), showed the influence of Otokar *Fischer. He also translated works about the history of Zionism and the poems of Franz *Werfel, Antoni *Slonimski, and a short poem by Franz *Kafka, "Praha." After the Nazi invasion in 1939, he escaped to London, where he served the Czechoslovak government-in-exile and became a close collaborator of Jan *Masaryk. His *Hovory s Janem Masarykem* ("Conversations with Jan Masaryk," 1952), published in Tel Aviv, was modeled on Karel Čapek's "Conversations with Thomas Masaryk" (1928–35) and was one of the first books reprinted in Czechoslovakia during the short-lived liberal era of 1967–68. Arriving in Israel in 1948, he joined the Israeli diplomatic service in 1950, serving as envoy to Yugoslavia and as ambassador to Poland, Norway, and Austria until his retirement in 1977. He was the *Encyclopaedia Judaica* departmental editor for Czechoslovak literature.

Dvorní šašci ("Court Clowns," 1990) was a novel about the suffering of Jews during the Holocaust. *Jeruzalémské povídky* ("Jerusalem Stories," 1991) evoked the atmosphere of post-1967 Jerusalem. Other novels included *Všichni moji strýčkové* ("All my Uncles," 1995); the autobiographical *Hrací hodiny* ("Musical Clock," 1996); *Loučení s Jeruzalémem* ("Farewell to Jerusalem," 1997); *Maškary v Benátkách* ("Masques in Venice," 1997); and *Žlutý dům* ("The Yellow House," 2003). All is prose works are written in a very poetic, clear style, in a beautiful Czech and full of warmth and optimism. A collection of poems, *Krása šedin* ("The Beauty of Grey Hair"), appeared in 1992. His translation of a number of books of the Old Testament from Hebrew into Czech was issued in 2002 under the title *Poezie Starého zákona* ("Poetry of the Old Testament"). Dagan's essays are collected in *Setkání* ("Encounters," 1994), bringing together portraits of Czech and other writers and politicians. He was awarded the T.G. Masaryk Order of Czechoslovakia in 1991 and of the Czech Republic in 1996, the Gratias Agit Prize in 2002, and the Jaroslav Seifert Prize in 2004.

BIBLIOGRAPHY: J. Kunc, *Slovník českých spisovatelů beletristů 1945–56* (1957); *Der Prager Kreis* (1966); *Jews of Czechoslovakia*, 1 (1968), index. **ADD. BIBLIOGRAPHY:** D. Emingerová, *Hovory s Viktorem Fischlem* (2002); M. Kaďůrková, *Setkání s Viktorem Fischlem* (2002); A. Mikulášek et al., *Literatura s hvězdou Davidovou*, 1 (1998); *Slovník českých spisovatelů* (1982).

[Milos Pojar (2nd ed.)]

DAGON (Heb. דָּגוֹן, Akk. **Dagān**), the Syrian and Canaanite god of seed, vegetation, and crops. Dagon first appears as an important and widely worshiped deity – but not as a god of crops – in documents of the dynasty of *Akkad (23rd century B.C.E.), which indicate that his cult was well established in the middle and upper regions of the Euphrates around the Balikh and Khabur rivers. This region was also called "the lands of Dagon," as Dagon was recognized there as the "god-king of the land." Temples of Dagon have been located in *Mari and Terqa, the chief cities of this region. There are a number of personal names from this region compounded with the name of Dagon.

During the period of the third dynasty of Ur (21st–20th centuries B.C.E.), the cult of Dagon was introduced into Sumer, perhaps by West Semites. It is significant that the chief "cattle-park" (or, better, "state bank") of the third dynasty of Ur, which was situated near Nippur and where thousands of animals were collected and distributed for various official uses, was called *Ṣilluš Dagan* ("in-the shelter-of-Dagon"; modern Drehem); on the evidence presented by personal names of various West Semites (*Amorites and Akkadians) active in *Ṣilluš Dagan*, it is possible that this economic center was originally established by them. Dagon's popularity among West Semites may also be reflected in the fact that his cult reached its height during the Isin dynasty, one of the successors of the third dynasty of Ur in the early Old-Babylonian period (19th century B.C.E.), of West Semitic origin. It is also significant that his cult was important in the time of *Hammurapi (First Babylonian Dynasty; Hammurapi calls Dagon "*baniya*" (my creator)). However, northern Mesopotamia remained his chief center. It is clear from the Mari documents of the 18th century that Dagon's cult flourished there, since lay and cultic ecstatic prophets from Terza (c. 43 mi. (70 km.) northwest of Mari) delivered the god's words, which they heard in dreams and other ecstatic circumstances, to the king of Mari.

The *Ugaritic documents (15th–14th centuries B.C.E.) are the first to shed light on the Dagon cult among the West Semites living in Syria. There and in Canaan, the etymology of his name alludes to his origins as a god of grain: Ugaritic *dgn*, Hebrew *dagan* ("grain"). On the other hand this term, as the Hebrew vocalization shows, was separated from the name of the deity. In the Ugaritic epics, one of Baal's epithets is "Son of Dagon," and there was an important temple in Ugarit dedicated to Dagon. Perhaps he was sometimes held by the Canaanites to be identical with Il, "the father of the gods." Philo of Byblos (first century C.E.), who described the Phoenician religion according to ancient sources, identifies Dagon with Chronos, the father of Greek gods.

A number of personal names in the *Alalakh and Ugarit texts are compounded with the element Dagon. The earliest personal name from central Syria is Dagan-takala (El-Amarna Letters, nos. 317–318), which, contrary to earlier suppositions, does not belong to southern Palestine but to central Syria. All the same, proof of the Dagon cult in Canaan and the coastal regions is found in the name of the two settlements of Beth-Dagon, which are mentioned in the Bible (Josh. 15:14; 19:27), one on the eastern border of the tribe of Asher, and the second in the territory of Judah. A third "*Bit Da-gan-na*" (Dagan) is mentioned by *Sennacherib as one of the conquests in his third campaign (against the west (701 B.C.E.), including Judah), together with *Jaffa (see D.D. Luckenbill, *The Annals of Sennacherib* (1924), p. 31, 69).

According to biblical evidence, the Philistines accepted Dagon as their god and set up temples to him in Gaza (Judg. 16:23) and Ashdod (I Sam. 5:1–7). The one in Ashdod was destroyed by the Hasmonean Jonathan (I Macc. 10:83–84). In Beth-Shean there is evidence of a Philistine presence in at least the 12th century B.C.E., mainly in the form of anthropoid clay sarcophagi (see *Philistines). These Philistine mercenaries, very possibly brought to Beth-Shean by Ramses III after his victory over them, established their rule there after the collapse of Egyptian sovereignty in Canaan. They apparently found a sanctuary of Dagon in the city (on the sanctuaries see *Beth-Shean). The cult of Dagon – and among others that of *Ashtoreth – was possibly established by the Canaanite inhabitants. It is to be noted that according to an El-Amarna letter (no. 289, lines 19–20), people from Ginti (i.e., Gath-Carmel, modern Gath in the Sharon) served as a local garrison in Beth-Shean. These soldiers possibly had a part in the transplanting of the cult of Dagon to this city, but it is also possible that it came directly from central Mesopotamia or Syria (cf. *Marduk). After the battle at Mt. Gilboa, the Philistines exposed the body of *Saul at the temple of Dagon, and his weapons at the sanctuary of Ashtaroth (see I Sam. 31:10, 12; I Chron. 10:10).

BIBLIOGRAPHY: H. Schmoekel, *Der Gott Dagan* (1928); N. Slouschz, *Oẓar ha-Ketovot ha-Fenikiyyot* (1942), 24, 27; Albright, Arch Rel, index; G. Dossin, in: A. Pasrat (ed.), *Studia Mariana*, 1 (1950), 49; F.J. Montalbano, in: CBQ, 13 (1951), 381–97; EM, 2 (1954), 623–5 (incl. bibl.); A. Malamat, in: *Eretz Israel*, 4 (1956), 78–84; S. Moscati (ed.), *Le antiche divinità semitiche* (1958), index; D.O. Edzard, in: H.W. Haussig (ed.), *Woerterbuch der Mythologie*, 1 (1965), 49–50; M.H. Pope and W. Roellig, *ibid.*, 276–8; P. Artzi, in: JNES, 27 (1968), 163–71. **ADD. BIBLIOGRAPHY:** J. Healey, IN: DDD, 216–19.

[Pinhas Artzi]

DAGON (Fishko), BARUKH (Asher David; c. 1885–1957), Hebrew short-story writer. He adopted the pseudonym of Barukh while active in the Russian underground. Dagon, who was born in the province of Pinsk, went to Warsaw at the end of the 19th century. He worked as a teacher there as well as in Lodz and other towns. In 1920 he immigrated to Palestine and taught in various settlements. His first stories were published in 1928 in *Davar* and dealt, as did most of his later writings, with the animal world. He published four books: *Nefesh Ḥayyah* (1943); *Ta'alumot ha-Ḥai* (1948); *Kanaf el Kanaf* (1956); and his autobiography *Gilgulei Ḥayyim* (1948).

BIBLIOGRAPHY: D. Sadan, *Avnei Boḥan* (1951), 252–4 (also in his *Bein Din le-Ḥeshbon* (1963), 253–4).

[Getzel Kressel]

DAHAN (**Adhan, Bendahan**), patronymic of several families originating in the Sahara regions of Morocco. The kabbalist SAADIAH DAHAN (c. 1630) wielded much influence in the region of Oued Ghéris. His son SOLOMON DAHAN (c. 1650) was a rabbi and a physician, and his grandson MASʿŪD DAHAN (c. 1680) was the *dayyan* of Tāfīlālet. The son of the latter, SOLOMON ADHAN (d. c. 1735), at first lived in Tetuán. He then left for Gibraltar and later for Amsterdam in 1720 to collect funds to redeem his family and synagogue, which had fallen into the hands of the nomad Arabs in the region of Tāfīlālet. He translated the work *Zekher Rav* of Solomon Sasportas from Hebrew to Spanish under the title *Memória de los 613 Preceptos* (Amsterdam, 1727), and wrote *Bi-Ne'ot Deshe* (Amsterdam, 1735), a book on ethics which has been frequently reprinted.

JACOB BENDAHAN (c. 1700) of Meknès wrote liturgical poems. His elder son MAIMON BENDAHAN (1756) was *dayyan* in Tetuán and his second son MOSES BENDAHAN (d. 1737) was *av bet din* in Meknès. Both brothers left many halakhic decisions, some of which were published in various Moroccan rabbinical works. *Piyyutim* by Moses are included in the *maḥzorim* of North Africa. JOSEPH BENDAHAN (d. c. 1820), *dayyan* in Tetuán, was the author of five works (commentaries, homilies, responsa, and *piyyutim*), one of which, entitled *Shufreih di-Yosef*, was published in Alexandria (1897) by his grandson JOSEPH NISSIM BENDAHAN, who added one of his own works, *Divrei Yosef*, to it. Joseph Nissim also wrote *Ma'aseh Bereshit* (Djerba, 1925).

BIBLIOGRAPHY: Kayeserling, Bibl, 8; J.M. Toledano, *Ner ha-Ma'arav* (1911), 132, 136, 146f., 162, 189, 211; J. Ben-Naim, *Malkhei Rabbanan* (1931), 58a, 68a, 81b, 84b, 88b, 100a, 118a.

[David Corcos]

DAHLBERG, EDWARD (1900–1977), U.S. novelist and critic. Born in Boston, Dahlberg was the illegitimate son of a Kansas City barber and had a miserable childhood, being committed first to a Catholic, and later to a Jewish, orphanage, remaining in the latter from the age of 12 until he was 17. For the next two years he led a vagabond existence, supporting himself by work in a wide range of occupations, from truck driver and cattle drover to dishwasher and clerk. He then studied at Berkeley (California) and Columbia universities, became a teacher, and moved to Europe, where he first began writing in 1926. Dahlberg's early experiences inspired the semi-autobiographical novels *Bottom Dogs* (1929) and *From Flushing to Calvary* (1932). *Those who Perish* (1934) dealt with the impact of Nazism, the rise of which he had seen in Germany, on a small American-Jewish community. With his later works – mainly "prophetic" criticism – the writer gained a considerable reputation as spokesman for the avant-garde, although he soon abandoned his political commitment to Communism. Dahlberg's other books include *Do These Bones Live* (1941); *Sing O Barren* (1947); *Flea of Sodom* (1950), an attack on modern civilization; *The Sorrows of Priapus* (1957), a study of three world cultures (illustrated by Ben *Shahn); *Truth Is More Sacred* (1961), correspondence with the English writer, Sir Herbert Read; and *The Carnal Myth* (1968). Dahlberg was considered an outstanding prose stylist and later taught at universities in the U.S., receiving various literary awards. His autobiography, *Because I Was Flesh*, appeared in 1963, and his letters, *Epitaphs of Our Times*, in 1967. Steven Moore edited *Samuel Beckett's Wake and Other Uncollected Prose* (1989), an anthology of Dahlberg's uncollected writings.

BIBLIOGRAPHY: H. Billings, *Edward Dahlberg* (1968); idem, *A Bibliography of Edward Dahlberg* (1971); F. Moramarco, *Edward Dahlberg* (1972); C. DeFanti, *Wages of Expectation: A Biography of Edward Dahlberg* (1978).

[Milton Henry Hindus]

DAIA (abbr. for Sp. **Delegación de Asociaciones Israelitas Argentinas**), umbrella organization and officially recognized representative body of Argentinian Jewry. Established in 1933 as a committee against the persecution of Jews in Germany, the organization became the Comité contra el Racismo y el Anti-semitismo in December 1934, and assumed its present name in 1935. The organization expanded from a confederation of 28 institutions from all Jewish ethnic groups, all of them in *Buenos Aires, to an institution comprising 130 organizations – congregational, political, economic, cultural, and welfare – throughout *Argentina. DAIA's principal objectives, to fight antisemitism and to represent the Jewish community vis-à-vis the world, have remained the same since its founding, and the organization's role in these two areas has been recognized by the government as well as by most Jews. From its inception, DAIA's policies supported Zionism and its leaders were Zionists. The Communists and their sympathizers refused to be a part of this framework and, except for the period 1946–53, they ran their own separate communal organization. In 1936 DAIA participated in the establishment of the *World Jewish Congress and since then has served as its representative in Latin America for many years. In 1964 the Latin American Jewish Congress was established at the initiative of the then president of DAIA, Itzhak Goldenberg.

Despite Argentina's political instability, DAIA has succeeded in its tasks and continued to survive, in great measure, because of its avoidance of any sort of political identification with any party involved in Argentina's domestic politics. At one point, during the period of the first presidency of General Juan Peron (1946–55), the Organización Israelita Argentina

(OIA), which was politically identified with the Peronist party, tried to use its influence to set itself up as the sole representative of Argentinean Jewry. Another competing organization, with much greater support than the OIA, was the Jewish Communists, who, as mentioned, had been totally disconnected from central community institutions since 1953. After DAIA's decision on Dec. 21, 1952, to denounce the *Slánský trials in Prague and to demand that all members endorse this position, the Communists and pro-Communists federated in IKUF refused to lend their voice to this condemnation, seceded, and remained detached from the organized Jewish community. From time to time the IKUF published condemnations of various actions of the State of Israel, supported Palestinian positions, and organized its own rallies in memory of the victims of the Holocaust in many cities in the country.

DAIA was the focus of later disputes within the Jewish community. In 1976–83, under the military dictatorship, the government systematically organized the "disappearance" of its opponents and thousands of people were kidnapped, tortured, and murdered. It is estimated that the number of Jews affected by these actions far exceeds their percentage in the general population. Nevertheless, the victims and their families, and some observers analyzing the events of this period, argue that DAIA did not speak out strongly enough on behalf of the regime's Jewish victims.

During the years of the Holocaust, DAIA fought against antisemitism in Argentina, emphasizing the loyalty of the Jews to the country and their contribution to its life. It participated in broad alliances with liberal and left-wing groups which fought antisemitism and racism in general, and especially against Nazi organizations. The DAIA also organized protection against attacks, both verbal and physical, by various antisemitic elements. In many stages of its existence DAIA leadership assumed a militant stand, e.g., on June 28, 1962, when a nationwide strike by Jewish commercial enterprises was declared to protest the government's inaction against spreading antisemitic violence.

Like similar organizations in other countries, DAIA has been active in protesting the injustice suffered by Jews in the Soviet Union and in Arab countries and in exerting influence in such Jewish matters as the reparations payments from Germany and Austria. Although DAIA is a member of the executive board of the *Jewish Colonization Association, and has participated in the *Conference on Jewish Material Claims, the Memorial Foundation of Jewish Culture, and the World Conference of Jewish Organizations, its main objectives are still fighting antisemitism, creating favorable public opinion toward Jews, and gaining the support of government officials.

In order to make its operation more effective, DAIA established local and regional branches throughout Argentina. The branches report local events to the leadership in Buenos Aires, and receive assistance when local action is insufficient.

The federative character of DAIA has been questioned in the recent years. Some political sectors in the community argue that the elections to its Board should be universal and not restricted to the electors in its General Assembly, in which each institution has one vote. They claim that it is not just for an institution with thousands of members to have no more influence than a small institution. Others wish to maintain the equal representation of all sectors in the community, regardless of their number.

DAIA has taken a strong public position regarding the prevention and punishment of discrimination. DAIA supported the Antidiscrimination Law prepared by the jurist Prof. Bernardo Beiderman and approved by the Congress in 1988. Since the establishment in 1997 in the Ministry of Justice of Argentina's National Institute Against Discrimination and Racism (INADI), DAIA has been a member of its advisory council.

To achieve its objectives more efficiently, DAIA has conducted sociological investigations and public opinion surveys, independently or together with other institutions like the American Jewish Committee. DAIA also issues information bulletins which have appeared sporadically since the organization's inception and are now distributed via the Internet. In an effort to reach intellectuals, it has since 1967 published more than 20 volumes of *Indice*, a compilation of essays and research articles devoted to the social sciences.

[Leon Perez / Efraim Zadoff (2nd ed.)]

DAICHES, rabbinical family, originating in Lithuania, settled in Britain. LOEB HIRSH ARYEH ẒEVI B. DAVID (d. 1891), *dayyan* and *rosh yeshivah* in Kovno, wrote a commentary on the New Year prayers, *Zivḥei Teru'ah* (1867). His son, ISRAEL ḤAYYIM (1850–1937), born in Darshunishek, Lithuania, studied at Lithuanian yeshivot and, after a short time as rabbi in a Lithuanian community, became rabbi in Leeds, England. Daiches founded the Union of Orthodox Rabbis of England. Often lenient in his opinions, Daiches tried to adapt to modern technological advances, and occasionally was subjected to strong criticism (see his *Mikveh Yisrael*, 1912). His published work mainly concerned the Jerusalem Talmud, on which he wrote annotations; the responsa of Isaac b. Sheshet (Ribash; 1879); *Ma'arḥot Yisrael*, on *Oraḥ le-Ḥayyim* by Ḥayyim Segal of Ratzki (1879); and notes added to Last's edition of *Magen Avot* by Menahem ha-Meiri (1909, 1958). Daiches also published responsa (1870) and sermons (*Imrei Yosher*, 1887), and *Derashot Maharyaḥ* (with autobiography, 1930). He edited a rabbinic journal, *Beit Va'ad la-Ḥakhamim*, during 1902–04.

His son SAMUEL (1878–1949) was a rabbinic and Oriental scholar. Born in Vilna, Samuel studied with his father and at the Berlin Rabbinical Seminary. After serving as rabbi at Sunderland, England, Daiches became lecturer in Bible, Talmud, and Midrash at Jews' College, London, in 1908. He also took an active part in the work of B'nai B'rith, the Anglo-Jewish Association, the British Board of Deputies, the Jewish Agency, and Jewish relief organizations. In his earlier days Daiches published works on Babylonian antiquity and its influence on Judaism, including *Altbabylonische Rechtsur-*

kunden (1903), *Talmudische und Midraschische Parallelen zum babylonischen Schoeffungsepos* (1903), *Babylonia and Hebrew Literature* (1904), *Balaam – A Babylonian Baru* (1909), *Jews in Babylonia in the Times of Ezra and Nehemiah According to Babylonian Inscriptions* (1910), and *Babylonian Oil Magic* (1913). His other studies include *Studies in Psalms* (1930), *Study of the Talmud in Spain* (1921), and *Divorce in Jewish Law* (1926). Daiches contributed to learned German and English journals and to the Hebrew *Ha-Shilo'aḥ*. A semi-jubilee volume, *Ye Are My Witnesses*, was published in his honor in 1936. His *Essays and Addresses*, a memorial volume, appeared in 1955.

SALIS (1880–1945), another son of Israel Ḥayyim, was also a rabbi and author. Like his brother, he was born in Vilna and received his rabbinic education from his father and at the Berlin Rabbinical Seminary. After serving as rabbi at Hull and Sunderland, England, he went to Edinburgh (1918), where he became the spiritual leader and spokesman of Scottish Jewry. He too was active in B'nai B'rith and the Zionist movement. He published a volume of selected essays, *Aspects of Judaism* (1928), and was one of the translators of the Soncino Talmud. David *Daiches (1912–), writer and critic, was his son.

BIBLIOGRAPHY: Israelsham-Weindow (eds.), *Ye Are My Witnesses* (1936), foreword by J.H. Hertz; *Essays and Addresses* (1955), with a memoir by G. Webber; Epstein, in: S. Federbush (ed.), *Ḥokhmat Yisrael be-Ma'arav Eiropah*, 1 (1958), 500–1; D. Daiches, *Two Worlds: An Edinburgh Jewish Childhood* (1956).

DAICHES, DAVID (1912–2005), English scholar and literary critic. A son of Rabbi Salis Daiches (1880–1945), he was born in Sunderland, and spent most of his youth in Edinburgh. After teaching at Chicago, Cornell, and Cambridge universities he was appointed professor of English and dean of the School of English and American Studies at the University of Sussex on its foundation in 1961. His works include *Robert Burns* (1952), *Poetry and the Modern World* (1940), and *Critical Approaches to Literature* (1956). He also published *Literary Essays*, *More Literary Essays*, and *The Novel and the Modern World* (all 1969), studies of Joseph Conrad, James Joyce, D.H. Lawrence, and Virginia Woolf. In his autobiography *Two Worlds: An Edinburgh Jewish Childhood* (1956), Daiches records his own rebellion against Orthodox Judaism, represented for him by his father, whom he deeply admired. Daiches maintained an interest in Hebraic matters in his scholarly writings, notably in his study *The King James Version of the English Bible* (1941). Daiches also produced another volume of autobiography, *Promised Lands: A Portrait of My Father* (1997).

ADD. BIBLIOGRAPHY: ODNB online for Salis Daiches.

[Murray Roston]

DAINOW, ẒEVI HIRSCH BEN ZE'EV WOLF (1832–1877), Russian preacher known as "the Maggid of Slutsk" after his native town Slutsk, in the district of Minsk. Dainow was regarded in his time as "the preacher of the Haskalah." He preached in favor of a combination of Torah with Haskalah and in popular Yiddish rebuked his compatriots for their estrangement from manual labor and stressed the need for reform in education, advocating that the *ḥeder* be abolished and Jewish children study in government schools. Dainow was widely known for his personal integrity; he was fearless in his preaching, favoring no one, not even the *maskilim*, though he regarded himself as close to them. This attitude and his criticism of the leaders of the old school roused against him widespread opposition, particularly in religious circles, and in many places the doors of the synagogue were closed to him. In his articles in the periodicals *Ha-Maggid* and *Ha-Mattif*, Dainow described the troubles and persecutions that were his lot. For a time Dainow was active throughout Russia on behalf of "The Society for the Promotion of Culture Among Jews of Russia." The Haskalah writers, including J.L. *Gordon, supported him and corresponded with him. The unremitting hostility of his opponents compelled him to leave Russia, and in 1874 he moved to London where he continued – as advised by J.L. Gordon – his role as preacher to the communities of Russian and Polish immigrants until his death. In London he was at first harassed by Chief Rabbi N.M. *Adler, but later was reconciled with him as the chief rabbi became convinced of his integrity. Dainow also founded a Hebrew school in London. One of his sermons, entitled *Kevod Melekh* in honor of Czar Alexander II, was published in 1869; he left other works in manuscript.

BIBLIOGRAPHY: J.M. Rosenthal, *Toledot Ḥevrat Marbei Haskalah be-Yisrael be-Ereẓ Rusyah*, 1 (1885), 69f.; 2 (1890), 207f; J.L. Gordon, *Iggerot* (1894), nos. 60, 62, 77, 78, 97, 98, 101, 107, 108, 111; J. Meisl, *Haskalah. Geschichte der Aufklaerungsbewegung unter den Juden in Russland* (1919), 174; J. Lipschitz, *Zikhron Ya'akov*, 2 (1927), 62–64, 194; Citron, in: *Hadoar*, 9–10 (1930–31), 60f., 75–77; S.J. Gliksberg, *Ha-Derashah be-Yisrael* (1940), 427; *Pinkas Slutsk u-Venoteha* (1962), 100, 307f.

[Yehoshua Horowitz]

DALESKI, HILLEL (1926–), scholar of English literature. Daleski was born in South Africa. In 1944 he joined the South African army and fought in Italy. In 1947 he graduated in English and history from Witwatersrand University in South Africa. In 1948 he volunteered for *MAHAL and fought in Israel's War of Independence. In 1952 he received his M.A. in English from Witwatersrand University and settled Israel with his wife and infant daughter. In 1963 he received his Ph.D. from the Hebrew University of Jerusalem, teaching there from 1954 and becoming a professor in 1976. He also served as provost of the School for Overseas Students in 1973–76 and was twice head of the English department, in 1968–70 and 1984–85. In 1985 he was president of the International Dickens Society. He was also professor in the English departments of Tel Aviv and Ben-Gurion universities and consultant in the establishment of the English department in Haifa University. Daleski became a member of the Israeli Academy of Sciences and Humanities in 1993 and an honorary member of the American Academy of Arts and Sciences in 1999. He published numerous essays and eight books dealing with D.H. Lawrence, Charles Dickens, Joseph Conrad, Thomas Hardy, and others. In 2000 he was awarded the Israel Prize for literature studies.

[Shaked Gilboa (2nd ed.)]

DALET (Heb. ד; דָּלֶת), the fourth letter of the Hebrew alphabet; its numerical value is 4. It is assumed that the earliest form of the *dalet* – as it appears in the Proto-Sinaitic inscriptions – was a pictograph of a fish (Heb. *dag*) ⊳◇. This developed in the South-Arabic script into 𐩵, and the early Phoenician *dalet* became a triangle ◁, which survived in the *delta* of the Greek alphabet: Δ. In the later Phoenician script the left angle was curved and the right stroke developed a downward tail 𐤃. The ancient Hebrew *dalet* also has an upper stroke drawn leftward 𐤃 and thus in Samaritan too: ࠃ.

While the Phoenician cursive tends to open the circular head at its lower part 𐤃, the Aramaic script opens the top of this letter 𐡃. This developed into the Jewish ד. As the *dalet* resembles the *resh*, it happens that both letters were written in the same way. Thus, in Syriac only diacritic marks distinguish between them. The Arabic د is an offshoot of the Aramaic *dalet*, which developed through the Nabatean cursive.

The modern cursive Hebrew dalet is a result of emphasizing the right upper angle, in order to distinguish it from the resh, and it developed as follows: ד → ד → ד → ד. See *Alphabet, Hebrew.

[Joseph Naveh]

DĀLIYAT AL-KARMIL, Druze village in Israel, on Mt. Carmel, 8 mi. (13 km.) south of Haifa. The village has existed at least since the early Middle Ages, but most of the present inhabitants' ancestors, hailing from the Lebanon, seem to have settled there under the rule of the Druze governor Fakhr al-Dīn in the 17th century. From 1882 to 1887, Lawrence *Oliphant lived there together with his secretary, Naphtali Herz *Imber. After 1948 Dāliyat al-Karmil progressed rapidly, receiving municipal council status in 1951 and attaining a population of 5,200 in 1968. Its economy was based on hill agriculture and local handicrafts, with many of the inhabitants employed as skilled laborers in Haifa or elsewhere. At the end of 2002 the population of Dāliyat al-Karmil was 13,300, with the village's jurisdiction extending over an area of 3.5 sq. mi. (9 sq. km.). In 2003 it was united with *Usafiyya as the city of Karmil.

[Efraim Orni / Shaked Gilboa (2nd ed.)]

DALIYYAH (Heb. דָּלִיָּה), kibbutz in Israel, in the Manasseh Hills of N.W. Samaria; affiliated with Kibbutz Arẓi ha-Shomer ha-Ẓair, founded as a "*tower and stockade" settlement on May 2, 1939, by pioneers from Romania and Germany. It constituted part of the "settlement bridge" between the two principal Jewish regions of the time – the Sharon Plain and the Jezreel Valley. In 1968 Daliyyah numbered 610 inhabitants; in 2002, 739. Its economy was based on intensive farming (field crops, orchards) and two industrial enterprises: "Arad" for the production of water meters and fine mechanical instruments, and "Zohar" for soaps and detergents. Dance festivals were held every few years at the kibbutz's open-air amphitheater, a tradition that ceased to exist. The name ("vine tendril" in Hebrew) was taken from Dāliyat al-Rūḥa, a former Arab village in the vicinity.

[Efraim Orni / Shaked Gilboa (2nd ed.)]

DALLAS, a financial and industrial center in North Texas and the second largest city in the state. First settled in 1844, the city had an estimated population of 1,188,580 in 1997, including a Jewish population of approximately 50,000. New figures released in 2003 estimate the total population for the 16-county North Texas region, which includes Dallas, to be almost six million.

The earliest Jewish settlement began in 1870 with the arrival of about 15 families. The first Jews were mainly retail merchants and several of them, among whom the Sanger and Kahn families were outstanding, played a vital role in the commercial development of the city. The first organized Jewish institution dates to 1872, when the Hebrew Benevolent Association was created; although it was primarily a charitable institution, it sponsored the first High Holiday services. A Jewish cemetery was dedicated the same year, and in 1873 a local B'nai B'rith chapter was formed.

Temple Emanu-El was Dallas' first congregation, founded in 1874 and allied with the Reform movement; it had a membership of 2,800 families in 2005. A second congregation, Shearith Israel, established as an Orthodox synagogue in 1884, became Conservative, and had 1,480 families. Another Orthodox congregation, Tiferet Israel, was founded in 1890 and had 325 families. Nearly 1,050 families belonged to the Reform Temple Shalom, which was organized in 1965. Dallas had 20 congregations – four Conservative, eight Reform, seven Orthodox, and one traditional. The Rabbinical Advisory Council founded in 1944 (now the Rabbinic Association of Greater Dallas) represents these synagogues.

There were seven Jewish day and high schools ranging from Orthodox to Reform, with a total attendance of more than 1,200 children. Thanks to a community-wide Capital Campaign which raised more than $55 million for the construction and renovation of ten agency facilities, many of these schools enjoyed new or refurbished buildings. Among them was a new state-of-the-art building for Solomon Schechter Academy and a new 8.5-acre campus for Akiba and Yavneh Academies which was slated to encompass Judaica and artwork by noted Jewish artist David Moss.

The Jewish Welfare Federation, now called the Jewish Federation of Greater Dallas, was organized in 1911 as a centralized agency for all Dallas Jewish social welfare services and fundraising for local, national, and overseas needs. It sponsors a Jewish Community Relations Council, composed of representatives of all major Jewish organizations, and a Leadership Development Group, founded in 1952. The Federation had a Jewish education department which provided teacher workshops, adult education initiatives, and programs such as Teen

Tour and Gift of Israel which enable students to travel to the Promised Land.

The Federation is a member of the United Way of Metropolitan Dallas, United Jewish Communities, the National Jewish Community Relations Advisory Council, and the Jewish Education Service of North America. Its Annual Campaign supported a network of more than 43 human and social service programs for Jews locally, nationally, in Israel, and overseas. The 2004 Annual Campaign raised an unprecedented $9.5 million for humanitarian needs.

There were three constituent agencies supported by the Federation: Jewish Family Service (JFS), the Legacy Senior Communities, Inc., and the Jewish Community Center of Dallas (the J). Jewish Family Service offered counseling, financial assistance, and job placement to both families and individuals. In 2004, 2,176 adults and children received food from the JFS food pantry. JFS relocated to new facilities in 2002 thanks to funds raised through the aforementioned Capital Campaign. The Legacy Senior Communities, Inc. is the parent company of Golden Acres-Dallas Home for Jewish Aged and the planned Legacy at Willow Bend. Golden Acres, opened in 1953, offers care and treatment for the elderly; it has adjacent apartment units for independent living and manages ECHAD, housing for low-income elderly. The Legacy at Willow Bend was planned as an up-and-coming premiere retirement community immersed in Jewish tradition and focused on independent living and an active lifestyle. The Julius Schepps Community Center, now the Jewish Community Center of Dallas, served more than 7,000 members. The J provided services which helped promote healthy individual and family living. Services included an early childhood program, programs for children and teens, an extensive physical education service, athletic leagues, a series of single adult activities, adult education classes, senior activities, cultural arts programs, and summer day camps. Funds from the Capital Campaign helped the J build a new natatorium and fitness center, which were completed in time for the Maccabi Games held in Dallas in summer of 2005. In addition to its three constituent agencies, the Federation also supported 11 local beneficiary agencies which provided a wide variety of humanitarian services.

By the 1970s, the old social and economic distinctions between the German-Jewish settlers who first came to Dallas and the later immigrants from Eastern Europe had largely been erased, and descendants of both groups participated on an equal basis in communal life and leadership. Also, the overall picture changed from the days when Jews were primarily merchants. Members of the Jewish community were engaged in a wide variety of business enterprises, including garment manufacturing, paper and air-conditioning companies, and finance. There were also a large number of Jewish professionals, including lawyers, doctors, engineers, technology professionals, and business consultants.

Jewish community relations had their stormy days in the 1920s, when the Ku Klux Klan was highly active. Even though relations improved, as late as the early 1980s there were still several social clubs that maintained an exclusionary policy toward Jews. In business and communal activities, however, the Jewish community has long been integrated into the Dallas community at large.

For more than 30 years, Southern Methodist University and Temple Emanu-El have sponsored the Community Course, which makes art, music, drama, and lecture programs available to the entire city. The Bridwell Library of the Perkins School of Theology houses two large collections of Judaica, the Sadie and David Lefkowitz Collection and the Levi A. Olan Collection. In Dallas' civic, cultural, and political life, too, Jews play a significant role. There have been Jewish presidents of the symphony orchestra, the chamber of commerce, and the Dallas Opera. In 1970 Stanley *Marcus, who was active in all of these, was a leader of the powerful Citizens' Council; Carl Flaxman was director of the Health, Education, and Welfare Office, which serves the entire southwest; and Julius Schepps was especially active in the Fair Park Association, which controls the famous Cotton Bowl (the New Year's Day football game). Dallas has also had three Jewish mayors: Adlene Harrison (1976), Annette Strauss (1987–91), and Laura Miller (elected 2002). Jewish city councilpersons in 2005 included Lois Finkelman and Mitchell Rasansky.

[Levi A. Olan / Jef Tngley (2nd ed.)]

BIBLIOGRAPHY: H. Cohen, in: AJHSP, 2 (1894), 139–56.

°**DALMAN, GUSTAF HERMANN** (until 1886 **G.A. Marx**; 1855–1941), German Protestant theologian, philologist, and Palestinologist. In his youth Dalman was closely associated with the Missionary Church Brotherhood ("Bruedergemeine") at Herrnhut and spent his last days with them. An important contact for him was Franz *Delitzsch, who recommended him in 1887 to the Institutum Judaicum in Leipzig, where Dalman taught for 15 years, from 1895 as assistant professor. He was the first director of the German Evangelical Institute for Antiquity in Jerusalem from 1902 to 1917 where he contributed a number of important papers and subsequently served as professor and head of the Institute of Palestinology in Greifswald (later the Gustav-Dalman-Institut). Dalman was a prolific writer in many fields including (1) Theology: *Der leidende und sterbende Messias* (1888); *Jesaja 53* (1914^2); *Worte Jesu* (1930^2); (2) Studies of Palestinian Aramaic (in which he included the Aramaic of Targum Onkelos): *Grammatik des juedisch-palaestinischen Aramaeisch* (1905^5, repr. 1989); *Aramaeische Dialektproben* (1927^2); *Aramaeisch-neuhebraeisches Woerterbuch* (1922^2, repr. 1967); (3) Historical geography and topography of Ereẓ Israel: *Petra* (1901); *Neue Petraforschungen* (1912); *Orte und Wege Jesu* (1924^2, repr. 1967; *Sacred Sites and Ways*, 1935), a study which also treats the talmudic sources on the sites where Jesus lived and taught; *Hundert Fliegerbilder aus Palaestina* (1925); *Jerusalem und sein Gelaende* (1930, repr. 1972), a comprehensive study of the Holy City, its terrain, names of sites, antiquities, topographic identifications, and descriptions of the contemporary Jerusalem community; (4) Palestinian folklore: *Palaestinensischer Diwan* (1901), a collection of Arabic folksongs from Palestine, Transjordan, and Syria; *Arbeit und Sitte in Palaestina* (7 vols., 1928–42; repr. 1964), dealing with all aspects of the Arab economy of Palestine, its terminology, and customs with continual references to the Bible and Talmud. From 1905 until 1926 Dalman was editor of the *Palaestinajahrbuch*. Dalman's autobiography was published in 1928. He had a profound knowledge of Jewish sources, especially the Mishnah and Talmud. Although he was (with Delitzsch) one of the few Christian theologians of the time who fought ardently against antisemitism, his position was always a missionary Christian one, convinced by the superiority of Christianity. His writings on post-biblical Judaism were especially marked by traditional anti-Judaic clichés, the Jewish denominations and intellectual trends in contemporary Germany seen only as developments leading to final conversion to Christianity.

ADD. BIBLIOGRAPHY: J. Maennchen, *Leben und Wirken* (1978); idem, *Dalman als Palaestinawissenschaftler* (1994); C. Wiese, *Wissenschaft des Judentums und protestantische Theologie* (1999), index.

[Irene Garbell / Marcus Pyka (2nd ed.)]

DALTON (Heb. דַּלְתּוֹן), moshav in central Upper Galilee, 4 mi. (7 km.) N. of Safed. During most of the Middle Ages, Dalton had a considerable Jewish population and it was believed that the tomb of R. *Yose ha-Gelili was located there. In the Crusader period, *Benjamin of Tudela noted a Jewish community at Dalton. The site has remnants of a synagogue of the talmudic period and numerous ancient rock tombs and prehistoric dolmens in its vicinity. The area of the Muslim-Arab village (Dallāta), abandoned in the 1948 War of Independence, was settled in 1950 by a Ha-Kibbutz ha-Dati group which had previously maintained the settlement of *Biriyyah. In 1953 settlers from Tripolitania set up a moshav affiliated to the Ha-Po'el ha-Mizrachi Moshavim Association. Dalton's economy was largely based on hill farming. In 1968 it had 610 inhabitants. In 2002 its population was 688. Dalton became known for its boutique winery (named after the moshav), producing about 700,000 bottles a year from nearby vineyards.

[Efraim Orni / Shaked Gilboa (2nd ed.)]

DALVEN, RACHEL (1905–1992), translator from Greek to English and historian of the Jews of Ioannina, Greece, where she lived from the age of five until early adulthood and which was the community of origin of her family. She translated the Greek poet Constantine Cavafy (*Complete Poems of Cavafy*, 1961) into English when he was unknown. She also translated her cousin Yosef Eliyia, the noted Greek Jewish poet from Ioannina. Her translations were first included in her anthology *Modern Greek Poetry* (1949, 1971). In 1977, she published her translation of the poet Yannis Ritsos, *The Fourth Dimension*.

Dalven received her Ph.D. from New York University and taught drama and English literature at Ladycliff College in Highland Falls, New York. She edited the academic journal *The Sephardic Scholar* at Yeshiva University and devoted over six decades of her life to the research of the Jews of Ioannina, Greece, the largest remaining Romaniote Judeo-Greek community of the 20th century. In 1990 she published *The Jews of Ioannina* with Cadmus Press of Philadelphia. She wrote numerous articles on the traditions, culture, and history of Ioanniote Jewry. She also wrote a biography of Anna Comnena and numerous plays, including *Our Kind of People* on Greek-Jewish immigrants in the United States. In 1973 she was the recipient of the Gold Key Award of the Columbia Scholastic Press Association of the Graduate School of Journalism of Columbia University.

BIBLIOGRAPHY: S. Bowman, "Rachel Dalven: An Appreciation," in: *Bulletin of Judaeo-Greek Studies*, 11 (Winter 1992), 34.

[Yitzchak Kerem (2nd ed.)]

DAMA, SON OF NETINA, according to the aggadah (TY Peah 1:1, 15c, Kidd. 1:7, 61b), a gentile council president (Gr. *patēr boulēs*) who lived in Ashkalon sometime in the first century C.E. According to R. Joḥanan, when R. *Eliezer was asked about the extent of the obligation to honor one's parents, he pointed to Dama as a perfect example of filial piety. The outline of the story as told in the Jerusalem Talmud is as follows: It happened once that one of the precious stones fell out of the High Priest's breastplate, and was lost. Seeking a replacement, the sages were referred to a certain Dama ben Netina who purportedly had the exact jewel they required in his possession. They offered him one hundred dinar, and Dama accepted their offer. When he went to fetch the jewel he discovered that he could not access it without waking his father. So he returned and informed his clients that he could not provide them with the item they sought. Assuming that he was trying to renegotiate the price, they increased their offer until they reached a sum of 1000 dinar. When his father finally woke up he brought them the jewel, and they were still willing to pay him their final offer of 1000 dinar. Dama, however, was only willing to accept their initial offer of one hundred, saying: "What? Do you think that I would sell the honor of my fathers for mere coins? I refuse to derive any tangible benefit from the honor of my fathers!" The Jerusalem Talmud goes on to ask what heavenly reward Dama received for such meritorious behavior. The answer given was that on that very night a pure red heifer – essential, according to Num. 19, for attaining ritual purity – was born to Dama's cow, and so the Jews purchased this extremely rare item from him for a small fortune.

In the past, Jewish historians have assumed that talmudic stories like these reflect accurate and reliable descriptions of events that occurred in the Land of Israel in the last decades before the destruction of the Second Temple. As a result some Jewish historians have sought to derive from this story, and from the parallel version in the Bavli (Kidd. 31a), important historical information concerning both the actions of the Sanhedrin (Büchler), and the forms of local Roman government (Krauss) during that period. Recent research has shown that these stories are often highly sophisticated literary works, reflecting multiple levels of editorial revision. Critical study of this story has shown that the literary and historical foundation of the tale lies in what might seem at first sight to be a secondary issue: the red heifer which was born to Dama's cow as a reward for his meritorious behavior.

In the earliest level of tannaitic literature (*Sifre Zuta*, Num. 19:2, p. 300) we find a dispute between R. Eliezer and his companions, in which R. Eliezer maintained that it is forbidden to purchase a red heifer from a gentile. His companions, who held that it is permissible, brought a legal precedent in order to support their position: "There was a case in which they bought a [red] heifer from the Arabs, and they called it *damat damat*, and it would run back and forth." In the parallel version in the Tosefta (Para 2:1, p. 631) the case is described somewhat differently: "There was a case in which they bought a [red heifer] from the Gentiles in Sidon, and it was called *doma*." Neither of these two versions informs us as to R. Eliezer's response, if any, to the legal precedent brought by his opponents, and which apparently refutes his position and permits the purchase of a red heifer from a gentile.

In the Jerusalem Talmud's version of the story cited above, a number of additional changes have been introduced into the narrative. First the story has moved from Sidon to Ashkelon. Second the name *doma* has ceased to be the name of the heifer, and has become *Dama*, the name of the heifer's gentile owner. Third, and most importantly, the dramatic focus of the story has shifted. It is no longer concerned with the halakhic issue of whether or not it is permissible to purchase a red heifer from a gentile. The central issue has moved to the moral and religious plane. The storyteller in the Jerusalem Talmud wants to know through what extraordinary act of righteousness did this gentile in Ashkelon merit the almost miraculous birth of a pure red heifer from his cow in the first place. In answering this question, he has told a tale of a man whose behavior reflected universal moral values – behavior recognized and rewarded by God because of its inherent worth, not because it was explicitly commanded, and with no regard to the religious affiliation of the man himself.

This basic story line was embellished and expanded in the Jerusalem Talmud, and further refined and elaborated in the Babylonian Talmud. It was told how his mother once humiliated him in public, striking him with her shoe while he was sitting in session as the head of the city council. Out of respect for his mother, he suffered the humiliation in silence, and even bent down to pick up the shoe which had fallen from her hand to return it to her (cf. Deut. R. 1:15). The Jerusalem Talmud goes on to say that Dama would never sit upon any stone that his father had sat upon, and that even after his father's death he would continue to treat the stone as an object of reverence. The Babylonian Talmud further develops the theme of this gentile's righteousness, stating that he limited the amount he was willing to take for the red heifer born into his flock to the sum that he had given up in the previous transaction over the jewel for the priestly breastplate, "although I know that you are prepared to pay all the money in the world for it" (Av. Zar. 23b).

BIBLIOGRAPHY: A. Büchler, *The Sanhedrin* (Heb., 1975), 88; A. Büchler, *Studies in the Period of the Mishnah and the Talmud* (Heb., 1968), 149; S. Krauss, *Persia and Rome in the Talmud and the Midrashim* (Heb., 1948), 120; J. Frankel, *Studies in the Intellectual World of the Aggadic Story* (Heb., 1981), 141–144; S. Valer, *Women and Femininity in the Stories of the Talmud* (Heb., 1993), 96–99, 134–137; S. Friedman, "On the Historical Figure of Dama ben Netina: A Chapter in the Study of Talmudic Aggadah," in: *The Jonah Frankel Jubilee Volume* (Hebrew, forthcoming).

[Stephen G. Wald (2nd ed.)]

DAMAGES.

Assessment

In Jewish law, once the tortfeasor's liability for the damage has been established and he is ordered to compensate for the loss, the measure of damages requires determination. This is done by assessing the market price of the damaged object prior to and subsequent to sustained damage (see BK 84b on injury suffered by an animal or person); the difference is the amount which the tortfeasor has to pay (BK 11a). In this way, the party who has suffered damage is enabled to purchase on the market an object such as was his before it was damaged, which damage is thereby annulled. If the damaged object is not sold separately on the market but as part of a larger unit only, the difference between the assessed market price of the unit – i.e., undamaged and with the damaged part – is the measure of compensation. Thus, for example, the owner of an animal which has consumed a row of unripe fruit in another's field, does not pay according to the value of the fruit eaten by his animal – as no one buys unripe fruit, which is valueless. Instead – it being customary for merchants to buy a large field of yet unripened fruit – the market price of the fruit in a large field is assessed, with and without the row in question respectively, and the difference is the measure of damages. Another opinion maintains that the measure is the difference between the respective market values of the land itself when sold with and without the row of fruit (see *Yam shel Shelomo* BK 6:18). The sages of the Talmud are divided on the question of the size of the field to be taken as the standard for valuing the damaged row, i.e., whether it should be 60 times the size of the row, or larger (BK 58b, 59b). Similarly, if injury is caused to the embryo of an animal, the measure of damages is the difference between the market values of the animal, pregnant and otherwise respectively, but the embryo itself is not assessed, for it is valueless – nor is it assessed as if it were already born (*Shitah Mekubbeẓet* BK 47a, s.v. *amar rava*).

In terms of this assessment, the tortfeasor does not compensate the injured party for any future loss of profits which result from the injury (Tos. to BK 34a, s.v. *shilmale*), nor for the loss of any benefits which could have been derived from the use of the damaged object, except insofar as such may already be accounted for in reducing the market price of the damaged object, at the time the damage was sustained. This rule is consistent with the principle that the tortfeasor is liable only for such damage as he ought to have foreseen at the time of his wrongful conduct, but not for any other or more extensive damage (see *Torts). The reason for this is that any loss of profits not reflected in the market price is a loss which is not foreseeable, and one which people accordingly do not make allowance for in the price they are prepared to pay on the market. For this reason too the tortfeasor does not compensate for any damage which the injured party could have avoided after suffering injury, since the former could not have foreseen that the latter would not do so. (Tos. to BK 10b, s.v. *lo*; BK 85b, on the failure to observe medical instructions in a case of personal injury.)

Where a person could not have foreseen that his conduct would cause damage, he is in the position of an *"anus"* (i.e., the consequences are caused by a mischance) and is absolved from liability (see *Torts); however if he benefits from the damage caused to another, as in the case where his animal eats vegetables left by another on a public road so that he does not have to feed it, he is liable to the injured party to the extent of the benefit derived (BK 20a:55b).

Assessment of Damages for Personal Injuries

A person who willfully, or by gross negligence (*karov la-mezid*), inflicts bodily harm (*ḥabbalah*) on another, must pay compensation to the latter, not only for the *nezek* ("loss," "damage") but also under four additional headings: *ẓa'ar* ("pain and suffering"), *rippui* ("medical expenses"), *shevet* ("loss of earnings"), and *boshet* ("humiliation"; detailed in ḤM 420). *Nezek* is assessed as in the case of damage to property, i.e., by comparing the injured party to a slave and estimating the respective prices he would fetch if sold as such on the market before and after the injury, the difference being the measure of compensation. This estimate takes account of the difference between the remuneration that could be earned for the heavy work he would have done if healthy and that which he shall earn for the work he can do having a disability (compare Abbaye's words *"shevet gedolah,"* BK 86a; and R. Isaac in TJ, BK 8:3, 6b). *Ẓa'ar* is assessed by estimating what a person, like the injured, would be prepared to pay to avoid the pain resulting from the injury as by way of narcotics or a drug; *rippui* is an estimate of the medical expenses to be incurred by the injured in order to be cured; *shevet* is the estimated loss of remuneration which the injured could have earned during the period of his illness; *boshet* is assessed according to the social position of both parties (BK 8:1). Because of the difficulty in measuring *boshet* in monetary terms, the sages at various times determined fixed measures for various acts of *boshet*, thus, e.g., 200 *zuz* for a slap on the face, 400 *zuz* for pulling a man's hair or spitting on him – the *tannaim* already being in dispute as to whether these measures were for the rich or for the poor (BK 8:6). Where the injured party suffers damage under one or some of the five headings only, the injuring party compensates him accordingly: thus if the injured party suffers *boshet* or *rippui* only, the latter compensates him under these headings alone.

Compensation for damage under the above four headings, excluding *nezek*, is payable only in the case of bodily harm inflicted willfully, or by gross negligence, caused by the wrongdoer's person (Rashi to BK end of 26a). There is no liability for *boshet* in the absence of an intention to harm or shame (BK 8:1). The interpretation of the commentators is that there is liability for *nezek* even when resulting from mischance (*ones*), and no liability under the other four headings except when resulting from negligent or willful conduct. But it may also be argued that there is liability for *nezek* in the case of negligence only, while a man is not liable under the other four headings unless the conduct is willful, or grossly negligent. It would seem that the reason for confining liability under the aforesaid four headings to the case where an injury is willfully inflicted by one person on the body of another (and not by a person on an animal or by an animal on a person), whereas for *nezek* there is liability in all the above cases, stems from the principle that the tortfeasor's liability for compensation is confined to such damage only as he could have foreseen at the time of causing the injury. Hence, inasmuch as damage under the said four categories of compensation varies from one injured party to another, the tortfeasor cannot be required to have foreseen the measures of each relevant to the particular injured party except when he has willfully inflicted a bodily injury by his own hand, because in such case, having seen the injured party to whom he was about to cause harm, he should have known the measure of *ẓa'ar*, rippui, shevet, and *boshet* peculiar to this particular injured person. Insofar as the said four categories of damage accompany every case of *ḥabbalah* and thus their scope should therefore be foreseen by the tortfeasor, they are apparently already included in the assessment of the *nezek*. Moreover, even where compensation is payable under all five headings specifically, payment is made to the extent of the foreseeable measure of each only and in no larger measure. Thus if an assessment of compensation for an injury has been made, this amount of damages only is payable, even if the health of the injured party should thereafter deteriorate unexpectedly (BK 91a).

Already in the talmudic period – in Babylonia, and certainly in other countries – many judges would not give judgment for damages under one or more of these five categories. Some would not award compensation for *boshet*, or even *nezek*; it was not necessary as a deterrent because damage of this type was not common, and the judges outside Ereẓ Israel, not being ordained by the rabbis of Ereẓ Israel, did not feel themselves qualified to deal with such matters (BK 84b). Also in the post-talmudic period damages were not awarded under one or more of these categories according to law (Sh. Ar., ḤM 1:2), but rather the tortfeasor would be placed under a ban or punished in some other manner until he effected a reconciliation with the injured party and reached agreement with him on an equitable compensation (*Piskei ha-Rosh* BK 8:3).

Payment of damages may be made in money or in chattels having a monetary value and sold on the market; land, to serve as a means of payment, must be "of the best" (*ibid.* BK 7a). The damages are looked upon as a debt due to the injured party, in the same way as a loan or any other debt. However there are traces in the Talmud of a view that payment of damages is a penalty serving to punish the wrongdoer for his conduct and is not merely compensation (Albeck, *Hashlamot ve-Tosafot* to his edition of the Mishnah BK 1:3). Some sages hold the opinion that payment of "half-damages" in the case of *shor tam* (ox that has not gored before – see *Avot Nezikin) is a fine (BK 15a), and therefore payment of "half-damages" was not sanctioned in Babylonia and in other countries as from the talmudic period (BK 15b).

The law of the State of Israel determines that the damages due to the injured party are the amount required to restore him, subjectively speaking, to the position in which he would have been but for suffering the injury. The measure of damages varies therefore not only according to the damage actually incurred, but also in accordance with the individual circumstances of the injured party.

[Shalom Albeck]

A Fixed Sum for Damages

PAYMENT. As noted above, for certain types of damage the Sages assessed and determined payment of a fixed sum.

The Jerusalem District Court adjudicated a case concerning a man who publicly hit another man in the face with his fist (CA [Jer] 507/00 *Silberg u Sha'ir*, 2 PSM (5760) 289). The parties requested that the Court adjudicate their case in accordance with Jewish Law. The assailant argued that payment in this kind of case fell into the category of a fine so that in accordance with Maimonides' ruling, he should only have to pay the fixed sum determined by the halakhah: "Many blows involve humiliation and some pain, but no irreparable bodily injury. The Sages previously assigned fixed sums for such blows… and all of them constitute fines. The fixed sum paid covers pain [*ẓa'ar*], embarrassment [*boshet*], medical expenses [*rpipui*] and lost work time [*shevet*]…" (Maim. Yad, Hovel u-Mazik 3.8)

The Court (Judge Y. Adiel) rejected the assailant's argument, relying on Bet Yosef (at Tur, ḤM 420.34;), who rules that Maimonides' comments only refer to a case in which the blow lacks the force required to cause severe bodily injury. Only then does the fixed sum replace individual compensation under each of the main headings of damage. In the case of a stronger blow, one liable to cause severe physical injury, even Maimonides would concur that compensation must be made for each of the relevant headings of damage, based upon a separate assessment for each heading.

In the case at hand, the Court determined that the blow was capable of causing severe bodily harm; hence, the payment of a fixed sum was not applicable. Even so, in the absence of any irreversible injury, compensation was only awarded under the four heads of damage. (Maim., ibid., 2.2; Sh. Ar., ḤM 420.5).

Damages – Li-Fenim mi-Shurat ha-Din (Beyond the Letter of the Law)

There are cases in Jewish law in which the strict law does not allow the court to impose payment on the assailant, yet the assailant is still liable under "the Law of Heaven" – that is, morally culpable. The authorities ruled that the practical import of such liability is that the Court must inform the guilty party that, while it cannot impose monetary payment on him, he is still morally obligated to discharge his liability and pay the plaintiff (R. Shlomo Luria, *Yam Shel Shlomo*, BK 6.6). Other authorities even ruled that he is disqualified as a witness until he pays, because he is in possession of stolen money (Me'iri, on BK 56a).

On occasion, the contemporary rabbinical courts obligate the assailant to pay part of the damages by choosing the path of compromise (see *Compromise). For example, when damage occurs by way of *gerama* (damage resulting indirectly from the assailant's action. See *Gerama and Garme). In such cases, the courts do not obligate the assailant to pay in the framework of damages, but instead rule that he must pay under the law of compromise. The rabbinical court ensures the execution of justice by resorting to the institution of compromise when the strict law does not provide a remedy (see, e.g., the rulings of the Kiryat Arba Regional Court, vol. 1, page 205, and the index there; Rabbi Z.N. Goldberg, "*Shivḥei ha-Pesharah*," in: *Mishpetei Areẓ* (2002).

As noted, another means of achieving the same goal is by the principle of *li-fenim mi-shurat ha-din* ("being more generous than the law requires"). This issue was adjudicated in the Israeli civil court. In the Kitan ruling (CA 350/77 *Kitan v.* Weiss, PD 33(2) 785), the Israeli Supreme Court reversed a lower court's award of compensation for damages in a claim submitted by the relatives of a man murdered by a worker in a factory. The worker killed the man with a gun given him by the factory for work purposes. The respondents argued that, due to the worker's problematic mental state, the factory should have foreseen that his possession of a weapon was fraught with danger. Hence, they argued, the factory should be required to compensate the victim's family. The appeal was rejected due to "lack of the required causal connection between the appellant's (i.e. the factory's) negligence, and the killing of the deceased (page 808 of the ruling).

In terms of strict law all three presiding judges (Justices Shamgar, Witkon, and Elon) concurred with this conclusion. In his ruling, Judge Elon added that it would be appropriate for the factory to go beyond the strict law and compensate the relatives of the deceased:

> For Judaism has a tradition, and there is a fundamental principle of Jewish Law, that along with strict liability, there is an additional obligation to act beyond the dictates of strict law (*li-fenim mi-shurat ha-din*). It is of particular significance here that this obligation found its chief expressions in the field of torts in a case relating to a problem identical to the one at hand. (*ibid.*, 809).

Judge Elon states further:

> In the development of the principle of "going beyond the letter of the law" in Jewish law, many halakhic authorities took the position that in certain circumstances this approach is mandatory. This is attested to by Rabbi Joel Sirkes, one of the leading

Sages in Poland at the end of the 16th and the first half of the 17th century, in his commentary Bayit Hadash (Baḥ) on the Tur: "It is customary in every Jewish court to compel the wealthy to pay where proper and appropriate, even where the letter of the law goes against it" (Baḥ on Tur, ḤM 12.4; see Menachem Elon, *Jewish Law,* 1:155f.).

This approach is anchored in the broader worldview of Jewish law, that finds expression, inter alia, in the well-known principle that "the giving of charity may be compelled" (TB, Ket. 49b), although this principle too is only exercised under certain conditions and circumstances. As is known, this rule constitutes the basis for the duty to provide maintenance for children and relatives under certain circumstances, even when this duty does not exist under strict law (see *Jewish Law,* 1:116f).

In the Israeli legal system, no person is compelled to act more generously than the law requires; such action is left to the [personal] initiative and will of the litigant. Yet under certain circumstances, it seems appropriate for the expression of such a wish to originate with the judge sitting on the dais-and here, too, the tradition of Jewish law provides a firm basis for this approach. In this context, Justice Elon wrote elsewhere that:

> The halakhic system clearly distinguishes between normative rulings, accompanied by judicially enforceable sanctions, and rulings lacking such sanction. Yet the source and background common to legal rulings and to moral imperatives have brought about the following substantive phenomenon within the world of *halakhah*: The legal system itself; in its role as such, occasionally makes reference to a moral imperative unaccompanied by coercion on the part of the court. Hence, even when there is no legal recourse to coercion, this does not absolve the Court of its judicial responsibility in the particular case. A rabbinical authority in his responsa, and Jewish courts in their rulings, should all include the moral imperative – to the extent that it exists – as part of their response or ruling on the matter under discussion. (*Jewish Law,* I. 145f.; cf ibid., 619–620).
>
> Personally, I would hope that the appellant, whose position is supported by strict law, will act more generously, and compensate the respondents, just as he originally proposed. This will fulfill what the wisest of all men taught us: "So follow the way of the good and keep to the paths of the just" (Prov. 2:20), this being the source for the principle of going beyond the letter of the law (*Jewish Law,* 1:809–10).

President Shamgar demurs from the aforementioned approach of Judge Elon "that seeks to elevate payment of compensation *li-fenim mi-shurat ha-din* to the status of a settled general principal of the law of torts," due to "the absence of clear standards"; [the danger of] "filing frivolous appeals"; and other reasons (*ibid.*, 805). This was also the position of Justice Witkon, who felt that granting compensation beyond the letter of the law should be left to the discretion of the person who would have to pay it. He explains, "I would not recommend blurring the boundaries between liability and non-liability" (*ibid.*, 807).

Further on in his judgment, Judge Elon added, in explaining his position:

> I believe that it is fitting, as I emphasized, that in certain circumstances the court should make such a request. As to the effect of that request, I completely agree with the following statement of my distinguished colleague, Justice Witkon, for whom I have the utmost respect: "I too will be happy if the respondents receive some measure of compensation, but the matter is entirely in the discretion of the appellant, and I would not propose to obscure the boundary between liability and non-liability."
>
> What are the particular circumstances in the matter before us? The District Court found the appellant liable, by law, to compensate the respondents. The appellant believed – and, it turned out, correctly – that by law he was not liable to compensate the respondents; but in consideration of the circumstances of the case he offered,to pay a certain sum *lifnim mi-shurat ha-din.* The majority of this Court held that, in fact, the appellant's negligence was proved, but that the causal connection between this negligence and the death of the respondents' relative was not proved; we therefore absolved the appellant, under the law, from liability to compensate the respondents. Why should we now refrain from expressing our wish that the appellant, who started to perform the *mitzvah* [lit. "commandment," and in colloquial usage "good deed"] of *li-fenim mi-shurat ha-din* continue and complete what he began
>
> These are the specific circumstances of the matter before us, and the Court should consider whether it is proper under the special circumstances of each case coming before it to express such a request. It need not be pointed out that appellants who think they can submit frivolous appeals will soon discover that not only will there be no suggestion by us that respondents do more than the law requires of them, but such appellants will also incur appropriate costs for conducting vexatious litigation against the respondents and for wasting the Court's time.
>
> I do not share the apprehension that it would engender confusion in the law were we to express our view and make the parties aware that in certain circumstances one should act more generously than the law requires. Courts regularly make decisions based on considerations of justice, equity, good faith, public welfare, equal protection, and locus *standi* in matters on which property and life itself depend. They are not deterred by fear that these standards are vague or, Heaven forbid, that on occasion they may reach an unfair result. It should therefore be presumed that the Courts will find their way in this matter where law and morality intersect and will be capable of soundly weighing up, in light of the circumstances of each case, whether to request – and it would be only a request – that the injured party be compensated *li-ferim mi-shurat ha-din.*
>
> If we are apprehensive about the danger of combining morality with law, we should be equally concerned with the manner in which the law itself is applied. My colleague points out that, in the case before us, the injury occurred in 1965 and the final judgment was given in 1979. How does the judgment look to the parties and to us when it is given – and to our sorrow this is not a rare occurrence – after the passage of two full sabbatical cycles [fourteen years], and we see [the injustice] yet are powerless to afford any remedy? Perhaps when parties recognize the value of acting *lifnim mi-shurat ha-din* in appropriate circumstances, there will even be a decrease in the innumerable legal actions for strictly legal relief, which are not always necessary, and thus the heavy burden on the courts may possibly be reduced somewhat (*ibid. 811*),

The gist of the aforementioned ruling was quoted again in a ruling rendered some time later (CA 842/79 *Ness and Others u Golda and Others*, PD 36(1) 204, by President Moshe Landau and Justices Menachem Elon and Dou Levin), per the comments of Justice Elon (220–221):

> There is a rule in Jewish law that when someone injures another person, and due to a lack of the required causal connection between the tortfeasor's negligence and the act itself; he is legally exempt from damage payments, under certain circumstances he will still be obligated to pay in order to "meet his Heavenly obligation" (see, for example, TB, BK 55b). It is therefore appropriate for the court to inform the litigants accordingly [i.e., of their obligation to meet their heavenly obligation] (see Ra'avan, BK 55b).
>
> This compensation for damage, whether total or partial, is likewise anchored in the great principle of *li-fenim mi-shurat ha-din*. The Sages, in fact, based that principle on a homily of the wisest of all men: 'That thou mayest walk in the way of good men, and keep the paths of the righteous' (Prov., 2:20)." (See TB. BM 83a; see *Kitan v. Weiss;* see *Ha-Mishpat ha-Ivri, ibid.*). As mentioned above, Golda's conduct provided no grounds to prevent their receiving the apartment back, for it had never left their ownership. It certainly provided no grounds to make them incur payment for the damage suffered by Davidman. Yet without a doubt, their own conduct as well played no small part, as detailed above, in making Davidman buy the apartment from Nes under his mistaken belief in good faith that Nes was the true owner. Under such circumstances, it would be appropriate for Golda to provide some compensation to Davidman for the damage caused him- his payment of £740,000 to Nes for the apartment. Ibis could be fulfilled by their returning to Davidman the entire sum that they had received from Nes for the apartment, which was now returned to them, including a sum of £50,000 lawfully owed them by Nes for having breached the contract with them. Under this strict law, C'Tolda is not bound by any such obligation. Rather, it is a request of them to act *li-fenim mi-shurat ha-din*. By such means they could "walk in the way of good men, and keep the paths of the righteous."

It would seem appropriate for this topic to emerge anew with the enactment of the Basic Laws of 1992, whose declared purpose is "to entrench within a Basic Law the values of the State of Israel as a Jewish and Democratic State." According to these laws, a prominent role is accorded to Jewish law within the values of the State of Israel as a Jewish State. A central issue in the process of combining Jewish and democratic values is the relationship between law and morality. According to these Basic Laws, Jewish values and the emphasis placed on them, precede the democratic values.

Under the law and in terms of propriety, in circumstances such as these, the Court should stress these values and incorporate them in its ruling, namely the duty stemming from these values to go beyond the letter of the law, and to compensate the victim for damages done to him.

For a detailed discussion of this, see the entry: *Law and Morality.

The Law in the State of Israel

The Civil Wrongs Ordinance (New Version) 1968 regulates the payment of compensation for damages. Section 76 provides that a victim is paid compensation "only in respect of such damage as would naturally arise in the usual course of events, and which directly arose from the defendant's civil wrong." This condition bears a certain resemblance to the position of Jewish law to the extent that it exempts the tortfeasor for indirectly caused damage (see *Gerama and Garme). On the other hand, the scope of liability in tort under section 76 is far broader than under Jewish law. Moreover, section 76 provides that awarding compensation is dependent upon the plaintiff specifying the damage he sustained.

Damages caused by traffic accidents are adjudicated under a special law – the Road Accident Victims (Compensation) Law, 5735 – 1975.

All of those laws will be interpreted in accordance with, and in light of, the values of the State of Israel as a Jewish and Democratic state, as elaborated in our discussion above.

[Menachem Elon (2nd ed.)]

BIBLIOGRAPHY: Gulak, Yesodei, 2 (1922), 14ff., 22ff., 31f., 211ff.; idem, *Le-Ḥeker Toledot ha-Mishpat ha-Ivri bi-Tekufat ha-Talmud*, 1 (*Dinei Karka'ot*) (1929), 28–30, 33n. 2, 34n. 2; idem, *Toledot ha-Mishpat be-Yisrael bi-Tekufat ha-Talmud*, 1 (*Ha-Ḥiyyuv ve-Shi'bbudav*) (1939), 43f., 95n.35, 109–11, 124, 141f., Herzog, Instit, 1 (1936), 211, 359; ET, 1 (1951³), 81f.; 2 (1949), 167; 3 (1951), 42–50, 161f.; 7 (1956), 376–82; Z. Karl, in: *Mazkeret Levi… Freund* (1953), 29–32, 46–52; S. Albeck, *Pesher Dinei ha-Nezikin ba-Talmud* (1965). **ADD. BIBLIOGRAPHY:** M. Elon, *Ha-Mishpat ha-Ivri* (1988), 1:129f., 258, 341f., 486f., 495, 532; 2:885; idem, *Jewish Law* (1994), 1:145f., 302, 410f.; 2:591f, 602, 648; 3:1078f.; idem, *Jewish Law* (*Cases and Materials*) (1999), 50–52; M. Elon, B. Lifshitz, *Mafte'aḥ ha-She'elot ve-ha-Teshuvot shel Ḥakhmei Sefarad u-Ẓefon Afrikah*, 2 (1986), 293, 299; S. Albeck, *Pesher Dinei Nezikin ba-Talmud* (1965); A. Guulak, *Yesodei*, (1922). 2:14ff., 22ff., 31f., 211ff.; idem, *Le-Ḥeker Toledot ha-Mishpat ha-Ivri bi-Tekufat ha-Talmud*, 1 (*Dinei Kurka'ot*) (1929), 28–30, 33 n. 2, 34 n. 2; idem, *Toledot ha-Mishpat be-Yisrael bi-Tekufat ha-Talmud*, (*Ha-Ḥiyyuv ve-Shibbudav*) (1939), 1:43f., 95n. 35, 109; 2:124, 141f.; Herzog, *Institutes*, 1(1936), 211, 359; ET, 1 (1951¹), 81f; 2 (1949), 167; 3 (1951), 42–50, 161f.; 7 (1956), 376–82; Z. Karl, in: *Mazkerethevi… Freund* (1953), 29–32, 46–52; B. Lifshitz, E. Shohetman, *Mafte'aḥ ha-She'elot ve-ha-Teshuvot shel Ḥakhmei Ashkenaz, Ẓarefat ve-Italya* (1997), 204–7; A. Sheinfeld, *Nezikin* (*Ḥok le-Yisrael*, N. Rakover (ed.)), 5752.

DAMANHŪR, name of several Egyptian cities in the Middle Ages. One Damanhūr is referred to by Maimonides in his responsa as a major community in Egypt at his time. He together with other *dayyanim* decreed that anybody could marry or divorce a woman in Damanhūr without the permission of Rabbi Halfon (Bar Ula), the *dayyan* of Damanhūr. It would appear that the reference is to the present Damanhūr, which is the principal city of the Buḥayra province. This Jewish community remained in existence until modern times. In the 19th century the community was subordinated to the Jewish court of law in Alexandria. In 1901 the rabbis of Cairo visited Damanhūr and declared there the new Qisushin regulation. In the 19th century there were no Jewish local institutions, probably because the majority of the Jewish population lived in the city only for a short time. In 1897 the community numbered 228 members, but in 1917 there were only 56. The decrease is probably accounted for by migration to nearby Alexandria. In spite of their small numbers, the Jews had many enemies in this city, and blood libels were brought against them in 1877 and 1882. The tomb of the kabbalist Jacob Abu Ḥasirah in Damanhūr was revered by the Jews of Egypt, and pilgrimages were made to it on festivals.

BIBLIOGRAPHY: Mann, Egypt, 2 (1922), 317; E. Ashtor, in: JJS, 19 (1968), 7. **ADD. BIBLIOGRAPHY:** Ashtor, Toledot, 1 (1944), 32, 326; 2 (1951), 358ff.; 3 (1970); J.M. Landau, *Jews in Nineteenth-Century Egypt* (1969), index; idem (ed.), *Toledot ha-Yehudim be-Miẓrayim ba-Tekufah ha-Ottemanit* (1988), index.

[Eliyahu Ashtor / Leah Bornstein-Makovetsky (2nd ed.)]

DAMARI, SHOSHANA (1922–2006), Israeli singer. Damari was born in the town of Damar, in Yemen, and moved to Palestine with her family at the age of two. She showed musical promise from an early age, accompanying her mother's singing at family and social gatherings on percussion. When she was 13 she joined the Shulamit school of drama in Tel Aviv and starred in her first concert in Tel Aviv three years later. In 1943 she was among the founding members of the Li La Lo theater company, and, one year later, appeared in the theater's debut production, "The Barber of Tel Aviv." Damari's principle contribution to the show was her rendition of "*Laylah ba-Gilboa*" ("A Night on Mount Gilboa") and, although the song was not a hit, Damari's soft Yemenite-inflected tones and richly textured voice stood out from the efforts of her European-born co-performers.

Damari came to national prominence following her performance in the theater company's second show, *Ra'ayon beli La Lo*, in which she sang "*Kalani'ot*" ("Anemones"), which was a huge hit and became Damari's signature song. The music for "*Kalani'ot*" was composed by Moshe *Wilensky, who, despite being born in Poland and a graduate of the Warsaw Academy of Music, incorporated Yemenite motifs in the song and in other material he wrote for Damari in subsequent years. Damari and Wilensky maintained their creative and fruitful partnership into the 1950s, when Wilensky began presenting a radio program called *Pizmon va-Zemer* ("Chorus and Song"). Every show included a song Wilensky wrote specially for Damari and was performed by her. These included such hits as "*Ha-Ro'ah ha-Ketanah min ha-Gai*" ("The Little Shepherdess from The Valley") and "*Le-Or ha-Zikhronot*" ("For the Memories").

In the mid-1950s Damari enjoyed a brief movie career, appearing in some of Israel's first movies, such as *Hill 24 Doesn't Answer* and *Be-Ein Moledet* ("Without a Homeland"), which told the story of the Damari family's move from Yemen to Palestine in the 1920s.

In the late 1940s Damari embarked on the first of many successful tours abroad. In 1947 she appeared at the famed Village Vanguard music club in New York and later performed in Canada and Cuba. In the 1960s and 1970s she appeared at many of the world's most prestigious music venues, including New York's Carnegie Hall and Lincoln Center. Despite being closely identified with her Yemenite roots, and classic Israeli songs, Damari also performed in other languages, including Spanish and even Yiddish.

In 1987 Damari's career was revived when she joined forces with crooner Boaz Sharabi, whose family also emigrated from Yemen, and the following year she received the country's ultimate accolade when she was awarded the Israel Prize. Damari subsequently appeared and recorded with Israel's other senior diva, Yaffa *Yarkoni, and with singer-songwriter Matti *Caspi. In 2005, the 83-year-old Damari surprised many by contributing two songs to young ethno-rock star Idan Reichel's second album *Mi-Ma'amakim* ("From the Deep").

Throughout her long career Damari set the standard for generations of young performers, both for her stage presence and her unparalleled vocal delivery.

[Barry Davis (2nd ed.)]

°**DAMASCIUS** (sixth century C.E.), the last head of the neoplatonist school. In his *Vita Isidori* he states that Theosebius, disciple of Hierocles, exorcised a demon from his master's wife by invoking the rays of the sun and the God of the Hebrews. He also tells in the same book that in the fifth century Marinus, successor of Proclus as chief of the neoplatonic school, was originally from Neapolis, modern Nablus (in the immediate vicinity of Shechem) a city built at the foot of Mount Gerizim, where there was a temple of Zeus Hypsistos which had been consecrated by Abraham, ancestor of the Hebrews. Marinus, he continues, was originally a Samaritan who later repudiated the doctrines of this sect (which he accused of having deviated from the faith of Abraham) and embraced Hellenism.

DAMASCUS, capital of Syria; in olden times a caravan center at an oasis in Southern Syria, on the principal crossroads between Mesopotamia-Syria and Palestine-Transjordan.

In the Bible

The name appears as דַּמֶּשֶׂק *Dammesek* (but once as דּוּמֶּשֶׂק *Dummesek*, II Kings 16:10) and דַּרְמֶשֶׂק *Darmesek*, as in Chronicles (e.g., II Chron. 16:2) and also in the Dead Sea Scrolls and rabbinic sources. The meaning of the name is obscure; derivations from Semitic sources have been suggested but the etymology of the name remains uncertain. In Assyrian documents of the first millennium B.C.E. *Dimašqi* is interchangeable with the peculiar epithet *ša imērišu*, the city or land "of his donkey," though the epithet most probably refers to the country only. The Egyptian Execration Texts and the *Mari documents (18th century B.C.E.) refer to the Damascus region as the "Land of Apum," ruled by West Semitic princes. Damascus is mentioned by name for the first time in the geographical lists of Thutmosis III (15th century B.C.E.). In the El-Amarna letters (14th century B.C.E.) Damascus is mentioned several times, once explicitly, as being in the "Land of Upe" (i.e., Apu[m]); at this time its rulers bore Indo-Aryan names. The patriarchal narratives twice mention Damascus in passing (Gen. 14:15; 15:2), and the biblical account includes it within the Land of Canaan (Num. 34). Though this region lay within the Egyptian dominion until Egypt's decline in the 12th century, the Hittites sporadically penetrated and held it.

The desert oasis of Damascus became an important center for the *Arameans shortly after their appearance in Syria toward the end of the second millennium. David, in his campaigns against the Aramean confederation, conquered the city and posted Israelite governors there (II Sam. 8:5–6). Damascus cast off the Israelite yoke during Solomon's reign and became the capital of the kingdom of *Aram Damascus, remaining so until its destruction by the Assyrians in 732 B.C.E. It reached its height in the ninth century as an important political, economic, and cultural center. Even so, Damascus was forced to grant Israelite merchants special rights in the city, as indicated by the Aramean king Ben-Hadad's submission to Ahab: "… you may establish bazaars for yourself in Damascus, as my father did in Samaria" (I Kings 20:34).

The city of Damascus was repeatedly attacked by Assyria, as the latter gained power. In 841 B.C.E. and again in 838 B.C.E., Shalmaneser III besieged it, destroying the vineyards and orchards surrounding the city; later Adad-Nirari III twice (or even three times) spared the city only after being paid a heavy tribute; in 773 B.C.E. Shalmaneser IV also campaigned against Damascus, weakening it sufficiently to allow Jeroboam II, king of Israel, to impose his suzerainty over it; and in 732 B.C.E. the final blow was delivered by Tiglath-Pileser III. Reduced to the status of the capital of an Assyrian province, Damascus was still mentioned in Assyrian sources in 727, 720, and 694 B.C.E. and even as late as the reign of Ashurbanipal (668–627 B.C.E.). In the Persian period, Damascus was an important administrative center, and may have been the capital of the satrapy of Trans-Euphrates (cuneiform, *ebir nāri*; Aram. *avar nahara* [Ezra:4:10, etc.]; Heb. *ever ha-nahar* [Ezra 8:36; Neh. 2:7, 9]). The geographical position of Damascus, dominating the major trade routes, led to an economic prosperity in the biblical period, as did the fertility of the desert oasis, as reflected in the Bible (II Kings 5:12; Ezek. 27:18, where its trade in wine and wool is specified). Damascus was a cultic center for the god Hadad (cf. *Ben-Hadad, the name typical of the Damascene kings), apparently worshiped locally under the name Rimmon (cf. "the house of Rimmon," II Kings 5:18). The ancient city of Damascus has not yet been uncovered. One of the few chance finds from the biblical period is a ninth-century B.C.E. basalt orthostat depicting a cherub/sphinx in Phoenician style, which had been built into a substructural wall of the Umayyad mosque. The latter building apparently stands on the site of the ancient temple of Hadad-Ramman (cf. II Kgs. 5:18). In addition, Damascus is mentioned in an Aramaic stele, fragments of which were uncovered at *Dan in northern Israel.

From the time of Alexander the Great's invasion of the Near East in 333 B.C.E., Damascus served as a Macedonian colony, later becoming the capital of Coele-Syria and Phoenicia (from 111 B.C.E.), and then eventually becoming incorporated into the Roman Empire. Very little archaeological data is known about the pre-Classical city of Damascus, except for a few chance finds. The general plan of the present Old City may have been modeled on the general plan of the Hellenistic city, as some scholars have proposed (including Sauvaget), but there is no certainty about this. Roman remains include the architectural remains and inscriptions of the Damascene Temple of Jupiter, and a very distinctive street running east-west, which may very well be the same as the "Street called Straight" mentioned in Acts 9:11. A church dedicated to John the Baptist, which may have housed his relic head, existed in the city in the Byzantine period. Most of the ancient buildings visible today in the city are Islamic, including the impressive Great Mosque built by Caliph al-Walid in 705–15.

[Abraham Malamat / Shimon Gibson (2nd ed.)]

Second Temple Period

With the advent of Alexander the Great in the east, Persian rule in Damascus was replaced by Macedonian, and later by that of Alexander's successors, the Diadochi, Seleucids, and Ptolemaids who alternately ruled over Damascus until its conquest by Pompey in 64 B.C.E. The city is mentioned several times in the Hasmonean era in connection with the conquests of Jonathan (I Macc. 11:62), who appointed his brother Simeon commander-in-chief at the Ladder of Tyre and after his conquest of Gaza in the south returned to Damascus. The army of Demetrius came to Kedesh in Galilee to thwart him but was defeated. Subsequently (*ibid.* 12:24–32) there is mention of another battle with the army of Demetrius in the land of Hamath, when Jonathan again was victorious and returned to Damascus. According to some scholars the sect known from the Covenant of *Damascus settled in the town or in its proximity after the capture of Damascus in the time of Pompey. "The land of Damascus" is mentioned several times in the book together with Damascus itself as the sect's place of residence. It may be assumed that this thickly populated commercial city situated at a major crossroads attracted Jews from various places.

Salome Alexandra attempted to extend her rule over Damascus which was threatened by Ptolemy of Chalcis but was unsuccessful (Jos., Ant., 13:418). In Damascus Pompey met with the emissaries of Hyrcanus and Aristobulus, the Hasmonean brothers who were contending for the throne, and from there he went in pursuit of Aristobulus (*ibid.*, 14:34f.). Damascus is also mentioned as Herod's place of refuge when, with the help of the high priest Hyrcanus, he fled Jerusalem when the members of the Sanhedrin were about to sentence him to death for having the Galilean rebels executed (*ibid.*, 14:177f.). In the course of time a large and important Jewish community was established in Damascus. The Jews of Damascus in the first century C.E. are mentioned in Acts 9 and 11

Corinthians 11:32. In Acts, Paul states that he requested letters from the high priest in Jerusalem addressed to the synagogues of Damascus asking that they hand over to him the adherents of the new sect in order to bring them to Jerusalem. On the eve of the Roman war the Jews of Damascus were murdered by the gentile inhabitants (Jos., Wars, 2:559–561; Life, 27).

In talmudic literature Damascus is mentioned only in the economic sphere; it is called "the gateway of the Garden of Eden" (Er. 19a), reference being made to its fertile land and produce: Damascene plums, wine of Senir, etc. The quality of the waters of the rivers of Damascus and their validity for ritual ablutions are also discussed (TJ, Beẓah 3:2, 62a; Parah 8:10, "Keramyon" and "Puga"). Apparently Judah ha-Nasi had possessions to the west and south of Damascus, and on his journeys to them he visited that city as well as the Jewish communities in the vicinity (Sanh. 5b), many of which are mentioned (Ḥovah, Kokheva, Kefar Avraham, Kefar Karinos, Rom, Beth-Anath, Aratris, Ifarkoris, Sakhuta, etc.). It may be assumed that on their way from Ereẓ Israel to Babylon scholars passed through these places, but there were no institutes of learning there or in the city of Damascus, and it may be inferred that the Jews of Damascus engaged in agriculture as well as in commerce and became well known in this respect.

Roman rule in Ereẓ Israel and Syria commenced in 64 B.C.E. and continued under the Eastern (Byzantine) Roman Empire until the first half of the seventh century. During these 300 years, the Roman and Persian empires were engaged in a struggle in the region, which changed hands several times. In 613, Damascus was again captured by the Persians. They retained it only for a short time. The despotic and often religiously fanatical Byzantine administration alienated the inhabitants, even the Christians, and they certainly did not succeed in gaining sympathizers among the Jews and Samaritans. As a result all the cities submitted to the Persian armies without any opposition.

From the descriptions of the Armenian historian Bishop Sebeos (seventh century) and the book of the monk Astrategius of Mar-Saba, among others, it is learned that the Jews collaborated with the Persian conquerors against the Christians. From Damascus the Persians proceeded to conquer Ereẓ Israel, coming there together with their Jewish supporters (according to Sophronius). It may be assumed that the alliance of the Jews with the Persians was motivated by the hope for a tolerant attitude and, perhaps, even of gaining autonomy for the Jewish communities of Syria and Ereẓ Israel, as had been attained by the large Jewish community of Babylonia. The alliance of the Jews of Damascus with the Persians and their participation in the punitive actions against the Christians are evidence of their difficult situation under Byzantine rule. Although the Christian population also suffered under Byzantine rule, the mention of the Jews' participation in the campaign of suppression against the Christians, and particularly those from Tyre, testifies to fierce rivalry, and perhaps also to additional privileges granted the Christians by the Byzantine emperors so as to oust the Jews of Damascus from their position.

[Abraham Lebanon]

Under Muslim Rule

According to one tradition, the Jews were mentioned in the terms of the capitulation in 635, according to which the city was handed over to the Arabs. It is certain that the conquerors granted the Jews the southeastern quarter of the city, where they had previously dwelt. By comparison with the oppression that they suffered under Byzantine rule, there was a definite improvement in their situation. During the reigns of the caliphs of the Umayyad dynasty (661–750), the Jews, as well as the Christians, enjoyed tolerant treatment. However, with the ascent to power of the Abbasid dynasty (750–1258), they suffered from decrees against them along with an increase in the taxes levied upon them. Even so, they could observe their religious rituals openly and the ties with the academies of Palestine and Babylonia were renewed. The Damascus community was affected by events which influenced the Jewish population of the Orient. Furthermore, the sectarian movements in Babylonia found sympathizers in Damascus. According to the Karaite author *Al-Kirkisānī, there were still in his days (first half of tenth century) some remnants of the ʿIsāwiyya sect (founded by Abū ʿĪsā al-Iṣfahānī) in Damascus. At the same time, the great Muslim caliphate began to disintegrate and Iraq, which was the center of its empire, suffered from the wars between various groups and military factions. These events also marked the beginning of an important emigration of Iraqi Jews towards other countries. Damascus, like other cities in Syria and Egypt, became the home of many Iraqi Jews who established their own synagogues in the city. One of the pages in the records of the Damascus *bet din* for the year 933 contains four betrothal documents of Iraqi Jews in three consecutive weeks.

After the conquest of Damascus by the *Fatimids in 969, a period of prosperity began for the Jewish community. The Fatimids were noted for their tolerant attitude towards non-Muslims and they appointed Jews and Christians to high positions. At the end of the tenth century, Manasseh ibn Ibrahim al-Qazzāz held the position of head of the financial administration of Fatimid Syria, and used all the means within his power to further the welfare of his coreligionists. The Jews of Damascus at that time were in close contact with the Jews of Cairo and the Palestinian academies. In Damascus there were distinguished scholars such as Samuel b. Hoshana (III) of the Palestinian academy, who was a hymnologist and probably also *av bet din*. As a result of its close ties with the Palestinian academies, the community of Damascus was dragged into disputes in Palestine. It was especially involved in the controversy between the *gaon* Solomon b. Judah and his opponent Nathan b. Abraham. In the **Genizah* there are a few documents about the immigrants from Damascus to Egypt during Fatimid rule.

With the conquest of the greater part of Palestine by the Crusaders, the Palestinian academy was transferred to

*Hadrach, near Damascus, and later to Damascus itself. The first head of the academy in Hadrach was Solomon b. Elijah, who held this position during the early 12th century. The academy was then headed by *Abraham b. Mazhir and his son Ezra. The 12th-century traveler Benjamin of Tudela, who visited Damascus in about 1173, relates that there were 3,000 Jews in the city. On the other hand, his contemporary Pethahiah of Regensburg, the German traveler, maintains that there were 10,000 Jews in Damascus. These numbers seem to be exaggerated and it is unlikely that the Damascus community consisted of more than 2,000 Rabbanite Jews and about 600 Karaites. Besides craftsmen and small tradesmen, there were also physicians and intellectuals who composed Hebrew poetry. The poet Judah *Al-Ḥarizi, who visited Damascus in 1217, mentions the exilarch R. Josiah b. Yishai (Jesse) and the physicians Moses b. Ṣadaga and Isaac b. Baruch as residents of the city.

Saladin, who conquered Damascus in 1174, and his descendants, the sultans of the *Ayyubid dynasty, were indeed fervent Muslims, but even so they treated the members of other religions with tolerance. They also befriended intellectuals and employed the services of physicians. In general, the Ayyubid rule (12th–13th century) brought prosperity for the whole city. Trade relations with the European countries were strengthened as a result of the establishment of colonies of Genoese and Venetian merchants in the coastal towns of the Latin principalities. It seems that the first nesi'im, descendants of the Exilarch who settled in Damascus, were Solomon and his son Yoshiyahu in the first half of the 12th century; and in the 1180s and 1190s Judah, the son of Yoshiyahu. At the beginning of the 13th century came his relative Yoshiyahu ben Ishai. These leaders received money from the public treasury and gave the community a sense of importance but did not have any official position in the city. They traveled often to Syrian communities, Ereẓ Israel, and Egypt and received money from the local communities. Yoshiyahu was mentioned by Alḥarizi who wrote about the leadership of the community in the last decade of the 12th century and at the beginning of the 13th century, including the great nagid Obadiah and Judah Abu Alrada. The title nagid of Damascus was later given to Hillel ben Moses. In the Cairo *Genizah one finds the appointment order given in 1193 by the *Mamluk Sultan al-Malik al-Fasl ʿAlī, the eldest son of Saladin, to Obadiah. He appointed him as the head of all the Jews, Rabbanite, Karaite, and Samaritan, in Damascus and all the communities in the area of Syria.

After the Mamluks defeated the *Mongols at the battle of ʿAyn Jālūt in 1260, Syria came under the domination of the Mamluk sultans of Cairo. These sultans, influenced by fanatical theologians, agreed to issue decrees against non-Muslims. In Damascus, where many Muslim theological colleges had been founded since the reign of Saladin, the theologians had considerable influence, which they used to implant religious hatred within the general population. As a result, during the Mamluk period there was much oppression and many decrees against non-Muslims, even more than in the other cities under Mamluk rule. In 1321 the Muslims destroyed a synagogue, in 1354 there was a general persecution of non-Muslims, and in 1365 there were searches for stores of wine, as many Muslims bought wine from the Jews in spite of the Koranic prohibition of alcohol. The authorities also renewed the requirements compelling Jewish women to wear one black and one red shoe, and compelling the men to blow on a whistle when entering the public bathhouses. Periodically, the Muslims brought accusations against the Jews and forced some of them to convert to Islam. In 1392 the Jews of Damascus were accused of having set fire to the central mosque. One Jew was then burnt alive, the community leaders were tortured, and a synagogue was converted into a mosque. However, after a lapse of two years, this synagogue was returned to the Jews. In 1286 the exilarch *Jesse (Yishai) b. Hezekiah excommunicated the kabbalists of Acre, who had criticized the works of *Maimonides. There is no further mention of these exilarchs during later generations; however, a deputy of the Egyptian *nagid* had his seat in Damascus. During the whole of this period, the Jews of Damascus maintained contacts with the Palestinian population and they were accustomed to make pilgrimages to Jerusalem, as *Naḥmanides and *Estori ha-Parḥi testify.

The short occupation of Damascus by Tamerlane in 1401, the ransom which the conqueror levied upon the city, and the looting in which he engaged brought great suffering to all in the city, and the community was slow in recuperating from this calamity. However, during the second half of the 15th century, the Jews of Damascus enjoyed a period of economic prosperity. There were wealthy merchants among them and cultural activities flourished at the same time. According to the reports of Jewish travelers who came from European countries toward the end of the 15th century, there were between 400 and 500 Jewish families in Damascus at that time, besides a small *Karaite community and a community of *Samaritans. In 1435 the Italian rabbi Elijah La Massa, who settled in Jerusalem, was answering halakhic questions for Damascus Jewry. Rabbi Joseph of Montagna visited Damascus in 1481 and found an organized community including many scholars. He had the impression that no poor Jews lived in the city. A student of Rabbi Obadiah of Bertinoro visited Damascus in 1495 and was the guest of the president of the community, Moses Makran. He mentioned that the Jewish population numbered 500 families, most of them merchants, workers, and moneylenders.

During the early 16th century, the Spanish refugees of 1492 began to arrive in Damascus. This immigration increased after 1516, when Syria became a part of the *Ottoman Empire. R. Moses *Basola found 500 refugee families in the city in 1521, as well as special synagogues belonging to the Jews of Spanish, Sicilian, and Iraqi origin. There were at first some conflicts between the Spanish and Iraqi Jews. The Spanish Jews formed a separate community with independent institutions, such as a separate cemetery. The Sicilians also acted in the same fashion. The split of the Damascus community into these three groups lasted a long time, and each congregation had its own

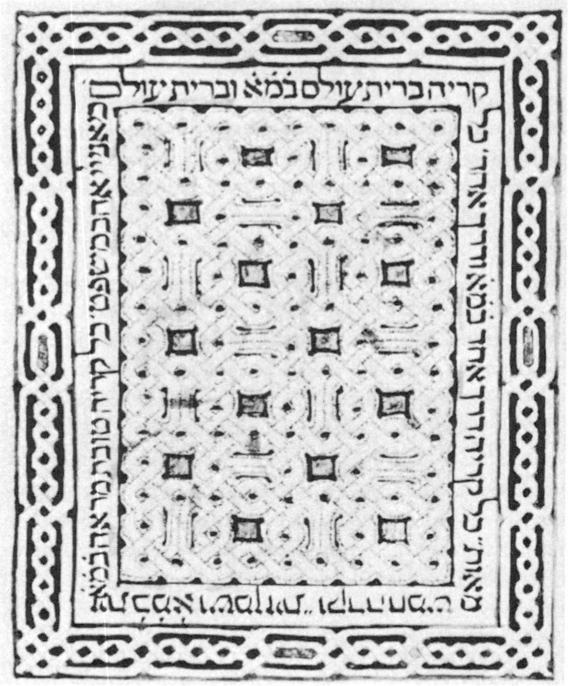

Carpet page from the Damascus Keter *Bible, Burgos, Spain, 1260. This was for many years in the possession of the Damascus Synagogue of Ḥushbasba Al'anabi. Jerusalem* J.N.U.L., *Ms. Heb. 4°790.*

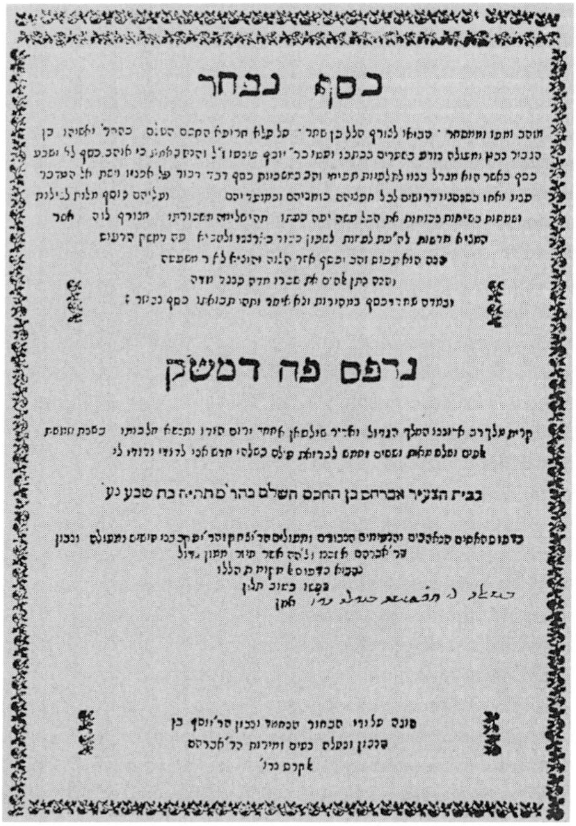

כסף נבחר

נדפס פה דמשק

Title page of the first edition of Kesef Nivḥar, *a book of sermons by the Damascus talmudist and kabbalist, Josiah b. Joseph Pinto, 1605.*

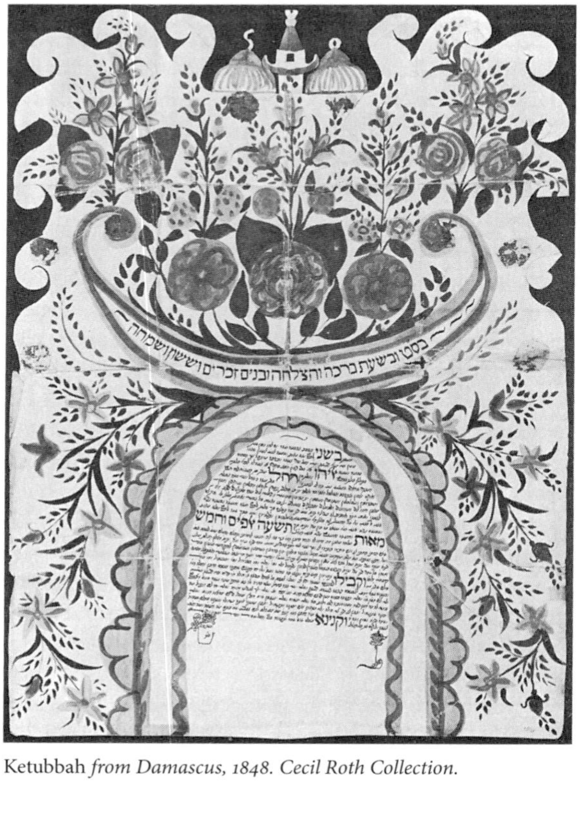

Ketubbah *from Damascus, 1848. Cecil Roth Collection.*

Fragment of the Damascus Document manuscript discovered by S. Schechter in the Cairo Genizah *collection and published by him in 1910 as* Fragments of the Zadokite Work.

rabbi, as well as a special *bet din*. However, in time these divisions were repaired. The influence of the Spanish Jews, among whom there were a number of scholars, increased as a result of their high cultural level. Furthermore, when the descendants of the original Spanish Jews ceased using Spanish, a major division between them and the rest of the community was removed. The Turkish authorities usually treated the Jews fairly. Some exceptions occurred, such as the destruction of the Iraqi Jews' synagogue in 1570 by a Turkish commissioner. However, even in this case the community was indemnified after a short while. The Jews of Damascus traded with other parts of the Ottoman Empire and maintained close ties with the rabbis of *Jerusalem and *Safed. Scholars from Jerusalem and Safed were appointed to rabbinical positions in Damascus and some of the rabbis of Damascus immigrated to Palestine in their old age. As a result of these contacts the study of the Kabbalah spread among the Jews of Damascus. In 1591 R. Moses *Alshekh from Safed visited Damascus as an emissary, returning a second time and serving as a dayyan in 1593. That year he returned to Safed and died soon after. R. Ḥayyim b. Joseph *Vital went to Damascus and lived there. A local rabbi in Damascus, Jacob Abulafia, was Vital's rival. R. Samuel b. Ḥayyim *Vital continued to propagate the teachings of his father in Damascus. In 1604 Safed was destroyed by the Druze and many of its Jews fled to Damascus. The influence of the kabbalists then became even more important. Two of the refugees, Isaac and Jacob, the sons of the Safed printer Abraham Ashkenazi, set up a Hebrew printing press in Damascus. In 1605 they printed *Kesef Nivḥar* ("Choice Silver"), the work of R. Josiah *Pinto, the rabbi of the Sephardi Jews in Damascus. R. Josiah Pinto wrote a series of works which reflected his kabbalistic outlook. At that time, there were also scholars and intellectuals in Damascus who wrote secular poems in Hebrew. The poet Israel *Najara settled in Damascus in 1579. In 1621 Rabbi Isaiah Halevi Horowitz (Ha-Shelah) passed through the city on his way to Ereẓ Israel and refused to serve as the local rabbi. Shabbetai *Ẓevi received some support from the Jews of Damascus. When his disciple Nathan of Gaza came to Damascus, many Jews in the city indicated that they still believed in the pseudo-messiah, despite the fact that he had already converted to Islam.

The wealthy merchants in Damascus in the middle of the 19th century (comprising around 24 merchant houses) were the richest class in the city and managed most of the local business of the *vilayet* of Damascus. There were also moneylenders who were the bankers of the city. The richest families were Levi-Stambouli, Angel, Lisbona, Farhi, Harari, Tovi, and Hason, philanthropists who helped the community.

The traveler *Benjamin II, who visited Damascus in 1848, estimated that the city had a Jewish population of 4,000, while the Austrian poet Dr. L.A. Frankl estimated that in about 1857 the population was 5,000. He mentioned the wealthiest Jew in Damascus, Raphael Stambouli, who was the host of Baron Alfonso de Rothschild in that year. He described the grandiose life of the community's elite, and noted the contempt of the Christian inhabitants for the Jews.

Frankl wrote in 1857 that the Karaite community in Damascus had been dissolved 50 years earlier. The Jewish community had eight synagogues, including "Frangi," which was the largest synagogue, founded by the Spanish settlers in Damascus; "Menesh," in which R. Hayim Vital had prayed; "Raki," in which the Farhi family had prayed (it was constructed in the middle of the 19th century); "Del Pasha"; "Halab"; "Midrash"; and "Dashabar" outside the city. Jews from Ereẓ Israel and Syria came to pray there. The great rabbi of Damascus in the second half of the 19th century was Rabbi Isaac Abulafia (died in Tiberias in 1910). Famous rabbis in the city were Nethanel Moses Chaboba, who was appointed head of the *bet din* in Damascus until his departure to Jerusalem in 1904 where he died the same year, Aaron Jacob, Solomon Sukari, and Meir Mashen. *The ḥakham bashi* in Damascus at this time was Rabbi Jacob Peretz. The massacre of Christians by Muslims and Druze in 1860 was followed by Christian accusations that the Jews had taken part in the violence and had bought their looted possessions. Many Jews were imprisoned as a result of these accusations, but later they were freed. The basic condition of the community did not change as a result of these events. However, after 1870 the economic situation deteriorated. This was due to the opening of the Suez Canal, which limited the international trade of Damascus, and the bankruptcy of the Ottoman Empire in 1875. Furthermore, local industries were ruined by the importation of manufactured goods from Europe. Economic decline was followed by a moral and cultural decline. At the turn of the century some Jewish girls became notoriously known as "singers," and the rabbis attempted to end this shame. In 1888 there was only one *talmud torah* in Damascus with 450 students, and in 1895 it was transferred to the Alliance Israélite Universelle. This organization had opened a school in Damascus in 1864, but it was closed after five years and reopened only in 1880. A school for girls was inaugurated by this organization in 1883. In 1910, 768 students were enrolled in these schools. In 1911 the Alliance Israélite Universelle withdrew its support from the schools. An 1883 report noted that 25% of the Jewish population was very poor, 50% was poor, 25% belonged to the middle class, and only one percent of community members were wealthy. Most of the Jewish inhabitants were simple workers. In 1895 there was a split in the community regarding the chief rabbinate. One group wished to dismiss the *ḥakham bashi* Rabbi Isaac Abulafia. Rabbi Solomon Eliezer Alafandari was appointed, but his 13 years in the city were marked by dissension. In 1909 he immigrated to Ereẓ Israel (and died in Jerusalem in 1930). In the second half of the 19th century there were about 20 Ashkenazi families from Europe which had assimilated into the older population of the community. In the 18th century Jews from Persia, Bukhara, India, and Iraq had settled in Damascus. In 1822 many Jews from Aleppo settled there after the earthquake in that city. It appears that the Jewish population in the city grew from 3,000 to 5,000. Many Jews from Hamah also immigrated to Damascus between 1832 and 1840. After 1860, Jews from Hasbiya settled there. At the end of the 19th century, many Jews from Damascus immigrated to Ereẓ Israel.

Emigration from Damascus up to 1870 was minimal, with most of the immigrants leaving for Egypt. But in the last two decades of the 19th century immigration was stepped up and in the first two decades of the 20th century it became a flood. Most of the emigrants were young people who settled in North and South America, where they hoped to improve their economic situation. According to the Ottoman census of the year 1882, there were 3,177 Jewish men and 3,088 Jewish women in Damascus at the time. The first regular elections for the Va'ad Gashmi were scheduled in Damascus for the end of the 19th century. From c. 1840 to the end of the century there had been a Va'ad Ruḥani with authority in religious affairs. During the second half of the 19th century, many local Jews abandoned Jewish tradition.

Throughout the Ottoman period Damascus had the second largest community in Syria after *Aleppo. In 1870 there was some incitement by the Christian inhabitants and the British consul, Richard Barton, against the Jews of Damascus, and the latter appealed to Sir Moses *Montefiore, Francis Goldschdmidt, Rabbi Adler of London, and Charles Netter to get the consul dismissed. He was ordered by his government to return to England in 1871. During World War I the city suffered a severe economic crisis. Eliyahu Sasson reported in 1921 that only 5% of community members were wealthy, most of them merchants, 25% were workers, and almost 70% were needy. The Protestant mission was active within the community but had only limited success.

The community was unsuccessful in its efforts at maintaining a Hebrew school. There was no increase in the population of the community due to the continuing emigration of Jews from Damascus to Beirut and to both North and South America. In 1900 Damascus had 10,000 Jews. In the first decade of the 20th century 1,500 young Jews emigrated from Damascus.

In 1930 the headmaster of the Alliance Israélite Universelle estimated the Jewish population at not more than 8,000 and noted the Zionist influence on Jewish society there. In 1926 the number was the same, and in 1943 there were only 6,000 Jews in the city. The Zionists founded two Hebrew schools in Damascus, in which a majority of the pupils came from the poorer strata of the community, but in 1925 these schools were closed. In the Jewish quarter many young Jews spoke French, which helped many of them who emigrated. A number of rabbis lived and were active in Damascus at the end of the 19th century and in the first half of the 20th century. Rabbi Jacob Hacohen Trab (d. 1923), who was born in Damascus, was appointed rabbi of Beirut in 1900. Rabbi Judah Ḥayyim Maslaton was the son of the community rabbi, Ezra Hacohen Trab Maslaton. He was born in Damascus in 1872 and immigrated after World War I to Egypt (d. 1946). Rabbi Joseph Judah Dana (died in Haifa in 1973) was a student of Rabbi Isaac Abulafia and served for many years as rabbi of Damascus. He immigrated c. 1948 to Israel. In Damascus social differences were marked, and the wealthy Jews lived on a very high standard. These had a Western orientation and many of them were Francos who had *capitulation rights. Among them were the Lisbona family, which enjoyed Austrian protection, and Jacob Levi Stambouli, who had British protection. The Jewish press in Europe emphasized the poverty of the Jewish majority. The *talmidei ḥakhamim* of Damascus were exempt from community taxes, but in 1875 the government ordered them to pay property taxes. In 1918 there were 15,000–17,000 Jews in Damascus. Only two families, Laniado and Totah, were wealthy, 300 families belonged to the middle class, and 600 families were needy. In 1919 most Jewish children were enrolled in Hebrew institutions headed by Abraham Elmaliah and Joseph Joel Rivlin. But in November 1919 the Jews of Damascus began to break off contact with the Committee of Deputies and the Zionist movement. The president of the community was Moses David Totah. In 1919 an orphanage was established and the Joint began to help the community. In 1924 there were 1,359 students in the Alliance Israélite Universelle institutions. There were also Jewish students from rich families who studied in Christian schools. In 1911 the new *ḥakham bashi* in Damascus, Rabbi Jacob Danon, invited his son-in-law, Abraham Elmaliah, to the city. Elmaliah changed the *talmud torah* to a Hebrew national school and invited teachers from Ereẓ Israel. Until 1917 it had 300 students and 200 more children in the kindergarten classes. In 1924, 150 poor Jewish students studied in Protestant Mission schools. In 1925 the Jewish quarter was sacked during the Druze rebellion against the French Mandate; some Jews were murdered and dozens were injured, while many buildings and shops were plundered.

The world economic crisis of the 1930s hurt also the Jews of Damascus. A large number were not employed and many immigrated to Ereẓ Israel and other countries. In 1936 they were accused of Zionism and Jews fled from Damascus. Zionist activity continued, however. In 1942 Tuviyyah Arazi described the dire economic circumstances of many of the children and youngsters there. Most of the children aged 10–12 worked and received no education. In that year the headmaster of the Alliance Israélite Universelle school was murdered.

[Alexander Astor / Leah Bornstein-Makovetsky (2nd ed.)]

Since 1948

The Jews of Damascus experienced fear and discrimination after the Israeli War of Independence. In July–August 1948 the Jewish quarter was bombed and dozens of Jews were killed and injured. Of the approximately 5,000 Jews in Damascus in 1948, and 3,500 in 1958, there remained only between 1,000 and 1,500 in 1968. Most Jews left for Lebanon immediately after the outbreak of the War of Independence, settling in Beirut; others went to Israel, Europe, and America. The vacant houses in the Jewish quarter were occupied by Palestinian Arab refugees whose presence caused constant tension and clashes with the remaining Jews. Many Jews fled from the city and secretly left for Israel and Lebanon. According to a report of the World Jewish Congress in 1954, the Jewish quarter in Damascus was full of Arab refugees. The head of the community committee was the banker Sabri Laniado, but the committee did not have any contact with the local authorities in Damascus. Only Jews who had special licenses could leave the city. Others were seized and imprisoned. The Jews were supported by the Beirut community and by the Joint Distribution Committee as well as by grants from Syrian Jews in other countries, such as Mexico, Argentina, the United States, and some in Eastern Europe. Most of the money was transferred to the authorities as bribes. Only a little of it reached the needy. Many Jews abandoned their property. In the Jewish talmud torah there were just 170 children with the funds for the school coming from the U.S. The Jews were persecuted by the authorities and frequently arrested, especially during the trial of the Israeli intelligence officer Eli *Cohen (1965) and during the Six-Day War (1967). The Muslim population also attacked Jews and planted a bomb in the synagogue in August 1949. The Jewish community suffered serious financial difficulties, most of its members being artisans or unemployed and living on the charity of the community council. A few Jews worked as clerks in the Banque de Commerce (which used to be the Zilkhah Bank), or in a Jewish-owned clothing factory. The number of conversions to Islam of Jewish girls marrying Muslims increased after the Jewish mass emigration. In 1968 the community's affairs were governed by a council of seven to nine members, whose main function was to support the needy with funds from Syrian Jews in America. Nissim Nedebo was rabbi of the community. The Alliance Israélite Universelle continued to run a school in Damascus, which had 420 pupils in 1965. Forty boys and girls attended government schools, and in 1965 there were eight Jewish students at Damascus University.

In an undercover operation in late 1994, 1,262 Syrian Jews were brought to Israel. The spiritual leader of the Syrian Jewish community from 1976 to 1994, Rabbi Abraham Hamra, was among those who left Syria and went to New York (and later Israel). Syria had granted exit visas on the condition that the Jews did not go to Israel. The decision to finally free the Jews came about largely as a result of pressure from the United States following the 1991 Madrid Peace Conference.

Many Jews worked as coppersmiths in Damascus. These artisans developed a style and technique of their own, creating masterpieces of metalwork in the course of the 20th century. With the immigration of the last artisans to Israel in 1992, this era came to an end in Damascus.

[Hayyim J. Cohen / Leah Bornstein-Makovetsky (2nd ed.)]

BIBLIOGRAPHY: ANCIENT TIMES: Albright, in: BASOR, 83 (1941), 30–36; 163 (1961), 46–47; Abd el-Kader, in: *Syria*, 26 (1949), 191–5; Malamat, in: *Tarbiz*, 22 (1950/51), 64; idem, *Near Eastern Archaeology in the Twentieth Century* (1970), 164–77; Speiser, in: JAOS, 71 (1951), 257–8; Gordon, in: IEJ, 2 (1952), 174–5; M.F. Unger, in: *Israel and the Arameans of Damascus* (1957); Tocci, in: RSO, 35 (1960), 129–33; Mazar, in: BA, 25 (1962), 98–120. **ADD. BIBLIOGRAPHY:** R. Vilk, *"Yehudei Surya Haselvekit,"* doctoral thesis (1987); B.Z. Luria, *Ha-Yehudim be-Surya bi-ymei Shivat Zion, ha-Mishnah ve-ha-Talmud* (1957); E. Bareket, *Shafrir Miẓrayim* (1995), 17, 23, 51, 60, 71, 76, 84, 89, 114, 149, 153–55, 158–60, 162, 186, 200; L. Rot-Garson, *Yehudei Suriya* (2000). MEDIEVAL AND MODERN PERIODS: Alḥarizi, *Taḥkemoni*, ed. by A. Kaminka (1899), index; Mann, Egypt, index; Rosanes, Togarmah, 1 (1930^2), 175ff.; 2 (1937/382), 140ff.; 3 (1938^2), 218ff.; 4 (1935), 297ff.; 5 (1938), 207ff.; Assaf, in: *Tarbiz*, 9 (1937/38), 26–27; idem, in: BJPES, 11, no. 3–4 (1943–45), 42–45; E. and J.Y. Rivlin, in: *Reshumot*, 4 (1926), 77–119; Baron, in: PAAJR, 4 (1932/33), 3–31; A.J. Brawer, in: *Zion*, 5 (1940), 294–7; 11 (1946), 83–108; Ashtor, Toledot, 1 (1944), 295ff., 321, 325, 334; 2 (1951), 9ff., 114ff., 158, 171, 423ff., 413ff.; 3 (1970), 6, 142ff., 149, 150, 152, 155; idem, in: JQR, 50 (1959/60), 61; Benayahu, in: *Sinai*, 24 (1949), 91–105; S. Landshut, *Jewish Communities in the Muslim Countries of the Middle East* (1950), 57–60. **ADD. BIBLIOGRAPHY:** L.A. Frankl, *Yerushalayma* (1860), 106–21; A.K. Rafeq, *The Province of Damascus 1723–1783* (1966); A. Yaʿari, Iggerot, index; N. Zenner, in: *Peʿamim*, 3 (1979), 45–58; M. Gil, in: B.Z. Kedar (ed.), *Perakim be-Toledot Yerushalayim bi-Yimei ha-Beinayim* (1979), 39–106; J.M. Landau and M. Maoz, in: *Peʿamim*, 9 (1981), 4–13; S. Schwarzfuchs, in: *Michael*, 7 (1982), 431–44; A. Cohen, in: *Sefunot*, 17 (1983), 99–104; J. Sutton, *Aleppo Chronicles: The Story of the Unique Sepharadeem of the Ancient Near East in Their Own Words* (1988); H. Abrahami, in: *Shorashim ba*-Mizraḥ (1989), 133–72; A. Rodrigue, *De L'instruction à l'émancipation* (1989), index; idem, *Ḥinukh, Ḥevrah ve-Historiyah* (1991), 240–42; N.A. Stillman, *The Jews of Arab Lands in Modern Times* (1991); N. Al-Qattan, in: T. Phillip (ed.), *The Syrian Land in the 18th and 19th Century* (1992), 196–216; Z. Zohar, *Massoret u-Temurah, Hitmodedut Ḥakhmei Yisrael be-Miẓrayim u-ve-Surya im Etgerei ha-Modernizaẓiyah 1880–1920* (1993); idem, in: *Peʿamim*, 44 (1990), 80–109; idem, in: *Peʿamim*, 66 (1996), 43–69; M. Harel, in: *Bein Shenei Olamot: Tenuʿot ha-Noʿar be-Arẓot ha-Islam* (1995); W.P. Zenner, in: W.P. Zenner (ed.), *Jews among Muslims: Communities in the Precolonial Middle East* (1996), 161–72, 173–86; M. Ben-Sasson, in: *Peʿamim*, 66 (1996), 5–19; Y. Harel, in: *Peʿamim*, 67 (1996), 57–95; idem, in: *Zion*, 61 (1996), 183–207; idem, in: *Peʿamim*, 67 (1996), 56–95; idem, *Bi-Sefinot shel Esh la-Maʿarav* (2003); idem, in: *Peʿamim*, 74 (1998), 131–55; idem, in: *Peʿamim*, 86–87 (2001), 67–123; M. Laskier, in: *Peʿamim*, 66 (1996), 70–127; J. Frankel, *The Damascus Affair: "Ritual Murder," Politics and the Jews in* 1840 (1997); M. Bar-Asher, in: *Peʿamim*, 67 (1997), 125–41; R. Lamdan, *A Separate People, Jewish Women in Palestine, Syria and Egypt in the 16th Century* (2000), index.

DAMASCUS, BOOK OF COVENANT OF (the **Zadokite Documents** or the **Damascus Document**; abbr. CD for Cairo Damascus), work presenting the views of the sect which is said to have left the Land of Judah and emigrated to the Land of Damascus. The work first became known through the discovery by Solomon *Schechter in 1896 of two fragmentary manuscripts of it (conventionally called A and B) in the *genizah* of a Karaite synagogue in Cairo. Schechter dated A to the 10th century C.E. and B to the 11th or 12th. They represent two different recensions of the work, to judge by the relatively small portions which overlap. When the Qumran texts were discovered in 1947 and the following years, an affinity between some of them and the Damascus Document was speedily recognized, and it soon became evident that the sect referred to in the

Damascus Document must be identified with the Qumran community. This conclusion was confirmed with the discovery of fragments of the Damascus Document in the Qumran caves – fragments of seven manuscripts in Cave 4 and further fragments in Cave 6 (6QD).

The book is written in biblical Hebrew, free from Aramaisms. The style is marked throughout by linguistic usages from the Bible; it contains also later idioms most of which are known from the Mishnah. It includes homilies in the spirit of the ancient Midrashim and material paralleled in such apocryphal and pseudepigraphic writings as the Book of Jubilees and the Testament of the Twelve Patriarchs.

The Admonition

The first part of the work, named "The Admonition" by C. Rabin, comprises moral instruction, exhortation, and warning addressed to members of the sect, together with polemic against its opponents; it serves as a kind of introduction to the second part, called "The Laws" by Rabin (see bibliography). Even in the Qumran manuscripts, these two parts are not treated as separate compositions but belong together as one work. The lack of continuity in several places in both parts suggests that the work as it now is known is an abridgment of a longer work, over and above the fact that the abridgment itself has survived in a fragmentary form.

The first part contains some details about the history of the sect as understood by the author. At the end of 390 years (cf. Ezek. 4:5) after the destruction of the First Temple there sprouted forth from "Israel and Aaron" a "planted root," the beginning of the sect. Twenty years later there arose the *Teacher of Righteousness (CD 1:11; in 20:14 he is called *moreh ha-yaḥid*, "the unique teacher" or "the teacher of the One" – or, if *ha-yaḥad* is read – "the teacher of the community"). He organized those who accepted and kept his teaching in a "new covenant." At the same time arose "the man of mockery" or "preacher of falsehood" who misled Israel; in consequence, many of those who had entered the covenanted community left it and were accordingly "delivered to the avenging sword of the covenant." "At the end of the destruction of the land," when the influence of the backsliders and adversaries of the sect became stronger, those who remained true to the covenant went out of the holy city and "escaped to the land of the north." The leader of those who "turned back [from impiety] in Israel and went out of the land of Judah to sojourn in the land of Damascus" was "the lawgiver who expounds the Torah," who enacted laws by which "those who entered into the new covenant in the land of Damascus" might regulate their lives "until the teacher of righteousness arises at the end of days." But there were also betrayers of the covenant who returned, together with the "people of mockery," and those and others like them are threatened with severe punishment.

The "people of mockery" are those who "build up an insecure wall and daub it with white plaster" (cf. Ezek. 13:10); by these the author seems to indicate the Pharisees who made a fence to the Torah (Ar. 1:2). These, he says, walked in the stubbornness of their heart (cf. Deut. 29:18; Jer. 3:17, etc.), followed the preacher of falsehood, and were caught in "fornication" – a term used by the author (and by those like-minded) of those who married two wives simultaneously or who married their nieces. To have two wives at once is, for the author, a breach of the ordinance of creation. The example of David cannot be pleaded as a defense, because in his day the Torah was inaccessible; it had been sealed and hidden in the Ark "until Zadok arose," i.e., Zadok the priest whose sons are "the chosen of Israel, men of renown." As for marrying the daughter of one's brother or sister, this is not explicitly forbidden in the Torah (for which reason it was permitted by the Pharisees), but in the circle to which the author belonged it was evidently regarded as forbidden by analogy with the prohibition of marriage between aunt and nephew (cf. Lev. 18:12–14). In addition to committing fornication in these two respects, the "people of mockery" are charged with failing to keep the laws of uncleanness as specified in the Torah; they profane the Temple and "speak abominations against the ordinances of God's covenant, saying that they are not right." Because the Temple was rendered unclean by them, those who had entered into the covenant undertook not to approach the Temple or bring sacrifices to it; that would be "kindling God's altar in vain" and they would do better to shut the Temple door altogether, in accordance with Malachi 1:10.

The Laws

The second part of the work deals with the laws of the sect and its social arrangements. These laws comprise regulations for judgment, the Sabbath, the altar, the synagogue and the city of the Temple, the attitude to worshipers of idols, forbidden foods, and uncleanness. Several of these regulations correspond to the accepted law, but others are in opposition to it and correspond rather to the laws accepted by the Samaritans and the Karaites, and all of them are inclined to be severe. The social arrangements that were fixed by the leaders of the sect put its members under a severe discipline. The members of the sect in all their "camps" are divided into four classes: priests, Levites, Israelites, and proselytes. Their names must be recorded in a book. At the head of each "camp" stands a priest who understands the "book of the *Hagu*" (a book of laws, apparently some composition of the character of the Manual of *Discipline, which seems to be older than the Damascus Document). Next to the priest stands the "inspector (*mevakker*) of the camp" whose responsibility it is to act as guide and educator of those in the camp. A distinction seems to be drawn between those who live in camps as members of a separated community and those "living in camps after the order of the earth" – which may denote associate members or sympathizers with the sect who pursued normal family life in the cities of Israel.

The Sect

Before the discovery and study of the Qumran community, many conjectures were expressed about the identity and date of the sect of the Damascus Document. Even when it has been set in a wider context, many such questions remain undecided. The internal testimony of the work indicates that the sect existed at a time when the Temple still stood. A particularly knotty problem is presented by the reference to Damascus: is this to be understood literally (as was usually taken for granted when the Damascus Document was the only one of its kind extant) or as a "prophetic name" (cf. Amos 5:27) for the wilderness of Judah to which they had withdrawn? (For the latter view see Y. North, in PEFQ, 87 (1955), 34ff.; F.M. Cross, *The Ancient Library of Qumran* (1958), 59f.). Murphy-O'Connor suggested alternatively that it might actually refer to Babylon.

If Damascus is taken literally, it appears that when the sect fled there, some of its adversaries and enemies went there too, and instigated a number of its members to betray and forsake it. From this it may be argued that at that time Jerusalem and Damascus were controlled by separate (if not indeed opposing) governments, so that it was possible for refugees from Judah to find asylum in or near Damascus: this situation corresponds only to the time of the Hasmoneans. (It is relevant to note that the oldest manuscript fragment of the Damascus Document from Qumran has been dated by some scholars on paleographical grounds to the pre-Roman period; cf. Cross, op. cit., 59, n. 46). The flight of both members of the sect and their adversaries from Judah to Damascus under the Hasmonean regime is best related to the reign of Alexander *Yannai, to the time when his enemies (as is known from Josephus and from the Talmud) fled from the Land of Israel after his decisive victory in the long civil war. Yannai would have hated the people of the sect because they opposed the Hasmonean assumption of the high priesthood, which in their view belonged exclusively to the descendants of Zadok; and it is possible that they also participated in the war of the Pharisees against Yannai. On this basis it is possible to suggest the following time-sequence in the history of the sect: The growth of the sect ("the root") began during the reign of John *Hyrcanus I (135–114 B.C.E.), when the opposition of the Pharisees to the Hasmonean kings' exercise of the high-priestly function became manifest. Twenty years (half a generation) later arose the "Teacher" who organized the sect in a covenant, and after his death, which occurred during Yannai's reign (103–76 B.C.E.), the people of the sect fled (at the end of the civil war) to the land of Damascus. During the peace which followed under *Salome Alexandra, the "people of mockery" returned to Jerusalem as did several of the people of the sect. In that case the Damascus Document would have been written originally after Salome's death (67 B.C.E.), during the war between her sons Hyrcanus II and Aristobulus II, when Pompey was preparing to march on Jerusalem (63 B.C.E.); his invasion may be hinted at by the author in the words "He is the head of the kings of Yavan, who is coming to wreak vengeance upon them." (Pompey was by this time the master of all the rulers in the Hellenistic states, which had fallen under the dominion of Rome.)

So much can be inferred from the Damascus Document taken by itself. How far this reconstruction can be correlated with the evidence of the other Qumran texts is a subject for continuing study. Certainly the basic ideas, as well as the language and style of the Damascus fragments, correspond from every point of view with those of the Qumran scrolls. Such leading personalities as the Teacher of Righteousness and the Man of Mockery are as prominent in some of the Qumran texts as they are in the Damascus Document. One possibility to be considered is that the Damascus sect was a special branch of the Qumran *yaḥad* whose history differed somewhat from that of the *yaḥad* as a whole; another is that the Damascus Document reflects a later development of the Qumran community than that represented by the Manual of Discipline.

BIBLIOGRAPHY: S. Schechter, *Documents of Jewish Sectaries*, 1 (1910); L. Rost, *Die Damaskusschrift* (1933); C. Rabin, *The Zadokite Documents* (19582); S. Zeitlin, *The Zadokite Fragments* (facsimile edition, 1952); H.H. Rowley, *The Zadokite Fragments and the Dead Sea Scrolls* (1952). **ADD. BIBLIOGRAPHY:** J. Murphy-O'Connor, "An Essene Missionary Document? CD II, 14-VI, 1," in: *Revue Biblique*, 77 (1970), 201–29; P.R. Davies, *The Damascus Covenant: An Interpretation of the "Damascus Document"* (1982); M. Broshi (ed.), *The Damascus Document Reconsidered* (1992); S.C. Reif, "Solomon Schechter and his Oxbridge Academic Friends," in: *Bulletin of the Anglo-Israel Archaeological Society* 21 (2003), 103–4.

[Michael E. Stone / Frederick Fyvie Bruce]

DAMASCUS AFFAIR, a notorious *blood libel in 1840 in which Christian antisemitism and popular Muslim anti-Jewish feelings came to a head and were aggravated by the political struggle of the European powers for influence in the Middle East. Syria was then ruled by Muhammad Ali of Egypt, who had rebelled against Turkey. France supported Muhammad Ali, while the other powers, especially Austria and Great Britain, were interested in preserving Turkish power and in preventing the extention of French influence.

On February 5, 1840, the Capuchin friar Thomas, an Italian who had long resided in Damascus, disappeared together with his Muslim servant Ibrahim ʿAmāra. The monk had been involved in shady business, and the two men were probably murdered by tradesmen with whom Thomas had quarreled. Nonetheless, the Capuchins immediately circulated the news that the Jews had murdered both men in order to use their blood for Passover. As Catholics in Syria were officially under French protection, the investigation should have been conducted, according to local law, by the French consul. But the latter, Ratti-Menton, allied himself with the accusers, and supervised the investigation jointly with the governor-general Sherif Padia; it was conducted in the most barbarous fashion. A barber, Solomon Negrin, was arbitrarily arrested and tortured until a "confession" was extorted from him, according to which the monk had been killed in the house of David Harari by seven Jews. The men whom he named were subsequently arrested; two of them died under torture, one of them converted to Islam in order to be spared, and the others were made to "confess." A Muslim servant in the service of David Harari related under duress that Ibrahim ʿAmāra was killed in the house of Meir Farḥi, in the presence of the latter and other Jewish notables. Most of those mentioned were arrested, but one of them, Isaac Levi Picciotto, was an Austrian citizen and thus under the protection of the Austrian consul; this eventually led to the intervention of Austria, England, and the United States in the affair. When some bones were found in a sewer in the Jewish quarter, the accusers proclaimed that they were those of Thomas, and buried them accordingly. An inscription on the tombstone stated that it was the grave of a saint tortured by the Jews. Then more bones were found, alleged to be those of Ibrahim ʿAmāra. But a well-known physician in Damascus, Dr. Lograso, refused to certify that they were human bones, and requested that they be sent to a European university for examination. This, however, met with the opposition of the French consul. The authorities then announced that, on the strength of the confessions of the accused and the remains found of the victims, the guilt of the Jews in the double murder was proved beyond doubt. They also seized 63 Jewish children so as to extort the hiding place of the victims' blood from their mothers.

The news of the atrocities in Damascus aroused the concern of the Jewish world. The first Jewish attempt to intervene in the tragic situation came from Alexandria in the form of a petition addressed to Muhammad Ali, as a result of the initiative of Israel *Bak, the Jerusalem printer. At the same time, the Austrian consul general in Egypt, A. Laurin, received a report from the Austrian consul in Damascus and also petitioned Muhammad Ali to stop the torture methods used by the investigators. Muhammad Ali agreed, and instructions were accordingly issued to Damascus by express courier. As a result, the use of torture came to an end on April 25, 1840. However, the accusation itself was not rescinded and the investigation against the Jews continued. Laurin tried to influence the consul general of France in Egypt to restrain Ratti-Menton, who was his subordinate, but he was unsuccessful. He then acted in a manner contrary to diplomatic practice by sending the report he had received from Damascus to James de Rothschild, the honorary Austrian consul in Paris. He also requested Rothschild to intervene with the French government. This did not bring any result. In order to alert public opinion in France and in the civilized world, James de Rothschild, without the authorization of Chancellor Metternich in Vienna, published the report in the press. In Vienna, his brother Solomon Rothschild approached Metternich on the issue. The latter reprimanded Laurin, but nevertheless consented to his activity, as it caused embarrassment to the representatives of France in Egypt and Syria. Laurin was then joined by the British consul general in Egypt, as well as by other European consuls, who supported him in his dispute with the French. As a result of his efforts, an order was sent to Damascus on May 3, 1840, requesting protection for the Jews from the violence of Muslim and Christian mobs.

In the meantime, Western Jewry had been shocked by what had happened, and vigorous protests were voiced. Western European Jews and, especially, the Jews of France and Britain, saw signs of a return to the darkness of the Middle Ages. The events also alarmed assimilated Jews, as was evident from their reactions, even of such Jews as the young *Lasalle, who had completely broken away from Judaism. Enlightened non-Jews also protested against the accusation through the press and mass meetings. A Jewish delegation, whose members included Moses *Montefiore, his secretary Louis *Loewe, Adolphe *Crémieux, and Solomon *Munk, left for Egypt and was received by Muhammad Ali. The delegation requested that the investigation should be abandoned by the Damascus authorities and transferred to *Alexandria for judicial clarification or that the case be considered by European judges. This request was not granted as war was imminent between Egypt and Turkey. Both Muhammad Ali and the French wished to prevent an investigation into the events in Damascus. The Jews, whose first concern was the release of their coreligionists, decided to accept the simple liberation of the prisoners without any judicial declaration of innocence. In the end it was, however, explicitly stated that their liberation was an act of justice and not merely a favor granted by the ruler. The liberation order was issued on August 28, 1840, and those prisoners who were still alive in Damascus were saved.

Montefiore and his delegation left Egypt for Constantinople, where they appealed to the sultan for the publication of a *firman* which would proclaim blood libels fallacious and prohibit the trial of Jews on the basis of such accusations. Nevertheless, the Catholics of Damascus continued to tell tourists, for many years, about the saint who had been tortured and murdered by the Jews, and how the Jews had been saved from the gallows by the intrigues of Jewish notables from abroad. The Damascus Affair also aroused Jewish awareness of the need for intercommunal cooperation, finally resulting in the establishment of the Alliance Israélite *Universelle.

[Abraham J. Brawer]

Broader Repercussions

What caused extraordinary anxiety among the Jews of the West in 1840 was not only the danger facing their co-religionists in the Middle East but also, and probably even more, the fact that the accusation of ritual murder in Damascus was initially accepted as proven fact by almost the entire press in the constitutional states of Continental Europe. Typical was a report appearing in innumerable newspapers in April declaring that "Today the truth is known: of the nine accused [Jews] … seven are united in admitting everything … the body [of Father Thomas] was suspended head down; one [of the Jews] held a tub to collect the blood while two others applied pressure to facilitate the flow. Then, once the source of blood had dried up, all of them, maddened, threw themselves on the corpse, cutting it to bits."

In Britain, such reports were treated with greater skepticism, but there the country's leading newspaper, *The Times*, persistently advanced the thesis that given the prima facie case against their religion, the onus of disproving the ritual murder charge fell squarely on the Jews. *The Times*, like the influential German *Leipziger Allgemeine Zeitung*, now extensively reproduced the arguments frequently elaborated upon in Christian polemics since the 13th century that passages in the Talmud prescribed the sacrifice of Gentiles. Thus, an editorial article in *The Times* in June 1840 could declare the affair to be "one of the most important cases ever submitted to the notice of the civilized world … Admitting for the moment [the accusation to be true] … then the Jewish religion must at once disappear from the face of the earth … We shall await the issue as the whole of Europe and the civilized world will do with intense interest."

Adding still further to the sense of embattlement and shock that now overtook large segments of European Jewry was the situation that had developed in France by the summer of 1840. Not only was the charge of ritual murder emanating from the French diplomatic delegation in Damascus persistently and vociferously supported by the entire ultramontane Catholic press led by the influential daily *l'Univers* but, making matters much worse, the French premier, Adolphe Thiers, likewise gave his – albeit more guarded – backing to the consul in Syria, the Comte de Ratti-Menton. (Replying in June to critics in the Chamber of Deputies he declared, for example, that "you protest in the name of the Jews and I protest in the name of a Frenchman who until now has carried out his duties with honor and loyalty.") It was in the wake of the debate in the French parliament that the representative bodies of Jewry in France and Britain, the Consistoire Central and the Board of Deputies, took the difficult decision to dispatch the high-level delegation led by Adolphe Crémieux and Moses Montefiore to the Middle East. It had become all too clear, stated one prominent member of the Anglo-Jewish community, that at stake was "whether the flame of persecution … lighted up in the East … be so fed with bigotry that it shall increase … and go forth like some monster, destroying and to destroy, until the very name of Jew should be heard only with horror and disgust and their persons shall sink under cruelty, oppression and contempt … It is not merely … for humanity [and] our oppressed brethren that we are called upon to act; it is our own battle we fight."

Jewish historiography (as typically in the above entry) tended to downplay severely the extent of the verbal battering unleashed against the Jews in Europe during the course of 1840, and likewise generally ignored the fact that two radically opposed versions of the Damascus Affair were passed down to posterity and to a large extent have continued to follow their own separate courses until today. In the Jewish narrative the crisis for the most part culminated in a "happy ending," with the release of the surviving prisoners in Damascus; the issue of the firman by the Sultan in Constantinople repudiating the ritual murder myth; and the triumphant return home of Montefiore and Crémieux. However, from very early on, an alternative Judeophobic version of the affair was put into circulation. In 1846 a two-volume book was published in Paris, written by Achille Laurent (almost certainly a pseudonym), *Relation historique des affaires de Syrie depuis 1840 jusqu'en 1842*, which contained the complete protocols of the interrogation undertaken by the local and French authorities in Damascus during their investigation of the (alleged) murder of Father Thomas and Ibrahim 'Amara, as well as a large collection of documents marshaled to reinforce the thesis that the ritual murder is prescribed by Judaism (or at least practiced traditionally by some Jewish sects). The entire collection clearly emanated from the coterie which had manned the French consulate in 1840, and thus could be seen as something close to an official publication. Containing as they did a series of confessions describing in great detail how and why the Jews of Damascus had committed the murders – but omitting all mention of the extensive use of torture – the protocols once in the public domain acted over time as an effective counterweight to the version of the affair preserved in Jewish historiography and collective memory.

In the coming years and decades, the protocols were published in various editions in German, Italian, Arabic, and Russian. The idea that the ritual murder case had been conclusively proved in Damascus and the prisoners only released for political reasons or because of bribery now became a key theme repeated at length in an extensive series of antisemitic journals and books, ranging from the Jesuit *Civiltà Cattolica* to *Der Stuermer*, and from Gougenot des Mousseaux's *Le juif, le judaïsme et la judaïsation des peuples chrétiens* to August Rohling's *Talmudjude* and to Henri Desportes' *Le mystère du sang chez les juifs de tous les temps*. In 1986 Mustafa Talas, the Syrian minister of defense, issued yet another edition of the protocols together with numerous documents related to the case. The idea that the ritual charge had been authenticated conclusively in Damascus in 1840 is repeated from time to time in Arabic-language media and by diplomats representing various Arab states. The tomb (allegedly) housing Father Thomas' remains still stands in the Franciscan Terra Sancta church in Damascus and carries the statement that he was "murdered by the Jews on February 5, 1840."

[Jonathan Frankel (2nd ed.)]

BIBLIOGRAPHY: S. Posener, *Adolphe Crémieux*, 1 (Fr. 1933), 197–247, 259–60; D. Salomons, *An Account of the Recent Persecutions of the Jews at Damascus* (1840); L. Loewe, *The Damascus Affair* (1940), diary 1840; Szajkowski, in: *Zion*, 19 (1954), 167–70; Brawer, *ibid.*, 5 (1940), 294–7; A. Galanté, *Documents officiels turcs concernant les Juifs de Turquie* (1931), 157–61, 214–40; Meisl, in: *Festschrift… S. Dubnow…* (1930), 226–36; J. Jacobs, in: *The Jewish Experience in America*, 2 (1969), 271–80; JHSET, index; Milano, Bibliotheca, nos. 2450–51; *Aceldama* (It., 1896), treats Thomas as martyr. **ADD. BIBLIOGRAPHY**: J. Frankel, *The Damascus Affair* (1997); Y. Harel, *Be-Sefinot shel Esh la-Ma'arav* (2003).

°D'AMATO, ALFONSE M. (1937–), U.S. politician. Born in Brooklyn, New York, and raised on Long Island, he got his start in politics in rough-and-tumble Nassau County. D'Amato was a United States senator from 1981 until 1999 after defeating New York icon, incumbent Senator Jacob *Javits. D'Amato was popular with his more generally liberal Jewish constituents as well as other New Yorkers. Like most New York senators, D'Amato was an ardent supporter of Israel. He was well known for serving the needs of his constituents. Among the many constituents he served with dedication and determination were Holocaust survivors and their heirs in their battle to recover dormant accounts in Swiss banks. In 1996, Senator D'Amato chaired a hearing on the Swiss bank controversy before the U.S. Senate Banking Committee. He was the first to testify before the House on the necessity of investigating what happened to billions of dollars in Swiss banks from funds deposited by Jews or Jewish property looted by Nazis in the World War II era. D'Amato's work, along with that of the World Jewish Congress, forced Switzerland to face its past, its myth of wartime neutrality, and its postwar actions and to take the beginning steps towards a measure of justice in the fight for Holocaust restitution.

[Beth Cohen (2nd ed.)]

DAMAVAND, town situated at the foot of Mount Damavand, E. of Teheran, Iran. An old cemetery and ruins of a synagogue in Damavand attest to the existence of a Jewish settlement there. In the 17th century the Jews of Damavand are mentioned by the Judeo-Persian chronicler *Babai ibn Luṭf among the 18 Jewish communities which were searched for kabbalistic writings and became victims of the then current wave of forced conversion. The Shabbatean agitation in Persia is connected with one Samuel b. Aaron Damavandi. The 1871 famine which swept over Persia severely affected the Jews of Damavand, but the Jewish traveler, E. *Neumark, found some Jews still living in Damavand in about 1883–85.

BIBLIOGRAPHY: I. Ben-Zvi, *Meḥkarim u-Mekorot* (1966), index.

[Walter Joseph Fischel]

DAMESHEK, WILLIAM (1900–1969), U.S. hematologist. Dameshek, who was born in Voronezh, Russia, graduated from Harvard Medical School in 1923 and became instructor in medicine there. In 1941 he became professor of medicine at Tufts College Medical School in Boston. Dameshek was appointed professor of medicine at the Mount Sinai School of Medicine and attending hematologist to the Mount Sinai Hospital, both in New York City, in 1966. He received several awards for his contributions in the field of hematology. Dameshek was founder and chief editor of *Blood*, the journal of hematology. Dameshek authored or coauthored many articles, monographs, and books. His principal studies were on agranulocytosis, acquired hemolytic anemia, hypersplenism, and Mediterranean anemia. His books include *The Hemorrhagic Disorders* (1955), *Leukemia* (1958), *Hemolytic Syndromes* (1949), and *Leukopenia and Agranulocytosis* (1944). He was president of the American Society of Hematology (1964) and the International Society of Hematology (1954–56).

[Suessmann Muntner]

°**DAMIAN, PETER** (**Petrus Damiani**; c. 1007–1072), theologian, canonized by the church. On the request of a correspondent named Honestus, probably a monk, Damian wrote an anti-Jewish polemic in two parts: *Antilogus contra Iudaeos* and *Dialogus inter Iudaerum requirentem et Christianum e contrario respondentem.* At first Damian had hesitated to undertake the work, for he said it would be useless, as the Jews had already almost completely disappeared from the world; he finally decided to write it lest the inexperience of Christians in religious discussion both strengthen the audacity of unbelievers and give rise to doubts in the hearts of the faithful. However, because of his lack of any real contact with Jews and ignorance of the actual subjects of the Judeo-Christian debate, Damian's work is artificial; at the end he admits that he has little hope of its proving effective with the Jews.

BIBLIOGRAPHY: PL, 145 (1853), 41–67; B. Blumenkranz, *Les auteurs chrétiens latins…* (1963), 265–72.

[Bernhard Blumenkranz]

DAMIETTA (Ar. **Dumyāt**; in the Bible: Jer. 47:4 – isle of Caphtor; and Isa. 30:4 – Hanes), city in Egypt, about eight miles from the Mediterranean Sea. In medieval times, Damietta was an important commercial town, through which goods were transferred from Europe to the Orient. Hence it had a relatively important Jewish community which is mentioned frequently in *Genizah* documents. During the tenth century emigrants from Iraq settled there.

The 11th and 12th centuries were a period of prosperity for the community. It had a regular *bet din* and supported the academy of Ereẓ Israel and other causes. At the beginning of the 11th century the Palestinian *gaon* Josiah addressed a letter to the *av bet din* Amran, the *dayyanim* Eleazar and Amram, and the other elders of the community requesting the continued support of the Damietta community for the Palestinian academy. Nathan ben Abraham, who wished to be the Palestinian *gaon*, wrote a letter from Damietta before traveling to Ereẓ Israel. Many *Genizah* documents deal with Jewish merchants who did business with Damietta in the middle of the 11th century. A mid-12th-century document recording the sums collected in various communities for a drive sponsored by the **nagid* Samuel b. Hananiah indicates that the Damietta community was of medium size. David, the son of the Palestinian *gaon* *Daniel ben Azariah, took control of the Damietta community in the second half of the 11th century. *Benjamin of Tudela reported in the 12th century that the city's population included 200 Jews. In the 12th century, when Damietta was a flourishing commercial town of international importance, Jews from Christian countries frequently visited the city.

The *Mamluks destroyed the city in the middle of the 13th century, and the mouth of the Nile was blocked to prevent attacks by European fleets. Despite the city's decline a small community of Jews continued to live there. Al-Sadīd al-Dumyāṭī (i.e., "of Damietta") was physician to the sultan al-Malik al-Nāṣir Muḥammad in the first half of the 14th century. Jews were living in the city in the 15th century and a flourishing community existed there in the first half of the 16th century. David *Reuveni was a guest in the home of a Damietta Jew in 1523, and *David b. Solomon ibn Abi Zimra mentions that Jews of Damietta were engaged in international trade in the 16th century. An Ottoman order from 1577 mentions a Jew named Shemuel who was head of the money house in the city and also served as a *multazim* (leaseholder) and the tax collector in the ports of *Alexandria and Damietta. In the 16th century only one *melamed* served in the community. Rabbi Ḥayyim *Capusi (d. 1631) lived for a time in Damietta. In 1670 the vice consul of Venice in Damietta was a Jew. The community continued to flourish in the 17th century. Rabbi *Ḥiyya Rofe (d. 1618) mentions a Jew who bought grain in Egypt and sent it with his servant via Damietta to Acre. Rabbi Ḥayyim Abraham de Boton from Jerusalem was in Damietta in 1676. A Jewish court of law sat in Damietta in 1676 and dealt with an *agunah*. The court of law was dependent on the *bet din* of *Cairo. This *bet din* in Cairo boycotted a person who served as *ḥazzan*, *melamed*, and *shoḥet* in Damietta. The Jews resided in a special quarter. In 1668 the members of the *Hevra Kaddisha* in Damietta, *Rosetta, and Cairo searched for Jewish bodies in order to bury them. Until 1769 there were Jews who served as customs officers in Damietta. In 1833, 300–400 Jews lived in the city. Jacob *Saphir reported that during the 19th century very few Jews remained in Damietta; most of them went to Alexandria, which had become a great city again. In the census of 1897 there were only nine Jews in the city; in 1907, one; and in 1936, three.

BIBLIOGRAPHY: J. Saphir, *Even Sappir*, 1 (1866), 3, 8; Mann, Egypt, 2 (1922), index; Assaf, in: *Tarbiz*, 9 (1937/38), 208–9; Strauss, in: *Zion*, 7 (1941/42), 145ff.; Ashtor, Toledot, 1 (1944), 248–9; 2 (1951), 423; 3 (1970), index; idem, in: JJS, 19 (1968), 2ff.; Baneth, in: *Sefer ha-Yovel… A. Marx* (1950), 86–88; Goitein, in: *Sinai*, 33 (1953), 227; idem, in: *Tarbiz*, 24 (1954/55), 21ff., 134ff.; 25 (1955/56), 393ff. **ADD. BIBLIOGRAPHY:** N. Golb, in: *Journal of Near Eastern Studies*, 24 (1965), 251–70; 33 (1974), 126; J.M. Landau, *Jews in Nineteenth-Century Egypt* (1969), index; S.D. Goitein, *Ha-Yishuv be-Ereẓ Yisra'el mi-Reshit ha-Islam u-vi-Tekufat ha-Ẓalbanim* (1980), 202, 256; idem, *A Mediterranean Society*, 6 vols., index; B.Z. Dinur, *Yisra'el ba-Golah*, 1, 279; 2, 194; 3, 76; 4, 52; J.M. Landau (ed.), *Toledot ha-Yehudim be- Miẓrayim ba-Tekufah ha-Ottomanit, 1517–1914* (1988), index; M. Littman, in: *Mi-Mizraḥ u-mi-Maʿarav*, 2 (1980), 53–66; M. Benayahu, in: *Yad le-Heiman, Kovetz Meḥkarim le-Zekher A.M. Habermann* (1984), 264–65; M. Ben-Sasson, *Yehudei Siẓilia, 825–1068* (1991), 381–87; E. Bareket, *Shafrir Miẓrayim* (1995), 18, 95.

[Eliyahu Ashtor / Leah Bornstein-Makovetsky (2nd ed.)]

DAMĪRA, city in Lower Egypt. A Jewish community existed there during the Middle Ages, which is mentioned in 11th- and 12th-century *Genizah* documents. It seems that *David b. Daniel first settled in this city when he arrived in Egypt. About 100 years later Maimonides addressed himself to the Jews of Damīra in a general letter to the communities of the Delta. The 12th-century traveler *Benjamin of Tudela stated that there were 700 Jews in this city; it was thus the third largest community in Egypt, after those of Cairo and Alexandria. However, the accuracy of this report is dubious because of the scarcity of documents concerning the city.

BIBLIOGRAPHY: Worman, in: JQR, 18 (1905/06), 10; Mann, Egypt, 1 (1920), 187; 2 (1922), 290, 317; S. Schechter, *Saadyana* (1903), 80–104; JJS, 18 (1967), 41–42.

[Eliyahu Ashtor]

°DAMOCRITUS (possibly first century B.C.E.), Greek historian who, according to Suda, wrote a work "On the Jews," in which he claimed that the Jews worshiped a golden ass' head, and that every seven years they captured a foreigner whom they sacrificed to their god – the first occurrence in literature of the *blood libel. *Apion has a similar account. Since the Romans of that time prohibited human sacrifice, the inference made by Damocritus is that Judaism condoned superstition and misanthropy.

BIBLIOGRAPHY: M. Stern, *Greek and Latin Authors on Jews and Judaism.*, vol. 1 (1974), 530–31.

[Shimon Gibson (2nd ed.)]

DAMPIERRE-DE-L'AUBE, locality in the Aube department, France, E. of Troyes. Situated a short distance from *Ramerupt, another medieval center of Jewish learning in *Champagne, Dampierre-de-l'Aube was the home of such eminent 12th- and 13th-century scholars as *Isaac b. Samuel the Elder (1120?–1185?), his son *Elhanan (martyred in 1184?), and *Isaac b. Abraham (d. c. 1209). The most important Jewish financier of Dampierre, Jacob, the son of Sanson Rufus, lent 450 livres to the Abbey of St. Loup in Troyes in 1220. Before 1224, the abbey also owed him two life annuities.

BIBLIOGRAPHY: Gross, Gal Jud, 160–70; C. Lalore (ed.), *Cartulaire… Saint-Loup de Troyes* (1875), 250ff., 260, 271ff.; Urbach, Tosafot, passim.

[Bernhard Blumenkranz]

DAMROSCH, family of musicians. LEOPOLD DAMROSCH (1832–1885), born in Posen (Poznan), was a conductor and composer. He took a medical degree but devoted himself to music and the violin. As orchestral leader in Magdeburg and Weimar, and conductor in Breslau, he cooperated with Liszt, Hans von Buelow, and others, in championing the cause of contemporary composers. Settling in New York (1871), he founded the Oratorio Society (1873) and the New York Symphony Society (1878), and directed the first German opera season (1884–85) at the Metropolitan Opera House. Among his compositions were the choral works *Ruth and Naomi* (1875) and *Sulamith* (1882), and works for the violin. FRANK HEINO DAMROSCH (1859–1937), born in Breslau, son of Leopold, was organist and school music supervisor (in Denver and New York), chorusmaster at the Metropolitan (1885–91), and director of choral societies. WALTER JOHANNES DAMROSCH (1862–1950), born in Breslau, younger son of Leopold, took over his father's conducting posts at the Metropolitan Opera and Oratorio Society, and conducted the New York Symphony Society from 1885 to 1927. He also directed his own opera company (1894–99). Walter Damrosch played an important part in the development of American concert life and its rise to world standards. He toured the U.S. widely, invited Tchaikovsky to America (1891), and gave the first American performances of many important works, including Tchaikovsky's last two symphonies. From 1927 he was music adviser to the National Broadcasting Corporation and did much educational work on the radio. He appeared in two films, *The Star Maker* and *Carnegie Hall* (1947), and wrote an autobiography, *My Musical Life* (1923, 1930^2).

BIBLIOGRAPHY: L.P. and R.P. Stebbins, *Frank Damrosch* (Eng., 1945); W.J. Henderson, in: *Musical Quarterly*, 18 (1932), 1–8 (on Walter); E.T. Rice, *ibid.*, 25 (1939), 129–34 (on Frank); 28 (1942), 269–75 (on Leopold); Riemann-Gurlitt; Baker, Biog Dict; Grove, Dict.

[Dora Leah Sowden]

DAN (Heb. דָּן).

(1) Biblical city in the Ḥuleh Valley near the sources of the Jordan. It was originally called Laish and was dominated by the Phoenicians of Sidon (Judg. 18:7, 27ff.). Laish is mentioned in the Egyptian Execration Texts of the early 18th century B.C.E. and in the list of cities conquered by Thutmose III (c. 1469 B.C.E.). Leshem is a variant spelling of Laish (Josh. 19:47). When the tribe of *Dan, under pressure from the Amorites, left their original territory and moved northward, they captured the city of Laish in a surprise raid and renamed it Dan. At the same time a sanctuary was established there with *Micah's idol and descendants of Moses acting as priests (Josh. 19:47; Judg. 1:34; 18:2ff.). The sanctuary continued to function until Tiglath-Pileser III's conquest in 733 B.C.E. and his exile of the inhabitants to Assyria (II Kings 15:29, where Dan, however, is not explicitly mentioned). The Bible anachronistically calls the city Dan already in the account of Abraham's pursuit of the four kings (Gen. 14:14) and when Moses before his death was shown "all the land, even Gilead as far as Dan" (Deut. 34:1). From the time of the Judges onward, Dan was regarded as the extreme northern point of Ereẓ Israel with Beer-Sheba as the southern (Judg. 20:1, etc.). Jeroboam erected a temple and set up a golden calf at Dan, and a second one at Beth-El (I Kings 12:29ff.); these rivals to Jerusalem were vehemently criticized by the prophets (Amos 8:14). During the reign of his successor Baasa, the city was sacked by Ben-Hadad, king of Aram-Damascus (I Kings 15:20). Dan was the gateway for all northern invasions of Ereẓ Israel (Jer. 4:15; 8:16). In the Hellenistic period it was apparently called Antioch; it marked the northernmost point of Alexander Yannai's conquests (Jos., Ant., 13:394; Wars, 1:105). The city subsequently failed to recover and remained a village called Kefar Dan in the Talmud (TJ, Dem. 1:1, 22c). Dan is identified with Tell al-Qāḍī (now Tell Dan) on one of the main sources of the Jordan.

Excavations begun in 1966 and directed by Avraham Biran have confirmed the identification of the site, with the discovery of a bilingual dedicatory inscription in Greek and Aramaic "To the God who is in Dan." The site was apparently first settled during the Neolithic period in the fifth millennium B.C.E. Strong fortifications and building remains from the Early Bronze Age have been uncovered; its name at that time may very well have been Laish (cf. Judges 18:29, which equates Laish with Dan). The Middle Bronze Age II at Dan is represented by massive fortifications, with earthen ramparts and a remarkably well-preserved mud-brick triple-arched gateway. The site prospered throughout the Middle and Late Bronze Ages. Mycenaean imports, including a complete charioteer vase, and a large quantity of vessels and ivory objects were found in a specially built tomb dated to the 14th century B.C.E. The Early Iron Age is represented at the site by a change in the character of the settlement, with vessels and other artifacts suggesting that the population was mixed, some local with others from Cyprus, Phoenicia, and southern Israel and Jordan. From the latter part of the Iron Age are the remains of a cultic high place (cf. the setting up of a golden calf at Dan by Jeroboam I of Israel; I Kings 12:20). The ninth century B.C.E. is well represented at the site by fortifications, gates, and a stone-paved piazza with standing stones (*maẓẓevot*). Fragments of an important stele inscribed in Aramaic and mentioning the "king of Israel" and the "house of David" were discovered in this area (for the various interpretations and discussions, see Bibliography below). Additional remains from the Iron Age II, as well as from the Persian, Hellenistic, and Roman periods, have also been uncovered at the site.

[Michael Avi-Yonah / Shimon Gibson (2nd ed.)]

(2) Kibbutz in northern Israel in the Ḥuleh Valley near the spring of the Dan River. The kibbutz, affiliated with Kibbutz Arẓi ha-Shomer ha-Ẓa'ir, was founded on May 4, 1939, one day after neighboring *Dafnah, as the second of the complex of settlements called the "Ussishkin fortress." Situated until 1967 directly on the Syrian border, Dan, together with Dafnah, had to repel enemy attacks in the early months of the War of Independence (1948). In the two subsequent decades it often came under Syrian artillery fire, particularly in the period preceding the Six-Day War. Its founders were pioneers from Romania, later joined by newcomers from various countries. The kibbutz economy was based on three industries: irrigation systems, polycarbonates, and PVC. Its farming was based mainly on fishery but also included field crops, orchards, and beehives. In the mid-1990s the population was approximately 560, dropping to 421 in 2002. Bet Ussishkin, a museum for vegetation, wildlife, antiquities, and settlement history of the region, is located there.

[Efraim Orni / Shaked Gilboa (2nd ed.)]

BIBLIOGRAPHY: J. Braslavski, *Ha-Yadata et ha-Areẓ*, 1 (1955^6), 176ff.; Avi-Yonah, in: BJPES, 10 (1943), 19–20; Dothan, in: *Eretz Israel*, 2 (1953), 166ff.; Aharoni, Land, index; Press, Ereẓ.; Albright, in: AASOR, 6 (1926), 16ff. **ADD. BIBLIOGRAPHY:** EXCAVATIONS: A. Biran, *Biblical Dan* (1994); idem, "Sacred Spaces: Of Standing Stones, High Places and Cult Objects at Tel Dan," in: *Biblical Archaeology Review*, 24:5 (1998), 38–45, 70; A. Biran, D. Ilan, and R. Greenberg, *Dan I: A Chronicle of the Excavations, the Pottery Neolithic, the Early Bronze Age, and the Middle Bronze Age* Tombs (1996); A. Biran and Rachel Ben-Dov, *Dan II: A Chronicle of the Excavations and* *the Late Bronze Age "Mycenaean Tomb"* (2002); D. Ilan, "Tel Dan in the Early Iron Age: A Cultural Crucible," in: *Bulletin of the Anglo-Israel Archaeological Society*, 22 (2004): 69. ARAMAIC STELE FRAGMENTS: A. Biran and J. Naveh. "An Aramaic Stele Fragment from Tel Dan," in: IEJ, 43 (1993), 81–98; idem, "The Tel Dan Inscription: A New Fragment," in: IEJ, 45 (1995), 1–18; E. Ben Zvi, "On the Reading '*bytdwd*' in the Aramaic Stele from Tel Dan," in: *Journal for the Study of the Old Testament*, 64 (1994) 25–32; F.H. Cryer, "On the Recently Discovered 'House of David' Inscription," in: *Scandinavian Journal of the Old Testament*, 8:1 (1994), 3–19; idem, "A '*Betdawd*' Miscellany: *Dwd, Dwd'* or *Dwdh?*" in: *Scandinavian Journal of the Old Testament*, 9:1 (1995), 52–58; idem, "King Hadad," in: *Scandinavian Journal of the Old Testament*, 9:2 (1995), 223–35; idem, "Of Epistemology, Northwest-Semitic Epigraphy and Irony: The 'BYTDWD/House of David' Inscription Revisited," in: *Journal for the Study of the Old Testament*, 69 (1996) 3–17; B.I. Demsky, "On Reading Ancient Inscriptions: The Monumental Aramaic Stele Fragment from Tel Dan," in: *Journal of the Ancient Near Eastern Society*, 23 (1995), 29–35; N.P. Lemche and T.L. Thompson. "Did Biran Kill David? The Bible in the Light Of Archaeology," in: *Journal for the Study of the Old Testament*, 64 (1994), 3–22; G.A. Rendsburg, "On the Writing of bytdwd in the Aramaic Inscription from Tel Dan," in: IEJ, 45 (1995), 22–25; V. Sasson, "The Old Aramaic Inscription from Tell Dan: Philological, Literary and Historical Aspects," in: JSS, 40 (1995), 11–30; W.M. Schniedewind, "Tel Dan Stela: New Light on Aramaic and Jehu's Revolt," in: BASOR, 302 (May 1996), 75–90; T.L. Thompson, "'House of David': An Eponymic Referent to Yahweh as Godfather," in: *Scandinavian Journal of the Old Testament*, 9:1 (1995), 59–74; idem, "Dissonance and Disconnections: Notes on the *bytdwd* and *hmlk.hdd* Fragments from Tel Dan," *Scandinavian Journal of the Old Testament*, 9:2 (1995), 236–40. **WEBSITE:** www.galil-elion.org.il

DAN (Heb. דָּן), the fifth son of Jacob and the firstborn of *Bilhah, Rachel's maid (Gen. 30:1–6).

The Name

The narrative attributes the origin of the name Dan to Rachel, who said: "God has vindicated me (*dananni*); indeed, He has heeded my plea and given me a son" (30:6). The name would thus be derived from the verb *dyn* ("to judge or vindicate"; cf. Gen. 49:16). Some scholars see in the name Dan the divine epithet *dayyan*, while others regard it as a divine name in itself. Most likely, however, the literal meaning intended by the biblical etymology is correct, and the name Dan should be regarded as a short form of Dan(ann)iel or the like.

The Tribe and Its Inheritance

Dan is listed first among the handmaid tribes in Jacob's blessing (Gen. 49:16–18), but second in the blessing of Moses (Deut. 33:22) and the Song of Deborah (Judg. 5:17). In tribal genealogies, only one clan is attached to Dan, Hushim (Gen. 46:23 or, by metathesis, Shuham, Num. 26:42). In the wilderness wanderings, the tribe encamped north of the Tabernacle together with Asher and Naphtali (Num. 2:25–29). It numbered 62,700 and 64,400 adult males respectively in the two censuses taken in this period (Num. 2:26; 26:43). The territorial inheritance of the tribe was decided by lot at Shiloh (Josh. 19:40–48). It is stated to have bordered the territory of Ephraim to the north, Benjamin to the east, and Judah to the south, and to have ex-

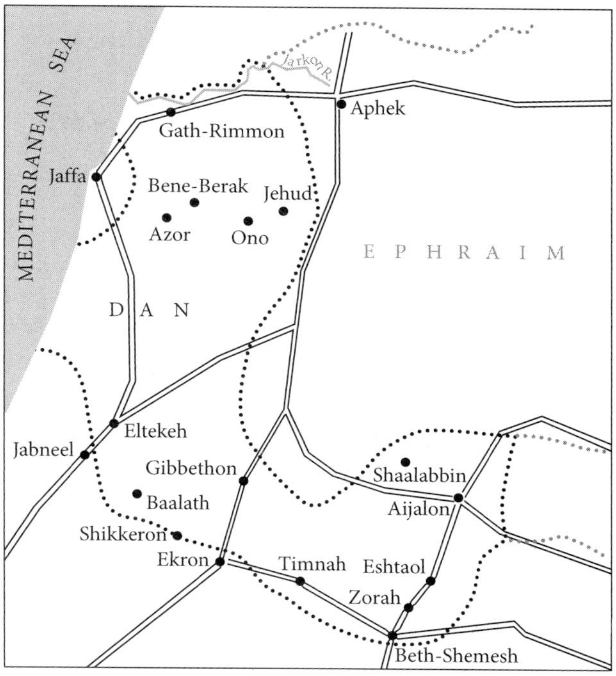

The allotted territory of the tribe of Dan. After Y. Aharoni, Lexicon Biblicum, *Dvir Co. Ltd, Tel Aviv.*

tended into the maritime plain. Seventeen settlements, most of which have been definitely identified, are included within the borders of Dan, but there is no unanimity as to whether the list reflects the Danite occupation before the migration northward, or a later period. Y. Kaufmann is convinced of the former, while A. Alt assigns the list of cities to the period of Josiah. Between these two extremes, B. Mazar steers a middle course by dating the list to the period of the United Kingdom. According to him, it reflects the historic and geographic development of the territory of Dan in the course of time. He divides the list of settlements into four groups or, more accurately, into four districts. The first includes Zorah, Eshtaol, and Ir-Shemesh (Beth Shemesh) in the southeast section of the coastal plain, and is the area of the initial settlement of the Danites. The second district includes Shaalabbin, Aijalon, Ithlah, and Elon in the Valley of Aijalon area. This constituted a mixed settlement, in which the struggle between the Israelites and the native population continued until the time of David. These two districts, including those cities which became Israelite, formed one administrative unit in the reign of David, and fell within the province of the second of Solomon's commissioners (I Kings 4:9). As to the two additional districts – Timnah, Ekron, Eltekeh, Gibbethon, and Baalath (i.e., the region of the Wadi Sorek and north of it), and Jehud, Bene-Berak, Gath-Rimmon, Me-Jarkon, and Rakkon, with its boundary close to Jaffa – they appear to have been annexed to the kingdom of Israel following the westward extension of its borders into Philistine territories. For these reasons, Mazar places the list of Joshua 19:40–48 in the period of Solomon.

According to Y. Aharoni, the list of Danite cities represents the earliest stage of Solomon's second administrative district, while I Kings 4:9 reflects the reduction in the region made toward the end of his reign. Four levitical cities situated in the territory of Dan are among the cities listed in Joshua 19:40–48, i.e., Aijalon, Gibbethon, Eltekeh, and Gath-Rimmon (Josh. 21:23–24). If the levitical cities were administrative centers and store cities built by Solomon in which he settled the levites "for all the work of the Lord and for the service of the king" (I Chron. 26:30–32), then this would support Mazar's dating of the list of Danite cities to the days of Solomon.

The History of the Tribe

Dan was the only one of the handmaid tribes originally to settle among the tribes of Leah and Rachel. Its inheritance bordered on Ephraim, Benjamin, and Judah. It would seem that, at first, its territory was limited to the area between Zorah and Eshtaol. Here, however, they were under pressure from Amorites on the west (Judg. 1:34), and perhaps also from the house of Joseph on the east (1:35). There may even have been pressure from *Judah (15:11). At any rate, the tribe of Dan was forced to search for a new area of settlement (18:1). The story of this second attempt is related in detail in a unique narrative which may have wider significance (Judg. 18). The Danite experience possibly constitutes the paradigm for all movements and migrations of the tribes of Israel during the period of settlement. The operation began with the dispatch of scouts (cf. Num. 13) to gather information about a suitable location. Five "able men" were sent from Zorah and Eshtaol "to spy out the land and to explore it" (Judg. 18:2). The spies found Laish and its environs to be adequate to their needs because it was fertile country, rich and spacious (18:9–10). Its conquest would present no great military problems since the city was isolated due to its distance from the Sidonian metropolis (18:7, 10, 27–28). Three references in ancient Hebrew poetry reflect the history of the Danites during the period of the Judges and the beginning of the monarchy. These are the allusions to be found in Jacob's blessing (Gen. 49), the blessing of Moses (Deut. 33), and the Song of Deborah (Judg. 5), short poetic utterances in which, however, there is more that is obscure than is clear. Jacob's blessing appears to reflect the earliest period in the history of the Danites, describing a tribe which, on the one hand, is struggling for recognition, participation, and responsibility within the tribal confederacy (Gen. 49:16) and, on the other, is fighting for its survival against nomadic tribes or even the Amorites (49:17). In the Song of Deborah the tribe is berated for not having participated in the war against the Canaanites. With biting irony the question is asked, "… and Dan, why did he abide with the ships?" (Judg. 5:17). It is not clear from this verse exactly where Dan resided at the time of Deborah's war, whether in the south across from Jaffa on the coast before the migration northward (cf. Josh. 19:46), or already in the north following the migration. Scholarly opinion generally favors the presence of Dan already in the north at this time, since it appears in the Song of Deborah together with the northern tribe of Asher. In the blessing of Moses it is clear that the tribe is in its northern location, since it is described as "a lion's whelp that leaps forth from Bashan" (Deut. 33:22), and is also coupled with the northern Naphtali, its "brother" tribe (cf. Gen. 30:6–8). The *Samson narratives indirectly give information concerning the Danite families which remained in their southern inheritance during the period of the Judges (Judg. 13–16). Those families in Mahaneh-Dan between Zorah and Eshtaol (Judg. 13:25) were subjugated by the Philistines together with the tribes of the house of Joseph and Judah, though they suffered more than the others since they were the first to be affected by the Philistine eastward expansion. Samson's guerrilla activities led to a hardening of Philistine rule (15:9). At the same time, Samson's experiences show that despite the attempt to preserve the purity of the family, tribe, and nation by not intermixing with the nations of the land (14:3), social contact and even marital ties were established between the Danite clans and the Philistines. According to Y. Yadin, the biblical references prove that at a certain stage of Dan's settlement the tribe enjoyed the closest relations with the Sea Peoples, that Dan was an ancient tribe that extended over the entire east, and that during this early period it had no connection with the confederacy of the tribes of Israel. It gradually moved closer to the tribes of Israel until it was accepted into the amphictyony and became one of them. Its original area of settlement was along the coast near Jaffa, in the region between the settlements of the Philistines and those of the Tjeker mentioned in Egyptian records. In Yadin's view there is a close relationship between the tribe of Dan and the tribe of Danaoi whose members were clearly seafarers who had a propensity for the worship of the sun and whose heroes excelled in their talent for solving riddles. Factions of the tribe wandered as fighting troops, spread to different places, and founded cities which they named for the patriarchs of the tribe. These groups of the tribe of the Danaoi were particularly attracted to the east Mediterranean coast in general and the Jaffa area in particular. The similarities between their history and that of the tribe of Dan led Yadin to suggest the identification of the two. It is possible, however, to explain the parallels as resulting from contact and influence. Moreover, there does not appear to have been any contact between the Sea Peoples and the tribe of Dan before the migration of the latter to the north under Amorite pressure (Judg. 1:34). The information about Dan from the period of the monarchy until the destruction is negligible. It would seem that with the founding of the monarchy the Danite clans in the south were assimilated into the kingdoms of Judah and Israel and lost their distinctiveness. As for those in the north, they appear to have been concentrated around the city of Dan, the importance of which increased after the division of the kingdom. Jeroboam son of Nebat, the first king of Israel, established a central royal sanctuary in Dan, the northern end of his kingdom, and placed in it one of the two golden calves for the worship of the God of Israel, in an attempt to renew the ancient cultic centers and to revive the early traditions, in order to remove the members of the northern kingdom from contact with Jerusalem and its Temple (I Kings 12:28–30). The Danite clans of the north apparently intermingled with their neighbors, especially the tribe of Naphtali (cf. I Kings 7:13 with II Chron. 2:13) and even with the people of Tyre (*ibid.*). The territory of Dan in the north constituted the northern flank of the kingdom of Israel and it suffered in the struggles and wars between Israel and Aram and between Israel and Assyria. In the time of King Baasha of Israel, the cities of Dan (Ijon, Dan, and Abel-Beth-Maacah) were conquered by Ben-Hadad, king of Aram, who had been hired by King Asa of Judah (I Kings 15:16–20). In the time of Pekah, king of Israel, the territory of Dan together with that of Naphtali and the whole of Galilee was conquered by Tiglath-Pileser III (732 B.C.E.), and its inhabitants were exiled to Assyria (II Kings 15:29). In this region, he established the Assyrian province of Megiddo.

[Isaac Avishur]

In the *Aggadah*

When Bilhah called her first son Dan ("judge"), she also prayed that it would be given to Samson, his descendant, to judge his people, and that they would not fall into the hands of the Philistines (Targ. Yer., Gen. 30:6). Similarly Jacob's deathbed blessing to Dan centered principally around Samson, who would bring victory to his people unaided (Gen. R. 98:13). In the same blessing Jacob ranked Dan equally with Judah, in that Samson's father would be of the tribe of Dan and his mother of Judah (*ibid.*; cf. Num. R. 10:5; 13:9), the Messiah to be descended from Dan on his mother's side. Dan, more than all his brothers, desired to slay Joseph hoping thereby that Jacob's love for Joseph would be turned to him (Test. Patr., Dan 1:4–7). Dan's only son was called Hushim ("rushes") because his children were destined to be as numerous as rushes (BB 143). Dan was one of Jacob's five weak sons (Rashi on BK 92a but see Gen. R. 95:4 for the opposite view). His descendants were all idol worshipers (PdRK 27b).

BIBLIOGRAPHY: A. Alt, in: PJB, 35 (1939), 38–39; Y. Kaufmann, *The Biblical Account of the Conquest of Palestine* (1953); Z. Kallai, in: VT, 8 (1958), 134–60; idem, *Naḥalot Shivtei Yisrael* (1967), 304–12; B. Mazar, in: BIES, 24 (1960), 8–16; Aharoni, Land, index; Y. Ben-Zvi, in: *Oz le-David Ben-Gurion* (1964), 177–82; Y. Yadin, in: Ha-Ḥevrah le-Ḥeker ha-Mikra (ed.), *Ma'aravo shel ha-Galil…* (1965), 42–55; A. Malamat, in: *Biblica*, 51 (1970), 1–16; Ginzberg, Legends, index.

DAN (Gurvich), FYODOR ILYICH (1871–1947), Russian Socialist and journalist. Born in St. Petersburg, Dan was a physician by profession. He joined the Socialist movement and in 1898 was banished to Siberia for three years. At the conference of the Social Democratic Workers party in 1902 he represented the underground newspaper *Iskra*, of which Lenin was one of the editors. In the following year he was rearrested and again sent to Siberia. This time he escaped abroad and joined the Menshevik wing of the party, in which he became a prominent figure. He returned to Russia in 1905, but in 1908 he was again forced to leave the country as a political exile. When he returned to Russia in 1912, he became editor of the newspaper *Rabochaya Gazeta*. In World War I, Dan served for a short time as an army doctor but in spite of his war service he was again sent to Siberia.

The February Revolution of 1917 set Dan free. He played an important role as a member of the presidium of the Petrograd Soviet and on the executive of the All-Russian Soviet, and opened the Second Congress in 1918. But unlike the Bolsheviks, he favored the continuation of the war, and opposed their policies. He was arrested in 1922 and after a year in prison was compelled to leave the Soviet Union. In 1923 he was a Menshevik delegate at the founding of the Labor and Socialist International (in Hamburg). He was one of the editors of *Sotsialisticheski vestnik* first in Berlin and then in Paris; and after the death of his brother-in-law Julius *Martov, in 1923, he became the leading figure in the Russian Social-Democratic movement in exile. In 1940 he settled in New York.

Dan wrote the essay "Die Sozialdemokratie Russlands nach dem Jahre 1908" in Martov's *Geschichte der russischen Sozialdemokratie* (1926). His own book, *Proiskhozhdenie bolshevizma* ("The Source of Bolshevism," New York, 1946), appeared shortly before his death. In the years 1941–47 he published the magazine *Novyi Put*. He was opposed to Zionism, but as early as 1904 published an article in *Iskra* denouncing antisemitism and supporting Jewish self-defense. In his last years he sympathized with the idea of a Jewish state.

DAN, JOSEPH (1935–), scholar and educator in Jewish Studies and Thought. Born in Bratislava, Czechoslovakia, he was taken to Palestine when he was three. His family settled in Jerusalem and Dan studied at the Hebrew University where he received a Ph.D. for his thesis on "The Theological Basis of the Ethical Thought of Ashkenazi Ḥasidism."

He began teaching at the Hebrew University in 1958, initially in the Department of Hebrew Literature and later in the Department of Jewish Thought where he was appointed professor of Kabbalah in 1978.

One of the most prominent researchers in the area of Jewish mysticism, Dan's research combined a historical, philological, and literary approach. The areas he concentrated on included the beginnings of the Kabbalah, the *Heikhalot* literature, the Ashkenazi Ḥasidic movement, and ethics and Ḥasidism.

In the teaching of Jewish Thought, he developed academic projects of wide public dimensions. He was the editor of *Jerusalem Studies in Jewish Thought* and wrote the Open University course "The Theology and Ethics of the Ashkenazi Ḥasidic Movement," bridging the gap between the purely academic sphere and the broader public.

He was a member of the editorial board of the quarterly *Tarbiz* from 1981 to 1986 and was director of the Jewish National and University Library 1984–1985.

He was responsible for writing and editing the catalogue of the 12,000-volume Scholem library which houses most of the books ever published in the area of Jewish mysticism. Dan published nearly 200 studies in various scholarly journals and articles in various encyclopedias including the *Encyclopaedia*

Judaica for which he was departmental editor for medieval Hebrew prose.

His books include *Ethical and Homiletical Literature* (Heb.; 1975), *The Ḥasidic Story* (Heb.; 1975), *The Teachings of Ḥasidism* (1983), and *Gershom Scholem and the Mystical Dimension in Jewish History* (1987). In 1998 and 1999 he published his four-volume *Jewish Mysticism*, a historical and comparative study.

In recognition of his great contribution to his field he was awarded the Israel Prize in 1997.

[Elaine Hoter]

DAN, LESLIE L. (1929–), Canadian entrepreneur and philanthropist. Dan was born in Budapest, Hungary. He survived the Holocaust as a teenager with the aid of false identity papers. Still a teenager when he arrived in Canada in 1947, Dan worked as a lumberjack and waiter to put himself though the University of Toronto, where he earned a B.Sc. in pharmacy in 1954 and an M.B.A. in 1959. He began an over-the-counter drug distribution company in 1960 and in 1965 created Novopharm. When he sold it to Israel's Teva Pharmaceuticals in 2000, the company was a world leader in pharmaceutical research and manufacture. While Dan remained on the Board of Teva he went on to develop and become chair of Viventia, which specializes in the discovery and development of products for the treatment of cancer.

A widely respected businessman, Dan also turned his expertise and personal fortune to battling disease worldwide. In 1985 he founded the Canadian Medicine Aid Programme (CAN-MAP) which provides millions of dollars of medicines and other aid to the sick in the developing world. He was a donor to Yad Vashem, and his generous support of the University of Toronto is evident in the Leslie Dan Faculty of Pharmacy and the Leslie L. Dan Pharmacy Building, which was completed in 2005. Toronto's Aish HaTorah's Dan Family Building is named in his honor, and he received honorary doctorates from several universities. He was also active on the boards of several Toronto hospitals and supported a wide range of health-oriented initiatives at Canadian universities. In 1996 Dan was awarded the Order of Ontario and made a Member of the Order of Canada.

[Paula Draper (2nd ed.)]

DAN, SERGIU (originally **I. Rossman**; 1903–1976), Romanian novelist and journalist. Born in Piatra-Neamt, Moldavia, Dan began his literary career by publishing original poems at the age of 19. He later wrote for such leading Romanian periodicals as *Contemporanul, Vremea*, and *Viata Româneasca*, and for *Bilete de Papagal*, a satirical magazine edited by the poet Tudor Arghezi. Dan was also for a time the political editor of the newspaper *Dreptatea*. His career in fiction began in 1929 when, in collaboration with Rumulus Dianu, he wrote *Viaţa minumată a lui Anton Pann* ("The Wonderful Life of Anton Pan"). His own first novel, *Dragoste şi moarte în provincie* ("Love and Death in the Provinces," 1931) won him a major Romanian literary prize. After this came two studies of middle-class life, *Arsenic* (1934) and *Surorile Veniamin* ("The Veniamin Sisters," 1935). In 1945 Dan published a novel, *Unde începe noaptea* ("When the Night Begins"), dealing with the fate of a Jewish family during the Hitler era and containing moving descriptions of life in the concentration camps. This was followed by *Roza şi ceilalţi* ("Rosa and the Others," 1947), an account of Jewish life in the provinces during the grim years of Fascist persecution. Both postwar novels are noteworthy for their penetrating psychological insight. During the next decade Dan published translations from French writers including Voltaire, Anatole France, and Aragon. Two later novels, *Taina Stolnicesei* (1958) and *Tase cel mare* ("Tase the Great," 1964), were of only minor literary significance.

BIBLIOGRAPHY: G. Călinescu, *Istoria literaturii romîne dela origini pînă în prezent* (1941), 713, 919.

[Abraham Feller]

°**DANBY, HERBERT** (1889–1953), English Hebraist. Danby went to Jerusalem in 1919, first as a librarian and later as a canon of the Anglican Cathedral of St. George, remaining there until he was appointed professor of Hebrew at Oxford in 1936. Although Danby devoted his efforts mainly to the translation of tannaitic legal codes and that of Maimonides, he was also a pioneer among Christian Hebraists in taking modern Hebrew seriously as both an academic and a literary medium, and in developing an assessment of Judaism that was not merely positive but also possessed of insight. Thus, in 1939 he published (with M.H. *Segal) an English and (modern) Hebrew dictionary. Danby's reputation rests on his English translation of *The Mishnah* (1933), which is considered a standard reference work. He also contributed books 9 ("Offerings") and 10 ("Cleanness") to the Yale English translation of Maimonides' *Mishneh Torah* (1950, 1954). He translated J. Klausner's *Jesus of Nazareth* (1925) and *History of Modern Hebrew Literature* (1932) as well as Ḥ.N. Bialik's *Biblical Legends* (1938). His first work had been a translation of the Mishnah and Tosefta of the tractate *Sanhedrin* (1919), and in 1927 he published *The Jew and Christianity*.

[Raphael Loewe]

DANBY, MICHAEL (1955–), Australian politician. Danby was born and educated in Melbourne, the son of a German Jew who fled to Australia after *Kristallnacht*. He worked for many years for the *Australia-Israel Review*, a Melbourne-based fortnightly magazine of which he was editor from 1986 to 1993, before entering the Australia parliament as the Labor member for Melbourne Ports, a heavily Jewish seat, in 1998, the only Jew in Australia's House of Representatives. He often defended Israel against critics of its policies, many from the left wing of his own party. From 2001 he served as an Opposition whip.

BIBLIOGRAPHY: G.B. Levey and P. Mendes (eds.), *Jews and Australian Politics* (2004).

[William D. Rubinstein (2nd ed.)]

DANCE.

In Ancient Israel

In the Bible, Mishnah, and Talmud, dance is referred to in various contexts as an important ritualized activity and as an expression of joy. None of these references, however, contain descriptions of how the dancers actually moved. Dancing is mentioned in connection with celebrations of military victories and in rituals such as the golden calf dance and the bringing of the Ark of the Covenant to Jerusalem.

The Bible contains many Hebrew verb roots employed to describe dancing activity, four of which were used in the description of the popular but religious event of the bringing of the Ark, which inspired King David and his subjects to dance before God. David not only danced in the ordinary sense of the word *saḥek* (שחק) but also rotated with all his might, *karker* (כרכר); and jumped, *pazez* (פזז) (II Sam. 6:5, 14, 16); a slightly different version appears in I Chronicles 15:29, mentioning that he skipped, *rakad* (רקד). The other verb roots used for describing dance are *daleg* (דלג), leap or jump; *kafotz* (קפץ), jump with both feet; *savav* (סבב), go around; *pase'aḥ* (פסח), skip; *ẓala'* (צלע), limp; *ḥagag* (חגג), dance in circle.

It is noteworthy that in addition to the textual descriptions we have some tangible evidence. This includes newly discovered iconographic features found in *Megiddo, *Lachish, the Negev, and other sites. For example, a number of cylinder seals from the second millennium B.C.E. show lines of dancers standing with their hands on one another's shoulders (*Near Eastern Archeology*, 66:3 (2003)). Figures on a late Bronze Age cylinder seal from Lachish have been interpreted as participants in a ritual or battle dance similar to the Arab folk "debka" still in use in our days. A. Mazar adds that "this posture is typical of seals showing dancers from various sites in Israel" (*ibid.*). T. Ilan in his study "Dance and Gender" (see Bibliography) describes dance represented in ancient iconography as an activity in which the two genders have specific defined roles.

VICTORY DANCES. Dancing to the accompaniment of drums is associated with the celebrations of military victories and welcoming home heroes who have routed an enemy. The women's role was to receive and extol the fighters. After the triumphant crossing of the Red Sea, "Miriam, the prophetess, the sister of Aaron, took a timbrel in her hand; and all the women went out after her with timbrels and with dances" (Ex. 15:20, 21). On his triumphant return from battle to Mizpah, Jephthah was greeted by his daughter with timbrels and dancing (Judg. 11:34). When David and Saul returned from the battle with the Philistines, "the women came out of all the cities of Israel, singing and dancing, to meet King Saul, with timbrels, with joy, and with rattles" (I Sam. 18:6). There is a detailed description of a victory parade, where Judith leads the women in the dance, to the accompaniment of a special thanksgiving song: "And all the women of Israel hurried to see her, and they praised her and made a dance for her… And she went out in the dance before all the people, leading all the women" (Judith 15:12, 13).

ECSTATIC DANCES. The most telling biblical evidence of the power of music inspiring ecstasy and prophetic vision is connected with King Saul. A passage from Samuel tells that Saul goes to the hill of God where he meets a group prophesizing while in motion, accompanied by several instruments. The text adds: "And the spirit of the Lord will come mightily upon thee, and thou shalt prophecy with them, and shalt be turned into another man" (I Sam. 10:5–6). There is no mention of dancing, which typically accompanies ecstatic practices, but the movement that is an inherent part of the situation described may well allude to its ritual nature.

David's dance before the Ark was an example of the religious ecstatic dance performed by men. The Psalms exhorted people to "praise God's name in the dance" – "praise Him with timbrels and dance" (Ps. 149:3; 150:4).

FOLK DANCES. Detailed descriptions have been handed down to us from the period of the Mishnah, from which we learn that there was folk dancing at religious celebrations. During the festival of Tabernacles, there was a daily procession around the altar in the Temple following the sacrifices. The celebrations reached a climax in the dances of the water-drawing festival: "Whoever has not witnessed the joy of the festival of the water-drawing has seen no joy in life. Pious men and men of affairs danced with torches in their hands, singing songs of joy and of praise, and the Levites made music with lyre and harp and cymbals and trumpets and countless other instruments" (Suk. 5:1b). During this celebration, R. Simeon b. Gamliel juggled eight lighted torches, and when he prostrated himself he dug his two thumbs into the ground, bent, kissed the ground, leaped up, and stood on his feet (Suk. 5:3a).

The Book of Judges (21:21), in describing the annual feast in Shiloh tells of the bride-choosing ceremonies. The story of the capture of brides by the surviving men of the tribe of Benjamin indicates that choosing brides during the vineyard dances was a recognized practice in Israel. Others believe it was the celebration of the vines on the Fifteenth of Av. According to the Mishnah, R. Simeon b. Gamaliel declared, "There were no holidays for Israel like the fifteenth of Av and the Day of Atonement, on which the daughters of Jerusalem went out in white dresses which were borrowed so that no one need be ashamed if she had none. And the daughters of Jerusalem went forth and danced in a circle in the vineyards. And what spake they? 'Youth, lift up thine eyes and behold her whom thou wouldst choose'" (Ta'an. 4:8).

In the Song of Songs (7:1), one finds the rather obscure mention of "the dance of the two companies," which seems to have been taken from a traditional wedding dance, and may imply two groups of dancers, a type of dancing that can still be seen at Bedouin festivities in the Middle East. In Talmudic literature (Ket. 17a) the bridal procession was regarded with great deference and was given priority on public thoroughfares requiring even a funeral procession to make way. Dancing in honor of the bride at a wedding was considered an act of religious devotion. Rabbis and scholars performed it joyously, each in his own manner. R. Judah b. Ilai would take a myrtle twig and dance before the bride singing. R. Samuel b. Isaac, even when he was old, would juggle three myrtle twigs as he sang and danced. R. Aḥa danced with the bride on his shoulder (*ibid.*).

In the Diaspora

During the dispersion, the dancing associated with the normal activities of a nation in its own country ceased. The rabbinical authorities often forbade dancing in public. The many discussions in the rabbinical literature and responsa about dancing include opinions ranging from lukewarm compromise to outright hostility. At weddings and bridal feasts and for the Sabbath and particularly on Purim and Simḥat Torah and Lag ba-Omer dancing continued while taking on new forms.

In European Jewry of the Middle Ages, dancing for pleasure was an end in itself. In the medieval ghettos of France, Germany, and Poland, where living quarters were crowded, almost every Jewish community had a wedding-house or *Tanzhaus* for festive occasions. Here the *Tanzfuehrer* (dance leader or caller) was aided by hired musicians. New humorous dances came into use, some of them reflecting the surrounding cultures. Among them were the *Maien Tanz, Umgehender Tanz, Spring Tanz, Judentanz, Adam Harischon Tanz, DoktorFoist [Faust] Tanz*, and *Fisch Tanz*. In Spain the children played with miniature wooden horses called *kurraj*. These toys resembled the pirate's wooden battle horses that were favorites among the adults.

During the Renaissance, Jews danced for recreation and entertainment. David Reuveni describes the dancing in the home of Jehiel Nissim of Pisa in 1524. They also danced in public as in the procession in Palermo celebrating the marriage of King Ferdinand of Castille and Isabella of Aragon in 1469. In Jewish homes in Italy the Hebrew teacher taught Bible and Talmud, music, and dancing. That Jews engaged extensively in the profession of teaching in that period is emphasized by the recurring laws closing schools of dance and music conducted by Jews, such as the edicts of 1443 in Venice, and 1466 in Parma. There were Jewish dancing teachers in Renaissance Italy, the most distinguished dance master of the time being *Guglielmo de Pesaro, author of a treatise on dance dated 1463. In the 16th century, another Jew, Jacchino *Massarano, won fame as a dance master and teacher in Rome.

Oriental Jewry's Dances

There are many communities, such as the Moroccans, Georgians, Libyans, and Ethiopians, in which spontaneous group folk dancing is important, yet the Jews of Yemen and Kurdistan Jewry are among the most prominent traditional cultures attributing dynamic importance to dance in the daily and festive life of the community.

Dance among the Jews born in Yemen comprises stylistic diversity characteristic of urban and rural settlements as well as including women and men. Dancing usually takes place during ceremonies and celebrations. Fundamentally, the men's dances are composed of steps and figures executed in a very small area. The dominant line is vertical – with agile, springy bending of the knees. The very expressive hands are used for an infinite variety of gestures. One or two singers, rhythm instruments, or hand clapping always accompany the dance but no melodic instruments were used. The women's dances are less variegated and more restrained. They are accompanied by the singing of the dancers themselves, or that of two female musicians who beat the rhythm respectively on copper plate and drum.

The dances of Jews from Kurdistan are distinguished from those of all other Jewish communities in that the men and women dance together. The dances are accompanied by songs and two instruments: the *zurna*, a nasal-sounding wind instrument similar to the oboe, and the *dola*, a large double-headed drum that is beaten on both sides, with one thick and one thin stick. Most Kurdish dances are based on open or closed circles, with couples or soloists taking turns in the center where they improvise figures and steps. Some of the men brandish short swords as they dance and the women wave colorful kerchiefs.

Ḥasidic Dances

With the rise of *Ḥasidism in Eastern Europe in the 18th century, dance assumed great importance for the Jewish masses. *Israel b. Eliezer Ba'al Shem Tov, the founder of Ḥasidism, used dance to attain religious enthusiasm (*hitlahavut*) and devoted adherence to the Almighty (*devekut*). He taught his followers that "the dances of the Jew before his Creator are prayers," and quoted the Psalmist, "All my bones shall say: 'Lord, who is like unto Thee?'" (Ps. 35:10). Ḥasidic dance assumed the form of the circle, symbolic of the ḥasidic philosophy that "every one is equal, each one being a link in the chain, the circle having no front or rear, no beginning or ending." The Ḥasidim would start their dancing in slow tempo, and as the music became faster they held arms upward and leapt in the air in an effort to reach spiritual ecstasy. The accompanying melodies were composed to brief texts from either the Bible or the Talmud. *Naḥman of Bratzlav, great-grandson of the Ba'al Shem Tov, believed that to dance in prayer was a sacred command, and he composed a prayer which he recited before dancing. He and other ḥasidic rabbis called for dancing on all festive occasions and even on the solemn days of the Ninth of Av, Rosh Ha-Shanah, and the Day of Atonement. During the celebrations on Simḥat Torah, the usual processions with the scrolls reached a climax in the rabbi's own dance. Wrapped in a prayer shawl, with a scroll held high in his hands, the rabbi danced with spiritual ecstasy as the Ḥasidim sang and clapped hands in a circle around him. The Ḥasidim danced on Friday nights around the rabbi's banquet table, and at twilight on Saturday they danced with mystic fervor. Ḥasidic dancing has influenced the celebrations at Jewish festivals generally, and has served as the basis and inspiration of choreography on Jewish themes in ballet.

HILLULA DANCES. The Aramaic word *hillula* implies a joyous celebration. Certain Orthodox Jewish sects use the term to describe the annual ritual of visiting the grave of a *ẓaddik* or ḥasid on the actual or reputed day of his death. Among those whose sanctification has been recognized by the entire nation is certainly *Simeon Bar Yoḥai. Lag ba-Omer, the traditional anniversary of his death, has long been commemorated in song and dance by pilgrims gathered at his tomb at Meron, near Safed. Naḥman of Bratzlav ordered his disciples to observe the anniversary of his death by studying a chapter of the Mishnah and dancing at his grave. The Bratzlav Ḥasidim fulfilled his wish for generations at the cemetery in Uman in the Ukraine. In Alkush, in the mountains of Kurdistan (northern Iraq), *Benjamin II, a 19th-century explorer, discovered an unusual form of celebration of Shavuot at the tomb of the prophet Nahum. Pilgrims joined in the reading of the Book of Nahum and circled the shrine singing while women came dancing around the catafalque. The next morning, the men went to the summit of a nearby hill, symbolizing Mount Sinai, read from the Torah, and then descended in warlike procession, clashing weapons and simulating the great combat heralding the coming of the Messiah. The women met the men with dancing and singing to the accompaniment of tambourines.

Life Cycle Dances

BIRTH AND CIRCUMCISION. A person's lifetime, from birth to death, is filled with a succession of special occasions, many of which are celebrated in song and dance. The first is birth. In many Eastern communities, the mother and newborn son were the center of special events. According to popular belief the demons – headed by *Lilith – are jealous of those blessed with a son who would soon fulfill the *mitzvah* of the circumcision; they are increasingly dangerous as the circumcision approaches. In Morocco, Jews would perform the *taḥdid* ceremony. The term is apparently derived from the word *ḥadid*, which means iron, so named in reference to the sword used the night before the circumcision to banish the evil spirits. The sword is brandished in all corners of the house and around the beds of the mother and child, while a selection of biblical verses and appropriate psalms are chanted. In Persia, the father would engage professional dancers for the night before the ceremony. Among the Sephardi Jews of North Africa, the Tray of Elijah, used in the circumcision rite, would be carried in procession with song and dance and lighted candles, from its last place of use to the home of the newborn. In Syria and Lebanon, on arrival of the tray, seven guests would be called on to dance with the tray in turn. In Kurdistan, the Chair of Elijah would be brought in procession from the synagogue and the guests would circle it with dances. In Aden, the guests would take turns to dance with the Chair of Elijah as if dancing with the prophet Elijah himself.

WEDDING. Of all family events, the wedding and its colorful attendant ceremonies probably is the most important in the life of the individual and the community. Dancing in honor of the bride gave rise to the *Mitzvah* dances. A 16th-century source published in Venice described the *Mitzvah* dance as a form of group dance in which the men danced with the bridegroom, and the women with the bride (*Sefer Minhagim*, Venice, 1590). This conformed to the prevalent practice and the restrictions against mixed dancing in Jewish communities. Later publications describe a modified *Mitzvah* dance. Men took turns to dance with the bride after wrapping something around the hand as a symbol of separation (J.M. Epstein, *Derekh ha-Yashar*, Frankfurt, 1704). By the beginning of the 19th century it became the practice for men to dance with the bride while separated by a handkerchief held at opposite ends. In the pattern of the *Mitzvah* dance, the bride was usually seated in the middle of a circle of chosen guests while the *badḥan* ("jester"), serving as master of ceremonies, called each guest by name to step forward and dance with the bride. First honors went to the parents of the couple and to the bridegroom; then scholars and important members of the community took turns. Each would extend to the bride the tip of a handkerchief or receive one from her, then circle with her once or twice to the accompaniment of music from the orchestra. During the wedding festivities, which lasted seven days, guests and neighbors took part in the dancing and even the beggars of the town had the right to dance with the bride. Other dances performed at weddings in East European communities were *Koilich Tanz*, a dance of salutation to the bride and bridegroom performed by a woman holding a twisted white loaf and some salt to wish them abundance; *Klapper Tanz*, a dance with much handclapping; *Redl, Frailachs, Karahod, Hopke*, vigorous circle dances done by men; *Besem Tanz*, a man dancing with a broom used as horse or musket; *Flash* [Bottle] *Tanz*, dance with a bottle on the head; *Bobes Tanz* for the grandmothers; *Mechutanem Tanz* for the relatives of both families; *Broyges Tanz*, a man and a woman portraying quarrel and reconciliation; *Sher, Sherele, Quadrille*, dances based on square and longways dances performed with partners; *Lancelot, Kutzatsky, Bulgar, Pas d'Espagne, Vingerka, Waltz*, forms of popular Russian, Polish, and Romanian dances. At ḥasidic weddings, an old practice was often revived of dancing in peasant costumes, animal skins, or even Cossack uniforms. Groups of young girls would also dance toward the seated bride from three directions singing *Keitzad merakkedim lifnei ha-kallah* ("How we dance before the bride"). The young men, meanwhile, would dance around the bridegroom.

Groups of professional women musicians called *tañaderas* (drummers) in the Balkan Sephardi communities, *mughnniyat* in Yemen, *mutribat* in Kurdistan (poet-singers), and *daqqaqat* (drummers) in Iraq, conducted the ceremonies and sang to the accompaniment of drums, amusing the women and making them dance. In Morocco, a small ensemble of male instrumentalists and a singer accompany the spontaneous dancing of women relatives and guests, performing individually gestures which call to mind the belly dance: the head tilted sideways and a kerchief in each hand. In Yemen, it was considered an honor for the women guests to dance with the *mazhera*, a bowl containing the henna dye with which the bride's hands were painted.

[Dvora Lapson / Amnon Shiloah (2nd ed.)]

Contemporary Period

Already at the early decades of the 20th century, when interest in ballet began to spread throughout the West, Jewish dancers once more made their mark. The Diaghilev Company, during its two decades in Western Europe (1909–29), had notable Jewish dancers (apart from its famous designer Leon *Bakst). The first to attract attention was Ida *Rubinstein, though she was known more for her beauty than for her skill as a dancer. More important were two women whose careers only began with Diaghilev. The first was Alicia *Markova, who became an internationally recognized ballerina. The second was Marie *Rambert, who founded one of the first classical companies in England. David *Lichine first made his name in Ida Rubinstein's company. The great Anna Pavlova (1881–1951) once confided to her American impresario, Sol *Hurok, that her father was Jewish but asked him not to reveal it before her death (see S. Hurok, *Impresario*, 1946). In Soviet Russia, Jews found opportunities that had been denied them in Czarist times. Outstanding among them was Asaf *Messerer, leading dancer and later teacher of the Bolshoi Ballet, and his sister Shulamith. His niece, Maya *Plisetskaya, became the company's prima ballerina. In America, Jewish teachers like Louis Chalif and Sandor Gluck trained performers for the classical ballet companies that formed in the U.S. in the 1930s and 1940s. Ballet Theater numbered three important women dancers of Jewish descent – Annabella Lyon, Melissa *Hayden, and Nora *Kaye, all notable not only for technical mastery but for the intensity of their dramatic portrayals. In the 1960s Bruce Marks became a leading dramatic male dancer with the company. Jewish choreographers also came to the fore at Ballet Theater. Both Michael *Kidd and Herbert *Ross, best known for their work in Broadway musical comedies, began their careers with Ballet Theater. Also from the ranks of this company came Jerome *Robbins, generally credited with winning attention for American dance in the wider world. Of major importance to American ballet was the work of Lincoln *Kirstein, founder of the New York City Ballet. The Jewish modern dancer has generally made more use of his Jewish heritage than his classical counterpart. Because the modern dance is based on the expression of individual emotion, rather than on the discipline that molds the individual to an established form (like the ballet), there emerged a search for identity through the exploration of ethnic background. Sophie *Maslow created *The Village I Knew*, depicting the life of Jews in Czarist Russia. Pearl Lang utilized her Jewish source in *Song of Deborah* and in *Legend*, based on An-Ski's *Dybbuk*; Helen *Tamiris portrayed with nostalgia the landmarks of Jewish family life in *Memoir*. Another Jewish choreographer, Anna *Sokolow, showed concern with the alienation of the individual in contemporary society. Her *Dreams* was an indictment of Nazi Germany. These Jewish choreographers made strong statements about their people and the plight of all humanity in their troubled times.

[Selma Jeanne Cohen]

Artistic Dance in Modern Israel

The pioneers of artistic dance in Ereẓ Israel in the early 20th century had to create dance "from scratch." *Ausdruckstanz* was the style that took root in a society based on socialist values. This dance style, standing for simplicity and freedom from tradition and opting for personal expression and social involvement, spoke to the heart of this generation of pioneers.

In 1920 Agadati presented a modern dance recital in Neveh Tzedek on the outskirts of Tel Aviv. Wishing to combine Middle Eastern and Western motifs, he turned to ḥasidic and Yemenite dances. Two years after Agadati's recital, Margalit Ornstein, who had immigrated to Ereẓ Israel from Vienna, established the first dance studio in Tel Aviv teaching Dalcroze Eurhythmics and Isadora Duncan's style. Rina *Nikova immigrated in 1924 from St. Petersburg and became ballerina in the Ereẓ Israeli Opera, founded that year by the conductor Mordechai Golinkin. She danced on a floor covered with Oriental rugs, usually accompanied by one man and three women who constituted the corps de ballet. In 1933, she founded the Yemenite Company, where young Yemenite girls performed dances on biblical themes. The company successfully toured Europe between 1936 and 1939.

The early 1930s saw the rise of the second generation of dancers. Among them were the twins Yehudit and Shoshana Ornstein, Deborah *Bertonoff, Dania Levin, and Yardena *Cohen.

Among the immigrants arriving in Ereẓ Israel following the Nazis' rise to power in 1933 were Tille Roessler, who had been a principal teacher at Gret Palucca's school in Dresden, and the dancers Else *Dublon, Paula Padani, and Katia Michaeli, who had danced in Mary Wigman's company. In 1935, at the peak of her artistic success as a notable dancer and creator in the *Ausdruckstanz* style in Central Europe, Gertrud *Kraus decided to immigrate to Ereẓ Israel. She gave many recitals and founded the Peoples' Dance Opera Company, which operated from 1941 to 1947. It was the first modern dance group in the world associated with an opera house.

By the end of the 1940s the third generation of dancers started performing. Prominent dancers included Naomi Aleskovsky, Rachel Nadav, Hilde Kesten, and Hassia *Levi-Agron, who later founded the faculty of dance at the Jerusalem Academy of Music and Dance.

As opposed to *Ausdruckstanz* which was favored among the settler community, classic ballet was rejected as representing bourgeois art. Despite this, Valentina Archipova-Grossman from Latvia founded in 1936 a classic ballet studio in Haifa, giving a start to many teachers. In 1938 Mia *Arbatova, a former ballerina at the Riga Opera, founded her ballet studio in Tel Aviv, in which many choreographers and artists studied.

During World War II, all cultural links to Europe were severed and the dance artists in the *yishuv* entered a period of cultural isolation extending up to Israel's War of Independence and the end of the austerity period of the early 1950s. Thus Israel, in absorbing the Jews as a safe haven from the Nazis, ironically became one of the only countries on the globe where *Ausdruckstanz* became not only acceptable but also dominant.

Side by side with universal issues concerning man and society, the newcomers created dances inspired by the landscape of the country and biblical themes, aiming to express the link between Modern and Ancient Israel. In the newly created State of Israel, many artistic endeavors were supported by the state, but not artistic dance, which was still viewed as elitist, while folk dances were considered acceptably socialist.

In the first half of the 1950s foreign dance groups began to tour Israel. American immigrants such as Ruth Harris, Rina Shaham, and Rena Gluck had brought awareness of American modern dance. Martha Graham's historic visit, by courtesy of the Baroness Bethsabee de Rothschild, struck waves and stimulated Israeli dancers to sign up for studies at her school in New York. At the same time, there was a rapid process of rejecting *Ausdruckstanz*.

At this critical juncture, Sara *Levi-Tannai founded in 1949 Inbal Dance Theater, an artistic Yemenite traditional-culture-inspired dance group. In the 1950s Noah Eshkol had invented the *Eshkol/Wachman Dance Notation. In 1971 Amos Hetz founded "Movements," a group that utilized the Dance Notation as a means of exploring new possibilities in movement.

All attempts to establish a permanent non-funded professional modern dance group had failed. (This was the case with the Israeli Ballet Theater founded by Kraus and the Lyric Theater founded by Anna *Sokolow.) In 1964, however, Bethsabee de Rothschild founded the *Batsheva Dance Company and during the 1970s several dance companies were established, such as *Bat-Dor by Rothschild (1967), the Israeli Ballet by Berta *Yampolsky and Hillel Markman (1968), the Kibbutz Contemporary Dance Company with its artistic director Yehudit Arnon (1969), and Kol Demamah by Moshe Efrati (1978), originally employing both deaf and hearing dancers.

Between 1964 and 1976, all professional dance activities in Israel took place in professional companies. This improved Israeli dancers' technical and teaching standards and their tours placed Israeli dance on the global map. Batsheva and Bat-Dor, the leading companies, competed for important choreographers from around the world and did not readily open their doors to Israeli choreographers; local creativity diminished.

In the mid-1970s, modern dance in Israel began to show signs of weariness. The dramatic, thematic approach as well as the movement idiom and artistic concept became repetitive. At that time, several young female choreographers who had studied abroad brought with them American post-modern influences. Post-modern dance gave the legitimacy to revolt against the canons of modern American dance as performed by the major dance companies in Israel. The first fringe generation included Ruth Ziv-Ayal, Ruth Eshel, Ronit Land, Heda Oren, Dorit Shimron, and Rina Schenfeld.

In 1981 Pina Bausch came to Israel with the Wuppertal Dance Theater for the first time, and the local dance community became familiar with the *Tanztheater* style. For about five years before that visit, experimental dance works had been created in Israel, some of them in the movement-theater style, and Bausch's visit reinforced this tendency, providing local creators with more tools. The creative upsurge following Bausch's visit to Israel was immediate. The following year, Nava Zuckerman founded the Temu-Na Theater and Oshra Elkayam founded her Movement Theater. In the 1980s fringe dance in Israel was enriched by more dancers and creators, including Mirali Sharon (who was among the few choreographers who created for Batsheva and Bat-Dor), Sally-Anne Friedland, Tami Ben-Ami, Yaron Margolin, Nir Ben-Gal, Liat Dror, Amir Kolben, and the Ramleh Dance Company in 1983 (later the Tamar Jerusalem Company).

Flamenco is very popular and there are several prominent dancers such as Silvia Doran, Neta Sheazaf, and Michal Natan. A manifestation of the relation between ethnic and artistic dance is the University of Haifa's Eskesta Dance Theater, which studies Ethiopian dance and creates artistic dance inspired by folklore. The yearly Karmiel Dance Festival in Galilee, established in 1988 and directed by Yonatan Karmon, draws thousands of people who come to dance folk dances for three days and nights. The festival program includes hall performances as well as mass dances in public parks and in the streets; folk dance, ethnic dance, and artistic dance are all combined.

In the past decade, a large group of young experienced Israeli creators and dancers have worked in established big companies and in marginal fringe frameworks. Among the most notable creators and companies are Ohad *Naharin (Batsheva Dance Company), Rami *Be'er (Kibbutz Contemporary Dance Company), Nir Ben-Gal and Liat Dror (The Group), Noa Wertheim and Adi Sha'al (Vertigo Dance Company), Anat Danieli Dance Company, Amir Kolben (Kombina Company), Ido Tadmor Dance Company, Tamar Borer, Yossi Yungman, Emanuel Gat, Noah Dar Dance Company – Holon, Muza Dance Company, Inbal Pinto Dance Company, Barak Marshal Dance, and Yasmeen Godder. The Inbal Dance Theater and the Israeli Ballet are still active. In 1998 Valery Panov established the Ashdod Ballet, where all the dancers are immigrants from the Former Soviet Union.

Increasing fringe activity brought about the establishment of the Shades in Dance project (1984), in which works by young fringe artists were exposed on a professional stage, and in 1990 the first of the Curtain Up events, premieres of works by known fringe creators, took place. In 1989 the Susan Dellal Center was founded, managed by Yair Vardi, and it became the main home of Israeli dance.

[Ruth Eshel (2nd ed.)]

Contemporary American Dance

Modern dance reflected American social conventions at the beginning of the 20th century complete with quotas restricting Jewish participation; this was true of Ruth St. Denis and Ted Shawn's Denishawn Co. and schools. Their main dancers, Martha *Graham, Doris Humphrey, and Charles Weidman, broke with Denishawn over their discriminatory policies. Apparently Isadora Duncan was not so exclusive for she and her staff trained Julia Levien, Mignon Garlin, Ruth Fletcher, and Hortense Kooluris. The Denishawn star, Martha Graham, became a favorite teacher at the heart of the Jewish world in New York's Lower East Side at the Neighborhood Playhouse. Built by Irene and Alice Lewisohn as both a philanthropic and artistic endeavor, the dance classes there offered an entree into modern American culture for the children of immigrants. Jewish teachers at the Neighborhood Playhouse included Blanche Talmud and Senia Gluck-Sendor. Students included leftist Edith Segal, and Helen Tamiris, who later directed the Federal Dance Project of the WPA with her husband/partner Daniel Nagrin, and their dances often dealt with brotherhood and emancipation. Tamiris's company included many Jewish dancers such Mura Dehn, Sue Ramos, and Pauline Bubrick Tish before Tamiris went on to choreograph for Broadway. Edith Segal, on the other hand, used her dances such as "The Belt Goes Red" and "Black and White" as vehicles for social protest at rallies. Other radical leftist dancers, of whom many trained by the German emigrée Hanya Holm, include Miriam Blecher, Lily Mehlman, Edna Ocko, and Muriel Mannings, who created the New Dance Group (both a school and center for performance). Hadassah Spira, born in Jerusalem, came to New York in 1938, created several solos including "Shuvi Nafshi" and headed the Ethnic Dance Dept. of the New Dance Group. In Hanya Holm's dance company, Eve Gentry was the most prominent Jewish dancer.

Of the mainstream modern dance companies, Graham's included the most remarkable number of Jewish dancers. Most notably among them were Anna *Sokolow, Lillian Shapero, and Sophie *Maslow. Among other Jewish Graham dancers were Bertram Ross, Robert Cohan, Stuart Hodes, Linda Margolis Hodes (who later moved to Israel to oversee Graham works in the Batsheva Dance Co), and Pearl *Lang. The drive to assimilate into American culture thrust some into glorifying American folk (such as Maslow's "Dust Bowl Ballads") though many maintained Jewish concerns for social justice and especially rights for workers' and Afro-Americans. Opposition to fascism was seen in dance concerts to support Spanish democracy during in the Spanish Civil War. Even Ruthanna *Boris from American Ballet Theater joined forces with modern dancers for this cause. So, too, did *Habimah-trained Benjamin *Zemach, who worked in both New York and Los Angeles. Bella Lewitzsky did not use Jewish material in her choreography or classes nor did Gloria Newman. Anna *Halprin (a.k.a. Ann), long an experimentalist with dance improvisation, community, and healing, was driven by social concerns. Her work for her 80th birthday in 2000, "Memories from my Closet, Grandfather Dance," has Jewish references and *klezmer* music. After World War II, both Pearl Lang and Sokolow did solos using Jewish male prayer symbols such as *tefillin.*

The Nazi regime destroyed all forms of dance by the mid-1930s: professional theater dance, dance in Yiddish theater, and dance in the folk and religious life of the Jewish communities of Europe. Stars such as Ruth Abrahamowitsch Sorel (trained by the German expressionist dancer Mary Wigman) performed at the Berlin State Opera house. Margarete Wallmann, who directed Wigman's Berlin school and that of the Vienna State Opera, fled Europe. So did Gertrud *Kraus, who immigrated to Palestine in 1935. Performers from Kraus's Viennese Company who escaped and reached America during World War II included Fred *Berk, Katya Delakova, and Claudia Vall, who taught dance in Hollywood after a brief touring stint with Berk. After partnership performing with Katya Delakova and their Jewish Dance Guild, Berk established the Jewish Dance Division at the 92nd St. Y., whose emphasis was on Jews living a pluralistic life in the U.S. Joyce Mollow, a modern dancer, was also concerned with Jewish themes; a yearly lectureship at Queens College on Jewish dance was established in her memory. Hans Wierner or Jan Veen, another dancer from Kraus's Co., had settled in Boston and taught at the New England Conservatory of Music. Truda Kashmann, also trained by Wigman, escaped Germany and directed a studio in Connecticut and trained Alwin Nikolais, a gentile talent who made an important home for dance in the Lower East Side. His lead dancers Murray Louis and Phyllis Lamhat became teachers and company directors in their own right. Pola Nirenska who was expelled from the Wigman Company in 1933 with the other Jewish performers, returned to her native Poland, escaped to London, and then the U.S., where she devoted herself to choreographing and teaching. Judith Berg, another Polish dancer trained by Wigman, was known in Warsaw for her dances on Jewish themes. She choreographed and danced the role of death in the Polish film of *The Dybbuk*. She escaped to the Soviet Union and with her partner Felix Fibich toured the provinces with a Yiddish revue. She reached the U.S. in 1950 where she continued to choreograph and perform in New York's Yiddish theater.

Elsie Salomons, who had danced in Kurt Joos's German Co., reached Canada, where she trained her niece Judith Marcuse who became an established performer and choreographer in Canada.

Eliot Feld, trained in ballet, performed in Jerome *Robbins' *West Side Story*, and later created "Tzaddik" for his contemporary Feld Ballet, though he is not known for dances on Jewish themes. His mentor, the prolific genius choreographer Robbins, and his collaborators, including Leonard *Bernstein, first considered portraying Jews and Catholics in conflict for Robbins' remake of the Romeo and Juliet tragedy, *West Side Story*. However, they changed their minds and shied away from religious conflict in favor of ethnic gangs. In 1964, Robbins directed and choreographed *Fiddler on the Roof* an enormous Broadway hit, which ran for almost eight years. On

The first female rabbi in Italy celebrates Ḥanukkah at Lev Chadash synagogue in Milan, 2004. © *Silvia Morara/Corbis.*

In 2005, the worldwide Jewish population was estimated to be close to 14 million persons, with its largest numbers in North America and Israel. Despite the large concentrations in these two geographical areas, there are Jews all over the world who come from a variety of racial and ethnic backgrounds. Here are a few faces that illustrate the diversity and vibrancy of Jewish life in its many world-scattered communities.

COMMUNITIES

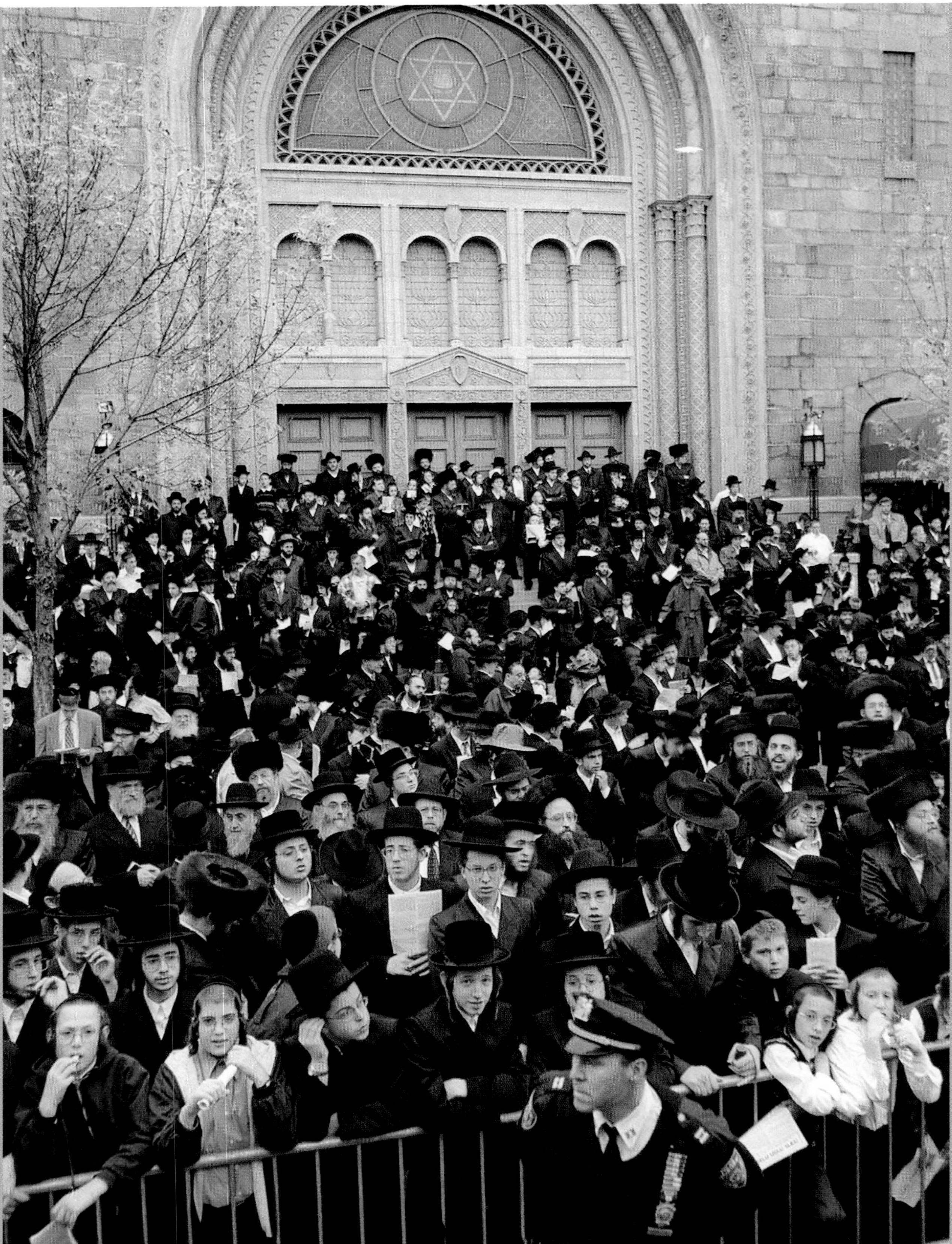

(opposite page):
A large gathering of Brooklyn's Orthodox Jewish community wait for the reading of Psalms in front of a synagogue in the Borough Park neighborhood in New York, 2000.
AP Images.

(this page):
Jewish man at the entrance of the synagogue in Bukhara, Uzbekistan.
Photo: Theodore Cohen, USA. By courtesy of Beth Hatefutsoth Photo Archive, Tel Aviv.

CELEBRANDO

(opposite page) TOP: A closing prayer during a *seder* at a Jewish Community Center in New York City, 2005. *AP Images.*

(opposite page) BOTTOM: In Havana, Cuba, teenagers play "Celebrating the Sabbath," a board game created by a member of the Jewish community there, 2005. *ADALBERTO ROQUE/AFP/Getty Images.*

(this page) ABOVE: Eliyahu Hanavi Synagogue; Alexandria, Egypt, 1994. *Photo: Shlomo Taitz, Israel. By courtesy of Beth Hatefutsoth Photo Archive, Tel Aviv.*

(this page) LEFT: Members of the Judah Hyam Hall Synagogue in New Delhi sing hymns during Sabbath service, 2003. *FINDLAY KEMBER/AFP/Getty Images.*

ABOVE: The rabbi and a few members of the oldest synagogue in Barcelona transport the gift of a medieval Torah scroll under a ḥuppah to their recently restored temple, Spain, 2005. *AP Images.*

(opposite page) TOP: Rejoicing at the Hillula (festivity) of R. Jacob Abi-Hasira; Damanhur, Egypt, 1994. *Photo: Shlomo Taitz, Israel. By courtesy of Beth Hatefutsoth Photo Archive, Tel Aviv.*

(opposite page) BOTTOM: A South African bride is lifted up on a chair by some of her wedding guests as her groom—in the background—is lifted as well at their reception in Johannesburg, 2005. *© Eitan Simanor/Alamy.*

LEFT: The contrast offered by Israeli society: Two young women, fashionably dressed, walk by two men wearing ***tallits*** (prayer shawls) and ***tefillin*** (phylacteries) in the city center of Jerusalem, 2000. *© Koren Ziv/Corbis Sygma.*

BELOW: Pilgrims process through the Hara, or Jewish quarter, on their way to El Ghriba synagogue on the Isle of Djerba, Tunisia, 2003. *FETHI BELAID/AFP/Getty Images.*

another occasion he turned to a Jewish theme creating "The Dybbuk Variations" for the New York City Ballet (1974); Sophie Maslow also choreographed her own "Dybbuk" as did Pearl Lang. Other choreographers have also been drawn to this spiritual story, including Bejart, whose company performed it in Israel. The Pilobolus Company, which specializes in group choreography, occasionally touched on a Jewish theme, especially when commissioned by the National Foundation for Jewish Culture, which sponsored their company piece called "Davenin." An offshoot of Pilobolus was Momix with Daniel Ezralow, which has choreographed for Batsheva.

Arnie Zane (1948–1988) collaborated with African-American Bill T. Jones and Zane occasionally used Jewish references in his work. Meredith Monk uses her own original music as well as choreography to encompass Jewish experience such as her epic to immigration, *Ellis Island*, or her ode to loss in World War II called *Quarry: An Opera* and *Book of Days* about the Middle Ages and Jewish life then and now. Liz Lerman has had a multi-generational, multi-racial dance company, the Liz Lerman Dance Exchange, since 1976 and often draws on Jewish themes for her dances including *The Hallelujah Project* and "Shehehianu." Like Monk, she was a MacArthur Prize recipient, a mark of American achievement, and in 2005 Lerman was commissioned by Harvard Law School to do a dance project on the Nuremberg Trials and genocide. Margalit *Oved, Ze'eva Cohen (both Israeli-American choreographer/dancers) with Risa Jaraslow, Ruth Goodman, Beth Corning, and Heidi Latsky are some who bring their Jewish experiences into their works.

David Gordon, David Dorfman, Danial Shapiro, and Stuart Pimsler use vestiges of burlesque and vaudeville in their humorous look at themselves as Jewish men through their own choreography, using autobiography and their Jewish families as a base for their choreography.

[Judith Brin Ingber (2nd ed.)]

Russian and European Dance

At the beginning of the 20th century, not a few Jews in Russia occupied a prominent place in classical ballet; yet, many of them did not reveal their Jewish origin. Sol *Hurok, the impresario of the great and most famous Diva Ana Pavlova (1881–1931), reports in his *Memories* that she told him she was the illegitimate daughter of the known Jewish banker Lazar Polakov, allowing him to disclose her origin only after her death.

The outstanding classical dancer, choreographer, and teacher Asaf *Messerer (1903–1992) belonged to a great artistic family. He was a legendary premier dancer with the Bolshoi Ballet Theater, where he performed the major roles in the most famous classical ballets. He also distinguished himself as a great choreographer and teacher, and staged ballets in Belgium. Hungary, and Poland, and he wrote two books on ballet technique.

His sister Sulamith Messerer (1908–) was a prima ballerina with the Bolshoi, where she danced leading roles in the 1930s and 1940s, often partnered by her brother Asaf. She moved to London in 1980 and was a ballet guest teacher with leading companies. Her niece, daughter of the cinema actress Rakhail (Raisa), is the legendary ballerina Maya *Plisteskaya (1925–), one of the most famous names in the history of ballet. She danced in many capitals and served as guest director at the Rome opera ballet (1984–86) and with Spanish National ballet (1987–90). She visited Israel several times.

In his autobiography *Dance – Imagination – Time*, Asaf Messerer refers to several Jewish dancers who began their career together with him, including Miriam Reisen, Lubov Bank, Raisa Stein, Feina Leisner, and others; they are all included in the *Russian Encyclopedia of Dance*.

A prominent and greatly gifted dancer was Michael Gabovitch (1905–1965), who danced leading roles with the Bolshoi, having for many years as a dance partner Galina Ulanova (1910–). In the years 1954–58 Gabovitch was the director of the Moscow choreographic school, and he is the author of books and articles on dance. His son, also called Michael, danced as soloist with the Bolshoi.

The star Alla Schelest (1919–1999) was for 25 years a tenured soloist with the St. Petersburg's Maryinsky Theater and the most appreciated dancer of the famous Jewish choreographer Leonid Yacobson (1904–1973).

The ballerina Nina Timofeyeva (1935–) made her debut with the Kirov-Maryinsky Theater in 1953 when she was 18 years old. In 1956 she became the leading soloist with the Bolshoi and was distinguished by her brilliant technique; she also made her mark in modern ballet. In 1991, she and her dancer daughter immigrated to Israel she and pursued her career in Jerusalem, first at the Rubin Academy and later, along with her daughter, she founded her own ballet company and school.

The famous Russian-born dancer Valery *Panov, who was a star with Kirov-Maryinsky in Moscow immigrated with his wife, dancer Galina, to Israel in 1974. After dancing in several Israeli venues, Valery became art director of the opera ballet in Bonn (1992–97) and also worked in South Africa. At the end of the 1990s he returned to Israel and founded his own ballet company and school in the town of Ashdod.

Another famous Russian dancer who immigrated to Israel was Alexander Lifchitz. He was a soloist with Kirov-Maryinsky Theater (1954–74), where he successfully distinguished himself with brilliant performances of character dances. After his immigration to Israel he directed a ballet school in Jerusalem until his premature death in 1998.

The prevailing antisemitism in Soviet Russia imprinted foremost the major theaters, which refused to enroll many excellent Jewish dancers; those who were lucky enough to be admitted preferred to conceal their Jewish origin; one finds among them such Jewish names as Violetta Bobet, Alexander Klein, Ella Fein, and others. Other dancers moved to cities like Novosibirsk, Kiev, and Riga, where they found recognition and favor as leading dancers

The choreographer and ballet director Boris Eifman (1946–) belongs to the generation of Soviet ballet masters who tried at the end of the 1960s and beginning of the 1970s to change traditional Russian ballet and make it more contemporary. Eifman, a spiritual disciple of Leonid Yacobson, endowed with a creative style of his own, is considered an important force in contemporary Russian culture as the director of his own dance theater.

Among the scholars and critics of Soviet dance, the Jews occupied important place. Akim Wolinsky (born Haim ben Lev Flakser in 1861) became famous among the most influential thinkers and writers on Russian ballet art. He was the author of several books and articles on all major personalities in dance. In 1921, he founded and directed a Russian dance school in Petersburg, where many of the prominent Soviet dancers studied. Another remarkable writer and critic is Vadim Gaievski, author of books on such celebrated artists as Petipa, Balanchine, Ulanova, Plisteskaya, and others.

After World War I and the Russian Revolution, many Russian dancers and choreographers settled in Central and Western Europe and where they enjoyed intense activity as dancers and choreographers. The most prominent were those associated with Diaghilev's *Ballets Russes*. The most famous among them is Ida *Rubinstein (1885–1960), who was the star of this prestigious company in the years 1909–11 and 1920. Rubinstein also founded and directed a company of her own (Paris, 1911–13) and then a second one with Bronislava Nijinska as choreographer (Paris, 1928–29, 1931, 1934).

Another outstanding artist is David Lishem (born David Lichtenstein in 1910). Although he left Russia at an early age he absorbed the Russian ballet tradition via L. Yegorva and Bronislava Nijinski, with whom he studied. He made his debut as a soloist with Ida Rubinstein's company and had as stage partner Ana Pavlova; he excelled in character dances. He immigrated in 1940 to the U.S. and danced there with the Ballet Theater.

Mentioned should be also made of the legendary Lituanian Sonia *Gaskel, who studied in Russia and Paris and founded the famous National Dutch company in Holland.

In her book *The Blue Maiden Dancer*, Nina Tichonova describes admirably the Parisian and Berlin's ballet in the period between the two world wars, mentioning the leading Russian names, which include not a few Jews. She also refers to the extraordinary phenomenon of the Russian Romantic Ballet Theater in Berlin, whose founders were Anatoli and his son Andre Shaikovitch, who also wrote books on ballet in French and German.

[Yossi Tavor (2nd ed.)]

The dancer, teacher, choreographer, and ballet director Marie (Cyvia Rambam) Rambert (1888–1982) was born in Poland and came to Paris in 1906 where she studied free dance with Raymond Duncan and later eurhythmics with Jacques Dalcrose in Geneva. In 1913, she was dancer and teacher of eurhythmics with Diaghilev's *Ballets Russes* and the musical adviser of dancer and choreographer Vaslav Nijinski when he created Stravisky's *Sacre du Printemps*. In 1912, she settled in London, where she pioneered classical ballet and was founder and director of the Rambert Ballet School (1920) and the Ballet Rambert (1935). Among her honors are the Queen Elizabeth Coronation Award (1956); Chevalier, Légion d'honneur (France, 1957), and Golf medal of the Order of Merit (Poland, 1979).

Another outstanding ballerina is the British-born Alicia (Alice Lilian Marks) *Markova (1910–2004), who danced at the Ballet Rambert. At the age of 15 she joined Diaghilev's *Ballets Russes*. Markova created many major roles in the ballets of Balanchine and in the 1950s was the prima ballerina of the London Festival Ballet. She was made a "Dame" (female equivalent of knighthood) by order of Queen Elizabeth.

The South African dancer, choreographer, and ballet director John *Cranko (1927–1973) came to London in 1945 and joined the Sadler Royal Ballet. This master of various styles of ballet was the artistic director of the Stuttgart Ballet and chief choreographer of the Bavarian State Opera in Munich.

The French dancer and choreographer Jean *Babilée (Gutmann), born in 1923, showed astonishing technique and natural grace as a child. He was the star of Roland Petit's *Les Ballets des Champs Elisées* (1945–50) and in 1955 earned the gold star for best dancer at the International Festival Dance in Paris.

[Amnon Shiloah (2nd ed.)]

BIBLIOGRAPHY: I. Abrahams, *Jewish Life in the Middle Ages* (1932), 91, 404–6, includes bibliography; W.O.E. Oesterley, *Sacred Dance* (1923), index, s.v. *Israelites and the nations of antiquity, Jewish custom, Jews, Ashkenazic* and *Jews, Sephardic*; C. Roth, *Jews in the Renaissance* (1959), 275–81, includes bibliography; F. Berk (ed.), *Jewish Dance, an Anthology of Articles* (1960). IN MODERN ISRAEL: Z. Friedhaber, in: *Tatzlil*, 2 (1962), 95–97; 4 (1964), 39–43; 5 (1965), 117–20. **ADD. BIBLIOGRAPHY:** N. Bahat-Ratzon (ed.), *Barefoot: Jewish-Yemenite Tradition in Israeli Dance* (1999); F. Berk (ed.), *Jewish Dance, an Anthology of Articles* (1960); A. Biran, "The Dancer from Dan," in: *Near Eastern Archeology*, 66:3 (2003), 128–32; Y. Cohen, *Be-Tof u-Maḥol* ("With Drum and Dance," 1963); idem, *Ha-Tof ve-ha-Yam* ("The Drum and the Sea," 1976); R. Eshel, *Dancing with the Dream: The Development of Artistic Dance in Israel 1920–1964* (1991); Z. Friedhaber, *Ha-Maḥol be-Am Yisrael* ("Dance among the Jewish People," 1984); idem, "*Ha-Maḥol bi-Kehillot Mantova*" ("Dance in the Jewish Communities of Mantua in the 17th and 18th Centuries"), in: *Peʿamim*, 37 (1988), 67–77; S. Cohen (ed.), *The International Encyclopedia of Dance* (1998); G. Kadman, "Yemenite Dances and their Influence on the New Israeli Folk Dances," in: *Journal of the International Folk Music Council*, 4 (1952), 27–30; G. Manor, *Inbal: Quest for a Movement-Language* (1975); idem, *Agadati – The Pioneer of Modern Dance in Israel* (1986); A. Mazar, "Ritual Dancing in the Iron Age," in: *Near Eastern Archeology*, 66:3 (2003), 126–27; W.O.E. Oesterley, *Sacred Dance*, index, s.v. (1923); T. Ilan, "Dance and Gender in Ancient Jewish Sources," in: *Near Eastern Archeology*, 66:3 (2003), 135–36; B.N. Cohen-Stratyner, *Biographical Dictionary of Dance* (1982); J.B. Ingber, *Victory Dances: The Life of Fred Berk* (1985); D. Nagrin, "Tamiris in Her Own Voice: Draft of an Autobiography," in: *Studies in Dance History* (Fall/Winter 1989), 1–162; J. Ingber, "Dance, Performance," in: *Jewish Women in America, An Historical Encyclopedia* (1997), 300–11; N.M. Jackson, *Converging Movements, Modern Dance and Jewish Culture at the 92nd St. Y* (2000); D. Jowitt, *Jerome Robbins: His Life, His Theater, His Dance* (2004); L. Worth, Libby and H.Poynor, *Anna Halprin* (2004).

DANGERFIELD, RODNEY (1921–2004), U.S. comedian. Born Jacob Cohen in Long Island, N.Y., Dangerfield was best known for his catchphrase, "I don't get no respect," and his self-deprecating routines which featured him sweating and fidgeting with his necktie. Dangerfield first started writing jokes at 15 and was performing at amateur nights by 17. In 1941, when he was not working as a singing waiter, he was performing as a stand-up comedian in nightclubs under the name Jack Roy. He married singer Joyce Indig in 1950 and one year later decided to quit the comedy circuit to get a steady job selling aluminum siding in New Jersey. "I dropped out of show business, but nobody noticed," he remarked. After the couple divorced in 1961, Dangerfield went back to stand-up, working a day job in an office and performing in clubs at night. Dangerfield eventually auditioned for television host Ed Sullivan, who immediately signed him to his program. He made 16 appearances on Sullivan's variety show and more than 60 appearances on *The Tonight Show* with Johnny Carson. He opened the comedy club Dangerfield's in Manhattan in 1969, and spent more than 20 years as a Las Vegas headliner. The 1970s found Dangerfield releasing books, *I Couldn't Stand My Wife's Cooking So I Opened a Restaurant* (1972) and *I Don't Get No Respect* (1973), and a variety of comedy albums. In 1978, he was selected as commencement speaker for Harvard University. His screen debut came with *The Projectionist* (1971), but it was his role as real estate developer Al Czervik in *Caddyshack* (1980) that launched his film career and which he followed with such features as *Easy Money* (1983), *Back to School* (1986), *Rover Dangerfield* (1991), *Ladybugs* (1992), *Natural Born Killers* (1994), *Meet Wally Sparks* (1997), and the Adam Sandler film *Little Nicky* (2000). Dangerfield won a Grammy Award in 1981 for his comedy album *No Respect*, a lifetime achievement award during the American Comedy Awards in 1994, and Comedy Central's first Comedy Idol award in 2003. In 2004, he released an album of love songs, *Romeo Rodney*, and published his autobiography, *It's Not Easy Bein' Me*. He died in Los Angeles from heart surgery complications.

[Adam Wills (2nd ed.)]

DANGLOW, JACOB (1880–1962), Australian rabbi. Born in England, Danglow was trained at Jews' College, London. In 1905 he became minister of St. Kilda Hebrew Congregation, Victoria, where he officiated for 52 years. Danglow served as chaplain of the Australian forces in France in World War I and later as senior Jewish chaplain in Australia. He was active in many communal institutions, especially the Montefiore Home for Aged Jews and the Jewish Young People's Association, and represented the community in many civic affairs, especially the hospital fund. Staunchly opposed to "political Zionism" prior to the establishment of the State of Israel, after Israeli independence Danglow became a champion of the Jewish state and visited it in 1956. Danglow was widely regarded as the most important Jewish religious leader in Australia, and presided at the state funeral of Australia's great Jewish general, Sir John Monash, in 1931, when one-third of Melbourne's population lined the streets of the funeral procession. John S. Levi's *Rabbi Jacob Danglow: 'The Uncrowned Monarch' of Australia's Jews* (1995) is a comprehensive biography.

ADD. BIBLIOGRAPHY: *Australian Dictionary of Biography*, 8, 204; H.L. Rubinstein, Australia I, 264–65, index; W.D. Rubinstein, Australia II, index.

[Israel Porush / William D. Rubinstein (2nd ed.)]

DANGOOR, EZRA SASSON BEN REUBEN (1848–1930), Iraqi rabbi. Dangoor studied in Baghdad and was a pupil of Abdallah *Somekh. Although he devoted much of his time to religious activity, he obtained his livelihood from business. From 1880 to 1886 he was in charge of documents issued by the Baghdad *bet din*. In 1894 he was appointed rabbi of Rangoon, Burma, but ill health compelled him to return a year later to Baghdad, where he was appointed chief of the *shoḥatim*. During 1923 to 1928 he served as chief rabbi of Baghdad but resigned office in consequence of communal disputes. Many books were published under his editorship in the Hebrew press he established in Baghdad in 1904, including festival prayer books according to the Baghdad rite; *Seder ha-ʿIbbur*, calendars for the years 5665–5683 (in other presses until 5691); *Birkhot Shamayim* (1905), on the blessings for precepts and for pleasures; *Sefer ha-Shirim* (1906), containing poems by different authors. There remain in manuscript in the Sassoon collection responsa, a history of Baghdad from the years 1793 to 1928, homilies, commentaries on biblical books, laws, customs, poems, and **piyyutim*. After his death, his children published a memorial volume (1931).

BIBLIOGRAPHY: Davidson, Oẓar, 4 (1933), 458; A. Yaari, *Ha-Defus ha-Ivri be-Arẓot ha-Mizraḥ*, 2 (1940), 104f., 131–48; A. Ben-Jacob, *Yehudei Bavel* (1965), 172–4; idem, *Shirah u-Fiyyut shel Yehudei Bavel ba-Dorot ha-Aḥaronim* (1970), index.

[Abraham David]

DANIEL (Heb. דָּנִיֵּאל,דָּנִאֵל, "God has judged, or vindicated").

(1) An evidently pre-Mosaic saint (Ezek. 14:14, 20) and sage (28:3) and, as such, of a type conceivable in any land (14:3ff.) and assumed by Ezekiel to have been heard of by the pagan prince of Tyre (28:1–3). The publication of the Ugaritic epic of Aqhat in 1936 showed the probability that the Phoenicians had a tradition about a man Daniel who was famed for both piety and wisdom. Aqhat's father, *Dnil*, is a devout worshiper of the gods and has their ear (especially that of Baal); he is also one who, either as an elder or king, "judges the case of the fatherless, adjudicates the cause of the widow." As Cassuto pointed out, this requires not only goodness but also wisdom (cf. I Kings 3:5ff.). It is perhaps no accident that in the great majority of Ezekiel manuscripts the name of this Daniel is written without *yod* (cf. the Ugaritic *dnil*, whereas the name of all the other biblical Daniels is written דניאל). It may be assumed that in the tradition known to Ezekiel this Daniel figured as a monotheist.

(2) The name of David's second son according to I Chronicles 3:1 (according to II Sam. 3:3, Chileab).

(3) The hero of the Book of Daniel; see the Book of *Daniel.

(4) A priest of post-Exilic times (Ezra 8:2; Neh. 10:7).

[Harold Louis Ginsberg]

In the Aggadah

Daniel (no. 3 above) was a scion of the House of David. He and his three companions, Hananiah, Mishael, and Azariah, were eunuchs at the royal palace and were thus able to exonerate themselves of the charges of immorality brought against them (Sanh. 93b; PdRE 52). Although the *Mekhilta de-R. Ishmael* (Pisḥa, 1) and Josephus (Ant., 10:266ff.) count Daniel among the prophets as do Christian sources (e.g., Matt. 24:15), the Talmud denies that he was a prophet. However, he was possessed of such great wisdom that he outweighed all wise men of the world (Yoma 77a). He was an expert in the interpretation of dreams and *Nebuchadnezzar trusted him at once (Tanḥ. B., Gen. 191). Despite the many dangers and difficulties at the royal court, Daniel conducted himself with the utmost piety. He refused to partake of wine or oil of the gentiles (Av. Zar. 36a). He was prepared to sacrifice his life rather than omit reciting the statutory prayers thrice daily, and he was cast into the lion's den as a punishment when the nobles surprised him reciting the *Minḥah* prayer. The mouth of the den was sealed with a huge stone which had rolled from Palestine to Babylon. Upon this stone sat an angel in the shape of a lion to protect Daniel against harassment by his enemies. When the following morning the king went to see Daniel's fate, he found him reciting the *Shema* (Mid. Ps. to 66). On another occasion Nebuchadnezzar tried to induce Daniel to worship an idol into whose mouth he placed the diadem (*ẓiẓ*) of the high priest bearing God's ineffable name, as a result of which the idol uttered the words "I am thy Lord." Daniel, however, did not yield. He conjured the idol not to desecrate God's name, whereupon the *ẓiẓ* passed to Daniel's mouth and the idol crumbled to pieces (Song. R. 7:9).

God revealed to Daniel the destiny of Israel and the date of the Last Judgment, which was not even revealed to Haggai, Zechariah, and Malachi (Dan. 10:7). Daniel, however, forgot the *keẓ* ("end") revealed to him (Gen. R. 98:2). Despite the fact that Daniel is lauded for his virtues of piety and charity (ARN[1] 4, 11), it is also stated that he was not rescued from the lion's den because of his own merits but through the merits of Abraham (Ber. 7b). Moreover, some regard him as a sinner who was punished because he gave good counsel to Nebuchadnezzar (BB 4a). Daniel is variously identified with the eunuch Hathach (Esth. 4:5, 6; Meg. 15a; BB 4a), Memucan (Esth. 1:16; Targ. Sheni), or Sheshbazzar (PR 6:23, *et al.*). According to *Josippon it was owing to Daniel's merit that Darius issued the orders that Jews should return to Palestine and rebuild the Temple (ch. 24). Daniel asked the king to appoint *Zerubbabel in his place. Opinions differ as to whether Daniel accompanied the returned exiles to Palestine. Some state that he returned after the proclamation of *Cyrus (Song. R. 5:5) while later sources (e.g., Josippon 9d–10a) state that he retired to *Shushan where he lived a pious life until his death and was buried there. The Talmud mentions "a synagogue of Daniel" situated three miles from the city of Barnish (Er. 21a).

In Islam

Muslim legend is acquainted with both biblical Daniels; the wise man mentioned in Ezekiel 14:14 and 28:3, and the hero of the Book of Daniel. Among the commentators of the Koran, some interpret the verses of Sura 85:4–5, "The fellows of the pit were slain," and "The fire with its kindling," as referring to Daniel (Dāniyāl) and his colleagues in the fiery furnace; nevertheless, this is only one of the many explanations to these obscure verses.

[Haïm Z'ew Hirschberg]

In the Arts

The hero of the Book of Daniel early attracted the attention of writers. One of the first examples of Anglo-Saxon poetry is a seventh-century paraphrase of the Book of Daniel, and he also appears later in the English miracle play, *Ordo Prophetarum*. In the 17th century the German tragicomedy *Der siegende Hofmann Daniel* (1671) dealt with the theme. After the English writer Hannah More, whose *Sacred Dramas* (1782) included a play about Daniel, literary treatments of the story became rare. Two 20th-century reinterpretations were *Daniel* (1907) by the Polish dramatist Stanislaw Wyspiański, and "*The Daniel Jazz*" (1920), the title poem in a collection by the U.S. writer Vachel Lindsay which imitates the dramatic sermons characteristic of the Afro-American churches.

In art, Daniel was a far more familiar figure, both because of the dramatic, visual quality of the biblical episodes in which he figures and because of his adaptability to Christian typology. Daniel in the lion's den was thought to prefigure Jesus in his sepulcher and was also seen as representing the saved soul, or man under God's protection. Daniel is usually portrayed as a young, beardless, and often naked youth, sometimes wearing the Phrygian bonnet. He is seen flanked by his lions, and occasionally accompanied by the ram of his apocalyptic vision. He is often associated with other figures from the Book of Daniel (and its apocryphal addition) in a narrative cycle: giving judgment in the case of *Susannah and the Elders; preceded in the ordeal by the Three Hebrews; and twice cast into the den of lions, under both Darius and Cyrus. The cycle of Nebuchadnezzar's dreams interpreted by Daniel shows the prophet more by implication than by presence, as does the apocalyptic cycle. A vast number of works of art depict the Daniel narrative in full, in part, or in isolated episodes. Daniel appears on fourth-century sarcophagi, fifth and sixth-century church doors, woven cloths, and belt-buckles in Spain, Germany, and Italy. In the seventh century, he is seen in the *Cosmas Indicopleustès* (Vatican Library) and, from the ninth century onward, on capitals and portals throughout the Romanesque world. Examples in miniature painting are to be found in the 11th-century Apocalypse of Saint-Sever (Paris,

Bibliothèque Nationale) and Spanish Beatus manuscripts, and later in 14th- and 15th-century Bibles. After the 13th century the theme was less popular. There is a Tintoretto Daniel in the Scuola di San Rocco, Venice, and Rubens painted Daniel and the lions (1618). Bernini's sculptures of Daniel and Habakkuk (1656) are to be seen in the Chigi chapel in S. Maria del Popolo, Rome. Delacroix painted Daniel and the lions in 1849. The Nebuchadnezzar dream cycle is illustrated by Guido Reni's 17th-century painting in Santa Maria Maggiore, Rome, and the apocalyptic cycle is referred to by Rembrandt in his "Vision of Daniel" (1650, Berlin). Some other portrayals are Michelangelo's fresco in the Sistine Chapel of the Vatican, and an 18th-century statue by Aleijadinho (Francisco Antônio Lisbôa) at Congonhas do Campo, Brazil. The subject of the Three Hebrews in the fiery furnace occurs in frescoes in Roman catacombs of the third and fourth centuries C.E. In the Middle Ages this theme is found in sculpture, mosaics, and manuscripts as well as frescoes. The three men were taken to represent the elect protected from all perils, including the flames of Hell. In early representations they are often nude, despite the fact that the Bible states that they were thrown into the flames fully clothed. They are also often depicted as children, their hands raised in an attitude of prayer.

In Music

The dramatic episodes of the "Daniel cycle," including and often combining the canonical and apocryphal parts, have always been favored by composers. While the music of the 12th-century Daniel play by Hilary of Poitiers has not survived, the contemporary *Ludus Danielis* from Beauvais Abbey is completely "scored" in the manuscript (British Museum, Ms. Egerton 2615, fols. 95r–108r) with a combination of composed songs and traditional church melodies. This has become known through a recording directed by Noah *Greenberg. Notable settings of the Daniel cycle are Caldara's opera and Hasse's oratorio (both presented at the Viennese court in 1731); Darius *Milhaud's *Les Miracles de la foi* (1951), a cantata for tenor, chorus, and orchestra based on passages from the Book of Daniel; and Benjamin Britten's modern "parable for church performance," *The Burning Fiery Furnace* (1966), with text by William Plomer. Vachel Lindsay's "*The Daniel Jazz*" was set to music in the jazz idiom by Louis *Gruenberg, for tenor and eight instruments (1923); and by Herbert Chappell (1963), for unison voices and piano. The Song of the Three Children (*Canticum trium Puerorum*, Vulg. Dan. 3:52–90), included in the Catholic liturgy, has inspired many fine musical settings. There is a notable setting by Josquin des Prés (15th century); a polychoral structure by Heinrich Schuetz and Michael Praetorius (17th century); and Karlheinz Stockhausen's *Gesang der drei Juenglinge* (1956) which dissolves and reconstitutes the human utterance by electronic manipulation. On the popular level is *Shadrack, Meshack, Abednego*, a composed spiritual by Robert MacGinney (often thought to be authentic), which was made famous by the jazz trumpeter and singer Louis Armstrong.

BIBLIOGRAPHY: Cassuto, in: EM, 2 (1954), 683–5; Ginsberg, in: Pritchard, Texts, 149–55 (English translation of the Aqhat epic); G.R. Driver, *Canaanite Myths and Legends* (1955), 48–60. IN THE AGGADAH: Ginzberg, Legends, index. IN ISLAM: Ṭabarī, *Tafsīr*, 30 (1329 A.H.), 85 (in the name of Ibn ʿAbbās); Thaʿlabī, *Qiṣaṣ* (1356 A.H.), 370 (in the name of Muqātil) A. Geiger, *Was hat Mohammed aus dem Judenthume aufgenommen* (1833), 189–90; J. Horovitz, *Koranische Untersuchungen* (1926), 92; G. Vajda, in: EI² s.v. *Dāniyāl*. IN THE ARTS: L. Réau, *Iconographie de l'art chrétien*, 2 pt. 1 (1956), 390–410; E. Kirschbaum (ed.), *Lexikon der christlichen Ikonographie*, 1 (1968), 469–73, includes bibliography; T. Ehrenstein, *Das Alte Testament im Bilde* (1923), 797–813; *The Bible in Art: The Old Testament* (1956), 232–3.

DANIEL, BOOK OF

DANIEL, BOOK OF, a book of the third division of the Hebrew Bible, the Hagiographa, named for a man Daniel whose fortunes and predictions are the subject of the book.

DIVISIONS AND CONTENTS

When the Book of Daniel is examined for content and literary character, it falls naturally into two roughly equal parts which may be designated Daniel A and Daniel B. Daniel A (chs. 1–6) comprises six stories, told in the third person, about the trials and triumphs of Daniel and his three companions; while Daniel B (chs. 7–12) consists of four accounts, cast in the first person, of as many apocalyptic revelations received by Daniel.

Summary of Daniel A (Dan. chs. 1–6)

CHAPTER 1. Nebuchadnezzar, the king of Babylon, took back with him from Judah several boys of good family, handsome looks, and promising intellect, and charged his grand vizier with the task, to be completed in three years, of rearing and educating them "in booklore and in the Chaldean tongue" (1:4) in order to qualify them for the king's service. Four of these boys, Daniel, Hananiah, Mishael, and Azariah – renamed Belteshazzar, Shadrach, Meshach, and Abed-Nego by the vizier – were so pious and so ingenious as to make an arrangement with the lower official to whom the vizier had assigned them whereby they exchanged with him the excellent rations they received from the king for raw vegetables. Finding, after a ten-day trial, that the four lads looked even healthier than the others, the official continued the arrangement indefinitely. At the end of their period of training, the king found them superior not only to their fellow students but to all the magicians and enchanters of his realm.

CHAPTER 2. Daniel came to the king's notice even before the three years were over. The king had had a dream which greatly perturbed him. He burned with eagerness to know what it meant, but reasoned that he could be sure that an interpretation was correct only if the interpreter was able to narrate the dream itself without being told it. Since none of his masters of occult lore was able to do this, the king ordered his captain of the guard to execute all the savants of Babylon. The officer proceeded to do so, and since Daniel and his companions came under the definition of savants, they were also to be put to death. On asking the captain of the guard for the reason and receiving his answer, Daniel persuaded him to discontinue the slaughter for a few hours and promised that at the end of that time he would come up with the answer to the king's questions. Then he and his companions prayed, and the solution was revealed to Daniel in a dream. Brought before the king, Daniel narrated the king's dream and interpreted it to mean that Nebuchadnezzar's domination of the whole world would be followed by the successive world ascendancies of three other monarchies, after which God would set up a fifth monarchy that would destroy the four previous monarchies and would endure forever. On hearing this, Nebuchadnezzar was so filled with admiration for Daniel and his God that he appointed Daniel both supreme administrator of the whole province of Babylon and supreme prefect over all the savants of Babylon; but at Daniel's request the supreme administrative office was divided among his three companions, while he retained only the advisory one (2:49).

CHAPTER 3:1–30. As high-ranking administrators, the three companions were affected by the decree which Nebuchadnezzar issued to all the top functionaries (3:2–3) to bow down to the image which he set up, but they ignored it. Certain Chaldeans thereupon denounced them to the king. They were doubtless functionaries, subordinate – and naturally jealous – colleagues of the Jewish administrators-in-chief. Nebuchadnezzar ordered Shadrach, Meshach, and Abed-Nego thrown into a blazing furnace; but not even their clothes were singed, and again he expressed his admiration for the God of the Jews and even further exalted the three Jewish top officials.

CHAPTERS 3:31–5:30. As for Daniel the sage, he interpreted a second dream of Nebuchadnezzar, the one that portended the king's seven years' lycanthropy, and a portent of a different nature – the famous writing on the wall – concerning Nebuchadnezzar's successor Belshazzar, who had not been aware of Daniel's extraordinary gifts until informed by the queen mother. Belshazzar thereupon bestowed upon Daniel, not an academic or advisory office, but the exalted administrative one of triumvir.

CHAPTER 6. Daniel remained a triumvir (though with a different title) under Belshazzar's successor Darius the Mede, and so distinguished himself in this capacity that the king placed him in sole charge of the empire. Then it was Daniel's turn to become the butt of professional jealousy. His rivals, taking advantage of Daniel's uncompromising piety, maneuvered the king into a position in which he was compelled, to his dismay, to order Daniel thrown into a lion pit. (The plotters persuaded the king to promulgate a decree forbidding anyone to address a petition to any being but the king for 30 days: a Jewish misunderstanding of the Babylonian superstition that food offerings – and hence the accompanying prayers – offered to one's personal god in the month of Tevet were unlucky. Surely a Jew's conscience need not deter him, in such circumstances, from abstaining for 30 days from all prayer, let alone ostentatious prayer; but the plotters knew that Daniel would

Illustrations from a missal, south Armenia, 1331, showing Daniel sleeping. Jerusalem, Library of the Armenian Patriarchate, Ms. 95, fol. 142r.

under no circumstances dispense with praying on his knees three times daily at open windows – not in a New York penthouse but less than ten feet above the ground.) After expressing to Daniel the hope that the God he served so faithfully will save him, the king departs for a supperless evening and a sleepless night in his palace. At the crack of dawn, he hurries back to the edge of the pit and calls in a broken voice, "O Daniel, servant of the living God, has the God whom you constantly worship been able to save you from the lions?" And what is his joy to hear Daniel's voice and be reassured! He promptly orders Daniel pulled up and his accusers cast down, and these the beasts give short shrift. Darius issues a decree that Daniel's God must be treated with awe and reverence throughout his realm, and Daniel continues to serve with distinction as vizier to Darius the Mede and to Cyrus the Persian.

Summary of Daniel B (Dan. chs. 7–12)

CHAPTER 7. The story of Daniel here reverts to the Chaldean period, the first year of King Belshazzar. The experience of Daniel related in this chapter has nothing to do with his character and career as a savant who interprets dreams and portents for kings or as a minister of state who is the victim of his rivals' intrigues. Instead, Daniel's role is that of an apocalyptist. Here, Daniel himself has a disturbing dream, and while the fact is stated in 7:1 in the third person, it is also stated there that Daniel himself wrote an account of the dream, and 7:2 ff. (apart from the introductory phrase at the beginning of verse 2) is simply the text of Daniel's first person narrative.

(The next two revelations, chapters 8 and 9, are narrated by Daniel in the first person without a third person introduction.) Daniel's dream in 7:1, like those of Nebuchadnezzar in chapters 2 and 4, is symbolic, but Daniel is as much at a loss to interpret the symbols as Nebuchadnezzar was to interpret those in his dreams; in the dream itself, however, Daniel asks an angel to enlighten him, and the angel obliges. In doing so, the angel sketches a succession of four transient monarchies and a fifth enduring one, similar to that which the sage Daniel sketched in his interpretation of Nebuchadnezzar's dream in chapter 2. In chapter 7, however, there is the additional feature of judgment and retribution: the beast which represents the first kingdom is annihilated ("taken from the earth") at the end of its period of ascendancy (verse 4, apart from the last two clauses, which are out of place – see below); the fourth, which is of a particularly oppressive character (7, 23) is annihilated at the conclusion of a solemn judgment by the divine tribunal (9–11); but the middle two are suffered to live on even after their loss of dominion (12). It is also made clear here that the fifth, world-wide, and everlasting, empire will be ruled by a people of "saints of the Most High," i.e., the Jews.

CHAPTER 8. Daniel relates that in the third year of the reign of Belshazzar he had a vision (rather than a dream). Again the features are symbolic, and their symbolism is explained to Daniel by an angel. Again the explanation involves a succession of monarchies, and this time they are identified by name: symbolized by a ram with two tall horns that sprout successively, the later one taller than the first, are the two Iranian monarchies, the Median and the Persian respectively. Symbolized by a he-goat with first one great horn which is broken and then four great horns that sprout in its stead, are respectively the united Greek world-kingdom (i.e., that of Alexander the Great) and its successor kingdoms; and symbolized by a smaller horn which branches off from one of the four successor horns is a particular king of one of the successor kingdoms (i.e., the Seleucid king Antiochus IV Epiphanes). This branch horn is represented as performing certain antics culminating in the banishing of the *tamid* ("the constant," i.e., the daily burnt offerings) from the "stand" (i.e., altar) of "the Commander of the Host [of Heaven]" (i.e., God) and the setting up of an "offense" on that stand (11–12).

CHAPTER 9. The apocalypse, dated in the first year of Darius the Mede, is neither a symbolic dream nor a symbolic vision. The angel Gabriel visits Daniel and communicates a "word" to him (9:21–24). As it happens, the designation *angelus interpres* would not be a misnomer if applied to Gabriel in this case, for if he does not interpret symbols, he does interpret Scripture. The occasion of his coming is Daniel's prayer for enlightenment on the meaning of Jeremiah's prediction (Jer. 25:11–12; 29:10) that "the ruins of Jerusalem" (Dan. 9:2) would endure 70 years. The interpretation is as follows: a period of 70 weeks of years was decreed for the expiation of the national guilt. At the end of the seventh week, an "anointed prince" (probably a high priest) will function again; at the end of another 62 weeks, an "anointed one" will be cut off. The remaining week will be one of religious persecution, and for the duration of its second half, sacrifice and oblation will be abolished and "an abomination of desolation" (called "offense" in 8:12) will occupy their "stand" (reading *kannam* for *kenaf* in 9:27).

CHAPTERS 10–12. As in chapter 7, Daniel is introduced briefly in the third person and then proceeds in the first person. The date of this apocalypse is given as the third year of the reign of King Cyrus of Persia, and like chapter 9 it consists entirely of a "word" (10:1 – three times) communicated to Daniel by an angel. It is vouchsafed him in response to prayer, but to judge by the content of the "word," the prayer was not for an exposition of scripture but simply for information on what was going to happen from the present (i.e., the third year of Cyrus) to the redemption of Israel, though occasionally, to be sure, the phrasing indicates that some old prophetic verse is being expounded. The angel then informs Daniel (11:2bff.) that Cyrus will be followed by three more Persian kings, but that after that the ascendancy will pass on to the Greeks. There will first be one mighty Greek king (obviously Alexander the Great), but his empire will split into a separate kingdom for each of the four points of the compass. First the king of the southern succession state (Ptolemy I) will be the most powerful, but then one of his officers, the king of the north (Seleucus I), will become stronger than he. There follows (verses 6–30) a remarkably accurate account of the wars and marriages between the dynasty of the north (the Seleucids) and that of the south (the Lagids) down to the Seleucid Antiochus IV and the joint Lagid kings Ptolemy VI and VII, with the Roman intervention which compelled Antiochus to withdraw from Egypt in the year 168 B.C.E., clearly hinted at at the beginning of verse 30. Then, Antiochus' measures against Judaism from the years 168 to 166 or 165 are described from verse 31 through verse 39 inclusive. The rest of the book is concerned with what is expected to happen after that.

DATES OF COMPOSITION AND CHARACTERISTICS OF THE PARTS

Traditional View

Both the rabbis of the Talmudic Age and the Christian Church Fathers accepted the book's own statements that the four apocalypses of Daniel B were written by a man named Daniel in the last years of the Babylonian Age and in the first ones of the Persian Age, i.e., approximately in the decade 545–535 B.C.E., and they did not question the historicity of any part of Daniel A.

Critical View

GENERAL CONSIDERATIONS. If prediction of events in detail of the far future is theoretically possible, it is, on the other hand, unexampled in the Torah and the Prophets, and events so far in the future would be of no discoverable relevance to the lives of his audience or readers. This is what struck the neoplationist pagan philosopher Porphyry (3rd century C.E.). His pertinent work has been lost, but the Latin Church Father

*Jerome (early 5th century C.E.) cites him occasionally in his commentary on Daniel, and at the beginning of his introduction to that commentary he quotes him as follows: "[The Book of Daniel] was composed by someone who lived in Judea in the reign of Antiochus who was surnamed Epiphanes, and he did not predict coming events but narrated past ones. Consequently, what he relates down to Antiochus embodies true history; but if he added any surmises about the future, he just invented them, for he did not know the future." Strange to say, Porphyry (according to Jerome) did not realize that the campaign described in Daniel 11:40 was an "added surmise," but asserted that Antiochus undertook a third campaign in Egypt, which is contrary to fact. Equally significant is the inaccuracy of the book's knowledge of pre-Hellenistic history. After Cyrus there reigned over the Persian Empire not a mere three kings (11:2) but ten (1 Cambyses, 2 Xerxeses, 3 Dariuses, 3 Artaxerxeses and 1 Arses). There never was a Darius the Mede (6:1; 9:1; 11:1), and Belshazzar (5:1, 2, 30; 7:1) never was king. Though Belshazzar deputized for his father King Nabonidus during the latter's prolonged absence from Babylon, documents continued to be dated there by regnal years of Nabonidus, and Belshazzar was never designated otherwise than as "the king's son." The most charitable view of the inaccuracy in Daniel 1:1, 2 is that "third year" is a mistake for "third month" and "Jehoiakim" for "Jehoiachin" (cf. II Kings 24:8ff.). However, Porphyry erred in ascribing all of the book to a person who lived in Judea in the reign of Antiochus IV (176/5–163 B.C.E.). Daniel B was indeed composed by such a person, or rather by four such persons (see infra). Daniel A, on the other hand, is unquestionably earlier, as was recognized by an impressive array of scholars in the first half of the 20th century (as a brief statement of the case, J.A. Montgomery, pp. 89–90 (see bibl.), is admirable). Since no anti-Epiphanian propaganda is discernible in Daniel chapters two or four, let alone in the story about King Darius in chapter six, it must be concluded that Daniel A chs. 1–6 (all summarized above) antedates Epiphanes' reign. A more precise dating of Daniel A is obtained through certain later additions to chapter two, viz. 2:42–43 and the expression "and the toes" in verse 41. These additions do not only add in the middle of the dream's original interpretation (vv. 36–45) a feature absent from the preceding narration of the dream (vv. 31–35), but they correct the original interpretation of the dream in which they occur. For first, the narration in 33b states merely that the feet of the image which Nebuchadnezzar saw in his dream were partly of iron and partly of clay. Secondly, according to the original interpretation of this in verse 41, verse 33b is explained to mean that the fourth kingdom will (ultimately) be a divided kingdom, but that something of the character of iron will permeate all its parts, since the two substances are combined in both feet. This is especially clear if we omit "and the toes" (which is missing in the versions anyway): "And as you saw the feet (and toes) partly of potter's clay and partly of iron, it shall be a divided kingdom; but some of the firmness of iron shall be in it, just as you saw iron mixed with the miry clay." However, verses 42–43, on the other hand, interpret a feature which is not found in the original narration. They assert that in the dream some of the toes were entirely of iron and some entirely of clay; this signifying that, in contradiction to verse 41, one part of the divided kingdom will be firm (throughout) and the other will be fragile (throughout). The feature on which verse 41 based its view, namely, that in the feet the iron and the earthenware are combined, is – so verses 42–43 assert – to be interpreted otherwise: it signifies that the two dynasties will attempt to fuse "by means of human seed," i.e., by biological union. However, the combination was not to endure, just as iron does not mix with earthenware. Such an avowed correction of an immediately preceding interpretation can only be an interpolation, and it can only have been occasioned by a dramatic upset of the balance of power. As it happens, such an upset of the balance of power, linked to an unsuccessful attempt by two dynasties to interbreed, is known from history. In the year 252 B.C.E. Antiochus II put aside his wife (she was also his sister) Laodice and espoused Berenice, daughter of Ptolemy II, and thus was born a son in whose veins coursed the blood of both dynasties. However, Antiochus became reconciled with Laodice. His sudden death was believed to have been caused by poisoning that Laodice ordered, and the subsequent murder of Berenice's child certainly was ordered by her. In the end she disposed of Berenice as well, thereby putting an end to the very attempt at "fusion." In the year 246, however, Berenice's brother Ptolemy III avenged her by invading the Seleucid Empire, reaching Bactria; although he permanently annexed only some islands and other coastal areas, as a result of his blows Asia Minor and the enormous satrapy of Media revolted and were not reconquered by the house of Seleucus for a quarter of a century. The interpolation in chapter two must therefore date from 246 or shortly after. Of course, the main text is earlier than the interpolation. It can be dated with considerable probability at around 304 B.C.E. In this respect, verses 44–45 are particularly significant. "(44) And in the days of those [i.e., the aforementioned four] kingdoms, the God of Heaven will raise up a kingdom which shall never be destroyed, and whose sovereignty shall never be left to another people. It [i.e., the fifth kingdom] shall pulverize and annihilate all those kingdoms but shall itself endure for evermore (45) inasmuch as you saw a stone rolling from the mountain unpropelled by hands and pulverizing the earthenware, the iron, the copper, the silver, and the gold…." It is the author of Daniel chapter two who first reasoned, from the fact that all the five substances in the dream endured until the impact of the stone, that none of the first three world-dominating monarchies would be destroyed by its successor but that all three would endure, though no longer dominant, until the fifth one appeared and destroyed both them and the fourth. The interpolation (as interpreted here) along with other indications identifies the fourth kingdom as the Greek; verses 37–38 identify the first as the Babylonian or Chaldean; and in the light of verse 30 and 6:1, 29 (cf. 8:1; 9:1; 10:1; 11:3, 5, 20–21), the two middle ones can only be the Median and the Persian. The question therefore arises, when did a post-imperial Babylonian monarchy, a post-imperial Median monarchy, and a post-imperial Persian monarchy exist side by side with a single but divided Greek imperial monarchy? The answer is that they existed together after Seleucus had returned to his satrapy of Babylon in 312 and had begun to call himself king (at first, only vis-à-vis his Oriental subjects, and in 305 or 304, vis-à-vis Hellenes as well), but only while he was still confined to southern Mesopotamia, and while Ptolemy, Antigonus, and others, though fighting each other, were fighting a civil war within a theoretically united realm, that is, before 301. By the latter date Seleucus, in getting rid of Antigonus in alliance with Ptolemy, had expanded into Syria; Seleucus and Ptolemy had more or less agreed on their common border; and Ptolemy and all the other successors had also donned crowns and proclaimed themselves kings. Within this period while Seleucus was only king of Babylonia, the territories representing the residual Median and Persian monarchies were Atropatene – which Strabo also calls Atropatian Media – and Persis respectively. These persisted as semiautonomous kingdoms, or principalities, not only throughout the Hellenistic period but well into the Roman. Chapter 2 may have been integrated into the collection which we have denominated Daniel A (at which time the initial and final verses were added to it) either before or after the interpolation verses 42–43, so that the collection Daniel A may be dated roughly in "the middle decades of the third century B.C.E."

THE FOUR AUTHORS OF DANIEL B. Daniel B is in its entirety a product of the reign of Antiochus IV, but it is not all from a single hand. It is the work of four apocalyptists, who have been designated as Apoc I, Apoc II, Apoc III, and Apoc IV. Apoc I comprises all of chapter 7 minus the verses and clauses which speak of an eleventh horn and an eleventh king (namely 8, 11a [minus בֵּאדַיִן plus חָזֵה הֲוֵית עַד דִּי], 11b, 20 [from וְאָחֳרִי on], 22, 24b–25). This apocalypse represents an updating of the dream and interpretation in chapter 2. For it, the fourth kingdom is not (as in ch. 2) the Greek kingdom (it is too far removed from the time when there was a single Greek kingdom either in fact or in theory), but the Seleucid kingdom. For it says of the fourth kingdom (24a), "And the ten horns – ten kings will arise from that kingdom." The Seleucids regarded themselves as the legitimate successors of Alexander the Great, and Berosus, a subject of Antiochus I, notes that the latter is the third king after Alexander. For him to be the third, one of the joint kings who was recognized by the generals after Alexander's death – his half brother Philip and his posthumous son Alexander – must be disregarded; probably it was Philip, who died some years before Seleucus returned to Babylon, unlike Alexander, who lived to about that date, so that Seleucus could be regarded as his successor. The first ten kings of Asia, were then, according to the Seleucid canon: (1) Alexander I; (2) Alexander II; (3) Seleucus I; (4) Antiochus I; (5) Antiochus II; (6) Seleucus II; (7) Seleucus III; (8) Antiochus III; (9) Seleucus IV; and (10) Antiochus IV. There is now available a Seleucid king list from Babylonia, which apparently counts no king at all from Alexander's death to the accession of Alexander II in 317 (see Pritchard, Texts[3], 567). The essential message of Apoc I is therefore this: The days of the wicked Seleucid kingdom are numbered; its present sovereign shall be its last. Yet Apoc I does not enlarge upon the wickedness of this particular king or hint at what his wickedness consisted of. This would hardly be conceivable after the paganization of the Temple and the outlawing of Judaism, which threatened it with early extinction. It would be conceivable, however, at any time from the beginning of Antiochus IV's reign, when he began to sell the high priesthood to the highest bidder and to encourage Hellenization, through the year 169 when he plundered the Temple down to the year 168 when he crushed a Jewish rebellion and abolished the temple state of Jerusalem, and established a pagan polis on the Akra and gave it control of the Temple. In fact its *terminus ante quem* is the paganization of the Temple and the proscription of Judaism at the very end of the year 167. After the latter developments, on the other hand, the absence of a specific allusion to them would be incomprehensible. That is why the author of the secondary matter (see above) in the chapter – who probably did not know the Seleucid king list – could not imagine that Antiochus IV was included among the ten kings of the original text and so added an eleventh. It is the author of Apoc IV who made all these additions (except perhaps verses 21–22, which may be from a still later hand), which we therefore designate by the siglum I–4. (For further characteristics of Apoc I, see above, the first paragraph under the heading "Daniel B.") Apoc II comprises the original matter in chapter 8, the secondary verses being 13–14, 16, 18–19, 26a, 27b. Verses 18–19 are from the author of Apoc III and are designated by the siglum II–3; the remaining interpolations are by the author of Apoc IV and are designated by the siglum II–4. Apoc II was written after the appalling developments of December 167, which it clearly reflects and the end of whose author it predicts. It adopts the form of a vision instead of a dream because the Hebrew word for "vision" (*ḥazon*) is the one used in the sense of "prediction" in Habakkuk 2:3, and the author wishes to stress that his *ḥazon* is, like Habakkuk's, for a future date (8:17). To Habakkuk, this circumstance is offered as a reason for the divine command to write down the *ḥazon*; in Apoc II it is further stressed that the future date in question is distant, and this, i.e., the fact that the *ḥazon* has no message for Daniel's contemporaries, is the reason which is given to Daniel (8:26) for the angel's instruction to "conceal" (to be discovered and opened in due course). Apoc III is the original part of chapters 10–12. Within this Apoc IV has transposed the two half verses 10:21b and 10:21a, and added 11:1–2a, 12:5–9, and 11–12 (unless, as is probable, verse 12 is still later). It is Apoc III who is the first to dispense with symbolic dreams or visions and to substitute a simple narration of future history by an angel who draws from memory upon "that which is inscribed in the Book of Truth" (10:21). Apoc III, like Apoc II, utilizes Habakkuk 2:3, but he departs further from its original sense. What he stresses is that more *ḥazon* (by which he means scheduled events) has yet to elapse until the final redemption

(10:14; 11:27), and he has even inserted a remark to that effect in the work of Apoc II (8:19 with 8:18; cf. 10:9). But Apoc III is particularly noteworthy for identifying, on the one hand, the Assyria of Numbers 24:24 and of Isaiah's prophecies with the Seleucid Empire, and the impious Assyrian king of Isaiah with Antiochus IV Epiphanes; and, on the other hand, as follows: (a) the servant of Isaiah 52:13–53:12 with those who, during the Epiphanian persecution, instructed (it is thus that he interprets the *yaskil* of Isa. 52:13) the not willingly apostate but despairing masses in the meaning of the ancient prophecies, thereby encouraging them to resist, or "justifying" them; (b) "the many" of Isaiah 52 with those despairing masses in Daniel 11:33–34 (the last word is to be deleted as a variant of the similar one in verse 32) and 12:3; and (c) the willing Hellenizers with the wicked of Isaiah 66:24 (Dan. 11:32; 12:2; note the word דֵּרָאוֹן, which is confined to Isa. 66:24 and Dan. 12:2). Because Isaiah represents Assyria as the staff of the Lord's indignation and as destined to oppress Judah until the indignation has spent itself, Apoc III not only employs the same language about Antiochus (cf. notably 11:36b with Isa. 10:23, 25) but infers from Isaiah 26:19ff. that the end of the indignation will be followed by a resurrection of some of the dead (Dan. 12:2) – the earliest formulation of a doctrine of resurrection. Since Apoc III knows nothing of Antiochus' departure for the East in the summer of 165 and expects instead a third expedition against Egypt, the summer of 165 is its *terminus ante quem*. Apoc IV, finally, is chapter 9. Its contribution (see above Daniel B) is the scheme of weeks of years, with the outlawing of Judaism falling in the middle of the last week. Apoc IV has interpolated this view into each of its three predecessors (7:26ff.; 8:14; 12:7, 11[12]). In the course of his interpolation in Apoc I, the author of Apoc IV betrays the fact that he postdates the expedition, in the summer of 165, to the East, which added Artaxias of Armenia to the two kings of Egypt whom Antiochus had defeated in 169 and 168 (7:24ff.). On the other hand, he does not know of the king's proclamation of amnesty in the winter of 164, still less of the rededication of the Temple in December 164 and of the king's death in the spring of 163; he therefore antedates these.

LITERARY GENRES AND MOTIFS

The genre to which Daniel B belongs is clearly apocalyptic. This type of literature arose in the Hellenistic period. The oldest parallel was pointed out by Eduard Meyer. It is a Demotic papyrus containing interpretations of obscure oracles. The author of these interpretations attributes them to the reign of the Pharaoh Tachos (360–359), to this king and to earlier ones who rebelled against the Persians. But he also alludes, in his interpretations, to persons and events from Tachos to his own time, which is the end of the third century B.C.E., and promises that the Greeks will be driven out of Egypt by a prince who will reign at Heracleopolis – a prediction which did not come true. The genre of Daniel A, on the other hand, is the courtier tale. There is in the Bible the story of the courtier Joseph, who was both an inspired interpreter of dreams and an admirable administrator: Daniel is the former in chapters 2 and 4 and the closely related interpreter of portents in chapter 5, and he is the latter in chapter 6. His three companions are also government officials in chapter 3. With the wise heathen courtier *Ahikar and the Jewish courtier *Mordecai, these Jewish ones have in common the trait of being plotted against by rivals who, however, are hoist with their own petard. Chapter 2 contains, so to speak, an apocalypse within a courtier tale, and the former is interesting for its utilization of borrowed motifs. The motif of four empires followed by a fifth is of Iranian origin. In the Iranian version, first the Assyrian kings ruled the world, then the Median, then the Persian, then the Greek (i.e., the Seleucid kings), but this fourth monarchy was destined to be supplanted by a fifth. No doubt the Iranians expected the fifth to be again a Persian kingdom, but the tradition reached Rome before 171 B.C.E. in a form which interprets Rome as the fifth empire. Daniel 2 merely says that the fifth kingdom will be set up by God, but no doubt it expects the Jewish people to occupy a position of honor in it. In addition, Daniel 2 substitutes Babylon or Chaldea for Assyria, which results in bad history, since the Median empire did not follow the Chaldean but coexisted with it, and, in fact, came to an end a decade before the other. The series gold, copper, silver, iron originally (as early as Hesiod, 8th century B.C.E.) symbolized the four ages of a progressively deteriorating world. The four monarchies which these metals symbolize in chapter 2, on the other hand, do not constitute a consistently descending series – the second is inferior to the first, but after that it is a rising series. Other probable and possible borrowed motifs are pointed out in recent commentaries.

THE LANGUAGE PROBLEM

In the book as it is now known, 1:1–2:4a and chapters 8–12 are Hebrew, the rest *Aramaic. Originally, it was entirely Aramaic. The popular story book Daniel A was composed in Aramaic because by the third century B.C.E. it was the language of the majority of Jews; and Daniel B, being a continuation of Daniel A, was written in the same language. That the Hebrew portions have a strong Aramaic tinge would not suffice by itself to prove that it was translated from Aramaic, but the occurrence of passages which can only be understood as translations of misread Aramaic does constitute such proof. A simple example is 12:8: "I heard but I did not understand, so I said: 'My Lord, what is the אַחֲרִית of all these things?'" The Hebrew word means "end," but "end" is pointless here. What Daniel wanted was the explanation of what he had heard. A glance at 5:12 suggests that behind אַחֲרִית is an Aramaic אַחֲוָיַת, "the explanation of," which had become corrupted to אַחֲרִית, or which the translator misread as אַחֲרִית (for further examples, see Ginsberg, in JBL, 68 (1949), 402–7).

BIBLIOGRAPHY: O. Eissfeldt, *The Old Testament, an Introduction* (1965), 512–3 (comprehensive listing of literature); idem, in: ZAW, 72 (1960), 134–48; idem, *Kleine Schriften*, 3 (1966), 513–25; J.A. Montgomery, *The Book of Daniel* (ICC, 1927); H.H. Rowley, *Darius the Mede and the Four World Empires in the Book of Daniel* (1935, 1959²);

Meyer, Ursp, 2 (1922), 184–99; E. Bickermann, *Der Gott der Makkabaeer* (1937); idem, *Four Strange Books of the Bible* (1967), 51–138; Swain, in: *Classical Philology*, 35 (1940), 1–21; H.L. Ginsberg, *Studies in Daniel* (1948); idem, in: VT, 3 (1953), 400–4; 4 (1954), 246–75; EM, 2 (1965), 686–97, 949–52; A.R. Emanuel Silva, *A Critical Analysis of the Historicity of the Book of Daniel* (1968). **ADD. BIBLIOGRAPHY:** L. Hartman and A. Di Lella, *The Book of Daniel* (AB; 1978); J. Collins, in: ABD II, 329–37; A.S. van der Woude (ed.), *The Book of Daniel in the Light of New Findings* (1993).

[Harold Louis Ginsberg]

DANIEL, BOOKS OF (Apocryphal), additions to the biblical Book of Daniel. Among the fragments found at *Qumran were three manuscripts (4QpsDan A, B, C) containing works pertaining to the Danielic literature. Two of these (A and B) are copies of the same composition, while the third may represent a different one. The texts are very fragmentary, but the work dealt, at least, with the Flood, the Exodus, sin and the first exile, the first of the four kingdoms (cf. Dan. 2:7, etc.), the Greek period, and the eschatological age. Another Dead Sea text associated with the Danielic literature is the *Prayer of Nabonidus* which presents a tradition close to, but in some respects earlier than, that found in the canonical Daniel.

A Daniel apocryphon is mentioned in early Christian lists, and extant Christian Daniel books include various forms of the work called in Armenian *The Seventh Vision of Daniel*. This is an apocalypse particularly noted for its description of the Antichrist. Texts are known in Armenian, Greek, Coptic, and Slavonic. The Greek and Armenian forms differ from one another in many respects, but their common source is quite apparent. The Slavonic represents the same text form as the Greek. A Persian work called *The History of Daniel* also contains similar materials, and further Daniel books also exist.

BIBLIOGRAPHY: Milik, in: RB, 63 (1956), 407–15; Freedman, in: BASOR, 145 (1957), 31–32; C.V. Tischendorf, *Apocalypses Apocryphae* (1860), xxx–xxxiii; E. Klosterman, *Analecta zur Septuaginta, Hexapla und Patristik* (1895), 113ff.; Kalemkiar, in: WZKM, 6 (1892), 109ff.; W. Bousset, *The Antichrist Legend* (1896), 66–72, 109–12; M.R. James, *Lost Apocrypha of the Old Testament* (1920), 70.

[Michael E. Stone]

DANIEL, DAN (Margowitz; 1890–1981), U.S. sportswriter, considered the dean of baseball writers in a career that spanned over 60 years. Born in New York City to immigrant parents, Daniel started his career in 1909 at the *New York Herald*, a year before graduating from the City College of New York. He came from a long line of doctors, and was even enrolled at Columbia's College of Physicians and Surgeons for a short time, but left to pursue a fulltime career as a sportswriter, when in 1911 he was offered $35 a week to work at the *New York Press* by sports editor Nat *Fleischer. It was there that Daniel became one of the first journalists to use a typewriter at a New York newspaper office.

When he was refused a byline early in his profession because of his Jewish surname, Daniel changed it to "By Daniel," using it in his long career at the *New York World-Telegram* and its successor, the *World-Telegram and Sun*, where he worked until the newspaper folded in 1966. He also wrote a column, "Daniel's Dope," and for 20 years conducted the well-known question and answer column "Ask Daniel" in the paper's sports section.

Daniels was by far America's most prolific baseball writer, best known for his 32 years of writing for the *Sporting News*, the Bible of baseball publications for the first half of the 20th century. Using the byline "By Dan Daniel" and "By Daniel M. Daniel," he contributed some 5,000 words a week by his estimate to that publication, having "more words published in the *Sporting News* than any other man," according to the newspaper's publisher.

Daniel was recognized as an authority on the history of the New York Yankees, having covered the club from the pre-Babe Ruth era through the days of Mickey Mantle. He was the first to recognize Lou Gehrig's consecutive games streak and was the official scorer for some 21 games during the 56-game hitting streak of Joe DiMaggio in 1941. Though there was criticism about Daniel's questionable role as the scorer in extending DiMaggio's streak in games 30 and 31, Daniel maintained, "There wasn't a hit he wasn't entitled to. I never favored him one iota and made him get his hits as I saw them."

Daniel was chairman of the Baseball Writers' Association of America, a member of baseball's rules committee, and served for many years on the Hall of Fame Committee on Baseball Veterans. In 1972, Daniel was recipient of the Baseball Writers' Association of America's J.G. Taylor Spink Award, the Baseball Hall of Fame's highest honor for sportswriters.

The versatile Daniel also covered football and was chairman of the Football Writers' Association. In addition, he wrote about boxing, serving as chairman of the Boxing Writers' Association, and was co-founder with Fleischer of *The Ring* magazine. Daniel was the author of *Babe Ruth: The Idol of the American Boy* (1930) and *The Mike Jacobs Story* (1950).

[Elli Wohlgelernter (2nd ed.)]

DANIEL, JEAN (1920–), French writer and journalist. Born in Blida (Algeria), Daniel grew up in Algeria where he completed graduate studies at the Algiers College of Humanities, going to Paris for postgraduate studies. After World War II, he was briefly attached to the Prime Minister's Office, and then turned to journalism. For ten years he was on the editorial board of the influential French weekly *L'Express*, leaving it in 1964 to launch a new paper, *Le Nouvel Observateur*, which took a radical stand on the burning issue at the time, the war in Algeria. Outspoken on civil rights and minorities, while being often the first with the news, the *Nouvel Observateur* was considered the leading magazine in France in the 1980s and was widely read abroad. Daniel was chairman of the board from 1978. Speaking for the moderate left, he often appeared on television and radio panels. He wrote several books, among them *L'Erreur* (1953); *Journal d'un journaliste* (1959); the autobiographical *Le Temps qui reste* (1973); *Le Refuge et la source* (1977); and *L'Ere des ruptures* (1979). His 2003 book *La Prison juive: humeurs et méditations d'un témoin* (*The Jewish Prison: A Rebellious Meditation on the State of Judaism*, 2005) is equally critical of Palestinian suicide bombers and Israeli settlers, faulting the Israeli government for the continuing occupation and not doing enough to create a viable Palestinian state. His collected writings on the Middle East were published in *La Guerre et la Paix: Israël-Palestine, Chroniques 1956–2003*.

ADD. BIBLIOGRAPHY: A. Schatz. "The Jewish Question," in: *New York Review of Books*, 52:14 (Sept. 22, 2005).

[Gideon Kouts]

DANIEL (Donyel), M. (pseudonym of **Mark** or **Mordechai Meyerovich**; 1900–1940), Soviet Yiddish fiction writer and dramatist; father of the Soviet-Russian writer Yuli *Daniel. Born in Latvia of poor parents, he became a laborer and later a tutor, after receiving a traditional Jewish education. During World War I Daniel was displaced to the Urals, which provided material for his first published work, a novella, *In a Tsayt Aza* ("In Such a Time," 1924). In 1921 Daniel moved to Moscow where he completed his education at the Yiddish department at the Second Moscow State University. His early stories, which are his best work, suggest the influence of Boris Pilnyak. Prominent among the civil war themes of the stories in *Oyfn Shvel* ("At the Threshold," 1928) is that of the role of the artist in the revolution. Daniel is best known for his novel *Yulis* (1930), whence the name of his son, and its dramatized version *Fir Teg* ("Four Days"), a "heroic tragedy" which played for over three years in the Yiddish state theaters of the Soviet Union. *Fir Teg* is a romantic treatment of the defeat and death of Yulis Shimeliovitsh and other Bolshevik leaders of the Vilna Workers' Council; they committed suicide while surrounded by Polish legionnaires who seized Vilna in 1919. Though the Bolsheviks are idealized, some Soviet critics were not pleased, claiming that revolution admits no tragedy, only heroism. Daniel died in Yalta of a protracted illness.

BIBLIOGRAPHY: Ch. Shmeruk et al. (eds.), *Pirsumim Yehudiyim bi-Verit ha-Mo'azot* (1961); A. Pomerantz, *Di Sovetishe Harugei Malkhus* (1962), 134–6, 464–5; LNYL, 2 (1958), 450–1.

[Leonard Prager]

DANIEL, MENAHEM SALIH (1846–1940), leader of the Baghdad community. Daniel's family, which was of Georgian origin, had left him large estates, mostly in the vicinity of the town of Hilla, Iraq. In 1876 he was elected to the Ottoman parliament, and in 1924 to the Iraqi parliament. In 1925 he was appointed representative of the Iraqi Jews in the senate, a post he retained until the early 1930s when he was succeeded by his son Ezra. His great influence in the Baghdad community was due to his great wealth, his close ties with the authorities, and especially his philanthropy. Both he and his son were opposed to Zionist activity in Iraq, fearing that it would incense the Arabs.

His son EZRA MENAHEM DANIEL (d. 1952) was a member of the Iraqi senate from the time he succeeded his father until his death. In the senate, he defended Iraqi Jews with great courage. In 1946 he refused to testify before the Anglo-American Commission of Inquiry (investigating the situation of the Jews in Palestine), despite the attempt of the Iraqi government to force him to do so.

BIBLIOGRAPHY: A. Ben-Jacob, *Yehudei Bavel* (1965), index (includes bibl. in English, Hebrew, and Arabic).

[Haim J. Cohen]

DANIEL, VISION OF, Hebrew apocalypse written in the Byzantine Empire. Scholars differ over its date: some place the work in the 13th century, after the Latin conquest of Constantinople (1204), while others maintain that it was written in the late tenth century. The "Vision" opens with the appearance of the angel Gabriel to the prophet Daniel, continues with historical narrative, and concludes with an apocalyptic vision. The main interest of the work is historiographic: it traces the policies of Byzantine emperors toward the Jews from Michael III to *Constantine VII Porphyrogenitus (ninth to mid-tenth centuries), supporting the assertion of *Megillat Aḥima'aẓ* (see *Ahimaaz b. Paltiel) that *Basil I attempted to convert the Jews, that his son Leo *VI rescinded the decree, and that Romanus I Lecapenus renewed the attempt, which finally was abandoned by Constantine VII. However, it also makes the unfounded allegations that Michael III persecuted the Jews, that Basil I began by rehabilitating the persecuted, and that Romanus "troubled them by expulsion but not through destruction." It may be that the writer of the "Vision" was influenced by the historiography of Constantine VII which exaggerated the virtues of his own Macedonian dynasty (founded by Basil I) and magnified the vices of the previous one, which ended with Basil's murder of Michael III. The writer's generally positive attitude toward the state indicates a marked improvement in the position of Jews in the Byzantine Empire which is further supported by the apocalyptic section of the work. Instead of the usual prophecy foretelling the annihilation of the Christian and Islamic kingdoms, the "Vision" concludes by postulating a final struggle between Rome and Constantinople from which Constantinople will emerge victorious and the Messiah will judge the nations of the world there.

BIBLIOGRAPHY: L. Ginzberg, *Ginzei Schechter*, 1 (1928), 313–23; Krauss, in: REJ, 87 (1929), 1–27; Y. Even-Shemuel (Kaufmann), *Midreshei Ge'ullah* (1954^2), 232–52; Baron, Social^2, 3 (1957), 179, 314–5; Sharf, in: *Bar Ilan, Sefer ha-Shanah*, 4–5 (1967), 197–208 (Eng. summary li–lii).

[Andrew Sharf]

DANIEL, YULI MARKOVICH (1925–1988), Soviet-Russian author, son of the Soviet Yiddish writer M. *Daniel. Although no original works by the younger Daniel had ever been published in the U.S.S.R., where he was known exclusively as a translator, mainly from Yiddish, and from Caucasian and Slavic languages, he acquired an international reputation as the author of a number of books smuggled out of the Soviet Union and published in the West in the early

1960s, under the pseudonym Nikolai Arzhak. These include the short novel *Govorit Moskva* ("This Is Moscow Speaking") and three short stories, *Ruki* ("Hands"), *Chelovek iz Minapa* ("The Man from Minap"), and *Iskupleniye* ("Atonement"). *This Is Moscow Speaking and Other Stories* appeared in an English translation in 1962. *This is Moscow Speaking*, a fanciful work describing a Soviet "public murder day" when citizens are free to kill one another, is the only work of his that treats a "Jewish" theme; a central character immediately ventures the guess that the "day" has been proclaimed to legalize anti-Jewish pogroms. Antisemitic motifs were prominent at the trial in February 1966 of Daniel and his friend and fellow "illegal" writer, Andrei Sinyavsky (who wrote under the pseudonym Abram Tertz). In spite of frail health resulting from wounds received while serving in the Red Army during World War II, Daniel was sentenced to five years' forced labor. The prosecutor and the authors of numerous articles published in the Soviet press before, during, and after the trial accused Daniel and Sinyavsky of slandering Soviet society by insinuating that it was not free of antisemitism. Andrei Sinyavsky, a non-Jew, had in fact devoted much attention to the problem of anti-Jewish prejudice in the U.S.S.R. Protests by leading Soviet intellectuals and strong international pressures failed to bring about the release of the two writers and Daniel's wife, Larissa Daniel-Bogoraz, herself received a prison sentence in the fall of 1968 for having participated in a street demonstration opposing the Soviet invasion of Czechoslovakia. Daniel continued to speak out even in prison camp, where he protested at the harsh conditions. He continued to write poems in prison which were published in the West. He was released from jail in 1970, lived in Moscow, and worked as a translator of literature under the pseudonym Yu. Prtrov.

BIBLIOGRAPHY: L. Labedz and M. Hayward (eds.), *On Trial; the Case of Sinyavsky (Tertz) and Daniel (Arzhak)* (1967).

[Maurice Friedberg]

DANIEL BEN AZARIAH (11th century), Palestinian *gaon*, 1051–62. Daniel was a descendant of one of the branches of the family of the *exilarch in Babylonia that had been banished. He succeeded Solomon b. Judah as *gaon* of Palestine on the latter's death in 1051, thus supplanting the sons of the *gaon* Solomon Ha-Kohen (b. Jehoseph). In a letter of that time he is called "*nasi* and *gaon* of Tiberias," even though the seat of the Palestinian academy was in Jerusalem. As a scion of the house of David, he was honored also in Egypt. The synagogue of the Palestinian community in Fostat (Old Cairo) was named in honor of him "Synagogue of our Lord Daniel, the Light of Israel, the Great Prince and Head of the Academy of the Majesty of Jacob." The *gaon* corresponded with R. Jehoseph, *nagid*, son of Samuel ha-Nagid of Spain, and bestowed titles of honor upon him; the latter was undoubtedly one of the supporters of the academy in Jerusalem. His son *David b. Daniel did not succeed him at his death because of his extreme youth, but in later years he was involved in a dispute over the succession to the gaonate.

BIBLIOGRAPHY: S. Schechter (ed.), *Saadyana* (Eng., 1903), 80–106; S. Poznański, *Babylonische Geonim* (1914), index; Mann, Egypt, 2 (1922), index; Mann, Texts, 2 (1935), index; idem, in: HUCA, 3 (1926), 283–8; idem, in: *Sefer Zikkaron... S.A. Poznański* (1927), 27–29.

[Tovia Preschel]

DANIEL BEN ELEAZAR BEN NETHANEL ḤIBBAT ALLAH, Babylonian *gaon*, late 12th–early 13th century. A book by the Arab historian Ibn al-Saʿī (1197–1275) contains the official letter of appointment dated 1208/9 given to Daniel by Caliph al-Naṣr bi-Dīn Allah. In it the caliph stated that he had learned that the *gaon* was "revered and praised by the members of his faith and has the qualities required for his office, and conducts himself with complete honesty, without flaw." It may be assumed that he took office approximately at the time of his official appointment; some scholars, however, identify him with Gaon Daniel b. R. Eleazar he-Ḥasid, whose letters of the period 1201–08 are extant, in which case he became *gaon* long before his official appointment by the caliph. It seems that Daniel died before 1220, as in approximately that year Judah *Al-Ḥarizi found Isaac b. Israel ibn al-Shuwayk holding the office of *gaon* in Baghdad. *Isaac b. Moses' *Or Zaru'a* and Zedekiah b. Abraham *Anav's *Shibbolei ha-Leket* quote a "R. Daniel Gaon" whom some scholars have identified with Daniel b. Eleazar.

BIBLIOGRAPHY: D.S. Sassoon, *History of the Jews of Baghdad* (1949), 73–75, 97; Mann, Texts, 1 (1931), 222–5; Assaf, Ge'onim, 129–30; idem, in: *Tarbiz*, 1:1 (1929), 110; S. Poznański, *Babylonische Geonim*... (1914), 37–42.

[Tovia Preschel]

DANIEL BEN ḤASDAI (d. 1175), *exilarch of Baghdad. Daniel inherited the office from his father, Ḥasdai b. David b. Hezekiah, and was already serving in this capacity before 1520, as is proved by a letter in which he confirms the appointment of *Nethanel b. Moses ha-Levi as head of "the great *bet din* in all the provinces of the land of Egypt." This letter, which was written in 1161, demonstrates his influence even in Egypt and contains many autobiographical details. He complains about his poverty, due to the political situation, and about the dissensions in his community. Later, however, it seems that his economic situation improved. The 12th-century traveler Benjamin of Tudela, who visited Baghdad a few years later, admiringly describes Daniel's personality and authority, his learning in Bible and Talmud, and his lavish hospitality. R. Abraham Ibn Ezra was also impressed by his personality. Since he had no son, after his death the leaders of the Baghdad Jewish community split into two camps over the choice of his successor (see *David b. Zakkai II).

BIBLIOGRAPHY: S. Poznański, *Babylonische Geonim* (1914), 117–9; Mann, Texts, 1 (1931), 228–36; idem, in: *Sefer Zikkaron ... S. Poznański* (1927), 23–24; Assaf, in: *Tarbiz*, 1:3 (1930), 66–77; 3 (1931/32), 343–4. **ADD. BIBLIOGRAPHY:** M. Gil, *Be-Malkhut Ishmaʿel bi-Tekufat ha-Geonim*, 1 (1997), 433–6.

[Tovia Preschel / Avraham David (2nd ed.)]

DANIEL BEN JEHIEL OF ROME (d. before 1101), rabbinical scholar, elder brother of *Nathan b. Jehiel. On the death of their father, in approximately 1070, he and Nathan became heads of the Rome yeshivah. Daniel wrote responsa, and many of the explanations of words in his brother's lexicon *Arukh* are quoted in his name. He also compiled a commentary on the Mishnah order of *Zera'im*. Zunz ascribes to him the authorship of the *piyyut* for the Sabbath of Ḥanukkah, beginning *Ahallel El be-Minnim ve-Ugav*, a poetical version of the Scroll of Antiochus.

BIBLIOGRAPHY: Rapoport, in: *Bikkurei ha-Ittim*, 10 (1829), 7, 19–20; Zunz, Lit Poesie, 163–4.

DANIEL BEN MOSES AL-QŪMISĪ (ninth-tenth centuries), Karaite scholar and leader of the *Avelei Zion ("Mourners of Zion"). He was born in Damghan, in the province of Qumis, northern Persia. Little is known about Daniel's life. He was evidently the first eminent Karaite author to settle in Jerusalem, where he died. Independent in theological outlook, Daniel even belittled the founder of Karaism, *Anan b. David, and dissented from certain of his halakhic principles, justifying himself by the maxim "those who come later will find the truth." Daniel also consistently maintained this principle in regard to himself. According to the Karaite scholar *Kirkisānī, "he would accept any conclusion arrived at by reasoning … and would acknowledge changes whenever they occurred in regard to opinions he had expressed in his writings…." In matters of law, Daniel was more rigorous than his fellow Karaites. On the other hand, he is said to have exempted males aged under 20 from the duty to observe all the biblical ordinances, and admitted the testimony of Muslims in matters connected with the determination of the Jewish calendar.

Daniel occupied himself to a considerable extent in biblical exegesis. While refraining from exhortation, he supplies brief comments intended to explain the simple meaning of the biblical text in a rationalistic manner. He interprets, for instance, the concept "angels" as natural forces, such as fire and water, sent as divine emissaries, and consequently negates the existence of angels. Daniel's commentaries on the Bible served him as a means of propagating his view on Karaism and asceticism. His most complete extant work, *Pitron Sheneim-Asar* (ed. by I. Markon, 1948, 1957), a commentary on the Minor Prophets, contains bitter criticism of the rabbinate and of the degeneration of the Jewish people through pursuit of worldly occupations and pleasures. Daniel blamed the prolongation of the Exile on the neglect of the divine truths – i.e., the Bible – due to the negative influence of the *Rabbanite "shepherds of the Diaspora." He especially condemned the arrogance of the rabbis and their officials, and their economic exploitation of the people. According to Daniel, the Torah was at first in the possession of a restricted group, "the priests and levites, together with the king." However, after the destruction of the First Temple it was handed over to the entire Jewish people in order that each individual should bear responsibility for his actions. Daniel became the leader and spokesman of the Avelei Zion; he was probably the author of their official program. He enjoined perpetual public mourning for the destruction of the Temple and constant supplication for redemption, all to be practiced while living in Jerusalem. He proposed the collection of funds from Karaites abroad to enable chosen members of the sect to live in Jerusalem and represent the community as mourners. "And if you do not come, because you yearn for your merchandise, send five people from each city supplied with means of subsistence, that we may form one association to appeal to God constantly from the mountains of Jerusalem."

Al-Qūmisī's homiletical commentaries (*derashot*) have been published (*Zion*, 3 (1929), 26–42), and of his brief commentary on the Bible, the part on the Minor Prophets has appeared, though its attribution to Daniel has been questioned (Marwick, in JBB, 5 (1961), 42ff.).

DAVID (ABU SULEIMAN) AL-QŪMISĪ (died c. 945), a Karaite scholar, was apparently his son. According to the Arabic scholar al-Masʿūdī, David lived in Jerusalem and translated the Bible into Arabic, with explanations. He is mentioned by *Japheth b. Ali in his commentary (to Lev. 23:p 5), as well as in an anonymous Arabic commentary on Leviticus (Oxford, Bodleian Library, Ms. Heb. d. 44).

BIBLIOGRAPHY: ON DANIEL: S. Pinsker, *Likkutei Kadmoniyyot* (1860), index; A. Harkavy, *Zikkaron la-Rishonim*, 8 (1903), 187–92; Marmorstein, in: *Ha-Ẓofeh le-Ḥokhmat Yisrael*, 8 (1924), 44–60, 321–37; 9 (1925), 129–45; Mann, in: JQR, 12 (1921/22), 273–91; Mann, Texts, index; L. Nemoy (ed.), *Karaite Anthology* (1952), index s.v. *al-Kūmisī, Daniel*; Z. Ankori, *Karaites in Byzantium* (1959), index. ON DAVID: Poznański, in: JQB, 8 (1896), 681; Steinschneider, *ibid.*, 11 (1899), 606.

DANIEL BEN PERAḤYAH HA-KOHEN (d. 1575), head of yeshivah and author. His family, which originated in Rome, claimed descent from *Josephus. From Rome his father moved to Salonika where, until his death in 1548, he was head of the yeshivah of the Italian community, being succeeded in that position by Daniel, who also served as a *dayyan*. In addition to his talmudic learning, Daniel studied philosophy, mathematics, medicine, and astronomy. A fire that broke out at Salonika in 1545 destroyed all his books, as well as most of his writings, of which only his commentary on *She'erit Yosef* by Joseph b. Shem Tov Ḥai on intercalation has been published (Salonika, 1568). To this work he appended material by himself on a variety of subjects, and also a work on intercalation by Abraham *Zacuto with his own commentary. With the rabbis of Salonika he was a signatory in 1573 to the ban against the physician Daud, the opponent of Don Joseph *Nasi. He was an intimate friend of Moses *Almosnino. On his death he was eulogized by the poet Saadiah *Longo. He had no sons and was succeeded by his brother Samuel.

BIBLIOGRAPHY: M. Molho, *Essai d'une monographie sur la famille Perahia à Thessaloniki* (1938), 14–20; Molho and Amarijlio, in: *Sefunot*, 2 (1958), 32–33, 35–36; I.S. Emmanuel, *Maẓẓevot Saloniki*, 1 (1963), 148–9.

[Abraham David]

DANIEL BEN SAADIAH HA-BAVLI (known as **Daniel ibn al-Amshata**; fl. c. 1200), Babylonian talmudist. Daniel was head of the "third yeshivah" in Baghdad when *Benjamin of Tudela was there c. 1170. In 1193 he was appointed "*segan ha-yeshivah*" ("vice president of the academy"), under *Zechariah b. Berachel. Some time later, after the death of his teacher *Samuel b. Ali ha-Levi (1193–94), he moved to Damascus. There he served as a preacher, his sermons making a profound impression. Judah *Al-Ḥarizi, who heard him there in 1220, praised him (*Taḥkemoni*, 46). Like Samuel b. Ali ha-Levi, he waged a bitter campaign against Maimonides' philosophical views. Forty-seven of his criticisms of *Mishneh Torah* and 13 of *Sefer ha-Mitzvot*, which he sent to Maimonides' son Abraham from Damascus in 1213, were published, together with Abraham's answers, in *Birkat Avraham* (1859), and with the Arabic original in *Ma'aseh Nissim* (1867). Much of his criticism of Maimonides' *Sefer ha-Mitzvot* is included in Naḥmanides' criticism of the same book. Daniel also wrote a commentary on Ecclesiastes, in which he again violently criticized Maimonides' views, though not mentioning him by name. When Abraham was urged by several rabbis to excommunicate Daniel, he refused to do so, both because of Daniel's distinction and because of his own lack of objectivity in the matter. The Maimonists finally prevailed upon the exilarch *David b. Samuel of Mosul to place Daniel under the ban. Eventually Daniel recanted his views.

BIBLIOGRAPHY: Abraham b. Moses b. Maimon, *Milḥamot ha-Shem*, ed. by R. Margaliot (1953); Graetz-Rabbinowitz, 5 (1897), 40ff; Poznański, in REJ, 33 (1896), 308–11; idem, *Babylonische Geonim im nachgaonaeischen Zeitalter* (1914), 120–1; Mann, Texts, 1 (1931), 401–11; D.J. Silver, *Maimonidean Criticism and the Maimonidean Controversy* (1965), index.

[Abraham David]

DANIEL BEN SAMUEL IBN ABĪ RABĪ' (**Ha-Kohen** (13th century)), Babylonian *gaon*. He was appointed in 1247 in succession to R. Isaac b. Israel (Abu al-Fath or Isḥaq ibn al-Shuwayk), by Abd al-Raḥman ibn al-Lamkhani, the Baghdad *qadi*. There was opposition to Daniel, especially by R. Eli b. Zechariah, who succeeded in persuading the vizier that the office of *gaon* was rightfully his and who was, in fact, appointed *gaon* in Daniel's place in 1250. *Eleazar b. Jacob ha-Bavli, the poet, praises Daniel in one of his poems. His son *Samuel also became *gaon*.

BIBLIOGRAPHY: S. Poznański, *Babylonische Geonim im nachgaonaeischen Zeitalter* (1914), 46–49, 68–70, 74f.; Mann, Texts, 1 (1931), 225–7; Fischel, in: MGWJ, 79 (1935), 310–5; Fischel, Islam, 131f; A. Ben-Jacob, *Yehudei Bavel* (1965), 33.

[Abraham David]

DANIEL ḤAYYATA ("the tailor"), Palestinian *amora*. He is quoted only a few times in midrashic literature. Thus he interprets Genesis 26:14 as teaching that a man who buys slaves should work together with them to spur them on to greater efficiency (Gen. R. 64:7). He is best known for a striking Midrash in which he interprets Ecclesiastes 4:1, "But I returned and considered all the oppressions that are done under the sun," as referring to *mamzerim* ("children of forbidden unions") who are oppressed "by the Great Sanhedrin" – though in accordance with the laws of the Torah – for the sins of their parents and who will be recompensed in the world to come (Lev. R. 32:8; Eccl. R. 4:1, 1). No biographical details are known of him, but, like the other rabbis mentioned in these midrashim, he was probably of the third or fourth century C.E.

BIBLIOGRAPHY: Bacher, Pal Amor, 3 (1899), 761; Hyman, Toledot, 334.

°**DANIEL-ROPS, HENRI** (pseudonym of **Jean Charles Henri Petiot**; 1901–1965), French historian and writer. A history schoolteacher by profession, Daniel-Rops was a prolific writer whose literary career extended over a period of 40 years. Among his more famous works are *Histoire sainte* or *Le peuple de la Bible* (1943; *Sacred History of Israel and the Ancient World*, 1949) and *Jesus en son temps* (1945; *Jesus in His Time*, 1955), and the 14-volume *Histoire de l'Eglise du Christ* (1948; *History of Church of Christ*, 1957–). These works, characterized by apologetics for the Catholic view of history, contain traditional anti-Jewish prejudices. On the other hand, Daniel-Rops acknowledged the bond of the Jewish people to the Holy Land and he expressed his admiration for the Zionist movement.

BIBLIOGRAPHY: M. Lobet, *A la rencontre de Daniel-Rops* (1949); P. Dournes, *Daniel-Rops, ou le réalisme de l'esprit* (1949); D. Feuerwerker, in: *Evidences* (Feb.–March 1951); *Cahiers de Savoie*, 4 (1965).

[Willehad Paul Eckert]

DANIELS, ALFRED (1924–1975), British painter. Daniels was born in the East End of London, and studied commercial art before World War II. While studying at the Royal College of Art, London, he was commissioned to execute a series of murals. Influenced by the American Jewish painter Ben *Shahn, Daniels always displayed a deep concern for ordinary people in everyday activity. He executed a number of paintings of East End Jewish life and combined in his work a concern for urban realism and a sense of stylization. Characteristic of his work was an exhibition devoted to buildings in London undergoing demolition, including the former Bayswater Synagogue. His work has much in common with such English painters as Stanley Spencer and Lowry, notably in the sympathetic humor with which he depicts everyday life. He was both a gifted draftsman and an active photographer, basing his compositions on these two forms of research. He exhibited regularly in London and abroad and received numerous commissions for murals and book illustrations. For some years he taught at the Hornsey College of Art, London. Daniels is represented in major collections throughout the world, including the Tel Aviv Museum.

[Charles Samuel Spencer]

DANIN (Suchowolsky), YEḤEZKEL (1867–1945), Ereẓ Israel pioneer. Danin was born in Bialystok, and settled in Ereẓ Israel in 1886, working first as a laborer in Rishon le-Zion, later in Jaffa where he started industrial plants that were among the first in the country. Danin was a member of *Benei Moshe and served as its representative in Jaffa in 1893. He was a founding member of *B'nai B'rith in Jaffa, and of the public library there (1890). His main interest was in promoting Hebrew education, and he helped found the first kindergarten in Jaffa. In 1903 Danin participated in the first conference of the *yishuv* in Zikhron Ya'akov (see *Israel, Historical Survey, 1880–1948). In 1906 he joined the Aḥuzat Bayit group which founded Tel Aviv in 1909. Danin was son-in-law of Yehoshua *Yellin. One of his sons, Ezra (1903–1984), was special adviser on Arab and Middle Eastern affairs to the Israel foreign minister for many years.

BIBLIOGRAPHY: Tidhar, 1 (1947), 480–1; R. Alper, *Korot Mishpaḥah Aḥat* (1955); Y. Churgin, *Yeḥezkel Danin* (Heb., 1943).

[Benjamin Jaffe]

DANKNER, AMNON (1946–), Israeli journalist and author. Born in Jerusalem, Dankner graduated in law from the Hebrew University. After a period as spokesman for the Ministry of Education, he entered journalism, becoming successively a columnist on *Davar, Ḥadashot*, and *Haaretz*, the last from which he was fired after writing a controversial column called "I have no Sister," which represented Sephardim in an unflattering light. He subsequently joined *Maariv* as a columnist, becoming editor in 2002. Formerly left-wing in outlook, Dankner moved towards the center and right, and once editor of *Maariv* he made corruption at the governmental and judicial levels a *cause célèbre* of the newspaper. He also wrote a number of novels, humorous works, screenplays, and nonfiction works. Most controversial was his biography of bohemian journalist and author Dahn *Ben-Amotz in 1992, alleging that Ben-Amotz had led a promiscuous life, including engaging in sex with minors, in which other well-known Israeli cultural figures had had a part. For the latter allegations he was sued for libel and apologized. He was also a permanent panel member of a popular television talkshow, *"Po-Politika,"* in the latter 1990s.

[Yoel Cohen (2nd ed.)]

DANON, ABRAHAM (1857–1925), scholar and writer. Danon studied at the Gheron yeshivah in Adrianople, his native city. His scholarly bent was nurtured by the Orientalist Joseph Halévy and Danon taught himself French, English, and German. He was one of the founders of Ḥevrat Shomerei Tushiyyah ("Society of the Friends of Wisdom"; also called Dorshei Haskalah, "Seekers of Enlightenment") in his city. In 1891 he headed the rabbinical seminary, which he had founded. During World War I he left Turkey for Paris, where he taught Hebrew at the Ecole Normale Orientale of the *Alliance Israélite Universelle and also engaged in research.

Danon edited the historical journal *Yosef ha-Da'at* (*El Progresso*), which was published in 1888 in Adrianople in Hebrew and Ladino, with the object of collating and publishing documentation relating to Oriental Jewry. He published in the *Revue des Etudes Juives, Journal Asiatique, Revue Hispanique*, etc., a number of scientific articles on the history, customs, sects, and literature of the Jews in Turkey, and translated poems and scholarly works into Hebrew. He also composed original poems. His works include *Maskil Leidan* (the latter word being the initials of his name), and *Toledot Benei Avraham*, a translation and adaptation of the *Histoire des Israélites* by Théodore Reinach, to which he added excerpts from the works of Jewish historians.

BIBLIOGRAPHY: A. Galanté, *Histoire des Juifs d'Istanbul*, 2 (1942), 99–100; Markus, in: *Sinai*, 29 (1951), 338–9; Yom Tov Bekhmoram (בכמהר"ם), *Toledot Ishim* (1935), 14–19; A. Elmaleh, in: *Mizraḥ u-Ma'arav* (1920), 365ff. (portrait). **ADD. BIBLIOGRAPHY:** A. Danon, "Trois poésies hebraïques," in: *Hamenora* (Istanbul), 2:2–3 (Feb.–Mar. 1924), 61.

[Simon Marcus]

°**DANTE ALIGHIERI** (1265–1321), Italy's greatest poet. Dante's *Divina Commedia* (c. 1307–21), generally regarded as the outstanding literary work of the Middle Ages, is in three parts: the *Inferno*, the *Purgatorio*, and the *Paradiso*. From biographical or autobiographical sources it cannot be proved for certain that Dante was in close touch with Jews or was personally acquainted with them. Jews are mentioned in his *Divina Commedia* mainly as a result of the theological problem posed by their historical role and survival. Such references are purely literary: the term *judei* or *giudei* designates "the Jews," a people whose religion differs from Christianity; while *ebrei* denotes "the Hebrews," the people of the Bible. Dante knew no Hebrew and the isolated Hebrew terms which appear in the *Commedia* – *Hallelujah, Hosanna, Sabaoth, El*, and *Jah* – are derived from Christian liturgy or from the scholastic texts of the poet's day. The *Commedia* contains no insulting or pejorative references to Jews. Although antisemites have given a disparaging interpretation to the couplet: "Be like men and not like foolish sheep, So that the Jew who dwells among you will not mock you" (*Paradiso*, 5:80–81), the Jews of Dante's time considered these lines an expression of praise and esteem. In the course of his famous journey through Hell, Dante encounters no Jews among the heretics, usurers, and counterfeiters whose sinful ranks Jews during the Middle Ages were commonly alleged to swell.

In the 19th century, scholars were convinced that Dante was on terms of friendship with the Hebrew poet *Immanuel of Rome. The latter and one of Dante's friends, Bosone da Gubbio, marked Dante's death by exchanging sonnets; and the death of Immanuel gave rise to another exchange of sonnets between Bosone and the poet Cino da Pistoia, in which Dante and Immanuel are mentioned together. Twentieth-century scholars, headed by M.D. (Umberto) Cassuto, showed that there is no basis for the alleged friendship between the two poets, but have proved Immanuel's dependence upon Dante's works. Important points of contact have also been discovered between Dante's conceptions and the views of R. *Hillel b. Samuel of Verona; hypotheses have been formulated on the resemblance of the notion of Hebrew as the perfect or original language in the *Commedia* and in the works of the kabbalist Abraham *Abulafia, and in general on the common neoplatonic element in Dante's theoretical and poetical works and in Kabbalah. Moreover, the *Questio de aqua et terra* probably written by Dante has a precedent in the discussion between Moses Ibn *Tibbon and Jacob ben Sheshet *Gerondi on the same subject a century before. Another parallel to Dante's outlook on the world may be found in the writings and translations of Immanuel's cousin, Judah b. Moses *Romano, who, within a few years of Dante's death, made a *Judeo-Italian version of some philosophical passages from the *Purgatorio* and the *Paradiso*, adding his own Hebrew commentary. Italian Jews quickly realized the lyrical and ideological value of the *Commedia* and an early edition was issued by a Jewish printer at Naples in 1477. Like Petrarch, Dante was widely quoted by Italian rabbis of the Renaissance in their sermons, and even by one or two Jewish scholars in their learned commentaries. The first actual imitation was that of Immanuel of Rome. His *Maḥberet ha-Tofet ve-ha-Eden* is the 28th and final section of his *Maḥberot* (Brescia, 1491). Here Immanuel also describes a journey to the next world, in which he is guided by Daniel, a friend or teacher who, in the opinion of some scholars, is Dante himself. A slight echo of the allegorical vision dealing with the soul's spiritual delight in the afterlife occurs in the *Maḥberet ha-Tene*, a rhymed prose work by R. *Ahitub b. Isaac of Palermo. Another important work openly inspired by the *Commedia* was *Mikdash Me'at* (written c. 1416), written by R. Moses b. Isaac *Rieti, in terza rima. This poetical meter was used for some decades by Hebrew Italian poets. By the 17th century Dante's influence on Jewish writers had weakened, and there is only a doubtful connection between the *Commedia* and Moses *Zacuto's verse-play *Tofteh Arukh* (Venice, 1715).

To mark the 600th anniversary of Dante's death, Samuel David *Luzzatto composed a Hebrew sonnet that became famous in scholarly circles throughout Europe. Many attempts have been made to translate the *Divina Commedia* into Hebrew. A translation of the first part by S. Formiggini was published in 1869; S. Sabbadini's Hebrew version of the other two parts remains in manuscript. Other partial translations were made into a more poetic and comprehensible Hebrew by Lelio della Torre (1871), V. Castiglioni (1912), E. Schreiber (1924), and V. *Jabotinsky (*Inferno*, chaps. 1, 3, 5, 33, in *Ha-Tekufah*, 19 (1923), 163–92). Immanuel *Olsvanger produced the first complete Hebrew translation of the *Commedia* (1943, 1953, 1956). Olsvanger also translated Dante's *Vita Nuova* (1957) while his *De monarchia* was translated into Hebrew by H. Merḥaviah (1961).

BIBLIOGRAPHY: F. Servi, *Dante e gli Ebrei* (1893); U. Cassuto, *Dante e Manoello* (1921, Heb. tr. 1965); J. Schirmann, in: YMḤSI, 1 (1933), 132–47; J. Sermoneta, in: *Romanica et Occidentalia, Etudes dédiées à la mémoire de Hiram Peri* (1963), 23–42; idem, in: *Studi Medievali*, 3rd series, 6 fasc. 2 (1965), 3–78; G. Rinaldi, in: *L'Alighieri: Rassegna Bibliografica Dantesca*, 7:2 (1966), 25–35; A. Cronbach, in: HUCA, 35 (1964), 193–212; R. Mondolfi, *Gli Ebrei. Qual luogo oltremondano sia per essi nella Commedia di Dante* (1904). **ADD. BIBLIOGRAPHY:** H. Rheinfelder, in: *Judenthum im Mittelalter* (1966), 442–57; idem, *Dante e la Bibbia* (1988); U. Eco, *The Search for the Perfect Language* (1995); B. Chiesa, in: *Henoch*, 23:2–3 (2001), 325–42; D. Bregman, in: *Prooftexts*, 23:1 (2003), 18–24; G. Battistoni, *Dante, Verona e la cultura ebraica* (2004); D. Stow, *Dante e la mistica ebraica* (2004).

[Joseph Baruch Sermoneta / Alessandro Guetta (2nd ed.)]

DANTO, LOUIS (1929–), *ḥazzan*. Danto was born in Suwalki, Poland, and sang in synagogue choirs there as a child, appearing with the *ḥazzanim* Steinberg and Berman. He spent WWII in Russia and studied voice development and cello at the Minsk conservatory. He also studied at music conservatories in Lodz, Poland, and in Italy, where his teachers included Beniamino Gigli and Tito Schipa. Danto specialized in bel canto and as such his voice is known for its rare beauty, purity, and breathtaking emotional expressivity. He immigrated to the United States and studied *ḥazzanut* under Leo Loeb and Herman Zalitz. After serving with a number of congregations in the United States, he became *ḥazzan* of the Toronto, Canada synagogue Beth Emeth–Bais Yehudah. He gave concerts of classical music and *ḥazzanut* throughout the United States and in Europe, South Africa, and Israel. Danto visited the Soviet Union and sang in the Great Synagogue of Moscow. In 1998, Danto received an honorary doctorate in music from the Jewish Theological Seminary in New York City. He has made 21 recordings of *ḥazzanut*, Yiddish songs, and classical vocal pieces. Numerous contemporary composers have written for and dedicated their works to Louis Danto. In addition, he is a researcher and a champion of rare and unusual repertoire. Most of his current recordings are available though Cadenza Records.

[Akiva Zimmerman / Raymond Goldstein (2nd ed.)]

°DANZ (Danzius), JOHANN ANDREAS (1654–1727), German Protestant theologian and Hebraist, born in Sundhausen, near Gotha. Danz was professor of Oriental languages and theology at the University of Jena from 1685 onward. One of the foremost Christian Hebraists of his time, Danz tried to present Hebrew grammar systematically but was only partially successful, since many of the constructions were artificial. His first work, *Kelippei Egozim* ("Nutshells"): *Nucifrangibulum Sanctam Scripturae Veteris Testamenti Linguam Ebraeam Enucleans* (Jena, 1686), is divided into two parts. The first part (later also published separately, under the title *Medakdek, sive Literator Ebraeo-Chaldaeus*, Jena, 1696) deals with the etymology of the Hebrew language. Here Danz developed his *Systema Trium Morarum* (the three-beat-syllable method), and he also explains Hebrew vocalization. In the second part of the book (later also published as a separate work, *Turgeman*, *sive Interpres Ebraeo-Chaldaeus*, Jena, 1694, and several editions) he is concerned with Hebrew syntax.

Aditus Syriae Reclusus (1689 and several republications) deals with difficult passages in Syriac. He also published *Spicilegium* (Jena, 1689); *Segulta de-Rabbanan, sive Rabbinismus Enucleatus* (Jena, 1699, and several editions); *Compendium Grammaticae Ebraicae-Chaldaicae* (Jena, 1699, and several editions), a Hebrew-Aramaic grammar, later translated into German by Georg David Kypke (Breslau, 1757); and *Sinceritas Scripturae Veteris Testamenti Praevalente keri Vacillans...* (Jena, 1713; annotations, *ibid.*, 1717), a book in defense of the masoretic text (*ketiv*).

BIBLIOGRAPHY: Wolf, Bibliotheca, 2 (1721), 591, 605; Steinschneider, Handbuch, 39; Fuerst, Bibliotheca, 1 (1863); ADB, 4 (1876), 751. **ADD. BIBLIOGRAPHY:** Gesenius, *Geschichte der hebraeischen Sprache*, 123ff. (1815); Steinschneider, in: ZHB, 2, 160 (1897), 124.

DANZIG (Danziger), ABRAHAM BEN JEHIEL MICHAL (1748–1820), codifier. Born in Danzig, he studied in Prague at the yeshivot of Joseph Liebermann and Ezekiel *Landau. True to his family tradition, he refused to derive any material gain from his studies and earned his livelihood as a merchant. Although required at times to travel long distances to trade fairs in Germany, he continued to learn with great devotion. From 1794 to 1812 he served as *dayyan* in Vilna, in an honorary capacity; only in his old age, after losing his possessions, was he obliged to accept remuneration for his services. Danzig wrote a number of halakhic works, but his fame rests upon two publications: (1) *Ḥayyei Adam* ("Man's Life"), covering all the laws of the Shulḥan Arukh dealing with daily conduct, based on the *Oraḥ Ḥayyim* sections, with an addendum called *Nishmat Adam*, in which he justified his decisions which were not in accordance with the accepted view (Vilna, 1810); and (2) *Ḥokhmat Adam* ("Man's Wisdom"), covering all the laws of the Shulḥan Arukh dealing with the dietary regulations, etc., contained in the *Yoreh De'ah* section, with an addendum called *Binat Adam*, which included discussions on various relevant halakhic subjects and responsa (Vilna, 1812). Both works were initially intended for youthful students and for educated laymen not fully versed in rabbinic literature who, in attempting to determine Jewish law, found themselves unable to grapple with the intricacies of the Shulḥan Arukh and with its maze of conflicting opinions. In these works, Danzig shows himself possessed of considerable pedagogical talent. He arranges the laws methodically, defines his terms lucidly and precisely, presents the various views and their sources, and renders his own decisions and his reasons for them – all in clear, simple language. The pleasant tenor of his writing, which is suffused with unquestioning faith and true piety, contributed largely toward the acceptance of his works.

Ḥayyei Adam appeared in almost a hundred editions. Groups called "Ḥevrot Ḥayyei Adam" were formed in several communities for the regular study of the code. Danzig's merits as a codifier were recognized also by renowned rabbis and codifiers, who gave due consideration to his decisions. His books include much of historical interest with regard to the daily life of Lithuanian Jewry in his generation.

BIBLIOGRAPHY: Abrahams, in: JQR, 3 (1890/91), 476f.; S.M. Chones, *Toledot ha-Posekim* (1910), 256ff.

[Simon S. Schlesinger]

DANZIGER, ITZHAK (1916–1977), Israeli sculptor. Danziger was born in Berlin to Felix Danziger and Malka Rozenblit. His father worked as a surgeon in Hamburg and was active in the Zionist movement. In 1923 the family settled in Jerusalem. As a child Danziger studied at schools in Tel Aviv, Haifa, Berlin, and England. He studied sculpture at the Slade School of Fine Art, University of London. During these years he concentrated on the study of ancient cultures: Asia, Egypt, Africa, and India, especially by copying sculptures in the British Museum. In 1938 Danziger returned to Tel Aviv, where he set up a studio in his father's hospital. His studio became a meeting place and a workshop for young artists. Over the years Danziger spent time both in Israel and abroad. He created sculptures and memorials and designed gardens and environments. In 1968 he was awarded the Israel Prize.

His best-known sculpture is *Nimrod* (1938–39), placed in the Israel Museum in Jerusalem. This sculpture may be seen as constituting a manifesto and indeed it became identified with the Canaanite movement although Danziger himself was never an official member of this movement. The source of this figure was the Bible: "Like Nimrod a mighty hunter before the Lord" (Gen: 10:9). The meaning of the name in Hebrew is "rebellion," so Nimrod represents rebellion against the Lord. His figure is an antithesis of the typical image of a Jewish scholar. It symbolized the search for an alternative image, a new representation of an Israeli figure. The style of the sculpture was influenced by Mesopotamian reliefs and the choice of Nubian sandstone created the connection to local space as well as to biblical time. In the sketch for this sculpture Danziger designed the figure as a muscular giant but the sculpture itself became, after obsessive work, completely different. Gazing up, it represented an ancient idol.

Danziger was the inspiration for the second generation of Israeli artists and was considered a central figure in Israeli sculpture. He organized ecological acts, in an attempt to revitalize nature. These acts expressed the artist's perception that he was the creator of a new order of nature in a place that had been damaged by man and by time (*Rehabilitation of the Nesher Quarry*, 1971). The gardens scattered across Israel captured Danziger's heart. His actions in these gardens expressed the connection with the local place and with its inhabitants and resulted in giving Israeli art a social aspect (*The Bustan at Al Kababir Village*, Carmel)

Danziger was killed on July 11, 1977, in a road accident on his way to Jerusalem.

BIBLIOGRAPHY: O. Mordechai, *Itzhak Danziger*, Tel Aviv Museum of Art and the Open Museum Industrial Park (1996).

[Ronit Steinberg (2nd ed.)]

DA-OZ, RAM (1929–), Israeli composer. Born in Berlin, he immigrated to Ereẓ Israel in 1934 and studied piano and oboe in Haifa. He lost his eyesight while fighting in the War of Independence (1948). After the war, he studied theory and composition privately with Hajos for three years, and graduated from the Tel Aviv Academy of Music in 1953. His early compositions show tendencies toward chromatic modulations and the influence of Prokofiev and Bartok. From the 1970s, Da-Oz employed traditional styles in combination with "free tonality." Among his works for piano are *Capriccio* (1960); *Aspects, Prologue, Variations and Epilogue*; *Changing Phantoms* for orchestra (1967); *Illuminations* for violin solo; three madrigals (1967); *Rhapsody on a Yemenite Jewish Melody* for orchestra (1971); *Jubilee Chants* for choir and orchestra (1984); *I Loved a Shepherdess: Fantasy on Sephardic Melodies* for violin and piano (1991); and *Two-Part Inventions* (1995). He also composed several Israeli folk songs.

BIBLIOGRAPHY: Grove online.

[Uri (Erich) Toeplitz and Yohanan Boehm / Gila Flam and Israela Stein (2nd ed.)]

DA PONTE, LORENZO (1749–1838), poet and librettist, best remembered for his work with Mozart. Born Emanuele Conegliano, Da Ponte was given the family name of his sponsor, the bishop of Ceneda, upon the family's baptism in 1763. He was educated for the priesthood and ordained, taught briefly, and embarked upon a writer's career. Banished from Venice after a period of dissipation and a scandal, he reached Vienna in 1783 and was appointed librettist to the Imperial Opera. His first meeting with Mozart apparently came about through the Jewish banker and patron of the arts, Raimund von *Wetzlar. Da Ponte's libretti for Mozart were *Lo sposo deluso* (1783, unfinished); the oratorio *Davidde penitente* (1785, of uncertain authorship; see *David, In Music); several concert arias; and the three great operas *Le nozze di Figaro* (1784), *Don Giovanni* (1787), and *Cosí fan tutte* (1789). *Don Giovanni*, although based on previous stage works, certainly owes a spiritual debt to Da Ponte's friendship with Casanova, whom he had known in Venice. In 1790 the emperor Joseph II died and Da Ponte, who had enjoyed his favor, was obliged to leave Vienna. In Trieste he abandoned his lightly borne clerical status by marrying Nancy (Anne Celestine) Grahl, the daughter of a German-English merchant. The ceremony was said to have been held "according to the Jewish rite," but the reports are ambiguous. After further wanderings and a stay in London, where he was a librettist at Drury Lane Theater, Da Ponte and his family went to the United States in 1805. He ultimately settled in New York, engaged unsuccessfully in various commercial ventures, and for some time taught Italian at Columbia College. He earned a place in American operatic history by persuading M. Garcia's visiting troupe to give the first American performance of *Don Giovanni* in 1825. He also raised money for building the Italian Opera House in New York in 1833. His autobiography, *Storia compendiosa della vita di Lorenzo da Ponte* (New York, 1807), was republished several times in a revised edition.

BIBLIOGRAPHY: P. Nettl, *Casanova und seine Zeit* (1949), 133–79; O. Schneider and A. Algatzi, *Mozart Handbuch* (1962), index; J.L. Russo, *Lorenzo da Ponte* (Eng., 1922); A. Fitzlyon, *Libertine Librettist* (1955); DAB, 5 (1930).

[Bathja Bayer]

DARABANI, small town in N.E. Romania. Jews from Galicia settled there in 1836. After them Jews from Russia also settled there. The location of Darabani on the commercial route connecting Bukovina and Moldavia attracted further Jewish settlement. However in 1875 and 1877 the owner of the land sued the Jews, and violence broke out. Anti-Jewish riots again occurred in 1907. There were 600 Jews living in Darabani in 1838; 638 (38% of the total population) in 1859; 2,472 in 1899; 2,387 (36.8%) in 1910; and 1,917 (17.8%) in 1930. The majority were merchants or artisans. Many of them were *ḥasidim* of the *admor* of Stefanesti. Between the two world wars the economic life of the town deteriorated because of the changes in borders and commercial routes. From the onset of communal life there was friction in the community. The Russian Jews established a separate synagogue in the 1840s; between the two world wars there was dissension in the community between artisans and merchants. In 1935–40, eight synagogues and five *ḥadarim* operated in Darabani. Among the rabbis was Nahum Shemaryahu Schechter (1908–30), author of some volumes of *derashot* and on Hebrew and Jewish names. He later immigrated to Israel and died in Jerusalem in 1976. The Hebrew and Romanian poet Shimon Haran (died in Jerusalem 2004) and the Yiddish and Romanian poet Sami Weinstein-Boiangiu (A. Ebion) were born in Darabani. A Zionist organization was established in Darabani in the 1930s. A branch of the Jewish party (Partidul Evreiesc, a political organization with a Zionist national trend) was active there and had representatives on the municipal council. Apart from the *ḥadarim* the community maintained its own school (1937).

[Yehouda Marton / Lucian-Zeev Herscovici (2nd ed.)]

Holocaust Period

In 1941 there were 1,854 Jews in Darabani. They were victimized by acts of terror as early as June 1940. On the pretext that the Jews were pro-Soviet and secretly preparing to greet the Soviet Army, Romanian army detachments and police daily attacked them in the streets, searched their houses, and arrested them. In June 1941, a few days before war against the Soviet Union broke out, all Jews were ordered to leave the town within half an hour and were allowed to take only their basic belongings with them. After the evacuation, their houses were plundered. The deportees had to walk to the railroad station, a distance of 22 mi. (35 km.) and were transported by freight car to *Dorohoi; the men were sent on to the concentration camp at Târgu-Jiu and the women and children to the small town of Turnu-Severin in western Romania. On Nov. 7, 1941, they were sent together with the men from Târgu-Jiu to *Transnistria, crossing the border in sealed freight cars and proceeding on foot to their destination, where most of them perished. At the end of 1943, a few of the survivors returned to Dorohoi and went from there to Darabani, where they were still subject to persecution. They were not permitted to engage in business, to walk in the streets, or buy food before 10 A.M., and Romanian inhabitants were forbidden to have any contact with them. After World War II survivors, joined by refugees from northern Bukovina, reorganized community life. In 1947, 990 Jews lived in Darabani, with five functioning synagogues in 1950, but their numbers diminished owing to emigration. Some ten Jewish families remained in the town by 1970 and maintained the synagogue. No Jews lived in Darabani in 1992. An association of Jews from Darabani is active in Israel, in the framework of the Association of Jewish Israelis from the former county of Dorohoi.

[Theodor Lavi / Lucian-Zeev Herscovici (2nd ed.)]

BIBLIOGRAPHY: PK Romanyah, 1 (1970), 102–3; M. Carp, *Cartea Neagră*, 1 (1946), 180; 3 (1947), 75; I. Herzig, in: *Renașterea Noastră*, 24 (1945), no. 250. **ADD. BIBLIOGRAPHY:** S. David (ed.), *Dorohoi-Săveni-Mihăileni-Darabani-Herța-Rădăuți Prut*, 1 (1992), 182–190 (Rom.), 205–46 (Heb.); 2 (1993), 327–36 (Rom.), 177–236 (Heb.); 3 (1996), 311–43 (Rom.), 283–336 (Heb.); 4 (1998), 347–58 (Rom.), 163–99 (Heb.); 5 (2000), 323–49 (Rom.), 147–238 (Heb.); S. Haran, *Darabani* (1992); C. Turliuc, in: SAHIR, 5 (2000), 163–73.

DARᶜĪ, MOSES BEN ABRAHAM (late 12th–early 13th century), Karaite poet. The assertion that Darᶜī was writing poetry as early as 843 is based on a forged date in the *Firkovich manuscript. The similarity between his poems and those of the Spanish school from Ibn Gabirol to Abraham Ibn Ezra can only be explained by his dependence upon them; Darᶜī, then, must have lived after Abraham Ibn Ezra. According to A. Neubauer, he lived at the end of the 13th century, because in his poems he prays for the deliverance of Jerusalem from the Muslims and the Christians, which points to a time when both sides were desperately contending for the city. The exact period of his life depends upon the correct identification of the poet's friends mentioned in his divan (a collection of poetry); it can, however, be stated that he must have been active about the year 1200. It is known that his parents had emigrated from Spain to Darᶜa (in Morocco), which accounts for the family name "Darᶜī." He himself was born in Alexandria, where he spent his youth. Steinschneider and Davidson assume that he was originally a Rabbanite and only later became a Karaite. In any case, his poems contain both violent outbursts against "the people of the distorted Mishnah" and tolerant utterances. He wrote his divan in Egypt; he is also known to have stayed in Damascus and to have undertaken a journey to Jerusalem. By profession he was a physician, as is evident from numerous acrostics in his poems. Two of Darᶜī's sons died during his lifetime. His poems have been preserved in a manuscript divan that originated in Jerusalem (Firkovich Collection, Leningrad). It consists of two parts: *Firdaws Azhār al-Qaṣāʾid wa al-Ashᶜār* ("Flower Garden of Qasidas and Songs"); and a "Supplement" (*Al-Mulḥaq li Dīwānihi al-Asbaq*), containing – both together – a collection of 544 poems. Another manuscript of the divan with 561 poems became known in 1837 (see Geiger, in: WZJT, 3 (1837), 443, no. 9–10). More recent copies of the divan (of the 19th–20th centuries) have been preserved in a manuscript acquired by I. Davidson as well as in the Asiatic Museum of Leningrad. Moreover, various religious poems of Darᶜī are preserved in manuscripts of song collections of Egypt and Damascus. Pinsker published more than 100 poems from the Firkovich manuscript in *Likkutei Kadmoniyyot* (1860), and also individual poems in the journal *Kokhevei Yiẓḥak* (26 (1861), 22ff; 27 (1862), 24–27; 28 (1862), 20–24); one poem was published by A. Neubauer (*Melekhet ha-Shir* (1865), 64). Davidson intended to publish the entire divan but only the first part appeared in *Horeb*, 3 (1936), 28–42. Both parts of the divan contain almost every poetical genre cultivated by the Spanish-Hebrew poets. To the secular poems belong epistles to friends, epithalamia, elegies, enigmas, epigrams, love lyrics, satires, etc. The religious poems are frequently arranged according to the sequence of the Sabbath reading of the Torah. Most of the poems are written in Hebrew and approximately ten are written in Arabic. Darᶜī signs most of the Hebrew poems "*Moshe Rofe Kara'i, Ḥazak.*" A special group comprises poems in both languages. A so-called *maqāma* (an address, sermon, or story, told in public and written in assonant prose), named the *Maqāma of Alexandria* (*Maḥberet No-Amon Miẓrayim*, ed. 1927 by I. Davidson), has been attributed to Darᶜī without any substantial reason. In general, Darᶜī's technical dexterity surpassed his poetical gifts. While the language and structure of his poems are in the best tradition of the Spanish school, the contents often betray a lack of individuality.

BIBLIOGRAPHY: S. Pinsker, *Likkutei Kadmoniyyot* (1860), 46–105, addenda 113–21; Schorr, in: *He-Ḥalutz*, 6 (1861), 57–59; Geiger, in: ZDMG, 15 (1861), 813–9; 16 (1862), 290; A. Neubauer, *Aus der Petersburger Bibliothek* (1866), 21–23, 115–7; Steinschneider, in: JZWL, 9 (1871), 172–83; idem, in: HB, 4 (1861), 6, 47, 144; idem, *Polemische und apologetische Literatur…* (1877), 287, 292, 331; idem, in: JQR, 10 (1897–98), 520–1; Frankl, in: J.S. Ersch and J.G. Gruber, *Allgemeine Encyklopaedie*, 33 (1883), 17; I. Sinani, *Istoriya vozniknoveniya i razvitiya karaimizma*, 2 (1889), 29–42; Kahana, in: *Oẓar ha-Sifrut*, 5 (1896), 90–95; idem, in: *Ha-Shiloʾaḥ*, 13 (1904), 435–42; Kohen, in: *Ha-Ẓefirah*, 25 (1898), 490, 518–9; M. Wiener, *Lyrik der Kabbalah* (1920), 154, 178; Davidson, in: *Maddaʿei ha-Yahadut*, 2 (1926–27), 297–308; idem, in: *Tarbiz*, 2 (1930), 118–9; Habermann, in: PAAJR, 33 (1965), 35–40 (Heb. sect.); Davidson, Oẓar, 4 (1933), 445–7, s.v. *Moshe Dari*; L. Nemoy (ed.), *Karaite Anthology* (1952), 133–46, 354–5.

[Jefim (Hayyim) Schirmann]

DARIUS (Heb. and Aram. (from the Elephantine papyri) דריוש; in the Elephantine papyri also דריוהוש, דריהוש; old Persian *darayavahus*), name of three Persian kings of the Achaemenid royal family.

DARIUS I (522–486 B.C.E.), a descendant of a collateral line of the Achaemenid royal family, followed Cambyses, son of Cyrus, on the throne of Persia after a period of political turmoil. He defeated Gaumata, who claimed to be Bardiya, brother of Cambyses, and rebels elsewhere in the empire. Darius gave his account of the struggle in the trilingual Behistun inscription (Old Persian, Elamite, and Babylonian; a fragmentary Aramaic version was found at Elephantine). This inscription, as well as that on his tomb at Naqsh-i Rustam, affords an insight into Persian religious beliefs of that period. Darius extended the empire to include Lybia, Thracia, Sogdiana, and India as its borders. His attempt to conquer Greece ended in defeat at Marathon in 490. He organized the empire into satrapies and set up a network of roads and a postal system. He also reformed the laws of the provinces and consolidated internal administration and taxation. According to Ezra 6:12 Darius forbade further obstruction to the rebuilding of the Temple in Jerusalem and supplied its needs: the Temple was completed in the second year of his reign (Haggai 1:15).

DARIUS II NOTHUS (442–404 B.C.E.), son of Artaxerxes I, was essentially a weak king whose rule over the western part of the empire was often lax. During his reign there was turmoil in Media, Lydia, Syria, and Egypt. Many of the Elephantine papyri are dated by his regnal years. During his fifth year the papyrus ordering the Jews of Elephantine to observe the Passover was issued in his name (Pritchard, Texts, 491), and it was in his 14th year (410 B.C.E.) that the Elephantine temple was destroyed. The reference to Darius the Persian in Nehemiah 12:22 is in all likelihood to Darius II and permits the dating of the list of priests given there.

DARIUS III CODOMANUS (336–330 B.C.E.), the last Achaemenian king, was defeated by Alexander the Great at Issus (333) and at Gaugamela (331), an event mentioned in I Maccabees 1:1. He was murdered by the satrap of Bactria.

BIBLIOGRAPHY: P.J. Junge, *Dareios I* (Ger., 1944); Olmstead, Hist, index; R.G. Kent, *Old Persian* (1953), 107–63, 189; B. Porten, *Archives from Elephantine* (1968), index.

[Jonas C. Greenfield]

DARIUS THE MEDE, Persian king. According to the Bible in Daniel 6:1 (cf. 11:1) Darius the Mede succeeded Belshazzar as king of Babylon. The reference is historically impossible and has caused much confusion. A possible explanation may be found in the recapture of Babylon in 520 B.C.E. by *Darius I and the loose use of the term Mede for Persian by the Greeks and Mineans. A more recent explanation is based on the Achaemenian Persian doctrine of three world monarchies of which Persia was the third. The Chaldeans were assumed to be the founders of the first great empire; they were followed by the Medes and finally by the Persians. The Jews substituted the Chaldeans for the Assyrians and the Persians. Darius, who conquered Babylon, was regarded by the Judean writer as Darius the Mede, successor to the Chaldean, Belshazzar, and as the predecessor of Cyrus the Persian.

BIBLIOGRAPHY: H.H. Rowley, *Darius the Mede and the Four World Empires in the Book of Daniel* (1935); H.L. Ginsberg, *Studies in Daniel* (1948), 5, 63–64, 69.

[Jonas C. Greenfield]

DARMESTETER, ARSÈNE (1846–1888), French philologist and authority in Romance languages. Darmesteter, who was born at Château-Salins (Lorraine), was appointed lecturer in Romance languages at the Ecole des Hautes Etudes in Paris in 1872. In 1877 he was appointed lecturer in French language and literature at the Sorbonne. He collaborated with Adolphe Hatzfeld in one of the most important modern dictionaries of the French language. He also taught at the Ecole Rabbinique, co-founded the Société des Etudes Juives, and the *Revue des Etudes Juives (1879), to which he contributed several articles.

Darmesteter's first contribution to Jewish scholarship was his *Le Talmud*, written in 1866 and published in *Reliques Scientifiques* (1890). He soon concentrated on the French words used by medieval Bible and Talmud commentators, *Rashi in particular. His *Glosses et Glossaires hebreux-français du moyen-âge* (in *Romania*, 1, 1872), was the first attempt to compile a dictionary of 11th-century French, based on these commentators. His most important work in this field is the dictionary of Rashi's **la'azim* in the Bible (*Les gloses françaises de Rashi dans la Bible*, 1909), and in his Talmud commentary *Les gloses françaises dans les commentaires talmudiques de Rashi* (1929). This was edited by D.S. *Blondheim, who published on his own a second volume of the work (1937). Darmesteter published the so-called *Deux élégies du Vatican*, commemorating the 13 Jewish martyrs of Troyes (1288), with a commentary (in *Romania*, 3, 1874). In 1890 his brother James published a three-part collection of Arsène's writings (*Reliques Scientifiques*), consisting of his general Jewish studies, his Judeo-French ones, and a memoir and bibliography.

His brother JAMES DARMESTETER (1849–1894), an Orientalist, was born at Château-Salins. He studied Oriental languages in Paris specializing in Indo-Iranian studies, and became professor at the Collège de France in 1886. Apart from many publications in this field, such as the translation of the *Zend-Avesta* (the sacred Books of the Zoroastrian religion) into French (1842) and English (1880), he published material on the relationship between Zoroastrianism and Judaism and a series of essays *Les Prophètes d'Israel* (1892), which was his credo. Darmesteter also prepared French editions of Shakespeare and Byron and wrote essays on English literature (1883).

BIBLIOGRAPHY: *Annuaire de l'Ecole pratique des Hautes Etudes* (1895), 17–40 (with James' bibliography); G. Paris, *Penseurs et Poètes* (1896), 1–6; A. France, in: *Vie Litteraire*, 4 (1888); A. Spire, *Quelques Juifs et demi-Juifs* (1913), 199–272.

DARMON (Garmon, Jarmon, Jarmona), North African family. JACOB B. ISAAC DARMON (1460) was *dayyan* of Mahdia (Tunisia) and one of the main correspondents of Ẓemaḥ b. Solomon *Duran. MORDECAI DARMON was a leading 17th-century merchant in Tunis, where the kabbalist MOSES DARMON (d. 1741) was *dayyan* of the Leghorn community. NEHORAI DARMON (1682–1760), talmudist, poet, and disciple of Isaac Lombroso, succeeded him. His literary works were destroyed when the Jewish and Christian houses were plundered by Algerian soldiers (1752). What had been saved was published under the title *Yeter ha-Baz* (Leghorn, 1787). MORDECAI DARMON, a wealthy scholar, was treasurer and adviser to the beys of Algeria before 1772. In 1783 he was sent on a diplomatic mission to Constantinople and later established the new Oran community for which he built a synagogue. He wrote *Ma'amar Mordekhai* (Leghorn, 1781), a collection of homiletic explanations on biblical and talmudic passages. His sons-in-law, the *dayyan* Masʿud and Judah Darmon, wrote many poems. The latter also wrote an important work on the *halakhah* entitled *Gur Aryeh* (Leghorn, 1851). The poet JOSEPH DARMON was coauthor with Solomon Zarka of Tunis of *Rinnah vi-Yshu'ah* (2 parts, 1856–57). The merchant ISAAC DARMON settled with his sons in Morocco. JACQUES DARMON represented England in Casablanca and VICTOR (Ḥayyim) DARMON was Spain's representative in Mazagan. As a result of a false testimony brought by the governor of the town, he was summarily executed (January 1844). The affair had wide repercussions in Europe and was one of the causes of the 1859–1860 Spanish-Moroccan war. DAVID DARMON (1885–?), musicologist and lawyer in Tunis, wrote several works and essays among which are *Le Réalisme dans la Musique* (1906) and *La Situation des Cultes en Tunisie* (1932^2) which contains much information on Tunisian Judaism.

BIBLIOGRAPHY: Simeon b. Ẓemaḥ Duran, *Yakhin u-Vo'az*, 1 (Leghorn, 1782), nos. 9–10, 25–49; Bloch, in: REJ, 13 (1886), 90–91; L. Godard, *Description et Histoire du Maroc*, 2 (1860), 611, 638; Miège, Maroc, 2 (1961), 87, 94–95, 186, 332; J. Lambert, *Choses et gens de Tunisie* (1912), 147; Hirschberg, Afrikah, 2 (1965), 132.

[David Corcos]

DARMON, AMRAM (1815–1878), French soldier. Darmon was born in Algiers and was a scion of the distinguished *Darmon family. He enthusiastically welcomed the French conquest of Algeria in 1830, and in 1834 joined the French army, enrolling in the spahis, and participated in all the subsequent campaigns. As a result of his knowledge of Arabic and French and of the country as a whole, he was appointed interpreter, serving in this capacity in the various campaigns, and in 1852 was given the official appointment of Interpreter, First Class. In December of that year he was named Chevalier of the Legion of Honor. From 1853 to 1868 he was head of the Arab Bureau in Mascara, where he died. Darmon took advantage of the decree of 1866 granting Algerian Jews the right of individual naturalization, four years before the Crémieux decree of 1870 which granted them automatic French citizenship.

DARMON, PIERRE (1934–), tennis player. Born in Tunis, Darmon was a top-ranked tennis player in France from 1956 through the 1970s, including No. 1 from 1956 to 1964, except in 1958, and was ranked in the top ten worldwide by various tennis publications in 1958, 1963, and 1964. In 1963 he lost in the singles finals at the French Open and reached the semifinals there in 1964 and the quarterfinals in 1958, 1962, and 1967. At Wimbledon, he reached the finals in doubles in 1963 and the quarterfinal in 1958. Darmon was also a singles semifinalist at the Italian Championships in 1957, and a singles quarterfinalist at the 1965 Australian Championships. Darmon won the French Championship nine times between 1956 and 1969, and represented France in 68 matches in Davis Cup competitions from 1956 to 1967, holding France's record for most total wins with 47 and most singles victories with 44. In 2002, he was named recipient of the Davis Cup Award of Excellence from the International Tennis Hall of Fame and the International Tennis Federation. Darmon was the director of the European Tennis Bureau of the Association of Tennis Professionals (ATP) in 1973, a member of the ATP Board of Directors from 1974 to 1979, and a member of the Men's International Professional Tennis Council from 1974 to 1979. He also served as tournament director of the French Open at Roland Garros from 1969 through 1978.

[Elli Wohlgelernter (2nd ed.)]

DARMSTADT, city in Hesse, Germany. Jews were mentioned there from the 16th century. They were subjected to the severe restriction of the *Judenordnung* enacted for the whole of *Hesse Jewry in 1585 and reimposed in 1629. In the 16th and 17th centuries Darmstadt Jews were compelled to attend Christian missionary sermons, like the other Hesse communities. They were granted permission to assemble for prayers only in 1695. A synagogue was erected in 1737, and the cemetery was established in 1709. The community numbered 200 persons in 1771. Its *Memorbuch* encompasses the years 1711 to 1863. The community flourished after the grant of civil rights to Jews.

About 2,000 Jews lived in Darmstadt in 1913, and 3,000 in 1933, many of them immigrants from Eastern Europe. A new synagogue was built in 1876. However, the local Orthodox members seceded and in 1906 founded an independent community and synagogue, which totaled approximately 110 families in 1925. The Orientalist Julius Landsberger served as rabbi of Darmstadt at the end of the 19th century. The last noted rabbi of the Reform community of the city was the scholar Bruno *Italiener. The poet Karl *Wolfskehl, the literary historian Friedrich *Gundolf, and the architect Alfred *Messel were all born in Darmstadt. Emigration after Hitler's rise to power reduced the community to fewer than 700 by August 1938. On Nov. 10, 1938, both the main synagogue, with its 30 Torah scrolls, and the Orthodox one were burned down. The remaining Jews were deported starting in December 1940. There were 70 Jews living in the city and 30 in the district in 1967. A new synagogue was inaugurated in 1988, when there were 116 community members. Due to the immigration of Jews from the former Soviet Union, their number rose to 670 in 2003.

BIBLIOGRAPHY: Lebermann, in: JJLG, 20 (1929), 181–252; A. Mueller, *Zur Geschichte der Judenfrage in den rechtsrheinischen Besitzungen der Landgrafschaft Hessen-Darmstadt in 16., 17. und 18. Jahrhundert…* (1937); *Darmstaedter israelitischer Kalender…* (1939); B. Postal and S.H. Abramson, *Landmarks of a People…* (1962);

H.W. Sabais (ed.), *Vom Geist einer Stadt...* (1956); FJW (1932–33), 378–9. **ADD. BIBLIOGRAPHY:** E.G. Franz, *Juden als Darmstaedter Buerger* (1984); B. Szklanowski, *Bet ha-Ḥayyim. Der juedische Friedhof in Darmstadt* (1988); R. Dreesen, *Darmstadt als Deportationsort* (2004).

[Edmund Meir / Stefan Rohrbacher (2nd ed.)]

DARMSTADT, JOSEPH (d. c. 1820), early settler of Richmond, Va. Darmstadt arrived in the United States as a sutler with the Hessian troops and was captured by Continental forces. Sent as a prisoner to Charlottesville, Virginia, he renounced his foreign allegiance, presumably recognizing the assets of a democratic government. Darmstadt settled in Richmond no later than 1786. He became a successful merchant because his knowledge of the language and customs of the large German colony in the mountains west of Richmond drew the people to trade in the capital city. A popular figure, he was elected to the exclusive Amicable Society in 1789. Darmstadt was active in Masonry and was the second Jewish Mason in Virginia. He was founder of Beth Shalome Congregation.

BIBLIOGRAPHY: H.T. Ezekiel and G. Lichtenstein, *History of the Jews of Richmond from 1769 to 1917* (1917); Rosenbloom, Biog Dict, 31.

[Simon Vega]

DAROCA, city in Saragossa province, N.E. Spain. During the period of Muslim rule the Jewish quarter of Daroca was situated on the slope of Mt. San Jorge at the eastern approach to the valley, with the Jewish cemetery nearby. After the reconquest of Daroca by Alfonso I of Aragon in 1122 Jews were granted the same rights as the Christian and Muslim residents in a *fuero* ("municipal charter"), endorsed by Count Ramon Berenguer IV in 1142. The Daroca community flourished during the 13th century. In 1210 the Jews of Daroca were exempted by Pedro II from paying certain tolls, notably those levied on entry to and exit from Moorish territory. An injunction was issued by James II in 1312 to stay the sale of property of Jews in Daroca under arrest for debt. The arrest of Jews on the Sabbath and Jewish holidays was also prohibited. Accusations were rife in 1321 that the Jews had poisoned the wells. Regulations concerning the institution and observance of the Jewish *oath in Daroca were introduced by Alfonso IV in 1330; the deponent was required to take the oath at the entrance to the synagogue, holding the Torah scroll, in the presence of three Christian witnesses only.

During the outbreaks of 1391 peasants in the neighborhood joined in the attacks on the Jews in Daroca and tried to force them to accept baptism. Although the king extended his protection to the community, only 27 taxpaying Jewish families remained in Daroca by 1398. The massacres of 1391 brought disaster to the Jews of Daroca. The Church increased its pressure on the survivors. The recovery was slow, but never complete. At the beginning of the 15th century the community of Daroca, like many others in the Crown of Aragon, was under great pressure from Christian society. The town physician at that time was Salamon Alconstantin. Joseph *Albo served as rabbi in Daroca and represented it at the disputation of *Tortosa in 1413–14, when the Jewish community was again attacked by the townspeople. By June 1414 many of the rabbinic figures of the Aragonese communities gave in and converted. Joseph Albo was one of the very few who had the courage and strength to withstand the Christians' pressure and remain Jewish. After the disputation, about 110 of the most eminent and affluent members of the Daroca Jewish community adopted Christianity. Under pressure of the Church many who belonged to the upper class, the *mano mayor,* converted. On Aug. 20, 1414, the apostates were exempted from communal fiscal liabilities by Ferdinand I. Subsequently the townsfolk of Daroca threatened to expel the remaining Jews unless they adopted Christianity; the municipal authorities seized a number of Jewish debtors on the pretext that they had been trying to abscond. The bailiff then proceeded to arrest all the Jews en masse. A number of the Jews let themselves down from the city walls by rope at night and made their escape. Of the 40 Jewish families, some 160 to 180 people, who had been living in Daroca, only nine or ten persons then remained, all in prison. Their names are known thanks to a trial initiated in January 1426. Following the mass conversion in Daroca and the flight of many Jews, a large part of the communal property and ritual objects were longer of any use. Some of the objects were put on sale. Some Jews of Daroca settled on baronial lands, such as Epila and Montalbán, or in villages in the surroundings of Daroca, Cariñena, Luco, and Anento. Some time after April 1414, the community or *aljama* ceased to exist as a juridical body. Joseph Albo left for Soria, in Castile. It seems that the majority of those who retained there Judaism came from the lower class of craftsmen.

The state of affairs evidently improved, however, and as result of Jewish immigration to the town, in 1458 the limits of the Jewish quarter were defined by John II in order to prevent Jews living alongside Christians. The Jewish community was living side by side with the Conversos, who were already showing signs of reverting to Judaism. In 1484 Ferdinand II issued a directive permitting Jews to be summoned to give evidence before the *Inquisition in cases where Conversos were accused of Judaizing. Jewish property in Daroca was looted after the issue of the edict of expulsion of the Jews from Spain in March 1492. By August the synagogue and hospital had been sold along with other Jewish communal property.

BIBLIOGRAPHY: Ashtor, Korot, 2 (1966), 166; H.C. Lea, *History of the Inquisition in Spain*, 1 (1904), 547; Baer, Urkunden, index; Baer, Studien, 132, 148; Baer, Spain, index; López de Meneses, in: *Sefarad*, 14 (1954), 108; Cabezudo Astrain, *ibid.*, 15 (1955), 107; Estéban Abad, in: *Teruel* (1959), 215–22, 361–72, 387–92. **ADD. BIBLIOGRAPHY:** M.A. Motis Dolader, in: *Proceedings of 10th WCJS,* Division B, vol. 2 (1990), 143–50

[Haim Beinart / Yom Tov Assis (2nd ed.)]

DAROFF, SAMUEL H. (1900–1967), Philadelphia clothing manufacturer; Jewish and civic leader. Daroff joined his father's clothing business, which grew into a nationally known firm. Daroff began his philanthropic career at the age of 27 in the Masonic Golden Slipper Club, and then gradually became known for his willingness to give time, money, and energy to good causes. He was campaign chairman of Philadelphia's Allied Jewish Appeal from 1945 to 1948. His period of communal leadership (1935–65) coincided with the coming of age and responsibility of the children of East European Jews, whom he represented in the succession to authority. One of his favorite organizations was the Philadelphia Jewish Armed Services Committee of the USO-JWB, to which he gave intense support long after interest in military and veterans' work had waned; another was the local branch of the American Jewish Congress. He was the second president of Philadelphia's Albert Einstein Medical Center (1953–57), which named its southern division for him, after his death. Daroff was active on the boards of a large number of national and international agencies and institutions. In Philadelphia he was interested in the work of the United Fund, Police Athletic League (which named one of its centers for him after his death), Hero Scholarship Fund, and Associated Hospital Service. Hundreds of honors were awarded to him, frequently in connection with fundraising efforts. Philadelphia honored him with the presidency of the Board of City Trusts, and in the state he was appointed chairman of the governor's Industrial Race Relations Committee and member of the Pennsylvania Fair Employment Practices Committee. While his personal inclinations were toward a traditional form of Judaism, Daroff was a member and supporter of many congregations – Orthodox, Conservative, and Reform.

[Bertram Wallace Korn]

°DARQUIER DE PELLEPOIX, LOUIS (1897–1980), French fascist and antisemite. Darquier, who served with distinction in World War I, became active in fascist organizations. In 1935 he was elected municipal councilor in Paris on a "national and anti-Jewish" platform. He was head of the Rassemblement Antijuif de France and published the fascist *La France Enchaînée*. On May 6, 1942, Pierre *Laval appointed him head of the General Commissariat of Jewish Affairs. He held this office until the end of February 1944, and collaborated closely with the Nazi occupation in the persecution of the Jewish population of France, which involved putting Jews "outside the law," spoliation of their property, and deportations. Upon the liberation of France, he escaped to Spain. He was convicted for high treason and condemned to death *in absentia* by the Haute Cour of France in 1946.

BIBLIOGRAPHY: J. Billig, *Le Commissariat Général aux questions juives (1941–44)*, 3 vols. (1955–60), index; IMT, *Trial of the Major War Criminals* (1949), index.

[Yehuda Reshef]

DARSHAN (Heb. דַּרְשָׁן), a professional or qualified expounder of Scripture. Originally a *darshan* expounded both halakhically and aggadically on all Scripture. *Ben Zoma, called "the last of the *darshanim*" (Sot. 9:15), is mentioned in one passage as a halakhic *darshan* (Ber. 1:5) and in another, where, with his colleague *Ben Azzai, he is referred to as a *darshan*, the exposition is mystical (Gen. R. 5:4). As the term *Midrash, which was originally applied both to *Midrash Halakhah* and *Midrash Aggadah*, came to refer to the latter only, so the term *darshan* came to be applied specifically to the homiletical interpreter of the Torah. The verse in Ecclesiastes (7:5) "It is better to hear the rebuke of the wise" is thus applied to *darshanim* in contrast to "the song of fools" referring to the **meturgemanim* who "raise their voice in song to make themselves heard by the people" (Eccl. R. ad loc.). Eleazar b. Simeon was eulogized as a "reader of Scripture, a Mishnah teacher, a *paytan*, and a *darshan*" (Lev. R. 30:1). In the Middle Ages, the word came to be applied to the professional preacher or the person who was an expert in preaching. In some of the larger Eastern European communities, a person was appointed to be the official preacher of the community, in contrast to the rabbi and the *dayyan* who occupied themselves with *halakhah*. Both the official and the itinerant preacher were usually given the title of **maggid*.

DARVAS, LILI (1906–1974), European and U.S. actress. Born in Budapest, Lili Darvas began her career in 1922 as Shakespeare's Juliet. She married the Hungarian playwright Ferenc *Molnar in 1922, and joined Max Reinhardt's company from 1926 to 1938. Immigrating to the U.S. in 1938, she played in Ferdinand Bruckner's *Criminals*. Her first English-speaking role was in *Soldier's Wife* in 1944. Subsequently, she appeared frequently on stage, screen, and television. She visited Budapest in 1965–66 to play the mother in *Olympia*, a drama that had originally been written for her by her husband.

DARWĪSH, SHALOM (1913–), Iraqi author. A lawyer by profession, Darwīsh was secretary of the Baghdad Jewish communal council (1931–44). His first volume of Arabic short stories dealt with the life of Iraq's masses and was followed by a second collection, *Baʿd al-Nās* ("One of the People," 1948). He immigrated to Israel in 1951 and settled in Haifa.

[Shmuel Moreh]

DASH, SAMUEL (1925–2004), U.S. attorney. Dash was born in Camden, New Jersey, his parents having emigrated from the Soviet Union. After graduating from Harvard Law School with a J.D. degree *cum laude*, he taught law at Northwestern University. Admitted to practice law in Illinois (1950) and Pennsylvania (1952), he was trial attorney in the U.S. Department of Justice (1951–52), and from 1952 to 1956 served in the district attorney's office in Philadelphia, rising from assistant district attorney to first assistant district attorney and ultimately to district attorney. Dash then entered private practice, specializing in criminal trial work. In 1965 he joined the law faculty of Georgetown University, Washington, D.C., and served as professor of law and director of the Institute of Criminal Law and Procedure at the Georgetown University Law Center.

As director of the Pennsylvania Bar Association Endowment Study of Wiretapping and Eavesdropping, in 1956–58 he developed material for his book *The Eavesdroppers* (1959; with R.E. Knowlton and R.F. Schwartz), a study that covers wiretapping practices, laws, devices, and techniques by law enforcement officers, and the wiretapping practices of big business, labor, and politics. The study helped change wiretapping law in America. Subsequently Dash's book *The Intruders: Unreasonable Searches and Seizures from King John to John Ashcroft* (2004) criticized the U.S. government's expanded search, seizure, and wiretapping powers following the September 11, 2001, terrorist attacks. Dash also published on *Readings in Criminal Justice* (with Bowman and Pye, 1968).

Dash served, among many other public offices, as director of the International League for the Rights of Man, which has consultative status with the United Nations, as chair of the American Bar Association's Criminal Justice Section, and as president of the National Association of Defense Lawyers in Criminal Cases. In 1973 Dash was appointed chief counsel to the U.S. Senate Committee investigating the Watergate scandal. His book *Chief Counsel: Inside the Ervin Committee – The Untold Story of Watergate* was published in 1976. Dash served in a number of other major inquiries as well. He made headlines while serving as ethics adviser to independent counsel Kenneth Starr during the Whitewater Investigation (1994–1998). He resigned in protest when Starr testified before the House Judiciary Committee to advocate for the impeachment of President Clinton. Dash, who had helped write the independent counsel law, felt that Starr's testimony exceeded his capacity as objective investigator.

As a member of the board of directors for the International League of Human Rights, Dash served on human rights missions to Northern Ireland (to investigate the 1972 Bloody Sunday incident), the Soviet Union, and Chile. In 1985 he was the first American the South African government allowed to visit Nelson Mandela in prison, and he took part in the mediation efforts that ultimately led to Mandela's release.

[Jacob Haberman / Ruth Beloff (2nd ed.)]

DASHEWSKI, PINḤAS (1879–1934), Russian Zionist activist. Dashewski came from an assimilated family in Korostyshev, Ukraine; his father was an army doctor. He joined a Zionist Socialist student circle in Kiev in 1902. After the *Kishinev pogrom Dashewski assaulted and wounded the chief instigator, P. *Krushevan, in St. Petersburg on June 4 (17), 1903. He was sentenced to five years' hard labor but was released in 1906. The incident, trial, and Dashewski's appearance in court acted as a protest against the regime, and a call for Jewish *self-defense. In 1910 Dashewski visited Ereẓ Israel. During the *Beilis case he took part in a delegation of Russian Jews to the U.S. Dashewski, who was a chemical engineer, worked in the Caucasus and Siberia. He remained a Zionist after the 1917 Revolution and was eventually arrested and died in prison.

BIBLIOGRAPHY: M. Singer, *Be-Reshit ha-Ẓiyyonut ha-Sozyalistit* (1957), 256–91; *Biografiya…* (Russ. and Yid., 1903), published by Young Israel, London; YE, s.v.

[Moshe Mishkinsky]

DA SILVA (Silverblatt), HOWARD (1909–1986), U.S. actor. Born in Cleveland, Da Silva at first worked as a stage actor. After learning the craft he worked at the Civic Repertory Theater in New York until 1934 and later, he played in many theatrical productions and Broadway musicals including *Alice in Wonderland, Waiting for Lefty, The World of Shalom Aleichem, Oklahoma*, and *Fiorello*. He also directed plays and wrote the Broadway comedy *The Zulu and the Zayde*. Da Silva appeared in numerous films from 1936 including *Abe Lincoln in Illinois, Nine Lives Are Not Enough, Lost Weekend, They Live by Night, David and Lisa, Topkapi, Nevada Smith, 1776* (as Benjamin Franklin), *The Great Gatsby, The Private Files of J. Edgar Hoover, Mommie Dearest*, and *Garbo Talks*.

[Jonathan Licht (2nd ed.)]

DASSAULT (originally **Bloch**), **DARIUS PAUL** (1882–1969), French army officer, born in Paris. Dassault graduated from the Ecole Polytechnique in 1903 and joined the army, serving in artillery units and at the general headquarters of the French army in the Near East during World War I. Between 1919 and 1933 he held posts in military schools including the Centre des Hautes Etudes Militaires and in 1933 was appointed head of the technical bureau of the French artillery. On the outbreak of World War II, Dassault was put in command of the Fifth Army Corps and following the French surrender in June 1940 he joined the Resistance. When France was liberated in 1944, he was raised to the rank of *général d'armée*, the highest rank in the French army, and appointed governor of Paris. From 1945 until he retired in 1948, Dassault was general inspector of artillery. His brother was Marcel *Dassault, owner of the aircraft factory of that name.

[Mordechai Kaplan]

DASSAULT, MARCEL (1892–1986), French aeronautical engineer and industrialist. Dassault was born Marcel Bloch in Paris, the son of a physician. He was one of the first graduates in aeronautical engineering (1914). In World War I he invented an improved propeller for the Spad fighter. In 1930 he founded the aircraft company Societé des Avions Marcel Bloch, where he designed a series of civil and military aircraft including the Bloch 152, the only French fighter aircraft potentially capable of opposing the Luftwaffe. The firm was nationalized in 1936 but he remained director. He was deported to Buchenwald in 1944, where he remained until the end of the war after his refusal to collaborate with the Germans on aircraft design. After the war he changed his name to Dassault, after his brother Paul's code name in the resistance "d'assault" (derived from the French phrase "char d'assault" for tank). In 1946 he founded the Societé des Avions Marcel Dassault. In 1967 Dassault's company merged with Breguet. The new company became the dominant supplier of French military aircraft. Dassault designed the Ouragan, and the Mystère and Mirage series of jet fighters. These aircraft made a prominent contribution to Israel's military campaigns. The Ouragan was used in the 1956 Sinai campaign and the Mystère IV in the 1967 Six-Day War.

An upgraded version of the Super Mystère B2 was employed in the 1973 Yom Kippur War. He also designed military transport aircraft and the Falcon series of private business jets. Subsequently the company greatly expanded and diversified its business interests in Dassault's later years and under the direction of his son and heir, Serge. Marcel Dassault served as a deputy in the French National Assembly (1951–55) and as a senator (1957–58). He was again elected a deputy in 1958.

[Michael Denman (2nd ed.)]

DASSIN, JULES (1911–), U.S. film director. Born in Middletown, Connecticut, Dassin attended high school in the Bronx, New York, and drama school in Europe. He started his career as an actor in the Yiddish Theatre in New York at age 25. In Hollywood, he worked his way up to a directorial position in MGM's short subjects unit, where he handled an inspired 20-minute adaptation of Edgar Alan Poe's *The Tell-Tale Heart* (1941). He then graduated to directing feature films for MGM, such as *Nazi Agent* (1942), *Reunion in France* (1942), and *The Canterville Ghost* (1944). He wrote radio plays, and directed film noir gangster movies such as *Brute Force* (1947) and *The Naked City* (1948) for Universal Studios. During the McCarthy period in the 1950s, Dassin started making films abroad. The last film he directed for a major American studio was 20th Century Fox's *Night and the City* (1950), which was shot in London. He moved to France, where he co-authored, directed, and acted in *Rififi* (1954), which is regarded as one of the most influential crime caper movies. During this period he directed the films *He Who Must Die* (1957), *La Loi* (1959), both of which he wrote, and the comedy thriller *Topkapi* (1964), which he also produced. Living in Greece, he became famous with the film *Never on Sunday* (1960), a humorous study of Greek seaport life, which he wrote and directed. In it, he played opposite Melina Mercouri, whom he later married. In 1967 he directed a documentary entitled *Survival* (screenplay by Irwin *Shaw) on the Six-Day Israel-Arab War. Dassin also wrote, produced, and directed *Phaedra* (1962), *10:30 P.M. Summer* (1966), *Up Tight* (1968), and *Promise at Dawn* (1970). He wrote and directed *A Dream of Passion* (1978) and directed *The Rehearsal* (1974) and *Circle of Two* (1980). As an actor, he appeared in *Phaedra*, *Promise at Dawn*, and *The Rehearsal*.

Although he was permitted back into the U.S. studio system in the mid-1960s, Dassin chose to remain in Europe. His son, JOE DASSIN (1938–1980), was one of France's most popular singers, with hits such as "L'eté indien" and "Aux Champs-Elysées."

ADD. BIBLIOGRAPHY: M. Mercouri, *I Was Born Greek* (1971).

[Linda Gutstein / Ruth Beloff (2nd ed.)]

DATHAN AND ABIRAM (Heb. דָּתָן, cf. Akk. *datnu*, "strong"; and Heb. אֲבִירָם, "my [or 'the'] father is exalted"), sons of Eliab of the tribe of Reuben, leaders of a revolt against the leadership of Moses (Num. 16; 26:9–11). According to these sources, they joined the rebellion of *Korah during the desert wanderings. Defying Moses' summons, they accused him of having brought the Israelites out of the fertile land of Egypt in order to let them die in the wilderness (16:12–14). Moses then went to the tents of Dathan and Abiram and persuaded the rest of the community to dissociate themselves from them. Thereafter, the earth opened and swallowed the rebels, their families, and property (16:25–33). Modern scholars generally regard this narrative as resulting from an editorial interweaving of originally distinct accounts of two separate rebellions against the authority of Moses. It is noted that verses 12–15 and 25ff. form a continuous, self-contained literary unit and that the former contains no mention of Korah, who is likewise omitted from the references in Deuteronomy 11:6 and Psalms 106:17. The event described served as a warning to Israel and as an example of divine justice (*ibid.*). Ben Sira (45:18), too, mentions it. However, no further details are given about the two rebels, and the narrative is clearly fragmentary. It is not unlikely that the rebellion was connected with the series of events that led to the tribe of Reuben's loss of its earlier position of preeminence.

[Nahum M. Sarna]

In the *Aggadah*

Dathan and Abiram are regarded as the prototype of inveterate fomenters of trouble. Their names are interpreted allegorically, Dathan denoting his violation of God's law, and Abiram his refusal to repent (Sanh. 109b). They were wholly wicked "from beginning to end" (Meg. 11a). They are identified with the two quarreling Israelites (Ex. R. 1:30) and it was they who caused Moses' flight from Egypt by denouncing him to Pharaoh for killing the Egyptian taskmaster, and revealing that he was not the son of Pharaoh's daughter (Yal., Ex. 167). They incited the people to return to Egypt (Ex. R. 1:29) both at the Red Sea and when the spies returned from Canaan (Mid. Ps. 106:5). They transgressed the commandment concerning the manna by keeping it overnight (Ex. R. 1:30). Dathan and Abiram became ringleaders of the rebellion under the influence of Korah, as a result of the camp of their tribe being next to that of Korah, and on this the rabbis base the statement "Woe to the wicked, woe to his neighbor" (Num. R. 18:5). When Moses humbly went to them in person in order to dissuade them from their evil designs, they were impertinent and insulting to him (MK 16a). In their statement to Moses, "we will not come up," they unconsciously prophesied their end, as they did not go up, but down to hell (Num. R. 18:10).

BIBLIOGRAPHY: J. Liver, in: *Scripta Hierosolymitana*, 8 (1961), 189–217, incl. bibl.; M.J. Perath, in: *Nederlands Theologisch Tijdschrift*, 16 (1961–62), 47–48; R. Gradwohl, in: ZAW, 75 (1963), 288–96; EM, 1 (1965), 33, incl. bibl.; 2 (1965), 773–4, incl. bibl.; Ginzberg, Legends, index.

DATO, MORDECAI BEN JUDAH (1525–1591/1601), Italian kabbalist. He annotated *Asis Rimmonim* by Elisha *Gallico (Venice, 1601). Dato's many writings are extant in numerous manuscripts. Two manuscripts of his *piyyutim*, collected in the work *Shemen Arev*, are found in the British Museum (645, 646), but they are not completely identical. The work published by A.W. Greenup (1910) contains the *piyyutim* of manuscript no. 645. Other manuscripts containing some of his *piyyutim* are found in: Moscow (Guenzburg 249), Cincinnati (230), Budapest (Kauffmann 414), London (Or. 10130 and 10471 = Mss. Gaster 318 and 251; and Ms. Adler 1825). The tract *Zimrat Yah* is found in Rome (Ms. Casenatense 116), and was copied by Dato's son, who transcribed his father's poems and their commentaries. Although the son claims to have written these commentaries on the basis of what he had heard from his father, there is practically no difference in the wording of these commentaries and those that were written by his father, except for a very small number of additions. This would explain the manner in which *Iggeret Levanon* was written. A work containing an entirely different kind of poem is *Sodot ha-Nekuddot* (Ms. Mantua 162, 4). Some of his *piyyutim* were included in *Ashmoret ha-Boker* (Venice, 1720/21; Leghorn, 1796), by *Aaron Berechiah of Modena.

His works include commentaries on biblical passages and sermons (Brit. Mus., Add. Ms. 27050, mainly in Italian; Ms. Add. 27007, also contains an index to the *Zohar); *Ma'amar Mordekhai*, a commentary on Esther (Ms. Add. 27097); a commentary on Habakkuk (Ms. Parma 1424); commentary on the Psalms (Moscow, Ms. Guenzburg 239) which is incomplete and is probably identical with *Shemen Sason*, which is mentioned in his other writings; a commentary on the *haftarot*, *Shemen ha-Mishḥah* (Ms. Parma 29); *Migdal David*, treating the Redemption (Bodleian Library, Ms. Opp. Add. 4ø 153); *Iggerot*, letters on Kabbalah to Ezra (perhaps Azariah da *Fano, Ms. Parma 130/5), and letters on halakhic matters to scholars in Italy (Moscow, Ms. Guenzburg, 129); *Iggeret Levanon*, containing memoirs of his visit to Safed written by his son but formulated by Dato himself; these were published by I. Tishby (*Sefunot*, 7 (1963), 137–66); *Processo* (Moscow, Ms. Guenzburg 159), on a lawsuit which he and his brother brought against the brothers Bordola.

BIBLIOGRAPHY: C. Roth, in: REJ, 80 (1925), 69–75; D. Tamar, in: *Sefunot*, 2 (1958), 66–70.

[Efraim Gottlieb]

DAUBE, DAVID (1909–1999), jurist and biblical scholar. Daube was born in Freiburg, Baden, and studied at the University of Goettingen and Cambridge and Oxford universities. From 1938–51 he was lecturer in law at Cambridge University, professor of jurisprudence at Aberdeen University, 1951–55, and Regius Professor of Civil Law at Oxford from 1955. From 1970 he was professor at the University of California at Berkeley. Daube was considered one of the world's leading authorities on Roman law, and he made important contributions to the understanding of the history of biblical and talmudic law. His published works included *Studies in Biblical Law* (1947), which compares Roman and Hebrew law; *New Testament and Rabbinic Judaism* (1956), which sheds light on many incidents and sayings in the New Testament with information from rabbinic and sectarian Jewish sources; *Sin, Ignorance and Forgiveness in the Bible* (1960), an examination of the plea of ignorance of the law as a defense; *Exodus Pattern in the Bible* (1963), analysis of the legal themes and terms used in the story of Exodus and other biblical tales of a similar pattern; *The Sudden in the Scriptures* (1964), which lists the terms for the sudden and the unexpected in both the Old and New Testaments with further elucidations drawn from rabbinic usage; *Collaboration with Tyranny in Rabbinic Law* (1965); and *Roman Law* (1969).

ADD. BIBLIOGRAPHY: ODNB online.

°DAUDET, LÉON (1867–1942), French writer and reactionary politician, codirector of L'*Action Française. He was born in Paris, the eldest son of Alphonse Daudet, and inherited his father's talent as a writer if not his moral sensitivity. A bigoted Catholic and anti-Republican from the start, Daudet was influenced by Charles *Maurras' neo-Royalist doctrines and associated with Edouard *Drumont, writing for the violently antisemitic *La Libre Parole*. He was elected to the Chamber of Deputies on an extreme right-wing policy (1919–24) and in 1940 supported the Vichy regime, welcoming its discriminatory policy toward the Jews. Daudet was probably the leading French pamphleteer of his day. He wrote around 100 books and innumerable articles, sometimes signed Rivarol, in which he frequently gave vent to his hatred of Republicans, Dreyfusards, Freemasons, or whoever else did not fit into his narrow and intolerant definition of a true French citizen. On the Jews he was especially virulent, as in his *La France en alarme* (1904), *L'avant-guerre…* (1913), and *Au temps de Judas* (1933). For Daudet, Jews were "goats with human faces, trafficking in gold and dung" whom he threatened with "the vengeance they deserve." Like Maurice *Barrès and Charles Maurras, Daudet subscribed to Drumont's contention that all Jews were potential traitors and the main source of political, social, and financial trouble in France.

BIBLIOGRAPHY: M. Hay, *Europe and the Jews* (1960), 178, 191–2, 197–8; P. Lucchini, *Léon Daudet* (Fr., 1964); P. Dresse, *Léon Daudet vivant* (1948).

DAUGAVPILS (until 1893 **Duenaburg**; Heb. **דינאבורג**; until 1920 **Dvinsk**), city in the Soviet Republic of Latvia, on the banks of the Western Dvina (Daugava) River, in 1940–91; within independent Latvia between 1920 and 1940 and from 1991. A Jewish community was organized in 1750–60. There were about 750 Jewish artisans in the town in 1805 (compared with 393 non-Jewish artisans). The Jewish population was 1,559 in 1815, growing to 2,918 in 1847. The town developed extensively from the 1860s, with the growth of the grain, flax, and timber trade, and after becoming a railroad junction. Its factories included the Zaks match factory, which employed 600–800 (mostly Jewish girls), sawmills, distilleries, tanneries, and three button factories which employed 600 workers, most of them Jews, at the beginning of the 20th century. In 1898 there were 4,862 Jewish artisans, including 2,193 masters, 1,760 journeymen, and 909 apprentices. Many Jews were employed in building the garrison complex and in services connected with it, railroad workshops, and the garment industry which was a source of livelihood for several thousands of Jews. Jews played a prominent part in the city's commerce and industry. Dvinsk became a center of activities of the Jewish workers' movements, principally the *Bund and *Po'alei Zion. A strong *self-defense organization was formed by the workers in 1903 which succeeded in deterring pogroms. In demonstrations during the 1905 revolution 30 people were killed or wounded, mostly Jews. Dvinsk was known as a center of Torah learning, and had a number of yeshivot. Two of Jewry's most prominent rabbis officiated there, Meir Simḥah *ha-Kohen, rabbi of the *Mitnaggedim* (1887–1926), and Joseph *Rozin, rabbi of the Ḥasidim (1889–1936). The community numbered 32,400 in 1897 (46% of the total population) and 56,000 (43%) in 1913. During World War I the city was severely damaged and was abandoned by most of its inhabitants. There were 11,838 Jews living in Daugavpils in 1921 (40.8% of the total population) and 11,106 (about 25%) in 1935. Noah *Meisel, who became a member of the Latvian parliament, headed the Bund. The Zionist movement, which had adherents in Dvinsk at the end of the 19th century and sent a delegate to the First Zionist Congress, grew considerably in the 1920s and 1930s, principally in the *Ẓe'irei Zion movement. A large section of youth was connected with Zionist youth organizations and *He-Ḥalutz, which maintained a farm for *hakhsharah*. Most Jewish children (over 2,000 at the beginning of the 1930s) attended the six Jewish schools of which five gave instruction in Hebrew or Yiddish. There were also a municipal Hebrew secondary school with several hundred pupils, a vocational training school maintained by *ORT, and a local Jewish sports organization. Communal institutions included a hospital, pharmacy, old-age home, orphanage, library, and three peoples' banks. Under the Soviets in 1940–41, all Jewish parties, organizations, and institutions were closed. Many activists and well-to-do Jews were exiled to Siberia. Instruction at Jewish schools was only allowed in the Yiddish language teaching a Soviet curriculum. When the Germans occupied Daugavpils on June 26, 1941, the Nazis, with the collaboration of the non-Jewish inhabitants, organized a pogrom on the Jews of the city. The synagogues were burned down or requisitioned by the army. During the first week of July 1,150 Jews were murdered. At the end of July a ghetto was set up at the abandoned cavalry barracks and 14,000–16,000 Jews from the city and the surrounding area were concentrated there. The first victims were the old and the sick, followed by thousands of refugees. On August 8–9, in two *Aktionen*, thousands of nonessential workers with their families and 400 orphans were murdered. By August 21, 9,012 Jews were dead. On November 7–9, 3,000–5,000 Jews were executed, including about 1,000 children. Five hundred Jews were killed on May 17, 1942, leaving alive a few hundred artisans. They were sent to the Riga ghetto in October 1943 and later confined in the Kaiserwald camp, where the Soviet army found 20 Jews on liberation day.

A community was reconstituted after the war. In the 1960s a small Jewish amateur drama group was in operation. In 1970 there were about 2,000 Jews in Daugavpils and one synagogue was still functioning. By the turn of the 21st century their number had dropped to around 400 after emigration.

BIBLIOGRAPHY: L. Berman, *In Loyf fun Yorn* (1945); M. Kaufmann, *Die Vernichtung der Juden Lettlands* (1947), 269–85; *Yahadut Latviyyah* (1953), 162–73, 225–32, 305–9, 335–6; P. Salzman-Frenkel, *Heftling Numer 94771* (1949). **ADD. BIBLIOGRAPHY:** L.M. Tsilevich (ed.), *Evrei v Daugavpilse: istoricheskie ocherk* (1993); Z.I. Yakub, *The Jews of Dunaburg* (1993); Y. Flior, *Dvinsk, the Rise and Fall of a Town* (1965); PK.

[Yehuda Slutsky / Shmuel Spector (2nd ed.)]

DAUPHINÉ, region and former province of S.E. France covering the present departments of Isère, Hautes-Alpes, and a small part of Drôme. The presence of Jews on its territory is confirmed from at least the beginning of the ninth century when they were to be found in *Vienne and its vicinity. Subsequently, and especially from the beginning of the 14th century, Jews are mentioned in at least 35 localities, including Briançon, *Crémieu, *Grenoble, Nyons, Serres, *Valence, Veynes, and Vizille. As a result of a *blood libel in Valréas in 1247 ten Jews were martyred there; in several other places Jews were imprisoned and their belongings were confiscated. However, when the Jews were expelled from France in 1306, the exiles were welcomed in Dauphiné, as were the Jews who arrived from the *Comtat-Venaissin in 1322. In 1348, the Jews were accused in several localities of Dauphiné of having spread the *Black Death.

In 1349, Dauphiné's existence as an independent state came to an end. In exchange for a considerable payment, the dauphin Humbert II ceded Dauphiné to the king of France, the eldest son of the king of France henceforth assuming the title of "dauphin." The undertaking to respect "the institutions and the customs of the country" was equally honored with regard to the Jews. Though they were now in the Kingdom of France, their residence in Dauphiné was not contested. In 1355 and 1404, it was explicitly stated that the Jews of newly-incorporated regions would continue to enjoy their former liberties and exemptions. However from 1355 the privileges which were granted to the Jews of Dauphiné were only valid for a limited period, even though they were renewable. These privileges specified in particular their freedom of residence, right to acquire houses, freedom of trade, and moneylending. Heavy financial burdens and the complaints against Jewish moneylending made many Jews leave Dauphiné, especially after 1390. The dauphin unsuccessfully attempted to restrain Jewish emigration by granting important fiscal advantages to the Jews who settled in the area, such as in the town of Crémieu in 1449. Yet, without any general expulsion decree ever having been applied and solely as a result of fiscal pressure and local vexations, Dauphiné appears to have had no Jews at the beginning of the 16th century after the continued emigration. At the beginning of the 18th century, some Jews, mainly from Comtat-Venaissin, attempted to settle in localities of Dauphiné, especially Grenoble. They were expelled by a decision of the Dauphiné parliament of Nov. 15, 1717. After the French Revolution Dauphiné ceased to exist as a separate administrative unit.

BIBLIOGRAPHY: B. Blumenkranz, *Juifs et Chrétiens…* (1960), index s.v. *Vienne*; Prudhomme, in: *Bulletin de l'Académie Delphinoise*, 17 (1881–82), 129ff.; idem, in: REJ, 9 (1884), 231ff.; G. Letonnelier, *Histoire du Dauphiné* (1958), passim; Z. Szajkowski, *Franco-Judaica* (1962), no. 310.

[Bernhard Blumenkranz]

DAUS, AVRAHAM (1902–1974), Israeli composer. Born in Berlin, he immigrated to Ereẓ Israel in 1936. Until 1940 he lived in Tel Aviv, and his overture to the *Sea-Gate Cantata*, performed by the then Palestine Orchestra, was one of the first local works performed by the "Philharmonic." From 1940 to 1964 Daus was a member of kibbutz Ḥefẓi-Bah, working as music teacher, composer, and choir conductor, but he eventually returned to Tel Aviv. Daus remained essentially European in style. When he returned to writing in dodecaphonic technique, his music lost none of its expressive character, as in *The Twelfth Sonnet* for cello solo. Daus's works include *Sea-Gate Cantata* (1937); *Variations on a Yemenite Theme for Flute and Piano* (1937); *String Quartet* (1953); *Concerto for Violin* (1957); *Four Dialogues for Violin and Cello* (1964); *The Twelfth Sonnet*, for cello solo (1967); *Four Improvisations while Reading the Song of Songs*, for guitar solo; and numerous songs and choral pieces.

[Uri (Erich) Toeplitz (2nd ed.), Yohanan Boehm (2nd ed.)]

DAVAR (Heb. דָּבָר), Hebrew daily newspaper of the *Histadrut ha-Ovedim. First published in Tel Aviv in 1925 under the editorship of B. *Katzenelson, *Davar* was the first daily of the entire Israel Labor Movement (although other periodicals by various Labor parties had appeared since 1907). As an organ for workers, the paper concerned itself with all the problems of the *yishuv*, Zionism, international Socialism, world politics, and the relations of the Histadrut with the Jewish and general Labor movement, devoting much space as well to Labor movement activities in the villages and the cities. In all public disputes in Israel and within the Histadrut itself, *Davar* officially took the stand of the Histadrut majority. Among its main contributors were B. Katzenelson, Z. Rubashov (later Z. *Shazar, the third president of the State of Israel), Moshe *Beilinson, David Zakay (d. 1978), Eliezer *Steinman (from 1935), and, for many years, N. *Alterman, with his column in verse "*Tur ha-Shevi'i*." After Katzenelson's death (1944), *Davar* had the following editors in chief: Zalman Shazar (who had actually fulfilled this function even previously), Haim *Shurer (from 1952), Yehudah Gotthelf (from 1966) and Ḥannah Zemer (from 1970).

Davar published many different supplements. These included a weekly English supplement, *Davar: Palestine Labour Weekly*, edited by Moshe Shertok (later *Sharett), 1929–31, and a German supplement, *Davar* (1931), at the beginning of the *aliyah* from Germany, under the editorship of Moshe Calvary. In 1931 publication of a children's supplement also began; it appeared in its later format as the weekly *Davar li-Yladim*. Others included *Ha-Meshek ha-Shittufi* (since 1932), on economic affairs; *Devar ha-Po'elet* (its editor from 1934–1966, Rachel Katzenelson-Shazar); evening newspapers, which appeared at various periods; and vocalized supplements (1935 and after). Vocalized columns within the body of the paper gave rise to *Hegeh* (1940–47), a vocalized Hebrew daily, the first of its kind in Ereẓ Israel. Its language was generally simple, translations being supplied for any difficult words. It was revived under the name *Omer* in 1951. In 1946 *Devar ha-Shavu'a*, an illustrated supplement, began appearing. In 1984 *Davar* began to publish the satirical newspaper *Davar Aḥer*, which gained much popularity. *Davar* also maintained the publishing house Am Oved, which, from its founding in 1927 until 1970, published nearly 200 books in all fields. In addition, from 1943 to 1956 *Davar* published an annual which dealt with literary and social problems and also included information on the events of the previous year.

The newspaper's downward slide began in the 1980s. With the loss of power of both the Labor Party and the Histadrut, many readers lost interest in *Davar* and the newspaper faced a severe financial crisis. In 1995 the newspaper appeared in a new format under the title *Davar Rishon*, with Ron Ben-Ishai as editor in chief, but ceased publication in 1996.

BIBLIOGRAPHY: G. Kressel, *Toledot ha-Ittonut ha-Ivrit be-Ereẓ-Yisrael* (1964), index; *Davar, Me'assef bi-Melot 25 Shanim* (1950); G. Kressel, in: *Davar, Tav Shin Yod Bet* (1951), 403–11; idem, in: *Davar, Tav Shin Tet Zayn* (1955), 421–36; *40 Shanah Davar: 1925–1965* (1965).

[Getzel Kressel / Shaked Gilboa (2nd ed.)]

DAVENPORT, MARCIA (1903–1996), U.S. novelist. Born in New York City, Marcia Davenport was the daughter of the lyric soprano Alma *Gluck. She herself became a music critic and joined the staff of *The New Yorker* magazine (1928–31), later working also for *Fortune* magazine. One of her marriages was to Russell Davenport, who became managing editor of *Fortune*. In 1930 she went to Prague in search of material on Mozart, whose biography she published as her first book in 1932. This was followed by two works that established her as a leading novelist: *Of Lena Geyer* (1936), the story of an opera singer, and *Valley of Decision* (1942), about life in the Pittsburgh steel mills, a bestseller that was made into a motion picture.

After the Nazi occupation of Czechoslovakia, Marcia Davenport became a close friend of the refugee Czech statesman, Jan Masaryk, and was active on behalf of the Czechoslovak cause during World War II. In 1945, at the invitation of President Beneš, she settled in Prague and remained there with Masaryk until the Communists seized power in 1948. She thereupon went to London, where she and Masaryk planned to be married as soon as he could join her but only a few days later he was found dead in mysterious circumstances. Returning to the U.S., Marcia Davenport resumed her literary career, and published *My Brother's Keeper* (1954) and *The Constant Image* (1960). Her autobiography, *Too Strong for Fantasy*, appeared in 1967.

[Milton Henry Hindus]

DA VERONA, GUIDO (1881–1939), Italian novelist. Da Verona sought to disguise his origin by changing his "Jewish" surname, Verona, to the more aristocratic Da Verona. His novels met with great success in the years which preceded and immediately followed World War I: he sold more than two million copies of his novels, thus becoming the harbinger of the new phenomenon of mass literature in Italy. Influenced by Gabriele d'Annunzio, Da Verona copied his prose style and dandyish ways; his stories are based on erotic themes, pervaded with an aestheticism in which he endeavored to create environments which were aristocratic, morbid, or exotic; hedonism and contempt for bourgeois morals satisfied the tastes of a large public whom he wished to please.

His best-known novels include *Colei che non si deve amare* (1911); *La vita comincia domani* (1912; *Life begins Tomorrow*, 1923); *Mimì Bluette, fiore del mio giardino* (1916; *Mimi Bluette*, 1929), his best book; *Sciogli le treccie, Maria Maddalena* (1920); and *Mata Hari* … (1927). In 1930 he published a parody of Alessandro Manzoni's masterpiece *I promessi sposi* (*The Betrothed*), in which one can recognize an implicit, but clear, satire of the Fascist régime. Progressively abandoned by his readers, victim of the anti-Jewish campaign of the late 1930s, he committed suicide.

ADD. BIBLIOGRAPHY: A. Arslan Veronese, "Guido da Verona," in: *Dizionario critico della letteratura italiana* (1986); T. Achilli, "Guido da Verona," in: G. De Donato and V. Gazzola-Stacchini (eds.), *I best seller del ventennio. Il regime e il libro di massa* (1991).

[Giorgio Romano / Alessandro Guetta (2nd ed.)]

DAVIČO, HAJIM S. (1854–1918), Serbian author and diplomat. Born into a patriotic Belgrade family, Davičo held consular posts in Munich, Salonika, and Trieste, but is mainly remembered as the pioneer of Jewish secular literature in Serbia. His two short story collections, *Perla* (1891) and *Sa Jalije* ("From Jalija," 1898), describe life among the Belgrade Sephardim and tensions between radicalism and Jewish tradition. He also engaged in business, acting as a supplier to Prince Milosh, and was a leading member of the Sephardi community. His signature appears on various petitions that Belgrade Jews addressed from time to time to the Serbian authorities.

ADD. BIBLIOGRAPHY: Ž. Lebl, *Do „konačnog rešenja" – Jevreji u Beogradu 1521–1942* (2001), 78, 92–93.

DAVIČO, LUJO (1908–1942), Yugoslav dancer and ballet teacher. Davičo was born in Belgrade (Serbia) of a large Sephardi family and studied ballet using Jacques Dalcroze's method in Geneva. In the 1930s he worked in Belgrade as a teacher and creator of dance performances following Dalcroze's method. He choreographed ballets accompanied by rhythm movements alone. Among his choreographies are **Kharaj* (meaning Muslim land tax), *Dalcroze March*, and *League of Nation*. His choreography also used folklore elements. As a freedom fighter opposing the Nazi-Italian occupation of Yugoslavia in 1941, he escaped to Montenegro and was killed participating in an attack on a group of Italian officers. A Belgrade ballet school was named after him. The Serbian National Ballet is named for him.

[Amnon Shiloah (2nd ed.)]

DAVIČO, OSCAR (1909–1989), Yugoslav poet and novelist. Born in Šabac, Serbia, Davičo was a high-school teacher but in 1932 was sentenced to five years' imprisonment for Communist activities. During World War II, he fought with the Yugoslav partisans against the Nazis. Before the war Davičo had been prominent in Belgrade as a surrealist writer and two of his early works were collections of verse, *Anatomija* (1930) and *Pesme* (1938). Davičo's postwar verse collections, notable for their nonconformism, their fantasy, and their erudite metaphors, include *Hana* (1951), *Čovekov čovek* ("A Man's Man," 1953), and *Trg eM* ("Square M," 1968). Although Davičo's rare references to his Jewish origin were made with a certain pride, his works displayed an increasingly anti-Zionist and anti-Israel bias. With *Pesma* (1952; *The Poem*, 1959), he published the first of a series of novels about the Nazi occupation, his own prison experiences, and his country's era of reconstruction. The later ones were *Beton i svici* ("Concrete and Glowworms," 1956), *Ćutnje* ("Silences," 1963), *Gladi* ("Hunger," 1963), *Tajne* ("Secrets," 1964), and *Begstva* ("Escapes," 1966). His novel *Gospodar zaborava* ("Master of Forgetfulness") appeared in 1980. Three of his novels were awarded Yugoslavia's highest literary prize. Davičo translated Thomas *Mann's novel *Buddenbrooks* into Serbo-Croat, and some of his own works have been translated into English and other languages. He was one of the editors of the literary periodical *Delo*. He also wrote a number of poems and other lyric compositions.

BIBLIOGRAPHY: Z. Gavrilovič, in: *Savremenik* (1956); *Lexikon der Weltliteratur im 20. Jahrhundert* (1960), 409; Finci, in: *Enciklopedija Jugoslavije*, 2 (1961), 668f.; M. Djilas, *Susreti*, 1 (1953), 128–32. **ADD. BIBLIOGRAPHY:** P. Palavestra, *Jevrejski pisci u srpskoj knjizevnosti* (1998); D. Katan Ben-zion, *Presence and Disappearance – Jews and Judaism in Former Yugoslavia in the Mirror of Literature* (2002), 261–66, 344–45 (Heb.).

[Zdenko Lowenthal]

DAVID (Heb. דָּוִד), youngest son of Jesse of the Ephrathite family that lived in Beth-Lehem in Judah (I Sam. 16:1; 20:27–28; I Chron. 2:13–15; cf. Micah 5:1).

In the Bible

SOURCES. I Samuel 16–II Kings 2 is our main source for David, supplemented by I Chronicles. Other texts name him, but in the main to emblematize either the dynasty in Jerusalem or a salvific ideal. He appears in superscriptions to many Psalms, on occasion (as Ps. 34:1) with historical references; but it is unclear whether this phenomenon originated as a historical or as a dramatic or musical notation.

Some scholars maintain that, like King Arthur, David is a late invention. But two stelae (Tel Dan, Mesha) indicate that by 830 or so Judah was identified as "the House of David." These stelae confirm that David was an earlier state-builder, and, according to ninth-century usage, the founder of its ruling dynasty. This ninth-century evidence explains his significance in the eighth and later centuries as an icon of Judah and as the progenitor of a line of kings whom YHWH adopted at accession (Isa. 9:5; cf. Ps. 2:6–7; 89:27–28). David's place in the dynastic liturgy long antedates the Exile.

Our sources in Samuel may be divided into three or more categories. In II Samuel, we have literature that is nearly contemporary with David himself, probably produced mainly in the court of Solomon. Some of this material is continuous with materials in I Samuel. Thus, it is certain that the materials admitting David's affiliation with Achish of Gath in I Samuel and the doublets – narratives with parallel narratives in another source about the same event evincing slight variation – pertaining thereto continue into II Samuel and issue ultimately into Solomon's ability to extract fugitives from Achish's Gath in I Kings 2:39–44. Thus, at a minimum, I Samuel 25–28:2; 29–30, belong to the same general source as does 2 Samuel. Conversely, I Samuel 23:19–24:23; 28:3–25; 31 all belong to another, parallel narrative.

I Samuel 8–15 represents itself as an account of the introduction of Saul's monarchy, while chaps. 16–31 concerns David's "rise" in interaction with Saul, of the tribe of Benjamin. This text consists of two parallel sources now in combination. A representative division yields narrative sources as follows:

A. I Sam. 9:1–10:13; 13:1–14:52; 17:12–31,41, 48b, 50, 55–58; 18:1–6a,10–11,17–19, 30; 20:1b–24:23; 28:3–25; 31.

B. II Sam. 8; 10:17–27; 11–12; 15–16; 17:1–11, 32–40, 42–48a, 49, 51–54; 18:6b–9, 12–16, 20–29; 19; 25–27; 28:1–2; 29–30; II Sam. 1ff.

Both sources contain legendary material, including one version of the account of David's slaying Goliath, which II Samuel 21:19 identifies as the victim of Elhanan (Ben-Dodo, the Bethlehemite; cf. I Chr. 20:5; Josephus, Ant. 7:302). Further legendary material shared by the sources is the etiology of the phrase, "Is Saul, too, among the prophets?" in 10:11, 19:24. This was originally a proverb, "Is it asked, too, among the prophets?" denoting problematic questions.

It is the material in the B source that seems to continue directly into II Samuel. Further, the B source concedes, while the A source denies, that David worked as a subordinate of the Philistines. Thus, whether or not the account of David's youth in this source is as early as the material in II Samuel, it seems to originate earlier than the A source in I Samuel. Arguably, both sources are composite, such that some material in each is early, other material later. All the same, the compilation of the A source postdates the compilation of the B source in this context.

Both sources cover David's youth. A's narrative focuses on Saul (chaps. 13–14; 28; 31). B's narrative shifts from Saul to David in I Samuel 16, and David remains its focus. B has been understood as an anti-monarchic source stemming from a very late period. It presents the monarchy, however, as an institution adopted by humans, and tolerated by YHWH, This view programmed later Israelite views of the monarchy (see Hos. 13:10; Deut. 17:14–15; Judg. 8:22–23). The A source, conversely, treats kingship as lowered from heaven. But, as it centers on Saul, and ends with his death at the Philistines' hands, its date, often thought to be early, is not clear. This source treats Saul's monarchy as an abortion, before the establishment of David's dynasty.

II Samuel, like the B source, evinces a date roughly contemporary with the events it reports. Foremost, it rebuts charges that David joined the Philistines in Saul's last battle, and incited the assassinations of Abner, Ishbaal, Absalom, Amasa, and all but one of Saul's descendants, not to mention Uriah the Hittite; these are figures whose political relevance, and, no doubt, memory had expired by the time of the Solomonic schism. Also, II Samuel makes very modest literal claims about David's conquests (see below, achievements), while later sources (Deuteronomy, Joshua, Chronicles, Josephus, and even II Kings 14:25) make much more grandiose claims. And, poetry preserved in II Samuel, such as David's laments over Saul and Abner, and his "last words," is unquestionably antique. The syntax of complex sentences in II Samuel is not, typically, that of later biblical prose. And the order of Israel's borders and components is different than in any later, standard, source. We may add that the settlement patterns, especially of the Negev and Philistia, reflected in the B source (I Sam. 27–30) and in II Samuel reflect realities of the 10th century, but not of subsequent eras. To take a particular example, I Samuel 27:6 claims that Ziklag remained subordinate to the kings of Judah. As Ziklag lay in the hinterland of Gath, it could not have belonged to kings of Judah after the eighth century B.C.E., and was probably not even settled in the ninth–eighth centuries. Finally, II Samuel starts a continuous reportage that ends at the end of II Kings in which reports of external contact are consistently corroborated and never falsified.

In II Samuel we learn of the death of Saul, David's accession in Judah and civil war with Ishbaal (I Chr. 8:33; 9:39, versus Ishboshet in Samuel – while most commentators believe the original name to have been altered in Samuel to avoid a reference to "Baal," a title rather than a name, that was used of YHWH in Israel, it is possible, despite the absence of the divine name from attested Israelite and Judahite epigraphs, that Samuel's version of the name is correct, and that it represents the Israelite equivalent of Egyptian *sbst*, "son of Bast," not to say "bastard"). David is then elected king of Israel; he conquers Jerusalem, and brings the ark there from the Gibeonite center, Kiryath-Jearim. YHWH then promises him an eternal dynasty. There follow accounts of foreign conquests, the Ammonite war and David's affair with Bath-Sheba, the Absalom revolt and its aftermath. Interspersed are details about David's offspring, officials, and army. A report about a census and the acquisition of the ground for the temple closes II Samuel.

I Chronicles 10–21 omits much from I Samuel 31–II Samuel 24. I Chronicles 22–29 reinterprets Solomon's designation as David's heir, stressing the planning of the temple and its liturgy. Chronicles does not speak of internal tensions, from Saul's time to the end of the Absalom revolt. It contains independent information about officials, but the text is usually derivative or projects later information into the past. However, Chronicles is important as a textual witness for reconstructing early readings in Samuel.

For David's sake, Samuel and Kings claim, YHWH forbears from destroying Judah (not Israel) because of a covenantal relationship. Kings also compares Judah's kings with and sometimes to David. Various prophets – Amos, Hosea, Isaiah, Jeremiah, and Ezekiel – refer to David as the emblem of the dynasty that will rule Israel in time. After the exile, so does Zechariah (chaps. 12–13). Ezra and Nehemiah, like Chronicles, remember David as a cult founder (for example, Ezra 3:10; 8:20; Neh. 12:24–46). Proverbs and Ecclesiastes cite David as an ancestor of their authors. Ruth presents itself as a story about David's ancestors and furnishes a genealogy to prove this. And, Song of Songs 4:4 mentions one of David's public works (similarly, in a way, II Kings 11:10, against which cf. II Kings 14:26–27; 10:16–17; II Sam. 8:7).

Finally, David appears in the superscriptions of numerous psalms, usually in an indeterminate setting. Several superscriptions stipulate particular conditions (as Ps. 52:2, 54:2) and in some cases psalms incorporate aspects of David's career or status (as 78, 89, 122, 132, 144). No reference is plainly early; Psalms 89, 132 address dynastic promises. Amos, however (6:5), already in the mid-eighth century, portrays David as a poet-courtier. Is the superscription "to David" musical, then, or dedicatory? Probably it has something to do with the king's role in the cult.

In the Tel Dan stela and probably the Mesha Stone, "the house of David" refers to the state administered in Jerusalem – Judah. The audience, learning that Israel "revolted against the house of David," thus (I Kings 12:19) probably took it to mean "revolted against (the state of) Judah." This is the only event in connection with which Kings mentions "the house of David"; the phrase is common, however, in Isaiah (7:2, 13; 22:22; cf. 9:6, 16:5, also 11:1–10) and in the post-exilic era.

NAME AND GENEALOGY. *Name.* At one time, scholars misidentified a cognate of David's name in Akkadian, and took it to mean, "leader". The root is *dwd*, usually "(paternal) uncle" or "beloved." However, no text contracts the diphthong. It is always spelled *dwd* or even *dwyd* (the *y* representing a vowel of the /i/-class), never *dd* (as "uncle" is sometimes written). The possibility of its meaning "beloved" as a bi-form of the root *ydd*, the root of Solomon's prophetically assigned name, Jedidiah, therefore remains. It is unlikely that there is any relation to the term for uncle.

Several other names are related to this one: *d(w)dw* (*Dodo*, Judg. 10:1; II Sam 23:9,24; I Chr. 11:12, 26; 27:4) and *Dodaw(y)ahu* (II Chr. 20:37), in which the diphthong is, however, contracted. Mesha, the late ninth century king of Moab, claims to have taken as booty the *'r'l dwdh*, the "Ariel" of (Ataroth's) *dwd*. He may also report removing the *'[r']ly yhwh*, two or more such objects dedicated to YHWH, from Nebo. The meaning of "Ariel" is unknown. It may be a sort of hero or statue or icon of a cult founder (for Moabites, II Sam 23:20 = I Chr. 11:22; also Isa. 29:1, 2, 7, as an epithet of Jerusalem). It also appears as a name (Gen. 46:16; Num. 26:17) and an altar (Ezek. 43:15–16).

Dwd in the Mesha stela is not proprietary to Judah. The inscription attests the fortification of Atarot and Nebo by Omri and Ahab, whose dynasty lent Israel its own dynastic name ("the house of Omri"). Nevertheless, the *dwd* of Ataroth was a significant item, as singular as YHWH. Since "paternal uncle" is rare as an element in Israelite names, David's name should be understood on Mesha's model. It probably is a divine epithet or hypostasis.

Antecedents. David's father is Jesse. The Hebrew, *y_š_y* (I Chr. 2:13 ʿ_š(y) is a hypocoristicon for a name name, like Ishbaal, "the Lord is (here)." The patronym is authentic: in direct discourse, David is called "the son of Jesse" only to derogate his claim to royalty. Of these contexts, one is Sheba's call to revolt (II Sam 20:1); the same cry recurs in I Kings 12:16, at the Solomonic schism: "We have no stake in David, nor legacy in the son of Jesse." It is first an outcry against David, but then against his dynasty (Sheba) and grandson (the Israelites at Shechem in I Kings 12). The antagonistic invocation of Jesse's name is evidence of David's paternity, as is the more positive reference to Jesse in Isaiah 11:1, 10. Finally, an archaic poem, David's Testament, describes him as "David son of Jesse" (II Sam 23:1), in terms comparable to the introduction of Balaam in oracular verse in Numbers and in the Deir Alla plaster inscriptions. Chronicles also refers to "David son of Jesse" in order to punctuate the narrative (I Chr. 10:14, 29:26; in poetry, I Chr. 12:18). However, the preservation of a patronymic suggest that David's father had an originally negative reputation of his own, or, minimally, had no proper claim to royal status. This inference dovetails with other information, concerning David's rise.

Later materials – the end of Ruth and I Chronicles 2:3–17 – trace David's ancestry back to the eponym Judah. The age of this tradition, which supplies the place of authentic royal ancestry, is probably reasonably old. It is difficult to imagine that the story of Judah's posterity in J (Gen. 38) is divorced from a concern to trace David's ancestry. Even more clearly, P, in the late seventh century, names David's ancestor, Nahshon, as a chief of Judah and husband of Aaron's sister (Ex. 6:23; Num 1:7). Some even argue that the story of David taking his parents to Moab for safekeeping (I Sam. 22:4) reflects the connection to Moab narrated in Ruth: the reverse is more likely: the admittedly peculiar reference in Samuel – which is of a piece with its account of David's relations with peripheral ethnicities – inspired the tale of Ruth.

Every tradition (Ruth; I Sam. 16, 17:15, 58, 20:6, 28) places David's family in Bethlehem. II Samuel 2:32 refers, unselfconsciously, to the ancestral tomb of Asahel, Joab's brother, there. Around 700 B.C.E., Micah 5:1 shares the tradition. Bethlehem, despite Rachel's tomb being associated with it (Gen. 35:19, 47:8; Jer. 41), was a backwater. David's affiliation with the village is thus secure.

YOUTH. I Samuel introduces David as designee to be the next king. He moves to Saul's court, and betroths one of Saul's daughters (Merab or Michal, depending on the source). In one version, David comes to Saul's court as a musician; in the other he arrives to fight Goliath, whom he dupes by promising close combat while using his sling at a distance. II Samuel 3 continues with a story of Michal's later delivery to David from her children and former husband, and her subsequent sequestration and childlessness.

During David's service to Saul, a ditty occasions Saul's anger: "Saul has slain his thousands, and David his myriads." At the time, David is Jonathan's armor-bearer. His later preservation of Jonathan's son, when allowing the extermination of Saul's offspring, attests this early relationship. Thus, Samuel makes David Saul's ally and a killer of Philistines. The aim of the earliest versions was to deny that he acted as a subordinate to the king of Gath, and that he remained a Philistine ally throughout his reign. David's protection of Jonathan's son Mephiboshet may therefore have been calculated policy, such that the special relationship with Jonathan may have been derived secondarily by an author of one of the two literary sources of II Samuel. It is uncertain whether David served Saul. No notice relating his men's deeds (II Sam 21:15–22, 23:6ff.) suggests that he did.

David *was* the vassal of Achish of Gath. One source claims that Achish rejected him (I Sam. 21:11–16). Another source admits that David worked for Achish but blunts the point of the embarrassment by alibiing David for the battle in which Saul perished. He *was* in the employ of the Philistine king of Gath, though driven there by Saul's rage, he *was* present, he *was* Achish's bodyguard, but was detailed to the rear; other Philistine kings dismissed him as a possible traitor; true, he was away from home, during the battle, but was chasing raiders around the south; and, he killed the messenger of Saul's death, who claimed to have killed him (I Sam. 27; 29–30; II Sam. 1).

David reigns seven years in Hebron (II Sam 2:2–4). Ishbaal reigns only two as Saul's successor. There was, however, no interregnum between Saul and Ishbaal (so II Sam 2:5–9: Abner crowns Ishbaal). Probably, David won northern constituencies after taking Jerusalem after Ishbaal's death. This explains why his alleged conflict with Philistia arises over Jerusalem. In Hebron, David's kingship was marginal, as the site's archaeology and the scant settlement of 11th century Judah suggest: he was a Philistine vassal. He was in name the same throughout his reign. But his taking of Jerusalem could be portrayed as the occasion of Israelite declarations of allegiance to him (II Sam. 5:1–3), and thus as his declaration of independence from Gath.

HISTORICAL RELATIONS WITH SAUL'S HOUSE. Reportedly on Saul's death, David penetrated into the hills of Judah (I Sam 30:1–2), establishing himself at Hebron. His expansion must reflect service to Achish, as the hills, previously, were virtually empty. From a base in Hebron, on the spine of the hills leading to Benjamin, David waged continued war with Ishbaal, Saul's son, and with Ishbaal's chief-of-staff, Abner (II Sam. 2–4). At the end of their conflict, Abner and 20 retainers brought Ishbaal's sister, Michal, to Hebron to be David's wife. (I Samuel claims she had been taken from David unjustly.) At the wedding banquet, David's general, Joab, ambushed Abner, and probably his escort. II Samuel 3 claims that Abner meant to betray Ishbaal, to hand David kingship over Israel. But here, as in the other cases in which Joab kills for David (Uriah, Absalom, Amasa), Joab suffers no penalty. Likewise, Samuel alleges that Michal was betrothed to David (I Sam 19:11–24) before being wed to Palti, an Israelite husband from whom Ishbaal delivered her to David. This narrative strategy transforms her delivery into the settlement of a contractual claim, and thus denies that it was the price of a peacemaking marriage alliance. Later, David sequestered Michal: he refused real alliance with Saul's house and limited the numbers of descendants of Saul. He also kept possession of Abner's corpse.

After Abner's murder, two "Gibeonites," from the town of Beeroth, brought Ishbaal's head to David, who thereafter maintained custody of it. David proclaimed his innocence in the matter and executed the assassins (II Sam. 4). The killers had good reason to expect a heartier reception; David had good reason for silencing them. Contemporaries must have accused him of ordering Abner's and Ishbaal's deaths.

Before Absalom's revolt, David sought an oracle about the cause of a famine. Conveniently, YHWH attributed it to Saul's war on the Gibeonites, which violated an earlier treaty (of which no one, one expects, had heard). David extradited Saul's surviving sons and grandsons for execution. Only after this did he return Saul's and Jonathan's corpses to the family tomb (II Sam. 21:1–14). His policy regarding Saulides was to export the living and import the dead.

David exempted only Saul's lame grandson, Jonathan's son. Mephiboshet (Meribbaal in I Chr. 8:34, 9:40) dwelled at the court, while a steward, Ziba, administered Saul's lands (II Sam. 4:4; 9). After the Absalom revolt, David awarded half the estate to Ziba (16:1–4, 19:25–31). The only other relation to survive the purge was Shimei, who accused David of murdering the entire family (II Sam. 16:5–10). Solomon later executed Shimei.

A final "Saulide" was David's son – if he was David's rather than Saul's – by Ahinoam of Jezreel, probably one of Saul's wives (below). Absalom assassinates Amnon, David's firstborn. Absalom's punishment is reasonably traditional, conforming to the pattern of expulsion for murder that is reflected in the punishments of Cain and Moses: three years in exile, and two after repatriation under house arrest. Still, this murder of Amnon removes the last vestige of Saul's dynasty, in the form of a wife's son, from the succession. The coincidence seems less coincidental when the narrative reports that David's nephew suggested the rape that Absalom avenged to Amnon (II Sam. 13:1–5).

David exterminated or permitted the extermination of Saul and his descendants. His hostages (Michal and Mephiboshet), and stories of his youth at Saul's court, friendship with Jonathan, and betrothal to Saul's daughters alibi him for the assassinations of Abner and Ishbaal and the executions of Saul's other descendants. All these presentations serve to insulate David against accusations that must have stemmed from his contemporaries. Any other explanation violates the nature of Near Eastern literary history, and will be too clever by half.

RISE TO KINGSHIP. David first became king in the town of Ziklag, as an appointee of Achish (probably Achaios, or "Achaean") of Gath. After Saul's death, since he is alibied regarding residence in Ziklag for that event, he seems to have claimed sovereignty over Judah from Hebron. Judah at the time was sparsely settled, especially outside the Shephelah. Pastoralists were probably traversing the Negev from Philistia to North Arabia at the time. Judah does not appear in

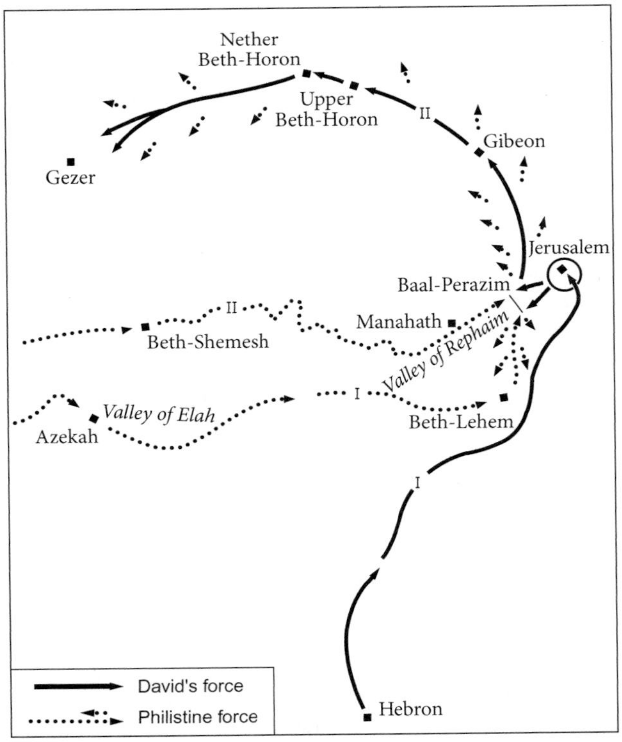

Map 1. David's conquest of Jerusalem and his wars against the Philistines. From Macmillan Bible Atlas, *Carta, Jerusalem, 1968.*

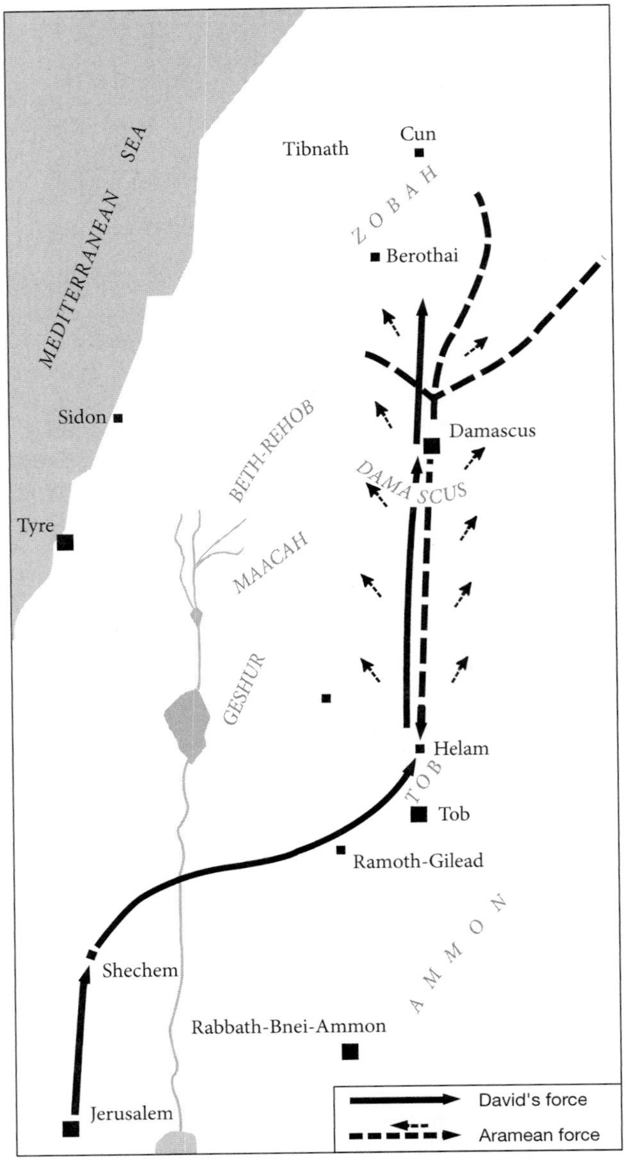

Map 2. David's conquest of Aram-Zobah and Aram-Damascus. From Macmillan Bible Atlas, *Carta, Jerusalem, 1968.*

any clearly premonarchic Israelite tradition (especially Judg. 5:13–18). No such defined geographical entity existed before David occupied Hebron. Benjamin, "the son of the south," was then the name for Israel's southlands, Judah included.

Even in Hebron, David continued to contain Israelites from reaching or threatening the Philistine plain in the Shephelah, particularly at Gath. He may have helped to project a threat against Ekron. He also engaged in marital diplomacy. His first wife, Ahinoam, was from Jezreel in the Jezreel Valley (the southern Jezreel was unoccupied). The Bible's only other Ahinoam was Jonathan's mother: David took her from Saul. Abigail, David's second wife, was probably David's sister. Her first husband, Nabal, was a man of parts in Judah (I Sam.

25; cf. II Sam. 17:25; I Kings 2:32; I Chr. 2:17). Marriages with Ahinoam and one of Saul's daughters (Michal/Merab) staked a claim on Saul's kingdom. Marriage with Abigail established a claim on Judah. A marital alliance with the king of Geshur (in the Golan) then surrounded Israel. David added appeals to Transjordan to defect from Ishbaal (II Sam. 2:5–7), made an early alliance with the Ammonites, and, late in his reign, made an alliance with Tyre. Combining the peripheral powers with alliances in Philistia, another border region, David engulfed the northern tribes. He enlisted Gibeonites north of Jerusalem and other mercenary elements, including "Gittites," some of whom stemmed from Kiryath-Jearim, a Gibeonite town. His coalition was directed almost exclusively against the denizens of Israel's heartland.

According to II Samuel 2, David asked Gileadites (elements in Transjordan) to recognize him as king. In Samuel the collaborators represent the whole of Israel. But the course of David's subjection of the north is far from perspicuous, and may have resulted in real control only after the Absalom result. That the coercion was an element of the process is clear from II Samuel's defense of Solomon's succession, and from Absalom's rebellion against David, including the tribes of Israel, and Jeroboam's successful revolt against Rehoboam's succession. David was, in the end, a Middle Eastern politician, and can only have ruled by division and terror.

ADMINISTRATION AND ACHIEVEMENTS. II Samuel identified David's officials by place of origin (Ittay the Gittite, for example, is probably Ittay son of Ribay from Kiryath-Jearim) or by ethnic or clan affiliations (Uriah the Hittite, among others). On the same model, I Samuel supplies a list of Saul's officers. I Kings 4 provides an even fuller list of Solomon's officials, mainly provincial administrators. Yet nothing comparable appears later in Kings, again distinguishing writing about the United Monarchy from that about its successor regimes. The reports about the course of bureaucratization attest the development of the state. Later titulature, attested in Kings and in epigraphs, indicates a far more extensive administrative apparatus.

Foreigners serving David as mercenaries, his collusion with Gibeonite aliens in exterminating Saul's house (and his enfranchisement of them in the army and the cult), and the patterns of his diplomacy, threatened Israel. I–II Samuel insist on his popular election. Still, only David's campaign for reelection after the Absalom revolt indicates a historical, not just literary, dependence on some measure of popular support. Notably, after the Absalom revolt, Joab undoes the compromise reflected in the appointment of Amasa, Absalom's commander-in-chief, to be David's chief of staff. The parallel to Abner's death will not have been lost on contemporary northerners.

The most diagnostic element of any narrative history is its omissions. Samuel is no exception. David introduced a new icon, the ark, into a new capital (II Samuel 6–7). He did not build a temple, and did not organize a centralized state.

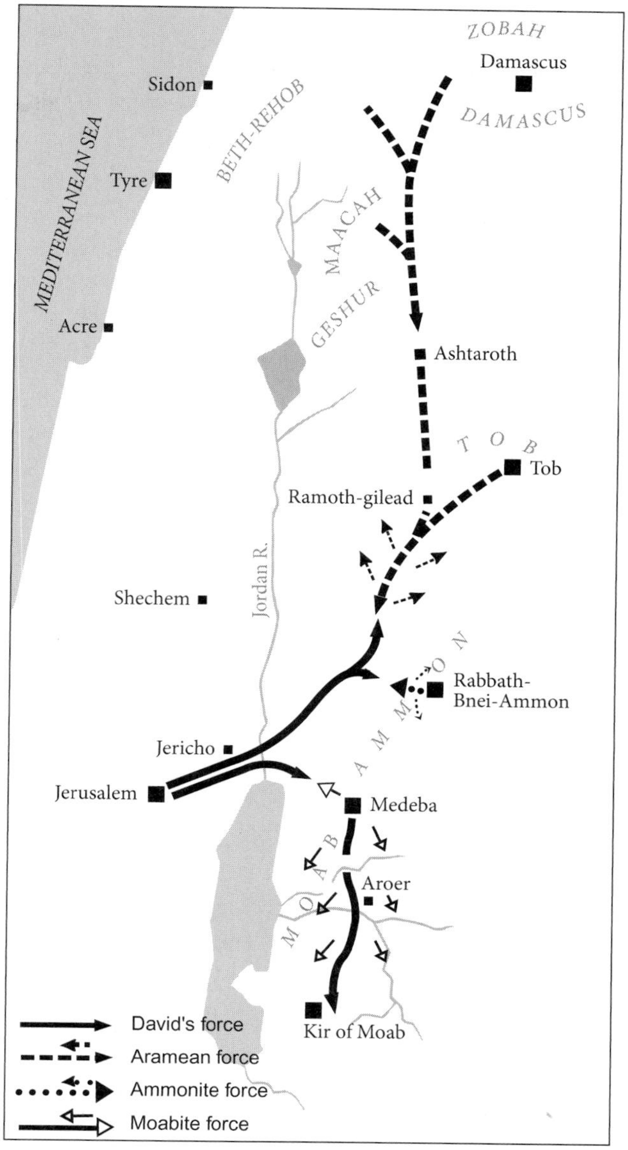

Map 3. David's wars against Moab, Aram and Ammon. From Macmillan Bible Atlas, *Carta, Jerusalem, 1968.*

He undertook no public works. Nor did he conquer any lowland fortresses. These silences speak legions about the nature of his bandit state.

David has left the imprint as a state-builder and conqueror on Western consciousness. Still, Samuel, the earliest source about his activity, alleges little in the way of conquest. He fails to expand to Gezer, or in Philistia proper: until Solomon's day, Gezer was "Canaanite." As king, David encounters Philistines only in the vicinity of Jerusalem. He subjects Aram-Zobah, but probably on the field in Transjordan (II Sam. 10) rather than campaigning to the north. He attacks some elements of population in Ammon, Moab, and Edom. But nothing suggests a campaign north of Dan. The northernmost activity in which David's troops are said to engage takes place at Abel Bet-Maacah. And in Transjordan his only clear achievement, by proxy, is the taking of Ammon's capital, sometime before the Absalom revolt. He garrisons some territory belonging to Damascus, not the city itself. He kills some Moabites. Only in the case of Edom is he said to have taken the whole territory – probably corresponding with the 50 or so caravan stations erected in the Negev in the 10th century.

The only instance in which a real policy history can be reconstructed is that of Ammon. David allied with its king, Nahash, an enemy of Saul's. When Nahash died, David took the capital, installing Hanun, a son of Nahash, as the latter's successor. Later, during Absalom's revolt, along with Gileadite allies, Hanun abetted David against the tribal militias of Israel and Judah. It is no coincidence, then, that Hanun's daughter became the mother of Solomon's successor, no fewer than two years before David's death. Ammon was in thrall to David, but was indispensable to his domestic authority.

Israel's expansion into the lowlands – which Solomon possessed, as texts and archaeological evidence attest – and into Transjordan should, at least in theory, have created a sense of "nationalism." Reality, however, differs from theory, and the narrative of the process of expansion covers the reality up. The mercenary base of the early monarchy kept countryside lineages in fear of losing autonomy. This fear undoubtedly fed Absalom's revolt, directed not against the dynasty, at least among the small population of Judah and that of Benjamin and southern Ephraim, but against David personally. It was a war concerning the succession.

Absalom's revolt was a war of Israel, and much of Judah, and probably parts of Philistia and Canaan, on David. Naturally, the narrative does not mention external enemies or allies – the Ammonites and Gileadites appear only to provision David in need, and the Gittites appear only in the form of David's mercenary army, not as outside supporters. Thus, the narrative does not represent the episode as involving anyone but Judah and Israel – a highly improbable scenario, but one useful for internal dissemination. II Samuel portrays the revolt as divine vengeance for the cuckolding and murder of Uriah the Hittite. This implies the rebels were on the side of the angels, so to speak. And, Absalom's daughter became Solomon's heir Rehoboam's first wife, clearly in a strategy of national reconciliation. Our text also insists that David actively campaigned for and earned reelection as king after the revolt (II Samuel 19), winning partly because he promised to replace his hatchet man, Joab, as national commander with the rebel general, Amasa. The text then blames Amasa's assassination, which follows immediately, on Joab, when Sheba son of Bichri revolts – a rebel without an army whose head is unceremoniously hurled over the wall of Abel BetMaacah, probably just then incorporated into the boundaries of David's Israel. With David's professional army dominant, the humiliating campaign for reelection and the appointment of Amasa suggest the importance of claiming popular support.

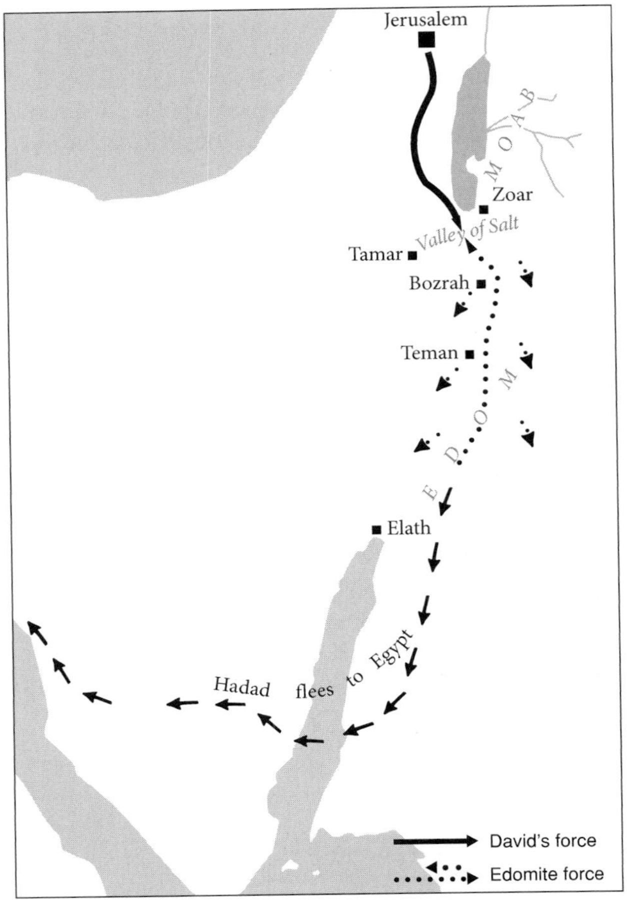

Map 4. David's conquest of Edom. From Macmillan Bible Atlas, *Carta, Jerusalem, 1968.*

David's religious policies are obscure. He adopted the ark from the Gibeonite city of Kiryath-Jearim as a state symbol. He also created two state priesthoods – one, from Judah, claiming descent from Aaron, and another from Shiloh, probably claiming descent from Moses. He naturally permitted countryside priests to continue as they had in the pre-monarchic period. While later temple liturgy (as Psalm 89) and the historiography (II Samuel 7) claim that YHWH endorsed eternal Davidic dynasty, alternative views (as Psalm 132) were fashioned in Judah to explain Israel's secession on Solomon's death.

One Davidic achievement was the establishment of control of movement in the Negev. Arabian caravan traffic to the coast assumed an immense importance at the end of the Late Bronze Age, and thereafter. The spices (including what we would call drugs, for the spice trade was in great measure the drug trade), crossed the Sinai and Negev at Egypt's expense, until Shishak's raid, five years after Solomon's death. Later, Necho, Josiah, and even Nabonidus would contest its direction.

David created a nation, Judah. His dynasty endured for almost 500 years. He also inevitably initiated a rift between popular and elite sovereignty, despite adhering, like Augustus in Rome, to the forms of popular election. Both before and after the Absalom revolt, according to the apology in II Samuel, David insisted on election by the people, or by the people's representatives. In appearance, David deferred to an Israelite mode of hinterland living that broke the traditional link between city-state monarchies and temple building, such that the shrine was not a permanent structure in the royal capital. In introducing the ark – which Saul had not embraced, and which had previously been tended by Gibeonites, against whom Saul actually waged campaigns – into the capital, David subverted this apparent deference, creating a state shrine. And yet, David's Jerusalem was not a proper city-state – it was more of a bolt hole. It was, in fact, not even a city, as its archaeological markers are all at least in large part absent.

Indeed, more than anything, what marks David's reign politically is an ongoing linkage with and reliance on foreigners, especially Gittites and Gibeonites, and a steady aversion to public works. II Samuel attributes almost no public building to him. Nor have archaeologists uncovered remains, with the possible exception of the "stepped stone structure" in Jerusalem, that could reasonably be attributed to him. It is true that Stratum VB at Megiddo is often attributed to his reign; however, it contains no clear monumental structure, and may well either antedate his conquest of Israel or reflect a very late period of his sovereignty.

In sum, David was never a builder, never an acolyte of monumental construction. His limited kingdom did not permit him to think of himself in these terms. It was left to his successor – perhaps the son of a mercenary named Uriah – to undertake the organization of states inside Israel and to impose heavy, or usual, taxation on them, so as to undertake construction in the countryside and in the capital. Only from Solomon's time do we have reports and archaeological reflexes of monumental construction.

SUCCESSION. David played the succession close to his vest. Of his sons, the third, Absalom, killed the eldest, Amnon, and was in turn killed by Joab in his, Absalom's, revolt. The second son, by Abigail, is never mentioned after his birth. The fourth, Adonijah, was widely expected to succeed.

The succession contest recapitulated the tensions of Absalom's revolt. Popular expectation focused (hopefully?) on Adonijah and Joab's support suggests that he was David's designee. Party to the Pretender was the Elide priest, Abiathar. Thus, traditional forces, in the court and at large, stood behind Adonijah's candidacy.

Solomon's succession, sympathetically presented, remains a coup. Behind Solomon stand: Zadok, the Judahite priest; Benaiah, the mercenary captain; and, the mercenaries of the capital, such as the Gittites. Solomon's administration, with its emphasis on public works and the exactions they required, colors the contrast with David. Yet conciliatory maneuvers early in Solomon's reign – Rehoboam's marriage to Absalom's daughter, the writing of II Samuel to exculpate David from political murders and Israel's population from treason because YHWH encouraged the revolt, and even the construction of the temple with its implications of tax relief for the laborers as a form of tax remission, all suggest that the transition was gradual. Solomon began by pursuing his father's course; only when a threat materialized from Egypt, in his 24th year, did the impulse to modernization assume urgency. For this reason, public works, for example at Megiddo, were not completed before the destruction of the Solomonic layer there. What is more, the Solomonic layers may in many cases have represented facades, at Hazor, Megiddo, and Gezer, in the first instance.

REASONS FOR DAVID'S PLACE IN TRADITION. David became the template for the future identification of Judah's king as the messiah, YHWH's "anointed": he was the adopted son of YHWH, a notion that derives from the temple royal ideology during the centuries leading up to the Babylonian exile. As a dynastic founder, David personified YHWH's reign over Judah, and, by extension, Israel. Later reinterpretation of the conception of David *redivivus* – adumbrated in the comparison of Judah's kings to him in the books of Kings and Psalms – and of the enthronement metaphor of his divine sonship led to their ratification as a future hope in a period without Davidic kings (the Restoration). In addition, the image of David as cult founder, full-blown in the presentation of I Chronicles, derives from the assignment to his reign of the dynastic charter, usually associated with temple building, and from the superscriptions to the Psalms.

While Israel's golden age is usually associated with Solomon, the Davidic figure, far more swashbuckling and more tragically human, naturally attracted the attention and the affection of later readers. The glory of David is thus in his commemoration, and in the reverberation of his image through the ages. The idea of a Messiah based on David, the idea of a David in the Psalms, the idea of a David as the progenitor of David – all these things are based on the reception in Judah of the literature, and particularly the historiography, about this king. Thus the literary presentation, starting with Samuel and continuing through Chronicles and into rabbinic literature, created an image that had enduring power throughout the ages.

[Baruch Halpern (2nd ed.)]

In the *Aggadah*

David's image in the *aggadah* is many-faceted. The unique status of his monarchy – in contrast to that of the other kings of Israel – is frequently emphasized: "The sovereignty of David shall never lapse" (Yal., Num. 771). The Midrash even declares that God "looks forward to David's being king until the end of the generations" (Gen. R. 88:7), and that "whoever contends against the sovereignty of the house of David deserves to be bitten by a snake" (Sanh. 110a). In this emphasis there is an echo of the dispute which, in its time, divided Judaism after the establishment of the dynasty of the Hasmoneans, who were not of Davidic descent (see *David, Dynasty of).

PHARISAIC SUPPORT OF DAVID'S DYNASTY. The Pharisees did not deny that, according to the *halakhah*, kings who were not of the house of David could be appointed (Hor. 13a; et al.); but they made a clear distinction between them by stressing that the dynasty of the House of David was eternal, and by placing limits upon the authority of the other kings: only kings of the House of David could judge and be judged themselves, and not kings of Israel (Sanh. 19a); kings of the House of David were anointed, but not kings of Israel (Hor. 11b); and even when kings of Israel were anointed (when the succession was in dispute), oil of balsam was to be used and not the prescribed anointing oil. It was also ruled: "In the Temple court, the kings of the House of David alone are permitted to sit" (Sot. 41b).

OPPONENTS OF THE DAVIDIC DYNASTY. On the other hand there were extremists who were opposed to the Davidic dynasty. Echoes of it are heard in the talmudic discussion (Yev. 76b–77a) dealing with the permission of Ammonite and Moabite women to intermarry with Jews: "Doeg the Edomite said to Abner, the son of Ner, 'Instead of inquiring whether he [David] is worthy to be king or not, inquire whether he is permitted to enter the assembly of Jews at all.' Why? 'Because he is descended from Ruth the Moabitess!' Abner said to him, 'We have been taught that only an Ammonite [is forbidden], but not an Ammonitess, a Moabite, but not a Moabitess'" (see: *Ammonites and Moabites in the *halakhah*). According to Aptowitzer, this passage alludes to the efforts of the Sadducees in the Sanhedrin of Hyrcanus to disqualify the House of David from reigning, an effort which they were compelled to abandon by use of force on the part of the Pharisees and their supporters outside the Sanhedrin. In Aptowitzer's opinion, the reference by Josephus (Wars, 1:54ff.) to a revolt in the days of Hyrcanus is to this incident. In this connection the Midrash states (Ruth R. 8:1): "David said before the Holy One, 'How long will they agitate against me, saying, Is he not of tainted descent? Is he not descended from Ruth the Moabitess?'" In order to impress the importance of the House of David upon the consciousness of the people, the rabbis laid down that, "Whoever does not mention the kingdom of the House of David in the blessing 'Who buildest Jerusalem' in the Grace after Meals, has not fulfilled his obligation" (Ber. 48b). In the **Amidah* prayer, too, they included a prayer for the restoration of the kingdom of the House of David.

DAVID'S PHYSICAL STRENGTH. Already as a youth David displayed extraordinary physical strength, one day slaying four lions and three bears (Mid. Sam. 20:5). With only one throw of his javelin he could kill 800 men (MK 16b). It was only as a simple shepherd, however, that he confronted Goliath. The five stones came to him of their own accord. They represented God, Aaron, and the three patriarchs (Mid. Sam. 21:1). One stone alone, which was guided by an angel, sufficed to kill Goliath (Mid. Ps. to 144). David waged 18 battles – five for his own benefit and 13 on behalf of Israel (Lev. R. 1:4), always attributing his victory to God (Mid. Ps. to 144). When he went to war, David made himself hard as steel (MK 16b).

DAVID AS A POET. The rabbis speak in superlatives of David's poetic genius. "While still dwelling in his mother's womb, he recited a poem … he contemplated the day of death and recited a poem" (Ber. 10a). The biblical account of David's playing the harp before Saul is enlarged in the *aggadah*: "a harp was suspended above his bed … as soon as midnight arrived, a north wind came and blew upon it and it played of itself" (Ber. 3b). The Talmud discusses the question of whether the psalms are to be regarded as entirely David's work or as a collection of compositions by various poets, including David, who edited them. R. Meir's view is: "All the praises stated in the Book of Psalms were uttered by David" (Pes. 117a). The statement (BB 14b) that "David wrote the Book of Psalms, including in it the work of 10 elders" is understood in the light of the Midrash (Eccl. R. 7:19 no. 4): "Although 10 men composed the Book of Psalms, it is named after none of them but after David." The rabbis perceived something of a contradiction between David's preoccupation with poetry and his involvement with Torah, saying, "This is what David meant: 'Midnight never found me asleep.' Until midnight he studied the Torah; thereafter he recited songs and praises" (Ber. 3b).

DAVID AS A SCHOLAR. David was exalted by the rabbis as a halakhic authority and a Torah scholar, his diligence being such that the Angel of Death was powerless over him because "his mouth did not cease from learning," the study of Torah protecting one from death. It was only when by a ruse the Angel of Death interrupted his study that he was able to claim him (TJ, Shab. 30). David's wish was: "May it be Thy will that words of Torah be repeated in my name in this world" (Yev. 96b). His great diligence is also reflected in the statement, "David said, 'Lord of the Universe! Every day I would think of going to a certain place or to a certain dwelling, but my feet would bring me to synagogues and to places of study'" (Lev. R. 35:1); and, "David said: 'The Holy One, blessed by He, has made a covenant with me that I shall master Scripture, Mishnah, Midrash, *halakhot*, and *aggadot*'" (Yal., II Sam. 165). David appears also as a halakhic authority and *av bet din* (Ber. 4a), and the decree forbidding a man to be alone with an unmarried woman is attributed to his *bet din* (Sanh. 21b; et al.). "Every one who went out in the wars of the house of David wrote a bill of divorce for his wife, so that she could remarry, should he fail to return and her status be uncertain" (Shab. 56a). He composed many prayers and it was he who set the number of priestly divisions at 24 (Ta'an. 27a).

THE BATH-SHEBA EPISODE. The rabbis are frequently openly critical of David. With reference to the episode of Bath-Sheba, however, the general tendency is to exonerate him from all blame, both in respect to the law itself since he decreed that "every one who goes out to war shall write a bill of divorce to his wife" (Shab. 56a), and Bath-Sheba was thus a divorcee; and because of his wholehearted remorse after the deed: "David said before the Holy One, blessed be He, 'Lord of the universe! Forgive me for that sin.' 'It is forgiven you,' He replied. 'Give me a sign during my lifetime,' he entreated. 'During your lifetime I shall not make it known,' He answered, 'But I shall make it known during the life of your son Solomon'" (Shab. 30a). Some go even further, saying: "Whoever says David sinned is mistaken ... he contemplated the act, but did not go through with it" (Shab. 56a).

RABBINIC CRITICISM OF DAVID. The rabbis enumerated other failings of David. In the opinion of the rabbis, it was David's overweening self-confidence which led him to beg God to put him to the test with Bath-Sheba so that he could prove himself comparable in that respect to Abraham, Isaac, and Jacob (Sanh. 107a). They maintained that his tongue was not free from taint. David, in his entreaty to Saul, says, "If it be the Lord that hath stirred thee up against me, let Him accept an offering" (I Sam. 26:19). The rabbis consider this an unbecoming allusion to God, and, in their opinion, David came to grief because of it in the matter of the census: "The Holy One said to David, 'You call me one who stirs up; I shall cause you to stumble over a thing which even schoolchildren know, that which is written, And when thou takest the sum of the children of Israel, according to their number, they shall give every man a ransom for his soul'" (Ber. 62b). Nor was he innocent of slander. He believed in Ziba's calumniation of his master Mephibosheth, that he intended treachery against David (Yoma 22b). He rejoiced at Saul's downfall: "The Holy One said to David, 'David, you sing a song at Saul's downfall? Were you Saul and he David, I would have destroyed many Davids before him'" (MK 16b). He employed inappropriate language in reference to Torah, referring to its words as "songs" (Sot. 35a), and he is responsible for the wrong path taken by his children. "Because David did not rebuke or chastise his son Absalom, he fell into evil ways and sought to slay his father ... David treated Adonijah similarly, neither rebuking nor punishing him, and therefore he became depraved, as it is written, 'His father had not grieved him'" (Ex. R. 1:1).

[Israel Moses Ta-Shma]

TOMB OF DAVID. According to the Bible, David was buried in the "city of David" presumably in the southeast of the present Siloam area (I Kings 2:10). Traditionally the later kings of the Davidic dynasty were also buried there and the Bible refers to the "sepulchers of the sons of David" (II Chron. 32:33), whose site was still known in the time of Nehemiah (Neh. 3:16). The tombs were in Jerusalem, but were never touched (Tos. B.B. 1:11). According to Josephus Herod broke into David's tomb to rob it, but when he tried to go into the inner chamber tongues of fire shot out (Jos., Ant., 16:7:1). The site is also mentioned in the New Testament (Acts 2:29). The tomb of David was probably destroyed at the time of the Bar Kokhba revolt (135 C.E.), and afterward the exact location of the site was forgotten. However, various sites were suggested by popular traditions over the ages and the one which became generally accepted was the place now called Mt. Zion. This tradition is about 1,000 years old, first being recorded in Crusader times, and was accepted in Jewish, Muslim, and Christian traditions. Benjamin of Tudela (c. 1173) reports a story about the miraculous discovery of David's tomb on Mt. Zion during the repairing of a church on the site. The site was in the hands of Muslims and Christians at various periods and came under Jewish control after the Israel War of Independence in 1948. It became a special center for Jewish pilgrims in the period from 1948 to 1967 because the most revered Jewish site, the Western Wall, was not accessible to Jews and David's Tomb was the closest point to the Old City of Jerusalem. Oriental Jews especially made pilgrimages to the site on all three festivals and particularly on Shavuot, the traditional date of David's death.

In the Liturgy

David figures in the liturgy both as the "sweet singer of Israel" and as the founder of the dynasty which according to Jewish tradition is eternal and is therefore destined to be restored. The concluding blessing to the extended **Pesukei de-Zimra* which are recited on Sabbaths and festivals – consisting as they do, both in the Ashkenazi and Sephardi rites, almost exclusively of psalms – states that it is the duty of all creatures to praise and extol God "even beyond the words of song and adoration of David the son of Jesse, Thine appointed servant." A similar reference is made in the *Kedusha* to the Sabbath morning *Amidah*. Much more prominent is the hope of the restoration of the Davidic dynasty, and, of course, it has messianic undertones. The subject of the 15th blessing of the *Amidah*, it is also implied in two passages of the *Grace after Meals. "Have mercy upon ... the kingdom of the House of David Thine anointed" and "showeth lovingkindness to His anointed, to David and his seed for evermore." (The addition to the Grace for the Intermediate Days of Sukkot also prays for God to "raise up the fallen tabernacle (*sukkah*) of David" (Amos 9:11)).

The most intriguing mention, however, is in the third of the four blessings which follow the reading of the *haftarah*: "Gladden us, O Lord our God ... with the kingdom of the House of David Thine anointed. Soon may he come and rejoice our hearts. Suffer not a stranger to sit upon his throne, nor let others any longer inherit his glory; for by Thy Holy Name Thou didst swear unto him that his light should not be quenched for ever. Blessed art Thou, O Lord, the Shield of David." The text of these blessings (with variations) is given in *Soferim* (13:13); that this blessing ends with "the Shield of David" is already mentioned in the Talmud (Pes. 117b). Various suggestions have been put forward to explain the connection between the prayer and the *haftarah*. It is bound up with the unsolved question as to the date and the circumstances of the introduction of the prophetic reading. Rabbi J.L. *Maimon (Fishman) puts forward the suggestion that it may have been a polemic against the Samaritans who denied both the sanctity of Jerusalem and the rights of the House of David (*Ha-Ẓiyyonut ha-Datit ve-Hitpatteḥutah* (1937), 68–69). If the view of *Abudarham, that the *haftarah* was instituted during the persecutions of *Antiochus Epiphanes as a substitute for the proscribed reading of the Pentateuch, can be accepted, it might equally have been a kind of protest against the royal aspirations of the *Hasmoneans, who were not of royal stock. A curious reference to David occurs in the liturgy of the Blessing of the New *Moon (*Kiddush Levanah*). It includes the phrase "David, King of Israel is alive and existing." The inclusion of this phrase is undoubtedly connected with an incident related in the Talmud (RH 25a) to the effect that R. Judah ha-Nasi sent R. Ḥiyya to sanctify the moon in a place called Ein Tov and send him the news that this had been done in these words. Moses *Isserles however states that the reason is "that his kingdom is compared to the moon (cf. Ps. 89:38) and like it will be renewed" (OḤ 426:2).

[Louis Isaac Rabinowitz]

In Kabbalah

The kabbalists saw in David the man who symbolized in the "quality of Kingdom" (*middat ha-Malkhut*), the tenth and last of the *Sefirot*. In Sefer ha-*Bahir, it is stated that this quality was offered to each of the three patriarchs, but they asked that they be given their own particular qualities and it was then given to David. David's name is the regular attribute of the *Sefirah Malkhut* which found its expression in his leadership. As a counterpart to the biblical King David, God has "another David" (*David aḥra*) who is in charge of all the inhabitants of the upper world, and he is the *Shekhinah* (Zohar, 3:84a). Together with Abraham, Isaac, and Jacob, David constitutes the "fourth leg of the *Merkabah"; or of the throne, in an extension of the midrashic saying: "It is the patriarchs who are the Merkabah" (Gen. R. 47:7). The symbolism of the "kingdom" as a *Sefirah* which has no light of its own but which receives its light from the other nine *Sefirot* above it, like the moon from the sun, has a basis in midrashic legends. There it is said that David was meant to live only a few hours, but Adam foresaw this and gave David 70 years of the thousand years which were allotted to him (Zohar). His constant study of the Torah, so that "his mouth never ceased reciting the Torah," is explained in *Sefer ha-Bahir* as his being a symbol for the attribute of "Oral Law," which is also the tenth *Sefirah*. In *Sefer ha-Peli'ah* the story of David, Uriah, and Bath-Sheba is explained as a symbolic repetition of the sin of Adam, performed in order to rectify that sin; i.e., the killing of Uriah, who symbolizes the primordial serpent, rectifies the sin, since King David is the reincarnation of the first man (the name Adam being interpreted as the initials of the names Adam, David, *Messiah). Evil and the *kelippah* (lit. "husk") also find their rectification (*tikkun*) in David in another way. David was ruddy, like the wicked Esau, but while the redness of Esau was "without any mixture of goodness and beauty," David's redness was rectified by his being "ruddy and withal of beautiful eyes"; for Esau inherited the sword and the shedding of blood, but David inherited the attribute of kingship "to act with mercy and charity and to kill according to the law" (Joseph *Gikatilla, *Sha'arei Orah*). His descent from Ruth the Moabitess is also repeatedly commented upon in the esoteric manner: David, the first Messiah, like the last Messiah, had of neccessity to descend from a mixture with the *sitra aḥra* ("other side," i.e., evil) so that he should be able to overcome the evil power which is rooted in the *sitra aḥra*; for man can only overcome that which is within himself (Joseph *Caro, *Maggid Mesharim*). When the custom of a *melavveh malkah* meal, i.e., a fourth meal at the end of the Sabbath day, became widespread (under the influence of Lurianic Kabbalah) this meal was named "King David's meal."

[Gershom Scholem]

In Christianity

David's importance for Christianity derives from the fact that Jesus was considered the Messiah, son of David. In the Gospels (Mark 12:35–37; Matt. 22:41–45; Luke 20:41–44), Jesus himself does not claim to be a descendant of the House of David, nor do his contemporaries know of such a connection (John 7:41–42). The title "Son of David," bestowed upon Jesus by sufferers turning to him for help, merely denotes the Messiah, a title also bestowed upon Bar Kokhba by Rabbi *Akiva. By Paul's generation, however, Christians already believed that Jesus was descended from the House of David (II Tim. 2:8; Heb. 7:17). Consequently two distinct and very artificial genealogies of Jesus were traced (Matt. 1:1–7; Luke 3:23–38).

David, like other biblical figures, was considered by Christian authors as a "type" of Jesus, and they explained biblical stories about David as referring to him. For medieval authors, David is the supreme example of the poet. He was the patron of the poets' guild (Meistersinger). The Christians considered David a prophet as well; according to the well-known church hymn *Dies irae*, he prophesied the End of Days. As David was also the embodiment of valor to the Christians, he was regarded in medieval times as an exemplary knight. In addition he was considered an exemplary king; Charlemagne liked his courtiers to call him "the new David." The Armenian Bagratid dynasty traced their lineage to David and Bath-Sheba, as Ethiopian monarchs do to Solomon the son of David. The Church regarded David as the prototype of a king obeying its precepts, and his anointment by Samuel was the basis for that of kings and emperors by the Church during the Middle Ages.

[David Flusser]

In Islam

David (Ar. Dā'ūd, also Dāwūd) was a figure known to the poets of Arabia during the *jāhiliyya* (heathen period before Muhammad). In their poems David was considered the inventor of coats of mail; they also knew of his connection with the *zabūr* (Psalms). Occasionally, his son Suleiman (Solomon) is also mentioned as the inventor of coats of mail – various characteristics were attributed to both of them. Muhammad also says that Allah taught David how to make armor (Sura 21:80), as well as how to soften iron (Sura 34:10). Muhammad, as well, mentions that Allah gave the *zabūr* (see Islam in the *Bible) to David (Sura 17:57).

David's victory over Jālūt (*Goliath) is mentioned in Sura 2:252. David was considered Allah's substitute (*khalīfa*) on earth in judging men with justice (Sura 38:35–38). Once, two men came to him to judge in their dispute. One of them owned 99 sheep and the second, only one; in spite of this the wealthy man also sought the sheep of the poor man (this seems to be an allusion to the episode of Uriah and the parable told by Nathan the prophet (II Sam. 11–12)). On another occasion Muhammad mentions a righteous judgment pronounced by David and Solomon in the matter of a field in which strangers pastured their flocks (Sura 21:78). The maximum brevity with which this judgment is mentioned shows that the story itself was very well known. The Midrash (Ex. R. 2:3) cites the test experienced by David who led his sheep through the wilderness, only in order to keep them from robbing [private fields]. Among the tales about David there is one which is influenced by Christianity. In Sura 5:82 it is related that David and Isa (Jesus) cursed a number of the people of Israel because they did not observe the precepts of God. The mention of David together with Jesus seems to indicate that Muhammad received this tradition from Christians. In the post-Koranic literature an important place is devoted to the life of David, which also served as a model in the elaboration of the biography of Muhammad. The events connected with the scheming of Tālūt (Saul), the revolt of Absalom, and the latter's death are cited. In Muslim legends of a later date, mention is also made of David's ties with Jerusalem and his tomb on Mount Zion. In Judeo-Arabic poetry the Davidic kingdom-to-come is referred to.

[Haïm Z'ew Hirschberg]

In Modern Hebrew Literature

David has fired the imagination of many modern Hebrew writers who have depicted different aspects of his life in a variety of literary genres. Haskalah literature did not create a character of depth. Romantic themes, whether it be romantic love or a pastoral yearning, dominated these Haskalah works. Thus the dramatis personae in *Melukhat Sha'ul ha-Melekh ha-Rishon al Yeshurun* ("The Reign of Saul the First King of Israel," 1794), a play by Joseph Ha-Efrati, primarily represent ideas and as such would tend to be one-faceted; the genius of the author however was in creating flesh and blood characters. David symbolizes the romantic yearning to return to the simple life of the shepherd and the peasant. Idealization of the rustic and the rural life is also found in the work of Shalom b. Jacob Cohen, *Matta'ei Kedem al Admat Ẓafon* ("Oriental Plants in the Soil of the North," 1807), which contains several poems on different episodes in the life of David. In one poem Barzillai rejects David's proposal to live in Jerusalem and David, at the height of his power and glory, comes to the tragic realization that a quiet rural life is preferable to the splendor and intrigues of the court. *Nir David* ("The Light of David," 1834), a romantic poem in 20 cantos, is a faithful rendering of the biblical story but shows no insight into the character or the events. The romantic yearning of the generation also finds voice in J.L. Gordon's Davidic poems: David is a sentimental romantic hero in *Ahavat David u-Mikhal* ("The Love of David and Michal," 1857), a historical epic which centers on the love of David the shepherd, later king, and the daughter of Saul. The theme is undying love portrayed through Michal. As in Shalom b. Jacob Cohen's poems, Gordon's *David u-Varzillai* ("David and Barzillai," 1851–56) portrays an older king whose scepter weighs heavy in his hand. Gordon's beautiful idyllic pastoral tableaus poignantly offset a tired king who, mourning his rebellious son's death, futilely yearns for a simple life. The national ballads of Abba Constantine Shapiro, *Me-Ḥezyonot Bat Ammi* ("The Visions of My People," 1884) mark a turning point in the ideational emphasis of David. The slumbering David, the redeemer (following the popular legend of David in the cave), awaits to be awakened so that he might save his people. Redemption is also the motif in Ya'akov Cahan's symbolic play *David Melekh Yisrael* ("David King of Israel," 1919–30, 1937). The redemptive theme, expressed in a lyrical vein, continues into the literature of the renascence period, e.g., in the poetry of Ya'akov Cahan – *Kinnor shel David* ("The Harp of David"); and of Jacob Fichmann – *Evel David* ("The Mourning of David," 1932), *Yo'av* ("Joab," 1934), and *Tefillat Erev le-David* ("Evening Prayer of David," 1960). Fichman did not choose the heroic pinnacles of David's life for subjects but rather the more human and tender episodes. *Evel David* and *Yo'av* are complementary works. The former is based on the legend that after his affair with Bath-Sheba David suffered deep melancholy for 20 years during which time he was deserted by the poetic muse. The poem, permeated by a deeply religious mood, skillfully describes the king's longing for his former state of innocence and poetic inspiration. In *Yo'av*, an older and wiser David has found his lost inspiration. His heart is again able to turn to God and his longing for God is expressed in poetry and song. But the blare of trumpets toward which Joab draws David's ear disturbs the king's regained idyll; the king's deep emotional conflict dissolves in his succumbing once again to the sound of war. Ḥ.N. Bialik in *Va-Yehi ha-Yom* ("On That Day," 1965) in the section *"Mi-Aggadot Melekh David"* ("From the Tales of King David") and Ya'akov Cahan in *Mishlei ha-Kedumim mi-Ymei ha-Melakhim* ("Tales of Ancient Times from the Times of the Kings," 1943) adapted legends, culled from folk tradition, into poetry and prose.

The more recent works on David do not follow any specific trend but are individualistic interpretations. They often are a reflection of the author's views of the fate of the Jewish people with which David has always been linked and of which he is many times the aspiring symbol. Some contemporary writers have portrayed David as a man of base qualities, others have drawn him as a man of majestic stature. *Yemei David* ("The Life of David," 1929), by Ari ibn Zahav, is a historical novel dealing mainly with David's youth, while in *Sha'ul Melekh Yisrael* ("Saul, King of Israel," 1944), a historical play by Max Brod and Sh. Shalom, David is a man whose actions are guided by the iron hand of fate. The David of Zalman Shneur's *Luḥot Genuzim* ("The Hidden Tablets," 1951) is a sly plotter, a man of intrigues and insatiable appetites. Uri Ẓevi Greenberg's majestic vision of the destiny of the Jewish people and the Land of Israel casts David and his wars (*Hod Malkhut*

David – "The Majesty of the Reign of David") as a mystical symbol of a glory to come; at the same time David is also the active symbol of an ideology culminating in the mystic symbol. Moshe Shamir's *Kivsat ha-Rash* ("The Lamb of the Poor Man," 1957), a historical novella on the life of David, centers mainly on Uriah, the Hittite, portrayed as a loyal subject who loves his king dearly. The underlying theme, explicitly stated in the epilogue by Uriah, is the poison of sin (symbolized by the poisoned arrow that killed Uriah) which seeps through the generations to come.

A number of plays in the 1960s have for theme Davidic episodes. The playwrights did not invest the characters with 20th century philosophy and social outlooks but stressed the use of language, thus illuminating a problem at the root of modern Israeli culture. Benjamin Galai's *Sippur Uriyyah* ("The Story of Uriah," 1967/8), a tragicomedy, simultaneously dramatizes the biblical tale and an apparently authentic Inca story on a similar theme with scenes alternating between the Incas and the Israelites. *Ha-Dov* ("The Bear"), later renamed and staged under the title *Mored ve-Melekh* ("The Rebel and the King," 1968), by Yisrael Eliraz, concentrates on the Absalom/David episode with David drawn as a decadent and weak king. Ya'akov Shabtai in *Keter ba-Rosh* ("A Crown on the Head," 1969) gave a comic interpretation to the biblical story. The plot, a series of intrigues, portrays in a comic-satirical vein the tension between David and his sons and the struggle between Solomon and Adonijah for the throne.

[Avie Goldberg]

In the Arts

LITERATURE. As king of Israel and psalmist, David has inspired innumerable poems and plays in many languages. Since David in Christian tradition was an ancestor of Jesus, he appeared as one of the so-called prophets in the medieval *Ordo Prophetarum*; and he also figured in the 15th-century French *Mistère du Viel Testament*. The motif gained wider popularity during the Renaissance, particularly in France, where David, with Homer and Virgil, was seen as one of the creators of the poetic art. Joachim Du Bellay (1522–1560) wrote *La Monomachie de Davidet de Goliath* (1560) and Guy *Le Fèvre de la Boderie constantly eulogized the psalmist in works such as *L'Encyclie des Secrets de l'Eternité* (1571) and *La Galliade* (1578) which include many verse paraphrases of psalms. La Boderie (in *La Galliade*, p. 112, citing the talmudic tractate *Bava Batra* 14b) also refers to the rabbinic tradition that David collected psalms composed from the time of Abraham onward. Two works by French Protestants were a dramatic trilogy by Loys Desmasures (c. 1515–1574?): *David Combattant; David Triomphant; David Fugitif* (1566), which alluded to the persecution and exile of the Huguenots; and Antoine de Montchrétien's play *David* (1601). In England George Peele's *The Love of King David and Fair Bathsabe* dealt more with Absalom than with the biblical romance.

Works of the 17th century include Abraham Cowley's verse epic *Davideis* (1656), one of the outstanding treatments of the theme, and Christian Weise's play *Vom verfolgten David* (1684). Literary interest in the figure of David was maintained in the 18th century, *Voltaire's subversive and mocking prose tragedy *Saül* (1763) dealing mainly with the second king of Israel, being balanced by *Saul* (1782), a noble and pious tragedy by the Italian poet and playwright Vittorio Alfieri. There is splendid imagery in *A Song to David* (1763), a hymn of praise to the psalmist by the English poet Christopher Smart. Some later works on the David theme were Friedrich Gottlieb Klopstock's German tragedy *David* (1722), a pious idyll; Friedrich Rueckert's drama *Saul und David* (1843); *Heine's poem "*Koenig David*" (in *Romanzero*, 1851); and the U.S. writer Joseph Holt Ingraham's religious romance *The Throne of David* (1860) which ends with Absalom's revolt. The story has retained its popularity in the 20th century, with works such as the U.S. poet Stephen Vincent Benét's *King David* (1923), and plays by D.H. Lawrence (*David*, 1926) and J.M. Barrie (*The Boy David*, 1936). Jewish writers have been prominent among modern interpreters of the motif. Lion *Feuchtwanger used the story of David and Bath-Sheba as the basis for his play *Das Weib des Urias* (1907) and Richard *Beer-Hofmann wrote a dramatic trilogy including *Der junge David* (1933). Two other plays by 20th-century Jewish writers were Israël *Querido's Dutch *Saul en David* (1914) and *Bathséba* (1940), a play by the Hungarian writer Károly *Pap.

On the whole, episodes of David's life, involving minor biblical characters, are of fairly recent date. They include Arnold *Zweig's three-act tragedy *Abigail und Nabal* (1913); *Abigail* (1916), a Yiddish play by David *Pinski; and *Abigail* (1924) by Grace Jewett Austin. An Oriental curiosity is *Abigail* (1923), a Marathi drama by Joseph *David of Bombay. Two works on related themes are "*Thamar y Amnón*," a ballad concluding the *Romancero gitano* (1928) of the Spanish poet and dramatist Frederico Lorca (1899–1936); and *Abiṣag* (1963), a dramatic poem about the Shunammite maiden who comforted the aged David, written by the Romanian Jewish author Enric Fortuna. Another work on this theme is Dan Jacobson's *Amnon and Tamar* (1970).

ART. David appears quite early in both Jewish and Christian art, where he has a major role, especially in illuminated manuscripts. As the traditional ancestor of Jesus, David is depicted from the sixth century C.E. in Byzantine manuscripts of the New Testament (Codex Rossanensis, Rossano Cathedral; Codex Synopensis, Paris, Bibliothèque Nationale, Suppl. Gr. 1286). Seventh-century Syriac Bibles portray scenes from the life of David in the Psalms, Samuel, and Kings (e.g., Paris, cod. Syr. 341). David the musician with a lyre, David the shepherd, David the lion-killer, and David the chosen anointed by Samuel became common subjects in Middle Byzantine psalters (e.g., Paris Psalter, Gr. 139). Their iconography stems mainly from late Antique, early Christian, and early Jewish art. The anointing of David is thus generally similar to the presentation in the wall painting of the third-century synagogue in *Dura Europos. Byzantine representations influenced most

West European illumination, from the Carolingian period (the Utrecht Psalter) through the Romanesques to the Gothic (St. Louis Psalter, Paris, Lat. 10525) and the Renaissance (the Breviary of Ecole D'Este, Modena, Estense Library, Lat, 424, Ms. v.G. 11). In Christian illumination, David was usually depicted as a main link in the representations of the Jesse tree. In Hebrew illuminated manuscripts, David is represented as wearing a crown and playing a lyre (e.g., Leipzig *Maḥzor*, Leipzig University manuscript v. 1102), and also as the founder of the royal House of David (e.g., Kennicott Bible, Bodleian Library, Ms. Ken. 1). In medieval art David frequently appears in media other than illuminated manuscripts. The wooden doors of S. Ambrosio of Milan (fourth century) present a narrative cycle, and scenes are represented in the ninth-century frescoes of S. Maria de Castel Seprio and many 12th-century portals, capitals, and windows at Moissac, Vézelay, Saint-Benoît sur Loire, Chartres, Bourges, and Amalfi.

[Bezalel Narkiss]

The young David triumphing over Goliath was a popular subject with the great sculptors of the Renaissance. The subject gave them an ideal opportunity to express the renewed pleasure which they found in the nude, a pleasure which they shared with the sculptors of classical antiquity to whom they turned for inspiration. Some examples are the sculptures of David by Donatello (1430–32, Florence, Bargello), Andrea del Verrocchio (1476, Florence, Bargello), and Michelangelo (1503, Florence, Accademia). Michelangelo's colossal marble statue has a vehement, heroic stance alien to its ancient prototypes. A baroque version of the subject was sculpted by Bernini (1623).

There are paintings of David and Goliath by Titian (1543–44) and Caravaggio (c. 1605–06, Borghese Rome Gallery), and David's triumphal return from the fight was depicted by Nicholas Poussin (1627, Madrid, Prado museum). A painting by *Rembrandt (1628) shows David presenting Saul with the head of Goliath. Another popular representation of the young David shows him playing the harp before Saul. The subject appears in medieval miniatures, and Rembrandt painted the subject twice, in 1630 and c. 1657 (The Hague, Mauritshuis). In the latter version, the angry monarch hides his face behind a curtain, moved to tears by the music. Josef *Israels also painted this subject in the 19th century. David as king and harpist has been painted by Rubens (1610–15, Frankfurt, Stadtmuseum), Rembrandt (1651, Mannheim), and Marc *Chagall (1951).

Of the episodes of David's middle career, the subject of Abigail pleading before David was especially popular in Italy and the Netherlands in the 17th century, and was painted by Rubens and by Simon Vouet (1590–1649). The bringing of the crown to David after Saul's death and his grief over the death of Saul were depicted by Jean Fiuquet, the 15th-century French artist, in a miniature illustrating the *Jewish Antiquities* of *Josephus (Paris, Bibliothèque Nationale, Ms. Fr. 247, fol 135v.). Standing in front of his massed army, David rends his garments. The story of David and Bath-Sheba has also inspired many artists. In medieval Christian iconography David symbolized Jesus, the coveted Bath-Sheba his bride (the Church undergoing purification by cleansing), and Uriah the Hittite symbolized the devil. In medieval representations of Bath-Sheba bathing, she is shown sometimes in the nude, sometimes half-dressed, and sometimes fully clothed, washing her feet in a tub. There are paintings of the subject by the Flemish artist Hans Memling (c. 1485, Stuttgart, Staatsgalerie), Lucas Cranach (1526, Berlin, Kaiser-Friedrichmuseum), Rubens (1635, Dresden), Rembrandt (1643, New York, Metropolitan, and 1654, Paris, Louvre), and Poussin (1633–34). In a later painting, Rembrandt shows the nude Bath-Sheba deep in thought with a note from King David in her hand.

MUSIC. In the Jewish and early Christian and Muslim traditions, King David is extolled as an ideal model of musical perfection. He is remembered as a poet and musician, or poet-musician who chanted the psalms he has composed for the Glory of God. Consequently, he has become known as "The sweet psalmist of Israel." The Kabbalah invokes his constant study of the Torah emphasizing the idea of rising at midnight to perform a nocturnal singing of psalms.

Interestingly, the great merit accorded to the nocturnal chanting of David's psalms is ardently extolled in the work *Ethicon* of the well-known scholar and archbishop of the Eastern Jacobite Church Bar Hebraeus (1226–1286). One also finds important references to the virtues assigned to the singing of psalms in writings of the Church's Fathers St. Basil, St. Chrysostom, Clement of Alexandria, and St. Jerome. In Islam, David, who is usually called the prophet Da'ud, is described in the Koran as having the most beautiful voice ever created by God. The development of this motif led to later interpretations associating David's beautiful voice with the powerful charm of his singing.

The different Davidic traditions reveal an interesting case of one ideal common model: David as poet-musician is represented as a symbol of divinely inspired music. Accordingly, this music embodies a kind of universal monistic religious spirituality, which enabled leaders of the three monotheistic religions to become inspired by it in order to support their respective dogmas by means of a special interpretation. Many prominent composers of the 17th and 18th centuries (notably A. Scarlatti, R. Keiser, A. Caldara, G. Ph. Telemann, and F. Veracini) wrote oratorios and operas on David. In the 19th century, the general decline of biblical oratorio and the politically suspect associations of the nationalistic themes inherent in the subject account for the relative paucity of music works about David. A certain renaissance occurred in the 20th century, although most of the works produced, not only by Jewish composers, were of transient interest. Two more important compositions are Arthur Honegger's *Le Roi David* and Darius *Milhaud's *David*. Honegger's anti-romantic "dramatic psalm," with minimal stage equipment and action, was written in 1921 to a text by René Morax. Milhaud's *David*, with French libretto by Armand *Lunel, was commissioned by the Koussevitzky Foundation for the 3,000th anniversary of the establishment of Jerusalem as David's capital in Jerusalem in 1954.

Descriptive compositions inspired by the figure of David include Menahem *Avidom's *David Symphony* (1947–48) and Paul Ben *Haim's *Sweet Psalmist of Israel* for orchestra (1956). David the dancer is depicted by *Castelnuovo-Tedesco in *Le danze del Re David* (piano solo, 1925). Schumann's *Davidsbuendlertaenze* (piano, op. 6, 1837) and the *March of the Davidsbuendler against the Philistines* (in *Carnival*, op. 9, piano, 1834–35) express his dislike of the musical philistinism around him. Zoltán Kodály's *Psalmus Hungaricus* (1923) for tenor, chorus, and orchestra is a poetic paraphrase of Psalm 55 combined with a 16th-century Hungarian poem. This work follows an old Hungarian biblical-historical tradition reflecting a contemporary political situation.

David was the patron of the Nuremberg Meistersinger and Hans Sachs's *Der klingende Ton* (1532) tells of Jonathan saving David from Saul's assassination attempt. Settings of David's lament over Saul and Jonathan include motets by Josquin des Prés, Pierre de la Rue, Clemens non Papa; an oratorio *David et Jonathas* (attributed to Carissimi); and Marc-Antoine Charpentier's stage music for Bretonneau's play in the 17th century. The oratorio *David's Lamentation over Saul and Jonathan* (1738) has been attributed to either John Christopher Smith or William Boyce. Johann Heinrich Rolle's oratorio *David and Jonathan*, based on Klopstock, was written in 1766. The fight between David and Goliath is commemorated in one of Johann Kuhnau's *Six Biblical Sonatas* (clavichord, 1700), while in the 20th century the theme is dealt with in Hanns *Eisler's *Goliath*, and Karel *Salmon's *David and Goliath* (1930). In folk music, an epic song with some dramatic action has been noted in the Kurdish Jewish tradition and in a Ladino ballad, "*Un pregón pregono el Rey*." The Afro-American spiritual "Li'l David play on your harp" has the David theme as its first verse and refrain. Some musical works about David, traditional or recently composed, have become Israeli folksongs. The best known of these is probably *David Melekh Yisrael Ḥai ve-Kayyam*.

The Bath-Sheba story occurs in the 18th-century oratorios (Georg Reutter, A. Caldera, Dittersdorf). Porpora's oratorio *Davide e Bersabea* (1734) was staged and written in London on the initiative of Handel's opponents. Mozart's cantata *Davidde penitente* (1785) was set to a libretto probably written by Lorenzo *Da Ponte and thus marks the start of their collaboration; the music (1782–83) is drawn largely from the Mass in C Minor (K. 427). On Abigail, the most noteworthy works are on oratorio by Francesco Durante (1736) and the oratoria *Nabal*, text by Morell, put together by J.C. Smith in 1764 with music taken from various Handel oratorios. Amnon and Tamar are the subject of a Ladino ballad, "*Un hijo tiene el Rey David*" (M.A. Attias, *Romancero Sefaradi* (1955), no. 75), and of an opera by Josef *Tal with text by Recha *Freier, which had its première in concert form in Jerusalem in 1960.

[Bathja Bayer / Amnon Shiloah (2nd ed.)]

BIBLIOGRAPHY: Bright, Hist, 171–90; Smith, in: JBL, 52 (1933), 1–11; Albright, Stone, 221–8; Alt, Kl Schr, 2 (1953), 66–75; Cazelles, in: PEQ, 87 (1955), 165–75; Morgenstern, in: JBL, 78 (1959), 322–5; Hodge, in: *Bibliotheca Sacra*, 119 (1962), 238–43; Mazar, in: *Essays… A.H. Silver* (1963), 235–44; idem, in: VT, 13 (1963), 310–20; idem, in: BA, 25 (1962), 98–120; E.H. Maly, *The World of David and Solomon* (1966); Wright, in: BA, 29 (1966), 83ff.; Weiser, in: VT, 16 (1966), 325–54; Malamat, in: JNES, 22 (1963), 1–17; idem, in: BA, 21 (1953), 96–102; idem, in: ZAW, 74 (1962), 145–64; Stoebe, in: BZAW, 77 (1958), 224–43; Bič, in: RHPR, 37 (1957), 156–62; Ap-Thomas, in: JNES, 2 (1943), 198–200; Eissfeldt, in: ZDPV, 66 (1943), 115–28; Mowinckel, in: ZAW, 45 (1927), 30–58; Nyberg, in: ARW, 35 (1938), 329–87; Speiser, in: BASOR, 149 (1959), 17–25; Vogt, in *Biblica*, 40 (1959), 1062–63; Elliger, in: PJB, 31 (1935), 29–75; Goldschmid, in: BJPES, 14 (1948–49), 122; Honeyman, in: JBL, 67 (1948), 13–25; Pákozdy, in: ZAW, 68 (1956), 257–9; Schofield, in: *The Expository Times*, 66 (1954–55), 250–2. **ADD. BIBLIOGRAPHY:** W.B. Barrick, "Saul's Demise, David's Lament and Custer's Last Stand," in: *Journal for the Study of the Old Testament*, 73 (1997), 25–41; W. Dietrich (ed.), *David und Saul im Widerstreit – Diachronie und Synchronie im Wettstreit: Beitraege zur Auslegung des ersten Samuelbuches* (2004); B. Halpern, *David's Secret Demons: Messiah, Murderer, Traitor, King* (2001); E.A. Knauf, "Saul, David and the Philistines: From Geography to History," in: *Biblische Notizen*, 109 (2001), 15–18; E. Mazar, "Excavating King David's Palace," in: BAR, 23:1 (1997), 50–57, 74; S.L. McKenzie, King David: *A Biography* (2000). IN THE AGGADAH: Ginzberg, Legends, index; A. Rosner, *Davids Leben und Charakter nach Talmud und Midrasch* (1908); V. Aptowitzer, *Parteipolitik der Hasmonaerzeit* (1927), index; Alon, Meḥkarim, 1 (1957), 17–18; J. Liver, *Toledot Beit David* (1959). TOMB OF DAVID: Z. Vilnay, *Maẓẓevot Kodesh be-Ereẓ Yisrael* (1951), 163–76. IN CHRISTIANITY: Meyer, Ursp, 2 (1921), 446; E. Hennecke, *Neutestamentliche Apokryphen* (1924^2), 108f.; J. Liver, in: *Tarbiz*, 26 (1956/57), 239–43. IN ISLAM: EI, s.v. *Dā'ūd*; G. Weil, *Biblische Legenden der Muselmaenner* (1845), 202–24; P. Jensen, in: *Der Islam*, 12 (1922), 84–97; J. Horovitz, *ibid.*, 184–9; H.Z. (J.W.) Hirschberg, *Der Dīwān des As-Samau'al ibn 'Adija'…* (1931), 25, 59–60; H. Speyer, *Biblische Erzaehlungen…* (1961), 369, 372, 375–82, 403; Tabarī, *Tafsīr*, 2 (1323 A.H.), 375–84; 17 (1327 A.H.), 34–37; 23 (1329 A.H.), 77–87; Tabārī, *Ta'rīkh*, 1 (1357 A.H.), 336–43; ibn Wathīma, *Qiṣaṣ*, Vatican Ms. Borgia 165, fols. 42v.–57v; Thaʿlabī, *Qiṣaṣ* (1356 A.H.), 227–47; Kisā'ī, *Qiṣaṣ*, ed. by I. Eisenberg (1922), 250–77. IN MODERN HEBREW LITERATURE: **ADD. BIBLIOGRAPHY:** M. Itzhaki, "David et Bethsabée: un récit biblique dans la poésie contemporaine," in: *Yod*, 8 (2002–3), 113–25; L. Perlemuter, "'La brebis du pauvre' Roman de l'écrivain israélien Moshe Shamir," in: *Yod*, 8 (2002–3), 97–111. IN THE ARTS: M. Roston, *Biblical Drama in England* (1968), s.v., includes bibliography; H. Steger, *David Rex et Propheta* (Ger., 1961), includes bibliography; L. Réau, *Iconographie de l'art chrétien*, 2 pt. 1 (1956), 254–86, 308–9 (a bibliography); D. Diringer, *The Illuminated Book: Its History and Production* (1967); E. Kirschbaum (ed.), *Lexikon der christlichen Ikonographie*, 1 (1968), 477–90 (includes bibliography).

DAVID, early Canadian family. LAZARUS DAVID (1734–1776), born in Swansea, Wales, arrived in Canada about 1760 and helped found the Shearith Israel Congregation in Montreal. His eldest son DAVID DAVID (1764–1824), born in Montreal, was a founder and member of the original board of directors of the Bank of Montreal. SAMUEL DAVID (1766–1824), second son of Lazarus David, married Sarah Hart, daughter of Aaron *Hart of Trois Rivières in 1810. He fought with the

British forces in the War of 1812. His diary (unpublished) reflects the conditions of Trois Rivières in the colonial period. AARON HART DAVID (1812–1882) was born in Montreal, the son of Samuel David. He earned a medical degree at Edinburgh in 1835 and practiced medicine in Montreal, becoming dean of the faculty of medicine at the University of Bishops College, president of the Natural History Society of Montreal, and general secretary of the Canadian Medical Association; he held numerous other important medical and scientific positions. Aaron David took a leading part in Jewish life in Quebec province and served as army surgeon in the 1837 Rebellion and the 1866 Fenian Raids. These and other members of the David family were closely involved in the affairs of the Shearith Israel Congregation of Montreal and served actively in the armed forces.

BIBLIOGRAPHY: B.G. Sack, *History of the Jews in Canada* (1965^2).

[Ben G. Kayfetz]

DAVID, DYNASTY OF. The genealogy of the House of *David as a royal dynasty and as a symbol of hope for future redemption has left its mark on Jewish history throughout the ages. One may distinguish six stages in its development: (a) its origin (until c. 1000 B.C.E.); (b) the reign of the House of David (until 587 B.C.E.); (c) the dynasty during the critical period of the Exile and the Return to Zion (until c. 400 B.C.E.); (d) its disappearance (about 100 C.E.); (e) the exilarchs and the *nesi'im* (until c. 900 C.E.); (f) the aftergrowths of the Davidic genealogy.

(a) From the account of Samuel's secret anointment of David (I Sam. 16), it appears that Jesse, David's father, was one of the elders of Bethlehem (cf. I Sam. 17:12). According to the genealogy at the end of the Book of Ruth (4:18ff.) and in I Chronicles 2:10ff., Jesse was a descendant of Boaz, who was a descendant of Nahshon the son of Amminadab, and chieftain (prince) of Judah, and thus a member of one of the most respected families in the tribe. In many passages David is called "the son of Jesse"; and in Isaiah 11:1 the remnant of the House of David is spoken of figuratively as "the stock of Jesse." In the Book of Ruth, the ancestry of David from the marriage of Boaz to Ruth the Moabite is especially emphasized and this matter undoubtedly is the climax of the story. It should not be assumed that the tradition of the genealogy of the House of David from Ruth is the result of the preaching against the divorce of foreign women during the time of Ezra, as scholars during the time of A. Geiger did. On the one hand, it is not correct to say that this story intends to emphasize the ancestry of David in the mixed families living in the country. The story of Ruth, which reflects life close to the beginning of the monarchy, is based on an historical tradition concerning the ancestry of the mother of the family of David (cf. I Sam. 22:3–4 on the mission of David's father and his mother to the king of Moab when David had fled from Saul). This story intends to stress that Ruth left her people and became a part of Israel and therefore God rewarded her and her son Obed was the father of Jesse, the father of David (Ruth 4:17).

Information about the pedigree of the Davidic dynasty appears in various biblical books – particularly in Samuel and Kings. But the comprehensive genealogical table of the House of David in biblical times appears in I Chronicles 2:10–17; 3:1–24. It consists of three separate parts: a) the genealogy of Jesse, a list of his children, and a list of the sons of David born in Hebron and Jerusalem (2:10–17; 3:1–9); b) a list of the kings of Judah, from Solomon to Josiah (3:10–14); c) the sons of Josiah and their descendants (3:15–24). The first section is only a partial parallel to the data found in the Former Prophets. Thus I Samuel 16:6ff. and 17:13–14 merely list David's three older brothers, with slightly different names; and the Book of Samuel states that Jesse had eight (not seven) sons (17:12; cf. 16:10–11). The list in Chronicles of David's sons born in Hebron parallels the list in II Samuel 3:2–5 with minor changes, but includes more names of sons born to David in Jerusalem than II Samuel 5:14–16 and diverges from it in other ways. Thus, the author of Chronicles did not copy his list from the Book of Samuel, but from another source which may have been common to both books. It is worth noting that it is only from the data in Chronicles that we learn that Joab and his brothers, the sons of Zeruiah, and Amasa, the son of Abigail, were sons of sisters of David.

(b) There is only minimal information about the House of David during its reign. In the Book of Kings there is only a list of the successive kings and the names of their mothers; similarly I Chronicles 3:10–14 contains only the names of the kings of Judah, from Solomon to Josiah. Chronicles records in addition the names of the sons of Rehoboam (II Chron. 11:18ff.) and the sons of Jehoshaphat (II Chron. 21:2ff.). The list of Solomon's governors mentions incidentally two of the married daughters of Solomon, Taphath and Basemath (I Kings 4:11, 15). In I Chronicles 3:15 the sons of Josiah are listed in a different chronological order from that in the Book of Kings, and the eldest, Johanan, is not known from other sources. It should be noted that the term "king's son" is an administrative title.

In Nathan's vision (II Sam. 7) the destiny of an eternal rule over Israel for the descendants of David is clearly expressed. This idea of the eternity of the royal House of David became more deeply rooted with the continuation of the dynasty's rule over Judah. In the course of time, the rule of the House of David became the symbol of God's love for His people. Even those prophets who sharply opposed the kings of their times saw in the future the destined leadership of a descendant of the House of David. A unique archaeological find made in 1993–94 at Tel Dan in northern Israel sheds light on the House of David. The find consists of fragments of a stele inscribed in Aramaic, mentioning a king of the House of David and a king of Israel (Jehoram?), and it is dated palaeographically and stratigraphically to the second half of the ninth century B.C.E. Much controversy has surrounded the interpretation of this find (see Bibliography below).

(c) The sources during the Exile and the return to Zion make very little mention of the House of David. The books of Ezra and Nehemiah do not even note that Zerubbabel was of the House of David, although in Haggai's prophecy he is depicted as the destined ruler of Israel (2:23). From the genealogical lists in I Chronicles 3, it emerges that Zerubbabel was a grandson of Jehoiachin. It is widely believed that Sheshbazzar, the chieftain (prince) of Judah at the beginning of the Return to Zion (Ezra 1:8), was also of the House of David, and that he is to be identified with Shenazzar son of Jehoiachin (Jeconiah; I Chron. 3:18).

The list in I Chronicles 3 enumerates the descendants of the House of David after the Return to Zion. According to the Septuagint, there are 11 generations after Zerubbabel, that is to say, counting 25 years to a generation, there is documentation of the existence of the House of David until the middle of the third century B.C.E. But according to the Hebrew text the number of generations is only five or six. The difficulty revolves around the generations between Zerubbabel and Hattush (third from the end of the list). If the latter is identical with the Hattush who is named in Ezra 8:2 as one of those who returned with Ezra from Babylon (457 B.C.E.), the genealogy ends two generations after Ezra's return, or at the beginning of the 4th century B.C.E. (It is unfortunately not possible to date with certainty the passage in Zech. 12:7–14.)

The rebuilding of the Temple under the leadership of Zerubbabel (520 B.C.E.) aroused hope, which finds expression in the prophecies of Haggai and Zechariah, for a renewal of the reign of the Davidic dynasty. Nonetheless, during the age of the Return to Zion, the House of David was in decline. The reasons for this are not known. It is possible that Zerubbabel was suspected of disloyalty and was therefore recalled to Babylon. It is clear, however, that he or his descendants did return to Babylon, for among those who came with Ezra was Hattush who is related to Zerubbabel. There is no information concerning the family's status in Babylon, nor why it (or part of it) returned to Judah with Ezra. After the beginning of the 4th century B.C.E. (the end of the list in I Chron. 3), the fate of the house of David is unknown.

The clash between the descendants of the House of David and the high priesthood over the leadership of Judah at the beginning of the Return to Zion ended with the victory of the priesthood. The weakened position of the Davidic dynasty also weakened the identification between them and the future fortunes of Israel. Even during the period of the Second Temple, Judaism did not relinquish the ideal of a redeemer from the House of David, but this now became an ideal for the distant future, and no longer exerted a decisive force in the formation of Jewish history.

(d) Information about the Davidic family after c. 400 B.C.E. is slight and fortuitous. Clermont-Ganneau and others have suggested that "Akabiah bar Elioenai" (a name incised on a tomb in the cemetery of Alexandrian mercenaries from the beginning of the Ptolomaic period) should be identified with Akkub ben Elioenai, a descendant of Zerubbabel (I Chron. 3:23–24). This identification is not possible for chronological reasons – at most, one may speculate whether the Akabiah of the inscription may have been a great-grandson of the Akkub in I Chronicles. In any event, the inscription indicates that this supposed descendant of David held a position of no particular importance. The Mishnah (Ta'an. 4, 5) lists the descendants of David among the families which used to offer the wood offering. It would appear that this Mishnah belongs to the Persian period, the time when Nehemiah established this sacrifice, for all the families mentioned are known from the books of Ezra and Nehemiah and are not mentioned thereafter. Until Roman rule, there is no primary source testimony about the descendants of David. One cannot attribute historical validity to the late work (apparently from the Middle Ages) attributed to Philo and known as *Breviarium Temporum* (in *Antiquities of Berosus Chaldaeus*), which contains a list of some of the descendants of Zerubbabel and claims that the Hasmonean dynasty was of the same Davidic line.

According to the New Testament, Jesus was of Davidic descent. Two of the Gospels, Matthew (1:1–7) and Luke (3:23–38), include a genealogy tracing him directly to David. The New Testament tells of afflicted people who address Jesus as "Son of David." These sources, which date from not later than the end of the 1st century C.E., reveal that a short time after the death of Jesus there was a current Christian tradition attributing Davidic descent to Jesus. However, no historical validity can be attributed to these New Testament genealogies which are mutually contradictory in their artificiality; they merely reflect the fact that at the end of the period of the Second Temple the belief in a *messiah from the House of David (a tradition whose roots are biblical) was strong in Israel, and that consequently those who believed that Jesus was the Messiah concluded that he must be descended from David. So, when R. *Akiva hailed *Bar Kokhba as the messiah, *Johanan b. Torta added, "Akiva, grass will grow upon your cheeks and still the son of David will not have come" (TJ Ta'an. 4:2, 17d). The evidence of Eusebius quoted in the name of Hegesippus about the persecutions of the descendants of the House of David by the Caesars Vespasian and Domitian refers to the family of Jesus; it is not to be regarded as independent testimony for the existence of descendants of David among the Jews of that period (*Historia Ecclesiastica*, 3:12, 19, 32.4).

A tradition from the period of the first *amoraim* (TJ Ta'an. 4:2; Gen. R. 98:8) tells of a genealogical table dating from the period before the destruction of the Temple which was found in Jerusalem, according to which Hillel and R. Ḥiyya the Great were related to the Davidic dynasty. But investigation of the account reveals that it includes names of sages from the 2nd and 3rd centuries C.E., and the midrashic character of some of the progress indicates that this is but one of many literary genealogical traditions which arose from the time of Judah ha-Nasi and concerned the relationship of the families of the *exilarchs in Babylonia and the *patriarchs in Palestine. There is no information concerning the House of David between the 4th century B.C.E. and the 2nd century C.E.

THE GENEALOGY OF THE HOUSE OF DAVID

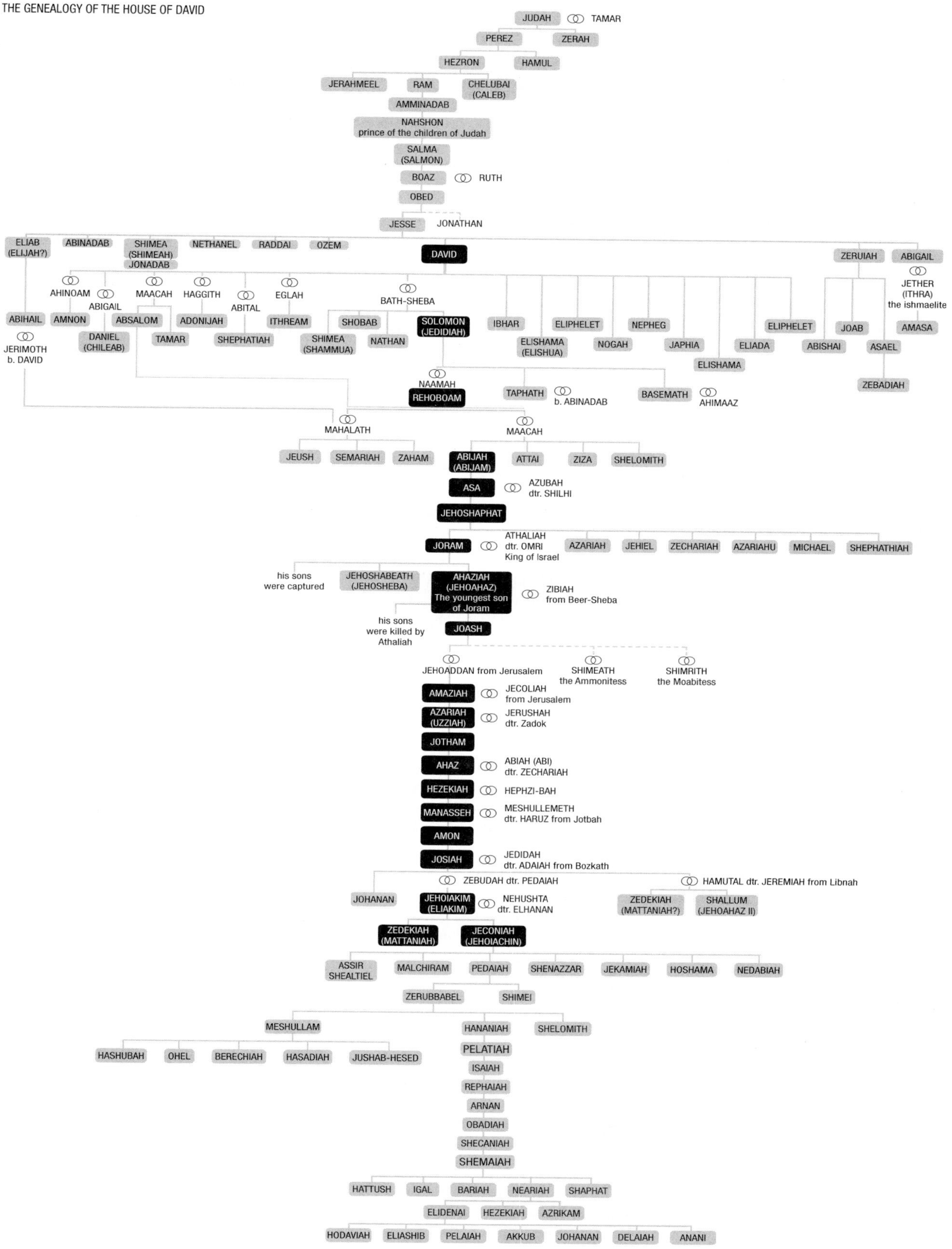

If descendants existed during this period, they played no role in the leadership of the people. The nation's disappointment after the excitement of Zerubbabel's days was critical, and expressions of hope for the renewal of the kingdom as well as promises of a future redeemer from the House of David appear only rarely in the sources following Zerubbabel's time. (The blessing found at the end of the Hebrew version of Ben Sira, "Praised be he who causes a horn to sprout for the House of David," is only a common liturgical formulation of the hope based on the biblical promises.) A weakening of the element of a king of the Davidic dynasty is observable in the eschatological and apocalyptic literature, such as the Book of Malachi and, later, Daniel and Enoch. In this literature, the figure of a superhuman redeemer appears, and replaces the figure of the future king of the House of David. This process of the Davidic expectation continued down to the days of the Hasmoneans.

With the decline of that dynasty, the hopes for "the end of days" and the messianic ferment, which had been the hallmarks of the sects during the Hasmonean period, became widespread. Roman oppression and the unhappiness that it caused evoked a religious ferment which was bound up with the revival of the messianic hopes for a redeemer from the House of David. Thus, the author of the Psalms of Solomon, which were written about the time of the capture of Jerusalem by Pompey (63 B.C.E.), is opposed to any ruler not of the House of David, and speaks evil of the Hasmoneans who had usurped the seat of David. There is no evidence that the writer of the Psalms of Solomon knew of the existence of descendants of David in his own period; Judaism then and to this day has assumed that the redeemer, when he appears, will prove his Davidic origin by his success. When Judea came under Roman rule, the messianic consciousness gained renewed impetus, though at this time no family in Ereẓ Israel had genealogical proof of descent from David.

(e) Testimonies to a relationship to the House of David in the period following the destruction of the Second Temple mainly involve the families of the exilarchs and *nesi'im*, particularly R. Judah ha-Nasi and his contemporary, the exilarch R. Huna, and are sparse, vague, and even contradictory (Ket. 62b; TJ, Kelim 89, 32b; TJ, Sot. 87, 22a; Hor. 11a–b; and their parallels). These relatively early documents do not contain even one genealogy. A genealogical list tracing the relationship of the exilarch family to Zerubbabel appears only at the beginning of the geonic period. Even the letter of R. Sherira Gaon, who was related to the family of the exilarch, contains no information about the exilarchs who preceded R. *Huna, the contemporary of Judah ha-Nasi.

The earliest attempt to reconstruct the relationship of the exilarchs to the Davidic kings was made in *Seder Olam Zuta*, a work attributed to the 5th century C.E. The writer connects Hezekiah, who lived after the destruction of the Second Temple, and was the grandfather or great-grandfather of R. Huna, to Jehoiachin by means of a confused version of the genealogy of descendants of Zerubbabel (I Chron. 3). It follows that this source also is able to trace the pedigree of the exilarchs for only two or three generations preceding R. Huna. *Seder Olam Zuta*, in turn, was used as the basis for later genealogies of the House of David, including the genealogical tables of the Karaites. The exilarchs are the principal links between the House of David and later times, and *Seder Olam Zuta* is the earliest attempt to reconstruct the chain backward.

The traditions concerning the relationship of Davidic descent from the family of the patriarchs are secondary to the traditions concerning the pedigree of the exilarchs. They probably originated in the desire of the Jews in Palestine (and perhaps of the patriarchs themselves) not to appear inferior to the exilarchs in terms of the origin and status of their leaders. From the beginning, the exilarchs had boasted of their descent from David, and on this pedigree they based the authority they assumed over the people (see TJ Sot. 87, 22a; Hor. 11a–b). There is no possibiltiy of deciding whether the genealogical tradition of the exilarchs is reliable despite the fact that they did not have a detailed genealogical tree, or whether the authority which they exerted preceded their adoption of a David pedigree. Conceivably, the rank of exilarch in Babylonia could date from a relatively early period and the exilarchs could be descended from Zerubbabel; however, it is difficult to reconcile the antiquity of the exilarchate in Babylon with the fact that nothing is heard about them until after the destruction of the Second Temple.

(f) On the aftergrowth of the Davidic genealogy, see *Genealogy.

BIBLIOGRAPHY: S. Klein, in: *Zion*, 4 (1938–39), 30–50, 177–8; S. Yeivin, in: *Zion*, 9 (1944), 49–69; Y. Kaufmann, *Molad* (1959), 331–8; J.W. Rothstein, *Genealogie des Koenigs Jojachin und seiner Nachfolger* (1902); W.F. Albright, JBL, 40 (1921), 104–24; G. Kuhn, in: ZNW, 22 (1923), 206–28; J. Liver, HTR, 52 (1959), 149–85; Genealogical table of the Davidic Dynasty according to biblical sources in EM, 2, after p. 640; Sh. Yeivin, in: EM, 2, 643–5. **ADD. BIBLIOGRAPHY:** ARAMAIC STELE FROM DAN MENTIONING "HOUSE OF DAVID": A. Biran and J. Naveh. "An Aramaic Stele Fragment from Tel Dan," in: IEJ, 43 (1993), 81–98; idem, "The Tel Dan Inscription: A New Fragment," in: IEJ, 45 (1995), 1–18; E. Ben Zvi, "On the Reading *'bytdwd'* in The Aramaic Stele from Tel Dan," in: *Journal for the Study of the Old Testament*, 64 (1994) 25–32; F.H. Cryer, "On the Recently Discovered 'House of David' Inscription," *Scandinavian Journal of the Old Testament*, 8:1 (1994), 3–19; idem, "A 'Betdawd' Miscellany: *Dwd, Dwd'* or *Dwdh*?" in: *Scandinavian Journal of the Old Testament* 9:1 (1995), 52–58; idem, "King Hadad," in: *Scandinavian Journal of the Old Testament*, 9:2 (1995), 223–35; idem, "Of Epistemology, Northwest-Semitic Epigraphy and Irony: The 'BYTDWD/House of David' Inscription Revisited," in: *Journal for the Study of the Old Testament*, 69 (1996), 3–17; B.I. Demsky, "On Reading Ancient Inscriptions: The Monumental Aramaic Stele Fragment from Tel Dan," in: *Journal of the Ancient Near Eastern Society*, 23 (1995), 29–35; N.P. Lemche and T.L. Thompson, "Did Biran Kill David? The Bible in the Light of Archaeology," in: *Journal for the Study of the Old* Testament, 64 (1994), 3–22; G.A. Rendsburg, "On the Writing of bytdwd in the Aramaic Inscription from Tel Dan," in: IEJ, 45 (1995), 22–25; V. Sasson, "The Old Aramaic Inscription from Tell Dan: Philological, Literary and Historical Aspects," in: JSS, 40 (1995) 11–30; W.M. Schniedewind, "Tel Dan Stela: New Light on Aramaic and Jehu's Revolt," in: BASOR, 302 (May 1996),

75–90; T.L. Thompson, "'House of David': An Eponymic Referent to Yahweh as Godfather," in: *Scandinavian Journal of the Old Testament*, 9:1 (1995), 59–74; idem, "Dissonance and Disconnections: Notes on the *bytdwd* and *hmlk.hdd*. Fragments from Tel Dan," in: *Scandinavian Journal of the Old Testament*, 9:2 (1995), 236–40.

[Jacob Liver]

DAVID, ERNEST (1825–1886), French writer on music. David was born in Nancy and died in Paris. His works include an essay on Jewish music, *La Musique chez les Juifs* (1873). The first part deals with the instruments in the Bible, the second with the post-biblical music of the synagogue. With M. Lussy, he wrote *Histoire de la notation musicale depuis ses orgines*, including non-European systems of notation. This work was awarded a prize by the Institut de France and published in 1882. He also published biographies of Bach (1882), Handel (1884), Mendelssohn, and Schumann (1886).

[Amnon Shiloah (2nd ed.)]

DAVID, FERDINAND (1810–1873), German violinist. David, who was born in Hamburg, was a pupil of Spohr. He made his first concert tour at the age of 15, accompanied by his sister Louise, who, as Madame Dulcken, became a well-known pianist. In Berlin he was a close friend of Felix *Mendelssohn, and in 1836 was appointed leader of the Leipzig Gewandhaus Orchestra, which Mendelssohn conducted. From 1843 he was instructor of violin at the Leipzig Conservatory. David helped Mendelssohn with technical advice on his violin concerto, and gave its first performance at a Gewandhaus concert on March 13, 1845. David's main importance was as a teacher. Some of the greatest violinists of the second half of the 19th century, including Joachim and Wilhelm, were his pupils. His *Violinschule* ("System for the Violin") and his violin studies continue to be used, but his important anthology of violin masterpieces from the Baroque period to the 19th century has lost its value because his editing became outdated. The popularity of David's own compositions – which included symphonies and five violin concertos – did not outlive him.

Bibliography: J. Eckardt, *Ferdinand David und die Familie Mendelssohn-Bartholdy* (1888); A. Bachmann, *Les Grands Violonistes du Passé* (1913); A. Moser, *Geschichte des Violinspiels* (1923); Baker, Biog Dict; Grove, Dict; MGG; Riemann-Gurlitt.

[Josef Tal]

DAVID, FILIP (1940–), Yugoslav author and stage producer. Born in Kragujevac, David studied in Belgrade, where he eventually produced plays for television. David often used Jewish themes and figures to present universal problems. He published two short story collections (1964, 1969); dramas such as *Balada o dobrim ljudima* ("A Ballad about Good Men," 1965); and plays for television, including *Balada o povratku* ("A Ballad of the Return," 1965), *Jednog dana, moj Jamele* ("One day, My Jamie," 1968), "Fountain in a Dark Forest" (1964), "Notes on What Is Real and What Is Abstract" (1969), "Prince of Fire" (1987), and "Pilgrims of Heaven and Earth" (1995).

DAVID, JEAN (1908–1993), Israeli painter. David was born in Bucharest and studied in France. In 1927 he studied art at the Beaux Art institution at Paris and in 1930 he took advanced studies at the Grande Chaumière Academy and André Lot Academy in Paris. In 1942 he escaped to Palestine on a small schooner. He served with the British Royal Navy from 1944 to 1947 and with the Israel Navy from 1949 to 1950. During the latter period he also served as adviser on industrial design to the Ministry of Commerce and Industry. In 1954 he was one of the founders of the Ein Hod artists' village in the north of Israel. He decorated walls in the Israel pavilion at the Brussels Exhibition of 1958 and at the Canadian Expo 1967. He represented Israel at various international exhibitions. His posters, especially those executed for the Government Tourist Office, earned him an international reputation as a graphic artist. David painted murals on the passenger ships of the Israel merchant marine. He also designed jewelry and enamels. Characteristic of David's painting is a lively sense of humor, a decorative use of color, an allusive use of ancient symbolism, and a deep feeling for the life of the sea derived from his experience as a sailor. In 1960 David received the Dizengoff Prize.

DAVID, JOSEPH (**Penker**; 1876–1948), Indian playwright and director; leading showman of Bombay, where he was born to a *Bene Israel family. He used the Urdu, Hindi, Gujarati, and Marathi languages with equal facility and was the author of more than 100 plays, among them tragedies and comedies based on religious and mythological themes. For 15 years he was the producer for the Parsi Imperial Theater Company and presented many plays which raised the standard of the Urdu-Hindi stage. In 1931 he wrote the screenplay of India's first full-length talking film, *Alam-Ara*, with a cast which included Elizer Kolet (also of the Bene Israel) in one of the leading roles.

DAVID, LARRY (1947–), U.S. comedian, producer, and comedy writer. Born in Brooklyn, N.Y., and a graduate of the University of Maryland in 1970, David served in the U.S. Army Reserve and spent more than a dozen years as a stand-up comedian and television comedy writer, with little success. Along the way he worked at several jobs, including an unsuccessful stint as a bra salesman, a subject he later reprised on television. In 1989 David teamed with another comedian, Jerry *Seinfeld, to create *The Seinfeld Chronicles*, a show famously "about nothing" that combined Seinfeld's relaxed, outer-directed humor with David's intense, inner-directed humor. Renamed *Seinfeld* and televised on the National Broadcasting Company network, the show, an outgrowth of the two comedians' conversations and personal experiences, became one of the most successful in television history. The weekly half-hour program ran successfully through the 1998 season with David exercising almost total creative control through the 1996 season, when he left, although he returned for the finale. The four key characters, Seinfeld, a comedian, George Costanza (portrayed by Jason *Alexander), the over-the-top Kramer, and Elaine

Benes (Julia *Louis-Dreyfus), a book editor, became fixtures in American homes. The bumbling Costanza character, David said, was modeled after himself. David appropriated the name of a neighbor, Kramer, who lived in his apartment building in New York, for the unpredictable Kramer figure.

David himself portrayed a number of characters on the program, including George Steinbrenner, principal owner of the New York Yankees, but he was never seen on screen. When the show was sold for syndication and reruns, David stood to earn more than $200 million.

In 2000, David created *Curb Your Enthusiasm*, an outrageous half-hour comedy series in which he starred with a number of his show-business friends. With largely improvised dialogue, the main character, Larry David, lives off the proceeds of *Seinfeld* while not doing much of anything about putting another show together. The plots were ludicrous and, because the program was televised on Home Box Office, a cable network, the language was crude and the story lines irritating, offensive, and satirically blunt. Few subjects, including the Holocaust, were out of bounds for comedy. One critic called David "the Philip Roth of situation comedy, unafraid to reveal just how devious, petty, annoying, argumentative, selfish, boorish and insensitive he can be." The show won many awards during its first four seasons.

[Stewart Kampel (2nd ed.)]

DAVID, MARTIN (1898–1986), legal historian and papyrologist. David was born in Poznan, then under German rule, but his family moved to Berlin during World War I. He was drawn to the study of cuneiform law and was appointed lecturer at Leipzig in 1930. On account of the Nazi persecution, David fled to Holland and became lecturer of Oriental legal history and papyrology at the University of Leiden in 1933. During World War II, David, together with his wife and three children, was imprisoned in the Westerbork and Theresienstadt concentration camps. After the liberation he became professor of comparative ancient legal history, director of the Leiden Institute of Papyrology, and member of the Royal Dutch Academy.

Among his major writings are *Die Adoption im altbabylonischen Recht* (1927); *Assyrische Rechtsurkunden* (1929; together with E. Ebeling); *Studien zur heredis institutio ex re certa...* (1930); *Vorm en wezen van de huwelijkssluiting naar de oud-oostersche rechtopvatting* (1934); *Der Rechtshistoriker und seine Aufgabe* (1937); *The Warren Papyri* (1941; together with van Groningen and van Oven); *Papyrological Primer* (1946, 1965[4]; together with van Groningen); *Gai, Institutionum commentarii*, 4 (1954; together with H.L.W. Nelson); *Berichtigungsliste der griechischen Papyrusurkunden aus Aegypten* (together with van Groningen et al.), 1–3 (1922–58).

David wrote a number of articles on the relations between biblical and cuneiform laws, emphasizing the basic differences in the social structures in which these two systems developed, hence denying that the former were influenced by the latter.

[Ze'ev Wilhem Falk]

DAVID, SAMUEL (1836–1895), composer. David studied with *Halévy and obtained the Rome Prize for his cantata *Jephté* (1858). From 1872 until his death, he was musical director of the synagogues in Paris. Among his works are the operas *Absalon* and *I Macabei*, operettas, cantatas (*Le Génie de la terre*, 1859), symphonies, and synagogal works. For the synagogues of Paris, David published a collection of religious music entitled *Po'al ḥayey adam: musique religieuse ancienne et moderne en usage dans les Temples consistoriaux israélites de Paris* (1895).

DAVID BEN AARON IBN ḤASSIN (**Hussein**; c. 1730–c. 1790), liturgical poet, disciple and son-in-law of R. Mordecai *Berdugo. He lived at Meknès (Morocco) and his numerous *piyyutim* were popular among Moroccan and other Oriental Jews. Some of his compositions were published, with a foreword by Raphael Berdugo, under the title *Tehillah le-David* (Amsterdam, 1807; enlarged edition, Casablanca, 1931). In addition to *piyyutim*, the collection includes wedding and friendship poems, elegies, and a poetic description of the precepts of ritual slaughter, *Mekoman shel Zevaḥim*.

BIBLIOGRAPHY: J.M. Toledano, *Ner ha-Ma'arav* (1911), 168, 187, 190; Davidson, Oẓar, 4 (1933), 374–5. **ADD. BIBLIOGRAPHY:** M. Sulam (ed.), *Yede Mosheh... be-Sofo Kuntres be-Shem Mekoman shel Zevaḥim shir ... al Dinei Sheḥitah ... she-Yasad David ben-Ḥasin ...* (2001).

[Samuel Abba Horodezky]

DAVID BEN ABRAHAM HA-LAVAN (c. 1300), kabbalist who lived in France or Spain. His grandfather was rabbi in Coucy, France. David wrote *Masoret ha-Berit*, a kabbalistic-philosophic tract distinguished by its radical formulation of kabbalistic doctrines. His method of argumentation resembled that of the neoplatonic philosophers and his system was not far removed from pantheism. All things existed in the Creator's mind "in a spiritual actuality" and the difference between their state in the Creator's mind and their current state is only the fact that they have been materialized, i.e., "they took on a material form in time." All creation out of nothing is either creation out of the essence of the Glory of God or out of His word, and in any case out of the power of the first source of emanation; this *ayin* ("nothingness") is more real in its existence than any other reality. The process of emanation of all created beings by action of the Will, even the minerals, and their return to the origin of their existence in the divine Will, is called "the secret of the true transmigration."

BIBLIOGRAPHY: Mekiẓe Nirdamim, *Kobez al Jad*, 1 (n.s. 1936); G. Scholem, in: *Gaster Anniversary Volume* (1936), 503–8.

[Gershom Scholem]

DAVID BEN ABRAHAM MAIMUNI (1222–1300), **nagid* of Egyptian Jewry and grandson of *Maimonides. David was only 15 years old when his father *Abraham b. Moses b. Maimon died (1237) and in spite of his youth, he was appointed **nagid* a few months later. A few years afterward opposition arose against him, possibly because of his youth, and he was deposed. In 1252 he was restored to his position, received government recognition, and remained in office for several decades. David had an extensive knowledge in all branches of Jewish literature and it seems that he was also competent in medicine. He maintained a correspondence with the leading scholars of Spain, Syria, and Italy, and is the author of three known works, which are extant in manuscript. The largest of them is a collection of commentaries on the weekly portions of the Torah and *haftarot* in Arabic. The commentary on the first portion of Genesis was published in Arabic under the title *Midrash Rabbenu David ha-Nagid* (Alexandria, 1914) and in Hebrew translation under the title *Midrash David* (Jerusalem, 1947). The commentaries on the books of Genesis and Exodus were translated into Hebrew as *Midrash Rabbi David ha-Nagid* (Jerusalem, 1964–68).

*Jacob b. Hananel ha-Sakili translated some of the sermons and inserted them in his *Torat ha-Minḥah*. These commentaries became popular among Egyptian Jewry and during many generations were read in synagogues. Some scholars have expressed doubt as to whether David was really the author. Nothing, however, in these sermons refutes the tradition that he is their author apart from the fact that he makes no mention of Maimonides being his grandfather. The writer follows the ideas of Maimonides (and moreover also quotes the Zohar, being probably the earliest known author to do so). It can be assumed that these sermons were delivered by David and were later recorded by one or several members of his audience. On the other hand, they probably include additions of the transcribers. The second work attributed to David is a commentary on *Avot* which was published in Arabic (Alexandria, 1901 and Cairo, 1932) and translated into Hebrew by Ben-Zion Krynfiss (*Sefer Midrash David*, Jerusalem, 1944). A commentary on the apocalypse, *Nevu'at ha-Yeled asher Ḥazah Naḥman…* ("The Prophecy of the Child Naḥman"), is also attributed to him and is said to have been written for the rabbis of Barcelona. He also wrote homilies to the Book of Lamentations under the title *Midrash Eikhah* which were published by A.I. Katsh in *Sinai*, 65 (1969), 251–80. In his old age some enemies slandered him to the governor of Egypt and David was compelled to flee to Acre, then under Crusader rule. In 1285 the physician al-Muhadhab Abul-Hassan b. al-Muwafak was appointed *nagid* in place of David. Abraham *Zacuto relates that David issued a ban against his slanderers and that many of them died (*Sefer Yuḥasin ha-Shalem*, p. 219). After his arrival in Acre, David was involved in a violent controversy with the conservative kabbalists who wanted to forbid the study of Maimonides' writings. The leader of this faction was Solomon *Petit, who had come to Palestine from France. David requested that the community leaders of the Oriental countries intervene. In consequence, in 1286–88, R. *Jesse b. Hezekiah, the exilarch of Damascus, R. *David b. Daniel, the *nasi* of Mosul, and *Samuel ha-Kohen b. Daniel Abu al-Rabi'a, the *rosh yeshivah* of Baghdad, issued a ban against anyone who insulted the memory of Maimonides. R. Solomon b. Abraham *Adret, the rabbi of Barcelona, also intervened and finally settled the controversy. In the interim David's supporters in Egypt succeeded in changing the government's attitude toward him and in about 1290 he returned to Egypt and was reinstated as *nagid*. The poet Joseph b. Tanḥum ha-Yerushalmi wrote enthusiastic poems on the occasion of his return, but David, tired from his troubles, appointed his son Abraham to share his duties. In a document from 1291 they jointly signed as *negidim*. David died in Egypt and his remains were brought to Palestine and interred in Tiberias near the tomb of Maimonides.

BIBLIOGRAPHY: Ashtor, Toledot, 1 (1944), 117–43; A.I. Katsh (ed.), *Midrash Rabbi David ha-Nagid* (1964), introd. to vol. on Genesis; idem, in: JQR, 48 (1957/58), 140–60; Goitein, in: *Tarbiz*, 34 (1964/65), 236–53; Hurwitz, in: *Sinai*, 59 (1966), 29–38.

[Eliyahu Ashtor]

DAVID BEN ARYEH LEIB OF LIDA (c. 1650–1696), rabbi and author; nephew of Moses b. Ẓevi Naphtali *Rivkes. He studied under *Joshua Hoeschel b. Jacob of Cracow, and in 1671 was called to the rabbinate in Lida. Subsequently he officiated as rabbi of Ostrog, Mainz (1677), and of the Ashkenazi community of Amsterdam (1681). There he was accused of Shabbatean leanings as well as of literary plagiarism in connection with his *Migdal David*, a commentary on the Book of Ruth (1680) which some ascribed to *Ḥayyim b. Abraham ha-Kohen. After being dismissed from his position, David returned to Poland, where he presented his case to the Council of the Four Lands and aired it in a pamphlet entitled *Be'er Esek* ("Well of Contention," 1684). The Polish rabbinate vindicated him and demanded his reinstatement. On his return to Amsterdam, however, his case was raised again, this time by the Sephardi rabbis, who subsequently likewise vindicated him. He returned to Poland shortly thereafter and died in Lvov. He was the author of numerous homiletic and kabbalistic works, including *Sod Adonai* (1680), on circumcision; *Shomer Shabbat* (1687), on the Shabbat; and *Ir Miklat* (1690), on the 613 commandments. A collection of 14 of his compositions was published under the title *Yad Kol Bo* in 1727. Another work on the Shulḥan Arukh *Oraḥ Ḥayyim* remains in manuscript. It is now clear that his first work, an ethical treatise, *Divrei David* (1671), was drawn from other sources, while the *Asarah Hillulim*, a commentary on Psalms (included in *Yad Kol Bo*), was incorrectly attributed to David by the publishers, having been taken from the commentary on Psalms by the Christian scholar, H.J. *Bashuysen. Much of the controversy which centered around David stemmed from his militancy and aggressiveness. Among his severest critics was Jacob *Emden.

BIBLIOGRAPHY: Michael, Or, no. 700; Freimann, in: *Sefer ha-Yovel … N. Sokolow* (1904), 459–80.

[Jacob S. Levinger]

DAVID BEN BOAZ (also called **David ha-Nasi** or **Abu Saʿid David ben Boaz**; 10th–11th centuries), Karaite scholar. According to Karaite tradition, David was a fifth generation removed from *Anan b. David b. Boaz. It is reported that his father died a martyr. One tradition relates that David and his brother Josiah took part in the polemic between *Saadiah Gaon and *David b. Zakkai (930–37). However another source places his activity half a century later. Possibly the reports are not contradictory, David living to a very old age. He was the head of the Karaites in Jerusalem, a position which he inherited from his father and grandfather and bequeathed to his son Solomon (who is known to have been living in 1016). His works, written in Arabic, include (1) a translation of the Pentateuch with a commentary of which only portions on Exodus, Leviticus, and Deuteronomy have been preserved (British Museum, Ms. Or. 2403, 2561, et al.; Ms. Leningrad); in this commentary David opposes certain opinions of Saadiah Gaon, but in a restrained manner; he also appends citations from the Talmud, explanatory notes to the biblical translations, and grammatical glosses; (2) a commentary on Ecclesiastes (British Museum, Ms. Or. 2552). A work on the tenets of faith (*Kitāb-al-Uṣūl*), no longer extant, has been attributed to David. His opinions and information about him are noted by many Karaite scholars. David is said to have been the first to reject the so-called catenary theory of forbidden marriages (*rikkub*) advocated by all his predecessors. He is thus the originator of the reform in this law which was effected by *Jeshua b. Judah in the 11th century.

BIBLIOGRAPHY: S. Pinsker, *Likkutei Kadmoniyyot*, 2 vols. (1860), index; S. Poznański, *Karaite Literary Opponents of Saadiah Gaon* (1908), 18–20; Mann, Egypt, index; Mann, Texts, index; L. Nemoy (ed.), *Karaite Anthology* (1952), 123, 231, 374; Z. Ankori, *Karaites in Byzantium* (1959), index.

[Yehoshua Horowitz]

DAVID BEN DANIEL (11th century), aspirant to Palestinian gaonate; son of the *gaon* *Daniel b. Azariah. In about 1078 David immigrated to Egypt, arriving there without any financial means. Maẓli'aḥ b. Japheth, a Damascus Jew living in Damira, supported him until he left for the Egyptian capital about a year later. In Cairo the community leaders, including the *nagid* Mevorakh, supported him, but the kindness was not appreciated. David's ambition to become exilarch of the Egyptian community led him to plot against Mevorakh. This resulted in the *nagid's* temporary deposition and expulsion from Cairo. David then became leader of the Egyptian Jews and also exerted authority over those communities of the coastal towns of Palestine and Syria that were still under the rule of the Fatimids. His request to be recognized as exilarch, as well as his struggle with the rabbis of the Palestinian yeshivah (transferred to Tyre in 1071), caused a great dispute. David attempted to succeed his father as *gaon* in Palestine, but his opponent Elijah b. Solomon ha-Kohen finally became *gaon*. All these disputes are described in the letters of both sides and preserved in the *Genizah (Megillat Evyatar (Abiathar))*. In 1094 David was deposed by his opponents. According to Mann, he wrote *piyyutim* (Mann, Egypt, 2 (1922), 224–5).

BIBLIOGRAPHY: S. Schechter (ed.), *Saadyana* (1903), 80–113; S. Poznański, *Babylonische Geonim* (1914), index; Mann, Egypt, 2 (1922), index; Mann, Texts, 2 (1935), index; idem, in: *Sefer Zikkaron … S.A. Poznański* (1927), 27–29.

[Tovia Preschel / Eliyahu Ashtor]

DAVID BEN DANIEL (fl. second half of the 13th century), exilarch in Mosul, Mesopotamia. David was descended from the exilarch Josiah b. Zakkai and a grandson of the exilarch *David b. Zakkai II. In 1288 David issued a threat of excommunication edict against R. Solomon b. Samuel (Petit), who came to Acre from France and revived the propaganda against Maimonides' works. David was supported by 11 rabbis, who accepted his authority and joined him in signing the edict.

BIBLIOGRAPHY: Mann, in *Sefer Zikkaron … S. Poznański* (1927), 23–25, 32; S. Poznański, *Babylonische Geonim* (1914), 120–2.

[Tovia Preschel]

DAVID BEN ḤAYYIM OF CORFU (d. 1530), rabbi and halakhic authority, known sometimes as MaHaRDaKh (**M**orenu **Ha**Rav **D**avid ha-**K**ohen). David was born on the island of Corfu. He studied under Judah *Minz in Padua and was much influenced by the Ashkenazi method of study. He served in the rabbinate in communities in Greece (including Corfu and Patras), and was in halakhic correspondence with distinguished contemporaries, among them Elijah *Mizraḥi, Moses *Alashkar, Jacob ibn *Ḥabib, and Joseph *Taitaẓak. Among his disciples were his son-in-law, David Vital, and Samuel *Kalai. He spent the last year of his life in Adrianople, where he died. Most of his works were destroyed in a conflagration there. A few responsa were rescued and published in Constantinople in 1537 by his son, Ḥayyim; they show him to be an outstanding halakhist, with a definite tendency toward stringency. In his vehement dispute from 1520 to 1525 with *Benjamin Ze'ev of Arta with regard to permission given to an *agunah* to remarry, he took an extreme stand in opposition to the lenient attitude adopted by other rabbis (see Res. *Benjamin Ze'ev* (Venice, 1539), nos. 1–17, 239, 246–9). He also declared that those Marranos who could have fled from their persecutors and did not do so were to be regarded as apostates.

BIBLIOGRAPHY: Conforte, Kore, 31–35; Graetz-Rabbinowitz, 6 (1898), 433–4; 7 (1899), 31, 36–37; H.J. Zimmels, *Die Marranen in der rabbinischen Literatur* (1932), 30–32; Rosanes, Togarmah, 1 (1930^2), 79–80.

[Abraham David]

DAVID BEN HEZEKIAH (d. before 1090), exilarch in Babylonia, son of the exilarch *Hezekiah b. David. David was in Jerusalem for a period during the gaonate of *Solomon b. Judah (1025–51). It seems that he wanted to be recognized as *nasi* in Ereẓ Israel, but did not succeed. Later, still during the lifetime of his father, he apparently visited Egypt. He then returned to Baghdad, and when his father died in 1058, succeeded him as exilarch. It is not known whether, like his father, he also acted as *rosh yeshivah* of Pumbedita. In 1090 his son Hezekiah is mentioned as exilarch. His grandson David b.

Hezekiah was also exilarch and was followed in the first half of the 12th century by his son Ḥasdai.

BIBLIOGRAPHY: S. Poznański, *Babylonische Geonim* (1914), 1–3; Mann, Egypt, 2 (1922), index; Mann, Texts, 1 (1931), 208; idem, in: *Sefer Zikkaron ... S.A. Poznański* (1927), 22f.

[Abraham David]

DAVID BEN HUSSEIN (**Ḥassūn, Ḥasan**), **ABU SULEIMAN** (second half of the tenth century), Karaite scholar. He is known only from a citation in the *Sefer ha-Mitzvot* (written c. 1007) of *Levi b. Japheth (sometimes wrongly attributed to his father, Japheth b. Ali). According to this, David compiled a manual of Karaite liturgy, also comprising homiletical, exegetical, and polemical material, and including strictures on certain Rabbanite traditions concerning *shi'ur komah* ("the measure of the body" of God). Though Pinsker's hypothesis that David's father was *Ḥasan (or Hussein) b. Mashi'aḥ is possible, there is as yet no factual proof to support it.

BIBLIOGRAPHY: S. Pinsker, *Likkutei Kadmoniyyot*, 1 (1860), 170; 2 (1860), 88–89, 92, 106; Steinschneider, in: JQR, 10 (1897/98), 539.

[Leon Nemoy]

DAVID BEN JOSHUA (d. 1647), head and emissary of the *Karaite community in Jerusalem. Originally from Egypt, David settled in Jerusalem in the early 17th century, where he helped to consolidate the Karaite community, later becoming its *parnas*. The anti-Jewish measures instituted by the harsh ruler Ibn Faruk in 1625–26 also affected the Karaite community. David was sent to Karaite congregations in Turkey and Crimea and succeeded in obtaining substantial assistance from them. At the end of that summer the situation of the community in Jerusalem deteriorated when new taxes were imposed. To pay them David was forced to borrow money and was imprisoned by his Arab creditors. When he was released, he resumed his missions to the Karaite communities in Crimea, Lithuania, and Poland, bearing a letter of recommendation also from the Rabbanites of Jerusalem. This stated that if speedy aid was not forthcoming there, the Arab creditors would seize the Karaite quarter and the entire community. David reached Luck (Lutsk), where he died in the fall of 1647.

BIBLIOGRAPHY: Mann, Texts, 2 (1935), index s.v. *David b. Yeshu'a*; Yaari, Sheluḥei, 172–4.

[Avraham Yaari]

DAVID BEN JOSHUA MAIMUNI (14th–15th centuries), **nagid* of Egyptian Jewry. David was the last of *Maimonides' descendants to occupy the position of *nagid*. He was a bibliophile who acquired a large library, and he encouraged the literary activity of others. It was under R. David's inspiration that R. Joseph Bonfils wrote his supercommentary *Ẓafenat Pa'ne'aḥ* ("Revealer of Secrets") to the commentary of R. Abraham *Ibn Ezra on the Torah. R. David wrote an essay in Arabic on the weights and measures of the Bible. For reasons so far unknown R. David was compelled to leave for Syria in the 1370s, writing a farewell letter to the Egyptian communities, which is still extant. He lived in *Aleppo, Syria, in 1375 and 1379, and also probably for some time in *Damascus. During his absence from Egypt, the position of *nagid* was occupied by R. Amram, who is mentioned in 1377 and 1380. At the beginning of the 15th century, R. David returned to Egypt and resumed office as *nagid*, as is learned from a document of 1409.

BIBLIOGRAPHY: Ashtor, Toledot, 1 (1944), 300–02; 2 (1951), 26–30; A.H. Freimann, in: *Minḥah li-Yhudah ... [Zlotnick]* (1950), 175–8.

[Eliyahu Ashtor]

DAVID BEN JUDAH (d. before 837?), exilarch in Babylonia. There was a controversy between the academies of Pumbedita and Sura concerning the candidate for the exilarchate. The academy of Pumbedita supported David b. Judah, while the academy of Sura supported his brother Daniel, supposedly a Karaite sympathizer. David b. Judah was finally appointed exilarch. This controversy degraded the prestige of the exilarchate and resulted in the decree of Caliph Ma'mun (813–33) authorizing the formation of independent religious sects. This decree strengthened the position of the Karaites, among others. In 833 David appointed R. Isaac b. R. Hunai (Ḥanina) as *rosh yeshivah* of Pumbedita. In a letter of 834 he stated that the sanctification of the new moon and the intercalation of the calendar were within the authority of the rabbis in Palestine. David's son Judah is mentioned as exilarch in 857.

BIBLIOGRAPHY: Mann, Egypt, 1 (1920), 53; 2 (1922), 41f.; Mann, Texts, 2 (1935), 130; Goode, in: JQR, 31 (1940/41), 158; Assaf, in: *Tarbiz*, 1:2 (1930), 66ff.; S. Assaf (ed.), *Sefer ha-Yishuv*, 2 (1944), 10, no. 6; Abramson, Merkazim, 11–14; Lazarus, in: MGWJ, 78 (1934), 279–88.

[Abraham David]

DAVID BEN JUDAH HE-ḤASID (early 14th century), Spanish kabbalist. He claimed to be the grandson of *Naḥmanides and a descendant of *Judah b. Samuel he-Ḥasid of Regensburg. David wrote several books which reflect the development of the different trends in Kabbalah after the publication of the *Zohar. Besides the teachings of Naḥmanides, these also included traditions that evolved from the sayings of the Castilian kabbalists, the Zohar, and the *Ḥasidei Ashkenaz. David was the author of the first extant commentary on one part of the Zohar, *Sefer ha-Gevul* (on *Idra Rabba*). He also wrote: *Marot ha-Ẓove'ot al ha-Torah* (preserved only in part), based on the Zohar, which he quotes in Hebrew translation, with the addition of numerous sayings from other sources; *Or Zaru'a*, a lengthy kabbalistic commentary on the order of the prayers; and treatises on the mysteries of the alphabet, on the Creation, and on *Merkabah mysticism. His works, extant only in several manuscripts, were quoted by many kabbalists even into the Safed period. *Sefer Livnat ha-Sappir* (1914), published under his name, was written in 1326 by R. Joseph Angelino, to judge from a comparison between it and David's works.

BIBLIOGRAPHY: Scholem, in: KS, 4 (1928), 302–27; D.S. Sassoon, *Ohel Dawid* (1932), nos. 1001–10; A. Marmorstein, in: MGWJ, 71 (1927), 39–48.

[Gershom Scholem]

DAVID BEN LEVI OF NARBONNE (latter half of the 13th century), scholar in Provence. Little is known about his life and personality other than that his principal teacher was Samuel b. Solomon Sekili, also a noted Provençal scholar. His few published responsa (in A. Sofer (ed.), *Teshuvot Ḥakhmei Provence*, 1967), show his importance as an authority. His decisions influenced French scholars to alter their verdicts in accordance with his opinions. R. David is known through his *Ha-Mikhtam* (after *Mikhtam le-David*, Ps. 16:1), which exerted a strong influence on the development of subsequent halakhic literature. In his work, a commentary covering many tractates of the Talmud, he bases himself on Alfasi. Many of his decisions which were included in the commentary were later incorporated in the *Orḥot Ḥayyim* of *Aaron b. Jacob ha-Kohen of Lunel, who often quoted David, sometimes anonymously. It was through the *Orḥot Ḥayyim* and the *Kol Bo*, which is dependent on it, that David's work became known to Joseph *Caro and Moses *Isserles, who made considerable use of these two books. The *Sefer ha-Mikhtam* quotes extensively from scholars of France, Provence, and Spain but relies primarily upon Rashi, Alfasi, Maimonides, Abraham b. David, Zerahiah ha-Levi, and Meshullam b. Moses. David's commentaries to the following tractates have been published: *Berakhot* (Jerusalem, 1967); *Rosh Ha-Shanah* (*ibid.*, 1963); *Megillah* (Lemberg, 1904); extracts on *Yoma* (in *Sam Ḥayyim*, Leghorn, 1801, which erroneously attributes them to Todros ha-Levi); *Sukkah, Mo'ed Katan, Pesaḥim*, and *Beẓah* (New York, 1959, simultaneously in two editions, A. Sofer and M. Blau, with the exception of *Beẓah* which is not included in Blau).

BIBLIOGRAPHY: Buber, in: *Sefer ha-Mikhtam* (1904), introduction; Sofer, in: *Sefer ha-Mikhtam* to *Sukkah*… (1959), introduction.

[Israel Moses Ta-Shma]

DAVID BEN MANASSEH DARSHAN (16th century), preacher and author in Poland. He was a pupil of *Isaac b. Bezalel, Moses *Isserles, and Solomon *Luria. In 1555, David visited Italy, and traveled among the communities there. He subsequently returned to Cracow, where he gained his livelihood by various means, occupying, as a lowly preacher, a humble and solitary position in Jewish society. Among other functions, he answered queries on treating the sick and wrote amulets and letters. David left for posterity a complete system for preserving the methods of biblical exposition which he practiced himself. He also drew up a program of study for yeshivot and for revising their administration, which was revolutionary for his day. He proposed establishing an original type of *bet midrash* where he himself would be available to deal with the problems of all who turned to him in order to dispense with the usual preoccupation with authority and prestige customary in the yeshivah. He undertook to give daily instruction on a text agreed upon with his hearers to people who were not regular Torah students and to accept the unlettered masses. Study in this yeshivah would be centered around a library with over 400 volumes which David had collected and was ready to donate to the proposed *bet midrash*. Another innovation he proposed was the recording and collection of the discussions among the scholars. David's utopian plan did not materialize, but it gives an interesting picture of the organization of the yeshivah in his day and the circles which frequented it. His two published works are *Shir ha-Ma'alot le-David* (Cracow, 1571), which contains references to several of his unpublished works, and *Ketav Hitnaẓẓelut le-Darshanim* (Lublin, 1574).

BIBLIOGRAPHY: H.H. Ben-Sasson, *Hagut ve-Hanhagah* (1959), index.

[Natan Efrati]

DAVID BEN MESHULLAM OF SPEYER (12th century), liturgical poet. His father was apparently the scholar R. Meshullam who lived in Mainz in 1034. On Feb. 19, 1090, David was received in Speyer by Emperor Henry IV as representative of the Jewish community, together with Judah b. Kalonymus and Moses b. Jekuthiel. In a remarkable *seliḥah* for the eve of the Day of Atonement, beginning *Elohim al Domi le-Dami* ("God! Be not silent on my blood"), still in use in the German and Polish rituals although the original text has been mutilated by censorship, he describes the horrors of the First Crusade.

BIBLIOGRAPHY: H. Bresslau, in: ZGJD, 1 (1887), 156–7; Germ Jud, 1 (1934), 329, 336; H. Brody and S. Wiener, *Mivḥar ha-Shirah ha-Ivrit* (1922), 221–3; S. Bernfeld, *Sefer ha-Dema'ot*, 1 (1924), 199–202; A.M. Habermann, *Gezerot Ashkenaz* (1945), 69–71; Davidson, Oẓar, 1 (1924), 211, no. 4626.

[Jefim (Hayyim) Schirmann]

DAVID (Tevele) BEN NATHAN OF LISSA (d. 1792), Galician rabbi. Born in Brody, David served as rabbi of Horochow and, from 1774 until his death, of Lissa. He was in halakhic correspondence with Ezekiel *Landau and Akiva b. Moses *Eger. In the controversy over the *Cleves *Get* he supported Israel *Lipschuetz; his responsum on this subject appears in *Or Yisrael*. Another of his responsa is found in the **Penei Aryeh* (no. 30) of Aryeh Leib b. Ḥayyim *Breslau. In 1774 David gave his approbation to the *Yein Levanon* of N.H. *Wessely, but when he realized the true aim of the educational reformers he attacked Wessely's plan in a sermon, accusing him of a desire "to stifle young children in the bud and shut the portals of Torah and faith against them" (1782). Wessely countered in letter 4 of *Divrei Shalom ve-Emet* (Berlin, 1785). Though Hirschel b. Aryeh Loeb Levin agreed to David's request to use his influence with the Berlin community to forbid the publicizing of Wessely's writings, Moses *Mendelssohn and David *Friedlaender prevented him from carrying it out. *Nefesh David*, comprising short sermons on the weekly scriptural readings, was published posthumously by David's grandson, A.S. Amkraut, in 1878. The second part, entitled *Mikhtav le-David*, consists of learned discussion on the Talmud and Codes. ZECHARIAH MENDEL (d. 1809), one of his three sons, was appointed *dayyan* of Lissa and, after his father's death, rabbi of Inowroclaw.

BIBLIOGRAPHY: Graetz, in: MGWJ, 20 (1871), 465–9; L. Lewin, *Geschichte der Juden in Lissa* (1904), 192–204; idem, in: JJLG, 12 (1918), 165–97; Waxman, Literature, 3 (1960²), 117f.; Z. Horowitz, *Kitvei ha-Ge'onim* (1928), 62f.; Gelber, in: *Arim ve-Immahot be-Yisrael*, 6 (1955), 57, 328.

[Yehoshua Horowitz]

DAVID BEN SAADIAH (11th century), Spanish scholar. David b. Saadiah was the author of *Mishpetei Shevu'ot* written in Arabic. Though he was famous as a *dayyan* in his time, the disappearance of his book has caused him to be virtually forgotten. A quotation from it is preserved in *Shitah Mekubbeẓet* (on BM 104b), from which it may be inferred that he also wrote a critical commentary on the *Halakhot Gedolot*. If he is to be identified with the R. David mentioned in the responsa of Moses b. Ḥanokh (Assaf in *Madda'ei ha-Yahadut*, 2 (1927), no. 23), as is almost certain, he also wrote commentaries on the Talmud. A fragment of *Mishpetei Shevu'ot* in the original Arabic was published by I. Friedlander in the *Israel Lewy Festschrift* (1911) where, however, it is ascribed in error to *Saadiah Gaon. It appears that *Sha'arei Shevu'ot* is merely an edited translation of David b. Saadiah's work written by Isaac b. Reuben. *Sha'arei Shevu'ot* had a very large circulation and many incomplete editions of it are extant. *Sefer Shevu'ot be-Ḥaruzim*, published by Assaf (1933), is also patterned for the most part after the *Sha'arei Shevu'ot*.

BIBLIOGRAPHY: Assaf, in: KS, 3 (1927), 295–7; idem, *Mi-Sifrut ha-Ge'onim* (1933), 12f.; Benedikt, in: KS, 25 (1948/49), 173; Abramson, in: *Talpioth*, 5 (1952), 773–80.

[Israel Moses Ta-Shma]

DAVID BEN SAMUEL (d. after 1201), exilarch in *Baghdad before 1195, although he is only mentioned as such from 1197. David succeeded his father, Samuel of Mosul, who held the position from 1175 to 1190. He secured his appointment only with some difficulty. The head of the Baghdad academy, *Samuel b. Ali, objected to the exilarchate and wished to abolish it. It was only as a result of the pressure of the Baghdad community that the position was maintained. Samuel b. Ali opposed the appointment of David b. Samuel as exilarch on the grounds that he was not sufficiently learned. It seems that *Maimonides was opposed to this view. It is doubtful whether R. David b. Samuel or R. David of Mosul excommunicated R. *Daniel b. Saadiah, the pupil of R. Samuel b. Ali, because he had violently criticized Maimonides' opinions a short while before 1235.

BIBLIOGRAPHY: Mann, in: *Sefer Zikkaron li-Khevod S.A. Poznański* (1927), 23f.; Mann, Texts, 1 (1931), index; Assaf, in: *Tarbiz*, 1 (1930), 126–8; Abramson, in: *Perakim*, 1 (1967–68), 16.

[Abraham David]

DAVID BEN SAMUEL HA-LEVI (known as the **Taz** from the initial letters of his work, *Turei Zahav*; 1586–1667), rabbi and halakhic authority. Born in Vladimir-Volynski (Lodomeria), Ukraine, he studied under his eldest brother, Isaac ha-Levi, and married the daughter of Joel *Sirkes. After his marriage he remained for some time in the house of his father-in-law and studied in his yeshivah. He established his own *bet midrash* in Cracow. He regarded the premature death of his children there as a punishment for establishing his home on top of the synagogue. David was appointed rabbi of Putalicze near Rawa (Galicia) in about 1618, and for 20 years he served as rabbi of Posen. About 1641 he was appointed rabbi of Ostrog in Volhynia, where he maintained a yeshivah. During the Chmielnicki pogroms (1648–49) he escaped to the fortress of Ulick. In the *seliḥot* (published in *Yalkut Menaḥem* of Menahem Mendel Biber, 1903) which he composed for the 26th of Sivan, he describes the miraculous escape of the Jews who gathered there for protection. He then went to Lublin, and finally, like many Polish scholars, wandered westward. He was consulted on halakhic problems in all the Moravian communities to which he came. When calm was partially restored in Poland, he returned there, and in 1654 was appointed rabbi of Lemberg to the community "outside the city." He participated in the meetings of the Council of the Four Lands and his signature appears on many of the rulings and resolutions issued by that body. His two sons, Mordecai and Solomon, were killed in the pogroms against the Jews of Lvov which broke out on May 3, 1664. During his last days he sent his son Isaiah and stepson Aryeh Leib b. Samuel Ẓevi to investigate the claims of *Shabbetai Ẓevi. They came back full of enthusiasm, bringing a letter and gifts for their aged father, who appears to have accepted their opinion. David died in Lvov.

His most important work, *Turei Zahav (Taz)*, is in the main a commentary on the four parts of the Shulḥan Arukh: *Even ha-Ezer* (reissued in full in Zolkiew, 1754) and *Ḥoshen Mishpat* (to section 246, Hamburg, 1692; the whole published in Berlin, 1766). The work is not a running commentary, but discussions on the *Tur* of Jacob b. Asher and the Talmud and its commentators. *Taz* on *Oraḥ Ḥayyim* was published in the margin of the Shulḥan Arukh, together with the commentary of Abraham Abele Gumbiner, under the combined title *Meginnei Ereẓ* (Dyhernfurth, 1692), *Magen David* being David's work and *Magen Avraham*, Gumbiner's. *Magen David* is a running commentary, but has a closer relationship to the *Tur* than to the Shulḥan Arukh. Various authors have written notes and glosses on this section of the *Taz*, the best-known being *Peri Megadim*, of Joseph b. Meir *Teomim. The most important and authoritative of the sections, however, is the *Taz* on *Yoreh De'ah* (Lublin, 1646). The second edition was published in the margin of the Shulḥan Arukh together with the commentary of *Shabbetai b. Meir ha-Kohen, the whole being called *Ashlei ha-Ravrevei* (Wilhelmsdorf, 1677). In the commentary David gives reasons for the rulings of the Shulḥan Arukh and examines the sources. This section became popular in all yeshivot as soon as it appeared and was accepted as authoritative by halakhists. At the end of the book he appended *Daf Aḥaron*, containing criticism of *Siftei Kohen* on *Yoreh De'ah* by Shabbetai b. Meir ha-Kohen. Many supercommentaries were also written on this section of *Taz*, the most important again being *Peri Megadim*. David added two books containing corrections and supplements to the *Taz* (*Haggahot ve-Ḥiddushim*, Halle, 1710; *Zahav Mezukkak*, Dyhernfurth, 1725). He also wrote *Divrei David* (*ibid.*, 1689), a supercommentary to that of *Rashi on the Pentateuch. The second edition of the *Taz* on *Even ha-Ezer* as well as a collection of responsa, which were available to scholars of the generation after his death, have not survived. David's works greatly influenced practical halakhic rulings during the succeeding generations. He is credited with halakhic contributions toward a synthesis of economic practice with the laws of the Torah. His rulings occasionally reflect a practical flexibility in the face of social and economic reality. The *Turei Zahav* synagogue in Lvov was named after him.

BIBLIOGRAPHY: Y.M. Zunz, *Ir ha-Ẓedek* (1874), 151–3; Fuenn, Keneset, 239; Ḥ.N. Dembitzer, *Kelilat Yofi*, 1 (1887, repr. 1960), 48–77; S. Buber, *Anshei Shem* (1895), 56–59; M.M. Biber, *Mazkeret li-Gedolei Ostraha* (1907), 53–58; S.M. Chones, *Toledot ha-Posekim* (1910), 266–70; Halpern, Pinkas (1945), index; H. Tchernowitz, *Toledot ha-Posekim*, 3 (1947), 139–41; Szulwas, in: I. Halprin (ed.), *Beit Yisra'el be-Polin*, 2 (1953), 20–21; J. Sasportas, *Ẓiẓat Novel Ẓevi*, ed. by I. Tishby (1954), 77–79; Ben-Sasson, in: *Zion*, 21 (1956), 183–206; Scholem, Shabbetai Ẓevi, 500–2.

[Shmuel Ashkenazi]

DAVID BEN SAUL (first half of 13th century), talmudic scholar who lived in Provence. David was a disciple of *Solomon b. Abraham of Montpellier and, together with him and *Jonah b. Abraham Gerondi, actively opposed Maimonides' philosophic writings. He is quoted in an anonymous commentary to *Bava Meẓia* in the responsa of Joseph b. David ibn Leb (3:60) and in those of Joseph di Trani (*Mahanit*, resp., vol. 2, YD 39).

[Joseph Elijah Heller]

DAVID BEN SHIMEON (1825–1879), Moroccan rabbi (known as "*Ẓuf Devash*"), founder of the Moroccan (Moghrabi) Jewish community of Israel. David b. Shimeon was born in Rabat, Morocco. In 1854 he left for Ereẓ Israel as part of the Moroccan immigration which had been growing continuously since the 1830s. These immigrants were mostly poor Jews who were motivated to leave by the deterioration of the position of the Jews in Morocco, the improvement of conditions in Ereẓ Israel, and messianic hopes. All attempts of the Moghrabis to establish themselves as a separate community, independent of the dominant Sephardi community, met with determined opposition on the part of the latter, who even leveled accusations at them before the Turkish and consular authorities, with the result that some of their leaders were imprisoned.

Aided by the Ashkenazim in Jerusalem, David finally succeeded in 1860 in establishing the separate Moghrabi community, arriving at an agreement with the Sephardim as to the allocation of the funds received by them from abroad. David applied himself vigorously to the needs of his community. He sent emissaries abroad on their behalf and built residential areas for them, including the suburb Maḥaneh Israel (1867), schools, and synagogues.

David b. Shimeon's works on *halakhah* and *aggadah* deal with the religious duty of settling in Ereẓ Israel. They include *Sha'ar he-Ḥaẓer* (1862) and *Sha'ar ha-Mifkad* (with additions by his son Raphael Aaron; 1908–9). His other works are no longer extant.

BIBLIOGRAPHY: A. Elmaleh, in: Luncz, *Luaḥ*, 14 (1909), 53–88; Y. Barnai, in: *Ha-Yishuv ha-Yehudi bi-Yerushalayim*.

[Jacob Barnai]

DAVID BEN SOLOMON (Abū al-Faḍl Dā'ūd ibn Abī al-Bayān Suleimān al-Isrā'īlī; 1161–after 1236), Karaite physician in Cairo. He was a pupil of and secretary to Ḥibat Allāh ibn Jumayʿ (or Jamīʿ), a Jewish convert to Islam, and personal physician to the sultan Saladin. David served as physician to the sultan al-Malik al-ʿAdil. He also served on the medical faculty of the Nāṣirī hospital in Cairo. Here he had among his students Ibn Abī Uṣaybiʿa, the author of the classical history of Arab physicians, who speaks of him in the highest terms as an outstanding diagnostician and therapeutist. David wrote *Al-Dustūr al-Bīmāristānī fī al-Adwiya al-Murakkaba* (ed. by P. Sbath, Cairo, 1933), a formulary of compound medicines for hospital use, and *Risālat al-Mujarrabāt*, a tract on well-tested medicines. Prescriptions by David are frequently quoted in the standard pharmaçopoeia (entitled *Minhāj al-Dukkān*) of the 13th-century Jewish apothecary Abū al-Minā al-Kūhīn al-ʿAṭṭār.

BIBLIOGRAPHY: Steinschneider, Arab Lit, 195f.; Brockelmann, Arab Lit, 1 (1898), 491, and Supplement 1 (1937), 896.

[Leon Nemoy]

DAVID BEN SOLOMON IBN ABI (Avi, Ben Abi) ZIMRA (known as **RaDBaZ** = **R**abbi **D**avid **B**en **A**bi **Z**imra; 1479–1573), talmudic scholar, halakhic authority, and kabbalist. Abi Zimra was born in Spain into a wealthy family, but by the age of 13 he was in Safed (possibly going via Fez – see Sambari in Neubauer's Chronicles, vol. 1 (1887), 157). The most eminent of his teachers was Joseph Saragossi of Sicily who left Spain in 1492 and eventually settled in Safed. Abi Zimra moved to Jerusalem but shortly before 1513 immigrated to Egypt, apparently due to bad economic conditions in Palestine. He remained there for 40 years, first in Alexandria, then in Cairo where he joined the *bet din* of the *nagid*, Isaac Sholal. After the conquest of Egypt by the Turks (1517) and the decline of the office of the *nagid*, Abi Zimra became the official head of Egyptian Jewry. He was not only *dayyan* but also head of a yeshivah, trustee of the *hekdesh*, and administrator of charity collections. He held all of these offices in an honorary capacity, as he was financially independent. Apart from his inherited wealth Abi Zimra was apparently successful in business and as a moneylender to non-Jews (S. Assaf, *Mekorot u-Meḥkarim* (1946), 199–203). His library, containing rare manuscripts, was famous. His was an open house; R. Isaac *Akrish lived there for many years and was the tutor of his children and grandchildren. Abi Zimra exercised a great influence upon his contemporaries which can be seen from his success in settling a quarrel between the Mustaʿrabs (the indigenous Jewish community) and the Maghrabis (the community with origins in other parts of North Africa), and in issuing many ordinances beneficial to Egyptian Jewry. The most famous of them are the abolition of the dating of legal documents according to the Seleucid era (*minyan shetarot*), and its replacement by dating according to the era of Creation (see *Calendar); formation of a *ḥevra kaddisha* (burial society; previously the dead had to be buried secretly to avoid attacks from the non-Jews); and the prohibition of the employment of non-Jews as dancers and musicians at Jewish weddings. He also tried to reintroduce into the public liturgy the recital of the *Amidah* by both the congregation and the reader (from the time of Maimonides this had been said by the reader only).

His reputation extended beyond the boundaries of Egypt and legal and religious questions were sent to him from many communities. Abi Zimra often engaged in disputations with Muslim and Karaite scholars, and his initially lenient attitude to the *Karaites became more stringent. Shortly before 1553 he decided to return to Palestine. He settled first in Jerusalem where he was dissatisfied with the local governor as well as with some of the Jews, and moved to Safed, where he remained until his death. Although Abi Zimra praised Jewish scholars who were versed in natural sciences and spoke with warm appreciation of the contribution of Jewish philosophers in promoting Jewish belief, he discouraged his students from studying philosophy (Resp. published by Assaf in *Minḥah le-David* (1935), 228–33). His negative attitude toward philosophy is more firmly expressed in his later works (Resp. no. 1616, *Migdal David* (1883), introd. and 34b; *Meẓudat David* (1862), no. 446). When asked which system of articles of faith (*Ikkarei ha-Dat*) he approved, he replied that he opposed any system, since each commandment was of paramount importance (Resp. no. 344). In Abi Zimra's view, the *aggadah*, which he regarded as equal in holiness to other parts of the Oral Law, can bear two meanings, one literal (*nigleh*) and one esoteric (*nistar*). He strongly criticized the Bible commentaries of Abraham *Ibn Ezra and David *Kimḥi who referred to a certain *aggadah* as "irrational." He believed in demons (Resp. no. 848) but strongly opposed superstitious practices, particularly those which conflict with religious laws. In some respects Abi Zimra was very stringent in religious practice, but he was also very humane and objected to imposing new restrictions.

His methods were scientific. He examined texts critically, comparing the different versions and tracing them back to their original sources, investigating their authenticity, and emending them only when necessary and no other solution could be found. A treatise on the methodology of the Talmud (*Kelalei ha-Gemara*, printed in *Me-Harerei Nemerim*, Venice, 1599; separately Zolkiew, 1749) was attributed to Abi Zimra, but modern scholarship doubts he is the author of this work. Nevertheless, a good number of his responsa are devoted to methodological principles.

Although he was a kabbalist, he introduced Kabbalah in decisions only when not in contradiction with the Talmud, or where no definite decision is laid down in the Talmud. When Kabbalah conflicted with the Talmud preference was to be given to the latter. When a young man, Abi Zimra wrote a kabbalistic work on the letters of the Hebrew alphabet (*Magen David*, Amsterdam, 1713) and in later years he composed works dealing more generally with Kabbalah. In his kabbalistic system *gematriot* ("numerical value of letters") and the doctrine of metempsychosis played important roles, the latter being reflected even in his legal decisions (e.g., on *ḥaliẓah*). He was one of the most open defenders of the doctrine of cosmic cycles in creation (*Shemittot*).

Abi Zimra's most important work is his collection of responsa (*Teshuvot ha-Radbaz*, 1882) in seven parts (see Boaz Cohen, in: *Ha-Ẓofeh le-Ḥokhmat Yisrael*, 14 (Budapest, 1930), 115–94, 211–356). Other of his responsa appear in the works of his contemporaries. Various individual responsa have been published from manuscript. A. Marx published one full of interest addressed to the Jewish community of Cochin, India, on the status of the black Jews (REJ, 89 (1930), 293–304). Eight more from the same manuscript were published by H.J. Zimmels (*Sefer ha-Yovel… S. Krauss* (1936), 178–87) and S. Assaf published a responsum in *Minḥah le-David* (*Kovez Ma'amarim le-Yovel… D. Yellin* (1935), 228–33). Abi Zimra's halakhic opinions were widely quoted throughout the centuries. Even in modern times, his responsa continue to have an impact on a wide variety of issues, including medical questions. Even though Abi Zimra was not a doctor, his medical knowledge was quite formidable and accurate. He was very sensitive to patients' needs and feelings, looking for leniencies wherever he could. Abi Zimra's opinion is much quoted regarding another modern issue, namely the halakhic status of Ethiopian Jewry; he affirms their Jewishness.

Abi Zimra's novellae are quoted by his pupil Bezalel *Ashkenazi in his *Shitah Mekubbeẓet* and he himself refers to his novellae to tractate *Shabbat* (*Magen David*, Introd.). His other published works are *Yekar Tiferet* (Smyrna, 1757), a commentary on those portions of Maimonides' *Mishneh Torah* on which there is no *Maggid Mishneh* commentary, i.e., on the sections *Hafla'ah, Zera'im, Kedushah*, and *Shofetim*, which were published in the Romm (Vilna) editions of the *Mishneh Torah*, and on *Sheluḥin ve-Shuttafin*, and *Avadim* by S.B. Werner (Jerusalem, 1945); *Meẓudat David* (written 1556, Zolkiew, 1862), an explanation of the traditional 613 commandments, both rational and kabbalistic; *Migdal David* (written 1560, Lemberg, 1883), a kabbalistic commentary on the Song of Songs; and *Keter Malkhut*, a *piyyut* for the Day of Atonement, which has been frequently published and is included in the Heidenheim *Maḥzor*. The remainder are still in manuscript.

BIBLIOGRAPHY: Azulai, 1 (1852), 44–45, no. 16; S. Hazzan, *Ha-Ma'alot li-Shelomo* (1894), 18a, no. 4; Rosanes, Togarmah, 1 (1930^2), 197ff.; 2 (1938), 151n, 181; 3 (1938), 326; H.J. Zimmels, *Rabbi David ibn abi Simra* (Ger., 1932); Ashtor, Toledot, 2 (1951), 458–70; Scheiber and Benayahu, in: *Sefunot*, 6 (1962), 125–34; Waxman, Literature, 2 (1960^2), 179–81; I.M. Goldman, *The Life and Times of Rabbi David Ibn Abi Zimra* (1971). **ADD. BIBLIOGRAPHY:** M. Shapiro, in: *Judaism*, 42:3 (1993), 332–43; A. Ophir Shemesh, in: *Asufot*, 14 (2002),125–54; Y. Shiloh, "*Kelalei ha-Talmud ve-Shittat Limud ha-Talmud shel Rabbi David ben Zimra*," dissertation, Bar-Ilan (2002); S. Morell, *Studies in the Judicial Methodology of Rabbi David ibn Ali Zimra* (2004).

[Hirsch Jacob Zimmels]

DAVID BEN ZAKKAI (I), exilarch in Iraq, 917–40. David became exilarch during a period of severe controversy, some five years after his uncle, *Ukva, had been removed from his position by the *rosh yeshivah* of Pumbedita, *Kohen Zedek, and his faction. David was appointed by the *rosh yeshivah* of Sura. The wealthy, who were influential in royal circles, were the principal opponents of the exilarchate. They probably wished to abolish the established leadership, which was based on lineage. David zealously watched over the dignity of his position and its income from distant provinces. Aided by government intervention, the exilarch collected a large sum of money from the Jews of Persia. *Nathan ha-Bavli's description of the installation ceremony of the exilarch and of his system of tax collection probably applies to David. In the early days of David's office the balance of authority in the autonomous Jewish leadership of Babylonia was disturbed by the decline of the yeshivah of Sura which was in danger of closing. Such a situation would have left Pumbedita, and the *gaon* at its head, as the only possible challenge to the authority of the exilarch. David showed initiative and a readiness to depart from traditional ways in order to save the ancient yeshivah and the double gaonate. He appointed *Saadiah ben Joseph as *gaon*, "who was not of the rabbinical body of the yeshivah, but from Egypt." David had become acquainted with him when, together, they had opposed the *gaon* *Ben Meir of Palestine over the issue of the independence of the Babylonian community in matters concerning the calendar. In this conflict Saadiah recognized David as a leader. It is related that David had been forewarned of Saadiah's irritable disposition, to which he replied: "My judgment and decision have already fallen in favor of him." The relations between David and Saadiah Gaon were satisfactory during the first two years following his appointment. Moreover, a document is extant in which the *gaon* lavishly praises the halakhic judgment of the exilarch. About 930, however, a dispute broke out between them. There are differing versions of the cause of the conflict, according to the two groups of supporters. It may be assumed that it was a struggle for the leadership between two resolute men, during a period of upheaval and tension among the ruling class of Babylonian Jewry. The consequences were grave: the wealthy supported Saadiah and appointed Josiah-Ḥasan, the brother of David, as exilarch. On the other hand, David appointed *Joseph b. Jacob as *gaon* of Sura. The struggle between the contending forces took the form of reciprocal accusations, bans, and counter-bans, and the case was even brought before the court of the caliph. David's party gained the upper hand; Josiah was expelled and Saadiah was removed from his position. David acted with excessive severity against his opponents. In the end the rivals reached a compromise (Purim, 937). David's life was a stormy one, but by the time of his death he had strengthened the authority of the exilarchate. His efforts had saved the yeshivah of Sura from extinction. Furthermore, his struggle for the prestige of his position and the maintenance of the traditional form of Jewish autonomous leadership prevented the rising wealthy class from seizing power.

BIBLIOGRAPHY: Neubauer, Chronicles, 2 (1888), 78–87; A. Harkavy, *Zikkaron le-Rishonim*, 1:4 (1892), 276–7, no. 555; B.M. Lewin (ed.) *Iggeret Sherira Ga'on* (1921), 117; Auerbach, in: *Juedische Studien Joseph Wohlgemuth…* (1928), 1–30; Baron, in: *Saadia Anniversary Volume* (1943), 9ff.; Abraham Ibn Daud, *Book of Tradition*, ed. by G.D. Cohen (1967), 54f., 58, 61, 130f.; H. Malter, *Saadia Gaon: His Life and Works* (1921), index.

[Haim Hillel Ben-Sasson]

DAVID BEN ZAKKAI (II) (d. c. 1216), exilarch in *Mosul, Mesopotamia. David and his cousin Samuel, descendants of the exilarch Josiah b. Zakkai, were community leaders in Mosul. *Pethahiah of Regensburg, who visited Mosul about 1175, states that they owned fields and vineyards and collected taxes from the local Jews. In 1174 after the exilarch *Daniel b. Ḥasdai died leaving no sons, there was a disagreement among the communal leaders in Baghdad over the choice of his successor. Some favored David, while others supported Samuel. Apparently Samuel was appointed exilarch in Baghdad and David in Mosul. It was either he or his kinsman David, son and successor of Samuel, who about 1215 complied with a request from Joseph ibn *Aknin, the disciple of Maimonides, to excommunicate *Daniel ha-Bavli for his attacks on his master. He was still alive in 1216, when he was visited in Mosul by the poet Judah *Al-Ḥarizi, but the date of his death is unknown. He was succeeded as exilarch in Mosul by his son Daniel and afterward, by Daniel's son *David ben Daniel.

BIBLIOGRAPHY: Mann, Texts, 1 (1931), index; idem, in: *Sefer Zikkaron … S. Poznański* (1927), 23, 25, 26–27, 37; S. Poznański, *Babylonische Geonim* (1914), index.

[Tovia Preschel]

DAVID D'BETH HILLEL, (d. 1846), traveler and scholar, author of *Travels from Jerusalem through Arabia, Kurdistan, Part of Persia and India to Madras 1824–32* (Madras, 1832). D'Beth Hillel left his native Vilna at the beginning of the 19th century, settled with other pupils of the Gaon of Vilna in *Safed around 1815, and began his long journey to the East in 1824. He traveled through *Palestine, *Syria, and remote regions of *Kurdistan and *Persia. After spending a year in Baghdad and other communities in Mesopotamia, he sailed from Bushire to India, landing at Bombay in October 1828. He then journeyed to Cochin (*Kochi) where he remained four months, returned to Bombay for a two-year sojourn, and then traveled through the Bombay presidency until he reached Madras in 1831. While waiting there for passage to return to Palestine, he taught Hebrew to some English clergymen, including the Anglican archdeacon T. Robinson to whom he dedicated his *Travels*. He returned to *Jerusalem in 1838, revisited India in 1845, and died the next year in Calcutta.

D'Beth Hillel was the first Jewish traveler since *Benjamin of Tudela to leave so detailed an account of the various Jewish communities in the Orient and of other Oriental sects and religions. His information and observations on the geographical distribution, the socio-economic structure, and the languages and dialects of the Jews in Palestine, Kurdistan, Persia, and India made his *Travels* an invaluable source of information on the Oriental Diaspora in the early 19th century. The book, published in an edition of only 300 copies, is extremely rare and has been used by only a few scholars.

BIBLIOGRAPHY: Yaari, in: *Sinai*, 4 (1939), 24–53 (Heb. tr. of chapters on Palestine); Fischel, *ibid.*, 5 (1940), 218–54 (Heb. tr. of chapters on Kurdistan, Babylonia, and Persia); idem, in: JSOS, 6 (1944), 195–226 (biographical details); idem, in: *Oriens*, 10 (1957), 240–47; idem, in: *In the Time of Harvest, Essays... H. Silver* (1963), 170–85.

[Walter Joseph Fischel]

DAVID-GORODOK (Pol. **Dawidgródek**; Heb. דוד קורדוק), town in Brest-Litovsk oblast, Belarus; until 1793 and from 1921 to 1939 within Poland. Jews are first known there from the middle of the 17th century. In 1667 David-Gorodok had an established community linked to that of *Pinsk. There were 408 Jews aged over one year living in David-Gorodok in 1766, and 386 in 1784. Main occupations were innkeeping, the sale of alcoholic liquor, trade in timber and forest produce, and cattle breeding. Jews were active in forest exploitation and the development of river navigation to the Ukraine and Baltic Sea which expanded in David-Gorodok in the 19th century, and the community increased. It numbered 1,572 in 1847, and 3,087 (40% of the total population) in 1897. In 1898, to offset the growing competition of the railroads, a number of Jewish carters there invested in a steamship. A further group founded a motorbus company in 1921. The majority in the community were **Mitnaggedim*. The local supporters of the *Bund (prominent among them A. *Litvak) and the Territorialist Socialist movement were active in the 1905 revolution and *self-defense against pogroms was organized in the community. The *Po'alei Zion party resumed activities in David-Gorodok in 1917. In the elections to the Russian Constituent Assembly in 1917, the local Zionist Organization received 740 votes and the Po'alei Zion 640 votes. The Jews in David-Gorodok suffered during the Revolution and the Polish-Soviet war (1917–1921). During Sukkot 1921 soldiers of the "White" General Bulak-Balakhovich who arrived with the Polish army were stationed there for several weeks, during which they went on a rampage of robbery, rape, and murder, receiving 100,000 rubles as ransom from the Jews. The Jewish population numbered 2,832 (28.1% of the total) in 1921. The *American Jewish Joint Distribution Committee provided considerable relief to the community. Jews owned sawmills, flour mills, and tanneries. They rented estates and lakes, and exported their products. Most of the retail trade was in Jewish hands. *He-Ḥalutz began activities in David-Gorodok in 1921, the *Mizrachi in 1925, and *Ha-Shomer ha-Ẓa'ir in 1927. A *Tarbut Hebrew elementary school was founded in 1924 (it numbered 400 pupils in 1934), and a Hebrew religious school, Yavneh, in 1927. The director of Tarbut, Abraham Olszanski, founded a group for Hebrew-speakers, Benei Yehudah, in 1931, which spread over Poland and became a movement. In 1928, when elections to the municipal councils were held in Poland under full democratic conditions, eight Jews were elected in David-Gorodok among the 24 members of the council.

[Arthur Cygielman]

Ḥasidism

There was a ḥasidic dynasty called after the township of the same name. The Ḥasidim of the Gorodok dynasty proper should be distinguished from the followers of *Menahem Mendel of Vitebsk, also sometimes called Ḥasidim of Gorodok (Yid. Horodok). The dynasty, whose followers came mainly from Polesia, was founded at the beginning of the 19th century by ZE'EV WOLFF GINSBURG (son of the ẓaddik Samuel of Kashivka (Volhynia)), the *av bet din* of David-Gorodok. He was followed by his son DAVID, his grandson ISRAEL JOSEPH HA-LEVI (d. c. 1899), the most influential member of the dynasty, and the latter's grandson ISAAC (d. 1908). The Ḥasidim of David-Gorodok were mostly artisans and simple people and their *ẓaddikim* behaved modestly. Their style of prayer was more sedate than that of most ḥasidim and they had special melodies. Isaac's descendants perished during the Holocaust.

[Wolf Zeev Rabinowitsch]

Holocaust Period

From Sept. 19, 1939, until July 5, 1941, the town was under Soviet rule and the Jewish population increased with the influx of refugees from German-occupied western Poland. The Soviet regime introduced drastic changes in economic, religious, and social life. Jewish community institutions were disbanded; the Hebrew *Tarbut school continued to function in Yiddish; private economic initiative was stifled; and artisans were organized into cooperatives. The Orthodox Jewish congregation made efforts to overcome difficulties imposed on their religious life. On the holidays, prayer services were held earlier in the morning so the men could appear at their places of work. In the summer of 1940 local Zionist and Revisionist leaders were arrested, followed in February 1941 by the arrest of over ten other community leaders. In April that year the young men were drafted into the Soviet army. When war broke out between Germany and the U.S.S.R. on June 22, 1941, Jewish groups attempted to flee to the Soviet interior. The Germans entered David-Gorodok on July 5, 1941. A local gentile delegation appeared before the Germans in Pinsk with a request to be allowed to attack the Jews. The Germans willingly acceded and issued orders for all Jewish males 14 years of age or older to appear in the square by the church. From there they were taken to the town of Hinowski where they had to dig the trenches in which they were murdered and buried. The Germans set up a ghetto for the surviving women and children. Sealed within, they suffered from disease and starvation. When the ghetto was liquidated in the summer of 1942, some of the inhabitants reached the partisans active in the vicinity. By the time Soviet forces reentered in 1944 no Jews were left alive in David-Gorodok. Later, very few survivors came back, mostly from the U.S.S.R. They all left David-Gorodok within a short time for the West and some of them settled in Israel.

[Aharon Weiss]

BIBLIOGRAPHY: W. Rabinowitsch, *Lithuanian Hasidism* (1970), 209–14, 227. **ADD. BIBLIOGRAPHY:** *Sefer Zikkaron David-Horodok* (1956).

DAVID IBN HAJJAR (12th century), Spanish talmudist and grammarian, and pupil of Isaac b. Jacob *Alfasi. Extracts from David's writings in Arabic on marriage contracts and divorce are cited in Hebrew translation in the collection of geonic responsa *Sha'arei Ẓedek* (1966, p. 33). Abraham *Ibn Ezra, in the introduction to his *Moznayim*, mentions David, the *dayyan*, in the list *ziknei leshon ha-kodesh* ("the sages of the Hebrew tongue"): "and R. David the *dayyan* ibn Hajjar, a Spaniard from Granada, also belongs to them, and decided to compose *Sefer ha-Melakhim*" – an Arabic work on Hebrew grammar. Ibn Hajjar is called Abu Suleiman ibn Muhagir by Moses *Ibn Ezra.

BIBLIOGRAPHY: W. Bacher, *Abraham ibn Ezra als Grammatiker* (1881), 185; idem, *Die hebraeische Sprachwissenschaft vom 10. bis zum 16. jahrhundert* (1892), 60.

DAVIDOFF, LEO MAX (1898–1975), U.S. neurosurgeon. Davidoff was born in Talsen, Latvia, and was taken to the United States in 1905. After his medical training he served as surgeon to the Byrd-Macmillan Arctic expedition of 1925. He headed the department of neurological surgery at the Jewish Hospital of Brooklyn (1937–45), the Montefiore Hospital (1945–49), and the Beth Israel Hospital (1949–54). From 1951 to 1956 he was neurosurgeon at the Mount Sinai Hospital and from 1954 to 1966 was director of neurological surgery at the Bronx Municipal Hospital Center. His academic appointments included the clinical professorship of neurological surgery at Columbia University's College of Physicians and Surgeons (1945–49) and the New York University College of Medicine (1949–54). In 1954 he began his association with the Albert Einstein College of Medicine of Yeshiva University, where he served as professor and chairman of the department of surgery (1954–58) and neurological surgery (1959–66). He was associate dean of the college from 1961 to 1966.

Davidoff was chairman of a number of medical training missions for the World Health Organization. He was a member of the medical advisory board of the *Hadassah organization and of the board of directors of the American Friends of the Hebrew University of Jerusalem. He was president of the Society of Neurological Surgeons (1951) and the Harvey Cushing Society (1957).

BIBLIOGRAPHY: Rudolf Virchow Medical Society, *Proceedings*, 26, suppl. (1968), 1–39.

[Fred Rosner]

DAVID OF MAKOW (d. 1814), *maggid* and *dayyan* in Makow, born in Rovno. In his youth he was an adherent of the ḥasidic leader *Menahem Mendel of Vitebsk, but after the Ḥasidim were excommunicated by *Elijah b. Solomon Zalman, the Gaon of Vilna, in 1772, David of Makow became one of his followers and joined the *Mitnaggedim* (opponents of Ḥasidism). He warned against the danger which he saw in the teachings of Ḥasidism, considering the way of life of the Ḥasidim as a threat to normative Judaism, and was harshly critical of Ḥasidism, blaming the courts of *ẓaddikim* for the spread of religious and moral anarchy. He took to task important Ḥasidim, including *Israel b. Eliezer Ba'al Shem Tov. Two anti-ḥasidic works attributed to him (though some consider that they were written by his son, Ezekiel of Radzymin) are *Zemir Ariẓim* (Warsaw, 1798) and a well-known treatise which exists in three versions: *Shever Poshe'im* (Jerusalem, National Library, Ms. 8° 2405), *Zot Torat ha-Kena'ot* (Oxford, Bodleian Library, Ms. Mich. 45, fols. 106–79), and *Zimrat ha-Areẓ* (Ms. Leningrad, Asiatic Museum). David of Makow also wrote commentaries on the Bible and the Mishnah which were never published; the manuscripts were destroyed in a fire in Serock in 1893. Two letters and his will, which are still extant, are anti-ḥasidic in content. David of Makow is the most noted polemicist against Ḥasidism in the years 1772 to 1798. His style and tone express the bitterness existing between the two camps. Echoes of this criticism of Ḥasidism are to be found in *Haskalah literature, as in the writings of Joseph *Perl and Peter *Beer. David's sons were Ezekiel of Radzymin (d. 1814) and Raphael, the father of Shabbetai, who copied *Zot Torat ha-Kena'ot*. His daughter Rachel married Joshua of Makow, who also took part in the struggle against Ḥasidism.

BIBLIOGRAPHY: Dubnow, Ḥasidut, index; E.R. Malachi, in: *Sefer ha-Yovel shel Hadoar* (1952), 286–300; M. Wilensky, in: PAAJR, 25 (1956), 137–56; idem, in: *Tarbiz*, 27 (1957/58), 550–5; idem, in: *Divrei ha-Congress ha-Olami ha-Revi'i le-Madda'ei ha-Yahadut*, 2 (1968), 237–51; idem, *Ḥasidim u-Mitnaggedim* (1970), index; A. Rubinstein, in: KS, 35 (1959/60), 240–9; idem, in: *Koveẓ Bar-Ilan*, 8 (1970), 225–43.

[Esther (Zweig) Liebes]

DAVID OF TALNA (David b. Mordecai Twersky; 1808–1882), *ẓaddik* living first at Vasilkov and afterward at Talna (Talnoye, Ukraine). He was the most celebrated of the eight sons of Menahem Nahum *Twersky, founder of the Chernobyl ḥasidic dynasty. Thousands of people came to his "court," which he maintained in luxurious style, even retaining a court jester. According to ḥasidic tradition his house contained a silver chair bearing the inscription in gold: *David Melekh Yisrael Ḥai ve-Kayyam* ("David, king of Israel, lives and is in existence"). This gave his opponents a means of denouncing him to the Russian authorities as a rebel against the government. He was thrown into prison and freed only after numerous appeals. In spite of his aristocratic way of life, he was a man of the people; his speech was flavored with popular proverbs so that it would be more readily understood by the common people. He was fond of music and brought to his court the most famous folk singers and musicians in the region. The Talna melodies became popular among both Ḥasidim and Jews in general. He wrote *Magen David* (1852), *Birkat David* (1862), and *Kehillat David* (1882).

BIBLIOGRAPHY: P. Minkowsky, in: *Reshumot*, 1 (1925), 109–22; M.S. Geshuri, *Ha-Niggun ve-ha-Rikkud ba-Ḥasidut*, 3 (1959), 319–40.

[Avraham Rubinstein]

DAVIDS, AARON ISSACHAR (Bernard) BEN NAḤMAN (1895–1945), chief rabbi of Rotterdam (Holland). Davids, a grandson of Joseph Hirsch *Duenner, was born in Amsterdam. In his youth Davids was very active in the Mizrachi movement and influenced young people in the spirit of Zionism. While studying at the rabbinical seminary and the university he was headmaster of the Amsterdam religious school. He was ordained rabbi in 1923 and immediately invited to serve as rabbi of Leeuwarden (Friesland). In 1927 he was appointed rabbi of Groningen and in 1930 chief rabbi of Rotterdam, a post he held until 1943. Despite the increase of Nazi persecutions in Holland, he refused to leave his community. In 1943, he was taken to a concentration camp in Holland, and sent to Bergen-Belsen where he died. In spite of his rigid Orthodoxy he maintained strong ties, and cooperated with, all Jewish circles in Holland.

BIBLIOGRAPHY: *Elleh Ezkerah*, 1 (1956), 77–81; F.J. Krop, *Rotterdams Jaarboekje* (1967), 206–7; L. Vorst, *ibid.* (1968), 144–7; S. de Jong, *Joodsch leven in de Friesche hoofdstad 1920–1945* (1970).

[Yehoshua Horowitz]

DAVIDSOHN, ISRAEL (1895–1979), U.S. pathologist. Born in Tarnopol, Austria, Davidsohn qualified in Europe before immigrating to the United States in 1923. He became pathologist and director of laboratories at Philadelphia's Mount Sinai Hospital (1926–30). He then moved to Mount Sinai Hospital, Chicago, where he was director of experimental pathology. He also taught at Rush Medical College (1934–41) and the University of Illinois College of Medicine (1941–47) and from 1947 to 1968 was professor and chairman of the pathology department at the University of Chicago Medical School. His main field of research was immunohematology.

DAVIDSOHN, ROBERT (1853–1937), historian of medieval Florence. Davidsohn engaged in business and journalism, being for a time coeditor of the liberal newspaper, the *Berliner Boersen-Courier*. He wrote an account of his early travels in *Vom Nordkap bis Tunis* (1884). When he was 33 he began to study history in earnest, and obtained a doctorate from Heidelberg in 1888. In the following year he settled in Florence and, inspired by the famous history of Rome in the Middle Ages written by his great friend, the German historian Gregorovius, decided to embark on similar study of his adopted city. The task took him over 30 years and his two most important works, *Forschungen zur Geschichte von Florenz* (4 vols., 1896–1908) and *Geschichte von Florenz* (4 vols., 1896–1927), established him as the leading authority on Florentine history. He was made an honorary citizen of the city, and an Italian translation of some of his works was published at public expense.

[Howard L. Adelson]

DAVIDSON, DAVID (1848–1933), U.S. Reform rabbi and educator. Davidson was born in Lauternburg, Germany, and immigrated to the United States in 1880 after having been educated at the University of Breslau and ordained in Europe. He served as rabbi of Congregation B'nai Jeshurun in Des Moines, Iowa, and Shearith Israel Congregation in Cincinnati, where he was invited by Isaac Mayer *Wise in 1885 to join the faculty of the recently established Union College (later renamed *Hebrew Union College). Davidson taught Talmud and exegesis at the Reform seminary from 1885 to 1892, when he was awarded a Doctor of Divinity degree by HUC and appointed rabbi of the Kahl-Montgomery Congregation in Montgomery, Alabama. In 1895, he was called to the prestigious Congregation Ahavath Chesed (later, Central Synagogue) in New York City, where he subsequently became the rabbi of Congregation Agudath Jeshurun.

Although recognized as a pioneer of Reform Judaism in America, Davidson also contributed significantly to the Conservative movement. In the early 1900s, he served as professor of rabbinics at the fledgling *Jewish Theological Seminary, without drawing a salary. There he befriended a number of students who were to make their own marks on American Jewish history, including Mordecai M. *Kaplan and Bernard C. *Ehrenreich as well as Stephen S. *Wise.

In 1901, Davidson left the active rabbinate in order to establish a private school – the Davidson Collegiate Institute, where he gave Morris Raphael Cohen his first teaching position – as well as a summer camp for boys in Pennsylvania. He was also a director of the Society for the Aid of Jewish Prisoners and lobbied for a Jewish Protectorate in Palestine. In 1931, he was elected an honorary member of the Central Conference of American Rabbis.

In addition to publishing sermons, plays, essays, and poems in both German and English, Davidson wrote several provocative works, including *Shall We Christianize the Constitution of the U.S.A.? Sabbath or Sunday?* (1889), and *The Moral Issue of the World War* (1915).

[Bezalel Gordon (2nd ed.)]

DAVIDSON, ISRAEL (1870–1939), scholar of medieval Hebrew literature. Davidson was born in Yonava, Lithuania; at a young age he became an orphan and went to live with his uncle in Grodno, Lithuania. In 1888, after a few years' study at Slobodka yeshivah, he immigrated to the United States. There he earned a living as a street vendor, then as a shop assistant and Hebrew teacher; at night he studied English and other subjects to meet college-entrance requirements. After completing his studies at Columbia University, he was director of the Hebrew Orphan Asylum and chaplain at the Sing Sing prison. In 1905 he began teaching Talmud at the Jewish Theological Seminary, New York, and in 1915 was appointed professor of medieval Hebrew literature.

Davidson's first major scholarly publication in English was *Parody in Jewish Literature* (1907, repr., 1967). Thereafter, he wrote and edited articles and books in both English and Hebrew. Among the most important works are his editions of Joseph *Ibn Zabara's *Sefer Sha'ashu'im* with an English introduction (1914; 1925[2] with Hebrew introduction); *Saadia's Polemic against Ḥīwī al-Balkhī* (1915); *Maḥzor Yannai* (1919), published from Greek palimpsests, Davidson recognizing *Yannai's *piyyut* in the superimposed writing; *Maḥberet mi-Shirei ha-Kodesh asher li-Shelomo ibn Gabirol* (1923), Ibn *Gabirol's sacred poetry with English translations by Israel Zangwill; *Ginzei Schechter* (vol. 3, 1928), poems and *piyyutim* from the Cairo *Genizah*; and *Sefer Milḥamot ha-Shem* (1934), the arguments of the Karaite *Salmon b. Yeroham against Saadiah Gaon. He was also responsible for preparing the critical edition of *piyyutim* for *Siddur R. Sa'adyah Ga'on* (with S. Assaf, 1941). His *Oẓar ha-Meshalim ve-ha-Pitgamim*, a treasury of medieval Jewish parables and maxims, on which Davidson had worked for many years, was published posthumously (1957).

Davidson's magnum opus is the *Oẓar ha-Shirah ve-ha-Piyyut* (*Thesaurus of Medieval Hebrew Poetry*, 4 vols. and supplement, 1925–38). In this gigantic work Davidson recorded in alphabetical order the initial words of more than 35,000 poems and prayers from post-biblical times to the beginning of the Haskalah period. Each entry contains information relating to the type and structure of the poem, its author, and all available information on its publication as well as the literature about it. An author index, containing over 2,800 names, and a subject index are included. In 1936 Davidson received the first Bialik Prize for this monumental work. Davidson's *Thesaurus* has remained an indispensable work of reference for scholars.

BIBLIOGRAPHY: A.M. Habermann, in: *Gilyonot*, 24 (1936/37), 109–12; 29 (1939), 180–81; Spiegel, in: *Hadoar* (May 16, 1930); Finkelstein, in: AJYB (1939), 35–56; O. Davidson, *Out of Endless Yearnings* (1946); S. Spiegel, in: *Menorah Journal*, 22 (1934), 69–72; S. Assaf (ed.), *Siddur Rav Sa'adyah Ga'on* (1941), 10–16.

[Abraham Meir Habermann]

DAVIDSON, JO (1883–1952), U.S. sculptor. Davidson was born in the ghetto of New York's Lower East Side to immigrant parents who had fled the Russian pogroms. Despite parental opposition, in his teens Davidson studied drawing in New York at the Educational Alliance's art school and at the Art Students' League. At 18 his parents sent him to New Haven to prepare for entrance to Yale Medical School. While in New Haven an admirer of Davidson's work showed the young man's drawings to the director of the art school. Impressed, the director allowed Davidson to take art classes at Yale free of charge. After accidentally walking into a sculpture room Davidson realized the direction his art was to take, and returned to New York to study sculpture. Further studies were undertaken in Paris, but he only remained at the École des Beaux-Arts for three weeks.

He received acclaim early on. Gertrude Vanderbilt Whitney, who later founded the Whitney Museum of American Art in New York, purchased a bust of a young girl in 1906. In 1909 Davidson had his first one-man show in New York, and in 1910 his 8-foot nude *La Terre* was exhibited and well received at the Salon d'Automne. Davidson soon began executing portrait busts of famous personalities, including military and political leaders. He sculpted presidents Woodrow Wilson (1916, bronze), Herbert Hoover (1921, bronze), Dwight D. Eisenhower (1948, bronze), and Franklin Delano Roosevelt (1933, bronze; 1951, stone). These works demonstrate Davidson's desire to provide a likeness of his sitter, and also to explore and distill the sitter's personality. His naturalistic approach combines with lively surface effects. Indeed, the vigorous and rapid modeling of clay remains apparent even after the sculpture has been cast in bronze.

Once established, Davidson traveled the world making bronze busts of figures as diverse as Gertrude Stein (1923), Charlie Chaplin (1925), Mahatma Gandhi (1931), Albert Einstein (c. 1937), and Helen Keller (1942 and 1945, half length). His nine-foot full-length bronze of the poet Walt Whitman is located at Bear Mountain State Park in New York (1936–39). Davidson visited Israel in 1951, at which time he made bronze likenesses of the country's major leaders, including Golda Meir (c. 1951), Chaim Weizmann (1951), and David Ben-Gurion (1951).

A large retrospective of Davidson's work was held in 1947, when 200 sculptures were displayed at the American Academy of Arts and Letters. Davidson's autobiography, *Between Sittings*, was published in 1951.

BIBLIOGRAPHY: *Jo Davidson: Portrait Sculpture* (1978); *Jo Davidson: American Sculptor, 1883–1952* (1983).

[Samantha Baskind (2nd ed.)]

DAVIDSON, LIONEL (1922–), English novelist. Davidson's thriller *The Night of Wenceslas* (1960) was followed by a romance, *The Rose of Tibet* (1962). Two visits to Israel inspired the story of an archaeologist's adventurous quest for "the true *menorah*," *A Long Way to Shiloh* (1966; published in the U.S. as *The Menorah Men*, 1966). *Making Good Again* (1968), a thriller set against the restitution process in Federal Germany, emphasized the ingrained Nazism of many "New Germans." Davidson settled in Israel in 1968. His *Kolmynsky Heights* (1994) was a bestseller.

DAVIDSON, MAX DAVID (1899–1977), U.S. Conservative rabbi. Davidson was born in Newark, New Jersey, and ordained at the *Jewish Theological Seminary in 1922, having received his B.A. degree from New York University in 1919. He spent his entire career as a pulpit rabbi in his native state of New Jersey, first in Asbury Park (Congregation Beth El, 1922–28) and then in Perth Amboy (Temple Beth Mordecai, 1929 until his death). Davidson rose to prominence as president both of the *Rabbinical Assembly (1950–52), after having served as treasurer and vice president of the organization during the previous three years, and the *Synagogue Council of America (1959–61), a body he had helped create. He also served as chairman of the *National Jewish Welfare Board's Division of Religious Activities, supervising chaplaincy affairs for the three major rabbinic groups in the U.S. armed services (1950–53); he had actively recruited Jewish chaplains during World War II, then spent the postwar years chairing the RA's Joint Placement Commission, in which capacity he secured congregational positions for demobilized military chaplains. As vice chairman of the RA's Membership Committee (1944–45), Davidson is credited with having streamlined the procedures for enrolling newly ordained Seminary graduates in the Rabbinical Assembly, leading to the expansion of the RA as the recognized professional association for Conservative rabbis. He subsequently chaired the Rabbinical Assembly's Ethics Committee and oversaw the adoption of the organization's Code of Professional Conduct. Even after his term as president, he continued to serve the RA as comptroller, archivist member of the Committee on Jewish Law and Standards, and chairman of the Joint Prayerbook Commission of the Rabbinical Assembly and the Synagogue Council of America. Throughout his many years in Rabbinical Assembly leadership roles, Davidson developed a reputation as a respected arbiter of disputes, a champion of freedom of conscience and diversity, and an outspoken critic of what he termed the "frightening" toll that congregational life had occasionally been shown to take on rabbinic colleagues.

BIBLIOGRAPHY: P.S. Nadell, *Conservative Judaism in America: A Biographical Dictionary and Sourcebook* (1988).

[Bezalel Gordon (2nd ed.)]

°**DAVIDSON, SAMUEL** (1806–1898), clergyman and Bible critic. Born in Northern Ireland, he was ordained as a Presbyterian minister in 1833 and was appointed the first professor of Bible criticism at the Royal College of Belfast (1835–41). After becoming a Congregationalist, he went to Lancashire Independent College, Manchester, in 1843, as professor of biblical criticism and Oriental languages. As a result of his visits to Germany, where he met and was influenced by J. Neander, H. *Hupfeld, and other leading Bible critics, Davidson translated Julius Fuerst's *Hebrew and Chaldee Lexicon of the Old Testament* (1867). However, he fell into disfavor with the college authorities because of his liberal views on the Bible. Despite this, he published *The Text of the Old Testament Considered* (1856, 1859²), a commentary on the Bible (especially the Pentateuch) pioneering new theories of Higher Criticism. The book was attacked by the Lancashire College committee, mainly because it denied the Mosaic authorship of the Pentateuch. After much controversy, he resigned the following year and retired to teach in a Cheshire school. In 1862 he moved to London where he was appointed Scripture examiner in London University and also served on the Old Testament Revision Committee. Among his major works on the Bible are *The Hebrew Text of the Old Testament Revised* (1855), in which he examined the Hebrew text and ancient translation; *Introduction to the Old Testament* (3 vols., 1862–63); and *On a Fresh Revision of the Old Testament* (1873), originally written for *Encyclopaedia Britannica*, but published separately since, according to Davidson, the original had been "mutilated" by the editors. His autobiography and diary were published in 1899 by his daughter Anne S. Davidson.

BIBLIOGRAPHY: J. Thompson, *Lancashire Independent College 1843–1893, Jubilee Memorial.*

[Mervyn M. Lewis]

DAVIDSON, WILLIAM (1922–), U.S. industrialist, philanthropist, sportsman. Born in Detroit, Mich., Davidson received a bachelor's degree in business administration from the University of Michigan in 1947 and a Juris Doctor degree in law from Wayne State University in 1949. Guardian Industries, a small, family windshield company owned by a relative, was 23 years old when Davidson joined it in 1955 after service in World War II and a short law career. In 1957 Davidson became president of Guardian, which bought glass and converted it into safety glass for windshields, and over the years Davidson transformed it into a multibillion-dollar, multinational company with more than 60 facilities on five continents. It now makes auto glass, fiberglass insulation, glass panels for office buildings, and other products as well as distributing building materials to retail stores. Davidson took Guardian public in 1968 and bought it back for himself in 1985. In the early 2000s it had 19,000 employees in 20 countries.

In addition, Davidson became majority owner of the Detroit Pistons professional basketball team in 1974; he owns the Detroit Shock of the Women's National Basketball Association, two arena professional football teams, the Tampa Bay Lightning professional hockey team, the DTE Energy Music Theater, the Meadow Brook Music Festival, and the Palace of Auburn Hills, the city where Guardian is headquartered. His hockey and basketball team won world championships one after the other in 2004, a fabulous achievement for a sportsman.

A high school track star, Davidson is a member of the Michigan Sports Hall of Fame and the Jewish Sports Hall of Fame. He is a longtime benefactor of the Detroit Symphony Orchestra. In 1992 he gave $30 million to the University of Michigan to set up the William Davidson Institute, which is dedicated to helping nations in Eastern Europe develop free-market economies.

Davidson gave millions to finance archaeological excavations around Jerusalem. In 1994, he gave the Jewish Theological Seminary of America $15 million for a graduate school of Jewish education, the largest donation made to a single institution of Jewish education in the United States. Davidson earlier was chairman of the United Jewish Appeal for Detroit and past president of Congregation Shaaray Zedek in Southfield, Mich.

[Stewart Kampel (2nd ed.)]

D'AVIGDOR (later **d'Avigdor-Goldsmid**), family that settled in England about the middle of the nineteenth century and became united with the prominent Jewish family Goldsmid. Among its members were ELIM D'AVIGDOR (1841–1895), engineer and author. He was the eldest son of count Salomon Henri d'Avigdor (whom Napoleon III created duke of Acquaviva) and grandson of Isaac Samuel d'Avigdor, member of the Great Sanhedrin. His mother RACHEL (1816–1896), noted for her charitable activities, was the daughter of Isaac Lyon *Goldsmid. D'Avigdor worked as an engineer in various parts of the world on construction projects, including railways in Syria and Transylvania. He wrote hunting stories under the pseudonym "Wanderer" and was publisher of the *Examiner* and *Yachting Gazette*. D'Avigdor was active in the Ḥovevei Zion (see *Ḥibbat Zion). As a member of the executive of the *Anglo-Jewish Association, he was responsible for the transference to its control of the Evelina de Rothschild school in Jerusalem, previously controlled by the Rothschild family. His son, SIR OSMOND D'AVIGDOR GOLDSMID (1877–1940), added the name Goldsmid on inheriting the estates of his cousin Sir Julian *Goldsmid. He devoted his life to public service. He received recognition for these services in 1934 when the hereditary baronetcy of Isaac Lyon Goldsmid was revived and awarded to him. In 1912 he was high sheriff of the county of Kent. Within the Jewish community, he served as president of the Anglo-Jewish Association (1921–26), president of the British *Board of Deputies (1926–33), chairman of the Jewish Colonization Association, and treasurer of the Jewish Memorial Council. Although not a Zionist, he was for many years chairman of the council of the British section of the Jewish Agency. His elder son, SIR HENRY JOSEPH D'AVIGDOR-GOLDSMID (1909–1976), the 2nd baronet, was a Conservative member of parliament from 1955 and parliamentary private secretary to the minister of housing and local government (1955–56). He was president of the Jewish Colonization Association, and chairman of the Anglo-Israel Bank. Another son, Brigadier General SIR JAMES ARTHUR D'AVIGDOR-GOLDSMID (1912–1987) headed the British Territorial Army. He later became major general and was a Conservative member of Parliament from 1970 to 1974.

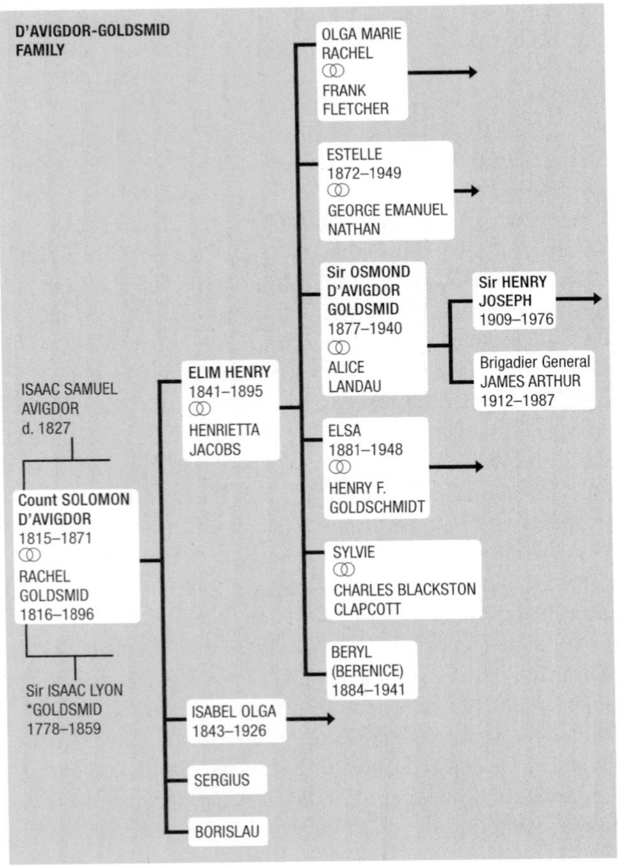

BIBLIOGRAPHY: JC (Feb. 15, 1895 and April 15, 1940); *The Times* (April 15, 1940); P. Emden, *Jews of Britain* (1943), 148–9; 536–7; JHSET, 17 (1951–52), 10. **ADD. BIBLIOGRAPHY:** C. Bermant, *The Cousinhood*, index; M. Jolles, *Biographical Directory of Prominent British Jews, 1830–1930* (2002), index; ODNB online.

[Vivian David Lipman]

DAVIN (David) DE CADEROUSSE (15th century), the first known Jew to attempt Hebrew *printing. While living in Avignon as a dyer, Davin de Caderousse met a Christian goldsmith from Prague named Procop Waldvogel. In 1446 the two entered into a notarial contract, Davin undertaking to teach the other the art of dyeing and Procop promising in return to provide him with the 27 letters of the Hebrew alphabet, cut in iron, and with the necessary instruments, in accordance with the "science and practise of writing," which he had been teaching him since 1444. The arrangement ultimately broke down, and no specimen of this earliest Hebrew printing press has survived.

BIBLIOGRAPHY: P. Requin, *Origines de l'imprimerie en France* (1891); C. Roth, *Jews in the Renaissance* (1959), 167–8.

[Cecil Roth]

DAVIS, ABEL (1878–1937), U.S. army officer. Born in Lithuania, Davis was taken to Chicago as a child and served in the Illinois National Guard during the Spanish-American War of 1898. He fought in France in World War I and won awards for gallantry in the battles before Amiens, St. Hilaire, and in the Argonne. He was later made a brigadier general in the Illinois National Guard. Davis was active in Jewish affairs as director of the Associated Jewish Charities and in 1921 was chairman of the American Jewish Relief Committee conference.

DAVIS, AL (1929–), principal owner and president of the Oakland Raiders football team, member of the Pro Football Hall of Fame. Born in Brockton, Massachusetts, Davis grew up in Brooklyn and graduated from Syracuse University in 1950, where he played football, basketball, and baseball. Davis was then named line coach at Adelphi College at age 21. He subsequently went into the U.S. Army, where he was assigned as head football coach at Ft. Belvoir, Virginia. Davis joined the staff of the NFL Baltimore Colts as a scout in 1954, and then served as line coach and chief recruiter at The Citadel in 1955–56. Afterwards he spent three years at the University of Southern California. Davis was then hired in 1960 by Sid *Gillman as an offensive coach for the Los Angeles Chargers in the newly formed American Football League.

In 1963, Davis was hired by the Oakland Raiders to be the team's head coach and general manager, after the team had only won three of their previous 28 games. Davis led the Raiders his first season to a 10–4–0 record, and was named AFL Coach of the Year by AP, UPI, *Sports Illustrated*, the *Sporting News*, and his fellow coaches. The nine-win turnaround from the previous season remains the greatest such accomplishment in pro football history. Davis coached three seasons for a 23–16–3 record, and was then named commissioner of the AFL in April 1966. Though Davis was acclaimed as an instrumental figure in the historic merger between the NFL and AFL, he was personally against it. Davis stepped down as commissioner two months later when Pete Rozelle was chosen to be commissioner of the new league, returning to the Raiders as general manager and principal owner.

Known for his dark glasses, slicked-back hair, Brooklyn accent, and ferocious competitiveness, Davis was regarded as a maverick owner. He moved the Raider franchise to Los Angeles in 1982 against the NFL's objections, winning the battle in Federal District Court, and then moved the team back to Oakland in 1995. Davis' Raiders played in five Super Bowls, winning in 1977, 1981, and 1984, with the team having the best record in pro sports from 1963 to 1991. It was a reflection of his often-quoted motto: "Just win, baby."

Davis was elected to the Pro Football Hall of Fame in 1992, the fourth Jew selected after Sid *Luckman, Sid *Gillman, and Ron *Mix, later joined by Marv *Levy and Benny *Friedman.

[Elli Wohlgelernter (2nd ed.)]

DAVIS, AL "BUMMY" (Avraham Davidoff; 1920–1945), U.S. welterweight boxer. Born in what was then the very Jewish Brownsville section of Brooklyn, Davis learned to fight on the neighborhood streets as a member of a teenage gang while plying his trade as a pushcart peddler. It was a neighborhood rife with members of the Jewish mafia known as "Murder, Inc.," including Abe "Kid Twist" Reles and "Pittsburgh Phil" Strauss, and Davis was the younger brother of both Willie Davidoff, a lieutenant to the famous mobster Louis "Lepke" *Buchalter, and Harry, who was also involved with the mob.

Davis was discovered by manager Johnny Attell while fighting as an amateur under the name Giovanni Pasconi. Called Vroomy, a derivative of Avraham, by his family, he was Boomy to his friends, a nickname that was finally changed to "Bummy" by Attell prior to Davis' first professional fight in May 1937. Known for his great left hook, Davis defeated his first 22 opponents, 16 by knockout including 10 in the first three rounds.

As the younger brother of two racketeers, Davis was tarred and feathered in the press as a mob-controlled lowlife, and found himself booed even by his home crowd for knocking out favorites such as Tony Canzoneri. Davis added to his legend in his most famous fight, against Fritzie Zivic on November 15, 1940. Zivic was infamous for his dirty tactics in the ring, and in the first round he repeatedly thumbed Davis in the eyes. When Zivic continued in the second round, Davis hit him below the belt at least ten times, refusing to stop. Davis was disqualified in the fight, fined $2,500, and suspended from the ring by New York State for life, but he was reinstated three years later. His final record was 66 wins (47 KOs), 10 losses, and 4 draws, and he was named No. 54 on *Ring* magazine's list of the 100 greatest punchers of all time.

Davis met a tragic end at the age of 25, when he was shot dead in Brownsville while breaking up a robbery at his former bar, called Dudy's. He is the subject of a biography, Ron Ross' somewhat fanciful *Bummy Davis vs. Murder, Inc.: The Rise and Fall of the Jewish Mafia and an Ill-Fated Prizefighter* (2003).

[Elli Wohlgelernter (2nd ed.)]

DAVIS, ALEXANDER BARNARD (1828–1913), Australian rabbi. Born in England, Davis served as headmaster of Westminster Jews' Free School, London, and minister of Kingston Congregation, Jamaica. From 1862 to 1904 he officiated as chief minister of the Great Synagogue in Sydney, and succeeded in reconciling opposing groups among the community. He founded the Sabbath School and the Sydney Jewish Education Board. Davis wrote several booklets on Jewish observance, the first of their kind to be published in Australia.

BIBLIOGRAPHY: JC (Sept. 16, 1898, Jan. 30 and Feb. 6, 1914). **ADD. BIBLIOGRAPHY:** I. Porush, *The House of Israel* (1977), index; H.L. Rubinstein, Australia, I, index; *Australian Dictionary of Biography*, 4, 34.

[Israel Porush]

DAVIS, DAVID BRION (1927–), U.S. historian. The son of writer Claude Brion Davis and Martha Wirt Davis, David Davis was educated at Dartmouth College, Oxford University, and Harvard University, where he received his Ph.D. in 1956. He acquired a wide range of cultural and intellectual experiences before his first appointment at Cornell University, where he taught until 1978. Well into his academic career, and after years of serious thought, Davis chose to convert to Judaism.

Davis is a pioneer in the effort to understand slavery and abolition. *The Problem of Slavery in Western Culture* (1967) reflects his effort to probe slavery as a "problem" in enlightened cultures rather than simply as an evil and aberrant institution. His earliest monograph was *Homicide in American Fiction, 1798–1860* (1957).

At his retirement from Yale in 2001, he was founding director of the Gilder-Lehrman Institute for the Study of Slavery and Sterling Professor of American History. Davis has served as visiting professor at numerous universities, and has won the Pulitzer Prize, the National Book Award, and the Bancroft Prize. In 1987–88 he served as president of the Organization of American Historians.

Known as a superb lecturer and teacher, Davis supervised 60 dissertations while on the Yale faculty, and fostered the careers of dozens of leading American scholars whose work extends far beyond studies of slavery, to include almost every phase of American history. His professional and personal confession is contained in his book of essays *In the Image of God* (2001), where he builds his case as an intellectual historian and an explorer of the human spirit, identifying the seminal experiences in his life that shaped his character. The essay at the beginning of the collection conveys his sense of where his conversion to Judaism meets his passion for understanding slavery in the broad spiritual sense. The essay also tracks his seminal experience with racism during his service in Europe during World War II.

While never an apologist for the role some Jews may have played in the industry of slavery, Davis has argued against any notion of collective Jewish guilt, or any attempts to see Jewish participation in the slave trade as disproportionate to the population as a whole. In fact, Davis used this myth to highlight the significant contributions of Jews to American business, letters, entertainment, and science (*New York Review of Books*, Dec. 1994, and *New Republic*, Apr. 12, 1993).

Other books by Davis include *Problem of Slavery in the Age of Revolution, 1770–1823* (1975); *Slavery and Human Progress* (1984); *From Homicide to Slavery: Studies in American Culture* (1986); and *The Problem of Slavery in the Age of Emancipation* (2005)

[William Cutter (2nd ed.)]

DAVIS, SIR EDMUND (1861–1939), mining magnate and art collector. Edmund Davis was born in Melbourne, Australia, and educated in Paris, where he studied art. From 1879 until 1889 he lived in the Cape Colony, where he built up a fortune in guano, copper, and railroads. He became an associate of Cecil Rhodes, engaged in mining exploration in various parts of southern Africa for many years. After 1889 he lived chiefly in London, and became an important financier in developing the minerals, especially the copper fields, of Northern Rhodesia (now Zambia). Rhodes made Davis a director of the British South Africa Company. He was also chairman or director of many other companies. He accompanied Rhodes on his visit to Kaiser William II of Germany in 1898 for discussions on the Cape-Cairo cable. Davis collected early and modern paintings, and in 1915 presented a selection of pictures of the modern British school to the Luxembourg Museum, Paris. Another collection was given to the South African Art Gallery in Cape Town. Davis later settled in England, and became sheriff of Kent in 1930. He was knighted in 1937. He left large bequests to hospitals and established scholarships at London University.

BIBLIOGRAPHY: P. Emden, *Jews of Britain* (1943), 429, 434. **ADD. BIBLIOGRAPHY:** ODNB online; DBB, 2, 24–28.

DAVIS, EDWARD ("Teddy the Jewboy," 1816–1841), Australian convict and one of a handful of Jewish bushrangers. Davis was born in England. In 1832, a London court convicted him of stealing a shopkeeper's till worth two shillings and five shillings worth of coins. His sentence was deportation to Australia for seven years. After a number of unsuccessful attempts at escape, as a result of which his sentence was increased by 48 months, he finally managed to escape in 1839 and organized a bushranger gang of ex-convicts like himself who, ranging on horseback over New South Wales, raided towns and settlements and robbed travelers on the desolate roads. Davis looked upon himself as a Robin Hood: he shared the spoils with the poor and would only countenance violence in self-defense. His downfall came in December 1840, when in the course of a raid on the township of Scone one of his gang, John Shea, killed a young shopkeeper. Shea, Davis, and four others were caught, convicted of murder, and sentenced to death. Davis' appeal was dismissed by the Executive Council and, accompanied by the *ḥazzan* of the Sydney synagogue, he went penitently to the gallows at the Old Sydney Gaol. A crowd of over a thousand gathered to see him hanged.

BIBLIOGRAPHY: *Australian Dictionary of Biography*; J.H.M. Abbott, *Newcastle Packets and the Hunter Valley* (1943); idem, *Castle Vane* (1920). **ADD. BIBLIOGRAPHY:** J.S. Levi and G.F.J. Bergman, *Australian Genesis: Jewish Convicts and Settlers, 1788–1860* (2002 edition), 242–59; H.L. Rubinstein, Australia, I, index.

[Morton Mayer Berman]

DAVIS, SIR ERNEST HYAM (1872–1962), New Zealand businessman and philanthropist. Davis was born in Nelson, the son of Moss Davis, an immigrant merchant, and developed his father's business, Hancock and Co., which controlled many of New Zealand's largest hotels. He was best known as one of the most important brewers in New Zealand, heading Captain Cook Brewery, the largest in the country, and was later prominent in founding the expanded New Zealand Breweries Ltd., as well as directing many other companies. Davis was one of the leaders of the anti-Prohibition movement in his country and, although a rich man, was a notable financial backer of the New Zealand Labour Party. He was mayor of Auckland from 1935 to 1941. During World War II he was chairman of the joint council of St. John and the Red Cross. His donations to Auckland included the Davis Marine Park, Davis Marine Lighthouse, and the Marion Davis Memorial Medical Library.

He also made large gifts to hospitals and other charities and to the Auckland Synagogue. Davis received a knighthood in 1937. At his death he was regarded as one of the towering figures in New Zealand's business life.

ADD. BIBLIOGRAPHY: G.W.A. Bush, "Ernest Hyam Davis," in: *Dictionary of New Zealand Biography.*

[Alexander Astor / William D. Rubinstein (2nd ed.)]

DAVIS, HENRY DAVID (1839–1915), British architect. Born in London, Davis became one of the first Jews to practice architecture in Britain, often in partnership with Barrow Emanuel (1842–1904), the son of Emanuel Emanuel (d. 1888), the first Jewish mayor of Portsmouth and the brother of Lady *Magnus. Their firm built the Clarence Pier in Portsmouth and many buildings in London, especially near Finsbury Square and in the East End, often dwellings for poor immigrants. They also built the West London Reform Synagogue (1870) and other Jewish buildings.

BIBLIOGRAPHY: ODNB online.

[William D. Rubinstein (2nd ed.)]

DAVIS, MARVIN H. (1925–2004), U.S. oil and entertainment businessman. Born in Newark, N.J., to immigrant parents (his father was a dress manufacturer), Davis moved with his family to Colorado, where he and his father bought oil and gas leases at low prices throughout the Rocky Mountains and then did extensive drilling. After taking over the business, Davis earned the nickname Mr. Wildcatter because he would drill thousands of wells in unexplored areas in search of oil or natural gas. He was a pioneer of the oil deal known as the "third for a quarter," in which an oil prospector insulates himself from risk by selling one-quarter of a well for one-third of the price of the well. Essentially, Davis drilled his own wells with other people's money. He also became a major real estate developer in Denver, acquiring a huge shopping center and office complex.

In 1981, when energy markets were peaking in the United States, he sold most of his oil and natural gas holdings for $600 million to the Canadian company Hiram Walker-Consumers Home Ltd., and turned his attention to undervalued entertainment businesses in Hollywood and real estate in California. With Marc *Rich, the financier who became a fugitive and was later pardoned by President Bill Clinton, he bought 20th Century Fox for $725 million. When he sold the company four years later to Rupert Murdoch's News Corporation, newspaper and magazine articles estimated that Davis earned a profit of $325 million. Davis also owned the Pebble Beach Company, which he sold in 1990 at a profit of millions of dollars, the Aspen Skiing Company, and the fabled Beverly Hills Hotel. He made highly publicized but unsuccessful bids on companies such as Northwest Airlines, United Airlines, CBS, and Resorts International. In 2002 he led a group of investors who tried to buy the American entertainment business of Vivendi Universal with an unsolicited bid of $20 billion but was rebuffed. In 2004, Forbes magazine listed Davis as the 30th richest person in the United States, estimating his wealth at $5.8 billion.

[Stewart Kampel (2nd ed.)]

DAVIS, MORTIMER B. (1866–1928), Canadian industrialist and philanthropist. Davis was born in Montreal, the third of seven children in a well-established Jewish family. His father was a founder of Montreal's first Reform congregation, Temple Emanu-El. After finishing Montreal High School, Davis went into the family's cigar business. As a young man he experimented in tobacco production and negotiated with the Imperial Tobacco Company of England to establish a subsidiary in Canada. Davis became the company's director and was soon involved in a variety of other Montreal business activities. He also took keen interest in charity and relief activities. Davis helped finance the integration of East European immigrants in Montreal and was one of the founders of the Mount Sinai Sanatorium, the first Jewish-community-funded hospital in the city. During World War I, Davis helped finance a Jewish battalion to fight with the British and in 1917 was rewarded with a knighthood by King George V, the first Canadian Jew to be so honored. After the war Davis, while not a religious man, was active in supporting Jewish schools in Montreal and donated a new building for the Montreal YMHA, soon known as the Davis Y. Sir Mortimer Davis died in 1928 but, feeling that Montreal should have a major Jewish hospital, he bequeathed 75 percent of his estate to be invested and used to build such a hospital. The Sir Mortimer Davis Jewish General Hospital, founded in 1934, was the result. In 1898 Davis married Henrietta Meyer of San Francisco but their marriage ended in divorce. Lady Davis, a keen businesswoman, became wealthy in her own right and remained a leading philanthropist in the Montreal Jewish community, supporting causes in both Canada and Israel.

[Gerald Tulchinsky (2nd ed.)]

DAVIS, MOSHE (1916–1996), historian and educator. Born in Brooklyn, New York, Davis was ordained a rabbi at the Jewish Theological Seminary in 1942, and was the first American to receive a doctoral degree from the Hebrew University of Jerusalem (1945). During 1946–50 he was dean of the Seminary's Teachers' Institute, then provost of the Seminary. One of the founders of Camp Massad, Davis also established the Leaders Training Fellowship and the Camp Ramah movement of the Teachers' Institute. He was the first program editor of the Seminary's radio program *Eternal Light* and the television program *Frontiers of Faith*. In 1959 Davis was founder and subsequently chairman in Israel of the Committee on Manpower Opportunities. An authority on contemporary Jewish life, especially American Jewry, Davis taught American Jewish history at the Jewish Theological Seminary, co-directed the Seminary's American Jewish History Center, and taught American Jewish history and institutions at the Hebrew University (from 1965). Having immigrated to Israel in 1959, he became the founder and head of the university's Institute of

Contemporary Jewry, the first of its kind in the world. In that capacity, he supervised studies, publications, and conferences dealing with centers of world Jewry. Within the institute he also founded the America–Holy Land Project, which became an academic sub-specialty of both American and Jewish history. Davis was the Stephen S. Wise Professor Emeritus of American Jewish History and Institutions at the Hebrew University. In 1974 he founded the International Center for the Academic Teaching of Jewish Civilization, under the sponsorship of the president of Israel.

Among his many honors, Davis garnered the Rothberg Prize in Jewish Education of the Hebrew University; the Speaker of the Knesset Quality of Life Award; and an honorary Ph.D. from the Jewish Theological Seminary of America. His publications include *Jewish Religious Life and Institutions in America* (1950); *Yahadut Amerikah be-Hitpatteḥutah* (1951); *Emergence of Conservative Judaism* (1963); *Journeys of the Children of Israel: A Guide to the Study of the Bible* (with I. Levy, 1966); *Beit Yisrael be-Amerikah* ("From Dependence to Mutuality: The American Jewish Community and World Jewry," 1970); *I Am a Jew* (1978); *Teaching Jewish Civilization: A Global Approach to Higher Education* (1995); and *America and the Holy Land* (1995). He was a consulting editor for the first edition of the *Encyclopaedia Judaica* (1971).

[Gladys Rosen / Ruth Beloff (2nd ed.)]

DAVIS, NATALIE ZEMON (1928–), U.S. historian of early modern France, scholar of women, gender, and film studies, academic leader and lecturer. Davis was born in Detroit, Michigan, daughter of Julian and Helen Lamport Zemon, both American-born children of immigrants from Eastern Europe. She grew up in a non-Jewish neighborhood and attended a private high school with few other Jewish students. Davis has suggested that this experience of mediating between two worlds may have contributed to her scholarly interest in issues of multiple and uncertain identities, fiction and storytelling, and the interplay between margins and center. After receiving her B.A. from Smith College and her Ph.D. from the University of Michigan, Davis taught at Brown University, the University of Toronto, the University of California at Berkeley, and was the Henry Charles Lea Professor of History at Princeton University from 1981 until her retirement in 1996. She received numerous honors and awards and was a fellow of the American Academy of Arts and Sciences and corresponding fellow of the British Academy. In 1987, she became the second woman to serve as president of the American Historical Association.

Davis expanded the boundaries of social history through her use of nontraditional archival sources and examinations of previously under-studied populations. She was a pioneer in cultural history and the incorporation of interdisciplinary approaches from anthropology and literature into historical scholarship. A prolific scholar, her books include *Society and Culture in Early Modern France* (1975); *The Return of Martin Guerre* (1983); *Fiction in the Archives: Pardon Tales and Their Tellers in Sixteenth-Century France* (1987); *The Gift in Sixteenth-Century France* (2000); and *Slaves on Screen: Film and Historical Vision* (2000). Davis also served as historical consultant for the successful film *Le Retour de Martin Guerre* (1982).

In the 1980s, Davis became increasingly interested in Jewish history. As in her investigations of women and gender, she wished to incorporate Jews into the broader historical narrative while demonstrating how doing so necessarily changes understandings of the past. Her insightful work on the autobiographical writings of Glikl bas Judah Leib in *Women on the Margins: Three Seventeenth Century Lives* (1995), as well as her collaboration on a volume devoted to the autobiography of Leon *Modena (*The Autobiography of a Seventeenth-Century Venetian Rabbi: Leon Modena's Life of Judah*, ed. Mark Cohen (1988)), brought together her interests in the Jewish experience and in narratives of self-fashioning.

BIBLIOGRAPHY: N.Z. Davis, *A Life of Learning,* American Council of Learned Societies Occasional Paper 39 (1997; http://www.acls.org/op39.htm); D. Snowman, "Natalie Zemon Davis," in: *History Today,* 52 (October 2002), 18–21; B. Wenger, "Davis, Natalie Zemon," in: P.E. Hyman and D.D. Moore (eds.), *Jewish Women in America,* 1 (1997), 315–17.

[Jennifer Sartori (2nd ed.)]

DAVIS, SAMMY JR. (1923–1990), U.S. singer, dancer, actor. Born in Harlem, New York, to performer Sammy Davis and dancer Elvira Sanchez, Sammy Davis, Jr. began his entertainment career at the age of three. He grew up on the road with his father, who belonged to the touring vaudeville group the Will Mastin Troupe, after his mother abandoned the family in 1928. As motion pictures increasingly killed demand for vaudeville acts, Davis and his father continued alongside Will Mastin in what inevitably become a trio. In 1943, he was drafted into the U.S. Army and sent to boot camp in Cheyenne, Wyoming, where he endured violent racism. He was eventually transferred to an entertainment division, which toured military bases around the United States. After his discharge from the service in 1945, Davis rejoined Mastin and his father, headlining with such acts as *Mel Torme, Mickey Rooney, and Frank Sinatra. On November 19, 1954, Davis was nearly killed in an automobile accident that took his left eye and shattered his face. As he recovered in a Los Angeles hospital, Davis began his conversion to Judaism. The publicity following his accident was intense and boosted Davis' career; even the controversy that followed his conversion had little impact. He performed in front of sold-out shows and released his first albums under the Decca label, *Starring Sammy Davis, Jr.* and *Just for Lovers*, in 1955. Davis' star climbed higher with the Broadway musical *Mr. Wonderful* (1956) and the film adaptation of George Gershwin's *Porgy and Bess* (1959). He married Loray White in 1958, but the couple divorced the following year. By 1960, Davis was a superstar. Frank Sinatra made him part of his "Rat Pack" along with Dean Martin, Joey Bishop, and others. He starred with fellow Rat Pack members in *Ocean's Eleven* (1960), *Sergeants 3* (1962), and *Salt and Pepper* (1968). His marriage to Swedish actress May Britt in 1960, who was Caucasian, made him a Ku Klux Klan target. In turn, Davis became a staunch supporter of the Black Power movement. B'nai B'rith named him man of the year in 1965, and he received Emmy nominations for *The Sammy Davis, Jr. Show* (1965) and *The Swinging World of Sammy Davis, Jr.* (1966). He divorced Britt in 1968 and in 1970 married Altovise Gore. Davis angered the political left in 1972 when he publicly supported Richard Nixon and performed in Vietnam. His Rat Pack drinking and drug abuse caught up with him in 1974, when Davis developed liver and kidney problems that required surgery and several months of rehabilitation. In the 1980s, Davis toured with Sinatra and Liza Minnelli. He made his final film appearance with Gregory Hines in *Tap* (1989), the same year doctors discovered his throat cancer, which would claim his life one year later.

[Adam Wills (2nd ed.)]

DAVIS, SUSAN A. (1944–), U.S. Democratic congresswoman representing California's 53rd Congressional District. Born in Cambridge, Massachusetts, Davis grew up in Richmond, California. Her father was a pediatrician; her husband is also a physician. She graduated from the University of California at Berkeley with a degree in sociology (1965). She then earned a master's degree in social work from the University of North Carolina (1968).

Between 1990 and 1994 she was the executive director of the Aaron Price Fellows Program, a program that teaches citizenship skills to multiethnic high school students, and then served on the City School Board in San Diego for nine years between 1983 and 1992, more than half of them as president or vice president. She was also active in the League of Women Voters of San Diego, eventually serving as its president.

She was elected to the California State Assembly in 1994. Her interests were in adolescence, and she championed legislation to protect medical privacy. Term-limited out, she was forced to run for another office and moved up when she was elected to the House of Representatives in 2000. Her Committee assignments in Congress reflected both her constituency and her interests. She served on the House Armed Services Committee – San Diego has major military installations – and the Education and the Workforce Committee. She focused on the issues of defense, education, environment, health care, and veterans' affairs. Defense and veterans' affairs are important concerns for the military families of San Diego, educational and health care were long-time interests of Davis.

Her primary area of concern in Congress reflected her local involvement as an educator. Like most Democrats she opposed the school voucher program but supported educational reform, most especially in areas that would improve teaching. She also endorsed increased evaluation programs for students and their teachers. In health care she supported the Patients Bill or Rights and Medicare. She was pro-choice.

[Michael Berenbaum (2nd ed.)]

DAVYDOV (Davidhof), KARL YULYEVICH (1838–1889), Russian cellist, composer, and teacher. Davydov, who was born in Goldingen, Courland, took a degree in mathematics at Moscow University in 1858, and then decided to pursue a musical career. In 1859, he became a professor at the Leipzig Conservatory and solo cellist at the Gewandhaus concerts. In 1862 Davydov returned to Russia as professor at the St. Petersburg Conservatory and joined the quartet of the Russian Music Society, with Leopold *Auer as his partner in recitals. He eventually succeeded Anton *Rubinstein as conductor of the St. Petersburg Conservatory orchestra and traveled extensively on concert tours abroad. Davydov's best known compositions are his cello works, which belong to the German romantic school. His main achievement was the establishment of the first cello school in Russia. The methods and advice given in his manual for cello students remain valid.

BIBLIOGRAPHY: L. Ginzburg, *K. Yu. Davydov* (Rus., 1950).

[Michael Goldstein]

DAWIDOWICZ, LUCY (1915–1990), U.S. historian and writer. Born Lucy Schildbret in New York City, she pursued her love for Yiddish culture as a research fellow at the YIVO Institute for Jewish Research in Vilna, Poland in 1938. On the eve of World War II she returned to New York, where the YIVO Institute was reestablished, and served as assistant to the research director of YIVO from 1940 to 1946. At the end of the war, she returned to Europe on behalf of the American Jewish Joint Distribution Committee to aid concentration camp survivors.

She returned to the United States in 1947, subsequently working as a research analyst and later research director for the American Jewish Committee. In 1969, she joined the faculty of Yeshiva University, serving as professor of Holocaust studies from 1970.

In 1967, she edited the anthology *The Golden Tradition: Jewish Life and Thought in Eastern Europe*, contributing an extensive and incisive introduction. *The War Against the Jews 1933–1945* (1975) contended that the Holocaust was not merely an antisemitic outburst but the final outcome of a ruthless totalitarian ideology whose central design was to eliminate the alien Jew.

In 1976, she edited *The Holocaust Reader*, which deals with Holocaust historiography. In *The Holocaust and the Historians* (1981), Dawidowicz attacked those who have attempted to deny the authenticity of the Holocaust.

[Susan Strul]

DAWIDSOHN, ḤAYYIM (1760–1854), merchant, community leader, and rabbi. Born in Pinczow, he was elected head of the *ḥevra kaddisha* in 1801. When the authorities dissolved the Warsaw *kehillah* in 1831 he was one of the three directors (*dozory*) appointed in its place. Himself a *Mitnagged* and Orthodox, Dawidsohn cooperated with the Ḥasidim and the assimilationists. With the incumbent rabbi of Warsaw, Solomon Zalman *Lipshitz, he opposed Jews joining the city guards during the insurrection of 1831, giving as a reason that they would have to shave. After the death of Lipshitz in 1839, Dawidsohn was elected rabbi of Warsaw despite his advanced years. He burned all his writings, mainly on *halakhah*, shortly before his death, considering that none of them was worthy of publication. His eldest son, Abraham Abele, was rabbi in Biala, and his second son, Naphtali, was a wealthy merchant.

BIBLIOGRAPHY: J. Shatzky, *Yidishe Bildungs Politik in Poyln fun 1806 bis 1860* (1943), index; D. Flinker, in: *Arim ve-Immahot be-Yisrael*, 3 (1948), 106–8; EG, 1 (1953), 297–8; A.B. Bromberg, *Mi Gedolei ha-Ḥasidut*, 15 (1959), 80–127; H. Seidman, in: *Velt Federatsye fun Poylishe Yidu, Yorbuch* (1964), 247–51.

DAWIDSOHN, JOSEPH (1880–1947), physician and Zionist leader in Poland. Born in Warsaw, he was a great-grandson of Ḥayyim *Dawidsohn. In 1913 he and Stefan Mendelson founded the first Jewish newspaper in Polish, *Przegląd Codzienny* ("Daily Review"). Dawidsohn also published *Nasz Kurier* ("Our Courier") in 1917, and *Nasze Słowo* ("Our Word") in 1931. In 1908 Dawidsohn founded the Bri'ut ("Health") association to fight tuberculosis among Jews and was its chairman until 1932. He was a member of the Polish Senate from 1928 to 1931. A year later he left for Ereẓ Israel, where he worked with the Jewish Agency's Immigration Department as inspector of medical services. He was the author of *Gminy żydowskie* (1931), a work on Jewish communities in Poland.

BIBLIOGRAPHY: *Żydzi w Polsce odrodzonej*, 2 (1932–33), 151–2, 160; EG, 1 (1953), 593; I. Gruenbaum, *Penei ha-Dor* (1958), 257–63. **ADD. BIBLIOGRAPHY:** J. Majchrowicz (ed.), *Kto byl kim w drugiej Rzeczypospolitej* (1994), 79.

DAWISON (Davidsohn), BOGUMIL (1818–1872), German actor, who was regarded as one of the great actors of his day. Dawison was born in Warsaw, where he also began his career. In 1839 he began working at the theater in Lemberg (Lvov), Galicia. From 1847 he acted in Hamburg, Germany. In 1849 he was invited to the Burgtheater in Vienna, and in 1854 to the Hoftheater in Dresden. From 1864 he toured Europe and the U.S., where he arrived in 1866. His acting was dynamic and innovative, and his characterizations had great vitality. Dawison's triumphs were in the Shakespearean roles of Richard III, Shylock, Lear, and Othello; as Franz Moor in Schiller's *The Bandits*; as Mephistopheles in Goethe's *Faust*; and as Harpagon in Molière's *The Miser*.

BIBLIOGRAPHY: E. Devrient, *Geschichte der deutschen Schauspielkunst* (1905); A. Winds, *Der Schauspieler* (1919); G.K. Gershuni, *Olam ha-Te'atron* (1962), 65–75. **ADD. BIBLIOGRAPHY:** P. Kollek, *Bugomil Dawison* (1978).

[Noam Zadoff (2nd ed.)]

DAYAN, family in Ereẓ Israel. SHEMUEL (1891–1968), pioneer of cooperative settlement in Ereẓ Israel. Dayan was born in Zhashkov, Ukraine, and joined the Zionist movement as a youth, settling in Ereẓ Israel in 1908. There he worked as a laborer in various agricultural settlements and was a founder of the kevuẓah *Deganyah Alef and later of Deganyah Bet. In 1921 he helped found the first *moshav ovedim, *Nahalal. A leader of the *Ha-Po'el ha-Ẓa'ir Party, and later of *Mapai, Dayan represented the moshav movement in *yishuv* institutions, in the Histadrut, and at Zionist Congresses. He was a leading member of the Histadrut Agricultural Center (Ha-Merkaz ha-Ḥakla'i) and a Mapai member in the First, Second, and Third Knessets. He published books and articles about Nahalal, Deganyah, and the moshav ovedim, including *Nahalal* (1936); *Moshav Ovedim* (1945); *Pioneers in Israel* (1961); and *Man and the Soil* (1965). His wife DEVORAH (née Zatolowsky; 1890–1956) was a leader of the women's labor movement and an editor of *Devar ha-Po'elet* (women workers' weekly). Her articles appearing in the labor press were collected in the books *Asapper* (1952) and *Be-Osher u-ve-Yagon* (1959; *Pioneer*, 1968). The elder son of Shemuel and Devorah was Moshe *Dayan (1915–1981), military commander and statesman. Their younger son ZOHAR (1926–1948) died in the Israeli War of Independence. A book of his poems and letters, *Be-Eragon: Shirim ve-Iggerot*, was published posthumously in 1950. Moshe's wife RUTH (née Schwartz; 1917–) was active in the development of home industries during the early years of Israel, and was head of the Crafts Department in the Ministry of Labor during 1953–54. She was founder and managing director of government-sponsored Maskit, which produces and markets Israeli handicrafts. His daughter Yael *Dayan (1939–) wrote the novels *New Face in the Mirror* (1959), *Envy the Frightened* (1961), *Dust* (1963), and *Death had Two Sons* (1965), as well as *Israel Journal, June 1967* (1967), and also served in the Knesset. His son Assaf (Assi) *Dayan (1945–) was a film actor and director.

[Abraham Aharoni]

DAYAN, ASSAF (**Assi**; 1945–), Israeli actor, director, and writer. The son of Moshe *Dayan, he was born in Nahalal. He starred in a number of classic Israeli films, including *Operation Thunderbolt* (1977), the story of the Entebbe rescue operation, and *Beyond the Walls* (1984), a prison drama about Israeli-Palestinian relations. He also appeared in Joseph *Cedar's popular *Campfire* (2004) and *Time of Favor* (*Ha-Hesder*, 2000). The left-leaning actor portrayed right-wing activists in both of Cedar's films. Early on in his film career, he was cast in John Huston's *A Walk with Love and Death* (1969), opposite Anjelica Huston, but from then on Dayan appeared mostly in Israeli films. The highlight of his directing career was *Life According to Agfa* (1992), a politically charged look at the regulars of a Tel Aviv pub. *Agfa* won the Israeli Academy of Film and Television's award for best picture and Dayan was voted best director. Dayan's writing and directing credits include *The Gospel According to God* (2004) and *Halfon Hill Doesn't Answer* (1975). He acted in more than 35 films, including *Open Heart* (2002), Amos *Gitai's *Zikhron Devarim* (1995), and *The Delta Force* (1986).

[Hannah Brown (2nd ed.)]

DAYAN, MOSHE (1915–1981), Israeli military commander and statesman, member of the Fourth to Tenth Knessets. The eldest son of Shemuel Dayan, who had been a member of the First Knesset, Dayan was born in kibbutz Deganya Alef, and raised in Nahalal. As a young man, he served as a watchman in Nahalal's fields, and later joined the Haganah. During the disturbances of 1936–39, he served with the special Jewish police force in the Jezreel Valley and Galilee. He was commander of a unit of the Haganah field squads in 1938, and participated in the operations of the special night squads commanded by Orde *Wingate. Dayan was arrested in 1939, in an illegal Haganah commanders' course, and was sentenced to ten years' imprisonment for possession of illegal firearms. Released in 1941, he joined an auxiliary force of the Haganah that cooperated with the British army in the conquest of the Lebanon from Vichy forces. In the course of this operation he was wounded, and lost his left eye. The eye patch Dayan started wearing from that time on, became his trademark. After joining the Palmaḥ, he helped British intelligence set up a broadcasting network, the purpose of which was clandestine operations behind enemy lines in the event that Palestine fell into German hands.

During the 1948–49 War of Independence, Dayan commanded the defense of Jewish settlements in the Jordan Valley. In the spring of 1948 he was named commander of a mechanized battalion that fought in Ramleh and Lydda, and helped halt the Egyptian forces on the Southern front. In August 1948 Dayan was appointed commander of the Jerusalem front and reached a local cease-fire agreement with the commander of the Arab Legion in the area. In this period Dayan was viewed as Mapai's answer to generals such as Yigal *Allon, who had emerged from *Mapam and *Aḥdut ha-Avodah. Dayan and Allon remained competitors, first in the military sphere and later in politics, for the rest of their lives.

In the spring of 1949 Dayan participated in the armistice agreement talks between Israel and Jordan at Rhodes.

In October 1949 he was appointed commander of the Southern Command, and in June 1952 commander of the Northern Command. In the same period he attended a senior officers' course in Great Britain. He was appointed chief of operations at General Headquarters in December 1952, and the following year was appointed as Israel's fourth chief of staff, a post he held until January 1958. As chief of staff, Dayan concentrated on improving the military capabilities of the IDF. With the intensification of *fedayeen* terrorist attacks in the course of 1955, Dayan organized a series of reprisal raids into Jordanian and Egyptian territory, to hit *fedayeen* bases there. He commanded the Israeli forces in the *Sinai Campaign, at the end of 1956, and emerged as a national hero. Dayan retired from active army service in 1958 and spent the following year attending courses at the universities of Tel Aviv and Jerusalem. In the fall of 1959 he was elected to the Fourth Knesset on the *Mapai list. In the government formed by David *Ben-Gurion after the election, Dayan was appointed minister of agriculture, a post he held until November 1964.

Dayan supported Ben-Gurion's position in the *Lavon Affair and resigned from Prime Minister Levi *Eshkol's government to join Ben-Gurion against this background. In July 1965 Dayan broke away with Ben-Gurion from Mapai, and was one of the founders of *Rafi and elected on its list to the Sixth Knesset. In August 1966 he made an independent study tour of war-torn Vietnam and wrote of his experience in a diary, which he published. Following public pressure, Dayan was appointed minister of defense on the eve of the outbreak of the *Six-Day War in June 1967, even though Prime Minister Eshkol, who had also served as minister of defense up to that point, had wanted to appoint Allon to the post. Dayan once again emerged from the war as a hero. After the war, as minister of defense, Dayan was responsible for administering the territories occupied by Israel. He devised a relatively liberal policy for the Palestinian population in the territories, following a policy of "open bridges" to Jordan, enabling the movement of both people and goods. Unlike Allon, who started to advocate a peace plan with Jordan based on territorial compromise and the establishment of a Jordanian-Palestinian state that would include most of the territories of the West Bank and Gaza Strip, Dayan preferred a functional solution that would create a Jordanian-Israeli condominium in the territories.

In the year after the Six-Day War Dayan actively supported the formation of the *Israel Labor Party by Mapai, Aḥdut ha-Avodah, and Rafi. Dayan was still minister of defense on the outbreak of the *Yom Kippur War of October 1973, and was widely blamed for the country's lack of preparedness. Even though the *Agranat Commission established to investigate the background to the outbreak of the war (or the *meḥdal*, as the failure was termed in Hebrew) did not criticize Dayan, and did not find anything wrong in his conduct, after Golda *Meir resigned as prime minister following the publication of the Committee's interim report, Yitzhak *Rabin, who formed a government in June 1974, did not include Dayan in it. Following the 1977 "political upheaval" (*mahapakh*) Dayan, elected to the Ninth Knesset on the Alignment list, decided to leave the Alignment and join the government formed by Menaḥem *Begin as foreign minister, remaining an independent MK in the Knesset until May 1981, when he formed the Telem parliamentary group. As foreign minister, Dayan played a major role in the peace talks with Egypt that led to the historic visit of Egyptian President Anwar *Sadat to Jerusalem in November 1977, to the signing of the Camp David Accords in September 1978, and to the signing of the Israeli-Egyptian Peace Treaty in March 1979. In October 1979 he resigned from the government in protest against the appointment of Joseph *Burg as head of the team to negotiate an autonomy plan for the Palestinians with the Egyptians. The new Telem Party that he formed towards the end of the Ninth Knesset advocated a continuation of the peace process on the basis of the Camp David Accords; continued Israeli military presence in areas vital for Israel's defense; opposition to any territorial compromise in the West Bank and the Gaza Strip, on the one hand,

and the extension of Israeli sovereignty to them, on the other; self-administration for the Palestinians in the territories, on the one hand, and continued Jewish settlement on State lands and land legally purchased. Telem received only two mandates in the elections to the Tenth Knesset.

Dayan passed away in October 1981, four months after the election, and was buried in Nahalal. His daughter, Yael *Dayan, was a novelist and a member of the Thirteenth to Fifteenth Knessets.

BIBLIOGRAPHY: N. Lau-Lavie, *Moshe Dayan: A Biography* (1968); P. Jurman (ed.), *Moshe Dayan, A Portrait* (1968). **ADD. BIBLIOGRAPHY:** I.I. Taslitt, *Soldier of Israel: The Story of General Moshe Dayan* (1969); Yehudah Harel, *Follow Me, the Story of Moshe Dayan* (1972); Shabtai Teveth, *Moshe Dayan: The Soldier, the Man, the Legend* (1974); Y. Harel, *Ha-Loḥem: Ḥayyav ve-Alilotav shel Moshe Dayan* (1978); Y. Dayan, *My Father, His Daughter* (1985); A. Falk, *Moshe Dayan: ha-Ish ve-ha-Aggadah – Biografiyah Psikho'analitit* (1985); R. Slater, *Warrior Statesman: The Life of Moshe Dayan* (1991); A. Bar-On, *Ḥotam Ishi: Moshe Dayan be-Milḥemet Sheshet ha-Yamim ve-Aḥareiha* (1997); E. Ben-Azar, *Ometz: Sippuro shel Moshe Dayan* (1998); A. Yadlin, G. Teren, et al., *Moshe Dayan: Bein Estrateg Li-Medina'i. Le-Zikhro shel Rav Aluf Moshe Dayan* (2003); M. Levi Van Creveld, *Moshe Dayan* (2004).

[Yehuda Slutsky / Susan Hattis Rolef (2nd ed.)]

DAYAN, YAEL (1939–), Israeli politician, writer, and peace activist, member of the Thirteenth to Fifteenth Knessets. Dayan was born in Nahalal. Her father was Moshe *Dayan and her grandfather Shemuel Dayan, a member of the First Knesset. Dayan first came to the public's notice in 1959, with the publication of her novel *New Face in the Mirror,* written in English and based on her army experiences. This was followed by *Envy the Frightened* (1961), *Dust* (1964), *A Soldier's Diary* (1967), *Death Had Two Sons* (1967), *Three Weeks in October* (1979), and *Avi, Bitoh* (*My Father, His Daughter,* 1986).

Dayan studied international relations at the Hebrew University of Jerusalem, and life sciences at the Open University.

She was first elected to the Thirteenth Knesset in 1992 on the *Israel Labor Party list and served in the Knesset until the Fifteenth Knesset. She was twice chairperson of the Knesset Committee for the Advancement of the Status of Women, where she fought relentlessly against the phenomenon of violence against women and violence in the family. Throughout her membership in the Knesset she also fought openly for the removal of the stigma and inequality of homosexuals and lesbians.

In the Labor Party primaries preceding elections to the Sixteenth Knesset, she did not finish high and together with Yossi *Beilin decided to run on the Meretz list, where she was placed 12th and therefore was not among the six Meretz candidates who won seats. In October 2003 Dayan ran successfully in the elections to the Tel Aviv municipality, subsequently serving as deputy mayor and holding the Welfare portfolio.

From the late 1970s Dayan was active in various peace movements, including *Peace Now, Bat Shalom, the International Center for Peace, and the Council for Peace and Security. She also became active in organizations fighting for human rights in general and the rights of women, homosexuals, and lesbians, in particular. She participated in many meetings with Palestinians, including meetings with Palestinian women. She was among the supporters of the Geneva Document signed by Yossi *Beilin and Yaser Abed Rabbo on December 1, 2003.

[Susan Hattis Rolef (2nd ed.)]

DAY AND NIGHT. The profound psychological effect made on man by the regular change from day to night is a theme in the *aggadah*, epitomized in Adam's fear upon watching the first sunset (Av. Zar. 8a). In the Scriptures and in the *aggadah*, night has negative associations. It is a time of fear and danger, a symbol of death and of the return to chaos (cf. Ps. 91:5–6; Song 3:8). Day has positive connotations. The converse view, however, is also expressed. The day comprehends dangers of its own ("the destruction that wasteth at noonday," Ps. 91:6), whereas night is a time for rest and the renewal of strength. God appears to man at night (Gen. 15:12; Job 4:13); it is "an acceptable time" for prayers also and most appropriate for meditation (Ps. 77:7; cf. "The night was created only for study," Er. 65a).

In contrast to pagan mythology, where sunrise represents a daily contention between opposing forces, in Jewish monotheism, the day-and-night cycle is attributed to a single God who "forms the light, and creates darkness" (Isa. 45:7), "who changes the times," and "who removes the light from before the darkness and the darkness from before the light" (beginning of the evening prayer). The special religious significance attached to this periodicity can be observed in the Temple rites of regular morning and evening sacrifices and in the benedictions over the daily cycle in the morning and evening prayers (the benediction "Creator of the luminaries" in the morning prayer, and the benediction "Who brings the nights" in the evening prayer). Every morning, when darkness disappears before the light, the initial act of creation is renewed. In biblical cosmogony, the concept that at first there was "darkness on the face of the abyss" compares with a similar view on the origin of the universe of other early cultures. In contrast to Greek mythology, however, it is not the darkness, or the abyss, that "gave birth" to the light. The day was created by the order: "Let there be light." The halakhic postulate "the day goes after the night" is based on this antecedence of darkness to light and of night to day (Gen. 1:5). The 24-hour cycle starts at sunset; Sabbath and festivals begin in the evening, and terminate at the start of the following night (a number of specific day-only fasts, however, start at dawn; see *Fast Days). Certain concepts, dating probably from the pre-biblical period, reflect the belief that day is the basis of all that is good; these concepts have entered the Bible (e.g., Ps. 104:2; Dan. 2:22; Isa. 30:26) and the Apocrypha, and more especially gnostic and other writings with a dualistic tendency. Traces of the dualist theory are found in Jewish folklore and it may be assumed that the belief that Jewish redemption will come in an era when there is perpetual day derives from it. The concept was accepted, at least poetically and symbolically, both in the Bible (Zech. 14:7) and in the *aggadah* (Ḥag. 12a).

During the talmudic and subsequent periods, many superstitious beliefs relating to night took root in Jewish folklore. *Lilith, known in Assyrian and Babylonian mythologies as a flying demon (e.g., in the Epic of Gilgamesh), was the most feared of the evil night spirits and a fiend especially dangerous to women in confinement. Although there is no relation between her name and the Hebrew word *laylah* ("night") the phonetic similarity converted her into a night-demon threatening the lives of newborn babies, especially uncircumcised males; she is also a succubus that clings to men sleeping alone (Shab. 151b). To stave her and other diabolic creatures off, the rabbis forbade people to go out alone at night, especially on Wednesdays and Fridays (Pes. 112b). Charms, amulets, adjurations, and potions, as means of protection against "the terror by night" (Ps. 91:5), were widespread in many Jewish communities until quite recently.

The *halakhah* attaches great importance to the day-and-night cycle. Many *mitzvot* may only be performed during the day, e.g., circumcision, the sounding of the **shofar*, putting on the *tefillin* (phylacteries), *lulav* ("the taking of the palm-branch"), the laying of the hands on, and the slaughtering of, sacrifices, genuflective prayer, testimony and judgment, the construction of the Temple, and others.

The Bible does not clearly define day and night or their divisions, such as "evening, morning, and noonday" (Ps. 55:18), the watches of the night (Ex. 14:24; Judg. 7:19), midnight or half the night (Ex. 11:4; 12:29), and the notion of "hour" is not mentioned at all. The duration of a "halakhic" day is from dawn until the appearance of the stars, i.e., a full solar day; it is divided into secondary periods, according to three systems:

(a) Every day (and every night) is divided into 12 "variable" ("זמניות") hours, no matter what season it occurs in; the duration of the hour is therefore dependent on the yearly season (Sanh. 38b). Ultra-Orthodox Jews in Israel follow this system to the present day.

(b) The entire day (day and night) is taken as one unit and is divided into 24 standard and fixed hours of 60 minutes each, as in the commonly accepted time system. The division of day and night into fixed hours, with a specific duration, is mentioned for the first time in the literature of the *tannaim* (see, e.g., Mekh. SbY to 12:29: "He is seated on the sundial [a time device probably introduced into Ereẓ Israel during the Hellenistic period] and shows the hours with an accuracy that is within a hair's breadth"). The notion of an "hour" as an undefined and not standardized lapse of time has, however, been maintained in the Mishnah ("The early pietists waited an hour…."; Ber. 5:1). Though it was only theoretical, there was also more detailed division; an *onah* ("term") is $1/24$ of an hour, an *et* ("period") is $1/24$ of an *onah*, and a *rega* ("moment") is $1/24$ of an *et* (Tosef., Ber. 1:3). In this classification the *rega* is approximately $1/4$ of a second. The rabbis, therefore, said that "a human being … does not know his *ittim* [plural of *et*], *rega'im* [plural of *rega*], and hours … but God … entered into it by a hair's breadth" (Gen. R. 10:9). A different, more precise calculation existed in Ereẓ Israel: "How much is a *rega* – $1/58{,}888$ of an hour" (Ber. 7a). A wide literature, notably the *Baraita de-Shemuel*, deals with such time calculations within the framework of astrological research. Another division of the hour is into 1,080 parts; this is also very ancient and is based on the lunar month.

(c) The solar day (alone) is divided according to the changes in the brightness of the sunlight. In this system, the day is divided as follows: dawn, the appearance of the first morning twilight, is the starting point when all precepts to be fulfilled during the day become obligatory. *Halakhah*, however, prefers sunrise to dawn because the commencement of the day presents problems of definition; *haneẓ ha-ḥammah* ("first appearance of the sun") occurs after dawn and precedes *zeriḥah* by the period of time it takes to walk a *mil* ("mile"). At that time, the pious read the *Shema. Zeriḥah* – full sunrise – is the moment when the entire sun appears over the horizon. Sunset is the moment when the entire sun disappears below the horizon. Evening twilight is the light after sunset and it is doubtful whether this period may be called day or night, and diverse opinions have been given by the *tannaim* as to its exact nature and time (Shab. 34b). According to Maimonides (Yad, Shabbat 5:4), the evening twilight begins with sunset and lasts until the appearance of three medium-sized stars, and from then on it is night. R. Tam argues that evening twilight begins from the period it takes to walk three and a quarter *mil* after sunset to the appearance of the stars. Until then, it is still day. In the Shulḥan Arukh (OḤ 261), this second opinion is accepted as binding. According to a third opinion, held by some of the early commentators, night begins immediately with sunset and the evening twilight is a period prior to sunset, lasting the time it takes to walk three and a quarter *mil*.

The *halakhah* used systems (a) and (b), while (c), which is the most ancient and is based on the direct observation of the movement of the celestial bodies, is only of secondary importance. All the hours and time concepts associated with the precepts are "variable." According to Mordecai *Jaffe's *Levush* and *Elijah ben Solomon of Vilna, the hours of the day are calculated from *zeriḥah* to *sheki'ah* (sunset); the majority of opinions, however, maintain that the calculation is from dawn until the appearance of the stars. The Shulḥan Arukh decides in favor of the second opinion. In the same way as the day, the night is divided into "variable" hours (there are three watches in three parts of the night), but this division is devoid of any practical importance, except for "the middle of the night," which is the time for reading *Tikkun Ḥaẓot* (the midnight prayer). "To keep a man away from sin," the rabbis limited to midnight the time for performing a number of precepts which otherwise could have been fulfilled during the whole night (Ber. 1:1).

The "standard" hours (according to system b) are used in *halakhah* to set related periods of time, such as "six hours" between the eating of meat and milk, "one hour" for the salting of meat, and many others.

BIBLIOGRAPHY: Bornstein, in: *Ha-Tekufah*, 6 (1920), 247–313; M. Tucazinsky, *Bein ha-Shemashot* (1929); Burstein, in: *Shanah be-Shanah*, 6 (1965–66), 101–35.

[Israel Moses Ta-Shma]

DAY OF ATONEMENT (Heb. יוֹם הַכִּפּוּרִים, *Yom ha-Kippurim*), one of the "appointed seasons of the Lord, holy convocations," a day of fasting and atonement, occurring on the Tenth of Tishri. It is the climax of the "*Ten Days of Penitence" and the most important day in the liturgical year.

In the Bible

All manner of work is forbidden on the Day of Atonement, as it is on the Sabbath (being likewise called "a Sabbath of solemn rest"), and the soul is to be "afflicted" ("from the evening of the ninth day of the seventh month until the evening of the morrow"), the punishment for transgressing these commandments being destruction and extirpation (Lev. 16:29–31; 23:27–32; Num. 29:7). Special additional offerings were to be brought (Num. 29:8–11), and, apart from these, a ceremony peculiar to the day (see **Avodah*) was solemnized in the Temple (Lev. 16:1–34). The essence of the day and the reasons for the ceremony are expressed by the verse: "For on this day shall atonement be made for you, to cleanse you; from all your sins shall ye be clean before the Lord" (Lev. 16:30). In the Jubilee year the *shofar* is to be sounded on the Day of Atonement to indicate the setting free of slaves and the restoration of the fields to their ancestral owners (Lev. 25:9–10).

In the Second Temple Period

The ritual performed by the high priest in the Temple was the central feature of the Day of Atonement (see **Avodah*; *Sacrifice). When the high priest, representative of the people (Yoma 1:5), "entered where he entered and stood where he stood" (5:3), while all feared for his life (5:1), he himself was enveloped in awe, holiness, and mystery; while when he had come out, he resembled, in his majesty, "a bright star emerging from between clouds" (Ecclus. 50:6ff.). It is certain that during the time of the Second Temple the Day of Atonement was already considered the greatest of the festivals. It is related that none of Israel's festive days compared with the Fifteenth of Av and the Day of Atonement, on which days the daughters of Jerusalem would go forth, dressed in white, and dance in the vineyards – "And what did they say? – 'Young man! Raise your eyes and behold what you choose for yourself'" (Ta'an. 4:8; and see below). According to the calendar of the Book of Jubilees, accepted by the *Dead Sea Sect, the Day of Atonement usually occurred on a different date from that kept by the remainder of Israel; and it is told that "the wicked priest" persecuted the members of the sect and "appeared amongst them just at the fixed time of the season of the rest of the Day of Atonement, to destroy them and to lead them astray on their fast day of Sabbath of rest" (Pesher Hab. 11:4–8).

In the *Halakhah*

The Pentateuch does not explain what is to be understood by "afflicting the soul" on the Day of Atonement. However, other passages in the Scriptures speak explicitly of afflicting the soul by fasting (Ps. 35:13; Is. 58:3, 5, 10; but cf., however, Num. 30:14; and see Yoma 74b). According to the sages, there are five ways in which the duty of afflicting the soul applies: by prohibitions against eating and drinking, washing oneself (for pleasure), anointing the body, wearing shoes (of leather), and cohabitation (Yoma 8:1; Yad, Shevitat Asor 1:4; 3:9). The penalty of extirpation, however, applies only to eating, drinking, and working (Yoma 74a). The same kinds of work are forbidden on the Day of Atonement as are forbidden on the Sabbath (Meg. 1:5), and danger to life (*pikku'aḥ nefesh*) overrides all the prohibitions of the Day of Atonement just as it does those of the Sabbath. Children are exempted from all modes of affliction, except the wearing of shoes. However, both in the time of the Second Temple, as well as in the Middle Ages, there were those who insisted that children also observe the "laws of affliction" in opposition to the view of the sages that it is one's duty to feed them with one's own hands (Tosef., Kippurim 4 [5]:1–2; Sof. 18:7; *Sefer ha-Yashar* of R. Tam responsa, ed. F. Roschthal (1898), 51:2, 52:2). Only a few years before they reach the age at which they are obliged to fulfill commandments (13 years for a boy and 12 years for a girl) should one begin to accustom them gradually to keep these laws. According to the *Karaites, children, too, are to be afflicted (*Eshkol ha-Kofer* of Judah Hadasi (1836), no. 135). Since the Day of Atonement is regarded as a "festive day," one is bound to honor it by wearing clean clothes (Shab. 119a; see below).

According to the sages, the goat dispatched to *Azazel as part of the Temple ritual on the Day of Atonement atones for all transgressions (Shev. 1:6), whereas after the destruction of the Temple, the Day itself atones (Sifra, Aḥarei Mot 8:1). However most of the sages are of the opinion that even the atonement of the goat was only effective for him who repented, for the Day only atones when accompanied by repentance (Yoma 8:8–9; cf. Yad, Teshuvah 1:2–4). This is the source of the custom of asking forgiveness of one another on the eve of the Day of Atonement. The sages hold that the fate of every person, which has been left pending from *Rosh Ha-Shanah, is finally determined on the Day of Atonement (Tosef., RH 1:13; cf. Yad, Teshuvah 3:3), and hence one should repent during the Ten Days of Penitence, and particularly on the Day of Atonement (*ibid.*, 2:7). The Day of Atonement is the only one of the appointed seasons which has no second day in the Diaspora. This is because of the extreme difficulty of fasting for two successive days. However, there were those who were strict and fasted both days (TJ, RH 1:4; RH 21a; Isaac b. Moses of Vienna, *Or Zaru'a*, 2 (1862), no. 281). The laws of the Day of Atonement remained essentially the same during the Middle Ages as they were in the days of the Second Temple and in the mishnaic and talmudic periods. Additions and variations were limited to the domain of customs and prayers.

Prayers

No definite knowledge is available about the Day of Atonement prayers during the period of the Second Temple. The few defective remnants of the Day of Atonement prayers among the writings of the Dead Sea Sect (Barthélemy-Milik, 1 (1955), 152–4) do not suffice to give a clear picture of the scope and content of the sect's prayers on this day. According to Philo (Spec. 2:196), it was already customary in the time of the Second Temple to spend the whole day, from morning to evening, in prayer. The Day of Atonement is the only day of the year which has five *Amidah* prayers: Evening, Morning, *Musaf*, Afternoon, and *Ne'ilat She'arim* ("Closing of the Gates," shortened to *Ne'ilah*). During the time of the Second Temple prayers were also said five times a day on *Fast days and *Ma'amadot* (Ta'an. 4:1). This is perhaps the source of the Muslim custom of praying five times a day (but see L. Ginzberg, *Peirushim ve-Ḥiddushim ba-Yerushalmi*, 1 (1941), lxxii). The prayers for the Day of Atonement begin in the evening with **Kol Nidrei*. The subject of the distinctive middle blessing of the *Amidah* prayer of the Day of Atonement is God's pardoning, forgiving, and granting atonement for Israel's iniquities (see, e.g., Sof. 19:4). The prayers of the Day of Atonement and of the New Year have many common features, and at times some of the prayers peculiar to the New Year have passed into the prayers of the Day of Atonement.

Especially characteristic of the Day of Atonement prayers is the duty of *confession. Though statutory on "the eve of the Day of Atonement close to nightfall," confession is made both prior to the last meal before the fast ("lest he become confused while eating and drinking"), and after it ("lest some mishap occurred during the meal"), as well as at each of the Day of Atonement services, the individual saying it after the *Amidah* proper and the reader in the middle of it (Tosef., Kippurim 4:14). Confession is now said once in the afternoon prayer on the eve of the Day of Atonement and ten times during the Day itself. Forms of confession are already to be found among the *amoraim* (Yoma 87b; TJ, Yoma 8:9, 45c), some of which are currently in use. Versions written alphabetically have been preserved from the early Middle Ages. The short form of confession ("We have trespassed, we have dealt treacherously," etc.) would appear to have originated already in the days of the *amoraim*, whereas the long form of confession ("For the sin wherein we have sinned," etc.) dates from a somewhat later period. However, it was already found in *Yannai (see **Al Ḥet*; **Ashamnu*).

In early times many *piyyutim*, especially *seliḥot* and *raḥamim* (entreating forgiveness and mercy), were added to the Day of Atonement prayers and acquired for themselves an important role as part of the "obligation of the day." The *piyyutim* of the **Avodah* ("Order of the Temple Service") occupy a central position in the prayers. Some added special psalms before the morning prayers. Although there are differences of opinion and custom with regard to the details of the *piyyutim* to be said on the Day of Atonement, some saying more and some less, the *piyyutim* and *seliḥot* have greatly endeared themselves to the public. However, there were also rabbis who were opposed to *piyyutim*, preferring in their stead "sermons on the laws of repentance, on religious topics, on wise opinions, and on true beliefs" (Menahem Ha-Meiri, in *Ḥibbur ha-Teshuvah*, ed. A. Sofer (1950), 532). The day concludes with the blowing of the *shofar*, a series of phrases in praise of God, and ends with "Next Year in Jerusalem."

The Reading of the Torah

In the morning service six people are called to the reading of the Torah (Meg. 4:2) from the portion *Aḥarei Mot* (Lev. 16; cf. Meg. 3:5), whose subject is the Day of Atonement. The **maftir* is the section in Numbers dealing with the additional sacrifices of the Day of Atonement (Num. 29:7–11; cf. Tosef., Meg. 4 [3]:7), and the *haftarah* is Isaiah 57, from verse 15 (or 14) until 58:14 (Meg. 31a), in which the prophet describes the ideal fast. During the afternoon service three men are called to the reading of the Torah of Leviticus 18, which deals with incest prohibitions (and which is a continuation of the morning reading of the Torah according to the ancient custom which still exists in Italy). The *haftarah* is the Book of Jonah and Micah 7:18–20, whose subject is ideal repentance and its effect, and God's forgiving mercy (Meg. 31a).

Customs

Many customs have their origin in the Middle Ages, especially among the Ashkenazi Jews. Thus it is customary to arrange the table for the eve of the Day of Atonement in the same manner as the Sabbath (*Sefer Ravyah*, ed. by V. Aptowitzer (1964^2), no. 528); to adorn the synagogue with beautiful drapery (Tur, OḤ 610); to wear white clothes, either in order to resemble the angels (*Sefer Ravyah*, no. 528) or because white is the color of shrouds and will thus inspire repentance by evoking death (Isserles to Sh. Ar., OḤ 610, 4). This last custom also passed into Italy and Provence, and it became a widespread custom to wear a white robe called *kittel*. Even a confirmed repentant is forbidden to wear sackcloth (*Sefer Ḥasidim*, ed. Freimann, 646). Very significant is the custom which originated in Germany in the days of the tosafists, and which became law, to light candles at home and recite a blessing over them. In addition to this candle and to that kindled (according to ancient custom) in order to prevent cohabitation, which is forbidden this day (Pes. 4:4), it has also become customary in some places to light a candle for the souls of the living (Abraham b. Nathan ha-Yarḥi, *Ha-Manhig* (1855), *Hilkhot Ẓom Kippur*, no. 71; cf. E.E. Urbach (ed.), *Arugat ha-Bosem* of Abraham b. Azriel, 3 (1962), 572, notes 35–36) and a candle for the souls of the dead (*Sefer ha-Minhagot* of Abraham b. Saul of Lunel in S. Asaf, *Sifran shel Rishonim* (1935), 152). It also became the custom "to mention the dead on the Day of Atonement and to donate charity in their memory" (Tanḥ., Ha'azinu 1, addendum). In northern France and Germany, after the reading of the Law, they used to publicly announce charitable donations "on behalf of the living and the dead: charity on behalf of the dead is not donated throughout Germany save on this Day" (*Maḥzor Vitry*, ed. S. Hurwitz (1923), 392). The custom of donating for charity was also adopted in Provence, Italy, and Spain, whereas the special prayer commemorating the dead was adopted only among the Ashkenazim and the Italians. Northern France is the place of the source of the custom of wearing a *tallit* also for the evening service, which is even put on while it is still day in order to be able to recite the blessing over it (Rashi, *Ha-Pardes*, ed. by Ehrenreich (1924), 234). In Germany it was fixed that in the evening, just at the beginning of the prayer, "absolution is granted from the ban against praying together with anyone guilty of transgressing any communal regulations" (*Sefer Ravyah*, no. 528). The formula "In the higher [i.e., celestial] assembly and in the lower assembly, with the consent of the Omnipresent and the consent of the congregation, we permit prayers being said together with transgressors" (Tur and Sh. Ar., OḤ 619) was adopted, with minor variations, throughout most of the Diaspora. It was customary, in the main, to recite the *She-Heḥeyanu* blessing in the synagogue on the night of the Day of Atonement before **Barekhu*. Some, however, said the blessing at home, or on the way to the synagogue, or even after the evening prayer. Women recite it when they kindle the festive candles. During the recital of the **Shema*, the words "Blessed be His glorious sovereign Name for ever and ever" are said aloud and not quietly as is usual (*Deuteronomy Rabbah*, ed. by S. Lieberman (1964^2), 69). In Germany the custom of saying the *Amidah* aloud was introduced, and from there comes also the custom that some remain standing during all the Day of Atonement prayers, and some even remain in the synagogue throughout the whole night, reciting psalms, hymns, and praises (*Sefer Ravyah*, 529). In many places, no break at all is made in the prayers during the course of the day, the *Minḥah* service following immediately after the *Musaf* service. Some places are most particular about the choice of a suitable reader, and some have had the custom of having two men stand one at each side of the reader during all the prayers. It is customary to smell spices, the enjoyment of pleasant odors not being forbidden.

The Eve of the Day of Atonement

A special importance was assigned to the day prior to the Day of Atonement, which was regarded already in the period of the Mishnah and Talmud not merely as a preparation for, but as an inseparable part of, the Day of Atonement. The statement, "Everyone who eats and drinks on the ninth [of Tishri] is considered by Scripture as having fasted on the ninth and tenth" (Ber. 8b) means that one should eat and drink well on the eve of the Day not merely to prepare for the fast but also to fulfill the command to rejoice in and to honor the festive day. From ancient times much meat, fowl, and fish was eaten on this day (see, e.g., Gen. R. 11:4), in which one spent less time in study and prayer. Little by little the eve of the Day of Atonement took on the character of a festival, some people desisting from doing any work then. It is customary to send gifts to the poor, and a duty to ask forgiveness from one another and to appease each other. During the geonic period, the custom of ritual immersion on the eve of the Day of Atonement after midday was introduced; this was usually performed before the *Minḥah* service, in any case before the final meal (*se'uddah mafseket*), but there were also other customs. Some said a blessing before the immersion. The opinion of most halakhic authorities, however, has been that a blessing should not be said. Even one who finds it difficult to immerse himself should endeavor to wash in hot water. It is also customary to trim the hair. In Germany and France it was customary after the *Minḥah* service to inflict 39 stripes, while the victim repeated the confession, and the one wielding the lash said "And He being full of compassion forgiveth iniquity" (*Ha-Orah* 1:95; et al.). This also became the custom among the Sephardim. Some visit the cemetery. In recent generations the custom originated in some places of blessing one's children before nightfall. (For customs from the geonic period which have an element of magic, see **Kapparot*, **Kol Nidrei*.)

Termination of the Day of Atonement

The termination of the Day of Atonement was also assigned a special status, similar to that of the eve of the Day. During the geonic era the custom of blowing the *shofar* at the conclusion of the Day of Atonement was adopted, there being differences of opinion about the number of blasts, the time (whether at the end of *Ne'ilah* or after the evening service and *Havdalah*), and the reason for blowing. There are those who contend that the purpose of the blowing is to call attention to the festive and joyous character of the termination of the Day of Atonement; in northern France and Germany, the termination of the Day was considered a festival, it being a religious duty to rejoice and eat abundantly. There were also special table-hymns for the end of the Day (*Sefer Ravyah*, no. 530; *Or Zaru'a* 2, no. 281); and there was also the custom of greeting people with the blessing "May you be answered and your entreaty granted"; "May you be inscribed for life and merit many years" (*Orḥot Ḥayyim*; cf. Judah Halevi, *Divan*, ed. by H. Brody, 3 (1910), 305, in a *seliḥah* for *Ne'ilah*: "May you merit many years, be answered, and have your entreaty granted"). Some have the custom to begin building the booths for *Sukkot as soon as the Day of Atonement terminates (Isserles to Sh. Ar., OḤ 624:5).

The Meaning of the Day – The Day of Atonement in Philosophic, Aggadic, and Belletristic Literature

In the Pentateuch there is no reference to mourning practices on the Day of Atonement. On the other hand, the Book of Jubilees maintains that the Day of Atonement, the one day in the year when forgiveness is granted to all who repent fully (Jub. 5:17–18), was established on the day that Jacob heard of Joseph's death and mourned for him. For this reason one should always be sad on this day (Jub. 34:17–18), and atonement is made with a male goat as a reminder of the male goat which Joseph's brothers slaughtered and in whose blood they dipped his shirt. This conception of the Day of Atonement as a day of sadness is peculiar to the author of the Book of Jubilees and does not appear elsewhere in Judaism except among many Karaites who instituted mourning practices on the Day of Atonement.

*Philo was the first author to discuss profoundly the significance of the Day of Atonement. In his opinion it is the greatest of the festivals as in it, being both a festival and a time of repentance and purification, true joy is to be found. In contrast to many other people, Philo maintained that true joy is not to be found in overeating and overdrinking, feasting and reveling, and dancing and music, which in reality only stir up man's lowest desires and lusts. The Day of Atonement, on the contrary, is defined by abstinence and devotion to praying from morning to night. The purpose of the fast is to purify the heart of people who pray without being disturbed by corporal desires, and entreat their Maker's forgiveness for their past sins and His blessing for the future. Philo testifies that all, not only those devoted to piety, but even those who are not distinguished at all on other days by the fear of heaven, fear the sanctity of the Day and observe it, evildoers standing together with the good in the struggle to subdue the evil inclination (Philo, Spec. 1:186–8; 2:193–203; Mos. 2:23–24).

The sages too regarded the Day of Atonement as the supreme festival and the greatest day of the year (Gen. R. 2:3), hence its names: "The Great Day" (or, in abbreviation, "The Day"), and "The Great Fast" (Ta'an. 4:8; Tosef., Ḥul. 5 [6]:9; Sifra, Aḥarei Mot 8:9, but cf. Men. 11:9; Sof. 19:4). A day of unparalleled joy, both for God, who gave it to Israel with love (SER 1), and for the children of Israel themselves (SEZ 4), the whole purpose of the Day of Atonement is to atone for those who repent and confess their iniquity. Even one who was far from his home the rest of the year endeavored to return to his wife and family in order to spend the day and the meal of its eve together with them (Ket. 62b, 63a; Shab. 127b). According to the *aggadah*, the Day of Atonement is the day the second Tablets of the Law were given to Moses (SOR 6), and also the day of Abraham's circumcision (PdRE 29); there is also a tradition that it is the day of the **Akedah*, the Binding of Isaac. It was said that even if all the other festivals were to be abrogated, the Day of Atonement, on which the children of Israel resemble the angels, would remain (*ibid.* 46). Satan has no power to accuse the children of Israel on this Day (Lev. R. 21:4). The assembly of Israel, sullied by sins during the whole year, is cleansed on the Day of Atonement (Song R. 1:5) since it is a day of pardon and forgiveness, and atonement is promised even to the completely wicked who repent, for their Maker desires their repentance and greatly rejoices in it. The Day of Atonement is thus regarded not just as a duty but still more as a right; and side by side with the feeling of the great transcendent distance between the sinner and God there manifests itself in an emphatic fashion the conception of His immanent nearness to all His creatures ("Thou dost reach out Thy hand to transgressors; Thy right hand is extended to receive repentant sinners").

During the Middle Ages, the character of the Day of Atonement as a joyful and a festive day did not change, but emphasis was also put upon its character as a day of judgment and justice and as the hour of "signing the verdict." As did Philo and the sages, the medieval philosophers also describe the Day of Atonement as a day when the soul, freed from corporal fetters, attains the peak of its perfection in the service of God (Judah Halevi, *Kuzari*, 3:5; Maim., *Guide*, 3:43; Ha-Meiri, *Ḥibbur ha-Teshuvah*, 427–8, 430, 442; according to Ha-Meiri 439–40, eating on the eve of the Day, too, serves this purpose).

In all generations halakhic sages, thinkers, and moralists deprecated lengthy praying when achieved at the cost of understanding and devotion. At the same time, it is the prayer of the Day of Atonement which expresses the perfection and greatness of the Day. In recent generations the Day of Atonement has become the last concrete bond with Judaism for many Jews.

The honored place allotted to the Day of Atonement in the various branches of the belletristic literature and art also testifies to its leading position both among Jews and among Gentiles who write about Jews. In modern Hebrew literature the Day of Atonement appears as a symbol of Judaism, both when depicting rebellion against Judaism (as for instance in the case of Naḥman, the hero of *Le-An* by M.Z. *Feuerberg), and when depicting the yearning for it. In *Sheloshah she-Akhlu*, D. *Frischmann depicts against the background of the Day of Atonement the wealth of meaning exhibited by the perfect world of Judaism, even from the standpoint of humanity as a whole, in contrast to the ludicrous emptiness of the world of the superficial *maskilim*. In his tale *Neshamot Illemot: 4 Nissim al ha-Yam*, I.L. *Peretz depicts the Day of Atonement as the only symbol of the simple faith of Satyah, the plain common Jew living among Gentiles. However, in his story "*Niggun Ḥadash*," the Day of Atonement expresses the contradiction between the bright, heavenly ideal and the gloomy, human reality. A.Z. *Rabinovitz in *Ḥalom* brings up the significance of the Day of Atonement in the consciousness of refugees saved from the pogroms, immigrating to Ereẓ Israel, in such a way that even God, as it were, is required by them on this day to justify His conduct of the world. The Day of Atonement plays a most important part in the works of S.Y. *Agnon. Reflected against the ideal and profound nature of the perfect Day of Atonement of the past (*Ba-Derekh; Zikkaron ba-Sefer* – the introduction to *Yamim Nora'im, Days of Awe*, 1965), Agnon brings up its problematic significance in a world broken and shattered both without and within (*Ore'aḥ Natah Lalun; Im Kenisat ha-Yom; Eineinu ha-Ro'ot*). On the one hand, the power of the Day of Atonement is so great that even the dead share a part in it with the living (*Bi-Meẓulot*); that man clothes himself with a different soul (*Eẓel Ḥemdat*); and that even his sick body is healed by it (*Lefi ha-Ẓa'ar ha-Sakhar*). On the other hand, however, not everything depends upon the Day itself, for a man could forfeit the Day of Atonement without Torah and prayer – an irrecoverable and irreplaceable loss (*Pi-Shenayim; Tallit Aḥeret*).

[Moshe David Herr]

Day of Atonement as Annual Day of Purgation in Temple Times

The Day of Atonement was the annual "day of purgation." The key to the meaning of the purging is the realization that (1) the sacrifices are of one type, called *ḥattat* or "purification offering" (actually designated *ḥattat ha-kippurim* in Ex. 30:10 and Num. 29:11); and (2) the three *ḥattat* animals employed are offered on behalf of two different groups: the bull is for the priesthood (Lev. 16:6, 11) and the two goats are for the people (16:5, 15).

FIRST PURPOSE: PURGING THE TEMPLE. According to the Mishnah: "All the goats make atonement for the impurity of the Temple and its sancta.... For impurity that befalls the Temple and its sancta through wantonness, atonement is made by the goat whose blood is sprinkled within [the shrine, or Holy of Holies] and by the Day of Atonement; for all other transgressions specified in the Torah – minor or grave, wanton or inadvertent, conscious or unconscious, of commission or omission ... the scapegoat makes atonement. The atonement is alike for Israelites, priests, or the anointed [high] priest ... the blood of the bull makes atonement for the impurity of the Temple and its sancta" (Shevu. 1:4–7). Despite the expansion and reinterpretation of the ritual of the Day of Atonement during the Second Temple period, the Mishnah is a reliable guide to the interpretation of the biblical account of the ritual, because the function of the sacrifice never changed. This Mishnah shows that an objective of the slain *ḥattat* animals was to purge the sanctuary of its impurity, and that the function of the live *ḥattat* goat, the one that was dispatched to *Azazel, was to purge the people of their sins. This distinction is corroborated by the biblical text expressly declaring that the purpose of the slain bull and goat is "to purge the shrine of impurities [*mi-tumot*] and transgressions" (Lev. 16:16, cf. 16:19), and that of the scapegoat is to carry off all their "iniquities" (*avonot*) and "transgressions" (*pesha'im*; Lev. 16:21). The Hebrew word *pesha'im*, which appears twice in this context, is found nowhere else in the entire priestly code. It has been suggested that this word has been borrowed from the world of politics where the verb פשע (*pasha*) means "to rebel" (e.g., II Kings 3:7; 8:20), and its application to the ritual of the Day of Atonement would point to a further basic function of the prescribed *ḥattat* offerings, alluded to by the Mishnah: to purge the Temple and the people of their *pesha'im*, their rebellious sins.

THE PRIESTLY TEMPLE THEOLOGY. The purpose of the purification offerings of the Day of Atonement could then only be understood in conjunction with two complementary postulates: (1) Whoever brazenly rebels against God is not eligible for sacrificial expiation (Num. 15:30–31), but the Temple must be purged of his sins and impurities. Moreover, the purging is urgent since his sins, committed wantonly, possess the additional power not only of contaminating the outer altar but of breaching the sanctuary and penetrating to the very shrine (Holy of Holies). Thus, on the Day of Atonement the entire Temple complex must be purged. (2) The private purification offering (Lev. 4; see also *Sacrifices) is presented for the *shegagah*, the inadvertent sin (and for severe physical impurity stemming from natural causes; Lev. 12–15).

THE TEMPLE AND AZAZEL. A third implication of the above Mishnah is that the two categories of purification offering – the slain, whose blood purges the Tabernacle, and the live, which expiates the people's sins – are two inseparable parts of a unified ceremonial. That this unity is not an anachronistic retrojection of rabbinic Judaism but is a verifiable biblical reality is confirmed by the coexistence of the two categories within the same ritual in both an ancient-Near-East and in another biblical ritual, which will be described below.

Temple purifications dominate the cultic landscape of Israel's environment. The ancient pagans feared impurity because they imputed to it demonic power. Impurity was an unending threat to the gods themselves, and to their temples, as revealed by the images of the protector gods (the *šêdu* and *lamassu* in Mesopotamia and the lion-gargoyles in Egypt) set before the entrances of temples and palaces and, above all, by the elaborate purgation rituals to rid the buildings of demons and prevent their return (examples from Pritchard, Texts: *Egyptian*: pp. 6–7, 12–14, 327 no. 6; *Hittite*: pp. 346, 351–3; *Mesopotamian*: pp. 33–34 lines 381–2, pp. 334–8 lines 14–16, pp. 60–72 tablet 1 lines 61–64, tablet 4 lines 61–62, 91, tablet 7 lines 32–33). The antiquity and ubiquity of the Azazel rite are even more striking. However, it has apparently not been observed that the two rites usually go together. Since impurity was demonic its exorcism was not enough: its power had to be removed. This was accomplished in one of three ways: curse, destruction, or banishment. The last was often used; rather than the evil being annihilated by curse or fire, it was banished to its place of origin (e.g., netherworld, wilderness), or to some place where either its malefic powers could work in the interests of the sender (e.g., enemy territory), or where it could do no harm at all (e.g., mountains, wilderness). Thus the scapegoat was sent to the wilderness which was considered uninhabited except by the satyr-demon *Azazel. A parallel example of banishment is found in the famous New Year festival in Babylon (Pritchard, Texts, p. 333 lines 345–61).

In these cases there is an integral connection between the actual purging (by aspersions, smearing, and incense) and the transfer of the released impurity onto a decapitated ram and its banishment via the river (see also Deut. 21:1–9). Similar motifs, common to Babylonian and biblical purification texts (especially in Lev. 14), indicate that the purgation-expulsion nexus essential to pagan magic could have obtained early in Israel's cult as well, but with a different meaning.

SECOND PURPOSE: PURGING THE PEOPLE. Though the purgation and Azazel rites of Israel's Day of Atonement differed little from their Near Eastern analogues, their meaning underwent a revolution. As scholars have noted, the rites are discrete: the slain *ḥattat* animals suffice to purge the Tabernacle, but the live *ḥattat* carries off the sins of the people. The reasons are clear: Israel, the holy people (Lev. 11:44; 19:2; 20:26), needs the same purification as the holy place for "they shall not contaminate their camp in whose midst I dwell" (Num. 5:3b). Moreover, the monotheistic dynamic is at work here: since the world of demons is nonexistent for Israel the only source of rebellion against God is in the heart of man, and it is there that cathartic renewal must constantly take place.

The Azazel ritual stipulates that "Aaron shall lay both his hands upon the head of the live goat and confess over it all the iniquities and transgressions of the Israelites, whatever their sins, putting them on the head of the goat; and it shall be sent off to the wilderness..." (Lev. 16:21). Ordinarily, the hand-laying and confession must be performed by the offerer himself (see *Sacrifices), but the perpetrator of *pesha*, rebellious sin, is barred from the sanctuary according to the priestly rules, and must be represented by the high priest. The latter's officiation should not be regarded as inherently efficacious; the people, though excluded from the rites, must submit to fasting and other acts of self-denial (Lev. 16:29; 23:27–32; Num. 29:7). The verbal confession of the high priest must be matched by the remorse of the people. Thus, repentance purges man, as the *ḥattat*-blood does the sanctuary. Unless man makes the initial effort toward his self-regeneration, the rite of Azazel is of no avail. Nor can his purgation by repentance be a perfunctory exercise (Yoma 8:9; see also below).

This ethical achievement is, thus far, unparalled in the ancient world. True, the Babylonian New Year calls for ritual of humiliation for the king, followed by his prayer of confession, but in contrast with Israel's high priest who in his confession specifies all the failings of his people, the Babylonian king appears arrogant and self-righteous. It was only the Jew who could say that "God ... has given to repentance the same honor as to innocence from sin" (Philo, Spec. 1:187).

Finally, atonement by sacrifice is only efficacious for sins against the Deity. This also holds true on the Day of Atonement. The Mishnah again has captured the ethical import: "For the sins between man and God, the Day of Atonement effects atonement, but for the sins between man and his fellow, the Day of Atonement will effect atonement only if he has appeased his fellow" (Yoma 8:9). That this spiritual principle is not an innovation of the rabbis but constitutes their legacy from biblical times is shown by its explicit presence in the *asham* offering, where restitution to man must precede sacrificial expiation from God (Lev. 5:20ff.).

THE EMERGENCE OF THE DAY. The Day of Atonement itself may not be as old as its individual ceremonial elements. For example, in distinction from all other festival prescriptions which give the date before the ritual (e.g., Lev. 23), here alone the date is not specified until the end (16:29) and the term "Day of Atonement" is lacking. It has been suggested that there is evidence that points to the evolution of an original rite for the purging of the sanctuary at an unspecified time one day a year (Lev. 16:34) into an annual day for the purging of the sanctuary and the atonement of individual Israelites (Lev. 16:29). An exact date for the named "Day of Atonement" appears in Lev. 23:27–28; 25:9.

Given the contentious nature of source analysis, scholars are not sure when the Day of Atonement came into being. Elements in the day's rituals have Hittite parallels that might point to great antiquity (COS I, 161–63). At the same time, given the general conservatism of ritual, late texts may preserve ancient elements while introducing new features, which, when identified, bring us closer to the actual time of composition. A formal indication that earlier material is being updated is the phrase *ḥukkat olam* (Lev. 16:31, 34; Knohl (1987), Sperling (1999)). Material evidence of lateness is indicated by the requirement of Aaron to wear breeches, or short trousers (*mikhnasayim*; Lev. 16:4). Trousers, mentioned only in the Priestly Code and Ezekiel, were an Iranian invention unlikely to have come to the attention of Jews before the sixth century (Sperling (1999)). Likewise indicative of lateness is the role of Aaron as priest. Although the original figure of Aaron is pre-exilic (e.g., Micah 6:4), scholars have long observed that Aaron is never identified as a priest in the prophetic literature of the pre-exilic period. Ezekiel, the priest-prophet of the exile, confers legitimacy only on the priestly line of Zadok (Ezek. 44:15–16), but knows nothing of Aaronide priests.

Yet another indication of the lateness of the Day of Atonement is its absence from the festival lists of Exodus 23, 34, and Deuteronomy 16.

The evidence from Ezra-Nehemiah is particularly significant because the book mentions Rosh Ha-Shanah and Sukkot but omits the Day of Atonement (Neh. 8–9). Inasmuch as the author of Ezra-Nehemiah was surely aware of much of the Priestly source, the Day of Atonement is most likely part of that source's latest stratum.

Thus, the Day of Atonement is later than the Exile.

[S. David Sperling (2nd ed.)]

BIBLIOGRAPHY: S. Landersdorfer, *Studien zum biblischen Versoehnungstag* (1924); Elbogen, Gottesdienst, 149–54; Idelsohn, Liturgy, 223–48; S.Z. Zevin, *Ha-Mo'adim ba-Halakhah* (1949^2), 62–89; T.H. Gaster, *Festivals of the Jewish Year* (1952), 135–86; D.Z. Hoffmann, *Sefer Va-Yikra* (1953), 298ff.; L. Jacobs, *Guide to Yom Kippur* (1957); Kaufmann, Y., Religion, 302–9; H. Schauss, *The Jewish Festivals* (1938), 119–42; idem, *Guide to Jewish Holy Days* (1962), passim; M. Arzt, *Justice and Mercy* (1963), 191–290, includes bibliography; E. Munk, *The World of Prayer*, 2 (1963), 169–209; M. Noth, *Leviticus* (Eng., 1965), 115–22; EM, 3 (1965), 595–600; S.Y. Agnon, *Days of Awe* (1965), 183–279, includes bibliography; K. Elliger, *Leviticus* (Ger., 1966), 200–17; H. Chamiel (ed.), *Yamim Nora'im* (1968); B.A. Levine, in: *Eretz Israel*, 9 (1969), 88–95 (Heb. sect.). **ADD. BIBLIOGRAPHY:** I. Knohl, in: HUCA, 58 (1987), 65–117; idem, *The Sanctuary of Silence* (1995); D. Wright, *On the Disposal of Impurity* (1987); idem, in: ABD II, 72–6; B. Levine, *JPS Torah Commentary Leviticus* (1989); J. Milgrom, *Leviticus 1–16* (AB; 1991); S.D. Sperling, *Original Torah* (1998), 103–19; idem, in: R. Chazan et al. (eds.), *Ki Baruch Hu* (Studies Baruch Levine; 1999), 373–85.

DAY OF THE LORD, a definite, though undetermined, point of time in the future, when God is expected to punish the wicked and justice will triumph. The term "Day of the Lord" serves as a key word in nine prophetic passages (Isa. 13:6–13; Joel 1:15; 2:1; 3:4; 4:14; Amos 5:18–20; Obad. 15; Zeph. 1:17–18; Mal. 3:23); in others it appears in some slightly varied form (see e.g., Isa. 2:12; Ezek. 30:3; Zech. 14:1–9). The prominent feature of these passages is a dramatic sense of doom, underlined by a few characteristic motifs, such as darkness and wailing. The usual message of these prophecies asserts that the Day of the Lord is near. From the polemic of Amos (5:18–20) against those who desire the Day of the Lord it is evident that the concept was well established by the time at which the so-called "writing" prophets started to function, and that an optimistic version was somewhat popular (presumably with patriotic overtones). Scholars have tried to utilize the term for their general theories on biblical *eschatology, or to find some hypothetical, non-prophetic origin of the concept. Thus according to Mowinckel and others, the Day of the Lord was originally a New Year festival; L. Černý suggests that it was a fateful, disastrous day; and von Rad presumes that in the early sacred wars of Israel, God was considered to reveal His will in battle, and therefore any battle was called a Day of the Lord. The last suggestion can find some support in Ezekiel 13:5, where a metaphorical battle, visualized as having taken place in the past, is referred to by the term Day of the Lord.

The main, though largely undiscussed, difficulty concerning the Day of the Lord is that of its significance. The passages do not convey a concept amenable to logical analysis, nor an eschatological doctrine. The warning is given that the Day of the Lord is near, but the more abstract idea involving history's drawing to a close is not indicated. The wicked will be punished, justice established, mankind confounded, and its destiny somehow definitely changed. However, none of this seems essential to the notion itself. Nor is the concept related to expectations of theophany. The prophets simply confront their listeners with the awful certainty of future Divine action. Thus in the expression "Day of the Lord" there is a rather vague but stark and powerful concept: God will indeed act – suddenly, decisively, and directly, in a single day, with vehemence and terror.

BIBLIOGRAPHY: D.H. Mueller, *Komposition und Strophenbau* (1907), 36–40; G. Hoelscher, *Die Urspruenge der juedischen Eschatologie*, 1 (1925), 13; H. Gressmann, *Der Messias* (1929), 75, 83, 84; Pedersen, Israel, 3–4 (1940), 546; J. Morgenstern, *Amos Studies*, 1 (1941), 408–13; A.S. Kapelrud, *Joel Studies* (1948), 54–57; W. Eichrodt, *Theologie des Alten Testaments* (1948), 233; L. Černý, *The Day of Yahweh and Some Relevant Problems* (1948); O. Procksch, *Theologie des Alten Testaments* (1950), 578; H.H. Rowley (ed.), *Old Testament and Modern Studies* (1951), 305; idem, *The Faith of Israel* (1956), 177–80; H.W. Robinson, *Inspiration and Revelation in the Old Testament* (1950), 135–47; S. Mowinckel, *He that Cometh* (1956), index; G. von Rad, in: JSS, 4 (1959), 97–108; Kaufmann, Y., Toledot, 2 (1960), 291–3, 516–7; 3 (1960), 157–9; M. Weiss, in: HUCA, 37 (1966), 29ff.

[Jacob Licht]

DAYTON, city in S.W. Ohio. Dayton's Jewish population in the mid-1990s was estimated to be 5,500 and by 2005 some 5,000 in a total population of around 160,000, down from around 7,500 in 1970. Like many smaller cities in Ohio, Dayton has been losing its Jewish population as manufacturing and other job opportunities open up in the South and the West, elderly Jews leave for warmer climates, and young natives who go off to college do not return home.

The first Jews to settle in Dayton came from Germany in the 1840s. They founded the first synagogue, Bnai Jeshuran, in 1850. The synagogue joined in the formation of the Union of American Hebrew Congregations in 1873 and adopted the Reform ritual. The first B'nai B'rith chapter was established in 1864. Traditional Judaism began in the 1890s with the arrival of Jewish immigrants from Eastern Europe. They established two synagogues, Beit Abraham and Beit Jacob, based upon the traditions of their native Lithuania and Romania. They also established a Hebrew school and Zionist societies. Gradually many other benefit societies, women's organizations, and landsmanschaften developed. The first Federation of Jewish Charities was formed in 1910. In 1944 the various social welfare agencies of the Jewish community were coordinated into the Jewish Community Council, which became the local agency of the United Jewish Appeal and the central organization for the Jewish Home for the Aged, the Jewish Community Center, the Community Relations Council, and the Dayton Community Hebrew School. The marked differences between German and Eastern European Jews gradually faded and all segments of the community worked together, especially on behalf of Israel and overseas Jewry.

Members of the Dayton Jewish community have made important contributions to the cultural life of the general community. Paul Katz was the longtime director of the Dayton Philharmonic; Sidney Kusworm served as a member of President Truman's Civil Rights Commission, and as a national officer of B'nai B'rith; Robert Nathan served as an adviser to four American presidents; Miriam Rosenthal served as a planner for the University of Dayton. Temple Israel, which was an outgrowth of Bnai Jeshuran Synagogue, was at one time an outpost of classical Reform but in recent years it has moved toward Jewish tradition. A second Reform synagogue, Congregation Beth Or, was established in 1984 in Washington Township. Beth Abraham has affiliated with the Conservative movement. There were two Orthodox synagogues, Beth Jacob and a Young Israel Synagogue, which closed in the early 21st century; the latter had been attended mainly by scientists and professionals who had settled in the community. Chabad also serviced the community and there were several ḥavurot. There were several synagogues in nearby communities. In 1961 the Hillel Academy, a widely recognized progressive Jewish day school combining religious and secular studies, was established at the Conservative synagogue.

Among the community's amenities is the Jewish Community Complex. The Complex serves as the central location for the Jewish Federation of Greater Dayton and its departments: Covenant House resident care facility, the Jewish Community Relations Council, the Dayton Jewish Community Center, the Dayton Jewish Education Commission, the *Dayton Jewish Observer,* Jewish Family Services, United Jewish Campaign, Women's Division, and the Dayton Jewish Federation Foundation.

In 1992, the Federation opened the JCC on Far Hills Ave. In the fall of 2002, the Federation expanded its services, with the opening of the Center for Jewish Culture and Education in Centerville to meet the needs of the South Jewish community.

Through the efforts of the community's leaders, recent years have been marked by a renewed spirit of unity among Dayton's Jewish congregations. Collaborative holiday celebrations, shared education programs, Hillel Academy Jewish day school, B'Yachad supplementary high school for Jewish studies, and the new Melton Adult Mini School are part of its educational matrix.

[Jack Reimer / Larry Skolnick (2nd ed.)]

DAYYAN, Syrian family claiming descent from King David. The Dayyan family's origin can be traced to a branch of the house of Josiah Ḥasan ben Zakkai, brother of the exilarch David (?917–940). One of his descendants, SOLOMON BEN AZARIAH, settled in *Aleppo, and his family there occupied the position of *nasi*, the title of the House of David. The first to be known with the family name is MOSES BEN SAADIAH DAYYAN in the 16th century. His son, MORDECAI (b. 1541), was a member of the *bet din* of Samuel *Laniado. Even after many Spanish refugee scholars settled in Aleppo, the Dayyan family continued to be held in great esteem. Some of them held key positions in religious and communal life.

One of the most important members of the family in Aleppo was ISAIAH (d. 1830), *ḥakham*, scribe, and *mohel.* His son ABRAHAM (d. 1876) was a distinguished rabbi and the author of *Shir Ḥadash* (1841), a commentary on Psalms; *Zikkaron la-Nefesh* (1842), ethical writings; *Holekh Tammim u-Fo'el Ẓedek* (1850), sermons and responsa; *Ta'am* (1867), sermons; and *Yosef Avraham* (1863), responsa. He also wrote sermons and commentaries on *Ein Ya'akov* and the Zohar, which are extant in manuscript. His son MOSES (d. 1901) wrote *Yashir Moshe* (1879), a homiletic commentary on Song of Songs; in the introduction to this work he traced the Dayyan family lineage. ISAIAH BEN MORDECAI (d. 1903) was head of the *bet din* in Aleppo. In 1888 he founded a Jewish press, which was administered after his death by his sons SAUL, SOLOMON, and ISAAC, and later by his grandson JOSEPH BEN EZRA. AARON (d. 1893) was chief rabbi of the community of Urfa, Turkey, during the 1880s. He was also a merchant and acted as Persian consul. He wrote a book of sermons, *Beit Aharon* (unpublished).

[Abraham David]

The best-known member of the branch of the family which moved to Ereẓ Israel was ḤIYYA BEN JOSEPH DAYYAN (late 17th century), scholar and emissary. His grandfather had emigrated from Damascus to Jerusalem where Ḥiyya was born and educated. He later moved to Hebron. As emissary of that community he traveled to North Africa (1665, 1669) and Italy (1673). While in Mantua, he met Moses *Zacuto who recommended him to his pupil, *Benjamin b. Eliezer ha-Kohen of Reggio. Both wrote poems dedicated to him. In Italy he strongly opposed the Shabbatean movement. Ḥiyya also went to Turkey and Persia as emissary for Jerusalem (1680–96). In 1696, while returning from Persia, he was attacked by robbers near Baghdad who took from him, besides his money and clothes, also the manuscript of his book *Adderet Eliyahu.* However, he found another copy he had made in Aleppo, which he took with him on his last mission to Morocco. In the introduction there is a description of his travels and an autobiography. One of his pupils in Meknès was R. Ḥayyim b. Moses *Attar the Elder.

[Avraham Yaari]

BIBLIOGRAPHY: Ashtor, Toledot, 2 (1951), 514–9; J.M. Toledano, *Oẓar Genazim* (1960), 219–25; J. Ben-Naim, *Malkhei Rabbanan* (1931), 32–33; D.Z. Laniado, *Li-Kedoshim Asher ba-Areẓ* (1952), 52–55, passim; Yaari, Sheluḥei, 301, 306, 466.

DAYYAN (Heb. דַּיָּן; pl. דַּיָּנִים, *dayyanim*), judge. In talmudic literature the word *dayyan* (from דִּין, judgment) completely replaces the biblical name for a judge, *shofet*. Although found twice in the Hebrew portion of the Bible (Ps. 68:6 where God is called "the *dayyan* of widows" and I Sam. 24:15), it is essentially an Aramaic word and is used consistently by the Targum for *shofet*. In the Aramaic Ezra 7:25 it is coupled with *shofetim*.

It was possibly this juxtaposition, suggesting a lower status to the *dayyan* as compared with the *shofet* (translated "magistrate" and "judge"), which determined the definition given to the term in the Middle Ages that has persisted to the present day. The term is confined to the members of the *bet din* other than the head of the *bet din*, who is accorded the title of *av bet din* or *rosh bet din*, whereas they are ordinary members of the court. Sometimes elders of the community or guild functionaries were given the title of *dayyan*. **Takkanot*, such as those of *Cracow of 1595 (JJLG, 10 (1912), 331–3), show that these communities maintained courts of *dayyanim* of various degrees of competence, in monetary suits according to the amount involved in the case. In modern times the *dayyan* was also referred to as *moreh ẓedek*, in particular in Eastern Europe. In some communities, like that of *Vilna, the rabbi did not serve on the *bet din* in the modern period, several *dayyanim* being appointed to this office. Only in England has the custom been adopted of according the title *dayyan*, which is regarded as higher than that of the ordinary rabbi, to members of the official religious law courts, particularly that of the chief rabbi.

In the State of Israel *shofet* is used for a judge in the civil courts and *dayyan* for the judge of the rabbinical courts.

BIBLIOGRAPHY: ET, s.v. *Bet Din*; Baron, Community, 2 (1942), 74, 84, 95.

[Louis Isaac Rabinowitz and Isaac Levitats]

DAYYEINU (Heb. דַּיֵּנוּ; "it would have satisfied us"), the refrain of a song of thanksgiving in the Passover **Haggadah*. The *Dayyeinu* song, in all rites, starts with the words: "How many are the favors that God has conferred upon us" and proceeds to enumerate 15 (in some rites 16) stages of the redemption of the Jews from Egyptian bondage, including their miraculous survival in the Sinai wilderness, their receiving the laws of Sabbath and the entire Torah, and finally, their being led into Ereẓ Israel and building the Temple. The origin of this litany is uncertain, although some scholars date it back to the late Second Temple period. No mention of it is made in the Talmud or in the Midrash, although some scholars see an indirect reference to it in *Shabbat* 32b. It first appears in the *siddur* of *Saadiah Gaon (ninth century C.E.). While some scholars believe that *Dayyeinu* was inspired by *Sifrei Deuteronomy* (337, 339, etc.), others hold the dependence to be in the opposite direction. The term "*dayyeinu*" is used ironically in Hebrew and in Yiddish and means "That's enough," "I've had enough."

BIBLIOGRAPHY: D. Goldschmidt, *Ha-Haggadah shel Pesaḥ ve-Toledoteha* (1960), 48–51; M. Kasher, *Haggadah Shelemah* (1967), 55–58; idem, *Israel Passover Haggadah* (1962), 134–41.

DEAD SEA (Heb. יָם הַמֶּלַח, *Yam ha-Melaḥ*; "Salt Sea"), an inland lake in central Ereẓ Israel. It was created in the Upper Pleistocene Age by the drying up of the Rift Valley Sea (except for the southern end which probably dates to historical times). The measurements of the sea are not constant; its length is about 50 mi. (80 km.), maximum width about 11 mi. (18 km.), and total area about 363 sq. mi. (940 sq. km.). It lies about 1,305 ft. (398 m.) below the level of the Mediterranean and is thus the lowest point on earth (for further details see *Israel: Mineral Resources, Dead Sea Minerals). In the Bible it is usually called *Yam ha-Melaḥ* ("Salt Sea"; Gen. 14:3; Num. 34:3; Josh. 15:2, etc.). The "bay" (Heb. *lashon*, "tongue") of the Dead Sea mentioned in the last citation probably refers to the bays on the northern and southern ends of the sea and not to the Lisān (Halashon) Peninsula which juts out from about the middle of its eastern shore. Alternative biblical names for the sea are *Yam ha-Aravah* ("Sea of the Aravah"; Deut. 3:17; Josh. 3:16; 12:3) and "eastern sea," a term used by the inhabitants of the country west of the Dead Sea to distinguish it from the Mediterranean (Ezek. 47:18; Joel 2:20). In biblical times the western shore of the Dead Sea was included within the Egyptian province of Canaan while the eastern shore was largely uninhabited until the establishment of the kingdoms of Moab and Edom in the 13th century B.C.E. With the Israelite conquest of Canaan, the eastern shore was divided between the tribe of Reuben and the Moabites, north and south of the Arnon, and the western shore was occupied by Judah (the tribe and the kingdom) until 586 B.C.E. After the Babylonian Exile, the entire eastern shore passed into the possession of the Nabateans and the western shore was divided between Judea and Idumea. The Nabateans extracted bitumen from the sea (mentioned in Gen. 14:10) and sold it to Egypt where it was used in embalming mummies. In the Hellenistic period the Dead

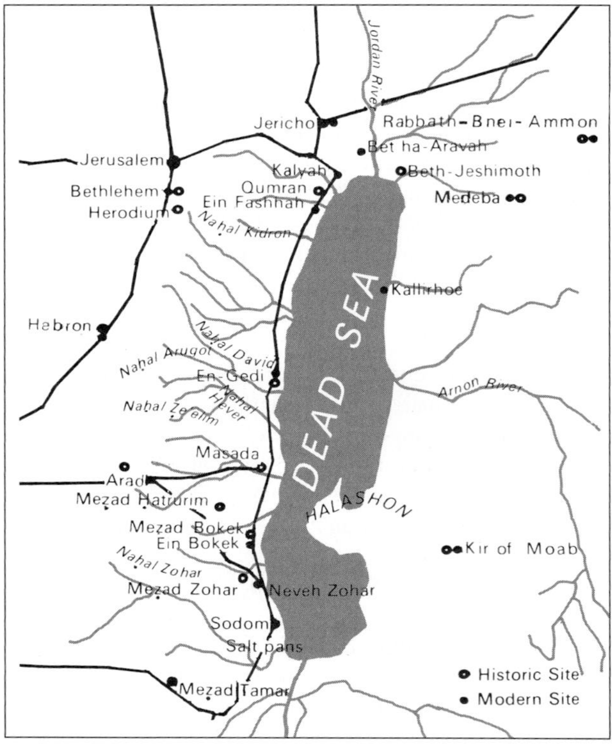

The Dead Sea and the surrounding areas.

Sea began to attract the attention of Greek scientists because of its peculiar natural phenomena. It is mentioned by Aristotle in his *Meteorology* (2:3, 39) and also by Strabo (5:2, 42). The common Latin name for the sea, Lacus Asphaltitis (Lake of Asphalt), is first recorded in this period. The successors of Alexander the Great, Antigonus and Demetrius, attracted by the wealth which the Nabateans derived from the sea, tried to subject them, but failed (Diodorus, 19:95–96). Alexander Yannai, on the other hand, succeeded in his military campaigns in conquering the entire area around the Dead Sea and thus secured for his kingdom the income from its products. Navigation developed on the sea in Hellenistic and Roman times; Vespasian's ships pursued the Jews fleeing by way of the sea during the Jewish War (66–70/73). The physical properties of the sea were well known by this time and are mentioned by Pliny, Tacitus, and Solinus. Vespasian ordered a bound man to be thrown into the sea to determine whether he would sink. In the Talmud the Dead Sea was called *Yammah shel Sedom*, "the Sea of Sodom"; according to R. Dimmi, "no one ever drowns in the Sea of Sodom" (Shab. 108b). It was considered the juridical boundary of Ereẓ Israel (TJ, Shev. 6:1, 36c). Throwing an object into the sea was suggested as a means of disposing of a religiously or morally undesirable advantage which a person had received unintentionally (Av. Zar. 3:9; Av. Zar. 49b; Tosef., Dem. 6:13, etc.). The name Dead Sea first appears in Roman times in writings of Pausanias (*Periegesis* 5:7, 4–5) and Galen, who made the most thorough study of the sea and its properties (*De simplicium medicamentorum facultatibus* 4:20). Documents from the time of the Bar Kokhba War (132–135) found in Dead Sea caves indicate that En-Gedi was the main supply port for the Jewish army during the final phase of the war. In Byzantine times the Dead Sea attracted pilgrims; on the Madaba Map two ships are depicted navigating the sea, one sailing northward with a cargo of salt and the second southward with wheat. The Arabs called the sea Buḥayrat Sadūm wa-ʿAmūra (the Sea of Sodom and Gemorrah) or Baḥr Zuʾār (the Sea of Zoar). The modern Arabic name for the Dead Sea, Baḥr Lūṭ (the Sea of Lot), first appears in the account of the Persian traveler Nasir-i Khusrau in 1047. In Crusader times navigation again increased on the sea; Idrīsī in 1154 mentions small boats sailing on it. Heavy customs duties were levied on goods transported across the sea; the Hospitalers obtained an exemption from them in 1152 which was renewed in 1177. The Dead Sea made a strong impression on European pilgrims who called it "the Devil's Sea." The Arab historian and geographer Yāqūt (1225) refers to it as al-Buḥayra al-Muntina, "the Stinking Sea." It was generally believed that deadly vapors emitted from the water prevented all life in its vicinity but at no time was the land along its shores wholly uncultivated. The large oasis of Zoar to the south was famous for its palm groves. A detailed account of the produce of these groves and of the methods used in their irrigation and cultivation are given in legal documents found in the *Judean Desert caves (second century C.E.) The southern part of the sea – the shallowest – was possibly created by an earthquake which occurred in historical times. This section has generally been regarded as the site of the biblical cities of Sodom and Gomorrah; some scholars, however, locate them farther north. The southern part of the western shore, although barren, was studded with fortifications, such as the Roman forts at Meẓad Bokek and Meẓad Zohar, and above all the fortress of Masada. The fertile oasis of En-Gedi north of Masada produced balsam and many kinds of semitropical fruits. On the northwestern shore the Essenes established themselves at *Qumran (Meẓad Hasimin) and Ein Feshkha. On the eastern shore are, from north to south, the oasis of Bet ha-Jeshimot (Khirbat al-Suwayma); the warm springs of Kallirhoe; a fort at Qaṣr al-ʿAsal; and a road station at Beit Nimrin (Rujm al-Numayra) where the road from Kerak to Zoar descends into the valley. Until 1830 a ford was reported to have existed between the Lisān Peninsula and the opposite shore but this later disappeared.

[Michael Avi-Yonah]

In the 19th and 20th Centuries

In the 19th and 20th centuries, the Dead Sea attracted many explorers and scholars. In 1806–07, the German U.J. Seetzen toured its shores and took notes on its morphology and climate. In 1837, the Irishman C. Costigan descended in a boat from Lake Kinneret to the Dead Sea, where he was caught in a storm, thrown up on the Lisān Peninsula, and died of hunger and thirst before aid could be brought. Between 1838 and 1872, the scholars E. Robinson, F. de Saulcy, and B. Tristram conducted research mainly into the region's historical geography. In 1847 the British naval officer T. Molyneux toured the Dead Sea, also going by boat from Lake Kinneret; he fell ill and died a few days later in Beirut. In 1848, an expedition of the American navy led by W.F. Lynch toured the Dead Sea area. Lynch named the two capes of the Lisān Peninsula "Cape Costigan" and "Cape Molyneux"; his own name was in turn commemorated by the German geographer C. Ritter who named the narrows connecting the southern with the northern basin "Lynch Straits." Further travelers who explored the Dead Sea include the geologists L. Lartet (France), M. Blanckenhorn (Germany), E. Hull and G.S. Blake (Great Britain; the latter was murdered by Arabs on the Dead Sea shore in 1940).

On the initiative of M. *Novomeysky, the first potash and bromine works were built in 1930 at Rabbat Ashlag near Kallia in the northwest corner of the Dead Sea by the Palestine Potash Company. A supplementary plant was opened in 1937 at the southern end of the western shore, at the foot of Mount Sedom. Among the pioneers working at both places was a group composed of members of Ha-Kibbutz ha-Meʾuḥad which called itself "Pelugat Yam ha-Melaḥ." A hotel was opened at Kallia in the 1930s. In 1939, the kibbutz *Bet ha-Aravah was established northeast of Rabbat Ashlag. In Israel's War of Independence, the Jewish workers of Rabbat Ashlag and Kallia and the settlers of Bet ha-Aravah found themselves completely cut off by the Transjordanian Arab Legion; during the night of May 19, 1948, they succeeded in evacuating the sites and sailing over the Dead Sea southward to reach the Sedom potash plant in whose defense they participated until the end of the war. In "Operation Lot" (October 1948) overland contact with Sedom was reestablished, and in March 1949 units of the Israeli Army moved along the Dead Sea shore north to the site of En-Gedi which had been allocated to the Jewish state in the 1947 UN partition plan. In 1955, the new Sedom potash plant of the Dead Sea Works began operating after the Beersheba-Sedom highway was completed. In 1995 a new plant for magnesium was established, a joint project of Israeli and German firms. Kibbutz En-Gedi was founded in 1953, and the motor road leading there from Sedom was built in 1956. The Dead Sea region was further integrated into Israel's communications network with the construction of the Arad-Sedom and Sedom-Eilat highways in 1964 and 1967 respectively. These not only aided production and marketing of the Dead Sea Works but also created conditions for the development of the tourism and recreation branch in the region. In the late 1960s a restaurant, hotel, picnic camps, and a museum of the Dead Sea Works were opened at Shefekh Zohar, two large hotels and bathing facilities at Ein Bokek making use of medicinal springs and thermal mud, a museum at the foot of Masada Rock, a nature reserve and nature study center at En-Gedi, youth hostels, etc. The occupation of the Judean Desert and the entire west coast of the Dead Sea by Israel in the Six-Day War made the region again easily accessible from Jerusalem.

According to measurements taken from 1818, the level of the Dead Sea waters rose, until 1898, by 36 ft. (11 m.), but since that time it has steadily fallen. Between 1930 and 1997, for example, the water level fell by 100 ft. (30 m.). One of the main reasons for the drop in the water level has been the use made of Jordan River water for agriculture and industry. Another reason is the water exploitation of Dead Sea industries, which have been drying out the sea in phosphate production. Up to 1977 the Dead Sea stretched over two basins, a large northern one and a smaller and shallower southern basin. In 1977, the water level was so low that a ribbon of dry land appeared between the two basins. The southern basin became a series of steaming pools, so that the present-day Dead Sea consists in effect of only the northern basin. Recently, as a result of the low water level, a new phenomenon, large suckholes, began to appear near the shore.

At the beginning of the 21st century 2,250 people were living in the area's kibbutzim, moshavim, and urban communities. The Shefekh Zohar and Ein Bokek area had about 1,550 hotel rooms and served as the center of the region's tourism. Tourist attractions were based on the sea itself, curative sites, and wildlife.

[Efraim Orni / Shaked Gilboa (2nd ed.)]

BIBLIOGRAPHY: J. Braslavi, *Ha-Yadata et ha-Areẓ*, 3 (1951); J. Almog-Eshel, *Ḥevel Yam ha-Melaḥ* (1956); Abel, Géog, 1 (1933), 498–505; Powell and Kelso, in: BASOR, 95 (1944), 14–18; C. Klein, *On the Fluctuations of the Level of the Dead Sea since the Beginning of the 19th Century* (Israel Water Commission, Hydrological Paper No. 7, 1960); W.F. Lynch, *Narrative of the United States Expedition to the River Jordan and the Dead Sea* (1850); A. Molyneux, in: *Journal of the Royal Geographical Society*, 18 (1848), 104–30; M. Novomeysky, *The Dead Sea* (1936).

DEAD SEA SCROLLS, the popular designation given to collections of manuscript material found in 1947 and the following years in various caves west of the Dead Sea, notably at *Qumran, *Murabbaʿāt, Khirbat Mird, together with *En-Gedi and *Masada. This entry concentrates on those found in the Qumran region (by far the greatest in bulk and probably in importance); those found at En-Gedi, Masada, and Murabbaʿāt are treated under these respective headings. For the Bar Kokhba Letters found in the Judean Desert see *Bar Kokhba, and for the *tefillin* of the Dead Sea Scrolls see **Tefillin*.

The Qumran Discoveries

Discovered by chance in 1947, the first scrolls, of which there were seven, some almost complete, came into the hands of dealers in antiquities, who offered them to scholars. The first scholar to recognize their antiquity was E.L. *Sukenik, who succeeded in acquiring three of them (the second Isaiah Scroll (B), the *Thanksgiving Hymns, the *War Scroll) for the Hebrew University. Between 1948 and 1950 he published specimens of them, his *editio princeps* of these scrolls appearing posthumously in 1955. The four other scrolls had been bought from a Bethlehem dealer (known as Kando) by Mar Athanasius Samuel, the Metropolitan of the Syrian Christian community, who had at first taken them to the American School of Oriental Research, where their importance was also recognized, in the absence of the school's director, Millar Burrows, by John Trever and William Brownlee. During the Israel War of Independence of 1948, these were brought to the United States, where they were studied by a group of scholars led by M. Burrows (d. 1980), who in 1950–51 published three of them – the first Isaiah Scroll, the **Pesher* (Commentary) on Habakkuk, and the Manual of *Discipline. Subsequently the Israel government bought these four scrolls, and thus all seven came to their permanent abode in the Israel Museum's Shrine of the Book in Jerusalem. Only after it reached Jerusalem was it possible to open the one hitherto unpublished scroll among the seven, the Genesis Apocryphon, which was published in 1956 by N. *Avigad and Y. *Yadin. In the meantime, with the West Bank now under Jordanian administration, the scrolls cave had been sought and identified, and, under the Jordanian Department of Antiquities, its director G. Lankester Harding and R. de *Vaux of the Ecole Biblique (in the then Jordanian part of Jerusalem) excavated it along with some 40 other caves in the vicinity of Khirbat Qumran and Ein Fashkha. Two years later, excavations began at the nearby ruins of Qumran, continuing until 1956, during which time the connections between the caves and the ruins became evident. Eleven more caves were discovered, some by the archeologists and some by the Bedouin, which contained scrolls, many of them highly fragmented. Many of these caves were man-made and lay on the edge of the plateau on which the settlement itself stood. By 1958 most of the material taken by the Bedouin had been purchased for the scholars, some through dealers in antiquities and sometimes with the assistance of overseas institutions. In view of the large quantity of material from cave 4, an international committee (understandably but regrettably excluding Jews) was appointed, under de Vaux, to publish the newly acquired materials in possession. Due to difficulties in deciphering, lack of funding and a declining level of enthusiasm, progress was slow, though a concordance of the Cave 4 scrolls was in fact completed in the late 1950s and early 1960s, yet was not made available, and then only to a limited circle of scholars, until 1989. Some texts were partly published in provisional articles in scholarly journals, and then gradually began to appear in definitive editions, in the series *Discoveries in the Judaean Desert* (Oxford). The first three volumes (1955, 1960, 1962) included the fragments from Cave 1, the documents from Murabba'at and the contents of caves 2–3 and 5–10 respectively. The intriguing and controversial *Copper Scroll had been unrolled in Manchester in 1956 and published, unofficially, by Allegro in 1960 (it has since resided in Amman). The disagreement between Allegro and his colleagues on the editorial committee foreshadowed disagreements that would later dog Scrolls scholarship. Allegro believed in rapid publication, even in provisional form, but also held controversial views about the Scrolls' significance, which he eagerly popularized. As a result he was marginalized. His views (for example, that the Scrolls helped to unmask Christianity as a fraud) have subsequently been rejected, though they have not perished; but his criticisms of the publication policy and practice of the editorial team were largely vindicated. In 1966, Sanders published the Psalms scrolls from Cave 11 (DJD 4) and in 1968 the first official edition of texts from Cave 4 appeared (Allegro, with Andersen: DJD 5). In 1967, the majority of the scrolls and fragments, which were held in Jerusalem's Rockefeller Museum, became available to Israeli scholars, and Y. Yadin also obtained a further important document, the *Temple Scroll, which he published in 1977 (English 1983). In 1971 De Vaux died and was succeeded as chief editor by Pierre Benoit, also of the Ecole Biblique, while further DJD volumes of Cave 4 texts appeared very slowly (de Vaux [posthumously] and Milik in 1977 and Baillet in 1982). Meanwhile, those outside the editorial team were denied access to the contents of unpublished material. When Benoit resigned in 1984, the Israeli Department of Antiquities appointed John Strugnell, one of the members of the original editorial team, to oversee a more rapid publication, and several new members, including Jewish and Israeli scholars, were co-opted. But although some Harvard doctoral students published editions entrusted to their dissertation directors, wider access remained forbidden to others. Increasing protest over this situation was answered in a series of dramatic developments that began in 1990. Strugnell was replaced by Emanuel Tov as editor in chief, and in the following year a computer-generated reconstruction from the concordance of cave 4 texts (which Strugnell had released) was published, followed by an unauthorized facsimile edition of plates of all the scrolls and, finally, a decision by the Huntington Library in California, which owned a set of plates of the unpublished scrolls, to make them publicly available broke the embargo. Since then, the DJD series has been completed, and Tov was able to resign, with his job done, in 2002.

[Jacob Licht]

Description

The Qumran manuscripts were mostly written on parchment, some on papyrus. Most are in Hebrew, some in Aramaic, a handful in Greek. The Qumran caves are numbered serially, 1 to 11, in the order in which the manuscript treasure contained in them came to light. A manuscript is defined as a single scroll, usually represented by one or more fragments. A document may be represented by one or several manuscripts, and the manuscripts may contain different versions of that document. Hence the designation "Community Rule" cannot refer simply, as it once did, to the cave 1 manuscript. A more accurate method of designation is the cave number and location, such as 1QS (= Serekh [ha-Yaḥad]). However, there are several different manuscripts of this document from Cave 4, giving rise to the labels 4QS^{a}, 4QS^{b}, etc. But the preferred method of designation is by cave, location and a unique number. Some of these numbers have changed over time, so that different manuscripts of the same document may form a sequence. Hence the document popularly referred to as the Halakhic Letter is also known as 4QMMT, but is strictly a (hypothetical, in this case!) reconstruction from fragments of the six manuscripts 4Q394–99. In addition, manuscripts in Aramaic have "ar" added (6QApoc ar), and *pesharim* have a "p" inserted (1QpHab). Scrolls are written in columns, and the method of citation is by column and line (CD [= Cairo Damascus] is an exception, being represented by two codices, having pages). However, in the case of a fragment of a manuscript that cannot be fitted into its place in the original scroll, individual column numbers are assigned. Thus, a citation from 4QPseudo-Jubilees^{a}, or 4Q225, might read 4Q225 frag. 22, col. 3 line 6 – or, more simply, 4Q225 22 iii 16. As more fragments become assigned to manuscripts and documents, either the enumeration will change, or, more probably, anomalies will enter the system. Indeed, the reordering of fragments of the Cave 1 Hodayoth manuscript (1QH) has already resulted in changes to the column numbering given in Sukenik's original edition.

Six caves (3, 5, 7, 8, 9, and 10) were discovered by archaeologists; the other five (and these included the most important in respect of their contents) were discovered by Bedouin of the Taʿamira tribe. There is strong evidence to connect these caves closely with the neighboring ruin of Khirbat Qumran; a reasonable assumption is that their contents formed part of the library belonging to a community, or a movement, to which the inhabitants of Khirbat Qumran belonged (see *Qumran). The nearly 900 manuscripts are commonly thought to have been hidden during the war with Rome from 66 to 70 C.E.; but they may not have been deposited in all 11 caves on the same occasion, for, whereas those in Cave 1 were carefully placed in covered cylindrical jars, those in other caves, and especially in Cave 4, which contained the greatest quantity of manuscripts, appear to have been dumped in haste. News of their discovery aroused intense interest throughout the world and considerable controversy, especially with regard to their dating. But paleographical and radiocarbon indications, together with the few historical allusions in the texts, point clearly to the 2nd century B.C.E.–1st century C.E. as the time of their writing, with a few manuscripts (according to radiocarbon dating) as early as the 4th century B.C.E. These dates mostly fit well with the period of occupation of the Qumran site in the Hellenistic era, which began in about 100 B.C.E. and ended in 68 C.E. The manuscripts were written over a period of several generations; in several cases (including the Damascus Document, Community Rule, and War Scroll) different recensions of the same work have been found (even in the same cave), enabling some deductions to be made concerning their history, and thus possibly the history of the sect that produced them. The Qumran scrolls are generally classified in three categories: "sectarian" works (200+ manuscripts); "biblical" manuscripts (also 200+); and other Jewish writings, whether previously known or otherwise (400+).

An extensive list of Qumran scrolls with their publications in English or Hebrew (including scrolls not mentioned in this article) appears in the Index Volume of this Encyclopaedia, in the list of bibliographical abbreviations under the letter Q.

Language, Orthography, and Spelling

The Dead Sea scrolls are mostly written in Hebrew, with some in Aramaic (a few fragments of a Greek translation of the Bible have also been found). Aspects of the evolution of ancient Hebrew from classical to Mishnaic remain disputed, in particular the relationship between written and spoken forms, and the question of dialects. The Hebrew of the non-biblical scrolls is not uniform: the majority of texts may represent a Judean dialect of spoken Hebrew or possibly a literary (scribal) language; the Damascus Document exhibits a Hebrew closer to biblical, while the Copper Scroll (and to some extent the Halakhic Letter) is very similar to Mishnaic Hebrew. As to orthography generally, the writing is often plene, characteristic forms being לוא, כיא, אמתכה. Thus the plural form of נגע is נגועים (or נגיעים); instead of הוא and היא we find הואה and היאה; קצור (= קצר), יושר (= ישר), מולאת (= מלאות), אנושי (= אנשי). Whether this points to a system of pronunciation different from that transmitted in the Tiberian masorah is not clear. Indications of weakening of the gutturals, as for example הנשי (= אנשי) probably does: but in other manuscripts, and commonly in the biblical manuscripts, the writing is defective, as in the Masoretic text. It has been suggested by Tov that the plene manuscripts come from a Qumran scribal school, though it is also found in some biblical manuscripts. Generally the square Hebrew script is used, in the stage of its development a little prior to the final one (the present day printed type). Thus the ה is closed and has a cross beam protruding slightly to the left; the ד has no protrusion to the right; the ז is a simple, straight line, sometimes with a small head on the right. The great majority of scribes make no distinction between a ו and a י (both of which resemble the numeral 1), a few however writing the י not shorter but wider. Several phases of the script can be distinguished, the three major categories being "Archaic" (as in First Temple period inscriptions) "Hasmonean" (c. 150–50 B.C.E.), and "Herodian" (50 B.C.E.–70 C.E.). In some scrolls the Divine Names (the Tetragrammaton YHWH and at times also *El*) are written in the archaic script, this being a characteristic feature of the commentaries, as also of the scroll of the Book of Psalms. The style of handwriting is also divided into formal, cursive, mixed, semicursive, and rounded. Paleography is a useful guide to the dating of the manuscripts, but because of their varied provenance, it cannot be translated into very precise dates, as is sometimes attempted. Scripts cannot be assumed to have developed uniformly in every place. Indeed, the script of an individual scribe does not necessarily change over his lifetime to reflect the latest custom, and if a scribe learns to write from a single teacher rather then in a school, he can only be assumed to continue the script that he was taught.

The Materials Used

The scrolls are written on parchment prepared from the hair side of the skin, while **tefillin* have been found written on parchment prepared from the flesh side of the skin. The skins were washed, soaked, depilated and sometimes tanned, then softened by beating, and cut. The length of a scroll varied, the longest (the Temple Scroll) being almost 9m. Longer scrolls were created by stitching skins together. Papyrus was made by cross-layering strips of the reed at right angles, gluing them together, scrubbing with pumice and cutting. Usually the surface was ruled with lines and margins to aid the scribe. Pens were fashioned from reeds, and about five inkwells (of clay, one of bronze) have been identified as coming from Qumran. The ink is almost invariably carbon-based, but ink of metallic origin was used for one scroll (the Genesis Apocryphon), which is consequently in a poor state of preservation, the ink having eaten into the parchment. In some scrolls the writing has become illegible, but various forms of photography, as well as computer enhancement, have recovered considerable areas of text. When completed, the scroll was rolled, with the beginning of the text on the outside. A tab was attached (if this had not been done during manufacture) and the scroll was bound together with a strap. Several scrolls were wrapped in linen, remnants of which have been found, and were placed in jars, some of them then sealed. However, the majority of the Qumran manuscripts were probably placed on shelves or in boxes (there are signs of shelving in Cave 4). They are now in small fragments and only a fraction of their content is preserved. Whether this fragmentary state is due only to the ravages of time and rodents, or human action, whether deliberate or accidental, ancient or more recent, can probably never be known. The matching of fragments and thus the restoration of original manuscripts was originally achieved by recognition of common content and handwriting, but another technique for correctly locating fragments within a manuscript analyzes the shape of damaged areas and matches them with the pattern of damage as reconstructed for the rolled-up scroll.

The Scrolls and Khirbat Qumran

The connection between the scrolls and the settlement at nearby Qumran, initially overlooked by the scroll hunters, has been almost universally taken for granted since excavations started there. There is no absolute proof of a connection, since the scrolls do not clearly allude to the site and the site itself contained no scrolls; but the circumstantial evidence is very strong. Two inscribed ostraca found in 1996 were claimed to contain the word *yaḥad*, the name of the sect in the Community Rule, but this has since been challenged, and no direct relation between these and the scrolls is proven. Evidence for the production and composition of scrolls at Qumran remains slight but not negligible. The suggestion by de Vaux that the nearby site of Ein Fashkha contained a tannery is now generally rejected. His view that an upper floor room of the eastern block of the Qumran settlement, whose floor had collapsed, was a *scriptorium* is still supported, though his reconstruction of a plaster table and writing benches now seems fanciful. The inhabitants of Qumran probably lived in the nearby caves; these inhabited caves show no evidence of scroll use; but cave 8 contained a collection of leather tabs, of the kind attached to the outer end of a scroll for aid in opening. It is now generally agreed that most of the scrolls were not written at Qumran, but taken there; however, the proximity of several caves to the site implies that their deposit was known to the inhabitants if not carried out by them. Several proposals have nevertheless been made that Qumran was not the site of a religious community but something else: a palace, fortress or trading post. The numerous cisterns are not all for immersion but probably for drinking water; those that were *miqva'ot* do not necessarily attest to an exceptional level of concern with purity, as the scrolls exhibit, but certainly inhabitants following standard Jewish purification practice. In retrospect, it has emerged that the initial interpretation of the site by de Vaux can be questioned, especially concerning the earliest phase of sectarian occupation and a possible period of abandonment late in the first century B.C.E. But despite several alternative theories about the nature of the settlement, his overall assessment still has its defenders (for further details see *Qumran).

[Philip Davies (2nd ed.)]

A BRIEF HISTORY OF RESEARCH

Introduction

Initial interest in the Scrolls, in which Christian involvement far outweighed Jewish, mostly for political reasons, focused on the identification and history of the Qumran sect and its relationship to the New Testament and early Christianity. With only the contents of Cave 1 published, it seemed possible to reconstruct with some clarity where and why the sect had been formed and what its major doctrines and its organization were. After a fairly brief period of debate, a consensus quickly emerged that the Dead Sea sect had been the Essenes, as described (though not without some contradictory details) by Philo and Josephus as well as the elder Pliny who, unlike the other two authors, specifically located them near the Dead Sea. It was also agreed that, like the Pharisees and Sadducees, this sect had arisen in the Hasmonean period. The founder of the sect had been a "Teacher of Righteousness" who had, as the Habakkuk *pesher* in particular described, been persecuted by a "Wicked Priest" and forced to flee to Qumran, where he established a community with his followers. The identity of this "Wicked Priest," was disputed, but the major contenders were the Hasmoneans Jonathan and Simon. During the 1970s this consensus was initially consolidated, and some important new data emerged. From the historical point of view the identification of the Qumran sect with the Essenes was supported by the excavations by P. Bar-Adon at Ein-el-Ghuweir, south of Qumran, uncovering a settlement from the same period as Qumran, also with large buildings suitable for communal activities. (Y. Hirschfeld has more recently claimed to find the Essene settlement to which Pliny refers overlooking En-Gedi.) The cemetery adjacent to the site displays the same peculiar form of burial found in the Qumran *cemetery (or cemeteries), including skeletons of women and children. The ongoing analysis of the Qumran literary documents received new impetus with the initial publication of several major texts. The most important of these is undoubtedly the Temple Scroll, the longest scroll yet found. Its publication marked the beginning of several important changes: Israeli and Jewish interest in the scrolls increased as the scrolls were now almost all now under Israeli control in Jerusalem, while the text itself, edited and published rapidly and expertly by Yigael Yadin, illustrated the importance of *halakhah* in understanding the Dead Sea scrolls, taking a good deal of emphasis away from Christian origins. However, Yadin's conclusion that the scroll was a product of the *yaḥad* provoked strong disagreement and reinvigorated discussion of the relationship between that community and the wider movement described in the Damascus Document. This in turn led to revised theories about the origins of the Qumran community, more complex than the Cave 1 scrolls had suggested. In particular, it began to be recognized that the *yaḥad* itself arose from a wider movement with well-established roots. Because of this, the problem of speaking simply of the "Qumran community" or "the sect" or even of "sectarian writings" has been more keenly appreciated. The publication of the fragments of 1 Enoch by Milik proved that the work was indeed originally composed in Aramaic and also highlighted the Enochic character of much of the scrolls' content. The question of the origins of the sect was to be complicated further by the Halakhic Letter, whose contents were revealed (originally as a "Letter from the Teacher of Righteousness") and discussed long before its official publication in 1994. In fact the editing and publication of this document were at the center of a controversy: a draft text and translation that had been informally circulating were printed and published by Z.J. Kapera of Cracow, who, under some kind of threat, had to destroy the remaining copies. But the *Biblical Archaeology Review* had printed a page from this edition, and E. Qimron, one of the official editors, sued that journal's editor for breach of copyright. His claim to be, effectively, the "author" of the Qumran document by virtue of his reconstruction was upheld on appeal and has set an unfortunate precedent. The Halakhic Letter lists a number of disagreements between its author and the recipient, who is apparently a Jewish ruler (king, high priest or both?). It prompts the suggestion that the origins of the sectarian movement may lie in conflicts between differing priestly traditions, which were debated before the decision to segregate into a sectarian lifestyle. A comparison of the Qumran *halakhah* with rulings ascribed to *ẓeduqim* in the rabbinic literature has also prompted some scholars to suggest that the sect may have been Sadducee rather than Essene, though the claim is based on a restricted number of cases. The publication of multiple texts of the Damascus Document and Community Rule has shown, too, how their complicated recensional history must be taken into account in any reconstruction of the history of the communities they describe. With each new publication of texts, it also became more difficult to fit all the contents of the scrolls into neat doctrinal systems. In general, the confident consensus that reigned between the 1950s and early 1970s has given way to a number of competing theories, to which doubts about the nature of the site of Qumran itself have added further confusion. The availability of all the texts has, nevertheless, led to a resurgence of interest in the texts, with a growing number of younger scholars now reexamining the very broad range of questions that the scrolls are generating. Much more knowledge has been accumulated, but with it rather less overall understanding of the phenomenon of Qumran and a better appreciation of the religious climate from which both rabbinic Judaism and Christianity grew.

Contents and Character of the Qumran Scrolls

SECTARIAN WRITINGS. It would be rash to conclude that all the books in any communal or private library reflect the beliefs and practices of the community or individual to whom they belong. It is also sometimes difficult to distinguish sectarian writings from those that come from the particular milieu (represented by such works as Enoch and Jubilees) from which they emerged. The sectarian scrolls can be classified generically (or functionally) as "Rules," "Halakhic," "Exegetical," "Parabiblical" "Wisdom" and "Liturgical". "Sectarian" writings are identified as those that share a common ideology and vocabulary with three of the "Rules" that explicitly describe a sectarian community: the Community Rule (Manual of Discipline), the Damascus (or "Zadokite") Document and Rule of the Congregation (though it is perhaps a description of an idealized future Israel). These further texts comprise the Thanksgiving Psalms, the War Scroll (another "Rule"), the Temple Scroll, the Halakhic Letter, the *pesharim* (biblical commentaries), some other midrashic (the Florilegium, the Melchizedek fragments) and halakhic (Ordinances, Tohorot) compositions, and perhaps the Angelic Liturgy (Songs of the Sabbath Sacrifice). The wisdom texts are an especially interesting category: they exhibit many of the terms and themes of biblical wisdom books, but their traditional virtues and rewards, the materialistic ethic and the empirical basis of knowledge have been imbued with an esoteric flavor: there are "secrets" and an eschatological reward. These texts are not necessarily strictly of sectarian origin (the book of Daniel exhibits similar features) but they do indicate movement towards what is the clearly sectarian ethic of other scrolls. In the case of liturgical works, it is sometimes difficult to determine whether the contents are strictly sectarian. They are in any case steeped in biblical language and ideas, especially from the Psalms. The case of the Thanksgiving Hymns (Hodayoth) seems clear, however, as these are imbued throughout with a consistent, dominant sectarian ideology, including dualistic language. The main themes are that mankind is evil, its flesh polluted, but the author has been elected by God, rescued from destruction, purged, endowed with wisdom and placed among the "holy ones" (angels). He has also founded a community and suffered persecution, elements that prompt many scholars to regard them – or some of them – as compositions of a spiritual leader, such as the Teacher of Righteousness, the persecuted hero of the *pesharim* who, according to the Damascus Document, founded, or more strictly, refounded the sect. It is highly likely that they were used in the sectarian liturgy and may have provided some of the biographical data used in the *pesharim*. The Pseudepigraphic Psalms, by contrast, contain some terminology characteristic of the sectarian writings, but no distinctive sectarian ideology is present. There is a high degree of dependence on, and quotation from, the biblical psalms; one manuscript (4Q236) even contains a highly variant version of Psalm 89. There are fragments of four manuscripts containing prayers for festivals, and three manuscripts of "Words of the Lights", apparently designed for each day of the week, and another manuscript containing morning and evening prayers (4Q503). It is a reasonable guess that the sectarians inherited a rich Jewish liturgical tradition of which we would otherwise be unaware, and in this respect the Qumran scrolls make an important contribution to our understanding of the evolution of Jewish worship. From Cave 11 comes a manuscript containing four psalms apparently designed for a healing liturgy (11QPsAp[a]). Finally, a number of hymn fragments (4Q434–39) contain the phrase *barki nafshi*, "Bless, o my soul," one of which (4Q434a) displays similarities with rabbinic blessings after meals and so may have fulfilled this function. Given the importance of the communal meal in the *yaḥad*, this is a plausible suggestion. Finally, a controversial hymn (contained within 4Q448) asks for blessing on "King Jonathan and for all the congregation of your people Israel who are in the four corners of heaven." This Jonathan was identified by the text's editors as the Hasmonean Alexander Jannaues (Jannai) who ruled from 103–76 B.C.E. However, he is generally considered to have been a likely enemy of the sect. G. Vermes has therefore proposed the Hasmonen Jonathan, brother of Judas (ruled 160–142 B.C.E.), who, he argues, may have once been favored by them. Alternatively, the text could be seen as originating from outside the sect: in which case, why was it copied and kept by them?

The Damascus Document, which was already known from two mediaeval manuscripts found in the Cairo *Genizah* as well as several Qumran copies, describes the origin, history and beliefs, together with its *halakhah* and organization and its rules of life, of a sectarian movement that is clearly related to, but not identical with, that described in the Community Rule. The latter contains mostly the doctrines, organization and disciplinary rules of a sect calling itself the *yaḥad* ("Union"), but without any account of its origins or history. Both texts are composite, and the various copies betray a recensional history. (For more details, see **Yaḥad*; *Dead Sea Sect; Book of Covenant of *Damascus.) One common feature of the sectarian texts seems to be the 364-day calendar that is also presented in 1 Enoch and Jubilees; the Temple Scroll in particular is constructed on this basis, and texts known as the *Mishmarot* (priestly courses) show the services of the priestly orders regulated according to a six-year cycle, which harmonizes the 26 annual courses of this calendar with the 24 of the lunar calendar. Another common thread is (temporary) alienation from the Jerusalem temple as a result of disagreement over the calendar and *halakhah* with its governing priesthood. The Angelic Liturgy (*Serekh Shirot Olat ha-Shabbat*) illustrates not only how the *yaḥad* maintained the ethos of the temple cult despite its (temporary, as it believed) abandonment of the Jerusalem sanctuary, but also throws important light on the community's beliefs about angels and its own mystical tradition in addition to four manuscripts from Cave 4 and a further one that came to light during the excavations at Masada. The document describes a weekly sabbath liturgy, over 13 weeks, in the heavenly temple. This text has opened up a new dimension in Jewish literature and religion of not only late Second Temple times, but subsequent Jewish mystical and angelic traditions while the Melchizedek midrash from Cave 11 features an angelic high priest who leads the struggle against Belial and his associates, but also effects the redemption of Israel at the end of the final era of history on the Day of Atonement. This work shows how the Genesis figure was interpreted in some circles (similar, but not identical, to the treatment in the Epistle to the Hebrews) and also sheds light on later Jewish speculation about heavenly redeemer figures: Melchizedek was later to be identified with both *Michael and *Metatron as the highest angelic figure below God. A further characteristic of the scrolls as a whole is a belief in the angelic origin of sin, as described in the Enochic "Book of Watchers," as a result of which humans remain subject to evil angelic powers, which will be destroyed at the end of days. The Flood that was sent upon the earth as a divine response to the angelic descent seems to have functioned as a prototype of the punishment to come, and Noah is prominent as the prototype of the righteous person (his illustrious birth is described in the Genesis Apocryphon). This view of the origin of sin, the differences in calendrical and halakhic matters, and the consequent breach with the Temple cult (minimal participation by the community in the Damascus Document, complete rejection in the case of the *yaḥad*) seem to combine into a kind of Judaism that has been called "Enochic" or "apocalyptic," but in fact it probably reflects very closely the views of the Priestly source within the Torah. The solar calendar is reflected in the P material in the Flood story (thirty-day months), and in the notion, expressed in that story, of a corruption of the earth by bloodshed (rectified in the Noachic covenant), P's doctrine of sin as a universal contagion and not just disobedience of the Torah, and the inclusion of the fallen angel 'Azazel in the Day of Atonement ritual (Lev. 16:21). If this observation is correct, the unresolved problem is to explain why this ideology came to be represented in a sectarian form in the second century B.C.E. The answer may lie in the intricacies of Hasmonean politics, but we cannot be certain. Yet it is evident that the ideology adopted by the writers of the scrolls is not a sudden reaction but the outcome of a longer process betraying differences within a Second Temple Judaism that was, before the discovery of the Scrolls, thought to be rather monolithic. Nevertheless, attempts to represent the so-called "apocalyptic" character of the Scrolls as in some way a forerunner of Christianity as against rabbinic Judaism have been frustrated by the prominence given in the scrolls to scrupulous observance of Torah, a high veneration of the temple, and an emphasis on a life of ritual purity.

Biblical Manuscripts

Most of these have survived only as fragments: all but two of the 24 books of the Jewish Scriptures are represented, the exceptions being Esther and Nehemiah (it cannot be said with certainty whether their absence is accidental or significant). The number of manuscripts of each books ranges from 36 (Psalms) to 1 (Chronicles). A few are written in the archaic Hebrew script. In addition, some Septuagint fragments have been identified: Cave 4 yielded fragments of two Septuagint manuscripts of Leviticus and one of Numbers; Cave 7, fragments of the Septuagint text of Exodus and of the Epistle of Jeremiah, a pseudepigraph commonly appended to the Book of Baruch. The most important Septuagint find made in the Dead Sea region comes not from Qumran but from the "Cave of Letters" in Naḥal Ḥever (see *Judean Desert Caves): It is a fragmentary copy of a Greek version of the Twelve Minor Prophets, identified as a new Greek revision, (now known as the Kaige or Proto-Theodotion revision), which apparently aimed at revising the LXX according to a Hebrew text close to the MT. Fragments of a Leviticus Targum were also found in Cave 4. A further contribution to the biblical material from Qumran is made by commentaries (see **Pesher*) and parabiblical compositions, or rewritings of the scriptural contents. Whereas the biblical texts from caves farther south which were occupied during the Bar Kokhba Revolt (132–5 C.E.) uniformly belong to the "proto-masoretic" type (the consonantal text to which the masorah was added from the sixth to the ninth centuries C.E.), those found in the Qumran caves reflect a variety of text-types (see below).

BIBLICAL TEXT AND CANON. As evidenced by the Minor Prophets scroll from Naḥal Ḥever (see above), between 70 C.E. and the Bar Kokhba Revolt, the biblical text appears to have been standardized during the first century C.E. But at Qumran there existed no uniformity of text. At first it had been concluded that the Hebrew biblical texts at Qumran fell into three types, corresponding to the forerunners of the Masoretic, Septuagint, and Samaritan texts, each originating from three regions: Babylonian, Egypt, and Palestine respectively. But the "local text" theory and the theory of "text types' have now been abandoned. Yet a more careful analysis shows that no such grouping is possible. There is too much variation even within the different textual types; for instance, the MT uses the short text for the Pentateuch but the longer one for the Later Prophets and Writings, while the LXX employs the longer text for the Pentateuch but a short one for Jeremiah. Again, MT and LXX Jeremiah are not so much different text types as variant editions. As for the Qumran manuscripts, the textual variations reflect much more a spectrum than a set of textual types, while the Psalms manuscripts display, like Jeremiah, a variant edition rather then a different text type. The problem was perhaps more acute as long as the scrolls were all thought to emanate from a small isolated community, but if, as now believed, they originated in different places, the variety is less surprising.

Whether there was a fixed canon is also disputed: While all but two books of the Masoretic canon (Esther and Nehemiah) are represented, the number of manuscripts of each book preserved (see above) may suggest that not all books were equally venerated. There are numerous manuscripts of Deuteronomy, Isaiah, and Psalms, but Chronicles and Ezra are extant in only one copy. The Halakhic Letter (C10) runs "… in the book (*sic*) of Moses, and the books of the Prophets and in David…," the last referring probably to a collection of Psalms. However, other works may have been regarded within the sect as of a similar status and authority, such as the Book of Jubilees (cited in the Damascus Document as "The Book of the Divisions of Times into their Jubilees and Weeks" (CD xvi:4) or the Enochic writings or even the Temple Scroll. The biblical manuscripts were usually copied in the regular square Hebrew script, except for the Holy Name being occasionally written in paleo-Hebrew characters. However, some biblical manuscripts were copied in this ancient script in their entirety, as for instance, Job and Leviticus (4QpaleoJob, 4QpaleoLev).

PENTATEUCH. Of the biblical manuscripts 86 are books of the Pentateuch, 30 of which are copies of Deuteronomy. While the Genesis and Leviticus manuscripts exhibit a stable text and a single manuscript tradition, Exodus is represented in two editions, one close to the MT and LXX, the other similar to the Samaritan text (but without the two most distinctive Samaritan variants relating to the Gerizim altar (Exodus 20:17 and Deut. 12:5, etc.)). The case of Numbers is similar to Exodus, though the non-MT edition is not specifically Samaritan, but only shares some features. Deuteronomy, the best represented of the Pentateuch, exists in a wider range of texts, and, in addition, there are some manuscripts apparently consisting of excerpts, presumably for liturgical purposes. In a few cases a Qumran reading is clearly superior to the MT: thus, for example, 4QDtq reads for Deuteronomy 32:8 *bny'l*, as does the LXX, instead of *bny ysr'l* of the MT.

FORMER PROPHETS. Joshua is represented by 2 (possibly 3) manuscripts, one of which (4QJosh[a]) has some interesting differences from the MT: the altar-building in Josh. 8:30 (in MT) comes before ch. 5 – a sequence also followed by Josephus. Samuel likewise includes some variant passages, for example, in the Goliath story (1 Sam. 17–18). The most ancient manuscript, 4QSam[b], is dated as the mid-third century B.C.E. and is related to the LXX of Samuel. The books of Judges and Kings have survived in small fragments only.

LATTER PROPHETS. The 21 manuscripts of Isaiah present a more complex picture than was initially drawn by the two cave 1 examples, where Isaiah A is reasonably close to the MT and Isaiah B even closer. But several manuscripts also support LXX readings. Both the MT and the shorter proto-LXX editions of Jeremiah are attested. Given its ideological influence on Qumran, Ezekiel is surprisingly poorly represented with three short manuscripts, on which little can be said, while the eight manuscripts of the Minor Prophets exhibit little diversity, though they do not betray the same conformity to the MT as the Naḥal Ḥever scroll.

WRITINGS. The 36 manuscripts of Psalm collections from Qumran make this the best represented of the scriptural books numerically. This is not surprising, given their influence on the other liturgical texts found in the caves. But none of the Psalms manuscripts' various sequences unambiguously supports the MT (and basically LXX) sequence. The best-preserved of the Psalms manuscripts from cave 11 (11QPs[a]) includes nine psalms not found in the MT, including what is Psalm 151 in the Septuagint, and also includes a list of "David's compositions," which attribute to him 3,600 psalms, 364 other songs, plus 52 for Sabbath offerings and yet more for festivals. (Perhaps these refer also to the so-called "Apocryphal Psalm" collections also found at Qumran.) The other Cave 11 Psalm manuscripts probably support this alternative sequence. Job has only four manuscripts, but, curiously, one is written in the archaic script, 4QpaleoJob. The eight Qumran fragments of Daniel do not include the apocryphal additions known from the LXX, and the points of transition from Hebrew to Aramaic and back are the same in the Qumran manuscripts as in the MT (Daniel 2:4 preserved in 1QDan[a] and 8:1 in 4QDan[a,b]).These manuscripts are, of course, likely to be fairly close in time to the autograph, probably composed in about 164 B.C.E.

PARABIBLICAL TEXTS. The quantity of Qumran texts that range between (but not including) biblical manuscripts and midrash is considerable, and the term "parabiblical" has been coined to denote them. They are excerpts, rewritings, paraphrases or compilations of biblical texts. To this category can be assigned *mezuzot* (8) and *tefillin* (30); these sometimes contain a text differing slightly from the MT. Another category is targums: a Targum to Job (Cave 11 with an additional fragment in Cave 4) and Leviticus, also from Cave 4 (it may be wondered why a community that read, and possibly spoke, Hebrew needed targums.) Both of these avoid the midrashic amplifications so common in other Targums. By contrast, the Genesis Apocryphon is reminiscent of the more expansionary targums, though it is not usually classified as such. The Cave 4 Testimonia is almost entirely biblical quotation (from Deuteronomy, Numbers and Joshua), apparently on the theme of leadership. The so-called "Genesis Commentary" (4Q252) is neither paraphrase nor commentary, but mixes both as it moves through the Genesis story, while the "Reworked Pentateuch" (four, maybe five manuscripts) combined topical juxtaposition with free composition. The Temple Scroll reorders biblical legislation (with some additions) into a more systematic form. A further text of this kind is a paraphrase of Joshua (4Q123), while the "New Jerusalem" text, difficult to fit easily into any of the categories, is perhaps best understood as a systematization of part of the contents of Ezekiel 40–48. While these are not biblical texts as such, they represent ways in which the biblical material was reorganized, sometimes to emphasize aspects of sectarian belief. The Book of Jubilees, also found in Hebrew at Qumran, is an excellent example. It is not believed to be sectarian, but it does emanate from the circles from which the sect emerged.

Other Jewish Writings

These may be divided (though the distinction is often accidental) between works previously known and those unknown. Among those known are a Greek portion of the Epistle of Jeremiah from Cave 7, fragments of Tobit from Cave 4 (three in Aramaic and one in Hebrew) and of Ecclesiasticus (the Wisdom of Ben Sira) from Cave 2 (in Hebrew). Fragments of this work were also found at Masada. The Book of Jubilees (ten Hebrew manuscripts from Caves 1, 2, and 4) and four of the five sections that make up 1 Enoch: The Parables or Similitudes are absent, but there is in addition an Enochic "Book of Giants" (eight Aramaic manuscripts from Cave 4). Both of these maintain the solar calendar that the sectarian writings also follow. Some of the Testaments of the Twelve Patriarchs – works extant in their entirety in a Greek recension exhibiting Christian influence – have also been identified: the Testament of Levi by some scraps from Cave 1 and fragments of three manuscripts from Cave 4 (all in Aramaic, with a text similar to that of fragments from the Cairo *Genizah*) and the Testament of Naphtali in Hebrew fragments from Cave 4. The Qumran text of both these Testaments is longer than the corresponding passages in the Greek recension.

The number of hitherto unknown works, attached to biblical figures, is impressive. They attest to a previously unsuspected richness and variety in Jewish literature during the Second Temple period. A group of writings is associated with the figure of Daniel: the Aramaic Prayer of Nabonidus (4QprNab) is assigned to the second century B.C.E. It relates events similar to Daniel 4, except that the central figure is that of Nabonidus (*nbny*) and the name Daniel does not occur. Another Aramaic work, a Daniel Apocryphon ($4QpsDanar^{a,b,c}$), recounts the history of Israel. A number of works are ascribed to patriarchal figures: An Aramaic work, the so-called Visions of Amram ($4QAmram^{a-e}$) tells about Amram's visions in which a figure called Milki-Resa' appears. In another Hebrew fragment (4Q280 2) the said Milki-Resa' is denounced as the head of the "Sons of Darkness." The name (unknown outside the Scrolls) is the opposite counterpart of Milki-Ṣedek, the eschatological judge who is the subject of another Hebrew work, the Midrash on *Melchizedek (11QMelch). Another Aramaic work, the Testament of Qahat (4QTQahat), is ascribed to Qahat the son of Levi. The Apocryphon of Joshua (previously known as the Psalms of Joshua) may represent a farewell speech ascribed to the hero, and it shares with the Testimonia Joshua's curse on the man who would rebuild Jericho.

The Copper Scroll

This most unusual document, found in Cave 3, consists of a single roll of almost pure copper, broken in antiquity into two parts, each of which was rolled before storage. Identified by K.G. Kuhn, even before opening, as a list of buried treasure, the rolls were brought to Manchester, England, by J. Allegro and sliced open. The identification of the contents was then confirmed, but despite Allegro's anxiety to publish it, the task was assigned to Milik and delayed. The delay may have been occasioned by fear of what sort of treasure hunt the disclosure of its contents might provoke, and Milik aired the view that the list was fictional. The general opinion today is that the treasure was real and must have belonged to the Temple. If so – and nothing suggests that its deposit was independent of the other scrolls – the presence of this document in a Qumran cave requires some explanation, and it supports the suggestion that at least some of the scrolls may have originally come from Jerusalem (the "chief of the [sectarian] camps" according to the Halakhic Letter).

[Philip Davies (2nd ed.)]

Khirbat Mird

Khirbat Mird is a ruined Christian monastery of the Byzantine period, on the site of the earlier fortress of Hyrcanion, north of Wadi al-Nār. Here, in July 1952, the Taʿāmira Bedouin discovered manuscript material of great interest but of considerably later date than the finds at Qumran and other sites near the western shore of the Dead Sea. It included papyrus fragments of private letters in Arabic from the seventh and eighth centuries C.E., a Syriac letter on papyrus written by a Christian monk, a fragment of Euripides' *Andromache* in Greek, and a number of Old and New Testament texts in Greek and Palestinian Syriac. The Greek texts included fragments of uncial codices of Wisdom, Mark, John, and Acts (fifth–eighth centuries C.E.); those in Palestinian Syriac included fragments of Joshua, Luke, John, Acts, and Colossians (many of these were palimpsests). All the Khirbat Mird manuscripts are of Christian origin.

[Frederick Fyvie Bruce]

BIBLIOGRAPHY: EDITIONS: *Discoveries in the Judaean Desert*, 39 vols. (1955–2002) M. Burrows, J.C. Trever and W.H. Brownlee, *Dead Sea Scrolls of St. Mark's Monastery*, 2 vols. (1950–51); E.L. Sukenik, *Dead Sea Scrolls of the Hebrew University* (1955); N. Avigad and Y. Yadin, *Genesis Apocryphon* (Eng. and Heb., 1956); Y. Yadin, *The War of the Sons of Light against the Sons of Darkness* (ET 1962); J.T. Milik, *The Books of Enoch* (1976); Y. Yadin, *The Temple Scroll* (ET 1983); J.H. Charlesworth (ed.), *The Dead Sea Scrolls: Hebrew, Aramaic, and Greek Texts with English Translations* (1994-); F. García Martínez and E.J.C. Tigchelaar, *The Dead Sea Scrolls Study Edition* (2 vols. 1997–98). TRANSLATIONS: G. Vermes, *The Complete Dead Sea Scrolls in English* (1997); M. Abegg, Jr., P. Flint and E. Ulrich, *The Dead Sea Scrolls Bible* (1999); M. Wise. M. Abegg, Jr., and E. Cook, *The Dead Sea Scrolls: A New Translation.* BIBLIOGRAPHIES: W.S. LaSor, *Bibliography of the Dead Sea Scrolls, 1948–1957* (1958); C. Burchard, *Bibliographie zu den Handschriften vom Toten Meer* (1959); C. Burchard, *Bibliographie zu den Handschriften vom Toten Meer II* (1965); M. Yizhar, *Bibliography of Hebrew Publications on the Dead Sea Scrolls, 1948–1964* (1967); B. Jongeling, *A Classified Bibliography of the Finds in the Desert of Judah 1958–69* (1971); F. García Martínez and D.W. Parry, *A Bibliography of the Finds in the Desert of Judah 1970–95* (1996); J.A. Fitzmyer, *The Dead Sea Scrolls, Major Publications and Tools for Study* (1990); A Pinnick, *The Orion Center Bibliography of the Dead Sea Scrolls (1995–2000)* (2001). See also the regularly updated bibliography at http://orion.mscc.huji.ac.il. See also the Encyclopedia of the Dead Sea Scrolls (2 vols: 2000). The following journals are devoted to Qumran: *Revue de Qumrân* (Paris); *Dead Sea Discover-*

ies (Leiden), *The Qumran Chronicle* (Cracow). INTRODUCTIONS: H. Stegemann, *The Library of Qumran* (ET 1998); J.C. VanderKam, *The Dead Sea Scrolls Today* (1994); L.H. Schiffman, *Reclaiming the Dead Sea Scrolls* (1994); N. Golb, *Who Wrote the Dead Sea Scrolls?* (1995); J.G. Campbell, *Deciphering the Dead Sea Scrolls* (2002); P.R. Davies, G.J. Brooke and P.R. Callaway, *The Complete World of the Dead Sea Scrolls* (2002). On the history of discovery and interpretation: N.A. Silberman, *The Hidden Scrolls. Christianity, Judaism, and the War for the Dead Sea Scrolls* (1994); on the archaeology: J. Magness, *The Archaeology of Qumran and the Dead Sea Scrolls* (2002); Y. Hirschfeld, *Qumran in Context: Reassessing the Archaeological Evidence* (2004); on the ostraca, F.M. Cross and E. Eshel, "Ostraca from Khirbet Qumran," IEJ, 47 (1997), 17–28 (1997); A. Yardeni, "A Draft of a Deed on an Ostracon from Khirbet Qumran," *IEJ* 47 (1997), 233–37; on the Jewish background: G. Boccaccini, *Beyond the Essene Hypothesis* (1998). For a review of major trends, see R.A. Kugler and E.M. Schuller (eds), *The Dead Sea Scrolls at Fifty* (1999). BIBLICAL TEXT AND CANON: F.M. Cross and Sh. Talmon (eds.), *Qumrān and the Story of the Biblical Text* (1975); E. Ulrich, *The Dead Sea Scrolls and the Origins of the Bible* (1999); P. Flint, *The Bible at Qumran* (2001); E. Tov, *Textual Criticism of the Hebrew Bible* (2001). OTHER STUDIES: *Script*: F.M. Cross, 'the Development of the Jewish Scripts' in G.E. Wright, *The Bible and the Ancient Near East* 170–264 (1965); *Language:* E. Qimron, *The Hebrew of the Dead Sea Scrolls* (1986); *Damascus Document:* P.R. Davies, *The Damascus Covenant* (1983); C. Hempel, *The Damascus Texts* (2000); *Community Rule:* J. Pouilly, *La Règle de la Communauté: son evolution littéraire* (1976); S. Metso, *The Textual Development of the Qumran Community Rule* (1997); *Rule of the Congregation:* L.H. Schiffman, *The Eschatological Community of the Dead Sea Scrolls* (1989); *War Scroll:* P.R Davies, *1QM, the War Scroll from Qumran* (1977); J. Duhaime, *The War Texts* (2004); *Pesharim:* M. Horgan, *The Pesharim* (1979); T. Lim, *The Pesharim* (2002); *Temple Scroll:* M.O. Wise, *A Critical Study of the Temple Scroll* (1990); S. White Crawford, *The Temple Scroll and Related Texts* (2000); *Halakhic Letter (4QMMT)*; J. Kampen and M.J. Bernstein (eds.), *Reading 4QMMT. New Perspectives on Qumran Law and History* (1996); *Florilegium:* A. Steudel, *Der Midrasch zur Eschatologie aus der Qumrangemeinde* (4QMidrESCH^{a,b}) (1994); *Copper Scroll:* J. Lefkovits, *The Copper Scroll (3Q15); A Re-Evaluation* (1999); G.J. Brooke and P.R. Davies (eds.), *Copper Scroll Studies* (2002); *Melchizedek:* P. Kobelski, *Melchizedek and Melchiresvac* (1981); see also C.A. Newsom, *The Songs of the Sabbath Sacrifice* (1985); E. Schuller, *Non-Canonical Psalms from Qumran: A Pseudepigraphic Collection* (1986); J.G. Campbell, *The Exegetical Texts* (2004); H.K. Harrington, *The Purity Texts* (2004); D. Harrington, *The Wisdom Texts from Qumran* (1996); B. Nitzan, *Qumran Pyare and Religious Poetry* (1994); J.C. VanderKam, *Calendars in the Dead Sea Scrolls* (1998). On the Essenes: G. Vermes and M.D. Goodman, *The Essenes According to the Classical Sources* (1989).

DEAD SEA SECT (also called **Qumran Sect** or **Qumran Community**). The name refers strictly to a Jewish community which lived in the Second Temple period and which adopted a strict and separatist way of life. It is so called because the main source of knowledge about it derives from the discovery of a settlement at Khirbat *Qumran, near the northwest shore of the Dead Sea, where it is believed to have lived, and where remnants, apparently of its library, were found in neighboring caves (see *Dead Sea Scrolls). The pottery and coins found there constitute the main external sources for establishing the date of the sect. From these, as well as from the fact that the library contains no work later than the Second Temple period, it appears that the settlement was inhabited (on the ruins of a much older settlement), from the beginning of the second century B.C.E. until its destruction by the Romans shortly after the fall of the Second Temple, around 70 C.E. The sect believed to have lived at Qumran called itself the *yaḥad* (or "Union"), and the Qumran scrolls describe its beliefs and organization. They also describe a related movement that lived in communities elsewhere. Although it has been suggested that these were offshoots of the Qumran community, the consensus is now that they represent a parent movement, from which the *yaḥad* split off, for reasons that are still debated. How much earlier that parent movement began is uncertain, though probably not more than a few decades. The occasional historical clues that the texts offer cannot be used with great confidence to describe the origins or growth of either the parent movement or the *yaḥad*, though it is possible to trace some outlines. In recent years, the suggestion has also been made that the scrolls are unconnected with the Qumran settlement, and that the site was not inhabited by a religious sect; but the circumstantial evidence linking the scrolls and the settlement is powerful if not conclusive. It has come to be realized, however, that many or even most of the scrolls were not, as once assumed, actually written at Qumran.

Its Views

The Qumran sect, like the broader Jewish movement from which it sprang, took a critical view of the established orthodoxy of its time, believing Israel to be under divine judgment, regarding itself as the true remnant of Israel and awaiting its imminent vindication at the "end of days." According to this worldview, the course of history and its epochs had been preordained by God. "… all the ages of God will come at the right time, as he established for them in the mysteries of his prudence" (Pesher Habakkuk 7:13–14). With its advent, evil would cease, the wicked would be destroyed, and the righteous would live under divine blessing. There is a strong predestinarian tone to many of the texts, which see the movement as an elect community, an "eternal [or righteous] planting," chosen and raised up by God. These views were carried to an extreme within the *yaḥad* (see also *Eschatology), which maintained that God had created mankind in two antagonistic camps of light and darkness, or truth and falsehood; each "lot" was under the dominion of an angelic figure: the "prince of light" and the "angel of darkness" (the latter also known as "Belial") respectively. Between these two, God had set "eternal enmity," which would cease only in the end of days with the destruction of the spirit of perversion and the purification of the righteous from its influence. Then the "children" of the "spirit of truth" would receive their reward. But although these "lots" are at first described as mutually exclusive, they are subsequently said to be apportioned differently among individuals: each person receives his portion, in accordance with which he is either righteous or wicked. Horoscope texts among the scrolls show that these proportions were also believed to correspond to physiological features. The dualistic teaching is contained in the *Manual of Discipline (or *Community Rule), from which the main evidence for the organization and doctrine of the *yaḥad* is drawn.

*In the Thanksgiving Psalms (Hodayoth) a different and more personal perspective is brought to the sect's anthropology. Here the emphasis is on the absolute iniquity and degradation of even one of the "elect of God." The author of these hymns describes humanity (including himself) as "a structure of dust shaped with water, his base is the guilt of sin, vile unseemliness, source of impurity, over which a spirit of degeneracy rules"; but God has chosen him, rescued his soul from the grave, purged his spirit from a great transgression, and granted him mercy that he might "take his place with the host of the holy ones" (the angels), given him a superior wisdom, and revealed to him "deep mysterious things." The basic feeling is one of the insignificance and lowliness of humanity, of its dependence on the loving-kindness of God, without which "the way of humanity is not established." Aversion from, and despair of, the human condition oscillate between sorrow at sin and joy at election.

According to the Community Rule, members of the *yaḥad* underwent a "covenant" (probably renewed annually) to observe the "law of Moses," but they also embraced the esoteric doctrines and practices of the sect concerning the maintenance of strict holiness and communion with angels, the latter expressed in the form of worship in the "heavenly Temple" alongside celestial beings (according to the contents of the Songs of the Sabbath Sacrifice). The parent movement, which is basically described in the Damascus (also known as "Zadokite") Document (see Covenant of *Damascus), also held to a predestinarian (though not dualistic) doctrine, constituted itself by a covenant and enforced strict obedience to the laws of Moses as it interpreted them, believing itself to be living in an age of divine wrath from which its strict adherence to God's will would earn it deliverance in the coming judgment. But it also seems to have lacked the mystical tendencies that the *yaḥad* exhibits.

Although it is commonly claimed that the community, and its parent, represented a reaction against the contemporary Hellenizing culture and, later, Roman political sovereignty, its writings are more concerned with the corruption of the Jerusalem priesthood and the abandonment by God of all Israelites outside its ranks. Hence relations between the *yaḥad* and the Temple were entirely cut off, though the parent movement maintained a minimum of participation in the Temple cult. Dealings with other Jews were also minimal in both cases, since these did not live as the law of God, according to the sect, required. The Halakhic Letter, which many regard as a key to the origins of the sectarian movement as a whole, specifies a number of differences between the Jewish religious leaders and the sect on mat-ters of purity. It is possible that these differences, which may go back to opposing priestly traditions, provide the immediate cause for the formation of the sectarian movement as a whole, whether through voluntary segregation or through expulsion by the religious authorities.

Though the sect and its parent movement lived under an intense eschatological expectation, it is unclear how exactly they envisaged the future. The Community Rule with its strong dualistic and predestinarian doctrine suggests that the "children of darkness" will be punished by fire and then annihilated by angels. However, it also hints at a process of divine purification of the "children of light." The War Scroll describes a 40-year battle, fought by a combination of angelic and human forces. In a mixture of dualistic and nationalistic perspectives, the war is both between "Israel" and the "nations" and between the forces of light and darkness, with the enemy including the "Kittim" (probably the Romans). This scenario seems to suggest a future restoration of Israel (including a restored Temple) and not merely of the sect, though the end of the document is missing. The "Rule of the Congregation" (1QSa) also seems to envisage a restored nation. But how a small, celibate and segregated group living in a condition of extreme purity would become the restored Israel is unclear. In the Rule of the Congregation the leadership of Israel is in the hands of two "messiahs," one priestly and one lay. In some other Qumran texts the lay messiah is referred to as the "Prince of the Congregation" and seems to be a Davidic figure. Both "messiahs" may possibly correspond to functions within the sect, or perhaps the parent movement. However, the Community Rule neither describes nor implies such figures, and other Qumran texts present other redeemer figures or even none: in the Melchizedek Fragments the "messianic" role is assumed by a heavenly high priest who will atone for the sins of Israel on the Day of Atonement at the end of days. There are also elsewhere echoes of the more prevalent apocalyptic concept of a revolution in the manifestations of nature itself, an earthquake and a flood of fire in the entire universe (Thanksgiving Psalms 3:26ff.). There is therefore no unanimity of views in the various writings of the sect about the nature of future redemption.

Modes of Life and Organization

The worldview of the sect formed the theoretical basis of its way of life, for from it proceeded the duty to be prepared for the coming of the end of days, which demanded a punctilious observance of the *mitzvot*, a separation from ordinary society, and maximum social cohesion. The members of the *yaḥad* (as described in the Community Rule) were to eat communally, bless communally, and take counsel communally. The *yaḥad* strictly observed the laws of ritual purity, regarded all non-members as ritually unclean, and insisted on a discipline which imposed on all members the obligation "that they show obedience of the lower to the higher." For this purpose members were listed according to their gradings. These were drawn up anew every year and laid down the order of their participation in ceremonies and assemblies. The leading places were, according to some copies of the Community Rule, reserved for "the priests the sons of Zadok." The "council of the community" (or "community of God" and other similar designations) may have constituted, perhaps at one phase of its history, an authoritative body within the sect, but in some places the term is apparently synonymous with the sect itself. However, in charge of instruction and of the daily conduct of affairs was the *maskil*. In the parent movement, as described in the Damascus Document, it was the *mebaqqer*, or "overseer" who took charge of discipline. The principal decisions in the *yaḥad* were made by the community of the members ("the many"). It was an exclusively celibate male community, forming a single social unit, and maintained entirely by the influx of new members (as in Pliny's account of the Essenes by the Dead Sea). When "volunteers" joined the community, they had to undergo a preliminary examination and then passed two successive stages of candidature, at the completion of each of which they ascended in the degree of purification. Only on the conclusion of their candidature were their possessions put into the communal pool. Offenses against internal discipline were punished in accordance with a disciplinary code (adapted from that of the parent movement), and sanctions included reduction of rations and temporary, or even permanent, exclusion from the "purity of the many," meaning they no longer belonged to the holy "body" that the sect constituted through its intensely communal life, and especially in sharing its meals. The organization described in the Damascus Document, on the other hand, contained both married and celibate settlements (called "camps"). The latter, at least, had a less monolithic social structure, being more like a "town" inhabited by households, allowing for private property, women, and children, as also for a child's reaching adolescence in the community. The organization as a whole was looser. There are no indications of whether these settlements were subject to any higher authority: Jerusalem, according to the Halakhic Letter, was a "chief camp," but perhaps only because of the city's sanctity. The *yaḥad* apparently followed the *halakhah* of its parent movement, i.e., it interpreted according to its own tradition the *mitzvot* accepted by the Jewish people as a whole, namely the "Law of Moses"; these are found in the Damascus Document, Halakhic Letter, and several other texts. Such *Halakhot* and halakhic Midrashim similar in character to those of rabbinic Judaism, but there seems to be some specific opposition in these to the teaching of the Pharisees (and thus, later, the rabbis). A major point of halakhic dispute is the sect's adoption of a calendar of 364 days (see *Calendar, Dead Sea Sect). How it was adjusted to a 365-day year we do not know, but it is probably both realistic and ancient (it can be detected within Genesis 6–9). This calendar is known from the Book of Jubilees and the Book of Enoch, and thus offers an important clue to the social and ideological background of the sect.

The Teacher of Righteousness

While the history of the *yaḥad* and its parent, and the development of their ideas, are unclear, some details are extant about the founder of the sect (or one of its first leaders), who was given the title *"teacher of righteousness," chiefly in the Damascus Document and the Habakkuk Pesher. Attempts to identify him with a known historical person remain debatable. The Damascus Document uses the title of a future, perhaps messianic figure, but also applies it to an individual who arose some time after the foundation of the movement itself. Apparently, he led a group of followers to form the *yaḥad*, while the remainder of the movement perhaps rejected him; his death is also noted. In the Pesher literature he is presented more as a founder figure who directly clashed with an opponent called the "wicked priest," who has been identified with a number of historical personages, all Hasmoneans, but who is completely absent from the Damascus Document. Some of the biographical details of the Teacher in the Pesharim reflect allusions in the Thanksgiving Hymns, which some scholars believe to have been written by the Teacher. But these details might simply have been borrowed from the Hymns by the authors of the Pesharim.

The Identification of the Sect with the Essenes

It is widely held that the wider parent movement, as well as the *yaḥad*, should be identified with the *Essenes described by *Josephus (War 1. 78–80; 2,119–161), *Philo (Quod omnis probus, 75–91) and the elder Pliny (Natural History 5.17, 4). While Pliny locates Essenes specifically near the Dead Sea, according to Josephus and Philo they lived throughout Judea. On the manner of initiation, attitudes to women and to the Temple there are strong similarities between Essenes and the larger sectarian movement, but opinion on the identification is not unanimous. In the light of a few halakhic parallels with details preserved in the Talmud, it has recently been suggested that the sect may have been related to the Sadducees. The identification with *Zealots, once proposed, is now largely rejected, though the sect probably sympathized with Jews who fought against Rome and may have joined them.

BIBLIOGRAPHY: J.M. Allegro, *The People of the Dead Sea Scrolls* (1959); G. Boccaccini, *Beyond the Essene Hypothesis* (1998); P.R. Davies, G.J. Brooke and P.R. Callaway, *The Complete World of the Dead Sea Scrolls* (2002); N. Golb, *Who Wrote the Dead Sea Scrolls?* (1995); Y. Hirschfeld, *Qumran in Context: Reassessing the Archaeological Evidence* (2004); J. Magness, *The Archaeology of Qumran and the Dead Sea Scrolls* (2002); F. García Martínez and E.J.C. Tigchelaar, *The Dead Sea Scrolls Study Edition* (1997); L.H. Schiffman, *Reclaiming the Dead Sea Scrolls* (1994).

DEAF-MUTE (Heb. חֵרֵשׁ, *ḥeresh*), always classed in the Talmud together with the minor and the imbecile as being irresponsible and of no independent will, from which stem all the restrictions and exemptions applying to him, both in law and the performance of *mitzvot*. They apply only to a deaf-mute, but not to one who is either deaf or dumb (Ter. 1:2). Nevertheless, it was realized that the mental capacity of the deaf-mute was superior to that of the imbecile, and a passage in the Talmud (Shab. 153a) grades the mental capacities of these three in the descending order of minor, deaf-

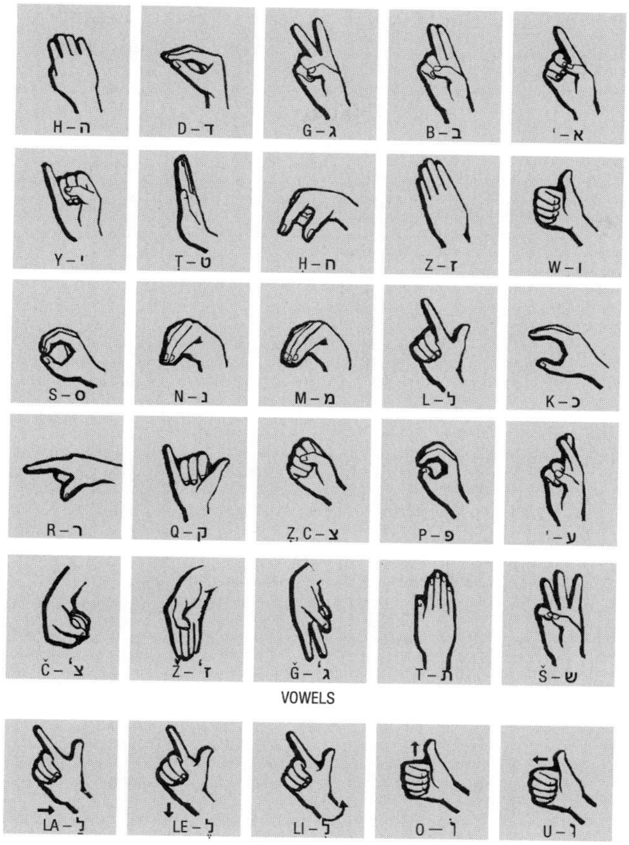

Hebrew manual alphabet of the deaf.

mute, and imbecile. In particular a definite relaxation was made in the case of the marriage and divorce of deaf-mutes, as regards marriage both to a normal person and to another deaf-mute (Yev. 14:1). In the discussion of the *Gemara* of the Babylonian Talmud on this Mishnah, it is laid down that he is of "feeble mind" or "partially normal and partially *non compos mentis*" (Yev. 113a and b). A marriage in which one of the parties is a *ḥeresh* is considered to be only of rabbinic validity, and the question of divorce is thus complicated. The details of the manner in which the marriage ceremony and the divorce take place are laid down in great detail, and have been the subject of a special work (*Melekhet Ḥeresh*, by Ezekiel Ḥefeẓ, 2 vols., 1874–85).

With the successful methods of modern treatment in overcoming the problem of communication with the deaf-mute, the tendency in the past and present centuries has been to remove the stigma of retardation from the deaf-mute in *halakhah* and to regard him as normal, in addition to the fact that once he has learned to speak he ceases to be the deaf-mute of the Talmud. It is now generally accepted that he may become bar mitzvah and be called up to the reading of the Torah. The subject has been dealt with in a halakhic brochure issued by the *bet din* of London, where all the relevant halakhic literature is quoted. (L. (A.L.) Grossnass, *Publications of the London Beth Din*, no. 10., 1963 (Heb.).)

Further Developments in the 1970s

The status of deaf-mutes, according to the *halakhah*, came to the fore in February 1977 when the district Bet Din of Tel Aviv, by a majority of 2 to 1, refused to accept a deaf-mute woman for conversion on the grounds that, according to the letter of the law, a deaf-mute is regarded as mentally retarded. An appeal had been lodged before the Supreme Bet Din against this decision. The Sephardi chief rabbi, Ovadiah Yosef, submitted a ruling in favor of deaf-mutes being counted in a *minyan*.

Another event was the first World Congress of Jewish Deaf held in Tel Aviv from July 1–31, 1977, under the auspices of the Association of the Deaf in Israel. The Ashkenazi chief rabbi of Israel, Rabbi Shlomo Goren, read a paper on "The Jewish Deaf and a New Approach to the *Halakhah*," in which he pointed out that the Jerusalem Talmud takes a more lenient view of the disabilities of the deaf according to the *halakhah* than does the Babylonian Talmud, and that this approach should be accepted.

A whole session at the Congress was devoted to papers on "The Religion and Jewish Tradition in the Life of the Jewish Deaf," which covered every aspect of the problem.

The amelioration in the status of the deaf-mute, according to the *halakhah*, depends upon the established fact that with technological advances in the teaching of deaf-mutes, their "lack of comprehension," which is the basis of their disabilities, can be overcome.

What may be termed the first breakthrough in the attitude previously adopted was given by Simhah Bunim Sofer (1842–1906) in his responsa *Shevet Sofer* (Even Ha-Ezer No. 21). He disagrees with the restrictive view given by his predecessors and adds: "Indeed I heard from my father, the author of the Responsa *Ketav Sofer* (Abraham Samuel Benjamin Wolf Sofer; 1815–1871), that after he paid a visit to an institution for deaf-mutes in Vienna, at the request of the authorities, and was thus enabled to see their tuition at first hand, he was so impressed by what he saw and the curriculum and behavior of the children, that he raised the question whether they should not be considered as truly normal and obliged to fulfill the commandments of the Torah. He told me that he instructed their teachers that they should be told to don phylacteries daily since 'their actions are evidence of their mental comprehension.'"

Chief Rabbi Ovadiah Yosef pointed out in his address to the congress, that both the former chief rabbis of Israel – Rabbi I. Herzog and Rabbi Ouziel – held similar views, and concluded that one can rely upon their decision.

Moreover, a distinction is made in *halakhah* between those who have only one of the two disabilities, deafness or dumbness – who are regarded as normal – on the one hand, and the totally deaf-mute, and the question as to whether the ability of the latter to converse in sign language can be regarded as removing their dumbness.

Nevertheless, some modern authorities maintain that there is a certain mental incapacity in deaf-mutes which prevents them from being regarded as being normal and the problem has been raised as to whether a deaf-mute widow may perform the duty of *ḥalizah despite the fact she is unable able to utter the formula (Deut. 25:7 and 9). The Israeli association has set up a halakhic committee to deal with the question.

In 1977 there appeared two volumes dealing with the deaf. The first, *A New Dictionary of Sign Language* in English by E. Cohen, L. Namir, and I.M. Schlesinger, professor of psychology at the Hebrew University, uses the Eshkol-Wachmann Movement Notation system and is intended for academics. The second, *A Dictionary of Sign Language for the Deaf in Israel* by L. Namir, I. Sella, M. Rimor, and I.M. Schlesinger, in Hebrew, is based upon the former work, is intended for field workers, and gives signs for some 1,200 Hebrew words.

In the U.S. there exist several congregations of deaf-mutes in which prayers are recited in sign language. There is every hope that these facts will be taken into consideration and the existing disabilities of deaf-mutes according to *halakhah* will be removed.

See: *Alphabet, Manual (Deaf); *Penal Law.

BIBLIOGRAPHY: *Piskei Din shel Batei ha-Din ha-Rabbani'im be-Yisrael*, 10:7, 193–209.

[Louis Isaac Rabinowitz]

°DEÁK, FERENCZ (1803–1876), Hungarian lawyer and liberal nationalist politician; minister of justice in the revolutionary government of 1848. In 1839 Deák opposed a bill prohibiting Jews from acquiring certain classes of immovable property from the nobility. In 1867, when he was active in framing the constitution, he advocated legal emancipation for the Jews. After the schism in Hungarian Jewry between the Reform and Orthodox in 1869, Deák supported the latter in their demand for a separate organization, regarding it as a matter of freedom of conscience.

BIBLIOGRAPHY: A. Csengery, *Franz Deák* (Ger., 1877); Gy. Szekfű, *Három nemzedék és ami utána következik* (1921^2), 213–9; I. Csetényi, in: *Emlékkönyv Dr. Hevesi Simon…* (1934), 85–89.

DEATH.

In the Bible

The Hebrew word for death is *mavet* (*mawet*) (*Heb.* מָוֶת) from the root *mvt* (*mwt*). For the Canaanites, *Mwt* (Mot) was the god of the underworld. Details of the myth of Mot are found in *Ugaritic literature. Mot fought against *Baal, the god of rain and of fertility; he was victorious and forced Baal to descend to his kingdom in the depths of the earth. But Anath, sister of Baal, avenged her brother and killed Mot. In the end Baal and Mot both returned to life, but at different times. Most commentators interpret this myth as a symbol of the changing seasons: Baal dies at the end of the rainy season, while Mot returns to life; the contrary happens when the rains begin again. In the Bible there are traces of such a myth in the belief that death is a destructive force distinct from God (see *Demons and Demonology) with its own messengers (e.g., war, sickness, plagues, cf. Hos, 13:14; Ps. 91:5–7; Prov. 16:14). In Jeremiah 9:20 it is said, "For Death (*mawet*) has climbed in through our windows, has entered our fortresses, cutting off children from the streets, young men from the squares." *Mawet* in this verse (see also Isa. 5:14; Hab. 2:5) may be compared to the Mesopotamian demon Lamashtu, who usually attacks children and pregnant women by climbing over the walls and entering through the windows (cf. Paul in bibl., where the widely held opinion that links this passage with the Baal myth is criticized). In the Bible there are two reasons given for man's death: the first states that God made man from the dust of the earth, and to dust he must return (Gen. 2:7; 3:19; Job 10:9). Genesis 3:22–24 gives a second reason: that of sin. By his expulsion from paradise, man was deprived of access to the tree of life, and thus eternal life was lost to him. The sentence of death passed on man in Genesis 3:19, "By the sweat of your face shall you get bread to eat until you return to the ground. For from it you were taken. For dust you are, and to dust you shall return," is opposed to other biblical passages that speak of the dead who go down into the tomb and enter the region of the dead (Isa. 14:9–12; Ezek. 32:17–32; etc.). Many names are given to this region: **she'ol*, always feminine and without a definite article as is usual in proper nouns, is found in no other language; *ʾereẓ* ("earth," "underworld"; e.g., I Sam. 28:13; Jonah 2:7; Job 10:21–22), which has the same meaning in Akkadian and Ugaritic; *kever (qever,* "grave"; Ps. 88:12), whose Akkadian parallel, *qabru*, is the normal form of designating the world of the dead; *ʿafar* ("dust"; Isa. 26:6, 19; cf. Gen. 3:19); *bor* ("pit"; e.g., Isa. 14:15, 38:18; Prov. 28:17; cf. Akk. *bûru); shaḥat* ("pit"; Ps. 7:16; cf. Akk. *šuttu*); *ʾavadon* ("Abaddon"; e.g., Job 28:22); *naḥalei beliyyaʿal*, "the torrents of Belial" (II Sam. 22:5,6). This region is in the depths of the earth; it is therefore called "the nether parts of the earth" (Ezek. 31:14); "the depths of the pit" (Lam. 3:55); "the land of darkness" (Job 10:21). Note the common Akkadian expressions for the region of the dead: "house of darkness" and "country of no return." The dead all inhabit this country, even those who were not buried (Gen. 37:35; Isa. 14:19; Ezek. 32:17–32; The Epic of Gilgamesh xii: 153). The dead are also called "*Rephaim" – in Ugaritic as well – but the origin of the word is obscure (Prov. 21:16). After death there is no contact between the dead man and his god (Ps. 30:10; 88:6, 12–13). Besides the idea that all the dead share the same unhappy situation, there is the notion that their fate depends on the attention bestowed on them by the living: whether or not they are properly buried, whether or not food or drink is brought to them (but not in the Bible), and, especially, whether or not their names are remembered. In the Bible great importance is placed on *burial, especially in the family tomb (Gen. 47:29–30; 49:29; 50:25; II Sam. 21:12–14). On the other hand, not to be buried at all is a serious punishment (cf. I Kings 14:11; et al.; note the Assyro-Babylonian malediction, "May he not be buried in the earth and may his spirit never be reunited with his loved ones."). Among the unfortunate beings in the next world, Akkadian texts name "the man who has no one to recall his name" (cf. II Sam. 18:18) and "he to whom neither food nor drink is brought"; he is reduced to "drinking fetid waters and eating the food that is thrown out by the living" (cf. The Epic of Gilgamesh xii: 154). Care of the dead is also inspired by self-interest because they can affect the world of the living either for good or for evil and can even foretell the future (I Sam. 28:15–20). In the Babylonian confessions, the spirits of the dead are mentioned along with the gods: "I honored the gods and the spirits of the dead." In the Bible, they were called spirits (lit. "gods"; I Sam. 28:13). The reticence of the Torah on matters concerning the dead is easily understandable. There is nothing about honoring the dead; on the contrary, there are prohibitions about mourning certain persons, and it is forbidden to give them alms (Deut. 26:14) and to consult them. The sacrifices to the dead, forbidden by Deuteronomy 26:14, are linked by Psalm 106:28 to idolatry: "They joined themselves also unto Baal-Peor, and ate the sacrifices of the dead." The custom of bringing meals to the dead did not however disappear, and during the Second Temple period, at least in certain devout circles, it was considered a pious work: "Pour out thy bread on the tomb of the just and do not give it to sinners" (Tob. 4:7). Ben-Sira attacks this belief (Ecclus. 30:18). For the Egyptians, the dead plow, harvest, eat, and drink – in short, do all they did while they were alive (The Book of the Dead, 110). This pessimism about the fate of man expressed in biblical and Mesopotamian texts can be most clearly felt in the words with which Siduri tries to convince Gilgamesh that there is no point in seeking eternal life, for "when the gods created mankind, Death for mankind they set aside, Life in their own hands retaining"; and she goes on advising him to enjoy this world (cf. Pritchard, Texts, 90; see also the parallel passage in Eccles. 9:7–10). The two exceptions to the biblical belief that man descends into *she'ol* and remains there forever are Enoch (Gen. 5:24) and Elijah (II Kings 2:11; cf. the fate of the hero of the Mesopotamian flood story Ziusudra/Utnapishtim). Perhaps this belief is the origin of the psalmist's hope that he would not descend to *she'ol* (Ps. 49:16). In a Ugaritic epic Anat proposes to give Aqhat immortality, but the latter does not believe in it. Similarly in an Akkadian myth it is related how immortality escapes Adapa because he follows the evil counsel of his father, Enki-Ea, and refuses to eat the bread of life and drink the water of life. Enki-Ea had led him to believe that they were the bread and the water of death (cf. Pritchard, Texts, 101–2). An epithet of Marduk in Babylonian texts is *muballiṭ mîti*, "he who gives life to the dead"; but the meaning of the expression is rather "he who cures the sick" (cf. *Ludlul bêl nemêqi* 2:47; II Sam. 9:8; 16:9). In the *Servant of the Lord poems, his sufferings are described as a death. *Resurrection in the true sense of the word is only found in Daniel 12:2, but here too resurrection is a reward and meant only for the people of Israel, while in Isaiah 66:24 punishment of the wicked is eternal, but is not connected with their resurrection. In Ezekiel 37:1–14, the return of Exiles is described as a resurrection from the dead. On the other hand, one should compare this to Genesis 2:19, which states that the body descends to the earth (cf. Ps. 104:29; Job 34:14–15). Whether the spirit of man ultimately goes upward is questioned in the late Book of Ecclesiastes 3:20–21, but 12:7 affirms that "the spirit of man returns to God, who gave it."

In Talmud and Midrash

Though so complex a subject as death was inevitably not dealt with by the rabbis in an unequivocal way, their discussions on the subject incorporate a series of closely interconnected doctrines. Death itself, though imbued with mystery – contact with the corpse, for instance, meant defilement in the highest degree – was thought of as that moment of transformation from life in this world to that of the beyond. In terms of the mishnaic image, "This world is like a corridor before the world to come" (Avot 4:16), death is the passing of the portal separating the two worlds, giving access to a "world which is wholly good" (Kid. 39b).

At death the soul leaves the body with a cry that reverberates from one end of the world to the other (Yoma 20b), to pass into a state of existence, the exact nature of which was a matter of considerable dispute amongst the rabbis (cf. Shab. 152b–153a; Ber. 18b–19a; Maim. Yad, Teshuvah 8:2, and the critical remark by Abraham b. David of Posquières (Rabad); see also *Afterlife, *Body and Soul, *World to Come). Whatever the nature of the world beyond, it was generally accepted that there the dead reap the deserts of the acts they performed while alive, that they were free from Torah and the commandments (Shab. 30b), and that death served as an atoning process (Sif. Num 112). One confession formula before death, particularly prescribed for the criminal about to be executed, is "May my death be an atonement for all my sins" (Sanh. 6:2). The atoning value of death received greater emphasis after the destruction of the Temple, with the abolition of sacrificial atonement, so that complete forgiveness for more serious sins was dependent, despite repentance, the Day of Atonement, and suffering, on the final atoning value of death (cf. the discussion in Urbach, *Ḥazal*, 380–3).

Death and birth are viewed as parallel processes: just as man is born with a cry, tears, and a sigh, so he dies. He is born with his fist clenched as if to say "the whole world is mine," and he dies with open hands as if to say, "I have inherited nothing from this world" (Eccles. R. 5:14). The rabbis considered that there were 903 forms of death, the most severe way of dying being from asthma, or croup, which is compared to a thorn being torn out of a ball of wool, and the lightest is described as "the kiss of death," specially reserved for the righteous, which is like a hair being removed from milk (Ber. 8a; BB 17a; see *Death, Kiss of). The way in which a person dies, and the day on which he dies, were thought to be significant as good or bad omens for the deceased. Thus, for example, should he die amid laughter, or on the Sabbath eve, it is a good sign, whereas to die amid weeping, or at the close of the Sabbath, is a bad omen (Ket. 103b). To die from a disease of the bowels is considered a good sign (Er. 41b), no doubt because the suffering involved was thought to cleanse a person of his iniquities. Thus it was said that many of the righteous died from bowel illness (Shab. 118b), this being an opportunity for any sins they may have accumulated to be purged before their entrance into the next world (cf., however, what was said above about the "kiss of death"). One description of the death process relates that when the dying man sees the angel of death, who is covered all over with eyes and stands above his pillow with drawn sword, he opens his mouth in fright, whereupon the angel lets fall a drop of gall suspended on the end of his sword. Swallowing this, the person dies, and because of this drop, his corpse gives off a bad odor (Av. Zar. 20b). At the moment of death the righteous man is vouchsafed a vision of the *Shekhinah*, the Divine Presence (Num. R. 14:22; Zohar, *Midrash ha-Ne'elam*, Gen. 98a).

Concerning the very necessity of death there was some dispute amongst the rabbis. On the one hand there is the rather extreme view, which did not win general acceptance, that death was the wages of sin: "There is no death without sin" (Shab. 55a), and it is the inevitable fate of man only in that no man is sinless, "… there is not a righteous man upon earth, that … sinneth not" (Eccles. 7:20). Even Moses and Aaron died because they had sinned (Shab. 55b). The few exceptions, the really righteous such as Elijah, were thought not to have died (Lev. R. 27:4; Eccles. R. 3:15), or in other cases to have died only as a consequence of the machinations of the serpent in Eden, who caused Adam to sin and thus bring death to the world (Deut. R. 9:8; Shab. 55a; in the Talmud this view is ascribed to those who maintain that death is not dependent on sin, but the impact of the original passage is unclear; see Urbach, op. cit., 376–7). In this vein it is said that "charity delivers from death, not merely from an unnatural death but from death itself" (Shab. 156b), and that did not the truly righteous request their own death, they would not die (Mid. Shoḥer Tov, Ps. 116).

On the other hand an older view, stemming from the tannaitic period, stresses the inevitability of death, its naturalness as part of the very fabric of the world since creation. Thus when God had completed the creation of the world He saw that "it was very good" (Gen. 1:31), concerning which R. Meir remarked, 'it was very good,' that is death" (Gen. R. 9:5; see Maimonides' comment on this passage in *Guide*, 3:10). The idea behind R. Meir's enigmatic statement would seem to be that death is an integral part of the natural order, making way for new life and continued creation. The naturalness of death is also explicit in the saying that the angel of death was created on the first day of creation (Tanḥ., Va-Yeshev 4; see also BB 10a, where death is described as the strongest thing in the world). The Mishnah in *Avot* (4:22) stresses: "Those who are born will of necessity die … for perforce you were created … born … live, and perforce you will die." According to this view sin only hastens death, but does not cause it in the first place. Lack of sin therefore either enables a man to reach his predetermined span of years, thus saving him from an untimely demise, or helps him to live longer than his allotted span (Shab. 156b).

These arguments concerning the inevitability of death or its dependence on sin turn on several factors, among them possible interpretations of the account of Adam's sin in Genesis. According to one view Adam brought death into the world by disobeying God and eating the forbidden fruit. The Children of Israel had an opportunity of overcoming the power of death when they received the Torah at Sinai, but they lost this opportunity when they sinned with the golden calf (Mekh., Ba-Ḥodesh 9; Ex. R. 32:1; cf. also Num. R. 9:45). The way Adam's sin was interpreted amongst the *amoraim* may have been influenced by apologetic considerations, particularly the need to negate the Pauline doctrine of original sin as an inheritance from Adam to all mankind (Rom. 5:12). Perhaps the view that each man's sin causes his own death is influenced by the need to stress individual responsibility as opposed to the Christian position that in Adam we have all sinned (*ibid.*).

That both the wicked and the righteous die was explained as follows. The wicked perish so that they should cease angering God, while the righteous die so that they may have rest from their continual struggle against the evil inclination which has no power over them after death (Gen R. 9:5). As noted, the process of dying also may serve the righteous as a means of ridding themselves of their sins (see also Tosef., Yoma 5 [4]:6). Nevertheless, though mortality affects both wicked and righteous alike, the rabbis were sure that the whole quality of their respective lives, on this earth and in the hereafter, differed greatly. For the wicked are considered as if dead while still alive, and the righteous even in death are called "living" (Ber. 18a, b; Tanh., Berakhah 7).

Laws and Customs

Jewish tradition emphasizes respect for the dying and the dead, and deference for the last wishes of a dying man, of adherence to such last wishes: the final requests of Jacob (Gen. 49:29), and Joseph (Gen. 50:25), and the advice of David (I Kings 2:1–9) were all faithfully heeded and observed. The Talmud states that the oral testament of a *goses* (גּוֹסֵס – the term applied to a dying man) has the same legal force as written and witnessed instructions (Git. 13a; see also *Gift, *Wills). The permission to transgress the Sabbath in order to ease the discomfort of the dying, however slender their chances of recovery, is not affected by the talmudic dictum that "most *gosesim* die" (Git. 28a). A dying person should not be left alone, and it is a great *mitzvah* to be present at *yeẓi'at neshamah* ("departure of the soul"). A candle is usually lit in the presence of the *goses* to symbolize the flickering of the human soul. A sick person, nearing his end, should be encouraged to confess his sins before God. He is urged: "Confess your sins. Many confessed their sins and did not die, and many who did not confess died; and as a reward, should you confess, you will live." (D 338:1; see also Sanh. 6:2, and Shab. 32a). Should he not know a formula of confession, he should be told to say, "May my death be an atonement" (see Sanh. 6:2). This rite may be performed on a Sabbath and on holy days, but should not take place in front of women and children because it would cause them distress and thus trouble the sick person (Sh. Ar., YD 338:1). One brief confession reads: "I acknowledge unto Thee, O Lord my God, and God of my fathers, that both my cure and my death are in Thy hands. May it be Thy will to send me a perfect healing. Yet if my death be fully determined by Thee, I will in love accept it at Thy hand. O may my death be an atonement for all my sins, iniquities, and transgressions of which I have been guilty against Thee" (Sh. Ar., YD 338:2). The confession should end with the recital of "Hear, O Israel: the Lord is our God, the Lord is One" (Deut. 6:4). The formulas of confession recited on the Day of Atonement are also used (see *Al Ḥet, *Ashamnu, *Confession). Death is presumed to occur when breathing appears to have stopped and when the absences of the peripheral pulse, the heartbeat, and the corneal reflex have been ascertained. Those present recite the blessing *Barukh Dayyan ha-Emet* ("Blessed be the true Judge"; *Bayit Ḥadash*, Tur, OḤ 223; see also Ber. 59b). The body must then be left untouched for about eight minutes. During this period, a feather is laid across the lips; those present watch carefully for the slightest sign of movement. When death is finally established, the eyes and mouth are gently closed by the eldest son or the nearest relative. Jacob was assured that Joseph would perform this final filial service (Gen. 46:4). The arms and hands are extended alongside the body, and the lower jaw is closed and bound before rigor mortis sets in. The body is placed on the floor, feet toward the door, and is covered with a sheet. A lighted candle is placed close to the head of the body. In the house of the dead it is customary to turn all the mirrors to the wall, or to cover them. Water standing in the vicinity of the corpse is poured out (Sh. Ar., YD 339:5). The custom may have originated in superstition; but it may also be a method of announcing the death to avoid actually having to articulate the bad news. None of these services discharged for the dead, however, should be performed for a *goses* (*ibid.*, 339:1). A dead body should not be left alone. It must be guarded constantly, whether on weekdays or the Sabbath, until the funeral, and, in pious circles, the Book of Psalms is continually recited. Various reasons have been advanced to explain the custom of watching the dead, which is apparently very ancient. It may have originated in a desire to keep away evil spirits, or to protect the body from rodents and body snatchers. It became a mark of respect for the dead who must not be left either defenseless or unattended.

[Harry Rabinowicz]

ORIENTAL CUSTOMS. In Tunis and other communities, the custom prevailed of putting a loaf of bread or a nail on the corpse immediately after death took place. In Yemen the *mezuzah* was removed from the door, and sacred books removed from the room of a dying man who was in great pain. It was believed that their presence weakened the power of the Angel of Death and that their removal would bring a speedier end to the suffering. Sometimes the *shofar* was sounded. The deceased was dressed in his best clothes (if a woman, in her wedding dress) under the shrouds because "he is going to meet the Messiah." Rose water was sprinkled on him and fragrant leaves put in his clothes. In Salonika the deceased was put in a coffin and his sons formally asked his forgiveness and kissed his hand. If the deceased was a rabbi the whole community did so. The custom of professional women mourners was widespread. Lime was sometimes put on the body to hasten decomposition.

[Reuben Kashani]

BIBLIOGRAPHY: ANCIENT TIMES: A. Heidel, *The Gilgamesh Epic and Old Testament Parallels* (1949^2), 137–223; H.H. Rowley (ed.), *Studies In Old Testament Prophecy* (1950), 73–81; idem, *The Faith of Israel* (1956), 150–76; M.R. Lehman, in: VT, 3 (1953), 361–71; H.L. Ginsberg, *ibid.*, 402–4; J. Blau, *ibid.*, 7 (1957), 98; W. Baumgartner, *Zum Alten Testament und seiner Umwelt* (1959), 124–46; J. Zandee, *Death as an Enemy According to Ancient Egyptian Conceptions* (1960); S.N. Kramer, in: *Iraq*, 22 (1960), 59–68; M. Dahood, in: *Biblica*. 41 (1960), 176–81; S.M. Paul, *ibid.*, 49 (1968), 373–6; S.E. Lowenstamm, in: EM, 4 (1962), 754–63. IN TALMUD AND MIDRASH: A. Buechler, *Studies in Sin and Atonement* (1928); G.F. Moore, *Judaism*, 3 vols. (1949); S. Schechter, *Aspects of Rabbinic Theology* (1909); E.E. Urbach, *Ḥazal* (1969). LAWS AND CUSTOMS: H. Rabinowicz, *A Guide to Life* (1964); J.J. Gruenwald, *Kol Bo al Avelut* (1947); Y.M. Tukaczynski, *Gesher ha-Ḥayyim* (1947); R. Yaron, *Gifts in Contemplation of Death in Jewish and Roman Law* (1960).

DEATH, KISS OF. Scripture records that "Aaron the priest ascended Mount Hor by the mouth of the Lord and died there" (Num. 33:38); and that "Moses the servant of the Lord died there in the land of Moab by the mouth of the Lord" (Deut. 34:5). The words "by the mouth of the Lord" were interpreted literally by the rabbis; they died there by the kiss of the Lord – which was given after Moses' soul absolutely refused to leave his body (Deut. R. 11:10) – and not through the agency of the Angel of Death, who was not granted dominion over them. Miriam and the three Patriarchs were said to have died in the same manner (BB 17a). Although only these six are named, sudden death after the age of 80 was also regarded as death through the kiss (MK 28a). Further, after his death R. *Naḥman b. Jacob appeared to Rabbah in a dream and told him that his death was as easy as drawing a hair out of milk; this is the way in which the kiss of death is described (*ibid.*). The description may be compared with that in the Koran (Sura 79:1) in the commentary of al-Bayḍāwī: "When a righteous person dies, the angel of death … makes the soul leave the body like a drop taken out of a bucket of water." The kiss is the easiest of the 903 kinds of death (the numerical value of תוצאות, *toẓa'ot*, in Ps. 68:21, "to God the Lord belong the issues [*toẓa'ot*] of death").

[Harry Freedman]

DEATH MARCHES, name given by prison inmates and retained by historians to the forced evacuations on foot of concentration and slave labor camps in the winter of 1944–45. With the onset of winter and Allied armies closing in on the Nazi concentration camps – the Soviets from the East and the British and Americans from the West – desperate SS officials attempted to evacuate the camps both to remove the eyewitnesses and to conceal the crimes that had been committed. Prisoners were moved westward in the dead of winter, forced to march toward the heartland of Germany, where their presence would be less incriminating. Daniel Goldhagen has called the death marches, "the ambulatory equivalent of the cattle car." Yet this time the prisoners were not being removed from Germany but moved back into Germany, perhaps to serve as labor, perhaps also to be used as fodder for a last stand.

On January 18, 1945, just days before the Red Army arrived at Auschwitz, 66,000 prisoners were marched to Wodzislaw, where they were put on freight trains to the Gross-Rosen, *Buchenwald, *Dachau, and *Mauthausen concentration camps. Almost one in four died en route. On January 20, 7,000 Jews, 6,000 of them women, were marched from Stutthof's satellite camps in the Danzig region. In the course of a 10-day march, 700 were murdered. Those who remained alive when the marchers reached the shores of the Baltic Sea were driven into the sea and shot. There were only 13 known survivors.

Death marches had been used before. In 1941, hundreds of thousands of Soviet prisoners of war had been herded along the highways of the Ukraine and Belorussia from one camp to another. They too were often walked to death. By 1942, with the pressures of a long war ahead of them, Soviet POWs were preserved as laborers. In 1942 Jews in Poland were marched from smaller ghettos to larger ones. Within a year many were deported by train to death camps. Elsewhere Romanians joined the Germans as Jews from Bessarabia and Bukovina were marched to Transnistria. Thousands died en route. On November 8, 1944, Adolf Eichmann initiated a death march of tens of thousands of Hungarian Jews from Budapest to the Austrian border. Impatient to deport Hungarian Jews, he could not wait for trains to arrive in Budapest. The march lasted a month. Those fortunate enough to survive were sent to Dachau and Mauthausen.

Characteristic of these death marches were that they occurred in the dead of winter, with few provisions for food or shelter and little opportunity to rest. Many died en route from starvation, cold, and exhaustion. For the Germans they were a means of moving a population from one place to another at a time of great scarcity and when entire systems were breaking down. They also were a way of literally walking the prisoners to death. Those who fell behind or who were too weak to continue were killed on the spot; their bodies were often left on the side of the road. Those fortunate enough to continue were shipped to concentration camps that were unable to handle them when they arrived; they had broken down from the sheer numbers of inmates and an infrastructure inadequate to the task. For the prisoners, the death marches were an unending marathon testing their endurance and will to live and pushing them beyond exhaustion. Most prisoners succumbed; the death rate was often more than 50 percent and sometimes only one in ten survived.

There were 59 different marches from Nazi concentration camps during the final winter of German domination, some covering hundreds of miles. Some had a specific destination; others were continued until liberation or death.

[Michael Berenbaum (2nd ed.)]

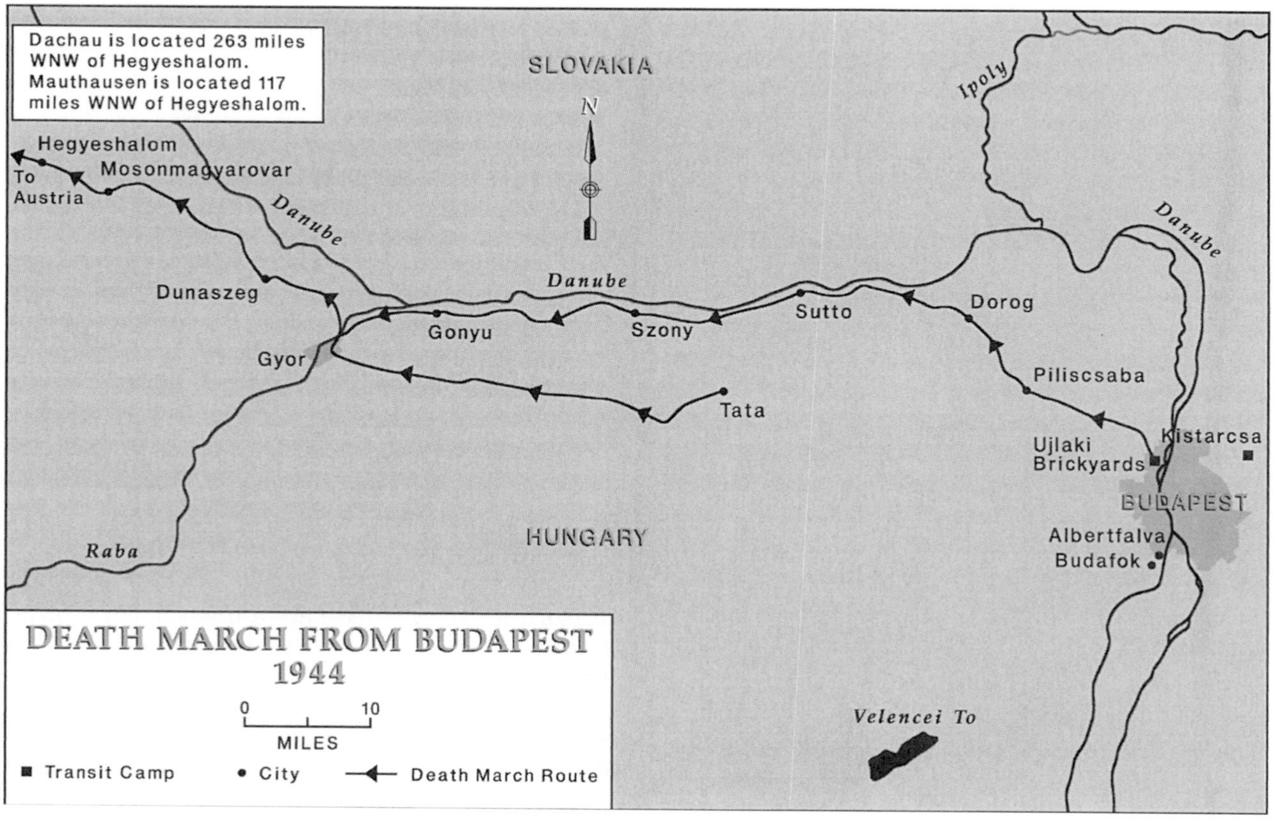

We worked in a labor camp called Christianstadt near Auschwitz in an ammunition factory. In the beginning of February 1945, we were told the commandant wanted us to get all our things together and leave. We are going to walk. The Russians are behind us and we have to get away from them.... We had no idea where we were going. The commandant said, "How many there will be at the end is not my responsibility. I am just supposed to bring you." Some were shot on this walk. They couldn't walk anymore and some tried to run away and were shot and others got away.

We had civilian winter coats and we had a little square striped piece on the back of the coat. A square hole was made into the coat and it was sewn into the coat. But most of us had – for some reason – scissors and a needle and thread in the camp, so when we had a little free time, we put a piece of material from our coat underneath that hole and then sewed the striped piece back on. It just seemed like somebody had the idea and we all copied it.

As we marched my girlfriend and I were talking. There were so many women you couldn't keep track of who is missing. We made the plans at night if there was an opportunity the next day to run off, what our names would be and what we would say to people. So as we gathered again in rows of five, the two of us ran. Nobody saw us. We took our scissors and we cut off these pieces of striped material. We threw them in the brook and we sang songs. We got stopped by a policeman and he said, "Aren't you two girls from the Jewish group that went by?" and we made the attempt to look very surprised. How could he think that we would be two Jewish girls? After that we stayed with some people overnight. We told everybody that we were cousins, and we changed our names. So we went on our way and we joined a troop of German refugees and we went to the Sudetenland in Germany. Our German helped us and there we took jobs with some families.

From the testimony of Eva Gestl Burns,
Gratz College Holocaust Oral History Archive

Death march of Dachau prisoners, April 1945. Yad Vashem, Jerusalem.

DEBDOU, town in N.E. *Morocco in the region of Oujda near the Algerian border whose Jewish population was largely comprised of Sephardi Jews from Seville who arrived in Morocco in 1391 and, apparently, also in 1492 following their expulsion from Spain. The Jewish community was governed by several influential families who engaged in internecine conflicts and power struggles over communal leadership. The most noted families in the disputes were the Cohen-Scalis, the Murcianos, the Benhamous, the Bensusans, the Benaims, the Ha-Cohens, and the Moralis. Toward the mid-18th century the community was ravaged by a cholera epidemic resulting in several deaths and the relocation of 300 families to other parts of Morocco. Thus the community was reduced from 630 families to 330. Nevertheless the Jews made up some two-thirds of the total population.

In 1903 the Debdou community encountered hostility from Muslims in nearby Oujda and local villagers. They were thus exposed to physical danger while, at the same time, the economic decline that affected much of Morocco rendered many of them helpless. They turned to the Paris headquarters of the *Alliance Israélite Universelle (which did not open a school in their community) and asked for financial assistance to ride out the difficult times. The Alliance responded favorably and assisted Debdou's Jews partially to overcome their problems. The inauguration of the French Protectorate in 1912 eliminated their security problems and improved their economic prospects.

Though other Moroccan Jewish communities made up one-fourth to one-third of the entire population of other cities and towns – notably Sefrou and Tangier – Debdou was the only area in Morocco where Jews remained the majority of the population well into the first half of the 20th century. In fact, Debdou was unique in the sense that it was doubtlessly the only Jewish community in Muslim lands where Jews formed a majority. David Cohen-Scali served as the unofficial governor of Debdou between 1895 and 1910.

Until the mid-1950s Debdou remained a vital center of Maghrebi Jewish life. Its scribes were famous for producing Scrolls of the Law for many of the Jewish communities of northern Morocco and Algeria. Debdou had more than a dozen synagogues, which preserved the religious rituals and customs of Spain. Like other Moroccan communities Debdou's Jewry engaged in craftsmanship and included small-scale merchants, tailors, and weavers. Some, however, were shepherds. After World War II as many as 1,000 Jews still lived in Debdou. They were organized for *aliyah* by the Jewish Agency's Immigration Department emissaries in 1955–56 and settled in the moshavim of Israel's southern and northern peripheries.

BIBLIOGRAPHY: B. Meakin, *Land of the Moors* (1901); N. Slouschz, *Travels in North Africa* (1927); A. Chouraqui, *Between East and West: A History of the Jews of North Africa* (1973); M.M. Laskier, *The Alliance Israélite Universelle and the Jewish Communities of Morocco: 1862–1962* (1983).

[Michael M. Laskier (2nd ed.)]

DE BENEDETTI, ALDO (1892–1970), Italian playwright. De Benedetti's light, sentimental comedies betray the influence of the French theater and of the Hungarian writers László Fodor and István Fekete. He made his reputation with the plays he wrote in the 1930s, including *La resa di Titti* (1932), *Lohengrin* (1933), and *Due dozzine di rose scarlatte* ("Two Dozen Red Roses," 1936). The latter, his greatest success, became widely known outside Italy. Almost all of his plays deal with attempts to escape from a stifling reality, to seek refuge in a romantic life. De Benedetti also worked for the cinema as a scriptwriter and director. His most successful motion pictures were *Marco Visconti* (1922), *Garibaldi* (1926), *Gli uomini, che mascalzoni* (1932), and *Mio figlio professore* (1946), which was written in collaboration with Vittorio De Sica. Due to the antisemitic laws of 1938, De Benedetti had to stop writing plays; but he wrote the scripts of some successful movies, such as *Maddalena, zero in condotta* (1941). After World War II, he dealt with more serious matters in *Lo sbaglio di essere vivo* (1945), a play reminiscent of Pirandello. In 1970 he committed suicide.

BIBLIOGRAPHY: G. Antonucci, *Storia del teatro italiano del Novecento* (1986), 116–121.

[Giorgio Romano / Alessandro Guetta (2nd ed.)]

DEBENEDETTI, GIACOMO (1901–1967), Italian critic and author. Born in Biella, Debenedetti studied mathematics at the University of Torino and afterwards received degrees in law and in literature. In 1920–30 he contributed to such important literary journals as *Il Baretti*, *Convegno*, *Solaria*, and *L'Italia letteraria*, and published his first book, a volume of stories, *Amedeo e altri racconti*, in 1926. In 1924 he gave a series of lectures on the prophets (*Profeti*, 1998), showing particular interest in the literary style of the Bible. He was also an important film critic, and from 1937 to 1943 he worked as a scriptwriter (anonymously from 1938 owing to the Fascist anti-Jewish laws). Debenedetti proved himself an outstanding critic in a number of essays in which he subjected the principal Italian writers of the 19th and 20th centuries, as well as historians of literature like Benedetto Croce, to penetrating analysis. Some of them were collected in *Saggi Critici* (1929; 1952^2). Analyzing the works of D'Annunzio and Pirandello in a second series of essays, *Saggi Critici* (1945; enlarged edition, 1955), Debenedetti proclaimed the need for committed, nonconformist critics to play an active part in politics. His literary criticism ended with a third volume of *Saggi Critici* (1959; 1963^2), which contains original judgments on three French writers, Gide, Proust, and Valéry. He also gave a series of lectures and wrote articles on the narrative structure of fiction (both in literature and cinema) in modern times (*Il personaggio uomo*, 1988). He taught Italian at the universities of Messina and Rome; his university courses were published posthumously (*La poesia italiana del Novecento*, 1974; *Il romanzo del novecento*, 1998), mainly by his wife. He was also an influential advisor for important publishing houses, and a translator (among others, of M. Proust, G. Eliot, K. Mansfield, J.-P. Sartre, H. Miller). Debenedetti fell victim to the Nazi persecution of the Jews when the Germans overran central and northern Italy late in World War II, and narrowly escaped deportation. He left two texts describing the Nazi persecution in Rome that are considered examples of engaged literature based on actual facts. In the first, *16 Ottobre 1943* (1945), he told the story of the roundup of the Jews of Rome and their deportation to the death camps. In the second, *Otto Ebrei* (1944; definitive edition, 1961), he described the notorious massacre in the Ardeatine Caves (see *Rome). In these works Debenedetti denounced not only the cruel and vile behavior of the German Nazis, but also the antifascist philosemitism of the postwar years, which continued to see the Jews as different from the rest of the Italians.

ADD. BIBLIOGRAPHY: C. Garboli (ed.), *Giacomo Debenedetti 1901–1967* (1968); R. Bertacchini, *Letteratura italiana. I critici*, 5 (1969), 3398–407, 3426ff.; idem, *Dizionario Biografico degli italiani* (1987), 360–65; R. Tordi (ed.), *Il Novecento di Debenedetti* (1991); A. Debenedetti, *Giacomino* (1994); W. Pedullà, *Il Novecento segreto di Giacomo Debenedetti* (2004).

[Joseph Baruch Sermoneta / Alessandro Guetta (2nd ed.)]

DEBIR (Heb. דְּבִיר).

(1) Canaanite royal city in the territory of Judah and originally inhabited by descendants of the Anakim ("giants?"; Josh. 12:13; 11:21). Debir is also called Kiriath-Sepher and Kiriath-Sannah (*ibid.* 15:15, 49). It was conquered by Joshua (*ibid.* 10:38–39; 12:13) but another biblical tradition attributes its capture to Othniel, son of Kenaz, Caleb's nephew (*ibid.* 15:15; Judg. 1:11–12). Debir is listed among the levitical cities (Josh. 21:15; I Chron. 6:43), which were apparently administrative centers under David. The Bible locates it in the southernmost district of the Judean hill country (Josh. 15:49). W.F. Albright's proposal to identify it with Tell Beit Mirsim, an important mound about 15 mi. (25 km.) southwest of Hebron, is usually accepted. Albright excavated the tell from 1926 to 1932, uncovering a series of strata dating from the late third millennium to the end of the monarchy. The city was strongly fortified in the Hyksos period and after a gap in occupation was resettled in the Late Bronze Age, suffering total destruction sometime in the latter part of the 13th century B.C.E. It was again occupied in the period of the Judges and provided with a casemate wall in the tenth century. Numerous dyeing plants for a textile industry were found in the city belonging to the period of the monarchy. The sequence of Bronze and Iron Age pottery found there still serves as the basis of the ceramic study of these periods. Some scholars reject Debir's identification with Tell Beit Mirsim arguing that this tell is actually located in the Shephelah ("lowland") whereas the Bible places Debir in the hill region of Judah, south of Hebron. K. Galling has suggested instead Khirbat Rābūḍ, about 8 mi. (13 km.) southwest of Hebron, an identification which appears probable following a survey by M. Kochavi which established that Khirbat Rābūḍ is a large tell of 60–70 dunams with prominent fortifications and remains dating mainly from the Late Bronze and Iron Ages (see also *Eglon).

(2) A locality on the northern boundary of Judah above the valley of Achor (Josh. 15:7). It is located near Ṭalʿat al-Damm between Jerusalem and Jericho. The ancient name may be preserved in Wadi al-Dabr.

(3) The king of the city of Eglon, south of Jerusalem, who was one of the five confederate kings in the Amorite coalition that attempted to halt Joshua's invasion (Josh. 10:3).

BIBLIOGRAPHY: (1) Albright, Arch Bib, 77ff.; Albright, Arch, index s.v. *Tell Beit Mirsim*; idem, in: AASOR, 12 (1932); 13 (1933); 17 (1938); 21–22 (1943), 155ff.; Abel, Geog, 2 (1938), 303–4; EM, 2 (1965), 588–90; Galling, in: ZDPV, 70 (1954), 135–41; Aharoni, Land, index.

[Michael Avi-Yonah]

DEBORAH (Heb. דְּבוֹרָה; "bee"), wife of Lappidoth; judge and prophet during the period of the *Judges. Deborah promoted the war of liberation from the oppression of *Jabin king of Canaan (Judg. ch. 4). She is cited as the primary author of the Song of Deborah (ch. 5). Unsuccessful efforts have been made to determine the exact time and place of Deborah's war within the general framework of the conquest of Canaan and the period of the Judges or to date the song by means of geography or the political situation reflected in it. Many scholars, however, place this period at about 1200–1125 B.C.E.

Deborah is unique among the Judges because she was a woman (cf. 5:7) and a prophet (4:4); according to the text, she is also the only one of the judges who actually judged (4:5). Although tribal affiliation is uncertain, her place of residence leads to the supposition that she was an Ephraimite (4:5) or that she may have come from Issachar (cf. 5:15). Both in the narration of the events and in the Song of Deborah, she appears as a national leader, as "judging Israel" (4:4), and as a "mother in Israel" (5:7). Her home and seat of justice was at the southern extremity of the hill-country of Ephraim, between *Beth-El and *Ramah under the "palm-tree of Deborah" (4:5), an unidentified site sacred to the people and possibly identified by popular tradition with Allon-Bacuth, the burial site of Deborah, Rebekah's nurse (Gen. 35:8). Some see in the image of Deborah the *kahin* (or *kahina*), known from the nomadic Arab tribes as a judge in a sanctified place, a magician and fortune-teller who aroused the warriors to battle with a song. The Bible tells nothing about Deborah's husband Lappidoth (Judg. 4:4).

The War of Deborah

This is the only war against the Canaanite oppression of the tribes of Israel described in the Book of Judges, and it may have been Israel's last campaign against the Canaanites. The relationship between this war against "Jabin king of Canaan, who reigned in Hazor" (Judg. 4:2) and the one against "Jabin king of Hazor" (Josh. 11:1ff.) has not yet been clarified. The sources imply a gap of several generations between the battle described in Joshua, which led to the conquest of Galilee, and the war of Deborah (cf. Judg. 2:10; 3:30; 4:3; 5:6). The narrative gives the distinct impression that the latter took place after the destruction of *Hazor itself, a problem already seen by the Radak (David *Kimḥi). Joshua's conquests had left many Canaanite enclaves in the interior of the country, especially in the northern plains (Judg. 1–3). The Canaanites' equipment included iron chariots, which the Israelites did not yet possess (1:19; 4:3), and this advantage enabled the enemy to control passage through the valleys (cf. 1:34). These Canaanite settlements in the valleys of Jezreel and Beth-Shean formed a barrier between the mountain tribes in the center of the land and those in the Galilee. In the days of Deborah, Jabin's military headquarters was located at *Harosheth-Goiim (4:2). With a force of "nine hundred chariots of iron" headed by *Sisera, Jabin "sorely oppressed the Israelites for twenty years" (4:3).

It is surprising that the initiative to engage in a war of liberation should have come from Deborah, who lived at a distance, at the southern extremity of the Canaanite kingdom, and that she should have summoned *Barak son of Abinoam from Kedesh-Naphtali in the northern extremity, also a considerable distance from the Canaanite kingdom. Deborah appointed Barak military commander and accompanied him to Kedesh-Naphtali, where he enlisted "ten thousand men from the tribe of Naphtali and the tribe of Zebulun" (4:6). Barak climbed Mount Tabor with his army while Sisera's camp moved from Harosheth-Goiim to the Kishon valley. Despite the considerable distance between the camps, Deborah ordered Barak to exploit the flooding of the Wadi Kishon as quickly as possible (5:21) and to move down from Mount Tabor and storm Sisera's camps. The battle was joined in "Taanach, by the waters of Megiddo" (5:19), a Canaanite town located near one of the tributaries of the Kishon, some 15 mi. (25 km.) southwest of Mount Tabor. Sisera's chariots sank deep into the mire and were totally disabled, and the Israelite army put "Sisera's entire camp to the sword until not one of them remained" (4:16). Sisera himself fled to the tent of *Jael, wife of *Heber the Kenite, who lived in friendship with Jabin (4:17), and was treacherously killed by Jael (4:17–22; 5:24–27). The victory marked the permanent decline of the Canaanite kingdom and ushered in a period of 40 years of tranquillity for Israel (4:23–24; 5:31).

Both accounts of the war of Deborah – the narrative and the poetic – concur in the main, giving a fairly complete picture of events, despite some discrepancies in details. In both accounts it is clearly a war of national liberation, not of isolated tribes. Nevertheless, the narrative indicates that only the two northern tribes – Zebulun and Naphtali – participated, whereas the song cites the names of many tribes (and clans), some praised for their participation, others condemned for their abstention (5:14–18), with Zebulun and Naphtali being generously acclaimed (5:18). It is difficult to ascertain whether these discrepancies constitute contradictory accounts or differing points of view of the same event. According to the song, the war of Deborah was a war of volunteers (5:2, 9), and the victory was a woman's victory, whether attributed to Deborah, the initiator, or to Jael, the slayer of the Canaanite commander.

The Song of Deborah

The song (Judg. ch. 5) is a paean of victory attributed to both Deborah and Barak. Among the most difficult, and, according to Bible scholars, among the earliest of Hebrew heroic poems, it was apparently sung antiphonally (cf. 5:12). The presence of many feminine images supports the view that the author was a woman. It opens with an invitation to kings and princes to listen (5:3) and a prologue (5:4–5) describing the trembling of the mountains in the face of Yahweh's triumphant march out of Seir. Section two (5:6–8) describes the wretched state of the people prior to the war. The period preceding the victory is called "the days of Shamgar son of Anath" and "the days of Jael" (5:6). The judge *Shamgar is known from another source (3:31), but a woman judge named Jael is mentioned nowhere else. It is hardly likely that the name Jael, the murderer of Sisera, is intended. The postwar change becomes evident in verses 9–11, which praise the "chieftains of Israel," i.e., the national leaders whose patriotism had achieved the victory. Section four (5:12–18) applauds the leading warriors and the tribes and clans that took part in the hostilities and, conversely, mocks those who remained apathetic. Praiseworthy are Ephraim, Benjamin, Machir (Manasseh?), Zebulun, Issachar, and Naphtali; discredited (apparently) are Reuben, Gilead (Gad?), Dan, and Asher; Judah and Simeon are not mentioned. Section five (5:19–22) recounts in highly figurative language the battle at Taanach against the "kings of Canaan" and Sisera and the role of nature therein.

Joyous clamor is interrupted between sections five and six (5:23) by a curse upon the settlement of Meroz for its failure to take part in the war. This serves as a dramatic antithesis to the blessings for Jael, which opens the next section. Section six (5:24–30) combines two scenes: the first describes the death of Sisera at the hand of Jael, the wife of Heber the Kenite; the second portrays the mother of Sisera in the company of "her ladies," who try to calm her as she waits in anxiety for her son to return from the battle. The song ends (5:31) with an exultant cry for the destruction of God's enemies and the supremacy of those who love Him.

The poetic form of the Song of Deborah is characterized by parallelism and the repetition of a word, or a combination of words, in various lines of most of the verses. Also characteristic is the frequency of the tricolon, that is, the three line verse (e.g., 5:2, 3b). According to tradition, the Song of Deborah is written in a form called "blank over script and script over blank," that is, a line of three hemistiches followed by a line of two longer hemistiches, and so on (similar to the form of the Song of Moses, Ex. 15). There is, however, no established tradition on the division of the words into hemistiches in the Song of Deborah. There is great similarity between this song and Psalm 68, which appears to have been composed under the former's influence. Tradition has assigned the Song of Deborah to the *haftarah* of the weekly portion of *Be-Shallaḥ*, whose central section is Moses' Song by the Sea (Ex. 15), which, in turn, bears a direct relationship in spirit, style, and content to the Song of Deborah.

[Jacob Liver]

In the *Aggadah*

Deborah was one of the seven prophetesses of the Bible. She dispensed justice in the open air under a palm tree to avoid being alone with a man in her house (Meg. 14a). Her husband Lappidoth is identified with Barak (SER 10), his name deriving from the fact that he made candles for the sanctuary (*lappid* = "torch"). According to one view this was his only merit because he was an ignorant man (*ibid.*). The rabbis criticize Deborah for her unbecoming arrogance in sending for Barak rather than going to him (Meg. 14b). Because of this and because of her conceit in boasting, "I arose, a mother in Israel" (cf. Judg. 5:7), she was given the unflattering name of Deborah ("bee"). The prophetic spirit departed from her for a time while she was composing her song (Pes. 66b); nevertheless she and Hannah were the two women in the world who composed praises to God unequaled by those written by men (Zohar, Lev. 19b). Deborah's great wealth enabled her to dispense justice without remuneration (Targ., Judg. 4:5).

In the Arts

The story of Deborah and the associated episode of Jael and Sisera have given rise to very few literary works. The French poet and Bible scholar Guy *Le Fèvre de la Boderie played on the Hebrew meaning of the name of the prophetess both in his epic *La Galliade* (1578) and in his poetic paraphrase of the Song of Deborah: "Debora gente Abeille / Reveille et leve toy, / Reveille toy reveille / Chante un Hymne au grand Roy…" (*Hymnes Ecclésiastiques*, 1578). From the 18th century onward, most works on these themes were texts designed for oratorios such as the *Deborah* of Handel. More attention has been paid to the motifs in the visual arts and in music. There are illustrations in 13th- and 14th-century manuscripts; the Psalter of St. Louis (French, 13th century) contains an illumination which shows the prophetess going forth with Barak and his men to make war on Sisera. In Ulm cathedral, Germany, Deborah, sword in hand, figures in the row of prophetesses on the choir stall (15th century). She also appears occasionally in baroque paintings, such as the work by Herrera Barnuevo (1619–1671) in the San Andrès church, Madrid. Jael has lent herself to even more plastic treatment, because of the dramatic qualities of her character. Usually artists have dealt with the slaying of Sisera, in which Jael, resembling Judith in appearance, wields a hammer in place of a sword. In Christian iconography she represents the Virgin's triumph over the devil or the Church triumphant, but in the misogynist art of the Middle Ages, Jael, like Delilah, exemplifies feminine duplicity. She appears in carvings and in manuscripts, including the Psalter of St. Louis (Bibliothèque Nationale, Paris) and the 14th-century Queen Mary Psalter (British Museum). There is also a fine drawing (c. 1430) after the Master of Flémalle (Brunswick Museum, Germany). During the Renaissance, Jael began to represent force and became a popular subject in Northern Europe. Some artistic treatments of this figure are a painting by the German artist Lucas Cranach, a wood-engraving by Albrecht Altdorfer, and an engraving by the Dutch artist Lucas van Leyden (all of the 16th century). Rembrandt made a pen drawing of Jael (1659), and there is a Gobelin tapestry illustrating the subject (Vienna Museum).

Deborah and Jael were popular with composers. About a dozen 17th- and early 18th-century oratorios on these themes are known, including some of historical interest, such as G. Fr. Rubini's *dialogo, Debora* (1656), which was the first demonstration of the reform of oratorio texts and structure proposed by its librettist, Spagna; and Porsile's *Sisara* (1719), Apostolo Zeno's first libretto. Handel's oratorio *Deborah*, with text by Samuel Humphreys (1739), is among the earliest works of his "oratorio period." Baldassare Galuppi's oratorio *Jahel* (Venice, 1747) featured an unusual item – an aria accompanied by two mandolins. Eighteenth-century compositions, mainly oratorios, were often performed in honor of politically active woman rulers, such as the empress Maria Theresa. Two successful later works were Josef Foerster's opera *Deborah* (1893; text after S. *Mosenthal) and Ildebrando Pizzetti's opera *Debora e Jaele* (composed 1915–21), first performed in Milan in 1922. Two settings of the verse "Thus may Thine Enemies Perish" from the Song of Deborah (Judg. 5:31) have been absorbed into the "corpus" of Israeli folksong: one by Uri Givon (with the textual variant "Thine Enemies, O Israel" instead of "O God") and another by Sara Levi-Tannai; both have also been made into folk dances. One of the Aramaic epic chants of the Jews of Kurdistan describes the story of Jael and Sisera (J.J. Rivlin, *Shirat Yehudei ha-Targum* (1959), 203–9).

BIBLIOGRAPHY: CHARACTER OF DEBORAH: J. Pedersen, *Studies in the Old Testament Prophecy* (1950), 127–42; Kaufmann Y., Toledot, 1 (1937), 700, 718; Brawer, in: BJPES, 8 (1941), 67–72. WAR OF DEBORAH: Albright, in: BASOR, 62 (1936), 26–31; Engberg and Albright, *ibid.*, 78 (1940), 4–9; Rabin, in: JJS, 6 (1955), 125–34; Alt, Kl Schr, 1 (1953), 256–73; Aharoni, in: J. Liver (ed.), *Historyah Ẓeva'it shel Ereẓ Yisrael…* (1964), 91–109; idem, *Hitnaḥalut Shivtei Yisrael ba-Galil ha-Elyon* (1957), 98–106; Malamat, in: B. Mazar (ed.), *Ha-Historyah shel Am Yisrael: Ha-Avot ve-ha-Shofetim* (1967), 221–3; Y. Kaufmann, *Sefer Shofetim* (1962), 113ff.; W. Richter, *Traditiongeschichtliche Untersuchungen zum Richterbuch* (1963), 29ff. THE SONG OF DEBORAH: S. Daiches, *The Song of Deborah* (1926); O. Grether, *Das Deboralied* (1941); W.F. Albright, *Yahweh and the Gods of Canaan* (1968), 1–25; Ackroyd, in: VT, 2 (1952), 160–2 (Eng.); Gerleman, *ibid.*, 1 (1951), 168–80 (Eng.); Goddard, in: *Westminster Theological Journal*, 3 (1941), 93–112; Sellin, in: *Procksch-Festschrift* (1934), 149–66; Slotki, in: JTS, 33 (1932), 341–54; Weiser, in: ZAW, 71 (1959), 67–97; Blenkinsopp, in: *Biblica*, 42 (1961), 61–71 (Eng.); Seale, in: JBL, 81 (1962), 343–7. IN THE AGGADAH: Ginzberg, Legends, index. IN THE ARTS: E. Kirschbaum (ed.), *Lexikon der christlichen Ikonographie*, 1 (1968), 490–1 (includes bibliography); T. Ehrenstein, *Das Alte Testament im Bilde* (1923), 469–72; L. Réau, *Iconographie de l'art chrétien*, 2 (1956), 327–8. **ADD. BIBLIOGRAPHY:** Y. Amit, *Judges* (1999), 82–91.

DEBORIN (Joffe), ABRAM MOISEYEVICH (1881–1963), Russian Marxist philosopher. Born into a poor family in Lithuania, Deborin found employment as a metalworker and got caught up in the revolutionary spirit of the time. In 1903 he sided with Lenin's Bolsheviks against the Menshevik faction. As a student in Switzerland he came under the influence of the founder of Russian Marxism, Georgi Plekhanov, and became a Menshevik. With the success of the Bolshevik Revolution of 1917, he quit the Mensheviks and turned again to Lenin, offering the regime his services as a philosopher. Lenin cautiously approved Deborin's appointment to the Sverdlov Communist University in 1921. By 1925 he controlled both the leading Soviet journal, *Pod znamenem marksizma* ("Under the Banner of Marxism"), and the philosophy section of the Institute of Red Professorship, the leading graduate school. In 1928 he joined the Communist Party, and became the most influential Soviet academic philosopher. However, in 1929 the second conference of Marxist-Leninist scholarly institutions adjudged Deborin's views "incorrect and un-Marxist." This, the first Soviet instance of the legislation of philosophic truth by party decree, came in the wake of a split – festering since 1924 – between the "mechanists," headed by L.I. Akselrod, who emphasized materialism, and what Stalin slightingly called the "Menshevizing idealists" headed by Deborin, who stressed Hegelian dialectics. In a sense, the Deborinists had been arguing for the integrity of dialectical materialism, and Deborin was condemned for failing to adjust from Leninism to Stalinism. After 1931 he played a modest role as philosophy member at Moscow's Academy of Science, which directed the work of some 260 Russian institutes. In 1937 many who were accused of "Menshevik idealism" were arrested and perished in camps and prisons. Deborin was spared this fate.

Deborin's earliest important work is *Vvedeniye v filosofiyu dialekticheskogo materializma* ("Introduction to the Philosophy of Dialectical Materialism," 1922). His later publications include the first volume of *Sotsialno-politicheskiye ucheniye novogo i noveyshego vremeni* ("Socio-political Doctrines of Modern Times," 1958; Sp. trans. *Las doctrinas político-sociales de la época moderna y contemporanea*, 1960), and a collection of articles, *Filosofiya i politika* (1961). In 1928, together with August Thalheimer, he published a volume for the 250th anniversary of *Spinoza's death, *Spinozas Stellung in der Vorgeschichte des dialektischen Materialismus.*

BIBLIOGRAPHY: D. Joravsky, *Soviet Marxism and Natural Science, 1917–1932* (1961), 119–29, 170–84; *Encyclopedia of Philosophy*, 2 (1967), 164–5, 309; 7 (1967), 266.

DEBRECEN, city in E. Hungary; following the Reformation it was a bastion of Calvinism (known as "Calvinist Rome"). Jews began to settle there from the beginning of the 19th century but without the agreement of the city council; official permission was eventually received in 1840. There are records of an organized community from 1851; synagogues were built in 1851 and 1865; a third – a monumental construction – was erected in 1895–97; the building was destroyed by fire in 1948. In 1870 the Debrecen community declared itself a *status-quo community; in 1886 a separate Orthodox community was formed. The Orthodox synagogue, still in use in 1970, was built in 1893. A Jewish secondary school, established in 1921, existed until 1944. The Jewish population numbered 118 in 1848; 544 in 1856; 6,200 in 1900; 8,400 in 1910; 10,170 in 1920; and 12,000 in 1940. Under the Nazi regime, the young men were sent to forced labor camps. Of these several hundred were burnt to death in the Dorosics hospital. About 7,500 persons were deported up to June 26–28, 1944: some to Auschwitz, and the rest – because the railway lines had been destroyed by bombing – to Austria.

Those who returned formed the largest community in the area, consisting of 4,640 members in 1946. In 1970 there were 1,200 Jews with rabbis and two synagogues. The status-quo community used a synagogue built in 1909–10. A small community remained at the outset of the 21st century, mostly aged and unaffiliated with Jewish organizations.

BIBLIOGRAPHY: *Magyar Zsidó Lexikon* (1929), 188–91; L. Zoltai, in: *Magyar Zsidó Szemle*, 51 (1934), 18–32; *Schlesinger Sámuel emlékezete* (Debrecen, 1938); UJE, 3 (1941), 505–6; E. Sós, in: *Magyar Zsidó Szemle*, 59–62 (1942–45), 61–80, includes bibliography in Hung.; I. Végházi, *Adatok a debreceni zsidóság történetéhez* (Buenos Aires, 1967).

[Alexander Scheiber]

DEBRECENJI (Brunner), JOŽEF (1905–), Yugoslav author and editor. Born in Budapest, Debrecenji began his career on the editorial staff of several Hungarian newspapers and periodicals. He spent World War II in concentration camps, an experience that strongly influenced his postwar writings. From 1945 Debrecenji became a full-time writer in Belgrade, publishing poems, short stories, novels, and literary criticism. His outstanding work, *Hladni krematorijum* ("The Cold Crematorium," 1951), first appeared in Hungarian as *Hideg krematórium* (1950). Debrecenji's later works, studies of human destiny in troubled times, include the drama *Smena* ("The Shift," 1953), and collections of short stories such as *Neverovatno leto* ("The Incredible Summer," 1955) and *Ljudsko meso* ("Human Flesh," 1962) which first appeared in Hungarian.

BIBLIOGRAPHY: *Enciklopedija Jugoslavije* (1956), s.v.

[Zdenko Lowenthal]

DECALOGUE (The Ten Commandments). The statements of God quoted by Moses in Deuteronomy 5:6–18 are entitled "the ten words, or utterances" (Heb. עֲשֶׂרֶת הַדְּבָרִים *aseret ha-devarim*; LXX δέκα ῥήματα [Deut. 4:13], δέκα λόγοι [10:4]). The same title in Exodus 34:28 has traditionally been referred to the "original" version of these statements in Exodus 20:2–14 [17] but see below). Mishnaic Hebrew עֲשֶׂרֶת הַדִּבְּרוֹת *aseret ha-dibberot* reflects the specialized use of דִּבֵּר *dibber* (cf. Jer. 5:13) for divine speech.

Problems of the Literary Setting

Exodus 19:9 announces a dialogue between God and Moses (or an address by God to Moses) to be held at Sinai and overheard by the people, for the purpose of making them believe Moses "ever after." Verse 19 tells of such a dialogue – the contents of which are not specified – amid smoke, quaking, and the blare of a horn (some exegetes identify it with the colloquy of verses 20–24, others, with the Decalogue). Again, after Moses descends to the people (19:25), God speaks ("to Moses," LXX A) the entire Decalogue (20:1ff.). Frightened by the thunder, the smoke, and the blaring horn, the people fall back and plead with Moses to be their intermediary; Moses reassures the people that God wants only to train them in the fear of Him, then approaches the cloud enshrouding God (20:15–18 (18–21)).

Deuteronomy represents God summoning the people at Horeb (Sinai) to let them hear His voice in order to train them in the fear of Him (4:10). He speaks to them "face to face" out of the fire – but Moses was standing between the people and God "to declare YHWH's word to you, because you were afraid of the fire and would not ascend the mountain" (5:4–5). After hearing the Decalogue, the frightened people plead with Moses to be their intermediary (5:20ff.).

The attempts to reconcile these accounts internally and with each other are not convincing. The accounts apparently combine different versions of the event: (a) God spoke with Moses, and the people overheard; (b) He spoke with Moses and then Moses transmitted His words to the people; (c) God spoke to the people directly. The relation of the Decalogue to God's purpose in speaking with Moses in the Exodus account is obscure; why He speaks it to the people in Deuteronomy is only slightly less so. Common to all versions, however, is the affirmation that at Sinai-Horeb the entire people heard God's voice (Ex. 19:9, 22 (?); Deut. 4:10ff., 33, 36; 5:19ff.; 9:10; Neh. 9:13). Medieval theologians deduced from the combination of the Decalogue and the motif of the people hearing God's voice, particularly in Exodus 19:9 and Deuteronomy 5:21, that God's purpose in proclaiming the Decalogue was achieved when "henceforth the people believed that Moses held direct communication with God, that his words were not creations of his own mind" (Judah Halevi, *Sefer ha-Kuzari*, 1:87), and hence, that the laws he subsequently communicated originated with God (Maim., Yad, Yesodei ha-Torah, 8:1f.). This is a likely interpretation of the present form of the Decalogue narrative.

The Decalogue comprised the stipulations of the *covenant between God and Israel (Deut. 4:13). It was engraved on both sides of two stone "tablets of the covenant" (לוּחֹת־הַבְּרִית or לֻחֹת הָעֵדֻת [עֵדוּת, traditionally rendered "testimony," is to be connected with Akkadian *adū* and Old Aramaic (עד(י, עדיא "treaty"] by the finger of God; Moses ascended Mount Sinai and there he remained, fasting forty days before receiving the tablets (Ex. 24:12, 18; 32:15–16; Deut. 9:9ff.). Furious over the *golden calf Moses broke the first pair of tablets (Ex. 32:19; Deut. 9:17), after which he again ascended Sinai, remaining another forty days pleading on behalf of the people. After God forgave the people, Moses was ordered to provide a second pair of stones on which God wrote exactly what was written on the first pair (Ex. 32:30ff.; 34:1ff., 28; Deut. 9:18–20; 10:1–2, 10). God commanded that this pair be placed inside the *Ark of the Covenant, which was housed first in the tent sanctuary, later in the Tabernacle at Shiloh, and ultimately in the *Temple in Jerusalem (Ex. 25:16, 21; 40:20; Deut. 10:2–5; I Kings 8:9). The Ark was conceived as God's footstool (I Chron. 28:2), which is comparable (Tur-Sinai, Haran) to the custom attested in Egypt and Hatti of depositing copies of pacts under the feet of gods who had witnessed them.

The account of these events is complicated in Exodus by the intervening presence, in 34:10–26, of another set of covenant stipulations, which Moses is also commanded to write down (34:27). These concern (1) alliances with the idolatrous Canaanites; (2) molten gods; (3) the festival of unleavened bread; (4) firstlings; (5) the Sabbath; (6) the festival of weeks; (7) the ingathering festival; (8) sacrifice; (9) first fruits; and (10) cooking a kid in its mother's milk. They are presented as the terms of God's renewed covenant with Israel, and repeat the injunctions from 23:23ff. and 34:10–19 touching on the chief offenses involved in the golden calf episode (other molten gods; an invented festival). In 34:27 and 28 references to the two distinct series of covenant stipulations are juxtaposed.

Critics have called the stipulations of Exodus 34 the "cultic decalogue," as distinguished from the traditional – or the "ethical" – decalogue, and regard it as the more ancient. This relative dating rests in large measure on the supposition that the "ethical decalogue" reflects the teachings of the literary prophets. Yet nothing of the peculiar emphases of literary prophecy (e.g., concern for the rights of the weak) appears in the "ethical decalogue," while its own ethical injunctions are found not only in pre-prophetic Israelite literature, but in extra-biblical sources as well (see below).

The interrelation of these two series of covenant stipulations is obscure; no less obscure is the relation of the Decalogue of Exodus 20 to the following law corpus (20:19–23 (22–26); 21–23) – "all the words of YHWH and all the rules" that Moses relayed to the people and wrote down in the "book of the covenant" (24:3–4, 7). Thus several entities called covenant documents appear in the formidably complex section, Exodus 19–34. Criticism has been unable to assign these documents convincingly to one or another of the narrative strands that have been analyzed in the Pentateuch (the Decalogue is often assigned to the "Elohist"). It is as likely as not that the covenant documents were preexisting entities incorporated more or less whole into the narrative. The Deuteronomic version of the Decalogue shows changes under the influence of its context and there is reason to believe that all of the covenant documents underwent changes (mostly accretions) before attaining their present form. (See Table: Decalogue 1.)

Versions of the Decalogue

In addition to the two versions of the Decalogue found in the masoretic text of Exodus and Deuteronomy, the Samaritan Pentateuch preserves slightly differing Hebrew texts. Its major innovation consists in counting, as the tenth "word," the injunction to publish the Decalogue on Mount *Gerizim – the sacred mountain of the *Samaritans (the injunction combines Deut. 11:29a, 27:2b–3a, 4a [Samaritan version], 5–7, and 11:30). This dogmatic accretion to the text reflects the notion, first attested in the Hellenistic-Jewish literature (see below), that the Decalogue is an epitome of the Law, a capsule of its chief injunctions. A Hebrew version of the Exodus Decalogue appears in the *Nash papyrus (c. second century B.C.E.) – evidently used in the liturgy, to judge from the **Shema*ʿ reading that immediately follows (see below). Nash is closely related to the Septuagint of Exodus, and is likely to be a copy from the Hebrew that underlies the Septuagint manuscript. A fragment

DECALOGUE

EXODUS | **DEUTERONOMY**

I YHWH am your God who brought you out of the land of Egypt: You shall have no other gods beside Me. You shall not make for yourself a sculptured image or (> D[1]) any likeness of what is in the heavens above, or on the earth below, or in the waters under the earth. You shall not bow down to them or serve them. For I YHWH your God am a jealous God, visiting the iniquity of fathers upon children (and D[2]) upon the third and upon the fourth generations of those who hate me, but showing kindness to the thousandth generation of those who love me and observe my commandments.

You shall not utter the name of YHWH your God for a vain thing; for YHWH will not clear one who utters his name for a vain thing.

Remember[3] the sabbath day to hallow it. Six days you shall labor and do all your work, but[4] the seventh day is a sabbath of YHWH your God; you shall not do any work[5] you and your son and your daughter, your male and your female slave[6] and[7] your[-6] cattle, and the stranger who is in your settlements. **For in six days YHWH made heaven and earth**[8] **the sea and all that is in them, and He rested on the seventh day; therefore YHWH blessed the sabbath**[9] **day and hallowed it.**

Observe the sabbath day to hallow it, as **YHWH your God commanded you.** Six days you shall labor and do all your work, but[4] the seventh day is a sabbath of YHWH your God; you shall not do any work[5] you and[10] your son and[10] your daughter, **and**[11] your male and your female slave **and**[11] **your ox and your ass** and **all**[10] your cattle, and the stranger who is in your settlements, **so that your male and female slave may rest as you do. You must remember that you were a slave in the land of Egypt and YHWH your God brought you out of there with a mighty hand and an outstretched arm; therefore YHWH your God has commanded you to make**[12] **the sabbath day.**[13]

Honor your father and your mother[14] that you may long endure on the[15] land that YHWH your God is giving you.

Honor your father and your mother **as YHWH your God commanded you,** [16-]that you may long endure **and that you may fare well**[-16] on the land that YHWH your God is giving you.

[17-]You shall not murder.

(And D[2]) You shall not commit adultery.

(And D[2]) You shall not steal[-17d]

(And D[2]) You shall not bear false (שקר) E; (שוא) (D) witness against your fellow.

You shall not have designs on your fellow's **house (-hold).**[18]

You shall not have designs[19] **on your fellow's wife,**[20] or[21] his male or his female slave, or[21] his ox, or his ass[22] or all that is your fellow's.

And[2] You shall not have designs on your fellow's **wife**[23]

And[2] **you shall not desire**[24] **your fellow's house,**[25 26] **his field** or[27] his male or[28] his female slave,[26] his ox, or[28] his ass,[29] or all that is your fellows.

Key to apparatus:
Dg = Greek Deut. (ed. Rahlfs)
Ds = Samaritan Deut. (ed. von Gall)
Eg = Greek Exod.
Es = Samaritan Exod.
N = Nash Papyrus
Q = 4Q Deut.m (see Bibl.)
+ = added matter in source(s) indicated
> = "is missing in"

1 + or Q, Ds, Dg
2 > Q, Ds, Dg
3 Observe Es
4 + on N, Q
5 + on it (*bh*) N, (bw) Q, Eg, Dg
6–6 your ox and your ass and all your N, Eg
7 > Es
8 + and Eg
9 seventh N, Eg
10 > Q
11 > Q, Ds, Dg
12 observe Q, Dg
13 + and to hallow it Dg; to hallow it, for in six days YHWH made heaven and earth, the sea all that is in them, and He rested on the seventh day; therefore YHWH blessed the sabbath day to hallow it Q
14 + that you may fare well and N, Eg
15 + good Eg
16–16 that you may fare well and that you may long endure Dg
17–17 adultery, steal, murder Eg; adultery, murder, steal N, Dg (Philo)
18 wife [N], Eg
19 *ttm?wh* N
20 house (or Eg) his field N, _Es, Eg
21 > Es
22 + or all his cattle Eg
23 house(hold) Ds
24 have designs on Q, Ds, Dg
25 wife Ds
26 + or Dg
27 > Q, Ds
28 > Q
29 + or all his cattle Dg

containing the Deuteronomic Decalogue has been found in *Qumran Cave 4 (4Q Deutm; c. first century B.C.E.).

A translation of the received Hebrew text of the Decalogue follows, paragraphed according to Norzi's Minḥat Shai. Minor divergences of D(euteronomy) from E(xodus) are in parentheses; where major divergences occur, E's version of the "word" appears on the left, D's on the right, with divergent matter in boldface. The divergences in early versions are in footnotes.

Divergences between the masoretic texts of E and D are wider than between each of them and their versions, or between the versional texts of E and D. This speaks for the priority of the masoretic text. The ground for the Sabbath in E is organically related to the opening command: reference to the Creation explains how the Sabbath is YHWH's, and why it is to be sanctified. Compared with it, D's ground – to give rest to slaves and remember the Exodus (cf. Deut. 15:15; 16:12; 24:18, 22; cf. Ex. 23:12) – is tangential. Rhetorical expansions in Deuteronomy's style occur in D's commands regarding the Sabbath and honoring parents (cf. 4:23; 20:17, and 5:26; 6:18; 12:25, etc.). The addition of ox and ass in its Sabbath command derives from the list in the last paragraph. A socioeconomic divergence appears in the last two paragraphs. E follows a general term (*bayit*; "household," as, e.g., in Gen. 18:19; 45:18; Deut. 25:9) with particulars in descending order, omitting real property. D includes real property, and so it puts wife first (as in E's particulars) and pairs *bayit*, taken as "house," with "field." D's divergences are thus of a piece with the rhetorical idiom of Deuteronomy, and reflect its post-settlement orientation.

The expansive and synthetic tendencies visible in D are carried even further in the versions, a climax being 4Q Deut. m's attachment of E's Sabbath ground onto D's (note 13). Ibn Ezra's remark on D's divergence from E applies to the entire recorded transmission of the Decalogue: "Words are like bodies, their meaning, like the soul; hence the custom of the wise… not to be too concerned with changing the words so long as their meaning stays the same."

The Division Into Ten "Words"

The entire passage in which (and in which only) God speaks in the first person is one long paragraph. *Sifrei* Numbers (112) calls it all "the first utterance" (concerning idolatry), though common opinion divides it into two (*Ḥizzekuni*: "The first two 'words' were said in a single utterance"). To make up ten, each sentence of the ban on coveting is counted a paragraph, though the cantillation connects them (cf. *Minḥat Shai* and Ibn Ezra, both of whom deprecate numbering the "words" according to the paragraphing).

Two sets of cantillations appear in the first paragraph and with the first four brief "You shall not's": the so-called "upper" set, which treats the whole paragraph as one long verse and breaks the "You shall not's" into four short ones, and the so-called "lower" set, which breaks the paragraph into four verses and unites the "You shall not's" into a single verse. The upper cantillation represents the traditional manner in which Israel heard the ten "words" at Sinai, and is used for the public synagogal reading of the Decalogue (some say, only on the Feast of Shavuot); the lower normalizes the verse-lengths, and is used on all other occasions (e.g., private reading; *Minḥat Shai, Ḥizzekuni*).

For Philo (Decal. 53ff., 66ff.) and Josephus (Ant., 3:91–92) the first "word" says that God is one and alone to be worshiped (i.e., "I YHWH" plus "You shall not make etc."). The Samaritans start the count with "You shall have no other gods" – which runs to the end of the paragraph, and adds a new tenth "word" (see above). The Samaritan notion that "I YHWH" stands outside the count had medieval Jewish proponents (see Ibn Ezra's commentary). The commonly held count makes "I YHWH" the first word (enjoining belief in God), "You shall have no other gods" to the end of the paragraph, the second (banning idolatry). The natural construction of the first sentence, however, subordinates it to the second (cf. Judg. 6:8–10; Hos. 13:2–4; Ps. 81:8–10), entailing the following count and characterization of the "words":

1. On the ground that it is He who liberated them from Egypt, God demands that Israel recognize as god no other divine beings (cf. Naḥmanides).

2. No image of any creature may be made for worship – no distinction being made between a symbol of another god and one used in the cult of YHWH. Any cult image is *ipso facto* "another god," an object of YHWH's jealousy (cf. Ex. 20:20 (23); Deut. 4:15ff.; the golden calf is in YHWH's honor, Ex. 32:5). This demand for an aniconic cult does not prohibit objects of religious art which are not intended as objects of worship (e.g., *cherubim, trees, lions, cattle (I Kings 6:23ff., 29; 7:25, 29)). If, however, such an object became venerated, it was then banned (II Kings 18:4).

3. Using God's name for a vain thing has traditionally been understood to mean false oaths (cf. Ps. 24:4; Targ.); but evil prayer (cf. Ps. 16:4) or sorcery might be intended too. Frivolous oaths (Philo, Josephus) and, finally, any idle use of God's name (e.g., as in an unnecessary benediction (Ber. 33a)) came to be included. Another possibility (Staples, Sperling) is that the phrase should be translated as: "You shall not speak the name of YHWH to that which is false." In other words, do not identify a false god with YHWH. Given the previous prohibition of having no other gods, Israelites might have been tempted to identify other gods with YHWH. To identify a false god with Yahweh was to commit a crime so severe that Yahweh would not acquit he offender.

4. Observance of the Sabbath rest, according to E, respects God's consecration of the day at the end of Creation. D's motive associates a purely ethical notion (cf. Ex. 23:12) with the general ground, expressed in the first "word," of Israel's duty to obey God's commands (cf. Deut. 6:21–24).

5. Honor is due to both father and mother (cf. Lev. 19:3; and Ex. 21:15, 17; Lev. 20:9; Deut. 21:18ff.; 27:16). Juxtaposition of this "word" to the preceding injunctions concerning God's honor was later explained by the parents' partnership

with God in creating offspring (Mekh. Sb-Y to 20:12, Naḥmanides; cf. Gen. 4:1).

6. "Murder" has traditionally rendered the Hebrew *razah* here; for, though the verb covers non-culpable homicide as well (Num. 35:11, 27, 30; Deut. 4:42), to construe it as an absolute ban on killing would bring this "word" into conflict with the death penalty prescribed by the law for many offenses. The injunction affirms the sanctity of human life.

7. The verb *na'af* denotes sexual relations with a married woman by anyone but her husband (Lev. 20:10; Jer. 29:23; Ezek. 16:32). The inviolateness of a married woman is the basis of a patrilineal society.

8. Tradition understands *ganav* here to denote kidnapping, i.e., a theft liable to capital punishment – an offense of the same order as the two preceding (Mekh., Yitro, 8). But to make the legal penalty determinative in a document that ignores legal penalties throughout is unwarranted. Stealing at large is banned; the right of possession is affirmed.

9. The ban on false witness seeks to protect all transactions that require the honesty of the citizenry in the marketplace (Jer. 32:12) as well as the court.

10. Traditional legal exegesis understands *ḥamad* to involve action (Mekh., Yitro, 8, comparing Deut. 7:25; Mekh., SBY to 20:17: "one who exerts pressure to get something"; cf. Levi b. Gershom, who compares Ex. 34:24 ["no man will endeavor to take it from you"] and Micah 2:2, and concludes that "one does not violate this prohibition until he does something to obtain the object"). But (as Ibn Ezra to Deut. 5:16 observes) the verb may also be merely mental (e.g., Prov. 6:25), so that one wonders whether the actional interpretation does not arise out of misplaced legalism, i.e., the wish to define the prohibition in terms amenable to law enforcement. Since *D* expressly substitutes *hitavvah* (*hit'awwah*, "desire") for *ḥamad* in the second sentence, it clearly regarded the injunction as banning guilty desires.

Original Form and Date: Critical View

The divergent grounds of the Sabbath command in *E* and *D*, the disparity caused by the uneven presence of motive clauses and particulars, and the shift from first to third person with reference to God in the third "word" and thereafter (whence the rabbinic theory that only the first two were heard "from the mouth of God" (Mak. 24a); but such shifts are common (e.g., Ex. 23:13–25; 34:11–26)) have given rise to the theory that the "words" were originally all terse and only later received, unequally, additional clauses. A representative attempt to reconstruct the original form of the "words" (Stamm and Andrew in bibl.) follows:

> I am YHWH your God:
> You shall have no other gods besides me.
> You shall not make yourself a graven image.
> You shall not take the name of YHWH in vain.
> Remember the Sabbath day.
> Honor your father and your mother.
> You shall not kill.
> You shall not commit adultery.
> You shall not steal (a person, i.e. kidnap).
> You shall not bear false witness.
> You shall not covet.

Criteria for dating even this shortened form of the Decalogue are wanting. Monolatry, aniconism (cf. the empty cherub throne over the ark), and the sanctity of the divine name are coeval with the beginnings of biblical religion. The Sabbath as a sacred day of rest is found in the manna-story (Ex. 16 [*J*, 11th–10th cent.]). The ethical values of the Decalogue are common to other ancient Near Eastern civilizations. Comparisons with the Egyptian "Protestation of Guiltlessness" (a guide for the deceased during his final judgment after death) have often been made: "… I have not stolen … I have not been covetous … I have not robbed … I have not killed men … I have not told lies … I have not committed adultery, etc." (Pritchard, Texts, 35). While there is no proof of Mosaic origin, there is no ideational or substantive objection to the Decalogue's originating in Moses' time. Literary influence of supposedly later Deuteronomic and priestly material has been found in the motive clauses; but even this is questionable in the light of the possibility that the influence may have run the other way. Reminiscences of the Decalogue have been detected in Hosea 4:2; 12:10; 13:4 and Jeremiah 7:9.

Structure and Arrangement

A dual structure can be seen in the Decalogue: items one through four deal with man's relation to God; six through ten with man's relation to man; and the fifth, with relation to parents, forming a bridge between the two (Philo). The first five "words," having particularly Israelite orientation, are furnished with additional motive clauses; and they alone each contain a reference to "YHWH your God." The last five "words" have neither – being universal ethical requirements (PR 21:99).

While the biblical text gives no indication of how the "words" were distributed on the tablets, it is commonly assumed that they stood five over against five. An ingenious homily based on this assumption correlates the "words" opposite each other on the tablets thus: Murder is an injury to God whose image man is – apostasy is equivalent to marital infidelity – stealing will lead to a false oath (cf. Zech. 5:3–4, Prov. 30:9) – the Sabbath-breaker attests falsely that God did not create the world in six days and rest on the seventh – he who covets his fellow's wife will end by fathering a child who rejects his true parent and honors another (Mekh., Yitro, 8).

The "words" are ranged in a fairly clear descending order from matters divine to matters human, and within each group from higher to lower values. Duties to God come first: the obligation to worship Him alone precedes treating His name with reverence, and both precede the symbolic piety of Sabbath rest. Respect for parental authority naturally follows respect for God. The purely ethical injunctions are ranged in an obvious hierarchy: life, the family, right of possession, reliability of public statements. The last "word" – the ban on guilty attempts or desires – deals with what is both least culpable and most ethically sensitive; it acts as a safeguard against infringing on any of the other ethical injunctions.

Setting in Life

In later times, the Decalogue pericope (Ex. 19–20) was part of the liturgy of the Feast of Shavuot – by tradition, the anniversary of the Sinai theophany (Meg. 31a; Tosef., Meg. 4:5). This provides an analogy to the modern theory that in ancient Israel a festival of "covenant renewal" existed, whose liturgy included the solemn recitation of the Decalogue (Deut. 31:11). Support for the theory has been sought in formal similarities between the categorical (apodictic) idiom of the Decalogue and passages in Hittite vassal treaties which, among other things, require regular public reading of the document. The absence of any reference to such a festival in the biblical calendars militates against the theory. Moreover, when a commemorative function is attached to a festival, it is invariably related to some mighty or redemptive act of God on behalf of man (*Creation, *Exodus), but the Sinai theophany is not counted among these acts until very late biblical times (Neh. 9:13–14). The analogy of Deuteronomy 31:11 suggests, on the contrary, that in biblical times the public recitation of covenant stipulations would have been a secondary adjunct to one of the major festivals. Only later, when the "gift of the Torah" was appreciated as a boon (not only a solemn obligation (a glimmer of this is seen in Deut. 4:8)), did it become the fit subject of a major commemorative festival.

Jeremiah 35:6–7 shows that the rule of an order (here the Rechabites) might be formally quite similar to the Decalogue. Like the founding father Jonadab ben Rechab, God defined the conduct required for the well-being of his "holy people" largely through prohibitions. Among such clusters of admonitions (cf. especially Lev. 19, "which contains the entire Decalogue" [Lev. R. 24:51] the Decalogue stands out for its generality and suggestiveness, and its balance of essential religious and ethical injunctions. Not much is known of the mode of transmission of the Decalogue and its setting in life before it was incorporated into the narratives of the Torah. The Decalogue came to be regarded as a summary of biblical law. Philo worked out the classes of law generated from each "word": the third "word," for example, covers all the rules of oaths; the fourth, all the sacred seasons and festivals; the fifth, all duties toward masters, elders, and rulers; the sixth, all sexual morality; the seventh, all bodily injury; the eighth, laws of debt, partnership, and robbery. This notion eventuated hymns for the Feast of Shavuot called *Azharot* ("Instructions"), in which the entire canon of 613 commandments was artfully distributed under the heads of each of the ten "words" (*Siddur R. Sa'adyah Ga'on*, ed. I. Davidson et al. (1941), 191–216; I. Elbogen, *Gottesdienst* (1924), 217–8).

The Nash papyrus reflects liturgical recitation of the Decalogue which was practiced in Egypt down to late times (J. Mann, in HUCA, 2 (1925), 283). **Tefillin* from Second Temple times found in the Qumran caves contain the Decalogue (see bibl.); and evidence that this practice was maintained among Babylonian Jews is found in Jerome (to Ezek. 24:15 [17]; see Habermann in bibl.).

[Moshe Greenberg]

In Rabbinical Literature

The problem of the two versions of the Decalogue did not constitute any difficulty for the rabbis. They maintained that "Remember" (Ex. 20:8) and "Observe" (Deut. 5:12), as well as all the other variations between the two versions, were uttered simultaneously, "something which transcends the capacity of the human mouth to utter and of the human ear to hear" (Shevu. 20b; RH 27a). The omission of "that it may go well with thee" (Deut. 5:16) from the Fifth Commandment in the first version was because the initial tablets were destined to be broken (BK 55a). Different opinions are expressed with regard to the number of commandments inscribed on each tablet. The prevailing opinion was that they were equally divided; the first five (relating to the duties of man to God) on one tablet and the next five (relating to the duties of man to man) on the second. Others held that each tablet contained the entire Decalogue. One interpretation of "they were written on both their sides; on the one side and on the other were they written" (Ex. 32:15) gives rise to the view that the entire Decalogue was written on both sides of the tablets (Song R. 5:14, no. 1). The Talmud, however (Shab. 104a), explains it to mean that the letters were incised right through the stone, which resulted in the comment that the *mem* and *samekh* which were in the tablets stood there by a miracle since they were completely closed letters and normally should have fallen out (Shab. 104a). As, however, the Jerusalem Talmud points out this applies only to the *ketav Ashuri* (the Assyrian script) whereas, if the Torah was written in the ancient Hebrew script, this would apply to the *ayin* (TJ, Meg. 1:11, 71c).

The first two commandments, which were stated in the first person, were heard directly from God by the people. The remaining commandments were transmitted by Moses (Mak. 24a). Every single Israelite felt as if God was announcing the commandments directly to him (Tanḥ. B. Ex., 79).

In the Liturgy

The Decalogue was originally included in the daily Temple service (Tam. 5:1). Outside the Temple, the people also wanted to include it in the daily service, but they were forbidden to do so in order to refute the contention of heretical sects (*minim*) that only the Ten Commandments were divinely given (Ber. 12a). The aggadic statement that all the 613 commandments were written on the tablets in the space between the Ten Commandments was probably also intended to dispel this view (Song R. 5:14, no. 2). As a result, the Decalogue does not form part of the statutory daily liturgy. The only emphasis given to it is that the congregation rises when it is read as part of the regular weekly portions (twice a year in the portions *Yitro* and *Va-Etḥannan*) and on the festival of Shavuot.

In some Oriental communities (e.g., in Libya), it was customary to read the Ten Commandments on Shavuot together with the Arabic translation. In many *Reform congregations, the solemn recital of the Ten Commandments is part of the confirmation ceremony which is generally celebrated on Shavuot. Likewise, at the bar mitzvah celebration in the synagogue, the boy or girl recites the Ten Commandments before the open *Ark as part of a solemn pledge of allegiance to the Jewish tradition.

For the Decalogue in *Tefillin* see *Tefillin and see also *Commandments, The 613.

[Aaron Rothkoff]

In Jewish Philosophy

In discussing the Decalogue, Jewish philosophers generally dealt with the following three topics: the nature of the Sinaitic phenomenon, the various enumerations of the Ten Commandments, and their philosophical message. The usual interpretation of the Sinaitic experience is that God willed that an incorporeal voice should come into being and pronounce the Ten Commandments in an audible and intelligible manner (*Philo, Decal. 9; *Judah Halevi, *Kuzari*, 1:89; *Levi b. Gershom, commentary to Ex. 20, etc.). Maimonides (*Guide*, 2:33) and Hermann *Cohen (*Die Religion der Vernunft* [1929], 44ff.) maintain that, since the Sinaitic experience was a prophetic one and thus could not have been experienced by those who were not qualified, it must follow that Moses alone heard and comprehended all the Ten Commandments. The people only heard an indistinguishable sound the meaning of which was explained to them by Moses. "I am the Lord" (Ex. 20:2) is generally accepted as the first commandment and the injunction against acknowledging the existence of other gods, making, or worshiping idols (Ex. 20:3–5) as the second. Philo, however, considers the prohibition of acknowledging other gods (Ex. 20:3) as the first commandment, and making or worshiping idols (Ex. 20:4–5) as the second. The Decalogue encompasses fundamental principles which contain the entire Mosaic teaching (S.D. *Luzzatto, commentary to Ex. 2; I. *Abrabanel, commentary to Ex. 20). Their aim is the perfection of the body and of the soul. Thus they include metaphysical truths and ethical rules of conduct (*Guide*, 3:17). Because of their greater importance, metaphysical truths are listed first in the first tablet (Joseph *Albo, *Sefer-ha-Ikkarim*, 3:26). The first three commandments teach the existence of God, His unity and incorporeality, His providence, revelation, and veneration (*ibid.*). The fourth commandment (Ex. 20:8–11; Deut. 5:12–15) enjoins a belief in creation, in the subordination of nature to God (*Guide*, 2:31), and in the equality of all men (H. Cohen, *Der Sabbath*, 1881). The last five commandments (Ex. 20:13–14; Deut. 5:16–18) aim at controlling emotions and desires in deeds, in words, and in intentions (Philo, Decal. 24ff.). *Abraham b. Ḥiyya, after placing the first command apart as comprehending all the others, divided the other nine (a) according to commands of thought, speech, and action, and (b) according to relations between man and God, man and his family, man and man, reaching the classification shown in Table: Decalogue 2.

Table 2. Abraham b. Ḥiyya's classification of the Decalogue

Relations between:	Man and God	Man and Family	Man and Man
Thought:	Second Command: "Thou shalt have no other God" – fear of God.	Fifth Command: "Honor thy father and thy mother."	Tenth Command: "Thou shalt not covet."
Speech:	Third Command: "Thou shalt not take the name of the Lord in vain."	Sixth Command: "Thou shalt not murder," especially one's family.	Ninth Command: "Thou shalt not bear false witness."
Action:	Fourth Command: "Remember the Sabbath Day."	Seventh Command: "Thou shalt not commit adultery."	Eighth Command: "Thou shalt not steal."

(see Abraham b. Ḥayyim, *Meditation of the Sad Soul*, tr. by G. Wigoder), 23–24, 130–9.

For Decalogue in Arts see *Moses in Arts.

[David Kadosh]

Bibliography: INTERPRETATION: M.M. Kasher, *Ḥumash Torah Shelemah*, 16 (1954); S. Goldman, *The Book of Human Destiny*, 3 (1958), 534–696; M. Noth, *Exodus* (Eng., 1962), 151–68. CRITICISM: J.J. Stamm and M.E. Andrew, *The Ten Commandments in Recent Research* (1967); E. Nielsen, *The Ten Commandments in New Perspective* (1968), incl. bibl.; A. Alt, *Essays on Old Testament History and Religion* (1966), 79–132; G. von Rad, *The Problem of the Hexateuch and Other Essays* (1966), 13–26; G.E. Mendenhall, in: BA, 17 (1954), 26–45, 50–75; D.J. Mc-Carthy, *Treaty and Covenant* (1963), 152–67 (critique of Mendenhall). ON THE TABLETS: N.H. Tur-Sinai, *Ha-Lashon ve-ha-Sefer*, 2 (1955), 54–61; M. Haran, in: IEJ, 9 (1959), 30–35, 89–92. ON THE NASH PAPYRUS: M.Z. Segal, *Masoret u-Vikkoret* (1957), 227–36. 4Q DEUT.: Smithsonian Institution (ed.), *Scrolls from the Wilderness of the Dead Sea* (1965), pl. 19 (cf. p. 31–32). **ADD. BIBLIOGRAPHY:** W. Staples, in: JBL, 58 (1939), 325–29; S.D. Sperling, *Original Torah* (1998), 63.

DECAPOLIS (Gr. "the ten cities"), league or administrative grouping of Syrian-Greek cities situated in southern Syria, the northern Jordan Valley, and in Transjordan in the Roman and Byzantine periods. The Decapolis which was originally attached to the Roman Province of Syria is already mentioned in the 1st century C.E. by Josephus (Wars, 3:446), who refers to Scythopolis as the largest of the cities of the Decapolis, and in the New Testament with Jesus at one point passing through the region of the Decapolis (Mark 7:31, cf. 5:20; Mathew 4:25). Pliny (*Natural History*, 5:74) indicated that the Decapolis adjoined the Province of Judaea and lists the following ten cities – *Damascus, Philadelphia (*Amman), Raphana (al-Rāfa), Scythopolis (*Beth-Shean), *Gadara (Gader, now Um-Qays), Hippus (*Susitha, now Qalʿat al-Ḥuṣn east of the Sea of Galilee), Dium/Dion (Tell al-Ashʿarī?), *Pella (Peḥal in the Talmud, now Khirbat Ṭabaqāt Fāḥil), *Gerasa/Galasa (Ge-

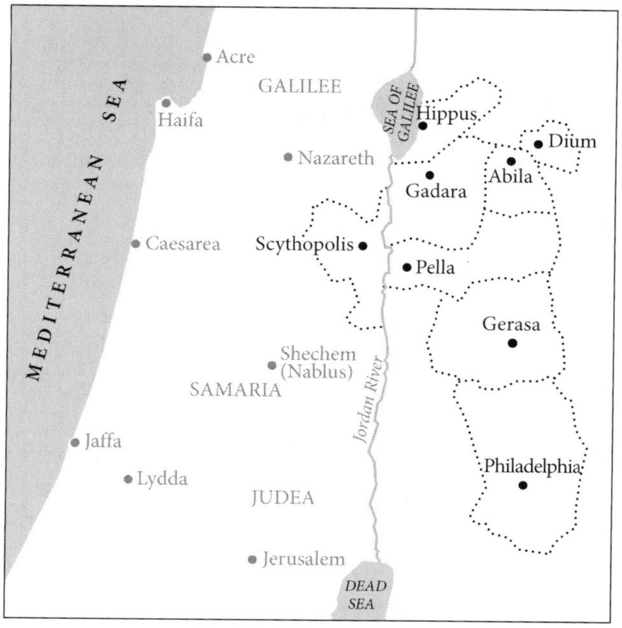

Map showing the eight cities constituting the continuous bloc of the Decapolis. Damascus and Kanatha lie north of this area.

resh), and Kanatha (Kenat, now al-Qanawāt in the Hauran). (See Map: Eight Cities of the Decapolis). Pliny admits, however, that other opinions existed concerning the composition of the Decapolis. Since most of the cities dated their civic eras from the time of Pompey's conquest of the area (63 B.C.E.), some scholars have suggested that Pompey founded the Decapolis when he freed the Greek cities which had been conquered by Alexander Yannai. In Hadrian's time Abila (Abel, Tell Ibil, north of Irbid) was also a member of the league. A different list of 18 cities of the Decapolis appears in the writings of the geographer Ptolemy (second century C.E.). It includes the cities mentioned by Pliny (excluding Raphana) and adds nine new places: Heliopolis, Abila, Saana, Hina, Abila Lysanias, Capitolias, Edrei, Gadora, and Samulis. In addition, the Decapolis was mentioned in the *Onomasticon* of Eusebius as a region situated near Peraea, and in the writings of Stephen of Byzantium (with a list of 14 cities).

Some of the cities of the Decapolis were situated on the sites of earlier cities (e.g. Damascus, Beth-Shean) while others were newly established in the Hellenistic period. Some claimed Greek origins (see a discussion of their foundation legends by Lichtenberger). Pompey incorporated the cities of the Decapolis into the province of Syria and granted them autonomy. In 30 B.C.E. Augustus gave Herod the cities of Gadara and Hippus; these were returned to the province of Syria after Herod's death. Kanatha and Raphana were under the control of Agrippa II. The other cities of the Decapolis were considered part of Syrian territory until 105–106 C.E. when Trajan transferred the cities in the far south to the newly established province of Arabia. In the Byzantine lists, some of the cities of the Decapolis are placed in Arabia and some in *Palaestina secunda*.

The cities of the league possessed autonomy in internal affairs as well as the right to mint coins. Only one inscription has been found to date that refers to the Decapolis. Damascus was granted the status of a Roman colony by Alexander Severus as was Gadara by Valens. Nothing is known of the legal aspects of the league in which the cities were united; at any rate, a reciprocal relationship existed between the various members. Each city had jurisdiction over an extensive area. With the exception of Damascus and Kanatha, the cities of the Decapolis constituted a continuous bloc south and southeast of the Sea of Galilee, extending from Philadelphia in the south to Hippus in the north. The cities of the league were important because they were situated along the trade routes between northern Arabia and Syria. Damascus served both economically and geographically as the northern assembling point for this trade and Scythopolis as the link connecting the trade routes with western Palestine. The cities of the Decapolis and their hinterlands formed a barrier against the Arabian desert-marauders and they also extended the agricultural belt to the east. At the same time they served as a Roman security ring around Palestine; during the Bar Kokhba War (132–135), Hadrian made Gerasa his base for attacking Judea. The establishment of the province of Arabia diverted the flow of trade from India, Arabia, and the Red Sea – which until then had passed through Petra to Gaza – northward to Damascus. This deflection increased the importance of the cities of the Decapolis and led to new economic prosperity, especially for the cities of Philadelphia, Gerasa, and Gadara. Their domination of the trade routes was further strengthened when the city of Tadmor (Palmyra) was destroyed by Aurelian in 273 C.E. In the 4th century, Gerasa and Philadelphia are described as "mighty cities" (Amianus Marcellinus).

Hellenistic culture flourished in the Decapolis in the Roman period. Among the famous residents of the cities were: Theodorus (teacher of the emperor Tiberius), Menippus the cynic, Oenomaus the stoic (who is perhaps identical with Avnimus the Gardi mentioned in the Talmud), and Meleager the poet, all from Gadara; Stephanus the historian, Plato the rhetorician, and Nikomachos the philosopher, from Gerasa; Aristotle the rhetorician came from Pella; and *Nicolaus the historian, one of Herod's ministers, from Damascus.

A large Jewish community existed in these cities at least from the time that most of them were conquered by Alexander Yannai. Some of the Jews were probably descendants of persons who had been converted by the Hasmonean king. In 44 C.E. a border dispute between the inhabitants of Jewish Transjordan and Philadelphia led to bloody clashes which were renewed on a large scale in most of the cities of the Decapolis at the outbreak of the Jewish War in 66 C.E. In Scythopolis 3,000 Jews were killed, in Damascus 10,000 or more, and there was mass slaughter in the other cities as well. According to Josephus, Gerasa was the only city which protected its Jewish inhabitants (Wars, 2:480), but remains of a synagogue found there show that it was destroyed even before the time of Hadrian. A large Jewish population nevertheless continued to live in the Decapolis cities for many generations after the destruction of the Temple, as is proved by remains of large synagogues in Hammath Gader and Gerasa and various statements in the Talmud (e.g., TJ, Dem. 2:1, 22d etc.). According to Eusebius a group of Jews who believed in Jesus fled from Jerusalem to Pella prior to the fall of Jerusalem to the Romans in 70 C.E.

BIBLIOGRAPHY: H.C. Butler, *Publications of the American Archaeological Expedition to Syria*, 4 vols. (1899–1900); University of Princeton, *Archaeological Expedition to Syria 1904–05*, 3 vols. (1907–16); Schuerer, Gesch, 2 (1907), 150–93; S. Klein, *Ever ha-Yarden ha-Yehudi* (1920); V. Tcherikover, *Ha-Yehudim ve-ha-Yevanim*, 2 (1930); idem, *Hellenistic Civilization and the Jews* (1959), 106 and index; idem, *Hellenistische Staedtegruendungen* (1925); A.H.M. Jones, *The Cities of the Eastern Roman Provinces* (1937), 260–1; M. Rostovtseff, *Social and Economic History of the Roman Empire*, 2 (1957), 664–5, n. 33, n. 34; Seyrig, in: *Syria: Revue d'art et d'Archéologie*, 36 (1959), 60–78; Bietenhard, in: ZDPV, 79 (1963), 24ff.; Avi-Yonah, Land. **ADD. BIBLIOGRAPHY:** S. Thomas Parker, "The Decapolis Reviewed," in: JBL, 94 (1975), 437–41; A. Spijkerman, *The Coins of the Decapolis and Provincia Arabia* (1978); B. Isaac, "The Decapolis in Syria: A Neglected Inscription," in: *Zeitschrift für Papyrologie und Epigraphik*, 44 (1981), 67–74; J.M.C. Bowsher, "Architecture and Religion in the Decapolis: A Numismatic Survey," in: PEQ, 119 (1987), 62; A. Segal, *Town Planning and Architecture in Provincia Arabia* (1988); F. Millar, *The Roman Near East 31 BC–AD 337* (1993), 408ff.; A. Lichtenberger, "City Foundation Legends in the Decapolis," in: *Bulletin of the Anglo-Israel Archaeological Society*, 22 (2004), 23–34.

[Shimon Applebaum / Shimon Gibson (2nd ed.)]

DE CASSERES, BENJAMIN (1873–1945), U.S. essayist. De Casseres began to write for Philadelphia newspapers at the age of 16 and continued as an essayist, book reviewer, editorial writer, and columnist for New York dailies. His first book of verse was *The Shadow-Eater* (1915) and his first book of prose, *Chameleon: Being a Book of My Selves* (1922). More than 20 books followed, including his collected works in three volumes (1939).

DECEMBRISTS (Dekabrists), group of revolutionaries in Russia. Drawn from the aristocracy and younger army officers, from 1816 it developed as a secret society and sought to abolish the despotic regime. After the death of Czar *Alexander I, the group attempted to foment a rebellion against his successor, *Nicholas I. The rebellion, which began on Dec. 26, 1825 (hence the name Decembrists), was unsuccessful and its participants were severely punished. It is assumed that most of the interest of the Decembrists in the Jewish problem was awakened by Grigori Peretz – a converted Jew among them. He was arrested and sentenced to exile. He spoke at length on the necessity of founding a society for the settlement of the Jews in Crimea or the Orient, where they would live as an autonomous nation. On his suggestion his group adopted the Hebrew word "*Ḥerut*" (freedom) as their motto. In his work *Russian Justice*, Pavel Pestel, one of the Decembrist leaders, devoted a paragraph to the Jewish problem. He negated the right of Jews to be citizens of the Russian state because "they are united by an excessive and incomparable solidarity" and "are unable to become integrated within any nation of the world." They are subjected to the rule of their rabbis and "await the arrival of the Messiah who will return them to their country." Pestel saw two ways of solving the Jewish problem: the first, "to destroy the unity among the Jews, which is harmful to the Russians" and to impose a strict supervision over them; the second, "to assist the Jews in establishing a special state somewhere in Asia Minor." For this purpose, Pestel suggested that all the Jews of Russia and Poland should be concentrated in one place and that an army be raised from their midst which would conquer a territory in Asiatic Turkey and establish a Jewish state. Another leader of the Decembrists, Nikita Muraviov, included full equality for the Jews in his proposed constitution.

BIBLIOGRAPHY: Dubnow, Hist Russ, 1 (1916), 409–13; S.M. Ginsburg, *Meshumodim in Tsarishn Russland* (1946), 48–50.

[Yehuda Slutsky]

DE CHAVES, AARON (d. 1705), Dutch painter and engraver; first Jewish artist recorded as working in England after the readmission of the Jews. De Chaves' painting *Moses and Aaron and the Ten Commandments* hung over the ark of the synagogue in Creechurch Lane, London, which was opened in 1656. This was the first new synagogue to be established. The painting is now in the possession of the Spanish and Portuguese Synagogue in London.

°DECKERT, JOSEPH (1846–1901), Catholic priest in Vienna and antisemitic agitator. He propagated the view that antisemitism was compatible with Catholicism. Resurrecting the *blood libel, he brought out a pamphlet on Simon of *Trent in 1893; later that year he published in *Vaterland* an account by the apostate Paulus *Meyer of a ritual murder which Meyer had allegedly witnessed in his native Ostrov in 1875. The rabbis whom he had named sued for libel, and Deckert, Meyer, and the journal's editor were found guilty and fined. Deckert's inflammatory sermons were the subject of frequent interpellations in parliament, and his travesty of the "Lord's Prayer" directed against the Jews was confiscated. However, in a trial for sedition (1896) he was acquitted. Deckert's antisemitic writings include *Kann ein Katholik Anti-semit sein* (1893) and *Tuerkennoth und Judenherrschaft* (1894^5).

BIBLIOGRAPHY: J.S. Bloch, *My Reminiscences*, 2 (1923), 365–575; F. Heer, *Gottes erste Liebe* (1967), 355, 375; H.L. Strach, *Das Blut* (1911), 126, 160–1; E. Weinzierl, in: K.H. Rengstorf (ed.), *Kirche und Synagoge*, 2 (1970), 510–3.

DECLARATION OF INDEPENDENCE, ISRAEL. During the five months that followed the UN Palestine partition resolution of November 29, 1947, repeated attempts were made by representatives of the U.S. State Department and others to prevent the establishment of the Jewish State. On March 19, 1948, it was announced that the U.S. Government would propose an international trusteeship over Palestine. This suggestion was categorically rejected by David *Ben-Gurion, then chairman of the Zionist Executive. At the beginning of April, the Zionist General Council and the Va'ad Le'ummi decided to establish a 13-member National Administration and a National Council of 37 members, which would, upon the departure of the British Mandatory forces, become the provisional government and legislature of the Jewish State.

On May 12 Moshe Shertok (*Sharett) returned from the United States and reported to the National Administration that Secretary of State George Marshall had revived the trusteeship proposal, though President Truman and public opinion still favored a Jewish state. Shertok proposed the formation of a government, rather than the establishment of a state, while Felix Rosenblueth (Pinḥas *Rosen) proposed the proclamation of a state within the framework of the UN decision. Ben-Gurion insisted that the proclamation should be only "on the basis" of the UN decision and opposed the demand of Rosenblueth and Bekhor *Shitreet that the frontiers of the state be specified, pointing out that the United States had not designated its own frontiers when declaring independence. If the Jews succeeded in repulsing the Arab attack, they would occupy Western Galilee and the Jerusalem Corridor, which would thus become part of the Jewish State. By a 5 to 4 majority, it was decided not to specify frontiers. A committee of five – David *Remez, Rosenblueth, Moshe Shapira, Shertok, and Aharon *Zisling – was appointed to draft the Declaration of Independence. The draft submitted by the committee on May 13 consisted of 22 articles, 12 of which began with "Inasmuch as…" It was criticized as too long and flowery, and the final wording was entrusted to Ben-Gurion, Rabbi Y.L. Fishman (*Maimon), A. Zisling, and M. Shertok. During the same evening Ben-Gurion prepared a final draft, which was approved by his colleagues on the committee.

The National Council met at 10 A.M. the next day. The Communist leader Meir Wilner proposed the addition of articles denouncing the British Mandate and opposing British military bases, but Shertok argued that such items were out of place in the Declaration. David Ẓevi Pinkas of the *Mizrachi proposed that the Declaration should begin: "The Land of Israel was promised to the Jewish people in the Torah and by the Prophets." Zisling objected to the term "*Ẓur Yisrael,*" a version of the name of God (literally "Rock of Israel"), in the final paragraph; *Mapai's Meir Grabovski (Argov) proposed the addition of the word "language" to the clause guaranteeing freedom of religion, conscience, education, and culture, to ensure that Arabic would have equal rights with Hebrew. Ben-Gurion agreed to Grabovski's proposal, but not to his reasoning. The language of the State must be Hebrew, but the Arabs would be free to use their language in all aspects of Israeli life. As to Zisling's objection, he said, everyone from Right to Left believed in the "Rock of Israel" in his own way. On a first vote, 16 voted for the draft and 8 abstained. The chairman reported that the members of the council who had been unable to leave Jerusalem, because of the battles, had met that morning and had approved the draft. He requested that the Declaration be adopted unanimously in a second vote, whatever objections members might have to a particular item or aspect, and this was done.

The council also approved a proposal submitted by Felix Rosenblueth, that the Provisional Council of State – as the National Council was to be called after independence – be the legislative authority, with the right to delegate its powers to the government for the purpose of urgent legislation. The White Paper of 1939 and the relevant Mandatory ordinances were to be repealed, but all other laws in existence on May 14, 1948, would remain in force in the State of Israel.

At 4:30 P.M. of the same day, Iyyar 5, 5708, the National Council met in the Tel Aviv Museum Hall. Among those present were representatives of the Jewish Agency, the Zionist Organization, the Va'ad Le'ummi, the Zionist funds, leaders of political parties, personalities in the various cultural fields, the chief rabbis, the Tel Aviv Town Council, the chief of staff of the *Haganah and his colleagues, and pioneers of Jewish settlement.

Ben-Gurion, who presided, announced: "I shall read you the Foundation Scroll of the State of Israel, which has been approved in first reading by the National Council." As he concluded with the appeal "Let us accept the Foundation Scroll of the Jewish State by rising," the entire audience rose. The chairman stated that any member who so desired would be able to make a statement at the next session. Rabbi Fishman thereupon pronounced the traditional blessing: "Blessed art Thou, O Lord, our God, King of the Universe, Who has kept us alive and preserved us and enabled us to reach this season." The chairman then read the resolution annulling the White Paper, which was unanimously adopted. He then signed the Declaration of Independence, and the secretary, Ze'ev Schaerf (*Sharef), read out the names of the council members in Hebrew alphabetical order. Amid enthusiastic applause, each member went up to the dais and signed, space being left for those still in Jerusalem to sign later. Ben-Gurion announced: "The State of Israel has arisen. This session is closed."

BIBLIOGRAPHY: Z. Sharef, *Three Days* (1962); *Kolot Esrim Shanah*, CBS record.

[David Ben-Gurion]

DE CORDOVA, JACOB (1808–1868), Texas pioneer. De Cordova was born in Spanish Town, Jamaica, and raised in Philadelphia. In 1834 he founded the Kingston *Daily Gleaner*, Jamaica's first daily paper, which his eldest brother's family has continued to publish. Returning to the United States in 1835, de Cordova was attracted to Texas by business, settled there, and became a citizen (1837). In 1842 he opened a large land agency. Thereafter he wrote guidebooks and lectured in New York, Philadelphia, and Manchester, England (1856–58), to attract settlers to Texas. Two years after Texas statehood (1845), de Cordova was elected to the Texas House of Representatives. Together with his brother Phineas (1819–1903), he published the semi-monthly *Texas Herald*, along with a weekly, the *Southwestern America* (1849–52), which helped stimulate railroad building in the state.

[Edward L. Greenstein]

°**DEEDES, SIR WYNDHAM** (1883–1956), British Zionist. During World War I he served at Gallipoli and, in 1915, was a member of the British Intelligence Service in Cairo. When Chaim *Weizmann reached Palestine in 1918 as head of the *Zionist Commission, Deedes was influenced by him and became a supporter of the Zionist cause. Herbert *Samuel, appointed high commissioner for Palestine in 1920, invited Deedes to become his chief secretary. In the early stages of the administration, Deedes proved an effective brake on the hostile attitude of the British civil servants to the policy based on the *Balfour Declaration. He unofficially recognized the Haganah and introduced Jews into the Palestine Police Force. In 1921 Deedes was instrumental in saving the Jewish settlement in *Reḥovot from destruction by a mob of 10,000 Arabs. He returned to England when his term of office ended in 1923 and subsequently visited several countries on Zionist missions. In 1943 he established the British Association for the Jewish National Home, and, upon the establishment of the State of Israel, formed the Anglo-Israel Friendship Association with both Jewish and Christian members. His Zionism was motivated by profound religious belief. He was one of the most outspoken non-Jewish supporters of Zionism in Britain. Deedes was knighted in 1921.

BIBLIOGRAPHY: Ch. Weizmann, *Trial and Error* (1966), index; G. Skelton (J. Presland), *Deedes Bey* (1942); N. Bentwich, *Sir Wyndham Deedes, a Christian Zionist* (1954); E. Elath et al. (eds.), *Memoirs of Sir Wyndham Deedes* (1958); E. Samuel, *Lifetime in Jerusalem* (1970). **ADD. BIBLIOGRAPHY:** B. Wasserstein, *Wyndham Deedes in Palestine* (1973); idem, *The British in Palestine: The Mandatory Government and the Arab-British Conflict* (1991); ODNB online.

[Getzel Kressel]

DEEP, THE. The ancient Hebrews believed that the earth lay across an all-encompassing ocean, which they called *tehom*. The term is used in the Bible either for the primordial waters *in toto* (Gen. 1:2) or for the upper or lower portion alone (cf. Ps. 42:8). Most frequently it denotes the latter, and it is then conventionally rendered "the deep." The Canaanite myths from Ras Shamra (Ugarit) speak similarly of "the two oceans" *(thmtm)*, i.e., the supernal and the infernal, the dwelling of the supreme god El being located at their confluence, i.e., on the horizon. In the Babylonian *Epic of Creation* the primordial ocean is personified as the monstrous Tiamat, who launches battle against the supreme god Anu, but is eventually subdued by Marduk and slit lengthwise "like an oyster," the two parts of her body forming, respectively, the vault of heaven and the bedrock of the earth. This myth is echoed in several passages of the Bible (Isa. 51:9–10; Hab. 3:8; Ps. 74:13–14; 89:9–10) which speak of a primeval combat between God and a monster variously styled Leviathan, Rahab ("Blusterer"), Tannin ("Dragon"), Yam ("Sea"), and Nahar ("Stream"). In the wake of Isaiah 27:1, post-biblical legend asserts that at the end of the world this monster will again break loose, and again be defeated – a notion which recurs in Iranian lore (Yashts 19:38–44; Bundahišn 29:9), and which also leaves traces both in the New Testament (Rev. 20:1–3) and in the Talmud (BB 75a). The personification of the primordial ocean as a monster is further echoed in Genesis 49:25, where Tehom is described as "crouching below," like a beast. Rivers and springs were believed to emanate from the nether *tehom* (Targ., Eccles. 1:7; cf. Weinsinck in bibl., p. 42), and the upsurging of it was partly responsible for the Deluge (Gen. 7:11). Ecclesiastes 1:7, as interpreted by Targum and Rashi, believes that after surging up from this nether *tehom* and flowing through streams into the sea, the water finds its way back to the *tehom* through tunnels and then surges up again to the springs and repeats the cycle. The rock on which the Temple was built at Jerusalem is said in later legend (Targ. Jon., Ex. 28:30) to have covered the mouth of the deep, and the stairs connecting the two courts of the Temple were called popularly "the stairs of Tehom" (Targ., Ps. 120). Similarly, the temple of Marduk at Babylon and that of E-ninu at Lagash rested reputedly on the nether ocean. Related to this is the belief that the supreme god sits enthroned over the waters of the nether flood. Thus, in a Hittite myth the god who conquers the dragon Illuyankas is subsequently installed "above the well," while in the second century C.E. Lucian was shown a spot in the temple at Hierapolis into which the waters of the Deluge were said to have gathered. This belief is, possibly, reflected in the words of Psalms 29:10: "The Lord sat enthroned over the flood" (see Gaster in bibl., pp. 750–1, 843–54, nos. 25–31). It is related in the Talmud (Ta'an. 25b) that the angel *Rdy'*, who is in charge of rain, stands midway between the upper and lower oceans, bidding the waters of the former to pour down, and of the latter to rise. In Ecclesiasticus 24:8 Wisdom is said to have walked primordially "in the depth of the abyss," and in Babylonian glossaries the name Apsu, by which the freshwater abyss is called, is fancifully etymologized as *ab-zu*, "abode of wisdom" (E. Dhorme, *Religion assyro-babylonienne* (1910), 73). Comparable is the classical notion that Proteus, the old man of the sea, is omniscient, while in ancient Mesopotamian folklore the seven sages (*apkallê*) who introduced civilization, emerge from the deep (Gaster, 324, no. 31). Job 28:12, 14 seems, however, to protest against this idea, while in Proverbs 8:24, Wisdom exists prior to the creation of the deep.

BIBLIOGRAPHY: A.J. Wensinck, *The Ocean in the Literature of the Western Semites* (1918); T.H. Gaster, *Myth, Legend and Custom in the Old Testament* (1969), 3–4, 323–5; H.L. Ginsberg, *The Five Megiloth and Jonah* (1969), on Eccles. 1:7.

[Theodor H. Gaster]

DEER. The *ayyal*, identified with the deer (*Cervus capreolus*), is mentioned among the seven species of permitted game that chew the cud and are cloven-footed (Deut. 14:5). The word occurs several times in the Bible in the feminine form *ayy-*

alah. The tribe of Naphtali was compared to a nimble deer ("a hind let loose") with branching horns ("he giveth *imrei shafer*," i.e., whose *amirim* ("antlers") are beautiful; Gen. 49:21). Since the hind has no horns, as pointed out by Rashi in his comment on the talmudic passage that "the hind's antlers branch out this way and that" (Yoma 29a), the reference here is to the hart, which in its first year has only one branch on its horns, growing two more later. Its height at the shoulder is about 30 in. (about 75 cms.). It is extremely beautiful and delicate (cf. Prov. 5:19). It survived in Ereẓ Israel until World War I but, despite its agility, it fell prey to hunters eager for its tasty meat. At present there are to be seen in Israel herds of *gazelle, which, although wrongly identified with *ayyal/ayyalah*, are in fact the biblical *ẓevi*, distinguished from the deer by its horns, which are hollow and do not branch out like those of the *ayyal*. Until the end of the 19th century the fallow deer (*Cervus dama mesopotamica*) was found in the Middle East. It is a larger deer, its height at the shoulder being about 35 in. (about 90 cms.), its horns broad, with five branches in those of an adult. Apparently this is the species called *yaḥmur* in the Bible. It is among the permitted game (Deut. 14:5) and was provided for Solomon's table (I Kings 5:3). In the Talmud it is identified with an important species of game akin to the deer (Bek. 7b), depicted frequently in ancient hunting scenes. In prehistoric times the European deer (*Cervus elaphus*), bones of which have been discovered in caves on Mount Carmel and in Lebanon, was also found in Ereẓ Israel.

BIBLIOGRAPHY: I. Aharoni, *Torat ha-Ḥai*, 1 (1923), 88–90; Lewysohn, Zool, 111–3; J. Feliks, *Animal World of the Bible* (1962), 10, 12.

[Jehuda Feliks]

DEGANYAH (Heb. דְּגַנְיָה), two kevuẓot – Deganyah Alef and Deganyah Bet – in Israel, on the Jordan-Yarmuk Plain south of Lake Kinneret, both affiliated to Iḥud ha-Kibbutzim. Deganyah Alef was founded in 1909 on land that was among the first holdings acquired by the *Jewish National Fund. The initiative came from seven pioneers of the Second Aliyah who were working as wage earners at the neighboring farm of *Kinneret and who applied to Arthur *Ruppin to farm a plot of land on their own responsibility. Ruppin decided to accord them a trial period on a part of the lands east of the Jordan named Umm Jūnī. Surprisingly, the experiment succeeded economically, although the group dispersed after a year. It was followed in 1911 by the "Ḥaderah Commune" whose members (pioneers from Russia) worked out the principles of collective settlement (see *Kibbutz movement) and made Deganyah the "Mother of the Kevuẓot." A.D. *Gordon, one of the early members, played an important part in laying the ideological foundations of communal living. In the initial years, the kevuẓah suffered from frequent attacks by Bedouin robbers encamped in the vicinity. After World War I, with the arrival of Third Aliyah immigrants, Deganyah's intensified farming created a need for more hands, but preferring to maintain the frame of the small "family" kevuẓah, the settlers ceded part of the land allocated to them for the establishment of another kevuẓah, which was built in 1920 and named Deganyah Bet. In time, the two settlements further intensified farming and recognized the need, both economic and social, to absorb more members, although they were able to give a part of their land for a third settlement, the kibbutz *Afikim. During the *War of Independence (1948), the Syrian army, having taken neighboring Ẓemaḥ, attempted to continue its advance across the Jordan westward; but on May 20, 1948, it was repulsed by the vigorous defense of Deganyah Alef. One of the Syrian tanks remained stuck in the settlement's perimeter; it remained there as a memorial. In memory of its fallen members, Deganyah laid out Gan ha-Meginnim (The Defenders' Park). In 1968 the two Deganyahs had a combined population of 960, in 2002 around 1,000, equally divided between the two. Both operated intensive, fully irrigated farming (avocado, bananas, date palms, dairy cattle, and poultry) based on the hot climate and abundance of water in the region. Deganyah Alef has operated the Toolgal industrial diamond plant since the early 1970s, while Deganyah Bet operates a guesthouse. The Bet Gordon Museum and Study Center for natural sciences and agriculture is located at Deganyah Alef. Levi *Eshkol and Kadish *Luz were members of Deganyah Bet. Arthur *Ruppin, Otto *Warburg, Leopold *Greenberg, and other personalities are buried at Deganyah Alef, alongside A.D. Gordon, Joseph *Busel, and other founders of the labor settlement movement. In 1981 Deganyah Alef was awarded the Israel Prize for special contribution to Israeli State and society. The name "Deganyah" (Cornflower) is based on the Arab designation of the land, Umm Jūnī, which in turn may have its origin in the village Kefar Gun of talmudic times.

BIBLIOGRAPHY: J. Baratz, *Village by the Jordan* (1954). **WEBSITE:** www.degania.org.il.

[Efraim Orni / Shaked Gilboa (2nd ed.)]

DEGGENDORF, city in Bavaria, Germany. In 1338 local burghers and members of the gentry, under the leadership of the ducal judge, set fire to the houses of the Jewish quarter and slaughtered the inhabitants. Duke Henry sanctioned the massacre by presenting the perpetrators with the Jews' property. As a result, the killing spread to 21 other places in Bavaria. The Deggendorf massacre occurred at a time of severe social unrest, which in previous years had led to waves of anti-Jewish rioting by the *Judenschlaeger* and *Armleder gangs in large parts of southern Germany. The slaughter of the Jews greatly benefited the impoverished townspeople, and a magnificent church was erected in place of the synagogue. Only at a later stage was the allegation of *Host desecration made to justify the massacre of the Jews. From the 15th century, relics of the supposed desecration were venerated in the church, and Deggendorf developed into a major place of pilgrimage in Germany. The last mass pilgrimage took place in 1843; the pictures in the church depicting the affair were covered up in 1967. In 1992 the pilgrimage was at last abolished. The small modern Jewish community (numbering 17 in 1910) was affiliated to that of *Straubing. Of the 500 inmates of the concentration camp established in Deggendorf on February 20, 1945, 400 were Jews. In 1946, 700 Jewish refugees were temporarily accommodated in a transit camp at Deggendorf. There is no postwar community in the city.

BIBLIOGRAPHY: Germ Jud, 2 (1968), 157; Salfed, Martyrol, 241. **ADD. BIBLIOGRAPHY:** M. Eder, *Die 'Deggendorfer Gnad'* (1992).

[Stefan Rohrbacher (2nd ed.)]

DE HAAS, JACOB (1872–1937), author, journalist, and Zionist. De Haas was born in London of Dutch parentage. In 1896, when Theodor *Herzl visited England to secure the support of British Jewry, de Haas, an active Zionist and editor of the *London Jewish World*, became an enthusiastic supporter of Herzlian Zionism. He was appointed "honorary secretary to Dr. Herzl," serving as the latter's spokesman and collaborator in Zionist affairs in Britain. In 1902, at the behest of Herzl, de Haas settled in the United States and was elected secretary of the Federation of American Zionists and editor of *The Maccabean*. Resigning in 1905 because of policy differences with the leadership, de Haas then moved to Boston, where he became publisher of the *Jewish Advocate*. In 1910 he met Louis D. *Brandeis and evoked his interest in Zionism, encouraging him to assume leadership of the Federation. When Brandeis was elected chairman of the Zionist Provisional Emergency Committee in 1914, he appointed de Haas director of its New England bureau. When Brandeis was appointed to the Supreme Court in 1916, de Haas returned to New York as executive secretary of the Committee to interpret and carry out the Brandeis policies. With the establishment of the Zionist Organization of America in 1918, he served as its leader until 1921 when the Brandeis administration was defeated. Subsequently, de Haas headed undertakings for Palestine launched by the Brandeis Zionist groups, including the Palestine Development Council and the Central Committee of the Palestine Development Leagues. In 1930, when the Brandeis faction regained a dominant role in the ZOA, de Haas again assumed command, but resigned within a year, realizing that the Brandeis economic program for Palestine was impractical because of the economic depression. Toward the end of his life he briefly took up the Revisionist cause. De Haas wrote *Theodor Herzl* (1927); *Louis D. Brandeis* (1927); *History of Palestine* (1934), and *The Great Betrayal* (1930, with Stephen *Wise) attacking the British Mandatory Government in Palestine. He edited the *Encyclopedia of Jewish Knowledge* (1934).

BIBLIOGRAPHY: *The New Palestine* (March 26, 1937), 1–3; L. Lipsky, *Gallery of Zionist Profiles* (1956), 166–75; A. Friesel, *Ha-Tenuah ha-Ẓiyyonit be-Arẓot ha-Berit ba-Shanim 1897–1914* (1970), index.

[Herbert Parzen]

DEHOK (**Dihok**), a town in the Iraqi part of Kurdistan. According to the official census of 1930, there were 843 Jews in the entire Dehok region. Their language was the *Aramaic spoken in the mountains, *Jabalī*. They were farmers, artisans, and weavers. The *ḥakhamim* who headed the community included Joseph b. Isaac, who in 1888 completed a book of homilies, and the kabbalist *ḥakham* Elijah Abraham Mizraḥi, who translated Kurdish-Aramaic poems into Hebrew. When the State of Israel was established, the entire community migrated there.

BIBLIOGRAPHY: A. Ben-Jacob, *Kehillot Yehudei Kurdistan* (1961), 56f.; Brawer, in: *Minḥah le-David* (1935), 248; Rivlin, in: *Zion Me'assef*, 4 (1930), 109–21.

[Abraham Haim]

DEINARD, EPHRAIM (1846–1930), bibliographer and Hebrew author. Born in Sasmakken, Latvia, Deinard wandered in his youth, collecting ancient manuscripts and books in many countries, and then established a bookshop in Odessa. In 1897 he tried unsuccessfully to found an agricultural settlement in Nevada (U.S.). An active Zionist, he settled in Palestine in 1913 where he investigated the possibilities of Jewish settlement. After being expelled by the Turks in 1916 he returned to the United States and continued his bibliographical work. His two most noteworthy bibliographical works are *Or Mayer: Catalogue of the Old Hebrew Manuscripts and Printed Books of the Library of the Hon. Mayer Sulzberger of Philadelphia* (1896) and *Koheleth America* (1926), a listing of Hebrew books published in America from 1735 to 1926. The first part of the latter work contains essays on the state of Hebrew literature in America, which are written in his unadorned, but typically acerbic, style. He laid the foundations of the Hebrew book and manuscript collections of the Library of Congress with the financial aid of Jacob *Schiff. A violent polemicist on many controversial subjects, he attacked Reform Judaism, Ḥasidism, Christianity, and Karaism. Deinard was a prolific Hebrew writer, producing more than 50 books and pamphlets often signed with his pseudonym, Adir. These included *Toledot Even Reshef* (1879; a biography of Abraham *Firkovich, whom he knew in the Crimea); *Sefer Massa Krim* (1878; on travels in Crimea); *Massa le-Ereẓ Kedem* (1883; travels in Palestine and Egypt); *Sefer Miflagot be-Yisrael* (1899; on the *Subbotniki* and *Ḥasidim); Zikhronot Bat Ammi* (1920; a history of Russian Jewry over the previous 70 years). He also published several short-lived Hebrew and Yiddish journals, among them *Ha-Le'ummi*, one of the earliest Hebrew periodicals in America.

BIBLIOGRAPHY: S. Berkowitz, "Ephraim Deinard – A Transitional Figure" (thesis, Columbia Univ., 1964); I. Schapiro, in: AJHSP, 34 (1937), 149–63 (incl. bio-bibliography); *Hadoar* (July 25, 1930); Waxman, *Literature*, 3 (1960^2), 599–601; 4 (1960^2), 1299.

[Getzel Kressel]

DEIR (**Dayr**) **AL-BALAḤ**, Arab town in southern Ereẓ Israel, 8½ mi. (13.7 km.) southwest of *Gaza. It appears to have existed since Byzantine times, when it bore the name Darom or Kefar Darom and Jews were among its inhabitants. Under the early caliphates, a fortress was constructed there. It was also a crusader fortress and administrative military center. The castle was described by William of Tyre. Toward the end of the Middle Ages, the place-name was changed to "Deir" (Monastery) with the added designation "al-Balaḥ" ("of Date

Palms"). Date palms still constitute the principal produce of the town, in addition to citrus fruits, almonds, pomegranates, and grapes. The town grew from 1,600 inhabitants in 1945 to 18,000 in 1967, of whom 7,000 lived in the local refugee camp. In 1997 the population increased to 42,839 inhabitants, two-thirds of whom were refugees. The original name was revived in 1946 by the religious kibbutz Kefar Darom, on the town's eastern outskirts, which had to be abandoned in the War of Independence but was reestablished further north in 1970 as *Benei Darom. From 1948 to 1967, it was in the *Gaza Strip under Egyptian control, coming under Israeli control in the Six-Day War and reverting to the *Palestinian Authority in 1994 under the terms of the Declaration of Principles initialed in Oslo and signed in Washington in 1993.

[Efraim Orni]

DEISTS, adherents of a rationalist movement that arose in the 17th and 18th centuries as an attempt to explain the Bible and create a theology based on the rules of logic and the sciences. Deism arose in the middle of the 17th century out of the rationalist criticism of the past, and especially the religious past, which had been one element of the thinking of the Renaissance and the Reformation. It was also a result of the inevitable de-emphasis on the uniqueness of Christian Europe and its special revelation, as corollary to increasing scientific and geographical discovery, which emphasized the multiplicity of cultures and man's reason and power. The Englishman who founded Deism, Lord Herbert of Cherbury (1583–1648), made the fundamental distinction between "natural religion" and the various positive faiths, which were judged by its standards (*De Religione Gentilium*, 1663). In 1670 Baruch *Spinoza published in Amsterdam his *Tractatus theologico-politicus…* (Treatise on Religious and Political Philosophy) which subjected the Bible and even the New Testament to criticism in the name of universal principles of reason and morality available to any man by his very nature. In this debate about the Bible, others and especially Pierre Bayle (1647–1706), in articles such as his famous *Dictionnaire Historique et Critique* (Rotterdam, 1697), helped establish as a first principle of the European Enlightenment not only that the Bible was not unique but that indeed it was morally and culturally inferior and obnoxious.

In England the immediate followers of Lord Herbert argued on the grounds of comparative religion, a discipline of which they were the founders, that the basic customs of Judaism had been taken over from the Egyptians. This question, whether the Jews had taught the Egyptians or the Egyptians had taught the Jews, had been at issue in antiquity between Hellenistic Jewish writers and such of their detractors as *Manetho. Learned men such as John Spencer (1630–1693) argued against the originality of the Jews and used all the remarks in the sacred literature of both Jews and Christians that attacked the "stiff-neckedness" of the biblical Jews to paint them in the most negative colors and to suggest that their laws were a punishment visited upon them (*De legibus Hebraeorum ritualibus et earum rationibus*, Cambridge, 1685). The sources in classic antiquity of this negative estimate of the biblical Jews are even more pronounced in the work of Charles Blount (1654–1693), who renewed the ancient charge of Greco-Roman antisemites that the Jews had been expelled from Egypt as lepers. Anthony Ashley Cooper, third Earl of Shaftesbury (1671–1713), declared that the Jews "were naturally a very cloudy people" (*Characteristics of Men, Manners, Opinions, Times*, 1 (London, 1711), 29); "they had certainly in Religion, as in everything else, the least Good Humor of any People in the world" (*ibid.*, 3 (1711), 116).

The attack on the credibility of the Bible and the character of the Jews was continued in England in the 18th century by such figures as Anthony Collins (1676–1729), who, in his *Discourse of Free-Thinking* (1713), devastated the belief in biblical prophecy and repeated that the Jews were "such an illiterate, barbarous, and ridiculous people," "crossgrained brutes," in dealing with whom God had to "use craft rather than reason" (*ibid.*, 157). Such opinions were held by most of the other spokesmen of Deism in England, including Thomas Chubb (1679–1747), Thomas Morgan (d. 1743), and Peter Annet (1693–1769). They were repeated by Henry St. John, first Viscount Bolingbroke (1678–1751), the English Deist by whom *Voltaire pretended to be most influenced. The judgment of this whole school of thought was given by its most redoubtable figure in the 18th century, Matthew Tindal (c. 1655–1733). In his *Christianity as Old as the Creation* (1730) the Jews are no longer depicted as being merely ignorant and barbaric; he suggests that human sacrifice was part of their religion and that the immorality of utterly destroying the Canaanites was indicative of their true character.

All of these attacks were leveled at the biblical Jews, and their function was primarily to discredit Christianity, but this Deistic criticism of the Bible had important effects on enlightened thinking about the estate of the contemporary Jew. The century of Enlightenment, and especially the Deistic believers in universal laws of nature, held that human character was continuous, and the Jews of today were therefore as their ancestors were held to have been. English Deistic thinking had substantial influence on the most important intellectual figure of the 18th century, Voltaire, and on such other figures as Nicolas Freret (1688–1749) and Baron Paul d'*Holbach. A post-Christian seemingly rational and historical outlook in the name of which Jews could be despised was thus defined. Even on Deistic foundations anti-Jewish conclusions were not the only possible ones. John Locke was not a Deist, but he was close to such figures as Bayle, he was the tutor of Bolingbroke in his youth, and Anthony Collins regarded himself as Locke's disciple. As early as 1689 Locke, in his *Letter Concerning Toleration*, had announced that no one, not even a Jew, "ought to be excluded from the civil rights of the Commonwealth because of his religion." Locke was followed in these pro-Jewish views by his Deistic disciple John *Toland, who accepted the opinion that Mosaic legislation was borrowed from the Egyptians, but that did not prevent him from arguing that the Code of Moses was the ideal civil constitution and that because of it the Jews had withstood their long exile to the present. Toland knew Jews personally, and as early as 1714 he published a work entitled *Reasons for Naturalizing the Jews in Great Britain and Ireland on the same foot with all other Nations, Containing also a Defence of the Jews against all vulgar Prejudices in all Countries*. Five years later, in *Nazarenus* (London, 1718, Appendix 1), he suggested, in one of the early "Zionist" statements, that the powers of the world ought to help restore the Jews to their own land. It was thus possible to see virtue in the ancient Jews and regard what was wrong with the modern ones as created by the persecution which had been visited upon them and hence to suggest that a change in their conditions would uncover the same universal human nature which is common to all men. This was the view of men such as Gotthold Ephraim *Lessing, the leading German Deist and man of letters in his time, and of a wide variety of people such as Comte de *Mirabeau the Younger, who helped create the atmosphere for the *emancipation of the Jews in France by the *French Revolution. The other opinion, that the character of the Jews was lasting and incorrigible, was the legacy of Deistic biblical criticism, especially in its recension by Voltaire, to modern secular antisemitism. With few exceptions, notably that of Toland, no one who followed Deism, or was seriously influenced by 17th–18th century rationalistic and critical currents, had any doubt that the Jews as they had been molded needed to be freed of their characteristics and traditions in order to join universal culture (which, despite its universalist self-image, was then really a Western classicizing paganism).

BIBLIOGRAPHY: S. Ettinger, in: *Zion*, 29 (1964), 182–207; L. Poliakov, *Histoire de l'antisémitisme*, 3 (1968), 73–85; A. Hertzberg, *French Enlightenment and the Jews* (1968); N.L. Torrey (ed. and tr.), *Voltaire and the Enlightenment* (1931); L. Stephen, *History of English Thought in the Eighteenth Century*, 2 vols. (1876, 1962^{4}).

[Arthur Hertzberg]

DEJ (Hung. **Dés**), town in central Transylvania, N. Romania; until the end of World War I and from 1940–44 within Hungary. In 1638 Dej became known through its connection with the history of the Transylvanian Sabbatarians (Judaizers). Although Jews were officially prohibited from living in Dej until 1848, by 1805 there were already 70 Jewish residents. Jewish settlement in Dej began in 1834; previously they had been allowed to live only in a few of the surrounding villages. After 1848 many immigrants from Galicia settled in Dej who made up the majority of the community which remained Orthodox with a strong ḥasidic following. The majority spoke Yiddish as well as Hungarian (and some also Romanian). Communal life was organized around the 1850s. Members of the *Panet family served as rabbis of Dej from the beginning of the community's establishment to its end in the Holocaust. The first synagogue was built in 1863 and another opened in 1907, beside many other synagogues and yeshivot. A state Jewish elementary school was established in 1884, remaining open until 1938; the language of instruction was Hungarian and Yiddish until 1919 and subsequently Romanian and Yiddish. Zionist organizations were active from 1918. Attempts to bring out periodicals in Yiddish, Hungarian, and even Hebrew proved short-lived. The physician Nathan Friedlaender (1819–1902) settled in Dej in 1864. Meir Jehuda Majrovitz (1895–1944), the Hungarian writer, was born in Dej. Also connected to the city is the well-known Holocaust historian Randolph *Braham, who lived there and was sent to forced labor during World War II.

The change of regime of 1919 – when the Hungarians were replaced by the Romanians – caused significant changes in the life of the local Jews, mostly for those strongly assimilated to Hungarian culture and language. They had to accustom themselves to the new antisemitism brought in by the Romanian authorities. However, the Jews tried hard to adapt to the new conditions and survive. More difficult to understand was the new situation after 1940, when the Hungarian Horthiite authorities who returned to Dej turned out to be quite different from those they had known and gotten along with before 1919; the disappointment was to be very severe.

The community numbered 3,360 in 1930 (22.2% of the total population), and 3,719 (22.8%) in 1941. During World War II, the Jews were subjected to many restrictions. Jewish males were mobilized for forced labor; a number of families who could not prove their citizenship were rounded up in the summer of 1941 and deported to Kamenets-Podolski, where they were murdered. In early May 1944 the remaining Jews were placed in a ghetto set up in a forest (the Bungur), located about two miles from the city. The ghetto was liquidated with the deportation of the Jews to Auschwitz in three transports between May 28 and June 8, 1944.

The survivors who returned, with Jews from other places, numbered approximately 1,000 in 1947. The community subsequently dwindled through emigration, many leaving for Israel. In 2004 there were fewer than ten Jews there.

BIBLIOGRAPHY: Z. Singer, *Dés*, 1 (Hung., 1970).

[Yehouda Marton / Paul Schveiger and Randolph Braham (2nd ed.)]

DE KLERK, MICHEL (1884–1923), Dutch architect. Born in Amsterdam, De Klerk became a leader of the architectural movement known as the "Amsterdam School." This school, which flourished from early in the century to the mid-1920s, proclaimed the beauty of unadorned materials and surfaces. Individual idiosyncrasy was encouraged, resulting in a rich variety of forms, and an Expressionist idiom was evolved, comparable to that developed in Germany during the same period.

The Amsterdam School became widely known through a series of low-cost housing projects. From 1911 onward De Klerk was engaged in designing workers' houses for the Eigen Haard Estate in the suburb of Amsterdam-Oost. The housing blocks were horizontal in emphasis, broken by sudden verticals, echoing the Dutch landscape. The use of brickwork created a richness of texture. Other features were the strangely shaped roofs with curious projections and whimsical details such as corner oriels in the shape of barrels. Despite the element of fantasy, the total effect of the scheme was quiet and controlled with a human warmth rare in the workers' housing schemes of the period.

BIBLIOGRAPHY: H.R. Hitchcock, *Architecture, 19th and 20th centuries* (1958), 357–9; Roth, Art, 734–5; R. Banham, *Guide to Modern Architecture* (1962), 53–56.

DELACRUT, MATTATHIAS BEN SOLOMON (mid-16th century), kabbalist and astronomer, born in Poland. In 1550 he went to Italy where he studied mathematics, natural sciences, astronomy, and Kabbalah in Bologna.

His works are (1) A commentary on Solomon b. Avigdor's Hebrew translation of Sacrobosco's *Tractatus de sphaera*, or *Aspectus circulorum* (*Marei Ofannim* or *Asfira ha-Gadol*, Offenbach, 1720), in which he made use of the Latin text and corrected the translation in several places. (2) *Ẓel ha-Olam* (Amsterdam, 1733), a translation of Gossouin's *Le Livre de Clergie* or *L'Image du Monde*, a treatise on astronomy and the natural sciences. On the title page Delacrut is named as the author; in his introduction he writes that this is the work of a gentile scholar which he has translated into Hebrew because of his zeal for Judaism. Some scholars believe that the work should be attributed to Ḥayyim Delacrut, a London rabbi, whose name was altered by the publisher to the better-known one of Mattathias Delacrut; others hold that Mattathias was either translator or editor. (3) A commentary on Joseph *Gikitilla's kabbalistic work *Sha'arei Orah* published posthumously by Delacrut's son Joseph (Cracow, 1600); Delacrut describes this work as eclectic but rather it is a popular exposition of kabbalist doctrines according to his individual interpretation. (4) A commentary on **Ma'arekhet ha-Elohut* (in Ms.). (5) A commentary on *Recanati (in Ms.), which Mordecai *Jaffe used in his commentary on Recanati, *Levushei Or Yekarot* (Lublin, 1595).

Delacrut was mainly absorbed in theoretical Kabbalah; at the core of his thinking lies the customary kabbalistic complex of questions concerning God, the Creation, and the relation of man to God. Man was created to serve the Creator, but not the contrary. Before the world was created, everything that was existed in the keeping of divine darkness. God accomplished the Creation by the agency of the *Sefirot*, which had always been a part of his essence and thus, in the act of creation, simply passed from the latent to the manifest plane. God created man in his own image; the soul of man acts in his body in the same way that God's qualities act in the world. The dualism of soul and body does not exist in man only but is present in the whole material world. Man stands at the median between the upper and lower world; he possesses free will and the power to decide between good or evil. Through purity of body and soul, man tries to approach nearer to God.

BIBLIOGRAPHY: Renan, Rabbins, 508; Guedemann, Gesch Erz, 1 (1880), 86; Steinschneider, Uebersetzungen, 590, 644; idem, *Sifrut Yisrael* (1897), 285; Ḥ.N. Dembitzer, *Kelilat Yofi*, 1 (1888), 27b, notes; Horodezky, Ḥasidut, 1 (1953[4]), xxv–xxvii (introd.).

[Samuel Abba Horodezky]

DE LA MOTTA, JACOB (1789–1845), antebellum southern U.S. physician. De la Motta was born in Savannah, Georgia. After getting a medical degree at the University of Pennsylvania in 1810 at the age of 21, he practiced in Charleston, South Carolina, until the outbreak of the War of 1812. Volunteering his services, De la Motta was commissioned as a surgeon in the U.S. Army. After the war he practiced in New York City and became an active Freemason, initiating his career as a leader in the medical, scientific, fraternal, political, cultural, and Jewish religious life of his times. In 1818 De la Motta set up practice in Savannah, where he did research on yellow fever, was active in politics, and continued his interest in Masonry. De la Motta returned to Charleston (1823), where he became a leading physician. He served as secretary of the Medical Society of South Carolina for ten years, as a trustee of the State Medical College, as assistant commissioner of health, and as physician for several public institutions. He set up a famous pharmacy called "Apothecaries Hall" and helped revise the *Pharmacopeia of the United States of America* (1830[2]). A Whig dissenter from the dominant nullification politics of antebellum Charleston, De la Motta ran for Congress but lost. President Harrison, whom he supported, appointed him receiver general for South Carolina in 1841. He achieved the highest Masonic office in Scottish Rite as grand commander of the Supreme Council (1844). Strongly Orthodox, De la Motta was a leading opponent of reform in Beth Elohim's ritual during the 1840s. He was a founder of the breakaway Orthodox congregation, Shearith Israel, and its first president.

BIBLIOGRAPHY: T.J. Tobias, in: *The Jewish Experience in America*, 2 (1969), 64–81.

[Thomas J. Tobias]

DELAUNAY-TERK, SONIA (1885–1979), French painter and fashion designer. She was born in Russia and in 1906 settled in Paris. In 1910 she married the painter Robert Delaunay. Her bold use of strong primary color was only fully revealed after 1912, when she and her husband invented a form of abstract painting known as "Orphism." This was based on "simultaneous color contrasts," often expressed in their paintings by circles of contrasting hues. Their innovation had a profound effect on the applied arts, including fashion, architecture, furnishings, and the theater. She illustrated books and became a celebrated designer of fabrics, scarves, and dresses.

BIBLIOGRAPHY: National Gallery of Canada, *Robert and Sonia Delaunay* (1965), exhibition catalog with introd. by B. Dorival.

DELAWARE, U.S. state located on the Middle Atlantic seaboard. The first to ratify the United States constitution in 1787, it is the state with the second smallest land mass and the sixth smallest population. In 2001, some 13,500 Jews lived in the state and accounted for 1.7 percent of the Delaware population.

Although Jewish fur traders were in the territory that became Delaware as early as 1655, only a handful of Jews, including Jacob Fiana, Abraham Judah, and Jacob and Daniel Solis,

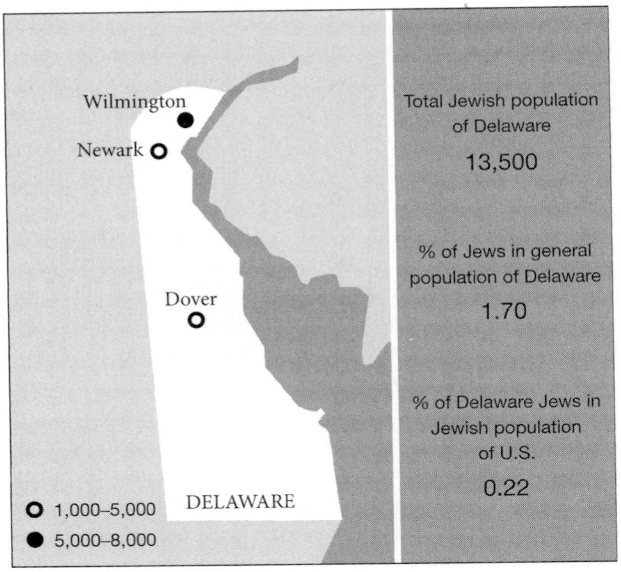

Jewish communities in Delaware. Population figures for 2001.

settled in the area before the middle of the 19th century when Jewish retailers from families in Philadelphia and Baltimore began opening stores in Wilmington. In 1879, 18 Jewish merchants formed Delaware's first Jewish organization, the Moses Montefiore Society, as a religious, educational, and charitable organization. Delaware became the last of the original colonies to have an organized Jewish community and worship services for the High Holidays.

Given Wilmington's prosperity and the influx of Jews from Eastern Europe, the Jewish population of Wilmington grew quickly reaching some 4,000 by 1920. The Jews formed numerous service organizations, including the Young Men's Hebrew Association (today's JCC), the Hebrew Charity Association (today's Jewish Family Service), and the Bichor Cholem Society (today's Kutz Home). By 1929, they had established three Orthodox synagogues, Adas Kodesch, Chesed Shel Emeth, and Machzikey Hadas; a Reform synagogue, Temple Beth Emeth; and a Conservative synagogue, Congregation Beth Sholom. These organizations and synagogues (Adas Kodesch and Chesed Shel Emeth merged in 1957) continued to serve the Wilmington population in 2005. Chabad-Lubavitch began conducting Sabbath services and educational activities in Wilmington and Newark in 1987.

A few Jewish students attended Delaware College, today's University of Delaware, at the end of the 19th century, but Jews did not settle in the college town of Newark until the early 20th century. The Hillel Foundation began activities at the university by 1948. In the early 21st century Hillel served some 800 students a year. The Newark Jewish Community, later known as Temple Beth El, the state's only Reconstructionist synagogue, was organized in 1954.

In the mid-19th century, a small number of Jewish retailers opened businesses in Dover, the state capital, and in several towns in southern Delaware. Jewish growth in the area was slower than in Wilmington, but by the early 20th century, Jewish retailers, peddlers, canners, distillers, and hotelkeepers lived in many towns of southern Delaware including Dover, Lewes, Georgetown, Milford, Millsboro, Seaford, and Smyrna. In 1897, with the aid of HIAS, the Isaac Benioff family settled in Kent County, becoming Delaware's first Jewish farmers. The Jewish Agriculture Society helped an additional 24 Jewish families establish farms in southern Delaware, primarily in Kent County, between 1912 and 1929. Religious services were held informally in homes until 1939 when the Jewish Congregation of Lower Delaware, a predecessor of today's Conservative synagogue, Congregation Beth Shalom, was incorporated.

In 1997, Jewish vacationers and retirees from Philadelphia, Baltimore, Washington, and Wilmington along with Jews from Lewes, Rehoboth, and the surrounding Delaware beach communities formed the Seaside Jewish Community. The group, which numbered more than 150 families in 2005, held religious services, educational programs including a Hebrew school, and social events.

Throughout the 20th century, most Delaware Jews continued to live in the Wilmington area, the focal point of Jewish life in Delaware. One Jewish federation, located in Wilmington, served the entire state. However, by the end of the 20th century, the demographics had shifted. A 1995 study estimated that 56% of Delaware's Jews lived in the Wilmington area, 32% in the Newark-Hockessin area, and 12% in southern Delaware.

Jews have become an integral part of life in all parts of the state. They have contributed to the arts, science, business, medicine, journalism, law, and public service. Irving *Shapiro became CEO of the Dupont Company in 1973 and chair of the Business Roundtable in 1976, Roxana Arsht became Delaware's first female judge in 1971, Daniel Herrmann became chief justice of the Delaware Supreme Court in 1973, and Jack Markell was Delaware's state treasurer in 2005.

BIBLIOGRAPHY: Ukeles Associates, Inc., *1995 Jewish Population Study of Delaware, Summary Report*; T. Young, *Becoming American, Remaining Jewish: The Story of Wilmington, Delaware's First Jewish Community 1879–1924* (1999); D. Geffen, *Jewish Delaware 1655–1976: History, Sites and Communal Services* (1976); T. Young (ed.), *Delaware and the Jews* (1979).

[Toni Young (2nd ed.)]

DEL BANCO, ANSELMO (**Asher Levi Meshullam**; d. 1532), head of the Jewish community in Venice. Owner of several loan-banks in the Venetian territories, Anselmo took refuge in Venice (from which the Jews had been hitherto excluded) when Padua was sacked by troops of the League of the Cambrai in 1509. From then on he acted as spokesman for Venetian Jewry and was largely responsible for securing rights of residence and taxation. He represented the community also in 1516 when the senate decided to establish a ghetto. He was also involved with the Jewish community of Jerusalem, sending money and helping those who sailed there from Venice.

He also corresponded with the famous kabbalist *Abraham ha-Levi of Jerusalem on messianic subjects, and his son Shimon covered the expenses of David *Reuveni in Venice. His daughter Diamant was married to Jehiel da Pisa.

His brother VITA (Hayyim) was also a wealthy banker and philanthropist. The family members were proprietors of one of the seven Venetian synagogues, known as the Scuola Meshulamim. Some of their descendants settled in Hamburg and were among the ancestors of the *Warburg family.

BIBLIOGRAPHY: N. Porgès, in: REJ, 77 (1923), 20–40; 78 (1924), 15–34; C. Roth, *Venice* (1930), 40–58, 141, 203; M. Sanuto, *Diarii* (1879–), indices. **ADD. BIBLIOGRAPHY:** A. David, in: *Shalem*, 6 (1992), 319–33 (Heb.); S. Simonsohn and M. Benayahu, *Seder Eliyahu Zuta*, 2 (1977), 215–327; B. Pullan, *Rich and Poor in Renaissance Venice* (1971), 479–88.

[Giorgio Romano / Moti Benmelech (2nd ed.)]

DEL BENE (Heb. מָה טוֹב, *Mah Tov*), **ELIEZER DAVID BEN ISAAC** (d. 1635), rabbinical author, born in Mantua. In his youth Del Bene won popularity as a preacher in the local synagogue; however, he provoked fierce opposition by frequently quoting Italian poets in his sermons and as a result was forced to retire from the pulpit. He then turned to talmudic studies, instructed by Menahem Azariah da *Fano, later becoming a member of the yeshivah of *Ferrara where he lived for 36 years until his death. His work *Ir David*, responsa, sermons, and novellae, remained unpublished.

BIBLIOGRAPHY: Kaufmann, in: JQR, 8 (1896), 513–24.

[Umberto (Moses David) Cassuto]

DEL BENE, JUDAH ASAHEL BEN DAVID ELIEZER (1615?–1678), rabbi and scholar who lived in Ferrara. Del Bene was considered by Isaac *Lampronti as one of the great talmudists of his time. He was the author of *Kisot le-Veit David* (Verona, 1646), a philosophical work in which he upheld basic Jewish teachings in the face of philosophical criticism. In the preface to *Kisot*, the author quotes from another, poetical work of his, *Yehudah Meḥokeki*.

BIBLIOGRAPHY: Wolf, Bibliotheca, 1 (1715), 452; G.B. de Rossi, *Dizionario Storico…*, 1 (1802), 98; Ghirondi-Neppi, 123; Zunz, in: *Liebermanns "Deutscher Volkskalender"* (1853), 67; F. Delitzsch, *Zur Geschichte der juedischen Poesie* (1836), 71; Steinschneider, Cat Bod, 1343–44; A. Pesaro, *Memorie storiche sulta comunità israelitica ferrarese* (1878), 48; Fuenn, Keneset, 411; Mortara, Indice, index.

DE LEE, JOSEPH B. (1869–1942), U.S. obstetrician and gynecologist. De Lee was professor of obstetrics and gynecology first at Northwestern University and later at the University of Chicago. He designed over 20 new obstetric instruments, the most important of which was the stethoscope to locate the easiest place for checking the heartbeat of the fetus. He also introduced the use of educational films to aid in teaching obstetrics. De Lee wrote three books which became standard texts in the field of obstetrics: *Notes on Obstetrics* (1904), *Obstetrics for Nurses* (1904; ten editions), and *Principles and Practice of Obstetrics* (1913; 11 editions). He also wrote numerous articles and monographs in his field. De Lee was the founder of the Chicago Lying-in Hospital and Dispensary and of the Chicago Maternity Center.

BIBLIOGRAPHY: S.R. Kagan, *Jewish Medicine* (1952), 482.

[Suessmann Muntner]

DE LEON, prominent early American Sephardi family.

DAVID CAMDEN DE LEON (1816–1872), first surgeon general of the Confederate Army, was born in Camden, South Carolina, eldest of three sons of MORDECAI H. DE LEON (1791–1848), a physician. David followed his father's profession, graduating from the University of Pennsylvania Medical School in 1836. He entered the U.S. Army as an assistant surgeon in 1838, serving in Florida during the Seminole War and then in frontier posts in the West. During the Mexican War De Leon was assigned to the invading American forces, entering Mexico City when it surrendered to General Scott. De Leon was twice cited for gallantry in action, gaining the sobriquet "the Fighting Doctor." In 1856 he was promoted to full surgeon with the rank of major. With the advent of the Civil War, De Leon, after considerable wrestling with his conscience, resigned from the U.S. Army and offered his services to the Confederacy. On May 6, 1861, he was appointed the first surgeon general of the Confederate Army but held the post only a few weeks. De Leon later served in Florida, Alabama, and Louisiana, and was named medical director of the army of Northern Virginia under General Lee, but resigned after a month. He has been characterized as an "unhappy and frustrated" man. After the war De Leon took refuge in Mexico and then returned to New Mexico, where he had been stationed and where he owned property. He planted, and also practiced private medicine until his death in Santa Fe. De Leon never married and is said to have ignored his Jewish origins.

EDWIN DE LEON (1828–1891), journalist, diplomat, Confederate agent, author, brother of David, was born in Charleston, South Carolina. Graduating from South Carolina College (now the University of South Carolina), De Leon became a journalist, and served as editor of several newspapers, including the Savannah *Republican*, the Columbia (S.C.) *Daily Telegraph*, and the Washington, D.C., *Southern Press*. In all of these he strongly advocated the institution of Negro slavery in the South. De Leon worked hard to help elect Franklin Pierce as president, and was rewarded by appointment as American consul general in Egypt, where he served ably for eight years under both Pierce and Buchanan. With the Civil War he resigned and reported to his old friend Jefferson Davis, who appointed him a confidential agent of the Confederate state department to stir up public opinion in Europe for the Confederate cause, and was given $25,000 to spend especially with the press. De Leon held no official title, representing himself as a "private citizen." His propaganda efforts failed to influence opinion in England and France, and his "gratuitous services" were ended in 1862. After the war De Leon was a freelance writer in New York. Later he returned to Egypt to live, and was involved in the installation of the Bell telephone system in Egypt about 1880. De Leon spoke and wrote on Egypt and the new South. His books include his memoirs, *Thirty Years of My Life on Three Continents* (1878), and *The Khedive's Egypt* (1878). He was buried in a Catholic cemetery in New York.

THOMAS COOPER DE LEON (1839–1914), author and editor, brother of David and Edwin, was born in Columbia, South Carolina. After attending Georgetown University, De Leon worked as a clerk in the bureau of typographical engineers in Washington. He served in the Confederate Army during the Civil War, apparently in the Confederate capitals, Montgomery and Richmond. His social and military observations were later the basis for a book, *Four Years in Rebel Capitals* (1890). After the war he edited *Cosmopolitan Magazine* in Baltimore, translated French novels, and wrote freelance articles. In 1868 he went to Mobile as managing editor (after 1877 editor) of the *Mobile Register*. In addition to his editorial work, De Leon was a versatile writer, poet, novelist, essayist, and playwright. His best-known book, Civil War reminiscences, was *Belles, Beaux and Brains of the '60s* (1907). He wrote a successful burlesque play which ran in New York, two parody plays, and two local-color novels. Although blind for the last 11 years of his life, De Leon remained active.

BIBLIOGRAPHY: DAVID CAMDEN: B.A. Elzas, *Jews of South Carolina* (1905), 271–3 and passim; S. Kagan, *Jewish Contributions to Medicine in America* (1934), 3, 43–44; J. Waring, *History of Medicine in South Carolina*, 2 (1967), 220–1; H. Simonhoff, *Jewish Participants in the Civil War* (1963), 229–31; *Appleton's Cyclopaedia of American Biography*, 2 (1888), 135. EDWIN: H.K. Hennig, "Edwin De Leon" (Thesis, University of South Carolina, 1928); C.P. Cullop, in: *Civil War History*, 8 (1962), 386–400; Edwin De Leon, manuscript papers and letters at University of South Carolina Library, Columbia, S.C. THOMAS COOPER: Wade, in: DAB, 5 (1930) 224.

[Thomas J. Tobias]

DE LEON, DANIEL (1852–1914), U.S. socialist leader. De Leon, who was born in Curaçao, Dutch West Indies, claimed descent from aristocratic, Spanish-Catholic stock. However, it is generally accepted as beyond doubt that he came from a Jewish family. He studied in Europe and went to New York in 1872. De Leon did not become concerned with labor matters until 1886, but by 1890 he had joined the Socialist Labor Party. From 1892 to his death, he edited the party's weekly *The People*, and from 1900 to 1914, the *Daily People*, becoming the single most important figure in the organization. De Leon vigorously rejected any compromise with the capitalist system, and attacked trade union leaders and socialists who were prepared to concentrate on the immediate demands of workers as enemies of the working class. He argued that only a minority would have the determination and spirit to lead the workers to Socialism, and this was the role that he assigned to the Socialist Labor Party. All who disagreed were forced from the party or left after bitter battles with De Leon. De Leon maintained that both political action and industrial unionism were necessary to spark revolutionary sentiments in the American worker. Until 1905 he laid heavy stress on political action through the Socialist Labor Party, but also organized the Socialist Trade and Labor Alliance in 1895 to provide a radical Socialist alternative to the American Federation of Labor. In 1905 De Leon helped organize the Industrial Workers of the World (IWW). At this time he placed increased emphasis on industrial unionism as a revolutionary tool. However, De Leon rejected the IWW's repudiation of political action in 1908, and he left that organization to form a rival group. Despite all disappointments, De Leon tirelessly insisted on the eventual victory of Socialism and the ultimate vindication of his methods and ideology.

BIBLIOGRAPHY: Mc-Kee, in: *Labor History*, 1 (1960), 264–97; A. Peterson, *Daniel De Leon*, 2 vols. (1941–53).

[Irwin Yellowitz]

DELFONT, BERNARD, LORD (1909–1994), British theatrical manager. Born in Russia, the son of Isaac Winogradsky, he grew up in England and entered theater management in 1941. He subsequently managed many West End theaters and controlled 30 companies with theatrical, film, television, music, and property interests. Delfont became particularly well known for organizing many Royal Variety Performances, the first in 1958. He was awarded a life peerage in Harold Wilson's resignation Honours List in 1976. He was the brother of Lord *Grade.

ADD. BIBLIOGRAPHY: B. Delfont with B. Turner, *East End, West End* (1990); ODNB online.

DE LIEME, NEHEMIA (1882–1940), Dutch Zionist. Born in The Hague, the son of a *shoḥet*, De Lieme was largely self-taught, mainly in the field of actuarial mathematics and economics. In 1904 he was one of the founders of the *Centrale Arbeiders Verzekeringsbank, the first Dutch workers' insurance company and bank. Legally still a minor, he became director of the bank, which largely due to him flourished after a difficult start, until his death. Although the Centrale was essentially a social democratic affair, De Lieme was throughout his life a convinced social liberal, at the same time emotionally involved with social problems and coolly business-like in the implementation of their solutions. He had great talent for organization. De Lieme joined the Zionist movement during the Zionist Congress in The Hague (1907). In 1912, after a crisis when its founder Jacobus *Kann endorsed Zionist propaganda among Christians, he became chairman of the Nederlandse Zionistenbond (NZB), the Dutch Zionist Federation. In 1914, when *Jewish National Fund headquarters were moved from Cologne to The Hague, De Lieme became its director. Because he managed the affairs of the JNF well through the difficult war years, he became a member of the Zionist Executive in London in 1920 and was one of the three members of the Zionist Reorganization Commission, which visited Palestine to report on the state of the Jewish settlements. While pioneers proudly wished to show their cattle and fields, De Lieme buried himself in their accounts and cemented his image as an unfeeling bookkeeper. He was highly critical of the financial management of the settlements, especially the delivery of subsidies without looking into the actual needs and into what he considered sound accounting. When the Executive in 1921 purchased the Jezreel Valley against his advice, he resigned. De Lieme's main objections were that the price of the Emek would inflate the land prices in Palestine and that *PICA already was negotiating with the owners about a purchase. With Jacobus *Kann and Siegfried *Van Vriesland, De Lieme now formed the "Hague Opposition," whose sentiments against *Weizmann's policies were shared by the *Brandeis Group in the United States: too much propaganda and bureaucracy, too little attention to the productiveness of Zionist enterprises in Palestine. For De Lieme especially the post-Balfour policy of engaging the whole Jewish and also the non-Jewish world in the building of the National Home meant a betrayal of Zionist principles. Though criticism of this opposition was largely shared by many Zionist figures in private, the Hague Opposition led a losing battle in the dynamics of the post-Balfour period, when the weak Zionist movement and scant Zionist funds required a good deal of political window dressing. De Lieme's standing within the NZB remained high despite only a brief chairmanship in 1924. He would strongly influence the Dutch Federation until 1940 in its criticism of Weizmann's policies, especially the establishment of the *Keren Hayesod and the *Jewish Agency, also later the immigration of Jewish refugees into Palestine, as would one of his successors, Fritz *Bernstein. In 1938 De Lieme, while he and his family already were preparing to immigrate to Palestine, publicly resigned from the Zionist Organization in protest against the Executive's decision to negotiate with the British Government on the partition of Palestine. From 1934 he took a great interest, financially and personally, in founding the International Institute for Social History in Amsterdam and in enabling it to purchase valuable archival material. De Lieme died shortly after the German invasion of Holland.

BIBLIOGRAPHY: *De Joodse Wachter* (June, 1952), special issue in memoriam; incl. bibl.; L. Giebels, *De zionistische beweging in Nederland 1899–1941* (1975); J.L.J.M. van Gerwen, *De Centrale Centraal. Geschiedenis van de NV De Centrale Arbeiders- en Verzekerings- en Deposito-Bank vanaf de oprichting in 1904 tot aan de fusie in de Reaal Groep in 1990* (1993).

[Ludy Giebels (2nd ed.)]

DELILAH (Heb. דְּלִילָה), a woman from the Valley of Sorek who was *Samson's mistress and who betrayed him to his enemies (Judg. 16:4ff.). The Philistine city kings offered her a handsome bribe to entice Samson to reveal the secret of his great strength. After three unsuccessful attempts, she finally induced her lover to disclose that it was his adherence to the Nazirite abstention from cutting the hair (cf. Judg. 13:5) of his head that made him so exceptional. She thereupon induced Samson to sleep, had him shorn of his long hair, and handed him over to the Philistines, who blinded and incarcerated him. The biblical narrative does not make it clear whether Delilah was herself a Philistine. It does not suggest that she was married to Samson, or that she was treacherously motivated from the first. The meaning of the name Delilah is uncertain. Two of the more plausible explanations are (1) "temptress," deriving, as does the parallel Safaitic name *Dllt*, from the Arabic root *dll*, meaning "to entice"; (2) a shortened theophoric name, akin to the Akkadian name Dalîl (or Dilîl) Ishtar, meaning "praises [or "majesty"] of Ishtar."

[Nahum M. Sarna]

In the *Aggadah*

The name Delilah is connected by the rabbis with *dalal* דלל ("to enfeeble") because "she enfeebled Samson's strength, she enfeebled his actions, and she enfeebled his determination" (Num. R. 9:24). To wrest his secret from him she disengaged herself from him at the moment of sexual consummation (Sot. 9b). She realized that Samson was finally telling the truth when he said: "I have been a Nazarene unto God" (Judg. 16:17), because she knew that he would not take the Lord's name in vain (Num. R. *ibid.*).

For Delilah in the arts, see *Samson.

DE LIMA, JOSEPH SUASSO (1791–1858), South African writer and journalist. Member of an Amsterdam family of Portuguese origin, he qualified in law, wrote for Amsterdam publishers, and in 1816 went on a government mission to Batavia. In 1818 he settled at the Cape as printer, publisher, and translator (of Hebrew, among other languages). One of the early South African literary figures to use Dutch, he wrote poems, plays, pamphlets, almanacs, and directories. His versatility and his lameness were both butts for the enemies he made in various controversies. He defended the form of colloquial Dutch spoken at the Cape, opened the first Dutch bookshop in South Africa, and ran the first weekly paper, the satirical *De Versamelaar*, for several years from 1825. His *Gedichten* appeared in Amsterdam in 1821; his *Nieuwe Gedichten* in 1840. In 1825 he published his brief *Geschiedenis van de Kaap de Goede Hoop*, the first manual of Cape history. De Lima joined the Dutch Reformed Church in 1833, but made a donation to the building fund of the first Cape synagogue in 1849.

BIBLIOGRAPHY: L. Herrman, *History of the Jews in South Africa* (1935), 94–97; Nienaber, in: *Jewish Affairs*, 7 (Johannesburg, 1952), 12–16.

°**DELITZSCH, FRANZ** (**Julius**; 1813–1890), German Protestant theologian, Bible and Judaica scholar. Inspired by Julius *Fuerst to devote himself to the study of Judaism, he was appointed professor of theology at the university of his native Leipzig in 1844. Later he taught at Rostock (1846), Erlangen (1850), and again in Leipzig (1867). Though Delitzsch was a devoted Christian and the most significant figure of the Lutheran "Mission to the Jews," believing in the supremacy of the New Testament over the Old, he maintained an extraordinary understanding of, and affection for, Judaism. Well versed in Hebrew and in Semitic languages, as well as in the Talmud and in medieval Jewish literature, Delitzsch was in close touch with the leading Jewish scholars of his time. As a devout Christian, he proselytized among the Jews, wrote several pamphlets for that purpose, and made a new translation of the New Testament into Hebrew (1877, 1901[12]; supposedly with the assistance of A.H. Weiss). In 1863 he founded the missionary magazine, *Saat auf Hoffnung* ("Seed on Hope"), which appeared regularly until 1935. In 1880 he established in Leipzig the *Institutum Judaicum* (renamed the "Delitzschianum" after his death), for the training of missionary workers among Jews, an institute which is still in existence in Muenster (Germany), but has been transformed into a purely scholarly institution. In 1884/85, a controversy erupted between Delitzsch and A. Berliner, who deplored the proselytizing spirit of his Protestant colleague's work. Delitzsch harshly silenced his criticism, asserting Christianity's theological superiority and accusing him of ingratitude with respect to his political solidarity with German Jewry. In general, his theological attitude towards Judaism implied strong traditional anti-Jewish elements, including his definition of Judaism as an obsolete stage of revelation, his verdict on "Jewish legalism," and his polemic against scholars like A. Geiger, whose criticism of Christianity appeared to him as an expression of presumptuous Jewish anti-Christianism. Despite his own ambivalent views on contemporary Judaism (*Christentum und jüdische Presse*, 1882), Delitzsch fought vehemently against defamations of the Talmud by antisemitic writers, especially against *Rohling's libelous pamphlet *Der Talmudjude* (1871). Delitzsch's first book, *Zur Geschichte der juedischen Poesie vom Abschluss der Heiligen Schriften des Alten Bundes bis auf die neueste Zeit* (1836), was the first comprehensive study of the history of Hebrew poetry and a serious attempt to deal with this subject with the accepted tools of literary criticism. In his Bible commentaries, the most important of which are those on Psalms (1859, 1894[5]), on Isaiah (1866–1889[4]), and on Ecclesiastes (1875), his approach was based upon philological analysis. He meticulously adhered to the masoretic text and, on principle, avoided critical emendations. He mitigated his traditional attitude only in his later writings, in which he accepted some of the tenets of the "source theory" of modern Bible criticism. To this subject he devoted his *Complutensische Varianten zum alttestamentischen Texte* (1878). Delitzsch assisted Seligmann *Baer in his edition of the Hebrew Bible, based upon the masoretic text. Delitzsch edited both Moses Ḥayyim *Luzzatto's *Migdal Oz* (1857) and the Karaite Aaron b. Elijah's *Ez Ḥayyim* (1841, with the assistance of M. *Steinschneider). He also wrote *Juedisches Handwerkerleben zur Zeit Jesu* ("Jewish Artisans in the Time of Jesus," 1868, 1879[2]) and *Juedisch-arabische Poesien aus vor-mohammedanischer Zeit* ("Pre-Islamic Jewish Poetry," 1874). His theological works and New Testament studies include *Die biblisch-prophetische Theologie* (1845); *System der biblischen Psychologie* (1855, 1861[2]); *Commentar zum Briefe an die Hebraeer* (1857); *Jesus und Hillel* (also in Hebrew; 1866, 1875[3]); *System der christlichen Apologetik* (1869). One of his missionary writings, *Ernste Fragen an die Gebildeten juedischer Religion* ("Serious Questions to the Educated Members of the Jewish Faith," 1888), which attempted to downplay the importance of Christology and the dogma of the Trinity in order to make it easier for Jews to convert to Christianity, also appeared in Hebrew under the title *Ha'amek She'elah* (1912[2]). The obituaries published in Jewish journals after his death reflect the ambivalence toward Delitzsch's work: scholars like D. Kaufmann expressed their deep admiration for his scholarly achievements but did not hide their resentment over not being accepted as academic equals and his denigration of contemporary Jewish identity.

BIBLIOGRAPHY: P.P. Levertoff, *Delitzsch-Bibliographie* (1913); A.M. Stengel, *Divrei Emet ve-Ahavah… le-Yom Hulledet… Professor Franz Delitzsch* (1884); A. Koehler, *Realencyclopedie fuer protestantische Theologie und Kirche*, 4 (1898), 565; Kaufmann, Schriften, 1 (1908), 290; E. Delitzsch, *Franz Delitzsch als Freund Israels* (1910); H.J. Kraus, *Geschichte der historisch-kritischen Erforschung des Alten Testaments* (1956), 210–21; NDB, 3 (1957), 581–2. **ADD. BIBLIOGRAPHY:** A.T. Levenson, in: JQR, 92, 383-420; S. Wagner, *Franz Delitzsch. Leben und Werk* (1978); C. Wiese, *Challenging Colonial Discourse. Jewish Studies and Protestant Theology in Wilhelmine Germany* (2005), 122–36, 150–58.

[Mordechai Breuer / Christian Wiese (2nd ed.)]

°**DELITZSCH, FRIEDRICH** (1850–1922), German Orientalist, son of Franz *Delitzsch. Delitzsch was the outstanding student of E. Schrader; he served as professor of Semitic languages and Assyriology in Leipzig (1877), in Breslau (1893), and from 1899 in Berlin. Delitzsch was among the founders of modern Assyriology. In addition to his purely Assyriological studies he investigated the Hebrew language in its relation to Akkadian and the Semitic languages in relation to the Indo-European languages in *Studien ueber indogermanisch-semitische Wurzelverwandtschaft* (1873), and *Prolegomena eines neuen hebraeisch-aramaeischen Woerterbuchs zum Alten Testament* (1886). Delitzsch also published in the field of Bible. His *Die Leseund Schreibfehler im Alten Testament…* (1920) is a valuable aid to textual criticism. More controversial are his comparative studies of Babylonian culture and the world of the Bible. Their motivation was not objectively scientific but blatantly antisemitic. In 1902, Delitzsch prepared a number of lectures on the topic "Babel and Bible" (*Babel und Bibel*, 1902–05; Eng. 1906), in which he claimed the absolute superiority of "Babylonia" over "Israel" and that the Bible, in and of itself, is devoid of religious and moral value. While his views were accepted by antisemites with joy, scholars and men of religion reacted sharply to the superficiality of his conclusions and to their evil intent. But Delitzsch, who was silenced for a while, repeated his claims after World War I, and this time in an open attack on the Hebrew Bible, Judaism, and the Jews in his book, *Die grosse Taeuschung* ("The Great Deception," 1921). His actions contributed not a little to the slogans of the antisemitic movements in Germany. The most important of the polemical works against Delitzsch is E. Koenig's work *Fried-*

rich Delitzsch's "Die grosse Taeuschung" kritisch beleuchtet* (1921).

BIBLIOGRAPHY: Lewin, in: *W. Feilchenfeld Festschrift* (1907), 47–65; H.J. Kraus, *Geschichte der historisch-kritischen Erforschung des Alten Testaments* (1956), 274–83; Price, in: *Beitraege zur Assyriologie*, 10 pt. 2 (1927), i–xii; Meissner, in: *Deutsches biographisches Jahrbuch*, 4 (1922), 31–35; Weissbach, in: *Reallexikon der Assyriologie*, 2 (1938), 198; Albright, in: ESS, 5 (1953), 68–69. **ADD. BIBLIOGRAPHY:** H. Huffmon, DBI I, 267; R. Lehmann, *Friedrich Delitzsch und der Babel-Bibel Streit* (1994); B. Arnold and D. Weisberg, in: JBL, 121 (2002), 441–57.

[Abraham Arzi]

DELL, EDMUND (1921–1999), British politician. An Oxford graduate and Labour member of Parliament from 1964 until 1979, Edmund Dell held a series of economic ministries in the 1964–70 and 1974–79 governments. Dell served as paymaster-general 1974–76 and then entered the cabinet as trade secretary from 1976 to 1978. After leaving Parliament, he became a company director. Dell was the author of ten books, including *A Hard Pounding* (1991), about the economic crises of 1974–79, and *The Chancellors: A History of the Chancellors of the Exchequer, 1945–90* (1996).

[William D. Rubinstein (2nd ed.)]

DELL, MICHAEL S. (1965–), U.S. computer entrepreneur. Born in Houston, Texas, Dell attended the University of Texas, intending to become a physician; instead, he became the dormitory millionaire. In 1984, with $1,000, Dell started a computer company called PC's Limited in his dormitory room. The company became successful enough for Dell to drop out of college at 19 to run the business full-time. Dell's idea was to sell computers directly to the consumer without going through retailers, and in the process design and deliver a computer based upon the customer's own specifications. Previously, buying a computer invariably involved a middleman. In addition to customization, Dell provided the industry's first support and service program. Today, the Dell corporation provides products and services in various information-technology and Internet-related sectors. Building to order, Dell has almost no inventory in computers or components, selling and delivering the completed PC units directly to consumers.

Dell is considered the most profitable PC manufacturer in the world, with sales of $35 billion and profits of $2 billion in 2002. Dell has 46,000 employees in more than 170 countries around the world. Dell is known for its ability to drive down prices and the company has a hold over its vendors. In addition, Dell has been able to leverage the power of the Internet to great advantage because it is the largest supplier of PCs over the Internet. Michael Dell ranks among the five wealthiest individuals in the United States. In 1999 Dell wrote *Direct From Dell: Strategies That Revolutionized an Industry,* which details the story of the rise of the company and the strategies he has refined that apply to all businesses.

Dell, through the foundation that bears his and his wife's name, has become active in philanthropy. One of their earliest gifts was $13 million toward building a new Austin (Texas) Museum of Art. The Dells gave $1 million for a new radiology center at the Children's Hospital of Austin, and the Dell Discovery Center at the Austin Children's Museum reflects the Dells' interests in children's causes. He also gave 40 acres, worth $2.5 million, in 1994 to the Jewish Federation of Austin as a site for a Jewish community center which bears his name.

[Stewart Kampel (2nd ed.)]

DELLA SETA, ALESSANDRO (1879–1944), Italian archaeologist. Della Setta was born in Rome to Giuseppe Della Seta and Rachele Rosselli. In 1901, he took a degree in archaeology and history of Greek and Roman art under Emanuel *Loewy's direction. In 1909, he qualified for university teaching in archaeology. In addition to his prolific and remarkable scientific production he worked as inspector of the National Museum of Villa Giulia, in Rome. In 1913, he held the chair of archaeology at the University of Genoa. During World War I, he attained the rank of artillery officer and received a War Cross. From 1919, for 20 years, Della Seta was head of the Italian Archaeological School of Athens. In 1926, his university chair was transferred from Genoa to Rome. In 1930, he was made a member of the Academy of the Lincei; he was also a member of the Greek Archaeological Society and a member of the technical committee of the *Enciclopedia Italiana*, directing the archaeological section from 1925 to 1930. The anti-Jewish laws of the Fascist regime put an end to his academic career as well as to his scientific production.

Della Seta was eminent both as a field archaeologist and as an art historian. In the 1930s he directed the important excavations at Paliochni, a site on the island of Lemnos, Greece. As an art historian he was particularly concerned with tracing the origins, development, and history of ancient classical art. Among his works are *La genesi dello scorcio nell'arte greca* (1907); *Religione e arte figurata* (1912); *Italia antica* (1922), a survey of Italian civilization from prehistory onward; *I monumenti dell' antichitā classica* (1926); and *Il nudo nell'arte* (1920).

BIBLIOGRAPHY: *Dizionario Biografico degli Italiani*, 37 (1989), 476–481 (includes bibliography).

[Massimo Longo Adorno (2nd ed.)]

DELLA TORRE, LELIO (**Hillel**; 1805–1871), Italian rabbi, teacher, and scholar. Born in Cuneo in Piedmont, he taught at the Collegio Colonna e Finzi in Turin from 1823 to 1829, serving as assistant rabbi from 1827. Two years later, with the opening of the Padua Rabbinical College (which trained the majority of Italian rabbis), he was made professor of Talmud. He gained renown for his teaching of homiletics and for his own preaching. Aside from his volumes of Hebrew poetry, *Tal Yaldut* and *Eglei Tal*, and numerous sermons, he published a commentary on the Pentateuch, translated and annotated the Psalms, and rendered the prayers according to Ashkenazi custom in Italian. His works on scholarly and current subjects, nearly 300 in Jewish publications alone, were published in the periodicals *Bikkurei ha-Ittim ha-Ḥadashim, Kerem Ḥemed, Kokhevei Yiẓḥak*, and *Avnei Nezer*, as well as in Italian, German, and French periodicals. Della Torre was honored by secular learned societies in Padua and Venice; his two-volume *Scritti Sparsi* appeared in 1908.

BIBLIOGRAPHY: Isaac Ḥayyim Castiglioni, in: *Oẓar ha-Sifrut*, 3 (1888–89), biography; idem, *Orazioni Postume* (1878), 187–202; E.S. Artom, in: *Italia*, 1 (Jerusalem, 1945), 8–13; Schirmann, Italyah, 501.

[Getzel Kressel]

DELMAR (De Le Mar; Lebhar, from Arabic *al-Baḥr*, "the sea"), Moroccan family of merchants and diplomats. The first known member of the family was JACOB LEBHAR of Safi (c. 1650). SHALOM DELMAR-LEBHAR (d. after 1775), "merchant of the sultan" of Morocco in Mogador, was known as a scholar and kabbalist. Of his five sons, MORDECAI was adviser to the sultan and in 1780 was put in charge of all commerce and the port of the city. Together with his brother JOSEPH of Mogador, he was an agent for the ransoming of Christian captives. MASʿŪD was appointed agent for the sultan in Amsterdam, where he negotiated the peace treaties of 1777. Later he went to London where he was received by George III; his negotiations resulted in the Anglo-Moroccan agreement of May 1783. His son ABRAHAM (c. 1826) was one of the directors of the *talmud torah* of Amsterdam.

BIBLIOGRAPHY: J.M. Toledano, *Ner ha-Maʿarav* (1911), 166–7; Hosotte-Reynaud, in: *Hesperis* (1957), 341; Hirschberg, *Afrikah*, 2 (1965), 292, 335, 367.

[David Corcos]

°**DEL MEDICO, HENRI E.** (1896–?), scholar, writer and translator. Del Medico was born in Constantinople into a banking family. He left Turkey in 1922 and studied Semitics first in France and during World War II at the Pontifical Institute at Rome. His main interests were Jewish literature of the Roman diaspora in the early centuries C.E.; the Hittites; the Ugaritic texts of Ras Shamra, which he translated, not quite satisfactorily, into French (*La Bible cananéene, découverte dans les textes de Ras Shamra*, 1950); and especially the Dead Sea Scrolls. On these Del Medico published a number of studies, some translated into English (*Riddle of the Scrolls*, 1958), Italian, and Spanish, in which he assumes a rather later date for their origin than the majority of scholars. He also published a number of studies in Byzantine civilization and translated German, English, Italian, and Spanish works into French.

[Rene Samuel Sirat]

DELMEDIGO, ELIJAH BEN MOSES ABBA (c. 1460–1497), philosopher and talmudist. Born in Candia, Crete, Delmedigo was also known as Elijah Cretensis. While still a young man he immigrated to Italy. He received a traditional Jewish education, and studied the classics of Islamic and Jewish philosophy, particularly the works of *Maimonides and *Averroes. In addition he became conversant with classical literature. His Jewish learning was recognized by his contemporaries as can be seen from an exchange of letters with Joseph *Colon, who addressed Delmedigo in terms of high regard (see Resp. Maharik, no. 54). Delmedigo served for a time as head of the yeshivah in Padua. He also delivered public lectures on philosophy in Padua and possibly other Italian cities. *Pico della Mirandola was among Delmedigo's Christian disciples and admirers. On the basis of his reputation as a philosopher, Delmedigo was chosen, under the patronage of the Venice authorities, to act as a mediator in a philosophic dispute which arose between two schools of Italian scholars, and his decision in favor of one side aroused hostility toward him on the part of the other. In addition to this animosity on the part of the Christians, a bitter controversy on a halakhic question developed between Delmedigo and the rabbi of Padua, Judah *Mintz, and after the death of his patron, Pico, in 1494, Delmedigo was compelled to leave Italy and return to his birthplace, where he was welcomed by Jews and Christians alike. There in 1496 he completed his major work, *Beḥinat ha-Dat* ("The Examination of Religion"), which he wrote at the request of one of his disciples Saul ha-Kohen *Ashkenazi. He remained in Crete until his death three years after his return.

The main subject of Delmedigo's *Beḥinat ha-Dat* (first published in 1629 in *Taʿalumot Ḥokhmah* of Judah Samuel *Ashkenazi; published a second time, together with a commentary, by I.S. *Reggio in 1833) is the relation between religion and philosophy. Basing himself on a text of Averroes, Delmedigo holds that the study of philosophy is permissible, affirming further that in cases of contradiction between religious faith and philosophic reasoning, the philosopher may interpret religious beliefs as to make them accord with philosophic truth. This, however, does not apply to the basic principles of faith. Every person, including the philosopher, is obligated to believe in the basic dogmas of religion, even when these appear to contradict philosophic truth. Recognizing the possible contradiction between religious principles and philosophic truths Delmedigo tended toward the double faith theory of the Christian Averroists. In *Beḥinat ha-Dat* Delmedigo also described rabbinic literature and attacked the Kabbalah. He argued against the antiquity of the Kabbalah, noting that it was not known to the sages of the Talmud, or to the *geonim*, or to *Rashi. He also denies that *Simeon b. Yoḥai was the author of the *Zohar, since that work mentions personalities who lived after the death of Simeon. In addition, he attacks the extreme allegorists among Jewish philosophers. In another section of his work he discusses the reasons underlying the commandments of the Torah (*taʿamei ha-mitzvot*). Delmedigo's importance in the history of philosophy rests in his making the teachings of Averroes known to the Italian scholars of the Renaissance, especially through his Latin translations of many of Averroes' works.

He composed the following translations: a translation, no longer extant, of Averroes' commentary on Plato's *Republic*; a translation of six of Averroes' questions on Aristotle's logic (Venice, 1497); a short translation of Aristotle's *Meteorologia*, and a translation of parts of Averroes' middle commentary on that work (Venice, 1488); a translation of parts one to seven of Averroes' middle commentary on Aristotle's *Metaphysics* (Venice, 1560); a translation of Averroes' introduction to his large commentary on Aristotle's *Metaphysics* (Paris, Bibliothèque Nationale, man. latin, Ms. no. 6508); a translation of Averroes' *De Spermate* (Venice, 1560). In addition to his translations, Delmedigo composed the following original works in Latin: *Questiones Tres*, consisting of three sections: *De Primo Motore, De Mundi Efficentia*, and *De Esse Essentia et Uno* (Venice, 1501); a commentary on Aristotle's natural philosophy (Venice, 1480); a Latin and Hebrew commentary on Averroes' *De Substantia Orbis*, in Hebrew, *Ma'amar be-Ezem ha-Galgal*, and two questions on Averroes' theory of the hylic intellect (Paris, Bibliothèque Nationale, Cod. héb., 968). A copy of Delmedigo's *Beḥinat ha-Dat* was found in the private library of *Spinoza, and it may be assumed that it influenced the development of Spinoza's ideas in the *Theologico-Political Treatise*.

BIBLIOGRAPHY: Guttmann, Philosophies, 258–9, 263; M.D. Geffen, *Faith and Reason in Elijah del Medigo's Behinat ha-Dat…* (1970); microfilm); U. Cassuto, *Ha-Yehudim be-Firenẓi bi-Tekufat ha-Renaissance* (1967), index, s.v. *Elia del Medigo*; Graetz, Hist, 4 (1894), 290–5; J.S. Delmedigo, *Maẓref la-Ḥokhmah* (1864), 10–11; Weiss, Dor, 5 (1904), 275–8; Munk, Mélanges, 510, n.2; Rippner, in: MGWJ, 20 (1871), 481–94; J. Dukas, *Recherches sur l'histoire littéraire du 15e siècle* (1876), 25–77; HB, 21 (1881), 60–71; A. Huebsch, in:MGWJ, 31 (1882), 555–63; idem, *ibid.*, 32 (1883), 28; J. Perles, *Beitraege zur Geschichte der hebraeischen und aramaeischen Studien* (1884), 196; M. Steinschneider, in: MGWJ, 37 (1893), 185–8; Guttmann, in: *Jewish Studies in Memory of Israel Abrahams* (1927), 192–208 (Ger.); A. Geiger, *Melo Chofnajim* (1840), xxii and xxiv.

[Jacob S. Levinger]

DELMEDIGO, JOSEPH SOLOMON (1591–1655), rabbi, philosopher, mathematician, and astronomer; also known as **Joseph Solomon Rofe** acronym **YashaR**) of Candia (Crete). A writer of extensive Jewish and secular learning and of encyclopedic range, he is the author of works whose number is estimated by some authorities at 30, by others at over 60. A member of a distinguished scholarly family, he was the son of Elijah Delmedigo, rabbi in Candia. In accordance with the family tradition, he was given a thorough Jewish and classical education. At the age of 15, he was admitted to the University of Padua, where he studied astronomy and mathematics under Galileo, and also medicine and philosophy, at the same time continuing his Jewish studies. While at Padua, he frequently visited Leone *Modena of the neighboring city of Venice, who, it appears, exercised a lasting influence on him. In 1613, he completed his studies at the University of Padua, and returned to Crete, where he began to practice medicine. From notes which he compiled during this period, he later began to compose his encyclopedic work *Ya'ar Levanon* ("Forest of Lebanon"), which he never brought to completion. In all likelihood he married in Candia, but there are indications that it was not a happy marriage. He soon found Candia too confining and left his homeland, never to return. Throughout his travels, he encountered misunderstanding and embitterment, since his ideas on the popularization of scientific knowledge aroused opposition and enmity.

His first stop after leaving Candia was Cairo. There he became acquainted with Ali b. Rahmadan, a renowned Arab mathematician, whom he refuted in a public disputation concerning spherical trigonometry. In Egypt, too, he met the physicist, Jacob the Alexandrian, head of the Karaite community there. Delmedigo was attracted to the Karaites by their love for secular learning and it is also possible that the hostility of Orthodox Jews caused him to turn occasionally to the Karaite sectaries for company. He was delighted to find in Egypt several works on Maimonides' *Guide*, as well as certain writings of Abraham ibn Ezra, whom he greatly admired. From Cairo, Delmedigo went to Constantinople, then a prominent center of learning. Here, again, he befriended several Karaite leaders, including Moses Mezordi, from whom he acquired many Karaite works. Here, too, he came to know some ardent followers of the Kabbalah, in particular Jacob ibn Nehemias. It may, however, be assumed that Delmedigo had already become acquainted with kabbalistic teachings while still at Padua. Yet, he approached its study more seriously during his stay in Poland. He immersed himself in the Kabbalah for two purposes: (1) To find in it solutions which philosophy could not offer, and (2) to criticize it. He wrote *Maẓref la-Ḥokhmah*, in which he allegedly refuted the attack on the Kabbalah made by his distant relative Elijah *Delmedigo, in his *Beḥinat ha-Dat.* Since, as Delmedigo himself explains, he was commissioned to write such a refutation, it is unclear whether the work reflects his true convictions. He says in this connection: "Do not presume that you can unravel the author's mind from his book" (ed. Odessa, 1864, p. 85). Leone Modena understood the *Maẓref la-Ḥokhmah* as a refutation of kabbalistic ideas, using it in his *Ari Nohem* ("Roaring Lion"), a systematic anti-kabbalistic treatise. Delmedigo next went to Poland, stopping off on the way in Romania, where he became friends with the kabbalist Solomon Arabi. In 1620, he was practicing medicine in Vilna, where he became the private physician of Prince Radziwill, and had many nobles for his patients. During the week, he used to make the circuit of the environs of Vilna to cure the sick, and on the Sabbath he would lecture in the synagogue. His nights were spent in scholastic pursuits. Though a conservative in many of his views, he was also a proponent of many new ideas. His scientific bent of mind having been stimulated by his early contact with Galileo, he was a pioneer in a number of aspects of scientific research. In astronomy, he parted company with the followers of Ptolemy to espouse the Copernician system. He was the first Jewish scholar to use logarithmic tables, which had just been invented. He preferred Platonic philosophy to Aristotelianism which had held almost unchallenged sway during the Middle Ages. In medicine and the natural sciences he emphasized the value of the empiric approach, although at an earlier stage he had criticized scientific empiricism. He spoke against the unsanitary conditions prevailing in the ghettos and the lack of organization and order. He wanted to uplift the people by a renaissance of science and learning of trades and professions. His knowledge of languages, acquired as tools for his scholarly research, encompassed Latin, Greek, Spanish, and Italian. He intended to study Arabic, but gave up the idea on finding that "everything that was beautiful in Arabic was taken, with few exceptions, from Greek writings." Coming to feel that he had been a failure in Eastern Europe, he left for Hamburg, Germany. From there he went to Amsterdam, where his first printed book, *Elim*, was published by *Manasseh Ben Israel (1629). This book was written as an answer to queries addressed to him by the Karaite scholar, *Zerah b. Nathan of Troki (near Vilna, Lithuania). Delmedigo named this work, which contained 12 general, and 70 specific queries, *Elim*, an allusion to the biblical Elim (Ex. 15:27) where there were 12 wells and 70 date trees. The questions concerned religious, metaphysical, and scientific matters.

In 1629–31, his *Ta'alumot Ḥokhmah*, a collection of kabbalistic treatises, was published by his disciple, Samuel Ashkenazi, in Basle, Switzerland. The first section, *Maẓref la-Ḥokhmah*, appeared in 1629, the second, *Novelot Ḥokhmah* ("Fallen Fruit of Wisdom"), in 1631. Except for these two books, the only other material that remains of Delmedigo's colossal output is the full text of his letter to Zerah of Troki, which was published together with a German translation in 1840 by Abraham Geiger in his *Melo Chofnajim*. It is known within the corpus of Delmedigo's published work under the name of *Iggeret Aḥuz*, after the first word of the letter. This letter is merely a precursory answer to Zerah's inquiries, and was written in 1624 or 1625. Delmedigo refers, in his writings, to a number of other works, which are no longer extant. Among these works are *Bosmat bat Shelomo* on arithmetic, geometry, astronomy, geography, logic, ethics, and metaphysics; *Ir gibborim*, divided into two parts: *Gevurot Adonai* on astronomy, and *Nifla'ot Adonai*, on chemistry and mechanics; and two medical works, *Refu'ot Te'alah*, and *Mekor Binah* which contains the Hebrew translation of the Latin aphorisms of Hippocrates. Toward the end of his life, Delmedigo settled at Frankfurt on the Main, where, as community physician, he again became part of ghetto life. Thereafter, he spent some years in Prague – a period about which little is known. On his tombstone in Prague are written the words: "He practiced what he preached – he was just to everyone – the glorified rabbi, scholar, divine philosopher, and mighty one among physicians."

BIBLIOGRAPHY: A. Geiger, *Melo Chofnajim* (1840), introduction, 1–95 (Ger. pt.) 1–29 (Heb. pt.); idem, *Nachgelassene Schriften*, 3 (1876), 1–33; G. Alter, *Two Renaissance Astronomers* (1958; = Československá Akademia Vd, *Rozprávy*, 68 (1958), 45–74, Eng.); L. Roth, in: *Chronicon Spinozanum*, 2 (1922), 54–66; C. Roth, *Life of Menasseh ben Israel* (1934), 132–4; Waxman, Literature, 2 (1960), 326–8; F. Kobler, *Treasury of Jewish Letters*, 2 (1952), 486–96.

[Jacob Haberman]

DEL MONTE, CRESCENZO (1868–1935), Italian poet. Del Monte, who first wrote sonnets in Romanesco, the *patois* of his native Rome, also composed poems in the *Judeo-Italian dialect. His aim was to preserve the folklore and language of a Jewish world that had begun to crumble after the abolition of the ghetto and the Jewish emancipation of 1870. Del Monte's sonnets resemble an impressionistic painting of the everyday life of the Roman ghetto in the 19th century, and portray the patriarchal life, religion, and superstitions of these "Romans more ancient than the Romans of today." He successfully conveyed the vitality and everyday speech of these Jews in verse notable for its powerful expression and nostalgia. His love for their dialect led Del Monte to investigate the philology of Judeo-Italian, with which he had become emotionally and artistically involved. On the assumption that Judeo-Italian constituted an early stage of the Italian language and that, unlike the Roman dialect, it had preserved the medieval character of the language, its ancient vocabulary and Latin structure, Del Monte reconstructed its grammar. He sought in the Roman prose of the 14th–17th centuries words and expressions which corresponded to those that he had used in his own poems. In this original philological research Del Monte came close to the poet Frédéric Mistral, who sought to revive Provençal. Recent studies indicate, however, that the language spoken by the Jews of Rome originated in southern Italy. Del Monte's sonnets are, nevertheless, of philological importance because of their linguistic richness. They were published in two volumes, *Sonetti Giudaico-Romaneschi* (1927) and *Nuovi sonetti Giudaico-Romaneschi* (1933). The second volume contains a Judeo-Italian grammar as well as extracts from the old Roman dialect and their translation into Judeo-Italian. A third and posthumous volume, *Sonetti postumi Giudaico-Romaneschi e Romaneschi* (1955), includes sonnets written in the Roman dialect and an introduction by the renowned philologist B. Terracini.

BIBLIOGRAPHY: B. Terracini, in: RMI, 21 (1955), 499–506. **ADD. BIBLIOGRAPHY:** C. Del Monte, "Un centenario da non dimenticare; Crescenzo Del Monte, poeta romano," in: RMI, 35 (1969), 123–35; B. Garvin, "Crescenzo del Monte; poet of the Roman ghetto," in: JQ, 7:2–3 (1979), 24–27; I. Di Nepi, "Roma e una sola e te lo dico: Crescenzo Del Monte," in: *Shalom*, 22 (1989), 43; M. Mancini, "Crescenzo Del Monte e il giudeo-romanesco," in: *Roma e Lazio* (1992), 203–7; idem, "Sulla formazione dell'identita linguistica giudeo-romanesca fra tardo medioevo e rinascimento," in: *Roma nel Rinascimento* (1993), 53–122; M. Mazzocchi Alemanni, "I "Sonetti giudaico-romaneschi" di Crescenzo Del Monte," in: *Italia Judaica*, 4 (1993), 327–35; S. Debenedetti Stow, "I sonetti di Crescenzo Del Monte," in: *Appartenenza e differenza. Ebrei d'Italia e Letteratura* (1998), 33–42.

[Joseph Baruch Sermoneta]

DELOS, a small island in the Cyclades, measuring just 3 miles (5 km.) north to south and nearly 1 mile (1.3 km.) east to west. Its earliest occupation dates to the third millennium B.C.E. The mythological birthplace of Apollo and Artemis, it had become the center of the Apollo cult by the seventh century B.C.E. It is mentioned in Homer's *Odyssey* and in a Homeric hymn to Apollo. In 478 B.C.E., Delos became the site of the treasury for the Delian League. By the end of the third century B.C.E., there was an influx of traders from all over the Aegean, many of whom established their ancestral cults and associations on the island. Delos also became one of the main centers of the Aegean slave trade. As a thriving cultic, trade, and slaving center, Delos was often raided and caught between local warring factions. By the mid-first century B.C.E., disruptions on Delos had taken their toll, leaving Delos outside the commercial loop. The priest of Apollo no longer lived on Delos, and only returned once a year for the annual ceremonial sacrifice prescribed by the cult. In the second century C.E., the Emperor Hadrian attempted (unsuccessfully) to revive the old Delian festivals but by then, according to Pausanias (8, 33:2), the island was very sparsely inhabited. Delos was abandoned around the fifth century C.E.

While there is some literary evidence relating to Jews on Delos, not a single piece of it refers to the existence of a synagogue. The earliest reference to Jews on Delos is found in I Maccabees (15:15–23). The other piece of literary evidence relating to Delos comes from Josephus (*Antiquities* 14:213–16) and, interestingly, mentions the Jews on Delos being prevented from following their traditional customs, but there is no mention of a synagogue.

It was André Plassart, of the Ecole française d'Athènes who, during excavations of 1912 and 1913, identified building GD80 on Delos as a synagogue. He relied on six Greek inscriptions, the principal one having been found some 100 yds. (90 m.) north of GD80 in a residential area near the stadium. The other five inscriptions were found scattered within the two main spaces of GD80. Plassart interpreted ID2329 as reading "Agathokles and Lysimachos for the synagogue," whereas it actually reads "Agathokles and Lysimachos for a prayer/votive." It is notable that no direct evidence was found in or around GD80 to identify it as a synagogue.

Plassart also considered that the internal configuration of GD80 was similar to that of later synagogues. However, there are other buildings on Delos with the same configuration as GD80, such as Sarapeion A (GD91) and C (GD100). Coincidentally, the names *Agathokles* and *Lysimachos* are mentioned in inscriptions relating to donations to both Sarapeia in IDS 2616 and 2618, raising further doubts about the validity of the ID2329 inscription as relating to a Jewish context.

In 1979, Philippe Fraisse of the Ecole française d'Athènes found two Samaritan inscriptions on Delos not far from GD80. Both inscriptions are in Greek and are dedicated by the "Israelites who offer to Holy Argarizein," clearly indicating the presence of a Jewish and/or Samaritan community on the island. The question is where on the island that community was based and whether or not it had a synagogue or some sort of community or association hall at all.

BIBLIOGRAPHY: J.R. Bartlett, *1 Maccabees* (1998); P. Bruneau, *Recherches sur les cultes de Délos à l'époque hellénistique et à l'époque impériale* (1970); P. Bruneau and J. Ducat, *Guide de Délos* (1970); M. Brunet, "Delos," in: *Bulletin de correspondence hellénique*, 114 (1990), 669–82; F. Durrbach, P. Roussel, A. Plassart et al., *Inscriptions de Délos* (1921–35); B.D. Mazur, *Studies on Jewry in Greece* (1935); M. Holleaux *Mélanges Holleaux. Recueil de mémoires concernant l'antiquité grecque* (1913); L. Matassa, "The Myth of the Synagogue on Delos," in: SOMA (2004; *British Archaeological Reports*, 2005); J. Overman, and R.S. MacLennan (eds.), *Diaspora Jews and Judaism. Essays in Honor of, and in Dialogue with, A. Thomas Kraabel* (1992); A. Plassart, "La synagogue juive de Délos," in: *Revue Biblique* (1914), 23.

[Lidia Domenica Matassa (2nd ed.)]

DELOUGAZ, PIERRE PINCHAS (1901–1975), educator and archaeologist. Born in Russia, he went as a child with his parents to Palestine. Later he studied in France and the United States. His activities as field archaeologist included excavations at *Nuzi (Iraq), 1928–29; at Khorsabad (Iraq), 1929–30, where he uncovered the famous colossal bull ("father of the elephant"); in 1931 he directed the excavations at Khafaje (Iraq); and in 1952 he directed excavations at Bet Yeraḥ (Israel). In 1944 he was appointed curator of the Oriental Institute Museum at Chicago, and in 1949 became a member of the faculty of the University of Chicago (professor at its Oriental Institute from 1960). His method of teaching and research combined archaeology and literature. He considered art objects as "social documents" to be used as "evidence" in interpretations. In addition to numerous articles he published several books, among them *The Temple Oval at Khafajah* (1940), *Pottery from the Diyala Region* (1952), *Plano-Convex Bricks… Treatment of Clay Tablets in the Field* (1933), *Pre-Sargonid Temples in the Diyala Region* (1942, with S. Lloyd). On Delougaz' method and the meaning of the term "Proto-literate period," coined by him in 1942, see: R.E. Braidwood, *The Near East and the Foundations of Civilization* (1952, 1962^2), 37, 45; I. Lloyd, *Mounds of the Near East* (1963), s.v. Delougaz, protoliterate; R.W. Ehrich (ed.), *Chronologies in Old World Archaeology* (1965), s.v. proto-literate.

[Penuel P. Kahane]

DELOUYA (**de Loya**), family of Spanish origin, which settled in *Marrakesh, south *Morocco. From this town, JAKI (ISAAC) DELOUYA (c. 1572) carried on trade relations with English merchants, to whom he was of great service. His descendants were especially distinguished as rabbis. Some of the writings of MEIR (c. 1625) were published in the works of Moroccan rabbis. ISAAC (d. 1711) was *av bet din* of Marrakesh from about 1680, heading a yeshivah which included among its pupils the talmudist Solomon Amar and the kabbalist Abraham Azulai. During the upheavals caused by the pretenders to the throne, he and his family were denounced to the sultan, Isaac was imprisoned for some time, and his two brothers, JUDAH and MOSES, died as a result (1701). MORDECAI BEN ISAAC, his son JACOB, and his grandson MEIR (c. 1780) were also scholars.

BIBLIOGRAPHY: SIHM, *Angleterre*, 1 (1918), 112–3; J.M. Toledano, *Ner ha-Ma'arav* (1911), 161; J. Ben-Naim, *Malkhei Rabbanan* (1931), passim.

[David Corcos]

DE LUCENA, family of freemen in colonial America. ABRAHAM HAIM DE LUCENA (d. 1725), New York merchant and cleric, was made a freeman of New York in 1708 and carried on a substantial business in general merchandise. In 1710 he unsuccessfully petitioned for the right to export wheat. De Lucena succeeded Saul *Brown as rabbi of the New York Jewish community, requesting Governor Robert Hunter in 1710 to exempt him from civic duties because he was a minister. The following year he donated money for the building of the Trinity Church steeple. His son SAMUEL (1711–?) was made freeman of New York in 1759. By 1782 he had a brokerage business in Philadelphia and was a contributor to the building of Congregation Mikveh Israel.

BIBLIOGRAPHY: J.R. Rosenbloom, *A Biographical Dictionary of Early American Jews* (1960), 101.

[Leo Hershkowitz]

DELVALLE, MAX SHALOM (1911–1979), Panamanian public figure. Born in Panama City, he entered politics in his late teens. He rapidly rose to prominence and was elected to the National Assembly. Delvalle became minister of public works and in 1964 vice president of the republic. In this latter capacity, Delvalle was the central figure of a constitutional crisis. In October 1967, President Marcos Robles announced the name of the candidate he would propose to succeed him in the 1968 elections. This led to a split in his party as the majority supported another candidate. In March 1968 the National Assembly, sitting as a court of justice, removed Robles and replaced him with Delvalle, who being the senior vice president was sworn in as president of the republic. In April, the Supreme Court decided that Robles was unconstitutionally deposed, but Delvalle denied its authority to overrule decisions of the legislature and continued to fill the presidency. In the following month, however, elections were held and a new president installed.

Max Delvalle was active in the Portuguese Jewish community of Panama, Kol Shearith Israel.

[Israel Drapkin-Senderey / Mordechai Arbell (2nd ed.)]

DELVALLE LEVI MADURO, ERIC ARTURO (1937–), Panamanian intellectual, businessman, and political activist. Nephew of the ex-president of Panama Max *Delvalle, Delvalle Levi Maduro is a member of one of the most prominent Portuguese Jewish families in Panama. He was active in democratic politics and as vice president replaced the president, Dr. Nicolas Ardito Barletta, in 1985. He served as president until 1987 and was deposed by the military dictatorship of General Manuel Noriega.

[Mordechai Arbell (2nd ed.)]

DEL VECCHIO, Italian family; according to one of its traditions, it ranks among the most ancient Jewish families of Italy. In Hebrew sources it is also referred to as Min ha-Zekenim ("the old ones" – a literal translation of Del Vecchio). Its members include SAMUEL MAHALALEL DEL VECCHIO (16th century), born in Ferrara where he served as rabbi. His name and knowledge of *halakhah* are mentioned in the responsa of Jehiel b. Azriel Trabot (in manuscript). He wrote *Sefer ha-Tikkunim* or *Haggahot ha-Rif*. ABRAHAM BEN SHABBETAI (d. 1654), born in Mantua, lived for some time in Sassuolo and served as rabbi of Mantua. He wrote a number of halakhic works; several of his responsa are included in works of contemporary scholars, such as Samuel Aboab in his responsa, *Devar Shemu'el* (Venice, 1702; no. 19). SOLOMON DAVID BEN MOSES (late 17th and early 18th century) was born in Lugo, near Ferrara, where he spent most of his life as rabbi of the town. He was a contemporary of Isaac *Lampronti, who mentions him with approval in his *Paḥad Yiẓḥak* and includes two of his responsa there. One of his responsa on the laying of *tefillin* during the intermediate days of the festival is quoted by Samson Morpurgo in his responsa *Shemesh Ẓedakah* (1, 4). His name is also mentioned with esteem in *Sefat Emet* by Nissim Mattathias Terni (1797, p. 16). His pupils included his grandson, Shabbetai Elhanan b. Elisha *Del Vecchio. SOLOMON MOSES (18th century) was rabbi in Sinigaglia. His name and erudition in *halakhah* are mentioned in Isaac Lampronti's *Paḥad Yiẓḥak*.

BIBLIOGRAPHY: Ghirondi-Neppi, 9, 325; L. Blau, *Kitvei Yehudah Aryeh mi-Modena* (1905), 99; M. Benayahu, in: *Sinai, Sefer Yovel* (1958), 493, 495; S. Simonsohn, *Toledot ha-Yehudim be-Dukkasut Mantovah*, 2 vols. (1963–65), index.

[Guiseppe Laras]

DEL VECCHIO (Min ha-Zekenim), SHABBETAI ELHANAN BEN ELISHA (1707–?), Italian rabbi, *posek*, and preacher. In his youth Del Vecchio studied under his grandfather, Solomon David Del Vecchio, who ordained him as rabbi. In 1727 he was ordained rabbi also by the rabbis of Ferrara who included Isaac *Lampronti, with whom he was on friendly terms from his youth. He was a teacher in several Italian communities: Leghorn, Ancona, and Lugo from 1730 to 1739, when he was appointed rabbi of the town of Casale. Del Vecchio was alone among his Italian contemporaries in that 20 of his responsa were included in the *Paḥad Yiẓḥak* of Lampronti. Del Vecchio used to sign his responsa as "Malkat Sheva" ("Queen of Sheba"; from **Sh**abbetai **B**en **E**lisha). He was also on friendly terms with Ḥ.J.D. *Azulai who visited him in Casale in 1755.

His writings are still in manuscript: *Yeled Zekunim*, a collection of letters sent to him by rabbis and emissaries with his replies, some of which were published by J. Nacht (see bibl.). His halakhic works are *Ir Miklat* on the precepts; *Mishpat ha-Morim; Da'at Zekenim; Ta'am Zekenim*; and *Penei Zekenim*. Responsa and additional letters are to be found in the Jewish Theological Seminary of New York (nos. 55–915–1044).

BIBLIOGRAPHY: Ghirondi-Neppi, 321f.; J. Nacht, in: *Mi-Ginzei Yerushalayim*, 25 (1932), 1–22; idem, in: *Zion*, 6 (1934), 114–38; B. Cohen, in: *Sefer ha-Yovel… A. Marx* (1943), 55 no. 155; M. Wilensky, in: KS, 23 (1946/7), 198–9; 27 (1950/1), 113; M. Benayahu, in: *Sinai, Sefer Yovel* (1958), 491–503; M. Benayahu, *Rabbi Ḥ.Y.D. Azulai* (Heb., 1959), index, s.v. *Min ha-Zekenim Shabbetai Elḥanan*.

[Abraham David]

°D'ELVERT, CHRISTIAN RITTER VON (1803–1896), Moravian historian and politician. He was mayor of Bruenn (Brno) from 1861 to 1863 and 1870 to 1876, and headed the historical section of the Moravian society for local research. The fourth volume of his *Beitraege zur oesterreichischen Rechtsgeschichte* entitled *Zur Geschichte der Juden in Maehren und Oesterreichisch-Schlesien* ("On the History of the Jews in Moravia and Austrian Silesia," 1895), with almost full bibliography, and his publication of the index numbers of all the documents in the archives of the Moravian regent concerning Jews, remain important for research on Moravian Jewry.

BIBLIOGRAPHY: *Oesterreichisches Biographisches Lexikon 1815–1950*, 1 (1957), 176–7; B. Bretholz, in: ADB, 47 (1903), 653–5.

DEMAI (Heb. דְּמַאי, דְּמַיי), agricultural produce about which there is a doubt whether it has been duly tithed; talmudic tractate. The precise etymology of this word has not been determined with certainty, and it appears that the rabbis of the Talmud were already unclear about it. The Jerusalem Talmud connects it to the root *dmy*, in the sense of "perhaps" as in: "perhaps he prepared it, perhaps he did not prepare it" (Sot. 9:12 (24b); end of *Ma'aser Sheni*, as interpreted by H. Yalon, *Pirkei Lashon*, 346), possibly as a morphological analogy to its opposite *vadai*, "certain." In practice, the term designates produce regarding which doubts exist as to whether all the "gifts" for the priests, Levites, etc. have been set aside properly, because it was acquired from an *am ha-areẓ* ("person of the land"), an individual whose trustworthiness on these matters is questionable. Owing to these doubts, the *ḥaver* is expected to set aside the gifts, though in a manner that minimizes the financial loss. Initially, the produce was subject to *terumah* for the priests, first tithe for the Levites (a tenth of which must be given to the priest) and, depending on the year in the sabbatical cycle, second tithe which can be consumed by the owner in Jerusalem, or poor tithe. Since the *am ha-areẓ* is relied on to obey the severe Torah-based precept of *terumah*, and there is no ritual prohibition against eating the tithes due to the Levites or the poor, the *demai* procedure involved designating the first tithe only so that the priestly portion could be taken from it and given to the kohen. Because neither the Levites nor the poor could prove their respective entitlement to their tithes (since *demai* is by definition a doubtful case), these remained the property of the owner. As a result, the actual financial loss borne by the owner by re-tithing *demai* was modest.

The institution of *demai* seems to date back to early in the Second Commonwealth era and evidently reflects the fundamental identity of the Pharisees as individuals who distinguished themselves from the less rigid ritual standards of the *ammei ha-areẓ*. A. Büchler argued that the Mishnah really reflects the clashes between Judean and Galilean cultures in the second century C.E. when the rabbis cited in the Mishnah were active and Judean rabbis were migrating northward in the aftermath of the Bar Kokhba revolt; however, his view has not been widely accepted. More recent scholarship has voiced considerable skepticism about the degree to which the conceptual picture that emerges from the Talmudic texts reflects the actual social or religious situation, especially as regards its assumptions about the normative status of rabbinic *halakhah*.

A rabbinic tradition (Mishnah Sotah end; Tosefta Sotah end of Ch. 13; TJ Sotah 9:11 and end of TJ Ma'aser Sheni) speaks of *demai* as being in force in the time of Johanan the High Priest; i.e., John Hyrcanus (135–104 B.C.E.), who enforced separation of the required gifts by the producers, thereby exempting the purchasers. The *baraita* in the Babylonian Talmud (Sotah 48a), on the other hand, describes Johanan as the person who first instituted *demai* upon discovering the laxity of tithe observance.

Demai is the tractate in the Mishnah, Tosefta and Jerusalem Talmud (but not the Babylonian) that deals with the halakhic concept of *demai*, doubtfully tithed produce. An exception to the normal pattern of arranging the sequence of tractates according to the numbers of their chapters, *Demai* (with seven chapters) appears third in the Mishnah and Jerusalem Talmud, and in most manuscripts of the Tosefta, before tractates with more chapters. The Mishnah tractate contains disputes between the Houses of Shammai and Hillel, sages from Yavneh, as well as much material from the generation of Usha.

Because *demai* is a rabbinic stringency that was instituted in response to a minority of unreliable individuals, the rabbis tended to interpret doubtful cases in a lenient manner. This is the theme of much the tractate, which deals with exemptions, such as for species of produce that are not normally kept as food (1:1), produce from outside the halakhic borders of Israel (1:3, 6:11), certain types of commercial purveyors (2:4, 5:1–4, 6), etc. Similarly, tithes that were separated as *demai* are not subject to all the restrictions that would apply to fully sacred produce (1:2), especially where it is used for the fulfillment of religious precepts, such as distribution to the poor (3:1), an *'eruv* (1:4), etc.

The Mishnah (2:2) discusses how a person may be certified as a *ne'eman* (one who is deemed trustworthy with respect to tithing); or as a full-fledged *ḥaver* who is trusted on matters of purity as well (2:3).

Historians are not in agreement whether the restrictions observed by the *ḥaver* were considered obligatory or voluntary expressions of extraordinary piety. At any rate, the tractate *Demai* is addressed to a target audience of *ḥaverim* who are assumed to be observing the highest standards or tithing and purity. Because the need for *demai* results from the acceptance by some Jews of stricter standards than those followed by others, the tractate deals extensively with the relationships and interactions between the *ḥaver* and other segments of the community who are less punctilious about those matters. Thus, it provides instruction for how to proceed when obtaining foodstuffs from non-*ḥaverim* (4:1), when transferring food to them (2:3, 3:5), when eating in each other's homes (4:2, 7:1), or when operating in partnership, as sharecroppers (6:1–8) or with family relations (3:6). The general tenor of the *halakhah* is pragmatic, in that it focuses on solutions to specific technical situations, while presuming the existence of normal social and economic relations between the various groups, rather than encouraging separation from the less observant segments of the populace.

BIBLIOGRAPHY: A. Büchler. *Der Galilèaische 'Am-Ha' Ares, Des Zweiten Jahrhunderts, Beitrèage Zur Innern Geschichte Des Palèastinischen Judentums in Den Ersten Zwei Jahrhunderten* (1906); idem, *Am ha-Arez ha-Gelili* (1964); A. Oppenheimer, *The 'Am Ha-Aretz: A Study in the Social History of the Jewish People in the Hellenistic-Roman Period*, Arbeiten zur Literatur und Geschichte des hellenistischen Judentums, 8 (1977); R.S. Sarason, *A History of the Mishnaic Law of Agriculture*: Section Three, a Study of Tractate Demai (1979); idem, *Demai*, Chicago Studies in the History of Judaism (1993) [= translation of TJ Demai].

[Eliezer L. Segal (2nd ed.)]

DEMALACH, YOEL (1924–), Israeli agriculturalist. Demalach was born in Italy and settled in Palestine in 1939. He joined kibbutz Revivim where he devoted himself to Negev agricultural development and invented irrigation methods for arid zone agriculture. In 1986 he received the Israel Prize for his investigation and teaching of arid region agriculture.

DEMBER, HARRY L. (1882–1943), German physicist. Born in Leimbach, Dember was at the Dresden Technische Hochschule (1905), where he was appointed professor of physics in 1914 and also director of the Physics Institute in 1923. Driven out by the Nazis, he held similar positions at the University of Istanbul from 1933 to 1941. He later immigrated to the United States and was visiting professor at Rutgers University, New Jersey, at the time of his death. His field was the photoelectricity of crystals and one aspect of his research in this area is known as the "Dember Effect."

DEMBITZ, LEWIS NAPHTALI (1833–1907), U.S. lawyer and Jewish leader. Dembitz was born in Zirke, province of Posen, Prussia, and went to the U.S. in 1849. He completed law studies in Cincinnati and then settled in Louisville, Kentucky, where he practiced law. Dembitz entered politics early and was elected to several Republican Party offices. He was a delegate to the Republican National Convention that nominated Lincoln in 1860. In 1888 he drafted the first Australian (secret ballot) voting system. Dembitz wrote a number of books on American law, including *Kentucky Jurisprudence* (1890); *Law Language for Shorthand Writers* (1892); and *Land Titles in the United States* (2 vols., 1895). Dembitz's affiliation with Jewish life was at first through the Reform movement, and he was a member of the commission on the plan of study for Hebrew Union College. But after that institution became openly Reform, and especially after the acceptance of the *Pittsburgh Platform, he joined the Conservative movement and helped to establish the Jewish Theological Seminary. Dembitz contributed several articles on Talmudic jurisprudence and on liturgy to the *Jewish Encyclopedia* and prepared the translations of Exodus and Leviticus which were incorporated into the revised English Bible of the Jewish Publication Society (1917). His volume *Jewish Services in Synagogue and Home* (1898) was widely used. His nephew, Louis *Brandeis, who admired him greatly, changed his middle name from David to Dembitz.

BIBLIOGRAPHY: M. Davis, *Emergence of Conservative Judaism* (1963), 333–5.

[Jack Reimer]

DEMBITZER, ḤAYYIM NATHAN (1820–1892), talmudist and historian. Dembitzer was born in Cracow and became a *dayyan* in his native city. Active in financial support of the old *yishuv* in Ereẓ Israel, Dembitzer urged scholars to renew their support for the R. Meir Ba'al ha-Nes Fund (1852). His first research was devoted to responsa literature and the tosafists. Dembitzer became noted for historical research and critical work in the field of talmudic and rabbinic literature and its leading personalities. As early as 1841 he had begun correspondence on biographical and historical subjects with such well-known rabbis as Solomon *Kluger and Ẓevi Hirsch ben Meir *Chajes. A visit to Germany in 1874 brought him in touch with such contemporary scholars as H. Graetz, Z. Frankel, L. Zunz, and D. Kaufmann, who influenced him to publish his work. His works include *Livyat Ḥen* (1882), notes and glosses on the work of Ravyah (R. Eliezer b. Joel ha-Levi); *Kelilat Yofi*, volume one (1888), a historical survey of the Lvov rabbis, and volume two (1893, repr. 1960), biographies of famous rabbis from Poland-Latvia from 1493 to 1692, including information on Polish Jewish independent government; essays on the Council of Four Lands; and *Torat Ḥen* (1895), halakhic responsa.

BIBLIOGRAPHY: Wettstein, *Toledot Meharḥan* (1893), reprinted in J. Mandelbaum, *Mafte'aḥ le-Sefer Kelilat Yofi* (1968), 11–35; Brann, in: MGWJ, 39 (1895), 142; B. Wachstein, *Die hebraeische Publizistik in Wien*, 3 (1930), 11; *Aḥi'asaf*, 1 (1893), 296 (obituary).

[Yehoshua Horowitz / Israel Halpern]

DEMBLIN, BENJAMIN (pseudonym of **Benjamin Teitelbaum**; 1897–1976), Yiddish writer. Born in Modzicz, Poland, Demblin immigrated to the U.S. in 1921 and began publishing in various Yiddish periodicals. Three of his novels deal with the *ḥalutzim: Tsvey un a Driter* ("Two and a Third," 1943), *Tsankendike Likht* ("Flickering Candles," 1958), and *Der Tate iz Gekumen* ("Father Has Come," included in the collection *Oyf Dray Kontinentn,* "Three Continents," 1963). His book-cycle *Erev Nakht* consists of five parts: *Erev Nakht* ("Before Night," 1954), *Oyf Eygenem Barot* ("On One's One," 1961), *In der Velt Arayn* ("Into the World," 1965), *A Fremde Velt* ("A Foreign World," 1973), and *In Nayem Land* ("In a New Land," 1973). His other books are *Afn Shvel* ("On the Threshold," 1933) and *Vest-Sayd* ("West Side," 1938; Heb. 1954). Demblin was a realist who depicted in epic style the social changes in Jewish and general life.

BIBLIOGRAPHY: B. Demblin, *In der Velt Arayn* (1965), 383–98 (bibliography by Y. Yeshurin); LNYL, 2 (1958), 534–5. **ADD. BIBLIOGRAPHY:** Kagan, Leksikon (1986), 201.

[Moshe Starkman / Tamar Lewinsky (2nd ed.)]

DEMBO, ISAAC (1846–1906), physician and communal worker, born in Ponevezh, Lithuania. He graduated from the military academy of medicine in 1870 and volunteered as a doctor in the Russian-Turkish War of 1877. Subsequently Dembo undertook a campaign to defend Jewish ritual slaughter against allegations of cruelty made by antisemites in Russia and abroad. He took part in a conference of the Russian Association for the Protection of Animals in 1891. To prove his point, Dembo also carried out experiments in Russia in the laboratory of the Russian physiologist I. Pavlov, and abroad in the laboratories of Du Bois-Reymond, Hoppe-Seyler, and Munk, among others, as well as in slaughterhouses. His *Das Schaechten* was translated into English (*The Jewish Method of Slaughter*, 1894), French, and Hebrew.

DEMETRIUS, earliest known Greco-Jewish writer. He lived during the reign of Ptolemy IV (221–204 B.C.E.). In ancient lists of Josephus and Clement of Alexandria, Demetrius is named first, followed by Philo (the Elder), and Eupolemus (Jos., Apion, 1:218; Clement, *Stromata* 1:141, 1). Without making clear whether these are Jewish or heathen, Josephus laments their inability to follow Hebrew records accurately (Josephus erroneously labels Demetrius as being from Phaleron).

Aside from Josephus' ambiguous testimony, seven remnants of Demetrius' work survive. Except for Fragment Six, cited by Clement of Alexandria, and Fragment Three, which reviews Clement's sources, the remaining texts have been salvaged in Eusebius' *Praeparatio Evangelica*, which quotes Alexander Polyhistor's monograph "On the Jews."

Fragment One, about ⁴⁄₅ of all Demetrius' texts, deals with patriarchal chronology, and reveals the great fervor with which biblical studies were pursued in the third century B.C.E. By a minute analysis of Genesis, as well as by some gratuitous assumptions, Demetrius chronicles the year and month of Jacob's travels and the birth of each of his 12 sons and daughter. Jacob stayed in Haran 20 years, during 14 of which he served for Laban's two daughters (Gen. 31:41). He married both sisters after the first seven years, and Demetrius maintains that all of his children (except Benjamin) were born during the next seven years. Thus, except for one interval, Leah bore her six sons and her daughter in an exact sequence of ten months. Demetrius then proceeds to record the age of each of the children in conjunction with the events of their father's life, the clan's eventual descent into Egypt, and the death of each member. The repetitiveness of the dates suggests that Demetrius aimed at the construction of a chronological canon of biblical history, with summaries stressing significant events, such as the birth of Abraham, Jacob's descent into Egypt, and the Exodus. Demetrius' chronology from Creation coincides remarkably with that preserved in the Septuagint version: the dating of the Flood in Demetrius is 2264 compared to 2262 according to the Septuagint and 1656 by the Hebrew; the birth of Abraham is set at 3334 as in the Septuagint compared to 1948 in the Hebrew, and the Exodus is dated as 3839 versus 3849 following the Septuagint and 2668 according to the Hebrew.

The first discrepancy is apparently due to Demetrius' counting the birth of Seth two years after the flood. The obvious conclusion is that Demetrius depended on the Greek version. It is conceivable, moreover, that Demetrius' chronological scheme solves the puzzle of how the texts of Genesis 5:11 and Exodus 12:40 were altered from the Hebrew numbers into those found in the Greek. It is now agreed that the alteration was deliberate. Demetrius may have studied with, possibly even was one of, the men who produced the Septuagint.

Fragment Two traces the genealogy of Zipporah, whom Demetrius identifies with the "Ethiopian woman" whom Moses married (Num. 12:1), a view adopted by *Ezekiel the poet and the Talmud (MK 16b). Demetrius traces her descent from Abraham and Keturah (Gen. 25:1–4), making her lineage more distinguished than that of Moses. She was the sixth generation after Abraham, Moses the seventh. The chronographer was apparently defending Moses against charges of having violated his own laws against intermarriage.

Demetrius did not restrict himself to chronography. Fragment Seven relates Abraham's binding of Isaac (Gen. 22). The miraculous sweetening of the bitter waters of the desert is reported in Fragment Four. The reasonable hypothesis that Demetrius represents a school of biblical exegesis is supported by Fragment Five, where he suggests that despite the statement in Exodus 13:18 to the contrary, the Jews came out of Egypt unarmed. He bases this on their statement that they were going for a journey of three days and that after sacrificing they would return (Ex. 5:3): "Where did they get their weapons from? It appears that they obtained the arms of the Egyptians who were drowned in the Red Sea." In spite of Fragment Three, which groups Demetrius with Aristobulus and Josephus, there is no reason to assume that he addressed himself to the pagan world. Demetrius wrote for students of the Bible without any trace of apologetics. There is no evidence of his influence in the Book of Jubilees, Philo, Josephus, or the rabbinic chronological treatise *Seder Olam*, but his impact on Philo (the Elder) and Eupolemus in matters relating to chronology, as well as on Ezekiel the poet, who adopted many scenes from Demetrius, is noteworthy.

BIBLIOGRAPHY: J. Freudenthal, *Hellenistische Studien*, 1 (1874), 35–82; Pauly-Wissowa, 8 (1901), 2813–14, no. 79; F. Jacoby (ed.), *Fragmente griechischer Historiker*, 3, C2 (1958), 666f., 110. 722.

[Ben Zion Wacholder]

DEMETRIUS, Jewish notable of *Alexandria (first century B.C.E.). He was the second husband of Mariamne, the daughter of Agrippa I. He "stood among the first in wealth and birth" among the Jews of Alexandria, and became *alabarch of that city. Mariamne left her husband Julius Archelaus to marry him. They had a son Agrippinus.

[Edna Elazary]

°DEMETRIUS I SOTER (162–150 B.C.E.), ruler of the Seleucid dynasty in Syria; son of *Seleucus IV. In his youth Demetrius was a hostage in Rome. When he became aware of the weakness of *Antiochus V and the governor *Lysias, he escaped, with the aim of wresting the Syrian crown from his cousin. Demetrius established his rule despite the opposition of the Roman Senate which did not wish to see an energetic ruler on the Seleucid throne. In consequence of the victory of his general *Bacchides over Judah Maccabee in 160 B.C.E., Demetrius reinstated the Syrian overlordship of Judea. He was also successful in crushing an insurrection in the eastern provinces led by Timarchus, governor of Babylonia. In the course of time, Demetrius, as a result of his tyranny, brought down upon himself the hatred of the Syrians. He also became embroiled with Attalus II of Pergamon and with Ptolemy V of Egypt. Finally the two kings joined forces against him in support of the pretender *Alexander Balas, who claimed to be the son of Antiochus IV. Jonathan the Hasmonean associated himself with Alexander, who appointed him high priest. The substantial concessions now made by Demetrius to the Jews availed nothing, as Jonathan did not trust him. In the end, Demetrius was defeated by Alexander and fell in battle (I Macc. 7:1–9; 10:20, 40–59; Jos., Ant., 12:389, 390, 393, 397, 400, 402–3, 415, 420; *ibid.*, 13:23, 35, 37, 39, 43–44, 47–48, 58–61).

BIBLIOGRAPHY: E.R. Bevan, *House of Seleucus*, 2 (1902), index; B. Niese, *Geschichte der griechischen und makedonischen Staaten…*, 3 (1903), 245ff., 263ff.; Schuerer, Hist, index; A.R. Bellinger, *End of the Seleucids* (1949), 75–76; Y. Yadin, *Ha-Megillot ha-Genuzot mi-Midbar Yehudah* (1958[2]), 119–20; T.H. Gaster, *Dead Sea Scriptures* (1956), 243.

[Abraham Schalit]

°DEMETRIUS II (Nicator) (141–125 B.C.E.), ruler of the Seleucid dynasty in Syria; son of *Demetrius I Soter. In 146/5, with the support of Ptolemy V of Egypt, he defeated Alexander Balas. Ptolemy succumbed to wounds received in this battle and Demetrius, having succeeded in getting the Egyptian army to leave Syria, seized control of the country. He now came to an agreement with Jonathan the Hasmonean, whereby the latter was confirmed in his high priesthood and his annexation of the three regions of Ephraim, Lydda, and Ramathaim was officially endorsed. On his side, Jonathan was compelled to raise the siege of Acre, to cede Jaffa and Ashdod which he had captured, and to promise a tribute of 300 talents. Relying upon his army of mercenaries, Demetrius embarked upon a tyrannical rule, which eventually led to the revolt of *Diodotus-Tryphon. Tryphon made use of the young son of Alexander Balas, who until then had been under the protection of the Nabatean governor, and was successful in winning over the Syrian populace. In the civil war between Demetrius and Tryphon that now ensued, Jonathan supported Demetrius, until the latter was taken prisoner in a campaign against the Parthians in 141. Against this background of Syrian weakness, the independence of Judea was achieved under Simeon the Hasmonean. During the imprisonment of Demetrius, his brother *Antiochus (VII) Sidetes reigned over Syria. He defeated Tryphon and also the Jews, but he too came to grief on his expedition against the Parthians in 130–129. Demetrius, whom the Parthians freed in order to stir up civil war in Syria, regained the kingdom in 129, but lost it again through revolution, when Ptolemy Physcon, king of Egypt, supported the claims of one Alexander who pretended to be the son of Alexander Balas. The war between Demetrius and this Alexander came to an end after two years. Demetrius attempted to escape to Tyre, but was captured and put to death in 126/5 (I Macc. 10:67–11:56; Jos., Ant., 13:86–87, 109–62, 174, 177, 180, 184–6, 218–9, 221–2, 253, 267–9, 271).

BIBLIOGRAPHY: E.R. Bevan, *House of Seleucus*, 2 (1902), index; B. Niese, *Geschichte der griechischen und makedonischen Staaten…*, 3 (1903), 245ff., 263ff.; Schuerer, Hist, index; A.R. Bellinger, *End of the Seleucids* (1949), 75–76; Y. Yadin, *Ha-Megillot ha-Genuzot mi-Midbar Yehudah* (1958[2]), 119–20; T.H. Gaster, *Dead Sea Scriptures* (1956), 243.

[Abraham Schalit]

°DEMETRIUS III EUKARIOS THEOS PHILOPATER SOTER (96–88 B.C.E.), ruler of the Seleucid dynasty in Syria; son of Antiochus Grypus, and one of the last kings of the Seleucid dynasty. On the initiative of Ptolemy Lathyrus, king of Egypt, Demetrius was appointed king of Syria, but civil wars prevented him from consolidating his rule over the whole country. From Damascus, his capital, Demetrius intervened in the affairs of Judea. When Alexander Yannai was waging war against the Arabs and the rulers of Transjordan, the rebellious Pharisees called in the aid of Demetrius against their king. Although Demetrius defeated the army of Yannai in a battle near Shechem, he was finally forced to leave the country. The memory of these events has apparently been preserved in the *Pesher Nahum* of the Dead Sea Scrolls: "…[Deme]trius, King of Greece, who sought to enter Jerusalem through the counsel of flatterers…" In the war against his brother Philip, Demetrius was captured and exiled to the court of Mithridates II, king of Pontus, where he died in captivity (Jos., Wars, 1:93–95; Jos., Ant., 13:370–1, 376–9, 384–6).

BIBLIOGRAPHY: E.R. Bevan, *House of Seleucus*, 2 (1902), index; B. Niese, *Geschichte der griechischen und makedonischen Staaten…*, 3 (1903), 245ff., 263ff.; Schuerer, Hist, index; A.R. Bellinger, *End of the Seleucids* (1949), 75–76; Y. Yadin, *Ha-Megillot ha-Genuzot mi-Midbar Yehudah* (1958[2]), 119–20; T.H. Gaster, *Dead Sea Scriptures* (1956), 243.

[Abraham Schalit]

DEMETZ, PETER (1922–), Czech scholar and writer. Born in Prague into a Czech-Jewish-German family, Demetz spent the last years of the war in a Nazi labor camp for *mischlinge*. After finishing his studies at Charles University in Prague, he went into exile in 1949. He settled in the United States, where in 1962 he became professor of German and comparative literature at Yale University, retiring in 1979. He lectured at many American and European universities and after 1989 also in the Czech Republic. In 2000 he was awarded the Medal of Merit by President Havel.

The existence of three cultures – Czech, German, and Jewish – in the Czech lands was always in the foreground of his research and literary activities. Among his works are *Franz Kafka a Praha* (1947; "Franz Kafka and Prague"), including "Franz Kafka and the Czech Nation," and studies of Rilke, such as *The Czech Themes of Rilke* (1952) and *René Rilkes Prager Jahre* (1953; "Prague Years of René Rilke"; Cz. tr., 1998).

Other works include *Die Literaturgeschichte Švejks* (1989; "The Literary History of Schweik") and *Über Literaten und sanfte Revolution in Berlin und Prag* (1991; "On Writers and the Velvet Revolution in Berlin and Prague"). *Böhmische Sonne, mährischer Mond: Essays und Erinnerungen* (1996; Cz., 1997) is a collection of essays on Hašek, Rilke, Kafka, Masaryk, and others. *Prague in Black and Gold. The History of a City* (1997; Cz., 1998) is a detailed history of Prague from the early Middle Ages until the period of T.G. Masaryk, with emphasis not only on its multicultural character but also on its longstanding tradition of rationality, realism, science, and the spirit of criticism.

Demetz returns to Franz Kafka in his study *The Air Show at Brescia, 1909* (2002; Cz., 2003), in which he explores the circumstances under which Kafka wrote his article "Die Aeroplane in Brescia," published in *Bohemia* in 1909. He includes the portraits of those who took part in the air show: Max *Brod and his brother Otto, Italian poet and novelist G. d'Annunzio, the composer Puccini, and the aviators.

Additional works of Demetz deal with German literary history, including *Marx, Engels und die Dichter* (1959; "Marx, Engels and the Poets"), *Formen des Realismus: Theodor Fontane* (1964, 1966; "Forms of Realism: Theodor Fontane"), *German Post-war Literature: A Critical Introduction* (1970, 1972), and many others.

Demetz also published old tales of Prague and many translations of well-known Czech authors into German (Božena Němcová, Jiří *Orten, Jaroslav Seifert, Ludvík Kundera, etc.).

BIBLIOGRAPHY: L. Nezdařil, "Zpráva o Petru Demetzovi," in: *Literární noviny* (1992, 1997).

[Milos Pojar (2nd ed.)]

DEMILLE, CECIL B. (1881–1959), U.S. film producer and director. DeMille was born in Ashfield, Massachusetts. His parents, Henry and Beatrice, were playwrights. His father was a minister, for whom his mother, born an English Jew, converted. After his father died, when DeMille was 12, he worked for several years at his mother's playhouse. In 1913, together with Jesse Lasky and Samuel Goldfish (later Goldwyn), DeMille formed the Jesse L. Lasky Feature Play Co., the basis for Paramount Pictures. The company's debut cinematic venture was *The Squaw Man* (1914), and the three were instrumental in Hollywood's becoming the film capital of the world. DeMille, who produced or directed as many as 70 films, and discovered such stars as Gloria Swanson, is renowned for his sweeping, epic style and frequent moral content, evident in films such as *The Ten Commandments* (1923, remade 1956), *The King of Kings* (1927), *Cleopatra* (1934), *Samson and Delilah* (1949), and *The Greatest Show on Earth* (1952). He also managed to weave a persona that matched the largeness of his films, hosting the popular radio series *Lux Radio Theater* every week for more than a decade, and frequently appeared in his movies as himself, well before the director Alfred Hitchcock employed the same tactic. Perhaps the most memorable example of DeMille's famous cameos occurs in *Sunset Boulevard* (1950), starring his protégé Gloria Swanson. During the McCarthy era of that same decade, DeMille temporarily fell out of favor for his adamant anti-Communist politics, but his views did not mar his legacy as a Hollywood legend.

[Casey Schwartz (2nd ed.)]

°**DEMJANJUK, JOHN** (**Ivan**; 1920–), Nazi death camp guard. Born in the Ukrainian village of Dub Macharenzi, Demjanjuk survived the famine in the Ukraine and was drafted into the Soviet Army at the start of World War II. Sustaining an injury to the back, he was treated in several hospitals before being returned to the front. During the battle of Kerch he was taken prisoner by the Germans. Recruited in a German prisoner-of-war camp, Demjanjuk was trained to be a Nazi camp guard, an auxiliary (watchman), at the Trawniki training camp in Lublin, Poland, where he was issued identity card 1393 and was dispatched to serve at several concentration and extermination camps until the war's end. Arriving in the United States in 1952, Demjanjuk concealed his Nazi service and gained admittance to the U.S. and eventually U.S. citizenship in 1958, living in Cleveland and working at a Ford auto plant.

In 1975, U.S. officials received information alleging that Demjanjuk had been a Nazi death camp guard at Sobibor. In 1976, his picture was sent to the Israeli police for investigation. Over the following years 18 Holocaust survivors would identify Demjanjuk as a guard at Treblinka, and several would identify him to police and in court as the gas chamber operator "Ivan" at the Treblinka death camp. Beginning in 1977, a series of legal actions ensued in the United States in which Demjanjuk was denaturalized and stripped of his U.S. citizenship (1981), ordered deported (1984), and extradited to stand trial in Israel for war crimes and crimes against humanity (1986), the first person to be so charged since Adolf Eichmann in 1961.

In 1987, the District Court of Israel put Demjanjuk on trial and broadcast the proceedings live on radio and on Israeli TV. Thousands attended the trial, giving an immediacy to the horrors of the Holocaust for a new generation. The trial lasted 18 months and involved the testimony of five Holocaust survivors and many experts on history as well as forensic experts who authenticated Demjanjuk's Nazi service ID card #1393, the original of which had been uncovered in Soviet archives and delivered to the Israeli authorities. In April 1988, Demjanjuk was convicted and sentenced to death. However, during the course of the appeal to Israel's Supreme Court, depositions of former Nazi guards tried in the Soviet Union in the late 1970s identified a different person named Ivan as the gas chamber operator at Treblinka. Even though the persons who gave the depositions were not known to be alive or cross-examined, the Supreme Court of Israel decided that this created enough of a doubt to reverse the decision against Demjanjuk. Although the court concluded that Demjanjuk himself was not innocent and had served the Nazis, nonetheless the Supreme Court of Israel ruled in 1993 that since the center of gravity of the case revolved around the six-month period between September 1942 and March 1943 when Demjanjuk was alleged to have been at Treblinka and Demjanjuk had not had a full opportunity to defend himself against charges of being at other death camps such as Sobibor, and that a new trial might contravene Israel's law against double jeopardy, and given that Demjanjuk had already spent eight years in Israeli prison in solitary confinement, the Supreme Court of Israel decided to release Demjanjuk and return him to the United States.

Back in the U.S., American courts found that U.S. prosecutors had known of these Russian testimonies and acted improperly. The courts vacated the extradition order against Demjanjuk, allowing him to remain in the U.S. (1993) and then set aside the decision to denaturalize him (1998). Accordingly, in 1999 the U.S. government filed a new denaturalization suit against Demjanjuk. In the intervening years, more Nazi era official documents had been unearthed which confirmed Demjanjuk's service at several concentration and extermination camps such as L.G. Okswo, Majdanek, Sobibor, and Flossenburg and further bolstered the authenticity of the Trawniki ID card #1393. Accordingly, Demjanjuk was again denaturalized (2002), which order was affirmed by the Sixth Circuit Court of Appeals in 2004. Demjanjuk, who continued to live in Cleveland, Ohio, appealed those decisions.

BIBLIOGRAPHY: *United States v. Demjanjuka*, 518 F. Supp. 1362 (N.D. Ohio 1981), revoking Demjanjuk's citizenship and naturalization; *Demajnjuk v. Petrovsky*, 612 F. Supp. 571 (N.D. Ohio 1985), allowing Demjanjuk to be extradited to Israel; *Demjanjuk v. Petrovsky*, 10 F.3d 338 (6th Circ. 1993), reopening the case after Demjanjuk was extradited to Israel and acquitted; *United States v. Demjanjuk* No. C77–923, 1998 U.S. Dist. LEXIS 4047 (N.S. Ohio 1998), setting aside Demjanjuk I, on the basis of prosecutorial misconduct; *United States v. Demjanjuk*, No. 1:99CV1193,2002 WL 544622 (N.D. Ohio Feb. 21, 2002); *United States v. Demjanjuk*, No. 1:99CV1193, 2002 WL 544623 (N.D. Ohio, Feb, 21, 2002), revoking Demjanjuk's citizenship and naturalization; *United States v. Demjanjuk*, No. 02–3539 (6th Circ. 2004), affirming the denaturalization; T. Teicholz, *The Trial of Ivan the Terrible: State of Israel vs. John Demjanjuk* (1990); A.F. Landau, *The Demjanjuk Appeal – Summary* (1993), at: Israel Ministry of Foreign Affairs, www.Israel-mfa.gov.il.

[Tom Teicholz (2nd ed.)]

DEMNAT (Fr. **Demnate**), town in the High Atlas Mountains of *Morocco, 70 miles (110 km.) east of the city of *Marrakesh. Demnat had an important Jewish community whose members settled there in the early 12th century. Living in a Berber-Muslim milieu, Demnat's Jewry engaged in agricultural activities, producing some of the best wine in Morocco, but were also craftsmen and artisans specializing in leather goods. Partial modernization and the spread of French language and culture gradually became embedded in Demnati Jewish life from the early 1930s due to the colonial presence as well as the work of the coeducational school of the *Alliance Israélite Universelle, founded in 1932. Many of the boys and girls who frequented this school subsequently adopted French names such as Robert, Jacques, Marcelle, Alice, and Jacqueline.

Judeo-Berber coexistence in Demnat remained harmonious, with no major violence against the Jews until the mid-19th century. From the early 1860s and into the mid-1880s, however, Jewish-Muslim relations were exacerbated as Jews faced a pogrom (1864) and were exposed to undue humiliations by the local governor, who instigated abuses (1884–85). Owing to the efforts of the Alliance teachers in *Fez, the French minister plenipotentiary in *Tangier, L.C. Féraud, was informed of the situation in Demnat and contacted Sultan Hasan I over the matter. Féraud's intercession led to the issuance of two *zahirs* (sultanic decrees) ordering cessation of the abuses. From the contents of the *zahirs* – for the year 1885 – it can be seen that the Jews had been compelled to buy goods from Muslims against their will, were recruited to work without receiving wages, had to give away their farm animals without receiving payment, and had to give up some of their most valuable products, particularly leather goods.

The status of the Jews improved markedly once again under French colonial domination. In the early 1950s, on the eve of communal self-liquidation and *aliyah*, conducted by the Jewish Agency for Palestine, 1,800 Jews were living in Demnat. The tides of radical nationalism, and the Moroccan struggle for independence from France beginning in August 1953, which took on a violent character in 1954–55, only hastened Jewish departures. By the early 1960s only a few Jews remained there.

BIBLIOGRAPHY: C. de Foucauld, *Reconnaissance au Maroc* (1888); P. Flamand, *Un mellah en pays berbère: Demnate* (1952); M.M. Laskier, *The Alliance Israélite Universelle and the Jewish Communities of Morocco: 1862–1962* (1983); M.M. Laskier, "Aspects of Change and Modernization: The Jewish Communities of Morocco's Bled," in: M. Abitbol (ed.), *Communautés juives des marges sahariennes du Maghreb* (1982), 329–64.

[Michael M. Laskier (2nd ed.)]

DEMOCRATIC FRACTION, radical opposition faction in the Zionist movement between the years 1901 and 1904 that demanded the democratization of Zionist institutions, the organization of cultural activities by the Zionist Organization, and immediate settlement in Ereẓ Israel. Its leaders were Leo *Motzkin and Chaim *Weizmann. Their demand that the Zionist Organization conduct cultural activities sharply contradicted the stand of the religious wing, which violently opposed such programs, fearing that they would be used for the dissemination of "secular" culture. During the Fourth *Zionist Congress (1900) it was decided at a Zionist student meeting to establish a democratic-progressive faction or party. A conference was held in Basle, a few days before the Fifth Zionist Congress (1901), attended by about 40 delegates, most of whom were Russian Zionist students from German, Swiss, and French universities. The conference decided to establish the Democratic Fraction, which would remain within the Zionist Organization but would have separate headquarters and independent cultural activities. It was also decided to create a Jewish statistical bureau and to conduct research into suitable ways of settling Ereẓ Israel, preferring the cooperative method. The conference also recommended the democratization of philanthropic organizations in the Diaspora and the establishment of cooperatives to provide economic self-help for workers, stressing the need to form a trade union for Jewish workers. Finally, it demanded the separation of Zionism and religion and condemned the Zionist movement's submission to its Orthodox wing. The Democratic Fraction, which appeared for the first time as an organized bloc at the Fifth Zionist Congress (1901), prompted the unification of those who opposed, for religious reasons, any cultural activities by the Zionist Organization.

An Information Bureau in Geneva headed by Chaim Weizmann served as the secretariat for the Democratic Fraction. Its activities centered around the development of the publishing house *Juedischer Verlag, the establishment of the statistical bureau, and the creation of a fund to found a Jewish university in Ereẓ Israel.

The organization of the Fraction was weak, and it did not even hold the planned annual conference. Only a consultation of 11 men (including Weizmann, Feiwel, and Martin *Buber) was held in January 1904. When they decided to join the emerging opposition to the *Uganda scheme, the Fraction practically ceased to exist. Thereafter, its members worked individually for the overall Zionist Organization.

BIBLIOGRAPHY: A. Bein, *Sefer Motzkin* (1939), 56–66; Ch. Weizmann, *Trial and Error* (1966), index; I. Klausner, *Oppoziẓyah le-Herzl* (1960); B. Feiwel, in: *Ost und West* (1902), 687–94.

[Israel Klausner]

DEMOCRATIC MOVEMENT FOR CHANGE (DMC; Heb. *Ha-Tenu'ah ha-Demokratit Le-Shinu'i*), political party formed in 1976 prior to the elections to the Ninth Knesset. The DMC was basically a protest party against the *Israel Labor. Its core group was made up of former chief of staff and archeology professor Yigael *Yadin, who headed the new party, *Shinu'i (a party formed by Amnon *Rubinstein in 1974), a group of former members of the Labor Party, headed by Major General (res.) Meir *Amit, a group of former members of the *Likud, headed by Shemuel *Tamir, as well as several Sephardi and Druze personalities.

The DMC participated in the elections to the Ninth Knesset on a platform that called for electoral reform to introduce a system of single-member constituencies; the passing of a Parties Law; a drastic paring of the government bureaucracy; the decentralization of the government system and the strengthening of local government; the preparation of a constitution (see *Governance); the establishment of a Ministry of Welfare; the reorganization of the education system in order to enhance social integration and reduce social gaps; a new housing policy based on building apartments for rental; strengthening the rule of law; preference for production over services; a fairer distribution of the tax burden; a fight against "black money" (unreported income); preservation of the Jewish character of the State of Israel and of Jerusalem as its capital; a willingness to accept a territorial compromise in return for true peace; opposition to the establishment of an additional state west of the Jordan River; the fixing of Israel's security border along the Jordan River; and continued Israeli control over areas vital for the State's security.

Most of the members of the new party were hoping to form a government with the Labor-Mapam Alignment after the elections. However, for the first time in Israel's history, the *Likud formed a government and commanded an absolute majority in the Knesset together with the religious parties, even without the DMC's 15 Knesset members (elected mainly at the expense of Labor); thus, despite its impressive electoral success, the DMC started its parliamentary life without real influence. The DMC joined the government formed by Menaḥem *Begin several months after it was sworn in, with Yadin becoming deputy prime minister, Tamir minister of justice, and Amit minister of transportation and communications. However, none of its ministers was directly involved in either the peace negotiations with Egypt or the liberalization of the economy. Within a year and four months of the elections to the Ninth Knesset the DMC broke up into several parliamentary groups. At the time of the elections to the Tenth Knesset in 1981 five of the DMC's 15 members were members of Shinu'i – the Center Party (the only splinter of the DMC that survived); two had joined the Labor Party; one had joined the Likud; one had joined Telem; four were independent members of the Knesset; and two were single-member parliamentary factions.

The dismal failure of the DMC to take root was a blow to all those who had hoped to form a strong Center Party. It was only in the elections to the Sixteenth Knesset in 2003 that the offshoot of the original Shinu'i managed to repeat the DMC's electoral success.

[Susan Hattis Rolef (2nd ed.)]

DEMOGRAPHY. This entry is arranged according to the following outline:

INTRODUCTION

SIZE AND GEOGRAPHICAL DISTRIBUTION OF WORLD JEWRY

Major Geographical Shifts of World Jewry

UP TO WORLD WAR I

1914 TO 1939

THE SHOAH

1948 TO 1970

1970 TO 2005

Dispersion and Concentration

URBANIZATION

POPULATION CHARACTERISTICS
- **Age composition**
- **Sex**
- **Origin Groups (Edot)**

INTRODUCTION

Jewish demography, like demography in general, deals essentially with the size and geographical distribution of the population, with its composition according to various characteristics (e.g., sex, age), and with population movements. The latter consist of natural movements or "*vital statistics" – births, deaths, marriages, and divorces; migratory movements (*migrations); and accessions to, or secessions from, the Jewish group. Demographic knowledge is based preponderantly on statistical data and their analysis; consequently data collection is an important part of demographic work. In recent decades, research has given increasing attention to the interrelation between demographic phenomena, in the narrow sense of the word, and cultural and economic phenomena. Since Diaspora Jews are scattered and everywhere in a minority status, and the very definition of Jewishness is today interpreted in differing ways, both the demographic profile and trends of the Jews and the study of the subject matter have peculiar aspects. Demographic work on Diaspora Jewry encounters special difficulties due to the lack of uniformity of available sources, and the need for data collection by Jewish institutions when official data are not available. Official statistics now exist only for a minority of Diaspora Jews, and even where they are forthcoming, they are mostly of a very general nature and insufficient for in-depth analysis (see *Vital Statistics).

SIZE AND GEOGRAPHICAL DISTRIBUTION OF WORLD JEWRY

Major Geographical Shifts of World Jewry

Over the last 125 years, the geography of the Jews has changed completely. As a result of the Shoah and of large-scale international migrations, many veteran Diaspora communities in Eastern and Central Europe, the Middle East, and North Africa virtually disappeared, or became small and precarious. Instead, two major demographic centers arose: the United States, whose Jewish stock arrived mainly in the period 1881–1924, and Israel, whose large-scale demographic expansion followed the establishment of the state in 1948. Several secondary Jewish population centers are now situated on either side of the Atlantic: in Western Europe, especially in France and England; in Canada, alongside the major Jewish Diaspora population in the U.S.; in South America, especially in Argentina; and in Australia.

These changes consisted largely of a westward shift of the world Jewish population. Only since 1948 was an eastward counterpull exercised by Israel. It has been calculated that, geographically, the virtual central point of world Jewry (considering both location and size of the various Jewish populations) was at the border of the Ukraine and Galicia in 1850. It shifted to a spot just west of Scotland in 1933 and toward the middle of the North Atlantic Ocean in 1960. It has since moved eastward reflecting the growing size and share of Jewish population In Israel. Likewise, the cultural-linguistic milieus in which the Jews live changed greatly. Until the onset of the modern migration movement toward the end of the 19th century, most Jews lived among peoples with Slavic languages, while other large Jewish populations had German-speaking surroundings in Europe and Arabic-speaking surroundings in Asia and Africa. All these milieus lost much of their importance for the Jews because of the Shoah and emigration. Correspondingly, there was a great rise in the proportion of Jews residing in countries whose official language is primarily English but also French or Spanish. With the growing demographic importance of Israel, Hebrew became the official as well as the everyday language of a considerable proportion of all Jews. On the other hand the diffusion of traditional Jewish languages of the Diaspora – Yiddish and Ladino – dramatically diminished in favor of the official languages of the various countries of Jewish residence. This reflected not only the special impact of emigration and the Shoah on the traditional centers of Yiddish and of Ladino in Eastern Europe and the Balkans, but also internal social and cultural processes among the Jews and changing relationships between them and the surrounding non-Jewish populations.

Table 1.
World Jewish Population, by Official Language of Country of Residence, 1931–2005 (Rough Percent Estimates)[a]

Official Language	1931	1967	2005
Total	100	100	100
English	32	50	47
Hebrew	2	17	40
French	2	4	4
Russian and other Slavic Languages	41	18	3
Spanish and Portuguese	3	5	3
German	4	1	1
Arabic	4	1	0
Other	12	4	2

a Ranked by frequency in 2005.

Finally, the "newness" of most of the numerically important Jewish populations of the various countries deserves to be emphasized. The majority of Jews now live in countries where, some generations ago, few or hardly any Jews were to be found. The countries with the 10 largest Jewish populations that accounted for about 95% of world Jewry in 2005, accounted only for a minor share in 1850. This has implications for the relationship between the Jews and the general population of the respective countries. In fact, most of those are immigration countries where not only the Jews but a large part of the population is of comparatively recent standing. In addition, the newness of many numerically important Jewish Diaspora groups affects the sphere of internal integration and organization, especially in view of the weakening over time of the religious factor (see *Community, Organization). The situation is obviously different in Israel, where common national aspirations and common practical needs generate stronger cohesive tendencies.

UP TO WORLD WAR I. During part of the 19th century, information on the number of Jews in various countries was unsatisfactory. Taking of official censuses was only gradually coming into use, and the completeness of some of the earlier censuses with regard to the Jews left much to be desired. There were virtually no censuses in Asia and Africa. In the Czarist Empire, which contained the largest number of Jews in the world, the first general census was taken only as late as 1897. In some countries of Western Europe and America, the Jews were not distinguished as such in the official statistics. Moreover, examination of the alleged number of Jews from successive official counts in Austria-Hungary and in some parts of the Czarist Empire makes the incompleteness of the earlier figures evident. This was apparently often due to a deliberate tendency on the part of many Jews to evade inclusion in official registrations and counts. Under these circumstances, comprehensive figures on the Jewish world population must be based partly on conjecture and cannot be viewed as more than very rough indications of an order of magnitude. A. *Ruppin estimated the total number of Jews at the end of the 18th century at 2,500,000. J. *Lestschinsky arrived at an estimate of about 3,250,000 Jews in 1825, of whom 2,750,000 (i.e., more than 80%) in Europe.

The figures on the subsequent development up to World War I, as presented in Table 2, are based (with some adaptations) on the studies of Lestschinsky.

World Jewish Population increased from about 4¾ million in 1850 to 13½ million in 1914, i.e., by 180% or by 16 per 1,000 annually. In comparison, during 1850–1900 the total world population is estimated to have grown by six-seven per 1,000 annually, and the population of Europe, North America, and Oceania by 11 per 1,000 annually. The faster growth of the Jews was due to their relatively larger natural increase, in consequence of the faster reduction of mortality among European Jewish communities. The proportion of Jews in Asia and Africa among all Jews in the world declined somewhat. This was due to their lower natural increase at that time, mainly because of higher mortality, as compared with the Jews in Europe and America (see *Vital Statistics).

A far more spectacular change in the geographical distribution of world Jewry was the increase in the proportion of Jews in America after 1880: from about 250,000 in that year to 1,175,000 in 1900 and nearly 3,500,000 in 1914, and from 3% to 11% and, by 1914, a quarter of world Jewry. The corresponding figures for the United States and Canada (together) were about 1,115,000 in 1900 and 3,360,000 in 1914. This rapid expansion of American Jewry was due to the migration of about 2,400,000 Jews during the years 1881–1914, of whom 2,150,000 went to the United States and Canada (see *Migration). Equally due to immigration, but on a much smaller scale, was the growth of the Jewish populations in South Africa and in Oceania.

While the proportion of European Jews among all the Jews in the world was reduced from 88% in 1880 to about two thirds in 1914, as a result of the heavy emigration, the absolute number of the Jews in Europe kept on growing from more than 4,000,000 in 1850 to 6,800,000 in 1880, 8,700,000 in 1900 and 9,100,000 in 1914. This numerical growth despite the heavy emigration drain – which, during the peak period of 1901–14, led to the departure of 1,600,000 Jews from Europe – is striking evidence for the natural increase of European Jews at that time. Even the number of Jews in Eastern Europe rose greatly from 1880 to 1900 and maintained itself from 1900 to 1914, though nearly all the overseas emigration consisted of persons originating from that region and there was, in addition, migration from Eastern to Central and Western Europe.

1914 TO 1939. During the period up to the outbreak of World War II, the Jewish population of the globe is estimated to have risen from about 13,500,000 to 16,500,000. The rate of growth was smaller than in the preceding period because of the reduction in natural increase caused by the spread of birth control among the Jews in Europe and America (see *Vital Statistics). The annual increase of world Jewry was about eight per 1,000. In comparison, total world population grew from 1920 to 1940 by ten per 1,000 annually, while the populations of Europe, North America, and Oceania, which underwent a demographic slowdown, grew by nine per 1,000 annually. Whereas the relative growth of the Jews had exceeded that of the peoples of Europe, North America, etc. in the 19th century, this was no longer so in the period between the two world wars.

The relative share of the European Jews among total world Jewry continued to decline from about two thirds in 1914 to 58% in 1939, mainly because of emigration to America, South Africa, Australia, and Ereẓ Israel. For the same reason and because of the reduced natural increase, the absolute number of Jews residing in Europe grew only a little between the two world wars. On the other hand, the proportion of American Jews among world Jewry grew from about a quarter in 1914 to a third in 1939. During this period, the relative growth of the number of Jews was much greater in Latin America and South Africa than in North America. This was due to the limitations imposed on immigration into the U.S., which very strongly affected the Jews (see *Migration).

On the other hand, there was a rise in the relative share of Jews in North Africa and, especially, in Asia. The main reasons were considerable Jewish migration to Ereẓ Israel, to the Asian territories of the U.S.S.R., and also to Egypt and an upward swing in the natural increase of the local Jewish population because of reduced mortality.

Table 2.
World Jewish Population by Major Regions, 1700–2005[a]

Region	1700	1800	1900	1939	1948[b]	1970[c]	2005[d]
				Thousands			
World total	**1,100**	**2,500**	**10,600**	**16,500**	**11,500**	**12,662**	**13,034**
Total Diaspora	**1,095**	**2,493**	**10,550**	**16,055**	**10,735**	**10,080**	**7,796**
Total Erez Israel	**5**	**7**	**50**	**445**	**650**	**2,582**	**5,238**
Europe	**720**	**2,020**	**8,765**	**9,500**	**3,750**	**3,241**	**1,520**
Western Europe[e]	180	363	1,230	1,425	1,035	1,119	1,066
Eastern Europe and Balkans[e]	265	803	3,450	4,680	765	216	94
Former USSR in Europe[f]	275	854	4,085	3,395	1,950	1,906	360
Asia	**200**	**260**	**440**	**1,000**	**1,275**	**2,944**	**5,277**
Palestine/Israel	5	7	50	445	650	2,582	5,238
Former USSR in Asia	} 195	} 253	} 390	165	350	262	20
Other Asia[g]				390	275	100	19
Africa	**175**	**212**	**340**	**600**	**700**	**207**	**79**
North Africa[h]	170	200	305	500	595	83	5
South Africa[i]	5	12	35	100	105	124	74
America-Oceania	**5**	**8**	**1,055**	**5,400**	**5,775**	**6,270**	**6,158**
North America[j]	} 5	} 8	1,000	4,940	5,215	5,686	5,652
Latin America			40	430	520	514	397
Oceania[k]	0	0	15	30	40	70	109
				Percent			
World total	**100.0**	**100.0**	**100.0**	**100.0**	**100.0**	**100.0**	**100.0**
Total Diaspora	**99.5**	**99.7**	**99.5**	**97.3**	**93.3**	**79.6**	**59.8**
Total Erez Israel	**0.5**	**0.3**	**0.5**	**2.7**	**5.7**	**20.4**	**40.2**
Europe	**65.5**	**80.8**	**82.7**	**57.6**	**32.6**	**25.6**	**11.7**
Western Europe[e]	16.4	14.5	11.6	8.6	9.0	8.8	8.2
Eastern Europe and Balkans[e]	24.1	32.1	32.5	28.4	6.7	1.7	0.7
Former USSR in Europe[f]	25.0	34.2	38.5	20.6	17.0	15.1	2.8
Asia	**18.2**	**10.4**	**4.2**	**6.1**	**11.1**	**23.3**	**40.5**
Palestine/Israel	0.5	0.3	0.5	2.7	5.7	20.4	40.2
Former USSR in Asia	} 17.7	} 10.1	} 3.7	1.0	3.0	2.1	0.2
Other Asia[g]				2.4	2.4	0.8	0.1
Africa	**15.9**	**8.5**	**3.2**	**3.6**	**6.1**	**1.6**	**0.6**
North Africa[h]	15.5	8.0	2.9	3.0	5.2	0.6	0.0
South Africa[i]	0.5	0.5	0.3	0.6	0.9	1.0	0.6
America-Oceania	**0.5**	**0.3**	**10.0**	**32.7**	**50.2**	**49.5**	**47.2**
North America[j]	} 0.5	} 0.3	9.4	29.9	45.3	44.9	43.4
Latin America			0.4	2.6	4.5	4.1	3.0
Oceania[k]	0.0	0.0	0.1	0.2	0.3	0.6	0.8

a Minor discrepancies due to rounding.
b May 15.
c December 31.
d January 1.
e Eastern European countries that joined the European Union included in Eastern Europe.
f Including Asian parts of Russian Republic. Including Baltic countries.
g Asian parts of Turkey included in Europe.
h Including Ethiopia.
i South Africa, Zimbabwe, and other sub-Saharan countries.
j U.S.A., Canada.
k Australia, New Zealand.

THE SHOAH. About six millions of Jews perished during the Nazi persecutions. In addition, there was a very low birth rate and survival of newborn among the Jews in the occupied territories. After the catastrophe, the total number of Jews was reduced by over one third. In consequence, a far-reaching change also took place in the geographical distribution of world Jewry. As the numerical strength of the European Jews waned, the relative shares of the Jews on the other continents rose. When it was again possible to do some statistical stocktaking in 1948, on the eve of the establishment of the State of Israel, less than a third of all Jews were found in Europe, as against more than a half in 1939. This change was essentially due to the enormous biological losses caused by the Shoah, but there was also some emigration from Europe in the early war years and again after the end of the war.

The Shoah was most devastating in the eastern parts of Europe occupied by the Nazis. In the years after the end of the war, a movement of *Displaced Persons also took place from Eastern to Central Europe. Therefore, if the regional distribution of the Jews inside Europe in 1948 is compared with that in 1939, an enormous reduction in absolute numbers is found everywhere, but the proportions of the various regions had changed greatly. Before the war, Eastern Europe, excluding the U.S.S.R., accounted for one half of European Jewry; by 1948 its share was diminished to less than a quarter, while the Jews in the U.S.S.R. constituted one half of all European Jews. Contributory causes for this development were the enlargement of the area of the U.S.S.R. after World War II and the departure of Displaced Persons from the other East European states; but the essential cause was the differential loss of life during the Shoah, when a much larger part of the Jews was spared in Russia than in the rest of Eastern Europe. Also the proportion of Jews in Western and Central Europe among all Jews of that continent was higher in 1948 (about a third) than in 1939 (about 20%). This happened, among other things, because the Jews in England had remained safe and because of the influx of Displaced Persons.

Table 3.
Jewish Populations in Europe, 1939–1945 (in thousands)

Country	1939	1945	Percent change
Eastern Europe and Balkans			
Estonia	5	} 66	-74
Latvia	95		
Lithuania	155		
Byelorussia	375	147	-61
Russia[a]	903	860	-5
Ukraine[b]	1,863	916	-51
Poland	3,225	100	-97
Czechoslovakia	357	42	-88
Hungary	404	180	-55
Romania	520	430	-17
Bulgaria	50	45	-10
Yugoslavia[c]	75	12	-84
Greece	75	8	-89
Turkey[d]	50	50	=
Western Europe			
Portugal, Spain[e]	6	9	+50
France	320	180	-44
Italy	47	29	-38
Switzerland	19	25	+31
Austria	60	7	-88
Germany	195	45	-77
Belgium[f]	93	32	-66
Netherlands	141	33	-77
United Kingdom[g]	345	350	+1
Scandinavia[h]	17	24	+41
Displaced persons	107	210	+96

a Including territory in Asia.
b Including Bessarabia/Moldavia.
c Including Albania.
d Territory in Europe only.
e Including Gibraltar.
f Including Luxembourg.
g Including Ireland.
h Denmark, Sweden, Norway, Finland.

As against the great drop in the share of European Jewry, the proportion of American Jewry rose from one third of world Jewry in 1939 to one half in 1948, and that of Asia including Palestine rose from 6 to 11%. There had been some immigration of Jews into these continents during the intervening years, but this was only a secondary factor in producing the marked changes in the respective proportions.

The direct outcome of the Shoah was the physical destruction of the majority of the Jews who had lived in Europe. Soon after the war came to an end, the vivid memory of the horrors, the renewed hostility of the non-Jews in some countries and, on the other hand, the creation of the State of Israel produced mass emigration of the survivors from Europe (see *Migration). The demographic aftereffects of the Shoah – particularly, distortions in the age and sex composition of the survivors – are conspicuous up to the present and will make themselves felt for a considerable time to come, not only in Europe, but also among those Jewish Diaspora populations elsewhere that have absorbed survivors from Europe. It has been estimated that if the expected growth of the generations that were destroyed and of those that were not born are factored in, the cumulative demographic impact of the Shoah might have ranged between 12 and 18 million lost people around the year 2000.

1948 TO 1970. After World War II, the statistical documentation available on the Jewish Diaspora based on official state sources greatly diminished. Before the War, the majority of world Jewry lived in countries (mainly in Europe) where official statistics furnished copious data on Jews. Now the situation was reversed: putting aside the State of Israel, over 70% of Diaspora Jews lived in countries without any official statistics on Jews, mainly in the United States. Besides, great conceptual problems emerged because of the growing frequency of "marginal Jews." On the other hand, over the years Jewish-sponsored efforts at collecting statistical information on Jewish populations produced a significant database for the study of Jewish demography (see *Vital Statistics). Under these circumstances, the quality of Jewish population estimates in many countries is unsatisfactory.

Since World War II, no assessment of Jewish demographic trends is possible without explaining what the data mean, particularly the statistical definition of "who is a Jew." The figures reported here usually relate to the concept of *core Jewish population*, i.e. *all those who, when asked, identify themselves as Jews; or, if the respondent is a different person in the same household, are identified by him/her as Jews*. This is an intentionally comprehensive approach, reflecting both subjective feelings and community norms and bonds. The definition is admittedly looser in the Diaspora than in Israel where personal status is subject to the ruling of the Ministry of the Interior. The *core Jewish population* broadly overlaps but does not necessarily coincide with the *halakhic* (rabbinic) definition of a Jew as someone who *is the child of a Jewish mother or converted by appropriate religious and legal procedure*. Inclusion in the *core* Jewish population does *not* depend on any measure of a person's Jewish commitment or behavior in terms of religiosity, beliefs, knowledge, communal affiliation, or otherwise. The *core* Jewish population includes all those who converted to Judaism, or decided to join the Jewish group informally and declare themselves Jewish. It excludes those of Jewish descent who have formally adopted another religion, as well as other individuals who did not convert out but currently refuse to recognize their Jewishness.

Concurrently, the concept of an *enlarged Jewish population* includes the sum of (a) the *core* Jewish population, (b) all other persons Jewish by birth or parentage who do *not* currently identify as Jews, and (c) all the respective *non-Jewish* household members (spouses, children, etc.). The *enlarged* Jewish population is by definition significantly larger than the *core* population.

The *Law of Return – Israel's distinctive legal framework for the eligibility and absorption of new immigrants – further extends its provisions to all current Jews, their Jewish or non-Jewish spouses, children, and grandchildren, and the respective spouses. As a result of its three-generation time perspective and lateral extension, the Law of Return applies to a much wider population than *core* and *enlarged* Jewish populations alike. The Law of Return, *per se*, does not effect a person's Jewish status, which, as noted, is adjudicated by Israel's Ministry of the Interior or rabbinical authorities. In practice, while the Law of Return defines objective, clear-cut normative rules for the attribution of certain rights and prerogatives, the initiative for being entitled to its provisions normally stems from people's subjective, individual awareness of belonging (directly or indirectly) to the Jewish collective. In Germany, since the 1990s, legislation similar to the principles of the Law of Return regulates the eligibility of Jewish immigrants.

The period from 1948 onward began during the "baby boom" of early postwar years; however, it was soon followed by a renewed decline in Jewish birth rates in Europe, America, and other Western countries. Jewish populations in Europe about which there is any statistical documentation reached a state of demographic stagnation and decline, with deaths consistently outnumbering births and additional losses to the Jewish population being occasioned by "withdrawals," whether in connection with frequent intermarriages or not. In the U.S., Canada, South Africa, and Australia, the only source of any Jewish population growth was international migration, but eventually in some cases this was insufficient to compensate for the deficit of internal demographic changes (see *Vital Statistics). Though there has been persistent natural increase in Israel, changes in the overall size of the Jewish world population have been rather limited.

Very conspicuous geographical shifts in the world Jewish population occurred over the years 1948–70. Throughout the period, the Jews in America accounted for about half of world Jewry. Nine-tenths of them resided in North America. But there were marked changes in the relative shares of other regions among world Jewry. The proportion of European Jews continued to decline from about a third of all Jews in 1948 to a quarter in 1970. It would have declined even somewhat further, were it not for an influx from North Africa. The relative share of Eastern Europe excluding the U.S.S.R. dropped both among total Jews in Europe (from more than 20 to less than 10%) and among world Jewry (from 7 to 2%). Throughout this period, the Jews in the European territories of the U.S.S.R. were one half or more of all Jews residing in Europe. The aggregate number and proportion of the Jews in other countries of Europe, i.e., mainly in the west and center of that continent, were first reduced by departures of Displaced Persons and others, most of whom went to Israel. But subsequently they were raised by intermittent immigration from countries of Eastern Europe and North Africa and the Middle East.

The proportion of Jews in North Africa and, consequently, in the whole of Africa, dropped drastically during 1948–70 (North Africa, from 5.5 to 0.5% of world Jewry). This was due to large-scale emigration from the Maghreb and other Arabic-speaking states. The emigrants went mainly to Israel and in the second place to France. The drain started after Israel's War of Independence (1948) and had come near to emptying North Africa of its once numerous Jewish population by the Six-Day War period (1967). A notable episode was the exodus of over 100,000 Jews from Algeria to France, together with the European population, in 1961–62.

Similarly, the share of Asia, excluding Israel and the Asian territories of the U.S.S.R., dropped from 3 to 1% of world Jewry during 1948–70. Most of the respective Jews had resided in Arabic-speaking countries; nearly all of them moved to Israel in a spectacular mass migration soon after the foundation of the new state.

On the other hand, the total share of Asia among world Jewry doubled from 1948 (11.5%) to 1967 (21.5%). This resulted essentially from the rapid growth of the Jewish population in Israel from 650,000 in May 1948 to almost 2,400,000 by the end of 1970. The number of Jews in the Asian territories of the U.S.S.R. also increased somewhat.

In all but one of the countries of Eastern and Central Europe, the number of Jews was very much smaller in 1970 than in 1939. This was due, of course, to the successive effects of the Shoah and of emigration. The most glaring instance in this respect is that of Poland, with 3,250,000 and only about 25,000 Jews, respectively (the latter figure relates to the reduced postwar territory). The one country in that region with a relatively smaller diminution in the number of Jews is the U.S.S.R., whose territory was only partly occupied by the Nazis during World War II and much enlarged after the war and where emigration is barred. The number of Jews in the European part of the U.S.S.R. amounted to 1,900,000 in 1959, according to the official census of that year. This number is probably below the actual figure, but there is no alternative statistical figure in existence. With regard to the 1939 figures in Table 2, those for Germany and Austria (at that time a German province) already showed the effects of Nazi rule: there were half a million Jews in Germany in 1933 and 190,000 in Austria in 1934. The number of Jews in 1939 on the enlarged post-World War II territory of the U.S.S.R. in Europe may be estimated at more than 4½ million.

In most countries of Western Europe, the number of Jews likewise declined, due to the Shoah and subsequent emigration. But the two notable exceptions are precisely the countries with the largest Jewish populations in that region. The Jews in England did not suffer directly from the Nazi persecutions; on the contrary, their numbers were swelled by the influx of refugees and survivors. The Jews in France did suffer from the Nazis and their number was estimated at only 180,000 in 1946, as compared with 320,000 in 1939. But the wartime losses were more than compensated by successive immigration from two sources: Eastern Europe (Displaced Persons, refugees after the Hungarian uprising of 1956, etc.), and North Africa, particularly Algeria.

As a result of all the demographic changes produced by the differential effects of the Shoah and of the subsequent migrations in the various European countries, a geographical polarization of the Jews in Europe has taken place. The main concentrations are now in the extreme east (the former U.S.S.R.) and in the extreme west (France, England). Over the postwar decades there was an increase in the number of Jews in nearly all countries of America, with the one conspicuous exception of Cuba, and in Oceania. The rise in the estimated Jewish population of the U.S. is shown in Table 4.

The number of Jews in South Africa increased, according to census figures, from 91,000 in 1936 to 115,000 in 1960. On the other hand, the number of Jews in each of the North African countries decreased reflecting the post-War de-colonization process.

Table 5 shows the expansion of the Jewish population in Ereẓ Israel.

The number of Jews in the Asian territories of the U.S.S.R. was, according to the official censuses, about 220,000 in 1939 and 370,000 in 1959. On the other hand, the two Arab countries in Asia with the largest Jewish populations had been Iraq and Yemen. To judge from the subsequent immigration to Israel, in the middle of 1948 there were about 125,000 Jews in Iraq and 50,000 in Yemen and Aden.

1970 TO 2005. Since 1970, significant changes affected the geographical distribution of world Jewry and the relative weight of communities in different regions of the world. The size of world Jewry at the beginning of 2005 was assessed at 13,034,000 (by the *core Jewish population* definition). World Jewry constituted 2.04 per 1,000 of the world's total population of 6,396 million. One in about 490 people in the world was a Jew. World Jewry's overall increase from 1970 through 2005 was about 3% (or 0.06% a year), as against an increase of over 70% in total world population (about 1.5% yearly). Significantly, Jewish zero population growth worldwide was the product of two entirely different trends compensating each other. The State of Israel and the rest of the world – or the Diaspora – are the two typological components of a contempo-

Table 4.
Jewish Population in the United States of America, 1790–2005

Year	Jews	Total US	% Jews
1790	1,500	4,000,000	0.04
1820	3,000	11,000,000	0.03
1830	6,000	15,000,000	0.04
1850	50,000	24,000,000	0.21
1860	150,000	30,000,000	0.50
1880	250,000	46,353,000	0.54
1890	400,000	59,974,000	0.67
1900	1,058,000	71,592,000	1.48
1910	1,777,000	85,817,000	2.07
1920	3,389,000	103,266,000	3.28
1930	4,228,000	119,038,000	3.55
1940	4,771,000	140,000,000	3.41
1950	5,000,000	157,813,000	3.17
1960	5,300,000	186,158,000	2.85
1970	5,400,000	210,111,000	2.57
1980	5,500,000	230,406,000	2.39
1990	5,515,000	254,776,000	2.16
2000	5,300,000	281,422,000	1.88
2005	5,280,000	293,600,000	1.80

Table 5.
Jewish Population of Erez Israel, 1856–2005

Year	Jews
1800	7,000
1856	10,000
1882	24,000
1895	47,000
1914	94,000
1922	84,000
1931	175,000
1947	630,000
1950	1,203,000
1960	1,911,000
1967	2,374,000
1975	2,979,000
1985	3,517,000
1995	4,522,000
2000	4,955,000
2005	5,238,000

rary world Jewish population that responds to two quite contrasting, if not conflicting, sets of demographic determinants and consequences. The Israeli component, approaching 40% of the world total in 2005, operates as the majority within its own sovereign state. The Diaspora, about 60% of world Jewry, consists of a large number of communities of different absolute sizes, each constituting a very small to minuscule share of the total population of the respective country.

In synthesis, Israel's Jewish population grew by more than two million between 1945 and 1970, and by another 2.6 million between 1970 and 2005. Diaspora Jewry diminished by about 400,000 between 1945 and 1970, and declined by another 2.3 million between 1970 and 2005. These changes reflect in part the net transfer of over 2.2 million Jewish migrants from the Diaspora to Israel over the whole period since World War II, including about one million since 1970. A substantial contribution to total population changes, however, comes from a very different balance of Jewish births and deaths, as well as to a different impact of accessions and secessions. Especially since the 1970s, these factors produced further substantial population increases in Israel, and visible declines in the aggregate of other Jewish communities.

Trends to growth, stability, or decline in the major Jewish communities were quite variable. The Jewish population in the United States increased by an estimated 100,000 between 1970 and 1990, from 5.4 to 5.5 million, less than might have been expected considering the total amount of known Jewish immigration to the U.S. Between 1990 and 2000, the number of U.S. Jews should have increased by an additional 200,000 only due to international migration. Instead, two new surveys undertaken in 2001, the NJPS and the AJIS, found a total of 5,200,000–5,350,000 or 150,000 to 300,000 less than in 1990. Substantial numbers of Jews did move to North America from the FSU, Israel, Latin America, South Africa, Iran, and other countries, but the internal interplay of demographic, social, and cultural forces balanced out much of the expected population increase and actually created a deficit.

The about 13 million Jews estimated worldwide at the dawn of the 21st century were intimately connected to several more millions of people. Some of the latter had Jewish origins or family connections but were not currently Jewish, whether because they changed their own identification, were the non-Jewish children of intermarried parents, or were non-Jewish members in intermarried households. These non-Jews shared the daily life experience, social and economic concerns, and cultural environment of their Jewish mates. The following examples indicate the extent of variation of *core* and *enlarged* Jewish populations in selected countries. The criteria followed in the ensuing comparison were not the same in each place.

In the Russian Republic in 2001, the Jewish population was estimated at 275,000 and the enlarged population including all non-Jewish members in the respective households was estimated at 520,000 – a difference of 89 percent. In the U.S. in 2001, based on two different surveys, a core Jewish population of 5,300,000 was part of an enlarged population estimated at 8.8 to 10 million – a difference of 69 to 89 percent. In the Netherlands, a 2000 survey found 30,000 Jews by matrilineal descent and another 13,000 by patrilineal descent – a 43 percent difference. In Brazil, according to the 1991 census, the reported Jewish population of 86,000 was part of an enlarged population of 117,000 in Jewish households – a difference of 36 percent. In France, according to a 2002 survey, 500,000 Jews had at least another 75,000 non-Jewish household members – a 15 percent difference. In Israel at the end of 2001, 5,025,000 Jews were accompanied by 275,000 non-Jewish family members, mostly in families that had immigrated from the F.S.U. – a difference of 5 percent. The gap between the numbers of individuals covered by the *enlarged* and *core* Jewish population definitions tended to increase in connection with growing rates of out-marriage. In some cases an increase in the *enlarged* population could be noted along with reduction of the respective *core*.

Recently, instances of accession or "return" to Judaism can be observed in connection with the absorption in Israel of immigrants from Eastern Europe and Ethiopia, and the comprehensive provisions of the Israeli Law of Return. The return or first-time access to Judaism of some of such previously unincluded or unidentified individuals contributed to slowing down the pace of decline of the relevant Diaspora Jewish populations and some gains for the Jewish population in Israel.

Table 6 gives an overall picture of Jewish population country by country for the beginning of 2005 as compared to 1970. The number of Jews in Israel rose from 2,582,000 in 1970 to 5,237,600 at the beginning of 2005, an increase of 2,655,600 people, or 102.9 percent (more than double the initial population). In contrast the estimated Jewish population in the Diaspora diminished from 10,063,200 to 7,796,500 – a decrease of 2,266,700 people, or 22.5 percent. These changes reflect the continuing Jewish emigration from the Former U.S.S.R. (FSU) and other countries, but also the internal decrease typical of the aggregate of Diaspora Jewry. While it took 13 years to add one million to world Jewry's postwar size, over 46 years were needed to add another million. The data also outline the slow Jewish population growth rate versus total population growth globally, and the declining Jewish share of world population. In 2005 the share of Jews per 1,000 world population was less than half what it was in 1945.

Table 6.
World Jewish Population, 1970 and 2005[a]

Country	1970	2005	Change %
World Total	**12,642,300**	**13,034,100**	**3.1**
Americas, total	**6,199,800**	**6,049,500**	**-2.4**
North America	**5,686,000**	**5,652,000**	**-0.6**
Canada	286,000	372,000	30.1
United States	5,400,000	5,280,000	-2.2
Central America	**46,800**	**51,900**	**10.9**
Bahamas	300	300	0.0

World Jewish Population, 1970 and 2005 (continued)

Country	1970	2005	Change %
Costa Rica	1,500	2,500	66.7
Cuba	1,700	600	-64.7
Dominican Republic	350	100	-71.4
Guatemala	1,900	900	-52.6
Jamaica	600	300	-50.0
Mexico	35,000	39,800	13.7
Netherlands Antilles	700	200	-71.4
Panama	2,000	5,000	150.0
Puerto Rico	1,200	1,500	25.0
Virgin Islands	200	300	50.0
Other	1,350	400	-70.4
South America	**467,000**	**345,600**	**-26.0**
Argentina	282,000	185,000	-34.4
Bolivia	2,000	500	-75.0
Brazil	90,000	96,700	7.4
Chile	30,000	20,800	-30.7
Colombia	10,000	3,300	-67.0
Ecuador	2,000	900	-55.0
Paraguay	1,200	900	-25.0
Peru	5,300	2,300	-56.6
Suriname	500	200	-60.0
Uruguay	32,000	19,500	-39.1
Venezuela	12,000	15,500	29.2
Europe, total	**3,241,200**	**1,519,600**	**-53.1**
European Union	**1,097,450**	**1,015,200**	**-7.5**
Austria	8,000	9,000	12.5
Belgium	32,500	31,200	-4.0
Denmark	6,000	6,400	6.7
Finland	1,450	1,100	-24.1
France[b]	530,000	494,000	-6.8
Germany[c]	30,000	115,000	283.3
Greece	6,500	4,500	-30.8
Ireland	5,400	1,200	-77.8
Italy	32,000	28,700	-10.3
Luxembourg	1,000	600	-40.0
Netherlands	30,000	30,000	0.0
Portugal	600	500	-16.7
Spain	9,000	12,000	33.3
Sweden	15,000	15,000	0.0
United Kingdom	390,000	297,000	-23.8
Other West Europe	**21,450**	**19,800**	**-7.7**
Gibraltar	600	600	0.0
Norway	750	1,200	60.0
Switzerland	20,000	17900	-10.5
Other	100	100	0.0
Former USSR (Europe)	**1,906,000**	**359,500**	**-81.1**
Belarus	148,000	21,000	-85.8
Estonia	5,300	1,900	-64.2
Latvia	36,700	9,500	-74.1
Lithuania	23,600	3,300	-86.0
Moldova	98,100	4,800	-95.1
Russia[d]	816,700	235,000	-71.2
Ukraine	777,400	84,000	-89.2
Other East Europe, Balkans	**216,300**	**94,100**	**-56.5**
Bulgaria	7,000	2,100	-70.0

Country	1970	2005	Change %
Czech Republic	7,000	4,000	-42.9
Hungary	70,000	49,900	-28.7
Poland	9,000	3,300	-63.3
Romania	70,000	10,300	-85.3
Slovakia	7,000	2,700	-61.4
Turkey[d]	39,000	17,900	-54.1
Former Yugoslavia[e]	7,000	3,900	-44.3
Other	300	0	-100.0
Asia, total	**2,944,200**	**5,277,100**	**79.2**
Israel	**2,582,000**	**5,237,600**	**102.9**
Former USSR (Asia)	**261,900**	**20,300**	**-92.0**
Armenia	1,000	0	-100.0
Azerbaijan	49,100	7,000	-85.7
Georgia	55,400	3,600	-93.5
Kazakhstan	27,700	3,800	-86.3
Kirghizstan	7,700	600	-92.2
Tajikistan	14,600	0	-100.0
Turkmenistan	3,500	300	-91.4
Uzbekistan	103,100	5,000	-95.2
Other Asia	**100,300**	**19,200**	**-80.9**
China[f]	200	1,000	400.0
India	15,000	5,100	-66.0
Iran	72,000	10,800	-85.0
Iraq	2,500	0	-100.0
Japan	500	1,000	100.0
Philippines	500	100	-80.0
Singapore	600	300	-50.0
Syria	4,000	100	-97.5
Thailand	100	200	100.0
Yemen	500	200	-60.0
Other	4,400	400	-90.9
Africa, total	**207,100**	**78,800**	**-62.0**
North Africa	**82,600**	**4,800**	**-94.2**
Egypt	1,000	100	-90.0
Ethiopia	25,000	100	-99.6
Morocco	45,000	3,500	-92.2
Tunisia	10,000	1,100	-89.0
Other	1,600	0	-100.0
Other Africa	**124,500**	**74,000**	**-40.6**
Kenya	200	400	100.0
South Africa	118,000	72,500	-38.6
Zaire	300	100	-66.7
Zimbabwe	5,200	400	-92.3
Other	800	600	-25.0
Oceania, total[g]	**70,000**	**109,100**	**55.9**
Australia	65,000	102,000	56.9
New Zealand	5,000	7,000	40.0

a Core Jewish population definition. See text.
b Including Monaco.
c In 1970: West Germany 28500; East Germany 1500.
d Including areas in Asia.
e Of which in 2005: Bosnia-Herzegovina 300; Croatia 1300; Macedonia 100; Serbia-Montenegro 1500; Slovenia 100.
f Including Hong Kong.
g Including other.

In 2005, over 47 percent of the world's Jews resided in the Americas, with over 43 percent in North America. Over 40 percent lived in Asia, including the Asian republics of the F.S.U. (but not the Asian parts of the Russian Republic and Turkey) – most of them in Israel. Europe, including the Asian territories of the Russian Republic and Turkey, accounted for about 12 percent of the total. Fewer than 2 percent of the world's Jews lived in Africa and Oceania.

Comparing the 2005 and 1970 Jewish geographical distributions, North America remained nearly unchanged, with some losses in the United States – mostly due to identificational assimilation – compensated by growth in Canada – mostly due to immigration. Communities in Central America had an overall increase of about 11 percent – mostly in Mexico, Panama, and Costa Rica, whereas other smaller communities diminished quite significantly. In South America there was an overall decrease of 26 percent. All countries registered a smaller Jewish population in 2005, most notably Argentina with a decrease of 34 percent. The exceptions were Brazil and Venezuela both of which, however, were past their peak and were experiencing some recent population attrition.

In Europe, the main event was the return of continental majority to Western European Jewish communities, after several centuries of East European predominance. The main determinant of such epochal change was the dissolution of the U.S.S.R. and the massive Jewish emigration that started in December 1989. Among the 15 countries of the European Union (before the enlargement of 2004 to 25 countries), between 1970 and 2005 Jewish population increased by 7.5 percent. This reflected very unequal patterns of change. Germany after reunification in 1991 experienced the most dramatic pace of growth of any Jewish community worldwide, increasing by 283 percent (nearly four times the initial size). Other communities in the EU and other Western European countries with some Jewish population increase included Austria, Denmark, Spain, and Norway. All other western countries experienced Jewish population decreases, most notably the United Kingdom with a decrease of 24 percent, and France with a 7 percent loss.

The European former Soviet republics lost overall 81 percent of their initial Jewish population in 1970. Decreases were most dramatic in Moldova (-95 percent), Ukraine (-89 percent), Lithuania (-86 percent), and Belarus (-86 percent), and somewhat less dramatic in Latvia (-74 percent), Russia (-71 percent), and Estonia (-64 percent). The Asian former Soviet republics lost overall 92 percent of their initial Jewish population. The most resilient community was in Azerbaijan, which nonetheless lost 83 percent of its Jewish population.

In other East European and Balkan countries, the Jewish population decreased overall by 56 percent, ranging between Hungary (-29 percent) and Romania (-85 percent).

The total Jewish population in Asia grew by 80 percent between 1970 and 2005, but this was due to Israel's more than doubling its Jewish population, and the rest of the continent's Jews (including the former Soviet republics) shrinking by 89 percent. In Central and Eastern Asia, the main change was a decline by 85 percent in the size of the Jewish community in Iran. Small Jewish communities tended to become established and expand in rapidly growing economic powers such as China, Japan, and South Korea.

In Africa, the total Jewish population diminished by 62 percent – 94 percent in North Africa (including Ethiopia), and 41 percent in Southern Africa, respectively. Finally, in Oceania the Jewish population increased by 56 percent – 57 percent in Australia and 40 percent in New Zealand, respectively.

In the course of time, Jewish population has become overwhelmingly concentrated in a relatively small number of countries. In 2005 two countries dominate the geography of world Jewry: the United States with about 5,280,000 *core Jewish population*, and the State of Israel with 5,235,000 (each accounting for about 40 percent of the world total). The remaining two and a half million Jews (20 percent), were highly dispersed. Four countries alone include more than one half of total non-U.S. and non-Israeli Jews: France (with an estimated 496,000 Jews in 2005), followed by Canada (372,000), the United Kingdom (297,000), and the Russian Republic (235,000). Further important Jewish communities lived in Argentina (estimated at 185,000 in 2005), Germany (115,000 in 1996), Australia (102,000), Brazil (97,000), Ukraine (84,000), and South Africa (73,000). Jewish populations of at least 100 existed in 93 countries.

To further understand the logic of the changes in geographical distribution in the course of the last quarter of a century, the main aspects of the intensive and manifold relationship that exists between Jewish communities and contemporary society at large deserve closer scrutiny. The Jewish presence – as expressed in absolute numbers and as a percentage of the total population – appears to be strongly related to major social and economic indicators of the world regions, individual countries, provinces, cities, and neighborhoods where they live. Jews simply do not move and redistribute at random, but their mobility patterns reflect the inherent attraction or repulsion of the main instrumental forces that operate in society at large.

During the early 2000s, 92 percent of the Jews globally lived in the highest ranked quintile of countries including most western nations and the state of Israel, 6.5 percent lived in the second best quintile of countries, whereas only 1.5 percent lived in the bottom three-fifths. By the same token, in the 1990s, over 59 percent of Jews in the European Union lived in the best fifth of economic regions, against 1 percent in the bottom fifth; and in 2000, 64 percent of Jews in the United States lived in the top fifth of states, against 1 percent in the bottom fifth. The different concentration of the Jewish presence out of the total population, by level of development of the environment, is thus very consistent and statistically significant, passing from densest in the wealthier and more sophisticated areas to scantiest in the poorest and more backward areas.

Dispersion and Concentration

For many centuries the Jews have been a dispersed people. Yet their dispersion was never uniform; there always developed major centers of Jewish residence with large absolute numbers of Jews and comparatively greater proportions among all Jews and among the respective general population. In this connection, the degree of urbanization of the Jews deserves particular attention. Both dispersion of the Jews and their relative concentration have been much altered in recent generations.

Dispersion of the Jews increased through the changes in geographical distribution produced by emigration from Europe and by the drastic reduction of European Jewry due to the Shoah. The intercontinental distribution of the Jews has undergone periods of growing dispersion and growing concentration. Whereas in 1880 one continent, Europe, accounted for nearly 90 percent of all Jews, during the 1960s the numerically most important continent of Jewish residence, America, contained barely one half of all Jews, while Europe and Asia comprised each more than 20 percent.

In keeping with these changes, the geographical distances involved in the dispersion of the larger Jewish populations increased greatly. Only in the 20th century did the dispersion of the Jews become a virtually global one, with the notable exceptions of East Asia and large parts of Africa. Since the 1970s the tendency of Jews to be regrouped in few countries became again predominant, with 80 percent of world Jewry residing in the United States and in Israel.

Before World War I, the Czarist empire contained 5¼ million Jews (census of 1897), Austria–Hungary, 2¼ million (census of 1910), and the number of Jews in the United States had risen from about 50,000 in 1850 to about 3¼ million at the beginning of the war. The next largest Jewish population in size, Germany, numbered about 600,000 in 1910. After the boundary changes that resulted from World War I, the United States became the country with the largest Jewish population, estimated at 4¼ million in 1927 and at 4¼ million in 1937. The Jews of Poland numbered 3¼ million (estimate for 1939; the census figure of 1931 was 3.1 million) and those in the U.S.S.R., 3 million (1939 census). The next-ranking country was Romania, with about 800,000 Jews in 1939. Germany had about half a million Jews when Hitler came to power, but far fewer on the eve of World War II. All other countries had considerably less than half a million Jews each.

The concentration of the Jews in a limited number of countries expresses itself clearly in the high proportion of the respective Jewish populations among world Jewry.

The concentration in the top group increased since the period before World War II. The three countries that then had more than one million Jews each comprised together 67 percent of world Jewry in 1931, whereas the two countries in that category now comprise over 80%. Moreover, there was and is a tendency for the countries with large populations, in absolute numbers, to also have a comparatively large percentage of Jews in relation to the general population; however, there were and are some exceptions. Before World War II, Poland was the European country with the largest number of Jews and had the highest share of Jews in the general population of all Diaspora countries (about 10 percent). Around 1970, of the ten countries with Jewish populations of 100,000 and over, nine had 0.5 percent or more Jews in their total population. The U.S. had both the largest number of Jews and the largest percentage of Jews among all inhabitants (nearly 3 percent), and the U.S.S.R., especially its European territories, came in next according to the relative frequency of Jews (1–2 percent of the total population).

The number of individual countries with sizable Jewish populations of 50,000 and over rose since the beginning of the modern Jewish migration movement in about 1880. In the last few decades, though, there has been a significant decrease in the number of those countries, as compared with the position prior to World War II, because of the effects of the Shoah and of emigration from Europe and from the Arabic-speaking countries. While in the late 1960s there were 41 countries with at least 5,000 Jews, this had diminished to 36 in 2005, in spite of the significant increase in the number of independent states following the dismemberment of the U.S.S.R., Yugoslavia, and Czechoslovakia.

Jewish population concentration occurred not only at the global level, but also regionally within countries. This partly reflected the tendency of Jews to congregate in the major cities of the various countries (see Urbanization below). In the Czarist empire, the Jews were largely segregated in the Polish provinces and in the so-called *Pale of Settlement along the western borders of Russia. According to the 1939 census of the Soviet Union, the percentage of Jews among all inhabitants varied in the main regions as follows: total, 1.8; all European Russia, 2:1; Belarus, 6.7; Ukraine, 4.9; rest of European Russia, 0.9; Asian Russia, 0.7. According to the 1959 census of the Soviet Union, three-quarters of the Jews were enumerated in the two most populous republics, the Russian S.F.S.R. and the Ukraine. The highest proportions of Jews in the general population were found in some of the republics lining the western border of the Soviet territory, in the Caucasus region, and in the Uzbek Republic in central Asia (where Bukhara is situated).

In Poland between the two world wars, concentration of the Jews was much heavier in the former Russian and Austrian provinces than in the areas previously belonging to the German empire. In the U.S., there long was a heavy concentration of the Jews in the northeastern region and particularly in New York since the inception of mass immigration. Only in the last few decades has the share of the Pacific region risen somewhat. In both 1937 and 1967, the State of New York accounted for about 45% of the entire Jewish population of the U.S., and the 10 states with the largest number of Jews comprised close to 90% of all Jews of the U.S. but somewhat less than one half of the general population of the U.S. In keeping with the rise of the total number of Jews in the U.S., the respective 10 states all had more than 100,000 Jews in 1967, while only eight did in 1937. On the whole, the respective 10 states were also those with a higher relative frequency of Jews among the general population. In 1937 the overall percentage of the Jews in the U.S. was 3.7 percent of the general population; the 10 states with the largest Jewish populations had each more than 2 percent Jews in their general population (and there were only five more such states); six of the 10 top-ranking states had more than 4 percent Jews in their population. By 1967 the overall share of the Jews in the U.S. had declined to about 2.9 percent, because of the slower growth of the Jews compared with the total population. The 10 states with the largest number of Jews all had at least 1.5 percent Jews among their general population (and there were only four more such states), while in seven of the 10 states the proportion of the Jews amounted to more than 3 percent (see Table 7). By the early 2000s, U.S. Jewry constituted less than 2 percent of total population, and the percent Jewish tended to decline all across the board of U.S. states.

In 2005, reflecting global Jewish population stagnation along with growing concentration in a few countries, 97 percent of world Jewry lived in the largest 15 communities, and, excluding Israel from the count, 96 percent lives in the 14 largest communities of the Diaspora, of which 68 percent were in the United States (see Table 8). There were at least 100 Jews in 93 different countries. Two countries had Jewish populations above 5 million individuals each (the U.S. and Israel), another seven had more than 100,000 Jews, three had 50,000–100,000, five had 25,000–50,000, ten had 10,000–25,000, and nine had 9 had 5,000–10,000. Another 57 countries had less than 5,000 and overall accounted for 1 percent of world Jewry; 22 had 1,000–5,000 Jews, and 35 had less than 1,000.

In only seven communities outside of Israel did Jews constitute at least about 5 per 1,000 (0.5 percent) of their country's total population (see Table 9). In descending order by the relative weight (not size) of their Jewish population they were Gibraltar (24.0 Jews per 1,000 inhabitants), the United States (18.0), Canada (11.7), France (8.2), Uruguay (5.7), Australia (5.1), and the United Kingdom (5.0).

By combining the two criteria of Jewish population size and density, for 2005 we obtain the following taxonomy of the 26 Jewish communities with populations over 10,000 (excluding Israel). There were five countries with over 100,000 Jews and at least 5 Jews per 1,000 of total population: the U.S., France, Canada, the U.K., and Australia; another three countries with over 100,000 Jews and at least 1 per 1,000 of total population: Argentina, Russia, and Germany; one country with 10,000–100,000 Jews and at least 5 per 1,000 of total pop-

Table 7.
Jewish Population of the United States of America, by Region and State, 1967–2001[a]

Regions and States	Jews		Percent distribution		Percent of Jews among general population	
	1967	2001	1967	2001	1967	2001
Total	**5,780,000**	**6,155,000**	**100.0**	**100.0**	**2.9**	**2.2**
NORTHEAST	**3,723,700**	**2,850,000**	**64.4**	**46.3**	**7.7**	**5.3**
New England	397,300	426,000	6.9	6.9	3.5	3.1
thereof: Massachusetts	257,700	275,000	4.5	4.5	4.8	4.3
Connecticut	102,900	111,000	1.8	1.8	3.5	3.2
Middle Atlantic	3,326,400	2,424,000	57.5	39.3	9.0	6.1
thereof: New York	2,520,100	1,657,000	43.6	26.9	13.7	8.7
New Jersey	363,000	485,000	6.3	7.9	5.2	5.7
Pennsylvania	443,300	282,000	7.6	4.6	3.8	2.3
MIDWEST	**733,600**	**706,000**	**12.7**	**11.4**	**1.3**	**1.1**
East North Central	598,400	574,000	10.4	9.3	1.5	1.3
thereof: Ohio	160,600	149,000	2.8	2.4	1.5	1.3
Illinois	283,500	270,000	4.9	4.4	2.6	2.2
West North Central	135,200	132,000	2.3	2.1	0.9	0.7
SOUTH	**590,600**	**1,265,000**	**10.2**	**20.6**	**1.0**	**1.3**
South Atlantic	460,400	1,071,000	8.0	17.4	1.6	2.1
thereof: Maryland	177,100	213,000	3.1	3.5	4.8	4.0
Florida	175,600	620,000	3.0	10.1	2.9	3.9
East South Central	41,400	40,000	0.7	0.6	0.3	0.2
West South Central	88,800	154,000	1.5	2.5	0.5	0.5
thereof: Texas	64,000	131,000	1.1	2.1	0.6	0.6
WEST	**731,000**	**1,334,000**	**12.7**	**21.7**	**2.2**	**2.1**
Mountain	53,100	250,000	0.9	4.1	0.7	1.4
Pacific	678,800	1,084,000	11.8	17.6	2.7	2.4
thereof: California	653,600	999,000	11.3	16.2	3.4	2.9

a Source: American Jewish Year Book. Data include unknown percentages of non-Jewish members of Jewish households, and some amount of duplication of multi-residential households.

ulation: Uruguay; nine more countries with 10,000–100,000 Jews and at least 1 per 1,000 of total population: Ukraine, South Africa, Hungary, Belgium, the Netherlands, Chile, Belarus, Switzerland, and Sweden; and eight countries with 10,000–100,000 Jews and less than 1 per 1,000 of total population: Brazil, Mexico, Italy, Turkey, Venezuela, Spain, Iran, and Romania.

URBANIZATION. In the traditional countries of Jewish residence in Europe, there was even in the past a strong tendency for the Jews to live in towns. The residential location of the Jews in towns was often imposed by the authorities, but also had strong links with the economic activities of the Jews and with their religious-communal organization. Exceptions existed in some regions of Central Europe, where the Jews had been banned from the towns and settled on the rural estates of the nobility. In Eastern Europe, a considerable proportion of the Jews lived in villages and in townlets very similar to villages. But even there the share of the Jews in the urban and semiurban population was much larger than in the village population. In many of the Islamic countries as well, a high proportion of the Jews used to live in towns.

In the second half of the 19th century, when middle-sized and large towns developed in the economic centers and capital cities of Central and Eastern Europe, the Jews, who by then had obtained civic rights and freedom to settle where they pleased, participated with particular intensity in this urban evolution. Both the absolute and relative frequency of the Jews rose rapidly in the expanding larger towns (except for central Russia, where Jewish residence continued to be virtually barred). On the other hand, there was a drain away from many customary local Jewish communities in small towns and (where applicable) in villages. In the course of time, the out-migration from the smaller localities led to the extinction of an ever increasing number of Jewish communities there, some of them centuries old. In regions of Jewish in-migration – Western Europe, overseas, and, after the Russian Revolution, also central Russia – the Jews tended to settle directly in the main economic centers and capital cities.

In the 20th century, high proportions of the Jews in the world as a whole and in many individual countries are found in large towns and particularly in the very largest towns (with more than 1,000,000 inhabitants), where those exist. The respective proportions are, as a rule, much larger among the Jews than among the non-Jews of the same country. The relative frequency of the Jews is, therefore, greater in the large localities than in smaller ones. All the same, before World War II the countries of Jewish residence could be divided roughly into three groups, according to the degree of urbanization of the Jews:

1. All but a small percentage of the Jews were town-dwellers in countries of recent immigration in Western Europe, America, and the like.

2. More than 10 percent of the Jews lived in the small localities of some countries of Central Europe.

3. In Eastern Europe, the proportion of Jews resident in small localities was about 20 percent or above, e.g., 25 percent in Poland (1931), 31 percent in Romania (1930).

Under very different conditions, the Jews of Ereẓ Israel also fell into this category at that time. There were also some other countries in Asia and Africa where a considerable percentage of the Jews lived in small localities.

Table 8.
Largest Jewish Populations, 2005

			% of Total Jewish Population			
		Jewish	In the World		In the Diaspora	
Rank	Country	Population	%	Cumulative %	%	Cumulative %
1	United States	5,280,000	40.5	40.5	67.7	67.7
2	Israel	5,237,600	40.2	80.7	=	=
3	France	494,000	3.8	84.5	6.3	74.1
4	Canada	372,000	2.9	87.3	4.8	78.8
5	United Kingdom	297,000	2.3	89.6	3.8	82.6
6	Russia	235,000	1.8	91.4	3.0	85.7
7	Argentina	185,000	1.4	92.8	2.4	88.0
8	Germany	115,000	0.9	93.7	1.5	89.5
9	Australia	102,000	0.8	94.5	1.3	90.8
10	Brazil	96,700	0.7	95.2	1.2	92.1
11	Ukraine	84,000	0.6	95.9	1.1	93.1
12	South Africa	72,500	0.6	96.4	0.9	94.1
13	Hungary	49,900	0.4	96.8	0.6	94.7
14	Mexico	39,800	0.3	97.1	0.5	95.2
15	Belgium	31,200	0.2	97.4	0.4	95.6

Table 9.
Distribution of the World's Jews, by Number and Proportion per 1,000 Population in Each Country, 2005

Number of Jews in Country	Total	Jews per 1,000 Population: 0.0–0.9	1.0–4.9	5.0–9.9	10.0–24.9	25.0+
		Number of Countries				
Total[a]	**93**	**62**	**23**	**4**	**3**	**1**
100–900	35	31	3	–	1	–
1,000–4,900	22	20	2	–	–	–
5,000–9,900	9	3	6	–	–	–
10,000–24,900	10	5	4	1	–	–
25,000–49,900	5	2	3	–	–	–
50,000–99,900	3	1	2	–	–	–
100,000–999,900	7	–	3	3	1	–
1,000,000 or more	2	–	–	–	1	1
		Jewish Population Distribution (Absolute Numbers)				
Total[a]	**13,034,100**	**304,900**	**925,400**	**912,500**	**5,652,600**	**5,237,600**
100–900	11,000	9,200	1,200	–	600	–
1,000–4,900	52,100	46,900	5,200	–	–	–
5,000–9,900	58,800	17,100	41,700	–	–	–
10,000–24,900	160,700	66,500	74,700	19,500	–	–
25,000–49,900	179,600	68,500	111,100	–	–	–
50,000–99,900	253,200	96,700	156,500	–	–	–
100,000–999,900	1,800,000	–	535,000	893,000	372,000	–
1,000,000 or more	10,517,600	–	–	–	5,280,000	5,237,600
		Jewish Population Distribution (Percent Distribution)				
Total[a]	**100.0**	**2.3**	**7.1**	**7.0**	**43.4**	**40.2**
100–900	0.1	0.1	0.0	0.0	0.0	0.0
1,000–4,900	0.4	0.4	0.0	0.0	0.0	0.0
5,000–9,900	0.5	0.1	0.3	0.0	0.0	0.0
10,000–24,900	1.2	0.5	0.6	0.1	0.0	0.0
25,000–49,900	1.4	0.5	0.9	0.0	0.0	0.0
50,000–99,900	1.9	0.7	1.2	0.0	0.0	0.0
100,000–999,900	13.8	0.0	4.1	6.9	2.9	0.0
1,000,000 or more	80.7	0.0	0.0	0.0	40.5	40.2

a Grand total includes countries with fewer than 100 Jews, for a total of 1,100 Jews. Minor discrepancies due to rounding. Israel includes West Bank and Gaza.

By 1925 Lestschinsky found that 23 percent of all Jews in the world lived in centers of over 1,000,000 inhabitants and 45 percent lived in centers of more than 100,000 inhabitants. Fifty-five percent of all Jews could be estimated to reside in about 166 localities, each comprising at least 10,000 Jews and 29 percent of all Jews in 15 localities having each more than 100,000 Jews. Of the 166 localities listed by Lestschinsky as containing at least 10,000 Jews each in 1925, 22 had a majority of Jewish inhabitants. These places were in Eastern Europe, with the exception of only two in Ereẓ Israel.

In the 1930s, 20 centers were estimated to have over 100,000 Jews. First and foremost among them ranked the uniquely large Jewish agglomeration of Greater New York, which was already estimated at about 2,000,000 persons – an eighth of world Jewry, exceeding the Jewish population of all but two individual countries outside the U.S. (namely Poland and the U.S.S.R.). It was estimated that the Jews formed nearly 30 percent of the total population of Greater New York. At a great interval, the next ranking group of cities had 3–400,000 Jews each: Chicago, Philadelphia, and Warsaw. Altogether, the 20 cities with more than 100,000 Jews each were geographically distributed as follows: Eastern Europe, 7 (5 in U.S.S.R., 2 in Poland); Central Europe, 3; Western Europe, 2; U.S., 6; South America, 1; Palestine, 1. The devastations of the Shoah, in terms of loss of life and uprooting of Jews; the geographical regrouping of the survivors returning to the original countries of residence; the large-scale emigration from Eastern Europe, as well as from Islamic countries – all affected the situation of the Jews with regard to urbanization. Under the new conditions, the previously existing tendency for Jews to congregate in the major towns was further accentuated. The scattered small Jewish communities and splinter groups in townlets and villages of Eastern Europe and of the Arabic-speaking countries virtually disappeared because the Jews flocked to the larger towns of those countries – for economic, cultural, and security reasons – or emigrated altogether. The great majority of the Jews who migrated to countries other than Israel settled directly in major cities, and even Israel provides only a partial exception to this rule.

An official population survey taken in the U.S. in 1957 showed that 96 percent of the (adult) Jews lived in urban localities and no fewer than 87 percent in urbanized areas of more than 250,000 inhabitants, while the corresponding proportions in the general population were only 64 and 37 percent respectively. In the U.S.S.R., according to the 1959 census, 95 percent of the Jews, but only 48 percent of the general population, lived in urban localities. Even in Israel, where 273,000 Jews lived in 705 rural localities in 1967, they constituted only 11 percent of the entire Jewish population, while 89 percent lived in urban localities of more than 2,000 inhabitants and 54 percent in towns of 50,000 and over. Also in virtually all other countries of Jewish residence, there is now a very high degree of urbanization of the Jews.

In 1967, there were 21 cities which (together with their outskirts) contained each more than 100,000 Jews. Greater New York continued to lead this array with an estimated number much above 2 million Jews. Next in size, at a long distance, comes Los Angeles, with 500,000 Jews. Of other towns, only four more had 300,000 Jews or over: Philadelphia, Buenos Aires, Paris, and Tel Aviv. The 21 major towns of Jewish residence were divided as follows according to geographical region: U.S.S.R., 4; Western Europe, 2; North America, 10 (thereof 9 in the U.S.); South America, 1; Israel, 4. In comparison with the distribution prior to World War II, the disappearance of the large Jewish populations in cities of Poland and Central Europe was conspicuous, as was the increased prominence of Israel.

In recent decades, many of the above-mentioned towns extended far beyond their municipal boundaries through the formation of conurbations that combined the main city as well as adjacent towns or suburbs into one continuous metropolitan area. These developments affected the Jewish population no less than the general one. One notable indicator of the sensitivity to global market forces of Jewish population distribution was the overwhelming concentration in major urban areas resulting from intensive international and internal migrations. The extraordinary urbanization of the Jews is evinced by the fact that in 2005, 52 percent of world Jewry lived in only five metropolitan areas – Tel Aviv, New York, Los Angeles, Jerusalem, and Haifa – and another 25 percent lived in the next 15 largest metropolitan areas (see Table 10). The Jewish population in the Tel Aviv urban conurbation extending from Netanyah to Ashdod (2,707,000) exceeded by far that in the New York Standard Metropolitan Area (2,051,000) extending from New York State to parts of Connecticut, New Jersey, and Pennsylvania. Of the 22 largest metropolitan areas of Jewish residence, 12 were located in the U.S. (in descending order New York, Los Angeles, Southeast Florida, Philadelphia, Chicago, Boston, San Francisco, Washington, Baltimore, Detroit, Cleveland, and Atlanta), four in Israel (the three mentioned plus Beersheba), two in Canada (Toronto and Montreal), and one each in France (Paris), the U.K. (London), Argentina (Buenos Aires), and Russia (Mos-

Table 10.
Metropolitan Areas with Largest Core Jewish Populations, 2005

Rank	Metro Area[a]	Country	Jewish Population	Share of World's Jews %	Cumulative %
1	Tel Aviv[b, c]	Israel	2,707,000	20.8	20.8
2	New York[d]	U.S.	2,051,000	15.7	36.5
3	Los Angeles[d]	U.S.	668,000	5.1	41.6
4	Jerusalem[e]	Israel	660,000	5.1	46.7
5	Haifa[b]	Israel	656,000	5.0	51.7
6	Southeast Florida[d, f]	U.S.	498,000	3.8	55.5
7	Be'er Sheva[b]	Israel	347,000	2.7	58.2
8	Philadelphia[d]	U.S.	285,000	2.2	60.4
9	Paris[g]	France	284,000	2.2	62.6
10	Chicago[d]	U.S.	265,000	2.0	64.6
11	Boston[d]	U.S.	254,000	1.9	66.6
12	San Francisco[d]	U.S.	218,000	1.7	68.2
13	London[h]	United Kingdom	195,000	1.5	69.7
14	Toronto[i]	Canada	180,000	1.4	71.1
15	Washington[j]	U.S.	166,000	1.3	72.4
16	Buenos Aires[k]	Argentina	165,000	1.3	73.6
17	Baltimore[j]	U.S.	106,000	0.8	74.5
18	Detroit[d]	U.S.	103,000	0.8	75.2
19	Moscow[l]	Russia	95,000	0.7	76.0
20	Montreal[i]	Canada	93,000	0.7	76.7
21	Cleveland[d]	U.S.	86,000	0.7	77.4
22	Atlanta[j]	U.S.	86,000	0.7	78.0

a Most metropolitan areas include extended inhabited territory and several municipal authorities around central city. Definitions vary by country. Some of the estimates may include non-core Jews.
b As newly defined in the 1995 Israeli Census.
c Includes Ramat Gan, Bene Beraq, Petach Tikvah, Bat Yam, Holon, Rishon Lezion, Netanya, and Ashdod, each with a Jewish population above 100,000.
d Consolidated Metropolitan Statistical Area (CMSA).
e Revised estimate. Includes the whole Jerusalem District and parts of Judea and Samaria District.
f Miami-Ft. Lauderdale and West Palm Beach-Boca Raton CMSA.
g Departments 75,77,78,91,92,93,94, 95.
h Greater London and contiguous postcode areas.
i Census Metropolitan Area.
j Metropolitan Statistical Area (MSA).
k Capital Federal and Gran Buenos Aires Partidos (AMBA).
l Territory administered by city council.

cow). In these central places of world economic and cultural significance, large numbers of Jews enjoy favorable and perhaps unprecedented standards of living and can bring to fruition high levels of professional specialization.

While these trends augur well for the Jews, and set the stage and expected rules of possible geographical changes in the future, they also portend a substantial amount of dependency of the Jewish minority upon the favorable conditions created by the majority. The new situation is radically different from the one that prevailed during most of modern Jewish history when Jews were tolerated or discriminated against, and often nurtured hopes for societal changes that would benefit their political and social status. Under the more stable and attractive contemporary conditions, Jewish interests tend to increasingly coincide with the established societal order. At the end of a long transformation which brought with it political emancipation and economic achievement, the Jews find themselves in a more conservative mood facing society at large. Under these conditions Jews also face the challenge of more intensive competition with and easy access to alternative, non-Jewish cultures and social networks. At least in the Diaspora, Jewish cultural continuity appears to be a more difficult target precisely where Jews are physically more secure and where socioeconomic achievement is more easily attainable.

To conclude the topic of the residential concentration of the Jews, it must be said that there have been numerous instances of the Jews living more densely in certain areas of a city or conurbation than in others. The ghettos and mellahs of the past were cases in point. In recent generations, the tendency for urban neighborhoods with greater-than-average density of the Jews has responded to religious, organizational, and social requirements of Jewish life in the Diaspora. It has also facilitated the economic absorption of Jewish in-migrants. Whereas in the earlier part of this century there were well-known cases of quarters with many poor Jews in the large towns, the picture has more recently shifted to residential areas, often suburban, preferred by middle-class or well-to-do Jews.

POPULATION CHARACTERISTICS

Age Composition

The age structure of a population depends on several factors. The first is the vital statistics pattern. High or low levels of fertility or mortality, and any changes in these levels, are reflected in the age distribution of populations. A reduction in births leads to a diminished proportion of children in the population. At first, this increases the relative weight of the adults at age groups typical for work and demographic reproduction. But if the birth rate is low over an extended period, a more advanced stage in the process of aging may be reached, when the relative share of elderly and old persons in the population rises considerably. The impact of a sudden rise in mortality, through calamities, is usually differential according to age and, therefore, affects the age structure of the survivors. The Shoah for example carried away relatively more children and old persons than young adults among the afflicted Jews.

In turn, young adults tend to participate in migrations relatively more than children or older people. Therefore it is usual to find that the proportion of young adults goes down in populations with a negative migration balance (i.e., an excess of emigrants over immigrants) and rises in populations with a positive migration balance. Conditions may be different in the rare cases where almost an entire population is transferred from one country to another, as happened with some Diaspora Jewries that were transplanted in Israel in the first years after the establishment of the Jewish state.

Withdrawals from a Jewish population, whether through conversion to another religion or otherwise, can also affect the age structure if the relative frequency of these withdrawals varies at different ages. Accessions to the Jewish group may exercise similar influences in the reverse. As time passes after changes in the age structure were produced by any of the above factors, the effects make themselves felt in ever higher age groups. Twenty-five years after the Shoah, the particularly heavy deficiency of children originally caused by the persecutions was felt in the age groups 25–40 of the survivors.

Since many Jewish populations have been influenced by stringent birth control, the Shoah, massive immigrations or emigrations, withdrawals, etc., their age structure tends to show distortions due to these various factors and to the time intervals at which they exercised their influence.

All Jewish communities throughout history and geography can be described within a common demographic framework by observing their evolving age composition. Notably, changes affecting different communities over time were not synchronic.

In the middle of the 19th century, large proportions of children (aged 0–14) were still found among the Jews all over Europe, where data are available. With the reduction in fertility, a diminution in the proportion of children set in followed after a while by a marked rise in the percentage of elderly persons. As the decline in fertility affected the Jews in various parts of Europe at different times, so did the consequent changes in the age structure. Both developments began and proceeded at earlier dates among the more assimilated Jews of Western and Central Europe than among the great bulk of traditional Jews in the eastern part of the continent. The movement went from west to east, but before the outbreak of World War II its effects were clearly also visible among the Jews of Eastern Europe. Insofar as sufficient statistical documentation is available, the gradual aging of the Jewish population in one country or town can be observed over successive decades. Since the Jews usually preceded the non-Jews, among whom they lived, in the reduction of fertility, they also preceded them with regard to the consequent changes in age structure. Among the Jews of one country, there were frequently differences in the speed of these transitions according to their varying degree of traditionalism or assimilation. This can be seen, in the data of Table 11, through comparison of the Jews in the various provinces of Czechoslovakia in 1930 and of Jews in Polish localities of different sizes in 1931: the Jews

Table 11.
Selected Jewish Populations, by Main Age Groups, 1897–2004

Country[a]	Year	Total	0–14	15–29	30–44	45–64	65+	Median age[b]
Traditional type								
Ethiopia	1991	100	51	20	13	11	5	14.7
Syria	1960	100	43	23	12	16	6	19.6
Russian Empire	1897	100	41	28	16	12	3	19.8
Romania	1899	100	40	26	19	12	3	20.8
Transitional type								
Poland	1921	100	34	30	16	15	5	23.0
Iran	1976	100	30	28	19	17	6	25.7
USSR	1926	100	29	34	18	15	4	29.4
Mexico	1991	100	24	27	20	22	7	35.0
Venezuela	1998	100	24	19	21	24	12	35.0
USA	1957	100	24	17	21	28	10	36.6
Ageing type								
USA	1990	100	19	19	26	19	17	37.6
Prussia	1925	100	18	25	24	25	8	34.4
United Kingdom	1986	100	17	19	19	21	24	41.1
USA	2001	100	16	20	19	26	19	41.5
Italy	1986	100	14	23	18	26	19	40.8
Russian Republic	1959	100	14	19	23	36	9	41.2
Terminal type								
Russian Republic	1970	100	10	16	23	31	20	45.5
Yugoslavia	1971	100	10	23	17	29	21	45.0
Russian Republic	1979	100	8	15	21	31	25	49.2
Russian Republic	2002	100	5	11	14	33	37	57.5
Romania	1979	100	5	11	10	34	40	59.1
Israeli type								
Palestine	1931	100	33	32	19	11	4	23.0
Israel	1948	100	29	26	26	15	4	27.1
Israel	1961	100	34	22	19	20	5	25.9
Israel	1985	100	30	24	20	16	10	27.5
Israel	2004	100	25	24	19	20	12	30.8

a Countries sorted by the descending percentage of population at age 0–14. The largest age group in each population is underlined.
b The median divides the population into two equal parts: one half having higher and one half having lower ages than the median age.

of Carpatho-Ruthenia in Czechoslovakia and the Jews of the smaller localities in Poland, who adhered to a more traditional mode of life in their respective country, had preserved higher percentages of children.

In the 1930s, the great decline in births occurred in the industrialized countries and made itself particularly felt among the Jews (see *Vital Statistics). As a result, the proportion of 0–14 year-olds in the Jewish populations of Central Europe and, where statistical data are available, of Western Europe dropped below 20 percent, while the proportion of the 60 year-olds and over rose considerably above 10 percent. In Eastern Europe aging was less pronounced, though it had slightly risen there too. In the whole of Poland, the relative share of children under 15 among the Jews declined from 34 percent in 1921 to somewhat less than 30 percent in 1931. At the latter date, it was 26 percent among the Jews of Warsaw. In some Diaspora countries that had absorbed considerable Jewish immigration, the proportion of children aged 0–14 among the Jews tended to be about 20 percent in the 1930s or 1940s – though with considerable variations due to the character of each such Jewish population and the year of the respective data. On the other hand, there were still relatively few old persons and consequently a high percentage of adults in the age range 15–59. This can be seen from Jewish community surveys taken at that time in various towns of the U.S. as well as from statistics of the Jews in Canada, South Africa, Australia, etc. Among the Jews of Palestine, the proportion of children remained relatively high, because the presence of many young adult immigrants had raised the birth figures. But owing to decreasing fertility, there also the percentage of the 0–14 year-old children declined.

The ravages of the Shoah were particularly heavy among the children and the elderly. Therefore, immediately after the war, unusually high proportions of young and middle-aged adults were found among the survivors. The deficiency of birth cohorts from about 1930 to 1945 continues to make itself strongly felt among the Jews of Europe. Because many survivors emigrated from Europe, the peculiarities of their age composition have influenced the absorbing Jewish populations, whether in Israel or elsewhere. Besides, smaller populations tend, in general, to have less regular age distributions. The drastic reduction in size of the Jewish groups extant in European countries and, particularly, in individual localities makes in itself for increased age distortions.

Outside Europe, the Jews of European origin did not suffer physical losses from the Shoah. Still, the 1930s and early 1940s were the time of the great slump in Jewish births in America and elsewhere (see *Vital Statistics). The deficiency of the birth cohorts of that time is reflected in the age distributions of the respective Jewish populations to this day. After World War II, the "baby boom" occurred among the Jews in Europe, America, Oceania, and Israel. This rise in births was similar to analogous developments in the industrialized societies of the world, but it was rather short-lived among the Jews. The bulge in the age distribution produced by the increased cohorts born in the second half of the 1940s or around 1950 still clearly appeared in many Jewish populations fifty year later. So were the effects of the subsequent renewed decline in Jewish births which led to a reduction of the child population. For example, in many Jewish populations studied in the 1960s, the 0–4 year-olds were less numerous than the 5–9 and 10–14 year-olds, respectively.

The overall age profile of Jews in Western Europe included fewer young children than adults and, more significantly, than elders in their mid-60s or early 70s. While there are some internal differences within the continent, it is quite an aging Jewish population. The age profile of Jews in the United States and Canada in the 1990s was somewhat younger. The proportion of children and young adults was larger, reflecting the rather large cohorts born during the *baby boom* of the 1950s and 1960s, and the *echo effect* of the generations born to the *baby-boomers* during the 1980s and 1990s. But ageing is well visible in the most recent North American data.

The age profile of East European Jewry, largely influenced by the FSU Jewish population, is striking. It points to the consequences for a population of prolonged very low levels of fertility, very high rates of assimilation, and selective emigration of a comparatively higher proportion of younger families, leaving behind a large share of the elderly and the very elderly. East European Jewry has lost most of its demographic basis for the future.

Because of their high fertility, the Jews in Asia and Africa used to have a younger age composition, with a high proportion (40 percent and over) of children aged 0–14 and a rather regular decrease of frequency in successively higher age groups, culminating in a small proportion (less than 5 percent) in ages 65 and over. These features can be seen in the age distributions of the Jews of Morocco and of the immigrants to Israel from Asia and Africa. Most of the Jews from Asia and Africa have left their traditional countries of residence and have settled elsewhere, especially in Israel and France. The lowering of fertility in the new surroundings (see *Vital Statistics) cannot but have its gradual effects on their age structure.

Finally, the age profile of the Jewish population in Israel provides the only example of a demographically balanced Jewish population with a larger basis of children sustaining gradually smaller shares of young adults, mature adults, and elders. This mainly reflects Israel's sustained birth rate, and to a minor extent the continuous influx of a high proportion of young adults among new immigrants.

Sex

In populations sufficiently large for standard biological trends to express themselves, there is a small surplus of males over females among the newborn, but the age-specific mortality rates are usually lower for females and, therefore, a surplus of females is to be expected in the adult population (unless external factors, such as migrations, exert a contrary influence). Where statistical data have been available, these general tendencies have been found to operate among the Jews also. Another widespread tendency is the larger participation of men than women in migrations. In this case, the proportion of males is, by the fact of migration, lowered in the population of origin and raised in the population of destination. Modern Jewish migrations have been less motivated by economic considerations and more by the search for refuge than those of most other nations, and this has reduced the sex differential; but in many cases a larger participation of men has also been found in migrations of Jews.

Jewish populations in the Diaspora are usually small, and this fact operates by itself to create irregularities in the sex-age composition. Besides, they have often been strongly influenced by migrations, withdrawals, and the aftereffects of the Shoah. Hence, distortions in the sex-age composition are frequent. For the Jewish population of entire countries, the ratio of males per 1,000 females (irrespective of age) has ranged in recent years from 833 in the U.S.S.R. (1959), where war losses of men were very heavy among the Jews (as among the general population), to more than 1,100 in some other Diaspora countries, e.g., Germany and Austria.

The sex-ratio is particularly significant in the principal ages of marriage, because under modern conditions, when the religious factor has been weakened, this ratio has an influence on the proportions of endogamic Jewish marriages and *intermarriages of Jews, respectively. It must be borne in mind, though, that on the average there is an age difference of several years between grooms and brides. When the ratio of Jewish men aged, say, 25–39 to 1,000 Jewish women aged 20–34 is calculated, marked disparities are found in some countries.

Origin Groups (Edot)

It has been customary to divide the Jewish world population into several groups, called *edot* ("communities") and distinguished according to a combination of historical, geographic, and linguistic criteria. These groups have somewhat differing liturgical usages. In countries where Jews of several origin groups resided, they sometimes established separate organizational frameworks for the maintenance of synagogues and other religious and communal services. This led to the term *edah*, or its equivalents in other languages, being sometimes used not from the demographic, but from the organizational viewpoint. There has never been a generally accepted classification of all Jewish origin groups. Yet it is usual to distinguish three main groups:

1. *Ashkenazim, who constitute the overwhelming majority of the Jews in Europe (except for Italy, Greece, Bulgaria, and parts of the former Yugoslavia), North and South America, South Africa, and Oceania. In the past, a large proportion of the Ashkenazim were Yiddish-speaking.

2. *Sephardim (in a narrow sense of the term of descendants of Jews from Spain), who were concentrated in Greece, Bulgaria, southern Yugoslavia, and western Turkey and formed a considerable proportion of the Jewish populations in Lebanon and Syria, Egypt and Northwest Africa. Sephardi communities were organized in several Latin American countries. Many of the Sephardim used to speak Ladino.

3. Oriental communities. The further breakdown of this group has varied among different scholars, but the principal divisions are the following:

a) Jews of Arabic-speaking countries, especially Syria, Iraq, Yemen, Libya, Tunisia, Algeria, Morocco. Migrants from these communities created new community centers in France, Latin America (especially Mexico and Venezuela), the United States, and other western countries.

b) Jews of Persia, Afghanistan, and Bukhara, speaking Persian or related languages. Emigrants from Iran created communities in the United States and other western countries.

c) Kurdish Jews, part of whom use an Aramaic dialect.

d) Jews of the Caucasus region. With the massive emigration of Jews from the former U.S.S.R., Jews from the Caucasus resettled in the United States, Germany, and other countries.

e) Indian Jews. These include the Bnei Israel, the Baghdadi community, and the Jews from Kochin.

f) Italian Jews include the descendants of an ancient core of early settlers who reached the south European shores before and during the period of the Roman Empire, long before the notions of Askhenaz and Sepharad had even developed.

g) Ethiopian Jews, including the Beta Israel and the Falashmura community of Jewish ancestry.

More refined divisions are uncertain, because of the smallness and instability of some of the groups distinguished.

These origin groups cannot be thought of as completely separated from one another. Migrations and/or marriages between Jews of different origin often led to transfers of individuals, even between the major divisions. Besides, the linguistic criterion for group affiliation lost much of its importance in recent generations, because of the increased importance of the official languages of the various countries for the respective Jewish populations.

Special difficulties exist with regard to the distinction of Sephardim and Oriental communities. Not all Sephardim were Ladino-speaking even some generations ago. The Sephardim established in Northwest Africa had long since gone over to the use of Arabic. Moreover, there has been a tendency to broaden the concept of Sephardim so as to make it include all Jews who are not Ashkenazim. This has been so both because of the prestige which the name Sephardim commands and because, organizationally, Sephardi institutions have often also comprised the Oriental elements in Jewish populations of mixed origin. About 1930, Ruppin estimated that there were roughly 1,300,000 Sephardim and Oriental Jews, constituting 8% of world Jewry. In the past, the proportion of this group was greater, but went down in the 19th and early 20th centuries because of the higher natural increase of the Ashkenazim, i.e., the European Jews, at that time. Of the 1,300,000 Sephardim and Oriental Jews in 1930, two thirds lived in Asia and Africa, but only 3% in Ereẓ Israel. Since then, the absolute and relative number of Sephardim and Oriental communities within Jewry has been altered. Around 2000, they were estimated at 3,400,000 or about 26 percent of all Jews. The increase in their proportion is due to the reduced number of Ashkenazim after the Shoah and to their own high natural increase during the last few decades, which recently greatly exceeded that of the Ashkenazim.

The geographical distribution of most origin groups changed completely. Two thirds of the Ashkenazim in 1930, but only about 30 percent in 1967 and 14 percent in 2000, lived in Europe. On the other hand, the share of America among the Ashkenazim rose over the same time interval from a third in 1930 to about 60 percent in 1967 and the same in 2000, and that of Ereẓ Israel from less than 1 percent in 1930 to about 10 percent in 1967 and 26 percent in 2000. Of the Ladino-speaking Sephardim, a small number remained in only one of their traditional countries of residence, Turkey. Most of the other Ladino-speaking Sephardim either perished in the Shoah (Greece, Yugoslavia) or moved to Israel (particularly those of Bulgaria). Of the Jews of the Arabic-speaking countries, nearly all those who lived in Asia and a great part of those from North Africa found new homes in Israel. Israel has also attracted many Jews from Turkey, Iran, India, etc. Around 2000, about two-thirds of all Sephardim and Oriental Jews were in-gathered in Israel, another large section moved to France, the rest were scattered over many countries in all continents. Some of the Oriental groups transferred almost in their entirety to Israel, e.g., Yemenites, "Babylonians" (i.e., from central and southern Iraq), the Kurdish Jews, several groups from Syria, the Libyan Jews.

While the division into the traditional origin groups reflected the geographical-cultural plurality of world Jewry before the upheavals and mass migrations of recent decades, its present value for indicating demographic differences other than mere origin is rapidly disappearing. The Sephardim of the Balkan countries showed in the recent past the same demographic patterns characteristic of European populations.

Most Oriental Jews after moving to Israel and France, respectively, were exposed to the rapidly modifying influences of the respective surroundings. Israel in particular provided the meeting ground of Jews of all origin groups. The life in common there and many intergroup marriages rapidly reduced and eventually annulled any previously existing demographic differences between the various origin groups. Factors other than mere origin, such as education, occupation, and place of residence, became increasingly important for differentiation in demographic behavior in a context of general convergence. The growing impact of out-marriage and assimilation further reduced the impact of *edot* on contemporary Jewish demography. Nonetheless, the relevance of separate traditions and community organizations continued to play a significant role in the patterns of Jewish identification among contemporary Jewry.

BIBLIOGRAPHY: U.O. Schmelz, in: AJYB, 70 (1969), 273–88; U.O. Schmelz and P. Glikson, *Jewish Population Studies, 1961–1968* (1970); AJYB (1899–); A. Ruppin, in: L. Finkelstein (ed.), *Jewish People Past and Present*, 1 (1946), 348–60; idem, *Soziologie der Juden*, 1 (1930); H.S. Halevi, *Hashpa'at Milḥemet ha-Olam ha-Sheniyyah al ha-Tekhunot ha-Demografiyyot shel Am Yisrael* (1963), Eng. introd. and summ.; J. Lestschinsky, in: *Weltwirtschaftliches Archiv*, 30 (1929), 123–365. **ADD. BIBLIOGRAPHY:** R. Bachi, *The Population of Israel* (1976); S. DellaPergola, in: *Holocaust and Genocide Studies*, 10:1 (1996), 34–51; idem, *World Jewry Beyond 2000: The Demographic* Prospects (1999); idem, in: *Pe'amim*, 93 (2002), 149–56; idem, in: AJYB, 105 (2005); S. DellaPergola, U. Rebhun, and M. Tolts, in: *Israel Studies*, 10:1 (2005), 61–95; M. Tolts, in: *Jews in Russia and Eastern Europe*, 1 (52), 37–63.

[Usiel Oscar Schmelz / Sergio DellaPergola (2nd ed.)]

DEMONS, DEMONOLOGY. A demon is an evil spirit, or devil, in the ordinary English usage of the term. This definition is, however, only approximate. In polytheistic religions the line between gods and demons is a shifting one: there are both good demons and gods who do evil. In monotheistic systems, evil spirits may be accepted as servants of the one God, so that demonology is bound up with angelology and theology proper, or they may be elevated to the rank of opponents of God, in which case their status as diabolic powers differs from that of the demons in polytheism. Moreover, in none of the languages of the ancient Near East, including Hebrew, is there any one general term equivalent to English "demon." In general, the notion of a demon in the ancient Near East was of a being less powerful than a god and less endowed with individuality. Whereas the great gods are accorded regular public worship, demons are not; they are dealt with in magic rites in individual cases of human suffering, which is their particular sphere.

Demonology in the Ancient Near East

Defense against evil spirits was a concern in Mesopotamia from earliest times, beginning with the Sumerians, to whom much of the terminology and praxis connected with demons may be traced. There is no qualitative difference between great gods and demons; one name for demon is "an evil god." Demons, however, have less power, though occasionally myths depict them as rebelling against the great gods, with some success. Incantations often list four, or even seven, classes of demons. Demons are messengers of the lord of the underworld, and march before him. They live in deserts and near graves, and many of them are ghosts, spirits of the dead, especially of those who died by violence or were not properly buried. Sickness may be thought of as caused by demonic possession, and some demons have the name of the specific disease they bring, thus "Headache," or "Fever." *Lamashtu* is the hag who kills children in the womb and newborn babies. Like many other demons, she is depicted as a composite monster. Lilitu, the Mesopotamian succubus, is mentioned once in the Bible as *Lilith (Isa. 34:14; see below), and in later Jewish demonology. Good demons are mentioned much less frequently.

In general features Canaanite demonology probably resembled that of Mesopotamia, to judge from the rather meager evidence preserved. In a mythological text from Ugarit, the father of the gods, El, is frightened almost to death by a demon "having two horns and a tail," like the devil in later representations. A Phoenician amulet of the seventh century B.C.E., from Arslan Tash, begins: "Incantations: O Flying One, O goddess, O Sasam… O god, O Strangler of Lambs! The house I enter you shall not enter; the court I tread you must not tread." Intended to protect women in childbirth, it goes on to invoke the protection of the gods, and contains depictions of the demons mentioned: a winged sphinx, labeled "Flying One, Lil[ith]," and a wolf devouring a child. Details of the text and iconography have close parallels in Mesopotamian, Arabic, classical, and later Jewish folklore, and illustrate the well-nigh universal character of many superstitions about demons (Gaster, in: *Orientalia*, 11 (1942), 41–79).

Demonology in the Bible

Israel's official religion contrasts sharply with contemporary polytheisms in the role assigned to demons, which in the Bible is practically nil. Magic was prohibited among the Israelites from very early times, for already the oldest collection of laws, the Book of the Covenant, contains the command: "You shall not tolerate a sorceress" (Ex. 22:17 [Eng. 22:18]; cf. Deut. 18:10–12), and Saul put the practitioners of necromancy out of the land (I Sam. 28:3). Since much of pagan magic was protective – intended to keep demons away or to expel them – obviously Israel's religion aimed at a very radical extirpation of traffic with demons. Calamities and illnesses were not from demons but from the Lord. "Shall there be evil in a city, and the Lord has not done it?" (Amos 3:6). Although God does not always accomplish His will immediately, but uses angels and spirits as agents, it is ordinarily made explicit that the spirits are under His control. The evil spirit which troubles Saul is "an evil spirit from the Lord" (I Sam. 16:14). Therefore, one must not overestimate the importance of the numerous small traces of belief in demons which survive in the Bible, or underestimate the difficulties involved in interpreting them. Most of the passages in question are poetic, and it is often impossible to be certain whether the demon named is part of living religious belief, or only part of traditional literary language. Just as some Mesopotamian demons have names which are also common nouns, so in biblical cases like *dever* and *mavet* (*mawet*; see below) it is hard to be sure when these are proper names and when not.

The Israelite conception of demons, as it existed in the popular mind or the literary imagination, resembled in some ways that held elsewhere. Demons live in deserts or ruins (Lev. 16:10; Isa. 13:21; 34:14). They inflict sickness on men (Ps. 91:5–6). They trouble men's minds (Saul; I Sam. 16:15, 23) and deceive them (I Kings 22:22–23) – but nevertheless these evil spirits are sent by the Lord. The mysterious being who attacks Jacob in Genesis 32:25ff. exhibits a trait which a very widespread belief associated with certain demons, who are spirits of the night and must perish at dawn. Even in Israelite popular religion, however, there seems to have been relatively little fear of the spirits of the dead. The Bible often mentions the shades of the dead, but "the congregation of the shades" (Prov. 21:16) carries on a shadowy existence below, and does not seem to trouble the living. Some features of the Israelite cult bear a formal resemblance to apotropaic measures employed in other religions. Thus, the bells on the robe of the high priest (Ex. 28:33–35) recall the use of bells in other cultures in the belief that their tinkling keeps off demons. So, also, horns (Ex. 19:16; Lev. 25:9; et al.), incense (Lev. 16:12–13), smearing of doorposts (Ex. 12:7), the color blue (Num. 15:38), written scripture-texts (phylacteries; Deut. 6:8; 11:18) – all have parallels elsewhere as devices to ward off evil spirits. In a given case, however, it is often extremely difficult to say to what extent any of these devices were consciously used for protection against demons at a particular period.

Specific Demons

Foreign gods are called *shedim* (Deut. 32:17; Ps. 106:37; cf. I Cor. 10:20), rendered "demons" or "devils" in most translations. The word is related to Akkadian *šêdu* ("demon"; good or evil).

SEʿIRIM ("hairy demons, satyrs") is also applied contemptuously to foreign deities (Lev. 17:7; II Chron. 11:15). These creatures haunt ruins, along with Lilith (Isa. 13:21; 34:14).

LILITH (Isa. 34:14; ultimately from Sumerian *lil*, "air," not Heb. *layl(ah)*, "night") was originally a succubus, believed to cohabit with mortals, but in the Arslan Tash incantation quoted above she is identified with the child-stealing demon, a character she retains in later folklore. The tradition that the name means "screech-owl" (in so many translations) reflects a very ancient association of birds, especially owls, with the demonic.

MAVET (*Mawet*), the ordinary Hebrew word for death, is also the proper name of a Canaanite underworld god (Mot), the enemy of Baal in a Ugaritic epic. The proper name, not the common noun, should probably be understood in Isaiah 28:15, 18: "We have made a covenant with Death," and Jeremiah 9:20 [Eng. 9:21]: "For Death is come up into our windows" (cf. Hos. 13:14; Job 18:13, "the firstborn of Death"; 28:22).

RESHEPH is another major god of the Canaanite religion who becomes a demonic figure in biblical literature. Resheph is known as the god of plague over much of the ancient Near East, in texts and artistic representations spanning more than a millennium from 1850 B.C.E. to 350 B.C.E. In Habakkuk 3:5, YHWH on the warpath is said to be preceded and followed by respectively Dever and Resheph. (This is similar to the picture of two divine attendants who escort major gods in ancient myths.) Just as some other names of deities are used as common nouns in biblical Hebrew (Dagon (*dagon*, "grain"); Ashtaroth (*ashtarot*, "increase [of the flock]"), etc.) so Reshef (*reshef*) has come to mean simply "plague" (Deut. 33:29; Ps. 78:48), and the fiery darts of the bow (Ps. 76:4 [Eng. 76:3]; Song 8:6), apparently from the common association of plague and arrows.

DEVER ("Pestilence") is the other demonic herald who marches with YHWH to battle (Hab. 3:5). Dever is also mentioned in Psalms 91:5–6: "Thou shalt not be afraid for the Terror (*Paḥad*) by night; Nor for the Arrow (*Ḥeẓ*) that flieth by day; Nor for the Pestilence (*Dever*) that walketh in the darkness; Nor for the Destruction (*Ketev*) that wasteth at noonday." Not only Dever but also the other words italicized above have been plausibly identified as names of demons. The "Arrow" is a familiar symbol in folklore, for disease or sudden pain, and *Ketev* (*Qetev*; cf. Deut. 32:24; Isa. 28:2; Hos. 13:14) is in this instance the personification of overpowering noonday heat, known also to Greek and Roman demonology.

*AZAZEL (*ʿAzʾazel*) occurs in the ritual for the *Day of Atonement (Lev. 16:8, 10, 26). Aaron casts lots over two goats, and the one "for *ʿAzʾazel*" is presented alive before the Lord, and then released into the wilderness. The ancient Greek and Latin versions understood *ʿAzʾazel* as "goat that departs," hence "the scapegoat" of some English versions. Most of the rabbinic commentators and some moderns take Azazel as the name of the place to which the goat is driven. The great majority of moderns regard Azazel as the personal name of a demon thought to live in the wilderness.

The vampire may be mentioned in Proverbs 30:15: "The *alukah (ʿaluqah)* hath two daughters, crying, 'Give, Give.'" Hebrew *ʿaluqah* may simply mean "leech," but since *ʿaulaq* occurs in Arabic literature as a name of a vampire, this fabulous creature and her two daughters may be referred to in this rather difficult passage.

Demons in Intertestamental Literature, Including the Dead Sea Scrolls

A great change had taken place in *angelology and demonology, at least in certain circles within Judaism, by the last centuries B.C.E. In this period the religion, while safeguarding its monotheistic character in various ways, nevertheless took on many traits of a dualistic system in which God and the forces of good and truth were opposed in heaven and on earth by powerful forces of evil and deceit. This seems to have been under the influence of Persian religion, with its opposition of Ormuzd the good god and Ahriman (Angra Mainyu) the evil god, but at the same time Jewish *dualism drew on older, native resources in constructing a more elaborate demonology. Ancient mythological themes, and figures from the Bible only potentially demonic, like Satan, were drawn in to fill out the enlarged conception of the role of evil spirits in the cosmos. It is characteristic of this period that the evil spirits are led by a prince, often called *Belial but also Mastemah, *Satan, or other names. The spirits of good and evil also struggled within the human soul, for in this period the role of demons is often conceived of as that of tempting men to evil rather than of inflicting physical harm. As a result, in many passages it is difficult to say whether "spirit" refers to a demon external to man or to a trait within the human soul. Belial (or Beliar, a corruption of the original form) is the most common name for the leader of the demons in the Dead Sea Scrolls, and occurs in other intertestamental literature and in II Corinthians 6:15. Belial (Heb. *Beliyya'al*) is a Hebrew compound word which etymologically means "no benefit" or "no thriving" and in liberal usage is often equivalent to "scoundrel." But already in the Bible "streams of *Beliyya'al*" means "streams of destruction" (II Sam. 22:5; Ps. 18:5). In the intertestamental literature Belial is "the spirit of perversion, the angel of darkness, the angel of destruction" and other spirits are subject to him. Mastemah, which as a common noun means approximately "enmity, opposition" in Hosea 9:7, 8 and in some passages in the Five Scrolls, is a demon "Prince Mastemah" in Jubilees (11:5, 11; 17:16; et al.), and perhaps also in the Damascus Document (16:5). Watchers (Aram. *ʿirin*) are a type of angel mentioned in Daniel 4:10, 14, 20. To this class the intertestamental literature assigns the angels who, according to Genesis 6:2, 4, cohabited with women before the flood and fathered the race of giants (Test. Patr., Reu. 5:6–7; Test. Patr., Napht. 3:5; cf. *Genesis Apocryphon*, ii 2:1, 16). *Asmodeus (Tobit 3:8, 17) is a demon who had slain the first seven husbands of Sarah, who becomes the wife of Tobias son of Tobit.

Demons in the New Testament

New Testament demonology in part reflects contemporary popular belief, which turns up also in rabbinic literature, and in part the dualism attested in the sectarian literature from Qumran. Demons are called "unclean spirits" or "evil spirits," as in rabbinic literature. They are believed to inhabit waste places. Possession by demons causes, or is associated with, various sicknesses, especially those in which there is a perversion of the human personality, so that the demon, not the man himself, directs his acts and speech (Mark 1:23, 26; 9:17–29). The story of how Jesus cured a demoniac by sending a legion of unclean spirits into a herd of swine (Matt. 8:28–34; Mark 5:1–20; Luke 8:26–39) illustrates vividly the persistence of very ancient popular belief, as does the parable of Matthew 12:43–45, in which the unclean spirit after wandering through the wilderness takes seven devils with him. On the other hand, in the New Testament lesser demons have little independent personality or power, but are subject to a prince, Beelzebul or Satan, and the demonic is often presented, not as something occasional and relatively harmless, but as a cosmic reality of great importance, the enemy of God and man (Eph. 6:12). Beelzebul (Beelzebub) is a name applied to the chief demon by both Jesus and his opponents (Matt. 10:25; 12:24, 27; Mark 3:22; Luke 11:15–19). The correct explanation of the name is much disputed, and new evidence from Ugarit has not completely cleared up the etymology. The spelling Beelzebub reflects identification of Beelzebul with Baal-Zebub, god of Ekron (II Kings 1:2). Possibly there were two different original forms, Beelzebul meaning "Baal is prince" or "Lord of the shrine," and Beelzebub "Lord of flies" (cf. Ugaritic *il dbb* [in Gordon, Textbook, *ʿnt* 3:43]).

[Delbert Roy Hillers]

In the Talmud

References are made to a belief in demonology during the tannaitic period. The *mazzikim* ("harmful spirits") are said to have been created on the eve of the Sabbath of creation (Avot 5:6) but this late reference is the only one made to demons in the entire Mishnah. Among the accomplishments of both Hillel (Sof. 16:9) and his disciple R. Johanan b. Zakkai was their knowledge of "the speech of the *shedim*" ("devils," Suk. 28a). The latter also gave the analogy of a *ru'aḥ tezazit* ("the demon of madness") entering a man and being exorcised, in order to explain to a heathen the anomaly of the laws of the *red heifer, although he agreed with his wondering disciples that it was but "putting him off with a straw" and that he himself did not accept it (PR 40a; Num. R. 19:4). Although these statements refer to Ereẓ Israel, the Jerusalem Talmud is markedly free from demonology, and in fact mentions only three general names for them – *mazzikim, shedim*, and *ruḥot*. A passage in the Babylonian Talmud specifically states that various beliefs connected with demons which were current in Babylon were ignored in Ereẓ Israel. Whereas in Ereẓ Israel they translated *shiddah* and *shiddot* (Eccles. 2:8) as "carriages," in Babylon they rendered them "male and female demons" (Git. 68a). The Palestinian R. Johanan stated that the *mazzikim* which used to hold sway in the world disappeared with the erection of the sanctuary in the wilderness (Num. R. 12:30). Demonology, however, is more prominent in the Palestinian Midrashim than in the Jerusalem Talmud. On the other hand the Babylonian Talmud is replete with demonology, obviously under the influence of the belief in demons which was widespread in Babylonia. In fact, in a responsum (published in Lewin, Oẓar, p. 20; cf. Assaf, Geonim, p. 262) *Hai Gaon states that the belief in demons was widespread in *Sura, since it was near to (old) Babylonia and to the house of Nebuchadnezzar, whereas in the more distant *Pumbedita they were far from such ideas. The Babylonian Jews lived in a world which was filled with demons and spirits, malevolent and sometimes benevolent, who inhabited the air, the trees, water, roofs of houses, and privies. They are invisible; "If the eye could see them no one could endure them. They surround one on all sides. They are more numerous than humans, each person has a thousand on his left and ten thousand on his right" and they are responsible for various inconveniences. Yet, by taking certain steps, in the morning one can see their footprints in the shape of those of a cock (Ber. 6a). Whereas in the Kabbalah there is an attempt to systematize demonology (see below) there is no sign of such an attempt in the talmudic literature. The material is vast and inchoate, scattered in profusion and without system throughout the whole Talmud and in the Midrashim. The following details, taken except where otherwise indicated from one passage of the Talmud (Pes. 110a–112b), may be taken as indicative.

Asmodeus is the king of the demons. The queen is *Agrath bat Mahalath, who has 10,000 demon attendants, each of whom can do harm. She haunts the air. Originally she held sway at all times, but Ḥanina b. Dosa, threatening to ban her from populated areas, relented in answer to her pleas and permitted her to be active on Wednesday nights and Sabbath eves. The Babylonian *amora* Abbaye later banished her from populated areas but she still lurks in the narrow alleys. Doing things in pairs, especially drinking an even number of cups, invites the malevolent activities of demons; an exception is the four cups enjoined in the *seder* on *Passover for which reason that occasion is called "a night of guarding" (Ex. 12:42), i.e., of protection from demons. Demons are especially harmful in and around palm trees, and their malevolent attention is invited by easing oneself between a palm tree and the wall, by passing between two palms, or by sleeping in the shadow of a palm tree. The demon Palga will affect a man easing himself on the stump of a palm tree; the demon Zereda him who leans his head on one. In general one should avoid many-branched or prickly trees, but there are special trees which are the favorite haunts of the spirits. In the caperbush there resides the eyeless Ruhe. Every sorb tree harbors demons in its shade and is especially dangerous when it is in the vicinity of a town. At least 60 demons haunt it, and they can be exorcised only by a "60 demon amulet." Demons called Rishpe live in the roots of trees. The demon *Ketev Meriri* (Deut. 32:34) is active in the mornings. It was seen by Abbaye when he was in the company of Papa and Huna b. Joshua. In the afternoon, its place is taken by *Ketev Yashud Ẓohorayim* (Ps. 91:6) which looks like a goat's horns, and has wings. Both these demons are particularly active from the 1st to the 16th of Tammuz.

According to the Midrash, however, *Ketev Meriri* is active during the period of mourning from the 17th of Tammuz to the Ninth of Av, between the fourth and ninth hours of the day. As late as the 13th century Zedekiah *Anav reports that in Rome pupils were not punished during these days and hours because of *Ketev Meriri* which held sway then (*Shibbolei ha-Leket*, 1:203). It is covered with scales and hairs; it has one eye in its heart and rolls like a ball between the sunlight and the shade. Whoever sees it, collapses and falls to the ground (Mid. Ps. 91:3; from the context however it appears that the reference should be to the *Ketev Yashud Ẓohorayim*). R. Joseph and R. Papa had friendly conversation with a demon called Joseph. Demons are prone to infest food and drink left under the bed, and one should refrain from drinking water on Wednesday and Sabbath eve or from pools and rivers at night. The demon Shabriri ("blindness" – cf. Targum Onkelos, Gen. 19:11) wreaks harm on those so doing, but an incantation, consisting of an abracadabra whereby the word is repeated, successively deducting one letter from the word (Shabriri, briri, riri, etc.), is an effective antidote. Solomon made use of male and female demons to build the Temple (Git. 68b) and to bring him water from India with which he was able to grow all kinds of exotic plants not otherwise growing in Ereẓ Israel (Eccles. R. to 2:5). Scholars were immune to the evil machinations of demons while they were engaged in study, but Rashi explains a passage of the Talmud to mean that, on the contrary, they are in need of special protection since the demons are envious of them (Ber. 62a). Psalm 91 is called "the Psalm of [protection against harmful] visitations." Moses is stated to have recited it when he ascended Mount Sinai "because of his fear of *mazzikim*… and angels of destruction." It is enjoined to be recited "because the whole world is full of evil spirits and *mazzikim*" (Tanḥ., Mishpatim, end) and the midrashic interpretations of this Psalm are a veritable treasure store of demonology lore (e.g., Mid. Ps. 91; Tanḥ., Mishpatim, end; Num. R. 12:3–4). The power of demons over man and his helplessness in face of it is illustrated by the fact that the talmudic metaphor for an act performed through *force majeure* is "as though a devil [*shed*] had compelled him" (e.g., RH 28a). The talmudic commentators and codifiers accepted the belief in demons; Maimonides alone opposed it.

[Louis Isaac Rabinowitz]

In Kabbalah

The kabbalists made use of all the motifs current in the Talmud and Midrash with regard to demons. New elements were developed or added, mainly in two directions: (1) the kabbalists attempted to systematize demonology so that it would fit into their understanding of the world and thus to explain demonology in terms derived from their understanding of reality; (2) new and varied elements were added from external sources, mainly from medieval Arabic demonology, from Christian demonology, and from the popular beliefs of the Germans and Slavs.

At times these elements were linked, more or less logically, to Jewish demonology and were thus "Judaized" to some extent. However, frequently the link was only external; material was incorporated into Jewish demonology with almost no explicit Jewish adaptation. This is particularly true with regard to the sources of practical Kabbalah. There, real kabbalistic beliefs mingled with folk beliefs which in fact originally had no connection with the beliefs of the kabbalists. This combination gives the late Jewish demonology its markedly syncretistic character. The material pertaining to this kind of demonology can be found in innumerable sources, many still in manuscript. Extensive research in this field and its development is one of the important desiderata of Jewish studies.

The works of the kabbalists also contain contradictory conceptions of the demons and the power of imagination. Traditions of the past as well as the cultural environment and the intellectual outlook of each individual kabbalist contributed toward the diversification of their beliefs. The ideas of the early Spanish kabbalists on this subject were formulated clearly in *Naḥmanides' commentary on Leviticus 17:7 and their influence is visible in all subsequent literature. In Naḥmanides' opinion the demons (*shedim*) are to be found in waste (*shedudim*), ruined, and cold places such as in the North. They were not created out of the four elements but only out of fire and air. They have subtle bodies, imperceptible by the human senses, and these subtle bodies allow them to fly through fire and air. Because they are composed of different elements, they come under the laws of creation and decay and they die like human beings. Their sustenance is derived from water and fire, from odors and saps; hence necromancers burned incense to demons. Despite the element of subtle fire which they contain, they are surrounded by a coldness that frightens off the exorcisers (this detail is singled out only in later sources). By means of their flight through air they are able to approach the "princes" of the zodiac who dwell in the atmosphere and thus hear predictions of the near but not the distant future.

Naḥmanides also hints (Comm. to Lev. 16:8) that the demons belong to the patrimony of Samael, who is "the soul of the planet Mars and Esau is his subject among the nations" (the angel of Edom or Christianity). The Castilian kabbalists, *Isaac b. Jacob ha-Kohen, Moses of *Burgos, and Moses de Leon (in his Hebrew works and in the *Zohar), linked the existence of demons with the last grade of the powers of the "left-side" emanation (the *sitra aḥra*, "other side," of the Zohar) which corresponds in its ten *Sefirot* of evil to the ten holy *Sefirot*. Their writings contain detailed descriptions of the way in which these powers emanated and explain the names of the supervisors of their hosts. Their ideas are mainly based on internal development in kabbalistic circles. In the various sources entirely different names are given to the upper grades of these demonic or Satanic powers. However, they all agree in linking the hosts of demons in the subhuman world, i.e., on earth, under the dominion of Samael and *Lilith who appear for the first time in these sources as a couple. Numerous details about these grades are found in *Sefer Ammud ha-Semali* by Moses of Burgos (*Tarbiz*, 4 (1933), 208–25).

In contrast, the Zohar, following a talmudic legend, stresses the origin of the demons in sexual intercourse between humans and demonic powers. Some demons, such as Lilith, were created during the six days of Creation, and in particular on the Sabbath eve at twilight, as disembodied spirits. They sought to take on the form of a body through association with humans, at first with Adam when he separated from Eve and then with all his descendants. However, the demons who were created out of such unions also long for this kind of intercourse. The sexual element in the relationship of man and demons holds a prominent place in the demonology of the Zohar, as well as that of several later kabbalistic works. Every pollution of semen gives birth to demons. The details of these relationships are remarkably similar to the beliefs current in Christian medieval demonology about succubi and incubi. They are based on the assumption (contrary to the talmudic opinion) that these demons have no procreating ability of their own and need the human semen in order to multiply. In the later Kabbalah it is pointed out that the demons born to man out of such unions are considered his illegitimate sons; they were called *banim shovavim* ("mischievous sons"). At death and burial they come to accompany the dead man, to lament him, and to claim their share of the inheritance; they may also injure the legitimate sons. Hence the custom of circling the dead at the cemetery to repulse the demons and also the custom (dating from the 17th century) in a number of communities of not allowing the sons to accompany their father's corpse to the cemetery to prevent their being harmed by their illegitimate step-brothers.

The terms *shedim* and *mazzikim* were often used as synonyms, but in some sources there is a certain differentiation between them. In the Zohar it is thought that the spirits of evil men become *mazzikim* after their death. However, there are also good-natured devils who are prepared to help and do favors to men. This is supposed to be particularly true of those demons who are ruled by Ashmedai (*Asmodeus) who accept the Torah and are considered "Jewish demons." Their existence is mentioned by the *Hasidei Ashkenaz as well as in the Zohar. According to legend, Cain and Abel, who contain some of the impurity of the serpent which had sexual relations with Eve, possess a certain demonic element and various demons came from them. But, in practice, the mating of female devils with human males and of male devils with female humans continued throughout history. These devils are mortal, but their kings and queens live longer than human beings and some of them, particularly Lilith and Naamah, will exist until the day of the Last Judgment (Zohar 1:55a). Various speculations were made on the death of the kings of the demons, in particular of Ashmedai (*Tarbiz*, 19 (1948), 160–3). One popular view is that Ashmedai is merely the title of the office of the king of the demons, just as Pharaoh is the title of the office of the king of Egypt, and "every king of the demons is called Ashmedai," as the word Ashmedai in gematria is numerically equivalent to Pharaoh. Long genealogies of the demons and their families are found in Judeo-Arabic demonology.

Apparently, the author of the Zohar distinguishes between spirits that have emanated from the "left-side" and were assigned definite functions in the "palaces of impurity" and devils in the exact sense who hover in the air. According to later sources, the latter fill with their hosts the space of the sky between the earth and sphere of the moon. Their activity takes place mainly at night, before midnight. Devils born out of nightly pollutions are called "the stripes of the children of men" (II Sam. 7:14). Sometimes the demons poke fun at men. They tell them lies about the future and mingle truth and lies in dreams. The feet of the demons are crooked (Zohar 3:229b). In numerous sources four mothers of demons are mentioned:

Lilith, Naamah, Agrath, and Mahalath (who is sometimes replaced by Rahab). The demons under their rule go out in their hosts at appointed times and constitute a danger to the world. At times, they gather on a particular mountain "near the mountains of darkness where they have sexual intercourse with Samael." This is reminiscent of the Witches' Sabbath in Christian demonology. Male and female witches also gather at this place, devote themselves to similar deeds, and learn the art of witchcraft from the arch-devils, who are here identical with the rebellious angels who have fallen from heaven (Zohar 3:194b, 212a). The author of the *Ra'aya Meheimna* in the Zohar (3:253a) distinguishes between three types of demons: (1) those similar to angels; (2) those resembling humans and called *shedim Yehuda'im* ("Jewish devils") who submit to the Torah; (3) those who have no fear of God and are like animals.

The distinction of demons according to the three main religions is found also in Arabic demonology as well as in sources of practical Kabbalah; it is mentioned in the full, uncensored text of a section of *Midrash Rut ha-Ne'lam* in the Zohar. Another division distinguishes between demons according to the various strata of the air in which they rule – an opinion common to the Zohar and to Isaac ha-Kohen who mentions details about this. On the other hand, the Zohar mentions *nukba di-tehoma rabba*, "the maw of the great abyss," as the place to which the devils return on the Sabbath when they have no power over the world. According to *Baḥya b. Asher, the devils also found refuge in Noah's ark, otherwise they would not have been saved from the Flood.

The kings of the devils were given names, but not the members of their hosts, who are known by the kings' names: "Samael and his host," "Ashmedai and his host," etc. Ashmedai is generally considered as the son of Naamah the sister of Tubal-Cain, but sometimes also as the son of King David and Agrath, the queen of the demons. Numerous names of demons have come from Arabic tradition. Among them should be mentioned Bilar (also Bilad or Bilid), the third king who succeeded Ashmedai. Bilar is merely a misspelling of *Satan's name "Beliar" in several Apocalypses and in early Christian literature, which thus returned to Jewish tradition via foreign sources. He plays an important role in "practical kabbalistic" literature and from it, disguised as Bileth, he came into German magic literature associated with the story of Doctor Faust. The seal of this king is described in detail in the book *Berit Menuḥah* (Amsterdam, 1648, 39b). The other demons too have seals, and those who know them can make them appear against their will. Their drawings are preserved in manuscripts of practical Kabbalah. The names of the seven kings of the demons in charge of the seven days of the week, very popular in later Jewish demonology, were derived from Arabic tradition. Prominent among them are Maimon the Black and Shemhurish, judge of the demons. Other systems originating in the Spanish Kabbalah put the three kings Ḥalama, Samael, and Kafkafuni at the head of the demons (*Sefer ha-Ḥeshek*, Ms. in Brit. Mus.; cf. *A. Freimann Jubilee*). Other systems of demonology are connected with lists of the angels and the demons in charge of the night hours of the seven days of the week, or with the demonological interpretation of diseases such as epilepsy. Such sources are *Seder Goral ha-Ḥoleh* and *Sefer ha-Ne'elavim* (G. Scholem, *Kitvei Yad be-Kabbalah* (1930), 182–5). These systems are not necessarily connected with kabbalistic ideas and some obviously preceded them. A complete system of kabbalistic demonology was presented, after the period of the Zohar, in *Sibbat Ma'aseh ha-Egel ve-Inyan ha-Shedim* (Ms. Sassoon 56), which develops internal Jewish motifs. A combination of the Zohar and Arab sources characterizes the book *Ẓefunei Ẓiyyoni* by Menahem Zion of Cologne (Ms. Oxford, late 14th century); it enumerates a long list of important demons and their functions while preserving their Arabic names. This book was one of the channels through which Arab elements reached the practical kabbalists among the Jews of Germany and Poland, and they recur often, albeit with errors, in collections of demonology in Hebrew and Yiddish. One of the most important among these is Schocken manuscript 102, dating from the end of the 18th century. Among North African and Near Eastern Jews, elements of kabbalistic and Arabic demonology were combined even without literary intermediaries; of particular interest is Sassoon manuscript 290. The collections of remedies and amulets composed by Sephardi scholars abound in this kind of material. An outstanding example of a complete mixture of Jewish, Arab, and Christian elements is found in the incantations of the book *Mafte'aḥ Shelomo* or *Clavicula Salononis*, a collection from the 17th century published in facsimile by H. Gollancz in 1914. King Zauba'a and Queen Zumzumit also belong to the Arab heritage. A rich German heritage in the field of demonology is preserved in the writings of *Judah he-Ḥasid and his disciples and in Menahem Zion's commentary on the Torah. According to the testimony of Naḥmanides, it was the custom of the Ashkenazi Jews to "dabble in matters concerning the demons, to weave spells and send them away, and they use them in several matters" (*Teshuvot ha-Rashba ha-Meyuḥasot la-Ramban*, no. 283). The *Ma'aseh Bukh* (in Yiddish; English translation by M. Gaster, 1934) lists numerous details about this Jewish-Ashkenazi demonology of the later Middle Ages. In addition to current popular beliefs, elements originating in scholarly magic literature as well as the names of demons whose origins were in Christian *magic were introduced from Christian demonology. These spread, not later than the 15th century, among the Jews of Germany. Demons such as Astarot, Beelzebub (in many forms), and their like became fixtures in incantations and lists of demons. A detailed kabbalistic system of demonology is found at the time of the expulsion from Spain in the book *Ha-Malakh ha-Meshiv*. These revelations were attributed to the kabbalist Joseph *Taitaẓak of Salonika. In this system, the hierarchy of the demons is headed by Samael the patron of Edom and Ammon of No (Alexandria), patron of Egypt, who also represents Islam. Ammon of No recurs in numerous sources in this period.

Ḥayyim *Vital tells about devils who are composed from only one of the four elements, in contrast to the opinion of

Naḥmanides mentioned above. This view probably has its origin in the European demonology of the Renaissance. Isaac *Luria's Kabbalah often mentions various *kelippot* ("shells") which have to be subdued via observance of the Torah and *mitzvot*, but it does not generally give them proper names or make them into devils as such. This process reached its peak in *Sefer Karnayim* (Zolkiew, 1709) by *Samson of Ostropol, who gives to many *kelippot* names which were not found in any ancient source. This book is the last original text in kabbalistic demonology.

Some details: according to *Isaac of Acre the devils have only four fingers and lack the thumb. The book *Emek ha-Melekh* (Amsterdam, 1648) mentions demons called *kesilim* ("fooling" spirits) who misguide man on his way and poke fun at him. Hence presumably the appellation *leẓim* ("jesters") occurring in later literature and in popular usage for the lower type of demons, those who throw about household goods and the like (poltergeists). From the beginning of the 17th century the demon called *Sh. D.* (ש״ד) is mentioned, i.e., *Shomer Dappim* ("guard of the pages"); he injures a man who leaves a holy book open. According to a popular belief of German Jews, the four queens of the demons rule over the four seasons of the year. Once every three months at the turn of the season, their menstrual blood falls into the waters and poisons them, and it is therefore forbidden to drink water at the change of the seasons. A special place in demonology is allotted to the Queen of Sheba, who was considered one of the queens of the demons and is sometimes identified with Lilith – for the first time in the Targum (Job, ch. 1), and later in the Zohar and the subsequent literature (*Tarbiz*, 19 (1948), 165–72). The motif of the battle between the prince and a dragon or a demonic reptile, representing the power of the *kelippah* who imprisoned the princess, is widespread in various forms in the demonology of the Zohar. Dragon is the name of the king of the demons who is also mentioned in *Sefer Ḥasidim*. According to Ḥayyim Vital, four queens of the demons rule over Rome (Lilith), over Salamanca (Agrath), over Egypt (Rahab), and over Damascus (Naamah). According to Abraham Galante, until the confusion of the languages there existed only two: the holy language (i.e., Hebrew) and the language of the demons. Belief in demons remained a folk superstition among some Jews in certain countries.

[Gershom Scholem]

BIBLIOGRAPHY: IN THE BIBLE: IDB, 1 (1962), 325–6, 332, 374, 3–24 (incl. bibl.); E. Ebeling and B. Meissner (eds.), *Reallexikon der Assyriologie*, 2 (1938), 107–13; I.J. Gelb et al., *The (Chicago) Assyrian Dictionary*, 1, pt. 1 (1964), 375–7 (s.v. *alû A*); 4 (1958), 397–401 (s.v. *eṭemmu*); F.M. Cross, *Ancient Library of Qumran* (1958), 156–61 (incl. bibl.); W. Foerster, *Theological Dictionary of the New Testament* (1964), s.v. *daimon*; S. Paul, in: *Biblica*, 49 (1968), 373–6. IN THE TALMUD: J. Trachtenberg, *Jewish Magic and Superstition* (1934); E.E. Urbach, *Ḥazal, Pirkei Emunot* (1969), 142–4. IN THE KABBALAH: M. Margalioth, *Malakhei Elyon* (1945), 201–94; G. Scholem, in: *Madda'ei ha-Yahadut*, 1 (1926), 112–27; idem, in: KS, 10 (1933/34), 68–73; idem, in: *Tarbiz*, vols. 3–5 (1932–34); idem, in: JJS, 16 (1965), 1–13; I. Tishby, *Mishnat ha-Zohar*, 1 (1957), 361–77; J.A. Eisenmenger, *Das entdeckte Judenthum*, 2 (1700), 408–68 (a mixture of talmudic and kabbalistic ideas); P.W. Hirsch, *Megalleh Tekufot… oder das schaedliche Blut, welches ueber die Juden viermal des Jahrs kommt* (1717); *Mitteilungen fuer juedische Volkskunde* (1898–1926) especially M. Grunwald, in vols. for 1900, 1906, 1907; *Jahrbuch fuer Juedische Volkskunde* (1923 and 1925); M. Weinreich, in: *Landau-Bukh* (1926), 217–38.

DENAZIFICATION, the efforts made by the Allies to remove active members of the former National Socialist Party from official public office and influential positions in Germany after World War II. At the Yalta Conference Franklin Delano Roosevelt, Winston Churchill, and Joseph Stalin proclaimed their desire to wipe out the Nazi party, institutions, organizations, laws, and cultural influences from German public and cultural life once they secured the surrender of Germany. This pledge was reaffirmed at Potsdam, which declared that "all members of the Nazi party who have been more than nominal participants … are to be removed from public or semi-public office and from positions of responsibility in important private undertakings." No guidelines were issued and the procedures and criteria were not clearly enunciated. Denazification was carried out on the basis of questionnaires about activities during the period of Nazi rule that the suspects had to fill out. The four Powers occupying Germany – the United States, U.S.S.R., Britain, and France – determined varied proceedings in each area of occupation, and the results were accordingly inconsistent and served national purposes. The French used this policy to weaken their traditional enemy Germany. The British were more pragmatic and thus more lenient in their enforcement of denazification and the Americans had two conflicting tendencies: first they had a general suspicion of all Germans; because of a sense of collective guilt, they could not easily distinguish between Nazis and other Germans, even at times anti-Nazis. Secondly, they sought to reeducate Germans for democracy, which took on added importance as the Cold War began. In the Soviet zone, the goal was to consolidate Communist rule and to eliminate capitalists and even take the property of the middle class. The results were diverse policies serving divergent goals. At first, denazification had important consequences as those who were not "rehabilitated" were not appointed to important offices or granted specific licenses (for example, to publish newspapers). To consolidate the policies five categories were established in 1946: (1) major offenders; (2) offenders; (3) lesser offenders; (4) followers; (5) persons exonerated. As political conditions and political needs changed the commitment to denazification diminished, amnesties were declared, and enforcement was transferred to the Germans themselves.

The extent of denazification was criticized in view of the multitude of cases of people who were "rehabilitated" in spite of their Nazi past. Among them were many who were active in the war against the Jews in a variety of ways, e.g., professors P.H. Seraphim (active in the "Final Solution"), H.F.K. Guenther (the outstanding racial scholar of the Nazi period), who published antisemitic literature, and Dr. Hans

Globke, co-author of the leading commentary on the Nuremberg Laws.

Still, despite the criticism, in the aftermath of the collapse of a totalitarian regime, occupying powers or successor governments look for ways to preserve the social, economic, cultural, and governmental structures of the given society while condemning the deeds and actors of a previous regime, and denazification is looked upon as an inviting precedent. It just could be that a fig leaf of procedural decontamination, however inadequate, is needed for a society to be rebuilt.

BIBLIOGRAPHY: C. Fitzgibbon, *Denazification* (1969); R. Seeliger (ed.), *Braune Universitaet: deutsche Hochschullehrer gestern und heute: eine Dokumentation*, nos. 1–6 (1964–68); T. Bower, *The Pledge Betrayed: America and Britain and the Denazification of Postwar Germany* (1982); W.E. Griffith, *The Denazification in the United States Zone of Germany* (1966).

[Jozeph Michman (Melkman) / Michael Berenbaum (2nd ed.)]

DENBURG, CHAIM (1918–1991), rabbi and scholar of *halakhah* and medieval Jewish philosophy. Denburg was born in Montreal, and received his B.A. from Yeshiva College as well as his rabbinic ordination from Rabbi Isaac Elchanan Theological Seminary in 1942. He spent his rabbinic career in Montreal at Congregations Chevra Kadisha (1942–49), Bnai Jacob (1949–56), and Shomrim Laboker (1956–91). He pursued graduate studies in medieval philosophy at the University of Montreal and received his doctorate from there in 1946 for a dissertation on "The Functional Value of Matter and Form in Maimonides." He subsequently taught in the Institute of Medieval Studies at the University of Montreal for over two decades. He published an annotated translation of portions of R. Joseph Caro's *Code of Jewish Law: Shulḥan Arukh* in two volumes (1954–55). He was president of the Board of Jewish Ministers of Montreal and active in the Rabbinical Council of Montreal and the Religious Welfare Committee of Canadian Jewish Congress.

BIBLIOGRAPHY: *Canadian Jewish News* (May 3, 1984); *Montreal Gazette* (Aug. 16, 1991).

[Ira Robinson (2nd ed.)]

DÉNES (Springer), BÉLA (1904–1959), Hungarian physician, author, and Zionist leader. Born in Budapest, Dénes was paralyzed in both legs from the age of four after an attack of poliomyelitis. He studied medicine at the universities of Pécs and Budapest, and during the 1927 antisemitic riots there was beaten up as a result of which he became deaf in one ear. He was forced to go to Brussels, where he graduated with distinction in medicine. Dénes received medical work upon his return to Budapest, but the appointment depended on his agreeing to abandon his religion. He thus ceased work as a physician and began writing political commentary in his newspaper, entitled *Független Szemle* ("Independent Review," 1933). Dénes was an active member of the Social Democratic Party but in 1933, after prolonged disagreement with its leaders, he joined *Po'alei Zion. During the Holocaust period he was arrested (1942) for concealing and supporting Jewish refugees, and in 1944 he went into hiding. When Budapest was conquered by the Soviet army (1945), he tried to found a Zionist newspaper, *Zsidó út* ("Jewish Way"), but it was stopped after three issues through Communist intervention. Between 1945 and 1948, Dénes was the leading Zionist figure in Hungary. In 1949, after the dissolution of the Zionist Federation, the authorities granted him a passport, but he was arrested and sentenced for "spying for Israel" and spent five years in prison. In 1957 he managed to go to Israel. His most famous essays are *A háború biológiája* ("The Biology of War," 1933), *Hogyan élnek, mit keresnek Magyarországon a tisztviselők* ("How the Clerks Live in Hungary and How They Find Their Sustenance," 1937), and *Hat évszázad kulturhistóriája* ("Six Centuries of Cultural History," 1938). His autobiography, within the diary of his prison period, is extant in manuscript form and in 1945–49 he was editor of *Johud-Mapaj Haoved* pamphlets.

[Baruch Yaron]

DENIA, seaport in Valencia, E. Spain. In the 11th century Denia became the capital of the powerful and tolerant Muslim kingdom of the al-Mujāhid dynasty. Various sources, including documents from the Cairo **Genizah*, tell about Jewish settlement in the town from the beginning of the 11th century, and it appears that in the middle of the century there was a substantial community there. The Jews of Denia engaged in trade both by land and by sea and established trading relations especially with Tunisian towns and with Alexandria. The correspondence of a prominent 11th-century merchant of Fostat (old Cairo), Nathan b. Naharai, attests Denia's commercial importance and the role of its Jews. The community included some of the highly respected families of Spanish Jewry, e.g., that of Ibn al-Khatūsh who also engaged in commerce and traveled to the East. In the middle of the 11th century Isaac *Ibn Yashush was the court physician. His contemporary, R. Samuel b. Joseph, was a scholar who came to Spain from Baghdad and corresponded with *Samuel ha-Nagid. The rabbi of the town, Isaac b. Moses ibn Sikhri, left Denia and moved to Babylonia where he was appointed head of the yeshivah of R. *Hai Gaon. He was succeeded in his position in the community of Denia by R. Isaac b. Reuben *Al-Bargeloni. The poet Ibn Khāzin, who lived in the town, exchanged poems with *Judah Halevi.

After the Christian conquest, only a few Jewish families, engaged in maritime trade, were left in Denia. In 1274 the Jews of Denia, together with the Jews of Orembloy, paid 100 solidos in the currency of Barcelona as an annual levy. There is no information on the fate of this community after the anti-Jewish riots of 1391.

In the Muslim period, the Jews of Denia lived in a quarter in the *alcazaba*, the old city. The place today is in complete ruins.

BIBLIOGRAPHY: Baer, Spain, 1 (1961), 31, 195; Baer, Urkunden, 1 (1929), 120, 391–2; H. Schirmann, in: YMḤSI, 6 (1946), 261; Ashtor, Korot, 2 (1966), 182–6.

[Haim Beinart]

°**DENIKIN, ANTON IVANOVICH** (1872–1947), one of the generals and organizers of the White Army in the Russian civil war of 1918–21. His name is associated with the savage pogroms perpetrated against the Jews by his officers and soldiers in Russia and the *Ukraine during these years. Made commander-in-chief of the armed forces of the White Army of south Russia in the spring of 1919, in the fall of that year Denikin embarked on a northward-bound campaign that brought his troops, with the pogroms accompanying them, to the town of Orel, approximately 180 mi. (300 km.) south of Moscow. This initial success was followed by military collapse and rapid retreat southward. The corruption and chaos which spread among Denikin's officers and soldiers as a result of the atrocities they committed against the Jews and the property they looted were among the reasons for the military collapse. In April 1920 the remnant of the White Army took to the Crimea. Denikin transferred his command to General Wrangel and left Russia.

According to available data, which is incomplete, Denikin's armies were responsible for 213 pogroms against 164 Jewish communities during their northward advance and subsequent retreat. The number of Jews massacred reached many thousands. Although outwardly expressing regret for the pogroms, mainly because of their adverse influence on the White cause, Denikin made no serious attempt to suppress the constant antisemitic agitation which was widely regarded by the political leaders of the White Army as their main propaganda weapon against the Soviet regime. When he received a delegation from the Jewish communities in the conquered territories in July 1919, Denikin claimed that he was unable to take any action against antisemitism since his "volunteer" army was composed of the "dregs of humanity" and he had to be satisfied that they at least obeyed his military orders.

BIBLIOGRAPHY: J. Schechtman, *Pogromy Dobrovolcheskoy armii na Ukraine* (1932); W. Latzki-Bertoldi, *Gzeyras Denikin* (1922); Y. Wilensky, *Perakim me-Ḥayyai ha-Ẓibburiyyim* (1968), 185–93.

[Yehuda Slutsky]

DENIS, ALBERTUS (also known as **Alavaro Diniz** and to his coreligionists as **Samuel Yahya**; c. 1580–c. 1645), court agent and mintmaster, one of the first members of the Portuguese Jewish community in Hamburg. In 1611, together with Andreas Falleiro and Ruy Fernando Cardoso, Denis purchased the Altona cemetery for the Portuguese Jews of Hamburg (the bill of sale was countersigned by him on May 31, 1611). A year later he was officially granted the right of residence in Hamburg; in the city register of 1614 he is listed as the donor of "*Twintig marck luebsch*" to the *Glueckstadt church. Denis acted as agent and mintmaster for Count Ernst of Schauenburg, and as such he incurred the enmity of the Hamburg authorities, who accused him of buying Reichsthaler coins minted in Hamburg and having them melted down in Altona. When the senate issued an order for his arrest, Denis took refuge in Altona and settled there under the protection of the count. In 1618 King Christian IV of Denmark put him in charge of the Glueckstadt mint, but it operated subsequently for only a few years. In Glueckstadt Denis also built and owned two houses and helped to introduce other Jews (see *Denmark). He remained a member of the Portuguese community of Hamburg; as their representative, he applied in 1637 to Count Otto of Schauenburg for a further extension of the cemetery privilege. Denis' minting activities contributed to the first "*Kipper und Wipper*" period of galloping inflation caused by corruption of the coinage.

With the stabilization of finances, Denis became a large-scale sugar importer and an exporter of grain through the ports of Luebeck and Danzig, where he tried to gain a foothold for his agents – often his relatives. In 1625 he obtained the right of settlement for Portuguese Jews in Troppau and Jaegerndorf in Silesia. In the 1630s he organized a news and information service for his Danish royal benefactor. His last activity was negotiating the 1643/4 settlement between Hamburg and Denmark, and he died in poverty soon after.

BIBLIOGRAPHY: H. Kellenbenz, *Sephardim an der unteren Elbe* (1958), index.

[Joseph Elijah Heller]

DENMARK, kingdom in N.W. Europe. It was the first of the three Scandinavian countries where Jews were permitted to settle. The first arrivals were invited by King Christian IV, who, on Nov. 22, 1622, at the request of his Jewish mintmaster Albertus *Denis, sent a message to the leaders of the Sephardi communities in Amsterdam and Hamburg inviting Sephardi Jews to settle in the recently established township of Glueckstadt on the eastern border of Elbe in his duchy of Holstein, offering them religious liberty and commercial privileges. A few accepted the invitation and began trading and manufacturing operations there. Other Sephardi Jews were also active in Denmark in the 17th century as financiers and jewelers to the royal family and members of the Danish nobility. Benjamin *Mussafia, author of the talmudic dictionary *Musaf ha-Arukh*, was appointed physician to the royal family in 1646. His son-in-law Gabriel Milan became governor of the Danish West Indies in 1684. Members of Sephardi families such as Abenzur, Franco, Granada, De Lima, Meldola, De Meza, Moresco, and Texeira de Mattos continued to engage in financial operations in Denmark during the 17th and 18th centuries, but gradually lost their mercantile significance in the state economy and their predominance in the Jewish community. Jewish communities existed in the duchies of Schleswig and Holstein, then under Danish rule, from the beginning of the 17th century, in Altona and Ottensen (now part of Altona). German Jews wishing to settle in the kingdom of Denmark proper had to produce royal authorization before entering the country. This was granted only to applicants in possession of sufficient capital to establish industrial enterprises, to deal in substantial amounts of Danish merchandise, or to build their own houses. Later, German Jews, mainly from Hamburg and Altona, who married Danish Jewesses were also permitted to settle in Denmark. Rabbis, teachers, and other communal

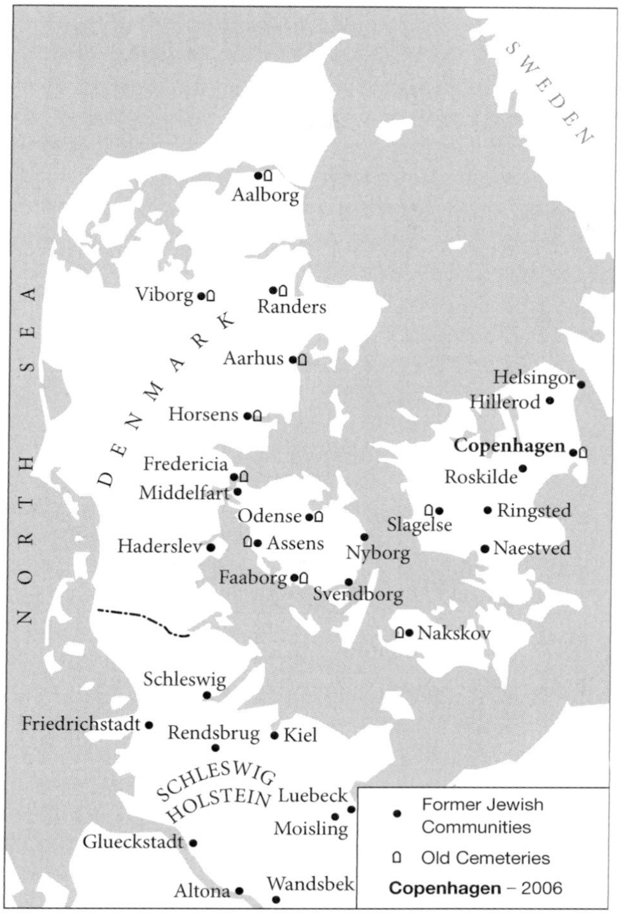

Danish Jewish communities in the 18th century and after World War II.

functionaries were permitted to practice in Denmark if guaranteed by leaders of the community. There were 1,830 Jews in Denmark in 1782 (1,503 in *Copenhagen).

The 19th century was a period of cultural, social, and economic progress for Danish Jewry, though there was a spate of anti-Jewish polemics between 1813 and 1819. Jews received Danish citizenship in 1814, and the last restrictive legislation was abolished in 1849 by the Danish constitution. While at the beginning of the 19th century the majority of Danish Jews were in poor circumstances, by about 1900 they mostly belonged to the middle and upper classes. The Jewish population increased steadily until, in the middle of the 19th century, there were about 4,200 Jews living in Denmark. The number subsequently declined to 3,500 in 1901 owing to intermarriage and a low birth rate. After the *Kishinev pogrom of 1903 a number of refugees from Eastern Europe entered Denmark, some in transit for the United States via Bremen and Hamburg. About 200 who arrived in 1904–05 obtained permanent residence, and their number subsequently increased to approximately 2,000. After some difficulties in social and cultural adjustment they gradually integrated into the old established Danish-Jewish society. The total Jewish population with the new immigrants numbered 6,000 in 1921 and has remained substantially the same.

On a footing of equality with their countrymen, the Jews in Denmark have been able to contribute to the development of their country in every sphere, and many have achieved international renown. They include the sculptor Kurt Harald Isenstein (see *Art), the literary critic Georg *Brandes, the botanist Nathanael *Wallich, the physicians and scientists Ludvig Levin *Jacobson, Adolph *Hannover, and Carl Julius *Salomonsen. Joseph Michaelsen, who served as postmaster-general, is considered the originator of the Universal Postal Union. Among outstanding politicians and high-ranking state officials were the minister of finance Edvard *Brandes, Herman Trier (1845–1925), a member of parliament and of Copenhagen municipal council, Moritz Levy (1824–1892), and Marcus Rubin (1845–1923), directors of the Danish National Bank, and Georg Cohn, who served as state adviser on international law. In the cultural sphere, contributions were made by the poets Meir Aaron *Goldschmidt, Henrik *Hertz, Henri *Nathansen, Louis *Levy, and Poul *Levin; the painters and sculptors Ernst Meyer, Joel *Ballin, Albert Gottschalk (1860–1906), and Theodor Philipsen (1840–1920); and the composers Fini Henriques (1867–1940), and Victor Bendix (1851–1926). Valuable contributions to science and learning in Denmark were made by the psychologist Edgar Rubin and the physicist Niels *Bohr.

Until the end of the 18th century the Jewish community remained strictly Orthodox. Influenced by the emancipation movement in Germany, however, a *Reform party was formed in Denmark by Mendel Levin *Nathanson who initiated several changes in the administration and educational system of the Jewish community of Copenhagen. The Danish Reform movement occasioned a schism within the Jewish community which was aggravated when Nathanson tried with the aid of Isaac Noah *Mannheimer, a young Danish Jewish theologian, to introduce a Reform service in Copenhagen. When Abraham Alexander *Wolff took office as chief rabbi (1829) he succeeded to some extent in reconciling the Orthodox and Reform parties. He was succeeded by David *Simonsen, the first native-born rabbi in Denmark; after ten years of office he retired to devote himself to Jewish studies and worldwide philanthropic activity. The Mahzike Hadas association was founded in connection with the retirement in 1910 of the strictly Orthodox chief rabbi Tobias Lewenstein. The succeeding chief rabbis were Max Schornstein and Moses Friediger, who was deported to Theresienstadt in 1943 but survived to return to Denmark, where he died in 1947. He was succeeded by Marcus *Melchior and in 1969 by his son Bent Melchior (1929–). The Zionist movement was introduced into Denmark in 1902 with the establishment of the Dansk Zionistforening. The World Zionist Congress headquarters moved to and operated from Copenhagen for the duration of the World War I period. Between 1933 and 1945 about 1,700 potential pioneers and members of Youth Aliyah from Central European countries received agricultural training with Danish farmers. The Danmark Loge of the B'nai B'rith was founded in 1912. Jewish periodicals in the Danish language have appeared in Denmark since 1907, except during the German occupation in World War II. Magazines in Yiddish appeared between 1911 and 1936, and a Yiddish daily, the *Folktsaytung*, appeared during World War I. A literary periodical *Tidsskrift for jødisk Historie og Litteratur,* sponsored by the Danmark Loge, was published in Copenhagen from 1917 to 1925.

[Julius Margolinsky / Rafael Edelman]

Holocaust Period

The fate of the Jewish community under German occupation was related to several factors: the attitude of the Germans to Denmark and its population and the attitude of the Danes to the Jews within their country. The German occupiers treated the Danes with respect, a dramatic difference compared with the way they related to occupied populations in Eastern Europe. Germany invaded Denmark on April 9, 1940, as part of its expansion westward. German occupation was limited: Danish institutions remained intact, even the Danish army and navy; only foreign affairs were no longer in Danish hands. Germany respected Danish sovereignty. The German occupation was administered by the Foreign Ministry and not the SS or the Gestapo and for internal bureaucratic reasons the Foreign Ministry wanted to keep it that way. Germany could not rule by decree in Denmark and thus there developed a policy of negotiation with Danish authorities, who collaborated within limits. Denmark had a long history of religious tolerance and did not perceive itself to have a "Jewish problem." The Danes regarded the Jewish question as a Danish problem rather than one of an isolated minority. They treated the Jews as fellow citizens. Throughout the 1930s, Denmark was reluctant to receive refugees but some Jews did manage to use Denmark as a country of transit and some 1,400 refugees from Germany, Austria, and Czechoslovakia and 300 children of *Youth Aliyah remained there.

For almost three and a half years, from the day of Denmark's occupation on April 9, 1940, to the major crisis in the Danish-German relationship at the end of August 1943, the Danish Jewish community, including the refugees, remained more or less unmolested. This unusual phenomenon can be explained by the fact that while the Danes collaborated with the Germans in the so-called policy of negotiation, they simultaneously extended full political, social, juridical, and personal protection to the Jews and to their property. So convincing was the steadfast behavior of the Danish authorities and the population that the Germans did not think it wise to injure the small Danish Jewish population as long as they were interested in the smooth operation of the Danish-German Agreement of April 9, 1940. Mounting Danish resistance during the summer of 1943 eventually destroyed the popular base of this agreement, which was eventually abolished by the Germans on Aug. 28, 1943. Emergency rule was declared. Until that time the civil representatives of the German Reich, Cécil von Renthe-Fink, as well as Werner Best, who succeeded him in office, did everything they could in order to avoid a conflict with the Danes over the issue of the Jews despite repeated attempts by Nazi authorities in Germany and small groups in Denmark to raise the issue. Best's role is perplexing as he was a known antisemite. He had served as deputy head of the Gestapo and worked as part of the German military bureaucracy to organize deportations to Auschwitz. His pragmatic behavior in Denmark may be explained by a difference in the attitude of the Danish population toward its own Jews. Martin Luther, Foreign Minister Joachim von *Ribbentrop's representative at the *Wannsee Conference in January 1942, stated that action against Jews in the Nordic countries had to be postponed. Public opinion in Denmark on the "Jewish" question was unanimous and had been expressed by the leader of the United Danish Youth Movement, Professor Hal Koch, just before the conference. Reacting to some incendiary declarations by Nazi newspapers in Denmark, he proclaimed that all suggestions to the effect that Danish Jews should be molested must be categorically rejected because the issue was one of both justice and respect for the Jews and the preservation of Danish freedom and law.

The Jewish community, anxious to cooperate with the Danish authorities, kept its members as inconspicuous as possible and refrained from all illegal activity, including escape. Only a group of *ḥalutzim* tried to escape illegally with partial success. Anxious to sustain his position in Berlin and to position himself for advance, Best advocated using this opportunity of emergency rule to deport the Jews. He was appealing to two very different audiences: Nazi colleagues anxious to deport the Jews and impose the "Final Solution" and the native population and its officialdom that regarded such acts as disruptive. His plan was opposed in German circles in Denmark, and several leading German personalities tried to ensure its cancellation. Ironically, Best, who was mainly interested in the additional police force transferred to Denmark to execute the deportation, was not very eager to carry out the order once Hitler approved it. He attempted to have it canceled and then leaked news of the operation through F.G. Dukwitz, the attaché for shipping affairs, who maintained good relations with leading Danish Social Democrats and informed them of the impending danger for the Jews. The warning was quickly spread and after a slight delay it was regarded as credible by the Jewish community, which canceled Rosh Ha-Shanah services, and by Danish citizens' organizations. The Lutheran Bishop of Copenhagen, H. Fuglsang-Damgaard, openly urged Danes to protect the Jews, proclaiming:

> Whenever persecutions are undertaken for racial or religious reasons, it is the duty of the Christian Church to protest against it for the following reasons:
>
> ...Because the persecution of the Jews is irreconcilable with the humanitarian concept of love of neighbors which follow from the message which the Church of Jesus Christ is commissioned to proclaim. With Christ there is no respect of persons, and he has taught us that every man is precious in the eyes of God.

> ...race and religion can never be in themselves a reason for depriving a man of his rights freedom or property. We shall therefore struggle to ensure the continued guarantee to our Jewish brothers and sisters [of] the same freedom which we ourselves treasure more than life.
>
> ...We are obliged by our conscience to maintain the law and to protest against any violation of human rights. Therefore we desire to declare unambiguously our allegiance to the word, we must obey God rather than man.

Seemingly overnight a rescue organization sprang up that helped 7,200 Jews and about 700 non-Jewish relatives escape to Sweden in less than three weeks. Danish captains and fishermen carried out this operation. What began as a spontaneous popular movement was developed into an organized action by the Danish resistance movement. Though the heroic nature of the rescue has become fable, still the fishermen charged for their services. The cost of the transfer amounted to about 12 million Danish crowns, of which the Jews themselves paid approximately 6½ to 7 million. The rest was provided out of private and public Danish contributions. Out of the action grew a regular flow of illegal traffic between Denmark and Sweden. Danish and Swedish Jews helped to organize it and kept it financially sound. This traffic continued until the end of the war and provided the Danish underground with a constant line of communication with the Allies.

The attitude of Sweden was also quite significant. It had informed the Germans of its willingness to accept the Jews and it made an announcement of its openness to these refugees on radio, thus independently encouraging the exodus of Jews across the narrow sea that separated Denmark from Sweden. By the fall of 1943, German troops were in retreat from El Alamein in North Africa to Stalingrad in the East. With reduced power came reduced influence.

During the night of the persecution (Oct. 1–2, 1943) and following it, less than 500 Jews were seized by the Germans. They were sent to *Theresienstadt and remained there until the spring of 1945, when they too were brought to Sweden by the action of the Swedish Red Cross, headed by Count *Bernadotte. The Danish rescue effort did not end in October 1943. Refugee property was carefully protected. Homes and their contents were inventoried and businesses placed in trust. Torah scrolls and holy objects were stored in churches and returned intact to the Jewish community after the war. Non-Jewish relatives who remained behind were supported. The Danish government was persistent in its inquiries about its citizens who were deported to *Theresienstadt. Packages were sent. In an attempt to alleviate Danish concerns, the Germans allowed a special Red Cross visit to the camp in 1944, even though what the visitors saw was a hoax. Danish Jews were the first prisoners to return home after liberation. Of the 464 Jews deported, only 51 perished. Upon their return from Sweden to Denmark at the end of the war, most of the Jews who escaped found their property intact. It may be estimated that approximately 120 people perished because of the persecution: about 50 in Theresienstadt and a few more in other camps. Close to the same number committed suicide or were drowned on their way to Sweden. Less than 2% of the Jewish population of Denmark perished.

After the war, unlike many other countries that did far less for their Jews, Denmark did not seek credit for the rescue. Yad Vashem's list of the Righteous Among the Nations of the World lists only one entry for Denmark, not one individual, but the Danish people. And Danish historians have been critical of the limited efforts to receive refugees and the improvised nature of the rescue. More should have been done, they have argued.

Why was Denmark different? The answer is still a matter of dispute though the exceptional character of Denmark is not. Danes at every level of society, from fishermen to high government officials, intellectuals to Church leaders alike have said that they simply treated Jews as the neighbors they were, and one does not allow the enemy who occupies one's country to deport neighbors. The explanation for their behavior may well be as simple as that.

[Leni Yahil / Michael Berenbaum (2nd ed.)]

Postwar Period

The Jewish population of Denmark at the end of 1968 was about the same as before World War II, i.e., between 6,000 and 7,000: 25% of the total population were descendants of the old established Danish Jews and 67% were emigrants from Eastern Europe and their descendants; 8% consisted of refugees from Germany and their children. Only 1% of the Jewish population resided outside Copenhagen. In the course of 1969 a further 1,500 Jewish refugees from Poland were taken into Denmark, mostly into the Copenhagen area. Almost all the Jews who were rescued during the war, as well as most of the deportees to *Theresienstadt and other camps, returned to Denmark at the end of the war. The birth rate continued to be low (only about 60 children born each year) and this was insufficient to keep the Jewish population at the same level. The good relations between Jews and non-Jews were maintained in the postwar period. Mutual goodwill was demonstrated on various occasions, such as the 10th and the 25th anniversaries of the rescue of Danish Jewry from Nazi persecution, or, in 1964, on the 150th anniversary of the granting of citizenship to Danish Jews, as well as by the sympathetic interest of the population in Jewish problems and in the State of Israel. Many Jews were prominent in the postwar period. Stephan *Hurwitz was appointed Ombudsman in 1955, when this high position in the administration was established; Henry *Grünbaum was minister of finance in the labor government from 1965 to 1968; and Erik Warburg was principal of the Copenhagen University from 1956 to 1958. The Jewish community was state-recognized and therefore entitled to assess all Jews in the country for taxation, unless they resigned formally from the community. This recognition also involved the rights of the rabbis to perform marriages and to register births and deaths. All community institutions were administered in a strictly traditional way. Most of the members of the Orthodox

Mahzike Hadas community belonged simultaneously to the larger Jewish community. Community affairs were directed by a board of seven members, elected by an assembly of 20, which in turn was chosen in general elections. In addition to all religious services the community maintained a Jewish day school and three kindergartens, homes for the aged, and a spacious community center. The community supported an active Zionist Federation, *WIZO, youth organizations, *B'nai B'rith, an organization of craftsmen, and two choirs. Danish Jewry participated in all efforts to aid the State of Israel and strengthened its ties with other Jewish communities through close cooperation with the *Conference on Jewish Material Claims, the *American Joint Distribution Committee, and Jewish communities in Europe.

Later Developments

It is estimated that some 3,000 Polish Jews fled to Denmark at the beginning of the 1970s as a result of antisemitism. Their arrival affected the development of Danish Jewry during the decade, although they included a comparatively high percentage in mixed marriages. Most of the Jews settled in and around Copenhagen, but hundreds were brought to Aarhus and Odense in the provinces and tried to organize some form of Jewish life in these towns. The Federation of Polish Jews in Denmark was established to represent the newcomers, but other organizations were also founded partly in opposition to the federation. A youth group with Zionist orientation called the Coordination Committee became active in organizing inter-Scandinavian seminars. Although many of the newcomers did join the Jewish community, at the elections for the Jewish Community Board in 1979 some Jews from Poland organized their own party and gained two out of the 20 seats of the Board.

The Jewish day school moved to new premises in 1974. At the end of the decade the number of pupils had risen to 325 with an additional 60 children in the kindergarten. With two other Jewish kindergartens almost 50% of the Jewish children in Copenhagen attended these day institutions. The 150th anniversary of the school was celebrated in 1980 in the presence of the minister of education and the mayor of Copenhagen; a *Festschrift* was published on the occasion.

After the death of Chief Rabbi Dr. Marcus *Melchior in December 1969, his son, Rabbi Bent *Melchior, was elected to succeed him. In 1972 he resigned because of a conflict with the board of the community after making some outspoken remarks about the tragic events at the Olympic Games in Munich. After six months of discussions, which threatened to sunder the Jewish community, a formula was found which enabled the chief rabbi to accept a new contract, and he was unanimously re-elected. Shortly after, an American-born assistant had to leave his post when he had admitted that he had traveled on an electric train on the Sabbath. He was succeeded by Danish-born Rabbi Bent *Lexner, the first rabbi of the community to be educated and ordained in Jerusalem. Upon Melchior's retirement in 1996, Lexner became chief rabbi.

The Bnei Akiva movement continued to be active in Jewish education of the young generation, and it inspired most of the *aliyah* movement. Another important educational activity was established through Dor Hemshech. Many young people were active in the work for Soviet Jewry, and the Actions Committee for Soviet Jewry succeeded in creating strong support among Danish public figures for this cause.

Arne *Melchior, for many years president of the Danish Zionist Federation, was elected in 1979 to a third term in the Danish parliament, representing the Center Democrats. The former minister of finance, Mr. Henry Gruenbaum, was also re-elected in the same elections, and a new member, Mr. Magnus Demsitz representing the Social Democrats, was elected. Dr. Rafael Edelmann, who for nearly 40 years headed the department of Hebraica and Judaica at the Royal Library in Copenhagen, resigned at the end of 1970 and went to Jerusalem, where he died in 1972. He was succeeded at the Royal Library by Ulf Haxen.

The traditional prayerbook with Danish translation was re-published in 1977. Among the very few changes was the inclusion of the prayer for the State of Israel and a new text for the special prayer used on Tisha be-Av. The same year the Jewish community began the publication of a new Danish translation of the Pentateuch, the work of Rabbi Bent Melchior.

Since the kings Christian IV and Frederick III invited the first Jews to enter Denmark in the 17th century, relations between the Danish royal family and the Jewish community have been very close. This continued during the reign of Queen Margrethe II. In 1983 she attended the festive service in the Copenhagen Synagogue on the occasion of the synagogue's 150th anniversary. A year later she participated in the celebrations of the 300th jubilee of the Copenhagen community. In 1987 the queen was host to an official state visit by Israel's president Chaim Herzog, and in 1992 she agreed to be the patron of the many 1993 events to mark the 50th anniversary of the unique rescue operation of Danish Jews in October 1943.

The good relations also reflect the general situation between Jews and Christians in the country. Although an increasing number of foreigners settled in Denmark during the 1980s and 1990s, leading to an unhappy rise in nationalistic outbursts against newcomers, the Jews in general were not affected by the negative feelings towards strangers. Many of the newcomers were Muslims, and not a few of them Arabs from the Middle East. Muslim immigration continued into the 21st century and there were occasional incidents involving young Arabs, but most have been regarded by the police as street brawls. In 2003 a leader of the Hizbut-Tahrir association in Denmark was sentenced to jail for disseminating slanderous pamphlets against Jews. The Jewish community joined forces with the majority fighting extreme right-wing forces. A small, insignificant Nazi party existed, but its "Fuehrer" fell in love with a Palestinian girl and had to resign. In 1996 the right-wing Dansk Folkeparti took the issue of *sheḥitah* to the Danish Parliament in a campaign against Jewish and Muslim ritual slaughter. Their bill was voted down but they have brought up the issue repeatedly over the years, and in early 2005 a new bill was introduced in Parliament. This time too a majority of MPs voted against it. There was in fact no Jewish ritual slaughter in Denmark at the time because the Danish Jewish community imported its meat from Ireland and poultry from France. Nonetheless, the bill's defeat was a very important victory for the Jewish community.

The PLO did not find it easier than the Nazis to establish themselves in Denmark. They opened an office in Copenhagen in the 1980s and many people on the political left were sympathetic toward the organization, in particular after the Lebanon war and during the first *intifada*. But a plan to assassinate the Danish chief rabbi and a few other prominent Danish Jews visiting Israel not only failed but also became the beginning of the end of the office. More successful was an Arab attempt in 1985 to bomb the Copenhagen Synagogue. Strong security measures have since then been maintained around Jewish institutions.

The Jewish community tried to fight the problem of assimilation in various ways. Strong connections with Israel were being maintained and there was steady immigration of young families. The percentage of Jews making *aliyah* remained one of the highest in all Western countries. A large number of Danish Jews now have close relatives in Israel, and Danish Jews visit Israel frequently. Another major effort was made in the educational field, but the small number of children born to Jewish families has led to a decrease in the number of children attending the Jewish day school.

The Danish Jewish community included a large number of elderly people. Since the 1960s two old-age homes for sick people have been established with the help of the municipality, and in 1992 a new building was erected with modern apartments for elderly Jews. The new institution is named after the famous Swede Raoul *Wallenberg, who saved tens of thousands of Hungarian Jews from Nazi persecution.

The comparatively small community, numbering 6,400 in 2005, nearly all in Copenhagen, participated in international Jewish organizations such as the World Zionist Organization, World Jewish Congress, and B'nai B'rith. Denmark's geographical position also called for an active contribution to the effort on behalf of Soviet Jewry, and until the removal of the Iron Curtain many Danish Jews visited the U.S.S.R. to bring Soviet Jews material on Judaism and support their political struggle for freedom. Since 1989 this work has changed in character. Strong cultural ties have been established with the Jewish population of the Baltic states, and in 1992 a big operation for relief work in St. Petersburg was started in an attempt to assist the large Jewish population of that city to survive physically.

[Bent Melchior]

Relations with Israel

The relations between Denmark and Israel have been friendly and warm. Denmark was among the countries that voted for the partition of Palestine, and thus the establishment of a Jewish state, on Nov. 29, 1947, and recognized Israel soon after its establishment. Formal diplomatic relations were established on the ambassadorial level. Denmark has usually supported Israel at the United Nations and other international organizations. Of special note was its active support for Israel's right to free passage through the Suez Canal and the Gulf of Eilat, expressed in the attempt of the Danish boat *Inge Toft* to transport Israeli cargo through the Suez Canal in 1959. Trade relations developed from a modest scope to over $9,500,000 in 1968, with a balance between imports and exports, and $220 million in 2003, with Israel importing twice as much as it exported. Tourism from Denmark to Israel grew substantially over the years. The two countries maintained active friendship leagues, which concern themselves with disseminating information, caring for tourists, exchange visits of public figures, scientists, artists, etc. In most of the cities of Israel, streets or squares are named in honor of Denmark. In Jerusalem a monument to the rescue of Danish Jewry was erected on the 25th anniversary of the operation, and a comprehensive school in that city is named in Denmark's honor, and there is a King Christian X hospital at Eitanim. From the beginning of the 1960s, many thousands of Danish youth went to Israel every year for visits extending to a number of months, mostly working on kibbutzim. This movement led to the creation of a Danish organization of youth who worked on kibbutzim.

The appointment of Carmi Gillon, former head of Israel's General Security Service (GSS), as ambassador to Denmark in 2001 sparked a minor diplomatic crisis when Danish Justice Minister Frank Jensen said that Gillon would be detained under suspicion "of having participated in, attempted, or assisted in torture" in his GSS role. Within a few months, however, the situation was defused.

[Yohanan Meroz]

BIBLIOGRAPHY: C.E. Cohen, *De Mosaiske Troesbekjenderes Stilling i Danmark…* (1837); M.L. Nathanson, *Historisk Fremstilling af Jødernes Forhold og Stilling i Danmark* (1860); J. Salomon and J. Fischer, *Mindeskrift i Anledning af Hundredaarsdagen for Anordningen af 29. Marts 1814* (1914); B. Balslev, *De Danske Jøders Historie* (1932); Moritzen, in: *Contemporary Jewish Record*, 3 (1940), 274–80; M. Hartvig, *Jøderne i Danmark i tiden 1600–1800* (1951); G. Hartmann and F. Schulsinger, *Physical and Mental Stress… Within the Jewish Population of Denmark* (1952); J. Margolinsky, *Gravspladserne på mosaisk vestre kirkegaard 1886–1955* (1955); idem, *Gravspladserne på mosaisk nordre kirkegaard i Møllegade 1693–1953* (1956); idem, *De jødiske kirkegaard i danske provinsbyer 1722–1956* (1957). HOLOCAUST PERIOD: L. Yahil, *The Rescue of Danish Jewry* (1969); idem, in: WLB (Oct. 1962), 73 (bibliography); Wilhelm, in: YLBI, 3 (1958), 313–32; *Yad Vashem Studies*, 6 (1967), 181–220; B. Outze (ed.), *Denmark during the German Occupation* (1946); Valentin, in: *YIVO Bleter*, 8 (1953), 224–51; Y. Haestrop, *From Occupied to Ally: Denmark's Fight for Freedom* (1963); idem, *Exposé, European Resistance Movement 1939–1945* (1960–64); A. Bertelsen, *October '43* (Eng. 1956); *Tid Landetz Beste*, 1 (1966); W. Lord, *A Night to Remember* (1967), novel; E. Arnold, *A Night of Watching* (1967), novel; R. Oppenheim, *The Door of Death* (1948), novel; H. Flender, *Rescue in Denmark* (1963). CONTEMPORARY PERIOD: A. Tartakower, *Shivtei Yisrael*, 2 (1966), 254–8; M. Melchior, *A Rabbi Remembers* (1968).

DENMARK, FLORENCE LEVIN (1931–), U.S. psychologist. Born and educated in Philadelphia, Florence Levin received her B.A. from the University of Pennsylvania; after her marriage to Stanley Denmark, she completed a Ph.D. in social psychology at the University of Pennsylvania in 1958. Denmark taught as an adjunct professor at Queens College while raising three young children. She began teaching at Hunter College in 1964, ultimately serving as director of the doctoral program in psychology at CUNY Graduate Center. In 1984, she was appointed Thomas Hunter Professor in the Social Sciences at Hunter and four years later she was named the first Robert Scott Pace Professor of Psychology at Pace University, where she also served as chair of the Department of Psychology.

Denmark published widely on prejudice and discrimination against women and minorities. She is internationally known for her pioneering research and contributions to the psychology of women, which she helped establish as a legitimate scholarly field. A victim of gender discrimination in the early phases of her career, Denmark was committed to empowering female students and colleagues through organizing conferences, training graduate students, and co-authoring important resource works. These include *Women: Dependent or Independent Variable?* (1975); *The Psychology of Women: Future Directions of Research* (1978); *Women's Choices, Women's Realities* (1983); and *Psychology of Women: A Handbook of Issues and Theories* (1993).

Denmark was among the founders of the Division on the Psychology of Women of the American Psychological Association in 1973 and served simultaneously as the fifth woman president of the APA (1981–82) and the president of Psi Chi, the psychology honors society. She received many honors for her outstanding contributions to psychology, including the Association for Women in Psychology Distinguished Career Award (1986); the APA Distinguished Contributions to Education and Training in Psychology Award (1987); and the APA Public Interest Award (1992). In 1985, the APA's Committee on Women in Psychology recognized Florence Denmark's achievements with a Distinguished Leadership Citation, commending her for "exceptional organizational skills, administrative expertise, political acumen, and humanitarian leadership to promote equality for women and ethnic minorities and to create new visions for psychologists."

BIBLIOGRAPHY: R. Unger, "Denmark, Florence Levin," in: P.E. Hyman and D. Dash Moore (eds.), *Jewish Women in America*, vol. 1 (1997), 326; M.A. Paludi and N.F. Russo, "Florence L. Denmark (1931–)," in: A.N. O'Connell and N.F. Russo (eds.), *Women in Psychology: A Bio-Bibliographic Sourcebook* (1990), 75–87; "Florence L. Denmark," in: A.N. O'Connell and N.F. Russo (eds.), *Models of Achievements: Reflections of Eminent Women in Psychology*, vol. 2 (1988), 279–93.

[Harriet Pass Freidenreich (2nd ed.)]

DENVER, capital of *Colorado, U.S.; also known as the "Mile High City" and "Queen City." Jews began settling in Denver, and elsewhere in Colorado, following the discovery of gold in 1858. While some Jews were afflicted with "gold fever," most saw economic opportunities in servicing those who streamed into the many new mining towns. By 1859, a dozen Jewish immigrants had arrived, originally from Germany and Central Europe; among them, the brothers Hyman and Fred Salomon, Leopold Mayer, and Abraham Jacobs.

In 1860, Denver's first Jewish organization, the Hebrew Burial and Prayer Society, was formed. It soon split into a B'nai B'rith lodge (1872), which is still active, and into Colorado's first synagogue, Temple Emanuel (Reform) (1874), today the State's largest Jewish house of worship. From these earliest efforts, the Jewish community grew in numbers, prosperity, and influence, creating organizations, synagogues, and institutions, many from necessity because of Denver's isolation from other American Jewish population centers.

While Denver's early Jewish settlers identified with Reform Judaism primarily, beginning in the 1880s, some 2.5 million (mostly traditionally religious) Jews emigrated from Eastern Europe to the United States. This migration changed the demographics of Denver. Many Orthodox Jews settled in Denver seeking a cure for tuberculosis, the "white plague." Two Jewish institutions were founded to respond to their needs and other sufferers of consumption from around the country. The National Jewish Hospital for Consumptives was opened in 1899. Its name was changed in 1985 to the *National Jewish Center for Immunology and Respiratory Medicine. It is now the National Jewish Medical and Research Center, with a worldwide reputation in the research and treatment of allergy and pulmonary diseases. The Jewish Consumptives Relief Society was established just outside of Denver in 1904 to serve the religious needs of suffering Orthodox Jews. In 1955, it changed its mission to other medical purposes.

In 1882, a farming colony of East European Orthodox Jews was settled by the Hebrew Immigrant Aid Society in Cotopaxi, Colorado. The experiment failed, with the immigrants moving to the West Side of Denver and founding its Orthodox community there. It established synagogues, *mikva'ot* (ritual baths), Jewish educational institutions, and a Yiddish theater. Descendants of many of the Cotopaxi families still occupy leadership positions in the community. Reform Jews, on the other hand, gravitated to the East Side of Denver, first to the Curtis Park area, then to Capitol Hill and Hilltop, where Temple Emanuel relocated in 1956. Emanuel founded Shwayder Camp in the Colorado Rockies in 1948.

Denver became a temporary haven for Yiddish poets who suffered from tuberculosis. Yehoash was treated from 1900–1910; H. Leivick, from 1932–33 and 1934–35. A legendary figure was Dr. Charles Spivak, long time director of the Jewish Consumptive Relief Society, a major figure in Yiddish and Jewish cultural life, and a founder of the *Intermountain Jewish News* in 1913. Rabbi Judah Leib Ginsburg, an immigrant from Dvinsk, Latvia, wrote and published major Hebrew works on the Bible and Mishnah in Denver. Max Goldberg became the leading figure in media in mid-20th century Denver. He brought network television to Colorado, pioneered in talk televison, wrote for the *Denver Post* and published the *Intermountain Jewish News*.

By the 1970s, when the Jewish population had reached 40,000, many Jews began dispersing to Denver's suburbs, but continued to utilize the many institutions they had established on both sides of the city. Among these were the Hebrew Educational Alliance (1920), Yeshiva Toras Chaim (1967), and Beth Jacob High School for Girls (1968) on the West Side; and, on the East Side, Beth HaMedrosh Hagadol Congregation (1897) and Beth Joseph Congregation (1922), which merged in 1997; Hillel Academy (1951); and Temple Sinai (1967). The Allied Jewish Federation of Colorado was organized as the Allied Jewish Council in 1942; the Jewish Family Service (so named in 1990) dates back to 1887; and Green Gables Country Club (1928) and the Jewish Community Center (1948) provide a social outlet for Denver Jews.

In the latter quarter of the 20th century, Dr. Stanley M. Wagner founded the Center for Judaic Studies at the University of Denver (1975) and its affiliates, the Rocky Mountain Jewish Historical Society, Beck Archives and the Holocaust Awareness Institute, and the Mizel Museum (of Judaica, originally) (1982). Shalom Park (1992), a state of the art Jewish nursing home and assisted living facility, was an outgrowth of the Beth Israel Hospital and old age home on the West Side (founded in 1905). The Denver Campus for Jewish Education (2002) merged Herzl Jewish Day School (1975) and the Rocky Mountain Hebrew Academy (1979).

Denver became the focus of a widespread controversy in Jewish life in 1983. The *Intermountain Jewish News* published a 12-page supplement, edited by Rabbi Hillel Goldberg. The supplement reported that the Rocky Mountain Rabbinical Council, composed of Reform, Conservative, Reconstructionist, and Orthodox rabbis, had discontinued a joint conversion program (established six years earlier). The program processed hundreds of converts, attempting to avoid a schism in the Jewish community. Personal and ideological factors brought its demise. Most Orthodox authorities around the world rejected the halakhic basis of the program despite a ruling from the Shalom Hartman Institute in Jerusalem supporting it. Some Reform and Conservative Rabbis throughout the country also opposed the idea of having to send converts to an exclusively Orthodox Beth Din. A number of years later, in January 1998, the Ne'eman Commission, established by the Israeli government to create a conversion process acceptable to all wings of Judaism, embraced a variation of the Denver program. Still, attempts to revive it failed.

Among the many persons who figured prominently in Denver Jewish history were Golda *Meir, who came to Denver in 1913, where she met her future husband, Morris Myerson; Sheldon K. Beren, an oilman, philanthropist and national president of Torah Umesorah; and Ruth M. Handler, creator of the Barbie Doll. Notable rabbis were Rabbi William S. Friedman, who served Congregation Emanuel, 1889-1938; Rabbi Charles E. H. Kauvar, who filled the Beth HaMedrosh Hagadol pulpit, 1902-1971; and Rabbi Manuel Laderman at the Hebrew Educational Alliance, 1932–1979. Jews were also active in the political life of the community. Wolfe Londoner became Denver's only Jewish mayor in 1889, Philip Winn became ambassador to Switzerland in 1986, and Larry Mizel and Norman Brownstein are major influences in, respectively, Republican and Democratic politics nationally. Robert Lazar Miller, Jesse Shwayder, A. B. Hirschfeld, and Louis Robinson, and their descendants, have been highly visible in the business community for generations. The "mother of Jewish charity work" was Francis Wisebart *Jacobs, whose portrait in a stained glass window graces the Colorado Hall of Fame in the rotunda of the State Capitol.

BIBLIOGRAPHY: I.L.Uchill, *Pioneers, Pioneers, Peddlers and Tsadikim* (1957); A.D. Breck, *Centennial History of the Jews of Colorado, 1859–1959* (1960), P. Goodstein, *Exploring Jewish Colorado* (1992); J. Abrams (ed.), *A Colorado Jewish Family Album 1859–1992* (1992); S.G. Freedman, *Jew vs. Jew* (2000), J. Abrams (ed.), *Rocky Mountain Jewish Historical Notes* (1986–); *Intermountain Jewish News* (1913–).

[Stanley M. Wagner (2nd ed.)]

DEPARTMENT STORES, an innovation first recognizable in mid-19th-century France. Similar contemporaneous developments were consumer cooperatives in Britain, and mail-order houses, chain stores, and "five-and-ten" stores in the United States. Only in Central Europe were department stores initiated and developed by Jewish entrepreneurs, except for the outstanding cases in Britain, South Africa, and the United States noted below. Of the five German department chain stores – *Schocken, *Tietz, *Wertheim, Karstadt, and Kaufhof – the first three were owned by Jews; although the last two were owned by non-Jews, they employed many Jews in top managerial positions. Jewish department stores were prominently situated in major cities; the N. Israel and Kadewe stores of Berlin and the Gerngross of Vienna were widely known. In addition, most medium and small towns had their own department stores, which were often Jewish-owned. The north German stores, founded in the last quarter of the 19th century for the sale of textiles, a field in which Jews were traditionally prominent, adapted to rapid industrialization and urbanization by expansion and diversification. Although department stores in Germany did not account for more than 4–5% of the total retail commerce, they aroused widespread and lasting hostility. The complaints and anxieties of small or specialized shopkeepers found support in conservative circles in general. Economic accusations of dishonest advertising and other unfair competitive practices merged with antisemitic attacks: the importance of the new type of Jewish shopkeeper was unpalatable to many; the very employment of Christian sales girls was distorted – they were pictured as being placed in danger of moral corruption by lustful Jewish bosses. In the late 19th and early 20th centuries this anti-department store pressure resulted in the levy of special taxes on department stores.

Under the Weimar Republic these laws were abolished and the stores entered a period of growth and expansion. Economic instability and unemployment, however, again made the stores a focus of popular resentment which the Nazis were quick to utilize. Before and especially after the Nazis seized power the stores were frequently sabotaged and their owners attacked in the streets. The nationwide *boycott of April 1, 1933, was specifically aimed against Jewish department stores, which continued to be harassed after the boycott was called off. Julius *Streicher, as *Gauleiter* of Franconia, led a vicious campaign against the Nuremberg Schocken store. The German government was eventually forced to ease the pressure for economic reasons and even to save the Tietz company from bankruptcy. On "*Kristallnacht*" (Nov. 9–10, 1938), the department stores, as symbols of Jewish economic oppression, were burned and looted along with the synagogues.

Jews played a major role in the development and ownership of department stores in the United States. The majority of such Jewish-owned stores originated with the 19th-century German-Jewish immigration to America. Many of these immigrants began their commercial careers as itinerant peddlers or small retailers in rural areas, where they enjoyed a virtual monopoly on merchandising; from there they expanded to large general stores, which eventually developed into the modern department stores of the late 19th and 20th centuries. A typical case was the *Gimbel family: after Adam Gimbel, a native of Germany, had opened a general store in the small town of Vincennes, Indiana, his seven sons established department stores first in Milwaukee, then in Philadelphia, and finally in New York, where Gimbels ultimately became one of the city's largest retail establishments. Its greatest competitor, Macy's, was not originally Jewish-owned, but was bought out in 1887 by the *Straus brothers, Isidore and Nathan, who had started by renting its basement to display the produce of the small glassware firm founded by their father Lazarus. In Brooklyn the brothers went into partnership with another German immigrant, Abraham *Abraham, to found Abraham & Straus. Bloomingdale's in New York grew out of a small drygoods store on Third Avenue owned by the *Bloomingdale brothers. Other New York department stores, such as B. Altman, Stern, Saks, S. Klein, and Ohrbach had similar histories, the latter two founded by 20th-century immigrants. Elsewhere in the U.S. large department store empires were also frequently the creation of Jews, such as I. Magnin and Levi *Straus on the West Coast, William *Filene's Sons Co. in the Boston area, Kauffmann Brothers in Pennsylvania, and Neimann & Marcus in Texas. The Chicago company of Sears, Roebuck, which came under the ownership of Julius *Rosenwald during the 1890s, became a vast mail order firm. Sears, Roebuck and other mail order firms, together with urban growth and the automobile, brought about the virtual extinction of countryside peddling as successfully practiced by Jewish immigrants. Jewish prominence in department store ownership continued, however. A highly successful chain of discount stores founded by a syndicate of young Jewish businessmen after the Korean War was E.J. Korvette, an acronym for "Eight Jewish Korean Veterans." Also prominent was the Farkas family, which owned Alexander's department store, a major entry in the New York market through the 1950s and 1960s.

By the early years of the 21st century, the retailing environment in the United States had changed, and most of the giant chains started years earlier by Jewish merchant families had disappeared like Korvette's or were absorbed in mergers and acquisitions. Federated Department Stores, for example, started in 1929 as a combination of Abraham & Straus of Brooklyn, Filene's of Boston, F&R Lazarus of Columbus, Ohio, and Bloomingdale's of New York. The stores operated independently for decades under the Federated umbrella and Federated also included Stern's, Burdine's, Rich's, Goldsmith's, and others, but in 2004 Federated, after gobbling up the May Company, decided to unite virtually all of its 400-odd stores under the Macy's brand name. The lone exception was Bloomingdale's, which grew from its New York origins to a high-end chain in several major American markets.

Nevertheless, other enterprising merchants entered the field, including Leslie H. *Wexner, who built The Limited, a chain in Columbus, Ohio, that specialized in women's clothing. By the late 1980s The Limited had become the parent of Henri Bendel, Lane Bryant, Victoria's Secret, Abercrombie & Fitch, and the Express stores and had a majority stake in Intimate Brands, which included Bath and Body Works and the White Barn Candle Company. The Wexner family was involved in many Jewish charities, supporting youth development programs, Jewish agencies, and temples and a long roster of organizations in the United States and Israel.

In Great Britain Simon *Marks and Israel *Sieff developed Marks and Spencer, famous for its high-quality, reasonably priced goods, and Sir Isaac *Wolfson founded Great Universal Stores. The *Cohen family of Liverpool established Lewis' chain of departmental stores in the north of England. In English-speaking countries public opinion was not hostile to department stores and recognized their advantages to the community. The leading Australian department store line was founded by Sidney (Simcha Baevski) *Meyer, founder of the Melbourne Myer Emporium. Jewish businessmen and industrialists played an important part in the development of the modern department store in South Africa, sometimes called there a "bazaar." In 1927, Sam *Cohen and Michael Miller, who had been in business together for 11 years, founded the O.K. Bazaars in Johannesburg and in time made it the largest chain-store business in South Africa. In 1931, Woolworths – independent of the company of similar name abroad – was started in Cape Town by Max Sonnenberg and developed with Elie Suzman to operate in other South African cities. In 1947 they became associated with Marks and Spencer of Britain. Other department stores such as Greatermans and the Belfast Warehouse were also developed by Jewish enterprise, while the countryside pharmacies of the South African Druggists Ltd. were largely the creation of Herman Karnovsky. Jewish involvement in department stores has undoubtedly diminished but new and notable entrepreneurs in retailing have arisen both in Britain (see *Green, Philip and *Kalms, Sir Stanley) and among Australian business leaders, many of whom are former refugees, operating chain stores and shopping centers.

In Israel the Histadrut developed a chain of small department stores called Ha-Mashbir la-Ẓarkhan. The first one opened in 1947 and by 1970 there were 14 branches throughout the country. A single large department store, Kol Bo Shalom, opened in Tel Aviv in 1965.

BIBLIOGRAPHY: H. Uhlig, *Die Warenhaeuser im Dritten Reich* (1956), incl. bibl.; G. Tietz, *Hermann Tietz* (Ger., 1965); K. Zielenziger, *Juden in der deutschen Wirtschaft* (1930), 206–20 (on Tietz); Reissner, in: YLBI, 3 (1958), 227–56 (on N. Israel); Moses, *ibid.*, 5 (1960), 73–104 (on Schocken); G. Rees, *St. Michael: A History of Marks and Spencer* (1969); M.C. Harrimann, *And the Price is Right* (1958); A. Marshall, *The Gay Provider* (1961); A. Briggs, *Friends of the People* (1956).

[Henry Wasserman / Stewart Kampel (2nd ed.)]

DE PASS, family of Sephardi Jews who settled in England in Cromwell's time. Some members migrated in the 19th century to South Africa, where they helped to develop the shipping, fishing, and sugar industries.

AARON DE PASS (1815–1877) arrived in Cape Town in 1846 with his family and his younger brother Elias, and became a merchant. He established the firm of De Pass Brothers in 1848 and, having acquired his own ships, engaged in the export of guano from islands on the southwest Cape coast. His ships developed the coastal trade as far north as Walvis Bay. In 1857 the firm, by then known as De Pass, Spence and Company, started the sealing and whaling industries. It built the first ship-repair facilities at the Cape and laid patent slipways for the government in Simonstown and Table Bay. A leading citizen of Cape Town, Aaron de Pass was appointed justice of the peace and commissioner of the municipality. He was an elder of Tikvath Israel, the first Hebrew congregation in *Cape Town. He brought the first *Sefer Torah* from England in 1847, and was founder and first *parnas* of its synagogue in 1849.

ELIAS DE PASS (1834–1913), Aaron's younger brother and partner. In 1848 he enlisted with the colonial troops in the war with the Xosa tribesmen on the eastern frontier. He served throughout the campaign and became a lieutenant. He was for a time honorary secretary of the Cape Town Hebrew Congregation and a founder-member of the first synagogue.

DANIEL DE PASS (d. 1921), son of Aaron, joined the family firm in 1860 and interested himself particularly in exploiting the Ichaboe guano islands under a government lease. He established fisheries in South-West Africa and was the first to work a copper mine there. He later acquired extensive diamond interests. He contested in the courts the German claims to the territory and succeeded in retaining the guano offshore islands and Walvis Bay for the Cape Colony. He made an important contribution to the Natal sugar industry by introducing from India a variety of sugar cane which became the mainstay of the industry. On a visit to England, Daniel De Pass raised money toward the building of the Durban synagogue, the first in Natal.

ALFRED DE PASS (1861–1952), Daniel's son, was born in Cape Town. Trained as a chemical engineer, he worked in the family business and developed its sugar interests in Natal. In Cape Town, where he spent the later part of his life, he was best known as a philanthropist and a patron and connoisseur of the arts. The De Pass collections of art treasures, donated during and after his lifetime, are to be found in South African and British galleries and museums. His bequests included sums for the upkeep of Jewish cemeteries in Cape Town and in Britain.

BIBLIOGRAPHY: L. Herrman, *History of the Jews in South Africa* (1935), index; G. Saron and L. Hotz, *Jews in South Africa* (1955), index; I. Abrahams, *Birth of a Country* (1955), index.

DE PHILIPPE (Phillips), EDIS (1918–1978), opera singer and founder-director of the Israel National Opera Company. Edis De Philippe was born in New York, and studied singing in the U.S., Italy, and France. At the age of 19 she appeared as Violetta in a gala performance of *La Traviata* in Washington before President Roosevelt. She went to Palestine in 1945 and set about founding an opera company backed by her own funds. She opened in 1947 with *Thaïs*, one of her outstanding roles. She continued single-mindedly to present opera regularly both in Tel Aviv and in other centers. From 1950 she devoted herself to production and direction, and added a ballet company in 1958.

[Dora Leah Sowden]

DE (DA) PIERA, MESHULLAM BEN SOLOMON (also called **En Vidas de Gerona**; first half of 13th century), Hebrew poet. Although Carmoly (in *Ha-Karmel*, 7, 1868/69) derived the family name of De Piera, who lived in northern Spain and southern France, from the city Fère in Burgundy, according to Neubauer it comes from the town Piera, in Catalonia, and this seems to be the most plausible explanation of the name. De Piera lived in the period of strife that raged around *Maimonides' *Guide of the Perplexed*. He first came under the influence of *Jonah b. Abraham Gerondi, the leader of the opposition, and his poems against the followers of the philosophical school stem from this period. He censured energetically all kinds of intellectualism and rationalism, and particularly that of the Maimonideans. For him, poetry was a way of defending the truth, a way to formulate his theological ideas about the most important issues in Judaism and to unmask the threat of the Maimonidean thinkers. His view of the foundations of Jewish faith brought him near to the Kabbalah and to the most traditional attitudes of Judaism. As a kind of champion of Orthodoxy and of the kabbalistic interpretation of Judaism, he even wrote against the Provençal Jews, seeing heretical trends in their ideas. He later changed his attitude however, perhaps on the advice of *Naḥmanides, and in one poem he begs his teacher, Isaac b. Zerahiah ha-Levi Gerondi, to forgive him for having opposed philosophy; the poor translations of the Arabic original, he claimed, had given him a false idea of the true content of the *Guide of the Perplexed*.

De Piera seems to have lived in Gerona for a long period and there belonged to a circle of mystics whom *Naḥmanides had gathered about him. Among his intimate friends was the Provençal poet, *Isaac b. Judah ha-Seniri of Beaucaire (c. 1220), and perhaps also Abraham *Ibn Ḥasdai of Barcelona. One of the most original Hebrew poets of his time, he abandoned many of the conventions of Andalusian poetry, dissenting from its ideological background, and even used a very different language, far from the pure biblical Hebrew used by the Andalusian poets. From the formal point of view, for example, he renounced the classical structure of the Arabic *qasida*. De Piera employs many unusual modes of structure, language, and subject-matter in his poems that, in the opinion of some scholars, can only partly be explained as due to the influence of Christian troubadour poetry, and in particular to the most obscure and difficult art of poetry which was at the time a particular fashion among the troubadours in southern France and in Catalonia; other scholars, however, prefer to explain his peculiarities as representing an internal development of Hebrew poetry. Abraham Bedersi, in his critical poem *Ḥerev ha-Mithappekhet* (published in *Ḥotam Tokhnit* (1865), 16 line 141), speaks of him with admiration. Only a part of De Piera's poetic work has been preserved (Neubauer, Cat, no. 1970 iv); a number of poems from this collection were edited by J. Patai, while an almost complete edition with introduction and commentaries was published by H. Brody (YMḤSI, 4 (1938), 1–117). As to the literary value of his poetry in the service of his theological ideology, there are very different opinions among scholars.

BIBLIOGRAPHY: Renan, Rabbins, 728–30; M. Steinschneider, in: *Kobez al Jad*, 1 (1885), 3, 23; J. Patai, in: HḤY, 5 (1921), 54–58, 129–33, 202–15; idem, *Mi-Sefunei ha-Shirah* (1933), 44–66; H. Brody, in: *Sefer Klausner* (1937), 267–73; J.N. Epstein, in: *Tarbiz*, 11 (1939/40), 218–9; Schirmann, Sefarad, 2 (1956), 295–318; Davidson, Oẓar, 4 (1933), 451. **ADD. BIBLIOGRAPHY:** J. Lehmann, in: *Prooftexts*, 1 (1981), 133–51; E. Fleischer, in: I. Twersky (ed.), *Rabbi Moses Nahmanides (Ramban): Exploration in His Religious and Literary Virtuosity* (1983), 35–49; J. Ribera, in: *Anuari de Filolologia*, 8 (1982), 177–88; 9 (1983), 187–93; 11–12 (1985–86), 73–84; Schirmann-Fleischer, *The History of Hebrew Poetry in Christian Spain and Southern France* (Heb., 1997), 293–322.

[Jefim (Hayyim) Schirmann / Angel Sáenz-Badillos (2nd ed.)]

DE PIERA, SOLOMON BEN MESHULLAM (c. 1342–c. 1418), Hebrew poet of the Kingdom of Aragon, descendant of Meshullam b. Solomon *de Piera. His family was an important Jewish family of Catalonia who had its origins in Piera, a municipality of Barcelona county. He was in Cervera in 1385 (he bought the right to a seat in the new synagogue) and in 1387 he visited or stayed in neighboring Monzon. At this time he was in contact with the school of talmudists and poets of Gerona. He relates that in 1391 people attacked his house and took his own still-unmarried children away. After his children's deaths, Solomon de Piera found refuge in Saragossa, where no unrest had occurred. There he was in the service of three generations of the De la Cavalleria family. He acted as secretary to Don Solomon de la Cavalleria (Abenlavi), the patriarch of the family; he fulfilled similar functions for his son, Don Benvenist de la Cavalleria; and he was the tutor of the latter's two sons. He gave himself over completely to the art of teaching how to write verses and compose poems. Thanks to Solomon de Piera, a completely new phenomenon appeared in the history of Hebrew poetry in Spain, for he was the leader of a group of poets who gave themselves the names of *kat ha-meshorerim*, "the group of poets," and *adat o ḥevrat nogenim* "band" or "troupe of musicians." They were poets like Vidal de la Cavalleria, son of Don Benvenist, Vidal Benvenist (or Abenvenist), the author of *Efer ve-Dinah;* Moses Abbas, Moses Gabbai, Samuel al-Rabi, Vidal al-Rabi, etc., who figure in the *Dîwân* of De Piera and maintained correspondence with him. All of them composed the same type of poetry. Just like the poets around them who wrote in Romance, they sent each other letters in the form of poems and took part in disputes and competitions. This "troupe of musicians," known also as the poets of the "Circle of Saragossa," started on its path after the terrible events of 1391, flowered during the reigns of the two last monarchs of the House of Barcelona, Juan I and his brother Martin the Humane, who died in 1396 and 1410, respectively; and began its decline with Fernando de Antequera's ascent to the throne of Aragon, because of his proselytizing zeal. It ceased to exist shortly after 1414, as a consequence of the Dispute of Tortosa and the conversion to Christianity of some of its most important members, including Vidal de la Cavalleria and De Piera himself. The most important work of Solomon de Piera was his *Dīwān,* composed and edited by himself. He added headings to the poems, written in the first person, explaining the circumstances under which the poems were composed and naming their authors or addressees. The preservation of the manuscripts of De Piera's poems is due to a later literary circle of a similar kind, which flourished in Salonika in the second half of the 16th century (Saadiah *Longo and others). There exist at least six manuscripts, dating from the 15th to the 17th centuries that claim to contain the *Dīwān* of De Piera, and many others (at least 21) with some of his poems and writings. About 362 poems of Solomon de Piera are preserved in his *Dīwān*. Most have a *qasida* structure and are in conventional meters, and 35 – nearly all, liturgical compositions – are *muwashshaḥāt*. In addition to the poems, there are many texts in rhymed prose – letters and other writings that are not independent compositions but form a single unit with the accompanying poems. The nature of this material has been obscured by the fact that S. Bernstein gave the title *The Diwan* (1942) to his collection of Solomon de Piera's poems. But De Piera's original *Dīwān* was neither an anthology nor a miscellaneous collection of poems like Bernstein's edition; it was a coherent work, in which all the above-mentioned materials appeared according to a definite structure and organization. At Don Benvenist's request, De Piera wrote a "manual for composing poetry," the *Imrei No'ash,* that has not been completely preserved or completely edited. His dictionary of rhymes, however, had wide distribution, as one can see from the large number of existing manuscripts. The introductory poem and the preface to this work were published by Tauber (Kiryat Sefer, 1924–25)*;* the section *Ḥelek ha-Millim ha-Meshuttafim* was published by M. Tama in *Maskiyyot Kesef* (Amsterdam (1785), 3–23). A collection of liturgical poems by De Piera was published by S. Bernstein (HUCA, 19, 1945). Commissioned by the Jewish community of Saragossa, De Piera wrote a number of circular letters to the communities of Aragon on such matters as taxation. He also wrote letters in prose to the poet Moses Abbas (A.M. Habermann, in: *Oẓar Yehudei Sefarad.* 1964).

BIBLIOGRAPHY: Schirmann, *Sefarad*, 2 (1959), 564–81, 698; Davidson, *Oẓar*, 4 (1933), 472–3; Brody, *Beitraege zu Salomo do Pieras Leben und Wirken* (1893); Vardi, "The 'Group of Poets,'" in: *Saragossa. Secular Poetry* (Heb., 1996); Schirmann-Fleischer, *The History of Hebrew Poetry in Christian Spain and Southern France* (1997), 580–600; Targarona-Scheindlin, in: *REJ*, (2001), 61–133.

[Judit Targarona (2nd ed.)]

°**DEPPING, GEORGES-BERNARD** (1784–1853), French historian of German origin. Depping was born and educated at Muenster, Westphalia, and settled in Paris, where he wrote on a variety of subjects. In 1823 he participated in a prize contest of the French Academy for an essay on "The Jews of France, Spain, and Italy," which he enlarged as a book in 1834 (*Les Juifs dans le moyen âge*). It was translated into German in the same year, and republished in French in 1844. Depping's work, while in some part based on original research in the published sources and generally sympathetic to the Jewish people, propagates many of the prejudices of earlier writers and his own time, which give a distorted, unjust picture of Jewish character and the economic role played by Jews in medieval Europe, and their legal position (corrected by O. *Stobbe). Depping has been used widely as a secondary source by historians, such as H. Graetz and W. Sombart, as well as antisemitic writers. He thus influenced the historical image of medieval Jewry.

BIBLIOGRAPHY: *Nouvelle Biographie Générale*, 13 (1866), 702–5; T. Oelsner, in: *YLBI*, 7 (1962), 189, no. 21.

[Toni Oelsner]

DEPUTIES OF THE JEWISH PEOPLE, representatives of Jewish communities in Russia to the government during the reign of *Alexander I (1801–25). After parts of *Poland-Lithuania had been annexed by Russia, the large communities sent *shtadlanim* to the court at St. Petersburg to represent them and defend their rights. Most of the *shtadlanim* were merchants or contractors who visited the city on business. When a committee was set up to frame a "Jewish constitution" in 1802–04 it was joined by several government-appointed Jewish advisers (N.N. *Notkin, A. *Peretz, and J.L. *Nevakhovich). The government also requested some important communities to send representatives to the committee. Together they tried to influence the committee in favor of Jewish rights. In 1807 the government appointed a "Jewish committee" to implement the inimical "Jewish constitution" of 1804 and proposed that the communities elect deputies to represent the Jews before the provincial governors. The memoranda of these deputies were referred to the "Jewish committee" in St. Petersburg and were influential in obtaining a temporary halt to the expulsion of Jews from the villages. It was also proposed to abolish the prohibition on the lease and sale of alcohol by Jews. During the invasion by Napoleon two "deputies of the Jewish people," Zundel Sonnenberg and Eliezer Dillon, accompanied Alexander's military headquarters in 1812–13, and acted as liaison between the czar and the large Jewish population in the combat area. They regularly presented memoranda and petitions concerning Jewish affairs to the court and transmitted its instructions to the Jewish communities. After the war an attempt was made to convert the committee of deputies into a permanent institution. The Jewish communities were requested to send representatives to St. Petersburg to maintain permanent contact with the ministries of religious affairs and popular education. On August 19, 1818, electors from the 12 districts (*gubernia*) of the *Pale of Settlement convened and elected three deputies, Zundel Sonnenberg, Beinush Lapkovski, and Michael Eisenstadt, and three deputy representatives. In order to raise funds to cover their expenses, which probably also included furnishing bribes, the assembly resolved that every Jew was to donate the silver headpiece of his prayer shawl. The change in Alexander's policy toward the Jews at the end of his reign reduced the importance and status of the deputies. Sonnenberg was dismissed because of "impudence toward the authorities." In 1825 the Jewish deputation was officially suspended "until the need arises for a new deputation," and the institution was thereby abolished and not renewed. However, the government continued to make use of Jewish representatives. In 1840 consultative committees, chosen from among "enlightened" Jews, were created and attached to governors in Kiev and five other towns. In 1844 the function of "Learned Jew" (*uchoni yevrei*) was created, meaning an expert and consultant in Jewish religious affairs attached to the district governers and responsible for education and interior affairs.

BIBLIOGRAPHY: J.I. Hessen (Gessen), *Yevrei v Rossii* (1906), 421–32; idem, in: *Yevreyskaya starina*, 2 (1909), 17–29, 196–206; S. Pen, in: *Voskhod*, nos. 1–3 (1905).

[Yehuda Slutsky / Shmuel Spector (2nd ed.)]

DERASH (or **Derush**) (Heb. דְּרַשׁ or דְּרוּשׁ from דָּרַשׁ, "to interpret"), a method of exposition of scriptural verses. In the Midrash the distinction between *derash* and the alternative method called **peshat* is not clearly defined and in parallel passages the terms are sometimes interchangeable (cf. Gen. R. 10:7 with Tanh., Ḥukkat 1). Only in the Middle Ages, probably under the influence of Rashi's Bible commentary, did *derash* come to be used for homiletical exposition in contrast to *peshat*, the literal interpretation. *Derashah* (Heb. דְּרָשָׁה) is the equivalent of the word "sermon" today. Originally it was confined to a sermon on a theme which was based on a homiletical interpretation of Scripture.

[Louis Isaac Rabinowitz]

DERASHOT HA-RAN (Heb. דְּרָשׁוֹת הָרַ"ן), a collection of 12 homiletic works. Traditionally, they are attributed to R. Nissim b. Reuben *Gerondi, one of the outstanding Jewish leaders in Christian Spain, known as רַ"ן ("Ran," from Rabbi Nissim). The prolific writings and information on Gerondi, however, do not prove his authorship, and there is nothing in the homilies themselves to identify the author. It is therefore necessary to assume that the first initial of the writer of the work was the Hebrew letter נ (*nun*), and that later scholars attributed it to the famous rabbi of Gerona.

The homilies in the collection (first edition probably Constantinople, c. 1533; second Venice, 1592, and many subsequent editions) belong to the tradition of philosophic homiletic literature, started by *Abraham b. Ḥiyya (12th century) and carried on by homiletic writers like Jacob *Anatoli and Isaac *Arama. Like other writers of homiletic philosophic works, the author of this collection does not exclusively follow one school of philosophy but is eclectic, basing himself on several schools. The work is nevertheless of some importance in the history of Jewish philosophy and it seems that *Ḥasdai Crescas was influenced by it in the formulation of his anti-Aristotelian philosophic system. The homilies are based on single verses from the Torah, each forming the theme of an individual homily. The method used is that of homiletic questioning of the form and content of the verses, as well as of some logical problems. The answers and homiletic interpretations are arrived at by way of the questioning itself, into which the author interweaves his moralistic and ethical system. He never approaches his ethical point directly and uses philosophic questions and answers as a bridge between the verses and the ethical conclusions. Among the philosophical problems he examines are the creation, the essence of nature, and in particular the nature of prophecy and the unique quality of the revelation to Moses (in the third and fifth homilies). In his ethical and moralistic teachings much emphasis is laid on the themes of the nature of the divine commandments, the relationship between rabbinic laws and the Torah, fear and love of God, and especially on the ways of repentance. The author took special pains to drive home to his audience that all the troubles the Jews were undergoing had some purpose in a divine design, whose end was good.

BIBLIOGRAPHY: Rosenmann, in: *Festschrift… Schwarz* (1917), 489–98; H.R. Rabinowitz, *Deyokna'ot shel Darshanim* (1967), 67–73.

[Joseph Dan]

DERAZHNYA, town in Khmelnitski district, Ukraine. A Karaite community existed there for many years and it suffered considerably during the *Chmielnicki uprising of 1648. The *Rabbanites settled there at the beginning of the 18th century. They suffered in a *Haidamack attack in 1734. There were 316 Jews living in Derazhnya in 1784, owning 50 houses, 3,333 in 1897 (68% of the total population), and 3,250 in 1926 (57.4%). *Shalom Aleichem placed the action of his short story "The German" there. A Jewish school with 140 pupils and a library was in operation at the beginning of the 20th century. Pogroms were unleashed on December 1, 1917, and in June 1919. Between the wars there were a Jewish council, a Jewish court, and a kolkhoz in Derazhnya. A Yiddish school attended by 90% (336) of the Jewish children in the town operated there. In 1939 the Jews numbered 2,651 (41% of the total population). The Germans occupied the town on July 11, 1941, and set up a closed ghetto, exacted heavy tributes, and confiscated all valuables. In September 1942, 4,080 Jews from Derazhnya and the surrounding settlements were murdered by the Germans. Two hundred skilled workers were executed later in the year in Letichev. The community was not refounded after World War II.

BIBLIOGRAPHY: *Yevrei v SSSR* (1929[4]), 48–51.

[Shmuel Spector (2nd ed.)]

DERBENT (former ***bāb al-Abwāb**), Caspian Sea port in Dagestan (Caucasus). Derbent has been erroneously identified with Terbent (טרבנת) mentioned in the Talmud (TJ, Meg. 4:5; 75b). Certainly Jews, evidently originally from Persia, were already settled in Derbent by the time that the kingdom of the *Khazars was established; some ascribe the first propagation of Judaism among the Khazars to Derbent Jews. Jewish-owned caravans used to pass through the city in this period. After the fall of the Khazar kingdom on the Volga in 969, a number of survivors took refuge in Derbent. Jews living there are mentioned in the 12th century by *Benjamin of Tudela, and in the 13th by the Christian traveler Wilhelm of Rubruquis. The first mention of Jews in Derbent in modern times is by the German traveler Adam Olearius in the 17th century. Derbent Jewry endured frightful sufferings during the wars in the 18th century; Nadir Shah of Persia forced many Jews to adopt Islam. After the Russian conquest many of the Jewish occupants of rural Dagestan fled to Derbent, which became the spiritual center of the *mountain Jews. The Jewish population numbered 2,200 in 1897 (15% of total population) and 3,500 in 1903. After the 1917 Revolution many Dagestan Jews deprived of their lands migrated to Derbent where they generally took up occupations in crafts or industry. A visitor to Derbent in the 1960s reported that some of the Jews were occupied in agriculture, principally vinegrowing. They were organized in four kolkhozes whose lands bordered on the town. The kolkhoz members lived in town; in general Jews tended to live in the same area.

BIBLIOGRAPHY: J.J. Chorny, *Sefer ha-Massa'ot* (1884), 278–322; I. Anisimov, *Kavkazskie Yevrei* (1888); E. Kozubsky, *Istoriya Goroda Derbenta* (1906); M. Artamonov, in: *Sovetskaya Arkheologiya*, 8 (1946), 121–44; idem, *Istoriya Khazar* (1962), index; Ben Ami, pseud. (A.L. Eliav), *Between Hammer and Sickle* (1967), 219–22 and passim.

[Yehuda Slutsky]

DEREKH EREẒ (Heb. דֶּרֶךְ אֶרֶץ; "way of the world"), desirable behavior of a man toward his fellows, in keeping with natural practice and accepted social and moral standards, including the rules of etiquette and polite behavior. This has become the common and accepted connotation of a term having several meanings in rabbinic literature:

(1) Natural and normal human behavior – "It is natural (*derekh ereẓ*) for the young to speak poetry; the middle-aged, proverbs; the old, despair at vanity" (Song R. 1:10).

(2) Worldly occupation – "It is appropriate to combine study of Torah with a trade" (*derekh ereẓ*) (Avot 2:2).

(3) A euphemism for sexual cohabitation – "'He saw our plight' (Deut 26:7) which means being cut off from sexual intercourse" (*derekh ereẓ*) (*Haggadah* of Passover; cf. Yoma 74b).

(4) Correct conduct and proper behavior – *derekh ereẓ* in this wide and general sense is much praised by the rabbis, and is the subject of a post-talmudic treatise, *Derekh Ereẓ* (see next entry). While its value is often equated to that of Torah itself, R. Ishmael b. Naḥman held that *derekh ereẓ*

preceded the Torah by 26 generations (i.e., the period between the creation of the world and the giving of the Torah; Lev. R. 9:3) – in other words, *derekh ereẓ* is part of the natural order of things.

Basic to *derekh ereẓ* are maintenance of family harmony and sensitive consideration for wife and family (Shab. 10b; MK 17a; et al.). The laws of *derekh ereẓ* demand that a man make it a rule to bear himself courteously toward his fellow (e.g., Avot 4:15; Ber. 6b; BM 87a), to exercise care in his words and claims, and especially to use "clean" speech (Pes. 3a). A man should eat less than his means allow (Ḥul. 84b). He should dress decently (Shab. 113a–114b, 145b). The rabbis stated "In whom mankind finds pleasure, God finds pleasure" (Avot 3:10). In agreement with this general principle, many specific instructions are found concerning proper behavior. Special stress is laid on putting the concerns of others before one's own (cf. Ḥag. 8a; et al.). Laws of *derekh ereẓ* also deal with definitions of modesty, particularly in relations between men and women, proper etiquette between teacher and pupil, table manners, reception of guests, etc. Scholars are to be particularly careful as regards *derekh ereẓ* since they serve as an example, and a fault in their behavior shames both them and the Torah. Maimonides' description based on halakhic and aggadic sources of the behavior befitting a scholar is in fact a summary of *derekh ereẓ*; it includes polite manners as well as the demand, "… he shall never in his lifetime trouble his fellow.…" It culminates in the counsel to prefer to be among the persecuted rather than the persecutors, among the humiliated rather than those who humiliate (cf. BK 93a). Such is the man described in the verse "And He said to me, 'You are My servant, Israel, in whom I will be glorified'" (Maim., Yad, De'ot 5).

Although the rabbis often found scriptural warrant for practices of *derekh ereẓ*, these were not generally included as formal laws in the great codes, since they were held to be recommendations rather than commandments, and often varied with time and place.

For "Torah with *derekh ereẓ*," see *Neo-Orthodoxy.

BIBLIOGRAPHY: ET, 7 (1956), 672ff.; W. Bacher, *Die exegetische Terminologie*, 1 (1889), 25; 2 (1905), 40–45.

[Simon S. Schlesinger]

DEREKH EREẒ (Heb. דֶּרֶךְ אֶרֶץ; lit. "way of the world"; "proper deportment"), one of the minor tractates of the Talmud, published in current editions of the Talmud at the conclusion of the fourth order, *Nezikin*. *Derekh Ereẓ*, as its name suggests, deals primarily with morals and customs. In its current printed edition, this treatise is divided into three sections: *Derekh Ereẓ Rabbah; Derekh Ereẓ Zuta*; and *Perek ha-Shalom*, which are basically independent units and were probably collated during the late Geonic period. It belongs to a genre of literature which represents the transition between earlier wisdom literature (Ben Sira, tractate *Avot*) and the mediaeval moralistic works (e.g., *Ma'alot ha-Middot* by Yeḥiel ben R. Yekutiel ha-Rofeh, 13th cent.; *Menorat ha-Maor*, by Israel Al-Nakawa, 14th cent., etc.). Related to this body of literature is also *Pseudo-Seder Eliyahu* Zuta, ed. M. Friedman, Jerusalem 1960, and *Masekhet Kallah*, ed. M. Higger, New York 1936.

Derekh Ereẓ Rabbah contains eleven chapters. It begins with a halakhic section on forbidden marriages, to which are appended some ethical maxims. The second chapter contains two entirely different sections, the first discussing 24 classes of people, 12 bad and 12 good; the second details the sins that cause eclipses of the sun and moon, concluding with mystical remarks about God and the 390 heavens. The third chapter contains moral reflections on the origins and destiny of man. Chapters 4 and 5 list rules of conduct for the sages and their disciples. Chapters 6 and 7 detail the proper mode of conduct in society and at the table; chapters 8 and 9 deal exclusively with rules of conduct while eating and drinking; and chapter 10 covers proper behavior in the bathhouse. The final chapter enumerates practices which are dangerous to life, concluding with blessings that are recited on various occasions. This short summary of the tractate's contents indicates that the first section, laws of forbidden marriages, is quite different from the rest of the work, which treats solely of ethical behavior and customs. *Elijah b. Solomon, the Vilna Gaon, was of the opinion that this first chapter is actually the last portion of the tractate **Kallah*, which precedes it in the printed editions and whose subject is marriage, and that it was wrongly taken from there and appended to *Derekh Ereẓ*.

There are ten chapters in *Derekh Ereẓ Zuta*. The name is misleading in one respect since the word *zuta* (lit. "small") could indicate that it is a shorter version of *Derekh Ereẓ Rabbah*. In reality, the two treatises have little in common, and the appellation *Zuta* is probably of later origin. The first nine chapters all possess a certain unity, in that they consist almost exclusively of exhortations to self-examination and modesty. Temperance, resignation, gentleness, patience, respect for age, and an attitude of forgiveness are urged. The moral and social duties of the scholars are stressed throughout. The first half of the tenth chapter is devoted to eschatology while the second half reverts to moral and ethical themes. Many of this tractate's statements are cogent and concise, such as, "if you have done much good let it seem insignificant in your eyes … but let a small kindness done for you appear great" (ch. 2). Appended to these tractates is the *Perek ha-Shalom* which extols the virtue of peace, and is a totally independent work, probably compiled during the Geonic period.

It may be that portions of these tractates were already redacted during the talmudic period. R. Judah's disciples requested that he teach them a section of the laws of *Derekh Ereẓ* (Ber. 22a). It also related that Simeon b. Ba waited on his master, R. Johanan, in accordance with the etiquette outlined in *Derekh Ereẓ* (TJ, Shab. 6:2, 8a). Nevertheless the present text of these treatises dates from the post-talmudic period, and more than one editor aided in its final redaction. These tractates are also known by other names in geonic and rabbinic literature. The first chapters of *Derekh Ereẓ Zuta* were also called the tractate on "Fear of Sin"; the third chapter of *Derekh Ereẓ Rabbah* was referred to as the "Chapter of Ben Azzai"; chapters 5–8 were called *Derekh Ereẓ Zeira,* and the first chapter of *Derekh Ereẓ Rabbah* was also known as the chapter of "Forbidden Relations." These treatises were widely read, and the fact that the tractate passed through so many hands partially accounts for the chaotic state of the texts. Eighteenth-century scholars did much, by means of glosses and commentaries, toward making the texts intelligible. A critical edition and English translation of these tractates was published by Michael Higger in 1935. Another English translation was issued in 1965.

BIBLIOGRAPHY: M. Higger (ed.), *Massekhtot Ze'irot* (1929); idem, *Massekhtot Derekh Ereẓ* (1935); D. Sperber (ed.), *Massekhet Derekh Ereẓ Zuta u-Perek ha-Shalom* (1994); idem, *A Commentary on Derekh Ereẓ Zuta, Chapters 5–8,* (1990); M. von Loopik, *The Ways of the Sages and the Way of the World* (1991).

[Daniel Sperber 2nd ed.]

DEREN, MAYA (**Eleanora Derenkowsky**; 1917–1961), U.S. avant-garde filmmaker. Born in Kiev, Deren moved with her family to New York in 1922 to escape antisemitic pogroms in the Ukraine; at that time the family changed its surname to Deren. Eleanora undertook an arts degree at New York University, completing her master's dissertation on symbolist poetry at Smith College in 1939. Following university, Eleanora managed and toured with Katherine Dunham's dance troupe.

Settling in Los Angeles in the 1940s, Deren changed her name to Maya and made the landmark experimental trance film *Meshes of the Afternoon* (1943) with Alexander Hammid. The film, set in Hollywood, unravels in a nightmarish narrative of repetition and symbolic displacement with objects magically appearing and transforming across the cut. Shot as a silent film, it was edited to Teiji Ito's drumbeat, generating a strong sense of rhythmic form and dynamic movement. In 1943 Deren collaborated with Marcel Duchamp to produce *Witch's Cradle*. The surviving fragments reveal themes that recur throughout Deren's films: the artist's role, the influence of nature, and a fascination with ritual. *At Land* (1944) shows Deren crawling across a dining table, oblivious to the diners. Its depiction of waves descending back into the sea subverts natural rhythms. In *A Study in Choreography for the Camera* (1945) the performer and the camera become dynamic forces as the dancer's twirls bridge disparate spaces. *Meditation on Violence* (1948) focuses on a Wu Tang ritual, juxtaposing violence and stillness. In *Ritual in Transfigured Time* (1946) Deren experiments with slowed footage of two wind-swept women immersed in ritualized wool looming. Her final film, *The Very Eye of Night* (1959), is an incomplete collaboration with the Metropolitan Opera Ballet School that synthesizes dance and Greek mythology against a background of blinking constellations.

Deren organized and presented lectures at universities across the United States and in Canada and Cuba to raise the profile of experimental films. Her innovations inspired the formation of Cinema 16 and Deren herself established the Creative Film Foundation to encourage independent filmmakers. Bridging the divide between praxis and theory, Deren wrote *An Anagram of Ideas on Art, Form and Film* (1946). In 1947 she won the Grand Prix Internationale for avant-garde film at the Cannes Film Festival and was awarded a Guggenheim Foundation Fellowship, a first for a motion picture artist. This allowed Deren to travel to Haiti to film voodoo rituals and write *Divine Horsemen: The Living Gods of Haiti* (1953; rep. 1983). To mark her untimely death the American Film Institute established the Maya Deren Award to inspire independent film and video artists.

BIBLIOGRAPHY: V.V.A. Clark, M. Hodson, and C. Neiman, *The Legend of Maya Deren: A Documentary Biography and Collected Works*, 2 vols. (1984, 1988); B.R. McPherson (ed.), *Essential Deren: Collected Writings on Film* (2005); B. Nicholls (ed.), *Maya Deren and the American Avant-Garde* (2001).

[Wendy Haslem (2nd ed.)]

DERENBURG (**Derenbourg**), family of scholars and writers. ẒEVI HIRSCH DERENBURG, an 18th-century Hebrew writer, was born in Offenbach. In 1789 he went to Mainz as a private tutor of Hebrew and also kept a restaurant. He wrote *Yoshevei Tevel* (Oftenbach, 1789), a didactic moral drama in the style of M.Ḥ. Luzzatto's *La-Yesharim Tehillah*. The eight *dramatis personae* were apparently modeled on living figures in the Mainz community, including the rabbi who is the play's hero. JOSEPH NAPHTALI DERENBOURG (1811–1895), son of Ẓevi Hirsch, was an Orientalist. Joseph lived as domestic tutor in Amsterdam (1835–38), and then settled in Paris, where he continued his Oriental studies, while maintaining, under the influence of A. *Geiger, his interest in Jewish studies. In 1843 he became a French citizen and added an "O" to the second part of his name. He taught German at the Lycée Henri IV in 1851, became corrector at the Imprimerie Nationale in 1852, and also cataloged the Hebrew manuscripts at the Bibliothèque Nationale. In 1857 he founded a Jewish high school for boys which he headed until 1864. Derenbourg was awarded the Légion d'Honneur in 1869 and in 1871 was elected to the Académie des Inscriptions et Belles Lettres. In 1877 a chair for rabbinic-Hebrew language and literature was created for him at the Ecole Pratique des Hautes Etudes. He succeeded Solomon *Munk on the central committee of the Alliance Israélite Universelle and served later as its vice president. From 1869 to 1872 he also served as member of the Paris Consistoire.

Among Derenbourg's major contributions in the field of Oriental languages and inscriptions are: *Les fables de Loqman le Sage* (1850); *Les inscriptions phéniciennes du Temple de Seti à Abydos* (1885; in collaboration with his son Hartwig); part four of *Corpus Inscriptionum Semiticarum* (on Himyaritic and Sabean inscriptions, in collaboration with his son; 2 pts., 1889–92). His most important contributions to Jewish scholarship were: *Essai sur l'histoire et la géographie de la Palestine d'après les Thalmuds et les autres sources rabbiniques* (1867); *Opuscules et traités d'Aboul Walid Merwan ibn Djanah de Cordoue* (in association with his son, 1880); *Deux versions hébraiques du livre Kalilah et Dimnah* (1881); *Le Livre des Par-*

terres Fleuris (Jonah ibn Janaḥ's Hebrew Grammar in Arabic, 1886); an edition of Maimonides' commentary on *Seder Tohorot* (Arabic text and Hebrew translation, 3 parts, 1887–89); and *Oeuvres complètes de R. Saadia b. Joseph al-Fayyoumi*, an edition of Saadiah's writings in Arabic, also in association with his son (5 vols., 1893–99), which was Derenbourg's most important work but remained unfinished. HARTWIG DERENBOURG (1844–1908), son of Joseph, was also an Orientalist. From 1875 he lectured in Arabic at the Ecole des Langues Orientales Vivantes and on Oriental languages at the Ecole Rabbinique. In 1885 Hartwig was appointed to the chair of Arabic at the Ecole des Hautes Etudes and to that of Islam, of which he was the first occupant. In 1900 he was elected a member of the Institut de France. Among his contributions to Jewish scholarship are the following: the editions and translations of Saadiah's Arabic version of Isaiah and Job (in association with his father and W. Bacher, 1896 and 1899; in manuscript at the British Museum). Derenbourg also compiled a catalog of Arabic manuscripts in Spanish libraries, which led him to discover the sources for a history of the Crusades and the Caliphate, published in 1895. A memorial volume, *Mélanges Hartwig Derenbourg* (1909), contains a full bibliography. For the German branch of the family, see *Dernburg.

BIBLIOGRAPHY: W. Bacher, *Joseph Derenbourg sa vie et son oeuvre* (1896); V. Scheil, *Notice sur la vie et les oeuvres de Hartwig Derenbourg* (1909); J. Fueck, *Die arabischen Studien in Europa* (1955), 249ff.

DERI, ARYEH (**Machluf**; 1959–), political leader of Shas in the years 1984–99. Member of the Thirteenth and Fourteenth Knessets. Deri was born in Meknès in Morocco, and immigrated to Israel with his family in 1968. He was educated in the Porat Yosef yeshivah and later in the Hebron yeshivah in Jerusalem. He was secretary of the *haredi* (ultra-Orthodox) settlement of Ma'aleh Amos, and in the years 1981–83 was a member of the Regional Council of *Gush Etzyon.

In 1984 Deri was instrumental in convincing Rabbi Ovadiah *Yosef, his mentor and patron, to establish Shas as a Sephardi *haredi* party, with the blessing of the Ashkenazi Rabbi Eliezer Menachem *Shach, against the background of feelings of discrimination within the Sephardi community. Deri did not stand for election to the Eleventh and Twelfth Knessets, concentrating instead on building the independent *El ha-Ma'ayan* Shas educational system, which soon provided education to tens of thousands of children from kindergarten age. In 1986 he was appointed director general of the Ministry of the Interior under a Shas minister.

Deri became minister of the interior in 1988, at the age of 29, even though he was not a member of the Knesset. In March 1990 he collaborated with the Israel Labor Party in bringing down the National Unity Government headed by Yitzhak *Shamir in a vote of no-confidence. However, after Shimon *Peres failed to form a government, he remained minister of the interior in the government formed by Shamir in June 1990. As minister of the interior he gained a reputation for his ability to make clearcut decisions on controversial issues, such as the abrogation of theater censorship or adjustment of the summer clock. He was subsequently elected to the Thirteenth Knesset, and was once again appointed minister of the interior in the government formed by Yitzhak *Rabin in July 1992, and as a result was ostracized by Rabbi Shach. Deri resigned from Rabin's government together with the other Shas ministers on the eve of the signature of the Declaration of Principles with the PLO in September 1993. At the same time criminal charges were brought against him, charging that he had transferred money from the Ministry of the Interior to various bodies established by Shas in breach of regulations, and that he had received bribes in the amount of $150,000, which he used to purchase apartments in Jerusalem, but which he claimed he had received as an inheritance from his wife's foster parents in the U.S.

The initial investigations lasted for close to three years, as Deri took advantage of his right to remain silent. Deri resigned from the government in September. The trial on the bribery charge opened in June 1994, and dragged on until March 1999, with Deri continuing to follow a strategy of remaining silent. Throughout the investigation and the trial Deri continued to lead Shas politically, and as his trial was viewed by many Sephardim as being based on discrimination, Shas won ten seats in the 1996 elections. Deri was finally found guilty of receiving bribes and sentenced by the District Court of Jerusalem in March 1999 to a four-year prison term and a fine of NIS 250,000. On appeal the sentence was reduced to three years. The affair turned Deri into a martyr within the Sephardi community. He was released from prison in July 2002. In September 2003 Deri was also found guilty of breach of trust for the illegal transfer of funds from the Ministry. However, he was not given another prison sentence.

Banned from returning to political life for a certain period, Deri resumed his religious studies. In the meantime a rift occurred between Deri and his former mentor Rabbi Ovadiah Yosef, against the background of Deri's conduct and Ovadiah's choice of Eliyahu Yishai to replace him as Shas' political leader.

BIBLIOGRAPHY: Y. Nir, *Aryeh Deri – Ha-Aliyah, ha-Mashber, ha-Ke'ev* (1999). **VIDEO RECORDING:** *Ani Ma'ashim* ("I Accuse," 1999).

[Susan Hattis Rolef (2nd ed.)]

DERNBURG, German family of jurists, editors, bankers, and statesmen. HEINRICH DERNBURG (1829–1907) was a jurist. He studied law at Giessen and Berlin and from 1854 to 1862 was professor of law at Zurich. In 1862 he became professor at Halle University which, in 1866, he represented in the Upper House of the Prussian parliament. In 1871 he became professor of Roman and Prussian law in Berlin. One of the outstanding exponents of the "Pandectic" in Roman law, his three-volume work *Pandekten* (1884–87) is still considered a classic. His books on Prussian private law, *Lehrbuch des preussischen Privatrechts, und der Privatrechtsnormen des Reichs*

(1877–80; 3 volumes), in which he emphasizes the importance of social and economic factors in the development of law, and *Das buergerliche Recht des Deutschen Reichs und Preussens* (1889–1915; 5 volumes), had a great influence on German jurisprudence. He was baptized when a child.

His brother FRIEDRICH (1833–1911) was editor of the Berlin *Nationalzeitung* and coeditor of the *Berliner Tageblatt*. He wrote travel sketches, plays, and novels. Friedrich's son BERNHARD DERNBURG (1865–1937) was trained to be a banker and began by working for the Berliner Handelsgesellschaft. Later he went to New York to join *Ladenburg, Thalman & Co., where he familiarized himself with U.S. business methods. Returning to Germany, he joined the Deutsche Bank. He became head of the bank's trust company and acquired a reputation as a reorganizer of companies in difficulties and as an efficiency expert. He then moved on to the Bank für Handel und Industrie and the Darmstaedter Bank. In 1906 he was appointed head of the German government department for the colonies and devoted his efforts to Germany's colonial expansion and, with the cooperation of leading German banks, to ensuring its financial basis. He traveled a great deal in order to increase his detailed and local knowledge of colonial problems. In 1912 he became a member of the Prussian upper house and in 1919, following Germany's collapse after World War I, served for a short time as cabinet minister. From 1920 to 1930 Bernhard Dernburg was a member of the Reichstag.

BIBLIOGRAPHY: T. Kipp, *Heinrich Dernburg* (Ger., 1908); E. Seckel, *Gedaechtnisrede auf Heinrich Dernburg* (1908); H. Sinzheimer, *Juedische Klassiker der Deutschen Rechtswissenschaft* (1938), 93–105a; S. Kaznelson, *Juden im deutschen Kulturbereich* (1959), 551–2, 747; Wininger, Biog, 2 (1927), 32–34; NDB, 3 (1956), 607–8, includes bibliography.

[Joachim O. Ronall]

DER NISTER (Yid. "the concealed one"; pseudonym of **Pinkhes Kahanovitsch**; 1884–1950), Yiddish writer. Born in Berdichev, Ukraine, he received a traditional Jewish education but also read secular works in Russian from an early age. His spiritual and literary growth was significantly influenced by his older brother, Aaron, a Bratzlaver Ḥasid whose personality and mysticism are echoed in the character of Luzi in Der Nister's realistic narrative, *Di Mishpokhe Mashber* ("The Family Mashber," vol. 1, Moscow, 1939; vol. 2, New York, 1948). In his youth Der Nister associated with Zionist socialist circles, some evidence of which, including his possible attendance at the Po'alei Zion conference (1905), as well as of his impression of Ber *Borochov at the conference, can be found in the novel *Fun Finften Yor* ("About the Fifth Year"), which remained in manuscript form in his literary legacy and was published in *Sovetish Heymland* (January 1964). Around 1905 he left Berdichev to avoid serving in the czarist army. Until World War I he led a fugitive existence, chiefly in Zhitomir, supporting himself by giving private Hebrew lessons. At 23, he published his first book, *Gedanken un Motivn – Lider in Proze* ("Thoughts and Motifs – Poems in Prose," 1907), which reveals what was to be a life-long preoccupation with such universal themes as the divine-satanic duality of humans, the eternal opposition between aspiration and reality, and the pendulum swings of human emotion. After having met Der Nister in 1910, I.L. *Peretz encouraged him to publish his short novel, *A Togbikhl fun a Farfirer* ("Diary of a Seducer"), which resembled a crime story, in his magazine, *Yudish*. Peretz was also instrumental in the publication of his next book of prose narratives, *Hekher fun der Erd* ("Higher Than the Earth," Warsaw, 1910), and his Kiev admirers David *Bergelson and Nachman *Mayzel assisted in publishing his first book of poetry, *Gezang un Gebet* ("Song and Prayer," Kiev, probably in 1910 or 1912). In 1917 he published a small collection of stories for children, *Mayselekh in Ferzn* ("Little Tales in Verse"; expanded and republished in 1917 and 1921 (with illustrations by Marc Chagall) and 1923). Living in Kiev, Der Nister contributed to *Eygns* (1918, 1920) and *Oyfgang* (1919), which belletristic collections served as the foundation of Soviet-Yiddish literature. In addition, he was a skilled translator of world literature; his rich fantasy and linguistic virtuosity displayed in his children's verse and stories have rarely been equaled.

In 1921 he left the Soviet Union, first for Kaunas (Kovno), then Berlin, a gathering point for literary emigrants. After some three years in Berlin, where he published *Gedakht* ("Imagined," 2 vols., 1922–3), the first collection of his visionary and fantastic tales, he moved to Hamburg where he worked for the Soviet trade mission in 1924–5. In 1926, while the Soviet Union was promoting Yiddish culture and attempting to lure émigré writers back, Der Nister returned to the Soviet Union, settling in Kharkov. Until 1929 Der Nister contributed to those periodicals still open to "fellow-traveling" writers. With the ascendancy of the "proletarian" critics in that year, his work came under sharp attack for its symbolism. For some time he published nothing, attempting in the years 1931–3 to find a place for himself on the hostile literary scene through writing *ocherki*, a form of reportage then regarded as progressive. Editing and translating continued to be the mainstays of his precarious livelihood. These were years of great anguish for Der Nister, who realized he could not adapt to the demands of realistic reportage nor abandon a style he had spent his life developing. Around the year 1935 he resolved to write his family saga, a resolve of desperation as well as a cunning stratagem on the part of a writer whose creative life was in danger. In a letter written around 1934 to his brother Motl, in Paris, Der Nister made his desperate position absolutely clear: "… the writing of my book is a necessity; otherwise I am nothing [*oys mentsh*]; otherwise I am erased from literature and from life…." The death sentence for Soviet-Yiddish literature may have been prepared as early as 1939, the year in which Der Nister won critical acclaim for the first volume of *Di Mishpokhe Mashber*, and the Soviet authorities suggested that Yiddish works appear only in translation, a danger sidetracked by the war, and one which Der Nister outspokenly opposed. The war years 1941–3 found Der Nister in Tashkent and Moscow, where he lived in great penury. During and immediately after the war he was close to the Jewish *Anti-Fascist

Committee in whose service he had accompanied Ukrainian Jewish immigrants to *Birobidzhan. There he had pressed parents to petition for Yiddish-language schools, which became one of the charges of anti-Soviet "nationalism" brought against him following the suppression of Jewish cultural life in the Soviet Union in November 1948. Not long thereafter Der Nister was arrested and died in a prison hospital.

Prior to 1929 Der Nister wrote as he wished; thereafter he worked under the shadow of repression. In the former period he wrote his highly original mystical visions and fantastic tales, developing a style unique in Yiddish literature. From the outset he had sought a universalist synthesis of the Jewish mystical tradition and world mythology, introducing into his earliest stories figures such as Buddha and the Virgin Mary, hitherto regarded as alien to Yiddish literature. His first volume, *Gedanken un Motivn*, reveals a tragic view of life wherein suffering is ultimately redeemed through love. Formally his "poetry in prose" is an attempt to combine rhymed and unrhymed passages. He employed this very peculiar compositional mixture until 1910, when many of his early works were published. His sense of the dual nature of humans finds expression in the antithetical pair of stories "Poylish" ("Polish") and "Kleopatra" (*Literarishe Monatsshriftn*, nos. 1 and 4, Vilna, 1908), where sanctified love and demonic lust are vividly contrasted through imagery derived from Jewish tradition on the one hand and classical tradition on the other. *Hekher fun der Erd* is filled with kabbalistic references and reveals Der Nister's mature literary language and reflections on the concept of creativity and its textual realization. The most intriguing composition of this volume, "Der Kadmen" ("The Original"), is a revision of the myth of creation, ending on a secularized cosmic evolutionary note. His tendency to express himself in mystical language is manifest in *Gezang un Gebet*, a volume of verse whose first poem, "Mir" ("We"), is a deeply felt meditation on the mystery of Jewishness and its destiny in the absence of spiritual guides. In these poems despair is countered by a vision of youth who rediscover the ancestral path.

Critics ignored Der Nister's first books, which they were unable to grasp; no reviews of his works were published until 1913, when the first two reviewers, Sh. *Niger and S. Rozenfeld, were essentially negative. David *Bergelson, a refined master of literary Yiddish himself, in a letter to Sh. Niger dated 1912, first recognized Der Nister's skill in shaping Yiddish language into original and innovative forms. Doubtless influenced by the criticism of Peretz, Der Nister, after 1912, de-emphasized description and introduced firm narrative structure into his visionary and fantastic tales, preserving their symbolic and ambiguous qualities while making them interesting as stories. Just as Peretz for his purposes renewed the ḥasidic hagiographic tale, so Der Nister revived the ḥasidic symbolic tale created by R. *Naḥman of Bratzlav, discovering, as had R. Naḥman before him, a popular and flexible medium for ideas which could not be broached directly. The years 1913–29, from the appearance of "A Mayse" ("A Story," in *Di Yidishe Velt*, no. 10, Vilna, 1913; later republished in *Gedakht*, vol. 1) to the sharply criticized "Unter a Ployt" ("Under a Fence," in *Di Royte Velt*, 5 no. 7, Kharkov, 1929) witnessed Der Nister's cultivation of a mode altogether congenial to him. This period marks the peak of his symbolist narrative achievement. Just as the characteristic symbols – e.g., the Well of Tradition and the Lonely Tower – and the mystic dualism of the Russian symbolists are reflected in his tales of this period, so too are the verb inversions and lyrical effects practiced by the Russian symbolists absorbed in Der Nister's Yiddish style. Set in space, in deep forests, at the margin of civilization, his stories are spun by characters without proper names, devils, wanderers, giants, drunkards, fools displaying a variety of archetypal relational patterns. Like those of his contemporary Franz *Kafka, they are paradigmatic representations of an alienated human condition. The hypnotic rhythms of his long sentences, their deliberate sound structure, the repeated use of "and" (possibly derived from the biblical conversive *vav*), and the archaic diction (derived from the *taytsh* tradition, i.e., from early Yiddish Bible translations) result in a dream-like, strangely compelling, at times surrealist atmosphere. The texture of his stories, interwoven with elements taken from the wondrous world of folk tales and, at times, of gothic fantasy, further heightens their enigmatic, unresolvable complexity. Most of the stories collected in the two volumes of *Gedakht* were reprinted in a revised one-volume edition (1929), when his last volume of symbolist stories, *Fun Mayne Giter* ("Of My Estates"), also appeared.

The extraordinarily complex "Unter a Ployt" represents Der Nister's covert protest against Soviet cultural regimentation as well as anguished self-accusation for abandoning his symbolic art. However, his subsequent efforts to write realistic reportage could not quell his characteristic impulse, and *Dray Hoyptshtet* ("Three Capitals," Kharkov, 1934) subtly resists the required orthodoxy. Aided by shifts in Party policy in the 1930s, Der Nister saved his artistic conscience by writing *Di Mishpokhe Mashber*, a family saga which appears to heed the requirements of realism while serving the author's own far from orthodox literary purposes. This novel, only two of whose three or more projected volumes have been published (a third volume may exist in manuscript somewhere in the Soviet Union), is perhaps the single greatest achievement of Soviet Yiddish prose. As suggested in its title, *Di Mishpokhe Mashber* (*mashber*, Hebrew "crisis") was conceived as the portrait of a traditional and rooted society in dissolution. Der Nister intended to portray East European Jewry from the 1870s to the revolutionary period. The two volumes published, which constitute Part One of the projected whole, cover less than a year during the 1870s in *Berdichev, the most Jewish of all Ukrainian towns. The view taken of Jewish life, and particularly the magnificent picture of Bratzlaver Ḥasidism, indicate deep sympathy rather than the prescribed anti-religious bias. What Der Nister has done in this supposedly "realistic" novel is to transform the nameless characters of his mystic tales into name-bearing particular persons. The central characters of the novel are precisely the same agonized seekers one finds in his tales and their concerns are the same. There is a remarkable continuity in Der Nister's creative career.

His war and postwar writings are impressive for the candor and courage with which strong national feeling is expressed, but undistinguished as literature. The informer of "Flora" (in *Dertseylungen un Eseyen* ("Stories and Essays") ed. N. Mayzel, New York, 1957) is a stereotyped villain, yet the story is of immense interest in its historical context. Nowhere else in Soviet Yiddish literature is a rabbi presented in so positive a light. Der Nister dared to envisage a Jewish future linked to the Jewish past. Unpublished manuscript material of Der Nister's from various periods appeared in *Sovetish Heymland* (no. 2, 1967), including a chapter from volume three of *Di Mishpokhe Mashber,* and in the collection *Vidervuks* ("New Growth," Moscow, 1969).

BIBLIOGRAPHY: Rejzen, Leksikon, 2 (1930^4), 580–4; LNYL, 5 (1965), 256–62; Y.Y. Kohn, *Pirsumim Yehudiyyim bi-Verit ha-Mo'aẓot 1917–1960* (1961), index; Ch. Shmeruk, in: Der Nister, *Ha-Nazir ve-ha-Gediyyah; Sippurim, Shirim, Ma'amarim* (transl. D. Sadan, 1963), 9–52; M. Piekarz, in: Ch. Shmeruk, (ed.), *A Shpigl oyf a Shteyn* (1964), 737–41; Ch. Shmeruk, in: *The Field of Yiddish*, 2 (1965), 263–87. **ADD. BIBLIOGRAPHY:** D. Bechtel, *Der Nister's Work 1907–1929: A Study of a Yiddish Symbolist* (1990); D. Mantovan, "Der Nister and His Symbolist Stories 1913–1929: Patterns of Imagination" (diss. 1993); D.G. Roskies, in: *A Bridge of Longing: The Lost Art of Yiddish Storytelling* (1995), 191–229.

[Leonard Prager and Chone Shmeruk / Daniela Mantovan (2nd ed.)]

°DE' ROSSI, GIOVANNI BERNARDO (1742–1831), Italian Christian Hebraist. De' Rossi was born in Villa Castelnuovo, Turin. He became a priest in 1766 and graduated in theology in Turin. He had a profound knowledge of Hebrew language and medieval Jewish literature, and held the chair of Oriental languages at Parma University from 1769 to 1821. De' Rossi's library of Jewish literature, one of the most valuable that has ever been brought together, comprised 1,432 manuscripts (some illuminated), and 1,442 printed books including many incunabula, some unique. It was purchased for 100,000 francs in 1816 by Marie Louise, duchess of Parma, who presented it to the Palatine library at Parma, where it still is. De' Rossi compiled a catalogue of his collection (*MSS. codices hebraici bibliothecae I.B. De' Rossi, accurate ab eodem descripti et illustrati*, 3 vols., Parma, 1803), and wrote valuable works on Jewish incunabula (*Annales hebraeo-typographici saeculi XV*, Parma, 1795) and 16th-century typography (*Annales hebraeo-typographici ab anno 1501 ad 1540*, Parma, 1799) as well as on other subjects of Jewish interest, including studies of variant biblical texts and polemical literature. His *Dizionario storico degli autori ebrei e delle loro opere* (2 vols., Parma, 1802; Ger. ed. Leipzig, 1839) is still of value, especially for the biographical notes on contemporary Jewish scholars.

BIBLIOGRAPHY: G.B. De' Rossi, *Memorie storiche sugli studi e sulle produzioni del Dottore G.B. De' Rossi* (Parma, 1809); A. Vaccari, *Scritti di erudizione e di filosofia*, 2 (1958), 459–69; Tamani, in: RMI, 32 (1966), 268–70; S.D. Luzzatto, *Opere del de' Rossi concernenti l'ebraica letteratura e bibliografia* (1868^2); Shunami, Bibl, index. **ADD. BIBLIOGRAPHY:** G. Busi, *Edizioni ebraiche del XVI secolo nelle Biblioteche dell'Emilia Romagna* (1987); F. Parente, in: *Dizionario Biografico degli Italiani*, 39 (1991), 205–14; B. Richler and M. Beit-Arie, *Hebrew Manuscripts in the Biblioteca Palatina in Parma* (2001).

[Ariel Toaff]

DERRIDA, JACQUES (1930–2004), French philosopher and literary critic. Derrida was born and raised in El-Biar, near Algiers. In 1942, he was expelled from school as result of antisemitic measures. In 1949 he moved to France and beginning in 1952 he studied at the École Normale Superieure, under Michel Foucault and Louis Althusser. He served in the French army in Algeria from 1957 until 1959 as a teacher of French and English. Until 1962 he hoped for the coexistence of the French of Algeria within an independent Algeria. In the same year Derrida resettled in Nice.

From 1960 to 1964, Derrida taught at the Sorbonne. From 1964 to 1984 he taught at the École Normale Superieure. In 1983, he founded the Collège International de Philosophie in Paris. In 1967 he published the first of a long series of books. He was not only a prolific writer, he also traveled extensively, lecturing and teaching. He was celebrated in the academic world, mostly in a number of American universities (e.g., Johns Hopkins, Yale, Cornell, City University of New York), but was almost excluded from the French university world. Nevertheless, his work was appreciated by many French academicians, among them Ph. Lacoue-Labarthe and J.L. Nancy, E. Levinas, and S. Kofman.

Derrida was an outspoken leftist intellectual. When visiting Israel, he had talks with Palestinian intellectuals. In 1981, he traveled to Prague for a clandestine seminar in support of the anti-totalitarian movement and was arrested by the police on the false accusation of drug possession. He was allowed to leave Czechoslovakia thanks to the intervention of François Mitterand and the French government. He also protested against apartheid in South Africa.

Among his many awards and honors he received the Nietzsche prize in 1988 and the Adorno Prize in 2001. His oeuvre has been translated into English, German, Spanish, Italian, Japanese, and other languages.

Derrida's Hermeneutics

Derrida developed a method, known as "deconstruction." Deconstructionism is neither nihilism nor destruction; it is affirmative openness towards the other. Derrida maintained that the written word is characterized by the absence of the original voice which gave it meaning. It is impossible, therefore, to know the intention behind the written word. Consequently, when one reads what is written, multiple meanings are possible: nobody has a monopoly on the "right" meaning. Letters and documents, from which the writer is absent, are open to endless interpretations, since there is no presence of the speaker who – face to face with the one who receives his words – eventually corrects his words or explains them. Texts are polyvalent and function as letters that did not reach their destination and are now read by whoever happens to read them.

Derrida studied at the Leuven Husserl Archive, and was long occupied with Husserl, whose phenomenology he deconstructed. Protesting against a metaphysics of presence and origin, where everything is transparent, Derrida showed the multiple fissures in texts and the indecidability that is implied in any text. He initiated a new hermeneutic. In a Heraclitian and anti-essentialist way, he showed how the meaning of a text changes all the time. The text is capable of infinite signification, and receives meaning not by reconstructing the intention of its writer, but through its autonomous function. The same book or letter can be read by different readers in different ways, and a second or third reading is not equal to the first. By limiting the text to one meaning, one excludes all other possible meanings. Meanings are produced through the different contexts of the reader and through the context in which a written document is placed.

A word also possesses several meanings. This is clear when one takes into account misunderstandings. One phonetic phenomenon can result in a proliferation of meanings, as is the case in the French homophone words l'est, l'é, lait, legs, or ontologie-hauntologie. The same word can also denote something completely different in another language, as in the case of the German "Gift," poison, that is the homophone of the English "gift," present.

Derrida and Postmodernism

Derrida is one of the most provocative thinkers of our time, and his thought is part of postmodern philosophy, which does not recognize universal truth and resists the imperialism of the sciences. In postmodernism, each text is a pretext for a multitude of interpretations and is open to the fantasy of the reader. The entire world is one big text and there is no limit to its explanations. Just as in medieval paintings cathedrals are carefully placed in biblical landscapes, the modern reader places his own point of view in every text. There is no absolute, objective truth, and the only truth that is recognized is that of the interpreting person. This does not mean that everyone has his own truth. It would be inaccurate to say that Derrida was a relativist. What he strove for is the advent of the wholly other outside the horizon of the same. In his numerous writings, there is a plenitude of associations, and in his books and articles he placed different texts next to each other, so that they began "speaking."

Derrida's Judaism as Refusal of Totality

Derrida admitted that he did not know Jewish culture. This non-knowledge was then elevated to a fundamental "not belonging." In this way, he thought of himself as "the last Jew" (*le dernier des juifs*): more Jewish than the Jews in his exemplary non-belonging. To be Jewish for Derrida is coterminous with the refusal of the same and the openness towards the wholly other. This non-identification is also what comes into the fore in his deconstructive method.

Derrida was French and Jewish. He thought that he was more French than the French people, because he is not a real Frenchman. In a parallel manner, he thought that he was more Jewish than every Jew, because he lacked a concrete engagement towards Judaism. In his view, he is and is not, at the same time.

Like Edmond Jabès, Derrida regarded the basic characterisitic of Judaism as a fundamental non-belonging to an all-absorbing totality. Jabès' oeuvre can be read as a poetic commentary on Derrida. Much has been written on the Jewish elements in the writings of such "non-Jewish Jews" (the term is from Deutscher) as Kafka, Marx, and Freud. This is also the case with Derrida, who saw his Jewishness as something contingent and denied that he belonged to any concrete Judaism, but conceived of this refusal as fundamentally Jewish.

Metaphoric Judaism: Deconstruction as Judaism

Derrida's Judaism is devoid of any concrete link to history, land, or law. It is at the same time a Judaism that believes because of its openness to the unabsorbable other, and is atheistic, without concrete content. Transcending his merely ethnic Jewishness, Derrida discussed Judaism, touching on many subjects: circumcision, bar mitzvah, the law, messianism, memory, and resurrection. Yet, again, the Judaism that Derrida encircles is without nation or religion. There is a link between Judaism and deconstruction: both are searching. Judaism becomes the example *par excellence* of his deconstructive method.

Derrida does not desert faith, nor does he exclude it. His deconstructionism affirms what is beyond the possible; it affirms the impossible, the coming of the wholly other (*tout autre*). It is an engagement, a certain faith, and a-theological hope for what is coming. Derrida alters religious sources by referring them to his expectation of what should come. Writing on religious notions like circumcision, confession, eschatology, or messianism, he divests these terms of their concrete, particular meaning and transcends them by translating them into something which is not present and which is hoped for. By reinventing these terms, he escapes the foreseeable and keeps the future (*l'à-venir*) open ended. In this sense, his method is not far from that of negative theology that refuses to define the wholly other.

Derrida's openness to the gift (*le don*) of justice and of the democracy to come lends to his work a touch of hope, in what was for him the best of Jewish tradition.

Derrida's works include *L'Ecriture et la différence* (1967), *La Voix et le phénomène* (1967), *De la Grammatologie (1967), La Dissémination* (1972), *Marge – de la philosophie* (1972), *Glas* (1974), and *Schibboleth* (1986). Later writings are collected in *Jacques Derrida and the Humanities: A Critical Reader,* ed. T. Cohen (2002).

BIBLIOGRAPHY: J.D. Caputo, *The Prayers and Tears of Jacques Derrida: Religion without Religion* (1997); L. Finas et al., *Ecarts: quatre essais à propos de Jacques Derrida* (1973); N. Garver and S.C. Lee, *Derrida & Wittgenstein* (1994); S. Handelman, *The Slayers of Moses:*

The Emergence of Rabbinic Interpretation in Modern Literary Theory (1982); I.H. Harvey, *Derrida and the Economy of Différance* (1986); C. Johnson, *System and Writing in the Philosophy of Jacques Derrida* (Cambridge Studies in French 40), (1993); P. Lacoue-Labarthe and JL. Nancy (eds.), *Les fins de l'homme – Colloque de Cérisy* (1981); J. Llewelyn, *Derrida on the Threshold of Sense* (1986); G.B. Madison (ed.), *Working through Derrida* (1993); M.C. Taylor, *Deconstructing Theology* (1982); Idem, *Erring(s): A Postmodern(ist) a/theolog*, (1984); E. Weber (ed.), *Questions au judaïsme, entretiens avec Elisabeth Weber* (1996); D. Wood and R. Bernasconi, *Derrida and Différance* (1988).

[Ephraim Meir (2nd ed.)]

DERSHOWITZ, ALAN M. (1938–), U.S. law professor and civil liberties lawyer. Dershowitz was born in Brooklyn, New York, graduated from Yeshiva University high school and Brooklyn College. He received his law degree from Yale Law School, where he was editor-in-chief of the *Yale Law Journal*. He was law clerk to Chief Judge David Bazelon, U.S. Court of Appeals, and Justice Arthur Goldberg of the U.S. Supreme Court. In 1967 he was appointed professor at Harvard Law School, where his special subjects were criminal law, psychiatry and law, and constitutional litigation. He served as consultant to the government of China on the revision of its criminal code, as a member of the President's Commission on Marijuana and Drug Abuse, the President's Commission on Causes and Prevention of Violence, and the President's Commission on Civil Disorders, and he was director of the National Institute of Mental Health. He was also chairman of the Civil Rights Commission for New England and of the Anti-Defamation League of B'nai B'rith, and was a prominent member of the board of directors of the American Civil Liberties Union.

Dershowitz lectured widely and wrote extensively (in books, magazines, and newspapers) on civil liberties and public affairs. He served as counsel in many important legal cases involving civil liberties, and became a public figure especially through his participation in television programs and interviews.

Dershowitz played a leading role in influencing Congress by promoting the theory of "presumptive sentencing," intended to obviate discrepancy in criminal sentencing for the same crimes.

Between 1967 and 1986 Dershowitz represented clients in 11 cases in the U.S. Supreme Court. Some of his cases attracted national attention, including those in which he represented Patricia Hearst, Claus von Bulow, the trial lawyer F. Lee Bailey, and Kenneth Tyson. Although stridently loyal to Jewish causes, he defended the constitutional right of the American Nazi party in 1977 to march in Skokie, Illinois, for he maintained that as a civil libertarian it was his duty to uphold the constitutional right of free speech, which includes the right to demonstrate peacefully. Dershowitz thinks of himself as a liberal in the tradition of John F. Kennedy and Hubert Humphrey. Although opposed to the philosophy and actions of the Jewish Defense League, in 1972 he successfully defended Sheldon Siegel, a member of the JDL, on a murder charge arising out of the blowing up of the offices of Sol Hurok to protest Hurok's sponsorship of Russian performers. Dershowitz succeeded at the trial of Siegel to expose the case as a police frame-up. *Time* magazine called him "the top lawyer of last resort in the country." He was on the defense team in the 1995 O.J. Simpson murder trial. *Newsweek* described Dershowitz as "the nation's most peripatetic civil liberties lawyer and one of its most distinguished defenders of individual rights."

In 2002 Dershowitz stirred up much controversy when he advocated the legalization of torture by means of a "torture warrant." He proposed that no torture be permitted without a warrant issued by a judge, his rationale being that it is practiced in any case, so better to create some parameters to monitor it. The application for such a warrant, he explained, would be "based on the absolute need to obtain immediate information in order to save lives, coupled with probable cause that the suspect had such information and is unwilling to reveal it."

From 1993, Dershowitz was Felix Frankfurter Professor of Law at Harvard Law School. His books include *The Best Defense* (1982); *Reversal of Fortune: Inside the von Bulow Case* (1982), which was made into a successful film; *Taking Liberties: A Decade of Hard Cases, Bad Laws and Bum Raps* (1988); his autobiography *Chutzpah* (1991); *Contrary to Popular Opinion* (1992); *Reasonable Doubts: The Criminal Justice System and the O.J. Simpson Case* (1997); *The Vanishing American Jew: In Search of Jewish Identity for the Next Century* (1997); *Sexual McCarthyism: Clinton, Starr, and the Emerging Constitutional Crisis* (2000); *Why Terrorism Works: Understanding the Threat, Responding to the Challenge* (2002); *Shouting Fire: Civil Liberties in a Turbulent Age* (2002); *The Case for Israel* (2003); *America Declares Independence* (2003); *Rights from Wrongs: The Origins of Human Rights in the Experience of Injustice* (2004); and *America on Trial: Inside the Legal Battles That Transformed Our Nation* (2004).

[Milton Ridvas Konvitz / Rohan Saxena and Ruth Beloff (2nd ed.)]

DÉRY (Deutsch), TIBOR (1894–1977), Hungarian author and poet. Déry's early work, which was naturalistic and romantic, was published in the journal *Nyugat* ("West"). He joined the Hungarian Communist Party in 1919. He left the country in the following year and eventually settled in Vienna, where he published verse influenced by the activist-surrealist school. His first major work, *Szemtől szembe* ("Face to Face"), a trilogy of interrelated short novels, was published in the early 1930s. In 1933 Déry began writing his trilogy *Befejezetlen mondat* ("Unfinished Sentence"), which depicts the problems of a young man of bourgeois origin seeking the road to Communism. As a result of his involvement in the workers' uprising of 1934, Déry was forced to leave Vienna and finally returned to Hungary, where he was forbidden to publish most of his work. He went into hiding during World War II, but when his works were published after the war, he won recognition both in Hungary and abroad. The works which he wrote between 1955 and 1956, short stories entitled *Szerelem* ("Love") and a short story, "Niki," were designed to expose the evils of the "cult of personality." For his part in the short-lived 1956 revolution, as a prominent member of the Petőfi Writers' Club, Déry was sentenced to nine years' imprisonment. He was released in 1961 and, after a short interval, was allowed to resume the publication of his work.

BIBLIOGRAPHY: *Magyar Irodalmi Lexikon*, 1 (1963), 250–1.

[Itamar Yaos-Kest]

°DERZHAVIN, GABRIEL ROMANOVICH (1743–1816), Russian administrator and poet; his investigation of the Jewish problem in his role as administrator influenced the status of the Jews in Russia and Russian policy toward the Jews from the beginning of the 19th century to the end of the czarist regime. Derzhavin was sent by the authorities in 1799/1800 to Belorussia, incorporated into Russia after the last partition of Poland, to investigate the conditions of Jewish life there in connection with a famine that had hit the peasants in the region. His conclusions were influenced both by the local Polish nobility, who blamed the Jews for the sufferings of the peasants, and by the Jew Nathan Note *Notkin, who advised Derzhavin to urge the government to direct the Jews from their traditional occupations and way of life to employment in crafts and colonization of "New Russia." The report Derzhavin submitted shows that he believed the allegations made against the Jews and the Jewish character. He suggested that the Jews should be divided into four estates according to income and place of residence, and that the steppes of Astrakhan and "New Russia" should be made available for Jewish agricultural colonization. Jews should be prohibited from keeping taverns and expelled from the villages in the old *Pale of Settlement.

BIBLIOGRAPHY: J.I. Hessen (Gessen), *Istoriya yevreyskogo naroda v Rossii*, 1 (1926), 132–6.

[Abba Ahimeir]

DESECRATION (Heb. חִלּוּל, *ḥillul*; lit., "desanctification" or "profanation").

In the Bible

Desecration occurs when the holy is replaced by the profane or impure, the difference between the two being that the impure must be purified before it can be resanctified (e.g., the purging and consecration of the altar on the *Day of Atonement, Lev. 16:19). The holy things which are subject to desecration or contamination are (1) objects, e.g., sacrifices (Lev. 19:8; 22:3), priestly dues (Num. 18:22), the sanctuary and its sancta (Lev. 21:12, 23; Ezek. 23:39; 44:7); (2) persons, e.g., priests (Lev. 21:4, 9); (3) sacred time, e.g., the Sabbath (Ex. 31:14); and (4) God's name (see below).

The paradigm of desecration is Ezekiel 22:26: "They [the priests] have desecrated My sancta: they did not differentiate between the holy and the profane and did not teach [distinguish] between the impure and pure ... so that I am profaned in their midst" (cf. Lev. 10:10; Ezek. 44:23). Thus, owing to priestly negligence in protecting the holy realm, the sancta, and even God, have been desecrated. Actually, there is but one cause for desecration: the illicit contact of the holy realm with the profane or impure, as in the case of the lay person's consuming sacred food reserved for the priests (Lev. 22:15; Num. 18:22); the priest incurring forbidden impurity (Lev. 21:4); the practicing of Moloch worship (Ezek. 23:29; cf. Lev. 20:3); and foreigners entering the temple area (Ezek. 44:7; cf. Ps. 74:7). By figurative extension, desecration is also applied to whoredom (Lev. 19:29; 21:9,14; Num. 25:1) and to the violation of God's injunctions (Lev. 22:9; Ps. 89:32) and covenant (Mal. 2:10). Legitimate desecration (lit., desanctification) takes place when the Nazirite (called "holy," Num. 6:8) ends his vow and brings a purification offering to return to his former profane state (Num. 6:14), and when the fourth-year fruit harvest is dedicated to the Lord (Lev. 19:24; cf. Deut. 20:6; Jer. 31:4). The sages logically applied the term to the redemption of all property given over ("sanctified," Lev. 27:14ff.) to the sanctuary (TJ, Naz. 2:1, 51 d). The sphere of holiness is identified with God's presence on earth. Any reduction in holiness is ipso facto a reduction in the divine domain; it is therefore a *ḥillul shem YHWH* ("a desecration of God's [power or] Name"). The desecrations described above are also desecrations of God's name, e.g., those connected with priests (Lev. 21:6; 22:2), sacrifices (Lev. 22:32; Mal. 1:12), altars (Amos 2:7–8), and Moloch worship (Lev. 18:21; 20:3). One other desecration falls exclusively within this category: the false oath (Lev. 19:12; Num. 30:3; Jer. 34:16). The prophets, moreover, not only condemn Israel on this charge but turn it back upon God in their lawsuit against Him. The exile, they argue, is a desecration of God's name (e.g., Isa. 48:11) not only because the nations look upon Israel's humiliation as a sign of their God's impotence (so pleads Moses, Num. 14:15–16), but because it constitutes a violation of God's promise of the land to the forefathers. In Ezekiel this argument is especially prominent. Basing himself on the priestly promise that God's covenanted oath is inviolable (Ezek. 20:44; cf. Lev. 26:42–45), the prophet affirms that Israel will be restored to its land (Ezek. 20:37ff.; 36:20–23; 39:7) though it does not merit it (Ezek. 20:44; 36:32). The principle of intention plays a part in the penalties prescribed for desecration; if the desecration is willful, it is punishable by death (e.g., Num. 18:32), but if caused by accidental tampering with sancta (Lev. 5:14–19) or by swearing falsely (Lev. 5:20ff.), it is expiable through proper remorse and sacrifice (*ʾasham*). See *Sacrifices.

[Jacob Milgrom]

After the Bible

In the Mishnah sacred things could often be profaned by reciting the correct formula, a procedure obviously adopted to simplify social and commercial intercourse. It enabled the scholar to dine at the home of the **am ha-areẓ* who was suspected of not tithing his produce, or to partake of his own produce that he had not managed to tithe before the Sabbath (Dem. 7:1–5). Incense donated to the Temple or left over from a previous year's allocation had to be temporarily "profaned" in order to make it available in the following year for use in the Temple service, which the rabbis insisted could not be financed by private offerings or surpluses. It was profaned by paying the salaries of the incense makers with it and then repurchasing it from them with the moneys from the obligatory annual *Shekel* contributions of the community. This was in fact a purely bookkeeping operation which, however, served to impress upon the people the highest standards of probity and ritual propriety when dealing with sacred things, which could permanently revert to lay use by payment to the Temple treasury in money only, but not in labor (Shek. 4:5, 6; Tosef., Shek. 2:9).

[Aryeh Newman]

DE-SHALIT, AMOS (1926–1969), Israeli scientist and educator. Born in Jerusalem, de-Shalit received his scientific training as a pupil of Joel *Racah at the Hebrew University, Jerusalem. De-Shalit's major field of research was theoretical physics concerning nuclear structure theory, and his most important contributions were on the nuclear shell theory. In 1963 he published, together with Igal *Talmi, *Nuclear Shell Theory*. De-Shalit headed the nuclear physics department of the *Weizmann Institute of Science, Reḥovot, from 1954 to 1964. He was scientific director of the Weizmann Institute from 1961 to 1963 and its director general from 1966 to 1968. He was elected a member of the Israel Academy of Science in 1963 and won the Israel Prize for Natural Sciences in 1965. He was an outstanding lecturer and had a tremendous enthusiasm for improved science teaching, which he succeeded in communicating to others. He believed that talented youngsters were in this technological age one of a nation's greatest assets, and that every effort should be made by the community to cultivate these talents. He believed that the future of higher education in the sciences was wholly dependent on the basis given at secondary education level. On his initiative the Israel Ministry of Education set up a committee for the promotion of the teaching of natural sciences in Israel in secondary schools and he served as chairman.

BIBLIOGRAPHY: *Europhysics News*, 6 (Nov. 1969), 8.

DESHEH, AVRAHAM (**"Pashanel"**; 1926–2004), Israeli producer. It is hard to imagine contemporary Israeli culture without the titanic influence of Avraham "Pashanel" Desheh. The number of bands and artists who owe their start in the entertainment business to Pashanel is enormous. The *Ha-Gashash ha-Ḥiver comedy trio, the seminal rock band Kaverret, the theater and singing troupe Green Onion, comedian Sefi Rivlin, and pop singer Yardenah Arazi are just some of the top acts who in all likelihood would not have made it had it not been for Pashanel.

Pashanel was born in Tel Aviv as Avraham Greenberg. His first encounter with the world of theater was as a taxi driver, after his release from the British army, when his fares included actors from the Cameri Theater. A career in theater soon became a burning ambition and he achieved his objective in 1957, when he was appointed director of the Zirah Theater. His first major stage success came in 1957 when, along with Chaim *Topol and Uri *Zohar, he created the popular Green Onion 13-member acting-singing troupe. Pashanel, Topol, and Zohar also put out a string of successful of musicals, including *Evita, Joseph and His Dreamcoat*, and *Fiddler On the Roof.*

After the break-up of Green Onion, in 1961, Pashanel and Zohar established the Amami theater production agency, which made a number of movies directed by Zohar, such as *Ḥor ba-Levanah* ("Hole In The Moon") and *Ha-Tarnegol* ("The Rooster"). Around this time Pashanel was also instrumental in establishing the Hammam music club in Jaffa and managed the hit pop group The Roosters, which included Yehoram *Gaon, Shaike Levi, Gavri Banai, and Israeli (Poli) Poliakov. Under Pashanel's guidance, the latter three later became the long-running seminal comic threesome Ha-Gashash ha-Ḥiver.

In his capacity as a producer, Pashanel was a leading force in all areas of the performing arts. He also had a well-developed knack for creating successful teams. The leading collaborations he initiated included the confluence of Ha-Gashash ha-Ḥiver with actor-writers Shaike *Ophir, Nissim *Aloni, and Yossi *Banai, and the all-female pop trio Shokolad Menta Mastik with director-producer Tzadi Tzarfati.

In his heyday, in the 1950s, 1960s, and early 1970s Pashanel was the undisputed king of the Israeli entertainment family. In 2002 he was given a Lifetime Achievement award in recognition of his contribution to Israeli theater, and he received a similar accolade for his movie work at the 2003 Jerusalem International Film Festival.

[Barry Davis (2nd ed.)]

DESKARTA (**Diskarta, Daskarta**), Babylonian town on the river Diala, about 55 mi. (90 km.) northeast of Baghdad. Arab writers ascribe the establishment of the town to Hormizd I (reigned 272–3), though he probably only fortified an already existing village. The town was of great importance for trade with Persia, and it may be assumed that a Jewish community existed there from its reestablishment. The earliest definite references to such a community are from the fourth century. A certain Judah of Deskarta, a disciple of Rava and teacher of Pappa, is frequently mentioned. R. Huna of Deskarta was another disciple of Rava, which leads to the supposition that the Jewish community of Deskarta came under the influence of the academy of Maḥoza. At the time of Chosroes II Parveg (590–628), the town became the Sassanid capital. It was destroyed by Heraclius in 628 and its ruins are still visible south of Shahraban. The name derives from Persian *das* ("district") and Aramaic *karta* ("town"), and is also used in talmudic literature as a name for a place in general, e.g., "the *deskarta* of slaves" (Git. 40a) and "the *deskarta* of the exilarch" (Er. 59a).

BIBLIOGRAPHY: Neusner, Babylonia, 2 (1966), 247; J. Obermeyer, *Landschaft Babylonien* (1929), 146–7.

[Yitzhak Dov Gilat]

DESMAESTRE, JONAH (late 14th century), Majorcan scholar. Desmaestre was the head of the local yeshivah. Despite his piety and full devotion to Torah and talmudic studies, he was well versed in philosophy and mysticism, mathematics and astronomy. Majorca was an important center of astronomical studies. He was the father-in-law of Simeon b. Ẓemaḥ *Duran, and his name is mentioned several times in the responsa of his descendants. In the documents of the kingdom of Aragon, he is called Biona del Maestre. Desmaestre studied in the yeshivah of Barcelona under Perez ha-Kohen. Considered one of the most pious men of his generation, Desmaestre received permission to travel to Aragon to make representations to the king on behalf of his community. With Ḥasdai *Crescas he did much to promote the interests of the Jews of the Kingdom of Aragon. He acted as the leader of the Jews of Majorca and joined forces with the leaders of the other communities in the Kingdom to improve the conditions of the Jews. In 1383, he succeeded in obtaining a grant of privilege from Pedro IV of Aragon, which reinforced the authority of the communal leadership and protected it from harassment by converts to Christianity. He vigorously defended the Jews of Lérida who had been accused of buying the consecrated Host. There is no evidence to confirm the report that Desmaestre died as a martyr in the persecution of 1391.

BIBLIOGRAPHY: Baer, Urkunden, 1 (1929), 542f., index s.v. *Biona del Maestre*; Baer, Spain, index s.v. *Jonah Desmaestre*; H. Jaulus, in: MGWJ, 23 (1874), 250.

DE SOLA, prominent Canadian family in the 19th and early 20th centuries. ABRAHAM DE SOLA (1825–1882), rabbi, author, educator, was born into a London family of limited means. He received his general education at the City of London School and Jewish education from his father, David Aaron, and linguist Louis Loewe, secretary and aide to Moses Montefiore.

De Sola applied to be Second Hazan at Bevis Marks, but David Piza of Montreal got the job. De Sola, in turn, assumed Piza's position at Montreal's Shearith Israel in January 1847 where he used his pulpit to assert the positive value of emancipation for the Jews. He was convinced that Jews, even as they embraced the opportunities which equality offered, need never compromise their beliefs or practices but could remain what he called "consistent" Jews. De Sola lived by this credo. Looking to create a strong Montreal Jewish community, he soon organized a Hebrew Philanthropic Society, then a congregational school modeled on that of Rebbeca Gratz in Philadelphia. He was active in later incarnations of the Philanthropic Society and assumed a leadership role in the fraternal organization Kesher shel Barzel. De Sola also entered the intellectual life of Anglo-Montreal. He joined the Natural History Society, and eventually became its president. In 1848 he was appointed a lecturer in Hebrew and rabbinic literature at McGill College and in 1853 was named a professor of Hebrew and Oriental literature. He was awarded an honorary doctor of laws in 1858.

De Sola was a prolific author. He revised a catechism for use in Jewish schools in 1853, and in 1854 co-authored a Jewish calendar for 50 years, which included up-to-date information on the Jewish communities of North America. In 1873 he purchased from Isaac Leeser's estate the copyright, plates, and some stock of Leeser's Bible translations, Leeser's edition of the Sephardi liturgy (which De Sola considered superior to the Ashkenazi) as well as other works. De Sola published a number of works on the compatibility of science with Bible and Rabbinic Judaism. He joined some of Montreal's leading scientists, most notably the principal of McGill College, J.W. Dawson, in proclaiming the principles of natural theology and disdain for Darwin. De Sola outlined his views on science and religion in his portrayals of Jewish intellectuals as well as in more specialized studies, most notably his 1852–53 serialized "Observations on the sanatory institutions of the Hebrews as bearing upon modern sanatory institutions," published in 1861. De Sola also had an interest in historical issues and published derivative studies on the Jews of France, Poland, and England.

Abraham de Sola joined Montreal's Jewish patricians when he married Esther Joseph in 1852. They had seven children.

[Richard Menkis (2nd ed.)]

Abraham de Sola's eldest son, AARON DAVID MELDOLA (1853–1918), who was born in Montreal, was a Zionist, and the first Canadian-born rabbi. He studied under his father's direction, became his assistant in 1876, and succeeded him on his death in 1882 as rabbi of the Spanish and Portuguese synagogue. He was a member of one of the commissions appointed to deal with the Jewish school question in Quebec as early as 1886. De Sola, who wrote many newspaper articles in defense of Orthodoxy, was appointed first vice president of the Orthodox convention in New York in 1898 and was one of the committee of three who drew up its declaration of principles. In 1902, as vice president of the Union of Orthodox Jewish Congregations, he issued a protest against the Central Conference of American Rabbis for discussing the transfer of the Sabbath to Sunday.

CLARENCE ISAAC (1858–1920), the third son of Abraham de Sola, was a Zionist and an industrialist. De Sola, who was born in Montreal, served as president of the Federation of Canadian Zionist Societies from its inception in 1899 until his death. He was also a member of the Zionist General Council of the World Zionist Organization. De Sola was a leading figure in the Canadian shipbuilding industry and general manager of the Comptoir Belgo-Canadien, the Belgium steel and construction trust. He was responsible for the establishment of a steamship service between Montreal and Antwerp. From 1904 until his death he was Belgian consul in Montreal.

BIBLIOGRAPHY: C.E.M. de Sola, *Jewish Ministers* (1905); JE, 11 (1905), 432–3; B.G. Sack, *History of the Jews in Canada*, 1 (1945), passim; C.E. Hart (ed.), *The Jew in Canada* (1926), passim. **ADD. BIBLIOGRAPHY:** G. Tulchinsky, *Taking Root* (1991), 40–60; R. Menkis, in: I.Y. Zinguer and S.W. Bloom (eds.), *L'antisémitisme éclairé* (2003), 313–31; A. Joseph, *Heritage of a Patriarch* (1995).

[Ben G. Kayfetz]

DE SOLA, JUAN BARTOLOMÉ (c. 1800–1858), Venezuelan general. Much confusion has existed about the place and date of birth of Juan De Sola. Presumably the son of Jeudah De Sola Nunes da Costa and of Sarah Ricardo, he was born c. 1800 on the island of St. Thomas. With the outbreak of the war for independence he joined the army of Gran Colombia (which included New Granada (Colombia) Venezuela, and Ecuador), obtaining the rank of lieutenant at the age of 19. In 1820 he was transferred to the "Bravos de Apure" Battalion, where he remained until the battle of Carabobo (1821). He was promoted to captain and decorated with the Coat of Arms of the "Vencedores de Carabobo" and with the bust of the liberator Simón Bolivar. To facilitate his marriage Juan embraced Catholicism in 1823. In the book where his conversion is registered one may read: "I proceeded to the instruction of Mr. Juan De Sola, Captain of the Battalion Apure, of the Hebrew nation, natural of St. Thomas […] I baptized him solemnly according to the Roman ritual and I imposed upon him the name of Juan Bartolomé de la Concepción." In 1830, Juan Bartolomé, then colonel of artillery, requested Venezuelan nationality, which was granted to him immediately. In 1837 he was appointed provisional governor of the Carabobo province. As president of the Provincial Delegation he sanctioned the ordinance that would create the public lighting system of the province. In 1858, he was promoted to the rank of brigadier general, but he died in Valencia (Venezuela) before he could take up the appointment.

[Jacob Carciente (2nd ed.)]

DESSAU, BERNARDO (1863–1949), Italian experimental physicist. Born in Offenbach, Germany, Dessau became an Italian citizen. He was a member of the Italian Academy of Sciences and professor at the University of Perugia (1904). He acted as *shoḥet* for the small Perugia Jewish community. An active Zionist, he founded *Il Vessillo Israelitico*, the first Italian Zionist periodical. He wrote books on wireless telegraphy, physical and chemical properties of alloys, and physics.

DESSAU, HERMANN (1856–1931), German historian and philologist. The son of the director of a Jewish school, Dessau studied under Theodor *Mommsen and became his collaborator at the *Corpus Inscriptionum Latinarum*. In 1884 he was appointed lecturer and in 1896 professor of ancient history at the University of Berlin; from 1900 he worked as the Latin epigraphist of the Prussian Academy. Dessau's principal studies were related to Latin inscriptions, the political and administrative problems of the Roman Empire, and Latin and patristic literature. He edited and published the basic book in the field of Latin inscriptions, *Inscriptiones Latinae Selectae* (5 vols. in 3, 1892–1916); his work on the Roman Empire, *Geschichte der roemischen Kaiserzeit*, remained incomplete, only the first two volumes being published (1924–30). Dessau was deeply attached to the traditional roots of Judaism. In 1919 he joined the council of the research department of the Akademie fuer die Wissenschaft des Judentums in Berlin. The last chapter of his book on the Roman Empire, entitled "Judaea und die Juden," was directed against the chapter bearing the same title in Mommsen's history of the Roman Empire. His mastery both of Roman history and of talmudic sources enabled him to attempt a reevaluation of the period of the Second Temple in the light of its Jewish character as well as in the context of general history.

BIBLIOGRAPHY: *Neue Deutsche Biographie*, 3 (1957), s.v. **ADD. BIBLIOGRAPHY:** *Enciclopedia Judaica Castellana*, 3 (1948), 473.

DESSAU, PAUL (1894–1979), German composer. The grandson of a cantor, Dessau was born in Hamburg. He was co-répétiteur in Hamburg (1912) and conducted operetta at the Tivoli Theatre, Bremen (1913). In 1919 he became co-répétiteur and conductor in Cologne. In 1925 he was appointed principal conductor at the Stätlische Oper, Berlin, and won the Schott Prize for his Violin Concertino. He left Germany in 1933 and visited Palestine. In 1939 he settled in New York and wrote a number of film scores (such as *Adamah* in 1947), but his political convictions led him to return to East Germany in 1948 and he made his home in East Berlin. Dessau composed in several fields. His vocal music, influenced by the concise verse of Bertolt Brecht (whom he met in New York in 1943), embraced almost every genre from political song to cantata and full-length opera. The latter include the operas *Mutter Courage und ihre Kinder* (1946), *Das Verhoer des Lukullus* (1951), *Puntila* (1957–59), *Lanzelot* (1969), *Einstein* (1971–73), and *Leonce and Lena* (1977–78). Dessau wrote also functional music for theater and radio. In 1936, he composed for the synagogue an oratorio, *Haggadah,* for which Max *Brod supplied the text. His early works were in free tonality; from 1936 he was influenced by the twelve-tone technique of *Leibowitz. After the rigorous separation of West and East Berlin, he remained one of the few artists allowed to commute between the two Germanys. He became a member of the East Berlin Deutsche Akademie der Künste in 1952 and was appointed professor in 1959. He was honored by both the East and West Berlin academies, he received an honorary doctorate from Leipzig University (1974), and four National Prizes of the German Democratic Republic (1953, 1956, 1965, 1974). Among his works are operas for children, the cantata *Requiem for Lumumba* (1963), and symphonic and chamber music.

ADD. BIBLIOGRAPHY: Grove online; MGG; *Baker's Biographical Dictionary*; F. Hennenberg, *Dessau-Brecht Musikalische Arbeiten* (1963), with bibl.; idem, *Paul Dessau* (1965); idem, *Für Sie porträtiert: Paul Dessau* (1974, 1981); J.J. Gordon, "Paul Dessau and his Opera *Einstein*," Ph.D. thesis, University College of Wales (1990).

[Peter Emanuel Gradenwitz / Israela Stein (2nd ed.)]

DESSAUER, FRIEDRICH (1881–1963), German engineer, biophysicist, and philosopher. Born in Aschaffenburg, Dessauer originally worked in the X-ray industry, and in 1921 became professor of biophysics at Frankfurt. He was a Center Party member of the Reichstag from 1924 to 1933, and editor of the *Rhein-Mainische Volkszeitung und Handelsblatt*. When the Nazis came to power he fled to Istanbul, where in 1934 he set up the biophysical and radiological institute. He became professor of experimental physics at Fribourg, Switzerland, 1937, but returned to Frankfurt in 1950 and was reappointed to a professorship there.

Dessauer wrote numerous scientific books and articles as well as many philosophical works. The chief of these were *Leben, Natur, Religion* (1924, 1926²), *Philosophie der Technik* (1927, 1933³), *Mensch und Kosmos* (1948), *Die Teleologie in der Natur* (1949), *Prometheus und die Weltuebel* (1959), and *Was ist der Mensch? Die vier Fragen des Immanuel Kant* (1959). He analyzed the assumptions of science and technology and their connections with philosophical and religious principles.

[Richard H. Popkin]

DESSLER, ELIJAH ELIEZER (1891–1954), one of the personalities of the *Musar movement. Dessler was born in Homel, Russia. His father, Reuben Baer, had been a pupil and subsequently one of the directors of the *bet ha-talmud* in the small town of Kelme (Lithuania), founded by Simḥah Zissel Ziv, the outstanding disciple of Israel *Lipkin (Salanter), founder of the Musar movement. Reuben Baer's home, however, was in Homel where he engaged in business, and there Dessler passed his early youth. At the Kelme *bet ha-talmud*, he pursued talmudic studies and his teachers included Ẓevi Hirsch Broda and Nahum Velvel Ziv, leading exponents of Musar. On the outbreak of World War I he returned to Homel, studying at the yeshivah established there by refugees from the Lithuanian yeshivot and administered by his father. In Homel he came close also to ḥasidic circles and was influenced by their ideas. In 1919 he married the daughter of Nahum Velvel Ziv and went to Riga where he engaged unsuccessfully in business. In 1929 he settled in London where he became the rabbi of a synagogue, first in East London and then in North-East London, and became the supervisor of a large *talmud torah*. He exercised a profound influence on the teaching of Musar, not only because of the profundity of his ideas but on account of his personal ethical conduct. In 1941 he accepted an invitation to become director of a *kolel* for advanced Talmud study in *Gateshead, England, where he also lectured on Musar. He served in an honorary capacity, earning his livelihood by giving private lessons. The *kolel* added to the prestige and development of the Gateshead yeshivah and his influence extended beyond England to other countries, through its graduates who served as heads of yeshivot. In 1947 Dessler accepted the invitation of Rabbi Joseph Kahaneman to become the spiritual supervisor of Ponevezh yeshivah in Bene-Berak, Israel, and there he remained until his death. His teachings were a harmonious combination of the doctrine of Musar, particularly as taught in Kelme, with the concepts of Jewish religious philosophy, *Kabbalah, and *Ḥasidism. Some of his ideas were published by his pupils, in part from his own manuscripts and in part from notes taken from his lectures, *Mikhtav me-Eliyahu* (3 vols., 1955–64). The work contains attempts at a confrontation between Jewish and general philosophy, arising from the problems raised by those of his pupils who had studied philosophy. A periodical named after him is published at irregular intervals in London by his followers, in which his ideas are discussed.

BIBLIOGRAPHY: L. Carmell, in: L. Jung (ed.), *Guardians of our Heritage* (1958), 675–99; *Mikhtav me-Eliyahu*, 1 (1955), biography at the beginning.

[Zvi Kaplan]

DESSOIR, LUDWIG (originally **Leopold Dessauer**; 1810–1874), German actor. He was born in Posen, the son of a merchant. Dessoir first appeared on the stage at the age of 14. From 1831 he acted in provincial theaters in character and heroic roles in classical repertoire (Shakespeare, Goethe, Schiller). He succeeded Karl August Devrients at the theater of Karlsruhe and was invited in 1849 to the Royal Theater in Berlin, where he continued his work for the next 23 years. His ability to analyze and interpret the spiritual content of a role enabled him to render many subtle characterizations. Dessoir was considered one of the finest Shakespearean actors of his time, not only on the German stage, but also in London, where he appeared in 1853. Lear, Othello, Hamlet, and Coriolanus, as well as Faust, Uriel Acosta, and Louis XI, were among his best portrayals.

BIBLIOGRAPHY: O.F. Genischen, *Berliner Hofschauspieler* (1872); G.H. Lewes, *On Actors and the Art of Acting* (1875). **ADD. BIBLIOGRAPHY:** C. Sander, *Ludwig Dessoir – Ein Schauspieler des 19. Jahrhunderts (Rekonstruktion einer Schauspielkunst)* (1967).

DESSOIR, MAX (1867–1947), German philosopher and psychologist, of Jewish origin (he described himself as a "*Vierteljude*"); son of Ludwig *Dessoir. Dessoir studied with Wilhelm Dilthey and received doctorates in philosophy and medicine. He was professor of philosophy in Berlin, 1897–1934 and taught until 1933. He only left Berlin in 1943 and returned to Germany in 1946 and taught at Frankfurt. Dessoir was particularly interested in marginal psychological phenomena, and in 1889 coined the term "parapsychology." He described and criticized the anthroposophy of Rudolph Steiner. Dessoir anticipated *Freud by introducing a theory of the subconscious, based on experiments carried out with hypnosis and dream analysis and psychological observation of daily life. Dessoir was also interested in aesthetics and "the general science of art" – a branch of study he founded. Aesthetic objects (or essences), in his view, include many phenomena in nature and in everyday life; while works of art have not only an aesthetic significance but also possess functions of meaning which embrace the whole range of culture: religious, moral, pedagogical, political, social functions, etc. Dessoir's aesthetics are mainly objectivist. He founded the *Zeitschrift fuer Aesthetik und allgemeine Kunstwissenschaft* in 1906 and was its editor for 30 years. His works include *Das Doppel-Ich* (1890); *Geschichte der neueren deutschen Psychologie* (1894); *Aesthetik und allgemeine Kunstwissenschaft* (1906); *Vom Jenseits der Seele* (1917); *Der Okkultismus in Urkunden*, 3 vols. (1925), ed. by M. Dessoir; *Beitraege zur allgemeinen Kunstwissenschaft*

(1929); *Die Rede als Kunst* (1940); *Buch der Erinnerung* (1946), an autobiography.

BIBLIOGRAPHY: C. Herrmann, *Max Dessoir, Mensch und Werk* (1927); W. Kuehne, *Max Dessoirs Methode…* (1922); A. Werner, in: *Philosophia*, 2 (Belgrade, 1937), 299–307 (Ger.). **ADD. BIBLIOGRAPHY:** A. Kurzweg, *Die Geschichte der Berliner "Gesellschaft für Experimental-Psychologie" mit besonderer Berücksichtigung ihrer Ausgangssituation und Wirkens Max Dessoir* (1976); R. Steiner, *Von Seelenrätseln – Max Dessoir über Antroposophie* (1983[5]).

DETENTION.

In the Bible

The Torah does not recognize the use of imprisonment as a punishment for criminal offenses (see *Imprisonment), but it explicitly mentions the placing of a person in detention as part of the procedure of making a legal determination in the case. Thus we read about the man found gathering wood on the Sabbath – a deed which was clearly considered a very serious offense – who was placed in detention pending completion of the clarification regarding the punishment that would be imposed upon him: "And they put him in custody, because it was not specified what should be done to him [what needed to be done with him]" (Lev. 15:34). The Aramaic translations of this verse interpret the meaning of the word "custody" as holding him in jail, i.e., detention. The Midrash explains that although it was clear that he was liable for the death penalty, it was still not clear by what means he was to be executed and therefore he was put in detention in the meantime (*Sifri*, *Numbers*, 114). Similarly, a man who blasphemed the name of God – another offense that was clearly extremely grave – was placed in detention until it was clarified what should be done with him: "And they put him in custody, that it might be declared unto them at the mouth of the Lord." (Lev. 24:12). Indeed, the punishment imposed on the offender in both cases, according to the command of God, was the death penalty (see *Capital Punishment).

In Talmudic Literature

DETENTION OF THOSE LIABLE FOR CAPITAL PUNISHMENT. On the basis of these sources, tannaitic literature expanded the provisions regarding detention and it was determined that the person condemned to capital punishment should be put in detention: "To teach us that all of those condemned to capital punishment are to be placed in detention" (Sifri, Numbers, 114); However, these words do not indicate the stage at which the offender is placed in detention – whether after the completion of his trial, or when he is still only a suspect; and if at the stage in which he is only a suspect – what kind of evidence is sufficient for this.

DETENTION OF SUSPECTS IN ORDER TO ESTABLISH THE IDENTITY OF THE OFFENDER. In the opinion of Rabbi Judah (second century), detention was also utilized in cases in which the offender is located among a group of innocent people, and it is not known which of them is the murderer. His view diverged from the Sages' view, according to which in such a case all are exempt from detention, in his opinion – "they are all placed in jail" until it becomes apparent which of them is the murderer (Sanhedrin 9:3).

DETENTION OF THOSE CONDEMNED TO DEATH. A person sentenced to death was placed in detention until the sentence was carried out. The Mishna (San. 11:4) and the Tosefta (Zuckermandel edition, San. 11:7) state that the sentence of the stubborn and rebellious son, the rebellious elder, the inciter, the one who leads others astray, the false prophet and the perjured witness is not implemented immediately after sentencing but rather "he is brought up to the High Court in Jerusalem and is kept in custody until the festival and he is executed during the intermediate days of the festival." This is the position of Rabbi Akiva, with which Rabbi Judah disagrees, and he states that in order not to cause the offender to suffer a delay of justice he is to be executed immediately.

DETENTION OF THE SUSPECT ONLY WHEN THERE IS EVIDENCE; HUMAN DIGNITY. In the beginning of the fourth century, the *amoraim* of Ereẓ Israel ruled that the judge may not place a suspect in detention unless there was solid evidence that he had committed the offense. Rabbi Yose, in the Jerusalem Talmud (San. 7, 8), rejects the notion that it is permissible to detain a person in the street only because of the suspicion that he has committed murder, insofar as such an act constitutes an affront to his dignity: "Can it be that we will seize someone in the marketplace and humiliate him?" On the basis of the Mishna in Tractate Sanhedrin (7:5) Rabbi Yose rules that a person suspect of having committed a capital crime is detained even prior to being judged, but only in cases in which there are witnesses who testify that the suspect committed the murder in which case it is permissible to arrest and detain him.

KEEPING A PERSON IN JAIL UNTIL THE RESULTS OF THE OFFENSE ARE CLARIFIED. In addition to the detention of a person suspected of having committed murder, talmudic literature provides that a person may be detained even prior to a determination of his liability for the death penalty, when it is absolutely certain that he committed the offense, and as a result of which it may subsequently transpire that he is liable for capital punishment. Regarding a person who strikes and injures another, the Torah states that, once the victim gets up from his sickbed and it is clear that he will not die from the assault, the perpetrator is only liable for the various heads of damages (see *Damages): "And if men strive together, and one smite another with a stone, or with his fist, and he die not, but keeps his bed: if he rise again, and walk abroad upon his staff, then shall he that struck him be acquitted: only he shall pay for the loss of his time, and shall cause him to be thoroughly healed" (Ex. 21:18–19). The *Mekhilta* (*Mekhilta of Rabbi Ishmael*, Horowitz edition, *Mishpatim*, *Parashah* 6) rejects the possibility that the attacker "will provide guarantors and go walking in the market" until the victim recovers and it provides that "he is detained until the victim recovers."

The Babylonian Talmud cites a similar interpretation of this verse in the name of the *Amora*, Rabba, according to whom it is not possible that the Torah is teaching us that if the victim recovers, the attacker will not be executed, because this is self-evident. Consequently, the purpose of the verse in the Torah must be to teach us that the attacker is held in jail until the fate of the victim is clear; if he died – the attacker is executed and if he recovered – the attacker will only pay damages (TB, Ket. 33, 2; San. 78, 2). According to Rashi's explanation (San., *ibid.*), the purpose of the detention is to prevent the attacker from fleeing.

In the Post-Talmudic Literature

HOLDING A PERSON IN DETENTION – MERELY A PROCEDURAL TOOL OR PART OF THE PUNISHMENT. Regarding the detention of a suspect in a criminal offense, we have found a dispute from the period of the *geonim*. Their dispute dealt with the question of whether it was permissible to detain a person on the Sabbath or a holy day, and from their words we learn of a different outlook regarding the essence of detention. Rav Paltoi Gaon (Pumbedita, ninth century; Halakhic Rulings [Miller], 135) answered that he must be put in detention but he should not be flogged because flogging constitutes a desecration of the Sabbath (see *Flogging). In his opinion, the detention is for the sole purpose of preventing him from fleeing, and it does not contain any punitive element. About 150 years later, *Sherira Gaon held in an opposing opinion, that "it is not permissible to put a person in jail on a holy day, and all the more so this is impermissible on the Sabbath …" (*Shibbolei ha-Leket*, 60); according to his view, the detention itself is part of the sentence and of the punishment, and therefore it is impermissible on the Sabbath. It should be noted that the halakhic authorities continued to consider this issue, which was also dealt with by Joseph Caro (Beit Yosef, OḤ, end of sec. 263), the Rama (Shulkhan Arukh, OḤ, 339, 4) and Jacob Reischer (Responsa *Shevut Yaakov* 1:14 Germany, the 18th century).

THE AMOUNT OF EVIDENCE NECESSARY IN ORDER TO KEEP A SUSPECT IN DETENTION. The discussion in the Jerusalem Talmud, *supra*, regarding the detention of a suspect from the moment that there is evidence against him, has been interpreted in various ways: R. Nissim Gerondi (*Ḥidushei Haran*, San. 56, 1) interprets that the mere existence of witnesses is insufficient in order to place the suspect in detention; rather they must actually appear and testify before the court adjudicating the matter, and only then will it be possible to place the suspect in detention. In an opposing opinion, Rabbi Moshe *Margoliot (*Penei Moshe*, Jerusalem Talmud, *ibid.*) interprets the words of the Jerusalem Talmud as providing that it is sufficient that the existence of witnesses has been established.

OVERALL SURVEY OF THE LAWS OF DETENTION AND RELEASE ON BOND – THE RESPONSUM OF THE RIBASH. R. Isaac bar Sheshet *Perfet (Responsa of the Ribash, sec. 236) received an inquiry from the heads of the community in the city of Tiroal in the Aragon region of Spain regarding the law applicable to a Jew who was suspected of being an informer and who was prosecuted before the rabbinical court in Tiroal. In the question posed to him various problems are raised, both substantive and procedural, regarding the crime of informing, including the issue of release of the suspect from jail upon the posting of bail. The Ribash replies in a clear and leading *responsum* on this subject, and sets forth the rules of the detention:

a. The detention is only in the case of a suspect in a criminal offense for which the punishment is "a sentence pertaining to the body of the guilty party," i.e., capital punishment or imprisonment, and not when the expectation is that he "will only be obligated to pay money."

b. The rabbinical court will order the detention of a suspect only if it was convinced that "the prosecutor's claims are substantiated" – in other words, that the evidence is sufficient to support a reasonable suspicion against him.

c. The legitimate grounds for detention are (1) to ensure that the suspect will stand trial; (2) to ensure that the suspect, if convicted, will serve his sentence; (3) it is unacceptable for the suspect to be "strolling about the marketplace" while the court is adjudicating his case. This rationale could be interpreted from the point of view of "public opinion," insofar as the public is likely to be disturbed by the contradiction inherent in the fact that, while a trial for a serious crime is underway, the suspect is free to go where he pleases. However, it seems that it should be interpreted in accordance with the accepted grounds for detention that are in use in the contemporary judicial system, according to which the suspect's "walking in the marketplace" may obfuscate evidentiary material, intimidate witnesses, endanger the public inasmuch as he may commit additional crimes, etc.

d. Regarding release on bail – a suspect who is held in detention cannot be released on the basis of bail posted by others, for the reason that if he flees and does not stand trial, on the one hand the obligation to try criminals will not be fulfilled, and, on the other hand, there is no reason for those who posted the bail to pay for a crime perpetrated by another.

From the words of the Ribash, therefore, it may be stated that a suspect may be placed in detention only if the crime he is suspected of having committed would render him subject to capital punishment or imprisonment, the court is satisfied that the prosecutor has solid grounds for charging him and there is concern that if he is not placed in detention the safety of the public will be jeopardized or that there will be an obstruction of justice.

DETENTION OF A PERSON UNTIL THE CONSEQUENCES OF HIS ACTION ARE CLARIFIED. Regarding one who strikes another, when it is still not known whether the victim will die or not, the Rambam held (Hilkhot Roẓe'aḥ, 4, 3) according to the words of the Babylonian Talmud cited above, that the court must evaluate the injury; if in its opinion the victim will die from it, then "the perpetrator is imprisoned immediately and they wait for this," to see if he will indeed die, in which case the perpetrator will be executed, and if he recovers, the perpetrator will only be liable to pay monetary damages.

In the State of Israel

In the State of Israel, the law regarding the problem of detentions has been the subject of controversy, and has even seen vicissitudes, and the provisions of Jewish law have had a decisive role in its formation. We will expand on this issue somewhat, insofar as we can learn from it the appropriate manner in which the Israeli legal system should absorb values from its roots planted in the heritage of Israel and in Jewish law, in particular regarding significant issues like detention, that have bearing on human dignity and freedom.

In the past, before governing legislation was adopted regarding this issue, there was an opinion that the court could arrest a suspect in a serious crime even if there was no apprehension regarding public safety or obstruction of justice. The main justification for this procedure was to ensure the public's trust in the effectiveness of the criminal justice system.

A thorough examination of the approach of Jewish law to the laws of detention is found in the decision of the Supreme Court in the Abukasis case (BSH 71/78, *State of Israel v. Rachel Abukasis*, 32(2) PD 240). In the wake of the appeal of the extension of the arrest order, the Court (Justice Menachem Elon) was asked to make a determination regarding the principles behind the laws of detention, and the Court discussed the position of Jewish law regarding this problem at length. The Court presented the principles that were set forth by the Ribash and adopted them, in order to rule, by way of judicial legislation, relying on "the democratic principles of our legal system and the principles of our historical and national law – the Jewish law" (BSHP 2169/92 *Suissa v. The State of Israel*, 46(3) PD 338, p. 342), that the seriousness of the crime is not sufficient in itself in order to hold a person in detention – except in cases of murder, etc., that were set forth in the legislation.

In 1988, the Knesset passed an amendment to the Rules of Criminal Procedure, which explicitly provided that the seriousness of the crime, in and of itself, would not serve as grounds for detention of a defendant prior to his trial, unless there was proof of a reasonable basis to fear that the public security would be endangered or that there would be an obstruction of justice, or, if as a result of the seriousness of certain crimes enumerated in the law, there was a presumption of such a danger.

In a later decision of the Supreme Court (the *Suissa* decision, *supra*), the Court (Justice Menachem Elon) emphasized that, in the wake of the legislation in the State of Israel of the Basic Law: Human Dignity and Freedom, whose stated goal is to solidify the values of the State of Israel as a Jewish and democratic state, "the justification for abrogating this basic right (of individual freedom) … is that if he goes free he will endanger the safety of the public or of an individual or will obstruct justice, and these alone. Our feelings of revulsion due to the seriousness of the crime or our concern regarding the effectiveness of the criminal system cannot justify abrogating a person's freedom and detaining him behind bars; the legislature designated alternatives to achieve these purposes, such as house arrest, and additional means" (*ibid.*, p. 347).

At present, the law in the State of Israel is set forth in the Rules of Criminal Procedure (Enforcement Powers – Arrests), 1996. Pursuant to this law, a judge may order the detention of a suspect before the filing of an indictment only when he is convinced that there is a reasonable suspicion that the person committed a crime whose punishment is more than three months' imprisonment, and in addition there is a reasonable basis to believe that if the suspect is not detained the result will be endangerment of the safety of an individual or of society at large or of State security or obstruction of justice or, if there are special reasons that necessitate detention, in order to carry out an investigation (sec. 13). Detention such as this, prior to the filing of an indictment, is limited in duration.

After the filing of an indictment, the Court is authorized to order the detention of a suspect until the completion of legal proceedings, when, as set forth above, there is reason to believe that otherwise an obstruction of justice will result or that the suspect presents a danger, and in addition to this, also in the case of the most serious crimes, involving serious violence, threat to public security or domestic violence (sec. 21).

A policeman is authorized to arrest a person even without a court order in circumstances in which he has a reasonable basis to believe that the person represents a threat to the security of the public or of a person, or that the failure to order his detention will result in an obstruction of justice (sec. 23). In all cases of arrest and detention by a policeman, a police officer must approve the arrest with a short time, and a judge must confirm the arrest within 24 hours.

The similarities between these detention provisions and the limits on holding a person in detention that the Ribash set out in his *responsum*, *supra* can be clearly seen.

As distinguished from the holding of the Ribash, who ruled that when there are grounds for detention the suspect may not be released on bail, the provisions of Israeli law set forth that, as long as it is possible to substitute release on bail or other restricting terms for the detention, it is obligatory to do so.

(See also *Imprisonment.)

BIBLIOGRAPHY: M. Elon, *Ha-Mishpat Ha-Ivri* (1988), 3:1464f., 1551ff.; idem, *Jewish Law* (1994), 4:1739f., 1843ff.; idem "Imprisonment in Jewish Law," in: *Jubilee Book in Honor of Pinchas Rosen* (1962); idem, "Basic Laws: Establishing the Values of a Jewish and Democratic State (Problems in Criminal Law)," in: *Mehkarei Mishpat (Bar-Ilan Law Studies)*, 13:1 (1996), 27–86; L. Kaminer, "Prison Sentences in Israel," in: *Tekhumin*, 9 (1988), 134–55.

[Menachem Elon (2nd ed.)]

DETROIT, largest city in Michigan, U.S., with a Jewish population of around 103,000 (with Ann Arbor) in 2001, comprising 1.9% of the city's total population. Part of the distinction of Detroit Jews derives from the nature and history of Detroit. Its economy, the first to emerge as distinctly 20th century American – that is, mobile, grounded in automobiles, roads, and related industries, and therefore suburbs, shopping centers, and massive industrial complexes like the Ford Rouge Plant – produced enormous wealth or the prospects of it. If Jewish immigration to the U.S. stopped in 1924, immigration to Detroit did not. Jews came from other American cities, seeking employment in the Ford factories or the related industries. Sometimes families that had been in this country for as many as 20 years picked up and left places like New York, Philadelphia, Indianapolis, Cleveland, or Baltimore to come to Detroit.

1760–1840

Jews had come to Michigan in the 18th century as fur traders and merchants. Chapman Abraham, Detroit's first known Jewish settler, arrived in Detroit in 1762 and became a successful trader for more than 20 years. Levi Solomons, partner of Chapman Abraham, was captured by the Indians near Detroit during the 1763 Pontiac Conspiracy. Chapman Abraham was captured during the 1763 Indian siege of Detroit, and after two harrowing months was released in exchange for an Indian chief. During the American Revolution Abraham fought in Canada against the invading Americans, remaining a loyalist all his life. Later records show he lived in Detroit in 1783. Hayman *Levy of New York, largest fur trader among the colonists and at one time a partner of Levi Solomons, carried on extensive business with Detroit merchants from 1774.

Ezekiel *Solomon, Michigan's first known Jewish settler, arrived in Fort Michilimackinac (today Mackinaw City) in 1761, and lived in Detroit in 1789. Moses David, of the well-known Montreal *David family, lived in Sandwich (now Windsor), Ontario, in 1792, when Sandwich and Detroit were still under British rule. Isaac *Moses joined Zion Lodge, Detroit's first Masonic lodge, in 1798, two years after Detroit's occupation by the Americans. Louis Benjamin was awarded a new plot of ground in 1808 to indemnify him for his loss in Detroit's great fire of 1805. Frederick E. Cohen, an English Jew, was in Detroit in 1837 during the Canadian rebellion, when he served in the Canadian militia. He became a prominent portrait painter, the first Jewish artist in Michigan. His self-portrait hangs in the Detroit Institute of Arts.

1840–1880

German Jews arrived in Detroit in significant numbers in the 1840s. Charles E. Bresler, a settler of the Ann Arbor-Ypsilanti area in the 1830s, moved to Detroit in 1844. He dealt in horses, furs, and wool, and made a fortune importing steel pens. He was one of the incorporators of Detroit's first Jewish congregation, Temple Beth El. Edward Kanter arrived in Detroit that same year, moving to Mackinac the following year where he was employed by the American Fur Company. Later he worked for the Leopold Brothers, pioneers on the island of Mackinac in the fishery business, and fur traders. Kanter returned to Detroit in 1852 and became Detroit's first Jewish banker and the first Michigan Jew to serve in the state legislature. Kanter Street is named after him. Simon Freedman, a settler of Adrian, Michigan, in the early 1840s, established a large dry goods business in Detroit around 1844, joined by his family. Like Besler, the Freedman brothers were among the founders of Beth El: Joseph was the first secretary of the congregation, Simon served as president, and Herman was president of the religious school board. In the 1870s David J. Wockum was the first Jew to serve on the Detroit Board of Education.

In 1850 Congregation Beth El was founded in the home of Sarah and Isaac Couzens by 12 German Jewish families. In 1851 a half acre of land on Champlain (later Lafayette) Street was purchased for a cemetery, the oldest Jewish congregational cemetery in Michigan. Beth El congregation's first rabbi, Samuel Marcus, was interred there in 1854 during a cholera epidemic. Originally an Orthodox congregation, Beth El became Reform in 1861, resulting in the withdrawal of 17 members who formed the Orthodox Shaarey Zedek congregation, later an important Conservative congregation. Beth El became a large and influential Reform Congregation, and among its leading rabbis was Kaufmann *Kohler (1869–71).

1880–1914

By 1880 there were approximately 1,000 Jews in Detroit, more than half from Eastern Europe, the others, German Jews. Detroit's Jewish population leaped during the so-called Great Migration from Eastern Europe, especially from 1880 to 1910 and from 1917 to 1924 when the government instituted its immigration restrictions. By 1920 the number of Jews in Detroit had reached almost 35,000, a 247% increase in 10 years while the general population of Detroit increased only 114%. There was one Reform congregation, Temple Beth El, and four Orthodox congregations, Shaarey Zedek, B'nai Israel (1871), B'nai Jacob (1875), and Beth Jacob (1878). Three charities existed: the Ladies' Society for the Support of Hebrew Widows and Orphans, popularly known as "Frauen Verein" (1863), Beth El Hebrew Relief Society, and Shaarey Zedek Jewish Relief Society. B'nai B'rith, Kesher Shel Barzel, and the Free Sons of Israel all had lodges in Detroit, and there was one flourishing social club, the Phoenix Social Club (1872).

Relations between the Ostjuden newcomers, most of whom were of the Orthodox tradition, and the more acculturated German Jews, primarily members of Temple Beth El, were ambivalent. Considerations of class, social standing, religious outlook, and degree of Americanization tended to keep the groups separate. However, the German community's sense of obligation to their less fortunate coreligionists overcame their feelings of antipathy, at least publicly, with the founding of two new charitable societies, the Hebrew Ladies' Sewing Society (1882) and the Self-Help Circle (1889), organized to assist the new immigrants, although many of them felt patronized. In 1896 a *Detroit News* article noted that "it is very rare that a German Israelite seeks relief from anybody," contrasting German Jews with East European Jews who needed charity. By 1903, however, a *Detroit Free Press* article pointed out that Russian Jews, while not so successful in business as German Jews, were "making their way upward." The article listed leading Jewish businessmen and four synagogues, the Division Street Talmud Torah, the House of Shelter, and the Hebrew Free Loan Office and concluded that Russian Jews were "intelligent, sensible, hard-working people, sober and religious, of good moral character and determined to get ahead in the world. They are men with characteristics that make any nation strong." Their German counterparts rarely agreed.

Some Eastern Europeans, conscious of the gulf between themselves and the city's German Jewish community, preferred to establish communal institutions more responsive to their special needs. The most important of these were the Talmud Torah Institute (1897), Hebrew Free Loan Association (1895), and Workman's Circle (Arbeter Ring) (1907). By 1917, Branch 156 of the Workmen's Circle was not only the largest secular Jewish organization in Detroit, but the largest Workmen's Circle branch in North America. It was the first of a wave of secular Jewish institutions that included Labor Zionist organizations, the Yiddish Sholom Aleichem Institute, Hayim Greenberg, and Farband Shule and the five IWO Communist-affiliated Hersh Leckert Schools. When the Farband Shule declared itself "the non-parteische" (non-partisan) school, it meant it was not a Hersh Leckert School.

Realizing that the profusion of Jewish charities resulted in unnecessary duplication and waste, Leo M. *Franklin, rabbi of Temple Beth El (1899–1941), united the Beth El Hebrew Relief Society, Hebrew Ladies' Sewing Society, Jewish Relief Society, and Self-Help Circle into the United Jewish Charities (1899). David W. Simons was the first president and Blanche Hart was superintendent until 1923. Despite differences, the German and the East European groups managed to cooperate in communal undertakings. This was exemplified when Temple Beth El, oldest and most prestigious congregation in the city, agreed to join the Kehilla (1911) organized by the Orthodox community. Prominent rabbis of the period included Leo Franklin; Judah Leib Levin, who was instrumental in organizing the United Orthodox Hebrew Congregations in the early 1900s, and founded the Yeshivah Beth Yehuda; and Abraham *Hershman of Conservative Shaarey Zedek (1908–46), an ardent Zionist.

Starting in the 1880s, Detroit's Jewish communities concentrated most heavily in the retail and wholesale clothing trades, mostly as proprietors of their own businesses, and in the clerical or white collar occupations as salesmen, insurance agents, and office workers. While Jews did not dominate any trade the way they did the garment industry in New York, a Jewish "monopoly" in Detroit's economic life did develop in the waste material and scrap metal business. By the late 1880s Jews outnumbered gentiles in this industry, and by the 1890s it had become almost solely a "Jewish" industry. This dominance was to continue after World War II.

Jews participated in the political life of Detroit during this period. Samuel Goldwater, a city alderman in 1894 and the Democratic Party's candidate for mayor in 1895, was the major force behind the organization of the Michigan Federation of Labor (1889). David E. Heineman served as a member of the state legislature (1896–1901) and Detroit's City Council (1902–09), and was city controller during 1910–13. In 1909 he was president of the American League of Municipalities; he also designed the flag of Detroit. Charles C. Simons was a state senator (1902). David W. Simons was a member of the first nine-man city council (1918).

1915–1940

The outbreak of World War I ended European immigration to Detroit until 1920. In 1915 the Jewish communities contained one Reform and 19 Orthodox congregations and by 1940 the Jewish population had risen to 85,000 as the number of congregations rose to 48. During these years the Jews of Detroit strengthened their communal organization. A survey of communal needs made in 1923 by the Bureau of Jewish Social Research of New York resulted in the organization, in 1926, of the Jewish Welfare Federation. Its first director was Morris D. *Waldman. Eventually housed in the Fred M. *Butzel Memorial Building, the Federation included among its affiliate agencies the Jewish Community Council, Jewish Community Center, Jewish Family and Children's Service, Jewish Home for the Aged, Fresh Air Society, Hebrew Free Loan Association, Federation Apartments, Jewish House of Shelter, Jewish Vocational Service and Community Workshop, Resettlement Service, Midrasha-College of Jewish Studies, Sinai Hospital and Shiffman Clinic, United Jewish Charities, and the United Hebrew Schools. The Jewish Community Council, organized in 1936, comprised 340 organizations and immediately took an active role in urban affairs, the civil rights movement, holding joint meetings with the NAACP and African American clergy. They would later offer staunch support of Israel. The first community-wide fund drive of the Jewish Welfare Federation in 1926 had 3,185 contributors; in 1940 there were 20,440 contributors; and in 1967 and 1969 the city's Allied Jewish Campaigns raised two of the highest per capita totals in the U.S.

Jewish education received a boost in 1919 when the United Hebrew Schools was organized by a merger of two *talmud torahs*. By 1940 the United Hebrew Schools had ten branches. In 1925 Congregation Beth El opened a College of Jewish Studies, and in 1940 an Institute on Judaism for Christian Clergymen. In addition to the various congregational Sunday and Hebrew schools and the secular schools, Jewish education had been fostered by the Beth Yehuda Day and Afternoon School, the Hillel Day School, and the Akiva Hebrew Day School.

If Detroit had become known for its modern, industrial achievements, it also gained a more infamous, less savory reputation that set it apart from other cities. It was unfortunately tarnished by its social and cultural blights. Racism and antisemitism may have been common features of the American cultural landscape in the 20th century, but their malevolence in Detroit was unmatched anywhere else. Father Charles Coughlin's vitriolic antisemitic national radio broadcasts in the 1930s, Henry Ford's anti-Jewish newspaper campaign in the *Dearborn Independent* during the 1920s, the Black Legion's night-riders and lynching, Gerald L.K. Smith and others, still evoke fear and anger in Detroit Jews. The 1930s also saw Detroit's German American Bund become fairly active. Along with news of the events in Europe, more subtle actions like department store ads from J.L. Hudson's that read "only Gentiles need apply," and public swimming pools that did not allow Jews to swim, or restrictive covenants that prevented Jews from purchasing or renting houses in Pleasant Ridge or Grosse Pointe or Birmingham, appreciably increased anxiety among Jews in Detroit.

The UJC 1923 Survey had noted: there appeared to be "no Jewish labor class consciousness in Detroit." While that lack of "labor class consciousness" may have been pervasive, organized Jewish groups, like the Jewish Community Council, the Workmen's Circle, the more than 80 *landsmannschaften*, supported the labor movement in Detroit. Perhaps the most notable example of this was the Detroit Laundry and Linen Drivers Association founded and led by Isaac Litwak in 1934. Within two years it had become Teamster Local 285 and in 1937 carried out no fewer than 12 major strikes. Unique among Jewish urban businesses, 25% of the laundry and linen workers in Detroit in 1936 were Jews. Locked out of other, more traditional Jewish enterprises like department stores because of antisemitism, Jews logically gravitated from tailoring and rag peddling to this trade. Nearly 90% of the laundry and linen industry was owned by Jews. Yet, in 1937, picket lines were attacked by goons, Litwak was severely beaten several times, once dragging himself to the line; he was arrested and joined in jail by Jimmy Hoffa, who made sure Litwak was not beaten or killed. The union triumphed in 1937 as it brought unorganized drivers earning $18/wk to contractual arrangements guaranteeing $95. The turmoil was typical of the early days of union organizing in Detroit, but with added emotional trauma in this case: although no charges were brought, it was clear that Jewish owners or their surrogates had hired Jewish hoodlums from the remnants of the notorious Jewish Purple Gang, to beat and break Jewish workers and their union.

Post-World War II

This period witnessed a growth in prosperity among the Jews of Detroit, and increasing mobility characterized by a steady move to the suburbs. The community's religious institutions were consolidated: by 1968 there were 23 Orthodox, six Conservative, four Reform, and one humanistic congregation founded by Rabbi Sherwin Wine, the Birmingham Temple, in the Detroit metropolitan area. Prominent in Jewish and general community affairs was Rabbi Morris *Adler, who served Congregation Shaarey Zedek from 1938 to 1966, when he was tragically shot in his pulpit and killed. A constant of Detroit Jewish history has been movement. By the time Jews began to move into Oak Park, the first suburb northwest of Detroit, beginning around 1948, an organized or identifiable Jewish presence in Detroit had existed for a hundred years. In that century, perhaps nothing characterized that people more than its movement – mytho-biblical in its quick, successive generational wanderings and in its group cohesion. It seemed that Jews moved en masse about every 20–30 (not to say 40) years. Morris Waldman, Federation's first executive director, who arrived in 1924, observing the rapid evacuation of the Hastings neighborhood in favor of the Westminster-Oakland area, called the phenomenon a *hegira*, a mass migration. The pattern of Jewish settlement in Detroit from 1840 to 1940 was a northwest exodus: from Lower Hastings to Upper Hastings, to Oakland between 1910 and 1940, to the Twlefth Street and Dexter areas just west of Oakland, to Northwest Detroit, from the late 1930s to the 1960s. After World War II, Oak Park, then Southfield became the greener pastures, where Jews could buy the typical brick ranch houses, in the midst of trees and open spaces, followed quickly by West Bloomfield and Farmington Hills. When correlated with generational, socio-economic upward mobility, such a prolonged series of moves seems to have sprung, in part, from a desire for larger homes, more space, and the pursuit of symbols of economic success. It mirrored the non-Jewish, upwardly mobile middle class abandonment of the central cities for the suburbs, the American dream of the 1950s: suburban life. As each generation of Jews became more educated, more successful, more American, and more assimilated, the wish to demonstrate all those features strengthened and took the form of new and bigger or better homes in new neighborhoods. Yet more than a quest for symbols of educational and economic achievement accounts for the regular relocation of whole communities. Federation surveys implied that, for all their tolerance, many Jews retained stereotypic views of African Americans and feared living in the same neighborhoods, although they often supported civil rights and defended blacks in that arena. In the Hastings Street neighborhood, long after Jews had moved their residences from there, they retained businesses. In the 1920s, 1930s, and 1940s often only Jewish merchants would allow blacks to shop in their stores. And only Jews would sell their businesses to blacks as white, non-Jewish racists grew more hostile to black neighbors – and to Jewish neighbors or businessmen. As black workers moved into Detroit, they occupied the areas in which Jews lived, and fears or prejudices on both sides fostered the Jewish moves.

A prominent Jewish community leader was Max M. *Fisher (d. 2005), long associated with the UJA, United Israel Appeal, and American Jewish Committee. As war seemed imminent in the Middle East in 1967, Fisher was flown from his yacht in the Aegean (where he was vacationing with Henry Ford II) to Tel Aviv, where he learned of Israel's needs and strategies. When he returned to his yacht, he convinced Ford to write a personal check for $100,000 and took Detroit by storm. Working with his friend Paul Zuckerman, who chaired the Israel Emergency Defense Fund, Fisher, just after a record-breaking UJA drive that had raised $5,627,136, cajoled, harangued, and convinced the Jews of Detroit to "give as you never gave before." Detroiters gave $4,700,000. Jewish Detroit had never been more united.

As Jewish professional success grew, and vestiges of anti-Jewish discrimination remained, Jews responded with specific actions. When Jewish physicians were blocked from practicing at some Detroit hospitals, Sinai Hospital was created; Jewish lawyers led the way in ending "restrictive covenants" in the Detroit metropolitan area and in reforming the civil rights codes in the Michigan Constitution. Jews were to be found in every area of the city's economic life, although despite the prominence of automobile manufacturing in Detroit, few Jews are employed in this industry. The occupational sphere where Jews have predominated is the waste industry, continuing their control of it from the 1890s. By the late 1960s almost 55 percent of those Jews who were employed could be classed in the manager or proprietor class. By 1970 almost 25 percent of the Jewish working force was in the professions, while 73 percent were white-collar workers. Less than 10 per cent of the Jewish population were blue-collar workers.

Jews prominent in political life included Melvin Ravitz, councilman (1969), and Sander *Levin, state senator and chairman of the State Democratic Committee (1969). Sander's brother, Carl, has served three terms in the U.S. Senate and Debbie Stabenow is Michigan's other senator (2000). Among noted civic leaders have been David A. *Brown (1875–1958); Max M. Fisher, who, after the Detroit Riots of 1967, led the foundation of New Detroit to try to reconstruct the city; Norman Drachler, superintendent of the Detroit Public Schools; Leonard N. Simons, president of the Detroit Historical Commission; Alfred A. May, president of the Detroit Round Table of Christians and Jews; Lawrence Fleischman, past president of the Detroit Institute of Arts Commission, and numerous others.

Detroit Jews have a distinguished record as jurists at the state and national level. Henry M. *Butzel was justice of the Supreme Court of Michigan; Charles C. Simons, a judge of the United States Circuit Court of Appeals; Lawrence Gubow and Theodore Levin, district court judges (1969); and S. Jerome Bronson and Charles Levin, judges of the state court of appeals (1969), and Avern Cohn, a federal judge. Jews of Detroit also play a prominent part in the cultural life of the city. When the Detroit Symphony Orchestra was organized in 1918, Ossip Gabrilowitsch became the principal conductor. He filled the post until his death in 1935 when Victor Kolar succeeded him. Mischa Mischakoff was concertmaster. Karl Haas was director of fine arts of radio station WJR and president of the Interlochen Arts Academy, a position then held by Robert Luby; concert pianist Mischa Kottler was director of music at radio station WWJ; Harry Weinberg hosted a long-lived Yiddish Radio Hour; Littman's People's Theatre featured everything from high drama with leading Yiddish speaking actors to burlesque. Albert *Kahn, world-renowned architect, built the city's General Motors Building, Fisher Building, and New Center Building, among many others. Charles E. Feinberg (d. 1988) was an internationally known collector of Jewish ceremonial art and authority on the poet Walt Whitman. Detroit's Jewish population remains a diverse and significant part of the city's culture.

BIBLIOGRAPHY: M. Tumin, *Intergroup Conflicts in Northwest Detroit* (1945); Katz, in: *Detroit Historical Society Bulletin* (Feb. 1950), 4–9; Meyer, in: JSOS, 2 (1940); *Detroit Jewish Chronicle*, 1–53 (1916–51); G.B. Catlin, *Story of Detroit* (1923); J.A. Miller, *Detroit Yiddish Theater, 1920–1937* (1967); I.I. Katz, *Beth El Story* (1955); Rockaway, in: *Michigan History*, 52 (1968), 28–36; Goldberg and Sharp, in: M. Sklare (ed.), *The Jews* (1958), 107–18; Meyer, in: S.M. Robison (ed.), *Jewish Population Studies* (1943), 109–30. **ADD. BIBLIOGRAPHY:** R.A. Rockaway, *The Jews of Detroit: 1762–1914* (1986); idem, *But He Was Good To His Mother: The Lives and Crimes of Jewish Gangsters* (2000); S. Bolkosky, *Harmony and Dissonance: Voices of Jewish Identity in Detroit, 1914–1967* (1991); S. Glazer, *Detroit* (1965); J. Levin Cantor, *Jews in Michigan* (2001); N. Baldwin, *Henry Ford and the Jews: The Mass Production of Hate* (2002).

[Irving I. Katz and Robert Rockaway / Sidney Bolkosky (2nd ed.)].

DEUEL, HANS ERWIN (1916–1962), Swiss agricultural chemist and expert on plant gums and pectins. He was born in Leipzig, Germany, and went to Switzerland in 1934. Deuel's entire working career was spent at the Technische Hochschule at Zurich where he became professor of agricultural chemistry in 1949. He was primarily interested in the polysaccarides, relating properties such as gelation and complex formation with their structural features. In the field of soil science he investigated the ion exchange properties of plant roots, organic weathering through the degradation of clays by orthodiphenols, carbohydrates in soils, and the chemistry of humic substances.

BIBLIOGRAPHY: Neukom, in: *Nature*, 193 (1962), 927.

[Samuel Aaron Miller]

DEUTCH, JOHN M. (1938–), director, U.S. Central Intelligence Agency (1995–96); deputy secretary of defense (1994–95). Born in Brussels, Belgium, Deutch came to the United States in 1940 with his family to escape Nazism and pursued a B.A. in history and economics from Amherst College as well as a B.S. in Chemical Engineering from Massachusetts Institute of Technology, where he earned his Ph.D. in physical chemistry (1965). He first served as a systems analyst at the Office of the Secretary of Defense and later as an assistant professor at Princeton (1967–70) before returning to MIT, where he was a professor of chemistry, dean of science, and provost (1982–90). He subsequently became an institute professor at MIT.

Deutch spent his career shuttling between academia and government service on the Cambridge-Washington axis. From 1977 to 1980 he served as director of Energy Research, acting assistant secretary for energy technology, and undersecretary of energy. In 1993, President Clinton nominated him as undersecretary of defense for acquisitions and technology. In March 1994 he became deputy secretary and then left the Defense Department to become director of the Central Intelligence Agency from May 1995 until the conclusion of Clinton's first term.

A significant security breach marred Deutch's sterling reputation. He stored top-secret information on unsecured home computers and kept private journals of his public work. Deutsch had his security clearance revoked. Criminal investigations were concluded when President Clinton pardoned him before leaving office in January 2001.

BIBLIOGRAPHY: L.S. Maisel and I. Forman, *Jews in American Politics* (2001).

[Michael Berenbaum (2nd ed.)]

DEUTERONOMY (Heb. סֵפֶר דְּבָרִים, *Sefer Devarim,* short for סֵפֶר וְאֵלֶּה הַדְּבָרִים, *Sefer ve-elleh ha-devarim*, "The Book of 'These Are the Words'"), the fifth book of the Pentateuch. The name Deuteronomy is derived from the Greek translation of מִשְׁנֵה הַתּוֹרָה *mishneh ha-torah* (Deut. 17:8) by Tò Δευτερονόμιον *Deuteronomion*, "the second law" or "the repeated law," whence the Latin *Deuteronomium*. Strictly speaking, *mishneh ha-torah* in its biblical context means "a copy of the law." Nonetheless, "second/repeated law" is an appropriate name for the book, inasmuch as Deuteronomy repeats law and history, known from what in our canon are the preceding books of the *Pentateuch. The appellation מִשְׁנֵה תּוֹרָה *mishneh torah* for Deuteronomy is also common in post-biblical Hebrew sources, and it seems that the Jewish tradition stands behind the Greek term. In contrast to their view of preceding books of the Pentateuch, critics take Deuteronomy to be, for the most part, an organic literary creation. It is presented as a long farewell speech of Moses, styled in the first person singular (except for a few small digressions: 4:41–49; 27:1–26; 31:7–9, 14ff.; 32:44–45). Deuteronomy interrupts the narrative flow of the Pentateuch by delaying the death of Moses from where it might have been expected in Numbers 27, to the Priestly resumption in Deut. 33:48–52; 34:1–6. In Deuteronomy 31:9, "this Torah," which is said to have been written by Moses and delivered into the custody of the levitical priests, refers to Deuteronomy, or some form of it; not to the entire Pentateuch.

Contents

A notice indicating time and place (1:1–5) precedes the introductory discourse. The discourse contains a historical retrospect of the Israelite journey, alluding to various incidents attending the perilous journey (spies, defeat at Hormah, conquest of Sihon and Og, and occupation of the whole territory of east Jordan). The discourse stresses the Providence that brought Israel through the desert. An appeal is made to the people to observe the statutes and ordinances of God (1:6–4:40). The second discourse, which is the principal part of the book, falls into two parts. The first (4:44–11:32) consists of a hortatory introduction opening with an exposition of the *Decalogue, and develops the first commandment at great length. The second section (ch. 12–26) is the Deuteronomic Code of Laws containing special laws or statutes that supplement the Decalogue. These statutes may be divided in three categories: (a) *Ceremonial laws*: centralization of worship (12), injunction against idolatry (13), pagan mourning rites (14:1–2), clean and unclean food (14:3–21), tithes (14:22–29), year of release (15:1–18), firstling offerings (15:19–23), and holy seasons (16:1–17). (b) *Civil Laws*: appointment of judges and supreme tribunal (16:18–20; 17:8–13), selection of a king (17:14–20), regulations concerning rights and revenues of priests and levites (18:1–8), rules concerning prophets (18:9–22). (c) *Criminal laws*: homicide (19:1–13), encroachment on property (19:14), false testimony (19:15–21). From Chapter 20 on we find regulations concerning laws of war (20:1–20), statement of family rights (21:15–21), sexual purity (22:13–29) and various others. Although many scholars see randomness in the arrangement of some of the laws, Stephen Kaufman argues strongly that the laws of chapters 12 through 25 reflect the order of the Decalogue. Chapter 26 ends the series with a conclusion to the law and a formula of commitment to the covenant. Chapter 27, which interrupts the discourse and is a narrative in the third person, contains the directions for the building of an altar on Mt. Ebal and a ceremonial blessing and cursing between Mt. Ebal and Mt. Gerizim. The following chapter (28) is a declaration of the blessings and curses which will overtake the people depending on whether they observe or neglect the prescribed statutes. Chapters 29–30 include Moses' third discourse, which insists on the fundamental duty of loyalty to God and embraces an appeal to Israel to accept the terms of the Deuteronomic covenant. Chapter 31 reports the appointment of Joshua (31:7–8, 14–15) and Moses' delivery of the Deuteronomic law to the levitical priests with instruction for it to be read publicly every seven years (31:9–13). Then follows the Song of Moses (Ch. 32), Moses' blessing (Ch. 33), and the final chapter (Ch. 34), which concludes the book with an account of the circumstances of Moses' death on Mt. Nebo.

Although no biblical source explicitly credits Moses with the composition of the entire Pentateuch, passages such as Deuteronomy 31:9 were read so expansively that Mosaic authorship was taken for granted in early Jewish tradition and the New Testament. Once Mosaic authorship became an article of faith for classical Judaism and Christianity the faithful found difficulty in the last eight verses of Deuteronomy, in which the death and burial of Moses are described. Some rabbis attributed the writing of these verses to Joshua; but another opinion had it that Moses wrote these verses too at God's dictation (BB 14b–15a). Medieval commentators, such as Abraham Ibn Ezra, were sensitive to some of the anachronistic passages in Deuteronomy incongruous to the time of Moses. The following are a few examples of difficult passages coped with by medieval commentators: (1) "beyond the Jordan" (1:1), a term generally employed by people living in Palestine could not properly be used by Moses who was then situated in Moab; (2) the expressions "at that time" (2:34; 3:4) and "unto this day" (3:14) imply that a long period of time has elapsed since the past spoken of; (3) the mention of Og's bedstead at Rabbath Ammon (3:11) as proof of Og's huge proportions and giant stature implies that Og was no longer alive to be used as living proof; (4) "As Israel did unto the land they were to possess" (2:12) refers to the conquest of Canaan which had not yet taken place according to the Bible; (5) the verse, "when Moses had put down in writing the words of this teaching to the very end, Moses charged the levites..." (31:24), probably refers only to certain chapters and not to the entire book since it is inconceivable that a book would relate the author's actions after the completion of the book. Ibn Ezra accepts the talmudic position of Mosaic authorship but probably felt that several verses were added to the book after Moses' death.

Critical Assessment

Deuteronomy is the only part of the Pentateuch called "the book of the law" (*Sefer ha-Torah*), i.e., the authoritative, sanctified guidebook of Israel. In the editorial framework of the Former Prophets, which is inspired by the book of Deuteronomy, it is designated by *Sefer Torat Moshe*, "the book of the law of Moses" (cf. Josh. 8:31; 23:6; II Kings 14:6). Deuteronomy is, in fact, the only book of the Pentateuch to be ascribed to Moses (Deut. 31:9; see above) and, according to most scholars, the first book to have been sanctified publicly (II Kings 23:1–3). Only after the other books were appended to Deuteronomy was the term "Torah" applied to the whole Pentateuch. The form of "testament" given to the book looks peculiar, but has its antecedents in the Egyptian method of diffusing wisdom and moral teachings. Addresses of kings and viziers to their successors in Egypt were couched in the form of a will, and this technique may have exerted an influence on Israel's literature, especially since there exist some affinities between Deuteronomy and the Wisdom Literature (see below). In spite of its apparent formal unity, the book is not a homogeneous piece of work. It has two introductions (1:1–4:40; 4:44–11:32), two different kinds of blessings and curses (27:11–26; 28:1–68), and appendices of various kinds (chapters 29ff.). The problem of the composite nature of the book has been dealt with by many modern scholars, and no final solution has been reached. There is general agreement in regard to chapters 5–26 and 28. It is believed that these chapters constituted the original book, which was later supplemented by an additional introduction (1:6–4:40) and by variegated material at the end of the book (27:1–8, 11–26; chapters 29–30). The rest of the material is to be divided into two categories: (1) the genuine Deuteronomic material dealing with the commissioning of Joshua (31:1–8); the writing of the Torah, its use in the future, and the depositing of it at the ark (31:9–13, 24–29; 32:45–47); and the death of Moses (chapter 34); and (2) ancient material appended to the book, such as the Song of Moses 32:1–43 with its introduction 31:14–23, the Blessing of Moses in chapter 33, and the later priestly passage in 32:48–52. According to M. Noth, Deuteronomy 1:1–4:40 and 31ff. is the work of the Deuteronomist who was responsible for editing the history of Joshua-Kings. In his opinion, this historian began with Deuteronomy 1 and incorporated Deuteronomy 4:44–30:20 into his work. His own material 1:1–4:40 and 31:1ff. is concerned with the preparations for the conquest and the commissioning of Joshua, which, in fact, serves as a good introduction for the conquest, opening the so-called Deuteronomic history of the Former Prophets. Some critics asserted that Deuteronomy 9:7–10:11, dealing with the events at Horeb (not the "Sinai" of the Priestly source), originally preceded the historical account in Deuteronomy 1:6ff. If this is correct, it lends support to the theory of Noth, because in this case there is a clear division of the book: the original code with its introduction on one hand, and the historical material added by the Deuteronomist on the other. However, as attractive as this theory may be, stylistically chapters 1–30 seem to be of the same stock and are different in nature from the Deuteronomic material of the Former Prophets. The composite nature of the book is recognizable not only in its framework but also in the code which forms the basic section of the book. Thus in chapter 12, two sets of prescriptions about centralization of cult are found: verses 1–12 and 13–25. The two sets may be distinguished by their style: in the former the people are addressed mainly in the second person plural, while in the latter the address is mainly in the second person singular. This distinction has been taken, since Steuernagel, as the basic criterion for distinguishing sources in Deuteronomy, in the code as well as in the framework. Steuernagel considered these as two different sources and thus he maintained that there were three strands in the chapter. In addition, Rofé (16–17) has demonstrated that within chapter 12 there is a difference between 12:13–19, which gives blanket permission for profane slaughter, and 12:20–28, which permits profane slaughter only if one is far from the chosen place. These last verses are what would later be called *halakhic* (legally orientated) Midrash in that they harmonize the blanket permission of profane slaughter of Deuteronomy 12:13–19 with its blanket prohibition in Leviticus 17:1–7. The combination of stylistic and linguistic clues together with indicators of historical and religious context are crucial to distinguishing sources.

DATE OF COMPOSITION. Deuteronomy gives its setting an antique flavor by providing ancient geographic and ethnic names, names of ancient giants and legendary peoples and details of ancient conquests (chapters 2–3). Yet the writers inform us that they are at some distance from the events related. For example, in order to write "there never again arose in Israel a prophet like Moses" (Deut. 34:10) it was necessary to know of a long line of prophets later than Moses. The first serious modern scholarly date for the composition of Deuteronomy was established by the pioneering work of de Wette in 1805. Trying to trace the historical circumstances underlying the book of Deuteronomy, de Wette found a correspondence between the reforms of *Josiah (640–609), which according to II Kings 22–23 were motivated by the discovery of a book of *torah* (see below), and the legislation of Deuteronomy. Before Josiah places of worship throughout the land were considered indispensable for the religious life of Israel, so that, for Elijah, destroying altars of YHWH was almost tantamount to slaying His prophets (I Kings 19:10, 14). In the legislative literature in Israel, however, the demand for cult centralization occurs for the first time in Deuteronomy. This book would therefore be an outcome, or a reflection, of the reforms of Josiah. These reforms are reflected in Deuteronomy not only in the law of centralization but also in: (1) the prohibition against pillars in the worship of YHWH (16:22), which according to the older sources is legitimate and even desirable (e.g., Gen. 28:18; 35:14; Ex. 24:4; Josh. 24:26); 2) the references to "astral worship" (*ṣeva ha-shamayim*; Deut. 4:19; 17:3), which is not mentioned in the previous books of the Pentateuch and seems to have been introduced into Judah through Arameo-Assyrian cultural influence in the eighth century B.C.E.; (3) the correspondence between the manner of celebrating Passover in the days of Hezekiah (II Chron. 30) and Josiah (see below) and the prescription in Deuteronomy 16:1–8. According to II Kings 23:22, Passover had not been celebrated in such a manner since the times of the Judges. No less important for the date of Deuteronomy is the unique style of this book, both in its phraseology and manner of discourse (rhetoric). Style such as that found in Deuteronomy (see below) is not found in any of the historical and prophetic traditions before the seventh century B.C.E. Conversely, from the seventh century onward almost all of the historical and the prophetical literature is permeated by this style. Theologically and stylistically Deuteronomy has become the archimedian point for dating the sources in the Pentateuch and the historical books of the Old Testament. On this analysis, the legal codes which do not presuppose centralization of cult must be from pre-Josianic times. In contrast, the editorial passages of Kings which evaluate the kings of Judah in accordance with their observance of centralization of cult, and those passages in Joshua-Judges which are styled in Deuteronomic phraseology cannot be from before the time of Josiah. An objective clue has thus been established for fixing the date of the editorial parts of the historic literature.

ANCIENT NEAR EASTERN TREATY FORMS AND DEUTERONOMY. A new dimension was added to the problem of the date of Deuteronomy by the discovery of the treaty between Esarhaddon king of Assyria (680–669 B.C.E.) and his eastern vassals (the longest Assyrian treaty as yet discovered). Affinities between ancient Near Eastern treaties and the biblical covenant in general had been stressed by Mendenhall in 1954 (see below), but the treaty of Esarhaddon, discovered in 1956, provided new material that is parallel only to that of Deuteronomy. The most important parallel is with the series of maledictions in Deuteronomy 28, which resemble strongly the Esarhaddon type of treaty (see Weinfeld 1965, in bibl.). The warnings against treason and inciting treason in Deuteronomy 13 closely resemble those found in the Esarhaddon succession treaty (Parpola in bibliography, 28–58) and in the contemporaneous Aramaic treaties. Especially striking is the warning against seduction by the prophet and cultic functionary, which has its parallel in the Assyrian treaty. The depiction of the scene of *Covenant and emphasis on the perpetual validity of the treaty as binding on all generations in Deuteronomy 29:9–14 also coincides with the description of the treaty scene in the Esarhaddon succession treaty and the earlier Aramaic treaty from Sefire (750–745 B.C.E.; COS II: 213–17). The stipulations demanding exclusive allegiance to the God of Israel in Deuteronomy are formulated in the conventional manner of state treaties and documents, especially those of the seventh and eighth centuries B.C.E. Thus the expression "to love with all your heart" is the standard term for being loyal to the sovereign, and, similarly, the biblical expressions: "to go after" (= to follow), "to fear" (= to revere), "to hearken to the voice of," "to do as He commands," "to act in complete truth," "to be sincere," have their exact parallels in the Esarhaddon treaties and also in the oaths of allegiance of the princes and officials of Esarhaddon and Ashurbanipal to their masters. It has been therefore supposed – e.g., by Frankena – that Josiah's covenant with God was considered a substitution for the former treaty with the king of Assyria, thereby expressing vassalship to YHWH instead of vassalship to the king of Assyria. Less convincing is K.A. Kitchen (*Ancient Orient and Old Testament*, 90 ff. and especially p. 99) who argues that "the Sinai covenant and its renewals must be classed with the late second millennium covenants."

The "Discovery" of the Book of the Law

In spite of the evidence established by the conventional theory for the date of Deuteronomy, it is hard to fix the exact date of its composition, and because of its complex nature, it is also difficult to mark the extent of its original form. The canonical book of Deuteronomy contains material ranging over centuries, from pre-monarchic material ignorant of Egyptian enslavement or the gift of the law at Sinai / Horeb (Deut. 33; Seeligmann; Rofé) to the realities of the Egyptian and other Jewish diasporas (Deut. 28–68; 29:27). There also Northern Israelite elements including the ceremonies at Mt. Gerizim and Ebal north of Shechem (Deut. 11:29–30; 27:4, 12–13), as well as the linguistic and doctrinal influences of *Hosea (Ginsberg). What is beyond doubt is that the "Book of the Law (*torah*)" was "discovered" in 622 B.C.E. (II Kings 22). The identification of the "Book of the Law" with Deuteronomy is based on the following:

1) As already indicated, the term "the Book of the Torah" is not mentioned anywhere aside from Deuteronomy, where it refers to the Book of Deuteronomy itself.

2) The abolition of high places and the centralization of the cult enacted by Josiah following the discovery of the book are prescribed only in Deuteronomy.

3) Astral worship, which is referred to in detail in Josiah's reform (II Kings 23:5, 11–12), is especially marked in Deuteronomy: "the host of heaven" (17:3).

4) The Passover celebrated in Jerusalem (II Kings 23:21–23) is performed in accordance with the commands of Deuteronomy 16:1–8, in contrast to the tradition reflected in Exodus 12, according to which it was to be celebrated at home.

5) The pledge taken by the people to keep the law of this

book (II Kings 23:3) is styled in the manner of the Deuteronomic injunctions of loyalty and allegiance to God.

It seems, however, that the book "discovered" was not identical with Deuteronomy in its present form. It is unlikely that a king would sponsor a program which made condescending and uncomplimentary references to the monarchy (Deut 17:20; 28:36). It is improbable that the book in its present form was read three times in one day: by Shaphan the scribe (II Kings 22:8), by the king (22:10), and presumably by Huldah the prophetess (22:13–14). Besides, though the prologues and epilogues of the code cannot be dated, it is nevertheless highly probable that a great amount of the material in the framework of the code is quite late and even post-Exilic (cf. e.g., Deut. 4:27–31; 30:1–10). The book could then consist mainly of a small introduction, a code (including above all chapters 12–19, which embody the principles of the reform), and the admonition of chapter 28 which may well explain the horror which befell the king at the recital of the book (II Kings 22:11ff.; Kimḥi to II Kings 22:11 quotes a rabbinic tradition that the scroll was found rolled to Deuteronomy 28:36 where the king's exile is predicted). If the idea of this basic Deuteronomy is accepted, the problem is when it was composed. The appropriate historical and religious background for the composition of this type of work is the time of Hezekiah and Josiah, with that of Josiah being more likely. Of the "good kings" only Hezekiah and Josiah are credited with both *Kultusreinheit* (cult-purification) and *Kultuseinheit* (cult-centralization). Although Hezekiah is credited with being the first king to implement the centralization of the cult, and he and his personnel are credited (like King Ashurbanipal of Assyria) with the collection of ancient literature (cf. Prov. 25:1), no book is cited as the motivation for Hezekiah's reform. The attribution of the book to Moses (directly in II Chronicles 34 and by implication in II Kings 22) would enable the proponents of centralization and purification to claim that their program was a restoration rather than an innovation. Earlier scholarship explained Josiah's religious reforms as directed against imposed Assyrian cults whose elimination was taken as political rebellion. For a number of reasons this view cannot be sustained. First, Assyria did not impose its cults on vassal states. Second, Josiah's actions were not directed against distinctively Assyrian cults but mainly against old local ones, including *Asherah. Third, in contrast to Hezekiah the Bible does not ascribe rebellion against Assyria to Josiah. Indeed, if we follow the chronology of Kings, by the time of Josiah's actions Assyria would have been in retreat. It is more likely that the religious reforms arose out of a genuine belief that Judah's troubles were due to infidelity to Yahweh. The "Yahweh-alone" movement could always adduce the fall of Samaria a century earlier in proof. No wonder, therefore, that the law book caused a national resurgence and led the people to turn back to God with great enthusiasm. The constant editing and reworking of Deuteronomy shows the great interest this book aroused. Furthermore, the religious upheaval of that time along with the contemporary antiquarian interest attested in Mesopotamia and Egypt gave impetus to the collecting of ancient traditions and putting them into a systematic historical framework. Though the so-called Deuteronomic history of the Former Prophets was not completed before the destruction of the Temple, its beginning, or the constituent stage of its crystallization, has to be sought in the Josianic period.

The Provenance of Deuteronomy

"History of Form," which opened up a new vista in biblical criticism, has also made a contribution in the field of research of Deuteronomy. The question of the "Sitz im Leben" of Deuteronomy, i.e., of the reality which gave birth to the style of its literary creation, was brought up by G. von Rad. By analyzing the peculiar structure of Deuteronomy: homily (chapters 1–11), laws (12:1–26:15), sealing of the covenant (26:16–19), and blessings and curses (27:11–26; chapter 28), he came to the conclusion that this combination of different literary genres could hardly have been invented. He assumed, therefore, that the complex literary structure must have been rooted in a cultic ceremony in which God's laws were recited by clergy. The recital opened with a homily and religious preaching and concluded with a public pledge sanctioned by blessings and curses. He claimed to find traces of an old cultic ceremony in Deuteronomy 27 and in the tradition of the Shechem covenant in Joshua 24. According to von Rad, Deuteronomy renews the cultic tradition of the old Shechem amphictyony, a theory that fits in well with the prevalent opinion about the affinities of Deuteronomy to northern traditions. As a matter of fact, in the previous century A. Klostermann had already conjectured that the homiletic style of Deuteronomy reflects a public recital, but he could not base his thesis on form-critical observations as did von Rad, and, therefore, did not connect it with the cult. In 1947 von Rad went a step further and identified the reciters of the law with the levites and moreover recognized them as the actual spokesmen of the Deuteronomic movement. He based this supposition mainly on Nehemiah 8:7, which speaks about the levites "instructing the people in law." According to von Rad's earlier study (1934), the sermons in Chronicles are the product of the levites of the post-Exilic period. Thus in seeking for the originators of the sermons in Deuteronomy, it was only natural for him to identify them also with the levites. However, Mendenhall in 1954 was the first to see the similarities between the Hittite treaties and the Israelite covenant. A treaty pattern with a common basic structure – historical introduction, stipulations, blessings and curses – was prevalent in the ancient Near East for a period of over 1,000 years. The structure of Deuteronomy would then follow a literary tradition of covenant writing rather than imitating a periodical cultic ceremony for which there is no evidence. Once it is unnecessary to assume a cultic ceremony for understanding the structure of Deuteronomy, the assumption that the levites preserved this cultic tradition becomes dubious too. If a literary pattern lies behind the form of Deuteronomy, it would be much more reasonable to assume that a literary circle familiar with treaty writing – in other words, court scribes – composed the book of Deuteronomy. Only scribes who dealt with literary and written documents and who had access to the court could have been familiar with the structure of treaties, and what is more important, with formulas originating in the Assyrian political milieu. The means that Deuteronomy used to foster its aims are identical with those employed by scribes-wise men in Israel and other ancient Near Eastern peoples. Like the sapiential teachers and pedagogues, the author of Deuteronomy also places great stress on the education of children. The author of the book repeatedly emphasizes that children must be taught the fear of God and that this is to be done by inculcation (6:7; 11:19), that is to say, by formal methods of education. The Book of Deuteronomy does indeed contain a wealth of didactic idioms that are not encountered in any other of the pentateuchal books, but that constitute part and parcel of the vocabulary of sapiential literature which, to be sure, was composed with a pedagogical object in mind. The author of Deuteronomy holds wisdom in esteem and sets it above other spiritual qualities. This becomes particularly evident when the traditions concerning the Mosaic appointment of judges in Exodus 18 are compared with Deuteronomy 1. According to Deuteronomy (1:13) the essential traits characterizing the judge and leader must be wisdom, understanding, and knowledge (*ḥokhmah, binah, da'at*), that is to say, the same intellectual traits possessed by the scribes, and not other personal characteristics such as social standing (e.g., *anshe ḥayil*), as in Exodus 18:21. The particular esteem with which Deuteronomy regarded wisdom explains the presence in this book of exhortations that have a sapiential character and formulation (cf. e.g., Deut. 19:14 with Prov. 22:28; Deut. 23:16 with Prov. 30:10; Deut. 25:13–16 with Prov. 20:10, 23). Wisdom has been styled "the humanism of the ancient Near East," and it is due to its impact that humanitarian laws, which have no counterpart in any other of the Pentateuchal books, found their way into the Book of Deuteronomy.

The Relation of Deuteronomy to the Tetrateuch

As to the relation of Deuteronomy to the Tetrateuch (i.e., the first four books of the Bible), critical work in Deuteronomy has indicated that this book depends on the historical and legal traditions of the preceding books of the Pentateuch, especially on the so-called Elohistic source. An exception, however, has to be made in regard to the priestly code which did not influence the laws of Deuteronomy, except its latest sections (e.g., Deut. 12:20–28). This is to be explained by the lateness of the priestly literature. Deuteronomy shows dependence especially on the *Book of the Covenant (Ex. 21–23; Deuteronomy itself also contains "the words of the Covenant," 28:69). The author makes it quite clear that at Horeb the Decalogue was proclaimed, whereas the law proper could have been given to Israel by Moses on the plains of Moab. In other words, Deuteronomy would be seen as complementing the old Book of the Covenant or supplementing it. It cannot be known whether the author of Deuteronomy had before him "the Book of the Covenant" in its present form or used a legal source in which laws of the type found in Exodus 21–23 were incorporated. What is clear is that Deuteronomy used laws identical in formulation with those of the Book of the Covenant and revised them according to its ideology. The parallels are:

Exodus 21:1–11	//	Deuteronomy 15:12–18
Exodus 22:15–16	//	Deuteronomy 22:28–29
Exodus 22:24–26	//	Deuteronomy 24:10–13
Exodus 23:4–5	//	Deuteronomy 22:1–4
Exodus 23:8	//	Deuteronomy 16:19
Exodus 23:15	//	Deuteronomy 16:3
Exodus 23:17	//	Deuteronomy 16:16
Exodus 23:18	//	Deuteronomy 16:4
Exodus 23:19b	//	Deuteronomy 14:21b

The parallels mainly pertain to the moral-religious section of the Book of the Covenant, the so-called apodictic law (Ex. 22:17–23:19). The civil section of the Book of the Covenant, the so-called casuistic law (Ex. 21:1–22:16), is not represented in Deuteronomy except for two laws (Ex. 21:1–11; 22:15–16). This may be explained in the following way: the civil law section in Exodus 21:1–22:16 constitutes the common law of the ancient Near East and has strong affinities to the Mesopotamian law codes. As in the neighboring codes, this section in the Book of the Covenant is mostly concerned with offenses against property, and even when dealing with human rights (injury, slaves etc.), it is the compensation for the damage that stands at the center of the discussion. Deuteronomy ignored these laws since the author's purpose was not to produce a civil law book like the Book of the Covenant treating of pecuniary matters but to set forth a code of laws securing the protection of the individual and particularly of those persons in need of protection. At the same time, Deuteronomy incorporated laws concerning the protection of the family and family dignity (22:11–19) which are not in the Book of the Covenant.

The only laws from the civil section of the Book of the Covenant employed by Deuteronomy are the law of the Hebrew slave (Ex. 21:1–11) and the law of the seduction of a virgin (Ex. 22:15–16). These two laws, which are located at the beginning and at the end of the section respectively, were incorporated by Deuteronomy because they contain moral implications aside from their civil aspect. Moreover, by the way these two laws are presented, Deuteronomy actually deprived them of their civil-financial character and turned them into purely moral-social laws. In Exodus 21:1–11 the rights of the master are protected no less than those of the slave (cf. the provision about the slaves born in the master's home belonging to the master, the master's right of keeping the slave in perpetuity, etc.), the main concern of the legislator there being to define the status of the slave. Deuteronomy, however, is concerned with only the slave, and, therefore, the obligations of the master to his slave (to bestow gifts, etc.) are stressed. By the same token, the law of the seduced virgin in Exodus 22:15–16 is discussed from the pecuniary point of view (the loss of the bride price) whereas Deuteronomy is concerned with the humiliation or moral degradation of the virgin and therefore does not deal explicitly with the bride price and does not grant the man who violated the virgin the right to refuse to marry her, but compels him to marry her forever.

In a similar way the author of Deuteronomy revised all the social and religious laws that he drew from the ancient lore. The social laws were elaborated and made to favor the distressed, as for example, the injunction not to enter the house of the debtor to take the pledge (Deut. 24:11) and the duty to take care of the loss until it is claimed by the owner (22:2), demands that seem utopian even in modern society. The religious-sacral laws were adapted to the new concept of centralization. Thus, for example, the law of the three annual pilgrimages in Deuteronomy 16:16, which is verbally identical with Exodus 23:17, is supplemented by the words "in the place that He will choose," which stresses the principle of centralization. The real meaning of the Deuteronomic law can be fully understood by comparing the religious institutions as reflected in Deuteronomy with those occurring in the other codes, including the priestly one. These show the uniqueness of the Deuteronomic law code. Though Deuteronomy deals basically with the same laws as the other codes, i.e., laws relating to sacrifices, the tithe, firstlings, the first fruits, festivals, the year of release, the cities of refuge, the judiciary, and the holy war, these appear here, according to some modern exegetes, in a completely new light and reflect a change not only in the institutions as such but in the religious concepts underlying them. Laws and institutions that have a substantially sacro-ritual character have in Deuteronomy undergone, it is held, a process of rationalization. Following the elimination of the provincial sanctuaries, the judiciary, which was closely associated with the sanctuary, was freed of its sacred ties and took on a more secular aspect. The cities of asylum that previously served as sacral places of refuge for the accidental homicide became in Deuteronomy secular cities whose exclusive function was to protect the manslayer from blood vengeance. Profane slaughtering which had been forbidden by the previous codes is allowed by Deuteronomy (12:13–19), a necessary consequence of the law of centralization. The year of release whose main essence in the earlier codes is the prohibition of the cultivation of the land (Ex. 23:10–11; cf. Lev. 25:1–7) is given here a new application, namely the remission of debts, and thus serves to ameliorate the condition of the poor (Deut. 5:1–11). All these innovations of the Deuteronomic Code, this theory maintains, revolutionized the religious life of the people, and, in fact, changed certain concepts in the faith of Israel. The sanctuary is here presented as a dwelling place of the name of God (e.g., 12:5, 11, 21), rather than the domicile of God Himself as in the ancient sources (cf. e.g., I Kings 8:13). Similarly the ark which in the previous sources is regarded as the seat of God or His chariot (e.g., Ex. 25:22; Num. 10:33–36; I Sam. 4:4) is seen in Deuteronomy only as the receptacle for the tablets (10:1ff.). A similar attitude is reflected in the descriptions of the revelation in Deuteronomy. According to Exodus 19, God went down to Mt. Sinai and from there made His voice heard to Moses and the people, whereas in Deuteronomy, God proclaimed His word from His seat in heaven, but it was transmitted to Israel through the great fire on the mount.

Deuteronomy is often characterized as monotheistic but the reality is more complex. Israelites must worship Yahweh exclusively (monolatry; Deut 5:7, 8; 6:4; 13:3–18; 28:15–20, 23–25; 30:17–18, etc.), but according to Deuteronomy 4:19, a verse that warns Israelites against worship of the heavenly bodies, it was Yahweh himself who designated the heavenly bodies as objects of worship for the Gentiles. Similarly subversive of monotheism, the belief that there is but one god in existence, is Deuteronomy 32:8–9, which informs us that when the Most High set up the boundaries of the nations he did so according to the numbers of the lesser divinities (Qumran *bny ʾl* or *bny ʾl[m]*). The existence of lesser divinities is acknowledged as well in Deuteronomy 10:17 where Yahweh is styled "god of gods and lord of lords." Deuteronomy 4:35, "It has been clearly demonstrated to you that Yahweh is God; there is none beside him," and Deuteronomy 4:39, "Know therefore this day and keep in mind that Yahweh alone is God in heaven above and on earth below; there is no other," are usually cited as denials of the existence of all other divinities. Yet the context of these verses cannot be ignored. Verse 34 asks rhetorically whether any god ever took another nation to himself as Yahweh has done for Israel. Verse 35 responds "Yahweh is THAT god; none beside him." The same sentiment is expressed in Deuteronomy 32:12: "Yahweh alone did guide him. No alien god at his (Yahweh's) side." Verse 39 is part of the same pericope, to be understood as "Know therefore … Yahweh alone is <the only> god in heaven above and on earth below, there is no other <who did these things.>"

STYLE AND PHRASEOLOGY. The style of Deuteronomy is distinguished by its simplicity, fluency, and lucidity and may be recognized by its phraseology and especially by its rhetorical character. The main characteristic of Deuteronomic phraseology is not the employment of new idioms and expressions, because many of these can be found in earlier sources and especially in the E source. Indeed, it cannot be said that in the seventh century a new vocabulary and new expressions were suddenly created. Language grows in an organic and natural way and it is not created artificially. What constitutes the novelty of the Deuteronomic style, therefore, is not new idioms and new expressions but a specific jargon reflecting the religious upheaval of this time. The Deuteronomic phraseology revolves around a few basic theological tenets such as:

1. the need to extirpate the native cults.
2. the centralization of the cult.
3. exodus, covenant, and election.
4. the repeated demand on Israel to serve Yahweh alone.
5. observance of the law and loyalty to the covenant.
6. inheritance of the land.
7. retribution and material motivation.

The editor of the Former Prophets, who was inspired by

Deuteronomy, uses the phraseology of Deuteronomy and even elaborates upon it. Like the Book of Deuteronomy so also the Deuteronomist makes use of speeches and discourses in order to express his ideology. Another branch of Deuteronomic writing may be recognized in Jeremiah's prose, where Deuteronomic phraseology is encountered and the oration is very common. According to this argument, therefore, the Deuteronomist, the editor of Joshua-Kings, and the editor of the prose sermons in Jeremiah are products of a continuous literary school starting in the middle of the seventh century and ending somewhere in the second half of the sixth century.

There are, however, less radical theories regarding the origin and date of Deuteronomy. These are reviewed in R.K. Harrison, *Introduction to the Old Testament* (1970), 631ff.

[Moshe Weinfeld / S. David Sperling (2nd ed.)]

Defenses of the Traditional View

The orthodox standpoint that Moses was the author of the Book of Deuteronomy as well as of the other books of the Pentateuch has been defended by a number of traditional scholars. These scholars maintain that the main theme of Deuteronomy is not centralization of worship, but opposition to idolatry. The struggle against idolatry could never have reached such intensity except in the age of Moses, the period of the formation of Israel's religion. It ideally fits into the period placed by tradition, immediately after Israel's apostasy to Baal of Peor (Num. 25), when the very existence of the new faith was threatened by contact with the Baal cult of Canaan. The centralization of the cult does not prove that Deuteronomy is of late origin since it may be argued that the law of a central sanctuary is quite early and primitive. Moreover, had a later author wished to impress the importance of cultic centralization he would have not failed to mention the city of Jerusalem, the main cultic center. Most of the laws repeated in Deuteronomy from the Book of the Covenant are found in one or more of the ancient Near Eastern codes, thereby testifying to their antiquity. As for the characteristic Deuteronomistic laws having no parallels in the Near Eastern codes, such as the law of release, the laws of kingship, appointment of judges, etc., there is nothing in these provisions incompatible with conditions and institutions of those early days. Not only the religious and legal but also the political background of Deuteronomy resembles that of the Mosaic and no other age. The order to destroy the Hittites, Amorites, Canaanites, Perizzites, Hivites, and Jebusites, the enemies of Israel (20:16–18), the denouncement of the inveterate enemies Ammon and Moab, the attitude toward the Edomites and Egyptians (23:8), and the omission of any mention of the Philistines or the division of the kingdom point to the political circumstances of the Mosaic age. The civil institutions are also of a nature approaching the primitive stage. There is no king. The elders of Israel are pictured sitting at the gate in judgment, while judges and clerks preside in trials in accordance with the advice of Jethro, Moses' father-in-law (Ex. 18). The book's covenantal structure fits ancient Near Eastern treaty forms; the Hittite vassal treaty form is a model by which the Book of Deuteronomy may be analyzed (see *Covenant). Linguistically, there is nothing against placing Deuteronomy in the days of Moses. Although the refined and polished style of the book may suggest a high state of development, it is probable that such a style existed in oratorical discourse, particularly in light of the perfect form of the 15th century B.C.E. Ras Shamra texts. Certain words are of an admittedly early period (נער for נערה, אל for אלה), and some of the ritual terms and practices such as *shalem* (peace offering), *kalil* (burnt offering), *maaser* (tithe), *tenufah* (wave offering), have their parallels in Ugaritic literature. Parallelism not only in poetry, but also in prose, accounts for many repetitions which higher criticism ascribes to different sources. Another principle of this sort is the change of person and the variation from singular to plural which higher critics take as a criterion for various sources, but is a general characteristic of the Bible and is common to all ancient Oriental composition. As to passages in the third person, they may be due to a late editor of the original book. Traditional scholars therefore believe that the best way to account for the book is to say that the bulk originated during the last days of Moses. The Israelites standing at the threshold of Canaan were about to graduate from a nomad group to a settled agricultural people and this change necessitated an amplification of the earlier codes of Exodus and Leviticus, which resulted in the book of Deuteronomy. The anachronisms and discrepancies may very well be explained by the reasonable assumption of later marginal notes by learned readers which in the course of time crept into the text itself and became an integral part thereof. Although the historical framework often lacks precision and strict sequence, as stated in the Talmud, "There is nothing prior or posterior in the Torah," for its chief aim is religious and moral and not purely historical.

BIBLIOGRAPHY: J. Wellhausen, *Prolegomena to the History of Ancient Israel* (1957); idem, *Die Composition des Hexateuchs…* (1899), 190ff.; G.R. Driver, *Deuteronomy* (ICC, 1902³); C. Steuernagel, *Deuteronomium* (1923²); M. Noth, *Ueberlieferungsgeschichtliche Studien* (1943), 3–110; G. von Rad, *Studies in Deuteronomy* (1953); Alt, Kl. Schr, 2 (1953), 250–75; G. Mendenhall, in: BA, 17 (1954), 50ff.; D.J. Wiseman, in: *Iraq*, 20 (1958), 1–99; D. McCarthy, *Treaty and Covenant* (1963); O. Eissfeldt, *The Old Testament, an Introduction* (1965), 219–33, 281–301; R. Frankena, in: OTS, 14 (1965), 122–54; A. Klostermann, *Der Pentateuch*, 2 (1907), 154ff.; M. Weinfeld, in: *Sefer Y. Kaufmann* (1960), 89–105; idem, in: *Tarbiz*, 30 (1960/61), 8–15; 31 (1961/62), 1–17; idem, in: JBL, 80 (1961), 241–7; 86 (1967), 249–62; idem, in: *Biblica*, 46 (1965), 417–27; M. Haran, in: *Tarbiz*, 37 (1967/68), 3–11; idem, in: *Biblica*, 50 (1969), 258–61; R.K. Harrison, *Introduction to the Old Testament* (1970); K.A. Kitchen, *Ancient Orient and Old Testament* (1966). **ADD. BIBLIOGRAPHY:** M. Smith, in: *Pseudepigrapha*, 1 (1971), 193–215; idem, *Palestinian Parties and Politics that Shaped the Old Testament* (1971); M. Weinfeld, *Deuteronomy and the Deuteronomic School* (1972); idem, *Deuteronomy 1–11* (AB; 1991), Bibliography, 85–122; idem, in: ABD II, 168–83; F. Cross, *Canaanite Myth and Hebrew Epic* (1973), 274–87; S. Kaufman, in, MAARAV, 1 (1978/9), 105–58; R. Freedman, in: B. Halpern and J. Levenson (eds.), *Turning Points.FS Cross* (1981), 167–92; H.L. Ginsberg, *The Israelian Heritage of Judaism* (1982); S. Parpola and K. Watanabe, *Neo-Assyrian Treaties and Loyalty Oaths* (1988); A. Rofé, *Introduction to Deuteronomy* (1988); M. Cogan and

H. Tadmor, *II Kings* (AB; 1988), 218–22, 293–300; I. Seeligmann, *Studies in Biblical Literature* (1992), 189–204; J. Tigay, *Deuteronomy* (JPS; 1996); S.D. McBride, in: DBI I, 273–94; B. Levinson, *Deuteronomy and the Hermeneutics of Legal Innovation* (1997); idem, in: J. Day, *In Search of Pre-exilic Israel* (2004), 272–375; K. van der Toorn, in: idem (ed.), *The Image and the Book* (1997), 229–48; G. Knoppers and J.G. McConville (eds.), *Reconsidering Israel – …Studies in Deuteronomistic History* (2000); M. Sweeney, *King Josiah of Judah the Lost Messiah of Israel* (2001), 64–76, 167–72; J. van Seters, *A Law Book for the Diaspora* (2002); R. Nelson, in: JSOT, 29 (2005), 319–37.

DEUTERONOMY RABBAH, aggadic Midrash on the Book of Deuteronomy.

Name

In medieval literature the work was also referred to as *Haggadat Elleh Ha-Devarim Rabbah* and *Devarim Rabbati*, the designation "*Rabbah*" being used to distinguish it from *Deuteronomy Zuta* (see **Genesis Rabbah; *Ruth Rabbah*).

Structure

Deuteronomy Rabbah is a homiletic Midrash (**Derash*). The printed version is divided into 11 sections according to the weekly pentateuchal readings, but the division is in fact into 27 homilies, according to the triennial cycle of the reading of the Torah customary in Ereẓ Israel in earlier times. *Deuteronomy Rabbah* is a characteristically **Tanḥuma-Yelammedenu* type of Midrash, even more so than those homilies on the Book of Deuteronomy contained in the printed editions of the *Tanḥuma* and in that of S. Buber (see below). Each homily is introduced by a halakhic question characteristic of the *Tanḥuma-Yelammedenu* type of Midrash and begins with the formula: *Halakhah adam me-Yisrael… Kakh shanu ḥakhamim* – "What is the *halakhah* for a man of Israel … thus our sages taught …" (here *halakhah* is used instead of the more usual *Yelammedenu rabbenu*, "Let our master teach us," of this type of Midrash). This is followed by a homily incorporating both *halakhah* and *aggadah*, the transition from *halakhah* to *aggadah* being introduced by the term: זה שאמר הכתוב ("This is what Scripture says"). Most of the homilies conclude with a message of consolation or redemption. The numerous transitions in lengthy homilies on the same subject are introduced by the formula *davar aḥer* … "another version…."

Different Versions

In 1895 S. Buber published from the Munich manuscript of *Deuteronomy Rabbah*, written in 1295, those homilies on the portion of *Devarim* which differ from the printed version, as well as addenda to the section *Niẓẓavim* (this manuscript omits the sections *Va-Etḥannan* and *Va-Yelekh* to the end of the Book of Deuteronomy, whereas all the remainder is identical with the printed version). A few years later a complete manuscript of *Deuteronomy Rabbah* in the possession of A. Epstein was found to be almost identical with the Munich manuscript and to contain homilies on *Va-Etḥannan* and *Va-Yelekh* different from those in the printed versions, addenda to *Ekev*, and homilies on *Ha'azinu* and *Ve-Zot ha-Berakhah* identical with those in the *Tanḥuma* Midrashim. In 1940 S. Lieberman published the Oxford manuscript of *Deuteronomy Rabbah*, which is similar to the Epstein manuscript, except for additional homilies from the *Tanḥuma* Midrashim on *Va-Etḥannan*. Manuscripts, therefore, contain homilies on *Devarim*, *Va-Etḥannan*, and *Va-Yelekh* different from those printed, as well as additional ones on *Ekev* and *Niẓẓavim*. This version is likewise mainly a homiletic Midrash of the *Tanhuma Yelammedenu* type, although several of its homilies have no halakhic introduction, and, even in those having halakhic introductions, they begin directly with the question without any *terminus technicus*, whereas the answer begins with כך שנו רבותינו ("Thus did our masters teach"). The aggadic proems are not all, as in the printed *Tanḥuma* Midrashim, anonymous; some begin with the name of an *amora*. In structure, language, and composition, the printed version of *Deuteronomy Rabbah* is a homogeneous Midrash. The same cannot be said for the manuscripts which contain a composition of several versions. It is certainly not a complete entity in itself. There were apparently extant several versions of the *Tanḥuma-Yelammedenu* Midrashim on the Book of Deuteronomy. One of these is that found in the printed edition as well as Buber's editions of *Tanḥuma*, another is the printed edition of *Deuteronomy Rabbah*, while several manuscripts of the latter work quote homilies on *Devarim, Va-Etḥannan*, and *Va-Yelekh*, and also additions to *Ekev* and *Niẓẓavim*, from another edition (C) of the *Tanḥuma-Yelammedenu* Midrashim, with homilies on *Ha'azinu* and *Ve-Zot ha-Berakhah* taken from the *Tanḥuma* Midrashim version (A). The version (C) of *Deuteronomy Rabbah* in the above-mentioned manuscripts was apparently known in the Middle Ages only to Spanish scholars (the first to cite it was Naḥmanides) and the manuscripts on which the printed version is based (B) only to the scholars of France and Germany (first being cited by Moses b. Jacob of Coucy). There were apparently manuscripts extant which contained further addenda from the *Tanḥuma-Yelammedenu* Midrashim, for medieval scholars sometimes quote statements in the name of *Deuteronomy Rabbah* which are not found in any existing version. On the other hand, they sometimes cite passages in the name of the *Tanḥuma* or *Yelammedenu* which are contained in one of the editions of *Deuteronomy Rabbah*.

Language

The language of the two versions of *Deuteronomy Rabbah* is rabbinic Hebrew combined with Galilean Aramaic and containing a liberal sprinkling of Greek words.

Redaction

Both versions of *Deuteronomy Rabbah* drew upon tannaitic literature, the Jerusalem Talmud, *Genesis Rabbah*, and *Leviticus Rabbah* (the printed version also apparently drew upon *Lamentations Rabbah*). The redaction of the material is characteristic of that of the *Tanḥuma-Yelammedenu* Midrashim. None of the sages mentioned in the work lived later than the fourth century C.E. Although certain homilies in the manuscripts are typical of earlier times, there seem also to be allusions to anti-Karaite polemics, which would date the final redaction of even the earliest (C) version as not earlier than 800 C.E. Likewise, homilies in the printed version, which draw upon Midrash *Petirat Moshe* and are typical of the period after the Muslim conquest, were apparently redacted in the ninth century C.E. To the same century also belong the combinations found in the manuscripts. The earliest manuscript upon which the printed version is based was copied in the 13th century.

BIBLIOGRAPHY: H.L. Strack, *Introduction to the Talmud and Midrash* (1931), 214; Zunz-Albeck, Derashot, 122–3; S. Lieberman, *Midrash Devarim Rabbah* (19652), iii–xxiii. **ADD. BIBLIOGRAPHY:** M. Rabinowitz, in: *Sinai 100 2* (1987), 731–736; M.B. Lerner, in: *Te'udah XI* (Hebrew) (1996), 107–145.

[Moshe David Herr]

DEUTSCH, ALADAR (1871–1949), chief rabbi of Prague under the Nazi occupation. He was a pupil of Solomon *Breuer in Frankfurt, and subsequently served as rabbi in several Prague synagogues, when he was active within the *Afike Jehuda association. From 1930 he served as acting chief rabbi; his appointment as chief rabbi under the Nazi regime was accompanied by all the humiliations to which Jewish leadership was then subjected. He was finally deported to *Theresienstadt, from where he returned, a broken man, to Prague. Deutsch published an essay on the Zigainer Synagogue (1907).

BIBLIOGRAPHY: *Věstnik židovské obcé náboženské v Praze*, 11 (1949), 100–1; *Afike Jehuda Festschrift* (1909), 35–44; (1929/30), 3–8.

DEUTSCH, ANDRE (1917–2000), British publisher. Born in Budapest, Deutsch moved to Switzerland after the German *Anschluss* of Austria (where he was living) and then to England. In 1945 he founded his own publishing firm, Allan Wingate, and, in 1951, his well-known firm of Andre Deutsch Ltd. His first bestseller was the memoirs of von Papen, Hitler's diplomat, but most of the famous works published by his firm were novels and other fiction, especially books by famous American writers like Norman Mailer, Jack Kerouac, Philip Roth, and John Updike, as well as the fiction of serious British novelists like V.S. Naipaul. Deutsch was one among a number of very prominent Jewish refugee publishers who emerged in Britain after World War II, such as Paul *Hamlyn and George *Weidenfeld.

BIBLIOGRAPHY: ODNB online.

[William D. Rubinstein (2nd ed.)]

DEUTSCH, BABETTE (1895–1982), U.S. poet. Born in New York, Babette Deutsch graduated from Columbia University, where she taught English from 1944. Her first poems were published while she was still a college student; two early books of verse were *Banners* (1919) and *Honey out of the Rock* (1925). Other volumes of poetry include *Fire for the Night* (1930), *Epistle to Prometheus* (1931), *One Part Love* (1939), and *Coming of Age* (1959). She published some novels, a number of children's books, and translations of German and Russian verse. One of the most notable of these translations was the version of Aleksandr Blok's epic poem about the Soviet Revolution, *Dvenadtsat* ("The Twelve," 1918), which she and her husband, Avrahm *Yarmolinsky, produced together in 1920. A sensitive and emotional writer whose poems often touch on social problems, Babette Deutsch also won distinction as a critic with such works as *Potable Gold* (1929), *This Modern Poetry* (1935; revised as *Poetry in Our Time*, 1952), and *The Reader's Shakespeare* (1946). Her later verse collections include *Animal, Vegetable, Mineral* (1954) and *Collected Poems, 1919–1962* (1963). A new edition of her *Collected Poems*, covering the years 1919–1969, appeared in 1969.

BIBLIOGRAPHY: J. Kunitz and H. Haycraft, *Twentieth Century Authors* (1942), 375–6, and supplement (1955), 277–8.

[Sol Liptzin]

DEUTSCH, BERNARD SEYMOUR (1884–1935), U.S. lawyer, public official, and communal leader. Deutsch was born in Baltimore. He began his career as a lawyer in 1905, attaining prominence and playing an active role in judicial reform. He served as president of the Bronx County Bar Association (1927–30) and participated in the 1930 investigation of abuses of legal ethics in New York. Deutsch, an independent Democrat, was elected on Fiorello La Guardia's Fusion Party ticket in 1933 as president of the Board of Aldermen. He displayed strong leadership in reviving the moribund aldermanic council. Together with La Guardia he worked to improve city services in such areas as transportation, home relief, and labor arbitration. Long active in Jewish affairs, Deutsch became president of the American Jewish Congress in 1929 and held that post until his death. In association with Stephen S. Wise, he led campaigns to arouse public opinion on behalf of the rights of German Jews.

BIBLIOGRAPHY: *New York Times* (Nov. 22, 1935), 1:8.

[Morton Rosenstock]

DEUTSCH, DAVID BEN MENAHEM MENDEL (1756–1831), Hungarian rabbi and author. Deutsch was a pupil of Ezekiel Landau. He served as rabbi of Jamnitz (1784–90), Frauenkirchen, Szerdahely, and, from 1810 until his death, of Waag-Neustadt. After he had published *Ohel David* (3 pts., Vienna, 1822), novellae on various tractates, he added various glosses to the work, and instructed that they be added to the passages indicated in every copy of the books. His novellae on *Yevamot* (Vienna, 1825) and on *Shevu'ot* (Pressburg, 1830; the latter published by his son Ezekiel, who also wrote an introduction) were brought to press through the efforts of his son-in-law, Meir Ash. Some of Deutsch's novellae were published by his grandson, Menahem Deutsch (Ungvar, 1867). Other novellae are to be found at the end of *She'elot u-Teshuvot ha-Ge'onim* (Pt. 1 responsa *Ge'onei Batra'ei*, Prague, 1816) and in part two of *Kedushat Yisrael* (Vienna, 1829) of Benjamin Wolf b. Leib (Lichtenstadt). Eleazar b. Aryeh Loeb Roke'aḥ,

Deutsch's colleague and intimate friend, mentions his responsa several times in his own work, *Shemen Roke'aḥ*.

BIBLIOGRAPHY: L. Muenz, *Rabbi Eleasar, genannt Schemen Rokeach* (1895), 42, 106–9; Hruschka, in: *Juden und Judengemeinden Maehrens…* (1929), 257 no. 8, 265 no. 82; M. Eisenstadt, *Zikhron Yehudah* (1900), 4a; P.Z. Schwartz, *Shem ha-Gedolim me-Ereẓ Hagar*, 1 (1913), 24b no. 21; J.J. (L.) Greenwald (Grunwald), *Ha-Yehudim be-Ungaryah* (1913), 75 no. 62; idem, in: *Oẓar ha-Ḥayyim*, 10 (1933/34), 122ff.

[Yehoshua Horowitz]

DEUTSCH, ELIEZER ḤAYYIM BEN ABRAHAM (1850–1916), Hungarian talmudist and author. Deutsch was born in Petra, near Kaschau. He studied under Menahem Eisenstadt of Ungvar, Judah Aszód, and Solomon *Ganzfried. In 1876 he was appointed rabbi of Hunfalu, and, in 1897, of the important community of Bonyhad, where he founded and headed a large yeshivah. Deutsch was a leader of Hungarian Orthodoxy, and a supporter of the "Moriah" association for the advancement of Orthodox Judaism, founded in 1905 by Meir Lerner in Altona.

A prolific writer, his books are (1) *Tevu'ot ha-Sadeh* in six parts (1892–1904), novellae on talmudic themes with responsa appended to each part; (2) *Ḥelkat ha-Sadeh* (1901), glosses and notes on the *Ara de-Rabbanan* of Israel Jacob *Algazi; (3) *Peri ha-Sadeh* in four parts (1906–15), responsa; (4) *Si'aḥ ha-Sadeh* (1914), aggadic novellae on the Torah and for festivals. Published posthumously were (5) *Ẓemaḥ ha-Sadeh* (1917), novellae and responsa on the problems of *agunot*; (6) *Duda'ei ha-Sadeh* (1929, published by his son, Moses), responsa and a selection of rulings with respect to the laws of mourning. In the *Yizraḥ Or* of David *Meldola, there is an appendix by Deutsch, *Omer ha-Sadeh*, that comprises the laws for determining the New Moon. Halakhic queries were addressed to Deutsch from many parts of the world.

BIBLIOGRAPHY: Deutsch, in: *Tevu'ot ha-Sadeh*, 5 (1902), introduction; S.N. Gottlieb, *Oholei Shem* (1912), 218; P.Z. Schwartz, *Shem ha-Gedolim me-Ereẓ Hagar*, 1 (1913), 196, no. 254; 3 (1915), s.v. book-titles; N. Ben-Menahem, *Mi-Sifrut Yisrael be-Ungaryah* (1958), 172, no. 95, 331, n. 3.

[Itzhak Alfassi]

DEUTSCH, EMANUEL OSKAR (Menahem; 1829–1873), Orientalist. Born in Neisse (Upper Saxony), Deutsch studied Jewish subjects with his uncle David Deutsch (see Israel *Deutsch) at Myslowice (Poland) and classics in Berlin. He became an assistant in the Oriental department of the British Museum in 1855. Deutsch, who possessed great ability in deciphering inscriptions, cooperated in W.S.A. Vaux's edition of *Phoenician Inscriptions* (1863) and in W. Smith's *Dictionary of the Bible* (1871) to which he contributed articles on the *Targumim*, the Samaritan Pentateuch, and other Bible versions. His essay on the Talmud in the *Quarterly Review* (October 1867) was translated into several languages. The article implied that the key to the understanding of Jesus was to be found in the study of his Palestinian background; this led to a renewed interest in the Talmud among Christians in England. A later article by Deutsch, on Islam, made less impact. He took a prominent part in the correspondence in the London *Times* which resulted from the discovery of the Mesha stele. He was also the paper's special correspondent to the Vatican Ecumenical Council 1869–70. Deutsch contributed nearly 200 articles to *Chambers' Encyclopaedia*. Some of his work was published posthumously in book form (*Literary Remains*, 1874) and edited by Lady Strangford.

BIBLIOGRAPHY: DNB, S.V.; JC (May 1873).

DEUTSCH, ERNST (1890–1969), German actor. At the age of 24, playing the main role in Hasenclever's *The Son*, Deutsch became one of the exponents of expressionism on the German stage. He had his most fruitful period at the Reinhardt Theater in Berlin, but could also be seen in films and on stage at the Burgtheater in Vienna. Deutsch played many Jewish roles, among them parts in Arnold Zweig's *Blood Libel in Hungary*, R. Beer-Hoffman's *Jacob's Dream*, and Galsworthy's *Loyalties*. With the rise of Hitler, Deutsch left Germany and worked in London and Hollywood. After World War II, he was invited to appear in Berlin and Vienna and in 1957 played in *Nathan the Wise*.

BIBLIOGRAPHY: J. Bab, *Schauspieler und Schauspielkunst*, 1928; A. Zweig, *Juden auf der deutschen Buehne* (1929). **ADD. BIBLIOGRAPHY:** G. Zivier, *Ernst Deutsch und das deutsche Theater: Fünf Jahrzehnte deutsche Theatergeschichte – Der Lebensweg eines großen Schauspielers* (1964).

DEUTSCH, FELIX (1884–1964), psychiatrist. Born in Vienna, Deutsch grew up in a liberal atmosphere without any formal religious background. Faced with the antisemitic environment of Vienna University, he joined the Zionist student organization Kadima, and became a leading figure with a reputation for fighting on the side of minority groups. He was a friend of Herzl and was one of the pallbearers at his funeral. In 1921 he lectured in medicine at Vienna University.

As early as 1919 Deutsch established a clinic for "organneuroses," a result of his scientific preoccupation with emotional factors in physical illness. This interest led him to psychoanalysis and to close association with Freud. As a result of his interest and influence, the first home of the Psychoanalytic Clinic was established in 1922 in Vienna. He produced many publications on the interaction of emotional and physical processes and became one of the pioneers of psychosomatic medicine. With the advent of Hitler, Deutsch immigrated to the United States in 1935, became research fellow in psychiatry at Harvard University, and held various teaching positions. From 1951 to 1954 he was president of the Boston Psychoanalytic Institute. He wrote articles on an astonishing variety of medical and psychoanalytical topics. Terms like "associative anamnesis," "sector psychotherapy," and "posturology" coined by him enriched the scientific language. In 1939, he published an essay on "The Production of Somatic Disease by Emotional

Disturbance," in *Inter-Relationship of Mind and Body* (published by the Association for Research in Nervous and Mental Disease), and in 1949, *Applied Psychoanalysis*. Deutsch never abandoned his Zionist ideals and his last project, cut short by his death, was a study of the art of children gathered in Israel from all corners of the world.

BIBLIOGRAPHY: G.W. Flagg, in: F. Alexander et al. (eds.), *Psychoanalytic Pioneers* (1966), 299–307; A. Grinstein, *Index of Psychoanalytic Writings*, 1 (1956), 380–4. **ADD. BIBLIOGRAPHY:** G. Hohendorf, "Felix Deutsch und die Entwicklung der psychosomatischen Medizin," in: C. Kaiser and M.-L. Wuensche (eds.), *Die "Nervosität der Juden" und andere Leiden an der Zivilisation und Konzepte individueller Krankheiten im psychiatrischen Diskurs um 1900* (2003), 207–26.

[Heinrich Zwi Winnik]

DEUTSCH, GOTTHARD (1859–1921), historian and theologian. Deutsch was born in Dolné Kounice (Kanitz), Moravia. He studied at the Breslau Jewish Theological Seminary and at Vienna University, and was ordained by Isaac Hirsch *Weiss. Deutsch first served as teacher of religion at Bruenn and as rabbi in Most (Bruex, Bohemia). In 1891 he accepted a position as professor of Jewish history and philosophy at Hebrew Union College, Cincinnati, where he became one of the leading spokesmen of Reform Judaism. Deutsch succeeded Isaac Meyer Wise as editor of the German-American monthly *Deborah* in 1901, and also contributed articles in English and German to several Jewish and general periodicals. Deutsch was known for his sympathies toward Orthodoxy despite his intellectual disagreement. He prayed at an Orthodox synagogue in Cincinnati. His German roots and appreciation of things German proved problematic at the beginning of World War I. As anti-German sentiment spread throughout the United States there was a move afoot to dismiss him from the HUC faculty. He belonged to the moderates in the Reform movement, and although not a Zionist he greatly sympathized with many aspects of Zionism. He was editor of the modern Jewish history division of the *Jewish Encyclopedia*. Deutsch, while in many ways an original historian who devoted meticulous attention to detail and motivations, did not write a major account of Jewish history, and most of his published work is in the form of essays and lectures. He wrote *Scrolls, Essays on Jewish History and Literature* (3 vols., 1917–20), *Memorable Dates of Jewish History* (1904), and *History of the Jews* (1904). Deutsch wrote a German novel, *Unloesbare Fesseln* (1903), and a historical play in English, *Israel Bruna* (1908). A son of Deutsch was HERMANN BACHER DEUTSCH (1889–1970), writer and journalist.

BIBLIOGRAPHY: *Hebrew Union College Monthly*, 8 (1922), 117–55; G.A. Dobbert, in: AJA, 20 (1968), 129–55; M. Raisin, *Great Jews I Have Known* (1952), 143–52; Bloch, in: *Sefer ha-Shanah li-Yhudei Amerikah*, 6 (1942), 451–61. **ADD. BIBLIOGRAPHY:** M.A. Cohen, "History," in: *Hebrew Union College-Jewish Institute of Religion at 100* (1976); K.M. Olitzsky, L.J. Sussman, and M.H. Stern (eds.), *Reform Judaism in America: A Biographical Dictionary and Sourcebook* (1993).

DEUTSCH, HELENE (née **Rosenbach**; 1884–1982), psychoanalyst and psychiatrist. Helene Deutsch was born in Przemysl, Poland, where her father, a lawyer, was at one time president of the Jewish community. Because of the restrictions on female education, she ran away to Vienna in order to train as a physician. In 1912 she married Felix *Deutsch. Helene Deutsch was the first woman assistant in Vienna University's psychiatric department, and was later made head of the female ward. After becoming acquainted with the ideas of Freud she gave up her academic career. She went through a training analysis by *Freud himself and became one of the leading figures of the so-called second generation of analysts. In 1923 she went to work with Karl *Abraham in Berlin for a year and on her return established the psychoanalytic training institute in Vienna along the lines of the Berlin institute, serving as its director until her departure for the U.S. in 1935. At the institute she introduced the "continuous case seminar," which became the clinical model for the presentation of psychoanalytical treatment. In the U.S. she settled in Boston, where she spent the rest of her career on the teaching staff of the Psychoanalytic Institute. The outstanding achievement in Helene Deutsch's scientific work is her exploration of the particularities of the female psyche, working on the basis of psychoanalytical theory and expanding the findings of Freud. Her publications in this field were summarized in two volumes entitled *Psychology of Women* (1944–45), a comprehensive monograph with arguments illustrated by numerous clinical cases from Helene Deutsch's own practice and from studies of the female character in world literature. The lucid case presentations and theoretical deductions in her *Psychoanalyse der Neurosen* (1930; *Psychoanalysis of the Neuroses*, 1932) make this one of the classics of psychoanalytic literature. Among her later publications are the book, *Neuroses and Character Types: Clinical Psychoanalytic Studies* (1965), and *Selected Problems of Adolescence* (1967).

BIBLIOGRAPHY: M.H. Briel, in: F. Alexander et al. (eds.), *Psychoanalytic Pioneers* (1966), 282–98.

[Heinrich Zwi Winnik]

DEUTSCH, IGNAZ (1808–1881), extremist leader of Austrian Jewish Orthodoxy. A native of Pressburg (Bratislava), he became a banker in Vienna and *gabbai* of the Polish synagogue there in 1848. To further Orthodox influence, he submitted numerous memoranda to the minister of religious affairs claiming that Orthodox Jews supported monarchical rule while Reform Jewry favored revolution. He urged the government to invest rabbis with the same powers as those enjoyed by Catholic clergymen under the concordat of 1855. In 1857 he appealed for government intervention in his unsuccessful attempt to secure the secession of Orthodox communities. Deutsch was prepared to give in to Catholics and the government over questions of Jewish rights, for instance, requesting rabbis not to support the Vienna community leadership's protest against the cancellation of the rights of Jews to own real estate (1853) and approving the pope's standpoint in the *Mortara case (1858). His denunciation (1860) of the *Alliance Israélite Universelle as subversive led to the founding of the independent Viennese *Allianz. In 1859 Deutsch had himself appointed representative in Austria by the Jews living in Jerusalem under the protection of the Austrian consul, but his request to be granted supervision of money collections for them was refused. However, he was recognized as supervisor (*Kurator*) of the affairs of Austrian Jews in Ereẓ Israel. He denounced L.A. *Frankl for introducing reforms in the synagogue attached to the Laemel school in Jerusalem.

Gerson *Wolf's publication (under the pen name of Israel Levi Kohn) in 1864 of several of Deutsch's applications to the ministry of religious affairs in *Beitrag zur Geschichte juedischer Tartueffe* (1864), after Deutsch had publicly denied that he had written them, the failure of his bank, and his circular to the Orthodox rabbis on the Mortara affair put an end to his public career. The leader of Vienna Orthodoxy, R. (Benjamin) Solomon *Spitzer, refused to cooperate with him. Deutsch achieved government recognition of the Pressburg (Bratislava) yeshivah as an academic institution of theological instruction.

BIBLIOGRAPHY: N.M. Gelber, *Aus zwei Jahrhunderten* (1924), 145–77.

DEUTSCH, ISRAEL (1800–1853), rabbi of Beuthen (Bytom). He and his brother DAVID (1810–1873), rabbi of Muslowitz (Myslowice) and Sohrau (Zory), Germany (now Poland), were militant champions of *Orthodoxy against *Reform. They opposed Abraham *Geiger's nomination as rabbi of Breslau and wrote jointly a pamphlet attacking his views (1843). David took a strong stand against rabbinical *conferences (*Asaf Asefah*, 1846) and the use of the organ in the synagogue. He published an annotated edition (with translation) of the Book of Habakkuk (1837) and Isaac of *Troki's *Ḥizzuk Emunah* (1865). Israel's letters to Abraham Muhr (*Zera Israel*, 1855, 26ff.), written between 1837 and 1846, are indicative of Orthodox thought in Germany at that time. The sermons of the two brothers were a synthesis between the old-style *derashah* and modern preaching. A third brother, ABRAHAM, was *dayyan* at Gleiwitz (Gliwice). The Orientalist Emanuel Oskar *Deutsch was their nephew.

BIBLIOGRAPHY: J. Nordin, *David Deutsch…* (Ger., 1902); W.G. Plant, *Rise of Reform Judaism* (1963), 257–8; Toury, in: BLBI, 8 (1965), 69–80.

DEUTSCH, JUDAH JOEL (c. 1870–1918), rabbi. He was a devoted disciple of Jekuthiel Judah *Teitelbaum, rabbi of Sighet (Máramarossziget). At the age of 20 he was appointed rabbi of Ganya in Máramaros. Invitations were extended to him to become rabbi of many Hungarian and Polish communities, but his invariable reply was: "Here I acquired my knowledge and here I wish to dispense it." He wrote important works on the Talmud, as well as many responsa, but almost all his writings were lost during World War I.

His son, MOSES DEUTSCH (1887–1944), succeeded him as rabbi. Endowed with an outstanding memory and a keen mind, he was an expert in Jewish monetary law, and was particularly conversant with the responsa of Moses Sofer (Schreiber), which he quoted freely. He perished in Auschwitz.

BIBLIOGRAPHY: P.Z. Schwartz, *Shem ha-Gedolim me-Ereẓ Hagar*, 1 (1914), 54b; O.Z. Rand, *Toledot Anshei Shem* (1950), 25; J.J. Greenwald, *Maẓẓevet Kodesh* (1952), 27.

[Naphtali Ben-Menahem]

DEUTSCH, LEO (**Lev Grigoryevich**; 1855–1941), Russian revolutionary. Deutsch was born in Tulchin (Kamenets Podolsk) and in the 1870s joined the Populist Narodniki. In 1877 he organized a revolt of farmers in the district of Chigirin (Ukraine); he was arrested but escaped to Switzerland. In 1879 he returned to Peterburg and was a member of the revolutionary organization Ẓemlia i Volia" ("Earth and Freedom"), and later of "Chornyi Peredel." In 1880 he immigrated to Switzerland, and with Plekhanov, Akselrod, and others in 1883 they founded "Osvobozhdenie Truda" ("Liberation of Labor"), the first Russian Marxist group abroad. In 1884 he was arrested in Germany and was handed over to the Russian government. After 16 years of hard labor he escaped to Switzerland again (1901). His experiences were published in *Sixteen Years in Siberia* (London, 1903; Russian ed. 1924), which was translated into many languages. He sided with the Mensheviks in 1903. In 1905 he returned to Russia, was arrested and escaped again, and lived in London from 1907 to 1911 and in the U.S. from 1911 to 1916. After the February Revolution he returned to Russia. Since his attitude toward the October Revolution was negative, he gave up politics. He concerned himself with editing Plekhanov's works. In his later years he was mainly occupied with the history of the Russian revolutionary movement. Only the first volume of his work *Rol yevreyev v russkom revolyutsionnom dvizhenii* ("The Role of the Jews in the Russian Revolutionary Movement," 1923) was ever published.

DEUTSCH, MORITZ (1818–1892), cantor and teacher. Deutsch, who was born in Nikolsburg, Moravia, was an infant prodigy in talmudic studies. Having a remarkable tenor voice, he went to Vienna to study music and cantorial singing. In 1842 he was appointed second cantor of the Liberal temple in Vienna, where Solomon *Sulzer was chief cantor. Two years later he became chief cantor at the Reform synagogue in Breslau. Here he formed and conducted a mixed choir. Deutsch taught cantorial music at the Breslau Theological Seminary for 30 years and in 1859 founded an institute for training cantors. He made original arrangements of liturgical music, aiming perhaps excessively at German choral style. His compositions include *Breslauer Synagogengesaenge* (1880) for soloist and choir, school songs, 12 preludes for organ and piano, and *Vorbeterschule* (1871).

BIBLIOGRAPHY: A. Friedmann, in: AZDJ, 75 (1911), 174–5, 199–201; Sendrey, Music, index; Idelsohn, *Melodien*, 6 (1932), 24; E. Zaludkowski, *Kulturtreger fun der yidisher Liturgye* (1930), 63–67.

[Joshua Leib Ne'eman]

DEUTSCH, OTTO ERICH (1883–1967), Austrian musicologist and bibliographer. He was for some time art critic of *Die Zeit* in Vienna, where he was born, and from 1926 to 1955, librarian of the important music collection of A. van Hoboken. After the *Anschluss* in 1938, he went to England, but returned to Vienna in 1956. Deutsch developed a form of "synthetic biography," which combined bibliographical and iconographical documentation. He devoted many years to the study of Schubert, producing *Schubert, A Documentary Biography* (1946) and *Schubert, Thematic Catalogue…* (1951). His later years were devoted to research on Mozart, which resulted in *Mozart – Die Dokumente seines Lebens* and *Mozart und seine Welt in zeitgenoessischen Bildern*, both in 1961. He also compiled a documentary biography of Handel (1954) and published reference works on early music printing. All Schubert's works are now designated by D (Deutsch) numbers, based on his 1951 catalog.

BIBLIOGRAPHY: MGG, s.v.; *Grove's Dict*, s.v. (see also suppl. vol.); Gerstenberg, in: *Die Musikforschung*, 21 (1968), 149–54.

[Judith Cohen]

DEUTSCH, SIMON (c. 1822–1877), Austrian revolutionary. Born in Nikolsburg, Deutsch lived in Vienna, where he studied for the rabbinate, cataloged Hebrew manuscripts at the Imperial Library, and published Menahem b. Jacob ibn Saruq's *Maḥberet*. He soon turned to Socialism and after the 1848 revolution was condemned to death, but escaped via Switzerland to France. In Paris, Deutsch entered business and became prosperous, opening branches in Belgium, Romania, and Turkey, but remained a radical and associated with Michelet and Proudhon. During the 1870 Franco-Prussian War, Deutsch served in the French army. In 1871 he took part in the Paris Commune as one of the leaders of the First Communist International. After the collapse of the Commune he was thrown into prison, but was saved from death by the Austrian ambassador. In 1874 he replaced Karl Marx at the directory committee of the International. From Paris, Deutsch moved to Turkey, where he was associated in the foundation of the Young Turk movement. He died in Constantinople.

BIBLIOGRAPHY: Nordmann, in: AZDJ, 47 (1883), 293–6. **ADD. BIBLIOGRAPHY:** *Enciclopedia Judaica Castellana*, 3 (1949), 473.

DEUTSCH DE LA MEURTHE, HENRI (1846–1919), French industrialist and philanthropist. Henri was born in Paris, and began his career as an industrialist with the Société des Pétroles, which his father, Alexander Deutsch (d. 1889), had founded. In 1866 Henri and his brother, Émile, took over joint management of the firm, and under their direction it became one of the leading French companies in the petroleum industry. Henri Deutsch de la Meurthe pioneered in advancing the commercial uses of petroleum. His work, *Le Pétrole et ses Applications* (1891), and the exhibit on the petroleum industry which he arranged at the 1889 World Fair in Paris, contributed greatly to a fuller understanding of the importance of petroleum in industry and commerce. In 1901 he encouraged the use of petroleum for aviation with an offer of a prize for a successful flight over Paris, which was won by Alberto Santos-Dumont. In 1906 he made a gift to the French government of the dirigible *Ville-de-Paris*, which Santos-Dumont had flown. He was the founder of the Aerotechnic Institute at St. Cyr for the University of Paris, and the donor of a chair in aeronautics at the Conservatoire National des Arts et Métiers. He wrote a lyric opera, *Icarus*, which was performed at the Paris Opera in 1911. He was an active member of the French Consistoire Central. A monument in his honor was erected at Ecquevilly, Seine-et-Oise, in 1923.

His brother ÉMILE (1847–1924), who also pioneered in the French petroleum industry, was born in Paris. He was the founder and first president of the Franco-American Brotherhood during World War I, and as its continuing head played an important role in giving assistance to nearly 300,000 French war orphans. In 1920 he set up the Émile and Louise de la Meurthe Foundation with an endowment of 10,000,000 francs, to build seven dormitories for impoverished students in Paris. Émile was also active in the Consistoire Central and was elected vice president of the Paris Consistory. He was a member of the central committee of the Alliance Israélite Universelle and founder of the Union Libérale Juive.

BIBLIOGRAPHY: *Dictionnaire de biographie française*, 11 (1967), 164.

DEUTSCHER, ISAAC (1907–1967), British Marxist historian and political scientist. Born in Cracow, Poland, Deutscher had a strictly Orthodox education and upbringing. In his youth he was a Hebrew-speaking Zionist and even translated modern Hebrew poetry into Polish. From 1926 he was a member of the illegal Communist Party in Poland, ultimately serving as the party's clandestine editor of several legal periodicals which secretly accepted Communist guidance. In 1932, when he disobeyed party orders and in the periodicals refused to brand the Social-Democrats as "Social-Fascists" and the principal enemies of the working class, he was expelled from the Communist Party. For several years he displayed leanings toward Trotskyism.

In 1939, before the outbreak of World War II, he went to London, where he was on the editorial staff of the *Economist* and the *Observer* (under the pen name "Peregrine"). Later he devoted himself to historical research and acquired an international reputation as the political biographer of *Stalin and *Trotsky and an expert on Soviet Russia and Communism. Deutscher remained a Marxist although he became famous for his writings and lectures in which he exposed the brutality of the Stalin regime. In 1953 he visited Israel and showed understanding and sympathy for Jewish national independence after the Nazi Holocaust. But later he became again sharply opposed to Zionism and lost no opportunity of attacking Israel for its ultranationalism and for being nationalist in a world becoming increasingly supranational. It has been said that Deutscher's attempt to secure a chair at Sussex

University in 1963 was thwarted by Sir Isaiah *Berlin, who spoke strongly against him as a member of the appointments panel. Deutscher never held a continuing position at a British university. In *The Non-Jewish Jew and Other Essays* (published posthumously, 1968) Deutscher discussed the heritage of European Jewry as he saw it and defined such personalities as *Spinoza, *Marx, *Freud, and Trotsky as "non-Jewish" Jews; the phrase has become proverbial. Despite this attitude, Deutscher in his essays treated life in the small Jewish towns with tenderness and sympathy and had a warm feeling for the Jewish working masses.

His works include *Stalin, a Political Biography* (1949), *Russia after Stalin* (1953), *The Great Contest: Russia and the West* (1960), a trilogy on the life of L. Trotsky – *The Prophet Armed* (1954), *The Prophet Unarmed* (1959), and *The Prophet Outcast* (1963) – and *Unfinished Revolution: Russia, 1917–1967* (1967). A collection of his essays, *Marxism, Wars, and Revolution: Essay from Four Decades,* edited by Tamara Deutscher, was published in 1984.

BIBLIOGRAPHY: D. Lazar, *Rashim be-Yisrael*, 2 (1955), 315–20; T. Deutscher, in: I. Deutscher, *The Non-Jewish Jew and other Essays* (1968), introd. and preface. **ADD. BIBLIOGRAPHY:** D.J. Horowitz, *Isaac Deutscher: The Man and His Work* (1971); ODNB online.

[Moshe Rosetti]

DEUTSCHER PALAESTINA-VEREIN, German society for the study of the Holy Land. It was founded by A. Socin, E. Kautzsch, and H. Guthe in 1877 on the model of the British Palestine Exploration Fund, its aim being the "advancement of the knowledge of the history of Palestine." The society, however, did not engage in excavations but concentrated on the publication of its journal, the *Zeitschrift des deutschen Palaestina-Vereins*. Many Jewish scholars contributed to the journal until 1933. Its publication stopped in 1943 and in the following year the archives and offices of the society were destroyed during the bombardment of Leipzig. From 1949 to 1951 it published the *Beitraege zur biblischen Landes-und Altertumskunde*. The society was reestablished at Bonn in 1952 and resumed the publication of its *Zeitschrift*. Its heads have included M. Noth, A. Kuschke, and K. Galling.

[Michael Avi-Yonah]

DEUTSCH-ISRAELITISCHER GEMEINDEBUND (DIGB), union of German Jewish communities; the first all-German Jewish association. Founded in 1869 at the Leipzig *synod, the DIGB began its activities only with the establishment of the German Empire (1871). Initially its headquarters were in Leipzig, but in 1882 they were moved to Berlin. The union gradually embraced most of the German communities, but internal dissensions and legal obstacles prevented it from becoming the representative body of German Jewry. Many of the Orthodox communities withheld their cooperation even though the DIGB's constitution precluded it from dealing with religious and political issues. After World War I, when the Weimar Republic permitted the unification of religious associations, a fresh attempt at effecting a joint representation of all communities had no practical results. Instead, separate communal associations were established in the different states, the largest of which was the Preussischer Landesverband der juedischen Gemeinden. A fully representative body, the *Reichsvertretung der deutschen Juden, was established only in 1933, as a result of the pressures of the Nazi regime.

The DIGB's activities were widespread. In particular it adopted small and financially weak communities, supporting the appointment of religious teachers, providing grants for communal buildings, planning curricula, and organizing Jewish teachers' conferences. One outcome of these efforts was the creation of the Jewish Teachers' Association of the German Empire. Funds were set up to provide for communal officials and charitable institutions, including homes for neglected and mentally retarded children, and a Jewish Workers' Colony for the rehabilitation of impoverished immigrants. In 1885 the DIGB founded the Historical Commission for Investigating the History of the Jews in Germany to gather and sift sources and records for scientific research into the Jewish past. The Commission included non-Jews, such as the legal historian Otto *Stobbe, one of its first chairmen. Only three volumes of the Commission's *Quellen zur Geschichte der Juden in Deutschland* (1888–98) were published. Another important publication was the *Zeitschrift fuer die Geschichte der Juden in Deutschland*, edited by Ludwig *Geiger and published for six years (1887–92). To cover German Jewry's more recent past the *Gesamtarchiv der deutschen Juden* (subsequently transferred to Israel; see Jewish *Archives) was set up, and a statistical yearbook was published. The DIGB attempted to combat antisemitism by disseminating explanatory literature, an activity later expanded by the *Centralverein deutscher Staatsbuerger juedischen Glaubens. Presidents of the DIGB included the renowned gynecologist S. *Kristeller and the historian Martin *Phillipson.

BIBLIOGRAPHY: A. Kober, in: JSOS, 9 (1947), 195–238; K. Wilhelm, in: YLBI, 2 (1957), 61–63; A. Sandler, *ibid.*, 76–84.

[Reuven Michael]

DEUTSCHKREUTZ (also **Cruez**; Hung. **Keresztúr** or **Németkeresztúr**, **Sopronkeresztúr**; Heb. **צלם, צעלם**), town in E. Austria. Its community, one of the "Seven Communities" of *Burgenland, increased mainly at the end of the 15th century. In 1526 it absorbed Jews expelled from *Sopron. The situation of the Jews in Deutschkreutz improved when the princes Esterházy took over Deutschkreutz in 1664. In 1701 an agreement was signed between them and the community, renewed several times against payment; Deutschkreutz Jews were permitted to do business in Sopron. A synagogue was built in 1747 and rebuilt in 1834. It was destroyed by the Nazis in 1941. The community was known for its Orthodoxy; its yeshivah became celebrated, especially under Menahem *Katz-Wannfried. The composer Karl *Goldmark grew up in Deutschkreutz. When in 1921 Burgenland was finally separated from Hungary, Deutschkreutz lost its hinterland, and the community decreased. It numbered 28 persons in 1672; 47 in 1725; 20 families in 1729; 222 persons in 1735; 100 families in 1780; 1,230 persons (37.8% of the total population) in 1880; 764 in 1911; 410 in 1929; and 433 (12.1%) in 1934. Immediately after the *Anschluss* in 1938 the Nazis expelled the Deutschkreutz Jews to Vienna. At the time there were 103 families (433 persons) there. In 1944 hundreds of Hungarian Jews were deported to Deutschkreutz to build the *Ostwall* fortifications. There were no Jews living in Deutschkreutz in 1970. A monument was erected on the site of the synagogue in 1949. The cemetery, including 286 gravesites of forced laborers from Hungary, has been fenced in and is cared for by the Vienna community. Part of the community archives has been preserved and transferred to the Burgenland state archives in Eisenstadt.

BIBLIOGRAPHY: L. Moses, in: JJLG, 18 (1927), 305–26; 19 (1928), 195–224; *Magyar Zsidó Lexikon* (1929) s.v. *Németkeresztúr*; MGWJ, 74 (1930), 92–93; Y. Gruenwald, *Mekorot le-Korot Yisrael* (1934), 91–99; MHJ, 2 (1937); 5, pt. 1 (1959); 5, pt. 2 (1960); 6 (1961); 7 (1963); 8 (1965); 10 (1967), index; N. Gergely, in: *Új Élet*, 14 (Dec. 15, 1969); A. Zistler, in: H. Gold (ed.), *Gedenkbuch der untergangenen Judengemeinden des Burgenlandes* (1970), 57–74; BJCE; PK. **ADD. BIBLIOGRAPHY:** S. Spitzer, *Die juedische Gemeinde von Deutschkreutz* (1995).

[Yehouda Marton]

DEUTSCHLAENDER, LEO (1888–1935), educationist and writer. Born in Berlin, he became head of Jewish education in Lithuania during World War I, first as appointee of the German occupation authorities. He was co-founder of the first Orthodox secondary school Yavneh in Kaunas (Kovno). When director of the Keren ha-Torah of *Agudat Israel, he helped Sara Schnirer to develop the *Beth Jacob Orthodox girls' education network, mainly in Poland, and headed its Teachers Training College for women in Cracow.

Deutschlaender's published work includes *West-Oestliche Dichterklaenge* (1919); *Goethe und das Alte Testament* (1923); *Biblisch-talmudische Sentenzen* (1931); *History of the Beth Jacob Girls Schools* (1933); and various textbooks for schools. He also wrote on education for the Hebrew and Yiddish periodicals published by Agudat Israel. He died in Vienna.

BIBLIOGRAPHY: Grunfeld-Rosenbaum, in; L. Jung (ed.), *Jewish Leaders* (1964), 426ff.; *Nachalath Z'wi*, 5 (1935), 344–5; LNYL, 2 (1958), 495–6.

[Judith Grunfeld-Rosenbaum]

DEUTZ, former town, now a suburb of *Cologne, Germany. Jews are first mentioned in Deutz as victims of the *Black Death persecutions (1348–49). It is unlikely that the expulsion of the Jews from Cologne in 1424 had a major impact on the development of the community in Deutz, which experienced significant growth only from the early 17th century. In 1631, during the Thirty Years War, the Jews of Deutz were permitted to deposit their wealth and pledges at Cologne. The Deutz *Memorbuch* for the years 1581–1784 records the prevention of anti-Jewish riots instigated by Cologne students in 1665. Throughout the 16th and 17th centuries celebrated Jewish physicians of Deutz practiced in Cologne. Noted 17th-century physicians, who were also talmudic scholars and community leaders, included Abraham Salomo (d. 1631), his son Isaac (d. 1657), and Levi Nathan (1616–1670). A synagogue is known to have existed in Deutz from the 16th century, but there is no evidence of a rabbinate before the mid-17th century. The first **Landesrabbiner* of the Electorate of Cologne to have officiated in Deutz was Herz Bruehl (d. 1656), who was succeeded in the 18th century by Judah Mehler (d. 1751) and Joseph Juspa Kossmann (d. 1758). In 1695 the Deutz community acquired a cemetery which was also used by the Cologne community from 1807 to 1867. In 1784 the old synagogue (built in the early 18th century) was destroyed by flood; it was rebuilt in 1786 and remained in use until 1914. A new synagogue was erected in 1915. The number of Jews in Deutz possessing rights of residence increased from four in 1616 to 17 in 1634 and 19 in 1764. In 1823, under Prussian rule, there were 238 Jews in Deutz, decreasing to 233 in 1840, and 206 in 1880. In 1928 the Deutz community was amalgamated with that of Cologne. The synagogue in Deutz was destroyed on **Kristallnacht*, Nov. 10, 1938.

BIBLIOGRAPHY: Germ Jud, 1 (1963), 86–87; 2 (1968), 161; K. Brisch, *Geschichte der Juden in Cöln und Umgebung...*, 2 vols. (1879–82); A. Kober, *Cologne* (Eng., 1940), passim; idem, in: *Festschrift zum 75 jaehrigen Bestehen des juedisch-theologischen Seminars*, 2 (1929), 173–236; idem, *Aus der Geschichte der Juden im Rheinland* (1931), 22–5; Salfeld, Martyrol, 287. **ADD. BIBLIOGRAPHY:** K.H.S. Schulte, *Familienbuch der Deutzer Juden* (1992); B. Klein, in: *Hirt und Herde* (2000), 251–78.

[Chasia Turtel / Stefan Rohrbacher (2nd ed.)]

DEUTZ, SIMON (1802–1852), French politician and son of Emmanuel Deutz (1763–1842). Emmanuel Deutz was rabbi of his native city of Coblenz then under French occupation. In 1806 and 1807 he was a member of the *Assembly of Jewish Notables and of the Napoleonic *Sanhedrin, and sat in the Central *Consistory formed in 1808. From 1822 until his death Deutz was *Grand Rabbin* of France.

Simon Deutz converted to Catholicism at the age of 23, but in his later years returned to the Jewish faith. Upon his conversion he adopted the name of Hyacinthe de Gonzague and worked for the amelioration of the condition of the persecuted Jews of Rome. Deutz was asked by Pope Leo XII to prepare a memorandum on the Jews of Rome, and he was secretary of a special commission appointed by Pius VIII to prepare a charter for them. However, the chairman, Cardinal Cappellari, known for his anti-Jewish views, consistently ignored Deutz's memoranda. In 1832 Deutz met the Duchess de Berry, then actively engaged in a legitimist conspiracy against Louis Philippe of France, and went to Spain and Portugal on her behalf to obtain arms and men. She also entrusted him with the delicate mission of securing a promise of Russian military assistance. In the end, however, Deutz, fearing civil war in France, denounced the duchess. Her arrest in 1832 was the signal for a public outcry against Deutz, the "Jewish traitor," few believing that he was activated by motives of loyalty to France. Adolphe *Crémieux asked Deutz's father to protest against his son's "shameful" act, on behalf of the Jewish community. The chief rabbi refused, but in 1835 Deutz published a memorandum *Arrestation de Madame* describing his conversion and his patriotic motives in his denunciation of the duchess. By this time Crémieux and others had become convinced of Deutz's sincerity.

BIBLIOGRAPHY: Szajkowski, in: JJS, 16 (1965), 53–67; C. Roth, *ibid.*, 17 (1966), 83f.; P. Klein, in: *Revue de la pensée juive*, 2:7 (1950/51), 87–103.

DEVEKUT (Heb. דְּבֵקוּת; lit. "cleaving"). The verb *dvk* occurs frequently in Deuteronomy (4:4, 10:20, 11:22, 13:5, 30:20) in the context of cleaving to God. The Talmud asks how it is possible for man to "cleave to God" Who is a "devouring fire" (Deut. 4:24) and answers that it is fulfilled by marrying the daughter of a scholar or assisting scholars materially (Ket. 111b). Elsewhere in answer to the same question, it answers that this is fulfilled by imitation of God, and emulating His attributes (the passage in Sotah 14a should obviously be based on the phrase "and cleave unto Him" in the verse quoted, and not on the words "Ye shall walk after the Lord your God").

Both the noun *devekut* and its verb *davok* have several theological and mystical meanings in kabbalistic literature. Sometimes it means no more than "being near to" or "to cleave." However, the most usual meaning of this term, if it can be said to have a usual meaning, is "communion with God," which is achieved mainly during the time of *prayer or meditation before prayer through using the right **kavvanot*, the mystical interpretations and meanings given to the words of prayer. Usually, *devekut* is described as the highest step on a spiritual ladder, which is reached after the believer has mastered the attitudes of fear of God, love of God, etc. The aspect in the divine world, according to the kabbalistic concept of the ten *Sefirot*, to which the mystic prays when he aspires to reach the state of *devekut*, is usually the **Shekhinah*, the tenth and lowest of the *Sefirot*, which is also the feminine element in the divine world. Usually, the kabbalists emphasize clearly that the communion achieved by the living mystic during prayer is transitory and incomplete in its nature. Only after death can a man hope that his soul will reach a complete and permanent state of *devekut* with God (again, usually with the *Shekhinah*), and the final state of bliss will not be achieved until the redemption, after the coming of the Messiah, when all just Jews will live together eternally in the state of *devekut*. This, the most conservative attitude, is expressed in the *Zohar several times (although other concepts are found in it too), and was widely accepted by the writers of kabbalistic ethical literature in the 16th–18th centuries, in Safed and in Eastern Europe. However, most kabbalists attempted to formulate a more ambitious concept of communion with God, which they described in many different symbols, revealing a wide range of spiritual attitudes toward the mystic's relationship with the divine powers.

One of the most common ideas to be found in kabbalistic literature is that *devekut* is itself a ladder, in which a man can climb from one *Sefirah* to another and raise his soul from one point to another in mystical contemplation. As the various portions and words of prayer and the various deeds that the commandments require correspond to different parts and powers in the divine worlds, so does the soul rise with the works and deeds toward the *Sefirah* to which it is intended. Thus the mystic may achieve *devekut* with the higher *Sefirot*, such as *yesod* (the ninth), *tiferet* (the sixth), *din* (fifth), and *ḥesed* (fourth) in the divine ladder. Kabbalists are more cautious when dealing with man's relationship with the highest *Sefirot*. However, there are expressions in kabbalistic literature which give the impression that *devekut* is possible even with them. In rare instances, *devekut* with the **Ein Sof*, the divine essence beyond all *Sefirot*, is also mentioned; and in some radical pronouncements (e.g., by *Isaac of Acre), it is possible to interpret the kabbalists' words as describing the possibility of achieving *devekut* with the *Ein Sof* while still living. The soul breaks all ties that bind it to the body and unites with the highest aspect of divinity. Such radical expressions, however, are very rare, and the exact meaning of *devekut* in such passages is open to different interpretations. Therefore *devekut* is not the Hebrew term corresponding to what the Christian mystic means by *unio mystica*. There are tendencies in some kabbalistic writings (and even in the Zohar itself) which point toward such a complete union with God, but usually the kabbalists were much more conservative, separating *devekut* from complete union by delaying it to the time after death and the end of days, and by limiting it to the lower parts of the divine worlds.

Early in the history of kabbalistic literature, there are expressions of contemplative, intellectual *devekut*, such as the *devekut ha-maḥashavah* ("the cleaving of thought to God"), which means the return of human thought to its origin in the divine wisdom; or the *devekut ha-raẓon* ("the cleaving of human will to God's"), achieved during prayer. However, in later kabbalistic writing, much more emphasis is placed on the union of the human soul with its spiritual origin in the world of the *Sefirot*. Sometimes there are some elements of ecstasy. The mystic's emotional state while approaching the state of *devekut* and while achieving it is described. In this case, the *devekut* is not an intellectual, contemplative state of mind, but a state of emotional exaltation. In such cases, there is sometimes a hint of a sexual element in the *devekut* between the mystic and the tenth *Sefirah*, the *Shekhinah*. However, such expressions are usually connected with the love of God, as the kabbalists interpreted it.

In most kabbalistic writings, there is a connection between the state of the *devekut* and prophecy, which is the outcome of such union between man and God. The fathers of the nation, Moses, and the prophets were described as people who achieved a lasting state of *devekut*. When *devekut* is achieved, *Ru'aḥ ha-Kodesh* ("The Holy Spirit") comes into contact with the mystic and gives him superhuman spiritual abilities. The idea of the *devekut* as the highest spiritual achievement in religious life was popularized by the writers of kabbalistic ethical literature, and numerous people who were not mystics became familiar with this concept. The last phase of this development was reached with the ḥasidic movement, where *devekut* became not only the supreme achievement of religious life but also its starting point. *Devekut*, according to *Ḥasidism, should be the believer's constant state of mind, even while he is dealing with everyday necessities of life and not only during the high points of prayer and religious activity.

[Joseph Dan]

The ideal of *devekut* as pointing to a complete mystical union between the human intellect and the Agent Intellect or God as an intellect is central in ecstatic Kabbalah as represented in the writings of Abraham *Abulafia. He draws upon the neo-Aristotelian theory of the identity between the knowing subject and its object during the process of intellection, but assumes that God may become the subject of human knowledge.

[Moshe Idel (2nd ed.)]

BIBLIOGRAPHY: Scholem, in: *Review of Religion*, 15 (1950), 115–139; Scholem, Mysticism, index; idem, in: MGWJ (1934), 494ff.; G. Vajda, *L'amour de Dieu dans la théologie juive de moyen âge* (1957), passim; I. Tishby, *Mishnat ha-Zohar*, 2 (1961), 289ff.; E. Gottlieb, in: *Proceedings of the Fourth World Congress for Jewish Studies*, 2 (1968), 203 (English section), and 327–334 (Hebrew section); G. Scholem, *Ursprung und Anfange der Kabbala* (1962), 265–71 and passim. **ADD. BIBLIOGRAPHY:** M. Idel, *Kabbalah: New Perspectives* (1988), 35–58; idem, *Studies in Ecstatic Kabbalah* (1988), 1–32; idem, *The Mystical Experience in Abraham Abulafia* (1988), 124–34; M. Pachter, *Roots of Faith and Devekut* (2004), 235–316.

DEVONS, ELY (1913–1967), British economist. Born in Wales and educated at Manchester University, Devons worked for the Joint Cotton Trades Organization from 1935 to 1940 when he was appointed to the cabinet's statistical office and subsequently to the economic office of the Ministry of Aircraft Production. In 1945 he returned to his native Manchester, where he held a chair until 1959 when he became professor of commerce (later economics) at the London School of Economics. His main fields were statistics, applied economics, and public policy. He questioned accepted economic theories and, because of his interest in public policy, was skeptical of the ability of governments to control and direct economic performance. His publications include *Planning in Practice* (1950), *An Introduction to British Economic Statistics* (1956), *Essays in Economics* (1961), and *Closed Systems and Open Minds* (1964), which he edited (with Max Gluckman).

ADD. BIBLIOGRAPHY: ODNB online.

[Joachim O. Ronall]

DE VRIES, ANDRÉ (1911–1996), Israel physician and medical scientist. De Vries, who was born in Leeuwarden, Holland, studied in Amsterdam. After holding various appointments in Holland, he immigrated to Palestine in 1940 and at first became a farmer. Persuaded to return to medicine, he joined the staff of Hadassah Hospital in Jerusalem in 1942. In 1954 he subsequently became director of the department of internal medicine and of the institute of medical research at Beilinson Hospital near Tel Aviv. In 1960 he was appointed clinical professor of medicine at the Hebrew University of Jerusalem. De Vries was one of the founders of the Faculty of Medicine at Tel Aviv University and in 1964 became dean of this faculty. In 1970 he was awarded the Israel Prize for medical science. His main research was on the methods of production of antivenins (notably snake venoms) and the epidemiology of kidney stones in sub-tropical climates.

[Joseph W. Davis]

DE VRIES, BENJAMIN (1905–1966), Israeli educator and talmudic scholar. De Vries, who was born in Leeuwarden, Holland, studied at the Amsterdam Rabbinical Seminary (where he later lectured), and at Leyden University. After immigrating to Palestine in 1934, he worked both as a teacher and an inspector of education in the religious state schools network. In 1955 he was appointed professor of Talmud at Tel Aviv University. De Vries published numerous articles on educational and religious subjects and made important contributions to the literary and legal study of the Talmud. He also wrote a volume in Dutch on *halakhah* development, *Hoofdlijnen en motieven in de ontwikkeling der Halachah* (1959); an introduction to the Talmud, *Mavo la-Talmud* (1951; 1962²); *Toledot ha-Halakhah ha-Talmudit* (1962; 1966²); and a collection of talmudic studies, *Meḥkarim be-Sifrut ha-Talmud* (1968).

BIBLIOGRAPHY: *Benjamin de Vries Memorial Volume* (1968), includes bibliography, 334–42.

[Ze'ev Wilhem Falk]

DE VRIES, M. (19th century), South African lawyer and politician. De Vries was state prosecutor of the Transvaal in 1868 and a member of the Volksraad (parliament) in 1871 and 1875. He was chairman of the session in 1872 and 1875. Since there was a shortage of suitable officials he rose to these positions despite a provision in the Transvaal constitution barring non-Protestants from holding public office.

DEW (Heb. טַל), condensation of water vapor on an object near the ground, whose temperature has fallen below the "dew point" of the surrounding air because of radiational cooling during the night. The conditions favoring the formation of dew are clear nights, moist air, and only light winds in the surface layers of the atmosphere.

The Bible places so much importance on dew as a source of water for plant life (Hos. 14:6–8) that in its absence a drought is considered to prevail (Ḥag. 1:10–11). Dew, like rain, is a symbol of life and God's beneficence (Zech. 8:12). (It should be noted, however, that in biblical Hebrew טל may also refer to rain.) As a figure of speech *dew* expresses a source of abundance (Gen. 27:28), silent and sudden-coming (II Sam. 17:12), and ephemeral (Hos. 13:3). Several verses referring to dew appear in the Bible, according to which the main season of dew is late spring–early summer, or harvest time (e.g., Hos. 14:6; Prov. 19:12; Isa. 18:4; Job 29:19; Song 5:2). Soon after harvest time in the Harod Valley, Gideon "wrung enough dew from the fleece to fill a bowl with water" (Judg. 6:38). This valley, however, does not receive much dew, and is situated near the hills of Gilboa which David, in his lament over the death of Saul and Jonathan, cursed to enjoy neither dew nor rain (II Sam. 1:21).

According to modern investigations, however, the value of dew in the water balance of plants is dubious. As for the distribution of dew, it is interesting to note that the Bible refers to many of the regions, on both sides of the Jordan, in which dew occurs. As some Bible scholars have pointed out, most verses which allude to dew in different regions employ similar phrases of dewiness for them. The average frequency of dew nights in Israel, according to measurements by the Duvdevani dew gauge in the period 1945–1952, was for Tel Shalom (on the Coastal Plain) 231 nights per year; at the Tavor Agr. School (Hill Region) 163; and at Dafnah (in the Jordan Valley) 115.

The largest annual number of dew nights is found in the central Coastal Plain and the northwestern Negev. The northern coastal region and Carmel beach are not favorable for dew formation. The Hill Region is not known for much dew. Mt. Carmel, being relatively low and the nearest hill to the Mediterranean, is the dewiest hill in Israel. The quantity and frequency of dew depend much on local topography: slopes receive little dew while level and concave areas receive it in abundance. In the low and level Valley of Jezreel there are many dew nights, but its western part is dewier than the eastern part, which descends to the Harod Valley. Dew is scarce in the Jordan Valley, particularly in its southern part (Jericho). However, in the flat and concave parts of the Ḥuleh and Beth-Shean valleys the conditions for dew formation are better.

A breakdown of the seasonal distribution of dew frequency in Israel indicates that the largest number of dew nights occurs in summer in the Coastal Plain and Hill Region, the lowest number occurs in winter, and an intermediate number occurs in spring and fall (see Table: Number of Dew Nights).

In the southern Jordan Valley, between the Beth-Shean Valley and the Dead Sea, the regimen of dew is opposite to that in the coastal and hill regions. Dew in the southern Jordan Valley is most frequent in winter, while in summer it is rare or absent in this low-lying region. In the northern Jordan Valley no one month shows a marked increase in the number of dew nights.

BIBLIOGRAPHY: S. Duvdevani, in: *Quarterly Journal of the Royal Meteorological Society*, 73 (1947), 282–96; D. Ashbel, in: *Geographical Review*, 39 (1949), 291–7; M. Gilead and N. Rosenan, in: IEJ, 4 (1954), 120–3; J. Neumann, in: *Archiv fuer Meteorologie, Geophysik und Bioklimatologie*, 9 (1956), 197–203; J. Katsnelson, in: *Enziklopedyah le-Ḥakla'ut*, 1 (1966), 27–62; U. Mané, in: *Atlas of Israel* (1970), sheet IV/1., maps R-T; N. Shalem, in: *Sinai*, 20 (1947), 119–35.

[Jacob Katsnelson]

DEW, PRAYER FOR, prayer incorporated into the liturgy because Ereẓ Israel depended on the moisture of *dew during the long, dry summers. As with rainfall, dew was held to be a heavenly blessing, and its absence a divine punishment (cf. Gen. 27:28, 39; Deut. 33:13; Judg. 6:37–40). The end of the rainy season and the beginning of summer is liturgically marked by a special prayer for dew, called *Tefillat Tal* (among Ashkenazim) or *Tikkun Tal* (among Sephardim), which forms part of the Additional Service (*Musaf*) of the first day of Passover, since it was held that the "stores of dew" are opened on this day (PdRE 32). The prayer is recited at the reader's repetition of the Additional Service *Amidah*. In the Ashkenazi ritual the prayer consists of a series of acrostic *piyyutim* (the central one *Taḥat Eilat Ofer* by Eleazar Kallir) and an invocation in six stanzas ending with: "For Thou art the Lord our God, who causes the wind to blow and the dew to descend," and with the plea: "For a blessing and not for a curse; For life and not for death; For plenty and not for famine; Amen." Nowadays, the *piyyutim* are generally omitted and in Israel the prayer is sometimes said after the Torah scrolls are returned to the ark and before the Additional Service. In Israel all rites have adopted the Sephardi custom of inserting the phrase: "Thou causest the dew to descend" (*morid ha-tal*) in every *Amidah* at the beginning of the second benediction in the period beginning with the first day of Passover and ending with Shemini Aẓeret when the Prayer for Rain is said. The Prayer for Dew and the Prayer for Rain are part of the service in all Jewish rituals including the Conservative and Reform trends who recite them, however, in shortened versions. In traditional Ashkenazi synagogues the reader wears a *kittel* ("shroud") for the Prayer for Dew (as he does on the Day of Atonement) and intones the *Kaddish* before the *Musaf* service in the melody of the Day of Atonement (Sh. Ar., OḤ 114).

BIBLIOGRAPHY: Davidson, Oẓar, 1 (1924), 236; 3 (1930), 526; Elbogen, Gottesdienst, 214f.; idem, in: HUCA, 3 (1926), 215–24.

DHAMĀR, one of the historic cities of Yemen; located on the road between Yarīm and Sana. Dhamār, a large town, was the seat of a famous *madrasa* ("school") of the ruling Zaydiyya sect and had a large Jewish community. The Jewish name for the city was Hadoram, according to the Judeo-Arabic translation ascribed to Saadia Gaon (Gen. 10:27). Dhamār was the main spiritual center of Yemenite Jewry in the 15th century (see R. *Zechariah ben Solomon Rofe). The community numbered about 300 families before the immigration to Israel on 1949–50. The local Jewish community continued to be the spiritual center for the surrounding Jewish communities, having seven synagogues and a permanent rabbinical court with three *dayyanim*. Prior to the Mawza' expulsion, the old Jewish quarter was within the walls of the city, but after the Jews returned from exile they built their new quarter outside the walls, later enclosed by a wall connecting it to the city. Uncharacteristically the head of the *bet din* also served as the temporal leader (*'āqil*), in charge of the poll tax (*jizyah*) and the *ṭuḥna* (compulsory milling of grain for the army). The Orphans Edict was strictly enforced, but community leaders managed to smuggle the young Jewish orphans via Sana to Aden. The socio-economic structure of the local Jewish community was the same as in other urban Jewish communities: silversmiths (about a third of all Jewish craftsmen), weavers, shoemakers, millers, tailors, builders, and wholesalers. The community possessed two famous Torah scrolls to which pilgrimages were made until the whole community immigrated to Israel.

BIBLIOGRAPHY: S. Yavnieli, *Massa Teman*, 17–18; S.Greidi, *Yamim Yedabberu* (1995); Y. Tobi, *Iyyunim bi-Megillat Teman* (1986), 155–56; idem, *"R. Hoter Ben Shlomo Ḥayyav u-Tekufato,"* in: D.R. Blumenthal, *The Philosophical Questions and Answers of Hoter Ben Shlomo* (1981), 279–93; M. Ẓaddok, *Yehudei Teman, Toledotehem ve-Orḥot Ḥayyeihem* (1967), 108–10.

[Yosef Tobi (2nd ed.)]

DHAMĀRĪ, MANṢUR SULEIMAN (Ibn al-Muʿallim, Heb. **Hoter ben Solomon**; first half of the 15th century), Yemenite scholar and author. Dhamārī's major work was *Sirāj al-ʿUqūl* ("Light of the Wise"), an early Yemenite midrashic compilation containing certain Midrashim unknown from other sources. He draws mainly on the Mishnah, the Talmud, the *Sifra* and *Sifrei* and also three post-talmudic scholars: Saadiah Gaon, Maimonides, and Nethanel b. Isaiah. An interesting innovation is his use of Arabic sources – poems, and philosophical essays – side by side with the Jewish sources. Most of the book is written in Arabic, with only about a third in Hebrew. Each chapter begins and ends with one or two poems. Dhamārī's method, similar to that of other Yemenite writers, is one of midrashic commentary, but he is noteworthy also for philosophical exposition. His quotations are, however, imprecise and interspersed with interpretations, some of which are very curious. Other known works by Dhamārī are *Sharḥ ʿalā al-Mishna*, a commentary on Maimonides' exposition of the Mishnah; *Sharḥ al-Qawāʿid*, a commentary on the 13 principles; and 100 responsa, mostly collected in 1423 (all unpublished).

BIBLIOGRAPHY: A. Kohut, *Manzûr al-Dhamâri's Hebrew-Arabic Philosophical Commentary on the Pentateuch* (n.d.); S. Lieberman, *Yemenite Midrashim* (1940); Y. Ratzaby, in: KS, 28 (1952/53), 261–78, 394–402, nos. 12, 127, 158, 231.

[Yehuda Ratzaby]

DHAMĀRĪ, SAʿID BEN DAVID (first half of the 15th century), Yemenite writer and scholar; author of *Midrash ha-Be'ur* (1441), a commentary on the Pentateuch and the *haftarot*, one of the early Yemenite Midrashim. The name of his work, he states, stems from the fact that it is an explanation (*be'ur*) of "the principles of the Torah and the oral tradition, as well as the sayings of the sages and stories about them." His sources were the Babylonian and Jerusalem Talmud, *Sifrei*, the *Mekhilta*, and Maimonides' works. Generally his teachings are identical to similar Yemenite Midrashim, but also contain important materials that Dhamārī took from earlier collections now lost. Of great significance are the differences in the versions transmitted by Dhamārī. The book as a whole is still in manuscript, but most of the weekly portion *Va-Yeẓe* was published by L. Finkelstein as an anonymous Midrash and subsequently identified by Ratzaby.

BIBLIOGRAPHY: Finkelstein, in: HUCA, 12–13 (1937–38), 523–57.

[Yehuda Ratzaby]

DHIMMA, DHIMMI, Arabic term referring to the status of Jews and Christians living in Islamic countries as protected people. This status does not apply to other peoples or religious groups, such as Hindus, for whom a strict policy of "conversion or death" is in force. The *dhimmi* must be humiliated, belittled, distinguished by his appearance: his distinctive dress indicates to the Muslim that the *dhimmi* is to be treated as an inferior.

Jewish and Christian religious leaders in Muslim lands may only serve with the permission of the Muslim authorities. The Muslim Arabs allowed the Babylonian Jews to keep an official head of the community and head of the yeshivot for several hundred years, but then abolished this office. The Turks continue to choose the Greek-Orthodox Patriarch and the Egyptian president chooses the head of the Coptic church.

It is a religious obligation of Muslims to degrade non-Muslims. When Jews used to live in Muslim lands, they could not own property. If they lived in cities, they had to pay a special tax to demonstrate their subservience. They could not serve in the army, nor carry weapons. Marrying a Muslim woman was punishable by death.

Dhimmitude is the Islamic system of governing populations conquered by holy (*jihād*) wars, encompassing all of the demographic, ethnic, and religious aspects of the political system. The word "dhimmitude" as a historical concept describes the legal and social conditions of Jews and Christians subjected to Islamic rule. *Dhimmi* was the name applied by the Arab-Muslim conquerors to indigenous non-Muslim populations who surrendered by a treaty (*dhimma*) to Muslim domination.

The Muslim empire incorporated numerous peoples which had their own religion, culture, land, and civilization. For centuries, these indigenous peoples constituted the great majority of the population in the Islamic lands. Although these populations differed, they were ruled by the same type of laws, based on the Shari'a.

This similarity, with its regional variations, created a uniform civilization developed through the centuries by all non-Muslim indigenous peoples who were vanquished by *jihād* wars and governed by Shari'a law. It is this civilization which is called Dhimmitude. It is characterized by the different strategies developed by each *dhimmi* group to survive as a non-Muslim entity in its Islamized country. Dhimmitude is not exclusively concerned with Muslim history and civilization. Rather, it investigates the history of those non-Muslim peoples conquered and colonized by *jihād*. It encompasses the relationship of Muslims and non-Muslims at the theological, social, political, and economic levels. It also encompasses the relationships among the numerous ethno-religious *dhimmi* groups and the type of mentality they have developed out of their particular historical condition, which lasted for centuries (in some Muslim countries, until today).

Dhimmitude is a complete, integrated system, based on Islamic theology. It cannot be judged from the circumstantial position of any one community, at a given time or in a given place. Dhimmitude must be appraised according to its laws and customs, irrespective of circumstances and political contingencies.

BIBLIOGRAPHY: S.D. Goitein, *Jews and Arabs* (1955); "Dhimma," in: EIS^2 2 (1965), 227–31 (includes bibliography); B. Ye'or, *The Dhimmi: Jews and Christians under Islam* (1985); Y. Courbage and P. Fargues, *Christians and Jews under Islam* (1988).

[Shlomo Alon (2nd ed.)]

DIAMAND, HERMAN (1860–1931), Polish Socialist politician. Born in Lvov into an assimilated family, as a student he was a member of the Zionist Zion Association but afterwards left it to join the PPS (Polish Socialist Party). Diamand was one of the founders of the Polish Social Democratic Party of Galicia and Silesia. He was a member of the party's executive committee from 1897 to 1899 and from 1904 to 1909 was a member of its directorate. In 1909 he represented the Polish Socialists at the International Bureau of the Second International. Diamand sat as a Galicia representative in the Austrian parliament from 1917 to 1918. After World War I he cooperated closely with Joseph Pilsudski in fighting for an independent Poland, and from 1919 until his death was a Socialist deputy in the Sejm (Polish parliament). Diamand was much concerned with the fate of the Jewish community of Lvov, and intervened many times with the authorities on its behalf.

ADD. BIBLIOGRAPHY: N.M. Gelber, *Toledot ha-Tenu'ah ha-Ẓiyyonit be-Galicia 1875–1918*, I–II (1958), index; H. Piasecki, *Sekcja zydowska PPSD i zydowska Partia Socjalno Demokratyczna* (1983), index; A. Tymieniecka, *Warszaska organizacja PPS, 1918–1939* (1982), index; I. Daszynski, *Pamietniki Diamanta z wyjatkow listow do zony zestawione* (1932); H. Diamand, *Polozenie gospodarcze Galicji przed wojna* (1915).

[Abraham Wein]

DIAMANT, PAUL JOSEPH (1887–1966), Israeli genealogist and historian of Austrian Jewry. Diamant, who was born in Vienna into a landowning family, was a devoted Zionist, and after World War I he turned his inherited estate into a training center for *ḥalutzim*. He subsequently became a leading member of the *Revisionist movement in Austria. After the *Anschluss* (1938), he took part in organizing illegal immigration. After his arrival in Palestine, he acquired a farm at Moẓa near Jerusalem. His interest in genealogy, heraldry, and history was stimulated by the fact that his family descended from Simon Michael and he was related to both Heinrich *Heine and Theodor *Herzl. He worked on a book (unpublished) on ennobled families of Jewish descent in order to refute the antisemitic *Semi-Gotha*. The material he gathered was deposited in the General *Archives for Jewish History. Diamant founded the short-lived *Archiv fuer juedische Familienforschung; Kunstgeschichte und Museumswesen* (1912–13), and in Jerusalem collaborated in establishing the Herzl Museum. He published a volume of letters written by Minna Diamant (1815–1840), *Ein Briefwechsel aus der Biedermeierzeit* (1962), and several articles in periodicals.

BIBLIOGRAPHY: I. Klausner, in: MB (June 10, 1966); B. Brilling, in: AWJD (July 5, 1966), 14.

DIAMOND, DAVID (**Leo**; 1915–), U.S. composer. Diamond taught himself to play the violin at an early age. In 1934 he studied at the New Music School in New York, and from 1937 to 1939 he studied with Boulanger in Paris. In 1951 he was appointed to a temporary professorship at the University of Rome. He was composer-in-residence for a year at the American Academy in Rome (1971) and was appointed professor of composition at the Juilliard School of Music (1973–86). His many honors include the Guggenheim Fellowship, the Prix de Rome (1942), the Paderewski Prize (1943), a National Institute of Arts and Letters grant (1944), the William Schuman Award (1985), the Gold Medal of the American Academy of Arts and Letters (1991), the Edward MacDowell Award (1991). Diamond's symphonic works are marked by an individual style in the advanced idiom of modern music. Despite the complexity of his harmonic and contrapuntal writing, he never abandoned the tonal system. His music is always marked by a strong rhythmic drive. The impression received from his music is that of cogency and lucidity. He composed 11 symphonies, three violin concertos, a cello concerto, a piano concerto, and *Rounds* for string orchestra. Diamond excelled in chamber music, often in unusual combinations, including *Quintet for flute, string trio and piano* (1937), and *Quintet for clarinet, two violas and two cellos* (1951). He also wrote vocal music – choral and song cycles. Of Jewish inspiration are his *Ahavah* for narrator and orchestra (1954) and *Kaddish* for cello and orchestra (1987–89).

ADD. BIBLIOGRAPHY: Grove online; MGG^2; *Baker's Biog Dict*, s.v.; V.J. Kimberling, *David Diamond: A Bio-Bibliography* (1987).

[Nicolas Slonimsky / Israela Stein (2nd ed.)]

DIAMOND, I.A.L. (**Itek Domnici**; 1920–1988), U.S. filmscriptwriter. Born in Ungheni, Romania, Diamond was taken to New York, where his father changed the family name. A mathematics prodigy in high school, he studied engineering at Columbia University but took up writing and added the initials I.A.L. to his name. He wrote four college musical shows, and at graduation received an offer from Paramount studios in Hollywood. He collaborated with Billy Wilder on the film comedies *Love in the Afternoon* (1957), *Some Like it Hot* (1959), *The Apartment* (1960), *One, Two, Three* (1961), *Irma la Douce* (1963), *Kiss Me, Stupid* (1964), *The Fortune Cookie* (1966), *The Private Life of Sherlock Holmes* (1970), *Avanti!* (1972), *The Front Page* (1974), *Fedora* (1978), and *Buddy Buddy* (1981).

Some of Diamond's other film writing credits include *That Certain Feeling* (1956); *Love in the Afternoon* (1957);

Merry Andrew (1958); and *Cactus Flower* (1969). In 1961 Diamond and Wilder won the Academy Award for Best Writing, Story and Screenplay for *The Apartment*. In 1980, the Writers Guild of America gave Diamond the Laurel Award for Screen Writing Achievement.

[Jonathan Licht / Ruth Beloff (2nd ed.)]

DIAMOND, JACK (1909–2001), Canadian businessman, thoroughbred breeder, racetrack owner, philanthropist. Born in Lubience in Galicia, Poland, Diamond learned about animals, including butchering, on his father's farm. He immigrated to Vancouver in 1926, several years after his brother. In 1939 he acquired the Pacific Meat Company and transformed it into the largest independent meat packer in western Canada. During the war he first served as a lobbyist in Ottawa for small meat packers, then as an adviser to the Wartime Prices and Trade Board on meat pricing and supplies. In 1964 he sold Pacific Meat and he and his sons established West Coast Reduction, a rendering operation. Within two decades the firm dominated rendering in western Canada. Jack Diamond was also enthralled with thoroughbred racing. In 1938 he set up his own stables and started buying and successfully breeding horses. After the war, he owned and operated two Vancouver race tracks, and in 1977 was inducted into the Canadian Horse Racing Hall of Fame.

Jack Diamond also worked for and contributed to a number of Jewish and non-Jewish causes. In the late 1940s he was instrumental in the building of a new synagogue for the Orthodox Schara Tzedeck, and also served as chair of the congregation's Cemetery Board for more than 40 years. He is credited with saving Vancouver's claim to the British Empire Games in 1954, was instrumental in the creation of the BC Heart Foundation, and served on the Board of Governors of Simon Fraser University (1967–73) and as chancellor (1975–78). Diamond and his family established the Diamond Foundation in 1984. The foundation supports, above all, local Jewish causes with an emphasis on education and has funded the Diamond Chair in Jewish Law and Ethics at the University of British Columbia, and has provided major support for a Jewish day school in the suburb of Richmond, and a Jewish high school in Vancouver. In 2005 the president of the Foundation was Jack's son Gordon and the executive director was his granddaughter Jill.

Diamond's many honors include his 2000 appointment as a Companion of the Order of Canada, the highest honor that Canada bestows on a citizen.

BIBLIOGRAPHY: G. Sirotnik, *Running Tough: The Story of Vancouver's Jack Diamond* (1988), published by the Diamond family.

[Richard Menkis (2nd ed.)]

DIAMOND, JACK (1932–), architect and teacher. Diamond was born and raised in South Africa. While he came from a long line of rabbis, he studied architecture. He earned a bachelor of architecture degree from the University of Capetown, a masters in politics, philosophy, and economics from Oxford University, and a masters in architecture from the University of Pennsylvania. He went on to teach architecture at the University of Pennsylvania and work for Philadelphia-based Louis Kahn, one of the foremost architects of the mid-20th century.

Diamond immigrated to Canada in 1964, where he inaugurated and directed the Master of Architecture program at the University of Toronto from 1964 to 1970. Diamond also held appointments at York University in Toronto and the University of Texas and taught at Harvard, Princeton, and the University of California at Berkeley.

Diamond began practicing architecture in Toronto in 1965, and in 1975 he joined in forming the firm of Diamond and Schmitt Architects, which won more than 90 design awards, including six Governor General's Awards for Architecture. Award-winning Diamond projects, including many theaters and university buildings, are found in Canada, Europe, the United States, and Asia. Among Diamond's more notable architectural achievements are the Four Seasons Centre for the Performing Arts in Toronto, the Max M. Fisher Music Center in Detroit, the Citadel Theatre in Edmonton, the Canadian Embassy in Prague, the Baycrest Centre for Geriatric Care in Toronto, and the Jewish Community Center in Manhattan. Diamond's Israeli projects include the Jerusalem City Hall, the School of Computer Science and Engineering Building at the Hebrew University in Jerusalem, and the Israel Foreign Ministry in Jerusalem.

From 1986 to 1989 Diamond served as a commissioner for the Ontario Human Rights Commission and in 1996 he was appointed commissioner of the Greater Toronto Area Planning Task Force. Diamond is an honorary fellow of the American Institute of Architects and was awarded the Royal Architectural Institute of Canada's Gold Metal and appointed to the Order of Canada.

[Harold Troper (2nd ed.)]

DIAMOND, JOHN, BARON (1907–1978), British politician. The son of a cantor in Leeds, Diamond qualified as a chartered accountant and entered Parliament in 1945 as Labour member for Gloucester. From 1964 to 1970 he was chief secretary to the Treasury (a post specially concerned with the control of government expenditure) and won wide respect in the House of Commons for his mastery of detail in financial legislation and his familiarity with business problems. From 1968 until 1970 he sat in the cabinet, and, following the 1970 election, was made a life peer. He was treasurer of the Sadler's Wells Operatic Trust and was actively concerned with Jewish youth work. His brother ARTHUR SIGISMUND DIAMOND (1897–1978), a lawyer, held the senior legal post of Master of the Supreme Court and was an authority on primitive law. He was president of the Jewish Historical Society, chairman of Leo Baeck College, and president of the West London Synagogue.

Their mother, HENRIETTA (née Beckermann; 1873–1957), was an active Zionist and one of the most active supporters of the Zebulun Seafaring Society for the training of Jewish sailors in Palestine.

ADD. BIBLIOGRAPHY: I. Finestein, "Arthur Sigismund Diamond, 1897–1978," in: JHSET, 26 (1974–78), 111–12.

[Vivian David Lipman]

DIAMOND, LOUIS KLEIN (1902–1999), U.S. hematologist. Diamond was born near Kishinev, Ukraine, and immigrated to New York City at the age of two. He graduated from Harvard Medical School, Boston (1927), where he progressed to professor of pediatrics (1967). He was medical director of the new U.S. National Blood Program for blood transfusion (1948–50). After retirement from Harvard (1968) he remained professionally active first at the University of California, San Francisco, and then at the University of California, Los Angeles Medical School into his nineties. Diamond was one of the founders of pediatric hematology. With Kenneth Blackfan he clarified the clinical manifestations and treatment of rhesus incompatibility disease in the newborn, and they described an unrelated form of congenital anemia named after them. He was a world-renowned clinician and teacher.

[Michael Denman (2nd ed.)]

DIAMOND, NEIL (1941–), U.S. singer and songwriter. Born in Brooklyn, New York, Diamond began his music career as a staff songwriter for Bang Records. He wrote hit songs for the Monkees, "I'm a Believer" (1965) and "A Little Bit Me, a Little Bit You" (1967), and then recorded his own smash single "Cherry Cherry." Diamond followed this up with a long series of Top Ten songs, including "Cracklin' Rosie," "Kentucky Woman," "Song Sung Blue," "Sweet Caroline," "I Am I Said," and "Solitary Man." He then scored the soundtrack for the movie *Jonathan Livingston Seagull* (1971) and wrote the number one single "You Don't Bring Me Flowers Anymore" (1979), which he recorded as a duet with Barbra Streisand. The two had known each other since they were students at Erasmus High School, where they had sung together in the school choir. In 1980 Diamond starred in a remake of the Al Jolson film classic *The Jazz Singer*, opposite Sir Laurence Olivier. Although the film was not a box office hit, the soundtrack album was very successful, spawning the singles "America," "Love on the Rocks," and "Hello Again." Diamond was not a hit as an actor either, becoming the first ever "winner" of a Razzie Award for Worst Actor. But he was in formidable company, having edged out such stars as Kirk Douglas, Anthony Hopkins, Michael Caine, Richard Dreyfuss, and Robert Blake for that dubious title that year. In 2000, the Songwriters Hall of Fame honored Diamond with the Sammy Cahn Lifetime Achievement Award. Diamond recorded some 75 albums and continued to go on concert tours worldwide, with members of his family performing in his back-up band.

[Jonathan Licht / Ruth Beloff (2nd ed.)]

DIAMOND, SIGMUND (1920–1999), U.S. sociologist. Born in Baltimore, Diamond graduated from Johns Hopkins University and joined the United Auto Workers Union. In 1945 he participated in a UAW-CIO-sponsored meeting for shop stewards in Tennessee. At night he violated state law by sleeping in a dormitory for blacks, thereby integrating public sleeping quarters in Tennessee for the first time since Reconstruction. The following year Diamond was a negotiator of the UAW-CIO contract with the Bendix Aviation Corp. When it was ratified, it became the first contract to give women equal pay for equal work.

In 1949 Diamond entered Harvard University, where he earned a Ph.D. in history. He was not granted a professorship there or at any other university he applied to in the United States because he had refused to cooperate with the FBI during the McCarthy period.

In 1955, however, Diamond was appointed to the first chair in historical sociology at Columbia University. A specialist in entrepreneurial and economic history, Diamond emphasized the sociological context of economic development. His major contribution to sociology lies in his analysis of the growth and transformation of new societies on the historically virgin soil of the Americas. He remained at Columbia until his retirement as Giddings Professor of Sociology and professor of history, emeritus, in 1986. Among his many activities during his years at Columbia were founding and directing the history department's program in social history and consulting on the American Jewish Committee oral history project on the Holocaust.

Diamond's publications include "From Organization of Society: Virginia in the Seventeenth Century" (*American Journal of Sociology*, 63:5, 1958); "An Experiment in Feudalism: French Canada in the Seventeenth Century" (*William and Mary Quarterly*, 1961); *Casual View of America: The Home Letters of Salomon de Rothschild 1859–1881* (1961); *The Creation of Society in the New World* (1963); *The Nation Transformed: The Creation of an Independent Society* (1963), a descriptive analysis of capitalistic development in America; *The Reputation of the American Businessman* (1966); *In Quest: Journal of an Unquiet Pilgrim* (1980); and *Compromised Campus: The Collaboration of Universities with the Intelligence Community 1945–1955* (1992). Diamond also edited the *Political Science Quarterly.*

[Werner J. Cahnman and Alvin Boskoff / Ruth Beloff (2nd ed.)]

DIAMOND TRADE AND INDUSTRY. Jews have been prominent in the trade and in working of precious stones, of which diamonds and pearls provided the bulk, from the Middle Ages to the modern era. They took an active part in opening up the diamond markets of India and Brazil, the resources of South Africa, the London diamond market, and the diamond industries of the Low Countries. Because the diamond trade routes corresponded with the links between Jewish centers in the Diaspora – in the Ottoman Empire, the Netherlands, in some of the cities of northwest Germany, and in Poland-Lithuania in the 16th to 18th centuries – the trade was particularly suited to Jewish enterprise. Additionally, as diamonds were still a relatively rare and new commodity in Europe up to the 16th century, this was a branch free of medieval trade and guild restrictions. Up to the 18th century the overwhelming majority of uncut diamonds came from India. Commerce and crafts pursued by Jews along the Indian Ocean trade routes, in Egypt, the Maghreb, and along the shores of southern Europe, included trade and workmanship in precious stones, pearls, and jewelry. The Fatimid caliphs were supplied with gems by the brothers *Abu Sa'd al Tustarī and Abu Naṣr al-Tustarī, influential bankers and diamond merchants in the 11th century at Cairo. As *moneylenders, Jews in Western and Central Europe had much to do with the assessment, repair, and sale of precious stones and jewelry which they received in pawn.

With the rise of *Amsterdam as a major center of the European diamond trade and industry in the 16th century, Dutch Jews, mostly members of the Portuguese Sephardi community who had been prominent in Portugal's diamond trade, played an important part in both. By the middle of the 17th century the preponderance of Jews in the newly developed trade was so marked that the resettlement of the Jews in England brought about a major shift in its structure. The Sephardi presence in London, combined with the growing ascendancy of England in the Eastern trade, resulted in the diversion of the greater part of Europe's diamond imports to England. A few years after the arrival of the first Jewish immigrants, the British East India Company, which had a monopoly of England's Indian trade, permitted independent merchants to import uncut diamonds under a system of individual licenses issued by India House. Until the end of the 18th century most Indian stones used by the European diamond industry were imported through London. The records of the East India Company show that the majority of the importers were Jewish and that they dominated the trade throughout most of this time. The diamond merchants exported silver and coral to India, the proceeds of which were invested in diamonds. The coral was first brought to London from Leghorn, mostly by Jewish merchants of that city who often had a direct share in the Indian diamond trade through Jewish agents in London. The Indian end of the trade was managed by agents of English firms – mainly English Jews who went out to India for this purpose. Around 1750 there were about ten Jewish diamond agents at *Madras.

In London the diamonds were usually sold to merchants who sent them to Amsterdam for cutting. Amsterdam remained throughout the 18th century the chief seat of the diamond industry, while *Antwerp, which was later to overshadow it, was of secondary importance, dealing mainly in stones of inferior quality. From Amsterdam the finished diamonds were distributed throughout Europe. From its inception, the diamond trade and industry of *Amsterdam was largely in Jewish hands. Portuguese Jewish diamond polishers are recorded in 1615; they later employed their poorer Ashkenazi brethren who gradually established their own businesses. Diamond cutting and polishing was a profitable profession, but suffered from the vicissitudes of an unstable market as well as an occupational disease – tuberculosis. The main demand for diamonds came from the courts of Europe, and jewel purveyance was both a stepping-stone to and a major part of the post of *Court Jew. An important stage in the transfer of precious stones from London to Amsterdam, and thence to the courts of Germany, was *Hamburg, where a sizable community of Sephardi Jews monopolized the diamond trade in the 17th and 18th centuries. One of the earliest Court Jews, *Lippold, was a supplier of gems and other luxury articles, as were almost all the Court Jews of the era. Aaron *Isaac of Sweden, the *Oppenheims of Vienna and Wuerttemberg, and the *Ephraim family all owed their success, at least initially, to their dealings in gems. *Glueckel of Hameln, a shrewd dealer in precious stones, gives a detailed picture in her autobiography both of the international commerce in precious stones and gold as well as of small-scale trading by German Jews in this sphere. After 1700 Ashkenazi Jews began to play an increasingly important role in the London center of the diamond trade. By the 1720s the investments of the Ashkenazi *Franks family in the Indian diamond trade were approximately equal to those of the biggest Sephardi enterprise – that of the brothers *Franco – and 60 years later the Ashkenazi merchant Israel Levin Salomons (Prager) attained a dominant position for a time.

The discovery of diamonds in Brazil around 1730 ended India's monopoly as a producer of uncut diamonds and for a time weakened the hold which London and its Jewish diamond merchants had on the import trade, though Brazilian stones were soon reaching London illegally in considerable quantities. In the long run this development diminished neither the prominence of Jews in the diamond trade and industry nor London's position as the chief international market for uncut diamonds. Jews continued to be dominant in the diamond-cutting industry of Amsterdam, and later of Antwerp, where in the late 19th century they constituted about one-fifth of the workers but three-quarters of the brokers and an even higher proportion of the factory owners. The diamond glut of the 1890s terminated a boom in the course of which the number of diamond workers had tripled through immigration of Jews from Eastern Europe. A period of reorganization followed, in which national and international diamond workers' unions in Belgium and Holland were organized under the leadership of Henry *Polak. The diamond workers' union spearheaded in 1893 a general strike in Belgium for a minimum wage.

The rise of Fascism in Europe created a crisis for Jews engaged in the diamond industry and trades. During World War II diamond-cutting centers were established in Ereẓ Israel (see below), Cuba, Brazil, Mexico, and the United States by Jewish refugees. The Nazi occupation authorities in Belgium and Holland made Jewish diamond merchants and industrialists their particular victims. By 1970 Jews had still not reattained their former dominance in the field in Amsterdam, although they had succeeded in doing so in Antwerp.

Jewish enterprise had a large share in the development of the South African diamond mines, which became the chief source of diamond supply after 1870, including the formation of De Beers Consolidated Mines Ltd. (1888), which in the 1960s controlled the production and marketing of the greater part of all uncut diamonds. German Jews were among the earliest pioneers of the South African diamond rush. Among the prospectors were many from London's East End, one of whom, Barney *Barnato, was a formidable rival and later partner of Cecil Rhodes. Alfred *Beit was the architect of the De Beers syndicate which S.B. *Joel first headed. Ernest *Oppenheimer and Harry Oppenheimer successfully followed in his footsteps.

[Gedalia Yogev / Henry Wasserman]

In Israel

A diamond industry was founded in Palestine before World War II by immigrants from the Low Countries, who brought with them the necessary technical skills and commercial connections.

During World War II Palestine replaced Belgium and the Netherlands as the gem diamond center of the free world. Palestine received its supplies of rough diamonds from the De Beers central selling organization ("The Syndicate") and sold its polished products mainly to the U.S. At its peak during this period, the industry employed some four thousand polishers, mainly in Netanyah. The value of the diamond exports reached some $16,000,000 a year.

The revival of the centers in Belgium and the Netherlands after the war, the diversion of raw material by the Syndicate to these countries, and the Israel War of Independence drastically contracted the diamond-cutting industry in Israel. By 1949 it was almost at a standstill. However, the industry revived in 1950 and, in the early 1960s, became the second largest diamond gem center in the world, after Belgium. Its share of the world trade in polished diamonds was between a quarter and a third, and it maintained the same proportion in the numbers of polishers employed.

The secure and steady supply of rough diamonds was a constant concern of the industry. The De Beers Syndicate directly controls the distribution of over 80% of the world output of rough diamonds. Between 1950 and 1959 its direct sales to Israel were frozen at approximately $7,000,000 a year. The industry had therefore to obtain its supplies from other sources, the proportion of which in the total import rose from 24% in 1950 to 84% in 1959. At the end of this period the special high premium of the indirect supplies was so severe that it endangered the prospects for further development.

Israeli agencies (among them *Pittu'aḥ* (Development), a company whose shares are owned by the Israeli government) were encouraged to exploit firsthand sources of supply in western Africa. Negotiations were conducted with the Syndicate with a view to assuring the industry in Israel an adequate share of the diamonds under the Syndicate's control. As a result, from 1961, the proportion of the supply from the Syndicate rose and gradually constituted more than half of the imports.

The Israel diamond industry concentrated on the cutting of melee stones, medium-sized octahedron-shaped rough stones, which are sawed in the middle. The two pyramid shaped parts are then polished by a chain of six polishers, each specializing in particular facets, to produce a round "brilliant" with 57 facets, suitable for setting. Some stones with particular shapes are cut into "fancies" (marquises, baguettes, etc.).

In the late 1960s the industry consisted of some 400 enterprises, about half of which employed fewer than 15 workers. Only 45 enterprises had more than 50 workers and only three more than 100 workers. Over half of the enterprises, and of the workers, were located in and around Tel Aviv (where the Diamond Exchange was also located), over a quarter in Netanyah, and the rest in Jerusalem and the development areas.

[Gideon Lahav]

In the 1970s Israel passed Antwerp as the world's largest diamond wholesaler, supplying over 50% of all cut and polished diamonds. A slump in the early 1980s led to the restructuring of the industry and the creation of around 800 new and smaller manufacturing units, with sales rising from $905 million in 1982 to $1.7 billion in 1986, representing 24% of Israel's total exports. By 2003 the figure had risen to $5.5 billion and further growth in 2004 of nearly 15% brought sales up to $6.3 billion. The United States imported 67% of the stones.

BIBLIOGRAPHY: S.D. Goitein, *A Mediterranean Society*, 1 (1967), s.v. *Jewelry, Pearls*; W.J. Fischel, *Ha-Yehudim be-Hodu* (1960), 41, 146–75; idem, in: *Sefunot*, 9 (1965), 249–62; idem, in: *Journal of Economic and Social History of the Orient*, 3 (1960), 78–107, 175–95; idem, in: REJ, 123 (1964), 433–98; Fischel, Islam, 72–78; H. Kellenbenz, *Sephardim an der unteren Elbe* (1958), 113, 133, 165, 168, 177, 191–8, 195, 458f.; S. Stern, *The Court Jew* (1950), 42–59; H. Schnee, *Die Hoffinanz und der moderne Staat*, 1 (1953), 38ff., 54, 59ff., 88ff., 146ff., 180, 244–53; 2 (1954), 19ff., 61f., 93f., 156f., 183ff.; 3 (1955), 23, 35f., 38f., 50, 75, 182ff., 194f.; 4 (1963), 124ff., 192, 188f.; C. Roth, *Venice* (1933), 182f.; JHSEM, 3 (1937), 100–3; R.J. D'Arcy Hart, *ibid.*, 57–75; L. Wolf, *ibid.*, 1 (1925), xxvi–xli; H. Heertje, *De diamantbewerkers van Amsterdam* (1936); H.I. Bloom, *The Economic Activity of the Jews of Amsterdam* (1937); S. Kleerekoper, in: *Studia Rosenthaliana*, 1 (1967), 75–80; K. Liberman, *L'Industrie et le commerce diamantaires belges* (1935); P.H. Emden, *Randlords* (1935); L. Herrmann, *A History of the Jews in South Africa* (1935), 226–36; E. Rosenthal, in: G. Saron and L. Hotz (eds.), *The Jews of South Africa* (1955), 105–20; N. Shapira, in: *Gesher*, 2 (1956), no. 2, 84–104; J. Gutwirth, in: JJSO, 10 (1968), 121ff. **IN ISRAEL:** Central Bureau of Statistics, *Survey of Employment and Equipment in Diamond Industry, 1961* (1962); Ministry of Commerce and Industry, Department of Diamonds, *Report, 1964, 1967* (1965, 1968; Hebrew); G. Lenzen, *Produktions- und Handelgeschichte des Diamanten* (1966). **WEBSITE:** www.diamond-il.co.il.

DIAS, LUIS (d. 1542), Marrano messianic pretender, known as the "Messiah of Setúbal," after the seaport south of Lisbon where he was born. Dias was poor and uneducated and his notions of Judaism were confused and rudimentary. Nevertheless, he came to regard himself as a prophet and eventually announced himself as the Messiah. He acquired fame as a miracle worker and had a following of both Old and *New Christians in Setúbal, Lisbon, and other places. People meeting him kissed his hand and many sent him mystical letters. His activities, including the rumors that he circumcised the children of his followers, led to his first arrest by the Inquisition. After confessing, he was reconciled to the Church, assigned various penances, and released. When it was discovered that he had reverted to his previous activities he was rearrested by the Inquisition and eventually burned as a relapsed heretic in 1542, with 83 of his followers. Under his influence a government official Gil Vaz Bugalho became a secret Jew and even prepared a booklet on religious practice for Judaizers before his death at the stake in 1551.

BIBLIOGRAPHY: J.L. D'Azevedo, *Historia dos Christaõs Novos Portugueses* (1921); idem, in: *Arquivo Historico Portugues*, 10 (1916), 442f.; J. Mendes dos Remedios, *Os Judeus em Portugal*, 2 (1928), 50f.; Roth, Marranos, index; A.Z. Aescoly, *Ha-Tenu'ot ha-Meshiḥiyyot be-Yisrael*, 1 (1956), 279, 412ff.

[Martin A. Cohen]

DIASPORA

Introduction

The word Diaspora, from the Greek διασπορά ("dispersion"), is used in the present context for the voluntary dispersion of the Jewish people as distinct from their forced dispersion, which is treated under *Galut. As such it confines itself to Jewish settlement outside Ereẓ Israel during the periods of Jewish independence or compact settlement in their land. It therefore applies to the period of the First Temple, the Second Temple, and that subsequent to the establishment of the State of Israel. The only dispersion during the period of the First Temple of which there is definite knowledge is the Jewish settlement in Egypt referred to in Jeremiah 44. (That in Babylon following the capture of Jehoiachin in 597 B.C.E., since it was forced and was the prelude to the complete Exile after the destruction of the Temple in 586, can be classified as an exile.) By the same definition, the Jewish communities in the world at present, after the establishment of the State of Israel, constitute a Diaspora, and since that event the custom has developed of referring to them in Hebrew as the *tefuẓot*, the Hebrew equivalent of Diaspora, in preference to the word previously used, *golah*, or *galut* ("exile"; for the concept of exile, see **Galut*). For the modern Diaspora, see Jewish *History and State of *Israel; for its demographic and statistical aspects, see *Demography, *Population, and *Vital Statistics; see contemporary periods of entries on the respective countries for the aspect of interrelation between Israel and the Jews living elsewhere.

By far the most important Diaspora during the period of the Second Temple was that of the Greco-Roman world. For the populous Babylonian Diaspora during this period, see *Babylonia.

In the Hellenistic-Roman Period

THE DISTRIBUTION OF JEWISH POPULATION. The existence of a Diaspora is one of the distinguishing features of the Jewish people in the Greco-Roman period. In part this Diaspora was a heritage from the preceding era; in part it was established only in the Hellenistic period with the rise of new Jewish groups as extensions of earlier ones. Among the various factors operating to enlarge the Diaspora geographically and increase it numerically were the banishments from Ereẓ Israel, political and religious pressures there, economic prospects emerging in prosperous countries such as *Egypt in the third century B.C.E., and the proselytizing movement, whose roots go back to the beginning of Second Temple times and which reached its zenith in the first century C.E, within the framework of the Roman Empire. As early as in the Hellenistic period the *Sibyl could sing of the Jewish nation "Every land is full of you, and every sea," and, in a reference to the first century B.C.E., the Greek geographer Strabo declared that it was difficult to find a place in the entire world to which the Jewish nation had not penetrated. Literary sources from the end of the Second Temple period (Philo, Acts) assert that the Jewish people had spread to all cities and lands.

The bulk of the Diaspora came under the sway of the Hellenistic and later of the Hellenistic-Roman civilization. Shaped first by the political, social, and economic changes which fashioned the character of the Mediterranean world in the period of "the balance of power" between the Hellenistic states, its development was afterward molded by the centralizing regime of the Roman Empire. Only one large Jewish group, that in Babylonia and in the countries of the Parthian Empire, was outside the sphere of Hellenistic or Roman political rule during the greater part of the period and developed its own forms of life, which in the course of time influenced Jewry as a whole. Two countries in particular bordering on Ereẓ Israel, namely Egypt and Syria (including Phoenicia), were influenced by their Jewish populations. Already in the Persian period, the Jewish inhabitants in Egypt were considerable in number. The fact that Ereẓ Israel was under the same rule at the beginning of the Hellenistic period encouraged the migration of Jews to the Nile Valley. Living in all the cities and border districts, from the capital *Alexandria in the north to Syene in the south of Upper Egypt, the Jews in Roman Egypt numbered by the first century C.E., according to Philo, a million souls. Alexandria became one of the largest Jewish centers in the world. From the beginning of the Jewish settlement in that city they had their own quarter, voluntarily established. Later they were also especially predominant in two of the city's five districts, although they were also to be found in the other three, in which they had synagogues. Other places in Lower Egypt distinguished for their Jewish populations were Schedia near Alexandria, Xenephiris, Athribis, and Nitrae, in all of which the Jews had synagogues. Particularly important was the concentration of the Jewish population in the Heliopolite nome, east of the Delta. Distinguished for its military spirit, it even erected its own temple, "the temple of Onias," headed by descendants of the high priest Onias III. The large number of papyri discovered in the villages and towns of the district of Fayyum (Magdola, Crocodilopolis, Psenyris,

Tebtunis, Berenice-Hormos, Philadelphia, Apollonias, Trikomia, Alexandrou-Nesos, etc.) afford valuable information on Jewish settlement in that area. Among the villages of Fayyum was one named Samaria (whose founders were undoubtedly immigrants from Samaria). During the whole Roman period Jews lived continuously in Oxyrhyncus. The ostraca found in excavations have shed light also on the life of the Jews in Apollinopolis Magna (Edfu) and in Thebes in Upper Egypt. The number of Jews in Egypt presumably reached its zenith in the period of the Julio-Claudian emperors. The revolt of the Jews in the days of *Trajan dealt a severe blow to the Jewish population of Egypt both in Alexandria and especially in the provincial cities and in the villages. In many places the Jews disappeared entirely, and it was only from the third century onward that they gradually began to resettle in them.

The Jewish settlement in Cyrenaica was, as it were, a direct extension of that of Egypt, having been largely under the same rule. There were considerable numbers of Jews in the principal cities – in *Cyrene, where already at the end of the Hellenistic period they constituted an important part of the city's population, and in *Berenice – as well as in the villages. In the life of the Jewish people the Jews of Cyrenaica filled a notable function and played a leading role in the revolt in the days of Trajan.

Josephus describes Syria as the country with the highest percentage of Jewish inhabitants, which is very probably on account of its proximity to Ereẓ Israel. There were particularly important Jewish centers in the capital *Antioch, in *Damascus, and in *Apamea. According to Philo, numerous Jews lived in Syria and in Asia Minor, where the settlement of Jews was greatly promoted by the policy of the Seleucid kings, whose rule extended over large areas of *Asia Minor. Thus it is known that Antiochus III (223–187 B.C.E.) settled 2,000 Babylonian Jewish families in Phrygia and Lydia. From the period of the Roman rule at the end of the republic and the beginning of the Julio-Claudian principate there is clear evidence of the existence of Jews in most of the important cities of Asia Minor, in Adramyttium, *Pergamum, *Sardis, *Ephesus, Tralles, *Miletus, Iasus, Halicarnassus, *Laodicea, Tarsus, and very many others, as well as in the regions of *Bithynia, Pontus, and *Cappadocia. Asia Minor was undoubtedly also a homeland, or at least a transit station, for the Jews who established the Jewish center on the northern bank of the Black Sea (Panticapaeum). No grave political crisis, such as the revolt of the Jews in Egypt and Cyrenaica, overtook the Jews of Asia Minor, and so their development in the cities of Asia could continue undisturbed. There were many Jews, too, in the various islands of the eastern Mediterranean. The first Jewish settlement there was undoubtedly in *Cyprus, close as it was to the coast of Ereẓ Israel. But the war of the Jews against the island's non-Jewish inhabitants in the days of Trajan led to the temporary break in Jewish settlement on the island. Many Jews also lived in *Crete, Delos, Paros, Melos, Euboea, and in other islands.

*Greece proper, which at the end of the Hellenistic period and during that of the Roman Empire suffered from a declining population and a stagnant economy, attracted fewer Jewish immigrants than did Egypt and Asia Minor. Nevertheless, there were Jews in all the important urban centers of Greece and *Macedonia. The first mention of Jews in Greece, a reference to a Jewish freedman, appears on a third-century inscription from the city of Oropus in Boeotia. Inscriptions of the second century B.C.E. mention the freeing of Jewish slaves in Delphi. In the days of Philo, Jews lived in most of the important districts of Greece (Thessaly, Boeotia, Macedonia, Aetolia, Attica, and most of the areas of the Peloponnesus). According to the Acts of the Apostles, there were Jewish communities in Thessalonica, in the Macedonian cities of Philippi and Beroea, and in the famed Greek cities of *Athens and *Corinth. Inscriptions also attest to Jewish settlements in various places in the Peloponnesus (the district of Laconia, the city of Patrae, Tegea), in Athens, and in Thessaly. From Greece the Jewish settlements spread northward to the Balkan peninsula (Stobi) and reached Pannonia.

A special position was held by the Jewish settlement in Italy and principally *Rome, which became the political capital of the entire Mediterranean world. As early as the second century B.C.E. Jews were found in Rome, from which they were expelled in 139 B.C.E. because of their attempts to propagate the Jewish religion there. However, even before Pompey's conquest of Jerusalem (63 B.C.E.) their number had increased in Rome, while the Jewish captives brought to the country by Pompey and subsequent Roman conquerors hastened the process of Jewish settlement in Italy. The Jewish slaves who, on being freed, had become Roman citizens constituted a not insignificant factor in the life of the capital. By 59 B.C.E. in his speech in defense of Flaccus, the governor of Asia, Cicero was complaining of the decisive Jewish influence in the assemblies of the Roman masses. *Julius Caesar allowed them to maintain their position, and under *Augustus and his successors the Jewish population in Rome numbered thousands and possibly even tens of thousands. The administrative measures taken by Tiberius and *Claudius were ineffective in hindering Jewish settlement in the capital, and they remained a permanent factor in the life of Rome throughout the whole period of the empire. Certain areas in the city were especially noted for their concentrations of Jewish inhabitants. Gradually Jewish settlements also arose in other cities in Italy, chiefly in the south, in the port of Puteoli, in Pompeii, in the cities of *Sicily, and in the course of time in northern Italy too. More slowly Jewish groups came into existence in the other provinces of the Latin west (*Gaul, *Spain, and *Germany). Of great importance was the Jewish settlement in *Africa and especially in *Carthage.

Special features distinguished the development of Jewry in the Parthian kingdom which included the Babylonian Jewish population and its extensions in Persia, Media, Elam, etc. This Jewry was not only ancient but extremely numerous, particularly in Babylonia proper, where in some regions and cities the Jews constituted the majority of the inhabitants. The centers of Jewish settlement in Babylonia at the end of Second Temple times were in the cities of *Nehardea and *Nisibis. There was also a considerable Jewish population in the large city of Seleucia on the Tigris, where the Jews were the counterpoise between the eastern-Syrian and the Greek inhabitants. Through the proselytization of the rulers of *Adiabene in the first century C.E. the Jewish population in the region of the Euphrates was greatly augmented.

OCCUPATIONS. The occupations of the Jews in the countries of the Hellenistic-Roman Diaspora were varied, and certainly they were not confined to only a few specified occupations, as was the case in the Middle Ages, and no restrictions were placed on them. In Judea, the Jews had been farmers from the earliest days, and, while the cultivation of the soil remained an important occupation of the Jews in the countries of the Diaspora, they also engaged in other pursuits. Numerous papyri in particular furnish considerable evidence of the part played by the Jews in the *agriculture of Egypt. Among the Jewish agriculturists in Ptolemaic Egypt were "royal farmers," tenant farmers, military settlers, and agricultural workers. There were also Jewish peasants and shepherds. Other documents show that there was a Jewish family of potters in "a Syrian village" in the Fayyum district, and also a Jewish weaver in Upper Egypt in the second century B.C.E. Jewish officials were prominent in government service, occupying positions in the police force, in the administration of the government banks, and particularly in the collection of taxes.

A similar diversity characterized the economic life of the Jews in Roman Egypt. In Roman Alexandria there were wealthy Jews, bankers with interterritorial connections, important merchants, and ship owners who filled a notable role in the Egyptian, and in the entire Mediterranean, economy. However, alongside these, Jewish artisans and poor Jews were no less prominent. The Jewish artisans in Roman Alexandria engaged in various trades, and even occupied places in the large synagogue according to their occupations. Among the Alexandrian Jews, some owned land in various places whereas others had difficulty in making a livelihood, as can be seen from the papyri of Abusir el Meleq. This picture is confirmed by documents relating to the provincial towns. Thus in Roman Egypt some Jews owned land, some engaged in cultivating the soil and in rearing sheep, some in transport on land or along the Nile where they loaded cargo for various parts of Egypt, while others were artisans. Only in military service and in the collection of taxes was there a decline in the activities of the Jews as compared with the preceding period, as a result of general changes in these spheres following the Roman conquest. More or less the same state of affairs existed in the other countries of the Mediterranean world. In Cyrenaica there were rich Jews who, after the Jewish War in 70 C.E., aroused the jealousy of the Roman governor; but there were also poor Jews, who were apparently adversely affected by the agricultural policy of the Roman regime in *Libya. There were likewise rich Jews in Puteoli and on the island of Melos. The vast sums of money which flowed to the Temple in Jerusalem from all parts of the Diaspora attest in some measure to the existence of wealthy circles among the Jews. It is however important to point out that at least in Rome itself at the zenith of the imperial period it was chiefly the poor and mendicant Jews, and not the rich ones, who attracted the attention of those who derided Jewry.

JEWISH LIFE IN THE HELLENISTIC KINGDOMS. In the period preceding the annexation to Rome of the Hellenistic kingdoms there was no uniformity in the political fortunes of the Jews in the Mediterranean Diaspora, since they lived under the rule of various states. Yet several general lines in the policy toward the Jews had already taken shape. Among these the most prominent were the toleration of the Jewish religion shown by the various Hellenistic kings, the right enjoyed by the Jews to organize themselves in their own communities, and the permission to maintain contact with the religious-national center in Jerusalem, which found expression in the contribution of the half *shekel to the Temple. Where their number permitted, such as in Egypt, the Jews also played an active part in the general political life of the country. Egypt is, in fact, the only land on which there is detailed information about the relations between the Hellenistic regime and the Jews. *Ptolemy II Philadelphus, the most renowned of the Ptolemaic kings in the third century B.C.E., was well disposed toward them. The Jewish slaves taken captive during his father's rule of Ereẓ Israel were freed, and Jewish tradition even ascribed the inception of the Septuagint to his initiative. Some deterioration occurred apparently during the reign of Ptolemy Philopator (222–204 B.C.E.), due both to the situation in Ereẓ Israel and to the king's religious policy in Alexandria itself; but the conflict was short-lived, and the political influence of the Jews in Ptolemaic Egypt reached its summit in the second century B.C.E. More than all the Ptolemaic kings, Ptolemy VI Philometor (180–145 B.C.E.) showed especial friendship toward the Jews. In his days the stream of emigration from Judea to Egypt increased as a result of the pressure of *Antiochus Epiphanes. Ptolemy Philometor was on intimate terms with the Alexandrian Jewish philosopher *Aristobulus, and prominent among his army commanders were men of Jewish origin. Well disposed to *Onias IV, the son of the Jerusalem High Priest Onias III, the king permitted him to build a temple in Egypt. The Jews in "the land of Onias" became in his time an organized military body and a not insignificant factor in Egyptian politics. After the death of Ptolemy Philometor, the Jewish army appeared in Alexandria to help *Cleopatra II in her struggle against her rival for the throne, Ptolemy Euergetes II (Ptolemy Physcon). As a result, the general position of the Egyptian Jews deteriorated for a time at the beginning of the rule of Ptolemy Physcon (145–116 B.C.E.). However, due to revolts and riots, the Egyptian kingdom was unable to forego the help of the Jews, and Ptolemy Physcon did not long persist in his anti-Jewish policy.

There is reason to assume that an appreciable number of Jews were granted Alexandrian citizenship by this king when his relations with the Greek population deteriorated. At the end of the second century B.C.E., in the struggle between Cleopatra III and Ptolemy Lathyrus, her son and rival for the throne, the Jews supported the queen, and Hilkiah and Hananiah, the sons of Onias IV, even commanded her army in the operations outside the borders of Egypt. At the beginning of the first century (88 B.C.E.) the Jews in Alexandria were persecuted. When Gabinius invaded Egypt the Jews on the frontier assisted the Roman army, as they also did when the army, which had come to extricate Caesar from dire straits in Alexandria, reached the gates of the country (47 B.C.E.). Their actions were undertaken under the influence of Hyrcanus II and Antipater, the rulers of Judea, who were friendly toward the Romans.

ROMAN RULE. Rome's domination of the entire Mediterranean world led to the concentration of the bulk of the Jewish people under homogeneous rule, so that the development of the various Jewish settlements followed a more uniform political pattern. The Roman regime, faced with the need to lay down a comprehensive approach to the Jewish people, based its policy on showing toleration toward the Jewish religion and doing nothing either directly or indirectly to its detriment. This Roman attitude stemmed from several factors:

(1) it was the prevailing Roman policy to refrain as far as possible from affronting the different religions in the empire;

(2) Roman conservatism tended to maintain the existing situation in the various states comprising the empire, and the Jewish community, from the period of the Hellenistic kingdoms, had been an element with its own status and claims, and toleration toward it was an established principle even before the Roman conquest;

(3) the important role played by the Jews in the life and economy of the empire and the comparatively high percentage of the Jewish population among the peoples of the empire, particularly in the east;

(4) the great unity prevailing among the various settlements of the Jews wherever they were, so that any serious attack on one of the great centers of Jewish population produced echoes in other Jewish groups;

(5) secondary factors, such as the ties of Herod and other rulers of his dynasty, and also some individual Jews, with the Roman Empire, on occasion influenced the steps taken by the governors;

(6) primarily the realization that the alternative facing Rome was either toleration or persecution, for the loyalty of the Jews to their religion was well-known, as was their readiness to suffer martyrdom for it. An attack on the Jewish religion was bound to provoke the Jews to revolt, and the emperors' tolerant policy toward the Jews constituted no injury to the empire.

This toleration found expression in several spheres: in the right granted to the Jews to organize themselves in their own institutions and to establish an autonomous system of internal administration and justice, to refrain from taking part in what they regarded as idolatry, and to be exempt from duties involving a transgression of Jewish religious precepts. The permission to refrain from idolatry also included the right to abstain from taking part in emperor worship, the chief expression of the loyalty of the peoples of the empire, abstention from which was generally regarded as treason. For this worship the Jews found a substitute by offering sacrifices in the Temple in Jerusalem for the well-being of the emperor and by prayers on his behalf recited in the various synagogues in Ereẓ Israel and in the Diaspora. Dispensation from duties conflicting with the Jewish religion included the right of Jews who were Roman citizens to be exempted from military service, since this precluded the observance of the Sabbath and other commandments. The architects of the defined Roman policy toward the Jews were Julius Caesar and Augustus, both of whom issued a series of orders to preserve the rights of the Jews and ensure their religious freedom. Caesar explicitly excluded the organizations of the Jews from the prohibition of maintaining *collegia* "except the ancient and legitimate ones," and the representatives of the Roman regime in the islands of the Mediterranean Sea and in Asia Minor acted within the area of their rule in accordance with Caesar's approach.

After Caesar's death, the two sides in the Roman civil war virtually competed with each other in granting privileges to the Jews. The consul Dolabella, ally of Mark Antony, confirmed the right of the Jews of Asia Minor to religious freedom and exemption from military service, and made his action known to the authorities of Ephesus, the most important city in Asia Minor. Marcus Brutus, one of Caesar's assassins, adopted a similar course.

Augustus, in particular, set an example to succeeding Roman rulers. Agrippa intervened to protect the rights of the Jews against the claims of the inhabitants of the Greek cities in Asia Minor, and Augustus instituted a general arrangement whereby the Jews were permitted to send money to the Temple in Jerusalem. Any attack on this money was regarded as sacrilege. This arrangement remained in force until the destruction of the Second Temple. In general, the framework of the relations with the Jews, laid down at the beginning of the Julio-Claudian principate, was preserved during the existence of the pagan Roman Empire. The Julio-Claudian emperors, from Tiberius onward, remained faithful to the policy of Augustus. In fact, it was only during the short reign of Gaius *Caligula (37–41 C.E.) that this policy was seriously challenged. Taking his divinity seriously, the insane emperor demanded of his Jewish subjects the full observance of emperor worship. In Alexandria the Greek enemies of the Jews took advantage of the new situation to incite riots against the Jews, the first "pogrom" in the history of the Roman Empire. Caligula's attempt to introduce his image into the Temple in Jerusalem almost led to an uprising of the entire Jewish nation. Due to the intervention of Agrippa I the immediate threat against the Temple was removed and the danger of a revolt passed, particularly after Caligula was murdered by conspirators in Rome, but the episode left a turbid sediment in the relations between the Roman regime and the Jews. At the beginning of Claudius' reign the riots in Alexandria were renewed, whereupon Jews from Ereẓ Israel and from the provincial towns of Egypt flocked to the assistance of their coreligionists. The intervention of the emperor restored the status quo, which remained undisturbed until the Jewish War. There were echoes of this war in the larger cities of the Diaspora. In Alexandria the riots between Jews and Greeks broke out again, and the Roman army under the command of the governor, Tiberius Julius Alexander, massacred numbers of Jews in the city. Difficulties were also placed in the way of the Jews in the cities of Syria: there were riots against the Jews of Damascus, and the non-Jewish inhabitants of Antioch attempted, after the destruction of the Second Temple, to deprive the Jews of their rights but were prevented from doing so by Titus' opposition. In Egypt and Cyrenaica, the remnants of the freedom fighters of Ereẓ Israel who had escaped to these countries tried to incite new riots, but their attempt was foiled by the opposition of the Jewish upper classes and the leading instigators of the revolt were executed by the Roman authorities. Nonetheless, wealthy Jews, too, suffered, especially in Cyrenaica, and many of them lost their lives in the brutal acts of the Roman governor there. In general, the destruction of the Second Temple turned Rome into a ruthless regime and an evil kingdom in the eyes of the Jews everywhere. The humiliating position to which the people had sunk in the Roman Empire found legal expression in the obligation imposed on all the Jews to pay, instead of the half shekel which they had contributed to the Temple before its destruction, a tax of two drachmas to the treasury of the temple of Jupiter Capitolinus ("the Jews' tax"). This tax, collected with particular severity under the emperor *Domitian (81–96 C.E.), continued to be an aggravating and humiliating burden on the Jews until the fourth century.

THE TRAJANIC REVOLT AND ITS AFTERMATH. The greatest crisis in the relations between the Roman Empire and the Jews of the Diaspora was the revolt in the days of Trajan. Encompassing a large part of the Jewish settlements in Mesopotamia and in the eastern basin of the Mediterranean Sea (in particular Egypt, Cyrenaica, and Cyprus), it was, in effect, the most dangerous agitation against the Roman regime in the east since the wars of Mithridates at the end of the republican period, for it jeopardized the very existence of Roman rule in the eastern lands. Various factors combined to cause the eruption. These were the hatred of Rome in consequence of the destruction of the Temple and of the humiliation suffered by the Jews, the persistent tension between the Jews and the Greek inhabitants of the large cities such as Alexandria, and eschatological-messianic expectations. The revolt continued for several years (115–117 C.E.). Apparently Cyrenaica served at first as a base of prime importance for the rebels, who were led by Andreas (or Lucuas). The war assumed large proportions. Thousands of the non-Jewish inhabitants of the country were killed, and extremely serious damage was caused to the temples and public buildings of Cyrene as well as to the entire economy of the province. In Egypt the Jewish uprising embraced all the Nile country, from Alexandria in the north to Thebes in the south. Fierce battles were fought in the capital, in the villages, and in the various provincial towns, and many years later (199–200 C.E.) the victory over the Jews was still celebrated at Oxyrhyncus in Middle Egypt. Papyri tell of the enormous dimensions of the material damage and the gravity of the war. Only after full-scale battles, in which considerable forces of Roman legions fought alongside the local population, was the revolt crushed. In Cyprus, too, a ruthless war was waged, at the outset of which the Jews, under the leadership of Artemion, massacred large numbers of the island's non-Jewish inhabitants and destroyed the city of Salamis. When the revolt was finally quelled, the death penalty was decreed against any Jew who set foot on the island. The riots in Mesopotamia were connected with Trajan's wars against the Parthians, and no direct connection has been established between these riots and the Jewish revolt in Cyrenaica and Egypt, the actions of the Jews in Mesopotamia being essentially part of the uprisings of the peoples of the east consequent on the Roman invasion of the Parthian kingdom. In any event, the Jews suffered severely from the riots, and the emperor's representative, the commander Lusius *Quietus, massacred many of the Jewish people in the region. The Jewish revolt in the days of Trajan undermined to a great extent the existence of the Jewish communities in Egypt and in Cyrenaica and for a long time put an end to the settlement of Jews in Cyprus. As a result of the revolt there was a certain decrease in the Jewish population in the east of the empire, the material basis of their existence was shaken, and their political and social influence declined.

During the reigns of Trajan and his successor *Hadrian (117–138 C.E.), suppressor of the Bar Kokhba revolt, the history of the Jews in the pagan Roman Empire reached its nadir. However, from the days of *Antoninus Pius (138–161 C.E.) a gradual improvement took place in their position. There were no more Jewish revolts in the lands of the Diaspora nor punitive actions by the imperial regime, and the Jews once more acquired a strong position in the economic life of the empire. Antoninus Pius permitted the Jews to practice circumcision, which had been forbidden under Hadrian, although with the aim of putting a stop to proselytization he prohibited them from circumcising non-Jews. This prohibition continued also under the emperor *Septimius Severus (193–211 C.E.) but in general the Severian period was marked by a reconciliation between the Jews and the imperial regime. The rights of the Jews were assured; the *nesi'im* of the family of Hillel exercised great influence over the Jewish nation throughout the Roman Empire and were officially recognized by the authorities. Alexander Severus (222–235 C.E.) was favorably disposed toward the Jewish religion, while under *Caracalla (212 C.E.) the masses of the Jews in the empire, like its other peoples, became in every respect Roman citizens. These more favorable relations between the Jewish people and the empire continued, in effect, until the beginning of the fourth century, when Christianity became dominant. The Jews certainly suffered during the political and economic crisis which affected all the inhabitants of the empire in the third century, from the frequent changes of rulers and the civil wars, the barbarian invasions, inflation, and the heavy burden of taxation and exactions, but under no circumstances did they suffer because they were Jews. They had become an accepted part of the society of the Roman Empire, although there is no evidence at this time of political activity by the Jews in the Diaspora.

ORGANIZATION OF THE JEWISH COMMUNITIES. In their various places of residence the Jews had the right of self-organization, recognized by the Hellenistic and Roman authorities. This measure of *autonomy was an expression of their religious freedom, and the background to promoting the Jewish religion and to the continued existence of the Jewish people in the Diaspora. Different names were given to the Jewish communities in different cities. At times the terms denoting them were taken from the general organizational terminology (such as the name *politeuma*), at others they were called simply "Jews," at others again they were designated "synagogue." Not only the name but also the form of organization differed among the Jews in the various cities and countries. In Alexandria, for example, as early as the Ptolemaic period, the Jews had established a unified organization, a community known as a *politeuma*, led by the elders. At the beginning of the Roman period the Alexandrian community was headed by a president (ethnarch) who enjoyed an independent status and supervised the juridical arrangements in the community. During the reign of Augustus, apparently, certain changes took place in the organization of the community, when the authority passed from the ethnarch to the **gerousia*, consisting of scores of members. In the city of Berenice, too, as shown by an inscription, the Jews were organized in a *politeuma*, headed by nine archons. In Rome the Jews were organized around their synagogues, but no proof has yet been discovered of a central organization embracing all the Jews in the city. Neither in the Hellenistic nor in the Roman imperial period did the Jews of the Diaspora have central, countrywide organizations. To the extent that there was a unified leadership for all the Jews of the empire, it was supplied by the Jewish rulers in Ereẓ Israel and the high priests, while these existed, and afterward by the *nesi'im* and the Sanhedrin at Jabneh and in Galilee. In marked contrast to the picture among Hellenistic-Roman Jewry was the Babylonian Jews' more stable organization, which had hereditary leadership in the person of the exilarch, who traced his descent from the Davidic dynasty, was accorded official recognition by the Parthian regime, and had extremely wide-ranging authority.

The communities of the Greco-Roman world exercised fairly extensive authority, the most important aspect of which was the right to maintain a system of *battei din* with autonomous jurisdiction not only in matters of worship and religion but also in civil cases. However, from papyri it is evident that in various places, even in Alexandria itself where there was a developed system of Jewish jurisdiction, the Jews nevertheless had occasion to turn to non-Jewish law courts. Hence recourse to Jewish autonomous jurisdiction in civil cases was not compulsory. A community also had the right to hold property as a corporate legal body and to collect money from its members, since various expenses, either current or exceptional, had to be met by the communities. The current expenditure included primarily that connected with maintaining religious services, the synagogues, and other Jewish public institutions, such as schools and cemeteries. One of the characteristic features of the community was supplying the needs of the local poor from a charity fund. Exceptional expenditure comprised that associated with building new synagogues, sending delegations to the authorities, ransoming captives, and so on. Here the Jewish community was often assisted by the generosity of individuals.

One of the grave problems requiring adjustment was the relation between Jewish self-organization and the institutions of the Greek cities in the Hellenistic-Roman east organized in the form of a *polis*. Since in any event not all the inhabitants of a city were its citizens, there are no grounds for assuming that all the Jews were citizens of the Hellenistic cities in which they lived. Nor was the position identical in all cities, and in any case everywhere there were Jews with a differing civic status. At least some members of the first groups of Jews who settled in a city at the time of its establishment undoubtedly enjoyed civic rights; thus in Alexandria there were Jews who were "Macedonians." In general, however, most of the Jews who arrived in the Greek cities were presumably either foreigners or enjoyed a special status laid down for the Jewish members of the *politeuma*. Where there were special arrangements with the Hellenistic kings and the Roman emperors, the practical consequences of the status granted to Jews was no less congenial than the grant of civic rights by the Greek city itself, and this status could even be tantamount to equal civic rights. Generally the position in this respect was flexible. At times the Greek cities tried to deprive the Jews of the rights granted to them by the kings and confirmed by the emperors. On the other hand, there were also attempts by Jews, mainly by those of the upper classes, to infiltrate into the body of the citizens in such places and at such times as seemed to them expedient. It must also be noted that those men whose activities caused them to rise in the scale of the municipal leadership or in the administrative hierarchy of the Hellenistic kingdoms or the Roman Empire very often severed themselves, to a greater or lesser extent, from the Jewish world and made concessions to idolatry. Indeed the Jews who in those years attained prominence actually forsook Judaism, such as Dositheus b. Drimylus in Ptolemaic Egypt, or Tiberius Julius Alexander, Philo's nephew, who became the governor of Egypt. In the Roman Empire the special citizenship of the Greek cities gradually lost its value; all Jews became Roman citizens, and in the various cities of the empire Jews also became members of the municipal councils, a position which by then was less of an honor than a heavy financial burden.

LINKS WITH EREẒ ISRAEL. In the days of the Second Temple, as also after its destruction, the Jews of the Diaspora maintained close ties with Ereẓ Israel which found expression in several ways. Many Diaspora Jews fulfilled the commandment of going on pilgrimage to the Temple, and during the festivals Jews from all parts of the world, from Parthia and Media in the east to Italy in the west, could be found in Jerusalem. Some came to study Torah in the renowned schools, as did, for example, the apostle Paul, who studied under Rabban Gamaliel the Elder. This situation also continued after the destruction of the Temple. The greatest scholars of Babylonian Jewry came to study in the academies of Ereẓ Israel; some settling and becoming active there, while others, returning to Babylonia, made that country a great spiritual center. Among the Jews of the Diaspora who settled permanently in Ereẓ Israel were some who shaped the character of Jewish society in Jerusalem at the end of the Second Temple period, the most prominent of these being the families of Boethus and Phiabi, houses of high priests whose members had immigrated from Egypt, and *Bet Hillel and the *Benei Bathyra, whose roots lay in the Babylonian Diaspora.

Material support from the Diaspora to Jerusalem consisted primarily of the half shekel contributed to the Temple. This money was sent by Jews and proselytes, not only from the Roman Empire but also from eastern Jewry under Parthian rule. The Jews of Babylonia sent their half shekels to Nehardea and Nisibis, from where a caravan, accompanied by many thousands of Jews to defend it against possible attack by brigands, transported the money to Jerusalem. Wealthy Jews in Alexandria also made liberal contributions to enhance the outward splendor of the Temple. During the years following the destruction of the Second Temple the Jews of the Diaspora continued their financial support of the patriarchate. Important, too, was the political assistance which the Diaspora rendered to the Jews of Ereẓ Israel. As early as in the days of Alexander Yannai, the intervention of Hananiah and Hilkiah, Jewish commanders in the Ptolemaic army, was a prime factor in the development of military events in Ereẓ Israel, where the Jews derived encouragement from the large numbers and steady loyalty of the Jews in the Diaspora during the Roman Empire.

CULTURE IN THE GRECO-ROMAN DIASPORA. Although the Jewish Diaspora gave rise to considerable spiritual creativity, only a small portion of the literary productions have been preserved. They were written mainly in Greek, which in the Hellenistic period had become the principal language of the Jews of the Roman Empire outside Ereẓ Israel. The characteristic feature of these works is that they are not Greek literature produced by authors of Jewish origin, but Jewish literature written in Greek, for Jewry. Jewish history and problems are the central themes, and not the subjects typical of Greek literature. Whether it chiefly aimed at satisfying the internal needs of Jewish society or whether it was partially of an apologetic nature, intended for external purposes, it must, restrained though it sometimes is, be regarded as polemical literature. In form, however, Jewish-Hellenistic literature adopted most of the types characteristic of Greek literary productions, and among its representatives were historians, philosophers, and dramatic and epic poets. In the Hellenistic-Roman period very few authors of Jewish origin achieved fame in general Greek works unrelated to Jewry. Among these was, apparently, *Caecilius of Calacte in Sicily, an author and literary critic who was a contemporary of Augustus. Only gradually and at a later period did Jewish names begin to appear in the fields of general medicine and science, literature and art. Most of the Jewish-Greek writers were from Egypt, but other places, too, such as Cyrene (where the historian Jason of *Cyrene lived), participated in these productions. The influence of Jewish-Hellenistic literature on the development of later Jewry was scant and it became generally known chiefly through the channels of the Christian Church.

BIBLIOGRAPHY: Schuerer, Gesch, 3 (1909$^{3/4}$), 1–188; M. Radin, *The Jews among the Greeks and Romans* (1915); A. Causse, *Les dispersés d'Israël* (1929); E.G. Kraeling, *Brooklyn Museum Aramaic Papyri* (1953); A. Schalit, in: JQR, 50 (1960), 289–318; H.J. Leon, *Jews of Ancient Rome* (1960); I. Ben-Zvi, in: *Eretz Israel*, 6 (1961), 130–48; V. Tcherikover, *Hellenistic Civilization and the Jews* (1959); idem, *Ha-Yehudim ve-ha-Yevanim ba-Tekufah ha-Hellenistit* (1963); idem; *Ha-Yehudim be-Miẓrayim ba-Tekufah ha-Hellenistit-ha-Romit le-Or ha-Papirologyah* (1963^{2}), Eng. Summary; idem, in: JJS, 14 (1963), 1–32; Juster, Juifs; Tcherikover, Corpus; Frey, Corpus; Neusner, Babylonia.

[Menahem Stern]

DIBBUK (Dybbuk). In Jewish folklore and popular belief an evil spirit which enters into a living person, cleaves to his soul, causes mental illness, talks through his mouth, and represents a separate and alien personality is called a *dibbuk*. The term appears neither in talmudic literature nor in the Kabbalah, where this phenomenon is always called "evil spirit." (In talmudic literature it is sometimes called *ru'aḥ tezazit*, and in the New Testament "unclean spirit.") The term was introduced into literature only in the 17th century from the spoken language of German and Polish Jews. It is an abbreviation of *dibbuk me-ru'aḥ ra'ah* ("a cleavage of an evil spirit"), or *dibbuk min ha-ḥiẓonim* ("*dibbuk* from the outside"), which is found in man. The act of attachment of the spirit to the body became the name of the spirit itself. However, the verb *davok* ("cleave") is found throughout kabbalistic literature where it denotes the relations between the evil spirit and the body, *mitdabbeket bo* ("it cleaves itself to him").

Stories about *dibbukim* are common in the time of the Second Temple and the talmudic periods, particularly in the Gospels; they are not as prominent in medieval literature. At first, the *dibbuk* was considered to be a devil or a demon which entered the body of a sick person. Later, an explanation common among other peoples was added, namely that some of the *dibbukim* are the spirits of dead persons who were not laid to rest and thus became *demons. This idea (also common in medieval Christianity) combined with the doctrine of

**gilgul* ("transmigration of the soul") in the 16th century and became widespread and accepted by large segments of the Jewish population, together with the belief in *dibbukim*. They were generally considered to be souls which, on account of the enormity of their sins, were not even allowed to transmigrate and as "denuded spirits" they sought refuge in the bodies of living persons. The entry of a *dibbuk* into a person was a sign of his having committed a secret sin which opened a door for the *dibbuk*. A combination of beliefs current in the non-Jewish environment and popular Jewish beliefs influenced by the Kabbalah form these conceptions. The kabbalistic literature of *Luria's disciples contains many stories and "protocols" about the exorcism of *dibbukim*. Numerous manuscripts present detailed instructions on how to exorcise them. The power to exorcise *dibbukim* was given to *ba'alei shem* or accomplished Ḥasidim. They exorcised the *dibbuk* from the body which was bound by it and simultaneously redeemed the soul by providing a *tikkun* ("restoration") for him, either by transmigration or by causing the *dibbuk* to enter hell. Moses *Cordovero defined the *dibbuk* as an "evil pregnancy."

From 1560 several detailed reports in Hebrew and Yiddish on the deeds of *dibbukim* and their testimonies about themselves were preserved and published. A wealth of material on actual stories of *dibbukim* is gathered in Samuel *Vital's *Sha'ar ha-Gilgulim*, in Ḥayyim *Vital's *Sefer ha-Ḥezyonot*, in *Nishmat Ḥayyim* by *Manasseh Ben Israel (book 3, chs. 10 and 14), in *Minḥat Eliyahu* (chs. 4 and 5) by *Elijah ha-Kohen of Smyrna, and in *Minḥat Yehudah* by Judah Moses Fetya of Baghdad (1933, pp. 41–59). The latter exorcised *Shabbetai Ẓevi and his prophet *Nathan of Gaza who appeared as *dibbukim* in the bodies of men and women in Baghdad in 1903. Special booklets on the exorcisms of famous spirits which took place in Korets have also been published (end of 17th century in Yiddish), in Nikolsburg (1696, 1743), in Detmold (1743), and in Stolowitz (1848). The last protocol of this kind, published in Jerusalem in 1904, concerns a *dibbuk* which entered the body of a woman and was exorcised by Ben-Zion Ḥazzan. The phenomena connected with the beliefs in and the stories about *dibbukim* usually have their factual background in cases of hysteria and sometimes even in manifestations of schizophrenia.

[Gershom Scholem]

In the Arts

There are a few significant treatments of the *dibbuk* theme in literature, one of the earliest being a story in the *Ma'aseh Book (1602; Eng. tr. 2 vols., 1934). The classic interpretation of the story is *Der Dibbuk* (1916), a play by S. *An-Ski, which inspired various artistic and musical treatments. An unusual adaptation of the old legend is the French novelist Romain *Gary's bitterly satirical *La Danse de Gengis Cohn* (1967; *The Dance of Genghis Cohn*, 1968), which tells of the haunting of an ex-Nazi by the spirit of a Jewish entertainer whom he murdered in World War II. In drama and music the *dibbuk* motif has mainly found expression in compositions associated with An-Ski's play, the *Habimah production of which, in Moscow in 1922, was both visually and dramatically a landmark. It was directed by Eugene Vakhtangov, who gave the play an expressionist interpretation; the stage sets were designed by Nathan *Altman, and Jacques *Chapiro collaborated in the production. A Yiddish film version of the play was made in Poland in 1938 and a Hebrew version in Israel in 1968.

Joel *Engel's music for An-Ski's play, like the play itself, dates from 1912, when the two men heard the old folktale from an innkeeper's wife. An-Ski constructed the play on the leitmotiv of the ḥasidic song *Mipnei mah* ("Why did the soul descend from the supreme height to the deep pit?"). The tune was used at the first performance of the play by the Vilna troupe, and was taken over by Engel. For the rest of the stage music, Engel drew on the folk melodies he had collected, mainly those of ḥasidic provenance. In 1926 Engel published an arrangement of the stage music as the Suite "*Hadibuk*" (op. 35). Bernhard Sekles wrote an orchestral prelude, *Der Dybuk* (publ. 1929). The opera *Il Dibuk* by Lodovico Rocca (text by Renato Simoni after An-Ski) had its premiere at La Scala, Milan, in 1934. Later settings include a ballet by Max Ettinger (1947), and two operas (both entitled *The Dybbuk*) by U.S. composers – David Tamkin (1951) and Michael Whyte (1962).

BIBLIOGRAPHY: *Sha'ar ha-Gilgulim* (1875), 8–17; Moses Zacuto, *Iggerot ha-Remez* (1780), no. 2; Moses Graff of Prague, *Kunteres Ma'aseh ha-Shem ki Nora Hu* (Fuerth, 1696); Moses Abraham b. Reuben Ḥayyat, *Sefer Ru'aḥ Ḥayyim*, (1785); M. Sassoon, *Sippur Nora shel ha-Dibbuk* (1966); Phinehas Michael, Av Bet Din of Stolowitz, *Ma'aseh Nora'ah*… (Yiddish, Warsaw, 1911); S.R. Mizraḥi, *Ma'aseh Nora shel ha-Ru'aḥ* (1904); M. Weinreich, *Bilder fun der Yidisher Literatur Geshikhte* (1928), 254–61; G. Scholem, in: *Leshonenu*, 6 (1934), 40–41.

DIBON (Heb. דִּיבֹן).

(1) An important Moabite city in Transjordan in the *mishor* ("table-land"), N. of the Arnon River. It was located on the King's Highway and was one of the stations of the Israelites on the way to the plains of Moab during the Exodus (Num. 33:45, as Dibon-Gad). The Bible also relates that Sihon, king of the Amorites, captured it from the first king of Moab (Num. 21:30). With the Israelite conquest, it was allotted to the tribe of Gad (Num. 32:3, 33), although it is also listed in the territory of Reuben (Josh. 13:17). Dibon is identified with modern Dhiban, 13 mi. (21 km.) east of the Dead Sea and 3 mi. (5 km.) north of the Arnon River. Dibon is mentioned in an inscription of Ramses II from Luxor, together with *Btrt*, another city in Moab. In the *Mesha Stele, discovered at Dibon in 1868, Mesha, king of Moab (II Kings 3:4), calls himself "the Dibonite." Dibon was his capital, and, after his rebellion against Israel (c. 850 B.C.E.), he built the "Qarḥoh," (apparently the main citadel of the city) with a *bamah* ("high place") to Chemosh, the god of Moab. Dibon henceforth continued to be part of Moab and the Bible refers to it as a Moabite city (Isa. 15:2; Jer. 48:18, 22). In 731 B.C.E. it came under As-

syrian domination, with tribute being paid to Tiglath-Pileser III, and this continued under subsequent rulers as well. In 582 the city fell at the time of the revolt against Nebuchanezzar.

Excavations began at Dibhan in the 1950s directed by Fred V. Winnett and subsequently by William H. Morton with A.D. Tushingham, bringing to light strata from the Early Bronze Age, Iron Age (Moabite), Nabatean, Roman, Byzantine and Umayyad periods. In one area of the excavations a palace from the Moabite level had an adjoining sanctuary, with cultic vessels, incense stand and fertility figurines. Especially noteworthy is a sequence of sacred buildings – a Roman temple built on the foundations of a Nabatean temple and a Byzantine church alongside them. Perhaps the high-place of the Temple of Kemosh, the Moabite deity, lay beneath the Nabatean temple. Dibon was an important place under the Nabateans; a Roman garrison occupied the area in the third century C.E. as the remains of a bath-house and a number of inscriptions testify. The plain of Dibon is mentioned in the Tosefta (*Shev.* 7:11); in the fourth century, Eusebius refers to it as a big village near the Arnon (*Onom.* 76:17ff.).

(2) A post-Exilic town in the Negev (Neh. 11:25). It is probably identical with *Dimonah in the Negev district of Judah (Josh. 15:22).

ADD. BIBLIOGRAPHY: A.D. Tushingham, "Dhiban Reconsidered: King Mesha and His Works," in: *Annual of the Department of Antiquities of Jordan*, 34 (1990), 183–91; P. Bienkowski (ed.), *Early Edom and Moab: The Beginning of the Iron Age in Southern Jordan* (1992); A.D. Tushingham and P.H. Pedrette, "Mesha's Citadel Complex (Qarḥoh) at Dhiban," in: *Studies in the History and Archaeology of Jordan*, vol. 5 (1995), 151–59.

[Yohanan Aharoni / Shimon Gibson (2nd ed.)]

DICHTER, MISHA (1945–), U.S. pianist. Dichter was born in Shanghai, where his Polish parents had fled at the outbreak of World War II. He moved with his family to Los Angeles in 1947 and began piano lessons at the age of six. Dichter studied with Aube Tzerko (a former *Schnabel student) and, later, with Rosina *Lhevinne at the Juilliard School of Music in New York. He also studied composition with Leonard Stein (a Schoenberg disciple). His crowning success came in 1966, when he won second prize in the Tchaikovsky International Piano Competition, Moscow, and he was particularly popular with Russian audiences.

After his London (June 1967) and New York (January 1968) debuts, Dichter toured widely. He performed with major American and European orchestras, and also in Israel and the Far East. An active chamber musician, Dichter frequently performed with his wife in duo-piano recitals. They gave the world premiere of Robert Starer's Concerto for Two Pianos with the Seattle Symphony. Dichter's master classes at Juilliard, Eastman, Yale, and Harvard were widely attended. A player of generous temperament and technique, he excelled in the Romantic piano repertory. Dichter's style reflects the German respect for structure and clarity and at the same time the Russian search for heroic proportion. His numerous recordings include works of Brahms, Liszt, Chopin, Mussorgsky, Schubert, Schumann, Stravinsky, and Tchaikovsky. As a writer, he contributed many articles to leading publications, including the *New York Times*.

BIBLIOGRAPHY: NG, s.v.; *Baker's Biographical Dictionary* (1997).

[Max Loppert / Naama Ramot (2nd ed.)]

°DICKENS, CHARLES (1812–1870), English novelist. One of his first full-length novels, *Oliver Twist* (1837–38), devoted to the evils of the poor-law system, introduces a Jewish villain, Fagin, a corrupter of youth and receiver of stolen goods. With Shakespeare's Shylock, Fagin is unquestionably the best-known Jewish figure depicted in the traditional canon of English literature. The young hero, Oliver, falls into Fagin's clutches but is saved from corruption by his own native innocence and by some good-hearted friends. Fagin, like the burglar Bill Sikes in the same novel, is one of Dickens' characters of monstrous evil, a literary stereotype larger than life. As for his Jewishness, Dickens claimed that "that class of criminal almost invariably was a Jew," but Fagin in fact lacks any recognizable Jewish traits. Dickens was challenged about his antisemitic prejudices, and in reply, claimed that he had always felt himself to be a friend of the Jews. As if to prove this, his last complete novel, *Our Mutual Friend* (1864–65), featured Mr. Riah, "the gentle Jew in whose race gratitude is deep." Jews appear in other novels of Dickens, notably *Pickwick Papers* (1836) and *Martin Chuzzlewit* (1843). Dickens' contradictory portrayal of Jews illustrates something of the ambiguity of the Jewish image in Victorian England, and also the deep contradictions in Dickens' own complex character.

BIBLIOGRAPHY: E. Johnson, *Dickens: His Tragedy and Triumph*, 2 vols. (1953); M.F. Modder, *Jew in the Literature of England* (1939), 217–36; E. Rosenberg, *From Shylock to Svengali* (1960), ch. 5. **ADD. BIBLIOGRAPHY:** P. Ackroyd, *Charles Dickens* (1990); J. Smole, *Charles Dickens* (2002); ODNB online.

[Harold Harel Fisch]

DICKENSTEIN, ABRAHAM (1902–1977), Israeli banker and industrialist. Dickenstein was born in Wishniewa, Poland, and immigrated to Ereẓ Israel in 1921.

From 1921 to 1924 he worked as an agricultural laborer but entered the world of finance in 1925, when he founded the Audit Union of Credit Co-operatives and the Audit Union of Consumers Co-operatives, and in 1927 the Transport Co-operatives. From 1924 to 1935 he was assistant director of Bank Hapoalim of which he later became managing director and visited the United States in 1936 to sell shares of the bank. Encouraged by his success, he conceived the idea of establishing an American financial corporation for the purpose of mobilizing finance and investment resources among United States Jewry for the purpose of expanding the industrial and agricultural economy of Israel. The outcome was the founding of AMPAL, the American Israel Corporation, in 1941, which, with a balance sheet of $400 million, was in the 1970s one of the most important financial organizations in Israel.

He also served as chairman of the board of the Israeli American Independent Development Bank.

DICKER-BRANDEIS, FREDERIKE (**Friedl**; 1898–1944), artist and teacher who spent the last two years of her life teaching art to children in the Theriesienstadt ghetto. Born in Vienna, Dicker-Brandeis's mother, Karolina Fanta, died by the time she was four years old. Her father, Simon Dicker, a stationery store employee, nurtured Friedl's early interest in art by providing her with supplies from his store. In her early teens, she studied graphic arts at the Experimental School of Graphics. In 1914 she began formal art lessons with Johannes Itten, a pioneer in the Bauhaus School. When Itten left in 1920 for the new State Bauhaus school of art and design in Weimar, Friedl followed him. This began a period of enormous creativity for the young woman. At the Bauhaus school, Friedl studied with Itten, Paul Klee, Georg Muche, and Lyonel Feininger. Her training and skills grew. She became accomplished in charcoals, oil painting, weaving, architecture, poster art, jewelry, bookbinding, and textiles. Because of her outstanding teaching abilities, Friedl was invited to teach Itten's basic course for freshman at Bauhaus while she was still student.

In 1923, Itten and a number of students, including Friedl, left Bauhaus. She and Franz Singer, a fellow student, opened the Workshops for Visual Arts. They designed and sold textiles, books, and jewelry. The following year, Friedl returned to Vienna and opened a new gallery. Singer followed her in 1926 and the Atelier Singer-Drucker became one of the most fashionable design houses in Vienna. In addition to interior design, the couple's business and staff expanded to include architects who designed the Montessori kindergarten and the Tennis Club in Vienna. The Atelier also worked in set design for Berthold Brecht's theater. During this time, Friedl began teaching art courses for kindergarten teachers as well.

In the early 1930s, Friedl became active in politics. She was arrested for Communist activities in 1934 and briefly imprisoned. After her release, she immigrated to Prague continuing both in art and politics. In Prague, Friedl devoted herself to more traditional modes of painting, worked as an interior designer, and taught children of German and Austrian refugees. There she also located her mother's family and, in 1936, married her cousin, Pavel Brandeis. After the Anschluss, Friedl received a visa for Palestine. Instead, she and Pavel moved to Hronov, a small town in Bohemia. As the situation worsened, Pavel and Friedl lost their jobs and were forced to move. On December 14, 1942, they were deported to Theresienstadt.

In Theresienstadt, Friedl lived in a home for girls, caring for and teaching them. She gave art lessons, lectured to art teachers, designed sets and costumes for children's productions, and, with Pavel, re-designed some of the girls' living quarters. Some of her students' artwork is included in *I Never Saw Another Butterfly*, a well-known collection of poetry and art created by children in Theresienstadt. Her work with the children is legendary and seen as the embodiment of spiritual defiance to the Nazis and the circumstances of their incarceration. When Pavel was deported to Auschwitz, Friedl volunteered for the next transport. She died in Auschwitz in October 1944.

BIBLIOGRAPHY: E. Markova: *Friedl Dicker-Brandeis, Vienna 1898–Auschwitz 1944: The Artist Who Inspired the Children's Drawings of Terezin* (2001); idem, *From Bauhaus to Terezin: Friedl Dicker-Brandeis and Her Pupils* (1990); S.G. Rubin, *Fireflies in the Dark: The Story of Friedl Dicker-Brandeis and the Children of Terezin* (2000).

[Beth Cohen (2nd ed.)]

DICKSTEIN, SAMUEL (1851–1939), mathematician and pedagogue, born in Warsaw. Author of many papers on mathematics and physics, from 1897 he edited *Wiadomości Matematyczne* ("Mathematical News"). One of the leaders of Polish Jewish assimilationism, he was its representative on the Warsaw Communal Council from 1884 to 1918. From 1891 to 1901 he was principal of a science-oriented secondary school (established in 1878) which had introduced Hebrew into its curriculum. It was closed by the Russian superintendent as being too Polish in orientation. In 1906 Dickstein was elected the first president of the Towarzystwo Rady Naukowej (Academic Council), the ruling body of the precursor of the Free Polish Polytechnic, and in 1915 became professor of mathematics at the University of Warsaw. His brother was the Polish Socialist Szymon *Dickstein.

BIBLIOGRAPHY: J. Shatzky, *Geshikhte fun Yidn in Varshe* (1953), index.

DICKSTEIN, SAMUEL (1885–1954), U.S. congressman. Dickstein, who was born in Vilna, Lithuania, was taken to the U.S. in 1887, when his family settled in New York's Lower East Side. In 1917 he was elected to the Board of Aldermen of New York City, and two years later to the State Legislature. In Albany he drafted several housing bills and drew up the first Kosher-Slaughtering Laws of New York State. Elected to the U.S. House of Representatives from the Lower East Side in 1922, Dickstein began a career there that spanned 22 years. As chairman of the House Immigration and Naturalization Committee, he lashed out constantly against alleged subversives both on the right and left during the 1930s and proposed that the naturalization and alien laws be used against them. A faithful member of the New York City Democratic political machine, Dickstein was elected a New York State Supreme Court justice in 1945, and served until his death.

[Richard Skolnik]

DICKSTEIN (Dykstajn), SZYMON (pseudonym **Jan Mlot**; 1858–1884), Polish naturalist and socialist theoretician. Born in Warsaw, he took special interest in new trends in natural science and was one of the translators of the works of Darwin and Spencer and was active in socialist circles. The growing repression of Polish socialists led him to immigrate in 1878 to Switzerland and later to France. Though at first influenced by anarchist ideas, Dickstein subsequently became a Marxist and joined the "First Proletariat" (the Polish Marxist Party). He maintained close ties with leading Russian revolutionaries including Plekhanov and devoted himself to popularizing Marxist socialism. In 1881 he published one of the first popular versions of Marx's *Kapital* and in the following year translated several works of Ferdinand Lassalle into Polish. His activities as a popularizer and press columnist had a great influence on the ideology of the first workers' parties in Poland.

[Abraham Wein]

°DIDEROT, DENIS (1713–1784), French man of letters. He was editor in chief of the celebrated *Encyclopédie ou Dictionnaire Raisonné des Sciences, des Arts et des Métiers* (1751–80), to which he also contributed many articles. His article *Juifs (Philosophie des)* constituted the major part of the article *Juif* in the encyclopedia (vol. 9 (1765), 24–51). In this Diderot writes with admiration about what he terms the two determining characteristics of the Jewish nation: its being the oldest nation still in existence and the only one which did not pass through the stage of polytheism. He also praises the "natural" religion of the patriarchs and the personality and ability of Moses. He later states, however, that all these attributes belong "more to the history of revelation than the history of philosophy." Diderot therefore provides a lengthy description of what he considers are the history and the principles of Jewish philosophy after the Babylonian captivity. The main points he made in his description of Jewish philosophy are that the Jews are a people almost unacquainted with science; and that "we cannot expect to find among the Jews exactitude of ideas or precision in style; in short, everything which characterizes a sound philosophy. On the contrary we find a confused mixture of principles of reason and of revelation, an affected and frequently impenetrable obscurity of principles, which cause fanaticism, a blind respect for the authority of the doctors and antiquity; in short, all the defects peculiar to an ignorant and superstitious nation."

BIBLIOGRAPHY: J. Assezat and M. Tourneaux (eds.), *Oeuvres complètes de Diderot*, 15 (1876), 318–400; 17 (1876), 431–3; Reinach, in: REJ, 8 (1844), 138–44; *Dictionnaire de biographie française*, 11 (1967), 266–9 (includes bibl.); A. Hertzberg, *The French Enlightenment and the Jews* (1968), 281–2, 310–2. **ADD. BIBLIOGRAPHY:** L. Schwartz, *Diderot and the Jews* (1981); D. Bourel, "Les rasés et les barbus: Diderot et le judaïsme," in: *Revue Philosophique* (1984), 333–58.

[Baruch Mevorah]

DIDI-HUBERMAN, GEORGES (1953–), French philosopher and art historian. Born in Saint-Etienne, an industrial city in the south of France, Didi-Huberman is the son of a painter of Tunisian descent who fought in the Forces Françaises Libres (FFL) Resistance group during the war and a mother of Polish descent who, together with her brother, was the sole survivor of the Holocaust in her family; her father, a workman who had come from the Warsaw ghetto to the mines of Saint-Etienne, died in Auschwitz. Georges' family played a decisive role in his intellectual career: "My childhood was placed under a dual influence. From my father, a painter, I learned the sense of beauty. His workplace was a place of colors. On my mother's side, it was the books – and the silence about the Shoah." After interrupted studies in the history of art and philosophy in Lyons and Paris, Didi-Huberman began a career in theater and dramaturgy, collaborating with André Engel or Jean-Pierre-Vincent, whom he assisted in creating a landmark staging of Bernard Chartreux's *Dernières nouvelles de la peste* at the festival of Avignon in 1983. This first career culminated with a position as playwright-in-residence at the prestigious Comédie-Française. But feeling the lack of a new language to bring to the stage, he resigned and returned to his former studies in the history of art, spending four years in Italy at the Villa Médicis in Rome, and in Venice. A disciple of Aby Warburg's school of thought, iconology, Didi-Huberman developed two main axes: specialization in the iconography of the Italian Renaissance and general, philosophical, and phenomenological reflection on the status of the image itself. From 1990, he taught at the EHESS (Ecole des Hautes Etudes en Sciences Sociales) in Paris, where he developed an anthropological approach to vision and the visual arts. His major works include *Fra Angelico: Dissemblance and Figuration* (1995); *L'image survivante: Histoire de l'art et temps des fantômes selon Aby Warburg* (2002); *Ninfa Moderna. Essai sur le drapé tombé* (2002); and *Invention of Hysteria: Charcot and the Photographic Iconography of the Salpêtrière* (2003). In 2001, after he published an essay for a Paris exhibition of photographs clandestinely taken at Auschwitz by members of the *Sonderkommando*, he entered into an acrimonious intellectual debate with Claude Lanzmann in the pages of *Les temps modernes* on the ability of images to represent the Holocaust and convey historical knowledge or ethical content. Didi-Huberman advocated a "philosophy of the unthinkable," which he related to the tradition inaugurated by Hannah *Arendt, where the visual arts and the image have a crucial role, whereas Lanzmann tended to discredit photography, relying on witnesses and documents. Didi-Huberman attempted to deal with Lanzmann's objections in *Images malgré tout* (2002), stressing the importance of image and cinematographic art in Lanzmann's own *Shoah* documentary. The relation of aesthetics to ethics was the crux of the controversy, which was reminiscent of Adorno's famous indictment of "poetry after Auschwitz."

[Dror Franck Sullaper (2nd ed.)]

DIDYMOTEIKHON (Didumotica, Demotika), city in W. Thrace, Greece. Dating from the Middle Ages, there was a *Romaniot synagogue in Constantinople named for the Jews of Demotikan origin. The oldest tombstone in the Jewish cemetery dates from 1456. The local Jews spoke Judeo-Spanish and maintained close relations with the Sephardi communities of nearby Edirne, Sofia, and Istanbul. In halakhic matters, the Jews were under the rabbinic authority of Edirne. In 1821, at the beginning of the Greek Revolution, there were several dozen Jewish families there. In 1897 an Alliance Israélite Universelle school was established, operating until the mid-1920s. When the Bulgarians captured the city on October 30, 1912, much Jewish property, including stores, were damaged. The economy deteriorated and the Turks captured the city on July 13, 1913. During World War I sovereignty returned to the Bulgarians, who ruled until 1919, when in accordance with the Neuilly Treaty the city came under Greek sovereignty. In about 1920, there were 900 Jews in Didymoteikhon out of a general population of 12,000. They included exporters of grains, silks, cheese, and wool, as well as small grocers. In 1920, the Solidarity youth group of school graduates was formed as an intellectual group and Zionist activity was held at the Cercle Israélite club. In 1922, a branch of B'nai B'rith was founded. In 1934–35, the later noted Athenian Rabbi Eli Barzilai was principal of the Jewish school and French was taught until 1936 when foreign language instruction was banned by dictator Ioannis Metaxas. In 1940 there were 1,000 Jews in Didymoteikhon, of whom 970 were deported during the Holocaust. In 1948, 38 Jews remained in the city, and in 1967, 21.

BIBLIOGRAPHY: N. Leven, *Cinquante ans d'histoire ...*, 2 (1920), 171–4; A. Galanté, *Les Synagogues d'Istanbul* (1937), 7, 10; J. Nehama, in: M. Molho (ed.), *In Memoriam*, 2 (1949), 164. **ADD. BIBLIOGRAPHY:** B. Rivlin (ed.), *Pinkas Kehillot Yavan* (1999), 86–92.

[Simon Marcus / Yitzchak Kerem (2nd ed.)]

DIE DEBORAH, German-language supplement of the English language weekly *The Israelite*, created by Isaac Mayer *Wise in Cincinnati in 1855. The first Jewish periodical in America devoted to women, *Die Deborah* appeared until 1902, two years after Wise's death. While ostensibly directed at women, the journal also served the larger needs of 19th century America's German-speaking Jewry, promoting a program of German identity, bourgeois culture, and Jewish Reform. The paper reported on Jewish affairs from all over the world and published essays on Jewish religion, culture, and history. It featured news from Germany and informed its readers on the cultural life of the German immigrant community in America. In particular, articles in *Die Deborah* discussed matters of schooling and education, and the journal prominently featured German literature, most commonly ghetto novels. *Die Deborah* promoted German culture, and it hailed the German concept of *Bildung* – the harmonious formation of the intellect and of the character – which was to inform true religiosity. The contributors to *Die Deborah* understood their Germanness not as an ethnic identity but as a legacy of cultural excellence, moral distinction, political progressiveness, and universalism which they wished to integrate into American society. *Die Deborah* promoted a Judaism based on a divinely inspired system of norms and values that encouraged free and rational thinking that was quite distinct from the patterns of male learning and halakhic observance of previous centuries. In this culture of middle-class propriety and enlightened German-Jewish sensitivity and religiosity, *Die Deborah* exalted the Jewish mother and wife as the pillar on which the Jewish religion rested. She instilled her children with faithfulness to Judaism and guaranteed the moral and cultural standards of Jewish family life. Domesticity, marriage, and motherhood remained central in *Die Deborah*, but the periodical also encouraged women's education, praised women's accomplishments in Jewish history, and encouraged women's activities outside the home, including professional careers. Thus, *Die Deborah* came to endorse the New Jewish Woman of the turn of the century and eventually supported women's suffrage. The importance of *Die Deborah* declined towards the end of the 19th century, as its readership achieved the integration into American society and the upward mobility that the journal had promoted.

BIBLIOGRAPHY: M.T. Baader, "From the 'Priestess of the Home' to the 'Rabbi's Brilliant Daughter': Concepts of Jewish Womanhood and Progressive Germanness in *Die Deborah* and the *American Israelite*, 1854–1900," in: *Leo Baeck Institute Year Book*, vol. 43 (1998), 47–72.

[Benjamin Maria Baader (2nd ed.)]

DIENCHELELE, from the Hebrew דיין כללי, *dayyan kelali* ("general judge"), an office instituted in Sicily in 1396 by King Martin I of Aragon. The holder of the office was both the judge and final court of appeal in cases judged according to Jewish law. The appointment was made from among those in special favor with the royal family, and since the *dienchelele* was often regarded as the actual representative of all the Jewish communities on the island, he was looked upon with suspicion by the Jews themselves. Joseph *Abenafia, personal physician to the king and queen, was appointed *dayyan kelali* in 1396 and held the office until 1407. In 1399, with the king's approval, Abenafia issued a series of ordinances that attempted to change and reform local customs. He forbade the marriage of underage girls, display of excessive grief at funerals, loaning money at interest, and gambling and he ordered that informers be punished. The holder of this office had wide powers in all matters governing community life: he appointed judges in all Sicilian communities, decided on the number of elected officials, and confirmed elections. This attempt at centralization was opposed by both the Jewish communities and the Sicilian cities because they feared it would infringe on their autonomy. Parallel to the institution of the general judge in the Kingdom of Sicily, another was appointed for the queen's lands (*Camera reginale*), an autonomous territory in the southeastern part of the island whose capital was Syracuse. The first judge appointed to this area was Rais de Ragusa, who remained in office until his death in 1414. After his death, Queen Bianca appointed Isaac son of David de Marsiglia, who was followed in 1416 by Sadone de Gaudio, all of them physicians. They, too, encountered the opposition of the local leadership. Although similar to the office of the court rabbis of Castile and Aragon, the Sicilian general judges did not enjoy the same power and they dealt only in matters concerning Jewish law, while criminal and civil jurisdiction was entrusted to a Christian official appointed as protector and judge of the Jews. In 1420 King Alfonso appointed Moses de Medici *Bonavoglia

(Hephetz) of Messina, a physician who completed his studies at the University of Padua, as general judge. His appointment was contested first by the city of Palermo, claiming that he had no jurisdiction as he was not a citizen of the city. Then, in 1421, at the request of the city councils of Palermo and Messina and their respective Jewish communities, the king revoked his appointment. Bonavoglia was reinstated in 1438 but only after a long process that necessitated the king's intervention. As a courtier, Bonavoglia intervened in 1431 to revoke the king's order of 1428 that the Jews of Sicily attend the sermons of the Franciscan Matteo Giummarra of Agrigento. Moses Bonavoglia died in 1446. He was succeeded by Joshua b. Nachrim de Manopelo of Randazzo. During his short stay in office he was accused of heresy for having summoned a priest to his sickbed and later denying the Christian faith; he was found innocent by a special commission ordered by the king. Joshua b. Nachrim was the last *dienchelele*. After having been twice in abeyance, the office was definitely abolished in 1447, at the request of the communities, in return for a heavy monetary payment.

BIBLIOGRAPHY: B. and G. Lagumina, *Codice diplomatico dei giudei di Sicilia* (1884), passim. **ADD. BIBLIOGRAPHY:** S. Simonsohn, *The Jews in Sicily*, III (2001), passim; S. Fodale, "Mosè Bonavoglia e il contestato *iudicatus generalis* sugli ebrei siciliani," in: N. Bucaria (ed.), *Gli ebrei in Sicilia, Studi in onore di Monsignor Benedetto Rocco* (1998), 99–109; H. Bresc, *Arabes de langue, juifs de religion. L'evolution du judaïsme sicilien dans l'environment latin, XIIe–XVe siècles* (2001), 303–12.

[Attilio Milano / Nadia Zeldes (2nd ed.)]

DIENEMANN, MAX (1875–1939), German Reform rabbi and author. Dienemann was born in Krotoszyn (now Poznań province, Poland), and studied at the Jewish Theological Seminary and university in Breslau. He served as rabbi in Ratibor, Upper Silesia, from 1903 to 1919, and at Offenbach from 1920 to 1938, when he immigrated to Palestine. Dienemann was one of the leaders of Reform in Germany and an active supporter of the World Union for Progressive Judaism. Dienemann wrote *Judentum und Christentum* (1914), *Liberales Judentum* (1935), *Galuth* (1939), and *Midrashim der Klage und des Zuspruchs ausgewaehlt und uebersetzt* (1935). He also published some sermons. Dienemann contributed articles to journals including *Der Morgen*, of which he was coeditor from 1931 to 1933. On his 60th birthday the Jewish community of Offenbach presented him with a *Festschrift (Minḥat Todah) Max Dienemann* (1935), and later his wife published a memorial volume, *Max Dienemann: ein Gedenkbuch, 1875–1935* (1946); both contain bibliographies. Selections from the *siddur*, in German translation, edited by S. Guggenheim and dedicated to Dienemann's memory, were published in 1948 as *Aus den Gebeten Israel.*

DIENNA, AZRIEL BEN SOLOMON (d. 1536), Italian rabbi and halakhic authority. Dienna, who came from a French family that had settled in Italy, studied under R. Nethanel Trabot. In his youth he was a teacher in Reggio and later moved to Pavia where he remained for 15 years. For a time, he also lived in Piedmont. In 1517, or possibly earlier, he became rabbi of Sabbioneta where he served until his death. He corresponded in *halakhah* with the great scholars of his generation. His works, which are still in manuscript, include a volume of responsa, several of which have been published in various periodicals. Many of them constitute a valuable source for the history, customs, and culture of the Jews of Italy, and they also demonstrate his strong personality and stormy temperament. He was sharp and sarcastic when replying to his opponents and took an active part in the communal disputes. He was involved in 1519 in the storm occasioned in the *Norsa-Finzi controversy, coming out in defense of Abraham Mintz. His responsum on this affair was published in *Pesak ha-Ḥerem shel ha-Rav Ya'akov Pollack*, appended to *Da'at Kedoshim* (1897–98) by I.T. Eisenstadt and S. Wiener.

In the scandal which arose in 1530–32 among his contemporaries over the dismissal of *Benjamin Ze'ev of Arta, Dienna supported those who expelled and excommunicated him. In 1532–36 he was the main instigator of the expulsion of Joseph of Arles from the *Ḥaverut* (a high grade of the Italian rabbinate) as well as from the rabbinate, pointing out that the latter's conduct did not conform with his rabbinical status. In his letter to Abraham ha-Kohen of Bologna in 1531 or 1535, Dienna dissociated himself from David *Reuveni who was greatly honored in many Italian communities, yet he expressed favorable sentiments about the false messiah Solomon *Molcho. Azriel's sons – Jacob, David, Samson, and Menahem – all served in the Italian rabbinate.

BIBLIOGRAPHY: Kaufmann, in: REJ, 30 (1895), 304–9; Loewenstein, *ibid.*, 31 (1895), 120–3; I. Sonne, in: MGWJ, 75 (1931), 127–9, 132–4; idem, in: REJ, 94 (1933), 197, 201–6; S. Assaf, in: KS, 15 (1938/39), 113–29; A.Z. Aešcoly, *Sippur David Re'uveni* (1940), index; A. (A.H.) Freimann, *Seder Kiddushim ve-Nissu'in* (1945), 132–3, 135–7; S. Simonsohn, *Toledot ha-Yehudim be-Dukkasut Mantovah*, 2 (1965), 515; E. Kupfer, in: KS, 41 (1965/66), 117–30.

[Abraham David]

DIESENDRUCK, ZEVI (1890–1940), philosopher, scholar. Born in Stryj, Galicia, he studied in Vienna. He also taught in Palestine (1913), attended the University of Berlin (1915), and in World War I joined the Austrian army. After the war, he served on the faculties of the Jewish Pedagogium (Vienna, 1918–27), the Jewish Institute of Religion (New York, 1927), the Hebrew University (Jerusalem, 1928–30), and the Hebrew Union College (Cincinnati, 1930–40), where he was professor of Jewish philosophy. Diesendruck showed a lifelong interest in Zionism, particularly the revival of the Hebrew language. He contributed to this revival with Hebrew essays, notably: the volume *Min ha-Safah ve-Lifnim* (1933); a Hebrew translation of Martin Buber's *Daniel;* Hebrew translations of Plato's *Phaedrus* (Warsaw, 1923), *Crito* (in: *Ha-Tekufah*, 24 (1924)), *Gorgias* (Berlin, 1929), and *The Republic* (Tel Aviv, 1935–36); and coedited (with G. Schoffmann) a Hebrew periodical *Gevulot* (1919). Diesendruck's chief interest was Jewish philosophy, particularly Maimonides' *Guide of the Perplexed.* Diesendruck's philosophic writings include "Maimonides Lehre von der Prophetie" (in: *Jewish Studies in Memory of Israel Abrahams*, 1927); "Die Teleologie bei Maimonides" (in: HUCA, 5 (1928), 415–534); "Samuel and Moses ibn Tibbon on Maimonides' Theory of Providence" (in: HUCA, 11 (1936), 341–66); "On the Date of the Completion of the *Moreh Nebukhim*" (in: HUCA, 12–13 (1937–38), 461–98); *Struktur und Charakter des platonischen Phaidros* (1927).

BIBLIOGRAPHY: G. Bader, *Medinah va-Ḥakhameha* (1934), 72; I. Cohen, *Demut el Demut* (1949), 2, 8–24; F. Lachower, *Shirah u-Maḥashavah* (1953), 164–84; S. Ẓemaḥ, *Adam im Aḥerim* (1954), 35–48; A. Kariv, *Iyyunim* (1950), 162–71; G. Schoffmann, *Kol Kitvei*, 4 (1960^3), 274f.

[Alvin J. Reines]

DIETARY LAWS, the collective term for the Jewish laws and customs pertaining to the types of food permitted for consumption and their preparation. The Hebrew term is *kashrut*, which is derived from the root כשר ("fit" or "proper"). The word appears in the Bible only three times (Esth. 8:5; Eccles. 10:10; 11:6) and even then not in connection with food.

Description of Permitted Foods

Although there are laws which qualify the consumption of agricultural produce (see *Mixed Species; **Terumah*; **Orlah*; *Wine; *Idolatry), from the point of view of the dietary laws all fruit and vegetables are permitted. This is in fact the force of the first dietary directive in the Bible: "Behold I have given you every herb yielding seed which is upon the face of the earth and every tree …" (Gen. 1:29). Vegetables may also be consumed with either meat or milk (see below, Milk and Meat). The dietary laws therefore concern themselves with what animals, birds, and fish may be eaten, the way in which they must be prepared for consumption, and the fact that meat must not be consumed or cooked together with milk or other dairy products.

ANIMALS. The Bible classifies those animals permitted for consumption as *tahor* ("clean"), and those prohibited as *tame* ("unclean"). The distinction is traced to the wording of Noah's instructions. "Of every clean beast thou shalt take to thee seven and seven, each with his mate; and of the beasts that are not clean, two (and two), each with his mate" (Gen. 7:2). The criterion seems to have been the animal's sacrificial suitability, rather than pagan taboos.

Animals that chew the cud and whose hooves are wholly cloven, are "clean" (Deut. 14:6). Ten such herbivorous animals, both wild and domestic, are specifically enumerated in the Pentateuch: the ox, the sheep, the goat, the hart, the gazelle, the roebuck, the wild goat, the pygarg, the antelope, and the mountain-sheep (Deut. 14:4–5). Animals that have only one of the required characteristics (like the camel, which does not have split hooves, or the pig, which does not chew the cud) are forbidden (Deut. 14:7–8). Altogether, the Bible enumerates 42 "unclean" animals (see Table: Clean and Unclean Animals).

BIRDS. Leviticus 11:13–19 lists 20 "unclean" birds, and Deuteronomy 14:12–18 enumerates 21. From these two lists, the rabbis compiled a total of 24 "unclean" birds (Ḥul. 63a–b). All birds of prey are forbidden, such as the vulture, the osprey, the kite, the falcon, the raven, and the hawk. The Bible does not list "clean" birds. According to the Mishnah (Ḥul. 3:6), "clean" birds must have a crop, a gizzard which can easily be peeled off, and an extra talon (see Table: Clean and Unclean Animals). Today, only those birds for which there is a tradition that they are "clean" are permitted (Ḥul. 63b). With regard to certain birds there is sometimes a difference of tradition; thus in some German communities, the pheasant was regarded as "clean" whereas in others it was forbidden. There are differences of opinion also with regard to the turkey (for a complete list and discussion see: *Sinai*, 64 (1969), 258–281). Since "anything which comes from the unclean is unclean" (Bek. 7a–b), the eggs of forbidden birds are also forbidden (Ḥul. 64b). The Talmud lists among the indications for such eggs the fact that they are round rather than oval, and that the yolk is often on the outside and the albumen on the inside (*ibid.* 64a). Even the eggs of permitted birds are forbidden if they have been fertilized (*ibid.* 64a–b). That is usually seen from the fact that there is a dark spot in certain parts of the albumen. However, since there are several opinions among the authorities as to where the "danger zone" is, any spot of blood in the egg renders it unfit for consumption unless it comes from a chicken run in which there is no cock (and cannot therefore have been fertilized); it may be eaten if the spot itself is removed.

FISH. Only aquatic creatures that have at least one fin and one easily removable scale (*kaskeset*) are "clean" and permitted (Lev. 11:9–12; see Table: Clean and Unclean Animals). The Committee of Laws and Standards of the Rabbinical Assembly of America (Conservative) has ruled that both the sturgeon and the swordfish are permitted, whereas in England the Ashkenazi authorities forbid sturgeon while the Sephardi permit it (see ET, 7 (1956), 208).

INSECTS. Leviticus 11:21–22 specifically permits the eating of four kinds of *locusts. "But all other flying creeping things, which have four feet, shall be an abomination unto you" (11:23). However, since even the permitted locusts cannot be easily identified today, they are not eaten by most communities. Although the bee is a forbidden insect, its honey is regarded as "transferred nectar" and may therefore be eaten (Bek. 7b).

**Sheḥitah* ("Ritual Slaughter")

Specific regulations govern the method by which an animal must be slaughtered before it is permitted. So complex and minute are the regulations that the slaughter must be carried out by a carefully trained and licensed *shoḥet*. It is his duty both to slaughter the animal, and to carry out an examination (*bedikah*). Should a defect be found in some of the organs, such as the brain, the windpipe, the esophagus, the heart, the lungs, or the intestines, the animal is *terefah*, and forbidden for consumption. Defects are normally classified under eight categories (Ḥul. 43a): *nekuvah*, perforated organ walls; *pesukah*, split pipes; *netulah*, missing limbs; *ḥaserah*, missing or defective organs; *keru'ah*, torn walls or membrane covers or organs; *derusah*, a poisonous substance introduced into the body, when mauled by a wild animal; *nefulah*, shattering by a fall; *shevurah*, broken or fractured bones. It is assumed in the Talmud that any of these defects would lead to the death of the animal within one year (Hul. 3:1; see below). Only if the animal has none of these injuries, is it pronounced *kasher*. After *sheḥitah*, it is suspended head down, so that as much blood as possible may drain.

Should various sections of the animal have been removed before the *bedikah* has taken place, the animal is usually considered *kasher*. This rule is based on the fact that the majority of animals are usually found, after *bedikah*, to be *kasher* (Ḥul. 11a–b). This rule, however, does not apply if the lung has been removed. Since a large minority of animals do suffer from lung diseases that portion of the body must always be examined and if that is impossible the animal is considered *terefah*.

Sheḥitah and *bedikah* of poultry is carried out in the same careful manner. The same laws of *terefah* apply but there is no need for examination except of the intestines. There are no specific rules concerning the method by which permitted fish are to be killed.

Koshering ("Preparation of Meat")

The prohibition against the consumption of blood (Lev. 7:26–27; 17:10–14) is the basis for the process of koshering meat. The purpose of the process is to draw out and drain the meat of non-veinal blood, before it is cooked. The blood can be removed either by salting the meat, or by roasting it over an open flame.

The salting process is begun by fully immersing the meat and bones in clean, cold water (in a vessel used exclusively for this purpose), for 30 minutes. The purpose of this operation is to open the pores, and remove any blood on the surface, thus enabling the salt to draw the blood out of the softened fibers of the meat. The meat is then laid out on a special grooved or perforated board, which is slanted, in order to allow the blood to flow down. It is then sprinkled with salt. The salt should be of medium texture; neither fine (which melts away), nor coarse (which falls off). Poultry should be opened and must be salted inside and out. The meat is then left to stand, for one hour, after which it is washed two or three times in cold water. In an emergency, i.e., when the meat is intended for a sick person or when time is short on the eve of Sabbath, the periods of immersion and salting may be reduced to 15 and 30 minutes respectively.

The salting process cannot be used if more than 72 hours have elapsed since the time of the *sheḥitah*. Such meat can only be koshered by roasting over an open flame, a process which is considered to be more effective in removing the blood than salting. It is, however, customary to salt the meat a little, even if it is to be roasted over an open flame.

Before koshering, the vein which runs along the front groove of the neck must be removed or cut in several places. The heart, too, is cut in several places and the tip is cut off so that the blood may drain. The gizzard is cut open and cleaned before koshering. Salting is not considered effective enough to kosher the liver, which is full of blood. It is therefore sprinkled with salt, cut across or pierced several times, and placed on or under an open flame, until it changes color, or a crust forms.

Other Regulations Regarding Meat

FORBIDDEN PORTIONS OF CLEAN ANIMALS. It is forbidden to eat certain portions of "clean" animals. The sciatic nerve (*nervus ischiadicus*; Heb. גִּיד הַנָּשֶׁה), for instance, must be removed before any animal, other than a bird, can be prepared for consumption. The prohibition is traced back to the blow inflicted upon Jacob: "Therefore the children of Israel eat not the sinew of the thigh-vein which is upon the hollow of the thigh unto this day" (Gen. 32:33).

The fat portions (*ḥelev*), attached to the stomach and intestines of an animal, sacrificed on the altar in biblical and Temple times, are also forbidden for consumption. They must be removed by porging (*nikkur*) the organs to which they are attached. The abdominal fat of oxen, sheep, or goats, unless it is covered by flesh, is forbidden (Lev. 3:17; 7:23–25).

NEVELAH AND *TEREFAH*. It is forbidden to eat either a *nevelah* (an animal that dies a natural death, or that has been killed by any method other than *sheḥitah*; Deut. 14:21), or a *terefah* (an animal that has been torn by a wild beast; Ex. 22:30). The term *terefah* is also applied to an animal suffering from an injury which may lead within a specific time to its death (see above). Such an animal is absolutely prohibited for consumption. The Talmud (Ḥul. Chap. 3) describes over 70 such injuries and lesions (see also Sh. Ar., YD 29–60; Maim., Yad, Sheḥitah 10:9), which Maimonides describes as "the limit" and which, he says "must not be increased even though it should be found by scientific investigation that other injuries are dangerous to the life of the animal" (Maim., Yad, *ibid.* 10:12), or diminished "even if it should appear by scientific investigation that some are not fatal; one must go only by what the sages have enumerated" (Maim., Yad, *ibid.* 10:13).

ADMIXTURE OF PERMITTED AND FORBIDDEN FOODS. It is forbidden to eat any amount (no matter how minute) of forbidden foods (Yoma 74a). In the case of an accidental mixture of a forbidden food with a permitted one, however, the latter is only considered to be "contaminated" if the quantity of forbidden food inserted is large enough to affect the taste. For practical purposes, it was decided that only if the quantity of forbidden food was less than 1/60 of the permitted food with which it became mixed, is it considered not to have affected the taste. If more, the whole mixture is forbidden. If the forbidden admixture is, however, a type which is intended to affect the taste, then the mixture is forbidden even if the admixture is less than 1/60. Any leaven which becomes mixed

Tables of Clean and Unclean Animals, Birds, Fish, etc.

General Note: The purpose of this table is to give a resume of clean and unclean animals from an academic point of view only. It does not purport to lay down the *halakhah.*

MAMMALS

Characteristics: Viviparous[1], suckle their young, breathe though lungs, hairs on the skin; the body temperature is constant, four-chambered heart (two auricles and two ventricles); the chest cavity is separated from the ventral by a diaphragm.

CLEAN

Ruminants with cloven hooves
Characteristics: herbivorous, they have incisors in their upper jaws. Ruminants, the stomach has four compartments. They have either hollow or solid horns[2]. They are cloven-hoofed, with two toes.
Examples: buffalo, kine, goat, sheep, ibex, gazelle, deer, antelope, wild ox, wild goat, giraffe(?)[3].

UNCLEAN

a) Cloven-hoofed but non-ruminants
Characteristics: They walk on their hooves, possess canine and incisor teeth.
Examples: pig, boar, hippopotamus.

b) Ruminants but not cloven-hoofed
Characteristics: They have very small hooves, like nails, walk on cushion-like pads which form the soles of their feet. They have tusk-like canines on both jaws and incisor teeth on the upper jaw. Their stomach has only three compartments.
Examples: camel, llama.

c) Solid-hoofed
Characteristics: They are herbivorous, have a single stomach, incisor teeth on both upper and lower jaws.
Examples: horse, ass, mule, onager, zebra.

d) Carnivorous
Characteristics: They have six incisors and two sharp canine teeth on both jaws. They have four or five toes with claws on each foot and walk either on their toes or on their paws.
Examples: cat, lion, leopard, dog, wolf, jackal, fox, hyena, bear.

e) Other mammals neither ruminants nor cloven-hoofed
Examples: hare[4], mouse[5], hyrax[6], bat[7], rat, elephant, ape, whale.

Notes:

1) *Mammals exist in Australia and New Zealand belonging to the order Monotermata, which lay eggs.*
2) *In this group the females have no horns. In the majority of species the males shed their horns annually. Some primitive species of cloven-hoofed ruminants are entirely without horns. There is some doubt as to whether they are clean.*
3) *The giraffe is a cloven-hoofed ruminant with a kind of horn, but there is no clear tradition as to whether it is kosher. Some hold that it is the tahash mentioned in the Bible and some the zemer of Deut. 14:5. The okapi belongs to the same family as the giraffe and has the same characteristics.*
4) *The hare is enumerated in the Bible (Lev. 11:6; Deut. 14:7) among the ruminants which are not cloven-hoofed. In point of fact it is not actually a ruminant although it appears to be one. See *Hare.*
5) *The mouse* (akhbar) *and the rat* (ḥoled) *are enumerated in the Bible (Lev. 11:29) among the "creeping things" which are forbidden for food and whose carcasses render unclean by contact. Six other "creeping things" which are not mammals but reptiles are mentioned in the same verse and context. See later.*
6) *The hyrax is listed (Lev. 11:5) with the non-cloven-hoofed ruminants. Systematically it does not belong to the ruminants but in its anatomical structure it is somewhat similar to them.*
7) *The bat is enumerated in the Bible (Lev. 11:19; Deut. 14:18) with birds, because it flies, but systematically it belongs to the mammals.*

BIRDS

Characteristics: Their bodies are covered with feathers, and their upper limbs are wing-shaped. They have no teeth, breathe through lungs, and have a constant body temperature. The heart is four-chambered (two auricles and two ventricles). They lay eggs which have a hard shell of calcium carbonate (chalk).

CLEAN

The Bible does not give the characteristics which distinguish clean birds from unclean, as it does in the case of mammals and fish. The Mishnah, however (Ḥul. 3:6), states that "a bird that seizes food in its claws is unclean; one which has an extra talon[1], a craw, and the skin of whose stomach can be peeled, is clean." To this the Talmud adds in the name of R. Nahman that "to anyone familiar with birds and their

UNCLEAN

a) Diurnal Birds of Prey
The Diurnal Birds of Prey mentioned in the Bible are from the family Falconidae which are carnivorous and Vulturidae which feed on carrion.
Falconidae: have hooked beaks and their talons are sharp and bent like hooks.
Examples: kestrel, hawk, eagle, kite, buzzard.

Tables of Clean and Unclean Animals, Birds, Fish, etc. (continued)

BIRDS (continued)

nomenclature, any bird which has one of these characteristics is clean, but to one unfamiliar with them it is unclean, but if it has the two characteristics it is clean" (Ḥul. 61b–62a). However, they also posited the rule "With regard to which birds are clean we rely upon tradition. A hunter is believed when he says "my master transmitted to me that this bird is clean." R. Johanan added, "provided he was familiar with birds and their nomenclature" (Ḥul. 63b). Already in the Talmudic period varying traditions are mentioned whereby certain birds were considered permitted in one locality and forbidden in another. For this reason, at the present day the custom has been adopted to eat only such birds as have all the signs of cleanliness, and about which there is a general tradition that they are clean. In the Bible and Talmud the following birds are mentioned as clean:

a) Columbiformes: pigeon, turtle dove, palm dove.
b) Galliformes[2]**:** hen, quail, partridge, peacock[3], pheasant[4].
c) Passerinae: house sparrow[5].
d) Anseriformes: domestic duck, domestic goose.

Vulturidae: The neck is usually bare, the bill thick and solid. The talons are blunt and only slightly inclined.
Examples: griffon vulture[6], black vulture, Egyptian vulture, bearded vulture.
b) Nocturnal Birds of Prey (Strigiformes)
Possessed of large head and eyes; they have four toes, two pointing forwards and two backwards. The Mishnah (Ḥul. 3:6) declares them unclean.
Examples: owl.
c) Water and Marsh Fowls
With the exception of the goose and the duck[7], they are all regarded as unclean.
Examples: stork, bittern, heron, crane, gull.
d) Various other Birds which either have no characteristics of a clean bird, or about which there is no tradition that they are permitted.
Examples: warblers, crow, swift, hoopoe, ostrich.

Notes:

1) *I.e., the rear talon is situated higher up on the leg than the other four, or the middle talon is longer than the others. This latter is characteristic of birds which eat grain and walk extensively on the ground (see *Eagle).*
2) *To this order belong two more domestic fowls: (a) the turkey which is today everywhere regarded as a clean bird, although a few generations ago there were localities where they refrained from eating it because of the lack of any tradition that it was clean, coming as it does from the New World. To this day the descendants of Isaiah Horowitz (the "Shelah") do not eat turkey; (b) the guinea-fowl which in some localities is regarded as clean while in others it is regarded as forbidden.*
3) *For the problem of its identification see *Peacock.*
4) *In many countries there is a tradition that the pheasant is a clean bird and permitted. See *Pheasant.*
5) *This is the "deror" of the Bible (Prov. 26:2; Ps 84:4). With regard to this bird also there is a tradition, particularly in Oriental countries, that it is a clean bird and permitted.*
6) *The signs of this bird are discussed in Ḥulin 61a et seq. see Tosafot,* ibid *63a, s.v.* nez, *as to its identification.*
7) *In some countries there is a tradition with regard to other species of birds belonging to this and other groups that they are clean and permitted.*

REPTILES

Characteristics: To this class belong creeping or crawling things which have short legs or none at all. As a result they move close to the ground or drag along it. They exist chiefly on dry land, and breathe with lungs. The majority lay eggs, but with a soft shell in which the white and the yolk[1] are mixed. They are cold-blooded, i.e., their temperature adjusts itself to the environment. Their skin is covered with scales or with heavy platelets.

CLEAN

None.

UNCLEAN

In the Bible reptiles are included in the general prohibition "and every creeping thing that creepeth upon the earth shall be an abomination; it shall not be eaten. Whatsoever goeth upon the belly and whatsoever goeth upon all four or whatsoever hath many feet among all creeping things that creep upon the earth, them ye shall not eat for they are an abomination." (Lev. 11:41–42)
The crocodile is forbidden in accordance with Lev. 11:12, which forbids "whatsoever hath no fins or scales in the water." Of the eight creeping things which are forbidden as food and whose carcasses defile on contact (*ibid.* 11:29–30), six belong to the class of Reptiles. They are the lizard, gecko, skink, monitor, tortoise and chameleon.
In addition all species of snakes are forbidden food though the laws of uncleanness on contact do not apply to them.
Examples: black snake viper, cobra.

Notes:

1) *This fact is mentioned in the Talmud (Ḥul. 64a) where a distinction is made between the eggs of birds and the eggs of reptiles.*

Tables of Clean and Unclean Animals, Birds, Fish, etc. (continued)

AMPHIBIANS

Characteristics: Vertebrates, born in water: when adult living on dry land, in water, or both media. During the early stages of metamorphosis (larva-tadpole) they breathe with gills; in the adult stage either with lungs or gills. The body temperature changes in accordance with the medium in which they live.

CLEAN	UNCLEAN
None.	a) Apoda (without legs). b) Tailed – salamander, newt. c) Tailless – toad, frog[1].

Notes:

1) *The frog, like all amphibians, is forbidden, but the Mishnah (Toh. 5:1) points out that its carcass, unlike the six reptiles mentioned above, does not convey uncleanness by contact.*

FISH

Characteristics: Vertebrates, living in water and breathing through gills[1]. In some species the body is covered with bony or teeth-like scales; others have no scales. All possess fins[2]. Their body temperature changes according to their environment. They reproduce either by laying eggs or by bringing forth their young alive[3].
Fish are divided into main classes:
a) Bony skeletons (about 30,000 species).
b) Cartilaginous (about 400 species).

CLEAN	UNCLEAN
According to the Bible those fish are permitted which have "fins and scales in the waters, in the seas and in the rivers" (Lev. 11:9; Deut. 14:9). In this category only Bony Skeletons are included, since they alone possess fins and scales. The scales must be real ones, i.e., they must overlap one another and be of bony origin and not a growth of the skin. Some scales are of minute proportions; for the fish to be clean the scales must be visible to the eye[4]. Some fish have scales while young but shed them later; they are clean. On the other hand there are fish which develop scales only when they grow to maturity; they are also clean[5]. *Examples*: carp, trout, salmon, herring.	**a) Cartilaginous** (Chondrichthytes) These fish either have no scales or have thick scales like teeth, which are not however true scales as they do not overlap. They give birth to their offspring alive, or lay eggs. To this group belong all the strange-shaped fish which inhabit the ocean depths, and all species of sharks. *Example*: shark, ray. **b) Cartilaginous – Bony** (Chondrostei) They also lack true scales. Their body is unprotected, except that it is partly covered with five long rows of protective matter. It is from these fish that caviar (mainly black in color) is derived. *Example*: sturgeon (controversial, see "Fish" in text). **c) Bony Skeletons** (Holostei) Fish which have no scales visible to the eye, or which have no fins. *Examples*: catfish, eel.

Notes:

1) *An exception are the fish with lungs (Dipnoi) through which they also breathe. They are able to exist out of water. Although they have both fins and scales it appears that they are not to be regarded as fish at all, but as "creeping things," and are therefore forbidden.*
2) *In some cases the fins are minute, while in others they are broad and are used by the fish to crawl on the seabed. Some even use them for flying.*
3) *In the Talmud (Bekh. 7b) it is stated that "an unclean fish breeds, whereas a clean fish lays eggs." This rule applies to Cartilaginous fish which bear their young alive and to all bony fish in Israel, which lay eggs. In other parts of the world however there are found fish, with fins and scales, which bear their young alive. To these, for instance, belong the species of Gambusia which have been introduced in various localities as ornamental fish or as devourers of insects.*
4) *Even those Bony Skeletons which are considered unclean have minute scales which can be seen only through a microscope. They are regarded as being without scales.*
5) *As the Talmud states (Av. Zar. 39a), "Fish which have no scales at the time, but grow them later … and those which have them but shed them when drawn out of the water … are permitted." The "baraita" lists, in this category, fish such as the* אַכְסְפְּטִיִּים *which is presumably the swordfish (Xiphias). This identification, however, is not absolutely certain and thus the permissibility of the swordfish is doubtful.*

INVERTERBRATES

Characteristics: To this group belongs the largest number of species in the animal kingdom. They have no bony skeleton. Their skin is either bare or covered with a calciferous shell or a thick chitinous membrane. They reproduce by simple division of the body, by laying eggs or by bringing forth their offspring alive. The smallest creatures of this group are the protozoa whose existence became known only with the invention of the microscope[1].

Tables of Clean and Unclean Animals, Birds, Fish, etc. (continued)

INVERTERBRATES (continued)

CLEAN	UNCLEAN
Of all the inverterbrates only a group apertaining to the order of locusts (Orthoptera) are permitted for food by the Bible. This order includes some hundreds of species (out of approximately a million other species of insects) and of it the Bible mentions only four, "Yet these may ye eat of every flying creeping thing that goeth upon all four[2], which have legs above their feet, to leap withal upon the earth; even these may ye eat, the locust after its kind, etc." (Lev. 11.21–22). The Rabbis interpret the word translated "after its kind" to include others of the same order and enumerate eight species of permitted Orthoptera (Ḥul. 65a–b cf. Maim. Yad, Ma'akhalot Asurot 1:21–22). The Mishnah gives four signs whereby permitted insects may be recognised: four legs, four wings, jointed legs and the wings covering the greater part of the body (Ḥul. 3:7). Insects of the order Orthoptera develop by stages. At first they have no wings and in the course of time they develop them. For this reason it is laid down that if they have no wings at the time but grow them later, they are permitted (Ḥul. 65a). This excludes such Orthoptera as have no wings at all. Even at the present day there are Jews in Israel from oriental countries who eat such locusts about which they have a tradition as to their permissibility.	All inverterbrates – with the exception of some Orthoptera – are forbidden[3]. Those which live in water are forbidden under the prohibition either of fish which lack fins and scales, or of "any living thing which is in the waters" (Lev. 11:10). Those which live on land are forbidden in accordance with the prohibition against "whatsoever goeth upon the belly, and whatsoever goeth upon all four, or whatsoever hath more feet" (ibid. 11:42). The main groups of forbidden inverterbrates are: **Leeches, Mollusks** (snail, oyster, squid). **Segmented Worms, Flatworms, Jellyfish, Sponges, Protozoa**.

Notes:

1) *Practically all protozoa are microscopic and invisible to the naked eye. it is obvious that food containing them is not thereby rendered forbidden. To the extent that they are visible, however, if it is clear that a certain food consists of protozoa, it would appear that one should refrain from eating it. Nevertheless it should be pointed out that until the last century the general opinion was that protozoa and insects are formed from non-living matter through spontaneous generation. This view is found in rabbinic literature with regard to certain insects, and on these grounds they regarded them as permitted.*

2) *All insects have six legs. The Bible disregards the two front legs which it regards as hands.*

3) *The Talmud lays down the rule with regard to all living things, including insects, "that which derives from an unclean animal is unclean," (Bekh. 1.2). The only exception is bee honey which, although it derives from the bee which is unclean, is nevertheless permitted as food, since " they gather it into their body but do not exude it from their body" (Bekh. 7b).*
Human milk is of course permitted (Maim. Yad, Ma'akhalot Asurot, 3:1).

[Jehuda Feliks]

with permitted food on Passover contaminates the whole, no matter how minute the amount (see **Ḥameẓ*).

Milk and Meat

"Thou shalt not seethe a kid in its mother's milk" is a prohibition repeated three times in the Pentateuch (Ex. 23:19; 34:26; Deut. 14:21). The rabbinical elaboration of this precept defines three distinct prohibitions: cooking meat and milk together; eating such a mixture; and deriving any benefit from such a mixture (Ḥul. 115b). Together these laws are known as the ordinances of *basar be-ḥalav* ("meat in milk"). "Milk" includes all dairy products, such as cheese, butter, sour cream, and fresh cream. To create a "fence around the law" the rabbis ordained that the separation of meat from milk must be as complete as possible. Thus, separate utensils, dishes, and cutlery must be used for dairy foods and meat (*milchig* and *fleishig*, respectively, in Ashkenazi parlance). These must be stored separately, and when washed, separate bowls (or preferably sinks), and separate dishcloths (preferably of different colors to avoid confusion), must be used. If meat and milk foods are cooked at the same time on a cooking range or even on an open fire in a closed oven, care should be taken that the dishes do not splash each other and that the pans are covered.

According to the Talmud (Ḥul. 105a) one may not eat milk after meat in the same meal. However, strict observance demands an interval of as long as six hours between eating meat and dairy dishes. Most West European Jews wait three hours, whereas the Dutch custom is to wait one hour. It is permitted to eat meat immediately after milk dishes, provided that the mouth is first rinsed and some bread eaten (Ḥul. *ibid.*). After hard cheese, however, it is customary to wait a longer period (Isserles to Sh. Ar., YD 89:2). Imitation "milk" derived from coconuts and soybeans may be used with meat. Fruit, vegetables, and eggs are all neutral (*parev* or *parve*), and may be eaten together with milk or meat dishes. Fish, too, is a neutral food. However, the rabbis prohibited the eating of fish and meat together, on the grounds that such a combination impairs the health.

Milk

Strictly observant Jews drink only *ḥalav Yisrael*, milk obtained and bottled under the supervision of a Jew (Av. Zar.

2:6). This ensures both that no other substances have been added to the milk, and, more particularly, that no milk of an unclean animal has been added. However, since such practices are today generally forbidden by state laws, and since, furthermore, "unclean" milk is more expensive than "clean," many authorities permit the consumption of milk which has not been supervised.

The dietary laws are exceedingly complex and a great deal of material in the Talmud is devoted to them. The tractate *Ḥullin* deals mainly with the subject and the *Yoreh De'ah*, one of the four sections of *Jacob b. Asher's *Tur* and the Shulḥan Arukh, deals exclusively with dietary laws.

History

IN PROPHETIC LITERATURE. The Hebrew prophets repeatedly refer to *kashrut*. *Isaiah (66:17) warned that those "eating swine's flesh and the detestable thing and the mouse, shall be consumed together." *Ezekiel (4:14), in his vision, claimed, "Ah, Lord God; behold my soul hath not been polluted, for from my youth up, even till now, have I not eaten of that which dieth of itself, or is torn of beasts; neither came there abhorred flesh into my mouth." *Daniel, together with his companions Ḥananiah, Mishael, and Azariah, refused to partake of the "king's food" and of the "wine which he drank" (Dan. 1:8).

THE SECOND TEMPLE TIMES. Jews endangered their lives by their faithful adherence to the dietary laws during the Syrian rule of Ereẓ Israel, especially in the reign of *Antiochus IV Epiphanes. I Maccabees (1:62–63) records, "Many of the people of Israel adhered to the law of the Lord. They would not eat unclean things, and chose rather to die." The eating of the "unclean things" was literally equated with apostasy: "*Eleazar, one of the principal scribes, a man already well stricken in years, was compelled to open his mouth and to eat swine's flesh. But he, welcoming death with renown, rather than life with pollution, advanced of his own accord to the instrument of torture" (II Macc. 6:18). During the same period, *Hannah and her seven sons chose martyrdom rather than contravene the dietary laws. "We are ready to die," they proclaimed, "rather than transgress the laws of our fathers" (*ibid.* 7:2). In the epic story of *Judith and Holofernes, Judith affirms, "I will not eat thereof, what I have brought with will be enough for me" (Judith 12:2).

The Book of *Tobit states that the dietary laws were specifically designed to set the children of Israel apart from their neighbors: "All my brethren, and those that were of my kindred, did eat of the bread of the gentiles, but I kept myself from eating of the bread of the gentiles" (Tob. 1:10–11).

Some tolerant gentile rulers not only permitted, but even facilitated, the observance of the dietary laws. Thus, in 44 B.C.E., Dolabella, the Roman governor of Syria, exempted the Jews of Ephesus from military service so that they would not be compelled to desecrate the Sabbath or eat forbidden food (Jos., Ant., 14:223–30). However, as Josephus' documentation of the barbarities committed during the Jewish revolt reveals, such remarkable instances of Roman tolerance were unfortunately rare. The *Essenes, on the contrary, were singled out for special savagery. "They were racked and twisted, burnt and broken, and made to pass through every instrument of torture in order to induce them to blaspheme their lawgiver and to eat some forbidden thing; yet they refused to yield to either demand, nor even once did they cringe to their persecutors or shed a tear. Smiling in their agonies, mildly deriding their tormentors, they cheerfully resigned their souls, confident that they would receive them back" (Jos., Wars, 2:152–3).

IN MEDIEVAL TIMES. Despite the difficulties, and even dangers, inherent in the observance of the dietary laws during subsequent periods of severe persecution, the Jews steadfastly remained faithful to *kashrut*. A Jewish chronicler of the period of the Crusades writes: "It is fitting that I should recount the praises of those who were faithful. Whatever they ate or drank, they did at the peril of their lives. They would ritually slaughter animals for food according to Jewish tradition and remove the fat and inspect the meat in accordance with the prescription of the sages. Nor did they drink the wine of the idol worshipers" (Chronicle of Solomon b. Samson, in: A.M. Habermann, *Gezerot Ashkenaz ve-Zarefat* (1945), 57). The heroism of the medieval *Marranos in defense of the dietary laws was matched by the devotion of the *Cantonists and the inmates of the Nazi concentration camps.

Attempts to Explain the Dietary Laws

Throughout the ages, many attempts have been made to explain the dietary laws. The Pentateuch itself does not explain them, although in three separate passages in the Bible they are closely associated with the concept of "holiness." Thus, Exodus 22:30 states: "And ye shall be holy unto Me; therefore ye shall not eat any flesh that is torn of beasts in the field; ye shall cast it to the dogs." Leviticus repeats the idea: "For I am the Lord your God; sanctify yourselves therefore, and be ye holy, for I am holy; neither shall ye defile yourselves with any manner of swarming thing that moveth upon the earth" (Lev. 11:44–45). Finally, Deuteronomy 14:21 states: "Ye shall not eat of any thing that dieth of itself; thou mayest give it unto the stranger that is within thy gates, that he may eat it; or thou mayest sell it unto a foreigner; for thou art a holy people unto the Lord thy God." The Pentateuch classifies the dietary laws as *ḥukkim*, "divine statutes," which by definition are not explained in the text (Yoma 67b). It has been variously suggested that the underlying motivation for the dietary laws are hygienic and sanitary, aesthetic and folkloric, or ethical and psychological.

MORAL EFFECTS. In Ezekiel 33:25, the prophet equates the eating of blood with the sins of idolatry and murder. One interpretation of this verse teaches that the dietary laws are ethical in intent, since abstention from the consumption of blood tames man's instinct for violence by instilling in him a horror of bloodshed. This is the view expressed in a letter by *Aristeas, an unknown Egyptian Jew (probably of the first century B.C.E.), who states that the dietary laws are meant to instill men with a spirit of justice, and to teach them certain moral lessons. Thus, the injunction against the consumption of birds of prey was intended to demonstrate that man should not prey on others (Arist. 142–7). *Philo, the Alexandrian Jewish philosopher, also suggests that creatures with evil instincts are forbidden lest men, too, develop these instincts (Spec. 4:118).

The rabbis of the Talmud rarely attempted to find rational explanations for the dietary laws, which they generally regarded as aids to moral conduct. "For what does the Holy One, Blessed be He, care whether a man kills an animal by the throat or by the nape of its neck. Hence its purpose is to refine man" (Gen. R. 44:1; Lev. R. 13:3). Commenting on the verse "and I have set you apart from the peoples, that ye should be mine" (Lev. 20:26), the *Sifra* (11:22), a halakhic Midrash on Leviticus, states, "Let not a man say, 'I do not like the flesh of swine.' On the contrary, he should say, 'I like it but must abstain seeing that the Torah has forbidden it.'"

EFFECTS ON THE SOUL OF MAN. Such mystics as Joseph *Gikatilla and Menahem *Recanati maintained that food affects not only the body but also the soul, clogging the heart and dulling man's finer qualities. Isaac b. Moses *Arama stated that, "The reason behind all the dietary prohibitions is not that any harm may be caused to the body, but that these foods defile and pollute the soul and blunt the intellectual powers, thus leading to confused opinions and a lust for perverse and brutish appetites which lead men to destruction, thus defeating the purpose of creation" (*Akedat Yiẓḥak, Sha'ar Shemini*, 60–end).

Samson Raphael *Hirsch wrote, "Just as the human spirit is the instrument which God uses to make Himself known in this world, so the human body is the medium which connects the outside world with the mind of man … Anything which gives the body too much independence or makes it too active in a carnal direction brings it nearer to the animal sphere, thereby robbing it of its primary function, to be the intermediary between the soul of man and the world outside. Bearing in mind this function of the body and also the fact that the physical structure of man is largely influenced by the kind of food he consumes, one might come to the conclusion that the vegetable food is the most preferable, as plants are the most passive substance; and indeed we find that in Jewish law all vegetables are permitted for food without discrimination" (*Horeb*, section 454, Eng. tr. by I. Gruenfeld (1962), 328).

HYGIENIC EXPLANATIONS. Maimonides (Guide, 3:48) noted that "These ordinances seek to train us in the mastery of our appetites. They accustom us to restrain both the growth of desire and disposition to consider the pleasure of eating as the end of man's existence." He also maintained, however, that all forbidden foods are unwholesome: "All the food which the Torah has forbidden us to eat have some bad and damaging effect on the body … The principal reason why the Law forbids swine's flesh is to be found in the circumstances that its habits and its food are very dirty and loathsome" (*ibid.*, 3:48). He gives an explanation entirely based on hygienic considerations, for the injunction against the consumption of sacrificial fat (*ḥelev*): "The fat of the intestines is forbidden because it fattens and destroys the abdomen and creates cold and clammy blood." Concerning the proscription of *basar be-ḥalav,* Maimonides states: "Meat boiled in milk is undoubtedly gross food, and makes a person feel overfull." He adds, however, "I think that most probably it is also prohibited because it is somehow connected with idolatry. Perhaps it was part of the ritual of certain pagan festivals. I find support for this view in the fact that two of the times the Lord mentions the prohibition, it is after the commandment concerning our festivals. 'Three times a year all your males shall appear before the Lord God' (Ex. 17:23–24; 23:17). That is to say, 'When you come before Me on your festivals, do not prepare your food in the manner in which the heathens do'" (*ibid.,* 3:48). Ancient inscriptions unearthed by archaeologists (e.g., at Ras Shamra-*Ugarit) tend to confirm that this was a fertility rite. J.G. Frazer, quoting a Karaite medieval author, writes: "There was a custom among the ancient heathens, who when they had gathered all the crop, used to boil a kid in its mother's milk" (*Folklore in the Old Testament*, 3 (1919), 117).

Abraham *Ibn Ezra maintained that the reason for the prohibition of *basar be-ḥalav* was "concealed," even from the eyes of the wise, although he added "But I believe it is a matter of cruelty to cook a kid in its mother's milk" (Commentary to Ex. 23:19; see: *Animals, Cruelty to). A contemporary interpretation, advanced by A.J. *Heschel, explains that the goat provides man with the perfect food – milk, which is the only food that can sustain the body by itself. It would, therefore, be an act of ingratitude to take the offspring of such an animal and cook it in the very milk which sustains us.

Many other scholars, however, followed in the footsteps of Maimonides. They pointed out that certain animals harbor parasites that create and spread disease. It was a fact that during the Middle Ages Jews were less prone than their neighbors to the many epidemics of the time. R. *Samuel b. Meir declared that "All cattle, wild beasts, fowl, fishes, and various kinds of locusts and reptiles which God has forbidden to Israel, are indeed loathsome and harmful to the body, and for this reason they are called 'unclean'" (Commentary to Lev. 11:3).

Commenting on the verse "Whatsoever hath fins and scales in the waters, in the seas, and in the rivers, them may ye eat" (Lev. 11:9), Naḥmanides states: "Now the reason for specifying fins and scales is that fish which have fins and scales get nearer to the surface of the water and are found more generally in freshwater areas … Those without fins and scales usually live in the lower muddy strata which are exceedingly moist and where there is no heat. They breed in musty swamps and eating them can be injurious to health." Many modern scholars give hygienic reasons for the dietary laws, since it is known that bacteria and spores of infectious diseases circulate through the blood.

Modern Views on the Dietary Laws

The dietary laws were on the agenda of the rabbinical conference held in Breslau on July 12–24, 1846. The Reform Movement appointed a committee consisting of S. Adler, D. Einhorn, L. Herzfeld, S. Hirsch, and S. Holdheim to examine this aspect of Jewish tradition. In his report published in *Sinai* (1859 and 1860), Einhorn stated that the dietary laws (with the exception of the prohibition to consume blood and animals that died a natural death) were directly related to the levitical laws of purity and the priestly laws of sacrifice and were, therefore, of a mere temporary ceremonial character and not essentially religious or moral laws. At the Pittsburgh Conference (November 16–18, 1885), the Reform Movement resolved: "We hold that all such Mosaic rabbinical laws as regarding diet ... originated in ages and under the influence of ideas entirely foreign to our present mental and spiritual state. They fail to impress the modern Jew with a spirit of priestly holiness; their observance in our days is apt rather to obstruct than to further modern spiritual elevation." However, the Pittsburgh Platform did not prevent Reform Jews and Reform congregations from adopting and observing the dietary laws and some have always done so. By the late 20th century, Reform Judaism had developed a more positive attitude towards observance of *kashrut* as part of a larger pattern of return to traditional practices. The basic Reform philosophy as stated in such Union of Reform Judaism publications as *Gates of Mitzvah* (ed. S. Maslin, 1979) is that it is a Reform Jew's responsibility to study and consider the laws of *kashrut* so as to develop a valid personal position. Publications of the URJ between 2000 and 2005 suggested that Reform Jews seriously consider their dietary choices and the rationales behind them and consider whether adopting some or all of the Jewish dietary laws would enhance their domestic practice of Judaism and their spiritual lives. Out of respect for the larger Jewish community as well as their own members who observe *kashrut*, many Reform synagogues now maintain kosher kitchens.

The Conservative position is set out in such publications as *The Jewish Dietary Laws*, by Samuel H. Dresner, and *A Guide to Observance*, by Seymour Siegel (both in one volume, 1966[2]). Dresner, for instance, maintains that "*kashrut* is one of the firmest ramparts of the pluralistic aspect of Judaism. It demands sacrifice, self-discipline and determination – but what that is really worthwhile in life does not? It demands the courage to turn our face against the powerful current of conformity that almost overcomes us daily. The goal of *kashrut* is holiness, a holy man and a holy nation. It is part of Judaism's attempt to hallow the common act of eating which is an aspect of our animal nature. It likewise sets us apart from the nations. Thus it achieves its objective, holiness in these two ways, both of which are implied in the Hebrew word *kadosh*: inner hallowing and outer separateness."

[Harry Rabinowicz / Rela Mintz Geffen (2nd ed.)]

Women and Dietary Laws

The scrupulous daily observance of *kashrut* in the home has necessarily been in the hands of women as preparation of meals was traditionally designated part of "women's work." Until contemporary times, observant Jews did not eat food outside their homes unless it was in the home of a relative or of another Jew whose observance was trusted or they were ill or found themselves in dangerous circumstances. Although supervision (*hashgaḥah*) of food for sale to the public was in the hands of men, as was slaughter (*sheḥitah*) in most cases, the maintenance of proper utensils, the purchase of food, the separation of meat and dairy, the ritual salting and soaking of meat, and the cooking and serving of the food were in the hands of women. Moreover, transmission both of mundane and esoteric knowledge of these domestic processes to the next generation of daughters was entrusted to their grandmothers, mothers, and other female relatives. Communities and families had to trust and rely on women for meticulous observance, particularly in the preparation for and during the holiday of Passover.

Eloquent testimony to the devotion of Jewish women to the maintenance of the dietary laws is found throughout Jewish history. Unfortunately, this often meant the willingness to suffer when various oppressors tried to break the will of Jews by forcing them to violate *kashrut*, particularly by eating pork, as in the examples of Hannah and her seven sons and of Judith in Second Temple times, cited above. Research into Inquisition documents has shown that women were strong defenders of domestic Judaism, including *kashrut*, and that even as *Crypto-Jews who had been forced into conversion they perpetuated some of the dietary laws whenever possible.

In later eras in Western Europe, when urbanization and secularization and the drive to rise in the society led to widespread acculturation and assimilation, particularly among middle class Jews, it was frequently the women in these families who were the last to give up observance of domestic ritual practices, including the dietary laws. A decline in traditional Jewish practice, including *kashrut*, accompanied the breakdown of traditional *shtetl* culture, growing urbanization in Eastern Europe, and the dislocations caused by immigration to America and other havens. Jewish leaders exhorted women to maintain *kashrut* in books, newspapers, and magazine articles in Yiddish and English that stressed female responsibility for maintaining the dietary laws. In the first decade of the 20th century Jewish women in New York City successfully organized a boycott of kosher butcher shops to counteract the precipitous rise in the price of kosher meat. Their actions became the model for kosher boycotts elsewhere, as well as other political activism of the time in support of suffrage and against exorbitant rents in immigrant neighborhoods, particularly the Lower East Side of Manhattan.

Food, Jewish law, and ritual are inextricably entwined at the very heart of the Jewish calendar and life cycle observances. In these arenas women were the facilitators rather than the public actors, even in the home. Wives arduously prepared Passover *seder* meals while husbands led the rituals. Somewhat ironically, the foods associated with various holidays as well as their modes of preparation have been shaped by the astonishing variety of societies, cultures, and areas of the world within which Jewish communities have been situated over the centuries. The women who have largely been responsible for Jewish cuisine have shown enduring creativity in adapting local delicacies and food ways to *kashrut*. Breads such as *mazzah* or *ḥallah* may be common to all, but the doughnuts fried in oil by Jewish women in the Ottoman Empire were a world away from the potato pancakes fried in oil to commemorate the miracle of Hanukkah in East European Jewish households. Even in 21st-century Israel, diverse laws governing the eating of *kitniyyot* (pulses and legumes including peas, rice, and corn) on Passover divide supermarkets and extended families in which Ashkenazi Jews have married Sephardi Jews.

Observance of the dietary laws by adults is an individual or couple's decision in an open society. However, because of the persistence of traditional gender role definitions in contemporary culture, it is generally Jewish women who continue to preside over the preparation of food, whether in households fully committed to the observance of Jewish law or in those where observance of the dietary laws is partial or mostly symbolic. Thus, the special historic connection of women to *kashrut* continues in the 21st century.

Dietary Laws and Jewish Culture

Jewish food, other than *mazzah*, was never standardized. In fact, in the contemporary world, the trend is to devise versions of a multitude of ethnic foods which comply with the laws of *kashrut*. Kosher pizza, Chinese, Japanese, and Indian food, or popular items such as sushi, *parve* ice cream, and margarine, and an American Thanksgiving dinner with the trimmings, may all be prepared in accordance with the dietary laws. Kosher restaurants specializing in a variety of cuisines are found in cities with substantial Jewish populations around the world and in the heart of Jerusalem, while recent kosher cookbooks offer recipes for dishes from many different ethnic fares.

Observance of the dietary laws, along with Sabbath observance connected to ritually infused meals, especially the Friday night dinner, are critical markers of Jewish identity in contemporary society. In the Diaspora in particular, they signal a willingness to maintain a particularistic identity in a multicultural society. For instance, in the demographic surveys through which American Jewish identification was analyzed from 1971 through 2001, observance of the dietary laws in the home is strongly associated with endogamy (in-marriage), other ritual observance, synagogue affiliation, providing children with formal Jewish education, and a feeling of connectedness to Israel and of responsibility for Jews around the world.

[Rela Mintz Geffen (2nd ed.)]

BIBLIOGRAPHY: S.H. Dresner, *The Jewish Dietary Laws* (1966²); H.M. Lazarus, *The Ways of her Household*, 1 (1923); *Outline of the Laws of Kashrut*, issued by the London Beth Din and Kashrut Commission; S.L. Rubinstein, *The Book of Kashrut* (1967); A. Wiener, *Die juedischen Speisegesetze* (1895); J. Gruenfeld, *The Philosophical and Moral Basis of the Jewish Dietary Laws* (1961). **ADD. BIBLIOGRAPHY:** H. Diner, *Hungering for America: Italian, Irish, and Jewish Foodways in the Age of Migration* (2002); P.E. Hyman, *Gender and Assimilation in Modern Jewish History* (1995); M.A. Kaplan, *The Making of the Jewish Middle Class: Women, Family, and Identity in Imperial Germany* (1994); R.L. Melammed, *Heretics or Daughters of Israel? The Crypto-Jewish Women of Castile* (1999); L. Stern, *How to Keep Kosher: A Comprehensive Guide to Understanding Jewish Dietary Laws* (2004).

°DIEZ MACHO, ALEJANDRO (1916–1985), Spanish Catholic priest and Bible scholar. Diez was born in Villafria de la Pena. After his ordination in 1939, he studied Semitic philology at the University of Barcelona. He joined the faculty of the same university in 1944 and occupied the chair of Hebrew language and rabbinic language and literature. His doctoral dissertation, *Mose ibn Ezra*, was published in 1953. Diez' main fields of interest, in which he published many articles, are medieval Hebrew literature and biblical research, especially the Aramaic translations of the Bible. In 1957 he began publishing a critical edition of the Targums in *Biblia poliglotta Matritensia*. Diez made important manuscript discoveries regarding both the Palestinian and Babylonian Targums; his rediscovery of the famous Targum manuscript *Neofiti* aroused considerable international attention.

BIBLIOGRAPHY: P.E. Kahle, *Cairo Geniza* (Eng., 1959²), passim; *Punta Europa* (March 3, 1956), 141–59. **ADD BIBLIOGRAPHY:** L. Díez Merino, in: D. Muñoz León (ed.), *Salvación en la palabra: ...en memoria del profesor Alejandro Díez Macho* (1986), 827–48.

[Victor A. Mirelman]

°DI GARA, GIOVANNI (16th century), Venetian printer of Hebrew books. Di Gara, who went to Venice from Riva del Garda (Trent), had apparently learned the art of Hebrew printing from Daniel *Bomberg; and after the latter's death he acquired most of Bomberg's type. Di Gara's printing activity spanned a half-century (1565–1610) and covered a wide range of Hebrew literature. Nearly 300 editions came out in this period, among them the *Turim* with Joseph Caro's commentary *Beit Yosef* (1565–94); Shulḥan Arukh (1593); a rabbinical Bible (1568); Judah Halevi's *Kuzari* (1594); Elijah de Vidas' *Reshit Ḥokhmah* (1578); Naḥmanides' *Torat ha-Adam* (1595); Isaac Aboab's *Menorat ha-Ma'or* (1595–1602); and a Mishnah (1609). He also printed some Yiddish and Latin books. There was close cooperation between Di Gara and the house of *Bragadini, and their printer's marks even appeared together on the same title page. That of Di Gara was a small single crown (in some cases he used two or three crowns as well); his title page is marked sometimes by a Roman arch whose pillars are garlanded with flowers and fruit; but he also imitated those of *Foa of Sabbioneta and of Meir Sofer of Mantua. The printer Asher *Parenzo, who worked for Bragadini, also worked for Di Gara. Others who were employed by him were Isaac Gerson of Safed, who introduced tables of contents and indexes; Samuel *Archivolti, author of the grammatical treatise *Arugat ha-Bosem*; Israel Zifroni and his son Elishama; and Leone Di *Modena. As typesetters, Di Gara had to employ Christians, which impaired the correctness of the editions. These have regularly the formula *con licentia dei superiori*. However, in 1592 Di Gara was accused by the Inquisition of having printed a book by Isaac Abrabanel without the required permission. At his death, Di Gara's types went to the Venetian printer Giovanni Cajon.

BIBLIOGRAPHY: D.W. Amram, *Makers of Hebrew Books in Italy* (1909), index; B. Friedberg, *Toledot ha-Defus ha-Ivri be-Italyah* … (1956), 72–73; A.M. Habermann, *Ha-Madpis Zuan Di Gara*, completed and edited by Y. Yudlov (1982); P.C. Ioly Zorattini, in: *Italia*, 1 (1976–78), 54–69; G. Busi, in: *Dizionario dei tipografi e degli editori italiani. Il Cinquecento*, 1 (1997), 378–79; J. Baumgarten, in: REJ, 159 (2000), 587–98.

[Giulio Busi (2nd ed.)]

DIGNE (Heb. דיגנייא), capital of the department of Basses-Alpes, S.E. France. By the end of the 13th century there was a sizable Jewish community there; the fact that in 1311 the market contained three kosher meat stalls is proof of its importance. Throughout the 14th century, the market stalls were the subject of frequent disputes, as were the Jews' right to use the municipal bath and their contribution to the municipal taxes. The Jews of Digne cultivated agricultural holdings around the town. By 1468 there were only 20 Jewish families left there and their number continued to decrease. After the expulsion from Provence in 1498, some of the Jews of Digne found refuge in Comtat-Venaissin where the surname Digne was common. Digne's best-known scholar was R. Baruch who, in 1305, vigorously contradicted Isaac ha-Kohen of Manosque and was excommunicated by him. At the beginning of the 20th century, Joseph *Reinach represented Digne in the National Assembly. There is still a Rue de la Juiverie in Digne, but there are no Jewish inhabitants.

BIBLIOGRAPHY: Gross, Gal Jud, 154–5; C. Arnaud, *Essai sur … Juifs en Provence* (1879), passim; F. Guichard, *Essai … ville de Digne* (1876), passim; E. Baratier, *Démographie provençale du 13e au 16e siècle* (1961), 72.

[Bernhard Blumenkranz]

DIJON, capital of Côte-d'Or department, E. central France. The first explicit evidence concerning the Jews there dates from 1196 when the Duke of Burgundy placed the Jews of Dijon under the jurisdiction of the commune, which he authorized to admit additional Jews. Ducal charters of 1197 and 1232 specified the authority of the town over the Jews of Dijon. They lived in the Rue de la Petite-Juiverie (today Rue Piron), the Rue de la Grande-Juiverie (Rue Charrue), and the Rue des Juifs (Rue Buffon). The synagogue and a "Sabbath house" were situated in the Petite-Juiverie, while the cemetery was in the present Rue Berlier. In this cemetery, which was confiscated after the Jews were expelled from France in 1306, over 50 tombstones were found about a century ago, apparently dating to the 13th century. Some Jews returned to Dijon in 1315, but, after the readmission of the Jews to the kingdom in 1359, a more important community was reestablished. When finally expelled in 1394, the Jews of Dijon left for *Franche-Comté. The only known scholars of Dijon are a certain R. Jacob and Simḥah Ḥazzan.

After 1789 Jews again settled permanently in Dijon, mainly from Upper Alsace. The Jewish population numbered 50 families in 1803, 100 in 1869, and about 400 persons in 1902. The community belonged to the Lyons *Consistory. Construction of the present synagogue in the rue de la Synagogue was begun in 1873; it was dedicated in 1879. The community also acquired land for a cemetery northwest of the city in 1789.

[Bernhard Blumenkranz]

Holocaust and Contemporary Periods

Dijon, an important railroad center, was under careful German surveillance during the Nazi occupation of World War II. The synagogue was emptied of its interior and served as a Nazi warehouse. Ninety Jews from Dijon perished in *Auschwitz. Dijon's returning Jews rapidly rebuilt their community after the war, and in 1960 the community was again flourishing. When Jews from North Africa settled in Dijon, the Jewish community increased to over 1,000 persons (1969) and owned a combined synagogue-communal center.

[Georges Levitte]

BIBLIOGRAPHY: Gross, Gal Jud, 151ff.; J. Garnier, *Chartes de communes … en Bourgogne* 1 (1867), nos. 19, 20, 41; Armand-Calliat, in: *Mémoires de la Société d'Histoire de Chalon-sur-Saône*, 34 (1956–57), 68, 73; Marilier, in: *Mémoires de la Commission des Antiquités de la Côte-d'Or*, 24 (1954–58), 171ff.; P. Milsand, *Rues de Dijon* (1874), passim; Gauthier, in: *Mémoires de la société d'émulation du Jura* (1914), 143ff.; Berg, in: *Journal des Communautés*, no. 109 (1954), 1–2; M. Clément-Janin, *Notice sur la Communauté Israélite de Dijon* (1879); M. Schwab, *Inscriptions hébraïques de la France* (1898); M. Gerson, in: REJ, 6 (1883), 222–9, and index in vol. 50.

DIK, ISAAC (Ayzik) MEIR (c. 1807–1893), first popular writer of Yiddish fiction, best known by the acronym **AMaD**. Born in Vilna, Dik received a traditional Jewish education and proved an able student. He began his literary activity around 1838 with a Hebrew story "*Zifronah*" and a Hebrew parody "*Massekhet Aniyyut*" ("Tractate on Poverty," in *Kanfei Yonah*, 1848). An adherent of the *Haskalah, Dik urged Jewish school and clothing reform, and in his early years corresponded to this end with the czarist minister of education. An admirer of the reforming zeal of Czar *Alexander II, Dik devoted his energy to promoting those reforms that would bring the Jews into modern European life as equal citizens. From 1861 he thus wrote only in Yiddish in order to instruct the unlearned in practical morality and ethics, becoming the author of over 300 stories and short novels. He is best known for introducing into Yiddish literature realistic tales with sound morals, many of which were subtle adaptations of other works. Dik knew that to teach, one must entertain, and he consistently used literature to popularize the ideas of the Haskalah which advocated both modern education and traditional learning. Since he was anxious to reach the widest possible audience without alienating pious traditionalists, he drew much material from traditional folklore. In 1865 he signed a contract with the Romm publishing house, agreeing to write a 48 page novelette each week. His engaging stories, which reveled in both sentimentality and melodrama, were eagerly read by men and women alike, who regularly bought nearly 100,000 copies of his works, many of which have not survived since they were literally read to shreds. Dik's work was characterized by the subtle use of narrative strategies and modes of discourse that worked against conventional expectations; his favorite modes were parody and satire in which he exposed the deficiencies of traditional Jewish society as he saw it. His purpose was to show Jewish people how to play productive roles in the modern world. The traditional values of Judaism nonetheless remained dear to him, and he himself remained strictly observant all his life. He popularized knowledge of the Bible, wrote on the *Haggadah*, composed a popular version of the *Shulḥan Arukh*, and published many stories on Ereẓ Israel, including a history of Jerusalem. Dik also summarized Jewish classical, medieval, and contemporary writings for the average Yiddish reader. His selected works, severely edited and modernized, were published in 1954 (*Geklibene Verk fun I.M. Dik*, ed. Sh. Niger).

BIBLIOGRAPHY: I.M. Dik, *R. Shemayah Mevarekh ha-Mo'adot* (1967), D. Sadan (ed. and tr.); Sh. Niger, in: *He-Avar*, 2 (1918), 140–54; M. Weinreich, *Bilder fun der Yidisher Literatur Geshikhte* (1928), 292–329; B. Rivkind, in: *YIVO Bleter*, 36 (1952), 191–230; LNYL, 2 (1958), 518–24; M. Kosover, in: JBA, 25 (1957/68), 241–8; C. Madison, *Yiddish Literature* (1968), 23f. **ADD. BIBLIOGRAPHY:** D. Roskies, *A Bridge of Longing: The Lost Art of Jewish Storytelling* (1995), 56–98; J. Sherman, *The Jewish Pope: Myth, Diaspora and Yiddish Literature* (2003), 83–105.

[Elias Schulman / Joseph Sherman (2nd ed.)]

DILLER, BARRY (1942–), U.S. media executive. Born in San Francisco, Calif., Diller was raised in Beverly Hills and had a good Jewish education. He skipped college and got his first job in show business in the mail room of the William Morris Agency. He moved to the programming department of the American Broadcasting Company in 1966 and was soon placed in charge of negotiating broadcast rights to feature films. He was promoted to vice president in charge of feature films and program development three years later and inaugurated the television network's Movie of the Week, which became the most popular movie series in the industry and helped ABC achieve parity with the National Broadcasting Company and the Columbia Broadcast System in the ratings. Abandoning conventional narratives like Westerns and crime melodramas, Diller ordered films that explored current issues like homosexuality, the Vietnam War, and drugs. The 90-minute films, sometimes called docudramas, were produced at the relatively low price of $350,000 each and probed current newspaper headlines and American popular culture for gripping topics aimed at young urban and adult audiences. By 1972 the genre had become an established network programming practice.

In 1974, at the age of 32, Diller was named chairman of Paramount Pictures and assembled a team that included Michael *Eisner and Jeffrey *Katzenberg. Diller had been hired by Charles Bluhdorn, head of Gulf & Western Industries, a sprawling conglomerate that had acquired Paramount in 1966. During Diller's 10-year tenure, Paramount produced such hit films as *Saturday Night Fever* and *Raiders of the Lost Ark* and such wildly successful TV shows as *Taxi* and *Cheers*. In 1984, Diller quit Paramount after a dispute with Martin S. *Davis, who had succeeded Bluhdorn, and went to work for Twentieth Century Fox. After Rupert Murdoch bought Fox, Diller was put in charge of developing the studio's new network. Starting with limited programming, Diller built Fox into a fourth network to compete with CBS, NBC, and ABC. He developed low-cost "reality" fare and balanced those shows with alternative and youth-oriented programming like *The Simpsons*.

In a surprise move, Diller quit Fox in 1992 to buy and run QVC, a television shopping network, with a $25 million stake. He made an unsuccessful bid to take over Paramount Communications in 1993 but lost to Sumner *Redstone of Viacom. Diller resigned from QVC in 1995 and acquired Silver King Communications, a small group of UHF stations, in an attempt to create a hybrid cable network that would offer a full schedule of entertainment, sports, and news. Also in 1995 he took over USA Interactive, which he expanded to include not only home shopping but a variety of successful companies that deal with interactive business on the Internet: Expedia, Inc., Hotels.com, and Ticketmaster. With these properties Diller became the leader of the online travel business. From May 2002 to March 2003 he served as chairman and chief executive of Vivendi Universal Entertainment. Diller served on the boards of several major corporations, including the Washington Post Company and the Coca-Cola Company.

[Stewart Kampel (2nd ed.)]

°**DILLMANN, AUGUST** (1823–1894), German Orientalist, Bible scholar, and theologian. Dillmann first studied Bible and theology and concentrated on Ethiopic studies at the universities of London, Paris, and Oxford in 1846–48. At Tuebingen he became professor extraordinary of theology (1853). He served as professor of Oriental languages at Kiel from 1854 to 1864, professor of theology at Giessen from 1864 to 1869, and at Berlin from 1869 until his death. Dillmann is best remembered for his long-standing attachment to Ethiopic studies. In 1847 and 1848 he published long neglected catalogs of Ethiopic manuscripts. He was responsible for pioneering studies on the various Ethiopic books of the Bible, Apocrypha, and Pseudepigrapha (from 1851 on). His Ethiopic grammar (*Grammatik der aethiopischen Sprache*, 1857, 1899^2), lexicon (*Lexicon linguae aethiopicae cum indice latino*, 1865), and chrestomathy (*Chrestomathia aethiopica*, 1866, 1950^2) were hailed as classics in the field. His most important works on the interpretation of the Bible are his commentaries on Genesis (1892^6) and Exodus-Leviticus (1897^3). An English translation of the one on Genesis came out in two volumes in 1897. He held that there were three independent sources in the Pentateuch (P, E, and J), and argued for the existence of an independent Deuteronomic source based on E. Unlike many higher biblical critics of his day, he maintained the priority of a pre-Exilic P over D. His posthumously published *Handbuch der alttestamentlichen Theologie* (1895) rejected J. *Wellhausen's philosophy of the development of Israel's religion and maintained that the religion of Israel, which was centered on holiness, was unique in the ancient world.

BIBLIOGRAPHY: W. Baudissin, *August Dillmann* (Ger., 1895); idem, in: *Realencyklopaedie fuer protestantische Theologie und Kirche*, 4 (1898), 662. **ADD. BIBLIOGRAPHY:** A. Amsalo, *Etymologischer Beitrag zu A. Dillmann Lexikon linguae Aethiopicae* (1962); E. Ullendorff, *Catalogue of the Ethiopian Manuscripts in the Bodleian Library* (1951).

[Zev Garber]

DILLON (Zuchowicki), ABRAHAM MOSES (1883–1934), Yiddish poet. Dillon was born in Russia. In 1909 he immigrated to the United States where he experienced years of hunger and hard physical labor. As a poet, he was affiliated with the New York impressionistic movement *Di Yunge*. His melancholy lyrics were published in anthologies and in the book *Gele Bleter* ("Yellow Leaves," 1919). A more complete edition of his work, *Lider fun A.M. Dillon*, appeared in 1935.

BIBLIOGRAPHY: Rejzen, Leksikon, s.v.; D. Ignatoff, *Opgerisene Bleter* (1957), 25–32; *Flowering of Yiddish Literature* (1963), 213ff.; M. Bassin, *Amerikaner Yidishe Poezye* (1940); S. Melzer, *Al Naharot* (1956); J. Leftwich, *Golden Peacock* (1939); S.I. Imber, *Modern Yiddish Poetry* (1927). **ADD. BIBLIOGRAPHY:** LNYL, 2 (1958), 501–2; M. Ravitch, *Mayn Leksikon* (1980), 4, 186–7.

[Melech Ravitch]

DIMANSTEIN, SIMON (1886–1937), Russian revolutionary and Communist leader. Son of a village peddler, Dimanstein studied at the Lubavitch yeshivah with the support of a distinguished Hebrew writer, Samuel Tchernowitz, and received his rabbinical diploma from Ḥaim Ozer Grodzensky. He joined the Bolshevik faction of the Russian Social Democratic Party in 1904 and actively opposed the Bund. Between 1906 and 1910 he was arrested on several occasions and finally banished to Siberia, but escaped and went to Paris. Dimanstein returned to Russia in 1917 following the February Revolution and, after the Bolsheviks seized power, became an assistant to Stalin, then Commissar for the Affairs of Nationalities. In January 1918 he became head of the Commissariat for Jewish Affairs, and from 1918 edited the Yiddish paper *Der Emess*. The newspaper was an instrument of Communist propaganda especially directed against religion, Zionism, and the Bund. With the creation of the *Yevsektsiya (the Jewish section of the Communist Party) Dimanstein was named chairman of its central committee from October 1918. In July 1919 he signed the order abolishing all Jewish parties, organizations, and institutions. He held various official posts, including commissar for education in Turkestan and head of the administration for political education in the Ukraine, and from 1924 was director of the nationalities sector in the Central Committee of the Communist Party. At the end of the 1920s he headed the OZET society for settling Jews on the land, and he played an important part in setting up the Jewish settlement in Birobidzhan. He was editor of the anthology "Yidn in FSSR" ("Jews in SSSR") in 1935. Dimanstein was arrested during the Stalin purges and died in prison, probably in 1937.

BIBLIOGRAPHY: Rejzen, Leksikon, 1 (1928), 694–7.

[Abba Ahimeir / Shmuel Spector (2nd ed.)]

DIMI (Avdimi Naḥota; fl. first half of the 4th century), Babylonian *amora*. Dimi was one of the *Neḥutei*, the scholars who traveled from Palestine to Babylonia and back, conveying the teachings of the Palestinian academies to Babylonia and bringing the *halakhot* of the Babylonian *amoraim* to Palestine. His statements in the Talmud are introduced by the formula, "When Rav Dimi came, he said ...." In particular, he transmitted the rulings of Johanan, *Resh Lakish, and Eleazar of the academy of Tiberias to the scholars of Pumbedita in the days of R. *Joseph and *Abbaye. Most of his statements are on halakhic topics, but he also transmits scriptural exegesis, midrashic *aggadot*, historical experiences (Ber. 44a, et al.), and particulars concerning the geography of Ereẓ Israel (Shab. 108b). He was painstakingly accurate in his reports; when he realized that he had been mistaken he sent word: "What I told you was erroneous, in fact it was said ..." (Shab. 63b). He made frequent use of the expression: "In the West (i.e., Ereẓ Israel) they say ...." For example, "When Rav Dimi came he said: In the West they say: 'Silence is worth twice as much as a word' (Meg. 18a). When Abbaye asked him: 'What do people avoid most in the West?' he replied: 'Putting others to shame. For R. Hanina said: "Only three categories of sinners do not reascend from Gehenna: he who commits adultery, he who publicly shames his neighbor, and he who calls his neighbor by a degrading nickname (even if the latter is accustomed to it)"'" (BM 58b). He reported, too, that in Ereẓ Israel it was customary to sing before a bride: "No powder and no paint and no styling of the hair – but she is still a graceful gazelle" (Ket. 17a). In the middle of the fourth century Dimi settled permanently in Babylonia, apparently because of the oppressive edicts of the emperor Constantine and the persecutions in the days of Gallus and Ursicinus (351).

BIBLIOGRAPHY: Hyman, Toledot, 327–31; Halevy, Dorot, 2 (1923), 467–73.

[Yitzhak Dov Gilat]

DIMI OF NEHARDEA (fl. 4th century), Babylonian *amora*, head of the academy of Pumbedita from 385 to 388. In his youth Dimi was a fruit merchant. The Talmud relates an anecdote concerning him which affords an insight into contemporary social practice. Dimi once brought dried figs to sell, apparently in the market of Maḥoza. As talmudic scholars were permitted to sell their produce before other merchants so as not to be detained too long from their studies, Rava, on the instigation of the exilarch, sent Adda b. Abba to test his scholarship and consequent right to the privilege. Adda put difficult questions to Dimi on the laws of ritual uncleanness and as Dimi could not answer, he was not granted the privilege (BB 22a). Little is known of his relations with his contemporaries. He is mentioned as engaging in halakhic disputes with Abbaye (Men. 35a) and with Rava. Whereas Rava preferred a teacher who taught much, even at the expense of accuracy, since "errors get corrected by themselves," Dimi preferred the more accurate if slower teacher, since "an error once implanted cannot be eradicated." Dimi himself, faithful to his principle, transmitted halakhic statements with great accuracy, his version at times differing from those of his colleagues (RH 20a; et al.). Whereas Rava held that a less qualified schoolteacher should not be replaced by a superior one since the latter, relying upon his talent, might neglect his duty and come to regard himself as indispensable, Dimi held that he should be replaced, for the need to prove his ability would inspire him to greater efforts (BB 21a). Though chiefly a halakhist, he is also known for his aggadic statement: "The dispensing of hospitality is more meritorious than early attendance at the *bet ha-midrash*" (Shab. 127a).

BIBLIOGRAPHY: Hyman, Toledot, 333; Weiss, Dor, 3 (1904^4), 182.

[Moshe Beer]

DIMITROVSKY, CHAIM ZALMAN (1920–), talmudist and historian. Born in Ereẓ Israel, Dimitrovsky was ordained in 1944. From 1951 he taught at the Jewish Theological Seminary in New York. In his historical writings, which deal mainly with the Jewish communities of Palestine and Italy in the 16th century, Dimitrovsky made use of halakhic works and unpublished documents in order to supplement and correct the accounts of historians and chroniclers. His analysis of a responsum and glosses concerning the legality of the renewal of *semikhah* (ordination) by the rabbis of Safed enabled him to reconstruct the facts of that controversy. Especially noteworthy historical contributions are his articles on the dispute between Joseph Caro and Moses Trani (in *Sefunot*, 6 (1962), 71–123) and on "Yeshivat *Rabbi Ya'akov Berab*" (*ibid.*, 7 (1963), 41–102). Dimitrovsky's writings in *halakhah* are devoted essentially to R. Solomon b. Abraham *Adret. He published Adret's novellae to the tractates *Megillah* and *Rosh ha-Shanah*, *Ḥiddushei Solomon ben Adret* … (1956 and 1961, respectively), and prepared an edition of his responsa.

[Shamma Friedman]

Dimitrovsky published (1980) *Seridei Bavli* consisting of 550 pages of a copy of the Babylonian Talmud printed in Spain between 1482 and 1497 based on an otherwise unknown version of the Talmud.

DIMONAH (Heb. דִּימוֹנָה), town in southern Israel, in the central Negev Hills, 21½ mi. (35 km.) southeast of Beer-Sheba and 25 mi. (40 km.) west of Sodom. It was founded in September 1955 to provide the employees of the *Sodom Dead Sea Works with homes in a healthy climate and at a convenient distance from their work. Laborers of the Oron phosphate field nearby also established permanent homes in Dimonah. The population grew to 3,500 in 1959 and by 1968 was 20,000. In 1969 the town received municipal status. Of the families resident at Dimonah in 1968, 65% were immigrants from North Africa, 20% from Europe, 10% from India, and the rest from Persia or born in Israel. Children below 15 years of age made up about half the population. Industry provided 65% of employment. During the 1980s the city's population began to decline, but thanks to the wave of immigration of the 1990s, it began to rise again. The population of Dimonah in the mid-1990s was approximately 30,000, rising further by 2002 to 33,700, making the city the third largest in the Negev. Its municipal area extended over 2.3 sq. mi. (6 sq. km.). At the turn of the 21st century the city's residents were employed in the textile, chemical, and electronic industries as well as in Dead Sea tourism. Some worked at the nearby atomic reactor and the new phosphate field of Ẓefa-Efeh. Income was considerably below the national average.

Dimonah is mentioned as one of the towns belonging to the tribe of Judah in the Negev (Josh. 15:22), but it is not certain whether the ancient site is identical with that of the present town.

[Efraim Orni / Shaked Gilboa (2nd ed.)]

DINA DE-MALKHUTA DINA (Aram. דִּינָא דְּמַלְכוּתָא דִּינָא), the halakhic rule that the law of the country is binding, and, in certain cases, is to be preferred to Jewish law. The problem of *dina de-malkhuta dina* is similar to – but not identical with – the problem of *conflict of laws in other legal systems.

The Historical Background

The original significance of this rule, which was laid down by the *amora* *Samuel, can be deduced from the historical events of that era. The conquest of Babylon from the Parthians by Ardashir I, king of the Sassanids in 226 C.E., brought an end to the period of tranquillity from which the Jews in *Babylonia had benefited. Losing their political and religious autonomy, they had to adapt themselves to the powerful and centralized rule of the Sassanids. In 241 Shapur I, son of Ardashir, succeeded to the throne and granted the minorities under his rule cultural and religious autonomy which also applied to the Jews. Samuel, their leader at that time, imbued Babylonian Jewry with the consciousness that they must become reconciled to the new government, and a personal friendship was apparently established between Samuel and Shapur (Neusner, Babylonia, vol. 2; 16, 27, 30, 45, 71). Consequently Samuel's rule had important political significance, since it recognized the new Sassanid kingdom as a civilized rule possessing good and equitable laws which Jews were bound to obey, as they were to pay the taxes it imposed (*ibid.*, 69, 95).

The Principle in the Talmud

Samuel's principle is cited only four times in the Talmud (Ned. 28a; Git. 10b; BK 113a; BB 54b and 55a). Three *halakhot* that are cited by *Rabbah (according to another reading by *Rava, fourth generation of Babylonian *amoraim*), in the name of the exilarch Ukban b. Nehemiah, and are attributed to Samuel deal with the relationship of Jews to the Persian government and with the relationship of Jewish to gentile law. These *halakhot* establish that the Persian law of the presumptive ownership of land is to be recognized even if it is opposed to Jewish law (see **Ḥazakah*); that the sale of land confiscated by the government for non-payment of tax on the land is valid, but only if the sale is because of non-payment of the land tax and not because of non-payment of the poll tax (BB 55a; et cf. BK 113b). Additional *halakhot* adopted in consequence of *dina de-malkhuta dina* are: recognition of the Persian rules for the transfer of land even if they are not in accordance with Jewish law (BB 54b and 55a); the right of the king to sell a person into slavery for evading payment of the poll tax and the option of a Jew to buy him from the government executive officers and to enslave him (Yev. 64a; BM 73b); a prohibition against cheating tax collectors and concealing assets from them, unless the taxes are illegal for the reasons mentioned in the Talmud (Ned. 28a; BK 113a); and the recognition of bills executed by, or endorsed by, non-Jewish courts despite their being invalid according to Jewish law. The Talmud records a dispute as to the scope of the last *halakhah*. One opinion is that every type of document is to be recognized except for bills of divorce and manumission; according to another view the recognition is granted only to declaratory bills serving as evidence, such as bills of debt, but not to constructive bills such as benefactions (Git. 10b). It may be assumed that the definite but restricted recognition of the government's right to punish wrongdoers was based in part on Samuel's principle, although this is not stated explicitly in the talmudic sources. His principle was accepted as definitive *halakhah*, in the talmudic era and later. In spite of the permissiveness of the *halakhah* in adopting a foreign statute, Jewish law remained dominant in Jewish society, as is amply testified by the great legal creativity of Babylonian Jewry in the talmudic era.

The Legal Basis of the Principle

No legal basis for Samuel's principle is given by the Talmud; nor, apparently, did this problem engage the attention of the *geonim*. In one responsum of the geonic period an effort was made to establish the principle for practical religious reasons. The responder, having regard to the realities before him – Jews under a foreign government – states that it is the will of God that Jews should obey the laws of their rulers, a verse from the book of Nehemiah (9:37) being quoted in support of this view (S. Assaf (ed.), *Teshuvot ha-Ge'onim* (1942), no. 66). Later a number of legal explanations were suggested for Samuel's principle. According to one, Jewish law is able in certain cases to accept non-Jewish law because non-Jews are commanded to enact laws to preserve orderly social life (see *Noachide Laws; Rashi, Git. 9b). According to another view the reason is contractual; i.e., the inhabitants have accepted the king's statutes or the king himself: "For all the citizens accept the king's statutes and laws of their own free will" (Rashbam BB 54b), or "For the inhabitants of that country have accepted him [the king] and take it for granted that he is their master and they are servants to him" (Maim. Yad, Gezelah 5:18). A third view that has been adopted, especially by later authorities, bases the rule *dina de-malkhuta dina* on the right of the court to expropriate a person's property (*hefker bet din hefker*, see **bet din* and **takkanot*); namely, that the halakhic scholars, by virtue of their authority to enact *takkanot* in monetary matters, even in opposition to the laws of the Torah, have in certain matters recognized the customs of the kingdom and its statutes (*Teshuvot Ba'alei ha-Tosafot* no. 12; *Devar Avraham*, vol. 1, no. 1). Some scholars have compared the right of non-Jewish kings to the power of a king of Israel (Nov. Ritba, BB 55a). Others take the view that the legality of the king's statutes derives from the simple fact that the land belongs to the king, who lays down the conditions of residence, and if Jews wish to dwell in his land they are obliged to obey his directions (Ran, Ned. 28a; *Or Zaru'a*, BK, no. 447; for an additional reason, similar but not identical, see *Or Zaru'a, ibid.* and *Devar Avraham*, vol. 1 no. 1). Still others see the halakhic validity of custom as the basis of *dina de-malkhuta dina (Aliyyot de-Rabbenu Yonah*, BB 55a). Most of these views reflect the sociopolitical outlook of the Middle Ages.

In recent times halakhic scholars have been occupied by the problem of whether the principle *dina de-malkhuta dina* derives from rabbinic or biblical law (see **Mishpat Ivri*). The accepted view is that it is of biblical authority and thus those consequences in the field of *halakhah* that derive from this conclusion must be applied to it (see *ibid.*; *Resp. Hatam Sofer*, YD, nos. 127 and 314; *Avnei Millu'im*, 28:2; *Devar Avraham*, vol. 1, no. 1).

The Nature of the Government and the Statute

The halakhic authorities did not accept every law and every kingdom for the purpose of applying the principle *dina de-malkhuta dina* and a series of conditions and qualifications were established.

(1) THE RECOGNIZED GOVERNMENT. There were scholars who held that the principle applied only where there existed a monarchist form of government (*Oraḥ la-Ẓaddik*, ḤM, no. 1). Others, however, were of the opinion that Samuel's rule included other types of authority. With changes in the forms of government and the increase of non-monarchic states, the second view gained acceptance (*Keneset ha-Gedolah*, Tur, ḤM 369).

(2) DINA DE-MALKHUTA DINA AND THE KINGDOM OF ISRAEL. Another problem is whether the principle applies to Jewish kings in the land of Israel. From talmudic sources it follows that a distinction must be made between the laws of Jewish kings and those of non-Jewish kings as far as *dina de-malkhuta dina* is concerned; this was also the opinion of most early halakhists (*Teshuvot Ba'alei ha-Tosafot* no. 12; Nov. Rashba, Ned. 28a). According to Solomon b. Abraham *Adret, those who believe that *dina de-malkhuta dina* does not apply to Jewish kings admit that it does apply to them if they rule outside Israel (Resp. Rashba, vol. 2, no. 134). This opinion corresponds with one of the reasons given for the prin-

ciple not applying to Jewish kings in Israel: "But the laws of Jewish kings are not valid because Israel was divided among [is the inheritance of] every individual Israelite and does not belong to the king, while in the case of non-Jews their law is that the whole land belongs to the king" (*Or Zaru'a*, BK, no. 447). In the course of time the school that held that Samuel's principle was to be applied to a Jewish government in Israel grew stronger (*Tashbez*, pt. 4, section 1, no. 14).

(3) THE PRINCIPLE OF EQUALITY. All agree that the law of the kingdom must apply equally to all its citizens (Maim. Yad, Gezelah, 5:14; Sh. Ar., ḤM 369:8). Resulting from the conditions of Jewish life in exile, the principle of equality was so interpreted that certain types of discrimination were recognized as valid. In one case it was decided that it is sufficient if the law does not discriminate between Jew and Jew despite the fact that Jews as a whole are adversely discriminated against (Resp. Maharik, no. 195). An additional loophole is: the king is permitted to enact special laws for "strangers, not of his own country" (*Ḥokhmat Shelomo* ḤM, 369:8).

The Scope of Laws Included in *Dina de-Malkhuta Dina*

(1) *ISSUR ("religious prohibitions") AND MONETARY LAW. All agree that the principle does not apply to religious or ritual observances (*issur ve-hetter*). This was so certain that it was not particularly stressed and is mentioned only in a few sources (*Tashbez*, pt. 1, no. 158).

(2) THE KING'S INTERESTS. Some scholars limited the application of *dina de-malkhuta dina* to such matters only as were the king's interests; namely, the needs of the kingdom and not matters of purely private law (*Sefer ha-Terumot, 46:*8) but most scholars believed that the principle is applicable even in matters of pure private law (*ibid., Maggid Mishneh, Malveh ve-Loveh* 27:1; Resp. Rashba, vol. 1, no. 895).

(3) "NON-JEWISH WAYS" AND NEW LAWS OF THE KING. Some halakhists affirm that the laws of the kingdom must be recognized but not "non-Jewish ways." This concept is somewhat obscure; in medieval times when it was first discussed, it apparently meant laws that were based on local customs whose source was not the laws of the kingdom but popular usage; these had no validity since the principle is that "the law of the king is binding but the laws of his people are not binding for us" (Rashba, Resp. vol. 6, no. 149; *Beit ha-Beḥirah*, BK 113b). On the other hand most medieval halakhists held that Samuel's rule does not apply to laws introduced by the kings themselves that were not previously the law of the land (*Teshuvot Ba'alei ha-Tosafot* no. 12; Nov. Ritba. BB 55a; Nov. Rashba, BB 55a). This was under the influence of the point of view prevailing in general medieval jurisprudence, which only recognized the validity of ancient laws. Despite the fact that most of the early halakhists held this view, since Maimonides and Asher b. Jehiel apparently disagreed with it (Alfasi does not discuss it at all), Joseph Caro decided the law in conformity with their opinion (see *Codification of Law), and in the Shulḥan Arukh he makes no mention of the restriction of *dina de-malkhuta dina* to ancient law. Joseph Caro's decision served in the following generations as the basis for the extension of Samuel's principle, an imperative necessity when medieval views on the static quality of law underwent sweeping changes and the main laws of the country were no longer based upon ancient statutes but on current legislation (Sh. Ar., ḤM 369:8–10).

(4) STATE LAWS IN OPPOSITION TO TORAH LAW. According to some halakhists the law of the state is binding only when it does not oppose Torah law; i.e., only when it relates to matters not explicitly dealt with in the Torah (A. Sofer (ed.), *Teshuvot Ḥakhmei Provinzyah* (1967), ḤM, no. 49; *Siftei Kohen*, ḤM 73, no. 39, *Ḥatam Sofer*, Resp. ḤM no. 44). This distinction is not sufficiently clear, since it is difficult to find the dividing line between what is available in Torah law and what constitutes a lacuna since, according to the point of view of halakhists, the solution of every problem is to be found in the *halakhah* itself.

Taxes

The king's right to collect taxes was already recognized in the Talmud, and was strengthened by all halakhists in the post-talmudic period. Evading payment of tax is considered robbery (Tashbeẓ, pt. 3 no. 46). The authorities, however, continued to differentiate between justified taxes and confiscations and those without justification (Sh. Ar., ḤM 369:6–11). In practice the way this distinction operated was decided in every individual case, in accordance with the conditions at the actual place and with the substance of the tax. According to the talmudic *halakhah* an unlimited tax is not to be recognized, but later it was declared valid by the *posekim* if it was for "great needs," such as financing a war (*Haggahot Mordekhai*, BB no. 659). Even taxes which were "wicked and cruel" were, from sheer necessity, at times recognized as legal. Thus it was decided that the rule that taxes which have no limit are not to be recognized is to be interpreted as referring to current constant taxes whose sum is at this time greater and beyond the usual amount; when the tax was *ab initio* not fixed, the king may place an arbitrary burden upon the community (*Terumat ha-Deshen*, no. 341).

Bills Executed in Non-Jewish Courts

Beginning with the period of the *geonim* and until the 13th century the aim of limiting the acceptance of bills executed by non-Jewish courts prevailed (S. Assaf (ed.), *Teshuvot ha-Ge'onim* (1942), no. 66; Maim. Yad, Malveh ve-Loveh 27:1), but after this period most halakhists extended acceptance of these documents (Ramban, Nov., BB 55a, Rashba, Nov., Git. 10b). This approach may be inferred from the communal *takkanot*. Communities which undertook to rule in all matters according to Maimonides' *Mishneh Torah* stipulated that in three *halakhot* his ruling was not to be followed, one of the three being Maimonides' *halakhah* that benefactions executed by non-Jewish courts were invalid (A.H. Hershman, *Rabbi Isaac ben Sheshet Perfet* (Eng., 1943), 88f.). Because of this tendency it was decided – in opposition to the *halakhah* of the geonic period that permitted the collection of bills executed by non-Jewish courts from free assets only (S. Assaf (ed.), *Teshuvot ha-Ge'onim* (1927), no. 123) – that such a bill is to be treated like any normal bill and can be collected also from property transferred by the debtor (see *Lien; Rashba, Resp. vol. 3, no. 69; *Piskei ha-Rosh*, Git. 1:10, 11). Likewise there was an extension of recognition of non-Jewish courts in which the bills were executed. The need to establish the honesty of the courts, mentioned by the early authorities (Rif. *Halakhot* Git. Ch. 1, no. 410; Maim. Yad, Malveh ve-Loveh 27:1), was to all intents and purposes no longer demanded, the tendency being to assume the uprightness of the courts until the contrary was proved (*Piskei ha-Rosh*, Git 1:10, 11). Not only were the judges recognized but also administrative officers like notaries (Ramban, Resp. no. 46), and among late authorities all kinds of documents issued by those authorities were recognized (*Be'er Yiẓḥak*, EH, 5:4; *Sho'el u-Meshiv* pt. 1, no. 10). See also **Shetar.*

Changes in the Value of the Coinage

Another problem frequently dealt with in connection with *dina de-malkhuta dina* is that of changes in the value of the coinage. Thus it was laid down that if the government decided that a debt is to be paid in a certain way this could be done despite the possibility of being involved in a breach of the prohibitions against usury or theft (*Sefer ha-Terumot*, 46:5; *Meisharim* 6:1; *Ḥatam Sofer*, Resp., ḤM, no. 58).

Appointments to Religious and Juridical Office by the Government

The question of *dina de-malkhuta dina* was also raised in connection with appointments by the government to juridical and religious office in the Jewish community. Some held that the principle applied to such appointments. The opinion that was accepted is that, though indeed there is basis for the principle even in these cases, it is the duty of one so appointed not to accept the appointment if it is against the will of the members of the Jewish community (Ribash, Resp. no. 271; Rema, ḤM 3:4; *Tashbeẓ*, pt. 1 nos. 158, 162; Rema, Resp. no. 123; *Hatam Sofer*, Resp. ḤM no. 19).

[Shmuel Shilo]

Scope and Limitations

We must bear in mind when discussing *dina de-malkhuta dina* ("the law of the kingdom is law") that it is an underlying principle in the subsequent development and creativity of Jewish law. It is apparent from the Talmud that this principle does not only govern the relationship between the individual and the authorities but also relates to civil cases between private parties. Indeed, during the talmudic era, as long as a central Jewish authority existed, this principle did not restrict Jewish law in any way. But, with the dispersion of the people to various centers and the cessation of central authority, from the tenth century onwards, Jewish law was in danger of turning into an academic subject, its development obstructed and creativity suppressed. The halakhic Sages were aware of this and prevented it by limiting the scope of the rule 'the law of the kingdom is law'. They subordinated the *halakha* to Gentile law only in particular cases and conditions and rejected its application to civil cases between private parties as discussed above. To this end, the talmudic sources implying the wider scope of the rule were harmonized and reinterpreted (*Sefer Haterumot* 46, 8, 5) and sometimes the apprehensions of undermining the Jewish legal system are explicitly stated (Meiri, *Beit ha-Beḥirah,* BK 113b). It might well be that the very limitations of the rule resulted that when it had been applied, the foreign legal elements were not merely recognized and validated but also integrated into Jewish law. (See Bibliography, Elon, (1988), 61–66; Elon (1994), 68–73.)

Criminal Jurisdiction by Non-Jewish Authorities Recognized by Jewish Law

The rule "the law of the kingdom is law" was employed for this purpose by the Israeli Supreme Court in the case of *Aloni* (HCJ, 852/86, *Aloni v. Ministry of Justice, judgment*, 41 (2), 1). The Supreme court was asked to decide whether to instruct the State to extradite to France a man charged with murder in a French court. The defendant was already declared extraditable according to Israeli Extradition Law and in accordance with the treaty between the two countries. But the Minister of Justice decided not to implement the extradition, due to the potential life-threatening situations that the defendant may face in the French jail from other prisoners. Justice Menachem Elon extensively discussed the approach of Jewish Law on the subject of extradition as it was treated throughout the Dispersion when the gentile authorities demanded from the Jewish congregations the handing over of Jews accused of severe criminal charges. The first part of Elon's opinion discussed whether Jewish Law enabled the extradition of one accused of serious crimes to gentiles on the grounds of the criminal accusation itself (pp. 76–90, of judgment; q.v. "Extradition").

The second part of the opinion relates to the issue of whether Jews have to inform the gentile authorities about criminal acts committed by Jews on the grounds that gentile jurisdiction to try all citizens is recognized within the framework of the rule "the law of the kingdom is law." The following is a brief summary of the main points of that decision. Solomon ben Abraham Adret (Rashba) in a Responsum quoted by the *Beit Yosef* commentary on *Tur* (ḤM 308/12) relates to a case in which the Jewish community was requested by the gentile authorities to investigate whether a certain Jew had committed a felony, in order that he be punished. Rashba relying on the principle of "the law of the kingdom is law" ruled that when a Jewish court was acting by license of the authorities, there was no need to observe the usual requirements of admissible evidence by Jewish law such as forewarning, competent witnesses etc. – even in capital cases because "if we do not say this, but insist on adherence to Biblical law in procedural law, the world would become a wasteland and murderers and their cronies would proliferate …" (*ibid.* according to the version published by Kaufmann in: JQR, 8 (1896), 228, 235–6; p. 90 in *Aloni* judgment).

R. Samuel *Medina (*Responsa Maharashdam*, ḤM, no. 55) upheld the opinion of a Responsum by Abraham ben David of Posquières (Rabad) and clearly states on the basis of "the law of the kingdom is law" that measures taken by the government to punish criminal felons were entirely justified, as it was within the authority of the government to legislate laws in its jurisdiction (p. 91, *Aloni* judgment).

In the 19th century R. Moses Schick (*Responsa Maharam Schick*, ḤM, no. 50) cites the abovementioned responsum by Rashba in a case where it was known, though not proved, in the Jewish community that a certain woman had murdered her husband. The question was whether to hand her over to the non-Jewish authorities. Rabbi Schick ruled that punishment meted out by the authorities was legitimate for "…all they do to improve social order is legitimate" (pp. 91–92, *Aloni* judgment).

In this context, Justice Elon also quotes R. Meir Dan Plotzki (Poland, 19th–20th cent.; *Kelei Ḥemdah*, *Mishpatim 1*) who says that the talmudic prohibition of seeking remedy in non-Jewish courts did not apply to European state courts of his time, and it was preferable to bring cases before them because *dina de-malkhuta dina*.

On the basis of these sources, Justice Elon ruled that the provision of Extradition Act 5714 – 1954 was congruent with Jewish Law which negates evasion of criminally charged suspects from standing trial, especially in capital cases, if the Jewish court was unable to adjudicate them. Numerous great halakhic authorities were of the opinion that such a suspect should be handed over to a court which had the authority to try him, either by the authority of Jewish Law itself, or under the authority of the principle *dina de-malkhuta dina*. (p. 96, *Aloni* judgment). Rabbi S. Israeli disagrees (see bibliography) with this conclusion. In his opinion the scope of 'the law of the kingdom is law' is limited to the particular country (and it cannot be invoked in an international situation). For a more extensive discussion see *Extradition.

The Validity of the Rule Concerning Israeli Law

Since the establishment of the State of Israel, rabbinical courts frequently address themselves to the relationship between Israeli Civil Law and Jewish Law. On many occasions, rabbinical courts have conferred binding authority on the state law within the halakhic discourse of Jewish Law on the basis of the rule *dina de-malkhuta dina*.

1. THE ADOPTION OF VARIOUS STATE LAWS BY RABBINICAL COURTS. The application of Israeli Law by rabbinical courts on various matters, and based on usage or community enactment, was discussed by the Israeli Supreme Court in the case of *Vilozhny* (HCJ 323/81 *Vilozhny* v. *The Great Rabbinical Court*, judgment 36(2) 733). The appellant requested the court to annul the decision of the Great Rabbinical Court which had ruled that the appellant had to vacate the apartment in which he lived with his wife, after having been granted a divorce, due to the violent behavior of the husband. The appellant argued that the court should have recognized that the apartment was occupied by him according to the Landlord and Tenant Law (Consolidated Version), 5732 – 1972, and thus not order the sale of the apartment as if it were vacant. The Rabbinical Court determined that its ruling did not contradict the landlord and tenant law "which was given the same halakhic validity as any usage or regulation enacted by the community." The Supreme Court (Justice M. Elon) relates to this comment of the Rabbinical Court, and adds that rabbinical courts in numerous instances tend to adopt Israeli Law, describing the various methods of adoption, illustrated by examples. We shall quote here implementations based on *dina de-malkhuta dina* in order to further clarify this point.

> During their decision-making process, Rabbinical Courts also make use from time to time of the principle of "the law of the kingdom is law" in order to validate various legal transactions, if they were not valid according to Jewish Law (e.g., concerning a bank guarantee defective in collaterals, app. 5725/47, RC judgment E 264, pp. 267–270; concerning the competence of a legal personality, the recognition of which was uncertain by traditional Jewish Law [in this case R.S. Dichovsky ruled that on the basis of "the law of the kingdom is law" it was possible to create new concepts in civil law, and even to create a new category of legal personalities] (case 11183/32, RC Judgment J 273, pp. 288–289); concerning entry of property at the land registry [in that case the court raised the question discussed above, whether "the law of the kingdom is law" applied in the Land of Israel]). The court ruled that since the registration was entered prior to the establishment of the State of Israel, in the time of British rule, there was no doubt about the validity of the rule (appeal 26/127, RC Judgment F 376, pp. 380–382). In some cases the Rabbinical Court even annulled transactions valid according to Jewish Law, if they have not met the requirements of the State Law (e.g., the requirement to enter a purchase in the land registry, though Jewish Law only requires an agreement (file 747/26, RC Judgment F 249 p. 252).

The court noted that "when the principle of 'the law of the kingdom is law' is evoked, the ruling by State Law is given binding validity, but it does not become a part of the Jewish Law" (p. 740 HCJ, Vilozhny).

It has to be noted that in a later ruling (file 307/38 RC judgment 12 279 p. 294) the Haifa District Rabbinical Court ruled (on the basis of Responsa Ḥatam Sofer, ḤM no. 44) that even though the applicability of *dina de-malkhuta dina* in the Land of Israel was a matter of controversy (see above), even the opponents concurred that, concerning usage and enactments with the aim of regulating trade to the public benefit, the rule applied also in the Land of Israel. Based on this principle, the court ruled that transfer of landed property which was not entered in the registry office was not valid, even if the act of acquisition had met the requirements of Jewish Law, because the law requiring registration as a precondition for a transaction of property intended to prevent fraud in land sales, and in such cases the rule of *dina de-malkhuta dina* was in force.

2. SPOUSES' JOINTLY OWNED PROPERTY PROCEDURES. A special case in which the question of using the rule of "the law of the kingdom is law" for the integration of State Law

and Supreme Court rulings into the legal system of rabbinical courts (see *bet din) was addressed, concerned the allocation of jointly owned property of couples about to be divorced. Israeli civil courts have ruled for numerous years to divide the property in equal shares (The Procedure of Spouses' Property). After subsequent legislation (The Property Relations Between Spouses Act 5733 – 1973), this ruling became State Law also binding for Rabbinical Courts (q.v. Matrimonial Property). In this context diverging opinions have been developed among contemporary halakhic authorities. In the opinion of R. Shlomo Dichovsky, judge of the Great Rabbinical Court (*Teḥumin*, 18 (1998), pp. 18–31; 19 (1999), pp. 205–20) rabbinical courts have to adjudicate according to the Spouses' Property Procedures, by the authority of the 'law of the kingdom is law' principle. In his opinion, judgments should be made on the assumption that the principle also obtained in the Land of Israel and applied also to laws enacted by the democratic government and to the precedents set by judicial legislation. Since the Israeli Supreme Court regards its own judgments as part of the binding law, there is no difference between a judgment and a law. Therefore, in his opinion, judgments of the Supreme Court should not be subjected to the distinction, of some authorities, between an explicit state law – to which *dina de-malkhuta dina* applies – and the legal precedent of a local court to which it does not. Since all citizens of the country are familiar with and conduct their affairs according to the Spouses' Property Procedure, and since it can be supported by Jewish usage, it has to be accepted by the authority of *dina de-malkhuta dina*. This is so with regard to presumption of jointly owned property, though it originates from court rulings, and the principle of 'the law of the kingdom is law' surely has to be applied to it and cases should be adjudicated accordingly in Rabbinical Courts.

A different view is expressed by R. Abraham Sherman, also a judge of the Great Rabbinical Court (*Teḥumin*, 18 (1988), pp. 32–40); 19 (1999), 205–20). His opinion is that laws and legal definitions not prompted by circumstances or social developments to improve the administration of proper order, but by *the ideological inclinations* of legislators or judges of the state courts, do not warrant the application of *dina de-malkhuta dina*, because it contradicts the principles of the Torah. Furthermore, it cannot be factually ascertained that the Spouses' Property Procedure was unanimously accepted, and therefore presume that all marriages take place with the assumption that the jointly owned property would be divided according to this procedure. Hence, it is difficult to find a halakhic basis for the Spouses' Property Procedure. So when the issue was the allocation of matrimonial assets rather than an enactment for the public benefit, 'the law of the kingdom is law' ought not to be evoked.

3. THE RELATIONSHIP BETWEEN JEWISH LAW AND THE ISRAELI STATE LAW. Justice Elon, in his opinion on the above-mentioned Vilozhny appeal, also discussed the desirable principles for the relationship between the State (secular) and the rabbinical legal systems. The main points are as follows (pp. 740–42 HC judgment):

We may distinguish between three possible methods by which Rabbinical Courts could confer binding validity on Israeli Civil Law. One way is the recognition of the binding validity, based on the principle of 'the law of the kingdom is law' as explained above. The other method is adoption – by means of the legal basis of a custom (or usage) in Jewish Law that integrates a certain law which then becomes an integral part of it. If there was an existing public usage of a certain legal norm, this norm may be recognized in certain circumstances as part of the Jewish legal system and may even be valid in spite of contradicting a particular law in Jewish civil law. Rabbinical courts make frequent use of the legal basis of usage (*situmta* in talmudic terminology) in order to absorb various principles and laws from other legal systems (**minhag*). The third method is *legislation*; the community or its leaders enjoy a limited measure of judicial authority and may make new laws in various legal spheres. In talmudic times this was called "the authority to impose punishments" (*mesi'in al kiztan*) but in later periods it has become known as "enactment of the public." These enactments have greatly enriched Jewish Law and became an integral part of it (**takkanot ha-kahal*).

From time to time, rabbinical courts make use of the principle of *dina de-malkhuta dina* or the recognition of common usage in order to validate or absorb laws from other legal systems. However, there are rare instances in which rabbinical courts recognize a state law on the basis of an "enactment of the public." This method has a fundamental and far-reaching importance, because as we said, the law of the state thus becomes part of the Jewish legal system. In the Vilozhny appeal, the Supreme Court noted that the ruling of the rabbinical court, to which the appeal related, made use of this method with regard to the Landlord and Tenant Act, since the rabbinical court stated that "it was given the same halakhic validity as any usage or regulation enacted by the community." The court also noted that with regard to the Landlord and Tenant Law a ruling had already been given by Rabbi Obadiah Hadayah, that it should be regarded as an enactment made by the leaders of the community since "here we are not concerned with foreign laws, but with laws enacted by the government for the benefit of the people of the country…" (Responsa Yaskil Avdi, 6, ḤM no. 8).

During its development and history, Jewish Law has many times met the need to confront other legal systems, created by foreign nations. The need to cope with a different legal system created by the Jewish people itself, whose legislative and judicial institutions do not recognize the authority of the *halakhah* as their guiding principle, is a new phenomenon in Jewish history. The recognition and validation of Israeli civil law on the basis of *dina de-malkhuta dina* or even based on the authority of common usage indicate an approach that conceived the state legal system as an entity without any inherent creative connection with Jewish Law. Conversely, halakhic recognition and validation of the Jewish state based on "enactments of the community" conceive the state legal system as a product of Jewish creativity, in accordance with one of the historical legal methods recognized by the Jewish legal system, and this is the preferable way for the future integration of Israeli and Jewish Laws.

[Menachem Elon (2nd ed.)]

BIBLIOGRAPHY: A. Rodriguez, *She'elot u-Teshuvot Oraḥ la-Ẓaddik* (1785), 586–74a; D. Hoffmann, *Mar Samuel, Rector der juedischen Akademie zu Nehardea in Babylonien* (1873); J. Newman, *Agricultural Life of the Jews in Babylonia between the Years 20* C.E. *and 500* C.E. (1932); J. Horovitz, in: MGWJ, 80 (1936), 215–31; A. Roth, in: *Ha-Soker*, 5 (1937–38), 110–25; F. Kern, *Kingship and Law in the Middle Ages* (1939); P. Biberfeld, *Dina de-Malkhuta Dina* (Schriftenreihe des Bundes Juedischer Akademiker, vol. 2, n.d.); T. Leibowitz, in: *Ha-Peraklit*, 4 (1947), 230–8; I.M. Horon, *Meḥkarim* (1951), 41–134; ET, 7 (1956), 295–308; S. Bendov, in: *Talpioth*, 7 (1960), 395–405; 8 (1963), 79–84, 526–30; 9 (1964), 230–7; S. Lieberman and Y. Kutscher, in: *Leshonenu*, 27 (1963), 34–39; S. Safrai, in: JJS, 14 (1963), 67–70; M. Beer, in: *Tarbiz*, 33 (1963/64), 247–58; S. Albeck, in: *Sefer Yovel… Abraham Weiss* (1964), 109–25; D. Daube, *Collaboration with Tyranny in Rabbinic Law* (1965); Neusner, Babylonia, 2 (1966); L. Landman, *Jewish Law in the Diaspora: Confrontation and Accomodation* (1968); Elon, Mafte'aḥ, 39f. **ADD. BIBLIOGRAPHY:** M. Elon, *Ha-Mishpat ha-Ivri* (1988), 1:16, 53, 58ff., 71, 117, 123, 175, 557, 566, 570, 602, 624, 654, 670, 747, 760, 765, 3:1325, 1486, 1529ff, 1633ff; idem, *Jewish Law* (1994), I:16, 59, 64ff., 79, 132, 139, 173, 194; 2:600, 677, 688, 700, 745; 771, 809, 828, 921, 941, 936; 4:1583, 1767, 1818f., 1944ff.; idem, *Jewish Law (Cases and Materials)* (1999), 391–98, 369–88; idem, "*Dinei Hasgara ba-Mishpat ha-Ivri*," in: *Teḥumin*, 8 (1986), 263; S. Yisraeli, *Hasgarat Avaryan le-Shiput Zar*, ibid, 287; M. Elon and B. Lifshitz, *Mafte'aḥ ha-She'elot ve-ha-Teshuvot shel Ḥahmei Sefarad u-Ẓefon Afrikah* (1986), 1:81–83; B. Lifshitz and E. Shohetman, *Mafteaḥ ha-She'elot ve-ha-Teshuvot shel Ḥakhmei Ashkenaz, Ẓarefat ve-Italyah* (1997), 52–53; S. Shilo, *Dina de-Malkhuta Dina* (1975); S. Dikhovsky, "*'Hilkhot Shittuf' – Ha-Im Dina Demalkhuta?*", in: *Teḥumin*, 18 (1998); A. Sherman, "*'Hilkhot Shittuf,' le-Or Mishpetei ha-Torah*," in: *Teḥumin*, 19 (1999), 205; Y. Rivlin, *Ha-Yerushah ve-ha-Ẓeva'a ba-Mishpat ha-Ivri* (1999) 293–304.

DINAH (Heb. דִּינָה), the daughter of *Jacob and his wife *Leah (Gen. 30:21). Of her life, the Bible records only that during her family's stay in the vicinity of *Shechem, she was raped by Shechem, the son of Hamor the Hivite. Jacob's sons, *Simeon and *Levi, avenged their sister by slaughtering the male population of Shechem, carrying off the women and children, and taking their goods and livestock as spoil (Gen. 34). The biblical narrative contains divergent appraisals of this act of revenge. On the one hand, Jacob strongly disapproves of his sons' deeds, and while his immediate reaction is based on a fear of reprisal by the local population (34:30), on his deathbed (49:5–7) he once again expresses disgust at their conduct, prophesying that their descendants would be scattered in later Israel. On the other hand, the story's emphatic ending ("Should our sister be treated like a whore?"; 34:31) appeals to the reader to understand their behavior and even to approve it. This ambivalence is reflected in later Jewish tradition as well (Judith 9:2–4; Gen. R. 80:12; Yal., Gen. 134–5).

Scholars who find a historical kernel in the story point to the absence of the tribes of Simeon and Levi from the tribal list of the Song of Deborah (Judges 5) and see in Genesis 34 and Genesis 49:5–7 an etiology of that absence. Others read the chapter from the anthropological perspective of ingroup versus outgroup marriage in proto-Israelite times. Still others (see Amit in Bibliography) understand the chapter as a hidden polemic of the post-exilic period directed against the practice of conversion to Judaism. Thanks to the feminist movement, more attention has been paid to the story of Dinah than in previous generations. The question raised recently of whether the story describes an actual rape is complicated by the absence of a single term for "rape" (post-biblical *anas*) from Biblical Hebrew.

The Bible relates nothing further of Dinah's life, nor of her progeny, after this episode, although she is numbered among those who immigrated to Egypt (Gen. 46:15).

[Jacob S. Levinger / S. David Sperling (2nd ed.)]

In the *Aggadah*

Dinah was destined to be a male, but Leah, out of compassion for her sister Rachel, prayed that she be a girl, so that of the 12 sons whom she knew Jacob was destined to beget, two would be born to her sister. Leah called her daughter Dinah because of the judgment (*din*) she had thus passed on herself (Ber. 60a). Both Jacob and Leah are held partly responsible for the tragedy of Dinah. Dinah, desiring to show off her beauty to the Canaanite (Tanḥ. B. on Gen. 34:1), "went out," in the same way that her mother "went out" (see Gen. 30:16), and "as the mother so was the daughter" (Gen. R. 80:1). According to another view, however, she never willingly left her tent. Shechem made her do so through a subterfuge (PdRE 38). Jacob was to blame in that he concealed Dinah from his brother. Because he refused to give her in marriage to the circumcised Esau, she was ravished by the uncircumcised Shechem (Gen. R. 80:4). Jacob was thereby punished for staying in Shechem and delaying his departure to Beth-El (Lev. R. 37:1). According to one view, Asenath, the wife of Joseph (Gen. 41:45), was a daughter of Dinah. Abandoned by Jacob and found and adopted by *Potiphar (Poti-Phera) in Egypt, she was recognized by Joseph by an amulet which Jacob had given her; she later became Joseph's wife (PdRE 38).

BIBLIOGRAPHY: E.A. Speiser, *Genesis* (1964), 262–8; de Vaux, Anc Isr, 368; Meisler (Mazar), in: BIES, 15 (1950), 84; EM, 2 (1965), 653–4 (incl. bibl.); Ginzberg, Legends, 1 (1925), 395–400; 5 (1925), 313–4. **ADD. BIBLIOGRAPHY:** C. Meyers, in: ADB, 2, 200; I. Sheres, *Dinah's Rebellion* (1990); D. Fewell and D. Gunn, in: JBL, 110 (1991), 193–211; A. Keefe, in: *Semeia*, 61 (1993), 79–97; L. Bechtel, in: JSOT, 62 (1994), 19–36; Y. Amit, in: M. Fox (ed.), *Texts, Temples, and Traditions* (FS Haran; 1996), 11–28; M. Gruber, in: *Beth Mikra*, 157 (1999), 119–27; E. van Wolde, in: VT, 52 (2002), 528–44.

DINE, JIM (1935–), U.S. painter, sculptor, printmaker, performance artist, book illustrator, stage designer, and poet. Cincinnati-born Jim Dine studied art at the Cincinnati Art Academy (1951–53), the Boston Museum School (fall 1955), and Ohio University (1954–57). He burst onto the art scene as a purveyor of artist performances known as Happenings after moving to New York City in 1958. The 32nd performance, *Smiling Workman* (1960), was followed by *The Vaudeville Show* (1960) and *Car Crash* (1960). At this time Dine also began making assemblages – canvases that incorporate found materials. *Lawnmower* from 1962 employs an actual lawnmower on a pedestal. The handlebars of this ordinary object lean against the canvas, which is mounted on the wall and painted with thick hues of green and yellow, suggesting grass and the sun. This kind of mixed-media work is one of many that utilize the everyday objects that continue to define Dine's oeuvre.

During the 1960s Dine was associated with Pop art, but the cold impartiality of the movement went against the artist's desire to imbue his work with elements of his own personality. Throughout the years, Dine instilled new layers of meaning in the varied objects which preoccupy his art, including hearts, trees, tools, gates, the Venus de Milo, and robes. These themes are reiterated in different media and in different styles. Tools have been painted, drawn, and created as prints, as well as used in assemblages. Similarly, bathrobes – introduced in 1964 – have been rendered in many media. The empty robes are meant to be self-portraits. Painted while in Jerusalem, *Light Comes upon the Old City* (1979) is a large canvas showing a dark empty robe suffused with golden light.

Ever restless and continually experimental, in 1966 the prolific Dine designed the costumes for the San Francisco Actor's Workshop production of *A Midsummer Night's Dream*, and in 1967–68 he designed costumes for a version of Oscar Wilde's *Picture of Dorian Gray* that never reached the stage. Several illustrated volumes of Dine's poems have been published (1969, 1987). He also illustrated a version of Guillaume Apollinaire's *The Poet Assassinated* (1968) and Sigmund Freud's *The Case of the Wolf-Man* (1993), among other books. In 1998 Dine designed a heart logo for the 67th General Assembly of the Jewish Council of Federations in Jerusalem.

BIBLIOGRAPHY: G.W.J. Beal, *Jim Dine: Five Themes* (1984); C.W. Glenn, *Jim Dine: Drawings* (1985); J.E. Feinberg, *Jim Dine* (1995); M. Livingstone, *Jim Dine: The Alchemy of Images* (1998); E. Carpenter, *Jim Dine Prints, 1985–2000: A Catalogue Raisonné* (2002).

[Samantha Baskind (2nd ed.)]

DINER, HASIA R. (1946–), scholar of American Jewish history. Born in Milwaukee, Wisconsin, the daughter of Morris and Ita Schwartzman, she received her Bachelor of Arts degree from the University of Wisconsin at Madison in 1968 and her doctorate from the University of Illinois in 1975. In 1975 Diner became an instructor in history at the University of Maryland, College Park; she served as a research associate at Radcliffe College from 1978 to 1980. From 1980 to 1984 she taught at the American University in Washington, D.C., and then from 1984 to 1996 was professor of history in the Department of American Studies at the University of Maryland.

In 1996 Diner became the Paul S. and Sylvia Steinberg Professor of American Jewish History at New York University, and she was appointed as director of the Goldstein-Goren Center for American Jewish History at New York University in 2003. She was a visiting lecturer at numerous academic conferences and universities, including Williams College, Michigan State University, the Jewish Theological Seminary, and the University of Munich.

Diner was a specialist in immigration history and the history of relations between American Jews and other ethnic and racial groups. Her many books and articles explore various aspects of immigration, identity, women's experience, and relationships between, for example, Jewish Americans and African Americans. Her works include *In the Almost Promised Land: American Jews and Blacks, 1915–1935* (1977); *A Time for Gathering: The Second Migration, 1820–1880* (1992); *Lower East Side Memories: The Jewish Place in America* (2000); *Hungering for America: Italian, Irish, and Jewish Foodways in the Age of Migration* (2002); *Her Works Praise Her: A History of Jewish Women in America from Colonial Times to the Present* (with Beryl Lieff Benderly, 2002); and *The Jews of the United States, 1645 to 2000* (2004). *Lower East Side Memories* received warm critical reception for its exploration of the transformation of the Lower East Side from a neighborhood of Jewish immigrants to a locale of nostalgia and myth within American Jewish memory.

One of 20 living women historians included in *American Women Historians, 1700s–1900s* (1998), Diner is a fellow of the American Academy for Jewish Research and a member of the Society of American Historians; she serves on the Executive Committee of the Academic Council of the American Jewish Historical Society and on the Executive Board of the Association for Jewish Studies. She was coeditor of the *Newsletter of the Association for Jewish Studies* from 1999. As an expert in Jewish immigration history, Diner served as a consultant to numerous films and public history projects, including *They Came for Good: A History of the Jewish People in America, Jews and Blacks in the Civil Rights Movement* and "Sitting Shiva with the Rogarshevkys" at the Lower East Side Tenement Museum.

[Dorothy Bauhoff (2nd ed.)]

DINES, ALBERTO (1932–), Brazilian journalist, author, biographer, and script writer. Dines was born in Rio de Janeiro. After starting at the *Jornal Israelita* in 1952, he advanced his career in journalism (writing mainly on cinema and politics) in prestigious Brazilian publications, also lecturing on journalism at universities in Brazil, Portugal, and the United States. In 1988 he published the biography *Morte no paraíso: A tragédia de Stefan Zweig*. In 1988–94 he lived in Portugal, where he carried out research on the Inquisition, published as *Vínculos de fogo: António José da Silva, o Judeu e outras histórias da Inquisição em Portugal e no Brasil* (1992). In Lisbon he also wrote *O baú de Abravanel. Uma crônica de sete séculos até Silvio Santos* (1990). The title story of his book *Posso?* (1972) describes the positive encounter between a Jew and a Christian on Christmas Eve. In 1979 he published a second book of short stories, *E por que não eu?* In 1996 Dines established *Observatório de Imprensa* (http://observatoriodaimprensa.com.br), an internet site on media criticism. He is director of LABJOR (Journalism Advanced Studies Laboratory) at Campinas University.

BIBLIOGRAPHY: M.A. Costa and A. Devalle, "Entrevista con Alberto Dines, 21/8/2002," at: www.tvebrasil.com.br/observatorio/sobre_dines/memoria.htm; D.B. Lockhart, *Jewish Writers of Latin America: A Dictionary* (1997).

[Florinda Goldberg (2nd ed.)]

DINESON, JACOB (1856–1919), Yiddish novelist. Dineson, who was born near Kovno (Kaunas), Lithuania, received a traditional Jewish education and was influenced by the Haskalah movement. Before turning to Yiddish, he wrote Hebrew articles in *Ha-Maggid, Ha-Meliz,* and *Ha-Shahar.* His first Yiddish novel, *Be-Ovoyn Oves* ("For the Parents' Sins," 1876), was banned by the Russian censor. Not until 13 years later and after rebutting H. *Graetz's denunciation of Yiddish, did he publish his second novel, which won the hearts of Yiddish readers and sold more than 200,000 copies: *Ha-Ne'ehovim ve-ha-Ne'imim oder der Shvartse Yungermantshik* ("The Beloved and the Pleasant or The Black Youth," 1877). He was the pioneer of the Yiddish sentimental novel, and retained the affection of the Yiddish reading public with his *Even Negef* ("Stumbling Block," 1890), *Hershele* ("Little Hershl," 1891), and *Yosele* ("Little Yosl," 1899). He also took the lead in modernizing elementary Jewish education through secular schools which were often called Dineson Schools. A close friend of I.L. Peretz, he helped establish the latter's fame.

BIBLIOGRAPHY: Rejzen, Leksikon, s.v.; LNYL, 2 (1958), 514–16; S. Niger, *Dertseyler un Romanistn*, 1 (1946), 78–83; S. Liptzin, *Flowering of Yiddish Literature* (1963), 78–83. **ADD. BIBLIOGRAPHY:** N. Meisel, *Noente un Eygene* (1957), 13–20.

[Chone Shmeruk / Samuel Spinner (2nd ed.)]

DININ, SAMUEL (1902–2005), U.S. educator. Born in Mogilev oblast, Russia, Dinin earned his bachelor's degree at the City College of New York in 1922 and received his master's degree and doctorate at Columbia University in 1923 and 1933, respectively. He was registrar and associate professor of education and history at the Manhattan-based Teachers Institute of the *Jewish Theological Seminary of America from 1926 to 1945. In 1945, he was appointed executive director of the Los Angeles Bureau of Jewish Education. Through his efforts in that capacity, the Bureau established the Los Angeles Hebrew High School in 1949. Elected dean of the University of Judaism in Los Angeles in 1957, he was named chairman of the faculty and vice president in 1963. He continued under the UJ's auspices as its chair of faculties and its vice president until 1974, when he retired to become the college's professor emeritus of education and history. Dinin played a key role in developing several institutional pillars of Jewish education in Los Angeles, including the West Coast's Bureau of Jewish Education (BJE) affiliate, the University of Judaism (UJ), and Camp Ramah. He wrote *Judaism in a Changing Civilization* (1933) and served as editor of *Jewish Education.*

[Leon H. Spotts]

DINITZ, SIMCHA H. (1929–2003), Israeli diplomat and politician, member of the Eleventh Knesset. Born in Tel Aviv, Dinitz served in the Haganah and the IDF. He studied political science at the University of Cincinnati in Ohio and received a B.Sc. in international relations and an M.Sc. in international law from the School of Foreign Service at Georgetown University in Washington, D.C. In 1958 he joined the Ministry of Foreign Affairs, first in the Information Department and from 1962 as deputy director general. In 1963 he was appointed as Golda Meir's political secretary and was twice a member of the Israeli delegation to the UN General Assembly. In 1966–68 he served in the Israeli Embassy in Rome and 1968–69 in Washington in charge of information. In 1972 Golda Meir appointed him director general of the Prime Minister's Office, and at the end of November 1972 he was appointed ambassador to the U.S., remaining in office through the Yom Kippur War and the beginning of the peace process with Egypt, playing an important role in arranging for the American airlift of weapons to Israel in the course of the Yom Kippur War and participating in the team that negotiated the Camp David Accord in September 1978. During his service in the U.S., Dinitz developed close relations with Henry *Kissinger when the latter served as President Nixon's national security advisor and then secretary of state. In the years 1979–84 Dinitz held the position of vice president of the Hebrew University of Jerusalem. In 1984 he was elected on the Alignment list to the Eleventh Knesset, but resigned from the Knesset in March 1988 after being elected chairman of the Executive of the World Zionist Organization and Jewish Agency, a position he held in 1986–5. In this period he oversaw the opening of the gates of the former Soviet Union to Jewish emigration, and Operation Solomon, in which 14,000 Ethiopian Jews were airlifted to Israel in a single day in May 1991.

Dinitz was forced to resign before his term was over due to charges brought against him for allegedly using a Jewish Agency credit card for personal purchases. In 1996 he was found guilty by the District Court of Jerusalem for fraudulently expropriating $22,000 in this manner, but the following year was exonerated by the Supreme Court on appeal.

[Susan Hattis Rolef (2nd ed.)]

DINITZ, SIMON (1926–), U.S. sociologist and criminologist. Dinitz received his Ph.D. from the University of Wisconsin at Madison in 1951. After his first teaching job there, Dinitz became professor of sociology at Ohio State University and research assistant in psychiatry. His special interest was the sociology of deviant behavior as expressed in delinquency and mental disorders, and he worked on the prevention of hospitalization for schizophrenics. He also served as senior fellow in the Academy of Contemporary Problems. He served as president of the American Society of Criminology (1971) as well as vice president (1968 and 1969). He capped his academic career as professor emeritus of sociology at Ohio State University.

A pioneer in the fields of sociology, psychology, criminal behavior, and public policy, Dinitz collaborated in writing such books as *Social Problems: Dissensus and Deviation* (1967); *Women after Treatment* (1968); *Critical Issues in the Study of Crime* (1968); *Schizophrenics in the Community: An Experiment in the Prevention of Hospitalization* (1967); *The Prevention of Juvenile Delinquency: An Experiment* (1972); *Schizophrenics in the New Custodial Community: Five Years After the Experiment* (1974); *In Fear of Each Other: Studies of Dangerousness in America* (1977); *The Mad, the Bad, and the Different* (1981); and *Introduction to Criminology: Order and Disorder* (1988). In acknowledgment of his lifelong dedication to improving the knowledge base of corrections and having trained many correctional practitioners, the Ohio Community Corrections Organizations created the Dr. Simon Dinitz Achievement Award, which is given to a community correctional practitioner who has made contributions to the improvement of community correction in Ohio. Similarly, the Ohio Department of Rehabilitation and Correction presents the Simon Dinitz Criminal Justice Research Award.

[Ruth Beloff (2nd ed.)]

DINUR (Dinaburg), BENZION (1884–1973), historian and educator. Dinur received his education in Lithuanian yeshivot, at Berne University, at the Berlin Hochschule, and at Petrograd University. He taught in several Jewish schools; at Jewish teachers' training colleges; and in "Oriental studies" courses. He was also active in the Zionist and Jewish Labor movements and in the problems of Jewish education. In 1921 Dinur settled in Ereẓ Israel and from 1923 to 1948 served as a teacher and later as head of the Jewish Teachers' Training College, Jerusalem. In 1936 he was appointed lecturer in modern Jewish history at the Hebrew University and became professor in 1948 and professor emeritus in 1952. Dinur was among the founders and editors of the bibliographical quarterly *Kirjath Sepher* (1924) and of the historical annual (later quarterly) *Zion* and of such historiographical projects as the *Sefer ha-Yishuv* (2 vols., 1939–44), *Sefer ha-Ẓiyyonut* (1938, 1954²), and *Toledot ha-Hagganah* (1954–59). He was elected to the first Knesset on the Mapai list and served as minister for education and culture from 1951 to 1955, when he was responsible for the 1953 State Education Law, which put an end to the prevailing party "trend" education system. From 1953 to 1959 Dinur was president of *Yad Vashem. In 1973 he was awarded the Israel Prize in education.

As a historian Dinur brought a Zionist approach to the understanding of Jewish history. Central to his historical studies is the idea of the fluctuation of the Jewish psyche and Jewish community structure between establishment in the Diaspora and a yearning for redemption, with Ereẓ Israel as the focus of these continuous tensions; this was the determining factor, which gave unity to the history of the people in the Diaspora and determined the change of periods and their character. Dinur's studies underline the national value of the Jewish communal presence in Ereẓ Israel from the capture of Jerusalem in 70 C.E. to the Arab conquest in 636 and its end in the Crusader period. For the historiography of modern Jewish history, he stressed the importance of research into the social ideology of Ḥasidism and of the Ḥovevei Zion movement. Dinur believed it best to let the sources speak for themselves, and in some of his major works, quotations, with his introductions and notes, are collected into literary unity. The subject of the division of Jewish history into periods occupied Dinur's mind a good deal, particularly the passage from the Middle Ages to modern times. According to him the latter period began in 1700, the year of the great immigration to Ereẓ Israel.

Among his major works are a history of the Jewish people divided into two series, of which the first part of the first series appeared under the title of *Yisrael be-Arẓo* (1938), and the second series under the title *Yisrael ba-Golah* (5 vols., 1926, 1958², 1961–66³); a history of Ḥibbat Zion, *Ḥibbat Ẓiyyon* (2 vols., 1932–34); see also *Mefallesei Derekh* (Pioneers, 1947); and *Arakhim u-Derakhim* (1958), a study of the educational and cultural problems of modern Israel. Dinur also edited the correspondence between A. Mapu and A. Kaplan (1929); the correspondence and the letters of Mapu (1970); of S.J. Rapoport with R. Kircheim, Z. Frankel and others (1928); and the Zionist writings of Hermann Schapira (1925). A collection of Dinur's miscellaneous studies appeared in 1955 under the title *Be-Mifneh ha-Dorot;* volume 1 of his memoirs under the title of *Be-Olam she-Shaka 1884–1914* appeared in 1958, and volume 2, *Bi-Ymei Milḥamah u-Mahpekhah 1914–21*, in 1960. A collection of essays, *Sefer Dinaburg*, in Dinur's honor was published by Y. Baer, J. Guttmann, and M. Schwabe in 1949 (with a bibliography up to 1948), and a volume of appreciation on the occasion of his 70th birthday (1954). In 1969 a volume of his essays appeared in English, *Israel and the Diaspora.*

BIBLIOGRAPHY: D.J. Cohen in: *Zion*, 18 (1955), 169–99; 23–24 (1958–59), 102–8; *Devarim al Prof. Benzion Dinur Sar ha-Ḥinnukh ve-ha-Tarbut bi-Melot Lo Shivim Shanah* (1954), includes biographical notes.

°**DIO CASSIUS** (c. 160–230 C.E.), author of a Roman history, written in Greek. Dio frequently records the religious zeal and self-sacrificing spirit of the Jews. "Such was the fervor of their piety that the first Jews made prisoners during the conquest of the Temple by *Sosius [governor of Syria under Antony, 37 B.C.E.] obtained by their supplications permission to reenter the sanctuary on the day of Saturn [Sabbath] and devote themselves with their compatriots to their temple ritual" (*Historia*, 49:22). In some respects, his account of the Jewish war (66–70 C.E.) is more favorable to the Jews than that given by *Josephus. According to Dio, during the siege of Jerusalem, Titus received an injury to his left shoulder causing permanent weakness to his left hand. Some Roman soldiers deserted to the Jews because they believed that the town was impregnable. Dio, in common with Tacitus, notes the bravery of the Jews and commented that they were happy to fall near the

Temple and in its defense. Although they were a few arrayed against the might of the Roman army, they only gave in when a part of the Temple was in flames. "All believed that it was not a disaster but victory, salvation, and happiness to perish together with the Temple" (*Historia*, 66:6). Neither Vespasian nor Titus wished to assume the title of "Judaicus" (possibly because that title might imply sympathy with Judaic teachings). Dio offers information about Jewish rebellions under Trajan and Hadrian. He loved the sensational and reports that the outbreak of Jewish revolts in the time of Trajan (115–117 C.E.) in Cyprus, Cyrene, and Egypt, was marked by scenes of stark horror (*Epitome*, 68:32). The Jews committed horrible outrages, as the papyri likewise suggest, "destroying both Greeks and Romans." The immediate cause of the Jewish revolt under *Bar Kokhba (132 C.E.) was Hadrian's intention to build a new city and temple on the ruins of Jerusalem as the official center of the colony of Aelia Capitolina. According to Dio, the defenders recruited soldiers from all countries of the Empire and beyond the Euphrates inhabited by their "fellow-nationals." The solidarity of Jews elsewhere in the Empire with the Judean rebels under Bar Kokhba is also stressed by Dio (*Epitome*, 69:13). In common with *Fronto, he reports that in the Bar Kokhba war the Romans sustained such severe losses that Hadrian, writing to the Senate, omitted the customary opening formula "I and my troops are well." Dio's remark that "all those who observe the Jewish law may be called Jews, from whatever ethnic group they derive," reflects the transformation of the Jewish nation into a worldwide religious community, with a steadily increasing number of proselytes. Like other writers of antiquity, he blames the Jews for their unsociable character and has little understanding for the practice of the Sabbath; but he pays homage to the Jews' imageless cult and their only and unique God. The Jews, he states "are distinguished from other nations by their whole mode of living, but particularly by the fact that they do not honor any of the other gods, adoring only one and with great fervor. There is no image of their divinity even in Jerusalem. They believe God to be ineffable and invisible, yet they devote to him a more fervent cult than all other mortals [see *Tacitus]. The Temple in Jerusalem is very large and beautiful. The day of Saturn on which they fulfill a number of particular rites and refrain from doing any serious work is consecrated to the Sanctuary." Dio Cassius repeats the commonplace (see *Plutarch) that Jerusalem was captured on the Sabbath because the Jews refrained from defending it on that day. He alluded to Jewish proselytism in his statement that Domitian had people put to death on the charge of "atheism," which in fact meant the acceptance of Jewish customs (*Epitome*, 67:14). The accusation of atheism was leveled against both Jews and Christians because they refused to share in the official heathen cult. Although, as mentioned, Dio Cassius shows contempt for Jewish observances and misunderstanding of the inner spirit of Judaism, he nevertheless admires the Jews' loyalty to their pure belief and their persistence in the face of repression. Jewish history in Rome may be summed up in the words of Dio Cassius: "Though often suppressed, they nevertheless mightily increase, so that they achieve even the free practice of their customs."

BIBLIOGRAPHY: Reinach, Textes, 179ff.; Bentwich, in: JQR, 23 (1932/33), 340ff.; Schuerer, Hist, 301ff.; Juster, Juifs, 2 (1914), 186ff. **ADD. BIBLIOGRAPHY:** M. Stern (ed.), *Greek and Latin Authors on Jews and Judaism*, vol. 2 (1980), 347–407.

[Solomon Rappaport]

°**DIO CHRYSOSTOM** ("golden-mouthed," called so for his eloquence; **Dio of Prusa**; c. 40–120 C.E.), orator. According to the testimony of his biographer, Synesius (c. 365–413/414; Bishop of Cyrene), in one of his speeches Dio described the *Essenes as a utopian-like community living "in the interior of Palestine" near the Dead Sea in the vicinity of Sodom.

BIBLIOGRAPHY: M. Stern (ed.), *Greek and Latin Authors on Jews and Judaism*. vol. 1 (1974), 538–40.

[Shimon Gibson (2nd ed.)]

°**DIOCLETIAN, CAIUS VALERIANUS**, Roman emperor 284–305 C.E. Diocletian is mentioned in Jewish sources on various occasions, particularly in the Jerusalem Talmud, and despite their aggadic embellishments they appear to contain at least a kernel of historical truth. Thus the fact that he was of lowly birth, the son of a humble scribe or of a slave (Eutropius, *Breviarium* 9:19, 2), is embellished in the Talmud to the effect that in his youth he was a swineherd, and the pupils of the Nasi Judah II used to mock and beat him. When he became emperor he sought to revenge himself on the Jews and summoned Judah to appear before him. Judah answered that they had derided Diocletian the swineherd but not Diocletian the emperor (TJ, Ter. 8:11, 46b). It is known that Diocletian was in Palestine, and in Tiberias, both in 286, during the patriarchate of Judah II, and during his campaign against the Persians (297–8), and it is probable that he had contact with the leading Jews there. Similarly there is an echo of the heavy taxation which he imposed in Palestine in the story that the inhabitants of Paneas went into exile as a result of these taxes, and returned only after 30 years (TJ, Shev. 9:2, 38d).

Diocletian showed a certain tolerance toward the Jews, one of the reasons probably being that Judaism – unlike Christianity – had been declared a *religio licita* by the Romans. Thus, when he imposed a tax to provide sacrifices to the gods – a fact explicitly mentioned in the Talmud (TJ, Av. Zar. 5:4, 44a) – he excluded the Jews, but not the Samaritans, from this impost. The Jews reacted favorably to this treatment. It is stated that Hiyya b. Abba, who was a kohen, crossed a cemetery in order to meet him (TJ, Ber. 3:1, 6a). Shortly after his stay in Tiberias he issued an edict against bigamy (Cod. Just. 5:5, 2) and against a man marrying his niece, but they do not appear to have been applied to the Jews. The Talmud quotes an inscription which Diocletian inscribed when he dedicated a market place to Hercules (or Heraclius) in Tyre (Av. Zar. 1:4, 39d) and that he instituted waterworks in Syria. Evidence of his stay there is confirmed from the Codex of Justinian (14:41, 9).

BIBLIOGRAPHY: T. Mommsen, *Juristische Schriften*, vol. 2, pp. 196ff.; idem, in: *Verhandlungen der Berliner Akademie* (1860), 417ff.; Rappoport, *Erekh Millin*, 1 (1914), s.v. *Erkulis*; Kohut, Arukh, Suppl., 49; Halevy, Dorot, 2, 337; M. Rostovtzev, *A Social and Economic History of the Roman Empire* (1926).

°**DIODORUS OF SICILY** (first century B.C.E.), author of a world history (called the "Library") in 40 books, from the creation of the world to Caesar's conquest of Britain in 54 B.C.E. Hecataeus of Abdera was the source for his account of the Jews (40. frag. 2). Diodorus notes that "Moyses" claimed to have received his laws from the god named Iao. He also provided a narrative on the capture of Jerusalem by the Romans in 63 B.C.E.

BIBLIOGRAPHY: J. Palm, *Über Sprache und Stil des Diodoros von Sizilien* (1955), pp. 167–89 in M. Stern (ed.), *Greek and Latin Authors on Jews and Judaism*, vol. 1 (1974).

[Shimon Gibson (2nd ed.)]

°**DIODOTUS-TRYPHON** (d. 137 B.C.E.), rebel against *Demetrius II, king of Syria. According to Strabo, Tryphon came from Casiana (according to Josephus from Apameia). He served in the army of Alexander Balas and when uprisings began against the rule of Demetrius II, he headed the insurgents in Larissa. Another step that won him wide support in Syria was his taking care of Antiochus, the minor son of Alexander *Balas, who at one time had been handed over to the Arab Malichus, ostensibly in order to prepare him for the throne. Tryphon appointed himself regent to the young king and assembled a large armed force. Demetrius was defeated by Tryphon and compelled to withdraw from Antiochia, whereupon Tryphon entered with the lad and gave him the title Antiochus VI. However the war between Demetrius and Tryphon continued.

In Judea Tryphon succeeded in attracting to his side *Jonathan the Hasmonean, whom he confirmed in the high-priesthood in the name of "king" Antiochus, and appointed his brother *Simeon strategus of the whole coast from the boundary with Tyre to the border of Egypt. Jonathan gave considerable aid to Tryphon. He won over to himself a large part of the army of Demetrius, and grew so powerful that he became suspect in the eyes of Tryphon. As far as can be seen Tryphon aimed at that time at deposing the young Antiochus and proclaiming himself king. Suspecting that Jonathan might stand in his way he decided to remove him. He encountered the high priest at the head of a large army in Beth-Shean. Unable to make an attack on Jonathan, Tryphon employed a subterfuge. He loaded him with many gifts and honors and persuaded him to send his main army away, and keep only a small force. When Jonathan came to Ptolemais with only 1,000 men, Tryphon fell upon him, murdered his men, and imprisoned him. He then proceeded to conquer Judea, but Jonathan's brother Simeon acted swiftly and with great energy, and was ready for battle when Tryphon arrived at the head of his army. Tryphon at first tried to negotiate and promised to release Jonathan in exchange for a ransom and hostages, but he did not fulfill his promises and war ensued. However Tryphon was unsuccessful in his efforts to reach Jerusalem and he retreated northward. On the way Jonathan was put to death. Tryphon also put to death the young Antiochus, who was no longer important for his purposes, and proclaimed himself king (142/143 B.C.E.). The war between him and Demetrius continued for some years, and this state of affairs was largely unchanged even after Demetrius was captured by the Parthians. Antiochus (Sidetes) seized the kingdom and succeeded in defeating Tryphon, who had fortified himself in Dora where he was besieged. Dora was compelled to submit to Antiochus, and Tryphon slipped away to Orthosia in Apamea where he committed suicide.

BIBLIOGRAPHY: I Macc. 11:39–15:39; Jos., Ant., 13:131ff.; Schuerer, Gesch, 1 (1901³/⁴), 172ff., 234ff.; E.R. Bevan, *The House of Seleucus*, 2 (1902), 226ff., 236ff.; B. Niese, *Geschichte der griechischen und makedonischen Staaten*, 3 (1903), 277ff., 281ff.

[Abraham Schalit]

°**DIOGENES LAERTIUS** (third century C.E.?), author of "Lives of the Philosophers" (*Vitae Philosophorum*), a eulogistic account of the ancient Greek philosophers. In the prologue (1, 9) he mentions the view of some writers which traces the origin of the Jews back to the Magi. In a separate work, "Life of Socrates," Diogenes mentions that the Jewish historian Justus of Tiberias is the authority in regard to Plato's appearance at the trial of Socrates.

BIBLIOGRAPHY: M. Stern (ed.), *Greek and Latin Authors on Jews and Judaism*, vol. 2 (1980), 332–34.

[Shimon Gibson (2nd ed.)]

°**DIONYSIUS VAN RYCKEL (Denis the Carthusian, Denys van Leeuwen**; 1402–1471), Christian theologian and mystic, born in Ryckel, Belgium. He studied at Cologne University and in 1424 joined the Carthusian order at Roermond (Holland). A prolific and popular writer, he wrote commentaries on the Bible, the works of Boethius, Peter Lombard, John Climacus, and Dionysius the Pseudo-Areopagite, and was acquainted with the works of Greek as well as Arab and Jewish philosophers. He was also the author of works on moral theology and religious discipline. His theories concerning the Jews and their destiny appear in the seventh book of his "Dialogue on the Catholic Faith," entitled "On the Proof of the Christian Faith Based Upon the Law and the Prophets, and on the Errors of the Jews" (in his *Opera*, 18 (1896), 471ff.). Although attacking the Jews as enemies of the Church and an offense to Jesus, Dionysius considers that they should be tolerated as part of God's holy design.

BIBLIOGRAPHY: Swenden, in: DHGE, 14 (1960), 256–60 (incl. bibl.); K. Schilling (ed.), *Monumenta Judaica, Handbuch* (1963), 148.

DIONYSUS, CULT OF, the cult of the Greek god of wine and fertility. The non-Jews of Alexandria and Rome alleged that the cult of Dionysus was widespread among Jews. Plutarch gives a Bacchanalian interpretation to the Feast of Tabernacles:

> "After the festival called 'the fast' [the Day of Atonement], during the vintage, the Jews place tables laden with different fruits in booths of thickets woven from vines and ivy. Their first festival is called by them *Sukkah* (σκηνή). A few days later, the Jews celebrate another festival, which one may simply call a Bacchanalian festival. For this is a festival on which the Jews carry fig branches and sticks adorned with ivy and carry them into the Temple. One does not know" – adds Plutarch – "what they do in the Temple. It seems reasonable to suppose that they practice rites in honor of Bacchus. For they blow small horns as the people of Argos do during the festival of Dionysus, and call upon their god. Others, who are called Levites, walk in front, either in allusion to Lysios (λύσιος) – perhaps 'the god who attenuates curses' – or because they call out 'Euius,' i.e., Bacchus."

According to Plutarch the subject of the connection between the Dionysian and Jewish cults was raised during a symposium held at Aidepsos in Euboea, with a certain Moiragenes linking the Jewish Sabbath with the cult of Bacchus, because "even now many people call the Bacchi 'Sabboi' and call out that word when they perform the orgies of Bacchus." Tacitus too thought that Jews served the god Liber, i.e., Bacchus-Dionysus, but "whereas the festival of Liber is joyful, the Jewish festival of Liber is sordid and absurd." According to Pliny, *Beth-Shean was founded by Dionysus after he had buried his wet nurse Nysa in its soil. His intention was to enlarge the area of the grave, which he surrounded with a city wall although there were as yet no inhabitants. Then the god chose the Scythians from among his companions, and in order to encourage them, honored them by calling the new city Scythopolis after them (Pliny, *Natural History* 5:18, 74). An inscription found at Beth-Shean dating from the time of Marcus Aurelius mentions that Dionysus was honored there as *ktistes*. Stephen of Byzantium reports a legend that connects the founding of the city of Rafa also with Dionysus (for the Dionysian foundation legends of cities in the region, see Lichtenberger's study). It is wrong to assume as some do that Plutarch took his account of the festival of Tabernacles from an antisemitic source, for despite all the woeful ignorance in his account it contains no accusation against, or abuse of, the Jews. It is more likely that Plutarch described the festival of Tabernacles from observation, interpreting it in accordance with his own philosophical outlook, which does not prevent him, however, from introducing into it features of the cult of the famous Temple of Jerusalem gleaned by him in his wide reading. The description as a whole, however, is of Tabernacles as it was celebrated in the Greek diaspora at the end of the first and the beginning of the second century C.E., and not as it was celebrated in the Temple, which had already been destroyed for more than a generation. The festival undoubtedly absorbed influences from the environment, so that Plutarch could indeed have witnessed what he recognized as customs of the Dionysian feast.

BIBLIOGRAPHY: Reinach, Textes, 142–7 (= Plutarch, *Moralia, Quaestiones Convivales* 4:671D–672B), 309 (= *Tacitus, Historiae*, 5:5); Buechler, in: rej, 37 (1898), 181–202; Schuerer, Gesch, 3 (1909[4]), 151. **ADD. BIBLIOGRAPHY:** M. Stern (ed.), *Greek and Latin Authors on Jews and Judaism*, vol. 1 (1974), 545ff.; A. Lichtenberger, "City Foundation Legends in the Decapolis," in: *Bulletin of the Anglo-Israel Archaeological Society* 22 (2004), 23–34.

[Abraham Schalit / Shimon Gibson (2nd ed.)]

°**DIOS** (**Dius**; c. 2nd century B.C.E.), historian, quoted by Josephus, who refers to him as "an accurate historian of Phoenicia" (Ant., 8:146–9; Contra Apionem, 1:112–5). Dios relates that King Solomon sent riddles to King Hiram ("Hirom") of Tyre, asking him to send him others in return, on the understanding that the one who failed to solve them would forfeit a sum of money. Hiram agreed and, unable to find the solutions, forfeited a large sum. Subsequently, however, with the aid of a Tyrian named Abdemon, Hiram not only solved Solomon's riddles but sent him others which Solomon could not solve. He had then to repay to Hiram more than he received. Dios also indicates that Hiram transformed Tyre by building up the eastern side with embanked fortifications and enlarging the town, linking it by a causeway to the off-shore island with a Temple of Zeus/Baal Shamin.

BIBLIOGRAPHY: M. Stern (ed.), *Greek and Latin* Authors *on Jews and Judaism*. vol. 1 (1974), 123–25.

[Shimon Gibson (2nd ed.)]

°**DIOSCORIDES PEDANIUS** (first century C.E.), pharmacologist from Anazarba in Cilicy, author of *De Materia Medica*. Dioscorides has a few references to materials of medical use found in Judaea, notably the balsam, the resin of the terebinth tree, asphalt (presumably from the Dead Sea), oil made from Ban (*Balanites aegyptica*), and scammony. He also makes reference to an item called the "Jewish stone," which, when dissolved and drunk with hot water, was thought to cure stones in the bladder. Dioscorides later exercised a great influence on medieval medicine. Ḥisdai ibn Shaprut took part in the revision of the Arabic translation of his work and Maimonides may have utilized it.

BIBLIOGRAPHY: M. Stern (ed.), *Greek and Latin Authors on Jews and Judaism*, vol. 1 (1974): 422–25.

[Shimon Gibson (2nd ed.)]

DIRINGER, DAVID (1900–1975), epigraphist and Orientalist. Born in Tłumacz (Galicia), Diringer studied at the University of Florence (Italy), where he later was appointed professor (1931–33). Diringer's main interest at first was the culture of the Etruscans. As a consequence of the anti-Jewish policy of Fascist Italy, Diringer moved in 1939 to England where he taught Semitic epigraphy at Cambridge University (1948). In England he specialized in Northwestern Semitic inscriptions and the history of the alphabet. At Cambridge he founded in his home a museum devoted to the history of writing systems, which he later transferred to Tel Aviv.

Among Diringer's publications, some scholarly and some for the general public, are *Le iscrizioni antico-ebraiche palesti-*

nesi (1934); *L'alfabeto nella storia della civiltà* (1937); *The Alphabet – A Key to the History of Mankind* (1953) together with R. Regensburger; *The Hand-Produced Book* (1953); *The Illuminated Book, Its History and Production* (1958); *Writing: Ancient Peoples and Places* (1962); *The Illuminated Book* (1967^2); *The Story of the Aleph Bet* (1960); *Writing* (1962); *The Alphabet* (2 vols., 1963); and *The Book Before Printing: Ancient, Medieval and Oriental* (1982).

[Meir Ydit]

DISCHE, ZACHARIAS (1895–1988), U.S. biochemist. Dische was born in Sambor (then Austria-Hungary, today Poland), the nephew of Leon *Reich. World War I broke out while Dische was studying at the University of Lvov and, after completing the first year of his medical studies, he was drafted into the Austrian army. He completed his medical degree in 1921 at the University of Vienna, where he became head of the chemistry laboratory of the physiological institute in 1931. Dische continued his research there until the *Anschluss* in 1938, when he was forced to flee Austria, first for Paris and later for the Medical School of Marseille. He reached America in 1941 and was appointed to the faculty at Columbia University in New York in 1947, becoming professor of biochemistry in 1957 and professor emeritus in 1963.

Dische discovered the basic reaction of the pentose phosphate cycle, the first example of feedback inhibition of a metabolic process. His contributions to scientific journals cover the biochemistry of sugars, the quantitative analysis of DNA sugars, polysaccharides in animal tissues, the cellular metabolism of blood and ocular tissues, and other biochemical topics. His analysis of the lens capsule was a model for basement membrane investigations in general. In 1965 he was awarded the Proctor Medal, the highest award in basic science in ophthalmology. He was elected to the National Academy of Sciences in 1976.

BIBLIOGRAPHY: Editorial, in: *Investigative Ophthalmology & Visual Science* (July 1988).

[Ruth Rossing (2nd ed.)]

DISCIPLINE, MANUAL OF ("The Sectarian Document" or "The Rule of the Community"; Heb. סֶרֶךְ הַיַּחַד, *Serekh ha-Yaḥad;* abbr. 1QS), one of the *Dead Sea Scrolls, found in the spring of 1947 near Qumran; now in the Israel Museum's Shrine of the Book in Jerusalem. The designation "Manual of Discipline" was coined by the American scholars Burrows, Trever and Brownlee – who were the first to study the scroll, and who published a facsimile edition in 1951 under that title. Since then at least ten fragmentary copies of the *Manual* have been discovered in two caves (IV and V) in the vicinity of the Qumran ruin where, according to most scholars, these and many other manuscripts were copied in Hellenistic and Roman times, before 70 C.E., by members of a Jewish religious community.

Description

The manuscript is about 6 ft. 2 in. (1.86 m.) long and c. 10 inches (24 cm.) high and is made up of five pieces of parchment sewn together. Originally other sheets of parchment were attached to 1QS; these fragments were later found in Cave 1 and have been labeled $1QS^a$ (usually appearing as superscript a) and $1QS^b$ (usually appearing as superscript b). 1QS has 11 columns of Hebrew writing (with an average of 26 lines to each column); the scroll is well preserved and contains only a few lacunae, but from the occurrence of some erasures and insertions it has been concluded that, in its present form, the text (slightly corrupt in some places) is the work of more than one scribe. The margins of the manuscript contain curious symbols some of which are also found in the First (Great) Isaiah Scroll ($1QIsa^a$) found together with the *Manual*; the meaning of these symbols is unknown.

Contents

1QS is first and foremost a religious document focused on various aspects of life within "the community" (Heb. הַיַּחַד, *ha-yaḥad*). 1QS 1:1–18a contains a series of statements about the ideal life to which the members pledged themselves at the annual renewal of the covenant which is described in 1:18b–3:12; on that occasion the "priests" and the "levites" pronounced (a) praises to God, (b) blessings of "all the men of God's lot," (c) curses against "all the men of Belial's lot," and (d) curses against unworthy members of the movement. A communal confession of sins was an important feature of this ceremony which was followed by the priests' pronouncement of an expanded version of the *Priestly Blessing (Num. 6:24–26). This liturgical part of 1QS ends with a warning to members not to rely on the efficacy of ablutions carried out mechanically for "it is by an upright and humble spirit that sin can be atoned" (3:8). Some scholars assume that baptismal rites formed part of this annual renewal of membership although this is not explicitly stated, 1QS 3:13–4:26 is a treatise which explains in theological terms the position of the members of the community in this world, as well as their destiny in the world to come. The basic theme of the sharp division of mankind into members and those outside – already clear from the preceding homiletic and liturgical parts – is here seen as ultimately due to God's providential planning of everything from the Creation on. He has given man two "spirits" (of "truth" and "iniquity") which struggle with each other in the heart of everyone (4:23). As a result of this conflict mankind is divided into sons of "truth," "righteousness," and "light" on the one hand, and of "iniquity" on the other. The two "spirits" are not to be taken as cosmic, dualistic principles (as in Zoroastrian theology), but in accordance with the use of "spirit" in Hebrew psychology (cf. within the pseudepigraphical books Test. Patr., Judah 20:1 which affords a close parallel to the *Manual* here). Nor is the "dualism" expressed here either absolute, physical, or cosmic but ethical and eschatological: God is in control from beginning to end, and "the angel of darkness," though in charge of the "sons of iniquity," is clearly inferior to God, in the same way as the "prince of lights" rules over the "sons of righteousness" in a capacity subordinate to God, who, for some unknown reason beyond human understanding ("according to His mysteries," 3:23), allows the "angel of darkness" enough power to cause the "sons of righteousness" to sin "during the period fixed by Him." Eventually, however, God will utterly destroy the spirit of iniquity from a part of mankind by a holy spirit (4:20ff.). The pious, chosen by God and yet responsible for their acts, will then enjoy "healing and great peace… together with everlasting blessings, endless gladness in everlasting life … in eternal light" (4:6ff.). The damned will suffer "eternal perdition … together with the disgrace of annihilation in the fire of murky Hell" (4:12ff.). Neither the Messiah nor the Resurrection is mentioned. The theory of Zoroastrian influence in this treatise, although accepted by many scholars, is rejected by others, who feel that the themes of the essay are satisfactorily explained against the general background of apocalyptic circles of the time. Apart from a penal code (6:24–7:25), which contains a list of punishments for various offenses (such as cursing God, telling a lie, rebelling against authority, guffawing, and spitting in the assembly), the section 5:1–9:25 is not easily divided into subsections. In a verbose and repetitive manner, often echoing biblical language, the author enumerates the ethical ideals of the members of the community (truth, unity, humility, righteousness, love, etc.; e.g., 5:4 and 8:2ff.), describes the community in quasi-poetical passages (e.g., metaphorically as a spiritual temple consisting of "Aaron" and "Israel," i.e., priestly and lay members, 5:6; 8:5ff.), and alludes to the perfect lives of the members as being capable of atoning for sins, not only their own (5:6; 8:3, 10; 9:4). From such homiletic passages, aimed at impressing the lofty vocation and status of the community on the reader, the author passes on to aspects of organization, admission of members (5:7ff.; 20ff., 6:13ff.; 8:16ff.), and communal activities such as meals and deliberations (6:2ff.); at the latter, problems of scriptural interpretation, as well as any matter of concern to the community, were discussed. This long section, indispensable for an understanding of the inner life and spiritual nature of the Qumran community or the religious movement centered there, ends with a summary of the virtues characteristic of the *maskil* ("the wise man"), the ideal member of the sect. Almost imperceptibly, transition is made to a set of at least three hymns of praise (10:1–8a; 10:8b–11:15a, and 11:15b–22) with which 1QS comes to an end. The main themes of these compositions are indicated in 10:23: "With thanksgiving hymns I will open my mouth, and the righteous deeds of God shall my tongue enumerate always, together with the faithlessness of man and his utter sinfulness." The author, as a human being, is sinful (11:9f.), but God has forgiven him and granted him "righteousness" (10:11; 11:12), and that is the reason for praising Him at all times (10:1ff.). (For the use of the word "righteousness" in the meaning of "Divine grace," see 11:14, 2.) These concluding hymns belong to the same literary genre as the compositions contained in the **Thanksgiving Psalms* (1QH) which were found in Cave I together with the *Manual*. Some scholars claim that these contents form a literary unit whereas others claim that 1QS contains a number of originally separate texts copied onto the same scroll. It is generally assumed, however, that the contents of the scroll all go back to the same religious circles; an exception to this view is that of Del Medico who has argued for the theory that 1QS not only is not a literary unit, but also that the various parts, of which in his view the text of the manuscript is made up, go back to different Jewish religious circles. It must be conceded, however, that there is a unity of language and style in the *Manual*; nor can it be said that the various sections are unrelated to each other, or that they have been put together in an entirely haphazard fashion. Furthermore, the fact mentioned above that other copies of the work are in existence suggests that a traditional form of it was copied and recopied through a fairly long period.

Language and Date

The language of the *Manual* is akin to biblical rather than mishnaic Hebrew, and its text must have been copied, or at least composed, at a time when there was little or no difference between the literary language of sacred writings (as attested by the consonantal text of the Hebrew Bible) and the spoken Hebrew of everyday life. Paleographically 1QS is dated by experts to around 100 B.C.E. and if these datings are correct other copies now lost were probably in circulation at an even earlier time (second century B.C.E.) among the many local groups within the religious movement for whom the document was intended. Linguistically 1QS is akin to the Great Isaiah Scroll (1QIsa[a]) which is supposed by many scholars to have originated in pre-canonical times, i.e., certainly before the first century C.E. – and long before the vocalization of the standard text by the masoretes in the early Middle Ages. The two manuscripts have some characteristic features in common, such as profuse application of vowel letters, a certain resemblance to Samaritan as regards pronominal suffixes, and – in the forms of nouns and verbs – a degree of influence from Aramaic which was then spoken in Palestine. Hebrew was undoubtedly spoken by the Jews in Palestine at this time, and therefore, the occurrence of words otherwise only known from late sources is not to be taken as pointing to a late date for the *Manual*.

Life and Identity of the Religious Circles Described in 1QS

No precise information about the history of the religious movement described in 1QS is available in either the document itself or in any other related text. However, the importance attached to the priestly element within the *Yaḥad* and the explicit reference to the "sons of Zadok," are usually taken to suggest that the *Yaḥad* originated in a schism within the Jerusalem priesthood in early Hasmonean times, as a result of which some Zadokite priests established a religious center at Qumran, possibly together with sympathizers among the *Hassideans. Cut off from the sacrificial cult at the central sanctuary they devoted themselves there to the study of the Scriptures (the Law and the Prophets), whose meaning was "found" or "revealed" by an allegorizing type of interpretation an example of which occurs in 8:13ff.: "When these become a community by these norms in Israel, they shall separate themselves from the session of the men of iniquity by going out into the wilderness in order to clear His way there; as it is written: 'In the wilderness make clear the way of.... [four dots are used in the manuscript to indicate the Tetragrammaton], level in the desert a highway for our God.' This alludes to the study of the Law which He has commanded through Moses to do, according to everything which has been revealed time and again, and according to that which the Prophets have revealed by His holy spirit." In this passage and elsewhere (5:1, 10; 8:10; 9:5, 9, 20ff.) the members are urged to "separate themselves" (verb נבדל) from iniquity, and a long passage (5: 11ff.) is devoted to a denunciation of the godless with whom the pious must have no dealings: they must not get involved in arguments with them, nor disclose any of their rules of conduct to them (9:16f.). The full members, whose exact place within the society was strictly defined according to seniority, learning, and behavior, ate, blessed and deliberated together (6:2ff.); new members, if approved by existing members and the inspector (*ha-mevakker* or *ha-pakid*), were admitted at the end of two years after which trial period they bound themselves by oath "to return to the Law of Moses ... according to everything which has been revealed from it to the sons of Zadok, the priests who keep the covenant and seek His pleasure" (6:8ff.). Their property was then pooled with the property of the community and they themselves were allocated a seat at the communal meals, and from then on they were entitled to take part in its deliberations (6:4). A degree of ownership of property is presupposed in some passages, and poverty does not in itself seem to have been regarded as an ideal. Women are not mentioned in 1QS, and most scholars assume that the members of the *Yaḥad* were unmarried; women are, however, referred to in other texts which were either found near Qumran or appear to have originated in related religious circles. Parts of the *Manual* (as, e.g., the liturgy of the annual renewal of the covenant) must refer to events which took place at the Qumran center; and in 8:1ff. a special group of 15 members (12 laymen and three priests) is mentioned who can hardly have lived anywhere else. It is clear, however, from 6:3, 6 that there were local groups – some of them consisting of no more than 10 members (the required minimum) – in various parts of the country, within which the levitical laws of purity were strictly observed and the Scriptures were intensely studied. Much in the *Manual* may be taken as referring to such "Qumranian" fellowships anywhere in the country, and some Jewish scholars have attempted to establish a connection between these and the *ḥavurot* ("fellowships") of the early Pharisees which are described in the Talmud in terms which are partly identical with those employed in 1QS of the Qumran *Yaḥad*. That is not to say, however, that the Qumran "sectarians" are necessarily identified with the Pharisees. None of the designations applied in 1QS to the members contains any clue as to their exact identity; it is clear that the movement was priestly, ritualistic, legalistic, with a bent toward secrecy, mysticism, and apocalypticism, but these qualifications do not in their totality fit any of the known Jewish religious groups in late Judaism, including the Essenes, although there are suggestive similarities (as well as some differences) between Josephus' description of the latter and the *Manual*. Most scholars accept the view that the Qumran *Yaḥad* was Essene. If the theory is correct, lQS, apart from enabling us to check Josephus' information on a number of points, adds considerably to the knowledge of a branch of Judaism which, even before the Scrolls were discovered, was thought by some to form the background out of which Christianity grew. Within the New Testament the most suggestive points of contact with the *Manual* are found in the Johannine group of writings and in the Epistle to the Hebrews.

Related Documents

A fragment containing the Hebrew title of 1QS ([סר]ך היחד; [ser]ekh *ha-yaḥad*), and 1QS^{a} and 1QS^{b} mentioned above, were all originally attached to 1QS. As, however, the bottom quarter of the last column of 1QS is left blank, the Manual clearly ends at 1QS 11:22, and has presumably always done so. That there is a literary relationship between 1QS^{a} ("the Rule of the Congregation"), 1QS^{b} (several fragments making up a collection of benedictions) and 1QS is certain in view of some degree of phraseological similarity (especially between 1QS^{a} 2:11ff. (the messianic banquet of the Congregation) and 1QS 6:4ff. (the daily meal of the members of the *Yaḥad*)). It is possible, however, that these texts do not all refer to the same religious circles because of differences in contents (1QS^{a}, e.g., is martial (possibly Hassidean) in character and deals with aspects of family life); it was perhaps from among the circles referred to in 1QS that the *Yaḥad* of the *Manual* arose; and at least the major part of another, larger document ("the Damascus Document," CD) also probably dates back to the time before the *Manual* was composed.

[Preben Wernberg-Møller]

A Theory of Composition

A general hypothesis of composition was proposed by J. Murphy O'Connor in 1969, with 1QS developing to meet the needs of the Community at different stages in its history, as follows: (1) 1QS 8:1–10a, 12b–16a, 9:3–10:8: with a Teacher of Righteousness proposing the establishment of the Community in the Wilderness, to serve as a spiritual temple and run by a priestly core; (2) 1QS 8:10–12a, 8:16b–9:2, interpolations relating to the attempt to deal with failures of obedience within the Community; (3) 1QS 5:1–13, 6:8–23, 6:24–7:25, the organizational redefinition of the Community as an institution, with new legislation for the assembly and for the admittance of new recruits; (4) 1QS 1:1–3:12, 3:13–4:23a, 4:23b–26, 10:9–11:22, with attempts being made to revitalize the spiritual life of the Community.

[Shimon Gibson (2nd ed.)]

BIBLIOGRAPHY: TEXT: M. Burrows et al., *The Dead Sea Scrolls of St. Mark's Monastery*, vol. 2, fasc. 2 (1951); TRANSLATIONS AND COMMENTARIES: W.H. Brownlee, *The Dead Sea Manual of Discipline* (1951); P. Wernberg-Møller, *The Manual of Discipline Translated and Annotated (Studies on the Texts of the Desert of Judah)*, ed. by J. van der Ploeg, 1 (1957); GENERAL WORKS: A. Dupont-Sommer, *The Jewish Sect of Qumran and the Essenes* (1954); H.H. Rowley, *The Zadokite Fragments and the Dead Sea Scrolls* (1952); Wernberg-Møller, in: *Annual of Leeds University Oriental Society*, 6 (1969), 56–8. **ADD. BIBLIOGRAPHY:** P.R. Davies, *Behind the Essenes: History and Ideology in the Dead Sea Scrolls* (1987); Charlesworth, J.H. (ed.), *The Dead Sea Scrolls: Hebrew, Aramaic, and Greek Texts with English Translations.* vol. 1: *Rule of the Community and Related Documents* (1994); THEORY OF COMPOSITION: J. Murphy O'Connor, "La genése litteraire de la Règle de la Communauté," in: *Revue Biblique* 76 (1969), 528–49; idem, "The Essenes and Their History," in: *Revue Biblique*, 81 (1974), 215–44.

DISCRIMINATION, distinguishing between people on the basis of the group to which the person belongs rather than individual characteristics. With rare exceptions, contemporary forms of discrimination against Jews were not based upon the type of legal device and sanction that reached its apotheosis with the *Nuremberg laws. The postwar disclosure of the details of the Holocaust generated such massive popular revulsion that legal forms of antisemitism became taboo, for the gas chambers and the concentration camps were the ultimate consequence of legalized anti-Jewish discrimination. Antisemitism continued to find expression in the contemporary world in non-legislative discriminatory patterns. Sophisticated formulations to mask the antisemitic intent of the pattern were elaborated, and in no case could the pattern appear to be overtly antisemitic. Even where complete or almost complete exclusion of Jews was practiced, the rationale for such action had to be explained on grounds other than religious or ethnic discrimination. The more characteristic pattern took the form of "tokenism" (i.e., the admission of one or a few Jews into a non-Jewish milieu) or a quota system, which restricted the number of Jews to a precise or approximate percentage of the total composition.

The overall pattern of discrimination was selective in character: not all or almost all Jews were the objects of discrimination and not all or almost all spheres of public life were the loci of the discriminatory pattern. There were, however, certain major postwar exceptions to the selective character of non-legislative discrimination. During the "Black Years" in the Soviet Union (1948–53), virtually all Jews were subject to some form of discrimination, and many were even more harshly treated. A similar phenomenon occurred in Poland during 1968, with the difference that Polish Jews were permitted and even encouraged to emigrate. These anti-Jewish campaigns were deliberately masked, however, in the first case as "anti-*Cosmopolitanism," and in the second as "anti-Zionism."

Soviet Union

The Soviet Union, where in 1970 approximately one-quarter of the world's Jewish population lived, offered a classic example of how antisemitic motivation on the highest level was expressed in either exclusion, tokenism, or quota techniques. Andrei D. Sakharov, the distinguished Soviet physicist and co-creator of the hydrogen bomb, acknowledged in 1968 that "in the highest bureaucratic elite of [the Soviet] government, the spirit of antisemitism was never fully dispelled after the 1930s." A burgeoning Russian nationalism, which fed upon traditional antisemitism and was reinforced by the determination to erect barriers against Western influences and contacts, provided the motivation for the policy, as Jews, characteristically, had family as well as spiritual and cultural links with the West. Sakharov specifically mentioned the Soviet Union's "appointments policy" as the device by which discrimination against Jews was effected. That "appointments policy" excluded Jews from all key policy-making positions. Whereas the percentage of Jews in the Central Committee of the Communist Party was 10.8% in 1939, over the course of years, the percentage was reduced to almost nil – only one Jew remained in the Central Committee in 1970. There were no Jews in the Politburo, the Orgburo, or the top levels of the Secretariat. In the sensitive areas of diplomacy, security, foreign trade, and military affairs there were virtually no Jews: at the top levels, there was none at all; elsewhere in the hierarchy there were less than a handful. The political sphere, which embraced soviets on various levels and which was manipulated by the Communist Party apparatus, was characterized by "tokenism," whereby a tiny percentage of Jews was selected by the party. In contrast with the composition of the Supreme Soviet in 1937, for example, when approximately 3.5% of the deputies were Jewish (before the new "appointments policy" had been instituted), at the end of the 1960s, with a membership of some 1,500, it contained a token number of Jews – 0.25%. The same percentage obtained in the Supreme Soviets of the 15 Union Republics, in which there were 14 out of some 5,300 deputies; one or two Jewish deputies were chosen for some of the Union Republic Supreme Soviets. On the bottom of the legislative scale, the local soviets, which comprised over 2,000,000 members, received a similar token number of Jews (about 8,000). The percentage on this level approximated that of Jews in the legislatures on the republic and national levels. The quota system was used in the various branches of administration. Yekaterina Furtseva, minister of culture from 1960, explained how the system was initiated. If "a heavy concentration of Jewish people" was found in a governmental department, "steps were taken to transfer them to other enterprises …" At about the same time, Canadian Communist Party leader J.B. Salsberg was told in Moscow that the "transfer" method was applied to Jews in the "once-backward" Union Republics in order to make room for the newly trained native cadres in the administrative apparatus. In December 1962, Premier Nikita Khrushchev told Soviet intellectuals that Kremlin policy was aimed at preventing too many Jews from holding prominent posts, and in June 1963, the Party's principal theoretical journal, *Kommunist*, admitted the widespread use of the quota system in the training and placement of cadres in the various Union Republics. The quota system was most clearly expressed in university admission practices. The Soviet *Bulletin of Higher Education* (December 1963) disclosed that "annually planned preferential admission quotas" prevailed in Soviet universities. Nicholas De Witt, a U.S. specialist on Soviet educational practices, explained that the quota system operated "to the particularly severe disadvantage of the Jewish population." In a study published in 1964, he found that "in those republics where Jews constitute an above-average proportion of the urban population, their representation among university students is well below the rate of the general population's access to higher education." Whereas in 1935 the Jewish enrollment in Soviet universities was 13% of the population, by the 1960s it dropped drastically to little more than 3%.

The pattern of discrimination against Jews in political and social life paralleled a policy that deprived the Jewish community of the ethnic and religious rights to which it was constitutionally entitled and that other Soviet ethnic and major religious groups enjoyed. It should be emphasized, however, that the pattern of discrimination, especially in the civic and political arenas, was not endemic to Communist societies. In other European Communist countries (including Poland until 1967–68), Jews held prominent positions at all levels of the party and state administration. Even in the U.S.S.R. the anti-Jewish pattern of discrimination did not extend to everyday channels of social life. Residential restrictions were nonexistent, and there were no barriers to membership and participation in the lower levels of the Communist Party, trade unions, armed forces, social services, and clubs. Employment opportunities, other than administration, in such fields as science, medicine, law, and the arts were widespread. Particularly in the crucial area of the sciences, Jews ranked high both in absolute and relative terms, although the quota system in university admission practices brought about a decline in the percentage of Jews in relation to other nationalities. With the disintegration of the Communist system, all forms of official antisemitism virtually came to an end in Russia and Eastern Europe, replaced in many cases by grassroots antisemitism.

United States

This Soviet pattern of discrimination was in striking contrast with the pattern prevailing in the United States, where in 1970 one-half of the world's Jewish population resided. Discrimination against Jews on the national political level was neither existent nor sanctioned. Jews played an important and active role in all areas of political, public, and community life, although to a lesser extent outside major population centers. Yet the chauvinism of an old, established patrician class, combined with a nativist-Populist tradition and an "in-group" phobia of those striving to protect their insecure status (in an extended period of upward social mobility), perpetuated patterns of social discrimination against Jews in non-government spheres – employment, housing, and social institutions. The techniques employed were exclusion, tokenism, and the quota system. Widespread patterns of discrimination in private industry were notable principally on the executive or management levels; no problem was apparent below that level. A study published in 1968 showed that comparatively few Jews were found in executive positions in the insurance, automobile, and shipping industries. A 1967 survey of 38 major companies in the New York City area, including utility and transportation companies, commercial banks, oil concerns, electronic firms, and stock exchanges, revealed that the proportion of Jews among the total number of executives was relatively small. Private employment agencies abetted the perpetuation of discrimination by responding positively to the real or imagined prejudices of their clients. Exclusive residential areas, both in suburbia and high-rental urban cooperatives, were often characterized by quota practices. By means of restrictive covenants, a complete ban on the sale of property to Jews could sometimes be effected. Even though the Supreme Court ruled that covenants were not legally enforceable, the device was still used, as, e.g., in certain choice locations in Washington, D.C. and Detroit. Resort hotels, especially in certain vacation areas, also erected barriers against Jews. A study in 1956–57 showed that one out of four hotels carried on such practices, with an even higher ratio in Arizona resort hotels. Particularly distinctive on the social landscape was the pattern of discrimination in country clubs and city social clubs. According to a 1961 survey, three-quarters of the former and 60% of the latter either excluded Jews or maintained quotas against them. A study released in 1969 emphasized that discrimination in these clubs led to an "almost insurmountable barrier" for Jews who strove for advancement in industry and finance. The reason for this crucial linkage between social-club discrimination and employment opportunities was the fact that top-level business executives frequented these clubs and "naturally turned to the ranks of those they knew." In local communities, social clubs were vital factors in the power structure, and the scope of Jewish participation in the local decision-making process was directly proportionate to the extent that they excluded or restricted Jews. Progress in removing barriers against Jews, however, was made gradually, especially in the employment field. Other private forms of social discrimination had greatly declined by 1970. Typical of this trend were university admission practices. An American Council on Education study in 1949 revealed that the average Jewish university applicant had considerably less chance of being accepted than a Catholic or Protestant of comparable scholastic ability. The technique generally used was a fixed quota. Since then, and especially from the 1960s, restrictions based upon religion or ethnic origin were significantly reduced, confining themselves largely to a few exclusive cooperatives, athletic or golf clubs, and law firms.

England

The American pattern of social discrimination was paralleled, at least to some extent, in the United Kingdom. In the early 1960s it was estimated that approximately one-half of British golf clubs prevented, as far as possible, the admission of Jews to membership. Usually a quota system was applied, although in Manchester nearly 100 clubs adhered to an unwritten "Aryan paragraph" providing for total exclusion. Whether and to what extent there was a decline in club discrimination from the middle and late 1960s was never studied. Private school (called "public" school in England) enrollment was also characterized by a form of snobbish discrimination effected by the quota system. A London newspaper study in the late 1950s showed that the best-known boys' "public" schools limited the number of Jewish students to 10–15%. Some girls' "public" schools excluded Jews entirely, while others placed a 10% quota on them. The absence of careful studies on "executive suite" discrimination made judgment about employment practices in England difficult, although in the 1960s relatively few Jews were found in finance and heavy industry. It can be surmised, however, that this problem and related forms of social discrimination were less pressing than in the United States. As in America, the political sphere was virtually devoid of discrimination. The basic motivation of discrimination in England appeared to be social, a vestige of patrician snobbishness perhaps reinforced by religious considerations. The extent to which the American pattern of social discrimination was present in other Western and Latin American countries was not made the object of any scientific study.

Arab Countries

Whereas antisemitism in most parts of the Jewish-populated world was expressed by subtler forms of discrimination, in the Arab countries the necessity for pretense was not felt, especially after the Six-Day War (1967). Discrimination against Jews was open, callous, and frequently brutal. Upon the establishment of the State of Israel, all the Jews in Iraq were classed as enemy aliens. This act was accompanied by the sequestration of Jewish property and businesses and the banning of emigration. In March 1950, when the ban was lifted for one year, almost all of Iraq's 120,000 Jews fled, leaving 6,000 in the country. Further anti-Jewish discriminatory legislation was enacted in the years that followed, while the outflow of Jews continued, and, as of May 1967, the 2,500 remaining Iraqi Jews faced sharp limitations in the areas of citizenship, travel, and property. The Six-Day War brought on even more repressive measures: all Jewish homes were placed under surveillance; telephones were disconnected; personal property could not be sold; assets were frozen; licenses were canceled; the dismissal of Jewish employees was ordered; and travel from their area of residence was forbidden. A complete ban on emigration made the discriminatory pressures under which Jews lived all the more burdensome. Several Jews were publicly hanged in Baghdad, together with Muslim opponents of the regime, as "imperialist and Zionist spies." The situation in Syria was similar. Even prior to the Six-Day War, Syrian Jews were forbidden to sell property and move about beyond a one-and-a-half-mile radius from their place of residence without a special permit. Jews were required to carry special identity cards, and after the war, the 4,000 Syrian Jews were not permitted to emigrate. Just prior to the Six-Day War, the UAR conducted a registration of its 2,500 Jews and, within two or three days of the outbreak of hostilities, ordered the imprisonment of the great majority of Jewish males. Most of these prisoners were released during 1968 but others were kept in prison until 1969 and 1970. Prior to the war, the 4,000-member Jewish community in Libya was subject to a variety of restrictions, including a ban on emigration. The outbreak of war unleashed popular violence against Jews. When the ban on emigration was lifted soon after the war ended, the entire Jewish community fled. The tiny Jewish community of Aden underwent a similar experience.

BIBLIOGRAPHY: E. Goldhagen (ed.), *Ethnic Minorities in the Soviet Union* (1968); S. Schwarz, *Jews in the Soviet Union* (1951); W. Korey, in: *Midstream*, 12 no. 5 (1966), 49–61; A.D. Sakharov, *Progress, Coexistence and Intellectual Freedom* (1968), AJYB, 69 (1968), N.C. Belth (ed.), *Barriers: Patterns of Discrimination against Jews* (1958); B.R. Epstein and A. Forster, *Some of My Best Friends* (1962); Rights, 7 no. 1 (Feb., 1968); B'nai B'rith International Council, *Survey, Report 64–1* (Jan., 1964); R.M. Powell, *The Social Milieu as a Force in Executive Promotion* (1969); M. Decter, in: *Foreign Affairs*, 41 (1963), 420–30; B.Z. Goldberg, *The Jewish Problem in the Soviet Union* (1961); N. De-Witt, *Education and Professional Employment in the U.S.S.R.* (1961); idem, *The Status of Jews in Soviet Education* (1964).

[William Korey]

DISEGNI, DARIO (1878–1967), Italian rabbi and educator. Born in Florence, he completed his general studies there, at the same time studying at the Rabbinical College under S.H. Margulies and H.Z. Chajes. He served as rabbi in several communities: Genoa (1902–06); Turin (1906–09); and Verona (1909–24). During World War I he was a military chaplain and in 1922 for a few months, the rabbi of the Sephardi congregation in Bucharest. From 1924 he was rabbi in Turin. From 1930 he was rabbi in Tripoli for six months. He was one of the organizers of the first Italian Rabbinical Federation in 1917 and the founder and director of the S.H. Margulies Rabbinical School. Some of his pupils there later taught in Israel. The school, which was of great importance in the Jewish life of Italy and for a certain time provided the Italian Rabbinical College with pupils, was subsequently directed by his successor, Sergio Joseph Sierra, and bore the name Margulies-Disegni Rabbinical School. Disegni edited prayer books for weekdays, the Sabbath, and holidays, with Italian translations and short notes. The texts are those of the communities in Milan, Rome, and Turin. Almost a century after S.D. Luzzatto's edition of the Italian text of the Bible, Disegni initiated a new Italian translation in four volumes (Turin, 1960–67), with the original text and short notes. As its editor, he obtained the collaboration of many Italian rabbis and himself contributed to the translation which met with enthusiastic approval also in non-Jewish circles. Disegni died in Turin. His writings include numerous articles in different journals and reviews. A *festschrift* in Italian and Hebrew was published in his honor in 1969.

BIBLIOGRAPHY: *Israel*, 52 (1966/67), nos. 14, 15, 16, 17; *Bollettino della Communità Israelitica di Milano*, no. 6 (1966/67); R. Bonfil, in: RMI, 33 (1967), 51–61; S. Sierra, in; *Miscellanea … D. Disegni* (1969); G. Romano, *ibid.*

[Alfredo Mordechai Rabello]

DISINTERMENT. Jewish law forbids the transfer of a dead body or of remnant bones from one grave to another, even when it is to a more respected site (Sh. Ar., YD 363:1; based upon Sem. 13:5–7; TJ, MK 2:4, 81b). This traditional prohibition is, however, lifted in the following cases: (a) If the dead person is to be reinterred alongside his parents or close relatives; the sanction is based on the concept that "It is seemly for a man to repose with his family, and in doing so, honor is conferred upon the deceased" (Sh. Ar., *ibid.*; Sem. 13:7). In Orthodox practice this is applicable where reinterment is in a family plot already in use, but not if a new site is acquired for future family use. Reform Judaism, however, permits disinterment for reburial in a family plot that is to be inaugurated and consecrated. Litigation on this subject took place in New York City in 1902 (*Cohn vs. Congregation She'arith Israel*) and the court sustained the congregation which refused to permit disinterment in accordance with traditional *halakhah* (see *The American Hebrew*, March 14, 21, 28, 1902, and *Jewish Exponent*, April 18, 1902). Most traditional halakhic authorities permit the removal of a dead body to a new family plot if the body was temporarily buried, i.e., with the intention of being later transferred to a family plot to be acquired. (b) Disinterment for the purpose of reburial in Ereẓ Israel was always regarded as a meritorious deed and a great honor for the deceased (Ket. 111a; Sh. Ar., *ibid.*). (c) The body of a Jew interred in a gentile cemetery may be exhumed for reburial in a Jewish cemetery. (d) Where a grave is in danger of water seepage or if it is not safe against robbers, etc., transfer is permitted.

In modern times, urban planning and the construction of railroads, highways, etc., frequently encroach on cemetery sites, necessitating disinterment by order of the authorities. Most halakhic authorities permit the transfer of the dead on condition that decent repose for the deceased is provided. A son may not be buried in a grave reserved for his father or in one vacated by his father through disinterment (Sanh. 47b; also Sh. Ar., YD 364:7); other persons, however, may be interred in a vacated grave, but it must not be used for other purposes (Sem. 13:9). On the day of the disinterment, members of the family are obliged to observe the customary mourning rites. (For the practice in talmudic times of "gathering the remnant bones" for reburial after 12 months, see **Likkut Aẓamot.*)

Under the halakhic direction of its chief rabbi, Shlomo *Goren, the Israel Defense Forces developed procedures for disinterments which are based upon those practiced during the wars fought during the period of the Second Commonwealth. Slain soldiers are temporarily buried in either nearby permanent or temporary military cemeteries (cf. Er. 17a; TJ, Er. 1:10, 19d). Only the military chaplaincy is present, and relatives do not participate in these funerals. There are no eulogies, and only a brief religious service is held. A declaration is made during this service that the interment is only temporary, and that it will therefore be permissible to rebury the deceased in a permanent cemetery. After a year has elapsed, the soldiers are reinterred in permanent military or civilian cemeteries in accordance with the wishes of their families (cf. TJ, Sanh. 6:12, 23d; Oho. 16:5). During the *Sinai Campaign of 1956, temporary cemeteries were consecrated by the military chaplaincy in the Northern and Central Negev. A year later, the remains of 132 soldiers were reinterred near their hometowns. During the *Six-Day War of 1967, temporary and permanent military cemeteries were used for the temporary burials. During June 1968, one year after the war, 475 military reinterments took place. During the reburials, special military and religious services were held in accordance with instructions issued by the army rabbinate.

BIBLIOGRAPHY: Eisenstein, Dinim, 338ff.; CCARY, 32 (1922), 41ff.; S.B. Freehof, *Reform Jewish Practice*, 1 (1948²), 149ff.

[Meir Ydit]

DISKIN, CHAIM (c. 1923–), Russian army doctor and Hero of the Soviet Union. Born in Korotkie, Bryansk district, RSFSR, Diskin was drafted into the Red Army in 1941 and served as an artillery gunner. In November 1942, in the battle of Moscow, wounded and cut off from his unit, he single-handedly destroyed seven German tanks. For this feat he was decorated as Hero of the Soviet Union. In 1947 he graduated from the Medical Military Academy and was later promoted from senior lecturer to head of department and professor. In October 1981 he received the rank of major-general in the Army Medical Corps. He retired from the army in July 1988.

BIBLIOGRAPHY: F.D. Sverdlov, *Yevrei Generaly vooruzhonnykh sil SSSR* (1993).

[Shmuel Spector (2nd ed.)]

DISKIN, MORDEKHAI (1844–1914), Ereẓ Israel pioneer. Diskin, born in Grodno, Russia, worked with his father as a market gardener. In 1882 he settled in Ereẓ Israel with his family and bought a holding in Petaḥ Tikvah that had been abandoned by earlier settlers because of malaria. He farmed there until his son shot and wounded a robber, and fear of vendetta caused him to move to Jerusalem. Diskin returned to Petaḥ Tikvah when it was resettled on the site of the neighboring village of Yehudiyyah. He became coachman in 1891, transporting passengers and goods between Petaḥ Tikvah and Jaffa, and taught Mishnah and Shulḥan Arukh in the evenings. Later he moved to Jaffa, still as a coachman, and his house became a free lodging for settlers who came to Jaffa for medical treatment. At the end of his life he became a shopkeeper, studying Torah and performing acts of charity. He was one of the founders of *talmud torah* Neẓaḥ Israel in Petaḥ Tikvah, the first modern religious school in the country. His monographs *Divrei Mordekhai* ("The Words of Mordekhai," 1889), *Ma'amar Mordekhai* ("Mordekhai's Essay," 1912), and *Yishuv ha-Areẓ* ("Settlement of the Land," 1913) are descriptions of the hardships of early agricultural settlement in Ereẓ Israel.

BIBLIOGRAPHY: Tidhar, 1 (1947), 439; M. Smilansky, *Mishpahat ha-Adamah*, 1 (1943), 99–103.

[Avraham Yaari]

DISKIN, MOSES JOSHUA JUDAH LEIB (1817–1898), rabbi, halakhist, and leader of the old *yishuv* in Jerusalem. Diskin was born at Grodno, where he achieved fame as a child prodigy. From 1844 he was rabbi successively at Lomza, Mezhirech, Kovno, and Shklov, and from 1873 at Brest-Litovsk (Brisk), hence his title the "Brisker Rov." As a result of a case in which he was implicated by the authorities, and in consequence of which he was imprisoned for a short period, he left Russia for France, and in the summer of 1877 immigrated to Ereẓ Israel. He settled in Jerusalem where he served as rabbi until his death, enjoying the esteem of the whole community, among sections of which he was even more highly respected than Samuel *Salant, the rabbi of Jerusalem. He was one of the most prominent rabbis of his generation, who, in addition to a life of Torah study, was in the vanguard of Orthodox activism, leading the fight against all expressions of modernity and modern culture in Ereẓ Israel and advocating complete dissociation of the religious from the irreligious. He repeatedly excommunicated the modern schools in Jerusalem, stating of the ban that "no one has the power to annul it, since renowned rabbis of former days ordained it.... It is, moreover, a fence around the Torah, and not even an assembly of all the rabbis is in any way able or allowed to abrogate it" (written in 1896, responsa, pt. 1, 8a, nos. 29, 30). He ruled against the controversial decision of leading rabbis in 1889 permitting the cultivation of fields during that year, which was a sabbatical year. On other occasions, however, he was reluctant to decide an issue on his own, and suggested that prominent rabbis be consulted (responsa, pt. 1, no. 47, p. 43a; no. 52, p. 45a). He was opposed to the indiscriminate use of *pilpul*, regarding it solely as an instrument to arrive at halakhic decision (pt. 1, no. 52, p. 43d; pt. 3, no. 13). He himself subjected *halakhot* to critical examination, applying himself particularly to the problem of permitting the remarriage of *agunot* (women whose husbands are missing but whose deaths have not been established).

Diskin was active in establishing several communal institutions in Jerusalem. In 1880 he founded the orphanage which still bears his name, his purpose being to "save" children from a similar institution in which foreign languages were taught, established at that time in Jerusalem. He actively supported the foundation in 1887 of the Joint Sheḥitah Board of the Ashkenazim, Perushim (the non-ḥasidic Ashkenazim), and Ḥasidim, and together with R. Salant headed that body, which abolished the separate *sheḥitah* arrangements of these communities. He directed the Ohel Moshe (now called Tiferet Yerushalayim) yeshivah, where he also taught; gave his approval to the establishment of a separate community for immigrants from America; and, initially, supported the founders of *Petaḥ Tikvah, even serving as official agent for their company. He severed all connections with them, however, when it became clear to him that the town was assuming the character of the newer settlements. In all his public activities in Jerusalem, Diskin was supported by his second wife, Sarah (Sonia) Rattner, who was known as the "Brisker *Rebbetzin.*" In some circles she was thought to dominate her husband to lead him to the adoption of extreme views; in the literature of the new settlers she was referred to disparagingly. After Diskin's death, the orphanage and later the yeshivah came under the directorship of his only son, Isaac Jeroham (born of his first wife), who, together with Rabbi *Sonnenfeld, was one of the ultra-Orthodox anti-Zionist leaders at the beginning of the national movement.

Among Moses Diskin's works are *Torat Ohel Moshe* (1902), novellae to Exodus and to the *aggadah*, including also some of the novellae of his father, Benjamin Diskin; *Likkut Omarim* (1922 and 1935), aggadic and halakhic novellae to Genesis and Exodus; and Responsa (1911), in three parts. Diskin's novellae were also published in the collection *Mafteḥot ha-Torah mi-Ẓiyyon* (1887–98). His novellae to the Babylonian Talmud – excerpted from his *Torat Ohel Moshe* – and responsa were republished in the *Hosafot le-Talmud Bavli* in two volumes (1964). Of the published eulogies on him, the following are noteworthy: B. Lempert, *Zekher Zaddik li-Verakhah* (1898) and J. Orenstein, *Allon Bakhut* (1899).

BIBLIOGRAPHY: J. Orenstein, *Torah mi-Ẓiyyon*, 3 (1898), no. 4, 31a–34b; *Lu'aḥ Aḥi'asaf*, 6 (1899), 347; *Sefer ha-Yovel shel Petaḥ Tikvah* (1929), 46, 75, 138, 426; Y. Press, in: *Minhah le-David* (1935), 129, 135f.; D. Yellin, *Ketavim Nivḥarim*, 1 (1936), 230–3; J.A. Weiss, *Bi-She'arayikh Yerushalayim* (1949), 39–41, 88–90; I. Sheinberger, *Ammud Esh* (1954); B.Z. Jadler, *Be-Tuv Yerushalayim* (1967), 339–55.

[Yehoshua Horowitz]

DISNA (Pol. **Dzisna**), town in former Vilno district, Poland, today Molodechno district, Belarus. It is assumed that the first Jews settled there in the 16th century, but an organized community was only formed in the late 18th century. The Jews numbered 412 in 1797, and many made their livings from the wholesale trade of agricultural products. The community numbered 1,880 in 1847; 4,617 in 1897 (68.3% of the total population); and 2,742 in 1921 (62% of the total). After WWI Disna was cut off from its markets in Russia (U.S.S.R.), the economy deteriorated, and the number of Jews in the town declined. Most children were enrolled in a Yiddish CYSHO school. Zionist youth movements were active, and many of their members made aliyah.

[Shmuel Spector (2nd ed.)]

Holocaust Period

Between the outbreak of World War II and the German-Soviet war, Disna was under Soviet occupation. When the German army entered on July 2, 1941, there were 6,000 Jewish inhabitants in the city, many of them refugees from central Poland. Soon after the arrival of the Germans, the synagogues were burned down. On July 14, ten Jews were murdered. On August 3, a ghetto was set up. The main *Aktion* was carried out on July 14–15, 1942, when the entire ghetto was destroyed. The inhabitants were all taken to Piaskowe Gorki where they were murdered. During the *Aktion* about 2,000 persons broke out of the ghetto and sought refuge in the forests. The Germans hunted down the escapees, but some succeeded in organizing partisan units, while other Disna Jews joined the Fourth Belorussian Partisan Brigade. On Jan. 22, 1943, 17 Jewish craftsmen, the sole survivors of the *Aktion* of June 1942 to remain in Disna, were murdered.

[Aharon Weiss]

BIBLIOGRAPHY: O. Hedemann, *Dzisna i Druja* (1934); B. Wasiutyński, *Ludność żydowska w Polsce …* (1930), 84.

DISPLACED PERSONS, term for the hundreds of thousands of Jewish refugees and millions of non-Jews uprooted by the devastation of World War II, a large proportion of whom wound up in Displaced Persons camps set up by the victorious Allied forces in Germany, Austria, and Italy. Today the term is often synonymous with Jewish Holocaust survivors, who in the early years after the war sometimes referred to themselves as DPs. As such it embraces both the Jewish survivors of the concentration and forced labor camps as well as those who survived the war by hiding or by fleeing east to the Soviet Union, a group that may have constituted a majority of the displaced persons.

The Allies estimated that in May 1945 the tumult of the war had displaced eight million people from their homes in virtually all the countries of Europe. But within a few months three out of every four found their way back to their cities and villages, reducing the scope of the problem significantly but still leaving masses of frail people to feed, shelter, and repatriate. Assembly centers designed for 3,000 people soon began to contain over 10,000, resulting in crowding, unsanitary conditions, and shortages of clothing and basic supplies. Historian Yehuda Bauer estimates that of the 200,000 Jews who emerged alive from the concentration or labor camps, 55,000 remained in occupied zones of Germany and Austria. Other historians say the number could be as high as 100,000. The Polish and Baltic Jews who found a wartime haven in the Soviet Union and then were allowed to repatriate more than doubled the refugee number so that at its peak in 1947 there were almost 250,000 displaced Jews in Europe.

The Jewish refugees, after learning how their families had been slaughtered and communities destroyed, could not or would not return to their hometowns and cities, and that feeling only hardened after the pogrom in the Polish town of *Kielce in July 1946 in which 41 Jews were massacred with police help. Many were helped to smuggle themselves across borders and reach the refugee camps in the Allied occupied zones by an organization of partisans and Zionists called *Beriḥah (Flight). Once in the DP camps, the refugees waited for permits that would admit them to Palestine, the United States, Canada, Australia, and a handful of countries that were willing, however grudgingly, to absorb refugees. But with immigration restrictions as stringent as they were the DPs often languished for years. As a result, camps initially set up as a short-term solution lingered as refugee settlements into the early 1950s, with one remaining open until 1957.

Initial conditions at the camps were squalid, reflecting either poor preparation by the Allies, plain negligence, or in more than a few cases outright contempt for the Jewish refugees. Some of the DP camps were set up on the very grounds of the concentration camps as they were at *Bergen-Belsen, where the German officers barracks were converted by the British for use by the refugees. Others were set up at prisoner-of-war barracks and institutional settings, though one was at a fancy hotel in the Austrian Alps. Many camps were surrounded with barbed wire as if it were the refugees who represented a threat to the neighboring population. DPs lacked underwear, shoes, toilet paper, toothbrushes and there were reports that refugees were being given less food per day than German prisoners of war had been given. Some American soldiers brought their antisemitic prejudices with them, manhandling Jewish DPs and encouraging them to return to their home countries. In some camps, German police, some of them ex-Nazis, were placed in charge, and in one famous incident in Stuttgart in 1946, 200 German policemen accompanied by dogs raided a Jewish assembly center in search of black market goods and killed one DP. Most appalling to the Jewish refugees was their intermingling in the camps with Poles, Lithuanians, Latvians, and others who had collaborated with the Nazis in the murder of Jews.

When reports about maltreatment filtered back to Congress, Earl G. Harrison, dean of the faculty of law at the University of Pennsylvania and a former commissioner of immigration, was appointed to investigate. He reported back on August 1, 1945, that conditions were so grim that "we appear to be treating the Jews as the Nazis treated them, except that we do not exterminate them." The camps under General George Patton in southern Germany were said to be particularly poorly managed. (Patton wrote in his diary in September 1945 that some believe that the Displaced Person is a human being, which he is not, and this applies particularly to the Jews, who are lower than animals.) In response to the Harrison report, a distressed President Harry S. Truman appointed an advisor to the military with sole responsibility for the camps. Jewish chaplains were also important in prodding the military to treat the refugees more humanely, as was pressure from relief workers for organizations like the *American Jewish Joint Distribution Committee and *HIAS (the Hebrew Immigrant Aid Society). A visit to the DP camps by David *Ben-Gurion, chairman of the Executive of the Jewish Agency, in October 1945 helped spur the army to concentrate Jews in their own camps and allow the entry of Jews from Poland. The United Nations Relief and Rehabilitation Administration, which had for months done an incompetent job of ministering to the refugees, was told to appoint Jewish refugees as camp administrators. Food was increased and conditions began to improve markedly.

While the discussion continued on what would be done with the DPs, whether they would be resettled in Palestine or in one of several Western countries, the refugees did not just remain idle. They started schools – including some 12,000 children at one point – and set up makeshift synagogues. They gave opera and theatrical performances and staged boxing matches. Despite the difficulty of obtaining printing presses and Hebrew type, they started some 70 newspapers, like *Unzer Shtimme* at Bergen-Belsen, the *Landsberger Lager Zeitung* and *Dos Fraye Wort* in Feldafing. Scores of writers and editors worked on those newspapers, many who had been human skeletons just months before or had been partisans staging ambushes against the Nazis. The more entrepreneurial traded in the black market that had cropped up in the occupied zones with the connivance of GIs and bureaucrats.

In many camps, the refugees took charge of their fate, setting up camp committees to run practical matters or aiding the Beriḥah network to smuggle people across a gauntlet of European borders to Palestine. Decades later, Menachem Rosensaft, a child of Bergen-Belsen and then a leader in the so-called Second Generation movement of children of survivors, recalled how his father, Joseph, an Auschwitz survivor, governed the Bergen-Belsen camp, organizing cultural and political activities, rooting out collaborators, and defying the British overseers, as he did when they attempted to transfer two groups of refugees to squalid camps. In effect, he said, from 1945 to 1950, his father had been the mayor of a largely autonomous Jewish community with its own schools, hospitals, and police force. In some instances, refugees directed the smuggling of arms to the *Haganah army in Palestine that was pressing the British to give Jews a state or trained for the Haganah using arms given to the refugee camp policemen.

Most importantly, the refugees revived family life, marrying and bearing children. The marriages were as often arranged out of convenience and desperate loneliness as out of romance, but that they took place at all signified a determination to carry on with life. The United States Holocaust Museum and Memorial has a singular wedding dress used by Lilly (Laks) Friedman, who survived Bergen-Belsen and was married in January 1946 near that camp. Because supplies were so scarce, her husband-to-be managed to scavenge a parachute from a German airman which Lily, trading her cigarette rations for the services of a dressmaker, converted to a dress. The dress was eventually borrowed by as many as 20 other refugee brides.

The DPs, most in their early twenties and thirties, also had thousands of children, making the DP camps, by some reckoning, the world's most fertile spot between 1946 and 1948. Historian Yehuda Bauer wondered decades later how the survivors summoned the strength and spirit to recapture life with such speed after spending years in the realm of death. Sam Norich, who was born in the Feldafing DP camp and went on to become the publisher of the *Forward* newspaper in the United States, offered a theory based on the Hebrew term originally used for the DPs, the *She'arit ha-Pleitah*, the surviving remnant. They saw themselves as the remnant that perpetuates, that redeems the family and the community as a whole, the community from which they came, he said in a speech in 2002.

It seems clear that the refugees were eager to see the establishment of a Jewish state, one that at a minimum would resolve their homelessness. In July 1945, 94 delegates from Jewish assembly centers held a conference at the St. Ottilien camp near Munich calling for the immediate establishment of a Jewish state in Palestine. More official entities also focused on this solution. Harrison proposed that the British accept 100,000 Jews into the territory of the British Mandate for Palestine and what was known as the Anglo-American Committee of Inquiry recommended in April 1946 that the British government immediately grant the Jewish refugees 100,000 immigration certificates to Palestine. Despite these pressures, the refugees in the British Zone were given only 6,000 immigration certificates until the establishment of the State of Israel and other zones received only 1,460. Therefore illegal immigration became the only option for most refugees.

The moral pressure of this mass of Jewish displaced persons – a problem that could not be solved without the creation of a Jewish homeland – is now regarded as having been crucial in persuading the British to hand over its mandate in Palestine to the United Nations in 1947 and in persuading President Harry S. Truman to push for the creation of Israel despite the resistance of his own State Department. Jewish leaders in Palestine agreed to settle for a partitioned country rather than a whole loaf of the land because of the unresolved situation of the refugees.

The creation of Israel did indeed begin solving the refugee problem. By the beginning of 1950, 75,000 Jewish DPs had made their way to Israel. Meanwhile, other countries like Australia and Canada opened their doors to take in refugees. In America, admission of Jewish refugees was notably grudging. One might have thought that given the failure of the United States to admit the imperiled Jews of Germany before the war and to admit refugees during the war that after the war the doors would have been opened generously. But that was not the case. Many in Congress believed that the DP camps were filled with Communist sympathizers; other legislators simply did not want to admit more Jews. President Truman issued a directive in December 1945 mandating preferential treatment in the immigration laws for displaced persons. But as of June 30, 1947, only 22,950 visas had been issued to DPs in Germany, just 15,478 to Jews. In 1948 Congress passed a law that gave preferential admission to DPs who had held that status as of December 22, 1945, a date that effectively excluded most Jews. Provisions in the law also gave preferences for entry to Baltics, Ukrainians, and ethnic Germans, some with collaborationist backgrounds, and people working at occupations like agriculture in which Jews were not heavily represented. The law was amended in 1950, with a later cutoff date, but still only 16 percent of the 365,000 visas issued to DPs between July 1, 1948, and June 30, 1952, were issued to Jews. All told, fewer than 100,000 Jewish DPs reached the United States as a result of the Truman directive and the two DP acts, historian Leonard Dinnerstein reported.

Still, the laws produced a fresh cohort of immigrants – 140,000 of them from all sources between 1946 and 1953 – who brought an unusual spice to the American stew. These Jews were different from the more established descendants of the so-called Lower East Side generation of the late 19th century in everything from accent to the depth of sorrowful experience. A study published in 1992 by the sociologist William B. Helmreich, *Against All Odds: Holocaust Survivors and the Successful Lives They Made in America*, found that despite the brutality of their wartimes experiences and the many years they lived in limbo afterwards, the survivors amassed an impressive record of achievement. At first the American DPs took jobs in the blue-collar industries like garment manufacturing and used their small nest eggs to purchase candy stores and laundromats, and a significant proportion went on to earn fortunes in real estate and other business enterprises. By 1989 more than 34 percent of the survivors reported earning $50,000 annually, far higher than the national average. They divorced less than American Jews and had more children. They formed strong friendships and social networks. Their children adjusted well, worked hard in school, and went on to successful lives of their own. Children of displaced persons who achieved national fame include Daniel Libeskind, who designed the Ground Zero replacement for the destroyed World Trade Center; Wolf *Blitzer, a leading anchor and correspondent for CNN; Hadassah Lieberman, wife of Senator Joseph *Lieberman of Connecticut, who ran unsuccessfully for the vice presidency of the United States often mentioning his wife's Holocaust roots; and Sam Gejdenson, who became a Democratic congressman from Connecticut. As a result, the story of the displaced persons may ultimately be seen as a story of the steely resilience of the human spirit and its ability to recover from the unspeakable.

BIBLIOGRAPHY: J. Berger, *Displaced Persons: Growing Up American After the Holocaust* (2001); L. Dinnerstein, *America and the Survivors of the Holocaust* (1982); H. Epstein, *Children of the Holocaust: Conversations with Sons and Daughters of Survivors* (1979); W.B. Helmreich, *Against All Odds: Holocaust Survivors and the Successful Lives They Made in America* (1992); A.L. Sachar, *The Redemption of the Unwanted: From the Liberation of the Death Camps to the Founding of Israel* (1983); D.S. Wyman, *The Abandonment of the Jews: America and the Holocaust, 1941–1945* (1984).

[Joseph Berger (2nd ed.)]

DISPUTATIONS AND POLEMICS. This entry is arranged according to the following outline:

In the Pagan Environment
- THE CHRISTIAN ENVIRONMENT AND MISSION
- DIALOGUE WITH TRYPHON
- CELSUS

In the Christian and Muslim Medieval Milieu
- GREGORY OF TOURS AND PRISCUS
- GILBERT CRISPIN
- CHRISTIAN RELIGIOUS DRAMA
- CHRONICLE OF AHIMAAZ
- 12TH CENTURY
- IN MUSLIM COUNTRIES
- THE 13TH-CENTURY DISPUTATIONS
- 15TH CENTURY

Renaissance and Reformation
- *HIZZUK EMUNAH*

Modern Times
- FRANKIST DISPUTATIONS
- MENDELSSOHN AND LAVATER
- ROSENZWEIG AND ROSENSTOCK
- BUBER AND SCHMIDT

Up to early modern times dialogue between members of different faiths attempted either to prove the superiority and absolute validity of one faith over the other, or to defend the totality of one faith and its Holy Scriptures, or elements in them, against questioning and criticism by believers in another faith. In some cases the representative of one side has been put on a quasi-legal trial to justify his convictions, as often happened to Jews in the Middle Ages. Disputations and polemics between believers of the three monotheistic faiths – Judaism, *Christianity, and *Islam – inevitably start from and return to the common ground of the Hebrew Bible and certain religious concepts held by all three, but always in order to confute the opposing view and prove the validity of the proponent's argument.

In recording the most open public disputation to take place in the Middle Ages, that of *Barcelona in 1263, the Christian account stresses that the object of the disputation was not to question the validity of Christianity, "which because of its certainty cannot be subjected to debate" (*que propter sui certitudinem non est in disputatione ponenda*).

This was to remain the ultimate standpoint of disputants throughout the centuries. As late as 1933, a representative of Protestant Christianity, Karl Ludwig Schmidt, declared to his Jewish partner, as representative of German Jewry, the Zionist and philosopher Martin *Buber, in a Christian-Jewish dialogue before a gathering of Jews: "The evangelical theologian who has to talk to you, must talk to you as a member of the Church of Jesus Christ, must endeavor to talk in a manner that will convey the message of the Church to Jewry. He must do this even if you would not have invited him to do so. The assertion of a mission to you may have a somewhat bitter taste as if intending an attack; but such an attack precisely involves caring about you as Jews – so that you may live with us as our brethren in our German fatherland as throughout the world" (*Theologische Blaetter*, 12 (1933), 258; and see below). This liberal German theologian found it necessary to declare at the outset of the debate the missionary character of Jewish-Christian disputation.

Despite the self-assurance and aggressiveness implicit in this attitude, both sides were inevitably influenced to a certain degree by the dialectics of their opponents. At a very early stage of the Jewish-Christian debate this challenge was perceived in a Midrash which relates that "the **minim* [i.e., early Christians] were continuously disputing with Rabbi Judah, the son of Nakosa: they would ask him and he would answer them … When he was called [to Heaven] his pupils said to him: Rabbi, you were helped from on High and were victorious. He said to them: '... Go and pray for this ... basket that was full of diamonds and pearls and now is full of burnt-out charcoal'" (Eccles. R. 1:8, no. 4).

Disputations sometimes started from a casual encounter, sparked off by an actual problem or object noticed. Sometimes, in particular from the 13th century in Europe, they were formally conducted in public. Authors of polemical literature like *Judah Halevi employed the artificial framework of the disputation to set forth their arguments. Alternatively, the dialectic climate of an actual disputation led to systematic theological formulations such as the *Sefer Ikkarim* (Book of Principles) of Joseph *Albo (see below) or *Cur Deus homo* ... of *Anselm of Canterbury. The reports and impressions of the actual disputations that have been preserved are conflicting. The same motifs tend to recur time after time, any variation reflecting the spirit of the times, personal interests, or particular circumstances.

The history of disputations and their content, while concomitantly a record of constant tension and deliberate animosity, is also a process of continuous mutual interpenetration of ideas and influence stimulated by this tension.

In the Pagan Environment

In biblical times, the pagan polytheism of the period precluded the holding of any discursive dialogue of this nature. Claims are made asserting the might of one deity or deities above those of others, usually uttered in the heat of war after victory. Jewish monotheistic prophecy makes frequent use of scathing and ironical polemics to denounce polytheism and idolatry.

However, in the cultural milieu of the Hellenistic Roman world, Jewish monotheism was challenged by missionary Hellenistic philosophy and beliefs. Thus the Mishnah records that pagans asked the elders (in Rome): "If God does not desire idolatry why does He not destroy it? They answered: If men had been worshipping objects unnecessary for the cosmos He would have destroyed them, but they worship the sun and moon and the stars and the planets. Should He destroy His world because of fools? They [the pagan questioners] said to them: Then let Him destroy those objects [of pagan worship] of which the cosmos has no need, and leave only those necessary for the cosmos. They answered: Then the arguments of the worshipers of those [necessary objects] would have been strengthened, for they would say: these are divinities, for they have not been destroyed" (Av. Zar. 4:7).

The exclusiveness and superiority claimed for Jewish monotheism against idolatry are developed in the following disputation: "A *philosophus* asked Rabban Gamaliel: Your Bible states 'for I the Lord thy God am a jealous God.' Is there any merit in idolatry to give rise to jealousy? A hero is jealous of a hero, a sage of a sage, a rich man of a rich man; hence there must be merit in idolatry since it provokes jealousy. He answered him: If a man called his dog by the name of his father, and wanting to take an oath takes it on the life of the dog, of whom would the father be jealous, of the son or of the dog?" (Mekh., Ba-Ḥodesh 9). Details of Jewish worship also enter the disputation, as when "a Gentile asked Rabban *Johanan ben Zakkai: Those things that you perform resemble a kind of magic – you take a cow, slaughter it and burn it, and keep its ashes; and when one of you has become defiled by contact with the dead they sprinkle him two or three times [with water mixed with the ashes] and say, 'You have been purified.'" In replying to the Gentile R. Johanan drew a comparison with similar rituals employed in exorcism. To his own pupils, however, he explained it as an act of faith: "The dead does not defile nor does water purify; it is just a decree of the King of Kings. The Almighty, Blessed be His Name, said: This is my order, this is my rule, and no man may transgress it" (PdRK 40a–b).

Gradually the motif of Jewish weakness and dispersion was introduced into the argument against Judaism. When a certain "heretic" stressed that although the Jews were at the mercy of Rome, the Gentiles refrained from destroying them, he was answered by R. *Hoshaiah: "This is because you do not know how to carry this out. If you [seek to] destroy us all, we are not all to be found within your borders. [If you seek to destroy] only those within your borders you would be reputed a maimed empire. [The heretic] answered: By the body of Rome, we are engaged constantly with this problem" (Pes. 87b). This last motif, in stressing the enmity of the Romans and the dispersion of the Jews in both the Roman and Persian empires, seems to sound the note of the emerging predominance of Christianity.

The Talmud sometimes ascribes legendary disputations to biblical figures, for instance between Abraham and Nimrod. There are also accounts of litigations, supposed to have taken place before courts of law and kings, between representatives of the Jewish people and other claimants to the Land of Israel. *Josephus tells about litigation that took place between the Jews of *Alexandria and the Samaritans "in the presence of Ptolemy himself, the Jews asserting that it was the Temple at Jerusalem which had been built in accordance with the laws of Moses, and the Samaritans that it was the Temple on Mount *Gerizim. And they requested the king to sit in council with his friends and hear their arguments on these matters" (Jos., Ant., 13:74–75; and see the argumentation, 75–79).

Some sages appear in talmudic literature as having engaged in disputations that not only concern the Jewish faith and way of life but also show to advantage the breadth of knowledge and acuity of Jewish scholarship, for instance, *Joshua b. Hananiah (see Ḥag. 5b; Ḥul. 59–60b; Bek. 8b–9a).

THE CHRISTIAN ENVIRONMENT AND MISSION The developing cleavage between Christianity and Judaism, until the final parting of the ways in the second century, led to increasing disputation between Christians and Jews. The lists of *testimonia* from the Hebrew Bible prepared by early Christian teachers consist of biblical quotations to be used not only to convince pagans but also, in most cases, to persuade Jews to accept the Christianity clauses. With the growing distance between Christian and Jewish theological concepts and ways of life, the disputations became more formal and were noted down. The early disputations in the form of independent treatises are written down by the Christian side although fragments and impressions of such disputations are on record in talmudic literature (Mekh. Shira, 7; Ba-Ḥodesh, 5; Kaspa, 3; Mekh. Sb Y, to Shemot, p. 2; Sif. Deut. 87–91, 306; TJ, Ber. 9:1, 12d–13b; TJ, Ta'an. 2:1, 65b; TJ, Sanh. 1:1, 18a; TJ (Venice, 1523), Sanh. 13:9, 23 c–d; TJ, Sanh. 10:1, 27d–28a; Ber. 7a, 10a, 12a–b; Shab. 88a–b, 116a–b; Pes. 56a; Er. 22a; Suk. 48b; Ta'an. 27b; Ḥag. 5b; Yev. 102b; Sot. 47a; Git. 57a; Sanh. 38b–39a, 43b (in *Ḥesronot ha-Shas* in "El ha-Mekorot" ed. of the Talmud, 1963), 98b–99a, 106a–b; Av. Zar. 4a, 6a–b, 17a; Tosef., Hul. 2:2; Eccles. R. 1:8, no. 4; 2:1, nos. 1, 2; 4:8, no. 1; Song R. 7:3). The challenges and pressures of these disputations in the world of the *amoraim* (third to fourth centuries) are projected in the explanation given by *Abbahu, the celebrated disputant with the Christians at Caesarea, to Christians who questioned the learning of a scholar from Babylonia: "We [i.e., the scholars of Ereẓ Israel] who are living with you regard it as our task to study [Scripture] thoroughly. They [the scholars of Babylonia] are not so well versed" in it (Av. Zar. 4a). Representing the Christian view is a work well-known by around 500, the *Altercatio Simonis Judaei et Theophili Christiani* (ed. by A. v. Harnack, Leipzig, 1883). Although the text was subsequently lost for centuries the form of the *Altercatio* and the arguments put forward there influenced later Christian presentations of disputations with Jews.

DIALOGUE WITH TRYPHON. Of fundamental importance both for the authority it carries and the arguments met there is *Justin Martyr's Dialogue with Tryphon held about the time of the *Bar Kokhba revolt and written down between 156 and 161. While the argument of general issues and detailed points is sharp and bitter in this early discussion between Christians and Jews, the relationship between the disputants is represented as one of mutual courtesy. They part with an acknowledgment by the Jewish debater that he has "been extraordinarily charmed with our intercourse," with Justin stating that the Jews "departed, finally praying for my deliverance both from the dangers of the sea, and from all ill. And I prayed also for them, saying: I can make no greater prayer for you, Gentlemen, than this, that …you may do in all respects the same as we, acknowledging that the object of our worship is the Christ of God" (Justin Martyr, *Dialogue,* 142:1–3, Eng. trans. by A.L. Williams (1930), 289).

Even so, politeness does not hinder Justin from hurling at the Jews their harsh fate, at a time of life and death struggle with Rome, which he saw as the punishment designated by their Law: "The circumcision according to the flesh, that was from Abraham, was given for a sign, that ye should be separated from the other nations and us, and that ye alone should suffer the things that ye are rightly suffering now, and that your lands should be desolate and your cities burned with fire, and that foreigners should eat up the fruits before your face, and none of you go up unto Jerusalem. For by nothing else are ye to be known from other men, save by the circumcision that is in your flesh …. All this has happened to you rightly and well. For ye slew the Just One and His prophets before Him, and now ye reject, and, as far as in you lies, dishonor those that set their hope on Him …, cursing in your synagogues them that believe in Christ" (*ibid.*, 16:2–4, pp. 32–33). He also frequently explains other precepts as having been given to the Jews to their detriment: "Now because of your sins and those of your fathers God charged you to keep the Sabbath as a sign … and has also given you His other ordinances" (*ibid.*, 21:1, p. 42). The true meaning of the Torah and commandments enjoined in the Prophets is to be found in their Christological, spiritual-figurative sense. Physical rest could not really be enjoined on Saturday, for "you see that Nature does not idle nor keep Sabbath. Abide as ye have been born" (*ibid.*, 23:3, pp. 47–48). The stubborn and sinful Jewish people continue in existence only because God "has not yet brought the Judgment, nor has begun to bring it, because He knows that every day some [of the Jews] are becoming disciples unto the name of His Christ, and are leaving the way of error" (*ibid.*, 39:2, p. 77). Justin categorically rejects any form of Judeo-Christianity (*ibid.*, 46:1–2, p. 90; 47:1–2, pp. 93–95; see Jewish *Christian sects). A large part of Justin's argumentation consists of *testimonia* from the Prophets adduced in evidence of the validity of Christianity. His methods of dialectic and manner of presentation became the prototype of later Christian argumentation against Jewry and Judaism.

Tryphon objects in principle to the method of adducing Christological *testimonia* from the Hebrew Bible: "Why do you select for citation only such parts as you choose out of the sayings of the Prophets, and make no mention of those [that do not fit the Christian view]," and brings examples to prove his point (*ibid.*, 27:1, p. 53). Justin was fully aware that the main concern of responsible Jews at this critical period was not discussion of Greek beliefs or philosophical debate. Thus he describes how "Tryphon's companions sat down opposite, and after one of them had made a remark about the war in Judea, they conversed about it" (*ibid.*, 9:3, p. 20). However, the Jew regards philosophical paganism as preferable to superstitious Christianity: "It were better for you to continue to hold the philosophy of Plato or of some other learned man … than to have been completely led away by false speeches, and to follow men of no account. For while you remained in that mode of philosophy and lived a blameless life, a hope was left you of a better fate, but when you forsook God, and placed your hope on a man, what kind of salvation yet remains for you?" (*ibid.*, 8:3, p. 17). The Christians suffer persecution for their credulity: "You people, by receiving a worthless rumor, shape a kind of messiah for yourselves, and for His sake are now blindly perishing" (*ibid.*, 8:4, p. 19). The true hope of salvation lies in strict fulfillment of the Law: "First be circumcised, then … keep the Sabbath and the Feasts and God's New Moons, and, in short, do all the things that are written in the Law, and then perchance you will find mercy from God" (*ibid.*, 8:4, p. 17).

Not only is the Christian method of citation and evidence seen as falsifying the words of the Hebrew Bible by removing them from their context and failing to have regard for the spirit of the Hebrew language, but many of the events related by Christians and the interpretations they give are regarded as blasphemous and foolish. When Justin insulted the Jew by quoting the words of the Bible according to the version of Paul, which stigmatizes the Jews as prophet-killers, and added the remark referred to above that the Jews are still permitted to exist because of those among them who convert to Christianity, Tryphon interjected: "I would have you know that you are out of your mind when you say all this" (*ibid.*, 39:1–3, p. 77). To the long list of *testimonia* cited by Justin on the prophecies relating to Jesus and his primordial divinity, the Jew reacts: "You say many blasphemous things, thinking to persuade us that this man who was crucified has been with Moses and Aaron, and has spoken to them in a pillar of cloud, that he then became man and was crucified, and has ascended into Heaven, and comes again on earth, and is to be worshipped" (*ibid.*, 38:1, p. 75). Belief in incarnation and crucifixion in relation to the preexistent Divinity is rejected as irrational: "For your assertion that this Christ existed, and was God, before all ages, then that He was even born and became man and suffered, and that He is not man by origin, seems to me to be not only strange but even foolish" (*ibid.*, 48:1, p. 95). The Christian claims for Jesus amount to an attempt to "prove to us that the existence of another God besides the Maker of the universe is recognized by the spirit of the Prophets" (*ibid.*, 55:1, p. 108; and see also 50:1, p. 100). The interpretation given by Justin to "*ha-almah*" in Isaiah 7:14 to mean "the Virgin" (*Dialogue*, 66, pp. 138–139) is corrected by Tryphon who states that its actual meaning is "the young woman" and places the prophecy in its historical context in the reign of King Hezekiah. He adds that the Christian concept of a virgin birth is pagan in origin and character: "Among the tales of those whom we call Greeks it is said that Perseus had been born of Danae, still a virgin, by him that they entitle Zeus flowing down upon her in the form of gold. And in fact you ought to be ashamed of saying the same sort of things as they, and should rather say that this Jesus was a man of human origin, and, if you prove from the Scriptures that He is the Christ, [say] that because of his perfect life under the Law he was deemed worthy to be chosen to be Christ. And do not dare to assert marvels, that you be not convicted of talking folly like the Greeks" (*ibid.*, 67, pp. 139–140). Hence it would seem, according to Justin's rendering, that Tryphon would have found some satisfaction in a Christianity which recognized Jesus as the human redeemer of the Gentiles alone. Tryphon tries at some length to elicit Justin's attitude regarding whether Judeo-Christians should observe the Law (*ibid.*, 46:1, p. 90; 47:1–2, p. 93; and see above Justin's rejection of the Judeo-Christians). According to Justin's account, Tryphon expressly proposed: "Let Him be recognized of you who are of the Gentiles as Lord and Christ and God, as the Scriptures signify, seeing also that you have all acquired the name of Christians from Him. But as for us, who are worshipers of God who made even Him [Jesus], we do not need to confess Him or worship Him." Anger at this proposition provoked Justin into a rare outburst of personal invective against his Jewish opponent (*ibid.*, 64:1–2, p. 133). Tryphon pointed out that the messiah awaited by the Jews was a king-savior, not a redeeming God: "For all of us Jews expect that the Christ will be a man of merely human origin, and that Elijah will come and anoint Him" (*ibid.*, 49:1, p. 97). The King will come to his people, the descendants of Abraham. When Justin quotes to him from *testimonia* that the messiah will come to Israel, Tryphon asks what that implies: "Are you Israel, and does He say all this about you?" (*ibid.*, 123:7, p. 256).

This relatively early encounter between a separated Christianity and Judaism establishes the main themes and groundwork of future Jewish-Christian *testimonia*, the polemical statements by Tertullian against the Jews in the same century, and the fragments of Jewish-Christian disputation found in tannaitic and amoraitic literature mentioned above. Constantly recurring subjects in disputation from the end of the second century, therefore, are the significance of "*Bereshit*" ("In the beginning") and of "*ad ki yavo Shiloh*" (Gen. 49:10). Are the Just Men and Patriarchs who lived before the giving of the Torah to be regarded as observers of the Law or not? Why was the Law given to the Jews? For their benefit, or as a punishment? Is the true meaning of the Law and the Prophets to be elicited by a "literal" or a "spiritual" interpretation? What is the significance of the use of the plural form in referring to the Divine in the Bible? Is it intended to convey the concept of Trinity? Who is "the suffering servant of God" in Isaiah 52 and following? What is the correct translation of "*ha-almah*"? Although variations of these questions occur, this was to remain the exegetical core of Jewish-Christian disputation. The fate of the Jewish people, the course of history and empires, and war and peace in the world enter and are developed in the debate at a later stage. Although as yet not clearly defined, certain attitudes are already embryonic: the Jewish objection to the concept of the Trinity as being inherently idolatrous, and to incarnation as insulting to the divine nature of God; the insistence on the Jewish side that understanding of Scripture should be based on a comprehensive knowledge of the original language without depriving the words of their literal meaning or isolating them from their context. There also emerge the mystic-fideistic standpoint of the Christian side, the critico-rationalistic approach of the Jewish side; the universalist-individualistic claims of Church spokesmen against the Jewish concept of Israel as a national "natural-historical cell," the "kingdom of priests and holy nation" entrusted in this social pattern to carry the Divine call to the world.

CELSUS. Also dating from the early period of the disputations are the somewhat dissimilar strands of anti-Christian argumentation quoted by *Celsus in his anti-Christian polemic written about 178. There the Jew is reported to have said: "I could say much about what happened to Jesus which is true, and nothing like the account which has been written by the disciples of Jesus" (in Origen; *Contra Celsum*, translated and edited by H. Chadwick (1953), 2:13, p. 78). Celsus' record, which contains numerous extra-New Testamentary details and innuendoes adverse to Jesus, in some way prefigures the later polemical version of Jesus' life and death, **Toledot Yeshu* (Origen; *Contra Celsum*), 1:28, pp. 27–28; 1:32, pp. 31–32; 1:38, p. 37; 1:67, p. 62; 2:8, pp. 71–72; 2:9, p. 73; 2:15, p. 81; 2:16, pp. 81–82; 2:26, p. 90; 2:27, p. 90; 2:32, p. 93; 2:34, p. 94; 2:44, p. 100; 2:46, p. 101; 2:55, p. 109; 2:70, p. 121). The Jew also repeats many of the anti-Christian arguments used by Tryphon and the *amoraim*. In addition, he is quoted as sharply condemning Jewish *apostasy to Christianity, saying: "Why do you take your origin from our religion? And then, as if you are progressing in knowledge, despise these things although you cannot name any other origin for your doctrine excepting our Law" (*ibid.*, 2:4, p. 69; and see also 2:1, pp. 66–67). He attacks the concept of the resurrection of Jesus, in particular comparing it to similar pagan legends (2:55, p. 109), and adds: "While he was alive he did not help himself, but after death he rose again and showed the marks of his punishment and how his hands had been pierced. But who saw this? A hysterical female, as you say, and perhaps some other one of those who were deluded by the same sorcery, who either dreamt in a certain state of mind and through wishful thinking had a hallucination due to some mistaken notion (an experience which has happened to thousands), or, which is more likely, wanted to impress the others by telling this fantastic tale, and so by this cock-and-bull story to provide a chance for other beggars" (*ibid.*). His attack on resurrection is continued by the argument: "But if he really was so great he ought, in order to display his divinity, to have disappeared suddenly from the cross" (*ibid.*, 2:68, p. 118). The Jew continues: "Where is he then, that we may see and believe?" (*ibid.*, 2:77, p. 126). He uses Jesus' rejection by the Jews as an argument against his divinity: "What God that comes among men is disbelieved, and that when he appears to those who were waiting for him? Or why ever is he not recognized by people who have been long expecting him?" (*ibid.*, 2:75, p. 123).

The problems raised here denote the type of argumentation used by Jews against Christians in the Christian-Judeo-Pagan triangle of the second half of the second century. When Judaism alone remained face to face with Christianity much argumentation of this category was omitted in the direct confrontation.

In the fourth century, the rise of Christianity to imperial dominion in the late Roman Empire, the shock of *Julian "the Apostate's" revolt against this domination, and the fire and smoke of internal Christian doctrinal battles, were accompanied by bitter and brutal denunciation of Judaism and the Jews, their character, and way of life by *John Chrysostom, *Eusebius, and other fathers of the Church. Not only was the concept of divine election now claimed for the Church only, as the "spiritual Israel," but it was categorically denied to the historical Jewish people, leaving the title only to those of the nation who were considered "Christians before Christ," like the Patriarchs and the Prophets. Much of the argumentation in the talmudic literature cited above was in answer to this mode of attack.

At the beginning of the seventh century, the tensions in Ereẓ Israel between Jews and Christians, the Persian invasion, and entanglement of a Jewish revolt in the Byzantine-Persian struggle (see also *Benjamin of Tiberias, *Heraclius; *Jerusalem) are reflected in the controversial tract *Doctrina Iacobi nuper baptizati,* written about 640 (ed. by N. Bonwetsch, Berlin, 1910).

In the Christian and Muslim Medieval Milieu

GREGORY OF TOURS AND PRISCUS. The changed atmosphere at the courts of the German Christian rulers in Europe, and the standpoint of an educated Jew there, emerge in the account of a disputation recorded by Bishop Gregory of Tours in his *Historiarum Libri decem* (6:5; ed. R. Buchner, pp. 8–13). The Jewish merchant *Priscus in 581 was confronted with the bishop in the presence of King Chilperic, who initiated the disputation, in an attempt to win the Jew to Christianity. Gregory rests his argument on chapter and verse while the Jew puts questions and cites contrary biblical testimony. Priscus said to the king: "God did not enter into marriage and did not bring forth a son, neither can he have a partner to his sovereignty, as Moses says: 'See now that it is I, even I, and there is no God with Me. I put to death and I make alive; I strike and I heal'" (*ibid.*). And again: "Can God be man, can He be born of woman? Can he suffer beatings and be sentenced to death?" (*ibid.*). At this point the bishop intervened to cite lengthy Christological *testimonia*, and the Jew asks: "What necessity was there for God to suffer in such a manner?" To the bishop's explanation that He did so in order to save mankind from sin and reconcile man with God, the Jew rejoined: "Could not God send prophets or apostles who would bring man back to the way of salvation? and had He only the means of humiliating himself in the flesh?" (*ibid.*).

With the growth of Christian power, its clash with the conquering armies of Islam, and the consequent changes in the Jewish fate, theological argument was increasingly related to the actual historical situation. The letters of Archbishop *Agobard of Lyons against the Jews include fragments of disputations he had with them. The conversion of the Christian priest *Bodo-Eleazar to Judaism not only provoked his own vituperative anti-Christian polemics but is also evidence of the meetings and disputations which took place between Jews and Christians at the court of Emperor *Louis the Pious.

A large portion of both Jewish and Christian biblical exegetical literature, and Jewish liturgical works – *piyyutim, seliḥot*, and *kinnot* – contain polemical argument with religious, historical, and social overtones.

Under Islam, in particular in *Baghdad of the tenth century where both Jews and Christians were in the position of a minority, disputations between the two, as well as between Jews and Muslims, are found taking place in a relatively open atmosphere. *Saadiah Gaon's Arabic work *Book of Beliefs and*

Opinions incorporates and summarizes much of the argument in these disputations. His works also convey the main line adopted in Jewish *Rabbanite controversy with the *Karaites. The writings of the Karaites *Daniel b. Moses al-Qūmisi, Abu-Yusuf Jacob al *Kirkisānī, *Sahl b. Maẓli'aḥ ha-Kohen, and *Salmon b. Jeroham contain the Karaite attack on Rabbanite tradition. Many of the Karaite arguments against the Talmud, the anthropomorphic legends, contradictions, and immoral views found there, later became part of the Christian arsenal for attack on the Talmud.

GILBERT CRISPIN. About five years before the catastrophe brought on Jewry by the First *Crusade a disputation took place in England between the abbot of Westminster, Gilbert *Crispin, and a Jewish scholar. The latter, who had studied at Mainz, came there both for business and in order to meet Gilbert, who regarded the Jew as a personal acquaintance (*mihi familiaris*). He records, "Each time that we would meet, immediately [*mox*] we would have a talk [*sermo*] in a friendly spirit [*amico animo*] about the Holy Scriptures and our faith." Gilbert noted that the answers of the Jew seemed logical and worthy to those present at the discussions to be preserved. He therefore wrote down both sides of the disputation, and sent the text to Anselm, archbishop of Canterbury (*Gisleberti Crispini Disputatio Judei et Christiani;* ed. by B. Blumenkranz, Utrecht (1956), 27–8). It was the wish of both sides to hold the talk "in a tolerant spirit" [*toleranti animo*], as the Jew phrased it, while Gilbert calls for discussion "in a patient spirit" [*animo patienti*] guaranteeing to dispute "for the cause of faith and out of love to thee" (*fidei causa et tui amore*, 28–29). The atmosphere of tolerance in which the disputation was held makes it a valuable record. In addition to the discussion of former points raised in disputations between Jews and Christians, the Jew stresses the anomaly of the position accorded to Jews in Christian countries: "If the Law is to be kept [as the Jew had argued previously], why do you regard its keepers like dogs, pushing them with sticks and persecuting them everywhere?" (*ibid.*, 28). The troubled state of the world is brought as evidence against accepting Jesus as the messiah, since it contradicts the words of the prophet: "and they shall beat their swords into plowshares …." He states: "The iron with difficulty suffices the smiths for the preparation of weapons. All over the world, nation fights with nation, neighbor oppresses his neighbor and kills him. One king wars with the other" (*ibid.*, 34). Apparently describing paintings that he has seen in the Church the Jew points out: "God Himself you paint as the Man of Sorrows, hanging on the cross, pierced with nails – a terrible sight and yet you adore it… Again sometimes you paint God enthroned on high gesturing with outstretched hand, and around him – as if for greater glory – an eagle and a man, a calf and a lion; yet all this is forbidden in Exodus 20:4" (*ibid.*, 65). There is evidence of a certain interpenetration of ideals. The Christian responds to the Jew's condemnation of the warlike society of his environment by holding up monastic ideals: "There are many men of war and wrath who have left fighting and temporal riches and have turned to serve God in poverty" (*ibid.*, 38). When the Jew claimed that the Law was given to be observed the abbot pointed to Christian asceticism: "There are many of us who abstain not only from eating pork but from meat altogether" (*ibid.*, 35). On the other hand, the Jew not only insists that all the precepts of the Law should be observed but also reconciles it with the figurative understanding of the Scriptures: "Shall we condemn the letter [of the Law] because we listen to its figurative sense? And because we obeyed the letter, is there any sense in condemning the figure? We follow the letter and perceive also the figurative sense of the letter" (*ibid.*, 32). Even scholars who consider this dialogue a literary fiction would have to concede that in tone and content it expresses the spirit of arguments exchanged between Jews and Christians in a friendly atmosphere on the eve of the First Crusade.

CHRISTIAN RELIGIOUS DRAMA. The development of Christian religious drama in the 12th and 13th centuries permitted disputation with Jews to be presented in a popular dramatic form. In the Latin mystery play *Ordo Prophetarum*, a "reader" summons the Jews before him in the introduction to the Birth of Christ. The prophets appear one after the other, range themselves around the "reader," and quote passages considered to be Christological in content. In these debates the Jews are often led by an *archisynagogus*, while the prophets are led by the "reader" who in many plays is identified with *Augustine. Later, from the middle of the 12th century, beginning with the German *Ludus de Antichristo*, the rival disputants receive personification as *Ecclesia and Synagoga. Basically, all these dramas are disputations. The tone imputed to the Jews, particularly in later versions, is coarse and jeering.

CHRONICLE OF AHIMAAZ. Certain motifs in Jewish polemical literature which developed and changed over the centuries originated in reaction to the impressive display made by Christian religious life. The southern Italian 11th-century Chronicle of *Ahimaaz b. Paltiel tells of a disputation supposed to have taken place between the Jew *Shephatiah b. Amittai of Oria (ninth century) and the Byzantine emperor *Basil I concerning the beauty and splendor of the Church of Hagia Sophia in Constantinople. The Jew quotes from Scripture to prove that Solomon's Temple was even greater and more magnificent: "Then did the king say: 'Rabbi Shephatiah has overcome me in his wisdom'; and Rabbi Shephatiah answered: 'My lord, Scripture has been victorious over you and not I'" (*Megillat Aḥima'aẓ*, ed. by B. Klar (1944), 21).

12TH CENTURY. From the 12th century, apparently, chance encounters between Christians and Jews might often flare up into religious arguments. Both Jewish and Christian writers prepared manuals for the use of simple people of their faith when encountering arguments of the other side. In Christian literature this led to a long line of polemical writings against the Jews (*Adversus Judaeos*, a type that originated much earlier), intended for this purpose, some in the form of a dialogue.

In Jewish literature, such manuals are generally entitled *Sefer Nizzaḥon*, being the outcome of former chance encounters and a preparation for future ones. The subject matter of these books and the methods employed by both sides largely follow traditional lines, although concrete situations and new themes may interpose themselves.

Joseph *Kimḥi not only defends the Jewish way of life of the 12th century (see *Apologetics) but also indicates how a Jewish patrician saw the mainly feudal Christian patterns of behavior: "You cannot claim that you are circumcised in heart, for he who ... murders and whores and robs and molests people, ridicules them and behaves like a brigand, is uncircumcised in heart. Hence you are uncircumcised both in heart and body and Israel is circumcised both in heart and body. For ye will not find a Jew whom they [the Jews] will hang, neither will they gouge out his eyes, nor will they mutilate one of his members for any transgression that he may have committed" (*Sefer ha-Berit*, in: *Milḥemet Ḥovah*, Constantinople, 1710, 26b). "You see with your own eyes that the Christian goes on the road to meet strangers, not to honor them but to seize all their provisions" (*ibid.*, 21a). "Even of your priests and bishops who do not take wives, it is well known that they whore" (*ibid.*, 21b).

In the 12th–13th-century *Sefer Nizzaḥon Yashan* there is a discussion in relation to the Cathedral of Speyer between Kalonymus and Emperor Henry II. Here the Jew again quotes chapter and verse to prove that the Temple surpassed the cathedral in greatness but the argument ended with an embittered denial of the sacredness of the cathedral precincts: "After Solomon built the Temple and finished it, it is written, 'the priests could not stand to minister by reason of the cloud; for the glory of the Lord filled the house of the Lord.' Yet if they were to load dung on a donkey and lead him through this cathedral nothing would happen to him" (J.C. Wagenseil (ed.), *Tela ignea Satanae* (1681), 41–42). Some arguments in this tract appear to be directed to Christian circles opposed to the Church establishment. The Jewish adversary is advised to cite certain verses in Isaiah to "those monks and priests that have taken into their hands the whole land ... that rise early and stay late in their church for their payment that is called praebenda" (*ibid.*, 82). The problem of saint adoration and miracles performed by saints is dealt with at length (*ibid.*, 128–32). The Jewish disputant is advised to tell his Christian adversaries that one proselyte to Judaism who accepts the Jewish way of life and the Jewish fate of humiliation and suffering achieves greater glory for Judaism than many apostates to Christianity who gain materially and socially by their apostasy (*ibid.*, 242–3). As treated by Jacob of Venice (*Yeshurun*, 6 (1875), 1–34) and *Jacob b. Reuben (*Milḥamot ha-Shem*, ed. J. Rosenthal, 1963), this type of manual acquires a personal imprint. The *Sefer ha-Mekanneh* (fragments of which have been published in various learned periodicals and articles) is ascribed to three members of the Official family: the father Nathan b. Joseph *Official and his sons Joseph and Asher.

With the rise of the *Dominican order and the development of Scholasticism, disputation became the principal method of learned disquisition and was frequently used to combat the *Albigenses in the south of France.

IN MUSLIM COUNTRIES. The disputations held in the countries of Islam were, as mentioned above, much more diversified than those taking place in Christian countries. The *dhimmī (protected minorities) numbered many sects and creeds. Philosophical schools also took part in such disputations. While the argument was predicated on almost complete agreement between Muslims and Jews concerning monotheism, and opposition to Christian concepts such as incarnation, the Trinity, and icon worship, a consistently held principle of Muslim argumentation was that the Jews had falsified the original text of the Bible, having added to or subtracted from it. *Samuel b. Moses al-Maghribī, an apostate to Islam, fastened the major responsibility on Ezra the Scribe, arguing that the Torah given to Moses, which originally had been in the possession of the levites only, and known orally to the priests, had been destroyed: "When Ezra saw that the Temple of the people was destroyed by fire, that their state had disappeared, their masses dispersed and their Book vanished, he collected some of his own remembrances and some still retained by the priests, and from this he concocted the Torah that the Jews now possess. That is why they hold Ezra in such high esteem and claim that a light appears over his tomb ... for he produced a book that preserves their religion. Now this Torah that they have is in truth a book by Ezra, and not a book of God. This shows that the person who collected the sections now in their possession was an empty man, ignorant of divine attributes. That is why he attributed anthropomorphism to God – regret over His past actions and the promise of abstention from similar acts in the future" (Samuel al-Maghribī, *Ifḥām al-Yahūd* ("Silencing the Jews"), ed. and tr. by M. Perlmann, in: PAAJR, 32 (1964), 55). This attitude caused *Maimonides to forbid all religious disputation with Muslims "according to what is known to you about their belief that this Torah was not given from Heaven" (J. Blau (ed.), *Teshuvot Rambam* (1958), no. 149).

Apart from this problem of the authenticity of the text, and the anthropomorphisms the Torah was said to contain in its present state, Muslim-Jewish disputation mainly centered around charges of *anthropomorphism in the Talmud and attacks on the Jewish way of life, as for example made by the Muslim theologian Ibn Ḥazm. On their side the Jews attacked *Muhammad as "a madman" and described the *Koran as a book full of follies fit only for simpletons. Muslim pride and their oppression of the Jews were also bitterly castigated, in particular after the shock of the *Almohad atrocities in the 12th century.

THE 13TH-CENTURY DISPUTATIONS. By the 13th century the arguments used in ancient Christian, Karaite, and Muslim debate, and current trends of dialectic, culminated in a series of public disputations between Jews and apostates arranged with ceremonial splendor before royalty and high dignitaries of the clergy. The first great debate of this type to be held was the disputation of *Paris (1240) between the apostate Nicholas *Donin and the tosafist *Jehiel b. Joseph of Paris, which centered on the Talmud. The arguments of the apostate were to a large extent a continuation and development of the anti-talmudic arguments of the Karaites. The Christian side regarded and conducted the disputation as a trial in which the Jews were called upon to defend their errors. It resulted in the burning of the Talmud. In 1263 there took place in Aragon the disputation of Barcelona. The apostate Pablo *Christiani led the Christian side. The Jewish side was represented by R. Moses b. Naḥman (*Naḥmanides). This disputation centered on the problem of the nature and coming of the messiah. A version of the disputation was recorded by Naḥmanides (published in various editions), who obtained the right to express himself freely in the debates. The apostate "said that he will prove from our Talmud that the messiah prophesied by the Prophets has already come." The nature and authority of **aggadah* were also a prominent issue. Naḥmanides, like the Jewish opponent of Gilbert Crispin and other Jewish disputants, not only stressed the warlike aspect of the world after the advent of Jesus but also added that war had become integral to feudal society: "And how difficult would it be for you, my lord the king, and for these your knights, if war was no longer learned." The Jew fearlessly questioned the nature of Christian authority and teaching: "The core of the contention and quarrel between the Jews and the Christians lies in that what you state concerning the dogma of the Divinity is a very bitter thing. And you, my lord king, are a Christian, the son of a Christian father and mother. You have listened all your life to what priests, Franciscans, and Dominicans tell about the birth of Jesus, and they have filled your mind, yea, your very bones, with this matter; and it has thus become ingrained in you through habit. Yet that which you believe – and it is the heart of your faith – reason cannot agree to, nature opposes, and the Prophets never said such a thing. Miracle also cannot extend to this ... that the Creator of Heaven and Earth and all that is in them shall become an embryo in the womb of a Jewess, shall grow there for seven months, shall be born a tiny creature, shall then grow up and later be given over to his enemies, and that they will sentence him to death and kill him. And you say that later he has risen from death and returned to his first place. Such beliefs cannot convince either a Jew or any other human being. Thus your speeches are made in vain and emptiness, for that belief lies at the heart of our quarrel. But let us also talk about the messiah, if you want it so" (*Kitvei R. Moshe b. Naḥman*, ed. by H.D. Chavel, 1 (1963), 310–1).

15TH CENTURY. The last of these great spectacles was the long drawn-out disputation of *Tortosa (1413–14). The many representatives of Judaism, who were compelled by official command to come to Tortosa and stay there during the disputation, defended themselves with acumen, and, in the difficult circumstances following the massacres in Spain of 1391, acquitted themselves with considerable courage against the attacks and calumnies of the apostate Maestro Hieronymus de Sancta Fide (Joshua *Lorki), a former champion of Judaism in discussion and writing. The *Sefer Ikkarim* of Joseph Albo (see above), who participated in this disputation, is largely a summing up of the Jewish position taken there. In 15th-century Spain, when the Jews were subjected to the pressure of constant persecution and missionary persuasion, an impassioned polemical exchange developed. The sermons and writings of Vincent *Ferrer represent the most influential and penetrating presentation of the Christian side. Jewish writings attest that the breakdown of Jewish existence in Christian Spain seemingly contributed historical testimony in support of Christian supremacy, in addition to the traditional Christological argumentation. The persuasiveness of this line of thinking had already been strikingly demonstrated in the 14th century with the conversion of *Abner of Burgos (and see *apostasy). In the 15th century a series of Jews crossed over to Christianity to wage a bitter war on Judaism. In addition to Joshua Lorki, one of the most prominent was the former Rabbi Solomon ha-Levi, who as *Pablo de Santa Maria became archbishop of Burgos. His writings, and the sermons and argumentation of others like him, ultimately sealed the fate of Spanish Jewry. The exchange of views between estranged brethren introduced the genre of letter-exchange into the area of disputation from the 14th century.

On the Jewish behalf arose a witty and penetrating polemicist and satirist, Profiat *Duran. In his *Kelimat ha-Goyim* ("Confusion of the Gentiles") he makes a systematic attempt to show that early Christianity was a conglomeration of mistaken conceptions held by naive persons, exploited by, and supplemented with, the tales and ideas of later-day Christian "deceivers" who had shaped the present form of Christianity. His satirical *Al Tehi ka-Avotekha* ("Be not Like Your Fathers"), addressed to an apostate, presents apostasy as a process of tiredness and reaction from Jewish rationalistic, intellectual inquiry, coupled with attraction to the mystic doctrines of Christianity. These views are voiced here by the apostate who attacks the Jews: "Your fathers have inherited falsehood and were following foolishness; through overmuch inquiry their intellect has become disturbed ... it appears to me [the Jew] that the Holy Spirit hovers over you [the apostate] in nightly vision and talks with you while awake .... Human reason does not draw you to its dwelling, the abode of darkness .... You regard it as alien, cruel as the serpent, the eternal enemy who injures faith ... It was a reprobate who said that reason and religion are two lights. Reason has no part with us ... it does not know the way towards light ... Faith alone soars upward" (*Al Tehi-ka-Avotekha,* in: *Kovez Vikkuḥim*, ed. by Isaac b. Abraham Akrish, Breslau, 1844, 6b–7a).

The physician Ḥayyim Ibn Musa around 1460 wrote a systematic manual for Jewish disputation, directed formally against the writings of *Nicholas of Lyra and the works of the persecuting apostates and influenced by similar earlier works of Ḥasdai *Crescas and others. He was faced with the weight of Christian cultural achievement and theological literature in

Spain in a disputation with a Christian scholar in the presence of the grandee whom he attended as physician: "It happened that we three were sitting together and suddenly the above-mentioned scholar said as an opening: 'Sir, surely you know that the Jews have one theological work only, called *Moreh Nevukhim*, whereas we have so many books on theology that even a palace as great as this would not contain them, if they were stacked from earth to heaven.' To this I remained silent. The lord ordered that I should answer him. Then I said, 'Jews have no need of such books; they need only a single page.'" Ḥayyim then briefly enumerates what he considers are the self-evident doctrines of Judaism, and continues: "In these doctrines all believe [i.e., Christians also]. Only concerning two or three dogmas is there some doubt. There is total difference in unity that you have made three ... As to incorporeity, you say that the son became incarnate, but after his death everything returned to one Divinity ... As to the changing of the Law, you say that he came to add and not to diminish, and our Torah says 'Ye shall not add to it neither diminish from it.' There is no quarrel between us that the messiah means salvation. Our dispute concerns only whether 'he has come' or 'he will come.' But to believe that God could not eradicate the Original Sin of Adam except through his own death, that He became incarnate in the womb of a woman, that His wisdom could not find a way to atone for this sin except through His death, that He suffered so much abuse and pain until He died – and that after all this and despite all this men still die and go to Hell, both Christians and the sinners, all the books in the world will not convince intelligent people, and in particular those who have grown up in the way of the Torah ... therefore the Jew requires only a single page for theology, for its plain meaning agrees entirely with reason" ... "Then both of us fell silent and the lord was amazed at this speech and ordered that we should not talk before him lest we should lead him to doubt; and we remained silent" (his *Magen va-Romaḥ*, Ms. Heb. Univ. Lib. Heb. 8° 787, pp. 67–68).

The 15th century was also a period of controversialist debate in troubled and divided Germany. The apostate monk Petrus *Nigri (Schwarz) preached to the Jews in Nuremberg and tried to dispute with them. Around 1410 Yomtov Lipmann *Muelhausen wrote his *Sefer Niẓẓaḥon* (Nuremberg and Altdorf, 1644), which sums up the traditional Jewish line of defense in disputation and also puts forward systematically the arguments for attacking Christian views. Written in a rationalistic vein, it evidences signs of the strains present in the Christian Church at this time. As often occurred, some of his argumentation shows the impress of Christian molds of thought. He writes: "The Christian mocked saying, females who are uncircumcised have no Jewish character. They [the Christian mockers] do not know that faith does not depend on circumcision but is in the heart; circumcision does not make a Jew of one who does not believe correctly, and one who believes correctly is a Jew even if he is not circumcised, although he is guilty of one transgression. And circumcision is not possible with women" (*Sefer Niẓẓaḥon*, p. 19).

Later in the 15th century, Johanan Luria represented the Jewish side in occasional disputations with courage and skill. Traces of Christian impressions of disputations with Jews are found in the writings of Hans Folz. John of *Capistrano complains that "the Jews say [apparently in disputations] that everyone can be saved in his own faith."

Renaissance and Reformation

At the Renaissance courts of Italy, in the atmosphere of excitement generated by Humanism on the eve of the *Reformation, Jewish-Christian encounters often resulted in religious argumentation; sometimes such disputations were formally arranged. Abraham *Farissol tells that "our Lord Ercole, the duke of Ferrara, and his wife and brother ... ordered me many times to come before their majesties to speak and dispute with two celebrated scholars of that time and place, of the Dominican and Minorite orders. I was compelled, on their order and with their permission, to step out publicly and speak before them many times, politely and temperately ... Against my will I obeyed the above-mentioned friars and the demand of certain other scholars, such as the sage bishop of Trani who compelled me to write down in detail, in a book in their language, the questions and answers during the disputation, exactly as they had asked and I had answered them. They said that they wished to see in writing whether there could be any substance in my answers so that they would be able to answer all of them, also in writing, and sum up in a book the evidence and strength of their point of view and prove their assumptions" (cf. HHY, 12 (1928), 286). The Hebrew version of his disputations, *Magen Avraham* (largely in manuscript), touches on a variety of subjects. It can be seen that Farissol was in close touch with both heretical "Judeo-Christian" circles among Jews, in particular among the exiles from Spain and Portugal, and heretical Christian "Judaizing," or anticlerical and anti-traditional, circles of Christian society. He quotes the opinions of such circles and sometimes gives information about their leaders. Farissol indicates that leadership is necessary for man's salvation, secular or spiritual (cf. REJ, 105 (1940), 37). In this context, for the sake of argument, under the heading "That the True Messiah to Israel has not yet come," he expresses the view: "I regard it a plausible possibility that they [i.e., the Christians] may call him [Jesus] their messiah and savior. For they as well as he say that after his coming and his teachings they were saved and cleansed from the stain of idolatry. And through him, and his apostles and companions, they have come very near to believing after a fashion in the unity of the First Cause, combining other assumptions and additions and innovations to believe in the Divine Law ... coming nearer to the truth than any others, for they have approached him from a very far distance, previously worshipping the dual forces that God hates" (*ibid.*, 38). Farissol proceeds to show at length that Jesus does not fulfill the conditions of the messiah promised to Israel (*ibid.*, 38–40). He also defends Jewish moneylending, arguing that in 16th-century society there could be no social or ethical reason for differentiation between income from money and income from other sources (HHY, 12 (1928), 290–7). He devoted a detailed chapter to criticism of the Bible translation of *Jerome (*ibid.*, 287–90).

With the rise and development of the Reformation in Central Europe, Martin *Luther and others among its originators made strenuous efforts to persuade the Jews to join their new brand of Christianity. Their failure turned Luther and *Martin Bucer (Butzer) into rabid enemies and persecutors of the Jews. From both the benevolent and the hostile standpoint they frequently had occasion to take issue with Judaism. An anonymous Jew, who early perceived the reliance placed on primary biblical sources in Lutheran argumentation, advised Jewish disputants as a preliminary to state that Jewish monotheism does not need support from texts: "The way of nature, through heart and through mind, obligates man to believe in pure monotheism. One has to believe it necessary that there be a Unity ruling the whole cosmos ... And so shall you speak to them in order to purify, cleanse them – if there were [no] book in the world, what could be done [to prove Christianity]? And how can you believe in it now? For their faith is founded on our Prophets and Holy Scriptures. If we have no Prophets, they have no testimony to adduce nor Scripture to expound. Whereas we have a root and foundation, even lacking every book or writing, in nature – for we believe in His unity and greatness as the Creator through His action in first place, and because whatever we do each day cannot be done, except by His will" (cf. Ḥ.H. Ben Sasson, in: HTR, 59 (1966), 388–9).

Not only do the writings of Jewish leaders and authors in the heart of Christian Europe, such as the communal leader *Joseph (Joselmann) b. Gershon of Rosheim, the chronicler *Joseph ha-Kohen, and the kabbalist *Abraham b. Eliezer ha-Levi, contain many impressions of the Reformation movement and its ideas and actions, sometimes in a polemical vein, but there are also remoter echoes of the Christian-Jewish debate. In the first half of the 16th century, the physician Abraham Ibn Migash, living in the Muslim capital of Constantinople, tells, "there came to my house an uncircumcised Spaniard, who esteemed himself wise, and he questioned me." The ensuing dispute on the initiative of the Christian, written down by the Jew, mainly includes traditional elements of "the exegetical core" of Christian-Jewish disputation. The Jew argues in principle against basing exegesis on translations of the biblical text: "Tell me, please, where do you find in any science or teaching that a word is isolated from its meaning, as understood in the language in which it is current and fixed within the frame of that language, to give it a separate meaning taken from an alien language?... This cannot be done, for if you do so the meanings of words and concepts will change and intermingle and will not be understood immediately. Communication will cease." The Christian complains of the pride displayed by Jews in their divine election. He argues that the Law concerning the election is not eternal, and bases his argumentation on talmudic quotations. The disputation shows that the Spaniard had knowledge of Hebrew and rabbinical sources and that the Jew was well acquainted with the principles of Christianity. He ends his written report with a prayer for the conversion of the Christian (*Kevod Elohim*, Constantinople, 1585, 128b–31b; and see also his anti-Christian remarks and tales, *ibid.*, 124b–8b).

HIZZUK EMUNAH. The medieval and Reformation Jewish anti-Christian disputation is brought to perfection in the *Ḥizzuk Emunah* (ed. by D. Deutsch, 1872) of Isaac b. Abraham *Troki. The criticism of the New Testament in this work profoundly influenced Voltaire, according to his own evidence. It was written to strengthen Jews in combating Christian argumentation, being the outcome of the questions that Isaac "disputed with bishops and lords .... My speech with them was mild, to influence and not to anger .... I said nothing for which I could not provide a true biblical quotation .... I am not afraid of the multitude in writing down words of truth and good taste, for the truth is loved by every wise man .... I intended to write down those arguments which are deemed by the uncircumcised to be strong as the work of a great artist, firm and true. With their refutation, the weaker arguments will fall of themselves .... My first proposition is to explain what caused the Christian scholars, with all their great learning in the sciences known to man, to hold beliefs which are foreign to the human intellect and without authentic evidence from the words of the Prophets" (*ibid.*, 9–13). Isaac not only defends the Jewish interpretation of the Bible and points out in detail discrepancies in the Gospels but also finds much to his advantage in the controversy within the Christian camp. The anti-Trinitarian arguments of Simon *Budny and others are used by him against the Trinitarians. The innovations of Lutheranism and Calvinism, the reciprocal persecution of Catholics and Reformers, the low status of the Greek Orthodox community in Catholic Poland, and the prosperity and power achieved by Islam, all these elements perceived on Isaac's horizon are used to rebut Christian argumentation based on Jewish weakness and suffering in the Exile.

Modern Times

The first disputation under conditions which assume a certain equality between the opponents took place in the Netherlands in 1686 between the Jew Isaac (Balthazar) *Orobio de Castro and the Christian Philipp van Limborch, written down and published as an exchange of letters by van Limborch under the title *De veritate religionis christianae; amica collatio cum erudito Judaeo* (Gouda, 1687). While the discussion largely follows traditional lines, there is a difference in tone; thus the Jewish argument based on the prevalence of war and strife in the world becomes internalized and psychologized. Orobio states that so far as he can see the Christian messiah has not changed men by enabling them to love their neighbors more than they could before his coming (*ibid.*, Ch. 17). Van Limborch, on the other hand, claims that true Christians do not consider Jesus as God, but state only that he was the "Son of God," meaning that he was greater than Moses, being both prophet and messiah.

FRANKIST DISPUTATIONS. In 1757, at Kamienec (*Kamenets), and in 1759, at *Lvov, a disputation took place between Jacob *Frank and his followers and the leaders of Polish Jewry. This essentially began as an internal quarrel within the Jewish camp, as the first phase of the debate, at Kamienec, proved conclusively. The theses of the Frankists in the second phase, at Lvov, were dictated to them by their Christian patrons and a result of their own frustration and bitterness. Hence they included, as their seventh point in the disputation, the charge that Jews require Christian blood for ritual purposes at Passover, thus giving currency to the old *blood libel. On this they were answered by the chief Jewish spokesman, Ḥayyim ha-Kohen Rapoport, who cited from Christian documents and authorities refuting the libel, supported by comparisons from outside Europe: "You adduce against us this seventh point and say that you are arguing not with evil intent or out of revenge but only through love of the truth. But this [the blood libel] is not a matter relating to the Catholic Church or its faith. Here we truly perceive your evil intent towards us and your passion for revenge … Can you supply thorough evidence in support of these false claims about a matter in opposition to man's habits and nature which supposes that we, the breed of Abraham, from whom we come and to whom we shall return (after death) require and use human blood? A charge that has not been heard of in Asia, in Africa, or in Europe, or in the whole world against any other nation (even the most heretical one). And this you intended to prove against us?" (M. Balaban, *Toledot ha-Tenu'ah ha-Frankit* (1935), 256).

MENDELSSOHN AND LAVATER. Moses *Mendelssohn was shocked and dismayed when he was called upon by J.C. Lavater in 1769 either to refute the "evidence for the truth of Christianity" that he, Lavater, had translated into German from the French and published, or to do "what Socrates would have done if he had read this work and found it irrefutable." Mendelssohn, who rejected in principle the demand for public disputation, at first stated that his continued adherence to Judaism, in its present state of humiliation, and his well-known constant search for philosophical truth furnished self-evident proof that he had investigated Judaism and found it worthy to adhere to and suffer for, and that he had found no reason for turning to Christianity, even though he was well aware that this would give him full civil rights and a better social life. He thus uses its humiliation as an argument for Judaism and its ability to confer material advantages on apostates as an argument against Christianity. Mendelssohn claimed that to hold a public disputation would endanger the present status of his brethren in Christian society. He also stated that Judaism is not missionary; the proselyte is warned before he joins it: "he who is not born under our Laws need not live according to them." Mendelssohn regarded missionary work as ridiculous when addressed to intelligent people and pictured it as trying to convert Confucius to Judaism or Christianity.

As the storm raised by Lavater grew, Mendelssohn reluctantly abandoned his opposition to controversial debate. In the spirit of medieval Jewish argumentation he told his adversaries: "A single Christian who agrees to be circumcised proves more for Judaism than a hundred Jews who agree to be baptized prove for the truth of Christianity." In another context Mendelssohn is ironical about the Christian conception that Jesus had abolished the Law given by God, while not having done so expressly. When the Crown Prince of Brunswick-Wolfenbuettel respectfully asked Mendelssohn to explain his position, Mendelssohn answered in a clear polemical vein, listing four principles that he would have to accept as a Christian and that reason rejects: "(1) a Trinity in the Divine essence; (2) the incarnation of a God; (3) the physical sufferings of a person of the Divinity which would contravene its Divine majesty; (4) the satisfaction of the first Person in the Divinity through the suffering and the death of the humiliated second Person." These, and similar principles of Christianity, Mendelssohn states, he would not believe even if they were vouched for in the Old Testament. He was also unable to accept the concept of Original Sin. In addition to contending that Jesus did not abolish the Law expressly, he also points out that he, Mendelssohn, was well acquainted with the Hebrew of the Bible and could not find Christological evidence there (M. Mendelssohn, *Gesammelte Schriften*, 7 (1930), in particular 7–13, 63, 91, 299–304, 321; see also 16, (1929), 142, 148, 150–1).

Relationships between Christians and Jews in the modern environment were faced with the paradox of *emancipation of the Jews on the one hand and modern-type *antisemitism on the other. Trends toward *assimilation were confronted with *Zionism. Jews entering the environing society encountered the romantic reaction of nationalist *Volksgeist* and "Christian state" conceptions. Christian-Jewish discussion enters a new phase in the 20th century. It is held in an arena where a plethora of diverse opinions, each claiming orthodoxy for itself and heresy for the others, are argued both informally and in the public eye.

ROSENZWEIG AND ROSENSTOCK. In this dynamic climate of tension there took place the friendly but trenchant disputation between an apostate devoted to Christianity, the legal historian, philosopher, and sociologist Eugen *Rosenstock-Heussy, and the great Jewish philosopher, Franz *Rosenzweig, then a young man. During their exchange of letters both were serving in the German army, writing almost from foxhole to foxhole. Between May and December 1916 they exchanged 21 letters, originating from a spirited conversation they had had in 1913. Although intended as a private exchange of views, the correspondence contains in a nutshell the dilemmas confronting a Jewish intellectual at that time. Later, in 1917, Rosenzweig described Rosenstock as "a persistent but inexperienced missionary" and stated in retrospect that the letters "cannot be made into a 'Dialogue,' for they were not; they were simply a bombardment between two learned canons with a lyrical urge." Hence, at least in the view of the Jewish participant, this was a disputation in the subjective medieval sense.

In his letters, Rosenstock-Heussy stresses the traditional Christian arguments that the Law had been abolished and salvation lay in Christianity. Inherent in the character of Jewish Law are self-righteousness and impassivity in contrast to the true spirituality and dynamics of Christianity. Rosenstock regards as presumption the Jewish reliance on their descent and on their continued history as an argument in favor of Judaism. The Jews had crucified Him who came to fulfill the Divine promise that all the Gentiles would come to Jerusalem. Christianity had liberated the individual from the bonds of family ties and national limitations. Present-day Jews live non-Jewish lives, as present-day Christians live non-Christian lives, but to the Christian this discrepancy between the ideal and its realization is part of the cross he has undertaken to carry. What, however, is the sense to a Jew who lives a non-Jewish life, "plays the organ and thinks in a non-Jewish way"; to a Jew without the Temple and without the Law, who does not marry at the age of 18, does not evade army service; to a Jew who makes his girl a Jewess so that he can marry her; where then remain the metaphysics of "the children of Abraham"? Rosenzweig pointed out in his answer that many elements in this attack on modern Jewish life in Germany were derived from a picture taking the "true Jewish life," to mean that represented by the Jews from Eastern Europe, the despised "Ost-Jude." Rosenstock compares the *akedah* of Isaac by Abraham, the sacrifice of a son, with the sacrifice according to the New Testament whereby he who fulfills the covenant with God sacrifices himself. This is the dividing line. The synagogue has talked for two thousand years about what she has, because she has nothing; Israel in this world assumes the pride of Lucifer. Judaism is in the age of blind senility: "I know that Judea will outlive all 'the Nations,' but you have no capacity for theology, for inquiry after truth, or for beauty. Thou shalt not make any image. At this price the Eternal Jew may live because he hangs on tenaciously to the life granted to him. But he is cursed to live by the sweat of his brow, taking loans everywhere, and making loans everywhere. The Jew dies for no fatherland and for no mission. He lives because his life does not approach the margin of life. He lives in a chimerical reflection of a real life that cannot be envisaged without the sacrifice of death and the nearness of the abyss. That Judea shall live on is dependent on the success of the individual Jew, on the number of his children. He is a paragraph of the Law, *c'est tout.* You may well believe that you have your own ship, but you do not know the sea at all, otherwise you would not speak in this way, you who are never shipwrecked.... You do not know that the world is movement and change; the Christian says there is day and there is night, but you are so moonstruck that you think that the night view is the only view that exists and you consider as the ideal conception the minimum of light, the night. You consider that this encompasses day and night" (F. Rosenzweig, *Briefe* (1935), 682). Subconsciously or consciously, Rosenstock the apostate combines medieval Jew-hatred with the images and expressions of modern social and economic antisemitism. He considers that "the emancipation of the Jews is a process of self-destruction, for Europe," in its modern phase. He is violently opposed to Zionism. Even if Hebrew is made into a living language it cannot be saved in the metaphysical sense.

To this attack Rosenzweig answers that "the serious acceptance in reality in which the theological principle about Jewish stubbornness is being worked out is Jew-hatred. You know as well as I that all the realistic explanations of this hatred are only so many fashionable dressings to hide the only true metaphysical reason, which is, metaphysically formulated, that we refuse to take part in the fiction of the Christian dogma that has gained world acceptance because (although reality) it is fiction (and *fiat veritas, pereat realitas,* for 'Thou God art truth'), and, formulated in the manner of enlightenment (by Goethe in *Wilhelm Meister*): that we deny the basis of present culture (and '*fiat regnum Dei, pereat mundus,*' for 'a kingdom of priests shall ye be unto me, and a holy people'); to formulate it in an unenlightened way: that we have crucified Christ and, believe me, we shall do it again any time, we alone in all the world (and *fiat nomen Dei Unius, pereat homo,* for 'whom shall you make equal to me that I will be equal')" (*ibid.*, 670–1). Thus Rosenzweig points out that the Church is obliged to formulate the concept of Jewish stubbornness; it is part of her dogma. "Do whatever you want, you cannot get rid of us. We live on, 'the Eternal Jew,' out of a feeling of duty to life and not because of hunger for it." He agrees that there is a contrast between the sacrifice of Isaac and the crucifixion, but in a different sense from the apostate's conception. Abraham sacrificed "not a child but the 'only' son and what is more: the son of the promise to the God of that promise ... the content of which is being made impossible according to human concepts through this sacrifice. We do not read this pericope on our most solemn Holy Days without reason. It is the prototypal sacrifice, not of one's own individuality (Golgotha) but of the folk existence of 'the son' and of all future sons ... Abraham sacrificed all that he could be; Christ all that he was" (*ibid.*, 689). Jewish life is not the way of life of the Polish Jew as depicted by Rosenstock. "Alongside this life, which is amoral in the deepest sense and external, there exists a purely Jewish life, which is internal, one that serves all that has to be worked out internally, not bought from externally, for the sake of the preservation of the people, its 'life.' To this realm belong the internal-Jewish leadership activity, here Jewish theology, here the art of the Synagogue (so even 'beauty'). However much these phenomena may hold of the alien, Judaism cannot but help assimilate them to itself. It does so of itself even if not intending to.... The extent to which the Jew takes part in the life of other nations is not determined for him by himself, but they dictate it for him" (*ibid.*, 691). Rosenzweig relates himself to the metaphor of the ship traveling eternally on high seas. He answers Rosenstock that the Jew may give up everything "except one: hope; before God's seat the Jew, so it is said, is asked only this: Have you hoped for salvation?" (*ibid.*, 693).

This dispute is marked by a deep interpenetration of problematics and symbolism. Rosenstock demands from a

Jew that he live a full Jewish life both personally and in family life. He attacks Zionism as an evil manifestation of Judaism. Rosenzweig even as a young man was deeply influenced by Christian symbolism, which permeated his thought. He wrote in 1913, "I thought that I had Christianized my Judaism, in reality I have Judaized Christianity.... I was envious of the Church scepter because I thought that the Synagogue clings to a broken scepter" (*ibid.*, 72). The image of the Synagogue created by Church art haunts Rosenzweig. He explains it as a kind of Jewish symbol: "The Synagogue, immortal, but with a broken staff and a scarf over her eyes, must renounce all worldly work and concentrate all her strength on keeping herself alive and pure from life.... The Synagogue had a scarf over her eyes; she didn't see the world – how could she have seen the idols in it? She looked and saw only with the prophetic eye of the internal, and therefore only the last things and the farthest ones" (*ibid.*, 74–5).

In this exchange of views, rich in symbols and intellectual allusions, the turbulent, disintegrating world of the German-Jewish intellectual of the early 20th century – still craving some sort of integration – is mirrored through its divided souls.

BUBER AND SCHMIDT. The agonized, semiformal disputation between Karl Ludwig Schmidt and Martin Buber took place as the fate of German Jewry hung in the balance, at the beginning of the road to the *Nuremberg laws and the *Holocaust. The Christian, who was fully aware of the predicament which Jewry was already facing at the time the disputation was held (Jan. 14, 1933), dismissed the crucial issue by saying: "It would be ostrich policy to attempt to deny the racial biological [*rassenbiologische*] and racial hygienic [*rassenhygienische*] problems which arise with the existence of the Jews among other people" (*Theologische Blaetter,* 12 (1933), 264). He rightly considered it a courageous act to invite Jews to brotherhood with Christians, which he repeatedly urged in this disputation, although only as sons of a Germany united through the Christian conception of the Church as the spiritual Israel (*ibid.*, 258, 259, 264, 272, 273). He was sure that "the Christian message says in this context: God has willed all this; Jesus, the Messiah rejected by his people, prophesied the destruction of Jerusalem. Jerusalem has been destroyed, so that it will never again come under Jewish rule. Until the present day the Jewish diaspora has no center" (*ibid.*, 262). Not only is the ancient Christian argument from Jewish suffering and loss of political existence invoked here in the year 1933 of the Christian era, but it was made with an eye on Zionism, which Schmidt looked upon as even worse than the old simple Judaism: "The modern world reacts to Zionism, which is national or even racist [*oder gar voelkischen*], on its own side in a racist way; of course it must not be forgotten that racist antisemitism in the modern world is pre-Zionist" (*ibid.*). Schmidt asks why the Jews participate so actively in revolutions when so much is said about their conservatism (*ibid.*, 263). He declares to the Jews, or perhaps warns them, "that the Church of Jesus Christ has again and again shown her want of this Jewry, demonstrating her patience by waiting in hope that finally the Jews also ... will be able to perceive that only the Church of the Messiah, Jesus of Nazareth, is the people of God, chosen by God, and that the Jews should become incorporated in it, if they indeed feel themselves as Israel" (*ibid.*, 264). He assures the Jews that "if and when the Church becomes more Christian than it is today, its conflict with Judaism will also become sharper, as it can and may do now. This sharp conflict has been present from the beginning of the history of Christianity." The conflict expresses the hurt and pain of the first Christians, Jews themselves, at the rejection of the Messiah by their brethren in the flesh (*ibid.*, 272). Schmidt strongly and courageously repudiates the racist attitude against the Jews and glorification of the State. To Buber's assertion that in the present condition of the world the signs of salvation are lacking, Schmidt answers with the hope of the second coming of Jesus (*ibid.*).

Toward the end of the disputation Buber answered the Christian from the plane of spiritual strength and pride derived from existential and material weakness and humiliation, in the ancient tradition of Jewish disputation: "I live not far from the city of Worms, to which I am bound by tradition of my forefathers; and, from time to time, I go there. When I go, I first go to the cathedral. It is a visible harmony of members, a totality in which no part deviates from perfection. I walk about the cathedral with consummate joy, gazing at it. Then I go over to the Jewish cemetery consisting of crooked, cracked, shapeless, random stones. I station myself there, gaze upward from the jumble of a cemetery to that glorious harmony, and seem to be looking up from Israel to the Church. Below, there is no jot of form; there are only the stones and the dust lying beneath the stones. The dust is there, no matter how thinly scattered. There lies the corporeality of man, which has turned to this. There it is. There it is for me. There it is for me, not as corporeality within the space of this planet, but as corporeality in my own memory, far into the depths of history, as far back as Sinai.

"I have stood there, have been united with the dust, and through it with the Patriarchs. That is a memory of the transaction with God which is given to all Jews. From this the perfection of the Christian house of God cannot separate me, nothing can separate me from the sacred history of Israel.

"I have stood there and have experienced everything myself; with all this death has confronted me, all the dust, all the ruin, all the wordless misery is mine; but the covenant has not been withdrawn from me. I lie on the ground, fallen like these stones. But it has not been withdrawn from me.

"The cathedral is as it is. The cemetery is as it is. But nothing has been withdrawn from us" (*ibid.*, 273).

Israel, strong and united in its national-religious continuity, cannot accept the Christian view that the world has been redeemed with the coming of Jesus. Buber in Nazi Germany declares: "We also know, as we know that there exists air that we take into our lungs, that there exists the plane on which we move; nay, deeper, more truly we know that world history has not yet been probed to its roots, that the world is not yet redeemed. We feel the unredeemability of the world" (*ibid.*, 267). Israel is both a nation and a religion, hence it is different from all other nations and religions. Man's confrontation with God demands nationality "as the precondition of the whole human answer to God. There must be a nation in which the human answer can be fulfilled in life in its entirety, to which public life also belongs. Not the individual as an individual, but only the community as a plurality and unity, working together ... can give God the full life-answer of man; therefore ... there is Israel" (*ibid.*, 268). The European community of nations has agreed, by accepting emancipation, to accept Jews as individuals. It rejects Jewish participation in creative life as a nation. Hence the stress placed by Zionism on the national aspect as a counter-balance to the prolonged denial of this aspect in modern times (*ibid.*, 270). To Schmidt's question, or insinuation, concerning Jewish conservatism and revolutionary activity, Buber answers that Jewish messianism calls forth both these aspects. Viewed from the standpoint of messianism, every state, however structured, is a problematical model of the divine state in the *eschaton.* But this same messianism always demands the Jew to see the other, questionable side of the state, its failure in realizations of the ideal: "Israel can never turn away its face from the state; it can never deny it; it must accept it; at the same time it must long for the perfection of the state, which is only so unsatisfactorily hinted at by every realization it achieves. Both the conservative and the revolutionary Jewish attitudes stem from the same [messianic feeling]" (*ibid.*, 271).

To the harsh and uncompromising postulate that the Jews can live in Europe only on acceptance of Christian conditions and conceptions Buber presents his thesis of open dialogue between Israel as a nation and religion, and Christianity as a religion for other nations. He proposes personally "to accept what others believe against our existence, against our consciousness of existence, as their religious reality, as a mystery. We cannot judge its meaning because we do not know it from the inside as we know ourselves from the inside" (*ibid.*, 266). "God's gates are open to all. The Christian need not come to them through Judaism. The Jew is not obliged to go to them through Christianity in order to arrive at God" (*ibid.*, 274). "No man that is not of Israel understands the mystery of Israel, and no man that is not of Christianity understands the mystery of Christianity; but unknowing they may acknowledge each other in mystery. How it can be possible that mysteries exist alongside each other is God's mystery" (*ibid.*, 267).

With these words Buber opened a way to divesting religious disputation of the polemical form it had assumed throughout most of its history and presenting it as an open and friendly meeting, ecumenical in the fullest sense. He had ancient Jewish ideological precedents for looking upon plurality of creeds and customs as "God's mystery" (notably the statements by various Jewish disputants in the 15th to 16th centuries and Maimonides' views on Christianity referred to above). Buber, however, reformulated this conception in modern terms, where it assumes a validity through anguish that disregarded fear, facing danger and humiliation.

Jewish-Christian disputation thus began in the meeting of Justin and Tryphon under the shadow of the Bar Kokhba revolt. The darkness and flames of the Holocaust and the light from Zion may illumine the pilgrimage to ecumenical conversation on equal terms, toward understanding and harmonious living, waiting for God to solve His own mystery in history.

BIBLIOGRAPHY: Baron, Social[2], 1 (1952), 188–207; 2 (1952), 71–88, 129–41, 151–62, 169–73, 187–91; 5 (1957), 82–137, 267–84; 8 (1958), 55–137; 9 (1965), 55–134; idem, in: *Diogenes*, 61 (1968), 32–51; J. Katz, *Exclusiveness and Tolerance* (1961); A.L. Williams, *Adversus Judaeos* (1935); J.W. Parkes, *Conflict of the Church and the Synagogue* (1964[2]), includes bibliography; O.S. Rankin, *Jewish Religious Polemic...* (1956); H.J. Schoeps, *Jewish-Christian Argument* (1963); A. Neubauer and S.R. Driver, *Fifty-Third Chapter of Isaiah ...*, 2 vols. (1876–77); Y. Baer, *Yisrael ba-Ammim* (1955); idem, in: *Tarbiz*, 2 (1930/31), 172–87; idem, in: *Zion*, 21 (1956), 1–49; 31 (1966), 117–45; Baer, Spain, 1 (1961), 150–9, 246–9; 2 (1966), 170–243; E.E. Urbach, *Ḥazal, Pirkei Emunot ve-De'ot* (1969), 466–502, 585–623 and passim; J.D. Eisenstein, *Oẓar Vikkuḥim* (1928); Dinur, Golah, 1 (1961), 282–379, 437–49; 2 (1966), 506–41; 4 (1969), 139–274; P. Browe, *Judenmission im Mittelalter und die Paepste* (1942), 55–130; H. Pflaum, *Die religioese Disputation in der europaeischen Dichtung des Mittelalters* (1935); M. Steinschneider, *Polemische und apologetische Literatur in arabischer Sprache* (1877); A. Posnanski, *Schiloh ... Geschichte der Messiaslehre* (1904); B. Blumenkranz, *Juden und Judentum in der mittelalterlichen Kunst* (1965); idem, *Juifs et Chrétiens dans le monde occidental 430–1096* (1965); idem, in: P. Wilpert (ed.), *Judentum im Mittelalter* (1966), 264–82; W.S. Seiferth, *Synagoge und Kirche im Mittelalter* (1964); A. Pacios Lopez, *La Disputa de Tortosa*, 2 vols. (1957); C. Roth, in: HTR, 43 (1950), 117–44; H.H. Ben-Sasson, *ibid.*, 59 (1966), 369–90; idem (ed.), *Toledot Am Yisrael*, 2 (1969), 34–36, 104–5, 164–70, 220–3, 309–11; idem, *Ha-Yehudim Mul ha-Reformazyah* (1969); M.A. Cohen, in: HUCA, 35 (1964), 157–92.

[Haim Hillel Ben-Sasson]

DISRAELI, BENJAMIN, EARL OF BEACONSFIELD (1804–1881), British statesman and novelist. His father, the historian and essayist Isaac *D'Israeli, quarreled with the London Sephardi community, and had his children baptized when Benjamin was 13 years old. Disraeli received a Christian upbringing, but his Jewish origins had a marked influence upon him. After unfortunate business ventures and after an abortive attempt to publish a morning newspaper, he wrote a number of satirical novels on English political society, starting with *Vivian Grey* (1826). This gave him an entry to London society, where his original dress and other extravagances made him a conspicuous figure. In 1828–31, an extensive tour of the Near East helped to determine his future attitude on foreign affairs and imperialism. A visit to Jerusalem made him conscious of the link between Judaism and Christianity and aroused his sympathy for the Ottoman Empire, where Jews were tolerantly treated. The literary harvest of this journey was *Alroy* (1833), a novel about Jewish messianism in the 12th century, in which the Jewish hero, David *Alroy, fails in his attempt to create a Jewish empire in Asia because it lacks the inspiration of Zion.

Disraeli's social ambitions drew him inevitably into politics, but it was not until 1837 that he was elected to Parliament as a Tory. Thereafter throughout his political career he followed a consistent line. His political philosophy is expressed in his *Vindication of the English Constitution* (1835), a development of the Conservative ideology evolved by Bolingbroke and Burke in the 18th century. On the one hand, he regarded the nation as a historically developed organism, whose well-being depended upon a balanced hierarchical structure of crown, church, and aristocracy. On the other hand, he wanted to restore the Tory party to its original historical role of leadership, guiding the way to national popular reform. He wished to transform the party from a purely aristocratic one to a popular movement embracing the working class. At first, Disraeli was met with suspicion and hostility, both within his party and outside, but within a few years he had made his mark as a brilliant parliamentary debater. In 1841, in reaction to his failure to receive an appointment in Peel's cabinet and in rejection of its bourgeois policy, he became leader of a group of young Conservative politicians, the "Young England" movement. A romantic party of revolt, which dreamed of gathering the people around the crown and the church under aristocratic leadership, it was hostile both to the middle class and to capitalism. Once again his personal experience found literary expression, this time in three major novels in which Disraeli's specific Tory outlook is the dominant theme. In *Coningsby* (1844), the rich banker Sidonia, who represents the outlook of the Jewish people, can be recognized as an idealized self-portrait merged into an idealized Rothschild. In the second, *Sybil* (1845), he warns against the contradiction between capital and labor, denounces the horror of the factory system and the division into two nations, rich and poor, mutually antagonistic. He looks back to a patriarchal medievalism with its natural aristocratic leadership and forward to the future with its demand for new thinking and new solutions. The hero of *Tancred* (1847), a young aristocrat, seeks to reestablish the harmony of English society. He goes to Palestine to restore to the Christian Church its Jewish foundations which are the bases of European civilization and to revive its moral and religious force.

The year 1846 was a turning-point in his political career. His opposition to the repeal of the Corn Laws, which protected the farmer whom he regarded as the backbone of English society, split the Conservative party; this led Prime Minister Peel to resign and left Disraeli as one of the acknowledged leaders of the Protectionist party.

When, in 1848, Baron Lionel de *Rothschild was elected to Parliament but was not permitted, as a Jew, to take his seat, Disraeli supported his right to be admitted. This he did not on the Liberals' grounds of religious tolerance, but rather because of the debt which Europe, and especially England, owed Jewry from whose midst the Christian savior had come. Although this angered high personages in his party, he boldly and constantly reminded them of his own Jewish origin and of their debt to this people.

Disraeli stressed his theory of the link between Judaism and Christianity in his biography of Lord George Bentinck (1852). He regarded the Semitic race as superior, and the Jews as its elite because of their spirituality. This spirituality, in his view, was ultimately and most finely embodied in the Church, in contrast to the materialism characteristic of the northern races. Disraeli attributed the preservation of Jewish vitality and power from ancient times to their purity of blood and their natural conservative attitude toward religion, aristocratic privilege, and property. With this theory he underlined his Toryism; on it he based his belief in the bond between the English people and the Jews. Moreover, the institutions and laws of English society, as well as those of Europe, were based on Semitic principles, and the debt owed to Jews had to be recognized and their proper place fully accorded them.

In 1852 the Tory party came to power under Lord Derby, and Disraeli became chancellor of the exchequer and leader of the House of Commons. He announced his party's rejection of protection but attempted to compensate the protectionists in his budget: when this was defeated after days of acrimonious debate, the government resigned. In 1858, he had another brief taste of power in Derby's second administration, and in June 1866 returned again to office. Disraeli's ideological views were reflected in his political career. Hence in 1867, as leader of the Commons, he proposed and carried an electoral reform bill extending the franchise to the industrial classes. This "leap in the dark" was in conformity with his view that the Conservative party should be popularly based. In 1868, on Lord Derby's resignation, Disraeli had his first brief term as prime minister and consolidated the warm friendship which he had already established with Queen Victoria. Ironically he was defeated at the general election based on the new suffrage. In 1874, he became prime minister once again after a decisive Conservative victory. During his six years of office, he applied the social principles for which he had always stood. He tried to bridge the gap between capital and labor by social and factory legislation directed toward a paternalistic rather than a modern welfare state. His foreign policy was guided by the desire to restore to England the glory which he thought had been weakened by Liberal pacifist policy. An important part of this policy was the attempt to enhance the British Empire, as the stronghold of culture, peace, and liberty. India was for him the heart of the Empire, and the acquisition of shares in the Suez Canal from the khedive of Egypt in 1875 with the financial help of the *Rothschilds was designed to ensure English control over the vital route to India.

In 1876 the Queen was proclaimed Empress of India and Disraeli was rewarded by being created Earl of Beaconsfield. In the ensuing developments, the central problem was Anglo-Russian rivalry. Disraeli adopted an aggressive policy, designed to check Russian penetration into the Mediterranean as well as to preserve the Ottoman Empire as a barrier. Critics of his policy asserted that its criterion was the attitude of these powers to Jews. When the Treaty of San Stefano (1878) resulted in the domination of Russia over the Balkans, he insisted that the agreement be submitted to the great powers, and at the subsequent Congress of *Berlin, Russia was forced to renounce all her acquisitions. This Congress was considered a personal triumph for Disraeli. He also supported the inclusion in the treaty of a clause granting rights to the Jews of the new Balkan countries. However, the anonymous memorandum prepared in 1878 for submission to the Congress, proposing the creation of a Jewish State in Palestine and once ascribed to Disraeli, is now proved to have been written by J.L. *Gordon. Economic crises and failures in Africa and Central Asia led to a Conservative defeat at the polls in 1880 followed by the resignation of the government. In his enforced leisure, Disraeli completed his *Endymion*, the most fascinating of his political novels.

The attitude of historians to Disraeli has been ambivalent. Some have seen him as an outstanding statesman, others as a political adventurer. He is now felt to have had a coherent philosophy and clearly defined political aims. The extravagant enthusiasms which marked his writings and his life, as well as his practical acumen, aroused suspicion. Yet despite many failures, Disraeli remained an optimist. His knowledge of Judaism was negligible, yet he gloried in his Jewish origin. His effort to prove that Christianity was a continuation of Judaism and his attempts to find a common denominator of Judaism and Christianity were misguided. His theory of race was wholly unscientific. A vaguely Zionist idea, that the Jew and Palestine are linked by destiny, runs through all his novels. A characteristic passage occurs in *Tancred:* "The vineyards of Israel have ceased to exist, but the eternal Law enjoins the children of Israel still to celebrate the vintage. A race that persists in celebrating their vintage although they have no fruits to gather, will regain their vineyards."

[Zvi Adiv]

As a Novelist

Disraeli's novels are closely related to his political career and ideology. They are not propaganda, but rather visionary statements of those same ideas and beliefs which underlay his special brand of Toryism. From a literary point of view, his works represent a somewhat strange mixture. They look back to the exotic Gothic novels of the late 18th century in their use of extravagant episode and high-pitched language. At the same time, they look forward to a new style later to be practiced by such writers as Mrs. Gaskell and Charles Kingsley, in which the novel deals with practical, social, and political issues with a view to righting wrongs.

In Disraeli's case, the inspiration is to be found in his desire to set up a new political movement (*Coningsby*, 1844), in his desire to improve the condition of the people in the new industrial towns (*Sybil*, 1845), and in his wish to revitalize the Church so as to make it a more effective moral and religious force (*Tancred*, 1847). There is also a certain Jewish strain of messianism in Disraeli's writing. In *Tancred* he proclaims his wish to set up a theocratic form of government, and his hero desires that the British might "conquer the world with angels at our head." Disraeli's conception of the British Empire is in fact

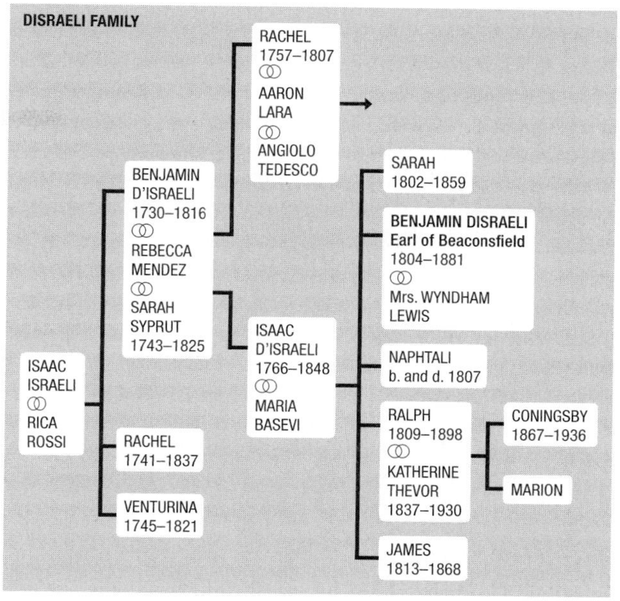

nourished – unconsciously no doubt – by Jewish sources, but his Judaism is reflected through a distorting glass. He sometimes speaks of Christianity as if it were a slightly modified form of Judaism.

Disraeli also directly discusses Jewish matters in a *Life* of his friend Lord George Bentinck (1852), as well as in *Alroy* (1833). In both *Coningsby* and *Tancred* he introduces the Jew Sidonia, who is always at hand to assist the hero with his wisdom, munificence, and vast international connections. In *Tancred* also, Disraeli speaks out energetically in favor of restoring national independence to the Jews, criticizing Jewish assimilationists "ashamed of their race and not fanatically devoted to their religion." Disraeli's style, through its extravagance and enthusiasm, provoked parodies by W.M. Thackeray and A. Trollope.

[Harold Harel Fisch]

It seems clear that Disraeli was obsessed by his Jewishness, just as were most of his contemporaries, for whom a Jewish political leader in Britain was a virtually unimaginable novelty. Historians have recently paid attention to the considerable antisemitic hostility faced by Disraeli, flowing from both the traditional Tory right wing and, more surprisingly, from many Victorian liberals, with an overt or covert evangelical Protestant worldview. Disraeli overcame all obstacles and prejudices to climb to "the top of the greasy pole." Probably only in Britain among Western nations in Victorian times was his career possible. That Disraeli was an iconic figure on the British right – not the left – the founder of the modern Conservative party, probably ensured to a significant degree that, in the troubled 20th century, British Conservatism never acquired an antisemitic tone or edge. In the final analysis, Disraeli's career was truly *sui generis.*

[William D. Rubinstein (2nd ed.)]

BIBLIOGRAPHY: There is a select bibliography on the life and the works of Disraeli in R. Blake, *Disraeli* (1967) and in P. Bloomfield, *Disraeli* (1961); W.F. Monypenny and G.E. Buckle, *The Life of Benjamin Disraeli, Earl of Beaconsfield*, 6 vols. (1910–20); N. Sokolow, *Ḥibbat Zion* (1935), index; C. Roth, *Benjamin Disraeli: Earl of Beaconsfield* (1952); E. Rosenberg, *From Shylock to Svengali* (1961), 290–2; H. Fisch, *Dual Image* (1959), 65–68; idem, in: *Essays… I. Brodie* (1967), 81–94; B. Jaffe, *Benjamin Disraeli* (Heb., 1960), 132–6 (incl. bibl.); R.W. Seton-Watson, *Disraeli, Gladstone and the Eastern Question…* (1963); G. Brandes, *Lord Beaconsfield: A Study* (1966); B.R. Jerman, *The Young Disraeli* (1960); S.R. Graubard, *Burke, Disraeli and Churchill* (1961). **ADD. BIBLIOGRAPHY:** S. Bradford, *Disraeli* (1983); T. Endelman and T. Kushner (eds.), *Disraeli's Jewishness* (2002); T. Endelman, "Disraeli's Jewishness Reconsidered," in: *Modern Judaism*, 5 (1985), 109–23; B. Jaffee, "A Reassessment of Benjamin Disraeli's Jewish Aspects," in: TJHSE, 27 (1982), 115–23; W.D. Rubinstein, *A History of the Jews in the English-Speaking World: Great Britain* (1996), 81–83, index; ODNB; M. Jolles, *Jews and the Carlton Club, with Notes on Benjamin Disraeli, Henri Louis Bischoffsheim and Saul Isaac, MP* (2002).

D'ISRAELI, ISAAC (1766–1848), English writer; father of Benjamin *Disraeli. In 1748 his father, a Sephardi Jew, settled in London, where Isaac was born. D'Israeli entered commerce, although he was financially independent. His *Curiosities of Literature* (1791, and often reprinted), which made him famous, reveals a remarkable acquaintance with the by-ways of English literature. His *Amenities of Literature* was completed in 1840, after he had become blind. Although he was a free-thinker, D'Israeli maintained a formal connection with the Spanish and Portuguese Synagogue in London. However, as a result of a dispute over a fine of £40 imposed on him by the Sephardi elders, he formally withdrew from that community in 1817 and had his children, including the future Earl of Beaconsfield, baptized as members of the Church of England. Although he did not become a Christian, his *Genius of Judaism* (1833), as well as some incidental remarks in his novel *Vaurien* (1797), testify to his estrangement from Judaism. D'Israeli's view of English history was pro-Tory. He defended the Stuart kings against the Whigs in a way which might well have influenced the outlook of his celebrated son. In his lifetime, D'Israeli was already a well-known and much admired name, a point which is often ignored by those who regard Benjamin Disraeli as a complete outsider.

BIBLIOGRAPHY: J. Ogden, *Isaac D'Israeli* (Eng., 1969); S. Kopstein, *Isaac D'Israeli* (Ger., 1939); W.F. Monypenny and G.E. Buckle, *The Life of Benjamin Disraeli, Earl of Beaconsfield*, 1 (1910), 1–27; C. Roth, *Benjamin Disraeli, Earl of Beaconsfield* (1952), 10–19; R. Blake, *Disraeli* (Eng., 1966). **ADD. BIBLIOGRAPHY:** Katz, England, 330–34; ODNB online.

[Harold Harel Fisch / William D. Rubinstein (2nd ed.)]

DISSENTCHIK, ARYEH (1907–1978), Israeli journalist. Born in Riga, Dissentchik worked in daily journalism in his home city. Active from his youth in the Revisionist movement, he served in Paris in the early 1930s as Ze'ev *Jabotinsky's secretary. After he immigrated to Palestine in 1934, he worked on the Revisionist newspaper *Ha-Yarden*, moving after its closure to the *Ha-Boker* newspaper. In 1948 Dissentchik joined *Maariv* as deputy editor to its founding editor-chief, Dr Azriel *Carlebach. When Carlebach died in 1956 Dissentchik replaced him, serving in the post until 1974. Dissentchik was a hardened newsman, widely connected with the Israeli political establishment, who ensured that *Maariv* maintained its dominant position as the country's largest-selling newspaper at the time as well as providing serious in-depth coverage and commentary. He was also the Israel correspondent of the Associated Press news agency for 10 years and a member of the world board of the International Press Institute. In 1978 he won the Sokolow Prize for outstanding journalism. One of his sons, Iddo, later became editor of *Maariv* as well.

[Yoel Cohen (2nd ed.)]

DITTENHOEFER, ABRAM JESSE (1836–1919), U.S. lawyer. Dittenhoefer, born in Charleston, South Carolina, son of German immigrants, was raised in New York City where he practiced law. A recognized authority on theatrical and copyright law, Dittenhoefer served as counsel to leading corporations and to the New York City Board of Aldermen. He was a judge of the City Court (1862–64). A lifelong Republican, Dittenhoefer cast an electoral vote in 1864 for Abraham Lincoln, was a delegate to Republican party national conventions, and served as chairman of the central committee of German Republicans for many years. He wrote *How We Elected Lincoln: Personal Recollections of Lincoln and Men of his Time* (1916).

BIBLIOGRAPHY: *National Cyclopaedia of American Biography*, 36 (1950), 147–8; *New York Times* (Feb. 24, 1919), 13 (obituary).

[Morton Rosenstock]

DIUM (**Dion**), city in Transjordan called after a Macedonian town and mentioned by Pliny (*Historia Naturalis*, 5:16). The city was captured by Alexander Yannai (Jos., Ant., 13:393) and later incorporated into the *Decapolis by Pompey (Ant., 14:75; Ptolemy, 5:14, 18). The coins of the city show that Zeus, identified with Baal-Hadad, was worshiped there. It should probably be identified with Tell al-Ashʿarī, 15 mi. (24 km.) northwest of Edrei; other suggestions, such as Dahāma or Tell al-Ḥusn, seem less likely.

BIBLIOGRAPHY: Alt, in: PJB, 29 (1933), 22 n.3; Abel, Geog, 2 (1938), 306–7; W.W. Wroth, *British Museum Catalogue of Coins … Syria* (1899).

[Michael Avi-Yonah]

DIVEKAR, SAMUEL EZEKIEL (**Samaji Hassaji Divekar**; d. 1797), soldier and benefactor of the Bene *Israel community in Bombay, India. Divekar enlisted with his brothers in a British native regiment where he rose to the rank of a native commandant or captain (*Subedar*). During the Anglo-Mysore wars he was taken prisoner by the notorious Tippoo Sultan, and according to one tradition was released through the intervention of some *Cochin Jews led by David Rahabi, who took him to Cochin. According to another legend, he was set free by Tippoo Sultan's mother who heard that he was a Bene-Israel.

Both stories state that he vowed to build a synagogue in Bombay for his own community in thanksgiving for his delivery. His "Sha'ar ha-Raḥamim" synagogue, the first in Bombay, was built in 1796 on present-day Samuel Street. It was renovated in 1860 and is still in use. Divekar was appointed *muqaddim* by his community and the office was assigned to his family on a hereditary basis. He died on a journey to Cochin, where he went to obtain Torah scrolls and liturgical appurtenances.

BIBLIOGRAPHY: S. Reinmann, *Masot Shelomo* (1884), 102–3; H.S. Kehimkar, *The History of the Bene Israel of India* (1937), 190ff., 255ff., 374; W.J. Fischel, *The Haggadah of the Bene Israel of India* (1968); D.S. Sassoon, *Ohel Dawid*, 2 (1932), 574f. **ADD. BIBLIOGRAPHY:** S.B. Isenberg, *India's Bene Israel, a Comprehensive Inquiry and Source Book* (1988); *The Israelite*, 3:3–4 (March–April 1919), 33; 7:7–8 (July–Aug. 1923).

[Walter Joseph Fischel / Yulia Egorova (2nd ed.)]

DIVIN (Pol. **Dywin**), town in Polesie district, Poland; now Brest-Litovsk district, Belarus, A small number of Jews lived there from the mid-16th century and an organized settlement existed from the end the century, as attested in a document from 1631. In 1634 the Polish king Wladislus IV ratified the ancient rights of Jews in Divin to acquire houses and building plots, and to engage in commerce. The local community owned a synagogue, a bath house, and a cemetery. In the framework of the Lithuanian Council, Divin was under the jurisdiction of the community of *Brest-Litovsk. In 1656 the Jews in the town were given one-third of the revenues from the municipal leases (they had requested one-half); supervision over these was entrusted to a committee consisting of two Christians and a Jew. There were 221 Jews living in Divin in 1756 and 556 in 1847. During the 19th century, the Jews there mainly engaged in small-scale commerce and crafts. The community numbered 1,094 in 1897 (3,737 the total population) and 786 in 1921 (34.1%). The laying of railways and roads at a great distance from Divin in the second half of the 19th century caused economic hardships and the Jewish population dropped. Divin was occupied by the Germans in the beginning of World War II. An open ghetto was established, and Jews from the villages were brought in, the number of its inhabitants reaching about a thousand. At the end of summer 1942 they were all murdered outside the town.

BIBLIOGRAPHY: B. Wasiutyński, *Ludność żydowska w Polsce* … (1930), 83. **ADD. BIBLIOGRAPHY:** S. Spector (ed.), *Pinkas Ha-Kehillot Polin*, vol.. 5, Volhynia and Polesie (1990).

[Arthur Cygielman / Shmuel Spector (2nd ed.)]

DIVINATION. Man, by nature, longs to know what the future holds for him, either out of inherent curiosity or in order to anticipate the dangers that await him. Therefore, in all ancient civilizations – and even in some cultures of today – there were diviners who used various methods to predict the future. It is possible to distinguish between practitioners who use external means to guess the future and persons who perceive the future simply through their own awareness. The prediction of the future through technical means is closely akin to *magic, and the line between them is sometimes blurred. What distinguishes the one from the other is that divination only attempts to predict future events, while magic also professes to influence and change them for good or bad. In any case, man believed that prediction of the future was possible, and that it was bound up with superhuman, demonic, or divine powers, from which the diviner received his knowledge either directly or indirectly. This belief rested on the assumption that there were powers – spirits or gods – that knew the future and with which man could communicate in order to receive this knowledge. It was believed that some men have a natural talent for receiving revelations, either in a waking state or in dreams, and in the manner in which the future is revealed to them, such men resemble the prophets, at least outwardly. Others, who predict the future through signs, had to learn the signs and the means by which to interpret them. Divination was of both general and individual concern. In Mesopotamia fortune-tellers first appear in the service of the community. Egyptian documents indicate that diviners served the needs of the country and the king, as well as the everyday needs of the individual. This is also the case in the biblical world. The Bible mentions that the *Urim and Thummim were consulted on the needs of the community (Num. 27:21; I Sam. 14:41; et al.), and the prophets for a prediction of the future (I Kings 22:5ff.; II Kings 3:11ff.); prophets were also sought after for the needs of the individual (I Sam. 9:10, 19). Among the masses, it was a widespread practice to seek false prophets and fortune-tellers, as is known from the polemics of the true prophets against them (Ezek. 13:17ff.; Micah 3:11; et al.).

The Prophet as a Mantic

There is a certain relationship, at least externally, between the mantic, who foretells the future by means of internal awareness, and the prophet (see *Prophets and Prophecy). Knowledge of mantics is drawn from Greek and Roman literature. The mantic achieved ecstasy through music, by use of intoxicating drugs, and by other means. Sometimes he ate the principal organs of a living animal upon which a magical act had been performed. Of all these methods only the use of music is found among the prophets, and that only twice: Saul is told that he will meet a band of prophets "with harp, tambourine, flute, and lyre before them, raving" (I Sam. 10:5); and when Elisha was asked to prophesy about the results of the war with Moab, he requested a minstrel – "And when the minstrel played, the power of the Lord came upon him" (II Kings 3:15). In some cases, the prophet performs the functions of the mantic. In Deuteronomy it is stressed that the prophet is to take the place of various types of fortune-tellers (Deut. 18:14ff.). The criterion given for distinguishing between true and false prophets is the fulfillment of the prophecy or its non-fulfillment (18:20–22). The prophets were also consulted on matters of a type that a mantic would answer. In the story of Saul and the asses, the servant says of Samuel the seer: "All that he says comes true" (I Sam. 9:6), i.e., the seer envisions the future and does not err. Jeroboam sent his wife to Ahijah of Shiloh to inquire whether his son would live (I Kings 14:1ff.), Jehoshaphat asked the prophets to tell him the outcome of the battle at Ramoth-Gilead (22:5ff.), and Elisha was asked to predict the outcome of the war with Moab (II Kings 3:11). This consultation of the prophets replaced the consultation of the *ephod found in earlier periods (cf. I Sam. 23:2–6, 9–12). Following Kuenen and Wellhausen, current theories hold that the early Israelite seer resembled the pre-Islamic Arab priest (*kāhin*), who understood omens and had dreams, but was not an ecstatic prophet. However, there is no evidence in the Bible that the Israelite men of God were ever guided by omens, and even the false prophets were not accused of this (although their prophecy is contemptuously called divination; Ezek. 13:7, 23; Micah 3:6, 7). The seer (Heb. *ro'eh*, as in I Sam. 9:9; I Chron. 9:22; II Chron. 16:7, 10; et al.; or *ḥozeh*, as in II Sam. 24:11; et al.) did not use technical means, although their use was customary among the priests, who wore the ephod under the breastplate upon which the Urim and Thummim were placed (see below).

Methods of Foretelling the Future in the Bible

In the Bible *dreams and consultation of the Urim and Thummim were considered valid means of inquiring into the future. The dream as a source of divine revelation was widespread in all ancient civilizations, and there are even books of dreams from Egypt and Mesopotamia. The dream informs the dreamer of what awaits him in the future, as in the examples of the dreams of Joseph (Gen. 37:5–9), the cup-bearer and the baker (40:5ff.), Pharaoh (41:1ff.), and many others; however, it does not explicitly reveal the future, and must be interpreted (41:8ff.). To do this, one must know what the phenomena in the dream symbolize and to what they are directed. Books of dreams were written in Egypt and Mesopotamia for the purpose of teaching the interpretations of dreams according to their symbols, and it is reasonable to assume that a system of dream-interpretation (oneiromancy) was also known in Israel. In some passages the phenomenon of the dream is negatively evaluated: "the dreamers tell false dreams, and give empty consolation" (Zech. 10:2), and "for when dreams increase, empty words grow many" (Eccles. 5:6; cf. v. 2).

The Urim and Thummim, a type of lot oracle, were placed in the breastplate over the ephod of the priest. He who consulted the Urim and Thummim sought to determine between only two possibilities, as in the case of David: "Will the men of Keilah surrender me into his hand? Will Saul come down? … And the Lord said, 'He will come down.'" (The Urim and Thummim answer only the second question.) "… Will the men of Keilah surrender me and my men into the hand of Saul? And the Lord said, 'They will surrender you'" (I Sam. 23:10–12). Egyptian documents indicate the manner in which the oracle worked. The appointed priest would call out to the divine oracle two answers to his question, and the god would react to one of them. By another method, the priest would call out a list of names of suspects to the god, who would react to the name of the guilty one. Thus, for example, in a description of consultation of the statue of Pharaoh Amenhotep I, who became a divine oracle after his death, the god is asked to clarify who is guilty of the theft of clothing belonging to the complainant. The priest called out the names of all the households in the village before the statue of the god, and the house of the thief was identified (cf. I Sam. 10:19ff.). In Egypt, the reply was given by the idol-bearers, who stepped backward to signify a negative answer, and forward for a positive one. Lucian relates a similar method of replying, in which the statue of Apollo carried in a chariot would gallop forward to indicate a positive answer (*De Dea Syria*, 36). Several terms for diviners, who are connected with the consultation of the spirits of the dead, appear in the Bible (Isa. 19:3): *ʾov*, *yiddeʿoni*, and *iṭṭim*. The Hebrew word *ʾov*, which is derived from the Hittite *a-a-bi*, means the pit from which the spirit of the dead rises, or the spirit of the dead which rises from the pit (cf. I Sam. 15:23; Isa. 29:4). The *yiddeʿoni* ("wizard") is apparently synonymous with the *baʿal ʾov* ("medium"), either because of his ability (*yadaʿ*, "to know") to call up the spirit of the dead or his knowledge of the future. *Iṭṭim* appears to be a synonym for *ʾov*, and is explained according to the Akkadian *eṭemmu*, the spirit of the dead. Consultation of the *terafim* is also mentioned in connection with divination (Judg. 17:5; 18:14; Ezek. 21:26; Hos. 3:4; Zech. 10:2). The word *terafim* is derived from Hittite *tarpi(sh)*. The primary sense of the word is "spirit," and from this it came to designate the object that served as the symbol of the spirit, e.g., a statue or statuette. The size of the *terafim* was not defined. Those which Rachel stole from Laban were small enough to be concealed in a camel-saddle (Gen. 31:34), while those in David's house were large enough for Michal to place in bed and delude Saul's messengers who came in search of David (I Sam. 19:13). Some scholars hold that the *meʿonen* or *ʿonen* ("soothsayer"; Deut. 18:10, 14; Isa. 57:3; Jer. 27:9; Micah 5:11) also consults the dead to foretell the future, and they explain the root *ʿnn* according to the Arabic *ʿanna* ("to appear"). The *meʿonen*, therefore, is one who causes the spirit of the dead to appear. However, since the *meʿonen* and his activity are mentioned a number of times together with divination (the Heb. verb *naḥesh* and noun *naḥash;* Lev. 19:26; Deut. 18:10; II Kings 21:6; II Chron. 33:6), the term possibly refers to a special type of divination.

The techniques of divining mentioned in the Bible are with a goblet, with arrows, by attaching a pre-agreed significance to the manner in which one was addressed, by the inspection of a liver (hepatoscopy), and by astrology. Divination by means of a goblet is mentioned in the story of Joseph who divined with his silver goblet (Gen. 44:5). This method was apparently based on the patterns formed by drops of water in a cup of oil (lecanomancy), or by beads of oil in a cup of water; in some cases they also divined from the patterns formed in a cup of wine. This type of divination is known from Babylonian documents dated as early as the 18th century B.C.E. Divination by arrows (balomancy) is explicitly mentioned in Ezekiel 21:26, according to which Nebuchadnezzar, king of Babylon, "shakes the arrows, he consults the teraphim…"

The word *qilqal* ("shakes, flings") shows that this method of divination involved the shaking of arrows. Mesopotamian documents indicate that it was customary to cast lots by flinging arrows into a quiver. Divination by arrows was practiced by Arab tribes before Islam and was prohibited by the Koran (Sura. 5:4, 92). According to the testimony of scribes, during the "period of ignorance" (*jāhiliyya*), the Arabs divined with blunt arrows in the sanctuary. They would place the arrows in a quiver and fling it until an arrow fell from it. The first arrow to fall was the one that expressed the will of the god. There is also evidence that the arrows were named according to the answers that they represented, and were cast before the statue of the god. It is possible to interpret the above passage concerning Nebuchadnezzar to mean that he consulted the *terafim* by casting lots with arrows in front of them. Bronze arrowheads of the 11th–10th centuries B.C.E., on which the word *ḥeẓ* ("arrow") was written, were found near Beth-Lehem, in Galilee, and in the Valley of Lebanon. S. Iwri interprets the word *ḥeẓ* here as "luck, good luck" (according to Arabic and Ugaritic), but this is only a surmise. The Bible also mentions fortune-telling or divination of the type known in Akkadian as *egirru* and in Greek as *klēdōn*, by which an interpretation was given to a conventional word that was seen as a sign. In this way, one can understand the peculiar sign conceived by Jonathan when he went to fight the Philistines: "If they say to us, 'wait until we come to you,' then we will stand in our place, and we will not go up to them. But if they say, 'come up to us,' then we will go up; for the Lord has given them into our hand. And this shall be the sign to us" (I Sam. 14:9–10; cf. v. 12). The same holds for the sign given by the servants of Ben-Hadad when they went to Ahab to beg for the life of their master (I Kings 20:32–33): "… and they went to the king of Israel and said, 'your servant, Ben-Hadad …' and he said, 'Does he still live? He is my brother.' Now the men were watching for an omen … and said, 'Yes, your brother Ben-Hadad.'"

Hepatoscopy and astrology were more advanced methods of divining the future. The study of the liver is mentioned in Ezekiel 21:26. This custom was widespread in Mesopotamia, in the land of Canaan, among the Hittites, Greeks, and Romans, and, in a later period, also among the Arabs. The qualified augur inspected, in an established order, all the internal organs of an animal sacrificed to a god, in particular the liver. According to the signs that he found in the liver, and which were learned in schools established for that purpose, he predicted the future. "The astrologers, the star-gazers," are mentioned in the prophecy concerning Babylon in Isaiah 47:13. Some scholars explain the Hebrew word for astrologers *hoverei shamayim*, according to the Arabic *habara* ("to cut into large parts"). That would indicate that astrologers divided the sky into star-families, as did Babylonian astrologers, and were identical with stargazers. Others interpret *hoverei shamayim* according to the Ugaritic *hbr* ("to bow") and consider *hoverei shamayim* to be those who bow to the celestial bodies; thus the passage connects the worship of stars with astrology. The observation of celestial bodies or other heavenly signs is referred to in Jeremiah 10:2: "Learn not the way of the nations, nor be dismayed at the signs of the heavens …"

The Biblical Attitude Toward Divination in General

Divination is included among the abominations of the nations which the Israelites were forbidden to learn and practice (Deut. 18:9–11). Leviticus 19:26, 31 also contains the prohibition against the use of magic to tell the future: "You shall not practice divination or soothsaying" and "Do not turn to ghosts and do not inquire of familiar spirits to be defiled by them." The punishment for those who do consult them is excommunication (20:6). However, in response to human nature, the Bible allowed consultation of the Urim and Thummim on the one hand and the prophets on the other, and considered them the only proper means of inquiring into the future. The Book of Deuteronomy designates the prophet to satisfy the needs that were met among the nations by fortune-tellers using systems of magic (Deut. 18:14ff.). The dream was also a proper method of prophesying the future (cf. I Sam. 28:6; et al.), since God would often reveal Himself to His chosen ones in a dream (See *Dreams). According to the prophets Jeremiah and Ezekiel, fortune-tellers and mantics predicted the future in the name of God (Jer. 27:9–10; 29:8–9; Ezek. 22:28; cf. 12:24; 13:6–9). They probably functioned in the area of popular religion, and the prophets saw them as falsifying the word of God and therefore fought them. That fortune-tellers were persecuted is known from the story of the medium and Saul, who removed the mediums and "wizards" and cut them off from the land (I Sam. 28:3, 9). In contrast to Saul's act, which he performed in accordance with the precepts of the Torah, Manasseh, king of Judah, introduced idolatry into Jerusalem: "[he] practiced soothsaying and augury, and dealt with mediums and with wizards" (II Kings 21:6; II Chron. 33:6). The cultic reform of Josiah put an end to these (II Kings 23:24).

[Shmuel Ahituv]

In the Talmud

The rabbis adopted an ambivalent attitude toward divination. On the one hand there is the clear prohibition of the Bible (see above); on the other the rabbis, particularly the Babylonian *amoraim*, lived in an environment which was the classic home of divination, where it was extensively practiced. To some extent they overcame the difficulty by distinguishing between *naḥash* (divination proper), which was forbidden, and *simanim* ("signs"), which were permitted.

The *Sifra Kedushim* 6 and the *Sifrei Deuteronomy* 171 give different examples of divination. The former merely talks of divination by "weasels, birds, and stars," apparently referring to the cry of the animal and the bird, the bird in flight, and the stars in their courses. The latter is more explicit, giving examples of a man regulating his conduct by omens, "For instance, if he says that bread has fallen from his mouth, his staff from his hand, a snake passed on his right and a fox on his left and his tail crossed his path [which are considered bad omens], or if he refuses to do something because it is the New Moon, or the eve of the Sabbath, or Saturday night." The same passage, however, includes the enchanter (*kosem*) in the category of divination: "the enchanter is one who seizes his staff [and decides according to the direction in which it falls] whether I will go or not." The Talmud (Sanh. 65b) combines these with some variations and adds other bad omens, e.g., if a raven croaks at a man or a deer crosses his path. These are enumerated in Maimonides (Yad, Akum 11:4).

The dividing line between divination and signs is indicated by the statement, "Any divination which is not as the divination of Eliezer the servant of Abraham at the well [Gen. 24:14] or Jonathan the son of Saul [I Sam. 14:9–10] is no divination" (Ḥul. 95b). There is, however, a curious difference of opinion among the medieval commentators as to the import of this statement. Maimonides (Yad, loc. cit.) regards it as meaning that divinations of this kind are forbidden. Abraham b. David of Posquières (ad loc.) roundly disagrees with him, stating emphatically that the passage means that this kind of divination is permitted. Similarly, the *tosafot* (Ḥul. 95b) agree with Maimonides, while Isserles adopts the view of Abraham b. David, though with reservations (Sh. Ar., YD 179:4). The former view seems to be more in accordance with the text and context, and the difference between divination and signs seems to be that in the cases of Eliezer and Jonathan the course of action taken was dependent on the happening, whereas a "sign" merely interprets an event as an omen for good or evil and is permitted.

Thus it is specifically stated in the name of R. Simeon b. Eleazar, "A house, a child, and a wife, though they do not constitute divination, do act as signs" (Ḥul. 95b); i.e., good or bad fortune immediately following the purchase of a house, the birth of a child, or marriage may be regarded as auguries of future success or failure. In the same context comes a special kind of divination which was regarded as permitted: the custom of asking a child to recite "his" biblical verse (Ḥag. 15a; Gitt. 57a et al.) and interpreting the answer as a sign. One interesting example is given by the Talmud (Ḥul. 95b). R. Johanan decided to visit Samuel in Babylon after the death of Rav. He asked a child to quote his verse and the child cited, "Now Samuel was dead" (I Sam. 28:3). Johanan took this as a sign but the Talmud adds, "It was not so. It was only that Johanan should not be put to the trouble of visiting him." The special importance of this form of divination is provided by two passages in the Talmud, one to the effect that "since the destruction of the Temple prophecy was taken from the prophets and given to fools and children" (BB 12b) and the other "if a man wakes up and finds that a scriptural verse has fallen into his mouth, it is a minor prophecy." David ha-Levi presumably combines these two sayings when he justifies this form of divination as "minor prophecy" (*Taz*, YD 179:4). The Talmud is replete with "signs" which do not belong to the category of divination, and the same applies to the Middle Ages, particularly in the *Sefer Ḥasidim* of Judah he-Ḥasid.

Nevertheless the distinction between divination and signs is sometimes so fine as to be almost imperceptible. When Rav was on a journey and came to a ford, if he saw the ferryboat coming toward him he regarded it as a good omen, if departing from him a bad one (Ḥul. 95b). Similarly it is difficult to decide whether the knowledge of "the language of birds" and "the language of the palm-trees" belongs to divination or not. Although, as has been stated, the *Sifra* specifically forbids divination by the cries of birds, and the third of the *Sibylline books (224) states, "the Jews do not consider the omens of flight as observed by the augurs," the Talmud tells the story of R. Ilish for whom the language of the raven was interpreted; he refused to obey it since the raven is a lying bird, but when a dove repeated the message he did (Git. 45a). Of *Johanan b. Zakkai it is related that among his accomplishments was a knowledge of "the language of palm-trees" (Suk. 28a; BB 134a). The following explanation is given by Nathan b. Jehiel in the *Arukh* (s.v. *si'aḥ*. The text here given is by B.M. Lewin (*Oẓar ha-Ge'onim*, 6 pt. 2 (1934)), Sukkah, no. 67, which is slightly different): "On a completely windless day, so still that even when a sheet is spread out it does not sway, he who understands the speech of the palms takes up his position between two adjacent palms and watches how their branches turn toward one another, and there is in this movement signs from which he can recognize many things." It is also said of R. Abraham Kabassi Gaon (who lived in the year 828) that he was an adept in the speech of the palms, and as a result used to communicate "great and wonderful things, the truth of which was attested by many."

Moses *Isserles qualifies the permissibility of such divinations as that of Eliezer and Johanan (see above) with the reservation, "But he who trusteth in the Lord, mercy compasseth him about" (Ps. 32:10), and the Talmud (Ned. 32a) states "He who refrains from practicing divination is brought within a [divine] barrier which even the ministering angels are not permitted to cross." Generally speaking, the view of the halakhic authorities is that divination, like all the other forms of superstitions mentioned in the Bible in this context, such as sorcery, necromancy, and "familiar spirits," is possible but forbidden. A strikingly different, rational, view is taken by Maimonides. After faithfully detailing their laws as found in the Talmud he concludes: "But all those things are lying and falsehood and it is with them that the ancient idolaters led astray the nations of the lands that they should follow them. It is not fitting that the people of Israel, who are wise and perspicuous, be attracted by those follies or imagine that they are of any effect, as it is said, 'For there is no enchantment with Jacob, neither is there any divination with Israel' (Num. 23:23); and it is also said, 'For these nations which thou art to dispossess, hearken unto soothsayers and unto diviners; but as for thee, the Lord thy God hath not suffered thee to do so' (Deut. 18:14). Whosoever believes in those matters and their like and imagines that they are true, and matters of wisdom, but the Torah has forbidden the practice of them, is but of the fools and the retarded and in the category of women and minors whose mind is not whole. Those who possess wisdom and are of wholesome mind, however, know clearly that all these things which the Torah has forbidden are not words of wisdom but confusions and vanity to which those lacking in knowledge are attracted and as a result they have forsaken all the ways of truth. For this reason the Torah, when it warns against all these follies, says (Deut. 18:13), 'Thou shalt be wholehearted with the Lord thy God'" (Yad, Akkum 11:16). *Elijah b. Solomon, Gaon of Vilna, however, criticized Maimonides for this rational approach, saying that "accursed philosophy led him astray."

[Louis Isaac Rabinowitz]

In the Middle Ages

OMENS. During the Middle Ages, both Jews and Christians readily read omens from bodily phenomena. The following passages by *Eleazar b. Judah of Worms seem to derive from non-Jewish sources: "Just as the astrologers foresee events from the stars, so there are some who can foretell the future from human signs. If the flesh under one's armpit quivers, they will be broaching a match to him soon ... If the sole of one's foot itches ... he will be journeying soon to a strange place ... if his palm, he will hold in his hand gold or silver ... itching in any part of the body is an omen ... God apprises man, through bodily phenomena, of what will transpire" (*Ḥokhmat ha-Nefesh*, 25d). Another powerful omen was sneezing. The behavior of animals was also regarded as a portent for the future. A dog howling mournfully is a clear sign that the angel of death is walking through a town; similarly, a dog dragging his hindquarters along the floor toward the door is an indication of the approach of death.

A number of occurrences betokened good or ill fortune; it was unlucky to open the day or the week with an action involving loss, for it was possible that this action could color the whole subsequent period. For this reason, it was considered undesirable to pay the tax-collector or repay a debt on the first day of the week. Other such superstitions include a seminal pollution on the Day of Atonement which was generally believed to herald death within a year, though the talmudic authorities differed in their interpretation of this; a Pentateuch falling to the ground was so bad an omen that it was customary to try to counter it by a period of fasting; making a mistake in prayer also heralded disaster; in the Rhineland it was believed that when the flames on the hearth leap unusually high, a guest will shortly arrive. If the fire is doused with water, the visitor will be drowned (Yoma 88a; Responsa Maharil, 83a–b, etc.; Balu, 149; Grimm, vol. 3,467, para. 889).

Particular tokens of good fortune were some foods. The main meal on Rosh Ha-Shanah included a number of foods symbolizing happiness and prosperity: a lamb's head, "that He may put us at the head and not the tail-end" of things; fat meats, and sweets such as apples dipped in honey, "that the new year may be prosperous and happy"; pomegranates, "that our merits may be as numerous as its seeds"; fish, which are proverbially symbols of fruitfulness, and others. The practice of eating on New Year's Day foods specially chosen for their good influence on the future probably initially reflected Roman custom, and it was also widespread in Christian Europe in the Middle Ages and modern times.

THE ART OF PREDICTION. The desire to know the future was not satisfied through interpretations of omens alone. The active creation of signs and portents was also widely practiced. Although, like leading non-Jewish thinkers, religious and lay, the rabbis forbade these practices on moral and religious grounds, their more or less open recognition that such "evils" bore results made all their prohibitions ineffectual. Medieval Jewry was acquainted with a considerable variety of means of divination deriving from Oriental and Greco-Roman sources as well as from contemporary Christian practice, and they resorted to many of these. One method was to place a lighted candle during the ten days between Rosh Ha-Shanah and the Day of Atonement (traditionally regarded as the period when the fate of each man is determined in heaven) where no draft could extinguish it. If the light went out, then the man in question would die before the year's end; if the candle burned to the end, then he could count on at least one more year of life.

On the night of *Hoshana Rabba, when it was believed that the decision concerning men's fate during the new year was finally and irrevocably set out in the heavenly book of records, it was a widespread practice among medieval Jews to go out into the moonlight to see if the shadows they cast were lacking heads, for the absence of a head was a certain sign that what had happened to the shadow would soon befall the body. The earliest Jewish reference to this custom is made by Eleazar of Worms, and Naḥmanides also mentions it, as well as many later German-Jewish writers.

Like Christians, Jews occasionally used the Bible as a method of divination. They followed the usual procedure of opening the Bible at random and taking as a portent the first word or sentence that met the eye, but in the Middle Ages they also adhered to a practice common in talmudic times of asking children what verses they had studied in school that day and taking them as good or bad omens.

Divination through casting lots was common throughout the Middle Ages. Although it was usual to employ simple devices like tossing a coin or throwing dice, even in these cases the procedure was complicated by rules governing when the operation could be performed, how the lot was to be held, and how the results should be interpreted, as well as prescribing what prayers or charms should be recited. The Hebrew "books of lots," like their Christian counterparts, were of Arabic origin; the Jewish versions seem to have been composed mainly in southern Europe and in the Orient.

The method of divination most common among Jews, which was well known in Oriental and classical antiquity, was also frequently practiced by medieval Christians. By this method a young child was made to gaze into a polished or reflecting surface until he saw figures that revealed the desired information. While this method of divination appears to have been most frequently used for detecting theft, it was also employed to divulge future events.

CALLING UP THE DEAD. Two kinds of necromancy are recognized in the Talmud, that of raising the dead man by naming him, and that of questioning him through the medium of a skull. Although both types were often referred to in the Middle Ages, it is doubtful if they were still employed. Other methods seem to have been more popular, such as the practice of two friends agreeing that the first to die should return to reveal the secrets of heaven to the other, appearing either in a dream, or during waking hours.

Other methods described in the sources include: (1) "incantations" at the grave, which were apparently frowned upon, for the word *laḥash* usually refers to a forbidden kind of magic; (2) spending the night on a grave, distinctively dressed and burning spices "until one hears an exceedingly faint voice from the grave responding to his questions"; this method was also considered unacceptable for it was included in the forbidden category of magic; (3) "A man and a woman station themselves at the head and foot of a grave, and on the earth between them they set a rattle, which they strike while they recite a secret invocation; then while the woman looks on the man puts the questions, and the deceased reveals the future to them"; (4) an apparently acceptable method which invoked the dead through the use of angelic names: "Stand before the grave and recite the names of the angels of the fifth camp of the first firmament, and hold in your hand a mixture of oil and honey in a new glass bowl, and say 'I conjure you, spirit of the grave, Nehinah, who rests in the grave upon the bones of the dead, that you accept this offering from my hand and do my bidding; bring me N son of N who is dead.'"

DIVINING TREASURE. It was widely believed in the Middle Ages, particularly in Germany, that treasure lay hidden in the earth. Many northern European folktales recount how a ghostly blue flame sometimes flickers on the ground above the hiding place of a hoard. However, since such capricious signs were a rare occurrence, people were not content to wait patiently for the chance appearance that would make them rich. A surer way of reaching the earth's treasures, therefore, was provided by the divining-rod. Several 15th-century Jewish formulas for making and using a divining-rod, which follow closely the texts of German recipes, have been printed. The language of spells, the names used in them, and the very belief on which they are based, are clear indications that they were borrowed from German originals. Not only buried treasure but also sought-after information could be revealed by this method. The preparation of the rods followed the same pattern, but the invocations were altered to suit the differing needs.

BIBLIOGRAPHY: T.W. Davies, *Magic, Divination and Demonology Among the Hebrews …* (1898); E.B. Taylor, *Primitive Culture*, 1 (1913[5]), 78–81, 117–33; J. Doeller, *Die Wahrsagerei im Alten Testament* (1923); J.G. Frazer, *The Golden Bough* (1935[3]), passim; Y. Kaufmann, Toledot, 1 (1937), 358ff.; idem, *Mi-Kivshonah shel ha-Yeẓirah ha-Mikra'it* (1966), 208–15; A. Guillaume, *Prophecy and Divination …* (1938); A.L. Oppenheim, in: AFO, 17 (1954–56), 49–55; idem, *Ancient Mesopotamia* (1964), 206–27, 366–9; de Vaux, Anc Isr, 349–53; H. Wohlstein, in: BZ, 5 (1961), 30–38; S. Iwry, in: JAOS, 81 (1961), 27–34; M. Vieyra, in: *Revue Hittite et Asiatique*, 69 (1961), 47–55; J. Nougayrol et al., *La divination en Mésopotamie ancienne* (1966); H. Hoffner, in: JBL, 86 (1967), 385–401; H.L. Ginsberg, in: VT supplement, 16 (1967), 74–75; idem, in: JNES, 27 (1968), 61–68; W.F. Albright, *Yahweh and the Gods of Canaan* (1968), 123–94. MIDDLE AGES: J. Trachtenberg, *Jewish Magic and Superstition* (1961); L. Blau, *Das altjuedische Zauberwesen* (1898); J. Grimm, *Deutsche Mythologie*, 3 vols. (1875–84); Gross, Gal Jud, 692–700; Grunwald, in: MGJV, 5 (1900), 1–87; 77 (1933), 161–71, 241–52, 467; Guedemann, *ibid.*, 24 (1875), 269f.; 60 (1916), 135–9; H.C. Lea, *A History of the Inquisition of the Middle Ages*, 3 (1911), 379–549; Lévi, in: REJ, 22 (1891), 332f.; 25 (1892), 1–13; 26 (1893), 69–74, 131–5; 29 (1894), 43–60; 47 (1904), 214; 61 (1911), 206–12; 68 (1914), 15–21; L. Thorndike, *The Place of Magic in the Intellectual History of Europe* (1905); idem, *History of Magic and Experimental Science*, 8 vols. (1923–58).

DIVINE PUNISHMENT. In a system of law based on divine revelation all punishment originally and ultimately derives from God. Even though human agencies may be entrusted with authority to inflict punishments in certain prescribed cases, God's own overriding punishing power remains unaffected, and the ways and means of divine punishment are as numerous and varied as they are of catastrophic unpredictability (cf. the punishments threatened for "rejecting God's laws and spurning His rules" in Lev. 26:14–43 and Deut. 28:15–68). God punishes whole peoples (the Flood: Gen. 6; Sodom and Gomorrah: Gen. 18; Egypt: Ex. 14:27–28; et al.) as well as individuals (Cain: Gen. 4:10–15; Aaron's sons: Lev. 10:1–2; Miriam: Num. 12:6–10; Korah and his company: Num. 16:28–35; et al.); and visits "the guilt of the fathers upon the children, upon the third and upon the fourth generations of those who reject" Him (Ex. 20:5; Deut. 5:9). The fear of God is inculcated in those tending to be cruel or callous (Ex. 22:26; Lev. 19:14, 32), and specific retaliatory punishments will be inflicted by God for mistreating widows and orphans (Ex. 22:21–23).

Originally, divine punishment was independent of and additional to judicial punishment; there are several biblical instances in which *capital punishment is prescribed for a particular offense and yet the threat of divine punishment is superadded (e.g., Ex 31:14). In one instance, the law explicitly states that where the prescribed capital punishment is not carried out, God will himself set His face "against that man and his kin and will cut off from among their people both him and all who follow him in going astray after Molech" (Lev. 20:2–5). This juxtaposition of divine and judicial punishments appears conclusively to disprove the view that *karet* ("cutting off") was not a divine punishment of death, but rather a judicial punishment of excommunication. While, in the nature of things, all judicial punishment is uncertain, depending on the offender being caught, evidence against him being available, and the "people of the land not hiding their eyes" from him (Lev. 20:4), divine punishment is certain and inescapable, and thus a much more effective deterrent; the omniscient God will not suffer His laws to be disobeyed with impunity (cf. Deut. 32:41). The fundamental injustice underlying the ideas of inherited guilt and deferred punishment and unbounded wrath is, from the point of view of penal policy, a lesser evil than God's failure to mete out deserved punishment.

For a good many offenses, the divine *karet* is the only punishment prescribed. It has been suggested that they are such offenses as are committed in private, for which eyewitnesses will not usually be available, such as, for instance, the eating of fat or blood (Lev. 7:25–27; 17:10, 14), or various sexual offenses (Lev. 20:17–18; 18:29), or the nonobservance of the Day of Atonement (Lev. 23:29–30) or of Passover (Ex. 12:15, 19). Others maintain that these offenses are mostly of a religious or sacerdotal character, such as failure to circumcise (Gen. 17:14) or to bring certain sacrifices (Num. 9:13), as well as the nonobservance of the religious festivals already mentioned; and that for such religious sins any judicial punishment was thought inappropriate (cf. Sifra 1:19). There are, however, some offenses, punishable by *karet* only, that do not fit into either of these categories as, for instance, public blasphemy (Num. 15:30–31). This fact – together with the gravity of some of the sexual offenses so punishable – led some scholars to assume that *karet*, even though a threat of divine punishment, was at the same time an authorization of judicial capital punishment (cf. Ibn Ezra, Lev. 18:29). This theory is strengthened by the fact that some of the offenses punishable with *karet* are stated to be also judicially punishable (Ex. 31:14; Lev. 20:6).

Apart from *karet*, divine punishment is expressed in terms of simple death (e.g., Num. 18:7) as well as of "bearing one's iniquity" or guilt (e.g., Lev. 5:1; 7:18; 17:16; 20:19; 24:15; Num. 5:31). Sometimes "he shall bear his guilt" is followed by "and he shall die" (Ex. 28:43; Num. 18:32); sometimes it is combined with the threat of *karet* (Lev. 19:8; 7:20), and sometimes joined with the threat of childlessness (Lev. 20:20). It has therefore been suggested that where the "bearing of guilt" stands alone, it is meant only as imposing the duty to bring a sacrifice to God (Tosef., Shevu. 3:1).

With the development of jurisprudence, it was sought to purge divine punishment from apparent injustice (Jer. 31:28–29; Ezek. 18:2–29), and it was later relegated altogether to the realm of homiletics; people were warned that premature death (at the age of 50), or death without leaving issues, were signs of the divine *karet* (Sem. 3:8; MK 28a; Rashi and Tos., Shab. 25a–b), and that every undetected murderer would meet with "accidental" death at the hands of God (Mak. 10b). By talmudic law, *karet*, though interpreted as divine capital punishment, was absolved by the human judicial punishment of *flogging (Mak. 13a–b; Yad, Sanh. 19:1); having been flogged, the offender has expiated even his divine capital crime (Mak. 3:15). This substitution of flogging for divine capital punishment was in legal theory founded on the notion that God would forgive offenders who had repented, and in His mercy refrain from punishing them; undergoing the flogging was regarded as tantamount to repentance. By being flogged, the offender could avoid divine punishment since he cannot be punished twice for the same offense (Mak. 13b). The recidivist, who after having twice been flogged again committed the same offense, was given up – presumably because the supposed repentance could not have been genuine – and was imprisoned and kept on a diet of barley until his belly burst (Sanh. 81b; Yad, Sanh. 18:4).

Where a lesser penalty, such as a *fine, is merged in the larger penalty for the same offense and will not therefore be recoverable, it is sometimes held that in order to satisfy divine law (*Dinei Shamayim*) as well as human law and not be liable to future divine retribution, one should pay also the lesser penalty, especially where it is payable to the victim (cf. BM 91a; Tos. to BK 70b–7 la; Tos. to Ḥul. 130b).

[Haim Hermann Cohn]

Divine Punishment in Civil Law

In the framework of the laws of damages, in a number of cases in which the strict letter of the law does not allow the court to impose payment on the damager, it has been stated that the tortfeasor incurs divine punishment. Tosefta (Zuckermandel Edition; Shebu. 3:2–3), quoting Rabbi Yehoshua, enumerates four such types of damage, regarding which "according to the strict letter of the law, there is no obligation to pay, yet Heaven will not forgive the damager until he pays." Following are the cases, in the manner in which they were explained by the sages of the Babylonian Talmud (BK 55b–56a) and brought down as law (Maim., Yad, Edut, 17:7; Nizkei Mamon, 14:14; Sh. Ar., ḤM, 28:1; 32:2; 418:11,17): (1) if someone knows testimony that can help his fellow yet does not provide it, either testimony in which one witness suffices, or in which two are required (see entry: *Witness); (2) if someone hires false witnesses to testify in favor of one's friend; (3) if someone trains his neighbor's field in the direction of a fire in such a way that an especially strong wind will make the field catch fire, or if he sees fires nearing his neighbor's field and he covers the field in such a manner that the one who lit the fire will be exempt from paying damages, and he thereby prevents the victim from receiving payment; (4) if someone breaches a rickety fence thereby enabling his neighbor's animal to leave, and it goes out and does damage.

The Babylonian Talmud (ibid.) enumerates other cases in which the damager is "exempt by human law but liable by divine law": (1) if someone does work with *mei chatat* [water earmarked for use with the Red Heifer in purifying people who had physical contact with the dead; such work disqualifies the water as a purifying agent (see *Red Heifer); (2) if someone sets poison before his neighbor's animal; (3) if someone leaves a burning ember in the charge of a deaf person, imbecile or minor; (4) if someone frightens his neighbor, without physical contact, and thereby causes him to become sick; (5) if someone's pitcher breaks in a public thoroughfare and he abandons the water and the broken shards, and someone else comes along and is injured by them (see Tosefta, [Zuckermandel edition], BK 6:16–17, where other cases are brought; see *Torts).

The legal responsibility of physicians is a special case. According to Tosefta (Zuckermandel, BK 6:17), "A licensed physician who, with the authority of *bet din* treated a patient [and committed an error], is exempt by human law but is subject to divine law." Nahmanides, himself a physician, explains that a physician who inadvertently commits injury will be liable by divine law only where he finds out that he has erred and knows what his error was. If, however, he never becomes aware of his error, he is not liable by divine law. Rabbi Simeon ben Zemah *Duran (Algiers, 14th century; Responsa *Tashbez*, 3:82) distinguishes between an inadvertent error during an operation, in which case he will be liable by divine law, and an error in prescribing medication, where not even liability by divine law is incurred. (See also *Assault.)

As far as the meaning of this incurrence within divine law, the *posekim* determined that a bet din has to inform the guilty party that, while the court cannot, in fact, sentence him to pay, he still incurs an obligation vis-à-vis divine law (Rabbi Shlomo Luria, *Yam Shel Shlomo*, BK 6:6). Some held that he is disqualified from bearing witness until he pays, because he is holding stolen money in his possession (Me'iri, Sofer Edition, BK 56a).

In the Kitan ruling (CA 350/77 *Kitan v. Weiss* PD 33(2) 785), the Israeli Supreme Court reversed a lower court's award of compensation for damages in a claim submitted by the relatives of a man murdered by a worker in a factory. The worker killed the man with a gun given him by the factory for work purposes. The respondents argued that, due to the worker's problematic mental state, the factory should have foreseen that his possession of a weapon was fraught with danger. Hence, they argued, the factory should be required to compensate the victim's family. The appeal was rejected because the causal connection between the appellant's (i.e., the factory's) negligence and the killing of the deceased was too weak. Judge Elon suggested in his ruling that the court should recommend to the factory to go beyond the letter of the law. In making this suggestion, Judge Elon relied on the principle of a divine punishment being incurred where, due to the lack of the causal connection required for a torts conviction, there is no possibility of sentencing by a human court. In the opinion of many Sages, under certain circumstances a human court can even force payment, going beyond the letter of the law, upon the defendant (Baḥ on Tur, ḤM 12:4). Even so, civil courts, in accordance with Israeli law, lack the authority to do this. Hence Judge Elon suggested to the defendants to follow this practice (ibid., pages 809–810). (See also CA 842/79 *Ness v. Golda*, PD 36(1) 204, page 220.)

In 1992, the Knesset adopted basic laws whose stated purpose was "to entrench within a Basic Law the values of the State of Israel as a Jewish and Democratic state." In accordance with these laws, a prominent role is accorded to Jewish law within the values of the State of Israel as a Jewish state. Today, all of this having occurred, the position of Jewish law should be given priority. It would appropriate for the courts to adopt this approach of making such recommendations to litigants, and under suitable conditions even of compelling them to go beyond the letter of the law.

For a detailed discussion of this, see *Damages; *Law and Morality.

[Menachem Elon (2nd ed.)]

BIBLIOGRAPHY: Rothschild, in: MGWJ, 25 (1876), 89–91; J. Lipkin, in: *Ha-Mishpat*, 3 (1928), 9–16; A. Buechler, *Studies in Sin and Atonement ...* (1928); ET, 7 (1956), 392–5; EM, 4 (1962), 330–2; B. Cohen, *Jewish and Roman Law*, 2 (1966), 740–4, 801. **ADD. BIBLIOGRAPHY:** M. Elon, *Ha-Mishpat Ha-Ivri* (1988), 1:129f, 496; idem, *Jewish Law* (1994), 1:145f; 2:604; idem, *Jewish Law (Cases and Materials)* (1999), 50–52; M. Elon and B. Lifshitz, *Mafte'aḥ ha-She'elot ve-ha-Teshuvot shel Ḥakhmei Sefarad u-Ẓefon Afrikah* (1986), 1:142–143; B. Lifshitz and E. Shohetman, *Mafte'aḥ ha-She-elot ve-ha-Teshuvot shel Ḥahmei Ashkenaz, Zarefat ve-Italyah* (1997), 94.

DIVORCE (Heb. גֵּרוּשִׁין), the formal dissolution of the marriage bond.

IN THE BIBLE

Divorce was accepted as an established custom in ancient Israel (cf. Lev. 21:7, 14; 22:13; Num. 30:10; Deut. 22:19, 29). In keeping with the other cultures of the Near East, a Hebrew in early biblical times could divorce his wife at will and send her from his home. This is reflected in the use of such terms as *shalle'aḥ* (e.g., Deut. 21:14; 24:1, 3), *garesh* (e.g., Lev. 21:7; Ezek. 44:22), and *hozi'* (Ezra 10:3; cf. Deut. 24:2) for divorce actions. It also accounts for the survival of the view down to the Christian era that "the woman goes out (*yoẓe'ah*) whether she pleases or not, but the husband sends her out (*moẓi'*) only if it so pleases him" (Yev. 14:1).

The biblical, like the Mesopotamian, law codes did not set down the law of divorce in all of its details. Instead, some of its provisions were stated in brief – almost in passing – within the context of a law restricting the right of a man to remarry his divorced wife (Deut. 24:1–4). Specifically, the husband was required to write her "a bill of divorce" (*sefer keritut*), hand it to her, and send her away from his house (Deut. 24:1; cf. Isa. 50:1; Jer. 3:8). The content of this document is unknown, though it has been conjectured that it contained the formula, "she is not my wife nor am I her husband" (Hos. 2:4). Z. Falk is probably right in assuming that biblical divorce remained essentially an oral declaration, witnessed by the writ. This accords with the actual Sumerian practice which required the husband to pronounce the formula "you are not my wife" and to pay his wife half a mina of silver before he dismissed her from his home. Moreover, as others have shown, the term *keritut* itself may be derived from the ancient Sumerian ceremony requiring the husband to cut the corner of his wife's garment to symbolize the severance of the marriage bond (cf. Ruth 3:9). In any event, biblical law was concerned with the finality of the divorce action and its attendant publicity, so that there might be no questions raised later with regard to the remarriage of the divorcée. Furthermore, the requirement that a bill of divorce be issued in writing and that the wife be formally sent out of her husband's house before the marriage was dissolved, kept him from acting rashly in a moment of anger. The prohibition of remarrying the same woman, if, in the interim, she had married another (Deut. 24:4; Jer. 3:1) acted, similarly, as a moderating influence. Finally, it has been suggested that a woman was entitled to some kind of a financial settlement in the event of an arbitrary divorce action. This is not clearly stipulated in the biblical texts. Still, the existence of such a requirement appears likely from its prominence in other Near Eastern codes (cf. e.g., *The Code of Hammurapi*, 137–140; in: Pritchard, Texts, 172). It also helps explain a husband's willingness to defame his wife despite the scandal to his household and the possible punishment to himself (Deut. 22:13–21), because presumably he could thus rid himself of her without any penalty. The Bible records only two types of situations in which the husband was stripped of his right of divorce. The first is the one just mentioned, in which he falsely accused his wife of prenuptial intercourse. The second resulted from his having ravished a virgin who had never been engaged to another man (Deut. 22:28–29). These instances and the requirements mentioned above were the only limitations set on a man's authority to dissolve his marriage. Bet Hillel was clearly correct in its interpretation of *ervat* (*ʿerwat*) *davar* (Deut. 24:1) as any kind of obnoxious behavior or mannerisms, and in concluding that a man was not restricted to grounds of sexual offense in seeking to divorce his wife (Git. 90a; cf. Deut. 23:15). Still, there are no instances in the Bible when a man sent his wife away lightly. On the contrary, Abraham is depicted as resisting the expulsion of his concubine (Gen. 21:11–12), Paltiel wept when he had to give up Michal (II Sam. 3:14–16), and Ezra encountered significant opposition when he called on the men to give up their foreign wives (Ezra 10:3ff.). The ideal of marriage was that of a permanent union (cf. Gen. 2:24) and conjugal fidelity was praised (Eccles. 9:9). Divorce did remain a necessary evil and was probably resorted to most often in the event of the barrenness of the marital union (cf. Gen. 30:1). There were instances, however, when living together must have been unbearable, and women did abandon their husbands (cf. Judg. 19:1–3; Jer. 3:20) since they had no legal recourse. The Torah did recognize, though, that a man had to discharge certain obligations toward his wife, and she, presumably, had the moral right to leave him if he refused to do so (cf. Ex. 21:10–11). The lot of the divorcée was not a pleasant one (cf. Isa. 54:6). Generally she returned to her father's home (Lev. 22:13), leaving her children with her former husband. Special arrangements were probably made for suckling infants; in later law, boys, at least, had to be returned to their father's home by the time they were six years old (Ket. 65b). The divorcée was free to remarry, but was prohibited to a priest (Lev. 21:7), indicating that some stigma was attached to her. Moral anguish speaks out of Malachi's denunciation of the frequency of divorce in Judea in the fifth century B.C.E. (2:13–16). At about the same time, the Jewish military colony in Elephantine seems to have adopted practices from their Egyptian neighbors which strengthened the woman's position in her marriage. In the three complete marriage contracts of this colony published to date (see bibl.: Cowley, 15, and Kraeling 2, 7), each spouse had full power to dissolve the marriage without establishing any grounds in "matrimonial offenses." The husband had to return his wife's dowry regardless of who had initiated the divorce proceedings, and he had to give her all of her possessions before she was required to depart from his home. These practices, however, had no basis in biblical law, though some scholars have found echoes of them during the talmudic period and later.

[David L. Lieber]

IN LATER JEWISH LAW

Talmudic literature also uses the terms *shalleʾaḥ*, *hoẓiʾ* (see above). Divorce must be distinguished from a declaration of nullity of marriage in which the court declares that no marriage ever came into existence so that all rights and duties flowing therefrom – personal or pecuniary – are rendered inoperative *ab initio* (i.e., in the case of a marriage prohibited on account of incest according to biblical law). It must also be distinguished from an annulment of marriage, i.e., the retroactive invalidation thereof by decree of the court (see **Agunah*; *Marriage). "A man takes a wife and possesses her. She fails to please him because he finds something obnoxious about her, and he writes her a bill of divorcement, hands it to her, and sends her away from his house" (Deut. 24:1). This verse, stated in relation to the prohibition against a man remarrying his divorced wife after her marriage to another man (see *Marriages, Prohibited), provides the basis for the system of divorce practiced according to Jewish law, i.e., there is no divorce other than by way of the husband delivering to his wife – and not vice versa – a bill of divorcement, in halakhic language called a *get pitturin* or simply *get* (a word having the meaning of *shetar*, or bill: see Maim. Comm. to Mishnah, Git. 2:5). The rabbis stated that "whosoever divorces his first wife, even the altar sheds tears" (Git. 90b; cf. Mal. 2:14–16), and therefore she should not be divorced unless "he found something obnoxious about her" – an expression whose exact meaning was the subject of a dispute between Bet Hillel, Bet Shammai, and Akiva (Yev. 112b; Git. 90a). However, in terms of a rabbinical enactment known as the *Ḥerem de-Rabbenu Gershom* (see also *Bigamy, *Monogamy) it became prohibited for the husband to divorce his wife against her will (*Rema* EH 119:6; for the text of the *ḥerem* in relation to divorce see PDR 1:198). In Jewish law, divorce is an act of the parties to the marriage, whereby it is to be fundamentally distinguished from divorce in many other systems of law, in which the essential divorce derives from a decree of the court. In Jewish law the function of the court – i.e., in the absence of agreement between the parties – is to decide the question whether and on what terms one party may be obliged to give, or the other receive, a *get*. Even after the court has thus decided, the parties nevertheless remain married until such time as the husband actually delivers the *get* to his wife. At the same time, it is the function of the court to ensure that all the formalities required for divorce are carried out according to law.

Divorce by Mutual Consent

Jewish law shows a further distinction from many other legal systems in that the mere consent of the parties to a divorce, without any need for the court to establish responsibility for the breakup of the marriage, suffices for its dissolution, i.e., for delivery of the *get*. It must be given or received by them, however, of their own free will and not out of fear that they may be obliged to fulfill any obligations which they undertook in the agreement in the event of their not being divorced (*Pitḥei Teshuvah* EH 134, n. 9; PDR 3:322–4; 4:353f.). Hence, if either party withdraws from the agreement and satisfies the court of a genuine desire for matrimonial harmony, the other party will likewise continue to be subject to all the recognized matrimonial obligations. In this case, however, the pecuniary conditions which the parties may have stipulated in the event of either of them failing to uphold the agreement may nevertheless be valid and enforceable (*Pitḥei Teshuvah* loc. cit.; PdR 2:9; 6:97; PD, 20, pt. 2 (1966), 6, 12f.). It is also customary to make provision in the divorce agreement for matters such as custody of the children and their maintenance, and in principle there is no reason why such conditions should not have binding validity vis-à-vis the legal relationships between the parties themselves (PDR 4:275, 281). On the question whether and to what extent such conditions are binding in respect of the children, see *Parent and Child.

Divorce other than by Consent

In the absence of an agreement between the parties to a divorce, the court is required to decide whether or not there is a basis for obliging or – in cases where this is permitted by law – for compelling the husband to give, or the wife to receive, a *get*.

The decision of the court is dependent upon the existence of any of the grounds recognized as conferring a right on the wife or husband to demand a divorce.

RIGHT OF THE WIFE TO DEMAND A DIVORCE. The wife is entitled to demand a divorce on the grounds of (a) physical defects (*mumim*) in her husband or (b) his conduct toward her.

Physical Defects as Grounds for Divorce. In order to obtain a divorce on the grounds of physical defects the wife must prove that these preclude him, or her, from the possibility of cohabition, e.g., because he suffers from a contagious and dangerous disease – "afflicted with boils and leprosy" – or because the defects are likely to arouse in her feelings of revulsion when in his proximity, and the like. In the case of the unreasonable refusal of the husband to comply with the judgment obliging him to give his wife a *get* of his own free will in these circumstances, the court may compel his compliance (Ket. 77a and codes; PDR 3:126). The question whether judicial coercion is possible in the case of epilepsy is disputed, and the practice of the courts is to oblige – but not compel – a divorce on this ground (PDR 1:65, 73f.; 2:188, 193), save in exceptional cases, e.g., where there is the danger of the wife becoming an *agunah* (PDR 4:164, 171–3). The wife is also entitled to a divorce if she is childless and claims that she wishes to have a child but that her husband is incapable of begetting children (Yev. 65a/b and codes; Resp. Rosh 43:4; PDR 1:5, 8; 2:150). The wife must satisfy the court, as a precondition to divorce on this ground, that she is not seeking the divorce for pecuniary reasons or because she has "set her eyes on another" (Yev. 117a and codes; Resp. Rosh 43:2; PDR 1:364, 369). Similarly, she must prove her claim that her husband is the cause of her childlessness; the lapse of ten years from the time of her marriage without her having been made pregnant by her husband establishes a presumption that there are no longer any prospects of her bearing her husband any children (Yev. 64a and codes; PDR 1:5, 9, 10, 369). If the husband claims that the cause does not lie with him, he may demand that the matter be clarified by submission of himself and his wife to a medical examination; if his claim is established, he is exempted from paying his wife's *ketubbah* (Yev. 65a; Resp. Rosh 43:12; Sh. Ar., EH 134; *Beit Shemu'el* 134, n. 14). A comparable cause of action arises from the wife's claim that her husband is impotent (i.e., he lacks *ko'aḥ gavra*; see *Marriage). The claim is grounded not on the wife's desire to raise a family but on her right to sexual relations as such, and it is therefore of no consequence that she already has children, nor is she required to wait for ten years (Yev. 65b and codes; PDR 1:5, 9, 55, 59, 82, 84; 5:154). If the evidence leaves room for the conclusion that medical treatment may possibly lead to the husband's recovery, the court will refrain from obliging the husband to give a *get* immediately (Yev. 65b and codes; PDR 1:81, 84–89; 5:239). In principle, the wife's claim as to her husband's impotence is accepted as trustworthy in terms of the rule that she is believed in matters between her husband and herself; however, corroboration of her statements is required (*Rema* EH 154:7, PDR loc. cit.). In the opinion of some authorities, a wife who succeeds in her claim would also be entitled to the sum mentioned in her *ketubbah*, since her trustworthiness extends also to the pecuniary aspect (*Pitḥei Teshuvah* EH 154:7; *Ha-Gra, ibid.*, n. 41); according to others, full proof is required with regard to the latter aspect (Tur and Sh. Ar., EH 154 and commentators thereto). However, should the wife have married her husband with knowledge of his defects, or if she acquired such knowledge after their marriage and nevertheless continued to live with him, she is considered to have waived her objections unless she is able to show that the defects became aggravated to an extent which she could not have foreseen (Ket. 77a and codes; PDR 1:5, 9, 10; 2:188, 192; 6:221, 223). If she is able to account for her delay on grounds which negate any waiver of rights on her part (such as failure to approach the court because of her embarrassment), her right to a divorce is likely to remain unaffected even if considerable time has elapsed since she first became aware of her husband's defects (PDR 1:11–12). No claim can be based on defects or circumstances which, however serious they may be, do not preclude the wife from cohabiting with her husband – e.g., his loss of a hand, leg, or an eye, etc. – whether occurring after the marriage or before, unless she proves that she did not know or, despite investigation, could not have known of the existence of the defect, and provided that she claims a divorce within a reasonable period after becoming aware thereof (Ket.

77a and codes; Resp. Rosh 42:2; *Maggid Mishneh* Ishut 25:11; *Beit Shemuel* 154 n. 2; PDR 1:5, 11, 65, 71).

Conduct of the Husband as a Ground for Divorce. Unjustified refusal of conjugal rights on the part of the husband entitled his wife to claim a divorce (Sh. Ar., EH 76:11; for her ancillary or alternative rights in this case, see **Moredet*). Similarly, the wife may claim a divorce on the ground of her husband's unjustified refusal to maintain her when he is in a position to do so, or could be if he was willing to work and earn an income. In this event she may also claim *maintenance without seeking a divorce (Ket. 77a, according to Samuel, contrary to Rav). The court will not decree that a divorce should be given on the husband's first refusal, but only if he persists in his refusal after being warned and obliged by the court to pay her maintenance (PDR 5:329, 332). Were the husband totally unable to provide her with the minimum requirements ("even the bread she needs"), some authorities are of the opinion that he can even be compelled to divorce her, whereas others hold that there is no room for compulsion since his default is due to circumstances beyond his control (Yad, Ishut 12:11; Sh. Ar., EH 70:3 and commentators; PDR 4:164, 166–70). The husband will not however be obliged to grant his wife a divorce if he maintains her to the best of his ability, even if this be the measure of "a poor man in Israel" and not in accordance with the rule that "she rises with him but does not go down with him" (see *Maintenance; Sh. Ar. and commentators, loc. cit., PDR loc. cit.). Unworthy conduct of the husband toward his wife with the result that she cannot any longer be expected to continue living with him as his wife constitutes a ground for her to claim a divorce ("a wife is given in order that she should live and not to suffer pain": Ket. 61; *Tashbeẓ*, 2:8). The ground is established when his conduct amounts to a continued breach of the duties laid down as a basis for conjugal life, i.e., "let a man honor his wife more than he honors himself, love her as he loves himself, and if he has assets, seek to add to her benefits as he would deal with his assets, and not unduly impose fear on her, and speak to her gently and not be given to melancholy nor anger" (Yad, Ishut 15:19, based on Yev. 62b; see also *Marriage). Thus the wife will have a ground for divorce if, e.g., her husband habitually assaults or insults her, or is the cause of unceasing quarrels, so that she has no choice but to leave the common household (*Rema* EH 154:3; *Ha-Gra, ibid.*, n. 10; *Tashbez*, loc. cit.; PDR 6:221). The same applies if the husband is unfaithful to his wife (Sh. Ar., EH 154:1 and commentators; PDR 1:139, 141); similarly, if he "transgresses the Law of Moses" – for instance when he causes her to transgress the dietary laws knowing that she observes them, or if he has intercourse with her against her will during her menstrual period (see **Niddah*; *Rema* EH 154:3; PDR 4:342). If the husband is able to persuade the court that his wife has condoned his conduct (PDR 1:139, 142), or of his genuine repentance, the court will not immediately oblige the husband to grant a divorce. The court will direct the parties to attempt living together for an additional period in order to ascertain whether a divorce is the only answer for them, unless it is satisfied that no purpose will be served by such delay (Sh. Ar. and commentators, loc. cit.; PDR 1:87–89; 3:346, 351; 4:257, 259).

RIGHT OF THE HUSBAND TO DEMAND A DIVORCE. The grounds on which the husband may demand a divorce (i.e., since the *Ḥerem de-Rabbenu Gershom*) are mainly similar to those which afford the wife this right against him, and previous awareness or condoning of these defects invalidates his claim (PDR 1:66).

Defects (or Disabilities) of the Wife. In addition, however, defects of the wife which provide the husband with grounds for a divorce are those which are peculiar to a woman as such, and which prevent the husband from cohabiting with her, or which render her unfit for or incapable of such cohabitation (Nid. 12b; Yad, Ishut 25:7–9; Resp.Rosh 33:2; Sh. Ar., EH 39:4 and 117:1, 2, 4; PDR 4:321; 5:131, 193). Included in such defects, according to the majority of the authorities, is epilepsy (Resp. Rosh 42:1; PDR 2:129, 134–6; 5:131, 194). If the husband was aware of such defects prior to the marriage or later became aware – or could have become aware – that they had existed before the marriage but still continued to cohabit with her, he will be considered to have condoned them and they will not avail him as grounds for divorce (Ket. 75 and codes; PDR 1:66; 5:193). Similarly a defect which becomes manifest in the wife only after the marriage does not provide the husband with a ground for divorce, unless she is afflicted with a disease carrying with it mortal danger, such as leprosy, or she has become incapable of cohabiting (Ket. loc. cit. and codes; PDR 2:129, 134–6; 5:131, 194). The husband may demand a divorce if his wife has failed to bear children within a period of ten years of their marriage, and he has no children (even from another woman), provided that he persuades the court of his sincere desire to have children (*Rema* EH 1:3; Sh. Ar., EH 154:1; see also *Oẓar ha-Posekim* EH 1, n. 13–60; PDR 4:353).

Conduct of the Wife. The husband will have ground for demanding a divorce if his wife knowingly misleads him into "transgressing the Law of Moses," as when she has sexual relations with him during her menstrual period and conceals this fact from him, or when she causes him to transgress the dietary laws, etc., knowing that he observes these laws (Ket. 72a and codes), but not if she acted inadvertently, or out of fear, or in ignorance of the law, or if the husband has by his own conduct shown that he is not particular about them (*Rema* EH 154:3; PDR 3:346, 350). Similarly, the husband may claim a divorce if his wife shows habitual immodesty or deliberately slights her husband's honor, as when she curses or assaults him, and generally any conduct on her part tending to disrupt normal family life in such manner as to convince the court that no further condonation and continuation of the matrimonial relationship can be expected of the husband (Ket. 72; Sot. 25a; codes; PDR *ibid.*). Condonation of the above also deprives him of his cause of action for divorce. A similar ground for divorce arises when the husband is able to prove, on the testimony of two witnesses, conduct on the part of his wife which gives rise to the strong suspicion that she has committed adultery, even if there is no evidence of actual adultery (Yev. 24b, 25a; Yad, Ishut 24:15; Sotah 2:13; Sh. Ar., EH 11:1). Where such proof is forthcoming, the husband is entitled to a judgment compelling his wife to accept a divorce (Sh. Ar. loc. cit. and commentators; *Rema* EH 115:4; PDR 1:51, 54; 2:125–8). If it is proved that the wife has committed adultery, of her own free will, she becomes prohibited to her husband and she will be unable to raise a plea of condonation on her husband's part, since there can be no consent to do what is prohibited by the law (Sot. 18b and 27b; Ket. 9a and codes; PDR 1:13). The wife can be compelled to accept a *get* against her will since she is not protected by the *Ḥerem de-Rabbenu Gershom* in this case. By virtue of the said prohibition, the wife herself may claim a divorce if her husband refrains from instituting action against her since he does not have the right to render her an *agunah*, because on the one hand he is prohibited from living with her and on the other she may not marry another man until divorced from her husband (*Oẓar ha-Posekim* EH 11, n. 1–54; PDR 5:154, 156); however, this is disputed by some authorities (PDR *ibid.*). In this case too the evidence of two witnesses is essential in terms of the rule that "in matters of incest (*ervah*) there cannot be less than two [witnesses]" (Yev. 24b; Kid. 66a; and codes). Thus, generally speaking, her confession alone will not suffice because of the suspicion that she has "set her eyes on another man" (Yev, 24b; Kid. 66a; PDR 3:260), nor will the evidence of one witness only, unless her husband states that he believes her or the single witness as he would two witnesses, and provided the court too is satisfied of the truth of the matter (Kid. 66a and codes). In this event the court will oblige but not compel the parties to divorce each other (Maim. loc. cit.; Sh. Ar. loc. cit.; PDR 4:160). A divorce on the grounds of adultery precludes the wife from remarrying her former husband – to whom she is prohibited by Pentateuchal law – and from marrying the man with whom she committed adultery – to whom she is prohibited by rabbinical law (Sot. 27b and codes). Moreover, she forfeits her *ketubbah* (Ned. 90b; Sh. Ar., EH 115:5). In cases of rape, the wife does not become prohibited to her husband unless he is a kohen (Yev. 56b and codes; see *Priest), nor does she lose her *ketubbah* (Ned. 91a and codes).

Divorce in the Case of a Prohibited Marriage

The court will always compel a divorce at the instance of either party to a prohibited marriage of the sort in which the marriage is valid when performed (see *Marriages, Prohibited), regardless of whether or not they had knowledge of the prohibition, as a matter of law or fact, and regardless of their continued cohabitation after becoming aware of the prohibition (Ket. 77a; Git. 88b; and codes).

The Will of Parties

THE HUSBAND. To be valid, a *get* must be given by the husband of his own free will and is therefore invalid if given while he is of unsound mind, or under duress contrary to law (Yev. 112b; Git. 67b, 88b; and codes). "Contrary to law" in this context means the exercise of compulsion against him when it is not permitted in any way by law, or its exercise in an invalid manner; for instance, if he gives the *get* in order to escape a payment imposed on him contrary to law, even by judgment of the court. Such a case may be when he is ordered to pay maintenance to his wife or children without being at all liable for this, or when he is ordered to pay an excessive amount (PDR 2:9–14). However, if the law specifically authorizes that he be compelled to give a *get* – as in the cases mentioned above – or if he is lawfully obliged to make a payment to his wife – e.g., when ordered to pay interim maintenance in an amount due to his wife pending the grant of a *get* and he has the option of escaping this obligation by granting the *get* – then the *get* will not be considered to have been given by him under unlawful duress, since his own prior refusal to give it was contrary to law (Yad, Gerushin 2:20; BB 48a; Sh. Ar., EH 134:5). In order to obviate any suspicion that the *get* may have been given under duress contrary to law, it is customary, before the *get* is written and before delivery therefore, for the husband to annul all *moda'ot*, i.e., declarations made by him before others in which he purported to have been compelled to give a *get* (*Beit Yosef* EH 134:1; Sh. Ar., EH 134:1–3).

THE WIFE. There must be free will on the part of the wife also to receive the *get* as laid down in the *Ḥerem de-Rabbenu Gershom*, in order to maintain the prohibition against polygamy (see *Bigamy) lest the husband circumvent the prohibition by divorcing his wife against her will and thus become free to take another wife. The wife was therefore given a right similar to that of the husband and cannot be divorced except with her consent (Resp. Rosh 42:1; *Rema* EH 119:2). This applies even in those communities which did not accept the said *ḥerem* against polygamy (cf. *Oẓar ha-Posekim* 1, n. 68, 12). Already according to talmudic law, it was forbidden to divorce a woman who had become of unsound mind, even though it was not prohibited to divorce a wife against her will. If her condition is such that she is "unable to look after her bill of divorcement," the latter will be invalid according to biblical law since it is enjoined that "he shall give it in her hand" (Deut. 24:1) and such a woman has no "hand" in the legal sense (Yev. 113b and codes). Where she "knows how to look after her *get*" even though she "does not know how to look after herself," she still cannot be divorced, but in this case by rabbinical enactment, lest advantage be taken of her and the husband will remain liable for all pecuniary obligations to her even if he should take another wife (*ibid.*). This is all the more so in terms of the aforesaid *ḥerem*, since in both cases the wife is incapable of receiving the *get* of her free will. Whereas talmudic law did not require the husband to obtain permission of the court before taking another wife, the *ḥerem* had the effect of prohibiting the husband from doing so, save with the permission of 100 rabbis. (On the question of the first wife's legal status after the grant of permission as aforesaid, see *Bigamy.)

Execution of the Divorce

Divorce is carried into effect by the bill of divorcement being written, signed, and delivered by the husband to his wife. It is written by a scribe upon the husband's instruction to write "for him, for her, and for the purpose of a divorce." The materials used in the writing must belong to the husband and the scribe formally presents them as an outright gift to the husband before writing the *get.* The strictest care must be taken with the formula of the *get*, most of it in Aramaic, and the text is, with minor differences, according to the wording given in the Talmud. To obviate errors, it is still the practice at the present day to write the bill in Aramaic, although writing in any other language is theoretically permissible (Git. 19b, 87b and codes; on the rules of writing a *get*, its form and language, and the effect of variations therein, see Sh. Ar., EH 120ff.; for the version customary in Ereẓ Israel, see ET, 5 (1953), 656; see also Yad, Gerushin 4:12; Sh. Ar., EH *"Seder ha-Get"* following n. 154). The following is a translation of an Ashkenazi *get*, according to the general usage in the Diaspora:

> On the ... day of the week, the ... day of the month of ..., in the year ... from the creation of the world according to the calendar reckoning we are accustomed to count here, in the city ... (which is also known as ...), which is located on the river ... (and on the river ...), and situated near wells of water, I, ... (also known as ...), the son of ... (also known as ...), who today am present in the city ... (which is also known as ...), which is located on the river ... (and on the river ...), and situated near wells of water, do willingly consent, being under no restraint, to release, to set free, and put aside thee, my wife, ... (also known as ...), daughter of ... (also known as ...), who art today in the city of ... (which is also known as ...), which is located on the river ... (and on the river ...), and situated near wells of water, who has been my wife from before. Thus do I set free, release thee, and put thee aside, in order that thou may have permission and the authority over thyself to go and marry any man thou may desire. No person may hinder thee from this day onward, and thou art permitted to every man. This shall be for thee from me a bill of dismissal, a letter of release, and a document of freedom, in accordance with the laws of Moses and Israel. ... the son of ..., witness. ... the son of ..., witness.

The bill of divorcement is composed of the *tofes*, i.e., the formula common to all such bills, and the *toref*, i.e., the specific part containing the details of the particular case, concluding with the declaration that the woman is henceforth permitted to any man. Care must be taken to write the correct date on which the bill is written, signed, and delivered, otherwise it can be invalidated as a bill which is "anticipatory" or "in arrear" of the true date of its writing or signature or delivery (Sh. Ar., EH 127). The husband should also be careful to avoid sexual relations with his wife between the time of writing and delivery of the bill since such a bill, called an "antiquated" one (*get yashan*), although valid in the final instance, may not be used in the first instance (Git. 79b; Sh. Ar., EH 148:1). Once the witnesses sign the *get*, it is delivered by the husband to his wife in the presence of "witnesses to the delivery" (generally the same witnesses as sign; Sh. Ar., EH 133:1). Delivery of the *get* in accordance with the regulations renders the wife divorced from her husband and free to marry any man save those to whom she is prohibited by law, e.g., a kohen or paramour (see *Marriages, Prohibited). It is customary that after the wife has received the *get* she gives it to the court, who presents her with a document stating that she has been divorced according to law. The court then tears the *get* in order to avoid any later suspicion that it was not absolutely legal and files it away in its torn state (*Beit Shemu'el* 135:2; Sh. Ar., EH 154 (*Seder ha-Get*), ch. 6; *Sedei Ḥemed, Asefat Dinim, Get* 1:23). The rules pertaining to the writing, signing, and delivery of a *get* are very formal and exact in order to avoid mistakes or a wrongful exploitation of the *get*, and they must therefore be stringently observed. (The exact details are to be found in Sh. Ar., EH 124–39.) As a result it was laid down that "no one who is unfamiliar with the nature of divorce (and marriage) may deal with them" (Kid. 13a). The Mishnah mentions a particular form of *get* which was customary in the case of kohanim, who were regarded as pedantic and hot-tempered and therefore likely to be hasty in divorcing their wives. This form of *get* – called a "folded" or "knotted" one as opposed to a "plain" *get* – consisted of a series of folds, each of which (called a *kesher*) was stitched and required the signature of three witnesses (two in the case of a "plain" *get*) who signed on the reverse side and not on the face, between each fold. All this was done to draw out the writing and signing of the *get* so that the husband might reconsider and become reconciled with his wife (BB 160ff.). The "folded" *get* was customary in ancient times only and the rules pertaining to it are omitted from most of the codes (e.g., Maim., Tur, Sh. Ar.).

Agency in Divorce

Although divorce in Jewish law is the personal act of the husband and wife, their presence in person is not a necessary requirement for its execution. Delivery and receipt of the bill of divorcement, like any regular legal act, may be effected through an agent in terms of the rule that "a man's agent is as himself" (see *Agency; Git. 62b and codes). Appointment of the agent is made before the court by way of a power of attorney (*harsha'ah*), i.e., a written document very carefully and formally prepared to include all the relevant details, in which the agent is empowered to delegate his authority to another, and the latter to another in turn, etc. (Sh. Ar., EH 140:3; 141:29–30). An agent appointed by the husband for the purpose of delivering the *get* to his wife is called "the agent of delivery" and the *get* takes effect only upon delivery thereof by the husband or his agent to the wife or her agent, the latter called "the agent of receipt" (Sh. Ar., *ibid.*). In the latter case the fact that the wife may not know exactly when the *get* takes effect is likely to result in complications and doubts and it has not therefore been customary to resort to agency of this kind (*Rema* EH 141:29). The wife may also appoint a "delivery" agent – i.e., to deliver the *get* to her (and not to receive it on her behalf) after receiving it from the husband or his agent – in such manner that she will become divorced only upon delivery thereof to herself. The latter agent is not an "agent of receipt" and is subject to the same rules as is an "agent of delivery" (Sh. Ar., EH 140:5). The rules of agency in divorce are of practical importance in cases where the parties live in different countries and wish to avoid the expense involved in the grant and delivery of a *get* in the presence of each other, or where they do not wish to confront one another. The same applies when one of the parties is an apostate. In these cases the husband is enabled to divorce his wife by way of "conferring" the *get* on her (*get zikkui*), i.e., by delivery thereof to an agent appointed by the court, the divorce taking effect upon the agent's receipt of the *get*. (According to some of the *posekim* the *get* must thereafter be delivered to the wife herself so as to avoid doubt.) This *halakhah*, that the court can appoint an agent for the wife without her explicit consent or knowledge, is based on the rule that "a benefit may be conferred on a person in his absence" (Yev. 118b; see *Agency), on the following reasoning: if the husband becomes an apostate, it is presumed that the Jewish woman will always prefer living as a divorcée to living with an apostate; if the wife becomes an apostate, it can only be to her advantage if she no longer remains tied to her Jewish husband and will thus no longer be liable if she cohabits with another (see *Rema* EH 1:10 and 140:4; *Oẓar ha-Posekim* EH 1, n. 81, 1–9).

Conditional *Get*

A *get* may be written and delivered conditionally, that is so as not to take effect except on fulfillment of a stipulated condition, e.g., if the husband should fail to return to his wife within a specified period or that no word from, or concerning him, shall be forthcoming until then. The condition must not contradict the basic nature of divorce, i.e., the absolute severance of the marriage relationship between the husband and wife. To have validity it is necessary that all the complicated laws pertaining to *conditions be observed at the time of its imposition. Similarly, it must later be carefully investigated whether all the facts required to establish fulfillment of the condition have been adequately proved, since there is at stake the random divorce of a married woman. The doubts and complications attaching to a conditional *get* are likely to be particularly severe in the light of a rabbinical enactment to the effect that a plea of accident (*force majeure*, see **Ones*) does not avail in divorce. Thus, contrary to the general rule that a person is not responsible for his act or omission resulting from accident, the husband cannot plead that the condition to which the validity of the *get* was subject was fulfilled only on account of accident – such as his failure to return in time due to an unforeseeable disruption of the means of transportation (Ket. 2b, 3a; Sh. Ar., EH 144:1; see also **Takkanot*). Hence in general the practice is not to permit a conditional *get* save in exceptional cases, and then the above-mentioned laws may be of great practical importance, e.g., in times of persecution or war when there is separation between husband and wife and the danger of her becoming an *agunah*. In such cases the practice is sometimes adopted of granting a *get* on condition, e.g., if the husband should fail to return from the war by a certain date the *get* shall be deemed to be effective, and the wife divorced and free to remarry without need for a levirate marriage or *ḥaliẓah*. Upon fulfillment of the condition, the *get* will take effect either immediately or retroactively to the time of its imposition, according to the terms thereof, and provided that everything had been done in strict conformity with all the requirements of the law (Sh. Ar., EH 143, 144, 147; see also **Agunah*, *Levirate Marriage). This aim may also be achieved by the conditional appointment of an agent, e.g., the appointment by the husband, before going to war, of an agent given written authority to write a *get* in his (the husband's) name and to deliver such to his wife, on condition that the power of attorney is not acted upon unless the husband should fail to return home within a stated period (Sh. Ar., EH 144:5, 6). The court itself may be thus appointed and may in turn, in terms of authority generally granted in the power of attorney, delegate its authority to a third party. A deathbed divorce (see *Wills) is also a conditional *get*, i.e., one given by a husband on his deathbed so as to free his wife from the requirement of a levirate marriage or *ḥaliẓah*. In practice such a *get* will also have no validity except if the husband dies, whereupon it will take effect retroactively from the date of its delivery (see Sh. Ar., EH 145).

Consequences of Divorce

Upon divorce, the parties are generally free to remarry as they please save as prohibited by law. The wife becomes entitled to the return of her own property from the husband, in accordance with the rules of law pertaining to the husband's liability therefor (see *Dowry). She is similarly entitled to payment of her *ketubbah* and dowry, save where she forfeits her *ketubbah*, e.g., because of her adultery. Divorce terminates the husband's legal obligation to maintain his wife, since this duty is imposed only during the subsistence of the marriage (Sh. Ar., EH 82:6). For charitable reasons, however, it is considered a *mitzvah* to sustain one's divorced wife more extensively than the poor at large (*Rema* EH 119:8). Upon divorce the parties are not permitted to continue their joint occupation of the former common dwelling, lest this lead to promiscuity (Sh. Ar., EH 6:7; 119:7, 11). If the dwelling belonged to one of them, whether owned or hired, it must be vacated by the other party and if it belonged to both it must be vacated by the wife (*ibid.*), as "the husband has greater difficulty in moving about than the wife" (Ket. 28a); although sometimes the courts, in order to settle financial matters between the parties, or in awarding compensation to the wife, will decide that the dwelling remain in her hands (see e.g., OPD, 158, 163 no. 6). If the divorced parties nevertheless continue to jointly occupy the dwelling, or later return thereto – as testified to by witnesses – they will be presumed to have cohabited together as husband and wife for the sake of a marriage constituted by their sexual intercourse (*kiddushei bi'ah*: see *Marriage). This follows from the rule that "a man does not have intercourse for the sake of promiscuity if he is able to do so in fulfillment of a precept," i.e., it will not be presumed that the parties wished to transgress since they were lawfully in a position to marry each other (Yad, Gerushin 10:17; Sh. Ar., EH 149:1). Hence they will be required to divorce each other once again if they should wish to marry third parties, i.e., a "*get* out of stringency" (*get mi-ḥumra*) at least and possibly even out of an undoubted *kiddushin* between them (Sh. Ar., EH 149:1, 2; PDR 7:35). If the wife marries another man without having first obtained a second *get* as aforesaid, this marriage will accordingly require dissolution, since she is regarded as being the wife of the first husband (Sh. Ar., loc. cit.; *Beit Shemu'el* thereto, n. 4). Since the aforesaid presumption is founded on the premise that the parties were in a position to be lawfully wedded, it will not apply in the reverse situation, e.g., in the case of a kohen who is prohibited from remarrying his divorced wife, or when the wife has meanwhile become the widow of or divorced from another husband, or if the husband has meanwhile taken another wife and hence become prohibited by the *ḥerem* from being married at the same time to another, i.e., his former wife. Consequently, according to some of the codes, no second *get* will be required in all the above cases (*Beit Shemu'el* loc. cit.; PDR loc. cit.).

IN THE STATE OF ISRAEL

In terms of the Rabbinical Courts Jurisdiction (Marriage and Divorce) Law, 5713–1953, matters of marriage and divorce between Jews, citizens or residents of the state, fall within the exclusive jurisdiction of the rabbinical courts, which jurisdiction extends to any matter connected with the suit for divorce, including maintenance for the wife and for the children of the couple (sec. 3(1)). Divorce for Jews is performed in accordance with Jewish law (sec. 2). In applying the *halakhah* the rabbinical courts have introduced an important innovation, namely the award of monetary compensation to a wife who is being divorced; this is done even when the divorce is not specifically attributable to the fault of the husband, but the court, after close scrutiny of all the facts, is persuaded that the situation prevailing between the parties does not, objectively speaking, allow for the continuation of their marriage. In this event, the court, upon the husband's demand that his wife be obliged to accept a *get*, will customarily oblige the former to pay a monetary or equivalent compensation to his wife – in addition to her *ketubbah* – in return for her willingness to accept the *get* (OPD 51–55; PDR 1:137). The extent of the compensation is determined by the court, having regard to all the circumstances, including the financial position of the parties and their respective contributions to the state of their assets.

[Ben-Zion (Benno) Schereschewsky]

ENFORCEMENT. The legal position in Israel regarding the enforcement of divorce may be divided into two periods, the first extending from 1953 to 1995, and the second from 1995 onwards.

The Legal Position from 1953. The Rabbinical Courts Jurisdiction (Marriage and Divorce) Law, 5713 – 1953 established the following procedure for enforcement of a judgment compelling the husband to grant a get to his wife, or compelling the wife to accept a *get* from her husband: "Where a rabbinical court, by final judgment, has ordered that a husband be compelled to grant his wife a *get*, or that a wife be compelled to accept a *get* from her husband, a district court may, upon expiration of six months from the day of the making of the order, on the application of the Attorney General, compel compliance with the order by imprisonment (sec. 6 of the Jurisdiction Law)."

This Law enumerates the following preconditions for imprisonment as a means of compelling the husband to grant a divorce: (a) the rabbinical court judgment ordering a compulsory *get* is a final one; where an appeal against the judgment is pending, it cannot be enforced; (b) the authority is granted exclusively where the judgment *compels* the giving of the *get*, and not where the ruling is that there is an *obligation* to give a *get* (HC 822/88 *Rozensweig Borochov v. Attorney General*, 42 (4) PD 759, 760); (c) six months have passed since the final judgment was given, and the *get* has not been given; (d) after that period, the Attorney General, and not the spouse, is authorized (at his own discretion – see HC 85/54 *Zada v. Attorney General*, 8 PD 738) to apply to the district court, requesting it to enforce compliance with the judgment, by way of imprisonment. The district court, and on appeal the Supreme Court, is the only legal instance empowered to compel the giving or receiving of a *get* by imprisonment of the spouse who refuses to comply with the judgment of the rabbinical court. The Law does not stipulate the length of the period, nor is it of fixed duration. The imprisonment terminates upon the granting of the *get*. In one case, the recalcitrant husband remained in prison for a number of decades until he died (CA 164/67 *Attorney General v. Yichhieh & Ora Avraham*, 22 (1) PD 29).

The power to determine whether there is a need to compel the granting of a *get* in a particular case is vested exclusively in the local rabbinical court, and in the Supreme Rabbinical Court, as an instance of appeal (see entries on *Bet Din* and *Appeal). The Jurisdiction Law of 1953 established a mechanism for dual civil supervision over the compulsion of a *get*: (a) the initiative was neither of the spouse nor of the rabbinical court, but rather of the Attorney General; (b) the judicial instance that actually decided on the imprisonment of the recalcitrant spouse was the civil instance (the district court) and not the rabbinical court. According to the decision of the Supreme Court sitting as the High Court of Justice, the rabbinical court was not permitted to circumvent this supervisory mechanism by way of "intimidatory maintenance" (excessively high maintenance payments as a way of pressuring the husband into granting a *get*). This is because the legislation explicitly provided that the only way of enforcing judgments to compel the granting of a *get* is by way of an application made by the Attorney General, followed by a decision of the civil court. It follows therefore that this power was not conferred on the rabbinical court. An attempt on the part of the rabbinical court to procure the compulsion of a *get* by way of "maintenance and intimidation" would be overstepping its authority, and its ruling would be annulled by the High Court of Justice (see: HC 54/55 *Rozensweig v. Head of Execution*, 9 PD 1542., per Silberg J.)

The Legal Position since 1995. About 40 years after the enactment of the Jurisdiction Law of 1953 – and in view of the surfeit of unresolved *agunah* cases as a result of the complex mechanism described above – the Knesset pioneered a solution to the problem by the enactment of a special law to deal with enforcement of divorce judgments: The Rabbinical Courts Law (Upholding Divorce Rulings) (Temporary Provision), 5755–1995 (see *Agunah for a brief description of this Law).

The Law was initially enacted as a temporary provision, but after a few years it became a permanent law. Over the years a number of additions and amendments were introduced in the wake of the lessons derived from its implementation.

The Law introduces the following innovations, in contrast with the situation that had existed since 1953: (1) the rabbinical court judgment need not be final (as in the 1953 law); even if the judgment can be appealed, the provisions of the 1995 Law apply; (2) the power to compel the granting of a *get* under the 1995 Law is not limited specifically to cases in which judgment was given for the compulsion of a *get* (as in the 1953 Law). Hence, section 1 of the 1995 Law provides: "For purposes of this section, it is immaterial if the judgment used the wording of compulsion, obligation, *mitzvah* (positive precept), suggestion or any other wording"; (3) moreover, the 1995 Law can be invoked 30 days after judgment is given for granting the *get*, and there is no need to wait six months, as was the situation under the 1953 Law; (4) the authority to compel the spouse to comply with the divorce judgment no longer rests with the civil authorities (the Attorney General and the district court) as under the 1953 Law; this authority has been conferred on the rabbinical court; (5) the procedure itself is initiated by the spouse, who is no longer dependent on the Attorney General's application to the district court; (6) the rabbinical court is permitted, at its own initiative, to impose or to amend restrictive orders; (7) under the 1995 Law, the period of coercive imprisonment cannot exceed five years, but, if necessary for the purpose of fulfilling the judgment, the rabbinical court is permitted to extend this period from time to time, provided that the total period of imprisonment does not exceed ten years (under the 1953 Law the imprisonment period was unlimited).

Another innovation of the 1995 Law was the establishment of a hierarchy of sanctions, collectively known as "restrictive orders," which the rabbinical court is authorized to impose on the recalcitrant husband (see *Agunah for a specification of the restrictive orders).

Regarding criminal inmates who refuse to give or accept a *get*, the Law establishes special provisions within the framework of restrictive orders, which include the denial of benefits generally granted to inmates, such as: receiving furloughs, sending letters, receiving visitors, work in prison, and the like. Similarly, the rabbinical court is authorized to issue an order stating that an inmate of this ilk will not be released on parole, or will not be entitled to an administrative release.

The aforementioned restrictive orders of the 1995 Law are a modern application of the *harḥakot* (sanctions) of Rabbenu Tam, which allow the ostracizing of husbands who refuse to grant a *get* by prohibiting all social contact with them (SHEZ 154:211 *Rema*, and see in further detail *Agunah). Indeed, the rabbinical courts have not regarded themselves as being limited to the specific restrictive orders enumerated in the 1995 Law, and in appropriate cases they added social-religious sanctions, such as not including the recalcitrant husband in a *minyan*, not giving him an *aliyah* to the Torah, prohibiting his burial in a Jewish cemetery, publicizing the entire matter, etc.

However, the most important and primary sanction established by the 1995 Law is the authority of the rabbinical court to imprison a person who refuses to comply with the divorce judgment. This imprisonment has proven to be particularly effective, and there have been quite a few cases in which the recalcitrant husband gave a *get* after just a short period in prison by order of the rabbinical court.

A special problem arises when the reluctant husband is in prison, serving a sentence for a criminal offense. How does one wield the imprisonment sanction against this kind of prisoner in order to compel him to give a *get* to his wife? The Law stipulates that, in such a case, service of the criminal sentence is discontinued, and from the date of the rabbinical court's order, the sentence being served by the inmate is regarded as being for his failure to give a *get*. After having given the *get*, he resumes the service of his criminal sentence (see section 47 of the Penal Law, 5737–1977).

Regarding inmates serving a sentence for a criminal offense, there may be cases in which the rabbinical court deems that imprisonment for compulsion of the *get* is not effective. In such cases, under section 3A of the 1995 Law, it is empowered to order that the inmate be held in solitary confinement for short, 14-day periods, and thereafter for seven-day periods, with intervals of seven days.

The rabbinical court has particularly broad discretionary powers under the 1995 Law. The Supreme Rabbinical Court supervises the rabbinical courts' implementation of the Laws by way of its power to stay execution of a restrictive order and within the framework of an appeal. This supervisory power applies both to restrictive orders and to the imprisonment that can be imposed on the husband refusing to give a *get*.

When recalcitrant husbands refusing to give a *get* petitioned the High Court of Justice, claiming that the imprisonment order issued by the rabbinical court violated their constitutional rights, their petitions were dismissed by dint of this brief and incisive argument: "The petitioner holds the key to his release from prison; when he gives the *get* to his wife, he will go free" (HC 3068/96 *Goldshmidt v. Goldshmidt and the Supreme Rabbinical Court*; HC 631/97 *Even Tzur v. Supreme Rabbinical Court*).

Originally, the 1995 Law regulated the manner of enforcing the *get* in cases where the *husband* is the party obliged to give the *get*. But the Law was amended shortly after its enactment, prescribing slightly different provisions for cases in which the *wife* refuses to accept a *get* from her husband. While the nature of the sanctions against the husband or the wife is essentially the same, with respect to their imposition on women, sections 1(c), (e), and (f) of the Law place the following two limitations: the first is the requirement of the advance approval of the president of the Supreme Rabbinical Court; the second is that, if restrictive orders against the wife have already been issued, the husband's application for permission to marry will not be adjudicated until three years have passed since the restrictive order was given.

It should be mentioned that the provisions of the 1995 Law do not detract from the provisions of the 1953 Law, and it is possible to enforce a divorce under either one of the two laws. However, in view of the effectiveness of the new law, since its enactment in 1995 it has been used exclusively, and the 1953 law is no longer applied.

Great importance is attached to the 1995 Law and the sanctions that have been imposed by rabbinical courts for enforcement of divorce judgments, and they have led to a significant reduction in the number of *agunot* in Israel. The rabbinical courts also relied upon the existence of enforcement measures in Israel as a justification for extending their jurisdiction to include Jewish couples with a limited connection to Israel, especially in cases in which they were civilly divorced abroad, and the woman requires a *get* according to the *halakhah* in order to be able to remarry (see judgments of the Supreme Rabbinical Court, *Appelbaum v. Appelbaum*, File 1239–53–1, and *Anon. v. Anon.*, judgment from 30.6.04). The latter judgment was adjudicated in HC 6751/04 *Sabag v. Supreme Rabbinical Court*. The majority view (Justices Procaccia and Adiel) was that the rabbinical courts in Israel do not have jurisdiction to adjudicate these cases. The minority view (Justice Rubinstein) was that the rabbinical court is competent to adjudicate the maintenance payments for a wife who is prevented from marrying due to the husband, even when the spouses are foreign residents, but Jewish. It should be noted that the Law was amended in 2005, and subject to a number of conditions stipulated in the amended Law, the Israeli Rabbinical Court now has jurisdiction over Jewish couples that were married abroad in accordance with *din torah*, and the 1995 Law applies to those couples as well (see in detail in the entry *Bet Din).

The aforementioned Knesset legislation of 1995 therefore makes an important contribution towards the resolution of the problem of the *agunah*, but the solution it provides is partial only, and the entire subject of the *agunah* still awaits an appropriate and desirable solution. The appropriate path for a comprehensive solution of the *agunah* problem is discussed in detail under **Agunah*.

In other dimensions too, the Israeli legal system operates in order to enforce the divorce and prevent a situation of *agunah*. For example, Elon opined that extradition abroad of a person suspected of murder could be delayed for at least one year in order to enable the rabbinical court to process the divorce of the parties involved, and thus prevent a situation in which the wife of the candidate for extradition would become an *agunah*; see HC 852/86 *Aloni v. Minister of Justice*, 41 (2) PD 1, 70 onwards (see 9 *Teḥumin*, 63 for the judgment of the rabbinical court).

There is now a new method for assisting in the enforcement of divorce judgments of the rabbinical courts if the wife receives a judgment obligating the husband to divorce her, and the husband refuses to comply: in such a case, the wife can sue him for the damage caused to her. In a recent ruling, the Jerusalem Family Court awarded damages in a case of this kind, basing itself on the general rules of negligence. The court ruled that the husband's failure to comply with the rabbinical cCourt's ruling, ordering him to give his wife a *get*, constituted a grave violation of the wife's autonomy and her right to self-realization. It violated her dignity and her freedom, causing her emotional damage by sentencing her to a life of loneliness, lack of partnership, intimacy, and sexual relations with a member of the other sex (FF 19270/03 *Anon. v. Anon.*: given by Judge Menahem Hacohen on 24.12.04).

[Moshe Drori (2nd ed.)]

STATISTICS

Europe

In 1897, the Russian Jews in the Pale of Settlement had a much higher divorce rate than other religious or ethnic groups. Jewish men in the relatively large cities had, on the average, 5.4 divorces per 1,000 males, while the others had only 2.2 per 1,000. In the case of the females the index was 19.1 and 5.4 respectively. Those who lived in smaller communities or rural places had a smaller percentage of divorces. It thus appears that the Jewish population had a much higher divorce rate than non-Jews. In both instances there was a larger percentage of divorces among the women than the men (since women are less likely to remarry) and those who lived in large cities had a higher divorce rate than their coreligionists in towns and rural communities. European Jewish communities witnessed in the years before World War I an upward trend in their divorce rate. One-eighth of those who were divorced or separated in Austria in the years 1882–89 were Jewish, but in the decade 1890–99 they constituted 15.8%, falling to 9.7% in the years 1900–12. Since in Austria the Jews formed only 4.8% of the population in 1890 and 4.6% in 1910, divorce was more prevalent among them than among other religious groups, many of whom were Roman Catholics. However, during this period, relating the number of divorces and separations to the number of marriages, the Jews had a lower rate of increase in divorces than others. The same was true of Prussia where during the same period the Jewish divorce rate continued to rise, but not as fast as the one of non-Jews. This suggests that the attitude of non-Jews to divorce was changing, and once this had occurred their divorce rate began to increase more rapidly than that of the Jews. The divorce rate of European Jews increased considerably in the years between World War I and World War II. The index of divorces per 1,000 living spouses of Jewish males in Polish cities increased from 2.8 in 1921 to 6.8 in 1931, while that of non-Jews in the same towns was 3.5 and 7.9. In the case of the females, the increases were from 9.6 to 17.3 and from 6.9 to 14.8 respectively. As in the case of Russia, the males had a relatively smaller number of divorces than the females, partly because of the difference in their remarriage rates. Because most of them were Roman Catholics, for whom remarriage was almost impossible, the non-Jewish males had a larger percentage of divorces than the Jewish group. Jewish women had a higher index of divorces because of the anti-divorce attitude of the Catholic Church. The Hungarian Jewish community, which had in 1930 a population of approximately 445,000, had a higher index of divorces than the Polish Jews and a larger increase in the decade 1920 to 1930. Urban Jews had a higher index than those in other localities; the Budapest community, for instance, had the largest percentage of divorces. The Jews in Czechoslovakia had a lower index of divorces than their coreligionists in Hungary. This may have been partly due to the fact that one-twelfth of the Czechoslovakian Jews were engaged in agriculture while only 2.7 were similarly employed in Hungary. German-born Jews in Prussia had in 1925 a larger percentage of divorces than their immigrant brethren. The index of divorces of the former was 14.0 for the males and 29.3 for the females; in the case of the immigrants the indices were 13.5 and 18.8 respectively. The differences were even more pronounced in Berlin, where the German-born males had an index of 24.8 and the females of 47.2 whereas the others had indices of only 18.8 and 23.4 respectively.

British Commonwealth

In Australia, where the number of divorces increased between 1911 and 1954, the male index rising from 7 to 38 and the female from 11.5 to 48.7, the Christians had in 1954 about the same percentage of divorces as the Jews. Canada had in 1931 a very small percentage of divorces, partly because those who had been separated from their spouses were not reported as such. Moreover, adultery was officially the only ground for divorce. The 1941 census report, however, had data on divorce and separation according to ethnic origin in cities with at least 30,000 inhabitants. Taking Montreal, Toronto, and Winnipeg, the three largest Jewish communities, the results were: the index for Jewish males was 14.8 and for Jewish females 24.8, while for the other males and females it was 26.3 and 40.7 respectively. The differences are mainly due to the fact that Jews have a low separation index.

Muslim Lands

Muslims usually have a large percentage of divorces. The Jews in Egypt had a much lower index of divorces than the Muslims. In and around Alexandria and Cairo, the index of divorces of the Muslim males in 1927 was 44.9 and that of the Jews 12.7; the corresponding female indices were 64.1 and 25.6. The Christians had about half as many divorces as the Jews. Twenty years later, the index of the Muslim males had dropped to 26.5 and that of the females to 49.7, while the Jewish indices had increased to 15.1 and 27.0. In 1951 in Morocco Jewish males had a relatively smaller number of divorces than Muslims, the indices being 14.4 and 22.6. However the female index of 57.6 was higher than that of Muslim females.

The U.S.

As far as the United States is concerned, it is difficult to assess the divorce rates of any of its religious or ethnic groups since the agencies which collect data on marriage and divorce do not use such classifications. Nor does the Bureau of the Census report the marital status of the population according to religious or ethnic origin. The only sources of information are surveys of Jewish communities or samples of the population in which Jews are included. As few attempts have been made to survey very large communities and some of the investigators do not use standard definitions or classifications, the results of these surveys and studies are suggestive rather than conclusive. Though the so-called family crisis at the beginning of the period of mass immigration was probably neither very serious nor of long duration, Jewish social agencies became very much interested in the family life of the immigrant. Studies made in the early 20th century showed that desertion was not as prevalent among Jews as among other ethnic and religious groups. An analysis of the Chicago Court of Domestic Relations in 1921 demonstrated that only 10.4% of the deserters whose religion was the same as their wives were Jewish. In 1929–35, when about one-tenth of Chicago's population was Jewish, only 5.5% of the non-support cases were Jewish couples, with those of Jewish origin whose spouses were not Jewish accounting for another 0.7%. In Philadelphia in the years 1937 to 1950, when Jews constituted about 16% of the white population, they accounted for 11.8% of the white couples who were divorced. Baltimore Jews also had low desertion and divorce rates. In 1936 and 1938, when at least one-tenth of the white population was Jewish, they formed only 5.3% of the white deserters. Similarly in the Detroit Jewish community broken homes were less prevalent than in other religious groups there. According to a metropolitan survey in 1958 only 4% of the Jewish respondents who had ever married reported that they had been divorced, as compared with 8% of the Catholics and 16% of the Protestants. However, a study made in 1955 reported that the Jews in several cities had a higher divorce and desertion rate than Protestants. Taken on the whole, these results show that divorce, separation, and desertion were less prevalent among American Jews than others, and surveys of Jewish communities made since 1946 showed that they have a relatively smaller number of broken homes than the rest of the white population. Divorce was more prevalent among those whose spouses are not Jewish than when both of them are of Jewish origin. (The above statistics are quoted by N. Goldberg in *Jews and Divorce* (see bibl.)). In more recent times Jewish divorce rates have followed the upward trend in the United States as a whole.

BIBLIOGRAPHY: GENERAL: J. Freid (ed.), *Jews and Divorce* (1968). IN THE BIBLE: Cowley, Aramaic, nos. 9, 15, 18; Pedersen, Israel, 1–2 (1926), 71, 232; L.M. Epstein, *The Jewish Marriage Contract* (1927), index; Epstein, Marriage, 41–42, 53; J. Patterson, in: JBL, 51 (1932), 161–70; C.H. Gordon, in: ZAW, 54 (1936), 277–80; I. Mendelsohn, in: BA, 11 (1948), 24–44; E. Neufeld, *The Hittite Laws* (1951), 146ff.; J.J. Rabinowitz, in: HTR, 46 (1953), 91–7; D.R. Mace, *Hebrew Marriage* (1953), 241–59; E.G. Kraeling, *The Brooklyn Museum Aramaic Papyri* (1953), nos. 2, 7, 14; A. van Selms, *Marriage and Family Life in Ugaritic Literature* (1954), 49ff.; R. Patai, *Sex and Family in the Bible and the Middle East* (1959), 112–21; de Vaux, Anc Isr, 34ff.; R. Yaron, *Introduction to the Law of the Aramaic Papyri* (1961), 44–65; J. Hemple, *Das Ethos des Alten Testaments* (1964), 70–71, 165ff.; B. Cohen, *Jewish and Roman Law*, 1 (1966), 377–408; Z. Falk, *Jewish Matrimonial Law in the Middle Ages* (1966), 113–43; B. Porten, *Archives from Elephantine* (1968), 35, 209ff., 223–4, 261–2; Pritchard, Texts (1969[3]), 159–98, 222–3. IN JEWISH LAW: D.W. Amram, *The Jewish Law of Divorce ...* (1896); L. Blau, *Die juedische Ehescheidung und der juedische Scheidebrief...* 2 vols. (1911–12); I.B. Zuri, *Mishpat ha-Talmud*, 2 (1921), 36–56; Gulak, Yesodei, 3 (1922), 24–30; B. Cohen, in: REJ, 92 (1932), 151–62; 93 (1934), 58–65; idem, in: PAAJR, 21 (1952), 3–34; republished in his: *Jewish and Roman Law* (1966), 377–408; addenda, *ibid.*, 781–3; ET, 5 (1953), 567–758; 6 (1954), 321–426; 8 (1957), 24–26; Elon, Mafte'aḥ, 26–37; M. Silberg, *Ha-Ma'amad ha-Ishi be-Yisrael* (1965[4]), 365–75; Berkovits, *Tenai be-Nissu'in u-va-Get* (1966); B. Schereschewsky, *Dinei Mishpaḥah* (1967[2]), 271–342; M. Elon, *Ḥakikah Datit...* (1967), 165–7; idem, in: ILR, 3 (1968), 432f. **ADD. BIBLIOGRAPHY:** M. Drori, "Enforcement of Divorce in the State of Israel at the End of the 20th Century," at: www.sanhedrin.co.il; A. Be'eri, "*Harḥakot Rabbeinu Tam*: New Approaches to Pressuring a Husband to Divorce His Wife," in: *Shenaton ha-Mishpat ha-Ivri*, 18–19 (2002–4), 65–106; "Individual versus Public Interest (Fear of *Agginot* as Opposed to an Extradition Order)," in: *Teḥumin*, 9 (1988), 63.

DIWAN, JUDAH BEN AMRAM (d. c. 1752), emissary of the communities in Ereẓ Israel to the Diaspora. He resided first in *Jerusalem and later in *Safed. In 1708, he was sent as a representative of Safed to *Iraq and *Persia. Upon his return, he was sent by the community of *Hebron on a mission to the same countries. In the course of this mission he preached in the communities of *Aleppo, *Hamadan, and *Tabriz, and issued responsa in *Baghdad and Hamadan. On his return journey, he learned of the financial pressure Arab creditors were exerting on the Jewish community in Jerusalem. He interrupted his trip and remained in Aleppo for some time where he lost his money in an unsuccessful business enterprise. Having heard that the leaders of the Constantinople community had arranged to settle the debts incurred by the Jerusalem community, Diwan went to Constantinople. There, in 1728, he printed his book *Zivḥei Shelamim* on the laws of *sheḥitah*. He then went on a further mission to several Oriental countries to collect contributions for Jerusalem. On his return, some of the wealthy members of the Constantinople community founded a yeshivah for him in Jerusalem, called Neveh Shalom Berit Avraham. In 1736, he was a signatory to the regulations of the community in Jerusalem. He sent the manuscript of his book *Ḥuṭ ha-Meshullash* to Constantinople where it was published in 1739. The book consists of sermons delivered and responsa issued while on his missions. The introduction includes an autobiography and the description of his three journeys. There are extant a number of *haskamot* ("declarations of approval") to books signed by Diwan.

BIBLIOGRAPHY: Yaari, Sheluḥei, index; Frumkin-Rivlin, 2 (1928), 164ff.; 3 (1929), addenda 29.

[Avraham Yaari]

DIYALA, province of eastern Iraq, 6,154 sq. mi. (15,754 sq. km.). There were formerly Jewish communities in eleven towns and villages of Diyala. According to the 1947 census, the total Jewish population was 2,850. The capital city, *Ba'quba, was inhabited by Jews as early as the 12th century. In *Khanaqin in 1845 there were twenty Jewish families; in 1932 there were 1,110 Jews, most of whom spoke Arabic, while a minority spoke Jebelic Aramaic. Most of the Khanaqin Jews were employed in the textile and iron trades. Some of them were also perfume and spice dealers. In 1911 a coeducational school was founded by the Alliance Israélite Universelle. The majority of the Jewish population of Diyala immigrated to Israel in 1950–51, while some went to America.

BIBLIOGRAPHY: A. Ben-Yaacob, *Yehudei Bavel* (1965), index.

[Abraham Ben-Yaacob]

DI-ZAHAV (Goldstein), EPHRAIM (1902–1957), *ḥazzan*. Di-Zahav was born in Jerusalem and after completing his basic education studied in London. When he returned to Palestine he became involved in journalism and literature. He was an official of the mandatory government. He graduated in music from the Jerusalem Conservatory, and participated in oratorios and musical performances in Jerusalem. For six years he held the position of cantor in the Jeshurun synagogue in Jerusalem. When the Palestine Broadcasting Service was established in 1936 he was among its first employees. He was responsible for numerous programs for the radio's Hebrew hour, and participated in broadcasts of cantorial music, regularly reading the cantillation. After the establishment of the State of Israel, he continued to participate in the traditional programs on both Kol Israel and the overseas broadcasts, Kol Zion Lagola. He published articles and stories in the Israeli press. Among his works are *Mi-Sippurei ha-Dod Efraim* (Uncle Ephraim's Tales) and *Ẓeror Aggadot* (An Anthology of Fables).

[Akiva Zimmerman (2nd ed.)]

DIZENGOFF, MEIR (1861–1936), a founder and first mayor of *Tel Aviv. Born in Akimovici, near Orgeyev, Bessarabia, he was active in Russian revolutionary circles in his youth, and was arrested in 1885. Later he became active in the Ḥovevei Zion movement. During the late 1880s he studied chemical engineering in France, specializing in glass production. He was sent to Ereẓ Israel in 1892 by Baron Edmond de Rothschild to establish a glass factory at Tantura (Dor) which was to supply bottles for the wines produced in the settlements. However, the factory was closed in 1894 when it became clear that the local sand was unsuitable. During his stay in Ereẓ Israel Dizengoff, together with others, tried to form a Jewish workers' organization. Returning to Russia in 1897, he settled in Odessa, went into business, and became active in the Zionist movement. He participated in Zionist Congresses and was among the opponents of the Uganda Scheme. Dizengoff was a founder of the Geulah Company, formed in 1904 to purchase land in Ereẓ Israel. As director of the company he returned to Ereẓ Israel in 1905 and settled in Jaffa. Dizengoff was one of the founders of the Aḥuzat Bayit Company for establishing a modern Jewish quarter near Jaffa. This quarter, later called Tel Aviv, was founded in 1909. In 1911 Dizengoff was elected head of the local council. Later, when Tel Aviv became a city (1921), Dizengoff was elected its first mayor and, except during 1925–28, served in that capacity until the end of his life. At the outbreak of World War I, Dizengoff headed a committee that assisted war sufferers and refugees. However, the Turkish authorities expelled him to Damascus, where he remained until the conquest of northern Palestine by the British at the end of 1918. In 1919 Dizengoff founded *Ha-Ezraḥ* ("The Citizen"), a first attempt at the political organization of the non-labor middle class. He was a member of the Zionist executive during 1927–29 and ran its trade and industry department. He donated his house on Tel Aviv's Rothschild Boulevard for the establishment of the Tel Aviv Museum in his wife Zina's name. Upon the outbreak of the Arab riots in 1936 Dizengoff urged that government offices be opened in Tel Aviv and succeeded in establishing a separate port at Tel Aviv independent of Jaffa and its port. Dizengoff published his memoirs, *Im Tel Aviv ba-Golah* ("With Tel Aviv in Exile"), in 1931.

BIBLIOGRAPHY: J. Yaari-Poleskin, *M. Dizengoff* (Heb., 1926); D. Smilansky, *Im Benei Dori* (1942), 89–107; Tidhar, 2 (1948), 794–6; M. Smilansky, *Mishpaḥat ha-Adamah*, 2 (1944), 180–7.

[Yehuda Slutsky]

DJERASSI, CARL (1923–), U.S. chemist. The son of a Bulgarian father and Austrian mother, both Jewish physicians, Djerassi was born in Vienna but immigrated to the U.S. with his mother in 1938 to escape from the Nazis. He was educated at the American College in Sofia and at Newark Junior College, New Jersey, before graduating with a B.A. from Kenyon College, Ohio (1942), and obtaining his Ph.D. in organic chemistry from the University of Wisconsin (1945). After working with the Ciba pharmaceutical company, he moved to Syntex in Mexico City (1949–52) before becoming a professor first at Wayne State University, Detroit, and subsequently at Stanford University (1959). He continued his association with Syntex as vice president for research. Djerassi made major contributions to organic chemistry, including elucidating the structure of complex natural products with innovative optical and spectrometric techniques, characterizing a vast range of sterols encountered in marine sponges and corals, synthesizing many novel steroids, and advancing alkaloid and terpenoid chemistry. As president of Syntex's offshoot company, Zoecon, he was concerned with new approaches to insect control. His best-known achievement is the first synthesis of a female oral contraceptive, "norethisterone." His prodigious scientific output is reported in over 1,200 original articles and seven scientific monographs. His many honors include election to the U.S. National Academy of Sciences (1961), the National Medal of Science (1973), the first Wolf Prize in Chemistry (1978), the National Medal of Technology (1991), the Priestley Medal (1992), and the Gold Medal of the American Institute of Chemists (2004).

Djerassi was deeply involved in scientific programs relevant to less-developed countries; he participated in Pugwash Conferences on Science and World Affairs and chaired the U.S. National Academy of Sciences Board for International Development. He was also concerned with the social and cultural problems of population control. His many other interests include writing fiction, poetry, and plays with a particular concern for the portrayal of scientists in fiction and drama. His well-known works include the plays *An Immaculate Misconception* (1999), *Calculus* (2003), *Ego* (2004) and five novels, two of which (*Menachem's Seed* and NO) are set in Israel. His interest in the visual arts inspired the foundation of the Resident Artists Program at Woodside, California, and his collection of Paul Klee's works.

[Michael Denman (2nd ed.)]

DJERBA (Jerba), island off the coast of Tunisia. In ancient times it was an important Phoenician trading center. According to the local tradition, the Jewish settlement there is very old. It maintains that the Jews came there during the reign of *Solomon and founded the present al-Ḥāra al-Kabīra (the "Big Quarter"). A family of priests fleeing Jerusalem in the year 70 C.E. is said to have transported one of the Temple gates to Djerba. It is believed to be enclosed in the Bezalel synagogue, known as al-Gharība (the "extraordinary") of the Ḥāra al-Ṣaghīra (the "Small Quarter"), which is situated in the center of the island. The Gharība was a much frequented place of pilgrimage. The Jewish population consisted mainly of *kohanim* (priests) with a small sprinkling of others, although there were no levites among the residents. According to tradition, the absence of levites on the island is the result of a curse against them by *Ezra because they refused to answer his request to send levites to Ereẓ Israel (cf. Ezra 8:15), and they all died. The history of the Jews of Djerba includes three serious persecutions: in the 12th century under the *Almohads; in 1519 under the Spanish; and in 1943 under the Nazis. In 1239 a colony of Jews from Djerba settled in *Sicily, where they obtained concessions to cultivate henna, indigo, and the royal palm groves. It was common for the male Jewish population of Djerba to look for livelihood abroad, but they kept returning to the island, where their families had remained. Exchange of goods with *Malta and *Italy was in the hands of the Jews, who grew the products and processed the commodities for export themselves. *Maimonides, in a letter to his son, expressed a low opinion of their superstitions and spiritual capacity, but praised them for their faith. In the 19th and 20th centuries the yeshivot of Djerba produced many rabbis and writers and they provided rabbis for the communities of North Africa. In 1976, some 300 youngsters received Jewish education. In the early 1990s, the American Jewish Joint Distribution Committee provided funding for Jewish education (including a girls' school) with a combined enrollment of 245. David Idan established a Hebrew printing press in Djerba in 1903, and many books, mainly Passover **Hagaddot* and liturgical items, were printed there. In 1946 there were some 4,900 Jews in Djerba, settled in al-Ḥara al-Ṣaghīra, al-Ḥāra al-Kabīra, and Houmt-Souk, the principal town of the island. Their number dwindled to about 1,500 by the late 1960s, about 1,000 in 1976, 800 in 1984, and 670 in 1993, the majority immigrating to Israel and settling in moshavim (many of them on moshav Eitan) or reaching France. Those remaining dealt in jewelry and commerce, but the Jewish neighborhoods lost their purely Jewish character as Muslims moved in and the community was the victim of several anti-Jewish incidents. In October 1980 a Jewish boy was sentenced to five years in prison (but released two months later) for destroying an Islamic religious manual during a 1978 schoolyard scuffle. Following the Israeli invasion of Lebanon in 1982, Jewish homes and shops in Djerba were ransacked and set on fire on Yom Kippur and several Jews were injured. The Tunisian government encourages the annual Lag ba-Omer pilgrimage to al-Gharība as a tourist attraction, even inviting Tunisian Jews from Israel to participate in May 1993. But al-Gharība suffered several attacks, with the pilgrimage temporarily decreasing. On May 9, 1979, a fire (labeled by the government an "accident") broke out, destroying seven Torah scrolls, the ark, and prayer books. During the Simḥat Torah prayers in October 1985, a Tunisian guard, posted by the government for protection, shot at the congregation, killing five (including a policeman) and wounding eleven. He was convicted and sentenced to a mental institution. On April 11, 2002, a natural gas truck exploded at the outer wall of al-Gharība, killing 21, mostly German tourists, with a group linked to al-Qaeda claiming responsibility.

BIBLIOGRAPHY: N. Slouschz, *Travels in North Africa* (1927), 251–68; R. Lachmann, *Jewish Cantillation and Song in the Isle of Djerba* (1940); R. Brunschwig, *La Berbérie orientale sous les Hafṣides*, 1 (1940), 399; Pinkerfeld, in: *Cahiers de Byrsa*, 7 (1957), 127–88; A.N. Chouraqui, *Between East and West* (1968), index s.v. *Djerba*. **ADD. BIBLIOGRAPHY:** *American Jewish Year Book*, 1972, 1978, 1985, 1994; H.Z. Hirschberg, *A History of the Jews in North Africa*, 2 vols. (1974–81), index; A.L. Udovitch and L. Valensi, *The Last Arab Jews: The Communities of Jerba, Tunisia* (1983); B. Haddad, *Sefer Jerbah Yehudit* (1978); Y. Mazouz, *Yahadut Jerbah* (1979); R. Attal, "Djerba, centre de diffusion du livre hébraïque," in: M. Abitbol (ed.), *Communautés juives des marges sahariennes du Maghreb* (1982), 469–78; G. Memmi, *Une île en Méditerranée* (1992); *Les Juifs de Jerba: 25 siècles d'histoire* (1990).

[David Corcos / Rachel Simon (2nd ed.)]

°DLUGOSZ, JAN (1415–1480), Polish cleric and annalist. He acted as secretary to Cardinal Zbigniew Oleśnicki in Cracow, who was violently anti-Jewish. After Oleśnicki's death in 1455, Dlugosz began a history of Poland, which he concluded in 1479. He was appointed archbishop of Lvov in 1478. A primary source for historical material, his annals include a firsthand account of the massacre of the Jews in Cracow in 1407 and the plunder, forcible conversions, and burnings of Jewish houses which accompanied it. His work set the anti-Jewish tone of medieval Polish historiography.

BIBLIOGRAPHY: Dubnow, Hist Russ, 1 (1916), 57.

[Natan Efrati]

DLUZHNOWSKY, MOSHE (Moyshe Dluzhnovski; 1906–1977), Yiddish novelist. Dluzhnowsky was born in Tomaszow Mazowiecki, Poland. His traditional *ḥeder* education was supplemented by autodidactic study of secular subjects. After his literary debut in 1925, he published short stories, novels, plays, essays, and reportage in the Yiddish press around the world. He immigrated in 1930 to Paris, where he described Jewish life in short stories and sketches. In 1940, he fled to Morocco and discovered in its *mellahs* a still unexplored field for Yiddish literature. His stories, and especially his novel *Vintmiln* ("Windmills," 1963), depicted the impoverished Berber-Arab-Jewish settlements. He went to the U.S. in 1941, where he contributed fiction to the Yiddish and English press. His works include a children's book *Der Raytvogn* ("The Chariot," 1958); a novel *Vi a Boym in Feld* ("As a Tree in the Field," 1958); and short story collections *Dos Rod fun Mazl* ("The Wheel of Fortune," 1949), *A Brunem Baym Veg* ("A Well by the Road," 1953), and *Tirn un Fentster* ("Doors and Windows," 1966). He also wrote several plays, some of them adapted from his novels. Most were produced in New York and South America, the most successful being *Di Eynzame Shif* ("The Lonely Ship," 1956).

BIBLIOGRAPHY: LNYL, 2 (1958), 526–8; B. Dimondstein, *Eseyen* (1958), 30–3; S.D. Singer, *Dikhter un Prozaiker* (1959), 224–9; Z. Zylbercweig, *Leksikon fun Yidishn Teater*, 4 (1963), 3653–7.

[Sol Liptzin / Eliezer Niborski (2nd ed.)]

°DMOWSKI, ROMAN (1864–1939), Polish politician and antisemite. He was leader of the Polish National Democratic party (ND: *Endecja) before 1914 in the Russian part of Poland and its chief representative in two of the *Dumas. Dmowski constantly propounded the view that antisemitism was an expression of the *Kulturkampf* between Jews and Poles; he adopted the anti-Jewish *boycott slogans introduced during the elections to the Duma in 1912. While on the Polish National Council between 1917 and 1918, which he headed as the representative of Poland to the Allied Powers, Dmowski discussed the future relations between Poles and Jews with the American Jewish leader Louis *Marshall in October 1918, particularly in view of the boycott then poisoning the atmosphere. Dmowski contended that Polish-Jewish relations would improve as the result of economic progress in an independent Poland, which would diminish the prevailing tensions. His readiness during the talks to listen to severe criticism of his antisemitic stand obviously only indicated his wish to alter his unfavorable image among American Jews so as to gain support in his activities as chairman of the Polish council. Dmowski served for a brief period in 1923 as foreign minister of Poland. After Józef *Pilsudski ousted Dmowski's party from all political power in 1926, Dmowski concentrated on writing articles in which he used antisemitism to rally right-wing opposition to Pilsudski's regime. With Hitler's rise to power Dmowski anticipated the collapse of world Jewry which in his view had hitherto depended on Germany. His "Downfall of Jewry" (1934) expresses the opinion that the 20th century will seal the fate of the Jewish people, which he considered to be an historical anachronism.

BIBLIOGRAPHY: J. Petrycki, *Roman Dmowski* (Pol., 1920); W. Feldman, *Dzieje polskiej myśli politycznej 1864–1914* (1933). **ADD. BIBLIOGRAPHY:** R. Dmowski, *Separatyzm zydowski i jego zrodla* (1909); S. Rudnicki, *Oboz narodowo radykalny* (1985), index; A. Micewski, *Z geografii politycznej II Rzeczypospolitej* (1966), 15–78; I. Openheim, "*Yaḥaso shel ha-Demokratiyah ha-Le'ummit h-Polanit (ha-Endecja) li-She'elah ha-Yehudit be-Shilhei ha-Me'ah ha-19 ve-Reshit ha-Me'ah ha-20*," in: *Galed*, 10 (1987), 87–119.

[Moshe Landau]

DNEPROPETROVSK (Yekaterinoslav until 1926), city and industrial center situated on the River Dnieper in Ukraine. Jews first settled there shortly after its foundation in 1778, and in 1804 the town was included in the *Pale of Settlement. The community numbered 376 in 1805 (total population 2,634) and 1,699 in 1847. With the growth of the city in the second half of the 19th century Jews began to move there from other parts of Russia, and played an important role in its commerce and industry. Apart from big flour mills Jews owned sawmills utilizing the timber sent down the Dnieper River. In the mid-19th century the railroad to Odessa was laid and Jews took a large part in the development of the grain trade and exports. Later, when the Donets Basin was linked to the city by railroad, Jews were involved in the metallurgical industry. Several Jewish agricultural colonies (see *Agriculture) were founded in the Yekaterinoslav province and in the neighborhood of the city itself between 1846 and 1855 with about 8,000 persons; some remained in existence until the German occupation in World War II. Apart from *ḥadarim* there was a *talmud torah* for poor children and seven private schools (1887), while 153 Jewish children studied in the local high school in 1882. The writer and lawyer Ilya *Orshanski together with others upgraded the curriculum of the *talmud torah* and the *heders* and organized food and clothing for destitute pupils. Pogroms occurred in Dnepropetrovsk and the vicinity on July 20–21, 1883, in which 350 homes and many Jewish shops were looted and destroyed. The losses were estimated at 600,000 rubles, and 2,870 persons lost their sources of income. By 1897 the Jewish population had increased to 41,240 (36.3% of the total population). It included 15,160 breadwinners (3,046 of them women), including 4,531 in trade, 2,969 in the garment industry, 1,426 artisans, and 1,714 in services and working in shops, with many professionals as well. Most of the shops and houses in the city center were owned by Jews. There were three *talmud torah* schools with 500 pupils, 885 studied in the *ḥadarim*, and a yeshivah and 16 private schools were in operation. In 1860 a hospital was founded with 14 beds, growing to 29 in 1886. In 1880 an old age home was opened for the poor. The community extended help in 1882 to 500 families (2,625 persons). There was also a small Karaite community in Dnepropetrovsk which had its own prayerhouse. They numbered 359 in 1897, dropping to 145 in 1926. Pogroms again broke out on October 21–23, 1905, and 74 Jews were killed, hundreds injured, and much property was looted and destroyed. Local *self-defense was organized in 1904, comprising 600 members, 2% of them Christians. It did much to protect the community. Revolutionary trends among the Jewish youth were strong, alongside Ḥasidism and Orthodoxy among the older generation of the community. Dnepropetrovsk was an important Zionist center where M. *Ussishkin (from 1891 to 1906) and Shemaryahu *Levin were active. The latter served there as a government-appointed rabbi from 1898 to 1904. The well-known lawyer Oscar *Grusenberg was born and raised in the city. He took part in the pogrom trials of Kishinev and Minsk and defended the accused in blood libels in Vilna and Kiev (the *Beilis Affair). Also living in the city was Hillel *Zlatopolsky, a Zionist activist and founder, with his daughter Shoshanah *Persitz, of the Omanut the publishing house (later Massadah). In World War I and the civil war in Russia, thousands of Jews took refuge in Dnepropetrovsk, which numbered 72,928 Jews in 1920. In the Civil War (1917–20) the city changed hands a number of times, suffering from tributes, looting, rape, and murder. In June 1919 the *Denikin army raped about 1,000 women and in May 1919 the Grigoryev band killed 150 Jews. After the establishment of Soviet rule, Jewish community life ceased there as elsewhere in the Soviet Union. Zionist activity was forbidden, and on September 18–22, 1922 about 1,000 were arrested. Only *He-Ḥalutz was allowed to function, until disbanded in summer 1926. The Jewish population numbered 62,073 in 1926 (26.9% of the total), with the following occupational structure: workers in factories and workshops: 6,397; office workers: 8,477; in professions: 425; in agriculture: 887; in trade: 2,194; artisans: 3,469; without professional status: 2,146; unemployed: 4,819. In 1924, 1,187 school-aged Jewish children studied in Yiddish schools and 4,064 in general schools. In the 1930s there were four Yiddish schools, a vocational high school for mechanics, and an industrial school at the Petrovski steel mill, where 500 Jews studied. An illegal Chabad yeshivah operated in the years 1929–35 with a few dozen students. According to the census of 1939 the Jewish population of the city was 89,525 (total population 526,000).

Dnepropetrovsk was occupied by the Germans on August 25, 1941. Thanks to evacuation and flight, only about 17,000 Jews remained. In September, 179 were killed. On October 2 a big tribute of 30 million rubles was imposed on the community and on October 13–14, 13,000–15,000 Jews were assembled and led to the botanical gardens, where they were murdered. The remaining 2,000 Jews were executed at the end of 1941 and the beginning of 1942. At the end of summer 1943 a unit of Operation Group 1005 opened the mass graves, burned the bodies, and dispersed the ashes. The city was liberated on October 25, 1943, and many Jews returned. According to the 1959 census there were 53,400 Jews living in Dnepropetrovsk. In 1963 antisemitic hooligans broke into a synagogue during the High Holiday services without interference from the police. In 1970 there was one synagogue still functioning in the city. During the High Holidays the synagogue street became filled with Jews and order was maintained by the police. J.L. Levin served as rabbi of Dnepropetrovsk before becoming chief rabbi of Moscow. Subsequent census figures put the Jewish population at 45,622 in 1979 and 17,869 in 1989. Immigration to Israel diminished the number significantly during the 1990s. The community offered wide-ranging communal and educational services. Shmuel Kaminetzky was chief rabbi.

BIBLIOGRAPHY: I. Halpern, *Sefer ha-Gevurah*, 3 (1950), 105, 162–79; M. Osherowitch, *Shtet un Shtetlekh in Ukraine*, 2 (1948), 99–111; Z. Harkavy, in: *He-Avar*, 5 (1957), 128–32; *Die Judenpogrome in Russland*, 2 (1910), 175–95; B. West, *Be-Ḥevlei Kelayah* (1963), 76. **ADD. BIBLIOGRAPHY:** Pinkas.

[Yehuda Slutsky / Shmuel Spector (2nd ed.)]

DO'AR HA-YOM (Heb. דֹּאַר הַיּוֹם; "Daily Mail"), Hebrew newspaper established in Jerusalem in 1919, under the editorship of Ithamar *Ben-Avi. The newspaper was designed primarily for those born in Ereẓ Israel and for the older *yishuv* circles (as emphasized by the programmatic leading article in the first issue). The tone of the paper, which was set by Ithamar Ben-Avi, followed that of the sensational French press. *Do'ar ha-Yom* introduced modern reportage in Hebrew. Many of its reporters were native Palestinian Jews, and it became the mouthpiece of the farmers and older settlers. Its editorial policy opposed the official Zionist movement. From December 1928 until the beginning of 1931 it supported the Revisionist movement and was edited by V. *Jabotinsky. Afterward, Ben-Avi returned as editor, but was later replaced. *Do'ar ha-Yom* ceased publication in 1936 and while no other daily newspaper imitated Ben-Avi's emotional and sensationalist style, the innovations he introduced influenced Israel journalism and many of the journalists influenced by Ben-Avi played important roles later on in the Israel press.

BIBLIOGRAPHY: I. Ben-Avi, *Im Shaḥar Aẓma'utenu* (1961), 367–82, 401–3, 505–13; G. Kressel, *Toledot ha-Ittonut ha-Ivrit be-Ereẓ-Yisrael* (1964), 197; G. Yardeni, *Hitpatteḥut ha-Ittonut ha-Ivrit* (1966).

[Getzel Kressel]

DOBIN, SHIMON (Shimoni; 1869–1944), writer, educator, and socialist in Russia. Born in Bobr, Belorussia, he joined the *Ḥibat Zion movement in Odessa as a young man. With B. *Borochov he became an early member of the *Po'alei Zion in Yekaterinoslav, and was a delegate to the Minsk convention of Russian Zionists in 1902. He continued to play an active role in Zionist workers' movements for some time, and was a founder of *Vozrozhdeniye and the *Zionist Socialist Workers' Party. In 1906–07 he edited *Folksshtimme*, the organ of the *Jewish Socialist Workers' Party. After imprisonment and exile for his political activities he joined the *Bund in Kiev in 1911. After the October Revolution he became active in "Ozet" and educational institutions, and contributed articles on Yiddish literature and language. He died in Sverdlovsk.

BIBLIOGRAPHY: *Eynikeyt* (June 8, 1944), 2; LNYL, 2 (1958), 430–1; *Iggerot B. Katznelson* (1961), 364–6; *Geshikhte fun Bund*, 2 (1962), index; *ibid.*, 3 (1966), index.

[Moshe Mishkinsky]

DOBKIN, ELIYAHU (1898–1976), Labor Zionist leader. Dobkin, who was born in Bobruisk, Belorussia, was a founder of the Zionist student organization, He-Ḥaver, in 1914 in Kharkov. He became general secretary of the *He-Ḥalutz movement in Warsaw in 1921. In 1932 he settled in Palestine. He served as a Mapai deputy-member of the Jewish Agency and Zionist Executive from 1937 to 1946, and thereafter as a full member. During World War II Dobkin was head of the Jewish Agency's immigration department, which dealt with rescue activities in Europe and later with "illegal" immigration. From 1951 to 1968 Dobkin served as head of the Agency's Youth and He-Ḥalutz Department, and was also chairman of Keren Hayesod ("United Israel Appeal") from 1951 to 1962. Dobkin was chairman of the Bezalel National Museum, Jerusalem. His writings include the book *Ha-Aliyyah ve-ha-Haẓẓalah bi-Shenot ha-Sho'ah* ("Rescue and Immigration during the Holocaust, 1946").

BIBLIOGRAPHY: Tidhar, 3 (1958^2), 1374.

[Benjamin Jaffe]

DOBRATH (Dovrat; Heb. דָּבְרַת).

(1) Levitical town of Issachar (Josh. 21:28; I Chron. 6:57). Dobrath/Daberath is located between Chisloth-Tabor and Japhia in the description of the border of Zebulun (Josh. 19:12). Some scholars see a connection between the names Dobrath and Deborah since the battle with the Canaanites took place in its vicinity. A Galilean village called Dabaritta is mentioned several times by Josephus (*Life*, 318); some of its inhabitants attacked and robbed a Herodian official (*Life*, 126; *Wars*, 2:595). In the Mishnaic period it was an administrative center as appears from a circular letter of the patriarch Gamaliel I; a Rabbi Matya of Dobrath is mentioned in the Talmud (TJ, Or. 1:1, 60d). In the fourth century Dabeira/Dabira was a Jewish village (Eusebius, *Onom.* 78:5; Jerome adds that it was small in size) in the territory of Diocaesarea (Sepphoris). Abel suggested identifying Dabbūriyya with Byzantine Helenopolis, but Bagatti believes it was at Kafr Kama instead. The Arab geographer Yakut mentions Dabbūriyya as a town in the province of Urdun. In the Middle Ages the place may have been known by the names Buria/Boria. It is the present-day Arab village of Dabbūriyya on the northern slopes of Mt. Tabor. It has been visited by many travelers and explorers since the 19th

century. Christian tradition places the location of Jesus' cure of the epileptic boy "having a dumb spirit" at Dabbūriyya (Luke 9:37–43; cf. Mark 9:28). The site is still largely unexcavated, although the remains of a ruined medieval chapel have been found – first reported on in the 19th century by Robinson and Guérin and eventually dug by Fathers Corbo and Loffreda in 1978. Others have noted the discovery at the site of a mosaic floor, tombs (including a decorated Roman stone door) and cisterns. Some travelers have associated the name Daburah with ruins situated in the northern part of the village, close to a path ascending to Mt. Tabor.

[Michael Avi-Yonah / Shimon Gibson (2nd ed.)]

(2) Kibbutz in Israel in the N.E. Jezreel Valley, W. of Mt. Tabor, affiliated with Iḥud ha-Kibbutzim. It was founded in 1946 by a group of immigrant youth who had previously settled temporarily near the En-Harod spring. Dovrat's economy is based on intensive farming (field crops, fruit orchards, poultry, and dairy cattle). The kibbutz also operates a small shopping center at the nearby gas station, a plant for organic fertilizers, and a computer laboratory. In 1968 its population was 290, in 2002 it was 278.

[Efraim Orni]

BIBLIOGRAPHY: Aharoni, Land, s.v. *Daberath;* G.A. Smith, *Historical Geography of the Holy Land* (1894⁴), 394; G. Dalman, *Sacred Sites and Ways* (1935), index; Neubauer, Géogr, 265; Avi-Yonah, Geog, 137; Abel, Geog, 2 (1938), 301. **ADD. BIBLIOGRAPHY:** E. Hoade, *Guide to the Holy Land* (1973), 861–62; E. Hareouveni, *The Settlements of Israel and Their Archaeological Sites* (1974), 103–4; Y. Tsafrir, L. Di Segni, and J. Green, *Tabula Imperii Romani. Iudaea – Palaestina. Maps and Gazetteer.* (1994): 106; B. Bagatti, *Ancient Christian Villages of Galilee* (2001), 226–27; G.S.P. Freeman-Grenville, R.L. Chapman and J.E. Taylor, *Palestine in the Fourth Century: The Onomasticon by Eusebius of Caesarea* (2003), 47, 125; Y. Elitzur, *Ancient Place Names in the Holy Land: Preservation and History* (2004): 222–31. **WEBSITE:** www.davrat.50g.com.

DOBROGEANU-GHEREA, CONSTANTIN (originally **Solomon Katz**; 1855–1920), Romanian literary critic and Socialist theoretician. Born in Slavianka, Ukraine, Katz became involved in revolutionary politics as a student at Kharkov University. His subsequent political career was colorful and adventurous. Pursued by the czarist police, he crossed into Romania in 1875, but three years later the Russian authorities found him masquerading as an American citizen, and he was kidnapped and taken back to Russia. After a year's imprisonment, Katz succeeded in making his way back to Romania, where he changed his name to Constantin Dobrogeanu-Gherea. He obtained the restaurant concession at the Ploieşti railway station, and the place became an asylum for writers and Romanian and Russian refugee socialists. As a literary theorist and critic, he succeeded in introducing into Romania a new perception of art as opposed to "art for art's sake." He insisted that art was a product of society and reflected the outlook of different social groups and classes. The articles he began publishing in various periodicals in 1885 were collected in his *Studii critice* (3 vols., 1890–97; 2 vols., 1925–27), to which a fourth volume was subsequently added. The work became the main guide to the materialist viewpoint in Romanian literature. As a political writer, Dobrogeanu-Gherea was the great popularizer of Marxist socialism in Romania. Outstanding among his political works are his *Concepţia materialistă a istoriei* ("The Materialist Concept of History," 1892), *Ce vor socialiştii romni* ("What do the Romanian Socialists Want," 1886; 1946), *Anarhism şi socialism* (1894), and *Socialismul n România*. In his social study *Neoiobăgia* ("The New Serfdom," 1910), he declared that even a bourgeois revolution had still to take place in Romania. In 1941, at the height of Antonescu's dictatorship, the Bucharest authorities exhumed Dobrogeanu-Gherea's remains and induced the Jewish community to rebury them in the Jewish cemetery. After World War II the new communist regime criticized his ideas, seeing in him a typical representative of the social democratic camp, and declared him guilty of "grave ideological errors."

BIBLIOGRAPHY: G. Călinescu, *Istoria literaturii române…* (1941), 484–8; F. Aderca, *Viaţa şi opera lui Dobrogeanu-Gherea* (1948); I. Peltz, *Cum i-am cunoscut* (1964), 145–56. **ADD. BIBLIOGRAPHY:** M. Iorgulescu (ed.), *C. Dobrogeanu-Gherea interpretat de…* (1975); Z. Ornea, *Viaţa lui C. Dobrogeanu-Gherea* (1982); M. Shafir, "Romania's Marx and the National Question: Constantin Dobrogeanu-Gherea," in: *History of Political Thought*, vol. 5, 11 (1984).

[Dora Litani-Littman]

DOBROVEN, ISSAY ALEXANDROVICH (1894–1953), conductor and composer. Dobroven was born in Nizhni-Novgorod, and was a child prodigy as a pianist. He later studied at the Moscow Conservatoire, and joined *Godowsky's master class in Vienna. Between 1917 and 1921 he was a professor at the Moscow Music Academy; in 1919 he became chief conductor at the Imperial Opera. He staged in Dresden (1923) the first German performance of Mussorgsky's *Boris Godunov*, the first step in a lifetime's pioneering of Russian music all over the world which led to his appointment as conductor at the Grosse Volksoper (1924) and of the Dresden symphony concerts. From then until World War II he was musical director of the Bulgarian State Opera, Sofia (1927–28) and guest conductor in the United States, Palestine, Italy, and of the Budapest Royal Opera. He spent the war years in Sweden, after which he resumed his international career. In operatic engagements Dobroven was his own producer and stage director. Outstanding among his many compositions was a piano concerto, the solo part of which he played all over Europe.

[Max Loppert (2nd ed.)]

DOBRUSCHKA, MOSES (1753–1794), Frankist and French revolutionary. Dobruschka was born in Bruenn into a family that belonged to the small circle of rich tax-farmers who largely controlled the tobacco administration during the regime of Maria Theresa. His mother, Schoendel, was the first cousin of Jacob *Frank, and her house served as a meeting place for the secret adherents of the sect. It was apparently this connection which caused Frank to settle in Bruenn (1773–86) after his release from prison in Czestochowa. Dobruschka received a talmudic education and was also initiated into the kabbalistic teachings of Shabbateanism. He began to study German literature and foreign languages as an adolescent. In 1773 he married the adopted daughter of Ḥayyim (Joachim) Popper, one of the richest Jews of Prague, and about the same time began writing in Hebrew and German in the spirit of the early *Haskalah, producing, among other books, *Sefer ha-Sha'ashu'a* (1775), a commentary on the *Beḥinat Olam* of Abraham *Bedersi. Dobruschka later engaged in business and amassed a considerable fortune as one of the chief army suppliers in the preparation of the war against the Turks. In 1778 he was ennobled by Emperor Joseph II, with whom he enjoyed some favor and to whom he dedicated enthusiastic poetic eulogies, taking the title of Franz Thomas Edler von Schoenfeld. He became active in the mystic circles of freemasonry, into which he introduced elements of Kabbalah, particularly of a Shabbatean nature, but retired from active participation in 1784. In the late 1780s he lived as a wealthy man with wide connections in the upper circles of Vienna and established contact with the famous writers of Germany, continuing to enjoy the favor of Leopold II, the successor of Joseph II. On the death of Jacob Frank in 1791, Dobruschka's name was mentioned as his possible successor as head of the Frankist sect.

Dobruschka (or Schoenfeld) became an ardent admirer of the ideals of the French Revolution, and his career is henceforth closely connected with it. Arriving in Strasbourg in March 1792, he changed his name to Gottlob Junius Frey, joined the Jacobin club, and immediately involved himself in French politics. He moved to Paris in June, joined the Jacobin club there, took part in the storming of the Tuileries, and wrote a philosophical and constitutional book *Philosophie sociale, dediée au peuple français* (1793), which was a spirited defense of Jacobinism and included a strong attack on Moses and Mosaic legislation. In January 1793 he made the acquaintance of François Chabot, a Jacobin demagogue who married his sister Leopoldine in October of that year. Shortly after he was denounced by Austrian and German émigrés as an Austrian agent and this, combined with a financial fraud in which he was involved, brought about his arrest, together with that of Chabot. He was charged with corruption and espionage, found guilty, and executed on April 5, 1794. A few months after his death some of his Austrian friends spread a rumor that he had been engaged on a secret mission to liberate the former queen, Marie-Antoinette, from prison.

BIBLIOGRAPHY: G. Scholem, in: *Zion*, 35 (1971), v–vii, 127–81.

DOBRUSCHKA-SCHOENFELD, family in Moravia. Its first known member, JACOB MOSES DOBRUSCHKA (Dobruska; d. 1763), bought the concession for the Jewish eatinghouse in Brno in 1734, and by 1750 held the tobacco monopoly in Moravia. His son SOLOMON (c. 1715–1774) in 1759 obtained permission to retain a "small Torah" in his home, and to hold services at the rear of his house. Solomon's wife, Schoendl (1735–1791), obtained the potash monopoly and other concessions, and by skillful management increased the family fortune. Wolf Eybeschuetz stayed in her home in 1761 where he was reputed to have worked miracles. Jacob *Frank used the alias "Dobruska" while staying in Brno (1773–86); Schoendl, his cousin and an admirer, presumably supported him financially. After Solomon's death, eight of their 12 children embraced Christianity. In 1778 six were ennobled receiving the title "Edler von Schoenfeld." Four became Austrian army officers. Other members of the family married into the Polish and Austrian nobility; only two of them remained Jews. Solomon's second son, Moses *Dobruschka MOSES (b. 1753), published in 1774 *Sefer Sha'ashu'a*, a commentary on the *Beḥinat Olam* of Jedaiah *ha-Penini, approved by leading rabbis and dedicated to Joachim *Popper whose niece he had married a year before. He subsequently wrote poems in German, dramas, and reviews, and translations from the Psalms. Moses, who had connections with Jacob Frank, was considered by some as a candidate for his successor. His sister, Franceska, married into the *Hoenigsberg family, notorious for its Frankist connections. In 1782 Moses (now Franz Thomas von Schoenfeld) moved to Vienna. He was one of the founders of the "Asiatische Brueder," a masonic lodge with predominantly Jewish members, and formulated its doctrines. With his brother EMANUEL (formerly David; b. 1765), he went to revolutionary France, where they appeared in Strasbourg in 1792 under a new name, Frey (Moses used the symbolic name, Siegmund Gottlob Junius Brutus Frey). The "Frey" brothers contributed magnanimously to patriotic causes and attracted many to their *salon* in Paris. Junius published two anti-Girondist pamphlets. The influential radical politician François Chabot married their youngest sister, Leopoldine, for the sake of her large dowry. Thereafter all three were caught bribing members of a parliamentary committee deciding the future of the Compagnie des Indes. Chabot lost his influence and the Frey brothers were suspected as Austrian spies. On April 5, 1794, they and their accomplices were guillotined, together with Danton.

BIBLIOGRAPHY: G. Scholem, in: H. Gold (ed.), *Max Brod. Ein Gedenkbuch* (1969), 77–92; E.E. Kisch, *Tales from Seven Ghettos* (1948), 21–41; H. Schnee, *Die Hoffinanz und der moderne Staat*, 4 (1963), 319, 355 n. 14; 5 (1965), 226–8, 276; Kwasnik-Rabinowicz, in: *Zeitschrift fuer die Geschichte der Juden in der Tschechoslowakei*, 1 (1930/31), 267–78; L. Kahn, *Les Juifs de Paris pendant la révolution* (1898), 248–66; L. Ruzicka, in: *Juedische Familienforschung*, 6:3 (1930), 282–9.

[Henry Wasserman]

DOBRUSHIN, YEKHEZKEL (1883–1953), Yiddish literary critic, poet, and playwright. Born in the Ukraine, he was educated privately and at the Sorbonne, where he was involved in *Territorialist circles. After his literary debut in 1912, he became a central figure among young Kiev-based Yiddish modernist writers, co-edited the Moscow literary journal *Der Shtrom* (1922–24), worked as one of the first university lecturers of Yiddish literature, and was the main literary consultant of the Moscow State Yiddish Theater, adapting works by Sholem Yankev *Abramovitsh, *Sholem Aleichem and A.

*Goldfaden, while various Yiddish theater troupes staged his plays. An enthusiast of Soviet Jewish colonization, he spent much time in villages built by Jewish colonists in the Crimea, one of which still bears his name: Dobrushino. He (co)authored several folklore collections and books of literary criticism, including his study *Dovid Bergelson* (1947). Together with other leading Jewish cultural activists of the Jewish *Anti-Fascist Committee he was arrested in 1949 and sent to a Siberian labor camp, where he died.

BIBLIOGRAPHY: Sh. Gordon, in: *Sovetish Heymland*, 8 (1988); Ch. Beider, in: *Di Pen*, 7 (1995); J. Veidlinger, *The Moscow State Yiddish Theater: Jewish Culture on the Soviet Stage* (2000); D. Shneer, *Yiddish and the Creation of Soviet Jewish Culture, 1918–1930* (2004); G. Estraikh, *In Harness: Yiddish Writers' Romance with Communism* (2005).

[Gennady Estraikh (2nd ed.)]

DOCTOROW, EDGAR LAWRENCE (1931–), U.S. novelist and editor. Born in the Bronx, New York, Doctorow began his career as a reader of fiction for TV and film studios. This led him into editorial work, first at New American Library (1959–1964) and then as editor-in-chief for Dial Press in the 1960s. His reading of mediocre film scripts for western movies helped inspire his first novel, *Welcome to Hard Times* (1960), a black comedy of the Wild West. His second novel, *Big as Life* (1966), a semi-science-fiction tale, described two huge, naked figures being introduced to New York. Several critics saw these figures as an allegory of the atom bomb.

In 1971, Doctorow published *The Book of Daniel*, a fictionalized account of the celebrated Rosenberg trial and its radical legacy. The novel is a portrait of the defendants' son "Daniel" who was profoundly affected by the death of his parents at the hands of a ruthless and indifferent society. The novel's style anticipates many of the innovative literary techniques employed in his later novels – juxtaposition of historical fact and fantasy and cinematic switches of tense, scene, and voice. The novel was made into a film.

Ragtime (1975) weaves a story around a host of early 20th century figures in the United States, among them Houdini, Freud, Jung, Emma Goldman, Theodore Roosevelt, Henry Ford, Woodrow Wilson, and Albert Einstein, together with ironic comment on their achievements and later effects. *Ragtime* was awarded the National Book Critics Circle Award in 1975. The film version was directed by Milos Forman. His *Loon Lake* (1980) dealt with life during the Depression; *World's Fair* (1985) culminates in a boy's visit to the New York World's Fair in 1939; and *Billy Bathgate* was made into a movie. Doctorow's fiction utilizes the past to explore parallel tendencies in the present and the inability of the present to learn from the past and escape its errors. His *City of God* (2000) is a theological novel. Its characters attempt to find the coherence of life and the significance of its representations through the events that have befallen them. Rich in its allusions and structure, the novel becomes an accounting for the spirit of things unseen within the city of man. *The March* (2005) is about Sherman's march to the sea in the American Civil War.

Doctorow also wrote a play, *Drinks Before Dinner* (1979), which was first produced at the New York Shakespeare Festival's Public Theater. He was a writer-in-residence at the University of California at Irvine and taught at Sarah Lawrence College in Bronxville, New York.

ADD. BIBLIOGRAPHY: C. Morris (ed.), *Conversations with E.L. Doctorow*, 1999; M. Tokarczyk, *E.L. Doctorow's Skeptical Commitment* (2000); H. Bloom (ed.), *E.L. Doctorow*, 2002.

[Susan Strul / Lewis Fried (2nd ed.)]

"DOCTORS' PLOT," the most dramatic anti-Jewish episode in the Soviet Union during *Stalin's regime involving the "unmasking" of a group of prominent Moscow doctors, mostly Jews, as conspiratorial assassins of Soviet leaders. It was a continuation of the "cosmopolitanism" accusations against Jewish scientists in the field of medicine. On January 13, 1953, *Pravda* and Radio Moscow announced that nine eminent doctors were under arrest and had confessed to murdering two Soviet leaders of the past, A.S. Shcherbakov and A.A. Zhdanov (who had died in 1945 and 1948, respectively). They were reported to have also admitted conspiring to murder a number of prominent figures in the Soviet armed forces, including the war minister, Marshal A.M. Vasilevski, the chief of staff, General S.M. Shtemenko, and the popular war hero, Marshal I.S. Konev. Six of the nine doctors were Jews. The number of arrested grew to 37 through 1952, of which 28 were doctors and the others family members. Among them were Professors Pevzner, Vinogradov, Ettinger, Vovsi, and others. "Most of the participants in the terrorist group," read the statement, "were connected with the international Jewish bourgeois nationalist organization, the 'Joint' (*American Jewish Joint Distribution Committee) established by American Intelligence … (in order to) conduct extensive espionage terrorist, and other subversive work in many countries including the Soviet Union."

These accusations unleashed panic among the Jews of the Soviet Union and were met by reactions of disbelief and foreboding in Western Europe, the U.S.A., and Israel. On January 19, the Israeli foreign minister, Moshe Sharett, bitterly condemned the Soviet action. A bomb exploded in the courtyard of the Soviet embassy in Tel Aviv on February 9, wounding four of the staff. Despite prompt apologies from the Israeli government, the U.S.S.R. immediately broke off diplomatic relations. The Soviet press now stepped up its attacks on Israel, the "Joint," Wall Street, Zionism, and imperialism. "The pack of mad dogs from Tel Aviv," wrote Yuri Zhukov in *Pravda*, Feb. 14, 1953, "is loathsome and vile in its thirst for blood." An article published in *Trud* on February 13 noted that the "Joint" had organized major anti-government conspiracies not only in the U.S.S.R. but in Hungary and Czechoslovakia as well – direct reference being made to the *Slansky Trial of November 1952.

Stalin died on March 5, and on April 3 *Pravda* announced that the doctors were not guilty and had been freed, and those responsible for using "impermissible means of investigation" had been arrested. On July 20 diplomatic relations between Israel and the Soviet Union were restored.

The Plot was apparently part of Stalin's plan for a new purge of the top Soviet leadership. It was probably directed against Lavrentii Beria, the minister of the interior (MVD), who had been responsible for security matters when Shcherbakov and Zhdanov had died. The *Pravda* editorial of January 13 specifically criticized "the agencies of state security" that had failed to "discover the doctors' wrecking, terrorist organization in time." (Moreover, the Plot was clearly modeled on the 1938 case of G.G. Yagoda, an earlier chief of the Secret Police who had been found guilty of recruiting medical specialists to murder such prominent citizens as Maxim Gorki.) Stalin's death enabled Beria to regain control of the Secret Police (MGB) and merge it with his ministry, the MVD. The release of the doctors and the arrest of their interrogators evidently formed part of Beria's desperate, but ultimately futile, effort to consolidate his power. Seen in broader perspective, the Plot proved to be the last of those macabre "conspiracies" that were manufactured during Stalin's reign but did not reappear in such a form in the subsequent Soviet regimes, though many of the anti-Jewish manifestations that had accompanied the Doctor's Plot were to reemerge later (see *Antisemitism in the Soviet Bloc).

In his secret speech at the Twentieth Party Congress (1956) Nikita Khrushchev blamed the Doctors' Plot on Stalin, but carefully ignored its antisemitic aspects and even took the opportunity to exonerate S.D. Ignatev, who had headed the MGB during the Plot, in early 1953. In fact, Ignatev was re-elected to the Party's Central Committee in 1956.

BIBLIOGRAPHY: R. Conquest, *Power and Policy in the USSR* (1962), index; B. Nicolaevsky, *Power and the Soviet Elite* (1965), passim; S. Schwarz, *Yevreyi v Sovetskom Soyuze s nachala vtoroy mirovoy voyny (1939–65)* (1966), passim. **ADD. BIBLIOGRAPHY:** G. Kostyrchenko, *V plenu u krasnovo faraona* (1994).

[Jonathan Frankel]

DÓCZY, LAJOS (1845–1918), Hungarian author, poet, and playwright, also known as L. Dux. Dóczy, who was born in Sopron, studied law at Vienna, and rose to a high position in the Austro-Hungarian government. He converted to Christianity and was made a baron. A founder of the neo-Romantic school of Hungarian drama, Dóczy became famous mainly as a writer of historical plays. One of these, *Az utolsó próféta* ("The Last Prophet," 1869), deals with the destruction of Jerusalem. Equally at home with German and Hungarian culture, Dóczy wrote in, and translated classical works into, both languages. His translations include a Hungarian version of Goethe's *Faust* and a German version of *Az ember tragédiája* ("The Tragedy of Man") by Imre Madách. Dóczy's most important plays are *Csók* ("Kiss," 1874), *Utolsó szerelem* ("Last Love," 1884), and *Széchy Mária* (1886).

BIBLIOGRAPHY: *Magyar Irodalmi Lexikon*, 1 (1963), 203–4; UJE, 31 (1941), 584–50.

[Baruch Yaron]

DOEBLIN, ALFRED (1878–1957), German poet, novelist, and physician. Born in Stettin, Doeblin was raised in poverty in Berlin in an assimilated family. After studying medicine in Berlin and Freiburg from 1900 he started working as a physician in 1905; later on he specialized in psychiatry, opening his own neurological practice in 1911. At the same time, Doeblin began publishing in the expressionistic journal *Der Sturm* and wrote his first stories, collected in *Die Ermordung der Butterblume* (1913). He gained fame with *Die drei Spruenge des Wang-lun* (1915; *Three Leaps of Wang-Lun*, 1991), a novel about a Chinese rebel who becomes the apostle of a new religion. With this and the following important novels *Wallenstein* (1920), *Berge, Meere und Giganten* (1924), and *Berlin-Alexanderplatz* (1929), Doeblin essentially initiated the modern novel in German literature, dealing with the central questions of his time such as war, technology, and the metropolis. Even though Doeblin left the Jewish community and converted to Catholicism, though not until living in exile in the U.S. in 1941, he never completely abandoned Judaism; on the contrary, particularly in the 1920s, traveling through Poland, he participated in the discourse on East European Judaism and Zionism. Already in *Zion und Europa* (1921) he opposed Western assimilated Judaism with East European Judaism, and even more so in his account of his travels through Poland, *Reise in Polen* (1926; *Journey to Poland*, 1991). After the attack of the Jews of the Berlin Scheunenviertel in 1923 he wrote even more strongly about Zionism, leaning, however, toward the Jewish Territorial Movement founded by Nathan *Birnbaum, with whom he was in personal contact (cf. *Zionismus und westliche Kultur,* 1924). Fleeing from Germany to Zurich and Paris in 1933 Doeblin again raised the question of the Jewish people in several essays (*Unser Dasein*, 1933; *Juedische Erneuerung*, 1933). Publishing also in Birnbaum's journals, *Der Ruf* and *Der juedische Volksgeist*, at that time, Doeblin still took the territorial position, arguing that the Jews should settle not only in Palestine but throughout the entire world, a position which he changed in favor of Zionism shortly afterwards, as reflected in his essay *Flucht und Sammlung des Judenvolks* (1935). After Birnbaum's death in 1937 and criticism by Ludwig *Marcuse, Doeblin abandoned the territorial position (cf. *Von Fuehrern und Schimmelpilzen*, 1938), though he still emphasized the right to a territorial home for the Jews. In 1940 he barely escaped from Paris to the United States, as he recounts in his autobiographical work *Schicksalsreise* (1949; *Destiny's Journey*, 1992). In exile from 1933, he published several important novels such as *Babylonische Wanderung* (1934) and *Pardon wird nicht gegeben* (1935) and began the trilogy *November 1918* (1938). In 1940, under the guidance of the Jesuits, he converted to Catholicism. He described his conversion in *Der unsterbliche Mensch; Ein religioeses Gespraech* (1946). After World War II, Doeblin returned to Europe, living in Paris and Germany, where he edited a literary periodical in Mainz and completed the trilogy *November 1918* with the novels *Verratenes Volk* (1948), *Heimkehr der Fronttruppen* (1949), and *Karl und Rosa* (1950). His last novel *Hamlet: oder Die lange Nacht* *nimmt ein Ende* (1956; *Tales of a Long Night*, 1984) underscores his religious journey.

BIBLIOGRAPHY: *Alfred Doeblin zum siebzigsten Geburtstag* (1948); R. Links, *Alfred Doeblin, Leben und Werk* (1965); H.-P. Bayerdoerfer, in: G. Grimm (ed.), *Im Zeichen Hiobs* (1986); K. Mueller-Salget, *Alfred Doeblin* (1988); T. Isermann, *Der Text und das Unsagbare* (1989); M. Prangel, in: S. Onderdelinden (ed.), *Interbellum und Exil* (1991), 162–80.

[Andreas Kilcher (2nd ed.)]

DOEG (Heb. דּוֹיֵג, דּוֹאֵג, דֹּאֵג), the Edomite, one of Saul's court officials and his trusted adviser (I Sam. 22:9). The epithet הָאֲדֹמִי (the Edomite; Ps. 52:2) points up Doeg's foreign origin. He was probably responsible for the king's property and his herds, as can be deduced from his title, "Saul's chief herdsman" (I Sam. 21:8; cf. I Chron. 27:28–31). Some read רצים (*raẓim*, "runners, guards") instead of רעים (*roʿim*, "herdsmen"), and believe that he headed a regiment of runners, i.e., the bodyguard of the king, who ran before his carriage and executed his orders (cf. II Sam. 15:1). It seems that Doeg attained his important position in the court of Saul after having held a senior appointment in Edom before his arrival in Israel. It could also be that his title *ʾabbir* (Heb. "chief") was the title of his Edomite office. This was in accordance with the policy of Saul and of David, both of whom chose experienced men from neighboring countries to conduct their administrative affairs. He doubtless adopted his master's religion (I Sam. 21:8).

His being an Edomite and a stranger among the servants of Saul explains his unswerving loyalty to the king. In contrast to the servants of the king who betrayed him and were ready to side with David in exchange for some benefits which they could gain, as Saul himself complained, and who refused to submit information on David's whereabouts, Doeg was the only one to inform the king of the assistance which had been extended by *Ahimelech, one of the priests of Nob, to David when he fled from Saul (I Sam. 22:7–10). He was also the only one of the royal runners who was ready to kill on the king's orders. He thus put to death 85 of the priests of Nob and destroyed the city to its foundations so that only Abiathar the son of Ahimelech succeeded in escaping the massacre and finding his way to David (I Sam. 22:17–20).

[Josef Segal]

In the *Aggadah*

Doeg was a man of great learning who, however, perverted his knowledge for base and selfish ends (Sanh. 106b). He was called "Adomi" (Edomite) because he made those who disputed with him blush (*adom*, "red") with shame at their ignorance (Mid. Ps. to 52:4). He suited the law to his own purposes when persuading Saul not to kill Agag (*ibid.*); when maintaining that Ahimelech's consultation of the *Urim and Thummim on David's behalf (I Sam. 22:11–19) was illegal (*ibid.*, 52:5); by convincing Saul that David's marriage to Michal had lost validity from the day David was declared a rebel (Gen. R. 32:1); and by attempting to refute David's legitimacy because of his descent from Ruth the Moabitess (Yev. 76b–77a). Doeg is rebuked, "Thou lovest evil more than good, and lying rather than to speak right" (Ps. 52:5), and God says to him, "Are you not a mighty man in Torah? Why than boastest thyself in mischief?" (Sanh. 106b). The variant spellings of Doeg's name in I Samuel 21:8 and 22:22 are explained: "At first God sits and is anxious (דּוֹאֵג, *doʾeg*) lest one go out on an evil course. But once he does so, He exclaims, 'Woe (דּוֹיֵג, *doyeg*) that he has entered on an evil path'" (Sanh. 106b). Eventually, Doeg's knowledge was taken from him. When he was 34 years old, he was confronted by three destroying angels, one of whom caused him to forget his learning, one burnt his soul, and the third scattered his ashes in the synagogues and schoolhouses (*ibid.*). According to another tradition, he was slain by his students when they saw that his wisdom had departed from him (Yalk. Sam. 131). His enmity toward David sprang from the fact that David chose a site for the Temple in preference to his own (Zev. 54b). Doeg deliberately praised David lavishly in Saul's presence (I Sam. 16:18) in order to arouse Saul's wrath against him (Sanh. 93b). As a result of his calumny Ahimelech, Abner, Saul, and Doeg himself lost their lives (TJ, Pe'ah 1:1). Doeg is one of the four commoners who have no place in the *olam ha-ba*, world to come (Sanh. 10:2), and one of those who set their eyes upon that which was not proper for them; what they sought was not granted to them, and what they possessed was taken from them (Sot. 9b).

BIBLIOGRAPHY: de Vaux, Anc Isr, 94, 219, 221; Ginzberg, Legends, 4 (1954), 74–76; 6 (1959), 241–2; I. Ḥasida, *Ishei ha-Tanakh* (1964), 100–02.

DOENMEH (**Dönme**), sect of adherents of *Shabbetai Ẓevi who embraced Islam as a consequence of the failure of the Shabbatean messianic upheaval in the *Ottoman Empire. After Shabbetai Ẓevi converted to Islam in September 1666, large numbers of his disciples interpreted his apostasy as a secret mission, deliberately undertaken with a particular mystical purpose in mind. The overwhelming majority of his adherents, who called themselves *maʾaminim* ("believers"), remained within the Jewish fold. However, even while Shabbetai Ẓevi was alive several leaders of the *maʾaminim* thought it essential to follow in the footsteps of their messiah and to become Muslims, without, as they saw it, renouncing their Judaism, which they interpreted according to new principles. Until Shabbetai Ẓevi's death in 1676 the sect, which at first was centered largely in Adrianople (*Edirne), numbered some 200 families. They came mainly from the Balkans, but there were also adherents from *Izmir, Brusa, and other places. There were a few outstanding scholars and kabbalists among them, whose families afterward were accorded a special place among the Doenmeh as descendants of the original community of the sect. Even among the Shabbateans who did not convert to Islam, such as *Nathan of Gaza, this sect enjoyed an honorable reputation and an important mission was ascribed to it. Clear evidence of this is preserved in the commentary on Psalms (written c. 1679) of Israel Ḥazzan of Castoria.

Many of the community became converts as a direct result of Shabbetai Ẓevi's preaching and persuasion. They were outwardly fervent Muslims and privately Shabbatean *ma'aminim* who practiced a type of messianic Judaism, based as early as the 1670s or 1680s on "the 18 precepts" which were attributed to Shabbetai Ẓevi and accepted by the Doenmeh communities. (The full text was published in English by G. Scholem, in: *Essays ... Abba Hillel Silver* (1963), 368–86.) These precepts contain a parallel version of the Ten Commandments. However, they are distinguished by an extraordinarily ambiguous formulation of the commandment "Thou shalt not commit adultery," which approximates more to a recommendation to take care rather than a prohibition. The additional commandments determine the relationship of the *ma'aminim* toward the Jews and the Turks. Intermarriage with true Muslims is strictly and emphatically forbidden.

After the death of Shabbetai Ẓevi the community's center of activities moved to *Salonika and remained there until 1924. Shabbetai's last wife, Jochebed (in Islam, ʿĀ'isha), was the daughter of Joseph Philosoph, one of the rabbis of Salonika, and she returned there from Albania after a brief sojourn in Adrianople. Later, she proclaimed her younger brother Jacob Philosoph, known traditionally as Jacob *Querido (i.e., "the beloved"), as the reincarnation of the soul of Shabbetai Ẓevi. So many different and contradictory traditions exist concerning the profound upheaval which affected the *ma'aminim* of Salonika around 1680 and afterward that, for the time being, it is impossible to say which is the most reliable. They all agree that there was considerable tension between the original Doenmeh community and the followers of Jacob Querido, among whom were several of the rabbis of Salonika. As a result of their propaganda, two to three hundred families, under the leadership of two rabbis, Solomon Florentin and Joseph Philosoph, and his son, underwent mass conversion to Islam. There are two contradictory accounts of this conversion. One dates it in the year 1683, and the other at the end of 1686. It is possible that there were two mass conversions, one after the other. Many mystical "revelations" were then experienced in Salonika, and several pamphlets were written reflecting the spiritual tendencies of the various groups. As time went on, most of the apostate families from other cities in Turkey migrated to Salonika and the sect was organized on a more institutional basis. During the 18th century the sect was joined by other Shabbatean groups, particularly from Poland. Jacob Querido demonstrated his outward allegiance to Islam by making the pilgrimage to Mecca with several of his followers – a course of action which the original Doenmeh community opposed. He died on his return from this journey in 1690 or 1695, probably in Alexandria.

Internal conflicts caused a split in the organization and resulted in the formation of two sub-sects: one, according to Doenmeh tradition, was called *Izmirlis* (*Izmirim*) and consisted of members of the original community, and the other was known as the *Ya'akoviyyim*, or in Turkish *Jakoblar*. A few years after Querido's death another split occurred among the *Izmirlis*, when around 1700 a new young leader, Baruchiah Russo, appeared among them and was proclaimed by his disciples to be the reincarnation of Shabbetai Ẓevi. In 1716 his disciples proclaimed him as the Divine Incarnation. Russo was apparently of Jewish birth and the son of one of the early followers of Shabbetai Ẓevi. After his conversion he was called "Osman Baba." A third sub-sect was organized around him. Its members were called *Konyosos* (in Ladino) or *Karakashlar* (in Turkish). This was considered to be the most extreme group of the Doenmeh community. It had the reputation of having founded a new faith with a leaning toward religious nihilism. Its adherents embarked on a new missionary campaign to the chief cities of the Diaspora. Representatives were sent to Poland, Germany, and Austria, where they were a source of considerable excitement between 1720 and 1726. Branches of this sect, from which the Frankists later emerged, were established in several places. Baruchiah Russo died in 1720 while still young and his grave was an object of pilgrimage for members of the sect until recent times. His son, who became the leader of this sect, died in 1781. During the period of the French Revolution a powerful leader of one of the sects (either the *Izmirim* or the Baruchiah sect), known as "Deverish Effendi," became prominent. He is perhaps to be identified with the Doenmeh preacher and poet, Judah Levi Tovah, several of whose poems and homiletical expositions in Ladino were preserved in manuscripts belonging to the Doenmeh and are now in a number of public collections.

It soon became clear to the Turkish authorities that these apostates, who had been expected to encourage the Jews to convert to Islam, had no intention of assimilating, but were determined to continue to lead a closed sectarian existence, although outwardly they strictly observed the practices of Islam, and were politically loyal citizens. From the beginning of the 18th century, they were called Doenmeh, meaning (in Turkish) either "converts" or "apostates." However, it is not clear whether this is a reference to their conversion from Judaism or to the fact of their not being true Muslims. The Jews called them *minim* ("sectarians") and among the writings of the Salonika rabbis there are several responsa dealing with the problems of how they are to be treated and whether they are to be regarded as Jews or not. They settled in specific quarters of Salonika, and their leaders were on friendly terms with Sufic circles, and with the dervish orders among the Turks, particularly the Baktashi. At the same time they maintained secret ties not only with those Shabbateans who had not converted, but also with several rabbis in Salonika, who, when knowledge of the Torah diminished among the Doenmeh, were paid for secretly settling points of law for them. These relationships were severed only in the middle of the 19th century. This double-faced behavior becomes clear only when their ambiguous attitude toward traditional Judaism is taken into account. On one level, they regarded the latter as void, its place being taken by a higher, more spiritual Torah, called *Torah de-Aẓilut* ("Torah of Emanation"). But on another level there remained certain areas in which they sought to conduct themselves according to the actual Torah of talmudic tradition, called *Torah di-Beri'ah* ("Torah of Creation").

The numerical strength of the Doenmeh is only approximately known. According to the Danish traveler, Karsten *Niebuhr, around 600 families lived in Salonika in 1774, and they married only among themselves. Before World War I their number was estimated to be between 10,000 and 15,000, divided more or less equally among the three sub-sects, with the *Konyosos* having a slight numerical majority. At first, knowledge of Hebrew was common among the Doenmeh and their liturgy was originally standardized in Hebrew. This can be seen in the part of their prayer book which is still extant (Scholem, in: KS, vols. 18 and 19). However, as time went on the use of Ladino increased, and both their homiletic and poetic literature was written in that tongue. They continued to speak Ladino among themselves up to about 1870 and it was only later that Turkish replaced it as the language of everyday speech.

As far as social structure is concerned, there were distinct differences among the three sub-sects which developed apparently between 1750 and 1850. The aristocrats of Doenmeh society were the *Izmirlis*, who were called *Cavalleros* in Ladino or *Kapanjilar* in Turkish. These included the great merchants and the middle classes, as well as most of the Doenmeh intelligentsia. They were also the first to show, from the end of the 19th century, a marked tendency toward assimilation with the Turks. The *Jakoblar* community of *Ya'akoviyyim* included a large number of lower- or middle-class Turkish officials, while the third and most numerous group, the *Konyosos* (according to the few available accounts), consisted as time went on mainly of the proletariat and artisan classes, e.g., porters, shoemakers, barbers, and butchers. Some say that for a long time practically all the barbers of Salonika belonged to this group. Each Doenmeh had a Turkish and a Hebrew name (for use in Turkish and Doenmeh society respectively). Furthermore, they preserved the original Sephardi family names, which are mentioned in poems composed in honor of the dead; many of these poems have survived in manuscript. Doenmeh cemeteries were used in common by all the sub-sects. In contrast, each sect had its particular synagogue (called *Kahal* – "congregation") at the center of its own quarter, concealed from the outsider.

Their liturgies were written in a very small format so that they could easily be hidden. All the sects concealed their internal affairs from Jews and Turks so successfully that for a long time knowledge of them was based only on rumor and upon reports of outsiders. Doenmeh manuscripts revealing details of their Shabbatean ideas were brought to light and examined only after several of the Doenmeh families decided to assimilate completely into Turkish society and transmitted their documents to friends among the Jews of Salonika and Izmir. As long as the Doenmeh were concentrated in Salonika, the sect's institutional framework remained intact, although several Doenmeh members were active in the Young Turks' movement which originated in that city. The first administration that came to power after the Young Turk revolution (1909) included several ministers of Doenmeh origin, including the minister of finance, *Javid Bey, who was a descendant of the Baruchiah Russo family and served as one of the leaders of his sect. One assertion that was commonly made by many Jews of Salonika (denied, however, by the Turkish government) was that *Kemal Atatürk was of Doenmeh origin. This view was eagerly embraced by many of Atatürk's religious opponents in Anatolia.

With the exchange of population that followed the Greco-Turkish war of 1924, the Doenmeh were compelled to leave Salonika. Most of them settled in Istanbul, and a few in other Turkish cities such as Izmir and Ankara. In the Turkish press at that time there was a lively debate about the Jewish character of the Doenmeh and their assimilation. When they were uprooted from the great Jewish center of Salonika, assimilation began to spread widely. Nevertheless, there is reliable evidence that the organizational framework of the *Konyosos* sect survived, and as late as 1960 many families still belonged to this organization. Among the Turkish intelligentsia, one of the professors at the University of Istanbul was widely regarded as the leader of the Doenmeh. Attempts to persuade them to return to Judaism and to immigrate to Israel have borne little fruit. Only a few isolated Doenmeh families were among the Turkish immigrants to Israel.

There is hardly any basic difference in religious opinions between the Doenmeh and the other sects who believed in Shabbetai Ẓevi. In their literature, as far as it is known, there is hardly a mention of their belonging to the Islamic fold. Their claim of being the true Jewish community is not unlike the claims of the early Christians and the Christian church. They preserved their faith in Shabbetai Ẓevi, who had abrogated the practical commandments of the material Torah and had opened up "the spiritual Torah" of the upper world as a substitute. The principle of the divinity of Shabbetai Ẓevi was firmly developed and accepted by the sect, as was the threefold nature of the upper forces of emanation, called *telat kishrei de-meheimanuta* ("the three bonds of faith"). In addition to their abrogation of the practical commandments and their mystical trinitarian belief, one factor in particular aroused great opposition among their contemporaries. This was their obvious inclination to permit marriages which were halakhically forbidden, and to conduct religious ceremonies which involved the exchange of wives and which, therefore, bastardized their issue according to Jewish law. Accusations of sexual licentiousness were made from the beginning of the 18th century, and although many have tried to belittle their importance there is no doubt that sexual promiscuity existed for many generations. The long sermon of Judah Levi Tovah (published by I.R. Molcho and R. Shatz, in: *Sefunot*, 3–4 (1960), 395–521) contains a spirited defense of the abrogation of the sexual prohibitions contained in the material "Torah of Creation." Orgiastic ceremonies in fact took place in the main on the Doenmeh *Ḥag ha-Keves* ("Festival of the Lamb") which fell on the 22nd of Adar and was recognized as a celebration of the beginning of spring. In addition, they celebrated other festivals, connected with the life of Shabbetai Ẓevi and particular events associated with their apostasy. They did not abstain from work on their festivals in order not to arouse outside curiosity. They contented themselves with rituals on the eve of their festivals. The Doenmeh liturgy for Tishah be-Av, the birthday of Shabbetai Ẓevi, called *Ḥag ha-Semaḥot* ("Festival of Rejoicing"), is extant in Hebrew and contains a Shabbatean adaptation of some of the High Holy Day prayers, with the addition of a solemn declaration of their Shabbatean creed, consisting of eight paragraphs (KS, vol. 18, 309–10).

BIBLIOGRAPHY: Scholem, in: *Numen*, 7 (1960), 93–122 (with bibl.); idem, in: *Sefunot*, 9 (1965), 195–207; idem, in: D.J. Silver (ed.), *In the Time of Harvest* (1963), 368–86; I. Ben-Zvi, *The Exiled and the Redeemed* (1957), 131–53; idem, in: *Sefunot*, 3–4 (1960), 349–94; G. Attias and G. Scholem, *Shirot ve-Tishbaḥot shel ha-Shabbeta'im* (1948).

[Gershom Scholem]

DOG. In the Bible the dog is usually spoken of disparagingly, the references being however to ownerless dogs which prowl in inhabited areas (Ps. 59:7, 15), feed off animal carcasses and human corpses (I Kings 23:38), and attack passersby (Ps. 22:17). "Dog" was a derogatory term (II Kings 8:13) and apparently was applied to a male temple-prostitute (cf. Deut. 23:19). However, shepherd dogs were bred (Isa. 56:11; Job 30:1). Divergent views were expressed by the sages on the rearing of dogs. The Mishnah says: "One should not rear a dog unless it is kept on a chain" (BK 7:7). There was also opposition to rearing dogs in Ereẓ Israel, R. Eleazar declaring that "he who rears dogs is like one who rears swine" (*ibid.* TB 83a). It was however permitted in a frontier town where "one keeps it chained during the daytime and looses it at night" (*ibid.*) and one *amora* even stated that a man should not live in a town "in which no dogs bark" (Pes. 113a). There is no explicit information extant on the breeds of dogs reared in biblical times. Pedigree dogs were probably raised alongside the local dog, *Canis familiaris putiatini*, of which there were different types. Various breeds of dogs appear in Assyrian and Egyptian monuments. The use of hunting dogs is attested by an ivory comb from Megiddo showing a dog hunting a mountain goat. Mosaics dating from mishnaic and talmudic times also depict dogs. The Mishnah distinguishes between a common dog, which resembles a wolf, and a village or wild dog, which resembles a jackal (Kil. 1:6; cf. Ber. 9b). Attacks by mad dogs were a common occurrence; the rabbis refer frequently to rabies and give the symptoms by which to recognize a mad dog (Yoma 83b, 84a).

BIBLIOGRAPHY: F.S. Bodenheimer, *Ha-Ḥai be-Ereẓ Yisrael* (1953), 264–8; idem, *Ha-Ḥai be-Arẓot ha-Mikra*, 2 (1956), 331–9; J. Feliks, *Kilei Zera'im ve-Harkavah* (1967), 121–3; Lewysohn, Zool, 82–89. **ADD BIBLIOGRAPHY:** Feliks, Ha-Ẓome'aḥ, 242.

[Jehuda Feliks]

DOHANJ, JULIJE (1884–1972), Yugoslav lawyer. Dohanj was born and studied in Budapest. He lived first in Karlovo Selo in the Banat region, moving later to Novi Sad, the capital of the Vojvodina province, where he had a successful career as an advocate. He was a Zionist and for a while even vice president of the Yugoslav Zionist Federation, but in the early 1930s he broke away and joined the Revisionist faction of Jabotinsky, which until then had had no adherents there. Under his influence the local Zionist group also broke away and became a center of Revisionism in Yugoslavia. Jabotinsky spoke at meetings in Zagreb, Belgrade, and Novi Sad, and the new movement, with its Betar youth sections, spread throughout the country. In 1935, after Jabotinsky left the Zionist organization, forming the New Zionist Organization, Dohanj presided over its Yugoslav branch. In that capacity, he helped organize "illegal" Jewish *immigration via the Danube River and, in cooperation with the British Embassy in Belgrade, attempted to warn the Yugoslav public of the Nazi danger.

Dohanj was married to a German woman. Despite this fact, or possibly because of it, he was arrested and interrogated, and was ultimately sent to the Gestapo headquarters in Berlin, where he was kept imprisoned throughout the war. Returning home after the liberation he reopened his office, but experiencing problems with the new Communist judiciary system he soon immigrated to the United States. He worked as a government employee and remarried, this time to an American. On his retirement in 1967 he moved to Israel, settling in Haifa.

[Zvi Loker (2nd ed.)]

°DOHM, CHRISTIAN WILHELM VON (1751–1820), German historian, economist, and diplomat. He was among the first to advocate "reformation" of the Jews and their customs, as well as improvement of their civil status. Dohm studied theology and law, and in 1779 entered the Prussian state service as royal archivist in Berlin where he met Moses *Mendelssohn. In 1786 and in 1797 he represented Prussia at the Congress of Rastatt, and in 1807 entered the service of the Kingdom of *Westphalia established by Napoleon. Dohm pursued the study of history and political science and wrote a number of books on these subjects.

His well-known work on the Jewish question, *Ueber die buergerliche Verbesserung der Juden* ("On the Improvement of the Jews as Citizens"; 1781, 1783^2), was undertaken at the instance of Mendelssohn who had asked him to draw up a memorandum in favor of the Jews of *Alsace. In this work Dohm reviews the history of the Jewish people in exile in order to point out the constant deterioration of their situation as a consequence of oppression and attacks. He argues that repression inevitably corrupts the character of the victim peoples as evidenced by the history of the Irish and the Gypsies. These examples are adduced to confirm his description of the Jewish character in his own time: "The Jews have wisdom, a sharp intellect, they are assiduous, persevering, and are able to find their way in every situation"; their ritual precepts, even though they encourage pettiness, educate them to fulfill their duty rigorously. On the other hand this nation has "an exaggerated tendency.... to look out for gain in every way, a love of usury … defects which are further aggravated in many of them by their self-imposed segregation owing to their religious precepts as well as rabbinical sophistry.… The breaking of the laws of the state restricting trade, the import and export of prohibited wares, the forgery of money and precious metals are the natural result" of these flaws of character. However, "if our reasoning is correct, we shall find that the oppression from which they still suffer and the restrictions imposed on the trades open to Jews are the true reasons for their shortcomings. Concomitantly we have also discovered the means by which they can be cured of this corruption so as to become better people and more useful citizens." Dohm finds no intrinsic evil in the Jewish religion and literature, and argues on this point against the anti-Jewish agitator Johann *Eisenmenger. He appreciates the enlightened Jewish intellectuals of his time, "these admirable men who attained eminence in the sciences and the arts." To eradicate the evil and abolish its consequences, Dohm suggests a series of measures for improving the situation of the Jews and hence their character. His proposals reproduce some of the ideas held by proponents of Enlightened Absolutism and in some points resemble the *Toleranzpatent* issued at that time by Emperor *Joseph II. Joseph Dohm plans to educate the Jews to identify themselves more closely to the state, and to serve it, by putting an end to oppression and by abolishing the economic restrictions imposed on them, as well as by encouraging them to participate in the culture of the environment. The educational effort and the grant of equal economic and civil opportunities to the Jews would be worthwhile to enlightened governments aiming at justice and the increase of their population. The Jews are preferable to new settlers since "they are more deeply rooted in the countries they inhabit than a foreigner can be, even after a considerable time; they know no other homeland besides the one which they already have and do not long for a home in a distant land."

Dohm thus voiced the climate of opinion prevailing in enlightened Christian and Jewish circles of Berlin. He aroused German public opinion to consider the Jewish problem as of political and social significance. His opinions had wide reverberations and provoked numerous and stormy debates. The antisemites accused him of being bought by the Jews. The Jewish *maskilim* were grateful to him for the way in which he described the situation of the Jews, and for his aims, with which they were basically in agreement.

BIBLIOGRAPHY: F. Reuss, *C.W. Dohms Schrift ueber die buergerliche Verbesserung der Juden…* (1891); M.W. Rapaport, *Chr. W. Dohm der Gegner der Physiocratie und seine Thesen* (1908); W. Cohn, in: ZGJD, 1 (1929), 255–61; Graetz, Gesch, 11 (1900), index; W. Gronau, *Chr. W. Dohm…* (Ger., 1824); B. Dinur, *Be-Mifneh ha-Dorot* (1955), index.

[Haim Hillel Ben-Sasson]

DOK, a fortress 3 mi. (5 km.) N. of Jericho where Simeon, the last of the Maccabean brothers, together with his wife and two sons, was murdered in 135 b.c.e. by his son-in-law, Ptolemy son of Habubu, governor (*stratêgos*) of Jericho (I Macc. 16:15). Josephus calls it Dagon (Ant., 13:230) and the place is also mentioned in the *Copper Scroll (265:19) found at one of the Qumran caves. A Byzantine monastery called Douka/Duca was founded in the vicinity of the site by St. Chariton. Dok is identified with Jebel Qarantal (Mons Quarantena); the Arabic names for the site are Duk and Dyuk, the first resembles the original name, but the second version stems from popular etymology (Dyuk = chickens). The name of the site is also preserved in the nearby village of ʿAyn al-Dūk (ancient *Naarah). The mountain of Qarantal commands a strategic situation overlooking Jericho to the east and has the remains of a small medieval chapel which was recorded by members of the Survey of Western Palestine in 1873. The site has not been thoroughly excavated, except for a few pits made by E. Netzer that revealed an ionic capital. Scattered architectural remains at the site, however, do attest to palatial buildings having existed at the site at the time of *Herod the Great and his successors, as well as during the Byzantine period (notably a Corinthian capital decorated with a cross). Roman siege works with towers have also been identified around the site by Z. Meshel, and a water system that was fed by an aqueduct was studied by D. Amit.

BIBLIOGRAPHY: Press, Ereẓ, 2 (1948), 181 s.v. *Dokim;* Van Kasteren, in: RB, 6 (1897), 99ff.; Alt, in: PJB, 23 (1927), 30–31; Abel, Geog, 1 (1933), 376. **ADD. BIBLIOGRAPHY:** W.J. Moutton, "A Visit to Quarn Sartabeh," *Bulletin of the American School of Oriental Research* 62 (1936): 141–8; Z. Meshel, "The Fortification System During the Hasmonean Period," in E. Schiller, *Zev Vilnay's Jubilee Volume*. Vol. I (1984): 2542–58. **ADD. BIBLIOGRAPHY:** D. Amit, "The Water System of Dok Fortress (Dagon)," in D. Amit, Y. Hirschfeld and J. Patrich (eds.), *The Aqueducts of Ancient Palestine* (1989), 223–28; D. Pringle, *The Churches of the Crusader Kingdom of Jerusalem. A Corpus:* Volume I: *A–K* (1993), 252–58; Y. Tsafrir, L. Di Segni, and J. Green, *Tabula Imperii Romani. Iudaea – Palaestina. Maps and Gazetteer.* (1994), 112–13; E. Netzer, *The Palaces of the Hasmoneans and Herod the Great* (2001), 70–72; Y. Elitzur, *Ancient Place Names in the Holy Land: Preservation and History* (2004), 358.

[Michael Avi-Yonah / Shimon Gibson (2nd ed.)]

DOKSHITSY (Pol. **Dokszyce**), town in Molodechno district, Belarus. It passed from Poland to Russia in 1793; was within Poland from 1921 to 1939; and afterwards was in the Belorussian SSR. The Jewish community probably started at the beginning of the 18th century and increased from 210 Jews in 1766 to 2,775 (49.1% of the total population) in 1878. It numbered 2,762 in 1897 (75.8%). The Jews traded in lumber and agricultural products, exporting to central Poland, Russia, and even Leipzig. They were also occupied in crafts and farming. In 1925 they numbered approximately 3,000. Between the two world wars, the Jews lost their markets and were required to pay heavy taxes, leading to economic decline. The loan fund sponsored by the *American Jewish Joint Distribution Committee had 250 members in 1925. There was a Hebrew Tarbut school which was the center of Zionist activities. The Germans occupied the town on June 22, 1941, creating a ghetto on September 30. During Passover 1942, 65 and later 350 Jews were executed. The liquidation of the ghetto commenced on May 29, 1942. It lasted 17 days and about 3,000 Jews were murdered. The community was not reestablished after World War II.

BIBLIOGRAPHY: J. Kermisz, *"Akcje"i Wysiedlenia* (1946), index.

[Shmuel Spector (2nd ed.)]

DOLGIN, SIMON ARTHUR (1915–2004), U.S. Orthodox rabbi and Mizrachi leader. Dolgin was born in Chicago and studied at the Hebrew Theological College there, where he was ordained in 1939, and received his doctorate in 1959. He also received a doctorate in theology from the University of Southern California in 1954. From 1939 until 1971, he served as rabbi of Beth Jacob Congregation, Beverly Hills, California; he was vice president of the Rabbinical Council of America from 1966 to 1968.

A prominent member of the Mizrachi, he was a member of the National Council of the Ha-Po'el ha-Mizrachi, 1943–55, and vice chairman of the National Council of Religious Zionists of America.

On immigrating to Israel in 1971 he was appointed director-general of the Ministry of Religious Affairs, holding the office until 1977, when he became head of the Midrashah Gevohah le-Torah in Jerusalem, serving simultaneously as rabbi of Ramat Eshkol in Jerusalem. In 1978 he was appointed chairman of the World Organization of Mizrachi-Ha-Po'el ha-Mizrachi.

DOLGINOVO (Pol. **Dołhinów**), town in Molodechno district, Belarus. It passed from Poland to Russia in 1793; was within Poland from 1921 to 1939; and was then in the Belorussian SSR. Jews settled there at the beginning of the 16th century but only formed a community in the 17th, numbering 485 in 1667. Apart from petty trade and crafts, the Jews also exported agricultural products through Danzig. A pogrom in 1881 resulted in the looting and destruction of shops and homes. The community numbered 1,194 in 1847; 2,559 in 1897 (out of a total population of 3,551); and 1,747 in 1921 (out of 2,671). During the interwar years, the loss of the agricultural hinterland (Russia) resulted in the decline of the economy. Some Jews earned a living by smuggling goods across the border with the Soviet Union. Most Jewish children studied in a Hebrew Tarbut school. In September 1939 the Soviets abolished all Jewish organizations and parties and nationalized the economy.

[Shmuel Spector (2nd ed.)]

Holocaust Period

The Jewish population of the city had increased to nearly 5,000 in 1941. From the outbreak of World War II in 1939 until the German-Soviet war the town was under Soviet occupation. On June 28, 1941, the German army captured it. In August 1941, 22 men, including the rabbi of the community, were murdered by the Germans. On March 3, 1942, in the first mass *Aktion* 1,500 Jews were shot to death and cremated on the outskirts of the town. On May 1, 1942, a ghetto was set up. During the *Shavuot* festival that year, the entire community was wiped out, except for 500 craftsmen who were spared from immediate death. In this period groups of Jews fled to the forests and joined the partisans operating in Nalibocka Puszcza. The few remaining members of the community were murdered in September 1942. Only about 200 persons survived the war as soldiers of the Soviet army drafted in the spring of 1941, others as members of partisan units, and a number who had gone into hiding. The community was not refounded after World War II.

[Aharon Weiss]

BIBLIOGRAPHY: *Eynikeit* (Dec. 3, 1945); material extant in Yad Vashem Archives.

DOLINA, town in Stanislavov district, Ukraine, in Poland between 1917 and 1939. Although Jews are mentioned in 1472, a community was only established in 1638, when they received a permit from the king to build a synagogue and cemetery and to trade, on condition that they pay taxes like the other burgers. After the Austrian annexation they suffered in the years 1772–1868 from severe restrictions and heavy and humiliating taxes. At the end of the 19th century many of the local Jews emigrated. The Jewish population was 2,654 in 1900 (29% of the total), 2,014 in 1921, and 2,488 in 1931. In the 1920s the economic conditions deteriorated. With the help of the Joint an orphanage, soup kitchen, and interest-free loan association were established. In the 1930s the economy improved after several factories reopened. Between September 1939 and June 1941 Dolina was under Soviet rule, with all public life terminated and industry and trade nationalized. Dolina was occupied by the Germans on July 2, 1941. In the beginning of August a group of Hungarian and local Jews was executed in a forest near the town. In July 1942 all the Jews from the environs were concentrated in Dolina and 3,000 people were murdered in ditches in the local cemetery. About 50 Jews joined the Babi partisan unit, but only five survived along with a few who hid in the forests.

BIBLIOGRAPHY: I. Schipper, *Kulturgeshikhte fun di Yidn in Poyln Beysn Mitlalter* (1926), index; *Sefer ha-Zikkaron li-Kedoshei Bolekhov* (1957).

[Shmuel Spector (2nd ed.)]

DOLITZKI, MENAḤEM MENDEL (1856–1931), Hebrew and Yiddish poet and novelist. Born in Bialystok, he received a traditional Orthodox education and, as a teenager, became interested in the ideas of the *Haskalah. At the age of 19 he wrote a long satiric poem, *Likkui Shenei ha-Me'orot, o Shenei Ẓaddikim she-Ḥibbelu Zeh ba-Zeh* ("The Eclipse of Both Luminaries, or Two Ẓaddikim Who Harmed One Another," published in *Ha-Shaḥar,* 1879, then in book form). In this poem he mockingly describes the way of life of the ḥasidic groups. He served as a Hebrew teacher in various towns and in 1881 was an eyewitness to pogroms in southern Russia, which had a profound effect on him. In his poem *Ha-Ikkar ve-ha-Noẓah* ("The Farmer and the Feather," 1884) and his stories *Be-Tokh*

Leva'im ("Among Lions," *Ha-Meliẓ*, 1884, also in book form) and *Mi-Bayit u-mi-Ḥuẓ* ("From Inside and Outside," *Ha-Meliẓ*, 1890–91, also in book form), he described the sufferings of the Jews in Russia. After the pogroms he joined the Ḥibbat Zion movement and wrote poems of yearning for Zion in the spirit of this movement. The poems are colorless and full of clichés but nevertheless exude warmth and innocent romanticism. From 1882 to 1892 he lived in Moscow where he worked as Hebrew secretary to the philanthropist K.Z. Wissotzky. He wrote a biography of Wissotzky called *Mofet le-Rabbim* ("An Example to Many," 1894). At the same time he published various collections of letters: *Shevet Sofer* ("Writer's Pen," 1883); *Niv Sefatayim* ("Fruit of the Lips," 1892); and later *Ha-Et* ("The Pen," 1906), which include some interesting letters of A. *Mapu and P. Smolenskin. In 1892, when the Jews were expelled from Moscow, Dolitzki emigrated to New York and was warmly received by the small band of Hebrew *maskilim* in the U.S. He began publishing descriptions of the persecution of Jews in Russia in the journal *Ha-Ivri*, mainly in poetic form. His epic poem dealing with the forced conscription of Jewish children *Ha-Ḥalom ve-Shivro* ("The Dream and its Meaning"), which he had started in Russia but could not publish there because of censorship, appeared in 1904. Despite the efforts of the Hebraists in the U.S. to assist him, he found no way of making a living from Hebrew writing. After working at various jobs he finally took up writing for the daily Yiddish press, turning out serialized novels which catered to the popular reader. He died in Los Angeles. In his youth he was highly regarded as a Hebrew writer and poet, and his poems and stories were very popular with the Hebrew reading public of his day. J.L. Gordon, in a poem dedicated to Dolitzki on his departure for America, views him as his heir in Hebrew poetry ("Here, take my pen, rise and inherit my place"). However, after his arrival in America a period of decline set in, from which he never recovered. His last years were spent in poverty, and he was quite forgotten. A list of his Hebrew works in translation appears in Goell, Bibliography, 20–21.

BIBLIOGRAPHY: Waxman, Literature, index; LNYL, 2 (1958), 444–6; A.R. Malachi, in: *Ha-Tekufah*, 34–35 (1950). **ADD. BIBLIOGRAPHY:** A. Ben-Or, *Toledot ha-Sifrut ha-Ivrit ha-Ḥadashah*, 2 (1951), 44–47.

[Gedalyah Elkoshi]

°**DOLLFUSS, ENGELBERT** (1892–1934), chancellor of Austria and leader of the *Christian Social party there. He served as chancellor from 1932 until his murder in an attempted Nazi putsch. An antisemite, Dollfuss had been instrumental in excluding from membership all students "tainted with Jewish blood" at a Catholic students' congress in 1920. During his chancellorship a number of covert anti-Jewish measures were introduced, and after the crushing defeat of the Social Democrats in February 1934 he refused to see a Jewish delegation, remarking that the Jews should be pleased that he was too busy to deal with Jewish affairs. However, Austrian Jewry regarded him as a "bulwark against persecution and the horrors of a Nazi regime" (JC, July 27, 1934) because of his energetic stand against Nazism. Dollfuss issued several statements against racial antisemitism and was not connected with any official action against Jews. His opponents considered the Jews one of the pillars of his regime. His murder made him the symbol of the fight against Nazism. After his murder the Zionist leadership of the Jewish community and Chief Rabbi David Feuchtwang praised Dollfuss as the renewer of the Austrian state and organized mourning services in the synagogues.

BIBLIOGRAPHY: Karbach, in: JSOS, 2 (1940), 255–9; G. Shepherd, *Dollfuss* (Eng., 1961); H. Greive, *Theologie und Ideologie, Katholizismus und Judentum in Deutschland und Oesterreich 1918–1935* (1969), index. **ADD. BIBLIOGRAPHY:** C.A. Gulick, *Austria from Habsburg to Hitler* (1948).

DOLMATOVSKI, YEVGENI ARONOVICH (1915–1994), Soviet poet and songwriter. Dolmatovski became known during World War II for his collections of patriotic verse, such as *Pesnya o Dnepre* ("Song of the Dnieper," 1942), and later wrote successful songs for postwar patriotic motion pictures. His other works include *Sozvezdiye* ("Constellation," 1947), praising the 16 republics of the U.S.S.R.; the anti-Western *Slovo o zavtrashnem dne* ("A Word about Tomorrow," 1949), which won the 1950 Stalin Prize; and *Iz zhizni poezii* ("From the Life of Poetry," 1965). Dolmatovski signed the 1970 manifesto opposing Jewish emigration from the Soviet Union.

DOLMENS ("stone table" in Breton, from *dol*, "table," and *men*, "stone"), ancient chambers built of a number of undressed vertical stone slabs (orthostats), usually weighing several tons, supporting a single flat capstone. In its original state the dolmen was covered over with a heaped-up mound of earth or small stones retained by an external ring of stones (tumulus). The disappearance of the encompassing mound since antiquity has given dolmens their typical table-like appearance. The stone chambers were intended to contain human remains and as such dolmens are regarded as places of burial. The dolmen is the most common of a series of monuments of proto-historic date called megaliths (structures built of massive undressed stone blocks), notably stone circles, standing stones (menhirs), and cists in cairns. Dolmens have been found across the world (see Joussaume) indicating that this form of burial was reinvented in different cultural centers. The idea that dolmens reflect patterns of diffusion (e.g., G. Elliot-Smith, who believed that the megaliths of Europe were built by wandering Egyptians) is no longer held by scholars. Burial in dolmens, or within stone cairns or tumuli, is characteristic of the southern Levant during much of the late fourth and third millennia B.C.E.

They are characteristic of regions where the geology does not provide natural caves or where the rock is difficult to quarry. Dolmens usually appear in groups ("fields") and they number in the hundreds. Some of the best examples are known from the Golan Heights and Transjordan (where there are fields of between 300 and 1000 each). In Palestine most of the dolmens have been found in the north, with isolated examples known further south (e.g., at Yiftahel). However, cairn and tumuli burials are known in southern Palestine as well, but their stone-built burial cists lack the monumental orthostats and massive capstones of the dolmens. An interesting field of tumuli with cist burials of this sort was investigated at Ramat ha-Nadiv in the Carmel Hill range. The oldest dolmens in the Near East are said to come from el-Adeimeh, 9 miles (15 kms.) southeast of Jericho, which was believed by Stekelis to be the cemetery of the Chalcolithic site of Tuleilat Ghassul, but there is uncertainty about this dating and they are more likely to be from the Early Bronze I. A series of extraordinary dolmens was investigated at Ala Safat in Transjordan, some of which had chambers that were accessed through stone slabs hewn with portholes. These too are dated to the Early Bronze Age. A correlation between the distribution of dolmen fields and Early Bronze Age settlements was pointed out by Vinitsky for the Golan. In the Golan a major study of dolmen fields was undertaken by Epstein, who noticed five types based on methods of construction and on the state of their preservation. Previous studies on dolmens have concentrated on typology, function, and date, but in-depth studies of dolmen landscapes have yet to be undertaken and may very well reveal evidence for various forms of social stratification. At er-Ramthaniyyeh in the Golan, for example, one "free-standing" type of dolmen existed within a field which otherwise only had *tumuli*-dolmens. Variation in monument type has also been noted by Greenberg within the dolmen fields of the Transjordan, as well as within the tumuli field at Ramat ha-Nadiv, suggesting the existence of a hierarchy within the populations they served. The general consensus of opinion is that dolmens served populations from a non-sedentary pastoralist background. Dolmens are notoriously difficult to date. The earliest artifacts found in them are dated to the Intermediate Bronze Age (EB IV; circa 2000 B.C.E.), but it seems likely that they were periodically reused or rebuilt for burial purposes throughout the protohistoric period, beginning with the Early Bronze I (late fourth millennium B.C.E.) and culminating with the Intermediate Bronze Age which was probably the last period in which the practice of dolmen construction persisted; this would account for the fact that most of the artifacts (mainly weapons, pottery, and some jewelry) found in dolmens date from this period.

BIBLIOGRAPHY: M. Stekelis, *Les monuments mégalithiques de Palestine* (1935); F. Turville-Petre, "Dolmen Necropolis Near Kerazeh, Galilee," in: *Palestine Exploration Fund Quarterly Statement*, 64 (1931), 155–66; D. Bahat, "The Date of the Dolmens Near Kibbutz Shamir," in: IEJ, 22 (1972): 44–46; C. Epstein, "Dolmens Excavated in the Golan", *'Atiqot* (English Series), 17 (1985): 20–58; K. Yassine, "The Dolmens: Construction and Dating Reconsidered," in: BASOR, 259 (1985), 63–69; R. Joussaume, *Dolmens for the Dead: Megalithic-Building Throughout the World* (1988), 251–58, Chap. 9: "The Near East"; M. Zohar, "Rogem Hiri: A Megalithic Monument in the Golan," in: IEJ, 39 (1989), 18–31; C. Dauphin and S. Gibson, "Ancient Settlements in their Landscapes: The Results of Ten Years of Survey on the Golan Heights (1978–1988)," in: *Bulletin of the Anglo-Israel Archaeological Society*, 12 (1992–1993): 7–31; L. Vinitsky, "The Date of the Dolmens in the Golan and Galilee: A Reassessment," in: *Tel Aviv*, 19 (1992), 100–12; R. Greenberg, "The Ramat Hanadiv Tumulus Field," in: Y. Hirschfeld (ed.), *Ramat Hanadiv Excavations* (2000), 583–614.

[Shimon Gibson (2nd ed.)]

DOLNI KOUNICE (Ger. **Kanitz**; Heb. קוניץ), small town in Moravia, Czech Republic. Jews were living there from the end of the 14th century. A "Jewish judge" is mentioned in 1581. The synagogue was destroyed by the Swedes in 1643; rebuilt immediately, it existed until the Holocaust. About the end of the 17th century several conventions of the Moravian communities were held in Dolni Kounice. Jews there were able to acquire real estate until the regulations imposing the *Familiants system were introduced in 1727; these also limited the number of families permitted to reside in the locality to 111. There were 16 "Jewish houses" registered in 1674 and 35 in 1823. Dolni Kounice was one of the political communities (**politische gemeinde*). The community numbered 595 in 1848; 206 in 1900; 71 in 1921; and 53 in 1930 (1.6% of the total population), of whom 41 declared their nationality as Jewish. The Jewish quarter was destroyed by fire in 1823, and in 1862 by flood. Dolni Kounice was the birthplace of the historian Gotthard *Deutsch. The historian Heinrich *Flesch was appointed rabbi there in 1894. The Jews in Dolni Kounice were deported to the Nazi death camps in 1942 and perished there. The synagogue equipment and *pinkas* (minute-book) of the *ḥevra kaddisha* were deposited in the central Jewish Museum in Prague. No community was reestablished after World War II. The synagogue building was restored by the authorities in 1969. Ancestors of Austrian chancellor Bruno *Kreisky were from Dolni Kounice.

BIBLIOGRAPHY: H. Gold (ed.), *Juden und Judengemeinden Maehrens…* (1929), 267–78; H. Flesch, in: JGGJČ, 2 (1930), 285–92; idem, in: M. Stein (ed.), *Jahrbuch des traditionstreuen Rabbiner-Verbandes in der Slowakei* (1923), 47–83; idem, in: *Jahrbuch zur juedischen Volkskunde*, 2 (1924/25), 617–18; I. Halpern, *Takkanot Medinat Mehrin* (1951), index, s.v. *Kuniẓ*.

[Meir Lamed]

DOLNI KUBIN (Slovak **Dolný Kubin**; Hung. **Alsókubin**), town in N. Slovakia, now Slovak Republic. According to existing documentation, Jews arrived in the city of Dolni Kubin, and in the Orava region, by the beginning of the 18th century, though it can be assumed that they were in the area earlier.

Moravian Jews were the pioneers of Jewish settlement in the entire region of northern upper Hungary, from Čadca to Bardejov. *Holešov Jewry, in northern Moravia, settled in many Jewish cities of this region, including Dolni Kubin in 1710. During their initial years in the city, the Jews rented houses from local inhabitants and were quick to exploit the city's strategic location between Cracow and Vienna for business purposes. In 1775 the Jews built their first synagogue. They also acquired land for a cemetery.

In 1780 there were 112 Jews in the Orava region; in 1801, 668; in 1840, 2,333; and in 1900, 3,197 (probably the peak). In the town of Dolni Kubin the Jewish population rose from 124 in 1835 to 680 in 1921 but then dropped to 248 in 1940 (of a total 2,005).

In 1870 the community split into an Orthodox and a *Neolog congregation. It was reunited as a *status quo community in 1886. The Zionist movement in Dolni Kubin was one of the first in Hungary. Moric Greunwald was among the founders of the World Mizrachi movement and was a personal friend of Theodor *Herzl. He participated in the second and third World Zionist Congresses. At the end of World War I a wave of pogroms shook the region. Jewish war veterans fought off threatening mobs.

In September 1938 Slovak autonomy was proclaimed, and on March 14, 1939, the independent Slovak state came under German protection. From the outset Jews were persecuted. On June 5, 1942, the Jews of Dolni Kubin and the vicinity were dispatched to the Zilina transit camp, and from there to extermination camps in Poland. In 1947, 27 Jews lived in Dolni Kubin, most of them leaving in 1948–49. The synagogue became a movie house. In 1991, a memorial to the victims of the Holocaust was erected in the presence of President Vaclav Havel. It was the first such ceremony since the fall of Communism in Slovakia.

BIBLIOGRAPHY: *Magyar Zsidó Lexikon* (1929), 32, s.v. *Alsókubin*; M. Lányi and H. Propperné Békefi, *A szlovenszkói zsidó hitközségek története* (1933), 225–9; *Monumenta Hungariae Judaica*, 7 (1963), 323–5; J. Bató, in: *Uj Kelet* (Feb. 11, 12, 13, 1969); B. Tomaschoff, *ibid.* (May 15, 1970).

[Yeshayahu Jelinek (2nd ed.)]

DOMALSKY, I. (Mikhail Davidovich Baytalsky; 1903–1978), Russian poet and publicist. Domalsky was born in the village of Chernovo in Odessa province. He participated in the Civil War and was a Komsomol (Communist Youth League) activist in the Ukraine. Together with M. Elko, he wrote the popular song "Po moryam – po volnam" ("Over the Seas – Over the Waves"). In the 1920s he worked as a journalist for newspapers in Kharkov and the Donbass. In 1930 he moved from the Donbass to Moscow where he worked on the staff of the newspapers *Vechernyaya Moskva* and *Izvestia.* Accused of Trotskyism, he was arrested and served two terms in forced labor camps in Vorkuta (1936–41 and 1950–56). He was a soldier in World War II and after his demobilization he worked as a metalworker in Eysk. While imprisoned Domalsky began to write poetry (c. from 1951) in which he expressed his passionate longing for Israel. The poems were smuggled out of the U.S.S.R. and published in Israel under the pseudonym D. Seter (Hebrew for "hidden") with parallel Hebrew translation. The book of poems was edited by Avraham Shlonsky and Moshe Sharett under the title *Pridet vesna moya* ("My Spring Will Come," 1962, 1975).

In 1956 Domalsky was rehabilitated. He then moved to Nal'chik where he began to write his memoirs, chapters of which appeared in Moscow in the *samizdat* (self-publishing) journal *Evrei v SSSR* ("Jews in the Soviet Union," 17, 1979) and in Israel in the journals *Vremya i my* ("Time and We," 11, 1978) and *22* (5, 1979).

In 1970 Domalsky moved to Moscow where, under various pseudonyms, he was actively involved both in the general democratic and Jewish *samizdats.* In 1975 his book *Russkie yevrei vchera i segodnya* ("Russian Jews Yesterday and Today") was published in Tel Aviv. In 1977 he wrote a sociological essay "Novoye v antisemitizme" ("What is New in Antisemitism?") which appeared in the collection *Antisemitizm v Sovetskom Soyuze. Yego korni i posledstviya* ("Antisemitism in the Soviet Union, its Roots and Consequences," Tel Aviv, 1979). In these publications Domalsky explained the mechanism of official Soviet antisemitism.

Domalsky died in Moscow. According to his wishes his remains were brought to Israel in 1979 and buried in kibbutz Gelil Yam near Herzliyyah.

[*The Shorter Jewish Encylopaedia* in Russian]

DOMBROVENI, Jewish agricultural colony in Bessarabia, founded in 1836 on 1,287 hectares (approx. 3,217 acres) of land bought by settlers from Podolia. It developed the most advanced level of farm economy in the Jewish colonies in the region. Of the 371 families (1,874 persons) living there in 1899, 139 owned land with an average holding of 9.2 hectares (approx. 32½ acres) per family; an additional 2,325 hectares (approx. 5,812 acres) were held on lease. The colony owned then 31 plows and 3,517 sheep and goats. A school was opened in 1900, to which the writer K.R. Abramowich-Ginzburg was appointed principal. Under the Romanian agrarian reform of 1922, 182 Jews in Dombroveni received 413 hectares (approx. 1,032 acres). The 303 members registered in the loan fund operating locally in 1925 included 225 farmers, 21 artisans, and 24 merchants. In 1930 there were in the colony 1,198 Jews (87.3% of the total population).

[Eliyahu Feldman]

Holocaust Period

After occupation by the Soviet army in June 1940, the rabbi and community leaders of Dombroveni were exiled to Siberia; Jewish property was confiscated in stages and all Zionist activity outlawed. In 1941, in the interval between the withdrawal of the Soviet forces and the entry of German-Romanian troops, Dombroveni was plundered by the inhabitants of the nearby villages, and the Jews fled to the outlying fields. When they were caught by the Romanian troops they were all concentrated in the school courtyard, robbed of their money and jewelry, and ordered to leave the place. Those who turned west were murdered by the Germans they met en route; others turned east and reached the Dniester, where some succeeded in crossing the river with the help of the remaining Soviet authorities and took refuge in the Soviet Union. Still others were caught by Romanians and dispatched to *Transnistria, where they were either killed or died of starvation and disease. The settlement itself was leased out and all the property seized and distributed among local peasants.

[Jean Ancel]

DOMENICO GEROSOLIMITANO (c. 1552–1621 or later), apostate and censor of Hebrew books. Born in Jerusalem, Domenico, whose Jewish name is unknown, received a talmudic and kabbalistic education at Safed and also studied mathematics and medicine. At first he was active as a rabbi, then practiced medicine in Cairo, and later became physician to the sultan in Constantinople. In 1593 he converted to Christianity and served the Inquisition as censor of Hebrew books first at Mantua and nearby towns, then at Monferrato, Milan, and Rome. In Rome Domenico became a member of the Collegio dei Neofiti, where he taught Hebrew in addition to his work as a censor. Parts of his Hebrew autobiography were published by Guidi (*Festschrift… A. Berliner,* 176ff.) and by G. Sacerdote. Domenico's writings, mostly in manuscript form, include an "Index Expurgatorius," the *Sefer ha-Zikkuk*, which lists all passages in Hebrew literature to which the Inquisition objected; a translation into Hebrew of the New Testament and the Apocrypha; and anti-Jewish, pro-Christian sermons in Italian.

BIBLIOGRAPHY: G. Bartolocci, *Bibliotheca magna rabbinica*, 2 (1678), 281–3; P.S. Medici, *Catalogo de' neofiti illustri…* (Florence, 1701), 13–15; Wolf, Bibliotheca, 3 (1727), 210; G. Sacerdote, in: REJ, 30 (1895), 257–83; W. Popper, *Censorship of Hebrew Books* (1899), index, s.v. *Sefer ha-Zikkuk*; I. Guidi, in: *Festschrift… A. Berliner* (1903), 176–9; N. Porges, *ibid.*, 273–95; I. Sonne, *Expurgation of Hebrew Books* (1943), 9–11.

[Alfredo Mordechai Rabello]

DOMESTIC PEACE (Heb. שְׁלוֹם בַּיִת, *shelom bayit*). The Jewish tradition visualizes God as seeking peace: in the heavenly spheres, between the nations on earth, and especially between *husband and wife. Since every man is considered a king in his own household, Scripture regards a man who establishes peace in his house as a sovereign who establishes peace in his dominion (ARN[1] 28:3). The rabbis sensed that the ultimate achievement of peace on earth depends upon its achievement in the smallest social unit – the *family. They also said that God's presence leads to peace in the home. However, the view that "Great is peace that reigns between husband and wife" had legal and moral consequences as well. It was permitted to tell a lie for the sake of domestic tranquility. God Himself had done this when He reported to Abraham on Sarah's soliloquy (Gen. 18:12–13 and BM 87a). Moreover, the practice of Jewish women to light candles every Sabbath eve, established by the rabbis as one of the principle commandments to be performed by females, is expressly for the purpose of promoting an atmosphere of warmth and peace on the holy day. The rabbis queried which of two commandments is to enjoy preference when there are insufficient funds for both, Sabbath or Ḥanukkah candles, and ruled that Sabbath candles were more important because they contributed to *shelom bayit* (Shab. 23b).

That God strongly desired *shelom bayit* was derived especially from the fact that according to the **sotah* ritual (Num. 5:11–31), He had permitted His holy name to be inscribed on parchment which was placed in water, though He knew that His name would thus be erased by the liquid. Yet He lent His name to this abuse that He might be a party to the restoration of marital tranquility. However, the rabbis in many places cautioned husbands not to make it necessary to resort to the ritual altogether. They should behave properly and not be tyrannical or jealous (Sot. 2b). Because of the principle that one cannot be expected to live with a snake under one roof, the rabbis ruled that the husband would not have the right to exact from his wife an accounting under oath with regard to her management of household goods (Ket. 86b). Either the relationship was one of trust, they stated, or it was better for it to be terminated. It is apparent from the Bible that the institution of polygamy was frowned upon because of *shelom bayit* long before it was abolished by the ban of R. *Gershom, in about the year 1000. The patriarchs Abraham and Jacob, who had more than one wife, had domestic strife; the prophet Samuel was born in such a home; and the kings suffered harmful intrigues because of their harems. There could hardly be *shelom bayit* when there was more than one mistress of the household, and the Bible proves this by its description of the relationship between the two wives of the same man by the word *ẓarah*, which also means misfortune and suggests that two wives of one husband can only bring grief to each other and to the home. Because of *shelom bayit*, husbands were urged to heed their wives' counsel (see the commentary of Me'iri on BM 59a) with regard to all household affairs, and especially the feeding and clothing of the sons and daughters. This, however, is only one of numerous rules involving the love and honor due to a wife from her husband and the husband's legal obligations because of the marital relationship. Moreover, for the sake of *shelom bayit*, a husband whose parents unjustly find fault with his wife is not required to please his parents by showing his agreement with them thereby angering his wife (*Sefer Ḥasidim*, 564). Thus even the fifth commandment of the Decalogue, to honor one's parents, is superseded by *shelom bayit*.

[Emanuel Rackman]

DOMESTIC VIOLENCE, behavior used by one partner to control the other; it can include verbal, emotional, sexual, and physical abuse and cuts across social strata. Although men can be abused, most victims are women. Children in abusive households are likely to have been abused or to have witnessed abuse. In recent decades, the term "domestic violence" has replaced "wife beating" or "wife battering"; such behavior is also referred to as "relationship violence," "domestic abuse," and "violence against a spouse."

Domestic violence is not a new issue among Jews. Although the word מכה (strike, blow, hit, beat) appears in the Bible, it is not associated with wife beating until talmudic times and even then it is not overtly discussed. The most useful source in the study of wife beating is responsa literature (ranging from geonic times to the present). There are a variety of attitudes towards domestic violence found in these texts, with some decisors who declare it unlawful while others justify it under certain circumstances. Gratuitous abuse, striking a wife without a reason, is unlawful and forbidden by all. However, the attitude of rabbinic sources toward perceived "bad wives" is ambivalent, and wife beating is occasionally sanctioned if it is for the purpose of chastisement or education.

Medieval Attitudes in the Muslim World

*Ẓemaḥ ben Paltoi, *gaon* of Pumbedita (872–90), allowed a man to flog his wife if she was guilty of assault. Rabbi *Yehudai b. Naḥman (Yehudai Gaon, 757–61) wrote that: "…when her husband enters the house, she must rise and cannot sit down until he sits, and she should never raise her voice against her husband. Even if he hits her she has to remain silent, because that is how chaste women behave" (*Oẓar ha-Ge'onim*, Ket. 169–70). The ninth-century *gaon* of Sura, *Sar Shalom b. Boaz (d. c. 859 or 864), distinguished between an assault on a woman by her husband and an assault on her by a stranger. The *gaon* of Sura's opinion was that the husband's assault on his wife should be judged less severely, since the husband had authority over his wife (*Oẓar ha-Ge'onim*, BK 62:198).

In his *Mishneh Torah*, Moses *Maimonides (1135–1204) recommended beating a bad wife as an acceptable form of discipline: "A wife who refuses to perform any kind of work that she is obligated to do, may be compelled to perform it, even by scourging her with a rod" (Ishut 21:10). The responsa of R. Solomon b. Abraham *Adret (Rashba, 1235–1310) include examples of husbands who occasionally or habitually use force; few of these men are brought to court for beating a wife in a moment of anger. However, there are instances in Rashba's responsa of wives who considered the rabbis as allies against violent husbands (Adret, vol. 5, no. 264; vol. 7, no. 477; vol. 8, no. 102; vol. 4, no. 113).

Medieval Attitudes in Ashkenaz

Responsa from 12th- and 13th-century France and Germany express a rejection of wife beating without any qualifications in a Jewish society in which women held high social and economic status. This attitude is reflected in a proposed *takkanah* (regulation supplementing the talmudic *halakhah*) of R. Perez b. Elijah, who believed that "one who beats his wife is in the same category as one who beats a stranger"; he decreed that "any Jew may be compelled on application of his wife or one of her near relatives to undertake by a *ḥerem* not to beat his wife in anger or cruelty so as to disgrace her, for that is against Jewish practice." If the husband refused to obey, the court could assign her maintenance according to her station and according to the custom of the place where she dwelled. It is not clear whether this *takkanah* ever received serious consideration.

Some Ashkenazi rabbis considered battering as grounds for forcing a man to give a *get*. Rabbi *Meir b. Baruch of Rothenburg (Maharam, c. 1215–1293) and R. *Simḥah b. Samuel of Speyer (d. 1225–1230) wrote that a man has to honor his wife *more* than himself and that is why his wife and not his fellow man should be his greater concern. R. Simḥah argued that like Eve, "the mother of all living" (Gen. 3:20), a wife is given to a man for living, not for suffering. She trusts him and thus it is worse if he hits her than if he hits a stranger. R. Simḥah lists all the possible sanctions. If these are of no avail, he not only recommends a compelled divorce, but allows one that is forced on the husband by gentile authorities. This is highly unusual since rabbis rarely endorse forcing a man to divorce his wife and it is even rarer to suggest that the non-Jewish community adjudicate internal Jewish affairs. Although many Ashkenazi rabbis quoted his opinions with approval, they were overturned by most authorities in later generations, starting with R. Israel b. Pethaḥiah *Isserlein (1390–1460) and R. *David b. Solomon Ibn Abi Zimra (Radbaz, 1479–1573). In his responsum, Radbaz wrote that R. Simḥah "exaggerated on the measures to be taken when writing that [the wifebeater] should be forced by non-Jews (*akum*) to divorce his wife … because [if she remarries] this could result in the offspring [of the illegal marriage, according to Radbaz] being declared illegitimate (*mamzer*)" (part 4, 157). Sixteenth-century responsa seem to acknowledge that wife beating is wrong, yet they avoid releasing the woman from the bad marriage. These evasive positions vis-à-vis relief for a beaten wife are part of *halakhah* and rest on the husband's dominant position in marriage.

Contemporary Perspectives

For many years there was a myth that domestic violence among Jewish families was infrequent. However, there is much data demonstrating that domestic abuse is a significant and under-recognized behavior in Jewish communities in Israel and the Diaspora. Jewish women typically take twice as long to leave battering relationships than other women for fear that they will lose their children and because they are aware of the difficulties in obtaining a *get*, the Jewish divorce decree which is dependent on the abusive husband's consent. The major halakhic stance in the early 21st century continues to support the central role and authority of the husband and domestic abuse is not automatic grounds for Jewish divorce. Rabbinic courts tend to favor men who promise to reform their behavior (*shelom bayit*) and often force women to return to their vicious husbands or lose their rights to maintenance and property and custody of children. An abused woman whose husband refuses to give her a divorce is considered an **agunah*, a chained or anchored woman.

The problem of domestic violence in Israel surfaced in the media during the first Gulf War in 1991 when soldiers were not mobilized and husbands and wives (and their children) were forced to be together in sealed rooms. Beginning in the 1990s the rate of husbands murdering wives spiralled upwards in Israel and this trend has continued, with over 200 spousal murders reported by 2002.

Jewish Women International (JWI) is among contemporary organizations addressing the plight of victims of domestic abuse. It has developed resources for Jewish women and an information guide for rabbis. JWI coordinated international conferences on Jewish domestic violence (2003 and 2005) addressing this behavior in the U.S., Israel, South America, and the FSU. An inter-denominational group, the Jewish Institute Supporting an Abuse-Free Environment (J-SAFE), promotes a Jewish community in which all institutions and organizations conduct themselves responsibly and effectively in addressing the wrongs of domestic violence. Its goal is to promote universal standards for training and policies that prevent abuse, that ensure that victims are treated supportively and appropriately, and that perpetrators are held accountable, thereby promoting a safer environment for all children and adults. In recent years, some rabbinic authorities, shocked by the growing murder rate, have made initial efforts to address the situation of women in abusive marriages.

BIBLIOGRAPHY: D. Gardsbane (ed.), *Healing and Wholeness: A Resource Guide on Domestic Abuse in the Jewish Community* (2002); N. Graetz, *Silence is Deadly: Judaism Confronts Wifebeating* (1998); A. Grossman, *Pious and Rebellious: Jewish Women in Europe in the Middle Ages* (Heb., 2001; Eng., 2004); C.G. Kaufman, *Sins of Omission* (2003); M. Scarf, *Battered Jewish Wives: Case Studies in the Response to Rage* (1988); J.R. Spitzer and Julie Ringold, *When Love in Not Enough: Spousal Abuse in Rabbinic and Contemporary Judaism* (1985, 1991, 1995); M.A. Straus and Richard J. Gelles, "Societal Change and Change in Family Violence from 1975 to 1985 as Revealed by Two National Surveys," in: *Journal of Marriage and the Family,* 48 (1986), 465–479; A. Twerski, *The Shame Born of Silence: Spouse Abuse in the Jewish Community* (1996).

[Naomi Graetz (2nd ed.)]

DOMICILE.

Definitions

In contrast to "residence," which is the place of physical abode, domicile is that place where a man has his true, fixed, and permanent home and principal establishment and to which whenever he is absent he has the intention of returning. For example, in matters governed by local custom, a man is bound to follow the practices of his place of domicile (*lex loci domicilii*) if they conflict with those of the locality in which he happens to be residing (Pes. 51a; Maim. Yad, Yom Tov, 8:20; see also **minhag*). There is also a distinction between "resident" and "inhabitant," the latter term implying a more fixed and permanent abode than the former and imposing privileges and duties to which a mere resident would not be subject. Thus, one who uttered a vow not to derive any benefit from the "inhabitants" of a certain city (*anshei ha-ir, benei ha-ir*) is forbidden to do so from those who have resided there more than 12 months, but is permitted to derive benefit from anyone residing there less than that. If, however, his vow was not to derive any benefit from the "residents" of the city (*yoshevei ha-ir*), he is forbidden to do so from anyone who has lived there for more than 30 days (BB 8a; Maim. Yad, Nedarim, 9:17).

Intention to Establish Domicile

Intention in the matter of establishing domicile may be avowed, implied, or construed. Occasionally, these types are in conflict with one another, and authorities have disagreed as to the relative strength of each type. A famous case is that of the observance of the second day of a festival. Inhabitants of the Land of Israel keep one day; those of the Diaspora keep two (see *Festivals). The settled law is that people traveling between the Land of Israel and the Diaspora follow the practice of the place to which they have arrived if their avowed intention is to establish domicile there (Sh. Ar., OḤ 496:3, and commentaries). But the following geonic responsum illustrates how implied intention or circumstantial factors can modify the settled law:

African Jews who have married in the Land of Israel and reside there: If 12 months have as yet not elapsed since they took up residence, they are obligated to keep two days following their place of origin; for this have the rabbis (BB 7b) taught, "How long must one reside in a city in order to be considered as one of its inhabitants? – 12 months." If, however, 12 months have elapsed, then thereafter – even if their avowed intention is to return – they follow the practice of the inhabitants of Jerusalem until they actually return to their homes.

The foregoing refers to people going to the Land of Israel from Africa. As for people, however, who go to the Land of Israel from Babylonia which has two talmudic academies:

If their avowed intention is to return – even though many years have elapsed – they keep the more stringent practices of both localities. If, however, they do not have the avowed intention of returning, they follow the practices of the Land of Israel whether this will make for more stringent or for more lenient observance (*Oẓar ha-Ge'onim*, ed. by B.M. Lewin, 3, pt. 2 (1930), 72, Pes. 51, no. 175).

Domicile as a Source of Obligations

The Talmud has a series of rules according to which the length of residence in a place determines the extent to which one becomes obligated to participate in local activities and to perform communal duties. Thirty days' residence carries with it the obligation to contribute to the communal soup kitchen maintained for the poor (*tamḥui*). It also renders one subject to the rules of the apostate city (*Ir ha-niddaḥat; Sanh. 112a). Three months' residence carries with it the additional obligation to contribute to the general charity fund of the community; six months' to the fund which provided clothing for the poor; nine months' to the fund which covered the funeral expenses of the poor. Twelve months' residence changes one's status to that of inhabitant and subjects one to all communal expenses, taxes, and imposts; in this respect, the purchase of a home has the equivalent effect of 12 months' residence (BB 7b–8a; Maim. Yad, Mattenot Aniyyim, 9:12, Shekhenim, 6:5).

Domicile of a Married Woman

According to the tannaitic sources, the domicile of a married woman is established by her husband. She could, with a few specified exceptions calculated to avoid undue hardship for her, be compelled to follow him on pain of divorce and loss of alimony rights (*ketubbah*). Thus, if they have been living in the country he may not compel her to move to the city, and if they have been living in the city he may not compel her to move to the country, "for in certain respects living in the country is preferable and in other respects living in the city is preferable." Another one of the exceptions to the general rule is taking up residence in the Holy Land. If a woman insists upon emigrating to the Land of Israel or, in Israel, to

Jerusalem, and her husband is adamant in his refusal, a divorce must be granted, and she retains her rights to alimony (Ket. 110b; Maim. Yad, Ishut, 13:17–20).

Concerning the domicile established by a rabbinic legal fiction, for the purpose of doubling the distance one might be permitted to walk outside the city limits on the Sabbath, see *eruv (eruv teḥumin).

With regard to restrictions on the freedom to establish domicile in the medieval communities of Europe, see *ḥerem ha-yishuv.

[Aaron Kirschenbaum]

The Establishment of Domicile as a Factor in the Determination of Subordination to Communal Enactments in Matters of Civil Law

This issue arose in a question put to R. Isaac B. Sheshet (Spain-Algiers fourteenth century) in the context of an enactment passed in a particular town requiring that marriage ceremony be conducted exclusively in the presence of communal trustees and in the presence of ten of them; otherwise the money transacted for *kiddushin* would be expropriated and the marriage annulled. This enactment was intended to prevent clandestine/secret marriages (see *Marriage, *Hefker, *Takkanot ha-Kahal, *Aguna). Ribash was asked whether the enactment could also apply to those who had taken up residence in the city after its enactment. Ribash responded that "even those who came from outside the town to reside there are subject to the same law as the people of the city and must abide by their enactments, and it is if they explicitly agreed to accept all of the communal enactments upon their arrival in the town, provided that they have no intention to leave. And they are even permitted with respect to matters that were forbidden in their own town because of the local custom, for as long as they do not intend to return, and if not forbidden in the town in which they came to live…" (see *Conflict of Laws).

On the other hand, in matters relating to the collection of taxes, a number of rulings in the responsa literature indicate that the community has no authority to subject a member of the community to a tax that was first levied prior to his becoming a member of the community. For example, if the community borrowed a certain sum of money, or if a tax was imposed by the ruler of the town, even if not by way of an enactment (Resp. Rashba, III, no.412) According to Ribash, a new resident can only be required to pay previous debts of the town when the enactment had already been made prior to his arrival in the town and the new resident already had notice of the enactment.

The State of Israel

ESTABLISHMENT OF DOMICILE FOR DETERMINATION OF RABBINICAL COURT'S JURISDICTION. The question of establishing a person's permanent place of residence is of crucial importance in the State of Israel, with respect to the jurisdiction of the rabbinical court in matters of personal status. The Rabbinical Courts Jurisdiction (Marriage and Divorce) Law 5713 – 1953 provides that "matters of marriage and divorce of Jews in Israel, being citizens or residents of the State, shall be under the exclusive jurisdiction of the rabbinical courts" (sec. 1). On a number of occasions, the Israeli Supreme Court was required to determine whether a Jewish couple was domiciled in Israel, this being the precondition for the jurisdiction of the rabbinical court. The general criterion adopted in Israeli common law is the criterion of "the center of a person's life." Where a Jewish couple was married in Israel and their life centered in Israel, the Israeli rabbinical court has jurisdiction over them, even if the couple went to live abroad (see in detail in entry *Bet Din*).

The Place of Residence for Determining a Minor's Domicile for Purposes of the Hague Convention

The determination of domicile is also of decisive importance in cases of child abduction (see entry: *Abduction). The Hague Convention, which regulates matters of jurisdiction in cases of child abduction (for the contracting states), was enacted as binding legislation in the State of Israel (The Hague Convention Law Return of Abducted Children, 1991). The Hague Convention compels the Court in whose jurisdiction the abducted child was found to order the return of the child to the state from which he was removed, so that the case can be adjudicated by the court of that State. Under section 3 (a) of the Convention, a condition for the Convention's applicability is that the child was habitually resident in the State (from which he was removed) immediately before the removal or the retention of the child. The Israeli Supreme Court determined that as a rule the habitual residence of the child is the place in which he lives his daily life. However, the view was also expressed that, when the parents have traveled abroad for a temporary period, the duration of which having been determined in advance, their temporary place of residence abroad will not be regarded as their domicile, and by extension, will not be regarded as the child's domicile.

In FA 575/04 (Jerusalem District Court) the Court was required to determine a child's habitual place of residence in order to determine whether the case was one of abduction, and as such was governed by the provisions of the Hague Convention. The Court addressed a number of parameters indicating that the parents' permanent place of residence was Israel. Their stay abroad was temporary, its duration having been determined in advance, and the return to Israel was one of the preconditions for the trip abroad. The couple had not purchased an apartment abroad, and on the other hand, they owned an apartment in Israel. They visited Israel on a regular basis, and the husband was attempting to find work in anticipation of their return. However, in the Court's view (Judge M. Drori), the central and clinching argument for viewing *Israel* as the parent's permanent place of residence was the fact that the husband, who was religiously observant, did not observe the Second Day of Festivals ordinarily observed by Jews living outside Israel.

The Court adduced extensive halakhic material from the *posekim* who dealt with the prohibition on residents of the

Land of Israel who traveled abroad from performing work on the second day of the Festival, as distinct from actions performed in private, which are permitted to them (Maim., Yad, Hilkhot Yom Tov, 8.2; Sh. Ar. OḤ, 496.3, Magen Avraham, ad loc. 4). The Court also cited at length a responsum of R. David b. Zimra (*Resp Ridbaz*, 4: 73), who distinguishes between three categories of people traveling from the Land of Israel abroad: One who goes abroad exclusively for business purposes belongs to the category of "intending to return immediately" and is therefore required to conduct himself in accordance with the strict law of the place to which he came, but only in public; one who travels for business purposes in order to make a profit, or to engage in his livelihood or to learn Torah, belongs to the category of "intending to return at a later stage" and therefore is required to behave in accordance with the strict law of his place of origin and the strict law of his current location, so as not to trigger dispute; and one who changed his place of residence together with his wife and children, even though he intends (in the future) to return to settle in Israel, and who is not referred to as one who "intends to return," and is therefore required to conduct himself in all matters as one of the local residents. With respect to the final category, R. Yisrael Meir Radin (*Mishna Berura*, 496.13) explains that "one who leaves his place of residence with his wife and children for the purpose of trading and profiting, even though at the time of his departure he intended to return, is considered as one who does not have the intention of returning, for presumably, having moved his entire family to a new residence, he will not move again for as long as he is engaged in a profitable livelihood in his new place of residence."

Based on these comments and the fact that the husband concerned was both observant and knowledgeable, the Court presumed that in these kinds of matters he had conducted himself in accordance with, and in awareness of, the *halakhah*. When abroad, the husband had treated the Second Day of the Festival for exiles as though it was a regular weekday. The Court ruled that this indicated that he did not intend to settle in England, and had every intention of returning to Israel. In the Court's view this was conclusive evidence that the habitual residence of the husband – the appellant – was in Israel, and it was as though on each festival the husband had made a public declaration that his habitual residence was in Israel.

[Menachem Elon (2nd ed.)]

ADD. BIBLIOGRAPHY: M. Elon, *Ha-Mishpat ha-Ivri*, vol. 1 (1988), 577, 593, 607, 614, 620f., 625, 627f; idem, *Jewish Law*, vol. 2 (1994), 711, 733, 751, 760, 767, 776.

DOMIN, HILDE (Hilde Loewenstein; 1909–), German poet and writer. Domin was born in Cologne, Germany. She studied law and economics, sociology, and philosophy in Heidelberg, Cologne, and Berlin. Among her teachers were Karl Jaspers and Karl Mannheim. In October 1932 she immigrated to Rome together with her future husband, the art historian Erwin Walter Palm. In 1935 she received her doctoral degree in the field of political science in Florence and taught languages in Rome. After the pact between Hitler and Mussolini she escaped with her husband in 1939 to England. In 1940 she settled in the Dominican Republic, where she worked as a translator and architectural photographer. From 1947 to 1952 she taught German at the University of Santo Domingo. After her mother's death, in 1951, she adopted the pseudonym Domin, as a reminder of the Dominican Republic.

In 1954 she moved back to West Germany, and three years later her first poems appeared. From 1961 she worked as a writer. Along with poems, stories, and one novel she wrote literary-scientific essays and worked as a translator and editor.

Her works reflect the emotional worlds of an individual caught between escape, exile, and return, with all the doubts and complexities involved.

Among her works are the poetry collections *Nur eine Rose als Stuetze* (1959), *Rueckkehr der Schiffe* (1962), *Der Baum blueht trotzdem* (1999), the novel *Das Zweite Paradies* (1968), and the autobiographical *Von der Natur nicht vorgesehen: Autobiographie* (1974) and *Aber die Hoffnung: Autobiographisches aus und ueber Deutschland* (1982).

Domin won numerous prizes, including the Droste-Preis der Stadt Meersburg (1971), Rainer-Maria-Rilke-Preis fuer Lyrik (1976), Nelly-Sachs-Preis der Stadt Dortmund (1983), Literaturpreis der Konard-Adenauer-Stiftung (1995), and received the Grosses Bundesverdienstkreuz (1994).

BIBLIOGRAPHY: B. v. Wagenheim (ed.), *Heimkehr ins Wort: Materialien zu Hilde Domin* (1982); M. Braun, *Exil und Engagement* (1993); B. Lermen and B.M. Braun, *Hilde Domin* (1997), incl. bibl.; B. v. Wagenheim (ed.), *Vokabular der Erinnerung* (1998).

[Noam Zadoff (2nd ed.)]

DOMINIC, ALEXANDRU (Avram Adolf Reichman; 1889–1942), Romanian poet and playwright. Born in Bucharest to a middle-class family, Dominic completed the local German-Evangelical secondary school and doctoral studies in law (Brussels) and in literature (Paris). While a student in France he had ties to an anarchist group and published articles in French periodicals, one of them *La société nouvelle*, under pen names. In 1912 he returned to Bucharest, where his poems appeared in Romanian periodicals. In 1920 he published his first volumes of expressionist and social poems, *Revolte si crucificari* ("Revolts and Crucifixions"). Well received by critics, Dominic was nominated for a Nobel Prize by the French review *Esope, journal d'action intellectuelle* in the same year. In 1921 he published the expressionist play *Sonata umbrelor* ("Sonata of the Shadows"), dealing with the problem of the intellectual. This play was staged at the National Theater in Bucharest (1920) and in German translation at Neues Theater am Zoo, Berlin (1922). In 1927, Dominic published a new volume of poems, *Clopote peste adancuri* ("Bells above Depths"). In 1924–25, together with the Romanian writer Liviu Rebreanu, Dominic edited the review *Miscarea literara*. His poem *Israel* (1920) deals with the theme of Jewish suffering. Dominic also published verses in the Zionist review *Puntea de fildes* (1925). In 1938 he visited Palestine, where he decided to send his son. Dominic died in Bucharest. His widow, Bertha, immigrated to Israel, where she established a prize in his memory. Some of his poems were translated into Hebrew.

BIBLIOGRAPHY: S. Leibovici-Lais and A. Zahareanu (eds.), *A. Dominic, Me'ah Shanah le-Holadat ha-Meshorer* (1987); A. Mirodan, *Dictionar neconventional*, 2 (1997), 111–32; A.B. Yoffe, *Bisdot Zarim*, 184–7, 445.

[Lucian-Zeev Herscovici (2nd ed.)]

Major centers of Jewish settlement in the Dominican Republic.

DOMINICAN REPUBLIC, republic in the Caribbean islands comprising two-thirds of the island of Hispaniola. This region (Santo Domingo) has quite a convoluted history. By the treaty of Ryswich (1607) it was given to Spain, but the treaty of Basel (1793) gave it to France, and in 1814 it reverted to Spain. Haiti occupied it from 1822 to 1844 when it became independent; it was then occupied by Spain until 1865, when it became independent once and for all.

In the first part of the sixteenth century those in charge of colonization of the Spanish colonies, the Converso Bishop Juan Rodriguez de Fonseca and the secretaries of King Ferdinand, Lope de Conchilles and Miguel Perez de Almazan, applied a policy of sending *Converso colonists to Santo Domingo. Historians deduce that in that period Santo Domingo was practically in Converso hands.

From 1781 to 1785 Jews arrived from the destroyed Jewish community on the Dutch island of St. Eustatius. During the French occupation (1795) Jews from Curaçao, occupied by England, began to settle there and were joined by Jews from St. Thomas and Jamaica, all holding foreign citizenship. Jews also arrived from Haiti after the slave rebellion there.

Under the Haitian occupation a cemetery for foreigners was established and the first Jewish grave is located in it – that of Jacob Pardo, dated December 6, 1826. The Jews dispersed in various areas, including the capital Santo Domingo and Puerto Plata, Monte Christi, La Vega, and S. Pedro de Macoris. They dealt mainly with the export of tobacco, timber, and jewelry and the importation of general merchandise from Curaçao, St. Thomas, and Europe through the Sephardi community of Hamburg.

The local population saw the Jews as a progressive, positive, and patriotic element. This is best demonstrated by the famous response by the first Dominican president, Santana (Sept. 16, 1846), to an anti-Jewish petition instigated by the Spaniards in the city of La Vega.

Jews actively helped in the revolution against Spain in 1865, and the new independent government immediately thanked Rafael de Mordecai de Marchena and other Dutch subjects for their active support in the War of Independence.

The number of Jews living there in that period cannot be effectively evaluated, since most of them lived as Dutch, Danish, or British citizens. No organized community existed, and one of them – Rafael Namias Curiel – acted as cantor and performed marriages until 1900. The second-generation Sephardi Jews assimilated almost completely into the local population in a phenomenon that was called by the historian Ucko "the fusion between the Sephardics and the Dominicans."

President Gregorio La Peron made an official proposal in 1882 for the settling in the Dominican Republic of Jews suffering from pogroms in Russia. After limited public debate, however, the proposal was abandoned without further investigation.

At the *Evian Conference on refugees, convened by President Franklin Roosevelt in 1938, the Dominican Republic offered to accept for settlement up to 100,000 refugees. The Dominican Republic Settlement Association Inc. (DORSA) – sponsored by the *American Jewish Joint Distribution Committee (JDC) – acquired from President Trujillo 22,230 acres of land in Sosúa on the northern coast, and the American Jewish Joint Agricultural Corp. (Agro-Joint) – a subsidiary of JDC – contributed a large sum in subsidies for the project. The agreement, signed by DORSA and the Dominican Republic and unanimously approved by parliament, assured the immigrants freedom of religion and facilitated immigration by offering tax and customs exemptions. DORSA, in turn, promised a policy of selective immigration and financial support for the settlers.

Despite the optimism of the government and the Agro-Joint, basic difficulties precluded the ultimate success of the project. Wartime conditions made travel, especially from occupied countries, extremely difficult. The first immigrants did not arrive until mid-1940; by 1942 there were only 472 settlers; and by 1947, 705 persons had passed through the settlement. Although the original objective of the project had been agricultural development, few of the settlers were agriculturists or even inclined toward it. Of the 373 people left in Sosúa in July 1947, only 166 were engaged in agriculture. The rest worked as businessmen and artisans. It is estimated that under the colonization scheme some 5,000 visas were actually issued, thus helping many of the beneficiaries to escape the Holocaust; but most of them never reached the Dominican Republic. The census taken in 1950 indicated the presence of 463 Jews in the Dominican Republic. Today most of the inhabitants of Sosúa have assimilated into the local population.

Descendants of Jews reached the highest strata of Dominican society. Francisco Henriquez y Carvajal, son of a

Jewish father and Converso mother, took office as president of the republic in 1916. His brother, the famous writer Federico Henriquez y Carvajal, wrote *La Hija del Hebreo* ("The Daughter of the Hebrew") on the problematics of mixed marriages. The president's son, Pedro Henriquez Urena, became one of the major linguists of the Spanish language. His other son, Max Henriquez Urena, as Dominican ambassador to the UN, made the welcoming speech when Israel was admitted to the *United Nations in 1949. The well-known writer Haim Horacio Lopez-Penha wrote the anti-Nazi book *Los Paisanos de Jesus* ("Jesus' Fellow Countrymen"). The composer Enrique de Marchena culminated his career with the concerto suite "Hebraicum," inspired by his visit to Israel.

In 2004 some 250 Jews lived in the Dominican Republic, which had two synagogues – one in Santo Domingo, the other in Sosúa; an active community, Centro Israelita de la Republica Dominicana; a bimonthly magazine, *Shalom;* and a Sunday school.

BIBLIOGRAPHY: *Comunidades Judías de Latinoamérica* (1968); A. Tartakower, *Megillat ha-Hityashevut*, 2 (1959), 268f., 272; M. Wischnitzer, in: JSOS, 4:1 (1942), 50–58; J. Shatzky, *Comunidades Judías en Latinoamérica* (1952), 163–5; L. Schapiro, in: L. Finkelstein (ed.), *The Jewish People Past and Present*, 2 (1948), 88. **ADD. BIBLIOGRAPHY:** M. Arbell, *The Jewish Nation of the Caribbean* (1994); C.E.Deive, "Los Judios en Santo Domingo y America durante el siglo XVI," in: A. Lockward, ed., *Presencia Judia en Santo Domingo* (1994), 195–92; E. Ucko, *La Fusion de los Sefardies con los Dominicanos* (1944).

[Benjamin (Benno) Varon (Weiser) / Mordechai Arbell (2nd ed.)]

DOMINICANS, Roman Catholic religious order, whose official name is *Ordo Fratrum Praedicatorum*, the Order of Friar Preachers. Often referred to as "Jacobins," after their Saint-Jacques Monastery in Paris, they were also popularly known as *domini canes*, "the [watch-] dogs of the Lord" because of their leading role in the *Inquisition. Founded by Saint Dominic and sanctioned by Pope Honorius III in 1216, the order's first mission was preaching against Christian heresies in the south of France. From 1232, the Dominicans (along with the *Franciscans) were also in charge of the Inquisition, which was initially an institution directed only against the Christian heresies of the *Albigenses and the Waldenses. Because of their duties in these and other spheres, the activity of the Dominicans soon became largely directed against the Jews.

When Popes Gregory X in 1274 and Nicholas IV in 1288 and 1290 reissued the *Turbato corde* bull of Clement IV (1267), which had likened to heretics those converted Jews who had later returned to Judaism together with those who had assisted them in the process (see Papal *bulls), they entrusted the Dominican and Franciscan inquisitors with the prosecution of such persons. The Dominicans proceeded with these prosecutions in southern France from the close of the 13th century. In his *Practica inquisitionis*, an Inquisition textbook written in about 1323, the Dominican Bernard Guy, inquisitor in Toulouse, inserted lengthy passages dealing with the Jews. The interrogatory model which he proposes was above all intended to uncover the accomplices of the converted Jews who had reverted to Judaism. Without any doubt, the cruelest role in the imposition of Inquisition policies against converted Jews was played by the Dominican Tomás de *Torquemada, inquisitor-general in Spain until his death in 1498.

The Dominicans also played a predominant role in the proceedings against the Talmud (see Burning of *Talmud) and the *censorship of other Jewish books following the denunciation by Nicholas *Donin in 1239; after the confiscation of March 3, 1240, these books were collected by the Dominicans (as well as by the Franciscans). When at this point one bishop came to the defense of the Jews, the Dominican Thomas de Cantimpré accused him of having been corrupted by the Jews. Both in order to be able to understand such books themselves, and also to be the better prepared for their spoken and written missionary activities among the Jews, the Dominicans introduced the study of Hebrew from the middle of the 13th century, a development in which the Spanish Dominican *Raymond de Peñaforte played an important part. Raymond *Martini, another Spanish Dominican, held a chair in Hebrew until his death (shortly after 1284), but at first it was mainly converted Jews who directed these studies. At the Council of Vienna in 1312, the Spanish Dominican Raymond Lully elicited a general decision calling for the teaching of languages (Hebrew and Arabic) for missionary activities. However, after the meeting of their general chapter in Rome in 1571, the Dominican attitude toward the teaching of Hebrew grew more reserved. On the insistence of the apostate Pablo *Christiani and Raymond de Peñaforte, the compulsory attendance of the Jews at Dominican missionary sermons was decreed in 1263 (see also *Sermons to Jews). In 1278, Pope Nicholas III ordered the grand master of the Dominicans to make such sermons and their compulsory attendance general practice. The Dominicans obtained the consent of Edward I of England for the introduction of such sermons in 1279; and subsequently many Dominicans, especially Vicente *Ferrer, and Peter *Schwarz, made widespread use of forced sermons to the Jews. The Dominicans were also in the forefront in organizing public *disputations, beginning with the one in *Paris in 1240, to which the Jews were compelled to send delegates. The disputation of *Barcelona in 1263 was convened on the initiative of Raymond de Peñaforte and Pablo Christiani.

Anti-Jewish polemics occupy an important place in Dominican writings. Raymond Martini drew up the *Capistrum Judaeorum* and the *Pugio fidei christianae* (Paris 1621, 1651; Leipzig, 1687), written in both Hebrew and Latin. Pierre de Janua, Martini's assistant, who was also well versed in Hebrew, wrote an *Opus adversus Judaeorum errores accuratum*. Alfonsus *Bonihominis, a Spaniard who lived for many years in Paris (d. 1353), claimed to have translated the *Epistola Rabbi Samuelis* (printed 1480?) from Arabic; however, it is probable that he composed the work himself. Other Dominican anti-Jewish works were *In sectam hebraicam* by the Italian Gratiadei Aesculanus (d. 1341); *Liber contra Judaeos nomine Thalamoth* (mid-14th century) attributed to Pierre de Pennis; and *Capistrum Judaeorum* (before 1418) by the Italian Lauterius de Batineis (or Laurentius de Valdinis, or de Ubaldinis). Theobaldius of Saxony (first half of the 15th century), one of the participants at the Council of Constance, wrote a *Refutatio errorum Thalmud*. The Spaniard Joannes Lopez (or Lupus, d. 1464) collected several anti-Jewish sermons and arguments under the title *Opus eruditum contra superstitiones Judaeorum*. The German Peter Schwarz, who appears to have learned Hebrew in a Jewish school in Spain and had attacked the Jews during a public disputation in Ratisbon, was the author of *Tractatus contra perfidos Judaeos de conditionibus veri Messiae… ex textibus hebraicis* which includes various appendices in Hebrew and a "reply to several Jewish arguments." Later authors were the Catalonian Gaspar Fayol, who wrote *Tractatus contra Judaeos* (end of the 15th century); John Baptist Theatinus, who knew some Hebrew, author of *De Trinitate et cognitione Dei contra philosophos et Judaeos* (early 16th century); and the Spaniard Cyprianus Benetus (d. 1522), to whom is attributed *Aculeus contra Judaeos*. Augustus Justiniani, who lived in northern Italy during the first half of the 16th century, translated several biblical texts from Hebrew, as well as Maimonides' *Guide of the Perplexed*, and translated the New Testament into Hebrew; he also published Victor Porcheti's pamphlet *Adversus impios Hebraeos*. On a more everyday plane, Sixtus Medices, who was in Venice during the second half of the 16th century, attacked the activity of Jewish moneylenders in *De foenore Judaeorum*. Antoninus Stabili (d. 1583) published in Italy *Fascicolo delle vanità Judaiche diviso in giornate sedeci*. In the older tradition of Dominican Hebrew scholars was Franciscus Donatus of Rome (d. c. 1653), who demonstrated his sound knowledge of the language in several works on Hebrew accents and abbreviations and made various translations from Hebrew.

Anti-Jewish polemics continued in the 17th century; especially prolific was the Italian Petrus Pichius, author of: *De partu virginis Deiparae adversus Judaeos; Epistola a gli Hebrei d'Italia nella quale si dimostra la vanità della loro penitenza ed aspetatione del Messia; Trattato della passione del Messia contra gli Ebrei; Stolte dottrine degli Ebrei con la loro confutazione*. The Italian Tommaso Campanella (d. 1639), author of about 80 works of all kinds, compiled *Adversus astrologos Judaeos*; and the Frenchman Johannes of Sancta Maria (1604–1660), in addition to a Hebrew grammar and commentaries on some of the prophets in which he made wide use of Hebrew sources, published the polemic, *De futura legalium apud Judaeos observatia post eorum ad Christi fidem conversionem*. Josephus Maria Ciantes of Rome (d. 1670), who had studied Hebrew and rabbinic literature and in 1625 had been appointed by Pope Urban VIII to "instruct" the Jews, was the author of *De sanctissima Trinitate contra Judaeos* and *De Sanctissima Christi incarnatione contra Judaeos*; the Hebrew translation of Thomas Aquinas' *Summa* is also his work. The Dominicans in Cologne, under their prior Jacob van Hoogstraaten, played a prominent and hostile role in the *Reuchlin-*Pfefferkorn controversy (1509–20) over the destruction of Hebrew books. In 1664, the general of the Dominicans, Giovanni Battista de' Manni, ordered members of the order in Poland to preach from the pulpit against the *blood libel. Although the Dominican Order continues to include in its ranks a considerable number of converted Jews, it has nevertheless given up all organized missionary activities among the Jews. Of late, the Dominicans have made important contributions to biblical studies and on the Dead Sea Scrolls at the Ecole Biblique et Archéologique Francaise de Jérusalem. They have adopted a positive attitude toward the State of Israel, where they have several monasteries and churches in Jerusalem.

BIBLIOGRAPHY: A.M. Walz, *Compendium Historiae Ordinis Praedicatorum* (1948²), 278ff., 291, 509; B. Altaner, *Die Dominikanermission des 13. Jahrhunderts* (1924), 94ff.; W. Eckert, in: K. Thieme (ed.), *Kirche und Synagoge* (1968), 217ff.; P. Browe, *Die Judenmission im Mittelalter…* (1942), index. **ADD. BIBLIOGRAPHY:** DOMINICANS IN THE HOLY LAND: S.P. Colby, *Christianity in the Holy Land* (1969); E. Schiller, *Christians and Christianity in Eretz-Israel* (2002); *Directory of the Catholic Church in the Holy Land* (2005).

[Bernhard Blumenkranz]

°**DOMITIAN (Titus Flavius Domitianus)**, Roman emperor, 81–96 C.E. Son of *Vespasian and brother of *Titus, Domitian attempted to establish an absolute monarchy against the senate, and resumed an expansionist policy. A rabid opponent of Oriental cults, he combated Judaism and Christianity, the latter then being considered a Jewish sect by the Romans. The triumphal arch dedicated to Titus for his victory in Palestine was erected in his reign. In the year 85, coins were issued with the inscription *Iudea Capta* or *Iudea Devicta*. In 95 he had his cousin *Flavius Clemens sentenced to death and the latter's wife, Flavia Domitilla, exiled, after having ensured their conviction for atheism on account of their adherence to Judaism (or Christianity). He stringently enforced the prohibition against conversion to Judaism and is said to have ordered the execution of all persons claiming to be descendants of the House of David (Euseb., Hist. Eccl. 3:19; Dio Cass., Hist. 69:23, 2), but it seems that he prevented the execution of a number of descendants of David who had been brought to him (Euseb., *ibid.* 3:20; Tertullianus Apol. 5:5). Under Domitian the *Fiscus Judaicus* was very strictly collected (*acerbissime actus est*) by means of informers (Suetonius, Domit. 12). The fiscal tribunal considered the cases not only of those who lived in accordance with Jewish custom, but also those who tried to hide their origin. Suetonius (*ibid.*) himself relates that he was present when a 90-year-old man was subjected to an examination in public, in order to see if he was circumcised (cf. Martial 7:55; 7:82). It was perhaps at that time that R. *Gamaliel went to Rome, together with three other rabbis, in the hope of being able to avert further persecutions.

BIBLIOGRAPHY: Schuerer, Hist, 289–300; A. Darmesteter, in: REJ, 1 (1880), 36–41; Weynand, in: Pauly-Wissowa, 12 (1909), 2541–96; P.E. Arias, *Domiziano* (1945); E.M. Smallwood, in: *Classical Philology*, 51 (1956), 1ff.; Halevy, Dorot, 1 (1923), 339ff.; R. Syme, in: *Journal of Roman Studies*, 20 (1930), 55–70; Alon, Toledot, 1, index; Baron, Social², index; H. Mantel, *Studies in the History of the Sanhedrin* (1962).

[Alfredo Mordechai Rabello]

DOMNINUS OF LARISSA (Laodicea in Syria; c. 415–485), philosopher and mathematician. He was a pupil of Syrian and a contemporary of Proclus Diadochus whose pupil Marinus mentions him frequently in his biography of Proclus. A neoplatonist of the Athenian school, he turned at times to the teachings of the Alexandrian school. Thus he criticized the metaphysical speculations of Syrian and Proclus, for which Damascius accused him of superficiality and of corrupting Platonic philosophy. Proclus is said to have directed against Domninus a work entitled "Restitution of Plato's Teaching." Damascius takes Domninus to task for having transgressed the prohibition against eating the meat of pigs when he visited the temple of Asclepius in order to effect the cure of a malady. On the other hand, Damascius praises Domninus as a mathematician. Domninus was also interested in problems of physical astronomy, such as the nature of comets, which he attempted to explain. Two of Domninus' mathematical works have been preserved: a mathematical handbook entitled ἐνχειρίδιον ἀριθμητικῆς εἰσαγωγῆς (in J. Boissonade (ed.), *Anecdota Graeca*, 4 (Paris, c. 1832), 413–29), and a treatise (ed. by C.E. Ruelle in *Revue de Philologie* (1883), 82ff., with French translation and a short commentary). In the *Encheiridion* Domninus mentions his intention to write a *Principle of Arithmetic*, but nothing further is known about this work. Domninus had a pupil Gesius, identical with Jasius, often cited by Arabic writers.

BIBLIOGRAPHY: S. Krauss, in: JQR, 7 (1894/95), 270; Pauly-Wissowa, 9 (1903), 1521; *Der kleine Pauly*, 2 (1967), 135ff.

DOMUS CONVERSORUM, home for converted Jews in London, established in 1232 by Henry III in New Street (now Chancery Lane). It could accommodate about 40 persons and paid pensions to others who lived outside. The home was governed by a warden and later a subwarden or presbyter, assisted by a chaplain. In 1280 Edward I devoted to its upkeep half of the property of converts, which legally escheated to the Crown, and for a period of seven years also the proceeds of the Jewish poll tax. From its foundation up to 1290 the total number of inmates and dependents was approximately 100. On the expulsion of the Jews from England in that year, there were as many as 80 at one time. Thereafter, its importance declined. However, it was hardly ever empty. It was continually resorted to by converts from France, Germany, Flanders, Italy, Spain, Portugal, or the Barbary States. From 1390 to the beginning of the 17th century, 38 men and ten women figure in its records. The last reference to an inmate appears in 1609, though for another 150 years converts from Judaism sometimes received crown pensions. The office of keeper was ultimately combined with the judicial office of Master of the Rolls. The last legal relic of the institution was abolished in 1891.

BIBLIOGRAPHY: Martin, in: JHSET, 1 (1893–94), 15–24; Adler, *ibid.*, 4 (1899–1901), 16–75; idem, *Jews of Medieval England* (1939), 277–379; Public Record Office, *Exhibition of Records (Jews in England)* (1957), 9–14.

[Cecil Roth]

DONALDA, PAULINE (1882–1970), Canadian soprano, teacher, administrator. Donalda was born Pauline Lightstone in Montreal into a Jewishly active East European immigrant home. As a child she attracted attention for the quality of her voice and studied music on scholarship at the Royal Victoria College. In 1902 she went to Paris on a grant from Donald Smith (Lord Strathcona), after whom she adopted the professional surname of Donalda. She made her London debut at Covent Garden in 1905 singing *Micaela* under the direction of Andre Messager, her Canadian debut in 1906 singing with her husband (Paul Seveilhac) in the Montreal Arena, and her New York debut later that same year in *Faust*. In the spring of 1910 Donalda opened the Covent Garden season and returned in 1912 singing in both *Les Huguenots* and *I Pagliacci*, again with her husband. She was about to leave Canada for a European tour when World War I broke out. She remained in Canada, often giving benefit concerts in support of the war effort. In 1917 she returned to Paris, where she sang in Balfe's *Le Talisman*, sharing the stage with her new husband, Mischa Leon (b. Haurowitz).

In 1922 Donalda left the stage to devote her life to teaching, opening a studio in Paris. She returned to Montreal in 1937, where she opened a studio, and in 1942 founded the Opera Guild, the company she directed until 1969. During her relatively short performing career, Donalda was recognized for the purity of her voice and for her musicality, fine diction, and powerful stage presence. She is remembered for the unfailing energy with which she promoted opera in Montreal and encouraged talented young Canadian singers. Donalda also was very active in support of Jewish music in Montreal and the study of music at the Hebrew University of Jerusalem.

[Joel Greenberg (2nd ed.)]

DONATH, ADOLPH (1876–1937), Austrian poet and art historian. Donath was born in Kremsier (Moravia) and, after studying law and philosophy at Vienna, began composing poetry on Jewish themes. The poems were published in the following year under the title *Tage und Naechte*, with a laudatory introduction by Georg *Brandes. Donath's early *Judenlieder* (1895) were set to music by Béla Nemes (1899, reprinted 1920). The poems in *Mensch und Liebe* (1901) bewailed the fate of the Jewish people without a homeland. From 1900 to 1904, Donath contributed regularly to the Viennese *Neue Freie Presse* and in 1904 he edited a *Festschrift* of Austrian poetry dedicated to poet Detlev von Liliencrons. In 1903, some of his poetry was included alongside those of Richard *Beer-Hofmann, Martin *Buber, and Stefan *Zweig in an anthology of Jewish poetry, entitled *Junge Harfen. Eine Sammlung jungjüdischer Gedichte*. In 1905 he moved to Berlin, where he devoted his writings mainly to art criticism, as well as the technique and psychology of art collecting. In 1910 he founded a bi-weekly art journal, *Der Kunstwanderer*, and from 1921 to 1925 edited the *Jahrbuch fuer Kunstsammler*; his book *Judenlieder* was published in 1920 in Vienna. After the advent of Nazism Donath moved to Prague, where he continued to write on art; his last book, *Wie die Kunstfaelscher arbeiten*, was published in 1937.

BIBLIOGRAPHY: Winninger, Biogr, 2 (1927), 66–67. **ADD. BIBLIOGRAPHY:** D. Bensimon, *Adolph Donath: parcours d'un intellectuel juif germanophobe: Vienne, Berlin, Prague* (2000); idem, *Adolph Donath. Ein juedischer Kunstwanderer in Wien, Berlin und Prag*, tr. C. Tudyka (2001).

[Sol Liptzin / Lisa Silverman (2nd ed.)]

DONATH, EDUARD (1848–1932), Austrian chemist. Donath was born in Wsetin, Moravia, and studied in Vienna. In 1876 he became a Christian. From 1888 he was professor of chemical technology and analysis at the Deutsche Technische Hochschule in Bruenn. Donath was a technologist, analyst, organic and inorganic chemist, geologist, and botanist. In particular, he worked on coal, metals, building materials, glass, water, rubber, dyestuffs, and the chemistry of food. His books include *Monographie der Alkohol-Gaehrung als Einleitung in das Stadium der Gaerungstechnik* (1874), *Die Pruefung der Schmiermaterialen* with K. Pollak (1879), *Neuerungen in der Chemie des Kohlenstoffes und seiner anorganischen Verbindungen* (1899), and *Das Wollfett…* with B.M. Margosches (1901). Donath was active in the development of technical universities at Brunswick, Vienna, Prague, and in the foundation of the Verein der Oesterreichischen Chemiker.

[Samuel Aaron Miller]

DONATH, LUDWIG (1900–1967), U.S. stage and screen actor. Born in Vienna, Donath became well known in pre-Hitler Germany and Austria in supporting roles. Later he was active in the anti-Nazi underground. He fled to the U.S. in 1940. In Hollywood, his mid-European accent typed him for Nazi roles, notably as the Fuehrer in *The Strange Death of Adolf Hitler* (1943). His talent soon brought him other parts: as Al Jolson's father in *The Jolson Story* (1947) and the psychiatrist in the Broadway success, *A Far Country* (1961).

DONATI, ANGELO (1885–1960), Resistance activist of the Holocaust period. Donati was born into a well-known Jewish family in Modena, Italy. After World War I he settled in Paris, where he created the Banco Italo-Francese di Credito while remaining an Italian citizen. In 1931 he brought *Jabotinsky together with the Italian government to open a naval school for *Betar in Civitavecchia. After the Germans occupied northern France in 1940, he found refuge in Nice, which was occupied by the Italians in November 1942. In Nice, he volunteered to help local Jewish organizations and eventually, in cooperation with the Roman Catholic priest Padre Maria Benedetto (Father *Marie Benoît), became active in rescuing Jews. Italian Police Inspector Guido Lo Spinoso, Italian commissioner for Jewish affairs, appointed Donati as his councilor. In turn, Donati introduced Padre Benedetto to Lo Spinoso in 1943 to persuade him to endorse a plan to rescue 30,000 Jews in Nice and the region in the event of a German occupation of the Italian-occupied zone. Padre Benedetto obtained an audience in Rome with Pope *Pius XII on July 16, 1943, in which he explained the plan to bring those Jews to northern Italy. After the fall of Mussolini on July 25, 1943, Donati negotiated with senior officials of the Italian Foreign Ministry and with the representatives of Great Britain and the United States at the Vatican in an attempt to transfer 30,000 Jews from France and another 20,000 from Italy to North Africa. The Italian government was ready to allocate four passenger ships, but the approval of Great Britain and the United States did not come. Though Italy's surrender in September 1943 frustrated these efforts, thousands of Jews managed to cross into Italy with the help of Italian authorities, and many were thus saved. Donati himself escaped in 1943 to Switzerland, where he continued rescue and assistance operations for Jews. He returned to Paris after the liberation in 1945, and was appointed as representative of the Italian Red Cross as well as ambassador of the small state of San Marino. He died in Paris. On April 25, 2004, Carlo Azeglio Ciampi, president of the Italian Republic, awarded Donati a posthumous Gold Medal of Civic Merit, referring to his "noble and enlightening example of eminent civic qualities."

BIBLIOGRAPHY: M. Benedetto, in: *Israel*, 3 (1961), 46; L. Poliakov and J. Sabille, *Jews under the Italian Occupation* (1955); M. Kahn-Woloch, *De l'oasis italienne au lieu du crime des Allemands* (2004); D. Carpi, *Between Mussolini and Hitler: The Jews and the Italian Authorities in France and Tunisia* (1994); O. Tarcali, *Retour à Erfurt, 1935–1945: Récit d'une jeunesse éclatée* (2001).

[Daniel Carpi / Sergio Itzhak Minerbi (2nd ed.)]

DONATI, ENRICO (1909–), Italian surrealist and abstract painter. He was born in Milan, and studied piano and composition before becoming a commercial artist and later a painter. In 1934 he moved to Paris, and subsequently to New York. Donati's art is largely inspired by geological phenomena. A collector of strange gems and ores, his paintings reflect their shifting, transparent colors. In 1949 he found a smooth, small stone on the beach at Dover in England. On breaking it open, he saw it contained a perfect fossil. From that time he became preoccupied with the theme of fossilization. At first he painted "moonscapes," depicting imaginary views down the center of a fossil, and then made a series of paintings depicting the surface of a fossilized plant or rock. Later he painted new themes, suggestive of immemorial antiquity: human imprints in sand and ancient inscriptions on cylinder seals and tablets.

BIBLIOGRAPHY: P. Selz, *Enrico Donati* (1965).

DONATI, LAZZARO (1926–1977), Italian painter, nephew of Angelo *Donati. He was born and lived in Florence. His painting is representational, but not literal. He painted on wood in thin, wet glazes and his favorite subjects were portraits of women, still lifes, city scenes, and landscapes. Donati's work is imbued with a purity of color and an atmosphere of poetic sensuality.

DONEN, STANLEY (1924–), U.S. film director. Born in Columbia, South Carolina, Donen trained as a dancer and while still in his teens began working with Gene Kelly on Broadway. He went with Kelly to Hollywood and joined MGM, where he worked closely with producer Arthur Freed. Donen's inventive choreography and directorial skills helped revitalize the musical during the 1940s and 1950s. For example, his filming of Fred Astaire dancing on the walls and ceiling of his London hotel room in *Royal Wedding* (1951) has become legendary. Donen directed some of the most successful and best-regarded musicals of the time, including *On the Town* (1949), *Singin' in the Rain* (1952), *Seven Brides for Seven Brothers* (1954), *It's Always Fair Weather* (1955), *Love Is Better than Ever* (1956), *Funny Face* (1957), *The Pajama Game* (1957), *Damn Yankees!* (1958), *The Little Prince* (1974), and *Movie Movie* (1978).

Donen also directed sophisticated comedies and thrillers, such as *Kiss Them for Me* (1957), *Indiscreet* (1958), *Once More, with Feeling* (1960), *Surprise Package* (1960), *The Grass Is Greener* (1960), *Charade* (1963), *Arabesque* (1966), *Two for the Road* (1967), *Bedazzled* (1967), *Staircase* (1969), *Lucky Lady* (1975), *Saturn 3* (1980), and *Blame It on Rio* (1984). In 1985 Donen directed the TV series *Moonlighting*, and in 1999 he directed the TV drama *Love Letters*, based on the play by A.R. Gurney.

Among his many honors, Donen has received the Career Achievement Award from the Los Angeles Film Critics Association (1989); a Lifetime Achievement Award from the Academy Awards "in appreciation of a body of work marked by grace, elegance, wit, and visual innovation" (1998); the Akira Kurasawa Award at the San Francisco International Film Festival (1995); the Opus Award from the ASCAP Film and TV Awards (2000); and the Career Golden Lion at the Venice Film Festival (2004).

BIBLIOGRAPHY: S.M. Silverman, *Dancing on the Ceiling: Stanley Donen and His Movies* (1996); J.A. Casper, *Stanley Donen* (1983).

[Ruth Beloff (2nd ed.)]

DONETSK (until 1924 **Yuzovka**, and until 1961 **Stalino**), industrial city in the Eastern Ukraine, established in 1869–70 when an iron mill and coal mines were opened. The Jewish population numbered 3,168 in 1897 (11.5% of the total). They were occupied as petty traders and artisans. In 1887 a magnificent synagogue was built, a *talmud torah* opened, and charity organizations were established. In 1887 the authorities prevented a pogrom against Jews and Englishmen, but during a pogrom which lasted for three days from October 20, 1905, many Jews were killed and wounded and synagogues and Jewish houses were destroyed. In 1910 there were three synagogues and five Jewish private schools. Zionism was active and a delegate was sent to the Sixth Zionist Congress. During World War I many refugees arrived and were helped by a local Jewish committee. Between the wars the general population grew by 400% and the Jewish population doubled. There were 11,300 Jews living in the town in 1926 (10.6% of the total population). In 1922 most of the Jews were artisans and were dominant in tailoring and hide production. In the second half of the 1920s there were 300 Jewish workers (among 12,000) in the big steel mill, 30 of them professionals. There were several hundred young Jews among the 4,000 workers employed in the construction of new steel mills. There was one Yiddish school with 320 pupils in Donetsk, and in 1935 it had six Yiddish and five Russian classes. In 1939 the Jews numbered 24,991 (total population 466,268). At the beginning of the German-Soviet war thousands of Jews were evacuated with their families by their factories or organizations, such as about 1,500 Jews employed at the Stalino Works who left with their families for the Urals. The town was occupied by the Germans from October 20, 1941, to September 8, 1943. A large ghetto was set up and its inhabitants were kept without food or medical aid, with hundreds dying every day. In December *Einzatzcommando* 6 murdered several hundred Jews. In April 1942 the liquidation of the ghetto commenced. The Germans took the Jews to the abandoned Maria mine and threw most of them down the shafts alive. They also used gas vans, throwing the bodies into the mine. Some 15,000 Jews were murdered there. According to the 1959 census, the Jewish population numbered 21,000 (3% of the total). There was a synagogue, a rabbi, and poultry slaughtering until 1959, when the synagogue was closed down during High Holiday services. In 1963 the militia clamped down on *minyanim* and confiscated religious articles, returning only prayer shawls. In 1970 the estimated Jewish population was 40,000. Many immigrated to Israel and the West in the 1990s but Jewish life was revived, with Pinchas Vyshedsky as chief rabbi from 1995 and a full range of religious, educational, and cultural services offered to the community.

BIBLIOGRAPHY: *Eynikeyt* (March 3, 1945), 2; S. Schwarz, *The Jews in the Soviet Union* (1951), index.

[Shmuel Spector (2nd ed.)]

DONIGER (O'FLAHERTY), WENDY (1940–), U.S. scholar of the history of religion. Born in New York City, educated at Radcliffe College (B.A., 1962), Harvard (M.A., 1963; Ph.D., 1968) and Oxford (D.Phil., 1973), Doniger taught at Harvard, the School of Oriental and African Studies of the University of London (1968–75), the University of California, Berkeley (1975–77), and the University of Chicago (from 1978), where from 1986 she was Mircea Eliade Distinguished Service Professor of the History of Religions at the Divinity School. She also held an appointment in the Department of South Asian Languages and Civilizations and was a member of the university's Committees on Social Thought and the Ancient Mediterranean World. In addition she was the director of the university's Martin Marty Center.

Doniger's work focuses primarily on the comparative historical study of religious mythology and its social and cultural meanings, with particular reference to gender relations, and on the history and culture of Hinduism, on which she is acknowledged to be among the greatest contemporary authorities. Her most important works include *Women, Androgynes, and Other Mythical Beasts* (1980), *Dreams, Illusions, and Other Realities* (1984), *Tales of Sex and Violence: Folklore, Sacrifice and Danger in the Jaimaniya Brahmana* (1985), *Other People's Myths: The Cave of Echoes* (1988), *The Implied Spider: Politics and Theology in Myth* (1998), *Splitting the Difference: Gender and Myth in Ancient Greece and India* (1999), and *The Bedtrick: Tales of Sex and Masquerade* (2000). She edited a number of important collections, including *Purana Perennis: Reciprocity and Transformation in Hindu and Jaina Texts* (1993), *Off With Her Head! The Denial of Woment's Identity in Myth, Religion, and Culture* (1995, with Howard Eilberg-Schwartz), and *Myth and Method* (1996, with Laurie L. Patton), and also published translations of culturally significant texts, including *The Rig Veda: An Anthology* (1981), the *Oresteia* (1989), and the *Kamasutra* (2002, with Sudhir Kakar), as well as *Mythologies* (1991), a translation of Yves Bonnefoy's landmark *Dictionnaire des Mythologies.*

[Drew Silver (2nd ed.)]

DONIN, HAYIM HALEVY (1928–1983), U.S. Orthodox rabbi and author. Donin was born Herman Dolnansky in New York City, legally changing his name in 1955. He earned his B.A. from Yeshiva University in 1948; his ordination from Yeshiva University in 1951; his M.A. from Columbia University in 1952; and his Ph.D. from Wayne State University in 1966. He served as rabbi of Congregation Kesher Israel in West Chester, Pennsylvania (1951–53), where he was also counselor of the B'nai B'rith Hillel Foundation at West Chester State Teachers College. In 1953, he became rabbi of Congregation B'nai David in Southfield, Michigan, where he remained until he immigrated to Israel in 1973.

Donin was Adjunct Professor of Judaic Studies at the University of Detroit (1969–73) and co-founder (with James Gordon) and first president of Akiva Hebrew Day School (1964), the first modern Orthodox day school in metropolitan Detroit. (Donin had previously started the Hebrew Academy of Oak Park, the forerunner of Yeshivat Akiva.) Donin also served as vice president of the Jewish Community Council of Detroit and chairman of the Board of License for Hebrew teachers in the Detroit area, and was a member of the Michigan Governor's Ethical and Moral Panel (1966–68). In 1961, he participated in the White House Conference on Aging, as Chairman of the Social Actions Commission of the Rabbinical Council of America, on whose National Executive Board he subsequently served (1967–8).

After publishing *Beyond Thyself* (1965), Donin wrote a highly acclaimed series of books on practicing Judaism from the Orthodox perspective: *To Be A Jew: A Guide to Jewish Observance in Contemporary Life* (1972); *To Raise a Jewish Child: A Guide for Parents* (1977); and *To Pray as a Jew: A Guide to the Prayer Book and Synagogue Service* (1980). Following the success of *To Be a Jew*, which was translated into seven languages, Donin moved to Jerusalem to write full-time, along with lecturing at Bar-Ilan University in Ramat Gan (1974–76). He was also one of the most popular teachers of conversion classes for non-Israelis sponsored jointly by the Rabbinical Council of America and the Chief Rabbinate of Israel. In 1999, Donin, who had already received Yeshiva University's Torah U'Mada Award, was honored posthumously by Yeshiva University with the Dr. Samuel Belkin Award for Excellence in Religion and Religious Education.

[Bezalel Gordon (2nd ed.)]

DONIN, NICHOLAS (13th century), apostate to Christianity; of La Rochelle. A pupil of R. *Jehiel b. Joseph of Paris, whose yeshivah he attended, he was excommunicated by his teacher for his heretical (Karaite?) ideas and repudiation of the Oral Law. Turning apostate and informer, he joined the *Franciscan Order, seeking revenge on his former coreligionists. Along with other converts, Donin compiled a list of 35 accusations against the Talmud – an indictment based on charges that the Talmud teaches that the Oral Law is superior to the Written Law, and that it is full of gross anthropomorphisms, obscenities, and blasphemies against Jesus, Mary, and Christianity. Donin was the main instigator of the famous disputation of Paris (1240), which in reality was a trial of the Talmud, himself appearing as the accuser with four rabbis called to be the defendants. Only two of them were given the opportunity to defend the Talmud: R. Jehiel and R. Judah b. David of Melun. As a result of the disputation the Talmud was condemned to be burned; 24 cart loads of talmudic works were burned in Paris in 1242. Donin was also said to be responsible for the spread of the *blood libel, although this accusation was not raised during the disputation. He is, however, not identical with the convert who instigated massacres of the Jews of *Anjou, *Poitou, and *Brittany in the year 1236. Although Donin continued his anti-Jewish activities for a long period, he was basically a rationalist who never became a good Christian. His name was mentioned in 1287 when he was condemned by the general of the Franciscans for a pamphlet attacking the order, which he wrote in 1279.

BIBLIOGRAPHY: M. Braude, *Conscience on Trial* (1952), 33–68; S. Grayzel, *Church and the Jews in the XIII Century* (1966^2), 29–32, 238–41, 276–7, 339–40; Baron, $Social^2$, 9 (1965), 80ff., 278; J.M. Rosenthal, in: JQR, 47 (1956/57), 58–76, 145–69; Dinur, Golah, 2 pt. 2 (1966^2), 521–34.

[Judah M. Rosenthal]

DONNOLO, SHABBETAI (913–c. 982), Italian physician and writer on medicine. He was born in Oria, Italy. The name Donnolo is Greek in origin but is common among Jews in its Arabic form "Dunash." Such details of his life as are known have come from an autobiographical sketch in the preface to his book *Sefer Ḥakhmoni*, a commentary on the Sefer *Yeẓirah. At the age of 12 he was captured by Saracen raiders, but was ransomed by relatives in Taranto and remained in southern Italy. Donnolo studied medicine under teachers who were acquainted with pharmacy, medicine, astronomy, and astrology.

He was well versed in the Talmud, and some geonic literature, knew Hebrew, Greek, Latin, and colloquial Italian, and acquired, copied and studied Greek and Latin medical manuscripts. He traveled a great deal, presumably visiting Salerno, but it appears that he never left Italy, for no mention of other countries is made in his autobiographical writings. There are erroneous references to Donnolo's having visited Modena in Lombardy, as he practiced as a physician and teacher of medicine in southern Italy only. *Rashi's reference to Donnolo residing in Lombardy is due to the fact that southern Italy was at that time also called Lombardy. In *Sefer ha-Mirkaḥot* ("Book of Remedies") Donnolo mentions the village of Martis near Russano, in Calabria.

In keeping with the practice of medieval Europe, Donnolo was both a pharmacist and a physician. He appears to have been an independent thinker and his works are neither translations nor copies, but the collected experience of 40 years of medical practice. Throughout his commentaries he stressed the importance of Hebrew writings and spread the knowledge of them. Donnolo was acquainted with the writings of *Asaph ha-Rofe. Many common features and identical Hebrew expressions are to be found in the works of the latter and Donnolo's "Book of Remedies." It is uncertain if Donnolo knew Arabic, even though the Saracens were then in Sicily. What is evident is that he was not acquainted with Arab medicine, as there is no reference to it in any of his writings. Donnolo's Hebrew is difficult. His terminology is Greek, Latin, and colloquial Italian. His use of Hebrew terms from the Bible and Talmud is rare and of Arabic rarer still, except when these terms already appear in the Talmud, the geonic writings, or the books of Asaph or else designate commodities imported from Arabia. Donnolo's statement in his commentary on the *Sefer Yeẓirah* that "you can foretell the future of the person from the lines and appearance of his face" indicates that he drew material from the same sources as *Hai Gaon. The parallelism of physiognomies and astrology is based on Donnolo's idea that the human body is an image of the macrocosm. As far as is known, Donnolo was the first person in Christian Europe to write on medicine in Hebrew. Apart from Asaph's book on medicine – which was not written in Europe – the "Book of Remedies" is probably the first Hebrew medical work. It has added importance in that it was probably the first serious medical book written in Italy after the fall of Rome. Donnolo wrote at the crossroads of the Greco-Latin and Arab cultures, and his works show that the Greek medicine of his time had not yet been affected by its Arab counterpart, despite the fact that the Salerno School (founded probably in Donnolo's time) is said to have taught in Hebrew, Latin, and Arabic. Donnolo was not a prolific writer, but the works he left helped to spread the Hebrew language and promote science. His works include the following: *Sefer ha-Mirkaḥot* ("Book of Remedies") – published by Steinschneider in Virchow's Archive in 1867 and republished in a more complete edition by Muntner in Jerusalem in 1950; *Sefer Ḥakhmoni* (1880); *Pizmon* – a ritual poem in primitive verse; *Sefer ha-Mazzalot* ("Book of Constellations") of which only a few sentences have survived; *Antidotarium* (in Ms.). Although his name does not appear on this work, Donnolo himself refers to it in the "Book of Remedies." In his commentary on the *Sefer Yeẓirah* he mentions another book on anatomy and physiology. Although the inscription *Sefer ha-Yakar* ("The Precious Book") appears on the title page of the "Book of Remedies" it would appear that this name was generic and included both the *Antidotarium* and a work on fevers. In any case it is followed by another more practical inscription: "The Book of Drugs, Liquids, Powders, Bandages, Applications and Ointments to rub on the Skin." It includes more than 100 simple remedies and the method of compounding them. The book deals with medical preparations, pharmacy, scents, and the use of honey and wax as auxiliaries and of balsams (resins) as preservative substances. All Donnolo's remedies derive from the vegetable world. The "Book of Remedies" is not, as Steinschneider believed, a fragment, but is both an independent book and at the same time an integral part of his work. The Donnolo Hospital in Jaffa bears his name.

[Suessmann Muntner]

Donnolo's Theology

Though there is no direct evidence that Donnolo knew *Saadiah Gaon's works, there are some close parallels between the theology of Donnolo and that of Saadiah who was his contemporary. Donnolo's theology is expressed in two of the three parts of his *Sefer Ḥakhmoni*, in his treatise on the verse "God created man in His image," and in his interpretation of the *Sefer Yeẓirah*. Donnolo's aim was to remove anthropomorphic elements in the concept of God by reinterpretation of the biblical verses which may give rise to such concepts; the same aim guided Saadiah in his *Emunot ve-De'ot*, though Donnolo's treatment of the subject is less systematic and conclusive. Donnolo, however, made use of his scientific knowledge while interpreting the anthropomorphic elements in the Bible and offering his own conclusions. Donnolo's thesis was that a verse which stresses, or appears to stress, the similarity between God Himself and man in fact refers to the relationship between man and the created world. Thus he introduced into Jewish thought the idea of man's being the microcosm in contrast to the created world, which is the macrocosm. Using all his scientific knowledge, Donnolo tried to prove that everything in man corresponds to some phenomenon in the world. Man's two eyes, for instance, correspond to the sun and the moon, and man's hair to the grass and forests which cover the earth. He gives a detailed study of the functions of the various parts of man's body, and then equates them with the function of the various powers and elements in the world. Man, therefore, was not created in the image of God, but in the image of God's creation.

God, according to Donnolo, cannot be seen, because He has no form. Therefore, some explanation has to be given to the phenomenon of prophecy and the various biblical passages describing the appearance of God to man. Though probably unaware of Saadiah's theology, Donnolo offered the same answer to this question as Saadiah had: God did not appear to the prophets, but His glory (*kavod*) did. Moreover, the *kavod*, according to Donnolo, appeared in various forms to various people, so as to prevent them from believing that God Himself has a human form. Donnolo attempted to give a scientific explanation of the creation of the world in the course of his interpretation of *Sefer Yeẓirah*, one of the earliest interpretations of this work. Subsequent interpreters, mainly the *Ḥasidei Ashkenaz, but to some extent the kabbalists as well, used Donnolo's views while constructing their own concept of the process of creation.

[Joseph Dan]

BIBLIOGRAPHY: D. Castelli (ed.), *Il commento di Sabbetai Donnolo sul Libro della creazione* (1880); H. Friedenwald, *Jews and Medicine* (1944), 148–52, 171–2, 223–4; Roth, Dark Ages, index; A. Geiger, *Melo Chofnajim* (1840), 29–33, 95–99; Muntner, in: *Atti del XIV Congresso internazionale di Storia della Medicina. Roma-Salerno 1954*, 2 (1956), 1100; idem, in: *Actes du VIIème Congrès International d'Histoire des Sciences. Jerusalem 1953* (1953); idem, in: RHMH, 32 (1956), 155–62; idem, in *Harofé Haivri*, 13 (1946), 86–97; idem, *Rabbi Shabbetai Donnolo* (Heb., 1949); G. Nebbia, *Donnolo, Medico e Sapiente Ebreo di Oria* (1963); Steinschneider, in: *Virchows Archive… praktische Medizin*, 38 (1867), 65–91; 40 (1867), 80–124; 42 (1868), 51–112.

DONSKOY, MARK SEMENOVICH (1901–1981), Soviet film director. Born in Odessa, he began working in films in 1926. Most of his films were made from his own scenarios. He became famous with *Pesnya o schast'e* ("Song of Happiness," 1934). His trilogy based on Maxim Gorky's autobiographical accounts: *Detstvo Gor'kogo* ("Gorky's Childhood," 1938), *Vlyudjakh* ("Among People," 1939), and *Moi universitety* ("My Universities," 1940) are distinguished by the vividness and precision of the depiction of Russian provincial life at the end of the 19th century and by the psychological acuteness of his presentation of character. The direct and candid depiction of suffering in the partisan movement in the Ukraine as seen in *Raduga* ("Rainbow," 1944) and *Nepokorennye* ("The Undefeated," 1945; according to B. Gorbatov's novella) made a strong impression and influenced the masters of the Italian neo-realistic cinema. In the second of these two films there is a particularly striking episode depicting the mass execution of Jews in a Nazi-occupied city. *Sel'skaya uchitel'nitsa* ("The Village School Mistress," 1947) enjoyed considerable popularity. Later films included one about Lenin's mother and screen versions of Gorky's novels *Mat'* ("The Mother," 1956) and *Foma Gordeev* ("Foma Gordeev," 1959).

Donskoy was awarded three Stalin Prizes and one State Prize, and the honorary titles of Peoples' Artist of the U.S.S.R. (1956) and Hero of Socialist Labor (1971).

[*The Shorter Jewish Encylopaedia* in Russian]

DON-YAḤIA (Donchin), YEHUDAH LEIB (1869–1941), rabbi, one of the earliest religious Zionists, a founder of the *Mizrachi movement. Don-Yaḥia was born in Drissa, Belorussia, and from 1902 was rabbi to various Russian communities. He began his Zionist activity while still a yeshivah student and in 1902 was one of the four rabbis who founded the Mizrachi movement. In 1901 he published *Ha-Ẓiyyonut mi-Nekuddat Hashkafat ha-Dat* ("Zionism from the Religious Point of View"), which ran into several editions. In it Don-Yaḥia attempted to prove to Orthodox circles that political Zionism and settlement in Ereẓ Israel were religious duties. He remained a Zionist even under the Soviet regime and settled in Tel Aviv in 1936. His responsa on matters of *halakhah*, sermons, and articles on topical subjects are collected in *Bikkurei Yehudah*, 2 vols. (1930–39).

His cousin SHABBETAI DON-YAḤIA (1909–1981) settled in Palestine in 1931 and became active in Ha-Po'el ha-Mizrachi. When the daily *Ha-Ẓofeh* was founded, he joined the staff as a columnist, becoming its editor in 1948.

BIBLIOGRAPHY: EẒD, 1 (1958), 637–43; Kressel, Leksikon, 1 (1965), 539–41.

[Getzel Kressel]

DOOR AND DOORPOST. The Bible distinguishes between the term *petaḥ*, which is the entrance to a house (Gen. 43:19), and *delet*, which is a device for closing and opening the entrance. Thus, while *petaḥ* applies to both the entrance to a tent (Gen. 18:1) and a house, the term *delet* is used only in connection with a built house. The door has two main components: a fixed frame and a moving board or slab. The frame has two doorposts (Heb. *mezuzot*), which are its vertical sides; a lintel (Heb. *mashqof*), its upper horizontal side; and a sill or threshold (Heb. *saf*), its lower horizontal side. Wider doorways occasionally had a third vertical beam on which two doorleaves, as implied by the dual form of the word *delata'im* ("paired doors"; Isa. 45:1), one attached to each of the doorposts, converged when shut. The doorway was constructed as part of the wall in question, but the doorposts, lintel, and threshold were built in after the construction of the building was completed. Finally, the door itself was set into this framework. At the top and bottom of each doorleaf was added a projecting hinge of wood, metal, or other material, to be received within depressions in the lintel and threshold respectively (cf. I Kings 7:50). Doors generally opened inward; they were prevented from swinging outward by ledges, stops at the outer edges of the lintel, and the threshold. Other methods of placing hinges were to suspend the door on some pliable material, such as leather or rope – these were fixed between the door and the doorpost at two points and served as hinges to enable the movement of the doors back and forth – or sometimes to put up special metal hinges that joined the door to the doorpost. A number of excavations have revealed the remains of metal coverings on hinges and sockets that served to protect them from wear. Excavations in Palestine have frequently uncovered sockets carved into the lintel and the threshold.

The threshold was of stone, either cut to size and laid slightly higher than the floor or built up from smaller stones. It was built slightly higher than the level of the floor and the street in order to keep out water and dirt. Doorposts were made either of wood or stone. The term *ʾammot* in Isaiah 6:4 probably refers to stone doorposts standing at both ends of the threshold. Doorposts made of wood are implied by the law about the Hebrew slave (Ex. 21:6; Deut. 15:17), according to which a Hebrew slave who, when the time of his release arrived, preferred slavery to freedom was to be placed against a doorpost and have his earlobe and the doorpost pierced with an awl as a symbol of his enslavement for life. Similarly, the lintel might be made either of stone or wood and was placed horizontally across the doorposts. The size of a doorway was related to the size of the building. Doorways to private dwellings from the Israelite period preserved in the Negev were lower than man's height, while the entrances to large buildings, such as palaces and temples, were proportionately higher and wider. Very large doors were erected at the gates of fortified cities (Judg. 16:3). The doors of luxurious buildings were made of special, expensive wood (I Kings 6:31, 34) or were overlaid with metal, usually copper, or even gold, like the doors of the Temple. Descriptions from various places on cylinder seals or monuments show single or double doors set within a decorative framework (Frankfurt, *The Art and Architecture…* (1954), Fig. 83). An integral part of the door was its bar or bolt, a device used to lock the door from the inside or the outside. The bar consisted of a movable horizontal beam which, when slid into a slot in the doorpost, prevented the door from opening. The lock was somewhat more complex and could be operated for locking or unlocking from the outside (II Sam. 13:17, 18). Another way to lock the door from inside was to put an iron bar on the inner side in a fitting depression. It seems that the Hebrew term for it is *bariʾaḥ* (cf. I Sam. 23:7). In the ancient world doorposts were marked in order to protect the people within the house from evil spirits and devils. That practice is reflected in Exodus 12:7, 22–23.

BIBLIOGRAPHY: Pritchard, Pictures, 219, pl. 675; Y. Kaplan, *Ha-Arkheʾologyah ve-ha-Historyah shel Tel Aviv-Yafo* (1959), 60, fig. 20, pls. 9–11; Y. Yadin et al., *Hazor*, 2 (1960), pl. 16:1.

[Zeʾev Yeivin]

DOR (**Dora**; Heb. דאר, דּוֹר, דֹּר), ancient harbor town on the coast of Carmel, 18 miles (29 km.) south of Haifa. The earliest known appearance of the name of Dor is from an Egyptian inscription from Nubia, dated to the time of Rameses II (13th century B.C.E.). According to Egyptian documents Dor fell into the hands of the Sikila/Tjekker, one of the Sea Peoples (Philistines), in the 12th/11th centuries B.C.E. Dor was one of the important Canaanite city-states in the league of Jabin, King of *Hazor (Josh. 11:2). It was among the cities of Manasseh in the territory of Asher, but according to Judges (1:27) it was not conquered by them. Solomon appointed the son of Abinadab as overseer of the region of Dor – the fourth district of his kingdom (I Kgs. 4:11). Under the name of Du'ru it belonged to the Assyrian province of the same name following the conquest of the region by Tiglath Pileser III in 732 B.C.E. In the Persian period (6th–4th centuries B.C.E.), when the cities on the coast were granted autonomy, Dor became a Sidonian colony. In the early Hellenistic period it was a Ptolemaic royal fortress. At the end of the second century B.C.E., Dora was in the hands of the tyrant Zoilus, who also ruled Strato's Tower (*Caesarea). Alexander Jannaeus acquired both cities by negotiation in the late second century B.C.E. After conquering the country (63 B.C.E.), Pompey restored Dora to its former owners, as was his policy with all cities that had formerly been autonomous. The city retained its freedom during the reign of Herod and his successors. According to Josephus (Ant. 19:300) a synagogue existed there before the destruction of the Second Temple. A change in status came about early in the second century C.E., when it was annexed to the province of *Phoenicia. In the late Roman period it became part of Palaestina Prima. Eusebius (*Onom.* 78:9; 136:16) states that the site is located 9 Roman miles from Caesarea. A fortified tower (*Merle*) was built on the southwestern edge of the mound in the Crusader period.

The site consists of a mound and a lower area used for occupation to the east, i.e. the upper and lower cities. Excavations were first undertaken in the mound in 1923 and 1924 by John Garstang on behalf of the British School of Archaeology in Jerusalem. Two test trenches were sunk on the northern and southern slopes, and a substantial area along the western slope in the area of the monumental temples with their impressive *podia* was cleared. Recent work has shown that these temples are undeniably Roman and apparently do not date back to the Hellenistic period as was once believed. Excavations on the tell were conducted by Ephraim Stern between 1980 and 2000 (current directors are Ilan Sharon and Ayelet Gilboa) and substantial structural remains from the Iron Age, Hellenistic, and Roman periods have been found. Excavations were first conducted in the lower city by J. Leibovitch in 1950–52, uncovering parts of a Roman theater and a Byzantine church, at the northern and southern ends of the city. The excavation of the Byzantine Church was resumed by Claudine Dauphin in 1979 and completed in 1994. A general survey of harbor installations along the edges of the tell and along the bays to the north and south has been undertaken by Avner Raban and others since the 1980s. Shipwrecks and other underwater features have been investigated by Raban, S. Wachsman, K. Raveh, and S. Kingsley. A survey of the aqueducts leading water to the site was made by Yuval Peleg. Regional surveys were conducted by Y. Olami, A. Siegelmann, A. Ovadiah, and others. A project of landscape archaeology was undertaken by Shimon Gibson and Sean Kingsley in 1994 with the investigation of settlements and fields, dating from the Chalcolithic, Early Bronze I, Middle Bronze Age IIA, Iron Age, Hellenistic, Roman, Byzantine, and medieval to Ottoman periods.

Several areas of the large 30-acre mound were examined during the excavations by Stern, and more recently by Sharon and Gilboa. In the upper level are remains of the Roman period. Below these lie the remains of a city wall of the Hellenistic period, which was apparently built in the latter part of the reign of Ptolemy II Philadelphus, and was still in use in the early Roman period. The wall, built of large ashlars, is still standing to a height of 7 feet, and it has a tower with a projection of 45 feet. It is built over the remains of a city wall of the Persian period, which is composed of large uncut stones and encloses a somewhat larger city. Beneath the Persian wall were sections of a brick Israelite city wall, at least 8 feet wide. Buildings remains were found within the wall. Whereas the buildings of the Persian and early Hellenistic period followed the Phoenician method of ashlar pillars alternating with a fill of undressed stones, the later Hellenistic walls were built of headers only. A dyeing installation of the Hellenistic period yielded large quantities of *murex* shells. Another monumental building of the Hellenistic period contained several plastered pools. The sections of the Hellenistic city examined revealed that it had been laid out according to the Hippodamian principles of town-planning, consisting of parallel intersecting streets, which formed a checkerboard pattern. Surprisingly, however, at Dor this method of town planning is dated to the Persian period. In the interior, adjacent to the wall, were shops opening onto a street. Little has remained of the underlying Persian level, except for pottery found in pits sunk into late Israelite levels. Inside the city were uncovered channels of an elaborate sewage system and of an aqueduct. From the city gate, a 30-foot-wide street led into the city, into an area which contained workshops of the Byzantine period. The gate of the Roman period has not been preserved. In deeper levels the gates of the Hellenistic and Persian periods were found, and beneath them an Israelite city gate, made of cyclopean boulders brought from Mt. *Carmel. In plan this gate resembles the gate of *Meggido IV-A. It consists of two guardrooms with paved squares at the front and back of the gate. Beneath this gate was a very solid gate of the four-chamber type, which is a unique example of Phoenician-Iron Age construction methods. One pilaster of the gate, facing the town, was made of polished orthostats. This gate is dated to the 9th–8th centuries B.C.E. and its destruction is ascribed to the Assyrians in 734 B.C.E. A massive fortification wall built of mud-brick along the eastern edge of the mound dates to the Early Iron Age (1150–1050 B.C.E.). These are associated with the Sikila/Tjekker settlement at the site. Only pottery and small finds are known from the Late Bronze Age. Several walls were dated to the 11th century B.C.E. The earliest remains of occupation at the site are buildings along the western edge of the site dating from the Middle Bronze IIA period.

The Byzantine-period town was apparently situated almost entirely in the area of the lower city immediately to the east of the mound that was no longer used for habitation purposes. The outline of the city is clearly visible in aerial photographs. Textual sources indicate that Dora was the seat of a bishop. The excavations by Dauphin have brought to light an episcopal basilica that was a center of pilgrimage and healing at the tomb of two saints and was erected in the fourth century over the ruins of a Graeco-Roman sanctuary.

[Shimon Gibson (2nd ed.)]

Modern Period

Modern Dor is a moshav, affiliated with Tenu'at ha-Moshavim, founded in 1949 by immigrants from Greece, some of whom had been stevedores in Salonika. These were joined by settlers from Iraq, Morocco, and other countries. Fishing, initially envisaged as a mainstay of the moshav's economy, was replaced by intensive farming and livestock as principal farm branches. A large plot of land was acquired at the site of the nearby Arab village Ṭanṭura (abandoned since 1948) by Baron Edmond de *Rothschild, who erected a glass factory in 1891 intended to exploit the fine shore sand for the production of bottles for the wine of Rishon le-Zion and Zikhron Ya'akov. The enterprise was unsuccessful. Dor was a partner with neighboring Kibbutz Naḥsholim in the Ḥof Dor recreation home. In 2002 its population was 321.

[Efraim Orni]

BIBLIOGRAPHY: G. Dahl, *The Materials for the History of Dor* (1951); S. Wachsmann and K. Raveh, "A Concise Nautical History of Dor/Tantura," in: International *Journal of Nautical Archaeology,* 13:3 (1984), 223–41; Y. Ayalon (ed.), *The Coast of Dor* (1988); K. Raveh and S. Kingsley, "The Status of Dor in Late Antiquity: A Maritime Perspective," in: *Biblical Archaeologist,* 54 (1991), 198–207; C. Dauphin and S. Gibson, "The Byzantine City of Dor/Dora Discovered," in: *Bulletin of the Anglo-Israel Archaeological Society,* 14 (1994–1995): 9–38; E. Stern et al., *Excavations at Dor. Final Report. Volumes I A-B* (1995); S.A. Kingsley and K. Raveh, *The Ancient Harbour and Anchorage at Dor, Israel,* BAR International Series 626 (1996); C. Dauphin, "On the Pilgrim's Way to the Holy City of Jerusalem: The Basilica of Dor in Israel," in: J.R. Bartlett (ed.), *Archaeology and Biblical Interpretation* (1997), 145–65; E. Stern, *Dor: Ruler of the Seas* (2000); A. Gilboa and I. Sharon, "An Archaeological Contribution to the Early Iron Age Chronological Debate: Alternative Chronologies for Phoenicia and Their Effects on the Levant, Cyprus, and Greece," in: BASOR, 332 (2003), 7–80; "Sea Peoples and Phoenicians along the Southern Phoenician Coast – A Reconciliation: An Interpretation of Sikila (SKL) Material Culture" in: BASOR, 337 (2005), 47–78.

DOR, MOSHE (1932–), Hebrew poet, essayist, and translator. Dor was born in Tel Aviv, served in the Haganah, and was a correspondent for the army weekly *Bamaḥaneh*. He later studied political science and history at Tel Aviv University and served many years as literary editor of *Maariv*. Dor was also cultural attaché at the Embassy of Israel in London and Distinguished Writer in Residence at the American University in Washington, D.C. A seminal figure in the "*Likrat*" literary circle in the 1950s, which strove to renew Hebrew poetry and free it from poetic verbosity and pathos, Dor published *Bisheloshah* in 1952 and the collection *Beroshim Levanim* ("White Cypresses") in 1954. This was followed by over a dozen other collections (including *Zahav va-Efer* ("Gold and Ashes," 1963), *Mivḥar Shirim* ("Selected Poems," 1970), *Ovrim et ha-Nahar* ("Crossing the River," 1989), and *Shetikat ha-Banai* ("Silence of the Builder," 1996)). In 2004 a volume of selected poems written over a period of 50 years appeared as *Shetaḥ Hefker*. Foregrounding the landscape, whether in Israel, London, or the United States, Dor coalesces feelings and sights, human experience and impressions. Dor has also published collections of essays and six books for children. Since the 1990s he has been living in Tel Aviv and in the U.S. Dor edited a number of collections in English, including: *The Burning Bush: Poems from Modern Israel* (with Nathan Zach; 1977), *The Stones Remember: Native Israeli Poetry* (with Barbara Goldberg and Giora Leshem; 1991), and *After the First Rain: Israeli Poems on War and Peace* (with Barbara Goldberg; 1998). A number of collections including Dor's own poetry have been published in English: *Maps of Time* (1978), *Crossing the River* (edited by Seymour Mayne; 1989), *Khamsin: Memoirs and Poetry by a Native Israeli* (1994).

BIBLIOGRAPHY: A. Sillitoe, Introduction, in: *Maps of Time*, 1978; H. Nagid, in: *Maariv* (March 7, 1980); A. Feinberg, "Moshe Dor's Kites on Hampstead Heath," in: *Modern Hebrew Literature*, 6 (1980); Z. Samir, in: *Yedioth Ahronoth* (August 6, 1993); I. Scheinfeld, in: *Haaretz, Sefarim* (July 14, 1993). **WEBSITE:** ITHL at www.ithl.org.il.

[Anat Feinberg (2nd ed.)]

DORATI, ANTAL (1906–1988), conductor and composer. Dorati was born in Budapest and entered the Budapest Royal Academy of Music at the age of 14, studying piano, conducting, and composition, and graduating at the age of 18. From 1924 to 1928 he was conductor at the Budapest Royal Opera House, subsequently becoming assistant to Fritz Busch at the Dresden State Opera, and at the same time conducting opera and concerts in other cities. In 1932 he became musical director of the Ballet Russe de Monte Carlo, with whom he toured widely and remained until 1940. Dorati's subsequent career focused principally on the United States: he was conductor of the Dallas Symphony Orchestra (1945–49) and of the Minneapolis Symphony Orchestra (1949–60), with whom he made many records. He was chief conductor of the BBC Symphony Orchestra from 1962 to 1966; and thereafter became musical director of the Stockholm Philharmonic Orchestra (from 1966) and later, concurrently, of the National Symphony Orchestra, Washington, D.C. (from 1969), with whom he had made his American debut, in 1937. Dorati's fine international reputation was based on his prowess as an orchestra builder; as a devoted advocate of contemporary music, with particular understanding of Bartok and Stravinsky; and as a conductor of many fine recordings. In 1973 he completed the formidable task of recording all the 107 Haydn symphonies, most of them for the first time. His many compositions include symphonies, a cello concerto, and choral and chamber music; he also made many ballet arrangements.

[Max Loppert (2nd ed.)]

DORFF, ELLIOT N. (1943–), U.S. rabbinical scholar. Born in Milwaukee, Wisc., Dorff was ordained by the Jewish Theological Seminary in 1970 and awarded a Ph.D. in philosophy by Columbia University in 1971. He then joined the faculty of the University of Judaism in Los Angeles. He later served as rector and distinguished professor of philosophy at the University and as a visiting professor at the UCLA School of Law.

The author of 10 books and over 150 articles on Jewish thought, law and ethics, Dorff assumed a leadership role in the community as well, serving as vice chair of the Conservative Movement's Committee on Jewish Law and Standards, co-editor of the halakhic commentary in *Etz Hayim*, the movement's edition of the Pentateuch, and president of the Society of Jewish Ethics and chair of the Academy of Jewish Philosophy and of the Jewish Law Association.

He was also deeply involved in public service. In the spring of 1993, he served on the Ethics Committee of then First Lady Hillary Rodham Clinton's Health Care Task Force. In 1999 and 2000 he was part of the U.S. Surgeon General's Commission to draft a Call to Action for Responsible Sexual Behavior; and from 2000 to 2002 he served on the National Human Resources Protections Advisory Commission, charged with reviewing and revising the federal guidelines for protecting human subjects in research projects.

In *Jewish Law and Modern Ideology* (1970), Dorff delineates the different approaches of the various Jewish religious movements to Jewish law and argues for the authenticity of the one adopted by the Conservative Movement. While he affirms his commitment to uphold the traditional *halakhah*, he also supports the right to adjust it to meet radically altered conditions of living and even to change it in keeping with new moral sensibilities.

Dorff's most extensive work on Jewish law is *A Living Tree* (1988), co-written with Arthur Rosett, which traces the development of Jewish law through the past three thousand years, paying special attention to the rabbinic and medieval periods. It explains the relationship between religion and law and the interaction of the latter with morality.

Dorff's stress on the importance of law is also evident in his most speculative work, *Knowing God* (1994). Acknowledging that, as a pluralist, he accepts the relativity of all truth claims, he nonetheless believes that there is an "objective reality" that serves as the ultimate criterion for the truth of any system of ideas. However, this reality can only be known by us through "the perspective of a perceiving community," which depends for its existence on a system of law to define its principles and concretize them. Since "it is the Jewish community of the past and the present that decides (for Jews) which events are revelatory and what … the implications of that revelation are," the most direct way to experience revelation is through the study of the classic Jewish religious texts.

Dorff has written three popular works *Matters of Life and Death* (1998), which deals with medical ethics; *To Do the Right and the Good* (2002) on Jewish social ethics; and *Love Your Neighbor and Yourself* (2003), devoted to personal ethics. His knowledge of the moral issues faced by current medical practitioners is impressive, as is his willingness to address controversial questions raised by infertility and death and dying.

While being quite traditional in his personal practice, giving the longstanding *halakhah* "the benefit of the doubt," he tends to be more liberal in his rulings on issues of gender equality and homosexuality, for example. His general view is that the *halakhah* embodies the highest moral standards. When he feels that it does not, he is prepared to modify it, though he exercises great care to maintain the integrity of the structure of Jewish law. In this, as in all his teaching, he demonstrates the Conservative Jewish regard for the law and the role it must play in keeping the Jewish community loyal to the covenant of Israel.

[David L. Lieber (2nd ed.)]

DORFMAN, JOSEPH (1904–1991), U.S. economist. Born in Russia and educated in the United States, Dorfman worked with the National Industrial Conference Board and joined the faculty at Columbia University in 1931. Economic methodology and history of economic thought were his main fields of study. His major publications included a five-volume work, *The Economic Mind in American Civilization* (1946–59); other studies deal with the economics of the Jacksonian era and the thought of Thorstein Veblen, the American social scientist. He also wrote *Thorstein Veblen and His America* (1934); *Early American Policy: Six Columbia Contributors* (1960); and *Institutional Economics: Veblen, Commons, and Mitchell Reconsidered* (1963). Dorfman was a distinguished fellow of the History of Economics Society. In 1990 the HES established an annual prize for the best dissertation in the history of economic thought. In 1992 the Dorfman family endowed a permanent fund for the award, which is now called the Joseph Dorfman Best Dissertation Award.

[Joachim O. Ronall / Ruth Beloff (2nd ed.)]

DORFMAN, JOSEPH (1940–), Israeli composer. Born in Odessa, Ukraine, Dorfman studied at the Stolyarsky School of Music (Odessa) and later at the Odessa Conservatory (1958–65) with Starkowa (piano) and Kogan (composition). In 1971 he received his Ph.D. in musicology at the Gnessin Musical Institute in Moscow. Already as a student he was engaged in a wide range of musical activities as a composer, lecturer, theoretician, coach, and conductor. During the 1960s, Dorfman was among the pioneers in performing and lecturing on contemporary Western music in the Soviet Union. A consistent field of interest was also Jewish music in all its aspects (art, liturgical, and folk). In 1973 he immigrated to Israel, where he was appointed professor of composition and theory at the Rubin Academy of Music (Tel Aviv University). There he also served as head of the Composition and Theory Department and head of the Academy. While continuing to promote both Jewish and contemporary Western music, he was artistic director of the International Festivals of Jewish Art Music and music director of the concert series "20th Century Music." Dorfman was also visiting professor at Columbia University, at the Hochschule fuer Musik und Darstellende Kunst in Frankfurt am Main, and at Johannes Gutenberg University, Mainz (Germany), as well as at Bar-Ilan University.

His early compositions of the Soviet period were influenced by early 20th century Russian music and by Hindemith. Later he moved in many directions, including recorded and live electro-acoustic improvisation, graphic notation, and various combinations of graphic and traditional forms of notation. His works include music for solo instruments, chamber ensembles and symphony orchestra, opera, ballet and oratorios, multimedia staging, and educational works. Dorfman was a prolific musician, performing as a solo pianist, a participant in various chamber groups, and conductor of concerts in several European festivals and radio programs.

BIBLIOGRAPHY: NG2.

[Yulia Kreinin (2nd ed.)]

DORFMAN, RALPH ISADORE (1911–1985), U.S. biochemist. Dorfman was born in Chicago. He joined the Worcester Foundation for Experimental Biology and became research professor of biochemistry, Boston University, in 1951. He was professor of chemistry at Clark University (1956), and later director of the Institute of Hormone Biology of Syntex Research Center in Palo Alto, California (1964). His books include *Metabolism of Steroid Hormones* (with F. Ungar, 1953) and *Androgens* (1956); he edited *Methods in Hormone Research* (5 vols., 1962–66).

[Bracha Rager (2nd ed.)]

DORI (Dostrovsky), YA'AKOV (1899–1973), military leader; first Israeli chief of staff. Dori, born in Odessa, Russia, was taken to Ereẓ Israel in 1906. After graduating from the Reali High School in Haifa, he served as a sergeant in the Palestinian Battalion of the Jewish Legion in World War I. When the Legion was disbanded, Dori joined the group of sergeants and soldiers who intended to form the nucleus for a Jewish unit within the Palestine Defense Force. The plan was canceled by the British authorities when this group of soldiers went to the defense of Tel Aviv in May 1921 during an attack by Arab rioters. Dori studied engineering in Belgium, and upon his return to Palestine joined the Haganah. From 1931 to 1939 he was Haganah commander of the Haifa district. Enhancing his military knowledge through self-education, Dori introduced systematic exercises and training in the Haifa branch of the Haganah, and formulated a plan for the defense of the town. He also participated in the training of commanders in nationwide courses. He was named head of the national command training bureau (Lishkat ha-Hadrakhah) upon its establishment. In September 1939 he became the first chief of staff of the Haganah, a post he held until the establishment of the State of Israel in 1948 (with an interval during 1945–47 to raise funds in the U.S. for the purchase of arms for the Haganah). With the establishment of Israel, Dori became the chief of staff of the Israel Defense Forces with the rank of *rav-alluf* (major general), a post he held until the end of the War of Independence. He served as president of the Haifa Technion from 1951 to 1965, contributing to its expansion and development as a center for technological and scientific training in Israel.

BIBLIOGRAPHY: Dinur, *Haganah*, 2 pt. 3 (1964), index; Tidhar, 3 (1958^2), 1120–21; 15 (1966), 4802–03; D. Lazar, *Rashim be-Yisrael*, 1 (1953), 152–8.

[Yehuda Slutsky]

DORIAN, DOREL (**Iancovici**; 1930–), Romanian writer. Dorian was born in Piatra-Neamt. Upon completion of secondary school he studied building engineering at the Politechnical Institute, Kiev, 1948–53. As a student he had begun to make literary contributions to *Revista elevilor* (1946) and to Communist youth journals, among them *Tanarul Muncitor* and *Scanteia Tineretului.* Upon his return to Romania he worked as a building engineer for several years until he became the editor of popular science publications, among them *Stiinta si tehnica.* In 1955 he published a volume of stories, *N-au inflorit inca merii* ("The Apple Trees Haven't Blossomed Yet"). In 1959, his first play, *Daca vei fi intrebat* ("If You Are Asked") was performed at the Bucharest Municipal Theater and his play *Secunda 58* ("The 58th Second") earned him a state prize. By 1985, ten of his plays had been performed in Romanian theaters and on TV, among them: *De n-ar fi iubirile* ("If There Was No Love," 1961); *Oricat ar parea de ciudat* ("As Strange as It Seems," 1965), judged the best of the year; *Teatru cu bile* ("Theater with Balls," 1970); and *Confesiune tarzie* ("Late Confession," 1985). His plays deal with problems of conscience under the Communist regime. Dorian also published science fiction and ecological and parapsychological essays, such as *Paranormal 2000* (1998). In the 1980s he became active in Jewish communal life. In 1996 he became the main editor of the bimonthly *Realitatea Evreiasca* and in 1997 editor of the series of cultural pamphlets published by the same review. He also published a play on a Jewish subject, *Foc in Calea Vacaresti* ("Fire on Vacareshty Street," 1999). From 1996 to 2004 he was a member of the Romanian Parliament as the representative of the Jewish minority.

BIBLIOGRAPHY: A. Mirodan, *Dictionar neconventional*, 2 (1997), 137–43; *Realitatea Evreiasca* (April 22, 2005).

[Lucian-Zeev Herscovici (2nd ed.)]

DORIAN, EMIL (1892–1956), Romanian poet and novelist. Born in Bucharest, Dorian practiced medicine there but devoted much of his time to writing. His works, published under such satirical pseudonyms as Michail Prunk and Dr. Knock, appeared in several important literary journals. Dorian's verse was later collected in *Cîntece pentru Lelioara* ("Songs for Lelioara," 1923), *In preajma serii* ("In the Twilight," 1924), and *De vorbă cu bălanul meu* ("A Talk with My White Horse," 1925). These poems, praised by the critics, display a serenity and love for mankind that later found expression in the novel *Vagabonzii* ("The Vagabonds," 1934). The leftist pacifism of this work provoked some hostile comment: the Romanian literary historian George Călinescu pointedly observed that only a Jew devoid of national feelings could so ruthlessly condemn a people's struggle. Other novels by Dorian were *Profeți și paiațe* ("Prophets and Clowns," 1933²) and *Otrava* ("Poison," 1946), the latter dealing with the anti-Jewish persecution under Antonescu's pro-Nazi regime. *Otrava* stressed the permanence of antisemitism and its persistence in all strata of society – including the proletariat. For this deviation Dorian's works were banned by the Communists and the writer was thereafter only allowed to publish poems and stories for children. He also translated Heine's *Buch der Lieder* and Eliezer Steinbarg's Yiddish fables.

BIBLIOGRAPHY: E. Lovinescu, in: *Critice*, vol. 7, p. 151; G. Călinescu, *Istoria literaturii romîne dela origini pînă în prezent* (1941), 766–7, 921; S. Albu, in: *Gazeta literară* (Bucharest, June 20, 1957).

[Abraham Feller]

DORIS (first century B.C.E.), first wife of *Herod the Great, whom he married (c. 47 B.C.E.) before he became king and while he was *strategos* of Galilee (Jos., Wars, 1:241, 432f., 448, 562, 590; Jos., Ant., 14:300; 17:68). The name Doris is Greek but was similar to Dorothea. Josephus refers to her as a Jerusalemite: "her family (γένος) being from Jerusalem" (War 1:432). Her precise background is unknown, but it is assumed she was Idumaean in origin and of Hellenized stock. On ascending the throne in 37 B.C.E. Herod dismissed her in order to marry the Hasmonean princess *Mariamne. Doris was now banished from the city together with her son Antipater II. Later Antipater was allowed back (c. 14 B.C.E.). Doris too was recalled and honored at the court, only to be dismissed again (c. 7/6 B.C.E.) with the discovery of her son's disloyalty and plotting against the king: "… he [Herod] stripped her of all the finery which he had bestowed upon her and for the second time dismissed her from court" (Wars 1: 590). She seems to have been as unscrupulous as her son, with whom she cooperated in all his crimes against the sons of Mariamne and against Herod himself.

BIBLIOGRAPHY: A. Schalit, *Namenwörterbuch zu Flavius Josephus* (1968); N. Kokkinos, *The Herodian Dynasty: Origins, Role in Society and Eclipse* (1998): 208–11; T. Ilan, *Lexicon of Jewish Names in Late Antiquity. Part I: Palestine 330 B.C.E.–200 CE* (2002): 316–17.

[Isaiah Gafni / Shimon Gibson (2nd ed.)]

DORMIDO, DAVID ABRABANEL (d. 1667), a founder of the modern English-Jewish community. Born in Spain of a Marrano family, as Manuel Martinez Dormido, he collected taxes in Andalusia and was a city councilor until arrested by the Inquisition in 1627. After appearing as a penitent in an auto-da-fé in 1632, he escaped to Bordeaux and in 1640 reached Amsterdam where he joined the Jewish community. Financially ruined by the Portuguese reconquest of Brazil he later accompanied Samuel Soeiro, son of *Manasseh Ben Israel, in 1654 to London where he petitioned Oliver Cromwell to assist him in recuperating his fortune and to readmit the Jews into England. Cromwell complied with the first request and apparently expressed sympathy with the second. Under the name David Abrabanel, Dormido signed the petition of the London Marranos for freedom of worship in 1656. When the Jewish community was formally organized in 1663 he was presiding warden. His son SOLOMON (ANTONIO) DORMIDO (1622–1700) was the first Jew to be admitted formally to the Royal Exchange in London. The statement that Dormido was Manasseh Ben Israel's brother-in-law has no authority.

BIBLIOGRAPHY: C. Roth, *Menasseh Ben Israel* (1934), 212–4, 219–21; D. Bueno de Mesquita, in: JHSET, 3 (1896–98), 88–93; 10 (1921–23), 235–7; L.D. Barnett, *Bevis Marks Records*, 1 (1940), index; A.M. Hyamson, *Sephardim of England* (1951), 24–26; A. Wiznitzer, *Jews in Colonial Brazil* (1960), 71, 137, 172. **ADD. BIBLIOGRAPHY:** Katz, England, 185–86.

[Cecil Roth]

DOROHOI, town in N.E. Romania, located on important trade routes between Poland, Bukovina, and Moldavia. Jews began to settle there in the 17th century. They were granted charters of privilege in 1799, 1808, and 1823. The Dorohoi community was organized, like other communities in Moldavia, as a *Breasla Jidovilor* ("Jewish guild"), first mentioned there in 1799 and existing until 1834. There were 600 Jewish families in Dorohoi in 1803, 3,031 persons in 1859 (50.1% of the total population), 6,804 in 1899 (53.6%), and 5,820 (36.6%) in 1930. The town was also a ḥasidic center, where *admorim* sometimes lived, among them Jehiel Michael Tierer and Hanoch Frenkel who died in Haifa. Among the town's rabbis were Mattitiyahu Kalman (d. 1824); Ḥayyim *Taubes (1847–1909) after serving in Sassov, Galicia, author of Torah commentaries and responsa; Dov Beer Drimer; and Pinhas Eliyahu Wasserman (1917–1996), who died in Jerusalem. Before the Holocaust 25 synagogues functioned in Dorohoi. A regular modern communal organization was set up in 1896. The community had a *talmud torah* and a secular Jewish school by 1895. A large number of refugees from persecutions in the vicinity arrived in Dorohoi in 1881–4. The community also suffered severely during the peasant revolt in 1907. The Jews were persecuted by the military authorities during World War I and suffered from economic restrictions between the two world wars. The Jews in Dorohoi were mainly occupied as artisans, manual workers, and petty shopkeepers. In 1920 the community established a hospital. Ḥovevei Zion groups became active in the last decades of the 19th century. Later various Zionist and other Jewish organizations also became active. Among the intellectuals born in Dorohoi were Romanian-language writers on general and Jewish themes, such as Ion Călugăru (1902–1956), Saşa Pană (1902–1979), and Ştefan Antim (1879–1944). Jewish periodicals in Yiddish and Romanian were also published there.

[Yehouda Marton / Lucian-Zeev Herscovici (2nd ed.)]

Holocaust Period

In 1941 there were 5,384 Jews living in Dorohoi, comprising about one third of the population. Antisemitic outbursts began in June 1940, when nearby Bessarabia and northern Bukovina were occupied by the Soviet Union. Romanian soldiers attacked the Jewish quarter, murdered about 200 Jewish inhabitants, and looted houses. The following day local peasants stripped the Jewish corpses that were still lying in the streets. The victims' families were forced to sign statements to the effect that their relatives had been murdered by "unknown wayfarers"; the public prosecutor, however, came to the conclusion that the soldiers had acted on instructions. The terror was renewed when Ion *Antonescu rose to power (September 1940), and many Jews were barred from commerce and the trades.

After the war with the Soviet Union broke out, 2,000 Jewish men from the towns and villages in the district were brought to the city and deported to *Transnistria on Nov. 7, 1941. Dorohoi's Jews were deported on November 12, and by November 14 two transports totaling 3,000 persons were dispatched. Many died in the sealed railroad cars before they reached their destination, *Ataki on the Dniester. Deportations were resumed on June 14, 1942, when 450 men were sent to Transnistria. They were later joined by their families in Mogilev and were sent from there to German camps on the banks of the Bug, where most of them met their deaths. In Dorohoi itself, only 2,000 Jews were left and they were forbidden to engage in any economic activity. In January 1943 the Antonescu government acceded to the request of the Dorohoi community and the leaders of the Association of Romanian Jewish Communities in *Bucharest to permit the return of the deportees; but it took until December 20 for this decision to go into effect. Of the 3,074 who had been deported, 2,000 came back to Dorohoi. In addition, 4,000 Jews from Transnistria who were not permitted to return to their original homes in the district also stayed in Dorohoi. In April 1944, the Soviet army occupied the city.

[Theodor Lavi]

Contemporary Period

After World War II the Jewish population of Dorohoi increased because of the refugees who settled there. In 1947, 7,600 Jews lived there. Community life was rebuilt. Jewish schools (including a secondary school) functioned until 1948. Later, Yiddish was taught in some public schools. In 1967 a kosher restaurant was opened and functioned until 1990. Dorohoi was presented as a model of the Jewish *shtetl* in Romania, with delegations of foreign Jewish organizations brought there to visit. In order to maintain this illusion Rabbi Pinhas Eliyahu Wasserman, the last rabbi of the community, was forced to remain in Dorohoi for some 20 years, even though the Jewish population had diminished through emigration, mainly to Israel. In 1956 there were 2,753 Jews in Dorohoi; in 1966, 1,013. In 2000, only 49 Jews remained in Dorohoi, with a functioning synagogue. An organization of Israeli Jews originating in Dorohoi is based in Kiryat Bialik, Israel. A forest dedicated to the memory of the Jews of the town and former county of Dorohoi is located at Shoresh, near Jerusalem, where annual memorial ceremonies are held.

[Lucian-Zeev Herscovici (2nd ed.)]

BIBLIOGRAPHY: M. Mircu, *Pogromurile din Bucovina şi Dorohoi* (1945), 132, 145; M. Carp, *Cartea neagră*, 1 (1940), index; F. Şaraga, in: *Sliha*, 11 (1956), 4; 1:12 (1956), 4; 1:13 (1956), 4; PK Romanyah, 1 (1970), 104–10. **ADD. BIBLIOGRAPHY:** S. David (ed.), *Dorohoi-Mihăileni-Darabani-Herţa-Rădăuţi Prut*, 5 vols. (1992–2000); M. Rozen, *Evreii din Judeţul Dorohoi* (2000); I. Wasserman, *Dobândeşte-ţi un rabin, câştigă-ţi un prieten* (2003), 278–345.

DORON, ABRAHAM (1929–), Israeli social worker specializing in the welfare state and social security system and considered the leading Israeli scholar in these fields. Doron was born in Radom, Poland, and immigrated to Israel in 1946. In 1951 he received his B.A. degree in social work and in 1954 completed his B.A. studies in history and sociology at the Hebrew University of Jerusalem. In 1961 he received his M.A. from the University of Chicago and in 1967 he received his Ph.D. at the London School of Economics and Political Science. From 1963 he taught at the Paul Baerwald School of Social Work of the Hebrew University. In 1979–81 he was head of the school. Doron served on various government planning committees and wrote numerous articles and books, including *The Welfare State in an Age of Change* (1985), *The Welfare State in Israel* (with Kremer, 1992), *For Universality – The Challenges of the Social Policy in Israel* (1992), and *The Work and Welfare Ministry – The Reunion which Never Existed* (1995). In 2004 he was awarded Israel Prize in social work.

[Shaked Gilboa (2nd ed.)]

DORON, HAIM (1928–), Israeli physician. Born in Buenos Aires, Argentina, he immigrated to Israel in 1953. He received his M.D. from the School of Medicine of the Buenos Aires University (1952) and M.P.H. from Public Health School, London School of Tropical Medicine and Hygiene, University of London, in 1961. From 1953 to 1960, he was a family physician in Beersheba and Negev settlement clinics, and from 1961 to 1968, medical director of the Sick Fund (Kuppat Ḥolim Kelalit), Negev District, and the Negev Central Hospital, Beer-Sheba. During those years of mass immigration he organized community health services in the Negev region and promoted the *aliyah* of physicians from Latin American and other countries. He was co-founder of the Ben-Gurion University of the Negev and, in partnership with Moshe *Prywes, of its medical school. From 1968 to 1976 he was head of the Medical Division, Kuppat Ḥolim Kelalit, and deputy chairman. During these years he initiated the reorganization of Kuppat Ḥolim Kelalit health services, developed regionalization and integration of hospital and community services, developed the physician/nurse team in primary care, and introduced social work service within the framework of the health community structure. He was appointed professor of Community Medicine at Tel Aviv University and Ben-Gurion University of the Negev. From 1989 to 1996 he headed the School of Health Professions, Sackler Faculty of Medicine, Tel Aviv University. Doron contributed to the social and cultural process in Beer-Sheba and the Negev during the years of mass immigration and the renaissance of family medicine in Israel.

[Bracha Rager (2nd ed.)]

DOROT (Heb. דּוֹרוֹת), kibbutz in southern Israel, 10½ mi. (17 km.) E. of Gaza, affiliated with Iḥud ha-Kibbutzim, founded in 1941 by immigrants from Germany in a move to spread Jewish settlement southward toward the Negev at a time when the Nazi armies were advancing on Egypt. In 1946 the kibbutz was severely damaged during a search for illicit arms by the British. Thorough soil reclamation work was necessary before farming became possible. Dorot engaged in farming (field crops and dairy cattle in partnership with nearby kibbutz *Ruḥamah), produced herbs, and operated a guest house. In 2002 its population was 500. Its name is composed of the initials of the labor leader Dov *Hos, his wife Rivkah, and his daughter Tirzah, who all died in a road accident.

WEBSITE: www.dorot.org.il.

[Efraim Orni]

DOROTHEUS, (1) son of Nethanel (c. 45 C.E.), member of the Jewish embassy sent to Rome to plead before Emperor *Claudius in a dispute regarding the custody of the high priest's vestments (Jos., Ant., 120:14). Following the intervention of *Agrippa II, the mission was successful. In the summer of 45 C.E., the emperor sent a letter officially entrusting the garments to the care of the Jews. (2) A grammarian in first-century B.C.E. Ascalon. (3) The name appears in Hebrew and Greek on ossuaries and a sarcophagus from Jerusalem (first century C.E.).

BIBLIOGRAPHY: A. Schalit, *Namenwörterbuch zu Flavius Josephus* (1968): 40; N. Kokkinos, *The Herodian Dynasty: Origins, Role in Society and Eclipse* (1998), 208–11; T. Ilan, *Lexicon of Jewish Names in Late Antiquity. Part 1: Palestine 330 BCE–200 CE* (2002): 276–77.

[Isaiah Gafni / Shimon Gibson (2nd ed.)]

DORPH, SHELDON (Shelly; 1941–), U.S. Jewish educator. Dorph was born in Philadelphia and completed undergraduate degrees from Temple University and Graetz College. After receiving rabbinical ordination from the Jewish Theological Seminary of America (JTS) in 1969, he was named director of Camp Ramah in the Berkshires, where he served for four years. He also served as principal of the Los Angeles Hebrew High School (1971–81) and as founding headmaster of the Golda Meir Day High School (1977–85). He published texts on biblical studies for high school students and edited the influential Shalav Hebrew textbook series for Behrman House Books. He earned a doctorate in religion and education from Teachers College, Columbia University, in 1976. He married Gail Zaiman Dorph, an important Jewish educator in her own right.

Dorph served as director of the Pacific Southwest Region of United Synagogue (1987–89) and helped guide the development of some 59 synagogues. But he was best known for his years as national director of the Ramah Camps, a position he held from 1989 to 2003. During that time Dorph oversaw a period of exceptional growth in the Ramah camping system, expanding to eight overnight camps and seven day camps in Canada, the U.S., and Israel and accommodating over 6,000 campers and 1,500 staff members each summer. While serving in the Ramah position he also taught in the education department at JTS.

In 1996 Dorph received the Shazar Prize from the Joint Authority for Jewish Education in the Diaspora for his work in Jewish education and Hebrew language. In 2004, Dorph received the Janice Coulter award for excellence in informal education from the North American Alliance for Jewish Youth and the Jewish Educators Assembly–Behrman House Books Award for Lifetime Achievement in Jewish Education.

[Barry W. Holtz (2nd ed.)]

DORTMUND (Heb. תירמוניא), city in Germany. A privilege issued by Emperor Henry IV to the city of *Worms in 1074 granted the Jews there trading rights in Dortmund market. In 1096 Mar Shemaryah, fleeing from the crusading mob, killed himself and his whole family in Dortmund. Records pointing to the existence of an organized Jewish settlement there date from the 13th century. The Jews paid a contribution of 15 marks to the imperial treasury from 1241 to 1250. They had their own quarter or street. While in 1250 it was the archbishop of Cologne who granted a privilege to the Jews of Dortmund and was responsible for their protection, these rights and duties had passed to the emperor by 1257, and from 1300 devolved on Count Eberhard of the Mark. By 1257 the community had a *Magistratus Judaeorum*, a rabbi (*clericus* or *papen*), a cantor, *shoḥet*, and a *Schulklopfer*, and possessed a synagogue, a communal center, a cemetery, and a *mikveh*, for which ground rent had to be paid. Jews participated in the guarding of the city walls.

In the *Black Death period the Jews were expelled from Dortmund (1350); the *Judenturm* ("Jews' Tower") was built with the spoils seized from them. They were readmitted in 1372 (for six- to ten-year periods) after making a payment to the count. Subsequently taxes were levied from individuals and not from the community; moneylenders were allowed to charge an interest rate of 36.1% on loans made within the city but twice as much outside. Jews could acquire property only with the permission of the municipality. There were no more than ten Jewish families living in Dortmund in 1380. Another expulsion seems to have taken place around the end of the 15th century as in 1543 the Jews were readmitted for an initial period of ten years, only to be expelled once more in 1596. A privilege granted in 1750 indicates the existence of a new community in Dortmund with elders elected every three years. Under French rule (1806–15) the Jews in Dortmund as elsewhere gained equal rights.

After its incorporation into Prussia in 1815, Dortmund expanded considerably as the result of the industrial revolution. The Jewish population also increased, from 120 in 1840 to 1,000 (1.5% of the total) in 1880, and 4,108 in 1933 (0.8%). The community built a modest synagogue around 1850 and a magnificent building in 1900. Benno *Jacob, the Bible scholar, became rabbi in Dortmund (1906–29); K. *Wilhelm served as rabbi from 1929 to 1933. The community had its own elementary school, apart from a religious school, and a variety of political, charitable, and social institutions, including a communal magazine. As the main congregation was *Reform, a small Orthodox congregation (*Adass Jisroel) was established, supported also by immigrants from Eastern Europe who arrived after World War I. The pattern of persecution in Dortmund followed the evolution of German policy. The Jewish population was 4,108 (out of 540,000) in 1933. The boycott was strictly enforced and sustained beyond April 1, 1933. More than 250 Jews were arrested in the initial year of the Nazi regime. The community tried to sustain its members, offering assistance to needy members, who grew in number. The Jewish school expanded to meet growing needs and then declined as Jews left. Unlike other cities, the community was forced to close its synagogue before *Kristallnacht*. By August 1938 the Jewish population was reduced to 2,600 through emigration. In October 600 Jews of Polish citizenship were expelled; Jewish businesses were Aryanized at a growing pace. On *Kristallnacht* 600 Jewish men were arrested and sent to Sachsenhausen; 500 more fled the city. On the outbreak of war the Jewish population was 1,222; the Jews soon became confined to "Jewish houses." Dortmund became an assembly point for deportations to the East, with about 40,000 deported in eight transports between 1942 and 1945. On April 27, 1942, between 700 and 800 Dortmund Jews were deported to Zamosc and then on to Belzec. On July 29, 1942, 331 elderly Jews were deported. By July 1944 only 334 were left, mainly partners of mixed marriages, but of those too the majority eventually suffered the same fate.

The post-war community, formed in 1945, numbered 351 in 1970, with a synagogue, communal center, and old-age home (opened in 1956). The Jewish community numbered 337 in 1989 and 3,800 in 2005 owing to immigration from the former Soviet Union. In 1998 the community center and synagogue were rebuilt. In 2003 a Jewish kindergarten was opened. From 2005 the community employed a rabbi. Dortmund is the seat of the Association of Jewish Communities in Westphalia.

BIBLIOGRAPHY: Germ Jud, 1 (1934, repr. 1963), 88–90; 2, pt. 1 (1968), 170–4; H.C. Meyer (ed.), *Aus Geschichte und Leben der Juden in Westfalen* (1962), includes bibliography; Kaiserling, in: MGWJ, 9 (1860), 81–91; B.N. Brilling, *Zur Geschichte der Juden in Dortmund* (1958). **ADD. BIBLIOGRAPHY:** U. Knipping, *Die Geschichte der Juden in Dortmund waehrend der Zeit des Dritten Reiches* (1977).

[Alexander Carlebach / Michael Berenbaum (2nd ed.)]

DOSA BEN HARKINAS (first–second centuries C.E.), Palestinian *tanna*. He is often referred to without patronymic, parallel passages showing that the Dosa referred to is Dosa b. Harkinas (cf., e.g., Eduy. 3:3 and Ḥul. 11:2 et al.). Dosa saw the Second Temple and survived its destruction, living until the time of *Gamaliel and *Akiva, i.e., the second decade of the second century. In Temple times, he engaged in halakhic dispute with *Akaviah b. Mahalalel and *Ḥanina Segan ha-Kohanim (Neg. 1:4). In a dispute concerning matrimonial law between Hanan, one of the judges of civil law, and the "sons of the high priests" he decided according to the latter, in opposition to Johanan b. Zakkai, who agreed with Hanan. He is mentioned 11 times in the Mishnah but more frequently in the *beraitot*. In the Mishnah (RH 2:8) it is related that Rabban Gamaliel accepted the testimony of two witnesses that they had seen the New Moon, despite the fact that Dosa was of the opinion that they were false witnesses, a view in which Joshua b. Hananiah concurred. Gamaliel did not take any steps against Dosa b. Harkinas, perhaps because of his age and honored status, but he ordered Joshua "to appear before me with your staff and your money on the day which according to your reckoning should be the Day of Atonement." Dosa advised Joshua to obey the *nasi*, since "If we call in question the decisions of the *bet din* of Rabban Gamaliel, we must call in question the decisions of every *bet din* which has existed since the days of Moses up to the present time" (RH 2:8–9). During the days of Akiva and Eleazar b. Azariah, the sages heard that Dosa had permitted the levirate marriage of a woman whose co-wife was the daughter of the levir. This was in conformity with the opinion of Bet Shammai against that of Bet Hillel, who forbade levirate marriage in such a case. When the sages heard of this ruling, "they were very disturbed, because he was a great scholar and his eyes were dim so that he was unable to come to the *bet midrash*." It was decided that Joshua b. Hananiah, Eleazar b. Azariah, and Akiva should call upon him to discuss the matter. Dosa explained that he too was of the opinion that the *halakhah* was in accordance with Bet Hillel, and the "son of Harkinas" who had permitted it was not he but his brother Jonathan, who was a disciple of Shammai (Yev. 16a; TJ, Yev. 1:6, 3a).

From a number of passages it appears that he was active in Jerusalem, but it is mentioned in the Tosefta (Mik. 6:2) that he appointed two scholars to investigate the ritual fitness of a **mikveh* between Usha and Shefaram. Dosa's maxim in *Avot* (3:10) is "Morning sleep, midday wine, children's talk, and sitting in the assemblies of the ignorant, put a man out of the world" (Avot 3:10).

BIBLIOGRAPHY: Frankel, Mishnah, index; Halevy, Dorot, 1 pt. 5 (1923), 219, 227, 340ff.; Hyman, Toledot, 322–4.

[Shmuel Safrai]

DOSA BEN SAADIAH (930–1017), head of the academy of Sura, and son of *Saadiah b. Joseph Gaon. It was not until 1013, 71 years after his father's death, that, at the age of 83, he became *gaon* of Sura. Though only a few of the responsa of Dosa have survived, the new spirit of *halakhah* introduced into the academy by his father, and by his predecessor R. *Samuel b. Ḥophni, is readily recognizable in them. During Dosa's lifetime Babylonia went into decline and Spanish scholars not only began to emancipate themselves from the authority of the *geonim* but even to compete with them. When R. *Samuel ha-Nagid wrote his commentary on complex talmudic subjects, in which he strongly criticized the explanations of Hai Gaon, Dosa hastened to Hai's support and vigorously defended him. At the request of Ḥasdai ibn Shaprut, Dosa wrote a monograph on his father's life, of which only fragments have survived. In addition to his responsa, Dosa wrote commentaries on the Talmud and philosophical works, none of which has been preserved. He studied the sciences and religious philosophy. One of his works was devoted to the problem of *creatio ex nihilo*.

BIBLIOGRAPHY: M. Margalioth, *Hilkhot ha-Nagid* (1962), 31ff.; Poznański, in: *Ha-Goren*, 6 (1905), 41; Levin, Oẓar, 12 (1943), 14; Assaf, in: *Tarbiz*, 6 (1934/35), 230; Mann, Texts, 1 (1931), 7, 116–7, 145, 153.

[Mordecai Margaliot]

DOSTAI BEN JUDAH (second century C.E.), *tanna* of the fifth generation. He is not mentioned in the Mishnah, but is quoted a number of times in the Tosefta and the tannaitic midrashim. In Tosef. Ḥul. 8:19 he transmits a *halakhah* in the name of R. Simeon. The tradition found in the printed editions of Bavli Mak. 7a, according to which a *tanna* by the name of Judah b. Dostai transmitted in the name of Simeon b. Shetaḥ.

A legal rule stating that a sentence passed by a Palestinian court over a person who later escaped abroad is not set aside for a new hearing, but in the case of a person who escaped to Palestine the sentence is set aside, is almost certainly a corruption of the reading found in the manuscripts "Dostai b. Judah said in the name of R. Simeon" (cf. Tosef. Ḥullin), as is confirmed by Tosef. Sanh 3:11, where the reading is "Dostai b. Judah said." Other occurrences of the name "Judah b. Dostai," as in BK 83b Vatican 116 and in Pesaḥim 70b Vatican 134 (both versus the readings of the majority of manuscripts) are also certainly scribal errors, e.g. in Pesaḥim 70b where the correct reading "Judah b. Dortai" was corrupted in various ways in several manuscripts (Friedman, Baraitot, 235 note 135). Therefore the "first century *tanna*" by the name of "Judah b. Dostai" should be removed from the lists of talmudic sages.

BIBLIOGRAPHY: Hyman, Toledot, 559; R. Rabinowitz, *Didqduqe Soferim*, Makkot 7a; S. Friedman, "Baraitot in the Babylonian Talmud: the Case of 'ben Tema' and 'ben Dortai'" (Hebrew), in: *Netiot le-David, Festschrift in Honor of David Weiss Halivni* (2004).

[Stephen G. Wald (2nd ed.)]

DOSTAI BEN YANNAI (fl. second half of second century), Palestinian *tanna*. The name Dostai is a form of the Greek Δοσίθεος corresponding to the Hebrew "Mattaniah." Only one brief *halakhah* is ascribed to Dostai himself (Tosef. Git. 7:11 = BB 11:10). In addition he reported a number of traditions in the name of the later *tannaim*, R. *Meir (Eruv. 5:4, Avot 3:8, Tos. Ber. 6:8), and R. *Yose b. Ḥalafta (Tos. Ṭoh. 5:8), as well as in the name of earlier figures like R. Eliezer (Tos, Shab. 14:16) and Bet Hillel and Bet Shammai (Tos. Ṭoh. 8:11). Like many relatively obscure tannaitic figures, the later talmudic tradition relates many colorful details concerning his adventures. Together with R. Yose b. Kippar he once went on a mission to Babylonia where they were ill-treated by the authorities. After their return to Palestine he defended himself before R. Aḥai b. Josiah for not having been able to protect his friend against the indignities they had suffered. This he did by giving a satirical description of the manners and vices of the Babylonian authorities (Git. 14a–b; TJ, Git. 1:6, 43d; TJ, Kid. 3:4, 64a). Some of the sayings ascribed to Dostai in the Talmud reflect a kind of humor, e.g., his answers to his pupils' questions on the differences between men and women (Nid. 31b). On the question "Why are the thermal springs of Tiberias not found in Jerusalem?" he replied that if Jerusalem had thermal springs the pilgrims would have come there for the pleasure of the baths and not for the sake of the pilgrimage (Pes. 8b). In another place, basing himself upon Psalms 17:15, he stated: "If a man gives but a penny to a beggar, he is deemed worthy of receiving the Divine Presence" (BB 10a).

BIBLIOGRAPHY: Bacher, Tann, 5 s.v.; Hyman, Toledot, 326.

DOSTÁL, ZENO (1934–1996), Czech writer and director. Dostál was born in Konice at Prostějov (Moravia). From 1944 he was hidden from Nazis by his relatives. In the 1950s his studies at the Faculty of Pedagogy were interrupted because of his father's imprisonment. In the 1960s, after working at manual labor, he was employed in a film studio in Prague, where he became an assistant director. He started publishing his "zodiac" stories in the 1980s: *Býk, Beran a Váhy* (1981; "A Taurus, an Aries and a Libra"), describing life in the author's native part of Moravia in the 1930s and during the Nazi occupation, followed by *Lev a Štír* (1983; "A Leo and a Scorpio"), *Vodnář* (1987; "An Aquarius"), *Vrata* (1987; "The Gate"), *Rekrut* (1989; "The Recruit"), *Labuť* (1991; "The Swan"), *Blíženci* (1993; "A Gemini"), and *Ryby* (1994; "A Pisces"), reflecting postwar Czech society and the situation of the Jews.

He directed the movies *Král Kolonád* (1990; "The King of Collonade"), after his story *Leo*; *Golet v údolí* (1995; "Galut in the Valley") based on the work of Ivan *Olbracht; and *Váhy* (1992; "A Libra") for Czech TV (based on his own screenplay).

From 1992 to his death in 1996, he was the chairman of the Prague Jewish community.

[Milos Pojar (2nd ed.)]

DOSTROVSKY, ARYEH (1887–1975), Israel dermatologist. Born in Caro, Russia, Dostrovsky studied medicine at several European universities before settling in Palestine in 1919. From 1920 to 1956 he was head of the Department of Skin and General Diseases at Hadassah Hospital, Jerusalem. He was the first dean of the Hebrew University-Hadassah Medical School (1948–53). Dostrovsky laid the foundation for the development of dermatology in Israel, and was a specialist in the problem of leprosy in Ereẓ Israel. He was a member of the expert advisory panel of the World Health Organization on venereal diseases and treponematosis and was coeditor of *International Dermatologica*.

DOSTROVSKY, ISRAEL (1918–), Israeli physicist. Dostrovsky was born in Odessa, Russia, and a year later immigrated with his parents to Ereẓ Israel. He studied in London, receiving his doctorate in physical chemistry in 1943, and from that year until 1948 was lecturer in chemistry at the University of North Wales. In 1948 he returned to Israel to join the staff of the Weizmann Institute, where he was head of the Isotope Research Department until 1965 and designed and constructed the isotope separation plant. From 1961 to 1964 he served as senior scientist at the Brookhaven National Laboratory in the United States. From 1965 to 1971 he was director general of the Israel Atomic Energy Commission. In 1971 Dostrovsky was appointed vice president of the Weizmann Institute and in 1972 acting president and chief executive officer. In November 1973 he was elected president. Dostrovsky made studies of the mechanism of chemical reactions and isotope effects in them and in the mechanisms of high-energy nuclear reactions: high-energy fission, spallation reactions and nuclear evaporation, fragmentation reactions, and nuclear transfer reactions. Later studies focused on solar energy. He founded the Weizmann Institute's solar energy research center, which utilizes unique equipment. He represented Israel in international organizations, such as the International Atomic Energy Agency, the International Energy Agency, and GALLEX, a program of the Neutrino Astrophysics Group for solar energy. Dostrovsky was a member of the Israeli Academy of Sciences and the New York Academy of Sciences. In 1995 he was awarded the Israel Prize for exact sciences.

[Shaked Gilboa (2nd ed.)]

DOTAN (Deutscher), ARON (1928–), Israeli scholar of the Hebrew language, the Masorah, biblical accentuation, and the history of Hebrew grammar. Born in Stuttgart, Germany, Dotan came to Palestine with his parents in 1934, and was raised and educated in Haifa. His academic studies at the Hebrew University of Jerusalem, begun in 1947, were interrupted by the War of Independence, during which Dotan served in the army and took part in battles in and around Jerusalem. He continued at the university after the war and was awarded a Ph.D. degree in 1963 for his study of *Dikdukei ha-Te'amim le-Rabbi Aharon ben Moshe ben Asher* (1963; see below). In 1961 he was appointed lecturer at Tel Aviv University (professor from 1969), where he continued to teach until his retirement in 1996. He also taught at Bar-Ilan University in Ramat Gan for most of this period, in addition to serving as a guest lecturer at the Sorbonne, at Yale University, and elsewhere. He was a member of the Academy of the Hebrew Language from 1966.

Dotan's research, as presented in several books and scores of articles, focuses mainly on the fields of the Masorah, biblical vocalization and accentuation, biblical manuscripts, and early Hebrew grammar. His *Sefer Dikdukei ha-Te'amim le-Rabbi Aharon ben Moshe ben Asher* ("The Dikdukei ha-Te'amim of Aaron ben Moses Ben-Asher") is a new critical edition of an early work by the outstanding tenth-century masorete Aaron ben Asher, with an introduction and extensive annotation. In another book, which inquires into Ben-Asher's religious affiliation, Dotan discredits the view that Ben-Asher was a Karaite (*Ben Asher's Creed: A Study of the History of the Controversy*, 1977). Dotan's intensive study of biblical manuscripts, of MS Leningrad (B19a) in particular, led to his publication in 1973 of a new edition of the Bible based entirely on this manuscript, which now serves as the Bible distributed to Israeli soldiers upon their conscription. A new edition of this Bible with a comprehensive introduction in English appeared under the title *Biblia Hebraica Leningradensia* (2001). Dotan's *Encyclopaedia Judaica* entry "Masorah" (1971; q.v.) provides a sweeping, detailed overview of the history of the Masorah and of the different systems of biblical accentuation.

Dotan's most important book in the field of early Hebrew grammar is *Or Rishon be-Ḥokhmat ha-Lashon* ("The Dawn of Hebrew Linguistics," 1997), a critical edition of *Saadiah Gaon's *Sefer Zahut Leshon ha-Ivrim* (in Arabic: *Kitāb Fasīh Lughat al-'Ibraniyyīn*), for which he was awarded the Bialik Prize for Jewish Thought in 1998. Alongside the Arabic original of this work, which is the first Hebrew grammar, this edition provides both an annotated Hebrew translation and a comprehensive introduction elucidating Saadiah's linguistic method.

In his *Min ha-Masorah el Reshit ha-Milona'ut ha-Ivrit* ("The Awakening of Word Lore: From the Masorah to the Beginnings of Hebrew Lexicography," 2004) Dotan shows that the Masorah comprised the basis of Hebrew lexicography. This approach is consistent with his thesis, demonstrated in a number of articles, that grammar was preceded by the Masorah.

[Chaim E. Cohen (2nd ed.)]

DOTHAN (Heb. דֹּתָן, דֹּתַיְן), city in the northern part of the territory of Manasseh near one of the north-south passes through the Carmel range. The author of Genesis locates the story of Joseph's sale to the *Ishmaelites-Midianites in this region (Gen. 37:17ff.). According to II Kings 6:13ff., Dothan was a walled city and the residence of the prophet Elisha. It is mentioned again in the apocryphal book of Judith (4:6; 7:3) among the cities in the Jezreel Valley near Holofernes' camp. Eusebius places it 12 mi. (20 km.) north of Samaria-Sebaste (Onom. 76:13). It is generally identified with Tell Dothan, 3 mi. (5 km.) south of Jenin and 13 mi. (22 km.) northwest of Shechem at the head of the valley of the same name. Excavations conducted there by J.P. Free, a professor at Wheaton College, between 1953 and 1960 uncovered remains from the Bronze and Iron Ages (Canaanite and Israelite periods) – walls, administrative buildings, private houses as well as tombs, rich in finds.

In 2005 an archaeological team from Wheaton College published the first volume of a series of final reports on the excavations. Their analysis revealed occupation from the Neolithic-Mameluke periods. Among the highlights, the Free excavations uncovered several sections of a large city wall dating to the EBII and EBIII, attended by several phases of walls and platforms, including a straddling tower, as well as monumental stairway and ramp, which probably led to a gate. The excavators found additional fortifications and a patrician house from the MBIIb-LBI periods. Dating from the LBII period, when the site was virtually uninhabited, some of the richest LB tombs in the region were excavated by Free's team. These family tombs lasted from LBIIA-Iron I and are an important example of continuity between the Bronze and Iron Ages in the highlands. The excavators uncovered a four-room Iron I period house surrounded by a large private precinct. Dating from the Iron II period, a massive exposure was excavated, which included seven buildings that were all variations on the four-room house. West of them a complex of buildings indicated an industrial area, showing evidence of smelting, weaving, and the production of oil and wine. In the southwest corner of the same area, the excavators uncovered a large administrative building, characterized by ashlar masonry, regular rooms grouped around a courtyard, pavements, drains, and dozens of identically sized small storage containers. These jars may have reflected the dry measure of a *seah*, for the purpose of redistribution. Along the western border of this area there was evidence of a typical Iron Age casemate wall. The Iron Age city underwent violent destruction, dated by radiocarbon analysis to the end of the ninth century. Some time later the tell was again used as a cemetery, after the region had been conquered by Assyria. From the Hellenistic period the fragmentary outline of a city *insula* was discovered, as well as a sizable collection of typical second century Rhodian stamped amphora handles. The Roman and Byzantine periods, confined to the top of the tell, contained massive architecture but few datable living surfaces. Finally, in the Mamluke period the top of the tell was reoccupied by a small farming village with typical Islamic courtyard houses.

BIBLIOGRAPHY: EM, 2 (1954), 772–3; Press, Ereẓ, s.v.; Aharoni, Land, index; Free, in: BASOR, 143 (1956), 11ff.; 152 (1958), 10ff.; 156 (1959), 22ff.; 160 (1960), 6ff. **ADD. BIBLIOGRAPHY:** D.M. Master, J.M. Monson, E.H.E. Lass, and G.A. Pierce (eds.), *Dothan I: Remains from the Tell (1953–1964)* (2005).

[Egon H.E. Lass and Daniel M. Master (2nd ed.)]

DOTHAN, MOSHE (1919–1999), Israeli archaeologist. After graduating from high school in his native Cracow, Dothan received an entry permit to study in Palestine at the Hebrew University of Jerusalem. He arrived in 1938 but his studies were soon interrupted by the outbreak of World War II. He spent two years in kibbutz Naḥshonim (today kibbutz Ma'apil) and then joined the British army in 1942. His service took him to Malta, North Africa, and Italy. When in Italy, he first felt an interest in archaeology.

In 1946 he returned to Palestine and completed a master's degree in archaeology and Jewish history and while working from 1950 in the Department of Antiquities in Jerusalem was able to conclude his doctorate. His thesis (1959) was on the Late Chalcolithic period (4000–3000 B.C.E.) and much of his research was based on his findings at Tel Asor (near Naḥal Iron), a site where a mass grave from that period was discovered.

He headed numerous excavations including Tel Afula (1951); Mezer in Naḥal Iron; the 1956 survey of Kadesh Barnea in northern Sinai of the Israelite town of the tenth century B.C.E.; Tel Mor, the ancient port dating from 1600 B.C.E. where Ashdod port stands today; the excavations of the important Philistine town of Ashdod (1960–77); Ḥammath Tiberias (1962) where the excavations revealed an early synagogue dated approximately 250 C.E. under other synagogues which had been constructed on top of it; and Tel Acre (1972–89) where he headed excavations whose finds went back to the tenth century B.C.E.

From 1972 to 1988 Dothan was a professor at Haifa University where he founded the department of maritime civilization and in 1976 the department of archaeology. He was the *Encyclopaedia Judaica* departmental editor for Bible realia.

He published over 150 articles, primarily in English. He was married to Trude *Dothan.

[Elaine Hoter]

DOTHAN, TRUDE (1922–), archaeologist, expert on the Philistines and Sea Peoples. Born in Vienna, Dothan moved to Jerusalem in 1925 with her parents, Grete Wolf Krakauer, a well-known painter, and Leopold Krakauer, one of the pioneers of modern Israeli architecture and a graphic artist. Dothan studied archaeology and biblical studies at the Hebrew University, eventually earning her M.A. in 1950 with a thesis on the Khirbet Kerak pottery of the EB III period, written under the guidance of Professor E.L. Sukenik. Following her post-graduate studies at the Oriental Institute, University of Chicago, in 1951–52, and at the Institute of Archaeology, University of London, in 1953, Dothan completed her Ph.D. in archaeology at the Hebrew University in Jerusalem in 1961. Having already excavated between 1945 and 1952 at Khirbet Kerak, Ein Gedi and Tel Qasile, Dothan became a field supervisor at the Hazor excavations in 1955–60, under Yigael Yadin, and later a co-director of excavations at Ein Gedi in 1961–62. In 1971–72, Dothan co-directed (with A. Ben-Tor) excavations at Athienou in Cyprus, as well as directing excavations at Deir el-Balah, near Gaza, at intervals between 1971 and 1982. From 1981 to 1996, Dothan co-directed a major archaeological project at Tel Miqne-*Ekron. Having taught archaeology at the Institute of Archaeology, Hebrew University, since 1962, earning her full professorship in 1974, Dothan gained an enormous amount of respect from her students and colleagues, for her enthusiasm and learning. Dothan is the author of numerous articles and books, notably *The Philistines and Their Material Culture* (1981), and *People of the Sea: In Search of the Philistines* (1992, with M. Dothan). A recipient of many fellowships and grants, Dothan was awarded the P. Schimmel Award in 1991 and the prestigious Israel Prize in 1998. A volume of essays, *Mediterranean Peoples in Transition* (eds. S. Gitin, A. Mazar and E. Stern), was presented in honor of Dothan in 1998. Trude Dothan was married to a distinguished archaeologist, the late Moshe *Dothan.

[Shimon Gibson (2nd ed.)]

DOUDTCHITZKY, DINORA (c. 1915–2004), Chilean engraver. Born in the Ukraine, Doudtchitzky's family emigrated to Argentina when she was 10 years old. In Buenos Aires she studied art and in 1939 she moved to Chile where she continued her studies in painting, murals, and engraving. In 1959 she became professor of engraving at the Catholic University.

DOUGLAS, KIRK (originally **Issur Danielovich Demsky**; 1916–), U.S. actor. Douglas was born in Amsterdam, N.Y. A good student and a keen athlete, he wrestled competitively during his time at St. Lawrence University. In 1939 he enrolled at the American Academy of Dramatic Arts in New York City. A small part in Broadway's *Wind Is Ninety* in 1945, as well as the help of former classmate Lauren *Bacall, brought him to the attention of Hollywood producer Hal B. Wallis, who chose him to play opposite Barbara Stanwyck in *The Strange Love of Martha Ivers* (1946). His performance received rave reviews, and more work quickly followed, including a role in the dramatic film *I Walk Alone* (1948). In it, he worked alongside Burt Lancaster. The chemistry between the two future screen legends was so strong that they ultimately appeared in seven films together, including *Gunfight at the O.K. Corral* (1957), *Seven Days in May* (1964), and *Tough Guys* (1986).

Douglas' portrayal in 1949 of a prizefighter in the film *Champion* confirmed his reputation as a leading dramatic artist. He had memorable roles in *Young Man with a Horn* (1950), *The Bad and the Beautiful* (1953), *Lust for Life* (1956), and *Lonely are the Brave* (1962).

Turning to production, he formed a film company that made the anti-war *Paths of Glory* (1957) and *Spartacus* (1960), in both of which Douglas starred. He identified himself with Israeli causes in the U.S. He starred in *The Juggler* (1953), which was filmed in Israel, and in 1966 played the lead in *Cast a Giant Shadow*, a film about Col. David (Mickey) *Marcus. Douglas celebrated his bar mitzvah twice: once when he was 13 years old, and the second time when he was 83.

Other films in the prolific actor's filmography include *My Dear Secretary* (1949), *A Letter to Three Wives* (1949), *The Glass Menagerie* (1950), *20,000 Leagues under the Sea* (1954), *Ulysses* (1955), *Man without a Star* (1955), *The Vikings* (1958), *Strangers When We Meet* (1960), *Town without Pity* (1961), *Two Weeks in Another Town* (1962), *The List of Adrian Messenger* (1963), *Is Paris Burning?* (1966), *The Arrangement* (1969), *There Was a Crooked Man* (1970), *The Fury* (1978), *The Man from Snowy River* (1982), *Greedy* (1994), *Diamonds* (1999), *It Runs in the Family* (2003), and *Illusions* (2004).

Douglas became a goodwill ambassador of the United Nations in 1983, and he also held the position of director of the Los Angeles chapter of the United Nations Association. He was a goodwill ambassador for the U.S. State Department from 1963. His efforts were rewarded in 1981 with the Presidential Medal of Freedom, and in 1983 with the Jefferson Award. France honored him by making him a Chevalier of the Legion of Honor. In 2002 he was awarded the UCLA Medal of Honor.

Douglas was inducted into the Hall of Great Western Performers of the National Cowboy and Western Heritage Museum in 1984. For his film work, he received the American Cinema Award (1987), the German Golden Kamera Award

(1987), the National Board of Review's Career Achievement Award (1989), a Life Achievement Award from the American Film Institute (1991), a Lifetime Achievement Award from the Academy of Motion Picture Arts and Sciences "for 50 years as a creative and moral force in the motion picture community" (1995), and a Lifetime Achievement Award from the American Film Institute (1999).

Kirk Douglas was voted the 36th Greatest Movie Star of all time by *Entertainment Weekly*.

He published his autobiography, *The Ragman's Son*, in 1988. He also wrote the novel *Dance with the Devil* (1990), the novel *The Gift* (1992), *Kirk Douglas Writes to Gary Cooper* (1992), the novel *Last Tango in Brooklyn* (1994), the novel *The Broken Mirror* (1997), *Climbing the Mountain: My Search for Meaning* (1997), *Young Heroes of the Bible: A Book for Family Sharing* (1999), and *My Stroke of Luck* (2002).

The actor Michael *Douglas is one of his four sons.

BIBLIOGRAPHY: *Current Biography Yearbook* 1952 (1953), 155–6. **ADD. BIBLIOGRAPHY:** T. Thomas, *The Films of Kirk Douglas* (1972); J. McBride, *Kirk Douglas: A Pyramid Illustrated History of the Movies* (1976); R. Lacourbe, *Kirk Douglas* (1980); M. Munn, *Kirk Douglas* (1985); S. Press, *Michael and Kirk Douglas* (1995); D.D. Darrid, *In the Wings: A Memoir* (1999).

[Stewart Kampel / Rohan Saxena and Ruth Beloff (2nd ed.)]

DOUGLAS, MELVYN (1901–1981), U.S. actor. Son of Edouard Hesselberg, a musician, Douglas first appeared on the New York stage in 1928 in *A Free Soul*. He went to Hollywood in 1931 to act in a screen version of *Tonight or Never*. After his army service in World War II, Douglas' Broadway appearances included *Two Blind Mice* (1949), *Inherit the Wind* (1955), *Waltz of the Toreadors* (1956), *The Best Man* (1960), and *Spofford* (1967). His films include *Counselor-at-Law* (1933), *The Shining Hour* (1938), *Ninotchka* (1939), *Billy Budd* (1962), *Hud* (1963), for which he received an Oscar for Best Supporting Actor, *The Americanization of Emily* (1964), *Hotel* (1967), *I Never Sang For My Father* (1970), *The Candidate* (1972), *The Tenant* (1976), and *Being There* (1979).

[Jonathan Licht (2nd ed.)]

DOUGLAS, MICHAEL (1944–), film actor and producer. Born in New Brunswick, New Jersey, Michael is the son of actor Kirk *Douglas. He received a B.A. from the University of California at Santa Barbara in 1968. Although his father tried to discourage him from entering show business, Michael would not be deterred. After graduating from university, he moved to New York City to continue his drama studies at the Neighborhood Playhouse and at the American Place Theatre.

Michael Douglas first made his mark in the television series *The Streets of San Francisco* (1972). He was the founder of Big Stick Productions and Stonebridge Entertainment. His first major success came as co-producer of the multi-Academy Award winning film *One Flew over the Cuckoo's Nest* (1975). His career as a movie star began with *Coma* (1978) and *Romancing the Stone* (1984). He won an Academy Award for best actor for his portrayal of a power-hungry New York stockbroker in the 1987 film *Wall Street*. Other leading roles were in *The China Syndrome* (1979), *Running* (1979), *Jewel of the Nile* (1985), A *Chorus Line* (1985), *Fatal Attraction* (1987), *Black Rain* (1989), *The War of the Roses* (1989), *Basic Instinct* (1992), *Shining Through* (1992), *Falling Down* (1993), *Disclosure* (1994), *The American President* (1995), *A Perfect Murder* (1998), *Wonder Boys* (2000), *Traffic* (2000), *One Night at McCool's* (2001), *The In-Laws* (2003), and *The Ride to Mt. Morgan* (2005).

The Michael Douglas Foundation, a non-profit organization, was established in 1991. Among its goals, the foundation seeks to better the living conditions of those in need of assistance, promote peace within and among nations, and protect the global ecosystem. Over the years, the foundation has contributed to more than 90 charities worldwide. In 1998 Douglas was named a United Nations Messenger of Peace because of his efforts to focus world attention on nuclear disarmament and human rights.

In 2000 he married actress Catherine Zeta-Jones.

ADD. BIBLIOGRAPHY: S. Press, *Michael and Kirk Douglas*, (1995).

[Jonathan Licht / Rohan Saxena and Ruth Beloff (2nd ed.)]

°DOUWES, ARNOLD (1906–1999), Righteous Among the Nations. The son of a Dutch pastor, Douwes was recruited for the underground by Johannes Post, a farmer and town councilor in the village of Nieuwlande (Drente), and immediately dedicated himself to saving Jews. Assisted by Max ("Nico") Leons, a Jew posing as a Protestant, Douwes systematically traversed great stretches of the Nieuwlande countryside on his bicycle, stopping at every house and farm to ask whether the inhabitants would be willing to lodge a Jewish child. When convincing failed, Douwes was not beyond, in some instances, forcing people to admit Jews for shelter, on the pretext that it was by order of the Resistance. His sometimes tactless methods produced good results – hundreds of Jews found shelter in the sprawling farms of the Nieuwlande region. Lou Gans, one of the many Jews assisted by Douwes, relates that when he arrived from Amsterdam, Douwes took him for a temporary stay with Jan Dekker, Nieuwlande's postman. He was then moved to the home of Hendrik Kikkert, a local farmer; then to Seine and Jans Otten, both of whom were teachers; and on to Simon Dijk, a housepainter (where counterfeit identity cards were printed), and Engel Bolwijn, a baker. "Our task was not easy," Douwes recalled. "The victims themselves were the main problem. It was very difficult to convince them. Many did not wish to acknowledge the dangers facing them.... We had to resort to lies in order to get the parents to give us their children!... When we told people 'one week,' it really meant until the liberation. When we said 'two days' we meant two years.... We used to contact people in Amsterdam and beg them to let their children go, assuring them that there were safe places waiting for them. There were really no such places. Our thinking was that we would somehow find suitable places the moment the children arrived. They had to be found and were indeed found: in homes, cellars, attics, or elsewhere." Douwes personally met the children in Amsterdam or at the train station when they arrived in the Nieuwlande region. Sixteen-year-old Haim Roet, one of those saved by Douwes, was brought by him by train from Amsterdam to Zwolle in eastern Holland and then by bicycle to Dedenswaart. There Haim was reunited with his brother, but when he fell ill, after about a month in hiding, and the local doctor refused to treat him, Douwes came to the rescue, taking him to a different doctor; then after Haim's recovery, bringing him back to Dedenswaart. When the German police staged raids in the area, Douwes spent the night on his bicycle, transferring children from one location to another right under their noses. "I well remember sitting on the back of Arnold's bike, riding the narrow lanes beside the canals that crisscrossed the area," Miriam Whartman relates. When she told Douwes that her host family in the village of Hollandse Veld was subtly trying to convert her, he immediately moved her to another household. Douwes kept a secret coded diary of the people rescued, their sheltering places and other vital information. An operation of such magnitude could not go long unnoticed, and the Gestapo was soon on the lookout for him. To avoid arrest he changed his appearance, sporting a mustache and wearing a hat and eyeglasses to hide his face as much as possible. Despite all his precautions, Douwes was arrested in December 1944. While awaiting execution, in an Assen prison, on December 11, 1944, the underground rescued him in a daring operation. He then went into hiding until the country's liberation. After the war he married Jet Reichenberger, one of the women saved by him, and the couple eventually settled in Israel with their three daughters, with Arnold resuming his previous profession as a landscape architect. Toward the end of his life, he returned to the Netherlands. It is estimated that Douwes was responsible for saving at least 500 Jews, including around 100 children. In 1965, Yad Vashem awarded him the title of Righteous Among the Nations.

BIBLIOGRAPHY: Yad Vashem Archives M31–56; I. Gutman, *Encyclopedia of the Righteous Among the Nations: Netherlands*, vol. 1 (2004), 223–24; M. Paldiel, *The Path of the Righteous* (1993), 138–41.

[Mordecai Paldiel (2nd ed.)]

DOV BAER (the Maggid) OF MEZHIRECH (d. 1772), one of the earliest and most important leaders of *Ḥasidism. As a youth, Dov Baer received a traditional religious education in the yeshivah of R. Jacob Joshua *Falk, author of *Penei Yehoshu'a*. He taught in Torchin and later became preacher in Korets and Rovno. Subsequently he moved to Mezhirech (Mezhirichi) in Volhynia, which became the center of the ḥasidic movement, and toward the end of his life he moved to Annopol (Hanipol). An erudite talmudic scholar, Dov Baer also made a profound study of Kabbalah, adopting the system of Lurianic Kabbalah (originated by Isaac *Luria) and an ascetic way of life. The mortifications to which he subjected himself eventually made him ill; he contracted a disease which affected his legs and he became bedridden. Tradition relates that he sought a cure from *Israel b. Eliezer (the Ba'al Shem Tov), the originator of modern Ḥasidism, whose reputation as a healer was widespread, and Dov Baer became one of his foremost disciples.

After the death of the Ba'al Shem Tov in 1760, Dov Baer was recognized as his successor to leadership of the movement although opposed by *Jacob Joseph of Polonnoye, the more senior disciple. The authority of Dov Baer as the main proponent of Ḥasidism was apparently only recognized in 1766, and even then there were a few notable exceptions such as Phinehas of Korets. Unlike his predecessor, Dov Baer was not a man of the people, and his illness made it difficult for him to associate with his disciples. He possessed charismatic qualities, however, and was an eloquent preacher and teacher. Solomon *Maimon, who visited Dov Baer during his youth, expressed great admiration for his spiritual endowments. Dov Baer was highly esteemed by his disciples, who not only derived spiritual sustenance from his teachings and utterances but also divined an inner significance in his daily life and actions. Thus, *Aryeh Leib Sarahs is said to have visited Dov Baer in order "to see how he put on his shoes and tied his shoelaces."

Dov Baer formulated a doctrine that provided Ḥasidism with a speculative-mystical system, introducing into it the concepts of Kabbalah and a specific pattern of organization. Dov Baer transferred the center of Ḥasidism from Podolia in the southeast to Volhynia in central Poland, and this facilitated its spread throughout the country. He endeavored to popularize Ḥasidism among new classes and in new areas, and sent emissaries to spread the new teaching in many places throughout Poland. His activity may be considered the beginning of Ḥasidism as a movement, while his personal conduct set the precedent in Ḥasidism, for the institution of the *Ẓaddik*, or saintly leader. Under his leadership, Ḥasidism spread in the Ukraine, Lithuania, and Poznania, and began to take root in central Poland. He also won respect and authority outside his own community, and his reputation as a talmudist led numerous people to appeal to him on legal matters, such as ownership and trespass. Dov Baer also took part in communal affairs and his emissary Aaron of Karlin succeeded in obtaining an amendment of the communal tax regulations. In Dov Baer's later years, his views on the Divinity, as well as his methods of leadership, aroused fierce opposition from many rabbis and those who did not accept Ḥasidism. Especial targets for their hostility were the ecstatic modes of religious worship, accompanied by violent bodily movement, adopted by the Ḥasidim of "Talk," the changes he introduced in the prayer ritual in adopting the Lurianic liturgy, the innovations in ritual slaughter, and the neglect of Torah study by the youth who abandoned the yeshivot and flocked to Mezhirech. The main problem confronting the rabbinical opposition was the authority assumed by the Ḥasidim to decide matters of belief and religious conduct. Eventually the ban of excommunication was pronounced on Ḥasidism in Vilna, the orthodox stronghold. According to tradition, the excommunication affected the health of Dov Baer and he died shortly afterward. After his death Ḥasidism remained without a single leader commanding the same authority and general support from all Ḥasidim, and the leadership was assumed by a number of his disciples. The doctrine of Dov Baer may only be ascertained from collections made of his interpretation of biblical passages and rabbinical literature which appear in several versions: *Maggid Devarav le-Ya'akov*, and *Likkutei Amarim* ("Collected Sayings," Lvov, 1697, falsified date), written down by Isaiah of Donovich; *Or ha-Emet* (Husiatyn, 1889), copied from the manuscript written by *Levi Isaac of Berdichev, and in Ms. 8°3282 in the Israel National Library, written by Levi Isaac of Berdichev. Additional sayings have been collected in *Likkutei Amarim* (Lvov, 1792).

Many of Dov Baer's homiletical observations are included in works written by his disciples, among whom were Samuel and Phineas *Horowitz, *Shneur Zalman of Lyady, Israel of *Kozienice, *Jacob Isaac of Lublin, Menahem Mendel of Vitebsk, Nahum of Chernobyl, *Elimelech of Lyzhansk, *Zusya of Annopol (Hanipol), Levi Isaac of Berdichev, Aaron of Karlin, and Aryeh Leib Sarahs.

His Doctrine

Dov Baer develops the doctrine of *devekut* ("devotion") out of a pantheistic and acosmic perception which describes the essence of God as penetrating all existence and embodying everything: "the whole earth is the Holy One, and it is the world which stands within the Creator." From this doctrine he formulated an approach to mankind which had as its basis an elevated appreciation of the metaphysical status of man. The divine emanation through all things renders possible, by means of inner reflection and contemplation, a close and direct relationship with the root of being, and the *ẓaddik* or the devoted man is thus a medium who enjoys direct contact with God. Since, in Dov Baer's theory, every man can achieve this direct contact with the Divine, the charismatic figure of the *ẓaddik* loses his function as the intermediary between the Ḥasid and God. From his acosmic and spiritualist outlook, Dov Baer speaks of *devekut* through the turning aside from conscious will and the negation of existence. The purpose of man is to abolish concrete cosmic reality and to return to the mystical *Ayin* ("Nothingness") which preceded creation ("God created existence out of nothing and He makes nothingness out of existence"). Thus the existence of man in this world is seen as a decline which must precede a rise, an existence which must precede nothingness. The soul descends from the heights in order to raise up the material existence through its spiritual exaltation and thus restore the unity which was disturbed by the work of creation. The *Sefirah* of *Ḥokhmah* ("Wisdom") or *Ayin* is the state which precedes creation as the object of the meditations of those in a state of *devekut*. In the words of the Maggid: "it is impossible for anything to pass from one existence to another, without it becoming nothing (*Ayin*) at the point of transition." (This is the Aristotelian theory of the "absence" in the transfer from potential to actual existence, which was transmuted from the physical realm to the metaphysical.) In all his extant writings there is a definitely acknowledged mingling between the sphere of the first *Sefirah* (*Keter, Ayin*) and the second (*Ḥokhmah*). Generally, Dov Baer does not distinguish between the two *Sefirot* – in various places they are treated as identical – and he transposes them in order to elucidate the true structure of the soul. He uses theosophic language and kabbalistic terminology when dealing with matters pertaining to the theory of the soul, from the principles of the doctrine of the *Sefirot*.

In his words on the essence of prayer, Dov Baer rejects the emphasis on the personal nature of supplication and advocates an attitude of indifference toward the results of the act, with no anticipation of an answer. Prayer is a psychological exercise in maximal concentration, a technique or ladder toward denial of the self. In the transfer from vocal prayer (speech) to prayer by thought, the human act is converted into divine speech (automatic speech).

The logical conclusion to be drawn from Dov Baer's monist approach, which lays down that God is to be found everywhere ("there is no place which is not occupied by Him") is that it is possible to worship Him with every act: "know Him in all thy ways" (he does not accept the Lurianic dualism which accentuates the extremes of evil and good; for him there is no absolute evil but only degrees of good). The idea of divine immanence and the Lurianic concept of the uplifting of the *niẓoẓot* ("sparks") are the theoretical basis for the principle of "worship through corporeality" (*avodah be-gashmiyyut*), i.e., the worship of God through *devekut* even during the performance of physical acts. Dov Baer was aware that such an emphasis on the value of the *devekut*, with its concomitant disregard of the precepts and halakhic principles, was likely to lead to anarchy and antinomianism; he therefore limited his approach to the spiritual sphere and emphasized the importance of the necessity for meticulous observance of the normative framework of the *mitzvot*. Because of his tendency toward spirituality, Dov Baer was a conservative in the field of *halakhah* and inclined toward conformity in practical areas. Worship through corporeality is difficult and only "outstanding men" can abide by it.

The concept of *ẓimẓum* ("contraction") in his doctrine contradicts in principle the Lurianic concept and returns to the ideological system of Moses *Cordovero. *Ẓimẓum* is not interpreted as a regression but as an abundance of emanation. The process of *ẓimẓum* is conceived as an act which differs in meaning with respect to the bestower and the recipients. From the aspect of the Divine Essence, *ẓimẓum* is an oblivion and a concealment, while from the aspect of the living creatures it is a manifestation and a revelation. *Ẓimẓum* is a form of cognition which compels God to appear according to the laws of the intellect. Dov Baer interprets the verse: "the king is held captive in the tresses" (Song 7:6), as "tresses of the mind" (*Maggid Devarav le-Ya'akov*). (The contraction of light and its embodiment in objects is conditional to perception, just as thought is revealed by its materialization – its *ẓimẓum* – in sound and speech.) By rejecting the Lurianic mythical personification, he blurs the origin of the fall of the *niẓoẓot* and dissociates himself from the notion of a crisis in the relationship of God with Himself and His relationship with the world. He does not interpret the *shevirah* ("breaking of the vessels") as a catastrophe within the divine world; its purpose is to illuminate, just as the tailor cuts in order to sew. The *shevirah* is expressed in allegoric fashion ("a broken heart") and is described as an internal event in the life of man.

Dov Baer's eschatological conception is not bound to any historical period. In it the emphasis is not on matters concerning messianism, as in Shabbateanism; rather the preredemption tension is slackened and the emphasis is placed on the road which leads to redemption instead of its consequences. Redemption has ceased to be a single national historical event and has become a continuous spiritual experience for the individual.

The main authority of the ḥasidic leader derived essentially from his direct connection with the heavenly powers, allied to his concern for the individual and the community. The *ẓaddik* is a man who struggles to attain a life of complete holiness, devoid of any personal benefit and untainted by any evil inclination. He supervises the scales of the world, watching over its moral equilibrium, and the social sphere is the lowest plane of his mystical activity. By the strength of his religious elevation, he is an intercessor for the bestowal of plenty and it is his task to put right the status of the worlds and redeem existence according to the Lurianic system of the uplifting of the "sparks" and the special *ḥasidic* method of the sublimation of evil thoughts, which transferred the scene of the struggle to the personal sphere and determined a process of internal individual restitution of the soul (*tikkun* of *Adam Kadmon* by means of *tikkun* of *Adam Taḥton*). Dov Baer differentiates between *ẓaddikim* who succeed in maintaining the dialectic tension between social life and the mystic life (and thus maintain a social and metaphysical link between themselves and the individual) and "*ẓaddikim* who are compelled to withdraw from the people" because their contact with society is liable to result in their downfall. His theory does not emphasize the doctrine of the *ẓaddik* and recognizes the possibility of ecstatic experiences without intermediaries. The doctrine of the *ẓaddik* was mainly developed by the disciples of Elimelech of Lyshansk (*ẓaddikut ma'asit*, the practical role of the *ẓaddik*) and was stressed in the Ḥasidism of Bratslav.

BIBLIOGRAPHY: R. Schatz, *Ha-Ḥasidut ke-Mistikah* (1968); M. Buber, *Der Grosse Maggid und seine Nachfolger* (1922); idem, *Tales of Hasidim* (1964), 98–112; G. Scholem, in: M. Buber and N. Rotenstreich (eds.), *Hagut* (1944), 147–51; idem, in: *Review of Religion*, 14 (1950), 115–39; Horodetzky, Ḥasidut, 75–102; Dubnow, Ḥasidut, 76–99; A.J. Heschel, in: *Sefer ha-Yovel shel ha-Do'ar* (1952), 279–85; J. Weiss, in: *Erkhei ha-Yahadut* (1953), 81–90; idem, in: HUCA, 31 (1960), 137–47.

[Esther (Zweig) Liebes]

DOVE (Heb. יוֹנָה, *yonah*), the domesticated (*Columba domestica*) as well as the wild pigeon, of which several species are found in Ereẓ Israel, in whose caves and rock clefts brood large flocks of rock pigeons (*Columba livia*), considered to be the original species of the domesticated variety. It builds its nest in the clefts of precipitous rocks inaccessible to birds and animals of prey (Jer. 48:28). Sepulchral chambers, hewn in caves in several places in Israel, are used by doves for brooding, and in the Bet Guvrin region there are columbaria consisting of tens of thousands of such chambers. Among the varieties of the rock pigeon is a wild variety found in Jerusalem which broods under the caves of houses and is known as the "loftdove" in contradistinction to the "cote dove" which is bred (Tosef., Beẓah 1:10). The Mishnah refers to the catching of wild doves in nets (BK 7:7). The dove, which is permitted as food, was brought as an offering by the poor (Lev. 5:7) and by the Nazirite (Num. 6:10). Because of their importance as a sacrifice, the state of the young doves' development was taken into account when intercalating the year (Sanh. 11a). The sages held that the dove was eligible for sacrifices because "there is none among the birds more persecuted than doves" (BK 93a). It is monogamous, the female following the male (cf. Hos. 7:11). At nesting time the males coo (Isa. 59:11). The dove symbolizes beauty, innocence, and purity (Song 1:15; 5:2). The "*benei yonah*" which were used as sacrifices are defined in the Talmud as tender young doves until "their feathers begin to glisten"; they are identical with the *gozal* (Gen. 15:9; cf. Kin. 2:1; Ḥul. 22b). Of a superior domestic stock were the "*hardesiot*" doves, a name derived, some contend, from that of King Herod who, according to Josephus, bred doves (Jos., Wars, 5:181; cf. Ḥul. 139b). Among those ineligible to act as witnesses is one who decoys doves from his neighbor's dovecote or who engages in pigeon races (Sanh. 25a). The first dove mentioned in the Bible is the one sent by *Noah which brought back an olive leaf (Gen. 8:8–11) – according to rabbinic tradition from the Mount of Olives.

BIBLIOGRAPHY: Lewysohn, Zool, 199ff.; Tristam, Nat Hist, 211–6; Y. Aharoni, *Torat ha-Ḥai*, 1 (1923), 103–5; F.S. Bodenheimer, *Ha-Ḥai be-Arẓot ha-Mikra*, 2 (1956), 385–92; J. Feliks, *Animal World of the Bible* (1962), 54. **ADD BIBLIOGRAPHY:** Feliks, Ha-Ẓome'aḥ, 238.

[Jehuda Feliks]

DOWRY (Heb. נְדֻנְיָה), the property a wife brings to her husband at marriage; the Yiddish equivalent, *nadn*, is from the same root. The custom of *nedunyah* became clearly defined and institutionalized only in the talmudic period. In biblical times, *mohar* (מֹהַר), whereby the groom bought his wife from her father (Gen. 24:53; Ex. 22:15–16; Hos. 3:2), was the accepted practice. It was then customary that the groom give the bride gifts, and that she bring certain property to her husband's home upon marriage: slaves, cattle, real estate, etc. (cf. Gen. 24:59–61; 29; Judg. 1:14ff.; I Kings 9:16). Evidence of the custom of *nedunyah* is to be found in Tobit (7:14; 8:21) and in the Assuan papyri (Cowley, Aramaic, nos. 15, 18). Gradually, *mohar* was superseded by the *ketubbah* custom according to which the husband merely assumed the responsibility of compensation to his wife in case he divorced her: he had to pay her 200 *zuzim* if she had been a virgin at the time of marriage, and 100 *zuzim* if a widow or divorcée (see **Ketubbah*).

By talmudic times, the institution of *nedunyah* was prevalent; the father gave a dowry to the bride since the daughter was excluded from paternal inheritance. Fifty *zuzim* (equivalent to the worth of 180 grams of silver) was the minimum amount a father was obliged to give to his daughter (Ket. 6:5). Parents usually gave much more, according to their social standing. Community funds provided the dowry for an orphan or a very poor girl (*ibid.*; cf. Sh. Ar., YD 251:8). In case of her father's death, the brothers of a minor girl were obliged to give her the minimum dowry, and the court estimated how much her father would have given her above the minimum dowry. The sum was then taken out of the father's estate and given to the daughter upon majority (Ket. 6:6; 68a–69b). In the absence of such an estimate, each daughter was entitled to receive one-tenth of the value of her father's estate in money, or in valuables (Yad, Ishut, 20:4–7; Sh. Ar., EH 113:4). If the father was unable or unwilling to pay the promised dowry at the betrothal ceremony, the groom could refuse to marry his bride (Ket. 13:5; Ket. 108b–109a). Insistence on exact payment of the promised dowry, however, was frowned upon by later rabbinic authorities (Rema to Sh. Ar., EH 2:1). In certain communities it was customary for the groom's father to make a dowry contribution equal to that of the bride's father (Ket. 102b). The dowry, whether given in real estate, slaves, money, or chattel was recorded in the marriage contract (the *ketubbah*) and in some instances one-third or one-fifth of the actual value of the dowry was added to the sum mentioned in the *ketubbah*. Based upon a decree enacted by *Simeon b. Shetaḥ (first century C.E.), the Talmud ruled that the husband and his entire property were liable for compensation as stipulated in the *ketubbah*, either in case he died (when she collected the sum specified in the *ketubbah* from the heirs) or in case he divorced his wife (Ket. 82b). For the status of the dowry and the husband's rights and obligations, see below. The rabbinic enactments (*Takkanot Shum*) by R. Jacob *Tam and by the rabbinic synod of the communities of Speyer, Worms, and Mainz (Germany) stipulated that if a woman died without children within the first year of her marriage, the whole dowry should be returned to her father or to his heirs, and if she died without children within two years of her marriage, one-half of her dowry should be returned to her father or his heirs. These stipulations were accepted by Jews all over Europe, as well as by some Oriental communities. A rabbinic conference at Slutsk (1761) modified these rules by decreeing that only after five years of marriage would the husband of a childless wife become the sole heir to his deceased wife's property.

The custom of dowry in its original sense prevailed until modern times, especially among Jews of Eastern Europe. In these communities, the dowry often consisted of full board granted to the groom for several years so that he might continue his talmudic studies free from financial care. The custom was called in Yiddish *kest* and the financial arrangements of the dowry were detailed in a document called *tena'im* ("stipulations"; "conditions") signed at the betrothal ceremony; *tenoim shraybn* is derived from the term *tena'im* (see Ket. 102a–b). Jews in Muslim countries never accepted the custom of *nedunyah*, but continued the practice of *mohar*. The money which the groom gave to the bride's father, however, was used to buy furniture and household goods for the newly married couple. In modern Israel, the Oriental practices of *mohar*, as well as the custom of *nedunyah*, tend to disappear gradually. On the other hand, in cases of divorce, when couples settle the material aspects before a rabbinic court, the court's judgment, which is guided by the principles of *halakhah*, is legally binding. Societies for providing dowries for poor or orphaned girls were prevalent (see **Hakhnasat Kallah*).

In Jewish Law

Dowry or *nedunyah*, apparently from the word *neden*, nedeh (i.e., gift – Ezek. 16:33 and commentaries), means all property of whatever kind brought by the wife to the husband upon their marriage (Yad, Ishut, 16:1 and *Maggid Mishneh* thereto). In its restricted and common meaning, the term is intended to refer to those assets of the wife which she of her own free will entrusts to her husband's responsibility, the equivalent whereof the husband of his own free will undertakes in the **ketubbah*, and in a sum of money specified therein as the *nedunyah*, to restore to his wife upon dissolution of their marriage (*Maggid Mishneh*, Ishut 16:1; Tur, EH 85; Sh. Ar., EH 66: 11a and 85:2, Isserles' gloss; 88:2). Such property is also called *nikhsei ẓon barzel*, to be distinguished from another category of the wife's property, called *nikhsei melog* (see below). It is the practice for the husband to undertake in the *ketubbah* to restore to his wife the dowry with an increment (the *tosefet nedunyah*) of one third or one half of the amount specified, subject to local custom. Both parts of the total amount may be stipulated together in an inclusive sum and this is the customary practice; to this inclusive sum is added the sum of the *ketubbah*, as fixed by the *halakhah*, and its increments (see **Ketubbah*), so that an overall sum is mentioned, but it is stressed that this sum is the aggregate of all the above-mentioned components (Sh. Ar., EH 66:11, and *Rema* thereto). The said obligation of the husband is treated in the same manner as any other pecuniary obligation (*Maggid Mishneh*, Ishut 16:1).

NIKHSEI ZON BARZEL. (lit. "the property of iron sheep") is a term derived from the name of a transaction in which one party entrusts property on certain terms to another, the latter undertaking responsibility therefor as he would for iron, i.e., for return of the capital value of the property as at the time of his receipt thereof, even if it should suffer loss or depreciation; since, generally, small cattle was the subject matter of such transactions, they came to be described by the above term (BM 69b and Rashi thereto). Hence the use of the term *ẓon barzel* for the property of the wife, to denote that part of her property given over to her husband's ownership but under his responsibility, i.e., subject to his undertaking to restore to her the value thereof as fixed in the *ketubbah* upon dissolution of the marriage. This obligation of the husband is governed by the rule that any appreciation or depreciation in the property is his, regardless of any change it may undergo, or even its loss (Tur and Sh. Ar., EH 85:2); on the other hand, this obligation remains constant despite any fluctuations in currency values (as distinguished from the fluctuations in the value of the property) and the husband remains liable for the sum specified in the *ketubbah* as the dowry equivalent at its value on the date of the marriage, but subject to calculation thereof in accordance with the local law prevailing at the time of its recovery (*Taz* EH 66, n. 6; *Rema* ḤM 74:7; Resp. *Ḥatam Sofer* EH 1:126). However, if at the time of its recovery, i.e., upon divorce or the husband's death (Sh. Ar., EH 66:11 and *Rema* EH 93:1), the actual property is still in existence and fit for the purpose assigned to it at the time of the marriage – generally the case in respect of real property – the wife is entitled to demand the return thereof in specie, as being "the luster of her father's home" (*shevaḥ beit aviha*), and neither the husband nor his heirs can compel her to accept money instead (Sh. Ar., EH 88:3; *Beit Shemu'el* 88: n. 4; *Taz* 88, n. 3).

NIKHSEI MELOG. (lit. "plucked property," i.e., usufruct) is a term derived from the word *meligah*, e.g., *meligat ha-rosh*, i.e., plucking of hair from the head which remains intact. Similarly, *melog* property is property of which the principal remains in the wife's ownership but the fruits thereof are taken by the husband so that he has no responsibility or rights in respect of the principal, both its loss and gain being only hers (*Rashbam* BB 149b; *Haggahot Maimoniyyot* Ishut 16:1), and upon dissolution of the marriage such property returns to the wife as it stands, in specie. This category embraces all the property of the wife falling outside the category of *nikhsei ẓon barzel* – save for property of the kind described in the next section – whether brought by her at the time of entering the marriage, or acquired thereafter, e.g., by way of inheritance or gift (Yad, Ishut 16:2; Tur and Sh. Ar., EH 85:7).

PROPERTY WHICH IS NEITHER ZON BARZEL NOR MELOG. A third category is property of the wife concerning which the husband has no rights at all, neither as to the principal nor the fruits thereof. This includes property acquired by her after the marriage by way of gift, the donor having expressly stipulated that it be used for a specific purpose (such as for her recuperation), or that it be used for any purpose of her choice without her husband having any authority thereover (Yad, Zekhi'ah 3:13, 14; Sh. Ar., EH 85:11), or property given to her as a gift by her husband, he being considered here to have waived his rights to the fruits thereof, in terms of the rule "whoever gives, gives with a generous mind" (BB 52b and *Rashbam* thereto; Sh. Ar., EH 85; 7; see also *Gifts).

THE HUSBAND'S RIGHTS TO THE PRINCIPAL. Since the wife is entitled to the ownership of her property – *melog*, because it has never ceased to be in her ownership, and *ẓon barzel*, in terms of the halakhic rule concerning "the luster of her father's home" (see above) – the husband is not entitled to deal therewith in any manner prejudicial to her right, e.g., sale, etc., and any such act is invalid with reference to both movable and immovable property (Sh. Ar., EH 90:13, 14; *Rema* to 14; *Beit Shemu'el* 90, n. 48; Resp. *Ribash* no. 150). In the case of money the position is different: if it falls within the category of *ẓon barzel* and therefore passes fully into the husband's ownership, he being responsible for returning the equivalent thereof as determined in the *ketubbah*, he is free to trade or otherwise deal therewith, as with his own money (*Ḥelkat Meḥokek* 85, n. 4; Resp. *Ribash* no. 150); if, however, the money is part of the *melog* property and therefore not in the husband's ownership, he is not entitled to trade therewith save with his wife's consent but may only – and even will be obliged to do so if so requested by his wife – invest the money in such manner that the principal is preserved for her, while the fruits will be his (Resp. *Ribash* no. 150; *Ḥelkat Meḥokek* 85 n. 42).

INCOME FROM THE WIFE'S PROPERTY. All the fruits of the wife's property, i.e., all benefits derived from her property in a manner leaving intact the principal and its continued capacity to provide benefits – such as natural or legal fruits, e.g., rental or the right of occupation or stock dividends – belong to the husband (Sh. Ar., EH 69:3, 85:1, 2, 13). In accordance with the regulations of the sages he is entitled to these in return for his obligation to ransom her should she be taken captive, in order to avoid the ill-feeling that would arise between them if he received no help from her (Ket. 47a–b and Codes). The wife cannot forego her right to be ransomed at her husband's expense with the object of depriving him of his right to the fruits of her property, lest she remain unransomed and become absorbed among the Gentiles (Sh. Ar., EH 85:1); for the same reason, the husband does not escape the obligation to ransom his wife by renouncing the fruits from her property (*ibid.*).

By virtue of this right, the husband is entitled to receive the fruits and to take all steps necessary for the realization thereof – such as collecting rent or demanding the ejection of a tenant – in his own name and without being specifically authorized thereto by his wife (Sh. Ar., ḤM 122:8; EH 85:4 and commentaries; PDRE 4:107); nor does he require any specific authority from his wife in order to recover and receive any money to which she is entitled, including the principal, in order that it may be available to him for its investment and his enjoyment of its fruits (Sh. Ar., ḤM 122:8; *Siftei Kohen*, ḤM 122, n. 33; *Rema ibid.*). On the other hand, the husband, being entitled to the fruits, has the corresponding obligation to defray thereof the expenses of the property (Sh. Ar., EH 88:7), and if the fruits do not suffice for the purpose and he has to invest of his own money and labor on the property, he generally will not be entitled to compensation, not even upon divorce, since he is considered to have waived any claim therefor, having invested them with a view to enjoying the fruits ("what he has expended, he has expended and what he has consumed, he has consumed" – Ket. 79b; Sh. Ar., EH 88:7).

The husband's ownership of the fruits is not absolute, since the object of the halakhic rule whence his right to the fruits of the wife's property is derived is "for the comfort of the home" Ket. 80b), i.e., for their mutual comfort in their home and so as to ease the burden of maintaining the household (see Yad, Ishut 22:20 and *Maggid Mishneh* thereto). Consequently he is not entitled to use the fruits for his personal advantage, and if he should invest them in a way showing that he is not using them for the comfort of the home, the investment will be considered the wife's property as capital forming part of her *nikhsei melog*, of which the fruits only may be taken by him, to be used for the comfort of the home (Tur, EH 85, *Perishah* n. 51; *Derishah* n. 2). For the same reason the husband's creditors, i.e., in respect of debts unconnected with the upkeep of the household, may not seize the fruits and recover their debt from the proceeds thereof since this would preclude them from being used for their assigned purpose (Sh. Ar., ḤM 97:26; commentaries to EH 85:17). On the other hand, since the fruits belong to the husband, the wife must not do anything which may deprive him of his right of usufruct. Hence her sale of the principal without her husband's consent will be invalid with regard to the fruits, as a sale of something not belonging to her and therefore the husband's right of usufruct is unimpaired thereby and he continues to enjoy the benefits thereof even if the principal is in the hands of the purchaser: "the husband may seize the fruits from the purchasers" (Sh. Ar., EH 90:9, 13). This does not mean, however, that Jewish law denies a married woman legal capacity, like an idiot or a minor, for the sale, as mentioned above, is invalid only in respect of the fruits, as being a sale of something that is not hers (*Rema* EH 90:9, 13; and *Ḥelkat Meḥokek* 90, n. 29); with reference to the principal, therefore, her ownership is not affected by the husband's usufruct and her sale is valid, to the extent that upon her divorce or the death of her husband, the purchaser will acquire, in addition to the principal, the fruits also of the property purchased by him without any need for novation or ratification of the sale. Upon the death of his wife the husband, indeed, is entitled to seize also the principal from the purchasers, but not because the sale is regarded as invalid for reasons of legal incapacity of the wife, but because the sages regulated that when a wife predeceases her husband, he is considered – *mi-ta'am eivah*, i.e., in order to avoid ill feeling between them – upon entering the marriage as the earliest purchaser of her property and therefore takes preference over any other purchaser ("*Takkanat Usha*" – see Ket. 50a, Rashi and Codes). The rule that "whatever the wife acquires, she acquires for her husband," therefore means no more than that he acquires the fruits but the principal is and remains her own (Git. 77a and *Rashi*; Sh. Ar., ḤM 249:3; on the question of the husband's right to the fruits when he is a *mored* ("rebellious spouse") see *Husband and Wife).

DOWRY AND THE MARRIAGE DEED. The wife may only recover her dowry at the same time as she does the *ketubbah*, i.e., upon divorce or the death of her husband (Sh. Ar., EH 66:11; *Rema* EH 93:1, Isserles). The two are distinct, however, since the amount of the *ketubbah* is payable from the husband's own pocket whereas the dowry is her own property. Hence, even in the case where the wife forfeits her *ketubbah* according to law (see *Divorce), she does not lose her dowry, save in case of any express halakhic rule to the contrary (Yad, Ishut 16:1; *Maggid Mishneh*, ibid.; PD 12: 1121, 1197–1201).

THE DAUGHTER'S RIGHT TO A DOWRY. See *Parent and Child.

IN THE STATE OF ISRAEL. The Supreme Court has interpreted section 2 of the Women's Equal Rights Law, 5711/1951, as directing that Jewish law is not to be followed in matters concerning the husband's rights to the fruits of his wife's property (PD 12:1528ff.). According to this interpretation there is complete separation between the property of the respective spouses with reference to both the principal and the fruits, and the fact of their marriage in no way affects the rights of either party with regard to his or her own property or the fruits thereof.

[Ben-Zion (Benno) Schereschewsky]

The Women's Equal Rights Law, 5711 – 1951, as interpreted by the Supreme Court (see HC 202/57 *Sidis v.Rabbinical Court of Appeals*, 12 PD 1528) had far reaching implications for those cases in which a woman sued her husband for support, while simultaneously earning income from her own property. Under Jewish Law, the husband was entitled in such a case to argue that the wife receive her support from the income from her property which, according to *halakhah*, belonged to the husband (File 5712/2921,4457, 1 PDR 239; File 5716/153, 2 PDR, 97). However, in its aforementioned ruling, the Supreme Court partially abrogated the network of reciprocal obligations, so that the husband's obligation to support his wife remained intact, whereas his right to the income from her property was annulled. This meant that the income from the wife's property could not be deducted from her maintenance. This result was harshly criticized, conflicting as it did with the trend towards equalization of reciprocal duties and rights between spouses under which, in cases where the woman had income from property, she was required to assist in the household expenses. The Supreme Court noted that "this situation is unsatisfactory" and recommended that the Legislature rectify the situation by way of appropriate legislation (CA 313/59 *Balban v.* Balban, 14 (1) PD 285, per Justice Yitzchak Olshan; CA *Rinat v.* Rinat, 20 (2) PD 21 per Justice Zvi Berenson). In another case (FH 23/69 *Yosef v.* Yosef, 24 (1) PD 792), the Supreme Court ruled that, when the wife worked and earned a living, her salary was to be deducted against the sum he owed her as support, because her income constituted "the wife's handiwork" (*ma'aseh yadeha*), which belongs to the husband (see entry: *HUSBAND and WIFE). In wake of that decision, the Court again called upon the Legislator to amend the existing legal position and to equate the law applying to income from the wife's real assets with the law applying to her income, so that both might be reckoned against the sum owed for her support (CA 61/71 *Cohen v. Cohen*, 25 (2) PD 327, per Justice Etzioni):

> The existing legal situation gives rise to blatant inequality between maintenance awarded to women who have income-producing property, and those whose income is derived from her wages. In the former case the Court does not consider her income in calculating the support her husband is required to provide, whereas in the case of the working woman, the Court does take her wages into account (her salary being considered "her handiwork"). This is an unacceptable state of affairs. The way to eliminate the inequality inherent in this state of affairs is [...] to apply to a women who owns *melog* (i.e., real property on which the husband enjoys usufruct) the same rule that applies to working woman when determining the amount of support (p. 332 of decision).

In response to the Supreme Court's recommendation to the legislature that the statute be amended, in 1976 a new clause, section 2a, was added to the Family Law Amendment (Maintenance) Law, providing that "Notwithstanding the provisions of the Women's Equal Rights Law, 5712 – 1951, in fixing the amount of support required to be paid to a spouse, the Court is entitled to take into account the income of the spouse from employment and from property, and if deemed appropriate – from any other source."

The Supreme Court (CA 596/89 *Hakak v.* Hakak, 45 (4) PD 749) ruled (per Justice M. Elon) that the amendment of the law restored the balance in Israeli law between the woman's right to support and the husband's halakhic right to his wife's handiwork:

> Had it been possible to rely exclusively on the personal law [based on *halakhah*], then with respect to Jewish spouses there would have been no need to amend the Maintenance Law, because according to Jewish Law, when fixing the amount of the support the wife's *melog* property is not taken into account – meaning that she does not have to sell her property in order to support herself. On the other hand, account *is* taken of her income from that property. However, as a result of the enactment of the Women's Equal Rights Law and its interpretation by the Supreme Court, this consideration for the wife's income from her property was abolished when fixing the amount of her support. This "incidental oversight" has now been rectified by the amendment in section 2a. Accordingly, section 2a begins with the provision: "Notwithstanding the provisions of the Women's Equal Rights Law" – the intention being to specify the name of the law requiring amendment, and to underscore that it was an amendment of that law. As a result of this amendment to the Women's Equal Rights Law, Jewish Law was "released" from the yoke of that "oversight" with respect to the fixing of the amount of support for the wife on the basis of the Women's Equal Rights Law as interpreted by the Supreme Court, and the crown of the original Jewish Law was restored (p. 778 of the decision) (see *Matrimonial Property).

[Menachem Elon (2nd ed.)]

BIBLIOGRAPHY: GENERAL: L.M. Epstein, *The Jewish Marriage Contract* (1927), 89–106; Tchernowitz, in: *Zeitschrift fuer vergleichende Rechtswissenschaft*, 29 (1913), 445–73. LEGAL ASPECTS: H. Tchernowitz, in: *Sefer Yovel... Naḥum Sokolow* (1904), 309–28; I.S. Zuri, *Mishpat ha-Talmud*, 2 (1921), 73–79; Gulak, Yesodei, 3 (1922), 44–60; Gulak, Oẓar, 56–65, 109f.; ET, 4 (1952), 88–91; B. Cohen, in: PAAJR, 20 (1951), 135–234; republished in his: *Jewish and Roman Law* (1966), 179–278; addenda *ibid.*, 775–7; idem, in: *Annuaire de l'Institut de Philologie et d'Histoire Orientales et Slaves*, 13 (1953), 57–85 (Eng.); republished in his: *Jewish and Roman Law* (1966), 348–76; addenda *ibid.*, 780f.; M. Silberg, *Ha-Ma'amad ha-Ishi be-Yisrael* (19654), 348ff.; M. Elon, *Ha-Mishpat Ha-Ivri* (1988), 1:192ff., 398, 466ff., 469, 537, 542; 3:1515ff; idem., *Jewish Law* (1994), 1:216ff.; 2:486, 568ff., 572, 654, 660; 4:1802ff.; B. Schereshewsky, *Dinei Mishpaha* (1993, 4th ed.) 115–16, 146–53, 171, 224–31. **ADD. BIBLIOGRAPHY:** M. Elon and B. Lifshitz, *Mafte'aḥ ha-She'elot ve-ha-Teshuvot shel Hakhmei Sefarad u-Ẓefon Afrikah* (1986), 1:45–47; 2:275–80; B. Lifshitz and E. Shohetman, *Mafte'aḥ ha-She'elot ve-ha-Teshuvot shel Ḥakhmei Ashkenaz, Ẓarefat ve-Italyah*, 32–33, 192–94.

°**DOZY, REINHART PIETER ANNE** (1820–1883), Dutch Arabist-Islamist. Having studied Semitics at Leiden, Dozy was appointed professor of medieval and modern history at the university. His scholarly activities concentrated on Arabic lexicography (cf. his *Supplément aux dictionnaires Arabes*, 2 vols. (1881)) and the history of Muslim Spain. His *Histoire des Musulmans d'Espagne, jusqu'a la conquête de l'Andalousie par les Almoravides 711–1110* (4 vols., 1861) was re-issued at least 20 times and became fundamental to the modern study of medieval Andalusia. In 1864 he published a Dutch volume on the Jews in Mecca, *De Israëliten te Mekka van Davids tijd tot in de vijfde eeuw onzer tijdrekening*. There he suggested that migrants from the tribe of Simeon had started the Meccan sanctuary in the days of David, and that a new wave of Hebrews during the Babylonian period had strengthened the Hebraic impact on Muslim ritual. This controversial theory was both applauded and criticized, the latter especially in German Jewish circles. (Dozy's Leiden colleague H. Oort continued the discussion in *The Worship of Baalim in Israel* (1865).) Contemporary Dutch Jewish scholars, too, followed Dozy's work with a keen interest.

BIBLIOGRAPHY: M. Jastrow, in: MGWJ, 13 (1864), 313–17; HB, 7 (1864), 103–6; K.H. Graf, in: ZDMG, 19 (1865), 330–51; G. Dugat, *Histoire des orientalistes de l'Europe*, 2 (1870), 44–65; M.J. de Goeje, *Biographie de R. Dozy* (1883); E.D. Pijzel, *Mannen van beteekenis in onze dagen* (1884), 263–300; G.J. Dozy, *De familie Dozy. Genealogie en geschiedenis* (1911), 151–55; P.C. Molhuysen et al., *Nieuw Nederlandsch Biografisch Woordenboek* I (1911), 749; J.W. Fueck, *Die arabischen Studien in Europa* (1955), 181–85; J. Brugman, in: W. Otterspeer, *Leiden Oriental Connections 1850–1940* (1989), 62–81; G. Martinez-Gros, in: *Studia Islamica*, 92 (2001), 113–26; J. Weststeijn, in: *Al-Masâq*, 16 (2004), 205–15.

[Irene E. Zwiep (2nd ed.)]

ABBREVIATIONS

GENERAL ABBREVIATIONS

This list contains abbreviations used in the Encyclopaedia (apart from the standard ones, such as geographical abbreviations, points of compass, etc.). For names of organizations, institutions, etc., in abbreviation, see Index. For bibliographical abbreviations of books and authors in Rabbinical literature, see following lists.

*	Cross reference; i.e., an article is to be found under the word(s) immediately following the asterisk (*).
°	Before the title of an entry, indicates a non-Jew (post-biblical times).
‡	Indicates reconstructed forms.
>	The word following this sign is derived from the preceding one.
<	The word preceding this sign is derived from the following one.

ad loc.	*ad locum*, "at the place"; used in quotations of commentaries.
A.H.	*Anno Hegirae*, "in the year of Hegira," i.e., according to the Muslim calendar.
Akk.	Addadian.
A.M.	*anno mundi*, "in the year (from the creation) of the world."
anon.	anonymous.
Ar.	Arabic.
Aram.	Aramaic.
Ass.	Assyrian.
b.	born; *ben, bar.*
Bab.	Babylonian.
B.C.E.	Before Common Era (= B.C.).
bibl.	bibliography.
Bul.	Bulgarian.
c., ca.	Circa.
C.E.	Common Era (= A.D.).
cf.	*confer*, "compare."
ch., chs.	chapter, chapters.
comp.	compiler, compiled by.
Cz.	Czech.
D	according to the documentary theory, the Deuteronomy document.
d.	died.
Dan.	Danish.
diss., dissert,	dissertation, thesis.
Du.	Dutch.
E.	according to the documentary theory, the Elohist document (i.e., using Elohim as the name of God) of the first five (or six) books of the Bible.
ed.	editor, edited, edition.
eds.	editors.
e.g.	*exempli gratia*, "for example."
Eng.	English.
et al.	*et alibi*, "and elsewhere"; or *et alii*, "and others"; "others."
f., ff.	and following page(s).
fig.	figure.
fl.	flourished.
fol., fols	folio(s).
Fr.	French.
Ger.	German.
Gr.	Greek.
Heb.	Hebrew.
Hg., Hung	Hungarian.
ibid	*Ibidem*, "in the same place."
incl. bibl.	includes bibliography.
introd.	introduction.
It.	Italian.
J	according to the documentary theory, the Jahwist document (i.e., using YHWH as the name of God) of the first five (or six) books of the Bible.
Lat.	Latin.
lit.	literally.
Lith.	Lithuanian.
loc. cit.	*loco citato*, "in the [already] cited place."
Ms., Mss.	Manuscript(s).
n.	note.
n.d.	no date (of publication).
no., nos	number(s).
Nov.	Novellae (Heb. *Ḥiddushim*).
n.p.	place of publication unknown.
op. cit.	*opere citato*, "in the previously mentioned work."
P.	according to the documentary theory, the Priestly document of the first five (or six) books of the Bible.
p., pp.	page(s).
Pers.	Persian.
pl., pls.	plate(s).
Pol.	Polish.
Port.	Potuguese.
pt., pts.	part(s).
publ.	published.
R.	Rabbi or Rav (before names); in Midrash (after an abbreviation) – *Rabbah.*
r.	recto, the first side of a manuscript page.
Resp.	Responsa (Latin "answers," Hebrew *She'elot u-Teshuvot* or *Teshuvot*), collections of rabbinic decisions.
rev.	revised.

Rom. Romanian.
Rus(s). Russian.

Slov. Slovak.
Sp. Spanish.
s.v. *sub verbo, sub voce*, "under the (key) word."
Sum Sumerian.
summ. Summary.
suppl. supplement.

Swed. Swedish.

tr., trans(l). translator, translated, translation.
Turk. Turkish.

Ukr. Ukrainian.

v., vv. *verso*. The second side of a manuscript page; also verse(s).

Yid. Yiddish.

ABBREVIATIONS USED IN RABBINICAL LITERATURE

Adderet Eliyahu, Karaite treatise by Elijah b. Moses *Bashyazi.
Admat Kodesh, Resp. by Nissim Ḥayyim Moses b. Joseph |Mizraḥi.
Aguddah, Sefer ha-, Nov. by *Alexander Suslin ha-Kohen.
Ahavat Ḥesed, compilation by *Israel Meir ha-Kohen.
Aliyyot de-Rabbenu Yonah, Nov. by *Jonah b. Avraham Gerondi.
Arukh ha-Shulḥan, codification by Jehiel Michel *Epstein.
Asayin (= positive precepts), subdivision of: (1) *Maimonides, *Sefer ha-Mitzvot;* (2) *Moses b. Jacob of Coucy, *Semag.*
Asefat Dinim, subdivision of *Sedei Ḥemed* by Ḥayyim Hezekiah *Medini, an encyclopaedia of precepts and responsa.
Asheri = *Asher b. Jehiel.
Aeret Ḥakhamim, by Baruch *Frankel-Teomim; pt, 1: Resp. to Sh. Ar.; pt2: Nov. to Talmud.
Ateret Zahav, subdivision of the *Levush*, a codification by Mordecai b. Abraham (Levush) *Jaffe; *Ateret Zahav* parallels Tur. YD.
Ateret Ẓevi, Comm. To Sh. Ar. by Ẓevi Hirsch b. Azriel.
Avir Ya'akov, Resp. by Jacob Avigdor.
Avkat Rokhel, Resp. by Joseph b. Ephraim *Caro.
Avnei Millu'im, Comm. to Sh. Ar., EH, by *Aryeh Loeb b. Joseph ha-Kohen.
Avnei Nezer, Resp. on Sh. Ar. by Abraham b. Ze'ev Nahum Bornstein of *Sochaczew.
Avodat Massa, Compilation of Tax Law by Yoasha Abraham Judah.
Azei ha-Levanon, Resp. by Judah Leib *Zirelson.

Ba'al ha-Tanya – *Shneur Zalman of Lyady.
Ba'ei Ḥayyei, Resp. by Ḥayyim b. Israel *Benveniste.
Ba'er Heitev, Comm. To Sh. Ar. The parts on OḤ and EH are by Judah b. Simeon *Ashkenazi, the parts on YD AND ḤM by *Zechariah Mendel b. Aryeh Leib. Printed in most editions of Sh. Ar.
Baḥ = Joel *Sirkes.
Baḥ, usual abbreviation for *Bayit Ḥadash*, a commentary on Tur by Joel *Sirkes; printed in most editions of Tur.
Bayit Ḥadash, see *Baḥ*.
Berab = Jacob Berab, also called Ri Berav.
Bedek ha-Bayit, by Joseph b. Ephraim *Caro, additions to his *Beit Yosef* (a comm. to Tur). Printed sometimes inside *Beit Yosef*, in smaller type. Appears in most editions of Tur.
Be'er ha-Golah, Commentary to Sh. Ar. By Moses b. Naphtali Hirsch *Rivkes; printed in most editions of Sh. Ar.
Be'er Mayim, Resp. by Raphael b. Abraham Manasseh Jacob.
Be'er Mayim Ḥayyim, Resp. by Samuel b. Ḥayyim *Vital.
Be'er Yiẓḥak, Resp. by Isaac Elhanan *Spector.
Beit ha-Beḥirah, Comm. to Talmud by Menahem b. Solomon *Meiri.
Beit Me'ir, Nov. on Sh. Ar. by Meir b. Judah Leib Posner.
Beit Shelomo, Resp. by Solomon b. Aaron Ḥason (the younger).
Beit Shemu'el, Comm. to Sh. Ar., EH, by *Samuel b. Uri Shraga Phoebus.
Beit Ya'akov, by Jacob b. Jacob Moses *Lorberbaum; pt.1: Nov. to Ket.; pt.2: Comm. to EH.
Beit Yisrael, collective name for the commentaries *Derishah*, *Perishah*, and *Be'urim* by Joshua b. Alexander ha-Kohen *Falk. See under the names of the commentaries.
Beit Yiẓḥak, Resp. by Isaac *Schmelkes.
Beit Yosef: (1) Comm. on Tur by Joseph b. Ephraim *Caro; printed in most editions of Tur; (2) Resp. by the same.
Ben Yehudah, Resp. by Abraham b. Judah Litsch (ליטש) Rosenbaum.
Bertinoro, Standard commentary to Mishnah by Obadiah *Bertinoro. Printed in most editions of the Mishnah.
[Be'urei] Ha-Gra, Comm. to Bible, Talmud, and Sh. Ar. By *Elijah b. Solomon Zalmon (Gaon of Vilna); printed in major editions of the mentioned works.
Be'urim, Glosses to Isserles *Darkhei Moshe* (a comm. on Tur) by Joshua b. Alexander ha-Kohen *Falk; printed in many editions of Tur.
Binyamin Ze'ev, Resp. by *Benjamin Ze'ev b. Mattathias of Arta.
Birkei Yosef, Nov. by Ḥayyim Joseph David *Azulai.
Ha-Buẓ ve-ha-Argaman, subdivision of the *Levush* (a codification by Mordecai b. Abraham (Levush) *Jaffe); *Ha-Buẓ ve-ha-Argaman* parallels Tur, EH.

Comm. = Commentary

Da'at Kohen, Resp. by Abraham Isaac ha-Kohen. *Kook.
Darkhei Moshe, Comm. on Tur Moses b. Israel *Isserles; printed in most editions of Tur.
Darkhei No'am, Resp. by *Mordecai b. Judah ha-Levi.
Darkhei Teshuvah, Nov. by Ẓevi *Shapiro; printed in the major editions of Sh. Ar.
De'ah ve-Haskel, Resp. by Obadiah Hadaya (see *Yaskil Avdi).*

Derashot Ran, Sermons by *Nissim b. Reuben Gerondi.
Derekh Ḥayyim, Comm. to *Avot* by *Judah Loew (Lob., Liwa) b. Bezalel (Maharal) of Prague.
Derishah, by Joshua b. Alexander ha-Kohen *Falk; additions to his *Perishah* (comm. on Tur); printed in many editions of Tur.
Derushei ha-Ẓelaḥ, Sermons, by Ezekiel b. Judah Halevi *Landau.
Devar Avraham, Resp. by Abraham *Shapira.
Devar Shemu'el, Resp. by Samuel *Aboab.
Devar Yehoshu'a, Resp. by Joshua Menahem b. Isaac Aryeh Ehrenberg.
Dikdukei Soferim, variae lections of the talmudic text by Raphael Nathan*Rabbinowicz.
Divrei Emet, Resp. by Isaac Bekhor David.
Divrei Ge'onim, Digest of responsa by Ḥayyim Aryeh b. Jeḥiel Ẓevi *Kahana.
Divrei Ḥamudot, Comm. on *Piskei ha-Rosh* by Yom Tov Lipmann b. Nathan ha-Levi *Heller; printed in major editions of the Talmud.
Divrei Ḥayyim several works by Ḥayyim *Halberstamm; if quoted alone refers to his Responsa.
Divrei Malkhi'el, Resp. by Malchiel Tenebaum.
Divrei Rivot, Resp. by Isaac b. Samuel *Adarbi.
Divrei Shemu'el, Resp. by Samuel Raphael Arditi.

Edut be-Ya'akov, Resp. by Jacob b. Abraham *Boton.
Edut bi-Yhosef, Resp. by Joseph b. Isaac *Almosnino.
Ein Ya'akov, Digest of talmudic *aggadot* by Jacob (Ibn) *Habib.
Ein Yiẓḥak, Resp. by Isaac Elhanan *Spector.
Ephraim of Lentshitz = Solomon *Luntschitz.
Erekh Leḥem, Nov. and glosses to Sh. Ar. by Jacob b. Abraham *Castro.
Eshkol, Sefer ha-, Digest of *halakhot* by *Abraham b. Isaac of Narbonne.
Et Sofer, Treatise on Law Court documents by Abraham b. Mordecai *Ankawa, in the 2nd vol. of his Resp. *Kerem Ḥamar.*
Etan ha-Ezraḥi, Resp. by Abraham b. Israel Jehiel (Shrenzl) *Rapaport.
Even ha-Ezel, Nov. to Maimonides' *Yad Ḥazakah* by Isser Zalman *Meltzer.
Even ha-Ezer, also called *Raban* of *Ẓafenat Pa'ne'aḥ,* rabbinical work with varied contents by *Eliezer b. Nathan of Mainz; not identical with the subdivision of Tur, Shulḥan Arukh, etc.
Ezrat Yehudah, Resp. by *Isaar Judah b. Nechemiah of Brisk.

Gan Eden, Karaite treatise by *Aaron b. Elijah of Nicomedia.
Gersonides = *Levi b. Gershom, also called Leo Hebraecus, or Ralbag.
Ginnat Veradim, Resp. by *Abraham b. Mordecai ha-Levi.

Haggahot, another name for *Rema.*
Haggahot Asheri, glosses to *Piskei ha-Rosh* by *Israel of Krems; printed in most Talmud editions.
Haggahot Maimuniyyot, Comm,. to Maimonides' Yad Ḥazakah by *Meir ha-Kohen; printed in most eds. of Yad.
Haggahot Mordekhai, glosses to *Mordekhai* by Samuel *Schlettstadt; printed in most editions of the Talmud after *Mordekhai.*
Haggahot ha-Rashash on Tosafot, annotations of Samuel *Strashun on the Tosafot (printed in major editions of the Talmud).
Ha-Gra = *Elijah b. Solomon Zalman (Gaon of Vilna).
Ha-Gra, Commentaries on Bible, Talmud, and Sh. Ar. respectively, by *Elijah b. Solomon Zalman (Gaon of Vilna); printed in major editions of the mentioned works.
Hai Gaon, Comm. = his comm. on Mishnah.
Ḥakham Ẓevi, Resp. by Ẓevi Hirsch b. Jacob *Ashkenazi.
Halakhot = Rif, *Halakhot.* Compilation and abstract of the Talmud by Isaac b. Jacob ha-Kohen *Alfasi; printed in most editions of the Talmud.
Halakhot Gedolot, compilation of *halakhot* from the Geonic period, arranged acc. to the Talmud. Here cited acc. to ed. Warsaw (1874). Author probably *Simeon Kayyara of Basra.
Halakhot Pesukot le-Rav Yehudai Ga'on compilation of *halakhot.*
Halakhot Pesukot min ha-Ge'onim, compilation of *halakhot* from the geonic period by different authors.
Ḥananel, Comm. to Talmud by *Hananel b. Ḥushi'el; printed in some editions of the Talmud.
Harei Besamim, Resp. by Aryeh Leib b. Isaac *Horowitz.
Ḥassidim, Sefer, Ethical maxims by *Judah b. Samuel he-Ḥasid.
Hassagot Rabad on Rif, Glosses on Rif, *Halakhot,* by *Abraham b. David of Posquières.
Hassagot Rabad [on Yad], Glosses on Maimonides, *Yad Ḥazakah,* by *Abraham b. David of Posquières.
Hassagot Ramban, Glosses by Naḥmanides on Maimonides' *Sefer ha-Mitzvot;* usually printed together with *Sefer ha-Mitzvot.*
Ḥatam Sofer = Moses *Sofer.
Ḥavvot Ya'ir, Resp. and varia by Jair Ḥayyim *Bacharach
Ḥayyim Or Zaru'a = *Ḥayyim (Eliezer) b. Isaac.
Ḥazon Ish = Abraham Isaiah *Karelitz.
Ḥazon Ish, Nov. by Abraham Isaiah *Karelitz
Ḥedvat Ya'akov, Resp. by Aryeh Judah Jacob b. David Dov Meisels (article under his father's name).
Heikhal Yiẓḥak, Resp. by Isaac ha-Levi *Herzog.
Ḥelkat Meḥokek, Comm. to Sh. Ar., by Moses b. Isaac Judah *Lima.
Ḥelkat Ya'akov, Resp. by Mordecai Jacob Breisch.
Ḥemdah Genuzah, , Resp. from the geonic period by different authors.
Ḥemdat Shelomo, Resp. by Solomon Zalman *Lipschitz.
Ḥida = Ḥayyim Joseph David *Azulai.
Ḥiddushei Halakhot ve-Aggadot, Nov. by Samuel Eliezer b. Judah ha-Levi *Edels.
Ḥikekei Lev, Resp. by Ḥayyim *Palaggi.
Ḥikrei Lev, Nov. to Sh. Ar. by Joseph Raphael b. Ḥayyim Joseph Ḥazzan (see article *Ḥazzan Family).
Hil. = Hilkhot … (e.g. *Hilkhot Shabbat).*
Ḥinnukh, Sefer ha-, List and explanation of precepts attributed (probably erroneously) to Aaron ha-Levi of Barcelona (see article *Ha-Ḥinnukh*).
Ḥok Ya'akov, Comm. to Hil. Pesaḥ in Sh. Ar., OḤ, by Jacob b. Joseph *Reicher.
Ḥokhmat Sehlomo (1), Glosses to Talmud, *Rashi* and Tosafot by Solomon b. Jehiel "Maharshal") *Luria; printed in many editions of the Talmud.
Ḥokhmat Sehlomo (2), Glosses and Nov. to Sh. Ar. by Solomon b. Judah Aaron *Kluger printed in many editions of Sh. Ar.
Ḥur, subdivision of the *Levush,* a codification by Mordecai b. Abraham (Levush) *Jaffe; *Hur (*or *Levush ha-Hur)* parallels Tur, OḤ, 242–697.
Ḥut ha-Meshullash, fourth part of the *Tashbeẓ* (Resp.), by Simeon b. Zemaḥ *Duran.

Ibn Ezra, Comm. to the Bible by Abraham *Ibn Ezra; printed in the major editions of the Bible *("Mikra'ot Gedolot").*
Imrei Yosher, Resp. by Meir b. Aaron Judah *Arik.
Ir Shushan, Subdivision of the *Levush,* a codification by Mordecai b. Abraham (Levush) *Jaffe; *Ir Shushan* parallels Tur, ḤM.
Israel of Bruna = Israel b. Ḥayyim *Bruna.
Ittur. Treatise on precepts by *Isaac b. Abba Mari of Marseilles.

Jacob Be Rab = *Be Rab.
Jacob b. Jacob Moses of Lissa = Jacob b. Jacob Moses *Lorberbaum.
Judah B. Simeon = Judah b. Simeon *Ashkenazi.
Judah Minz = Judah b. Eliezer ha-Levi *Minz.

Kappei Aharon, Resp. by Aaron Azriel.
Kehillat Ya'akov, Talmudic methodology, definitions etc. by Israel Jacob b. Yom Tov *Algazi.
Kelei Ḥemdah, Nov. and *pilpulim* by Meir Dan *Plotzki of Ostrova, arranged acc. to the Torah.
Keli Yakar, Annotations to the Torah by Solomon *Luntschitz.
Keneh Ḥokhmah, Sermons by Judah Loeb *Pochwitzer.
Keneset ha-Gedolah, Digest of *halakhot* by Ḥayyim b. Israel *Benveniste; subdivided into annotations to *Beit Yosef* and annotations to Tur.
Keneset Yisrael, Resp. by Ezekiel b. Abraham Katzenellenbogen (see article *Katzenellenbogen Family).
Kerem Ḥamar, Resp. and varia by Abraham b. Mordecai *Ankawa.
Kerem Shelmo. Resp. by Solomon b. Joseph *Amarillo.
Keritut, [Sefer], Methodology of the Talmud by *Samson b. Isaac of Chinon.
Kesef ha-Kedoshim, Comm. to Sh. Ar., ḤM, by Abraham *Wahrmann; printed in major editions of Sh. Ar.
Kesef Mishneh, Comm. to Maimonides, *Yad Ḥazakah,* by Joseph b. Ephraim *Caro; printed in most editions of *Yad Ḥazakah.*
Keẓot ha-Ḥoshen, Comm. to Sh. Ar., ḤM, by *Aryeh Loeb b. Joseph ha-Kohen; printed in major editions of Sh. Ar.
Kol Bo [*Sefer*], Anonymous collection of ritual rules; also called *Sefer ha-Likkutim.*
Kol Mevasser, Resp. by Meshullam *Rath.
Korban Aharon, Comm. to *Sifra* by Aaron b. Abraham *Ibn Ḥayyim; pt. 1 is called: *Middot Aharon.*
Korban Edah, Comm. to Jer. Talmud by David *Fraenkel; with additions: *Shiyyurei Korban;* printed in most editions of Jer. Talmud.
Kunteres ha-Kelalim, subdivision of *Sedei Ḥemed,* an encyclopaedia of precepts and responsa by Ḥayyim Hezekiah *Medini.
Kunteres ha-Semikhah, a treatise by *Levi b. Ḥabib; printed at the end of his responsa.
Kunteres Tikkun Olam, part of *Mispat Shalom* (Nov. by Shalom Mordecai b. Moses *Schwadron).

Lavin (negative precepts), subdivision of: (1) *Maimonides, *Sefer ha-Mitzvot;* (2) *Moses b. Jacob of Coucy, *Semag.*
Leḥem Mishneh, Comm. to Maimonides, *Yad Ḥazakah,* by Abraham [Ḥiyya] b. Moses *Boton; printed in most editions of *Yad Ḥazakah.*
Leḥem Rav, Resp. by Abraham [Ḥiyya] b. Moses *Boton.
Leket Yosher, Resp and varia by Israel b. Pethahiah *Isserlein, collected by *Joseph (Joselein) b. Moses.
Leo Hebraeus = *Levi b. Gershom, also called Ralbag or Gersonides.
Levush = Mordecai b. Abraham *Jaffe.
Levush [Malkhut], Codification by Mordecai b. Abraham (Levush) *Jaffe, with subdivisions: [*Levush ha-] Tekhelet* (parallels Tur OḤ 1–241); [*Levush ha-] Ḥur* (parallels Tur OḤ 242–697); [*Levush] Ateret Zahav* (parallels Tur YD); [*Levush ha-Buẓ ve-ha-Argaman* (parallels Tur EH); [*Levush] Ir Shushan* (parallels Tur ḤM); under the name *Levush* the author wrote also other works.
Li-Leshonot ha-Rambam, fifth part (nos. 1374–1700) of Resp. by *David b. Solomon ibn Abi Zimra (Radbaz).
Likkutim, Sefer ha-, another name for *[Sefer] Kol Bo.*

Ma'adanei Yom Tov, Comm. on *Piskei ha-Rosh* by Yom Tov Lipmann b. Nathan ha-Levi *Heller; printed in many editions of the Talmud.
Mabit = Moses b. Joseph *Trani.
Magen Avot, Comm. to *Avot* by Simeon b. Ẓemaḥ *Duran.
Magen Avraham, Comm. to Sh. Ar., OḤ, by Abraham Abele b. Ḥayyim ha-Levi *Gombiner; printed in many editions of Sh. Ar., OḤ.
Maggid Mishneh, Comm. to Maimonides, *Yad Ḥazakah,* by *Vidal Yom Tov of Tolosa; printed in most editions of the *Yad Ḥazakah.*
Maḥaneh Efrayim, Resp. and Nov., arranged acc. to Maimonides' *Yad Ḥazakah* , by Ephraim b. Aaron *Navon.
Maharai = Israel b. Pethahiah *Isserlein.
Maharal of Prague = *Judah Loew (Lob, Liwa), b. Bezalel.
Maharalbaḥ = *Levi b. Ḥabib.
Maharam Alashkar = Moses b. Isaac *Alashkar.
Maharam Alshekh = Moses b. Ḥayyim *Alashekh.
Maharam Mintz = Moses *Mintz.
Maharam of Lublin = *Meir b. Gedaliah of Lublin.
Maharam of Padua = Meir *Katzenellenbogen.
Maharam of Rothenburg = *Meir b. Baruch of Rothenburg.
Maharam Shik = Moses b. Joseph Schick.
Maharash Engel = Samuel b. Ze'ev Wolf Engel.
Maharashdam = Samuel b. Moses *Medina.
Maharḥash = Ḥayyim (ben) Shabbetai.
Mahari Basan = Jehiel b. Ḥayyim Basan.
Mahari b. Lev = Joseph ibn Lev.
Mahari'az = Jekuthiel Asher Zalman Ensil Zusmir.
Maharibal = *Joseph ibn Lev.
Mahariḥ = Jacob (Israel) *Ḥagiz.
Maharik = Joseph b. Solomon *Colon.
Maharikash = Jacob b. Abraham *Castro.
Maharil = Jacob b. Moses *Moellin.
Maharimat = Joseph b. Moses di Trani (not identical with the Maharit).
Maharit = Joseph b. Moses *Trani.
Maharitaẓ = Yom Tov b. Akiva Ẓahalon. (See article *Ẓahalon Family).
Maharsha = Samuel Eliezer b. Judah ha-Levi *Edels.
Maharshag = Simeon b. Judah Gruenfeld.
Maharshak = Samson b. Isaac of Chinon.
Maharshakh = *Solomon b. Abraham.
Maharshal = Solomon b. Jeḥiel *Luria.
Mahasham = Shalom Mordecai b. Moses *Sschwadron.
Maharyu = Jacob b. Judah *Weil.
Maḥazeh Avraham, Resp. by Abraham Nebagen v. Meir ha-Levi Steinberg.
Maḥazik Berakhah, Nov. by Ḥayyim Joseph David *Azulai.

*Maimonides = Moses b. Maimon, or Rambam.
*Malbim = Meir Loeb b. Jehiel Michael.
Malbim = Malbim's comm. to the Bible; printed in the major editions.
Malbushei Yom Tov, Nov. on *Levush,* OḤ, by Yom Tov Lipmann b. Nathan ha-Levi *Heller.
Mappah, another name for *Rema.*
Mareh ha-Panim, Comm. to Jer. Talmud by Moses b. Simeon *Margolies; printed in most editions of Jer. Talmud.
Margaliyyot ha-Yam, Nov. by Reuben *Margoliot.
Masat Binyamin, Resp. by Benjamin Aaron b. Abraham *Slonik
Mashbir, Ha- = *Joseph Samuel b. Isaac Rodi.
Massa Ḥayyim, Tax *halakhot* by Ḥayyim *Palaggi, with the subdivisions *Missim ve-Arnomiyyot* and *Torat ha-Minhagot.*
Massa Melekh, Compilation of Tax Law by Joseph b. Isaac *Ibn Ezra with concluding part *Ne'ilat She'arim.*
Matteh Asher, Resp. by Asher b. Emanuel Shalem.
Matteh Shimon, Digest of Resp. and Nov. to Tur and *Beit Yosef,* ḤM, by Mordecai Simeon b. Solomon.
Matteh Yosef, Resp. by Joseph b. Moses ha-Levi Nazir (see article under his father's name).
Mayim Amukkim, Resp. by Elijah b. Abraham *Mizraḥi.
Mayim Ḥayyim, Resp. by Ḥayyim b. Dov Beresh Rapaport.
Mayim Rabbim, , Resp. by Raphael *Meldola.
Me-Emek ha-Bakha, , Resp. by Simeon b. Jekuthiel Ephrati.
Me'irat Einayim, usual abbreviation: *Sma* (from: *Sefer Me'irat Einayim*); comm. to Sh. Ar. By Joshua b. Alexander ha-Kohen *Falk; printed in most editions of the Sh. Ar.
Melammed le-Ho'il, Resp. by David Ẓevi *Hoffmann.
Meisharim, [*Sefer*], Rabbinical treatise by *Jeroham b. Meshullam.
Meshiv Davar, Resp. by Naphtali Ẓevi Judah *Berlin.
Mi-Gei ha-Haregah, Resp. by Simeon b. Jekuthiel Ephrati.
Mi-Ma'amakim, Resp. by Ephraim Oshry.
Middot Aharon, first part of *Korban Aharon,* a comm. to *Sifra* by Aaron b. Abraham *Ibn Ḥayyim.
Migdal Oz, Comm. to Maimonides, *Yad Ḥazakah,* by *Ibn Gaon Shem Tov b. Abraham; printed in most editions of the *Yad Ḥazakah.*
Mikhtam le-David, Resp. by David Samuel b. Jacob *Pardo.
Mikkaḥ ve-ha-Mimkar, Sefer ha-, Rabbinical treatise by *Hai Gaon.
Milḥamot ha-Shem, Glosses to Rif, *Halakhot,* by *Naḥmanides.
Minḥat Ḥinnukh, Comm. to *Sefer ha-Ḥinnukh,* by Joseph b. Moses *Babad.
Minḥat Yiẓḥak, Resp. by Isaac Jacob b. Joseph Judah Weiss.
Misgeret ha-Shulḥan, Comm. to Sh. Ar., ḤM, by Benjamin Ze'ev Wolf b. Shabbetai; printed in most editions of Sh. Ar.
Mishkenot ha-Ro'im, Halakhot in alphabetical order by Uzziel Alshekh.
Mishnah Berurah, Comm. to Sh. Ar., OḤ, by *Israel Meir ha-Kohen.
Mishneh le-Melekh, Comm. to Maimonides, *Yad Ḥazakah,* by Judah *Rosanes; printed in most editions of *Yad Ḥazakah.*
Mishpat ha-Kohanim, Nov. to Sh. Ar., ḤM, by Jacob Moses *Lorberbaum, part of his *Netivot ha-Mishpat;* printed in major editions of Sh. Ar.
Mishpat Kohen, Resp. by Abraham Isaac ha-Kohen *Kook.
Mishpat Shalom, Nov. by Shalom Mordecai b. Moses *Schwadron; contains: *Kunteres Tikkun Olam.*
Mishpat u-Ẓedakah be-Ya'akov, Resp. by Jacob b. Reuben *Ibn Ẓur.
Mishpat ha-Urim, Comm. to Sh. Ar., ḤM by Jacob b. Jacob Moses *Lorberbaum, part of his *Netivot ha-Mishpat;* printed in major editons of Sh. Ar.
Mishpat Ẓedek, Resp. by *Melammed Meir b. Shem Tov.
Mishpatim Yesharim, Resp. by Raphael b. Mordecai *Berdugo.
Mishpetei Shemu'el, Resp. by Samuel b. Moses *Kalai (Kal'i).
Mishpetei ha-Tanna'im, Kunteres, Nov on *Levush,* OḤ by Yom Tov Lipmann b. Nathan ha-Levi *Heller.
Mishpetei Uzzi'el (Uziel), Resp. by Ben-Zion Meir Hai *Ouziel.
Missim ve-Arnoniyyot, Tax *halakhot* by Ḥayyim *Palaggi, a subdivision of his work *Massa Ḥayyim* on the same subject.
Mitzvot, Sefer ha-, Elucidation of precepts by *Maimonides; subdivided into *Lavin* (negative precepts) and *Asayin* (positive precepts).
Mitzvot Gadol, Sefer, Elucidation of precepts by *Moses b. Jacob of Coucy, subdivided into *Lavin* (negative precepts) and *Asayin* (positive precepts); the usual abbreviation is *Semag.*
Mitzvot Katan, Sefer, Elucidation of precepts by *Isaac b. Joseph of Corbeil; the usual, abbreviation is *Semak.*
Mo'adim u-Zemannim, Rabbinical treatises by Moses Sternbuch.
Modigliano, Joseph Samuel = *Joseph Samuel b. Isaac, Rodi (Ha-Mashbir).
Mordekhai (Mordecai), halakhic compilation by *Mordecai b. Hillel; printed in most editions of the Talmud after the texts.
Moses b. Maimon = *Maimonides, also called Rambam.
Moses b. Naḥman = Naḥmanides, also called Ramban.
Muram = Isaiah Menahem b. Isaac (from: Morenu R. Mendel).

Naḥal Yiẓḥak, Comm. on Sh. Ar., ḤM, by Isaac Elhanan *Spector.
Naḥalah li-Yhoshu'a, Resp. by Joshua Ẓunẓin.
Naḥalat Shivah, collection of legal forms by *Samuel b. David Moses ha-Levi.
*Naḥmanides = Moses b. Naḥman, also called Ramban.
Naẓiv = Naphtali Ẓevi Judah *Berlin.
Ne'eman Shemu'el, Resp. by Samuel Isaac *Modigilano.
Ne'ilat She'arim, concluding part of *Massa Melekh* (a work on Tax Law) by Joseph b. Isaac *Ibn Ezra, containing an exposition of customary law and subdivided into *Minhagei Issur* and *Minhagei Mamon.*
Ner Ma'aravi, Resp. by Jacob b. Malka.
Netivot ha-Mishpat, by Jacob b. Jacob Moses *Lorberbaum; subdivided into *Mishpat ha-Kohanim,* Nov. to Sh. Ar., ḤM, and *Mishpat ha-Urim,* a comm. on the same; printed in major editions of Sh. Ar.
Netivot Olam, Saying of the Sages by *Judah Loew (Lob, Liwa) b. Bezalel.
Nimmukei Menaḥem of Merseburg, Tax *halakhot* by the same, printed at the end of Resp. Maharyu.
Nimmukei Yosef, Comm. to Rif. *Halakhot,* by Joseph *Ḥabib (Ḥabiba); printed in many editions of the Talmud.
Noda bi-Yhudah, Resp. by Ezekiel b. Judah ha-Levi *Landau; there is a first collection *(Mahadura Kamma)* and a second collection *(Mahadura Tinyana).*
Nov. = Novellae, Ḥiddushim.

Ohel Moshe (1), Notes to Talmud, *Midrash Rabbah,* Yad, *Sifrei* and to several Resp., by Eleazar *Horowitz.

Ohel Moshe (2), Resp. by Moses Jonah Zweig.
Oholei Tam. Resp. by *Tam ibn Yaḥya Jacob b. David; printed in the rabbinical collection *Tummat Yesharim.*
Oholei Ya'akov, Resp. by Jacob de *Castro.
Or ha-Me'ir Resp by Judah Meir b. Jacob Samson Shapiro.
Or Same'aḥ, Comm. to Maimonides, *Yad Ḥazakah,* by *Meir Simḥah ha-Kohen of Dvinsk; printed in many editions of the *Yad Ḥazakah.*
Or Zaru'a [the father] = *Isaac b. Moses of Vienna.
Or Zaru'a [the son] = *Ḥayyim (Eliezer) b. Isaac.
Or Zaru'a, Nov. by *Isaac b. Moses of Vienna.
Orah, Sefer ha-, Compilation of ritual precepts by *Rashi.
Oraḥ la-Ẓaddik, Resp. by Abraham Ḥayyim Rodrigues.
Oẓar ha-Posekim, Digest of Responsa.

Paḥad Yiẓḥak, Rabbinical encyclopaedia by Isaac *Lampronti.
Panim Me'irot, Resp. by Meir b. Isaac *Eisenstadt.
Parashat Mordekhai, Resp. by Mordecai b. Abraham Naphtali *Banet.
Pe'at ha-Sadeh la-Dinim and Pe'at ha-Sadeh la-Kelalim, subdivisions of the *Sedei Ḥemed,* an encyclopaedia of precepts and responsa, by Ḥayyim Hezekaih *Medini.
Penei Moshe (1), Resp. by Moses *Benveniste.
Penei Moshe (2), Comm. to Jer. Talmud by Moses b. Simeon *Margolies; printed in most editions of the Jer. Talmud.
Penei Moshe (3), Comm. on the aggadic passages of 18 treatises of the Bab. and Jer. Talmud, by Moses b. Isaiah Katz.
Penei Yehoshu'a, Nov. by Jacob Joshua b. Ẓevi Hirsch *Falk.
Peri Ḥadash, Comm. on Sh. Ar. By Hezekiah da *Silva.
Perishah, Comm. on Tur by Joshua b. Alexander ha-Kohen *Falk; printed in major edition of Tur; forms together with *Derishah* and *Be'urim* (by the same author) the *Beit Yisrael.*
Pesakim u-Khetavim, 2nd part of the *Terumat ha-Deshen* by Israel b. Pethahiah *Isserlein' also called *Piskei Maharai.*
Pilpula Ḥarifta, Comm. to *Piskei ha-Rosh, Seder Nezikin,* by Yom Tov Lipmann b. Nathan ha-Levi *Heller; printed in major editions of the Talmud.
Piskei Maharai, see *Terumat ha-Deshen,* 2nd part; also called *Pesakim u-Khetavim.*
Piskei ha-Rosh, a compilation of *halakhot,* arranged on the Talmud, by *Asher b. Jehiel (Rosh); printed in major Talmud editions.
Pitḥei Teshuvah, Comm. to Sh. Ar. by Abraham Hirsch b. Jacob *Eisenstadt; printed in major editions of the Sh. Ar.

Rabad = *Abraham b. David of Posquières (Rabad III.).
Raban = *Eliezer b. Nathan of Mainz.
Raban, also called *Ẓafenat Pa'ne'aḥ* or *Even ha-Ezer,* see under the last name.
Rabi Abad = *Abraham b. Isaac of Narbonne.
Radad = David Dov. b. Aryeh Judah Jacob *Meisels.
Radam = Dov Berush b. Isaac Meisels.
Radbaz = *David b Solomon ibn Abi Ziumra.
Radbaz, Comm. to Maimonides, *Yad Ḥazakah,* by *David b. Solomon ibn Abi Zimra.
Ralbag = *Levi b. Gershom, also called Gersonides, or Leo Hebraeus.
Ralbag, Bible comm. by *Levi b. Gershon.
Rama [da Fano] = Menaḥem Azariah *Fano.
Ramah = Meir b. Todros [ha-Levi] *Abulafia.
Ramam = *Menaham of Merseburg.
Rambam = *Maimonides; real name: Moses b. Maimon.
Ramban = *Naḥmanides; real name Moses b. Naḥman.
Ramban, Comm. to Torah by *Naḥmanides; printed in major editions. ("Mikra'ot Gedolot").
Ran = *Nissim b. Reuben Gerondi.
Ran of Rif, Comm. on Rif, *Halakhot,* by Nissim b. Reuben Gerondi.
Ranaḥ = *Elijah b. Ḥayyim.
Rash = *Samson b. Abraham of Sens.
Rash, Comm. to Mishnah, by *Samson b. Abraham of Sens; printed in major Talmud editions.
Rashash = Samuel *Strashun.
Rashba = Solomon b. Abraham *Adret.
Rashba, Resp., see also; *Sefer Teshuvot ha-Rashba ha-Meyuḥasot leha-Ramban,* by Solomon b. Abraham *Adret.
Rashbad = Samuel b. David.
Rashbam = *Samuel b. Meir.
Rashbam = Comm. on Bible and Talmud by *Samuel b. Meir; printed in major editions of Bible and most editions of Talmud.
Rashbash = Solomon b. Simeon *Duran.
*Rashi = Solomon b. Isaac of Troyes.
Rashi, Comm. on Bible and Talmud by *Rashi; printed in almost all Bible and Talmud editions.
Raviah = Eliezer b. Joel ha-Levi.
Redak = David *Kimḥi.
Redak, Comm. to Bible by David *Kimḥi.
Redakh = *David b. Ḥayyim ha-Kohen of Corfu.
Re'em = Elijah b. Abraham *Mizraḥi.
Rema = Moses b. Israel *Isserles.
Rema, Glosses to Sh. Ar. by Moses b. Israel *Isserles; printed in almost all editions of the Sh. Ar. inside the text in Rashi type; also called *Mappah* or *Haggahot.*
Remek = Moses Kimḥi.
Remakh = Moses ha-Kohen mi-Lunel.
Reshakh = *Solomon b. Abraham; also called Maharshakh.
Resp. = Responsa, *She'elot u-Teshuvot.*
Ri Berav = *Berab.
Ri Escapa = Joseph b. Saul *Escapa.
Ri Migash = Joseph b. Meir ha-Levi *Ibn Migash.
Riba = Isaac b. Asher ha-Levi; Riba II (Riba ha-Baḥur) = his grandson with the same name.
Ribam = Isaac b. Mordecai (or: Isaac b. Meir).
Ribash = *Isaac b. Sheshet Perfet (or: Barfat).
Rid= *Isaiah b. Mali di Trani the Elder.
Ridbaz = Jacob David b. Ze'ev *Willowski.
Rif = Isaac b. Jacob ha-Kohen *Alfasi.
Rif, *Halakhot,* Compilation and abstract of the Talmud by Isaac b. Jacob ha-Kohen *Alfasi.
Ritba = Yom Tov b. Abraham *Ishbili.
Riẓbam = Isaac b. Mordecai.
Rosh = *Asher b. Jehiel, also called Asheri.
Rosh Mashbir, Resp. by *Joseph Samuel b. Isaac, Rodi.

Sedei Ḥemed, Encyclopaedia of precepts and responsa by Ḥayyim Ḥezekiah *Medini; subdivisions: *Asefat Dinim, Kunteres ha-Kelalim, Pe'at ha-Sadeh la-Dinim, Pe'at ha-Sadeh la-Kelalim.*
Semag, Usual abbreviation of *Sefer Mitzvot Gadol,* elucidation of precepts by *Moses b. Jacob of Coucy; subdivided into *Lavin* (negative precepts) *Asayin* (positive precepts).
Semak, Usual abbreviation of *Sefer Mitzvot Katan,* elucidation of precepts by *Isaac b. Joseph of Corbeil.

Sh. Ar. = *Shulḥan Arukh*, code by Joseph b. Ephraim *Caro.
Sha'ar Mishpat, Comm. to Sh. Ar., ḤM. By Israel Isser b. Ze'ev Wolf.
Sha'arei Shevu'ot, Treatise on the law of oaths by *David b. Saadiah; usually printed together with Rif, *Halakhot;* also called: *She'arim of R. Alfasi.*
Sha'arei Teshuvah, Collection of resp. from Geonic period, by different authors.
Sha'arei Uzzi'el, Rabbinical treatise by Ben-Zion Meir Ha *Ouziel.
Sha'arei Ẓedek, Collection of resp. from Geonic period, by different authors.
Shadal [or Shedal] = Samuel David *Luzzatto.
Shai la-Moreh, Resp. by Shabbetai Jonah.
Shakh, Usual abbreviation of *Siftei Kohen*, a comm. to Sh. Ar., YD and ḤM by *Shabbetai b. Meir ha-Kohen; printed in most editions of Sh. Ar.
Sha'ot-de-Rabbanan, Resp. by *Solomon b. Judah ha-Kohen.
She'arim of R. Alfasi see *Sha'arei Shevu'ot.*
Shedal, see Shadal.
She'elot u-Teshuvot ha-Ge'onim, Collection of resp. by different authors.
She'erit Yisrael, Resp. by Israel Ze'ev Mintzberg.
She'erit Yosef, Resp. by *Joseph b. Mordecai Gershon ha-Kohen.
She'ilat Yavez, Resp. by Jacob *Emden (Yavez).
She'iltot, Compilation arranged acc. to the Torah by *Aḥa (Aḥai) of Shabḥa.
Shem Aryeh, Resp. by Aryeh Leib *Lipschutz.
Shemesh Ẓedakah, Resp. by Samson *Morpurgo.
Shenei ha-Me'orot ha-Gedolim, Resp. by Elijah *Covo.
Shetarot, Sefer ha-, Collection of legal forms by *Judah b. Barzillai al-Bargeloni.
Shevut Ya'akov, Resp. by Jacob b. Joseph Reicher.
Shibbolei ha-Leket Compilation on ritual by Zedekiah b. Avraham *Anav.
Shiltei Gibborim, Comm. to Rif, *Halakhot*, by *Joshua Boaz b. Simeon; printed in major editions of the Talmud.
Shittah Mekubbeẓet, Compilation of talmudical commentaries by Bezalel *Ashkenazi.
Shivat Ẓiyyon, Resp. by Samuel b. Ezekiel *Landau.
Shiyyurei Korban, by David *Fraenkel; additions to his comm. to Jer. Talmud *Korban Edah;* both printed in most editions of Jer. Talmud.
Sho'el u-Meshiv, Resp. by Joseph Saul ha-Levi *Nathanson.
Sh[ulḥan] Ar[ukh] [of Ba'al ha-Tanyal], Code by *Shneur Zalman of Lyady; not identical with the code by Joseph Caro.
Siftei Kohen, Comm. to Sh. Ar., YD and ḤM by *Shabbetai b. Meir ha-Kohen; printed in most editions of Sh. Ar.; usual abbreviation: *Shakh.*
Simḥat Yom Tov, Resp. by Tom Tov b. Jacob *Algazi.
Simlah Ḥadashah, Treatise on *Sheḥitah* by Alexander Sender b. Ephraim Zalman *Schor; see also *Tevu'ot Shor.*
Simeon b. Ẓemaḥ = Simeon b. Ẓemaḥ *Duran.
Sma, Comm. to Sh. Ar. by Joshua b. Alexander ha-Kohen *Falk; the full title is: *Sefer Me'irat Einayim;* printed in most editions of Sh. Ar.
Solomon b. Isaac ha-Levi = Solomon b. Isaac *Levy.
Solomon b. Isaac of Troyes = *Rashi.

Tal Orot, Rabbinical work with various contents, by Joseph ibn Gioia.
Tam, Rabbenu = *Tam Jacob b. Meir.
Tashbaẓ = Samson b. Zadok.
Tashbeẓ = Simeon b. Zemaḥ *Duran, sometimes also abbreviation for Samson b. Zadok, usually known as Tashbaẓ.
Tashbeẓ [Sefer ha-], Resp. by Simeon b. Ẓemaḥ *Duran; the fourth part of this work is called: *Ḥut ha-Meshullash.*
Taz, Usual abbreviation of *Turei Zahav*, comm., to Sh. Ar. by *David b. Samnuel ha-Levi; printed in most editions of Sh. Ar.
(Ha)-Tekhelet, subdivision of the *Levush* (a codification by Mordecai b. Abraham (Levush) *Jaffe); *Ha-Tekhelet* parallels Tur, OḤ 1-241.
Terumat ha-Deshen, by Israel b. Pethahiah *Isserlein; subdivided into a part containing responsa, and a second part called *Pesakim u-Khetavim* or *Piskei Maharai.*
Terumot, Sefer ha-, Compilation of *halakhot* by Samuel b. Isaac *Sardi.
Teshuvot Ba'alei ha-Tosafot, Collection of responsa by the Tosafists.
Teshjvot Ge'onei Mizraḥ u-Ma'aav, Collection of responsa.
Teshuvot ha-Geonim, Collection of responsa from Geonic period.
Teshuvot Ḥakhmei Provinẓyah, Collection of responsa by different Provencal authors.
Teshuvot Ḥakhmei Ẓarefat ve-Loter, Collection of responsa by different French authors.
Teshuvot Maimuniyyot, Resp. pertaining to Maimonides' *Yad Ḥazakah;* printed in major editions of this work after the text; authorship uncertain.
Tevu'ot Shor, by Alexander Sender b. Ephraim Zalman *Schor, a comm. to his *Simlah Ḥadashah*, a work on *Sheḥitah.*
Tiferet Ẓevi, Resp. by Ẓevi Hirsch of the "AHW" Communities (Altona, Hamburg, Wandsbeck).
Tiktin, Judah b. Simeon = Judah b. Simeon *Ashkenazi.
Toledot Adam ve-Ḥavvah, Codification by *Jeroham b. Meshullam.
Torat Emet, Resp. by Aaron b. Joseph *Sasson.
Torat Ḥayyim, , Resp. by Ḥayyim (ben) Shabbetai.
Torat ha-Minhagot, subdivision of the *Massa Ḥayyim* (a work on tax law) by Ḥayyim *Palaggi, containing an exposition of customary law.
Tosafot Rid, Explanations to the Talmud and decisions by *Isaiah b. Mali di Trani the Elder.
Tosefot Yom Tov, comm. to Mishnah by Yom Tov Lipmann b. Nathan ha-Levi *Heller; printed in most editions of the Mishnah.
Tummim, subdivision of the comm. to Sh. Ar., ḤM, *Urim ve-Tummim* by Jonathan *Eybeschuetz; printed in the major editions of Sh. Ar.
Tur, usual abbreviation for the *Arba'ah Turim* of *Jacob b. Asher.
Turei Zahav, Comm. to Sh. Ar. by *David b. Samuel ha-Levi; printed in most editions of Sh. Ar.; usual abbreviation: *Taz.*

Urim, subdivision of the following.
Urim ve-Tummim, Comm. to Sh. Ar., ḤM, by Jonathan *Eybeschuetz; printed in the major editions of Sh. Ar.; subdivided in places into *Urim* and *Tummim.*

Vikku'aḥ Mayim Ḥayyim, Polemics against Isserles and Caro by Ḥayyim b. Bezalel.

Yad Malakhi, Methodological treatise by *Malachi b. Jacob ha-Kohen.

Yad Ramah, Nov. by Meir b. Todros [ha-Levi] *Abulafia.
Yakhin u-Vo'az, Resp. by Ẓemaḥ b. Solomon *Duran.
Yam ha-Gadol, Resp. by Jacob Moses *Toledano.
Yam shel Shelomo, Compilation arranged acc. to Talmud by Solomon b. Jehiel (Maharshal) *Luria.
Yashar, Sefer ha-, by *Tam, Jacob b. Meir (Rabbenu Tam); 1st pt.: Resp.; 2nd pt.: Nov.
Yaskil Avdi, Resp. by Obadiah Hadaya (printed together with his Resp. *De'ah ve-Haskel).*
Yavez = Jacob *Emden.
Yehudah Ya'aleh, Resp. by Judah b. Israel *Aszod.
Yekar Tiferet, Comm. to Maimonides' *Yad Ḥazakah,*by David b. Solomon ibn Zimra, printed in most editions of *Yad Ḥazakah.*
Yere'im [*ha-Shalem*], [*Sefer*], Treatise on precepts by *Eliezer b. Samuel of Metz.
Yeshu'ot Ya'akov, Resp. by Jacob Meshullam b. Mordecai Ze'ev *Ornstein.
Yiẓhak Rei'aḥ, Resp. by Isaac b. Samuel Abendanan (see article *Abendanam Family).
Ẓafenat Pa'ne'aḥ (1), also called *Raban* or *Even ha-Ezer,* see under the last name.
Ẓafenat Pa'ne'aḥ (2), Resp. by Joseph *Rozin.
Zayit Ra'anan, Resp. by Moses Judah Leib b. Benjamin Auerbach.
Ẓeidah la-Derekh, Codification by *Menahem b. Aaron ibn Zerah.
Ẓedakah u-Mishpat, Resp. by Ẓedakah b. Saadiah Huẓin.
Zekan Aharon, Resp. by Elijah b. Benjamin ha-Levi.
Zekher Ẓaddik, Sermons by Eliezer *Katzenellenbogen.
Ẓemaḥ Ẓedek (1) Resp. by Menaham Mendel Shneersohn (see under *Shneersohn Family).
Zera Avraham, Resp. by Abraham b. David *Yiẓḥaki.
Zera Emet Resp. by *Ishmael b. Abaham Isaac ha-Kohen.
Ẓevi la-Ẓaddik, Resp. by Ẓevi Elimelech b. David Shapira.
Zikhron Yehudah, Resp. by *Judah b. Asher
Zikhron Yosef, Resp. by Joseph b. Menahem *Steinhardt.
Zikhronot, Sefer ha-, Sermons on several precepts by Samuel *Aboab.
Zikkaron la-Rishonim . . ., by Albert (Abraham Elijah) *Harkavy; contains in vol. 1 pt. 4 (1887) a collection of Geonic responsa.
Ẓiẓ Eliezer, Resp. by Eliezer Judah b. Jacob Gedaliah Waldenberg.

BIBLIOGRAPHICAL ABBREVIATIONS

Bibliographies in English and other languages have been extensively updated, with English translations cited where available. In order to help the reader, the language of books or articles is given where not obvious from titles of books or names of periodicals. Titles of books and periodicals in languages with alphabets other than Latin, are given in transliteration, even where there is a title page in English. Titles of articles in periodicals are not given. Names of Hebrew and Yiddish periodicals well known in English-speaking countries or in Israel under their masthead in Latin characters are given in this form, even when contrary to transliteration rules. Names of authors writing in languages with non-Latin alphabets are given in their Latin alphabet form wherever known; otherwise the names are transliterated. Initials are generally not given for authors of articles in periodicals, except to avoid confusion. Non-abbreviated book titles and names of periodicals are printed in *italics.* Abbreviations are given in the list below.

AASOR	*Annual of the American School of Oriental Research* (1919ff.).
AB	*Analecta Biblica* (1952ff.).
Abel, Géog	F.-M. Abel, *Géographie de la Palestine,* 2 vols. (1933-38).
ABR	*Australian Biblical Review* (1951ff.).
Abr.	Philo, *De Abrahamo.*
Abrahams, Companion	I. Abrahams, *Companion to the Authorised Daily Prayer Book* (rev. ed. 1922).
Abramson, Merkazim	S. Abramson, *Ba-Merkazim u-va-Tefuẓot bi-Tekufat ha-Ge'onim* (1965).
Acts	Acts of the Apostles (New Testament).
ACUM	*Who is who in ACUM* [*Aguddat Kompozitorim u-Meḥabbrim*].
ADAJ	*Annual of the Department of Antiquities, Jordan* (1951ff.).
Adam	Adam and Eve (Pseudepigrapha).
ADB	*Allgemeine Deutsche Biographie,* 56 vols. (1875–1912).
Add. Esth.	The Addition to Esther (Apocrypha).
Adler, Prat Mus	1. Adler, *La pratique musicale savante dans quelques communautés juives en Europe au XVIIe et XVIIIe siècles,* 2 vols. (1966).
Adler-Davis	H.M. Adler and A. Davis (ed. and tr.), *Service of the Synagogue, a New Edition of the Festival Prayers with an English Translation in Prose and Verse,* 6 vols. (1905–06).
Aet.	Philo, *De Aeternitate Mundi.*
AFO	*Archiv fuer Orientforschung* (first two volumes under the name *Archiv fuer Keilschriftforschung)* (1923ff.).
Ag. Ber	*Aggadat Bereshit* (ed. Buber, 1902*).*
Agr.	Philo, *De Agricultura.*
Ag. Sam.	*Aggadat Samuel.*
Ag. Song	*Aggadat Shir ha-Shirim* (Schechter ed., 1896).
Aharoni, Ereẓ	Y. Aharoni, *Ereẓ Yisrael bi-Tekufat ha-Mikra: Geografyah Historit* (1962).
Aharoni, Land	Y. Aharoni, *Land of the Bible* (1966).

Ahikar	Ahikar (Pseudepigrapha).
AI	*Archives Israélites de France* (1840–1936).
AJA	*American Jewish Archives* (1948ff.).
AJHSP	*American Jewish Historical Society – Publications* (after vol. 50 = AJHSQ).
AJHSQ	*American Jewish Historical (Society) Quarterly* (before vol. 50 =AJHSP).
AJSLL	*American Journal of Semitic Languages and Literature* (1884–95 under the title *Hebraica,* since 1942 JNES).
AJYB	*American Jewish Year Book* (1899ff.).
AKM	Abhandlungen fuer die Kunde des Morgenlandes (series).
Albright, Arch	W.F. Albright, *Archaeology of Palestine* (rev. ed. 1960).
Albright, Arch Bib	W.F. Albright, *Archaeology of Palestine and the Bible* (1935^{3}).
Albright, Arch Rel	W.F. Albright, *Archaeology and the Religion of Israel* (1953^{3}).
Albright, Stone	W.F. Albright, *From the Stone Age to Christianity* (1957^{2}).
Alon, Meḥkarim	G. Alon, *Meḥkarim be-Toledot Yisrael bi-Ymei Bayit Sheni u-vi-Tekufat ha-Mishnah ve-ha Talmud,* 2 vols. (1957–58).
Alon, Toledot	G. Alon, *Toledot ha-Yehudim be-Ereẓ Yisrael bi-Tekufat ha-Mishnah ve-ha-Talmud,* I (1958^{3}), (1961^{2}).
ALOR	Alter Orient (series).
Alt, Kl Schr	A. Alt, *Kleine Schriften zur Geschichte des Volkes Israel,* 3 vols. (1953–59).
Alt, Landnahme	A. Alt, *Landnahme der Israeliten in Palaestina* (1925); also in Alt, Kl Schr, 1 (1953), 89–125.
Ant.	Josephus, *Jewish Antiquities* (Loeb Classics ed.).
AO	*Acta Orientalia* (1922ff.).
AOR	*Analecta Orientalia* (1931ff.).
AOS	American Oriental Series.
Apion	Josephus, *Against Apion* (Loeb Classics ed.).
Aq.	Aquila's Greek translation of the Bible.
Ar.	*Arakhin* (talmudic tractate).
Artist.	Letter of Aristeas (Pseudepigrapha).
ARN^{1}	*Avot de-Rabbi Nathan,* version (1) ed. Schechter, 1887.
ARN^{2}	*Avot de-Rabbi Nathan,* version (2) ed. Schechter, 1945^{2}.
Aronius, Regesten	I. Aronius, *Regesten zur Geschichte der Juden im fraenkischen und deutschen Reiche bis zum Jahre 1273* (1902).
ARW	*Archiv fuer Religionswissenschaft* (1898–1941/42).
AS	*Assyrological Studies* (1931ff.).
Ashtor, Korot	E. Ashtor (Strauss), *Korot ha-Yehudim bi-Sefarad ha-Muslemit,* 1(1966^{2}), 2(1966).
Ashtor, Toledot	E. Ashtor (Strauss), *Toledot ha-Yehudim be-Miẓrayim ve-Suryah Taḥat Shilton ha-Mamlukim,* 3 vols. (1944–70).
Assaf, Ge'onim	S. Assaf, *Tekufat ha-Ge'onim ve-Sifrutah* (1955).
Assaf, Mekorot	S. Assaf, *Mekorot le-Toledot ha-Ḥinnukh be-Yisrael,* 4 vols. (1925–43).
Ass. Mos.	Assumption of Moses (Pseudepigrapha).
ATA	Alttestamentliche Abhandlungen (series).
ATANT	Abhandlungen zur Theologie des Alten und Neuen Testaments (series).
AUJW	*Allgemeine unabhaengige juedische Wochenzeitung* (till 1966 = AWJD).
AV	Authorized Version of the Bible.
Avad.	*Avadim* (post-talmudic tractate).
Avi-Yonah, Geog	M. Avi-Yonah, *Geografyah Historit shel Ereẓ Yisrael* (1962^{3}).
Avi-Yonah, Land	M. Avi-Yonah, *The Holy Land from the Persian to the Arab conquest (536 B.C. to A.D. 640)* (1960).
Avot	*Avot* (talmudic tractate).
Av. Zar.	*Avodah Zarah* (talmudic tractate).
AWJD	*Allgemeine Wochenzeitung der Juden in Deutschland* (since 1967 = AUJW).
AZDJ	*Allgemeine Zeitung des Judentums.*
Azulai	Ḥ.Y.D. Azulai, *Shem ha-Gedolim,* ed. by I.E. Benjacob, 2 pts. (1852) (and other editions).
BA	*Biblical Archaeologist* (1938ff.).
Bacher, Bab Amor	W. Bacher, *Agada der babylonischen Amoraeer* (1913^{2}).
Bacher, Pal Amor	W. Bacher, *Agada der palaestinensischen Amoraeer* (Heb. ed. *Aggadat Amora'ei Ereẓ Yisrael),* 2 vols. (1892–99).
Bacher, Tann	W. Bacher, *Agada der Tannaiten* (Heb. ed. *Aggadot ha-Tanna'im,* vol. 1, pt. 1 and 2 (1903); vol. 2 (1890).
Bacher, Trad	W. Bacher, *Tradition und Tradenten in den Schulen Palaestinas und Babyloniens* (1914).
Baer, Spain	Yitzhak (Fritz) Baer, *History of the Jews in Christian Spain,* 2 vols. (1961–66).
Baer, Studien	Yitzhak (Fritz) Baer, *Studien zur Geschichte der Juden im Koenigreich Aragonien waehrend des 13. und 14. Jahrhunderts* (1913).
Baer, Toledot	Yitzhak (Fritz) Baer, *Toledot ha-Yehudim bi-Sefarad ha-Noẓerit mi-Teḥillatan shel ha-Kehillot ad ha-Gerush,* 2 vols. (1959^{2}).
Baer, Urkunden	Yitzhak (Fritz) Baer, *Die Juden im christlichen Spanien,* 2 vols. (1929–36).
Baer S., Seder	S.I. Baer, *Seder Avodat Yisrael* (1868 and reprints).
BAIU	*Bulletin de l'Alliance Israélite Universelle* (1861–1913).
Baker, Biog Dict	*Baker's Biographical Dictionary of Musicians,* revised by N. Slonimsky (1958^{5}; with Supplement 1965).
I Bar.	I Baruch (Apocrypha).
II Bar.	II Baruch (Pseudepigrapha).
III Bar.	III Baruch (Pseudepigrapha).
BAR	*Biblical Archaeology Review.*
Baron, Community	S.W. Baron, *The Jewish Community, its History and Structure to the American Revolution,* 3 vols. (1942).

Baron, Social	S.W. Baron, *Social and Religious History of the Jews*, 3 vols. (1937); enlarged, 1-2(1952^{2}), 3-14 (1957–69).
Barthélemy-Milik	D. Barthélemy and J.T. Milik, *Dead Sea Scrolls: Discoveries in the Judean Desert*, vol. 1 *Qumram Cave* I (1955).
BASOR	*Bulletin of the American School of Oriental Research.*
Bauer-Leander	H. Bauer and P. Leander, *Grammatik des Biblisch-Aramaeischen* (1927; repr. 1962).
BB	(1) *Bava Batra* (talmudic tractate). (2) *Biblische Beitraege* (1943ff.).
BBB	Bonner biblische Beitraege (series).
BBLA	*Beitraege zur biblischen Landes- und Altertumskunde* (until 1949–ZDPV).
BBSAJ	*Bulletin*, British School of Archaeology, Jerusalem (1922–25; after 1927 included in PEFQS).
BDASI	*Alon* (since 1948) or *Hadashot Arkhe'ologiyyot* (since 1961), bulletin of the Department of Antiquities of the State of Israel.
Begrich, Chronologie	J. Begrich, *Chronologie der Koenige von Israel und Juda* (1929).
Bek.	*Bekhorot* (talmudic tractate).
Bel	Bel and the Dragon (Apocrypha).
Benjacob, Oẓar	I.E. Benjacob, *Oẓar ha-Sefarim* (1880; repr. 1956).
Ben Sira	see Ecclus.
Ben-Yehuda, Millon	E. Ben-Yedhuda, *Millon ha-Lashon ha-Ivrit*, 16 vols (1908–59; repr. in 8 vols., 1959).
Benzinger, Archaeologie	I. Benzinger, *Hebraeische Archaeologie* (1927^{3}).
Ben Zvi, Eretz Israel	I. Ben-Zvi, *Eretz Israel under Ottoman Rule* (1960; offprint from L. Finkelstein (ed.), *The Jews, their History, Culture and Religion* (vol. 1).
Ben Zvi, Ereẓ Israel	I. Ben-Zvi, *Ereẓ Israel bi-Ymei ha-Shilton ha-Ottomani (1955).*
Ber.	*Berakhot* (talmudic tractate).
Beẓah	*Beẓah* (talmudic tractate).
BIES	Bulletin of the Israel Exploration Society, see below BJPES.
Bik.	*Bikkurim* (talmudic tractate).
BJCE	Bibliography of Jewish Communities in Europe, catalog at General Archives for the History of the Jewish People, Jerusalem.
BJPES	Bulletin of the Jewish Palestine Exploration Society – English name of the Hebrew periodical known as: 1. *Yedi'ot ha-Ḥevrah ha-Ivrit la-Ḥakirat Ereẓ Yisrael va-Attikoteha* (1933–1954); 2. *Yedi'ot ha-Ḥevrah la-Ḥakirat Ereẓ Yisrael va-Attikoteha* (1954–1962); 3. *Yedi'ot ba-Ḥakirat Ereẓ Yisrael va-Attikoteha* (1962ff.).
BJRL	*Bulletin of the John Rylands Library* (1914ff.).
BK	*Bava Kamma* (talmudic tractate).
BLBI	*Bulletin of the Leo Baeck Institute* (1957ff.).
BM	(1) *Bava Meẓia* (talmudic tractate). (2) *Beit Mikra* (1955/56ff.). (3) British Museum.
BO	*Bibbia e Oriente* (1959ff.).
Bondy-Dworský	G. Bondy and F. Dworský, *Regesten zur Geschichte der Juden in Boehmen, Maehren und Schlesien von 906 bis 1620*, 2 vols. (1906).
BOR	*Bibliotheca Orientalis* (1943ff.).
Borée, Ortsnamen	W. Borée *Die alten Ortsnamen Palaestinas* (1930).
Bousset, Religion	W. Bousset, *Die Religion des Judentums im neutestamentlichen Zeitalter* (1906^{2}).
Bousset-Gressmann	W. Bousset, *Die Religion des Judentums im spaethellenistischen Zeitalter* (1966^{3}).
BR	*Biblical Review* (1916–25).
BRCI	*Bulletin of the Research Council of Israel* (1951/52–1954/55; then divided).
BRE	*Biblical Research* (1956ff.).
BRF	*Bulletin of the Rabinowitz Fund for the Exploration of Ancient Synagogues* (1949ff.).
Briggs, Psalms	Ch. A. and E.G. Briggs, *Critical and Exegetical Commentary on the Book of Psalms*, 2 vols. (ICC, 1906–07).
Bright, Hist	J. Bright, *A History of Israel* (1959).
Brockelmann, Arab Lit	K. Brockelmann, *Geschichte der arabischen Literatur*, 2 vols. 1898–1902), supplement, 3 vols. (1937–42).
Bruell, Jahrbuecher	*Jahrbuecher fuer juedische Geschichte und Litteratur*, ed. by N. Bruell, Frankfurt (1874–90).
Brugmans-Frank	H. Brugmans and A. Frank (eds.), *Geschiedenis der Joden in Nederland* (1940).
BTS	*Bible et Terre Sainte* (1958ff.).
Bull, Index	S. Bull, *Index to Biographies of Contemporary Composers* (1964).
BW	*Biblical World* (1882–1920).
BWANT	*Beitraege zur Wissenschaft vom Alten und Neuen Testament* (1926ff.).
BZ	*Biblische Zeitschrift* (1903ff.).
BZAW	*Beihefte zur Zeitschrift fuer die alttestamentliche Wissenschaft*, supplement to ZAW (1896ff.).
BŻIH	*Biuletyn Zydowskiego Instytutu Historycznego* (1950ff.).
CAB	*Cahiers d'archéologie biblique* (1953ff.).
CAD	*The* [*Chicago*] *Assyrian Dictionary* (1956ff.).
CAH	*Cambridge Ancient History*, 12 vols. (1923–39)
CAH^{2}	*Cambridge Ancient History*, second edition, 14 vols. (1962–2005).
Calwer, Lexikon	*Calwer, Bibellexikon.*
Cant.	Canticles, usually given as Song (= Song of Songs).

Cantera-Millás, Inscripciones	F. Cantera and J.M. Millás, *Las Inscripciones Hebraicas de España* (1956).
CBQ	*Catholic Biblical Quarterly* (1939ff.).
CCARY	Central Conference of American Rabbis, *Yearbook* (1890/91ff.).
CD	*Damascus Document* from the Cairo *Genizah* (published by S. Schechter, *Fragments of a Zadokite Work*, 1910).
Charles, Apocrypha	R.H. Charles, *Apocrypha and Pseudepigrapha* . . ., 2 vols. (1913; repr. 1963–66).
Cher.	Philo, *De Cherubim*.
I (or II) Chron.	Chronicles, book I and II (Bible).
CIG	*Corpus Inscriptionum Graecarum*.
CIJ	*Corpus Inscriptionum Judaicarum*, 2 vols. (1936–52).
CIL	*Corpus Inscriptionum Latinarum*.
CIS	*Corpus Inscriptionum Semiticarum* (1881ff.).
C.J.	Codex Justinianus.
Clermont-Ganneau, Arch	Ch. Clermont-Ganneau, *Archaeological Researches in Palestine*, 2 vols. (1896–99).
CNFI	*Christian News from Israel* (1949ff.).
Cod. Just.	Codex Justinianus.
Cod. Theod.	Codex Theodosinanus.
Col.	Epistle to the Colosssians (New Testament).
Conder, Survey	Palestine Exploration Fund, *Survey of Eastern Palestine*, vol. 1, pt. I (1889) = C.R. Conder, *Memoirs of the . . . Survey*.
Conder-Kitchener	Palestine Exploration Fund, *Survey of Western Palestine*, vol. 1, pts. 1-3 (1881–83) = C.R. Conder and H.H. Kitchener, *Memoirs*.
Conf.	Philo, *De Confusione Linguarum*.
Conforte, Kore	D. Conforte, *Kore ha-Dorot* (1842^2).
Cong.	Philo, *De Congressu Quaerendae Eruditionis Gratia*.
Cont.	Philo, *De Vita Contemplativa*.
I (or II) Cor.	Epistles to the Corinthians (New Testament).
Cowley, Aramic	A. Cowley, *Aramaic Papyri of the Fifth Century B.C.* (1923).
Colwey, Cat	A.E. Cowley, *A Concise Catalogue of the Hebrew Printed Books in the Bodleian Library* (1929).
CRB	*Cahiers de la Revue Biblique* (1964ff.).
Crowfoot-Kenyon	J.W. Crowfoot, K.M. Kenyon and E.L. Sukenik, *Buildings of Samaria* (1942).
C.T.	Codex Theodosianus.
DAB	*Dictionary of American Biography* (1928–58).
Daiches, Jews	S. Daiches, *Jews in Babylonia* (1910).
Dalman, Arbeit	G. Dalman, *Arbeit und Sitte in Palaestina*, 7 vols.in 8 (1928–42 repr. 1964).
Dan	Daniel (Bible).
Davidson, Oẓar	I. Davidson, *Oẓar ha-Shirah ve-ha-Piyyut*, 4 vols. (1924–33); Supplement in: HUCA, 12–13 (1937/38), 715–823.

DB	J. Hastings, *Dictionary of the Bible*, 4 vols. (1963^2).
DBI	F.G. Vigoureaux et al. (eds.), *Dictionnaire de la Bible*, 5 vols. in 10 (1912); Supplement, 8 vols. (1928–66)
Decal.	Philo, *De Decalogo*.
Dem.	*Demai* (talmudic tractate).
DER	*Derekh Ereẓ Rabbah* (post-talmudic tractate).
Derenbourg, Hist	J. Derenbourg *Essai sur l'histoire et la géographie de la Palestine* (1867).
Det.	Philo, *Quod deterius potiori insidiari solet*.
Deus	Philo, *Quod Deus immutabilis sit*.
Deut.	Deuteronomy (Bible).
Deut. R.	*Deuteronomy Rabbah*.
DEZ	*Derekh Ereẓ Zuta* (post-talmudic tractate).
DHGE	*Dictionnaire d'histoire et de géographie ecclésiastiques*, ed. by A. Baudrillart et al., 17 vols (1912–68).
Dik. Sof	*Dikdukei Soferim*, variae lections of the talmudic text by Raphael Nathan Rabbinovitz (16 vols., 1867–97).
Dinur, Golah	B. Dinur (Dinaburg), *Yisrael ba-Golah*, 2 vols. in 7 (1959–68) = vols. 5 and 6 of his *Toledot Yisrael*, second series.
Dinur, Haganah	B. Dinur (ed.), *Sefer Toledot ha-Haganah* (1954ff.).
Diringer, Iscr	D. Diringer, *Iscrizioni antico-ebraiche palestinesi* (1934).
Discoveries	*Discoveries in the Judean Desert* (1955ff.).
DNB	*Dictionary of National Biography*, 66 vols. (1921–222) with Supplements.
Dubnow, Divrei	S. Dubnow, *Divrei Yemei Am Olam*, 11 vols (1923–38 and further editions).
Dubnow, Ḥasidut	S. Dubnow, *Toledot ha-Ḥasidut* (1960^2).
Dubnow, Hist	S. Dubnow, *History of the Jews* (1967).
Dubnow, Hist Russ	S. Dubnow, *History of the Jews in Russia and Poland*, 3 vols. (1916 20).
Dubnow, Outline	S. Dubnow, *An Outline of Jewish History*, 3 vols. (1925–29).
Dubnow, Weltgesch	S. Dubnow, *Weltgeschichte des juedischen Volkes* 10 vols. (1925–29).
Dukes, Poesie	L. Dukes, *Zur Kenntnis der neuhebraeischen religioesen Poesie* (1842).
Dunlop, Khazars	D. H. Dunlop, *History of the Jewish Khazars* (1954).
EA	El Amarna Letters (edited by J.A. Knudtzon), *Die El-Amarna Tafel*, 2 vols. (1907 14).
EB	*Encyclopaedia Britannica*.
EBI	*Estudios biblicos* (1941ff.).
EBIB	T.K. Cheyne and J.S. Black, *Encyclopaedia Biblica*, 4 vols. (1899–1903).
Ebr.	Philo, *De Ebrietate*.
Eccles.	Ecclesiastes (Bible).
Eccles. R.	*Ecclesiastes Rabbah*.
Ecclus.	Ecclesiasticus or Wisdom of Ben Sira (or Sirach; Apocrypha).
Eduy.	*Eduyyot* (mishanic tractate).

EG	*Enziklopedyah shel Galuyyot* (1953ff.).
EH	*Even ha-Ezer.*
EHA	*Enẓiklopedyah la-Ḥafirot Arkheologiyyot be-Ereẓ Yisrael,* 2 vols. (1970).
EI	*Enzyklopaedie des Islams,* 4 vols. (1905–14). Supplement vol. (1938).
EIS	*Encyclopaedia of Islam,* 4 vols. (1913–36; repr. 1954–68).
EIS^{2}	*Encyclopaedia of Islam, second edition (1960–2000).*
Eisenstein, Dinim	J.D. Eisenstein, *Oẓar Dinim u-Minhagim* (1917; several reprints).
Eisenstein, Yisrael	J.D. Eisenstein, *Oẓar Yisrael* (10 vols, 1907–13; repr. with several additions 1951).
EIV	*Enẓiklopedyah Ivrit* (1949ff.).
EJ	*Encyclopaedia Judaica* (German, A-L only), 10 vols. (1928–34).
EJC	*Enciclopedia Judaica Castellana,* 10 vols. (1948–51).
Elbogen, Century	I Elbogen, *A Century of Jewish Life* (1960^{2}).
Elbogen, Gottesdienst	I Elbogen, *Der juedische Gottesdienst ...* (1931^{3}, repr. 1962).
Elon, Mafte'aḥ	M. Elon (ed.), *Mafte'aḥ ha-She'elot ve-ha-Teshuvot ha-Rosh* (1965).
EM	*Enẓiklopedyah Mikra'it* (1950ff.).
I (or II) En.	I and II Enoch (Pseudepigrapha).
EncRel	*Encyclopedia of Religion*, 15 vols. (1987, 2005^{2}).
Eph.	Epistle to the Ephesians (New Testament).
Ephros, Cant	G. Ephros, *Cantorial Anthology,* 5 vols. (1929–57).
Ep. Jer.	Epistle of Jeremy (Apocrypha).
Epstein, Amora'im	J N. Epstein, *Mevo'ot le-Sifrut ha-Amora'im* (1962).
Epstein, Marriage	L M. Epstein, *Marriage Laws in the Bible and the Talmud* (1942).
Epstein, Mishnah	J. N. Epstein, *Mavo le-Nusaḥ ha-Mishnah,* 2 vols. (1964^{2}).
Epstein, Tanna'im	J. N. Epstein, *Mavo le-Sifruth ha-Tanna'im.* (1947).
ER	*Ecumenical Review.*
Er.	*Eruvin* (talmudic tractate).
ERE	*Encyclopaedia of Religion and Ethics,* 13 vols. (1908–26); reprinted.
ErIsr	*Eretz-Israel*, Israel Exploration Society.
I Esd.	I Esdras (Apocrypha) (= III Ezra).
II Esd.	II Esdras (Apocrypha) (= IV Ezra).
ESE	*Ephemeris fuer semitische Epigraphik*, ed. by M. Lidzbarski.
ESN	*Encyclopaedia Sefaradica Neerlandica,* 2 pts. (1949).
ESS	*Encyclopaedia of the Social Sciences,* 15 vols. (1930–35); reprinted in 8 vols. (1948–49).
Esth.	Esther (Bible).
Est. R.	*Esther Rabbah.*
ET	*Enẓiklopedyah Talmudit* (1947ff.).
Eusebius, Onom.	E. Klostermann (ed.), *Das Onomastikon* (1904), Greek with Hieronymus' Latin translation.
Ex.	Exodus (Bible).
Ex. R.	*Exodus Rabbah.*
Exs	Philo, *De Exsecrationibus.*
EẒD	*Enẓiklopeday shel ha-Ẓiyyonut ha-Datit* (1951ff.).
Ezek.	Ezekiel (Bible).
Ezra	Ezra (Bible).
III Ezra	III Ezra (Pseudepigrapha).
IV Ezra	IV Ezra (Pseudepigrapha).
Feliks, Ha-Ẓome'aḥ	*J. Feliks, Ha-Ẓome'aḥ ve-ha-Ḥai ba-Mishnah* (1983).
Finkelstein, Middle Ages	L. Finkelstein, *Jewish Self-Government in the Middle Ages* (1924).
Fischel, Islam	W.J. Fischel, *Jews in the Economic and Political Life of Mediaeval Islam* (1937; reprint with introduction "The Court Jew in the Islamic World," 1969).
FJW	*Fuehrer durch die juedische Gemeindeverwaltung und Wohlfahrtspflege in Deutschland* (1927/28).
Frankel, Mevo	Z. Frankel, *Mevo ha-Yerushalmi* (1870; reprint 1967).
Frankel, Mishnah	Z. Frankel, *Darkhei ha-Mishnah* (1959^{2}; reprint 1959^{2}).
Frazer, Folk-Lore	J.G. Frazer, *Folk-Lore in the Old Testament,* 3 vols. (1918–19).
Frey, Corpus	J.-B. Frey, *Corpus Inscriptionum Iudaicarum*, 2 vols. (1936–52).
Friedmann, Lebensbilder	A. Friedmann, *Lebensbilder beruehmter Kantoren*, 3 vols. (1918–27).
FRLT	*Forschungen zur Religion und Literatur des Alten und Neuen Testaments* (series) (1950ff.).
Frumkin-Rivlin	A.L. Frumkin and E. Rivlin, *Toledot Ḥakhmei Yerushalayim*, 3 vols. (1928–30), Supplement vol. (1930).
Fuenn, Keneset	S.J. Fuenn, *Keneset Yisrael,* 4 vols. (1887–90).
Fuerst, Bibliotheca	J. Fuerst, *Bibliotheca Judaica,* 2 vols. (1863; repr. 1960).
Fuerst, Karaeertum	J. Fuerst, *Geschichte des Karaeertums,* 3 vols. (1862–69).
Fug.	Philo, *De Fuga et Inventione.*
Gal.	Epistle to the Galatians (New Testament).
Galling, Reallexikon	K. Galling, *Biblisches Reallexikon* (1937).
Gardiner, Onomastica	A.H. Gardiner, *Ancient Egyptian Onomastica,* 3 vols. (1947).
Geiger, Mikra	A. Geiger, *Ha-Mikra ve-Targumav*, tr. by J.L. Baruch (1949).
Geiger, Urschrift	A. Geiger, *Urschrift und Uebersetzungen der Bibel* 1928^{2}).
Gen.	Genesis (Bible).
Gen. R.	*Genesis Rabbah.*
Ger.	*Gerim* (post-talmudic tractate).
Germ Jud	M. Brann, I. Elbogen, A. Freimann, and H. Tykocinski (eds.), *Germania Judaica,* vol. 1 (1917; repr. 1934 and 1963); vol. 2, in 2 pts. (1917–68), ed. by Z. Avneri.

GHAT	*Goettinger Handkommentar zum Alten Testament* (1917–22).
Ghirondi-Neppi	M.S. Ghirondi and G.H. Neppi, *Toledot Gedolei Yisrael u-Ge'onei Italyah ... u-Ve'urim al Sefer Zekher Ẓaddikim li-Verakhah . . .*(1853), index in ZHB, 17 (1914), 171–83.
Gig.	Philo, *De Gigantibus.*
Ginzberg, Legends	L. Ginzberg, *Legends of the Jews,* 7 vols. (1909–38; and many reprints).
Git.	*Gittin* (talmudic tractate).
Glueck, Explorations	N. Glueck, *Explorations in Eastern Palestine,* 2 vols. (1951).
Goell, Bibliography	Y. Goell, *Bibliography of Modern Hebrew Literature in English Translation* (1968).
Goodenough, Symbols	E.R. Goodenough, *Jewish Symbols in the Greco-Roman Period,* 13 vols. (1953–68).
Gordon, Textbook	C.H. Gordon, *Ugaritic Textbook* (1965; repr. 1967).
Graetz, Gesch	H. Graetz, *Geschichte der Juden* (last edition 1874–1908).
Graetz, Hist	H. Graetz, *History of the Jews,* 6 vols. (1891–1902).
Graetz, Psalmen	H. Graetz, *Kritischer Commentar zu den Psalmen,* 2 vols. in 1 (1882–83).
Graetz, Rabbinowitz	H. Graetz, *Divrei Yemei Yisrael,* tr. by S.P. Rabbinowitz. (1928 1929²).
Gray, Names	G.B. Gray, *Studies in Hebrew Proper Names* (1896).
Gressmann, Bilder	H. Gressmann, *Altorientalische Bilder zum Alten Testament* (1927²).
Gressmann, Texte	H. Gressmann, *Altorientalische Texte zum Alten Testament* (1926²).
Gross, Gal Jud	H. Gross, *Gallia Judaica* (1897; repr. with add. 1969).
Grove, Dict	*Grove's Dictionary of Music and Musicians,* ed. by E. Blum 9 vols. (1954⁵) and suppl. (1961⁵).
Guedemann, Gesch Erz	M. Guedemann, *Geschichte des Erziehungswesens und der Cultur der abendlaendischen Juden,* 3 vols. (1880–88).
Guedemann, Quellenschr	M. Guedemann, *Quellenschriften zur Geschichte des Unterrichts und der Erziehung bei den deutschen Juden* (1873, 1891).
Guide	Maimonides, *Guide of the Perplexed.*
Gulak, Oẓar	A. Gulak, *Oẓar ha-Shetarot ha-Nehugim be-Yisrael* (1926).
Gulak, Yesodei	A. Gulak, *Yesodei ha-Mishpat ha-Ivri, Seder Dinei Mamonot be-Yisrael, al pi Mekorot ha-Talmud ve-ha-Posekim,* 4 vols. (1922; repr. 1967).
Guttmann, Mafte'aḥ	M. Guttmann, *Mafte'aḥ ha-Talmud,* 3 vols. (1906–30).
Guttmann, Philosophies	J. Guttmann, *Philosophies of Judaism* (1964).
Hab.	*Habakkuk* (Bible).
Ḥag.	*Ḥagigah* (talmudic tractate).
Haggai	*Haggai* (Bible).
Ḥal.	*Ḥallah* (talmudic tractate).
Halevy, Dorot	I. Halevy, *Dorot ha-Rishonim,* 6 vols. (1897–1939).
Halpern, Pinkas	I. Halpern (Halperin), *Pinkas Va'ad Arba Araẓot* (1945).
Hananel-Eškenazi	A. Hananel and Eškenazi (eds.), *Fontes Hebraici ad res oeconomicas socialesque terrarum balcanicarum saeculo XVI pertinentes,* 2 vols, (1958–60; in Bulgarian).
HB	*Hebraeische Bibliographie* (1858–82).
Heb.	Epistle to the Hebrews (New Testament).
Heilprin, Dorot	J. Heilprin (Heilperin), *Seder ha-Dorot,* 3 vols. (1882; repr. 1956).
Her.	Philo, *Quis Rerum Divinarum Heres.*
Hertz, Prayer	J.H. Hertz (ed.), *Authorised Daily Prayer Book* (rev. ed. 1948; repr. 1963).
Herzog, Instit	I. Herzog, *The Main Institutions of Jewish Law,* 2 vols. (1936–39; repr. 1967).
Herzog-Hauck	J.J. Herzog and A. Hauch (eds.), *Real-encyklopaedie fuer protestantische Theologie* (1896–1913³).
HḤY	*Ha-Ẓofeh le-Ḥokhmat Yisrael* (first four volumes under the title *Ha-Ẓofeh me-Ereẓ Hagar)* (1910/11–13).
Hirschberg, Afrikah	H.Z. Hirschberg, *Toledot ha-Yehudim be-Afrikah ha-Zofonit,* 2 vols. (1965).
HJ	*Historia Judaica* (1938–61).
HL	*Das Heilige Land* (1857ff.)
ḤM	*Ḥoshen Mishpat.*
Hommel, Ueberliefer.	F. Hommel, *Die altisraelitische Ueberlieferung in inschriftlicher Beleuchtung* (1897).
Hor.	*Horayot* (talmudic tractate).
Horodezky, Ḥasidut	S.A. Horodezky, *Ha-Ḥasidut ve-ha-Ḥasidim,* 4 vols. (1923).
Horowitz, Ereẓ Yis	I.W. Horowitz, *Ereẓ Yisrael u-Shekhenoteha* (1923).
Hos.	Hosea (Bible).
HTR	*Harvard Theological Review* (1908ff.).
HUCA	*Hebrew Union College Annual* (1904; 1924ff.)
Ḥul.	*Ḥullin* (talmudic tractate).
Husik, Philosophy	I. Husik, *History of Medieval Jewish Philosophy* (1932²).
Hyman, Toledot	A. Hyman, *Toledot Tanna'im ve-Amora'im* (1910; repr. 1964).
Ibn Daud, Tradition	Abraham Ibn Daud, *Sefer ha-Qabbalah – The Book of Tradition,* ed. and tr. By G.D. Cohen (1967).
ICC	International Critical Commentary on the Holy Scriptures of the Old and New Testaments (series, 1908ff.).
IDB	*Interpreter's Dictionary of the Bible,* 4 vols. (1962).
Idelsohn, Litugy	A. Z. Idelsohn, *Jewish Liturgy and its Development* (1932; paperback repr. 1967)
Idelsohn, Melodien	A. Z. Idelsohn, *Hebraeisch-orientalischer Melodienschatz,* 10 vols. (1914 32).
Idelsohn, Music	A. Z. Idelsohn, *Jewish Music in its Historical Development* (1929; paperback repr. 1967).

IEJ	*Israel Exploration Journal* (1950ff.).
IESS	*International Encyclopedia of the Social Sciences* (various eds.).
IG	*Inscriptiones Graecae,* ed. by the Prussian Academy.
IGYB	*Israel Government Year Book* (1949/50ff.).
ILR	*Israel Law Review* (1966ff.).
IMIT	*Izraelita Magyar Irodalmi Társulat Évkönyv* (1895 1948).
IMT	International Military Tribunal.
INB	*Israel Numismatic Bulletin* (1962–63).
INJ	*Israel Numismatic Journal* (1963ff.).
Ios	Philo, *De Iosepho.*
Isa.	Isaiah (Bible).
ITHL	Institute for the Translation of Hebrew Literature.
IZBG	*Internationale Zeitschriftenschau fuer Bibelwissenschaft und Grenzgebiete* (1951ff.).
JA	*Journal asiatique* (1822ff.).
James	Epistle of James (New Testament).
JAOS	*Journal of the American Oriental Society* (c. 1850ff.)
Jastrow, Dict	M. Jastrow, *Dictionary of the Targumim, the Talmud Babli and Yerushalmi, and the Midrashic literature,* 2 vols. (1886 1902 and reprints).
JBA	*Jewish Book Annual* (19242ff.).
JBL	*Journal of Biblical Literature* (1881ff.).
JBR	*Journal of Bible and Religion* (1933ff.).
JC	*Jewish Chronicle* (1841ff.).
JCS	*Journal of Cuneiform Studies* (1947ff.).
JE	*Jewish Encyclopedia,* 12 vols. (1901–05 several reprints).
Jer.	Jeremiah (Bible).
Jeremias, Alte Test	A. Jeremias, *Das Alte Testament im Lichte des alten Orients* 1930^{4}).
JGGJČ	*Jahrbuch der Gesellschaft fuer Geschichte der Juden in der Čechoslovakischen Republik* (1929–38).
JHSEM	Jewish Historical Society of England, *Miscellanies* (1925ff.).
JHSET	Jewish Historical Society of England, *Transactions* (1893ff.).
JJGL	*Jahrbuch fuer juedische Geschichte und Literatur* (Berlin) (1898–1938).
JJLG	*Jahrbuch der juedische-literarischen Gesellschaft* (Frankfurt) (1903–32).
JJS	*Journal of Jewish Studies* (1948ff.).
JJSO	*Jewish Journal of Sociology* (1959ff.).
JJV	*Jahrbuch fuer juedische Volkskunde* (1898–1924).
JL	*Juedisches Lexikon,* 5 vols. (1927–30).
JMES	*Journal of the Middle East Society* (1947ff.).
JNES	*Journal of Near Eastern Studies* (continuation of AJSLL) (1942ff.).
J.N.U.L.	Jewish National and University Library.
Job	Job (Bible).
Joel	Joel (Bible).
John	Gospel according to John (New Testament).
I, II and III John	Epistles of John (New Testament).
Jos., Ant	Josephus, *Jewish Antiquities* (Loeb Classics ed.).
Jos. Apion	Josephus, *Against Apion* (Loeb Classics ed.).
Jos., index	*Josephus Works,* Loeb Classics ed., index of names.
Jos., Life	Josephus, *Life* (ed. Loeb Classics).
Jos, Wars	Josephus, *The Jewish Wars* (Loeb Classics ed.).
Josh.	Joshua (Bible).
JPESB	Jewish Palestine Exploration Society Bulletin, see BJPES.
JPESJ	Jewish Palestine Exploration Society Journal – Eng. Title of the Hebrew periodical *Kovez ha-Ḥevrah ha-Ivrit la-Ḥakirat Erez Yisrael va-Attikoteha.*
JPOS	*Journal of the Palestine Oriental Society* (1920–48).
JPS	Jewish Publication Society of America, *The Torah* (1962, 1967^{2}); *The Holy Scriptures* (1917).
JQR	*Jewish Quarterly Review* (1889ff.).
JR	*Journal of Religion* (1921ff.).
JRAS	*Journal of the Royal Asiatic Society* (1838ff.).
JHR	*Journal of Religious History* (1960/61ff.).
JSOS	*Jewish Social Studies* (1939ff.).
JSS	*Journal of Semitic Studies* (1956ff.).
JTS	*Journal of Theological Studies* (1900ff.).
JTSA	Jewish Theological Seminary of America (also abbreviated as JTS).
Jub.	Jubilees (Pseudepigrapha).
Judg.	Judges (Bible).
Judith	Book of Judith (Apocrypha).
Juster, Juifs	J. Juster, *Les Juifs dans l'Empire Romain,* 2 vols. (1914).
JYB	*Jewish Year Book* (1896ff.).
JZWL	*Juedische Zeitschift fuer Wissenschaft und Leben* (1862–75).
Kal.	*Kallah* (post-talmudic tractate).
Kal. R.	*Kallah Rabbati* (post-talmudic tractate).
Katz, England	*The Jews in the History of England, 1485-1850 (1994).*
Kaufmann, Schriften	D. Kaufmann, *Gesammelte Schriften,* 3 vols. (1908 15).
Kaufmann Y., Religion	Y. Kaufmann, *The Religion of Israel* (1960), abridged tr. of his *Toledot.*
Kaufmann Y., Toledot	Y. Kaufmann, *Toledot ha-Emunah ha-Yisre'elit,* 4 vols. (1937 57).
KAWJ	*Korrespondenzblatt des Vereins zur Gruendung und Erhaltung der Akademie fuer die Wissenschaft des Judentums* (1920 30).
Kayserling, Bibl	M. Kayserling, *Biblioteca Española-Portugueza-Judaica* (1880; repr. 1961).
Kelim	*Kelim* (mishnaic tractate).
Ker.	*Keritot* (talmudic tractate).
Ket.	*Ketubbot* (talmudic tractate).

Kid.	*Kiddushim* (talmudic tractate).
Kil.	*Kilayim* (talmudic tractate).
Kin.	*Kinnim* (mishnaic tractate).
Kisch, Germany	G. Kisch, *Jews in Medieval Germany* (1949).
Kittel, Gesch	R. Kittel, *Geschichte des Volkes Israel,* 3 vols. (1922–28).
Klausner, Bayit Sheni	J. Klausner, *Historyah shel ha-Bayit ha-Sheni,* 5 vols. (1950/512).
Klausner, Sifrut	J. Klausner, *Historyah shel haSifrut ha-Ivrit ha-Ḥadashah,* 6 vols. (1952–582).
Klein, corpus	S. Klein (ed.), *Juedisch-palaestinisches Corpus Inscriptionum* (1920).
Koehler-Baumgartner	L. Koehler and W. Baumgartner, *Lexicon in Veteris Testamenti libros* (1953).
Kohut, Arukh	H.J.A. Kohut (ed.), *Sefer he-Arukh ha-Shalem,* by Nathan b. Jehiel of Rome, 8 vols. (1876–92; Supplement by S. Krauss et al., 1936; repr. 1955).
Krauss, Tal Arch	S. Krauss, *Talmudische Archaeologie,* 3 vols. (1910–12; repr. 1966).
Kressel, Leksikon	G. Kressel, *Leksikon ha-Sifrut ha-Ivrit ba-Dorot ha-Aḥaronim,* 2 vols. (1965–67).
KS	*Kirjath Sepher* (1923/4ff.).
Kut.	*Kuttim* (post-talmudic tractate).
LA	Studium Biblicum Franciscanum, *Liber Annuus* (1951ff.).
L.A.	Philo, *Legum allegoriae.*
Lachower, Sifrut	F. Lachower, *Toledot ha-Sifrut ha-Ivrit ha-Ḥadashah,* 4 vols. (1947–48; several reprints).
Lam.	Lamentations (Bible).
Lam. R.	*Lamentations Rabbah.*
Landshuth, Ammudei	L. Landshuth, *Ammudei ha-Avodah* (1857–62; repr. with index, 1965).
Legat.	Philo, *De Legatione ad Caium.*
Lehmann, Nova Bibl	R.P. Lehmann, *Nova Bibliotheca Anglo-Judaica* (1961).
Lev.	Leviticus (Bible).
Lev. R.	*Leviticus Rabbah.*
Levy, Antologia	I. Levy, *Antologia de liturgia judeo-española* (1965ff.).
Levy J., Chald Targ	J. Levy, *Chaldaeisches Woerterbuch ueber die Targumim,* 2 vols. (1967–68; repr. 1959).
Levy J., Nuehebr Tal	J. Levy, *Neuhebraeisches und chaldaeisches Woerterbuch ueber die Talmudim . . .,* 4 vols. (1875–89; repr. 1963).
Lewin, Oẓar	Lewin, *Oẓar ha-Ge'onim,* 12 vols. (1928–43).
Lewysohn, Zool	L. Lewysohn, *Zoologie des Talmuds* (1858).
Lidzbarski, Handbuch	M. Lidzbarski, *Handbuch der nordsemitischen Epigraphik,* 2 vols (1898).
Life	Josephus, *Life* (Loeb Classis ed.).
LNYL	*Leksikon fun der Nayer Yidisher Literatur* (1956ff.).
Loew, Flora	I. Loew, *Die Flora der Juden,* 4 vols. (1924 34; repr. 1967).
LSI	*Laws of the State of Israel* (1948ff.).
Luckenbill, Records	D.D. Luckenbill, *Ancient Records of Assyria and Babylonia,* 2 vols. (1926).
Luke	Gospel according to Luke (New Testament)
LXX	Septuagint (Greek translation of the Bible).
Ma'as.	*Ma'aserot* (talmudic tractate).
Ma'as. Sh.	*Ma'ase Sheni* (talmudic tractate).
I, II, III, and IVMacc.	Maccabees, I, II, III (Apocrypha), IV (Pseudepigrapha).
Maimonides, Guide	Maimonides, *Guide of the Perplexed.*
Maim., Yad	Maimonides, *Mishneh Torah (Yad Ḥazakah).*
Maisler, Untersuchungen	B. Maisler (Mazar), *Untersuchungen zur alten Geschichte und Ethnographie Syriens und Palaestinas,* 1 (1930).
Mak.	*Makkot* (talmudic tractate).
Makhsh.	*Makhshrin* (mishnaic tractate).
Mal.	Malachi (Bible).
Mann, Egypt	J. Mann, *Jews in Egypt in Palestine under the Fatimid Caliphs,* 2 vols. (1920–22).
Mann, Texts	J. Mann, *Texts and Studies,* 2 vols (1931–35).
Mansi	G.D. Mansi, *Sacrorum Conciliorum nova et amplissima collectio,* 53 vols. in 60 (1901–27; repr. 1960).
Margalioth, Gedolei	M. Margalioth, *Enẓiklopedyah le-Toledot Gedolei Yisrael,* 4 vols. (1946–50).
Margalioth, Ḥakhmei	M. Margalioth, *Enẓiklopedyah le-Ḥakhmei ha-Talmud ve-ha-Ge'onim,* 2 vols. (1945).
Margalioth, Cat	G. Margalioth, *Catalogue of the Hebrew and Samaritan Manuscripts in the British Museum,* 4 vols. (1899–1935).
Mark	Gospel according to Mark (New Testament).
Mart. Isa.	Martyrdom of Isaiah (Pseudepigrapha).
Mas.	Masorah.
Matt.	Gospel according to Matthew (New Testament).
Mayer, Art	L.A. Mayer, *Bibliography of Jewish Art* (1967).
MB	*Wochenzeitung* (formerly *Mitteilungsblatt*) *des Irgun Olej Merkas Europa* (1933ff.).
MEAH	*Miscelánea de estudios árabes y hebraicos* (1952ff.).
Meg.	Megillah (talmudic tractate).
Meg. Ta'an.	*Megillat Ta'anit* (in HUCA, 8 9 (1931–32), 318–51).
Me'il	*Me'ilah* (mishnaic tractate).
MEJ	*Middle East Journal* (1947ff.).
Mehk.	*Mekhilta de-R. Ishmael.*
Mekh. SbY	*Mekhilta de-R. Simeon bar Yoḥai.*
Men.	*Menaḥot* (talmudic tractate).
MER	*Middle East Record* (1960ff.).
Meyer, Gesch	E. Meyer, *Geschichte des Alterums,* 5 vols. in 9 (1925–58).
Meyer, Ursp	E. Meyer, *Urspring und Anfaenge des Christentums* (1921).
Mez.	*Mezuzah* (post-talmudic tractate).
MGADJ	*Mitteilungen des Gesamtarchivs der deutschen Juden* (1909–12).
MGG	*Die Musik in Geschichte und Gegenwart,* 14 vols. (1949–68).

MGG²	*Die Musik in Geschichte und Gegenwart, 2nd edition (1994)*
MGH	*Monumenta Germaniae Historica* (1826ff.).
MGJV	*Mitteilungen der Gesellschaft fuer juedische Volkskunde* (1898–1929); title varies, see also JJV.
MGWJ	*Monatsschrift fuer Geschichte und Wissenschaft des Judentums* (1851–1939).
MHJ	*Monumenta Hungariae Judaica,* 11 vols. (1903–67).
Michael, Or	H.Ḥ. Michael, *Or ha-Ḥayyim: Ḥakhmei Yisrael ve-Sifreihem,* ed. by S.Z. Ḥ. Halberstam and N. Ben-Menahem (1965²).
Mid.	*Middot* (mishnaic tractate).
Mid. Ag.	*Midrash Aggadah.*
Mid. Hag.	*Midrash ha-Gadol.*
Mid. Job.	*Midrash Job.*
Mid. Jonah	*Midrash Jonah.*
Mid. Lek. Tov	*Midrash Lekaḥ Tov.*
Mid. Prov.	*Midrash Proverbs.*
Mid. Ps.	*Midrash Tehillim* (Eng tr. *The Midrash on Psalms* (JPS, 1959).
Mid. Sam.	*Midrash Samuel.*
Mid. Song	*Midrash Shir ha-Shirim.*
Mid. Tan.	*Midrash Tanna'im* on Deuteronomy.
Miége, Maroc	J.L. Miège, *Le Maroc et l'Europe,* 3 vols. (1961 62).
Mig.	Philo, *De Migratione Abrahami.*
Mik.	*Mikva'ot* (mishnaic tractate).
Milano, Bibliotheca	A. Milano, *Bibliotheca Historica Italo-Judaica* (1954); supplement for 1954–63 (1964); supplement for 1964–66 in RMI, 32 (1966).
Milano, Italia	A. Milano, *Storia degli Ebrei in Italia* (1963).
MIO	*Mitteilungen des Instituts fuer Orientforschung* 1953ff.).
Mish.	Mishnah.
MJ	*Le Monde Juif* (1946ff.).
MJC	see Neubauer, Chronicles.
MK	*Mo'ed Katan* (talmudic tractate).
MNDPV	*Mitteilungen und Nachrichten des deutschen Palaestinavereins* (1895–1912).
Mortara, Indice	M. Mortara, *Indice Alfabetico dei Rabbini e Scrittori Israeliti ... in Italia ...* (1886).
Mos	Philo, *De Vita Mosis.*
Moscati, Epig	S, Moscati, *Epigrafia ebraica antica* 1935–1950 (1951).
MT	Masoretic Text of the Bible.
Mueller, Musiker	[E.H. Mueller], *Deutsches Musiker-Lexikon* (1929)
Munk, Mélanges	S. Munk, *Mélanges de philosophie juive et arabe* (1859; repr. 1955).
Mut.	Philo, *De Mutatione Nominum.*
MWJ	*Magazin fuer die Wissenshaft des Judentums* (18745 93).
Nah.	Nahum (Bible).
Naz.	*Nazir* (talmudic tractate).
NDB	*Neue Deutsche Biographie* (1953ff.).
Ned.	*Nedarim* (talmudic tractate).
Neg.	*Nega'im* (mishnaic tractate).
Neh.	Nehemiah (Bible).
NG²	*New Grove Dictionary of Music and Musicians* (2001).
Nuebauer, Cat	A. Neubauer, *Catalogue of the Hebrew Manuscripts in the Bodleian Library ...,* 2 vols. (1886–1906).
Neubauer, Chronicles	A. Neubauer, *Mediaeval Jewish Chronicles,* 2 vols. (Heb., 1887–95; repr. 1965), Eng. title of *Seder ha-Ḥakhamim ve-Korot ha-Yamim.*
Neubauer, Géogr	A. Neubauer, *La géographie du Talmud* (1868).
Neuman, Spain	A.A. Neuman, *The Jews in Spain, their Social, Political, and Cultural Life During the Middle Ages,* 2 vols. (1942).
Neusner, Babylonia	J. Neusner, *History of the Jews in Babylonia,* 5 vols. 1965–70), 2nd revised printing 1969ff.).
Nid.	*Niddah* (talmudic tractate).
Noah	Fragment of Book of Noah (Pseudepigrapha).
Noth, Hist Isr	M. Noth, *History of Israel* (1958).
Noth, Personennamen	M. Noth, *Die israelitischen Personennamen. ...* (1928).
Noth, Ueberlief	M. Noth, *Ueberlieferungsgeschichte des Pentateuchs* (1949).
Noth, Welt	M. Noth, *Die Welt des Alten Testaments* (1957³).
Nowack, Lehrbuch	W. Nowack, *Lehrbuch der hebraeischen Archaeologie,* 2 vols (1894).
NT	New Testament.
Num.	Numbers (Bible).
Num R.	*Numbers Rabbah.*
Obad.	Obadiah (Bible).
ODNB online	*Oxford Dictionary of National Biography.*
OḤ	*Oraḥ Ḥayyim.*
Oho.	*Oholot* (mishnaic tractate).
Olmstead	H.T. Olmstead, *History of Palestine and Syria* (1931; repr. 1965).
OLZ	*Orientalistische Literaturzeitung* (1898ff.)
Onom.	Eusebius, *Onomasticon.*
Op.	Philo, *De Opificio Mundi.*
OPD	*Osef Piskei Din shel ha-Rabbanut ha-Rashit le-Ereẓ Yisrael, Bet ha-Din ha-Gadol le-Irurim* (1950).
Or.	*Orlah* (talmudic tractate).
Or. Sibyll.	Sibylline Oracles (Pseudepigrapha).
OS	*L'Orient Syrien* (1956ff.)
OTS	*Oudtestamentische Studien* (1942ff.).
PAAJR	*Proceedings of the American Academy for Jewish Research* (1930ff.)
Pap 4QSᵉ	A papyrus exemplar of IQS.
Par.	*Parah* (mishnaic tractate).
Pauly-Wissowa	A.F. Pauly, *Realencyklopaedie der klassichen Alertumswissenschaft,* ed. by G. Wissowa et al. (1864ff.)

PD	*Piskei Din shel Bet ha-Mishpat ha-Elyon le-Yisrael* (1948ff.)
PDR	*Piskei Din shel Battei ha-Din ha-Rabbaniyyim be-Yisrael.*
PdRE	*Pirkei de-R. Eliezer* (Eng. tr. 1916. (1965^{2}).
PdRK	*Pesikta de-Rav Kahana.*
Pe'ah	*Pe'ah* (talmudic tractate).
Peake, Commentary	A.J. Peake (ed.), *Commentary on the Bible* (1919; rev. 1962).
Pedersen, Israel	J. Pedersen, *Israel, Its Life and Culture,* 4 vols. in 2 (1926–40).
PEFQS	*Palestine Exploration Fund Quarterly Statement* (1869–1937; since 1938–PEQ).
PEQ	*Palestine Exploration Quarterly* (until 1937 PEFQS; after 1927 includes BBSAJ).
Perles, Beitaege	J. Perles, *Beitraege zur rabbinischen Sprach- und Alterthumskunde* (1893).
Pes.	*Pesaḥim* (talmudic tractate).
Pesh.	Peshitta (Syriac translation of the Bible).
Pesher Hab.	Commentary to Habakkuk from Qumran; see 1Qp Hab.
I and II Pet.	Epistles of Peter (New Testament).
Pfeiffer, Introd	R.H. Pfeiffer, *Introduction to the Old Testament* (1948).
PG	J.P. Migne (ed.), *Patrologia Graeca,* 161 vols. (1866–86).
Phil.	Epistle to the Philippians (New Testament).
Philem.	Epistle to the Philemon (New Testament).
PIASH	*Proceedings of the Israel Academy of Sciences and Humanities* (1963/7ff.).
PJB	*Palaestinajahrbuch des deutschen evangelischen Institutes fuer Altertumswissenschaft,* Jerusalem (1905–1933).
PK	*Pinkas ha-Kehillot,* encyclopedia of Jewish communities, published in over 30 volumes by Yad Vashem from 1970 and arranged by countries, regions and localities. For 3-vol. English edition see Spector, *Jewish Life.*
PL	J.P. Migne (ed.), *Patrologia Latina* 221 vols. (1844–64).
Plant	Philo, *De Plantatione.*
PO	R. Graffin and F. Nau (eds.), *Patrologia Orientalis* (1903ff.)
Pool, Prayer	D. de Sola Pool, *Traditional Prayer Book for Sabbath and Festivals* (1960).
Post	Philo, *De Posteritate Caini.*
PR	*Pesikta Rabbati.*
Praem.	Philo, *De Praemiis et Poenis.*
Prawer, Ẓalbanim	J. Prawer, *Toledot Mamlekhet ha-Ẓalbanim be-Ereẓ Yisrael,* 2 vols. (1963).
Press, Ereẓ	I. Press, *Ereẓ-Yisrael, Enẓiklopedyah Topografit-Historit,* 4 vols. (1951–55).
Pritchard, Pictures	J.B. Pritchard (ed.), *Ancient Near East in Pictures* (1954, 1970).
Pritchard, Texts	J.B. Pritchard (ed.), *Ancient Near East Texts* ... (1970^{3}).

Pr. Man.	Prayer of Manasses (Apocrypha).
Prob.	Philo, *Quod Omnis Probus Liber Sit.*
Prov.	Proverbs (Bible).
PS	*Palestinsky Sbornik* (Russ. (1881 1916, 1954ff).
Ps.	Psalms (Bible).
PSBA	*Proceedings of the Society of Biblical Archaeology* (1878–1918).
Ps. of Sol	Psalms of Solomon (Pseudepigrapha).
IQ Apoc	The *Genesis Apocryphon* from Qumran, cave one, ed. by N. Avigad and Y. Yadin (1956).
6QD	*Damascus Document* or *Sefer Berit Dammesk* from Qumran, cave six, ed. by M. Baillet, in RB, 63 (1956), 513–23 (see also CD).
QDAP	*Quarterly of the Department of Antiquities in Palestine* (1932ff.).
4QDeut. 32	Manuscript of Deuteronomy 32 from Qumran, cave four (ed. by P.W. Skehan, in BASOR, 136 (1954), 12–15).
4QEx^{a}	Exodus manuscript in Jewish script from Qumran, cave four.
4QEx$^{\alpha}$	Exodus manuscript in Paleo-Hebrew script from Qumran, cave four (partially ed. by P.W. Skehan, in JBL, 74 (1955), 182–7).
4QFlor	*Florilegium,* a miscellany from Qumran, cave four (ed. by J.M. Allegro, in JBL, 75 (1956), 176–77 and 77 (1958), 350–54).).
QGJD	*Quellen zur Geschichte der Juden in Deutschland* 1888–98).
IQH	*Thanksgiving Psalms* of *Hodayot* from Qumran, cave one (ed. by E.L. Sukenik and N. Avigad, *Oẓar ha-Megillot ha-Genuzot* (1954).
IQIs^{a}	Scroll of Isaiah from Qumran, cave one (ed. by N. Burrows et al., *Dead Sea Scrolls* ..., 1 (1950).
IQIs^{b}	Scroll of Isaiah from Qumran, cave one (ed. E.L. Sukenik and N. Avigad, *Oẓar ha-Megillot ha-Genuzot* (1954).
IQM	The *War Scroll* or *Serekh ha-Milḥamah* (ed. by E.L. Sukenik and N. Avigad, *Oẓar ha-Megillot ha-Genuzot* (1954).
4QpNah	Commentary on Nahum from Qumran, cave four (partially ed. by J.M. Allegro, in JBL, 75 (1956), 89–95).
IQphyl	Phylacteries *(tefillin)* from Qumran, cave one (ed. by Y. Yadin, in *Eretz Israel,* 9 (1969), 60–85).
4Q Prayer of Nabonidus	A document from Qumran, cave four, belonging to a lost Daniel literature (ed. by J.T. Milik, in RB, 63 (1956), 407–15).
IQS	*Manual of Discipline* or *Serekh ha-Yaḥad* from Qumran, cave one (ed. by M. Burrows et al., *Dead Sea Scrolls* ..., 2, pt. 2 (1951).

IQS[a]	The *Rule of the Congregation or Serekh ha-Edah* from Qumran, cave one (ed. by Burrows et al., *Dead Sea Scrolls ...*, 1 (1950), under the abbreviation IQ28a).
IQS[b]	*Blessings* or *Divrei Berakhot* from Qumran, cave one (ed. by Burrows et al., *Dead Sea Scrolls ...*, 1 (1950), under the abbreviation IQ28b).
4QSam[a]	Manuscript of I and II Samuel from Qumran, cave four (partially ed. by F.M. Cross, in BASOR, 132 (1953), 15–26).
4QSam[b]	Manuscript of I and II Samuel from Qumran, cave four (partially ed. by F.M. Cross, in JBL, 74 (1955), 147–72).
4QTestimonia	Sheet of Testimony from Qumran, cave four (ed. by J.M. Allegro, in JBL, 75 (1956), 174–87).).
4QT.Levi	*Testament of Levi* from Qumran, cave four (partially ed. by J.T. Milik, in RB, 62 (1955), 398–406).
Rabinovitz, Dik Sof	See Dik Sof.
RB	*Revue biblique* (1892ff.)
RBI	*Recherches bibliques* (1954ff.)
RCB	*Revista de cultura biblica* (São Paulo) (1957ff.)
Régné, Cat	J. Régné, *Catalogue des actes . . . des rois d'Aragon, concernant les Juifs* (1213–1327), in: REJ, vols. 60 70, 73, 75–78 (1910–24).
Reinach, Textes	T. Reinach, *Textes d'auteurs Grecs et Romains relatifs au Judaïsme* (1895; repr. 1963).
REJ	*Revue des études juives* (1880ff.).
Rejzen, Leksikon	Z. Rejzen, *Leksikon fun der Yidisher Literature,* 4 vols. (1927–29).
Renan, Ecrivains	A. Neubauer and E. Renan, *Les écrivains juifs français ...* (1893).
Renan, Rabbins	A. Neubauer and E. Renan, *Les rabbins français* (1877).
RES	*Revue des étude sémitiques et Babyloniaca* (1934–45).
Rev.	Revelation (New Testament).
RGG[3]	*Die Religion in Geschichte und Gegenwart,* 7 vols. (1957–65[3]).
RH	*Rosh Ha-Shanah* (talmudic tractate).
RHJE	*Revue de l'histoire juive en Egypte* (1947ff.).
RHMH	*Revue d'histoire de la médecine hébraïque* (1948ff.).
RHPR	*Revue d'histoire et de philosophie religieuses* (1921ff.).
RHR	*Revue d'histoire des religions* (1880ff.).
RI	*Rivista Israelitica* (1904–12).
Riemann-Einstein	*Hugo Riemanns Musiklexikon,* ed. by A. Einstein (1929[11]).
Riemann-Gurlitt	*Hugo Riemanns Musiklexikon,* ed. by W. Gurlitt (1959–67[12]), Personenteil.
Rigg-Jenkinson, Exchequer	J.M. Rigg, H. Jenkinson and H.G. Richardson (eds.), *Calendar of the Pleas Rolls of the Exchequer of the Jews,* 4 vols. (1905–1970); cf. in each instance also J.M. Rigg (ed.), *Select Pleas ...* (1902).
RMI	*Rassegna Mensile di Israel* (1925ff.).
Rom.	Epistle to the Romans (New Testament).
Rosanes, Togarmah	S.A. Rosanes, *Divrei Yemei Yisrael be-Togarmah,* 6 vols. (1907–45), and in 3 vols. (1930–38[2]).
Rosenbloom, Biogr Dict	J.R. Rosenbloom, *Biographical Dictionary of Early American Jews* (1960).
Roth, Art	C. Roth, *Jewish Art* (1961).
Roth, Dark Ages	C. Roth (ed.), *World History of the Jewish People,* second series, vol. 2, *Dark Ages* (1966).
Roth, England	C. Roth, *History of the Jews in England* (1964[3]).
Roth, Italy	C. Roth, *History of the Jews in Italy* (1946).
Roth, Mag Bibl	C. Roth, *Magna Bibliotheca Anglo-Judaica* (1937).
Roth, Marranos	C. Roth, *History of the Marranos* (2nd rev. ed 1959; reprint 1966).
Rowley, Old Test	H.H. Rowley, *Old Testament and Modern Study* (1951; repr. 1961).
RS	*Revue sémitiques d'épigraphie et d'histoire ancienne* (1893/94ff.).
RSO	*Rivista degli studi orientali* (1907ff.).
RSV	Revised Standard Version of the Bible.
Rubinstein, Australia I	*H.L. Rubinstein, The Jews in Australia, A Thematic History, Vol. I (1991).*
Rubinstein, Australia II	*W.D. Rubinstein, The Jews in Australia, A Thematic History, Vol. II (1991).*
Ruth	Ruth (Bible).
Ruth R.	*Ruth Rabbah.*
RV	Revised Version of the Bible.
Sac.	Philo, *De Sacrificiis Abelis et Caini.*
Salfeld, Martyrol	S. Salfeld, *Martyrologium des Nuernberger Memorbuches* (1898).
I and II Sam.	Samuel, book I and II (Bible).
Sanh.	*Sanhedrin* (talmudic tractate).
SBA	Society of Biblical Archaeology.
SBB	*Studies in Bibliography and Booklore* (1953ff.).
SBE	*Semana Biblica Española.*
SBT	*Studies in Biblical Theology* (1951ff.).
SBU	*Svenkst Bibliskt Uppslogsvesk,* 2 vols. (1962–63[2]).
Schirmann, Italyah	J.Ḥ. Schirmann, *Ha-Shirah ha-Ivrit be-Italyah* (1934).
Schirmann, Sefarad	J.Ḥ. Schirmann, *Ha-Shirah ha-Ivrit bi-Sefarad u-vi-Provence,* 2 vols. (1954–56).
Scholem, Mysticism	G. Scholem, *Major Trends in Jewish Mysticism* (rev. ed. 1946; paperback ed. with additional bibliography 1961).
Scholem, Shabbetai Ẓevi	G. Scholem, *Shabbetai Ẓevi ve-ha-Tenu'ah ha-Shabbeta'it bi-Ymei Ḥayyav,* 2 vols. (1967).
Schrader, Keilinschr	E. Schrader, *Keilinschriften und das Alte Testament* (1903[3]).
Schuerer, Gesch	E. Schuerer, *Geschichte des juedischen Volkes im Zeitalter Jesu Christi,* 3 vols. and index-vol. (1901–11[4]).

Schuerer, Hist	E. Schuerer, *History of the Jewish People in the Time of Jesus,* ed. by N.N. Glatzer, abridged paperback edition (1961).
Set. T.	*Sefer Torah* (post-talmudic tractate).
Sem.	*Semaḥot* (post-talmudic tractate).
Sendrey, Music	A. Sendrey, *Bibliography of Jewish Music* (1951).
SER	*Seder Eliyahu Rabbah.*
SEZ	*Seder Eliyahu Zuta.*
Shab	*Shabbat* (talmudic tractate).
Sh. Ar.	J. Caro Shulḥan Arukh. OḤ – *Oraḥ Ḥayyim* YD – *Yoreh De'ah* EH – *Even ha-Ezer* ḤM – *Ḥoshen Mishpat.*
Shek.	*Shekalim* (talmudic tractate).
Shev.	*Shevi'it* (talmudic tractate).
Shevu.	*Shevu'ot* (talmudic tractate).
Shunami, Bibl	S. Shunami, *Bibliography of Jewish Bibliographies* (1965[2]).
Sif.	*Sifrei Deuteronomy.*
Sif. Num.	*Sifrei Numbers.*
Sifra	*Sifra* on Leviticus.
Sif. Zut.	*Sifrei Zuta.*
SIHM	Sources inédites de l'histoire du Maroc (series).
Silverman, Prayer	M. Silverman (ed.), *Sabbath and Festival Prayer Book* (1946).
Singer, Prayer	S. Singer *Authorised Daily Prayer Book* (1943[17]).
Sob.	Philo, *De Sobrietate.*
Sof.	*Soferim* (post-talmudic tractate).
Som.	Philo, *De Somniis.*
Song	Song of Songs (Bible).
Song. Ch.	Song of the Three Children (Apocrypha).
Song R.	*Song of Songs Rabbah.*
SOR	*Seder Olam Rabbah.*
Sot.	*Sotah* (talmudic tractate).
SOZ	*Seder Olam Zuta.*
Spec.	Philo, *De Specialibus Legibus.*
Spector, Jewish Life	*S. Spector (ed.), Encyclopedia of Jewish Life Before and After the Holocaust (2001).*
Steinschneider, Arab lit	M. Steinschneider, *Die arabische Literatur der Juden* (1902).
Steinschneider, Cat Bod	M. Steinschneider, *Catalogus Librorum Hebraeorum in Bibliotheca Bodleiana,* 3 vols. (1852–60; reprints 1931 and 1964).
Steinschneider, Hanbuch	M. Steinschneider, *Bibliographisches Handbuch ueber die . . . Literatur fuer hebraeische Sprachkunde* (1859; repr. with additions 1937).
Steinschneider, Uebersetzungen	M. Steinschneider, *Die hebraeischen Uebersetzungen des Mittelalters* (1893).
Stern, Americans	M.H. Stern, *Americans of Jewish Descent* (1960).
van Straalen, Cat	S. van Straalen, *Catalogue of Hebrew Books in the British Museum Acquired During the Years 1868–1892* (1894).
Suárez Fernández, Docmentos	L. Suárez Fernández, *Documentos acerca de la expulsion de los Judios de España* (1964).
Suk.	*Sukkah* (talmudic tractate).
Sus.	Susanna (Apocrypha).
SY	*Sefer Yeẓirah.*
Sym.	Symmachus' Greek translation of the Bible.
SZNG	*Studien zur neueren Geschichte.*
Ta'an.	*Ta'anit* (talmudic tractate).
Tam.	*Tamid* (mishnaic tractate).
Tanḥ.	*Tanḥuma.*
Tanḥ. B.	*Tanḥuma.* Buber ed (1885).
Targ. Jon	Targum Jonathan (Aramaic version of the Prophets).
Targ. Onk.	Targum Onkelos (Aramaic version of the Pentateuch).
Targ. Yer.	Targum Yerushalmi.
TB	Babylonian Talmud or Talmud Bavli.
Tcherikover, Corpus	V. Tcherikover, A. Fuks, and M. Stern, *Corpus Papyrorum Judaicorum,* 3 vols. (1957–60).
Tef.	*Tefillin* (post-talmudic tractate).
Tem.	*Temurah* (mishnaic tractate).
Ter.	*Terumah* (talmudic tractate).
Test. Patr.	Testament of the Twelve Patriarchs (Pseudepigrapha). Ash. – Asher Ben. – Benjamin Dan – Dan Gad – Gad Iss. – Issachar Joseph – Joseph Judah – Judah Levi – Levi Naph. – Naphtali Reu. – Reuben Sim. – Simeon Zeb. – Zebulun.
I and II	Epistle to the Thessalonians (New Testament).
Thieme-Becker	U. Thieme and F. Becker (eds.), *Allgemeines Lexikon der bildenden Kuenstler von der Antike bis zur Gegenwart,* 37 vols. (1907–50).
Tidhar	D. Tidhar (ed.), *Enẓiklopedyah la-Ḥalutẓei ha-Yishuv u-Vonav* (1947ff.).
I and II Timothy	Epistles to Timothy (New Testament).
Tit.	Epistle to Titus (New Testament).
TJ	Jerusalem Talmud or Talmud Yerushalmi.
Tob.	Tobit (Apocrypha).
Toh.	*Tohorot* (mishnaic tractate).
Torczyner, Bundeslade	H. Torczyner, *Die Bundeslade und die Anfaenge der Religion Israels* (1930[3]).
Tos.	*Tosafot.*
Tosef.	Tosefta.
Tristram, Nat Hist	H.B. Tristram, *Natural History of the Bible* (1877[5]).
Tristram, Survey	Palestine Exploration Fund, *Survey of Western Palestine,* vol. 4 (1884) = *Fauna and Flora* by H.B. Tristram.
TS	*Terra Santa* (1943ff.).

TSBA	*Transactions of the Society of Biblical Archaeology* (1872–93).
TY	*Tevul Yom* (mishnaic tractate).
UBSB	United Bible Society, *Bulletin.*
UJE	*Universal Jewish Encyclopedia*, 10 vols. (1939–43).
Uk.	*Ukẓin* (mishnaic tractate).
Urbach, Tosafot	E.E. Urbach, *Ba'alei ha-Tosafot* (1957²).
de Vaux, Anc Isr	R. de Vaux, *Ancient Israel: its Life and Institutions* (1961; paperback 1965).
de Vaux, Instit	R. de Vaux, *Institutions de l'Ancien Testament*, 2 vols. (1958 60).
Virt.	Philo, *De Virtutibus.*
Vogelstein, Chronology	M. Volgelstein, *Biblical Chronology (1944).*
Vogelstein-Rieger	H. Vogelstein and P. Rieger, *Geschichte der Juden in Rom*, 2 vols. (1895–96).
VT	*Vetus Testamentum* (1951ff.).
VTS	*Vetus Testamentum* Supplements (1953ff.).
Vulg.	Vulgate (Latin translation of the Bible).
Wars	Josephus, *The Jewish Wars.*
Watzinger, Denkmaeler	K. Watzinger, *Denkmaeler Palaestinas*, 2 vols. (1933–35).
Waxman, Literature	M. Waxman, *History of Jewish Literature*, 5 vols. (1960²).
Weiss, Dor	I.H. Weiss, *Dor, Dor ve-Doreshav*, 5 vols. (1904⁴).
Wellhausen, Proleg	J. Wellhausen, *Prolegomena zur Geschichte Israels* (1927⁶).
WI	*Die Welt des Islams* (1913ff.).
Winniger, Biog	S. Wininger, *Grosse juedische National-Biographie ...*, 7 vols. (1925–36).
Wisd.	Wisdom of Solomon (Apocrypha)
WLB	*Wiener Library Bulletin* (1958ff.).
Wolf, Bibliotheca	J.C. Wolf, *Bibliotheca Hebraea*, 4 vols. (1715–33).
Wright, Bible	G.E. Wright, *Westminster Historical Atlas to the Bible* (1945).
Wright, Atlas	G.E. Wright, *The Bible and the Ancient Near East* (1961).
WWWJ	*Who's Who in the World Jewry* (New York, 1955, 1965²).
WZJT	*Wissenschaftliche Zeitschrift fuer juedische Theologie* (1835–37).
WZKM	*Wiener Zeitschrift fuer die Kunde des Morgenlandes* (1887ff.).
Yaari, Sheluḥei	A. Yaari, *Sheluḥei Ereẓ Yisrael* (1951).
Yad	Maimonides, *Mishneh Torah (Yad Ḥazakah).*
Yad	*Yadayim* (mishnaic tractate).
Yal.	*Yalkut Shimoni.*
Yal. Mak.	*Yalkut Makhiri.*
Yal. Reub.	*Yalkut Reubeni.*
YD	*Yoreh De'ah.*
YE	*Yevreyskaya Entsiklopediya*, 14 vols. (c. 1910).
Yev.	*Yevamot* (talmudic tractate).
YIVOA	*YIVO Annual of Jewish Social Studies* (1946ff.).
YLBI	*Year Book of the Leo Baeck Institute* (1956ff.).
YMḤEY	See BJPES.
YMḤSI	*Yedi'ot ha-Makhon le-Ḥeker ha-Shirah ha-Ivrit* (1935/36ff.).
YMMY	*Yedi'ot ha-Makhon le-Madda'ei ha-Yahadut* (1924/25ff.).
Yoma	*Yoma* (talmudic tractate).
ZA	*Zeitschrift fuer Assyriologie* (1886/87ff.).
Zav.	*Zavim* (mishnaic tractate).
ZAW	*Zeitschrift fuer die alttestamentliche Wissenschaft und die Kunde des nachbiblishchen Judentums* (1881ff.).
ZAWB	*Beihefte* (supplements) to ZAW.
ZDMG	*Zeitschrift der Deutschen Morgenlaendischen Gesellschaft* (1846ff.).
ZDPV	*Zeitschrift des Deutschen Palaestina-Vereins* (1878–1949; from 1949 = BBLA).
Zech.	Zechariah (Bible).
Zedner, Cat	J. Zedner, *Catalogue of Hebrew Books in the Library of the British Museum* (1867; repr. 1964).
Zeitlin, Bibliotheca	W. Zeitlin, *Bibliotheca Hebraica Post-Mendelssohniana* (1891–95).
Zeph.	Zephaniah (Bible).
Zev.	*Zevaḥim* (talmudic tractate).
ZGGJT	*Zeitschrift der Gesellschaft fuer die Geschichte der Juden in der Tschechoslowakei* (1930–38).
ZGJD	*Zeitschrift fuer die Geschichte der Juden in Deutschland* (1887–92).
ZHB	*Zeitschrift fuer hebraeische Bibliographie* (1896–1920).
Zinberg, Sifrut	I. Zinberg, *Toledot Sifrut Yisrael*, 6 vols. (1955–60).
Ẓiẓ.	*Ẓiẓit* (post-talmudic tractate).
ZNW	*Zeitschrift fuer die neutestamentliche Wissenschaft* (1901ff.).
ZS	*Zeitschrift fuer Semitistik und verwandte Gebiete* (1922ff.).
Zunz, Gesch	L. Zunz, *Zur Geschichte und Literatur* (1845).
Zunz, Gesch	L. Zunz, *Literaturgeschichte der synagogalen Poesie* (1865; Supplement, 1867; repr. 1966).
Zunz, Poesie	L. Zunz, *Synogogale Posie des Mittelalters*, ed. by Freimann (1920²; repr. 1967).
Zunz, Ritus	L. Zunz, *Ritus des synagogalen Gottesdienstes* (1859; repr. 1967).
Zunz, Schr	L. Zunz, *Gesammelte Schriften*, 3 vols. (1875–76).
Zunz, Vortraege	L. Zunz, *Gottesdienstliche vortraege der Juden ...* 1892²; repr. 1966).
Zunz-Albeck, Derashot	L. Zunz, *Ha-Derashot be-Yisrael*, Heb. Tr. of Zunz Vortraege by H. Albeck (1954²).

TRANSLITERATION RULES

HEBREW AND SEMITIC LANGUAGES:

	General	*Scientific*
א	not transliterated[1]	ʾ
בּ	b	b
ב	v	v, ḇ
גּ	g	g
ג		ḡ
דּ	d	d
ד		ḏ
ה	h	h
ו	v – when not a vowel	w
ז	z	z
ח	ḥ	ḥ
ט	t	ṭ, t
י	y – when vowel and at end of words – i	y
כּ	k	k
כ, ך	kh	kh, ḵ
ל	l	ḻ
מ, ם	m	m
נ, ן	n	n
ס	s	s
ע	not transliterated[1]	ʿ
פּ	p	p
פ, ף	f	p, f, ph
צ, ץ	ẓ	ṣ, ẓ
ק	k	q, k
ר	r	r
שׁ	sh[2]	š
שׂ	s	ś, s
תּ	t	t
ת		ṯ
ג׳	dzh, J	ğ
ז׳	zh, J	ž
צ׳	ch	č
ָ		å, o, ȯ (short) â, ā (long)
ַ	a	a
ֲ		a, ª
ֵ		e, ẹ, ē
ֶ	e	æ, ä, ę
ֱ		œ, ĕ, ᵉ
ְ	only *sheva na* is transliterated	ə, ĕ, e; only *sheva na* transliterated
ִ, ִי	i	i
ֹ, וֹ	o	o, o, o
ֻ, וּ	u	u, ŭ û, ū
ֵי	ei; biblical e	
‡		reconstructed forms of words

1. The letters א and ע are not transliterated.
An apostrophe (') between vowels indicates that they do not form a diphthong and are to be pronounced separately.
2. *Dagesh ḥazak* (forte) is indicated by doubling of the letter, except for the letter שׁ.
3. Names. Biblical names and biblical place names are rendered according to the Bible translation of the Jewish Publication Society of America. Post-biblical Hebrew names are transliterated; contemporary names are transliterated or rendered as used by the person. Place names are transliterated or rendered by the accepted spelling. Names and some words with an accepted English form are usually not transliterated.

YIDDISH

א	not transliterated
אַ	a
אָ	o
בּ	b
בֿ	v
ג	g
ד	d
ה	h
ו, וּ	u
וו	v
וי	oy
ז	z
זש	zh
ח	kh
ט	t
טש	tsh, ch
י	(consonant) y (vowel) i
יִ	i
יי	ey
ײַ	ay
כּ	k
כ, ך	kh
ל	l
מ, ם	m
נ, ן	n
ס	s
ע	e
פּ	p
פֿ, ף	f
צ, ץ	ts
ק	k
ר	r
ש	sh
שׂ	s
תּ	t
ת	s

1. Yiddish transliteration rendered according to U. Weinreich's Modern *English-Yiddish Yiddish-English* Dictionary.
2. Hebrew words in Yiddish are usually transliterated according to standard Yiddish pronunciation, e.g., חזנות = *khazones*.

LADINO

Ladino and Judeo-Spanish words written in Hebrew characters are transliterated phonetically, following the General Rules of Hebrew transliteration (see above) whenever the accepted spelling in Latin characters could not be ascertained.

ARABIC

ا ء	a[1]	ض	ḍ
ب	b	ط	ṭ
ت	t	ظ	ẓ
ث	th	ع	c
ج	j	غ	gh
ح	ḥ	ف	f
خ	kh	ق	q
د	d	ك	k
ذ	dh	ل	l
ر	r	م	m
ز	z	ن	n
س	s	ه	h
ش	sh	و	w
ص	ṣ	ي	y
ـَ	a	ـَا ى	ā
ـِ	i	ـِي	ī
ـُ	u	ـُو	ū
ـَو	aw	ـِّ	iyy[2]
ـَي	ay	ـُوّ	uww[2]

1. not indicated when initial
2. see note (f)

a) The EJ follows the *Columbia Lippincott Gazetteer* and the *Times Atlas* in transliteration of Arabic place names. Sites that appear in neither are transliterated according to the table above, and subject to the following notes.

b) The EJ follows the *Columbia Encyclopedia* in transliteration of Arabic names. Personal names that do not therein appear are transliterated according to the table above and subject to the following notes (e.g., Ali rather than ʿAlī, Suleiman rather than Sulayman).

c) The EJ follows the *Webster's Third International Dictionary, Unabridged* in transliteration of Arabic terms that have been integrated into the English language.

d) The term "Abu" will thus appear, usually in disregard of inflection.

e) Nunnation (end vowels, *tanwīn*) are dropped in transliteration.

f) Gemination (*tashdīd*) is indicated by the doubling of the geminated letter, unless an end letter, in which case the gemination is dropped.

g) The definitive article *al-* will always be thus transliterated, unless subject to one of the modifying notes (e.g., El-Arish rather than al-ʿArīsh; modification according to note (a)).

h) The Arabic transliteration disregards the Sun Letters (the antero-palatals (*al-Ḥurūf al-Shamsiyya*).

i) The *tā-marbūṭa* (o) is omitted in transliteration, unless in construct-stage (e.g., *Khirba* but *Khirbat Mishmish*).

These modifying notes may lead to various inconsistencies in the Arabic transliteration, but this policy has deliberately been adopted to gain smoother reading of Arabic terms and names.

GREEK

Ancient Greek	*Modern Greek*	*Greek Letters*
a	a	*Α; α; ᾳ*
b	v	*Β; β*
g	gh; g	*Γ; γ*
d	dh	*Δ; δ*
e	e	*Ε; ε*
z	z	*Ζ; ζ*
e; e	i	*Η; η; ῃ*
th	th	*Θ; θ*
i	i	*Ι; ι*
k	k; ky	*Κ; κ*
l	l	*Λ; λ*
m	m	*Μ; μ*
n	n	*Ν; ν*
x	x	*Ξ; ξ*
o	o	*Ο; ο*
p	p	*Π; π*
r; rh	r	*Ρ; ρ; ῥ*
s	s	*Σ; σ; ς*
t	t	*Τ; τ*
u; y	i	*Υ; υ*
ph	f	*Φ; φ*
ch	kh	*Χ; χ*
ps	ps	*Ψ; ψ*
o; ō	o	*Ω; ω; ῳ*
ai	e	*αι*
ei	i	*ει*
oi	i	*οι*
ui	i	*υι*
ou	ou	*ου*
eu	ev	*ευ*
eu; ēu	iv	*ηυ*
–	j	*τζ*
nt	d; nd	*ντ*
mp	b; mb	*μπ*
ngk	g	*γκ*
ng	ng	*νγ*
h	–	ʽ
–	–	ʼ
w	–	*Ϝ*

RUSSIAN

А	A
Б	B
В	V
Г	G
Д	D
Е	E, Ye[1]
Ё	Yo, O[2]
Ж	Zh
З	Z
И	I
Й	Y[3]
К	K
Л	L
М	M
Н	N
О	O
П	P
Р	R
С	S
Т	T
У	U
Ф	F
Х	Kh
Ц	Ts
Ч	Ch
Ш	Sh
Щ	Shch
Ъ	omitted; see note [1]
Ы	Y
Ь	omitted; see note [1]
Э	E
Ю	Yu
Я	Ya

1. Ye at the beginning of a word; after all vowels except ***Ы***; and after ***Ъ*** and ***Ь***.
2. O after ***Ч***, ***Ш*** and ***Щ***.
3. Omitted after ***Ы***, and in names of people after ***И***.

A. Many first names have an accepted English or quasi-English form which has been preferred to transliteration.
B. Place names have been given according to the *Columbia Lippincott Gazeteer*.
C. Pre-revolutionary spelling has been ignored.
D. Other languages using the Cyrillic alphabet (e.g., Bulgarian, Ukrainian), inasmuch as they appear, have been phonetically transliterated in conformity with the principles of this table.

GLOSSARY

Asterisked terms have separate entries in the Encyclopaedia.

Actions Committee, early name of the Zionist General Council, the supreme institution of the World Zionist Organization in the interim between Congresses. The Zionist Executive's name was then the "Small Actions Committee."

*__Adar__, twelfth month of the Jewish religious year, sixth of the civil, approximating to February–March.

*__Aggadah__, name given to those sections of Talmud and Midrash containing homiletic expositions of the Bible, stories, legends, folklore, anecdotes, or maxims. In contradistinction to **halakhah*.

*__Agunah__, woman unable to remarry according to Jewish law, because of desertion by her husband or inability to accept presumption of death.

*__Aharonim__, later rabbinic authorities. In contradistinction to **rishonim* ("early ones").

Ahavah, liturgical poem inserted in the second benediction of the morning prayer *(*Ahavah Rabbah)* of the festivals and/or special Sabbaths.

Aktion (Ger.), operation involving the mass assembly, deportation, and murder of Jews by the Nazis during the *Holocaust.

*__Aliyah__, (1) being called to Reading of the Law in synagogue; (2) immigration to Ereẓ Israel; (3) one of the waves of immigration to Ereẓ Israel from the early 1880s.

*__Amidah__, main prayer recited at all services; also known as *Shemoneh Esreh* and *Tefillah*.

*__Amora__ (pl. **amoraim**), title given to the Jewish scholars in Ereẓ Israel and Babylonia in the third to sixth centuries who were responsible for the **Gemara*.

Aravah, the *willow; one of the *Four Species used on *Sukkot ("festival of Tabernacles") together with the **etrog, hadas*, and **lulav*.

*__Arvit__, evening prayer.

Asarah be-Tevet, fast on the 10th of Tevet commemorating the commencement of the siege of Jerusalem by Nebuchadnezzar.

Asefat ha-Nivḥarim, representative assembly elected by Jews in Palestine during the period of the British Mandate (1920–48).

*__Ashkenaz__, name applied generally in medieval rabbinical literature to Germany.

*__Ashkenazi__ (pl. **Ashkenazim**), German or West-, Central-, or East-European Jew(s), as contrasted with *Sephardi(m).

*__Av__, fifth month of the Jewish religious year, eleventh of the civil, approximating to July–August.

*__Av bet din__, vice president of the supreme court (*bet din ha-gadol*) in Jerusalem during the Second Temple period; later, title given to communal rabbis as heads of the religious courts (see **bet din*).

*__Badḥan__, jester, particularly at traditional Jewish weddings in Eastern Europe.

*__Bakkashah__ (Heb. "supplication"), type of petitionary prayer, mainly recited in the Sephardi rite on Rosh Ha-Shanah and the Day of Atonement.

Bar, "son of . . . "; frequently appearing in personal names.

*__Baraita__ (pl. **beraitot**), statement of **tanna* not found in *Mishnah.

*__Bar mitzvah__, ceremony marking the initiation of a boy at the age of 13 into the Jewish religious community.

Ben, "son of . . . ", frequently appearing in personal names.

Berakhah (pl. **berakhot**), *benediction, blessing; formula of praise and thanksgiving.

*__Bet din__ (pl. **battei din**), rabbinic court of law.

*__Bet ha-midrash__, school for higher rabbinic learning; often attached to or serving as a synagogue.

*__Bilu__, first modern movement for pioneering and agricultural settlement in Ereẓ Israel, founded in 1882 at Kharkov, Russia.

*__Bund__, Jewish socialist party founded in Vilna in 1897, supporting Jewish national rights; Yiddishist, and anti-Zionist.

Cohen (pl. **Cohanim**), see Kohen.

*__Conservative Judaism__, trend in Judaism developed in the United States in the 20th century which, while opposing extreme changes in traditional observances, permits certain modifications of *halakhah* in response to the changing needs of the Jewish people.

*__Consistory__ (Fr. *consistoire*), governing body of a Jewish communal district in France and certain other countries.

*__Converso(s)__, term applied in Spain and Portugal to converted Jew(s), and sometimes more loosely to their descendants.

*__Crypto-Jew__, term applied to a person who although observing outwardly Christianity (or some other religion) was at heart a Jew and maintained Jewish observances as far as possible (see Converso; Marrano; Neofiti; New Christian; Jadīd al-Islām).

*__Dayyan__, member of rabbinic court.

Decisor, equivalent to the Hebrew *posek* (pl. **posekim*), the rabbi who gives the decision (*halakhah*) in Jewish law or practice.

*__Devekut__, "devotion"; attachment or adhesion to God; communion with God.

*__Diaspora__, Jews living in the "dispersion" outside Ereẓ Israel; area of Jewish settlement outside Ereẓ Israel.

Din, a law (both secular and religious), legal decision, or lawsuit.

Divan, diwan, collection of poems, especially in Hebrew, Arabic, or Persian.

Dunam, unit of land area (1,000 sq. m., c. ¼ acre), used in Israel.

Einsatzgruppen, mobile units of Nazi S.S. and S.D.; in U.S.S.R. and Serbia, mobile killing units.

*__Ein-Sof__, "without end"; "the infinite"; hidden, impersonal aspect of God; also used as a Divine Name.

*__Elul__, sixth month of the Jewish religious calendar, 12th of the civil, precedes the High Holiday season in the fall.

Endloesung, see *Final Solution.

*__Ereẓ Israel__, Land of Israel; Palestine.

*__Eruv__, technical term for rabbinical provision permitting the alleviation of certain restrictions.

*__Etrog__, citron; one of the *Four Species used on *Sukkot together with the **lulav, hadas*, and *aravah*.

Even ha-Ezer, see Shulḥan Arukh.

*__Exilarch__, lay head of Jewish community in Babylonia (see also *resh galuta*), and elsewhere.

*__Final Solution__ (Ger. *Endloesung*), in Nazi terminology, the Nazi-planned mass murder and total annihilation of the Jews.

*__Gabbai__, official of a Jewish congregation; originally a charity collector.

*__Galut__, "exile"; the condition of the Jewish people in dispersion.

*Gaon (pl. geonim), head of academy in post-talmudic period, especially in Babylonia.
Gaonate, office of *gaon.
*Gemara, traditions, discussions, and rulings of the *amoraim*, commenting on and supplementing the *Mishnah, and forming part of the Babylonian and Palestinian Talmuds (see Talmud).
*Gematria, interpretation of Hebrew word according to the numerical value of its letters.
General Government, territory in Poland administered by a German civilian governor-general with headquarters in Cracow after the German occupation in World War II.
*Genizah, depository for sacred books. The best known was discovered in the synagogue of Fostat (old Cairo).
Get, bill of *divorce.
*Ge'ullah, hymn inserted after the *Shema* into the benediction of the morning prayer of the festivals and special Sabbaths.
*Gilgul, metempsychosis; transmigration of souls.
*Golem, automaton, especially in human form, created by magical means and endowed with life.
*Ḥabad, initials of *ḥokhmah, binah, da'at*: "wisdom, understanding, knowledge"; ḥasidic movement founded in Belorussia by *Shneur Zalman of Lyady.
Hadas, *myrtle; one of the *Four Species used on Sukkot together with the *etrog*, *lulav*, and *aravah*.
*Haftarah (pl. haftarot), designation of the portion from the prophetical books of the Bible recited after the synagogue reading from the Pentateuch on Sabbaths and holidays.
*Haganah, clandestine Jewish organization for armed self-defense in Ereẓ Israel under the British Mandate, which eventually evolved into a people's militia and became the basis for the Israel army.
*Haggadah, ritual recited in the home on *Passover eve at seder table.
Haham, title of chief rabbi of the Spanish and Portuguese congregations in London, England.
*Hakham, title of rabbi of *Sephardi congregation.
*Hakham bashi, title in the 15th century and modern times of the chief rabbi in the Ottoman Empire, residing in Constantinople (Istanbul), also applied to principal rabbis in provincial towns.
Hakhsharah ("preparation"), organized training in the Diaspora of pioneers for agricultural settlement in Ereẓ Israel.
*Halakhah (pl. halakhot), an accepted decision in rabbinic law. Also refers to those parts of the *Talmud concerned with legal matters. In contradistinction to *aggadah*.
Ḥaliẓah, biblically prescribed ceremony (Deut. 25:9–10) performed when a man refuses to marry his brother's childless widow, enabling her to remarry.
*Hallel, term referring to Psalms 113-18 in liturgical use.
*Ḥalukkah, system of financing the maintenance of Jewish communities in the holy cities of Ereẓ Israel by collections made abroad, mainly in the pre-Zionist era (see *kolel*).
Ḥalutz (pl. ḥalutzim), pioneer, especially in agriculture, in Ereẓ Israel.
Ḥalutziyyut, pioneering.
*Ḥanukkah, eight-day celebration commemorating the victory of *Judah Maccabee over the Syrian king *Antiochus Epiphanes and the subsequent rededication of the Temple.
Ḥasid, adherent of *Ḥasidism.
*Ḥasidei Ashkenaz, medieval pietist movement among the Jews of Germany.
*Ḥasidism, (1) religious revivalist movement of popular mysticism among Jews of Germany in the Middle Ages; (2) religious movement founded by *Israel ben Eliezer Ba'al Shem Tov in the first half of the 18th century.
*Haskalah, "enlightenment"; movement for spreading modern European culture among Jews c. 1750–1880. See *maskil*.
*Havdalah, ceremony marking the end of Sabbath or festival.
*Ḥazzan, precentor who intones the liturgy and leads the prayers in synagogue; in earlier times a synagogue official.
*Ḥeder (lit. "room"), school for teaching children Jewish religious observance.
Heikhalot, "palaces"; tradition in Jewish mysticism centering on mystical journeys through the heavenly spheres and palaces to the Divine Chariot (see Merkabah).
*Ḥerem, excommunication, imposed by rabbinical authorities for purposes of religious and/or communal discipline; originally, in biblical times, that which is separated from common use either because it was an abomination or because it was consecrated to God.
Ḥeshvan, see Marḥeshvan.
*Ḥevra kaddisha, title applied to charitable confraternity (*ḥevrah*), now generally limited to associations for burial of the dead.
*Ḥibbat Zion, see Ḥovevei Zion.
*Histadrut (abbr. For Heb. Ha-Histadrut ha-Kelalit shel ha-Ovedim ha-Ivriyyim be-Ereẓ Israel). Ereẓ Israel Jewish Labor Federation, founded in 1920; subsequently renamed Histadrut ha-Ovedim be-Ereẓ Israel.
*Holocaust, the organized mass persecution and annihilation of European Jewry by the Nazis (1933–1945).
*Hoshana Rabba, the seventh day of *Sukkot on which special observances are held.
Ḥoshen Mishpat, see Shulḥan Arukh.
Ḥovevei Zion, federation of *Ḥibbat Zion, early (pre-*Herzl) Zionist movement in Russia.
Illui, outstanding scholar or genius, especially a young prodigy in talmudic learning.
*Iyyar, second month of the Jewish religious year, eighth of the civil, approximating to April-May.
I.Ẓ.L. (initials of Heb. *Irgun Ẓeva'i Le'ummi; "National Military Organization"), underground Jewish organization in Ereẓ Israel founded in 1931, which engaged from 1937 in retaliatory acts against Arab attacks and later against the British mandatory authorities.
*Jadīd al-Islām (Ar.), a person practicing the Jewish religion in secret although outwardly observing Islām.
*Jewish Legion, Jewish units in British army during World War I.
*Jihād (Ar.), in Muslim religious law, holy war waged against infidels.
*Judenrat (Ger. "Jewish council"), council set up in Jewish communities and ghettos under the Nazis to execute their instructions.
*Judenrein (Ger. "clean of Jews"), in Nazi terminology the condition of a locality from which all Jews had been eliminated.
*Kabbalah, the Jewish mystical tradition:
Kabbala iyyunit, speculative Kabbalah;
Kabbala ma'asit, practical Kabbalah;
Kabbala nevu'it, prophetic Kabbalah.
Kabbalist, student of Kabbalah.
*Kaddish, liturgical doxology.
Kahal, Jewish congregation; among Ashkenazim, *kehillah*.

*Kalām (Ar.), science of Muslim theology; adherents of the Kalām are called *mutakallimūn*.
***Karaite**, member of a Jewish sect originating in the eighth century which rejected rabbinic (*Rabbanite) Judaism and claimed to accept only Scripture as authoritative.
***Kasher**, ritually permissible food.
Kashrut, Jewish *dietary laws.
***Kavvanah**, "intention"; term denoting the spiritual concentration accompanying prayer and the performance of ritual or of a commandment.
***Kedushah**, main addition to the third blessing in the reader's repetition of the *Amidah* in which the public responds to the precentor's introduction.
Kefar, village; first part of name of many settlements in Israel.
Kehillah, congregation; see *kahal*.
Kelippah (pl. **kelippot**), "husk(s)"; mystical term denoting force(s) of evil.
***Keneset Yisrael**, comprehensive communal organization of the Jews in Palestine during the British Mandate.
Keri, variants in the masoretic (*masorah) text of the Bible between the spelling (*ketiv*) and its pronunciation (*keri*).
***Kerovah** (collective plural (corrupted) from **kerovez̩**), poem(s) incorporated into the **Amidah*.
Ketiv, see *keri*.
***Ketubbah**, marriage contract, stipulating husband's obligations to wife.
Kevuz̩ah, small commune of pioneers constituting an agricultural settlement in Erez̩ Israel (evolved later into *kibbutz).
***Kibbutz** (pl. **kibbutzim**), larger-size commune constituting a settlement in Erez̩ Israel based mainly on agriculture but engaging also in industry.
***Kiddush**, prayer of sanctification, recited over wine or bread on eve of Sabbaths and festivals.
***Kiddush ha-Shem**, term connoting martyrdom or act of strict integrity in support of Judaic principles.
***Kinah** (pl. **kinot**), lamentation dirge(s) for the Ninth of Av and other fast days.
***Kislev**, ninth month of the Jewish religious year, third of the civil, approximating to November-December.
Klaus, name given in Central and Eastern Europe to an institution, usually with synagogue attached, where *Talmud was studied perpetually by adults; applied by Ḥasidim to their synagogue ("*kloyz*").
***Knesset**, parliament of the State of Israel.
K(c)ohen (pl. **K(c)ohanim**), Jew(s) of priestly (Aaronide) descent.
***Kolel**, (1) community in Erez̩ Israel of persons from a particular country or locality, often supported by their fellow countrymen in the Diaspora; (2) institution for higher Torah study.
Kosher, see *kasher*.
***Kristallnacht** (Ger. "crystal night," meaning "night of broken glass"), organized destruction of synagogues, Jewish houses, and shops, accompanied by mass arrests of Jews, which took place in Germany and Austria under the Nazis on the night of Nov. 9–10, 1938.
***Lag ba-Omer**, 33rd (Heb. **lag**) day of the **Omer* period falling on the 18th of *Iyyar; a semi-holiday.
Leḥi (abbr. For Heb. ***Loḥamei Ḥerut Israel**, "Fighters for the Freedom of Israel"), radically anti-British armed underground organization in Palestine, founded in 1940 by dissidents from *I.Z.L.
Levir, husband's brother.
***Levirate marriage** (Heb. *yibbum*), marriage of childless widow (*yevamah*) by brother (*yavam*) of the deceased husband (in accordance with Deut. 25:5); release from such an obligation is effected through *ḥaliz̩ah*.
LHY, see Leḥi.
***Lulav**, palm branch; one of the *Four Species used on *Sukkot together with the **etrog*, *hadas*, and *aravah*.
***Ma'aravot**, hymns inserted into the evening prayer of the three festivals, Passover, Shavuot, and Sukkot.
Ma'ariv, evening prayer; also called **arvit*.
***Ma'barah**, transition camp; temporary settlement for newcomers in Israel during the period of mass immigration following 1948.
***Maftir**, reader of the concluding portion of the Pentateuchal section on Sabbaths and holidays in synagogue; reader of the portion of the prophetical books of the Bible (**haftarah*).
***Maggid**, popular preacher.
***Maḥzor** (pl. **maḥzorim**), festival prayer book.
***Mamzer**, bastard; according to Jewish law, the offspring of an incestuous relationship.
***Mandate, Palestine**, responsibility for the administration of Palestine conferred on Britain by the League of Nations in 1922; mandatory government: the British administration of Palestine.
***Maqāma** (Ar. pl. **maqamāt**), poetic form (rhymed prose) which, in its classical arrangement, has rigid rules of form and content.
***Marḥeshvan**, popularly called Ḥeshvan; eighth month of the Jewish religious year, second of the civil, approximating to October–November.
***Marrano(s)**, descendant(s) of Jew(s) in Spain and Portugal whose ancestors had been converted to Christianity under pressure but who secretly observed Jewish rituals.
Maskil (pl. **maskilim**), adherent of *Haskalah ("Enlightenment") movement.
***Masorah**, body of traditions regarding the correct spelling, writing, and reading of the Hebrew Bible.
Masorete, scholar of the masoretic tradition.
Masoretic, in accordance with the masorah.
Meliz̩ah, in Middle Ages, elegant style; modern usage, florid style using biblical or talmudic phraseology.
Mellah, *Jewish quarter in North African towns.
***Menorah**, candelabrum; seven-branched oil lamp used in the Tabernacle and Temple; also eight-branched candelabrum used on *Ḥanukkah.
Me'orah, hymn inserted into the first benediction of the morning prayer (*Yoz̩er ha-Me'orot*).
***Merkabah**, *merkavah*, "chariot"; mystical discipline associated with Ezekiel's vision of the Divine Throne-Chariot (Ezek. 1).
Meshullaḥ, emissary sent to conduct propaganda or raise funds for rabbinical academies or charitable institutions.
***Mezuzah** (pl. **mezuzot**), parchment scroll with selected Torah verses placed in container and affixed to gates and doorposts of houses occupied by Jews.
***Midrash**, method of interpreting Scripture to elucidate legal points (*Midrash Halakhah*) or to bring out lessons by stories or homiletics (*Midrash Aggadah*). Also the name for a collection of such rabbinic interpretations.
***Mikveh**, ritual bath.
***Minhag** (pl. **minhagim**), ritual custom(s); synagogal rite(s); especially of a specific sector of Jewry.
***Minḥah**, afternoon prayer; originally meal offering in Temple.

*__Minyan__, group of ten male adult Jews, the minimum required for communal prayer.

*__Mishnah__, earliest codification of Jewish Oral Law.

Mishnah (pl. **mishnayot**), subdivision of tractates of the Mishnah.

Mitnagged (pl. ***Mitnaggedim**), originally, opponents of *Ḥasidism in Eastern Europe.

*__Mitzvah__, biblical or rabbinic injunction; applied also to good or charitable deeds.

Mohel, official performing circumcisions.

*__Moshav__, smallholders' cooperative agricultural settlement in Israel, see moshav ovedim.

Moshavah, earliest type of Jewish village in modern Ereẓ Israel in which farming is conducted on individual farms mostly on privately owned land.

Moshav ovedim ("workers' moshav"), agricultural village in Israel whose inhabitants possess individual homes and holdings but cooperate in the purchase of equipment, sale of produce, mutual aid, etc.

*__Moshav shittufi__ ("collective moshav"), agricultural village in Israel whose members possess individual homesteads but where the agriculture and economy are conducted as a collective unit.

Mostegab (Ar.), poem with biblical verse at beginning of each stanza.

*__Muqaddam__ (Ar., pl. **muqaddamūn**), "leader," "head of the community."

*__Musaf__, additional service on Sabbath and festivals; originally the additional sacrifice offered in the Temple.

Musar, traditional ethical literature.

*__Musar movement__, ethical movement developing in the latter part of the 19th century among Orthodox Jewish groups in Lithuania; founded by R. Israel *Lipkin (Salanter).

*__Nagid__ (pl. **negidim**), title applied in Muslim (and some Christian) countries in the Middle Ages to a leader recognized by the state as head of the Jewish community.

Nakdan (pl. **nakdanim**), "punctuator"; scholar of the 9th to 14th centuries who provided biblical manuscripts with masoretic apparatus, vowels, and accents.

*__Nasi__ (pl. **nesi'im**), talmudic term for president of the Sanhedrin, who was also the spiritual head and later, political representative of the Jewish people; from second century a descendant of Hillel recognized by the Roman authorities as patriarch of the Jews. Now applied to the president of the State of Israel.

*__Negev__, the southern, mostly arid, area of Israel.

*__Ne'ilah__, concluding service on the *Day of Atonement.

Neofiti, term applied in southern Italy to converts to Christianity from Judaism and their descendants who were suspected of maintaining secret allegiance to Judaism.

*__Neology__; **Neolog**; **Neologism**, trend of *Reform Judaism in Hungary forming separate congregations after 1868.

*__Nevelah__ (lit. "carcass"), meat forbidden by the *dietary laws on account of the absence of, or defect in, the act of **sheḥitah* (ritual slaughter).

*__New Christians__, term applied especially in Spain and Portugal to converts from Judaism (and from Islam) and their descendants; "Half New Christian" designated a person one of whose parents was of full Jewish blood.

*__Niddah__ ("menstruous woman"), woman during the period of menstruation.

*__Nisan__, first month of the Jewish religious year, seventh of the civil, approximating to March-April.

Niẓoẓot, "sparks"; mystical term for sparks of the holy light imprisoned in all matter.

Nosaḥ (**nusaḥ**) "version"; (1) textual variant; (2) term applied to distinguish the various prayer rites, e.g., *nosaḥ Ashkenaz*; (3) the accepted tradition of synagogue melody.

*__Notarikon__, method of abbreviating Hebrew works or phrases by acronym.

Novella(e) (Heb. **ḥiddush* (*im*)), commentary on talmudic and later rabbinic subjects that derives new facts or principles from the implications of the text.

*__Nuremberg Laws__, Nazi laws excluding Jews from German citizenship, and imposing other restrictions.

Ofan, hymns inserted into a passage of the morning prayer.

*__Omer__, first sheaf cut during the barley harvest, offered in the Temple on the second day of Passover.

Omer, Counting of (Heb. *Sefirat ha-Omer*), 49 days counted from the day on which the *omer* was first offered in the Temple (according to the rabbis the 16th of Nisan, i.e., the second day of Passover) until the festival of Shavuot; now a period of semi-mourning.

Oraḥ Ḥayyim, see Shulḥan Arukh.

*__Orthodoxy__ (Orthodox Judaism), modern term for the strictly traditional sector of Jewry.

*__Pale of Settlement__, 25 provinces of czarist Russia where Jews were permitted permanent residence.

*__Palmaḥ__ (abbr. for Heb. *peluggot maḥaẓ*; "shock companies"), striking arm of the *Haganah.

*__Pardes__, medieval biblical exegesis giving the literal, allegorical, homiletical, and esoteric interpretations.

*__Parnas__, chief synagogue functionary, originally vested with both religious and administrative functions; subsequently an elected lay leader.

Partition plan(s), proposals for dividing Ereẓ Israel into autonomous areas.

Paytan, composer of **piyyut* (liturgical poetry).

*__Peel Commission__, British Royal Commission appointed by the British government in 1936 to inquire into the Palestine problem and make recommendations for its solution.

Pesaḥ, *Passover.

*__Pilpul__, in talmudic and rabbinic literature, a sharp dialectic used particularly by talmudists in Poland from the 16th century.

*__Pinkas__, community register or minute-book.

*__Piyyut__, (pl. **piyyutim**), Hebrew liturgical poetry.

*__Pizmon__, poem with refrain.

Posek (pl. ***posekim**), decisor; codifier or rabbinic scholar who pronounces decisions in disputes and on questions of Jewish law.

*__Prosbul__, legal method of overcoming the cancelation of debts with the advent of the *sabbatical year.

*__Purim__, festival held on Adar 14 or 15 in commemoration of the delivery of the Jews of Persia in the time of *Esther.

Rabban, honorific title higher than that of rabbi, applied to heads of the *Sanhedrin in mishnaic times.

*__Rabbanite__, adherent of rabbinic Judaism. In contradistinction to *Karaite.

Reb, rebbe, Yiddish form for rabbi, applied generally to a teacher or ḥasidic rabbi.

*__Reconstructionism__, trend in Jewish thought originating in the United States.

*__Reform Judaism__, trend in Judaism advocating modification of *Orthodoxy in conformity with the exigencies of contemporary life and thought.

Resh galuta, lay head of Babylonian Jewry (see exilarch).

Responsum (pl. ***responsa**), written opinion (*teshuvah*) given to question (*she'elah*) on aspects of Jewish law by qualified authorities; pl. collection of such queries and opinions in book form (*she'elot u-teshuvot*).

***Rishonim**, older rabbinical authorities. Distinguished from later authorities (**aḥaronim*).

***Rishon le-Zion**, title given to Sephardi chief rabbi of Ereẓ Israel.

***Rosh Ha-Shanah**, two-day holiday (one day in biblical and early mishnaic times) at the beginning of the month of *Tishri (September–October), traditionally the New Year.

Rosh Hodesh, *New Moon, marking the beginning of the Hebrew month.

Rosh Yeshivah, see *Yeshivah.

***R.S.H.A.** (initials of Ger. *Reichssicherheitshauptamt*: "Reich Security Main Office"), the central security department of the German Reich, formed in 1939, and combining the security police (Gestapo and Kripo) and the S.D.

***Sanhedrin**, the assembly of ordained scholars which functioned both as a supreme court and as a legislature before 70 C.E. In modern times the name was given to the body of representative Jews convoked by Napoleon in 1807.

***Savora** (pl. **savoraim**), name given to the Babylonian scholars of the period between the **amoraim* and the **geonim*, approximately 500–700 C.E.

S.D. (initials of Ger. *Sicherheitsdienst*: "security service"), security service of the *S.S. formed in 1932 as the sole intelligence organization of the Nazi party.

Seder, ceremony observed in the Jewish home on the first night of Passover (outside Ereẓ Israel first two nights), when the *Haggadah is recited.

***Sefer Torah**, manuscript scroll of the Pentateuch for public reading in synagogue.

***Sefirot, the ten**, the ten "Numbers"; mystical term denoting the ten spheres or emanations through which the Divine manifests itself; elements of the world; dimensions, primordial numbers.

Selektion (Ger.), (1) in ghettos and other Jewish settlements, the drawing up by Nazis of lists of deportees; (2) separation of incoming victims to concentration camps into two categories – those destined for immediate killing and those to be sent for forced labor.

Seliḥah (pl. ***seliḥot**), penitential prayer.

***Semikhah**, ordination conferring the title "rabbi" and permission to give decisions in matters of ritual and law.

Sephardi (pl. ***Sephardim**), Jew(s) of Spain and Portugal and their descendants, wherever resident, as contrasted with *Ashkenazi(m).

Shabbatean, adherent of the pseudo-messiah *Shabbetai Ẓevi (17th century).

Shaddai, name of God found frequently in the Bible and commonly translated "Almighty."

***Shaḥarit**, morning service.

Shali'aḥ (pl. **sheliḥim**), in Jewish law, messenger, agent; in modern times, an emissary from Ereẓ Israel to Jewish communities or organizations abroad for the purpose of fund-raising, organizing pioneer immigrants, education, etc.

Shalmonit, poetic meter introduced by the liturgical poet *Solomon ha-Bavli.

***Shammash**, synagogue beadle.

***Shavuot**, Pentecost; Festival of Weeks; second of the three annual pilgrim festivals, commemorating the receiving of the Torah at Mt. Sinai.

***Sheḥitah**, ritual slaughtering of animals.

***Shekhinah**, Divine Presence.

Shelishit, poem with three-line stanzas.

***Sheluḥei Ereẓ Israel** (or **shadarim**), emissaries from Ereẓ Israel.

***Shema** ([Yisrael]; "hear… [O Israel]," Deut. 6:4), Judaism's confession of faith, proclaiming the absolute unity of God.

Shemini Aẓeret, final festal day (in the Diaspora, final two days) at the conclusion of *Sukkot.

Shemittah, *Sabbatical year.

Sheniyyah, poem with two-line stanzas.

***Shephelah**, southern part of the coastal plain of Ereẓ Israel.

***Shevat**, eleventh month of the Jewish religious year, fifth of the civil, approximating to January–February.

***Shi'ur Komah**, Hebrew mystical work (c. eighth century) containing a physical description of God's dimensions; term denoting enormous spacial measurement used in speculations concerning the body of the **Shekhinah*.

Shivah, the "seven days" of *mourning following burial of a relative.

***Shofar**, horn of the ram (or any other ritually clean animal excepting the cow) sounded for the memorial blowing on *Rosh Ha-Shanah, and other occasions.

Shoḥet, person qualified to perform **sheḥitah*.

Shomer, *Ha-Shomer, organization of Jewish workers in Ereẓ Israel founded in 1909 to defend Jewish settlements.

***Shtadlan**, Jewish representative or negotiator with access to dignitaries of state, active at royal courts, etc.

***Shtetl**, Jewish small-town community in Eastern Europe.

***Shulḥan Arukh**, Joseph *Caro's code of Jewish law in four parts:
Oraḥ Ḥayyim, laws relating to prayers, Sabbath, festivals, and fasts;
Yoreh De'ah, dietary laws, etc;
Even ha-Ezer, laws dealing with women, marriage, etc;
Ḥoshen Mishpat, civil, criminal law, court procedure, etc.

Siddur, among Ashkenazim, the volume containing the daily prayers (in distinction to the **maḥzor* containing those for the festivals).

***Simḥat Torah**, holiday marking the completion in the synagogue of the annual cycle of reading the Pentateuch; in Ereẓ Israel observed on Shemini Aẓeret (outside Ereẓ Israel on the following day).

***Sinai Campaign**, brief campaign in October–November 1956 when Israel army reacted to Egyptian terrorist attacks and blockade by occupying the Sinai peninsula.

Sitra aḥra, "the other side" (of God); left side; the demoniac and satanic powers.

***Sivan**, third month of the Jewish religious year, ninth of the civil, approximating to May–June.

***Six-Day War**, rapid war in June 1967 when Israel reacted to Arab threats and blockade by defeating the Egyptian, Jordanian, and Syrian armies.

***S.S.** (initials of Ger. *Schutzstaffel*: "protection detachment"), Nazi formation established in 1925 which later became the "elite" organization of the Nazi Party and carried out central tasks in the "Final Solution."

***Status quo ante** community, community in Hungary retaining the status it had held before the convention of the General Jewish Congress there in 1868 and the resultant split in Hungarian Jewry.

*Sukkah, booth or tabernacle erected for *Sukkot when, for seven days, religious Jews "dwell" or at least eat in the *sukkah* (Lev. 23:42).

***Sukkot**, festival of Tabernacles; last of the three pilgrim festivals, beginning on the 15th of Tishri.

Sūra (Ar.), chapter of the Koran.

Ta'anit Esther (Fast of *Esther), fast on the 13th of Adar, the day preceding Purim.

Takkanah (pl. ***takkanot**), regulation supplementing the law of the Torah; regulations governing the internal life of communities and congregations.

***Tallit (gadol)**, four-cornered prayer shawl with fringes (*ẓiẓit*) at each corner.

***Tallit katan**, garment with fringes (*ẓiẓit*) appended, worn by observant male Jews under their outer garments.

***Talmud**, "teaching"; compendium of discussion on the Mishnah by generations of scholars and jurists in many academies over a period of several centuries. The Jerusalem (or Palestinian) Talmud mainly contains the discussions of the Palestinian sages. The Babylonian Talmud incorporates the parallel discussion in the Babylonian academies.

Talmud torah, term generally applied to Jewish religious (and ultimately to talmudic) study; also to traditional Jewish religious public schools.

***Tammuz**, fourth month of the Jewish religious year, tenth of the civil, approximating to June-July.

Tanna (pl. ***tannaim**), rabbinic teacher of mishnaic period.

***Targum**, Aramaic translation of the Bible.

***Tefillin**, phylacteries, small leather cases containing passages from Scripture and affixed on the forehead and arm by male Jews during the recital of morning prayers.

Tell (Ar. "mound," "hillock"), ancient mound in the Middle East composed of remains of successive settlements.

***Terefah**, food that is not *kasher*, owing to a defect on the animal.

***Territorialism**, 20th century movement supporting the creation of an autonomous territory for Jewish mass-settlement outside Ereẓ Israel.

***Tevet**, tenth month of the Jewish religious year, fourth of the civil, approximating to December–January.

Tikkun ("restitution," "reintegration"), (1) order of service for certain occasions, mostly recited at night; (2) mystical term denoting restoration of the right order and true unity after the spiritual "catastrophe" which occurred in the cosmos.

Tishah be-Av, Ninth of *Av, fast day commemorating the destruction of the First and Second Temples.

***Tishri**, seventh month of the Jewish religious year, first of the civil, approximating to September–October.

Tokheḥah, reproof sections of the Pentateuch (Lev. 26 and Deut. 28); poem of reproof.

***Torah**, Pentateuch or the Pentateuchal scroll for reading in synagogue; entire body of traditional Jewish teaching and literature.

Tosafist, talmudic glossator, mainly French (12–14th centuries), bringing additions to the commentary by *Rashi.

***Tosafot**, glosses supplied by tosafist.

***Tosefta**, a collection of teachings and traditions of the *tannaim*, closely related to the Mishnah.

Tradent, person who hands down a talmudic statement on the name of his teacher or other earlier authority.

***Tu bi-Shevat**, the 15th day of Shevat, the New Year for Trees; date marking a dividing line for fruit tithing; in modern Israel celebrated as arbor day.

***Uganda Scheme**, plan suggested by the British government in 1903 to establish an autonomous Jewish settlement area in East Africa.

***Va'ad Le'ummi**, national council of the Jewish community in Ereẓ Israel during the period of the British *Mandate.

***Wannsee Conference**, Nazi conference held on Jan. 20, 1942, at which the planned annihilation of European Jewry was endorsed.

Waqf (Ar.), (1) a Muslim charitable pious foundation; (2) state lands and other property passed to the Muslim community for public welfare.

***War of Independence**, war of 1947–49 when the Jews of Israel fought off Arab invading armies and ensured the establishment of the new State.

***White Paper(s)**, report(s) issued by British government, frequently statements of policy, as issued in connection with Palestine during the *Mandate period.

***Wissenschaft des Judentums** (Ger. "Science of Judaism"), movement in Europe beginning in the 19th century for scientific study of Jewish history, religion, and literature.

***Yad Vashem**, Israel official authority for commemorating the *Holocaust in the Nazi era and Jewish resistance and heroism at that time.

Yeshivah (pl. ***yeshivot**), Jewish traditional academy devoted primarily to study of rabbinic literature; *rosh yeshivah*, head of the yeshivah.

YHWH, the letters of the holy name of God, the Tetragrammaton.

Yibbum, see levirate marriage.

Yiḥud, "union"; mystical term for intention which causes the union of God with the **Shekhinah*.

Yishuv, settlement; more specifically, the Jewish community of Ereẓ Israel in the pre-State period. The pre-Zionist community is generally designated the "old yishuv" and the community evolving from 1880, the "new yishuv."

Yom Kippur, Yom ha-Kippurim, *Day of Atonement, solemn fast day observed on the 10th of Tishri.

Yoreh De'ah, see Shulḥan Arukh.

Yoẓer, hymns inserted in the first benediction (*Yoẓer Or*) of the morning **Shema*.

***Ẓaddik**, person outstanding for his faith and piety; especially a ḥasidic rabbi or leader.

Ẓimẓum, "contraction"; mystical term denoting the process whereby God withdraws or contracts within Himself so leaving a primordial vacuum in which creation can take place; primordial exile or self-limitation of God.

***Zionist Commission (1918)**, commission appointed in 1918 by the British government to advise the British military authorities in Palestine on the implementation of the *Balfour Declaration.

Ẓyyonei Zion, the organized opposition to Herzl in connection with the *Uganda Scheme.

***Ẓiẓit**, fringes attached to the **tallit* and **tallit katan*.

***Zohar**, mystical commentary on the Pentateuch; main textbook of *Kabbalah.

Zulat, hymn inserted after the **Shema* in the morning service.